Baseball america®
2008 ALMANAC

BASEBALL AMERICA INC. • DURHAM, N.C.

Baseball america®
2008 ALMANAC

A Comprehensive Review of the 2007 Season, Featuring Statistics and Commentary

PUBLISHED BY
Baseball America Inc.

EDITOR
Will Lingo

CONTRIBUTING EDITORS
Ben Badler, J.J. Cooper, Matt Eddy, Aaron Fitt, Chris Kline, Josh Leventhal, John Manuel, Alan Matthews, Nathan Rode

CONTRIBUTING WRITER
John Perrotto

INTERNS
David Ely, Jim Shonerd, Travis Young

DESIGN & PRODUCTION
Daniel BeDen, Sara Hiatt, Linwood Webb

STATISTICAL CONSULTANTS
Major League Baseball
Advanced Media

Baseball america

PRESIDENT/CEO Catherine Silver
VICE PRESIDENT/PUBLISHER Lee Folger
EDITORS IN CHIEF Will Lingo, John Manuel
DESIGN & PRODUCTION DIRECTOR Sara Hiatt

COVER PHOTO by Bill Nichols

Distributed by Simon & Schuster
ISBN 1-932391-18-5

EDITOR'S NOTE
• Major league statistics are based on final, unofficial 2007 averages.
• The organization statistics, which begin on page 43, include all players who participated in at least one game during the 2007 season. Pitchers' batting statistics are not included, nor are the pitching statistics of field players who pitched in less than two games. For players who played with more than one team in the same league, the player's cumulative statistics appear on the line immediately after the player's statistics with each team.
• Innings pitched have been rounded off to the nearest full inning.

TABLE OF CONTENTS

LARRY GOREN

MAJOR LEAGUES

2007 IN REVIEW

Bonds leads the charge in Year of the Milestone

BY JOHN PERROTTO

The ball sailed deep into the Bay Area night and into the right-center field stands at San Francisco's AT&T Park, a majestic drive worthy of being a record-setting home run.

With that blast on Aug. 7, Giants left fielder Barry Bonds broke what is considered the most hallowed record in sports. It was home run No. 756, breaking the all-time mark held for 33 years by Hank Aaron.

Fireworks went off overhead as Bonds circled the basis and the adoring crowd shook the beautiful waterfront ballpark. It was a joyous occasion in a city where Bonds' father once starred and where Barry grew up then returned to as a free agent in 1993.

Yet while the celebration endured in the Bay Area, fans nearly everywhere else had mixed emotions. Some were indifferent and others were incensed that Bonds had become the game's home run king because of compelling evidence that the slugger had used performance-enhancing drugs. Bonds was also under a third grand jury investigation for perjury, the government believing he had lied to them during the 2006 investigation of the Bay Area Laboratory Co-Operative (BALCO), during which he testified that he had never knowingly used steroids.

While the record-breaking home run came in a swirl of controversy, it was one of a multitude of significant milestones reached during the 2007 season. In fact, it would be appropriate to label 2007 as the Year of the Milestone considering:

■ Rangers DH Sammy Sosa hit his 600th career home run, while Blue Jays DH Frank Thomas, Yankees third baseman Alex Rodriguez and White Sox DH Jim Thome all reached 500.

■ Astros second baseman Craig Biggio recorded his 3,000th hit.

■ Mets lefthander Tom Glavine won his 300th game and Yankees righthander Roger Clemens notched career victory No. 350.

■ Padres righthander Trevor Hoffman became the first closer to eclipse 500 saves, one season after setting the all-time record.

While those milestones all were significant, they all lacked the drama and prologue of Bonds' pursuit of Aaron. After he connected for No. 756 off Nationals lefty Mike Bacsik, Bonds was defiant when asked if the record has been stained in any way.

"This record is not tainted at all. At all. Period," Bonds said.

Commissioner Bud Selig seemed uncomfortable with Bonds breaking the record of his close friend Aaron. Selig

BILL NICHOLS

Barry Bonds connected for his record-breaking 756th career home run off Mike Bacsik on Aug. 7

occasionally followed Bonds as he chased 756 and watched him tie the record three nights earlier in San Diego with a homer off the Padres righthander Clay Hensley, while some fans in Petco Park held up signs with asterisks. Selig, however, was not in attendance the night the record fell.

Instead, Selig sent MLB executive vice president Jimmie Lee Solomon and Hall of Fame outfielder Frank Robinson as emissaries. He subsequently released a statement that alluded to the potential stain on the record—though the commissioner did deign to phone Bonds immediately after the game.

"While the issues which have swirled around this record will continue to work themselves toward resolution, today is a day for congratulations on a truly remarkable achievement," Selig said in the statement.

Aaron maintained for months that he had no urge to witness his record being broken, and he did not attend. The 73-year-old all-time great did congratulate Bonds in a taped message played on the stadium scoreboard in the aftermath of No. 756, though some thought it stiff and forced.

"It is a great accomplishment which required skill,

longevity and determination," Aaron said in the video. "Throughout the past century, the home run has held a special place in baseball and I have been privileged to hold this record for 33 of those years. I move over now and offer my best wishes to Barry and his family on this historic achievement.

"My hope today, as it was on that April evening in 1974, is that the achievement of this record will inspire others to chase their own dreams."

Bonds seemed genuinely touched as he watched Aaron's message.

"When I saw Hank Aaron, that made everything," Bonds said. "We've always loved him. He's always the home run king."

Bonds stood at home plate as the ball sailed over the fence, then raised both arms over his head with fists clenched before circling the bases. His 17-year-old son Nikolai, the Giants' batboy, greeted him at home plate and the two embraced. Bonds' wife, two daughters and mother joined them. As did his godfather Willie Mays, the Hall of Fame outfielder who himself starred for the Giants and hit 660 home runs, the fourth-most ever.

The home run also was a dream come true in a bizarre way for Bascik, a journeyman who had been out of the majors for three years before earning a spot on the Nationals' roster.

"I dreamed about it as a kid, but when I dreamed about it, I was the one hitting the home run and not giving it up," Bacsik said. "I didn't really want to be part of history as a bad part, but I am. I'm OK with it."

The record-setting home run turned out to be a last hurrah for Bonds, as the Giants informed him with a week left in the season that they did not plan to re-sign him as a free agent, signaling the end of his 15-year run in San Francisco. Still, he left his hometown worshippers with something to remember.

"This is the greatest record in all of sports," Giants manager Bruce Bochy said. "We are all fortunate to witness it. It's awesome. This road to history has been a lot of fun."

Other Feats Of Strength

The 2007 season was also fun for many other home run hitters who reached milestones.

One of them was Sosa, whose career appeared to be over after an injury-plagued 2005 season with the Orioles that began when he testified in front of the Congressional subcommittee investigating the use of steroids in baseball. He received only one contract offer for the 2006 season, from the Nationals—with no guaranteed money. Sosa declined, and sat out the season.

However, needing just 12 home runs to join Aaron, Bonds, Babe Ruth and Mays as the only members of the 600-homer club, Sosa agreed to go to 2007 spring training with the Rangers as a non-roster invitee. He made the team, and started as DH on Opening Day. Sosa broke in with the Rangers in 1989 before being traded to the White Sox later that year.

Sosa hit .252/.311/.468 with 21 home runs as a part-time player, connecting for No. 600 on June 20 against—appropriately—Cubs righthander Jason Marquis at Ameriquest Field in Arlington. Sosa had spent his best seasons with the Cubs, winning National League MVP honors in 1998 and clubbing 66 homers in 1998, 63 in 1999 and 64 in 2001.

Sosa did his trademark bounce out of the batter's box as his solo shot to right-center cleared the fence.

"It was something that cannot be explained," Sosa said.

500 HOME RUNS

Rodriguez and Thomas joined the 500-home run club in 2007, while Sosa became just the fifth player ever to reach 600 on June 20. Rodriguez was the youngest player ever to hit his 500th, at 32 years, 8 days, surpassing Jimmie Foxx's old mark by nearly 11 months. Manny Ramirez (490) and Gary Sheffield (480) likely will become the 26th and 27th players to hit 500 in 2008.

1.	**Barry Bonds**★	762	13. Mickey Mantle#	536
2.	Hank Aaron	755	14. Jimmie Foxx	534
3.	Babe Ruth★	714	15. Willie McCovey★	521
4.	Willie Mays	660	Ted Williams★	521
5.	**Sammy Sosa**	609	**17. Alex Rodriguez**	518
6.	Ken Griffey★	593	**18. Frank Thomas**	513
7.	Frank Robinson	586	19. Ernie Banks	512
8.	Mark McGwire	583	Eddie Mathews★	512
9.	Harmon Killebrew	573	21. Mel Ott★	511
10.	Rafael Palmeiro★	569	**22. Jim Thome★**	507
11.	Reggie Jackson★	563	23. Eddie Murray#	504
12.	Mike Schmidt	548		

300 WINS

With the Mets' 8-3 victory against the Cubs on Aug. 5, Glavine became just the fifth lefthander to reach 300 wins, and the 23rd pitcher overall. Randy Johnson (284) stands to become the sixth and 24th sometime in 2008 or 2009.

1.	Cy Young	511	13. Eddie Plank★	326
2.	Walter Johnson	417	14. Nolan Ryan	324
3.	Pete Alexander	373	Don Sutton	324
	Christy Mathewson	373	16. Phil Niekro	318
5.	Pud Galvin	364	17. Gaylord Perry	314
6.	Warren Spahn★	363	18. Tom Seaver	311
7.	Kid Nichols	361	19. Charley Radbourn	309
8.	**Roger Clemens**	354	20. Mickey Welch	307
9.	**Greg Maddux**	347	21. **Tom Glavine★**	303
10.	Tim Keefe	342	22. Lefty Grove★	300
11.	Steve Carlton★	329	Early Wynn	300
12.	John Clarkson	328		

3,000 STRIKEOUTS

Martinez notched strikeout No. 3,000 in his first start of the 2007 season—though that start was delayed until Sept. 3 while he recovered from rotator-cuff surgery. John Smoltz (2,975) should attain his 3,000th strikeout early in the 2008 season.

1.	Nolan Ryan	5,714	9. Walter Johnson	3,509
2.	**Roger Clemens**	4,672	10. Phil Niekro	3,342
3.	Randy Johnson★	4,616	11. **Greg Maddux**	3,273
4.	Steve Carlton★	4,136	12. Fergie Jenkins	3,192
5.	Bert Blyleven	3,701	13. Bob Gibson	3,117
6.	Tom Seaver	3,640	14. **Curt Schilling**	3,116
7.	Don Sutton	3,574	15. **Pedro Martinez**	3,030
8.	Gaylord Perry	3,534		

400 SAVES

One season after passing Smith for the all-time lead, Hoffman collected his 500th save on June 6, becoming the first player to reach the milestone. Durability has been Hoffman's calling card, as he's saved 30 or more games in 12 of the past 13 seasons, with a high of 53 in 1998. Assuming health, Billy Wagner (358) is poised to become the fifth pitcher to notch 400 saves.

1.	**Trevor Hoffman**	524
2.	Lee Smith	478
3.	**Mariano Rivera**	443
4.	John Franco★	424

Trevor Hoffman

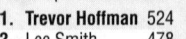
Active players in bold. ★Bats lefthanded. #Switch-hitter.

3,000 HITS

Biggio recorded hit No. 3,000 on June 28 and passed seven other players before sailing off into the sunset after the season. Barry Bonds (2,935) could join Biggio in 2008, but no other player was particularly close to 3,000, with 40-somethings Omar Vizquel (2,598) and Julio Franco (2,586) next in line.

1.	Pete Rose#	4,256	15.	George Brett*	3,154
2.	Ty Cobb*	4,189	16.	Paul Waner*	3,152
3.	Hank Aaron	3,771	17.	Robin Yount	3,142
4.	Stan Musial*	3,630	18.	Tony Gwynn*	3,141
5.	Tris Speaker*	3,514	19.	Dave Winfield	3,110
6.	Carl Yastrzemski*	3,419	20.	**Craig Biggio**	3,060
7.	Cap Anson	3,418	21.	Rickey Henderson	3,055
8.	Honus Wagner	3,415	22.	Rod Carew*	3,053
9.	Paul Molitor	3,319	23.	Lou Brock*	3,023
10.	Eddie Collins*	3,315	24.	Rafael Palmeiro*	3,020
11.	Willie Mays	3,283	25.	Wade Boggs*	3,010
12.	Eddie Murray#	3,255	26.	Al Kaline	3,007
13.	Nap Lajoie	3,242	27.	Roberto Clemente	3,000
14.	Cal Ripken	3,184			

600 DOUBLES

While Biggio gained more attention for scaling the all-time hits list in 2007, his showing on the doubles list is equally impressive—if not more so. He passed four Hall of Famers on his way to fifth on the all-time list, in the process becoming the top doubles-hitting righthanded batter in history. Luis Gonzalez (570) and Jeff Kent (537), both Dodgers in 2007, were next on the active list.

1.	Tris Speaker*	792	8.	Carl Yastrzemski*	646
2.	Pete Rose#	746	9.	Honus Wagner	640
3.	Stan Musial*	725	10.	Hank Aaron	624
4.	Ty Cobb*	724	11.	Paul Molitor	605
5.	**Craig Biggio**	668		Paul Waner*	605
6.	George Brett*	665	13.	Cal Ripken	603
7.	Nap Lajoie	657	14.	**Barry Bonds***	601

Active players in bold. *Bats lefthanded. #Switch-hitter.

Alex Rodriguez became the youngest player ever to hit his 500th home run at 32 years, eight days

"Getting my 600th against the Chicago Cubs, and my first team was the Texas Rangers. It's like everything clicked."

Sosa also felt vindicated after being written off by many in baseball.

"People that know baseball know that I was retired for one year. And to put everything together and come back, that's big," Sosa said. "That's why hitting 600 home runs is a great thing."

Hitting 500 home runs is also a great thing. Thomas was the first of three to attain that mark when he went deep on June 28 in Minneapolis against Twins righthander Carlos Silva, sending a pitch into the left-field stands.

Thomas received a standing ovation from the Metrodome crowd and pointed toward his wife, three children and father-in-law sitting in the suites down the right-field line as he crossed home plate. Incidentally, Thomas' first home was hit in the Metrodome, on Aug. 28, 1990.

Thomas blasted his homer just in the nick of time, as his family had to leave for the airport at 1:45 p.m. Thomas connected in the first inning of the mid-week, afternoon game.

"My daughter said, 'Dad, you've got to do it in the first couple of at-bats,' " Thomas said.

Thomas was ejected from that game in the ninth inning after being called out on strikes for the second time.

"I'm probably the first to get 500 home runs and get thrown out of the ballgame," Thomas said. "That's something I didn't want to happen, but the moment just got the best of me."

Just eight days after his 32nd birthday, Rodriguez became the youngest player to reach 500 home runs when he connected off Royals righthander Kyle Davies on Aug. 4 at Yankee Stadium. The third baseman hit 54 homers during the season, but he sat on 499 for 10 days before finally going deep with a drive that just stayed inside the left-field foul pole.

"I acted like a goofball running around the bases, but you only hit 500 once," Rodriguez said. "I haven't hit one in so long I didn't know if it was going to be foul. It was awesome. And then you kind of get that high school reception when you hit a home run and all of the guys are out of the dugout."

Rodriguez ended the season with 518 homers, putting him in position to challenge Bonds' all-time record.

Thome's 500th home run was more than just a milestone: It was a two-run blast in the bottom of the ninth inning to give the White Sox a 9-7 win against the Angels at U.S. Cellular Field on Sept. 16. Righthander Dustin Moseley was the victim. Thome became the 23rd player to reach 500, but the first to do so in walk-off fashion.

"Just can't believe it. I really can't," Thome said. "I would never have imagined doing that as a walk-off. Just amazing to see your teammates standing there. It's like a movie script.

"I tried to tell myself, 'Relax, relax, just let it happen, let it happen.' In that situation, especially tied, you're looking for a ball to drive."

Three players hit their 500th career home run in 2007, something that had never happened before. Red Sox left fielder Manny Ramirez was left on the doorstep at 490. He managed to hit just 20 home runs in an injury-plagued year for his lowest total since he was a rookie with the Indians in 1994.

CONTINUED ON PAGE 11

On the Money

PLAYER OF THE YEAR

BY GEORGE KING

TAMPA

Only in the crazy Yankees universe could the best player in baseball have three years remaining on his contract and leave $91 million on the table to become a free agent.

Rodriguez had 10 days following the World Series to opt out of the contract and test the free agent waters. But he didn't need that long.

Agent Scott Boras announced during Game Four of the World Series that Rodriguez would, indeed, test free agency, where Boras believed a 12-year deal in the $30 million a year range was attainable.

This despite general manager Brian Cashman's challenge to Rodriguez: opt out and you are out of The Bronx.

"If Alex Rodriguez opts out of his contract then we will not participate in free agency," Cashman said. "That is accurate and that is definitive."

Rodriguez batted .314/.422/.645 and led the majors with 54 home runs, 156 RBIs and 143 runs scored in 2007. His production made him an easy choice to win Baseball America's 2007 Major League Player of the Year award, the third time he's been bestowed with the honor.

Showering Rodriguez in praise for his remarkable production doesn't broach the major topic of the times, however. What's he's done in the past has been awe-inspiring, but what happens next has become the matter at hand.

Boras says Rodriguez getting a 12-year deal isn't out of the question, and painted a picture where the team committing a dozen seasons to his client would make money with Rodriguez.

"In 2000 the YES network didn't exist," said Boras, who insists regional sports networks have changed the financial landscape of baseball, providing deep revenue streams. "Now it's worth $3 billion to $3.5 billion easily. What is it going to be worth in 12 years when Alex will be at the end of his career, chasing records and people wanting to say, 'I saw him play.'

"The key thing for Alex and his family is that he wants to be in the place where he is going to end his career," Boras said. "He wants to be in one spot with a positive chance to win a World (Series) championship."

The Yankees were interested in talking about an extension before Rodriguez hit free agency, because the Rangers were set to pay $21 million of his salary from 2008 to 2010—part of the price they paid for unloading the shortstop after the 2003 season.

To make his point about Rodriguez' ability to pay for himself, Boras invented IPN, which stands for Iconic magnetism, historic Performance and Network value. The historic performance points mostly to Rodriguez' pursuit of Barry Bonds' new home run record. A-Rod

has hit 518 homers compared with Bonds' 762, and while Bonds isn't quite done yet, Rodriguez figures to chase him down over the course of his next contract.

When the talk was about a seven-year deal for $210 million, the Angels were mentioned as the leading candidate to land A-Rod. They have looked into a regional sports network but haven't signed a deal with one (or created one). The Red Sox and Mets, who have their own networks, surfaced as candidates, though it's unclear how serious their interest is.

As for Rodriguez' year, it was special from the start and turned the ocean of 2006 boos into chants of "MVP, MVP, MVP."

So enamored with Rodriguez were Yankee Stadium fans that not one boo was heard during the Division Series in which the Yankees, for the third straight season, were eliminated. Rodriguez, who was 3-for-29 (.103) in the previous two ALDS meltdowns, went 4-for-15 (.267) and hit a home run in the deciding Game Four loss.

Alex Rodriguez

In four seasons with the Yankees, Rodriguez has had some of the best seasons ever by a righthanded hitter in Yankee Stadium. He's averaged 43 home runs per season in New York, has never posted an on-base percentage below .375 and even has racked up 88 stolen bases over that span.

However, the Yankees won only one playoff series in that span and have lost their last four postseason series, including the historic collapse in the 2004 AL Championship Series, when they blew a three-game lead to the Red Sox. This year, for the first time since 1997, the Yankees didn't win the AL East and had to settle for the wild card.

As a Yankee, Rodriguez has hit .245 with 21 strikeouts, three home runs and just six RBIs in 94 at-bats in 20 playoff games. After the season, Rodriguez has respectable career postseason numbers of .279/.361/.483 in 39 games (147 at-bats), with seven home runs. In the regular season, he's a career .306/.389/.578 hitter.

Rodriguez' departure leaves unanswered questions: Who replaces him at third? And who takes over the cleanup spot?

The answer might not come from within the Yankees organization. Strong-armed second baseman Robinson Cano and his emerging power can be shifted from second to third. Or the Yankees could sign Mike Lowell—originally drafted by the Yankees back in 1996—away from the Red Sox. Also, the White Sox' Joe Crede, who had back surgery this summer, will be on the trade market and likely dealt before he becomes a free agent following the 2008 season.

PREVIOUS WINNERS

1998—Mark McGwire, 1b, Cardinals	**2001**—Barry Bonds, of, Giants	**2004**—Barry Bonds, of, Giants
1999—Pedro Martinez, rhp, Red Sox	**2002**—Alex Rodriguez, ss, Rangers	**2005**—Albert Pujols, 1b, Cardinals
2000—Alex Rodriguez, ss, Mariners	**2003**—Barry Bonds, of, Giants	**2006**—Johan Santana, lhp, Twins

But Wait, There's More

Biggio helped ensure June 28 would be a day to remember in baseball history. Just hours after Thomas slugged his 500th home run, the Astros second baseman collected his 3,000th hit in front of the home fans at Houston's Minute Maid Park. In that game, Biggio recorded just the second five-hit game of his 20-year career.

Hit No. 3,000 came on a single to center off Rockies righthander Aaron Cook, though he was thrown out at second while trying to stretch the hit into a double. That was Biggio's third hit of the game. His fifth was an 11th-inning single coming ahead of Carlos Lee's grand slam that gave the Astros an 8-5 victory.

"I couldn't have scripted it any better," said Biggio, who became the 27th player in history with 3,000 hits. "There are a lot of things that have happened over the past 20 years, but this is the best."

Fireworks went off. The counter in left-center field ticked to 3,000. A giant banner with his picture and the number 3,000 was unveiled after the hit.

Biggio had one more dramatic moment left, and that came June 25 when he announced plans to retire at the end of the season, all 20 of which were spent with the Astros. He then hit a grand slam that night off Dodgers righthander Rudy Seanez.

Biggio finished his career with a .281/.363/.433 batting line, 3,060 hits (20th all time), 291 home runs, 1,175 RBIs, 1,844 runs (13th) and 414 stolen bases while playing catcher, second base and center field at various points in his career. Just as significantly, he hit 668 doubles, three more than Hall of Fame third baseman George Brett and the fifth-highest total of all time.

Perhaps if Biggio had played one more season he would have surpassed Hughie Jennings on the all-time hit by pitch list. He finished two shy, with 285.

Glavine notched his 300th win on Aug. 5 in an 8-3 Mets win against the Cubs at Wrigley Field. The feat nearly got lost on a monumental weekend in which Bonds tied Aaron's record and Rodriguez hit his 500th home run the day before.

Glavine pitched 6⅓ innings, allowing two runs and six hits to become the first 300-game winner since former Braves teammate Greg Maddux reached that mark in 2004.

Craig Biggio finished with 3,060 hits (20th all time), 668 doubles (fifth) and 285 hit by pitches (second)

Only one other active pitcher was within 50 wins of 300, and that pitcher, Diamondbacks lefty Randy Johnson, finished the 2007 season on the disabled list after having his second back surgery in less than a year. The 44-year-old Johnson had 284 wins.

"I'm not saying I want to be the last one. I would love for someone to have this feeling and this sense of accomplishment," Glavine said. "If I was the last one, I guess it would be pretty cool to be the last one to do something in the game."

Clemens became the eighth pitcher to reach 350 wins when his Yankees beat the Twins on July 2. That came nearly two months after Clemens announced that he had signed a one-year contract with the Yankees on May 6.

He had also signed an in-season contract with the Astros

AMERICAN LEAGUE STANDINGS

EAST	W	L	PCT	GB	Manager	General Manager	Attendance	Average	Last Penn.
Boston Red Sox	96	66	.593	—	Terry Francona	Theo Epstein	2,970,755	36,676	2007
★New York Yankees	94	68	.580	2	Joe Torre	Brian Cashman	4,271,083	52,729	2003
Toronto Blue Jays	83	79	.512	13	Josh Gibbons	J.P. Ricciardi	2,360,644	29,144	1993
Baltimore Orioles	69	93	.426	27	S.Perlozzo/D.Trembley	Mike Flanagan	2,164,822	27,060	1983
Tampa Bay Devil Rays	66	96	.407	30	Joe Maddon	Andrew Friedman	1,387,603	17,131	None
CENTRAL	**W**	**L**	**PCT**	**GB**	**Manager**	**General Manager**	**Attendance**	**Average**	**Last Penn.**
Cleveland Indians	96	66	.593	—	Eric Wedge	Mark Shapiro	2,275,912	28,449	1997
Detroit Tigers	88	74	.543	8	Jim Leyland	Dave Dombrowski	3,047,133	37,619	2006
Minnesota Twins	79	83	.488	17	Ron Gardenhire	Terry Ryan	2,296,383	28,350	1991
Chicago White Sox	72	90	.444	24	Ozzie Guillen	Ken Williams	2,684,395	33,141	2005
Kansas City Royals	69	93	.426	27	Buddy Bell	Dayton Moore	1,616,867	19,961	1985
WEST	**W**	**L**	**PCT**	**GB**	**Manager**	**General Manager**	**Attendance**	**Average**	**Last Penn.**
Los Angeles Angels	94	68	.580	—	Mike Scioscia	Bill Stoneman	3,365,632	41,551	2002
Seattle Mariners	88	74	.543	6	M.Hargrove/J.McLaren	Bill Bavasi	2,672,223	32,990	None
Oakland Athletics	76	86	.469	18	Bob Geren	Billy Beane	1,921,844	23,726	1990
Texas Rangers	75	87	.463	19	Ron Washington	Jon Daniels	2,353,862	29,423	None

*Won wild card.

PLAYOFFS: Division Series: Boston defeated Los Angeles 3-0 and Cleveland defeated New York 3-1 in best-of-five series.
Championship Series: Boston defeated Cleveland   4-3 in best-of-seven series.

in June 2006.

After breaking Lee Smith's all-time saves record late in the 2006 season, Hoffman notched his 500th save on June 7 when the Padres closer pitched a scoreless ninth to finish out a 5-2 win against the Dodgers.

"It just throws, in a sense, a number out there that becomes sought after," Hoffman said. "I'm respectful of the fact that it is a number that hasn't been achieved, but in the same right, it's only 22 saves beyond what Lee Smith did."

However, his teammates were impressed, particularly Maddux, in his first year with the Padres.

"To have 500 saves is pretty impressive," Maddux said. "He's raised the bar for relievers. He's taken it to a level that the game has never been seen, and it's up to the guys behind him to shoot for. Good luck trying to get there."

Several other milestones were attained in 2007, but got lost in the fray.

Giants shortstop Omar Vizquel, Reds right fielder Ken Griffey Jr., Tigers DH Gary Sheffield and Dodgers left fielder Luis Gonzalez all got to 2,500 hits, while Braves third baseman Chipper Jones and Yankees left fielder Johnny Damon notched their 2,000th hits. Yankees righthander Mike Mussina won his 250th game, and Braves righthander John Smoltz and Yankees lefthander Andy Pettitte each recorded victory No. 200.

Three no-hitters were thrown after none were recorded during the 2006 season.

White Sox lefthander Mark Buehrle threw the first on April 18 against the Rangers at Chicago's U.S. Cellular Field. The only thing that kept Buehrle from a perfect game was a fifth-inning walk to Sosa, whom Buehrle then picked off first base. He faced the minimum 27 batters in the 6-0 win.

"Obviously, I never in a million years thought I'd be able to have this happen," Buehrle said.

Tigers righthander Justin Verlander pitched his gem June 12 in a 4-0 win against the Brewers at Detroit's Comerica Park. His fastball reached speeds as high as 100 mph during a 12-strikeout performance.

Red Sox rookie righthander Clay Buchholz threw his no-hitter in just his second major league start Sept. 1, after being recalled from Triple-A Pawtucket earlier that day

Grady Sizemore, one of the AL's most exciting players, appeared in all 162 games for the second time

LARRY GOREN

when the rosters expanded to 40.

Buchholz became the 17th rookie to throw a no-hitter and the third pitcher since 1900 to throw a no-hitter in his first or second major league start. Bobo Hollomon did it in his first start on May 6, 1953, for the St. Louis Browns against the Philadelphia Athletics, and Wilson Alvarez did it in his second start on Aug. 11, 1991, for the White Sox against the Orioles.

Steroid Use Again Grabs Headlines

As fan reaction to Bonds' home run chase so vividly pointed out, the specter of performance-enhancing drugs continued to hang over the game in 2007.

NATIONAL LEAGUE STANDINGS

EAST	W	L	PCT	GB	Manager	General Manager	Attendance	Average	Last Penn.
Philadelphia Phillies	89	73	.549	—	Charlie Manuel	Pat Gillick	3,108,325	38,374	1993
New York Mets	88	74	.543	1	Willie Randolph	Omar Minaya	3,853,955	47,580	2000
Atlanta Braves	84	78	.519	5	Bobby Cox	John Schuerholz	2,745,207	33,891	1999
Washington Nationals	73	89	.451	16	Manny Acta	Jim Bowden	1,943,812	23,998	None
Florida Marlins	71	91	.438	18	Fredi Gonzalez	Larry Beinfest	1,370,511	16,920	2003
CENTRAL	**W**	**L**	**PCT**	**GB**	**Manager**	**General Manager**	**Attendance**	**Average**	**Last Penn.**
Chicago Cubs	85	77	.525	—	Lou Piniella	Jim Hendry	3,252,462	40,154	1945
Milwaukee Brewers	83	79	.512	2	Ned Yost	Doug Melvin	2,869,144	35,422	None
St. Louis Cardinals	78	84	.481	7	Tony La Russa	Walt Jocketty	3,552,180	43,854	2006
Houston Astros	73	89	.451	12	P.Garner/C.Cooper	Tim Purpura/Tal Smith	3,020,405	37,289	2005
Cincinnati Reds	72	90	.444	13	J.Narron/P.Mackanin	Wayne Krivsky	2,058,593	25,415	1990
Pittsburgh Pirates	68	94	.420	17	Jim Tracy	Dave Littlefield	1,749,142	22,141	1979
WEST	**W**	**L**	**PCT**	**GB**	**Manager**	**General Manager**	**Attendance**	**Average**	**Last Penn.**
Arizona Diamondbacks	90	72	.556	—	Bob Melvin	Josh Byrnes	2,325,249	28,707	2001
*Colorado Rockies	90	73	.552	½	Clint Hurdle	Dan O'Dowd	2,376,250	28,979	2007
San Diego Padres	89	74	.546	1½	Bud Black	Kevin Towers	2,790,074	34,445	1998
Los Angeles Dodgers	82	80	.506	8	Grady Little	Ned Colletti	3,857,036	47,618	1988
San Francisco Giants	71	91	.438	19	Bruce Bochy	Brian Sabean	3,223,215	39,793	2002

*Won wild card.

PLAYOFFS: Division Series: Arizona defeated Chicago 3-0 and Colorado defeated Philadelphia 3-0 in best-of-five series.
Championship Series: Colorado defeated Arizona 4-0 in best-of-seven series.

A number of players were implicated when the Albany, N.Y., district attorney targeted a network of anti-aging clinics and online pharmacies for alleged illegal sales of steroids and growth hormone, including Indians right-hander Paul Byrd, Cardinals right fielder Rick Ankiel, Blue Jays third baseman Troy Glaus, Angels center fielder Gary Matthews Jr., Orioles left fielder Jay Gibbons, Mets lefthander Scott Schoeneweis and Rangers utilityman Jerry Hairston Jr.

The biggest bombshell hit on the day of Game Seven of the American League Championship Series when the San Francisco Chronicle reported that investigators had found that Byrd bought nearly $25,000 worth of human growth hormone (HGH) from 2002 to 2005. Thus, Byrd was forced to face the media and explain the situation just hours before his team lost to the Red Sox.

That Byrd's name was associated with performance-enhancing drugs was shocking because the slight right-hander had a hard time reaching 90 mph with his fastball. Byrd acknowledged using HGH for a medical condition, but claimed he never injected the banned drug without a doctor's prescription.

"I have nothing to hide," Byrd said. "Everything has been done out in the open. I have a reputation. I speak to kids. I speak to churches. I do not want the fans of Cleveland or honest, caring people to think that I cheated, because I didn't."

Baseball did not ban HGH until Jan. 13, 2005. Byrd made his final purchase of HGH a week earlier, the newspaper reported. Byrd claimed he took the drugs because he had a tumor at the base of his pituitary gland that caused insomnia.

Rick Ankiel   The New York Daily News reported in September that Ankiel bought HGH, tainting what had been an engaging comeback story by the pitcher-turned-outfielder.

Ankiel returned to the major leagues on Aug. 9 for the first time since washing out as a pitcher three years earlier. He hit 32 home runs in 102 minor league games with Triple-A Memphis, and proceeded to hit .285 with 11 homers and 39 RBIs in 47 games with the Cardinals.

Ankiel won 11 games as a rookie pitcher in 2000 but then was beset with severe control problems that in 2005 persuaded the Cardinals to convert him into an outfielder. He then missed the entire 2006 season with a serious knee injury he sustained in spring training.

Meanwhile, MLB's investigation into steroid use stretched into its second year under the direction of George Mitchell, the former Senate majority leader. Yankees first baseman Jason Giambi became the first known active player to agree to talk with Mitchell, after facing the possibility of suspension when he admitted to USA Today that he had a "personal history regarding steroids."

Giambi escaped punishment from Selig, though, because of his charitable work and cooperation with Mitchell.

"It's over and done with. I'm thrilled with it. He did what he needed to do. Now I can go forward," Giambi said.

"He's doing a lot of public-service work, and I think that's terribly important," Selig said. "I think it's more important for us to keep getting the message out. He was, I thought, very frank and candid with Senator Mitchell, at least that was the senator's conclusion. Given everything, this is an appropriate decision."

AMERICAN LEAGUE: BEST TOOLS

A Baseball America survey of American League managers, conducted at midseason 2007, ranked players with the best tools:

BEST HITTER
1. Ichiro Suzuki, Mariners
2. Derek Jeter, Yankees
3. Magglio Ordonez, Tigers

BEST POWER
1. Alex Rodriguez, Yankees
2. Justin Morneau, Twins
3. Vladimir Guerrero, Angels

BEST BUNTER
1. Ichiro Suzuki, Mariners
2. Kenny Lofton, Rangers
3. Luis Castillo, Twins

BEST STRIKE-ZONE JUDGMENT
1. Travis Hafner, Indians
2. Bob Abreu, Yankees
3. Placido Polanco, Tigers

BEST HIT-&-RUN ARTIST
1. Placido Polanco, Tigers
2. Derek Jeter, Yankees
3. Orlando Cabrera, Angels

BEST BASERUNNER
1. Ichiro Suzuki, Mariners
2. Brian Roberts, Orioles
3. Derek Jeter, Yankees

FASTEST BASERUNNER
1. Carl Crawford, Devil Rays
2. Ichiro Suzuki, Mariners
3. Joey Gathright, Royals

MOST EXCITING PLAYER
1. Ichiro Suzuki, Mariners
2. Grady Sizemore, Indians
3. Carl Crawford, Devil Rays

BEST PITCHER
1. Johan Santana, Twins
2. Dan Haren, Athletics
3. Josh Beckett, Red Sox

BEST FASTBALL
1. Justin Verlander, Tigers
2. Joel Zumaya, Tigers
3. Felix Hernandez, Mariners

BEST CURVEBALL
1. Josh Beckett, Red Sox
2. Justin Verlander, Tigers
3. Francisco Rodriguez, Angels

BEST SLIDER
1. Jeremy Bonderman, Tigers
2. Scott Kazmir, Devil Rays
3. C.C. Sabathia, Indians

BEST CHANGEUP
1. Johan Santana, Twins
2. James Shields, Devil Rays
3. Daisuke Matsuzaka, Red Sox

BEST CONTROL
1. Paul Byrd, Indians
2. Johan Santana, Twins
3. Roy Halladay, Blue Jays

BEST PICKOFF MOVE
1. Andy Pettitte, Yankees
2. Kenny Rogers, Tigers
3. Mark Buehrle, White Sox

BEST RELIEVER
1. Jonathan Papelbon, Red Sox
2. J.J. Putz, Mariners
3. Mariano Rivera, Yankees

BEST DEFENSIVE C
1. Ivan Rodriguez, Tigers
2. Joe Mauer, Twins
3. Jason Varitek, Red Sox

BEST DEFENSIVE 1B
1. Mark Teixeira, Rangers
2. Carlos Pena, Devil Rays
3. Casey Kotchman, Angels

BEST DEFENSIVE 2B
1. Luis Castillo, Twins
2. Placido Polanco, Tigers
3. Brian Roberts, Orioles

BEST DEFENSIVE 3B
1. Eric Chavez, Athletics
2. Adrian Beltre, Mariners
3. Mike Lowell, Red Sox

BEST DEFENSIVE SS
1. Derek Jeter, Yankees
2. Orlando Cabrera, Angels
3. Yuniesky Betancourt, Mariners

BEST INFIELD ARM
1. Adrian Beltre, Mariners
2. Brandon Inge, Tigers
3. Yuniesky Betancourt, Mariners

BEST DEFENSIVE OF
1. Ichiro Suzuki, Mariners
2. Torii Hunter, Twins
3. Vernon Wells, Blue Jays

BEST OUTFIELD ARM
1. Ichiro Suzuki, Mariners
2. Vladimir Guerrero, Angels
3. Delmon Young, Devil Rays

BEST MANAGER
1. Jim Leyland, Tigers
2. Mike Scioscia, Angels
3. Ron Gardenhire, Twins

In late April, former Mets clubhouse assistant Kirk Radomski pleased guilty to felony charges of distributing steroids to major leaguers and to laundering money. While no names leaked out from that investigation by the federal government, Radomski, who worked for the Mets from 1985 to 1995, did agree to cooperate with Mitchell.

"This individual was a major dealer of anabolic steroids, including human growth hormones, whose clientele was focused almost exclusively on major league players," said

CONTINUED ON PAGE 15

Record-setting bat propels Braun

BY TOM HAUDRICOURT

MILWAUKEE

ROOKIE OF THE YEAR

It's almost as if there are two Ryan Brauns.

There's Ryan Braun, the offensive prodigy, a slugger who never blinked an eye when facing major league pitching for the first time and seemingly could do whatever he wanted at the plate.

Then there's Ryan Braun, third baseman-in-training, capable of making errors on the easiest of plays while also showing his athleticism with web gems on occasion.

Add it all up, and the offensive fireworks overshadow the defensive shortcomings and make the Brewers determined to keep Braun at third base until proven otherwise. It also made him our Rookie of the Year.

"He shouldn't even look at a bat this winter," manager Ned Yost said. "Instead, he should take 100, 150 ground balls a day. It's a matter of repetition and experience over there."

When they selected Braun with the fifth pick of the 2005 draft, the Brewers knew he needed fine-tuning at third base.

"You always knew he would be a pretty good player," Brewers scouting director Jack Zduriencik said. "But honestly, for anybody to do what he has done this quickly is a pleasant surprise. To see him doing the things he has been doing, we're all proud."

The Brewers opened the season with a platoon of veterans, Craig Counsell and Tony Graffanino, at third base, but both struggled mightily at the plate. Meanwhile, Braun, 23, was taking apart Pacific Coast League pitching, batting .344/.418/.701 in 34 games.

Unable to wait any longer, the Brewers summoned Braun on May 25 and plugged him into the starting lineup. All they were asking of him was to bat third for a club leading the NL Central and looking for its first playoff berth in 25 years.

Batting ahead of NL home run champ Prince Fielder no doubt helped, but Braun seemed impervious to slumps, rarely going more than a game or two without a hit. When the smoke cleared at the end of the season, he had hit .324/.370/.634 in 113 games, with 26 doubles, six triples, 34 homers and 97 RBIs.

Braun's slugging percentage was the highest by a rookie in major league history (minimum 400 at-bats), easily topping the mark of .618 established by Oakland's Mark McGwire in 1987. He absolutely crushed lefties, batting .450/.516/.964 with 15 homers in 111 at-bats.

"He's got tremendously quick hands and really hits through the ball," Brewers hitting coach Jim Skaalen said. "He stays on the ball as well as anyone we've got. You watch his swing in slow motion and it's so long after contact, which is what we try to get everybody to do."

Braun finished with 26 errors in 111 starts at third base, including one dreadful three-error game against the Padres in the final series of the season. He finished with a .895 fielding percentage.

"I think Braunie's biggest problem is reading the ball off the bat," Brewers coach Dale Sveum said. "He's gotten a lot better on the routine plays, has gotten a lot better with his throws."

Ryan Braun posted a rookie-record .634 slugging

DAVID STONER

TOP 20 ROOKIES

1. Ryan Braun, 3b, Brewers
2. Troy Tulowitzki, ss, Rockies
3. Dustin Pedroia, 2b, Red Sox
4. Chris Young, of, Diamondbacks
5. Hunter Pence, of, Astros
6. Daisuke Matsuzaka, rhp, Red Sox
7. Tim Lincecum, rhp, Giants
8. Jeremy Guthrie, rhp, Orioles
9. James Loney, 1b, Dodgers
10. Kevin Kouzmanoff, 3b, Padres
11. Yovani Gallardo, rhp, Brewers
12. Brian Bannister, rhp, Royals
13. Delmon Young, of, Devil Rays
14. Mark Reynolds, of, Diamondbacks
15. Joakim Soria, rhp, Royals
16. Kyle Kendrick, rhp, Phillies
17. Alex Gordon, 3b, Royals
18. Micah Owings, rhp, Diamondbacks
19. Yunel Escobar, ss, Braves
20. Josh Hamilton, of, Reds

Tulowitzki

Matsuzaka

PREVIOUS WINNERS

1989—Gregg Olson, rhp, Orioles	1995—Hideo Nomo, rhp, Dodgers	2001—Albert Pujols, of/3b/1b, Cardinals
1990—Sandy Alomar, c, Indians	1996—Derek Jeter, ss, Yankees	2002—Eric Hinske, 3b, Blue Jays
1991—Jeff Bagwell, 1b, Astros	1997—Nomar Garciaparra, ss, Red Sox	2003—Brandon Webb, rhp, D'backs
1992—Pat Listach, ss, Brewers	1998—Kerry Wood, rhp, Cubs	2004—Khalil Greene, ss, Padres
1993—Mike Piazza, c, Dodgers	1999—Carlos Beltran, of, Royals	2005—Huston Street, rhp, Athletics
1994—Raul Mondesi, of, Dodgers	2000—Rafael Furcal, ss/2b, Braves	2006—Justin Verlander, rhp, Tigers

NATIONAL LEAGUE: BEST TOOLS

A Baseball America survey of National League managers, conducted at midseason 2007, ranked players with the best tools:

BEST HITTER
1. Matt Holliday, Rockies
2. Albert Pujols, Cardinals
3. Miguel Cabrera, Marlins

BEST POWER
1. Prince Fielder, Brewers
2. Ryan Howard, Phillies
3. Adam Dunn, Reds

BEST BUNTER
1. Juan Pierre, Dodgers
2. Willy Taveras, Rockies
3. Omar Vizquel, Giants

BEST STRIKE-ZONE JUDGMENT
1. Barry Bonds, Giants
2. Todd Helton, Rockies
3. Albert Pujols, Cardinals

BEST HIT-&-RUN ARTIST
1. Paul LoDuca, Mets
2. Mark Loretta, Astros
3. David Eckstein, Cardinals

BEST BASERUNNER
1. Jose Reyes, Mets
2. Hanley Ramirez, Marlins
3. Juan Pierre, Dodgers

FASTEST BASERUNNER
1. Jose Reyes, Mets
2. Willy Taveras, Rockies
3. Rafael Furcal, Dodgers

MOST EXCITING PLAYER
1. Jose Reyes, Mets
2. Hanley Ramirez, Marlins
3. Matt Holliday, Rockies

BEST PITCHER
1. Jake Peavy, Padres
2. Brad Penny, Dodgers
3. John Smoltz, Braves

BEST FASTBALL
1. Billy Wagner, Mets
2. Brad Penny, Dodgers
3. Derrick Turnbow, Brewers

BEST CURVEBALL
1. Ben Sheets, Brewers
2. Roy Oswalt, Astros
3. Cole Hamels, Phillies

BEST SLIDER
1. John Smoltz, Braves
2. Jake Peavy, Padres
3. Carlos Zambrano, Cubs

BEST CHANGEUP
1. Trevor Hoffman, Padres
2. Tom Glavine, Mets
3. Cole Hamels, Phillies

BEST CONTROL
1. Greg Maddux, Padres
2. John Smoltz, Braves
3. Ben Sheets, Brewers

BEST PICKOFF MOVE
1. Chris Capuano, Brewers
2. Doug Davis, Diamondbacks
3. Jason Simontacchi, Nationals

BEST RELIEVER
1. Trevor Hoffman, Padres
2. Takashi Saito, Dodgers
3. Francisco Cordero, Brewers

BEST DEFENSIVE C
1. Russell Martin, Dodgers
2. Yadier Molina, Cardinals
3. Brad Ausmus, Astros

BEST DEFENSIVE 1B
1. Derrek Lee, Cubs
2. Adrian Gonzalez, Padres
3. Albert Pujols, Cardinals

BEST DEFENSIVE 2B
1. Orlando Hudson, Diamondbacks
2. Chase Utley, Phillies
3. Freddy Sanchez, Pirates

BEST DEFENSIVE 3B
1. Scott Rolen, Cardinals
2. Ryan Zimmerman, Nationals
3. David Wright, Mets

BEST DEFENSIVE SS
1. Jose Reyes, Mets
2. Omar Vizquel, Giants
3. Jimmy Rollins, Phillies

BEST INFIELD ARM
1. Jose Reyes, Mets
2. Rafael Furcal, Dodgers
3. Troy Tulowitzki, Rockies

BEST DEFENSIVE OF
1. Andruw Jones, Braves
2. Carlos Beltran, Mets
3. Mike Cameron, Padres

BEST OUTFIELD ARM
1. Jeff Francoeur, Braves
2. Carlos Beltran, Mets
3. Shane Victorino, Phillies

BEST MANAGER
1. Bobby Cox, Braves
2. Tony La Russa, Cardinals
3. Ned Yost, Brewers

"I have a very strong feeling about it since (Bonds) was on the program. And like everyone else, the program consisted of the clear," Arnold told HBO Sports, referring to one of the steroids-based creams he devised for BALCO. "To me, it was implicit that whoever (Conte) worked with was on the program."

MLB began suspending players for amphetamine use in 2007, with Tigers infielder Neifi Perez the first to be penalized in July. He was suspended twice, the first time for 25 days and the second time for 80 days. Players did not incur suspensions until their second failed test, so Perez' suspensions were the result of his second and third failed tests.

Padres center fielder Mike Cameron became the second player suspended on Oct. 31, the day after he filed for free agency.

The only major leaguer suspended for using a performance-enhancing substance was Devil Rays righthander Juan Salas, who received a 50-game penalty.

NL Races Go Down To The Wire

While the postseason turned out to be one of the dullest in history, the regular season had plenty of thrilling finishes in the National League. None of the four playoffs spots were clinched until the second-to-last-day of the season, and the Rockies and Padres needed a one-game playoff to determine the wild card winner.

That game was a thriller, at least, as the Padres scored two runs in the top of the 13th inning only to lose in the bottom half when Hoffman, baseball's all-time saves leader, coughed up three runs. Left fielder Matt Holliday scored the winning run as he raced home from third base on Jamey Carroll's shallow sacrifice fly, giving the Rockies a 9-8 victory and their second playoff berth in 15 seasons.

The Rockies won 14 of their last 15 games to make the playoffs, overcoming a 5½-game deficit in the wild card race with two weeks left in the season.

The Phillies clinched their first NL East title and playoff berth in 14 years on the final day of the season, taking advantage of a monumental collapse by the Mets, who held a seven-game lead with 17 games to play.

Tied going into the final day of the season, the Phillies prevailed when they beat the Nationals at home 6-1 while the Mets got crushed by the Marlins 8-1 at home.

The Cubs became the first NL team to clinch a playoff spot, claiming the Central Division by two games over the Brewers. They defeated the Reds 6-0 in Cincinnati on the second-to-last day of the season to clinch, completing a worst-to-first leap in the division after spending nearly $300 million on free agents the previous winter.

Fitting for the wacky NL races, the Diamondbacks won the Western Division on the penultimate night of the season despite getting thumped 11-1 at Colorado. That didn't prevent Diamondbacks righthander Livan Hernandez from purchasing six $400 bottles of Cristal champagne to celebrate.

In 2006, the Diamondbacks and Rockies tied for last place in the division.

What the AL playoff races lacked in drama they made up for with superior teams. All four of the league's postseason participants were determined by the middle of the final week; not coincidentally, the teams boasted the four best records in baseball.

The Red Sox ended the Yankees' run of nine straight AL East titles, but the Yankees themselves overcame a 21-29 start and 9½-game deficit in the wild card race as of July 7.

"It's as good as it gets," Red Sox owner John Henry said

Matt Parrella, a federal prosecutor in San Francisco.

According to a search warrant executed by investigators, Radomski became a major source of performance-enhancing drugs for baseball players after federal investigators shut down BALCO in Burlingame, Calif. The same federal investigators who netted guilty pleas from BALCO founder Victor Conte and Bonds' personal trainer, Greg Anderson, were handling the Radomski case.

Bonds and Sheffield were previously implicated as steroid users by Patrick Arnold, a chemist who went to jail for distributing steroids to athletes in the case stemming from the 2003 raid of BALCO.

Though he hit just .237, Chris Young slugged 32 home runs, nearly becoming the first 30-30 rookie

after the franchise won its first division title in 12 years. "To win the division, that's what you want to do."

The Yankees, meanwhile, celebrated the wild card berth as much as any of their division titles. It was an emotional comeback for the Yankees as they clinched their 13th consecutive playoff berth despite the awful start.

"Everybody counted us out. Everybody," closer Mariano Rivera said. "But we hung in there."

The Indians captured their first AL Central title in six years, one year after finishing 18 games out of first. Things started slowly for Cleveland as they were snowed out of their first three home games then had to move their next three games against the Angels to Milwaukee because of the inclement weather.

"Somewhere among the snow, the craziness and the injuries, this team became a family," pitcher Paul Byrd said.

The Angels won their third AL West crown in four years, winning their division despite the inability to land a big hitter during the previous offseason. However, they got a boost from such second-year regulars as righthander Jered Weaver and second baseman Howie Kendrick.

"A lot of things we planned on over the winter didn't really materialize," Angels manager Mike Scioscia said. "We had an incredible amount of injuries. I think that all the young kids that are in that room at any time, they kept us going."

Individual Achievement

The extra day added to the NL season because of the tie between the Rockies and Padres for the wild card also carried the race for the league's batting title into extra innings.

Holliday finished at .340, three points ahead of Chipper Jones. But heading into game No. 162, Holliday's advantage was practically the slimmest possible, .3397 to .3392. He put distance between them by going 1-for-3 against the Diamondbacks then 2-for-6 in the playoff against the

ROOKIE WONDERS

20 HOMERS, 20 STEALS

Young narrowly missed becoming baseball's first 30-30 rookie, falling three stolen bases short. Note that six of the eight 20-20 rookies did it in eras of high offense—in 1987 when everybody was hitting homers or post-1995 when run scoring climbed to near-historic heights.

Player, Team	Year	Age	HR	SB
Chris Young, Diamondbacks	2007	23	32	27
Carlos Beltran, Royals#	1999	22	22	27
Nomar Garciaparra, Red Sox	1997	23	30	20
Marty Cordova, Twins	1995	25	24	20
Devon White, Angels#	1987	24	24	32
Ellis Burks, Red Sox	1987	22	20	27
Mitchell Page, Athletics★	1977	25	21	42
Tommie Agee, White Sox	1966	23	22	44

★Bats lefthanded. # Switch-hitter.

HOME RUN LEADERS

It's hard to believe with the great rookie classes we've seen recently, but Braun and Young became just the second and third rookies to swat 30 or more homers in a season since 1987, when both McGwire and Nokes did.

No.	Player, Team	Year	Age	HR
1.	Mark McGwire, Athletics	1987	23	49
2.	Wally Berger, Braves	1930	24	38
	Frank Robinson, Reds	1956	20	38
4.	Al Rosen, Indians	1950	26	37
	Albert Pujols, Cardinals	2001	21	37
6.	Hal Trosky, Indians★	1934	21	35
	Rudy York, Tigers	1937	23	35
	Ron Kittle, White Sox	1983	25	35
	Mike Piazza, Dodgers	1993	24	35
10.	Ryan Braun, Brewers	2007	23	34
	Walt Dropo, Red Sox	1950	27	34
12.	Jimmie Hall, Twins★	1963	25	33
	Earl Williams, Braves	1971	22	33
	Jose Canseco, Athletics	1986	21	33
15.	Chris Young, Diamondbacks	2007	23	32
	Tony Oliva, Twins★	1964	25	32
	Matt Nokes, Tigers★	1987	23	32

★Bats lefthanded.

200 STRIKEOUTS

Though Matsuzaka's season seemed like a mild disappointment because he went just 5-6, 5.19 in the second half, he became the 11th rookie since 1946 to strike out 200 batters in a season.

No.	Pitcher, Team	Year	Age	SO
1.	Dwight Gooden, Mets	1984	20	276
2.	Herb Score, Indians★	1955	22	245
3.	Hideo Nomo, Dodgers	1995	26	236
4.	Kerry Wood, Cubs	1998	21	233
5.	John Montefusco, Giants	1975	25	215
6.	Don Sutton, Dodgers	1966	21	209
7.	Gary Nolan, Reds	1967	19	206
	Bob Johnson, Royals	1970	27	206
9.	Mark Langston, Mariners★	1984	23	204
10.	Daisuke Matsuzaka, Red Sox	2007	26	201
11.	Tom Griffin, Astros	1969	21	200

★Throws lefthanded.

Padres. Jones finished with an 0-for-5 showing against the Astros to wind up at .337.

"Winning the batting title was great, but making the playoffs was better," Holliday said.

Tigers right fielder Magglio Ordonez took the AL batting crown with a .363 average to easily outdistance Mariners center fielder Ichiro Suzuki, who hit .351.

"It means a lot. To tell you the truth, I don't know how

I did it, but I did it," Ordonez said. "You always have your goals, but sometimes you don't get your goals. But this time I surpassed my goal and it was amazing."

Rodriguez won his fifth AL home run title with 54, giving him the third-most titles in league history behind Babe Ruth's 11 and Harmon Killebrew's six. Brewers first baseman Prince Fielder won his first NL home run crowd with 50 and joined his father Cecil, who belted 51 for Detroit in 1990, in becoming the first father-son tandem to reach 50. At 23, Prince Fielder also became the youngest player ever to hit 50. Willie Mays was 24 when he reached that plateau in 1955.

Rodriguez also led the AL with 156 RBIs, joining Ruth, Hack Wilson, Jimmie Foxx and Sammy Sosa as the only players with 50 homers and 150 RBIs in a season. With 137 RBIs, Holliday tallied one more than Phillies first baseman Ryan Howard, again using the wild card playoff to his advantage. Holliday drove in two runs in the Rockies' 163rd game.

Rodriguez' 143 runs topped the AL and were most in the league since Rickey Henderson scored 146 in 1985. Phillies shortstop Jimmy Rollins paced the NL with 139 and also shattered the major league record with 716 at-bats, eclipsing the old mark of 705 set by Willie Wilson in 1980.

Suzuki led the AL in hits for the fourth time in his career with 238, while Holliday was first in the NL with 216.

Cardinals first baseman Albert Pujols became the first player to hit .300 with 30 home runs and 100 RBIs in each of his first seven seasons. He finished with a .327 average, 32 homers and 103 RBIs.

Tigers center fielder Curtis Granderson became the first major leaguer to hit as many as 23 triples in 58 years. Dale Mitchell also hit 23 in 1949. Granderson also carved out a unique place in history by accumulating 20 or more doubles, triples, homers and stolen bases, becoming the third player ever to do so. Rollins joined him a few weeks later as the fourth player.

Mets shortstop Jose Reyes easily led the major leagues with 78 stolen bases (in 99 tries), marking the third straight year he paced the NL. Devil Rays left fielder Carl Crawford and Orioles second baseman Brian Roberts tied for the AL crown with 50. Crawford had led the league outright in 2003, 2004 and 2006.

Bonds set a major league record by leading the NL in walks for the 12th time in his career (and in seven of the last eight seasons), drawing 132 bases on balls. Ruth had held the record with 11 walks titles. Red Sox DH David Ortiz led the AL for the second straight season with 111. Howard broke the major league record with 199 strikeouts, surpassing the previous mark of 195 set by Adam Dunn in 2004.

Padres righthander Jake Peavy led the NL with a 2.54 ERA, a title he also won in 2004, while Angels righthander John Lackey topped the AL with a 3.01 mark. Red Sox righthander Josh Beckett went 20-7, 3.27 to become the major leagues' first 20-game winner since 2005. Peavy finished 19-6 to lead the NL. Diamondbacks righthander Brandon Webb led the major leagues with four complete games, the lowest figure ever to lead a league.

Peavy started the wild card playoff game, in which he recorded six strikeouts, giving him the edge needed to lead the majors with 240. Devil Rays lefthander Scott Kazmir held that distinction after 162 games, but he fell one short at 239.

The Diamondbacks led the NL with 90 wins, the fewest ever by the league leader since the 162-game schedule took effect in 1961. The 1974 Orioles and 1983 Los Angeles

BILL NICHOLS

Joe Torre stepped down as Yankees manager having won four World Series in 12 seasons at the helm

Dodgers shared the previous low with 91. The Pirates went 68-94 for the franchise's 15th consecutive losing season, one short of the major league record set by the Phillies from 1933 to 1948.

For the only the second time in history, no team finished with a winning percentage of .600 or higher or a losing percentage of .400 or lower. The other time that occurred was in 2000.

Changes At The Top

It was a year of upheaval with managers and general manager. Eight managers either quit or were fired, and eight clubs made GM changes.

The most fascinating managerial change involved Joe Torre's departure from the Yankees after 12 seasons, each of which included a trip to the postseason. He quickly accepted the same job with the Dodgers following Grady Little's resignation a month after the season.

Torre turned down a one-year contract offer from the Yankees that would have guaranteed him $5 million with $1 million in performance bonuses for winning the AL Division Series, AL Championship Series and World Series. A World Series appearance also would have automatically trigged an option year for 2009.

Coming off a three-year, $19.2 million contract that paid him $7.5 million in 2007, Torre was insulted and rejected the offer. The Yankees said they offered the incentive-based contract because they had not been to the World Series since 2003, and had not won since 2000, despite having baseball's highest payroll each season.

"The fact that somebody is reducing your salary is just telling me they're not satisfied with what you're doing," said Torre, who had a 1,942-1,173 (.605) regular season record and won four World Series and six pennants as Yankees' manager from 1996 to 2007. "There really was no negotiation

CONTINUED ON PAGE 19

Good things come to those who wait

BY TRACY RINGOLSBY

DENVER

ORGANIZATION OF THE YEAR

Rookie shortstop Troy Tulowitzki played a large role in the Rockies return to relevance

After 10 years of wondering what a September that mattered would feel like, Rockies first baseman Todd Helton found out.

It was as good as he ever imagined, and then some.

And for his teammates, what made the Rockies' strong finish to claim the National League wild card so special was what a postseason appearance meant to Helton.

"When you have a player who has meant as much to a franchise as Todd has to the Rockies, and you realize he has never had a chance to be in a playoff, it makes what we are going through mean that much more to me," Rockies left fielder Matt Holliday said. "Most of us have been around three, four years, and we think about the struggles we've been through. Todd's been playing 10 years, waiting for this."

Helton has meant a lot to the Rockies, and it extends past his on-field accomplishments, which include a batting title, five all-star selections and three Gold Gloves.

"Todd is the guy who used to call me in the minor leagues, back when I was in the lower levels, when most people thought I was a crappy player, and he'd tell me how good I was going to be," Holliday said. "He's the guy who would talk about someday we'd be hitting third, fourth in the lineup. He would tell me when that happens we'd have a chance to win."

Looks like Helton may have been right when he was offering encouragement to that prospect who never hit more than 16 home runs in a minor league season.

Here's Holliday, who led the NL in batting and RBIs, hitting third, and Helton hitting fourth. And here are the Rockies, not only a postseason team, but one that could be starting a long run of success.

For their build-from-within mindset, the Rockies became our latest Organization of the Year honoree.

Six of the Rockies' eight everyday positions were manned by homegrown players: Helton, Holliday, shortstop Troy Tulowitzki, third baseman Garrett Atkins, right fielder Brad Hawpe and the center fielder, whether it's Ryan Spilborghs or Cory Sullivan. And three of the four starting pitchers were original Rockies—Jeff Francis, Franklin Morales and Ubaldo Jimenez—as well as closer Manny Corpas.

And all were key factors in the Rockies putting on the most dramatic late-season push in history, winning 14 of their final 15 games, including a tiebreaker against the Padres.

"Obviously a lot of people disagreed with the approach and were upset with it," manager Clint Hurdle said. "But I think (winning the wild card) is a tangible sign that we are headed in the right direction."

Helton had played in 1,578 games before his postseason debut, which ranked third among active players this year. (Interestingly, Jeff Cirillo, who was the leader with 1,617 games, also had his streak ended with the Diamondbacks in 2007.) He has been with the Rockies since his career started, and has taken his responsibility to the team seriously.

"We are all enjoying this, but it is more special because of Todd," Hawpe said. "A few years ago when the organization decided to go with (young players), he stood by us, and endorsed the plan, saying he felt we had a good future. Every one of us appreciated that."

The irony is the Rockies came close to trading Helton in the offseason. He agreed to waive his no-trade if a deal could be worked out with the Red Sox. When the talks fell through, however, Helton said he would not consider any future trades. He said he wanted to finish his career where it began, with the Rockies.

"I want to be in a postseason, and most of all, I want to be part of a postseason with the Rockies," Helton said at the time.

PREVIOUS WINNERS

1982—Oakland Athletics	1989—Texas Rangers	1996—Atlanta Braves	2003—Florida Marlins
1983—New York Mets	1990—Montreal Expos	1997—Detroit Tigers	2004—Minnesota Twins
1984—New York Mets	1991—Atlanta Braves	1998—New York Yankees	2005—Atlanta Braves
1985—Milwaukee Brewers	1992—Cleveland Indians	1999—Oakland Athletics	2006—Los Angeles Dodgers
1986—Milwaukee Brewers	1993—Toronto Blue Jays	2000—Chicago White Sox	
1987—Milwaukee Brewers	1994—Kansas City Royals	2001—Houston Astros	
1988—Montreal Expos	1995—New York Mets	2002—Minnesota Twins	

involved. I was hoping there would be but there wasn't."

Former Marlins manager Joe Girardi, who was deposed in Florida the same season he won NL manager of the year honors, was hired as Torre's replacement.

Citing personal reasons, Little claimed reports that the Dodgers were courting Torre had nothing to do with his resignation. The Dodgers lost 11 of their last 14 games to finish 82-80 after winning the NL West the year before. Little went 170-154 in two seasons in Los Angeles.

The Orioles, 29-40 and on an eight-game losing streak, fired Sam Perlozzo on June 18, kicking off the managerial firing season. Bullpen coach Dave Trembley replaced Perlozzo and was given the job on a permanent basis Aug. 22. The Orioles finished 69-93 in their 10th straight losing season.

Perlozzo's firing followed by less than a month the hiring of former Cubs and Twins general manaer Andy MacPhail as Orioles' president of baseball operations. At the end of the season, Orioles vice president Jim Duquette, who served as the de facto GM, left the organization after ceding much of his power to MacPhail.

The Reds fired Jerry Narron on July 1 and replaced him with advance scout Pete Mackanin on an interim basis. Cincinnati went 31-51 under Narron. Though Mackanin led the Reds to a 41-39 record the rest of the way, Cincinnati hired former Giants and Cubs manager Dusty Baker following the season.

Also on July 1, Mike Hargrove surprisingly resigned as Mariners' manager, even though the club was on an eight-game winning streak and in contention for the AL West crown with a 45-33 record. Bench coach John McLaren was given the job for the remainder of the year and, though the Mariners slipped to 43-41 after he took over, received a two-year contract extension at season's end. Hargrove said his passion had begun to fade after 16 seasons as manager for the Indians, Orioles and Mariners.

"There are no dark, sinister reasons for this decision. This has been my decision," Hargrove said. "I have no reason to lie. I don't expect people to understand it. I really don't. Because at times I don't understand it myself."

The Astros fired manager Phil Garner and GM Tim Purpura on Aug. 27, less than two years after the duo led the Astros to their first World Series appearance in 2005. The Astros were 58-73 on their way to a 73-89 finish. Bench coach Cecil Cooper was promoted to interim manager then given a two-year contract at the end of the season. Former Phillies GM Ed Wade, who had been working as a scout for the Padres, was hired to replace Purpura.

"I had a wonderful time with the Astros," said Garner, who had previously managed the Brewers and Tigers. "They reinvigorated my interest in baseball and really gave me a great opportunity to reinvigorate my career. I'm more grateful for the job they gave me than I am saddened and upset by the firing."

Royals manager Buddy Bell announced Aug. 1 that he was stepping down at the end of the season, which Kansas City finished with a 69-93 record. He had successfully beaten throat cancer the previous offseason and said he wanted to spend more time with his family. Bell, who also managed the Tigers and Rockies, then joined the White Sox as director of minor league instruction. Trey Hillman, who spent the previous five seasons managing the Nippon Ham Fighters in Japan, replaced Bell.

Jim Tracy was fired as Pirates' manager at the end of the season after going 135-189 in two years on the job. That came after GM Dave Littlefield was shown the door on Sept.

Phil Rizzuto, Hall of Fame shortstop and longtime Yankees broadcaster, died in August at age 89

THE SPORTS GROUP

7 and replaced by Neal Huntington, a special assistant to the GM with the Indians. The Pirates named John Russell, who had managed the Phillies' Triple-A affiliate in Ottawa in 2007, as Tracy's replacement.

Longtime Braves GM John Schuerholz stepped down after 17 years on the job to become club president, handing the reins to assistant GM Frank Wren. Under Schuerholz the Braves won a major league record 14 division titles from 1991-2005 and the World Series in 1995. The 67-year-old Schuerholz had also spent nine years as the Royals' GM, winning a World Series in 1985. He admitted the grind of the job had worn him down and that his only disappointment was winning just one World Series with the Braves.

"What else is there?" Schuerholz said. "It would have been, unequivocally, the complete validation of the grand nature of this franchise. Nobody could have said anything about the Atlanta Braves and ended the sentence with the word 'but.' "

"John Schuerholz is an unbelievable judge of talent," Braves third baseman Chipper Jones said. "It almost seems like he has a crystal ball."

Schuerholz' move came in a year in which the Braves were the only franchise sold, going to Liberty Media Corp. from Time Warner, Inc., in a deal worth a reported $450 million. It was part of a transaction in which Time Warner transferred the Braves, a group of craft magazines and $1 billion for about 60 million shares of Liberty stock.

One year after winning the World Series, the Cardinals fired GM Walt Jocketty and promoted assistant GM John Mozeliak. The Cardinals made the postseason seven times during Jocketty's 13-year tenure, but he became disenchanted with the front office structure under chairman Bill DeWitt Jr. Jocketty felt that Jeff Luhnow, promoted from a consultant position to head of the Cardinals' player development and scouting departments, had been given too much power and only communicated with him through third parties.

CONTINUED ON PAGE 21

Outfielder Curtis Granderson broke out in a big way, hitting 38 doubles, 23 triples and 23 homers

Righthander Brandon Webb bettered his numbers from 2006, when he won the Cy Young award

FIRST TEAM

POS	PLAYER, TEAM	AVG	OBP	SLG	AB	R	H	2B	3B	HR	RBI	SB	CS	BB	SO
C	Jorge Posada, Yankees	.338	.426	.543	506	91	171	42	1	20	90	2	0	74	98
1B	Prince Fielder, Brewers	.288	.395	.618	573	109	165	35	2	50	119	2	2	90	121
2B	Chase Utley, Phillies	.332	.410	.566	530	104	176	48	5	22	103	9	1	50	89
3B	Alex Rodriguez, Yankees	.314	.422	.645	583	143	183	31	0	54	156	24	4	95	120
SS	Jimmy Rollins, Phillies	.296	.344	.531	716	139	212	38	20	30	94	41	6	49	85
LF	Matt Holliday, Rockies	.340	.405	.607	636	120	216	50	6	36	137	11	4	63	126
CF	Curtis Granderson, Tigers	.302	.361	.552	612	122	185	38	23	23	74	26	1	52	141
RF	Magglio Ordonez, Tigers	.363	.434	.595	595	117	216	54	0	28	139	4	1	76	79
DH	David Ortiz, Red Sox	.332	.445	.621	549	116	182	52	1	35	117	3	1	111	103

	PITCHER, TEAM	W	L	ERA	G	GS	CG	SV	IP	H	BB	SO	HR	G/F	AVG
SP	Jake Peavy, Padres	19	6	2.54	34	34	0	0	223	169	68	240	13	1.24	.208
SP	Brandon Webb, Diamondbacks	18	10	3.01	34	34	4	0	236	209	72	194	12	3.34	.237
SP	C.C. Sabathia, Indians	19	7	3.21	34	34	4	0	241	238	37	209	20	1.35	.259
SP	Josh Beckett, Red Sox	20	7	3.27	30	30	1	0	201	189	40	194	17	1.29	.245
RP	J.J. Putz, Mariners	6	1	1.38	68	0	0	40	72	37	13	82	6	1.01	.153

SECOND TEAM

POS	PLAYER, TEAM	AVG	OBP	SLG	AB	R	H	2B	3B	HR	RBI	SB	CS	BB	SO
C	Victor Martinez, Indians	.301	.374	.505	562	78	169	40	0	25	114	0	0	62	76
1B	Carlos Pena, Devil Rays	.282	.411	.627	490	99	138	29	1	46	121	1	0	103	142
2B	Placido Polanco, Tigers	.341	.388	.458	587	105	200	36	3	9	67	7	3	37	30
3B	David Wright, Mets	.325	.416	.546	604	113	196	42	1	30	107	34	5	94	115
SS	Hanley Ramirez, Marlins	.332	.386	.562	639	125	212	48	6	29	81	51	14	52	95
LF	Adam Dunn, Reds	.264	.386	.554	522	101	138	27	2	40	106	9	2	101	165
CF	Ichiro Suzuki, Mariners	.351	.396	.431	678	111	238	22	7	6	68	37	8	49	77
RF	Vladimir Guerrero, Angels	.324	.403	.547	574	89	186	45	1	27	125	2	3	71	62
DH	Chipper Jones, Braves	.337	.425	.604	513	108	173	42	4	29	102	5	1	82	75

	PITCHER, TEAM	W	L	ERA	G	GS	CG	SV	IP	H	BB	SO	HR	G/F	AVG
SP	Fausto Carmona, Indians	19	8	3.06	32	32	2	0	215	199	61	137	16	3.28	.248
SP	John Lackey, Angels	19	9	3.01	33	33	2	0	224	219	52	179	18	1.25	.254
SP	Erik Bedard, Orioles	13	5	3.16	28	28	1	0	182	141	57	221	19	1.47	.212
SP	Johan Santana, Twins	15	13	3.33	33	33	1	0	219	183	52	235	33	0.92	.225
RP	Jonathan Papelbon, Red Sox	1	3	1.85	59	0	0	37	58	30	15	84	5	0.53	.146

Organization of the Year: Colorado Rockies **Executive of the Year:** Jack Zduriencik, Brewers **Player of the Year:** Alex Rodriguez, Yankees. **Rookie of the Year:** Ryan Braun, Brewers. **Manager of the Year:** Terry Francona, Red Sox

EXECUTIVE OF THE YEAR

JACK ZDURIENCIK, BREWERS

Zduriencik

The first-ever scouting director to be named our executive of the year, Zduriencik helped build the Brewers from the ground up. Players drafted by Zduriencik and his staff began paying dividends in 2005, when the franchise snapped its steak of 12 straight losing seasons, and continued into 2007 as the Brewers challenged for the NL Central title.

The Brewers have identified one regular in each of Zduriencik's first six drafts—though it was too early to evaluate his 2006 and 2007 efforts.

2000: Right fielder Corey Hart (11th round)
2001: Shortstop J.J. Hardy (2nd)
2002: First baseman Prince Fielder (1st)
2003: Second baseman Rickie Weeks (1st)
2004: Righthander Yovani Gallardo (2nd)
2005: Third baseman Ryan Braun (1st)

PREVIOUS WINNERS

Year	Executive, Team	Year	
1998	Doug Melvin, Rangers	2002	Billy Beane, Athletics
1999	Jim Bowden, Reds	2003	Brian Sabean, Giants
2000	Walt Jocketty, Cardinals	2004	Terry Ryan, Twins
2001	Pat Gillick, Mariners	2005	Mark Shapiro, Indians
		2006	Dave Dombrowski, Tigers

MANAGER OF THE YEAR

TERRY FRANCONA, RED SOX

Francona

Francona capped his fourth season at the helm with his second World Series title, becoming the 21st manager in history to win the big prize more than once. One of the others, Bill Carrigan, skippered the Sox to back-to-back titles in 1915 and 1916. (See chart in Postseason, Page 35.)

Among Francona's other accomplishments:

■ His .579 winning percentage ranks second in franchise history, behind only Joe McCarthy (.606 from 1948-50), for Red Sox managers of two or more seasons.

■ He emerged as winning manager from two seven-game AL Championship Series; the first with the Yankees in 2004 included a dramatic comeback from a three-game deficit.

PREVIOUS WINNERS

Year	Manager, Team	Year	
1998	Larry Dierker, Astros	2002	Mike Scioscia, Angels
1999	Jimy Williams, Red Sox	2003	Jack McKeon, Marlins
2000	Dusty Baker, Giants	2004	Bobby Cox, Braves
2001	Lou Piniella, Mariners	2005	Ozzie Guillen, White Sox
		2006	Jim Leyland, Tigers

Despite his club's annual success, Angels GM Bill Stoneman stepped down at the end of the season and was replaced by player development director Tony Reagins. Like so many other GMs, Stoneman, the architect of the franchise's only World Series winning team in 2002, cited the ever-increasing demands of the job as his reason for taking a reduced role as a special adviser to Angels owner Arte Moreno.

That, too, was the reason cited for Twins GM Terry Ryan's move into a senior adviser role after 13 years on the job. Longtime assistant GM Bill Smith was promoted to replace Ryan, who led the small-revenue Twins to four AL Central titles from 2002 to 2006.

Marlins GM Larry Beinfest, like Schuerholz, was promoted to club president. Assistant GM Michael Hill was named as successor to Beinfest, who built the Marlins' 2003 World Series winner.

Passing Of A Yankee Legend

Tragedy struck baseball early on the morning of April 29 when Cardinals righthander Josh Hancock was killed in an automobile accident in St. Louis.

Hancock's sport utility vehicle slammed into the back of a flatbed tow truck that was parked in the left lane on Interstate-64 with its lights flashing while assisting another car that had crashed. The 29-year-old Hancock was intoxicated and talking on his cell phone at 12:35 a.m.

It was the second time in five years that a Cardinals pitcher died during the season. Darryl Kile died in his sleep in a Chicago hotel room in 2002.

"This has obviously been a very difficult time," Cardinals righthander Braden Looper said. "Josh was a great teammate and a great friend to everybody, and he was a key part of our success."

Three days before Hancock's death, the Cardinals got a scare that some teammates said reminded them of Kile, as Hancock overslept and showed up late for a day game in St. Louis. Hancock told the St. Louis Post-Dispatch he thought the starting time was later and didn't get up until the "20th call" from anxious teammates.

Hancock spent six seasons in the major leagues with the Red Sox (2002), Phillies (2003-04), Reds (2004-05) and Cardinals (2006-07), compiling a 9-7, 4.20 record with one save in 102 games, including 12 starts. He pitched in the 2006 postseason with the World Series winning Cardinals.

Hall of Fame shortstop Phil Rizzuto died of pneumonia in his sleep on Aug. 13 at a nursing home in West Orange, N.J., at the age of 89. While Rizzuto made it to the Hall of Fame for his 13 seasons with the Yankees, from 1941-56, "The Scooter" won the hearts of Yankees fans for four decades as a broadcaster.

"I guess heaven must have needed a shortstop," Yankees owner George Steinbrenner said. "He epitomized the Yankee spirit—gritty and hard charging—and he wore the pinstripes proudly."

Rizzuto was the oldest living Hall of Famer and his Cooperstown plaque noted how the 5-foot-6 shortstop "overcame diminutive size." Winner of the 1950 AL MVP award, Rizzuto was a member of seven World Series-winning Yankees teams and was a five-time all-star. He batted .273/.351/.355 with 38 home runs, 563 RBIs and 149 stolen bases in 1,661 games.

Rizzuto's No. 10 was retired by the Yankees, and the club wore his number on its left sleeves for the remainder of the season.

Rizzuto delighted TV and radio listeners with his native Brooklyn accent. He went repeatedly to his catch phrase, exclaiming "Holy Cow!" when Roger Maris hit his 61st home run in 1961, for example—and often used the term huckleberry in a playfully derisive manner.

"He didn't try to act like an announcer," Hall of Fame lefthander and Rizzuto teammate Whitey Ford said. "He just said what he thought. It added fun to the game."

Bowie Kuhn, who served as commissioner from 1969 to 1983 and oversaw baseball's transformation to a business of free agents with multi-million dollar contracts, also died of pneumonia March 15. He was 80.

"He led our game through a great deal of change and controversy," Selig said. "Yet, Bowie laid the groundwork for the success we enjoy today."

When Kuhn took over from William Eckert on Feb. 4, 1969, baseball had just completed its last season as a 20-team sport, a reserve clause and an average salary of just under $19,000.

By the time Peter Ueberroth succeeded Kuhn on Oct. 1, 1984, the major leagues had 26 teams in four divisions, a designated hitter in the AL, the first night World Series games, free agency and an average salary of nearly $330,000.

"I want it to be remembered that I was commissioner during a time of tremendous growth in the popularity of the game," Kuhn said, "and that it was a time in which no one could question the integrity of the game."

Hall of Fame broadcaster Herb Carneal, who called Twins games for 45 years in his soothing baritone voice, died on April 1 at 83 of congestive heart failure.

Carneal joined the Twins in 1962 during the franchise's second year in Minneapolis. He also broadcast Philadelphia Athletics and Orioles games before coming to Minnesota.

"To hear that voice was magic," said former Twins first baseman Kent Hrbek, who grew up in Bloomington, Minn. "When I was a kid, it meant school was almost out and spring was coming."

Hall Of Fame Class Exemplified

Two of the baseball's least controversial superstars, Cal Ripken Jr. and Tony Gwynn, were inducted into the Hall of Fame in Cooperstown, providing contrast in a year in which Bonds chased the all-time home run record.

"This day shouldn't be all about us," Ripken said. "Today is about celebrating the best that baseball has been and the best it can be. This is a symbol it's alive, popular. Whether you like it or not, as big leaguers, we are role models. The only question is, will it be positive or will it be negative?"

Gwynn expressed the same thoughts during his induction speech.

"I think the fans felt comfortable enough in us, they could trust us and how we played the game, especially in this era of negativity," he said. "I don't think there's any question about that. When you sign your name on the dotted line, it's more than just playing the game of baseball. You've got to be responsible and make decisions and show people how things are supposed to be done."

An estimated 75,000 fans turned out for the induction, many coming by bus from Maryland and wearing the black and orange of the Orioles, the team for which Ripken spent his entire 21-year career from 1981 to 2001. Like Ripken, Gwynn spent his entire career with one team, playing 20

STEVE MOORE

Tom Glavine joined Roger Clemens and Greg Maddux as the only active pitchers with 300 wins

seasons with the Padres from 1982 to 2001.

Best known for playing in 2,632 consecutive games and breaking Lou Gehrig's record of 2,130, Ripken hit .276/.340/.447 with 3,184 hits, 431 home runs and 1,695 RBIs in 3,001 games. He was a two-time AL MVP and a 19-time all-star.

Gwynn finished with 3,141 hits and won eight NL batting titles, while hitting .338/.388/.459 with 135 homers and 1,138 RBIs in 2,440 games.

Rick Hummel, longtime baseball writer for the St. Louis Post-Dispatch, received the J.G. Taylor Spink Award for meritorious writing, and Royals announcer Denny Matthews received the Ford C. Frick Award for broadcasting excellence.

After the veterans committee failed to elect anyone for a third straight election, the Hall of Fame's board of directors voted to cut the size of the committee and number of players it will consider for future enshrinement, while also altering the procedures for electing long-retired players, managers, umpires and executives.

Under the new rules, only the 63 living Hall of Famers will cast ballots for players, and a committee of 16—comprised of Hall of Famers, veteran writers, executives and historians—will vote for managers and umpires. Previously, past winners of the Frick and Spink awards were allowed to cast ballots, raising the number of voters to more than 80.

A historical overview committee appointed by the Baseball Writers' Association of America will narrow the list of players to be considered to 20 instead of 200, and a screening committee of six Hall of Famers will identify five players each. That slate of 20-25 players, depending on duplicate selections, will be narrowed to just 10 names by the veterans committee.

Committee members will be allowed to vote for four

CONTINUED ON PAGE 24

AL extends All-Star win streak to 10

ALL-STAR GAME

Ichiro Suzuki has been breaking new ground ever since he made his major league debut in 2001.

The Mariners center fielder became the first position player to come to the United States from Japan. He also set the single-season hit record with 262 in 2004.

So it was fitting Suzuki would hit the first inside-the-park home run in All-Star Game history to lead the American League to a 5-4 win over the National League in the 2007 midsummer classic at AT&T Park in San Francisco. He went 3-for-3 and was named the game's MVP.

Suzuki's two-run homer in the fifth inning came off Padres righthander Chris Young, the game's losing pitcher, and hit an advertisement on the right-center field wall in an area know as the arcade. Instead of bouncing straight back, it caromed toward right field as Reds right fielder Ken Griffey Jr. gave chase.

By the time Griffey finally retrieved the ball, Suzuki was at third and easily made it home with the first inside-the-parker of his major league career. That gave the AL a 2-1 lead they never relinquished in recording its 10th consecutive All-Star victory.

"I thought it was going to go over the fence," Suzuki said through an interpreter. "When it didn't, I was really bummed."

Cubs left fielder Alfonso Soriano hit a two-out home run in the ninth inning to cut the AL lead to 5-4. The NL then loaded the bases on three consecutive walks before Angels righthander Francisco Rodriguez got the last out by inducing Phillies center fielder Aaron Rowand to fly out to right field.

Indians catcher Victor Martinez and Devil Rays left fielder Carl Crawford also homered for the AL, while Red Sox righthander Josh Beckett was the winning pitcher. Mets shortstop Jose Reyes had three hits for the NL.

—JOHN PERROTTO

Shortstop Jose Reyes collected three hits and a stolen base in a losing effort by the NL

BILL NICHOLS

July 10 in San Francisco
American League 5, National League 4

AMERICAN	AB	R	H	BI	NATIONAL	AB	R	H	BI
Suzuki, cf	3	1	3	2	Reyes, ss	4	1	3	0
Hunter, cf	2	0	0	0	Hardy, ss	0	0	0	0
Rodriguez, p	0	0	0	0	Bonds, lf	2	0	0	0
Jeter, ss	3	0	1	0	Hamels, p	0	0	0	0
Sabathia, p	0	0	0	0	Lee, 1b	2	0	1	0
Lowell, 3b	1	1	1	0	Beltran, cf	3	1	1	0
Ortiz, 1b	2	0	0	0	Hudson, 2b	1	0	0	0
Morneau, 1b	2	0	0	0	Griffey, rf	2	0	1	2
Rodriguez, 3b	3	0	1	0	Rowand, cf	2	0	0	0
Verlander, p	0	0	0	0	Wright, 3b	3	0	1	0
Sizemore, rf-cf	1	0	0	0	Sanchez, 3b	1	0	0	0
Guerrero, rf	3	0	0	0	Fielder, 1b	1	0	0	0
Santana, p	0	0	0	0	Young, p	0	0	0	0
Martinez, ph	1	1	1	2	Cordero, p	0	0	0	0
Papelbon, p	0	0	0	0	Holliday, ph-rf	2	0	0	0
Putz, p	0	0	0	0	Martin, c	3	0	0	0
Rios, rf	0	0	0	0	McCann, c	1	0	0	0
Ordonez, lf	2	0	0	0	Utley, 2b	2	0	0	0
Crawford, lf	2	1	1	1	Saito, p	0	0	0	0
Rodriguez, c	2	0	1	0	Lee, ph	1	0	0	0
Guillen, ss	2	0	0	0	Wagner, p	0	0	0	0
Polanco, 2b	1	0	0	0	Hoffman, p	0	0	0	0
Roberts, 2b	2	1	0	0	Young, ph	1	1	1	0
Haren, p	0	0	0	0	Peavy, p	0	0	0	0
Ramirez, ph	1	0	0	0	Penny, p	0	0	0	0
Beckett, p	0	0	0	0	Cabrera, ph	1	0	0	0
Posada, ph-c	3	0	1	0	Sheets, p	0	0	0	0
					Soriano, lf	3	1	1	2
Totals	**36**	**5**	**10**	**5**	**Totals**	**35**	**4**	**9**	**4**

American	000	021	020—5
National	100	001	002—4

LOB—American 5, National 9. **2B**—Posada, Reyes. **3B**—Beltran. **HR**—Suzuki, Crawford, Martinez, Soriano. **GIDP**—Jeter. **SF**—Griffey. **SB**—Rodriguez, Reyes, Lee. **PB**—Posada. **E**—Fielder.

AMERICAN	IP	H	R	ER	BB	SO	NATIONAL	IP	H	R	ER	BB	SO
Haren	2	2	1	1	1	2	Peavy	1	1	0	0	0	0
Beckett W	2	1	0	0	0	2	Penny	1	0	0	0	0	0
Sabathia	1	1	0	0	0	0	Sheets	1	2	0	0	0	0
Verlander	1	2	1	1	0	0	Hamels	1	2	0	0	0	0
Santana	1	0	0	0	0	2	Young BS, L	1	1	2	2	1	0
Papelbon	1	1	0	0	0	2	Cordero	1	1	1	1	0	0
Putz	⅔	2	2	2	1	1	Saito	1	0	0	0	0	0
Rodriguez S	⅓	0	0	0	2	0	Wagner	1	2	2	2	0	1
							Hoffman	1	1	0	0	0	0

Umpires: HP—Bruce Froemming. **1B**—Charlie Reliford. **2B**—Mike Winters. **3B**—Kerwin Danley. **LF**—Ted Barrett. **RF**—Bill Miller. **T**—3:06. **A**—43,965.

BILL NICHOLS

All-Star Game MVP Ichiro Suzuki hit the first inside-the-park home run in the game's history

players and the standard for induction remains 75 percent of the vote.

Players will be voted on every two years in odd years starting in 2009, while a ballot for managers and umpires will be offered every two years instead of every four years beginning in 2008. A BBWAA-appointed committee also will narrow the list of eligible manager/umpire candidates to 10. A board-appointed committee comprised of Hall of Famers, executives and veteran writers will review the ballot of executives.

The Hall of Fame also made 1943 a dividing line. Beginning in 2009, players whose careers began in 1942 or earlier will be reviewed every five years by a board-appointed committee of 12 Hall of Famers, veteran writers, and historians.

Slight Modifications

MLB enacted a new penalty in 2007 in which any position player who scuffs or defaces a baseball would be ejected and receive an automatic 10-game suspension. Previously, the penalty was to call the pitch a

STEVE MOORE

Pedro Martinez

ball and warn the player. For pitchers, umpires were given the discretion to issue only a warning if they determine the pitcher's actions weren't intended to alter the characteristics of a pitch.

As part of the first changes to baseball rules since 1996, MLB's rules committee also approved a recommendation from general managers to largely eliminate tie games.

Prior to 2007, when an official game was called due to weather and the score was tied, the statistics counted and a new game was replayed from the start. Under the change, when a game is tied in the bottom of the fifth inning or later and is called because of weather, it will be suspended and resumed before the next scheduled game between the teams at the same ballpark.

If no more games remain between the teams at the same ballpark, it will be resumed when the teams meet at the visitor's ballpark. If it is the final scheduled meeting between the teams, it will be replayed from the start if it is needed to determine a postseason berth.

Under another change, a player may no longer step into a dugout to catch a foul ball. He still will be allowed to reach into a dugout.

A batter running to first base also will be allowed to exit the three-foot lane in foul territory "for the sole purpose

of touching first base," and a batter will lose the ability to run to first on a dropped third strike if he leaves the dirt circle around home plate unless he does so while trying to reach first base. Previously, a player could run to first until he reached the dugout or his defensive position.

In another change, a batter who hits an apparent game-ending home run with less than two outs would be allowed to circle the bases if a runner ahead of him doesn't continue to home plate, thinking the game is over. If there are two outs when the play begins, however, the runner who abandons trying for home plate would be the third out and the home run would not count.

Another change allows pitchers to wear a multicolored glove if the umpire determines it isn't distracting. Also, a pitcher in the stretch position instead of the windup with no runners on base will no longer have to come to a complete stop. With no runners on, a pitcher will be required to pitch to the plate within 12 seconds, the timing starting when the pitcher is in possession of the ball and the batter is in the batter's box, alert to the pitcher.

Meanwhile, owners approved seven-year "Extra Innings" out-of-market television contracts with DirecTV and iN Demand, deals that guarantee the clubs an average of $80 million annually. Owners also approved the launch of the MLB Network, which Selig said will be available to at least 47 million homes when it starts broadcasting on Jan. 1, 2009.

"That will exceed any other cable channel launch in cable television history by almost 20 million homes," MLB executive vice president Tim Brosnan said, adding that the current high was set by MSNBC, which was available in 28 million homes a year after its launch in 1996.

The MLB Network will broadcast baseball programming 24 hours a day, including a weekly Saturday night live game during the regular season. Brosnan said affiliation agreements were in place with 33 multi-system operators of cable television networks to carry the MLB Network on their widest digital tier. Baseball owns two-thirds of the network, DirecTV owns one-sixth and Comcast, Cox and Time Warner Cable own the remaining sixth.

MLB originally reached an exclusive "Extra Innings" deal with DirecTV that was criticized by some. The deal was a $400 million, four-year contract that gave the company a $300 million, three-year option.

Baseball said goodbye to RFK Stadium for a second time on Sept. 23 as the Nationals, who relocated from Montreal three years earlier, played their final game in their temporary home and beat the Phillies 5-3. The Washington Senators also spent 10 years there from 1962 to 1971 before moving to Texas and becoming the Rangers in 1972.

OFF THE HOT SEAT

Eight teams made managerial changes during or after the 2007 season, headlined by the Yankees decision to part ways with Joe Torre, who managed New York to the playoffs in all 12 of his seasons at the helm.

Team	2007 Manager	Years	PCT	Fate	Date	Interim	2008 Manager
Orioles	Sam Perlozzo	3	.427	Fired	June 18	Dave Trembley	Dave Trembley
Reds	Jerry Narron	3	.467	Fired	July 1	Pete Mackanin	Dusty Baker
Mariners	Mike Hargrove	3	.478	Resigned	July 1	John McLaren	John McLaren
Royals	Buddy Bell	3	.399	Resigned	Aug. 1	None	Trey Hillman
Astros	Phil Garner	4	.524	Fired	Aug. 27	Cecil Cooper	Cecil Cooper
Pirates	Jim Tracy	2	.417	Fired	Oct. 5	None	John Russell
Yankees	Joe Torre	12	.605	Resigned	Oct. 20	None	Joe Girardi
Dodgers	Grady Little	2	.525	Resigned	Oct. 30	None	Joe Torre

ARIZONA DIAMONDBACKS
Barden, Brian	April 3
Bonifacio, Emilio	Sept. 2
Murphy, Bill	Sept. 3
Owings, Micah	April 6
Peguero, Jailen	June 8
Reynolds, Mark	May 16
Schultz, Mike	April 20
Upton, Justin	Aug. 2

ATLANTA BRAVES
Acosta, Manny	Aug. 12
Ascanio, Jose	July 13
Escobar, Yunel	June 2
Jones, Brandon	Sept. 16
Reyes, Jo-Jo	July 7
Saltalamacchia, Jarrod	May 2
Sammons, Clint	Sept. 12

BALTIMORE ORIOLES
Doyne, Cory	June 16
Hernandez, Luis	July 8
Liz, Radhames	Aug. 25
Olson, Garrett	July 4

BOSTON RED SOX
Bailey, Jeff	July 6
Buchholz, Clay	Aug. 17
Ellsbury, Jacoby	June 30
Matsuzaka, Daisuke	June 10
Moss, Brandon	Aug. 6
Okajima, Hideki	June 9

CHICAGO CUBS
Cherry, Rocky	April 23
Fox, Jacob	July 19
Fuld, Sam	Sept. 5
Gallagher, Sean	June 9
Hart, Kevin	Sept. 4
Patterson, Eric	Aug. 6
Petrick, Billy	June 27
Pie, Felix	April 17
Pignatiello, Carmen	Aug. 16
Rapada, Clay	June 14

CHICAGO WHITE SOX
FBroadway, Lance	Sept. 7
Danks, John	June 13
Day, Dewon	June 15
Gonzalez, Andy	April 25
Lucy, Donny	Sept. 5
Molina, Gustavo	April 2
Phillips, Heath	Sept. 30
Richar, Danny	July 28
Wassermann, Ehren	Sept. 28

CINCINNATI REDS
Bailey, Homer	June 8
Burton, Jared	April 4
Coutlangus, Jon	April 7
Dumatrait, Phil	Aug. 2
Hamilton, Josh	April 2
Hanigan, Ryan	Sept. 9
McBeth, Marcus	June 6
Salmon, Brad	May 1
Shearn, Tom	Aug. 26
Votto, Joey	Sept. 4

CLEVELAND INDIANS
Cabrera, Asdrubal	Aug. 8
Francisco, Ben	May 1
Laffey, Aaron	Aug. 4
Lewis, Jensen	July 16

COLORADO ROCKIES
Arias, Alberto	May 1
Barker, Sean	June 6
Bellorin, Edwin	Aug. 7
Clarke, Darren	May 18
Koshansky, Joe	Sept. 1
McClellan, Zach	April 16
Morales, Franklin	Aug. 18
Newman, Josh	Sept. 12
Smith, Seth	Sept. 16
Stewart, Ian	Aug. 11

DETROIT TIGERS
De La Cruz, Eulogio	June 18
Jurrjens, Jair	Aug. 15
Maybin, Cameron	Aug. 17
Vasquez, Virgil	May 13

FLORIDA MARLINS
Barone, Daniel	Aug. 10
Carroll, Brett	June 17
De Aza, Alejandro	April 2
Garcia, Harvey	Sept. 3
Lindstrom, Matt	April 4
Seddon, Chris	Sept. 3
Vanden Hurk, Rick	April 10
Wolf, Ross	Aug. 10
Zarate, Mauro	Aug. 7

HOUSTON ASTROS
Anderson, Josh	Sept. 2
Gutierrez, Juan	Aug. 19
McLemore, Mark	May 24
Patton, Troy	Aug. 25
Paulino, Felipe	Sept. 5
Pence, Hunter	April 28
Towles, J.R.	Sept. 5

KANSAS CITY ROYALS
Buckner, Billy	Aug. 25
Butler, Billy	May 1
Gordon, Alex	April 2
Hochevar, Luke	Sept. 8
Musser, Neal	June 19
Soria, Joakim	May 2

LOS ANGELES ANGELS
Brown, Matt	May 10
Budde, Ryan	July 31
Evans, Terry	June 17
Gorneault, Nick	June 30
Gwyn, Marcus	July 29
Haynes, Nathan	May 28
Thompson, Rich	Sept. 1
Wood, Brandon	April 26

LOS ANGELES DODGERS
Abreu, Tony	May 22
Hu, Chin-Lung	Sept. 1
Hull, Eric	July 24
LaRoche, Andy	May 6
Meloan, Jonathan	Sept. 1

MILWAUKEE BREWERS
Braun, Ryan	May 25
Gallardo, Yovani	June 18
Parra, Manny	July 20
Stetter, Mitch	Sept. 1
Stocker, Mel	Sept. 1

MINNESOTA TWINS
Blackburn, Nick	Sept. 3
Buscher, Brian	July 27
DePaula, Julio	May 16
Jones, Garrett	May 15
Miller, Jason	May 26
Morales, Jose	Sept. 8
Slowey, Kevin	June 1
Watkins, Tommy	Aug. 10

NEW YORK METS
Collazo, Willie	Sept. 5
Gomez, Carlos	May 13
Muniz, Carlos	Sept. 25
Smith, Joe	April 1

NEW YORK YANKEES
Basak, Chris	June 9
Chamberlain, Joba	Sept. 16
Clippard, Tyler	May 20
DeSalvo, Matt	May 7
Duncan, Shelley	July 20
Gonzalez, Alberto	Sept. 1
Hughes, Phil	April 26
Igawa, Kei	June 22
Kennedy, Ian	Sept. 1
Ohlendorf, Ross	Sept. 11
Ramirez, Edwar	July 3
Sardinha, Bronson	Sept. 15
Wright, Chase	April 17

OAKLAND ATHLETICS
Barton, Daric	Sept. 10
Blevins, Jerry	Sept. 16
Braden, Dallas	April 24
Buck, Travis	April 2
Marshall, Jay	June 8
Melillo, Kevin	June 24
Putnam, Danny	April 23
Robertson, Connor	May 17
Suzuki, Kurt	June 12

Joba Chamberlain

DIAMOND IMAGES

PHILADELPHIA PHILLIES
Bisenius, Joe	April 5
Garcia, Anderson	July 7
Happ, J.A.	June 30
Hernandez, Yoel	May 5
Kendrick, Kyle	June 13
Segovia, Zack	April 8
Zagurski, Mike	May 25

PITTSBURGH PIRATES
Davidson, Dave	Sept. 6
Kelly, Don	April 2
Kuwata, Masumi	June 14
Morgan, Nyjer	Sept. 1
Pearce, Steven	Sept. 1
Sanchez, Romulo	Aug. 26

ST. LOUIS CARDINALS
Cate, Troy	May 27
Cavazos, Andy	June 7
Dove, Dennis	April 30
Esposito, Brian	June 2
Jimenez, Kelvin	April 27
Ryan, Brendan	June 2

SAN DIEGO PADRES
Cameron, Kevin	April 5
Cassel, Jack	Aug. 10
Headley, Chase	June 15
Macias, Drew	Sept. 29
Morton, Colt	Sept. 21
Stansberry, Craig	Aug. 25
Thatcher, Joe	July 26

SAN FRANCISCO GIANTS
Giese, Dan	Sept. 8
Lincecum, Tim	May 6
Rodriguez, Guillermo	June 13
Schierholtz, Nate	June 11
Threets, Erick	Sept. 12
Velez, Eugenio	Sept. 5

SEATTLE MARINERS
Balentien, Wladimir	Sept. 4
Clement, Jeff	Sept. 4
Johnson, Rob	Sept. 4
Morrow, Brandon	June 8
Rowland-Smith, Ryan	June 22
White, Sean	April 4

TAMPA BAY DEVIL RAYS
Dukes, Elijah	April 2
Iwamura, Akinori	April 2
Ridgway, Jeff	Sept. 17
Ruggiano, Justin	Sept. 19
Sonnanstine, Andy	June 10

TEXAS RANGERS
Galarraga, Armando	Sept. 15
Mahar, Kevin	May 16
Mendoza, Luis	Sept. 8
Metcalf, Travis	May 19
Murray, A.J.	May 16
White, Bill	Sept. 5

TORONTO BLUE JAYS
Banks, Josh	Sept. 11
De Jong, Jordan	June 10
Gronkiewicz, Lee	June 19
Litsch, Jesse	May 20
Thigpen, Curtis	June 6
Vermilyea, Jamie	April 22
Wolfe, Brian	May 30

WASHINGTON NATIONALS
Albaladejo, Jonathan	Sept. 5
Casto, Kory	April 3
Chico, Matt	April 4
Detwiler, Ross	Sept. 7
Flores, Jesus	April 4
Hanrahan, Joel	July 28
Lannan, John	July 26
Maxwell, Justin	Sept. 5
Speigner, Levale	April 2

CLUB BATTING

	AVG	G	AB	R	H	2B	3B	HR	RBI	BB	SO	SB	CS	OBP	SLG
New York	.290	162	5717	968	1656	326	32	201	929	637	991	123	40	.366	.463
Detroit	.287	162	5757	887	1652	352	50	177	857	474	1054	103	30	.345	.458
Seattle	.287	162	5684	794	1629	284	22	153	754	389	861	81	30	.337	.425
Los Angeles	.284	162	5554	822	1578	324	23	123	776	507	883	139	55	.345	.417
Boston	.279	162	5589	867	1561	352	35	166	829	689	1042	96	24	.362	.444
Baltimore	.272	162	5631	756	1529	306	30	142	718	500	939	144	42	.333	.412
Cleveland	.268	162	5604	811	1504	305	27	178	784	590	1202	72	41	.343	.428
Tampa Bay	.268	162	5593	782	1500	291	36	187	750	545	1324	131	48	.336	.433
Minnesota	.264	162	5522	718	1460	273	36	118	671	512	839	112	30	.330	.391
Texas	.263	162	5555	816	1460	298	36	179	768	503	1224	88	25	.328	.426
Kansas City	.261	162	5534	706	1447	300	46	102	660	428	1069	78	44	.322	.388
Toronto	.259	162	5536	753	1434	344	24	165	719	533	1044	57	22	.327	.419
Oakland	.256	162	5577	741	1430	295	16	171	711	664	1119	52	20	.338	.407
Chicago	.246	162	5441	693	1341	249	20	190	667	532	1149	78	45	.318	.404

CLUB PITCHING

	ERA	G	CG	SHO	SV	IP	H	R	ER	HR	BB	SO	AVG
Boston	3.87	162	5	13	45	1438.2	1350	657	618	151	482	1149	.247
Toronto	4.00	162	11	9	44	1448.2	1383	699	644	157	479	1067	.251
Cleveland	4.05	162	9	9	49	1462.2	1519	704	658	146	410	1047	.268
Minnesota	4.18	162	5	8	38	1436.2	1505	725	663	185	420	1094	.269
Los Angeles	4.23	162	5	9	43	1435	1480	731	674	151	477	1156	.266
Oakland	4.30	162	4	9	36	1448	1468	758	689	138	530	1036	.263
Kansas City	4.50	162	2	6	36	1437.1	1547	778	716	168	520	993	.277
New York	4.50	162	1	5	34	1450.2	1498	777	724	150	578	1009	.268
Detroit	4.58	162	1	9	44	1447.1	1498	797	735	174	566	1047	.266
Texas	4.76	162	0	6	42	1430	1525	844	755	155	668	976	.274
Chicago	4.77	162	9	9	42	1440.2	1556	839	763	174	499	1015	.276
Seattle	4.77	162	6	12	43	1434.1	1578	813	754	147	546	1020	.281
Baltimore	5.19	162	4	9	30	1438.2	1491	868	827	161	696	1087	.268
Tampa Bay	5.53	162	2	2	28	1429.2	1649	944	879	199	568	1194	.290

CLUB FIELDING

	FPCT	PO	A	E	DP		FPCT	PO	A	E	DP
Baltimore	.987	4316	1690	79	15	Minnesota	.984	4310	1611	95	15
Boston	.986	4316	1538	81	14	Toronto	.984	4346	1853	102	16
Cleveland	.985	4388	1697	92	16	Los Angeles	.983	4305	1550	101	15
New York	.985	4352	1588	88	17	Chicago	.982	4322	1604	108	16
Oakland	.985	4344	1687	90	15	Kansas City	.982	4312	1553	106	16
Seattle	.985	4303	1656	90	16	Tampa Bay	.980	4289	1548	117	15
Detroit	.984	4342	1635	99	14	Texas	.980	4290	1744	124	17

INDIVIDUAL BATTING LEADERS (MINIMUM 3.1 PA/TEAM GAME)

	AVG	G	AB	R	H	2B	3B	HR	RBI	BB	SO	SB
Ordonez, Magglio, Detroit	.363	157	595	117	216	54	0	28	139	76	79	4
Suzuki, Ichiro, Seattle	.351	161	678	111	238	22	7	6	68	49	77	37
Polanco, Placido, Detroit	.341	142	587	105	200	36	3	9	67	37	30	7
Posada, Jorge, New York	.338	144	506	91	171	42	1	20	90	74	98	2
Ortiz, David, Boston	.332	149	549	116	182	52	1	35	117	111	103	3
Figgins, Chone, Los Angeles	.330	115	442	81	146	24	6	3	58	51	81	41
Lowell, Mike, Boston	.324	154	589	79	191	37	2	21	120	53	71	3
Guerrero, Vladimir, Los Angeles	.324	150	574	89	186	45	1	27	125	71	62	2
Jeter, Derek, New York	.322	156	639	102	206	39	4	12	73	56	100	15
Pedroia, Dustin, Boston	.317	139	520	86	165	39	1	8	50	47	42	7

INDIVIDUAL PITCHING LEADERS (MINIMUM 1 IP/TEAM GAME)

	W	L	ERA	G	GS	CG	SHO	SV	IP	H	R	ER	BB	SO
Lackey, John, Los Angeles	19	9	3.01	33	33	2	2	0	224	219	87	75	52	179
Carmona, Fausto, Cleveland	19	8	3.06	32	32	2	1	0	215	199	78	73	61	137
Haren, Dan, Oakland	15	9	3.07	34	34	0	0	0	223	214	91	76	55	192
Bedard, Erik, Baltimore	13	5	3.16	28	28	1	1	0	182	141	66	64	57	221
Sabathia, C.C., Cleveland	19	7	3.21	34	34	4	1	0	241	238	94	86	37	209
Beckett, Josh, Boston	20	7	3.27	30	30	1	0	0	201	189	76	73	40	194
Santana, Johan, Minnesota	15	13	3.33	33	33	1	1	0	219	183	88	81	52	235
Escobar, Kelvim, Los Angeles	18	7	3.4	30	30	3	1	0	196	182	79	74	66	160
Kazmir, Scott, Tampa Bay	13	9	3.48	34	34	0	0	0	207	196	91	80	89	239
Buehrle, Mark, Chicago	10	9	3.63	30	30	3	1	0	201	208	86	81	45	115

AWARD WINNERS

Selected by Baseball Writers Association of America.

MOST VALUABLE PLAYER

Player	1st	2nd	3rd	Total
Alex Rodriguez, New York	26	2	—	382
Magglio Ordonez, Detroit	2	22	4	258
Vladimir Guerrero, L.A.	—	3	10	203
David Ortiz, Boston	—	1	11	177
Mike Lowell, Boston	—	—	1	126
Jorge Posada, New York	—	—	—	112
Victor Martinez, Cleveland	—	—	—	103
Ichiro Suzuki, Seattle	—	—	—	89
Carlos Pena, Tampa Bay	—	—	2	64
Curtis Granderson, Detroit	—	—	—	51
Derek Jeter, New York	—	—	—	17
Grady Sizemore, Cleveland	—	—	—	15
J.J. Putz, Seattle	—	—	—	12
C.C. Sabathia, Cleveland	—	—	—	11
Torii Hunter, Minnesota	—	—	—	5
Orlando Cabrera, L.A.	—	—	—	5
Bobby Abreu, New York	—	—	—	4
John Lackey, L.A.	—	—	—	4
Placido Polanco, Detroit	—	—	—	4
Justin Morneau, Minnesota	—	—	—	3
Chone Figgins, L.A.	—	—	—	3
Josh Beckett, Boston	—	—	—	2
Fausto Carmona, Cleveland	—	—	—	1
Frank Thomas, Toronto	—	—	—	1

CY YOUNG AWARD

Player	1st	2nd	3rd	Total
C.C. Sabathia, Cleveland	19	8	—	119
Josh Beckett, Boston	8	14	4	86
John Lackey, L.A.	1	5	16	36
Fausto Carmona, Cleveland	—	1	4	7
Eric Bedard, Baltimore	—	—	1	1
Roy Halladay, Toronto	—	—	1	1
Johan Santana, Minnesota	—	—	1	1
Justin Verlander, Detroit	—	—	1	1

ROOKIE OF THE YEAR

Player	1st	2nd	3rd	Total
Dustin Pedroia, Boston	24	4	—	132
Delmon Young, Tampa Bay	3	12	5	56
Brian Bannister, Kansas City	1	8	7	36
Daisuke Matsuzaka, Boston	—	2	6	12
Reggie Willits, L.A.	—	2	5	11
Hideki Okajima, Boston	—	—	3	3
Josh Fields, Chicago	—	—	1	1
Joakim Soria, Kansas City	—	—	1	1

MANAGER OF THE YEAR

Player	1st	2nd	3rd	Total
Eric Wedge, Cleveland	19	6	3	116
Mike Scioscia, L.A.	4	11	9	62
Joe Torre, New York	5	8	12	61
Terry Francona, Boston	—	3	4	13

GOLD GLOVE AWARDS

Selected by AL managers

C—Ivan Rodriguez, Detroit. 1B—Kevin Youkilis, Boston. 2B—Placido Polanco, Detroit. 3B—Adrian Beltre, Seattle. SS—Orlando Cabrera, Los Angeles. OF—Torii Hunter, Minnesota; Grady Sizemore, Cleveland; Ichiro Suzuki, Seattle. P—Johan Santana, Minnesota.

SILVER SLUGGER AWARDS

Selected by AL managers, coaches

C—Jorge Posada, New York. 1B—Carlos Pena, Tampa Bay. 2B—Placido Polanco, Detroit. 3B—Alex Rodriguez, New York. SS—Derek Jeter, New York. OF—Vladimir Guerrero, Los Angeles; Magglio Ordonez, Detroit; Ichiro Suzuki, Seattle. DH—David Ortiz, Boston.

DEPARTMENT LEADERS

BATTING

GAMES
Sizemore, Grady, Indians	162
Young, Delmon, Devil Rays	162
Markakis, Nick, Orioles	161
Rios, Alex, Blue Jays	161
Suzuki, Ichiro, Mariners	161

AT-BATS
Suzuki, Ichiro, Mariners	678
Young, Delmon, Devil Rays	645
Rios, Alex, Blue Jays	643
Jeter, Derek, Yankees	639
Young, Michael, Rangers	639

RUNS
Rodriguez, Alex, Yankees	143
Abreu, Bobby, Yankees	123
Granderson, Curtis, Tigers	122
Sizemore, Grady, Indians	118
Ordonez, Magglio, Tigers	117

HITS
Suzuki, Ichiro, Mariners	238
Ordonez, Magglio, Tigers	216
Jeter, Derek, Yankees	206
Young, Michael, Rangers	201
Polanco, Placido, Tigers	200

TOTAL BASES
Rodriguez, Alex, Yankees	376
Ordonez, Magglio, Tigers	354
Ortiz, David, Red Sox	341
Granderson, Curtis, Tigers	338
Rios, Alex, Blue Jays	320

DOUBLES
Ordonez, Magglio, Tigers	54
Ortiz, David, Red Sox	52
Hill, Aaron, Blue Jays	47
Guerrero, Vladimir, Angels	45
Hunter, Torii, Twins	45

TRIPLES
Granderson, Curtis, Tigers	23
Iwamura, Akinori, Devil Rays	10
Crawford, Carl, Devil Rays	9
DeJesus, David, Royals	9
Guillen, Carlos, Tigers	9

EXTRA-BASE HITS
Ortiz, David, Red Sox	88
Rodriguez, Alex, Yankees	85
Granderson, Curtis, Tigers	84
Ordonez, Magglio, Tigers	82
Pena, Carlos, Devil Rays	76

HOME RUNS
Rodriguez, Alex, Yankees	54
Pena, Carlos, Devil Rays	46
Ortiz, David, Red Sox	35
Thome, Jim, White Sox	35
2 players	31

RUNS BATTED IN
Rodriguez, Alex, Yankees	156
Ordonez, Magglio, Tigers	139
Guerrero, Vladimir, Angels	125
Pena, Carlos, Devil Rays	121
Lowell, Mike, Red Sox	120

SACRIFICES
Patterson, Corey, Orioles	13
Vazquez, Ramon, Rangers	12
McDonald, John, Blue Jays	12
Willits, Reggie, Angels	11
2 players	10

SACRIFICE FLIES
Cabrera, Orlando, Angels	11
Martinez, Victor, Indians	11
Matsui, Hideki, Yankees	10
4 players	9

Magglio Ordonez

LARRY GOREN

HIT BY PITCHES
DeJesus, David, Royals	23
Rodriguez, Alex, Yankees	21
Garko, Ryan, Indians	20
Guillen, Jose, Mariners	19
Sizemore, Grady, Indians	17

WALKS
Ortiz, David, Red Sox	111
Cust, Jack, Athletics	105
Pena, Carlos, Devil Rays	103
Hafner, Travis, Indians	102
Sizemore, Grady, Indians	101

David Ortiz

MORRIS FOSTOFF

INTENTIONAL WALKS
Guerrero, Vladimir, Angels	28
Hafner, Travis, Indians	17
Ramirez, Manny, Red Sox	13
Suzuki, Ichiro, Mariners	13
3 players	12

STOLEN BASES
Crawford, Carl, Devil Rays	50
Roberts, Brian, Orioles	50
Figgins, Chone, Angels	41
Patterson, Corey, Orioles	37
Suzuki, Ichiro, Mariners	37

CAUGHT STEALING
Figgins, Chone, Angels	12
Crawford, Carl, Devil Rays	10
Sizemore, Grady, Indians	10
3 players	9

STRIKEOUTS
Cust, Jack, Athletics	164
Sizemore, Grady, Indians	155
Upton, B.J., Devil Rays	154
Inge, Brandon, Tigers	150
Peralta, Jhonny, Indians	146

TOUGHEST TO STRIKE OUT
(At-bats per strikeout)
Polanco, Placido, Tigers	19.57
Pedroia, Dustin, Red Sox	12.38
Johjima, Kenji, Mariners	11.83
Betancourt, Yuniesky, Mariners	11.17
Kotchman, Casey, Angels	10.3

GROUNDED INTO DOUBLE PLAYS
Teahen, Mark, Royals	23
Young, Delmon, Devil Rays	23
4 players,	22

MULTIPLE-HIT GAMES
Suzuki, Ichiro, Mariners	76
Polanco, Placido, Tigers	65
Cabrera, Orlando, Angels	63
3 players	61

ON-BASE PERCENTAGE
Ortiz, David, Red Sox	.445
Ordonez, Magglio, Tigers	.434
Posada, Jorge, Yankees	.426
Rodriguez, Alex, Yankees	.422
Pena, Carlos, Devil Rays	.411

SLUGGING PERCENTAGE
Rodriguez, Alex, Yankees	.645
Pena, Carlos, Devil Rays	.627
Ortiz, David, Red Sox	.621
Ordonez, Magglio, Tigers	.595
Thome, Jim, White Sox	.563

ON-BASE PLUS SLUGGING
Rodriguez, Alex, Yankees	1.067
Ortiz, David, Red Sox	1.066
Pena, Carlos, Devil Rays	1.037
Ordonez, Magglio, Tigers	1.029
Thome, Jim, White Sox	.973

PITCHING

WINS
Beckett, Josh, Red Sox	20
Carmona, Fausto, Indians	19
Lackey, John, Angels	19
Sabathia, C.C., Indians	19
Wang, Chien-Ming, Yankees	19

LOSSES
Cabrera, Daniel, Orioles	18
Contreras, Jose, White Sox	17
Jackson, Edwin, Devil Rays	15
Washburn, Jarrod, Mariners	15
3 players	14

DEPARTMENT LEADERS

GAMES
Downs, Scott, Blue Jays	81
Walker, Jamie, Orioles	81
Bradford, Chad, Orioles	78
Vizcaino, Luis, Yankees	77
2 players	74

GAMES STARTED
Blanton, Joe, Athletics	34
Cabrera, Daniel, Orioles	34
Gaudin, Chad, Athletics	34
Haren, Dan, Athletics	34
Kazmir, Scott, Devil Rays	34
Meche, Gil, Royals	34
Pettitte, Andy, Yankees	34
Sabathia, C.C., Indians	34

COMPLETE GAMES
Halladay, Roy, Blue Jays	7
Sabathia, C.C., Indians	4
4 players	3

SHUTOUTS
Byrd, Paul, Indians	2
Contreras, Jose, White Sox	2
Lackey, John, Angels	2
Weaver, Jeff, Mariners	2
19 players	1

GAMES FINISHED
Putz, J.J., Mariners	65
Jenks, Bobby, White Sox	62
Nathan, Joe, Twins	60
Rivera, Mariano, Yankees	59
Borowski, Joe, Indians	58

SAVES
Borowski, Joe, Indians	45
Jenks, Bobby, White Sox	40
Putz, J.J., Mariners	40
Rodriguez, Francisco, Angels	40
Jones, Todd, Tigers	38

INNINGS PITCHED
Sabathia, C.C., Indians	241
Blanton, Joe, Athletics	230
Halladay, Roy, Blue Jays	225.1
Lackey, John, Angels	224
Haren, Dan, Athletics	222.2

HITS ALLOWED
Blanton, Joe, Athletics	240
Byrd, Paul, Indians	239
Pettitte, Andy, Yankees	238
Sabathia, C.C., Indians	238
2 players	232

RUNS ALLOWED
Contreras, Jose, White Sox	134
Cabrera, Daniel, Orioles	133
Jackson, Edwin, Devil Rays	116
Garland, Jon, White Sox	114
Millwood, Kevin, Rangers	111

EARNED RUNS ALLOWED
Cabrera, Daniel, Orioles	126
Contreras, Jose, White Sox	117
Jackson, Edwin, Devil Rays	103
Blanton, Joe, Athletics	101
Weaver, Jeff, Mariners	101

HOME RUNS ALLOWED
Santana, Johan, Twins	33
Vazquez, Javier, White Sox	29
Danks, John, White Sox	28
Shields, Jamie, Devil Rays	28
3 players	27

WALKS
Cabrera, Daniel, Orioles	108
Gaudin, Chad, Athletics	100
Kazmir, Scott, Devil Rays	89
Jackson, Edwin, Devil Rays	88
Batista, Miguel, Mariners	85

WALKS PER NINE INNINGS
Byrd, Paul, Indians	1.31
Sabathia, C.C., Indians	1.38
Shields, Jamie, Devil Rays	1.51
Blanton, Joe, Athletics	1.57
Silva, Carlos, Twins	1.6

HIT BATSMEN
Verlander, Justin, Tigers	19
Contreras, Jose, White Sox	15
Cabrera, Daniel, Orioles	15
Matsuzaka, Daisuke, Red Sox	13
2 players	12

STRIKEOUTS
Kazmir, Scott, Devil Rays	239
Santana, Johan, Twins	235
Bedard, Erik, Orioles	221
Vazquez, Javier, White Sox	213
Sabathia, C.C., Indians	209

STRIKEOUTS PER NINE INNINGS
Bedard, Erik, Orioles	10.93
Kazmir, Scott, Devil Rays	10.41
Santana, Johan, Twins	9.66
Burnett, A.J., Blue Jays	9.56
Vazquez, Javier, White Sox	8.85

Scott Kazmir

STEVE MOORE

STRIKEOUTS PER NINE INNINGS (RELIEVERS)
Rodriguez, Francisco, Angels	12.03
Putz, J.J., Mariners	10.3
Soria, Joakim, Royals	9.78
Nathan, Joe, Twins	9.67
Benoit, Joaquin, Rangers	9.55

PICKOFFS
Pettitte, Andy, Yankees	5
Buehrle, Mark, White Sox	5
4 players	4

WILD PITCHES
Verlander, Justin, Tigers	17
Batista, Miguel, Mariners	15
McGowan, Dustin, Blue Jays	13

Bonderman, Jeremy, Tigers	12
4 players	10

OPPONENT BATTING AVERAGE
Bedard, Erik, Orioles	.212
Burnett, A.J., Blue Jays	.214
Santana, Johan, Twins	.225
McGowan, Dustin, Blue Jays	.230
Verlander, Justin, Tigers	.233

WORST ERA
Contreras, Jose, White Sox	5.57
Cabrera, Daniel, Orioles	5.55
Millwood, Kevin, Rangers	5.16
Bonser, Boof, Twins	5.10
Bonderman, Jeremy, Tigers	5.01

FIELDING

PITCHER
FPCT	10 players tied at	1.000
PO	Shields, Jamie, Devil Rays	30
A	Carmona, Fausto, Indians	39
E	Contreras, Jose, White Sox	6
TC	Carmona, Fausto, Indians	64
DP	Marcum, Shaun, Blue Jays	6

CATCHER
FPCT	Pierzynski, A.J., White Sox	.998
	Mauer, Joe, Twins	.998
	Johjima, Kenji, Mariners	.998
PO	Varitek, Jason, Red Sox	937
A	Laird, Gerald, Rangers	75
E	Navarro, Dioner, Devil Rays	14
TC	Varitek, Jason, Red Sox	982
DP	Johjima, Kenji, Mariners	15
PB	Pierzynski, A.J., White Sox	14
CS%	Mauer, Joe, Twins	53%

FIRST BASE
FPCT	Youkilis, Kevin, Red Sox	1.000
PO	Morneau, Justin, Twins	1189
A	Pena, Carlos, Devil Rays	130
E	Saltalamacchia, Jarrod, Rangers	9
TC	Morneau, Justin, Twins	1296
DP	Konerko, Paul, White Sox	131

SECOND BASE
FPCT	Polanco, Placido, Tigers	1.000
PO	Cano, Robinson, Yankees	320
A	Hill, Aaron, Blue Jays	560
E	Kinsler, Ian, Rangers	17
TC	Cano, Robinson, Yankees	830
DP	Cano, Robinson, Yankees	136

THIRD BASE
FPCT	Iwamura, Akinori, Devil Rays	.975
PO	Beltre, Adrian, Mariners	121
A	Inge, Brandon, Tigers	325
E	Inge, Brandon, Tigers	18

	Beltre, Adrian, Mariners	18
TC	Inge, Brandon, Tigers	434
DP	Lowell, Mike, Red Sox	34

SHORTSTOP
FPCT	Cabrera, Orlando, Angels	.983
PO	Peralta, Jhonny, Indians	249
A	Peralta, Jhonny, Indians	452
E	Bartlett, Jason, Twins	26
TC	Peralta, Jhonny, Indians	720
DP	Betancourt, Yuniesky, Mariners	110

OUTFIELD
FPCT	Crisp, Coco, Red Sox	.998
	Suzuki, Ichiro, Mariners	.998
PO	Granderson, Curtis, Tigers	428
A	Cuddyer, Michael, Twins	19
E	Guerrero, Vladimir, Angels	9
TC	Granderson, Curtis, Tigers	443
DP	Teahen, Mark, Royals	7
	Young, Delmon, Devil Rays	7

CLUB BATTING

	AVG	G	AB	R	H	2B	3B	HR	RBI	BB	SO	SB	CS	OBP	SLG
Colorado	.280	163	5691	860	1591	313	36	171	823	622	1152	100	31	.354	.437
Atlanta	.275	162	5689	810	1562	328	27	176	781	534	1149	64	30	.339	.435
Los Angeles	.275	162	5614	735	1544	276	35	129	706	511	864	137	55	.337	.406
New York	.275	162	5605	804	1543	294	27	177	761	549	981	200	46	.342	.432
Philadelphia	.274	162	5688	892	1558	326	41	213	850	641	1205	138	19	.354	.458
St. Louis	.274	162	5529	725	1513	279	13	141	690	506	909	56	33	.337	.405
Chicago	.271	162	5643	752	1530	340	28	151	711	500	1054	86	33	.333	.422
Cincinnati	.267	162	5607	783	1496	293	23	204	747	536	1113	97	31	.335	.436
Florida	.267	162	5627	790	1504	340	38	201	749	521	1332	105	34	.336	.448
Pittsburgh	.263	162	5569	724	1463	322	31	148	694	463	1135	68	30	.325	.411
Milwaukee	.262	162	5554	801	1455	310	37	231	774	501	1137	96	32	.329	.456
Houston	.260	162	5605	723	1457	293	30	167	700	547	1043	65	33	.33	.412
Washington	.256	162	5520	673	1415	309	31	123	646	524	1128	69	23	.325	.390
San Francisco	.254	162	5538	683	1407	267	37	131	641	532	907	119	33	.322	.387
San Diego	.251	163	5612	741	1408	322	31	171	704	557	1229	55	24	.322	.411
Arizona	.250	162	5398	712	1350	286	40	171	687	532	1111	109	24	.321	.413

CLUB PITCHING

	ERA	G	CG	SHO	SV	IP	H	R	ER	HR	BB	SO	AVG
San Diego	3.72	163	1	20	45	1484.2	1406	666	611	119	474	1136	.25
Chicago	4.04	162	2	10	39	1446.2	1340	690	650	165	573	1211	.246
Atlanta	4.11	162	1	6	36	1456.1	1442	733	665	172	537	1106	.259
Arizona	4.13	162	7	12	51	1441	1446	732	662	169	546	1088	.262
Los Angeles	4.20	162	4	6	43	1450	1443	727	677	146	518	1184	.261
San Francisco	4.20	162	5	10	37	1453.2	1442	720	677	133	593	1057	.261
New York	4.27	162	2	10	39	1452.1	1415	750	687	165	570	1134	.255
Colorado	4.32	163	4	7	39	1472	1497	758	706	164	504	967	.266
Milwaukee	4.44	162	3	6	49	1444.1	1513	776	708	161	507	1174	.269
Washington	4.58	162	0	6	46	1446.2	1502	783	736	187	580	931	.269
St. Louis	4.67	162	2	8	34	1435.2	1514	829	741	168	509	945	.271
Houston	4.70	162	2	6	38	1464.2	1566	813	761	206	510	1109	.273
Philadelphia	4.76	162	5	5	42	1458.1	1555	821	767	198	558	1050	.276
Pittsburgh	4.94	162	4	5	32	1447.2	1627	846	793	174	518	997	.288
Cincinnati	4.95	162	6	7	34	1449.2	1605	853	796	198	482	1068	.282
Florida	4.96	162	0	4	40	1443.2	1617	891	793	176	661	1142	.285

CLUB FIELDING

	FPCT	PO	A	E	DP		FPCT	PO	A	E	DP
Colorado	.989	4416	1842	68	180	Atlanta	.983	4369	1657	107	141
Philadelphia	.986	4375	1723	89	162	Houston	.983	4394	1689	103	128
Pittsburgh	.986	4343	1721	83	190	New York	.983	4357	1518	101	124
San Francisco	.986	4361	1666	88	148	Milwaukee	.982	4333	1529	109	144
San Diego	.985	4454	1766	92	147	Washington	.982	4340	1567	109	153
Chicago	.984	4340	1535	94	134	Los Angeles	.981	4350	1651	114	160
Cincinnati	.984	4349	1517	95	155	St. Louis	.980	4307	1672	121	155
Arizona	.983	4323	1635	106	157	Florida	.977	4331	1510	137	159

INDIVIDUAL BATTING LEADERS (MINIMUM 3.1 PA/TEAM GAME)

	AVG	G	AB	R	H	2B	3B	HR	RBI	BB	SO	SB
Holliday, Matt, Colorado	.340	158	636	120	216	50	6	36	137	63	126	11
Jones, Chipper, Atlanta	.337	134	513	108	173	42	4	29	102	82	75	5
Utley, Chase, Philadelphia	.332	132	530	104	176	48	5	22	103	50	89	9
Renteria, Edgar, Atlanta	.332	124	494	87	164	30	1	12	57	46	77	11
Ramirez, Hanley, Florida	.332	154	639	125	212	48	6	29	81	52	95	51
Pujols, Albert, St. Louis	.327	158	565	99	185	38	1	32	103	99	58	2
Wright, David, New York	.325	160	604	113	196	42	1	30	107	94	115	34
Cabrera, Miguel, Florida	.320	157	588	91	188	38	2	34	119	79	127	2
Helton, Todd, Colorado	.320	154	557	86	178	42	2	17	91	116	74	0
Young, Dmitri, Washington	.320	136	460	57	147	38	1	13	74	44	74	0

INDIVIDUAL PITCHING LEADERS (MINIMUM 1 IP/TEAM GAME)

	W	L	ERA	G	GS	CG	SHO	SV	IP	H	R	ER	BB	SO
Peavy, Jake, San Diego	19	6	2.54	34	34	0	0	0	223	169	67	63	68	240
Webb, Brandon, Arizona	18	10	3.01	34	34	4	3	0	236	209	91	79	72	194
Penny, Brad, Los Angeles	16	4	3.03	33	33	0	0	0	208	199	75	70	73	135
Smoltz, John, Atlanta	14	8	3.11	32	32	0	0	0	206	196	78	71	47	197
Young, Chris, San Diego	9	8	3.12	30	30	0	0	0	173	118	66	60	72	167
Oswalt, Roy, Houston	14	7	3.18	33	32	1	0	0	212	221	80	75	60	154
Hudson, Tim, Atlanta	16	10	3.33	34	34	1	1	0	224	221	87	83	53	132
Hamels, Cole, Philadelphia	15	5	3.39	28	28	2	0	0	183	163	72	69	43	177
Perez, Oliver, New York	15	10	3.56	29	29	0	0	0	177	153	90	70	79	174
Cain, Matt, San Francisco	7	16	3.65	32	32	1	0	0	200	173	84	81	79	163

AWARD WINNERS

Selected by Baseball Writers Association of America.

MOST VALUABLE PLAYER

Player	1st	2nd	3rd	Total
Jimmy Rollins, Philadelphia	16	7	4	353
Matt Holliday, Colorado	11	18	1	336
Prince Fielder, Milwaukee	5	6	17	284
David Wright, New York	—	1	4	182
Ryan Howard, Philadelphia	—	—	2	112
Chipper Jones, Atlanta	—	—	1	107
Jake Peavy, San Diego	—	—	—	97
Chase Utley, Philadelphia	—	—	1	89
Albert Pujols, St. Louis	—	—	—	50
Hanley Ramirez , Florida	—	—	—	49
Eric Byrnes, Arizona	—	—	—	43
Alfonso Soriano, Chicago	—	—	1	39
Aramis Ramirez, Chicago	—	—	—	36
Jose Valverde, Arizona	—	—	—	19
Miguel Cabrera , Florida	—	—	—	18
Jose Reyes, New York	—	—	—	16
Brandon Webb, Arizona	—	—	—	15
Troy Tulowitzki, Colorado	—	—	1	13
Carlos Lee, Houston	—	—	—	7
Adrian Gonzalez, San Diego	—	—	—	6
Carlos Beltran, New York	—	—	—	6
Brandon Phillips, Cincinnati	—	—	—	3
Aaron Rowand, Philadelphia	—	—	—	3
Brad Hawpe, Colorado	—	—	—	2
Ryan Braun, Milwaukee	—	—	—	2
Carlos Marmol, Chicago	—	—	—	1

CY YOUNG AWARD

Player	1st	2nd	3rd	Total
Jake Peavy, San Diego	32	—	—	160
Brandon Webb, Arizona	—	31	1	94
Brad Penny, Los Angeles	—	—	14	14
Aaron Harang, Cincinnati	—	1	7	10
Carlos Zambrano, Chicago	—	—	3	3
Cole Hamels, Philadelphia	—	—	2	2
John Smoltz, Atlanta	—	—	2	2
Jose Valverde, Arizona	—	—	2	2
Jeff Francis, Colorado	—	—	1	1

ROOKIE OF THE YEAR

Player	1st	2nd	3rd	Total
Ryan Braun, Milwaukee	17	14	1	128
Troy Tulowitzki, Colorado	15	17	—	126
Hunter Pence, Houston	—	—	15	15
Chris Young, Arizona	—	—	10	10
Kyle Kendrick, Philadelphia	—	1	4	7
Yunel Escobar, Atlanta	—	—	1	1
James Loney, Los Angeles	—	—	1	1

MANAGER OF THE YEAR

Player	1st	2nd	3rd	Total
Bob Melvin, Arizona	19	7	3	119
Charlie Manuel, Philadelphia	7	11	8	76
Clint Hurdle, Colorado	4	10	8	58
Lou Piniella, Chicago	2	3	6	25
Bud Black, San Diego	—	1	1	4
Manny Acta, Washington	—	—	4	4
Ned Yost, Milwaukee	—	—	2	2

GOLD GLOVE AWARDS

Selected by NL managers
C—Russell Martin, Los Angeles. **1B**—Derrek Lee, Chicago. **2B**—Orlando Hudson, Arizona. **3B**—David Wright, New York. **SS**—Jimmy Rollins, Philadelphia. **OF**—Carlos Beltran, New York; Jeff Francoeur, Atlanta; Andruw Jones, Atlanta; Aaron Rowand, Philadelphia. **P**—Greg Maddux, San Diego.

SILVER SLUGGER AWARDS

Selected by NL managers, coaches
C—Russell Martin, Los Angeles. **1B**—Prince Fielder, Milwaukee. **2B**—Chase Utley, Philadelphia. **3B**—David Wright, New York. **SS**—Jimmy Rollins, Philadelphia. **OF**—Carlos Beltran, New York; Matt Holliday, Colorado; Carlos Lee, Houston. **P**—Micah Owings, Arizona.

DEPARTMENT LEADERS

BATTING

GAMES
Francoeur, Jeff, Braves	162
Lee, Carlos, Astros	162
Pierre, Juan, Dodgers	162
Rollins, Jimmy, Phillies	162
Zimmerman, Ryan, Nationals	162

AT-BATS
Rollins, Jimmy, Phillies	716
Reyes, Jose, Mets	681
Pierre, Juan, Dodgers	668
Zimmerman, Ryan, Nationals	653
Phillips, Brandon, Reds	650

RUNS
Rollins, Jimmy, Phillies	139
Ramirez, Hanley, Marlins	125
Holliday, Matt, Rockies	120
Reyes, Jose, Mets	119
2 players	113

HITS
Holliday, Matt, Rockies	216
Ramirez, Hanley, Marlins	212
Rollins, Jimmy, Phillies	212
Pierre, Juan, Dodgers	196
Wright, David, Mets	196

TOTAL BASES
Holliday, Matt, Rockies	386
Rollins, Jimmy, Phillies	380
Ramirez, Hanley, Marlins	359
Fielder, Prince, Brewers	354
Cabrera, Miguel, Marlins	332

DOUBLES
Holliday, Matt, Rockies	50
Uggla, Dan, Marlins	49
Ramirez, Hanley, Marlins	48
Utley, Chase, Phillies	48
Gonzalez, Adrian, Padres	46

TRIPLES
Rollins, Jimmy, Phillies	20
Reyes, Jose, Mets	12
Johnson, Kelly, Braves	10
5 players	9

EXTRA-BASE HITS
Holliday, Matt, Rockies	92
Rollins, Jimmy, Phillies	88
Fielder, Prince, Brewers	87
Ramirez, Hanley, Marlins	83
Uggla, Dan, Marlins	83

HOME RUNS
Fielder, Prince, Brewers	50
Howard, Ryan, Phillies	47
Dunn, Adam, Reds	40
Holliday, Matt, Rockies	36
3 players	34

RUNS BATTED IN
Holliday, Matt, Rockies	137
Howard, Ryan, Phillies	136
Cabrera, Miguel, Marlins	119
Fielder, Prince, Brewers	119
Lee, Carlos, Astros	119

SACRIFICES
Pierre, Juan, Dodgers	20
Vizquel, Omar, Giants	14
Maine, John, Mets	14
3 players	13

SACRIFICE FLIES
Lee, Carlos, Astros	13
Uggla, Dan, Marlins	11
Greene, Khalil, Padres	11
3 players	10

Prince Fielder

Chipper Jones

HIT BY PITCHES
Utley, Chase, Phillies	25
Rowand, Aaron, Phillies	19
Willingham, Josh, Marlins	16
3 players	14

WALKS
Bonds, Barry, Giants	132
Helton, Todd, Rockies	116
Burrell, Pat, Phillies	114
Howard, Ryan, Phillies	107
Dunn, Adam, Reds	101

INTENTIONAL WALKS
Bonds, Barry, Giants	43
Howard, Ryan, Phillies	35
Cabrera, Miguel, Marlins	23
Pujols, Albert, Cardinals	22
Fielder, Prince, Brewers	21

STOLEN BASES
Reyes, Jose, Mets	78
Pierre, Juan, Dodgers	64
Ramirez, Hanley, Marlins	51
Byrnes, Eric, Diamondbacks	50
Rollins, Jimmy, Phillies	41

CAUGHT STEALING
Reyes, Jose, Mets	21
Pierre, Juan, Dodgers	15
Ramirez, Hanley, Marlins	14
Harris, Willie, Braves	11
3 players	9

STRIKEOUTS
Howard, Ryan, Phillies	199
Uggla, Dan, Marlins	167
Dunn, Adam, Reds	165
Cameron, Mike, Padres	160
2 players	141

TOUGHEST TO STRIKE OUT
(At-bats per strikeout)
Pierre, Juan, Dodgers	18.05
Loretta, Mark, Astros	11.22
Theriot, Ryan, Cubs	10.74
Vizquel, Omar, Giants	10.69
Wilson, Jack, Pirates	10.37

GROUNDED INTO DOUBLE PLAYS
Pujols, Albert, Cardinals	27
Lee, Carlos, Astros	27
Phillips, Brandon, Reds	26
Zimmerman, Ryan, Nationals	26
Holliday, Matt, Rockies	23

MULTIPLE-HIT GAMES
Rollins, Jimmy, Phillies	63
Ramirez, Hanley, Marlins	62
Holliday, Matt, Rockies	59
Pierre, Juan, Dodgers	59
Pujols, Albert, Cardinals	59

ON-BASE PERCENTAGE
Bonds, Barry, Giants	.480
Helton, Todd, Rockies	.434
Pujols, Albert, Cardinals	.429
Jones, Chipper, Braves	.425
Wright, David, Mets	.416

SLUGGING PERCENTAGE
Braun, Ryan, Brewers	.634
Fielder, Prince, Brewers	.618
Holliday, Matt, Rockies	.607
Jones, Chipper, Braves	.604
Howard, Ryan, Phillies	.584

ON-BASE PLUS SLUGGING
Jones, Chipper, Braves	1.029
Fielder, Prince, Brewers	1.013
Holliday, Matt, Rockies	1.012
Pujols, Albert, Cardinals	.997
Utley, Chase, Phillies	.976

LARRY GOREN

ED WOLFSTEIN

DEPARTMENT LEADERS

PITCHING

WINS
Peavy, Jake, Padres	19
Webb, Brandon, Diamondbacks	18
Zambrano, Carlos, Cubs	18
Francis, Jeff, Rockies	17
3 players	16

LOSSES
Wells, Kip, Cardinals	17
Cain, Matt, Giants	16
5 players	15

GAMES
Rauch, Jon, Nationals	88
Rivera, Saul, Nationals	85
Beimel, Joe, Dodgers	83
Broxton, Jonathan, Dodgers	83
2 players	81

GAMES STARTED
Willis, Dontrelle, Marlins	35
11 players	34

COMPLETE GAMES
Webb, Brandon, Diamondbacks	4
Lowe, Derek, Dodgers	3
Morris, Matt, 2 teams	3
7 players	2

SHUTOUTS
Webb, Brandon, Diamondbacks	3
13 players	1

GAMES FINISHED
Weathers, David, Reds	60
Cordero, Chad, Nationals	59
Valverde, Jose, Diamondbacks	59
Cordero, Francisco, Brewers	58
Dempster, Ryan, Cubs	58

SAVES
Valverde, Jose, Diamondbacks	47
Cordero, Francisco, Brewers	44
Hoffman, Trevor, Padres	42
Saito, Takashi, Dodgers	39
Cordero, Chad, Nationals	37

INNINGS PITCHED
Webb, Brandon, Diamondbacks	236.1
Harang, Aaron, Reds	231.2
Hudson, Tim, Braves	224.1
Peavy, Jake, Padres	223.1
Zambrano, Carlos, Cubs	216.1

HITS ALLOWED
Hernandez, Livan, Diamondbacks	247
Suppan, Jeff, Brewers	243
Willis, Dontrelle, Marlins	241
Morris, Matt, 2 teams	240
Francis, Jeff, Rockies	234

RUNS ALLOWED
Olsen, Scott, Marlins	134
Willis, Dontrelle, Marlins	131
Morris, Matt, 2 teams	123
Moyer, Jamie, Phillies	118
Eaton, Adam, Phillies	117

EARNED RUNS ALLOWED
Willis, Dontrelle, Marlins	118
Olsen, Scott, Marlins	114
Eaton, Adam, Phillies	113
Hernandez, Livan, Diamondbacks	112
Moyer, Jamie, Phillies	111

HOME RUNS ALLOWED
Williams, Woody, Astros	35
Hernandez, Livan, Diamondbacks	34
James, Chuck, Braves	32
Eaton, Adam, Phillies	30
Moyer, Jamie, Phillies	30

WALKS
Zambrano, Carlos, Cubs	101
Davis, Doug, Diamondbacks	95
Lowry, Noah, Giants	87
Willis, Dontrelle, Marlins	87
Olsen, Scott, Marlins	85

WALKS PER NINE INNINGS
Maddux, Greg, Padres	1.14
Harang, Aaron, Reds	2.02
Smoltz, John, Braves	2.06
Hamels, Cole, Phillies	2.11
Bush, Dave, Brewers	2.13

HIT BATSMEN
Kim, Byung-Hyun, 3 teams	16
Willis, Dontrelle, Marlins	14
Zambrano, Carlos, Cubs	14
Owings, Micah, Diamondbacks	14
4 players,	13

STRIKEOUTS
Peavy, Jake, Padres	240
Harang, Aaron, Reds	218
Smoltz, John, Braves	197
Webb, Brandon, Diamondbacks	194
Hill, Rich, Cubs	183

STRIKEOUTS PER NINE INNINGS
Peavy, Jake, Padres	9.67
Perez, Oliver, Mets	8.85
Hamels, Cole, Phillies	8.69
Young, Chris, Padres	8.69
Smoltz, John, Braves	8.62

Jake Peavy

MORRIS FOSTOFF

STRIKEOUTS PER NINE INNINGS (RELIEVERS)
Marmol, Carlos, Cubs	12.46
Lidge, Brad, Astros	11.82
Turnbow, Derrick, Brewers	11.12
Broxton, Jonathan, Dodgers	10.87
Wagner, Billy, Mets	10.54

PICKOFFS
Davis, Doug, Diamondbacks	7
Rodriguez, Wandy, Astros	6
Simontacchi, Jason, Nationals	5
4 players	4

WILD PITCHES
Harang, Aaron, Reds	12
Snell, Ian, Pirates	12
Cain, Matt, Giants	12
3 players	10

OPPONENT BATTING AVERAGE
Young, Chris, Padres	.192
Peavy, Jake, Padres	.208
Perez, Oliver, Mets	.229
Zambrano, Carlos, Cubs	.233
Hill, Rich, Cubs	.235

WORST ERA
Olsen, Scott, Marlins	5.81
Wells, Kip, Cardinals	5.70
Belisle, Matt, Reds	5.32
Williams, Woody, Astros	5.27
Willis, Dontrelle, Marlins	5.17

FIELDING

PITCHER
FPCT	18 players tied at	1.000
PO	Hudson, Tim, Braves	27
	Sampson, Chris, Astros	27
A	Maddux, Greg, Padres	51
E	Webb, Brandon, Diamondbacks	5
	Willis, Dontrelle, Marlins	5
TC	Webb, Brandon, Diamondbacks	75
DP	Suppan, Jeff, Brewers	7

CATCHER
FPCT	Snyder, Chris, Diamondbacks	.999
PO	Martin, Russell, Dodgers	1065
A	Martin, Russell, Dodgers	85
E	Martin, Russell, Dodgers	14
TC	Martin, Russell, Dodgers	1164
DP	Martin, Russell, Dodgers	11
PB	Olivo, Miguel, Marlins	16
	Molina, Bengie, Giants	16
CS%	Molina, Yadier, Cardinals	54%

FIRST BASE
FPCT	Helton, Todd, Rockies	.999
PO	Gonzalez, Adrian, Padres	1470
A	Gonzalez, Adrian, Padres	140
E	Fielder, Prince, Brewers	14
TC	Gonzalez, Adrian, Padres	1620
DP	LaRoche, Adam, Pirates	154

SECOND BASE
FPCT	Phillips, Brandon, Reds	.990
PO	Phillips, Brandon, Reds	341
A	Phillips, Brandon, Reds	433
E	Johnson, Kelly, Braves	14
E	Kent, Jeff, Dodgers	14
TC	Phillips, Brandon, Reds	782
DP	Sanchez, Freddy, Pirates	121

THIRD BASE
FPCT	Feliz, Pedro, Giants	.973
PO	Zimmerman, Ryan, Nationals	140
A	Zimmerman, Ryan, Nationals	348
E	Braun, Ryan, Brewers	26
TC	Zimmerman, Ryan, Nationals	511
DP	Zimmerman, Ryan, Nationals	39

OUTFIELD
FPCT	Five players tied at	.995
PO	Jones, Andruw, Atlanta Braves	396
A	Francoeur, Jeff, Atlanta Braves	19
	Soriano, Alfonso, Chicago Cubs	19
E	Burrell, Pat, Philadelphia Phillies	10
TC	Rowand, Aaron, Philadelphia Phillies	405
DP	Five players tied at	4

SHORTSTOP
FPCT	Tulowitzki, Troy, Rockies	.987
PO	Tulowitzki, Troy, Rockies	262
A	Tulowitzki, Troy, Rockies	561
E	Ramirez, Hanley, Marlins	24
TC	Tulowitzki, Troy, Rockies	834
DP	Tulowitzki, Troy, Rockies	114

2007
POSTSEASON

Red Sox' Series sweep caps bland playoff slate

BY JOHN PERROTTO

Few postseasons have had as little to offer as the one in 2007.

Five of the seven series were sweeps, including the World Series for the third time in four years. Another series went only one game over its limit and only one went the distance.

There were no signature moments and no memorable games. All in all, it was a blah run of October games.

Yet, it would be hard convincing the Red Sox that it wasn't an exciting postseason. Not when they captured their second World Series title in four seasons after enduring an 86-year championship drought.

The Red Sox punctuated their season with a four-game sweep of the red-hot Rockies in the World Series, and the party lasted late into a cool evening in Denver.

Red Sox manager Terry Francona, the coaches, players, owners and front-office workers celebrated on the field at

Josh Beckett gave up four runs in 30 postseason innings, improving his career mark to 6-0, 1.73

TWICE THE GLORY

With his second World Series title in four years, Red Sox skipper Terry Francona became the 21st manager ever to win it all more than once. Interestingly, both Billy Martin (94 games) and Dick Howser (one) spent time as manager for the World Series-winning 1978 Yankees, but Bob Lemon was manager during the playoffs, so he gets the credit. Had Martin (who won with the 1977 Yankees) or Howser (1985 Royals) kept the job, he would appear on the list below.

No.	Manager	WS Wins
1	Joe McCarthy, Yankees	7
	Casey Stengel, Yankees	7
3	Connie Mack, Athletics	5
4	Walter Alston, Dodgers	4
	Joe Torre, Yankees	4
6	Sparky Anderson, Reds/Tigers	3
	Miller Huggins, Yankees	3
	John McGraw, Giants	3
9	Bill Carrigan, Red Sox	2
	Frank Chance, Cubs	2
	Terry Francona, Red Sox	2
	Cito Gaston, Blue Jays	2
	Bucky Harris, Senators/Yankees	2
	Ralph Houk, Yankees	2
	Tom Kelly, Twins	2
	Tony La Russa, Athletics/Cardinals	2
	Tommy Lasorda, Dodgers	2
	Bill McKechnie, Pirates/Reds	2
	Danny Murtaugh, Pirates	2
	Billy Southworth, Cardinals	2
	Dick Williams, Athletics	2

Denver's Coors Field for a full two hours after righthander Jonathan Papelbon got pinch-hitter Seth Smith to swing through a high fastball for the final out. Demonstrating that Red Sox Nation has no qualms about traveling two time zones away, nearly 5,000 fans stood in the lower seating bowl and alternately cheered and chanted.

"Look at this scene. We have 16 million people in Red Sox Nation," said righthander Curt Schilling, referring to the population of New England. "We have a responsibility like no other team to our fans because we're the best-supported franchise in baseball. That's why the goal is to win the World Series every year, and it's so sweet when we're able to do it."

It was generally assumed the Red Sox could never enjoy a World Series title more than the one they captured in 2004 by sweeping the Cardinals. That year Boston rallied from a 3-0 deficit to beat the archrival Yankees in the American League Championship Series.

"This one is just as special in my book," Schilling said. "I don't know how you can compare one with the other. It's like if you have two children. They're both very special to you and you're not going to love one more than the other."

"Each season presents a different set of circumstances and that's why this one is as special as the one we won in '04," Francona said. "It's just hard to say this one is more special than that one or vice versa. You get so caught up in the moment and living in the present that you don't really take time to think about comparing what happened in the past to what is happening now.

"I know this much, though, when that final out is made and you're the champion, there is no other feeling like it in the world. To know you're the last team standing is pretty special."

The Red Sox emphatically made sure they were the last team standing, as they swept the Angels in three games in the AL Division Series then rallied from a 3-1 deficit to beat the Indians in an ALCS that went the full seven games. Then they put away the Rockies, who entered the World Series on one of the biggest late-season rolls in baseball history, with 21 wins in their previous 22 games.

The Red Sox outscored the Rockies 29-10 in the Series and out-hit them .333-.218, as they finished with the second-highest batting average ever in a World Series behind the .338 by the Yankees in 1960. The Yankees lost that series in seven games to the Pirates, but the Red Sox pitch-

World Series MVP Mike Lowell hit .400 in 15 at-bats with a home run and three doubles

ing staff made sure it would not squander that kind of offense in this series. They posted a 2.50 ERA.

"It all comes down to who executed better and I think there is little doubt that the Red Sox executed much better than we did in this series," Rockies manager Clint Hurdle said. "They played great. They were the better team in this series. I don't think anyone would dispute that."

One player who executed throughout the series was Red Sox third baseman Mike Lowell, winner of Series MVP honors for hitting .400 (6-for-15) with one double and a leadoff home run in the seventh inning of Game Four that chased Rockies starter Aaron Cook. The run proved critical as the Red Sox held on for a 4-3 victory.

Lowell also played on a World Series winner in 2003 when the Marlins knocked off the Yankees as heavy underdogs. For his part, Lowell said he felt a lot more pressure this time.

"In '03, we were kind of beating the odds each time we won, but I think it's a little different when from the outset a lot of people are expecting you to win a world championship. And if you don't, then it's a disappointing year," Lowell said. "For us to come through and do what we thought we were capable of doing is unbelievable."

The Red Sox were unbelievable from the get-go, as they rolled to a 13-1 victory in Game One at Fenway Park, setting a record for most runs and largest victory margin in an opener.

The Sweep, Blow By Blow

Red Sox righthander Josh Beckett allowed one run and six hits in seven innings, with one walk and nine strikeouts. He improved to 4-0, 1.20 in four postseason starts. More impressively, Beckett moved to 6-2, 1.73 in 10 career postseason games. Rookie second baseman Dustin Pedroia

EXPANSION-ERA PENNANTS

Baseball started small, adding the Angels and the Senators (second iteration) to the American League in 1961, and the Astros and Mets to the National in 1962, bringing the total number of teams to 20. By 1998, 10 additional expansion teams had been introduced to all four corners of North America and into all four time zones.

Seeing as three of the four '90s expansion teams already have won pennants and that nearly 50 percent (14 of 30) of all teams today are expansion teams, it doesn't make sense to take the long view of history when talking about World Series glory. To level the playing field, a look at pennant distribution in 47 years of the expansion era, 1961 through 2007:

Team	Years Active	W	L	Pennants
Yankees	All	8	6	14
Cardinals	All	4	4	8
Dodgers	All	4	4	8
Athletics	All	4	2	6
Orioles	All	3	3	6
Reds	All	3	3	6
Red Sox	All	2	3	5
Braves	All	1	4	5
Mets	46	2	2	4
Tigers	All	2	1	3
Twins	All	2	1	3
Phillies	All	1	2	3
Giants	All	0	3	3
Blue Jays	31	2	0	2
Marlins	15	2	0	2
Pirates	All	2	0	2
Royals	39	1	1	2
Indians	All	0	2	2
Padres	39	0	2	2
Angels	All	1	0	1
Diamondbacks	10	1	0	1
White Sox	All	1	0	1
Astros	46	0	1	1
Brewers	39	0	1	1
Rockies	15	0	1	1

No pennants: Cubs, Devil Rays, Mariners, Nationals and Rangers.
W = World Series won. L = World Series lost.

became only the second player to lead off a World Series with a home run.

The Red Sox then won a 2-1 squeaker in Game Two, as Lowell hit a tie-breaking double in the fifth inning. Schilling gave up only one run in 5⅓ innings for the win, while lefthander Hideki Okajima and Papelbon finished with a combined 3⅔ scoreless relief innings.

Game Three marked the first World Series game ever played in Denver but the Red Sox spoiled the mile-high party with a 10-5 win that put them on the brink of a sweep. Center fielder Jacoby Ellsbury, another rookie, had four hits and Pedroia added three. They became the first rookies to hit 1-2 in the batting order in a World Series game.

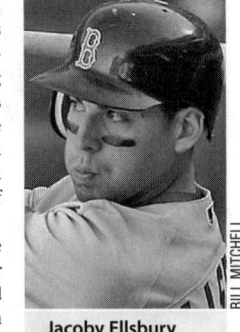

Jacoby Ellsbury

BILL MITCHELL

The Red Sox turned to lefthander Jon Lester in Game Four and he delivered 5⅓ scoreless innings for the win. A year ago at the time, Lester was undergoing chemotherapy treatments in his successful fight against lymphoma,.

Pinch-hitter Bobby Kielty homered in the eighth in his first World Series appearance to give the Red Sox a 4-1 lead. As it turned out, they needed that cushion because Rockies third baseman Garrett Atkins' two-run homer in the bottom of the inning drew the Rockies within a run. That's as far as they got. Papelbon retired the final five batters for the save.

Rocky Mountain High

The Rockies had been the story of the postseason until the World Series.

They were 5½ games out in the NL wild card race with 15 days remaining, but rattled off 13 wins in 14 games to force a one-game playoff with the Padres in Denver. The Padres scored two runs in the top of the 12th at Coors Field to take an 8-6 lead, but the Rockies rallied with three in the bottom of the inning against all-time saves leader Trevor Hoffman.

AMERICAN LEAGUE CHAMPIONS, 1901–2007

	PENNANT	PCT		PENNANT	PCT		PENNANT	PCT		PENNANT	PCT
1901	Chicago	.610	1918	Boston	.595	1935	Detroit	.616	1952	New York	.617
1902	Philadelphia	.610	1919	Chicago	.629	1936	New York	.667	1953	New York	.656
1903	Boston	.659	1920	Cleveland	.636	1937	New York	.662	1954	Cleveland	.721
1904	Boston	.617	1921	New York	.641	1938	New York	.651	1955	New York	.623
1905	Philadelphia	.622	1922	New York	.610	1939	New York	.702	1956	New York	.630
1906	Chicago	.616	1923	New York	.645	1940	Detroit	.584	1957	New York	.636
1907	Detroit	.613	1924	Washington	.597	1941	New York	.656	1958	New York	.597
1908	Detroit	.588	1925	Washington	.636	1942	New York	.669	1959	Chicago	.610
1909	Detroit	.645	1926	New York	.591	1943	New York	.636	1960	New York	.630
1910	Philadelphia	.680	1927	New York	.714	1944	St. Louis	.578	1961	New York	.673
1911	Philadelphia	.669	1928	New York	.656	1945	Detroit	.575	1962	New York	.593
1912	Boston	.691	1929	Philadelphia	.693	1946	Boston	.675	1963	New York	.646
1913	Philadelphia	.627	1930	Philadelphia	.662	1947	New York	.630	1964	New York	.611
1914	Philadelphia	.651	1931	Philadelphia	.704	1948	Cleveland	.626	1965	Minnesota	.630
1915	Boston	.669	1932	New York	.695	1949	New York	.630	1966	Baltimore	.606
1916	Boston	.591	1933	Washington	.651	1950	New York	.636	1967	Boston	.568
1917	Chicago	.649	1934	Detroit	.656	1951	New York	.636	1968	Detroit	.636

DIVISION ERA (1969-1993)

*Won pennant. ^ Won first half; defeated Milwaukee 3-2 in playoff. ^^ Won first half, defeated Kansas City 3-0.

	EAST	PCT	WEST	PCT	LCS		EAST	PCT	WEST	PCT	LCS
1969	Baltimore★	.673	Minnesota	.599	3-0		Milwaukee	.585	Kansas City	.566	
1970	Baltimore★	.667	Minnesota	.605	3-0	1982	Milwaukee★	.586	California	.574	3-2
1971	Baltimore★	.639	Oakland	.627	3-0	1983	Baltimore★	.605	Chicago	.611	3-1
1972	Detroit	.551	Oakland★	.600	3-2	1984	Detroit★	.642	Kansas City	.519	3-0
1973	Baltimore	.599	Oakland★	.580	3-2	1985	Toronto	.615	Kansas City★	.562	4-3
1974	Baltimore	.562	Oakland★	.556	3-1	1986	Boston★	.590	California	.568	4-3
1975	Boston★	.594	Oakland	.605	3-0	1987	Detroit	.605	Minnesota★	.525	4-1
1976	New York★	.610	Kansas City	.556	3-2	1988	Boston	.549	Oakland★	.642	4-0
1977	New York★	.617	Kansas City	.630	3-2	1989	Toronto	.549	Oakland★	.611	4-1
1978	New York★	.613	Kansas City	.568	3-1	1990	Boston	.543	Oakland★	.636	4-0
1979	Baltimore★	.642	California	.543	3-1	1991	Toronto	.562	Minnesota★	.586	4-1
1980	New York	.636	Kansas City★	.599	3-0	1992	Toronto★	.593	Oakland	.593	4-2
1981	New York★^	.607	Oakland^^	.587	3-0	1993	Toronto★	.586	Chicago	.580	4-2

WILD CARD ERA (1994—2007)

*Won pennant. † Lost ALCS.

	EAST	PCT	CENTRAL	PCT	WEST	PCT	WILD CARD	PCT	LCS
1994	New York	.619	Chicago	.593	Texas	.456	None		
1995	Boston	.597	Cleveland★	.694	Seattle†	.545	New York (E)	.549	4-2
1996	New York★	.568	Cleveland	.615	Texas	.556	Baltimore (E)†	.543	4-1
1997	Baltimore†	.605	Cleveland★	.534	Seattle	.556	New York (E)	.593	4-2
1998	New York★	.704	Cleveland†	.549	Texas	.543	Boston (E)	.568	4-2
1999	New York★	.605	Cleveland	.599	Texas	.586	Boston (E)†	.580	4-1
2000	New York★	.540	Chicago	.586	Oakland	.565	Seattle (W)†	.562	4-2
2001	New York★	.594	Cleveland	.562	Seattle†	.716	Oakland (W)	.630	4-1
2002	New York	.640	Minnesota†	.584	Oakland	.636	Anaheim (W)★	.611	4-1
2003	New York★	.623	Minnesota	.556	Oakland	.593	Boston (E)†	.586	4-3
2004	New York†	.623	Minnesota	.568	Anaheim	.568	Boston (E)★	.605	4-3
2005	New York	.586	Chicago★	.611	Los Angeles†	.586	Boston (E)	.586	4-1
2006	New York★	.599	Minnesota	.593	Oakland†	.574	Detroit (C)★	.586	4-0
2007	Boston★	.593	Cleveland†	.593	Los Angeles	.580	New York (E)	.580	4-3

The winning run scored when outfielder Matt Holliday dashed home from third base on Jamey Carroll's sacrifice fly to shallow right field.

The Rockies then joined the 1976 Cincinnati Reds as the only teams to win their first seven postseason games, sweeping the Phillies in three games in the NLDS and the Diamondbacks in four games in the NLCS. The Diamondbacks had swept the Cubs in three games in the other NLDS.

Holliday was the NLCS MVP for going 5-for-15 (.333) with two homers and four RBIs.

The Rockies had eight days off before the start of the World Series, the longest idle spell ever for a league champion. It was fair to speculate that the layoff may have contributed to their World Series struggles. At the very least, the magic had worn off.

"There is no reason to hang our heads, because we accomplished a lot this season," said first baseman Todd Helton, who made it to the postseason for the fist time after playing in 1,578 regular-season games with the Rockies.

"We have no reason to be upset. We made the World Series. We did a lot this year. We came a long way."

After polishing off the Angels in the ALDS, the Red Sox had to come a long way back against the Indians in the ALCS, but did so in grand fashion by outscoring Cleveland 30-5 in winning the final three games.

Boston found themselves in a 3-1 hole after dropping one game at home and two more in Cleveland, but battled back against the Indians' top two starters—lefthander C.C. Sabathia and righthander Fausto Carmona—to win the series in seven games. The Indians made it to the ALCS by downing the Yankees in four games in their ALDS.

The Red Sox then carried that momentum right on into the World Series, finishing the postseason on a seven-game winning streak, which was reminiscent of their closing run in 2004 in which they won the final four games against the Yankees in the ALCS and then swept the Cardinals in the World Series.

"This team's got a lot of heart," Red Sox catcher and captain Jason Varitek said. "We worked really hard. We had to battle like crazy to beat Cleveland then we beat a very, very good team in the Rockies. An excellent team. We had to do the little things to win and we did."

NATIONAL LEAGUE CHAMPIONS, 1901–2007

	PENNANT	PCT		PENNANT	PCT		PENNANT	PCT		PENNANT	PCT
1901	Pittsburgh	.647	1918	Chicago	.651	1935	Chicago	.649	1952	Brooklyn	.627
1902	Pittsburgh	.741	1919	Cincinnati	.686	1936	New York	.597	1953	Brooklyn	.682
1903	Pittsburgh	.650	1920	Brooklyn	.604	1937	New York	.625	1954	New York	.630
1904	New York	.693	1921	New York	.614	1938	Chicago	.586	1955	Brooklyn	.641
1905	New York	.686	1922	New York	.604	1939	Cincinnati	.630	1956	Brooklyn	.604
1906	Chicago	.763	1923	New York	.621	1940	Cincinnati	.654	1957	Milwaukee	.617
1907	Chicago	.704	1924	New York	.608	1941	Brooklyn	.649	1958	Milwaukee	.597
1908	Chicago	.643	1925	Pittsburgh	.621	1942	St. Louis	.688	1959	Los Angeles	.564
1909	Pittsburgh	.724	1926	St. Louis	.578	1943	St. Louis	.682	1960	Pittsburgh	.617
1910	Chicago	.675	1927	Pittsburgh	.610	1944	St. Louis	.682	1961	Cincinnati	.604
1911	New York	.647	1928	St. Louis	.617	1945	Chicago	.636	1962	San Francisco	.624
1912	New York	.682	1929	Chicago	.645	1946	St. Louis	.628	1963	Los Angeles	.611
1913	New York	.664	1930	St. Louis	.597	1947	Brooklyn	.610	1964	St. Louis	.574
1914	Boston	.614	1931	St. Louis	.656	1948	Boston	.595	1965	Los Angeles	.599
1915	Philadelphia	.592	1932	Chicago	.584	1949	Brooklyn	.630	1966	Los Angeles	.586
1916	Brooklyn	.610	1933	New York	.599	1950	Philadelphia	.591	1967	St. Louis	.627
1917	New York	.636	1934	St. Louis	.621	1951	New York	.624	1968	St. Louis	.599

DIVISION ERA (1969—1993)

*Won pennant. ^ Won first half; defeated Milwaukee 3-2 in playoff. ^^ Won first half, defeated Kansas City 3-0.

	EAST	PCT	WEST	PCT	LCS		EAST	PCT	WEST	PCT	LCS
1969	New York★	.617	Atlanta	.574	3-0		Philadelphia	.618	Houston	.623	
1970	Pittsburgh	.549	Cincinnati★	.630	3-0	1982	St. Louis★	.568	Atlanta	.549	3-0
1971	Pittsburgh★	.599	San Francisco	.556	3-1	1983	Philadelphia★	.556	Los Angeles	.562	3-1
1972	Pittsburgh	.619	Cincinnati★	.617	3-2	1984	Chicago	.596	San Diego★	.568	3-2
1973	New York★	.509	Cincinnati	.611	3-2	1985	St. Louis★	.623	Los Angeles	.586	4-2
1974	Pittsburgh	.543	Los Angeles★	.630	3-1	1986	New York★	.667	Houston	.593	4-2
1975	Pittsburgh	.571	Cincinnati★	.667	3-0	1987	St. Louis★	.586	San Francisco	.556	4-3
1976	Philadelphia	.623	Cincinnati★	.630	3-0	1988	New York	.625	Los Angeles★	.584	4-3
1977	Philadelphia	.623	Los Angeles★	.605	3-1	1989	Chicago	.571	San Francisco★	.568	4-1
1978	Philadelphia	.556	Los Angeles★	.586	3-1	1990	Pittsburgh	.586	Cincinnati★	.562	4-2
1979	Pittsburgh★	.605	Cincinnati	.559	3-0	1991	Pittsburgh	.605	Atlanta★	.580	4-3
1980	Philadelphia★	.562	Houston	.571	3-2	1992	Pittsburgh	.593	Atlanta★	.605	4-3
1981	Montreal^	.566	Los Angeles★^^	.632	3-2	1993	Philadelphia★	.599	Atlanta	.642	4-2

WILD CARD ERA (1994—2007)

*Won pennant. † Lost ALCS.

	EAST	PCT	CENTRAL	PCT	WEST	PCT	WILD CARD	PCT	LCS
1994	Montreal	.649	Cincinnati	.593	Los Angeles	.509	None		
1995	Atlanta★	.625	Cincinnati†	.590	Los Angeles	.542	Colorado (W)	.535	4-2
1996	Atlanta★	.593	St. Louis†	.543	San Diego	.562	Los Angeles (W)	.556	4-3
1997	Atlanta†	.623	Houston	.519	San Francisco	.556	Florida (E)★	.568	4-2
1998	Atlanta†	.654	Houston	.630	San Diego★	.605	Chicago (C)	.552	4-2
1999	Atlanta★	.636	Houston	.599	Arizona	.617	New York (E)†	.595	4-2
2000	Atlanta	.586	St. Louis†	.586	San Francisco	.599	New York (E)★	.580	4-1
2001	Atlanta†	.543	Houston	.574	Arizona★	.568	St. Louis (C)	.574	4-1
2002	Atlanta	.631	St. Louis†	.599	Arizona	.605	San Francisco (W)★	.590	4-1
2003	Atlanta	.623	Chicago†	.543	San Francisco	.621	Florida (E)★	.562	4-3
2004	Atlanta	.593	St. Louis★	.648	Los Angeles	.574	Houston (C)†	.568	4-3
2005	Atlanta	.556	St. Louis†	.617	San Diego	.506	Houston (C)★	.549	4-2
2006	New York†	.599	St. Louis★	.516	San Diego	.543	Los Angeles (W)	.543	4-3
2007	Philadelphia	.549	Chicago	.525	Arizona†	.556	Colorado (W)★	.552	4-0

THE WORLD SERIES — YEAR-BY-YEAR

No Series played on 1994

Year	Winner	Manager	Loser	Manager	Result	MVP
1903	Boston (AL)	Jimmy Collins	Pittsburgh (NL)	Fred Clarke	5-3	None Selected
1904	NO SERIES					
1905	New York (NL)	John McGraw	Philadelphia (AL)	Connie Mack	4-1	None Selected
1906	Chicago (AL)	Fielder Jones	Chicago (NL)	Frank Chance	4-2	None Selected
1907	Chicago (NL)	Frank Chance	Detroit (AL)	Hugh Jennings	4-0	None Selected
1908	Chicago (NL)	Frank Chance	Detroit (AL)	Hugh Jennings	4-1	None Selected
1909	Pittsburgh (NL)	Fred Clarke	Detroit (AL)	Hugh Jennings	4-3	None Selected
1910	Philadelphia (AL)	Connie Mack	Chicago (NL)	Frank Chance	4-1	None Selected
1911	Philadelphia (AL)	Connie Mack	New York (NL)	John McGraw	4-2	None Selected
1912	Boston (AL)	Jake Stahl	New York (NL)	John McGraw	4-3-1	None Selected
1913	Philadelphia (AL)	Connie Mack	New York (NL)	John McGraw	4-1	None Selected
1914	Boston (NL)	George Stallings	Philadelphia (AL)	Connie Mack	4-0	None Selected
1915	Boston (AL)	Bill Carrigan	Philadelphia (NL)	Pat Moran	4-1	None Selected
1916	Boston (AL)	Bill Carrigan	Brooklyn (NL)	Wilbert Robinson	4-1	None Selected
1917	Chicago (AL)	Pants Rowland	New York (NL)	John McGraw	4-2	None Selected
1918	Boston (AL)	Ed Barrow	Chicago (NL)	Fred Mitchell	4-2	None Selected
1919	Cincinnati (NL)	Pat Moran	Chicago (AL)	Kid Gleason	5-3	None Selected
1920	Cleveland (AL)	Tris Speaker	Brooklyn (NL)	Wilbert Robinson	5-2	None Selected
1921	New York (NL)	John McGraw	New York (AL)	Miller Huggins	5-3	None Selected
1922	New York (NL)	John McGraw	New York (AL)	Miller Huggins	4-0	None Selected
1923	New York (AL)	Miller Huggins	New York (NL)	John McGraw	4-2	None Selected
1924	Washington (AL)	Bucky Harris	New York (NL)	John McGraw	4-3	None Selected
1925	Pittsburgh (NL)	Bill McKechnie	Washington (AL)	Bucky Harris	4-3	None Selected
1926	St. Louis (NL)	Rogers Hornsby	New York (AL)	Miller Huggins	4-3	None Selected
1927	New York (AL)	Miller Huggins	Pittsburgh (NL)	Donie Bush	4-0	None Selected
1928	New York (AL)	Miller Huggins	St. Louis (NL)	Bill McKechnie	4-0	None Selected
1929	Philadelphia (AL)	Connie Mack	Chicago (NL)	Joe McCarthy	4-1	None Selected
1930	Philadelphia (AL)	Connie Mack	St. Louis (NL)	Gabby Street	4-2	None Selected
1931	St. Louis (NL)	Gabby Street	Philadelphia (AL)	Connie Mack	4-3	None Selected
1932	New York (AL)	Joe McCarthy	Chicago (NL)	Charlie Grimm	4-0	None Selected
1933	New York (NL)	Bill Terry	Washington (AL)	Joe Cronin	4-1	None Selected
1934	St. Louis (NL)	Frankie Frisch	Detroit (AL)	Mickey Cochrane	4-3	None Selected
1935	Detroit (AL)	Mickey Cochrane	Chicago (NL)	Charlie Grimm	4-2	None Selected
1936	New York (AL)	Joe McCarthy	New York (NL)	Bill Terry	4-2	None Selected
1937	New York (AL)	Joe McCarthy	New York (NL)	Bill Terry	4-1	None Selected
1938	New York (AL)	Joe McCarthy	Chicago (NL)	Gabby Hartnett	4-0	None Selected
1939	New York (AL)	Joe McCarthy	Cincinnati (NL)	Bill McKechnie	4-0	None Selected
1940	Cincinnati (NL)	Bill McKechnie	Detroit (AL)	Del Baker	4-3	None Selected
1941	New York (AL)	Joe McCarthy	Brooklyn (NL)	Leo Durocher	4-1	None Selected
1942	St. Louis (NL)	Billy Southworth	New York (AL)	Joe McCarthy	4-1	None Selected
1943	New York (AL)	Joe McCarthy	St. Louis (NL)	Billy Southworth	4-1	None Selected
1944	St. Louis (NL)	Billy Southworth	St. Louis (AL)	Luke Sewell	4-2	None Selected
1945	Detroit (AL)	Steve O'Neill	Chicago (NL)	Charlie Grimm	4-3	None Selected
1946	St. Louis (NL)	Eddie Dyer	Boston (AL)	Joe Cronin	4-3	None Selected
1947	New York (AL)	Bucky Harris	Brooklyn (NL)	Burt Shotton	4-3	None Selected
1948	Cleveland (AL)	Lou Boudreau	Boston (NL)	Billy Southworth	4-2	None Selected
1949	New York (AL)	Casey Stengel	Brooklyn (NL)	Burt Shotton	4-1	None Selected
1950	New York (AL)	Casey Stengel	Philadelphia (NL)	Eddie Sawyer	4-0	None Selected
1951	New York (AL)	Casey Stengel	New York (NL)	Leo Durocher	4-2	None Selected
1952	New York (AL)	Casey Stengel	Brooklyn (NL)	Chuck Dressen	4-3	None Selected
1953	New York (AL)	Casey Stengel	Brooklyn (NL)	Chuck Dressen	4-2	None Selected
1954	New York (NL)	Leo Durocher	Cleveland (AL)	Al Lopez	4-0	None Selected

Year	Winner	Manager	Loser	Manager	Result	MVP
1955	Brooklyn (NL)	Walter Alston	New York (AL)	Casey Stengel	4-3	Johnny Podres, p, Brooklyn
1956	New York (AL)	Casey Stengel	Brooklyn (NL)	Walter Alston	4-3	Don Larsen, p, New York
1957	Milwaukee (NL)	Fred Haney	New York (AL)	Casey Stengel	4-3	Lew Burdette, p, Milwaukee
1958	New York (AL)	Casey Stengel	Milwaukee (NL)	Fred Haney	4-3	Bob Turley, p, New York
1959	Los Angeles (NL)	Walter Alston	Chicago (AL)	Al Lopez	4-2	Larry Sherry, p, Los Angeles
1960	Pittsburgh (NL)	Danny Murtaugh	New York (AL)	Casey Stengel	4-3	Bobby Richardson, 2b, New York
1961	New York (AL)	Ralph Houk	Cincinnati (NL)	Fred Hutchinson	4-1	Whitey Ford, p, New York
1962	New York (AL)	Ralph Houk	San Francisco (NL)	Alvin Dark	4-3	Ralph Terry, p, New York
1963	Los Angeles (NL)	Walter Alston	New York (AL)	Ralph Houk	4-0	Sandy Koufax, p, Los Angeles
1964	St. Louis (NL)	Johnny Keane	New York (AL)	Yogi Berra	4-3	Bob Gibson, p, St. Louis
1965	Los Angeles (NL)	Walter Alston	Minnesota (AL)	Sam Mele	4-3	Sandy Koufax, p, Los Angeles
1966	Baltimore (AL)	Hank Bauer	Los Angeles (NL)	Walter Alston	4-0	Frank Robinson, of, Baltimore
1967	St. Louis (NL)	Red Schoendienst	Boston (AL)	Dick Williams	4-3	Bob Gibson, p, St. Louis
1968	Detroit (AL)	Mayo Smith	St. Louis (NL)	Red Schoendienst	4-3	Mickey Lolich, p, Detroit
1969	New York (NL)	Gil Hodges	Baltimore (AL)	Earl Weaver	4-1	Donn Clendenon, 1b, New York
1970	Baltimore (AL)	Earl Weaver	Cincinnati (NL)	Sparky Anderson	4-1	Brooks Robinson, 3b, Baltimore
1971	Pittsburgh (NL)	Danny Murtaugh	Baltimore (AL)	Earl Weaver	4-3	Roberto Clemente, of, Pittsburgh
1972	Oakland (AL)	Dick Williams	Cincinnati (NL)	Sparky Anderson	4-3	Gene Tenace, c, Oakland
1973	Oakland (AL)	Dick Williams	New York (NL)	Yogi Berra	4-3	Reggie Jackson, of, Oakland
1974	Oakland (AL)	Alvin Dark	Los Angeles (NL)	Walter Alston	4-1	Rollie Fingers, p, Oakland
1975	Cincinnati (NL)	Sparky Anderson	Boston (AL)	Darrell Johnson	4-3	Pete Rose, 3b, Cincinnati
1976	Cincinnati (NL)	Sparky Anderson	New York (AL)	Billy Martin	4-0	Johnny Bench, c, Cincinnati
1977	New York (AL)	Billy Martin	Los Angeles (NL)	Tom Lasorda	4-2	Reggie Jackson, of, New York
1978	New York (AL)	Bob Lemon	Los Angeles (NL)	Tom Lasorda	4-2	Bucky Dent, ss, New York
1979	Pittsburgh (NL)	Chuck Tanner	Baltimore (AL)	Earl Weaver	4-3	Willie Stargell, 1b, Pittsburgh
1980	Philadelphia (NL)	Dallas Green	Kansas City (AL)	Jim Frey	4-2	Mike Schmidt, 3b, Philadelphia
1981	Los Angeles (NL)	Tom Lasorda	New York (AL)	Bob Lemon	4-2	Cey/Guerrero/Yeager, L.A.
1982	St. Louis (NL)	Whitey Herzog	Milwaukee (AL)	Harvey Kuenn	4-3	Darrell Porter, c, St. Louis
1983	Baltimore (AL)	Joe Altobelli	Philadelphia (NL)	Paul Owens	4-1	Rick Dempsey, c, Baltimore
1984	Detroit (AL)	Sparky Anderson	San Diego (NL)	Dick Williams	4-1	Alan Trammell, ss, Detroit
1985	Kansas City (AL)	Dick Howser	St. Louis (NL)	Whitey Herzog	4-3	Bret Saberhagen, p, Kansas City
1986	New York (NL)	Dave Johnson	Boston (AL)	John McNamara	4-3	Ray Knight, 3b, New York
1987	Minnesota (AL)	Tom Kelly	St. Louis (NL)	Whitey Herzog	4-3	Frank Viola, p, Minnesota
1988	Los Angeles (NL)	Tom Lasorda	Oakland (AL)	Tony La Russa	4-1	Orel Hershiser, p, Los Angeles
1989	Oakland (AL)	Tony La Russa	San Francisco (NL)	Roger Craig	4-0	Dave Stewart, p, Oakland
1990	Cincinnati (NL)	Lou Piniella	Oakland (AL)	Tony La Russa	4-0	Jose Rijo, p, Cincinnati
1991	Minnesota (AL)	Tom Kelly	Atlanta (NL)	Bobby Cox	4-3	Jack Morris, p, Minnesota
1992	Toronto (AL)	Cito Gaston	Atlanta (NL)	Bobby Cox	4-2	Pat Borders, c, Toronto
1993	Toronto (AL)	Cito Gaston	Philadelphia (NL)	Jim Fregosi	4-2	Paul Molitor, dh, Toronto
1995	Atlanta (NL)	Bobby Cox	Cleveland (AL)	Mike Hargrove	4-2	Tom Glavine, p, Atlanta
1996	New York (AL)	Joe Torre	Atlanta (NL)	Bobby Cox	4-2	John Wetteland, p, New York
1997	Florida (NL)	Jim Leyland	Cleveland (AL)	Mike Hargrove	4-3	Livan Hernandez, p, Florida
1998	New York (AL)	Joe Torre	San Diego (NL)	Bruce Bochy	4-0	Scott Brosius, 3b, New York
1999	New York (AL)	Joe Torre	Atlanta (NL)	Bobby Cox	4-0	Mariano Rivera, p, New York
2000	New York (AL)	Joe Torre	New York (NL)	Bobby Valentine	4-1	Derek Jeter, ss, New York
2001	Arizona (NL)	Bob Brenly	New York (AL)	Joe Torre	4-3	Johnson, p/Schilling, p, Arizona
2002	Anaheim (AL)	Mike Scioscia	San Francisco (NL)	Dusty Baker	4-3	Troy Glaus, 3b, Anaheim
2003	Florida (NL)	Jack McKeon	New York (AL)	Joe Torre	4-2	Josh Beckett, p, Florida
2004	Boston (AL)	Terry Francona	St. Louis (NL)	Tony La Russa	4-0	Manny Ramirez, of, Boston
2005	Chicago (AL)	Ozzie Guillen	Houston (NL)	Phil Garner	4-0	Jermaine Dye, of, Chicago
2006	St. Louis (NL)	Tony La Russa	Detroit (AL)	Jim Leyland	4-1	David Eckstein, ss, St. Louis
2007	Boston (AL)	Terry Francona	Colorado (NL)	Clint Hurdle	4-0	Mike Lowell, 3b, Boston

WORLD SERIES BOX SCORES

GAME ONE OCTOBER 24, 2007

BOSTON RED SOX 13, COLORADO ROCKIES 1

Colorado	ab	r	h	bi	bb	so	Boston	ab	r	h	bi	bb	so
Taveras, cf	4	0	0	0	0	2	Pedroia, 2b	5	1	1	2	1	0
Matsui, 2b	4	0	1	0	0	1	Youkilis, 1b	5	3	2	1	1	1
Holliday, lf	4	0	0	0	0	2	Ortiz, dh	5	2	3	2	0	0
Helton, 1b	4	0	2	0	0	1	a-Hinske, ph-dh	1	0	0	0	0	1
Atkins, 3b	4	1	1	0	0	1	Ramirez, lf	4	3	3	2	1	0
Hawpe, rf	4	0	0	0	0	4	Crisp, cf	1	0	0	0	0	0
Tulowitzki, ss	3	0	2	1	0	0	Lowell, 3b	3	1	1	0	2	0
Torrealba, c	3	0	0	0	0	1	Varitek, c	4	1	2	2	1	2
Spilborghs, dh	2	0	0	0	1	0	Drew, rf	5	1	2	2	0	1
							Lugo, ss	4	0	3	1	1	0
							Cora, ss	0	0	0	0	0	0
							Ellsbury, cf-lf	4	1	0	1	1	1
TOTALS	**32**	**1**	**6**	**1**	**1**	**12**	**TOTALS**	**41**	**13**	**17**	**13**	**8**	**6**

```
Colorado   010 000 000—1
Boston     310 270 00x—13
```

a-Struck out for Ortiz in the 8th.

LOB—Rockies 5, Red Sox 12. **2B**—Atkins (1), Tulowitzki 2 (2), Helton (1), Youkilis 2 (2), Drew (1), Ortiz 2 (2), Ramirez (1), Varitek (1), Lowell (1). **HR**—Pedroia (1).

COLORADO	IP	H	R	ER	BB	SO	BOSTON	IP	H	R	ER	BB	SO
Francis L	4	10	6	6	3	3	Beckett W	7	6	1	1	1	9
Morales	⅔	6	7	7	1	0	Timlin	1	0	0	0	0	2
Speier	0	0	0	3	0	Gagne	1	0	0	0	0	1
Herges	1⅓	0	0	0	1	1							
Affeldt	1	1	0	0	0	0							
Hawkins	1	0	0	0	0	2							

Speier pitched to 3 batters in the 5th.

Balk—Morales. **IBB**—Ramirez (by Francis), Lowell (by Francis).

Umpires: HP—Ed Montague. 1B—Laz Diaz. 2B—Ted Barrett. 3B—Chuck Meriwether. LF—Mike Everitt. RF—Mike Reilly.
T—3:30. **A**—36,733.

GAME TWO OCTOBER 25, 2007

BOSTON RED SOX 2, COLORADO ROCKIES 1

Colorado	ab	r	h	bi	bb	so	Boston	ab	r	h	bi	bb	so
Taveras, cf	3	1	0	0	0	1	Pedroia, 2b	4	0	1	0	1	0
Matsui, 2b	4	0	0	0	0	2	Youkilis, 1b	3	0	0	0	2	0
Holliday, lf	4	0	4	0	0	0	Ortiz, dh	3	1	0	0	1	1
Helton, 1b	3	0	0	1	1	1	Ramirez, lf	4	0	1	0	0	1
Atkins, 3b	4	0	0	0	0	0	Lowell, 3b	3	1	1	1	1	0
Hawpe, rf	4	0	1	0	0	2	Drew, rf	2	0	2	0	1	0
Tulowitzki, ss	2	0	0	0	1	1	Varitek, c	3	0	0	1	0	2
Torrealba, c	2	0	0	0	0	0	Ellsbury, cf	3	0	1	0	1	0
Spilborghs, dh	3	0	0	0	0	3	Lugo, ss	3	0	0	0	0	0
TOTALS	**29**	**1**	**5**	**1**	**2**	**10**	**TOTALS**	**28**	**2**	**6**	**2**	**7**	**3**

```
Colorado   100 000 000—1
Boston     000 110 00x—2
```

LOB—Rockies 5, Red Sox 12. **2B**—Lowell (2). **S**—Lugo. **SF**—Varitek. **SB**—Ellsbury (1). **PO**—Holliday. **E**—Lowell (1).

COLORADO	IP	H	R	ER	BB	SO	BOSTON	IP	H	R	ER	BB	SO
Jimenez L	4⅓	3	2	2	5	2	Schilling W	5⅓	4	1	1	2	4
Affeldt	0	0	0	0	1	0	Okajima	2⅓	0	0	0	0	4
Herges	1	1	0	0	1	0	Papelbon S	1⅓	1	0	0	0	2
Fuentes	2	1	0	0	0	1							
Corpas	⅓	0	0	0	0	0							

Affeldt pitched to 1 batter in the 5th.

Pickoff: Papelbon (Holliday at 1st base). **HBP**—Drew (by Jimenez), Taveras (by Schilling).

T—3:39. **A**—36,730.

GAME THREE OCTOBER 27, 2007

BOSTON RED SOX 10, COLORADO ROCKIES 5

Boston	ab	r	h	bi	bb	so	Colorado	ab	r	h	bi	bb	so
Ellsbury, cf-lf	5	2	4	2	0	0	Matsui, 2b	5	1	3	0	0	1
Pedroia, 2b	5	1	3	2	0	0	Tulowitzki, ss	4	1	1	0	1	1
Papelbon, p	0	0	0	0	0	0	Holliday, lf	5	1	3	0	0	0
Ortiz, 1b	4	1	1	1	0	2	Helton, 1b	4	1	1	0	1	1

Rockies lefthander Jeff Francis went 17-9, 4.22 on the year, but lasted just four innings in Game One
BILL MITCHELL

Youkilis, 1b	1	0	0	0	0	0	Atkins, 3b	2	1	0	0	2	1
Ramirez, lf	4	0	0	1	1	1	Hawpe, rf	5	0	2	1	0	2
Lowell, 3b	5	2	2	2	0	1	Torrealba, c	5	0	2	1	0	0
Drew, rf	4	0	1	0	0	1	Sullivan, cf	2	0	0	0	0	0
Okajima, p	0	0	0	0	0	0	b-Spilborghs, ph-cf	2	0	0	0	0	0
Delcarmen, p	0	0	0	0	0	0	Fogg, p	0	0	0	0	0	0
Cora, 2b	0	0	0	0	0	0	Morales, p	1	0	0	0	0	1
Varitek, c	4	1	1	1	0	1	a-Smith, ph	1	0	1	0	0	0
Lugo, ss	3	2	1	0	2	0	Affeldt, p	0	0	0	0	0	0
Matsuzaka, p	3	0	1	2	0	1	c-Baker, ph	1	0	0	0	0	0
Lopez, p	0	0	0	0	0	0	Herges, p	0	0	0	0	0	0
Timlin, p	0	0	0	0	0	0	Fuentes, p	0	0	0	0	0	0
Crisp, cf	1	1	1	0	0	0	d-Taveras, ph	1	0	0	0	0	0
							Hawkins, p	0	0	0	0	0	0
TOTALS	**39**	**10**	**15**	**10**	**3**	**7**	**TOTALS**	**38**	**5**	**11**	**5**	**4**	**7**

```
Boston     006 000 031—10
Colorado   000 002 300—5
```

a-Singled for Morales in the 5th. b-Flied out for Sullivan in the 6th. c-Lined out for Affeldt in the 6th. d-Lined out for Fuentes in the 8th.

LOB—Red Sox 7, Rockies 11. **2B**—Lugo (1), Ellsbury 3 (3), Ortiz (3), Drew (2), Pedroia (1). **3B**—Hawpe (1). **HR**—Holliday (1). **S**—Cora. **SF**—Varitek. **SB**—Lowell (1). **E**—Drew (1). **SB**—Matsui (1). **A**—Holliday.

BOSTON	IP	H	R	ER	BB	SO	COLORADO	IP	H	R	ER	BB	SO
Matsuzaka W	5⅓	3	2	2	3	5	Fogg L	2⅔	10	6	6	2	2
Lopez	0	2	0	0	0	0	Morales	2⅓	1	0	0	0	1
Timlin	⅔	2	2	2	0	0	Affeldt	1	0	0	0	0	1
Okajima	1	2	1	1	0	2	Herges	1	0	0	0	0	3
Delcarmen	⅔	1	0	0	1	0	Fuentes	1	3	3	3	1	0
Papelbon S	1⅓	1	0	0	0	0	Hawkins	1	1	1	1	0	0

Lopez pitched to 2 batters in the 6th.
Timlin pitched to 2 batters in the 7th.

IBB—Ramirez (by Fogg). **HBP**—Atkins (by Matsuzaka).
T—4:19. **A**—49,983.

GAME FOUR OCTOBER 28, 2007

BOSTON RED SOX 4, COLORADO ROCKIES 3

Boston	ab	r	h	bi	bb	so	Colorado	ab	r	h	bi	bb	so
Ellsbury, cf-lf	4	1	2	0	0	1	Matsui, 2b	4	0	1	0	0	1

BOSTON

Player, Pos.	AB	R	H	RBI	BB	SO
Pedroia, 2b	4	0	0	0	0	0
Ortiz, 1b	3	0	1	1	1	0
1-Crisp, pr-cf	0	0	0	0	0	0
Ramirez, lf	4	0	0	0	0	1
Okajima, p	0	0	0	0	0	0
Papelbon, p	0	0	0	0	0	0
Lowell, 3b	4	2	2	1	0	0
Drew, rf	4	0	0	0	1	0
Varitek, c	4	0	2	1	0	0
Lugo, ss	3	0	1	0	0	0
Lester, p	2	0	0	0	0	1
Delcarmen, p	0	0	0	0	0	0
Timlin, p	0	0	0	0	0	0
a-Kielty, ph	1	1	1	1	0	0
Youkilis, 1b	0	0	0	0	0	
TOTALS	33	4	9	4	1	4

COLORADO

Player, Pos.	AB	R	H	RBI	BB	SO
Corpas, p	0	0	0	0	0	0
c-Smith, ph	1	0	0	0	0	1
Tulowitzki, ss	4	0	0	0	0	3
Holliday, lf	4	0	0	0	0	1
Helton, 1b	4	1	2	0	0	0
Atkins, 3b	3	1	1	2	1	0
Spilborghs, cf	3	0	0	0	1	1
Hawpe, rf	3	1	1	1	1	0
Torrealba, c	4	0	0	0	1	0
Cook, p	2	0	1	0	0	0
Affeldt, p	0	0	0	0	0	0
b-Sullivan, ph	1	0	1	0	0	0
Fuentes, p	0	0	0	0	0	0
Carroll, 2b	1	0	0	0	0	0
TOTALS	34	3	7	3	3	7

Boston 100 010 110—4
Colorado 000 000 120—3

a-Homered for Timlin in the 8th. 1-Ran for Ortiz in the 8th.
b-Singled for Affeldt in the 7th. c-Struck out for Corpas in the 9th.

LOB—Red Sox 3, Rockies 7. 2B—Ellsbury (4), Lowell (3), Helton (2), Matsui (1). HR—Lowell (1), Kielty (1), Hawpe (1), Atkins (1).

BOSTON	IP	H	R	ER	BB	SO
Lester W	5⅔	3	0	0	3	3
Delcarmen	⅔	2	1	1	0	1
Timlin	⅔	0	0	0	0	2
Okajima	⅓	2	2	0	0	0
Papelbon S	1⅓	0	0	0	0	1

COLORADO	IP	H	R	ER	BB	SO
Cook L	6	6	3	3	0	2
Affeldt	1	1	0	0	0	1
Fuentes	⅔	2	1	1	1	0
Corpas	1⅓	0	0	0	0	1

Cook pitched to 1 batter in the 7th.

T—3:35. A—50,041.

BOSTON VS. COLORADO COMPOSITE BOX

COLORADO

Player, Pos.	AVG	G	AB	R	H	2B	3B	HR	RBI	BB	SO	SB
Garrett Atkins, 3b	.154	4	13	3	2	1	0	1	2	3	2	0
Jeff Baker, rf	.000	1	1	0	0	0	0	0	0	0	0	0
Jamey Carroll, 2b	.000	1	1	0	0	0	0	0	0	0	0	0
Aaron Cook, p	.500	1	2	0	1	0	0	0	0	0	0	0
Brad Hawpe, rf	.250	4	16	1	4	0	1	1	2	1	8	0
Todd Helton, 1b	.333	4	15	2	5	2	0	0	1	2	3	0
Matt Holliday, lf	.294	4	17	1	5	0	0	1	3	0	3	0
Kazoo Matsui, 2b	.294	4	17	1	5	1	0	0	0	0	5	1
Franklin Morales, p	.000	1	1	0	0	0	0	0	0	0	1	0
Seth Smith, ph	.500	2	2	0	1	0	0	0	0	0	1	0
Ryan Spilborghs, dh	.000	4	10	0	0	0	0	0	0	2	4	0
Cory Sullivan, cf	.333	2	3	0	1	0	0	0	0	0	0	0
Willy Taveras, cf	.000	3	8	1	0	0	0	0	0	0	3	0
Yorvit Torrealba, c	.143	4	14	0	2	0	0	0	1	0	1	0
Troy Tulowitzki, ss	.231	4	13	1	3	2	0	0	1	2	5	0
Totals	.218	4	133	10	29	6	1	3	10	10	36	1

BOSTON

Player, Pos.	AVG	G	AB	R	H	2B	3B	HR	RBI	BB	SO	SB
Coco Crisp, cf	.500	3	2	1	1	0	0	0	0	0	0	0
J.D. Drew, rf	.333	4	15	1	5	2	0	0	2	1	3	0
Jacoby Ellsbury, cf	.438	4	16	4	7	4	0	0	3	2	2	1
Eric Hinske, ph	.000	1	1	0	0	0	0	0	0	0	1	0
Bobby Kielty, ph	1.000	1	1	1	1	0	0	1	1	0	0	0
Jon Lester, p	.000	1	2	0	0	0	0	0	0	0	1	0
Mike Lowell, 3b	.400	4	15	6	6	3	0	1	4	3	1	1
Julio Lugo, ss	.385	4	13	2	5	1	0	0	1	3	0	0
Daisuke Matsuzaka, p	.333	1	3	0	1	0	0	0	2	0	1	0
David Ortiz, dh	.333	4	15	4	5	3	0	0	4	2	3	0
Dustin Pedroia, 2b	.278	4	18	2	5	1	0	1	4	2	0	0
Many Ramirez, lf	.250	4	16	3	4	1	0	0	2	2	2	0
Jason Varitek, c	.333	4	15	2	5	1	0	0	5	1	5	0
Kevin Youkilis, 1b	.222	4	9	3	2	2	0	0	1	3	1	0
Totals	.333	4	141	29	47	18	0	3	29	19	20	2

Pitcher	W	L	ERA	G	GS	SV	IP	H	R	ER	BB	SO
Jeremy Affeldt	0	0	0.00	4	0	0	3.0	2	0	0	1	2
Aaron Cook	0	1	4.50	1	1	0	6.0	6	3	3	0	2
Many Corpas	0	0	0.00	2	0	0	1.2	1	0	0	0	1
Josh Fogg	0	1	20.25	1	1	0	2.2	10	6	6	2	2
Jeff Francis	0	1	13.50	1	1	0	4.0	10	6	6	3	3
Brian Fuentes	0	0	9.82	3	0	0	3.2	6	4	4	2	1
LaTroy Hawkins	0	0	4.50	2	0	0	2.0	1	1	1	0	2
Matt Herges	0	0	0.00	3	0	0	3.1	1	0	0	2	4
Ubaldo Jimenez	0	1	3.86	1	1	0	4.2	3	2	2	5	2
Franklin Morales	0	0	21.00	2	0	0	3.0	7	7	7	1	1
Ryan Speier	0	0	0.00	1	0	0	0.0	0	0	0	3	0
Totals	0	4	7.68	4	4	0	34.0	47	29	29	19	20

Pitcher	W	L	ERA	G	GS	SV	IP	H	R	ER	BB	SO
Josh Beckett	1	0	1.29	1	1	0	7.0	6	1	1	1	9
Many Delcarmen	0	0	6.75	2	0	0	1.1	3	1	1	1	1
Eric Gagne	0	0	0.00	1	0	0	1.0	0	0	0	0	1
Jon Lester	1	0	0.00	1	1	0	5.2	3	0	0	3	3
Javier Lopez	0	0	0.00	1	0	0	2.0	0	0	0	0	0
Daisuke Matsuzaka	1	0	3.38	1	1	0	5.1	3	2	2	3	5
Hideki Okajima	0	0	7.36	3	0	0	3.2	4	3	3	0	6
Jonathan Papelbon	0	0	0.00	3	0	3	4.1	2	0	0	0	3
Curt Schilling	1	0	1.69	1	1	0	5.1	4	1	1	2	4
Mike Timlin	0	0	7.71	3	0	0	2.1	2	2	2	0	4
Totals	4	0	2.50	4	4	3	36.0	29	10	10	10	36

E—Lowell, Drew. DP—Boston 3, colorado 2. LOB—Boston 34, colorado 28. CS—None. S—Cora, Lugo, Torrealba. SF—Varitek (2). HBP—Drew (Jimenez), Taveras (Schilling), Atkins (Matsuzaka). IBB—Ramirez (Francis, Fogg), Lowell (Francis). WP—None. PB—None. BK—Morales

SCORE BY INNINGS

Colorado 110 002 420—10
Boston 416 390 141—29

BOSTON VS. LOS ANGELES COMPOSITE BOX

LOS ANGELES

Player, pos.	AVG	G	AB	R	H	2B	3B	HR	RBI	BB	SO	SB
Garret Anderson, lf	.222	3	9	0	2	1	0	0	0	1	2	0
Orlando Cabrera, ss	.250	3	12	0	3	1	0	0	1	1	1	0
Chone Figgins, rf	.231	3	13	1	3	2	0	0	1	0	4	0
Vladimir Guerrero, rf	.200	3	10	0	2	0	0	0	0	1	0	0
Nathan Haynes, ph	.000	1	1	0	0	0	0	0	0	0	1	0
Maicer Izturis, 3b	.333	3	12	1	4	2	0	0	0	0	2	2
Howie Kendrick, 2b	.200	3	10	0	2	0	0	0	1	0	1	0
Casey Kotchman, 1b	.000	2	5	1	0	0	0	0	0	2	1	0
Jeff Mathis, c	.000	2	3	0	0	0	0	0	1	0	0	0
Kendry Morales, dh	.111	3	9	1	1	0	0	0	0	0	2	0
Mike Napoli, c	.167	3	6	0	1	0	0	0	0	0	3	0
Robb Quinlan, ph	.000	1	1	0	0	0	0	0	0	0	0	0
Juan Rivera, dh	.333	2	3	0	1	0	0	0	0	1	1	0
Reggie Willits, cf	.000	3	4	0	0	0	0	0	0	1	2	1
Totals	**.192**	**3**	**99**	**4**	**19**	**6**	**0**	**0**	**4**	**7**	**20**	**5**

Pitcher	W	L	ERA	G	GS	SV	IP	H	R	ER	BB	SO
Kelvim Escobar	0	0	5.40	1	1	0	5.0	4	3	3	5	5
John Lackey	0	1	6.00	1	1	0	6.0	9	4	4	2	4
Dustin Moseley	0	0	0.00	1	0	0	1.0	1	0	0	0	1
Darren Oliver	0	0	27.00	1	0	0	0.2	2	2	2	0	0
Francisco Rodriguez	0	0	54.00	1	0	0	0.1	1	2	2	1	1
Ervin Santana	0	0	0.00	1	0	0	2.0	0	0	0	0	2
Scot Shields	0	0	2.25	2	0	0	4.0	0	1	1	4	4
Justin Speier	0	1	27.00	2	0	0	1.2	4	5	5	1	0
Jered Weaver	0	1	3.60	1	1	0	5.0	4	2	2	3	5
Totals	**0**	**3**	**6.66**	**3**	**3**	**0**	**25.2**	**25**	**19**	**19**	**16**	**22**

BOSTON

Player, Pos.	AVG	G	AB	R	H	2B	3B	HR	RBI	BB	SO	SB
Coco Crisp, cf	.200	3	10	0	2	0	0	0	0	2	1	3
J.D. Drew, rf	.182	3	11	1	2	0	0	0	3	0	1	0
Jacoby Ellsbury, lf	.000	2	1	1	0	0	0	0	0	0	0	0
Eric Hinske, ph	.000	1	1	0	0	0	0	0	0	0	1	0
Mike Lowell, 3b	.333	3	9	1	3	2	0	0	3	1	0	0
Julio Lugo, ss	.300	3	10	2	3	0	0	0	0	1	4	1
David Ortiz, dh	.714	3	7	5	5	0	0	2	3	6	1	0
Dustin Pedroia, 2b	.154	3	13	2	2	2	0	0	1	1	2	0
Manny Ramirez, lf	.375	3	8	3	3	0	0	2	4	5	2	0
Jason Varitek, c	.182	3	11	1	2	1	0	0	1	0	4	0
Kevin Youkilis, 1b	.250	3	12	3	3	1	0	1	2	1	4	0
Totals	**.269**	**3**	**93**	**19**	**25**	**6**	**0**	**5**	**19**	**16**	**22**	**2**

Pitcher	W	L	ERA	G	GS	SV	IP	H	R	ER	BB	SO
Josh Beckett	1	0	0.00	1	1	0	9.0	4	0	0	0	8
Manny Delcarmen	0	0	0.00	1	0	0	1.1	0	0	0	1	0
Eric Gagne	0	0	9.00	1	0	0	1.0	1	1	1	0	1
Javier Lopez	0	0	0.00	1	0	0	0.1	0	0	0	0	0
Daisuke Matsuzaka	0	0	5.79	1	1	0	4.2	7	3	3	3	3
Hideki Okajima	0	0	0.00	2	0	0	2.1	1	0	0	1	2
Jonathan Papelbon	1	0	0.00	1	0	0	1.1	0	0	0	2	1
Curt Schilling	1	0	0.00	1	1	0	7.0	6	0	0	1	4
Totals	**3**	**0**	**1.33**	**3**	**3**	**0**	**27.0**	**19**	**4**	**4**	**7**	**20**

SCORE BY INNINGS

Los Angeles	030 000 001—4
Boston	303 210 073—19

E—Lowell. **DP**—Boston 7, Anaheim 1. **LOB**—Boston 11, Anaheim 23. **CS**—Lugo. **S**—None. **SF**—Lowell, Youkilis, Kendrick. **HBP**—Guerrero (Delcarmen). **IBB**—Ortiz (Escobar, Rodriguez). **WP**—Lackey, Beckett, Matsuzaka, Gagne. **PB**—None. **BK**—None

CLEVELAND VS. NEW YORK COMPOSITE BOX

NEW YORK

Player, Pos.	AVG	G	AB	R	H	2B	3B	HR	RBI	BB	SO	SB
Bobby Abreu, rf	.267	4	15	1	4	1	0	1	2	2	3	1
Melky Cabrera, cf	.188	4	16	2	3	0	0	1	2	0	1	0
Robinson Cano, 2b	.333	4	15	3	5	1	0	2	3	1	1	0
Johnny Damon, lf	.278	4	18	2	5	0	0	2	5	1	5	0
Shelley Duncan, 1b	.500	3	4	1	2	0	0	0	0	0	1	0
Jason Giambi, dh	.250	3	4	0	1	0	0	0	0	2	0	0
Derek Jeter, ss	.176	4	17	0	3	0	0	0	1	0	4	0
Hideki Matsui, lf	.182	4	11	4	2	0	0	0	0	5	2	0

Yankees righthander Chien-Ming Wang took two of the club's two ALDS losses, posting a 19.06 ERA

Player, Pos.	AVG	G	AB	R	H	2B	3B	HR	RBI	BB	SO	SB
Doug Mientkiewicz, 1b	.000	4	6	0	0	0	0	0	0	1	0	0
Jorge Posada, c	.133	4	15	1	2	1	0	0	0	2	3	0
Alex Rodriguez, 3b	.267	4	15	2	4	0	0	1	1	2	6	0
Totals	**.228**	**4**	**136**	**16**	**31**	**3**	**0**	**7**	**14**	**14**	**28**	**1**

Pitcher	W	L	ERA	G	GS	SV	IP	H	R	ER	BB	SO
Joba Chamberlain	0	0	4.91	2	0	0	3.2	3	2	2	3	4
Kyle Farnsworth	0	0	0.00	1	0	0	1.0	1	0	0	0	2
Phil Hughes	1	0	1.59	2	0	0	5.2	3	1	1	0	6
Mike Mussina	0	0	3.86	1	0	0	4.2	4	2	2	4	3
Ross Ohlendorf	0	0	27.00	1	0	0	1.0	4	3	3	1	0
Andy Pettitte	0	0	0.00	1	1	0	6.1	7	0	0	2	5
Mariano Rivera	0	0	0.00	3	0	0	4.2	2	0	0	1	6
Jose Veras	0	0	0.00	2	0	0	0.2	1	0	0	1	1
Ron Villone	0	0	0.00	1	0	0	0.1	0	0	0	0	0
Luis Vizcaino	0	1	13.50	1	0	0	0.2	2	1	1	2	0
Chien-Ming Wang	0	2	19.06	2	2	0	5.2	14	12	12	4	2
Totals	**1**	**3**	**5.89**	**4**	**4**	**0**	**36.2**	**45**	**24**	**24**	**20**	**30**

CLEVELAND

Player, Pos.	AVG	G	AB	R	H	2B	3B	HR	RBI	BB	SO	SB
Casey Blake, 3b	.118	4	17	1	2	1	0	0	2	0	5	0
Asdrubal Cabrera, 2b	.176	4	17	3	3	0	0	0	2	1	4	0
Ryan Garko, 1b	.364	3	11	3	4	0	0	1	3	1	1	0
Franklin Gutierrez, rf	.200	4	10	2	2	0	0	0	0	2	5	0
Travis Hafner, dh	.250	4	16	4	4	0	0	1	2	5	3	0
Kenny Lofton, lf	.375	4	16	2	6	1	0	0	4	2	1	1
Victor Martinez, c	.353	4	17	2	6	1	0	1	4	1	3	0
Jason Michaels, rf	1.000	1	1	0	1	1	0	0	0	0	0	0
Trot Nixon, rf	.500	1	4	1	2	1	0	1	2	0	1	0
Jhonny Peralta, ss	.467	4	15	2	7	3	0	0	2	4	3	1
Kelly Shoppach, c	.667	1	3	1	2	2	0	0	0	0	0	0
Grady Sizemore, cf	.375	4	16	3	6	0	1	1	1	4	4	1
Totals	**.315**	**4**	**143**	**24**	**45**	**10**	**1**	**6**	**22**	**20**	**30**	**3**

Pitcher	W	L	ERA	G	GS	SV	IP	H	R	ER	BB	SO
Rafael Betancourt	0	0	0.00	2	0	0	2.0	1	0	0	0	3
Joe Borowski	0	0	4.50	2	0	0	2.0	1	1	1	2	1
Paul Byrd	1	0	3.60	1	1	0	5.0	8	2	2	2	2
Fausto Carmona	0	0	1.00	1	1	0	9.0	3	1	1	2	5
Aaron Fultz	0	0	0.00	1	0	0	1.0	2	0	0	1	1
Jensen Lewis	0	0	0.00	2	0	0	2.0	0	0	0	0	4

	W	L	ERA	G	GS	SV	IP	H	R	ER	BB	SO
Rafael Perez	1	0	1.50	3	0	0	6.0	3	1	1	1	6
C.C. Sabathia	1	0	5.40	1	1	0	5.0	4	3	3	6	5
Jake Westbrook	0	1	10.80	1	1	0	5.0	9	6	6	0	1
Totals	3	1	3.41	4	4	1	37.0	31	16	14	14	28

SCORE BY INNINGS

New York	112 154 101 00	—16
Cleveland	632 252 030 01	—24

E—A. Cabrera, Nixon, cano. **DP**—Cleveland 5, Yankees 6 . **LOB**—Cleveland 39, Yankees 24. **CS**—Cano, Sizemore, Lofton. **S**—Michaels, A Cabrera (3), Blake, Mientkiewicz. **SF**—None. **HBP**—Sizemore (Wang), Shoppach (Wang). **IBB**—Rodriguez (Sabathia), Matsui (Fultz), Martinez (Rivera), Garko (Rivera), Hafner (Mussina), Sizemore (Veras). **WP**—Chamberlain (2), Hughes. **PB**—Posada. **BK**—None.

NATIONAL LEAGUE DIVISION SERIES

ARIZONA VS. CHICAGO COMPOSITE BOX

CHICAGO

Player, Pos.	AVG	G	AB	R	H	2B	3B	HR	RBI	BB	SO	SB
Mark DeRosa, 2b	.333	3	9	2	3	0	0	0	0	2	2	0
Cliff Floyd, rf	.000	2	5	0	0	0	0	0	0	2	2	0
Mike Fontenot, ph	.000	2	2	0	0	0	0	0	0	0	1	0
Rich Hill, p	.000	1	1	0	0	0	0	0	0	0	0	0
Jacque Jones, cf	.222	3	9	1	2	1	0	0	0	3	1	0
Jason Kendall, c	.250	1	4	0	1	0	0	0	1	0	1	0
Derrk Lee, 1b	.333	3	12	1	4	0	0	0	0	1	4	0
Ted Lilly, p	.000	1	2	0	0	0	0	0	0	0	2	0
Matt Murton, p	.250	1	4	1	1	0	0	0	0	0	0	0
Felix Pie, ph	.000	1	1	0	0	0	0	0	0	0	1	0
Aramis Ramirez, 3b	.000	3	12	0	0	0	0	0	0	1	5	0
Alfonso Soriano, lf	.143	3	14	0	2	0	0	0	0	1	4	0
Geovany Soto, c	.167	2	6	1	1	0	0	1	2	2	1	0
Ryan Theriot, ss	.250	3	12	0	3	0	0	0	1	1	1	1
Daryle Ward, ph	.500	3	2	0	1	1	0	0	2	1	1	0
Carlos Zambrano, p	.333	1	3	0	1	0	0	0	0	0	1	0
Totals	.194	3	98	6	19	3	0	1	6	14	27	1

Pitcher	W	L	ERA	G	GS	SV	IP	H	R	ER	BB	SO
Ryan Dempster	0	0	0.00	1	0	0	1.0	0	0	0	0	2
Scott Eyre	0	0	0.00	1	0	0	0.0	1	0	0	0	0
Kevin Hart	0	0	18.00	1	0	0	1.0	0	2	2	2	2
Rich Hill	0	1	9.00	1	1	0	3.0	6	3	3	2	3
Bob Howry	0	0	0.00	2	0	0	3.0	1	0	0	0	3
Ted Lilly	0	1	16.20	1	1	0	3.1	7	6	6	4	4
Carlos Marmol	0	1	9.00	2	0	0	3.0	3	3	3	3	6
Kerry Wood	0	0	3.00	2	0	0	3.0	3	1	1	0	2
Michael Wuertz	0	0	0.00	2	0	0	1.2	0	0	0	1	2
Carlos Zambrano	0	0	1.50	1	1	0	6.0	4	1	1	1	8
Totals	0	3	5.76	3	3	0	25.0	25	16	16	13	35

ARIZONA

Player, Pos.	AVG	G	AB	R	H	2B	3B	HR	RBI	BB	SO	SB
Eric Byrnes, lf	.250	3	12	1	3	0	1	1	3	1	4	1
Jeff Cirillo, ph	.000	1	1	0	0	0	0	0	0	0	0	0
Tony Clark, 1b	.000	3	6	0	0	0	0	0	0	0	2	0
Doug Davis, p	.000	1	1	0	0	0	0	0	1	0	1	0
Stephen Drew, ss	.500	3	14	4	7	1	1	2	4	0	5	1
Livan Hernandez, p	.333	1	3	0	1	0	0	0	0	0	1	0
Conor Jackson, 1b	.125	3	8	0	1	0	0	1	1	3	0	0
Miguel Montero, c	.000	1	2	1	0	0	0	0	0	1	0	0
Augie Ojeda, 2b	.444	3	9	1	4	1	0	0	1	1	1	0
Mark Reynolds, 3b	.200	3	10	2	2	0	0	1	1	2	4	0
Jeff Salazar, rf	.000	2	3	0	0	0	0	0	0	1	2	0
Chris Snyder, c	.143	3	7	2	1	0	0	0	1	2	0	0
Justin Upton, rf	.600	2	5	2	3	0	0	0	1	3	0	1
Brandon Webb, p	.000	1	2	0	0	0	0	0	0	0	2	0
Chris Young, p	.273	3	11	3	3	0	0	0	2	4	3	1
Totals	.266	3	94	16	25	3	2	6	16	13	35	4

Pitcher	W	L	ERA	G	GS	SV	IP	H	R	ER	BB	SO
Juan Cruz	0	0	0.00	1	0	0	0.1	1	0	0	0	1
Doug Davis	1	0	6.35	1	1	0	5.2	5	4	4	4	8
Livan Hernandez	1	0	1.50	1	1	0	6.0	5	1	1	5	2
Brandon Lyon	0	0	0.00	3	0	0	3.0	1	0	0	1	1
Tony Pena	0	0	0.00	2	0	0	2.0	2	0	0	0	0
Jose Valverde	0	0	0.00	3	0	1	3.0	1	0	0	1	6
Brandon Webb	1	0	1.29	1	1	0	7.0	4	1	1	3	9
Totals	3	0	2.00	3	3	1	27.0	19	6	6	14	27

Rockies outfielder Matt Holliday hit .289/.319/.622 in the postseason, with five homers and 10 RBIs

LARRY GOREN

SCORE BY INNINGS

Chicago	020 103 000	—6
Arizona	240 421 201	—16

E—Drew, Ojeda, Reynolds. **DP**—Chicago 5, Arizona 4. **LOB**—Chicago 27, Arizona 20. **CS**—None. **S**—Davis (2). **SF**—Jackson. **HBP**—Floyd (Hernandez), Ojeda (Hill), DeRosa (Webb). **IBB**—None. **WP**—Webb, Hart, Wuertz. **PB**—Snyder. **BK**—None.

PHILADELPHIA VS. COLORADO COMPOSITE BOX

COLORADO

Player, Pos.	AVG	G	AB	R	H	2B	3B	HR	RBI	BB	SO	SB
Garrett Atkins, 3b	.231	3	13	3	3	2	0	0	1	0	1	0
Jeff Baker, ph	1.000	1	1	0	1	0	0	0	0	0	0	0
Josh Fogg, p	.000	1	1	0	0	0	0	0	0	0	0	0
Jeff Francis, p	.000	1	2	0	0	0	0	0	0	0	0	0
Brad Hawpe, rf	.273	3	11	1	3	0	0	0	2	5	0	0
Todd Helton, 1b	.083	3	12	1	1	0	1	0	0	1	2	0
Matt Holliday, lf	.231	3	13	2	3	0	0	2	3	0	3	0
Ubaldo Jimenez, p	.000	1	1	0	0	0	0	0	0	0	0	0
Kazuo Matsui, 2b	.417	3	12	5	5	1	2	1	6	2	2	0
Franklin Morales, p	.000	1	0	0	0	0	0	0	0	0	1	0
Seth Smith, ph	.500	2	2	1	1	0	0	0	0	0	0	0
Ryan Spilborghs, cf	.250	3	8	2	2	0	0	0	0	3	3	0
Yorvit Torrealba, c	.500	3	10	3	5	1	0	0	3	2	0	0
Troy Tulowitzki, ss	.167	3	12	1	2	1	0	1	2	1	5	0
Totals	.267	3	101	16	27	5	3	4	16	11	22	0

Pitcher	W	L	ERA	G	GS	SV	IP	H	R	ER	BB	SO
Jeremy Affeldt	0	0	9.00	1	0	0	1.0	1	1	1	0	2
Manny Corpas	0	0	0.00	3	0	3	3.1	2	0	0	0	3
Josh Fogg	1	0	0.00	1	0	0	2.0	1	0	0	1	0
Jeff Francis	1	0	3.00	1	1	0	6.0	4	2	2	2	8
Brian Fuentes	1	0	0.00	3	0	0	2.1	1	0	0	3	4
LaTroy Hawkins	0	0	0.00	1	0	0	1.0	0	0	0	1	0
Matt Herges	0	0	0.00	1	0	0	0.2	0	0	0	0	0
Ubaldo Jimenez	0	0	1.42	1	1	0	6.1	3	1	1	4	5
Franklin Morale	0	0	9.00	1	1	0	3.0	3	3	3	2	3
Ryan Speier	0	0	0.00	1	0	0	1.1	1	0	0	0	0
Totals	3	0	2.33	3	3	3	27.0	16	8	7	12	26

Indians righthander Jake Westbrook pitched 12⅔ ALCS innings and got the nod in Game Seven

PHILADELPHIA

Player, Pos.	AVG	G	AB	R	H	2B	3B	HR	RBI	BB	SO	SB
Michael Bourn	.000	2	1	0	0	0	0	0	0	0	0	0
Pat Burrell, lf	.182	3	11	1	2	0	0	1	1	2	3	0
Chris Coste, ph	.000	1	1	0	0	0	0	0	0	0	0	0
Greg Dobbs, 3b	.000	3	3	0	0	0	0	0	0	1	1	0
Cole Hamels, p	.500	1	2	0	1	0	0	0	0	0	0	0
Wes Helms, 3b	.000	2	1	0	0	0	0	0	0	1	0	0
Ryan Howard, 1b	.250	3	12	1	3	0	0	1	1	0	7	0
Tadahito Iguchi, 2b	.000	3	1	0	0	0	0	0	0	2	0	0
Kyle Kendrick, p	.000	1	1	0	0	0	0	0	0	0	0	0
Jamie Moyer, p	.000	1	2	0	0	0	0	0	0	0	0	0
Abraham Nunez, 3b	.000	3	2	0	0	0	0	0	0	0	0	0
Jimmy Rollins, ss	.182	3	11	1	2	0	1	1	4	2	3	1
Aaron Rowand, cf	.083	3	12	1	1	0	0	0	1	0	4	0
Carlos Ruiz, c	.333	3	9	1	3	1	0	0	1	1	1	0
Chase Utley, 2b	.182	3	11	0	2	0	0	0	0	2	5	0
Shane Victorino, rf	.222	3	9	2	2	0	0	1	1	0	1	1
Jayson Werth, lf	.000	2	3	0	0	0	0	0	0	1	1	0
Totals	.172	3	93	8	16	1	1	5	8	12	26	3

Pitcher	W	L	ERA	G	GS	SV	IP	H	R	ER	BB	SO
Antonio Alfonseca	0	0	0.00	1	0	0	1.0	1	0	0	0	0
Clay Condrey	0	0	5.40	1	0	0	1.2	4	1	1	0	2
Tom Gordon	0	0	4.50	2	0	0	2.0	2	1	1	1	4
Cle Hamels	0	1	4.05	1	1	0	6.2	3	3	3	4	7
Kyle Kendrick	0	1	12.27	1	1	0	3.2	5	5	5	2	2
Kyle Lohse	0	0	6.75	1	0	0	1.1	1	1	1	0	1
Jose Mesa	0	0	81.00	1	0	0	0.1	3	3	3	2	0
Jamie Moyer	0	0	1.50	1	1	0	6.0	5	1	1	2	2
Brett Myers	0	0	0.00	2	0	0	1.1	2	0	0	0	3
J.C. Romero	0	1	4.50	3	0	0	2.0	3	1	1	0	1
Totals	0	3	5.54	3	3	0	26.0	27	16	16	11	22

SCORE BY INNINGS

Colorado	230 414 110—16
Philadelphia	120 021 200—8

E—Torrealba. DP—Colorado 2, philadelphia 3. LOB—Colorado 20, philadelphia 17. CS—Tulowitzki. S—Francis, Jimenez. SF—None. HBP—Howard (Morales). IBB—Matsui (Gordon 2), Torrealba (Kendrick). WP—Fuentes. PB—None. BK—None

---

AMERICAN LEAGUE CHAMPIONSHIP SERIES

BOSTON VS. CLEVELAND COMPOSITE BOX

CLEVELAND

Player, Pos.	AVG	G	AB	R	H	2B	3B	HR	RBI	BB	SO	SB
Casey Blake, 3b	.346	7	26	4	9	2	0	1	2	1	7	0
Asdrubal Cabrera, 2b	.241	7	29	2	7	0	0	0	4	1	8	0
Ryan Garko, 1b	.292	6	24	4	7	2	1	0	2	0	5	0
Chris Gomez, ph	.000	1	1	0	0	0	0	0	0	0	1	0
Franklin Gutierrez, rf	.211	6	19	3	4	0	0	1	4	3	6	0
Travis Hafner, dh	.148	7	27	2	4	1	0	1	2	2	12	0
Kenny Lofton, lf	.222	7	27	2	6	2	0	1	2	1	3	1
Victor Martinez, c	.296	7	27	4	8	1	0	1	3	3	5	0
Jason Michaels, pR	.000	1	0	1	0	0	0	0	0	0	0	0
Trot Nixon, rf	.429	3	7	0	3	0	0	0	1	0	1	0
Jhonny Peralta, ss	.259	7	27	4	7	2	0	2	8	1	8	0
Kelly Shoppach, c	.333	1	3	0	1	0	0	0	0	0	2	0
Grady Sizemore, cf	.222	7	27	6	6	2	0	1	2	4	5	1
Totals	.254	7	244	32	62	12	1	8	30	16	63	3

Pitcher	W	L	ERA	G	GS	SV	IP	H	R	ER	BB	SO
Rafael Betancourt	0	0	6.75	5	0	0	8.0	6	7	6	1	6
Joe Borowski	0	0	4.50	4	0	1	4.0	6	2	2	3	1
Paul Byrd	1	0	3.60	1	1	0	5.0	6	2	2	0	4
Fausto Carmona	0	1	16.50	2	2	0	6.0	10	11	11	9	7
Aaron Fultz	0	0	0.00	1	0	0	0.0	0	0	0	2	0
Aaron Laffey	0	0	0.00	1	0	0	4.2	1	0	0	1	3
Jensen Lewis	0	0	6.35	5	0	0	5.2	6	4	4	0	3
Tom Mastny	1	0	0.00	3	0	0	4.2	2	0	0	2	3
Rafael Perez	0	0	45.00	3	0	0	1.0	7	8	5	2	0
C.C. Sabathia	0	2	10.45	2	2	0	10.1	17	12	12	7	9
Jake Westbrook	1	1	3.55	2	2	0	12.2	16	5	5	4	7
Totals	3	4	6.82	7	7	1	62.0	77	51	47	31	43

BOSTON

Player, Pos.	AVG	G	AB	R	H	2B	3B	HR	RBI	BB	SO	SB
Coco Crisp, cf	.143	7	21	2	3	1	0	0	0	6	1	1
J.D. Drew, rf	.360	7	25	5	9	1	0	1	6	1	2	0
Jacoby Ellsbury, cf	.250	5	8	3	2	0	0	0	1	1	1	1
Eric Hinske, pR	.000	1	0	1	0	0	0	0	0	0	0	0
Bobby Kielty, rf	.400	2	5	1	2	0	0	0	2	1	2	0
Mike Lowell, 3b	.333	7	27	3	9	2	0	1	8	2	3	0
Julio Lugo, ss	.200	7	25	3	5	2	0	0	2	1	5	0
Doug Mirabelli, c	.000	1	2	0	0	0	0	0	0	0	1	0
David Ortiz, dh	.292	7	24	7	7	3	0	1	3	6	5	0
Dustin Pedroia, 2b	.345	7	29	8	10	3	0	1	5	3	5	0
Many Ramirez, lf	.409	7	22	5	9	1	0	2	10	9	5	0
Jason Varitek, c	.269	7	26	3	7	3	0	1	4	2	5	0
Kevin Youkilis, 1b	.500	7	28	10	14	1	1	3	7	5	3	0
Totals	.318	7	242	51	77	17	1	10	48	31	43	2

Pitcher	W	L	ERA	G	GS	SV	IP	H	R	ER	BB	SO
Josh Beckett	2	0	1.93	2	2	0	14.0	9	3	3	1	18
Many Delcarmen	0	0	16.20	3	0	0	1.2	4	3	3	2	3
Eric Gagne	0	0	7.71	3	0	0	2.1	3	2	2	4	0
Jon Lester	0	0	4.91	2	0	0	3.2	3	2	2	1	5
Javier Lopez	0	0	18.00	3	0	0	2.0	3	4	4	2	0
Daisuke Matsuzaka	1	1	5.59	2	2	0	9.2	12	6	6	2	9
Hideki Okajima	0	0	0.00	3	0	0	5.0	4	0	0	2	3
Jonathan Papelbon	0	0	0.00	3	0	1	5.0	3	0	0	2	3
Curt Schilling	1	0	5.40	2	2	0	11.2	15	7	7	0	8
Mike Timlin	0	0	0.00	3	0	0	3.1	1	0	0	0	3
Tim Wakefield	0	1	9.64	1	1	0	4.2	5	5	5	2	7
Totals	4	3	4.57	7	7	1	63.0	62	32	32	16	63

SCORE BY INNINGS

Cleveland	330	4(11)2	110 07—32
Boston	71(15)	065	36(11) 00—51

E—Garko, cabrera, Blake, Youkilis, Beckett, Lugo. DP—Cleveland 5, Boston 14. LOB—Cleveland 44, Boston 46. CS—None. S—Lugo, pedroia. SF—Lowell (2), Ortiz (2), Ramirez, peraltz, cabrera, Sizemore. HBP—Ortiz (Sabathia), Varitek (Sabathia), Lowell (Sabathia), Garko (Beckett), Shoppach (Wakefield), Martinez (Lopez, papelbon). IBB—Kielty (Sabathia), Ramirez (Westbrook), Ellsbury (Betancourt), Sizemore (Okajima). WP—Matsuzaka (2), Beckett, Lopez, Sabathia. PB—Martinez. BK—None.

NATIONAL LEAGUE CHAMPIONSHIP SERIES

ARIZONA VS. COLORADO *COMPOSITE BOX*

COLORADO

Player, Pos.	AVG	G	AB	R	H	2B	3B	HR	RBI	BB	SO	SB
Garrett Atkins, 3b	.143	4	14	0	2	0	0	0	0	2	2	0
Jeff Baker, ph	.500	2	2	0	1	0	0	0	0	0	1	0
Jamey Carroll, 3b	.000	2	1	0	0	0	0	0	0	1	0	0
Josh Fogg, p	.000	1	1	0	0	0	0	0	0	1	0	0
Jeff Francis, p	.000	1	2	0	0	0	0	0	0	0	0	0
Brad Hawpe, rf	.333	4	12	2	4	0	0	0	2	5	3	0
Todd Helton, 1b	.214	4	14	3	3	0	0	0	1	2	4	0
Matt Holliday, lf	.333	4	15	3	5	0	0	2	4	1	6	0
Ubaldo Jimenez, p	.000	1	2	0	0	0	0	0	0	0	2	0
Kazoo Matsui, 2b	.235	4	17	2	4	0	0	0	2	1	5	1
Franklin Morales, p	.000	1	1	0	0	0	0	0	0	0	0	0
Seth Smith, ph	.500	2	2	1	1	0	0	0	2	0	0	0
Ryan Spilborghs, cf	.500	2	2	1	1	0	0	0	0	0	0	0
Cory Sullivan, cf	.000	1	1	0	0	0	0	0	0	0	1	0
Willy Taveras, cf	.167	4	18	3	3	1	0	0	1	2	5	1
Yorvit Torrealba, c	.200	4	15	2	3	1	0	1	4	2	5	0
Troy Tulowitzki, ss	.188	4	16	1	3	0	0	0	0	1	5	0
Totals	**.222**	**4**	**135**	**18**	**30**	**3**	**0**	**3**	**16**	**18**	**39**	**2**

Pitcher	W	L	ERA	G	GS	SV	IP	H	R	ER	BB	SO
Jeremy Affeldt	0	0	0.00	2	0	0	1.1	0	0	0	0	0
Many Corpas	1	0	1.69	4	0	2	5.1	3	1	1	0	3
Josh Fogg	1	0	1.50	1	1	0	6.0	7	1	1	1	3
Jeff Francis	1	0	1.35	1	1	0	6.2	7	1	1	1	4
Brian Fuentes	0	0	7.36	4	0	0	3.2	7	3	3	0	6
LaTroy Hawkins	0	0	0.00	2	0	0	2.0	1	0	0	0	1
Matt Herges	1	0	0.00	3	0	0	3.0	1	0	0	1	2
Ubaldo Jimenez	0	0	1.80	1	1	0	5.0	5	1	1	4	6
Franklin Morales	0	0	2.25	1	1	0	4.0	5	1	1	1	2
Ryan Speier	0	0	0.00	1	0	1	1.0	0	0	0	0	1
Totals	**4**	**0**	**1.89**	**4**	**4**	**3**	**38.0**	**36**	**8**	**8**	**8**	**28**

ARIZONA

Player, Pos.	AVG	G	AB	R	H	2B	3B	HR	RBI	BB	SO	SB
Eric Byrnes, lf	.176	4	17	0	3	1	0	0	2	1	3	0
Alberto Callaspo, ph	.000	2	2	0	0	0	0	0	0	0	0	0
Jeff Cirillo, 2b	.400	3	5	0	2	0	0	0	0	0	0	0
Tony Clark, 1b	.222	3	9	0	2	1	0	0	0	1	1	0
Doug Davis, p	1.000	1	1	1	1	0	0	0	0	0	0	0
Stephen Drew, ss	.294	4	17	2	5	0	0	0	0	1	2	0
Livan Hernandez, p	.500	1	2	0	1	0	0	0	0	0	0	0
Conor Jackson, 1b	.333	3	9	1	3	0	0	0	1	0	0	0
Miguel Montero, c	.400	3	5	0	2	0	0	0	0	0	0	0
Augie Ojeda, 2b	.167	4	12	0	2	0	0	0	0	0	2	0
Micah Owings, p	.333	2	3	1	1	0	0	0	0	0	0	0
Mark Reynolds, 3b	.125	4	16	1	2	0	0	1	1	0	5	0
Jeff Salazar, rf	.143	4	7	0	1	0	0	0	0	0	1	0
Chris Snyder, c	.333	3	12	1	4	2	0	1	3	1	4	0
Justin Upton, rf	.222	4	9	0	2	1	1	0	0	0	3	0
Brandon Webb, p	.500	1	2	0	1	0	0	0	0	0	1	0
Chris Young, cf	.286	4	14	1	4	1	0	0	1	4	5	0
Totals	**.254**	**4**	**142**	**8**	**36**	**7**	**1**	**2**	**8**	**8**	**28**	**0**

Pitcher	W	L	ERA	G	GS	SV	IP	H	R	ER	BB	SO
Juan Cruz	0	0	0.00	3	0	0	4.0	0	1	0	3	8
Doug Davis	0	0	1.80	1	1	0	5.0	5	2	1	4	5
Livan Hernandez	0	1	6.35	1	1	0	5.2	8	4	4	2	4
Brandon Lyon	0	0	0.00	2	0	0	3.0	0	0	0	0	4
Dustin Nippert	0	0	0.00	2	0	0	2.1	1	0	0	0	2
Micah Owings	0	1	4.91	1	1	0	3.2	6	6	2	2	2
Tony Pena	0	0	0.00	3	0	0	3.1	1	0	0	0	7
Doug Slaten	0	0	0.00	3	0	0	1.1	0	0	0	2	1
Jose Valverde	0	1	5.40	1	0	0	1.2	1	1	1	3	2
Brandon Webb	0	1	6.00	1	1	0	6.0	7	4	4	2	4
Totals	**0**	**4**	**3.00**	**4**	**4**	**0**	**36.0**	**30**	**18**	**12**	**18**	**39**

Rockies rookie righthander Ubaldo Jimenez was the team's most consistent starter in the playoffs

BILL MITCHELL

SCORE BY INNINGS

Colorado	123 019 100	01—18
Arizona	102 100 031	00—7

E—Jackson (2), Reynolds, Matsui, Hawkins . DP—Arizona 6, colorado 1. LOB—Arizona 32, colorado 31. CS—Young (2). S—Francis, Matsui. SF—Helton. HBP—Reynolds (Francis), Upton (Francis), Young (Corpas), Holliday (Owings). IBB—Clark (Jimenez), Atkins (Slaten), . WP—Webb, Slaten, cruz, Jimenez. PB—Snyder. BK—None

ORGANIZATION STATISTICS

Arizona Diamondbacks

BY JACK MAGRUDER

The Arizona Diamondbacks may have stepped up a little earlier than even some in the organization expected by winning the 2007 NL West pennant, but their ascension was seen as just a matter of time.

The Diamondbacks blended career years from Eric Byrnes, Brandon Webb and Jose Valverde with contributions from a gifted pool of young talent to serve notice that this could be only the beginning.

"We like our team. It is a group that has shown they know how to win games," general manager Josh Byrnes said two days after the Diamondbacks lost to Colorado in the NLCS while predicting few changes in the offseason.

"We knew we could compete. I don't know that we would have placed bets to the level of 90 wins and the division title, but we certainly thought we'd be there until the end," team president Derrick Hall said.

The D-Backs, 90-72, did not make it easy on themselves. They had the lowest batting average in the NL and the lowest batting average with runners in scoring position in the majors while becoming the sixth team in major league history to make the postseason—and have the best record in the league—with a negative run differential, scoring 712 runs while giving up 732.

Byrnes was an offensive catalyst while posting his second consecutive career year since joining the D-Backs, and his game-winning single on Opening Day was a harbinger—15 different Diamondbacks had go-ahead or game-winning hits from the seventh inning on as the team posted 42 come-from-behind victories.

Byrnes, 31, became just the 11th player in major league to hit 20 home runs and steal 50 bases. He stole No. 50 when the Diamondbacks clinched their first postseason appearance since 2002 in a 4-2 victory Sept. 28 in Colorado, the last time the Rockies lost until the World Series.

Webb, the defending NL Cy Young Award winner, won his career-high 18th game that night to cap a regular season in which he also set personal bests in strikeouts and innings pitched. Webb threw three straight shutouts during a mid-summer streak of 42 consecutive scoreless innings, tying for the 12th longest streak in major league history. He anchoring a staff that was fourth in the NL in quality starts and was backed by the best bullpen, statistically, in the majors.

Valverde simplified his repertoire while shattering the franchise record and leading the major leagues with 47 saves in 54 opportunities. Former closer Brandon Lyon and up-and-coming Tony Pena provided a dominant bridge from the starters to Valverde. Lyon led the majors with 35 holds and Pena had 30 as the Diamondbacks finished with the most saves in the majors and the highest save percentage in the NL.

Center fielder Chris Young, one of 12 rookies the Diamondbacks used this season and the centerpiece of the trade that sent Javier Vazquez to the White Sox in the winter of 2005, emerged as a two-way weapon.

Young, 24, was the first rookie in major league history with at least 30 homers and 25 stolen bases and showed Steve Finley-like range in center field. Young's signature moment came when he leaped over the fence in center field to take a potential grand slam away from Mike Cameron in a 9-5 victory over San Diego on Aug. 1 during a second-half stretch in which the Diamondbacks went 21-6 to take over

MAJOR LEAGUE: BRANDON WEBB, RHP

The 2006 Cy Young Award winner's 3.01 ERA tied for the second-lowest in baseball this year. He led all of baseball with three shutouts, and his 236 innings ranked second. Webb also led the team with 18 wins, four complete games, 194 strikeouts, 34 games started and a .643 winning percentage. He allowed only 12 home runs all year.

MINOR LEAGUE: JUSTIN UPTON, OF

The top pick in 2005, Upton tore through two minor league levels before becoming the major league's youngest player this season as a 19-year-old. Between high Class A and Double-A, Upton hit .319/.410/.551 with 18 home runs, 23 doubles, six triples and 19 stolen bases in 385 at-bats.

ORGANIZATIONAL LEADERS

BATTING		★Minimum 250 at-bats
★AVG	Brito, Javier, Mobile	.327
R	Bonifacio, Emilio, Mobile	84
H	Parra, Gerardo, South Bend/Visalia	171
TB	Carter, Chris, Tucson	262
2B	D'Antona, Jamie, Tucson	43
3B	Perales, Daniel, South Bend	10
HR	Miller, Brad, South Bend	22
RBI	Perales, Daniel, South Bend	92
BB	Brashear, Justin, South Bend	81
SO	Mena, Steve, South Bend	134
SB	Bonifacio, Emilio, Mobile	41
★OBP	Brito, Javier, Mobile	.433
★SLG	Upton, Justin, Visalia/Mobile	.551
PITCHING		^Minimum 75 innings
W	Green, Matthew, Mobile	12
	Torra, Matt, Visalia	12
L	Carrasco, D.J., Tucson	14
^ERA	Vasquez, Esmerling, Mobile	2.99
G	Choate, Randy, Tucson	55
	Schultz, Mike, Tucson	55
CG	Smith, Greg, Mobile/Tucson	3
SV	Harville, Chad, Tucson	25
IP	Vasquez, Esmerling, Mobile	165
BB	Gonzalez, Enrique, Tucson	61
SO	Vasquez, Esmerling, Mobile	151
^AVG	Vasquez, Esmerling, Mobile	.217

first place in the NL West.

Young was not the only rookie to step up. Third baseman Mark Reynolds, recalled from Double-A Mobile on May 16, showed light-tower power by hitting 17 home runs. Righthander Micah Owings, who went 8-8, 4.30, also showed big-time pop as a hitter. He had two four-hit games, hitting two homers and a double while driving in six in a 12-6 victory over Atlanta on Aug. 18.

Veteran slugger and clubhouse leader Tony Clark had 17 home runs in 221 at-bats, a ratio exceeded by only Ryan Howard and Prince Fielder among NL qualifiers.

Clark summarized the season by saying: "You always hear the cliché, if you have 25 guys pulling in the same direction, anything can happen. We found a way."

General Manager: Josh Byrnes. **Farm Director:** A.J. Hinch. **Scouting Director:** Tom Allison

Class	Team	League	W	L	PCT	Finish*	Manager	Affiliate Since
Majors	Arizona	National	90	72	.556	1st (16)	Bob Melvin	—
Triple-A	Tucson Sidewinders	Pacific Coast	75	67	.528	5th (16)	Bill Plummer	1998
Double-A	Mobile BayBears	Southern	71	68	.511	5th (10)	Brett Butler	2007
High A	Visalia Oaks	California	.77	30	.550	1st (10)	Hector de la Cruz	2007
Low A	South Bend Silver Hawks	Midwest	68	70	.493	9th (14)	Mark Haley	1997
Short-season	Yakima Bears	Northwest	33	43	.434	8th (8)	Mike Bell	2001
Rookie	Missoula Osprey	Pioneer	27	49	.355	7th (8)	Damon Mashore	1999
Overall 2007 Minor League Record			**351**	**327**	**.518**	**9th**		

* Finish in overall standings (No. of teams in league) ^League champion

ORGANIZATION STATISTICS

ARIZONA DIAMONDBACKS

NATIONAL LEAGUE

BATTING	B-T	HT	WT	DOB	AVG	vLH	vRH	G	AB	R	H	2B	3B	HR	RBI	BB	HBP	SH	SF	SO	SB	CS	SLG	OBP
Barden, Brian	R-R	5-11	185	4-2-81	.083	.000	.143	8	12	0	1	0	0	0	0	0	0	0	0	3	0	0	.083	.083
2-team (15 St. Louis)					.171	—	—	23	35	6	6	1	0	0	2	0	0	0	7	0	0	.200	.216
Bonifacio, Emilio	B-R	5-11	180	4-23-85	.217	.200	.222	11	23	2	5	1	0	0	2	4	0	0	3	0	1	.261	.333
Byrnes, Eric	R-R	6-2	210	2-16-76	.286	.248	.297	160	626	103	179	30	8	21	83	57	10	1	4	98	50	7	.460	.353
Callaspo, Alberto	B-R	5-10	175	4-19-83	.215	.219	.214	56	144	10	31	8	0	0	7	9	1	1	1	14	1	1	.271	.265
Cirillo, Jeff	R-R	6-1	205	9-23-69	.200	.167	.214	28	40	6	8	4	0	0	6	4	0	0	0	6	0	0	.300	.273
Clark, Tony	B-R	6-7	245	6-15-72	.249	.219	.254	113	221	31	55	5	1	17	51	21	0	0	3	59	0	0	.511	.310
DaVanon, Jeff	B-R	6-0	200	12-8-73	.154	.000	.182	13	26	5	4	2	0	1	5	1	0	1	8	1	1	.231	.303
Drew, Stephen	L-R	6-1	185	3-16-83	.238	.246	.235	150	543	60	129	28	4	12	60	60	3	5	8	100	9	0	.370	.313
Hairston, Scott	R-R	6-0	200	5-25-80	.222	.230	.217	76	176	21	39	13	1	3	16	19	1	3	0	37	2	0	.358	.301
2-team (31 San Diego)					.243	—	—	107	263	37	64	18	2	11	36	26	1	3	1	55	2	0	.452	.313
Hammock, Robby	R-R	5-10	185	5-13-77	.244	.286	.208	34	45	5	11	2	0	0	3	1	0	0	7	0	0	.289	.306
Hudson, Orlando	B-R	6-0	185	12-12-77	.294	.281	.298	139	517	69	152	28	9	10	63	70	2	5	7	87	10	2	.441	.376
Jackson, Conor	R-R	6-2	225	5-7-82	.284	.320	.270	130	415	56	118	29	1	15	60	53	4	2	3	50	2	2	.467	.368
Montero, Miguel	L-R	5-11	195	7-9-83	.224	.286	.218	84	214	30	48	7	0	10	37	20	3	1	6	35	0	0	.397	.292
Ojeda, Augie	B-R	5-8	170	12-20-74	.274	.250	.292	57	113	16	31	2	2	1	12	15	0	2	2	13	1	0	.354	.354
Quentin, Carlos	R-R	6-2	220	8-28-82	.214	.172	.230	81	229	29	49	16	0	5	31	18	11	1	4	54	2	2	.349	.298
Reynolds, Mark	R-R	6-1	200	8-3-83	.279	.278	.279	111	366	62	102	20	4	17	62	37	5	1	5	129	0	1	.495	.349
Sadler, Donnie	R-R	5-6	175	6-17-75	.000	—	.000	1	1	0	0	0	0	0	0	0	0	0	0	0	0	0	.000	.000
Salazar, Jeff	L-L	6-0	190	11-24-80	.277	.300	.274	38	94	13	26	6	1	1	10	9	0	0	0	19	2	0	.394	.340
Smith, Jason	L-R	6-3	200	7-24-77	.250	—	.250	2	4	0	1	0	0	0	0	0	0	0	0	2	0	0	.250	.250
Snyder, Chris	R-R	6-3	230	2-12-81	.252	.316	.215	110	326	37	82	20	0	13	47	40	7	3	4	67	0	1	.433	.342
Tracy, Chad	L-R	6-2	200	5-22-80	.264	.174	.287	76	227	30	60	18	2	7	35	29	1	0	3	43	0	0	.454	.346
Upton, Justin	R-R	6-3	205	8-25-87	.221	.200	.230	43	140	17	31	8	3	2	11	11	1	0	0	37	2	0	.364	.283
Young, Chris	R-R	6-2	180	9-5-83	.237	.246	.234	148	569	85	135	29	3	32	68	43	6	1	5	141	27	6	.467	.295

PITCHING	B-T	HT	WT	DOB	W	L	ERA	G	GS	CG	SV	IP	H	R	ER	HR	BB	SO	AVG	vLH	vRH	K/9	BB/9
Choate, Randy	L-L	6-1	195	9-5-75	0	0	—	2	0	0	0	3	0	0	0	0	0	0	1.000	1.000	.000	—	—
Cirillo, Jeff	R-R	6-1	205	9-23-69	0	0	0.00	1	0	0	0	1	0	0	0	0	2	1	.000	.000	.000	9.00	18.00
Cruz, Juan	R-R	6-2	155	10-15-78	6	1	3.10	53	0	0	0	61	45	28	21	7	32	87	.205	.269	.143	12.84	4.72
Davis, Doug	R-L	6-4	215	9-21-75	13	12	4.25	33	33	0	0	193	211	100	91	21	95	144	.281	.252	.290	6.73	4.44
Durbin, J.D.	R-R	6-0	210	2-24-82	0	0	94.50	1	0	0	0	1	7	7	7	0	1	1	.778	.750	.800	13.50	13.50
2-team (18 Philadelphia)					6	5	6.06	19	10	1	1	65	78	49	44	6	37	40	—	—	—	5.51	5.10
Eveland, Dana	L-L	6-1	240	10-29-83	1	0	14.40	5	1	0	0	5	8	8	8	0	5	3	.364	.500	.313	5.40	9.00
Gonzalez, Edgar	R-R	6-0	225	2-23-83	8	4	5.03	32	12	0	0	102	110	61	57	18	28	62	.276	.313	.237	5.47	2.47
Gonzalez, Enrique	R-R	5-10	210	7-14-82	0	0	13.50	1	0	0	0	2	4	4	3	0	1	0	.400	.500	.333	0.00	4.50
Hernandez, Livan	R-R	6-2	245	2-20-75	11	11	4.93	33	33	1	0	204	247	116	112	34	79	90	.308	.295	.320	3.96	3.48
Johnson, Randy	R-L	6-10	225	9-10-63	4	3	3.81	10	10	0	0	57	52	26	24	7	13	72	.245	.182	.257	11.44	2.06
Kennedy, Joe	R-L	6-4	250	5-24-79	0	0	20.25	3	0	0	0	3	4	7	6	0	2	1	.333	.333	.333	3.38	6.75
Kim, Byung-Hyun	R-R	5-9	175	1-19-79	0	1	23.62	2	2	0	0	3	11	9	7	1	2	3	.611	.556	.667	10.12	6.75
3-team (3 Colorado, 23 Florida)					10	8	6.08	28	22	0	0	118	131	90	80	20	68	107	—	—	—	8.14	5.17
Lyon, Brandon	R-R	6-1	195	8-10-79	6	4	2.68	73	0	0	2	74	70	25	22	22	40	.251	.233	.267	4.86	2.68
Medders, Brandon	R-R	6-1	190	1-26-80	1	2	4.30	30	0	0	0	29	30	16	14	9	16	23	.273	.186	.328	7.06	4.91
Murphy, Bill	L-L	5-11	215	5-9-81	0	0	5.68	10	0	0	0	6	9	4	4	0	7	2	.346	.462	.231	2.84	9.95
Nippert, Dustin	R-R	6-8	225	5-6-81	1	1	5.56	36	0	0	0	45	48	30	28	5	16	38	.267	.238	.290	7.54	3.18
Ojeda, Augie	B-R	5-8	170	12-20-74	0	0	0.00	1	0	0	0	1	0	0	0	0	0	0	.000	.000	.000	0.00	0.00
Owings, Micah	R-R	6-5	220	9-28-82	8	8	4.30	29	27	2	0	153	146	81	73	20	50	106	.253	.265	.240	6.25	2.95
Peguero, Jailen	R-R	6-0	195	1-4-81	1	0	9.20	18	0	0	0	15	17	15	15	2	13	9	.309	.240	.367	5.52	7.98
Pena, Tony	R-R	6-2	220	1-9-82	5	4	3.27	75	0	0	2	85	63	36	31	8	31	63	.207	.245	.176	6.64	3.27
Petit, Yusmeiro	R-R	6-0	230	11-22-84	3	4	4.58	14	10	0	0	57	58	30	29	12	18	40	.260	.274	.250	6.32	2.84
Schultz, Mike	R-R	6-2	220	11-28-79	0	0	0.00	1	0	0	0	1	1	0	0	0	1	0	.333	1.000	.000	9.00	9.00
Slaten, Doug	L-L	6-5	200	2-4-80	3	2	2.72	61	0	0	0	36	41	15	11	4	14	28	.275	.268	.284	6.94	3.47
Valverde, Jose	R-R	6-4	255	7-24-79	1	4	2.66	65	0	0	47	64	46	21	19	7	26	78	.196	.202	.189	10.91	3.64
Webb, Brandon	R-R	6-2	230	5-9-79	18	10	3.01	34	34	4	0	236	209	91	79	12	72	194	.237	.272	.199	7.39	2.74
Wickman, Bob	R-R	6-1	240	2-6-69	0	1	1.35	8	0	0	0	7	6	2	1	0	1	2	.240	.500	.067	2.70	1.35
2-team (49 Atlanta)					3	4	3.58	57	0	0	20	50	54	24	20	4	21	37	—	—	—	6.62	3.75

FIELDING

Catcher	PCT	G	PO	A	E	DP	PB
Hammock	1.000	12	41	6	0	0	1
Montero	.984	73	340	30	6	5	5
Snyder	.999	106	722	58	1	9	9

First Base	PCT	G	PO	A	E	DP
Cirillo	1.000	2	1	1	0	0
Clark	.996	83	432	32	2	50
Hammock	1.000	1	1	0	0	1
Jackson	.988	108	859	48	11	86
Snyder	1.000	2	1	0	0	0
Tracy	.992	18	122	5	1	9

Second Base	PCT	G	PO	A	E	DP
Bonifacio	.960	6	9	15	1	6
Callaspo	1.000	10	4	12	0	4
Cirillo	—	2	0	0	0	0
Hudson	.985	137	258	387	10	96

	PCT/AVG	G	PO	A	E	DP
Ojeda	1.000	26	29	70	0	18
Reynolds	1.000	2	1	0	0	0
Sadler	1.000	1	1	0	0	0

Third Base	PCT	G	PO	A	E	DP
Barden	1.000	3	0	2	0	1
Callaspo	.971	18	11	23	1	5
Cirillo	1.000	11	5	13	0	2
Hammock	.667	4	0	2	1	0
Jackson	1.000	2	1	0	0	0
Ojeda	1.000	7	0	3	0	0
Reynolds	.951	104	55	157	11	21
Tracy	.962	48	29	73	4	6

Shortstop	PCT	G	PO	A	E	DP
Callaspo	.947	9	11	25	2	3
Drew	.973	147	212	409	17	98
Ojeda	1.000	12	18	23	0	3

	PCT	G	PO	A	E	DP
Smith	1.000	1	0	2	0	0

Outfield	PCT	G	PO	A	E	DP
Byrnes	.986	160	351	12	5	1
Callaspo	1.000	10	15	1	0	0
DaVanon	.917	8	11	0	1	0
Hairston	.969	52	90	3	3	1
Hammock	1.000	7	7	0	0	0
Jackson	1.000	2	3	0	0	0
Quentin	.993	76	141	2	1	0
Reynolds	1.000	2	1	0	0	0
Salazar	1.000	30	52	3	0	1
Snyder	—	1	0	0	0	0
Upton	.930	42	65	1	5	0
Young	.984	146	354	6	6	2

TUCSON SIDEWINDERS

TRIPLE-A

PACIFIC COAST LEAGUE

BATTING	B-T	HT	WT	DOB	AVG	vLH	vRH	G	AB	R	H	2B	3B	HR	RBI	BB	HBP	SH	SF	SO	SB	CS	SLG	OBP
Ball, Jarred	B-R	6-0	185	4-18-83	.346	.278	.382	23	52	8	18	9	1	2	14	5	0	3	1	11	0	1	.673	.397
Barden, Brian	R-R	5-11	185	4-2-81	.269	.303	.257	83	286	36	77	9	2	2	25	31	7	5	0	56	2	3	.336	.355
2-team (20 Memphis)					.263	—	—	103	354	43	93	12	2	4	37	36	8	5	3	69	2	3	.342	.342
Brown, Dee	L-R	6-0	220	3-27-78	.282	.327	.256	41	131	25	37	7	0	2	24	13	1	0	0	24	1	1	.382	.352
2-team (62 Sacramento)					.293	—	—	103	376	72	110	21	0	16	78	37	3	0	6	76	3	1	.476	.355
Callaspo, Alberto	B-R	5-10	175	4-19-83	.341	.288	.356	59	226	48	77	15	2	5	30	28	1	0	6	17	1	2	.491	.406
Carter, Chris	L-L	6-0	210	9-16-82	.324	.292	.336	126	503	74	163	39	3	18	84	50	4	0	6	68	2	0	.521	.383
D'Antona, Jamie	R-R	6-2	210	5-12-82	.308	.390	.277	128	483	79	149	43	5	13	86	40	4	0	6	57	3	2	.499	.362
DaVanon, Jeff	B-R	6-0	200	12-8-73	.333	.250	.364	5	15	3	5	0	0	0	1	1	0	0	2	0	0	.333	.412
2-team (7 Sacramento)					.326	—	—	12	43	10	14	1	0	1	2	8	1	0	0	7	1	3	.419	.442
Erickson, Matt	L-R	5-11	190	7-30-75	.299	.240	.315	77	231	38	69	13	2	1	33	22	5	2	3	33	3	1	.385	.368
Gonzalez, Carlos	L-L	6-1	200	10-17-85	.310	.294	.320	10	42	9	13	5	0	1	5	1	0	0	0	6	1	0	.500	.396
Hammock, Robby	R-R	5-10	185	5-13-77	.325	.317	.328	67	246	34	80	17	1	4	35	43	2	0	2	34	3	2	.451	.427
Johnson, Mark	L-R	6-0	180	9-12-75	.320	.500	.294	80	244	37	78	10	0	4	34	52	2	1	2	21	0	2	.410	.440
Krynzel, Dave	L-L	6-1	185	11-7-81	.232	.250	.226	23	69	11	16	2	0	3	9	5	3	2	2	20	2	3	.391	.304
Merrill Jr., Ronnie	B-R	6-1	185	11-13-78	.264	.313	.243	14	53	7	14	4	1	0	9	4	1	0	1	13	1	0	.377	.322
Morgan, Matthew	R-R	6-2	195	8-10-81	.213	.266	.172	70	216	16	46	6	0	0	16	21	1	4	0	38	1	0	.241	.286
Ojeda, Augie	B-R	5-8	170	12-20-74	.323	.429	.282	32	99	20	32	8	0	0	17	10	3	4	2	11	1	0	.404	.395
Quentin, Carlos	R-R	6-2	220	8-28-82	.348	.250	.379	33	115	30	40	12	1	4	27	9	9	0	2	14	0	1	.574	.430
Richar, Danny	L-R	6-0	170	6-9-83	.285	.253	.299	66	267	40	76	20	4	8	46	27	0	3	2	47	4	5	.479	.348
Romero, Alex	L-R	6-1	185	9-9-83	.310	.265	.328	131	535	82	166	32	6	5	66	37	1	8	3	53	12	10	.421	.354
Sadler, Donnie	R-R	5-6	175	6-17-75	.214	.163	.246	52	112	19	24	1	5	2	17	22	1	2	0	26	5	0	.366	.348
Salazar, Jeff	L-L	6-0	190	11-24-80	.299	.277	.307	108	402	76	120	31	9	10	68	56	5	2	7	56	18	5	.495	.385
Smith, Jason	L-R	6-3	200	7-24-77	.315	.286	.319	14	54	9	17	3	1	3	10	0	1	0	2	11	0	2	.574	.316
Thompson, Rich	L-R	6-3	185	4-23-79	.295	.325	.286	111	325	60	96	18	6	3	41	28	5	9	0	49	15	2	.415	.360
Tracy, Chad	L-R	6-2	200	5-22-80	.467	.200	.600	3	15	3	7	2	0	1	4	0	0	0	0	1	0	0	.800	.467

PITCHING	B-T	HT	WT	DOB	W	L	ERA	G	GS	CG	SV	IP	H	R	ER	HR	BB	SO	AVG	vLH	vRH	K/9	BB/9
Bass, Adam	R-R	6-6	210	7-31-81	3	1	2.16	19	4	0	0	50	43	13	12	3	16	35	.230	.316	.167	6.30	2.88
Carrasco, D.J.	R-R	6-1	215	4-12-77	5	14	6.68	34	22	1	0	137	185	121	102	16	60	103	.321	.311	.328	6.75	3.93
Choate, Randy	L-L	6-1	195	9-5-75	3	1	2.98	55	0	0	3	63	68	27	21	3	16	61	.270	.242	.286	8.67	2.27
Cruz, Juan	R-R	6-2	155	10-15-78	0	0	0.00	1	0	0	0	2	0	0	0	0	0	5	.000	.000	.000	22.50	0.00
Daigle, Casey	R-R	6-5	250	4-4-81	10	5	6.59	42	16	0	0	109	156	84	80	18	31	95	.333	.345	.323	7.82	2.55
Eveland, Dana	L-L	6-1	240	10-29-83	1	0	1.95	7	5	0	0	28	29	7	6	0	10	15	.271	.261	.274	4.88	3.25
Fruto, Emiliano	R-R	6-3	230	6-6-84	0	1	2.45	6	0	0	0	11	8	3	3	0	10	14	.216	.200	.227	11.45	8.18
Glant, Dustin	R-R	6-2	200	7-20-81	0	1	6.03	17	1	0	0	31	42	26	21	3	13	15	.321	.234	.369	4.31	3.73
Gonzalez, Enrique	R-R	5-10	210	7-14-82	8	10	5.15	27	27	0	0	154	186	105	88	11	61	118	.300	.300	.299	6.91	3.57
Harville, Chad	R-R	5-9	190	9-16-76	6	4	3.71	47	0	0	25	53	45	23	22	6	21	46	.228	.282	.198	7.76	3.54
Howard, Adam	R-R	6-4	200	8-16-83	1	0	0.00	1	0	0	0	3	3	1	0	0	0	4	.214	.333	.125	10.80	0.00
Johnson, Randy	R-L	6-10	225	9-10-63	1	0	3.00	2	2	0	0	12	15	5	4	1	2	10	.326	.222	.351	7.50	1.50
MacLane, Evan	L-L	6-2	185	11-4-82	7	7	7.70	32	19	0	0	116	190	117	99	21	37	53	.373	.388	.367	4.12	2.88
Medders, Brandon	R-R	6-1	190	1-26-80	5	3	4.69	35	0	0	5	48	55	28	25	3	24	38	.286	.342	.252	7.12	4.50
Murphy, Bill	L-R	5-11	215	5-9-81	3	3	3.68	54	9	0	1	100	93	53	41	10	43	102	.246	.214	.258	9.15	3.86
Nippert, Dustin	R-R	6-8	225	5-6-81	0	3	4.75	10	8	0	0	36	23	19	19	3	23	46	.189	.175	.200	11.50	5.75
Owings, Micah	R-R	6-5	220	9-28-82	0	0	0.00	1	1	0	0	5	1	0	0	0	1	7	.250	.364	.000	12.60	1.80
Peguero, Jailen	R-R	6-0	195	1-4-81	6	2	1.89	53	0	0	4	67	47	19	14	5	26	68	.201	.222	.188	9.18	3.51
Petit, Yusmeiro	R-R	6-0	230	11-22-84	8	4	4.04	17	17	0	0	94	83	47	42	11	38	60	.237	.271	.210	5.77	3.65
Sadler, Donnie	R-R	5-6	175	6-17-75	0	1	—	1	0	0	0	2	2	2	2	1	0	0	1.000	1.000	1.000	—	—
Schultz, Mike	R-R	6-7	220	11-28-79	4	5	3.92	55	1	0	4	78	85	38	34	4	36	50	.285	.298	.277	5.77	4.15
Smith, Greg	L-L	6-2	190	12-22-83	4	2	3.78	10	10	1	0	52	61	27	22	4	18	34	.296	.228	.322	5.85	3.10

FIELDING

Catcher	PCT	G	PO	A	E	DP	PB
D'Antona	.971	21	125	7	4	2	7
Hammock	.997	40	305	17	1	2	4
Johnson	.988	62	402	26	5	9	5
Morgan	.990	30	179	21	2	1	2

First Base	PCT	G	PO	A	E	DP
Barden	1.000	2	17	1	0	1
Carter	.978	89	680	43	16	73
D'Antona	.984	47	332	26	6	41
Hammock	1.000	12	95	7	0	9
Johnson	.979	5	45	2	1	2
Morgan	.943	6	32	1	2	5

Second Base	PCT	G	PO	A	E	DP
Barden	.952	18	32	48	4	18
Callaspo	.989	20	36	53	1	16
Erickson	.959	25	48	68	5	12
Merrill Jr.	1.000	3	7	7	0	2
Morgan	.954	26	46	58	5	18
Ojeda	1.000	1	0	3	0	0

	PCT	G	PO	A	E	PB
Richar	.967	50	99	134	8	39
Sadler	.960	8	10	14	1	2
Smith	1.000	3	3	15	0	3

Third Base	PCT	G	PO	A	E	DP
Barden	.971	50	34	99	4	5
Callaspo	.875	3	2	5	1	0
D'Antona	.909	67	35	114	15	14
Erickson	.971	13	14	19	1	2
Hammock	.885	12	6	17	3	2
Merrill Jr.	1.000	5	4	11	0	0
Morgan	.875	4	4	3	1	0
Sadler	1.000	2	1	2	0	0
Tracy	1.000	2	2	7	0	0

Shortstop	PCT	G	PO	A	E	DP
Barden	.926	16	16	59	6	10
Callaspo	.973	36	46	99	4	21
Erickson	.942	25	34	64	6	16
Merrill Jr.	.923	5	7	17	2	4
Ojeda	.993	29	37	102	1	21

	PCT	G	PO	A	E	PB
Richar	.914	16	18	35	5	8
Sadler	.974	17	29	45	2	10
Smith	1.000	10	11	34	0	13

Outfield	PCT	G	PO	A	E	DP
Ball	1.000	13	22	1	0	0
Brown	.971	15	32	1	1	0
Carter	1.000	23	26	3	0	0
DaVanon	1.000	5	2	0	0	0
Erickson	—	1	0	0	0	0
Gonzalez	1.000	10	20	1	0	0
Hammock	1.000	5	6	1	0	0
Krynzel	1.000	20	34	2	0	1
Morgan	—	2	0	0	0	0
Quentin	.949	31	53	3	3	0
Romero	.981	124	250	8	5	4
Sadler	.929	11	13	0	1	0
Salazar	.993	106	262	4	2	2
Thompson	1.000	90	159	11	0	2

MOBILE BAYBEARS

DOUBLE-A

SOUTHERN LEAGUE

BATTING	B-T	HT	WT	DOB	AVG	vLH	vRH	G	AB	R	H	2B	3B	HR	RBI	BB	HBP	SH	SF	SO	SB	CS	SLG	OBP
Avlas, Phil	R-R	5-11	183	12-17-82	.202	.151	.226	89	228	28	46	3	1	1	16	27	1	2	3	44	3	1	.237	.286
Ball, Jarred	B-R	6-0	185	4-18-83	.252	.325	.210	77	218	30	55	14	1	0	23	16	2	3	0	35	11	3	.326	.309
Bonifacio, Emilio	B-R	5-11	180	4-23-85	.285	.293	.281	132	551	84	157	21	5	2	40	38	2	4	1	105	41	13	.352	.333
Brito, Javier	R-R	6-3	210	3-25-83	.327	.353	.314	127	440	72	144	29	2	11	72	78	6	1	3	90	1	0	.477	.433
Castillo, Wilkin	B-R	6-0	190	6-1-84	.302	.289	.309	109	410	50	124	31	3	6	46	17	3	16	3	62	18	14	.437	.333
Cunningham, Aaron	R-R	5-11	195	4-24-86	.288	.250	.308	31	118	25	34	8	3	5	20	12	2	0	0	27	1	3	.534	.364
Ford, Josh	R-R	6-2	235	1-17-83	.265	.238	.277	76	257	30	68	13	0	3	29	31	3	0	1	58	0	1	.350	.349
Gonzalez, Carlos	L-L	6-1	200	10-17-85	.286	.213	.326	120	458	63	131	33	3	16	75	32	1	2	6	103	9	5	.476	.330
Merrill Jr., Ronnie	B-R	6-1	185	11-13-78	.253	.328	.210	99	324	53	82	13	4	13	47	41	4	4	2	69	13	4	.438	.342
Murillo, Agustin	R-R	6-3	195	5-5-82	.306	.250	.353	19	62	3	19	1	0	0	7	2	1	0	0	9	3	0	.323	.338
Nicolas, Cesar	R-R	6-4	230	4-17-82	.245	.232	.251	109	310	53	76	18	0	9	52	47	16	3	6	78	2	7	.390	.367
Rahl, Chris	R-R	6-0	185	12-5-83	.259	.303	.238	119	432	64	112	26	5	8	51	15	3	3	5	87	15	5	.398	.286
Reynolds, Mark	R-R	6-1	200	8-3-83	.306	.362	.276	37	134	28	41	9	2	6	22	20	0	1		32	2	1	.537	.394
Ryal, Rusty	R-R	6-2	195	3-16-83	.238	.174	.262	47	168	18	40	6	2	0	21	8	5	5	1	42	4	3	.405	.291
Sosa, Ricardo	R-R	6-1	213	5-24-84	.000	.000	.000	8	6	0	0	0	0	0	0	2	0	0	2	0	0		.000	.250
Upton, Justin	R-R	6-3	205	8-25-87	.309	.282	.322	71	259	48	80	17	4	13	53	37	5	0	5	51	10	7	.556	.399
Zeringue, Jon	R-R	6-2	215	3-29-83	.143	.048	.190	24	63	5	9	2	0	2	10	6	2	0	2	21	1	1	.270	.233

PITCHING	B-T	HT	WT	DOB	W	L	ERA	G	GS	CG	SV	IP	H	R	ER	HR	BB	SO	AVG	vLH	vRH	K/9	BB/9
Brown, Brooks	L-R	6-3	205	6-20-85	4	4	3.66	12	12	0	0	66	64	30	27	2	36	54	.261	.280	.244	7.33	4.88
Castellanos, Jonathan	R-R	6-0	214	9-17-81	5	6	3.82	13	13	0	0	68	81	38	29	5	19	38	.291	.281	.299	5.00	2.50
Castillo, Osbek	R-R	6-3	195	1-29-81	1	3	5.72	29	6	0	1	68	55	44	43	6	52	59	.221	.192	.248	7.85	6.92
Elliott, Matt	R-R	6-0	175	4-6-84	1	6	4.29	46	1	0	5	63	60	40	30	6	33	69	.248	.207	.286	9.86	4.71
Glant, Dustin	R-R	6-2	200	7-20-81	5	2	3.61	30	0	0	5	47	50	21	19	4	13	44	.276	.346	.223	8.37	2.47
Goocher, Clint	L-L	6-2	195	6-15-82	5	4	3.42	52	0	0	6	76	70	37	29	7	23	66	.241	.204	.261	7.78	2.71
Green, Matthew	R-R	6-5	195	1-5-82	12	6	3.95	28	28	0	0	148	151	75	65	15	55	128	.265	.280	.252	7.78	3.34
Kinsey, Chris	R-R	6-3	230	10-18-82	4	7	4.51	28	22	0	0	122	136	69	61	10	60	88	.290	.321	.262	6.21	4.44
Mahon, Reid	R-R	6-3	215	6-1-83	1	0	1.29	6	0	0	2	7	7	2	1	0	1	4	.241	.500	.059	5.14	1.29
Rosen, Mark	L-L	5-11	200	6-30-84	4	4	3.12	50	0	0	7	66	80	36	23	6	22	78	.303	.260	.327	10.58	2.98
Scherzer, Max	R-R	6-3	190	7-27-84	1	4	3.91	14	14	0	0	74	64	38	32	3	40	76	.235	.242	.227	9.29	4.89
Shappi, A.J.	R-R	6-2	195	10-16-82	1	7	3.66	40	2	0	2	76	76	37	31	6	17	57	.258	.261	.255	6.72	2.00
Smith, Greg	L-L	6-2	190	12-22-83	5	3	3.36	12	12	2	0	70	64	30	26	7	14	62	.251	.207	.274	8.01	1.81
Stange, Daniel	R-R	6-3	185	12-22-85	1	0	5.40	5	0	0	1	7	9	4	4	1	2	5	.321	.313	.333	6.75	2.70
Vasquez, Esmerling	R-R	6-1	154	11-7-83	10	6	2.99	29	29	0	0	165	125	61	55	11	60	151	.217	.233	.203	8.22	3.27
Wilkinson, Matthew	L-R	6-3	205	10-25-77	0	0	5.93	11	0	0	0	14	18	10	9	1	7	13	.310	.435	.229	8.56	4.61
Woody, Abe	R-R	5-10	195	11-9-82	8	6	4.58	48	0	0	5	73	88	41	37	7	25	48	.302	.299	.305	5.94	3.10

FIELDING

Catcher	PCT	G	PO	A	E	DP	PB
Avlas	.944	2	17	0	1	0	0
Castillo	.985	70	548	57	9	5	10
Ford	.989	73	502	53	6	6	10

First Base	PCT	G	PO	A	E	DP
Avlas	1.000	1	9	0	0	1
Ball	—	1	0	0	0	0
Brito	.991	106	864	65	8	81
Nicolas	.991	40	293	23	3	27

Second Base	PCT	G	PO	A	E	DP
Avlas	.942	16	27	38	4	8
Bonifacio	.972	78	130	216	10	42
Castillo	.927	19	31	58	7	8

	PCT	G	PO	A	E	DP
Reynolds	.955	6	12	9	1	1
Ryal	.978	26	56	76	3	12

Third Base	PCT	G	PO	A	E	DP
Avlas	.909	4	3	7	1	0
Brito	1.000	1	0	1	0	0
Castillo	.938	6	3	12	1	0
Merrill Jr.	.978	19	16	28	1	5
Murillo	.920	17	10	13	2	1
Nicolas	.912	53	23	91	11	4
Reynolds	.882	31	24	58	11	3
Ryal	.886	21	15	24	5	2

Shortstop	PCT	G	PO	A	E	DP
Bonifacio	.957	56	93	153	11	26

	PCT	G	PO	A	E	DP
Castillo	.925	10	17	32	4	9
Merrill Jr.	.985	78	125	194	5	49

Outfield	PCT	G	PO	A	E	DP
Avlas	.976	29	40	1	1	0
Ball	.949	58	92	2	5	1
Brito	1.000	8	4	0	0	0
Castillo	1.000	1	1	0	0	0
Cunningham	1.000	31	52	4	0	0
Gonzalez	.952	117	225	12	12	4
Rahl	.982	112	158	6	3	1
Upton	.966	67	138	4	5	1
Zeringue	1.000	19	31	1	0	0

CALIFORNIA LEAGUE

BATTING	B-T	HT	WT	DOB	AVG	vLH	vRH	G	AB	R	H	2B	3B	HR	RBI	BB	HBP	SH	SF	SO	SB	CS	SLG	OBP
Bruce, Derek	R-R	6-2	190	8-3-82	.264	.311	.248	111	417	58	110	20	4	7	40	32	6	4	5	63	2	8	.381	.322
Burgess, Brandon	B-R	6-4	225	2-24-83	.260	.287	.249	90	331	56	86	19	4	17	56	33	17	0	4	103	5	2	.495	.353
Byrne, Bryan	L-R	6-3	200	4-30-84	.310	.297	.313	128	478	75	148	25	5	13	74	66	7	1	5	78	4	1	.464	.397
Ciriaco, Pedro	R-R	6-0	150	9-27-85	.251	.213	.262	119	463	61	116	14	5	3	39	20	4	5	3	81	20	11	.322	.286
Cunningham, Aaron	R-R	5-11	195	4-24-86	.358	.419	.337	29	123	25	44	11	2	3	20	5	2	3	2	23	5	3	.553	.386
Curreri, Frank	L-R	6-4	215	12-4-82	.330	.327	.331	62	209	29	69	10	2	4	36	39	0	0	5	43	5	2	.455	.427
DaVanon, Jeff	B-R	6-0	200	12-8-73	.333	.429	.314	12	42	5	14	5	1	1	5	10	0	0	0	3	1	3	.571	.462
Hankerd, Cyle	R-R	6-3	180	1-24-85	.285	.379	.251	103	386	55	110	27	1	8	54	35	19	0	6	60	2	3	.422	.368
Hester, John	R-R	6-4	210	9-14-83	.263	.292	.253	79	297	38	78	16	1	10	43	22	1	0	0	64	4	2	.424	.316
Mercado, Orlando	R-R	5-10	215	3-13-85	.256	.266	.252	69	211	27	54	12	0	6	37	51	9	2	2	42	2	2	.398	.418
Milons, Jereme	R-R	6-2	185	2-5-83	.307	.342	.296	77	309	39	95	18	2	4	46	17	1	3	3	71	17	9	.417	.342
Parra, Gerardo	L-L	5-11	197	5-6-87	.284	.250	.300	24	102	11	29	2	1	2	14	4	0	3	0	17	2	3	.382	.303
Ryal, Rusty	R-R	6-2	195	3-16-83	.301	.262	.312	70	276	46	83	15	3	11	46	16	8	0	2	47	2	4	.496	.354
Santana, Mayo	R-R	6-3	190	8-23-81	.235	.276	.212	44	162	25	38	12	1	2	19	12	1	0	3	27	0	1	.358	.287
Septimo, Leyson	L-L	6-0	150	7-7-85	.271	.197	.290	100	362	54	98	18	2	5	42	23	6	5	3	67	12	6	.373	.322
Sharpe, Blake	R-R	6-2	185	9-10-83	.300	.214	.333	14	50	4	15	3	0	1	6	4	2	2	0	8	1	0	.420	.375
Smith, Jason	L-R	6-3	200	7-24-77	.444	.000	.500	3	9	4	4	0	0	1	5	2	1	0	0	1	0	0	.778	.583
Thomson, Gregory	L-L	6-1	205	6-13-84	.285	.239	.301	112	459	72	131	22	9	9	52	29	11	3	6	67	18	9	.431	.339
Upton, Justin	R-R	6-3	205	8-25-87	.341	.423	.320	32	126	27	43	6	2	5	17	19	3	0	2	28	9	4	.540	.433

PITCHING	B-T	HT	WT	DOB	W	L	ERA	G	GS	CG	SV	IP	H	R	ER	HR	BB	SO	AVG	vLH	vRH	K/9	BB/9
Ambriz, Hector	L-R	6-1	210	5-24-84	10	8	4.08	28	26	2	0	150	137	79	68	12	50	133	.241	.259	.220	7.98	3.00
Anderson, Brett	L-L	6-4	215	2-1-88	3	3	4.85	9	9	0	0	39	50	23	21	6	11	40	.311	.250	.326	9.23	2.54
Bongiovanni, Vincent	R-R	6-5	215	1-11-83	5	2	4.13	45	0	0	5	70	58	37	32	10	32	65	.221	.238	.207	8.40	4.13
Brown, Brooks	L-R	6-3	205	6-20-85	6	3	2.81	14	14	0	0	80	66	30	25	2	23	74	.224	.252	.191	8.33	2.59
Bruce, Derek	R-R	6-2	190	8-3-82	0	0	0.00	1	0	0	0	0	0	0	0	0	0	0	.000	.000	.000	0.00	0.00
Buck, Dallas	R-R	6-2	195	11-11-84	4	4	3.41	16	16	0	0	98	84	49	37	10	31	88	.231	.215	.247	8.11	2.86
Castillo, Osbek	R-R	6-3	195	1-29-81	0	1	4.66	2	2	0	0	10	11	5	5	1	6	6	.289	.267	.304	5.59	5.59
Cory, Forrest	R-L	6-3	205	10-13-83	8	1	3.35	41	0	0	3	78	72	38	29	12	28	55	.240	.210	.256	6.35	3.23
Cupps, Anthony	R-R	6-3	198	5-31-83	4	13	6.01	28	25	1	0	138	165	100	92	13	60	71	.306	.318	.296	4.64	3.92
Doherty, Ryan	R-R	7-1	255	2-2-84	0	0	3.00	3	0	0	0	3	1	2	1	1	0	3	.083	.167	.000	9.00	0.00
Enright, Barry	R-R	6-3	200	3-30-86	0	0	0.00	4	0	0	1	5	3	1	0	0	2	4	.167	.333	.000	7.20	3.60
Evans, Cody	R-R	6-5	190	9-3-83	7	6	5.40	35	0	0	2	72	95	45	43	7	17	60	.328	.352	.309	7.53	2.13
Eveland, Dana	L-L	6-1	240	10-29-83	0	0	0.00	2	2	0	0	5	1	1	0	0	2	9	.059	.000	.077	16.20	3.60
Guerrero, Hipolito	L-L	6-0	149	6-13-83	1	1	3.96	33	3	0	1	64	60	30	28	5	30	50	.251	.338	.251	7.07	4.24
Howard, Adam	R-R	6-4	200	8-16-83	4	2	3.52	23	11	0	1	84	87	38	33	6	23	74	.270	.238	.304	7.90	2.45
Johnson, Randy	R-L	6-10	225	9-10-63	0	0	3.00	1	1	0	0	6	4	2	2	0	0	4	.182	.000	.190	6.00	0.00
Mahon, Reid	R-R	6-3	215	6-1-83	1	1	1.29	11	0	0	8	14	10	3	2	1	2	9	.196	.100	.258	5.79	1.29
Newby, Kyler	R-R	6-4	225	2-22-85	1	0	1.50	9	0	0	2	12	7	3	2	0	2	10	.156	.250	.103	7.50	1.50
Pohlman, Daniel	R-R	6-1	215	1-1-82	1	0	5.68	16	0	0	3	25	28	19	16	5	14	11	.280	.289	.273	3.91	4.97
Santana, Mayo	R-R	6-3	190	8-23-81	0	0	0.00	1	0	0	0	2	2	3	0	0	1	1	.250	.000	.286	5.40	5.40
Scherzer, Max	R-R	6-3	190	7-27-84	2	0	0.53	3	3	0	0	17	5	1	1	0	2	30	.089	.033	.154	15.88	1.06
Stange, Daniel	R-R	6-3	185	12-22-85	4	5	3.19	38	0	0	16	42	37	26	15	3	18	53	.230	.260	.205	11.27	3.83
Torra, Matthew	R-R	6-3	225	6-29-84	12	10	6.01	28	28	0	0	159	186	115	106	15	43	137	.292	.320	.266	7.77	2.44
Wright, Kyle	R-R	6-3	170	4-27-83	4	3	4.33	36	0	0	3	60	62	43	29	8	22	60	.254	.262	.248	8.95	3.28

FIELDING

Catcher	PCT	G	PO	A	E	DP	PB
Curreri	.988	33	287	29	4	4	7
Hester	.977	59	393	32	10	1	9
Mercado	.982	51	355	36	7	4	9

First Base	PCT	G	PO	A	E	DP
Burgess	1.000	1	10	2	0	3
Byrne	.990	126	1030	91	11	73
Curreri	1.000	4	41	2	0	4
Santana	1.000	11	93	6	0	8

Second Base	PCT	G	PO	A	E	DP
Bruce	.986	90	163	261	6	35
Ryal	.964	31	45	89	5	12

Santana	.972	7	13	22	1	5
Sharpe	.955	14	26	38	3	8

Third Base	PCT	G	PO	A	E	DP
Burgess	.901	79	45	127	19	8
Ryal	.933	38	28	69	7	2
Santana	.903	24	12	53	7	5
Smith	—	1	0	0	0	0

Shortstop	PCT	G	PO	A	E	DP
Bruce	.926	20	35	52	7	16
Ciriaco	.938	118	164	324	32	51
Ryal	.750	2	1	2	1	0
Smith	1.000	1	1	2	0	1

Outfield	PCT	G	PO	A	E	DP
Burgess	.000	1	0	0	1	0
Cunningham	.983	27	56	1	1	1
Curreri	.889	4	8	0	1	0
DaVanon	1.000	6	13	1	0	0
Hankerd	.957	95	124	9	6	1
Milons	.976	55	122	2	3	0
Parra	.982	23	53	2	1	1
Septimo	.955	92	158	11	8	3
Thomson	.984	98	246	5	4	1
Upton	.958	28	66	2	3	0

MIDWEST LEAGUE

BATTING	B-T	HT	WT	DOB	AVG	vLH	vRH	G	AB	R	H	2B	3B	HR	RBI	BB	HBP	SH	SF	SO	SB	CS	SLG	OBP
Brashear, Justin	L-R	6-2	215	1-19-85	.194	.158	.205	82	252	44	49	10	1	3	22	81	4	0	2	68	1	2	.278	.395
Byrne, Shane	B-R	6-3	190	9-14-83	.125	.333	.077	7	16	1	2	0	0	0	0	1	1	1	0	2	0	0	.125	.222
Conner, Clayton	R-R	6-3	210	10-8-86	.143	.000	.200	11	42	2	6	0	0	1	3	1	1	0	1	16	0	0	.214	.178
Curreri, Frank	L-R	6-4	215	12-4-82	.305	.214	.324	26	82	7	25	5	1	0	10	21	0	0	0	20	0	4	.390	.447
Ferrer, Manuel	R-R	5-9	201	2-15-85	.216	.224	.213	71	218	25	47	10	1	1	27	31	2	5	1	42	5	2	.284	.317
Harbin, Taylor	R-R	5-9	175	2-13-86	.214	.000	.273	3	14	2	3	1	0	0	1	0	0	0	0	2	0	0	.286	.214
Jones, Tyler	L-L	6-0	176	12-29-83	.277	.250	.284	69	242	29	67	6	3	2	16	20	3	6	1	40	10	7	.351	.338
McFeely, Shea	R-R	6-0	229	4-21-84	.234	.271	.221	55	188	26	44	8	0	4	14	19	6	1	0	36	3	1	.340	.324
Mena, Steve	R-R	6-2	230	1-24-85	.253	.213	.267	132	482	65	122	26	2	15	48	49	10	0	3	134	1	4	.409	.333

	B-T	HT	WT	DOB	AVG	vLH	vRH	G	AB	R	H	2B	3B	HR	RBI	BB	HBP	SH	SF	SO	SB	CS	SLG	OBP
Mercado, Richard	R-R	6-0	220	5-23-83	.263	.253	.267	77	270	25	71	16	0	6	40	29	1	2	5	50	0	1	.389	.331
Miller, Brad	R-R	6-5	245	6-25-83	.262	.262	.262	135	500	71	131	24	3	22	91	67	9	0	5	116	0	0	.454	.356
Oxendine, Matthew	R-R	6-0	187	10-13-83	.251	.205	.264	88	323	41	81	17	1	1	30	25	4	3	3	60	5	3	.319	.310
Parra, Gerardo	L-L	5-11	197	5-6-87	.320	.328	.317	110	444	64	142	25	4	6	57	30	8	1	5	51	24	8	.435	.370
Perales, Daniel	L-L	5-10	176	3-18-85	.282	.271	.285	136	554	80	156	32	10	16	92	42	8	0	5	100	7	7	.462	.338
Sanchez, Yunesky	B-R	6-2	212	5-3-84	.282	.262	.289	110	408	49	115	16	2	3	37	25	2	6	4	36	6	6	.353	.323
Side, Joey	R-R	6-1	186	12-4-83	.291	.274	.297	129	478	76	139	25	7	1	51	53	15	6	5	72	5	6	.379	.376
Sosa, Ricardo	R-R	6-1	213	5-24-84	.202	.211	.200	24	84	11	17	3	0	0	7	7	1	1	0	19	0	0	.238	.272

PITCHING	B-T	HT	WT	DOB	W	L	ERA	G	GS	CG	SV	IP	H	R	ER	HR	BB	SO	AVG	vLH	vRH	K/9	BB/9
Anderson, Brett	L-L	6-4	215	2-1-88	8	4	2.21	14	14	0	0	81	76	26	20	3	10	85	.248	.197	.261	9.41	1.11
Barnette, Tony	R-R	6-1	192	11-9-83	8	8	3.60	26	25	1	1	160	160	74	64	11	28	108	.262	.264	.260	6.08	1.58
Beck, Chad	R-R	6-4	251	1-17-85	1	2	4.33	31	0	0	1	52	53	27	25	5	20	48	.264	.256	.269	8.31	3.46
Butler, Eric	R-R	6-4	243	12-26-83	5	4	3.61	27	7	0	0	67	67	27	27	4	20	64	.264	.188	.310	8.55	2.67
Christianson, Chase	R-R	6-5	220	12-11-84	0	1	7.41	15	0	0	0	17	22	14	14	1	9	12	.310	.348	.292	6.35	4.76
Dove, Shane	L-L	6-2	185	7-22-84	1	3	6.33	15	0	0	0	21	31	16	15	2	7	15	.333	.310	.344	6.33	2.95
Enright, Barry	R-R	6-3	200	3-30-86	0	0	0.00	1	0	0	1	2	1	0	0	0	0	1	.167	—	.167	4.50	0.00
Howard, Adam	R-R	6-4	200	8-16-83	1	2	1.32	7	0	0	0	14	11	2	2	0	1	8	.220	.250	.200	5.27	0.66
Mahon, Reid	R-R	6-3	215	6-1-83	4	4	1.77	32	0	0	11	46	34	15	9	1	8	28	.204	.209	.200	5.52	1.58
Neighborgall, Jason	R-R	6-5	205	12-19-83	0	0	108.00	5	0	0	0	1	3	12	12	0	12	2	.429	.333	.500	18.00	108.00
Nippert, Derik	R-R	6-8	237	5-6-81	5	2	1.91	12	9	0	0	47	49	18	10	2	14	37	.265	.244	.282	7.09	2.68
Norberto, Jordan	L-L	6-0	195	12-8-86	6	7	5.28	21	21	0	0	102	102	67	60	10	46	111	.266	.225	.275	9.76	4.05
Perez, Jorge	R-R	5-11	167	1-16-86	3	4	3.41	40	0	0	4	69	65	37	26	6	28	81	.246	.258	.240	10.62	3.67
Pfautz, Craig	R-L	6-3	209	9-13-84	3	5	4.94	41	0	0	1	62	80	39	34	5	14	47	.313	.316	.311	6.82	2.03
Romanczuk, Mark	L-L	6-1	215	9-24-83	4	3	3.73	33	6	0	1	72	77	32	30	6	30	59	.279	.266	.300	7.34	3.73
Romero, Eddie	L-L	5-10	206	11-7-85	8	8	4.45	27	26	0	0	146	182	78	72	18	48	93	.312	.255	.324	5.75	2.97
Sanchez, Ramon (Perez)	R-R	6-2	222	6-6-84	2	2	4.69	39	0	0	5	56	46	36	29	6	32	60	.219	.244	.205	9.70	5.17
Scribner, Evan	R-R	6-3	190	7-19-85	1	0	2.61	5	0	0	0	10	7	3	3	1	5	13	.184	.176	.190	11.32	4.35
Urquidez, Jason	R-R	6-0	177	9-12-82	1	1	0.43	13	0	0	3	21	19	4	1	0	3	7	.244	.241	.245	3.00	1.29
Valdez, Cesar	R-R	6-2	200	3-17-85	7	10	3.41	25	25	2	0	148	130	63	56	11	32	106	.235	.250	.223	6.45	1.95

FIELDING

Catcher	PCT	G	PO	A	E	DP	PB
Brashear	.995	72	491	54	3	6	9
Curreri	.980	13	86	14	2	2	3
Mercado	.989	54	403	33	5	5	9

First Base	PCT	G	PO	A	E	DP
Brashear	1.000	1	0	1	0	0
McFeely	1.000	4	41	1	0	3
Mena	1.000	6	46	1	0	6
Miller	.985	130	1116	103	18	104

Second Base	PCT	G	PO	A	E	DP
Ferrer	.983	41	67	102	3	22
Harbin	1.000	3	6	5	0	2

	PCT	G	PO	A	E	DP
McFeely	1.000	1	2	1	0	0
Mena	.920	14	18	28	4	6
Oxendine	.974	82	158	211	10	64

Third Base	PCT	G	PO	A	E	DP
Conner	.842	9	3	13	3	0
McFeely	.918	38	25	100	10	7
Mena	.929	87	61	174	18	20
Mercado	1.000	1	1	2	0	0
Sosa	.839	4	5	21	5	2

Shortstop	PCT	G	PO	A	E	DP
Ferrer	.966	28	36	79	4	19
Mena	1.000	1	1	0	0	0

	PCT	G	PO	A	E	DP
Oxendine	.957	4	6	16	1	5
Sanchez	.966	106	140	310	16	47

Outfield	PCT	G	PO	A	E	DP
Byrne	1.000	5	9	0	0	0
Jones	.980	54	92	7	2	2
Mena	.951	26	31	8	2	1
Parra	.959	105	222	10	10	2
Perales	.970	119	222	5	7	2
Side	.970	114	219	8	7	1

YAKIMA BEARS   *SHORT-SEASON*

NORTHWEST LEAGUE

BATTING	B-T	HT	WT	DOB	AVG	vLH	vRH	G	AB	R	H	2B	3B	HR	RBI	BB	HBP	SH	SF	SO	SB	CS	SLG	OBP
Ayers, Joseph	R-R	6-0	190	9-26-84	.198	.222	.188	35	121	17	24	3	0	2	14	10	3	1	1	45	8	2	.273	.274
Batten, Joseph	R-R	5-10	175	12-14-84	.290	.333	.274	63	224	36	65	17	0	1	21	37	4	0	2	45	12	6	.379	.397
Beshenich, Andrew	R-R	6-2	200	2-25-88	.167	.128	.187	36	114	11	19	4	0	0	8	6	5	1	1	42	5	2	.202	.238
Byrne, Shane	B-R	6-3	190	9-14-83	.269	.253	.277	63	242	28	65	10	4	3	32	22	1	1	2	58	3	2	.380	.330
Conner, Clayton	R-R	6-3	210	10-8-86	.351	.380	.339	45	171	35	60	12	4	9	45	11	5	0	3	44	0	0	.626	.400
Easley, Ed	R-R	6-1	180	12-21-85	.250	.290	.237	33	124	21	31	1	1	6	20	9	5	0	3	30	1	0	.419	.319
Frey, Evan	L-L	6-0	170	6-7-86	.309	.207	.340	58	246	48	76	8	6	0	21	27	3	1	0	42	13	10	.390	.384
Hallberg, Mark	R-R	5-11	170	12-9-85	.313	.299	.319	58	233	44	73	15	1	6	32	22	8	1	5	21	12	1	.464	.384
Hanke, Aaron	R-R	6-0	195	12-3-84	.245	.271	.232	47	184	28	45	15	3	4	26	17	1	0	2	35	3	1	.424	.309
Mee, Michael	L-R	6-0	190	10-14-83	.304	.277	.313	54	191	30	58	10	1	0	27	28	5	1	4	28	3	1	.366	.399
Melendez, Joel	R-R	5-11	170	9-18-85	.104	.167	.067	16	48	13	5	1	0	0	1	11	1	0	0	17	12	0	.125	.283
Parra, Julio	R-R	6-0	200	6-12-86	.178	.000	.232	23	73	5	13	2	0	0	4	7	1	0	0	18	0	0	.205	.259
Pimentel, Johan	R-R	5-11	175	7-13-89	.321	.600	.261	9	28	6	9	1	0	0	2	3	1	0	4	0	0	0	.357	.387
Ramirez, Ramon	B-R	6-2	170	2-22-86	.277	.309	.262	65	253	33	70	12	2	2	32	14	4	0	2	48	1	2	.364	.322
Rodriguez, Miguel	B-R	6-1	175	7-25-86	.133	.100	.143	38	128	6	17	3	0	0	11	11	2	2	0	41	0	4	.156	.213
Schmidt, Konrad	R-R	6-2	225	8-2-84	.250	.193	.280	45	164	19	41	10	0	6	24	4	6	0	1	38	1	0	.421	.291
Sharpe, Blake	R-R	6-2	185	9-10-83	.250	.333	.000	1	4	1	1	1	0	0	0	1	0	0	0	0	0	0	.500	.250
Smith, Anthony	L-L	6-1	175	3-28-85	.000	.000	.000	4	11	0	0	0	0	0	1	0	0	0	0	6	0	0	.000	.083
Wheeless, Chance	L-L	6-5	220	9-28-84	.341	.300	.382	12	44	4	15	3	0	1	4	6	0	0	0	15	0	0	.477	.420

PITCHING	B-T	HT	WT	DOB	W	L	ERA	G	GS	CG	SV	IP	H	R	ER	HR	BB	SO	AVG	vLH	vRH	K/9	BB/9
Arif, Omar	L-L	5-10	170	9-3-84	1	2	4.56	24	3	0	0	49	62	38	25	4	17	32	.310	.400	.267	5.84	3.10
Caro, Luis	R-R	5-11	183	8-15-85	3	6	5.98	11	11	0	0	56	69	48	37	5	21	36	.305	.324	.290	5.82	3.40
Christianson, Chase	R-R	6-5	220	12-11-84	4	5	3.77	16	11	0	1	72	81	40	30	6	29	67	.285	.268	.297	8.41	3.64
Collmenter, Joshua	R-R	6-4	235	2-7-86	6	3	2.71	14	12	0	0	66	60	22	20	4	21	57	.244	.250	.238	7.73	2.85
Enright, Barry	R-R	6-3	200	3-30-86	0	0	0.00	5	0	0	0	8	4	0	0	0	3	12	.148	.100	.176	13.50	3.38
Fournier, Daniel	R-R	6-4	205	5-19-85	6	5	4.08	15	15	0	0	82	89	46	37	2	34	61	.284	.295	.274	6.72	3.75
Harrington, Ian	L-L	6-1	190	4-23-85	1	4	6.94	21	5	0	0	47	74	56	36	8	22	38	.354	.459	.296	7.33	4.24
Maine, Scott	L-L	6-3	195	2-2-85	1	0	6.10	8	0	0	1	10	6	9	7	0	12	20	.154	.000	.240	17.42	10.45
Morgan, Sean	R-R	6-3	215	1-15-86	1	1	5.46	17	0	0	0	28	31	19	17	3	15	29	.277	.360	.210	9.32	4.82
Neighborgall, Jason	R-R	6-5	205	12-19-83	0	0	17.47	11	0	0	0	6	5	11	11	0	25	2	.238	.364	.100	3.18	39.71
Ortega, Alvaro	R-R	5-11	192	1-22-86	1	3	5.96	19	4	0	0	54	64	41	36	6	24	46	.292	.330	.259	7.62	3.98

	B-T	HT	WT	DOB	W	L	ERA	G	GS	CG	SV	IP	H	R	ER	HR	BB	SO	AVG	vLH	vRH	K/9	BB/9
Roemer, Wes	R-R	6-0	190	10-7-86	1	0	4.50	8	0	0	0	12	11	6	6	1	2	18	.234	.118	.300	13.50	1.50
Rosen, Danny	R-R	6-0	180	5-17-85	0	0	0.93	7	0	0	1	10	7	3	1	0	5	5	.206	.333	.160	4.66	4.66
Spottiswood, William	R-R	6-3	208	4-24-85	2	3	2.49	26	0	0	10	43	37	16	12	2	8	45	.224	.173	.267	9.35	1.66
Thompson, Bryant	R-R	6-2	190	8-26-85	2	7	8.17	15	12	0	0	54	61	58	49	2	38	58	.281	.289	.275	9.67	6.33
Urquidez, Jason	R-R	6-0	177	9-12-82	1	0	2.93	10	0	0	1	15	12	6	5	0	4	11	.203	.263	.175	6.46	2.35
Vasquez, Daniel	R-R	6-0	195	3-4-86	3	4	3.94	21	3	0	2	48	41	23	21	2	24	46	.230	.190	.263	8.62	4.50

FIELDING

Catcher	PCT	G	PO	A	E	DP	PB
Easley	.987	20	127	20	2	2	0
Parra	.971	18	157	12	5	0	6
Pimentel	.981	8	47	5	1	1	3
Schmidt	.969	36	249	29	9	2	3

First Base	PCT	G	PO	A	E	DP
Conner	1.000	9	89	3	0	4
Mee	.995	43	367	28	2	31
Ramirez	1.000	17	136	10	0	11
Wheeless	.985	8	58	7	1	5

Second Base	PCT	G	PO	A	E	DP
Ayers	.978	29	53	82	3	16

Batten	.927	33	58	94	12	15
Rodriguez	.907	15	33	35	7	7
Sharpe	1.000	1	3	1	0	0

Third Base	PCT	G	PO	A	E	DP
Conner	.890	27	17	48	8	2
Ramirez	.894	41	25	85	13	7
Rodriguez	.833	9	3	17	4	1

Shortstop	PCT	G	PO	A	E	DP
Ayers	.889	6	10	14	3	1
Hallberg	.944	58	107	162	16	26
Rodriguez	.897	15	22	30	6	8

Outfield	PCT	G	PO	A	E	DP
Batten	.927	27	33	5	3	0
Beshenich	.964	27	23	4	1	1
Byrne	.980	60	96	3	2	1
Frey	.972	58	133	4	4	0
Hanke	.970	42	56	8	2	2
Melendez	.971	15	31	3	1	0
Smith	1.000	4	1	2	0	0

MISSOULA OSPREY   ROOKIE

PIONEER LEAGUE

BATTING	B-T	HT	WT	DOB	AVG	vLH	vRH	G	AB	R	H	2B	3B	HR	RBI	BB	HBP	SH	SF	SO	SB	CS	SLG	OBP
Bustamante, Gerardo	R-R	5-8	184	6-10-86	.216	.278	.203	30	97	15	21	3	0	3	13	12	0	3	0	21	0	1	.340	.303
Clifford, Peter	L-R	6-0	195	12-20-83	.280	.256	.286	63	225	42	63	16	2	10	40	36	2	0	4	51	8	1	.502	.378
Coughlin, Sean	L-R	6-1	215	5-14-85	.245	.262	.239	54	184	23	45	13	0	5	32	26	5	1	3	52	0	1	.397	.349
Dijol, Jose	R-R	6-2	186	11-7-84	.152	.136	.159	23	66	4	10	3	0	1	9	6	1	0	1	16	1	0	.242	.230
Estevez, Victor	R-R	5-11	183	9-8-88	.184	.333	.143	35	98	15	18	2	1	0	5	12	3	1	1	31	0	2	.224	.289
Fie, Andrew	R-R	6-3	205	10-25-87	.235	.293	.215	44	162	19	38	5	0	3	12	11	1	0	1	60	3	1	.321	.286
Harbin, Taylor	R-R	5-9	175	2-13-86	.276	.264	.279	63	243	42	67	15	2	10	42	20	5	1	2	38	5	4	.477	.341
Janes, Connor	R-R	6-4	225	8-27-83	.267	.000	.364	5	15	3	4	2	0	1	5	0	1	0	2	0	0		.600	.313
Musselman, William	R-R	6-2	210	11-1-84	.182	.200	.175	25	77	11	14	2	0	0	8	14	1	1	2	20	1	1	.208	.309
Navarro, Reynaldo	B-R	5-10	175	12-22-89	.250	.149	.279	60	212	21	53	4	0	1	17	6	2	2	3	41	6	3	.283	.274
Principe, Jimmy	R-R	6-2	185	3-11-86	.239	.310	.213	54	218	28	52	4	1	5	26	11	2	2	1	65	6	3	.362	.280
Rumler, Elijah	R-R	5-8	185	12-30-84	.271	.375	.243	51	188	29	51	13	0	2	24	10	13	2	0	39	5	4	.372	.351
Smith, Anthony	L-L	6-1	205	3-28-85	.298	.157	.341	56	218	39	65	15	0	6	29	17	3	0	3	32	1	1	.450	.353
Summers, Houston	R-	5-10	180	8-20-87	.227	.333	.188	9	22	1	5	1	0	0	2	1	1	0	5	0	2		.273	.320
Urena, Ariel	R-R	5-11	170	1-29-86	.218	.324	.182	41	133	16	29	9	1	2	12	6	0	0	0	33	1	2	.346	.252
Walker, Derrick	R-R	6-4	215	10-10-85	.291	.362	.267	63	230	37	67	17	3	5	39	27	6	0	2	61	9	7	.457	.377
Wheeless, Chance	L-L	6-5	220	9-28-84	.217	.250	.208	48	161	22	35	9	0	4	16	24	3	0	2	40	1	1	.348	.326
Worthington, Tyrell	R-R	6-0	190	8-2-88	.135	.200	.111	13	37	6	5	0	1	0	2	5	0	0	0	11	1	0	.189	.238

PITCHING	B-T	HT	WT	DOB	W	L	ERA	G	GS	CG	SV	IP	H	R	ER	HR	BB	SO	AVG	vLH	vRH	K/9	BB/9
Augenstein, Bryan	R-R	6-5	225	7-11-86	0	2	3.38	10	2	0	0	21	20	13	8	2	7	16	.250	.286	.231	6.75	2.95
Baez, Santo	R-R	6-1	155	12-16-88	3	4	6.42	14	7	0	0	41	46	40	29	5	20	21	.269	.234	.290	4.65	4.43
Beltre, Cristian	R-R	6-1	195	5-10-85	3	8	5.20	15	15	0	0	71	86	51	41	14	22	38	.290	.280	.296	4.82	2.79
Blake, Josh	L-L	6-4	205	10-17-84	1	4	4.81	23	3	0	3	58	61	36	31	7	19	46	.266	.313	.248	7.14	2.95
Castro, Ramon	R-R	5-11	145	10-5-86	0	0	6.00	4	0	0	0	6	11	6	4	0	3	3	.393	.200	.435	4.50	4.50
Davis, Ty	R-R	6-6	225	9-11-84	3	2	3.97	21	0	0	1	48	52	29	21	3	19	62	.274	.239	.294	11.71	3.59
Durst, Jason	R-R	6-2	183	8-28-87	1	9	7.97	15	14	0	0	64	90	66	57	13	30	49	.331	.346	.321	6.85	4.20
Ellis, Josh	R-R	6-1	190	8-7-84	2	2	6.50	24	0	0	3	36	32	30	26	1	29	43	.234	.296	.193	10.75	7.25
Henry, Bryan	R-R	6-3	205	2-15-85	5	3	5.28	12	12	0	0	58	71	40	34	13	12	61	.302	.274	.321	6.36	1.86
Layne, Thomas	L-L	6-3	185	11-2-84	4	8	4.63	16	16	0	0	80	94	49	41	9	23	66	.296	.308	.291	7.46	2.60
Ortega, Yonata	R-R	6-1	165	11-11-86	0	2	6.40	19	0	0	1	32	38	32	23	6	18	26	.275	.283	.272	7.24	5.01
Peralta, Wascar	L-L	6-2	208	10-30-87	0	0	9.82	3	0	0	0	4	5	4	4	1	4	4	.353	.250	.385	9.82	9.82
Prihoda, Luke	R-R	6-5	230	8-10-84	3	2	7.88	22	0	0	1	38	58	38	33	10	9	25	.343	.338	.346	5.97	2.15
Reynolds, Brett	R-R	6-3	195	9-28-84	1	2	10.30	7	7	0	0	25	38	30	29	8	10	16	.349	.341	.354	5.68	3.55
Scribner, Evan	R-R	6-3	190	7-19-85	0	1	2.92	18	0	0	2	37	35	13	12	1	9	48	.243	.291	.213	11.68	2.19
Sena, Giornale	R-R	6-3	186	5-28-86	0	0	17.18	9	0	0	0	11	13	23	21	1	24	5	.295	.118	.407	4.09	19.64
Summers, Houston	R-R	5-10	180	8-20-87	1	0	4.95	13	0	0	0	36	39	26	20	0	19	12	.279	.260	.289	2.97	4.71

FIELDING

Catcher	PCT	G	PO	A	E	DP	PB
Bustamante	.982	30	190	31	4	2	11
Coughlin	1.000	26	156	11	0	2	4
Musselman	.990	24	186	19	2	3	4
Summers	1.000	1	1	0	0	0	0

First Base	PCT	G	PO	A	E	DP
Coughlin	.944	9	80	5	5	4
Dijol	.983	10	54	5	1	9
Smith	.984	15	119	7	2	14
Wheeless	.983	47	409	41	8	39

Second Base	PCT	G	PO	A	E	DP
Estevez	.889	15	23	17	5	4

Harbin	.951	56	121	173	15	36
Rumler	.950	13	17	40	3	9

Third Base	PCT	G	PO	A	E	DP
Estevez	.833	20	12	18	6	3
Fie	.912	40	22	82	10	6
Rumler	.938	18	15	30	3	6
Summers	.667	4	2	4	3	0

Shortstop	PCT	G	PO	A	E	DP
Harbin	1.000	4	5	9	0	1
Navarro	.913	58	114	179	28	37
Rumler	.922	20	28	55	7	7

Outfield	PCT	G	PO	A	E	DP
Clifford	.955	54	78	7	4	0
Janes	1.000	2	2	0	0	0
Principe	.959	52	87	6	4	0
Smith	.935	26	43	0	3	0
Summers	1.000	3	2	0	0	0
Urena	.959	41	65	6	3	3
Walker	.933	58	108	3	8	1
Worthington	.889	7	8	0	1	0

DOMINICAN SUMMER LEAGUE

BATTING	B-T	HT	WT	DOB	AVG	vLH	vRH	G	AB	R	H	2B	3B	HR	RBI	BB	HBP	SH	SF	SO	SB	CS	SLG	OBP
Arias, Pedro	R-R	6-1	195	9-8-88	.194	.000	.233	12	36	2	7	3	0	0	4	3	2	0	0	4	1	1	.278	.293
Asencio, Isaias	R-R	6-0	169	12-31-87	.091	.000	.125	8	22	1	2	2	0	0	1	4	2	0	1	4	2	0	.182	.276
Brito, Luis	R-R	6-4	215	8-27-89	.187	.095	.222	27	75	8	14	3	0	2	10	16	0	0	0	36	0	0	.307	.330
Carmona, Jose	B-R	6-0	160	11-20-88	.137	.079	.153	59	175	14	24	6	0	1	16	32	0	3	2	41	0	6	.189	.268
Castillo, Ramon	R-R	5-11	190	9-6-88	.253	.436	.197	52	166	23	42	12	0	3	19	20	11	0	2	21	0	0	.380	.367
Corniel, Jorge	R-R	5-8	180	1-4-88	.161	.143	.167	30	93	13	15	5	1	0	18	15	1	1	0	19	0	2	.237	.284
Diaz, Alberto	R-R	6-1	180	9-3-88	.257	.322	.236	64	241	46	62	12	2	1	21	24	9	3	0	39	19	7	.336	.347
Hilario, Rafael	R-R	5-10	175	1-28-88	.261	.088	.305	52	165	13	43	7	0	1	9	12	5	0	4	21	1	2	.321	.323
Inciarte, Astolfo	L-L	5-8	170	2-9-88	.287	.440	.241	36	108	18	31	5	1	0	14	18	0	1	3	20	2	1	.352	.380
Mariano, Ramon	B-L	6-1	187	11-1-87	.179	.167	.183	51	179	18	32	8	0	1	19	19	7	0	2	35	0	2	.240	.280
Marte, Alfredo	R-R	6-1	170	3-31-89	.328	.333	.327	67	265	30	87	19	4	4	45	17	5	0	2	37	3	1	.475	.377
Martich, Mesael	R-R	6-0	170	1-10-86	.333	.667	.000	2	6	2	2	0	1	0	0	1	1	0	0	1	0	0	.667	.500
Noboa, Michael	R-R	5-8	160	6-21-87	.157	.222	.127	43	115	6	18	0	1	0	9	15	6	1	1	24	4	5	.174	.285
Perez, Rossmel	B-R	5-10	180	8-26-89	.306	.154	.353	39	111	8	34	4	1	0	5	28	6	0	0	19	2	3	.360	.469
Rodriguez, Danny	R-R	6-1	174	4-15-87	.200	.135	.217	54	180	14	36	6	0	1	14	12	8	1	1	52	3	1	.250	.279
Rodriguez, Roberto	L-L	6-0	156	3-22-89	.240	.282	.229	54	179	34	43	5	3	1	9	34	3	5	0	41	4	4	.318	.370
Taveras, Damil	B-R	6-0	185	2-5-89	.147	.190	.137	37	116	8	17	2	0	0	7	11	1	0	0	40	3	1	.164	.227
Zarate, Luis	R-R	6-0	180	10-30-88	.077	.067	.083	29	39	10	3	1	0	0	1	5	3	2	0	13	2	0	.103	.234

PITCHING	B-T	HT	WT	DOB	W	L	ERA	G	GS	CG	SV	IP	H	R	ER	HR	BB	SO	AVG	vLH	vRH	K/9	BB/9
Adino, Hector	R-R	5-11	155	6-14-88	3	4	1.89	18	2	0	1	38	17	13	8	0	19	25	.137	.154	.133	5.92	4.50
Brea, Ariel	L-L	5-10	155	5-14-89	0	0	4.86	12	0	0	0	17	24	12	9	2	9	22	.324	.333	.324	11.88	4.86
Cespedes, Jesus	R-R	6-2	200	12-24-88	2	5	2.66	16	13	0	0	71	62	36	21	1	21	45	.231	.210	.238	5.70	2.66
De Jesus, Cesse	R-R	5-11	155	5-16-90	0	0	4.86	14	0	0	1	17	17	12	9	1	8	22	.279	.455	.240	11.88	4.32
De La Rosa, Winfil	R-R	6-3	190	11-17-87	0	2	8.38	9	0	0	0	10	10	12	9	0	12	7	.263	.667	.229	6.52	11.17
Ferrera, Xadiel	R-R	6-2	175	5-24-88	1	0	5.23	13	0	0	1	21	18	17	12	1	18	11	.234	.250	.230	4.79	7.84
Gomez, Eduardo	R-R	6-0	165	12-31-89	0	0	1.80	7	0	0	0	10	10	5	2	0	6	9	.256	.000	.313	8.10	5.40
Jabalera, Jairo	L-L	5-11	160	11-18-85	0	1	36.00	4	1	0	0	2	3	11	8	0	10	3	.273	—	.273	13.50	45.00
Marte, Jonny	R-R	6-1	175	12-12-87	0	2	1.56	27	0	0	16	35	24	8	6	1	9	25	.196	.231	.189	6.49	2.34
Martinez, Gustavo	R-R	6-2	162	3-13-90	0	2	5.11	5	3	1	0	12	13	9	7	0	10	15	.283	.167	.324	10.95	7.30
Peralta, Jose	R-R	6-1	190	8-28-89	0	1	10.38	3	1	0	0	4	6	5	5	0	5	3	.353	.333	.364	6.23	10.38
Quezada, Rafael	R-R	6-3	180	11-21-86	3	2	3.74	14	13	0	0	67	65	31	28	0	33	55	.255	.255	.260	7.35	4.41
Rodriguez, Randy	L-L	6-0	155	1-6-88	1	7	3.39	16	13	0	0	72	68	35	27	1	24	58	.249	.250	.249	7.28	3.01
Rojas, Bryan	L-L	6-0	172	3-10-87	2	1	5.22	19	0	0	2	29	29	19	17	2	16	30	.264	.500	.259	9.20	4.91
Rosario, Diogenes	R-R	6-0	170	9-1-88	3	2	4.75	12	8	0	0	42	42	31	22	2	26	24	.263	.297	.252	5.18	5.62
Rosario, Amado	R-R	5-11	160	12-17-87	4	3	2.83	14	10	0	0	54	54	29	17	0	27	50	.261	.188	.274	8.33	4.50
Sosa, Kenny	L-L	6-0	167	3-26-87	4	4	2.40	20	0	0	0	45	30	18	12	1	27	53	.188	.000	.194	10.60	5.40
Taveras, Ricardo	R-R	6-2	210	10-17-87	0	1	0.43	5	4	0	0	21	17	3	1	0	6	18	.218	.227	.214	7.71	2.57
Zepeda, Bayron	L-L	5-10	185	8-29-87	7	3	3.31	23	2	0	0	52	57	20	19	1	11	37	.289	.133	.302	6.45	1.92

FIELDING

Catcher	PCT	G	PO	A	E	DP	PB
Arias	.985	10	49	17	1	1	3
Corniel	.992	26	203	35	2	3	4
Perez	.976	39	276	47	8	0	10
Zarate	1.000	1	1	0	0	0	0

First Base	PCT	G	PO	A	E	DP
Castillo	.987	27	221	6	3	17
Mariano	.977	44	362	19	9	29
D. Rodriguez	1.000	7	34	2	0	2

Second Base	PCT	G	PO	A	E	DP
Hilario	.937	33	69	50	8	15
Noboa	.914	42	93	77	16	16

	PCT	G	PO	A	E	DP	PB
Rodriguez	.955	7	10	11	1	3	

Third Base	PCT	G	PO	A	E	DP
Carmona	1.000	1	0	3	0	0
Hilario	.886	6	10	21	4	2
D. Rodriguez	.867	18	16	75	14	4
R. Rodriguez	1.000	1	0	1	0	0
Taveras	.903	35	24	78	11	2

Shortstop	PCT	G	PO	A	E	DP
Carmona	.919	58	87	162	22	28
Diaz	1.000	1	0	2	0	0
Hilario	.955	18	27	37	3	5
D. Rodriguez	1.000	2	3	5	0	1

Outfield	PCT	G	PO	A	E	DP
Arias	.500	1	1	0	1	0
Asencio	1.000	7	7	0	0	0
Brito	.967	22	28	1	1	0
Diaz	1.000	62	143	7	0	0
Hilario	1.000	1	1	0	0	0
Inciarte	.900	15	8	1	1	0
Mariano	1.000	2	2	0	0	0
Marte	.926	53	79	9	7	2
D. Rodriguez	1.000	3	2	0	0	0
R.Rodriguez	.913	50	61	2	6	0
Zarate	.944	18	17	0	1	0

ORGANIZATION STATISTICS

Atlanta Braves

BY BILL BALLEW

After 14 straight postseason appearances, the Braves found themselves on the outside looking in during October for the second straight year. A solid April and late September served as bookends for four months of mediocrity, leading to a third-place finish in the National League East for the second time in as many seasons.

Yet despite their on-field failure, the biggest news of the year came a few weeks after the season concluded when general manager John Schuerholz announced he was resigning from the position after 17 years. Assistant GM Frank Wren took over for Schuerholz. Wren served Baltimore's GM in 1999 after eight years as an assistant GM with Florida, and takes the reins in Atlanta during a tumultuous period, highlighted by plans not to re-sign free agent center fielder Andruw Jones.

Since joining the Braves in October 1990, Schuerholz, 67, guided the team to 14 consecutive division titles, five National League pennants and one World Series crown.

Amid their inconsistencies, the Braves stayed in the postseason hunt by winning 9-of-11 games during the final two weeks of the season, yet had dug too deep a hole to climb into the playoffs. Injuries played a crucial role in the Braves' inability to record long winning streaks. The loss of lefthander Mike Hampton to surgery on his left elbow for the second straight year crippled the rotation after the top two—righthanders Tim Hudson and John Smoltz. Hudson led the team with 16 wins while Smoltz, 40, ranked fourth in the NL with a 3.11 ERA. Otherwise, the Braves resorted to rotation roulette, with Chuck James, Buddy Carlyle, Jo-Jo Reyes and a host of others firing more blanks than bullets.

Schuerholz spent the previous winter trying to bolster the bullpen, and the efforts proved fruitful. Righthander Rafael Soriano and rookie righthander Peter Moylan each showed closer potential. The Braves' primary closer, Bob Wickman was released in late August after complaining about pitching more than the ninth inning. Former Pirates closer Mike Gonzalez pitched only six weeks before undergoing Tommy John surgery in mid May.

The Braves were a run-scoring machine at times. Atlanta tied for second in the NL with a .275 batting average and placed third with 810 runs scored Again, injuries played a huge role in preventing all cogs from operating in unison. Jones and shortstop Edgar Renteria challenged for the league batting crown, yet both missed more than a month—Jones in May and June with bruised hands and Renteria in August and early September with a high right ankle sprain. Those ailments coupled with the disappointing output of center fielder Andruw Jones, played significant roles in the Braves' inability to take over first place from the late-sliding Mets.

The overall lack of success did not occur from a lack of effort. Schuerholz made what proved to be his final blockbuster deal as Atlanta's GM when he acquired first baseman Mark Teixeira from the Rangers at the trading deadline for five top prospects—catcher/first baseman Jarrod Saltalamacchia, shortstop Elvis Andrus lefthanders Matt Harrison and Beau Jones and righthander Neftali Feliz. Teixeira held up his end of the bargain by giving the Braves a significant power presence in the middle of the order, but again the surrounding cast was unable to cooperate.

Playoff pushes were commonplace in Atlanta's farm system. Triple-A Richmond won the International League wild

card before defeating Scranton/Wilkes-Barre and Durham in the postseason to win the Governors' Cup. The R-Braves lost an 8-1 decision to Sacramento in the Bricktown Showdown in Oklahoma City. Left fielder Brandon Jones paced the organization with 100 RBIs and shortstop Brent Lillibridge led Atlanta farmhands with 42 stolen bases.

Mississippi won the Southern League's first-half crown in the South Division to reach the playoffs, while East Division champion Danville met Elizabethton for the Appalachian League crown for the third consecutive year.

Center fielder Jordan Schafer, who split the season between low Class A Rome and high Class A Myrtle Beach, was tabbed the top prospect in the Carolina League after leading the minors with 176 hits and ranking third with 49 doubles.

General Manager: Frank Wren. **Farm Director:** Paul Snyder. **Scouting Director:** Roy Clark

Class	Team	League	W	L	PCT	Finish*	Manager	Affiliate Since
Majors	Atlanta	National	84	78	.519	7th (30)	Bobby Cox	—
Triple-A	Richmond Braves	International	77	64	.546	4th (14)^	Dave Brundage	1966
Double-A	Mississippi Braves	Southern	67	72	.482	5th (10)	Phillip Wellman	2005
High A	Myrtle Beach Pelicans	Carolina	59	80	.424	7th (8)	Rocket Wheeler	1999
Low A	Rome Braves	South Atlantic	66	74	.471	11th(16)	Randy Ingle	2003
Rookie	Danville Braves	Appalachian	48	20	.706	2nd (9)	Paul Runge	1993
Rookie	GCL Braves	Gulf Coast	17	43	.283	15th(16)	Luis Ortiz	1998
Overall 2007 Minor League Record			**334**	**353**	**.486**	**20th**		

* Finish in overall standings (No. of teams in league) ^League champion

ORGANIZATION STATISTICS

ATLANTA BRAVES

NATIONAL LEAGUE

BATTING	B-T	HT	WT	DOB	AVG	vLH	vRH	G	AB	R	H	2B	3B	HR	RBI	BB	HBP	SH	SF	SO	SB	CS	SLG	OBP
Diaz, Matt	R-R	6-1	205	3-3-78	.338	.356	.318	135	358	44	121	21	0	12	45	16	4	1	5	63	4	0	.497	.368
Escobar, Yunel	R-R	6-2	200	11-2-82	.326	.355	.303	94	319	54	104	25	0	5	28	27	5	2	4	44	5	3	.451	.385
Franco, Julio	R-R	6-1	210	8-23-58	.250	.250	.250	15	40	1	10	3	0	0	8	4	0	0	1	10	0	0	.325	.311
2-team (40 New York)					.222	—	—	55	90	8	20	3	0	1	16	14	0	0	2	23	2	1	.289	.321
Francoeur, Jeff	R-R	6-4	220	1-8-84	.293	.317	.281	162	642	84	188	40	0	19	105	42	5	0	7	129	5	2	.444	.338
Harris, Willie	L-R	5-9	170	6-22-78	.270	.191	.283	117	344	56	93	20	8	2	32	40	3	1	3	71	17	11	.392	.349
Johnson, Kelly	L-R	6-1	205	2-22-82	.276	.272	.278	147	521	91	144	26	10	16	68	79	4	2	2	117	9	5	.457	.375
Jones, Andruw	R-R	6-1	210	4-23-77	.222	.225	.221	154	572	83	127	27	2	26	94	70	8	0	9	138	5	2	.413	.311
Jones, Brandon	L-R	6-1	210	12-10-83	.158	.500	.067	5	19	0	3	1	0	0	4	0	1	0	1	8	0	0	.211	.190
Jones, Chipper	B-R	6-4	210	4-24-72	.337	.274	.378	134	513	108	173	42	4	29	102	82	0	0	5	75	5	1	.604	.425
Langerhans, Ryan	L-L	6-3	205	2-20-80	.068	.000	.079	20	44	3	3	1	0	0	1	6	1	0	1	16	0	1	.091	.192
2-team (103 Washington)					.170	—	—	123	206	27	35	7	2	6	23	28	2	1	2	79	3	1	.311	.273
McCann, Brian	L-R	6-3	210	2-20-84	.270	.264	.273	139	504	51	136	38	0	18	92	35	5	2	6	74	0	1	.452	.320
Miller, Corky	R-R	6-1	245	3-18-76	.259	.250	.263	12	27	3	7	2	0	1	4	1	1	0	0	5	0	0	.444	.310
Orr, Pete	L-R	6-1	185	6-8-79	.200	.000	.228	57	65	11	13	1	0	0	2	3	0	1	0	14	1	0	.215	.235
Pena, Brayan	B-R	5-11	210	1-7-82	.212	.222	.200	16	33	2	7	0	0	1	3	0	0	0	0	3	0	1	.303	.212
Prado, Martin	R-R	6-1	190	10-27-83	.288	.211	.429	28	59	5	17	3	0	0	2	3	0	0	0	6	0	0	.339	.323
Renteria, Edgar	R-R	6-1	200	8-7-75	.332	.349	.323	124	494	87	164	30	1	12	57	46	1	2	0	77	11	2	.470	.390
Saltalamacchia, Jarrod	B-R	6-4	195	5-2-85	.284	.290	.278	47	141	11	40	6	0	4	12	10	1	0	1	28	0	0	.411	.333
Sammons, Clint	R-R	6-0	200	5-15-83	.667	1.000	.500	2	3	0	2	1	0	0	0	0	0	0	0	0	0	0	1.000	.667
Teixeira, Mark	B-R	6-3	220	4-11-80	.317	.342	.303	54	208	38	66	9	1	17	56	27	4	0	1	46	0	0	.615	.404
Thorman, Scott	L-R	6-3	235	1-6-82	.216	.176	.228	120	287	37	62	18	0	11	36	14	3	1	2	70	1	1	.394	.258
Wilson, Craig	R-R	6-2	215	11-30-76	.172	.200	.067	24	58	6	10	2	0	1	2	8	3	0	0	25	0	0	.259	.304
Woodward, Chris	R-R	6-0	190	6-27-76	.199	.229	.167	92	136	16	27	6	1	1	8	10	0	4	1	29	1	0	.279	.252

PITCHING	B-T	HT	WT	DOB	W	L	ERA	G	GS	CG	SV	IP	H	R	ER	HR	BB	SO	AVG	vLH	vRH	K/9	BB/9
Acosta, Manny	R-R	6-4	170	5-1-81	1	1	2.28	21	0	0	0	24	13	6	6	2	14	22	.165	.250	.093	8.37	5.32
Ascanio, Jose	R-R	6-0	170	5-2-85	1	1	5.06	13	0	0	0	16	17	11	9	3	6	13	.254	.280	.238	7.31	3.38
Barry, Kevin	R-R	6-2	235	8-18-78	0	0	22.50	1	0	0	0	2	6	5	5	0	2	4	.500	.500	.500	18.00	9.00
Bennett, Jeff	R-R	6-3	200	6-10-80	2	1	3.46	3	2	0	0	13	14	5	5	3	3	14	.269	.357	.237	9.69	2.08
Boyer, Blaine	R-R	6-3	215	7-11-81	0	0	3.38	5	0	0	0	5	10	3	2	0	1	3	.417	.500	.357	5.06	1.69
Carlyle, Buddy	L-R	6-3	185	12-21-77	8	7	5.21	22	20	0	0	107	117	67	62	19	32	74	.284	.343	.229	6.22	2.69
Colyer, Steve	L-L	6-4	235	2-22-79	0	1	4.91	7	0	0	0	4	9	2	2	1	4	4	.500	.429	.545	9.82	9.82
Cormier, Lance	R-R	6-1	200	8-19-80	2	6	7.09	10	9	0	0	46	56	38	36	16	22	27	.303	.257	.333	5.32	4.34
Davies, Kyle	R-R	6-2	205	9-9-83	4	8	5.76	17	17	0	0	86	92	61	55	12	44	59	.272	.255	.286	6.17	4.60
Devine, Joey	R-R	5-11	205	9-19-83	1	0	1.08	10	0	0	0	8	7	1	1	0	8	7	.241	.300	.211	7.56	8.64
Dotel, Octavio	R-R	6-0	210	11-25-73	0	0	4.70	9	0	0	0	8	5	5	4	1	1	12	.172	.143	.182	14.09	1.17
Gonzalez, Mike	R-L	6-2	215	5-23-78	2	0	1.59	18	0	0	2	17	15	3	3	0	8	13	.246	.333	.189	6.88	4.24
Hudson, Tim	R-R	6-1	170	7-14-75	16	10	3.33	34	34	1	0	224	221	87	83	10	53	132	.261	.261	.261	5.30	2.13
James, Chuck	L-L	6-0	170	11-9-81	11	10	4.24	30	30	0	0	161	164	77	76	32	58	116	.265	.252	.268	6.47	3.24
Ledezma, Wilfredo	L-L	6-4	210	1-21-81	0	2	7.71	12	0	0	0	9	12	10	8	1	4	7	.300	.231	.333	6.75	3.86
2-team (9 San Diego)					0	2	6.85	21	1	0	0	24	32	21	18	3	12	23	—	—	—	8.75	4.56
Lerew, Anthony	L-R	6-3	220	10-28-82	0	2	7.71	3	3	0	0	12	14	10	10	4	7	9	.298	.222	.345	6.94	5.40
Mahay, Ron	L-L	6-2	190	6-28-71	1	0	2.25	30	0	0	0	28	19	8	7	1	16	23	.194	.095	.268	7.39	5.14
McBride, Macay	L-L	5-11	210	10-24-82	1	0	3.60	18	0	0	0	15	14	9	6	1	15	17	.237	.160	.294	10.20	9.00
Moylan, Peter	R-R	6-2	200	12-2-78	5	3	1.80	80	0	0	1	90	65	27	18	6	31	63	.208	.242	.184	6.30	3.10
Paronto, Chad	R-R	6-5	250	7-28-75	3	1	3.57	41	0	0	1	40	47	20	16	1	19	14	.307	.333	.287	3.12	4.24
Redman, Mark	L-L	6-5	245	1-5-74	0	4	11.63	6	5	0	0	22	38	29	28	4	11	13	.380	.227	.423	5.40	4.57
2-team (5 Colorado)					2	4	7.62	11	8	0	0	41	59	37	35	6	17	27	—	—	—	5.88	3.70
Reyes, Jo-Jo	L-L	6-2	230	11-20-84	2	2	6.22	11	10	0	0	51	55	39	35	9	30	27	.286	.129	.317	4.80	5.33
Ring, Royce	L-L	6-0	220	12-21-80	0	0	0.00	11	0	0	0	3	2	0	0	0	3	4	.133	.100	.200	7.20	5.40
2-team (15 San Diego)					1	0	2.70	26	0	0	0	20	13	8	6	1	17	21	—	—	—	9.45	7.65
Smoltz, John	R-R	6-3	220	5-15-67	14	8	3.11	32	32	0	0	206	196	78	71	18	47	197	.249	.262	.237	8.62	2.06
Soriano, Rafael	R-R	6-1	220	12-19-79	3	3	3.00	71	0	0	9	72	47	26	24	12	15	70	.181	.164	.197	8.75	1.88
Villarreal, Oscar	L-R	6-0	215	11-22-81	2	2	4.24	51	0	0	1	76	75	40	36	6	32	58	.260	.315	.220	6.84	3.77
Wickman, Bob	R-R	6-1	240	2-6-69	3	3	3.92	49	0	0	20	44	48	22	19	4	20	35	.267	.250	.281	7.21	4.12
2-team (8 Arizona)					3	4	3.58	57	0	0	20	50	54	24	20	4	21	37	—	—	—	6.62	3.75
Yates, Tyler	R-R	6-4	240	8-7-77	2	3	5.18	75	0	0	2	66	64	44	38	6	31	69	.251	.310	.213	9.41	4.23

FIELDING

Catcher	PCT	G	PO	A	E	DP	PB
McCann	.987	132	907	53	13	9	6
Miller	1.000	11	49	3	0	1	1
Pena	1.000	10	52	2	0	1	1
Saltalamacchia	.993	25	138	12	1	3	2
Sammons	1.000	2	5	1	0	0	0

First Base	PCT	G	PO	A	E	DP
Diaz	1.000	2	3	1	0	1
Franco	1.000	10	101	10	0	11
Saltalamacchia	.981	14	96	9	2	7
Teixeira	.992	54	494	30	4	46
Thorman	.991	84	571	56	6	46
Wilson	.993	20	133	10	1	15
Woodward	.967	6	28	1	1	3

Second Base	PCT	G	PO	A	E	DP
Escobar	.963	21	28	49	3	10
Johnson	.978	133	227	383	14	83
Orr	1.000	4	9	3	0	2
Prado	.941	10	14	34	3	3
Woodward	1.000	11	12	16	0	4

Third Base	PCT	G	PO	A	E	DP
Escobar	.923	22	20	28	4	4
Harris	.800	1	2	4	0	0
C. Jones	.971	126	75	226	9	17
Orr	.944	14	4	13	1	1
Prado	1.000	9	4	7	0	0
Woodward	.875	24	5	16	3	2

Shortstop	PCT	G	PO	A	E	DP
Escobar	.977	53	59	113	4	22
C. Jones	1.000	1	1	1	0	0
Renteria	.977	121	147	322	11	71
Woodward	.931	13	7	20	2	5

Outfield	PCT	G	PO	A	E	DP
Diaz	.988	98	158	4	2	1
Francoeur	.986	162	327	19	5	2
Harris	.983	100	173	4	3	1
A. Jones	.995	154	396	3	2	1
B. Jones	1.000	5	5	0	0	0
Langerhans	1.000	19	18	0	0	0
Orr	—	1	0	0	0	0

RICHMOND BRAVES   TRIPLE-A

INTERNATIONAL LEAGUE

BATTING	B-T	HT	WT	DOB	AVG	vLH	vRH	G	AB	R	H	2B	3B	HR	RBI	BB	HBP	SH	SF	SO	SB	CS	SLG	OBP
Bigbie, Larry	L-R	6-4	210	11-4-77	.253	.135	.282	59	186	28	47	11	2	2	24	20	0	0	2	38	5	0	.366	.322
Blanco, Gregor	L-L	5-11	170	12-12-83	.282	.246	.296	124	464	81	131	18	5	3	35	63	2	14	2	85	23	18	.362	.369
Bohn, T.J.	R-R	6-5	200	1-17-80	.241	.190	.262	46	145	20	35	8	0	1	14	21	2	1	1	41	8	4	.317	.343
Canizares, Barbaro	R-R	6-3	210	11-21-79	.344	.442	.308	49	163	24	56	13	1	3	34	12	3	0	4	28	0	0	.491	.390
Clark, Doug	L-R	6-2	205	3-5-76	.275	.269	.277	134	451	75	124	23	4	15	69	59	3	2	5	91	20	5	.443	.359
Escobar, Yunel	R-R	6-2	200	11-2-82	.333	.327	.336	46	180	20	60	10	3	2	29	14	0	0	1	27	3	5	.456	.379
Franco, Iker	R-R	6-2	240	3-3-81	.220	.220	.221	60	177	16	39	8	0	2	27	20	1	2	1	33	0	2	.299	.302
Franco, Julio	R-R	6-1	210	8-23-58	.286	.000	.333	4	14	2	4	0	0	1	3	0	0	0	0	6	0	0	.286	.412
Harris, Willie	L-R	5-9	170	6-22-78	.362	.292	.412	17	58	17	21	7	2	1	7	8	3	0	1	6	7	3	.603	.457
Holt, J.C.	L-R	5-9	175	12-8-82	.292	.167	.333	13	48	10	14	4	0	0	3	4	0	1	0	8	3	1	.375	.346
Jones, Brandon	L-R	6-1	210	12-10-83	.300	.341	.287	44	170	26	51	12	1	4	26	17	1	1	2	36	5	0	.453	.363
Koonce, Graham	L-L	6-4	230	5-15-75	.224	.205	.229	58	183	22	41	9	1	10	42	25	4	0	3	53	0	0	.448	.326
Lillibridge, Brent	R-R	5-11	190	9-18-83	.287	.301	.282	87	321	47	92	14	2	10	41	20	3	8	3	59	28	5	.436	.331
McCarthy, Bill	R-R	6-2	205	12-2-79	.224	.196	.237	49	165	19	37	7	2	5	18	14	6	1	0	45	2	2	.382	.308
Mendez, Carlos	R-R	6-0	225	6-18-74	.278	.306	.258	82	263	29	73	19	0	6	35	8	3	0	3	37	0	2	.418	.303
Miller, Corky	R-R	6-1	245	3-18-76	.210	.236	.198	64	181	12	38	8	0	4	25	25	13	0	3	26	4	0	.320	.342
Orr, Pete	L-R	6-1	185	6-8-79	.240	.161	.260	43	154	26	37	6	4	1	8	14	1	0	0	39	7	3	.351	.308
Pena, Brayan	B-R	5-11	210	1-7-82	.301	.341	.287	94	345	42	104	20	2	6	48	19	2	3	1	38	5	7	.423	.341
Prado, Martin	R-R	6-1	190	10-27-83	.316	.340	.308	103	395	61	125	23	3	4	41	34	4	7	3	41	5	4	.420	.374
Rozema, Mike	L-R	6-2	180	9-16-81	.154	.333	.100	8	13	3	2	2	0	0	3	1	0	0	0	3	0	0	.308	.214
Schuerholz, Jonathan	R-R	5-11	190	6-25-80	.215	.154	.231	51	130	19	28	7	0	3	19	14	2	4	3	23	7	1	.338	.295
Serrano, Ray	R-R	5-8	221	1-19-81	.000	.000	.000	1	3	0	0	0	0	0	0	0	0	0	0	0	0	0	.000	.000
Timmons, Wes	R-R	6-0	190	7-12-79	.256	.237	.264	120	355	47	91	18	0	5	52	25	19	2	6	29	8	5	.349	.333

PITCHING	B-T	HT	WT	DOB	W	L	ERA	G	GS	CG	SV	IP	H	R	ER	HR	BB	SO	AVG	vLH	vRH	K/9	BB/9
Acosta, Manny	R-R	6-4	170	5-1-81	9	3	2.26	40	0	0	12	60	46	18	15	0	35	56	.218	.260	.194	8.45	5.28
Baerlocher, Ryan	R-R	6-5	240	8-6-77	2	4	4.25	10	9	0	0	53	60	25	25	3	14	32	.290	.312	.265	5.43	2.38
Barry, Kevin	R-R	6-2	235	8-18-78	5	7	4.14	24	22	0	0	113	118	59	52	13	41	83	.277	.284	.270	6.61	3.27
Basner, Ryan	R-R	6-3	230	7-15-81	4	5	4.31	29	4	0	1	79	88	43	38	11	26	70	.288	.304	.275	7.94	2.95
Bennett, Jeff	R-R	6-3	200	6-10-80	3	5	3.35	36	6	0	1	86	84	32	32	5	34	45	.266	.270	.263	4.71	3.56
Boyer, Blaine	R-R	6-3	215	7-11-81	4	3	4.30	21	12	0	2	73	76	40	35	1	50	62	.288	.280	.298	7.61	6.14
Bueno, Francisley	L-L	5-11	200	3-5-81	1	0	2.79	3	3	0	0	19	19	6	6	3	3	19	.247	.391	.185	8.84	1.40
Bush, Paul	R-R	6-1	175	10-5-79	1	0	1.74	5	0	0	1	10	5	2	2	0	5	10	.147	.143	.150	8.71	4.35
Carlyle, Buddy	L-R	6-3	185	12-21-77	5	2	2.59	9	9	1	0	49	40	15	14	5	9	56	.225	.174	.257	10.36	1.66
Colyer, Steve	L-L	6-4	235	2-22-79	0	0	0.00	2	0	0	0	2	2	0	0	0	1	1	.250	.667	.000	4.50	0.00
Cormier, Lance	R-R	6-1	200	8-19-80	4	2	3.46	10	10	1	0	52	56	22	20	4	15	31	.287	.211	.384	5.37	2.60
Cormier, Rheal	L-L	5-10	195	4-23-67	1	0	1.17	5	0	0	0	8	4	1	1	0	3	7	.154	.375	.056	8.22	3.52
Davies, Kyle	R-R	6-2	205	9-9-83	0	1	4.50	2	2	0	0	10	11	5	5	1	6	12	.289	.300	10.80	5.40
Devine, Joey	R-R	5-11	205	9-19-83	3	0	1.64	17	0	0	4	22	15	5	4	2	13	27	.188	.250	.125	11.05	2.45
Hernandez, Moises	R-R	6-1	168	3-18-84	0	1	7.71	1	1	0	0	5	3	4	4	0	4	1	.167	.167	.167	1.93	7.71
Hernandez, Buddy	R-R	5-9	180	3-3-79	9	3	3.13	47	1	0	3	75	76	30	26	7	18	71	.264	.277	.253	8.56	2.17
Hodges, Trey	R-R	6-3	195	6-29-78	6	6	4.72	30	20	0	1	122	125	70	64	10	63	81	.269	.294	.243	5.98	4.65
Hyde, Lee	R-L	6-2	185	2-14-85	0	0	0.00	2	0	0	0	2	0	0	0	0	3	0	.333	.000	.400	0.00	13.50
Johnson, Jonathan	R-R	6-0	180	7-16-74	1	4	6.45	10	9	0	0	45	57	33	32	7	21	26	.322	.309	.333	5.24	4.23
Lerew, Anthony	L-R	6-3	220	10-28-82	1	0	1.37	5	5	0	0	26	20	5	4	0	8	15	.211	.225	.200	5.13	2.73
McBride, Macay	L-L	5-11	210	10-24-82	1	2	3.13	7	5	0	0	23	26	10	8	3	7	24	.274	.214	.284	9.39	2.74
2-team (5 Toledo)					2	2	3.19	12	5	0	0	31	35	14	11	4	12	30	—	—		8.71	3.48
Miller, Corky	R-R	6-1	245	3-18-76	0	0	—	1	0	0	0	1	0	0	0	0	0	0	1.000	1.000		—	
Moylan, Peter	R-R	6-2	200	12-2-78	0	0	0.00	2	0	0	1	2	0	0	0	0	1	3	.000	.000	.000	13.50	4.50
Nelson, Brad	R-R	6-3	200	1-5-82	1	1	2.53	3	1	0	0	11	9	5	3	1	6	6	.237	.167	.269	5.06	5.06
Paronto, Chad	R-R	6-5	250	7-28-75	0	0	3.78	11	0	0	2	17	18	8	7	1	4	11	.277	.250	.297	5.94	2.16
Redman, Mark	L-L	6-5	245	1-5-74	1	0	0.00	1	1	0	0	6	5	0	0	0	2	6	.250	.000	.250	9.53	3.18
2-team (4 Syracuse)					1	2	3.96	5	5	0	0	25	31	18	11	3	14	16	—	—		5.76	5.04
Reyes, Jo-Jo	L-L	6-2	230	11-20-84	4	0	1.00	6	6	0	0	36	25	7	4	2	12	39	.192	.148	.204	9.75	3.00
Ring, Royce	L-L	6-0	220	12-21-80	1	2	5.68	15	0	0	1	13	17	9	8	2	7	14	.333	.158	.438	9.95	4.97
Scalamandre, Rich	R-R	5-11	195	8-20-80	0	4	5.60	22	0	0	1	35	40	26	22	4	15	18	.296	.292	.300	4.58	3.82
Schreiber, Zach	R-R	6-1	200	6-24-82	1	1	2.43	24	0	0	1	33	26	10	9	1	11	38	.205	.189	.217	10.26	2.97
Smith, Dan	L-L	6-5	250	9-9-83	3	5	5.43	14	11	0	0	58	58	35	35	6	39	39	.267	.303	.252	6.05	6.05
Startup, Will	L-L	6-0	195	8-4-84	3	2	2.19	43	0	0	1	49	39	13	12	3	18	49	.219	.262	.197	8.94	3.28
Stevens, Jake	L-L	6-2	215	3-15-81	1	0	0.00	1	0	0	0	5	3	2	0	0	2	3	.188	.000	.214	5.79	3.86
Stockman, Phil	R-R	6-8	250	1-25-80	1	0	1.72	9	0	0	0	16	7	3	3	1	6	15	.132	.208	.069	8.62	3.45
Sturtze, Tanyon	R-R	6-5	230	10-12-70	0	1	6.75	4	0	0	0	4	5	3	3	1	5	3	.333	.500	.222	6.75	11.25
Winkelsas, Joe	R-R	6-3	188	9-14-73	1	0	3.97	5	0	0	0	11	10	6	5	0	5	7	.250	.286	.231	5.56	3.97

FIELDING

Catcher	PCT	G	PO	A	E	DP	PB
I. Franco	.991	57	388	36	4	6	4
Miller	.994	62	408	51	3	5	10
Pena	.995	32	205	13	1	3	1
Serrano	1.000	1	6	1	0	0	0

First Base	PCT	G	PO	A	E	DP
Canizares	.980	36	281	20	6	31
J. Franco	.895	3	16	1	2	2
Koonce	.991	39	292	26	3	33
Mendez	.997	40	286	23	1	26
Pena	.984	22	172	12	3	16
Timmons	1.000	12	65	4	0	4

Second Base	PCT	G	PO	A	E	DP
Harris	.955	5	10	11	1	2
Holt	.964	12	12	42	2	5

	PCT	G	PO	A	E	DP
Orr	.983	14	25	32	1	5
Prado	.995	87	191	229	2	65
Rozema	.952	5	9	11	1	2
Schuerholz	.991	25	47	59	1	16

Third Base	PCT	G	PO	A	E	DP
Harris	.955	8	6	15	1	1
Orr	.929	10	3	10	1	0
Pena	1.000	4	3	7	0	0
Prado	.933	9	4	10	1	0
Rozema	—	1	0	0	0	0
Schuerholz	.898	16	8	36	5	6
Timmons	.972	109	77	165	7	20

Shortstop	PCT	G	PO	A	E	DP
Escobar	.964	46	69	116	7	24
Lillibridge	.975	85	140	208	9	57

	PCT	G	PO	A	E	DP
Orr	1.000	3	6	9	0	2
Prado	1.000	7	7	13	0	2
Schuerholz	1.000	4	8	9	0	3

Outfield	PCT	G	PO	A	E	DP
Bigbie	.986	36	67	4	1	2
Blanco	.981	120	295	8	6	3
Bohn	.989	43	86	6	1	1
Clark	.984	124	238	7	4	1
Harris	1.000	4	6	0	0	0
Jones	.949	43	70	5	4	3
McCarthy	.985	38	64	3	1	0
Orr	1.000	19	23	0	0	0
Pena	1.000	17	19	2	0	0

MISSISSIPPI BRAVES

SOUTHERN LEAGUE

DOUBLE-A

BATTING	B-T	HT	WT	DOB	AVG	vLH	vRH	G	AB	R	H	2B	3B	HR	RBI	BB	HBP	SH	SF	SO	SB	CS	SLG	OBP
Bennett, Paul	R-R	5-11	180	9-6-83	.000	.000	.000	12	17	0	0	0	0	0	0	2	0	0	0	9	0	0	.000	.105
Bohn, T.J.	R-R	6-5	200	1-17-80	.224	.250	.215	23	85	15	19	3	0	1	6	14	1	0	1	23	3	0	.294	.337
Britton, Phillip	R-R	6-0	180	9-25-84	.000	—	.000	2	5	1	0	0	0	0	0	0	0	0	0	1	0	0	.000	.000
Burrus, Josh	R-R	5-11	190	8-20-83	.213	.171	.250	91	239	30	51	10	0	6	32	32	4	3	3	82	8	3	.331	.313
Creek, Greg	L-R	6-3	225	8-29-82	.246	.193	.263	72	232	30	57	15	0	1	17	27	2	0	4	58	2	5	.323	.325
Esquivel, Matt	R-R	6-2	225	12-17-82	.247	.330	.210	98	372	66	92	16	2	19	70	46	3	0	5	97	15	2	.454	.331
Hernandez, Diory	R-R	5-11	170	4-8-84	.307	.333	.297	115	433	50	133	25	1	7	59	29	14	5	0	68	22	20	.418	.370
Holt, J.C.	L-R	5-9	175	12-8-82	.312	.315	.310	94	385	47	120	17	5	0	22	40	3	8	1	77	20	8	.382	.380
Jones, Brandon	L-R	6-1	210	12-10-83	.293	.347	.266	94	365	58	107	21	6	15	74	44	3	0	6	84	12	7	.507	.368
Jurich, Mark	L-L	5-10	195	12-29-80	.268	.194	.295	114	373	46	100	32	3	7	63	36	3	1	5	62	1	2	.426	.333
Kaaihue, Kala	R-R	6-2	230	3-29-85	.127	.105	.138	33	118	14	15	5	1	0	8	11	2	0	2	51	0	0	.186	.211
Lillibridge, Brent	R-R	5-11	190	9-18-83	.275	.366	.226	52	204	31	56	8	3	3	17	20	6	6	1	60	14	7	.387	.355
Loadenthal, Carl	L-L	5-11	185	12-27-81	.300	.326	.289	129	476	72	143	17	5	0	31	62	4	6	4	80	40	18	.357	.383
Lunar, Fernando	R-R	6-0	190	5-25-77	.111	.167	.083	6	18	1	2	0	0	0	0	1	0	0	0	7	0	0	.111	.158
Pope, Van	R-R	6-0	200	2-26-84	.223	.270	.203	123	421	48	94	23	4	6	43	36	9	5	1	77	10	5	.340	.298
Rozema, Mike	L-R	6-2	180	9-16-81	.265	.288	.255	69	189	25	50	5	2	5	25	15	0	1	1	42	6	2	.392	.317
Saltalamacchia, Jarrod	B-R	6-4	195	5-2-85	.309	.227	.339	22	81	18	25	7	0	6	13	13	0	0	0	17	2	0	.617	.404
Sammons, Clint	R-R	6-0	200	5-15-83	.243	.300	.222	83	296	27	72	10	0	5	36	26	1	2	3	72	1	1	.338	.304
Schuerholz, Jonathan	R-R	5-11	190	6-25-80	.182	.167	.188	12	22	2	4	0	0	0	0	2	0	0	0	9	1	0	.182	.308
Serrano, Ray	R-R	5-8	221	1-19-81	.301	.238	.333	35	123	21	37	12	2	3	15	9	2	0	1	20	2	0	.504	.356
Young, Matt	L-R	5-8	175	10-3-82	.242	.208	.254	33	95	6	23	4	1	0	15	10	0	1	2	18	0	3	.305	.308

PITCHING	B-T	HT	WT	DOB	W	L	ERA	G	GS	CG	SV	IP	H	R	ER	HR	BB	SO	AVG	vLH	vRH	K/9	BB/9
Ascanio, Jose	R-R	6-0	170	5-2-85	2	2	2.54	44	1	0	10	78	66	26	22	1	18	71	.234	.225	.240	8.19	2.08
Baerlocher, Ryan	R-R	6-5	240	8-6-77	2	1	3.57	7	7	0	0	45	51	18	18	4	7	31	.302	.289	.312	6.15	1.39
Basner, Ryan	R-R	6-3	230	7-15-81	0	0	0.00	7	0	0	0	12	6	1	0	0	4	9	.143	.167	.133	6.75	3.00
Bennett, Jeff	R-R	6-3	200	6-10-80	0	0	4.15	6	0	0	0	9	7	4	4	0	6	7	.212	.231	.200	7.27	6.23
Bueno, Francisley	L-L	5-11	200	3-5-81	4	6	3.67	22	19	0	0	113	132	55	46	8	26	77	.293	.325	.280	6.15	2.08
Bullock, Tyler	R-R	6-3	225	1-22-84	1	0	7.36	9	0	0	0	18	24	21	15	2	9	8	.333	.433	.262	3.93	4.42
Bush, Paul	R-R	6-1	175	10-5-79	0	0	0.00	1	0	0	0	1	1	0	0	0	0	2	.250	—	.250	18.00	0.00
Cormier, Lance	R-R	6-1	200	8-19-80	1	1	4.50	2	2	0	0	8	8	4	4	1	0	6	.267	.222	.333	6.75	0.00
Devine, Joey	R-R	5-11	205	9-19-83	2	4	2.06	33	0	0	16	35	26	9	8	1	13	51	.211	.283	.169	13.11	3.34
Gunderson, Kevin	R-L	5-10	165	9-16-84	0	0	2.25	2	0	0	0	4	8	1	1	0	2	0	.471	.600	.417	0.00	4.50
Harrison, Matt	L-L	6-5	205	8-16-85	5	7	3.39	20	20	0	0	117	118	51	44	6	34	78	.264	.288	.255	6.02	2.62
Hernandez, Moises	R-R	6-1	168	3-18-84	2	2	5.94	10	10	0	0	50	60	39	33	8	27	20	.294	.351	.245	3.60	4.86
Hyde, Lee	R-L	6-2	185	2-14-85	1	0	1.80	1	1	0	0	5	2	1	1	0	1	4	.111	.000	.133	7.20	1.80
Jung, Sung Ki	R-R	5-10	161	8-6-79	0	1	1.93	7	0	0	1	9	9	2	2	0	1	8	.273	.263	.286	7.71	0.96
Medlen, Kris	B-R	5-10	175	10-7-85	0	0	11.57	3	0	0	1	2	4	3	3	0	2	2	.444	.667	.333	7.71	7.71
Morton, Charlie	R-R	6-5	218	11-12-83	4	6	4.29	41	6	0	0	80	80	41	38	3	37	67	.270	.276	.265	7.57	4.18
Nelson, Brad	R-R	6-3	200	1-5-82	5	1	3.77	29	5	0	0	76	69	34	32	4	20	51	.240	.256	.228	6.01	2.36
Nix, Michael	R-R	6-5	235	5-21-83	4	6	2.33	44	0	0	0	70	57	25	18	2	30	73	.226	.245	.212	9.43	3.88
Parr, James	R-R	6-1	185	2-27-86	4	5	4.59	18	16	0	0	98	111	51	50	8	25	75	.295	.277	.312	6.89	2.30
Payano, Nelson	L-L	6-2	180	11-13-82	1	1	4.91	4	0	0	0	4	3	2	2	0	3	3	.214	.000	.300	7.36	9.82
Reyes, Jo-Jo	L-L	6-2	230	11-20-84	8	1	3.56	13	13	0	0	73	63	31	29	5	35	71	.240	.234	.241	8.71	4.30
Scalamandre, Rich	R-R	5-11	195	8-20-80	3	2	4.95	16	0	0	2	20	24	15	11	3	9	11	.300	.226	.347	4.95	4.05
Schreiber, Zach	R-R	6-1	200	6-24-82	3	5	2.22	34	0	0	5	45	26	13	11	3	22	38	.173	.188	.163	7.66	4.43
Smith, Dan	L-L	6-5	250	9-9-83	4	2	1.94	9	9	0	0	51	37	14	11	1	20	41	.204	.333	.176	7.24	3.53
Stockman, Phil	R-R	6-8	250	1-25-80	1	0	0.59	12	0	0	3	15	8	2	1	0	7	17	.148	.292	.033	9.98	4.11
Sturtze, Tanyon	R-R	6-5	230	10-12-70	0	2	21.60	2	2	0	0	2	3	4	4	0	4	2	.375	.400	.333	10.80	21.60
Villa, Kelvin	L-L	5-10	160	12-14-85	8	12	5.39	28	28	0	0	144	169	94	86	14	66	121	.294	.296	.293	7.58	4.13
Wilkerson, Wes	R-R	6-4	215	9-11-76	1	3	7.67	18	0	0	1	27	40	25	23	3	10	21	.345	.354	.338	7.00	3.33
Winkelsas, Joe	R-R	6-3	188	9-14-73	1	2	2.55	14	0	0	0	25	22	13	7	0	9	21	.232	.306	.186	7.66	3.28

ORGANIZATION STATISTICS

FIELDING

Catcher	PCT	G	PO	A	E	DP	PB
Britton	1.000	1	7	0	0	0	0
Lunar	1.000	6	37	5	0	0	1
Saltalamacchia	.972	20	159	15	5	0	1
Sammons	.995	82	559	63	3	3	7
Serrano	1.000	33	244	22	0	4	1

First Base	PCT	G	PO	A	E	DP
Britton	1.000	1	3	0	0	0
Creek	.990	57	464	38	5	48
Jurich	.996	56	423	27	2	39
Kaaihue	.993	33	262	13	2	25

Second Base	PCT	G	PO	A	E	DP
Bennett	.000	1	0	0	1	0
Hernandez	.994	33	67	96	1	28

	PCT	G	PO	A	E	DP
Holt	.985	94	169	234	6	54
Rozema	.913	12	16	26	4	4
Schuerholz	1.000	2	4	8	0	2
Young	.917	1	8	3	1	2

Third Base	PCT	G	PO	A	E	DP
Creek	1.000	2	0	2	0	0
Hernandez	1.000	1	1	0	0	0
Pope	.964	121	82	243	12	21
Rozema	.818	22	12	24	8	3
Sammons	1.000	1	1	0	0	0
Schuerholz	1.000	1	0	4	0	0

Shortstop	PCT	G	PO	A	E	DP
Bennett	.500	2	0	1	1	0
Hernandez	.966	79	120	197	11	44

Lillibridge	PCT	G	PO	A	E	DP
Lillibridge	.945	51	82	141	13	36
Pope	1.000	1	1	0	0	0
Rozema	.906	9	10	19	3	4
Schuerholz	1.000	1	0	2	0	1

Outfield	PCT	G	PO	A	E	DP
Bohn	1.000	23	68	2	0	1
Burrus	.956	48	83	4	4	1
Esquivel	.953	97	214	9	11	3
Jones	.984	88	176	6	3	2
Jurich	.977	29	39	3	1	0
Loadenthal	.993	120	284	8	2	1
Young	.982	25	52	4	1	3

MYRTLE BEACH PELICANS

HIGH CLASS A

CAROLINA LEAGUE

BATTING	B-T	HT	WT	DOB	AVG	vLH	vRH	G	AB	R	H	2B	3B	HR	RBI	BB	HBP	SH	SF	SO	SB	CS	SLG	OBP
Alvarez, Roberto	R-R	5-11	190	8-30-83	.291	.278	.295	101	385	49	112	20	3	6	50	24	2	0	2	80	6	3	.405	.334
Andrus, Elvis	R-R	6-0	185	8-26-88	.244	.330	.214	99	385	59	94	20	3	3	37	44	6	3	2	88	25	7	.335	.330
Arnold, Derrick	B-R	5-10	165	8-3-83	.219	.230	.215	104	333	37	73	14	1	3	23	14	4	4	2	64	11	4	.294	.258
Bennett, Paul	R-R	5-11	180	9-6-83	.225	.250	.215	59	173	20	39	9	1	1	13	35	4	4	2	58	9	3	.306	.364
Cabrera, Willie	R-R	5-11	185	8-3-86	.251	.295	.242	68	251	28	63	7	1	2	24	24	0	0	1	31	2	2	.311	.315
Camarena, Jose	B-R	5-10	170	5-29-84	.225	.130	.261	81	276	29	62	13	0	5	37	31	2	5	2	75	4	3	.326	.305
Campbell, Eric	R-R	6-0	190	8-6-85	.221	.267	.206	81	298	47	66	13	0	14	49	36	5	1	4	48	6	3	.406	.312
Davis, Quentin	L-R	5-10	170	3-7-83	.261	.256	.262	134	495	55	129	10	11	4	65	31	0	18	6	73	37	21	.349	.301
Fisher, Michael	B-R	6-2	188	3-22-85	.250	.100	.280	30	120	15	30	4	0	1	13	10	3	2	0	21	0	2	.308	.323
Fontaine, Chase	L-R	6-2	185	10-22-85	.205	.214	.203	22	78	6	16	4	0	0	7	8	1	0	1	26	1	0	.256	.284
Hernandez, Diory	R-R	5-11	170	4-8-84	.313	.333	.309	17	64	9	20	8	2	0	9	2	1	0	0	11	2	2	.500	.343
Kaaihue, Kala	R-R	6-2	230	3-29-85	.298	.317	.291	89	309	57	92	20	1	22	61	53	9	0	5	92	0	1	.583	.410
Marcial, Robert	R-R	5-10	170	4-21-84	.205	.250	.170	16	44	4	9	1	0	0	4	5	0	2	1	5	1	1	.227	.280
Monk, Brandon	R-R	5-11	180	2-22-87	.375	.375	.375	13	40	3	15	1	0	0	2	0	2	0	0	8	0	0	.400	.405
Roberts, J.D.	L-R	6-4	225	8-8-81	.199	.145	.215	81	246	18	49	8	0	2	20	19	2	3	2	72	2	5	.256	.260
Rozema, Mike	L-R	6-2	180	9-16-81	.294	.214	.315	20	68	10	20	1	1	2	15	9	2	2	2	13	1	2	.426	.383
Sammons, Clint	R-R	6-0	200	5-15-83	.269	.583	.212	23	78	13	21	6	0	4	13	10	2	0	1	14	1	1	.500	.363
Schafer, Jordan	L-L	6-1	190	9-4-86	.294	.299	.292	106	436	70	128	34	8	10	43	40	1	3	1	95	19	11	.477	.354
Stevens, Jeff	R-R	6-3	215	3-28-84	.245	.429	.214	14	49	4	12	5	0	1	6	3	0	0	0	13	0	0	.408	.288
Terrazas, Ivan	B-R	5-11	168	11-11-83	.200	—	.200	5	15	1	3	0	0	0	4	1	0	0	0	6	0	0	.200	.250
Verastegui, Jerry	L-R	5-10	210	1-26-83	.213	.171	.230	41	122	11	26	4	0	0	10	10	1	1	1	19	0	2	.246	.276
Williams, Larry	L-R	6-2	205	4-6-85	.287	.188	.300	31	108	9	31	5	0	1	15	3	0	1	1	22	1	0	.361	.304
Young, Matt	L-R	5-8	175	10-3-82	.280	.278	.280	65	243	29	68	7	3	1	18	37	4	1	2	36	14	7	.346	.381

PITCHING	B-T	HT	WT	DOB	W	L	ERA	G	GS	CG	SV	IP	H	R	ER	HR	BB	SO	AVG	vLH	vRH	K/9	BB/9
Acosta, Jorge	L-L	5-11	185	9-18-83	2	2	6.56	21	0	0	0	36	37	31	26	2	35	35	.276	.182	.322	8.83	8.83
Arnold, Derrick	B-R	5-10	165	8-3-83	0	0	8.53	5	0	0	0	6	6	6	6	3	5	3	.261	.375	.200	4.26	7.11
Bullock, Tyler	R-R	6-3	225	1-22-84	2	2	4.73	33	0	0	1	46	39	26	24	1	30	33	.235	.295	.200	6.50	5.91
Butts, Brett	R-R	6-1	190	4-24-86	0	1	3.18	2	0	0	0	6	7	3	2	0	1	1	.318	.500	.000	1.59	1.59
Cho, Jang Ji	R-R	6-1	210	7-11-83	1	1	7.32	12	0	0	0	20	25	17	16	4	11	11	.305	.407	.255	5.03	5.03
Cuevas, Jairo	R-R	6-2	217	1-24-84	6	12	3.55	25	25	0	0	132	113	74	52	9	71	116	.225	.197	.241	7.91	4.84
Drese, Ryan	R-R	6-3	235	4-5-76	0	3	6.88	6	6	0	0	17	29	13	13	2	6	7	.387	.400	.380	3.71	3.18
Dumesnil, Bryan	R-L	6-3	210	9-19-83	1	1	2.89	7	0	0	0	19	22	6	6	2	3	19	.286	.200	.316	9.16	1.45
Evans, Dustin	R-R	6-3	200	9-24-84	2	10	4.70	21	21	0	0	100	111	68	52	11	35	72	.285	.212	.328	6.50	3.16
Gunderson, Kevin	R-L	5-10	165	9-16-84	4	5	3.08	44	0	0	7	53	51	23	18	3	31	47	.256	.213	.270	8.03	5.30
Hanson, Thomas	R-R	6-6	210	8-28-86	3	3	4.20	11	11	0	0	60	53	33	28	10	32	64	.243	.253	.237	9.60	4.80
Heath, Deunte	R-R	6-4	205	8-28-85	2	4	5.82	11	11	0	0	56	64	45	36	8	31	47	.284	.343	.259	7.60	5.01
Hernandez, Moises	R-R	6-1	168	3-18-84	10	3	3.66	15	15	0	0	91	94	43	37	10	26	51	.265	.328	.229	5.04	2.57
Hyde, Lee	R-L	6-2	185	2-14-85	0	0	4.50	3	0	0	0	6	6	3	3	0	5	6	.300	.333	.294	9.00	7.50
Jones, Beau	L-L	6-1	195	8-25-86	0	0	15.26	5	1	0	0	8	10	15	13	0	14	3	.294	.273	.304	3.52	16.43
Jung, Sung Ki	R-R	5-10	165	8-6-79	0	1	1.15	33	0	0	22	39	22	6	5	2	12	49	.164	.111	.111	11.31	2.77
Lyman, Jeffrey	R-R	6-3	215	1-14-87	0	5	8.90	8	2	0	0	31	39	42	31	4	20	17	.295	.283	.304	4.88	5.74
Medlen, Kris	B-R	5-10	175	10-7-85	2	0	1.13	18	0	0	2	24	22	7	3	1	7	28	.239	.174	.261	10.50	2.62
Nelson, Brad	R-R	6-3	200	1-5-82	3	0	0.00	9	0	0	0	14	10	0	0	0	3	26	.208	.235	.194	5.27	1.98
Nix, Michael	R-R	6-5	235	5-21-83	0	0	10.12	3	0	0	0	2	3	3	3	1	2	5	.300	.333	.286	16.88	6.75
Parr, James	R-R	6-1	185	2-27-86	3	4	3.18	8	8	1	0	40	36	14	14	1	6	37	.252	.273	.239	8.39	1.36
Payano, Nelson	L-L	6-2	180	11-13-82	4	4	3.56	39	1	0	0	61	45	28	24	2	51	83	.207	.185	.215	12.31	7.57
Reynoso, Ryne	R-R	6-2	215	3-15-85	0	0	0.00	2	0	0	0	2	1	0	0	0	4	4	.125	.000	.333	15.43	15.43
Santiago, Jose	R-R	6-4	180	8-1-81	0	1	12.60	5	0	0	0	5	6	10	7	0	9	10	.286	.200	.384	10.80	16.20
Sencion, Carlos	L-L	6-6	170	11-17-84	2	2	2.81	19	6	0	0	64	53	23	20	6	52	76	.225	.231	.223	10.69	7.31
Stanley, Adam	L-L	6-0	201	11-20-84	3	2	5.53	28	0	0	1	57	64	35	35	7	37	28	.288	.291	.287	4.42	5.84
Stevens, Jake	L-L	6-2	215	3-15-85	6	8	5.54	23	13	0	0	88	109	62	54	9	40	50	.302	.284	.319	5.13	4.11
Valenzuela, Sergio	R-R	6-2	190	9-15-84	0	0	6.88	18	2	0	0	35	47	33	27	3	18	19	.318	.263	.352	4.84	4.58
Venters, Jonathan	R-L	6-3	188	3-20-85	3	3	3.39	17	12	0	1	80	60	39	30	4	38	64	.210	.145	.228	7.23	4.29
Vines, Chris	R-R	6-5	215	2-26-85	0	3	11.66	6	5	0	0	15	26	20	19	1	12	8	.413	.323	.500	4.91	7.36
Wilson, Tyler	L-L	6-1	210	7-11-86	0	0	0.00	4	0	0	0	5	2	0	0	0	5	4	.125	.200	.091	6.75	8.44

FIELDING

Catcher	PCT	G	PO	A	E	DP	PB
Camarena	.993	75	544	47	4	2	14
Sammons	.981	19	132	25	3	1	3
Stevens	.984	14	115	10	2	2	1
Verastegui	.984	36	231	22	4	4	9

First Base	PCT	G	PO	A	E	DP
Alvarez	.985	16	124	10	2	7
Bennett	.958	9	64	4	3	3
Camarena	1.000	1	5	0	0	1
Kaaihue	.991	83	701	43	7	72
Roberts	.980	21	141	7	3	15
Rozema	1.000	2	10	0	0	0
Terrazas	1.000	4	29	0	0	2
Williams	1.000	12	84	5	0	4

Second Base	PCT	G	PO	A	E	DP
Arnold	.968	66	103	173	9	31
Bennett	.973	33	63	81	4	16

Fontaine	.846	3	7	4	2	1
Hernandez	1.000	15	34	40	0	11
Marcial	1.000	14	24	34	0	10
Monk	.889	3	2	6	1	2
Rozema	1.000	1	1	1	0	0
Young	.944	12	14	20	2	3

Third Base	PCT	G	PO	A	E	DP
Arnold	.962	21	9	41	2	3
Bennett	.897	9	8	18	3	0
Campbell	.953	78	50	151	10	14
Fontaine	.848	10	3	25	5	1
Monk	.950	9	6	13	1	0
Roberts	.500	3	1	2	3	0
Rozema	.933	14	15	27	3	3

Shortstop	PCT	G	PO	A	E	DP
Andrus	.949	98	174	296	25	63
Arnold	1.000	9	15	21	0	4

Bennett	1.000	1	1	0	0	0
Fisher	.910	30	48	63	11	11
Rozema	1.000	2	0	8	0	0

Outfield	PCT	G	PO	A	E	DP
Alvarez	1.000	41	62	1	0	1
Arnold	1.000	4	0	1	0	0
Cabrera	.963	59	98	7	4	2
Davis	.978	127	252	14	6	2
Fontaine	1.000	4	4	0	0	0
Marcial	—	1	0	0	0	0
Roberts	.985	36	63	1	1	0
Schafer	.988	101	232	12	3	3
Terrazas	1.000	1	1	0	0	0
Williams	.800	3	4	0	1	0
Young	1.000	54	112	2	0	2

ROME BRAVES
LOW CLASS A
SOUTH ATLANTIC LEAGUE

BATTING	B-T	HT	WT	DOB	AVG	vLH	vRH	G	AB	R	H	2B	3B	HR	RBI	BB	HBP	SH	SF	SO	SB	CS	SLG	OBP
Brezeale, Danny	R-R	5-11	200	5-13-86	.228	.202	.234	117	404	53	92	27	0	9	56	15	17	3	8	124	3	6	.361	.279
Britton, Phillip	R-R	6-0	180	9-25-84	.287	.286	.287	89	345	54	99	22	3	10	44	9	9	1	0	44	4	4	.455	.322
Cabrera, Willie	R-R	5-11	185	8-3-86	.262	.216	.273	65	260	28	68	17	1	3	30	11	2	0	3	28	2	1	.369	.293
Flowers, Tyler	R-R	6-4	220	1-24-86	.298	.306	.297	106	389	65	116	34	2	12	70	49	3	0	4	74	3	4	.488	.378
Fontaine, Chase	L-R	6-2	185	10-22-85	.288	.323	.279	95	313	60	90	14	6	3	26	58	2	2	0	75	10	9	.399	.402
Franco, Julio	R-R	6-1	210	8-23-58	.308	.500	.273	4	13	3	4	0	0	0	2	1	2	0	0	2	1	0	.308	.438
Hernandez, Victor	R-R	6-1	170	1-17-85	.255	.200	.265	46	137	7	35	5	0	1	18	9	2	0	1	33	1	1	.314	.309
Hicks, Brandon	R-R	6-2	200	9-14-85	.313	.263	.321	37	128	26	40	11	0	4	15	27	1	0	1	26	5	3	.492	.433
Jones, Travis	R-R	5-9	190	11-10-85	.256	.222	.266	46	164	34	42	5	1	10	27	34	5	1	2	36	6	4	.482	.395
Lundahl, Chad	R-R	6-2	190	8-18-84	.215	.267	.199	88	311	31	67	13	0	3	33	17	2	1	4	63	0	1	.286	.257
Marcial, Robert	R-R	5-10	170	4-21-84	.232	.278	.223	74	220	28	51	8	1	1	20	16	1	7	0	52	4	4	.291	.287
Mejia, Ernesto	R-R	6-6	190	12-2-85	.307	.310	.306	36	137	17	42	9	2	4	24	4	1	0	1	30	2	1	.489	.329
Miles, Cole	B-R	5-8	165	3-24-87	.245	.231	.250	16	53	6	13	1	0	0	2	5	0	1	1	10	4	0	.264	.305
Monk, Brandon	R-R	5-11	180	2-22-87	.174	.154	.179	19	69	4	12	4	0	0	2	2	1	0	1	17	0	1	.232	.216
Morris, Joshua	R-R	6-5	230	5-11-85	.165	.188	.157	34	121	11	20	8	0	1	10	12	2	1	0	36	0	1	.256	.252
Owings, Jon	R-R	6-4	192	4-4-85	.256	.276	.251	107	403	62	103	19	2	16	51	34	5	1	3	94	10	7	.432	.319
Rodriguez, Concepcion	R-R	6-2	170	9-19-86	.206	.278	.187	123	427	51	88	24	0	7	50	54	5	2	5	82	11	6	.311	.299
Schafer, Jordan	L-L	6-1	190	9-4-86	.372	.222	.412	30	129	16	48	15	2	5	20	16	0	0	1	31	4	4	.636	.441
Silva, Yohan	B-R	5-11	175	1-30-85	.236	.200	.244	104	339	62	80	10	4	10	43	59	2	6	2	72	11	5	.378	.351
Stevens, Jeff	R-R	6-3	215	3-28-84	.083	.000	.111	3	12	0	1	1	0	0	0	0	0	0	0	2	0	0	.167	.083
Verastegui, Jerry	L-R	5-10	210	1-26-83	.243	.222	.250	11	37	3	9	1	0	0	1	4	0	0	0	6	0	0	.270	.317
Williams, Larry	L-R	6-2	205	4-6-85	.270	.232	.278	89	337	25	91	16	2	3	23	25	2	0	2	57	2	1	.320	.322

PITCHING	B-T	HT	WT	DOB	W	L	ERA	G	GS	CG	SV	IP	H	R	ER	HR	BB	SO	AVG	vLH	vRH	K/9	BB/9
Acosta, Jorge	L-L	5-11	185	9-18-83	0	2	3.70	16	0	0	2	24	20	12	10	1	15	34	.222	.138	.262	12.58	5.55
Brezeale, Danny	R-R	5-11	200	5-13-86	0	0	0.00	1	0	0	0	1	0	0	0	0	0	0	.000	.000	.000	13.50	0.00
Broadway, Michael	R-R	6-5	190	3-30-87	11	6	5.25	29	11	0	0	96	125	65	56	5	33	50	.314	.333	.299	4.69	3.09
Butts, Brett	R-R	6-1	190	4-24-86	1	3	3.47	9	0	0	1	23	21	10	9	2	5	17	.244	.281	.222	6.56	1.93
Chapman, Jaye	R-R	6-0	180	5-22-87	3	1	6.27	20	0	0	0	37	31	26	26	4	19	42	.225	.321	.159	10.12	4.58
Cho, Jang Ji	R-R	6-1	210	7-11-83	0	0	15.00	3	0	0	0	3	6	5	5	0	1	0	.429	.286	.571	0.00	3.00
Cofield, Kyle	R-R	6-5	190	1-23-87	4	8	3.86	25	16	0	1	112	96	56	48	7	56	90	.236	.232	.240	7.23	4.50
Cormier, Lance	R-R	6-1	200	8-19-80	0	0	4.50	1	1	0	0	2	5	1	1	0	0	4	.455	.000	.556	18.00	0.00
Curtis, James	R-R	6-1	205	5-6-86	3	5	7.21	27	3	0	1	49	67	43	39	6	27	39	.337	.316	.350	7.21	4.99
Dumesnil, Bryan	R-L	6-3	210	9-19-83	0	0	2.08	3	0	0	0	4	4	1	1	0	1	4	.250	.000	.286	8.31	2.08
Gustafson, Timothy	R-R	6-3	185	12-29-84	3	8	5.01	22	20	1	0	111	135	78	62	1	31	93	.305	.324	.296	7.52	2.51
Hanson, Thomas	R-R	6-6	210	8-28-86	2	6	2.59	15	14	0	0	73	51	28	21	6	26	90	.194	.173	.203	11.10	3.21
Heath, Deunte	R-R	6-4	205	8-28-85	2	3	2.03	16	9	0	0	71	59	19	16	1	19	47	.225	.288	.184	5.96	2.41
Johnson, Joseph	R-R	6-4	210	8-10-84	1	1	4.87	17	0	0	0	20	24	12	11	1	15	20	.304	.435	.250	8.85	6.64
Jones, Beau	L-L	6-1	195	8-25-86	5	0	2.96	21	0	0	3	49	38	17	16	1	12	46	.210	.270	.194	8.51	2.22
Lyman, Jeffrey	R-R	6-3	215	1-14-87	5	8	4.59	20	20	0	0	104	122	64	53	10	39	77	.295	.273	.308	6.66	3.38
McMillan, Clayton	L-L	6-3	180	9-19-86	0	1	3.38	3	0	0	0	8	8	3	3	1	1	0	2	.300	.250	.333	10.12	6.75
Medlen, Kris	B-R	5-10	175	10-7-85	0	1	0.87	17	0	0	8	21	13	4	2	1	3	33	.169	.172	.167	14.37	1.31
Mehlich, Michael	R-R	6-3	180	9-5-87	1	0	1.50	4	0	0	0	6	5	2	1	0	3	3	.217	.231	.200	4.50	4.50
Pruneda, Benino	R-R	5-9	170	8-8-88	0	0	7.71	3	0	0	2	2	4	2	2	0	0	3	.364	.333	.500	11.57	0.00
Railsback, Cody	R-R	6-4	175	6-3-87	0	2	10.57	3	1	0	0	8	9	9	7	0	8	4	.281	.467	.118	4.70	9.39
Ramirez, Wiliam	R-R	6-3	171	7-8-85	0	2	4.91	2	1	0	0	7	8	9	4	0	0	4	.258	.316	.167	4.91	0.00
Reid, Rico	R-R	5-11	218	9-24-88	0	0	2.45	2	0	0	0	4	3	5	1	0	2	5	.200	.250	.143	12.27	4.91
Reynoso, Ryne	L-R	6-2	215	3-15-85	3	4	1.98	40	0	0	9	59	48	19	13	0	32	71	.221	.162	.248	10.83	4.88
Richmond, Jamie	R-R	6-3	185	3-23-86	7	6	3.05	25	24	0	0	139	141	71	47	9	25	98	.255	.293	.235	6.36	1.62
Rohrbough, Cole	L-L	6-3	205	5-23-87	2	0	1.29	6	6	0	0	28	13	7	4	1	12	38	.138	.125	.148	12.21	3.86
Sencion, Carlos	L-L	6-6	170	11-17-84	2	1	3.72	14	0	0	0	39	31	19	16	1	17	50	.215	.161	.230	11.64	3.96
Shaffer, Jared	R-R	6-3	200	2-28-87	0	0	2.28	9	2	0	1	24	25	8	6	0	14	15	.281	.311	.250	5.70	5.32
Silva, Yohan	B-R	5-11	175	1-30-85	0	0	0.00	2	0	0	0	1	1	0	0	0	0	0	.500	.000	.500	0.00	54.00
Sturtze, Tanyon	R-R	6-5	230	10-12-70	0	1	5.40	4	4	0	0	5	7	3	3	0	1	1	.333	.333	.333	1.80	1.80
Valenzuela, Sergio	R-R	6-0	175	9-15-84	1	2	7.12	14	3	0	0	37	55	33	29	5	19	19	.350	.355	.347	4.66	4.66
Vines, Chris	R-R	6-5	215	2-26-85	2	0	1.00	6	5	0	0	18	9	2	2	0	3	17	.143	.217	.100	8.50	1.50
Wilson, Tyler	L-L	6-1	210	7-11-86	6	4	3.40	37	0	0	5	50	38	20	19	2	28	70	.211	.321	.165	12.52	5.01

FIELDING

Catcher	PCT	G	PO	A	E	DP	PB
Britton	.990	81	622	82	7	8	7
Flowers	.991	15	105	11	1	0	3
Hernandez	.993	41	254	43	2	2	3
Stevens	1.000	3	21	2	0	0	1
Verastegui	.981	11	92	11	2	2	3

First Base	PCT	G	PO	A	E	DP
Brezeale	1.000	4	5	0	0	0
Flowers	.988	69	533	41	7	48
Franco	1.000	1	8	0	0	1
Lundahl	1.000	1	3	0	0	0
Mejia	.981	20	143	16	3	12
Morris	.995	24	205	8	1	11
Williams	.986	36	246	30	4	24

Second Base	PCT	G	PO	A	E	DP
Fontaine	.936	51	93	126	15	17
Jones	.956	45	79	118	9	23
Lundahl	.889	4	6	10	2	3
Marcial	1.000	2	31	66	0	13
Miles	.873	15	25	37	9	5
Monk	1.000	10	17	28	0	6

Third Base	PCT	G	PO	A	E	DP
Brezeale	.917	110	76	188	24	18
Fontaine	.800	4	0	4	1	0
Hernandez	1.000	2	2	1	0	0
Lundahl	.818	10	7	11	4	1
Marcial	.865	25	11	34	7	2
Monk	1.000	6	3	12	0	0
Silva	1.000	1	0	3	0	0

Shortstop	PCT	G	PO	A	E	DP
Brezeale	—	2	0	0	0	0
Fontaine	.833	14	18	37	11	4
Hicks	.964	37	52	107	6	22
Lundahl	.943	74	116	163	17	33
Marcial	.934	20	24	47	5	10
Monk	.846	3	3	8	2	1

Outfield	PCT	G	PO	A	E	DP
Brezeale	1.000	1	0	0	0	0
Cabrera	.977	59	122	5	3	1
Fontaine	.750	2	3	0	1	0
Marcial	1.000	10	10	1	0	0
Owings	.981	95	194	10	4	4
Rodriguez	.984	115	178	10	3	2
Schafer	1.000	30	44	1	0	1
Silva	.974	99	213	10	6	0
Williams	.978	31	42	2	1	0

DANVILLE BRAVES   ROOKIE

APPALACHIAN LEAGUE

BATTING	B-T	HT	WT	DOB	AVG	vLH	vRH	G	AB	R	H	2B	3B	HR	RBI	BB	HBP	SH	SF	SO	SB	CS	SLG	OBP
Anderson, Chris	R-R	6-0	210	10-27-85	.286	.333	.275	22	49	10	14	3	0	2	7	14	0	1	1	17	0	1	.469	.438
Carmona, Eliazar	R-R	6-1	170	12-12-85	.242	.273	.235	51	120	23	29	5	1	0	7	6	1	5	1	27	4	1	.300	.281
Coe, Adam	R-R	6-0	190	6-7-88	.257	.171	.277	58	218	25	56	16	0	3	24	17	2	2	2	51	4	0	.372	.314
Dixon, Dennis	L-R	6-4	190	1-11-85	.100	.000	.111	4	10	1	1	0	0	0	1	0	0	0	0	0	0	0	.100	.182
Dominguez, Javier	B-R	6-1	150	7-14-85	.191	.400	.129	42	110	19	21	3	1	3	11	5	3	1	1	28	1	1	.318	.244
Fisher, Michael	B-R	6-2	188	3-22-85	.325	.407	.303	33	126	22	41	11	1	2	27	15	1	0	2	27	0	3	.476	.396
Garcia, Steven	R-R	5-11	190	9-7-86	.250	.000	.286	21	48	6	12	3	0	1	8	2	0	2	1	21	0	1	.375	.275
Gress, Randy	R-R	6-3	180	12-6-84	.216	.250	.207	18	37	4	8	4	0	0	2	4	0	0	0	9	1	0	.324	.293
Heyward, Jason	L-L	6-4	220	8-9-89	.313	.667	.231	4	16	3	5	1	0	0	1	1	0	0	0	5	0	0	.375	.353
Hicks, Brandon	R-R	6-2	200	9-14-85	.224	.267	.209	18	58	14	13	3	1	3	13	12	2	1	1	18	1	1	.466	.370
Johnson, Benjamin	R-R	6-1	190	7-17-86	.282	.130	.325	32	103	13	29	2	0	1	12	9	1	0	2	23	3	2	.330	.351
Johnson, Cody	L-R	6-4	195	8-18-88	.305	.245	.321	63	243	51	74	18	5	17	57	26	1	0	0	72	7	0	.630	.374
Jones, Travis	R-R	5-9	190	11-10-85	.271	.273	.270	13	48	9	13	2	0	2	7	6	3	0	2	9	1	1	.438	.373
Lee, Carlos	R-R	6-3	195	8-12-84	.245	.250	.243	60	188	34	46	10	1	3	23	16	6	5	1	49	2	3	.356	.322
Lundahl, Chad	R-R	6-2	190	8-18-84	.295	.267	.299	32	112	13	33	6	0	0	12	10	0	0	1	13	0	0	.348	.350
Mejia, Ernesto	R-R	6-6	190	12-2-85	.339	.375	.329	29	109	17	37	8	2	5	24	6	5	0	3	24	6	0	.587	.390
Miles, Cole	B-R	5-8	165	3-24-87	.333	.378	.323	60	234	40	78	6	4	2	27	23	4	5	3	28	11	4	.419	.398
Monk, Brandon	R-R	5-11	180	2-2-87	.063	.167	.000	8	16	0	1	0	0	0	1	0	0	0	1	5	0	0	.063	.059
Morris, Joshua	R-R	6-5	230	5-11-85	.282	.324	.273	55	202	31	57	18	1	4	35	10	11	1	0	51	2	2	.441	.350
Parliament, Adam	R-R	6-4	220	12-16-85	.244	.222	.250	25	45	7	11	3	0	0	8	4	1	0	0	10	0	1	.311	.320
Shults, Stephen	R-R	6-2	190	12-24-87	.271	.135	.303	59	192	34	52	19	0	6	25	16	8	0	1	67	2	3	.464	.350
Stevens, Jeff	R-R	6-3	215	3-28-84	.407	.333	.420	25	59	10	24	5	0	1	13	4	7	0	0	10	0	0	.542	.500

PITCHING	B-T	HT	WT	DOB	W	L	ERA	G	GS	CG	SV	IP	H	R	ER	HR	BB	SO	AVG	vLH	vRH	K/9	BB/9
Barrett, Eric	L-L	6-2	180	12-19-86	2	0	2.28	5	3	0	0	24	14	9	6	0	9	25	.173	.167	.174	9.51	3.42
Beck, Casey	R-R	6-1	215	3-28-87	1	2	7.71	13	0	0	1	16	15	15	14	1	19	22	.242	.235	.244	12.12	10.47
Butts, Brett	R-R	6-1	190	4-24-86	2	0	0.73	5	0	0	0	12	8	4	1	1	3	12	.178	.182	.176	8.76	2.19
Castro, Yeliar	R-R	6-3	180	12-3-87	1	1	6.55	5	1	0	0	11	14	8	8	0	5	6	.333	.211	.435	4.91	4.09
Chapman, Jaye	R-R	6-0	180	5-22-87	0	1	1.23	9	0	0	1	7	6	3	1	1	1	13	.200	.182	.211	15.95	1.23
Cho, Jang Ji	R-R	6-1	210	7-11-83	0	0	45.00	1	0	0	0	1	6	6	5	2	0	2	.600	.333	.714	18.00	0.00
Evarts, Steve	L-L	6-3	180	10-13-87	4	0	1.95	8	7	0	0	37	29	11	8	0	4	34	.213	.103	.243	8.27	0.97
Feliz, Neftali	R-R	6-3	180	5-2-88	2	0	1.98	8	7	0	0	41	28	8	6	0	12	28	.191	.250	.167	9.22	3.95
Fellman, Nicholas	L-R	6-3	190	8-29-85	1	0	2.25	22	0	0	16	28	16	8	7	1	7	46	.157	.182	.145	14.79	2.25
Figueroa, Steven	R-R	6-0	215	5-1-88	1	0	3.60	1	1	0	0	5	6	2	2	0	3	2	.300	.375	.250	3.60	5.40
Gearrin, Cory	R-R	6-3	200	4-14-86	1	1	4.44	18	0	0	0	26	21	14	13	1	16	37	.214	.214	.214	12.65	5.47
Gonzalez, Raul	R-R	6-2	155	7-12-85	3	1	3.80	10	0	0	0	21	25	9	9	1	6	16	.291	.393	.241	6.75	2.53
Ladd, Tim	L-L	5-11	175	11-2-85	1	2	4.88	14	1	0	1	31	37	23	17	3	15	25	.289	.357	.270	7.18	4.31
Locke, Jeffrey	L-L	6-2	180	11-20-87	7	1	2.66	13	11	0	1	61	48	23	18	2	8	74	.213	.188	.210	10.92	1.18
Lundahl, Chad	R-R	6-2	190	8-18-84	0	0	4.50	2	0	0	0	2	2	1	1	0	0	0	.250	.000	.333	0.00	0.00
Mehlich, Michael	R-R	6-2	180	9-5-87	0	0	1.80	9	0	0	2	15	13	4	3	1	14	16	.228	.333	.190	9.60	8.40
Ortegano, Jose	L-L	6-1	145	8-5-87	6	1	1.48	13	9	0	0	61	44	14	10	3	11	55	.199	.280	.189	8.16	1.63
Osuna, Edgar	L-L	6-1	165	11-25-87	5	3	2.47	13	6	0	2	55	55	19	15	4	11	66	.258	.406	.232	10.87	1.81
Palica, Thomas	L-L	6-3	215	7-21-87	4	2	4.91	12	2	0	1	37	43	23	20	2	11	31	.291	.379	.269	7.61	2.70
Paulino, Angelo	R-R	6-4	190	12-15-86	1	0	1.80	1	1	0	0	5	2	1	1	1	3	6	.118	.000	.200	10.80	5.40
Ramirez, Wiliam	R-R	6-3	171	7-8-85	0	2	4.28	12	2	0	2	34	44	23	16	2	15	33	.310	.385	.282	8.82	4.01
Rodgers, Chad	L-L	6-3	185	11-23-87	3	1	3.88	11	10	0	1	49	40	21	21	2	11	46	.220	.362	.170	8.51	2.03
Rohrbough, Cole	L-L	6-3	205	5-23-87	3	2	1.08	8	7	0	0	33	20	8	4	1	8	58	.167	.250	.141	15.66	2.16

FIELDING

Catcher	PCT	G	PO	A	E	DP	PB
Anderson	.992	16	116	12	1	0	1
Dominguez	.975	23	140	19	4	1	5
Garcia	.990	16	92	8	1	2	3
B. Johnson	1.000	16	117	16	0	1	7
Stevens	.989	25	154	20	2	3	0

First Base	PCT	G	PO	A	E	DP
Dominguez	1.000	2	2	0	0	0
Mejia	.987	17	140	8	2	12
Morris	.990	53	467	24	5	25
Shults	1.000	1	7	1	0	1

Second Base	PCT	G	PO	A	E	DP
Fisher	—	1	0	0	0	0
Jones	1.000	8	14	29	0	3
Lundahl	1.000	7	5	6	0	0
Miles	.957	55	77	145	10	29
Monk	.833	7	5	10	3	1

Third Base	PCT	G	PO	A	E	DP
Coe	.909	54	27	93	12	4
Fisher	.895	8	3	14	2	1
Shults	.783	12	5	13	5	0

Shortstop	PCT	G	PO	A	E	DP
Fisher	.949	24	36	57	5	7
Gress	.963	16	16	36	2	5
Hicks	.947	10	14	22	2	4
Lundahl	.967	28	37	79	4	12

Outfield	PCT	G	PO	A	E	DP
Carmona	.972	46	63	6	2	0
Dixon	1.000	4	2	0	0	0
Dominguez	.952	17	16	4	1	1
Heyward	1.000	4	6	0	0	0
C. Johnson	.931	51	49	5	4	0
Lee	.974	60	93	2	2	0
Miles	1.000	2	5	0	0	0
Parliament	.955	25	20	1	1	0
Shults	.982	38	52	3	1	1

GULF COAST LEAGUE

ORGANIZATION STATISTICS

BATTING

BATTING	B-T	HT	WT	DOB	AVG	vLH	vRH	G	AB	R	H	2B	3B	HR	RBI	BB	HBP	SH	SF	SO	SB	CS	SLG	OBP
Berres, David	L-R	6-1	185	12-16-86	.169	.211	.150	45	118	14	20	0	0	0	3	11	3	3	0	36	6	3	.169	.258
Bohn, T.J.	R-R	6-5	200	1-17-80	.355	.000	.524	11	31	8	11	5	0	1	5	5	5	0	1	8	1	2	.613	.432
Canizares, Barbaro	R-R	6-3	210	11-21-79	.545	.667	.400	4	11	1	6	0	0	1	2	4	0	0	1	0	0	0	.818	.667
Dixon, Dennis	L-R	6-4	190	1-11-85	.188	.091	.238	24	64	7	12	1	1	0	6	14	1	0	0	18	5	0	.234	.342
Elorriaga-Matra, Daniel	R-R	6-0	185	12-28-88	.143	.071	.179	17	42	1	6	1	0	0	3	2	1	0	1	9	1	0	.167	.196
Freeman, Frederick	L-R	6-5	220	9-12-89	.268	.227	.285	59	224	24	60	7	0	6	30	7	2	0	1	33	1	2	.379	.295
Fuller, Chais	R-R	5-11	200	8-11-84	.175	.280	.139	36	97	11	17	5	0	0	4	7	4	1	0	24	1	3	.227	.259
Gilmore, Jon	R-R	6-3	195	8-23-88	.284	.295	.280	43	162	11	46	5	1	1	29	4	0	0	3	28	0	0	.346	.296
Gress, Randy	R-R	6-3	180	12-6-84	.103	.130	.086	25	58	6	6	1	0	1	6	4	2	0	2	15	1	0	.172	.182
Hamaoka, Takumi	L-R	6-1	185	9-4-86	.212	.185	.224	41	85	11	18	3	0	0	6	3	0	1	1	20	1	0	.247	.236
Henry, Rashod	R-R	5-11	175	8-26-88	.279	.200	.317	21	61	6	17	1	0	0	2	0	0	2	0	13	7	4	.295	.279
Heyward, Jason	L-L	6-4	220	8-9-89	.296	.300	.294	8	27	1	8	4	0	1	5	2	1	0	1	4	1	1	.556	.355
Kennelly, Mathew	R-R	6-1	180	3-21-89	.215	.296	.188	39	107	10	23	4	0	2	10	5	3	0	0	19	0	0	.308	.270
Maddox, Chadwick	R-R	5-11	190	4-5-86	.186	.156	.200	35	102	4	19	3	0	0	5	8	2	0	1	21	1	1	.216	.257
Miles, Kuyaunnis	L-R	5-11	175	5-15-87	.128	.160	.119	43	109	4	14	2	1	0	3	3	3	0	1	57	8	2	.165	.172
Monk, Brandon	R-R	5-11	180	2-22-87	.182	.200	.176	8	22	2	4	1	0	0	1	3	0	0	0	8	0	0	.227	.280
Parra, Camilo	R-R	6-3	170	11-9-86	.217	.222	.215	41	92	16	20	1	0	3	7	5	4	0	0	31	2	0	.326	.287
Redden Jr., Ray	R-R	6-2	200	1-3-84	.125	.000	.200	10	8	0	1	0	0	0	0	1	0	0	0	2	0	0	.125	.222
Reyes, Cesar	R-R	5-11	205	4-7-83	.111	.000	.154	14	18	0	2	0	0	0	1	0	0	0	0	5	0	0	.111	.111
Shimabukuro, Ryohei	L-R	6-0	205	9-1-89	.198	.250	.175	34	81	10	16	3	0	3	8	2	0	0	14	0	0	.346	.217
Sime, Samuel	R-R	6-2	180	4-20-87	.295	.317	.287	56	217	35	64	15	0	5	33	7	1	0	5	28	10	2	.433	.313
Spiers, Joseph	R-R	5-9	190	1-17-86	.225	.214	.230	39	102	18	23	1	0	0	4	18	2	1	0	21	9	3	.235	.352
Sucre, Jesus	R-R	6-0	200	4-30-88	.221	.235	.214	40	104	8	23	5	0	0	14	7	0	1	2	10	1	1	.269	.265

PITCHING

PITCHING	B-T	HT	WT	DOB	W	L	ERA	G	GS	CG	SV	IP	H	R	ER	HR	BB	SO	AVG	vLH	vRH	K/9	BB/9
Barrett, Eric	L-L	6-2	180	12-19-86	1	2	1.36	8	5	0	0	33	33	14	5	0	11	46	.262	.310	.247	12.55	3.00
Brewer, Caleb	R-R	6-3	205	2-2-89	0	1	4.68	11	4	0	0	33	31	22	17	3	24	23	.248	.256	.244	6.34	6.61
Castro, Yeliar	R-R	6-3	180	12-3-87	1	1	2.79	8	6	0	0	29	28	14	9	2	10	20	.246	.220	.266	6.21	3.10
Cho, Jang Ji	R-R	6-1	210	7-11-83	0	0	0.00	2	0	0	0	3	1	0	0	0	0	5	.100	.000	.167	15.00	0.00
Davis, Kevin	R-R	6-1	205	2-13-84	1	1	2.25	14	0	0	0	24	22	8	6	0	16	23	.244	.216	.264	8.62	6.00
Figueroa, Steven	R-R	6-0	215	5-1-88	2	5	5.63	12	9	0	0	48	47	32	30	10	13	44	.257	.321	.202	8.25	2.44
Garcia, Ysidro	R-R	6-0	165	5-15-87	0	4	8.16	11	0	0	0	14	24	20	13	2	14	5	.333	.273	.385	3.14	8.79
Gonzalez, Raul	R-R	6-2	155	7-12-85	1	0	9.75	5	0	0	0	12	18	13	13	1	5	8	.353	.429	.300	6.00	3.75
Gress, Randy	R-R	6-3	180	12-6-84	0	0	0.00	1	0	0	0	1	0	0	0	0	0	0	.500	1.000	.000	0.00	0.00
Hyde, Lee	R-L	6-2	185	2-14-85	0	1	1.50	3	3	0	0	6	3	1	1	0	1	6	.158	.000	.188	9.00	1.50
Kent, Steve	L-L	6-0	170	5-8-89	3	2	3.86	13	10	0	0	56	52	31	24	10	12	44	.241	.200	.246	7.07	1.93
Lagua, Eligio	R-R	6-4	180	3-29-87	0	3	5.28	14	2	0	0	29	36	21	17	3	17	22	.308	.326	.297	6.83	5.28
McMillan, Clayton	L-L	6-3	180	9-19-86	1	1	4.50	10	0	0	2	14	19	10	7	4	4	13	.322	.333	.321	8.36	2.57
Murillo, Eliezer	R-R	6-4	200	10-21-88	1	2	7.18	15	0	0	1	26	21	23	21	4	15	14	.221	.268	.185	4.78	5.13
Parra, Camilo	R-R	6-3	170	11-9-86	0	0	—	1	0	0	0	3	3	0	0	0	5	0	.000	.000	—	—	
Paulino, Angelo	R-R	6-4	190	12-15-86	2	4	4.71	12	8	0	0	42	39	26	22	5	22	46	.241	.247	.235	9.86	4.71
Pruneda, Benino	R-R	5-9	170	8-8-88	0	0	0.00	3	0	0	0	6	6	0	0	0	1	8	.273	.200	.333	12.00	1.50
Railsback, Cody	R-R	6-4	175	6-3-87	1	3	3.95	7	1	0	0	14	14	9	6	2	5	14	.264	.318	.226	9.22	3.29
Reid, Rico	R-R	5-11	218	9-24-88	0	0	0.00	1	0	0	0	2	1	0	0	0	1	3	.167	.000	.200	13.50	4.50
Rodriguez, Santos	L-L	6-5	180	1-2-88	0	1	6.67	12	0	0	2	28	29	25	21	3	21	35	.248	.087	.287	11.12	6.67
Rojas, Junior	R-R	6-2	175	4-8-87	3	3	4.26	7	6	0	0	32	33	15	15	3	10	28	.270	.154	.325	7.96	2.84
Shaffer, Jared	R-R	6-2	170	3-27-86	0	1	3.20	8	0	0	2	20	22	8	7	1	10	15	.289	.370	.245	6.86	4.58
Small, Matthew	R-R	6-3	185	12-29-87	0	3	4.91	10	0	0	1	15	15	12	8	0	6	18	.250	.273	.237	11.05	3.68
Smith, Dan	L-L	6-5	250	9-9-83	0	1	1.80	2	2	0	0	5	3	2	1	0	0	5	.158	.000	.167	9.00	0.00
Stockman, Phil	R-R	6-8	250	1-25-80	0	0	7.20	3	0	0	0	5	5	4	4	0	1	9	.250	.429	.154	16.20	1.80
Sturtze, Tanyon	R-R	6-5	230	10-12-70	0	2	27.00	2	2	0	0	1	2	2	2	0	2	1	.667	.000	1.000	13.50	27.00
Wohlever, Terrence	L-L	5-11	200	1-10-87	0	2	12.00	7	0	0	0	9	18	12	12	2	3	15	.400	.286	.421	15.00	3.00

FIELDING

Catcher

Catcher	PCT	G	PO	A	E	DP	PB
Elorriaga	1.000	11	52	3	0	0	3
Kennelly	.996	31	205	19	1	1	3
Redden Jr.	1.000	4	6	1	0	0	1
Reyes	1.000	12	23	1	0	0	1
Sucre	.985	33	170	24	3	1	6

First Base

First Base	PCT	G	PO	A	E	DP
Canizares	1.000	1	5	1	0	0
Freeman	.995	51	391	22	2	52
Fuller	1.000	1	4	0	0	1
Shimabukuro	.988	14	77	2	1	2

Second Base

Second Base	PCT	G	PO	A	E	DP
Fuller	.980	16	14	34	1	9
Gress	.979	14	16	31	1	9
Monk	.966	8	15	13	1	3
Parra	—	1	0	0	0	0
Spiers	.945	34	46	91	8	22
Sucre	1.000	1	1	0	0	0

Third Base

Third Base	PCT	G	PO	A	E	DP
Freeman	.786	5	3	8	3	0
Fuller	—	1	0	0	0	0
Gilmore	.841	40	19	55	14	6
Sime	.860	15	8	29	6	5
Sucre	.750	1	0	3	1	0

Shortstop

Shortstop	PCT	G	PO	A	E	DP
Fuller	.954	15	22	40	3	12
Gress	.935	8	13	16	2	5
Sime	.904	40	72	97	18	23
Spiers	1.000	1	1	1	0	1

Outfield

Outfield	PCT	G	PO	A	E	DP
Berres	.986	42	71	2	1	0
Bohn	1.000	7	15	0	0	0
Dixon	.976	24	41	0	1	0
Hamaoka	.957	31	44	1	2	0
Henry	1.000	14	23	0	0	0
Heyward	1.000	6	11	1	0	1
Maddox	.921	30	35	0	3	0
Miles	.955	36	41	1	2	0
Parra	.980	37	50	0	1	0

ORGANIZATION STATISTICS

DOMINICAN SUMMER LEAGUE

BATTING	B-T	HT	WT	DOB	AVG	vLH	vRH	G	AB	R	H	2B	3B	HR	RBI	BB	HBP	SH	SF	SO	SB	CS	SLG	OBP
Almanzar, Ricardo	L-L	6-3	200	11-5-88	.264	.240	.270	42	140	9	37	9	0	1	15	10	3	0	1	36	1	1	.350	.325
Berroa, Nilson	R-R	5-11	156	12-30-87	.224	.237	.221	62	210	28	47	7	0	0	17	29	10	3	1	37	11	3	.257	.344
Campusano, Albaro	R-R	5-11	175	12-14-86	.349	.333	.352	31	109	21	38	2	0	2	15	17	4	1	1	12	3	3	.422	.450
Caraballo, Eduardo	R-R	6-0	170	6-14-87	.248	.269	.243	47	137	22	34	5	2	1	14	13	3	3	0	40	14	3	.336	.327
Concepcion, Angelito	R-R	5-11	168	8-27-89	.182	.500	.111	5	11	3	2	1	0	0	2	2	0	0	0	6	2	0	.273	.308
De Los Santos, Ramon	R-R	6-0	187	12-26-89	.109	.200	.089	21	55	5	6	0	0	0	2	12	4	0	0	12	1	1	.109	.310
Estevez, Juan	R-R	6-2	145	9-27-87	.273	.231	.278	32	110	15	30	3	2	2	14	10	5	0	0	25	5	2	.391	.360
Falcon, Daniel	R-R	6-1	195	12-27-88	.272	.314	.264	60	213	29	58	8	3	6	31	18	7	0	1	67	5	4	.423	.347
Feliz, Anthony	R-R	6-2	195	10-7-87	.279	.310	.273	51	190	31	53	16	4	3	30	10	10	1	0	33	3	1	.453	.348
Garibaldi, Abdiel	B-R	6-0	175	2-8-89	.272	.294	.266	31	81	12	22	4	0	0	7	5	6	0	0	13	1	0	.321	.359
Hernandez, Deivi	R-R	6-3	180	9-3-86	.194	.125	.207	29	98	12	19	5	0	1	11	9	3	0	0	31	1	2	.276	.282
Martinez, Andrewis	R-R	5-10	175	2-14-88	.278	.370	.247	36	108	15	30	3	1	0	8	8	3	4	0	25	5	3	.324	.345
Marval, Osman	B-R	6-1	185	11-26-86	.308	.231	.327	53	133	22	41	10	2	0	21	26	0	0	2	17	3	0	.414	.416
Medina, Erick	R-R	6-0	170	7-15-87	.244	.350	.229	50	164	29	40	15	2	0	14	5	8	3	2	29	6	0	.360	.296
Odreman, Alberto	R-R	6-3	194	3-12-89	.250	.412	.213	29	92	6	23	7	0	0	10	7	2	0	1	20	1	2	.326	.314
Puello, Ramon	R-R	6-3	185	8-31-88	.067	.083	.061	17	45	3	3	1	0	0	4	0	1	0	2	18	1	0	.089	.083
Rivera, Wilson	R-R	6-0	170	10-30-89	.221	.310	.196	41	131	27	29	5	1	0	6	19	0	1	1	30	7	3	.275	.318
Severino, Miguel	B-R	5-11	200	6-22-87	.255	.300	.244	34	98	9	25	5	0	0	10	13	5	0	1	25	1	4	.306	.368
Theran, Miguel	R-R	5-9	150	1-5-90	.158	.143	.167	8	19	1	3	2	0	0	2	1	1	0	0	7	2	1	.263	.238
Vizcaya, Johnder	R-R	6-0	176	2-18-89	.352	.190	.386	34	122	19	43	7	0	1	15	17	1	1	0	25	4	2	.434	.436

PITCHING	B-T	HT	WT	DOB	W	L	ERA	G	GS	CG	SV	IP	H	R	ER	HR	BB	SO	AVG	vLH	vRH	K/9	BB/9
Acosta, Jose	R-R	6-7	184	10-15-88	1	1	5.68	15	0	0	0	19	17	18	12	1	13	13	.210	.263	.194	6.16	6.16
Alvarez, Danilo	R-R	6-0	190	1-14-90	4	2	2.72	18	1	0	0	40	29	21	12	1	15	25	.195	.211	.189	5.67	3.40
Avilan, Luis	L-L	6-2	165	7-19-89	6	3	2.44	14	13	0	0	70	54	23	19	4	16	71	.213	.364	.206	9.13	2.06
de Luna, Luis	R-R	6-1	175	6-18-90	0	0	5.29	9	3	0	1	17	20	13	10	1	10	9	.299	.200	.316	4.76	5.29
Delgado, Dimaster	L-L	6-2	180	3-3-89	3	3	2.43	13	12	0	0	59	49	31	16	1	12	86	.217	.333	.209	13.04	1.82
Delgado, Randall	R-R	6-3	165	2-9-90	1	2	2.00	11	10	0	0	45	34	12	10	2	12	50	.213	.162	.228	10.00	2.40
Diaz, Grabiel	R-R	6-2	190	2-11-88	3	3	2.75	26	0	0	12	36	29	16	11	0	9	29	.220	.273	.202	7.25	2.25
Escobar, Reidy	R-R	6-4	170	11-27-89	1	0	27.00	1	0	0	0	1	3	3	3	1	0	0	.500	.500	.500	0.00	0.00
Garcia, Ysidro	R-R	6-0	165	5-15-87	1	1	1.20	10	0	0	2	15	6	2	2	0	5	9	.120	.111	.122	5.40	3.00
Herrera, Saskuel	R-R	6-1	175	11-15-89	0	0	9.39	8	0	0	0	8	7	10	8	0	9	5	.219	.250	.208	5.87	10.57
Lopez, Daniel	R-R	6-1	170	5-16-87	3	4	1.17	16	2	0	3	46	20	15	6	1	15	37	.130	.119	.134	7.19	2.91
Nunez, Edwin	R-R	6-2	146	1-18-89	4	0	3.38	14	1	0	0	19	17	10	7	2	15	7	.233	.154	.250	3.38	7.23
Paulino, Jorge	R-R	6-2	200	7-8-89	0	1	1.29	5	1	0	0	7	3	3	1	0	3	7	.136	.000	.167	9.00	3.86
Reyes, Marcos	R-R	6-1	168	11-16-88	0	2	4.15	9	0	0	0	17	9	10	8	1	16	18	.158	.083	.178	9.35	8.31
Rodriguez, Junior	R-R	6-0	189	2-8-89	0	4	5.23	22	2	0	1	33	30	34	19	2	28	22	.238	.250	.235	6.06	7.71
Surinach, Julio	R-R	6-1	157	7-29-88	4	2	2.11	15	9	0	0	60	35	22	14	1	15	49	.170	.179	.167	7.39	2.26
Vargas, Adrian	R-L	6-4	165	5-7-88	2	1	3.12	20	3	0	0	40	38	26	14	1	25	34	.241	.273	.238	7.59	5.58
Vega, Manuel	R-R	6-2	157	9-14-89	4	2	2.40	12	11	0	0	56	53	25	15	0	10	41	.252	.244	.254	6.55	1.60

FIELDING

Catcher	PCT	G	PO	A	E	DP	PB
De Los Santos	.994	21	138	21	1	1	5
Delgado	1.000	2	6	1	0	0	0
Garibaldi	.985	30	171	23	3	1	4
Marval	.972	32	211	28	7	1	7
Severino	1.000	1	1	0	0	0	0

First Base	PCT	G	PO	A	E	DP
Almanzar	.980	27	188	7	4	10
Caraballo	1.000	1	1	0	0	0
Estevez	.962	11	71	5	3	2
Garibaldi	1.000	1	0	1	0	0
Marval	.991	23	112	3	1	6
Puello	1.000	1	2	0	0	0

	PCT	G	PO	A	E	DP
Severino	.971	31	224	14	7	16
Vizcaya	1.000	1	4	0	0	0

Second Base	PCT	G	PO	A	E	DP
Berroa	1.000	9	15	14	0	1
Campusano	.936	29	66	80	10	13
Martinez	.892	16	32	34	8	5
Vizcaya	.885	20	38	39	10	5

Third Base	PCT	G	PO	A	E	DP
Campusano	.875	3	3	4	1	0
Estevez	.821	7	6	17	5	0
Falcon	.813	60	36	133	39	8
Vizcaya	1.000	2	2	4	0	0

Shortstop	PCT	G	PO	A	E	DP
Berroa	.944	53	90	130	13	18
Concepcion	.833	4	3	7	2	2
Estevez	.914	15	27	37	6	4

Outfield	PCT	G	PO	A	E	DP
Caraballo	.979	42	44	2	1	1
Feliz	.946	46	65	5	4	0
Hernandez	.941	26	30	2	2	1
Medina	.952	45	59	1	3	0
Odreman	.967	24	27	2	1	0
Puello	1.000	9	6	1	0	0
Rivera	.968	36	55	5	2	1

Baltimore Orioles

BY ROCH KUBATKO

With so little changing for the Orioles in the American League East standings, they decided certain aspects of the organization no longer could stay the same. Gone are pitching coach Leo Mazzone, bench coach Tom Trebelhorn and first-base coach Sam Mejias. Gone is vice president of baseball operations Jim Duquette, who resigned in October.

The shake-up began during the summer, with bullpen coach Dave Trembley replacing Sam Perlozzo as manager and Andy MacPhail joining the front office as president of baseball operations. But nothing could prevent the Orioles from suffering a 10th consecutive losing season.

Trembley, who never managed or coached in the majors until joining Perlozzo's staff this season, took over on June 18. The Orioles went 21-15 through July 31, but finished 19-38 after Aug. 1.

Having the 12th-highest payroll in baseball did little for the Orioles, whose 69-93 record was their worst since 2002 and tied for third-worst in the majors. They finished fourth for the ninth time in 10 seasons. An 11-28 skid came immediately after the Orioles removed Trembley's interim tag.

"I wish it would have turned out different for a lot of reasons and a lot of people," Trembley said. "Mainly for the fans and the players, not for me."

Injuries attacked the rotation with vigor and forced the team to use 27 pitchers, leading to a 5.17 ERA that ranked 13th in a 14-team league. The Orioles posted a 6.89 ERA in September, the majors' worst mark in that month in 51 seasons.

Lefthander Erik Bedard was on a Cy Young pace before missing the last five weeks with a strained oblique muscle. His 221 strikeouts eclipsed Mike Mussina's single-season team record of 218. Rookie righthander Jeremy Guthrie was sidelined by the same injury. Lefthander Adam Loewen was placed on the disabled list May 4 and had surgery to repair a fractured left elbow. Righthander Steve Trachsel didn't pitch from June 30 to July 20, and later was traded to the Cubs.

By the final month, the Orioles' rotation included journeymen righthanders Victor Zambrano and Victor Santos whose contracts were purchased from other clubs out of desperation. Rookie righthander Radhames Liz was rushed from Double-A Bowie and made four starts among his nine appearances.

The Orioles spent $42 million on four relievers over the winter, but they released Scott Williamson and got very little from set-up man Danys Baez (0-6, 6.44) before he underwent Tommy John surgery on his right elbow. Closer Chris Ray also is expected to miss 2008 after undergoing the same procedure. The bullpen's 5.71 ERA n 2007 was the highest in team history and second-worst in the majors.

A 1-8 homestand that began June 8 cost Perlozzo his job, but the Orioles sank even lower. They went 1-9 from Aug. 21-30, the worst 10-game homestand in club history. They allowed a club-record 100 runs, 30 of them coming in an historic loss to the Rangers. The Orioles allowed 10 runs or more in 18 games and five runs or more in an inning 24 times.

Shortstop Miguel Tejada's consecutive-games streak, the longest active in the majors, ended at 1,152 when the Orioles placed him on the DL June 22 with a fractured left wrist. He didn't play again until July 27, and hinted again that he'd prefer to be traded with two years remaining on his contract.

PLAYERS OF THE YEAR

MAJOR LEAGUE: ERIK BEDARD, LHP

Before a strained right oblique ended his season in late August, Bedard was a strikeout machine, leading all of baseball 10.93 strikeouts per nine innings. His 221 strikeouts ranked fourth in baseball, and his 3.16 ERA ranked third in the American League. Bedard also led the Orioles with 13 wins, and 6.97 hits per nine innings.

MINOR LEAGUE: RADHAMES LIZ, RHP

Armed with a 100 mph fastball, Liz struck out 161 batters in 137 innings for Double-A Bowie. His strikeouts ranked second in the Eastern League, while his 3.22 ERA was third in the EL. The crowning jewel of his year came when Liz threw a no-hitter against Harrisburg.

ORGANIZATIONAL LEADERS

BATTING		★Minimum 250 at-bats
★AVG	House, J.R., Norfolk	.298
R	Figueroa, Daniel, Delmarva	75
H	Cervenak, Mike, Norfolk	157
TB	Salazar, Oscar, Bowie	263
2B	Salazar, Oscar, Bowie	39
3B	Fahey, Brandon, Norfolk	8
HR	Jimenez, Luis A., Bowie	22
HR	Salazar, Oscar, Bowie	22
RBI	Salazar, Oscar, Bowie	96
BB	Figueroa, Daniel, Delmarva	68
SO	Cepicky, Matt, Norfolk/Bowie	118
SB	Figueroa, Daniel, Delmarva	35
★OBP	Figueroa, Daniel, Delmarva	.398
★SLG	Tripp, Brandon, Delmarva	.531

PITCHING		^Minimum 75 innings
W	Anderson, Craig, Bowie/Norfolk	12
L	Johnson, Jim, Norfolk	12
^ERA	Olson, Garrett, Norfolk	3.16
G	Green, Steve, Norfolk	52
G	Miller, Jim, Bowie/Norfolk	52
CG	Spoone, Chorye, Frederick	3
SV	Doyne, Cory, Norfolk	29
IP	Anderson, Craig, Bowie/Norfolk	167
BB	Waters, Chris, Norfolk/Bowie	89
SO	Hernandez, David, Frederick	168
^AVG	Spoone, Chorye, Frederick	.200

Second baseman Brian Roberts batted .290/.377/.432 with 42 doubles and shared the league lead with 50 stolen bases. Right fielder Nick Markakis hit .300/.362/.485 with 23 home runs and 112 RBIs was named most valuable Oriole in his second major league season.

Only one of the Orioles' minor league affiliates qualified for the playoffs, but high Class A Frederick made it count by winning the Carolina League championship. Righthander Chorye Spoone threw two complete games to win MVP honors, allowing two runs in 18 innings. Liz was chosen as the organization's minor league pitcher of the year after going 11-4, 3.22 with 161 strikeouts in 137 innings. Low Class A Delmarva outfielder Brandon Tripp was the organization's player of the year.

General Manager: Mike Flanagan. **Farm Director:** David Stockstill. **Scouting Director:** Joe Jordan

Class	Team	League	W	L	PCT	Finish*	Manager	Affiliate Since
Majors	Baltimore	American	69	93	.426	11th (14)	Tom Trebelhorn	—
Triple-A	Norfolk Tides	International	69	74	.483	9th (14)	Gary Allenson	2007
Double-A	Bowie Baysox	Eastern	72	68	.514	4th (12)	Bien Figueroa	1993
High A	Frederick Keys	Carolina	64	74	.464	5th (8)^	Tommy Thompson	1989
Low A	Delmarva Shorebirds	South Atlantic	68	68	.500	9th (16)	Gary Kendall	1997
Short-season	Aberdeen IronBirds	New York-Penn	34	42	.447	9th (14)	Andy Etchebarren	2002
Rookie	Bluefield Orioles	Appalachian	32	36	.471	6th (9)	Alex Arias	1958
Overall 2007 Minor League Record			**339**	**362**	**.484**	**21st**		

* Finish in overall standings (No. of teams in league) ^League champion

ORGANIZATION STATISTICS

BALTIMORE ORIOLES

AMERICAN LEAGUE

BATTING	B-T	HT	WT	DOB	AVG	vLH	vRH	G	AB	R	H	2B	3B	HR	RBI	BB	HBP	SH	SF	SO	SB	CS	SLG	OBP
Bako, Paul	L-R	6-2	205	6-20-72	.205	.192	.208	60	156	13	32	3	1	1	8	15	1	1	1	50	0	1	.256	.277
Bynum, Freddie	L-R	6-1	190	3-15-80	.260	.263	.260	70	96	21	25	8	2	2	11	2	2	1	0	30	8	1	.448	.290
Castillo, Alberto	R-R	6-0	215	2-10-70	.161	.263	.000	11	31	5	5	2	0	1	3	3	0	1	1	10	0	0	.323	.229
Fahey, Brandon	L-R	6-2	170	1-18-81	.167	.000	.200	40	54	10	9	1	1	0	1	2	0	0	0	9	2	1	.222	.196
Gibbons, Jay	L-L	6-0	195	3-2-77	.230	.283	.219	84	270	28	62	14	0	6	28	15	2	0	3	52	0	0	.348	.272
Gomez, Chris	R-R	6-1	185	6-16-71	.302	.290	.310	73	169	17	51	10	1	1	16	10	0	5	1	20	1	2	.391	.339
2-team (19 Cleveland)					.297			92	222	21	66	12	1	1	21	10	0	6	2	26	1	2	.374	.325
Hernandez, Luis	B-R	5-10	180	6-26-84	.290	.300	.286	30	69	5	20	2	0	1	7	1	0	1	0	10	2	2	.362	.300
Hernandez, Ramon	R-R	6-0	235	5-20-76	.258	.250	.261	106	364	40	94	18	0	9	62	36	6	0	3	59	1	3	.382	.333
House, J.R.	R-R	5-10	210	11-11-79	.211	.077	.280	19	38	5	8	2	0	3	3	1	2	0	0	11	0	0	.500	.268
Huff, Aubrey	L-R	6-4	235	12-20-76	.280	.305	.272	151	550	68	154	34	5	15	72	48	1	0	4	87	1	1	.442	.337
Knott, Jon	R-R	6-3	240	8-4-78	.214	.000	.600	7	14	3	3	0	0	1	4	4	0	0	1	3	0	0	.429	.368
Markakis, Nick	L-L	6-2	215	11-17-83	.300	.274	.311	161	637	97	191	43	3	23	112	61	5	1	6	112	18	6	.485	.362
Millar, Kevin	R-R	6-0	215	9-24-71	.254	.250	.256	140	476	63	121	26	1	17	63	76	8	0	2	94	1	1	.420	.365
Molina, Gustavo	R-R	6-0	220	2-24-82	.222	—	.222	7	9	1	2	1	0	0	0	0	0	0	0	3	0	0	.333	.222
2-team (10 Chicago)					.111			17	27	1	3	1	0	0	1	1	0	1	1	7	0	0	.148	.138
Moore, Scott	L-R	6-2	195	11-17-83	.255	.000	.279	17	47	2	12	2	0	1	11	1	0	2	2	15	0	1	.362	.260
Mora, Melvin	R-R	5-11	200	2-2-72	.274	.254	.280	126	467	67	128	23	1	14	58	47	3	5	5	83	9	3	.418	.341
Patterson, Corey	L-R	5-9	175	8-13-79	.269	.310	.251	132	461	65	124	26	2	8	45	21	4	13	4	65	37	9	.386	.304
Payton, Jay	R-R	5-10	205	'11-22-72	.256	.285	.244	131	434	48	111	21	5	7	58	22	3	5	6	42	5	2	.376	.292
Redman, Tike	L-L	5-11	175	3-10-77	.318	.133	.373	40	132	23	42	9	2	2	16	5	0	1	1	18	7	1	.462	.341
Roberts, Brian	B-R	5-9	180	10-9-77	.290	.268	.299	156	621	103	180	42	5	12	57	89	0	2	4	99	50	7	.432	.377
Stern, Adam	L-R	5-11	185	2-12-80	—	—	—	2	0	0	0	0	0	0	0	0	0	0	0	0	0	0	—	—
Tejada, Miguel	R-R	5-9	215	5-25-76	.296	.323	.287	133	514	72	152	19	1	18	81	41	10	0	3	55	2	1	.442	.357

PITCHING	B-T	HT	WT	DOB	W	L	ERA	G	GS	CG	SV	IP	H	R	ER	HR	BB	SO	AVG	vLH	vRH	K/9	BB/9
Baez, Danys	R-R	6-1	235	9-10-77	0	6	6.44	53	0	0	3	50	50	36	36	8	29	29	.259	.346	.200	5.19	5.19
Bedard, Erik	L-L	6-1	195	3-6-79	13	5	3.16	28	28	1	0	182	141	66	64	19	57	221	.212	.229	.208	10.93	2.82
Bell, Rob	R-R	6-5	215	1-17-77	4	3	5.94	30	0	0	0	53	73	37	35	7	24	28	.327	.391	.282	4.75	4.08
Birkins, Kurt	L-L	6-2	190	8-11-80	1	2	8.13	19	2	0	0	34	52	31	31	3	14	30	.340	.345	.337	7.86	3.67
Bradford, Chad	R-R	6-5	205	9-14-74	4	7	3.34	78	0	0	2	65	77	28	24	1	16	29	.294	.321	.282	4.04	2.23
Burres, Brian	L-L	6-1	180	4-8-81	6	8	5.95	37	17	0	0	121	140	81	80	14	66	96	.288	.306	.281	7.14	4.91
Cabrera, Daniel	R-R	6-9	270	5-28-81	9	18	5.55	34	34	1	0	204	207	133	126	25	108	166	.265	.294	.236	7.31	4.76
Cabrera, Fernando	R-R	6-4	220	11-16-81	0	0	12.60	9	0	0	1	10	12	14	14	2	9	9	.293	.313	.280	8.10	8.10
2-team (24 Cleveland)					1	2	7.21	33	0	0	1	44	50	36	35	9	31	48	—	—	—	9.89	6.39
Cherry, Rocky	R-R	6-5	225	8-19-79	0	0	7.71	10	0	0	0	16	17	14	14	3	13	10	.279	.179	.364	5.51	7.16
Doyne, Cory	R-R	6-2	240	8-13-81	0	0	14.73	5	0	0	0	4	7	7	7	3	2	5	.412	.462	.250	4.91	7.36
Guthrie, Jeremy	R-R	6-1	195	4-8-79	7	5	3.70	32	26	0	0	175	165	78	72	23	47	123	.249	.255	.243	6.31	2.41
Hoey, Jim	R-R	6-6	210	12-30-82	3	4	7.30	23	0	0	0	25	25	21	20	2	18	18	.272	.351	.218	6.57	6.57
Johnson, Jim	R-R	6-5	245	6-27-83	0	0	9.00	1	0	0	0	2	3	2	2	0	2	1	.375	.333	.400	4.50	9.00
Leicester, Jon	R-R	6-3	220	2-7-79	2	3	7.59	10	5	1	0	32	36	27	27	3	13	16	.283	.242	.328	4.50	3.66
Liz, Radhames	R-R	6-2	185	6-10-83	0	2	6.93	9	4	0	0	25	25	19	19	3	23	24	.260	.244	.275	8.76	8.39
Loewen, Adam	L-L	6-5	225	4-9-84	2	0	3.56	6	6	0	0	30	27	14	12	1	26	22	.239	.227	.246	6.53	7.71
Olson, Garrett	R-L	6-1	195	10-18-83	1	3	7.79	7	7	0	0	32	42	28	28	4	28	28	.326	.261	.340	7.79	7.79
Parrish, John	L-L	5-11	210	11-26-77	2	2	5.40	45	0	0	0	42	41	26	25	2	33	36	.252	.270	.236	7.78	7.13
2-team (8 Seattle)					2	2	5.71	53	0	0	0	52	63	34	33	2	37	41	—	—	—	7.10	6.40
Ray, Chris	R-R	6-3	215	1-12-82	5	6	4.43	43	0	0	16	43	35	22	21	5	18	44	.222	.233	.212	9.28	3.80
Santos, Victor	R-R	6-2	205	10-2-76	0	2	8.16	4	3	0	0	14	20	13	13	5	10	4	.364	.348	.375	2.51	6.28
Shuey, Paul	R-R	6-3	215	9-16-70	0	1	9.82	25	0	0	1	26	33	28	28	3	21	22	.317	.355	.301	7.71	7.36
Trachsel, Steve	R-R	6-4	205	10-31-70	6	8	4.48	25	25	1	0	141	151	73	70	16	69	45	.279	.248	.303	2.88	4.41
Walker, Jamie	L-L	6-2	195	7-1-71	3	2	3.23	81	0	0	7	61	57	25	22	6	17	41	.244	.216	.268	6.02	2.49
Williams, Todd	R-R	6-3	210	2-13-71	0	2	7.53	14	0	0	0	14	19	12	12	2	4	9	.328	.429	.270	5.65	2.51
Williamson, Scott	R-R	6-0	195	2-17-76	1	0	4.40	16	0	0	0	14	12	8	7	1	8	16	.235	.353	.176	10.05	5.02
Wright, Jaret	R-R	6-2	245	12-29-75	0	3	6.97	3	3	0	0	12	12	11	8	1	9	7	.308	.300	.316	6.10	7.84
Zambrano, Victor	B-R	6-0	205	8-6-75	0	1	9.49	5	2	0	0	12	12	13	13	1	11	11	.261	.294	.241	8.03	8.03
2-team (8 Toronto)					0	3	10.17	13	4	0	0	23	32	26	26	6	22	16	—	—	—	6.26	8.61

FIELDING

Catcher

Catcher	PCT	G	PO	A	E	DP	PB
Bako	.989	57	324	24	4	5	8
Castillo	1.000	11	92	7	0	1	1
R. Hernandez	.990	104	636	44	7	4	9
House	1.000	9	31	2	0	0	1
Molina	1.000	7	12	2	0	0	0

First Base

First Base	PCT	G	PO	A	E	DP
Gomez	1.000	36	131	9	0	7
R. Hernandez	—	1	0	0	0	0
House	1.000	1	2	0	0	0
Huff	.993	51	424	24	3	41
Millar	.999	101	852	66	1	94
Moore	1.000	3	19	2	0	1

Second Base

Second Base	PCT	G	PO	A	E	DP
Bynum	1.000	4	2	7	0	0
Fahey	1.000	9	10	15	0	4
Gomez	1.000	6	8	20	0	6
Hernandez	1.000	2	4	3	0	1
Roberts	.991	154	278	457	7	110

Third Base

Third Base	PCT	G	PO	A	E	DP
Fahey	.500	2	0	1	1	0
Gomez	.948	25	13	42	3	9
House	—	2	0	0	0	0
Huff	.971	15	9	24	1	1
Moore	1.000	12	6	12	0	2
Mora	.971	120	79	260	10	18

Shortstop

Shortstop	PCT	G	PO	A	E	DP
Bynum	.967	15	13	16	1	2
Fahey	1.000	18	11	24	0	5
Gomez	1.000	10	13	31	0	9
L. Hernandez	.965	23	31	52	3	17
Tejada	.971	124	149	358	15	77

Outfield

Outfield	PCT	G	PO	A	E	DP
Bynum	1.000	27	36	2	0	0
Fahey	1.000	7	7	0	0	0
Gibbons	.975	45	78	1	2	1
L. Hernandez	—	1	0	0	0	0
Knott	1.000	2	4	0	0	0
Markakis	.994	161	303	13	2	4
Millar	1.000	3	1	0	0	0
Moore	—	1	0	0	0	0
Patterson	.990	132	281	8	3	1
Payton	.976	129	281	3	7	2
Redman	.990	37	94	1	1	1
Stern	—	2	0	0	0	0

NORFOLK TIDES

TRIPLE-A

INTERNATIONAL LEAGUE

BATTING	B-T	HT	WT	DOB	AVG	vLH	vRH	G	AB	R	H	2B	3B	HR	RBI	BB	HBP	SH	SF	SO	SB	CS	SLG	OBP
Alvarez, Gerardo	R-R	5-10	185	10-31-79	.000	.000	.000	5	13	0	0	0	0	0	1	2	0	1	0	3	0	0	.000	.133
Boucher, Sebastien	L-R	6-0	190	10-19-81	.217	.300	.170	23	83	13	18	2	0	1	11	10	1	0	2	20	3	2	.277	.302
Brown, Travis	R-R	5-11	180	8-1-80	.159	.235	.111	16	44	5	7	0	0	0	3	5	1	3	0	10	0	0	.159	.260
Castillo, Alberto	R-R	6-0	215	2-10-70	.271	.250	.277	64	203	24	55	6	0	3	24	32	0	3	2	34	0	0	.345	.367
Cepicky, Matt	L-R	6-2	215	11-10-77	.212	.100	.261	12	33	3	7	3	0	1	4	3	0	0	1	6	0	0	.394	.270
Cervenak, Mike	R-R	5-11	195	8-17-76	.283	.284	.283	140	554	69	157	25	4	15	78	22	7	0	6	80	2	0	.424	.316
Clendenin, Morgan	L-R	6-0	187	10-2-81	.250	.500	.214	6	16	2	4	2	0	1	0	0	1	0	0	2	0	0	.563	.294
Crespo, Cesar	B-R	5-11	190	5-23-79	.244	.221	.253	101	340	32	83	14	1	3	35	38	0	10	2	68	11	7	.318	.318
Dubois, Jason	R-R	6-5	245	3-26-79	.251	.279	.241	104	378	40	95	23	0	13	42	28	2	0	4	96	0	0	.415	.303
Fahey, Brandon	L-R	6-2	170	1-18-81	.236	.185	.255	91	343	37	81	8	8	2	28	30	3	4	3	46	12	5	.324	.301
Hart, Bo	R-R	5-11	175	9-27-76	.214	.235	.208	23	70	6	15	3	1	0	5	4	1	0	1	10	0	0	.286	.263
Hernandez, Luis	B-R	5-10	180	6-26-84	.273	.167	.296	9	33	4	9	0	0	0	3	0	0	1	0	5	0	0	.273	.273
House, J.R.	R-R	5-10	210	11-11-79	.298	.333	.287	110	419	52	125	32	2	11	66	43	4	0	5	59	1	5	.463	.365
Hubele, Ryan	R-R	5-11	200	9-9-80	.327	.353	.313	15	49	8	16	4	0	1	6	4	1	2	1	10	1	0	.469	.382
Knott, Jon	R-R	6-3	240	8-4-78	.250	.231	.257	87	288	42	72	15	2	13	34	48	1	0	3	80	4	2	.451	.356
Majewski, Val	L-L	6-2	220	6-14-81	.210	.182	.216	36	124	16	26	6	1	2	11	17	1	1	0	30	7	1	.323	.310
Montanez, Luis	R-R	6-2	200	12-15-81	.259	.329	.225	69	212	27	55	11	0	7	26	22	2	3	2	35	1	3	.410	.332
Payton, Jay	R-R	5-10	205	11-22-72	.250	.333	.200	2	8	3	2	1	0	0	0	1	0	0	0	1	0	0	.375	.333
Redman, Tike	L-L	5-11	175	3-10-77	.304	.203	.335	80	296	53	90	15	6	2	27	32	2	3	3	24	25	8	.416	.372
Stern, Adam	L-R	5-11	185	2-12-80	.270	.247	.278	78	289	40	78	11	6	1	23	24	1	6	2	65	17	6	.360	.326
Tiffee, Terry	B-R	6-3	225	4-21-79	.272	.263	.274	124	475	45	129	26	1	10	55	24	2	0	4	53	0	1	.394	.307
Torres, Andres	B-R	5-9	175	1-16-83	.267	.274	.265	108	393	38	105	16	0	4	41	24	1	12	5	56	22	11	.338	.307
Whiteside, Eli	R-R	6-2	220	10-22-79	.180	.235	.159	18	61	5	11	1	0	2	6	1	2	2	1	12	1	1	.295	.215
Yan, Ruddy	B-R	6-0	160	1-13-82	.149	.077	.176	14	47	4	7	0	0	0	4	1	1	0	3	5	0		.149	.231

PITCHING	B-T	HT	WT	DOB	W	L	ERA	G	GS	CG	SV	IP	H	R	ER	HR	BB	SO	AVG	vLH	vRH	K/9	BB/9
Anderson, Craig	L-L	6-3	180	10-30-80	7	3	2.98	15	15	0	0	97	85	38	32	7	16	57	.237	.299	.211	5.31	1.49
Bell, Rob	R-R	6-5	215	1-17-77	4	3	2.97	10	10	0	0	67	61	25	22	5	17	59	.241	.268	.215	7.96	2.30
Beltran, Francis	R-R	6-6	255	11-29-79	2	9	4.70	47	0	0	8	59	73	35	31	2	15	47	.298	.226	.362	7.13	2.28
Birkins, Kurt	L-L	6-2	190	8-11-80	8	4	3.07	20	19	0	0	106	102	39	36	6	38	98	.255	.145	.304	8.35	3.24
Burres, Brian	L-L	6-1	180	4-8-81	1	0	2.25	2	0	0	0	4	2	1	1	1	1	5	.143	.000	.222	11.25	2.25
Cabrera, Fernando	R-R	6-4	220	11-16-81	0	0	3.00	3	0	0	0	3	1	1	1	0	2	2	.125	.250	.000	6.00	6.00
Doyne, Cory	R-R	6-2	240	8-13-81	0	1	2.23	42	0	0	29	44	23	11	11	0	16	49	.152	.159	.148	9.95	3.25
Green, Steve	R-R	6-2	200	1-26-78	2	4	4.81	52	0	0	3	67	72	37	36	6	37	69	.280	.246	.309	9.22	4.95
Hoey, Jim	R-R	6-6	210	12-30-82	0	2	1.33	20	0	0	2	27	15	4	4	1	10	21	.167	.157	.167	13.67	3.33
Johnson, Jim	R-R	6-5	245	6-27-83	6	12	4.07	26	25	2	0	148	164	79	67	15	48	109	.278	.283	.273	6.63	2.92
Kester, Tim	R-R	6-4	202	12-1-71	9	9	4.82	28	23	0	1	127	142	76	68	10	29	69	.287	.324	.258	4.89	2.06
Leicester, Jon	R-R	6-3	220	2-7-79	3	3	2.22	13	11	0	0	65	48	22	16	5	22	54	.209	.229	.197	7.48	3.05
McCurdy, Nick	R-R	6-3	185	1-24-80	1	2	5.93	17	1	0	0	27	34	20	18	7	7	20	.293	.304	.286	6.59	2.30
Miller, Jim	R-R	6-1	200	4-28-82	1	2	4.23	22	0	0	3	28	25	13	13	3	16	30	.234	.229	.237	9.76	5.20
Mitchell, Andy	R-R	6-3	205	9-10-78	8	8	3.96	39	12	0	0	116	123	59	51	6	40	70	.276	.306	.248	5.43	3.10
Moreno, Victor	R-R	6-0	240	6-10-79	2	5	5.06	39	1	0	3	64	69	40	36	4	32	52	.279	.328	.237	7.31	4.50
Olson, Garrett	R-L	6-1	195	10-18-83	9	7	3.16	22	22	1	0	128	95	49	45	13	39	120	.208	.179	.217	8.44	2.74
Penn, Hayden	R-R	6-3	200	10-13-84	2	1	5.14	4	4	0	0	21	26	12	12	2	5	20	.313	.429	.224	8.57	2.14
Salazar, Richard	L-L	5-11	191	10-6-81	1	0	11.74	8	0	0	0	8	11	10	10	2	5	7	.333	.250	.412	8.22	5.87
Shuey, Paul	R-R	6-3	215	9-16-70	0	0	4.70	21	0	0	1	23	30	14	12	2	9	24	.313	.361	.283	9.39	3.52
Tiffee, Terry	B-R	6-3	225	4-21-79	0	0	9.00	1	0	0	1	1	1	1	1	0	1	1	.250	.000	.500	9.00	0.00
Tracey, Sean	L-R	6-1	205	11-14-80	0	1	7.53	14	0	0	0	14	12	14	12	2	17	11	.218	.357	.171	6.91	10.67
Waters, Chris	L-L	6-0	170	8-17-80	0	0	3.00	1	1	0	0	6	9	2	2	0	3	3	.360	.333	.375	4.50	4.50
Williams, Todd	R-R	6-3	210	2-13-71	1	0	0.00	9	0	0	1	12	7	1	0	0	1	7	.171	.214	.148	5.40	0.77

FIELDING

Catcher	PCT	G	PO	A	E	DP	PB
Castillo	.996	63	470	29	2	4	9
Clendenin	.974	5	37	1	1	1	0
House	.992	51	337	26	3	4	5
Hubele	.988	14	79	5	1	0	0
Whiteside	.993	15	128	10	1	0	2

First Base	PCT	G	PO	A	E	DP
Cepicky	.889	1	8	0	1	1
Cervenak	.994	96	858	60	6	64
Dubois	1.000	1	1	0	0	0
House	.987	24	218	17	3	22
Knott	.976	13	112	9	3	9
Tiffee	1.000	11	100	9	0	7

Second Base	PCT	G	PO	A	E	DP
Alvarez	.889	1	1	7	1	1
Crespo	.994	33	57	111	1	23
Fahey	.982	15	19	35	1	7

	PCT	G	PO	A	E	DP
Hart	.982	23	38	72	2	18
Torres	.974	76	110	194	8	35

Third Base	PCT	G	PO	A	E	DP
Alvarez	1.000	3	2	9	0	1
Brown	.900	3	3	6	1	0
Cervenak	.941	24	18	46	4	1
Crespo	.833	2	3	12	3	1
Tiffee	.962	109	86	215	12	21

Shortstop	PCT	G	PO	A	E	DP
Brown	1.000	14	22	47	0	7
Crespo	.951	21	27	51	4	15
Fahey	.965	75	97	207	11	31
Hernandez	1.000	9	19	26	0	8
Torres	.972	31	41	96	4	20

Outfield	PCT	G	PO	A	E	DP
Alvarez	—	1	0	0	0	0

	PCT	G	PO	A	E	DP
Boucher	1.000	23	56	1	0	0
Cepicky	1.000	2	4	0	0	0
Cervenak	1.000	2	5	0	0	0
Crespo	1.000	38	72	3	0	2
Dubois	.989	57	88	3	1	0
Fahey	1.000	2	3	0	0	0
Hubele	.667	1	2	0	1	0
Knott	1.000	63	102	7	0	1
Majewski	.970	31	63	2	2	0
Montanez	.981	64	102	3	2	1
Payton	—	1	0	0	0	0
Redman	.980	75	143	3	3	1
Stern	.987	75	150	5	2	2
Yan	.963	12	26	0	1	0

BOWIE BAYSOX

DOUBLE-A

EASTERN LEAGUE

BATTING

	B-T	HT	WT	DOB	AVG	vLH	vRH	G	AB	R	H	2B	3B	HR	RBI	BB	HBP	SH	SF	SO	SB	CS	SLG	OBP
Andrews, Robert	R-R	6-0	200	12-23-83	.281	.667	.241	13	32	4	9	0	0	0	3	0	3	1	0	8	1	1	.281	.343
Bass, Bryan	B-R	6-1	190	4-12-82	.227	.235	.224	107	339	51	77	18	0	11	36	34	3	7	2	116	16	4	.378	.302
Bock, Brian	R-R	6-1	210	8-24-81	.203	.333	.145	24	79	6	16	3	0	0	5	5	1	1	1	10	0	0	.241	.256
Brown, Travis	R-R	5-11	180	8-1-80	.087	.111	.071	10	23	2	2	2	0	0	3	3	1	1	0	8	0	0	.174	.222
Bynum, Freddie	L-R	6-1	190	3-15-80	.000	—	.000	1	3	0	0	0	0	0	0	0	0	0	0	2	0	0	.000	.000
Cepicky, Matt	L-R	6-2	215	11-10-77	.240	.179	.262	104	362	46	87	21	4	15	54	41	1	0	6	112	1	2	.445	.315
Clendenin, Morgan	L-R	6-1	187	10-2-81	.221	.200	.224	20	68	3	15	3	0	1	9	1	1	0	1	17	0	0	.309	.239
Davis, Blake	L-R	5-11	160	12-22-83	.209	.111	.227	35	115	12	24	7	0	0	10	9	0	4	1	25	1	1	.270	.264
Figueroa, Paco	R-R	5-11	182	2-19-83	.280	.240	.291	95	350	60	98	19	2	1	19	43	4	9	0	52	15	11	.354	.365
Fiorentino, Jeff	L-R	6-1	185	4-14-83	.282	.217	.303	126	436	68	123	18	4	15	65	44	1	10	5	89	8	4	.445	.346
Hernandez, Luis	B-R	5-10	180	6-26-84	.242	.303	.219	92	364	42	88	15	6	0	37	18	1	6	4	50	6	5	.316	.276
Hubele, Ryan	R-R	5-11	200	9-9-80	.206	.273	.175	63	209	30	43	9	1	6	21	13	1	4	3	44	2	1	.344	.252
Jimenez, Luis Antonio	L-L	6-4	205	5-7-82	.328	.284	.340	90	320	57	105	18	0	22	79	41	0	0	5	71	1	1	.591	.399
Maestrales, Pete	B-R	5-11	190	7-4-79	.217	.000	.227	8	23	3	5	3	0	0	2	2	0	0	0	5	0	0	.348	.280
Majewski, Val	L-L	6-2	220	6-19-81	.295	.319	.286	91	332	49	98	23	3	3	42	31	4	1	4	65	6	4	.410	.358
Molina, Gustavo	R-R	6-0	220	2-24-82	.364	.389	.356	22	77	5	28	4	0	0	6	3	0	0	10	0	0	.416	.388
Montanez, Luis	R-R	6-2	200	12-15-81	.339	.414	.315	31	121	24	41	2	0	3	11	10	2	2	0	16	3	2	.430	.398
Pulley, Matthew	L-R	6-3	200	5-15-85	.000	—	.000	1	3	1	0	0	0	0	0	0	0	0	0	2	0	0	.000	.250
Reimold, Nolan	R-R	6-4	207	10-12-83	.306	.341	.296	50	186	30	57	15	0	11	34	17	0	0	0	47	2	3	.565	.365
Salazar, Oscar	R-R	6-1	205	6-27-78	.289	.232	.307	136	532	73	154	39	2	22	96	26	3	1	4	77	3	3	.494	.324
Sing, Brandon	R-R	6-5	215	3-13-81	.187	.185	.188	64	214	17	40	10	0	2	14	13	0	0	2	57	3	1	.262	.231
Tejada, Miguel	R-R	5-9	215	5-25-76	.000	—	.000	1	3	0	0	0	0	0	0	0	0	0	0	0	0	0	.000	.000
Whiteside, Eli	R-R	6-2	220	10-22-79	.291	.226	.309	42	141	18	41	7	4	4	30	8	2	3	2	32	0	3	.482	.333
Yan, Ruddy	B-R	6-0	160	1-13-82	.263	.239	.270	98	373	52	98	14	3	3	22	32	1	4	2	39	10	10	.340	.321

PITCHING

	B-T	HT	WT	DOB	W	L	ERA	G	GS	CG	SV	IP	H	R	ER	HR	BB	SO	AVG	vLH	vRH	K/9	BB/9
Alvarez, Oscar	L-L	6-0	165	9-17-80	11	7	5.20	25	24	0	0	135	131	88	78	16	57	67	.256	.213	.271	4.47	3.80
Anderson, Craig	L-L	6-3	180	10-30-80	5	1	5.27	13	13	0	0	70	85	42	41	11	21	38	.315	.271	.327	4.89	2.70
Baez, Danys	R-R	6-1	235	9-10-77	0	0	2.25	3	0	0	0	4	3	1	1	1	1	2	4	.231	.125	.400	9.00	4.50
Basilio, Manny	R-R	6-3	218	10-20-79	0	0	0.00	2	0	0	0	1	1	0	0	0	0	2	.200	.000	.250	13.50	0.00
Brown, Travis	R-R	5-11	180	8-1-80	0	0	0.00	1	0	0	0	0	0	0	0	0	0	0	.000	.000	.000	0.00	0.00
Deza, Fredy	R-R	6-2	175	12-11-82	7	8	4.43	36	16	0	0	124	131	70	61	22	43	101	.270	.279	.261	7.33	3.12
Garcia, Rosman	R-R	6-2	215	1-3-79	3	5	5.97	33	8	0	1	86	108	68	57	6	38	57	.309	.292	.324	5.97	3.98
Haehnel, David	L-L	6-4	200	7-21-82	2	1	6.00	40	0	0	0	69	70	54	46	8	47	57	.260	.267	.258	7.43	6.13
Hale, Beau	R-R	6-2	202	12-1-78	6	5	5.15	15	15	0	0	72	92	48	41	7	28	44	.317	.279	.357	5.53	3.52
Hoey, Jim	R-R	6-6	210	12-30-82	1	0	0.00	20	0	0	14	19	13	0	0	0	4	28	.200	.125	.273	13.50	1.93
Jimenez, Luis Antonio	L-L	6-4	205	5-7-82	0	0	0.00	1	0	0	0	1	0	0	0	0	0	1	.000	—	.000	9.00	0.00
Lebron, Luis	R-R	6-1	172	3-15-85	0	0	3.86	2	0	0	0	2	1	1	1	0	1	4	.125	.000	.250	15.43	3.86
Lewis Jr., Rommie	L-L	6-6	200	9-2-82	5	5	5.35	47	1	0	0	69	80	44	41	10	29	64	.294	.293	.295	8.35	3.78
Liz, Radhames	R-R	6-2	185	10-30-83	11	4	3.22	25	25	2	0	137	101	60	49	13	70	161	.204	.204	.203	10.58	4.60
McCrory, Bob	R-R	6-1	205	5-3-82	1	2	3.91	22	0	0	13	23	23	17	10	0	16	22	.247	.277	.217	8.61	6.26
McCurdy, Nick	R-R	6-3	185	1-24-80	2	4	1.66	28	1	0	3	49	36	11	9	1	15	45	.205	.250	.170	8.32	2.77
Miller, Jim	R-R	6-1	200	4-28-82	2	3	2.79	30	0	0	4	39	26	13	12	0	25	49	.188	.246	.148	11.41	5.82
Perez, Carlos	L-L	6-1	185	5-20-82	0	2	5.40	3	2	0	0	12	20	8	7	0	7	12	.370	.500	.325	9.26	5.40
Rleal, Sendy	R-R	6-1	190	6-21-80	5	3	3.40	29	0	0	1	45	34	20	17	5	19	35	.210	.259	.160	7.00	3.80
Roman, Orlando	R-R	6-1	210	11-28-78	1	1	4.24	7	3	0	0	17	19	9	8	2	11	17	.275	.308	.233	9.00	5.82
Romero, Felix	R-R	6-1	192	6-18-80	2	7	4.13	46	1	0	0	81	77	40	37	8	43	96	.250	.278	.223	10.71	4.87
Salazar, Richard	L-L	5-11	191	10-6-81	0	0	5.68	5	0	0	0	6	8	4	4	1	4	9	.308	.200	.375	12.79	5.68
Shuey, Paul	R-R	6-3	215	9-16-70	0	0	0.00	1	0	0	0	1	0	0	0	0	0	0	.000	.000	—	0.00	0.00
Waters, Chris	L-L	6-0	170	8-17-80	8	9	4.49	27	27	0	0	152	144	83	76	17	86	117	.250	.255	.249	6.91	5.08
Williamson, Scott	R-R	6-0	195	2-17-76	0	1	27.00	1	1	0	0	2	5	6	6	0	1	4	.455	.333	.500	18.00	4.50
Wright, Jaret	R-R	6-2	245	12-29-75	0	0	3.00	3	2	0	0	3	3	1	1	0	0	4	.273	.286	.250	12.00	0.00

FIELDING

Catcher	PCT	G	PO	A	E	DP	PB
Bock	.984	24	165	16	3	1	3
Clendenin	.968	11	83	8	3	0	2
Hubele	.990	48	360	20	4	4	3
Molina	.977	21	166	6	4	0	1
Whiteside	.988	40	294	27	4	6	4

First Base	PCT	G	PO	A	E	DP
Cepicky	.946	13	63	7	4	6
Clendenin	1.000	4	30	3	0	2
Hubele	.875	1	7	0	1	0
Jimenez	.976	55	418	30	11	42
Salazar	1.000	18	133	4	0	13
Sing	.993	57	388	42	3	43

Second Base	PCT	G	PO	A	E	DP
Bass	.936	18	30	43	5	10

	PCT	G	PO	A	E	DP
Brown	1.000	2	2	0	0	0
Figueroa	.972	92	191	230	12	67
Hernandez	1.000	1	3	1	0	0
Maestrales	1.000	3	5	2	0	0
Salazar	.988	21	37	42	1	12
Yan	.930	11	16	24	3	6

Third Base	PCT	G	PO	A	E	DP
Bass	.911	70	42	111	15	11
Hubele	1.000	2	3	3	0	0
Maestrales	—	1	0	0	0	0
Salazar	.910	79	48	114	16	13

Shortstop	PCT	G	PO	A	E	DP
Bass	.889	10	12	12	3	5
Brown	.929	6	9	17	2	7
Bynum	1.000	1	1	4	0	1

	PCT	G	PO	A	E	DP
Davis	.965	35	53	86	5	22
Hernandez	.969	90	125	247	12	47
Salazar	1.000	1	3	1	0	0
Tejada	1.000	1	0	3	0	0

Outfield	PCT	G	PO	A	E	DP
Andrews	1.000	11	23	1	0	1
Bass	.900	9	9	0	1	0
Cepicky	1.000	40	57	2	0	0
Fiorentino	.993	117	269	13	2	3
Hubele	1.000	4	11	0	0	0
Majewski	.987	90	215	7	3	3
Montanez	.963	30	73	4	3	1
Reimold	.978	48	87	3	2	0
Salazar	1.000	2	0	1	0	0
Yan	.982	82	153	9	3	2

FREDERICK KEYS

HIGH CLASS A

CAROLINA LEAGUE

BATTING	B-T	HT	WT	DOB	AVG	vLH	vRH	G	AB	R	H	2B	3B	HR	RBI	BB	HBP	SH	SF	SO	SB	CS	SLG	OBP
Alvarez, Gerardo	R-R	5-10	185	10-31-79	.180	.190	.175	74	206	23	37	10	0	3	22	16	11	6	2	32	3	6	.272	.272
Amador, Chris	R-R	5-10	167	12-14-82	.269	.222	.278	45	160	30	43	7	1	6	27	21	3	4	1	42	14	1	.438	.362
Bock, Brian	R-R	6-1	210	8-24-81	.227	.254	.214	64	216	28	49	9	0	5	23	19	1	1	5	32	3	4	.338	.286
Brown, Travis	R-R	5-11	180	8-1-80	.191	.224	.174	60	173	20	33	4	1	1	18	30	3	3	1	29	6	3	.243	.319
Bynum, Freddie	L-R	6-1	190	3-15-80	.235	.333	.214	5	17	3	4	0	1	0	2	1	1	0	0	4	0	0	.353	.316
Clendenin, Morgan	L-R	6-0	187	10-2-81	.275	.400	.250	16	40	8	11	4	0	1	4	3	0	1	1	8	0	0	.450	.318
Davis, Blake	L-R	5-11	160	12-22-83	.291	.292	.291	93	357	49	104	24	3	4	28	35	5	8	1	71	11	13	.409	.362
Davison, Todd	R-R	5-10	175	10-7-83	.212	.167	.238	15	33	3	7	1	0	0	2	4	0	1	0	8	0	1	.242	.297
Dillon, Zachary	L-R	5-10	210	5-18-83	.275	.264	.278	92	305	33	84	27	2	5	41	35	2	4	2	32	0	4	.426	.352
Duncan, Jacob	L-L	5-11	190	11-20-81	.256	.185	.276	90	308	38	79	13	1	2	31	19	3	14	2	46	9	2	.325	.304
Duran, Carlos	L-L	6-1	165	12-27-82	.175	.043	.228	28	80	6	14	6	0	2	8	3	0	0	0	11	2	0	.325	.205
Finan, Ryan	L-R	6-5	220	1-5-82	.284	.260	.292	113	380	52	108	24	1	10	64	55	9	1	2	74	0	3	.432	.386
Fleisher, Mark	R-R	6-4	235	9-18-83	.247	.336	.202	108	364	52	90	24	0	16	58	31	6	0	6	85	0	2	.445	.312
Henson, Tyler	R-R	6-1	190	12-15-87	.059	.000	.077	6	17	0	1	0	0	0	1	1	0	0	1	8	0	0	.059	.105
Hernandez, Ramon	R-R	6-0	235	5-20-76	.333	.500	.250	2	6	0	2	1	0	0	0	0	1	0	0	2	0	0	.500	.429
Johnson, Justin	L-R	6-1	180	11-7-82	.178	.200	.167	34	90	7	16	5	1	0	4	7	0	0	1	26	1	0	.256	.235
Jones, Kennard	L-L	5-11	185	9-8-81	.252	.202	.271	134	457	59	115	21	5	4	48	60	1	5	0	95	26	15	.346	.340
Krause, Brent	R-R	6-3	215	11-2-81	.275	.400	.241	39	138	22	38	9	0	5	20	14	2	0	0	43	1	4	.449	.351
Madera, Sandy	R-R	6-2	198	8-11-80	.262	.250	.269	12	42	4	11	3	1	1	6	5	2	0	0	5	0	1	.452	.367
Maestrales, Pete	B-R	5-11	190	7-4-79	.237	.191	.255	113	384	42	91	20	1	4	38	60	1	0	4	68	10	8	.326	.339
Nowicki, Joseph	L-L	6-2	210	11-12-82	.667	1.000	.000	1	3	0	2	0	0	0	0	0	1	0	0	0	0	0	.667	.750
Pulley, Matthew	L-R	6-3	200	1-5-82	.197	.200	.196	22	66	3	13	5	0	0	6	7	0	1	1	16	0	1	.273	.272
Rivas, Arturo	R-R	6-0	205	2-2-84	.317	.303	.322	37	123	16	39	12	1	3	17	16	1	0	1	26	2	1	.504	.397
Stephen, Jedidiah	R-R	6-2	195	4-30-84	.214	.300	.188	14	42	4	9	2	0	1	5	2	0	1	0	11	0	3	.333	.244
Tejada, Miguel	R-R	5-9	215	5-25-76	1.000	—	1.000	1	2	1	2	0	0	1	1	0	0	0	0	0	0	0	2.500	1.000
Tucker, Jonathan	R-R	5-7	170	7-2-83	.260	.258	.261	124	446	67	116	18	2	2	41	62	2	15	3	45	20	8	.323	.351
Winterling, Paul	R-R	6-3	220	7-31-83	.206	.219	.194	21	68	9	14	5	0	4	14	7	0	1	0	19	2	3	.456	.280
Yount, Dustin	L-R	6-1	198	10-27-82	.030	.000	.042	13	33	2	1	1	0	0	1	4	1	0	1	9	0	0	.061	.154

PITCHING	B-T	HT	WT	DOB	W	L	ERA	G	GS	CG	SV	IP	H	R	ER	HR	BB	SO	AVG	vLH	vRH	K/9	BB/9
Allar, Brent	R-R	6-3	230	3-1-85	0	0	9.64	3	0	0	0	5	5	5	5	1	3	3	.263	.222	.300	5.79	5.79
Alvarez, Gerardo	R-R	5-10	185	10-31-79	0	0	0.00	1	0	0	0	2	2	0	0	0	0	1	.286	.000	.667	4.50	0.00
Bascom, Timothy	R-R	6-1	205	1-4-85	1	0	3.00	2	1	0	0	6	6	2	2	0	0	4	.250	.214	.300	6.00	0.00
Basilio, Manny	R-R	6-3	218	10-20-79	2	8	6.22	19	4	0	0	51	62	36	35	6	15	40	.300	.267	.325	7.11	2.66
Baysinger, Trent	L-L	6-0	185	9-1-81	0	0	6.75	15	0	0	0	17	26	14	13	1	9	13	.338	.053	.431	6.75	4.67
Bergesen, Bradley	L-R	6-2	205	9-25-85	3	6	5.75	10	10	1	0	56	78	38	36	4	9	35	.332	.324	.335	5.59	1.44
Berken, Jason	R-R	6-0	175	11-27-83	9	9	4.53	27	26	2	0	151	160	90	76	12	49	124	.274	.280	.270	7.39	2.92
Blasko, Chadd	R-R	6-6	215	3-9-81	0	0	7.33	17	2	0	0	27	22	23	22	5	24	30	.224	.265	.203	10.00	8.00
Burch, Jason	R-R	6-5	215	10-15-82	2	0	3.06	15	0	0	5	18	16	8	6	0	8	19	.262	.211	.286	9.68	4.08
Clark, Zach	R-R	6-0	195	7-11-83	0	1	11.05	3	1	0	0	7	14	11	9	2	5	13	.438	.533	.353	1.23	3.68
Erbe, Brandon	R-R	6-4	180	12-25-87	6	8	6.26	25	25	0	0	119	127	95	83	14	62	111	.273	.297	.261	8.37	4.68
Fleisher, Mark	R-R	6-4	235	9-18-83	0	0	9.00	5	0	0	0	5	7	5	5	2	3	5	.333	.167	.400	9.00	5.40
Hernandez, David	R-R	6-3	214	5-13-85	7	11	4.95	28	27	0	0	145	130	86	80	16	47	168	.249	.271	.235	10.40	2.91
Horner, Tag	L-L	6-3	220	11-12-82	0	2	5.68	36	0	0	1	51	55	36	32	6	20	17	.272	.242	.287	3.02	3.55
Jan, Carlos	L-L	5-11	165	11-3-79	0	0	4.82	5	0	0	0	9	6	5	0	1	7	6	.265	.375	.231	6.75	9.64
Lonsberry, Daniel	R-R	6-4	200	7-6-83	6	2	3.49	43	0	0	2	67	61	33	26	3	26	65	.245	.222	.258	8.73	3.49
Maestrales, Pete	B-R	5-11	190	7-4-79	0	1	13.50	1	0	0	0	2	4	3	3	0	1	2	.444	.800	.000	9.00	4.50
McCrory, Bob	R-R	6-1	205	5-3-82	0	0	1.23	22	0	0	14	22	16	4	3	1	12	22	.205	.188	.217	9.00	4.91
Ouellette, Ryan	R-R	5-11	185	10-4-85	0	2	6.00	7	0	0	0	12	11	10	8	1	6	5	.234	.278	.207	3.75	4.50
Owen, Blake	R-R	6-3	215	10-29-83	1	1	6.21	23	0	0	2	42	54	31	29	9	20	29	.323	.359	.301	6.21	4.29
Perez, Carlos	L-L	6-1	185	5-20-82	9	7	3.80	29	11	0	4	90	84	42	38	5	44	73	.256	.190	.272	7.30	4.40
Potter, Joshua	R-R	6-4	175	4-8-83	2	4	4.87	46	3	0	1	85	103	54	46	12	23	55	.298	.280	.308	5.82	2.44
Rleal, Sendy	R-R	6-1	190	6-21-80	0	1	1.80	4	0	0	0	5	4	1	1	1	1	4	.200	.143	.231	7.20	1.80
Salazar, Richard	L-L	5-11	191	10-6-81	4	0	3.35	35	0	0	2	54	56	31	20	5	19	48	.271	.172	.309	8.05	3.19
Spoone, Chorye	R-R	6-1	215	9-16-85	10	9	3.26	26	25	3	0	152	108	65	55	8	67	133	.200	.189	.205	7.88	3.97
Thall, Chad	L-L	6-4	220	8-2-85	0	0	0.00	1	0	0	0	1	1	0	0	0	0	2	.250	.500	.000	18.00	0.00
Trachsel, Steve	R-R	6-4	205	10-31-70	0	1	2.57	1	1	0	0	7	7	3	2	0	1	4	.259	.188	.364	5.14	1.29
Williamson, Scott	R-R	6-0	195	2-17-76	0	1	13.50	2	1	0	0	2	4	3	3	0	0	2	.444	.000	.500	9.00	4.50
Wright, Jaret	R-R	6-2	245	12-29-75	0	0	1.93	1	1	0	0	3	3	1	1	0	2	6	.188	.000	.333	11.57	3.86

FIELDING

Catcher	PCT	G	PO	A	E	DP	PB
Bock	.992	46	331	35	3	3	6
Clendenin	1.000	2	11	2	0	0	0
Dillon	.986	68	502	54	8	3	16
Hernandez	1.000	1	7	0	0	0	0
Johnson	.995	26	162	20	1	0	2
Madera	1.000	1	6	1	0	0	1
Pulley	1.000	8	38	2	0	0	1
Winterling	—	1	0	0	0	0	0

First Base	PCT	G	PO	A	E	DP
Alvarez	1.000	1	1	0	0	1
Amador	1.000	1	1	0	0	0
Bock	1.000	1	1	0	0	0
Clendenin	.938	3	13	2	1	3
Dillon	1.000	1	2	0	0	0
Finan	.986	28	134	11	2	15
Fleisher	.985	98	850	57	14	82
Maestrales	.980	15	93	6	2	5
Pulley	.982	6	52	3	1	6
Yount	.963	10	75	3	3	8

Second Base	PCT	G	PO	A	E	DP
Alvarez	.980	25	39	57	2	18
Amador	1.000	4	1	3	0	0
Brown	.984	15	20	42	1	9
Bynum	.917	2	3	8	1	2
Davison	.944	10	10	24	2	4
Henson	1.000	2	3	2	0	2
Maestrales	.934	17	24	33	4	7
Stephen	1.000	1	1	2	0	0
Tucker	.973	82	157	199	10	48

Third Base	PCT	G	PO	A	E	DP
Alvarez	.930	28	10	30	3	3
Bock	—	1	0	0	0	0
Brown	.929	14	6	20	2	4
Davison	1.000	3	1	2	0	0
Finan	.923	88	50	154	17	7
Henson	.750	3	0	3	1	0
Maestrales	.895	16	7	27	4	1
Pulley	.000	2	0	0	1	0
Stephen	.862	10	4	21	4	2
Tucker	1.000	4	1	6	0	0

Shortstop	PCT	G	PO	A	E	DP
Alvarez	1.000	4	4	7	0	0
Brown	.945	32	44	112	9	27
Bynum	1.000	1	0	1	0	0
Davis	.958	91	136	299	19	54
Davison	.667	1	1	1	1	0
Henson	.714	2	0	5	2	0
Stephen	.667	1	1	1	1	0
Tejada	1.000	1	1	3	0	0
Tucker	.938	19	28	62	6	16

Outfield	PCT	G	PO	A	E	DP
Alvarez	1.000	23	25	3	0	1
Amador	.971	40	67	1	2	0
Bynum	1.000	2	8	0	0	0
Clendenin	1.000	1	1	0	0	0
Duncan	.974	71	106	7	3	0
Duran	1.000	27	38	5	0	0
Jones	.978	130	258	9	6	1
Krause	.969	37	62	1	2	0
Maestrales	.978	39	42	3	1	0
Nowicki	1.000	1	1	0	0	0
Rivas	.922	35	55	4	5	1
Tucker	1.000	24	35	4	0	2
Winterling	1.000	17	30	1	0	0
Yount	1.000	2	1	0	0	0

DELMARVA SHOREBIRDS

LOW CLASS A

SOUTH ATLANTIC LEAGUE

BATTING	B-T	HT	WT	DOB	AVG	vLH	vRH	G	AB	R	H	2B	3B	HR	RBI	BB	HBP	SH	SF	SO	SB	CS	SLG	OBP
Abreu, Miguel	R-R	6-0	190	11-14-84	.267	.311	.255	124	486	71	130	28	5	13	60	9	4	7	2	64	22	7	.426	.285
Andrews, Robert	R-R	6-0	200	12-23-83	.249	.220	.255	84	281	47	70	10	3	2	26	25	6	8	1	55	15	7	.327	.323
Bynum, Freddie	L-R	6-1	190	3-15-80	.000	—	.000	1	1	0	0	0	0	0	0	0	0	0	0	1	0	0	.000	.500
Cash, David	B-R	6-3	180	11-22-85	.262	.218	.273	112	409	49	107	19	2	1	51	20	2	9	6	91	20	8	.325	.295
Castillo, Victor	B-R	5-11	222	9-12-84	.294	.380	.271	81	231	22	68	7	0	1	27	27	3	1	3	33	3	1	.338	.371
Davison, Todd	R-R	5-10	175	10-7-83	.234	.289	.217	57	197	27	46	10	3	2	30	27	3	8	1	39	9	5	.345	.333
Figueroa, Daniel	R-R	5-11	182	2-19-83	.278	.281	.277	116	396	75	110	14	5	0	28	68	14	10	4	91	35	11	.338	.398
Florimon Jr., Pedro	B-R	6-2	165	12-10-86	.197	.200	.196	111	371	50	73	14	1	4	34	28	3	13	3	107	16	6	.272	.257
Gonzalez, Franklin	R-R	6-0	160	4-7-86	.214	—	.214	5	14	3	3	0	0	0	0	2	1	0	0	3	0	0	.214	.353
Howell, Joey	R-R	6-1	205	9-22-85	.179	.176	.179	19	56	11	10	4	0	1	5	6	4	0	0	15	3	1	.304	.303
Musslewhite, Stuart	R-R	5-11	195	3-20-82	.182	.231	.168	58	176	15	32	6	0	0	13	8	0	8	3	26	0	4	.216	.214
Pierce, Michael	R-R	6-3	185	4-19-84	.232	.320	.207	82	224	20	52	18	0	5	21	26	2	3	2	86	0	0	.379	.315
Rowell, Billy	L-R	6-5	205	9-10-88	.273	.185	.299	91	352	47	96	21	3	9	57	31	3	0	2	104	3	2	.426	.335
Silveren, Pedro	R-R	6-0	160	9-2-84	.234	.190	.250	26	77	10	18	4	0	0	5	1	2	0	1	16	5	1	.286	.298
Snyder, Brandon	R-R	6-2	210	11-23-86	.283	.267	.288	118	448	63	127	23	3	11	58	44	6	1	2	107	0	2	.422	.354
Tripp, Brandon	L-R	6-2	200	4-2-85	.288	.297	.287	104	371	72	107	25	4	19	79	43	13	1	5	112	7	1	.531	.377
Vinyard, Christopher	R-R	6-4	230	12-15-85	.269	.273	.268	129	480	61	129	34	0	16	82	48	9	0	10	115	1	0	.440	.340
Winterling, Paul	R-R	6-3	220	7-31-83	.320	.333	.313	29	100	19	32	8	2	4	11	14	0	0	2	30	5	0	.560	.397

PITCHING	B-T	HT	WT	DOB	W	L	ERA	G	GS	CG	SV	IP	H	R	ER	HR	BB	SO	AVG	vLH	vRH	K/9	BB/9
Allar, Brent	R-R	6-3	230	3-1-85	0	0	5.85	20	0	0	3	20	18	14	13	0	19	24	.247	.333	.162	10.80	8.55
Andrews, Robert	R-R	6-0	200	12-23-83	0	0	27.00	1	0	0	0	1	4	3	3	0	2	2	.571	1.000	.400	0.00	18.00
Bascom, Timothy	R-R	6-1	205	1-4-85	3	3	3.74	12	12	0	0	67	60	30	28	6	24	55	.229	.244	.217	7.35	3.21
Beato, Pedro	R-R	6-6	230	10-27-86	7	8	4.05	27	27	0	0	142	139	75	64	10	59	106	.256	.253	.258	6.70	3.73
Bergesen, Bradley	L-R	6-2	205	9-25-85	7	3	2.19	15	15	1	0	94	75	30	23	3	17	73	.214	.258	.179	6.96	1.62
Bordes, Brett	L-L	5-10	175	11-30-83	3	2	3.09	32	0	0	2	44	32	19	15	0	37	34	.212	.196	.221	7.01	7.63
Clark, Zach	R-R	6-0	195	7-11-83	2	3	3.10	10	9	1	0	58	57	30	20	2	9	37	.258	.326	.209	5.74	1.40
De Nabal, Fernando	R-R	6-3	180	6-16-84	0	4	9.00	6	4	0	0	14	13	16	14	0	27	16	.265	.294	.250	10.29	17.36
Esposito, Joseph	L-R	5-11	220	5-15-85	0	0	0.00	1	0	0	0	3	2	0	0	0	4	3	.222	.286	.000	9.00	12.00
Gallaway, Bruce	R-L	6-3	200	9-17-82	4	6	5.46	39	0	0	1	61	61	48	37	4	46	61	.256	.228	.270	9.00	6.79
Hamblet, Reid	R-R	6-1	205	9-11-83	9	3	5.54	30	6	0	1	89	91	60	55	6	63	67	.269	.291	.251	6.75	6.35
Horner, Tag	L-L	6-3	220	11-12-82	0	1	3.55	11	0	0	2	13	15	8	5	1	3	9	.294	.222	.333	6.39	2.13
Jevne, Zachary	R-R	6-7	220	8-9-82	1	0	3.00	1	1	0	0	6	2	2	2	0	3	2	.111	.143	.000	3.00	4.50
Lebron, Luis	R-R	6-1	172	3-15-85	1	2	5.04	46	0	0	5	55	48	35	31	1	55	86	.233	.209	.252	13.99	8.95
Maria, Jose	L-L	6-3	175	6-14-83	2	5	7.01	19	3	0	0	35	45	33	27	3	17	21	.315	.390	.284	5.45	4.41
Mattaliano, Mick	R-R	6-3	200	11-11-85	1	0	1.93	3	0	0	0	5	3	1	1	1	1	2	.286	.300	.273	3.86	1.93
McCurry, Cole	L-L	6-2	180	9-25-85	2	0	1.80	2	1	0	0	10	7	2	2	1	3	8	.200	.222	.192	7.20	2.70
Moore, Jeffrey	R-R	6-1	195	3-26-83	6	4	2.45	18	18	0	0	99	73	41	27	7	43	66	.206	.242	.174	6.00	3.91
Ouellette, Ryan	R-R	5-11	185	10-14-84	2	1	2.10	18	0	0	0	34	28	13	8	1	11	29	.222	.189	.247	7.60	2.88
Owen, Blake	R-R	6-3	215	10-29-83	2	2	5.40	13	0	0	0	28	32	20	17	1	17	19	.296	.357	.258	6.04	5.40
Perez, Wilfredo	L-L	6-0	145	8-12-84	5	3	1.67	27	8	0	5	81	53	18	15	3	28	108	.183	.230	.163	12.00	3.11
Schmidt, Kyle	R-R	6-3	220	8-25-83	6	8	3.37	23	23	0	0	131	125	60	49	12	38	145	.252	.289	.220	9.96	2.61
Soriano, Julio	R-R	6-2	160	9-24-83	1	2	7.45	8	0	0	0	10	12	12	8	1	13	10	.300	.214	.346	9.31	12.10
Tamba, Josh	L-R	6-2	200	11-15-84	0	3	5.82	14	10	0	0	56	63	49	36	6	32	32	.288	.275	.300	5.17	5.17
Thall, Chad	L-L	6-4	220	8-2-85	3	5	4.14	48	0	0	17	63	63	33	29	4	18	59	.259	.297	.243	8.43	2.57
Williamson, Scott	R-R	6-0	195	2-17-76	1	0	4.50	1	0	0	0	2	2	1	1	0	1	2	.250	.333	.200	9.00	4.50

FIELDING

Catcher	PCT	G	PO	A	E	DP	PB
Castillo	.971	75	503	58	17	5	11
Musslewhite	1.000	11	62	1	0	0	6
Pierce	.972	79	515	34	16	2	10

First Base	PCT	G	PO	A	E	DP
Castillo	1.000	1	4	0	0	0
Davison	1.000	4	13	0	0	2
Musslewhite	1.000	2	3	0	0	0
Snyder	.982	64	569	34	11	48
Vinyard	.986	74	604	32	9	52

Second Base	PCT	G	PO	A	E	DP
Abreu	.960	120	238	368	25	62

	PCT	G	PO	A	E	DP
Davison	.971	18	25	43	2	10
Musslewhite	.900	2	3	6	1	1
Silveren	1.000	1	2	3	0	1

Third Base	PCT	G	PO	A	E	DP
Davison	.875	10	5	9	2	1
Gonzalez	.800	2	0	4	1	0
Musslewhite	.953	31	14	47	3	3
Rowell	.888	82	30	137	21	5
Silveren	.766	23	9	27	11	3

Shortstop	PCT	G	PO	A	E	DP
Davison	.940	19	38	41	5	11
Florimon Jr.	.929	109	185	289	36	62

	PCT	G	PO	A	E	DP
Gonzalez	.917	3	4	7	1	2
Musslewhite	.982	11	20	36	1	11

Outfield	PCT	G	PO	A	E	DP
Abreu	—	1	0	0	0	0
Andrews	.934	77	118	9	9	3
Bynum	1.000	1	2	0	0	0
Cash	.983	103	169	6	3	3
Davison	1.000	2	5	0	0	0
Figueroa	.992	114	228	8	2	1
Howell	1.000	15	35	1	0	0
Musslewhite	.500	3	1	0	1	0
Tripp	.988	96	154	5	2	0
Winterling	.938	22	43	2	3	2

ABERDEEN IRONBIRDS

SHORT-SEASON

NEW YORK-PENN LEAGUE

BATTING	B-T	HT	WT	DOB	AVG	vLH	vRH	G	AB	R	H	2B	3B	HR	RBI	BB	HBP	SH	SF	SO	SB	CS	SLG	OBP
Adams, Ryan	R-R	6-0	195	4-21-87	.236	.250	.232	67	246	29	58	10	2	3	22	18	4	2	2	63	8	3	.329	.296
Angle, Matthew	L-R	5-10	175	9-10-85	.301	.347	.289	66	236	60	71	4	4	0	14	47	2	2	0	40	34	4	.352	.421
Bent, Brian	R-R	6-2	210	9-11-85	.172	.200	.163	22	64	5	11	1	0	0	3	3	1	1	2	14	0	0	.188	.214
Binick, Kraig	R-L	5-10	180	2-10-85	.409	.250	.444	6	22	3	9	1	0	0	5	1	1	0	1	0	2		.455	.458
Crancer, Wally	L-R	6-0	215	7-7-84	.241	.292	.228	67	237	36	57	7	3	5	31	28	2	0	6	47	1	1	.359	.319
Gioioso, Michael	R-R	6-0	190	2-14-85	.000	.000	.000	3	10	1	0	0	0	0	1	1	1	0	4	0	0		.000	.167
Gonzalez, Franklin	R-R	6-0	160	4-7-86	.202	.417	.175	39	109	13	22	4	1	1	12	5	6	0	0	30	0	1	.284	.275
Henson, Tyler	R-R	6-1	190	12-15-87	.289	.297	.286	67	256	44	74	18	4	5	31	22	5	3	3	68	20	2	.449	.353
Hernandez, Ramon	R-R			5-20-76	.500	.000	.500	2	4	2	2	1	0	0	0	0	0	0	0	1	0	0	.750	.750
Johnson, Justin	L-R	6-1	180	11-7-82	.250	.300	.243	25	80	12	20	4	2	2	12	3	0	1	0	12	0	0	.425	.277
Mahoney, Joseph	L-L	6-7	255	2-1-87	.269	.294	.262	65	242	31	65	10	2	9	44	19	4	0	2	57	1	1	.438	.330
Martinez, Anthony	R-R	6-3	240	12-19-83	.296	.370	.273	65	230	30	68	13	0	4	50	24	4	0	6	50	1	1	.404	.364
Nowicki, Joseph	L-L	6-2	210	11-12-82	.283	.204	.307	69	230	35	65	7	2	8	41	21	4	0	7	63	5	2	.435	.344
Reinhardt, Douglas	R-R	6-3	210	10-22-85	.205	.235	.185	18	44	3	9	1	0	0	3	5	2	3	2	18	0	0	.227	.302
Silveren, Pedro	R-R	6-0	160	9-2-84	.200	.500	.154	4	15	3	3	0	0	0	0	0	0	0	0	3	0	0	.200	.200
Stephen, Jedidiah	R-R	6-2	195	4-30-84	.317	.414	.280	28	104	14	33	5	3	3	14	7	1	1	1	22	1	2	.510	.363
Trammell, Bubba	R-R	6-2	220	11-6-71	.143	.000	.148	9	28	2	4	1	0	0	3	1	1	0	0	9	0	0	.179	.200
Tucker, Matthew	B-R	6-2	185	6-5-83	.211	.182	.219	30	95	14	20	9	0	0	12	14	6	0	1	22	0	1	.305	.345
Widlansky, Robbie	L-R	6-2	210	11-6-84	.181	.241	.165	48	144	14	26	6	0	2	17	10	4	0	1	26	1	0	.264	.252
Wolf, Jordan	R-R	6-1	195	5-5-85	.198	.200	.197	36	106	13	21	3	3	1	14	14	0	0	2	15	1	1	.311	.287

PITCHING	B-T	HT	WT	DOB	W	L	ERA	G	GS	CG	SV	IP	H	R	ER	HR	BB	SO	AVG	vLH	vRH	K/9	BB/9
Allar, Brent	R-R	6-3	230	3-1-85	0	0	1.69	5	0	0	3	5	6	4	1	0	2	6	.286	.143	.357	10.12	3.38
Britton, Zachary	L-L	6-2	172	12-22-87	6	4	3.68	15	15	0	0	64	64	33	26	1	22	45	.256	.210	.271	6.36	3.11
Clark, Zach	R-R	6-0	195	7-11-83	3	1	1.03	5	4	0	0	26	19	6	3	1	7	20	.194	.237	.167	6.84	2.39
De Nabal, Fernando	R-R	6-3	180	6-16-84	0	1	4.28	16	0	0	0	34	30	21	16	1	22	35	.227	.229	.226	9.36	5.88
Esposito, Jason	L-R	5-11	220	5-15-85	5	3	2.79	23	0	0	3	52	39	20	16	1	19	53	.209	.200	.214	9.23	3.31
Jevne, Zachary	R-R	6-7	220	8-9-82	3	4	2.84	12	12	0	0	57	51	34	18	6	12	51	.235	.178	.276	8.05	1.89
Kirbis, Anthony	R-R	6-2	220	2-16-85	0	0	2.70	2	0	0	0	7	8	5	2	1	3	5	.286	.222	.316	6.75	4.05
Leicester, Jon	R-R	6-3	220	2-7-79	0	0	3.18	2	2	0	0	6	7	2	2	0	2	6	.318	.300	.333	9.53	3.18
Mariotti, John	L-R	6-0	225	8-19-84	2	2	1.46	12	4	0	2	37	27	18	6	3	12	25	.197	.212	.188	6.08	2.92
Mathews, Shane	R-R	6-3	210	3-28-85	0	3	3.06	15	0	0	1	18	14	10	6	1	17	12	.222	.105	.273	6.11	8.66
Mattaluno, Mick	R-R	6-3	200	1-17-85	1	0	1.69	11	0	0	1	16	12	5	3	1	2	13	.207	.238	.189	7.31	1.12
Miller, Aubrey	R-R	6-4	215	9-22-83	3	5	4.91	16	10	0	0	55	66	42	30	2	17	40	.293	.350	.248	6.55	2.78
Mueller, Scott	R-R	6-3	175	6-9-86	0	2	7.04	21	0	0	5	23	27	20	18	2	10	37	.290	.382	.237	14.48	3.91
Nery, Nathan	R-L	6-4	210	8-25-85	5	4	4.08	22	8	0	0	64	70	34	29	4	18	42	.279	.355	.254	5.91	2.53
Noel, Luis	R-R	6-1	175	9-29-87	0	0	12.86	3	0	0	0	7	13	10	10	4	8		.382	.500	.300	10.29	3.86
Ouellette, Ryan	R-R	5-11	185	10-4-85	0	1	2.25	6	0	0	0	8	6	2	2	0	1	8	.214	.286	.190	9.00	1.12
Parker, Brian	R-R	6-4	195	8-21-85	0	0	0.93	4	0	0	0	10	7	1	1	0	3	9	.194	.500	.077	8.38	2.79
Penn, Hayden	R-R	6-3	200	10-13-84	0	1	4.50	1	1	0	0	4	4	4	2	1	2	5	.235	.286	.200	11.25	4.50
Salberg, Chris	L-L	6-1	185	5-8-84	0	0	54.00	1	1	0	0	1	5	4	4	1	1	2	.714	1.000	.667	27.00	13.50
Schindling, Andrew	R-R	6-2	165	8-15-86	0	3	5.72	14	7	0	0	39	45	28	25	4	15	36	.281	.329	.241	8.24	3.43
Smith, Jacob	L-L	6-4	210	10-1-85	1	0	4.66	7	0	0	0	10	9	7	5	1	6	6	.265	.308	.238	5.59	5.59
Soriano, Julio	R-R	6-2	160	9-24-83	1	0	6.75	5	0	0	0	13	11	10	10	1	12	19	.229	.222	.233	12.83	8.10
Stadanlick, Ryan	R-R	6-3	210	8-3-84	2	1	6.83	16	0	0	0	28	34	28	21	0	15	27	.286	.275	.294	8.78	4.88
Tamba, Josh	L-R	6-2	210	11-15-84	1	5	9.23	13	12	0	0	40	58	52	41	2	30	31	.331	.313	.342	6.98	6.75
Touchatt, Kyle	R-R	6-2	200	11-22-84	1	2	4.40	23	0	0	3	29	31	18	14	1	12	15	.290	.333	.265	4.71	3.77
Tracey, Sean	L-R	6-1	205	11-14-80	0	0	13.50	3	0	0	0	2	3	4	3	0	4	0	.429	.000	.600	0.00	18.00

FIELDING

Catcher	PCT	G	PO	A	E	DP	PB
Bent	.988	22	148	17	2	0	8
Hernandez	1.000	1	6	1	0	0	0
Johnson	.977	24	151	21	4	0	3
Wolf	.993	34	257	27	2	0	6

First Base	PCT	G	PO	A	E	DP
Mahoney	.982	39	366	22	7	24
Martinez	.980	39	319	17	7	32

Second Base	PCT	G	PO	A	E	DP
Adams	.946	58	79	185	15	32
Gioioso	1.000	3	9	13	0	3
Gonzalez	.937	16	19	40	4	8

	PCT	G	PO	A	E	DP
Reinhardt	1.000	1	1	1	0	0
Silveren	.885	4	11	12	3	3

Third Base	PCT	G	PO	A	E	DP
Gonzalez	.894	19	13	29	5	0
Henson	.500	1	0	1	0	0
Reinhardt	.733	6	2	9	4	0
Stephen	.943	24	19	47	4	7
Tucker	.857	29	22	50	12	3

Shortstop	PCT	G	PO	A	E	DP
Adams	.900	9	18	27	5	6
Gonzalez	1.000	3	0	1	0	0
Henson	.911	65	102	185	28	35

	PCT	G	PO	A	E	DP
Stephen	.852	4	8	15	4	6

Outfield	PCT	G	PO	A	E	DP
Angle	.985	66	130	5	2	1
Binick	1.000	6	11	0	0	0
Crancer	.947	61	85	5	5	0
Mahoney	.800	6	4	0	1	0
Nowicki	.958	66	108	6	5	1
Reinhardt	.833	2	5	0	1	0
Stephen	—	1	0	0	0	0
Trammell	1.000	5	5	0	0	0
Widlansky	.962	29	24	1	1	0

BLUEFIELD ORIOLES

ROOKIE

APPALACHIAN LEAGUE

BATTING	B-T	HT	WT	DOB	AVG	vLH	vRH	G	AB	R	H	2B	3B	HR	RBI	BB	HBP	SH	SF	SO	SB	CS	SLG	OBP
Binick, Kraig	R-L	5-10	180	2-10-85	.292	.319	.282	67	250	52	73	9	6	6	36	30	12	0	2	39	15	1	.448	.391
Black, Dustin	R-R	6-0	205	12-8-86	.274	.344	.247	33	113	20	31	12	0	0	14	21	2	1	0	28	0	0	.381	.397
Chmiel, Paul	L-R	6-5	200	5-17-87	.297	.375	.271	18	64	11	19	2	0	3	12	14	0	0	1	22	0	1	.469	.418
Crowley, Malcolm	L-R	5-10	180	3-19-87	.258	.385	.167	9	31	3	8	2	0	0	4	4	0	0	0	7	0	0	.323	.343
D Oleo, Richard	L-L	6-2	165	5-5-86	.240	.236	.242	51	183	31	44	6	4	3	32	19	1	6	4	48	3	2	.366	.309
DiGeronimo, Joe	R-R	5-10	175	9-11-84	.067	.000	.071	5	15	1	1	0	0	0	1	2	0	0	0	3	0	0	.067	.176
Gioioso, Michael	R-R	6-0	190	2-14-85	.203	.218	.197	57	177	17	36	3	1	0	14	22	5	1	1	48	3	1	.232	.307
Heller, Daniel	L-L	6-3	210	1-11-87	.179	.205	.169	47	168	9	30	6	0	1	11	10	0	0	1	51	0	0	.232	.223
Julius, Jacob	L-L	6-0	185	3-13-86	.210	.234	.201	59	181	35	38	10	4	5	22	49	4	2	1	59	5	3	.392	.387
Lopez, Luis	R-R	6-0	180	11-24-87	.150	.300	.000	5	20	1	3	0	0	0	0	1	0	0	0	10	0	0	.150	.190
Monaghan, Brendan	R-R	6-2	190	4-11-85	.277	.132	.320	49	166	34	46	8	3	4	38	21	4	2	2	27	1	0	.434	.368
Pehrson, Preston	L-R	6-2	215	9-21-85	.118	.182	.093	24	76	2	9	3	1	0	7	2	1	0	1	27	0	0	.184	.150
Perlozzo, Eric	R-R	5-9	175	9-7-84	.247	.261	.243	55	182	24	45	8	2	1	16	21	2	6	2	33	1	1	.330	.329
Pope, Kieron	R-R	6-1	195	10-3-86	.197	.267	.176	20	66	4	13	2	0	0	5	5	3	0	2	22	0	1	.227	.284
Silveren, Pedro	R-R	6-0	160	9-2-84	.301	.135	.353	40	153	23	46	9	0	2	21	16	1	0	1	37	10	2	.399	.368
Tucker, Matthew	B-R	6-2	185	6-5-83	.312	.294	.322	38	141	30	44	14	3	4	35	23	4	0	3	33	4	2	.539	.415
White, Jason	L-R	6-1	175	6-7-84	.282	.329	.264	63	252	49	71	24	3	1	32	27	2	1	1	73	5	2	.413	.355

PITCHING	B-T	HT	WT	DOB	W	L	ERA	G	GS	CG	SV	IP	H	R	ER	HR	BB	SO	AVG	vLH	vRH	K/9	BB/9
Basta, Samuel	L-L	6-0	165	2-21-86	2	3	6.32	13	4	0	0	31	47	29	22	2	17	17	.338	.385	.333	4.88	4.88
Cooney, Brandon	R-R	6-6	240	8-2-85	4	2	4.58	11	10	0	0	53	63	33	27	4	14	36	.301	.303	.301	6.11	2.38
Egan, Pat	R-R	6-8	225	10-25-84	2	4	4.95	13	11	0	0	60	78	42	33	0	18	39	.311	.312	.310	5.85	2.70
Flagello, Clifford	R-R	5-10	200	1-3-85	5	5	4.83	13	9	0	0	54	65	38	29	6	19	56	.295	.300	.293	9.33	3.17
Garcia, Adolfito	R-R	6-2	170	1-31-85	1	2	5.12	19	1	0	2	39	43	24	22	3	17	43	.283	.295	.278	10.01	3.96
Gleason, Sean	L-R	6-0	190	8-21-85	5	4	2.93	14	10	0	0	68	78	22	22	3	14	61	.288	.307	.279	8.11	1.86
Kirbis, Anthony	R-R	6-2	220	2-16-85	0	0	4.85	17	0	0	3	39	43	27	21	1	12	27	.270	.387	.242	6.23	2.77
Lee, Bryan	R-R	6-5	200	1-24-85	0	4	8.53	12	4	0	0	25	22	25	24	2	38	26	.232	.226	.234	9.24	13.50
Mills, Jason	R-R	6-4	215	3-22-84	0	0	1.35	5	0	0	1	7	5	1	1	0	0	8	.200	.125	.250	10.80	0.00
Parker, Brian	R-R	6-4	195	8-21-85	3	0	2.18	15	0	0	6	21	14	6	5	1	2	15	.187	.182	.189	6.53	0.87
Procner, Stephen	L-L	6-2	200	12-27-84	3	3	4.07	13	13	0	0	55	64	29	25	2	17	36	.287	.172	.304	5.86	2.77
Robert, Bernard	R-R	6-0	188	2-17-85	3	2	5.09	20	1	0	1	35	39	24	20	4	21	37	.275	.250	.284	9.42	5.35
Selen, Ezequiel	R-R	6-3	170	7-14-85	2	2	6.10	16	0	0	2	31	31	25	21	2	20	27	.263	.421	.188	7.84	5.81
Williamson, Henry	R-R	6-5	225	11-1-85	2	5	4.13	16	5	0	2	61	55	34	28	1	17	68	.228	.233	.226	10.03	2.51

FIELDING

Catcher	PCT	G	PO	A	E	DP	PB
Black	.990	28	177	29	2	1	5
Monaghan	1.000	36	258	27	0	1	7
Pehrson	.983	12	51	6	1	0	3

First Base	PCT	G	PO	A	E	DP
Chmiel	.966	16	160	12	6	14
Gioioso	1.000	1	9	0	0	1
Heller	.972	14	133	6	4	8
Julius	.978	28	258	8	6	16
Pehrson	.989	9	87	6	1	3
Perlozzo	1.000	1	4	1	0	0

Second Base	PCT	G	PO	A	E	DP
Crowley	.867	6	16	23	6	7

	PCT	G	PO	A	E	DP
DiGeronimo	1.000	5	9	17	0	3
Gioioso	.983	43	64	114	3	21
Perlozzo	.985	16	24	40	1	6
Silveren	.929	3	4	9	1	0
Tucker	1.000	2	5	5	0	1

Third Base	PCT	G	PO	A	E	DP
Gioioso	.750	7	4	11	5	1
Perlozzo	.600	1	1	2	2	0
Silveren	.909	37	18	82	10	3
Tucker	.863	25	19	50	11	2

Shortstop	PCT	G	PO	A	E	DP
Gioioso	.969	5	6	25	1	2
Tucker	.800	1	1	3	1	0

White	.949	63	93	206	16	35

Outfield	PCT	G	PO	A	E	DP
Binick	.978	67	127	7	3	1
D Oleo	.979	23	44	2	1	0
Heller	1.000	30	29	2	0	0
Julius	.962	29	23	2	1	0
Lopez	1.000	5	6	1	0	0
Monaghan	.917	9	11	0	1	0
Pehrson	1.000	1	1	0	0	0
Perlozzo	.981	40	47	4	1	0
Tucker	.941	11	15	1	1	0

GCL ORIOLES

ROOKIE

GULF COAST LEAGUE

BATTING	B-T	HT	WT	DOB	AVG	vLH	vRH	G	AB	R	H	2B	3B	HR	RBI	BB	HBP	SH	SF	SO	SB	CS	SLG	OBP
Bernardo, Luis	R-R	6-0	170	1-16-88	.225	.160	.247	32	102	10	23	6	0	0	8	7	2	1	1	16	1	2	.284	.316
Bonevacia, Arthur	B-R	5-9	160	5-16-88	.272	.333	.250	21	81	10	22	4	0	1	10	8	2	0	1	15	0	0	.358	.348
Cardona, Rodolfo	R-R	5-10	155	11-27-86	.283	.263	.289	40	159	25	45	12	3	2	30	12	4	2	3	35	8	2	.434	.343
Carolus, Levi	R-R	6-0	160	9-22-87	.222	.162	.238	47	167	23	37	11	2	4	26	10	2	3	1	44	6	2	.383	.272
DiGeronimo, Joe	R-R	5-10	175	9-11-84	.279	.207	.305	32	111	11	31	1	0	0	12	4	3	0	1	14	9	4	.288	.319
Ellis, Lee	R-R	6-2	210	7-22-84	.219	.173	.234	55	210	33	46	8	3	2	18	19	5	0	2	58	2	2	.314	.297
Kolodny, Tyler	R-R	6-2	210	3-9-88	.318	.359	.304	43	151	33	48	10	2	6	30	15	8	1	1	30	6	0	.530	.406
Lester, Calvin	B-R	6-1	180	12-23-83	.209	.222	.205	51	191	36	40	9	0	0	8	43	1	4	0	43	16	7	.257	.357
Martin, Justin	R-R	6-0	185	3-18-88	.216	.300	.185	12	37	6	8	3	0	1	6	4	2	0	1	5	0	0	.378	.318
Mora, Melvin	R-R	5-11	200	2-2-72	.286	1.000	.167	2	7	1	2	1	0	0	1	0	0	0	0	1	0	0	.429	.286
Polanco, Elvin	B-L	6-3	190	3-3-87	.318	.352	.307	54	217	35	69	18	0	5	37	14	4	0	2	39	3	0	.470	.367
Polo, Winter	R-R	6-1	160	5-10-85	.750	1.000	.667	1	4	1	3	1	0	0	1	0	0	0	0	1	0	0	1.250	.750
Ray, Nicholas	L-L	6-0	185	11-5-85	.246	.292	.229	52	179	30	44	8	2	1	13	31	4	0	3	65	9	5	.330	.364
Reimold, Nolan	R-R	6-4	207	10-12-83	.233	.000	.292	9	30	4	7	4	1	0	8	6	3	0	0	4	0	0	.433	.410
Tarnow, Joshua	R-R	6-0	180	11-4-84	.221	.077	.255	22	68	7	15	4	0	0	8	9	1	1	0	12	1	1	.279	.321
Tropiano, Ralph	B-R	5-10	180	7-19-84	.167	.231	.118	14	30	3	5	1	0	0	3	7	0	1	1	9	2	0	.200	.316
Vasquez, Robert	R-R	6-0	160	11-8-86	.230	.121	.265	40	135	13	31	6	0	1	16	16	1	1	1	42	3	1	.304	.316

PITCHING	B-T	HT	WT	DOB	W	L	ERA	G	GS	CG	SV	IP	H	R	ER	HR	BB	SO	AVG	vLH	vRH	K/9	BB/9
Achil, Miguel	R-R	6-4	145	3-18-88	1	1	7.23	11	0	0	0	19	20	16	15	0	20	8	.294	.357	.250	3.86	9.64
Allen, Colin	R-R	6-1	175	10-14-86	0	0	0.00	1	0	0	0	2	2	1	0	0	1	2	.333	.000	.500	9.00	4.50
Almanzar, Jorge	R-R	6-2	160	7-25-86	0	1	2.42	12	0	0	5	22	18	7	6	0	17	19	.234	.233	.234	7.66	6.85
Barrows, Derek	R-R	6-1	187	11-20-80	0	0	5.02	8	0	0	0	14	18	10	8	1	3	10	.295	.300	.293	6.28	1.88
Burch, Jason	R-R	5-5	215	10-15-82	0	0	2.57	5	0	0	0	7	6	2	2	1	1	8	.231	.250	.222	10.29	1.29
Cole, Zachary	R-R	6-4	185	1-18-85	0	0	5.84	9	0	0	2	12	13	10	8	1	11	11	.277	.211	.321	8.03	8.03
Conklin, Andrew	R-R	6-2	215	7-8-87	1	1	4.35	8	0	0	0	21	23	12	10	0	13	15	.288	.233	.320	6.53	5.66
Desten, Geraldo	R-R	6-3	195	8-10-86	1	2	4.18	9	4	0	1	24	24	13	11	3	12	17	.270	.303	.250	6.46	4.56
Esposito, Joseph	L-R	5-11	220	5-15-85	0	0	0.00	1	0	0	0	1	1	0	0	0	2	2	.333	—	.333	18.00	0.00
Finch, Eric	R-R	6-4	215	9-27-87	0	0	0.93	7	0	0	0	10	2	1	1	0	1	10	.067	.182	.000	9.31	1.86
Huches, Leonardo	R-R	6-2	195	11-9-85	3	3	6.75	15	0	0	5	23	32	21	17	1	12	19	.333	.350	.321	7.54	4.76
Leicester, Jon	R-R	6-3	220	2-7-79	0	0	2.25	2	2	0	0	4	3	1	1	0	2	7	.200	.333	.111	15.75	4.50

Madrigal, Leonardo	L-L	6-3	140	1-12-87	2	1	1.65	5	2	0	0	16	12	4	3	0	7	11	.218	.333	.175	6.06	3.86
McCurry, Cole	L-L	6-2	180	9-25-85	6	5	3.07	15	10	0	0	67	57	27	23	6	11	62	.228	.317	.200	8.29	1.47
Mercedes, Juan	R-R	6-4	170	9-18-85	0	0	13.50	2	0	0	0	3	6	7	4	1	3	3	.375	.571	.222	10.12	10.12
Moore, Justin	R-R	6-3	190	7-26-89	1	0	0.00	3	0	0	1	7	1	0	0	0	0	5	.043	.000	.063	6.43	0.00
Mueller, Scott	R-R	6-3	175	6-9-86	0	0	0.00	1	0	0	0	1	0	0	0	0	0	1	.000	.000	.000	9.00	0.00
Noel, Luis	R-R	6-1	175	9-29-87	6	2	3.18	14	11	0	1	65	64	30	23	3	16	51	.258	.302	.230	7.06	2.22
Odom, Aaron	L-L	6-0	165	9-24-84	1	2	1.74	8	5	0	0	21	19	9	4	0	6	23	.232	.192	.250	10.02	2.61
Orman, Conrad	L-L	6-2	180	5-1-87	8	2	4.97	14	6	0	0	54	56	35	30	1	29	30	.271	.233	.286	4.97	4.80
Penn, Hayden	R-R	6-3	200	10-13-84	0	0	2.40	5	5	0	0	15	17	6	4	0	4	17	.279	.250	.289	10.20	2.40
Rivero, Raul	R-R	6-0	165	5-6-86	2	3	3.63	12	10	1	0	67	77	33	27	4	8	48	.293	.277	.300	6.45	1.07
Smith, Jacob	L-L	6-4	210	10-1-85	0	0	4.50	1	0	0	0	2	3	1	1	0	1	4	.333	.250	.400	18.00	4.50
Taveras, Sam	R-R	6-3	180	1-4-88	0	1	2.51	6	1	0	1	14	8	4	4	0	7	8	.170	.200	.156	5.02	4.40
Tropiano, Ralph	B-R	5-10	180	7-19-84	0	0	0.00	1	0	0	0	1	1	0	0	0	0	1	.250	—	.250	9.00	0.00

FIELDING

Catcher	PCT	G	PO	A	E	DP	PB
Bernardo	.978	29	178	42	5	1	15
Lester	1.000	1	9	3	0	0	0
Martin	.983	9	56	3	1	0	1
Tarnow	.987	20	141	16	2	5	7

First Base	PCT	G	PO	A	E	DP
Carolus	1.000	1	3	0	0	0
Kolodny	1.000	4	11	0	0	1
Polanco	.988	53	472	27	6	44
Vasquez	.909	2	8	2	1	0

Second Base	PCT	G	PO	A	E	DP
Cardona	.962	9	16	34	2	9
Carolus	.917	11	23	32	5	7
DiGeronimo	1.000	5	11	12	0	2
Tropiano	.972	9	13	22	1	7
Vasquez	.961	29	56	42	4	15

Third Base	PCT	G	PO	A	E	DP
Carolus	.911	17	6	35	4	3
Kolodny	.875	36	26	79	15	9
Tropiano	.000	1	0	0	2	0
Vasquez	.933	5	3	11	1	2

Shortstop	PCT	G	PO	A	E	DP
Cardona	.929	29	55	89	11	15
Carolus	.800	1	1	3	1	1
DiGeronimo	.980	25	54	91	3	19
Vasquez	.778	1	2	5	2	0

Outfield	PCT	G	PO	A	E	DP
Bernardo	1.000	1	1	0	0	0
Bonevacia	1.000	13	24	1	0	1
Ellis	.982	51	106	4	2	4
Lester	.966	49	83	3	3	1
Polo	1.000	1	4	0	0	0
Ray	1.000	49	83	2	0	1
Reimold	.923	5	12	0	1	0
Vasquez	—	1	0	0	0	0

DSL ORIOLES — ROOKIE

DOMINICAN SUMMER LEAGUE

BATTING	B-T	HT	WT	DOB	AVG	vLH	vRH	G	AB	R	H	2B	3B	HR	RBI	BB	HBP	SH	SF	SO	SB	CS	SLG	OBP
Batista, Luiyi	R-R	6-1	170	4-22-88	.000	.000	.000	3	10	0	0	0	0	0	1	0	0	0	0	4	0	0	.000	.000
Casamayor, Omar	B-R	5-11	170	11-3-86	.344	.383	.333	58	215	40	74	12	4	1	29	20	8	5	1	19	18	8	.451	.418
Cruz, Daniel	R-R	6-2	186	5-3-88	.037	.143	.000	16	27	1	1	0	0	0	1	4	1	0	0	21	0	0	.037	.188
De La Cruz, Donis	R-R	6-2	160	2-25-87	.121	.000	.143	14	33	10	4	1	0	0	3	3	2	0	0	12	1	0	.152	.237
Gonzalez, Grolmann	R-R	6-1	180	10-12-88	.285	.366	.265	64	207	44	59	12	3	3	37	24	4	2	3	41	19	6	.415	.366
Guerrero, Janensis	R-R	6-0	170	5-21-89	.247	.294	.232	27	73	8	18	4	1	0	11	6	1	1	0	20	1	0	.329	.313
Hodge, Humberto	R-R	6-4	170	11-6-87	.088	.000	.120	15	34	2	3	1	0	0	2	0	1	1	1	14	0	1	.118	.111
Mejia, Francisco	R-R	6-1	150	2-27-86	.196	.235	.189	39	107	13	21	5	0	2	14	8	1	0	1	29	5	0	.299	.256
Melenciano, Jaynnertt	R-R	6-1	170	11-13-87	.236	.286	.225	48	157	35	37	7	1	1	16	15	6	10	0	37	12	1	.312	.326
Meyer, Edinho	R-R	6-2	170	2-7-88	.273	.333	.254	48	154	24	42	15	0	4	28	20	10	2	1	32	1	1	.448	.389
Nivar, Jose	B-R	6-1	170	2-28-89	.182	.077	.203	28	77	8	14	3	1	0	11	5	4	0	1	22	1	0	.247	.264
Polanco, Joel	R-R	6-2	190	9-27-85	.194	.071	.213	44	103	8	20	2	0	0	11	26	7	2	2	17	0	0	.214	.384
Ramirez, Luis	L-L	6-3	170	4-24-88	.236	.267	.227	45	140	25	33	7	1	5	22	14	4	3	0	32	4	3	.407	.323
Ricardo, Dashenko	R-R	6-0	160	3-1-90	.297	.343	.276	38	111	15	33	7	1	1	19	8	2	2	2	32	2	0	.405	.350
Rivera, Larry	B-R	6-1	170	5-26-88	.144	.133	.148	52	118	22	17	3	0	1	11	16	10	2	0	30	8	2	.195	.299
Rodriguez, Rubby	R-R	6-1	180	8-25-87	.178	.100	.200	17	45	3	8	0	0	1	6	5	3	1	1	18	0	1	.244	.296
Rosa, Garabez	R-R	6-2	166	10-12-89	.275	.311	.265	58	200	31	55	10	2	2	17	3	3	15	4	44	7	4	.375	.290
Santana, Javier	B-R	6-1	160	7-31-87	.231	.182	.244	61	208	41	48	7	0	1	18	46	7	2	0	62	5	12	.279	.387
Tejeda, Anyi	R-R	6-3	173	1-19-89	.161	.261	.129	31	93	14	15	3	0	1	9	2	2	4	1	33	0	0	.226	.194
Wilson, Edwin	R-R	6-1	170	5-11-87	.265	.316	.258	52	147	19	39	10	0	1	19	17	5	4	0	44	7	5	.354	.361

PITCHING	B-T	HT	WT	DOB	W	L	ERA	G	GS	CG	SV	IP	H	R	ER	HR	BB	SO	AVG	vLH	vRH	K/9	BB/9
Abad, Leonaldo	R-R	6-3	193	1-17-87	1	4	4.82	14	0	0	0	28	36	21	15	2	18	15	.321	.273	.342	4.82	5.79
Batista, Luiyi	R-R	6-1	170	4-22-88	3	3	0.72	17	0	0	2	25	16	8	2	0	15	25	.172	.250	.160	9.00	5.40
Cespedes, Angel	R-R	6-2	170	8-27-89	2	4	5.01	14	12	0	0	56	65	48	31	3	15	29	.285	.205	.304	4.69	2.43
De La Cruz, Donis	R-R	6-2	160	2-25-87	0	0	1.64	12	0	0	0	22	18	10	4	0	8	22	.214	.188	.221	9.00	3.27
De La Cruz, Jario	R-R	6-3	183	7-15-87	3	0	3.99	20	0	0	3	50	45	27	22	2	29	62	.242	.258	.239	11.23	5.26
Hodge, Humberto	R-R	6-4	170	11-6-87	0	0	0.00	2	0	0	0	3	2	0	0	0	1	3	.222	.000	.286	10.12	3.38
Jimenez, Enrico	L-L	6-3	195	2-7-89	3	3	3.94	18	7	0	2	59	61	31	26	2	27	72	.265	.200	.270	10.92	4.10
Madrigal, Leonardo	L-L	6-3	140	1-12-87	1	1	8.31	5	5	0	0	13	13	17	12	1	15	23	.241	.333	.235	15.92	10.38
Nunez, Eduardo	R-R	6-2	170	11-29-89	1	5	4.70	18	3	0	1	44	47	27	23	2	16	44	.285	.393	.263	9.00	3.27
Ramirez, Eiri	R-R	6-0	173	2-2-88	1	1	4.00	6	4	0	0	18	18	8	8	0	12	17	.265	.000	.290	8.50	6.00
Reyes, Jeancarlos	R-R	6-1	150	6-22-87	5	3	3.65	15	14	1	0	67	56	33	27	2	26	83	.222	.282	.211	11.20	3.51
Rivera, Larry	B-R	6-1	170	5-26-88	0	0	—	1	0	0	0	0	2	3	3	0	2	0	1.000	1.000	1.000	—	—
Salas, Jhon	B-R	6-1	190	11-4-84	2	4	4.12	19	0	0	1	55	57	33	25	1	25	46	.265	.277	.262	7.57	4.12
Santana, Wascar	L-L	6-4	150	7-29-87	0	4	8.36	14	3	0	0	38	37	43	35	1	41	34	.268	1.000	.263	8.12	9.80
Sosa, Jose	R-R	6-4	190	4-2-87	1	4	7.31	17	0	0	0	32	27	32	26	1	28	49	.223	.111	.243	13.78	7.88
Tavarez, Daurin	R-R	6-6	160	2-8-89	2	6	4.07	14	14	0	0	55	56	33	25	4	31	58	.258	.321	.238	9.43	5.04
Taveras, Sam	R-R	6-3	180	1-4-88	0	2	4.40	8	8	0	0	31	29	21	15	0	16	43	.244	.160	.266	12.62	4.70
Yan, Yormi	R-R	6-5	190	5-27-86	1	0	7.27	6	0	0	0	9	15	10	7	2	7	6	.349	.250	.371	6.23	7.27

FIELDING

Catcher	PCT	G	PO	A	E	DP	PB
Guerrero	.949	25	162	25	10	0	9
Polanco	.979	18	126	14	3	0	2
Ricardo	.992	32	214	27	2	2	13
Rodriguez	.974	17	130	21	4	0	5

First Base	PCT	G	PO	A	E	DP
Cruz	1.000	2	2	0	0	0
Gonzalez	1.000	1	2	0	0	1
Hodge	1.000	4	6	0	0	0
Meyer	.974	37	257	8	7	22
Polanco	.962	18	97	3	4	4
Santana	1.000	1	1	0	0	0
Wilson	.969	25	145	10	5	17

Second Base	PCT	G	PO	A	E	DP
Casamayor	.953	17	32	29	3	2
Hodge	1.000	2	0	2	0	0
Rivera	—	1	0	0	0	0
Santana	.948	56	138	100	13	29

Third Base	PCT	G	PO	A	E	DP
Batista	.667	1	1	1	1	0
Casamayor	.832	35	32	47	16	7
Ciriaco	.829	12	10	19	6	1
Cruz	.571	7	5	3	6	0
De La Cruz	.846	6	6	16	4	0
Hodge	.880	7	7	15	3	1
Tejeda	.947	10	3	15	1	2

Shortstop	PCT	G	PO	A	E	DP
Batista	1.000	1	1	2	0	0
Casamayor	.889	2	3	5	1	1
Cruz	1.000	1	0	1	0	0
Rosa	.876	52	63	142	29	25
Santana	.889	3	5	3	1	0
Tejeda	.914	22	28	57	8	5

Outfield	PCT	G	PO	A	E	DP
Cruz	1.000	1	1	0	0	0
Gonzalez	.951	58	93	5	5	1
Mejia	1.000	24	26	2	0	0
Melenciano	.908	42	53	6	6	1
Nivar	.885	21	23	0	3	0
Ramirez	.951	37	54	4	3	1
Rivera	.955	40	40	2	2	0
Wilson	.903	21	25	3	3	0

Boston Red Sox

BY ALEX SPEIER

In just four seasons, the Red Sox have explored the full spectrum of the life cycle.

Until 2004, New Englanders spent the better part of 86 years insisting that a peaceful entry into the great beyond depended on seeing their team win a single title. Now, after a second World Series crown in four years, the same fans are greeting championships as a birthright.

That ruddy optimism became understandable as the Red Sox plowed through the regular season and October. A familiar ensemble of superstars and a precocious group still in its big league infancy led the team's march to victory.

The 2007 season marked the culmination of GM Theo Epstein's much heralded scouting and player development machine. Much of the team's personality was defined by players barely old enough to drink the celebratory champagne.

Righthander Clay Buchholz, 23, produced the most electrifying moment of the regular season when he threw a no-hitter in his second career start but was left off the postseason roster due to shoulder concerns.

Second baseman Dustin Pedroia, 24, punctuated his rookie campaign (.317/.380/.442) with October excellence. Center fielder Jacoby Ellsbury, also 24, enjoyed a brilliant callup and made a case for World Series MVP after going 7-for-16.

The final contest of the World Series sweep over the Rockies, meanwhile, was bookended by the excellence of lefthander Jon Lester, 23, and second-year closer Jonathan Papelbon, 26, who reeled off 10.2 scoreless postseason innings.

Yet the Sox were also clearly more than just a patchwork of homegrown talent, ranking as the most expensive champion in baseball history.

The grand ambitions of the Sox season, after all, were unhatched with an Ed McMahon-sized check almost immediately following the 2006 World Series. In the early days of last November, the Sox posted a $51.1 million fee for the rights to righthander Daisuke Matsuzaka, and then signed him to a contract for another $52 million over six years.

An additional $106 million brought free agent shortstop Julio Lugo and right fielder J.D. Drew into the mix.

The rotation seemed poised for dominance, with Matsuzaka joining Opening Day starter Curt Schilling and emergent ace Josh Beckett. The apparent depth of a lineup that included David Ortiz, Manny Ramirez, Mike Lowell and Kevin Youkilis inspired visions of a return to the run-scoring peaks of 2003-05, when the Sox led the majors in offense for three straight years.

Papelbon switched from the rotation back to closer in spring training and teamed with Hideki Okajima, the middle-relief revelation who surprisingly surpassed Matsuzaka in regular season impact. The result was a balanced Sox team that burst out of the gate, claiming sole possession of first place on Apr. 18 and maintaining a stranglehold on that position for the final 166 days of the regular season.

While the Sox were occasionally pushed by the Yankees, who moved within two games for a fleeting moment in September, their playoff position was never challenged. Thanks to a division lead that swelled to double digits by May 20, the team was able to position itself for October. The Sox carefully regulated the workloads of their pitchers.

Beckett (20-7, 3.27), thanks to a precautionary disabled list trip in May for a skin tear on his finger, dominated the regular season and proved transcendent in the playoffs

PLAYERS OF THE YEAR

MAJOR LEAGUE: DAVID ORTIZ, DH

Ortiz battled through injuries but his production still ranked among the best in baseball, as he led the Red Sox to their first division title since 1995. His .445 on-base percentage was first in the American League, and his .621 slugging average ranked third. Ortiz also led the Red Sox with 35 home runs, 52 doubles, 116 runs and 111 walks.

MINOR LEAGUE: CLAY BUCHHOLZ, RHP

Buchholz showcased excellent stuff and put up huge numbers in the minors, which would have been enough to win this award. His 171 strikeouts ranked fifth in the minor leagues, and his 12.34 strikeouts per nine innings ranked first. His no-hitter against the Orioles was the icing on the cake.

ORGANIZATIONAL LEADERS

BATTING		★Minimum 250 at-bats
★AVG	Bell, Bubba, Lancaster/Portland	.337
R	Daeges, Zachary, Lancaster	124
H	Daeges, Zachary, Lancaster	170
TB	Daeges, Zachary, Lancaster	298
2B	Daeges, Zachary, Lancaster	55
3B	Hall, Michael, Greenville/Lancaster	9
HR	Bates, Aaron, Lancaster/Portland	28
RBI	Daeges, Zachary, Lancaster	113
BB	Still, Jon, Greenville/Lancaster	105
SO	Place, Jason, Greenville	160
SB	Ellsbury, Jacoby, Portland/Pawtucket	41
★OBP	Bates, Aaron, Lancaster/Portland	.435
★SLG	Bell, Bubba, Lancaster/Portland	.584
PITCHING		^Minimum 75 innings
W	Beazley, Travis, Greenville/Lancaster	13
L	Steinocher, Brian, Greenville	12
^ERA	Buchholz, Clay, Portland/Pawtucket	2.44
G	Papelbon, Josh, Greenville	62
CG	Lester, Jon, Green./Pawtucket/Portland	2
SV	Hughes, Travis, Pawtucket	24
IP	Beazley, Travis, Greenville/Lancaster	156
BB	Barnes, John, Lancaster/Portland/Pawtucket	88
SO	Buchholz, Clay, Portland/Pawtucket	171
^AVG	Buchholz, Clay, Portland/Pawtucket	.193

(4-0, 1.20). Okajima, who was shut down for two weeks in September, and Papelbon, both became multi-inning bullpen forces in October.

Even the lineup reached peak efficiency in the playoffs. Ramirez recovered from a September oblique strain to become a postseason monster (.346, 4 HRs, 16 RBIs). He combined with Ortiz, Lowell and Youkilis to forge a .365 average, 1.153 OPS, 13 homers and 51 RBIs in the playoffs.

That quartet helped Boston outscore the Angels, Indians and Rockies by a combined count of 99-46.

Boston's cupboard is hardly bare, with several prospects on the verge of joining Pedroia, Ellsbury and Buchholz in Boston. Jed Lowrie appears ready to take over at shortstop or third base, righthander Justin Masterson could join the back end of the rotation or the bullpen by the end of 2008 and Brandon Moss should add outfield depth.

2007 PERFORMANCE

General Manager: Theo Epstein. **Farm Director:** Mike Hazen. **Scouting Director:** Jason McLeod

Class	Team	League	W	L	PCT	Finish*	Manager	Affiliate Since
Majors	Boston	American	96	66	.593	1st (14)	Terry Francona	—
Triple-A	Pawtucket Red Sox	International	67	75	.472	10th (14)	Ron Johnson	1973
Double-A	Portland Sea Dogs	Eastern	71	72	.497	6th (12)	Arnie Beyeler	2003
High A	Lancaster JetHawks	California	83	57	.593	1st (10)	Chad Epperson	2007
Low A	Greenville Drive	South Atlantic	58	81	.417	14th (16)	Gabe Kapler	2005
Short-season	Lowell Spinners	New York-Penn	40	36	.526	5th (14)	Jon Deeble	1996
Rookie	GCL Red Sox	Gulf Coast	30	26	.536	6th (16)	Dave Tomlin	1993
Overall 2007 Minor League Record			**349**	**347**	**.501**	**13th**		

* Finish in overall standings (No. of teams in league) ^League champion

ORGANIZATION STATISTICS

BOSTON RED SOX

AMERICAN LEAGUE

BATTING	B-T	HT	WT	DOB	AVG	vLH	vRH	G	AB	R	H	2B	3B	HR	RBI	BB	HBP	SH	SF	SO	SB	CS	SLG	OBP
Bailey, Jeff	R-R	6-2	200	11-19-78	.111	.167	.000	3	9	1	1	0	0	1	1	0	0	0	0	1	0	0	.444	.111
Cash, Kevin	R-R	6-0	190	12-6-77	.111	.077	.143	12	27	2	3	1	0	0	4	4	1	0	1	13	0	0	.148	.242
Clayton, Royce	R-R	6-0	200	1-2-70	.000	.000	.000	8	6	1	0	0	0	0	0	0	0	0	0	3	0	0	.000	.000
2-team (69 Toronto)					.246	—	—	77	195	24	48	14	0	1	12	14	1	3	3	53	2	1	.333	.296
Cora, Alex	L-R	6-0	200	10-18-75	.246	.179	.257	83	207	30	51	10	5	3	18	7	9	7	2	23	1	1	.386	.298
Crisp, Coco	B-R	6-0	180	11-1-79	.268	.270	.267	145	526	85	141	28	7	6	60	50	1	9	5	84	28	6	.382	.330
Drew, J.D.	L-R	6-1	200	11-20-75	.270	.224	.286	140	466	84	126	30	4	11	64	79	1	0	6	100	4	2	.423	.373
Ellsbury, Jacoby	L-L	6-1	185	9-11-83	.353	.346	.356	33	116	20	41	7	1	3	18	8	1	0	2	15	9	0	.509	.394
Hinske, Eric	L-R	6-2	235	8-5-77	.204	.200	.205	84	186	25	38	12	3	6	21	28	3	0	1	54	3	0	.398	.317
Kielty, Bobby	B-R	6-1	225	8-5-76	.231	.308	.154	20	52	6	12	2	0	1	9	5	1	0	3	17	0	0	.327	.295
2-team (13 Oakland)					.218	—	—	33	87	10	19	3	0	1	12	8	2	0	4	26	0	0	.287	.287
Lowell, Mike	R-R	6-3	210	2-24-74	.324	.323	.325	154	589	79	191	37	2	21	120	53	3	0	8	71	3	2	.501	.378
Lugo, Julio	R-R	6-1	175	11-16-75	.237	.226	.241	147	570	71	135	36	2	8	73	48	0	8	4	82	33	6	.349	.294
Mirabelli, Doug	R-R	6-1	220	10-18-70	.202	.250	.194	48	114	9	23	3	0	5	16	11	1	1	0	41	0	0	.360	.278
Moss, Brandon	L-R	6-0	205	9-16-83	.280	.250	.286	15	25	6	7	2	1	0	1	4	0	0	0	6	0	0	.440	.379
Murphy, David	L-L	6-4	215	10-18-81	.500	.500	.000	3	2	1	1	0	0	0	0	0	0	0	0	1	0	0	.500	.500
2-team (43 Texas)					.343	—	—	46	105	17	36	12	2	2	14	7	0	0	0	20	0	0	.552	.384
Ortiz, David	L-L	6-4	230	11-18-75	.332	.308	.343	149	549	116	182	52	1	35	117	111	4	0	3	103	3	1	.621	.445
Pedroia, Dustin	R-R	5-9	180	8-17-83	.317	.348	.303	139	520	86	165	39	1	8	50	47	7	5	2	42	7	1	.442	.380
Pena, Wily Mo	R-R	6-3	245	1-23-82	.218	.282	.165	73	156	18	34	9	1	5	17	14	2	0	0	58	0	1	.385	.291
Ramirez, Manny	R-R	6-0	200	5-30-72	.296	.344	.279	133	483	84	143	33	1	20	88	71	7	0	8	92	0	0	.493	.388
Varitek, Jason	B-R	6-2	230	4-11-72	.255	.264	.252	131	435	57	111	15	3	17	68	71	1	8	0	122	1	4	.421	.367
Youkilis, Kevin	R-R	6-1	220	3-15-79	.288	.290	.287	145	528	85	152	35	2	16	83	77	15	0	5	105	4	2	.453	.390

PITCHING	B-T	HT	WT	DOB	W	L	ERA	G	GS	CG	SV	IP	H	R	ER	HR	BB	SO	AVG	vLH	vRH	K/9	BB/9
Beckett, Josh	R-R	6-5	220	5-15-80	20	7	3.27	30	30	1	0	201	189	76	73	17	40	194	.245	.255	.235	8.70	1.79
Buchholz, Clay	L-R	6-3	190	8-14-84	3	1	1.59	4	3	1	0	23	14	6	4	0	10	22	.184	.217	.133	8.74	3.97
Corey, Bryan	R-R	6-0	170	10-21-73	1	0	1.93	9	0	0	0	9	6	2	2	0	4	6	.231	.167	.286	5.79	3.86
Delcarmen, Manny	R-R	6-2	190	2-16-82	0	0	2.05	44	0	0	1	44	28	11	10	4	17	41	.183	.167	.194	8.39	3.48
Donnelly, Brendan	R-R	6-3	245	7-4-71	2	1	3.05	27	0	0	0	21	19	8	7	0	5	15	.235	.212	.250	6.53	2.18
Gabbard, Kason	L-L	6-3	205	4-8-82	4	0	3.73	7	7	1	0	41	28	17	17	3	18	29	.196	.147	.211	6.37	3.95
2-team (8 Texas)					6	1	4.65	15	15	1	0	81	68	42	42	8	41	55	—	—	—	6.09	4.54
Gagne, Eric	R-R	6-0	240	1-7-76	2	2	6.75	20	0	0	0	19	26	14	14	1	9	22	.325	.325	.325	10.61	4.34
2-team (34 Texas)					4	2	3.81	54	0	0	16	52	49	22	22	3	21	51	—	—	—	8.83	3.63
Hansack, Devern	R-R	6-2	180	2-5-78	0	1	4.70	3	1	0	0	8	9	5	4	2	5	5	.273	.333	.167	5.87	5.87
Lester, Jon	L-L	6-2	190	1-7-84	4	0	4.57	12	11	0	0	63	61	33	32	10	31	50	.257	.231	.267	7.14	4.43
Lopez, Javier	L-L	6-4	220	7-11-77	2	1	3.10	61	0	0	0	41	36	16	14	3	18	16	.240	.293	.176	5.75	3.98
Matsuzaka, Daisuke	R-R	6-0	185	9-13-80	15	12	4.40	32	32	1	0	205	191	100	100	25	80	201	.246	.238	.253	8.84	3.52
Okajima, Hideki	L-L	6-1	195	12-25-75	3	2	2.22	66	0	0	5	69	50	17	17	6	17	63	.202	.236	.182	8.22	2.22
Papelbon, Jonathan	R-R	6-4	230	11-23-80	1	3	1.85	59	0	0	37	58	30	12	12	5	15	84	.146	.104	.200	12.96	2.31
Pineiro, Joel	R-R	6-1	200	9-25-78	1	1	5.03	31	0	0	0	34	41	20	19	3	14	20	.293	.317	.275	5.29	3.71
Romero, J.C.	B-L	5-11	205	6-4-76	1	0	3.15	23	0	0	1	20	24	7	7	2	15	11	.308	.297	.317	4.95	6.75
Schilling, Curt	R-R	6-5	235	11-14-66	9	8	3.87	24	24	1	0	151	165	68	65	21	23	101	.275	.274	.277	6.02	1.37
Snyder, Kyle	B-R	6-8	215	9-9-77	2	3	3.81	46	0	0	0	54	45	29	23	7	32	41	.223	.195	.242	6.79	5.30
Tavarez, Julian	L-R	6-2	195	5-22-73	7	11	5.15	34	23	0	0	135	151	89	77	14	51	77	.281	.260	.300	5.15	3.41
Timlin, Mike	R-R	6-4	210	3-10-66	2	1	3.42	50	0	0	1	55	46	23	21	7	14	31	.232	.173	.274	5.04	2.28
Wakefield, Tim	R-R	6-2	210	8-2-66	17	12	4.76	31	31	0	0	189	191	104	100	22	64	110	.264	.246	.277	5.24	3.05

FIELDING

Catcher	PCT	G	PO	A	E	DP	PB
Cash	.985	12	56	8	1	2	0
Mirabelli	.995	46	194	19	1	4	6
Varitek	.994	125	937	39	6	8	4

First Base	PCT	G	PO	A	E	DP
Bailey	1.000	3	16	2	0	1
Cora	.500	1	1	0	1	0
Hinske	.989	43	256	22	3	25
Ortiz	1.000	7	37	3	0	3
Youkilis	1.000	135	990	90	0	101

Second Base	PCT	G	PO	A	E	DP
Cora	.994	47	67	95	1	20
Pedroia	.990	137	259	360	6	78

Third Base	PCT	G	PO	A	E	DP
Clayton	1.000	3	0	2	0	0
Lowell	.961	154	105	264	15	34
Youkilis	.921	13	5	30	3	4

Shortstop	PCT	G	PO	A	E	DP
Clayton	.750	1	0	3	1	0
Cora	.969	33	25	69	3	18

Lugo	.968	145	214	360	19	70

Outfield	PCT	G	PO	A	E	DP
Crisp	.998	144	408	7	1	4
Drew	.974	135	224	3	6	1
Ellsbury	1.000	33	75	0	0	0
Hinske	1.000	35	42	1	0	0
Kielty	1.000	20	28	1	0	0
Moss	1.000	15	12	1	0	0
Murphy	1.000	2	2	0	0	0
Pena	.965	67	79	3	3	1
Ramirez	.990	120	182	8	2	0

INTERNATIONAL LEAGUE

BATTING	B-T	HT	WT	DOB	AVG	vLH	vRH	G	AB	R	H	2B	3B	HR	RBI	BB	HBP	SH	SF	SO	SB	CS	SLG	OBP
Bailey, Jeff	R-R	6-2	200	11-19-78	.245	.264	.237	115	404	64	99	22	1	15	60	59	13	0	2	99	9	6	.416	.358
Borowiak, Zach	R-R	6-1	185	5-18-81	.118	.333	.071	8	17	0	2	1	0	0	1	3	0	0	0	9	0	0	.176	.250
Brown, Dusty	R-R	6-0	180	6-19-82	.185	.364	.063	8	27	1	5	2	0	0	3	2	0	0	0	10	0	0	.259	.241
Carter, Chris	L-L	6-0	210	9-16-82	.234	.217	.250	12	47	6	11	1	0	1	4	4	1	0	0	7	0	0	.319	.308
Cash, Kevin	R-R	6-0	190	12-6-77	.176	.186	.171	59	176	22	31	7	0	7	25	23	2	5	2	56	0	0	.335	.276
Clark, Brady	R-R	6-2	200	4-18-73	.263	.200	.286	5	19	2	5	2	0	0	3	3	1	0	1	1	0	1	.526	.375
Clayton, Royce	R-R	6-0	200	1-2-70	.143	.158	.111	7	28	2	4	3	0	0	3	2	0	0	0	10	0	0	.250	.200
Ellsbury, Jacoby	L-L	6-1	185	9-11-83	.298	.265	.312	87	363	66	108	14	5	2	28	32	4	1	1	47	33	6	.380	.360
Jimenez, Luis Antonio	L-L	6-4	205	5-7-82	.148	.200	.141	25	81	4	12	2	0	1	7	9	0	0	1	21	1	0	.210	.231
Keylor, Cory	L-R	6-3	195	8-25-79	.188	1.000	.133	4	16	1	3	0	0	0	3	0	0	0	1	7	0	0	.188	.176
Kielty, Bobby	B-R	6-1	225	8-3-76	.237	.222	.241	10	38	7	9	1	0	2	5	5	0	0	0	14	0	0	.421	.326
Kottaras, George	L-R	6-0	185	5-16-83	.241	.292	.225	87	294	32	71	22	0	9	39	32	2	2	4	71	1	4	.408	.316
Lowrie, Jed	B-R	6-0	180	4-17-84	.300	.333	.282	40	160	21	48	16	1	5	21	12	3	0	2	33	0	1	.506	.356
McEwing, Joe	R-R	5-11	170	10-19-72	.268	.231	.281	122	477	50	128	23	2	8	49	26	6	8	1	104	6	9	.385	.316
Moss, Brandon	L-R	6-0	205	9-16-83	.282	.292	.277	133	493	66	139	41	2	16	78	61	3	0	2	148	15	4	.471	.363
Murphy, David	L-L	6-4	215	10-18-81	.280	.224	.300	100	400	50	112	20	5	9	47	41	1	0	2	68	8	1	.423	.347
Ochoa, Alex	R-R	6-0	200	3-29-72	.138	.107	.153	24	87	2	12	1	0	0	3	4	0	0	1	17	0	1	.149	.174
Prieto, Alex	R-R	5-11	205	6-19-76	.242	.250	.239	59	182	22	44	11	2	3	21	19	1	3	0	32	2	3	.374	.317
Pritz, Bryan	R-R	5-10	180	5-5-82	.188	.333	.100	5	16	0	3	0	0	0	2	2	0	0	0	5	1	0	.188	.278
Robinson, Kerry	L-L	6-0	175	10-3-73	.250	.250	.250	7	28	3	7	2	0	0	2	1	0	0	0	4	1	0	.321	.276
Rogers, Ed	R-R	6-3	190	8-29-78	.249	.267	.243	111	405	41	101	16	0	6	35	20	5	6	4	66	9	5	.333	.290
Scales, Bobby	B-R	6-0	170	10-4-77	.294	.313	.286	122	432	64	127	28	8	11	57	50	8	3	6	94	14	3	.472	.373
Sheely, Matt	R-R	5-9	160	8-30-86	.429	.500	.000	2	7	3	3	0	0	0	2	0	0	0	0	2	0	0	.429	.429
Spann, Chad	R-R	6-1	195	10-25-83	.223	.183	.239	74	251	22	56	9	0	4	17	24	2	2	1	77	1	3	.307	.295
Spivey, Junior	R-R	6-0	200	1-28-75	.241	.150	.269	25	87	13	21	5	0	2	14	11	1	0	0	24	2	1	.368	.333
Tucker, Michael	L-R	6-2	210	6-25-71	.224	.194	.236	72	237	28	53	16	0	6	26	49	3	1	1	64	1	2	.367	.362

PITCHING	B-T	HT	WT	DOB	W	L	ERA	G	GS	CG	SV	IP	H	R	ER	HR	BB	SO	AVG	vLH	vRH	K/9	BB/9
Alvarez, Abe	L-L	6-2	190	10-17-82	5	8	4.77	25	16	0	0	100	102	57	53	9	45	69	.268	.221	.285	6.21	4.05
Barnes, John	R-R	6-2	210	4-24-76	1	1	2.25	3	3	1	0	20	11	6	5	1	13	15	.164	.111	.226	6.75	5.85
Borowiak, Zach	R-R	6-1	185	5-18-81	0	0	0.00	1	0	0	0	1	1	0	0	0	0	1	.250	1.000	.000	9.00	0.00
Breslow, Craig	L-L	6-0	185	8-8-80	2	3	4.06	49	1	0	1	69	70	38	31	6	25	73	.262	.286	.250	9.57	3.28
Buchholz, Clay	L-R	6-3	190	8-14-84	1	3	3.96	8	8	0	0	39	32	21	17	5	15	55	.221	.198	.250	12.80	3.03
Burns, Mike	R-R	6-1	210	7-14-78	4	9	4.66	35	15	1	3	112	125	69	58	15	29	80	.282	.295	.266	6.43	2.33
Corey, Bryan	R-R	6-0	170	10-21-73	6	8	3.69	58	0	0	3	68	57	31	28	6	20	67	.228	.191	.259	8.82	2.63
Delcarmen, Manny	R-R	6-2	190	2-16-82	3	2	3.38	20	0	0	0	29	28	13	11	1	14	37	.243	.289	.214	11.35	4.30
Farnsworth, Jeff	R-R	6-2	190	10-6-75	0	0	4.50	1	0	0	0	2	3	1	1	0	0	1	.333	.500	.000	4.50	0.00
Gabbard, Kason	L-L	6-3	205	4-8-82	7	2	3.24	14	14	0	0	75	66	29	27	10	25	64	.235	.235	.235	7.68	3.00
Hansack, Devern	R-R	6-2	180	2-5-78	10	7	3.61	25	23	0	0	140	126	62	56	16	40	131	.240	.271	.204	8.44	2.58
Hansen, Craig	R-R	6-5	185	11-15-83	3	1	3.86	40	0	0	3	51	58	29	22	2	32	48	.275	.324	.223	8.42	5.61
Hernandez, Runelvys	R-R	6-1	250	4-27-78	0	3	3.06	7	7	0	0	35	31	17	12	5	12	24	.233	.250	.213	6.11	3.06
3-team (6 Scranton/Wilkes-Barre, 4 Indianapolis)					1	7	4.35	17	17	0	0	83	98	61	40	14	29	51	—	—	—	5.55	3.16
Hertzler, Barry	R-R	6-2	215	2-15-81	1	1	16.31	10	0	0	0	16	35	29	29	0	14	4	.449	.417	.500	2.25	7.88
Holdzkom, Lincoln	R-R	6-5	245	3-23-82	1	0	1.59	12	0	0	0	17	19	5	3	0	14	13	.279	.294	.265	6.88	7.41
Hughes, Travis	R-R	6-5	235	5-25-78	7	6	1.91	57	0	0	24	75	61	25	16	3	29	72	.227	.235	.218	8.60	3.46
Lester, Jon	L-L	6-2	190	1-7-84	4	5	3.89	14	14	2	0	72	67	32	31	4	31	51	.250	.250	.250	6.40	3.89
Lonergan, Scott	B-R	6-4	200	12-6-83	0	0	6.23	1	0	0	0	4	3	4	3	0	2	3	.188	.250	.125	6.23	4.15
Lopez, Javier	L-L	6-4	220	7-11-77	2	1	3.78	17	0	0	0	17	19	7	7	0	8	15	.302	.310	.294	8.10	4.32
Martinez, Edgar	R-R	6-0	220	10-23-81	2	6	5.16	42	0	0	1	68	69	46	39	11	28	58	.264	.230	.295	7.68	3.71
Pauley, David	R-R	6-2	185	6-17-83	6	6	4.33	27	26	0	0	154	164	90	74	18	49	110	.269	.255	.283	6.44	2.87
Pineiro, Joel	R-R	6-1	200	9-25-78	0	0	2.25	2	2	0	0	8	3	2	2	0	4	3	.125	.214	.000	3.38	4.50
Schilling, Curt	R-R	6-5	235	11-14-66	0	0	0.00	3	3	0	0	15	8	0	0	0	0	18	.157	.114	.250	10.80	0.00
Smith, Chris	R-R	6-2	200	4-9-81	0	0	1.80	1	0	0	0	5	12	5	1	1	0	2	.444	.333	.533	3.60	0.00
Timlin, Mike	R-R	6-4	210	3-10-66	0	0	4.15	8	2	0	0	9	9	4	4	0	3	3	.281	.333	.214	3.12	3.12
Zink, Charlie	R-R	6-1	190	8-26-79	2	3	5.89	8	8	0	0	47	51	37	31	8	27	23	.267	.255	.281	4.37	5.13

FIELDING

Catcher	PCT	G	PO	A	E	DP	PB
Brown	.970	8	60	5	2	1	5
Cash	.995	58	393	36	2	4	10
Kottaras	.985	83	621	41	10	4	8

First Base	PCT	G	PO	A	E	DP
Bailey	.987	85	718	58	10	54
Carter	1.000	12	97	13	0	11
Jimenez	1.000	7	56	3	0	6
Moss	1.000	5	48	2	0	4
Scales	.989	31	255	17	3	25
Tucker	1.000	5	47	3	0	2

Second Base	PCT	G	PO	A	E	DP
Borowiak	.750	1	3	0	1	0
Lowrie	.933	7	11	17	2	4
McEwing	.989	64	116	160	3	36
Prieto	.975	16	25	54	2	8
Rogers	.980	22	40	60	2	11
Scales	.965	33	48	91	5	11

Spivey	.960	9	23	25	2	5

Third Base	PCT	G	PO	A	E	DP
Borowiak	1.000	2	0	4	0	0
Cash	1.000	1	0	1	0	0
Lowrie	.889	2	2	6	1	0
McEwing	.951	34	21	56	4	3
Prieto	1.000	3	0	2	0	0
Rogers	.955	28	22	41	3	3
Scales	1.000	4	0	4	0	0
Spann	.930	73	65	149	16	15

Shortstop	PCT	G	PO	A	E	DP
Borowiak	1.000	2	3	1	0	0
Clayton	.840	6	6	15	4	2
Lowrie	.973	31	36	108	4	21
McEwing	.938	5	4	11	1	1
Prieto	.959	40	59	104	7	24
Rogers	.965	62	74	172	9	24
Scales	.889	3	1	7	1	1

Outfield	PCT	G	PO	A	E	DP
Bailey	1.000	13	21	0	0	0
Clark	1.000	4	5	1	0	0
Ellsbury	.983	84	171	1	3	1
Keylor	.909	4	9	1	1	0
Kielty	.929	7	13	0	1	0
McEwing	1.000	5	10	1	0	0
Moss	.992	122	238	5	2	2
Murphy	.966	97	189	9	7	2
Ochoa	.917	14	21	1	2	0
Pritz	1.000	4	8	0	0	0
Robinson	1.000	7	10	1	0	0
Rogers	—	1	0	0	0	0
Scales	.986	41	66	7	1	0
Sheely	1.000	2	1	0	0	0
Spivey	.955	16	21	0	1	0
Tucker	1.000	12	19	1	0	0

ORGANIZATION STATISTICS

PORTLAND SEA DOGS

DOUBLE-A

EASTERN LEAGUE

BATTING	B-T	HT	WT	DOB	AVG	vLH	vRH	G	AB	R	H	2B	3B	HR	RBI	BB	HBP	SH	SF	SO	SB	CS	SLG	OBP
Bacani, David	R-R	5-7	170	7-30-79	.308	.333	.300	4	13	3	4	2	0	1	2	3	1	0	0	2	0	0	.692	.471
Bates, Aaron	R-R	6-4	232	3-10-84	.198	.167	.205	27	91	16	18	9	0	4	13	17	4	0	0	29	0	0	.429	.348
Bell, Bubba	L-R	6-0	195	10-9-82	.265	.176	.292	34	147	23	39	5	2	4	22	14	2	0	0	17	4	0	.408	.337
Borowiak, Zach	R-R	6-1	185	5-18-81	.232	.233	.232	79	254	41	59	6	0	3	31	22	4	5	3	42	3	0	.291	.300
Brown, Dusty	R-R	6-0	180	6-19-82	.268	.255	.271	69	254	43	68	16	2	9	43	28	2	0	1	64	0	0	.453	.344
Corsaletti, Jeffrey	L-R	6-0	190	2-22-83	.266	.259	.269	123	462	93	123	21	3	6	58	83	9	2	4	87	20	7	.364	.385
Crozier, Eric	L-L	6-4	200	8-11-78	.236	.140	.260	63	220	37	52	11	1	9	44	35	1	0	3	81	1	0	.418	.340
Ellsbury, Jacoby	L-L	6-1	185	9-11-83	.452	.346	.511	17	73	16	33	10	2	0	13	6	4	0	0	7	8	1	.644	.518
Granadillo, Tony	B-R	5-10	165	8-10-84	.333	.250	.348	9	27	4	9	3	0	0	4	3	0	0	0	3	0	1	.444	.400
Johnson, Jay	R-R	6-2	185	12-19-82	.265	.271	.264	109	411	47	109	27	4	5	64	44	3	3	2	79	5	3	.387	.339
Keylor, Cory	R-R	6-3	195	8-25-79	.246	.348	.216	111	398	53	98	24	6	9	47	41	5	1	6	109	7	3	.405	.320
Lowrie, Jed	B-R	6-0	180	4-17-84	.297	.352	.276	93	337	61	100	31	7	8	49	65	1	3	2	58	5	3	.501	.410
Natale, Jeff	R-R	5-9	180	8-24-82	.270	.295	.262	119	404	66	109	28	1	5	64	88	21	1	10	36	5	3	.381	.417
Otness, John	R-R	5-11	200	9-15-81	.227	.269	.212	71	251	17	57	10	2	0	24	8	4	1	2	31	1	1	.283	.260
Paniagua, Salvador	R-R	6-1	240	5-21-83	.262	.000	.333	14	42	6	11	3	1	2	6	4	0	0	0	14	0	0	.524	.326
Pinckney, Andrew	B-R	6-1	195	4-7-82	.264	.280	.260	125	458	72	121	28	4	14	64	41	4	0	5	100	4	7	.434	.327
Pritz, Bryan	R-R	5-10	180	5-5-82	.292	.231	.309	101	356	50	104	22	3	7	47	39	1	1	5	53	4	1	.430	.359
Reddick, Josh	L-R	6-2	180	2-19-87	.000	—	.000	1	1	0	0	0	0	0	0	0	0	0	0	0	0	0	.000	.000
Spann, Chad	R-R	6-1	195	10-25-83	.250	.269	.243	24	96	13	24	8	0	4	26	8	1	0	4	32	0	1	.458	.303
Suarez, Iggy	R-R	5-11	165	5-3-81	.253	.289	.240	105	352	53	89	17	2	4	33	36	2	2	1	89	7	1	.347	.325
Youngbauer, Scott	B-R	6-1	175	1-14-79	.167	.000	.195	13	48	4	8	2	1	0	3	5	0	1	0	12	1	0	.250	.245

PITCHING	B-T	HT	WT	DOB	W	L	ERA	G	GS	CG	SV	IP	H	R	ER	HR	BB	SO	AVG	vLH	vRH	K/9	BB/9
Almanzar, Carlos	R-R	6-2	200	11-6-73	0	0	2.25	3	0	0	0	4	3	1	1	0	1	4	.214	.250	.167	9.00	2.25
Bajoczky, Tony	R-R	6-0	170	9-24-84	0	0	5.40	1	1	0	0	5	6	3	3	1	1	2	.300	.333	.286	3.60	1.80
Barnes, John	R-R	6-2	210	4-24-76	1	2	2.76	4	3	0	0	16	10	8	5	0	20	11	.185	.259	.111	6.06	11.02
Bowden, Michael	R-R	6-3	215	9-9-86	8	6	4.28	19	19	1	0	97	105	51	46	9	33	82	.279	.299	.261	7.63	3.07
Buchholz, Clay	L-R	6-3	190	8-14-84	7	2	1.77	16	15	1	0	87	55	18	17	4	22	116	.180	.149	.210	12.05	2.28
Cox, Bryson	R-R	6-4	205	8-10-84	1	1	4.91	9	0	0	0	15	15	14	8	1	11	3	.273	.154	.379	1.84	6.75
Diaz, Felix	R-R	6-1	190	7-27-80	4	4	5.59	9	9	1	0	47	50	32	29	7	12	49	.270	.268	.272	9.45	2.31
Dobies, Andrew	L-L	6-1	180	4-20-83	4	3	5.35	34	10	0	0	76	90	50	45	10	28	70	.297	.279	.304	8.33	3.33
Fernandes, Kyle	L-L	6-0	190	9-12-85	0	0	6.75	1	0	0	0	3	6	2	2	0	0	2	.500	.667	.444	6.75	0.00
Goodson, Matthew	R-R	6-3	195	9-26-82	1	1	4.76	5	5	0	0	23	14	14	12	0	16	24	.177	.222	.140	9.53	6.35
Haigwood, Daniel	R-L	6-2	200	11-19-83	3	5	5.74	17	16	0	0	69	68	51	44	12	49	72	.257	.375	.225	9.39	6.39
Hertzler, Barry	R-R	6-2	215	2-15-81	3	2	2.98	30	0	0	1	54	54	23	18	4	12	24	.261	.313	.213	3.98	1.99
Holdzkom, Lincoln	R-R	6-5	245	3-23-82	4	1	3.47	30	0	0	1	47	35	23	18	5	30	41	.211	.261	.175	7.91	5.79
Hottovy, Thomas	L-L	6-1	195	7-9-81	4	10	5.61	24	23	0	0	120	144	78	75	17	49	69	.304	.277	.315	5.16	3.66
Jackson, Kyle	R-R	6-3	190	4-9-83	4	9	5.99	42	0	0	1	71	69	54	47	9	48	83	.254	.291	.228	10.57	6.11
James, Michael	R-R	6-1	185	6-2-81	2	3	3.77	55	0	0	22	57	56	28	24	8	37	60	.255	.220	.279	9.42	5.81
Johnson, Jay	R-R	6-2	185	12-19-82	0	0	9.00	1	0	0	0	1	2	1	1	0	1	0	.400	.333	.500	0.00	9.00
Jones, Christopher	R-R	6-3	205	6-9-84	0	1	27.00	1	0	0	0	2	5	6	6	1	1	3	.500	.400	.600	13.50	4.50
Jones, Hunter	L-L	6-4	235	1-10-84	2	1	3.19	23	0	0	2	42	35	17	15	3	16	43	.226	.243	.220	9.14	3.40
Lester, Jon	L-L	6-2	190	1-7-84	1	0	1.50	1	1	0	0	6	5	1	1	0	4	4	.217	.333	.200	6.00	6.00
Masterson, Justin	R-R	6-6	250	3-22-85	4	3	4.34	10	10	0	0	58	49	29	28	4	18	59	.225	.312	.160	9.16	2.79
Maxwell, Blake	R-R	6-5	255	8-1-84	0	0	3.38	1	0	0	0	3	3	1	1	0	0	3	.273	.167	.400	10.12	0.00
Nall, T.J.	R-R	6-1	175	11-4-80	0	2	9.00	2	1	0	0	6	8	7	6	2	6	4	.333	.364	.308	6.00	9.00
2-team (12 Harrisburg)					3	11	5.18	14	13	0	0	75	96	53	43	12	28	48	—	—	—	5.79	3.38
Povich, Chad	R-R	6-0	185	6-13-86	0	0	0.00	1	0	0	0	3	2	0	0	0	1	1	.222	.000	.286	3.38	3.38
Shoemaker, Scott	R-R	6-4	210	9-21-81	0	0	10.80	2	0	0	0	3	7	5	4	0	2	2	.438	.300	.667	5.40	5.40
Smith, Chris	R-R	6-2	200	4-9-81	6	9	4.41	30	14	0	1	104	126	57	51	10	42	80	.309	.302	.315	6.92	3.63
Vaquedano, Jose	R-R	6-4	167	7-9-81	2	1	3.96	22	0	0	0	39	37	17	17	5	18	23	.255	.327	.211	5.35	4.19
Vaughan, Beau	B-R	6-4	230	6-4-81	1	2	3.34	42	0	0	6	59	52	25	22	2	31	64	.228	.267	.197	9.71	4.70
Zink, Charlie	R-R	6-1	190	8-26-79	9	3	3.98	16	16	1	0	93	92	50	41	6	44	55	.265	.280	.251	5.34	4.27

FIELDING

Catcher	PCT	G	PO	A	E	DP	PB
Brown	.991	69	500	57	5	6	15
Otness	.996	65	475	36	2	5	6
Paniagua	.990	12	92	4	1	0	4

First Base	PCT	G	PO	A	E	DP
Bates	.989	24	172	9	2	22
Borowiak	1.000	5	31	4	0	3
Crozier	.995	52	388	33	2	47
Natale	.990	41	291	21	3	34
Otness	1.000	5	48	5	0	5
Spann	.983	13	110	5	2	9
Youngbauer	1.000	4	42	2	0	3

Second Base	PCT	G	PO	A	E	DP
Bacani	1.000	3	2	9	0	0
Borowiak	.976	46	90	115	5	33
Granadillo	.962	8	14	11	1	4
Lowrie	1.000	2	2	3	0	0
Natale	.981	37	80	76	3	18
Suarez	.967	48	78	124	7	34
Youngbauer	.750	2	5	4	3	2

Third Base	PCT	G	PO	A	E	DP
Borowiak	.969	22	10	53	2	5
Pinckney	.935	114	77	212	20	26
Spann	1.000	5	3	13	0	4
Suarez	1.000	1	0	1	0	0

	PCT	G	PO	A	E	DP
Youngbauer	1.000	1	2	0	0	0

Shortstop	PCT	G	PO	A	E	DP
Borowiak	1.000	7	6	11	0	4
Lowrie	.961	85	130	190	13	48
Suarez	.972	55	90	150	7	37

Outfield	PCT	G	PO	A	E	DP
Bell	.988	30	76	4	1	0
Corsaletti	.986	117	213	6	3	1
Ellsbury	.962	17	50	0	2	0
Johnson	1.000	85	139	5	0	1
Keylor	.982	96	159	3	3	0
Pritz	.990	88	185	10	2	4

LANCASTER JETHAWKS

HIGH CLASS A

CALIFORNIA LEAGUE

BATTING	B-T	HT	WT	DOB	AVG	vLH	vRH	G	AB	R	H	2B	3B	HR	RBI	BB	HBP	SH	SF	SO	SB	CS	SLG	OBP
Anderson, Lars	L-L	6-4	215	9-25-87	.343	.333	.348	10	35	13	12	2	0	1	9	11	0	0	1	9	0	0	.486	.489
Bates, Aaron	R-R	6-4	232	3-10-84	.332	.345	.329	98	373	89	124	21	2	24	88	69	19	0	4	83	0	1	.592	.456
Bell, Bubba	L-R	6-0	195	10-9-82	.370	.354	.374	76	322	95	119	27	1	22	83	48	5	0	3	39	10	4	.665	.455
Correll, Brad	R-R	6-2	205	6-17-81	.344	.424	.315	59	250	69	86	13	3	23	80	19	3	0	4	34	4	0	.696	.391
Daeges, Zachary	L-R	6-4	225	11-16-83	.330	.256	.352	127	515	124	170	55	5	21	113	82	8	0	9	97	4	1	.579	.423

	B-T	HT	WT	DOB	AVG	vLH	vRH	G	AB	R	H	2B	3B	HR	RBI	BB	HBP	SH	SF	SO	SB	CS	SLG	OBP
Farkes, Zak	R-R	5-11	190	5-30-83	.275	.205	.298	40	153	29	42	7	0	10	33	9	0	0	0	36	1	0	.516	.315
Garrabrants, Steve	R-R	5-10	170	11-18-81	.288	.270	.295	37	125	32	36	8	2	9	32	24	3	0	1	29	1	0	.600	.412
Granadillo, Tony	B-R	5-10	165	8-10-84	.326	.379	.311	109	445	104	145	36	7	8	63	54	13	0	4	65	2	0	.492	.411
Hall, Michael	L-L	6-1	195	5-20-85	.301	.200	.330	82	266	59	80	19	7	11	43	49	2	0	2	78	0	1	.549	.411
Jeroloman, Chuck	R-R	6-1	190	9-14-82	.155	.000	.188	17	58	9	9	4	1	1	6	5	2	0	0	22	0	0	.310	.246
Johnson, Jay	R-R	6-2	185	12-19-82	.282	.500	.207	25	110	16	31	7	0	1	17	13	1	0	1	20	0	1	.373	.360
Khoury, Ryan	R-R	5-10	180	3-19-84	.300	.293	.302	98	380	82	114	29	1	11	69	49	8	0	7	78	3	1	.468	.385
Lara, Christian	R-R	5-11	150	4-11-85	.238	.298	.220	99	366	73	87	18	7	9	53	48	2	2	5	106	1	4	.399	.325
Negron, Kristopher	R-R	6-0	180	2-1-86	.182	.000	.333	3	11	3	2	0	0	0	0	2	0	0	0	2	0	0	.182	.308
Paniagua, Salvador	R-R	6-1	240	5-21-83	.286	.297	.284	46	185	33	53	13	1	11	42	8	5	0	3	56	1	0	.546	.328
Sheely, Matt	R-R	5-9	160	8-30-86	.231	.200	.250	5	13	3	3	1	0	0	2	2	0	1	1	4	0	0	.308	.313
Soto, Luis	B-R	6-1	179	12-7-85	.221	.231	.217	70	263	39	58	7	1	8	33	28	2	0	1	62	0	2	.346	.299
Still, Jon	R-R	6-2	210	11-16-84	.288	.267	.292	22	80	19	23	4	0	4	19	18	2	0	3	18	0	1	.488	.417
Suarez, Iggy	R-R	5-11	165	5-3-81	.379	.364	.382	18	66	15	25	8	1	0	15	13	0	0	1	17	0	1	.530	.475
Turner, Christopher	R-R	5-11	195	12-2-83	.160	.000	.206	22	81	12	13	1	0	5	9	8	1	0	1	40	0	1	.358	.242
Wagner, Mark	R-R	6-1	205	6-11-83	.318	.342	.312	95	368	71	117	35	1	14	82	55	3	0	5	46	0	1	.533	.406
White, Scott	R-L	6-3	196	10-18-83	.256	.234	.261	117	465	79	119	29	1	21	98	56	12	0	6	103	4	3	.458	.347
Yema, Yahmed	L-L	6-0	195	9-3-84	.229	.050	.270	28	109	13	25	3	0	6	16	10	0	0	1	16	1	0	.404	.257

PITCHING	B-T	HT	WT	DOB	W	L	ERA	G	GS	CG	SV	IP	H	R	ER	HR	BB	SO	AVG	vLH	vRH	K/9	BB/9
Bard, Daniel	R-R	6-4	195	6-25-85	0	2	10.13	5	5	0	0	13	21	23	15	2	22	9	.350	.259	.424	6.07	14.85
Barnes, John	R-R	6-2	210	4-24-76	4	4	6.96	12	12	0	0	63	61	57	49	11	55	57	.254	.223	.281	8.10	7.82
Beazley, Travis	R-R	6-0	175	6-17-83	7	2	4.17	10	10	0	0	54	57	30	25	8	13	34	.268	.212	.321	5.67	2.17
Blackey, Jason	R-R	6-4	206	4-11-83	4	0	5.40	41	0	0	0	73	71	50	44	8	21	48	.251	.229	.267	5.89	2.58
Bowden, Michael	R-R	6-3	215	9-9-86	2	0	1.37	8	8	0	0	46	35	10	7	1	8	46	.212	.169	.256	9.00	1.57
Casillas, Ismael	R-R	6-3	215	12-8-82	4	4	6.14	35	0	0	3	66	65	48	45	10	34	61	.257	.243	.267	8.32	4.64
Cox, Adam	L-L	6-4	170	6-27-80	2	1	5.85	6	6	0	0	32	35	23	21	6	13	21	.282	.242	.297	5.85	3.62
Cox, Timothy	R-L	5-10	165	7-8-86	1	1	6.18	11	0	0	0	28	40	23	19	6	8	18	.345	.400	.326	5.86	2.60
Fernandes, Kyle	L-L	6-0	190	9-12-85	2	0	7.61	13	0	0	0	24	31	21	20	3	13	19	.320	.355	.303	7.23	4.94
Goodson, Matthew	R-R	6-3	195	9-26-82	4	5	6.88	11	11	0	0	52	75	43	40	12	24	38	.336	.362	.314	6.54	4.13
Guyette, Kevin	R-R	6-4	215	12-3-82	5	2	3.95	21	3	0	2	57	51	30	25	6	23	42	.241	.270	.220	6.63	3.63
Johnson, Kristofer	L-L	6-4	170	10-14-84	9	7	5.56	27	27	0	0	136	148	91	84	20	57	100	.279	.282	.278	6.62	3.77
Jones, Hunter	L-L	6-4	235	1-10-84	4	1	2.11	24	0	0	0	47	35	16	11	2	21	40	.212	.273	.182	7.66	4.02
Large, T.J.	R-R	6-4	185	5-28-83	6	4	3.19	32	0	0	9	54	58	25	19	4	20	54	.275	.224	.310	9.06	3.35
Masterson, Justin	R-R	6-6	250	3-22-85	8	5	4.33	17	17	0	0	96	103	56	46	4	22	56	.275	.299	.253	5.24	2.07
Maxwell, Blake	R-R	6-5	255	8-1-84	6	3	6.04	40	0	0	3	70	87	49	47	10	27	39	.309	.321	.300	5.01	3.47
McAllister, Cody	R-R	6-2	190	3-21-84	0	0	5.97	14	0	0	1	29	36	19	19	5	9	22	.305	.278	.328	6.91	2.83
Nall, T.J.	R-R	6-1	175	11-4-80	1	4	6.57	11	11	0	0	62	68	51	45	9	24	38	.278	.284	.272	5.55	3.50
Pena, Mario	L-L	6-4	170	12-7-84	1	1	12.21	4	2	0	0	14	27	20	19	2	6	0	.422	.476	.395	0.00	3.86
Rhoades, Chad	R-R	5-10	175	3-10-83	3	2	4.34	49	0	0	16	64	75	38	31	7	23	63	.298	.353	.250	8.81	3.22
Richardson, Dustin	L-L	6-5	195	1-9-84	4	0	2.74	4	4	0	0	23	14	8	7	1	5	25	.173	.148	.185	9.78	1.96
Rozier, Michael	L-L	6-5	210	7-4-85	4	9	7.74	23	23	0	0	107	160	113	92	20	50	83	.346	.299	.364	6.98	4.21
Vaquedano, Jose	R-R	6-4	167	7-9-81	2	0	5.40	14	1	0	0	28	32	19	17	4	9	23	.286	.333	.257	7.31	2.86
Zink, J.T.	R-R	6-2	195	5-6-85	0	0	216.00	1	0	0	0	0	6	8	8	1	2	0	.857	—	.857	0.00	54.00

FIELDING

Catcher	PCT	G	PO	A	E	DP	PB
Farkes	.993	17	134	12	1	4	7
Paniagua	.984	37	236	18	4	1	7
Still	1.000	7	52	3	0	0	2
Wagner	.993	82	527	61	4	5	9

First Base	PCT	G	PO	A	E	DP
Anderson	1.000	8	66	10	0	8
Bates	.992	87	771	68	7	98
Daeges	.987	10	66	10	1	6
Farkes	.962	3	21	4	1	1
Still	.965	10	72	11	3	4
White	.992	27	217	26	2	17

Second Base	PCT	G	PO	A	E	DP
Garrabrants	.964	13	17	36	2	6
Granadillo	.983	91	185	286	8	72
Jeroloman	.889	5	12	12	3	4

	PCT	G	PO	A	E	DP
Khoury	.938	27	59	78	9	23
Negron	.941	2	6	10	1	2
Suarez	1.000	4	11	11	0	5

Third Base	PCT	G	PO	A	E	DP
Daeges	.667	1	1	1	1	0
Farkes	.889	5	2	6	1	0
Garrabrants	1.000	9	7	13	0	2
Granadillo	.909	15	16	34	5	1
Jeroloman	1.000	5	6	5	0	2
Khoury	.899	47	25	99	14	7
White	.913	62	52	105	15	12

Shortstop	PCT	G	PO	A	E	DP
Granadillo	.923	2	5	7	1	3
Jeroloman	1.000	6	10	12	0	2
Khoury	.967	21	33	54	3	7
Lara	.954	99	165	293	22	75

	PCT	G	PO	A	E	DP
Negron	.833	1	1	4	1	1
Suarez	.957	14	22	45	3	8

Outfield	PCT	G	PO	A	E	DP
Bell	.972	74	170	2	5	0
Correll	.984	55	119	6	2	3
Daeges	.968	78	117	5	4	2
Garrabrants	1.000	12	22	0	0	0
Hall	.974	81	175	12	5	2
Johnson	1.000	25	35	3	0	1
Khoury	1.000	1	2	0	0	0
Sheely	1.000	4	9	0	0	0
Soto	.910	59	69	2	7	1
Turner	.919	22	34	0	3	0
Yema	.970	28	61	3	2	1

GREENVILLE DRIVE

LOW CLASS A

SOUTH ATLANTIC LEAGUE

BATTING	B-T	HT	WT	DOB	AVG	vLH	vRH	G	AB	R	H	2B	3B	HR	RBI	BB	HBP	SH	SF	SO	SB	CS	SLG	OBP
Anderson, Lars	L-L	6-4	215	9-25-87	.288	.269	.295	124	458	69	132	35	3	10	69	71	2	0	2	112	2	4	.443	.385
Arambarris, Manuel	R-R	6-0	178	8-25-85	.284	.314	.274	85	345	46	98	11	4	4	37	17	0	0	3	61	2	0	.374	.315
Chambers, Michael	R-R	6-0	175	1-20-84	.157	.259	.120	43	102	5	16	4	0	0	4	7	0	1	0	25	0	0	.196	.211
Chiang, Chih-Hsien	L-R	6-2	170	2-21-88	.262	.226	.275	97	355	35	93	27	2	5	41	22	4	0	3	81	1	1	.392	.310
Cooney, Matthew	R-R	5-11	255	12-26-85	.111	.333	.000	5	9	0	1	0	0	0	0	0	0	0	0	4	0	0	.111	.273
Diaz, Argenis	R-R	5-11	175	2-12-87	.279	.278	.279	99	405	62	113	25	5	2	40	36	4	0	2	92	5	9	.380	.342
Egan, Jonathan	R-R	6-4	210	10-12-86	.206	.227	.200	63	204	26	42	10	1	9	31	28	5	0	1	79	0	0	.397	.315
Engel, Reid	L-L	6-3	190	5-7-87	.292	.272	.298	112	411	60	120	20	6	9	49	38	9	1	5	78	13	4	.436	.361
Exposito, Luis	R-R	6-3	210	1-20-87	.233	.167	.278	9	30	3	7	0	0	0	2	2	0	0	0	5	0	0	.233	.281
Farkes, Zak	R-R	5-11	190	5-30-83	.181	.200	.172	24	83	13	15	2	0	4	10	8	2	0	0	23	0	0	.349	.269
Fernandez-Oliva, Carlos	B-R	6-1	175	9-23-86	.234	.314	.198	47	167	24	39	6	0	0	16	14	2	0	3	44	2	1	.269	.296
Hall, Michael	L-L	6-1	195	5-20-85	.213	.375	.143	24	80	15	17	5	2	0	7	14	0	0	0	21	2	1	.325	.330
Jones, Michael	L-R	6-3	220	6-14-85	.276	.318	.259	22	76	7	21	4	2	0	10	12	0	0	2	17	0	0	.382	.367
Negron, Kristopher	R-R	6-0	180	2-1-86	.226	.214	.230	112	403	61	91	14	3	4	29	46	13	5	0	97	29	7	.295	.325
Place, Jason	R-R	6-3	205	5-8-88	.214	.205	.216	129	459	60	98	23	4	12	55	52	4	0	2	160	19	4	.359	.298
Reddick, Josh	L-R	6-2	180	2-19-87	.306	.330	.298	94	369	60	113	17	6	18	72	26	3	0	5	51	8	5	.531	.352

	B-T	HT	WT	DOB	AVG	vLH	vRH	G	AB	R	H	2B	3B	HR	RBI	BB	HBP	SH	SF	SO	SB	CS	SLG	OBP
Reza, Aaron	R-R	5-7	180	6-25-85	.220	.188	.233	20	59	4	13	3	0	0	4	10	3	0	0	8	1	1	.271	.361
Sheely, Matt	R-R	5-9	160	8-30-86	.300	.293	.303	40	140	25	42	9	2	2	21	9	1	1	1	22	11	1	.436	.344
Smyth, Paul	R-R	6-2	205	4-25-83	.317	.469	.274	43	145	24	46	10	1	7	26	7	5	0	2	30	0	1	.545	.365
Still, Jon	R-R	6-2	210	11-16-84	.292	.258	.304	102	360	71	105	25	1	21	79	87	4	0	3	85	2	0	.542	.432
Vasquez, Pedro	R-R	6-0	167	6-29-86	.224	.207	.232	35	98	16	22	5	0	1	9	9	2	0	0	24	5	1	.306	.303

PITCHING	B-T	HT	WT	DOB	W	L	ERA	G	GS	CG	SV	IP	H	R	ER	HR	BB	SO	AVG	vLH	vRH	K/9	BB/9
Bard, Daniel	R-R	6-4	195	6-25-85	3	5	6.42	17	17	0	0	62	55	49	44	3	56	38	.250	.276	.233	5.55	8.17
Beattie, Eric	R-R	6-3	190	4-2-83	0	0	5.00	10	0	0	0	9	7	9	5	1	17	6	.206	.250	.182	6.00	17.00
Beazley, Travis	R-R	6-0	175	6-17-83	6	7	5.22	18	15	1	0	102	111	61	59	12	12	92	.279	.323	.257	8.14	1.06
Blackley, Adam	L-L	6-1	220	2-22-85	1	0	6.75	17	0	0	0	32	31	26	24	3	21	34	.248	.296	.235	9.56	5.91
Chambers, Michael	R-R	6-0	175	1-20-84	0	0	0.00	0	0	0	0	1	1	0	0	0	0	1	.250	.000	.500	9.00	0.00
Cox, Bryson	R-R	6-4	205	8-10-84	1	1	5.40	21	0	0	0	33	31	23	20	4	10	24	.238	.216	.253	6.48	2.70
Craft, Jordan	R-R	6-3	200	6-5-85	1	3	10.80	12	7	0	0	25	35	30	30	3	18	23	.337	.265	.371	8.28	6.48
Doubront, Felix	L-L	6-2	166	10-23-87	3	7	8.93	11	11	0	0	42	63	49	42	8	17	22	.337	.400	.320	4.68	3.61
Fernandes, Kyle	L-L	6-0	190	9-12-85	2	1	4.50	26	0	0	1	50	51	26	25	4	19	33	.271	.326	.254	5.94	3.42
Guerra, Joseph	R-R	5-11	178	9-4-86	2	0	4.02	6	6	0	0	31	40	16	14	0	6	6	.308	.242	.368	1.72	1.72
James, Jimmy	R-R	6-2	175	10-16-84	2	5	5.59	10	0	0	0	47	54	35	29	6	24	29	.287	.273	.300	5.59	4.63
Jones, Christopher	R-R	6-3	205	6-9-84	7	7	4.70	31	18	0	3	113	122	69	59	9	35	120	.271	.256	.280	9.56	2.79
Large, T.J.	R-R	6-4	185	5-28-83	1	2	3.65	17	0	0	0	25	25	12	10	3	5	25	.253	.150	.322	9.12	1.82
Lentz, Richard	R-R	6-2	210	8-6-84	0	1	4.04	31	0	0	1	49	45	22	22	3	42	52	.249	.256	.243	9.55	7.71
Lester, Jon	L-L	6-2	190	1-7-84	0	0	2.08	3	3	0	0	13	11	3	3	2	2	15	.229	.125	.250	10.38	1.38
McAllister, Cody	R-R	6-2	190	3-21-84	0	1	1.84	10	0	0	3	15	11	7	3	2	5	14	.200	.158	.222	8.59	3.07
New, Brantley	R-R	6-3	215	5-1-84	1	2	8.31	10	0	0	0	26	39	26	24	1	11	16	.355	.511	.238	5.54	3.81
Papelbon, Josh	R-R	6-1	210	6-24-83	5	8	3.91	62	0	0	18	76	86	41	33	4	21	57	.289	.296	.284	6.75	2.49
Phillips, Ryan	L-L	6-4	210	5-29-84	3	4	4.17	22	13	0	0	78	67	43	36	3	46	80	.233	.350	.203	9.27	5.33
Povich, Chad	R-R	6-0	185	6-13-86	1	1	10.47	10	0	0	0	16	32	21	19	4	8	14	.410	.467	.375	7.71	4.41
Province, Christopher	R-R	6-3	220	1-20-85	3	2	4.91	15	0	0	2	33	41	24	18	1	8	23	.311	.333	.295	6.27	2.18
Richardson, Dustin	L-L	6-5	195	1-9-84	5	7	3.34	21	21	0	0	100	86	46	37	4	47	98	.235	.235	.235	8.85	4.24
Rodriguez, Jorge	R-R	6-1	160	3-11-85	5	1	6.45	34	0	0	0	75	100	69	54	13	38	41	.321	.325	.318	4.90	4.54
Socolovich, Miguel	R-R	6-1	155	7-24-86	2	2	6.65	11	0	0	0	22	30	20	16	4	10	21	.323	.303	.333	8.72	4.15
Steinocher, Brian	R-R	6-1	190	8-1-84	4	12	5.78	29	18	0	1	125	152	84	80	12	30	64	.306	.335	.286	4.62	2.17
Ventura, Felix	R-R	5-11	165	4-27-84	0	2	9.00	3	0	0	0	5	8	7	5	2	4	3	.364	.333	.385	5.40	7.20

FIELDING

Catcher	PCT	G	PO	A	E	DP	PB
Cooney	.960	4	22	2	1	1	1
Egan	.984	59	392	30	7	4	12
Exposito	.985	9	61	4	1	0	3
Farkes	.989	10	81	5	1	1	2
Smyth	.980	32	181	15	4	4	3
Still	.983	39	261	22	5	1	11

First Base	PCT	G	PO	A	E	DP
Anderson	.990	113	943	93	10	90
Chambers	.980	15	96	4	2	6
Cooney	—	1	0	0	0	0
Farkes	1.000	2	24	3	0	1
Jones	.987	10	69	8	1	4
Still	.969	9	55	7	2	7

Second Base	PCT	G	PO	A	E	DP
Chambers	1.000	9	7	11	0	2
Chiang	.963	86	120	189	12	38
Negron	.982	41	77	145	4	29
Reza	1.000	3	9	7	0	2
Vasquez	1.000	14	22	40	0	7

Third Base	PCT	G	PO	A	E	DP
Arambarris	.913	81	48	163	20	10
Chambers	.778	10	4	10	4	1
Farkes	1.000	6	2	13	0	1
Negron	.933	31	31	39	5	3
Reza	.839	16	7	19	5	1
Smyth	—	1	0	0	0	0
Vasquez	.667	5	2	6	4	0

Shortstop	PCT	G	PO	A	E	DP
Diaz	.952	99	167	305	24	62
Negron	.969	40	64	124	6	24
Vasquez	.964	10	7	20	1	1

Outfield	PCT	G	PO	A	E	DP
Chambers	—	1	0	0	0	0
Engel	.976	102	152	9	4	0
Fernandez-Oliva	.907	43	62	6	7	1
Hall	.978	24	41	4	1	1
Negron	1.000	5	3	0	0	0
Place	.969	127	263	14	9	6
Reddick	.966	93	182	19	7	3
Sheely	.980	29	46	2	1	0
Smyth	1.000	8	11	3	0	0

LOWELL SPINNERS   SHORT-SEASON

NEW YORK-PENN LEAGUE

BATTING	B-T	HT	WT	DOB	AVG	vLH	vRH	G	AB	R	H	2B	3B	HR	RBI	BB	HBP	SH	SF	SO	SB	CS	SLG	OBP
Brooks, Deshaun	R-R	6-4	230	10-25-84	.208	.200	.211	34	101	17	21	2	1	2	12	7	4	0	0	30	0	0	.307	.286
Cabreja, Rafael	L-R	5-9	160	4-14-87	.250	.250	.250	61	216	23	54	11	3	2	25	35	2	4	4	42	7	3	.356	.354
Dent, Ryan	R-R	6-0	190	3-15-89	.178	.125	.189	11	45	5	8	1	0	0	3	1	0	0	0	13	4	1	.200	.196
Fernandez-Oliva, Carlos	B-R	6-1	175	9-23-86	.307	.406	.276	70	267	35	82	17	1	2	42	26	0	7	4	40	6	3	.401	.364
Jimenez, Jorge	L-R	6-1	210	9-12-84	.303	.214	.330	68	238	38	72	23	3	4	44	32	16	0	5	18	4	7	.475	.412
Jones, Michael	L-R	6-3	220	6-14-85	.340	.293	.355	45	162	25	55	7	1	2	16	26	1	0	0	31	1	0	.432	.434
Kalish, Ryan	L-L	6-1	205	3-28-88	.368	.286	.394	23	87	27	32	4	1	3	13	16	1	0	0	12	18	3	.540	.471
Keowen, Kade	R-R	6-5	215	4-18-86	.207	.250	.195	39	145	18	30	11	0	1	15	8	4	0	3	47	0	0	.303	.263
Lewis, Brett	R-R	5-10	192	3-16-85	.213	.176	.224	29	75	10	16	2	0	0	8	14	3	2	1	14	1	1	.240	.355
Lin, Che-Hsuan	R-R	6-0	180	9-21-88	.163	.000	.212	11	43	7	7	2	0	0	3	5	1	1	0	10	3	2	.209	.265
Marks, David	R-R	6-0	190	3-23-87	.241	.154	.250	58	174	30	42	9	1	1	14	30	7	1	1	59	10	3	.322	.373
Milano, Dan	R-R	6-1	210	8-25-85	.273	.375	.240	10	33	4	9	1	0	1	6	2	2	0	1	8	1	0	.394	.342
Navarro, Yamaico	R-R	5-11	170	10-31-87	.289	.353	.270	62	225	36	65	10	1	5	37	22	3	1	2	52	12	6	.409	.357
Reza, Aaron	R-R	5-7	180	6-25-85	.180	.250	.170	20	61	6	11	2	1	0	5	6	2	0	1	11	3	1	.246	.271
Segovia, Luis	B-R	5-10	150	7-19-86	.118	.214	.097	32	76	12	9	0	0	0	6	4	4	4	1	25	3	3	.118	.218
Stanley, Jered	R-R	6-3	220	9-18-84	.059	.000	.063	5	17	1	1	0	0	0	0	0	0	0	0	7	0	0	.059	.059
Tejeda, Oscar	R-R	6-1	177	12-26-89	.298	.348	.282	22	94	14	28	5	2	0	12	6	1	0	0	26	4	1	.394	.347
Vasquez, Pedro	R-R	6-0	167	6-29-86	.224	.283	.208	58	219	28	49	7	0	5	23	20	3	2	0	52	10	5	.324	.298
Vazquez, William	R-R	6-2	190	2-22-85	.203	.130	.239	28	69	7	14	3	0	0	8	11	3	2	0	19	0	0	.246	.337
Weeden, Tyler	R-R	6-2	220	9-26-87	.251	.344	.232	54	183	23	46	10	1	5	24	16	4	0	2	68	0	0	.399	.322

PITCHING	B-T	HT	WT	DOB	W	L	ERA	G	GS	CG	SV	IP	H	R	ER	HR	BB	SO	AVG	vLH	vRH	K/9	BB/9
Bajoczky, Tony	R-R	6-0	170	9-24-84	0	2	5.68	4	1	0	1	13	15	10	8	2	3	7	.300	.292	.308	4.97	2.13
Beattie, Eric	R-R	6-3	190	4-2-83	0	1	10.02	18	0	0	0	21	16	27	23	2	40	20	.219	.179	.244	8.71	17.42
Blackley, Adam	L-L	6-1	220	2-22-85	2	2	4.70	23	0	0	0	38	40	27	20	3	18	66	.255	.364	.212	15.50	4.23
Capellan, Jose	L-L	6-2	170	7-18-86	4	3	3.69	14	14	0	0	76	68	35	31	1	11	71	.238	.260	.230	8.44	1.31
Clay, Caleb	R-R	6-2	180	2-15-88	1	0	2.14	5	5	0	0	21	23	10	5	0	6	9	.280	.324	.250	3.86	2.57
Craft, Jordan	R-R	6-3	200	6-5-85	7	3	3.31	15	10	0	0	65	43	28	24	4	28	64	.187	.146	.220	8.82	3.86

Player	B-T	HT	WT	DOB	W	L	ERA	G	GS	CG	SV	IP	H	R	ER	HR	BB	SO	AVG	vLH	vRH	K/9	BB/9
Doubront, Felix	L-L	6-2	166	10-23-87	1	3	5.66	8	8	0	0	35	41	24	22	2	11	25	.283	.333	.258	6.43	2.83
Gonzalez, Carlos	R-R	6-2	175	3-10-86	0	1	3.97	5	0	0	0	11	9	7	5	1	1	11	.220	.238	.200	8.74	0.79
Guerra, Joseph	R-R	5-11	178	9-4-86	1	3	5.48	10	7	0	0	43	67	30	26	5	6	28	.360	.371	.353	5.91	1.27
Hagadone, Nick	L-L	6-5	230	1-1-86	0	1	1.85	10	10	0	0	24	14	5	5	1	8	33	.163	.226	.127	12.21	2.96
James, Jimmy	R-R	6-2	175	10-16-84	2	0	0.47	4	4	0	0	19	10	2	1	0	1	19	.152	.200	.111	9.00	0.47
Lawson, Ryne	L-R	6-2	180	6-21-85	4	4	4.76	16	2	0	1	51	53	33	27	4	23	34	.270	.337	.221	6.00	4.06
Lonergan, Scott	B-R	6-4	200	12-6-83	1	1	4.79	14	0	0	0	21	27	11	11	4	6	19	.325	.343	.313	8.27	2.61
Miller, Ryne	R-R	6-4	230	9-25-85	0	0	3.00	1	0	0	0	3	4	2	1	0	0	4	.267	.143	.375	12.00	0.00
Mills, Adam	R-R	5-11	190	11-19-84	3	1	2.04	14	1	0	1	35	32	14	8	3	9	37	.235	.269	.214	9.42	2.29
Mota, Willy	R-R	6-1	165	10-25-85	5	3	2.60	17	0	0	1	28	23	9	8	2	15	22	.225	.261	.196	7.16	4.88
New, Brantley	R-R	6-3	215	5-1-84	2	0	0.90	4	0	0	0	10	6	4	1	0	2	5	.162	.250	.095	4.50	1.80
Pineiro, Joel	R-R	6-1	200	9-25-78	0	0	0.00	1	1	0	0	1	0	0	0	0	0	2	.000	.000	.000	18.00	0.00
Portice, Eammon	R-R	6-2	185	6-18-85	0	2	5.29	14	0	0	0	32	28	22	19	2	17	43	.226	.320	.162	11.97	4.73
Povich, Chad	R-R	6-0	185	6-13-86	1	1	3.52	5	0	0	1	8	9	4	3	0	2	10	.281	.154	.368	11.74	2.35
Province, Christopher	R-R	6-3	220	1-20-85	0	0	0.00	3	0	0	1	5	2	0	0	0	2	4	.125	.167	.100	6.75	3.38
Reza, Aaron	R-R	5-7	180	6-25-85	0	0	0.00	1	0	0	0	1	0	0	0	0	0	2	.000	—	.000	18.00	0.00
Segovia, Luis	B-R	5-10	150	7-19-86	0	0	0.00	1	0	0	0	2	1	0	0	0	1	1	.143	.000	.200	4.50	4.50
Socolovich, Miguel	R-R	6-1	155	7-24-86	5	4	3.56	14	13	0	0	68	55	31	27	7	34	51	.224	.262	.194	6.72	4.48
Ventura, Felix	R-R	5-11	165	4-27-84	1	1	2.10	28	0	0	14	34	27	9	8	0	11	45	.208	.298	.137	11.80	2.88

FIELDING

Catcher	PCT	G	PO	A	E	DP	PB
Lewis	.974	24	176	10	5	1	1
Milano	1.000	1	9	0	0	0	0
Vazquez	1.000	13	95	7	0	1	2
Weeden	.997	44	350	35	1	5	8

First Base	PCT	G	PO	A	E	DP
Brooks	.968	16	109	12	4	5
Jimenez	1.000	10	63	6	0	4
Jones	.983	44	390	24	7	32
Segovia	1.000	1	2	0	0	0
Vazquez	.976	12	77	6	2	9

Second Base	PCT	G	PO	A	E	DP
Dent	1.000	10	24	21	0	5

	PCT	G	PO	A	E	DP
Navarro	—	1	0	0	0	0
Reza	1.000	16	29	44	0	6
Segovia	.938	19	29	46	5	6
Vazquez	.950	35	73	117	10	27

Third Base	PCT	G	PO	A	E	DP
Jimenez	.958	52	36	102	6	14
Navarro	.935	16	19	24	3	1
Reza	1.000	3	0	8	0	0
Segovia	1.000	3	1	3	0	0
Vazquez	.727	4	4	4	3	0

Shortstop	PCT	G	PO	A	E	DP
Navarro	.928	41	55	112	13	27
Segovia	1.000	1	0	1	0	0

	PCT	G	PO	A	E	DP
Tejeda	.910	19	18	43	6	7
Vasquez	.925	19	16	46	5	5

Outfield	PCT	G	PO	A	E	DP
Cabreja	.957	58	103	7	5	1
Fernandez-Oliva	.949	65	103	9	6	3
Kalish	.959	23	46	1	2	0
Keowen	.935	35	53	5	4	2
Lin	.971	11	33	0	1	0
Marks	1.000	36	38	1	0	1
Segovia	1.000	4	2	1	0	0
Stanley	1.000	2	4	1	0	0
Vazquez	—	2	0	0	0	0

GCL RED SOX ROOKIE

GULF COAST LEAGUE

BATTING	B-T	HT	WT	DOB	AVG	vLH	vRH	G	AB	R	H	2B	3B	HR	RBI	BB	HBP	SH	SF	SO	SB	CS	SLG	OBP
Arambarris, Manuel	R-R	6-0	178	8-25-85	.118	.000	.167	4	17	1	2	0	0	0	0	1	0	0	0	3	1	0	.118	.167
Beltre, Engel	L-L	6-1	169	11-1-89	.208	.225	.202	34	125	20	26	3	3	5	13	12	7	0	1	44	6	3	.400	.330
Blocker, Darren	R-R	6-0	200	2-23-87	.257	.244	.264	34	113	25	29	13	0	2	17	13	6	0	0	21	2	0	.425	.373
Burgos, Ricardo	L-R	5-10	170	6-23-87	.268	.200	.307	42	138	27	37	8	0	7	23	23	1	0	2	39	1	0	.478	.372
Cooney, Matthew	R-R	5-11	215	12-26-85	.148	.095	.175	19	61	2	9	0	0	1	7	1	1	1	0	17	0	0	.197	.175
Dening, Mitch	L-R	6-1	165	8-17-88	.301	.379	.265	47	176	21	53	8	1	1	18	19	2	0	2	26	11	6	.375	.372
Dent, Ryan	R-R	6-0	190	3-15-89	.371	.435	.250	10	35	7	13	1	2	1	2	5	1	1	0	5	4	3	.600	.463
Egan, Jonathan	R-R	6-4	210	10-12-86	.107	.286	.050	9	28	1	3	1	0	0	4	0	0		2	15	0	0	.143	.206
Gil, Rafael	R-R	6-0	165	10-3-85	.200	.263	.182	25	75	8	15	3	0	2	8	2	6	0	0	18	1	0	.320	.277
Gilardo, Peter	R-R	6-0	205	11-19-85	.255	.269	.241	20	55	5	14	2	0	1	3	5	0	0	0	14	2	1	.345	.317
Huang, Chih-Hsiang	R-R	6-1	185	11-18-87	.207	.119	.260	34	116	11	24	8	0	0	9	10	1	0	1	27	1	1	.276	.273
Lin, Che-Hsuan	R-R	6-0	180	9-21-88	.263	.238	.279	43	175	33	46	10	6	4	22	17	3	0	5	42	14	3	.457	.330
Mailman, David	L-L	6-2	180	10-7-88	.227	.154	.333	6	22	5	5	0	0	1	2	3	0	0	0	6	0	1	.364	.320
Rizzo, Anthony	L-L	6-3	220	8-8-89	.286	.273	.300	6	21	6	6	0	0	1	3	1	2	0	0	2	0	0	.429	.375
Roque, Kenneth	L-R	5-11	162	9-20-89	.145	.136	.150	24	62	8	9	0	0	0	4	11	0	3	1	21	2	4	.145	.270
Serrano, Victor	R-R	5-10	150	6-30-86	.260	.243	.267	34	123	13	32	6	0	0	9	1	1	2	2	22	11	5	.309	.268
Solano, Emmanuel	B-R	5-8	160	8-26-82	.274	.265	.279	28	95	11	26	4	0	0	9	6	1	0	3	15	6	6	.316	.314
Stanley, Jered	R-R	6-3	220	9-18-84	.304	.308	.300	8	23	4	7	3	0	2	9	3	0	0	1	7	0	0	.696	.370
Sumoza, Luis	R-R	6-0	170	7-15-88	.253	.250	.248	53	190	21	48	17	4	3	31	17	1	1	1	58	2	1	.432	.316
Tapia, Levi	R-R	5-10	200	4-21-87	—	—	—	1	0	0	0	0	0	0	0	0	0	0	0	0	0	0	—	1.000
Tejeda, Oscar	R-R	6-1	177	12-26-89	.295	.293	.289	45	173	23	51	13	1	1	21	15	0	1	4	27	6	2	.399	.344
Vazquez, William	R-R	6-2	190	2-22-85	.294	.250	.308	5	17	3	5	1	2	0	4	1	0	0	1	1	0	0	.588	.316

PITCHING	B-T	HT	WT	DOB	W	L	ERA	G	GS	CG	SV	IP	H	R	ER	HR	BB	SO	AVG	vLH	vRH	K/9	BB/9
Almanzar, Carlos	R-R	6-2	200	11-6-73	0	0	0.00	4	2	0	0	7	5	0	0	0	0	10	.208	.250	.167	13.50	0.00
Alvarez, Jose	L-L	5-11	150	5-6-89	4	1	1.84	11	9	0	0	49	36	24	10	4	14	38	.202	.200	.203	6.98	2.57
Bajoczky, Tony	R-R	6-0	170	9-24-84	4	2	1.91	8	6	0	0	38	36	13	8	0	1	29	.247	.308	.213	6.93	0.24
Blue, William	R-R	6-2	215	4-5-87	0	1	14.29	5	0	0	0	6	10	11	9	0	10	2	.385	.429	.333	3.18	15.88
Buller, Daniel	R-L	6-0	205	12-25-84	0	0	4.00	12	0	0	1	18	25	9	8	0	8	16	.333	.240	.380	8.00	4.00
Colvin, Ryan	R-R	6-2	165	4-12-87	2	3	4.59	12	9	0	0	49	55	29	25	3	10	37	.286	.250	.308	6.80	1.84
Galue, Victor	R-R	6-0	160	8-3-87	0	3	4.58	14	0	0	3	20	23	20	10	1	8	11	.280	.323	.255	5.03	3.66
Gil, Alberto	R-R	6-2	170	7-9-85	4	1	5.55	15	0	0	2	24	24	17	15	0	7	16	.261	.194	.304	5.92	2.59
Gonzalez, Carlos	R-R	6-2	175	3-10-86	1	3	2.60	15	0	0	6	17	12	7	5	0	3	9	.179	.172	.184	4.67	1.56
Guerrero, Emilis	R-R	6-2	162	12-26-85	3	0	2.91	9	5	0	0	34	35	11	11	2	5	32	.257	.313	.208	8.41	1.32
Haigwood, Daniel	R-L	6-2	200	11-19-83	1	0	1.23	2	2	0	0	7	6	1	1	0	3	10	.231	.200	.250	12.27	3.68
Huntzinger, Brock	R-R	6-3	200	7-2-88	0	1	2.57	4	3	0	0	7	5	3	2	0	0	8	.192	.091	.267	10.29	0.00
Jimenez, Arbert	L-L	6-0	145	12-12-87	1	1	4.30	13	2	0	0	29	42	19	14	2	4	29	.344	.371	.333	8.90	1.23
Latimer, Adam	L-L	6-4	190	12-4-85	1	0	5.40	2	0	0	0	3	3	2	2	1	4	1	.231	.000	.273	2.70	10.80
Mendez, Mauricio	R-R	6-6	198	9-22-85	2	1	1.55	17	0	0	0	29	23	6	5	0	12	24	.221	.189	.239	7.45	3.72
Miller, Ryne	R-R	6-4	230	9-25-85	0	1	1.88	10	0	0	5	14	9	3	3	0	6	13	.191	.158	.214	8.16	3.77
Paulino, Aregnis	R-R	6-6	205	12-12-85	1	1	6.44	14	1	0	0	29	36	25	21	1	14	16	.313	.304	.319	4.91	4.30
Perez, Pedro	R-R	6-4	170	5-3-88	4	4	2.98	12	9	0	0	45	42	19	15	0	12	30	.232	.286	.192	5.96	2.38
Povich, Chad	R-R	6-0	185	6-13-86	0	0	0.00	3	0	0	1	4	3	1	0	0	1	5	.188	.333	.100	11.25	2.25

	B-T	HT	WT	DOB	W	L	ERA	G	GS	CG	SV	IP	H	R	ER	HR	BB	SO	AVG	vLH	vRH	K/9	BB/9
Rozier, Michael	L-L	6-5	210	7-4-85	0	1	6.00	2	2	0	0	3	6	3	2	0	0	1	.429	.500	.400	3.00	0.00
Strickland, Hunter	R-R	6-5	200	9-24-88	0	2	6.04	9	6	0	0	25	40	21	17	3	4	22	.357	.367	.349	7.82	1.42
Zerpa, Armando	L-L	5-11	175	2-13-87	2	0	1.98	13	0	0	0	27	19	11	6	0	12	26	.192	.200	.190	8.56	3.95

FIELDING

Catcher	PCT	G	PO	A	E	DP	PB
Cooney	.990	14	90	13	1	3	4
Egan	1.000	1	11	0	0	0	1
Gil	.994	25	141	17	1	1	5
Gilardo	.951	19	123	14	7	0	6
Tapia	1.000	1	2	0	0	0	0
Vazquez	1.000	4	26	2	0	1	2

First Base	PCT	G	PO	A	E	DP
Burgos	.987	35	296	19	4	19
Dening	.978	15	127	9	3	14
Rizzo	1.000	6	48	6	0	4

Second Base	PCT	G	PO	A	E	DP
Huang	.941	12	14	34	3	1
Roque	.861	19	40	47	14	9
Serrano	.937	14	35	39	5	10
Solano	.958	12	30	38	3	9

Third Base	PCT	G	PO	A	E	DP
Arambarris	.667	2	0	2	1	0
Blocker	.875	31	24	60	12	3
Huang	.824	16	8	20	6	2
Serrano	.906	10	4	25	3	1

Shortstop	PCT	G	PO	A	E	DP
Dent	.846	8	6	16	4	4

	PCT	G	PO	A	E	DP
Roque	.727	2	2	6	3	1
Serrano	.909	3	6	4	1	0
Tejeda	.930	44	83	131	16	24

Outfield	PCT	G	PO	A	E	DP
Beltre	.951	33	55	3	3	0
Dening	1.000	24	41	3	0	1
Lin	.986	42	66	7	1	4
Mailman	.933	6	12	2	1	0
Serrano	1.000	1	2	0	0	0
Solano	.909	12	20	0	2	0
Stanley	1.000	8	20	2	0	0
Sumoza	.981	48	94	7	2	0

DSL RED SOX   ROOKIE

DOMINICAN SUMMER LEAGUE

BATTING	B-T	HT	WT	DOB	AVG	vLH	vRH	G	AB	R	H	2B	3B	HR	RBI	BB	HBP	SH	SF	SO	SB	CS	SLG	OBP
Avila, Jackvid	R-R	6-0	160	3-9-89	.207	.200	.208	24	87	7	18	6	0	0	8	4	5	0	0	19	2	1	.276	.281
Bermudez, Ronald	R-R	6-1	165	6-6-88	.349	.388	.339	65	229	37	80	19	3	3	39	42	3	1	1	34	12	9	.498	.455
Bonifacio, Juan	R-R	6-2	168	12-7-88	.221	.286	.205	47	145	24	32	9	1	5	22	17	6	1	0	60	7	3	.400	.327
Bonilla, Nelson	R-R	6-4	195	7-6-87	.203	.158	.217	44	158	20	32	8	0	3	26	16	2	0	2	50	1	1	.310	.281
Chourio, Pedro	R-R	6-2	211	3-13-90	.191	.200	.189	30	94	8	18	4	0	0	7	12	4	1	0	44	1	0	.234	.309
De La Nieve, Marcial	R-R	5-11	185	7-10-88	.172	.333	.130	13	29	6	5	2	0	0	5	5	1	1	0	6	1	0	.241	.314
Diaz, Luis	R-R	6-0	155	9-26-88	.176	.095	.203	48	165	20	29	14	3	0	11	13	3	2	0	48	2	1	.297	.249
Feliz, Roberto	R-R	6-1	180	12-30-87	.304	.254	.320	64	240	35	73	13	1	7	55	23	7	0	0	50	6	6	.454	.381
Gonzalez, Pedro	L-L	6-0	185	3-17-90	.220	.276	.202	39	123	17	27	3	2	0	9	13	2	1	0	29	1	2	.276	.304
Lora, Eddie	B-L	6-2	228	3-21-89	.222	.213	.225	65	216	28	48	5	2	4	19	48	3	0	3	92	4	3	.319	.367
Meregildo, Miguel	R-R	6-0	164	11-22-88	.121	.000	.159	29	58	14	7	0	0	0	3	12	6	0	1	22	4	2	.121	.325
Pichardo, Wilfred	B-R	5-9	146	10-21-89	.241	.221	.248	68	270	55	65	7	7	0	14	37	6	5	2	63	33	6	.319	.343
Pinto, Derwin	R-R	5-10	196	2-20-90	.220	.067	.254	28	82	14	18	2	1	0	13	19	3	1	0	24	1	0	.268	.385
Reyes, German	B-R	6-1	182	6-5-88	.122	.067	.134	31	82	13	10	2	0	2	6	14	0	0	1	33	1	2	.220	.247
Sanchez, Maykol	R-R	5-11	176	5-30-88	.221	.333	.184	42	131	11	29	3	0	0	9	18	6	1	2	23	2	2	.244	.338
Santana, Wilfi	R-R	6-0	185	11-8-88	.234	.162	.252	53	188	12	44	6	1	0	16	7	4	1	1	38	5	2	.277	.275

PITCHING	B-T	HT	WT	DOB	W	L	ERA	G	GS	CG	SV	IP	H	R	ER	HR	BB	SO	AVG	vLH	vRH	K/9	BB/9
Batista, Anatanaer	R-R	5-10	150	2-2-89	3	0	2.19	6	5	0	0	25	19	8	6	0	8	32	.207	.161	.230	11.68	2.92
Cabral, Cesar	L-L	6-3	175	2-11-89	5	4	1.76	14	14	0	0	66	55	22	13	0	21	58	.218	.206	.220	7.87	2.85
Castillo, Yeiper	R-R	6-3	158	9-6-88	2	2	1.83	13	8	0	1	54	35	14	11	0	22	59	.182	.203	.171	9.83	3.67
Consuegra, Randy	R-R	6-2	211	10-04-89	4	2	2.59	14	8	1	1	49	39	18	14	1	30	38	.223	.214	.227	7.03	5.55
De La Cruz, Victor	R-R	6-0	168	10-10-88	1	3	3.31	13	2	0	1	33	31	27	12	0	27	23	.237	.231	.239	6.34	7.44
Gonzalez, Alberto	R-R	6-2	181	4-16-88	2	2	4.71	11	1	0	0	29	25	20	15	0	20	30	.240	.242	.239	9.42	6.28
Jimenez, Javier	R-R	6-3	143	7-28-89	2	4	3.46	15	7	0	0	39	37	20	15	2	24	28	.264	.327	.231	6.46	5.54
Jimenez, Manuel	R-R	5-11	177	1-6-87	3	0	1.16	11	0	0	0	23	13	4	3	0	7	19	.167	.074	.216	7.33	2.70
Lastreto, Nestor	L-L	6-0	160	9-28-89	2	1	3.27	13	0	0	0	22	21	10	8	0	5	15	.244	.556	.208	6.14	2.05
Lopez, Edwin	L-L	6-1	165	12-11-87	0	3	5.17	14	0	0	3	31	24	20	18	2	15	28	.209	.154	.216	8.04	4.31
Marin, Leandro	R-R	5-11	165	11-9-88	0	0	2.70	3	0	0	0	3	3	1	1	0	4	3	.273	.333	.250	8.10	10.80
Neuman, Dennis	R-R	5-11	185	10-18-89	1	3	1.91	21	0	0	7	33	19	11	7	0	16	32	.171	.222	.147	8.73	4.36
Pimentel, Stolmy	R-R	6-3	186	2-1-90	3	1	2.90	14	13	0	0	62	44	20	20	2	22	60	.202	.235	.180	8.71	3.19
Reyes, Ernesto	L-L	6-0	190	7-31-90	2	0	5.40	5	0	0	0	5	1	4	3	0	11	4	.063	.000	.071	7.20	19.80
Rivera, Manuel	L-L	6-0	170	9-1-89	3	2	1.04	20	0	0	6	35	24	5	4	0	17	37	.197	.300	.188	9.61	4.41
Rosario, Charlie	R-R	5-10	158	7-23-88	3	3	3.66	14	12	0	0	64	54	32	26	2	12	56	.222	.267	.197	7.88	1.69
Ulloa, Brandon	R-R	6-2	170	2-9-89	2	1	2.63	14	0	0	1	38	30	22	11	2	21	36	.216	.220	.213	8.60	5.02

FIELDING

Catcher	PCT	G	PO	A	E	DP	PB
De La Nieve	.972	13	60	9	2	0	0
Pinto	.991	27	185	38	2	2	5
Sanchez	.997	42	310	34	1	2	5

First Base	PCT	G	PO	A	E	DP
Bonilla	1.000	1	6	0	0	0
Gonzalez	.953	5	36	5	2	4
Lora	.991	65	603	31	6	50

Second Base	PCT	G	PO	A	E	DP
Pichardo	.947	68	140	184	18	37
Reyes	.833	2	6	4	2	2

Third Base	PCT	G	PO	A	E	DP
Bonilla	.969	42	34	89	4	6
Chourio	.813	30	23	55	18	5

Shortstop	PCT	G	PO	A	E	DP
Diaz	.914	48	66	146	20	24
Reyes	.856	25	37	64	17	16

Outfield	PCT	G	PO	A	E	DP
Avila	.750	8	9	0	3	0
Bermudez	1.000	63	110	7	0	1
Bonifacio	.925	29	36	1	3	1
Feliz	.962	19	24	1	1	1
Gonzalez	1.000	1	2	0	0	0
Gonzalez	.970	31	29	3	1	0
Meregildo	.867	26	25	1	4	0
Santana	.937	53	57	2	4	1

Chicago Cubs

BY JEFF VORVA

Sure, there were a fair amount of Cubs fans who were happy to see the team go from worst (66-96 in 2006) to first (85-77 in 2007) in the National League Central.

But they were fairly quiet in October. The loudest fans were the angriest.

Second baseman Alfonso Soriano flew out to right field to conclude Arizona's sweep of the Cubs in the National League Division series, leaving a long-suffering fan base nearly 100 years without a World Series title.

"This is just the start," manager Lou Piniella said. "We're going to get better. No matter how far you go up the ladder in baseball, if you don't win the World Series you're going to find disappointment along the way."

The Cubs are near the top rungs of the ladder but not quite there yet. Some of their top stars (Soriano, third baseman Aramis Ramirez, first baseman Derrek Lee, righthanders Carlos Zambrano and Jason Marquis and lefthander Ted Lilly) are locked up in big deals and are scheduled to be back in 2008.

Who the Cubs surround those players with during the offseason could be the tricky part, in light of their contract situation and the team's ownership being in limbo.

Piniella took a last-place team and stewed when it struggled in April and May (22-29). He stewed but he didn't stand pat.

He moved guys around the field and in the lineup. He had some shipped off to the minors or other teams. In the end, he had a team he was comfortable with and the Cubs made it to the playoffs by beating out Milwaukee by two games in what was considered a weak division.

Things turned around in early June, when Zambrano fought with then-Cubs catcher Michael Barrett and Piniella kicked dirt on an umpire. But it's tough to find anyone in the organization who will admit those two events were the catalyst for the turnaround.

Soriano showed his star power by hitting 14 homers in September, including seven to lead off games—the most by any major leaguer in one month. However he hit just .143 in the playoffs. Lee hit for average but lost some power. Ramirez was solid all around but had no postseason hits or RBIs.

Ryan Theriot unseated veteran Cesar Izturis for the starting job at shortstop and appears to be a mainstay at that position for the next couple of years. Mark DeRosa played several positions during the season and hit a solid .293/.371/.420. Outfielders Cliff Floyd and Jacque Jones combined for a meek 14 homers in 2007.

Zambrano (18-13), Lilly (15-8), Marquis (12-9) and righthander Rich Hill (11-8) each posted double-digit wins and are slated to return in 2008. The Cubs will be in search of a fifth starter and it's possible that rookie righthander Kevin Hart (0.82 ERA in eight relief appearances for the Cubs after going 12-6, 3.99 between Double-A Tennessee and Triple-A Iowa) or closer Ryan Dempster could fill that role if the Cubs don't find a starter from outside the organization.

Carlos Marmol (1.43 ERA) was lights-out as a setup man although he struggled in the playoffs. Bob Howry (3.32 ERA) was also solid helping to set up Dempster (28 saves in 31 opportunities) while also picking up eight saves when Dempster was injured for close to a month.

The minor leagues helped contribute to the Cubs postseason run. General manager Jim Hendry liberally dipped into

the Double-A Tennessee and Triple-A Iowa pools for talent while Piniella was figuring out the makeup of his team.

Among Chicago prospects making their major league debut in 2007 were: catcher Jake Fox, outfielders Sam Fuld and Felix Pie, second baseman Eric Patterson, righthanders Rocky Cherry, Sean Gallagher, Hart and Billy Petrick and lefthanders Carmen Pignatiello and Clay Rapada.

Pacific Coast League MVP Geovany Soto, who hit .353/.424/.652 with 26 homers and 109 RBIs for Iowa, was also impressive enough in two stints with the parent club (.389/.443/.667 in 54 at-bats) that he started two playoff games over veteran Jason Kendall, and will be considered for regular play in 2008.

General Manager: Jim Hendry. **Farm Director:** Oneri Fleita. **Scouting Director:** Tim Wilken

Class	Team	League	W	L	PCT	Finish*	Manager	Affiliate Since
Majors	Chicago	National	85	77	.525	6th (16)	Lou Piniella	—
Triple-A	Iowa Cubs	Pacific Coast	79	65	.549	3rd (16)	Buddy Bailey	1981
Double-A	Tennessee Smokies	Southern	73	65	.529	3rd (10)	Pat Listach	2007
High A	Daytona Cubs	Florida State	57	80	.416	11th (12)	Jody Davis	1993
Low A	Peoria Chiefs	Midwest	71	68	.511	7th (14)	Ryne Sandberg	2005
Short-season	Boise Hawks	Northwest	37	39	.487	3rd (8)	Tom Byers	2001
Rookie	AZL Cubs	Arizona	27	29	.482	6th (9)	Ricardo Medina	1997
Overall 2007 Minor League Record			**344**	**346**	**.499**	**14th**		

* Finish in overall standings (No. of teams in league) ^League champion

ORGANIZATION STATISTICS

CHICAGO CUBS

NATIONAL LEAGUE

BATTING	B-T	HT	WT	DOB	AVG	vLH	vRH	G	AB	R	H	2B	3B	HR	RBI	BB	HBP	SH	SF	SO	SB	CS	SLG	OBP
Barrett, Michael	R-R	6-3	210	10-22-76	.256	.262	.254	57	211	23	54	9	0	9	29	17	0	0	3	36	2	2	.427	.307
2-team (44 San Diego)					.244	—	—	101	344	29	84	17	0	9	41	19	0	0	4	57	2	2	.372	.281
Blanco, Henry	R-R	5-11	220	8-29-71	.167	.050	.235	22	54	3	9	3	0	0	4	2	0	1	1	12	0	0	.222	.193
Bowen, Rob	B-R	6-3	225	2-24-81	.065	.067	.063	10	31	3	2	1	0	0	2	4	0	0	1	13	0	0	.097	.167
2-team (30 San Diego)					.212	—	—	40	113	15	24	9	0	2	13	17	1	1	2	41	1	2	.345	.316
Cedeno, Ronny	R-R	6-0	180	2-2-83	.203	.176	.225	38	74	6	15	2	0	4	13	3	0	2	1	18	2	1	.392	.231
DeRosa, Mark	R-R	6-1	205	2-26-75	.293	.283	.297	149	502	64	147	28	3	10	72	58	7	3	4	93	1	2	.420	.371
Floyd, Cliff	L-R	6-4	230	12-5-72	.284	.303	.281	108	282	40	80	11	0	9	45	35	5	0	0	47	0	0	.422	.373
Fontenot, Mike	L-R	5-8	170	6-9-80	.278	.212	.297	86	234	32	65	12	4	3	29	22	0	1	3	43	5	4	.402	.336
Fox, Jacob	R-R	6-0	210	7-20-82	.143	.200	.000	7	14	3	2	2	0	0	1	1	0	0	0	2	0	0	.286	.200
Fuld, Sam	L-L	5-10	180	11-20-81	.000	.000	.000	14	6	3	0	0	0	0	0	3	0	0	0	3	0	0	.000	.333
Hill, Koyie	B-R	6-0	190	3-9-79	.161	.182	.155	36	93	7	15	4	0	2	12	8	1	1	2	18	0	0	.269	.231
Izturis, Cesar	B-R	5-9	190	2-10-80	.246	.178	.267	65	191	15	47	11	0	0	8	13	1	2	0	16	3	0	.304	.298
2-team (45 Pittsburgh)					.258	—	—	110	314	31	81	14	2	0	16	19	1	3	0	19	3	3	.315	.302
Jones, Jacque	L-L	5-10	200	4-25-75	.285	.295	.283	135	453	52	129	33	2	5	66	34	2	3	3	70	6	3	.400	.335
Kendall, Jason	R-R	6-0	205	6-26-74	.270	.244	.278	57	174	21	47	10	1	1	19	19	6	3	0	15	0	3	.356	.362
Lee, Derrek	R-R	6-5	245	9-6-75	.317	.339	.312	150	567	91	180	43	1	22	82	71	9	0	3	114	6	5	.513	.400
Monroe, Craig	R-R	6-1	205	2-27-77	.204	.182	.250	23	49	6	10	4	0	1	4	6	0	0	0	13	0	1	.347	.291
Moore, Scott	L-R	6-2	195	11-17-83	.000	—	.000	2	5	0	0	0	0	0	0	0	0	0	0	0	0	0	.000	.000
Murton, Matt	R-R	6-1	220	10-3-81	.281	.319	.257	94	235	35	66	13	0	8	22	26	0	0	0	39	1	0	.438	.352
Pagan, Angel	B-R	6-1	180	7-2-81	.264	.236	.289	71	148	21	39	10	2	4	21	10	0	1	2	32	4	1	.439	.306
Patterson, Eric	L-R	5-11	170	4-8-83	.250	—	.250	7	8	0	2	1	0	0	0	1	0	0	0	3	0	0	.375	.250
Pie, Felix	L-L	6-2	170	2-8-85	.215	.111	.241	87	177	26	38	9	3	2	20	14	0	2	1	43	8	1	.333	.271
Ramirez, Aramis	R-R	6-1	215	6-25-78	.310	.395	.286	132	506	72	157	35	4	26	101	43	4	0	5	66	0	0	.549	.366
Soriano, Alfonso	R-R	6-1	180	1-7-76	.299	.254	.311	135	579	97	173	42	5	33	70	31	4	0	3	130	19	6	.560	.337
Soto, Geovany	R-R	6-1	230	1-20-83	.389	.444	.333	18	54	12	21	6	0	3	8	5	0	0	1	14	0	0	.667	.433
Theriot, Ryan	R-R	5-11	175	12-7-79	.266	.286	.260	148	537	80	143	30	2	3	45	49	0	8	3	50	28	4	.346	.326
Ward, Daryle	L-L	6-2	240	6-27-75	.327	.250	.333	79	110	16	36	13	0	3	19	22	0	0	1	23	0	0	.527	.436

PITCHING	B-T	HT	WT	DOB	W	L	ERA	G	GS	CG	SV	IP	H	R	ER	HR	BB	SO	AVG	vLH	vRH	K/9	BB/9
Cherry, Rocky	R-R	6-5	225	8-19-79	1	1	3.00	12	0	0	0	15	13	6	5	1	6	13	.224	.143	.250	7.80	3.60
Cotts, Neal	L-L	6-1	200	3-25-80	0	1	4.86	16	0	0	0	17	15	9	9	1	9	14	.246	.240	.250	7.56	4.86
Dempster, Ryan	R-R	6-2	215	5-3-77	2	7	4.73	66	0	0	28	67	59	36	35	8	30	55	.240	.259	.224	7.42	4.05
Eyre, Scott	L-L	6-1	215	5-30-72	2	1	4.13	55	0	0	0	52	59	26	24	3	35	45	.294	.253	.317	7.74	6.02
Gallagher, Sean	R-R	6-2	225	12-30-85	0	0	8.59	8	0	0	1	15	19	15	14	3	12	5	.317	.294	.346	3.07	7.36
Guzman, Angel	R-R	6-3	195	12-14-81	0	1	3.56	12	3	0	0	30	32	12	12	2	9	26	.278	.333	.218	7.71	2.67
Hart, Kevin	R-R	6-4	215	11-29-82	0	0	0.82	8	0	0	0	11	7	1	1	0	4	13	.189	.000	.292	10.64	3.27
Hill, Rich	L-L	6-5	205	3-11-80	11	8	3.92	32	32	0	0	195	170	89	85	27	63	183	.235	.191	.247	8.45	2.91
Howry, Bob	L-R	6-5	220	8-4-73	6	7	3.32	78	0	0	8	81	76	31	30	8	19	72	.245	.192	.283	7.97	2.10
Lilly, Ted	L-L	6-1	190	1-4-76	15	8	3.83	34	34	0	0	207	181	91	88	28	55	174	.236	.258	.230	7.57	2.39
Marmol, Carlos	R-R	6-2	180	10-14-82	5	1	1.43	59	0	0	1	69	41	11	11	3	35	96	.169	.209	.146	12.46	4.54
Marquis, Jason	L-R	6-1	210	8-21-78	12	9	4.60	34	33	1	0	192	190	111	98	22	76	109	.256	.274	.242	5.12	3.57
Marshall, Sean	L-L	6-7	205	8-30-82	7	8	3.92	21	19	0	0	103	107	52	45	13	35	67	.267	.203	.280	5.84	3.05
Miller, Wade	R-R	6-2	210	9-13-76	0	1	10.54	3	3	0	0	14	24	16	16	5	6	6	.381	.412	.345	3.95	3.95
Ohman, Will	L-L	6-2	205	8-13-77	2	4	4.95	56	0	0	1	36	42	20	20	3	16	33	.282	.236	.325	8.17	3.96
Petrick, Billy	R-R	6-6	240	4-29-84	0	0	7.45	8	0	0	0	10	8	8	8	3	7	6	.229	.154	.273	5.59	6.52
Pignatiello, Carmen	R-L	6-0	205	9-12-82	0	0	4.50	4	0	0	0	2	3	1	1	1	0	3	.375	.500	.000	13.50	0.00
Rapada, Clay	R-L	6-5	200	3-9-81	0	0	0.00	1	0	0	0	0	0	0	0	0	0	0	.000	.000	—	0.00	0.00
Trachsel, Steve	R-R	6-4	205	10-31-70	1	3	8.31	4	4	0	0	17	25	16	16	3	7	11	.368	.267	.447	5.71	3.63
Wood, Kerry	R-R	6-5	225	6-16-77	1	1	3.33	22	0	0	0	24	18	9	9	0	13	24	.207	.148	.233	8.88	4.81
Wuertz, Michael	R-R	6-3	205	12-15-78	2	3	3.48	73	0	0	0	72	64	30	28	8	35	79	.234	.238	.233	9.83	4.35
Zambrano, Carlos	B-R	6-5	255	6-1-81	18	13	3.95	34	34	1	0	216	187	100	95	23	101	177	.233	.268	.200	7.36	4.20

FIELDING

Catcher	PCT	G	PO	A	E	DP	PB
Barrett	.988	55	389	18	5	2	8
Blanco	1.000	14	102	4	0	1	2
Bowen	.988	9	78	3	1	1	0
Hill	.995	31	190	11	1	3	1
Kendall	.987	52	362	24	5	2	5
Soto	1.000	16	109	10	0	0	0

First Base	PCT	G	PO	A	E	DP
Blanco	1.000	2	8	1	0	0
DeRosa	.980	9	49	0	1	9
Fox	1.000	1	3	0	0	2
Lee	.994	147	1165	87	7	99
Moore	1.000	1	10	1	0	1
Ward	.990	16	90	5	1	12

Second Base	PCT	G	PO	A	E	DP
Cedeno	1.000	8	10	14	0	3

Second Base	PCT	G	PO	A	E	DP
DeRosa	.984	93	168	193	6	45
Fontenot	.976	62	112	128	6	33
Soriano	—	1	0	0	0	0
Theriot	.992	37	47	70	1	17

Third Base	PCT	G	PO	A	E	DP
Cedeno	1.000	4	3	3	0	1
DeRosa	.958	37	24	68	4	3
Ramirez	.972	126	88	260	10	19
Theriot	.857	8	5	7	2	0

Shortstop	PCT	G	PO	A	E	DP
Cedeno	.959	15	14	33	2	5
DeRosa	1.000	1	1	1	0	0
Fontenot	.500	3	2	0	2	0
Izturis	.964	60	57	130	7	28
Theriot	.980	108	126	260	8	56

Outfield	PCT	G	PO	A	E	DP
DeRosa	1.000	23	30	1	0	0
Floyd	1.000	79	101	1	0	0
Fox	1.000	3	2	0	0	0
Fuld	1.000	8	9	1	0	1
Hill	—	1	0	0	0	0
Jones	.986	122	272	8	4	0
Monroe	1.000	17	22	0	0	0
Murton	.967	68	115	3	4	1
Pagan	1.000	60	80	0	0	0
Patterson	1.000	2	1	0	0	0
Pie	1.000	82	121	1	0	0
Soriano	.980	134	273	19	6	4
Theriot	1.000	5	5	0	0	0
Ward	1.000	11	25	1	0	0

IOWA CUBS   TRIPLE-A

PACIFIC COAST LEAGUE

BATTING	B-T	HT	WT	DOB	AVG	vLH	vRH	G	AB	R	H	2B	3B	HR	RBI	BB	HBP	SH	SF	SO	SB	CS	SLG	OBP
Blanco, Henry	R-R	5-11	220	8-29-71	.200	.667	.000	3	10	2	2	0	0	0	1	0	0	0	0	3	0	0	.200	.200
Cedeno, Ronny	R-R	6-0	180	2-2-83	.359	.409	.337	75	287	52	103	15	3	10	37	30	2	7	1	46	6	4	.537	.422
Coats, Buck	L-R	6-3	195	6-9-82	.303	.311	.300	123	455	81	138	21	3	11	59	44	2	1	6	74	18	2	.435	.363
Cortes, Jorge	L-L	5-10	195	10-17-80	.333	1.000	.000	8	6	3	2	1	0	0	1	3	0	0	0	0	0	0	.500	.556
Craig, Matt	B-R	6-2	200	4-16-81	.273	.310	.259	31	110	16	30	7	1	4	25	10	0	0	1	29	0	0	.464	.331
Fontenot, Mike	L-R	5-8	170	6-9-80	.336	.350	.331	55	211	46	71	17	4	6	34	16	1	2	1	32	3	1	.540	.384
Fox, Jacob	R-R	6-0	210	7-20-82	.283	.333	.261	25	99	18	28	7	0	6	19	5	4	0	0	23	2	0	.535	.343
Fuld, Sam	L-L	5-10	180	11-20-81	.269	.077	.333	14	52	13	14	4	1	1	2	9	2	0	0	5	2	0	.442	.397
Garcia, Alberto	R-R	6-1	180	6-5-83	.500	1.000	.429	3	8	2	4	1	0	0	2	1	0	0	1	0	0	0	.625	.556
Hart, Bo	R-R	5-11	175	9-27-76	.188	.300	.107	19	48	3	9	2	0	0	2	2	0	2	0	14	2	0	.229	.220
Hill, Koyie	B-R	6-0	190	3-9-79	.322	.385	.309	47	149	22	48	16	0	2	24	11	0	0	2	23	1	1	.470	.364
Hoffpauir, Micah	L-L	6-3	195	3-1-80	.319	.278	.338	82	310	56	99	24	0	16	73	24	2	0	6	34	2	1	.552	.365
Kinkade, Mike	R-R	6-1	210	5-6-73	.308	.303	.310	33	120	26	37	6	1	7	29	9	7	0	1	14	2	0	.550	.387
Kroeger, Josh	L-L	6-3	220	8-31-82	.263	.304	.244	51	175	27	46	7	0	10	31	21	0	0	2	38	0	1	.474	.338
Machado, Albenis	B-R	6-0	170	3-20-79	.100	.154	.059	19	30	6	3	0	0	0	3	7	0	0	1	8	0	1	.100	.263
Mahoney, Mike	R-R	6-0	200	12-5-72	.244	.286	.226	19	45	4	11	1	0	3	5	1	0	0	7	0	0	.267	.277
McGehee, Casey	R-R	6-1	195	10-12-82	.173	.067	.216	18	52	3	9	2	1	0	5	3	1	0	1	10	0	1	.269	.228
Moore, Scott	L-R	6-2	195	11-17-83	.265	.200	.290	103	321	61	85	19	4	19	69	48	9	1	3	100	4	3	.526	.373
Murton, Matt	R-R	6-1	220	10-3-81	.331	.357	.321	39	151	30	50	16	1	6	27	18	2	0	1	18	1	0	.570	.407
Nelson, John	R-R	6-1	190	3-3-79	.244	.191	.265	54	160	26	39	7	0	10	30	17	1	0	2	46	0	1	.475	.317
2-team (47 Memphis)					.211	—	—	101	265	37	56	10	0	15	44	27	2	0	4	87	0	1	.419	.285
Pagan, Angel	B-R	6-1	180	7-2-81	.250	.273	.243	33	116	18	29	4	3	3	9	10	0	1	0	20	6	1	.414	.310
Patterson, Eric	L-R	5-11	170	4-8-83	.297	.275	.305	128	516	94	153	28	6	14	65	54	2	4	6	85	24	9	.455	.362
Pie, Felix	L-L	6-2	170	2-8-85	.362	.190	.428	55	229	51	83	9	5	9	43	19	0	1	1	40	9	6	.563	.410
Richie, Anthony	R-R	6-1	215	2-9-82	.244	.196	.262	62	197	20	48	6	0	9	27	11	2	1	4	30	2	1	.411	.285
Rojas, Carlos	R-R	6-1	175	1-11-84	.268	.357	.236	69	213	21	57	12	1	0	18	13	3	4	0	29	2	0	.333	.319
Simokaitis, Joe	R-R	6-1	200	12-27-82	.223	.208	.226	38	130	18	29	7	1	1	10	7	3	0	2	27	0	1	.315	.275
Soto, Geovany	R-R	6-1	230	1-20-83	.353	.328	.365	110	385	75	136	31	3	26	109	53	1	1	9	94	0	0	.652	.424
Walker, Christopher	B-R	5-8	170	7-3-80	.192	.146	.210	57	172	12	33	3	0	1	11	5	0	1	3	40	5	3	.227	.211
Ward, Daryle	L-L	6-2	240	6-27-75	.077	.333	.000	4	13	0	1	1	0	0	1	0	0	0	0	2	0	0	.154	.077

PITCHING	B-T	HT	WT	DOB	W	L	ERA	G	GS	CG	SV	IP	H	R	ER	HR	BB	SO	AVG	vLH	vRH	K/9	BB/9
Almonte, Hector	R-R	6-1	220	10-17-75	0	1	12.71	4	0	0	0	6	9	8	8	2	6	6	.391	.000	.450	9.53	9.53
Baez, Federico	R-R	6-2	190	8-4-81	2	0	8.84	16	0	0	0	18	30	18	18	4	12	16	.366	.417	.326	7.85	5.89
Bailey, Cory	R-R	6-1	210	1-24-71	5	3	2.86	44	7	0	5	91	100	33	29	6	16	61	.276	.260	.287	6.01	1.58
Cherry, Rocky	R-R	6-5	225	8-19-79	2	0	4.59	43	1	0	7	51	50	27	26	5	18	56	.250	.323	.217	9.88	3.18
Christl, Michael	R-R	6-4	185	9-2-84	0	0	0.00	1	0	0	0	2	0	0	0	0	1	1	.000	.000	.000	4.50	4.50
Cotts, Neal	L-L	6-1	200	3-25-80	2	2	4.83	24	6	0	0	50	43	28	27	4	30	48	.236	.369	.162	8.58	5.36
Dempster, Ryan	R-R	6-2	215	5-3-77	0	0	0.00	2	1	0	0	2	1	0	0	0	1	4	.143	.200	.000	18.00	4.50
Gallagher, Sean	R-R	6-2	225	12-30-85	3	1	2.66	8	8	0	0	41	33	12	12	1	13	37	.232	.250	.214	8.19	2.88
Guzman, Angel	R-R	6-3	195	11-29-81	0	2	12.19	3	3	0	0	10	14	14	14	1	6	7	.318	.333	.300	6.10	5.23
Hart, Kevin	R-R	6-4	215	11-29-82	4	1	3.54	9	8	1	0	56	56	23	22	6	23	39	.271	.297	.250	6.27	3.70
Henderson, Jim	L-R	6-5	190	10-21-82	3	0	5.54	8	0	0	0	13	16	8	8	2	6	6	.308	.500	.167	4.15	4.15
Howard, Ben	R-R	6-2	200	1-15-79	6	9	4.28	55	0	0	2	82	84	41	39	13	24	68	.270	.330	.238	7.46	2.63
Jones, Geoffrey	L-L	6-5	230	8-10-79	0	2	5.87	11	0	0	0	15	25	12	10	0	8	13	.373	.316	.396	7.63	4.70
Mahoney, Mike	R-R	6-0	200	12-5-72	0	0	9.00	2	0	0	0	2	4	2	2	1	2	1	.500	.500	.500	4.50	9.00
Marmol, Carlos	R-R	6-2	180	10-14-82	4	1	3.95	8	7	0	0	41	30	18	18	4	12	48	.204	.271	.143	10.54	2.63
Marshall, Sean	L-L	6-7	205	8-30-82	2	0	1.82	4	4	0	0	25	17	6	5	2	8	15	.191	.211	.186	5.47	2.92
Mateo, Juan	R-R	6-2	220	12-17-82	2	3	4.05	8	7	0	0	40	50	26	18	8	11	29	.299	.378	.237	6.52	2.48
Mathes, J.R.	L-L	6-3	205	11-9-81	10	8	5.58	27	27	1	0	152	204	111	94	20	37	86	.325	.260	.349	5.10	2.20
Miller, Wade	R-R	6-2	210	9-13-76	0	1	3.21	3	3	0	0	14	12	5	5	0	6	12	.235	.185	.292	7.71	3.86
Nannini, Mike	R-R	5-11	190	8-9-80	0	0	3.18	5	0	0	1	11	12	8	4	1	5	14	.267	.368	.192	11.12	3.97
O'Malley, Ryan	R-L	6-1	205	4-9-80	3	9	7.76	19	19	0	0	87	133	84	75	19	34	48	.361	.405	.349	4.97	3.52
Ohman, Will	L-L	6-2	205	8-13-77	0	0	2.70	9	0	0	0	7	7	2	2	0	5	9	.292	.444	.200	12.15	6.75
Petrick, Billy	R-R	6-6	240	4-29-84	1	1	5.11	9	0	0	0	12	17	8	7	3	2	7	.354	.238	.444	5.11	1.46
Pignatiello, Carmen	R-L	6-0	205	9-12-82	1	0	2.76	45	0	0	2	49	40	20	15	5	16	44	.216	.173	.250	8.08	2.94
Prinz, Bret	R-R	6-3	210	6-15-77	1	1	5.14	8	0	0	0	14	15	10	8	3	6	15	.294	.353	.265	9.64	3.86
Rapada, Clay	R-L	6-5	200	3-9-81	7	2	3.58	55	0	0	17	55	55	24	22	4	25	50	.272	.159	.331	8.13	4.07
Redmond, Cedric	R-R	6-3	180	8-30-88	0	0	0.00	1	0	0	0	1	0	0	0	0	0	0	.000	1.000	.000	0.00	0.00
Santo, Joel	R-R	6-3	194	6-4-84	0	0	4.70	1	1	0	0	8	7	4	4	2	0	5	.250	.250	.250	5.87	0.00
Schappert, Paul	L-L	6-5	215	12-21-81	0	0	1.69	3	0	0	0	5	6	1	1	1	3	3	.316	.143	.417	5.06	5.06

Name	B-T	HT	WT	DOB	W	L	ERA	G	GS	CG	SV	IP	H	R	ER	HR	BB	SO	AVG	vLH	vRH	K/9	BB/9
Walrond, Les	L-L	6-3	205	11-7-76	11	5	4.77	27	24	0	0	138	167	82	73	13	48	93	.308	.305	.308	6.08	3.14
Webb, John	R-R	6-3	220	5-23-79	4	6	5.18	31	9	0	1	80	98	53	46	5	38	53	.301	.271	.323	5.96	4.27
Wells, Randy	R-R	6-5	230	8-28-82	5	6	4.52	40	9	0	0	96	100	54	48	11	41	101	.268	.227	.297	9.50	3.86

FIELDING

Catcher	PCT	G	PO	A	E	DP	PB
Blanco	1.000	3	7	0	0	0	1
Hill	.986	30	199	17	3	2	0
Mahoney	1.000	3	16	0	0	0	1
Richie	.986	45	323	24	5	2	1
Soto	.994	74	471	38	3	6	7

First Base	PCT	G	PO	A	E	DP
Craig	1.000	8	54	3	0	5
Fox	.983	6	55	2	1	8
Garcia	1.000	1	1	0	0	1
Hart	1.000	4	32	2	0	5
Hill	1.000	3	18	1	0	1
Hoffpauir	.992	70	558	46	5	60
Kinkade	1.000	2	9	6	0	0
Kroeger	.953	10	57	4	3	4
Mahoney	1.000	3	18	5	0	1
McGehee	1.000	4	25	1	0	3
Moore	1.000	3	29	1	0	0
Nelson	.989	26	171	17	2	29
Soto	.994	22	159	15	1	23
Ward	1.000	3	27	4	0	3

Second Base	PCT	G	PO	A	E	DP
Fontenot	.988	19	36	48	1	13
Hart	1.000	4	4	10	0	4
Machado	1.000	5	8	13	0	2
Patterson	.969	83	165	211	12	60
Rojas	.979	38	81	104	4	33
Simokaitis	.955	5	11	10	1	3

Third Base	PCT	G	PO	A	E	DP
Craig	.947	22	15	39	3	5
Fontenot	.968	15	6	24	1	3
Hart	.917	7	3	8	1	3
Kinkade	1.000	7	4	18	0	2
Machado	1.000	2	0	1	0	0
McGehee	.944	12	11	23	2	1
Moore	.941	79	45	129	11	17
Nelson	.909	20	6	24	3	3
Rojas	1.000	2	1	3	0	0

Shortstop	PCT	G	PO	A	E	DP
Cedeno	.957	75	113	219	15	59
Fontenot	.978	24	27	63	2	9
Hart	—	1	0	0	0	0
Machado	1.000	6	5	7	0	2

	PCT	G	PO	A	E	DP
Moore	.750	2	2	4	2	2
Rojas	.934	25	32	53	6	14
Simokaitis	.974	30	40	108	4	28

Outfield	PCT	G	PO	A	E	DP
Coats	.997	116	274	15	1	1
Cortes	1.000	3	2	0	0	0
Fontenot	—	1	0	0	0	0
Fox	1.000	19	33	1	0	0
Fuld	.962	13	21	4	1	1
Garcia	1.000	3	3	0	0	0
Hoffpauir	.923	13	12	0	1	0
Kinkade	1.000	20	41	3	0	2
Kroeger	.968	38	60	0	2	0
Mahoney	.333	4	1	0	2	0
Moore	1.000	19	27	0	0	0
Murton	1.000	38	64	3	0	1
Pagan	.986	30	68	2	1	0
Patterson	1.000	40	82	3	0	0
Pie	.978	55	130	3	3	2
Richie	—	1	0	0	0	0
Simokaitis	1.000	2	3	1	0	0
Walker	1.000	47	65	3	0	1

TENNESSEE SMOKIES

DOUBLE-A

SOUTHERN LEAGUE

BATTING	B-T	HT	WT	DOB	AVG	vLH	vRH	G	AB	R	H	2B	3B	HR	RBI	BB	HBP	SH	SF	SO	SB	CS	SLG	OBP
Camp, Matt	L-R	6-0	175	5-29-84	.063	.000	.071	8	16	0	1	0	0	0	0	1	0	0	0	1	3	1	0	.063	.059
Cates, Gary	R-R	5-7	155	7-3-81	.262	.282	.254	97	343	29	90	11	1	2	27	18	1	14	3	44	16	7	.318	.299
Chirinos, Robinson	R-R	6-1	185	6-5-84	.220	.231	.218	42	127	11	28	4	2	2	16	13	1	5	0	31	1	1	.331	.298
Colvin, Tyler	L-L	6-3	190	9-5-85	.291	.233	.316	62	247	34	72	11	2	9	31	5	3	1	1	54	7	1	.462	.313
Cortes, Jorge	L-L	5-10	195	10-17-80	.293	.140	.323	112	348	58	102	19	2	2	38	56	3	11	2	56	7	2	.376	.394
Craig, Matt	B-R	6-2	200	4-16-81	.326	.352	.302	87	276	41	90	20	1	10	44	40	4	1	2	58	1	0	.514	.416
Dopirak, Brian	R-R	6-4	235	12-20-83	.218	.241	.204	21	78	2	17	1	0	1	4	3	0	0	0	19	0	0	.269	.247
Fox, Jacob	R-R	6-0	210	7-20-82	.284	.318	.264	91	359	60	102	23	1	18	60	17	8	0	4	72	6	2	.504	.327
Fuld, Sam	L-L	5-10	180	11-20-81	.290	.247	.305	90	335	56	97	23	2	2	27	41	5	8	3	38	10	3	.388	.372
Garcia, Alberto	R-R	6-1	180	6-5-83	.238	.231	.250	11	21	3	5	0	1	0	3	0	0	0	0	6	0	0	.333	.238
Kroeger, Josh	L-L	6-3	220	8-31-82	.382	.289	.430	66	225	40	86	14	2	11	50	27	2	0	2	35	8	3	.609	.449
McGehee, Casey	R-R	6-1	195	10-12-82	.273	.294	.264	105	384	53	105	26	2	9	54	40	0	5		73	1	2	.422	.338
Reynolds, Kyle	L-R	6-2	190	9-1-83	.281	.300	.277	35	139	24	39	9	0	9	35	8	1	0	1	29	2	2	.540	.322
Richie, Anthony	R-R	6-1	215	2-9-82	.217	.250	.200	9	23	1	5	1	0	0	1	0	0	0	0	4	0	0	.261	.250
Rick, Alan	L-R	6-3	205	9-8-83	.238	.250	.237	29	63	11	15	4	0	2	10	11	2	1	1	21	0	0	.397	.364
Robinson, Chris	R-R	6-0	200	5-12-84	.263	.351	.206	89	289	29	76	18	0	1	27	21	1	7	2	69	3	0	.336	.313
Rojas, Carlos	R-R	6-1	175	1-11-84	.198	.081	.261	38	106	10	21	2	0	0	8	14	0	5	0	21	2	0	.217	.292
Salas, Issmael	R-R	5-10	175	7-25-82	.247	.234	.253	110	344	46	85	19	0	8	53	27	5	8	3	36	2	2	.352	.309
Simokaitis, Joe	R-R	6-1	200	12-27-82	.257	.230	.272	76	210	24	54	9	0	3	15	28	2	4	3	50	1	3	.343	.346
Spearman, Jemel	R-R	6-0	190	12-27-80	.259	.279	.248	115	355	53	92	16	7	7	41	29	0	3	3	54	8	2	.403	.313
Spears, Nate	L-R	5-11	165	5-3-85	.298	.143	.320	38	114	22	34	2	2	4	11	13	3	4	1	19	2	0	.456	.382
Walker, Christopher	B-R	5-8	170	7-3-80	.295	.381	.226	24	95	11	28	3	0	2	13	7	0	1	0	16	7	4	.389	.343

PITCHING	B-T	HT	WT	DOB	W	L	ERA	G	GS	CG	SV	IP	H	R	ER	HR	BB	SO	AVG	vLH	vRH	K/9	BB/9
Atkins, Mitch	R-R	6-3	230	10-1-85	1	1	5.54	7	4	0	0	26	30	18	16	5	11	18	.288	.298	.281	6.23	3.81
Avery, Matt	R-R	6-6	230	9-7-83	2	2	4.22	31	1	0	0	49	50	26	23	8	18	36	.269	.274	.265	6.61	3.31
Berg, Justin	R-R	6-4	220	6-7-84	7	7	4.95	27	26	0	0	140	157	88	77	4	69	69	.293	.339	.261	4.44	4.44
Blevins, Jerry	L-L	6-6	185	9-6-83	2	2	1.53	23	0	0	3	29	23	5	5	1	8	37	.215	.176	.233	11.35	2.45
Cates, Gary	R-R	5-7	155	7-3-81	0	0	0.00	1	0	0	0	3	0	0	0	0	0	2	.000	.000	.000	6.00	0.00
Estrada, Jesse	R-R	6-8	260	10-27-83	1	0	0.00	2	0	0	0	2	2	0	0	0	1	3	.286	.500	.200	13.50	4.50
Gallagher, Sean	R-R	6-2	225	12-30-85	7	2	3.39	11	11	0	0	61	54	25	23	3	24	54	.233	.222	.239	7.97	3.54
Hart, Kevin	R-R	6-5	215	11-29-82	8	5	4.24	18	17	0	0	102	100	59	48	13	27	92	.255	.327	.208	8.12	2.38
Henderson, Jim	L-R	6-5	190	10-21-82	4	3	1.86	42	0	0	10	58	50	15	12	7	25	49	.239	.304	.200	7.60	3.88
Holliman, Mark	R-R	6-0	195	9-19-83	10	11	3.57	27	26	2	0	161	157	68	64	15	57	108	.257	.254	.259	6.02	3.18
Johnson, Grant	R-R	6-6	220	5-26-83	1	1	4.37	28	0	0	3	47	36	26	23	5	20	43	.207	.245	.190	8.18	3.80
Jones, Geoffrey	L-L	6-5	230	8-10-79	4	2	1.02	39	0	0	9	44	32	8	5	0	12	57	.203	.132	.225	11.57	2.44
Layden, Tim	L-L	6-2	180	12-22-82	0	1	6.00	3	0	0	0	15	27	13	10	1	9	11	.380	.412	.370	6.60	5.40
Mendez, Adalberto	R-R	6-2	160	2-22-82	3	4	4.83	40	0	0	1	60	52	36	32	10	33	50	.233	.284	.208	7.54	4.98
Miller, Wade	R-R	6-2	210	9-13-76	0	1	10.38	2	1	0	0	9	13	10	10	1	4	7	.351	.250	.439	7.27	4.15
Mueller, Jon	R-R	6-4	180	5-12-84	0	0	0.00	3	0	0	0	3	5	1	0	0	4	2	.313	.000	.556	5.40	10.80
Nannini, Mike	R-R	5-11	190	8-9-80	1	1	4.22	8	3	0	0	21	17	11	10	2	15	17	.224	.237	.211	7.17	6.33
O'Malley, Ryan	R-L	6-1	205	4-9-80	2	0	4.79	10	5	0	0	36	38	19	19	6	5	25	.268	.296	.261	6.31	1.26
Petrick, Billy	R-R	6-6	240	4-29-84	1	1	2.37	18	0	0	2	30	22	10	8	3	8	33	.202	.229	.189	9.79	2.37
Pignatiello, Carmen	R-L	6-0	205	9-12-82	1	0	0.00	5	0	0	2	7	2	0	0	0	2	6	.080	.143	.056	8.10	2.70
Reinhard, Gregory	L-R	6-2	215	8-11-83	1	1	4.25	20	0	0	0	30	28	14	14	5	16	26	.250	.216	.267	7.89	4.85
Roquet, Rocky	R-R	6-2	210	11-6-82	4	0	3.63	28	0	0	7	40	32	16	16	4	18	42	.224	.216	.228	9.53	4.08
Samardzija, Jeff	R-R	6-5	220	1-23-85	3	3	3.41	6	6	0	0	34	33	15	13	8	9	20	.250	.282	.213	5.24	2.36
Schappert, Paul	L-L	6-5	215	12-21-81	3	7	7.51	24	11	0	0	77	98	66	64	19	28	29	.316	.319	.315	3.40	3.29
Simokaitis, Joe	R-R	6-1	200	12-27-82	0	0	0.00	1	0	0	0	1	0	0	0	0	0	0	.250	.333	.000	0.00	0.00
Veal, Donald	L-L	6-4	215	9-18-84	8	10	4.97	28	27	0	0	130	126	80	72	11	73	131	.256	.320	.240	9.05	5.04
Wood, Kerry	R-R	6-5	225	6-16-77	0	0	0.00	1	0	0	0	2	0	0	0	0	0	1	.000	.000	.000	0.00	0.00

FIELDING

Catcher	PCT	G	PO	A	E	DP	PB
Fox	.978	13	84	6	2	0	1
McGehee	.990	48	362	32	4	2	10
Richie	1.000	7	45	3	0	0	0
Rick	1.000	5	18	2	0	0	0
Robinson	.989	77	479	46	6	3	2

First Base	PCT	G	PO	A	E	DP
Craig	.990	36	264	20	3	29
Dopirak	.994	20	150	7	1	12
Fox	.991	38	299	29	3	27
Garcia	1.000	2	13	0	0	1
McGehee	1.000	4	7	3	0	1
Reynolds	.963	10	72	6	3	7
Rick	.989	14	81	7	1	6
Salas	1.000	36	236	27	0	15

Second Base	PCT	G	PO	A	E	DP
Camp	1.000	1	2	4	0	0

	PCT	G	PO	A	E	DP
Cates	.988	78	133	194	4	38
Salas	.969	21	44	49	3	13
Simokaitis	—	1	0	0	0	0
Spearman	.961	29	35	39	3	9
Spears	.967	34	54	65	4	17

Third Base	PCT	G	PO	A	E	DP
Craig	.922	42	22	72	8	6
Fox	—	1	0	0	0	0
McGehee	.955	52	33	95	6	14
Reynolds	.938	23	21	39	4	4
Rojas	1.000	1	1	0	0	0
Salas	.955	18	12	30	2	2
Simokaitis	.941	9	3	13	1	1
Spearman	.833	11	4	16	4	2

Shortstop	PCT	G	PO	A	E	DP
Cates	.982	22	18	36	1	4
Chirinos	.949	39	56	112	9	17

	PCT	G	PO	A	E	DP
Rojas	.936	34	48	99	10	18
Salas	1.000	5	6	4	0	2
Simokaitis	.969	63	87	132	7	27

Outfield	PCT	G	PO	A	E	DP
Camp	1.000	6	12	0	0	0
Cates	1.000	1	1	0	0	0
Colvin	1.000	59	143	4	0	1
Cortes	.984	101	177	7	3	3
Fox	.985	35	61	5	1	0
Fuld	.987	87	208	13	3	4
Garcia	1.000	7	7	1	0	0
Kroeger	1.000	53	99	6	0	1
Salas	1.000	26	28	1	0	1
Spearman	.959	59	93	0	4	0
Walker	.982	24	56	0	1	0

DAYTONA CUBS
HIGH CLASS A

FLORIDA STATE LEAGUE

BATTING	B-T	HT	WT	DOB	AVG	vLH	vRH	G	AB	R	H	2B	3B	HR	RBI	BB	HBP	SH	SF	SO	SB	CS	SLG	OBP
Adduci, James	L-L	6-2	185	5-15-85	.121	.333	.100	12	33	2	4	1	0	0	1	0	0	1	0	13	0	1	.152	.121
Amador, Chris	R-R	5-10	167	12-14-82	.260	.273	.255	87	319	63	83	11	5	13	34	17	7	2	2	80	19	6	.448	.310
Camp, Matt	L-R	6-0	175	5-29-84	.311	.364	.291	30	119	18	37	8	0	0	7	6	0	1	1	16	10	3	.378	.341
Carter, Yusuf	B-R	6-2	205	2-6-85	.190	.188	.190	58	195	17	37	9	2	6	28	10	0	1	1	64	4	2	.349	.228
Chirinos, Robinson	R-R	6-1	185	6-5-84	.259	.284	.248	79	239	35	62	14	2	3	20	37	12	5	0	48	8	5	.372	.385
Clevenger, Steven	L-R	6-0	185	4-5-86	.323	.265	.348	43	164	21	53	8	1	2	24	13	1	1	4	5	0	0	.421	.368
Colvin, Tyler	L-L	6-3	190	9-5-85	.306	.296	.309	63	245	38	75	24	3	7	50	10	3	0	4	47	10	4	.514	.336
Culpepper, Jeff	L-R	6-1	190	12-30-81	.406	.500	.375	8	32	6	13	3	0	0	6	3	0	0	0	5	0	1	.500	.457
Dopirak, Brian	R-T	6-4	235	12-20-83	.277	.227	.293	94	347	49	96	23	0	17	64	23	4	0	5	91	1	1	.490	.325
Garcia, Alberto	R-R	6-1	180	6-5-83	.262	.271	.256	67	195	18	51	6	2	5	19	9	2	2	1	36	2	3	.390	.300
Harvey, Ryan	R-R	6-5	240	8-30-84	.246	.259	.241	59	224	30	55	10	1	11	35	7	1	0	2	53	0	1	.446	.269
Joseph, Alfred	R-R	5-11	190	7-25-86	.220	.500	.189	24	59	7	13	1	0	0	4	5	1	0		14	1	1	.237	.324
Lopez, Andrew	R-R	6-1	185	1-18-87	.167	.111	.200	9	24	3	4	1	0	1	3	3	1	0	0	8	0	0	.333	.286
Matulia, Matt	B-R	6-0	185	5-24-84	.249	.213	.263	128	457	70	114	18	8	3	38	56	10	10	2	91	16	7	.344	.343
Mota, Jonathan	R-R	6-0	165	6-1-87	.231	.250	.223	38	134	20	31	8	1	1	17	11	2	3	1	21	4	3	.328	.297
Mottram, William	L-R	6-0	195	11-14-84	.138	.200	.132	19	58	4	8	1	0	0	7	7	0	4	1	13	0	1	.155	.227
Muyco, Jake	R-R	6-0	190	9-16-84	.180	.137	.203	71	206	13	37	7	0	1	15	18	1	5	1	52	1	3	.228	.248
Norwood, Ryan	R-L	6-4	220	2-18-83	.217	.229	.212	35	120	10	26	2	0	0	15	9	3	0	2	24	1	0	.233	.284
Rea, Jeffrey	L-R	5-8	160	7-10-84	.335	.293	.351	43	155	25	52	6	3	0	11	16	0	2	0	22	7	1	.413	.398
Reed, Mark	L-R	5-11	175	4-13-86	.184	.156	.189	88	228	25	42	8	1	0	18	13	1	4	0	57	6	5	.228	.231
Reynolds, Kyle	L-R	6-2	190	9-1-83	.282	.262	.286	74	248	30	70	13	2	12	44	15	0	0	2	53	7	2	.496	.321
Rick, Alan	L-R	6-3	205	8-19-82	.231	.143	.236	55	147	17	34	7	1	5	22	22	4	1	1	45	1	1	.395	.345
Samson, Nate	R-R	6-0	170	8-19-87	.500	.500	.500	3	6	3	3	1	0	0	3	1	0	1	0	2	0	0	.667	.571
Spears, Nate	L-R	5-11	165	5-3-85	.261	.270	.258	78	249	36	65	13	3	1	26	28	6	15	2	44	4	1	.349	.347
Valdez, Jesus	R-R	6-2	170	11-2-84	.250	.268	.244	83	288	36	72	11	4	1	39	18	4	0	3	40	2	3	.326	.300
Walker, Christopher	B-R	5-8	170	7-3-80	.368	.286	.417	5	19	3	7	0	0	0	0	3	0	1	0	6	1	1	.368	.455

PITCHING	B-T	HT	WT	DOB	W	L	ERA	G	GS	CG	SV	IP	H	R	ER	HR	BB	SO	AVG	vLH	vRH	K/9	BB/9
Atkins, Mitch	R-R	6-3	230	10-1-85	8	7	3.13	20	20	1	0	115	99	51	40	14	31	88	.255	.251	.224	6.89	2.43
Avery, Matt	R-R	6-6	230	9-7-83	1	1	1.61	19	0	0	7	22	17	5	4	1	8	15	.213	.185	.226	6.04	3.22
Blackford, Todd	L-R	6-4	215	6-10-85	1	0	5.40	5	5	0	0	25	25	15	15	1	10	13	.275	.250	.288	4.68	3.60
Blevins, Jerry	L-L	6-6	185	9-6-83	1	0	0.38	15	0	0	6	24	13	1	1	0	5	32	.159	.250	.129	12.17	1.90
Clipp, Brad	R-R	6-2	180	8-15-84	1	0	2.84	3	0	0	0	6	3	2	2	0	2	7	.150	.375	.000	9.95	2.84
Cooper, Michael	R-R	6-6	230	1-29-84	0	2	2.70	3	0	0	0	3	4	3	1	0	0	2	.286	.600	.111	5.40	0.00
Cuevas novas, Miguel	R-R	6-9	260	8-11-83	0	0	0.00	1	1	0	0	3	2	1	0	0	0	5	.200	.000	.333	13.50	10.12
Downs, Darin	R-L	6-3	176	12-26-84	3	7	4.11	34	2	0	2	61	61	39	28	10	17	65	.255	.214	.272	9.54	2.49
Estrada, Jesse	R-R	6-8	260	10-27-83	4	5	4.58	31	18	2	0	132	138	71	67	13	37	103	.273	.323	.240	7.04	2.53
Garcia, Alberto	R-R	6-1	180	6-5-83	0	1	9.00	1	0	0	0	2	1	1	0	0	0	0	.400	.333	.500	0.00	0.00
Johnson, Grant	R-R	6-6	220	5-26-83	1	1	3.57	16	0	0	0	23	19	12	9	2	11	25	.221	.310	.175	9.93	4.37
Koerber, Scott	L-L	6-4	215	9-30-82	4	6	4.13	39	6	0	3	89	97	45	41	10	28	52	.280	.267	.284	5.24	2.82
Layden, Tim	L-L	6-2	180	12-22-82	1	6	5.40	34	0	0	9	47	61	33	28	4	24	40	.311	.283	.322	7.71	4.63
Marshall, Sean	L-L	6-7	205	8-30-82	1	0	3.00	1	1	0	0	6	7	2	2	1	1	4	.304	.667	.250	6.00	1.50
Mendez, Adalberto	R-R	6-2	160	2-22-82	0	2	5.67	5	5	0	0	27	30	19	17	6	16	16	.283	.318	.258	5.33	5.33
Meyer, Scott	R-R	6-3	220	10-8-85	0	1	7.56	6	0	0	0	8	12	8	7	0	5	5	.333	.385	.304	5.40	6.48
Mueller, Jon	R-R	6-4	180	5-12-84	5	2	5.27	23	2	0	0	41	53	31	24	7	13	25	.308	.238	.349	5.49	2.85
Petrick, Billy	R-R	6-6	240	4-29-84	0	1	3.09	6	0	0	0	12	12	4	4	0	2	10	.267	.059	.393	7.71	1.54
Phelps, Michael	R-R	6-4	190	5-26-84	1	3	6.09	24	0	0	2	34	42	30	23	2	17	23	.304	.340	.282	6.09	4.50
Platt, Charles	R-R	6-2	235	10-12-82	1	0	4.29	21	1	0	1	36	40	22	17	4	15	16	.276	.313	.258	4.04	3.73
Reinhard, Gregory	L-R	6-2	215	8-11-83	4	4	5.40	15	15	1	0	65	82	50	39	8	30	49	.308	.275	.336	6.78	4.15
Roquet, Rocky	R-R	6-2	210	11-6-82	1	0	1.50	3	0	0	0	6	5	1	1	0	1	9	.217	.250	.200	13.50	1.50
Samardzija, Jeff	R-R	6-5	220	1-23-85	3	8	4.95	24	20	1	0	107	142	69	59	8	35	45	.323	.335	.316	3.77	2.93
Santo, Joel	R-R	6-3	194	6-4-84	8	9	5.15	27	22	0	0	124	122	79	71	16	72	78	.260	.273	.252	5.66	5.23
Schappert, Paul	L-L	6-5	215	12-21-81	3	0	4.50	5	1	0	1	30	36	17	15	5	9	14	.290	.235	.311	4.20	2.70
Shaver, Chris	L-L	6-7	235	8-21-81	0	0	5.79	1	1	0	0	5	5	4	3	0	4	5	.263	.286	.250	9.64	7.71
Taylor, Scott	R-R	6-3	240	12-28-86	4	11	5.74	26	13	0	0	94	130	68	60	11	19	43	.330	.323	.333	4.12	1.82
Tuero, Yusdel	R-R	5-11	180	3-7-82	0	2	2.93	14	0	0	2	15	14	10	5	0	7	9	.246	.286	.222	5.28	4.11
Walters, Donald	R-R	6-1	195	7-18-86	1	1	5.06	4	0	0	0	5	6	3	3	2	5	3	.286	.333	.267	5.06	8.44

FIELDING

Catcher	PCT	G	PO	A	E	DP	PB
Clevenger	1.000	7	50	5	0	0	1
Muyco	.991	67	397	61	4	5	4
Reed	.979	67	333	48	8	6	3
Rick	.972	8	34	1	1	0	1

First Base	PCT	G	PO	A	E	DP
Adduci	1.000	1	12	0	0	1
Clevenger	1.000	23	174	6	0	14
Dopirak	1.000	35	230	16	0	26
Garcia	.990	30	194	11	2	14
Mottram	1.000	2	6	0	0	0
Norwood	.990	35	286	21	3	25
Reed	1.000	7	10	3	0	1
Reynolds	.933	2	14	0	1	1
Rick	.989	26	161	12	2	14

Second Base	PCT	G	PO	A	E	DP
Camp	.946	12	27	26	3	5

Chirinos	1.000	9	20	24	0	6
Matulia	.975	27	58	61	3	13
Mota	1.000	1	2	6	0	2
Rea	.967	20	41	47	3	11
Reed	—	2	0	0	0	0
Spears	.973	73	149	208	10	41

Third Base	PCT	G	PO	A	E	DP
Chirinos	.909	5	2	8	1	0
Matulia	.947	52	37	88	7	6
Mota	1.000	4	4	4	0	0
Mottram	.850	16	8	26	6	4
Reed	—	1	0	0	0	0
Reynolds	.887	67	39	110	19	11

Shortstop	PCT	G	PO	A	E	DP
Chirinos	.960	58	94	173	11	30
Matulia	.950	51	75	151	12	25
Mota	.951	33	49	88	7	12

Samson	1.000	3	3	2	0	1

Outfield	PCT	G	PO	A	E	DP
Adduci	1.000	9	14	0	0	0
Amador	.969	86	181	7	6	1
Camp	.985	19	64	2	1	0
Carter	.939	57	104	4	7	1
Colvin	.994	61	172	3	1	1
Culpepper	.750	3	2	1	1	0
Garcia	.962	31	51	0	2	0
Harvey	.982	48	103	5	2	1
Joseph	.946	18	33	2	2	0
Lopez	1.000	5	11	0	0	0
Muyco	—	1	0	0	0	0
Rea	.960	21	48	0	2	0
Rick	—	1	0	0	0	0
Valdez	.973	78	135	9	4	4
Walker	1.000	5	13	0	0	0

PEORIA CHIEFS
LOW CLASS A
MIDWEST LEAGUE

BATTING	B-T	HT	WT	DOB	AVG	vLH	vRH	G	AB	R	H	2B	3B	HR	RBI	BB	HBP	SH	SF	SO	SB	CS	SLG	OBP
Adduci, James	L-L	6-2	185	5-15-85	.292	.292	.292	107	401	54	117	18	2	2	48	30	3	1	1	98	20	6	.362	.345
Barney, Darwin	R-R	5-10	175	11-8-85	.273	.182	.303	44	176	27	48	9	3	2	21	11	3	0	2	22	5	2	.392	.323
Blanco, Henry	R-R	5-11	220	8-29-71	.316	.400	.286	8	19	3	6	1	0	1	5	3	1	0	1	3	0	0	.526	.417
Camp, Matt	L-R	6-0	175	5-29-84	.249	.234	.255	91	333	52	83	15	1	2	35	31	4	2	4	51	31	6	.318	.317
Canepa, Matthew	R-R	6-1	195	6-3-85	.168	.225	.148	48	155	9	26	1	0	0	8	10	2	1	2	44	2	0	.174	.225
Canzler, Russell	R-R	6-2	215	4-11-86	.270	.262	.273	125	460	60	124	24	2	7	54	35	2	1	5	88	12	8	.376	.321
Carter, Yusuf	B-R	6-2	205	2-6-85	.258	.250	.261	68	252	37	65	9	5	10	41	10	0	2	2	84	11	4	.452	.284
Castillo, Wellington	R-R	6-0	200	4-24-87	.271	.323	.249	98	317	41	86	11	2	11	44	23	8	3	2	77	1	3	.423	.333
Hardman, Clark	L-R	6-2	200	8-8-85	.153	.091	.164	19	72	3	11	2	0	0	7	5	0	0	0	14	0	2	.181	.208
Heredia, Valerio	B-R	5-10	150	3-14-86	.000	.000	.000	5	18	1	0	0	0	0	0	0	0	0	0	10	0	0	.000	.000
Johnson, Leon	L-L	6-1	185	6-11-85	.198	.240	.186	33	111	23	22	3	0	1	11	21	1	4	0	30	10	3	.252	.331
Johnston, Dylan	L-R	6-0	180	3-25-87	.169	.070	.215	43	136	14	23	4	1	3	16	15	1	0	1	59	8	5	.279	.255
Joseph, Alfred	R-R	5-11	190	7-25-86	.246	.306	.219	77	268	41	66	6	1	2	24	17	6	0	1	32	11	5	.299	.305
Lalli, Blake	R-R	6-2	210	5-12-83	.295	.298	.294	77	268	29	79	13	0	4	33	18	3	2	1	43	3	1	.388	.345
Lansford, Josh	R-R	6-2	220	7-3-84	.273	.247	.283	84	322	29	88	17	0	3	42	16	0	6	3	33	2	7	.354	.305
Leclerc, Brian	L-R	5-10	175	1-12-85	.246	.321	.217	39	126	10	31	7	2	0	13	5	1	0	1	20	0	1	.333	.278
Lewis, DJ	R-R	6-0	180	8-25-85	.195	.143	.222	37	123	12	24	3	0	2	12	13	0	0	1	26	0	2	.268	.270
Lopez, Andrew	R-R	6-1	185	1-18-87	.258	.200	.286	17	62	7	16	5	1	1	9	1	2	1	1	25	1	0	.419	.288
Malone, Ryne	L-R	5-11	180	1-6-85	.245	.163	.262	73	245	41	60	15	1	3	21	30	4	1	2	42	1	1	.351	.335
Mota, Jonathan	R-R	6-0	165	6-1-87	.277	.246	.290	67	220	35	61	17	1	2	16	24	1	5	1	42	9	5	.391	.350
Norwood, Ryan	R-L	6-4	220	2-18-83	.253	.238	.259	22	75	6	19	3	0	0	5	6	0	0	1	11	0	1	.293	.305
Samson, Nate	R-R	6-0	170	8-19-87	.246	.244	.246	61	183	19	45	6	1	0	19	21	3	4	4	25	1	4	.290	.327
Schermerhorn, Derek	R-R	6-2	215	4-29-84	.222	.196	.239	39	117	10	26	3	0	1	10	7	3	0	0	23	3	2	.248	.283
Smith, Marquez	R-R	5-10	210	3-20-85	.297	.471	.234	18	64	13	19	3	0	3	14	7	1	0	0	8	0	1	.484	.375
Wright, Ty	R-R	6-0	200	2-26-85	.284	.176	.316	19	74	5	21	1	0	2	5	5	0	0	0	15	5	1	.378	.329

PITCHING	B-T	HT	WT	DOB	W	L	ERA	G	GS	CG	SV	IP	H	R	ER	HR	BB	SO	AVG	vLH	vRH	K/9	BB/9
Alburquerque, Al	R-R	6-0	150	6-10-86	1	4	9.24	11	4	0	0	25	36	29	26	5	12	20	.330	.292	.386	7.11	4.26
Bartek, Michael	R-R	5-11	165	2-28-84	0	1	7.13	17	4	0	0	42	52	37	33	2	29	28	.299	.284	.312	6.05	6.26
Bernard, Oscar	R-R	6-2	170	6-27-83	1	3	8.10	19	0	0	1	30	41	32	27	7	24	14	.318	.308	.325	4.20	7.20
Billek, Mike	R-R	6-4	235	3-4-84	0	1	24.75	2	1	0	0	4	11	11	11	0	3	2	.500	.750	.444	4.50	6.75
Carrillo, Marco	R-R	5-11	200	2-1-87	7	6	4.07	31	20	0	0	130	117	68	59	9	57	94	.240	.243	.238	6.49	3.94
Castillo, Julio	R-R	6-3	212	10-6-87	0	0	7.27	7	0	0	0	9	8	7	7	0	15	2	.258	.286	.235	2.08	15.58
Ceda, Jose	R-R	6-4	205	1-28-87	2	2	3.11	21	6	0	0	46	14	18	16	1	31	66	.093	.065	.112	12.82	6.02
Clipp, Brad	R-R	6-2	180	8-15-84	1	0	3.48	4	0	0	0	10	10	4	4	2	3	12	.244	.263	.227	10.45	2.61
Cuevas novas, Miguel	R-R	6-9	260	8-11-83	0	1	5.40	7	3	0	0	22	21	13	13	2	18	24	.256	.212	.286	9.97	7.48
Dolis, Rafael	R-R	6-3	180	1-10-88	3	1	1.80	6	6	0	0	30	23	7	6	1	16	24	.223	.260	.189	7.20	4.80
Hempy, Arik	R-L	6-4	245	7-19-84	0	1	24.00	2	2	0	0	3	8	8	8	1	7	3	.471	.444	.500	9.00	21.00
Hernandez, Robert	R-R	6-1	165	10-7-88	8	9	4.34	20	20	0	0	104	106	60	50	11	28	71	.266	.277	.257	6.16	2.43
Lalli, Blake	R-R	6-1	210	5-12-83	0	0	0.00	1	0	0	0	4	1	0	0	0	4	1	.077	.000	.167	6.75	0.00
Lambert, Casey	L-L	5-11	175	12-11-85	1	0	2.70	18	0	0	1	33	21	12	10	0	13	33	.178	.111	.207	8.93	3.51
Maestri, Alessandro	R-R	5-11	180	6-1-85	6	3	2.26	48	4	0	12	84	57	24	21	7	15	83	.186	.258	.139	8.93	1.61
Maradeo, Matt	R-R	6-5	210	6-30-83	0	3	2.96	18	0	0	2	46	27	19	15	2	16	45	.165	.300	.087	8.87	3.15
Mateo, Juan	R-R	6-2	220	12-17-82	2	1	5.24	6	6	0	0	22	27	14	13	1	8	14	.303	.375	.245	5.64	3.22
Miller, Wade	R-R	6-2	210	9-13-76	0	0	6.00	1	1	0	0	3	4	2	2	0	0	5	.333	.333	.333	15.00	0.00
Muldowney, Billy	R-R	6-1	185	8-9-84	2	3	5.24	6	6	1	0	22	29	19	13	3	6	24	.299	.378	.231	9.67	2.42
Papelbon, Jeremy	R-L	6-1	205	6-24-83	7	6	3.11	39	8	0	3	107	95	39	37	7	30	99	.235	.231	.237	8.33	2.52
Pawelek, Mark	L-L	6-3	190	8-18-86	0	0	6.75	2	0	0	0	4	2	3	3	0	4	3	.167	.000	.400	6.75	9.00
Pina, Jose	R-R	6-2	150	11-2-85	5	8	4.29	23	19	0	0	107	107	56	51	16	37	71	.261	.259	.262	5.97	3.11
Platt, Charles	R-R	6-2	235	10-12-82	2	1	2.73	13	0	0	0	33	27	11	10	4	7	22	.223	.273	.195	6.00	1.91
Renshaw, Jacob	R-R	6-3	215	4-29-86	12	8	4.33	23	22	0	0	112	113	61	54	12	42	96	.263	.253	.268	7.69	3.36
Roquet, Rocky	R-R	6-2	210	11-6-82	0	0	0.36	19	0	0	11	25	17	1	1	0	11	29	.200	.235	.176	10.44	3.96
Ruhlman, Jayson	L-L	6-1	180	8-17-84	5	3	2.88	51	0	0	6	91	86	37	29	2	36	85	.249	.260	.245	8.44	3.57
Russell, James	L-L	6-4	205	1-8-86	0	0	0.00	2	2	0	0	7	3	0	0	0	4	9	.136	.000	.143	11.57	5.14
Shaver, Chris	L-L	6-7	235	8-21-81	1	0	1.32	3	3	0	0	14	13	3	2	0	6	11	.245	.083	.293	7.24	3.95
Siegfried, Chris	L-L	6-5	195	10-20-84	1	0	5.59	10	1	0	0	19	14	13	12	0	16	23	.200	.100	.275	10.71	7.45
Walters, Donald	R-R	6-1	195	7-18-86	0	3	4.30	7	0	0	0	15	14	10	7	1	8	13	.246	.167	.303	7.98	4.91
Wood, Kerry	R-R	6-5	225	6-16-77	1	0	0.00	3	1	0	0	3	1	0	0	0	1	3	.100	.000	.143	9.00	3.00

FIELDING

Catcher	PCT	G	PO	A	E	DP	PB
Blanco	1.000	7	43	2	0	1	0
Canepa	.992	45	326	31	3	2	3
Castillo	.978	86	591	74	15	5	13
Lalli	1.000	10	76	8	0	0	1
Mota	.978	20	35	53	2		13
Samson	.976	38	69	95	4		20

First Base	PCT	G	PO	A	E	DP
Canzler	.989	98	770	47	9	67
Lalli	.986	9	62	6	1	3
Lewis	1.000	6	49	4	0	7
Norwood	.990	12	92	4	1	3
Schermerhorn	.994	23	148	12	1	10

Second Base	PCT	G	PO	A	E	DP
Camp	.977	40	98	110	5	30
Malone	.963	50	89	117	8	21

Third Base	PCT	G	PO	A	E	DP
Lansford	.942	84	75	154	14	18
Malone	.976	19	12	28	1	3
Mota	1.000	14	12	21	0	3
Schermerhorn	.971	10	7	26	1	2
Smith	.881	16	15	22	5	1

Shortstop	PCT	G	PO	A	E	DP
Barney	.957	44	69	108	8	20
Johnston	.892	43	58	90	18	15
Mota	.954	34	47	98	7	15
Samson	.925	23	35	63	8	17

Outfield	PCT	G	PO	A	E	DP
Adduci	.960	99	166	4	7	1
Camp	.971	50	130	6	4	2
Canzler	1.000	16	29	2	0	1
Carter	.959	65	113	3	5	0
Hardman	1.000	19	38	2	0	0
Heredia	1.000	5	10	0	0	0
Johnson	.942	31	45	4	3	2
Joseph	.940	68	105	5	7	0
Leclerc	.964	30	51	3	2	1
Lewis	.926	16	23	2	2	0
Lopez	.909	12	19	1	2	1
Malone	1.000	1	3	0	0	0
Wright	.972	19	34	1	1	0

BOISE HAWKS   SHORT-SEASON

NORTHWEST LEAGUE

BATTING	B-T	HT	WT	DOB	AVG	vLH	vRH	G	AB	R	H	2B	3B	HR	RBI	BB	HBP	SH	SF	SO	SB	CS	SLG	OBP
Andersen, Cliff	L-L	6-2	185	7-24-87	.000	.000	.000	2	3	1	0	0	0	0	1	0	0	0	1	2	0	0	.000	.000
Baez, Sammy	R-R	6-2	175	12-10-84	.182	.250	.143	3	11	1	2	0	0	0	0	1	0	0	0	3	0	1	.182	.250
Bautista, Luis	R-R	6-4	232	9-19-84	.313	.231	.333	23	64	9	20	3	0	0	11	10	0	0	0	17	0	1	.359	.405
Burke, Kyler	L-L	6-3	205	4-20-88	.254	.293	.241	63	224	35	57	11	1	10	41	24	6	3	2	63	1	3	.446	.340
Clevenger, Steven	L-R	6-0	185	4-5-86	.373	.412	.364	22	83	10	31	9	0	0	18	4	0	0	1	6	0	0	.482	.398
Donaldson, Joshua	R-R	6-0	195	12-8-85	.346	.452	.321	49	162	37	56	11	2	9	35	37	2	0	1	34	6	2	.605	.470
Guyer, Brandon	R-R	6-1	210	1-28-86	.268	.100	.295	19	71	9	19	1	0	0	14	6	3	7	1	9	5	0	.282	.346
Johnston, Dylan	L-R	6-0	180	3-25-87	.237	.276	.224	62	232	35	55	18	4	3	16	24	2	1	0	74	7	5	.388	.314
Leclerc, Brian	L-R	5-10	175	1-12-85	.500	.000	1.000	1	2	1	1	0	0	0	0	2	0	0	0	0	0	0	.500	.750
Made, Jose	R-R	5-8	172	10-23-85	.192	.346	.141	39	104	15	20	5	1	1	8	6	1	2	0	29	1	0	.288	.243
Mercedes, Mario	R-R	5-10	160	11-22-86	.271	.222	.288	32	107	16	29	7	0	0	8	2	1	1	1	11	1	1	.336	.331
Moss, Bill	R-R	6-0	194	6-26-84	.171	.184	.165	45	123	11	21	7	2	1	14	14	3	2	3	25	3	2	.285	.266
Mottram, William	L-R	6-0	195	11-14-84	.171	.059	.203	22	76	9	13	3	0	2	11	8	1	0	0	26	0	1	.289	.259
Rosa, Jovan	R-R	6-2	180	10-26-87	.250	.273	.243	14	48	3	12	0	0	0	5	3	2	0	0	12	0	1	.250	.321
Rundle, Andrew	L-L	6-4	180	11-5-87	.199	.159	.213	48	166	28	33	6	1	2	20	21	2	1	0	61	3	2	.283	.296
Sawyer, Marc	L-L	6-3	210	10-2-85	.203	.213	.200	61	207	19	42	10	1	1	22	19	1	4	0	55	2	1	.275	.273
Schermerhorn, Derek	R-R	6-2	215	4-29-84	.276	.182	.333	8	29	3	8	3	0	0	1	1	0	0	0	5	0	0	.379	.300
Smith, Marquez	R-R	5-10	210	3-20-85	.275	.245	.286	54	193	37	53	11	1	5	41	37	0	0	6	40	1	2	.420	.381
Thomas, Tony	R-R	5-10	180	7-10-86	.308	.318	.304	46	182	44	56	12	8	5	33	25	5	1	1	41	28	2	.544	.404
Vitters, Josh	R-R	6-3	200	8-27-89	.190	.000	.250	7	21	2	4	0	0	0	3	1	0	0	0	5	1	1	.190	.261
Wright, Ty	R-R	6-0	200	2-26-85	.317	.372	.301	52	189	40	60	12	2	8	44	23	8	1	3	22	6	2	.529	.408
Wyatt, Jonathan	L-R	5-10	180	9-6-84	.306	.361	.288	66	245	61	75	18	4	4	41	42	3	7	4	47	12	6	.461	.408

PITCHING	B-T	HT	WT	DOB	W	L	ERA	G	GS	CG	SV	IP	H	R	ER	HR	BB	SO	AVG	vLH	vRH	K/9	BB/9
Acosta, Ryan	R-R	6-2	170	11-4-88	0	2	3.00	3	3	0	0	12	9	4	4	2	3	8	.209	.222	.200	6.00	2.25
Alburquerque, Al	R-R	6-0	150	6-10-86	3	2	3.73	10	6	0	1	41	42	20	17	2	17	49	.266	.241	.291	10.76	3.73
Ashwood, Zachary	B-L	6-4	202	5-20-86	4	3	3.28	18	10	0	0	58	58	28	21	2	21	49	.265	.283	.260	7.65	3.28
Bernard, Oscar	R-R	6-2	170	6-27-83	2	1	7.40	16	0	0	0	21	23	24	17	0	24	16	.277	.351	.217	6.97	10.45
Bunton, Michael	L-L	6-3	195	10-23-85	0	1	6.35	3	3	0	0	11	14	8	8	1	7	7	.318	.250	.344	5.56	5.56
Cabrera, Alberto	R-R	6-4	170	10-25-88	3	3	5.40	9	9	0	0	38	41	24	23	4	18	33	.287	.220	.333	7.75	4.23
Castillo, Julio	R-R	6-3	212	10-6-87	0	4	5.48	7	7	0	0	23	24	21	14	4	15	12	.270	.270	.269	4.70	5.87
Chen, Hung-Wen	R-R	5-11	195	2-3-86	1	0	3.60	2	0	0	0	5	3	2	2	1	1	2	.188	.143	.222	3.60	1.80
Hatley, Marcus	R-R	6-5	190	3-26-88	1	0	3.86	3	0	0	1	5	3	2	2	1	2	3	.167	.125	.200	5.79	3.86
Hempy, Arik	R-L	6-4	245	7-19-84	1	3	4.70	9	7	0	0	31	27	19	16	4	11	33	.227	.269	.215	9.68	3.23
Higgins, Yuri	R-R	5-8	182	2-26-85	2	1	2.50	10	0	0	1	18	16	9	5	1	8	15	.250	.138	.343	7.50	4.00
Huseby, Christopher	R-R	6-5	220	1-11-88	2	5	3.39	15	15	0	0	66	61	39	25	7	31	53	.245	.252	.239	7.19	4.21
Lambert, Casey	L-L	5-11	175	12-11-85	1	0	2.25	4	0	0	0	8	5	2	2	0	2	14	.167	.500	.143	15.75	2.25
Latham, Jordan	R-R	6-1	180	9-25-86	2	0	3.74	20	0	0	1	46	45	28	19	3	26	47	.250	.173	.305	9.26	5.12
Lee, Simon	R-R	6-2	210	7-14-83	0	0	6.75	3	0	0	1	3	4	2	2	0	0	1	.333	.333	.333	3.38	0.00
McCormick, Andrew	R-R	6-6	210	8-9-84	0	1	16.62	5	1	0	0	9	22	18	16	1	5	3	.449	.286	.571	3.12	5.19
Moss, Bill	R-R	6-0	194	6-26-84	0	0	0.00	1	0	0	0	1	0	0	0	0	0	0	.000	.000	—	0.00	0.00
Muller, John	L-R	6-2	200	7-28-84	2	3	5.15	25	0	0	3	44	41	27	25	7	26	51	.252	.282	.228	10.51	5.36
Parker, Blake	R-R	6-3	220	6-19-85	1	0	3.18	8	0	0	0	11	15	5	4	0	7	10	.319	.368	.286	7.94	5.56
Pawelek, Mark	L-L	6-3	190	8-18-86	1	2	9.24	8	1	0	0	13	13	13	13	1	10	10	.277	.267	.281	7.11	7.11
Santana, Audy	R-R	6-3	160	11-10-86	4	2	3.28	26	0	0	0	47	42	24	17	4	24	58	.232	.229	.235	11.19	4.63
Sasser, Dustin	L-L	6-0	200	9-13-85	3	4	4.59	14	14	0	0	65	64	37	33	4	24	51	.262	.232	.271	7.10	3.34
Schermerhorn, Derek	R-R	6-2	215	4-29-84	0	0	0.00	1	0	0	0	1	0	0	0	0	1	1	.250	.000	.333	9.00	9.00
Siegfried, Chris	L-L	6-5	195	12-12-85	0	1	2.35	14	0	0	0	23	23	12	6	2	9	17	.250	.273	.243	6.65	3.52
Taylor, Brandon	R-R	6-1	200	7-26-82	1	0	9.92	6	0	0	0	16	26	19	18	0	9	6	.366	.439	.267	3.31	4.96
Tolentino, Harol	R-L	6-4	165	11-8-88	1	0	9.00	10	0	0	1	13	14	13	13	3	13	10	.286	.077	.361	6.92	9.00
Vento, Stephen	R-R	6-3	210	3-28-86	2	1	4.86	22	0	0	3	33	34	26	18	6	21	29	.262	.263	.260	7.83	5.67

FIELDING

Catcher	PCT	G	PO	A	E	DP	PB
Bautista	1.000	6	35	1	0	0	0
Clevenger	.988	11	70	11	1	2	3
Donaldson	.990	42	345	39	4	5	11
Mercedes	.988	25	149	16	2	2	4

First Base	PCT	G	PO	A	E	DP
Bautista	.942	9	45	4	3	3
Clevenger	.984	7	58	3	1	7
Mottram	1.000	3	18	0	0	2
Sawyer	.985	61	491	30	8	46
Schermerhorn	.976	5	34	7	1	3

Second Base	PCT	G	PO	A	E	DP
Made	.957	15	32	35	3	11

	PCT	G	PO	A	E	DP
Moss	.990	25	42	62	1	13
Mottram	1.000	1	0	2	0	0
Thomas	.959	40	91	119	9	24

Third Base	PCT	G	PO	A	E	DP
Moss	.857	8	1	11	2	0
Mottram	.846	10	9	13	4	3
Rosa	.929	13	8	18	2	0
Smith	.921	45	18	99	10	5
Vitters	.882	5	3	12	2	0

Shortstop	PCT	G	PO	A	E	DP
Johnston	.885	56	81	134	28	25
Made	.944	19	24	43	4	12
Moss	.966	12	13	43	2	5

Outfield	PCT	G	PO	A	E	DP
Andersen	1.000	2	1	0	0	0
Baez	1.000	2	2	0	0	0
Burke	.976	57	77	5	2	1
Guyer	.941	18	30	2	2	0
Leclerc	1.000	1	2	0	0	0
Rundle	.986	44	70	2	1	1
Wright	.938	45	56	4	4	0
Wyatt	.980	64	135	9	3	4

AZL CUBS
ARIZONA LEAGUE

ROOKIE

ORGANIZATION STATISTICS

BATTING

	B-T	HT	WT	DOB	AVG	vLH	vRH	G	AB	R	H	2B	3B	HR	RBI	BB	HBP	SH	SF	SO	SB	CS	SLG	OBP
Andersen, Cliff	L-L	6-2	185	7-24-87	.298	.276	.308	45	178	24	53	11	7	1	17	9	3	3	0	59	3	0	.455	.342
Barney, Darwin	R-R	5-10	175	11-8-85	.444	.333	.500	5	18	6	8	3	0	0	2	4	0	0	0	0	0	0	.611	.545
Bautista, Luis	R-R	6-4	232	9-19-84	.368	.600	.286	5	19	5	7	3	0	1	5	2	0	1	0	1	0	0	.684	.429
Brooks, Patrick	R-R	6-0	185	7-4-85	.203	.268	.169	36	118	14	24	8	0	0	8	8	2	1	1	29	1	2	.271	.264
Donaldson, Joshua	R-R	6-0	195	12-8-85	.182	.400	.000	4	11	1	2	2	0	0	2	0	0	0	0	4	0	1	.364	.308
Gonzalez, Marwin	B-R	6-1	186	3-14-89	.288	.250	.302	17	59	12	17	3	3	1	10	9	1	0	0	10	1	2	.492	.391
Guyer, Brandon	R-R	6-1	210	1-28-86	.222	.118	.255	17	72	10	16	4	1	1	5	5	4	0	0	16	6	2	.347	.309
Guzman, Gian	R-R	6-2	180	5-26-89	.243	.226	.250	47	177	21	43	6	4	0	16	12	1	2	1	35	7	5	.322	.293
Hardman, Clark	L-R	6-2	200	8-8-85	.351	.333	.357	15	57	9	20	1	1	0	7	4	2	1	1	8	4	0	.404	.406
Harvey, Ryan	R-R	6-5	240	8-30-84	.118	.000	.182	4	17	1	2	0	0	0	1	1	0	0	0	7	0	0	.118	.167
Hudgins, Matt	L-R	6-4	220	8-8-84	.203	.214	.200	20	64	5	13	2	0	2	9	1	0	0	1	20	1	0	.328	.212
Johnson, Leon	L-L	6-1	185	6-11-85	.433	.393	.462	18	67	26	29	5	5	1	11	12	1	1	0	7	13	1	.701	.525
Lara, Elvis	R-R	5-11	160	11-19-86	.267	.216	.297	31	101	9	27	2	1	1	8	3	1	0	1	11	3	2	.337	.292
Lopez, Andrew	R-R	6-1	185	1-18-87	.174	.000	.222	6	23	3	4	0	0	1	2	1	1	0	0	7	1	0	.304	.240
Perez, Carlos	R-R	6-1	180	10-18-87	.338	.302	.359	43	145	20	49	10	3	2	31	14	2	2	2	28	1	2	.490	.399
Perez, Nelson	L-R	6-3	215	11-16-87	.252	.245	.255	44	155	20	39	5	4	4	21	6	2	0	0	46	1	4	.413	.288
Rea, Jeffrey	L-R	5-8	160	7-10-84	.341	.357	.333	11	41	9	14	2	0	0	5	5	0	0	1	4	2	1	.390	.404
Reyes, Jesus	R-R	6-1	215	3-26-86	.413	.563	.333	13	46	9	19	3	2	0	8	1	0	0	0	8	0	1	.565	.426
Rosa, Jovan	R-R	6-2	180	10-26-87	.340	.271	.375	39	144	25	49	7	1	3	26	10	2	1	1	34	0	1	.465	.389
Sabates, Roberto	R-R	6-4	210	10-11-84	.272	.250	.278	33	103	10	28	7	3	0	13	9	1	0	1	26	0	2	.398	.333
Sommer, Luke	L-L	6-3	190	6-22-85	.237	.237	.197	49	177	25	42	11	6	2	31	12	5	2	3	36	0	3	.401	.299
Thomas, Tony	R-R	5-10	180	7-10-86	.176	.000	.273	5	17	7	3	0	2	0	6	2	1	0	1	5	0	0	.412	.286
Valentin, Cesar	R-R	5-11	155	10-19-88	.242	.263	.234	27	66	5	16	4	1	0	6	5	0	1	1	11	0	2	.333	.292
Vitters, Josh	R-R	6-3	200	8-27-89	.067	.000	.100	7	30	0	2	0	0	0	2	1	0	0	1	9	0	0	.067	.094
Walker, Christopher	B-R	5-8	170	7-3-80	.429	.625	.308	6	21	3	9	0	0	0	1	5	0	1	0	2	2	3	.429	.538
Wen, Chih-Hsiang	R-R	6-1	190	11-17-84	.176	.222	.167	20	51	6	9	0	0	0	1	9	1	2	0	26	5	3	.176	.311

PITCHING

	B-T	HT	WT	DOB	W	L	ERA	G	GS	CG	SV	IP	H	R	ER	HR	BB	SO	AVG	vLH	vRH	K/9	BB/9
Acosta, Francisco	R-R	6-4	170	8-7-88	0	1	16.20	3	0	0	0	3	8	8	6	0	5	1	.444	.200	.538	2.70	13.50
Acosta, Ryan	R-R	6-2	170	11-4-88	0	0	3.00	3	1	0	0	6	5	2	2	0	3	6	.263	.167	.308	9.00	4.50
Bachman, Corey	R-R	6-1	190	5-24-85	3	0	5.40	13	0	0	0	23	32	21	14	1	11	19	.337	.333	.339	7.33	4.24
Bartek, Michael	R-R	5-11	165	2-28-84	0	0	1.50	3	0	0	0	6	4	1	1	0	2	7	.222	.400	.154	10.50	3.00
Bunton, Michael	L-L	6-3	195	10-23-85	4	3	2.79	12	5	0	0	42	45	19	13	1	15	21	.280	.262	.286	4.50	3.21
Castillo, Julio	R-R	6-3	212	10-6-87	1	0	1.89	6	3	0	0	19	15	6	4	0	4	17	.217	.286	.188	8.05	1.89
Ceda, Jose	R-R	6-4	205	1-28-87	0	0	2.45	2	1	0	0	4	2	1	1	0	3	3	.182	.500	.000	7.36	7.36
Chen, Hung-Wen	R-R	5-11	195	2-3-86	0	0	10.12	2	1	0	0	3	3	3	3	0	0	3	.273	.200	.333	10.12	0.00
Cherry, Rocky	R-R	6-5	225	8-19-79	0	0	0.00	2	2	0	0	2	0	0	0	0	0	1	.000	.000	.000	4.50	0.00
Christl, Michael	R-R	6-4	185	9-2-84	1	2	4.03	15	0	0	0	22	17	13	10	2	21	23	.205	.138	.241	9.27	8.46
Clipp, Brad	R-R	6-2	180	8-15-84	0	1	7.00	5	2	0	0	9	10	10	7	1	4	11	.286	.455	.208	11.00	4.00
Cuevas novas, Miguel	R-R	6-9	260	8-11-83	1	0	3.24	4	1	0	0	8	10	4	3	0	4	11	.286	.214	.333	11.88	4.32
Guzman, Angel	R-R	6-3	195	12-14-81	0	1	0.00	4	4	0	0	5	1	1	0	0	1	3	.059	.167	.000	5.40	1.80
Harben, Adam	R-R	6-5	210	8-19-83	0	1	1.80	3	3	0	0	5	2	1	1	0	4	6	.133	.000	.182	10.80	7.20
Hatley, Marcus	R-R	6-5	190	3-26-88	1	3	3.82	13	6	0	0	38	36	19	16	0	12	26	.254	.295	.235	6.21	2.87
Hempy, Arik	R-L	6-4	245	7-19-84	0	0	5.40	1	1	0	0	2	4	1	1	0	1	1	.500	.000	.667	5.40	5.40
Higgins, Yuri	R-R	5-8	182	2-26-85	1	0	6.75	1	0	0	0	1	1	1	1	0	1	1	.200	.000	.333	9.00	6.75
Kreier, Kevin	R-R	6-4	195	8-31-87	0	1	11.78	12	0	0	1	18	33	25	24	6	9	10	.384	.294	.442	4.91	4.42
Lami, Junniol	R-R	6-1	160	1-1-88	0	0	4.24	11	0	0	0	17	14	10	8	1	14	18	.215	.121	.313	9.53	7.41
Lee, Simon	R-R	6-2	210	7-14-83	0	2	1.47	10	0	0	0	18	15	6	3	0	4	20	.227	.238	.222	9.82	1.96
Martinez, Oswaldo	R-R	6-0	180	9-25-88	2	0	3.60	6	3	0	0	20	18	9	8	1	2	20	.250	.304	.224	9.00	0.90
McCormick, Andrew	R-R	6-6	210	8-9-84	1	0	2.65	10	0	0	0	17	20	7	5	0	8	20	.290	.250	.311	10.59	4.24
Meyer, Scott	R-R	6-3	220	10-8-85	3	0	2.28	10	0	0	0	28	22	8	7	0	1	19	.218	.229	.212	6.18	0.33
Muldowney, Billy	R-R	6-1	185	8-9-84	0	1	3.00	2	2	0	0	3	3	4	1	1	0	2	.250	.250	.250	6.00	0.00
Muschko, Craig	R-R	6-2	192	8-17-85	0	2	6.86	14	0	0	1	21	27	16	16	1	14	17	.325	.364	.300	7.29	6.00
Parker, Blake	R-R	6-3	220	6-19-85	1	0	1.80	11	0	0	2	15	10	6	3	0	3	14	.185	.167	.194	8.40	1.80
Pawelek, Mark	L-L	6-3	190	8-18-86	0	0	0.00	1	0	0	0	1	2	1	0	0	1	1	.400	.000	.500	9.00	9.00
Redmond, Cedric	R-R	6-3	180	3-30-84	1	0	6.00	10	0	0	2	21	27	17	14	1	7	30	.314	.270	.347	12.86	3.00
Rivera, Christopher	R-R	6-4	200	3-4-84	1	1	3.57	13	0	0	0	23	22	13	9	0	8	14	.256	.194	.300	5.56	3.18
Russell, James	L-L	6-4	205	1-8-86	0	0	0.00	2	0	0	0	2	0	0	0	0	0	0	.000	.000	.000	0.00	0.00
Suarez, Larry	R-R	6-4	245	12-20-89	1	4	5.31	14	9	0	0	41	37	33	24	4	26	35	.248	.344	.176	7.75	5.75
Taylor, Brandon	R-R	6-1	200	7-26-82	1	0	2.61	5	0	0	0	10	8	5	3	1	7	5	.211	.000	.333	4.35	6.10
Tolentino, Harol	R-L	6-4	165	11-8-88	1	1	5.82	7	4	0	0	22	20	16	14	0	10	27	.280	.192	.273	11.22	4.15
Tuero, Yusdel	R-R	5-11	180	3-7-82	1	3	4.00	5	2	0	0	18	21	10	8	1	4	18	.280	.286	.277	9.00	2.00
Vento, Stephen	R-R	6-3	210	3-28-86	0	0	0.00	3	0	0	0	3	0	0	0	0	0	3	.200	.000	.300	5.40	0.00
Walters, Donald	R-R	6-1	195	7-18-86	0	1	6.75	2	1	0	0	3	5	2	2	1	1	1	.455	.500	.429	3.38	3.38
Wood, Kerry	R-R	6-5	225	6-16-77	0	1	2.25	4	4	0	0	4	4	0	1	0	1	5	.250	.333	.143	11.25	2.25

FIELDING

Catcher	PCT	G	PO	A	E	DP	PB
Bautista	1.000	1	4	1	0	0	1
Donaldson	.889	3	6	2	1	0	0
Hudgins	.915	9	50	4	5	1	4
Perez	.993	34	240	35	2	1	7
Sabates	.955	25	154	16	8	2	5

First Base	PCT	G	PO	A	E	DP
Bautista	.955	3	20	1	1	2
Brooks	.990	14	101	3	1	6
Gonzalez	1.000	2	8	1	0	0
Hudgins	.864	2	19	0	3	0
Perez	.983	6	56	2	1	11
Perez	1.000	1	1	0	0	0
Reyes	.973	13	104	6	3	12
Rosa	1.000	3	13	1	0	2
Sabates	1.000	3	37	2	0	4
Sommer	.982	20	159	9	3	22

Second Base	PCT	G	PO	A	E	DP
Brooks	.944	15	26	41	4	11
Gonzalez	.750	2	0	3	1	0
Guzman	.935	6	13	16	2	8
Lara	.952	24	35	65	5	12
Rea	1.000	5	10	13	0	4
Thomas	.867	4	5	8	2	1
Valentin	1.000	10	10	15	0	2

Third Base	PCT	G	PO	A	E	DP
Brooks	.857	7	4	14	3	0
Gonzalez	.938	8	1	14	1	3
Guzman	.875	3	1	6	1	0
Lara	1.000	3	0	3	0	0
Rosa	.922	36	35	72	9	11
Valentin	.714	4	2	3	2	1
Vitters	.727	4	1	7	3	0

Shortstop	PCT	G	PO	A	E	DP
Barney	1.000	5	8	13	0	3

	PCT	G	PO	A	E	DP
Gonzalez	.927	7	11	27	3	6
Guzman	.934	37	69	130	14	26
Lara	1.000	1	0	0	0	0
Thomas	—	1	0	0	0	0
Valentin	.949	9	16	21	2	4

Outfield	PCT	G	PO	A	E	DP
Andersen	.930	38	49	4	4	0
Guyer	.971	17	30	4	1	2
Hardman	.943	15	32	1	2	0
Harvey	1.000	2	3	0	0	0
Johnson	1.000	16	23	2	0	1
Lopez	1.000	5	6	0	0	0
Perez	.947	42	60	11	4	5
Rea	.917	6	10	1	1	0
Reyes	1.000	1	1	0	0	0
Sommer	.978	29	42	2	1	1
Walker	.875	6	6	1	1	0
Wen	1.000	5	7	0	0	0

DSL CUBS

ROOKIE

DOMINICAN SUMMER LEAGUE

BATTING

	B-T	HT	WT	DOB	AVG	vLH	vRH	G	AB	R	H	2B	3B	HR	RBI	BB	HBP	SH	SF	SO	SB	CS	SLG	OBP
Bautista, Robert	B-R	6-1	165	8-20-88	.222	.203	.229	62	216	31	48	10	2	1	21	32	3	3	2	61	13	7	.301	.328
Castro, Starlin	R-R	6-1	160	3-24-90	.299	.344	.281	60	221	47	66	6	2	2	31	23	4	2	3	24	13	2	.371	.371
Contreras, John	R-R	6-0	185	4-17-86	.272	.329	.247	68	254	40	69	12	2	8	47	14	9	0	1	53	5	4	.429	.331
Gonzalez, Miguel	R-R	6-0	180	10-30-89	.178	.143	.208	14	45	5	8	0	1	0	4	3	0	0	0	8	0	1	.222	.229
Hernandez, Albert	R-R	6-1	170	2-25-89	.263	.277	.257	46	152	22	40	9	3	2	10	18	4	0	0	24	4	2	.401	.356
Herrera, Edgar	R-R	6-2	200	1-15-86	.217	.250	.214	16	46	4	10	2	0	0	6	1	3	0	0	15	6	3	.261	.280
Jimenez, Elvin	R-R	6-1	175	10-6-87	.083	.000	.118	17	48	7	4	1	0	0	4	6	0	0	0	21	2	0	.104	.185
Lake, Junior	R-R	6-3	175	3-27-90	.274	.350	.245	62	223	41	61	16	2	3	30	16	7	3	0	53	9	3	.404	.341
Magallanes, Herasmo	B-R	5-11	166	11-25-85	.235	.174	.253	35	102	11	24	7	0	1	3	12	3	0	0	34	1	4	.333	.333
Mejia, Alexander	R-R	6-0	179	1-18-86	.286	.289	.285	60	182	26	52	13	4	3	24	32	2	2	1	22	8	3	.451	.396
Pierre, Nelson	B-R	6-0	160	12-23-87	.270	.217	.288	29	89	8	24	1	1	0	5	9	0	2	0	15	10	4	.303	.337
Quezada, Andres	B-R	5-11	175	3-15-86	.270	.258	.276	53	185	34	50	9	4	1	24	22	5	1	2	42	12	9	.378	.360
Ramirez, Pedro	R-R	6-1	185	9-9-87	.160	.091	.194	34	100	10	16	4	1	0	6	8	3	2	1	33	1	0	.220	.241
Sosa, Alvaro	L-R	6-0	181	6-7-86	.284	.294	.281	63	211	23	60	11	4	1	30	16	5	1	2	33	6	4	.389	.346
Soto, Andy	R-R	5-10	170	8-5-86	.270	.315	.252	60	185	29	50	8	2	1	19	12	3	4	2	27	10	9	.351	.322
Vigay, Jose	R-R	5-10	185	12-10-88	.303	.379	.267	34	89	7	27	4	0	1	15	9	0	2	0	22	0	3	.382	.367

PITCHING

	B-T	HT	WT	DOB	W	L	ERA	G	GS	CG	SV	IP	H	R	ER	HR	BB	SO	AVG	vLH	vRH	K/9	BB/9
Antigua, Jeffry	R-L	6-1	170	6-23-90	7	2	3.15	14	14	0	0	71	72	33	25	2	14	55	.259	.238	.261	6.94	1.77
Beltre, Bienvenido	R-R	6-1	190	4-26-88	2	3	5.73	12	0	0	0	22	22	17	14	2	8	12	.262	.059	.313	4.91	3.27
Carmona, Rogelino	R-R	6-3	210	8-30-89	1	2	4.41	15	9	0	0	49	54	27	24	2	16	30	.284	.250	.295	5.51	2.94
De La Cruz, Alejandro	R-R	6-2	170	6-5-88	2	1	6.67	16	1	0	1	27	29	22	20	1	9	14	.290	.412	.265	4.67	3.00
de Leon, Manolin	R-R	6-0	175	11-23-86	2	1	2.89	26	0	0	9	37	40	15	12	2	9	27	.288	.200	.312	6.51	2.17
Florentino, Arturo	R-R	6-4	170	1-3-85	0	1	3.48	23	0	0	14	21	24	10	8	1	5	16	.300	.250	.313	6.97	2.18
Garcia, Wily	R-R	6-3	190	7-10-88	0	0	0.00	2	1	0	0	1	1	0	0	0	1	1	.333	.000	.333	13.50	13.50
Gonzalez, Yohan	R-R	6-4	210	4-15-90	0	1	2.84	10	4	0	0	25	23	10	8	0	10	23	.242	.250	.241	8.17	3.55
Gonzalez, Miguel	R-R	6-0	180	10-30-89	0	0	54.00	1	0	0	0	0	2	2	2	0	2	0	.000	.000	.000	0.00	54.00
Mota, Pacheco	R-R	6-4	200	7-13-90	2	2	5.34	19	1	0	0	30	35	24	18	3	16	25	.282	.364	.265	7.42	4.75
Nunez, Dionis	R-R	6-4	170	9-28-88	4	3	5.24	16	4	0	0	34	32	25	20	3	29	11	.246	.265	.240	2.88	7.60
Paulino, Francis	L-L	6-5	216	10-9-87	0	0	4.50	5	0	0	0	8	6	5	4	0	5	7	.194	.000	.200	7.88	5.62
2-team (10 DSL)					1	2	2.15	15	0	0	2	29	23	11	7	1	12	22	—	—	—	6.75	3.68
Pena, Julio	R-R	6-3	185	3-1-89	2	5	3.42	15	15	0	0	68	70	34	26	1	13	32	.267	.173	.290	4.21	1.71
Pena, Lenny	R-R	6-4	191	4-27-86	0	0	4.15	3	0	0	0	4	5	2	2	0	2	1	.313	.500	.286	2.08	4.15
Perez, Marcos	L-R	6-1	175	1-1-90	2	1	2.86	11	6	0	0	44	34	15	14	3	13	22	.217	.194	.223	4.50	2.66
Pineda, George	R-R	6-3	175	7-19-88	2	1	4.33	18	0	0	1	27	21	16	13	1	18	22	.210	.154	.230	7.33	6.00
Rache, Ramon	R-R	6-0	180	3-22-88	3	3	2.67	14	0	0	1	30	25	12	9	0	8	36	.219	.136	.239	10.68	2.37
Reyes, Ramon	B-R	6-3	185	1-2-89	3	2	3.13	10	4	0	0	23	16	9	8	2	8	18	.198	.105	.226	7.04	3.13
Severino, Jose	R-R	5-11	165	8-13-89	7	2	2.33	13	12	0	0	66	56	25	17	2	6	42	.224	.204	.229	5.76	0.82
Sierra, Miguel	R-R	6-5	170	7-28-88	2	0	5.02	19	0	0	2	29	34	20	16	0	13	12	.304	.303	.304	3.77	4.08

FIELDING

Catcher	PCT	G	PO	A	E	DP	PB
Gonzalez	.978	14	78	12	2	0	2
Sosa	.978	57	249	59	7	2	5
Vigay	.963	16	71	7	3	0	6

First Base	PCT	G	PO	A	E	DP
Castro	1.000	1	4	0	0	0
Contreras	1.000	3	12	0	0	2
Lake	1.000	2	18	1	0	1
Magallanes	.967	14	108	8	4	10
Mejia	.991	30	199	15	2	22
Ramirez	.996	27	224	8	1	15
Sosa	.980	12	89	7	2	8
Vigay	1.000	4	22	1	0	1

Second Base	PCT	G	PO	A	E	DP
Bautista	.939	24	65	59	8	17
Castro	.979	7	20	27	1	6

Lake	.964	36	109	79	7	22
Mejia	1.000	2	5	4	0	2
Pierre	.950	4	9	10	1	4
Sosa	1.000	1	1	2	0	0
Soto	—	1	0	0	0	0
Vigay	—	1	0	0	0	0

Third Base	PCT	G	PO	A	E	DP
Bautista	1.000	3	1	3	0	0
Castro	—	2	0	0	0	0
Contreras	.930	65	68	198	20	16
Lake	1.000	3	0	3	0	0
Magallanes	.750	3	0	6	2	1
Ramirez	1.000	1	0	3	0	0
Soto	.667	1	0	2	1	0

Shortstop	PCT	G	PO	A	E	DP
Bautista	.914	32	46	102	14	18

Castro	.943	21	35	64	6	10
Lake	.907	18	32	56	9	12
Mejia	.000	1	0	0	1	0
Pierre	.500	1	0	1	1	0
Soto	1.000	1	4	4	0	0

Outfield	PCT	G	PO	A	E	DP
Castro	1.000	1	1	0	0	0
Hernandez	.964	39	51	2	2	1
Herrera	.958	16	22	1	1	1
Jimenez	.944	17	15	2	1	1
Mejia	.907	34	34	5	4	1
Pierre	.902	25	33	4	4	1
Quezada	.975	53	111	6	3	1
Soto	.980	57	90	6	2	1

VSL TWINS/CUBS

ROOKIE

VENEZUELAN SUMMER LEAGUE (STATISTICS FOR THIS TEAM ARE ON PAGE 187)

Chicago White Sox

BY PHIL ROGERS

Crash.

Two years after winning the World Series—and one year after completing their first back-to-back 90-win seasons since Al Lopez' teams strung together three in a row in the mid-1960s—the White Sox received a rude awakening by barely avoiding last place in the American League Central.

Injuries, a combustible bullpen and a woeful lack of run production from an offense built around sluggers Paul Konerko, Jim Thome and Jermaine Dye, combined to leave the White Sox at 72-90—a record boosted by an 11-6 finish.

Third baseman Joe Crede, left fielder Scott Podsednik, center fielder Darin Erstad and valued utility man Pablo Ozuna all missed significant time, exposing the team's lack of depth. With almost one-quarter of the season at-bats going to a group of unproven players headed by outfielders Andy Gonzalez and Jerry Owens and second baseman Danny Richar, the Sox hit .246 as a team and scored only 4.3 runs per game—the third worst average in the majors and almost one run a game less than AL Central champion Cleveland.

"No excuses, but if all those guys were healthy, it would have been different," Thome said. "Things have just not gone our way."

The problems of 2007 were first revealed in late 2006. From the start of 2005 through July 6, 2006, the White Sox went 166-93, including an 11-1 waltz through the 2005 playoffs. That's a .641 winning percentage, which would drop to .447 over the next 237 games, including the 34-41 finish in 2006 that kept the Sox from returning to the playoffs.

While Thome blamed injuries, there was no singular development that marked the line of demarcation between the winning White Sox and the losing White Sox.

General manager Ken Williams deemed that manager Ozzie Guillen was not culpable, rewarding him with a contract extension that runs through 2013. Ace Mark Buehrle, right-hander Javier Vazquez, catcher A.J. Pierzynski and Dye also signed contract extensions over the course of the season.

Williams was critical of several of his moves, including a retooling of the bullpen that backfired. Seeking power arms, he built a staff that included Mike MacDougal, Matt Thornton, David Aardsma, Andrew Sisco and Nick Masset in front of closer Bobby Jenks. While Jenks pitched well, the bullpen went 19-25, 5.47 in 2007, ranking 12th in the AL. It could have been worse, but Guillen actually used his bullpen less than any other AL manager. Guillen got 1,016 innings out of Buehrle, Vazquez, righthanders Jon Garland and Jose Contreras in addition to rookie lefthander John Danks.

Williams also left Guillen with limited production in left field, sticking with Scott Podsednik as the regular, and in center field, where he imported only Darin Erstad as an alternative to Brian Anderson.

The climate wasn't much better in the farm system. Longtime scouting director Duane Schaffer was fired midway through a season in which the six clubs combined for a 334-369 record, with only Rookie-level Great Falls (Pioneer) reaching the playoffs.

The most positive development for the organization was the emergence of third baseman Josh Fields, who led American League rookies with 23 home runs after being pro-

PLAYERS OF THE YEAR

MAJOR LEAGUE: JAVIER VAZQUEZ, RHP

While the White Sox struggled to score runs, the starting pitching was solid, and Vazquez was a key cog in the rotation. He led the White Sox with 216 2/3 innings and 15 wins. His 213 strikeouts were a team-high and ranked fourth in the American League. His 4.26-to-1 strikeout-to-walk ratio was a team-best and fifth in the majors.

MINOR LEAGUE: GIO GONZALEZ, LHP

Gonzalez led the minor leagues with 185 strikeouts, one year after finishing 12th in the minors with 166. Gonzalez went 9-7, 3.18 for Double-A Birmingham, putting him fourth in the Southern League in ERA. Gonzalez was both effective and durable, allowing just 116 hits in 150 innings.

ORGANIZATIONAL LEADERS

BATTING		★Minimum 250 at-bats
★AVG	Bourgeois, Jason, Birmingham/Charlotte	.306
R	Cook, David, Winston-Salem/Birmingham	92
H	Bourgeois, Jason, Birmingham/Charlotte	153
TB	Schnurstein, Micah, Winston-Salem	258
2B	Allen, Brandon, Kannapolis	39
3B	Shelby, John, Kannapolis	9
HR	Carter, Christopher, Kannapolis	25
HR	Schnurstein, Micah, Winston-Salem	25
RBI	Allen, Brandon, Kannapolis	93
RBI	Carter, Christopher, Kannapolis	93
BB	Cook, David, Winston-Salem/Birmingham	75
SO	Collaro, Thomas, Birmingham/Charlotte	158
SB	Bourgeois, Jason, Birmingham/Charlotte	38
★OBP	Cook, David, Winston-Salem/Birmingham	.388
★SLG	Cook, David, Winston-Salem/Birmingham	.531
PITCHING		**^Minimum 75 innings**
W	Rodriguez, Derek,Winston-Salem	14
L	Haeger, Charlie, Charlotte	16
^ERA	De Los Santos, Fautino, Kannapolis/Winston-Salem	2.65
G	Hernandez Jr., Fernando, Birmingham	60
CG	Haeger, Charlie, Charlotte	3
SV	Perez, Oneli, Birmingham	16
SV	Texeira, Kanekoa, Kannapolis	16
IP	Phillips, Heath, Charlotte	174
BB	Broadway, Lance, Charlotte	78
SO	Gonzalez, Gio, Birmingham	185
^AVG	De Los Santos, Fautino, Kannapolis/Winston-Salem	.163

moted to replace the injured Crede in June. He delivered 33 homers and 104 RBIs between Triple-A and the big leagues.

Dominican righthander Fautino de los Santos was a revelation in his first season in the States, going 10-5, 2.65 with 11.3 strikeouts per nine innings and a .163 opponent average between low Class A Kannapolis and high Class A Winston-Salem. Relocating from third to first base, 20-year-old Chris Carter had a breakout season at Kannapolis, batting .291/.383/.522 with 25 homers and 93 RBIs. Lefthander Heath Phillips (13-7, 4.30) and righthanders Jack Egbert (12-8, 3.06) and Gio Gonzalez (9-7, 3.18) were among the pitching leaders in the International and Southern Leagues.

General Manager: Ken Williams. **Farm Director:** Alan Regier. **Scouting Director:** Doug Laumann

Class	Team	League	W	L	PCT	Finish*	Manager	Affiliate Since
Majors	Chicago	American	72	90	.444	10th (14)	Ozzie Guillen	—
Triple-A	Charlotte Knights	International	63	80	.441	13th (14)	Marc Bombard	1999
Double-A	Birmingham Barons	Southern	62	78	.443	8th (10)	Rafael Santana	1986
High A	Winston-Salem Warthogs	Carolina	64	74	.464	5th (8)	Tim Blackwell	1997
Low A	Kannapolis Intimidators	South Atlantic	69	70	.496	7th (16)	Chris Jones	2001
Rookie	Great Falls White Sox	Pioneer	51	24	.680	1st (8)	Chris Cron	2003
Rookie	Bristol Sox	Appalachian	25	43	.368	8th (9)	Omer Munoz	1995
Overall 2007 Minor League Record			**334**	**369**	**.475**	**24th**		

* Finish in overall standings (No. of teams in league) ^League champion

ORGANIZATION STATISTICS

CHICAGO WHITE SOX

AMERICAN LEAGUE

BATTING	B-T	HT	WT	DOB	AVG	vLH	vRH	G	AB	R	H	2B	3B	HR	RBI	BB	HBP	SH	SF	SO	SB	CS	SLG	OBP
Anderson, Brian	R-R	6-2	220	3-11-82	.118	.000	.222	13	17	3	2	1	0	0	0	2	0	0	0	7	0	0	.176	.211
Cintron, Alex	B-R	6-1	205	12-17-78	.243	.238	.244	68	185	23	45	7	1	2	19	9	1	0	1	35	2	1	.324	.281
Crede, Joe	R-R	6-2	230	4-26-78	.216	.206	.218	47	167	13	36	5	0	4	22	10	0	0	1	24	0	1	.317	.258
Dye, Jermaine	R-R	6-5	240	1-28-74	.254	.292	.241	138	508	68	129	34	0	28	78	45	4	0	4	107	2	1	.486	.317
Erstad, Darin	L-L	6-2	220	6-4-74	.248	.157	.282	87	310	33	77	13	1	4	32	28	0	6	1	44	7	2	.335	.310
Fields, Josh	R-R	6-1	215	12-14-82	.244	.321	.213	100	373	54	91	17	1	23	67	35	1	6	3	125	1	1	.480	.308
Gonzalez, Andy	R-R	6-2	190	12-15-81	.185	.185	.185	67	189	17	35	6	0	2	11	25	0	1	0	61	1	5	.249	.280
Hall, Toby	R-R	6-3	240	10-21-75	.207	.288	.141	38	116	8	24	4	0	0	3	3	0	0	1	12	0	0	.241	.225
Iguchi, Tadahito	R-R	5-10	200	12-4-74	.251	.202	.272	90	327	45	82	17	4	6	31	44	2	1	3	65	8	1	.382	.340
Konerko, Paul	R-R	6-2	215	3-5-76	.259	.296	.244	151	549	71	142	34	0	31	90	78	3	0	6	102	0	1	.490	.351
Lucy, Donny	R-R	6-3	210	8-8-82	.200	.500	.154	8	15	0	3	0	0	0	0	0	0	0	0	6	0	0	.200	.200
Mackowiak, Rob	L-R	5-11	195	6-20-76	.278	.297	.275	85	237	34	66	11	2	6	36	23	6	0	2	53	3	1	.418	.354
Molina, Gustavo	R-R	6-0	220	2-24-82	.056	.000	.125	10	18	1	1	0	0	1	0	1	1	0	1	4	0	0	.056	.100
2-team (7 Baltimore)					.111	—	—	17	27	1	3	1	0	0	1	1	1	0	1	7	0	0	.148	.138
Owens, Jerry	L-L	6-3	190	2-16-81	.267	.235	.274	93	356	44	95	9	2	1	17	27	3	3	0	63	32	8	.312	.324
Ozuna, Pablo	R-R	5-11	190	8-25-74	.244	.256	.231	27	78	9	19	3	0	0	3	3	1	3	0	9	3	0	.282	.280
Pierzynski, A.J.	L-R	6-3	240	12-30-76	.263	.252	.266	136	472	54	124	24	0	14	50	25	8	1	3	66	1	1	.403	.309
Podsednik, Scott	L-L	6-1	190	3-18-76	.243	.279	.229	62	214	30	52	13	4	2	11	13	4	4	0	36	12	5	.369	.299
Richar, Danny	L-R	6-0	170	6-9-83	.230	.205	.236	56	187	30	43	9	3	6	15	16	0	2	1	33	1	3	.406	.289
Sweeney, Ryan	L-L	6-4	215	2-20-85	.200	.167	.205	15	45	5	9	3	0	1	5	4	0	0	0	5	0	1	.333	.265
Terrero, Luis	R-R	6-3	205	5-18-80	.231	.196	.258	61	117	18	27	2	0	5	12	12	9	1	0	35	4	3	.376	.348
Thome, Jim	L-R	6-3	250	8-27-70	.275	.196	.315	130	432	79	119	19	0	35	96	95	6	0	3	134	0	1	.563	.410
Uribe, Juan	R-R	6-0	220	3-22-79	.234	.257	.225	150	513	55	120	18	2	20	68	34	4	7	5	112	1	9	.394	.284

PITCHING	B-T	HT	WT	DOB	W	L	ERA	G	GS	CG	SV	IP	H	R	ER	HR	BB	SO	AVG	vLH	vRH	K/9	BB/9
Aardsma, David	R-R	6-4	205	12-27-81	2	1	6.40	25	0	0	0	32	39	24	23	4	17	36	.300	.283	.310	10.02	4.73
Broadway, Lance	R-R	6-2	210	8-20-83	1	1	0.87	4	1	0	0	10	5	2	1	0	5	14	.143	.188	.105	12.19	4.35
Buehrle, Mark	L-L	6-2	220	3-23-79	10	9	3.63	30	30	3	0	201	208	86	81	22	45	115	.269	.314	.258	5.15	2.01
Bukvich, Ryan	R-R	6-2	250	5-13-78	1	0	5.05	45	0	0	0	36	36	23	20	5	24	18	.257	.209	.278	4.54	6.06
Contreras, Jose	R-R	6-4	245	12-6-71	10	17	5.57	32	30	2	0	189	232	134	117	21	62	113	.304	.333	.270	5.38	2.95
Danks, John	L-L	6-1	200	4-15-85	6	13	5.50	26	26	0	0	139	160	92	85	28	54	109	.289	.281	.292	7.06	3.50
Day, Dewon	R-R	6-4	210	9-29-80	0	1	11.25	13	0	0	0	12	19	15	15	1	9	7	.352	.375	.333	5.25	6.75
Floyd, Gavin	R-R	6-4	225	1-27-83	1	5	5.27	16	10	0	0	70	85	45	41	17	19	49	.299	.314	.286	6.30	2.44
Garland, Jon	R-R	6-6	215	9-27-79	10	13	4.23	32	32	2	0	208	219	114	98	19	57	98	.270	.259	.281	4.23	2.46
Haeger, Charlie	R-R	6-1	220	9-19-83	0	1	7.15	8	0	0	0	11	17	11	9	3	8	1	.354	.286	.407	0.79	6.35
Jenks, Bobby	R-R	6-3	275	3-14-81	3	5	2.77	66	0	0	40	65	45	20	20	2	13	56	.198	.237	.169	7.75	1.80
Logan, Boone	R-L	6-5	200	8-13-84	2	1	4.97	68	0	0	0	51	59	30	28	7	20	35	.298	.221	.357	6.22	3.55
MacDougal, Mike	B-R	6-3	180	3-5-77	2	5	6.80	54	0	0	0	42	50	37	32	3	33	39	.291	.298	.288	8.29	7.02
Masset, Nick	R-R	6-4	235	5-17-82	2	3	7.09	27	1	0	0	39	52	33	31	2	26	21	.323	.338	.312	4.81	5.95
Myers, Mike	L-L	6-3	225	6-26-69	1	0	11.20	17	0	0	0	14	21	19	17	3	7	6	.356	.250	.452	3.95	4.61
2-team (55 New York)					4	0	4.80	72	0	0	0	54	59	33	29	6	23	27	—	—	—	4.47	3.81
Phillips, Heath	L-L	6-3	205	3-24-82	1	1	3.68	6	0	0	0	7	10	3	3	1	4	2	.333	.375	.318	2.45	4.91
Prinz, Bret	R-R	6-3	210	6-15-77	0	0	8.10	4	0	0	0	3	4	3	3	1	2	1	.286	.333	.250	2.70	5.40
Sisco, Andrew	L-L	6-10	270	1-13-83	0	1	8.36	19	0	0	0	14	19	13	13	2	11	13	.306	.250	.367	8.36	7.07
Thornton, Matt	L-L	6-6	230	9-15-76	0	0	4.79	68	0	0	2	56	59	31	30	4	26	55	.269	.283	.260	8.79	4.15
Vazquez, Javier	R-R	6-1	210	7-25-76	15	8	3.74	32	32	2	0	217	197	95	90	29	50	213	.242	.230	.253	8.85	2.08
Wassermann, Ehren	B-R	6-0	185	12-6-80	1	1	2.74	33	0	0	0	23	20	9	7	0	7	14	.238	.533	.174	5.48	2.74

FIELDING

Catcher	PCT	G	PO	A	E	DP	PB
Hall	.985	37	187	10	3	1	5
Lucy	1.000	5	27	1	0	0	0
Molina	1.000	9	41	1	0	0	1
Pierzynski	.998	130	796	46	2	6	14

First Base	PCT	G	PO	A	E	DP
Erstad	.995	22	174	14	1	18
Gonzalez	1.000	5	7	0	0	1
Konerko	.996	141	1180	71	5	131
Mackowiak	1.000	5	23	1	0	2
Thome	1.000	1	2	0	0	0

Second Base	PCT	G	PO	A	E	DP
Cintron	.939	14	22	24	3	6
Gonzalez	1.000	4	4	4	0	1

	PCT	G	PO	A	E	DP
Iguchi	.986	90	188	247	6	66
Ozuna	1.000	3	12	10	0	3
Richar	.988	56	103	139	3	37

Third Base	PCT	G	PO	A	E	DP
Cintron	.878	19	7	27	5	3
Crede	.971	46	36	97	4	18
Fields	.958	79	47	159	9	13
Gonzalez	.864	25	15	42	9	6
Mackowiak	—	1	0	0	0	0
Ozuna	.824	9	5	9	3	0

Shortstop	PCT	G	PO	A	E	DP
Cintron	.975	17	34	45	2	14
Gonzalez	—	1	0	0	0	0
Ozuna	—	1	0	0	0	0

	PCT	G	PO	A	E	DP
Uribe	.976	150	245	443	17	102

Outfield	PCT	G	PO	A	E	DP
Anderson	.900	8	9	0	1	0
Dye	.990	135	284	9	3	3
Erstad	.993	63	132	2	1	0
Fields	.947	21	34	2	2	0
Gonzalez	1.000	32	62	2	0	1
Mackowiak	.975	68	112	4	3	1
Owens	.991	89	213	1	2	1
Ozuna	.929	7	13	0	1	0
Podsednik	.966	56	110	4	4	1
Sweeney	1.000	14	25	1	0	1
Terrero	.989	57	84	2	1	1

INTERNATIONAL LEAGUE

BATTING	B-T	HT	WT	DOB	AVG	vLH	vRH	G	AB	R	H	2B	3B	HR	RBI	BB	HBP	SH	SF	SO	SB	CS	SLG	OBP
Anderson, Brian	R-R	6-2	220	3-11-82	.255	.300	.236	57	200	29	51	8	2	8	31	19	1	0	3	47	3	2	.435	.318
Bourgeois, Jason	R-R	5-9	185	1-4-82	.311	.287	.324	88	338	51	105	18	3	7	34	29	3	3	1	49	23	6	.444	.369
Castillo, Javier	R-R	6-2	180	8-29-83	.100	—	.100	3	10	0	1	0	0	0	0	0	0	0	0	0	0	0	.100	.182
Collaro, Thomas	R-R	6-4	216	4-4-83	.291	.275	.302	27	103	9	30	7	0	4	13	7	0	0	0	29	0	1	.476	.336
Erstad, Darin	L-L	6-2	220	6-4-74	.128	.222	.069	12	47	3	6	0	0	0	2	5	0	0	0	14	0	0	.128	.212
Fields, Josh	R-R	6-1	215	12-14-82	.283	.293	.280	56	205	28	58	14	0	10	37	39	1	0	4	60	8	5	.498	.394
Gonzalez, Andy	R-R	6-2	190	12-15-81	.242	.217	.248	35	124	15	30	7	1	3	17	22	1	0	1	39	6	1	.387	.358
Gonzalez, Wiki	R-R	5-11	205	5-17-74	.260	.306	.239	69	235	25	61	8	0	10	41	15	2	1	0	19	1	1	.421	.310
Hall, Toby	R-R	6-3	240	10-21-75	.263	.200	.286	5	19	3	5	0	0	2	7	2	0	0	0	3	0	0	.579	.333
Kelly, Kenny	R-R	6-2	190	1-26-79	.256	.263	.253	78	246	39	63	7	0	9	28	30	0	5	0	61	12	3	.394	.337
Lopez, Pedro	R-R	6-1	160	4-28-84	.242	.152	.266	41	161	20	39	7	0	2	11	15	0	5	0	26	1	3	.323	.307
2-team (34 Louisville)					.284	—	—	75	285	40	81	13	1	3	28	28	0	9	2	38	4	3	.368	.346
Lucy, Donny	R-R	6-3	210	8-8-82	.200	.250	.176	19	75	5	15	3	0	0	3	3	0	0	0	25	0	0	.240	.231
Molina, Gustavo	R-R	6-0	220	2-24-82	.209	.256	.188	43	139	13	29	4	0	2	9	9	2	5	1	27	0	2	.281	.265
Owens, Jerry	L-L	6-3	190	2-16-81	.284	.310	.276	59	232	39	66	10	0	3	21	29	1	1	4	37	23	8	.366	.361
Perez, Kenny	B-R	6-2	190	9-28-81	.270	.322	.251	64	226	24	61	10	2	6	26	16	0	3	3	38	2	3	.412	.314
Perez, Tomas	B-R	5-11	185	12-29-73	.265	.295	.248	88	344	42	91	15	0	4	41	20	1	4	2	54	4	1	.343	.305
Podsednik, Scott	L-L	6-1	190	3-18-76	.288	.167	.347	20	73	12	21	5	0	1	6	10	2	0	2	15	2	3	.397	.379
Richar, Danny	L-R	6-0	170	6-9-83	.346	.273	.382	32	133	21	46	5	4	5	15	10	2	0	0	24	4	0	.556	.400
Ricks, Adam	B-R	5-10	195	3-24-82	.153	.043	.204	22	72	3	11	4	0	0	8	4	0	2	0	12	0	0	.208	.197
Rogowski, Casey	L-L	6-3	230	5-1-81	.245	.259	.239	137	453	62	111	28	0	14	54	61	6	2	3	109	17	5	.400	.340
Sanchez, Alex	L-L	5-8	155	8-26-76	.359	.378	.348	24	103	12	37	4	1	3	7	3	0	2	0	11	3	3	.505	.377
Smith, Jason	R-R	5-10	195	5-20-79	.136	.154	.130	33	103	3	14	1	0	1	3	1	3	1	3	32	0	0	.175	.167
Snyder, Earl	R-R	6-0	210	5-6-76	.221	.216	.224	73	280	39	62	16	0	9	37	24	1	0	5	66	0	0	.375	.281
2-team (43 Louisville)					.215	—	—	116	404	53	87	21	0	13	53	37	3	0	5	95	0	1	.364	.283
Sweeney, Ryan	L-L	6-4	215	2-20-85	.270	.241	.285	105	397	50	107	17	2	10	47	48	1	2	2	71	8	5	.398	.348
Terrero, Luis	R-R	6-3	205	5-18-80	.231	.125	.265	20	65	7	15	4	0	4	9	1	1	0	0	15	3	1	.477	.254
Thome, Jim	L-R	6-3	250	8-27-70	.214	.200	.222	5	14	2	3	1	0	0	5	6	0	0	0	3	0	0	.286	.450
Wilson, Craig	R-R	6-2	225	11-30-76	.180	.167	.189	15	61	8	11	2	0	1	5	7	1	0	0	28	0	0	.262	.275
Young, Ernie	R-R	6-1	230	7-8-69	.214	.250	.201	107	374	44	80	12	0	13	42	38	9	0	9	99	0	0	.350	.302

PITCHING	B-T	HT	WT	DOB	W	L	ERA	G	GS	CG	SV	IP	H	R	ER	HR	BB	SO	AVG	vLH	vRH	K/9	BB/9
Aardsma, David	R-R	6-4	205	12-27-81	3	2	4.33	28	0	0	15	35	26	18	17	7	11	45	.198	.176	.213	11.46	2.80
Babula, Shaun	B-L	5-11	183	5-21-77	3	3	4.70	37	6	0	0	61	61	36	32	6	30	45	.260	.226	.278	6.60	4.40
Broadway, Lance	R-R	6-2	210	8-20-83	8	9	4.65	26	26	2	0	155	155	86	80	17	78	108	.264	.264	.264	6.27	4.53
Bukvich, Ryan	R-R	6-2	250	5-13-78	1	3	2.89	23	0	0	9	28	24	9	9	2	9	32	.226	.295	.177	10.29	2.89
Childers, Jason	R-R	6-0	160	1-13-75	3	2	3.91	46	0	0	0	53	53	26	23	6	21	38	.265	.241	.282	6.45	3.57
Day, Dewon	R-R	6-4	210	9-29-80	0	2	6.28	14	0	0	0	14	10	10	10	2	20	15	.192	.286	.129	9.42	12.56
Floyd, Gavin	R-R	6-4	225	1-27-83	7	3	3.12	17	17	0	0	107	93	39	37	9	35	96	.234	.251	.216	8.10	2.95
Haeger, Charlie	R-R	6-1	220	9-19-83	5	16	4.08	24	23	3	0	148	138	82	67	16	67	126	.250	.267	.235	7.68	4.08
Logan, Boone	R-L	6-5	200	8-13-84	0	1	2.16	4	0	0	1	8	8	2	2	1	4	11	.250	.250	.250	11.88	4.32
MacDougal, Mike	B-R	6-3	180	3-5-77	2	0	0.00	8	0	0	0	9	7	1	0	0	2	11	.219	.364	.143	11.42	2.08
Malone, Corwin	R-L	6-3	200	7-3-80	0	1	7.63	11	1	0	1	15	21	15	13	4	10	14	.323	.333	.320	8.22	5.87
Masset, Nick	R-R	6-4	235	5-17-82	0	4	4.57	11	9	0	0	45	51	26	23	6	9	33	.285	.348	.222	6.55	1.79
Nunez, Vladimir	R-R	6-4	240	3-15-75	4	10	5.42	29	14	0	1	111	113	71	67	15	46	78	.265	.267	.264	6.31	3.72
Phillips, Heath	L-L	6-3	205	3-24-82	13	7	4.30	28	28	1	0	174	198	90	83	23	56	108	.287	.319	.276	5.60	2.90
Pollok, Dwayne	R-R	6-3	195	11-12-80	1	1	3.33	18	1	0	1	24	28	11	9	0	6	12	.280	.341	.237	4.44	2.22
Prinz, Bret	R-R	6-3	210	6-15-77	0	1	0.56	15	0	0	1	16	10	2	1	0	9	16	.179	.056	.237	9.00	5.06
2-team (14 Indianapolis)					0	1	0.90	29	0	0	7	30	23	4	3	0	16	31	—	—	—	9.30	4.80
Reynoso, Paulino	L-L	6-3	200	8-10-80	3	0	4.09	21	0	0	0	22	26	12	10	1	20	18	.295	.143	.367	7.36	8.18
Robbins, Jake	R-R	6-5	220	5-23-76	0	0	5.11	20	0	0	0	25	31	14	14	0	17	12	.330	.300	.352	4.38	6.20
Sierra, Eduardo	R-R	6-3	185	4-15-82	1	2	4.01	18	3	0	0	25	20	14	11	2	15	19	.230	.256	.208	6.93	5.47
Sisco, Andrew	L-L	6-10	270	1-13-83	3	6	4.35	23	15	0	0	79	76	43	38	10	44	76	.259	.221	.275	8.69	5.03
Vasquez, Carlos	L-L	6-3	230	12-6-82	4	3	3.05	41	0	0	2	62	50	27	21	2	33	43	.227	.319	.185	6.24	4.79
Wassermann, Ehren	B-R	6-0	185	12-6-80	2	4	2.11	38	0	0	5	43	34	13	10	0	18	33	.230	.290	.186	6.96	3.80

FIELDING

Catcher	PCT	G	PO	A	E	DP	PB
W. Gonzalez	.984	65	441	36	8	6	9
Hall	1.000	4	17	1	0	0	0
Lucy	.994	19	139	16	1	1	5
Molina	.985	29	176	27	3	2	8
Smith	.992	31	227	27	2	2	12

First Base	PCT	G	PO	A	E	DP
Erstad	.944	2	17	0	1	1
Perez	1.000	4	36	0	0	2
Perez	.917	3	9	2	1	0
Rogowski	.995	121	964	68	5	98
Wilson	1.000	7	53	3	0	4
Young	.993	19	137	3	1	13

Second Base	PCT	G	PO	A	E	DP
Bourgeois	.960	44	92	101	8	26
A. Gonzalez	.969	20	40	54	3	14
W. Gonzalez	.909	3	4	6	1	1
Lopez	.960	5	9	15	1	5

	PCT	G	PO	A	E	DP
Perez	.985	28	61	71	2	21
Perez	.980	19	44	55	2	18
Richar	.991	26	43	73	1	16
Ricks	1.000	2	1	1	0	0

Third Base	PCT	G	PO	A	E	DP
Bourgeois	.750	1	2	1	1	0
Castillo	.778	3	2	5	2	1
Fields	.955	53	54	93	7	9
Molina	.963	14	7	45	2	6
Perez	1.000	1	1	0	0	0
Ricks	.960	18	17	31	2	4
Snyder	.937	57	32	131	11	14

Shortstop	PCT	G	PO	A	E	DP
Fields	.900	4	2	7	1	1
A. Gonzalez	.927	12	20	31	4	11
Lopez	.981	36	51	100	3	23
Perez	1.000	1	0	3	0	0
Perez	.970	69	106	182	9	32

	PCT	G	PO	A	E	DP
Richar	.935	6	13	16	2	6
Snyder	.966	19	21	36	2	8

Outfield	PCT	G	PO	A	E	DP
Anderson	1.000	38	79	3	0	1
Bourgeois	1.000	39	84	3	0	0
Collaro	.961	27	46	3	2	0
Erstad	.944	10	17	0	1	0
A. Gonzalez	1.000	3	5	0	0	0
Kelly	.984	63	112	10	2	3
Owens	.984	59	118	3	2	0
Perez	1.000	10	21	0	0	0
Podsednik	.955	20	21	0	1	0
Rogowski	.969	20	30	1	1	0
Sanchez	1.000	23	56	1	0	0
Sweeney	1.000	105	251	13	0	4
Terrero	.973	19	36	0	1	0
Wilson	1.000	8	12	0	0	0
Young	1.000	1	2	0	0	0

SOUTHERN LEAGUE

BATTING	B-T	HT	WT	DOB	AVG	vLH	vRH	G	AB	R	H	2B	3B	HR	RBI	BB	HBP	SH	SF	SO	SB	CS	SLG	OBP
Aldridge, Cory	L-R	6-1	225	6-13-79	.259	.229	.274	124	421	60	109	33	5	9	58	70	3	0	6	117	4	3	.425	.364
Armstrong, Cole	L-R	6-3	210	8-24-83	.239	.118	.278	22	71	2	17	6	0	1	12	3	1	2	2	20	0	0	.366	.273
Bourgeois, Jason	R-R	5-9	185	1-4-82	.296	.274	.315	43	162	25	48	10	3	2	20	16	1	2	3	20	15	3	.432	.357
Collaro, Thomas	R-R	6-4	216	4-4-83	.257	.294	.239	109	436	55	112	26	2	19	67	27	5	0	3	129	7	3	.456	.306
Cook, David	R-R	5-11	195	7-21-81	.293	.303	.288	29	99	19	29	5	2	8	25	24	2	0	1	22	2	2	.626	.437
Frost, Jeremy	R-R	6-2	215	11-19-79	.239	.216	.255	70	238	28	57	5	1	6	21	16	2	4	4	64	2	1	.345	.288
Garrett, Shawn	B-R	6-3	220	11-2-78	.292	.262	.306	55	212	28	62	18	0	3	28	21	1	0	3	49	4	4	.420	.354
Getz, Chris	L-R	6-0	175	8-30-83	.299	.323	.285	72	278	40	83	10	2	3	29	36	2	2	1	30	13	7	.381	.382
Hollis, Eric	R-R	6-2	225	9-26-82	.308	.250	.400	8	13	0	4	1	0	0	2	1	0	0	0	3	1	0	.385	.357
Kelly, Christopher	R-R	6-1	195	2-23-82	.231	.214	.239	123	459	36	106	19	0	5	44	18	4	7	8	97	0	0	.305	.262
Lucy, Donny	R-R	6-3	210	8-8-82	.269	.250	.278	87	290	42	78	17	0	6	27	30	3	2	1	59	13	1	.390	.343
Mercedes, Victor	B-R	5-11	184	4-15-79	.276	.178	.317	83	341	49	94	21	2	6	31	24	1	8	2	57	7	7	.402	.323
Myers, Michael	R-R	6-1	194	12-11-79	.180	.228	.161	94	278	28	50	10	1	3	32	33	3	7	2	61	5	7	.255	.272
Nanita, Ricardo	L-L	6-1	180	6-12-81	.260	.261	.260	123	427	45	111	21	0	5	42	33	5	4	6	53	10	8	.344	.316
Perez, Kenny	B-R	6-2	190	9-28-81	.265	.455	.211	25	98	9	26	4	2	1	17	4	0	1	0	9	0	0	.378	.294
Shabala, Adam	L-R	6-1	190	2-6-78	.251	.256	.250	51	187	32	47	6	0	3	13	32	2	3	0	46	7	4	.332	.367
Smith, Sean	R-R	6-0	194	8-24-82	.219	.274	.190	86	269	26	59	4	0	1	14	18	4	10	1	63	13	7	.245	.277
Valido, Robert	R-R	6-2	180	5-16-85	.177	.265	.125	70	266	23	47	8	1	0	17	9	3	7	3	43	10	6	.214	.210
West, Jeremy	R-R	6-0	200	11-8-81	.274	.258	.287	52	190	19	52	3	0	0	18	15	5	0	1	28	1	1	.289	.341

PITCHING	B-T	HT	WT	DOB	W	L	ERA	G	GS	CG	SV	IP	H	R	ER	HR	BB	SO	AVG	vLH	vRH	K/9	BB/9
Bittner, Tim	L-L	6-2	210	6-9-80	2	4	4.46	48	0	0	0	67	92	39	33	7	30	30	.342	.318	.354	4.05	4.05
Day, Dewon	R-R	6-4	210	9-29-80	2	3	3.60	20	0	0	3	25	26	13	10	1	12	48	.257	.214	.288	17.28	4.32
Egbert, Jack	L-R	6-3	205	5-12-83	12	8	3.06	28	28	0	0	162	138	63	55	3	44	165	.232	.242	.221	9.19	2.45
Fields, Joshua	R-R	6-1	180	1-20-80	0	2	9.00	9	0	0	0	9	15	12	9	2	6	4	.375	.294	.435	4.00	6.00
Gonzalez, Gio	R-L	5-11	185	9-19-85	9	7	3.18	27	27	0	0	150	116	57	53	10	57	185	.216	.224	.212	11.10	3.42
Hernandez Jr., Fernando	R-R	5-11	190	7-31-84	1	3	3.06	60	0	0	9	85	73	30	29	4	23	84	.230	.220	.237	8.86	2.43
Honel, Kris	R-R	6-5	190	11-7-82	2	2	5.79	17	12	0	0	61	56	46	39	6	52	44	.243	.308	.190	6.53	7.71
Malone, Corwin	R-L	6-3	200	7-3-80	2	6	5.40	32	3	0	0	62	77	44	37	1	33	65	.309	.348	.294	9.49	4.82
McCulloch, Kyle	R-R	6-3	180	3-20-85	1	2	6.41	6	6	0	0	27	38	25	19	4	11	16	.333	.393	.276	5.40	3.71
Perez, Oneli	R-R	6-2	190	5-26-83	6	2	2.10	59	0	0	16	77	62	19	18	5	20	89	.219	.230	.212	10.40	2.34
Russell, Adam	R-R	6-8	250	4-14-83	9	11	4.80	38	20	0	1	139	159	81	74	8	58	95	.290	.339	.251	6.17	3.76
Sierra, Eduardo	R-R	6-3	185	4-15-82	1	5	4.74	29	0	0	2	38	39	29	20	1	22	42	.262	.290	.241	9.95	5.21
Torres, Carlos	R-R	6-2	180	10-22-82	2	2	3.70	36	0	0	1	56	57	26	23	3	22	59	.269	.309	.244	9.48	3.54
Vasquez, Carlos	L-L	6-3	230	12-6-82	0	0	1.23	11	0	0	2	15	8	2	2	0	3	14	.160	.071	.194	8.59	1.84
Wesley, John	R-R	6-6	263	10-14-80	1	2	4.11	13	0	0	0	15	17	7	7	1	3	18	.288	.233	.345	10.57	1.76
Whisler, Wes	L-L	6-5	240	4-7-83	6	13	5.00	28	27	0	0	157	195	107	87	10	42	74	.305	.316	.301	4.25	2.41
Wing, Ryan	L-L	6-2	170	2-1-82	6	6	3.24	35	17	0	0	114	89	44	41	8	46	93	.211	.239	.201	7.34	3.63

FIELDING

Catcher	PCT	G	PO	A	E	DP	PB
Armstrong	.995	21	176	17	1	3	1
Frost	.986	37	250	26	4	3	4
Hollis	1.000	7	14	0	0	0	0
Lucy	.992	84	692	56	6	6	10

First Base	PCT	G	PO	A	E	DP
Armstrong	1.000	1	1	0	0	0
Frost	.993	27	250	23	2	21
Garrett	.982	46	399	28	8	41
Hollis	1.000	1	5	0	0	1
Kelly	.967	6	54	4	2	5
Myers	.990	32	294	14	3	26
Perez	1.000	2	13	1	0	0
Shabala	1.000	1	1	0	0	0
West	.978	30	251	17	6	29

Second Base	PCT	G	PO	A	E	DP
Bourgeois	.955	12	19	44	3	5
Getz	.975	69	112	198	8	46
Mercedes	.969	24	54	103	5	23
Myers	.961	26	54	68	5	13
Perez	.969	14	24	39	2	10
Shabala	—	1	0	0	0	0

Third Base	PCT	G	PO	A	E	DP
Bourgeois	.667	4	1	3	2	1
Kelly	.914	114	53	225	26	24
Myers	.913	13	6	15	2	2
Perez	.923	4	0	12	1	1
Shabala	.857	11	6	12	3	2

Shortstop	PCT	G	PO	A	E	DP
Mercedes	.962	60	95	181	11	36
Myers	.919	12	12	22	3	6
Perez	.700	4	5	9	6	2
Valido	.959	70	97	232	14	46

Outfield	PCT	G	PO	A	E	DP
Aldridge	1.000	44	60	1	0	1
Bourgeois	1.000	21	47	0	0	0
Collaro	.994	101	167	6	1	3
Cook	.983	28	58	1	1	0
Myers	1.000	12	17	1	0	0
Nanita	.983	116	172	6	3	2
Shabala	.984	37	60	1	1	1
Smith	.988	85	170	1	2	0

CAROLINA LEAGUE

BATTING	B-T	HT	WT	DOB	AVG	vLH	vRH	G	AB	R	H	2B	3B	HR	RBI	BB	HBP	SH	SF	SO	SB	CS	SLG	OBP
Allen, Rod	R-R	6-2	210	9-21-82	.209	.241	.191	76	249	23	52	11	0	4	23	11	4	2	1	62	10	4	.301	.253
Armstrong, Cole	L-R	6-3	210	8-24-83	.288	.269	.295	80	285	35	82	17	0	12	39	23	2	3	3	69	1	1	.474	.342
Castillo, Javier	R-R	6-2	180	8-29-83	.288	.277	.291	116	403	41	116	28	2	9	62	35	3	1	6	82	9	6	.434	.345
Cook, David	R-R	5-11	195	7-21-81	.279	.228	.295	93	340	73	95	22	3	16	50	51	3	0	6	77	10	8	.503	.373
Cunningham, Aaron	R-R	5-11	195	4-24-86	.296	.288	.296	67	252	51	74	12	5	8	37	34	4	8	8	39	22	8	.476	.376
Gartrell, Maurice	R-R	6-2	220	1-14-84	.288	.375	.263	20	73	13	21	1	1	2	6	6	2	0	0	17	2	0	.411	.358
Hudson, Robert	R-R	6-0	170	8-31-83	.263	.281	.257	72	255	35	67	10	2	1	18	12	2	2	0	47	14	10	.329	.301
Johnson, Brandon	L-R	6-0	190	7-23-84	.195	.294	.177	81	215	21	42	12	0	0	13	15	0	10	2	62	18	2	.251	.246
Lang, C.J.	R-R	5-9	170	4-12-84	.272	.329	.242	85	243	33	66	12	1	0	20	29	2	9	3	26	6	3	.329	.350
McCarthy, Ryan	R-R	6-3	195	9-4-82	.231	.222	.233	28	78	8	18	2	0	0	4	13	3	2	0	21	0	0	.256	.362
Mercedes, Victor	B-R	5-11	184	4-15-79	.245	.137	.286	46	184	20	45	6	4	4	24	14	1	1	1	23	5	9	.408	.300
Orlando, Paulo	R-R	6-3	165	11-1-85	.253	.281	.245	102	391	49	99	16	4	8	34	19	4	10	1	84	20	7	.376	.294
Reves, Tyler	R-R	5-11	208	1-15-84	.220	.234	.216	89	286	23	63	17	2	6	23	20	1	2	2	73	5	2	.315	.272
Ricks, Adam	B-R	5-10	195	9-24-82	.264	.212	.278	51	148	22	39	11	0	2	21	20	0	0	0	25	2	2	.378	.351
Roberts, Daron	R-R	6-0	215	2-25-83	.281	.313	.272	108	377	40	106	23	2	12	59	12	12	2	4	90	19	7	.448	.321
Schnurstein, Micah	R-R	6-1	207	7-18-84	.274	.281	.271	135	508	83	139	36	4	25	84	54	9	0	7	103	7	8	.508	.349
Sharp, Matt	L-R	6-0	205	8-3-82	.250	.250	.250	18	48	7	12	3	0	0	7	9	1	0	0	9	0	0	.313	.368
Valido, Robert	R-R	6-2	180	5-16-85	.252	.239	.255	57	234	30	59	8	0	3	16	14	1	4	1	36	20	3	.325	.296

PITCHING

PITCHING	B-T	HT	WT	DOB	W	L	ERA	G	GS	CG	SV	IP	H	R	ER	HR	BB	SO	AVG	vLH	vRH	K/9	BB/9
Bakker, Garry	R-R	6-2	208	3-28-83	2	7	3.67	31	11	0	0	83	79	47	34	5	45	64	.251	.213	.282	6.91	4.86
Brooks, Richard	R-R	6-3	180	7-18-84	0	0	1.93	15	0	0	0	19	21	7	4	0	7	14	.280	.364	.245	6.75	3.38
Cassel, Justin	R-R	6-1	190	9-25-84	4	2	2.27	10	6	0	0	40	31	13	10	1	17	31	.215	.303	.141	7.03	3.86
Chirino, Israel	L-L	6-1	200	11-8-83	0	3	2.70	34	0	0	1	33	36	14	10	1	19	23	.290	.256	.309	6.21	5.13
De Los Santos, Fautino	R-R	6-0	205	2-15-86	1	1	3.65	5	5	0	0	25	20	12	10	3	7	32	.220	.176	.246	11.68	2.55
Gannon, Joe	L-R	6-1	195	3-15-75	0	1	13.50	3	2	0	0	7	12	12	11	1	6	8	.364	.176	.563	9.82	7.36
Hudson, Robert	R-R	6-0	170	8-31-83	0	0	0.00	1	0	0	0	1	1	0	0	0	2	2	.250	.000	.333	18.00	18.00
Link, Jon	R-R	6-2	205	3-23-84	1	0	2.55	14	0	0	3	18	16	5	5	1	4	19	.246	.261	.238	9.68	2.04
Lujan, John	R-R	6-1	220	5-10-84	2	5	3.73	49	1	0	11	82	76	44	34	7	37	90	.241	.293	.211	9.88	4.06
McCulloch, Kyle	R-R	6-3	180	3-20-85	7	7	3.64	22	22	0	0	121	116	62	49	7	42	88	.251	.256	.247	6.55	3.12
Omogrosso, Brian	R-R	6-3	230	4-26-84	8	8	3.74	40	14	1	5	120	94	60	50	7	57	108	.211	.249	.178	8.08	4.26
Rice, Jason	R-R	6-0	190	5-13-86	3	3	5.68	23	1	0	0	32	22	28	20	3	36	43	.191	.143	.227	12.22	10.23
Richard, Clayton	L-L	6-5	225	9-12-83	8	12	3.63	28	27	1	0	161	159	86	65	11	59	99	.262	.180	.285	5.52	3.29
Rodriguez, Derek	R-R	6-1	190	5-17-83	14	5	3.69	28	28	1	0	161	164	80	66	10	55	124	.269	.257	.278	6.93	3.07
Rodriguez, Ryan	L-L	6-4	233	7-10-84	4	8	5.70	34	12	0	1	85	114	66	54	9	29	67	.323	.295	.333	7.07	3.06
Santeliz, Clevelan	R-R	6-0	160	9-1-86	2	1	4.30	14	0	0	0	15	10	7	7	3	9	18	.192	.188	.194	11.05	5.52
Torres, Carlos	R-R	6-2	180	10-22-82	0	2	3.72	19	0	0	3	36	33	16	15	0	10	41	.248	.177	.310	10.16	2.48
Torres, Joseph	L-L	6-2	193	9-3-82	2	0	3.58	21	0	0	2	33	23	16	13	1	16	39	.190	.178	.197	10.74	4.41
Wesley, John	R-R	6-6	263	10-14-80	1	2	2.84	19	0	0	7	25	22	9	8	3	14	32	.237	.229	.241	11.37	4.97
Zaleski, Matthew	R-R	6-0	205	12-2-81	5	7	5.21	35	9	0	0	95	109	63	55	10	39	54	.289	.291	.288	5.12	3.69

FIELDING

Catcher	PCT	G	PO	A	E	DP	PB
Armstrong	.980	73	477	50	11	6	7
Hudson	—	1	0	0	0	0	0
Lang	1.000	1	1	0	0	0	0
Reves	.989	37	239	24	3	0	8
Ricks	.994	26	147	18	1	4	3
Sharp	.986	17	126	11	2	0	8

First Base	PCT	G	PO	A	E	DP
Hudson	1.000	1	3	0	0	0
Reves	.994	19	134	20	1	13
Ricks	.667	1	2	0	1	0
Schnurstein	.986	123	1148	92	17	111

Second Base	PCT	G	PO	A	E	DP
Hudson	.951	37	67	107	9	29

	PCT	G	PO	A	E	DP
Johnson	.942	47	82	112	12	29
Lang	.985	36	43	91	2	19
Mercedes	.970	34	75	116	6	32
Ricks	1.000	1	0	1	0	0
Valido	1.000	1	0	2	0	0

Third Base	PCT	G	PO	A	E	DP
Castillo	.897	106	48	204	29	18
Hudson	1.000	3	1	0	0	0
Johnson	.818	5	3	6	2	1
Lang	.968	16	5	25	1	1
Mercedes	.882	11	3	27	4	3
Schnurstein	.846	7	3	8	2	0

Shortstop	PCT	G	PO	A	E	DP
Castillo	1.000	5	2	5	0	0

	PCT	G	PO	A	E	DP
Hudson	.972	30	39	101	4	16
Lang	.934	28	35	79	8	18
McCarthy	.917	28	51	93	13	22
Mercedes	1.000	1	1	2	0	0
Valido	.956	56	84	178	12	41

Outfield	PCT	G	PO	A	E	DP
Allen	.967	56	87	2	3	0
Cook	.967	85	140	5	5	1
Cunningham	.961	60	71	3	3	0
Gartrell	1.000	15	31	1	0	0
Hudson	—	1	0	0	0	0
Johnson	.917	17	10	1	1	0
Orlando	.972	101	203	8	6	0
Roberts	.979	90	132	5	3	1

KANNAPOLIS INTIMIDATORS

LOW CLASS A

SOUTH ATLANTIC LEAGUE

BATTING

BATTING	B-T	HT	WT	DOB	AVG	vLH	vRH	G	AB	R	H	2B	3B	HR	RBI	BB	HBP	SH	SF	SO	SB	CS	SLG	OBP
Allen, Brandon	L-R	6-2	235	2-12-86	.283	.226	.303	129	516	84	146	39	5	18	93	39	4	0	2	124	7	4	.483	.337
Anderson, John	L-R	5-11	190	1-18-77	.281	.308	.274	53	196	35	55	11	0	0	20	16	1	5	2	24	0	2	.337	.335
Carter, Christopher	R-R	6-4	210	12-18-86	.291	.271	.276	126	467	84	136	27	3	25	93	67	6	0	5	112	3	2	.522	.383
Cruz, Lee	R-R	6-2	190	6-13-83	.277	.281	.276	108	415	55	115	31	5	10	56	15	5	1	3	57	3	4	.448	.308
Gartrell, Maurice	R-R	6-2	220	1-14-84	.301	.286	.307	95	339	67	102	20	3	12	57	37	4	1	2	77	12	2	.484	.374
Gilbert, Archie	R-R	5-8	180	7-8-83	.289	.279	.294	101	342	66	99	17	6	9	49	37	9	4	2	39	35	13	.453	.372
Gomes, Anderson	R-R	6-1	185	3-12-85	.300	.287	.306	79	283	50	85	17	1	7	47	34	1	1	6	55	2	3	.442	.370
Grace, Michael	R-R	6-1	220	4-27-84	.252	.282	.239	120	425	54	107	27	4	8	59	35	3	9	3	109	3	1	.391	.311
Hernandez, Francisco	B-R	5-9	160	2-4-86	.277	.326	.254	80	271	42	75	23	1	4	36	35	2	1	1	29	0	1	.413	.362
Hudson, Robert	R-R	6-0	170	8-31-83	.250	.270	.238	25	100	10	25	5	0	0	7	2	1	2	1	17	6	1	.300	.269
Killian, Billy	L-R	6-1	190	6-12-86	.281	.444	.255	19	64	13	18	5	0	0	4	0	0	1	0	11	2	0	.359	.281
Madsen, Scott	R-R	6-0	178	4-23-82	.200	.198	.201	83	265	44	53	5	2	0	23	14	12	5	2	62	17	5	.234	.270
Miranda, Sergio	B-R	5-9	169	3-5-87	.282	.222	.303	61	238	45	67	9	2	1	30	37	3	4	1	27	5	3	.349	.384
Sharp, Matt	L-R	6-0	205	8-3-82	.223	.200	.231	37	121	19	27	4	0	2	13	20	0	0	0	17	1	0	.306	.333
Shelby, John	R-R	5-10	185	8-6-85	.301	.285	.307	122	488	83	147	35	9	16	79	35	5	6	4	77	19	8	.508	.352
Tavares, Reymundo	B-R	5-10	165	2-7-83	.203	.160	.222	27	79	7	16	2	0	0	3	10	0	3	0	10	3	3	.228	.292
Vargas, Hancer	B-R	5-11	174	12-5-88	.189	.158	.197	29	95	11	18	0	0	0	5	8	0	3	0	21	2	1	.189	.252

PITCHING

PITCHING	B-T	HT	WT	DOB	W	L	ERA	G	GS	CG	SV	IP	H	R	ER	HR	BB	SO	AVG	vLH	vRH	K/9	BB/9
Brooks, Richard	R-R	6-3	180	7-18-84	3	6	5.15	14	11	0	0	58	73	39	33	3	22	49	.311	.333	.292	7.65	3.43
De Los Santos, Fautino	R-R	6-0	205	2-15-86	9	4	2.40	21	15	0	0	98	49	33	26	5	36	121	.148	.153	.144	11.15	3.32
Dubee, Michael	R-R	6-2	177	1-12-86	3	0	4.09	8	6	0	0	33	34	16	15	3	13	35	.272	.250	.286	9.55	3.55
2-team (30 Lakewood)					7	4	3.96	38	6	0	1	89	86	41	39	5	35	89	—	—	—	9.03	3.55
Edwards, Justin	L-L	5-11	170	9-7-87	6	9	5.79	27	21	0	0	115	128	81	74	10	44	87	.280	.355	.252	6.81	3.44
Long, Matthew	R-R	6-5	220	2-23-84	9	3	5.54	26	18	1	0	104	130	71	64	12	31	73	.313	.309	.317	6.32	2.68
Perez, Carlos	L-L	6-2	175	2-19-84	4	6	5.66	37	10	0	0	97	127	75	61	10	33	66	.314	.302	.320	6.12	3.06
Rasner, Jacob	R-R	6-4	195	12-4-86	7	11	6.83	28	28	0	0	140	185	118	106	15	64	112	.316	.333	.304	7.22	4.12
Rice, Jason	R-R	6-0	190	5-13-86	3	2	4.54	12	7	0	0	38	36	29	19	0	29	32	.257	.259	.256	7.65	6.93
Rocco, Michael	R-R	6-2	180	8-19-85	0	4	5.67	24	1	0	3	46	57	37	29	5	20	41	.297	.213	.357	8.02	3.91
Rodriguez, Noe	L-L	6-0	165	8-8-84	5	2	3.95	43	0	1	6	68	78	35	30	4	37	82	.286	.305	.275	10.80	4.87
Rote, Ryan	R-R	6-4	225	8-8-82	3	3	4.42	50	0	6	6	75	74	53	37	10	41	66	.250	.227	.263	7.88	4.90
Santeliz, Clevelan	R-R	6-0	160	9-1-86	1	4	6.69	27	0	0	0	38	40	35	28	4	27	37	.274	.339	.233	8.84	6.45
Shirek, Charles	R-R	6-4	180	10-25-85	0	0	5.40	6	0	0	1	7	5	5	4	2	2	3	.217	.429	.125	4.05	2.70
Spurgeon, Steven	R-R	6-2	190	8-22-83	5	2	5.36	43	0	0	0	84	96	57	50	8	32	66	.281	.277	.283	7.07	3.43
Texeira, Kanekoa	R-R	6-2	190	2-6-86	5	2	3.69	39	0	0	16	54	49	24	22	0	22	58	.239	.218	.252	9.73	3.69
Torres, Joseph	L-L	6-2	193	9-3-82	1	0	3.86	3	0	0	0	5	2	2	2	0	5	5	.133	.250	.091	9.64	9.64
Wesley, John	R-R	6-6	263	10-14-80	1	0	0.79	11	0	0	5	11	7	2	1	1	7	17	.179	.154	.192	13.50	5.56
Winn, Joseph	R-R	6-0	195	9-1-84	0	1	9.00	11	0	0	0	15	21	20	15	3	7	15	.318	.333	.310	9.00	4.20
Zazueta, Jose	R-R	6-0	204	2-24-87	4	11	5.35	25	22	1	0	106	111	73	63	7	71	66	.270	.266	.272	5.60	6.03\

FIELDING

Catcher	PCT	G	PO	A	E	DP	PB
Hernandez	.978	70	480	60	12	9	7
Killian	.958	17	110	4	5	0	1
Sharp	.997	37	278	23	1	1	8
Tavares	.961	25	176	23	8	0	3

First Base	PCT	G	PO	A	E	DP
Allen	.995	66	517	26	3	52
Carter	.983	73	611	27	11	47

Second Base	PCT	G	PO	A	E	DP
Anderson	.973	50	90	127	6	25
Grace	1.000	4	1	5	0	1

Madsen	.960	35	56	88	6	16
Shelby	.936	54	107	126	16	31

Third Base	PCT	G	PO	A	E	DP
Grace	.898	119	68	196	30	20
Hernandez	.900	10	6	12	2	0
Hudson	1.000	1	1	1	0	0
Madsen	.963	12	7	19	1	1
Tavares	—	1	0	0	0	0

Shortstop	PCT	G	PO	A	E	DP
Hudson	.966	24	33	79	4	15
Madsen	.910	31	46	75	12	13

Miranda	.944	60	85	170	15	25
Vargas	.887	27	32	70	13	13

Outfield	PCT	G	PO	A	E	DP
Cruz	.954	92	137	7	7	1
Gartrell	.973	92	172	7	5	2
Gilbert	.972	99	204	6	6	2
Gomes	.974	79	148	2	4	1
Madsen	.857	3	6	0	1	0
Shelby	.981	68	144	7	3	0

BRISTOL SOX   ROOKIE

APPALACHIAN LEAGUE

BATTING

	B-T	HT	WT	DOB	AVG	vLH	vRH	G	AB	R	H	2B	3B	HR	RBI	BB	HBP	SH	SF	SO	SB	CS	SLG	OBP
Andrade, Jorge	R-R	6-1	210	10-1-85	.216	.239	.200	37	116	8	25	6	0	0	3	5	0	0	0	29	0	1	.267	.248
Avila, Jesus	R-L	6-0	165	11-26-88	.195	.238	.182	33	87	10	17	4	0	0	11	7	3	1	3	19	2	0	.241	.270
Cheatham, Jordan	L-L	5-10	185	11-2-87	.287	.333	.273	50	157	24	45	8	4	3	26	28	1	1	0	39	4	3	.446	.398
Gerst, Kent	L-R	5-10	170	2-6-88	.280	.257	.291	57	225	34	63	5	2	1	15	20	2	1	0	39	17	9	.333	.344
Gilbert, Kenneth	L-L	6-2	185	2-6-89	.203	.364	.175	26	74	6	15	2	0	0	7	6	3	0	0	32	2	0	.230	.289
Guillen, Oney	R-R	5-9	155	1-25-86	.122	.103	.131	32	90	6	11	2	0	0	4	5	1	0	1	23	1	1	.144	.175
Hash, Kylee	B-R	6-2	205	3-31-88	.155	.083	.174	21	58	3	9	1	0	1	8	6	0	1	2	21	0	0	.224	.227
Johnson, Logan	L-R	5-9	175	11-22-83	.280	.256	.288	53	164	25	46	16	0	3	22	24	15	0	0	40	1	1	.433	.419
Luna, Miguel	L-R	5-10	165	11-20-84	.264	.375	.244	22	53	9	14	1	1	0	5	1	0	0	0	15	0	0	.321	.278
Mahin, Nick	R-R	6-2	230	8-19-85	.298	.327	.287	52	181	29	54	10	3	9	33	10	3	0	2	34	2	2	.536	.342
Martinez, Jose	R-R	6-5	170	7-25-88	.282	.243	.297	65	245	34	69	11	3	7	37	22	4	2	2	53	12	2	.437	.348
Matthews, Jedon	R-R	6-2	190	12-7-87	.253	.273	.233	33	87	14	22	6	3	1	11	11	2	0	0	36	3	3	.425	.350
Morales, Sergio	R-R	6-1	190	12-17-87	.270	.276	.268	55	196	35	53	8	2	6	24	14	3	0	2	67	11	3	.423	.326
Pena, Ramon	R-R	5-10	153	9-22-85	.202	.125	.242	36	94	6	19	1	0	0	7	11	1	2	1	14	0	1	.213	.290
Santos, Orlando	R-R	6-0	187	12-10-86	.230	.167	.250	24	74	7	17	3	0	2	8	3	0	0	1	22	0	0	.351	.256
Vargas, Hancer	B-R	5-11	174	12-5-88	.255	.320	.231	51	184	29	47	3	0	0	10	14	2	4	1	40	12	8	.272	.313
Yapor, Duarte	R-R	5-11	190	9-22-86	.167	.156	.174	31	78	6	13	5	2	0	13	12	1	3	1	14	0	0	.282	.283

PITCHING

	B-T	HT	WT	DOB	W	L	ERA	G	GS	CG	SV	IP	H	R	ER	HR	BB	SO	AVG	vLH	vRH	K/9	BB/9
Albritton, Daniel	R-R	6-0	200	11-10-84	1	3	5.16	20	0	0	3	23	30	15	13	0	4	31	.316	.400	.286	12.31	1.59
Burdie, Charlis	R-R	6-1	185	9-8-85	3	5	4.53	15	11	0	0	54	54	30	27	2	27	60	.258	.283	.250	10.06	4.53
Cassel, Justin	R-R	6-1	190	9-25-84	0	0	6.75	2	2	0	0	3	5	2	2	0	0	3	.357	.167	.500	10.12	0.00
Corley, Tyson	R-R	6-6	200	1-26-86	0	0	0.00	9	0	0	1	17	7	3	0	0	5	17	.119	.000	.152	9.00	2.65
Doan, Joey	R-R	6-0	160	9-27-83	1	1	7.16	9	0	0	0	16	22	15	13	1	2	10	.314	.286	.321	5.51	1.10
Griffith, Nevin	R-R	6-2	165	3-23-89	0	0	5.19	8	1	0	0	9	14	8	5	0	6	7	.359	.357	.360	7.27	6.23
Guzman, Luis	R-R	6-1	165	6-13-87	2	3	7.96	17	2	0	0	37	64	41	33	7	12	35	.362	.411	.339	8.44	2.89
Infante, Gregory	R-R	6-2	185	7-10-87	2	3	4.01	10	8	0	0	34	25	17	15	1	23	33	.207	.244	.188	8.82	6.15
Johnson, Garrett	L-L	6-10	205	9-2-87	2	0	8.10	15	0	0	0	20	28	22	18	0	12	23	.329	.286	.338	10.35	5.40
Jones, Nathan	R-R	6-5	190	1-28-86	0	4	5.13	13	10	0	0	47	44	33	27	4	29	42	.250	.268	.244	7.99	5.51
Lin, Po-Yu	R-R	6-0	221	9-16-86	6	5	3.30	14	11	0	0	63	71	33	23	6	17	65	.280	.218	.307	9.34	2.44
Lubisich, Nik	L-L	6-2	195	4-19-79	0	0	5.73	5	3	0	0	11	16	8	7	0	2	8	.340	.286	.350	6.55	1.64
Paniagua, Onarkys	R-R	6-3	170	1-28-86	1	10	7.29	13	10	0	0	54	75	61	44	9	21	37	.314	.304	.317	6.13	3.48
Ramirez, Ronald	L-L	5-11	148	10-17-85	1	0	2.35	4	0	0	0	8	6	2	2	0	0	1	.222	.167	.238	1.17	0.00
Rojas, Wilmer	L-L	6-0	163	10-12-86	1	1	2.43	21	0	0	11	30	23	9	8	1	13	40	.221	.583	.174	12.13	3.94
Rosario, Frank	R-R	6-2	162	10-31-85	2	5	5.84	13	7	0	0	45	54	40	29	6	25	47	.295	.222	.326	9.47	5.04
Santiago, Hector	R-L	6-0	210	12-16-87	1	1	1.65	17	0	0	0	33	19	7	6	1	16	38	.176	.182	.175	10.47	4.41
Tollefson, Adam	L-L	5-8	181	12-2-86	4	0	3.11	17	0	0	0	38	26	14	13	1	13	43	.190	.111	.209	10.27	3.11
Torres, Joseph	L-L	6-2	193	9-3-82	0	0	9.00	1	0	0	0	1	2	1	1	0	0	1	.400	.000	.500	9.00	0.00
Viola, Frank	R-R	6-4	188	6-19-84	0	0	4.96	11	3	0	0	16	27	13	9	4	7	10	.346	.286	.368	5.51	3.86

FIELDING

Catcher	PCT	G	PO	A	E	DP	PB
Hash	.990	21	182	9	2	1	8
Santos	.983	22	143	26	3	0	9
Yapor	.984	29	209	37	4	3	7

First Base	PCT	G	PO	A	E	DP
Andrade	.976	35	265	19	7	23
Mahin	.980	38	278	14	6	26

Second Base	PCT	G	PO	A	E	DP
Avila	.949	26	37	57	5	17

Guillen	.907	32	45	62	11	15
Johnson	1.000	4	2	3	0	1
Luna	.917	5	5	6	1	2
Pena	1.000	11	14	21	0	6

Third Base	PCT	G	PO	A	E	DP
Avila	.500	2	0	1	1	0
Johnson	.870	49	40	101	21	10
Matthews	.879	22	11	40	7	4

Shortstop	PCT	G	PO	A	E	DP
Johnson	1.000	1	1	0	0	0

Luna	1.000	1	1	0	0	0
Pena	.951	25	27	51	4	8
Vargas	.886	47	55	131	24	26

Outfield	PCT	G	PO	A	E	DP
Cheatham	.971	28	31	3	1	0
Gerst	.972	57	99	5	3	1
Gilbert	1.000	20	29	3	0	1
Mahin	.938	9	14	1	1	0
Martinez	.957	53	87	2	4	1
Morales	.955	42	63	0	3	0

GREAT FALLS WHITE SOX   ROOKIE

PIONEER LEAGUE

BATTING

	B-T	HT	WT	DOB	AVG	vLH	vRH	G	AB	R	H	2B	3B	HR	RBI	BB	HBP	SH	SF	SO	SB	CS	SLG	OBP
Curtis, John	L-R	6-2	210	11-22-84	.177	.133	.184	37	113	18	20	6	1	1	9	19	1	1	0	22	1	1	.274	.301
Estill, Lyndon	R-R	6-3	215	3-29-87	.247	.302	.231	54	186	34	46	8	7	7	38	21	5	3	1	84	3	5	.478	.338
Gallagher, Jim	L-L	6-1	195	9-3-85	.332	.362	.325	67	247	52	82	21	1	9	44	35	6	1	6	38	7	4	.534	.418
Hunter, Joe	R-R	6-1	190	12-2-83	.143	.125	.154	5	21	2	3	0	0	0	3	0	0	0	0	8	0	0	.143	.250
Inouye, Matt	R-R	5-10	185	5-20-84	.309	.286	.318	40	123	29	38	9	2	5	28	13	7	1	2	17	5	1	.537	.400
Jordan, Danny	R-R	6-0	190	5-9-86	.235	.250	.231	32	85	9	20	2	0	4	13	12	2	0	2	31	0	0	.400	.337
Marrero, Christian	L-L	6-1	185	7-30-86	.305	.356	.290	69	269	53	82	21	6	12	63	36	2	0	6	43	3	2	.561	.383

Player	B-T	HT	WT	DOB	AVG	vLH	vRH	G	AB	R	H	2B	3B	HR	RBI	BB	HBP	SH	SF	SO	SB	CS	SLG	OBP
Mead, Andrew	R-R	6-1	190	4-17-84	.300	.286	.306	45	150	27	45	12	1	2	22	11	4	3	2	26	7	2	.433	.359
Miranda, Sergio	B-R	5-9	169	3-5-87	.464	.000	.542	7	28	2	13	3	1	0	1	3	0	1	0	4	1	2	.643	.516
Mollenhauer, Dale	L-R	5-10	170	6-26-86	.276	.353	.256	69	246	41	68	12	2	0	33	23	0	5	3	36	13	5	.341	.335
Morgan, Josh	R-R	6-2	215	7-20-84	.299	.250	.311	60	231	39	69	16	0	4	35	18	1	1	5	48	7	0	.420	.345
Paiml, Greg	R-R	6-0	185	8-3-84	.310	.340	.302	67	226	36	70	17	3	3	34	26	4	1	3	55	7	3	.451	.386
Persichina, Joe	L-R	6-0	190	12-14-84	.281	.375	.258	46	160	35	45	11	1	0	16	19	6	2	1	24	5	1	.363	.376
Retherford, C.J.	R-R	5-10	180	8-14-85	.318	.246	.338	61	261	53	83	30	4	13	48	24	8	3	3	45	2	3	.613	.389
Sanchez, Salvador	R-R	6-6	195	9-13-85	.343	.397	.329	70	283	57	97	16	10	7	51	18	7	1	2	59	18	13	.544	.394
Turner, Steven	R-R	6-1	190	8-9-84	.281	.125	.333	20	32	9	9	2	1	0	5	3	2	1	0	16	3	3	.406	.378

PITCHING	B-T	HT	WT	DOB	W	L	ERA	G	GS	CG	SV	IP	H	R	ER	HR	BB	SO	AVG	vLH	vRH	K/9	BB/9
Bowling, Adam	R-R	6-4	180	1-16-84	3	2	6.41	17	0	0	2	27	36	19	19	3	6	39	.316	.375	.284	13.16	2.02
Carter, Anthony	L-R	6-2	170	4-4-86	5	3	3.93	15	15	0	0	71	78	34	31	6	17	62	.280	.264	.291	7.86	2.15
Corley, Tyson	R-R	6-6	200	1-26-86	0	1	8.31	5	0	0	0	9	14	16	8	1	8	4	.341	.308	.357	4.15	8.31
Doan, Joey	R-R	6-0	160	9-27-83	1	0	2.25	6	0	0	1	8	9	4	2	0	1	2	.290	.111	.364	2.25	1.12
Ely, John	R-R	6-1	190	5-17-86	6	1	3.86	13	12	0	0	56	55	26	24	6	14	56	.259	.238	.279	9.00	2.25
Fields, Joshua	R-R	6-1	180	1-20-86	1	0	0.00	8	0	0	1	11	8	0	0	1	1	10	.216	.111	.250	8.44	0.84
Hunt, Leroy	R-R	6-6	240	11-28-87	2	0	3.82	14	0	0	0	31	31	17	13	2	18	30	.254	.265	.247	8.80	5.28
Lowe, Johnnie	R-R	6-5	220	3-21-85	4	2	4.57	15	15	0	0	65	67	37	33	4	22	56	.262	.287	.245	7.75	3.05
Mabee, Henry	R-R	6-4	230	7-10-85	3	2	1.88	18	0	0	8	24	15	6	5	1	9	22	.185	.172	.192	8.25	3.38
Maxwell, Levi	R-R	6-2	200	12-22-84	3	2	4.11	23	0	0	4	31	30	15	14	1	14	32	.254	.263	.250	9.39	4.11
Morales, Ronald	L-L	6-3	195	1-22-85	2	0	3.32	23	0	0	2	38	40	16	14	3	14	28	.286	.195	.323	6.63	3.32
Moreno, Juan	R-R	6-3	176	11-29-86	6	4	2.39	16	16	0	0	90	83	29	24	4	11	77	.246	.310	.208	7.67	1.10
Perez, Wander	L-L	6-3	168	1-5-85	1	0	3.98	28	0	0	1	43	44	23	19	3	22	62	.259	.313	.238	12.98	4.60
Poreda, Aaron	L-L	6-6	240	10-1-86	4	0	1.17	12	8	0	0	46	29	7	6	1	10	48	.181	.171	.185	9.32	1.94
Ramirez, Ronald	L-L	5-11	148	10-17-85	0	0	0.00	3	0	0	4	2	0	0	0	0	1	2	.167	.000	.222	4.15	2.08
Segura, Wascar	R-R	6-3	180	7-4-85	2	0	6.86	16	0	0	0	21	22	19	16	2	18	18	.275	.313	.250	7.71	7.71
Skogley, Kevin	L-L	6-6	203	9-24-84	2	5	4.72	18	9	0	1	55	65	37	29	7	21	45	.298	.239	.314	7.32	3.42
Woodson, Alexander	L-L	6-0	190	10-10-85	6	2	4.93	20	1	0	1	42	56	29	23	0	8	43	.309	.239	.333	9.21	1.71

FIELDING

Catcher	PCT	G	PO	A	E	DP	PB
Curtis	.985	32	238	22	4	2	5
Inouye	.992	33	218	24	2	1	5
Jordan	.976	25	178	23	5	1	7

First Base	PCT	G	PO	A	E	DP
Jordan	1.000	1	2	0	0	0
Marrero	.988	52	480	28	6	47
Morgan	.989	18	169	7	2	11
Persichina	.958	10	86	5	4	7

Second Base	PCT	G	PO	A	E	DP
Mollenhauer	.969	60	103	174	9	45

	PCT	G	PO	A	E	DP
Persichina	.933	23	29	54	6	9

Third Base	PCT	G	PO	A	E	DP
Paiml	.842	7	1	15	3	2
Persichina	.848	9	4	24	5	0
Retherford	.912	60	31	125	15	13

Shortstop	PCT	G	PO	A	E	DP
Miranda	.872	7	12	22	5	7
Mollenhauer	.900	10	12	24	4	4
Paiml	.951	59	86	205	15	34
Persichina	.875	3	2	5	1	0

Outfield	PCT	G	PO	A	E	DP
Estill	.987	51	72	2	1	0
Gallagher	1.000	59	68	6	0	0
Hunter	1.000	3	5	0	0	0
Marrero	1.000	8	10	2	0	1
Mead	1.000	42	51	4	0	1
Persichina	1.000	2	2	0	0	0
Sanchez	.964	63	98	9	4	3
Turner	1.000	13	18	0	0	0

DSL WHITE SOX 1

ROOKIE

DOMINICAN SUMMER LEAGUE

BATTING	B-T	HT	WT	DOB	AVG	vLH	vRH	G	AB	R	H	2B	3B	HR	RBI	BB	HBP	SH	SF	SO	SB	CS	SLG	OBP
Aguasvivas, Nestor	R-R	6-1	187	9-19-87	.263	.186	.279	66	247	39	65	13	0	5	35	29	3	0	3	57	5	4	.377	.344
Brazoban, Rafael	R-R	6-1	200	12-12-87	.225	.000	.246	35	71	7	16	0	0	0	5	8	3	0	0	27	0	3	.225	.329
De La Cruz, Edgar	R-R	6-0	190	7-26-89	.202	.200	.202	36	104	7	21	5	0	0	7	9	1	1	0	27	2	2	.250	.272
De La Cruz, Luis	R-R	5-11	172	10-12-87	.220	.261	.213	55	150	23	33	3	1	0	15	45	4	2	2	23	3	6	.253	.408
Ferreiras, Angel	R-R	6-1	184	8-12-88	.143	1.000	.000	2	7	2	1	0	0	0	1	0	0	0	3	1	0	.143	.250
2-team (49 DSL)					.223	—		51	166	21	37	7	3	2	15	11	3	0	1	46	2	2	.337	.282
Garcia, Josue	R-R	6-2	190	10-29-84	.272	.231	.279	27	81	15	22	7	1	2	13	20	6	1	1	25	8	6	.457	.444
Garcia, Miguel	R-R	6-1	150	5-16-90	.095	.500	.075	16	42	2	4	0	0	0	3	2	1	0	1	6	0	2	.095	.152
2-team (17 DSL)					.153	—		33	72	7	11	0	0	0	6	4	2	1	1	14	1	2	.153	.215
Ladera, Kevin	R-R	6-0	155	6-2-89	.242	.200	.250	35	128	16	31	5	0	0	7	17	4	2	0	20	9	3	.281	.349
2-team (16 DSL)					.239	—		51	156	24	36	7	0	0	11	25	4	2	0	31	9	5	.273	.346
Lora, Ronald	R-R	6-1	180	3-31-89	.185	.273	.176	37	119	17	22	3	1	0	12	13	2	1	0	45	6	4	.227	.276
Lugo, Antoni	R-R	6-1	187	6-16-88	.230	.241	.228	59	187	23	43	5	0	1	19	15	9	4	4	31	5	5	.273	.312
Marte, Abrahan	R-R	6-2	205	8-6-87	.226	.250	.222	39	124	14	28	5	2	1	15	10	5	0	0	27	1	2	.323	.309
Marte, Victor	R-R	6-0	180	9-15-89	.175	.250	.157	25	63	7	11	1	0	0	4	10	1	1	0	20	2	3	.190	.297
Moreno, Pedro	R-R	5-11	165	7-30-85	.273	.500	.222	3	11	3	3	2	0	0	1	2	0	0	0	3	0	0	.455	.385
Moya, Carlos	R-R	6-4	175	8-15-86	.250	.292	.238	36	108	15	27	6	1	2	9	10	4	2	0	30	4	1	.380	.336
Peguero, Anneury	R-R	5-11	170	6-4-87	.314	.152	.352	50	175	29	55	3	2	1	14	32	5	1	0	28	12	4	.371	.434
Pimentel, Francisco	R-R	6-1	195	11-13-87	.184	.190	.183	47	125	16	23	1	0	3	19	30	5	1	3	38	0	2	.264	.356
Ramos, Luis	R-R	6-3	185	6-19-88	.253	.395	.223	65	249	32	63	11	3	2	31	20	7	3	1	62	7	6	.345	.325
Rivas, Daniel	R-R	6-0	190	10-30-86	.500	.000	.667	4	4	4	2	0	0	0	0	3	0	0	0	1	0	.500	.500
Silfo, Fernando	R-R	6-1	195	11-18-85	.200	.222	.190	11	30	4	6	0	0	0	0	3	1	0	0	6	0	1	.200	.294
Tavarez, Misael	R-R	6-5	190	12-6-87	.272	.159	.298	67	235	35	64	15	1	3	40	22	13	0	4	68	13	5	.383	.361

PITCHING	B-T	HT	WT	DOB	W	L	ERA	G	GS	CG	SV	IP	H	R	ER	HR	BB	SO	AVG	vLH	vRH	K/9	BB/9
Bruno, Keuri	R-R	6-0	180	1-20-87	3	2	3.96	14	1	0	1	36	37	23	16	3	13	17	.268	.100	.315	4.21	3.22
Cueva, Jorge	R-R	6-3	205	3-24-89	0	2	10.62	10	1	0	0	20	25	29	24	2	17	23	.281	.250	.302	10.18	7.52
Hernandez, Wandy	R-R	6-3	189	8-26-85	4	2	1.64	15	0	0	0	44	24	17	8	2	12	28	.158	.179	.150	5.73	2.45
Juma, Ronny	L-R	6-2	182	10-26-88	1	3	5.87	12	0	0	0	23	23	24	15	1	18	14	.256	.200	.259	5.48	7.04
Medina, Aneuris	L-L	6-2	170	5-21-87	0	6	5.21	13	13	0	0	57	64	52	33	3	27	55	.270	.133	.279	8.68	4.26
Mercedes, Raffy	R-R	6-1	185	12-17-88	1	8	5.63	13	13	0	0	62	86	54	39	6	15	48	.322	.234	.358	6.93	2.17
Payano, Luis	R-R	6-1	176	3-31-87	1	7	7.28	18	9	1	0	59	93	69	48	3	25	56	.352	.375	.345	8.49	3.79
Perez, Augusto	R-R	6-1	168	4-20-86	2	8	3.88	17	7	0	0	65	72	46	28	4	26	66	.274	.262	.277	9.14	3.60
Reyes, Luis	R-R	6-0	177	6-21-89	0	1	10.38	4	0	0	0	4	9	8	5	0	2	3	.391	.667	.350	6.23	4.15
2-team (5 DSL)					0	1	4.50	9	0	0	0	16	23	17	8	0	8	11	—	—	—	6.19	4.50

	B-T	HT	WT	DOB	W	L	ERA	G	GS	CG	SV	IP	H	R	ER	HR	BB	SO	AVG	vLH	vRH	K/9	BB/9
Rivas, Daniel	R-R	6-0	174	10-30-86	0	2	10.22	18	0	0	0	25	39	37	28	3	10	23	.358	.458	.329	8.39	3.65
Rodriguez, Francisco	L-L	6-2	160	10-5-84	0	2	2.00	4	3	0	0	9	10	5	2	0	3	9	.270	.500	.257	9.00	3.00
Rodriguez, Yovan	R-R	6-0	180	7-12-86	3	2	5.03	15	0	0	1	39	48	37	22	1	11	40	.289	.382	.265	9.15	2.52
Ruiz, Diogenes	R-R	6-2	185	10-1-88	0	0	7.71	16	0	0	0	19	24	24	16	2	15	14	.300	.357	.269	6.75	7.23
Teis, Luis	R-R	6-5	180	6-6-87	1	3	3.73	18	11	0	1	60	60	33	25	3	24	52	.269	.292	.263	7.76	3.58
Zabala, Carlos	L-L	6-2	180	11-4-85	1	7	5.61	14	12	1	0	69	83	60	43	4	24	77	.287	.333	.283	10.04	3.13

FIELDING

Catcher	PCT	G	PO	A	E	DP	PB
E. De La Cruz	.950	27	155	35	10	2	19
Peguero	—	1	0	0	0	0	0
Pimentel	.969	46	333	39	12	4	20
Rivas	1.000	1	1	0	0	0	0
Silfo	.935	9	53	5	4	0	2

First Base	PCT	G	PO	A	E	DP
Aguasvivas	.977	36	278	19	7	15
Garcia	1.000	2	14	0	0	1
Lugo	.971	4	32	2	1	2
Marte	.967	6	28	1	1	1
Moya	.981	28	198	4	4	17

Second Base	PCT	G	PO	A	E	DP
E. De La Cruz	.800	1	1	3	1	1

	PCT	G	PO	A	E	DP
L. De La Cruz	.897	33	72	59	15	11
Ladera	1.000	1	1	0	0	0
Marte	.897	11	16	19	4	0
Peguero	.950	31	73	60	7	13

Third Base	PCT	G	PO	A	E	DP
Aguasvivas	.847	16	17	33	9	3
L. De La Cruz	.750	8	4	11	5	0
Lugo	.868	53	46	105	23	5

Shortstop	PCT	G	PO	A	E	DP
Garcia	.866	16	21	50	11	4
Ladera	.934	34	38	104	10	13
Lugo	1.000	1	0	2	0	0
Marte	.667	1	1	1	1	0
Marte	.733	10	5	28	12	3

	PCT	G	PO	A	E	DP
Moreno	.714	3	6	9	6	1
Peguero	.758	14	28	22	16	4

Outfield	PCT	G	PO	A	E	DP
Aguasvivas	1.000	16	12	1	0	0
Brazoban	.918	31	44	1	4	0
Ferreiras	1.000	1	0	1	0	0
Garcia	.881	23	30	7	5	0
Lora	.868	30	32	1	5	0
Marte	1.000	6	5	0	0	0
Ramos	.928	63	130	11	11	2
Rivas	—	1	0	0	0	0
Tavarez	.913	62	83	11	9	4

DSL WHITE SOX2 ROOKIE

DOMINICAN SUMMER LEAGUE

BATTING	B-T	HT	WT	DOB	AVG	vLH	vRH	G	AB	R	H	2B	3B	HR	RBI	BB	HBP	SH	SF	SO	SB	CS	SLG	OBP
Acuna, Luis	B-R	6-0	160	4-17-85	.239	.300	.226	37	113	11	27	3	0	2	15	4	4	0	1	27	1	2	.319	.287
Buckridge, Shaydron	R-R	5-10	170	5-12-88	.325	.103	.374	55	160	26	52	8	0	0	25	28	6	4	2	19	7	3	.375	.439
Cabrera, Raldy	R-R	6-0	180	9-25-89	.124	.167	.112	47	113	15	14	3	0	0	7	18	2	1	0	57	2	4	.150	.256
Celis, Johny	L-R	6-0	165	3-26-86	.289	.395	.265	68	232	38	67	11	0	8	52	50	10	0	3	37	6	6	.440	.431
Escobar, Eduardo	B-R	5-10	150	1-5-89	.291	.214	.307	64	247	56	72	5	4	0	18	22	5	6	2	45	19	14	.344	.359
Ferreiras, Angel	R-R	6-1	184	8-12-88	.226	.273	.214	49	159	19	36	7	3	2	14	10	3	0	1	43	1	2	.346	.283
2-team (2 DSL)					.223	—	—	51	166	21	37	7	3	2	15	11	3	0	1	46	2	2	.337	.282
Garcia, Miguel	R-R	6-1	150	5-16-90	.233	.000	.304	17	30	5	7	0	0	0	3	2	1	2	0	8	1	0	.233	.303
2-team (16 DSL)					.153	—	—	33	72	7	11	0	0	0	6	4	2	2	1	14	1	2	.153	.215
Ladera, Kevin	R-R	6-0	155	6-2-89	.229	.111	.256	16	48	8	11	1	0	0	4	8	0	0	0	11	0	2	.250	.346
2-team (35 DSL)					.239	—	—	51	176	24	42	6	0	0	11	25	4	0	2	31	9	5	.273	.346
Linares, Josue	R-R	6-1	185	3-17-88	.091	.100	.083	7	22	0	2	0	0	0	0	4	0	1	0	12	0	0	.091	.231
Parra, Carlos	L-R	6-0	188	2-24-90	.211	.261	.198	42	114	20	24	5	0	0	8	26	3	0	2	30	4	0	.254	.346
Patino, Jeffer	R-R	5-10	163	10-8-88	.297	.278	.301	64	219	44	65	9	3	2	34	29	6	11	0	36	5	6	.393	.394
Robles, Abraham	R-R	6-2	170	3-15-90	.188	.222	.179	31	85	8	16	2	0	0	7	11	2	0	0	30	0	2	.212	.296
Rosales, Yeikler	R-R	6-1	180	6-5-88	.173	.320	.139	51	133	8	23	1	1	0	9	5	5	7	0	46	8	7	.195	.231
Sierra, Luis	R-R	5-11	150	7-23-87	.301	.241	.308	68	246	52	74	17	0	6	51	28	13	6	4	29	10	0	.443	.395
Trujillo, Rather	R-R	6-0	185	2-23-89	.196	.200	.195	65	189	30	37	4	2	0	18	27	16	4	3	35	18	6	.238	.340
Vega, Juan	R-R	6-1	165	3-9-89	.241	.265	.232	38	133	16	32	6	2	0	29	2	15	1	3	22	6	3	.316	.320

PITCHING	B-T	HT	WT	DOB	W	L	ERA	G	GS	CG	SV	IP	H	R	ER	HR	BB	SO	AVG	vLH	vRH	K/9	BB/9
Aguilera, Hector	R-R	6-3	185	3-26-90	4	4	5.01	17	4	1	1	47	50	35	26	3	22	33	.289	.421	.273	6.36	4.24
Carrillo, Marco	R-R	5-10	155	4-3-89	4	1	5.47	18	3	0	2	49	51	31	30	4	30	37	.287	.229	.301	6.75	5.47
Duque, Jean	R-R	6-3	190	7-17-89	2	2	3.73	12	8	0	0	41	40	24	17	1	21	44	.256	.214	.266	9.66	4.61
Gouvea, Murillo	R-R	6-2	190	9-15-88	3	5	4.33	14	8	0	1	44	37	28	21	3	29	56	.242	.240	.242	11.54	5.98
Gutierrez, Santiago	L-L	6-1	205	2-26-86	1	4	4.56	19	0	0	5	51	55	28	26	3	23	36	.289	.750	.280	6.31	4.03
Martinez, Joucer	R-R	6-2	160	2-3-86	4	5	2.38	16	15	1	0	83	65	32	22	3	23	73	.215	.210	.217	7.88	2.48
Merejildo, Jose	R-R	6-1	185	3-19-86	1	7	2.92	18	6	0	2	49	51	28	16	3	28	38	.282	.343	.267	6.93	5.11
Mota, Arismendy	R-R	6-2	165	2-16-87	4	3	4.61	15	13	0	0	68	75	40	35	3	27	42	.291	.313	.286	5.53	3.56
Ortega, Yorvix	R-R	5-11	175	8-1-89	4	7	7.77	19	2	0	3	46	53	48	40	3	25	37	.294	.361	.278	7.19	4.86
Reyes, Luis	R-R	6-0	177	6-21-89	0	0	2.31	5	0	0	0	12	14	9	3	0	6	8	.286	.250	.293	6.17	4.63
2-team (4 DSL)					0	1	4.50	9	0	0	0	16	23	17	8	0	8	11	—	—		6.19	4.50
Rienzo, Andre	R-R	6-3	160	6-5-88	1	1	7.63	7	3	0	0	15	16	15	13	1	11	22	.286	.200	.304	12.91	6.46
Rodriguez, Alvin	R-R	6-2	174	10-5-87	0	0	6.11	13	1	0	1	28	25	25	19	1	33	23	.243	.417	.190	7.39	10.61
Tejada, Silvio	R-R	6-6	190	9-6-88	0	1	4.57	11	6	0	0	41	40	28	21	0	23	20	.270	.286	.267	4.35	5.01
Trinidad, Geurys	R-R	6-4	185	1-31-87	3	0	8.85	13	0	0	2	20	19	22	20	2	24	15	.244	.438	.194	6.64	10.62

FIELDING

Catcher	PCT	G	PO	A	E	DP	PB
Acuna	.944	14	103	16	7	1	13
Buckridge	.975	41	257	54	8	1	11
Parra	.969	21	142	12	5	1	7
Vega	1.000	1	3	1	0	0	1

First Base	PCT	G	PO	A	E	DP
Acuna	1.000	1	5	0	0	2
Celis	.991	63	532	22	5	45
Ferreiras	1.000	1	1	0	0	0
Linares	1.000	1	4	0	0	0
Sierra	1.000	5	46	1	0	6

Second Base	PCT	G	PO	A	E	DP
Escobar	.800	2	3	1	1	1

	PCT	G	PO	A	E	DP
Garcia	.920	10	11	12	2	2
Ladera	1.000	12	24	22	0	6
Patino	.964	57	127	114	9	28

Third Base	PCT	G	PO	A	E	DP
Acuna	1.000	1	2	1	0	1
Linares	.952	6	5	15	1	1
Patino	1.000	5	3	9	0	0
Robles	1.000	2	1	3	0	0
Sierra	.964	58	50	139	7	14

Shortstop	PCT	G	PO	A	E	DP
Escobar	.940	57	82	167	16	30
Garcia	1.000	2	1	7	0	0
Ladera	—	1	0	0	0	0

	PCT	G	PO	A	E	DP
Linares	—	1	0	0	0	0
Robles	.771	15	20	34	16	6
Sierra	1.000	3	3	4	0	1

Outfield	PCT	G	PO	A	E	DP
Buckridge	—	1	0	0	0	0
Cabrera	.879	39	27	2	4	0
Celis	1.000	7	5	1	0	0
Escobar	—	1	0	0	0	0
Ferreiras	.928	43	61	3	5	1
Parra	—	1	0	0	0	0
Rosales	.962	51	69	7	3	0
Trujillo	.979	65	132	9	3	1
Vega	.925	34	47	2	4	1

Cincinnati Reds

BY JOHN FAY

The Reds had hoped 2007 was the year they'd take the next step and break through with a winning season. Instead, they took a big step backward, posting the club's seventh consecutive losing season. As a result, the Reds start next season with their fifth different manager since 2003.

The downward spiral that led to Jerry Narron being fired and replaced by interim manager Pete Mackanin began almost as soon as the season began. The result was disappointing for CEO Bob Castellini and GM Wayne Krivsky, who had made progress in their first year running the club.

The Reds were 13-13 on May 1. But a major bullpen implosion led to a 5-20 record through most of May. That put the Reds 10½ games back in the National League Central. Krivsky brought in Mike Stanton, Kirk Saarloos and Rheal Cormier to shore up the bullpen, but the Reds still tied for last in the majors by converting just 55 percent of their save opportunities.

The club—which had been in contention until the second to last day of the 2006 season—was essentially done before June began.

The club turned to Mackanin, who had been a major league advance scout, in early July.

"It comes down now to the performance of the team," Krivsky said at the time. "I share in that, but being the manager, you've got the direct responsibility there handling the team on a day-to-day basis. My job is to acquire talent, bring in talent, and he does what he can with what he has available to him. There's no perfect scenarios.

"In my opinion, being around the team, I felt like we needed a change of voice, a change of maybe attitude or approach, and based on the results, we felt a change was needed in those areas."

The club played well under Mackanin. But the fact that the club ultimately chose Dusty Baker over Mackanin for the full-time post indicates it was trying to show fans they are headed in a different direction.

The Reds went 41-39 under Mackanin with his record tainted by a weak finish in which the Reds lost eight of their last nine. The club was 2-8 after Ken Griffey Jr.'s season-ending groin injury and 1-5 after Adam Dunn's season-ending knee surgery.

Mackanin was seriously considered for the full-time post, but Baker was considered a more proven commodity.

"He's a winner," Castellini said, "a proven winner."

Baker comes in with some parts to work with.

■ Righthander Aaron Harang developed into the 200-inning, 200-strikeout horse at the front of the rotation the Reds have been looking for since Jose Rijo. The Reds were 24-10 in games Harang started—a remarkable statistic for a team so far under .500.

■ Second baseman Brandon Phillips had a breakout year and became the first Red since Barry Larkin to hit 30 home runs and steal 30 bases.

■ Rule 5 pick Josh Hamilton returned to professional baseball after a near four-year absence and hit for power (.922 on-base plus slugging percentage) but was limited to just 90 games because of a variety of injuries.

■ The club's other Rule 5 pick, Jared Burton overcame a rough start to the year and showed an ability to lock down the eighth inning during the second half of the season, when he went 4-1, 1.83 in 34 innings.

PLAYERS OF THE YEAR

MAJOR LEAGUE: ADAM DUNN, OF

Dunn had another big year with the Reds, leading the team with a .386 on-base percentage and a .554 slugging percentage. His 40 home runs also were a team-high and were the third-most in the National League. Dunn also led the Reds with 106 RBIs, 101 walks and 69 extra-base hits. His 165 strikeouts were also a team-high.

MINOR LEAGUE: JAY BRUCE, OF

A five-tool player, Bruce finished the year as Baseball America's Minor League Player of the Year. Bruce went all the way from high Class A Sarasota to Triple-A Louisville, and had an OPS higher than .900 at each level. He hit a combined .319/.375/.587 with 26 home runs, 46 doubles and eight triples.

ORGANIZATIONAL LEADERS

BATTING		★Minimum 250 at-bats
★AVG	Bruce, Jay, Sarasota/Chatt./Louisville	.319
R	Rosales, Adam, Sarasota/Chattanooga	98
H	Griffin, Michael, Sarasota/Chattanooga	171
TB	Bruce, Jay, Sarasota/Chatt./Louisville	306
2B	Bruce, Jay, Sarasota/Chatt./Louisville	46
3B	Rosales, Adam, Sarasota/Chattanooga	11
HR	Bruce, Jay, Sarasota/Chatt./Louisville	26
RBI	Votto, Joey, Louisville	92
BB	DeJesus, Michael, Sarasota	78
SO	Dickerson, Chris, Chattanooga/Louisville	162
SB	Dickerson, Chris, Chattanooga/Louisville	30
★OBP	Gutierrez, Tonys, Chattanooga/Sarasota	.399
★SLG	Bruce, Jay, Sarasota/Chatt./Louisville	.587
PITCHING		^Minimum 75 innings
W	Thompson, Daryl, Dayton/Sarasota	14
L	Four players tied at	10
^ERA	Cueto, Johnny, Sarasota/Louisville/Chatt.	3.07
G	Lutz, Derrik, Chattanooga/Sarasota	61
CG	Jukich, Ben, Sarasota	2
SV	Roenicke, Josh, Sarasota/Chattanooga	24
IP	Cueto, Johnny, Sarasota/Louisville.Chatt.	161
BB	Webb, Travis, Dayton	62
SO	Cueto, Johnny, Sarasota/Louisville/Chatt.	170
^AVG	Ramirez, Ramon, Sarasota/Chatt./Louisville	.229

■ Dunn raised his average nearly 30 points, drove in a career-high 106 runs and cut his errors from 17 to six.

The farm system is loaded at the top with talent ready to make a major league impact but lacks significant depth. Minor League Player of the Year Jay Bruce, who hit 26 home runs at three levels but did not receive a big league callup, should compete for a spot in the Reds' outfield in 2008. He was the top-rated prospect in the Triple-A International League and was joined on the list by righthander Homer Bailey (No. 2), who showed flashes of brilliance after a midseason promotion to Cincinnati, and first baseman Joey Votto (No. 10), who ranked fourth in the IL in home runs and second in RBIs.

Righthander Johnny Cueto was the fourth-rated prospect in the Double-A Southern League and compiled a 170-34 strikeout-walk ratio at three levels.

General Manager: Wayne Krivsky. **Farm Director:** Terry Reynolds. **Scouting Director:** Chris Buckley

Class	Team	League	W	L	PCT	Finish*	Manager	Affiliate Since
Majors	Cincinnati	National	72	90	.444	13th (16)	Jerry Narron/Pete Mackanin	—
Triple-A	Louisville Bats	International	74	70	.514	7th (14)	Rick Sweet	2000
Double-A	Chattanooga Lookouts	Southern	67	73	.479	7th (10)	Jayhawk Owens	1988
High A	Sarasota Reds	Florida State	81	59	.579	3rd (12)	Joe Ayrault	2005
Low A	Dayton Dragons	Midwest	78	62	.557	6th (14)	Billy Gardner	2000
Rookie	Billings Mustangs	Pioneer	37	38	.493	4th (8)	Joe Krunzel	1974
Rookie	GCL Reds	Gulf Coast	15	41	.268	16th (16)	Pat Kelly	1999
Overall 2007 Minor League Record			**352**	**343**	**.506**	**T-11th**		

* Finish in overall standings (No. of teams in league) ^League champion

ORGANIZATION STATISTICS

CINCINNATI REDS

NATIONAL LEAGUE

BATTING	B-T	HT	WT	DOB	AVG	vLH	vRH	G	AB	R	H	2B	3B	HR	RBI	BB	HBP	SH	SF	SO	SB	CS	SLG	OBP
Bellhorn, Mark	B-R	6-1	205	8-23-74	.071	.250	.000	13	14	2	1	0	0	0	1	4	0	0	0	5	0	0	.071	.278
Cantu, Jorge	R-R	6-3	200	1-30-82	.298	.241	.357	27	57	8	17	8	0	1	9	7	2	0	2	10	0	0	.491	.382
Castro, Juan	R-R	5-11	190	6-20-72	.180	.226	.155	54	89	5	16	5	0	0	5	4	0	3	2	21	0	0	.236	.211
Coats, Buck	L-R	6-3	195	6-9-82	.206	.500	.083	20	34	2	7	4	0	0	2	3	0	0	1	15	0	0	.324	.263
Conine, Jeff	R-R	6-1	225	6-27-66	.265	.266	.264	80	215	23	57	11	1	6	32	20	0	1	6	28	4	0	.409	.320
2-team (21 New York)					.254	—	—	101	256	25	65	13	1	6	37	27	0	2	7	36	4	0	.383	.317
Cruz, Enrique	R-R	6-1	205	11-21-81	.000	—	.000	1	1	0	0	0	0	0	0	0	0	0	0	0	0	0	.000	.000
Dunn, Adam	L-R	6-6	275	11-9-79	.264	.239	.278	152	522	101	138	27	2	40	106	101	5	0	4	165	9	2	.554	.386
Ellison, Jason	R-R	5-10	180	4-4-78	.188	.111	.393	37	48	7	9	1	0	1	2	5	1	2	0	15	1	0	.271	.278
Encarnacion, Edwin	R-R	6-1	215	1-7-83	.289	.284	.291	139	502	66	145	25	1	16	76	39	14	0	1	86	8	1	.438	.356
Freel, Ryan	R-R	5-10	185	3-8-76	.245	.143	.315	75	277	44	68	13	3	3	16	18	7	2	0	47	15	8	.347	.308
Gil, Jerry	R-R	6-3	200	10-14-82	—	—	.000	1	0	0	0	0	0	0	0	0	0	0	0	0	0	0	—	—
Gonzalez, Alex	R-R	6-0	200	2-15-77	.272	.234	.287	110	393	55	107	27	1	16	55	24	8	2	3	75	0	1	.468	.325
Griffey Jr., Ken	L-L	6-3	230	11-21-69	.277	.236	.300	144	528	78	146	24	1	30	93	85	1	0	9	99	6	1	.496	.372
Hamilton, Josh	L-L	6-4	235	5-21-81	.292	.222	.314	90	298	52	87	17	2	19	47	33	4	0	2	65	3	3	.554	.368
Hanigan, Ryan	R-R	6-0	195	8-16-80	.300	.000	.429	5	10	3	3	1	0	0	2	1	0	0	0	2	0	0	.400	.364
Hatteberg, Scott	L-R	6-1	210	12-14-69	.310	.205	.323	116	361	50	112	27	1	10	47	49	3	1	3	35	0	0	.474	.394
Hopper, Norris	R-R	5-10	210	3-24-79	.329	.351	.324	136	121	307	51	101	14	2	0	14	20	1	6	1	33	14	6	.388	.371
Jorgensen, Ryan	R-R	6-2	220	5-4-79	.200	.143	.250	4	15	3	3	0	0	2	6	0	0	0	0	5	0	0	.600	.200
Keppinger, Jeff	R-R	6-0	180	4-21-80	.332	.362	.320	67	241	39	80	16	2	5	32	24	4	6	1	12	2	1	.477	.400
Lopez, Pedro	R-R	6-1	160	4-28-84	.178	.125	.200	14	45	1	8	2	0	0	1	1	0	0	0	10	0	0	.222	.213
Moeller, Chad	R-R	6-3	215	2-18-75	.167	.263	.103	30	48	6	8	1	0	1	2	0	0	1	0	17	0	0	.250	.167
2-team (7 Los Angeles)					.161	—	—	37	56	8	9	1	0	1	2	0	1	1	0	18	0	0	.232	.175
Phillips, Brandon	R-R	6-0	195	6-28-81	.288	.341	.266	158	650	107	187	26	6	30	94	33	12	2	5	109	32	8	.485	.331
Ross, David	R-R	6-2	240	3-19-77	.203	.248	.175	112	311	32	63	10	0	17	39	30	0	5	2	92	0	0	.399	.271
Valentin, Javier	B-R	5-10	215	9-19-75	.276	.290	.274	97	243	19	67	21	0	2	34	19	1	0	2	25	0	0	.387	.328
Votto, Joey	L-R	6-3	220	9-10-83	.321	.269	.345	24	84	11	27	7	0	4	17	5	0	0	1	15	1	0	.548	.360
Wise, Dewayne	L-L	6-1	195	2-24-78	.200	—	.200	5	5	1	1	0	1	0	1	0	0	0	1	0	0	0	.600	.333

PITCHING	B-T	HT	WT	DOB	W	L	ERA	G	GS	CG	SV	IP	H	R	ER	HR	BB	SO	AVG	vLH	vRH	K/9	BB/9
Arroyo, Bronson	R-R	6-5	195	2-24-77	9	15	4.23	34	34	1	0	211	232	109	99	28	63	156	.280	.274	.285	6.66	2.69
Bailey, Homer	R-R	6-4	205	5-3-86	4	2	5.76	9	9	0	0	45	43	32	29	3	28	28	.257	.284	.233	5.56	5.56
Belisle, Matt	R-R	6-3	230	6-6-80	8	9	5.32	30	30	1	0	178	212	111	105	26	43	125	.301	.298	.303	6.33	2.18
Bray, Bill	L-L	6-3	220	6-5-83	3	3	6.28	19	0	0	1	14	16	10	10	1	5	14	.281	.158	.342	8.79	3.14
Burton, Jared	R-R	6-5	230	6-2-81	4	2	2.51	47	0	0	0	43	28	15	12	2	22	36	.187	.130	.219	7.53	4.60
Coffey, Todd	R-R	6-5	255	9-9-80	2	1	5.82	58	0	0	0	51	70	36	33	12	19	43	.323	.343	.313	7.59	3.35
Cormier, Rheal	L-L	5-10	195	4-23-67	0	0	9.00	6	0	0	0	3	4	3	3	1	1	1	.364	.200	.500	3.00	3.00
Coutlangus, Jonathan	L-L	6-1	185	10-21-80	4	2	4.39	64	0	0	0	41	38	22	20	3	27	38	.250	.231	.264	8.34	5.93
Dumatrait, Phil	R-L	6-2	200	7-12-81	0	4	15.00	6	6	0	0	18	39	30	30	6	12	9	.448	.471	.443	4.50	6.00
Gosling, Mike	L-L	6-2	210	9-23-80	2	0	4.91	23	0	0	0	33	42	22	18	5	28	32	.318	.260	.354	8.73	7.64
Guardado, Eddie	R-L	6-0	225	10-2-70	0	0	7.24	15	0	0	0	14	16	11	11	2	4	8	.286	.333	.273	5.27	2.63
Harang, Aaron	R-R	6-7	275	5-9-78	16	6	3.73	34	34	2	0	232	213	100	96	28	52	218	.242	.237	.246	8.47	2.02
Livingston, Bobby	L-L	6-3	205	9-3-82	3	3	5.27	10	10	0	0	56	77	35	33	8	8	27	.325	.341	.321	4.31	1.28
Lohse, Kyle	R-R	6-2	210	10-4-78	6	12	4.58	21	21	2	0	132	143	76	67	16	33	80	.280	.279	.282	5.47	2.26
2-team (13 Philadelphia)					9	12	4.62	34	32	2	0	193	207	109	99	22	57	122	—	—	—	5.70	2.66
Majewski, Gary	R-R	6-1	220	2-26-80	0	4	8.22	32	0	0	0	23	43	22	21	3	3	10	.398	.333	.420	3.91	1.17
McBeth, Marcus	R-R	6-2	195	8-23-80	3	2	5.95	23	0	0	0	20	22	13	13	2	7	17	.286	.273	.295	7.78	3.20
Milton, Eric	L-L	6-3	220	8-4-75	0	4	5.17	6	6	0	0	31	39	21	18	4	9	18	.298	.300	.297	5.17	2.59
Ramirez, Elizardo	B-R	6-0	190	1-28-83	0	2	7.71	4	3	0	0	16	20	14	14	5	8	8	.313	.258	.364	4.41	4.41
Saarloos, Kirk	R-R	6-0	180	5-23-79	1	5	7.17	34	3	0	0	43	54	36	34	8	19	27	.305	.338	.284	5.70	4.01
Salmon, Brad	L-R	6-4	225	1-3-80	0	1	4.13	26	0	0	0	24	22	11	11	3	10	22	.244	.310	.213	8.25	3.75
Santos, Victor	R-R	6-2	205	10-2-76	1	4	5.14	32	0	0	0	49	51	28	28	10	23	44	.276	.260	.287	8.08	4.22
Shearn, Tom	R-R	6-4	230	8-28-77	3	0	4.96	7	6	0	0	33	32	18	18	8	13	16	.262	.200	.306	4.41	3.58
Stanton, Mike	L-L	6-1	215	6-2-67	1	3	5.93	69	0	0	0	58	75	39	38	6	18	40	.315	.306	.321	6.24	2.81
Stone, Ricky	R-R	6-1	195	2-28-75	0	0	10.13	5	0	0	0	5	7	6	6	4	0	3	.318	.143	.625	5.06	0.00
Weathers, David	R-R	6-3	235	9-25-69	2	6	3.59	70	0	0	33	78	67	33	31	4	27	48	.233	.254	.218	5.56	3.13

FIELDING

Catcher	PCT	G	PO	A	E	DP	PB
Hanigan	1.000	3	16	0	0	0	0
Jorgensen	.968	4	29	1	1	0	0
Moeller	1.000	17	72	5	0	0	0
Ross	.993	108	662	50	5	7	6
Valentin	.997	73	341	19	1	4	8

First Base	PCT	G	PO	A	E	DP
Cantu	1.000	14	86	4	0	7
Conine	.993	56	390	21	3	50
Hatteberg	.996	96	657	50	3	66
Keppinger	1.000	1	2	0	0	0
Valentin	1.000	1	3	0	0	1
Votto	1.000	17	107	11	0	15

Second Base	PCT	G	PO	A	E	DP
Bellhorn	1.000	1	0	1	0	1
Cantu	1.000	1	1	3	0	0

Castro	.846	8	6	5	2	0
Freel	1.000	2	3	3	0	1
Keppinger	1.000	3	10	7	0	2
Lopez	1.000	1	1	1	0	1
Phillips	.990	156	341	433	8	113

Third Base	PCT	G	PO	A	E	DP
Bellhorn	1.000	2	0	4	0	0
Cantu	—	1	0	0	0	0
Castro	.944	17	8	9	1	0
Conine	—	1	0	0	0	0
Encarnacion	.953	137	112	212	16	21
Freel	.958	19	17	29	2	3
Keppinger	.968	13	7	23	1	3

Shortstop	PCT	G	PO	A	E	DP
Castro	1.000	16	10	27	0	5
Cruz	.000	1	0	0	1	0

Gonzalez	.963	103	147	264	16	73
Keppinger	.989	47	62	124	2	27
Lopez	.979	12	23	24	1	10
Phillips	1.000	1	0	1	0	0

Outfield	PCT	G	PO	A	E	DP
Coats	.952	12	18	2	1	0
Conine	1.000	1	1	0	0	0
Dunn	.976	144	244	4	6	0
Ellison	1.000	26	44	1	0	0
Freel	.986	60	136	3	2	0
Griffey Jr.	.974	133	291	5	8	2
Hamilton	.981	84	200	7	4	2
Hopper	.995	92	197	5	1	1
Keppinger	1.000	2	6	1	0	0
Votto	.933	6	14	0	1	0
Wise	1.000	4	6	0	0	0

LOUISVILLE BATS   TRIPLE-A

INTERNATIONAL LEAGUE

BATTING	B-T	HT	WT	DOB	AVG	vLH	vRH	G	AB	R	H	2B	3B	HR	RBI	BB	HBP	SH	SF	SO	SB	CS	SLG	OBP
Bannon, Jeff	R-R	6-3	180	8-21-79	.240	.337	.195	93	313	33	75	13	1	4	41	22	2	5	3	61	3	0	.326	.291
Bellhorn, Mark	B-R	6-1	205	8-23-74	.255	.266	.250	98	326	38	83	23	0	12	57	63	6	1	3	93	0	0	.436	.382
Bolivar, Luis	B-R	6-0	180	2-15-81	.262	.091	.323	13	42	7	11	1	0	1	7	4	1	2	0	11	3	0	.357	.340
Boscan, J.C.	R-R	6-2	215	12-26-79	.286	.400	.250	8	21	0	6	0	0	1	5	0	0	1	0	5	0	0	.286	.407
Bruce, Jay	L-L	6-2	218	4-3-87	.305	.298	.307	50	187	28	57	12	2	11	25	15	1	0	1	48	2	2	.567	.358
Cantu, Jorge	R-R	6-3	200	1-30-82	.309	.273	.319	24	94	12	29	9	0	2	13	5	3	0	0	15	0	0	.468	.363
2-team (24 Durham)					.276	—	—	48	185	24	51	14	1	3	23	13	3	0	1	36	0	0	.411	.332
Coats, Buck	L-R	6-3	195	6-9-82	.438	.250	.500	4	16	1	7	2	0	0	4	1	0	0	0	5	2	0	.563	.471
Conway, Dan	R-R	6-2	220	10-13-79	.158	.222	.138	24	76	7	12	1	0	1	5	8	2	1	1	23	0	1	.211	.253
Crosby, Bubba	L-L	5-11	195	8-11-76	.128	.071	.160	13	39	4	5	1	1	1	5	6	1	1	0	11	1	1	.282	.261
Dickerson, Christopher	L-L	6-3	225	4-10-82	.260	.250	.263	104	354	58	92	11	6	13	44	52	5	3	2	131	23	5	.435	.361
Edwards, Mike	R-R	6-1	200	11-24-76	.256	.212	.278	46	160	25	41	12	0	2	21	14	0	6	2	26	5	0	.369	.313
2-team (3 Indianapolis)					.251	—	—	49	167	26	42	12	0	2	21	14	1	6	2	26	5	0	.359	.310
Encarnacion, Edwin	R-R	6-1	215	1-7-83	.413	.364	.429	11	46	12	19	3	0	3	7	1	0	0	0	4	1	0	.674	.426
Freel, Ryan	R-R	5-10	185	3-8-76	.333	.333	.333	8	33	6	11	2	0	0	3	2	0	0	2	2	0	.394	.389
Godwin, Tyrell	L-R	6-0	200	7-10-79	.241	.238	.241	26	108	12	26	7	1	0	10	7	0	0	2	18	3	2	.324	.287
2-team (15 Columbus)					.234	—	—	41	145	14	34	8	1	0	11	9	0	0	24	4	3	.303	.279
Gutierrez, Jesse	R-R	6-2	195	6-16-78	.276	.338	.254	88	268	31	74	16	1	7	34	20	3	0	3	46	0	1	.422	.330
Hamilton, Josh	L-L	6-4	235	5-21-81	.350	.333	.360	11	40	9	14	1	0	4	8	5	0	0	0	9	3	0	.675	.422
Hanigan, Ryan	R-R	6-0	195	8-16-80	.252	.353	.236	41	127	16	32	5	0	1	9	14	2	6	1	15	0	0	.315	.333
Herr, Aaron	R-R	6-0	205	3-7-81	.274	.303	.264	132	507	75	139	31	5	19	83	39	4	0	5	144	9	4	.467	.328
Hopper, Norris	R-R	5-10	210	3-24-79	.267	.000	.308	4	15	2	4	0	0	0	1	1	0	0	1	2	0	.267	.353
Janish, Paul	R-R	6-2	190	10-12-82	.221	.327	.187	55	199	20	44	8	1	3	19	14	2	11	1	31	2	0	.317	.278
Jorgensen, Ryan	R-R	6-2	205	5-4-79	.237	.194	.251	73	249	29	59	16	0	2	26	21	0	5	4	52	1	0	.325	.292
Keppinger, Jeff	R-R	6-0	180	4-21-80	.368	.446	.337	57	228	31	84	15	1	2	18	23	1	6	3	14	1	1	.469	.424
Lopez, Pedro	R-R	6-1	160	4-28-84	.339	.327	.347	34	124	20	42	5	1	1	17	13	0	4	2	12	3	0	.427	.396
2-team (41 Charlotte)					.284	—	—	75	285	40	81	13	1	3	28	28	0	9	2	38	4	3	.368	.346
Machado, Anderson	L-R	5-11	160	1-25-81	.223	.186	.230	107	278	45	62	7	4	4	25	54	2	7	1	73	11	3	.320	.352
Moeller, Chad	R-R	6-3	215	2-18-75	.250	.250	.250	16	48	5	12	5	0	3	10	4	0	0	0	12	0	0	.542	.308
Ross, David	R-R	6-2	240	3-19-77	.222	.333	.000	3	9	0	2	1	0	0	1	0	0	1	0	0	0	0	.333	.364
Snyder, Earl	R-R	6-0	210	5-6-76	.202	.294	.167	43	124	14	25	5	0	4	16	13	2	0	0	29	0	1	.339	.288
2-team (73 Charlotte)					.215	—	—	116	404	53	87	21	0	13	53	37	3	0	5	95	0	1.364.283	
Votto, Joey	L-R	6-3	220	9-10-83	.294	.242	.311	133	496	74	146	21	2	22	92	70	5	0	9	110	17	10	.478	.381
Wise, Dewayne	L-L	6-1	195	2-24-78	.251	.237	.254	54	207	34	52	11	7	7	20	8	2	4	1	56	8	2	.473	.284

PITCHING	B-T	HT	WT	DOB	W	L	ERA	G	GS	CG	SV	IP	H	R	ER	HR	BB	SO	AVG	vLH	vRH	K/9	BB/9
Bailey, Homer	R-R	6-4	205	5-3-86	6	3	3.07	12	12	0	0	67	49	29	23	4	32	59	.204	.165	.237	7.89	4.28
Belisle, Matt	R-R	6-3	230	6-6-80	0	1	3.00	1	1	0	0	6	7	4	2	0	2	7	.269	.200	.364	10.50	3.00
Bray, Bill	L-L	6-3	220	6-5-83	1	2	4.26	18	0	0	0	19	19	10	9	1	6	29	.247	.133	.319	13.74	2.84
Bumatay, Mike	L-L	6-0	170	10-9-79	0	0	20.25	3	0	0	0	1	3	3	3	0	3	1	.500	1.000	.400	6.75	20.25
Burton, Jared	R-R	6-5	230	6-2-81	1	0	0.64	10	0	0	1	14	11	1	1	0	4	13	.224	.222	.226	8.36	2.57
Coffey, Todd	R-R	6-5	255	9-9-80	2	0	1.33	19	0	0	1	27	17	4	4	0	5	25	.185	.205	.170	8.33	1.67
Coutlangus, Jonathan	L-L	6-1	185	10-21-80	2	0	6.35	9	0	0	0	11	14	9	8	3	7	14	.311	.313	.310	11.12	5.56
Cueto, Johnny	R-R	5-10	198	2-15-86	2	1	2.05	4	4	0	0	22	22	5	5	2	2	21	.259	.262	.256	8.59	0.82
DeJesus, Misael	R-R	6-3	190	11-4-84	0	0	0.00	1	0	0	0	1	1	1	0	0	1	3	.200	.333	.000	27.00	9.00
Donaldson, Daniel	R-L	6-4	180	7-23-84	0	0	21.00	2	0	0	0	3	4	7	7	0	6	3	.333	.250	.375	9.00	18.00
Dumatrait, Phil	R-L	6-2	200	7-12-81	10	6	3.53	22	22	0	0	125	114	57	49	10	49	76	.242	.248	.239	5.47	3.53
Gardner, Richie	R-R	6-2	201	2-1-82	4	5	5.71	13	13	0	0	65	82	43	41	10	20	41	.318	.339	.300	5.71	2.78
Gosling, Mike	L-L	6-2	210	9-23-80	5	3	3.00	13	13	0	0	78	71	31	26	7	23	65	.242	.195	.259	7.50	2.65
Guardado, Eddie	R-L	6-0	225	10-2-70	0	0	4.50	9	0	0	0	8	11	4	4	2	4	3	.355	.444	.318	3.38	4.50
Guerrero, Daniel	R-R	6-1	190	7-21-85	1	0	3.60	1	1	0	0	5	3	2	2	1	0	2	.176	.200	.143	3.60	0.00
Kelly, Steven	R-R	6-0	210	9-30-79	1	6	7.57	20	8	1	0	52	76	50	44	7	27	27	.349	.323	.369	4.64	4.64
Kershner, Jason	L-L	6-2	190	12-19-76	5	4	4.00	39	3	0	1	63	57	28	28	7	19	42	.253	.277	.244	6.00	2.71
Livingston, Bobby	L-L	6-3	205	9-3-82	3	4	3.80	17	16	1	0	104	123	47	44	7	17	63	.299	.198	.334	5.43	1.47
Majewski, Gary	R-R	6-1	220	2-26-80	1	1	3.96	38	0	0	4	39	33	17	17	2	15	30	.239	.302	.200	6.98	3.49
Mallett, Justin	R-R	6-6	211	11-11-81	1	0	0.00	1	1	0	0	5	4	2	0	0	1	5	.222	.143	.273	9.00	1.80
Maloney, Matthew	L-L	6-4	220	1-16-84	2	1	3.18	3	3	0	0	17	10	6	6	2	6	23	.169	.091	.188	12.18	3.18
Manon, Julio	R-R	6-0	200	6-10-73	1	0	0.00	5	0	0	1	4	3	1	0	0	3	4	.100	.000	.111	12.00	9.00
McBeth, Marcus	R-R	6-2	195	8-23-80	1	1	2.56	30	0	0	12	32	33	12	9	2	7	29	.260	.304	.225	8.24	1.99
Medlock, Calvin	R-R	5-10	195	11-8-82	2	1	5.63	13	0	0	0	16	17	10	10	0	14	17	.270	.154	.351	9.56	7.88
2-team (9 Durham)					4	1	4.55	22	0	0	0	32	26	17	16	2	23	25	—	—	—	7.11	6.54
Pelland, Tyler	R-L	6-0	198	10-9-83	1	1	3.04	19	0	0	0	24	17	9	8	1	7	27	.213	.111	.242	10.27	2.66

ORGANIZATION STATISTICS

Name	B-T	HT	WT	DOB	W	L	ERA	G	GS	CG	SV	IP	H	R	ER	HR	BB	SO	AVG	vLH	vRH	K/9	BB/9
Ramirez, Elizardo	B-R	6-0	190	1-28-83	4	3	3.74	12	12	0	0	65	71	28	27	4	19	44	.280	.239	.314	6.09	2.63
Ramirez, Ramon	R-R	5-10	172	9-16-82	1	0	0.00	5	2	0	0	15	7	0	0		6	16	.149	.200	.091	9.82	3.68
Saarloos, Kirk	R-R	6-0	180	5-23-79	0	2	3.95	18	5	0	0	41	47	19	18	3	9	28	.287	.329	.253	6.15	1.98
Salmon, Brad	L-R	6-4	225	1-3-80	2	2	3.56	37	0	0	4	43	41	19	17	3	17	40	.253	.309	.213	8.37	3.56
Santos, Victor	R-R	6-2	205	10-2-76	1	1	1.11	8	4	0	0	24	24	6	3	1	5	15	.258	.190	.314	5.55	1.85
Shackelford, Brian	L-L	6-1	205	8-30-76	0	5	4.96	41	0	0	1	33	34	20	18	0	13	14	.272	.296	.254	3.86	3.58
2-team (11 Durham)					0	5	4.47	52	0	0	1	44	45	24	22	3	17	21	—	—	—	4.26	3.45
Shearn, Tom	R-R	6-4	230	8-28-77	7	10	4.20	26	24	0	0	144	153	72	67	9	51	109	.276	.252	.298	6.83	3.19
Stone, Ricky	R-R	6-1	195	2-28-75	5	6	1.87	59	0	0	16	63	50	15	13	4	11	39	.219	.202	.231	5.60	1.58
Till, Brock	R-R	5-10	210	7-1-80	0	0	6.23	4	0	0	0	4	11	3	3	0	1	5	.500	.636	.364	10.38	2.08
Wilkerson, Wes	R-R	6-4	215	9-11-76	2	1	3.93	26	0	0	0	37	35	18	16	3	18	21	.246	.222	.266	5.15	4.42

FIELDING

Catcher	PCT	G	PO	A	E	DP	PB
Boscan	1.000	7	50	5	0	2	1
Conway	1.000	23	132	11	0	0	1
Hanigan	1.000	34	213	32	0	4	1
Jorgensen	.983	72	489	42	9	2	2
Moeller	1.000	11	85	4	0	1	1
Ross	1.000	3	16	2	0	0	1

First Base	PCT	G	PO	A	E	DP
Cantu	.988	11	74	6	1	9
Gutierrez	.997	40	284	22	1	30
Hanigan	1.000	2	10	1	0	3
Keppinger	.933	5	24	4	2	2
Snyder	.969	6	58	4	2	8
Votto	.989	94	823	79	10	94

Second Base	PCT	G	PO	A	E	DP
Bannon	1.000	1	0	3	0	0
Bellhorn	.972	50	97	145	7	34
Bolivar	1.000	5	10	13	0	1
Cantu	1.000	12	26	36	0	8
Herr	.986	56	119	161	4	48
Keppinger	1.000	21	45	59	0	11
Machado	.974	11	15	23	1	4

Third Base	PCT	G	PO	A	E	DP
Bannon	1.000	7	5	7	0	3
Bolivar	1.000	7	3	19	0	3
Edwards	.000	1	0	0	1	0
Encarnacion	.900	11	7	20	3	1
Freel	1.000	1	0	1	0	0
Gutierrez	—	1	0	0	0	0
Herr	.919	70	39	142	16	11
Keppinger	.923	22	14	34	4	7
Machado	.952	15	12	28	2	6
Snyder	.954	28	9	53	3	7

Shortstop	PCT	G	PO	A	E	DP
Bannon	.800	2	4	4	2	1
Bellhorn	.929	13	19	33	4	9
Janish	.953	55	62	159	11	32
Keppinger	1.000	3	0	3	0	1
Lopez	.958	33	37	99	6	20
Machado	.979	54	90	141	5	39
Snyder	1.000	1	1	0	0	0

Outfield	PCT	G	PO	A	E	DP
Bannon	.969	81	123	3	4	0
Bruce	.975	50	111	6	3	2
Coats	1.000	4	13	0	0	0
Crosby	1.000	10	24	0	0	0
Dickerson	.960	104	215	2	9	0
Edwards	.989	44	88	2	1	0
Freel	1.000	5	9	1	0	1
Godwin	.955	25	42	0	2	0
Hamilton	.895	9	17	0	2	0
Hopper	.833	4	5	0	1	0
Keppinger	1.000	15	11	1	0	1
Machado	.929	19	24	2	2	0
Votto	.961	41	70	4	3	3
Wise	.992	54	119	3	1	0

CHATTANOOGA LOOKOUTS   DOUBLE-A

SOUTHERN LEAGUE

BATTING	B-T	HT	WT	DOB	AVG	vLH	vRH	G	AB	R	H	2B	3B	HR	RBI	BB	HBP	SH	SF	SO	SB	CS	SLG	OBP
Anderson, Drew	B-R	5-9	170	2-2-83	.250	.282	.237	128	516	76	129	31	8	11	57	50	1	10	3	121	11	6	.405	.316
Bolivar, Luis	B-R	6-0	180	2-15-81	.297	.287	.303	109	350	48	104	21	9	3	42	24	7	3	2	72	13	5	.434	.352
Boscan, J.C.	R-R	6-2	215	12-26-79	.198	.214	.190	30	86	7	17	1	0	1	9	24	0	0	1	21	1	0	.244	.369
Bruce, Jay	L-L	6-2	218	4-3-87	.333	.286	.356	16	66	10	22	7	1	4	15	8	0	0	0	20	2	1	.652	.405
Castro, Jose	B-R	5-8	160	11-5-86	.278	.364	.256	13	54	5	15	2	1	0	1	2	2	1	0	8	1	0	.352	.328
Conway, Dan	R-R	6-2	220	10-13-79	.231	.167	.286	5	13	0	3	1	0	0	0	1	0	1	0	2	0	0	.308	.286
Cosme, Caonabo	R-R	6-2	160	3-18-79	.276	.299	.265	92	293	42	81	19	2	12	53	11	0	2	3	84	5	0	.478	.300
Cruz, Enrique	R-R	6-1	205	11-21-81	.267	.336	.235	128	484	60	129	29	1	7	62	42	0	7	6	116	12	4	.374	.321
Cumberland, Shaun	L-R	6-2	185	8-1-84	.301	.167	.326	31	113	11	34	9	0	1	17	7	3	0	1	20	1	1	.407	.355
2-team (99 Montgomery)					.259	—		130	467	44	121	23	2	7	51	36	4	2	3	91	4	9	.362	.316
Dickerson, Christopher	L-L	6-3	225	4-10-82	.272	.167	.321	30	114	11	31	4	1	1	11	7	2	0	0	31	7	2	.351	.325
Dorn, Daniel	L-L	6-2	205	7-20-84	.311	.100	.338	26	90	20	28	6	1	8	21	15	3	0	1	23	1	0	.667	.422
Garthwaite, Jay	R-R	6-2	220	11-26-80	.238	.230	.242	89	252	25	60	10	0	10	37	19	2	1	2	83	1	1	.421	.295
Godwin, Tyrell	L-R	6-0	200	7-10-79	.249	.275	.242	79	245	35	61	14	0	7	30	35	2	0	0	51	6	6	.392	.348
Griffin, Michael	R-R	5-10	182	10-1-83	.327	.339	.321	47	165	19	54	10	4	3	21	10	1	0	2	26	5	0	.491	.365
Gutierrez, Jesse	R-R	6-2	195	6-16-78	.325	.455	.276	16	40	4	13	4	0	1	5	1	1	0	1	7	0	0	.500	.349
Gutierrez, Tonys	L-L	6-1	220	8-18-83	.274	.267	.275	53	135	12	37	7	0	2	17	24	1	0	3	35	5	1	.370	.380
Hanigan, Ryan	R-R	6-0	195	8-16-80	.299	.354	.282	60	197	30	59	14	1	3	27	41	3	2	4	30	0	2	.426	.420
Henry, Sean	R-R	5-10	154	8-18-85	.241	.364	.213	14	58	9	14	3	2	0	2	6	2	1	0	11	1	1	.345	.333
Janish, Paul	R-R	6-2	190	10-12-82	.244	.315	.216	88	324	46	79	21	2	1	20	50	9	5	3	54	10	3	.330	.358
Perez, Miguel	R-R	6-3	190	9-25-83	.269	.333	.261	8	26	3	7	1	0	3	4	0	0	0	3	0	0	.654	.269
Piepkorn, Jeremiah	R-R	6-3	200	2-18-81	.158	.222	.100	7	19	1	3	0	0	1	1	1	0	0	0	1	0	0	.316	.200
Purdom, John	R-R	6-2	230	5-28-81	.000	.000	.000	1	4	1	0	0	0	0	0	3	0	0	2	1	0	0	.000	.000
2-team (15 Carolina)					.231	—	—	16	39	4	9	1	0	1	10	3	0	0	2	7	0	0	.333	.273
Rosales, Adam	R-R	6-1	193	5-20-83	.278	.241	.295	67	255	51	71	18	6	13	31	37	5	2	3	66	4	4	.549	.377
Strait, Cody	R-R	6-1	180	5-28-83	.216	.179	.228	58	218	31	47	15	0	7	29	17	4	1	2	64	11	2	.381	.282
Tatum, Craig	R-R	6-0	217	3-18-83	.231	.224	.235	46	173	21	40	10	1	2	22	17	1	0	3	49	0	1	.335	.299
Williams, Marland	R-R	5-9	185	6-22-81	.215	.243	.202	104	321	38	69	6	6	11	44	34	2	1	1	143	14	7	.374	.293

PITCHING	B-T	HT	WT	DOB	W	L	ERA	G	GS	CG	SV	IP	H	R	ER	HR	BB	SO	AVG	vLH	vRH	K/9	BB/9
Asadoorian, Rick	R-R	6-2	198	7-23-80	1	1	3.59	37	0	0	0	53	40	23	21	5	28	48	.209	.270	.171	8.20	4.78
Avery, James	R-R	6-1	210	6-10-84	11	10	5.22	27	27	0	0	147	162	96	85	16	59	96	.287	.274	.297	5.89	3.62
Bohorquez, Carlos	R-R	5-10	195	10-6-81	3	2	4.02	22	0	0	0	31	28	14	14	1	19	23	.239	.277	.214	6.61	5.46
Bumatay, Mike	L-L	6-0	170	10-9-79	1	1	4.74	25	0	0	2	25	26	13	13	1	10	30	.268	.167	.313	10.95	3.65
Burton, Jared	R-R	6-5	230	6-2-81	0	1	11.81	9	0	0	0	5	10	7	7	0	5	3	.400	.375	.412	5.06	8.44
Cosme, Caonabo	R-R	6-2	160	3-18-79	1	0	9.00	1	0	0	0	1	1	1	1	0	1	1	.250	.000	.500	9.00	9.00
Cueto, Johnny	R-R	5-10	198	2-15-86	6	3	3.10	10	10	0	0	61	52	24	21	6	11	77	.231	.231	.231	11.36	1.62
Fisher, Carlos	R-R	6-3	215	2-22-83	5	9	4.29	21	21	0	0	113	127	61	54	11	42	94	.291	.340	.248	7.46	3.34
Flannery, Mike	R-R	6-1	195	9-20-79	0	1	7.08	17	0	0	1	20	24	17	16	2	12	21	.293	.308	.286	9.30	5.31
Gardner, Richie	R-R	6-2	201	2-1-82	2	1	1.82	6	6	0	0	35	27	10	7	1	8	33	.214	.286	.179	8.57	2.08
Guevara, Carlos	R-R	5-11	190	3-18-82	1	2	2.32	51	0	0	16	62	51	17	16	4	23	87	.226	.183	.256	12.63	3.34
Kelly, Steven	R-R	6-0	210	9-30-79	0	3	4.78	7	5	0	0	26	36	18	14	2	7	19	.336	.333	.339	6.49	2.39
Lecure, Sam	R-R	6-1	190	5-4-84	7	5	4.17	21	21	0	0	110	119	55	51	12	46	104	.281	.295	.267	8.51	3.76
Lockwood, Luke	L-L	6-3	170	7-21-81	1	7	5.53	14	12	0	0	70	90	53	43	8	22	52	.320	.236	.341	6.69	2.83
Lutz, Derrik	R-R	6-0	210	4-22-85	1	0	1.13	7	0	0	0	8	2	1	1	0	2	5	.154	.300	.063	5.62	2.25
Mallett, Justin	R-R	6-6	210	11-11-81	3	6	4.73	44	0	0	1	91	82	50	48	7	46	88	.247	.293	.216	8.67	4.53
Maloney, Matthew	L-L	6-4	220	1-16-84	2	2	2.57	4	4	0	0	28	17	9	8	4	3	39	.175	.222	.157	12.54	0.96
Medlock, Calvin	R-R	5-10	195	11-8-82	2	2	2.64	29	0	0	2	48	35	14	14	3	5	59	.202	.161	.225	11.14	0.94

				W	L	ERA	G	GS	CG	SV	IP	H	R	ER	HR	BB	SO	AVG	vLH	vRH	K/9	BB/9
Pelland, Tyler	R-L	6-0	198	10-9-83	5	4	3.95	35	5	0	2	66	63	40	29	6	32	71	.251	.154	.285	9.68	4.36
Ramirez, Ramon	R-R	5-10	172	9-16-82	5	1	4.60	16	0	0	1	31	30	16	16	3	12	35	.254	.231	.273	10.05	3.45
Roenicke, Josh	R-R	6-3	195	8-4-82	1	1	0.95	19	0	0	8	19	12	3	2	0	6	15	.185	.242	.125	7.11	2.84
Ruzic, Dushan	R-R	6-8	277	1-5-82	1	2	4.24	13	0	0	0	23	19	13	11	3	12	19	.232	.244	.216	7.33	4.63
Till, Brock	R-R	5-10	210	7-1-80	4	1	3.56	38	0	0	1	43	42	22	17	1	15	25	.256	.310	.226	5.23	3.14
Vazquez, Camilo	L-L	6-0	180	10-3-83	4	8	5.14	21	21	0	0	112	133	75	64	9	42	85	.296	.354	.283	6.83	3.38
Viola, Pedro	L-L	6-1	185	6-29-83	0	0	0.95	14	0	0	2	19	12	3	2	2	6	17	.176	.167	.184	8.05	2.84

FIELDING

Catcher	PCT	G	PO	A	E	DP	PB
Boscan	.996	30	248	22	1	4	0
Conway	1.000	3	25	2	0	0	0
Hanigan	.992	56	463	41	4	4	1
Perez	1.000	6	43	4	0	1	0
Purdom	1.000	1	5	0	0	0	0
Tatum	.983	46	372	44	7	4	5

First Base	PCT	G	PO	A	E	DP
Bolivar	1.000	2	11	1	0	2
Cosme	.997	30	281	21	1	31
Garthwaite	.973	9	66	7	2	6
J. Gutierrez	1.000	10	72	4	0	2
T. Gutierrez	.988	34	238	13	3	13
Hanigan	1.000	2	14	0	0	0
Piepkorn	1.000	5	29	3	0	3
Rosales	.988	57	459	41	6	46

Second Base	PCT	G	PO	A	E	DP
Anderson	.972	101	184	260	13	51
Bolivar	.990	22	39	57	1	11
Cosme	.900	6	9	9	2	4
Griffin	1.000	2	3	4	0	0
Janish	.964	13	21	33	2	7

Third Base	PCT	G	PO	A	E	DP
Bolivar	.930	15	6	34	3	4
Cosme	.895	7	3	14	2	1
Cruz	.924	105	64	178	20	6
Griffin	.900	8	5	13	2	0
Janish	1.000	4	14	0	1	0
Rosales	1.000	3	2	5	0	1

Shortstop	PCT	G	PO	A	E	DP
Bolivar	.896	17	26	34	7	8
Castro	.982	13	23	33	1	10
Cosme	.941	29	44	67	7	21
Cruz	.962	16	18	33	2	7
Janish	.974	68	93	205	8	37
Rosales	1.000	2	4	8	0	3

Outfield	PCT	G	PO	A	E	DP
Anderson	.977	25	42	1	1	1
Bolivar	.963	35	50	2	2	0
Bruce	1.000	15	27	1	0	1
Cumberland	.945	30	68	1	4	1
Dickerson	.968	30	60	1	2	0
Dorn	1.000	14	25	2	0	2
Garthwaite	.978	35	44	1	1	0
Godwin	.989	64	87	2	1	0
Griffin	.981	31	50	2	1	0
T. Gutierrez	.667	3	1	1	1	0
Henry	.974	14	38	0	1	0
Rosales	1.000	2	6	1	0	1
Strait	.992	55	107	10	1	2
Williams	1.000	84	194	9	0	2

SARASOTA REDS
HIGH CLASS A
FLORIDA STATE LEAGUE

BATTING	B-T	HT	WT	DOB	AVG	vLH	vRH	G	AB	R	H	2B	3B	HR	RBI	BB	HBP	SH	SF	SO	SB	CS	SLG	OBP
Bruce, Jay	L-L	6-2	218	4-3-87	.325	.298	.337	67	268	49	87	27	5	11	49	24	2	0	4	67	4	4	.586	.379
Cabrera, Gerardo	R-R	6-0	190	12-23-83	.213	.160	.232	34	94	9	20	3	0	1	9	12	0	0	1	20	1	1	.277	.299
DeJesus, Michael	L-R	5-8	173	7-16-83	.261	.237	.271	113	417	76	109	12	2	4	29	78	3	8	2	52	4	6	.329	.380
Dorn, Daniel	L-L	6-2	205	7-20-84	.281	.214	.303	92	338	49	95	21	1	12	66	32	12	0	5	69	3	1	.456	.359
Esquer, Anthony	R-R	6-1	215	9-3-84	.182	.000	.211	9	22	0	4	0	0	0	1	0	0	0	0	5	0	0	.182	.182
Eymann, Eric	R-R	6-2	191	2-9-84	.246	.239	.249	130	491	61	121	28	4	8	53	23	4	4	5	103	3	3	.369	.283
Griffin, Michael	R-R	5-10	182	10-1-83	.303	.324	.295	90	386	65	117	24	2	7	45	21	2	2	7	47	12	6	.430	.337
Gutierrez, Tonys	L-L	6-1	220	8-18-83	.302	.304	.302	66	225	41	68	8	2	1	25	42	1	0	3	36	1	0	.369	.410
Heisey, Chris	R-R	6-0	200	12-14-84	.349	.214	.414	12	43	6	15	1	0	1	5	4	0	1	1	6	3	1	.442	.396
Holden, Josh	L-L	6-0	219	12-10-80	.251	.268	.247	77	219	21	55	2	4	0	17	18	5	2	1	47	15	5	.297	.321
Hopper, Norris	R-R	5-10	200	3-24-79	.294	1.000	.250	4	17	1	5	0	0	0	2	0	0	0	0	2	0	0	.294	.294
Kainer, Carson	R-R	6-1	210	10-27-84	.290	.250	.310	18	62	10	18	5	1	1	8	5	0	1	0	16	0	0	.452	.343
Kendrick, Wayne	R-R	5-6	160	2-11-85	.261	.500	.211	9	23	3	6	2	0	0	1	0	0	0	0	1	0	1	.348	.261
Keppinger, Jeff	R-R	6-0	180	4-21-80	.333	.400	.286	3	12	1	4	2	0	0	1	0	0	0	0	1	0	0	.500	.308
Kroski, Chris	L-R	6-1	218	5-17-82	.281	.310	.275	70	224	32	63	18	2	6	29	27	5	0	2	42	0	1	.460	.368
Perez, Miguel	R-R	6-3	190	9-25-83	.324	.276	.342	30	108	12	35	5	0	4	18	6	0	0	2	19	0	0	.481	.353
Piepkorn, Jeremiah	R-R	6-3	200	2-18-81	.256	.226	.267	61	223	29	57	14	1	8	35	13	3	2	1	54	1	1	.435	.304
Purdom, John	R-R	6-2	230	5-28-81	.077	.000	1.000	7	13	0	1	1	0	0	3	2	0	0	0	1	0	0	.154	.200
2-team (44 Jupiter)					.255	—		51	157	12	40	7	0	3	31	16	0	3	2	21	1	1	.357	.320
Rosales, Adam	R-R	6-1	193	5-20-83	.294	.299	.293	69	248	47	73	23	5	8	48	31	13	2	6	46	9	2	.488	.393
Strait, Cody	R-R	6-1	180	5-28-83	.241	.360	.213	69	266	39	64	15	4	7	39	17	3	1	3	56	15	7	.406	.291
Suarez, Gabriel	R-R	6-0	188	12-14-84	.000	.000	.000	1	3	0	0	0	0	0	0	0	0	0	0	0	0	0	.000	.000
Szymanski, Brandon	B-R	6-5	210	10-1-82	.242	.257	.237	123	434	63	105	17	4	14	59	28	3	1	3	153	9	4	.396	.291
Tablado, Raul	R-R	6-2	195	3-3-82	.143	.111	.167	8	21	1	3	2	0	0	2	5	0	0	0	4	0	0	.238	.308
Tatum, Craig	R-R	6-0	217	3-18-83	.320	.242	.353	58	219	29	70	15	0	10	39	9	1	1	1	41	0	1	.525	.348
Tordi, Justin	R-R	6-1	208	4-9-84	.221	.190	.232	25	77	6	17	5	0	0	6	2	0	0	0	18	0	0	.286	.294
Turner, Justin	R-R	5-11	190	11-23-84	.200	.333	.176	6	20	2	4	0	0	0	2	0	0	0	0	2	0	0	.200	.238
Valaika, Chris	R-R	6-1	200	8-14-85	.253	.240	.257	57	217	26	55	9	1	2	23	13	6	2	3	42	0	3	.332	.310
Witt, Paul	R-R	5-11	180	12-8-82	.048	.000	.077	16	21	1	1	0	0	0	0	3	1	1	0	8	0	0	.048	.200

PITCHING	B-T	HT	WT	DOB	W	L	ERA	G	GS	CG	SV	IP	H	R	ER	HR	BB	SO	AVG	vLH	vRH	K/9	BB/9
Asadoorian, Rick	R-R	6-2	198	7-23-80	0	0	1.29	12	0	0	0	14	11	2	2	0	9	12	.229	.353	.161	7.71	5.79
Bailey, Homer	R-R	6-4	205	5-3-86	0	1	10.13	2	2	0	0	8	15	9	9	2	5	7	.385	.318	.471	7.88	5.62
Bohorquez, Carlos	R-R	5-10	195	10-6-81	2	1	5.77	23	0	0	1	39	51	31	25	1	18	30	.309	.313	.306	6.92	4.15
Bray, Bill	L-L	6-2	220	6-5-83	0	0	0.00	2	0	0	0	2	0	0	0	0	1	2	.000	.000	.000	9.00	4.50
Cueto, Johnny	R-R	5-10	198	2-15-86	4	5	3.33	14	14	1	0	78	72	34	29	3	21	72	.238	.252	.230	8.27	2.41
Denham, Dan	R-R	6-2	195	12-24-82	3	1	4.61	12	0	0	0	27	24	20	14	2	17	22	.229	.178	.267	7.24	5.60
Donaldson, Daniel	R-L	6-4	180	7-23-84	0	2	2.55	10	0	0	0	18	18	5	5	1	12	17	.261	.192	.302	8.66	6.11
Fisher, Carlos	R-R	6-3	215	2-22-83	4	1	2.20	7	7	0	0	41	34	12	10	1	7	41	.221	.243	.202	9.00	1.54
Gardner, Richie	R-R	6-2	201	2-1-82	5	1	1.65	7	7	0	0	44	29	10	8	1	9	25	.187	.169	.200	5.15	1.85
Gressick, Anthony	R-R	6-3	200	1-1-84	0	0	12.15	5	0	0	0	7	10	9	9	0	8	5	.323	.333	.313	6.75	10.80
Gunter, Kevin	R-R	6-3	210	11-5-83	1	0	1.93	7	0	0	0	9	10	4	2	0	2	8	.270	.250	.280	7.71	1.93
Jukich, Ben	L-L	6-4	190	10-17-82	8	2	3.55	14	14	2	0	76	59	33	30	2	27	71	.215	.226	.212	8.41	3.20
Lanier, Bo	R-R	5-11	167	11-20-82	2	0	7.50	11	0	0	0	12	10	10	10	2	17	8	.217	.083	.265	6.00	12.75
Lecure, Sam	R-R	6-1	190	5-4-84	1	0	1.80	1	1	0	0	5	2	1	1	0	0	8	.125	.125	.125	14.40	0.00
Lutz, Derrik	R-R	6-0	210	4-22-85	3	5	3.15	54	0	0	23	60	63	27	21	2	21	49	.274	.244	.289	7.35	3.15
Manon, Julio	R-R	6-0	200	6-10-73	0	0	18.00	1	0	0	0	1	3	2	2	0	0	0	.500	.000	.750	0.00	0.00
Manuel, Robert	R-R	6-3	197	7-9-83	6	5	4.03	33	11	0	1	98	100	47	44	3	22	93	.265	.267	.263	8.51	2.01
Medina, Ruben	R-R	5-11	157	7-28-86	5	3	1.78	44	0	0	1	66	53	20	13	2	30	53	.226	.267	.201	7.26	4.11
Montano, Luis	R-R	6-0	180	3-20-85	2	1	6.75	5	0	0	1	9	12	6	6	2	6	12	.340	.588	.200	9.00	4.50
Ondrusek, Logan	R-R	6-7	209	2-13-85	7	10	4.43	31	22	0	1	124	131	72	61	4	48	86	.278	.385	.210	6.24	3.48
Pauly, Thomas	R-R	6-2	208	7-28-81	0	0	5.79	13	1	0	0	19	16	12	12	2	15	15	.235	.286	.213	7.23	7.23
Pointer, Adam	R-R	5-11	190	9-21-84	0	0	9.00	2	0	0	0	2	2	2	2	0	4	1	.333	.000	.500	4.50	18.00
Rafael, Juan	R-R	6-2	165	12-4-85	1	1	2.65	7	2	0	1	17	16	5	5	1	7	13	.250	.179	.306	6.88	3.71

Name	B-T	HT	WT	DOB	W	L	ERA	G	GS	CG	SV	IP	H	R	ER	HR	BB	SO	AVG	vLH	vRH	K/9	BB/9
Ramirez, Ramon	R-R	5-10	172	9-16-82	5	2	4.05	15	12	0	1	73	64	37	33	5	25	86	.232	.193	.259	10.55	3.07
Roenicke, Josh	R-R	6-3	195	8-4-82	2	1	3.25	27	0	0	16	28	23	10	10	1	15	41	.225	.154	.270	13.34	4.88
Rojas, Jose A.	R-R	5-11	195	3-2-83	1	2	4.32	23	0	0	0	33	30	20	16	2	23	41	.242	.280	.216	11.07	6.21
Ruzic, Dushan	R-R	6-8	277	1-5-82	2	1	2.82	30	0	0	1	45	42	16	14	2	14	44	.249	.254	.245	8.87	2.82
Smit, Alexander	L-L	6-3	210	10-2-85	0	2	3.71	4	3	0	0	17	12	10	7	0	8	19	.207	.222	.200	10.06	4.24
2-team (18 Fort Myers)					1	6	5.32	22	11	0	1	68	74	50	40	4	34	57	—	—	—	7.58	4.52
Tabor, Lee	L-L	6-2	175	12-17-84	1	0	5.02	10	0	0	0	14	17	12	8	1	9	11	.288	.067	.364	6.91	5.65
Thompson, Daryl	R-R	6-1	183	11-2-85	9	5	3.77	22	22	0	0	105	106	51	44	19	31	97	.262	.288	.241	8.31	2.66
Viola, Pedro	L-L	6-1	185	6-29-83	0	1	0.90	10	0	0	2	20	14	2	2	0	7	28	.187	.091	.226	12.60	3.15
Watson, Sean	R-R	6-2	220	7-24-85	4	4	5.43	14	10	0	0	55	54	34	33	8	21	50	.257	.253	.260	8.23	3.46
Wood, Travis	R-L	5-11	166	2-6-87	3	2	4.86	12	12	0	0	46	49	33	25	6	27	54	.268	.273	.267	10.49	5.24

FIELDING

Catcher	PCT	G	PO	A	E	DP	PB
Esquer	.983	9	54	5	1	2	0
Kroski	.991	55	400	32	4	2	7
Perez	.984	28	225	14	4	1	9
Purdom	1.000	3	9	0	0	0	0
Tatum	.985	55	436	33	7	6	11

First Base	PCT	G	PO	A	E	DP
Gutierrez	.987	64	490	26	7	42
Kroski	—	1	0	0	0	0
Piepkorn	.996	28	215	18	1	25
Rosales	.991	49	407	22	4	35
Witt	1.000	3	12	0	0	0

Second Base	PCT	G	PO	A	E	DP
DeJesus	.979	109	200	277	10	57
Griffin	1.000	6	9	20	0	5

	PCT	G	PO	A	E	DP
Kendrick	.960	8	10	14	1	6
Keppinger	1.000	1	2	5	0	0
Tordi	.980	14	20	29	1	7
Turner	1.000	5	10	8	0	2
Witt	1.000	2	3	4	0	2

Third Base	PCT	G	PO	A	E	DP
Eymann	.934	48	35	93	9	5
Griffin	.946	77	54	120	10	4
Keppinger	1.000	2	0	2	0	0
Piepkorn	.667	1	1	1	1	0
Tablado	1.000	5	1	5	0	1
Tordi	.913	12	3	18	2	2

Shortstop	PCT	G	PO	A	E	DP
Eymann	.977	82	117	229	8	53
Rosales	1.000	2	1	3	0	0

	PCT	G	PO	A	E	DP
Suarez	1.000	1	1	3	0	0
Tablado	.800	3	3	5	2	2
Valaika	.956	51	67	127	9	25
Witt	.850	9	6	11	3	0

Outfield	PCT	G	PO	A	E	DP
Bruce	.963	67	154	4	6	1
Cabrera	.986	30	68	0	5	0
Dorn	.991	87	105	5	1	0
Griffin	1.000	2	3	0	0	0
Heisey	.938	11	14	1	1	0
Holden	1.000	41	50	0	0	0
Hopper	1.000	3	3	0	0	0
Kainer	1.000	7	8	0	0	0
Piepkorn	1.000	1	1	0	0	0
Strait	.975	67	148	10	4	3
Szymanski	.950	118	237	8	13	2

DAYTON DRAGONS — LOW CLASS A

MIDWEST LEAGUE

BATTING

Name	B-T	HT	WT	DOB	AVG	vLH	vRH	G	AB	R	H	2B	3B	HR	RBI	BB	HBP	SH	SF	SO	SB	CS	SLG	OBP
Cabrera, Gerardo	R-R	6-0	190	12-23-83	.235	.220	.242	41	136	18	32	6	0	1	8	6	0	0	0	30	1	0	.301	.268
Cozart, Zachary	R-R	6-1	185	8-12-85	.239	.226	.244	53	184	28	44	7	2	2	18	11	2	3	1	36	3	1	.332	.288
Encarnacion, Fernando	R-R	6-0	185	7-23-85	.250	—	.250	1	4	1	1	0	0	0	1	2	0	0	0	0	0	0	1.000	.250
Esquer, Anthony	R-R	6-1	215	9-3-84	.217	.294	.185	52	175	21	38	5	0	0	18	15	1	1	2	27	0	1	.246	.280
Francisco, Juan	B-R	6-2	180	6-24-87	.268	.281	.262	135	534	69	143	21	4	25	90	23	0	2		161	12	6	.463	.301
Frazier, Todd	R-R	6-3	215	2-12-86	.318	.333	.308	6	22	4	7	3	0	2	5	2	0	0	0	4	0	0	.727	.375
Heisey, Chris	R-R	6-0	200	12-14-84	.289	.287	.290	104	374	60	108	24	2	9	46	25	10	5	0	57	19	5	.436	.350
Jones, Keltavious	L-S	5-9	170	9-21-85	.212	.167	.219	24	85	10	18	7	1	0	8	4	3	0	0	23	1	0	.318	.272
Kainer, Carson	R-R	6-1	210	10-27-84	.280	.292	.275	59	225	35	63	10	0	2	33	16	2	0	3	51	2	3	.351	.329
Long, Jacob	R-R	6-1	180	4-17-86	.174	.286	.125	7	23	2	4	1	0	0	1	2	0	1	0	7	0	0	.217	.240
Louwsma, Jason	R-R	6-2	210	9-9-83	.247	.307	.211	99	340	44	84	17	0	7	44	23	7	1	2	68	8	3	.359	.306
Parker, Logan	L-L	6-3	215	7-18-84	.269	.231	.282	115	405	48	109	18	3	9	50	57	0	0	4	95	13	1	.395	.356
Phipps, Denis	R-R	6-2	176	7-22-85	.238	.293	.213	125	450	65	107	14	2	9	53	41	10	0	4	98	18	6	.338	.313
Rodriguez, Eddy	R-R	6-0	205	12-1-85	.236	.247	.230	83	280	32	66	15	0	6	33	16	4	0	2	61	1	1	.354	.285
Rojo, Billy	R-R	5-8	177	4-23-83	.227	.254	.214	61	194	21	44	9	1	1	21	9	3	4	2	43	8	3	.299	.269
Stubbs, Drew	R-R	6-4	200	10-4-84	.270	.242	.283	129	497	93	134	29	5	12	43	69	6	1	2	142	23	15	.421	.364
Tordi, Justin	R-R	6-1	208	4-9-84	.209	.300	.170	24	67	10	14	2	1	0	4	3	1	0	0	14	0	0	.269	.254
Turner, Justin	R-R	5-11	190	11-23-84	.311	.313	.310	117	466	70	145	26	4	10	59	39	9	0	2	72	12	8	.446	.374
Valaika, Chris	R-R	6-1	200	8-14-85	.307	.301	.310	79	300	38	92	20	3	10	56	17	8	0	6	72	1	4	.493	.353
Waring, Brandon	R-R	6-4	195	1-2-86	1.000	—	1.000	1	1	0	1	0	0	0	0	0	0	0	0	0	0	0	1.000	1.000

PITCHING

Name	B-T	HT	WT	DOB	W	L	ERA	G	GS	CG	SV	IP	H	R	ER	HR	BB	SO	AVG	vLH	vRH	K/9	BB/9
Arneson, Jamie	L-L	6-5	195	11-5-85	1	3	4.88	14	13	0	0	59	54	33	32	10	56	54	.251	.204	.267	8.24	8.54
DeJesus, Misael	R-R	6-3	190	11-4-84	6	3	3.73	43	0	0	1	82	81	38	34	5	30	92	.254	.222	.280	10.10	3.29
Donaldson, Daniel	R-L	6-4	180	7-23-84	0	1	4.94	14	0	0	0	27	32	15	15	3	16	20	.296	.333	.282	6.59	5.27
Geronimo, Ramon	R-R	6-0	185	10-8-83	7	3	2.45	49	0	0	12	66	56	20	18	2	14	49	.230	.194	.255	6.68	1.91
Gonzalez, Rafael	R-R	6-1	232	3-21-86	13	5	3.53	25	25	1	0	135	131	65	53	18	56	75	.256	.246	.266	5.00	3.73
Gressick, Anthony	R-R	6-3	200	1-1-84	5	8	4.30	26	13	0	0	90	81	49	43	6	47	82	.235	.200	.265	8.20	4.70
Guardado, Eddie	R-L	6-0	225	10-2-70	0	0	0.00	3	0	0	1	3	2	0	0	0	0	3	.182	.000	.286	9.00	0.00
Guerrero, Daniel	R-R	6-1	190	7-21-85	5	4	4.00	18	18	0	0	90	102	43	40	9	23	85	.291	.320	.265	8.50	2.30
Gunter, Kevin	R-R	6-3	210	11-5-83	0	2	3.08	19	0	0	2	38	35	17	13	1	10	32	.241	.164	.289	7.58	2.37
Louwsma, Jason	R-R	6-2	210	9-9-83	0	0	18.00	1	0	0	0	1	3	2	2	0	1	0	.600	1.000	.333	0.00	9.00
Mateo, Marcos	R-R	6-1	199	4-18-84	2	4	3.50	41	0	0	6	72	68	29	28	2	24	63	.260	.291	.239	7.88	3.00
Rojas, Jose A.	R-R	5-11	195	3-2-83	1	2	3.60	5	0	0	11	37	30	16	15	4	13	53	.219	.180	.250	12.89	3.16
Smit, Alexander	L-L	6-3	210	10-2-85	2	2	1.19	5	5	0	0	23	19	7	3	1	8	19	.235	.182	.254	7.54	3.18
Smith, Jordan	R-R	6-4	200	2-4-86	10	8	3.84	26	26	0	0	134	133	74	57	8	40	96	.258	.272	.244	6.46	2.69
Stanton, Mike	L-L	6-1	215	6-2-67	1	1	9.00	1	1	0	0	1	1	1	1	0	2	2	.250	1.000	.000	18.00	9.00
Tabor, Lee	L-L	6-2	175	12-17-84	4	2	2.69	33	0	0	2	64	51	24	19	7	23	71	.215	.141	.262	10.04	3.25
Thompson, Daryl	R-R	6-1	183	11-2-85	5	0	0.96	5	5	0	0	28	16	3	3	1	2	24	.165	.132	.186	7.71	0.64
Valiquette, P.	L-L	6-0	175	2-14-87	1	2	6.75	7	0	0	0	11	17	9	8	1	2	8	.347	.200	.385	6.75	1.69
Viola, Pedro	L-L	6-1	185	6-29-83	3	1	1.87	22	0	0	2	43	29	14	9	3	17	49	.190	.200	.184	10.18	3.53
Watson, Sean	R-R	6-2	220	7-24-85	5	2	1.88	13	13	0	0	72	58	20	15	7	13	85	.226	.240	.213	10.67	1.63
Webb, Travis	L-L	6-4	200	8-2-84	7	5	3.45	28	21	0	0	115	105	50	44	9	62	114	.246	.293	.233	8.95	4.87
Young, Terrell	R-R	6-3	175	8-7-85	1	4	4.08	23	0	0	0	35	27	16	16	2	22	33	.216	.229	.208	8.41	5.60

FIELDING

Catcher	PCT	G	PO	A	E	DP	PB
Encarnacion	1.000	1	12	2	0	0	0
Esquer	.996	52	406	42	2	3	3
Long	.985	7	61	3	1	0	0
Rodriguez	.982	82	606	84	13	3	4
Tordi	1.000	2	11	0	0	0	1

First Base	PCT	G	PO	A	E	DP
Louwsma	1.000	3	30	2	0	27
Parker	.983	104	859	70	16	73

Second Base	PCT	G	PO	A	E	DP
Cozart	1.000	6	7	20	0	4
Rojo	.958	46	75	85	7	18
Turner	.973	98	163	265	12	63

Third Base	PCT	G	PO	A	E	DP
Francisco	.923	117	86	188	23	19
Louwsma	.959	22	13	34	2	1
Tordi	1.000	3	0	6	0	0
Turner	1.000	1	0	1	0	0

Shortstop	PCT	G	PO	A	E	DP
Cozart	.956	46	70	124	9	25
Frazier	.973	6	16	20	1	6
Tordi	.967	13	11	18	1	8
Turner	.961	10	18	31	2	6

Valaika	.946	73	87	174	15	33
Outfield	PCT	G	PO	A	E	DP
Cabrera	1.000	27	45	1	0	0
Heisey	.989	99	171	8	2	1
Jones	1.000	20	30	0	0	0

Kainer	.984	35	60	1	1	0
Louwsma	1.000	3	2	0	0	0
Phipps	.963	121	224	12	9	2
Stubbs	.983	126	269	15	5	2

BILLINGS MUSTANGS ROOKIE

PIONEER LEAGUE

BATTING	B-T	HT	WT	DOB	AVG	vLH	vRH	G	AB	R	H	2B	3B	HR	RBI	BB	HBP	SH	SF	SO	SB	CS	SLG	OBP
Baker, Ryan	R-R	5-11	190	11-6-83	.179	.000	.208	10	28	7	5	3	0	0	2	3	0	0	0	5	1	0	.286	.258
Bartles, Brett	R-R	6-1	180	8-20-86	.312	.316	.310	39	154	26	48	6	6	5	26	14	1	0	2	37	4	3	.526	.368
Bour, Jason	R-R	6-3	215	7-2-86	.287	.211	.311	42	157	15	45	9	0	1	22	7	2	0	0	38	1	0	.363	.325
Cabrera, Angel	R-R	6-0	185	10-14-85	.291	.429	.250	53	182	37	53	12	0	1	21	19	1	1	1	44	4	0	.374	.360
Feiner, Kevyn	R-R	6-1	170	6-11-87	.247	.200	.259	23	73	11	18	2	1	2	7	6	0	1	0	16	1	1	.384	.304
Frazier, Todd	R-R	6-3	215	2-12-86	.319	.206	.349	41	160	29	51	6	5	5	25	18	7	0	1	22	3	3	.513	.409
Gualdron, Jose	R-R	5-11	165	7-18-87	.167	.143	.174	9	30	2	5	0	0	0	2	0	0	1	0	3	0	0	.167	.167
Hauschild, Tyler	R-R	6-0	210	11-24-85	.192	.250	.175	19	52	5	10	3	1	0	3	1	1	0	0	17	0	0	.288	.250
Jones, Keltavious	L-L	5-9	170	9-21-85	.318	.290	.325	38	157	31	50	11	2	3	25	13	4	3	2	21	7	4	.471	.381
Jones, Michael	R-R	6-3	180	11-19-86	.256	.300	.238	60	203	31	52	7	3	4	28	7	0	2	3	43	7	4	.379	.277
Kendrick, Wayne	R-R	5-6	160	2-11-85	.246	.250	.244	22	65	7	16	3	0	0	7	3	0	1	0	6	2	0	.292	.279
Long, Jacob	R-R	6-1	180	4-17-86	.275	.208	.294	33	109	20	30	7	0	3	10	15	5	1	1	22	0	0	.422	.385
Maunus, Kyle	R-R	6-4	210	2-26-85	.281	.267	.286	53	185	38	52	11	1	6	27	21	3	0	2	40	3	1	.449	.360
McKennon, Michael	L-L	6-3	210	3-31-85	.286	.310	.279	73	287	44	82	25	2	11	54	17	3	0	1	65	0	2	.502	.331
Meade, Francis	R-R	6-1	215	9-27-85	.211	.158	.231	25	71	12	15	3	1	2	11	14	1	0	0	23	0	0	.366	.349
Menchaca, Brandon	R-R	5-11	195	4-15-85	.261	.240	.267	63	241	51	63	9	7	7	45	31	6	1	1	70	16	6	.444	.358
Mendez, Carlos	R-R	6-0	175	9-15-86	.280	.625	.118	7	25	2	7	1	0	0	3	0	1	0	1	1	0	0	.320	.308
Penniall, William	B-R	5-11	165	9-3-83	.071	.000	.125	9	14	0	1	0	0	0	1	3	0	0	0	5	0	1	.071	.235
Reed, Justin	L-R	5-11	179	11-29-87	.250	.318	.231	28	100	22	25	4	2	3	15	13	4	0	2	41	4	4	.420	.353
Rimes, Eli	L-L	6-0	210	6-7-85	.059	.143	.000	5	17	1	1	0	0	0	1	1	0	0	0	3	0	0	.059	.111
Tordi, Justin	R-R	6-1	208	4-9-84	.214	.235	.208	19	70	6	15	3	1	1	9	6	2	1	0	17	0	0	.329	.295
Waring, Brandon	R-R	6-4	195	1-2-86	.311	.217	.338	68	267	63	83	17	2	20	61	21	5	0	2	83	1	0	.614	.369

PITCHING	B-T	HT	WT	DOB	W	L	ERA	G	GS	CG	SV	IP	H	R	ER	HR	BB	SO	AVG	vLH	vRH	K/9	BB/9
Bowman, Andrew	R-L	6-4	190	11-8-85	1	5	7.19	14	14	0	0	51	78	54	41	3	19	41	.355	.368	.352	7.19	3.33
Carroll, Scott	R-R	6-5	210	9-24-84	0	1	2.93	6	5	0	0	15	14	8	5	0	5	15	.226	.207	.242	8.80	2.93
Del Rosario, Enerio	R-R	6-2	165	10-16-85	5	4	3.97	15	15	0	0	70	77	40	31	6	30	40	.288	.274	.300	5.12	3.84
Donaldson, Daniel	R-L	6-4	180	7-23-84	0	1	19.29	1	0	0	0	2	7	5	5	0	2	1	.500	.750	.400	3.86	7.71
Gaffney, Scott	R-R	6-3	190	3-13-86	1	2	6.00	20	0	0	5	24	32	18	16	2	12	34	.333	.452	.277	12.75	4.50
Hauschild, Tyler	R-R	6-0	210	11-24-85	0	1	13.50	1	0	0	0	1	1	1	1	0	1	0	.000	.000	.000	0.00	13.50
Honeycutt, Harris	R-R	6-1	200	12-18-84	2	2	5.03	12	6	0	0	39	49	26	22	3	15	48	.304	.348	.272	10.98	3.43
Horst, Jeremy	L-L	6-4	225	10-1-85	3	2	3.18	16	0	0	2	40	34	15	14	2	22	51	.234	.283	.212	11.57	4.99
Jeffords, Raymond	R-R	6-1	200	11-4-84	1	1	6.46	16	0	0	1	24	19	18	17	4	27	33	.211	.125	.242	12.55	10.27
Klinker, Matthew	R-R	6-5	220	10-8-84	2	2	5.44	15	2	0	0	41	55	30	25	6	10	39	.322	.354	.309	8.49	2.18
Krebs, Joseph	L-L	6-0	0	9-14-84	3	2	3.98	10	0	0	1	20	23	9	9	2	10	20	.288	.300	.283	8.85	4.43
Lotzkar, Kyle	L-R	6-4	200	10-24-89	0	0	1.13	2	2	0	0	8	1	1	1	1	3	12	.040	.125	.000	13.50	3.38
Montano, Luis	R-R	6-0	180	3-20-85	8	4	3.62	15	13	0	0	82	81	37	33	7	20	64	.256	.273	.241	7.02	2.20
Partch, Curtis	R-R	6-5	200	2-13-87	1	0	3.29	12	1	0	1	27	21	11	10	3	21	22	.221	.233	.212	7.24	6.91
Pointer, Adam	R-R	5-11	190	9-21-84	1	1	4.42	14	0	0	1	18	21	11	9	0	5	20	.296	.269	.311	9.82	2.45
Ravin, Joshua	R-R	6-4	195	1-21-88	1	5	8.55	13	13	0	0	40	44	46	38	7	41	39	.284	.333	.250	8.78	9.22
Rhoden, Tyler	R-R	6-3	222	12-23-84	2	0	4.50	7	1	0	0	20	21	14	10	2	5	17	.259	.308	.214	7.65	2.25
Romero, Anthony	R-R	6-2	210	8-24-84	0	3	6.83	14	3	0	0	29	35	24	22	3	9	19	.289	.341	.263	5.90	2.79
Valiquette, Phillippe	L-L	6-0	175	2-14-87	3	1	1.77	11	0	0	3	41	31	17	8	0	11	29	.214	.175	.229	6.42	2.43
Wandless, Nicholas	R-R	6-2	220	11-15-83	1	0	7.39	19	0	0	0	32	42	27	26	6	14	27	.321	.271	.361	7.67	3.98
Zeffiro, Dan	R-R	6-3	175	8-13-85	2	1	4.34	17	0	0	0	37	37	22	18	3	12	33	.250	.300	.224	7.96	2.89

FIELDING

Catcher	PCT	G	PO	A	E	DP	PB
Bour	1.000	2	148	16	0	3	3
Hauschild	.988	13	81	4	1	0	2
Long	.977	30	239	18	6	2	6
Meade	.993	18	130	17	1	1	0

First Base	PCT	G	PO	A	E	DP
Bour	1.000	1	1	2	0	0
Maunus	1.000	8	48	3	0	3
McKennon	.992	70	579	46	5	57
Mendez	1.000	2	14	2	0	1
Rimes	1.000	1	1	0	0	0

Second Base	PCT	G	PO	A	E	DP
Baker	.889	3	7	9	2	3

Cabrera	.966	33	59	82	5	21
Feiner	.931	21	38	57	7	11
Gualdron	1.000	2	4	5	0	2
Kendrick	.970	21	38	58	3	16

Third Base	PCT	G	PO	A	E	DP
Bartles	.714	4	1	4	2	2
Cabrera	.941	7	7	9	1	1
Mendez	.846	4	2	9	2	0
Waring	.921	63	46	130	15	13

Shortstop	PCT	G	PO	A	E	DP
Baker	.957	6	2	20	1	1
Cabrera	.908	11	20	39	6	7
Feiner	—	2	0	0	0	0

Frazier	.938	35	44	93	9	13
Gualdron	.895	6	5	12	2	2
Tordi	.965	19	33	76	4	17
Waring	.750	1	1	2	1	1

Outfield	PCT	G	PO	A	E	DP
Bartles	.957	17	21	1	1	0
Hauschild	—	1	0	0	0	0
K. Jones	.917	37	55	0	5	0
M. Jones	.942	57	95	2	6	0
Maunus	.953	33	39	2	2	0
Menchaca	.977	57	125	4	3	1
Mendez	—	1	0	0	0	0
Penniall	1.000	7	5	0	0	0
Reed	.978	26	43	0	1	0

GCL REDS ROOKIE

GULF COAST LEAGUE

BATTING	B-T	HT	WT	DOB	AVG	vLH	vRH	G	AB	R	H	2B	3B	HR	RBI	BB	HBP	SH	SF	SO	SB	CS	SLG	OBP
Bartles, Brett	R-R	6-1	180	8-20-86	.379	.500	.348	9	29	6	11	0	1	0	2	2	1	0	0	5	0	0	.448	.438
Bastardo, Jose	R-R	5-11	165	11-16-85	.219	.175	.243	37	114	21	25	6	3	3	13	11	5	2	0	30	3	3	.404	.315
Brown, Tony	L-L	6-0	190	1-28-86	.246	.277	.234	51	171	26	42	8	0	7	23	20	5	0	1	56	1	2	.415	.340
Cech, Petr	L-R	5-10	185	10-13-87	.308	.000	.348	12	26	3	8	3	0	0	3	1	0	0	0	7	0	1	.423	.333
Encarnacion, Fernando	R-R	6-0	185	7-23-85	.286	.000	.667	4	7	0	2	2	0	0	1	0	0	0	0	1	0	0	.571	.286
Feiner, Kevyn	R-R	6-1	170	6-11-87	.286	.222	.308	10	35	3	10	2	0	0	1	1	0	1	0	6	3	1	.343	.306
Gualdron, Jose	R-R	5-11	165	7-18-87	.265	.184	.306	41	147	24	39	8	0	2	12	4	5	2	1	18	2	4	.361	.306

Mendez, Carlos	R-R	6-0	175	9-15-86	.227	.231	.226	40	132	12	30	3	0	2	14	12	1	0	3	8	2	1	.295	.291
Mesoraco, Devin	R-R	6-1	200	6-19-88	.219	.206	.223	40	137	16	30	4	0	1	8	15	3	0	0	26	2	0	.270	.310
Moreta, Radhames	R-R	6-0	165	10-28-86	.227	.238	.223	43	154	17	35	6	0	0	14	7	1	1	2	27	2	4	.266	.262
Oliveras, Alexis	L-R	6-0	180	3-29-89	.191	.130	.216	47	162	14	31	4	3	0	13	10	1	2	2	45	1	0	.253	.240
Perez, Miguel	R-R	6-3	190	9-25-83	.417	.600	.286	4	12	4	5	1	0	1	3	1	0	0	0	2	0	0	.750	.462
Pullen, Brodie	R-R	6-0	195	10-26-88	.211	.300	.169	32	95	8	20	3	0	0	10	10	0	0	0	29	0	1	.242	.286
Reed, Justin	L-R	5-11	179	11-29-87	.310	.292	.314	32	129	20	40	5	4	1	11	13	3	1	0	31	9	3	.434	.386
Sanchez, Rafael	L-R	6-1	190	8-1-86	.163	.063	.188	24	80	10	13	3	0	1	1	8	1	0	0	18	1	1	.238	.247
Scott, David	L-R	6-2	220	3-29-85	.293	.262	.306	43	140	14	41	7	1	2	22	15	0	0	1	34	1	1	.400	.359
Soto, Neftali	R-R	6-2	180	2-28-89	.303	.366	.279	40	152	18	46	7	5	2	28	11	2	1	1	31	2	0	.454	.355
Waller, Todd	R-R	6-1	195	4-26-87	.146	.067	.182	21	48	3	7	0	0	0	1	6	0	0	0	12	1	0	.146	.241
Wideman, Jordan	R-R	5-11	200	3-14-89	.213	.267	.196	21	61	8	13	2	0	0	5	6	3	0	0	14	0	1	.246	.314
Wise, Dewayne	L-L	6-1	195	2-24-78	.333	.000	.500	2	6	2	2	1	0	0	0	0	0	0	0	2	1	0	.500	.333

PITCHING	B-T	HT	WT	DOB	W	L	ERA	G	GS	CG	SV	IP	H	R	ER	HR	BB	SO	AVG	vLH	vRH	K/9	BB/9
Arneson, Jamie	L-L	6-5	195	11-5-85	2	3	4.50	5	5	0	0	20	17	13	10	1	18	25	.236	.167	.271	11.25	8.10
Beal, Josh	R-R	6-2	220	10-21-87	1	4	5.48	21	0	0	3	21	27	16	13	1	12	25	.303	.367	.271	10.55	5.06
Chiu, Tzu-Kai	L-L	6-0	220	9-14-87	3	4	3.42	12	11	0	0	53	49	23	20	3	8	47	.239	.177	.266	8.03	1.37
Conatser, Jonathan	R-R	6-3	180	12-4-85	0	2	4.79	8	2	0	0	21	22	16	11	0	4	22	.278	.242	.304	9.58	1.74
Fiebig, Thomas	R-R	6-3	200	3-24-89	1	0	6.17	19	0	0	0	23	29	18	16	1	10	15	.309	.268	.340	5.79	3.86
Gonzalez, Aguido	L-L	5-10	185	9-19-86	0	1	6.75	11	0	0	0	9	12	7	7	0	10	10	.316	.250	.333	9.64	9.64
Horst, Jeremy	L-L	6-4	225	10-1-85	0	0	4.50	1	0	0	0	2	3	4	1	0	2	4	.300	1.000	.222	18.00	9.00
Hotchkiss, Jordan	R-R	6-4	210	4-3-86	0	1	1.89	13	0	0	1	19	13	9	4	0	11	9	.191	.208	.182	4.26	5.21
Lotzkar, Kyle	L-R	6-4	200	10-24-89	0	2	3.86	7	7	0	0	21	21	10	9	2	7	24	.263	.261	.263	10.29	3.00
Marizan, Jose	L-L	6-1	170	2-7-88	0	4	10.02	11	5	0	0	21	26	26	23	3	26	18	.317	.364	.310	7.84	11.32
Medina, Jose	R-R	6-3	165	3-19-87	3	0	6.45	15	0	0	0	22	26	17	16	1	18	15	.292	.275	.306	6.04	7.25
Navarro, Victor	R-R	6-3	180	11-7-89	0	1	18.32	12	0	0	0	9	19	22	19	2	12	8	.422	.370	.500	7.71	11.57
Nickols, Robert	L-L	6-5	215	3-4-86	0	0	9.90	12	0	0	1	10	14	21	11	1	15	12	.304	.308	.303	10.80	13.50
Otterness, Steven	L-L	6-4	210	10-30-84	0	5	3.94	12	11	0	0	48	52	28	21	1	17	35	.275	.270	.276	6.56	3.19
Partch, Curtis	R-R	6-5	200	2-13-87	0	0	1.29	5	0	0	2	7	2	4	1	0	7	4	.083	.000	.133	5.14	9.00
Pauly, Thomas	R-R	6-2	208	7-28-81	0	0	3.38	3	0	0	0	3	3	3	1	0	0	3	.250	.250	.250	10.12	0.00
Rafael, Juan	R-R	6-2	165	12-4-85	1	3	2.33	8	7	0	0	39	30	13	10	0	7	34	.211	.180	.235	7.91	1.63
Rhodes, Ricky	R-R	6-7	205	5-30-89	0	1	10.13	7	0	0	0	5	5	8	6	0	11	3	.238	.000	.294	5.06	18.56
Rice, Brandon	R-R	6-4	210	1-11-88	2	3	4.50	13	3	0	0	46	49	29	23	6	12	17	.277	.297	.262	3.33	2.35
Rodriguez, Efrain	R-R	6-2	175	11-22-89	2	3	2.30	10	4	0	0	31	27	18	8	3	10	18	.231	.195	.250	5.17	2.87
Snowden, Charles	L-L	6-1	150	10-6-88	0	2	3.51	10	1	0	0	26	24	17	10	1	5	30	.231	.375	.188	10.52	1.75
Vinyard, Jeremy	R-R	6-1	165	8-10-88	0	2	10.61	6	0	0	0	9	14	15	11	2	11	6	.350	.364	.345	5.79	10.61

FIELDING

Catcher	PCT	G	PO	A	E	DP	PB
Cech	1.000	4	11	0	0	0	0
Encarnacion	—	1	0	0	0	0	0
Mesoraco	.975	28	173	26	5	1	3
Perez	.968	4	27	3	1	0	0
Waller	.987	10	73	4	1	0	0
Wideman	.962	19	115	12	5	1	1

First Base	PCT	G	PO	A	E	DP
Mendez	.987	20	144	7	2	11
Sanchez	.959	18	133	9	6	10
Scott	.966	20	163	10	6	9

Second Base	PCT	G	PO	A	E	DP
Feiner	.906	7	14	15	3	5
Gualdron	.972	23	50	56	3	8
Moreta	.948	28	50	60	6	13

Third Base	PCT	G	PO	A	E	DP
Bartles	.857	5	0	6	1	0
Gualdron	1.000	4	4	10	0	0
Mendez	.833	14	9	31	8	2
Pullen	.892	29	16	42	7	3
Sanchez	.882	5	6	9	2	1
Soto	.692	4	2	7	4	1
Waller	1.000	1	0	1	0	0

Shortstop	PCT	G	PO	A	E	DP
Bartles	—	1	0	0	0	0
Gualdron	.906	12	15	33	5	5
Moreta	.833	14	17	28	9	4
Soto	.913	32	43	93	13	11

Outfield	PCT	G	PO	A	E	DP
Bartles	1.000	4	2	1	0	0
Bastardo	.976	37	79	3	2	0
Brown	.953	48	78	3	4	0
Feiner	1.000	2	4	0	0	0
Gualdron	1.000	1	1	0	0	0
Mendez	1.000	7	7	0	0	0
Oliveras	.964	47	80	0	3	0
Reed	.952	32	59	1	3	1
Scott	—	1	0	0	0	0
Waller	—	1	0	0	0	0
Wise	1.000	2	2	0	0	0

DSL REDS — ROOKIE

DOMINICAN SUMMER LEAGUE

BATTING	B-T	HT	WT	DOB	AVG	vLH	vRH	G	AB	R	H	2B	3B	HR	RBI	BB	HBP	SH	SF	SO	SB	CS	SLG	OBP
Arrendell, Kelvin	R-R	6-0	180	10-4-86	.173	.308	.128	27	52	9	9	1	0	1	8	10	0	0	1	20	0	1	.250	.302
Contreras, Efrain	R-R	6-1	165	2-6-87	.378	.200	.400	12	45	6	17	0	2	0	8	1	4	1	0	7	6	1	.467	.440
De La Cruz, Raul	R-R	6-1	190	12-1-85	.283	.231	.300	43	106	14	30	5	0	1	10	15	1	1	0	32	13	5	.358	.377
Felipe, Ayeudi	R-R	6-1	175	3-12-90	.192	.206	.186	41	120	9	23	2	1	1	9	9	3	0	0	28	4	2	.250	.265
Gomez, Luis	R-R	6-4	180	6-25-86	.157	.048	.194	30	83	10	13	2	0	0	7	6	2	0	1	12	0	3	.181	.228
Guerrero, Sergio	R-R	6-0	179	11-13-87	.203	.200	.205	64	236	34	48	12	1	6	26	17	3	2	2	60	6	5	.339	.264
Meran, George	R-R	5-10	153	12-5-89	.237	.278	.227	38	93	12	22	4	3	0	5	10	2	0	0	14	1	3	.344	.324
Moreno, Michael	R-R	6-3	200	10-21-87	.205	.200	.206	42	117	11	24	4	0	0	9	15	0	0	0	37	3	0	.239	.295
Perez, Jorge	R-R	6-0	160	12-21-87	.274	.267	.276	67	263	43	72	13	5	1	28	27	3	1	2	36	7	7	.373	.346
Pimentel, Mauricio	B-R	6-0	165	11-12-88	.264	.309	.251	68	250	48	66	4	4	0	23	42	4	4	2	58	29	14	.312	.376
Restrepo, Alberto	R-R	5-9	160	6-8-88	.114	.200	.100	18	35	5	4	1	0	0	0	6	1	1	0	14	0	0	.143	.262
Rodriguez, Henry	B-R	5-10	150	2-9-90	.235	.000	.308	7	17	3	4	0	0	0	4	1	0	0	1	1	1	0	.235	.263
Rodriguez, Miguel	R-R	6-0	199	2-4-87	.289	.271	.295	58	204	23	59	7	3	2	35	13	8	2	4	36	1	3	.382	.349
Rodriguez, Roberto	R-R	5-8	163	3-15-86	.208	.261	.192	50	101	18	21	0	0	1	8	15	3	0	1	22	4	4	.238	.325
Rojas, Miguel	R-R	5-9	160	2-24-89	.250	.000	.267	7	16	3	4	1	0	0	0	3	0	3	0	0	1	0	.313	.368
Schiavoni, Mauro	R-R	5-8	190	8-6-86	.246	.182	.260	24	61	10	15	3	1	0	1	7	0	0	0	10	1	0	.328	.324
Sosa, Humberto	R-R	5-9	210	10-13-85	.275	.250	.282	67	240	24	66	19	1	3	46	32	5	1	7	41	1	1	.400	.363
Vasquez, Samuel	R-R	6-0	175	2-6-87	.262	.216	.274	63	237	34	62	16	2	1	28	9	4	0	5	49	12	8	.359	.294

PITCHING	B-T	HT	WT	DOB	W	L	ERA	G	GS	CG	SV	IP	H	R	ER	HR	BB	SO	AVG	vLH	vRH	K/9	BB/9
Albino, Reinaldo	R-R	6-2	165	3-16-89	1	1	1.99	16	3	0	0	32	25	11	7	0	16	25	.216	.250	.202	7.11	4.55
Almonte, Ramon	R-R	6-0	165	6-20-88	1	3	3.33	10	6	0	0	24	19	16	9	0	17	28	.209	.300	.183	10.36	6.29
Aquino, Juan	R-R	6-1	175	12-27-87	8	3	2.76	13	9	0	0	62	42	25	19	2	12	62	.185	.283	.160	9.00	1.74
Castro, Oscar	R-R	6-2	165	3-29-89	1	0	3.86	2	0	0	0	5	6	2	2	0	4	3	.316	.167	.385	5.79	7.71
Ceballos, Rafael	R-R	6-2	190	3-17-89	1	1	0.41	12	0	0	2	22	12	2	1	0	14	12	.164	.222	.145	4.91	5.73
De La Rosa, Rafael	L-L	6-0	180	5-12-88	7	3	2.35	19	15	0	0	80	70	26	21	0	16	59	.236	.143	.243	6.61	1.79
Duarte, Francisco	R-R	6-1	160	2-24-87	2	1	3.27	22	1	0	0	55	51	25	20	1	16	22	.248	.319	.226	3.60	2.62
Gomera, Ivan	L-L	6-2	160	7-26-85	1	3	1.62	33	0	0	21	39	27	9	7	0	19	28	.197	.375	.186	6.46	4.38
Infante, Ezequiel	L-L	5-10	152	8-31-88	3	3	2.57	26	2	0	1	56	54	21	16	0	19	33	.262	.188	.268	5.30	3.05
Machuca, Luis	R-R	6-1	190	3-16-88	7	3	2.00	14	13	0	0	81	67	24	18	1	10	54	.225	.243	.219	6.00	1.11

	B-T	HT	WT	DOB	W	L	ERA	G	GS	CG	SV	IP	H	R	ER	HR	BB	SO	AVG	vLH	vRH	K/9	BB/9
Marizan, Jose	L-L	6-1	170	2-7-88	1	0	1.64	3	2	0	0	11	9	3	2	0	5	11	.225	.000	.243	9.00	4.09
Martinez, Junior	R-R	6-0	210	4-30-86	1	1	5.10	19	1	0	0	30	28	22	17	0	24	26	.250	.273	.241	7.80	7.20
Mercedes, Elvin	R-R	6-4	150	3-2-89	1	1	3.28	14	0	0	0	25	22	13	9	1	15	11	.242	.389	.205	4.01	5.47
Rodriguez, Ramon	R-R	6-2	182	2-14-88	3	4	5.64	13	11	0	0	45	46	34	28	3	27	44	.267	.277	.264	8.87	5.44
Ruiz, Jesus	R-R	6-7	180	8-3-87	0	1	13.50	8	0	0	0	7	11	11	11	0	14	5	.355	.200	.385	6.14	17.18
Santana, Hector	R-R	6-1	186	2-4-88	0	1	6.75	1	1	0	0	1	2	1	1	0	0	0	.400	—	.400	0.00	0.00
Silvestre, Elvin	R-R	6-1	166	10-8-89	1	1	4.20	11	5	0	0	30	35	19	14	2	17	25	.297	.371	.265	7.50	5.10

FIELDING

Catcher	PCT	G	PO	A	E	DP	PB
De La Cruz	1.000	15	69	11	0	0	4
Restrepo	.968	13	53	7	2	1	2
Schiavoni	.992	19	107	14	1	0	4
Sosa	.984	37	212	29	4	2	5

First Base	PCT	G	PO	A	E	DP
Arrendell	.976	15	79	2	2	8
De La Cruz	.974	15	110	2	3	6
De La Rosa	1.000	1	10	0	0	0
M. Rodriguez	.974	21	176	11	5	22
Sosa	.987	29	226	7	3	17

Second Base	PCT	G	PO	A	E	DP
Meran	.968	15	31	29	2	5
Perez	.982	15	27	28	1	6

	PCT	G	PO	A	E	DP
Pimentel	.962	31	79	71	6	20
H. Rodriguez	.966	5	11	17	1	4
R. Rodriguez	.977	11	26	17	1	4
Rojas	1.000	2	7	5	0	2

Third Base	PCT	G	PO	A	E	DP
De La Cruz	1.000	1	2	3	0	1
Meran	.906	11	3	26	3	3
Perez	.843	24	17	53	13	6
H. Rodriguez	1.000	1	1	4	0	1
M. Rodriguez	.919	26	29	50	7	1
R. Rodriguez	.923	14	10	26	3	3

Shortstop	PCT	G	PO	A	E	DP
Meran	—	1	0	0	0	0
Perez	.928	29	37	91	10	15
Pimentel	.913	39	62	74	13	13
Rojas	1.000	6	5	16	0	3

Outfield	PCT	G	PO	A	E	DP
Contreras	.958	11	22	1	1	1
De La Cruz	—	1	0	0	0	0
Felipe	.950	39	56	1	3	1
Gomez	.969	22	30	1	1	0
Guerrero	.951	63	109	8	6	1
Moreno	1.000	22	24	0	0	0
R. Rodriguez	.500	12	1	0	1	0
Vasquez	.960	62	161	9	7	3

VSL REDS/DEVIL RAYS

ROOKIE

VENEZUELAN SUMMER LEAGUE (C=CINCINNATI, T= TAMPA BAY)

BATTING	B-T	HT	WT	DOB	AVG	vLH	vRH	G	AB	R	H	2B	3B	HR	RBI	BB	HBP	SH	SF	SO	SB	CS	SLG	OBP
Alvarez, Jhonder (C)	R-R	5-10	160	11-27-88	.253	.154	.292	32	91	10	23	2	0	0	4	11	4	0	0	25	2	0	.275	.358
Cabrera, Orlando (T)	R-R	5-11	165	10-25-89	.158	.087	.189	23	76	5	12	0	0	1	4	4	2	1	0	27	0	1	.197	.220
Cedeno, Julio (T)	R-R	6-2	185	8-25-89	.300	.224	.326	51	190	27	57	13	2	5	32	16	9	0	0	39	5	1	.468	.381
Chacoa, Miguel (C)	B-R	5-11	165	11-27-88	.349	.370	.339	25	83	20	29	3	0	1	13	13	1	1	0	14	12	3	.422	.443
Colmenares, Cesar (C)	B-R	6-1	160	6-26-90	.188	.200	.182	52	160	13	30	1	0	0	13	14	0	2	3	40	1	2	.194	.249
Contreras, Efrain (C)	R-R	6-1	165	2-6-87	.315	.328	.310	65	241	54	76	14	0	11	36	30	12	0	2	35	25	5	.510	.414
Figueroa, Carlos (C)	B-R	6-1	175	10-12-89	.176	.188	.173	28	68	5	12	3	0	0	8	10	2	0	3	20	0	0	.221	.289
Gonzalez, Argenis (C)	R-R	6-1	190	3-30-87	.333	.214	.377	33	105	11	35	5	1	0	13	15	1	0	0	16	3	2	.400	.421
Guerra, Omar (T)	R-R	5-11	173	12-29-86	.188	.115	.213	31	101	11	19	1	0	1	6	14	0	2	0	15	5	2	.198	.333
Hernandez, David (C)	R-R	6-1	155	3-24-87	.344	.357	.340	59	209	38	72	13	1	3	27	18	4	2	1	27	4	4	.459	.405
Martinez, Mario (C)	R-R	6-1	165	12-5-87	.213	.063	.267	14	61	8	13	2	1	1	15	1	1	1	0	6	0	0	.328	.238
Nagahashi, Mauricio (T)	R-R	6-1	165	4-12-90	.202	.105	.224	36	104	13	21	3	0	0	3	7	5	0	0	26	3	1	.231	.284
Nakandakare, Lucas (T)	R-R	6-2	215	9-18-89	.302	.129	.385	33	96	7	29	2	1	0	13	24	1	2	0	17	0	2	.344	.446
Omana, Gustavo (C)	B-R	6-0	200	9-24-85	.321	.300	.331	57	193	29	62	10	0	2	37	19	4	3	3	19	0	0	.404	.388
Rodriguez, Henry (C)	B-R	5-10	150	2-9-90	.267	.288	.257	54	206	30	55	14	5	3	25	28	3	1	1	29	4	2	.427	.361
Rojas, Miguel (C)	R-R	5-9	160	2-24-89	.228	.267	.211	30	101	12	23	5	0	2	9	14	3	1	1	11	1	1	.337	.336
Torres, Alejandro (T)	R-R	6-1	178	9-30-88	.234	.225	.238	38	145	15	34	3	0	0	13	8	2	0	0	18	5	0	.255	.284
Ugueto, Eliecer (T)	R-R	6-1	163	9-18-88	.137	.171	.126	47	146	18	20	3	0	3	10	24	4	0	0	69	4	3	.219	.276

PITCHING	B-T	HT	WT	DOB	W	L	ERA	G	GS	CG	SV	IP	H	R	ER	HR	BB	SO	AVG	vLH	vRH	K/9	BB/9
Amador, Renny (C)	L-L	6-0	185	2-26-88	1	1	6.61	18	1	0	0	31	23	31	23	2	48	37	.202	.231	.198	10.63	13.79
Andrade, Francisco (C)	L-L	5-9	150	8-9-90	1	3	7.03	15	1	0	0	24	36	19	19	4	4	13	.350	.167	.361	4.81	1.48
Bencomo, Omar (T)	R-R	6-1	168	2-10-89	2	3	2.89	12	8	0	0	47	53	24	15	2	6	31	.288	.286	.289	5.98	1.16
Bocaranda, Wilfredo (C)	L-L	6-3	185	11-27-87	0	1	2.76	20	2	0	1	46	43	22	14	4	20	26	.247	.083	.259	5.12	3.94
Calderon, Hugo (C)	R-R	6-1	170	9-19-87	4	2	4.35	28	0	0	1	52	57	31	25	4	31	41	.289	.367	.264	7.14	5.40
Contreras, Yoel (C)	R-L	6-3	180	1-1-86	1	6	5.95	16	13	0	0	59	65	47	39	4	37	39	.283	.273	.283	5.95	5.64
Crespo, Ali (T)	R-R	6-4	209	2-1-90	1	2	4.35	11	0	0	0	21	21	15	10	3	18	10	.280	.286	.278	4.35	7.84
Duarte, Hugo (T)	R-R	6-1	169	1-7-90	0	5	5.66	19	4	0	0	41	41	28	26	3	18	26	.266	.191	.299	5.66	3.92
Duenas, Carlos (T)	L-L	5-11	165	12-28-87	1	1	10.50	3	2	0	0	6	10	8	7	0	5	4	.345	.000	.400	6.00	7.50
Espana, Luis (T)	R-R	6-4	172	3-27-89	1	5	6.25	19	7	0	0	40	32	41	28	2	30	18	.215	.194	.221	4.02	6.69
Figuera, Jose (T)	R-R	6-5	175	9-16-89	0	1	6.62	8	7	0	0	18	19	15	13	0	17	6	.284	.333	.269	3.06	8.66
Gonzalez, Fernando (C)	R-R	6-3	175	5-19-89	0	2	5.40	22	0	0	0	40	33	30	24	6	33	24	.231	.143	.259	5.40	7.42
Lopez, Kevin (T)	R-R	6-2	173	10-22-89	0	0	2.08	2	1	0	0	4	1	1	1	0	5	6	.077	.333	.000	12.46	10.38
Martinez, Daniel (C)	L-L	6-2	170	6-4-90	0	3	5.53	14	13	0	0	41	41	31	25	2	30	41	.268	.615	.236	9.07	6.64
Mujica, Juan (T)	L-L	5-10	185	3-21-90	0	0	4.50	4	2	0	0	8	6	4	4	0	11	1	.214	.000	.222	1.12	12.38
Palencia, Juan (C)	R-R	5-11	150	6-20-90	0	0	3.12	3	0	0	1	9	5	3	3	1	5	5	.172	.125	.190	5.19	5.19
Parra, Fray (T)	L-L	6-0	154	9-18-88	0	1	60.75	2	1	0	0	1	2	9	9	0	13	1	.400	.000	.400	6.75	87.75
Quinonez, Eduar (T)	R-R	6-3	169	8-9-89	0	4	9.69	16	2	0	1	26	37	34	28	2	16	15	.336	.333	.337	5.19	5.54
Rodriguez, Wilking (T)	R-R	6-1	160	3-24-90	3	2	1.95	17	0	0	2	32	23	7	7	1	14	28	.200	.306	.152	7.79	3.90
Sanchez, Daniel (T)	R-R	6-2	180	5-29-89	1	5	17.85	17	2	0	0	20	25	41	39	1	41	13	.329	.300	.339	5.95	18.76
Yendis, Luis (T)	R-R	6-3	178	7-19-89	1	4	4.80	16	2	0	0	30	37	20	16	2	15	15	.311	.419	.273	4.50	4.50

FIELDING

Catcher	PCT	G	PO	A	E	DP	PB
Cabrera	.961	9	42	7	2	1	1
Figueroa	1.000	13	64	14	0	0	3
Gonzalez	1.000	12	58	8	0	0	4
Nakandakare	.963	8	44	8	2	0	2
Omana	.962	18	108	18	5	4	0
Torres	.958	19	96	19	5	1	3

First Base	PCT	G	PO	A	E	DP
Cabrera	1.000	2	18	0	0	0
Figueroa	1.000	2	2	0	0	0
Gonzalez	.973	13	66	6	2	4
Hernandez	1.000	6	16	2	0	0
Nakandakare	.994	18	157	5	1	15
Omana	.977	28	237	13	6	32
Torres	1.000	12	99	5	0	8
Ugueto	—	1	0	0	0	0

Second Base	PCT	G	PO	A	E	DP
Alvarez	.917	3	6	5	1	0
Hernandez	.988	16	39	45	1	14
Rodriguez	.957	46	114	109	10	28
Rojas	1.000	2	4	4	0	1
Ugueto	1.000	6	11	13	0	4

Third Base	PCT	G	PO	A	E	DP
Alvarez	—	1	0	0	0	0
Cedeno	.877	47	37	106	20	11
Chacoa	.667	3	2	2	2	0
Figueroa	.800	2	3	1	1	1
Hernandez	.897	18	18	34	6	1
Omana	.867	5	7	6	2	0

Shortstop	PCT	G	PO	A	E	DP
Alvarez	.636	3	2	5	4	0
Colmenares	—	1	0	0	0	0

	PCT	G	PO	A	E	DP
Hernandez	.929	16	28	51	6	14
Rojas	.955	27	50	78	6	16
Ugueto	.872	31	48	81	19	13

Outfield	PCT	G	PO	A	E	DP
Alvarez	.952	24	37	3	2	1
Cedeno	1.000	1	1	0	0	0
Chacoa	.950	22	16	3	1	1
Colmenares	.943	46	80	2	5	0
Contreras	.989	65	160	12	2	3
Guerra	.921	30	31	4	3	0
Hernandez	.875	10	14	0	2	0
Martinez	.962	14	23	2	1	1
Nagahashi	1.000	7	1	0	0	0
Rojas	—	1	0	0	0	0
Torres	1.000	6	9	2	0	0
Ugueto	1.000	5	7	1	0	0

Cleveland Indians

BY ANDY CALL

The Indians returned to the playoffs for the first time since 2001, but the pleasant memories from the first 170 games will forever be tainted by the disappointing outcome of the final three.

"The body of work is 96 wins," GM Mark Shapiro said. "My hope is, we'll benefit from the final failure and build off the success of the 96 wins."

The Indians saw a 3-1 AL Championship Series lead evaporate as the Red Sox rallied to win in seven games.

"If you're not the team that wins your last game, no matter what level you get to, you feel that sense of bitterness and disappointment," Shapiro said. "The backdrop of that is, 96 wins, the most in the major leagues, the fact we experienced the postseason for the first time in a long time, we won a (Division Series) in Yankee Stadium and we took the Red Sox to Game Seven."

The core of young players the Indians had been developing since the Bartolo Colon trade in 2002 finally reached full maturity in 2007,

There was snow, injuries and no shortage of craziness, yet the Indians pulled away from defending AL champion Detroit and earned the team's first division title in seven years.

The Indians overcame those challenges through excellent starting pitching, solid work by the bullpen and offensive help from some unexpected sources.

"We handled the peaks and valleys," manager Eric Wedge said.

Shapiro made some key moves before the season began to strengthen the club's weak spots, particularly a bullpen that had ranked 14th in the AL a year earlier. Relief pitchers Joe Borowski, Keith Foulke, Aaron Fultz and Roberto Hernandez were all signed to free agent contracts.

The first challenge came on the first day of spring training when Foulke, projected to be the team's closer, called to say he was retiring. Injuries sidelined lefthander Cliff Lee for all of April and righthander Jake Westbrook for all of May. Another starter, lefthander Jeremy Sowers, couldn't regain the form that made him one of the best rookies in 2006.

The first home series of the season was snowed out, and weather forced three more home games to be shifted to Milwaukee. On April 19, Borowski gave up six runs in the ninth inning of an 8-6 loss at Yankee Stadium. Five starting position players were batting .222 or worse at the end of April. Starting third baseman Andy Marte was in the minor leagues by the end of May.

The season could have gone south quickly. Instead, the Indians spent most of the first two months in first or second place, going 14-8 in April and 19-11 in May.

Righthander Fausto Carmona came up from the minors, won 19 games and finished second in the league in ERA. Foulke stayed home, but Borowski led the league in saves. Hernandez was a flop, but rookie lefthander Rafael Perez and righthander Jensen Lewis became late-inning mainstays.

Veteran Travis Hafner struggled all season in the three hole, but No. 4 hitter Victor Martinez had the best year of his career. Free agent outfielders Trot Nixon and David Dellucci offered little help, but Franklin Gutierrez showed signs of becoming an everyday big league outfielder. Josh Barfield lost his second-base job to 21-year-old rookie Asdrubal Cabrera, who sparkled offensively and defensively.

The Indians had some solid team efforts in the minor leagues as well. Double-A Akron played its way into the Eastern League finals. High Class A Kinston won its division in both halves of the Carolina League schedule before falling in the playoffs.

Triple-A Buffalo outfielder Ben Francisco won the International League batting title and hit a game-winning home run in his first big league start. Akron first baseman Jordan Brown was named MVP and rookie of the year in the Eastern League. Five low Class A Lake County pitchers combined to throw two no-hitters against Delmarva in a 10-day span. First baseman Todd Martin set a short-season Mahoning Valley franchise record for batting average while leading the Scrappers to the New York-Penn League crown.

PLAYERS OF THE YEAR

MAJOR LEAGUE: C.C. SABATHIA, LHP

Everything came together this year for Sabathia, who led all of baseball with 241 innings and a 5.65-to-1 strikeout-walk ratio. His 3.21 ERA was a career low, and his 209 strikeouts ranked fifth in the American League. His 19 wins ranked second in the AL and his four complete games were the second most in baseball.

MINOR LEAGUE: JORDAN BROWN, 1B

Brown led the Eastern League in hitting with a .333 average for Double-A Akron, and his 161 hits led the league. Brown showed remarkable plate discipline, finishing third in the EL with a .421 on-base percentage and drawing more walks (63) than strikeouts (56). Brown also stole 11 bases in 13 attempts.

ORGANIZATIONAL LEADERS

BATTING		★Minimum 250 at-bats
★AVG	Brown, Jordan, Akron	.333
R	Davis, Adam, Lake County	95
	Whitney, Matthew, Lake County/Kinston	95
H	Brown, Jordan, Akron	161
TB	Whitney, Matthew, Lake County/Kinston	279
2B	Head, Stephen, Kinston/Akron	38
3B	Inglett, Joe, Buffalo	9
	Rodriguez, Joshua, Kinston	9
HR	Whitney, Matthew, Lake County/Kinston	32
RBI	Whitney, Matthew, Lake County/Kinston	113
BB	Weglarz, Nicholas, Lake County/Kinston	83
SO	Pena, Roman, Lake County	138
SB	Constanza, Jose, Kinston	39
★OBP	Brown, Jordan, Akron	.421
★SLG	Whitney, Matthew, Lake County/Kinston	.545

PITCHING		^Minimum 75 innings
W	Laffey, Aaron, Akron/Buffalo	13
L	Nottingham, Shawn, Akron	12
^ERA	Deters, James, Buffalo/Kinston	2.5
G	Newsom, Randy, Kinston/Akron	57
CG	Herrmann, Frank, Kinston	3
SV	Roehl, Scott, Akron/Kinston	24
IP	Lofgren, Chuck, Buffalo/Akron	151
BB	Lofgren, Chuck, Buffalo/Akron	71
SO	Lofgren, Chuck, Buffalo/Akron	130
^AVG	Deters, James, Buffalo/Kinston	.236

2007 PERFORMANCE

General Manager: Mark Shapiro. Farm Director: Ross Atkins. Scouting Director: John Mirabelli

Class	Team	League	W	L	PCT	Finish*	Manager	Affiliate Since
Majors	Cleveland	American	96	66	.593	1st (14)	Eric Wedge	—
Triple-A	Buffalo Bisons	International	75	67	.528	6th (14)	Torey Lovullo	1995
Double-A	Akron Aeros	Eastern	80	61	.567	3rd (12)	Tim Bogar	1997
High A	Kinston Indians	Carolina	87	52	.626	1st (8)	Mike Sarbaugh	1987
Low A	Lake County Captains	South Atlantic	64	74	.464	12th (16)	Chris Tremie	2003
Short-season	Mahoning Valley Scrappers	New York-Penn	37	37	.500	7th (14)	Tim Laker	1999
Rookie	GCL Indians	Gulf Coast	28	31	.475	8th (16)	Rouglas Odor	2006
Overall 2007 Minor League Record			371	322	.535	5th		

* Finish in overall standings (No. of teams in league) ^League champion

ORGANIZATION STATISTICS

CLEVELAND INDIANS

AMERICAN LEAGUE

BATTING	B-T	HT	WT	DOB	AVG	vLH	vRH	G	AB	R	H	2B	3B	HR	RBI	BB	HBP	SH	SF	SO	SB	CS	SLG	OBP
Barfield, Josh	R-R	6-0	190	12-17-82	.243	.211	.255	130	420	53	102	19	3	3	50	14	3	3	4	90	14	5	.324	.270
Blake, Casey	R-R	6-2	210	8-23-73	.270	.256	.276	156	588	81	159	36	4	18	78	54	10	5	5	123	4	5	.437	.339
Cabrera, Asdrubal	B-R	6-0	170	11-13-85	.283	.340	.259	45	159	30	45	9	2	3	22	17	2	5	3	29	0	0	.421	.354
Choo, Shin-Soo	L-L	5-11	205	7-13-82	.294	.000	.357	6	17	5	5	0	0	0	5	2	0	0	1	5	0	1	.294	.350
Dellucci, David	L-L	5-11	195	10-31-73	.230	.167	.240	56	178	25	41	11	2	4	20	17	1	0	3	40	2	1	.382	.296
Francisco, Ben	R-R	6-1	190	10-23-81	.274	.286	.273	25	62	10	17	5	0	3	12	3	0	0	1	19	0	2	.500	.303
Garko, Ryan	R-R	6-2	225	1-2-81	.289	.310	.281	138	484	62	140	29	1	21	61	34	20	0	3	94	0	1	.483	.359
Gomez, Chris	R-R	6-1	185	6-16-71	.283	.300	.273	19	53	4	15	2	0	0	5	0	0	1	1	6	0	0	.321	.278
2-team (73 Baltimore)					.297	—	—	92	222	21	66	12	1	1	21	10	0	6	2	26	1	2	.374	.325
Gutierrez, Franklin	R-R	6-2	180	2-21-83	.266	.330	.232	100	271	41	72	13	2	13	36	21	1	5	3	77	8	3	.472	.318
Hafner, Travis	L-R	6-3	240	6-3-77	.266	.274	.261	152	545	80	145	25	2	24	100	102	7	0	5	115	1	1	.451	.385
Lofton, Kenny	L-L	5-11	190	5-31-67	.283	.231	.293	52	173	24	49	9	3	0	15	17	0	4	2	23	2	3	.370	.344
2-team (84 Texas)					.296	—	—	136	490	86	145	25	6	7	38	56	2	6	5	51	23	7	.414	.367
Marte, Andy	R-R	6-1	190	10-21-83	.193	.278	.154	20	57	3	11	4	0	1	8	2	1	0	0	9	0	0	.316	.233
Martinez, Victor	B-R	6-2	195	12-23-78	.301	.289	.307	147	562	78	169	40	1	25	114	62	10	0	11	76	0	0	.505	.374
Michaels, Jason	R-R	6-0	205	5-4-76	.270	.287	.261	102	259	36	70	9	1	7	39	20	3	2	3	50	3	4	.397	.324
Nixon, Trot	L-L	6-2	215	4-11-74	.251	.224	.256	99	307	30	77	17	0	3	31	44	0	0	3	59	0	0	.336	.342
Peralta, Jhonny	R-R	6-1	195	5-28-82	.270	.275	.269	152	574	87	155	27	1	21	72	61	4	1	7	146	4	4	.430	.341
Rivas, Luis	R-R	5-11	190	8-30-79	.273	.667	.125	4	11	3	3	0	1	1	4	0	0	0	0	6	0	0	.727	.273
Rouse, Mike	L-R	5-11	190	4-25-80	.119	.000	.143	41	67	7	8	1	0	0	4	7	0	1	1	20	1	1	.134	.200
Shoppach, Kelly	R-R	6-0	220	4-29-80	.261	.265	.260	59	161	26	42	13	0	7	30	11	1	3	1	56	0	0	.472	.310
Sizemore, Grady	L-L	6-2	200	8-2-82	.277	.284	.274	162	628	118	174	34	5	24	78	101	17	0	2	155	33	10	.462	.390

PITCHING	B-T	HT	WT	DOB	W	L	ERA	G	GS	CG	SV	IP	H	R	ER	HR	BB	SO	AVG	vLH	vRH	K/9	BB/9
Betancourt, Rafael	R-R	6-2	200	4-29-75	5	1	1.47	68	0	0	3	79	51	13	13	4	9	80	.183	.241	.147	9.08	1.02
Borowski, Joe	R-R	6-2	225	5-4-71	4	5	5.07	69	0	0	45	66	77	39	37	9	17	58	.289	.293	.286	7.95	2.33
Byrd, Paul	R-R	6-1	190	12-3-70	15	8	4.59	31	31	2	0	192	239	107	98	27	28	88	.301	.322	.280	4.12	1.31
Cabrera, Fernando	R-R	6-4	220	11-16-81	1	2	5.61	24	0	0	0	34	38	22	21	7	22	39	.286	.321	.263	10.43	5.88
2-team (9 Baltimore)					1	2	7.21	33	0	0	1	44	50	36	35	9	31	48	—	—	—	9.89	6.39
Carmona, Fausto	R-R	6-4	220	12-7-83	19	8	3.06	32	32	2	0	215	199	78	73	16	61	137	.248	.275	.216	5.73	2.55
Davis, Jason	R-R	6-6	225	5-8-80	0	0	4.76	8	0	0	0	11	13	6	6	1	5	5	.283	.160	.429	3.97	7.15
2-team (16 Seattle)					2	0	5.84	24	0	0	0	37	42	27	24	4	25	19	—	—	—	4.62	6.08
Fultz, Aaron	L-L	6-0	210	9-4-73	4	3	2.92	49	0	0	0	37	31	12	12	2	18	28	.228	.191	.265	6.81	4.38
Hernandez, Roberto	R-R	6-4	245	11-11-64	3	1	6.23	28	0	0	0	26	33	21	18	2	16	18	.308	.261	.344	6.23	5.54
Koplove, Mike	R-R	5-11	175	8-30-76	0	0	6.00	5	0	0	0	6	6	4	4	0	2	4	.261	.125	.333	6.00	3.00
Laffey, Aaron	L-L	6-0	185	4-15-85	4	2	4.56	9	9	0	0	49	54	26	25	2	12	25	.287	.322	.271	4.56	2.19
Lara, Juan	R-L	6-2	205	1-26-81	0	0	13.50	1	0	0	0	1	2	2	1	1	2	2	.333	.500	.250	13.50	6.75
Lee, Cliff	L-L	6-3	190	8-30-78	5	8	6.29	20	16	1	0	97	112	73	68	17	36	66	.284	.327	.267	6.10	3.33
Lewis, Jensen	R-R	6-3	195	5-16-84	1	1	2.15	26	0	0	0	29	26	8	7	1	10	34	.234	.244	.229	10.43	3.07
Mastny, Tom	R-R	6-6	225	2-4-81	7	2	4.68	51	0	0	0	58	63	30	30	6	32	52	.283	.282	.283	8.12	4.99
Miller, Matt	R-R	6-3	215	11-23-71	0	0	0.00	2	0	0	0	1	2	0	0	0	0	0	.400	.000	.500	0.00	0.00
Mujica, Edward	R-R	6-2	220	5-10-84	0	0	8.31	10	0	0	0	13	19	12	12	3	2	7	.333	.320	.344	4.85	1.38
Perez, Rafael	L-L	6-3	185	5-15-82	1	2	1.78	44	0	0	1	61	41	15	12	5	11	62	.187	.145	.213	9.20	2.23
Sabathia, C.C.	L-L	6-7	290	7-21-80	19	7	3.21	34	34	4	0	241	238	94	86	20	37	209	.259	.203	.275	7.80	1.38
Sowers, Jeremy	L-L	6-1	180	5-17-83	1	6	6.42	13	13	0	0	67	84	49	48	10	21	24	.308	.206	.338	3.21	2.81
Stanford, Jason	L-L	6-1	205	1-23-77	1	1	4.78	8	2	0	0	26	32	15	14	1	7	16	.296	.407	.259	5.47	2.39
Westbrook, Jake	R-R	6-3	200	9-29-77	6	9	4.32	25	25	0	0	152	159	78	73	13	55	93	.276	.288	.263	5.51	3.26

FIELDING

Catcher	PCT	G	PO	A	E	DP	PB
Martinez	.995	121	779	53	4	8	6
Shoppach	.987	58	287	28	4	6	2

First Base	PCT	G	PO	A	E	DP
Blake	1.000	12	39	5	0	4
Garko	.993	125	1073	71	8	115
Gomez	1.000	8	25	2	0	2
Hafner	1.000	11	97	4	0	8
Martinez	.995	30	187	13	1	18

Second Base	PCT	G	PO	A	E	DP
Barfield	.975	120	242	338	15	73
Cabrera	.995	40	70	119	1	28

Gomez	1.000	4	12	9	0	3
Rivas	1.000	2	3	4	0	0
Rouse	.978	14	21	24	1	4

Third Base	PCT	G	PO	A	E	DP
Blake	.962	145	99	258	14	24
Cabrera	1.000	1	0	1	0	0
Gomez	1.000	6	6	16	0	3
Marte	.915	19	16	27	4	2
Rouse	.938	14	4	11	1	3

Shortstop	PCT	G	PO	A	E	DP
Cabrera	1.000	7	8	21	0	5
Peralta	.974	152	249	452	19	106

Rivas	.800	1	0	4	1	0
Rouse	.977	11	10	32	1	5

Outfield	PCT	G	PO	A	E	DP
Blake	1.000	7	13	2	0	2
Choo	1.000	5	10	1	0	1
Dellucci	1.000	51	97	3	0	0
Francisco	1.000	19	32	0	0	0
Gutierrez	.994	95	154	3	1	1
Lofton	1.000	51	84	3	0	1
Michaels	.993	101	147	4	1	0
Nixon	.971	87	129	4	4	2
Sizemore	.995	160	399	4	2	2

INTERNATIONAL LEAGUE

BATTING	B-T	HT	WT	DOB	AVG	vLH	vRH	G	AB	R	H	2B	3B	HR	RBI	BB	HBP	SH	SF	SO	SB	CS	SLG	OBP
Barton, Brian	R-R	6-3	187	4-25-82	.264	.231	.279	25	87	9	23	3	0	1	7	7	2	0	0	18	1	1	.333	.333
Branyan, Russell	L-R	6-3	195	12-19-75	.000	.000	.000	1	4	0	0	0	0	0	0	0	0	0	0	3	0	0	.000	.000
Cabrera, Asdrubal	B-R	6-0	170	11-13-85	.316	.333	.310	9	38	6	12	3	0	0	3	2	0	0	0	8	2	0	.395	.350
Choo, Shin-Soo	L-L	5-11	205	7-13-82	.260	.292	.245	59	208	34	54	11	2	3	26	21	3	0	6	40	10	3	.375	.328
Cooper, Jason	L-L	6-2	215	12-6-80	.260	.277	.253	103	339	60	88	26	8	10	51	51	2	0	3	81	9	2	.472	.357
Durrington, Trent	R-R	5-10	190	8-27-75	.226	.217	.228	71	195	30	44	5	2	1	20	26	3	5	2	41	15	5	.287	.323
Francisco, Ben	R-R	6-1	190	10-23-81	.318	.274	.337	95	377	60	120	27	2	12	51	36	4	6	2	66	22	8	.496	.382
Ginter, Keith	R-R	5-10	195	5-5-76	.247	.231	.254	106	369	50	91	15	1	15	62	63	9	1	7	68	3	3	.415	.364
Gutierrez, Franklin	R-R	6-2	180	2-21-83	.341	.361	.333	30	129	29	44	7	0	4	16	8	1	0	0	20	7	3	.488	.384
Haad, Yamid	R-R	6-2	220	9-2-77	.301	.278	.312	35	113	14	34	4	0	2	14	9	0	1	2	22	2	0	.389	.347
Inglett, Joe	L-R	5-10	180	6-29-78	.253	.228	.263	107	392	45	99	15	9	4	57	40	7	9	7	62	7	12	.367	.327
Larkin, Shaun	L-R	5-9	175	9-7-79	.000	—	.000	3	1	0	0	0	0	0	0	0	0	0	0	0	0	0	.000	.000
Luna, Hector	R-R	6-1	190	2-1-80	.251	.216	.267	83	323	39	81	18	0	6	35	21	2	0	4	48	4	4	.362	.297
2-team (18 Syracuse)					.267			101	390	54	104	25	1	8	43	30	5	0	4	62	4	4	.397	.324
Marte, Andy	R-R	6-1	190	10-21-83	.267	.261	.270	96	352	47	94	17	1	16	60	21	2	0	4	64	0	0	.457	.309
Mulhern, Ryan	R-R	6-2	205	11-29-80	.290	.293	.289	130	476	67	138	36	2	16	76	40	6	1	4	133	1	3	.475	.350
Panther, Nathan	L-L	6-0	180	7-12-81	.400	.500	.000	2	5	1	2	0	0	0	0	0	0	0	0	0	0	0	.400	.400
Rivas, Luis	R-R	5-11	190	8-30-79	.263	.248	.269	105	410	58	108	17	3	11	43	42	7	4	2	69	13	7	.400	.341
Rose, Mike	B-R	6-1	225	8-25-76	.262	.268	.260	88	290	37	76	18	1	7	36	34	1	5	5	71	1	4	.403	.336
Rouse, Mike	L-R	5-11	190	4-25-80	.277	.278	.277	20	65	11	18	4	1	0	3	9	1	3	1	8	1	1	.369	.368
Snyder, Brad	L-L	6-3	200	5-25-82	.263	.203	.289	86	259	41	68	12	3	10	35	36	2	4	2	91	12	0	.448	.355
Van Every, Jonathan	L-L	6-1	195	11-27-79	.272	.319	.252	51	158	17	43	5	1	8	23	23	2	2	1	57	2	3	.468	.370
Wallace, David	R-R	6-2	230	10-17-79	.115	.036	.147	33	96	9	11	1	0	3	4	11	1	2	0	3	4	1	.219	.213

PITCHING	B-T	HT	WT	DOB	W	L	ERA	G	GS	CG	SV	IP	H	R	ER	HR	BB	SO	AVG	vLH	vRH	K/9	BB/9
Beverlin, Jason	L-R	6-5	220	11-27-73	1	1	4.50	4	0	0	0	6	4	3	3	1	7	6	.211	.000	.364	9.00	10.50
Buzachero, Edward	R-R	5-11	180	6-13-81	4	7	5.24	42	3	0	1	67	74	48	39	8	21	42	.280	.325	.247	5.64	2.82
Deters, James	R-R	6-4	180	6-4-83	0	0	12.00	1	0	0	0	3	5	5	4	1	4	5	.333	.222	.500	15.00	12.00
Dittler, Jake	R-R	6-4	220	11-24-82	3	1	5.23	7	1	1	0	21	25	13	12	1	5	9	.313	.385	.278	3.92	2.18
DuBose, Eric	L-L	6-3	235	5-15-76	4	3	4.24	11	8	0	0	57	65	29	27	6	23	41	.294	.269	.305	6.44	3.61
Durrington, Trent	R-R	5-10	190	8-27-75	1	0	0.00	2	0	0	0	1	1	0	0	0	2	0	.200	.250	.000	0.00	13.50
Elarton, Scott	R-R	6-7	260	2-23-76	1	0	2.50	9	0	0	0	18	17	7	5	2	5	14	.246	.194	.303	7.00	2.50
Harris, Jeff	R-R	6-1	215	7-4-74	6	9	4.68	27	22	1	0	138	145	77	72	24	36	83	.266	.279	.250	5.40	2.34
Koplove, Mike	R-R	5-11	175	8-30-76	4	2	2.50	51	0	0	14	54	49	16	15	3	22	44	.243	.248	.237	7.33	3.67
Koronka, John	L-L	6-1	180	7-3-80	3	3	3.54	9	9	1	0	48	62	25	19	2	17	29	.312	.266	.342	5.40	3.17
Laffey, Aaron	L-L	6-0	185	4-15-85	9	3	3.08	16	15	2	0	96	89	36	33	5	23	75	.243	.250	.240	7.01	2.15
Lara, Juan	R-L	6-2	205	1-26-81	4	3	3.88	52	0	0	2	58	53	28	25	3	27	50	.245	.280	.227	7.76	4.19
Lee, Cliff	L-L	6-3	190	8-30-78	1	3	3.51	8	8	0	0	41	32	17	16	1	25	50	.206	.196	.212	10.98	5.49
Lewis, Jensen	R-R	6-3	195	5-16-84	1	0	1.38	10	0	0	1	13	5	2	2	1	4	12	.116	.053	.167	8.31	2.77
Lofgren, Chuck	L-L	6-4	215	1-29-86	0	1	10.80	1	1	0	0	5	7	6	6	1	3	7	.350	.000	.500	12.60	5.40
Miller, Adam	R-R	6-4	200	11-26-84	5	4	4.82	19	11	1	0	65	68	39	35	4	21	68	.265	.275	.252	9.37	2.89
Miller, Matt	R-R	6-1	215	11-23-71	0	1	2.89	38	0	0	1	37	25	16	12	4	21	36	.200	.196	.203	8.68	5.06
Mujica, Edward	R-R	6-2	220	5-10-84	2	1	5.02	34	0	0	14	38	35	22	21	4	9	44	.248	.304	.194	10.51	2.15
Niesel, Christopher	R-R	5-11	195	11-18-82	0	0	4.50	1	0	0	0	2	2	1	1	0	0	2	.250	.250	.000	0.00	0.00
Perez, Rafael	L-L	6-2	185	5-15-82	3	3	3.66	8	7	0	0	47	53	27	19	3	11	31	.298	.325	.290	5.98	2.12
Pesco, Nick	R-R	6-6	195	9-17-83	0	0	24.55	2	0	0	0	4	11	10	10	0	6	4	.500	.500	.500	9.82	14.73
Rundles, Rich	L-L	6-5	180	6-3-81	2	4	2.70	17	0	0	0	27	28	15	8	1	16	19	.259	.175	.309	6.41	5.40
Sikorski, Brian	R-R	6-1	190	7-27-74	0	1	3.52	13	0	0	2	15	11	7	6	2	7	21	.193	.129	.269	12.33	4.11
Slocum, Brian	R-R	6-3	210	3-27-81	2	2	4.15	5	5	0	0	26	21	13	12	3	16	28	.208	.204	.213	9.69	5.54
Smith, Sean	R-R	6-4	195	10-13-83	9	7	4.25	24	21	1	0	133	130	67	63	16	58	90	.260	.265	.256	6.07	3.91
Sowers, Jeremy	L-L	6-1	180	5-17-83	4	5	4.10	15	15	1	0	97	112	56	44	6	24	61	.288	.236	.308	5.68	2.23
Stanford, Jason	L-L	6-1	205	1-23-77	5	1	4.11	18	14	0	0	88	84	45	40	8	34	60	.256	.308	.240	6.16	3.49
Warden, Jim Ed	R-R	6-7	195	5-7-79	1	1	7.33	16	0	0	0	23	38	25	19	2	12	20	.369	.362	.375	7.71	4.63
Westbrook, Jake	R-R	6-3	200	9-29-77	0	1	8.44	2	2	0	0	5	9	7	5	0	5	5	.375	.600	.214	8.44	8.44

FIELDING

Catcher	PCT	G	PO	A	E	DP	PB
Durrington	1.000	3	2	0	0	0	0
Haad	.983	34	217	17	4	5	6
Rose	.993	84	568	37	4	10	8
Wallace	.996	32	212	13	1	1	4

First Base	PCT	G	PO	A	E	DP
Durrington	.947	6	17	1	1	1
Ginter	1.000	26	202	15	0	23
Larkin	1.000	2	3	1	0	1
Luna	1.000	10	71	8	0	4
Mulhern	.992	106	872	63	8	89

Second Base	PCT	G	PO	A	E	DP
Cabrera	1.000	4	3	4	0	1
Durrington	.957	22	39	50	4	12

Ginter	1.000	2	4	7	0	0
Inglett	.976	59	123	164	7	45
Luna	.897	13	25	36	7	6
Rivas	.967	49	81	122	7	29

Third Base	PCT	G	PO	A	E	DP
Durrington	.846	7	3	8	2	0
Ginter	.958	48	32	105	6	13
Luna	.944	8	5	12	1	2
Marte	.936	87	63	187	17	21

Shortstop	PCT	G	PO	A	E	DP
Cabrera	1.000	5	8	12	0	3
Ginter	1.000	1	0	1	0	0
Inglett	.972	9	13	22	1	4
Luna	.946	53	84	144	13	38

Rivas	.943	59	72	145	13	22
Rouse	.909	20	27	43	7	9

Outfield	PCT	G	PO	A	E	DP
Barton	.964	25	53	0	2	0
Choo	1.000	41	58	2	0	0
Cooper	1.000	77	144	5	0	0
Durrington	1.000	9	17	1	0	1
Francisco	.984	85	175	4	3	1
Gutierrez	.987	29	73	3	1	0
Inglett	.987	40	74	4	1	0
Panther	1.000	2	2	1	0	1
Rose	1.000	1	2	0	0	0
Snyder	.980	80	144	6	3	3
Van Every	1.000	50	144	5	0	2

EASTERN LEAGUE

BATTING	B-T	HT	WT	DOB	AVG	vLH	vRH	G	AB	R	H	2B	3B	HR	RBI	BB	HBP	SH	SF	SO	SB	CS	SLG	OBP
Arnal, Cristo	R-R	6-0	177	9-17-85	.000	.000	—	1	4	0	0	0	0	0	0	0	0	0	0	1	0	0	.000	.000
Aubrey, Michael	L-L	6-0	195	4-15-82	.248	.200	.261	52	206	22	51	11	0	7	34	10	3	0	2	35	0	0	.403	.290
Barton, Brian	R-R	6-3	187	4-25-82	.314	.303	.317	106	389	56	122	18	2	9	59	41	28	2	1	99	20	9	.440	.416

ORGANIZATION STATISTICS

	B-T	HT	WT	DOB	AVG	vLH	vRH	G	AB	R	H	2B	3B	HR	RBI	BB	HBP	SH	SF	SO	SB	CS	SLG	OBP
Brown, Jordan	L-L	6-0	205	12-18-83	.333	.333	.333	127	483	85	161	36	2	11	76	63	11	0	1	56	11	2	.484	.421
Cabrera, Asdrubal	B-R	6-0	170	11-13-85	.310	.265	.323	96	368	78	114	23	3	8	54	45	3	2	7	42	23	7	.454	.383
Camacaro, Armando	R-R	5-11	215	4-6-79	.333	.200	.375	6	21	3	7	1	0	1	6	0	0	0	0	3	0	0	.524	.333
Choy Foo, Rodney	B-R	6-1	190	12-12-81	.251	.283	.240	111	367	46	92	15	4	12	46	67	3	1	6	80	13	4	.411	.366
Crowe, Trevor	B-R	6-0	190	11-17-83	.259	.285	.251	133	518	87	134	26	4	5	50	62	4	2	3	71	28	9	.353	.341
Cumberbatch, Cirilo	B-R	6-2	185	7-11-86	.250	—	.250	2	8	1	2	2	0	0	2	0	0	0	0	0	0	0	.500	.250
De La Cruz, Chris	B-R	6-0	165	5-3-82	.341	.143	.378	15	44	11	15	0	1	0	1	5	0	3	0	3	1	2	.386	.408
Gimenez, Chris	R-R	6-2	190	12-27-82	.221	.333	.191	30	113	20	25	6	0	6	12	9	1	0	0	31	1	0	.434	.285
Goleski, Ryan	R-R	6-3	215	3-19-82	.257	.289	.246	128	471	50	121	18	4	9	73	51	6	1	8	101	9	9	.369	.332
Head, Stephen	L-L	6-3	220	1-13-84	.276	.192	.306	26	98	13	27	9	0	3	18	8	0	0	0	18	1	0	.459	.330
Herrera, Javi	R-R	6-1	200	10-8-81	.167	.000	.191	18	54	2	9	1	0	0	6	2	2	0	3	10	0	0	.185	.213
2-team (39 Harrisburg)					.228	—	—	57	167	19	38	5	0	4	23	25	5	0	5	26	1	2	.329	.337
Larkin, Shaun	L-R	5-9	175	9-7-79	.422	.455	.412	13	45	7	19	4	0	2	11	6	0	0	0	1	0	0	.644	.490
McBride, Matt	R-R	6-2	215	5-23-85	.571	—	.571	2	7	2	4	2	0	0	0	0	0	1	0	0	0	0	.857	.625
Osborn, Pat	R-R	6-4	210	2-27-81	.230	.279	.214	55	183	16	42	7	0	1	19	19	3	2	4	24	6	2	.284	.306
Panther, Nathan	L-L	6-1	180	7-12-81	.164	.231	.143	16	55	2	9	2	2	1	1	4	8	0	1	0	10	0	2	.291	.270
Pinckney, Brandon	R-R	5-10	165	4-12-82	.270	.356	.230	79	278	41	75	13	2	3	36	20	1	12	5	34	0	2	.363	.316
Reyes, Argenis	B-R	5-10	165	9-25-82	.278	.316	.269	125	467	65	130	21	4	3	32	23	1	11	1	56	27	8	.360	.313
Toregas, Wyatt	R-R	5-11	200	12-2-82	.250	.274	.243	86	284	36	71	16	0	6	39	27	4	2	7	45	3	1	.370	.317
Van Every, Jonathan	L-L	6-1	195	11-27-79	.344	.348	.344	44	151	27	52	14	5	4	34	19	1	3	2	48	4	5	.583	.416
Wallace, David	R-R	6-4	230	10-17-79	.214	.267	.185	26	84	14	18	2	0	5	13	13	2	0	1	30	0	0	.417	.330

PITCHING	B-T	HT	WT	DOB	W	L	ERA	G	GS	CG	SV	IP	H	R	ER	HR	BB	SO	AVG	vLH	vRH	K/9	BB/9
Brownlie, Robert	R-R	6-0	220	10-5-80	1	2	3.17	9	8	0	0	48	42	21	17	5	14	37	.227	.207	.247	6.89	2.61
Burton, T.J.	L-R	6-3	185	7-30-83	2	2	3.86	28	0	0	0	37	47	24	16	2	21	30	.303	.274	.323	7.23	5.06
Buzachero, Edward	R-R	5-11	180	6-13-81	2	1	6.10	10	0	0	2	10	15	7	7	0	0	9	.349	.375	.333	7.84	0.00
Cevette, Dan	L-L	6-4	205	10-19-83	0	1	9.00	1	1	0	0	4	6	4	4	0	3	4	.353	.571	.200	9.00	6.75
Collins, Kyle	R-R	6-1	165	8-17-81	0	2	8.10	10	0	0	1	13	18	13	12	4	6	8	.300	.280	.314	5.40	4.05
Dittler, Jake	R-R	6-4	220	11-24-82	6	1	4.25	20	9	0	0	72	77	37	34	4	26	40	.286	.301	.271	5.00	3.25
DuBose, Eric	L-L	6-3	235	5-15-76	1	2	9.61	4	4	0	0	20	26	21	21	4	12	17	.306	.273	.327	7.78	5.49
Finocchi, Mike	R-R	6-0	190	4-28-85	2	1	4.67	15	0	0	2	17	16	9	9	1	5	16	.254	.231	.270	8.31	2.60
Fultz, Aaron	L-L	6-0	210	9-4-73	0	0	0.00	1	1	0	0	1	0	0	0	0	0	1	.000	.000	.000	9.00	0.00
Gomez, Mariano	L-L	6-6	190	9-12-82	3	3	4.05	48	1	0	2	67	54	30	30	6	24	53	.230	.250	.219	7.15	3.24
Laffey, Aaron	L-L	6-0	185	4-15-85	4	1	2.31	6	6	0	0	35	29	13	9	2	7	24	.225	.194	.237	6.17	1.80
Lara, Juan	R-L	6-2	205	1-26-81	0	0	0.00	2	0	0	0	1	1	0	0	0	2	2	.167	.000	.250	13.50	0.00
Lee, Cliff	L-L	6-3	190	8-30-78	1	0	0.00	1	1	0	0	5	2	0	0	0	1	7	.111	.333	.000	12.60	1.80
Lewis, Jensen	R-R	6-3	195	5-16-84	2	0	1.85	24	0	0	1	39	27	12	8	2	13	49	.196	.227	.167	11.31	3.00
Lewis, Scott	B-L	6-0	185	9-26-83	7	9	3.68	27	25	0	0	135	135	58	55	13	34	121	.262	.222	.275	8.09	2.27
Lofgren, Chuck	L-L	6-4	215	1-29-86	12	7	4.37	26	26	0	0	146	153	79	71	14	68	123	.270	.310	.257	7.56	4.18
Martin, J.D.	R-R	6-4	205	1-2-83	2	3	4.25	9	9	0	0	42	42	22	20	4	16	23	.259	.253	.267	4.89	3.40
Ness, Joe	R-R	6-5	230	11-4-83	4	3	6.18	26	8	0	0	71	79	52	49	7	44	61	.282	.273	.292	7.70	5.55
Newsom, Randy	R-R	6-2	200	5-6-82	4	1	3.12	46	0	0	18	49	52	18	17	3	17	22	.283	.385	.208	4.04	3.12
Nottingham, Shawn	L-L	6-1	190	1-22-85	9	12	4.77	27	26	1	0	149	157	88	79	11	59	96	.275	.212	.296	5.80	3.56
Panther, Nathan	L-L	6-1	180	7-12-81	0	0	0.00	1	0	0	0	2	1	0	0	0	1	1	.167	.000	.200	4.50	4.50
Pesco, Nick	R-R	6-6	195	9-17-83	0	1	6.52	4	0	0	0	10	11	8	7	1	11	4	.297	.357	.261	3.72	10.24
Politte, Cliff	R-R	5-10	195	2-27-74	0	0	6.75	8	3	0	0	8	8	6	2	5	10	7	.267	.278	.250	11.25	5.62
Roehl, Scott	R-R	6-1	195	8-19-81	0	0	0.00	2	0	0	0	2	1	0	0	0	1	3	.125	.167	.000	13.50	4.50
Rundles, Rich	L-L	6-5	180	6-3-81	3	0	1.83	23	2	0	2	34	27	10	7	0	10	29	.216	.205	.221	7.60	2.62
Santos, Reid	L-L	6-1	170	8-24-82	8	3	2.72	39	10	0	2	96	80	39	29	10	30	85	.223	.216	.226	7.97	2.81
Stevens, Jeff	R-R	6-1	220	9-5-83	3	1	3.17	34	0	0	2	48	40	17	17	4	16	65	.223	.167	.257	12.10	2.98
Valdez, Luis	R-R	6-4	175	3-11-84	0	0	0.00	1	0	0	0	1	1	0	0	0	0	1	.250	.500	.000	9.00	0.00
Warden, Jim Ed	R-R	6-7	195	5-7-79	4	4	2.81	40	0	0	6	51	50	19	16	4	16	48	.246	.215	.273	8.42	2.81
Westbrook, Jake	R-R	6-3	200	9-29-77	0	1	15.43	1	1	0	0	2	5	4	4	0	3	1	.500	.500	.500	3.86	11.57

FIELDING

Catcher	PCT	G	PO	A	E	DP	PB
Camacaro	1.000	6	37	3	0	0	0
Gimenez	1.000	10	82	6	0	0	2
Herrera	1.000	19	99	9	0	0	1
McBride	1.000	2	17	0	0	0	0
Toregas	.989	84	597	44	7	9	3
Wallace	.995	25	177	9	1	2	2

First Base	PCT	G	PO	A	E	DP
Aubrey	.988	32	230	16	3	22
Brown	.990	95	700	60	8	74
Choy Foo	1.000	5	29	4	0	4
Head	1.000	8	72	8	0	7
Larkin	.973	4	34	2	1	1
Osborn	.972	5	33	2	1	5

Second Base	PCT	G	PO	A	E	DP
Cabrera	1.000	1	1	2	0	0
Choy Foo	1.000	9	16	19	0	3
De La Cruz	1.000	4	7	9	0	1
Pinckney	.984	15	24	39	1	9
Reyes	.983	113	244	287	9	82

Third Base	PCT	G	PO	A	E	DP
Choy Foo	.941	74	54	136	12	12
De La Cruz	—	2	0	0	0	0
Gimenez	.955	15	10	32	2	2
Larkin	1.000	2	2	2	0	0
Osborn	.930	48	30	89	9	8
Pinckney	1.000	4	0	4	0	1

Shortstop	PCT	G	PO	A	E	DP
Cabrera	.960	91	126	233	15	57
De La Cruz	.917	4	5	17	2	3
Pinckney	.955	49	59	134	9	26

Outfield	PCT	G	PO	A	E	DP
Barton	.990	97	189	3	2	0
Brown	.900	10	9	0	1	0
Crowe	.979	129	317	7	7	2
Cumberbatch	.667	2	2	0	1	0
Gimenez	.750	2	3	0	1	0
Goleski	.982	122	206	15	4	2
Head	1.000	18	33	0	0	0
Panther	1.000	16	25	0	0	0
Reyes	1.000	2	4	0	0	0
Van Every	.962	31	100	0	4	0

KINSTON INDIANS   HIGH CLASS A

CAROLINA LEAGUE

BATTING	B-T	HT	WT	DOB	AVG	vLH	vRH	G	AB	R	H	2B	3B	HR	RBI	BB	HBP	SH	SF	SO	SB	CS	SLG	OBP
Arnal, Cristo	R-R	6-0	177	9-17-85	.100	.000	.111	3	10	0	1	0	0	0	0	0	0	0	0	3	0	0	.200	.100
Aubrey, Michael	L-L	6-0	195	4-15-82	.400	.571	.333	13	50	15	20	5	0	5	11	6	3	0	0	7	0	0	.800	.492
Butia, Mike	L-R	6-2	215	11-29-82	.215	.215	.215	99	325	46	70	16	0	7	47	53	3	3	5	73	2	1	.329	.326
Camacaro, Armando	R-R	5-11	215	4-6-79	.233	.182	.250	28	90	12	21	6	0	6	19	7	2	3	1	19	1	0	.500	.300
Constanza, Jose	B-L	5-9	150	9-1-83	.274	.232	.288	112	445	71	122	13	4	2	34	39	2	10	2	80	39	9	.335	.334
De La Cruz, Chris	B-R	6-0	165	5-3-82	.318	.329	.313	63	242	40	77	15	0	1	26	28	1	5	2	28	2	3	.393	.388
Drennen, John	L-L	6-0	190	8-26-86	.254	.153	.292	131	496	72	126	25	2	13	77	53	10	2	4	104	6	6	.391	.336
Finegan, Brian	R-R	6-0	190	12-15-81	.253	.264	.248	69	229	36	58	16	0	1	21	33	7	1	2	51	8	2	.336	.362

BATTING	B-T	HT	WT	DOB	AVG	vLH	vRH	G	AB	R	H	2B	3B	HR	RBI	BB	HBP	SH	SF	SO	SB	CS	SLG	OBP
Gimenez, Chris	R-R	6-2	190	12-27-82	.283	.299	.275	83	269	56	76	14	1	20	54	50	8	2	3	55	3	2	.565	.406
Goedert, Jared	R-R	6-1	180	5-25-85	.256	.222	.270	35	125	23	32	9	0	4	23	23	0	0	1	25	1	0	.424	.369
Head, Jerad	R-R	6-1	195	11-15-82	.266	.252	.275	83	252	39	67	17	3	5	32	29	17	2	1	56	7	3	.417	.378
Head, Stephen	L-L	6-3	220	1-13-84	.251	.277	.241	102	387	73	97	29	0	13	61	40	13	1	6	71	5	0	.426	.336
Hodges, Wes	R-R	6-2	180	9-14-84	.288	.317	.277	104	393	60	113	22	3	15	71	44	8	0	5	90	0	0	.473	.367
Mills, Beau	L-R	6-3	220	8-15-86	.275	.000	.355	10	40	7	11	6	0	1	5	4	3	0	1	8	0	0	.500	.375
Panther, Nathan	L-L	6-1	180	7-12-81	.287	.214	.305	67	209	43	60	13	3	10	28	42	5	3	0	41	6	4	.522	.418
Ramirez, Max	R-R	5-11	170	10-11-84	.303	.247	.332	77	277	46	84	20	0	12	62	53	6	0	6	63	1	0	.505	.418
Realini, Dustin	R-R	6-2	200	5-14-84	.407	.462	.357	8	27	8	11	4	0	0	3	3	0	0	0	5	0	0	.556	.467
Rodriguez, Joshua	R-R	6-0	175	12-18-84	.262	.248	.267	133	493	84	129	20	9	20	82	68	2	1	4	95	21	8	.460	.351
Romero, Niuman	B-R	6-0	160	1-24-85	.350	.231	.407	12	40	5	14	2	0	0	6	4	0	0	1	9	1	0	.400	.400
Weglarz, Nicholas	L-L	6-3	215	12-16-87	.143	.000	.250	2	7	1	1	0	0	1	1	1	0	0	0	3	0	0	.571	.250
Whitney, Matthew	R-R	6-4	200	2-13-84	.288	.290	.287	57	226	43	65	11	0	16	49	22	0	0	3	59	1	0	.549	.347
Wu, Chao Kuan	L-R	6-3	192	5-25-84	.280	.250	.286	13	25	2	7	0	0	0	1	3	0	0	0	3	0	0	.280	.357

PITCHING	B-T	HT	WT	DOB	W	L	ERA	G	GS	CG	SV	IP	H	R	ER	HR	BB	SO	AVG	vLH	vRH	K/9	BB/9
Burton, T.J.	L-R	6-3	185	7-30-83	5	0	1.75	20	0	0	0	26	24	7	5	2	8	29	.235	.176	.265	10.17	2.81
Cevette, Dan	L-L	6-4	205	10-19-83	2	0	4.45	13	3	0	0	30	30	15	15	3	16	32	.263	.348	.242	9.49	4.75
Collina, Kyle	R-R	6-2	185	1-21-84	0	0	0.00	2	0	0	0	2	2	0	0	0	1	1	.286	.000	.333	4.50	4.50
Collins, Kyle	R-R	6-1	165	8-17-81	2	3	6.52	23	0	0	1	29	40	24	21	3	27	22	.331	.370	.299	6.83	8.38
Deters, James	R-R	6-4	180	6-4-83	12	4	2.24	33	10	0	1	112	101	36	28	9	21	66	.232	.243	.227	5.29	1.68
Dixon, Kevin	R-R	6-3	225	12-16-83	10	4	3.72	28	22	0	2	133	143	73	55	9	41	72	.272	.280	.266	4.87	2.77
Edell, Ryan	L-L	6-1	215	7-6-83	11	6	3.70	31	17	0	1	122	122	54	50	12	31	109	.262	.241	.266	8.06	2.29
Finocchi, Mike	R-R	6-0	190	4-28-85	3	2	2.84	30	0	0	3	57	56	24	18	0	26	36	.249	.167	.298	5.68	4.11
Herrmann, Frank	L-R	6-4	220	5-30-84	11	5	4.01	26	26	3	0	146	163	75	65	15	28	88	.285	.285	.285	5.42	1.73
Huff, David	L-L	6-2	190	8-22-84	4	2	2.72	11	11	0	0	60	57	23	18	4	15	46	.251	.314	.240	6.94	2.26
Lee, Cliff	L-L	6-3	190	8-30-78	0	0	0.00	1	1	0	0	2	1	0	0	0	0	4	.143	.000	.167	18.00	0.00
Meyer, Matt	L-L	6-4	210	1-17-85	3	4	4.32	32	0	0	3	50	50	28	24	4	32	58	.258	.254	.260	10.44	5.76
Newsom, Randy	R-R	6-2	200	5-6-82	0	1	1.50	11	0	0	0	12	11	2	2	1	1	9	.234	.250	.231	6.75	0.75
Niesel, Christopher	R-T	5-11	195	11-18-82	4	1	3.00	23	0	0	1	45	36	16	15	1	9	36	.222	.242	.210	7.20	1.80
Panther, Nathan	L-L	6-1	180	7-12-81	0	0	0.00	1	0	0	0	1	1	0	0	0	2	1	.000	.000	.000	13.50	27.00
Pesco, Nick	R-R	6-6	195	9-17-83	0	0	0.00	1	0	0	0	1	0	0	0	0	3	1	.000	.000	.000	9.00	27.00
Roehl, Scott	R-R	6-1	195	8-19-81	4	0	2.66	44	0	0	24	47	48	15	14	3	18	42	.264	.209	.296	7.99	3.42
Stevens, Jeff	R-R	6-1	220	9-5-83	3	2	2.31	15	0	0	0	35	18	13	9	2	9	37	.150	.209	.117	9.51	2.31
Stiller, Erik	R-R	6-5	200	7-10-84	3	6	2.89	25	5	0	4	62	56	24	20	6	13	49	.236	.291	.205	7.07	1.88
Tomlin, Josh	R-R	6-1	175	10-19-84	1	1	3.58	6	5	0	0	28	24	13	11	0	12	20	.231	.333	.176	6.51	3.90
Tseng, Sung-Wei	R-R	5-10	195	12-28-84	6	9	4.05	26	26	0	0	140	130	71	63	10	47	92	.250	.224	.268	5.91	3.02
Wagner, Neil	R-R	6-0	195	1-1-84	0	0	3.00	16	0	0	0	24	17	8	8	2	6	18	.198	.171	.222	6.75	2.25
Wright, Steven	R-R	6-2	205	9-30-84	3	2	7.13	13	13	0	0	48	64	47	38	3	22	39	.320	.359	.287	7.31	4.12
Wu, Chao Kuan	L-R	6-3	192	5-25-84	0	0	9.00	1	0	0	0	1	1	1	1	0	2	0	.333	1.000	.000	0.00	18.00

FIELDING

Catcher	PCT	G	PO	A	E	DP	PB
Camacaro	.990	27	186	15	2	1	
Gimenez	.993	45	257	25	2	2	7
Ramirez	.984	66	451	27	8	8	9
Wu	1.000	12	37	2	0	0	2

First Base	PCT	G	PO	A	E	DP
Aubrey	1.000	8	76	5	0	2
Camacaro	1.000	1	5	0	0	0
Gimenez	1.000	10	72	3	0	5
S. Head	.997	70	648	48	2	42
Mills	1.000	3	34	3	0	2
Realini	.974	7	36	1	1	3
Whitney	.987	46	361	27	5	26

Second Base	PCT	G	PO	A	E	DP
Arnal	1.000	2	2	7	0	1

(2B)	PCT	G	PO	A	E	DP
De La Cruz	.973	50	103	152	7	27
Finegan	.966	49	96	131	8	23
Goedert	.980	31	54	94	3	14
J. Head	.950	12	18	20	2	4
Romero	1.000	1	2	0	0	0

Third Base	PCT	G	PO	A	E	DP
Arnal	1.000	1	0	2	0	1
De La Cruz	.903	9	7	21	3	2
Finegan	1.000	7	7	5	0	0
Gimenez	—	1	0	0	0	0
Goedert	.917	3	2	9	1	0
J. Head	.921	11	6	29	3	1
Hodges	.922	97	55	169	19	10
Mills	1.000	3	2	9	0	0
Realini	.800	2	1	3	1	0
Romero	1.000	8	3	20	0	2

Shortstop	PCT	G	PO	A	E	DP
De La Cruz	1.000	4	3	7	0	0
Finegan	.933	11	20	36	4	7
Rodriguez	.943	125	163	371	32	56
Romero	1.000	3	2	8	0	1

Outfield	PCT	G	PO	A	E	DP
Butia	.983	57	112	4	2	0
Constanza	.983	108	225	7	4	1
Drennen	.983	121	225	3	4	2
Finegan	1.000	3	2	0	0	0
Gimenez	.889	7	7	1	1	1
J. Head	.966	57	109	3	4	2
S. Head	1.000	17	36	0	0	0
Panther	.979	60	136	6	3	1
Weglarz	—	2	0	0	0	0

LAKE COUNTY CAPTAINS

LOW CLASS A

SOUTH ATLANTIC LEAGUE

BATTING	B-T	HT	WT	DOB	AVG	vLH	vRH	G	AB	R	H	2B	3B	HR	RBI	BB	HBP	SH	SF	SO	SB	CS	SLG	OBP
Alcombrack, Robert	R-R	6-0	205	6-10-88	.143	1.000	.000	2	7	1	1	0	0	0	0	0	0	0	0	3	0	0	.143	.143
Alvarado, Ramon	R-R	6-1	185	6-3-85	1.000	—	1.000	1	1	0	1	0	0	0	0	0	0	0	0	0	0	0	1.000	1.000
Arnal, Cristo	R-R	6-0	177	9-17-85	.229	.375	.185	12	35	7	8	2	0	0	2	4	1	1	0	5	1	2	.286	.325
Castillo, Alex	R-R	6-0	168	11-29-85	.195	.158	.206	27	87	6	17	3	0	1	9	7	1	5	1	19	1	0	.264	.260
Cumberbatch, Cirilo	B-R	6-2	185	7-11-86	.300	.289	.304	82	290	46	87	13	2	6	43	34	11	3	5	50	5	1	.421	.388
Davis, Adam	B-R	5-9	185	10-15-84	.266	.255	.270	127	500	95	133	23	8	6	41	74	6	2	1	113	22	11	.380	.367
Denham, Jason	L-L	6-0	170	5-1-86	.255	.266	.251	112	440	76	112	11	3	7	43	57	3	5	4	105	29	10	.341	.341
Flores, Osiel	R-R	6-0	194	6-1-84	.000	—	.000	2	3	0	0	0	0	0	0	0	0	0	0	2	0	0	.000	.000
Garcia, Felipe	R-R	6-3	225	5-15-83	.242	.316	.209	19	62	9	15	2	0	1	6	5	5	1	2	12	0	0	.323	.338
Goedert, Jared	R-R	6-1	180	5-25-85	.364	.308	.381	46	165	44	60	10	0	16	51	35	2	1	2	29	0	1	.715	.475
Hernandez, Ramon	R-R	6-0	170	8-25-86	.162	.200	.146	23	68	6	11	3	0	1	10	8	1	1	0	19	1	0	.250	.260
Juhl, Brian	R-R	6-0	205	9-22-85	.235	.125	.295	21	68	10	16	2	0	1	7	13	3	1	2	20	1	0	.309	.372
Lytle, Andrew	R-R	6-1	165	9-15-82	.152	.167	.148	13	33	5	5	1	0	0	6	3	0	0	1	9	1	1	.182	.256
McBride, Matt	R-R	6-2	215	5-23-85	.283	.353	.255	105	421	66	119	35	2	8	66	38	6	0	7	54	1	0	.432	.348
Mills, Beau	L-R	6-3	220	8-15-86	.271	.321	.248	44	177	32	48	12	1	5	36	14	4	0	3	38	0	0	.435	.333
Montero, Lucas	B-R	5-11	180	10-18-84	.252	.321	.229	34	111	13	28	5	4	1	15	9	2	0	0	26	1	0	.396	.308
Pacheco, Fernando	L-L	6-1	205	10-1-84	.180	.250	.160	38	122	10	22	2	0	4	10	8	2	0	0	43	0	0	.295	.242
Pena, Roman	L-L	6-0	190	9-2-86	.240	.265	.231	123	455	58	109	20	6	7	70	60	12	4	2	138	2	4	.356	.342
Realini, Dustin	R-R	6-2	200	5-14-84	.222	.263	.210	24	81	9	18	3	1	1	7	9	1	1	0	27	0	0	.321	.308
Rivero, Carlos	R-R	6-3	198	5-20-88	.261	.245	.266	115	436	59	114	26	0	7	62	47	1	2	4	84	1	2	.369	.332

	B-T	HT	WT	DOB	AVG	vLH	vRH	G	AB	R	H	2B	3B	HR	RBI	BB	HBP	SH	SF	SO	SB	CS	SLG	OBP
Romero, Niuman	B-R	6-0	160	1-24-85	.209	.167	.224	69	215	31	45	10	2	1	24	44	5	2	3	45	3	1	.288	.352
Tavarez, Argenis	B-R	5-11	165	2-19-84	.212	.455	.146	17	52	5	11	5	0	0	7	4	0	2	0	9	1	1	.308	.268
Uribes, David	R-R	5-11	170	12-22-84	.220	.341	.174	49	159	22	35	1	0	1	11	20	2	0	3	17	6	4	.245	.310
Weglarz, Nicholas	L-L	6-3	215	12-16-87	.276	.284	.272	125	439	75	121	28	0	23	82	82	7	1	3	129	1	1	.497	.395
Whitney, Matthew	R-R	6-4	205	2-13-84	.308	.366	.288	71	286	52	88	19	0	16	64	31	4	0	5	62	0	1	.542	.377

PITCHING

	B-T	HT	WT	DOB	W	L	ERA	G	GS	CG	SV	IP	H	R	ER	HR	BB	SO	AVG	vLH	vRH	K/9	BB/9
Archer, Christopher	R-R	6-2	165	9-26-88	0	0	9.00	1	0	0	0	4	5	4	4	0	3	5	.333	.400	.300	11.25	6.75
Brech, Alan	L-L	6-0	195	9-10-84	4	0	2.62	21	0	0	0	34	28	10	10	4	12	21	.222	.297	.191	5.50	3.15
Bunkelman, Cody	R-R	6-3	225	2-6-85	1	2	6.93	24	0	0	1	38	40	30	29	3	32	30	.272	.290	.259	7.17	7.65
Collina, Kyle	R-R	6-2	185	1-21-84	1	0	0.00	4	2	0	0	14	5	0	0	0	2	18	.109	.105	.111	11.85	1.32
Creps, Austin	R-R	6-2	175	2-23-85	1	3	6.11	25	0	0	1	46	70	40	31	5	11	33	.340	.351	.330	6.50	2.17
Eisenberg, Michael	L-R	6-7	200	2-19-85	1	5	6.96	8	8	0	0	32	40	27	25	4	22	34	.305	.200	.382	9.46	6.12
Espino, Paolo	R-R	5-10	190	1-10-87	4	5	3.66	33	13	0	0	108	95	53	44	20	31	116	.231	.219	.239	9.64	2.58
Frias, Santo	R-R	6-3	189	12-8-87	0	0	4.32	2	1	0	0	8	7	4	4	0	5	8	.233	.400	.150	8.64	5.40
Fultz, Aaron	L-L	6-0	210	9-4-73	0	0	0.00	1	0	0	0	1	0	0	0	0	0	0	.000	.000	.000	9.00	0.00
Gomez, Jeanmar	R-R	6-3	168	10-2-88	11	7	4.80	27	27	1	0	141	152	84	75	19	46	94	.278	.214	.328	6.01	2.94
Jones, Christopher	L-L	6-2	165	9-19-88	0	1	6.75	1	1	0	0	4	4	3	3	1	3	2	.286	.000	.364	4.50	6.75
Lytle, Andrew	R-R	6-1	165	9-15-82	0	0	0.00	1	0	0	0	1	1	0	0	0	0	0	.200	1.000	.000	0.00	0.00
Meyer, Matt	L-L	6-4	210	1-17-85	0	0	0.50	11	0	0	0	18	12	6	1	1	5	20	.182	.118	.204	10.00	2.50
Montero, Joanniel	R-R	6-5	191	2-2-86	0	0	4.38	4	2	0	0	12	10	6	6	0	4	7	.222	.118	.286	5.11	2.92
Morris, Ryan	L-L	6-3	175	1-10-88	0	2	5.22	9	9	0	0	40	31	23	23	2	23	31	.217	.147	.239	7.03	5.22
Pacheco, Fernando	L-L	6-1	205	10-1-84	0	0	0.00	1	0	0	0	1	0	0	0	0	0	1	.000	.000	.000	9.00	0.00
Perdomo, Luis	R-R	6-0	170	4-27-84	4	6	3.27	56	0	0	10	66	43	28	24	6	26	81	.181	.247	.138	11.05	3.55
Pontius, Mike	R-R	6-2	235	10-26-87	0	3	5.84	13	0	0	0	25	22	22	16	5	12	27	.232	.140	.308	9.85	4.38
Robinson, Matthew	R-R	6-1	190	12-20-83	1	4	8.44	17	0	0	0	27	38	30	25	2	8	21	.336	.465	.257	7.09	2.70
Rondon, Hector	R-R	6-3	165	2-26-88	7	10	4.37	27	27	0	0	136	143	78	66	13	27	113	.269	.288	.255	7.48	1.79
Smith, Carlton	L-R	6-1	200	1-23-86	11	6	4.22	31	18	0	0	122	125	67	57	13	33	79	.260	.249	.267	5.84	2.44
Sumner, Scott	R-R	6-2	185	7-21-83	1	0	6.11	17	0	0	1	28	38	20	19	2	21	33	.322	.391	.278	10.61	6.75
Tomlin, Josh	R-R	6-1	175	10-19-84	10	3	3.30	26	15	0	0	104	103	44	38	10	19	89	.255	.242	.264	7.73	1.65
Turek, Travis	R-R	6-1	170	9-2-87	0	2	13.14	7	0	0	0	12	21	19	18	2	9	2	.389	.417	.367	1.46	6.57
Valdez, Luis	R-R	6-4	175	3-11-84	2	3	4.71	40	0	0	2	71	70	47	37	4	27	64	.254	.263	.249	8.15	3.44
Wagner, Neil	R-R	6-0	195	1-1-84	1	4	3.68	34	0	0	11	44	41	21	18	3	11	49	.246	.265	.232	10.02	2.25
Westbrook, Jake	R-R	6-3	200	9-29-77	0	1	7.20	1	1	0	0	5	6	5	4	0	0	5	.286	.125	.385	9.00	0.00
Wright, Steven	R-R	6-2	205	9-30-84	4	7	4.61	14	14	0	0	66	61	37	34	9	15	75	.243	.248	.239	10.18	2.04

FIELDING

Catcher	PCT	G	PO	A	E	DP	PB
Alcombrack	1.000	2	16	2	0	0	0
Castillo	.973	26	194	20	6	0	7
Flores	1.000	1	5	1	0	0	0
Juhl	.987	19	148	7	2	0	2
McBride	.988	87	644	43	8	2	16
Tavarez	.984	7	57	6	1	1	1

First Base	PCT	G	PO	A	E	DP
Flores	1.000	1	1	0	0	0
Garcia	1.000	7	57	2	0	3
Lytle	1.000	4	12	0	0	2
Mills	.994	17	159	7	1	11
Pacheco	.984	36	288	13	5	24
Realini	.976	8	71	9	2	8
Romero	.952	6	36	4	2	3
Tavarez	.923	3	10	2	1	0

Uribes	1.000	4	27	2	0	1
Whitney	.973	63	545	33	16	51

Second Base	PCT	G	PO	A	E	DP
Arnal	1.000	4	14	13	0	4
Davis	.977	104	165	305	11	63
Goedert	.946	8	18	17	2	2
Romero	1.000	1	3	1	0	0
Tavarez	1.000	1	0	3	0	0
Uribes	.981	29	40	63	2	12

Third Base	PCT	G	PO	A	E	DP
Arnal	.667	4	1	1	1	0
Davis	.903	25	15	41	6	1
Goedert	.919	34	28	63	8	4
Lytle	.909	7	1	9	1	1
Mills	.914	22	20	33	5	4
Realini	.824	12	2	12	3	2

Romero	.956	43	25	83	5	6

Shortstop	PCT	G	PO	A	E	DP
Lytle	1.000	2	0	3	0	0
Rivero	.951	112	142	343	25	65
Romero	.955	20	30	54	4	9
Uribes	.909	7	9	11	2	3

Outfield	PCT	G	PO	A	E	DP
Alvarado	—	1	0	0	0	0
Arnal	1.000	2	2	0	0	0
Cumberbatch	.961	65	114	9	5	2
Denham	.991	101	208	7	2	2
Hernandez	.953	22	40	1	2	0
Montero	.952	19	18	2	1	0
Pena	.968	112	230	10	8	3
Weglarz	.942	105	160	3	10	1

MAHONING VALLEY SCRAPPERS

SHORT-SEASON

NEW YORK-PENN LEAGUE

BATTING

	B-T	HT	WT	DOB	AVG	vLH	vRH	G	AB	R	H	2B	3B	HR	RBI	BB	HBP	SH	SF	SO	SB	CS	SLG	OBP
Alvarado, Ramon	R-R	6-1	185	6-3-85	.250	.286	.240	10	32	3	8	0	0	0	1	4	1	0	0	12	0	1	.250	.351
Arnal, Cristo	R-R	6-0	177	9-17-85	.250	.136	.282	31	100	21	25	3	0	0	4	8	0	2	0	13	6	2	.280	.306
Brown, Matthew	L-R	6-1	183	2-21-85	.250	.188	.275	63	224	22	56	14	3	0	31	25	2	1	4	41	6	1	.339	.325
Castillo, Alex	R-R	6-0	168	11-29-85	.259	.240	.267	48	166	20	43	7	1	1	23	14	3	3	3	36	7	1	.331	.323
Douglas, Stephen	L-R	6-2	185	5-10-85	.140	.333	.108	12	43	4	6	0	0	0	2	5	0	0	0	10	3	1	.140	.229
Flores, Osiel	R-R	6-0	194	6-1-84	.239	.400	.196	24	71	5	17	2	0	1	5	9	0	0	2	22	0	0	.310	.325
Hehr, Jeffrey	R-R	6-0	180	7-27-85	.234	.211	.240	50	167	18	39	4	0	0	18	12	5	1	2	28	4	1	.257	.301
Infante, Jansy	B-R	6-1	170	2-27-86	.292	.300	.288	63	240	39	70	10	0	2	23	30	3	7	0	40	4	4	.333	.377
Jenkins, Justin	R-R	6-2	210	6-3-83	.230	.179	.245	48	178	16	41	11	2	3	22	10	2	0	0	42	3	2	.365	.279
Martin, Todd	L-L	6-3	210	6-25-83	.360	.333	.369	54	197	27	71	8	1	8	40	23	2	0	5	40	0	0	.533	.423
Mills, Beau	L-R	6-3	220	8-15-86	.179	.273	.118	28	28	5	5	2	0	0	1	3	2	0	0	7	0	0	.250	.303
Montero, Lucas	B-R	5-11	180	10-18-84	.333	.000	.400	3	12	1	4	1	0	0	1	0	0	0	0	2	0	0	.417	.385
Nash, Chris	R-R	6-4	230	2-22-87	.274	.304	.256	16	62	4	17	4	1	0	12	7	1	0	1	18	0	0	.371	.352
Pacheco, Fernando	L-L	6-1	205	10-1-84	.188	.222	.143	6	16	3	3	1	0	0	3	3	0	0	0	3	0	0	.250	.316
Petrucci, Nicholas	R-R	6-1	190	7-16-85	.192	.200	.189	49	177	21	34	6	3	3	18	9	1	1	1	40	1	0	.311	.234
Realini, Dustin	R-R	6-2	200	5-14-84	.205	.111	.229	15	44	1	9	1	0	0	6	5	0	0	2	0	1	12	.227	.294
Sanchez, Karexon	B-R	5-11	175	8-22-87	.333	.333	.333	11	33	2	11	2	2	0	9	8	0	0	0	3	9	2	.515	.488
Thompson, Mark	R-R	5-9	165	11-26-84	.240	.243	.239	71	250	35	60	9	2	0	24	25	17	3	3	60	11	2	.292	.346
Valadez, Michael	R-R	6-1	220	5-31-86	.240	.217	.247	27	100	9	24	2	0	0	6	3	1	0	0	19	0	0	.260	.269
Valdes, Juan	B-R	6-0	150	6-22-85	.319	.300	.329	34	119	29	38	5	1	4	26	20	1	1	2	29	8	1	.479	.415
White, Adam	B-R	5-10	190	4-21-85	.260	.310	.242	57	219	39	57	9	5	1	10	26	9	3	0	45	22	8	.361	.362

PITCHING

	B-T	HT	WT	DOB	W	L	ERA	G	GS	CG	SV	IP	H	R	ER	HR	BB	SO	AVG	vLH	vRH	K/9	BB/9
Brech, Alan	L-L	6-0	195	9-10-84	1	0	0.00	2	1	0	0	7	8	1	0	0	2	3	.296	.500	.280	4.05	2.70
Brettl, James	L-L	6-0	180	2-21-84	3	0	2.50	20	0	0	0	36	30	11	10	1	8	20	.236	.237	.236	5.00	2.00

Name	B-T	HT	WT	DOB	W	L	ERA	G	GS	CG	SV	IP	H	R	ER	HR	BB	SO	AVG	vLH	vRH	K/9	BB/9
Bunton, Nathan	R-R	6-1	205	6-1-84	0	2	7.71	11	0	0	0	12	12	11	10	0	10	6	.261	.250	.265	4.63	7.71
Campfield, Garrison	R-R	6-1	200	5-29-84	1	0	0.00	6	0	0	0	11	5	0	0	0	3	5	.152	.100	.174	4.22	2.53
Carlin, Brett	L-L	5-11	180	4-3-85	0	0	0.82	7	0	0	1	11	10	2	1	0	5	8	.250	.167	.265	6.55	4.09
Cawiezell, Dallas	R-R	6-6	255	9-4-85	0	1	3.46	8	0	0	1	13	12	6	5	0	5	13	.273	.200	.333	9.00	3.46
Collina, Kyle	R-R	6-2	185	1-21-84	0	2	4.15	10	0	0	0	17	12	10	8	1	7	21	.185	.235	.167	10.90	3.63
De La Cruz, Kelvin	L-L	6-5	187	1-8-88	2	4	3.98	12	12	0	0	54	41	27	24	5	34	53	.216	.313	.183	8.78	5.63
Delage, William	L-L	6-1	170	7-12-84	0	4	4.38	14	6	0	0	37	37	22	18	4	16	38	.272	.122	.337	9.24	3.89
Eisenberg, Michael	L-R	6-7	200	2-19-85	4	7	4.08	15	15	0	0	79	76	41	36	7	17	50	.252	.312	.210	5.67	1.93
Frega, Daniel	R-R	6-5	195	11-16-84	6	2	3.49	15	10	0	0	57	64	33	22	3	26	43	.291	.346	.259	6.83	4.13
Holt, Jonathan	L-R	6-2	210	3-10-86	2	3	4.32	16	4	0	4	33	36	22	16	5	4	27	.261	.267	.256	7.29	1.08
Judy, Josh	R-R	6-4	200	2-9-86	0	0	0.00	4	1	0	1	11	7	0	0	0	3	7	.194	.278	.111	5.73	2.45
Landis, Kyle	R-R	6-1	185	5-30-86	1	0	0.33	20	0	0	6	27	17	4	1	1	10	37	.170	.114	.200	12.18	3.29
Miller, Ryan	L-L	6-0	195	12-14-86	0	2	18.69	3	3	0	0	4	9	10	9	1	8	3	.409	1.000	.381	6.23	16.62
Montero, Joanniel	R-R	6-5	191	2-2-86	7	3	3.69	14	10	0	0	63	61	28	26	3	7	21	.258	.232	.277	2.98	0.99
Morales, Daniel	R-R	6-3	230	1-28-85	2	1	4.63	15	0	0	0	23	25	14	12	2	11	21	.281	.313	.263	8.10	4.24
Pestano, Vinnie	R-R	6-0	205	2-20-85	1	1	3.57	21	0	0	6	23	17	9	9	5	7	27	.198	.303	.132	10.72	2.78
Rieck, Garrett	L-L	6-2	175	9-4-85	3	1	2.00	18	0	0	1	36	38	11	8	0	4	31	.275	.395	.230	7.75	1.00
Rodrigues, Mark	R-R	6-2	165	4-6-83	1	1	6.75	12	0	0	0	24	31	19	18	4	13	12	.313	.278	.333	4.50	4.88
Rodriguez, Mark	R-R	6-0	200	6-1-83	0	0	27.00	1	0	0	0	1	4	5	4	2	2	1	.444	.000	.500	6.75	13.50
Taylor, Heath	L-L	5-11	220	5-26-86	3	3	2.35	12	12	0	0	57	53	18	15	0	15	38	.248	.304	.228	5.97	2.35

FIELDING

Catcher	PCT	G	PO	A	E	DP	PB
Castillo	.986	41	253	30	4	3	5
Flores	1.000	11	56	6	0	0	3
Valadez	.990	24	180	21	2	3	5

First Base	PCT	G	PO	A	E	DP
Arnal	.600	1	3	0	2	1
Martin	.984	42	352	22	6	40
Mills	1.000	3	25	3	0	3
Nash	.970	15	123	7	4	14
Pacheco	.977	5	39	3	1	7
Petrucci	1.000	10	55	4	0	5
Realini	.939	5	29	2	2	2

Second Base	PCT	G	PO	A	E	DP
Arnal	1.000	8	14	12	0	1

	PCT	G	PO	A	E	DP	PB
Hehr	.979	49	95	133	5	39	
Infante	.989	20	42	48	1	13	
Realini	1.000	1	2	2	0	1	
Sanchez	1.000	1	3	4	0	2	

Third Base	PCT	G	PO	A	E	DP
Arnal	.833	12	7	18	5	1
Infante	.939	39	11	66	5	7
Mills	1.000	3	2	5	0	1
Petrucci	.750	12	10	17	9	1
Realini	1.000	7	6	17	0	2
Sanchez	.714	6	3	7	4	0

Shortstop	PCT	G	PO	A	E	DP
Arnal	1.000	5	11	11	0	3
Hehr	.750	1	3	0	1	0

		G	PO	A	E	DP
Thompson	.952	70	113	222	17	49

Outfield	PCT	G	PO	A	E	DP
Alvarado	1.000	6	6	1	0	0
Arnal	1.000	3	4	0	0	0
Brown	.984	59	115	12	2	2
Douglas	1.000	11	28	0	0	0
Jenkins	.978	33	44	0	1	0
Martin	1.000	2	7	1	0	0
Montero	1.000	3	6	1	0	0
Petrucci	.927	25	38	0	3	0
Valdes	.985	30	64	1	1	1
White	1.000	56	131	5	0	4

GCL INDIANS

GULF COAST LEAGUE

ROOKIE

BATTING	B-T	HT	WT	DOB	AVG	vLH	vRH	G	AB	R	H	2B	3B	HR	RBI	BB	HBP	SH	SF	SO	SB	CS	SLG	OBP
Alcombrack, Robert	R-R	6-0	205	6-10-88	.244	.258	.240	38	127	20	31	10	0	7	23	14	6	0	1	41	2	0	.488	.345
Armstrong, Corteze	L-R	5-11	180	6-9-84	.265	.259	.267	37	113	12	30	5	0	0	14	12	5	0	1	33	10	1	.310	.359
Choo, Shin-Soo	L-L	5-11	205	7-13-82	.200	.000	.250	2	5	0	1	1	0	0	2	1	0	0	0	1	0	0	.400	.333
Douglas, Stephen	L-R	6-2	185	5-10-85	.333	.500	.310	9	33	4	11	2	1	0	6	1	0	0	1	10	5	1	.455	.343
Finegan, Brian	R-R	6-0	190	12-15-81	.071	—	.071	5	14	1	1	0	0	0	2	0	0	0	0	4	0	1	.071	.188
Greenwell, Bo	L-L	6-0	185	10-15-88	.215	.158	.236	37	144	12	31	5	0	0	8	16	1	0	0	24	5	4	.250	.298
Hernandez, Ramon	R-R	6-1	170	8-25-86	.221	.220	.221	51	163	26	36	7	1	3	23	17	3	3	3	38	8	2	.331	.301
King, Daryl	R-R	6-4	228	1-21-88	.149	.222	.132	21	47	7	7	2	0	1	5	6	0	0	0	30	0	0	.255	.245
Martinez, Richard	R-R	6-0	186	6-19-87	.250	.316	.232	27	88	11	22	2	0	0	14	12	2	0	1	18	1	0	.273	.350
Nash, Chris	R-R	6-4	230	2-22-87	.313	.279	.325	47	166	28	52	16	0	3	21	17	1	0	4	35	4	1	.464	.372
Nilsson, Jay	R-R	6-1	185	11-1-87	.229	.059	.273	26	83	21	19	6	0	2	9	14	10	1	0	27	0	0	.373	.340
Rincon, Luis	R-R	6-1	200	4-30-87	.228	.355	.188	34	127	12	29	4	0	4	20	4	0	1	0	20	2	1	.354	.252
Rivas, Ronald	R-R	6-2	184	1-16-88	.245	.158	.266	26	98	15	24	4	0	1	11	8	3	0	1	19	6	2	.316	.318
Rodriguez, Angel	L-L	6-0	176	7-10-87	.288	.209	.318	41	153	19	44	5	2	0	17	11	1	0	1	29	7	3	.346	.337
Rucker, Kevin	R-R	6-1	185	9-14-89	.281	.250	.300	11	32	3	9	1	0	0	8	4	2	0	0	8	0	0	.313	.361
Sanchez, Karexon	B-R	5-11	175	8-22-87	.273	.279	.271	48	176	29	48	7	0	3	21	16	2	0	1	42	10	1	.364	.338
Smit, Jason	R-R	6-0	185	10-27-89	.214	.120	.239	35	117	10	25	6	0	1	15	10	4	0	1	35	0	0	.291	.295
Velasquez, Isaias	R-R	5-11	155	5-7-88	.277	.227	.296	47	159	33	44	8	0	0	18	16	4	1	1	29	22	3	.327	.356
Willard, Matthew	R-R	5-11	177	12-31-85	.244	.286	.226	26	90	14	22	4	0	0	6	9	3	1	0	25	12	0	.289	.333

PITCHING	B-T	HT	WT	DOB	W	L	ERA	G	GS	CG	SV	IP	H	R	ER	HR	BB	SO	AVG	vLH	vRH	K/9	BB/9
Archer, Christopher	R-R	6-2	165	9-26-88	1	7	5.64	12	11	0	0	53	56	36	33	4	21	48	.271	.313	.242	8.20	3.59
Arias, Carlos	R-R	6-2	178	7-4-85	0	1	4.35	16	0	0	4	21	16	10	10	2	5	17	.211	.205	.216	7.40	2.18
Bolivar, Julio	R-R	6-3	168	2-28-87	0	1	8.49	8	0	0	0	12	12	17	11	2	11	11	.250	.133	.303	8.49	8.49
Bunkelman, Cody	R-R	6-3	225	2-6-85	1	1	2.84	9	0	0	1	13	8	5	4	2	4	12	.174	.250	.115	8.53	2.84
De La Cruz, Kelvin	L-L	6-5	187	1-8-88	3	0	0.50	3	3	0	0	18	7	1	1	1	2	20	.117	.059	.140	10.00	1.00
Diaz, Kelvin N.	R-R	6-4	189	2-7-87	0	0	13.50	1	0	0	0	1	1	1	1	0	2	1	.333	.500	.000	13.50	27.00
Frias, Santo	R-R	6-3	189	12-8-87	2	3	1.88	9	9	0	0	48	36	17	10	1	8	47	.207	.244	.194	8.81	1.50
Gaub, John	R-L	6-2	200	4-28-85	0	0	2.25	4	0	0	0	4	4	1	1	0	4	4	.308	1.000	.182	9.00	9.00
Harper, Kyle	R-R	6-4	220	2-10-85	0	0	6.75	6	1	0	0	5	8	4	4	1	5	4	.333	.500	.250	6.75	8.44
Jesus, Candido	L-L	6-1	170	10-5-85	1	1	4.55	16	0	0	0	28	22	15	14	2	19	25	.222	.231	.221	8.13	6.18
Jones, Christopher	L-L	6-2	165	9-19-88	0	0	2.45	1	1	0	0	4	4	1	1	0	2	5	.267	.250	.273	12.27	4.91
Judy, Josh	R-R	6-4	200	2-9-86	1	2	0.63	9	0	0	0	14	11	4	1	0	8	14	.204	.100	.265	8.79	5.02
Mahalic, Joseph	R-R	6-3	205	11-28-88	2	0	4.88	7	4	0	0	24	28	16	13	0	7	21	.277	.231	.293	7.88	2.62
Martinez, Anillins	L-L	6-2	176	4-6-87	2	0	3.30	16	0	0	0	30	27	13	11	1	17	27	.235	.087	.272	8.10	5.10
Miller, Ryan	L-L	6-0	195	12-14-86	4	2	2.40	9	9	0	0	45	26	15	12	1	12	44	.160	.250	.130	8.80	2.40
Morris, Ryan	L-L	5-11	180	11-8-88	3	0	1.80	5	5	0	0	25	13	6	5	0	8	22	.149	.176	.132	7.92	2.88
Niesel, Christopher	R-R	5-11	195	11-18-82	0	0	0.00	1	0	0	0	1	1	0	0	0	1	1	.250	.000	.333	9.00	9.00
Pontius, Mike	R-R	6-2	235	10-26-87	0	0	2.89	7	0	0	2	9	11	4	3	1	1	13	.282	.222	.300	12.54	0.96
Ramirez, Wilfredo	L-R	6-4	210	11-24-87	1	1	2.60	16	0	0	0	28	26	8	8	2	4	27	.243	.250	.241	8.78	1.30
Robinson, Matthew	R-R	6-1	190	12-20-83	0	2	8.76	6	2	0	0	12	20	14	12	1	4	9	.351	.263	.395	6.57	2.92

ORGANIZATION STATISTICS

					W	L	ERA	G	GS	CG	SV	IP	H	R	ER	HR	BB	SO	AVG	vLH	vRH	K/9	BB/9
Rosario, Gregorio	R-R	6-4	180	8-26-88	4	7	5.55	11	10	0	0	49	57	36	30	3	14	39	.292	.289	.294	7.21	2.59
Turek, Travis	R-R	6-1	170	9-2-87	2	1	1.59	14	0	0	1	28	19	12	5	0	6	18	.184	.222	.171	5.72	1.91
Urena, Jose	L-L	6-2	186	3-14-88	1	2	5.04	8	4	0	0	25	28	19	14	0	12	21	.280	.083	.307	7.56	4.32

FIELDING

Catcher	PCT	G	PO	A	E	DP	PB
Alcombrack	.990	35	261	23	3	3	10
Martinez	.984	24	164	21	3	4	6
Rincon	1.000	3	19	0	0	0	3

First Base	PCT	G	PO	A	E	DP
Nash	.986	41	338	20	5	30
Rincon	.973	19	133	10	4	9
Velasquez	.667	1	2	0	1	0

Second Base	PCT	G	PO	A	E	DP
Finegan	1.000	3	6	6	0	0
Rivas	1.000	2	8	2	0	0
Sanchez	.951	31	60	77	7	16

Smit	.933	10	15	27	3	4
Velasquez	.983	16	21	36	1	6

Third Base	PCT	G	PO	A	E	DP
Nilsson	.864	18	15	36	8	3
Sanchez	.875	14	10	32	6	2
Smit	.808	10	3	18	5	1
Velasquez	.893	20	8	42	6	1

Shortstop	PCT	G	PO	A	E	DP
Rivas	.898	22	30	49	9	7
Smit	.944	9	10	24	2	1
Velasquez	1.000	4	7	9	0	5
Willard	.898	26	46	60	12	13

Outfield	PCT	G	PO	A	E	DP
Armstrong	.973	34	66	5	2	1
Choo	1.000	1	2	0	0	0
Douglas	.938	9	15	0	1	0
Greenwell	.970	35	62	2	2	0
Hernandez	.988	47	80	2	1	0
King	1.000	18	21	0	0	0
Nilsson	—	1	0	0	0	0
Rincon	1.000	1	1	0	0	0
Rodriguez	.960	38	46	2	2	1
Rucker	.941	10	16	0	1	0

DSL INDIANS

ROOKIE

DOMINICAN SUMMER LEAGUE

BATTING	B-T	HT	WT	DOB	AVG	vLH	vRH	G	AB	R	H	2B	3B	HR	RBI	BB	HBP	SH	SF	SO	SB	CS	SLG	OBP
Abreu, Abner	R-R	6-3	170	10-24-88	.303	.213	.335	56	228	34	69	13	7	4	41	18	1	0	2	46	5	4	.474	.353
Aponte, Juan	R-R	6-0	185	3-2-88	.291	.317	.282	65	237	27	69	18	0	6	39	22	17	0	3	41	2	1	.443	.387
Basabe, Lurvin	B-R	5-8	179	9-23-89	.284	.302	.277	60	208	38	59	4	3	1	24	45	3	6	4	30	19	14	.346	.412
Brito, Jesus	R-R	6-1	160	12-25-87	.210	.224	.205	61	210	24	44	17	1	1	25	37	4	2	3	55	1	3	.314	.335
Burdier, Jose	R-R	5-11	185	8-24-86	.224	.241	.218	45	116	22	26	2	1	0	12	10	1	2	0	22	9	4	.259	.291
Camargo, Jose	R-R	6-0	175	9-6-89	.238	.184	.257	54	193	28	46	11	0	1	18	23	7	6	4	26	3	4	.311	.335
Cid, Delvi	R-R	6-2	170	7-19-89	.302	.338	.287	65	262	37	79	8	2	1	24	28	5	6	1	49	21	15	.359	.378
Diaz, Kelvin	R-R	5-11	184	8-22-87	.315	.234	.345	68	238	40	75	19	2	8	41	37	12	1	4	29	8	5	.513	.426
Polonia, Luis	B-R	5-8	170	11-29-85	.305	.371	.283	50	141	18	43	6	2	0	19	16	0	1	1	16	2	5	.376	.373
Quintero, Rafael	R-R	6-1	145	9-3-87	.228	.130	.250	43	123	19	28	3	0	2	12	25	2	1	0	16	2	1	.301	.367
Read, Darling	R-R	6-1	190	5-29-88	.194	.179	.200	61	216	29	42	5	1	3	22	23	2	6	3	71	3	2	.269	.275
Santos, Cesar	R-R	5-10	168	8-6-86	.206	.185	.212	43	126	18	26	6	0	1	9	10	4	2	2	32	6	1	.278	.282

PITCHING	B-T	HT	WT	DOB	W	L	ERA	G	GS	CG	SV	IP	H	R	ER	HR	BB	SO	AVG	vLH	vRH	K/9	BB/9
Barrios, Angel	R-R	6-3	186	1-3-88	1	3	10.26	8	2	0	0	17	24	22	19	0	19	12	.348	.333	.353	6.48	10.26
Burdier, Jose	R-R	5-11	185	8-24-86	0	1	2.79	8	0	0	0	10	10	5	3	1	5	9	.278	.333	.267	8.38	4.66
Diaz, Juan	R-R	6-2	170	3-13-87	7	4	1.48	16	1	0	0	49	46	15	8	0	16	37	.251	.293	.239	6.84	2.96
Flores, Jose	R-R	6-3	185	6-4-89	0	7	6.04	14	12	0	0	48	46	38	32	2	26	23	.256	.316	.228	4.34	4.91
Jimenez, Francisco	L-L	5-11	164	10-2-88	0	0	13.50	3	0	0	0	4	7	8	6	0	3	4	.318	.000	.318	9.00	6.75
Jimenez, Jose	R-L	6-3	190	11-5-85	0	2	5.09	22	0	0	0	46	51	36	26	2	33	23	.270	.250	.278	4.50	6.46
Mendez, Sandy	R-R	6-3	183	10-9-85	5	1	2.96	16	0	0	2	52	43	21	17	1	3	39	.222	.143	.239	6.79	0.52
Montano, Francisco	R-R	6-1	175	6-4-89	2	1	7.39	16	0	0	0	35	53	36	29	5	14	17	.349	.308	.357	4.33	3.57
Montero, Denny	R-R	6-4	200	4-29-88	1	0	6.00	3	0	0	1	6	8	6	4	1	4	8	.308	.750	.227	12.00	6.00
Morales, Alexander	R-R	6-0	161	7-26-89	0	8	5.03	14	13	1	0	54	52	39	30	4	21	35	.254	.265	.251	5.87	3.52
Pena, Jose	R-R	6-4	192	6-23-87	1	2	4.97	14	1	0	0	42	40	27	23	0	22	40	.248	.255	.246	8.64	4.75
Perez, Alexander	R-R	6-2	156	7-24-89	1	2	2.90	13	10	0	0	50	41	18	16	3	13	64	.218	.145	.248	11.60	2.36
Quintero, Jesus	R-R	6-2	165	5-16-89	1	3	2.20	4	2	0	0	16	18	10	4	0	6	9	.273	.381	.222	4.96	3.31
Quintero, Rafael	R-R	6-1	145	9-3-87	0	1	4.50	3	2	0	0	8	12	6	4	0	1	2	.353	.556	.280	2.25	1.12
Salazar, Danny	R-R	6-0	180	1-11-90	5	3	1.96	14	14	0	0	64	52	25	14	1	12	49	.221	.149	.239	6.85	1.68
Salazar, Yobanis	R-R	6-2	199	4-27-89	0	1	7.20	4	1	0	0	5	5	6	4	0	4	4	.227	.222	.231	7.20	7.20
Solano, Luis	R-R	5-11	160	1-27-87	3	1	2.28	26	0	0	7	51	40	14	13	1	16	52	.216	.195	.222	9.12	2.81
Soto, Franklin	R-R	6-2	170	9-18-89	0	2	5.70	13	11	0	0	43	43	32	27	0	26	37	.259	.167	.279	7.80	5.48

FIELDING

Catcher	PCT	G	PO	A	E	DP	PB
Aponte	.984	44	262	48	5	7	10
Quintero	.984	35	223	29	4	2	4

First Base	PCT	G	PO	A	E	DP
Aponte	.994	24	170	8	1	17
Brito	.993	23	137	7	1	11
Burdier	.985	21	125	10	2	6
Diaz	.975	5	36	3	1	2
Polonia	1.000	1	1	0	0	1
Quintero	.987	9	72	3	1	7
Santos	1.000	3	11	1	0	2

Second Base	PCT	G	PO	A	E	DP
Abreu	.939	11	18	13	2	3

Basabe	.961	32	75	71	6	16
Brito	.966	15	24	33	2	8
Camargo	.938	15	46	30	5	5
Polonia	1.000	5	2	2	0	0

Third Base	PCT	G	PO	A	E	DP
Abreu	.882	21	22	45	9	2
Brito	.867	4	3	10	2	0
Burdier	1.000	1	1	1	0	0
Camargo	1.000	1	2	0	0	0
Diaz	.884	46	60	123	24	14
Quintero	1.000	1	1	2	0	0

Shortstop	PCT	G	PO	A	E	DP
Abreu	.883	15	21	32	7	8

Basabe	.806	22	35	52	21	7
Brito	1.000	2	1	0	0	0
Camargo	.912	37	54	102	15	12

Outfield	PCT	G	PO	A	E	DP
Brito	.913	28	37	5	4	0
Burdier	.895	12	16	1	2	0
Cid	.986	65	132	4	2	2
Polonia	.983	31	51	8	1	3
Read	.951	61	94	4	5	1
Santos	.919	27	33	1	3	1

Colorado Rockies

BY JACK ETKIN

Their stumble in the World Series in no way diminished the historic journey the Rockies took to get there. In the process, a franchise with next to no success and whose minuscule national identity was bound up in missteps, thin air and losing took a giant step forward in 2007.

In 14 previous seasons, the Rockies never won more than 83 games and reached the postseason once, as the wild card in 1995. They won a franchise-record 90 games— it was just their fifth winning season and first since 2000—including a one-game tiebreaker with San Diego that sent the Rockies into the postseason with 14 wins in their final 15 games.

The Rockies swept the Phillies in a division series and the Diamondbacks in the National League Championship Series, making it 21 wins in 22 games before losing four straight to the Red Sox in the World Series after an eight-day layoff, the second longest in postseason history.

"We knocked a lot off our to-do list this season," manager Clint Hurdle said. "We have one big item that remains."

Sixteen of the 25 players on their Series roster were homegrown as the Rockies grew into a good team.

The Rockies regained their dominance at Coors Field, where their 51-31 record was the second best in franchise history. They set a franchise record by going 39-42 on the road.

But what made the Rockies run so improbable was that until mid-September they seemed headed toward incremental improvement. The Rockies reached the postseason despite sharing first or second place in the NL West for just seven days and became just the sixth team in major league history to fall nine games below .500 and reach the Series.

Indeed, the Rockies were 18-27 and seven games behind after games of May 21. Beginning the following day, the Rockies went 72-46 (.610), which was the best record in the NL in that stretch and the second best in the majors behind only the Yankees, who went 74-45 (.622).

Yet the Rockies path was anything but a straight shot upward. Fresh off a three-game sweep of the Yankees at Coors Field, the Rockies lost their first eight games on what became a 1-9 road trip June 22-July 1. Lefthanded reliever Brian Fuentes blew four saves and suffered four of the losses, just before a strained side muscle sidelined him until mid-August.

Fuentes' slide cost him his closer's job. But righthander Manny Corpas anchored a successfully retooled bullpen that included the likes of righthanders Matt Herges and Jorge Julio. Corpas converted 19-of-20 save opportunities beginning with his debut as the closer July 7.

Matt Holliday was an offensive bulwark all season and led the league in batting, RBIs, hits and doubles.

Rookie shortstop Troy Tulowitzki solidified the infield and took on a leadership role. His 24 home runs were the most ever by an NL rookie shortstop. Moreover, Tulowitzki led all major league shortstops in fielding percentage (.987), chances (834) and assists (561) and made just 11 errors.

Lefthander Jeff Francis, 17-9, 4.22, tied the franchise record for victories in one season, and his role became paramount as the rotation sustained a series of injuries.

Righthander Jason Hirsh missed all but two days of July with an ankle injury and in his second start back Aug. 7, was hit with a line drive that felled him for the season with a broken right leg.

Righthander Rodrigo Lopez made his final start of the season July 26 and a month later underwent elbow sur-

gery. And righthander Aaron Cook suffered a strained left oblique muscle Aug. 10 that sidelined him until Oct. 28 when he started Game Four of the World Series.

Rookie righthander Ubaldo Jimenez and lefthander Franklin Morales stepped in and made huge contributions. Jimenez went 0-1, 2.25 in three postseason starts; Morales went 3-2, 3.43.

Righthander Greg Reynolds dominated at Double-A Tulsa through mid-May, making one more start before undergoing shoulder surgery in late August.

Brandon Hynick of high Class A Modesto was California League pitcher of the year and shortstop Chris Nelson, after two years at low Class A Asheville, had a breakthrough season.

2007 PERFORMANCE

General Manager: Dan O'Dowd. **Farm Director:** Marc Gustafson. **Scouting Director:** Bill Schmidt

Class	Team	League	W	L	PCT	Finish*	Manager	Affiliate Since
Majors	Colorado	National	90	73	.552	^2nd (16)	Clint Hurdle	—
Triple-A	Colorado Springs Sky Sox	Pacific Coast	69	75	.479	11th (16)	Tom Runnells	1993
Double-A	Tulsa Drillers	Texas	69	69	.500	4th (8)	Stu Cole	2003
High A	Modesto Nuts	California	76	64	.543	3rd (10)	Jerry Weinstein	2005
Low A	Asheville Tourists	South Atlantic	80	58	.580	4th (16)	Joe Mikulik	1994
Short-season	Tri-City Dust Devils	New York-Penn	37	39	.487	3rd (8)	Fred Ocaio	2001
Rookie	Casper Rockies	Pioneer	22	53	.293	8th (8)	Tony Diaz	2001
Overall 2007 Minor League Record			**353**	**358**	**.496**	**T-15th**		

* Finish in overall standings (No. of teams in league) ^League champion

ORGANIZATION STATISTICS

COLORADO ROCKIES

NATIONAL LEAGUE

BATTING	B-T	HT	WT	DOB	AVG	vLH	vRH	G	AB	R	H	2B	3B	HR	RBI	BB	HBP	SH	SF	SO	SB	CS	SLG	OBP
Atkins, Garrett	R-R	6-3	215	12-12-79	.301	.286	.307	157	605	83	182	35	1	25	111	67	2	0	10	96	3	1	.486	.367
Baker, Jeff	R-R	6-2	210	6-21-81	.222	.246	.205	85	144	17	32	2	2	4	12	13	2	0	0	40	0	0	.347	.296
Barker, Sean	R-R	6-3	220	5-26-80	.000	—	.000	3	2	0	0	0	0	0	0	0	1	0	1	0	0	0	.000	.333
Barmes, Clint	R-R	6-0	210	3-6-79	.216	.444	.143	27	37	5	8	3	0	1	1	0	1	0	1	0	13	0	0	.297	.237
Bellorin, Edwin	R-R	5-9	225	2-21-82	.000	.000	.000	3	2	0	0	0	0	0	0	0	0	0	0	0	0	0	.000	.000
Carroll, Jamey	R-R	5-9	170	2-18-74	.225	.262	.194	108	227	45	51	9	1	2	22	38	4	6	3	34	6	2	.300	.317
Finley, Steve	L-L	6-2	195	3-12-65	.181	.267	.165	43	94	9	17	3	0	1	2	8	0	0	0	4	0	0	.245	.245
Gil, Geronimo	R-R	6-3	240	8-7-75	.071	.000	.125	5	14	1	1	0	0	0	0	1	0	1	0	5	0	0	.071	.133
Hawpe, Brad	L-L	6-3	205	6-22-79	.291	.214	.315	152	516	80	150	33	4	29	116	81	3	1	5	137	0	2	.539	.387
Helton, Todd	L-L	6-2	210	8-20-73	.320	.285	.334	154	557	86	178	42	2	17	91	116	0	2	0	74	0	1	.494	.434
Holliday, Matt	R-R	6-4	235	1-15-80	.340	.301	.351	158	636	120	216	50	6	36	137	63	10	0	4	126	11	4	.607	.405
Iannetta, Chris	R-R	6-0	205	4-8-83	.218	.204	.223	67	197	22	43	8	3	4	27	29	5	1	2	58	0	0	.350	.330
Koshansky, Joe	L-L	6-4	225	5-26-82	.083	.000	.091	17	12	0	1	1	0	0	2	2	0	0	1	5	0	0	.167	.200
Mabry, John	L-R	6-4	210	10-17-70	.118	.000	.121	28	34	4	4	1	0	1	5	5	0	0	0	10	0	0	.235	.231
Matsui, Kazuo	B-R	5-10	185	10-23-75	.288	.271	.291	104	410	84	118	24	6	4	37	34	0	8	1	69	32	4	.405	.342
Quintanilla, Omar	L-R	5-9	190	10-24-81	.229	.100	.250	27	70	6	16	4	0	0	5	5	0	0	0	15	0	0	.286	.280
Smith, Seth	L-L	6-3	215	9-30-82	.625	.000	.625	7	8	4	5	0	1	0	0	0	0	0	1	0	0	0	.875	.625
Spilborghs, Ryan	R-R	6-1	190	9-5-79	.299	.356	.271	97	264	40	79	14	1	11	51	28	2	0	6	45	4	1	.485	.363
Stewart, Ian	L-R	6-3	205	4-5-85	.209	.100	.242	35	43	3	9	4	0	1	9	1	2	0	0	17	0	0	.372	.261
Sullivan, Cory	L-L	6-0	180	8-20-79	.286	.353	.276	72	140	19	40	6	1	2	14	9	2	1	1	25	2	0	.386	.336
Taveras, Willy	R-R	6-0	160	12-25-81	.320	.371	.304	97	372	64	119	13	2	2	24	21	7	7	1	55	33	9	.382	.367
Torrealba, Yorvit	R-R	5-11	200	7-19-78	.255	.264	.252	113	396	47	101	22	1	8	47	34	6	6	1	73	2	1	.376	.323
Tulowitzki, Troy	R-R	6-3	205	10-10-84	.291	.333	.278	155	609	104	177	33	5	24	99	57	9	5	2	130	7	6	.479	.359

PITCHING	B-T	HT	WT	DOB	W	L	ERA	G	GS	CG	SV	IP	H	R	ER	HR	BB	SO	AVG	vLH	vRH	K/9	BB/9
Affeldt, Jeremy	L-L	6-4	225	6-6-79	4	3	3.51	75	0	0	0	59	47	26	23	3	33	46	.226	.250	.211	7.02	5.03
Arias, Alberto	R-R	5-11	155	10-14-83	1	0	4.91	6	0	0	0	7	8	4	1	5	3	.308	.385	.231	3.68	6.14
Bautista, Denny	R-R	6-5	190	8-23-80	2	1	12.46	9	1	0	0	9	18	12	12	0	4	8	.429	.480	.353	8.31	4.15
Buchholz, Taylor	R-R	6-4	220	10-13-81	6	5	4.23	41	8	0	0	94	105	47	44	8	20	61	.288	.268	.306	5.86	1.92
Clarke, Darren	R-R	6-8	235	3-18-81	0	0	0.00	2	0	0	0	1	2	0	0	0	1	1	.333	1.000	.000	6.75	6.75
Cook, Aaron	R-R	6-3	215	2-8-79	8	7	4.12	25	25	2	0	166	178	87	76	15	44	61	.279	.263	.295	3.31	2.39
Corpas, Manny	R-R	6-3	170	12-3-82	4	2	2.08	78	0	0	19	78	63	20	18	6	20	58	.224	.234	.214	6.69	2.31
Dessens, Elmer	R-R	5-11	200	1-13-71	1	1	7.58	5	5	0	0	19	21	16	16	3	9	10	.276	.343	.220	4.74	4.26
2-team (12 Milwaukee)					2	2	7.15	17	5	0	0	34	45	32	27	6	12	22	—	—	—	5.82	3.18
Fogg, Josh	R-R	6-0	205	12-13-76	10	9	4.94	30	29	0	0	166	194	99	91	23	59	94	.293	.279	.305	5.11	3.21
Francis, Jeff	L-L	6-5	205	1-8-81	17	9	4.22	34	34	1	0	215	234	103	101	25	63	165	.278	.242	.289	6.90	2.63
Fuentes, Brian	L-L	6-4	230	8-9-75	3	5	3.08	64	0	0	20	61	46	26	21	6	23	56	.206	.204	.207	8.22	3.38
Harikkala, Tim	R-R	6-2	185	7-15-71	0	0	8.10	1	1	0	0	3	9	3	3	0	1	2	.500	.500	.500	5.40	2.70
Hawkins, LaTroy	R-R	6-5	215	12-21-72	2	5	3.42	62	0	0	0	55	52	21	21	6	16	29	.252	.237	.266	4.72	2.60
Herges, Matt	L-R	6-0	210	4-1-70	5	1	2.96	35	0	0	0	49	34	17	16	4	15	30	.198	.176	.184	5.55	2.77
Hirsh, Jason	R-R	6-8	250	2-20-82	5	7	4.81	19	19	1	0	112	103	63	60	18	48	75	.243	.236	.250	6.01	3.85
Jimenez, Ubaldo	R-R	6-4	200	1-22-84	4	4	4.28	15	15	0	0	82	70	46	39	10	37	68	.228	.244	.212	7.46	4.06
Julio, Jorge	R-R	6-1	225	3-3-79	0	3	3.93	58	0	0	0	53	50	25	23	6	20	50	.256	.205	.287	8.54	3.42
2-team (10 Florida)					0	5	5.23	68	0	0	0	62	68	39	36	8	31	56	—	—	—	8.13	4.50
Keppel, Bob	R-R	6-5	205	6-11-82	0	0	11.25	4	0	0	0	4	6	5	5	1	3	1	.353	.222	.500	2.25	6.75
Kim, Byung-Hyun	R-R	5-9	175	1-19-79	1	2	10.50	3	1	0	0	6	6	7	7	2	4	2	.286	.500	.000	3.00	6.00
3-team (2 Arizona, 23 Florida)					10	8	6.08	28	22	0	0	118	131	90	80	20	68	107	—	—	—	8.14	5.17
Lopez, Rodrigo	R-R	6-1	185	12-14-75	5	4	4.42	14	14	0	0	79	83	43	39	11	21	43	.273	.270	.276	4.88	2.38
Martin, Tom	L-L	6-1	205	5-21-70	0	0	4.91	26	0	0	0	26	32	14	14	4	9	10	.302	.289	.309	3.51	3.16
McClellan, Zach	R-R	6-5	190	11-25-78	1	0	5.79	12	0	0	0	14	20	9	9	0	5	13	.351	.394	.292	8.36	3.21
Morales, Franklin	L-L	6-0	170	1-24-86	3	2	3.43	8	8	0	0	39	34	15	15	2	14	26	.241	.249	.235	5.95	3.20
Morillo, Juan	R-R	6-3	190	11-5-83	0	0	9.82	4	0	0	0	4	3	4	4	1	1	3	.214	.111	.400	7.36	2.45
Newman, Josh	L-L	6-1	200	6-11-82	0	0	4.50	2	0	0	0	2	2	1	1	0	0	3	.250	.000	.667	13.50	0.00
Ortiz, Ramon	R-R	6-0	175	5-23-73	1	0	7.62	10	0	0	0	13	15	11	11	4	7	7	.306	.333	.290	4.85	4.85
Ramirez, Ramon	R-R	5-11	190	8-31-81	2	2	8.31	22	0	0	0	17	21	16	16	2	6	15	.313	.240	.357	7.79	3.12
Redman, Mark	L-L	6-5	245	1-5-74	2	0	3.20	5	3	0	0	20	21	8	7	2	6	14	.269	.273	.268	6.41	2.75
2-team (6 Atlanta)					2	4	7.62	11	8	0	0	41	59	37	35	6	17	27	—	—	—	5.88	3.70
Serafini, Dan	B-L	6-1	190	1-25-74	0	0	54.00	1	0	0	0	0	3	2	2	0	2	0	.000	.000	.000	0.00	54.00
Speier, Ryan	R-R	6-7	210	7-24-79	3	1	4.00	20	0	0	0	18	20	8	8	1	8	13	.299	.333	.279	6.50	4.00

FIELDING

Catcher	PCT	G	PO	A	E	DP	PB
Bellorin	1.000	2	3	0	0	0	0
Gil	1.000	4	21	3	0	0	1
Iannetta	.997	60	301	27	1	1	4
Torrealba	.991	112	679	56	7	7	4

First Base	PCT	G	PO	A	E	DP
Atkins	.971	10	31	3	1	3
Baker	.976	20	120	2	3	12
Helton	.999	153	1448	95	2	153
Koshansky	1.000	3	9	0	0	0

Second Base	PCT	G	PO	A	E	DP
Barmes	1.000	5	1	5	0	0
Carroll	.992	60	81	164	2	37
Matsui	.992	102	200	311	4	84

	PCT	G	PO	A	E	DP
Quintanilla	1.000	25	39	49	0	15
Third Base	**PCT**	**G**	**PO**	**A**	**E**	**DP**
Atkins	.963	154	84	252	13	34
Baker	1.000	2	0	3	0	0
Barmes	—	1	0	0	0	0
Carroll	.900	35	5	13	2	5
Mabry	.875	4	3	4	1	0
Stewart	1.000	11	5	16	0	0
Shortstop	**PCT**	**G**	**PO**	**A**	**E**	**DP**
Barmes	.952	8	8	12	1	3
Carroll	1.000	11	10	22	0	5
Quintanilla	1.000	2	1	2	0	0
Tulowitzki	.987	155	262	561	11	114

Outfield	PCT	G	PO	A	E	DP
Baker	1.000	18	27	1	0	0
Barker	1.000	2	1	0	0	0
Barmes	.750	5	3	0	1	0
Carroll	1.000	3	2	0	0	0
Finley	1.000	28	46	1	0	1
Hawpe	.977	142	246	6	6	1
Holliday	.990	157	296	7	3	0
Mabry	1.000	1	0	0	0	0
Smith	—	1	0	0	0	0
Spilborghs	.992	72	115	2	1	1
Sullivan	1.000	52	77	1	0	1
Taveras	.982	86	212	7	4	0

COLORADO SPRINGS SKY SOX

TRIPLE-A

PACIFIC COAST LEAGUE

BATTING	B-T	HT	WT	DOB	AVG	vLH	vRH	G	AB	R	H	2B	3B	HR	RBI	BB	HBP	SH	SF	SO	SB	CS	SLG	OBP
Baker, Jeff	R-R	6-2	210	6-21-81	.231	.364	.133	7	26	3	6	1	0	1	2	1	0	0	0	8	0	0	.385	.259
Barker, Sean	R-R	6-3	220	5-26-80	.330	.289	.351	72	261	52	86	23	2	6	46	14	6	1	3	65	13	5	.502	.373
Barmes, Clint	R-R	6-0	210	3-6-79	.299	.331	.284	108	428	68	128	20	6	11	44	22	22	4	1	52	8	6	.451	.364
Bellorin, Edwin	R-R	5-9	225	2-21-82	.326	.381	.304	59	221	38	72	18	0	9	45	16	2	0	5	28	1	0	.529	.369
Bernier, Douglas	R-R	5-11	175	6-24-80	.310	.276	.329	97	216	27	67	15	0	2	27	31	1	2	2	51	4	2	.407	.396
Cabrera, Jolbert	R-R	6-1	215	12-8-72	.329	.280	.356	19	70	11	23	9	0	2	13	1	2	0	1	5	0	0	.543	.351
2-team (45 Memphis)					.265	—	—	64	200	21	53	14	1	4	21	8	6	5	3	28	0	2	.405	.309
Colina, Alvin	R-R	6-3	210	12-26-81	.195	.143	.221	80	272	22	53	19	0	5	35	17	2	0	5	69	0	0	.320	.243
Duenas, Tomas	R-R	5-11	205	7-16-81	.000	.000	—	1	2	0	0	0	0	0	0	0	0	0	0	1	0	0	.000	.000
Gaetti, Joe	R-R	5-11	205	10-16-81	.270	.312	.245	74	244	40	66	14	5	11	32	23	4	0	2	88	3	4	.504	.341
Garcia, Lino	R-R	6-3	192	10-12-83	.227	.273	.182	16	44	6	10	2	0	0	2	3	1	0	0	5	2	0	.273	.292
Gomez, Alexis	L-L	6-2	180	8-8-78	.298	.291	.300	102	329	40	98	21	5	8	40	18	1	1	2	77	6	3	.465	.334
Iannetta, Chris	R-R	6-0	225	4-8-83	.296	.125	.433	16	54	8	16	3	0	1	7	7	2	0	0	6	0	0	.407	.397
Koshansky, Joe	L-L	6-4	225	5-26-82	.295	.276	.305	136	498	79	147	30	2	21	99	67	2	0	2	128	4	3	.490	.380
Macri, Matt	R-R	6-2	200	5-29-82	.667	—	.667	3	9	1	6	2	0	1	4	0	0	0	0	1	0	1	01.222	.667
Matsui, Kazuo	B-R	5-10	185	10-23-75	.500	—	.500	2	6	1	3	0	0	0	2	0	0	0	0	1	1	0	.500	.625
Menechino, Frank	R-R	5-8	200	1-7-71	.222	.000	.286	4	9	2	2	0	0	0	1	3	0	0	1	0	0	0	.222	.417
2-team (34 Portland)					.375	—	—	38	128	25	48	16	1	3	21	14	0	0	1	19	2	0	.586	.434
Nix, Jayson	R-R	5-11	185	8-26-82	.292	.277	.299	124	439	80	128	33	2	11	58	31	4	7	2	79	24	8	.451	.342
Olson, Tim	R-R	6-2	200	8-1-78	.270	.250	.280	20	37	3	10	1	0	1	3	1	0	0	0	7	1	0	.378	.289
Paulk, Mike	L-L	6-2	195	4-23-84	.250	.600	.000	3	12	0	3	1	0	0	0	0	0	0	0	2	0	0	.333	.250
Quintanilla, Omar	L-R	5-9	190	10-24-81	.319	.313	.321	98	348	54	111	30	4	3	43	31	5	6	3	65	3	1	.454	.380
Sanchez, Tino	B-R	6-0	175	2-2-79	.278	.000	.357	5	18	4	5	1	0	0	1	1	0	0	0	0	0	0	.333	.316
Smith, Seth	L-L	6-3	215	9-30-82	.317	.262	.340	129	451	68	143	32	6	17	82	39	10	1	4	73	7	3	.528	.381
Spilborghs, Ryan	R-R	6-1	190	9-5-79	.323	.326	.321	34	124	25	40	7	1	5	17	18	1	1	1	19	4	3	.516	.410
Stewart, Ian	R-R	6-3	205	4-5-85	.304	.328	.294	112	414	72	126	23	2	15	65	49	3	4	4	92	11	2	.478	.379
Sullivan, Cory	L-L	6-0	180	8-20-79	.262	.259	.263	53	206	29	54	9	3	1	21	18	1	3	0	44	4	3	.350	.324
Taveras, Willy	R-R	6-0	160	12-25-81	.357	.333	.375	4	14	0	5	0	0	0	1	0	0	1	0	2	1	2	.357	.400

PITCHING	B-T	HT	WT	DOB	W	L	ERA	G	GS	CG	SV	IP	H	R	ER	HR	BB	SO	AVG	vLH	vRH	K/9	BB/9
Arias, Alberto	R-R	5-11	155	10-14-83	2	2	3.76	10	3	0	0	26	32	12	11	1	8	15	.317	.313	.321	5.13	2.73
Bautista, Denny	R-R	6-5	190	8-23-80	3	2	2.92	51	0	0	0	65	54	22	21	1	31	63	.228	.286	.196	8.77	4.31
Beckstead, Jentry	R-R	6-0	175	6-9-80	0	0	5.11	9	0	0	0	12	13	7	7	2	8	3	.295	.316	.280	2.19	5.84
Cook, Aaron	R-R	6-3	215	2-8-79	0	1	27.00	1	1	0	0	1	4	3	3	0	1	0	.667	.750	.500	0.00	9.00
De Paula, Jorge	R-R	6-1	210	11-10-78	8	6	6.41	19	18	0	0	100	126	87	71	16	44	53	.310	.300	.317	4.79	3.97
DeJean, Mike	R-R	6-2	200	9-28-70	0	3	7.86	17	3	0	0	26	36	24	23	9	8	21	.327	.310	.333	7.18	2.73
Dessens, Elmer	R-R	5-11	200	1-13-71	1	0	0.00	1	0	0	0	3	1	0	0	0	1	1	.111	.000	.200	3.00	3.00
2-team (3 Nashville)					2	0	1.23	4	3	0	0	15	8	2	2	0	1	11	—	—	—	6.75	0.61
DuBose, Eric	L-L	6-3	235	5-15-76	0	3	7.83	7	5	0	0	23	33	22	20	2	11	20	.359	.367	.355	7.83	4.30
Esposito, Mike	R-R	6-0	190	9-27-81	5	5	6.05	27	11	1	1	103	134	81	69	16	38	49	.318	.352	.298	4.30	3.33
Fogg, Josh	R-R	6-0	205	12-13-76	0	1	3.60	1	1	0	0	5	6	3	2	0	3	2	.273	.300	.250	5.40	0.00
Fuentes, Brian	L-L	6-4	230	8-9-75	0	0	0.00	2	1	0	0	2	2	0	0	0	2	3	.286	.000	.400	9.00	0.00
Gallo, Mike	L-L	6-0	175	4-2-77	5	2	5.10	56	0	0	6	60	64	37	34	7	29	44	.272	.250	.287	6.60	4.35
Harikkala, Tim	R-R	6-2	185	7-15-71	3	1	4.18	8	5	0	0	32	39	17	15	2	11	15	.305	.340	.284	3.66	3.05
Hawkins, LaTroy	R-R	6-5	215	12-21-72	1	0	2.25	4	0	0	0	4	2	1	1	0	2	5	.154	.000	.222	11.25	4.50
Herges, Matt	L-R	6-0	210	4-1-70	2	1	1.27	32	0	0	1	35	24	6	5	2	10	33	.194	.125	.237	8.41	2.55
Hirsh, Jason	R-R	6-8	250	2-20-82	1	2	4.85	3	3	0	0	13	16	8	7	1	4	7	.314	.400	.258	4.85	2.77
Jimenez, Ubaldo	R-R	6-4	200	1-22-84	8	5	5.85	19	19	1	0	103	110	74	67	9	62	89	.279	.263	.293	7.78	5.42
Kaiser, Marc	R-R	6-2	205	5-7-82	6	7	5.96	27	19	0	0	131	168	97	87	14	79	48	.331	.329	.333	3.29	5.41
Keppel, Bob	R-R	6-5	205	6-11-82	8	10	5.48	26	23	0	0	138	162	95	84	14	60	64	.298	.295	.300	4.17	3.91
Kim, Byung-Hyun	R-R	5-9	175	1-19-79	1	1	2.96	5	5	0	0	24	21	10	8	2	11	31	.233	.217	.250	11.47	4.07
Lawrence, Brian	R-R	6-0	195	5-14-76	0	2	8.69	3	3	1	0	20	32	19	19	3	5	10	.376	.373	.385	4.58	2.29
2-team (13 New Orleans)					8	5	4.73	16	16	2	0	105	120	57	55	9	14	67	—	—	—	5.76	1.20
Lopez, Rodrigo	R-R	6-1	185	12-14-75	1	0	2.38	2	2	0	0	11	4	3	3	0	4	8	.108	.143	.063	3.18	3.18
Martin, Tom	L-L	6-1	205	5-21-70	0	0	7.20	5	0	0	0	5	6	4	4	1	4	4	.286	.250	.308	7.20	1.80
McClellan, Zach	R-R	6-5	195	11-25-78	1	0	0.00	3	0	0	0	4	2	0	0	0	3	5	.154	.222	.000	6.75	0.00
Morales, Franklin	L-L	6-0	170	1-24-86	0	2	3.71	3	3	0	0	17	20	8	7	1	13	16	.323	.375	.315	8.47	6.88
Morillo, Juan	R-R	6-3	190	11-5-83	0	1	3.72	7	0	0	0	10	9	4	4	0	8	9	.200	.167	.167	11.17	3.72
Newman, Josh	L-L	6-1	200	6-11-82	3	2	4.06	55	0	0	6	62	73	34	28	3	30	49	.292	.189	.355	7.11	4.35
Olson, Tim	R-R	6-2	200	8-1-78	0	0	—	1	0	0	0	0	4	4	1	0	0	0	1.000	1.000	1.000	—	—
Ramirez, Ramon	R-R	5-11	190	8-31-81	4	0	2.28	25	0	0	0	28	18	8	7	0	16	35	.182	.256	.133	11.39	5.20
Redman, Mark	L-L	6-5	245	1-5-74	0	0	2.92	2	2	0	0	12	17	4	4	1	4	5	.354	.200	.395	3.65	2.92
2-team (9 Oklahoma)					2	4	4.90	11	11	1	0	68	87	38	37	4	25	33	—	—	—	4.37	3.31

Rivera, Oscar	L-L	6-2	185	4-13-81	1	1	4.66	2	2	0	0	10	10	5	5	1	3	7	.256	.267	.250	6.52	2.79
Serafini, Dan	B-L	6-1	190	1-25-74	0	1	3.48	11	3	0	1	21	18	8	8	0	9	12	.240	.353	.207	5.23	3.92
Speier, Ryan	R-R	6-7	210	7-24-79	1	4	4.38	50	0	0	33	49	47	26	24	3	23	40	.253	.261	.248	7.30	4.20
Veres, Dave	R-R	6-2	220	10-19-66	0	0	9.64	5	0	0	0	5	7	6	5	1	1	5	.318	.375	.286	9.64	1.93
Walker, Kevin	L-L	6-4	190	9-20-76	4	6	5.31	15	12	1	0	80	96	52	47	6	20	39	.304	.304	.304	4.41	2.26
Williams, Todd	R-R	6-3	210	2-13-71	1	1	7.11	6	0	0	0	6	10	5	5	2	2	4	.400	.200	.533	5.68	2.84

FIELDING

Catcher	PCT	G	PO	A	E	DP	PB
Bellorin	1.000	57	320	34	0	2	2
Colina	.987	75	416	39	6	3	6
Duenas	1.000	1	3	0	0	0	1
Iannetta	1.000	14	81	4	0	0	1
Sanchez	1.000	2	10	1	0	0	1

First Base	PCT	G	PO	A	E	DP
Baker	1.000	2	16	1	0	3
Bernier	1.000	12	72	6	0	11
Koshansky	.988	131	1267	86	17	166
Olson	1.000	1	2	0	0	0
Paulk	1.000	3	21	2	0	4
Spilborghs	1.000	3	11	0	0	3

Second Base	PCT	G	PO	A	E	DP
Barmes	1.000	2	4	1	0	0
Bernier	1.000	9	12	22	0	6

	PCT	G	PO	A	E	DP
Cabrera	1.000	1	3	4	0	0
Matsui	1.000	2	3	3	0	1
Menechino	.929	2	6	7	1	3
Nix	.986	107	234	404	9	124
Olson	1.000	2	6	1	0	0
Quintanilla	.967	27	50	98	5	30

Third Base	PCT	G	PO	A	E	DP
Barmes	1.000	1	1	1	0	0
Bernier	.967	30	30	57	3	12
Cabrera	1.000	5	4	11	0	2
Macri	1.000	2	1	2	0	0
Nix	.875	5	1	6	1	0
Olson	1.000	3	2	1	0	0
Stewart	.914	108	66	212	26	23

Shortstop	PCT	G	PO	A	E	DP
Barmes	.982	90	157	327	9	90

Bernier	.983	16	18	39	1	12
Quintanilla	.976	48	90	155	6	51

Outfield	PCT	G	PO	A	E	DP
Baker	1.000	1	1	0	0	0
Barker	.992	64	123	3	1	0
Barmes	1.000	9	7	0	0	0
Bernier	.500	1	1	0	1	0
Cabrera	1.000	13	12	4	0	1
Gaetti	.965	67	104	7	4	1
Garcia	1.000	13	21	1	0	0
Gomez	.970	83	121	9	4	0
Smith	.983	123	219	16	4	7
Spilborghs	.960	29	47	1	2	0
Sullivan	.991	52	103	3	1	0
Taveras	1.000	3	3	0	0	0

TULSA DRILLERS   DOUBLE-A

TEXAS LEAGUE

BATTING	B-T	HT	WT	DOB	AVG	vLH	vRH	G	AB	R	H	2B	3B	HR	RBI	BB	HBP	SH	SF	SO	SB	CS	SLG	OBP
Colonel, Christian	R-R	6-2	210	12-25-81	.309	.358	.288	134	527	78	163	47	0	17	84	46	1	0	6	80	6	4	.495	.362
Czarniecki, Jordan	R-R	6-1	175	10-4-80	.281	.242	.298	128	427	74	120	31	0	13	58	55	7	7	5	75	18	4	.445	.368
Dragicevich, Jeffrey	R-R	6-2	200	8-1-82	.248	.292	.217	36	117	12	29	7	0	5	19	11	3	1	2	39	0	1	.436	.323
Duenas, Tomas	R-R	5-11	205	7-16-81	.213	.217	.211	68	216	19	46	8	0	6	32	10	3	1	3	54	1	0	.333	.254
Frey, Christopher	L-L	6-1	180	8-11-83	.295	.264	.308	132	474	65	140	30	6	1	34	36	9	9	3	61	12	7	.390	.354
Gaetti, Joe	R-R	5-11	205	10-16-81	.232	.220	.235	49	177	24	41	11	0	8	28	21	4	0	2	52	2	1	.429	.324
Guarno, Rick	R-R	6-0	185	8-16-82	.258	.253	.260	75	248	28	64	15	0	6	37	17	12	4	4	67	4	0	.391	.331
Herrera, Jonathan	R-R	5-9	150	11-3-84	.257	.218	.272	131	509	65	131	24	4	3	40	36	8	17	3	69	18	12	.338	.315
Macri, Matt	R-R	6-2	200	5-29-82	.298	.418	.250	79	275	46	82	23	0	11	33	20	2	0	1	58	4	4	.502	.349
Miller, Matt	R-R	6-2	210	12-26-82	.262	.271	.259	126	446	59	117	22	2	11	61	42	10	0	4	69	1	4	.395	.337
Olson, Tim	R-R	6-2	200	8-1-78	.290	.364	.250	11	31	3	9	0	1	1	8	1	0	0	0	8	0	0	.452	.313
Rifkin, Aaron	L-L	6-3	220	3-12-79	.272	.264	.275	123	453	61	123	36	0	15	76	38	8	0	3	119	3	1	.450	.337
Sanchez, Tino	B-R	6-0	175	2-2-79	.175	.375	.143	32	57	4	10	3	0	1	8	8	0	1	0	10	0	0	.281	.277
Sardinha, Duke	R-R	6-0	200	12-9-80	.261	.296	.241	76	222	31	58	12	1	10	34	19	3	2	2	51	1	3	.459	.325
Wimberly, Corey	B-R	5-8	180	10-26-83	.268	.303	.252	92	365	63	98	15	1	4	33	19	12	4	4	52	36	9	.348	.323

PITCHING	B-T	HT	WT	DOB	W	L	ERA	G	GS	CG	SV	IP	H	R	ER	HR	BB	SO	AVG	vLH	vRH	K/9	BB/9
Asahina, Jonathan	B-R	6-1	190	12-31-80	3	5	5.07	10	10	0	0	50	58	32	28	8	25	15	.289	.281	.295	2.72	4.53
Beckstead, Jentry	R-R	6-0	175	6-9-80	3	1	5.01	36	0	0	0	59	64	34	33	6	24	48	.286	.294	.278	7.28	3.64
Bright, Adam	L-L	6-0	180	8-11-84	1	3	3.72	52	0	0	0	46	44	21	19	3	26	41	.260	.174	.320	8.02	5.09
Casadiego, Gerardo	R-R	6-0	180	12-19-80	1	0	3.12	6	0	0	0	9	8	3	3	2	2	10	.242	.267	.222	10.38	2.08
Clarke, Darren	R-R	6-8	235	3-18-81	1	1	1.64	10	1	0	0	11	5	2	2	1	1	16	.139	.154	.130	13.09	0.82
Daley, Matt	R-R	6-2	175	6-23-82	2	6	3.49	43	10	0	0	95	83	40	37	12	22	84	.228	.228	.228	7.93	2.08
De Paula, Jorge	R-R	6-1	210	11-10-78	1	0	3.60	1	1	0	0	5	6	2	2	0	3	2	.400	.583	.125	3.60	5.40
Deduno, Samuel	R-R	6-1	156	7-2-83	5	8	5.44	21	21	1	0	124	120	90	75	13	66	121	.251	.277	.222	8.78	4.79
DeJean, Mike	R-R	6-2	220	9-28-70	0	0	6.23	3	0	0	0	4	8	4	3	1	1	3	.421	.333	.500	6.23	2.08
Esposito, Mike	R-R	6-0	190	9-27-81	1	1	1.29	1	1	1	0	7	7	1	1	2	3	6	.250	.313	.167	3.86	3.86
Grube, Jarrett	R-R	6-4	220	11-5-81	7	3	2.53	52	0	0	0	68	58	20	19	4	21	61	.229	.248	.217	8.11	2.79
Johnson, Alan	R-R	6-1	180	8-24-83	2	0	0.00	2	2	0	0	13	7	0	0	0	2	7	.159	.222	.059	4.85	1.38
Lo, Ching Lung	R-R	6-6	190	8-20-85	8	8	5.61	26	26	1	0	140	162	95	87	20	66	87	.300	.306	.295	5.61	4.25
Mattheus, Ryan	R-R	6-3	215	11-10-83	9	11	5.56	26	26	1	0	159	182	100	98	13	55	102	.294	.304	.285	5.79	3.12
Morales, Franklin	L-L	6-0	170	1-24-86	3	4	3.48	17	17	1	0	96	77	41	37	8	45	77	.226	.239	.221	7.24	4.23
Morillo, Juan	R-R	6-3	190	11-5-83	6	4	2.35	46	0	0	0	57	44	19	15	2	27	59	.210	.153	.259	9.26	4.24
Olson, Tim	R-R	6-2	200	8-1-78	0	1	9.00	1	0	0	0	1	1	2	1	1	0	2	.333	.500	.000	18.00	0.00
Parker, Zack	R-L	6-2	205	8-19-81	2	1	6.55	16	5	0	0	33	35	28	24	4	25	19	.282	.278	.284	5.18	6.82
Redman, Mark	L-L	6-5	245	1-5-74	0	0	9.00	1	1	0	0	5	5	5	5	2	2	7	.250	.286	.231	12.60	3.60
Register, Steven	R-R	6-1	170	5-16-83	1	3	4.03	60	0	0	37	58	63	27	26	3	16	48	.279	.293	.268	7.45	2.48
Reynolds, Greg	R-R	6-7	225	7-3-85	4	1	1.42	8	8	0	0	51	32	10	8	2	9	35	.180	.198	.165	6.22	1.60
Rivera, Oscar	L-L	6-2	185	4-13-81	0	1	0.00	1	1	0	0	3	1	3	0	2	0	2	.100	.000	.125	6.00	6.00
Sardinha, Duke	R-R	6-0	200	12-9-80	0	1	9.00	1	0	0	0	1	2	1	1	1	0	0	.500	.667	.000	0.00	0.00
Songster, Judd	R-R	6-3	195	12-26-79	5	5	4.30	42	1	0	2	67	71	37	32	7	31	55	.275	.281	.270	7.39	4.16
Thompson, Sean	L-L	5-11	170	10-13-82	5	1	4.06	9	9	0	0	67	67	33	30	6	26	80	.248	.263	.244	4.47	3.05
2-team (16 San Antonio)					9	8	3.73	24	23	1	0	133	124	61	55	11	56	81	—	—	—	5.49	3.80
Williams, Todd	R-R	6-3	210	2-13-71	0	0	0.00	2	0	0	0	2	2	1	0	0	0	0	.286	.000	.500	0.00	0.00

ORGANIZATION STATISTICS

FIELDING

Catcher	PCT	G	PO	A	E	DP	PB
Duenas	.991	65	416	36	4	5	6
Guarno	.993	74	496	59	4	6	8
Sanchez	1.000	3	19	2	0	0	0

First Base	PCT	G	PO	A	E	DP
Colonel	1.000	1	11	0	0	1
Rifkin	.996	107	956	62	4	102
Sanchez	1.000	1	2	0	0	0
Sardinha	.994	36	298	14	2	31

Second Base	PCT	G	PO	A	E	DP
Dragicevich	.981	21	42	59	2	11

Macri	.990	21	46	55	1	12
Olson	.930	8	18	22	3	8
Sardinha	.947	8	10	26	2	7
Wimberly	.962	87	162	264	17	68

Third Base	PCT	G	PO	A	E	DP
Colonel	.941	102	68	219	18	14
Dragicevich	1.000	9	10	21	0	1
Macri	.937	33	19	55	5	4
Sardinha	1.000	1	0	1	0	0

Shortstop	PCT	G	PO	A	E	DP
Dragicevich	1.000	5	4	12	0	3

Herrera	.964	127	192	400	22	99
Macri	.905	12	12	26	4	5

Outfield	PCT	G	PO	A	E	DP
Colonel	1.000	27	38	1	0	0
Czarniecki	1.000	119	192	17	0	1
Frey	.993	121	294	11	2	5
Gaetti	.986	44	69	1	1	1
Miller	.995	114	178	5	1	1
Olson	—	1	0	0	0	0
Sardinha	—	1	0	0	0	0

MODESTO NUTS HIGH CLASS A

CALIFORNIA LEAGUE

BATTING	B-T	HT	WT	DOB	AVG	vLH	vRH	G	AB	R	H	2B	3B	HR	RBI	BB	HBP	SH	SF	SO	SB	CS	SLG	OBP
Becktel, Travis	R-R	6-1	201	4-3-83	.233	.210	.239	108	374	59	87	20	6	8	46	37	6	3	2	103	15	7	.382	.310
Blumenthal, Kyle	L-R	5-10	195	1-11-83	.172	.235	.156	57	169	28	29	7	2	4	21	27	0	4	3	50	1	1	.308	.281
Cabrera, Everth	B-R	5-8	160	11-17-86	.267	.333	.222	4	15	3	4	0	1	0	2	2	2	1	0	7	1	0	.400	.421
Carte, Daniel	R-R	6-0	190	5-18-84	.283	.293	.281	111	427	52	121	35	5	14	71	13	10	3	4	130	4	4	.487	.317
Cook, Christopher	R-R	6-4	222	7-3-83	.107	.200	.087	8	28	2	3	1	0	0	2	3	2	0	0	10	0	0	.143	.242
Cuadrado, Phillip	B-R	6-1	210	11-4-83	.215	.333	.189	37	130	19	28	5	2	3	19	13	4	0	1	29	0	1	.354	.304
Dragicevich, Jeffrey	R-R	6-2	200	8-1-82	.310	.286	.318	8	29	6	9	1	0	1	3	3	1	0	0	4	1	0	.448	.394
Fowler, Dexter	B-R	6-4	173	3-22-86	.273	.302	.264	65	245	43	67	7	5	2	23	44	7	2	1	64	20	11	.367	.397
Garcia, Lino	R-R	6-3	192	10-12-83	.254	.308	.233	57	185	27	47	8	2	7	17	11	4	7	0	61	3	1	.432	.310
Garner, Cole	R-R	6-2	210	12-15-84	.213	.242	.201	96	319	39	68	18	4	8	33	20	7	5	1	115	7	5	.370	.274
Haley, Nick	L-R	5-11	185	5-25-84	.301	.297	.302	50	163	35	49	8	1	0	15	32	2	5	0	26	3	4	.362	.421
Kindel, Jeff	L-L	6-3	205	9-1-83	.317	.337	.311	126	477	79	151	34	7	14	83	41	7	3	6	81	3	4	.505	.375
Nelson, Christopher	R-R	5-11	176	9-5-85	.289	.281	.292	133	529	97	153	42	7	19	99	55	7	0	9	92	27	5	.503	.358
Nelson, Justin	L-L	6-3	205	4-23-83	.319	.444	.294	60	213	36	68	14	1	13	53	41	2	0	7	69	3	3	.577	.422
Robledo, Nelson	R-R	6-1	180	6-13-84	.278	.205	.301	53	180	24	50	9	0	0	21	15	2	3	2	27	0	2	.328	.337
Valdez, Jose	L-R	6-1	152	9-6-83	.258	.204	.267	85	322	39	83	21	1	3	54	29	2	3	3	54	5	4	.357	.320
Van Kooten, Jason	R-R	6-0	170	9-1-84	.181	.167	.186	27	83	7	15	2	0	0	6	4	0	0	1	19	3	2	.205	.216
Wilson, Neil	R-R	6-1	190	12-7-83	.255	.261	.253	94	353	54	90	25	3	10	70	32	2	1	6	62	4	1	.428	.319
Young Jr., Eric	B-R	5-10	180	5-25-85	.291	.268	.297	130	540	113	157	29	11	8	63	46	13	12	2	105	73	18	.430	.359

PITCHING	B-T	HT	WT	DOB	W	L	ERA	G	GS	CG	SV	IP	H	R	ER	HR	BB	SO	AVG	vLH	vRH	K/9	BB/9
Arnold, David	R-R	6-1	220	3-6-86	1	0	13.50	12	0	0	0	15	28	23	22	1	17	11	.394	.340	.426	6.75	10.43
Burok, James	R-R	6-3	212	11-16-82	0	0	10.80	4	0	0	0	3	4	4	4	0	3	1	.286	.333	.250	18.90	8.10
Cedeno, Xavier	L-L	6-1	165	8-26-86	6	8	5.09	23	23	0	0	117	121	78	66	6	61	83	.266	.262	.268	6.40	4.71
Deduno, Samuel	R-R	6-1	156	7-2-83	1	1	6.55	2	2	0	0	11	9	8	8	1	7	8	.214	.167	.233	6.55	5.73
Durden, Brandon	R-L	6-3	215	7-20-84	8	9	4.70	26	26	0	0	157	176	103	82	12	42	93	.279	.260	.287	5.33	2.41
George, Jon	R-R	6-4	220	7-6-84	5	4	3.97	49	1	0	3	66	66	31	29	2	20	35	.256	.220	.286	4.80	2.74
Huerta, Edgar	L-L	5-11	200	10-21-79	1	0	5.19	12	0	0	0	17	17	11	10	3	9	20	.254	.182	.289	10.38	4.67
Hynick, Brandon	R-R	6-3	205	3-7-85	16	5	2.52	28	28	3	0	182	170	64	51	13	31	136	.243	.273	.222	6.71	1.53
Johnson, Alan	R-R	6-1	180	8-24-83	14	7	2.99	26	26	1	0	169	162	69	56	9	47	119	.254	.218	.288	6.35	2.51
Johnston, Andrew	R-R	6-5	205	4-30-84	3	6	5.51	55	0	0	13	64	71	43	39	10	22	29	.291	.322	.264	4.10	3.11
Merrell, Darric	R-R	6-4	210	1-22-82	2	1	6.33	38	2	0	0	64	72	49	45	11	32	54	.282	.196	.340	7.59	4.50
Patton, David	R-R	6-3	175	5-18-84	5	5	4.52	49	0	0	1	68	73	37	34	6	34	59	.283	.259	.303	7.85	4.52
Roe, Chaz	R-R	6-5	180	10-9-86	7	11	4.33	29	29	2	0	170	148	93	82	17	73	131	.235	.233	.238	6.92	3.86
Santiago, Tomas	R-R	6-4	210	10-30-81	2	4	4.70	35	3	0	8	54	45	31	28	4	29	65	.227	.286	.170	10.90	4.86
Strickland, Brett	R-R	6-0	170	2-15-83	0	1	6.75	4	0	0	0	5	7	4	4	0	1	5	.333	.222	.417	8.44	1.69
Strop, Pedro	B-R	6-0	160	6-13-85	5	2	4.28	48	0	0	7	55	43	28	26	4	29	75	.215	.198	.228	12.35	4.77
Trent, Matthew	R-R	6-2	220	8-7-82	0	0	1.08	5	0	0	0	8	7	1	1	0	2	2	.233	.083	.333	2.16	2.16
Weathers, Casey	R-R	6-1	205	6-10-85	0	0	0.00	1	0	0	0	1	0	0	0	0	2	2	.000	.000	.000	18.00	18.00
Zimmermann, Rob	R-R	6-5	245	11-17-81	0	0	6.43	12	0	0	0	14	12	12	10	1	17	11	.222	.273	.188	7.07	10.93

FIELDING

Catcher	PCT	G	PO	A	E	DP	PB
Blumenthal	.988	41	230	15	3	1	3
Robledo	.980	40	272	25	6	1	4
Wilson	.996	68	452	59	2	2	9

First Base	PCT	G	PO	A	E	DP
Cook	.986	7	65	4	1	4
Cuadrado	.984	8	58	5	1	2
Haley	1.000	1	9	2	0	2
Kindel	.984	119	1046	71	18	107
Robledo	.985	9	62	3	1	5

Second Base	PCT	G	PO	A	E	DP
Cabrera	1.000	4	5	13	0	2

Haley	1.000	7	11	24	0	7
Valdez	1.000	2	3	10	0	2
Van Kooten	.750	1	0	3	1	1
Young Jr.	.964	126	277	389	25	83

Third Base	PCT	G	PO	A	E	DP
Blumenthal	.944	8	3	14	1	3
Carte	1.000	1	0	1	0	0
Cuadrado	.905	16	5	33	4	4
Dragicevich	1.000	7	1	13	0	1
Haley	.891	27	13	44	7	9
Valdez	.925	71	46	139	15	10
Van Kooten	.957	18	17	28	2	8

Shortstop	PCT	G	PO	A	E	DP
Nelson	.947	130	201	348	31	69
Valdez	.957	7	16	29	2	8
Van Kooten	.941	5	7	9	1	1

Outfield	PCT	G	PO	A	E	DP
Becktel	1.000	106	234	7	0	2
Carte	.980	91	136	11	3	2
Fowler	.975	62	157	2	4	0
Garcia	.981	56	104	2	2	0
Garner	.978	76	132	3	3	1
Haley	1.000	4	4	0	0	0
Nelson	.959	42	68	3	3	1

SOUTH ATLANTIC LEAGUE

BATTING	B-T	HT	WT	DOB	AVG	vLH	vRH	G	AB	R	H	2B	3B	HR	RBI	BB	HBP	SH	SF	SO	SB	CS	SLG	OBP
Agustin, Jhaysson	R-R	6-0	170	3-16-85	.189	.170	.194	59	212	24	40	14	1	5	35	13	4	0	3	73	2	2	.335	.246
Berglund, Bret	R-R	6-4	210	12-9-82	.275	.169	.308	82	273	46	75	19	2	9	43	42	9	1	2	78	20	5	.458	.387
Cox, Jay	L-R	6-0	200	10-30-84	.277	.297	.272	120	437	71	121	37	7	8	73	48	2	2	4	104	14	8	.449	.348
Ferrante, Victor	R-R	6-3	215	12-6-84	.269	.263	.271	100	346	54	93	20	4	16	69	37	13	0	6	110	5	8	.488	.356
Gomez, Hector	R-R	6-1	157	3-5-88	.266	.300	.257	124	534	89	142	34	8	11	61	29	5	2	120	20	10	.421	.309
Jackson, Anthony	B-R	5-7	170	6-17-84	.244	.290	.232	121	464	84	113	21	12	6	42	51	5	6	3	111	34	5	.379	.323
Mayora, Daniel	R-R	5-11	145	7-27-85	.312	.271	.323	127	516	88	161	42	1	14	78	41	6	5	3	124	26	9	.479	.367
McKenry, Michael	R-R	5-10	210	3-4-85	.287	.180	.317	113	408	79	117	35	1	22	90	66	6	3	2	84	8	9	.539	.392
Nagy, Spence	B-R	5-11	185	6-14-85	.190	.158	.199	54	179	15	34	7	1	0	14	12	3	0	2	51	12	3	.240	.250
Nazario, Radames	R-R	6-0	166	6-14-87	.196	.125	.211	14	46	1	9	0	0	0	4	3	1	3	0	14	0	3	.196	.260
Paulk, Mike	L-L	6-2	195	4-23-84	.303	.267	.313	130	491	91	149	34	4	11	93	65	2	1	8	90	14	9	.456	.382
Repec, Matt	R-R	6-1	190	8-30-83	.276	.284	.274	86	322	52	89	30	3	10	48	25	5	2	3	80	8	4	.481	.335
Strickland, Geoff	B-R	5-10	180	7-1-84	.267	.242	.273	100	326	73	87	23	9	9	47	71	2	5	0	100	23	15	.475	.401
Van Kooten, Jason	R-R	6-0	170	9-1-84	.154	.000	.167	3	13	1	2	0	0	0	1	0	1	0	0	2	0	0	.154	.214
Wiens, Logan	R-R	6-6	210	1-13-86	.264	.154	.300	28	106	10	28	12	1	3	26	8	0	0	0	26	0	0	.481	.316

PITCHING	B-T	HT	WT	DOB	W	L	ERA	G	GS	CG	SV	IP	H	R	ER	HR	BB	SO	AVG	vLH	vRH	K/9	BB/9
Baker, Craig	R-R	6-1	210	1-31-85	3	1	3.35	36	0	0	5	51	58	23	19	6	18	48	.284	.273	.291	8.47	3.18
Baumgardner, Tommy	L-L	6-3	220	10-15-83	3	2	2.31	51	0	0	15	51	44	15	13	2	8	52	.229	.204	.238	9.24	1.42
Burok, James	R-R	6-3	212	11-16-82	4	1	1.72	41	0	0	1	47	28	13	9	1	18	51	.168	.242	.119	9.77	3.45
Ferrer, Simon	B-R	5-10	175	6-24-80	7	11	5.22	30	26	1	0	167	203	109	97	21	60	88	.307	.318	.299	4.73	3.23
Fuentes, Brian	L-L	6-4	230	8-9-75	0	0	0.00	1	0	0	1	0	0	0	0	0	2	0	.000	—	.000	18.00	0.00
Graham, Andy	R-R	6-4	210	6-29-84	10	10	5.39	26	25	1	1	139	168	88	83	11	43	140	.304	.297	.308	9.09	2.79
Harris, William	R-R	6-4	225	8-28-84	1	2	1.32	38	0	0	1	48	38	10	7	2	13	68	.212	.211	.213	12.84	2.45
Jarrett, Sean	R-R	6-5	210	4-26-83	0	1	1.15	15	0	0	5	16	11	5	2	1	4	12	.183	.120	.229	6.89	2.30
Katz, Ethan	R-R	6-5	210	7-4-83	3	2	2.96	19	0	0	1	27	28	13	9	2	7	23	.259	.295	.234	7.57	2.30
Kreidermacher, A.	B-R	6-2	195	1-27-83	2	2	2.27	22	4	0	0	44	49	22	11	4	13	28	.285	.253	.309	5.77	2.68
Marbry, Michael	R-R	6-3	185	9-3-84	0	0	14.54	5	0	0	0	4	10	7	7	2	3	2	.476	.417	.556	4.15	6.23
Parker, David	R-R	6-0	180	12-5-82	3	1	5.74	17	0	0	0	31	34	23	20	5	16	29	.283	.318	.263	8.33	4.60
Rodriguez, Aneury	R-R	6-3	180	12-13-87	9	9	5.15	28	28	1	0	152	182	105	87	19	48	160	.298	.314	.288	9.47	2.84
Rogers, Esmil	R-R	6-1	146	8-14-85	7	4	3.75	19	18	1	0	118	125	60	49	6	42	90	.272	.272	.271	6.88	3.21
Simons, Zach	L-R	6-3	200	5-23-85	8	2	4.52	42	0	0	1	70	69	37	35	6	31	62	.261	.300	.241	8.01	4.00
Sullivan, Josh	R-R	6-4	215	7-5-84	3	2	3.26	13	9	0	0	50	42	23	18	3	25	45	.223	.253	.202	8.15	4.53
Weathers, Casey	R-R	6-1	205	6-10-85	0	1	4.61	13	0	0	2	14	6	7	7	2	7	19	.130	.091	.167	12.51	4.61
Weiser, Keith	R-L	6-2	190	9-21-84	17	7	3.75	28	28	1	0	175	195	86	73	18	30	126	.283	.349	.265	6.47	1.54

FIELDING

Catcher	PCT	G	PO	A	E	DP	PB
Agustin	.982	55	408	29	8	5	18
McKenry	.979	85	650	63	15	5	8

First Base	PCT	G	PO	A	E	DP
Nagy	1.000	2	5	0	0	0
Paulk	.984	85	701	47	12	83
Repec	.988	37	306	19	4	18
Wiens	.974	16	141	7	4	15

Second Base	PCT	G	PO	A	E	DP
Mayora	.972	119	217	330	16	80
Nagy	.973	9	13	23	1	2

	PCT	G	PO	A	E	DP	PB
Nazario	1.000	1	0	3	0	1	
Strickland	1.000	10	21	36	0	6	

Third Base	PCT	G	PO	A	E	DP
Nagy	.896	30	19	41	7	5
Nazario	1.000	10	10	21	0	3
Repec	.944	37	27	58	5	6
Strickland	.923	60	59	109	14	12
Van Kooten	1.000	2	2	5	0	0

Shortstop	PCT	G	PO	A	E	DP
Gomez	.933	121	182	359	39	68
Nagy	.967	12	18	41	2	12

	PCT	G	PO	A	E	DP
Nazario	.933	3	3	11	1	5
Strickland	.857	5	0	6	1	0

Outfield	PCT	G	PO	A	E	DP
Berglund	.982	80	155	9	3	0
Cox	.976	115	154	8	4	0
Ferrante	.973	86	126	17	4	4
Jackson	.979	120	271	11	6	3
Paulk	1.000	3	8	1	0	0
Strickland	1.000	17	30	1	0	0

NORTHWEST LEAGUE

BATTING	B-T	HT	WT	DOB	AVG	vLH	vRH	G	AB	R	H	2B	3B	HR	RBI	BB	HBP	SH	SF	SO	SB	CS	SLG	OBP
Aguailar, Brian	L-R	5-11	185	4-29-84	.088	.000	.100	11	34	2	3	0	0	0	2	5	1	0	0	10	0	0	.088	.225
Anderson, Nate	L-R	6-2	220	10-22-83	.144	.067	.160	27	90	10	13	6	0	0	12	9	0	2	0	24	2	0	.211	.222
Banda, Joshua	R-R	6-1	195	9-7-85	.254	.275	.244	32	118	17	30	6	0	5	20	6	0	0	0	29	1	3	.432	.290
Bell, Josh	R-R	6-0	220	7-3-84	.154	.250	.111	4	13	2	2	0	0	0	3	1	0	0	1	9	0	0	.154	.200
Bowden, Johnny	R-R	6-3	205	8-15-84	.179	.237	.156	22	67	9	12	7	0	1	9	8	2	1	2	27	1	0	.328	.278
Cabrera, Everth	B-R	5-8	160	11-17-86	.300	.264	.320	42	150	29	45	8	3	1	23	27	8	1	0	24	12	5	.413	.432
Clark, Kevin	L-L	6-0	195	12-10-85	.251	.119	.285	61	207	34	52	15	0	7	25	28	0	4	0	58	4	3	.425	.340
Cuadrado, Phillip	B-R	6-1	210	11-4-83	.355	.389	.348	31	110	19	39	9	0	4	22	18	4	1	3	18	1	4	.545	.452
Davis, Lars	L-R	6-4	215	11-7-85	.219	.279	.201	52	187	17	41	5	3	3	27	14	5	1	5	49	2	4	.326	.284
Holcomb, Darin	R-R	5-11	205	12-7-85	.303	.354	.288	74	277	46	84	23	1	12	51	31	12	2	5	30	7	1	.523	.391
Kinzler, Derek	L-R	6-0	176	11-27-84	.208	.200	.211	18	48	6	10	0	0	0	2	5	1	1	0	8	5	1	.208	.296
Lapin, Brian	R-R	6-6	230	5-24-85	.255	.286	.240	41	145	21	37	5	5	1	14	13	2	1	1	23	2	5	.379	.323
Loupadiere, Maruis	R-R	6-0	180	4-28-85	.254	.179	.293	32	114	20	29	6	1	4	15	4	5	1	0	28	4	2	.430	.309
Mitchell, Michael	R-R	5-11	185	8-24-85	.259	.211	.278	70	247	39	64	3	3	0	25	31	8	9	3	71	32	11	.296	.356
Nazario, Radames	R-R	6-0	166	6-14-87	.152	.077	.200	11	33	1	5	2	1	0	3	3	2	2	0	5	1	1	.273	.263
Nelson, Justin	L-L	6-3	205	4-23-83	.286	.250	.333	2	7	0	2	0	0	0	2	2	0	0	0	2	0	0	.286	.444
Pacheco, Jordan	R-R	6-0	190	1-30-86	.258	.429	.208	8	31	5	8	2	0	0	3	1	2	0	0	6	0	0	.323	.324
Reichert, Brandon	R-R	6-2	210	12-1-83	.222	.260	.197	39	126	18	28	5	1	2	11	10	1	1	0	27	3	0	.325	.285
Rike, Brian	L-L	6-2	220	12-13-85	.296	.364	.275	49	186	36	55	13	1	4	29	32	3	0	2	54	7	3	.441	.404
Schaeffer, Warren	R-R	6-0	180	1-28-85	.000	.000	.000	1	4	0	0	0	0	0	0	0	0	0	0	1	0	0	.000	.000
Velazquez, Helder	R-R	6-3	165	10-14-88	.262	.310	.243	73	317	44	83	19	4	1	43	5	5	3	5	62	13	5	.356	.280
Wiens, Logan	R-R	6-6	210	1-13-86	.188	.267	.152	13	48	3	9	1	0	1	5	3	1	0	0	11	0	0	.271	.250

ORGANIZATION STATISTICS

PITCHING

PITCHING	B-T	HT	WT	DOB	W	L	ERA	G	GS	CG	SV	IP	H	R	ER	HR	BB	SO	AVG	vLH	vRH	K/9	BB/9
Arias, Agustin	R-R	5-10	165	5-28-85	2	2	4.38	24	0	0	3	25	27	13	12	0	11	33	.293	.278	.304	12.04	4.01
Arnold, David	R-R	6-1	220	3-6-86	1	0	5.40	19	0	0	0	23	31	18	14	3	7	18	.320	.311	.327	6.94	2.70
Billings, Bruce	R-R	6-0	200	11-18-85	4	2	2.97	15	15	0	0	79	59	30	26	8	16	89	.208	.176	.235	10.18	1.83
Chambliss, Austin	L-R	6-2	185	2-19-87	4	3	6.35	22	1	0	0	28	33	20	20	2	10	40	.300	.439	.217	12.71	3.18
Coffey, Drew	L-L	6-0	205	11-2-85	2	5	4.50	15	10	0	1	58	59	33	29	3	15	41	.266	.306	.254	6.36	2.33
Collis, Devin	L-L	6-2	180	4-27-84	0	0	1.93	7	0	0	0	9	6	2	2	0	2	8	.188	.286	.160	7.71	1.93
Duarte, Marco	R-R	6-2	185	8-19-86	2	2	5.21	12	6	0	0	48	57	36	28	6	7	41	.288	.200	.347	7.63	1.30
Durst, Kenneth	B-L	6-0	195	10-1-85	0	0	18.00	5	0	0	0	4	5	8	8	0	5	7	.294	.500	.231	15.75	11.25
Fabian, Robinson	R-R	6-3	152	2-10-86	4	6	3.96	15	15	0	0	77	85	42	34	5	26	67	.281	.292	.272	7.80	3.03
Graham, Connor	R-R	6-6	235	12-30-85	1	0	2.37	6	4	0	0	19	23	7	5	2	6	18	.303	.250	.361	8.53	2.84
Groves, Andrew	R-R	6-2	190	10-6-84	0	3	4.97	21	0	0	0	29	28	18	16	0	17	31	.259	.318	.219	9.62	5.28
Kuo, Sheng-An	R-R	6-2	190	1-1-86	5	4	4.69	15	14	0	0	71	73	41	37	4	32	58	.271	.306	.237	7.35	4.06
Miller, Brandon	L-L	6-2	195	11-24-84	0	1	7.20	9	0	0	0	15	23	14	12	1	1	9	.359	.286	.395	5.40	0.60
Pena, Riquy	R-R	6-2	162	6-17-85	1	1	2.93	31	0	0	16	31	20	11	10	2	19	29	.183	.231	.140	8.51	5.58
Reynolds, Matthew	L-L	6-5	240	10-2-84	1	4	3.60	20	0	0	0	35	37	21	14	4	4	27	.264	.250	.272	6.94	1.03
Riordan, Cory	R-R	6-4	200	5-25-86	2	3	4.25	14	11	0	0	66	69	34	31	5	17	65	.265	.242	.288	8.91	2.33
Rodriguez, Craig	L-R	6-4	210	6-27-85	3	3	3.74	23	0	0	0	34	33	15	14	0	8	29	.268	.333	.227	7.75	2.14
Williamson, Joseph	R-R	6-2	210	1-28-86	5	0	5.96	17	0	0	0	23	23	16	15	2	6	33	.253	.300	.216	13.10	2.38

FIELDING

Catcher	PCT	G	PO	A	E	DP	PB
Aguailar	1.000	5	42	0	0	0	0
Anderson	1.000	8	72	9	0	0	2
Bell	1.000	3	32	4	0	0	1
Bowden	.987	20	128	19	2	1	0
Davis	.988	46	365	31	5	4	7

First Base	PCT	G	PO	A	E	DP
Anderson	1.000	13	90	4	0	8
Cuadrado	1.000	16	114	8	0	11
Holcomb	.917	4	29	4	3	1
Reichert	.994	38	283	23	2	26
Wiens	.992	13	108	16	1	10

Second Base	PCT	G	PO	A	E	DP
Cabrera	.968	32	55	97	5	18

	PCT	G	PO	A	E	DP
Cuadrado	.984	15	26	34	1	5
Kinzler	.935	18	22	36	4	8
Nazario	1.000	2	1	2	0	0
Pacheco	1.000	4	2	13	0	3
Schaeffer	1.000	1	3	4	0	2
Velazquez	1.000	10	22	27	0	8

Third Base	PCT	G	PO	A	E	DP
Cuadrado	1.000	1	0	1	0	0
Holcomb	.940	69	34	106	9	11
Nazario	.889	3	2	6	1	1
Velazquez	.909	6	2	18	2	1

Shortstop	PCT	G	PO	A	E	DP
Cabrera	.951	11	13	26	2	4
Cuadrado	1.000	1	2	1	0	0

	PCT	G	PO	A	E	DP
Nazario	.950	5	7	12	1	1
Pacheco	.867	4	4	9	2	2
Schaeffer	—	1	0	0	0	0
Velazquez	.948	57	74	146	12	30

Outfield	PCT	G	PO	A	E	DP
Banda	.900	6	9	0	1	0
Clark	.928	42	61	3	5	0
Lapin	.961	35	72	2	3	0
Loupadiere	.900	30	49	5	6	0
Mitchell	.981	69	156	0	3	0
Nelson	.800	2	3	1	1	0
Rike	.920	48	76	5	7	2

CASPER ROCKIES   ROOKIE

PIONEER LEAGUE

BATTING

BATTING	B-T	HT	WT	DOB	AVG	vLH	vRH	G	AB	R	H	2B	3B	HR	RBI	BB	HBP	SH	SF	SO	SB	CS	SLG	OBP
Bowman, Bo	L-L	6-2	200	9-22-84	.272	.214	.286	46	147	19	40	7	2	0	17	29	3	0	1	38	6	5	.347	.400
Christensen, David	R-R	6-1	195	2-11-88	.223	.259	.211	62	229	31	51	11	1	9	21	15	5	2	1	95	7	3	.397	.284
Cuadrado, Phillip	B-R	6-1	210	11-4-83	.294	.250	.308	5	17	3	5	1	0	1	2	2	0	0	0	5	0	0	.529	.368
Cunningham, Jeffrey	L-R	6-3	220	3-22-86	.254	.297	.244	59	193	27	49	14	0	8	29	29	5	0	2	71	5	3	.451	.362
Kinzler, Derek	L-R	6-0	176	11-27-84	.277	.294	.267	15	47	6	13	1	1	0	1	4	1	0	0	7	0	2	.340	.346
Lembeck, Chad	R-R	6-2	195	11-2-84	.234	.216	.246	31	94	13	22	4	2	4	14	9	1	1	0	37	2	3	.447	.308
Lowe, Shane	B-R	6-3	184	8-14-87	.170	.171	.170	40	135	10	23	4	1	1	5	7	5	1	1	79	4	2	.237	.236
Martinez, Carlos	R-R	5-11	182	9-12-88	.200	.209	.196	45	140	15	28	2	1	1	10	3	5	3	1	37	2	4	.250	.242
Murry, Zack	R-R	6-0	185	6-12-87	.286	.357	.269	58	213	24	61	8	0	1	22	15	4	4	0	34	8	6	.338	.345
Pacheco, Jordan	R-R	6-1	190	1-30-86	.292	.275	.298	55	192	27	56	10	2	3	29	21	7	3	1	36	3	1	.411	.380
Rauch, Andrew	R-R	6-3	210	3-30-86	.200	.239	.183	43	150	19	30	10	0	5	21	16	5	1	0	67	1	1	.367	.298
Reyes, Leonardo	R-R	6-0	165	8-2-88	.260	.357	.237	41	146	17	38	8	1	0	15	18	1	2	0	27	7	3	.329	.345
Robinson, Scott	R-R	6-0	185	7-6-88	.240	.208	.252	50	196	33	47	3	4	5	25	7	4	3	1	51	10	3	.372	.279
Rosario, Wilin	R-R	5-11	180	2-23-89	.209	.265	.185	34	115	11	24	4	0	2	9	11	1	0	0	38	2	2	.296	.283
Sandoval, Orlando	R-R	6-0	185	1-22-86	.264	.250	.273	37	106	10	28	5	1	1	12	4	0	0	0	39	2	3	.358	.291
Schaeffer, Warren	R-R	6-0	180	1-28-85	.187	.158	.198	44	134	19	25	4	0	1	13	10	5	2	0	23	3	1	.216	.268
Seabury, Beau	R-R	6-1	190	6-13-85	.304	.323	.296	32	112	16	34	6	0	3	11	12	1	1	0	39	1	0	.438	.376
Sims, James	R-R	6-0	180	4-11-86	.125	.000	.154	17	48	5	6	0	0	0	5	5	2	1	0	24	0	2	.125	.236
Vasami, Christopher	R-R	6-4	230	3-7-85	.259	.256	.262	24	81	7	21	4	1	2	17	4	2	0	2	20	1	1	.407	.303

PITCHING

PITCHING	B-T	HT	WT	DOB	W	L	ERA	G	GS	CG	SV	IP	H	R	ER	HR	BB	SO	AVG	vLH	vRH	K/9	BB/9
Aristil, Jonnathan	R-R	6-1	160	11-30-86	1	3	4.95	22	0	0	0	36	35	28	20	4	21	32	.246	.224	.273	7.93	5.20
Campos, Jose	R-R	6-1	160	12-4-84	1	4	5.76	5	5	0	0	25	32	21	16	2	8	13	.302	.254	.362	4.68	2.88
Chacin, Jhoulys	R-R	6-1	188	1-7-88	6	5	3.13	16	16	0	0	92	85	45	32	5	26	77	.248	.273	.225	7.53	2.54
Duarte, Marco	R-R	6-2	185	8-19-86	3	1	3.21	5	0	0	0	14	10	5	5	1	2	11	.200	.100	.267	7.07	1.29
Durst, Kenneth	B-L	6-0	195	10-1-85	0	1	4.50	15	0	0	0	22	26	12	11	2	7	25	.299	.444	.261	10.23	2.86
Escalona, Edgmer	R-R	6-4	175	10-6-86	1	1	4.05	18	0	0	0	27	22	17	12	1	13	20	.212	.239	.190	6.75	4.39
Fischer, Jeff	R-R	6-5	200	12-2-85	0	10	5.77	15	15	0	0	73	94	60	47	18	17	63	.307	.293	.321	7.73	2.09
Frazier, Parker	R-R	6-5	159	11-11-88	3	5	10.07	16	10	0	0	45	78	54	50	8	18	22	.386	.465	.311	4.43	3.63
Froneberger, Isaiah	L-L	5-8	200	6-23-89	0	0	8.00	9	0	0	1	9	13	8	8	2	13	.351	.375	.333	13.00	2.00
Lively, Mitchell	R-R	6-5	230	9-7-85	1	0	1.35	6	0	0	0	7	4	2	1	0	2	3	.182	.250	.143	4.05	2.70
Lopez, Leonel	R-R	6-2	153	8-12-85	0	1	4.00	7	0	0	0	9	10	4	4	1	0	14	.263	.261	.267	14.00	1.00
Lopez, Ronny	R-R	6-2	185	8-12-86	0	1	6.75	4	0	0	0	5	7	4	4	0	4	7	.304	.300	.308	11.81	6.75
Marrero, Andres	R-R	6-1	190	7-8-88	0	0	9.14	17	0	0	1	22	36	26	22	4	16	16	.371	.431	.304	6.65	6.65
Miller, Brandon	L-L	6-2	195	11-24-84	2	1	4.43	8	0	0	0	43	53	21	21	3	7	26	.310	.268	.323	5.48	1.48
Molina, Jonathan	R-R	5-11	125	6-6-86	1	2	5.45	24	0	0	0	36	48	34	22	5	20	38	.308	.347	.274	9.41	4.95
Nicasio, Juan	R-R	6-3	190	8-31-86	0	3	4.36	13	8	0	0	43	48	32	21	3	13	33	.276	.349	.205	6.85	2.70
Noboa, Luis	R-R	6-2	148	2-26-85	0	1	6.48	4	0	0	0	17	18	19	12	2	10	23	.269	.222	.300	12.42	5.40
Parker, David	R-R	6-0	180	12-5-82	0	2	1.04	6	0	0	0	9	8	2	1	0	1	6	.258	.400	.190	6.23	1.04
Paschal, Bobby	L-L	6-0	180	4-3-84	0	5	6.27	16	6	0	0	33	36	27	23	1	28	30	.283	.265	.290	8.18	7.64
Sandes, Jorge	B-R	6-0	170	2-25-85	0	0	13.50	3	0	0	0	3	8	6	5	2	0	0	.500	.556	.429	0.00	0.00
Shao, Stephen	L-L	6-0	170	3-24-85	2	1	4.88	14	0	0	0	28	35	17	15	3	11	17	.307	.194	.359	5.53	3.58

Player	B-T	HT	WT	DOB	W	L	ERA	G	GS	CG	SV	IP	H	R	ER	HR	BB	SO	AVG	vLH	vRH	K/9	BB/9
Taylor, Randall	R-R	6-1	185	5-23-85	1	4	1.13	24	0	0	5	24	16	7	3	3	7	29	.184	.125	.234	10.88	2.62
Vicaro, Mike	R-R	6-0	185	8-13-83	0	1	5.73	7	0	0	0	11	15	10	7	2	3	11	.313	.304	.320	9.00	2.45
Williamson, Joseph	R-R	6-2	210	1-28-86	0	0	0.00	1	0	0	1	2	0	0	0	0	0	4	.000	.000	.000	15.43	0.00
Zink, J.T.	R-R	6-2	195	5-6-85	0	1	5.21	5	4	0	0	19	27	13	11	2	4	19	.321	.341	.302	9.00	1.89

FIELDING

Catcher	PCT	G	PO	A	E	DP	PB
Rauch	.978	26	197	26	5	1	6
Rosario	.964	23	139	23	6	1	12
Seabury	.988	29	203	37	3	3	10

First Base	PCT	G	PO	A	E	DP
Bowman	1.000	3	23	1	0	1
Cunningham	.976	57	464	31	12	50
Vasami	.976	23	188	19	5	13

Second Base	PCT	G	PO	A	E	DP
Kinzler	1.000	5	9	14	0	5
Martinez	.902	14	27	28	6	8

	PCT	G	PO	A	E	DP
Murry	.938	56	92	133	15	29
Pacheco	.974	7	13	24	1	5

Third Base	PCT	G	PO	A	E	DP
Cuadrado	1.000	3	0	4	0	0
Kinzler	.833	5	0	5	1	2
Lowe	.810	30	20	61	19	5
Pacheco	.929	37	25	67	7	5
Schaeffer	.833	3	2	8	2	1

Shortstop	PCT	G	PO	A	E	DP
Martinez	.917	28	40	82	11	16
Pacheco	.905	12	18	20	4	0

	PCT	G	PO	A	E	DP
Schaeffer	.965	42	68	126	7	32

Outfield	PCT	G	PO	A	E	DP
Bowman	.981	32	50	1	1	0
Christensen	.971	54	101	0	3	0
Kinzler	1.000	3	4	0	0	0
Lembeck	.923	28	34	2	3	0
Reyes	.903	35	54	2	6	0
Robinson	.920	43	80	0	7	0
Sandoval	.929	34	46	6	4	2
Sims	1.000	11	15	1	0	0
Vasami	1.000	2	2	0	0	0

DSL ROCKIES   ROOKIE

DOMINICAN SUMMER LEAGUE

BATTING	B-T	HT	WT	DOB	AVG	vLH	vRH	G	AB	R	H	2B	3B	HR	RBI	BB	HBP	SH	SF	SO	SB	CS	SLG	OBP
Castillo, Engels	R-R	6-3	194	7-25-90	.190	.125	.213	46	121	13	23	2	2	0	9	13	4	1	2	52	2	1	.240	.286
Charles, Moises	R-R	5-11	168	12-1-88	.245	.208	.257	64	253	41	62	3	3	1	21	30	13	7	1	47	11	11	.292	.354
Crousset, Juan	L-L	5-11	193	4-30-90	.176	.184	.169	51	176	19	31	6	1	0	9	11	5	2	0	51	2	2	.222	.245
De La Cruz, Robert	R-R	5-11	189	10-10-89	.227	.158	.257	57	207	18	47	3	1	3	22	12	5	2	1	38	1	0	.295	.284
Gomez, Leuris	R-R	6-0	170	10-20-86	.303	.203	.328	69	261	34	79	14	1	1	28	27	6	12	1	38	23	16	.375	.380
Gonzalez, Jose	R-R	6-2	165	6-23-87	.202	.207	.203	61	208	26	42	8	2	2	24	34	9	6	1	62	3	1	.288	.337
Nina, Angelys	R-R	5-11	165	11-16-88	.323	.290	.333	66	254	33	82	19	3	3	43	23	6	8	2	23	24	8	.457	.387
Peralta, Angelo	B-R	5-11	175	7-11-88	.197	.213	.190	40	127	19	25	5	1	1	15	25	1	5	1	41	0	2	.276	.331
Perez, Miguel	B-R	6-0	156	9-9-88	.276	.298	.264	68	283	41	78	9	7	1	31	17	7	10	4	33	33	10	.367	.328
Ramirez, Michael	R-R	5-10	165	4-27-90	.248	.281	.232	36	129	10	32	3	0	0	9	5	4	4	0	28	1	2	.271	.297
Sandoval, Orlando	R-R	6-0	185	1-22-86	.000	.000	.000	2	8	0	0	0	0	0	0	0	0	0	0	2	0	0	.000	.000
Santos, Yarody	R-R	6-2	165	9-5-89	.171	.140	.182	62	211	20	36	9	0	0	11	18	2	3	1	60	0	2	.213	.241
Valdez, Fausto	R-R	6-2	220	5-9-88	.154	.171	.152	44	130	12	20	6	0	2	7	13	8	1	0	47	0	0	.246	.272

PITCHING	B-T	HT	WT	DOB	W	L	ERA	G	GS	CG	SV	IP	H	R	ER	HR	BB	SO	AVG	vLH	vRH	K/9	BB/9
Alvarado, Diego	R-R	6-1	160	7-6-90	2	2	4.62	19	3	0	1	51	56	37	26	1	17	33	.279	.228	.299	5.86	3.02
Brito, Leomar	R-R	6-5	172	7-17-88	0	0	3.38	3	0	0	0	3	3	1	1	0	1	2	.273	.333	.250	6.75	3.38
Castillo, Juan	R-R	6-4	200	11-3-88	1	1	4.91	13	2	0	0	15	9	11	8	0	17	11	.173	.182	.171	6.75	10.43
Charagua, Wilmer	R-R	6-1	170	7-31-86	4	3	1.08	28	0	0	0	67	57	13	8	1	8	53	.244	.190	.261	7.15	1.08
De La Cruz, Julio	R-R	6-1	162	1-28-88	0	1	6.75	8	0	0	0	8	9	6	6	0	8	3	.296	.500	.261	3.38	9.00
Dominguez, Felito	R-R	5-9	179	3-2-86	5	1	2.05	38	1	0	20	57	37	18	13	1	9	40	.188	.231	.177	6.32	1.42
Ferrer, Ricardo	R-R	6-2	174	10-11-89	2	1	1.13	4	4	0	0	16	11	3	2	0	6	10	.216	.333	.190	5.62	3.38
Garcia, Joan	L-L	6-2	158	3-26-89	1	3	2.81	14	2	0	1	32	28	20	10	1	22	21	.228	.333	.225	5.91	6.19
Gonzalez, Juan	R-R	6-2	206	4-5-90	0	2	3.38	6	3	0	0	16	15	8	6	0	10	12	.242	.083	.280	6.75	5.62
Gonzalez, Nelson	R-R	6-1	168	2-15-90	3	1	3.23	15	7	0	0	47	40	23	17	1	19	22	.227	.171	.244	4.18	3.61
Mayo, Vianney	R-R	6-2	165	4-6-90	0	3	5.75	12	5	0	0	20	18	16	13	0	17	12	.234	.158	.259	5.31	7.52
Morillo, Scarly	R-R	6-1	175	6-17-89	2	2	2.63	16	11	0	0	48	37	25	14	0	21	47	.214	.317	.182	8.81	3.94
Noboa, Luis	R-R	6-2	148	2-26-85	2	0	1.42	6	4	0	0	25	11	4	4	0	12	17	.139	.278	.098	6.04	4.26
Perez, Juan	R-R	6-1	151	4-28-86	3	2	2.05	25	0	0	1	53	42	21	12	0	16	27	.223	.143	.242	4.61	2.73
Sacramento, Lowin	R-R	6-6	203	9-4-87	2	3	2.49	15	1	0	0	25	17	8	7	1	9	15	.191	.429	.147	5.33	3.20
Sanchez, Miguel	R-R	6-2	190	6-12-90	0	0	3.14	8	2	0	0	14	10	6	5	1	9	6	.192	.167	.200	3.77	5.65
Suarez, Carlos	R-R	6-2	170	11-24-87	2	2	3.17	16	5	0	0	48	46	18	17	3	10	38	.247	.172	.261	7.08	1.86
Suarez, Rafael	R-R	6-0	200	5-14-89	3	3	3.53	10	9	0	0	51	44	23	20	2	25	48	.247	.194	.261	8.47	4.41
Vargas, Jonathan	L-L	6-2	150	5-29-89	5	3	3.09	12	11	0	0	47	40	22	16	0	28	36	.238	.000	.248	6.94	5.40

FIELDING

Catcher	PCT	G	PO	A	E	DP	PB
Gonzalez	.982	60	397	91	9	1	8
Peralta	1.000	6	28	8	0	0	5
Ramirez	.978	6	41	3	1	1	0

First Base	PCT	G	PO	A	E	DP
Gonzalez	1.000	1	6	1	0	0
Peralta	.987	32	280	18	4	25
Perez	.984	12	119	4	2	13
Valdez	.989	34	267	13	3	31

Second Base	PCT	G	PO	A	E	DP
Nina	.988	55	156	161	4	43

	PCT	G	PO	A	E	DP
Perez	.899	18	48	41	10	12

Third Base	PCT	G	PO	A	E	DP
Gomez	.926	68	68	206	22	21
Nina	.833	3	4	1	1	0

Shortstop	PCT	G	PO	A	E	DP
Nina	.956	8	15	28	2	5
Perez	.667	1	0	4	2	0
Santos	.898	62	131	203	38	37
Valdez	1.000	1	0	2	0	0

Outfield	PCT	G	PO	A	E	DP
Castillo	1.000	37	45	2	0	0

	PCT	G	PO	A	E	DP
Charles	.986	62	135	9	2	2
Crousset	.918	37	41	4	4	0
De La Cruz	1.000	2	2	0	0	0
De La Cruz	.983	41	56	2	1	0
Peralta	—	1	0	0	0	0
Perez	.946	42	51	2	3	0
Sandoval	1.000	2	1	0	0	0

Detroit Tigers

BY JON PAUL MOROSI

The Tigers won 88 games last season but fell short of their expectations.

It had been almost 20 years since a Detroit team could have said that.

"We've reached a point in the organization where (we) want to contend in the postseason," Tigers general manager Dave Dombrowski said in a year-end meeting with the media. "If that doesn't happen—anything short of winning a world championship—there's going to be a little short of total satisfaction. There's a fine line between making the postseason and not."

Still, Detroit seems well positioned for long-term success after a 2007 season in which it drew 3 million fans for the first time in franchise history.

The team's payroll is in excess of $90 million and its leadership is in place for the foreseeable future. Dombrowski is under contract through 2011, and manager Jim Leyland signed an extension through 2009 two days after the season ended.

Dombrowski didn't need to make big changes after a 2006 season in which Detroit reached its first World Series since 1984. The Tigers lost only one veteran from their postseason roster—lefthanded reliever Jamie Walker—and added slugger Gary Sheffield to address the need for an impact bat.

Sheffield's presence alone seemed to make the 2007 Tigers better than the 2006 Tigers, and many experts picked Detroit to win the World Series. But that was before the Tigers' disabled list started looking like an all-star roster.

Lefthander Kenny Rogers, who had thrown 23 scoreless postseason innings the previous autumn, went on the disabled list at the end of spring training because of an arterial blood clot. He went 3-4, 4.43 in 63 innings over 11 starts after winning 17 games the year before.

Joel Zumaya, an overpowering set-up man in 2006, missed nearly four months after rupturing a tendon in his right middle finger. Fernando Rodney, another key reliever, had two separate stays on the disabled list. Jeremy Bonderman and Nate Robertson, who were part of the previous year's postseason rotation, missed starts because of arm trouble. Top prospects Andrew Miller and Jair Jurrjens came up as reinforcements, but also spent time on the DL.

Vance Wilson, a valuable back-up catcher, missed the entire season with elbow issues that ultimately required Tommy John surgery. First baseman Marcus Thames strained his left hamstring just when he was at the top of his game.

The most significant health issue, though, was Sheffield's ongoing right shoulder pain. When he injured the shoulder on July 21, Detroit had the best record in baseball. But the Tigers went 30-37 thereafter and finished eight games behind Cleveland in the AL Central.

Even with the painful finish, many Tigers enjoyed unprecedented individual success:

■ Magglio Ordoñez won the batting title and might have been AL MVP if it had not for Alex Rodriguez.

■ Ordoñez and Placido Polanco became the first Detroit teammates in 70 years to finish with 200 or more hits in the same season. Polanco became the first everyday second baseman in modern history to have an errorless season.

■ Curtis Granderson became the third major leaguer with at least 20 doubles, 20 triples, 20 home runs, and 20 steals in a

PLAYERS OF THE YEAR

MAJOR LEAGUE: MAGGLIO ORDONEZ, OF

At age 33, Ordonez had the best year of his career. Ordonez hit .363/.434/.595, leading all of baseball in average, and finishing second in the American League in on-base percentage and fourth in slugging. His 54 doubles were the most in baseball. In the AL, he ranked second in hits (216), RBIs (139) and total bases (354).

MINOR LEAGUE: JAIR JURRJENS, RHP

The fifth-youngest player to play in the major leagues in 2007, Jurrjens filled in when the Tigers needed him to shore up an injury-plagued rotation. He spent most of the season with Double-A Erie, where his 3.20 ERA ranked second in the Eastern League. Jurrjens walked 31 batters in 112 2/3 innings.

ORGANIZATIONAL LEADERS

BATTING		★Minimum 250 at-bats
★AVG	Scram, Deik, West Michigan/Lakeland	.311
R	Thomas, Clete, Erie	97
H	Perez, Timo, Toledo	151
TB	Hernandez, Michael, Lakeland/Erie	234
	Larish, Jeff, Erie	234
2B	Perez, Timo, Toledo	39
3B	Torres, Andres, Erie/Toledo	20
HR	Hessman, Mike, Toledo	31
RBI	Hernandez, Michael, Lakeland/Erie	106
BB	Larish, Jeff, Erie	87
SO	Hessman, Mike, Toledo	153
SB	Suero, Ovandy, Lakeland	75
★OBP	Hannahan, Jack, Toledo	.422
★SLG	Hessman, Mike, Toledo	.540
PITCHING		**^Minimum 75 innings**
W	Bonine, Eddie, Erie/Toledo	15
L	French, Lucas, Lakeland	14
^ERA	Badenhop, Burke, Lakeland/Erie	2.92
G	Jensen, Brett, West Michigan	56
CG	Badenhop, Burke, Lakeland/Erie	3
CG	Trahern, Dallas, Toledo/Erie	3
SV	Lopez, Aquilino, Toledo	26
IP	Trahern, Dallas, Toledo/Erie	169
BB	Gagnier, Lauren, West Michigan	60
SO	Below, Duane, West Michigan	160
^AVG	Below, Duane, West Michigan	.236

year. (Philadelphia's Jimmy Rollins later became the fourth.)

■ Justin Verlander, the lone pitcher to remain in the rotation all year, threw a no-hitter on June 12 and had the best winning percentage among AL starters (18-6, .750).

Meanwhile, injuries in Detroit created opportunities for 15 players who began the year in the Tigers farm system.

Outfielder Cameron Maybin, the organization's top prospect, spent just one week at Double-A Erie before a mid-August promotion and homered off Roger Clemens in only his second big league game. Ryan Raburn came up from Triple-A Toledo in early July and hit .304 in 49 games while showing good versatility in the field. He played all three outfield positions, as well as second and third base, and likely earned a big league job for 2008.

General Manager: Dave Dombrowski. **Farm Director:** Dan Lunetta. **Scouting Director:** David Chadd

Class	Team	League	W	L	PCT	Finish*	Manager	Affiliate Since
Majors	Detroit	American	88	74	.543	4th (14)	Jim Leyland	—
Triple-A	Toledo Mud Hens	International	82	61	.573	2nd (14)	Larry Parrish	1987
Double-A	Erie SeaWolves	Eastern	81	59	.579	2nd (12)	Matt Walbeck	2001
High A	Lakeland Flying Tigers	Florida State	53	87	.379	12th (12)	Kevin Bradshaw	1967
Low A	West Michigan Whitecaps	Midwest	83	57	.593	1st (14)^	Tom Brookens	1997
Short-season	Oneonta Tigers	New York-Penn	44	32	.579	4th (14)	Andy Barkett	1999
Rookie	GCL Tigers	Gulf Coast	28	32	.467	9th (16)	Benny Castillo	1995
Overall 2007 Minor League Record			**371**	**328**	**.531**	**6th**		

* Finish in overall standings (No. of teams in league) ^League champion

ORGANIZATION STATISTICS

DETROIT TIGERS

AMERICAN LEAGUE

BATTING	B-T	HT	WT	DOB	AVG	vLH	vRH	G	AB	R	H	2B	3B	HR	RBI	BB	HBP	SH	SF	SO	SB	CS	SLG	OBP
Casey, Sean	L-R	6-4	235	7-2-74	.296	.365	.285	143	453	40	134	30	1	4	54	39	2	0	2	42	2	2	.393	.353
Clevlen, Brent	R-R	6-2	190	10-27-83	.100	.167	.000	13	10	2	1	0	0	0	0	0	0	0	0	7	0	0	.100	.100
Granderson, Curtis	L-R	6-1	185	3-16-81	.302	.160	.337	158	612	122	185	38	23	23	74	52	5	5	2	141	26	1	.552	.361
Guillen, Carlos	B-R	6-1	215	9-30-75	.296	.302	.295	151	564	86	167	35	9	21	102	55	3	0	8	93	13	8	.502	.357
Hessman, Mike	R-R	6-5	215	3-5-78	.235	.208	.259	17	51	7	12	0	0	4	12	5	0	0	1	17	0	0	.471	.298
Infante, Omar	R-R	6-0	180	12-26-81	.271	.281	.265	66	166	24	45	6	1	2	17	9	0	2	1	29	4	1	.355	.307
Inge, Brandon	R-R	5-11	190	5-19-77	.236	.333	.209	151	508	64	120	25	2	14	71	47	11	7	4	150	9	2	.376	.312
Maybin, Cameron	R-R	6-4	205	4-4-87	.143	.000	.200	24	49	8	7	3	0	1	2	3	1	0	0	21	5	0	.265	.208
Monroe, Craig	R-R	6-1	205	2-27-77	.222	.302	.190	99	343	47	76	19	0	11	55	20	2	1	6	94	0	3	.373	.264
Ordonez, Magglio	R-R	6-0	215	1-28-74	.363	.410	.351	157	595	117	216	54	0	28	139	76	2	0	5	79	4	1	.595	.434
Perez, Neifi	B-R	6-0	175	6-2-73	.172	.217	.146	33	64	5	11	3	0	1	6	4	0	3	0	8	0	0	.266	.221
Perez, Timo	L-L	5-9	180	4-8-75	.389	.429	.386	29	90	12	35	9	2	0	13	6	0	0	0	6	1	1	.533	.427
Polanco, Placido	R-R	5-10	195	10-10-75	.341	.326	.345	142	587	105	200	36	3	9	67	37	11	2	4	30	7	3	.458	.388
Rabelo, Mike	B-R	6-1	200	1-17-80	.256	.276	.252	51	168	14	43	10	2	1	18	6	5	5	1	41	0	0	.357	.300
Raburn, Ryan	R-R	6-0	185	4-17-81	.304	.259	.338	49	138	28	42	12	2	4	27	8	0	1	1	33	3	0	.507	.340
Rodriguez, Ivan	R-R	5-9	195	11-30-71	.281	.302	.274	129	502	50	141	31	3	11	63	9	1	1	2	96	2	2	.420	.294
Santiago, Ramon	B-R	5-11	175	8-31-79	.284	.300	.281	32	67	10	19	5	1	0	7	1	3	3	0	10	3	0	.388	.324
Sheffield, Gary	R-R	6-0	215	11-18-68	.265	.245	.271	133	494	107	131	20	1	25	75	84	9	0	6	71	22	5	.462	.378
Thames, Marcus	R-R	6-2	220	3-6-77	.242	.310	.209	85	269	37	65	15	0	18	54	13	1	0	1	72	2	1	.498	.278

PITCHING	B-T	HT	WT	DOB	W	L	ERA	G	GS	CG	SV	IP	H	R	ER	HR	BB	SO	AVG	vLH	vRH	K/9	BB/9
Bazardo, Yorman	R-R	6-2	220	7-11-84	2	1	2.28	11	2	0	0	24	19	7	6	2	5	15	.218	.289	.143	5.70	1.90
Bonderman, Jeremy	R-R	6-2	220	10-28-82	11	9	5.01	28	28	0	0	174	193	105	97	23	48	145	.278	.268	.291	7.49	2.48
Byrdak, Tim	L-L	5-11	195	10-31-73	3	0	3.20	39	0	0	1	45	38	23	16	3	26	49	.230	.176	.268	9.80	5.20
Capellan, Jose	R-R	6-4	235	1-13-81	0	1	6.43	10	0	0	0	14	18	13	10	5	3	12	.305	.444	.244	7.71	1.93
De La Cruz, Eulogio	R-R	5-11	175	3-12-84	0	0	6.75	4	0	0	0	7	10	8	5	1	4	5	.357	.250	.438	6.75	5.40
Durbin, Chad	B-R	6-2	200	12-3-77	8	7	4.72	36	19	0	1	128	133	71	67	21	49	66	.268	.281	.255	4.65	3.45
Grilli, Jason	R-R	6-5	225	11-11-76	5	3	4.74	57	0	0	0	80	81	46	42	5	32	62	.263	.237	.275	7.00	3.62
Jones, Todd	L-R	6-3	230	4-24-68	1	4	4.26	63	0	0	38	61	64	29	29	3	23	33	.267	.265	.269	4.84	3.38
Jurrjens, Jair	R-R	6-1	160	1-29-86	3	1	4.70	7	7	0	0	31	24	16	16	4	11	13	.220	.262	.167	3.82	3.23
Ledezma, Wilfredo	L-L	6-4	210	1-21-81	3	1	4.79	23	0	0	0	36	38	21	19	4	26	24	.277	.340	.241	6.06	6.56
Lopez, Aquilino	R-R	6-3	185	4-21-75	0	0	5.19	10	0	0	1	17	18	10	10	2	6	7	.273	.258	.286	3.63	3.12
Maroth, Mike	L-L	6-0	190	8-17-77	5	2	5.06	13	13	0	0	78	97	47	44	15	33	28	.319	.304	.323	3.22	3.79
McBride, Macay	L-L	5-11	210	10-24-82	0	1	6.11	20	0	0	0	18	19	12	12	3	10	13	.275	.344	.216	6.62	5.09
Mesa, Jose	R-R	6-3	235	5-22-66	1	1	12.34	16	0	0	0	12	19	16	16	3	6	9	.365	.375	.361	6.94	4.63
Miller, Andrew	L-L	6-6	210	5-21-85	5	5	5.63	13	13	0	0	64	73	43	40	8	39	56	.282	.175	.312	7.88	5.48
Miner, Zach	R-R	6-3	200	3-12-82	3	4	3.02	34	1	0	0	54	56	22	18	3	22	34	.273	.207	.317	5.70	3.69
Rapada, Clay	R-L	6-5	200	3-9-81	0	0	11.57	4	0	0	0	2	3	3	3	2	2	4	.300	.167	.500	15.43	7.71
Robertson, Nate	R-L	6-2	225	9-3-77	9	13	4.76	30	30	0	0	178	199	98	94	22	63	119	.283	.296	.278	6.03	3.19
Rodney, Fernando	R-R	5-11	220	3-18-77	2	6	4.26	48	0	0	1	51	46	27	24	5	21	54	.238	.247	.231	9.59	3.73
Rogers, Kenny	L-L	6-1	190	11-10-64	3	4	4.43	11	11	0	0	63	65	36	31	8	25	36	.264	.197	.289	5.14	3.57
Seay, Bobby	L-L	6-2	215	6-20-78	3	0	2.33	58	0	0	1	46	38	12	12	1	15	38	.228	.209	.250	7.38	2.91
Tata, Jordan	R-R	6-6	220	9-20-81	1	1	7.71	3	3	0	0	14	16	12	12	1	8	8	.302	.375	.241	5.14	5.14
Vasquez, Virgil	R-R	6-3	205	6-7-82	0	1	8.64	5	3	0	0	17	27	16	16	7	5	7	.360	.400	.325	3.78	2.70
Verlander, Justin	R-R	6-5	200	2-20-83	18	6	3.66	32	32	1	0	202	181	88	82	20	67	183	.233	.232	.234	8.17	2.99
Zumaya, Joel	R-R	6-3	210	11-9-84	2	3	4.28	28	0	0	1	34	23	16	16	3	17	27	.189	.271	.135	7.22	4.54

FIELDING

Catcher	PCT	G	PO	A	E	DP	PB
Rabelo	.982	49	246	21	5	5	3
Rodriguez	.993	127	834	50	6	7	7

First Base	PCT	G	PO	A	E	DP
Casey	.998	131	992	42	2	87
Guillen	.995	36	185	17	1	15
Hessman	1.000	12	74	0	0	15
Thames	.990	33	180	15	2	17

Second Base	PCT	G	PO	A	E	DP
Infante	.986	20	30	38	1	8
N. Perez	1.000	7	7	14	0	5
Polanco	1.000	141	294	389	0	101

	PCT	G	PO	A	E	DP
Raburn	.973	10	10	26	1	5

Third Base	PCT	G	PO	A	E	DP
Hessman	1.000	4	1	5	0	0
Infante	.966	9	6	22	1	1
Inge	.959	150	91	325	18	25
N. Perez	.923	3	2	10	1	0
Raburn	1.000	3	1	1	0	0

Shortstop	PCT	G	PO	A	E	DP
Guillen	.955	132	160	352	24	79
Infante	.941	14	15	17	2	5
N. Perez	.952	24	13	27	2	7
Santiago	.978	31	29	62	2	12

Outfield	PCT	G	PO	A	E	DP
Clevlen	1.000	12	4	0	0	0
Granderson	.989	157	428	10	5	4
Hessman	1.000	1	1	0	0	0
Infante	1.000	19	23	0	0	0
Maybin	1.000	15	32	0	0	0
Monroe	.983	97	163	6	3	1
Ordonez	.996	143	261	4	1	2
T. Perez	.958	24	44	2	2	0
Raburn	1.000	38	55	1	0	1
Sheffield	1.000	12	25	1	0	0
Thames	.975	46	77	1	2	1

INTERNATIONAL LEAGUE

BATTING	B-T	HT	WT	DOB	AVG	vLH	vRH	G	AB	R	H	2B	3B	HR	RBI	BB	HBP	SH	SF	SO	SB	CS	SLG	OBP
Almonte, Erick	R-R	6-2	180	2-1-78	.276	.296	.271	38	123	14	34	5	1	1	19	26	0	2	2	28	3	1	.358	.397
Blue, Vincent	L-R	6-2	180	2-8-83	.167	.250	.150	11	24	3	4	2	0	0	0	5	0	0	0	9	1	0	.250	.310
Clevlen, Brent	R-R	6-2	190	10-27-83	.220	.254	.212	90	322	33	71	14	5	7	36	39	1	1	3	113	4	4	.360	.304
Espinosa, David	B-R	6-2	190	12-16-81	.204	.250	.189	111	372	43	76	17	5	5	49	34	0	9	4	93	12	2	.317	.268
Graham, Andrew	R-R	6-4	215	4-22-82	.208	.286	.187	36	96	12	20	3	1	1	8	7	2	4	1	26	1	2	.292	.274
Hannahan, Jack	L-R	6-2	205	3-4-80	.295	.259	.307	101	336	56	99	20	1	13	63	76	1	0	4	92	5	5	.476	.422
Hessman, Mike	R-R	6-5	215	3-5-78	.254	.228	.262	117	422	71	107	24	2	31	101	64	6	1	5	153	6	11	.540	.356
Hollimon, Mike	B-R	6-1	185	6-14-82	.211	.200	.214	5	19	2	4	1	1	0	2	1	0	0	0	4	0	0	.368	.250
Hooper, Kevin	R-R	5-10	160	12-7-76	.301	.297	.302	60	246	46	74	11	0	1	19	16	3	6	2	25	11	4	.358	.348
Infante, Omar	R-R	6-0	180	12-26-81	.368	.125	.433	10	38	3	14	2	0	0	4	4	0	0	1	2	1	0	.421	.419
Leon, Maxwell	B-R	5-11	190	6-28-84	.333	.000	.400	2	6	1	2	1	0	0	0	1	0	0	0	2	0	1	.500	.429
Maples, Chris	R-R	5-10	180	10-31-79	.188	.244	.169	65	181	17	34	7	1	0	15	18	3	1	2	68	3	1	.238	.270
Mateo, Henry	B-R	6-0	175	10-14-76	.257	.274	.253	96	311	44	80	16	2	3	20	34	5	8	2	55	24	10	.350	.338
Perez, Timo	L-L	5-9	180	4-8-75	.309	.297	.313	122	489	76	151	39	1	13	69	35	4	7	5	47	13	6	.472	.356
Perry, Jason	L-R	6-0	200	8-18-80	.184	.000	.222	20	16	49	10	9	3	0	2	3	8	1	0	16	0	0	.367	.310
Raburn, Ryan	R-R	6-0	185	4-17-81	.292	.306	.288	85	315	60	92	21	3	17	64	51	4	0	3	73	12	4	.540	.394
Roa, Joel	R-R	6-0	175	1-2-84	.000	.000	.000	3	6	0	0	0	0	0	0	0	0	0	0	4	0	0	.000	.000
Santiago, Ramon	B-R	5-11	175	8-31-79	.263	.247	.268	91	365	40	96	19	4	3	30	16	9	11	1	61	8	9	.362	.309
Sardinha, Dane	R-R	6-0	215	4-8-79	.202	.247	.188	117	381	38	77	15	1	10	47	25	4	5	6	98	2	0	.325	.255
Shelton, Chris	R-R	6-0	215	6-26-80	.269	.255	.273	139	498	75	134	31	1	14	65	83	9	1	3	141	4	2	.420	.381
Thames, Marcus	R-R	6-2	220	3-6-77	.375	1.000	.286	2	8	2	3	0	0	1	2	0	0	0	1	0	0	0	.750	.375
Torres, Andres	B-R	5-10	190	1-26-78	.292	.273	.296	42	168	23	49	6	9	4	17	11	4	4	1	39	5	6	.506	.348
Wilson, Vance	R-R	5-11	215	3-17-73	.273	—	.273	3	11	2	3	0	0	0	0	0	0	1	0	0	2	0	0	.273	.333

PITCHING	B-T	HT	WT	DOB	W	L	ERA	G	GS	CG	SV	IP	H	R	ER	HR	BB	SO	AVG	vLH	vRH	K/9	BB/9
Bazardo, Yorman	R-R	6-2	220	7-11-84	10	6	3.75	23	21	2	0	137	134	66	57	8	43	69	.263	.248	.277	4.54	2.83
Bonine, Eddie	R-R	6-5	220	6-6-81	1	0	2.25	1	1	0	0	8	7	2	2	0	1	4	.233	.333	.000	4.50	1.12
Byrdak, Tim	L-L	5-11	195	10-31-73	1	0	2.59	17	0	0	0	24	22	7	7	3	8	30	.247	.242	.250	11.10	2.96
Capellan, Jose	R-R	6-4	235	1-13-81	0	1	5.79	9	0	0	3	9	12	7	6	1	5	5	.308	.429	.240	4.82	0.96
Chiavacci, Ron	R-R	6-0	240	9-5-77	12	6	3.39	26	23	0	0	151	148	64	57	14	43	126	.258	.237	.277	7.49	2.56
Colon, Roman	R-R	6-6	225	8-13-79	0	1	3.60	6	0	0	0	10	10	4	4	0	8	6	.263	.313	.227	5.40	7.20
Connolly, Jonathan	R-L	6-0	205	8-24-83	1	1	3.91	4	4	1	0	23	18	11	10	4	4	15	.228	.278	.213	5.87	1.57
Darensbourg, Vic	L-L	5-8	175	11-13-70	6	2	1.72	50	0	0	0	52	43	11	10	0	17	42	.235	.247	.225	7.22	2.92
De La Cruz, Eulogio	R-R	5-11	175	3-12-84	3	0	3.52	22	1	0	0	38	41	17	15	0	18	25	.289	.239	.333	5.87	4.23
Hamman, Corey	L-L	6-2	198	4-12-80	1	6	4.44	31	7	0	0	73	92	41	36	10	23	35	.325	.368	.303	4.32	2.84
Johnson, Jeremy	R-R	6-3	170	7-19-82	3	3	3.44	39	2	0	2	68	64	28	26	4	23	45	.258	.219	.287	5.96	3.04
Karnuth, Jason	R-R	6-2	190	5-15-76	2	2	3.41	30	0	0	6	37	36	18	14	5	7	27	.261	.275	.253	6.57	1.70
Lambert, Chris	R-R	6-1	205	3-8-83	0	0	0.00	1	1	0	0	2	1	0	0	0	2	10	.053	.000	.200	15.00	3.00
Larrison, Preston	R-R	6-4	235	11-19-80	2	2	3.84	45	0	0	1	59	54	28	25	2	29	37	.248	.250	.246	5.68	4.45
Lopez, Aquilino	R-R	6-3	185	4-21-75	3	5	2.35	48	0	0	26	54	46	18	14	5	11	58	.227	.278	.186	9.73	1.84
Martinez, Anastacio	R-R	6-2	180	11-3-78	4	4	4.24	14	6	1	0	40	36	21	19	2	22	33	.242	.274	.218	7.36	4.91
2-team (9 Columbus)					6	7	4.46	23	11	1	0	73	67	46	36	5	43	61	—	—	—	7.56	5.33
McBride, Macay	L-L	5-11	210	10-24-82	1	0	3.38	5	0	0	0	8	9	4	3	1	5	6	.310	.250	.333	6.75	5.62
2-team (7 Richmond)					2	2	3.19	12	5	0	0	31	35	14	11	4	12	30	—	—	—	8.71	3.48
Mesa, Jose	R-R	6-3	235	5-22-66	0	0	0.00	1	1	0	0	2	2	0	0	0	1	1	.250	.333	.200	4.50	0.00
Miller, Andrew	L-L	6-6	210	5-21-85	0	0	9.00	2	2	0	0	6	6	6	6	0	5	9	.250	.250	.250	13.50	7.50
Miner, Zach	R-R	6-3	200	3-12-82	1	4	4.88	11	8	0	0	52	43	30	28	4	22	33	.228	.202	.250	5.75	3.83
O'Brien, Matt	R-R	6-3	215	8-10-82	1	0	1.50	1	1	0	0	6	3	1	1	0	1	3	.143	.167	.111	4.50	1.50
Ostlund, Ian	R-L	6-1	200	10-17-78	2	1	4.50	15	0	0	0	18	21	10	9	2	2	15	.292	.250	.313	7.50	1.00
Rapada, Clay	R-L	6-5	200	3-9-81	0	0	11.57	2	0	0	0	2	5	3	3	0	1	3	.417	.200	.571	11.57	3.86
Rodney, Fernando	R-R	5-11	220	3-18-77	0	0	0.00	4	0	0	3	4	0	0	0	0	2	4	.308	.400	.250	12.00	6.00
Rogers, Kenny	L-L	6-1	190	11-10-64	0	0	0.00	1	1	0	0	4	3	0	0	0	0	2	.231	.500	.111	4.91	0.00
Tankersley, Dennis	R-R	6-2	215	2-24-79	10	7	4.41	24	24	0	0	139	167	74	68	13	51	80	.308	.335	.285	5.19	3.31
Tata, Jordan	R-R	6-6	220	9-20-81	4	5	3.05	14	14	0	0	83	67	31	28	8	28	50	.220	.190	.262	5.44	3.05
Tomey, Anthony	R-R	6-4	245	8-17-81	1	0	6.00	5	0	0	0	6	8	4	4	0	7	4	.320	.429	.278	6.00	10.50
Trahern, Dallas	R-R	6-3	190	11-29-85	1	0	2.84	1	1	0	0	6	3	2	2	0	2	2	.217	.250	.200	2.84	4.26
Vasquez, Virgil	R-R	6-3	205	6-7-82	12	5	3.48	25	25	2	0	155	139	64	60	18	33	127	.241	.254	.227	7.37	1.92
Zumaya, Joel	R-R	6-3	210	11-9-84	0	0	6.75	3	0	0	0	3	3	2	2	0	2	2	.273	.200	.333	6.75	6.75

FIELDING

Catcher	PCT	G	PO	A	E	DP	PB
Graham	.981	35	200	10	4	2	3
Roa	1.000	3	9	0	0	0	0
Sardinha	.992	116	732	54	6	9	6

First Base	PCT	G	PO	A	E	DP
Hannahan	1.000	7	67	2	0	7
Hessman	.900	1	9	0	1	0
Maples	.947	10	68	4	4	6
Shelton	.993	130	1202	82	9	144
Thames	1.000	1	14	1	0	3

Second Base	PCT	G	PO	A	E	DP
Hannahan	.985	37	74	118	3	30
Hooper	.990	52	118	172	3	48
Infante	1.000	1	6	4	0	2

Leon	1.000	1	2	3	0	0
Mateo	.989	60	121	159	3	43
Raburn	1.000	1	1	3	0	1
Santiago	1.000	1	1	4	0	2

Third Base	PCT	G	PO	A	E	DP
Almonte	1.000	5	2	7	0	0
Hannahan	1.000	21	16	55	0	9
Hessman	.975	115	81	264	9	34
Leon	.500	1	0	1	1	0
Maples	1.000	2	0	5	0	0

Shortstop	PCT	G	PO	A	E	DP
Almonte	.975	29	53	100	4	23
Hollimon	1.000	5	7	15	0	3
Hooper	.980	9	14	34	1	9

Infante	.932	9	13	28	3	4
Mateo	1.000	4	8	10	0	4
Santiago	.976	88	136	302	11	69

Outfield	PCT	G	PO	A	E	DP
Blue	.941	9	16	0	1	0
Clevlen	.985	89	184	8	3	0
Espinosa	.958	79	111	3	5	2
Maples	.972	24	33	2	1	1
Mateo	.905	28	37	1	4	1
Perez	.977	80	120	8	3	2
Perry	.960	15	22	2	1	0
Raburn	.986	85	201	10	3	3
Torres	.990	42	98	2	1	1

ERIE SEAWOLVES

DOUBLE-A

EASTERN LEAGUE

BATTING	B-T	HT	WT	DOB	AVG	vLH	vRH	G	AB	R	H	2B	3B	HR	RBI	BB	HBP	SH	SF	SO	SB	CS	SLG	OBP
Almonte, Erick	R-R	6-2	180	2-1-78	.293	.368	.256	50	174	25	51	12	0	3	25	28	0	1	1	32	3	3	.414	.389
Cotto, Pedro	L-L	5-11	175	5-26-82	.252	.161	.269	69	202	27	51	7	2	0	17	13	0	4	1	26	2	2	.307	.296
Dlugach, Brent	R-R	6-4	195	3-3-83	.292	.233	.333	22	72	12	21	4	3	1	7	6	0	0	0	25	1	1	.472	.346
Haley, Adam	L-R	6-0	171	9-4-80	.200	—	.200	2	5	1	1	0	0	0	0	0	0	0	0	0	0	0	.200	.200
Hernandez, Michael	R-R	6-0	175	12-18-83	.250	.263	.244	18	64	11	16	2	0	4	19	4	0	0	3	15	1	0	.469	.282
Hollimon, Mike	B-R	6-1	185	6-14-82	.282	.271	.289	127	471	91	133	34	8	14	76	64	5	7	5	121	17	6	.478	.371
Joyce, Matthew	L-R	6-2	185	8-3-84	.257	.252	.259	130	456	61	117	33	3	17	70	51	3	1	3	127	4	6	.454	.333
Kirkland, Kody	R-R	6-4	200	6-9-83	.202	.189	.208	123	411	57	83	22	3	14	51	41	10	4	9	127	9	6	.372	.285
Larish, Jeff	L-R	6-2	200	10-11-82	.267	.280	.260	132	454	71	121	25	2	28	101	87	9	0	6	108	6	2	.515	.390
Maybin, Cameron	R-R	6-4	205	4-4-87	.400	.667	.353	6	20	9	8	1	0	4	8	6	0	0	0	6	0	0	1.050	.538
McIntyre, Nick	B-R	5-10	185	3-11-81	.209	.272	.177	90	278	33	58	9	1	2	18	13	5	4	2	72	5	0	.270	.255
Melian, Jackson	R-R	6-2	205	1-7-80	.310	.357	.284	88	319	47	99	15	2	14	65	30	6	0	6	67	7	6	.502	.374
Ramirez, Wilkin	R-R	6-2	190	10-25-85	.215	.225	.210	34	121	15	26	3	1	2	14	8	2	1	1	38	6	2	.306	.273
Rhymes, William	L-R	5-9	155	4-1-83	.265	.194	.282	39	155	21	41	6	0	1	21	6	2	6	2	20	5	1	.323	.297
Roa, Joel	R-R	6-0	175	1-2-84	.167	.125	.183	31	84	10	14	2	0	2	8	2	0	2	1	22	0	0	.262	.184
Thomas, Clete	L-R	5-11	195	11-14-83	.280	.256	.292	137	528	97	148	30	6	8	53	59	7	3	2	110	18	11	.405	.359
Torrealba, Steve	R-R	6-0	220	2-24-78	.232	.268	.214	90	298	38	69	11	0	10	45	25	4	6	4	63	1	0	.366	.296
Torres, Andres	B-R	5-10	190	1-26-78	.292	.295	.290	85	305	53	89	15	11	6	35	38	2	12	2	66	17	4	.472	.372
Trzesniak, Nick	R-R	6-0	210	11-19-80	.299	.414	.256	33	107	16	32	5	0	3	16	9	0	0	2	17	0	1	.430	.347
Worth, Daniel	R-R	6-1	180	9-30-85	.429	.667	.250	5	14	4	6	2	1	0	4	1	0	0	1	1	1	0	.714	.438

PITCHING	B-T	HT	WT	DOB	W	L	ERA	G	GS	CG	SV	IP	H	R	ER	HR	BB	SO	AVG	vLH	vRH	K/9	BB/9
Ardoin, Kevin	R-R	6-1	167	8-6-82	3	5	4.02	34	0	0	0	47	52	35	21	7	25	19	.280	.290	.269	3.64	4.79
Badenhop, Burke	R-R	6-5	220	2-8-83	2	0	1.45	3	3	2	0	19	8	3	3	1	3	12	.127	.194	.063	5.79	1.45
Bierd, Randor	R-R	6-4	190	3-14-84	3	2	3.35	27	3	0	1	46	31	18	17	1	10	52	.188	.181	.195	10.25	1.97
Bonine, Eddie	R-R	6-5	220	6-6-81	14	5	3.90	25	25	2	0	155	159	77	67	13	24	73	.265	.256	.274	4.25	1.40
Colon, Roman	R-R	6-6	225	8-13-79	2	0	5.91	5	1	0	1	11	11	7	7	3	5	10	.262	.250	.273	8.44	4.22
Connolly, Jonathan	R-L	6-0	205	8-24-83	7	7	4.58	21	19	0	1	112	127	66	57	16	29	68	.280	.347	.261	5.46	2.33
De La Cruz, Eulogio	R-R	5-11	175	3-12-84	4	5	3.41	11	11	2	0	66	54	31	25	5	19	57	.224	.226	.222	7.77	2.59
Dolsi, Freddy	R-R	6-0	160	1-9-83	0	0	0.00	1	0	0	0	1	1	0	0	0	1	0	.250	.000	.500	0.00	9.00
Finigan, P.J.	R-R	6-0	185	9-30-82	0	0	8.18	9	0	0	1	11	13	10	10	2	4	12	.277	.381	.192	9.82	3.27
Gerbe, Jeff	R-R	6-3	190	7-4-84	0	1	4.50	2	2	1	0	12	8	8	6	1	6	5	.190	.083	.233	3.75	4.50
Hamman, Corey	L-L	6-2	198	4-12-80	0	3	7.59	4	2	0	1	11	16	13	9	4	6	13	.348	.200	.389	10.97	5.06
Johnson, Jeremy	R-R	6-3	170	7-19-82	2	0	3.38	2	0	0	0	5	2	2	2	0	2	4	.111	.000	.286	6.75	3.38
Jurrjens, Jair	R-R	6-1	160	1-29-86	7	5	3.20	19	19	1	0	113	112	43	40	7	31	94	.257	.248	.269	7.51	2.48
Kown, Andrew	L-R	6-7	210	10-7-82	6	8	4.13	27	19	1	1	120	127	64	55	9	36	86	.272	.327	.220	6.45	2.70
Miller, Andrew	L-L	6-6	210	5-21-85	2	0	0.59	4	4	0	0	31	22	3	2	2	5	24	.208	.263	.195	7.04	1.47
Mills, Adam	B-R	6-1	195	10-18-66	1	1	2.79	29	0	0	23	29	21	9	9	1	11	22	.204	.136	.254	6.83	3.41
Miner, Zach	R-R	6-3	200	3-12-82	0	0	4.50	2	0	0	0	2	4	1	1	0	1	2	.400	.250	.500	9.00	4.50
Ostlund, Ian	R-L	6-1	200	10-17-78	0	0	2.18	14	0	0	1	21	16	7	5	3	5	25	.211	.182	.222	10.89	2.18
Righter, Matthew	R-R	6-5	190	8-7-81	3	4	4.80	19	5	0	0	54	63	31	29	9	16	37	.294	.260	.322	6.13	2.65
Robertson, Nate	R-L	6-2	225	9-3-77	1	0	0.00	1	1	0	0	6	0	0	0	0	1	6	.000	.000	.000	9.00	1.50
Rusch, Matthew	R-R	5-11	180	5-20-83	6	1	3.40	40	0	0	3	53	42	20	20	4	18	55	.218	.237	.200	9.34	3.06
Sleeth, Kyle	R-R	6-5	205	12-30-81	0	1	10.66	8	0	0	1	13	24	19	15	0	9	6	.407	.444	.375	4.26	6.39
Tomey, Anthony	R-R	6-4	245	8-17-81	3	0	1.97	32	0	0	2	46	31	11	10	2	21	46	.194	.176	.209	9.07	4.14
Trahern, Dallas	R-R	6-3	190	11-29-85	12	6	3.87	26	26	3	0	163	177	81	70	12	51	92	.284	.308	.258	5.09	2.82
Wise, Brendan	L-R	6-2	190	1-9-86	1	0	5.40	2	0	0	0	2	4	1	1	0	1	1	.500	.500	.500	5.40	5.40
Zell, Danny	L-L	6-5	210	11-27-81	2	5	3.56	47	0	0	2	48	47	22	19	5	8	53	.253	.183	.296	9.94	1.50

FIELDING

Catcher	PCT	G	PO	A	E	DP	PB
Roa	.974	31	172	12	5	0	5
Torrealba	.980	89	538	49	12	7	10
Trzesniak	.990	32	181	14	2	0	3

First Base	PCT	G	PO	A	E	DP
Almonte	1.000	5	35	3	0	6
Cotto	.987	17	139	9	2	18
Larish	.994	120	1113	86	7	94
McIntyre	1.000	1	7	1	0	0
Torrealba	1.000	1	1	0	0	0

Second Base	PCT	G	PO	A	E	DP
Haley	—	1	0	0	0	0
Hollimon	.980	95	188	308	10	62

McIntyre	.984	12	16	47	1	1
Rhymes	.962	38	62	117	7	27

Third Base	PCT	G	PO	A	E	DP
Almonte	.750	2	1	2	1	0
Kirkland	.923	119	72	265	28	22
McIntyre	.941	21	8	40	3	4

Shortstop	PCT	G	PO	A	E	DP
Almonte	.947	38	36	108	8	18
Dlugach	.929	20	25	54	6	12
Haley	—	1	0	0	0	0
Hollimon	.935	31	44	99	10	23
McIntyre	.965	54	75	148	8	33
Worth	.933	5	4	10	1	1

Outfield	PCT	G	PO	A	E	DP
Cotto	1.000	43	63	1	0	0
Haley	1.000	1	1	1	0	0
Hernandez	1.000	10	11	1	0	0
Joyce	.987	119	203	20	3	5
Maybin	1.000	5	11	0	0	0
McIntyre	1.000	3	3	0	0	0
Melian	1.000	22	31	1	0	0
Ramirez	.929	18	25	1	2	0
Thomas	.964	129	274	17	11	4
Torres	.978	84	173	6	4	2

LAKELAND FLYING TIGERS

HIGH CLASS A

FLORIDA STATE LEAGUE

BATTING	B-T	HT	WT	DOB	AVG	vLH	vRH	G	AB	R	H	2B	3B	HR	RBI	BB	HBP	SH	SF	SO	SB	CS	SLG	OBP
Bourquin, Ron	L-R	6-3	205	4-29-85	.192	.111	.217	26	78	9	15	2	0	0	3	14	2	0	1	25	1	0	.218	.326
Casanova, Adrian	R-R	6-1	210	5-6-83	.233	.188	.243	27	90	6	21	3	1	0	10	8	1	0	2	13	0	0	.289	.297
Collet, Cody	R-R	6-0	195	1-22-85	.185	.174	.190	31	81	7	15	3	0	0	7	11	0	1	1	28	0	0	.222	.280
Cotto, Pedro	L-L	5-11	175	5-26-82	.200	1.000	.143	5	5	1	1	0	0	0	0	0	0	0	0	2	0	0	.267	.200
Haske, Mark	L-R	5-10	165	5-28-83	.209	.255	.200	103	316	34	66	5	2	3	27	45	1	2	3	76	6	4	.266	.307
Hernandez, Michael	R-R	6-0	175	12-18-83	.260	.216	.273	116	427	60	111	25	4	20	87	41	4	0	6	102	1	3	.478	.326
Iorg, Cale	R-R	6-2	190	9-6-85	.278	.333	.250	5	18	3	5	2	0	0	5	1	0	0	0	5	0	0	.389	.316
Justice, Justin	L-L	6-0	185	2-19-85	.258	.132	.290	112	383	42	99	23	7	6	44	40	4	1	3	100	10	3	.402	.333
Kunkel, Jeffrey	B-R	5-11	200	3-11-83	.203	.300	.167	25	74	3	15	2	0	0	1	1	0	1	0	17	0	0	.230	.213
Leon, Maxwell	B-R	5-11	190	6-28-84	.299	.238	.321	96	321	50	96	16	2	1	30	33	2	13	2	41	14	1	.371	.366

ORGANIZATION STATISTICS

	B-T	HT	WT	DOB	AVG	vLH	vRH	G	AB	R	H	2B	3B	HR	RBI	BB	HBP	SH	SF	SO	SB	CS	SLG	OBP
Linares, Miguel	R-R	6-2	180	12-16-83	.157	.205	.125	39	108	6	17	2	0	0	2	4	1	2	1	28	0	1	.176	.193
Maybin, Cameron	R-R	6-4	205	4-4-87	.304	.189	.342	83	296	58	90	14	5	10	44	43	4	1	6	83	25	6	.486	.393
Mendez, Rafael	R-R	6-0	190	4-24-84	.188	.146	.200	59	176	11	33	8	1	2	18	14	0	2	1	50	0	0	.278	.246
Ramirez, Carlos	R-R	5-11	190	9-1-85	.083	.167	.000	4	12	1	1	0	0	0	0	0	0	0	0	6	0	0	.083	.083
Ramirez, Wilkin	R-R	6-0	190	10-25-85	.273	.200	.295	88	319	48	87	7	4	10	41	20	1	0	3	86	28	6	.414	.315
Rhymes, William	L-R	5-9	155	4-1-83	.304	.270	.313	88	326	43	99	12	2	4	35	44	2	12	1	38	24	3	.390	.389
Roa, Joel	R-R	6-0	175	1-2-84	.167	.308	.118	35	102	8	17	2	0	0	0	0	0	0	0	28	0	1	.186	.167
Roberson, Ryan	R-R	6-5	240	8-1-83	.268	.330	.248	100	366	47	98	28	1	15	51	28	5	0	3	107	3	0	.473	.326
Roof, Shawn	R-R	5-10	175	8-3-84	.217	.265	.198	37	115	7	25	3	0	0	15	7	1	0	1	27	0	1	.243	.266
Ryan, Dusty	R-R	6-4	230	9-2-84	.214	.270	.194	46	145	17	31	0	0	7	22	18	3	0	2	52	0	1	.359	.310
Scram, Deik	L-R	6-2	180	2-1-84	.283	.273	.286	41	152	25	43	9	4	3	13	17	0	0	0	29	7	3	.454	.355
Suero, Ovandy	B-R	5-10	160	6-20-82	.252	.281	.240	116	433	58	109	12	2	1	23	32	3	6	3	95	75	21	.296	.306
Wells, Casper	R-R	6-2	210	11-23-84	.500	.500	—	2	2	0	1	0	0	0	0	0	0	0	0	1	0	0	1.000	.500
Worth, Daniel	R-R	6-1	180	9-30-85	.251	.275	.244	51	171	22	43	9	2	2	21	18	1	1	1	39	6	0	.363	.325

PITCHING	B-T	HT	WT	DOB	W	L	ERA	G	GS	CG	SV	IP	H	R	ER	HR	BB	SO	AVG	vLH	vRH	K/9	BB/9
Aponte, Eleazar	R-R	6-1	160	3-4-85	5	9	4.85	23	20	0	1	111	128	71	60	11	39	75	.288	.283	.292	6.06	3.15
Ardoin, Kevin	R-R	6-1	167	8-6-82	0	3	12.34	5	3	0	0	12	24	20	16	1	8	6	.421	.435	.412	4.63	6.17
Badenhop, Burke	R-R	6-5	220	2-8-83	10	6	3.13	23	23	1	0	135	130	61	47	5	34	78	.251	.264	.242	5.19	2.26
Benitez, Gabriel	R-R	6-4	165	3-1-83	1	6	7.31	42	2	0	0	60	79	52	49	3	47	54	.322	.394	.278	8.06	7.01
Castro, Angel	R-R	5-11	200	11-14-82	4	2	3.79	13	13	1	0	74	71	34	31	6	26	35	.259	.294	.238	4.28	3.18
Clelland, Edward	L-L	6-0	165	6-27-82	1	1	7.58	16	0	0	1	19	25	19	16	2	15	17	.321	.500	.250	8.05	7.11
Cody, Christopher	L-L	6-0	180	1-7-84	0	1	6.00	2	2	0	0	6	8	4	4	0	2	3	.348	.000	.348	4.50	3.00
2-team (5 Brevard County)					2	2	4.15	7	7	0	0	26	26	12	12	2	8	26	—	—	—	9.00	2.77
Denney, Kyle	R-R	6-2	190	7-27-77	2	0	5.75	5	4	0	0	20	22	13	13	0	7	17	.278	.316	.244	7.52	3.10
Dolsi, Freddy	R-R	6-0	160	1-9-83	5	3	3.48	48	0	0	23	52	52	24	20	3	17	44	.267	.346	.211	7.66	2.96
Figaro, Alfredo	R-R	6-0	173	7-7-84	0	2	4.76	5	4	0	0	23	26	15	12	0	6	6	.292	.390	.208	2.38	2.38
French, Lucas	L-L	6-4	220	9-13-85	5	14	4.05	27	27	0	0	149	172	94	67	10	47	93	.291	.233	.304	5.62	2.84
Garcia, Ramon	L-L	6-2	165	10-30-84	0	1	27.00	1	1	0	0	2	8	7	7	1	1	1	.615	.600	.625	3.86	3.86
Hammond, Paul	L-L	5-11	205	9-20-82	2	1	5.12	23	0	0	0	32	47	23	18	1	12	24	.346	.348	.344	6.82	3.41
Kown, Andrew	L-R	6-7	210	10-7-82	0	0	6.23	1	1	0	0	4	7	6	3	0	0	2	.318	.286	.375	4.15	0.00
Lewis, Jeremy	R-L	6-4	180	9-12-80	0	2	2.04	12	0	0	0	18	10	4	4	1	5	16	.172	.190	.162	8.15	2.55
2-team (16 Brevard County)					0	3	4.50	28	0	0	1	40	37	22	20	2	14	32	—	—	—	7.20	3.15
Mendez, Rafael	R-R	6-0	190	4-24-84	0	0	0.00	2	0	0	0	1	0	0	0	0	2	2	.000	.000	.000	13.50	13.50
Miller, Andrew	L-L	6-6	210	5-21-85	1	4	3.48	7	7	2	0	41	43	21	16	1	15	28	.264	.159	.303	6.10	3.27
Miller, Justin	R-R	6-4	220	7-20-84	0	0	0.00	2	2	0	0	2	2	0	0	0	1	1	.250	.000	.286	4.50	4.50
Moscoso, Guillermo	R-R	6-1	165	11-14-83	0	0	0.00	1	1	0	0	3	2	0	0	0	1	4	.182	.400	.000	12.00	3.00
O'Brien, Matt	R-R	6-3	215	8-10-82	0	3	7.59	7	6	0	0	32	47	28	27	1	12	9	.343	.365	.329	2.53	3.38
Piccola, Zachary	R-L	6-3	225	3-27-85	0	0	21.21	7	0	0	0	5	16	11	11	0	4	3	.593	.600	.588	5.79	7.71
Rainwater, Josh	R-R	6-1	220	4-9-85	2	2	3.02	19	4	0	0	48	45	22	16	2	21	34	.253	.286	.231	6.42	3.97
Ramos, Jacob	L-L	5-9	170	5-18-83	5	2	3.46	20	0	0	0	26	28	18	10	3	19	25	.272	.343	.235	8.65	6.58
Righter, Matthew	R-R	6-5	190	8-7-81	3	2	6.14	17	2	0	0	37	43	26	25	4	12	19	.285	.254	.310	4.66	2.95
Santos, Adriano	R-R	6-2	170	9-8-84	0	0	0.00	3	0	0	0	5	2	0	0	0	3	4	.125	.167	.100	7.20	5.40
Sleeth, Kyle	R-R	6-5	205	12-20-81	1	8	7.62	17	15	0	0	65	83	62	55	13	31	40	.309	.333	.295	5.54	4.29
Steik, Ricky	L-R	6-4	220	1-24-84	3	9	5.63	38	0	0	1	64	74	49	40	7	32	60	.282	.264	.295	8.44	4.50
Tomey, Anthony	R-R	6-4	245	8-17-81	0	0	0.00	5	0	0	0	5	3	0	0	0	4	9	.158	.167	.154	15.19	6.75
Vasquez, Sendy	B-R	6-1	160	8-10-82	0	3	8.20	4	0	0	0	19	25	22	17	0	11	12	.329	.433	.261	5.79	5.30
Wise, Brendan	L-R	6-2	190	1-9-86	1	2	3.12	31	0	0	3	35	28	14	12	4	10	18	.226	.341	.169	4.67	2.60
Witt, Derek	R-R	6-1	180	12-31-83	2	1	3.15	41	1	0	1	71	71	33	25	3	21	41	.260	.264	.257	5.17	2.65

FIELDING

Catcher	PCT	G	PO	A	E	DP	PB
Casanova	.994	27	171	9	1	0	7
Collet	.987	31	138	11	2	2	7
Kunkel	.975	16	74	5	2	1	4
Mendez	.987	18	69	6	1	3	5
Roa	.994	30	154	11	1	2	5
Roberson	1.000	1	7	0	0	0	1
Ryan	.985	35	186	13	3	1	5

First Base	PCT	G	PO	A	E	DP
Cotto	.976	4	40	1	1	4
Haske	.956	6	41	2	2	3
Mendez	.984	35	286	21	5	30
W. Ramirez	1.000	1	9	0	0	0
Roberson	.985	99	861	61	14	107

Second Base	PCT	G	PO	A	E	DP
Haske	.971	28	59	76	4	23
Mendez	.667	1	0	2	1	0
C. Ramirez	.833	1	3	2	1	2
Rhymes	.971	86	172	258	13	67
Roof	.951	18	45	53	5	18
Suero	.957	9	17	27	2	4

Third Base	PCT	G	PO	A	E	DP
Bourquin	.929	26	11	54	5	0
Haske	1.000	3	1	3	0	1
Justice	1.000	1	3	3	0	0
Kunkel	.833	3	3	2	1	0
Leon	.921	93	55	190	21	23
Linares	.844	22	5	33	7	3
C. Ramirez	1.000	1	1	2	0	0
Roa	1.000	1	0	1	0	1

Shortstop	PCT	G	PO	A	E	DP
Haske	.937	61	102	212	21	44
Iorg	1.000	4	7	12	0	4
Linares	.926	18	26	62	7	18
Rhymes	.750	1	1	2	1	0
Roof	.892	13	18	40	7	9
Worth	.967	48	68	165	8	41

Outfield	PCT	G	PO	A	E	DP
Cotto	1.000	1	2	0	0	0
Hernandez	.962	78	143	7	6	4
Justice	.973	90	171	6	5	4
Kunkel	—	1	0	0	0	0
Leon	1.000	1	1	0	0	0
Maybin	.969	71	183	4	6	1
Mendez	1.000	7	10	0	0	0
C. Ramirez	1.000	2	5	1	0	0
W. Ramirez	.969	79	148	8	5	2
Roof	1.000	7	2	0	0	0
Scram	.970	41	60	5	2	1
Suero	.917	55	104	6	10	1
Wells	—	1	0	0	0	0

WEST MICHIGAN WHITECAPS

LOW CLASS A

MIDWEST LEAGUE

BATTING	B-T	HT	WT	DOB	AVG	vLH	vRH	G	AB	R	H	2B	3B	HR	RBI	BB	HBP	SH	SF	SO	SB	CS	SLG	OBP
Bertram, Michael	L-R	6-2	220	2-25-84	.251	.200	.258	77	247	24	62	16	2	2	32	19	3	3	3	39	2	2	.356	.309
Boesch, Brennan	L-L	6-5	185	4-12-85	.267	.260	.269	126	513	52	137	19	4	10	86	23	1	0	5	81	15	4	.378	.297
Ciriaco, Audy	R-R	6-3	195	6-16-87	.224	.228	.221	121	434	42	97	18	4	4	39	18	1	4	3	78	8	3	.311	.254
De Leon, Santo	R-R	6-2	175	11-1-83	.261	.275	.256	109	398	38	104	13	3	4	43	15	9	5	0	65	10	6	.344	.300
Hernandez, Gorkys	R-R	6-0	175	9-7-87	.293	.286	.296	124	481	84	141	25	5	4	50	36	5	4	7	69	54	11	.391	.344
Kunkel, Jeffrey	B-R	5-11	200	3-11-83	.230	.235	.227	29	100	6	23	2	1	0	4	5	3	1	0	19	1	0	.270	.287
Laster, Jeramy	R-R	6-1	185	4-5-85	.276	.280	.275	110	391	68	108	21	3	16	72	37	8	1	4	141	16	7	.468	.348
Newton, Jordan	R-R	5-10	185	8-29-85	.269	.298	.253	37	134	17	36	6	2	3	16	9	3	1	1	32	5	2	.410	.327
Ott, Louis	B-R	6-0	185	2-22-85	.271	.444	.230	43	140	24	38	4	1	2	16	19	3	0	1	28	2	3	.357	.368

	B-T	HT	WT	DOB	AVG	vLH	vRH	G	AB	R	H	2B	3B	HR	RBI	BB	HBP	SH	SF	SO	SB	CS	SLG	OBP
Scram, Deik	L-R	6-2	180	2-1-84	.327	.316	.330	73	266	45	87	14	6	2	24	40	2	3	2	54	14	5	.447	.416
Sizemore, Scott	R-R	6-0	185	1-4-85	.265	.274	.262	125	438	78	116	33	5	4	48	73	9	4	6	60	16	10	.390	.376
Skelton, James	L-R	5-11	165	10-28-85	.309	.307	.309	101	353	60	109	24	2	7	52	55	2	4	3	53	18	5	.448	.402
Strieby, Ryan	R-R	6-6	220	8-9-85	.253	.303	.235	123	443	65	112	23	2	16	76	63	5	0	8	78	6	5	.422	.347
Timm, Brandon	R-R	6-2	200	12-4-84	.249	.288	.231	82	253	31	63	14	3	0	19	19	4	2	2	66	8	4	.328	.309
Tucker, Joseph	R-R	5-11	170	1-25-84	.261	.237	.271	35	134	14	35	6	0	1	12	8	2	1	1	30	6	3	.328	.310

PITCHING	B-T	HT	WT	DOB	W	L	ERA	G	GS	CG	SV	IP	H	R	ER	HR	BB	SO	AVG	vLH	vRH	K/9	BB/9
Aponte, Eleazar	R-R	6-1	160	3-4-85	0	0	7.88	2	1	0	0	8	14	7	7	0	4	9	.400	.500	.370	10.12	4.50
Below, Duane	L-L	6-2	205	11-15-85	13	5	2.97	26	26	0	0	146	128	54	48	6	58	160	.236	.286	.220	9.89	3.58
Bierd, Randor	R-R	6-4	190	3-14-84	1	1	2.05	15	0	0	0	22	17	8	5	1	6	29	.210	.172	.231	11.86	2.45
Castro, Angel	R-R	5-11	200	11-14-82	7	4	3.01	14	12	0	0	78	66	29	26	10	23	43	.230	.292	.173	4.98	2.67
Cedano, Kelvin	R-R	6-0	175	11-3-85	2	2	4.23	13	0	0	0	28	26	13	13	2	19	24	.257	.208	.302	7.81	6.18
Clelland, Edward	L-L	6-0	165	6-27-82	2	0	0.79	24	0	0	6	34	16	4	3	0	6	23	.134	.077	.151	6.09	1.59
Cody, Christopher	L-L	6-0	180	1-7-84	5	5	1.77	14	14	0	0	91	70	22	18	1	15	92	.215	.149	.232	9.07	1.48
Fien, Casey	R-R	6-2	195	10-21-83	6	1	3.10	39	0	0	6	61	55	28	21	4	10	77	.233	.302	.193	11.36	1.48
Fragoso, Jose	R-R	6-0	175	11-12-84	0	2	7.82	6	0	0	0	13	18	11	11	4	4	12	.340	.423	.259	8.53	2.84
Furbush, Charles	L-L	6-5	215	4-11-86	4	1	2.17	8	7	0	0	46	40	14	11	2	11	46	.237	.158	.260	9.07	2.17
Fyvie, Dan	R-R	6-0	207	8-12-82	0	3	5.50	14	0	0	1	18	21	11	11	0	7	13	.300	.250	.342	6.50	3.50
Gagnier, Lauren	R-R	6-2	210	2-28-85	5	11	4.57	28	22	1	0	144	142	85	73	14	60	119	.261	.269	.254	7.45	3.76
Garcia, Ramon	L-L	6-2	165	10-30-84	0	1	5.52	5	4	0	0	15	17	10	9	0	4	13	.283	.222	.294	7.98	2.45
Gerbe, Jeff	R-R	6-3	190	7-4-84	2	2	2.34	19	9	0	2	73	65	26	19	2	12	40	.243	.282	.218	4.93	1.48
Gil, Luis	R-R	6-1	170	2-12-84	0	0	4.91	3	0	0	0	4	6	2	2	0	4	2	.375	.333	.385	4.91	9.82
Jensen, Brett	R-R	6-7	180	11-29-83	5	1	1.79	56	0	0	23	60	52	12	12	2	8	66	.227	.248	.211	9.85	1.19
Marte, Luis	R-R	5-11	170	8-26-86	1	2	2.83	15	2	0	3	35	28	13	11	2	11	36	.220	.259	.188	9.26	2.83
Moscoso, Guillermo	R-R	6-1	165	11-14-83	0	0	1.13	1	1	0	0	8	5	1	1	0	1	7	.185	.091	.250	7.88	0.00
Napolitan, Phil	R-R	6-1	185	1-29-82	4	2	6.25	27	0	0	1	45	67	36	31	6	8	42	.344	.350	.339	8.46	1.61
Nickerson, Jonah	R-R	6-0	210	3-9-85	11	7	4.24	25	25	2	0	151	156	74	71	8	38	116	.271	.271	.271	6.93	2.27
O'Brien, Matt	R-R	6-3	215	8-10-82	7	2	2.19	12	12	0	0	82	83	29	20	5	14	41	.263	.282	.247	4.48	1.53
Piccola, Zachary	R-L	6-3	225	3-27-85	1	2	6.18	20	0	0	0	28	31	26	19	3	22	28	.279	.250	.287	9.11	7.16
Rainwater, Josh	R-R	6-1	220	4-9-85	7	2	2.32	16	4	0	0	43	34	16	11	2	13	39	.217	.245	.202	8.23	2.74
Rogers, Kenny	L-L	6-1	190	11-10-64	0	1	1.80	1	1	0	0	5	7	3	1	0	2	4	.333	1.000	.300	7.20	3.60
Witt, Derek	R-R	6-1	180	12-31-83	0	0	4.50	2	0	0	0	2	2	1	1	1	0	0	.286	.000	.400	0.00	0.00

FIELDING

Catcher	PCT	G	PO	A	E	DP	PB
Bertram	1.000	6	7	0	0	0	0
Kunkel	.991	29	207	25	2	2	2
Newton	.996	29	235	21	1	3	1
Ott	.960	8	21	3	1	0	0
Skelton	.990	84	615	56	7	4	8

First Base	PCT	G	PO	A	E	DP
Bertram	.987	29	215	6	3	24
De Leon	.974	5	32	5	1	5
Skelton	1.000	3	2	0	0	0
Strieby	.993	114	962	70	7	76
Timm	—	1	0	0	0	0

Second Base	PCT	G	PO	A	E	DP
Ott	.964	14	17	37	2	2
Sizemore	.971	116	193	313	15	82
Tucker	.968	16	19	42	2	5

Third Base	PCT	G	PO	A	E	DP
Bertram	.945	35	26	60	5	3
De Leon	.929	104	84	190	21	18
Ott	.800	5	2	10	3	3
Tucker	1.000	2	1	10	0	1

Shortstop	PCT	G	PO	A	E	DP
Ciriaco	.951	121	163	303	24	63
Ott	.927	11	12	26	3	7

Tucker	.951	12	14	25	2	3

Outfield	PCT	G	PO	A	E	DP
Boesch	.987	114	225	4	3	2
Hernandez	.979	121	277	6	6	2
Laster	.954	89	134	10	7	3
Scram	.986	38	68	0	1	0
Timm	.982	70	106	5	2	1
Tucker	1.000	1	1	0	0	0

ONEONTA TIGERS
SHORT-SEASON

NEW YORK-PENN LEAGUE

BATTING	B-T	HT	WT	DOB	AVG	vLH	vRH	G	AB	R	H	2B	3B	HR	RBI	BB	HBP	SH	SF	SO	SB	CS	SLG	OBP
Bourquin, Ron	L-R	6-3	205	4-29-85	.325	.290	.341	57	194	31	63	13	3	2	28	31	3	1	2	35	2	2	.454	.422
Bowen, Joseph	B-R	6-1	190	9-25-87	.040	.125	.000	9	25	0	1	0	0	0	0	0	0	0	0	12	0	0	.040	.040
Carlson, Christopher	R-R	6-4	230	1-7-84	.291	.253	.306	72	258	44	75	21	1	10	51	29	9	0	4	34	0	1	.496	.377
Casanova, Adrian	R-R	6-1	210	5-6-83	.161	.261	.103	21	62	7	10	1	0	0	8	7	2	2	2	12	0	0	.177	.260
Flores, Angel	R-R	6-0	195	8-16-86	.224	.217	.226	31	85	10	19	3	0	0	7	15	2	0	0	24	0	0	.259	.353
Henry, Justin	L-R	6-3	180	4-30-85	.340	.337	.341	67	250	49	85	11	2	1	31	33	5	4	4	22	14	7	.412	.421
Kaiser, Kody	B-R	5-9	185	4-6-85	.266	.270	.264	70	271	42	72	17	3	5	39	39	3	0	2	78	15	4	.406	.341
Linares, Miguel	R-R	6-2	180	12-16-83	.152	.000	.179	12	33	4	5	1	0	0	3	2	1	0	1	13	0	0	.182	.216
Middleton, Cory	R-R	6-1	185	10-3-85	.266	.186	.296	60	218	25	58	10	2	6	39	15	4	1	0	61	4	1	.413	.325
Patino, Jorge	R-R	5-10	150	1-25-84	.254	.306	.229	59	193	21	49	9	0	1	20	11	6	3	0	18	4	3	.316	.314
Peter, Kyle	L-R	6-2	185	2-4-86	.274	.325	.256	45	157	29	43	4	2	0	14	21	4	3	1	28	14	3	.325	.372
Rochelle, Kristopher	R-R	6-2	190	9-22-84	.000	.000	.000	4	10	0	0	0	0	0	0	1	4	1	0	1	0	0	.000	.333
Rodriguez, Orlando	R-R	6-0	180	8-29-85	.151	.167	.143	19	53	6	8	0	0	1	5	3	1	1	0	11	1	0	.208	.211
Seawell, Ryan	R-R	6-2	225	7-16-85	.278	.241	.300	33	79	18	22	8	0	0	7	12	4	0	0	22	1	1	.380	.400
Sullivan, Michael	L-R	6-2	190	12-16-83	.254	.245	.257	59	189	28	48	8	5	0	16	32	2	3	2	48	6	3	.349	.364
Thomas, Devin	B-R	5-10	195	2-22-85	.227	.143	.245	33	119	17	27	4	1	6	27	14	0	0	3	27	2	0	.429	.301
Wells, Casper	R-R	6-2	210	11-23-84	.265	.333	.233	67	260	46	69	18	11	9	47	18	6	0	4	64	8	7	.523	.323
White, Christopher	B-R	5-11	170	11-12-87	.197	.238	.175	17	61	12	12	3	1	0	4	6	0	0	0	16	1	1	.279	.269

PITCHING	B-T	HT	WT	DOB	W	L	ERA	G	GS	CG	SV	IP	H	R	ER	HR	BB	SO	AVG	vLH	vRH	K/9	BB/9
Brackman, Mark	R-R	6-7	230	3-23-85	4	4	4.05	14	14	0	0	73	75	42	33	6	22	47	.261	.280	.250	5.77	2.70
Crichton, Erik	R-R	5-10	190	6-6-85	4	0	1.56	26	0	0	2	35	24	7	6	2	14	39	.192	.255	.149	10.12	3.63
Darrow, Rudy	R-R	5-10	180	2-11-84	4	3	2.41	26	0	0	1	37	30	11	10	0	10	39	.222	.259	.198	9.40	2.41
Figaro, Alfredo	R-R	6-0	173	7-7-84	4	2	3.38	11	11	0	0	53	56	23	20	1	16	40	.269	.300	.241	6.75	2.70
Finefrock, Sean	R-R	6-5	200	2-11-87	3	5	5.98	12	10	0	0	53	59	44	35	5	21	30	.281	.271	.288	5.13	3.59
Fragoso, Jose	R-R	6-0	175	11-12-84	2	4	3.77	25	1	0	2	43	36	23	18	2	21	53	.225	.167	.266	11.09	4.40
Garcia, Wilton	R-R	6-1	165	4-12-85	1	0	0.00	4	0	0	0	7	3	1	0	0	4	10	.136	.250	.071	13.50	5.40
Gil, Luis	R-R	6-1	170	2-12-84	1	1	6.33	17	0	0	0	27	29	20	19	1	11	14	.274	.308	.254	4.67	3.67
Hammond, Paul	L-L	5-11	205	9-20-82	0	0	9.00	4	0	0	0	4	9	5	4	0	1	5	.409	.600	.250	11.25	2.25
Homer, Chris	R-R	6-1	190	3-6-81	1	1	3.14	11	0	0	0	14	13	10	5	0	12	11	.250	.333	.194	6.91	7.53

	B-T	HT	WT	DOB	W	L	ERA	G	GS	CG	SV	IP	H	R	ER	HR	BB	SO	AVG	vLH	vRH	K/9	BB/9
Johnson, Brandon	R-R	6-5	210	3-9-87	0	1	5.23	3	2	0	0	10	10	6	6	1	9	8	.250	.235	.261	6.97	7.84
Kibler, Jonathan	L-L	6-5	210	8-10-86	0	0	2.38	2	2	0	0	11	8	3	3	0	3	11	.200	.333	.161	8.74	2.38
Krol, Noah	B-R	6-2	185	6-6-84	0	0	2.20	28	0	0	17	29	20	8	7	1	11	39	.190	.156	.217	12.24	3.45
Mahoney, Collin	R-R	6-4	245	12-26-82	2	1	6.39	20	0	0	1	25	22	24	18	2	30	14	.227	.211	.237	4.97	10.66
Miguelez, Emmanuel	L-L	6-2	200	11-16-85	0	1	4.91	2	2	0	0	7	5	5	4	0	5	7	.200	.200	.200	8.59	6.14
Moscoso, Guillermo	R-R	6-1	165	11-14-83	8	2	2.37	14	14	2	0	80	75	25	21	3	15	68	.248	.338	.175	7.68	1.69
Nardozzi, Paul	R-R	6-0	200	3-14-85	1	1	4.91	10	5	0	0	29	27	18	16	5	13	22	.239	.189	.283	6.75	3.99
Ramos, Jacob	L-L	5-9	170	5-18-83	1	1	5.40	5	0	0	0	5	8	3	3	0	1	0	.381	.333	.444	0.00	1.80
Santos, Adriano	R-R	6-2	170	9-8-84	2	0	3.57	18	0	0	1	23	27	10	9	0	18	19	.293	.333	.271	7.54	7.15
Sborz, Jay	R-R	6-4	210	1-24-85	0	0	5.40	5	1	0	0	10	10	10	6	1	6	9	.263	.389	.150	8.10	5.40
Vasquez, Sendy	B-R	6-1	160	8-10-82	6	5	4.23	14	14	0	0	77	68	43	36	3	48	61	.242	.274	.220	7.16	5.63

FIELDING

Catcher	PCT	G	PO	A	E	DP	PB
Bowen	.979	5	43	3	1	0	1
Casanova	.987	20	132	18	2	1	3
Flores	.976	28	176	25	5	2	7
Rochelle	1.000	4	30	4	0	3	7
Thomas	.977	22	161	12	4	2	7

First Base	PCT	G	PO	A	E	DP
Bourquin	.905	3	15	4	2	1
Carlson	.989	71	599	39	7	44
Flores	1.000	1	5	1	0	0
Middleton	1.000	1	8	2	0	0
Seawell	.967	6	29	0	1	6

Second Base	PCT	G	PO	A	E	DP
Henry	.974	62	119	179	8	34
Kaiser	.949	14	29	45	4	4
Patino	1.000	3	3	7	0	0
White	1.000	1	0	1	0	0

Third Base	PCT	G	PO	A	E	DP
Bourquin	.905	53	32	92	13	6
Kaiser	.800	5	2	6	2	1
Linares	.833	3	2	3	1	0
Middleton	.930	21	17	36	4	5
Seawell	1.000	1	1	0	0	0
Sullivan	1.000	1	0	1	0	0

Shortstop	PCT	G	PO	A	E	DP
Kaiser	.922	16	28	43	6	10
Linares	.920	9	8	15	2	3
Patino	.972	58	88	157	7	27

Outfield	PCT	G	PO	A	E	DP
Henry	1.000	2	3	0	0	0
Kaiser	.985	32	61	4	1	1
Middleton	1.000	6	9	1	0	0
Peter	.966	44	83	2	3	0
Rodriguez	1.000	18	24	1	0	0
Seawell	1.000	12	13	1	0	0
Sullivan	.989	55	86	1	1	0
Wells	.960	60	88	7	4	0
White	.885	15	23	0	3	0

GCL TIGERS   ROOKIE

GULF COAST LEAGUE

BATTING	B-T	HT	WT	DOB	AVG	vLH	vRH	G	AB	R	H	2B	3B	HR	RBI	BB	HBP	SH	SF	SO	SB	CS	SLG	OBP
Arlet, Luis	R-R	5-11	174	11-8-84	.312	.238	.358	30	109	22	34	2	2	5	16	3	4	0	0	26	2	3	.505	.353
Bowen, Joseph	B-R	6-1	190	9-25-87	.238	.216	.247	40	126	13	30	4	1	4	16	14	3	1	0	38	1	0	.381	.329
Clevlen, Brent	R-R	6-2	190	10-27-83	.313	.286	.324	14	48	10	15	1	0	2	8	3	0	0	1	8	1	0	.458	.346
Guzman, Joaquin	B-R	6-0	170	9-22-86	.205	.167	.223	44	151	17	31	4	1	2	25	12	0	4	2	31	5	3	.285	.261
Harrigan, Brandon	R-R	6-0	215	1-26-85	.179	.320	.113	28	78	12	14	1	0	0	7	11	2	0	2	23	1	1	.192	.290
Harryman, Eric	R-R	5-10	170	10-6-84	.130	.333	.074	22	69	6	9	1	0	1	7	3	3	1	2	23	1	0	.188	.195
Iorg, Cale	R-R	6-2	190	9-6-85	.182	.500	.111	3	11	1	2	0	0	0	1	1	0	0	0	6	0	0	.182	.308
Lamont, Wade	L-R	6-2	230	6-25-84	.189	.083	.220	32	106	17	20	3	0	1	7	12	2	1	0	29	1	0	.245	.283
Lehrman, Derek	L-R	6-1	205	12-11-84	.225	.367	.140	24	80	6	18	3	1	1	8	7	0	1	0	23	0	1	.325	.287
Maddox, Craig	L-R	5-10	190	4-10-85	.240	.136	.283	25	75	12	18	1	0	3	13	8	1	1	0	20	1	0	.373	.321
Maybin, Cameron	R-R	6-4	205	4-4-87	.571	1.000	.500	2	7	1	4	0	0	0	1	2	0	0	0	2	0	0	.571	.667
McBratney, Marc	L-R	5-10	175	12-26-84	.313	.235	.346	44	115	17	36	5	2	1	12	20	0	4	0	24	4	1	.417	.415
Parrott, Hayden	R-R	6-1	195	4-11-88	.291	.328	.273	52	196	21	57	6	0	2	21	8	1	2	1	30	2	2	.352	.320
Peter, Kyle	L-R	6-2	185	2-4-86	.500	1.000	.429	3	8	4	4	1	0	0	3	0	0	0	0	2	0	0	.625	.636
Ramirez, Carlos	R-R	5-11	190	9-1-85	.270	.308	.250	46	148	24	40	9	3	4	26	13	4	0	0	52	1	1	.453	.345
Roberson, Ryan	R-R	6-5	240	8-1-83	.235	.500	.200	7	17	2	4	0	0	0	4	1	0	0	0	5	1	0	.235	.409
Rochelle, Kristopher	R-R	6-2	190	9-22-84	.333	.500	.000	4	3	1	1	0	0	0	0	1	0	0	0	2	0	0	.333	.500
Rodriguez, Orlando	R-R	6-0	180	8-29-85	.283	.258	.293	32	113	15	32	5	0	2	12	6	0	1	0	22	3	4	.381	.319
Roof, Shawn	R-R	5-10	175	8-3-84	.250	.143	.308	15	40	7	10	1	0	0	3	5	1	0	0	8	0	0	.275	.423
Ryan, Dusty	R-R	6-4	230	9-2-84	.063	.000	.111	6	16	1	1	0	0	0	0	4	0	0	0	5	0	0	.063	.250
Taylor, Londell	R-R	6-2	200	9-13-88	.156	.214	.129	17	45	2	7	1	0	0	3	2	0	0	0	12	2	1	.178	.191
Tomas, Roger	B-R	5-8	185	4-17-86	.243	.175	.282	32	111	14	27	6	1	2	13	9	1	0	1	18	1	0	.369	.303
Tucker, Joseph	R-R	5-11	170	1-25-84	.257	.357	.190	9	35	3	9	3	0	0	3	2	0	0	0	5	2	0	.343	.297
Vaughn, D'Andre	R-R	5-11	190	9-7-88	.167	.154	.176	12	30	7	5	2	0	0	2	2	0	0	0	8	1	0	.233	.265
White, Christopher	B-R	5-11	170	11-12-87	.279	.267	.285	50	183	25	51	9	2	3	22	20	2	2	0	36	15	4	.399	.356

PITCHING	B-T	HT	WT	DOB	W	L	ERA	G	GS	CG	SV	IP	H	R	ER	HR	BB	SO	AVG	vLH	vRH	K/9	BB/9
Aponte, Eleazar	R-R	6-1	160	3-4-85	2	0	1.50	3	0	0	0	12	9	2	2	1	3	11	.209	.250	.185	8.25	2.25
Carvajal, Dario	R-R	6-1	165	4-17-85	0	2	3.77	7	3	1	1	29	25	15	12	1	13	23	.234	.192	.247	7.22	4.08
Cedano, Kelvin	R-R	6-0	175	11-3-85	1	0	3.09	4	0	0	0	12	9	5	4	0	1	9	.191	.083	.229	6.94	0.77
Chestnut, Nolan	R-L	6-3	210	5-29-84	0	2	4.00	8	0	0	0	9	11	10	4	1	5	6	.289	.167	.313	6.00	5.00
Finefrock, Sean	R-R	6-5	200	2-11-87	0	0	2.84	2	2	0	0	6	4	2	2	0	2	2	.182	.333	.158	2.84	2.84
Franco, Santo	L-L	5-11	157	5-7-85	0	0	0.83	22	0	0	12	22	14	2	2	0	17	26	.192	.250	.175	10.80	7.06
Fuhrman, Aaron	L-L	6-0	185	4-2-88	2	7	5.25	12	11	1	0	60	61	40	35	5	22	56	.268	.280	.264	8.40	3.30
Furbush, Charles	L-L	6-5	215	4-11-86	2	0	2.81	4	3	0	0	16	11	5	5	2	3	23	.186	.111	.200	12.94	1.69
Garcia, Wilton	R-R	6-1	165	4-12-85	3	1	3.64	22	0	0	0	47	50	24	19	4	13	29	.275	.271	.276	5.55	2.49
Hamilton, Brandon	R-R	6-2	205	12-25-88	1	1	3.10	7	3	0	0	20	12	9	7	2	12	23	.171	.192	.159	10.18	5.31
Hess, Andrew	R-R	6-4	210	11-6-84	0	0	0.00	3	0	0	0	3	2	0	0	0	1	5	.200	.143	.333	15.00	3.00
Homer, Chris	R-R	6-1	190	3-6-81	0	2	5.59	9	0	0	0	10	14	9	6	2	5	11	.318	.200	.379	6.52	2.79
Johnson, Brandon	R-R	6-5	210	3-9-87	4	5	2.58	12	11	0	0	59	59	31	17	3	11	45	.252	.207	.279	6.83	1.67
Kibler, Jonathan	L-L	6-5	210	8-10-86	3	2	2.43	7	5	0	0	30	26	10	8	0	6	23	.241	.174	.259	6.98	1.82
Lewis, Jeremy	R-L	6-4	180	9-12-80	0	0	10.38	3	0	0	1	4	7	5	5	2	1	3	.389	.000	.412	6.23	2.08
Marte, Luis	R-R	5-11	170	8-26-86	2	0	0.75	2	1	0	0	12	8	1	1	0	1	12	.186	.158	.208	9.00	0.75
Mieses, Santo	R-R	5-11	185	4-15-85	3	3	4.04	25	0	0	1	36	30	22	16	1	12	36	.229	.308	.177	9.08	3.03
Miguelez, Emmanuel	L-L	6-2	200	11-16-85	2	4	4.20	10	9	0	0	45	51	24	21	1	14	38	.293	.212	.312	7.60	2.80

	B-T	HT	WT	DOB	W	L	ERA	G	GS	CG	SV	IP	H	R	ER	HR	BB	SO	AVG	vLH	vRH	K/9	BB/9
Miller, Justin	R-R	6-4	220	7-20-84	2	1	0.74	16	0	0	0	24	19	7	2	1	8	13	.209	.414	.113	4.81	2.96
Perinar, Gary	R-R	6-0	200	2-10-86	0	0	13.50	1	0	0	0	1	2	1	1	0	2	1	.500	1.000	.333	13.50	27.00
Putkonen, Luke	R-R	6-6	200	5-10-86	0	1	4.15	3	3	0	0	9	8	5	4	0	0	9	.229	.100	.280	9.35	0.00
Sborz, Jay	R-R	6-4	210	1-24-85	1	1	2.61	5	2	0	0	10	9	4	3	0	2	8	.237	.357	.167	6.97	1.74
Villareal, Brayan	R-R	5-10	140	5-10-87	0	0	6.23	1	1	0	0	4	4	4	3	0	3	5	.235	.333	.214	10.38	6.23
Zumaya, Richard	R-R	6-0	180	11-10-89	0	0	4.08	8	1	0	1	18	10	9	8	1	8	16	.169	.167	.171	8.15	4.08

FIELDING

Catcher	PCT	G	PO	A	E	DP	PB
Bowen	.986	38	262	29	4	3	6
Harrigan	1.000	13	70	7	0	0	2
Lehrman	.972	6	34	1	1	0	0
Maddox	1.000	7	35	2	0	0	1
Rochelle	—	2	0	0	0	0	0
Ryan	.975	5	36	3	1	0	2

First Base	PCT	G	PO	A	E	DP
Lamont	.996	31	263	6	1	25
Ramirez	.986	28	190	17	3	16
Roberson	1.000	4	25	2	0	1

Second Base	PCT	G	PO	A	E	DP
Harrigan	1.000	1	0	1	0	0

Harryman	.941	20	40	56	6	14
Parrott	.833	1	1	4	1	0
Ramirez	.923	5	5	7	1	2
Roof	.947	5	11	7	1	1
Tomas	.988	24	43	42	1	12
Tucker	1.000	9	13	19	0	3

Third Base	PCT	G	PO	A	E	DP
Parrott	.844	51	27	92	22	8
Ramirez	.895	12	9	25	4	2
Roof	.500	1	0	1	1	0

Shortstop	PCT	G	PO	A	E	DP
Guzman	.946	44	64	111	10	20
Harryman	1.000	2	0	4	0	0

Iorg	1.000	2	2	7	0	2
Roof	.975	8	9	30	1	6
Tomas	.964	7	9	18	1	3

Outfield	PCT	G	PO	A	E	DP
Arlet	.983	29	53	4	1	0
Clevlen	1.000	10	17	0	0	0
Maybin	1.000	1	1	0	0	0
McBratney	1.000	42	46	0	0	0
Peter	1.000	3	4	0	0	0
Rodriguez	.949	32	54	2	3	1
Taylor	.957	17	21	1	1	0
Vaughn	1.000	11	16	0	0	0
White	.992	50	115	5	1	2

DSL TIGERS   ROOKIE

DOMINICAN SUMMER LEAGUE

BATTING	B-T	HT	WT	DOB	AVG	vLH	vRH	G	AB	R	H	2B	3B	HR	RBI	BB	HBP	SH	SF	SO	SB	CS	SLG	OBP
Aguasvivas, Juaner	R-R	6-3	225	9-15-89	.224	.333	.200	60	214	34	48	5	0	2	34	27	4	3	3	75	2	1	.276	.319
Bautista, Pedruin	R-R	5-11	162	5-12-84	.296	.325	.288	64	203	55	60	14	5	2	46	48	10	3	3	30	33	7	.443	.447
Constanza, Jose	B-R	5-10	150	1-30-88	.299	.286	.302	60	184	50	55	6	3	0	31	57	0	2	2	34	19	9	.364	.461
Cruz, Jose	B-R	5-11	170	9-4-84	.217	.200	.220	20	46	14	10	1	2	0	9	18	0	1	1	10	2	1	.326	.431
Dionicio, Victor	L-L	6-1	180	2-10-90	.207	.200	.209	33	87	18	18	3	0	0	9	14	2	1	0	40	1	1	.241	.330
Grullon, Luis	R-R	6-3	200	9-12-87	.292	.321	.283	38	120	29	35	9	0	5	34	25	10	0	1	43	2	1	.492	.449
Guzman, Jose	L-L	6-1	185	3-23-87	.211	.056	.247	41	95	19	20	4	0	1	8	24	4	0	3	30	3	0	.284	.381
Heredia, Santos	B-L	5-8	170	10-15-89	.288	.280	.291	35	104	28	30	4	2	1	9	32	4	0	0	31	8	5	.394	.471
Montesino, Isidro	R-R	6-0	170	9-9-86	.250	.450	.202	35	104	26	26	2	1	0	7	13	5	1	0	27	5	2	.288	.361
Nunez, Gustavo	B-R	5-10	148	2-8-88	.284	.302	.279	64	243	50	69	10	3	0	42	32	3	10	3	45	9	7	.350	.370
Pena, Herison	R-R	6-1	210	3-10-89	.191	.000	.290	20	47	6	9	1	0	0	7	5	7	0	1	15	0	1	.213	.350
Rijo, Samir	R-R	6-2	205	6-26-90	.189	.212	.184	55	185	24	35	4	1	0	23	26	2	1	3	63	0	2	.222	.292
Rodriguez, Julio	R-R	6-2	200	3-8-89	.263	.348	.246	39	137	17	36	9	0	0	29	6	2	1	3	12	0	0	.328	.297
Soto, Elvin	L-R	6-2	190	5-6-89	.222	.184	.232	54	180	36	40	6	3	7	39	40	5	0	1	66	1	1	.406	.376
Suazo, Juan	R-R	6-0	185	12-11-87	.148	.154	.146	20	61	10	9	2	0	1	3	8	1	3	0	23	0	1	.230	.257

PITCHING	B-T	HT	WT	DOB	W	L	ERA	G	GS	CG	SV	IP	H	R	ER	HR	BB	SO	AVG	vLH	vRH	K/9	BB/9
Bautista, Pedruin	R-R	5-11	162	5-12-84	0	0	32.40	1	0	0	0	2	7	7	6	0	2	1	.583	1.000	.375	5.40	10.80
Collado, Sergio	R-R	5-11	165	5-19-86	0	0	4.00	3	2	0	0	9	5	5	4	0	13	8	.172	.000	.227	8.00	13.00
De La Cruz, Sandy	R-R	6-1	180	6-11-87	1	1	2.28	25	0	0	15	28	19	9	7	0	13	26	.192	.250	.181	8.46	4.23
Diaz, Robert	L-L	6-2	180	2-12-89	2	1	3.78	15	2	0	0	33	18	17	14	1	29	33	.164	.000	.171	8.91	7.83
Duran, Darlin	L-L	6-0	160	3-3-89	7	0	2.09	11	7	0	0	47	31	19	11	0	27	38	.189	.333	.178	7.23	5.13
Guzman, Jose	L-L	6-1	185	3-23-87	0	0	4.50	1	0	0	0	2	2	3	1	1	2	0	.250	—	.250	0.00	9.00
Herrera, Gabriel	R-R	6-0	190	5-8-86	2	0	1.85	20	0	0	3	44	36	14	9	1	21	61	.218	.080	.243	12.57	4.33
Herrera, Jean	R-R	6-0	170	3-28-86	0	0	0.00	3	0	0	1	3	2	0	0	0	2	4	.167	.000	.222	12.00	6.00
Lebron, Ramon	R-R	6-1	180	2-1-89	0	0	10.80	2	2	0	0	3	5	6	4	0	3	3	.333	.000	.385	8.10	8.10
Martinez, Joel	R-R	6-4	190	6-20-85	2	3	7.36	14	3	0	1	26	32	28	21	1	11	26	.291	.273	.293	9.12	3.86
Martinez, Jose	R-R	6-2	170	1-26-89	1	0	3.38	5	2	0	0	16	10	6	6	0	7	14	.179	.143	.184	10.12	3.94
Mendez, Alejandro	R-R	6-1	190	9-8-85	5	4	1.37	15	14	2	0	79	52	23	12	1	30	103	.189	.181	.192	11.78	3.43
Moreno, Crucito	R-R	6-3	175	5-3-88	9	4	5.48	24	0	0	0	43	45	32	26	3	27	42	.268	.310	.259	8.86	5.70
Nunez, Marcos	R-R	6-5	210	7-10-89	3	0	5.58	12	3	0	0	31	34	27	19	0	13	14	.268	.259	.270	4.11	3.82
Ortiz, Vladimir	R-R	6-2	186	3-24-89	4	0	4.70	11	2	0	1	23	16	14	12	1	16	18	.200	.214	.192	7.04	6.26
Reynoso, Edward	L-L	6-0	150	9-5-88	9	0	0.76	13	13	1	0	71	36	10	6	0	23	110	.150	.136	.151	14.01	2.93
Severino, Raul	L-L	6-3	195	5-7-87	0	0	5.59	10	1	0	2	19	21	21	12	0	20	21	.280	.000	.296	9.78	9.31
Sierra, Waldy	R-R	6-2	190	8-23-86	4	2	3.92	14	14	0	0	62	49	34	27	0	32	72	.217	.206	.219	10.45	4.65
Zapata, Jose	L-L	5-11	155	3-27-86	0	0	0.00	2	0	0	0	1	1	3	0	0	6	1	.167	—	.167	6.75	40.50

FIELDING

Catcher	PCT	G	PO	A	E	DP	PB
Pena	.970	17	113	15	4	0	5
Rodriguez	.971	36	297	39	10	0	5
Suazo	.985	19	188	15	3	1	1

First Base	PCT	G	PO	A	E	DP
Aguasvivas	.981	41	344	12	7	28
Cruz	1.000	1	4	0	0	1
Grullon	.990	24	185	12	2	13
Guzman	1.000	1	2	0	0	0

Second Base	PCT	G	PO	A	E	DP
Bautista	.959	31	56	62	5	18

Constanza	.951	14	18	21	2	5
Heredia	.957	31	40	49	4	8

Third Base	PCT	G	PO	A	E	DP
Bautista	.824	29	16	54	15	2
Soto	.867	37	29	82	17	8
Suazo	1.000	1	0	2	0	0

Shortstop	PCT	G	PO	A	E	DP
Montesino	.833	2	1	4	1	0
Nunez	.920	64	95	171	23	26

Outfield	PCT	G	PO	A	E	DP
Constanza	.937	47	56	3	4	0

Cruz	.870	19	20	0	3	0
Dionicio	.917	33	19	3	2	0
Guzman	.868	37	31	2	5	0
Montesino	.941	31	44	4	3	1
Rijo	.909	55	46	4	5	2

ORGANIZATION STATISTICS

VENEZUELAN SUMMER LEAGUE

BATTING	B-T	HT	WT	DOB	AVG	vLH	vRH	G	AB	R	H	2B	3B	HR	RBI	BB	HBP	SH	SF	SO	SB	CS	SLG	OBP
Caldera, Ciro	R-R	5-10	175	6-16-86	.229	.233	.227	45	131	16	30	6	0	1	16	18	5	3	2	11	3	1	.298	.340
Castillo, Luis	R-R	5-11	160	5-15-89	.232	.286	.211	66	241	33	56	11	1	2	35	27	3	6	1	24	8	5	.311	.316
De Los Santos, Wondy	B-R	5-9	154	1-3-90	.217	.286	.193	58	184	26	40	3	2	1	18	22	6	3	0	39	7	1	.272	.321
Diaz, Alvaro	R-R	5-11	188	3-30-88	.000	.000	.000	3	6	0	0	0	0	0	0	0	0	0	0	1	0	0	.000	.000
Espinoza, Alexis	R-R	6-1	180	12-20-88	.268	.233	.284	43	138	25	37	6	1	12	27	9	9	1	0	34	6	0	.587	.353
Espinoza, Ivan	R-R	6-0	165	1-16-89	.280	.356	.245	43	143	26	40	6	1	1	12	15	2	5	1	20	10	5	.357	.354
Gomez, Gilbert	R-R	6-0	165	4-30-90	.138	.136	.139	20	58	5	8	0	0	2	6	3	2	1	1	28	1	1	.241	.203
Gonzalez, Jhoe	L-L	6-1	162	6-29-89	.215	.318	.175	37	79	9	17	5	0	0	2	13	2	0	0	11	1	1	.278	.340
Gonzalez, Orlando	R-R	5-10	165	8-30-85	.319	.319	.318	70	251	32	80	9	1	5	48	24	10	0	4	16	3	3	.422	.394
Guanipa, Dick	R-R	6-0	180	6-20-90	.213	.071	.255	24	61	5	13	3	0	1	8	6	5	0	0	29	0	0	.311	.333
Leiva, Raul	B-R	6-2	185	1-30-90	.208	.150	.222	39	101	12	21	4	0	0	8	5	4	1	1	25	0	1	.248	.270
Palacios, Luis	R-R	5-10	162	7-7-89	.307	.291	.315	69	257	44	79	16	0	3	27	35	6	4	2	34	8	5	.405	.400
Salas, Luis	R-R	6-0	172	1-2-89	.272	.351	.237	68	243	29	66	18	0	2	40	25	6	0	4	44	13	5	.370	.349
Stephenson, Zuriel	R-R	6-1	198	5-8-89	.192	.216	.182	46	125	17	24	4	0	0	8	18	2	2	0	41	3	0	.224	.303
Torrealba, Ronald	R-R	5-11	145	6-1-90	.178	.217	.162	67	202	30	36	3	0	0	13	40	9	7	2	22	3	8	.193	.336

PITCHING	B-T	HT	WT	DOB	W	L	ERA	G	GS	CG	SV	IP	H	R	ER	HR	BB	SO	AVG	vLH	vRH	K/9	BB/9
Cachutt, Carlos	R-R	6-0	165	11-11-88	3	4	4.70	11	9	0	0	38	35	23	20	2	17	32	.246	.250	.245	7.51	3.99
Celis, Fernando	R-R	6-1	165	3-27-89	2	1	4.28	17	2	0	1	27	30	24	13	4	15	19	.263	.179	.291	6.26	4.94
Diaz, Jose	R-R	6-0	160	4-20-89	0	2	5.26	11	7	0	0	39	54	28	23	2	11	19	.320	.327	.316	4.35	2.52
Gonzalez, Eduardo	R-R	6-3	152	11-2-88	1	1	9.27	16	1	0	0	22	41	29	23	1	14	11	.394	.419	.384	4.43	5.64
Larez, Victor	R-R	6-3	160	5-28-87	3	0	2.20	19	0	0	0	45	40	16	11	4	11	38	.237	.278	.217	7.60	2.20
Lozano, Juan	L-L	6-0	175	4-8-89	1	0	4.62	17	0	0	1	25	25	17	13	1	17	11	.250	.250	.250	3.91	6.04
Mendoza, Clemente	R-R	6-0	170	7-24-90	1	4	4.97	16	5	0	0	38	49	31	21	1	18	27	.310	.304	.313	6.39	4.26
Oliveros, Lester	R-R	5-11	178	5-28-88	2	0	1.41	27	0	0	19	38	25	6	6	0	13	59	.181	.118	.202	13.85	3.05
Ortega, Jose	R-R	5-11	165	10-12-88	0	0	2.45	10	0	0	0	11	9	3	3	1	3	11	.209	.182	.219	9.00	2.45
Ortiz, Jose Francisco	L-L	6-0	166	7-19-85	4	3	5.18	14	8	0	1	49	59	32	28	5	17	37	.314	.313	.314	6.84	3.14
Palacios, Wilsen	R-R	6-3	180	12-15-89	2	2	4.91	10	4	0	0	29	37	20	16	1	12	17	.314	.250	.333	5.22	3.68
Robles, Mauricio	L-L	5-9	142	3-5-89	3	6	3.26	14	14	0	0	69	60	33	25	4	27	83	.237	.200	.242	10.83	3.52
Salcedo, Gustavo	L-L	6-0	150	1-30-86	6	2	2.98	21	1	0	1	45	37	20	15	3	21	36	.231	.231	.231	7.15	4.17
Sanz, Luis	R-R	6-1	152	11-19-87	6	3	3.58	14	13	0	0	73	69	36	29	4	32	41	.265	.291	.254	5.05	3.95
Siso, Jose	L-L	5-11	155	3-22-89	1	2	11.05	16	3	0	0	22	31	27	27	3	22	22	.344	.357	.342	9.00	9.00
Torrealba, Michael	R-R	5-11	150	11-19-89	2	2	5.65	15	3	0	0	29	27	19	18	0	20	19	.255	.206	.278	5.97	6.28

FIELDING

Catcher	PCT	G	PO	A	E	DP	PB
Caldera	.982	32	183	31	4	2	4
O. Gonzalez	.986	30	184	22	3	3	4
Leiva	.985	19	117	11	2	1	2

First Base	PCT	G	PO	A	E	DP
Caldera	.947	8	53	1	3	8
A. Espinoza	1.000	2	3	0	0	1
J. Gonzalez	.951	15	70	7	4	2
O. Gonzalez	.979	24	221	8	5	17
Guanipa	1.000	7	38	2	0	5
Leiva	.962	13	97	4	4	9
Stephenson	.994	21	152	5	1	8

Second Base	PCT	G	PO	A	E	DP
De Los Santos	.959	55	90	120	9	28
O. Gonzalez	.765	2	5	8	4	1
Palacios	1.000	5	6	13	0	5
Torrealba	.974	14	31	44	2	11

Third Base	PCT	G	PO	A	E	DP
O. Gonzalez	.935	15	10	33	3	3
Guanipa	.893	13	7	18	3	0
Palacios	.938	52	51	115	11	12

Shortstop	PCT	G	PO	A	E	DP
Palacios	.935	20	33	53	6	10
Torrealba	.924	54	86	170	21	30

Outfield	PCT	G	PO	A	E	DP
Caldera	—	1	0	0	0	0
Castillo	.992	64	107	12	1	2
A. Espinoza	.892	25	29	4	4	0
I. Espinoza	.964	41	51	2	2	0
J. Gonzalez	.875	11	13	1	2	0
O. Gonzalez	1.000	3	3	0	0	0
Salas	.976	63	115	6	3	2
Stephenson	.826	22	19	0	4	0

Florida Marlins

BY MIKE BERARDINO

A season that began with lefthander Scott Olsen suggesting the Marlins rotation could produce 80 combined victories—16 apiece—instead fell to pieces amid a torrent of injuries and under performance.

Sixty percent of the game's brightest young rotation landed on the disabled list, with righthanders Josh Johnson (elbow reconstruction) and Anibal Sanchez (shoulder) succumbing to season-ending surgeries. In addition, promising righthander Ricky Nolasco worked just 55 innings (including the minors) due to elbow problems.

That trio went from 33 wins in 2006 to three in 2007.

Even the holdovers who managed to stay healthy struggled to put up decent numbers. Olsen and staff leader Dontrelle Willis made a combined 68 starts but together went 20-30, 5.47. Olsen also struggled through a midseason arrest and alcohol-related charges. He later received counseling and vowed to put his career back on track.

As a result, the Marlins saw their starters combine to go 42-63, 5.58—the worst mark in the majors.

A year after they won 78 games and chased a wild-card spot to the season's final two weeks, the Marlins slumped to 71 wins and fifth place in the NL East. It was their first appearance in last place since the dark days of 1999. First-year manager Fredi Gonzalez remembered that year all too well. He was third-base coach for John Boles, but the pain of 2007 was much worse for the ever-optimistic Gonzalez.

Not only was he trying to establish himself in the dugout after four years on the Braves' big league staff, but he was attempting to follow a popular figure in the fired Joe Girardi, who became the first NL Manager of the Year not to return the following season. Gonzalez seemed to hold up well throughout the season and the Marlins even got a chance to play spoiler on the final weekend when they knocked the Mets out of the playoffs.

Yet there were still individual bright spots in 2007.

Reigning NL Rookie of the Year Hanley Ramirez turned in an even better season. He threatened to join the rare 50 double/50 stolen base club before falling two doubles short, but he led the team in runs created and solidified his place as one of the game's most exciting young players. He did all this despite a nagging shoulder injury that required surgery at season's end.

Third baseman Miguel Cabrera put up another big season, pounding out careers bests of 34 home runs and 119 RBIs. He has driven in at least 112 runs in each of his four full seasons.

Second baseman Dan Uggla increased his home run total by four, finishing with 31 and a .479 slugging percentage. Left fielder Josh Willingham produced solid numbers for the second straight year, and right fielder Jeremy Hermida, after an injury-plagued first half, turned in a strong final two months.

On the mound, righthander Kevin Gregg stepped into the closer's void created by Jorge Julio's failure and finished with 32 saves in 36 chances. Righthanded set-up man Matt Lindstrom, voted the team's top rookie by South Florida baseball writers, posted a 3.09 ERA.

Loria also made the impressive move of locking up his entire baseball operations staff through 2015. As the offseason began, he announced GM Larry Beinfest would be promoted to president of baseball operations, assistant

PLAYERS OF THE YEAR

MAJOR LEAGUE: MIGUEL CABRERA, 3B

Cabrera and shortstop Hanley Ramirez formed perhaps the most offensively potent left side of the infield in 2007. Cabrera hit .320/.401/.565, and his 34 home runs tied for fifth in the National League. Cabrera led the team in on-base percentage and slugging, as well as RBIs (119) and walks (79). His 332 total bases ranked fifth in the NL.

MINOR LEAGUE: RICK VANDEN HURK, RHP

Vanden Hurk cruised through Double-A, but struggled in his first major league season. Still, Vanden Hurk's minor league numbers were inspiring. He struck out 61 in 53 2/3 innings for Double-A Carolina, posting a 3.52 ERA along the way. He also struck out 14 in 12 innings for Triple-A Albuquerque.

ORGANIZATIONAL LEADERS

BATTING		★Minimum 250 at-bats
★AVG	Raynor, John, Greensboro	.333
R	Raynor, John, Greensboro	110
H	Andino, Robert, Albuquerque	166
TB	Seabol, Scott, Albuquerque	290
2B	Sanchez, Gaby, Jupiter	40
3B	Andino, Robert, Albuquerque	13
HR	Pascucci, Valentino, Albuquerque	34
RBI	Seabol, Scott, Albuquerque	105
BB	Mitchell, Lee, Carolina	72
SO	Mitchell, Lee, Carolina	153
SB	Raynor, John, Greensboro	54
★OBP	Raynor, John, Greensboro	.429
★SLG	Abercrombie, Reggie, Albuquerque	.584
PITCHING		^Minimum 75 innings
W	Taylor, Graham, Greensboro/Jupiter	12
	Volstad, Christopher, Jupiter/Carolina	12
L	Three players tied at	11
^ERA	Taylor, Graham, Greensboro/Jupiter	2.99
G	Garcia, Harvey, Carolina/Albuquerque	60
CG	McCall, Derell, Greensboro/Jupiter	3
CG	Taylor, Graham, Greensboro/Jupiter	3
SV	Doolittle, Todd, Jupiter	28
IP	Taylor, Graham, Greensboro/Jupiter	174
BB	George, Chris, Albuquerque	68
SO	Taylor, Graham, Greensboro/Jupiter	138
^AVG	Taylor, Graham, Greensboro/Jupiter	.232

GM Michael Hill moving up to general manager while player personnel vice president Dan Jennings and scouting and development VP Jim Fleming received identical extensions.

In the minors, the Marlins again struggled to produce victories as many of their top prospects were pushed along or even promoted to the majors. The farm system went 323-367 (.468), with no affiliates reaching the playoffs.

On draft day, the Marlins picked 12th and added a player who could be Cabrera's eventual successor: California prep third baseman Matt Dominguez. They signed Dominguez for $1.8 million just before the Aug. 15 deadline.

The Marlins have never failed to sign their top draft pick, a streak dating to their first draft in 1992.

2007 PERFORMANCE

General Manager: Larry Beinfest. **Farm Director:** Brian Chattin. **Scouting Director:** Stan Meek

Class	Team	League	W	L	PCT	Finish*	Manager	Affiliate Since
Majors	Florida	National	71	91	.438	14th (16)	Fredi Gonzalez	—
Triple-A	Albuquerque Isotopes	Pacific Coast	72	70	.507	8th (16)	Dean Treanor	2003
Double-A	Carolina Mudcats	Southern	60	80	.429	10th (10)	Brandon Hyde	2003
High A	Jupiter Hammerheads	Florida State	63	76	.453	9th (12)	Luis Dorante	2002
Low A	Greensboro Grasshoppers	South Atlantic	71	69	.507	8th (16)	Edwin Rodriguez	2003
Short-season	Jamestown Jammers	New York-Penn	28	47	.373	13th (14)	Daren Everson	2002
Rookie	GCL Marlins	Gulf Coast	29	25	.537	7th (16)	Tim Cossins	1992
Overall 2007 Minor League Record			**323**	**367**	**.468**	**XXth**		

* Finish in overall standings (No. of teams in league) ^League champion

ORGANIZATION STATISTICS

FLORIDA MARLINS

NATIONAL LEAGUE

BATTING	B-T	HT	WT	DOB	AVG	vLH	vRH	G	AB	R	H	2B	3B	HR	RBI	BB	HBP	SH	SF	SO	SB	CS	SLG	OBP
Abercrombie, Reggie	R-R	6-3	215	7-15-81	.197	.162	.231	35	76	16	15	3	0	2	5	2	2	0	0	22	7	1	.316	.238
Amezaga, Alfredo	B-R	5-10	180	1-16-78	.263	.224	.269	133	400	46	105	14	9	2	30	35	4	4	5	52	13	7	.358	.324
Andino, Robert	R-R	6-0	170	4-25-84	.385	.333	.400	7	13	0	5	1	0	0	0	0	0	0	0	2	0	0	.462	.385
Boone, Aaron	R-R	6-2	200	3-9-73	.286	.213	.310	69	189	27	54	11	0	5	28	21	13	1	4	41	2	0	.423	.388
Borchard, Joe	B-R	6-4	230	11-25-78	.196	.188	.197	85	179	20	35	9	0	4	19	21	2	0	0	60	4	0	.313	.287
Cabrera, Miguel	R-R	6-4	240	4-18-83	.320	.364	.309	157	588	91	188	38	2	34	119	79	5	1	7	127	2	1	.565	.401
Carroll, Brett	R-R	6-0	190	10-3-82	.184	.240	.125	23	49	10	9	1	0	0	2	3	0	1	0	15	0	0	.204	.231
De Aza, Alejandro	L-L	6-0	175	4-11-84	.229	.313	.205	45	144	14	33	8	2	0	8	6	1	5	2	37	2	0	.313	.261
Gall, John	R-R	6-0	195	4-2-78	.000	.000	.000	3	4	0	0	0	0	0	0	0	1	0	0	1	0	0	.000	.200
Hermida, Jeremy	L-R	6-3	210	1-30-84	.296	.292	.297	123	429	54	127	32	1	18	63	47	4	1	3	105	3	4	.501	.369
Hoover, Paul	R-R	6-1	210	4-14-76	.375	.667	.200	3	8	1	3	0	0	0	0	0	0	0	0	2	0	0	.375	.375
Jacobs, Mike	L-R	6-3	215	10-30-80	.265	.290	.257	114	426	57	113	27	2	17	54	31	2	0	1	101	1	2	.458	.317
Linden, Todd	B-R	6-3	220	6-30-80	.271	.225	.270	85	129	15	35	7	1	1	8	14	1	0	0	36	4	0	.364	.347
2-team (30 San Francisco)					.245	—	—	115	184	21	45	8	1	1	11	19	1	0	0	59	4	0	.315	.319
Olivo, Miguel	R-R	6-0	220	7-15-78	.237	.295	.221	122	452	43	107	20	4	16	60	14	2	0	1	123	3	2	.405	.262
Ramirez, Hanley	R-R	6-3	200	12-23-83	.332	.399	.312	154	639	125	212	48	6	29	81	52	7	4	4	95	51	14	.562	.386
Reed, Eric	L-L	6-0	170	12-2-80	.100	.000	.118	18	20	3	2	0	0	0	1	0	0	0	6	1	0	.100	.143
Ross, Cody	R-L	5-9	205	12-23-80	.335	.385	.306	66	173	35	58	19	0	12	39	20	3	0	1	38	2	0	.653	.411
Treanor, Matt	R-R	6-0	210	3-3-76	.269	.245	.280	55	171	16	46	7	1	4	19	19	5	2	1	29	0	0	.392	.357
Uggla, Dan	R-R	5-11	200	3-11-80	.245	.245	.245	159	632	113	155	49	3	31	88	68	13	4	11	167	2	1	.479	.326
Willingham, Josh	R-R	6-2	215	2-17-79	.265	.218	.281	144	521	75	138	32	4	21	89	66	16	0	1	122	8	1	.463	.364
Wood, Jason	R-R	6-1	170	12-16-69	.239	.244	.236	98	117	11	28	6	0	3	26	8	0	1	1	38	0	0	.368	.286

PITCHING	B-T	HT	WT	DOB	W	L	ERA	G	GS	CG	SV	IP	H	R	ER	HR	BB	SO	AVG	vLH	vRH	K/9	BB/9
Barone, Daniel	R-R	6-2	185	4-24-83	1	3	5.71	16	6	0	0	41	50	29	26	11	19	18	.311	.258	.347	3.95	4.17
Benitez, Armando	R-R	6-4	260	11-3-72	2	5	5.73	36	0	0	9	33	32	28	21	5	20	39	.258	.255	.260	10.64	5.45
2-team (19 San Francisco)					2	8	5.36	55	0	0	9	50	49	37	30	8	29	57	—	—	—	10.19	5.19
Carvajal, Marcos	R-R	6-4	175	8-19-84	0	0	6.75	3	0	0	0	4	8	4	3	0	2	2	.381	.364	.400	4.50	4.50
Field, Nate	R-R	6-2	205	12-11-75	0	0	27.00	1	0	0	0	1	3	3	3	0	1	2	.500	.750	.000	18.00	9.00
Garcia, Harvey	R-R	6-2	170	3-16-84	0	1	4.38	8	0	0	0	12	14	6	6	3	7	15	.298	.409	.200	10.95	5.11
Gardner, Lee	R-R	6-0	220	1-16-75	3	4	1.94	62	0	0	2	74	72	19	16	2	18	52	.254	.308	.208	6.30	2.18
Gregg, Kevin	R-R	6-6	240	6-20-78	0	5	3.54	74	0	0	32	84	63	34	33	7	40	87	.206	.162	.247	9.32	4.29
Johnson, Josh	L-R	6-7	230	1-31-84	0	3	7.47	4	4	0	0	16	26	17	13	1	12	14	.388	.419	.361	8.04	6.89
Julio, Jorge	R-R	6-1	225	3-3-79	0	2	12.54	10	0	0	0	9	18	14	13	2	11	6	.400	.292	.524	5.79	10.61
2-team (58 Colorado)					0	5	5.23	68	0	0	0	62	68	39	36	8	31	56	—	—	—	8.13	4.50
Kensing, Logan	R-R	6-1	185	7-3-82	3	0	1.35	9	0	0	0	13	11	2	2	0	7	13	.224	.250	.190	8.78	4.73
Kim, Byung-Hyun	R-R	5-9	175	1-19-79	9	5	5.42	23	19	0	0	110	114	74	66	17	62	102	.266	.296	.235	8.37	5.09
3-team (2 Arizona, 3 Colorado)			10		86.08	28	22	0	0	118	131	90	80	20	68	107	—	—	—	8.14	5.17		
Lindstrom, Matt	R-R	6-4	210	2-11-80	3	4	3.09	71	0	0	0	67	66	27	23	2	21	62	.258	.263	.255	8.33	2.82
Martinez, Carlos	R-R	6-3	200	5-26-82	0	0	13.50	2	0	0	0	3	4	4	3	1	2	3	.333	.333	.333	6.75	3.38
Messenger, Randy	R-R	6-6	240	8-13-81	1	1	2.66	23	0	0	1	24	27	7	7	0	9	12	.303	.308	.300	4.56	3.42
2-team (37 San Francisco)					2	4	4.20	60	0	0	1	64	85	30	30	4	21	34	—	—	—	4.76	2.94
Miller, Justin	R-R	6-2	200	8-27-77	5	0	3.65	62	0	0	0	62	53	27	25	5	24	74	.228	.324	.184	10.80	3.50
Mitre, Sergio	R-R	6-3	225	2-16-81	5	8	4.65	27	27	0	0	149	180	88	77	9	41	80	.303	.271	.332	4.83	2.48
Nolasco, Ricky	R-R	6-2	220	12-13-82	1	2	5.48	5	4	0	0	21	26	16	13	3	9	11	.321	.293	.350	4.64	3.80
Obermueller, Wes	R-R	6-2	210	12-22-76	2	3	6.56	18	7	0	0	59	72	49	43	7	36	35	.306	.309	.304	5.34	5.49
Olsen, Scott	L-L	6-5	215	1-12-84	10	15	5.81	33	33	0	0	177	226	134	114	29	85	133	.315	.331	.311	6.78	4.33
Owens, Henry	R-R	6-3	230	4-23-79	2	0	1.96	22	0	0	4	23	19	7	5	3	10	16	.216	.262	.174	6.26	3.91
Pinto, Renyel	L-L	6-4	215	7-8-82	2	4	3.68	57	0	0	1	59	45	25	24	7	32	56	.222	.210	.227	8.59	4.91
Ramirez, Erasmo	L-L	6-0	190	4-29-76	0	0	5.40	4	0	0	0	3	4	2	2	0	2	1	.286	.286	.286	2.70	5.40
Sanchez, Anibal	R-R	6-0	180	2-27-84	2	1	4.80	6	6	0	0	30	43	17	16	3	19	14	.341	.329	.357	4.20	5.70
Seddon, Chris	L-L	6-3	220	10-13-83	0	2	8.83	7	4	0	0	17	29	19	17	2	5	10	.349	.214	.377	5.19	2.60
Tankersley, Taylor	L-L	6-1	220	3-7-83	6	1	3.99	67	0	0	1	47	42	22	21	4	29	49	.246	.179	.301	9.32	5.51
VandenHurk, Rick	R-R	6-5	195	5-22-85	4	6	6.83	18	17	0	0	82	94	63	62	15	48	82	.294	.289	.298	9.04	5.29
Willis, Dontrelle	L-L	6-4	225	1-12-82	10	15	5.17	35	35	0	0	205	241	131	118	29	87	146	.294	.123	.320	6.40	3.81
Wolf, Ross	R-R	6-0	180	10-18-82	0	1	11.68	14	0	0	0	12	24	16	16	4	3	6	.393	.269	.486	4.38	2.19
Wood, Jason	R-R	6-1	170	12-16-69	0	0	0.00	1	0	0	0	1	0	0	0	0	0	0	.000	.000	.000	0.00	0.00
Zarate, Mauro	R-R	6-1	180	2-8-83	0	0	10.80	4	0	0	0	5	11	7	6	3	1	3	.393	.333	.438	5.40	1.80

FIELDING

Catcher	PCT	G	PO	A	E	DP	PB
Hoover	1.000	2	12	0	0	0	0
Olivo	.986	119	787	64	12	9	16
Treanor	.993	53	385	16	3	2	3

First Base	PCT	G	PO	A	E	DP
Amezaga	1.000	4	4	1	0	0
Boone	.987	48	352	26	5	34
Hoover	1.000	1	1	0	0	0
Jacobs	.992	108	793	45	7	91
Wood	.976	45	112	10	3	16

Second Base	PCT	G	PO	A	E	DP
Amezaga	.955	11	21	21	2	7
Uggla	.985	158	323	402	11	111

	PCT	G	PO	A	E	DP
Wood	1.000	2	2	0	0	1
Third Base						
Amezaga	1.000	12	11	6	0	0
Boone	1.000	12	6	9	0	0
Cabrera	.941	154	100	266	23	33
Wood	1.000	7	1	1	0	0
Shortstop						
Amezaga	.981	18	16	35	1	4
Andino	1.000	3	3	4	0	1
Ramirez	.963	151	225	392	24	98
Outfield						
Abercrombie	.984	19	60	2	1	0
Amezaga	.978	91	211	8	5	1

	PCT	G	PO	A	E	DP
Borchard	.979	46	93	1	2	1
Carroll	.958	20	45	1	2	1
De Aza	.989	35	85	3	1	0
Gall	1.000	1	1	0	0	0
Hermida	.966	116	247	7	9	1
Linden	1.000	30	40	0	0	0
Reed	1.000	4	4	0	0	0
Ross	.974	61	109	5	3	4
Willingham	.987	137	211	9	3	0
Wood	—	1	0	0	0	0

ALBUQUERQUE ISOTOPES   TRIPLE-A
PACIFIC COAST LEAGUE

BATTING	B-T	HT	WT	DOB	AVG	vLH	vRH	G	AB	R	H	2B	3B	HR	RBI	BB	HBP	SH	SF	SO	SB	CS	SLG	OBP
Abercrombie, Reggie	R-R	6-3	215	7-15-81	.323	.291	.333	93	353	71	114	23	9	17	55	11	11	2	2	95	41	6	.584	.361
Andino, Robert	R-R	6-0	170	4-25-84	.278	.297	.270	142	598	85	166	25	13	13	50	40	1	2	3	129	21	13	.428	.322
Arlis, Patrick	R-R	6-0	215	12-18-80	.000	.000	.000	1	2	0	0	0	0	0	0	1	0	0	0	0	0	0	.000	.333
Ashby, Chris	R-R	6-2	215	12-15-74	.224	.262	.198	51	152	19	34	6	0	5	23	24	0	0	1	30	0	1	.362	.328
Baker, John	L-R	6-1	210	1-20-81	.285	.254	.294	89	270	35	77	15	0	8	41	28	4	0	1	58	2	0	.430	.360
Beattie, Andrew	B-R	5-8	175	2-28-78	.277	.314	.269	74	206	34	57	8	2	13	46	34	1	1	3	58	6	4	.524	.377
Borchard, Joe	B-R	6-4	230	11-25-78	.355	.235	.390	22	76	19	27	3	0	8	28	15	0	0	2	12	1	2	.711	.452
Carroll, Brett	R-R	6-0	190	10-3-82	.314	.391	.286	88	318	60	100	21	6	19	70	18	7	0	3	69	0	4	.597	.361
Davis, Brad	R-R	6-2	185	12-29-82	.500	—	.500	1	2	0	1	1	0	0	1	1	0	0	0	0	0	0	1.000	.667
Gall, John	R-R	6-0	195	4-2-78	.300	.325	.291	113	413	75	124	28	3	13	58	38	3	0	2	49	10	4	.477	.362
Hermansen, Chad	R-R	6-2	190	9-10-77	.283	.292	.279	89	293	46	83	15	3	9	44	30	3	1	3	84	9	2	.447	.353
2-team (27 New Orleans)					.281	—	—	116	392	56	110	19	3	11	57	38	4	1	4	112	11	3	.429	.347
Hermida, Jeremy	L-R	6-3	210	1-30-84	.200	.000	.250	2	5	1	1	0	0	0	0	2	1	0	0	1	0	0	.200	.286
Hoover, Paul	R-R	6-1	210	4-14-76	.292	.321	.279	31	96	11	28	7	1	4	21	7	0	0	2	18	0	1	.510	.333
Labandeira, Josh	R-R	5-7	180	2-25-79	.301	.328	.284	93	292	33	88	19	1	2	35	28	4	3	2	54	1	4	.394	.368
Linden, Todd	B-R	6-3	220	6-30-80	.375	.389	.367	14	48	10	18	3	1	1	10	8	1	0	0	12	0	1	.542	.474
Martinez, Sandy	L-R	6-0	240	10-8-70	.000	.000	.000	3	9	0	0	0	0	0	0	1	0	0	0	2	0	0	.000	.100
Moore, Frank	L-R	6-2	213	7-2-78	.358	.333	.366	28	53	8	19	4	1	0	6	5	0	1	0	10	0	2	.472	.414
Pascucci, Valentino	R-R	6-6	235	11-17-78	.284	.313	.275	132	447	93	127	27	1	34	98	67	12	0	3	123	9	1	.577	.389
Phillips, Jason	R-R	6-1	220	9-27-76	.185	.200	.176	8	27	2	5	0	0	0	2	5	0	0	1	2	0	0	.185	.179
Raburn, John	B-R	6-0	164	2-16-79	.292	.357	.265	21	48	10	14	4	0	0	6	6	0	0	0	5	2	1	.375	.370
Reed, Eric	L-L	6-0	170	12-2-80	.285	.203	.311	95	302	54	86	10	12	0	20	17	2	7	4	58	30	3	.397	.323
Seabol, Scott	R-R	6-4	200	5-17-75	.300	.369	.276	139	503	100	151	29	7	32	105	56	2	2	10	95	6	2	.577	.366
Sears, Todd	L-R	6-6	205	10-23-75	.302	.353	.283	33	63	8	19	4	0	1	10	13	0	0	1	10	1	1	.413	.416
Sorensen, Zach	B-R	6-0	190	1-3-77	.227	.333	.211	11	22	2	5	0	0	0	1	8	0	1	0	4	0	1	.227	.433

PITCHING	B-T	HT	WT	DOB	W	L	ERA	G	GS	CG	SV	IP	H	R	ER	HR	BB	SO	AVG	vLH	vRH	K/9	BB/9
Barone, Daniel	R-R	6-2	185	4-24-83	7	0	4.09	10	10	0	0	62	60	30	28	6	14	31	.256	.289	.221	4.52	2.04
Baugh, Kenny	R-R	6-4	190	2-5-79	7	9	8.19	21	19	1	0	97	134	95	88	14	60	59	.333	.340	.326	5.49	5.59
Beattie, Andrew	B-R	5-8	175	2-28-78	0	0	0.00	3	0	0	0	3	2	0	0	0	0	1	.200	.000	.286	3.38	0.00
Corcoran, Roy	R-R	5-10	175	5-11-80	4	4	3.54	53	0	0	15	61	63	30	24	1	33	52	.270	.294	.250	7.67	4.87
Dorman, Rich	R-R	6-2	210	9-30-78	1	1	5.06	8	0	0	2	16	15	10	9	1	5	15	.246	.286	.158	8.44	2.81
Etherton, Seth	R-R	6-1	200	10-17-76	0	2	7.88	2	2	0	0	8	17	12	7	5	4	4	.436	.417	.467	4.50	4.50
Field, Nate	R-R	6-2	205	12-11-75	6	6	3.50	44	0	0	11	46	37	20	18	6	17	45	.211	.268	.161	8.74	3.30
Fulchino, Jeff	R-R	6-5	250	11-26-79	6	6	5.83	16	16	0	0	88	108	63	57	13	39	55	.298	.352	.253	5.62	3.99
Garcia, Harvey	R-R	6-2	170	3-16-84	4	1	6.19	42	0	0	1	48	59	35	33	9	22	45	.303	.325	.288	8.44	4.12
Gardner, Lee	R-R	6-0	220	1-16-75	0	2	4.73	9	0	0	1	13	10	8	7	0	2	10	.222	.200	.240	6.07	1.35
George, Chris	L-L	6-2	185	9-16-79	7	11	5.56	26	26	0	0	139	157	94	86	21	68	95	.287	.288	.286	6.14	4.39
Julianel, Ben	B-L	6-2	180	9-4-79	2	2	6.23	27	1	0	0	39	49	32	27	4	22	34	.310	.224	.374	7.85	5.08
Kensing, Logan	R-R	6-1	185	7-3-82	0	1	4.00	8	0	0	0	9	7	4	4	0	7	8	.212	.222	.208	8.00	7.00
Labandeira, Josh	R-R	5-7	180	2-25-79	0	0	0.00	2	0	0	0	2	1	0	0	0	1	0	.143	.250	.000	9.00	0.00
Martinez, Carlos	R-R	6-3	200	5-26-82	0	0	6.75	3	0	0	0	1	3	1	1	0	1	2	.429	.500	.400	13.50	6.75
McGinley, Blake	R-L	6-1	175	8-2-78	0	0	10.80	1	0	0	0	5	6	3	3	0	3	2	.409	.400	.412	3.60	3.60
Mildren, Paul	R-L	6-1	195	5-3-84	5	7	5.86	21	21	0	0	106	115	78	69	16	52	65	.282	.254	.296	5.52	4.42
2-team (3 Omaha)					6	8	6.28	24	24	0	0	119	135	92	83	18	60	76	—	—	—	5.75	4.54
Miller, Justin	R-R	6-2	200	8-27-77	0	0	1.50	11	0	0	6	12	9	3	2	0	4	20	.196	.200	.192	15.00	3.00
Mobley, Chris	R-R	5-11	170	8-16-83	0	0	3.00	1	0	0	0	3	2	1	1	0	1	2	.200	.250	.167	6.00	3.00
Molldrem, Craig	R-R	6-6	205	9-17-81	0	0	3.00	6	0	0	0	9	11	6	3	0	3	5	.275	.333	.250	5.00	3.00
Nolasco, Ricky	R-R	6-2	220	12-13-82	0	2	14.09	4	4	0	0	15	29	26	24	6	4	15	.392	.516	.302	8.80	2.35
Obermueller, Wes	R-R	6-2	210	12-22-76	4	1	4.55	11	11	0	0	63	67	36	32	6	27	45	.271	.252	.295	6.39	3.84
Ramirez, Erasmo	L-L	6-0	190	4-29-76	2	1	3.74	22	0	0	1	22	27	10	9	3	4	10	.314	.278	.340	4.15	1.66
2-team (19 Sacramento)					5	1	2.51	41	0	0	3	43	45	13	12	3	6	21	—	—	—	4.40	1.26
Rodriguez, Eddy	R-R	6-1	215	8-8-81	0	1	12.00	2	0	0	0	3	5	4	4	0	1	3	.357	.375	.333	9.00	3.00
Rodriguez, Ricardo	L-R	6-3	190	5-21-78	2	4	6.43	14	10	0	0	56	78	44	40	5	14	31	.331	.301	.369	4.98	2.25
Serrano, Jimmy	R-R	5-10	170	5-9-74	1	1	9.00	4	0	0	0	13	22	16	13	4	5	9	.373	.300	.410	6.23	3.46
Silva, Jesus	R-R	6-0	199	12-24-82	0	1	5.68	3	2	0	0	19	21	12	12	4	6	3	.276	.302	.242	3.79	1.42
Tankersley, Taylor	L-L	6-1	220	3-7-83	0	1	4.76	7	0	0	0	6	3	3	3	1	2	5	.167	.167	.167	7.94	3.18
Ungs, Nic	R-R	6-2	220	9-3-79	5	5	4.98	29	18	0	1	112	122	73	62	17	45	66	.282	.252	.306	5.30	3.62
VandenHurk, Rick	R-R	6-5	195	5-22-85	2	0	2.25	2	2	0	0	12	6	3	3	3	4	14	.150	.167	.136	10.50	3.00
Villafuerte, Brandon	R-R	5-11	195	12-17-75	1	0	0.00	3	0	0	0	3	1	0	0	0	0	3	.091	.000	.200	8.10	0.00
Wolf, Ross	R-R	6-0	180	10-18-82	4	3	3.42	45	0	0	2	47	54	24	18	5	17	23	.293	.294	.293	4.37	3.23
Young, Chris	R-R	6-4	218	4-19-81	0	2	6.17	32	0	0	0	35	51	32	24	6	12	13	.325	.292	.353	3.34	3.09
Yourkin, Matt	R-L	6-3	225	7-4-81	0	0	2.92	26	0	0	0	25	26	12	8	0	11	16	.268	.409	.151	5.84	4.01
Zarate, Mauro	R-R	6-1	180	2-8-83	2	0	2.38	25	0	0	0	34	29	9	9	2	12	23	.238	.241	.234	6.09	3.18

ORGANIZATION STATISTICS

FIELDING

Catcher	PCT	G	PO	A	E	DP	PB
Arlis	1.000	1	7	1	0	0	0
Ashby	.986	36	203	14	3	1	12
Baker	.986	77	391	35	6	3	7
Davis	1.000	1	4	1	0	0	0
Hoover	.989	29	168	13	2	2	1
Martinez	1.000	3	20	1	0	0	0
Phillips	1.000	8	65	3	0	0	0

First Base	PCT	G	PO	A	E	DP
Abercrombie	1.000	1	5	1	0	0
Ashby	1.000	9	51	3	0	4
Baker	1.000	3	10	0	0	0
Gall	.983	29	162	13	3	15
Moore	.958	4	23	0	1	4
Pascucci	.994	112	934	77	6	104
Seabol	—	1	0	0	0	0
Sears	.977	5	40	2	1	6

Second Base	PCT	G	PO	A	E	DP
Andino	.833	1	1	4	1	0
Beattie	.966	60	104	148	9	43
Labandeira	.972	77	132	216	10	46
Moore	1.000	7	9	19	0	3
Raburn	.953	11	19	22	2	5
Seabol	1.000	1	1	0	0	0
Sorensen	.947	9	10	26	2	5

Third Base	PCT	G	PO	A	E	DP
Hoover	—	1	0	0	0	0
Labandeira	.923	11	2	22	2	1
Pascucci	—	1	0	0	0	0
Seabol	.957	136	105	247	16	31

Shortstop	PCT	G	PO	A	E	DP
Andino	.950	141	226	402	33	88
Labandeira	.963	9	13	13	1	5

Outfield	PCT	G	PO	A	E	DP
Abercrombie	.945	86	144	10	9	2
Ashby	.800	4	8	0	2	0
Borchard	.969	19	30	1	1	0
Carroll	.972	86	191	14	6	4
Gall	.993	85	144	2	1	0
Hermansen	.977	66	124	1	3	0
Hermida	1.000	1	1	0	0	0
Linden	1.000	13	33	1	0	0
Moore	1.000	2	4	0	0	0
Pascucci	1.000	1	1	0	0	0
Raburn	.667	4	2	0	1	0
Reed	.987	85	232	4	3	3

CAROLINA MUDCATS   DOUBLE-A

SOUTHERN LEAGUE

BATTING	B-T	HT	WT	DOB	AVG	vLH	vRH	G	AB	R	H	2B	3B	HR	RBI	BB	HBP	SH	SF	SO	SB	CS	SLG	OBP
Arlis, Patrick	R-R	6-0	215	12-18-80	.087	.059	.103	15	46	0	4	1	0	0	2	7	0	1	1	16	0	1	.109	.204
Bear, Ryan	R-R	6-2	220	1-26-81	.255	.336	.211	112	357	47	91	18	0	10	50	34	6	2	3	82	3	1	.389	.328
Brinkley, Dante	R-R	5-11	180	8-21-81	.257	.258	.257	95	311	47	80	18	1	11	33	30	12	0	1	114	15	7	.428	.345
Campusano, Jose	B-R	5-11	165	12-19-83	.259	.200	.273	35	108	15	28	3	2	1	2	3	1	1	0	26	9	2	.352	.286
Carroll, Brett	R-R	6-0	190	10-3-82	.270	.226	.290	30	100	9	27	13	0	3	12	12	3	0	2	20	0	2	.490	.359
Davis, Brad	R-R	6-2	185	12-29-82	.287	.297	.283	45	150	13	43	16	1	3	20	18	2	2	1	39	0	1	.467	.368
De Aza, Alejandro	L-L	6-0	175	4-11-84	.350	.667	.294	5	20	7	7	2	0	2	3	3	0	0	0	2	0	0	.750	.435
Harrison, Vince	R-R	5-11	222	11-29-79	.264	.362	.159	40	91	10	24	4	0	3	15	9	1	0	1	14	1	1	.407	.333
Hayes, Brett	R-R	6-1	200	2-13-84	.234	.313	.209	74	273	22	64	16	0	3	31	18	0	2	2	51	2	0	.326	.280
Jacobs, Mike	L-R	6-3	215	10-30-80	.300	.250	.333	4	10	1	3	0	0	1	2	0	0	0	0	3	0	0	.600	.300
Lambin, Chase	B-R	6-2	195	7-7-79	.283	.222	.308	116	434	64	123	31	6	15	59	45	5	5	5	111	3	6	.486	.354
McCann, Brad	R-R	6-3	190	12-9-82	.250	.167	.286	10	20	3	5	0	0	2	3	0	0	0	1	9	0	0	.550	.238
Miller, Jai	R-R	6-4	195	1-17-85	.261	.273	.255	129	406	54	106	26	2	14	58	55	5	4	3	127	12	5	.438	.354
Mitchell, Lee	R-R	6-1	198	4-21-82	.282	.216	.309	135	451	73	127	29	2	20	73	72	13	0	3	153	2	1	.488	.393
Moore, Frank	L-R	6-2	213	7-2-78	.225	.208	.228	70	182	21	41	9	1	4	23	17	0	3	3	49	2	0	.352	.287
Ochoa, Brad	R-R	6-0	180	9-5-85	.200	.250	.000	3	5	1	1	0	0	0	1	0	0	0	2	0	0	.200	.333
Psomas, Grant	R-R	6-3	210	9-2-82	.238	.168	.271	129	442	66	105	28	4	18	57	53	10	0	4	119	9	6	.441	.330
Purdom, John	R-R	6-2	230	5-28-81	.257	.300	.240	15	35	3	9	1	0	1	10	3	0	0	2	6	0	0	.371	.300
2-team (1 Chattanooga)					.231	—		16	39	4	9	1	0	1	10	3	0	0	2	7	0	0	.333	.273
Raburn, John	R-R	6-0	164	2-16-79	.241	.215	.251	96	324	48	78	9	5	2	23	44	3	1	1	61	20	5	.318	.336
Randel, Kevin	L-R	6-1	180	6-11-81	.184	.118	.209	42	125	13	23	8	0	2	7	27	1	0	0	43	4	1	.296	.333
Riggs, Eric	B-R	6-2	190	8-19-76	.293	.260	.304	81	297	54	87	25	5	11	50	33	7	4	2	44	3	3	.522	.375
Rundgren, Rex	R-R	6-1	170	11-20-80	.208	.200	.212	86	250	22	52	4	1	2	21	16	0	5	4	48	1	3	.256	.252

PITCHING	B-T	HT	WT	DOB	W	L	ERA	G	GS	CG	SV	IP	H	R	ER	HR	BB	SO	AVG	vLH	vRH	K/9	BB/9
Barone, Daniel	R-R	6-2	185	4-24-83	1	3	3.86	13	13	0	0	75	68	35	32	7	18	60	.245	.240	.249	7.23	2.17
Brauer, James	R-R	6-4	210	7-16-82	0	3	4.02	6	4	0	0	16	20	8	7	1	5	8	.317	.333	.308	4.60	2.87
Delgado, Jesus	R-R	6-1	200	4-19-84	5	7	4.80	31	16	0	1	94	97	59	50	6	45	75	.266	.302	.239	7.21	4.32
Dorman, Rich	R-R	6-2	210	9-30-78	0	0	1.80	5	0	0	0	5	1	1	1	0	4	5	.067	.125	.000	9.00	7.20
Garcia, Harvey	R-R	6-2	170	3-16-84	2	2	4.07	18	0	0	0	24	21	14	11	3	17	25	.231	.273	.207	9.25	6.29
Gogal, Jeff	R-L	6-2	195	6-10-82	0	0	10.12	2	0	0	0	3	5	3	3	0	2	5	.417	.200	.571	16.88	6.75
Hernandez, Gaby	R-R	6-3	215	5-21-86	9	11	4.22	28	28	1	0	154	144	87	72	14	56	113	.245	.269	.225	6.62	3.28
Johnson, Josh	L-R	6-7	230	1-31-84	0	0	1.74	2	2	0	0	10	8	2	2	0	5	9	.216	.273	.192	7.84	4.35
Julianel, Ben	B-L	6-2	180	9-4-79	0	0	3.68	9	1	0	0	15	11	6	6	2	6	17	.204	.167	.222	10.43	3.68
Kensing, Logan	R-R	6-1	185	7-3-82	0	0	3.00	3	0	0	0	3	2	1	1	0	1	6	.182	.000	.250	18.00	3.00
Koehler, Kurt	R-R	6-1	190	9-5-84	1	1	6.12	21	0	0	5	25	29	18	17	0	11	10	.296	.265	.313	3.60	3.96
Letson, Wes	L-L	6-0	200	9-13-82	0	0	0.00	5	0	0	0	5	5	0	0	0	3	3	.278	.286	.273	5.79	5.79
Martinez, Carlos	R-R	6-3	200	5-26-82	1	1	3.38	19	0	0	0	21	21	12	8	2	5	18	.247	.382	.157	7.59	2.11
McGinley, Blake	R-L	6-1	175	8-2-78	6	9	4.26	42	8	0	1	76	71	36	36	9	28	63	.249	.267	.239	7.46	3.32
Mobley, Chris	R-R	5-11	170	8-16-83	7	2	4.42	37	0	0	11	39	47	19	19	2	13	26	.311	.333	.291	6.05	3.03
Molldrem, Craig	R-R	6-0	205	9-17-81	5	4	4.84	47	0	0	0	61	59	38	33	7	36	49	.254	.326	.212	7.19	5.28
Nestor, Scott	R-R	6-4	225	8-20-84	2	4	4.44	58	0	0	1	75	65	44	37	5	41	86	.233	.220	.241	10.32	4.92
Nolasco, Ricky	R-R	6-2	220	12-13-82	0	1	6.00	1	1	0	0	3	2	3	2	0	1	2	.182	.000	.333	6.00	3.00
Olivera, Manuel	R-L	5-11	205	12-8-77	0	4	5.97	7	6	0	0	29	33	23	19	2	18	16	.311	.300	.314	5.02	5.65
Raburn, John	B-R	6-0	164	2-16-79	0	0	0.00	1	0	0	0	0	0	0	0	0	0	0	.000	—	.000	0.00	0.00
Rundgren, Rex	R-R	6-1	170	11-20-80	0	0	9.00	1	0	0	0	1	2	1	1	0	1	1	.500	1.000	.667	9.00	9.00
Russ, James	R-R	6-4	210	10-24-80	1	6	3.83	21	16	0	1	89	77	42	38	8	31	60	.237	.225	.246	6.04	3.12
Santos, Jarrett	R-R	6-4	215	8-18-81	3	1	3.32	22	2	0	0	43	49	17	16	4	20	26	.293	.222	.327	5.40	4.15
Seddon, Chris	L-L	6-3	220	10-13-83	3	6	4.33	14	14	0	0	69	65	37	33	6	25	58	.252	.235	.260	7.60	3.28
2-team (12 Montgomery)					6	10	4.64	26	26	0	0	140	136	77	72	13	48	98	—	—	—	6.32	3.09
Serrano, Jimmy	R-R	5-10	170	5-9-76	4	2	3.70	20	8	0	0	58	54	26	24	4	16	38	.248	.229	.265	5.86	2.47
Silva, Jesus	R-R	6-0	199	12-24-82	1	4	7.88	7	5	0	0	24	39	29	21	2	8	12	.364	.438	.305	4.50	3.00
Tyler, Scott	R-R	6-5	265	8-20-82	0	2	8.80	28	0	0	1	31	26	31	30	2	44	33	.230	.368	.160	9.68	12.91
VandenHurk, Rick	R-R	6-5	195	5-22-85	2	2	3.52	9	9	0	0	54	42	23	21	5	21	61	.219	.228	.212	10.23	3.52
Villafuerte, Brandon	R-R	5-11	195	9-17-75	0	0	0.87	9	0	0	4	10	8	2	1	0	1	6	.211	.313	.136	5.23	0.87
Volstad, Christopher	R-R	6-7	190	9-23-86	4	2	3.16	7	7	0	0	43	41	19	15	4	10	25	.252	.250	.253	5.27	2.11
Young, Chris	R-R	6-4	218	4-19-81	0	1	4.22	10	0	0	1	11	16	10	5	1	3	6	.333	.471	.258	5.06	2.53
Yourkin, Matt	R-L	6-3	225	7-4-81	1	1	5.29	26	0	0	0	32	33	21	19	3	13	32	.266	.208	.303	8.91	3.62
Zarate, Mauro	R-R	6-1	180	2-8-83	0	1	1.40	17	0	0	1	26	14	7	4	2	9	32	.152	.171	.137	11.22	3.16

FIELDING

Catcher	PCT	G	PO	A	E	DP	PB
Arlis	.991	14	101	11	1	3	2
Davis	.992	45	336	24	3	3	2
Hayes	.989	71	514	36	6	4	8
Ochoa	1.000	1	10	0	0	0	0
Purdom	.986	13	65	6	1	0	1

First Base	PCT	G	PO	A	E	DP
Bear	.980	5	47	1	1	2
Hayes	.917	1	10	1	1	1
Jacobs	.944	4	17	0	1	1
Lambin	1.000	1	0	1	0	0
McCann	1.000	5	33	2	0	1
Moore	1.000	12	73	3	0	5
Psomas	.993	114	927	91	7	80
Riggs	1.000	14	105	6	0	8

Second Base	PCT	G	PO	A	E	DP
Harrison	1.000	2	2	4	0	1
Lambin	.950	46	72	118	10	25
Moore	1.000	1	3	1	0	1
Raburn	1.000	9	19	16	0	2
Randel	.945	36	80	76	9	21
Rundgren	1.000	1	4	3	0	1

Third Base	PCT	G	PO	A	E	DP
Harrison	.750	4	3	3	2	0
Mitchell	.970	126	81	247	10	17
Moore	.750	4	1	2	1	0
Psomas	1.000	7	5	6	0	1
Randel	1.000	1	0	1	0	0
Riggs	1.000	5	4	7	0	0

Shortstop	PCT	G	PO	A	E	DP
Lambin	.945	57	76	147	13	31
Raburn	.949	18	22	52	4	10
Riggs	.938	3	5	10	1	3
Rundgren	.962	67	92	212	12	33

Outfield	PCT	G	PO	A	E	DP
Bear	.974	85	142	8	4	1
Brinkley	.984	76	116	4	2	1
Campusano	.946	27	49	4	3	1
Carroll	.969	30	59	4	2	3
De Aza	1.000	4	9	0	0	0
Harrison	1.000	11	12	1	0	0
Lambin	.923	5	12	1	1	0
Miller	.969	123	271	7	9	1
Moore	.971	32	33	0	1	0
Raburn	.981	58	100	4	2	0

JUPITER HAMMERHEADS

HIGH CLASS A

FLORIDA STATE LEAGUE

BATTING	B-T	HT	WT	DOB	AVG	vLH	vRH	G	AB	R	H	2B	3B	HR	RBI	BB	HBP	SH	SF	SO	SB	CS	SLG	OBP
Boone, Aaron	R-R	6-2	200	3-9-73	.000	—	.000	1	3	1	0	0	0	0	1	0	0	0	0	0	0	0	.000	.000
Brinkley, Dante	R-R	5-11	180	8-21-81	.349	.250	.387	12	43	11	15	2	0	5	12	6	2	0	0	12	4	2	.744	.451
Coghlan, Chris	L-R	6-1	190	6-18-85	.200	.103	.228	34	130	17	26	5	3	2	18	15	0	0	3	19	5	1	.331	.277
DAntonio, Trent	B-R	5-9	180	8-14-85	.285	.259	.290	57	151	20	43	5	0	0	12	24	2	4	0	32	7	4	.318	.390
Davis, Brad	R-R	6-2	185	12-29-82	.163	.300	.043	14	43	0	7	2	0	0	3	9	0	0	1	11	0	0	.209	.302
De Aza, Alejandro	L-L	6-0	175	4-11-84	.500	.500	.500	2	8	1	4	1	1	0	0	1	0	0	0	1	0	1	.875	.556
Fulton, Jonathan	R-R	6-4	200	12-1-83	.217	.212	.219	99	337	25	73	10	0	3	26	17	4	3	5	78	4	2	.273	.259
Gendron, Steve	R-R	6-3	195	11-25-81	.183	.200	.178	18	60	4	11	1	0	0	3	3	1	0	9	2	1	.200	.234
Guerrero, James	R-R	5-7	175	6-8-84	.242	.318	.198	56	182	26	44	7	0	2	19	35	3	3	2	33	3	5	.313	.369
Harrison, Vince	R-R	5-11	222	11-29-79	.297	.160	.367	22	74	8	22	1	0	2	13	5	0	1	3	12	0	0	.392	.329
Harvey, Kris	R-R	6-2	195	1-5-84	.238	.258	.229	116	420	52	100	16	3	12	55	34	6	4	5	100	6	3	.376	.301
Hayes, Brett	R-R	6-1	200	2-13-84	.338	.333	.341	17	65	10	22	3	1	1	11	9	0	0	1	10	2	3	.462	.413
Hermida, Jeremy	L-R	6-3	210	1-30-84	.333	.000	.364	3	12	4	4	0	1	2	5	1	0	0	4	0	01.000	.385
Jacobs, Mike	L-R	6-3	215	10-30-80	.167	.250	.125	3	12	2	2	0	0	1	3	1	0	0	2	0	0	.417	.231
Jenkins, Andrew	R-R	6-0	205	7-23-83	.289	.256	.303	112	425	51	123	20	3	4	54	24	1	1	4	74	1	1	.379	.326
Langley, Torre	R-R	5-9	175	10-9-87	.161	.250	.105	12	31	2	5	3	0	0	2	0	0	0	5	1	0	.258	.161
Martinez, Guillermo	R-R	6-0	180	10-5-84	.200	.000	.333	4	5	2	1	0	0	0	1	0	0	0	0	0	0	.200	.333
Martinez, Osvaldo	R-R	5-10	170	5-7-88	—	—	.000	1	0	0	0	0	0	0	0	1	0	0	0	0	0	0	—	1.000
McCann, Brad	R-R	6-3	190	12-9-82	.246	.263	.240	37	138	10	34	6	0	6	21	2	0	2	2	42	1	0	.420	.254
Molina, Angel	R-R	6-2	226	11-4-81	.253	.125	.299	29	91	10	23	8	0	1	12	14	3	0	0	18	0	1	.374	.370
Ontiveros, Emilio	R-R	5-11	170	1-2-85	.333	.333	.333	9	24	4	8	0	0	0	2	1	0	0	1	6	0	0	.333	.346
Piste, Carlos	B-R	6-1	179	3-8-85	.000	.000	.000	4	8	0	0	0	0	0	0	2	1	0	4	0	0	.000	.200
Purdom, John	R-R	6-2	230	5-28-81	.271	.267	.273	44	144	12	39	6	0	3	28	14	0	3	2	20	1	1	.375	.331
2-team (7 Sarasota)					.255	—		51	157	12	40	7	0	3	31	16	0	3	2	21	1	1	.357	.320
Randel, Kevin	L-R	6-1	180	6-11-81	.304	.256	.316	78	214	34	65	22	5	2	35	36	1	3	1	40	3	1	.537	.405
Restko, J.T.	R-R	6-5	190	12-15-84	.265	.235	.278	107	374	42	99	19	2	7	40	26	10	2	1	73	0	1	.382	.328
Roberson, Colin	R-R	6-5	205	7-15-83	.213	.214	.213	84	216	23	46	12	3	5	32	15	0	0	1	67	11	2	.366	.263
Ross, Cody	R-L	5-9	205	12-23-80	.261	1.000	.227	7	23	2	6	1	0	2	3	1	0	0	0	6	0	0	.565	.292
Sanchez, Gaby	R-R	6-2	225	9-2-83	.279	.288	.276	133	473	89	132	40	3	9	70	64	6	0	4	74	6	6	.433	.369
Scott Jr., Lorenzo	L-L	6-3	210	3-1-82	.258	.228	.268	132	399	74	103	15	5	4	31	47	5	10	1	120	38	14	.351	.343
Septimo, Agustin	L-R	5-11	170	5-27-84	.192	.212	.184	113	354	63	68	9	5	5	35	37	5	15	8	81	26	5	.288	.272
Taylor, JR	B-R	5-8	170	11-6-82	.223	.214	.227	37	103	15	23	3	0	0	3	22	0	4	0	16	2	3	.252	.360

PITCHING	B-T	HT	WT	DOB	W	L	ERA	G	GS	CG	SV	IP	H	R	ER	HR	BB	SO	AVG	vLH	vRH	K/9	BB/9
Basurto, Eric	R-R	6-3	200	4-17-86	1	0	9.00	2	0	0	0	3	2	3	3	0	4	2	.222	.333	.167	6.00	12.00
Beato, Benito	R-R	6-2	190	3-21-85	0	1	1.23	4	0	0	0	7	7	5	1	1	5	4	.250	.214	.286	4.91	6.14
Brauer, James	R-R	6-4	210	7-16-82	0	5	6.75	11	10	0	0	52	76	45	39	3	11	22	.342	.372	.324	3.81	1.90
Cowley, Tom	L-L	6-3	190	12-30-83	0	1	11.25	2	2	0	0	8	13	11	10	3	2	5	.371	.333	.391	5.62	2.25
Doolittle, Todd	R-R	5-10	175	11-1-82	3	5	3.68	51	0	0	28	51	56	26	21	5	23	61	.275	.297	.262	10.69	4.03
Etherton, Seth	R-R	6-1	200	10-17-76	1	1	1.80	1	1	0	0	5	5	2	1	0	1	3	.263	.250	.273	5.40	1.80
Gogal, Jeff	R-L	6-2	195	6-10-82	4	3	2.27	35	1	0	0	48	30	15	12	2	13	58	.174	.152	.189	10.95	2.45
Hutchinson, Trevor	R-R	6-5	220	10-8-79	1	3	4.85	7	6	0	0	30	42	21	16	1	10	13	.328	.453	.240	3.94	3.03
Iehl, Jason	R-R	6-2	185	4-23-84	0	2	4.66	16	2	0	0	29	29	19	15	1	14	22	.261	.244	.271	6.83	4.34
Ingoglia, Christopher	B-L	6-2	205	8-23-85	0	0	0.00	1	0	0	0	3	2	0	0	0	1	2	.182	.000	.286	6.00	3.00
Jarrett, Jason	R-R	6-5	195	5-26-84	0	1	3.27	8	0	0	0	11	10	4	4	0	8	2	.244	.211	.273	1.64	6.55
Johnson, Josh	L-R	6-7	230	1-31-84	0	0	0.79	3	3	0	0	11	9	2	1	0	0	13	.220	.118	.292	10.32	0.00
Julio, Jorge	R-R	6-1	225	3-3-79	0	1	3.60	2	2	0	0	5	11	7	2	0	1	6	.407	.385	.429	10.80	1.80
Kensing, Logan	R-R	6-1	185	7-3-82	0	0	27.00	1	0	0	0	1	4	2	2	1	0	2	.667	.667	.667	27.00	0.00
Koehler, Kurt	R-R	6-1	190	9-5-84	3	1	4.79	25	1	0	1	36	46	20	19	2	19	26	.324	.383	.295	6.56	4.79
Letson, Wes	L-L	6-0	200	9-13-82	2	2	4.20	21	3	0	0	45	53	24	21	4	15	22	.296	.273	.310	4.40	3.00
Liersemann, Ross	R-R	6-4	205	8-14-83	0	0	9.00	1	0	0	0	3	6	3	3	0	2	4	.400	.250	.455	12.00	6.00
Marceaux, Jacob	R-R	6-1	195	2-14-84	3	5	5.22	30	0	0	0	40	35	26	23	0	23	29	.238	.216	.250	6.58	5.22
Martinez, Carlos	R-R	6-3	200	5-26-82	0	0	4.50	2	0	0	0	2	3	1	1	0	1	1	.333	.400	.250	4.50	0.00
McCall, Derell	R-R	6-2	229	9-22-81	5	3	3.21	13	10	2	0	73	68	29	26	6	21	40	.243	.227	.257	4.93	2.59
Mitre, Sergio	R-R	6-3	225	2-16-81	1	0	0.00	1	1	0	0	9	5	1	0	0	4	6	.147	.222	.063	4.00	0.00
Mobley, Chris	R-R	5-11	170	8-16-83	0	0	2.66	15	0	0	0	24	21	10	7	2	5	16	.236	.214	.246	6.08	1.90
Nolasco, Ricky	R-R	6-2	220	12-13-82	1	1	0.75	5	3	0	0	12	10	3	1	1	9	9	.217	.304	.130	6.75	0.75
Owens, Henry	R-R	6-3	230	4-23-79	1	0	0.00	3	0	0	0	3	1	0	0	0	0	5	.100	.000	.167	15.00	0.00
Roberts, Joshua	R-R	6-5	230	5-12-84	0	0	0.00	1	0	0	0	2	0	0	0	0	1	3	.000	.000	.000	13.50	4.50
Santos, Jarrett	R-R	6-4	215	8-18-81	2	2	5.02	8	4	0	1	29	35	19	16	1	10	16	.304	.302	.306	5.02	3.14
Silva, Jesus	R-R	6-0	199	12-24-82	6	5	4.18	17	11	0	1	75	76	43	35	4	31	45	.259	.257	.259	5.38	3.70

Player	B-T	HT	WT	DOB	W	L	ERA	G	GS	CG	SV	IP	H	R	ER	HR	BB	SO	AVG	vLH	vRH	K/9	BB/9
Sinkbeil, Brett	R-R	6-2	170	12-26-84	6	4	3.42	14	14	1	0	79	82	41	30	8	14	49	.268	.306	.242	5.58	1.59
Talbott, Travis	L-L	5-11	175	5-23-82	1	3	3.83	37	0	0	0	52	45	26	22	2	29	42	.247	.174	.292	7.32	5.05
Tankersley, Taylor	L-L	6-1	220	3-7-83	1	0	6.75	4	0	0	0	4	4	3	3	1	0	5	.250	.200	.273	11.25	0.00
Taylor, Graham	L-L	6-3	225	5-25-84	1	1	8.10	2	2	0	0	10	16	9	9	0	5	3	.356	.400	.343	2.70	4.50
Taylor, JR	B-R	5-8	170	11-6-82	0	0	27.00	1	0	0	0	1	1	1	1	0	0	0	.500	.500	.000	0.00	0.00
Thompson, Aaron	L-L	6-3	195	2-28-87	4	6	3.37	20	19	0	0	115	121	64	43	2	35	84	.266	.281	.260	6.57	2.74
Tucker, Ryan	R-R	6-2	190	12-6-86	5	8	3.71	24	24	1	0	138	142	64	57	6	46	104	.264	.289	.246	6.77	2.99
Tyler, Scott	R-R	6-5	265	8-20-82	0	0	4.50	1	0	0	0	2	1	1	1	0	2	4	.143	.333	.000	18.00	9.00
Volstad, Christopher	R-R	6-7	190	9-23-86	8	9	4.50	21	20	2	0	126	152	76	63	8	37	93	.293	.318	.278	6.64	2.64
Wood, Timothy	R-R	6-1	185	11-16-82	0	2	3.81	17	0	0	0	26	24	14	11	1	8	26	.245	.308	.203	9.00	2.77
Zabala, Felix	R-R	5-10	150	7-1-84	0	0	0.00	1	0	0	0	1	0	0	0	0	0	0	.000	—	.000	0.00	0.00
Zarate, Mauro	R-R	6-1	180	2-8-83	2	2	2.42	14	0	0	1	26	19	7	7	1	11	20	.213	.258	.190	6.92	3.81

FIELDING

Catcher

Catcher	PCT	G	PO	A	E	DP	PB
DAntonio	.987	53	278	20	4	1	7
Davis	.980	14	91	9	2	0	0
Hayes	.990	16	91	11	1	0	1
Jenkins	1.000	16	86	12	0	1	4
Langley	.962	12	43	8	2	0	0
Purdom	.986	44	267	20	4	4	8
Sanchez	1.000	3	16	2	0	0	2
Gendron	.947	15	23	31	3	2	
Guerrero	.981	47	97	158	5	25	
Harrison	1.000	7	9	14	0	3	
Martinez	1.000	2	0	2	0	0	
Ontiveros	1.000	7	6	11	0	5	
Piste	.889	3	6	10	2	1	
Randel	.960	31	59	86	6	19	
Scott Jr.	1.000	1	2	2	0	1	
Taylor	1.000	14	22	41	0	5	
Guerrero	.964	10	13	40	2	5	
Martinez	1.000	2	3	4	0	0	
Martinez	1.000	1	1	0	0	0	
Ontiveros	1.000	4	2	11	0	1	
Septimo	.937	110	176	329	34	65	
Taylor	.916	20	27	71	9	17	

First Base

First Base	PCT	G	PO	A	E	DP
Boone	1.000	1	4	1	0	1
Jacobs	.968	3	29	1	1	5
Jenkins	1.000	29	236	10	0	16
McCann	.965	14	100	9	4	9
Molina	.500	1	1	0	1	1
Randel	1.000	1	6	2	0	1
Sanchez	.990	104	937	67	10	79

Third Base

Third Base	PCT	G	PO	A	E	DP
Fulton	.916	94	37	203	22	9
Harrison	1.000	10	4	14	0	0
Jenkins	.857	11	7	23	5	2
Randel	.945	32	20	49	4	3
Sanchez	.929	8	2	11	1	2
Taylor	1.000	1	0	1	0	0

Outfield

Outfield	PCT	G	PO	A	E	DP
Brinkley	.824	12	14	0	3	0
De Aza	1.000	1	1	0	0	0
Gendron	1.000	2	1	0	0	0
Harvey	.959	114	178	11	8	3
Hermida	1.000	2	3	0	0	0
Jenkins	.978	34	40	4	1	1
Molina	.935	28	43	0	3	0
Randel	1.000	1	1	0	0	0
Restko	.944	65	82	3	5	1
Roberson	.961	75	90	8	4	2
Ross	1.000	4	7	0	0	0
Scott Jr.	.975	130	270	4	7	0

Second Base

Second Base	PCT	G	PO	A	E	DP
Coghlan	.974	32	77	107	5	28

Shortstop

Shortstop	PCT	G	PO	A	E	DP
Gendron	.929	5	3	10	1	1

GREENSBORO GRASSHOPPERS — LOW CLASS A

SOUTH ATLANTIC LEAGUE

BATTING	B-T	HT	WT	DOB	AVG	vLH	vRH	G	AB	R	H	2B	3B	HR	RBI	BB	HBP	SH	SF	SO	SB	CS	SLG	OBP
Blackwood, Jacob	R-R	6-0	195	9-14-85	.245	.266	.238	122	490	54	120	26	1	10	78	17	3	0	4	53	0	0	.363	.272
Burns, Gregory	L-L	6-2	185	11-7-86	.280	.318	.267	120	414	70	116	21	4	7	54	40	4	7	3	122	39	6	.401	.347
Coghlan, Chris	L-R	6-1	190	6-18-85	.325	.333	.321	81	305	60	99	26	4	10	64	47	5	0	3	43	19	4	.534	.419
Cousins, Scott	L-L	6-2	190	1-22-85	.292	.352	.272	110	421	69	123	25	0	18	74	38	7	3	3	92	16	7	.480	.358
Garcia, Daniel	R-R	6-0	165	12-27-87	.228	.242	.222	105	351	49	80	22	2	9	34	26	1	5	2	109	2	4	.379	.282
Guerrero, James	R-R	5-7	175	6-8-84	.263	.238	.271	45	160	30	42	6	2	3	13	25	6	2	0	29	6	3	.381	.382
Hatcher, Chris	B-R	6-2	180	1-12-85	.242	.213	.252	102	356	62	86	23	1	15	50	34	5	0	6	104	8	6	.438	.312
Howard, Adam	R-R	6-2	195	10-3-85	.251	.352	.209	69	243	29	61	10	0	12	42	15	1	0	2	67	2	1	.440	.295
Kaats, Dustin	R-R	6-0	175	12-18-86	.136	.000	.176	5	22	2	3	2	0	0	1	1	0	0	0	8	0	0	.227	.174
Martinez, Guillermo	R-R	6-0	180	10-5-84	.263	.250	.266	44	99	12	26	4	0	1	7	10	0	1	1	19	0	0	.333	.327
McDougall, Spike	R-R	6-3	180	2-7-84	.262	.313	.246	126	446	82	117	30	1	21	77	63	11	0	5	143	28	4	.475	.364
Mense, Hunter	L-L	5-11	185	8-30-84	.273	.000	.500	3	11	2	3	0	2	0	2	2	1	0	0	3	0	0	.818	.333
Morrison, Logan	L-L	6-2	215	8-25-87	.267	.195	.291	128	453	71	121	22	2	24	86	48	7	0	5	96	2	2	.483	.343
Ochoa, Blake	R-R	6-0	180	9-5-85	.191	.214	.180	33	89	5	17	4	0	2	9	7	1	2	1	20	0	1	.303	.255
Ontiveros, Emilio	R-R	5-11	170	1-2-85	.225	.077	.254	25	80	9	18	1	0	0	10	10	2	4	0	14	2	1	.238	.326
Piste, Carlos	B-R	6-1	179	3-8-85	.200	.250	.188	22	60	7	12	2	0	1	8	2	1	0	0	20	2	3	.283	.238
Raynor, John	R-R	6-2	185	1-4-84	.333	.410	.303	116	445	110	148	28	8	13	57	66	11	2	2	98	54	8	.519	.429
Roberson, Colin	R-R	6-5	205	7-15-83	.333	.250	.400	3	9	4	3	0	0	2	5	2	0	0	0	4	1	0	1.000	.455
Santin, Daniel	L-L	6-3	205	11-7-84	.264	.261	.264	32	110	9	29	5	0	3	11	2	2	0	0	13	0	0	.391	.289
Webb, Justin	R-R	6-1	175	11-5-82	.170	.170	.170	81	206	17	35	9	0	3	16	28	6	4	2	66	4	1	.257	.285

PITCHING	B-T	HT	WT	DOB	W	L	ERA	G	GS	CG	SV	IP	H	R	ER	HR	BB	SO	AVG	vLH	vRH	K/9	BB/9
Beato, Benito	R-R	6-2	190	3-21-85	0	0	4.50	8	0	0	0	12	12	10	6	2	8	10	.235	.267	.222	7.50	6.00
Buente, Jay	R-R	6-2	185	9-28-83	5	2	3.75	42	0	0	2	60	58	36	25	6	19	71	.245	.205	.264	10.65	2.85
Correa, Hector	R-R	6-3	165	3-18-88	1	5	9.29	8	8	0	0	31	55	40	32	7	16	20	.401	.375	.420	5.81	4.65
Cowley, Tom	L-L	6-3	190	12-30-83	5	6	4.66	21	19	0	0	100	117	54	52	15	28	73	.298	.286	.301	6.55	2.51
Czyz, Don	R-R	6-2	200	9-16-83	3	5	4.61	47	0	0	1	66	74	42	34	5	15	72	.281	.284	.280	9.77	2.04
Encarnacion, Rodolfo	R-R	5-11	180	5-8-86	2	1	4.93	36	2	0	0	46	47	34	25	3	37	51	.267	.328	.232	10.05	7.29
Faria, Carlos	R-R	6-1	185	10-7-84	0	2	6.75	3	2	0	0	8	10	6	6	0	5	11	.345	.308	.375	12.38	5.62
Goyen, Matthew	R-L	6-5	220	1-19-83	1	1	5.91	6	5	0	0	21	25	15	14	5	5	31	.291	.200	.310	13.08	2.11
Hyle, Michael	R-R	6-3	195	2-20-82	4	6	5.65	23	16	0	0	88	109	58	55	10	23	77	.307	.384	.265	7.90	2.36
Iehl, Jason	R-R	6-2	185	4-23-84	0	0	6.75	10	0	0	0	9	9	9	9	1	5	10	.351	.333	.364	7.50	3.75
Jackson, Andy	L-L	6-1	185	8-8-83	2	3	8.14	15	0	0	0	21	25	21	19	2	8	21	.281	.154	.333	9.00	3.43
Jones, Blake	R-R	6-2	205	4-15-81	5	6	2.94	47	0	0	19	52	39	22	17	5	14	42	.205	.250	.180	7.27	2.42
Leroux, Christopher	L-R	6-6	210	4-14-84	2	3	4.14	46	0	0	0	72	72	38	33	6	29	76	.261	.319	.231	9.54	3.64
Lewis, Marc	L-L	6-0	205	10-3-84	2	1	4.74	4	0	0	0	19	22	12	10	1	7	14	.289	.316	.281	6.63	3.32
Madden, Corey	R-R	6-1	195	3-30-84	0	0	12.00	8	0	0	0	12	25	18	16	2	7	11	.439	.524	.389	8.25	5.25
Martinez, Cristhian	R-R	6-1	160	3-6-82	9	5	4.08	18	18	0	0	97	97	55	44	16	18	74	.259	.274	.253	6.87	1.67
McCall, Derell	R-R	6-2	229	9-22-81	4	6	4.08	16	13	1	0	75	87	52	34	11	17	56	.284	.261	.299	6.72	2.04
Rasowky, Avi	L-L	6-1	195	5-17-83	2	1	3.15	25	0	0	1	40	38	17	14	4	14	40	.232	.318	.200	9.00	3.15
Roberts, Joshua	R-R	6-5	230	5-12-84	1	0	3.38	6	0	0	0	11	9	4	4	0	4	6	.225	.286	.192	5.06	3.38
Rosario, Sandy	R-R	6-1	170	8-22-85	0	1	9.82	2	2	0	0	7	11	8	8	1	2	7	.355	.385	.333	8.59	2.45
Santos, Jarrett	R-R	6-4	215	8-18-81	1	2	3.26	7	6	0	0	39	38	17	14	3	1	26	.252	.253	.250	6.05	0.23
Stone, Bradley	R-R	6-3	190	5-20-84	3	6	2.31	39	1	0	3	58	53	24	15	2	15	44	.233	.329	.185	6.79	2.31
Taylor, Graham	L-L	6-3	225	5-25-84	11	3	2.68	25	25	3	0	164	135	59	49	16	18	135	.222	.191	.230	7.39	0.99
Winters, Kyle	R-R	6-4	190	4-22-87	8	4	3.95	19	19	1	0	112	105	55	49	13	20	68	.245	.219	.264	5.48	1.61

FIELDING

Catcher	PCT	G	PO	A	E	DP	PB
Buente	1.000	1	1	0	0	0	0
Hatcher	.991	96	658	80	7	6	14
Howard	1.000	3	10	2	0	0	1
Ochoa	.979	32	202	26	5	0	6
Santin	.988	24	155	11	2	1	0
Webb	1.000	3	8	1	0	0	0

First Base	PCT	G	PO	A	E	DP
Blackwood	1.000	5	26	0	0	0
Hatcher	1.000	2	10	1	0	0
Howard	.981	20	143	9	3	18
McDougall	.989	12	88	4	1	9
Morrison	.990	119	987	52	11	76
Ochoa	1.000	1	4	0	0	0

Second Base	PCT	G	PO	A	E	DP
Coghlan	.964	78	146	233	14	53
Guerrero	.980	45	79	121	4	26
Martinez	1.000	7	6	8	0	2
Ontiveros	.933	4	4	10	1	0
Webb	.986	20	29	43	1	10

Third Base	PCT	G	PO	A	E	DP
Blackwood	.892	114	59	230	35	18
Howard	1.000	3	2	0	0	0
Martinez	.643	7	4	5	5	0
Piste	.741	15	6	14	7	2
Webb	1.000	22	12	42	0	1

Shortstop	PCT	G	PO	A	E	DP
Garcia	.870	82	101	206	46	35

	PCT	G	PO	A	E	DP
Martinez	.977	25	26	59	2	10
Ontiveros	.951	20	22	55	4	12
Piste	1.000	2	3	3	0	1
Webb	.955	29	30	76	5	12

Outfield	PCT	G	PO	A	E	DP
Burns	.985	119	255	9	4	1
Cousins	.965	105	214	9	8	2
Hatcher	.750	3	3	0	1	0
Howard	1.000	10	16	0	0	0
Kaats	1.000	4	7	0	0	0
McDougall	.955	69	104	3	5	0
Mense	1.000	3	10	2	0	1
Raynor	.978	114	163	15	4	1
Roberson	1.000	3	7	0	0	0
Webb	1.000	10	8	1	0	0

JAMESTOWN JAMMERS   SHORT-SEASON

NEW YORK-PENN LEAGUE

BATTING	B-T	HT	WT	DOB	AVG	vLH	vRH	G	AB	R	H	2B	3B	HR	RBI	BB	HBP	SH	SF	SO	SB	CS	SLG	OBP
Anetsberger, Ryan	R-R	6-2	210	7-22-85	.266	.283	.260	61	222	34	59	11	4	7	29	15	8	1	3	39	1	1	.446	.331
Belcher, Tyler	R-R	5-11	215	7-22-85	.184	.269	.153	33	98	5	18	2	0	0	3	5	1	0	1	14	0	0	.204	.229
Crockett, Marcus	L-L	5-10	190	1-20-87	.192	.143	.211	17	52	4	10	1	1	0	3	7	0	0	0	24	5	1	.250	.288
Cummins, Morgan	R-R	6-0	210	4-16-85	.279	.308	.262	29	68	10	19	4	2	1	8	13	2	0	1	19	0	0	.441	.405
Curry, Ryan	R-R	5-10	185	4-18-85	.308	.333	.297	62	224	38	69	13	0	8	27	17	10	0	5	33	2	4	.473	.375
Dominguez, Matt	R-R	6-2	180	8-28-89	.189	.267	.136	10	37	3	7	2	0	1	4	1	0	0	0	12	0	0	.324	.211
Dunn, Christopher	R-R	5-10	180	3-8-84	.103	.091	.107	20	39	3	4	0	0	0	2	4	3	0	2	9	0	1	.103	.229
Hickman, Thomas	L-L	6-1	180	4-18-88	.183	.303	.153	51	164	15	30	7	1	1	17	19	3	1	4	63	3	0	.256	.278
Jacobs, Justin	R-R	6-1	180	7-31-88	.203	.234	.192	53	177	14	36	5	0	3	14	30	1	1	1	36	11	4	.282	.321
Kaats, Dustin	R-R	6-0	175	12-18-86	.181	.184	.181	60	204	20	37	11	2	6	25	25	7	1	1	81	8	5	.343	.291
Langley, Torre	R-R	5-9	175	10-9-87	.265	.255	.268	58	204	20	54	11	0	8	33	6	0	2	5	30	0	0	.436	.279
Lasater, Ben	R-R	6-3	195	5-25-84	.258	.238	.263	61	198	20	51	13	2	4	19	19	5	2	1	43	0	0	.404	.336
Martinez, Osvaldo	R-R	5-10	170	5-7-88	.184	.167	.190	38	114	8	21	5	0	0	6	11	1	4	0	25	8	2	.228	.262
Petersen, Bryan	L-R	6-0	200	4-9-86	.250	.339	.214	57	216	27	54	13	1	5	24	18	4	1	1	53	11	2	.389	.318
Piste, Carlos	B-R	6-1	179	3-8-85	.255	.231	.265	43	137	18	35	11	2	5	9	25	0	1	0	48	6	4	.474	.370
Rojas, Jeison	B-R	6-1	170	7-16-86	.000	.000	.000	3	6	0	0	0	0	0	0	0	0	0	0	4	0	0	.000	.000
Silverio, Rigoberto	B-R	6-1	156	7-2-86	.244	.250	.241	28	78	14	19	4	0	0	6	9	2	1	0	14	6	0	.295	.337
Smith, Jameson	L-R	5-11	190	10-9-86	.188	.250	.167	5	16	1	3	1	0	0	3	0	0	0	0	4	0	0	.250	.316
Stanton, Michael	R-R	6-5	205	11-8-89	.067	.125	.045	9	30	2	2	1	0	1	2	3	0	1	1	15	0	0	.200	.147
Waters, Lucas	R-R	6-0	185	8-24-86	.187	.231	.173	40	107	12	20	8	0	0	4	9	2	0	0	30	4	3	.262	.263

PITCHING	B-T	HT	WT	DOB	W	L	ERA	G	GS	CG	SV	IP	H	R	ER	HR	BB	SO	AVG	vLH	vRH	K/9	BB/9
Alsup, Andrew	R-R	6-2	180	2-3-83	0	1	3.47	22	0	0	0	36	34	15	14	1	27	32	.246	.317	.216	7.93	6.69
Badgley, Mark	R-R	6-3	200	12-5-83	1	0	4.70	20	0	0	0	31	27	18	16	4	11	26	.231	.217	.239	7.63	3.23
Battisto, Andrew	R-R	6-0	193	9-30-83	3	3	5.00	22	0	0	0	36	31	22	20	5	13	39	.230	.220	.235	9.75	3.25
Blacksher, Derek	R-R	6-0	210	3-1-85	0	1	4.91	5	0	0	0	7	7	4	4	2	8	8	.241	.313	.154	9.82	2.45
Campbell, Adam	R-R	6-1	215	9-21-84	0	1	9.00	2	0	0	0	3	5	3	3	1	1	2	.385	.000	.556	9.00	3.00
Cishek, Steven	R-R	6-6	200	6-18-86	1	2	1.95	25	0	0	0	32	20	13	7	1	19	30	.175	.268	.123	8.35	5.29
Correa, Hector	R-R	6-3	165	3-18-88	6	2	3.22	11	11	0	0	59	61	25	21	5	13	83	.261	.216	.292	12.73	1.99
Faria, Carlos	R-R	6-1	185	10-7-84	1	3	7.25	11	3	0	0	22	26	21	18	3	10	17	.286	.250	.314	6.85	4.03
Galbizo, Rafael	R-R	6-1	185	2-18-85	2	1	4.13	11	3	0	0	33	30	19	15	3	16	29	.242	.390	.169	7.94	4.41
Hammons, Kevin	L-L	6-4	190	9-28-84	3	0	3.63	12	2	0	0	22	14	9	9	1	16	16	.194	.136	.220	6.45	6.45
Ingoglia, Christopher	B-L	6-2	205	8-23-85	0	4	8.49	4	4	0	0	12	16	11	11	1	7	7	.333	.571	.293	5.40	5.40
Jackson, Andy	L-L	6-1	185	8-8-83	0	1	4.65	15	0	0	0	31	38	24	16	1	10	31	.297	.258	.309	9.00	2.90
Lewis, Marc	L-L	6-0	205	10-3-84	2	4	2.08	9	0	0	0	39	29	12	9	1	18	26	.213	.333	.175	6.00	4.15
Linares, Kristhiam	L-L	6-1	175	5-17-86	1	3	6.88	4	4	0	0	17	22	15	13	1	5	12	.301	.077	.350	6.35	2.65
Madden, Corey	R-R	6-1	195	3-30-84	1	0	2.73	19	0	0	0	33	23	10	10	4	9	37	.193	.195	.190	10.09	2.45
Parcell, Garrett	R-R	6-5	220	7-12-84	4	1	1.24	22	0	0	0	36	26	11	5	1	10	36	.197	.182	.208	8.92	2.48
Sanabia, Alejandro	R-R	6-1	165	9-8-88	2	6	5.13	15	15	1	0	67	73	45	38	5	17	69	.271	.347	.212	9.32	2.30
Snow, Anthony	R-R	6-4	210	1-20-84	1	6	6.29	16	8	0	0	49	69	45	34	5	16	29	.340	.357	.331	5.36	2.96
Van Looy, Jonathan	L-L	6-2	210	8-11-88	0	1	4.12	5	0	0	0	20	23	12	9	1	10	10	.288	.357	.273	4.58	4.58
Voss, Jay	L-L	6-4	195	4-22-87	0	7	7.63	15	11	0	0	48	78	45	41	5	21	35	.364	.417	.344	6.52	3.91

FIELDING

Catcher	PCT	G	PO	A	E	DP	PB
Belcher	.986	30	190	22	3	2	6
Cummins	1.000	5	5	1	0	0	0
Langley	.987	45	338	30	5	2	5
Smith	.974	4	36	2	1	0	2

First Base	PCT	G	PO	A	E	DP
Anetsberger	1.000	9	59	5	0	5
Cummins	1.000	13	95	7	0	12
Lasater	.990	58	451	39	5	30
Rojas	1.000	3	10	0	0	0
Silverio	1.000	1	2	0	0	1

Second Base	PCT	G	PO	A	E	DP
Curry	.981	48	80	129	4	20
Martinez	.943	16	24	42	4	8
Piste	.800	1	2	2	1	1
Silverio	.934	17	22	35	4	6
Waters	1.000	2	2	7	0	3

Third Base	PCT	G	PO	A	E	DP
Anetsberger	.916	47	27	82	10	4
Dominguez	.929	10	6	20	2	1
Martinez	.600	2	0	3	2	0
Silverio	.667	8	0	8	4	0
Waters	.864	14	4	15	3	3

Shortstop	PCT	G	PO	A	E	DP
Curry	1.000	3	2	4	0	1
Martinez	.916	20	25	51	7	13

	PCT	G	PO	A	E	DP
Piste	.956	40	57	94	7	16
Waters	.926	19	22	53	6	6

Outfield	PCT	G	PO	A	E	DP
Crockett	.882	11	15	0	2	0
Curry	1.000	5	9	1	0	0
Dunn	1.000	13	33	0	0	0
Hickman	.956	41	64	1	3	0
Jacobs	.972	46	67	2	2	1
Kaats	.950	51	90	5	5	1
Martinez	1.000	1	1	0	0	0
Petersen	.959	53	89	4	4	0
Stanton	1.000	9	20	0	0	0
Waters	1.000	1	4	0	0	0

GULF COAST LEAGUE

BATTING	B-T	HT	WT	DOB	AVG	vLH	vRH	G	AB	R	H	2B	3B	HR	RBI	BB	HBP	SH	SF	SO	SB	CS	SLG	OBP
Alcantara, Milciades	R-R	6-0	176	10-16-89	.138	.125	.143	11	29	2	4	1	0	0	2	4	0	1	0	7	0	2	.172	.242
Arias, Rene	R-R	6-0	182	6-22-87	.219	.286	.200	26	64	9	14	2	0	0	6	1	0	1	0	13	0	0	.250	.231
Banks, Ernie	R-R	6-4	220	5-14-86	.324	.222	.357	22	74	8	24	4	0	0	10	6	1	0	0	11	2	0	.378	.383
Ceballos, Jose	R-R	6-0	190	12-27-89	.149	.100	.167	29	74	5	11	2	0	0	5	7	1	1	2	22	0	0	.176	.226
Crockett, Marcus	L-L	5-10	190	1-20-87	.267	.238	.275	27	101	20	27	10	2	3	16	16	0	1	0	33	5	3	.495	.368
De Aza, Alejandro	L-L	6-0	175	4-11-84	.667	.000	.667	4	9	2	6	2	0	0	1	2	1	0	0	1	2	2	.889	.750
Dominguez, Matt	R-R	6-2	180	8-28-89	.100	.167	.071	5	20	0	2	0	0	0	2	1	0	0	1	2	0	0	.100	.136
Dunn, Christopher	R-R	5-10	180	3-8-84	.277	.150	.317	21	83	12	23	2	0	0	8	4	3	3	0	19	5	2	.301	.333
Escalona, Raul	R-R	5-10	184	2-21-88	.276	.186	.304	50	181	24	50	9	0	3	25	17	5	0	3	23	2	1	.376	.350
Hoover, Paul	R-R	6-1	210	4-14-76	.440	.500	.435	7	25	7	11	5	0	0	4	0	0	0	1	5	0	0	.640	.423
Lawler, Brett	R-R	6-3	200	7-30-84	.250	.273	.244	20	52	10	13	1	0	0	1	7	2	0	0	13	0	1	.269	.361
MacDonald, Mitch	L-R	5-11	185	6-8-87	.246	.167	.267	22	57	10	14	7	0	0	6	17	4	0	1	17	0	0	.368	.443
Martinez, Felix	R-R	6-2	200	8-16-84	.218	.167	.238	33	87	10	19	5	0	0	8	9	1	1	1	20	5	1	.276	.296
Mercedes, Luis	R-R	5-10	165	4-9-86	.180	.261	.156	37	100	16	18	1	0	0	9	13	2	2	3	25	2	4	.190	.280
Molina, Angel	R-R	6-2	226	11-4-81	.412	.455	.400	13	51	6	21	4	0	3	11	3	0	0	0	9	1	1	.667	.444
Noel, Ketnold	R-R	6-3	188	1-14-88	.176	.136	.186	36	108	10	19	9	1	1	17	9	3	0	3	42	1	1	.306	.252
Ontiveros, Emilio	R-R	5-11	170	1-21-85	.111	.200	.077	7	18	2	2	0	0	0	1	3	0	0	1	5	0	0	.111	.227
Pasek, Michael	R-R	5-9	160	9-8-89	.214	.212	.215	43	140	14	30	4	0	1	13	11	4	2	1	42	6	1	.243	.288
Rojas, Jesus	B-R	6-1	170	7-16-86	.348	.395	.333	52	181	33	63	14	0	4	30	27	0	4	3	32	1	0	.492	.425
Sears, Todd	L-R	6-6	205	10-23-75	.409	.000	.450	7	22	3	9	1	0	0	4	1	0	0	0	3	0	0	.455	.519
Short, Joshua	R-R	6-2	220	4-1-87	.225	.269	.211	35	102	15	23	4	1	4	18	15	7	1	1	30	2	0	.402	.360
Smith, Jameson	L-R	5-11	190	10-9-86	.167	.333	.083	6	18	3	3	1	0	0	1	0	0	0	0	6	0	0	.222	.211
Stanton, Michael	R-R	6-5	205	11-8-89	.269	.100	.375	8	26	6	7	2	0	0	1	1	1	0	0	6	0	0	.346	.321
Vargas, Elvin	R-R	6-4	210	5-29-84	.140	.091	.154	24	50	6	7	2	0	0	7	5	8	0	0	8	1	0	.180	.317
White, Ray	R-R	5-8	160	6-25-87	.221	.333	.188	37	104	20	23	10	0	1	7	21	3	2	0	30	5	3	.346	.367

PITCHING	B-T	HT	WT	DOB	W	L	ERA	G	GS	CG	SV	IP	H	R	ER	HR	BB	SO	AVG	vLH	vRH	K/9	BB/9
Allen, Cody	R-R	6-2	190	9-19-86	0	1	2.89	9	0	0	0	9	14	5	3	1	3	12	.341	.444	.313	11.57	2.89
Barrow, Brandon	L-L	6-4	195	4-18-89	0	3	3.94	9	9	0	0	32	32	20	14	3	12	30	.258	.222	.268	8.44	3.38
Basurto, Eric	R-R	6-3	200	4-17-86	2	0	3.60	11	0	0	0	15	11	6	6	1	2	16	.204	.154	.220	9.60	1.20
Beato, Benito	R-R	6-2	190	3-21-85	3	1	2.57	12	0	0	4	14	8	6	4	0	8	12	.157	.000	.211	7.71	5.14
Benjamin, Ramon	R-R	6-2	180	6-14-87	4	3	2.82	16	2	0	0	38	25	13	12	0	20	32	.187	.195	.183	7.51	4.70
Blacksher, Derek	R-R	6-0	210	3-1-85	3	1	0.49	15	0	0	9	18	12	2	1	0	7	25	.185	.278	.149	12.27	3.44
Brauer, James	R-R	6-4	210	7-16-82	0	0	0.00	1	1	0	0	3	2	0	0	1	4	.200	.000	.250	12.00	3.00
Dorman, Rich	R-R	6-2	210	9-30-78	0	0	0.00	3	2	0	0	6	1	0	0	0	1	10	.059	.200	.000	15.00	1.50
Durand, Brett	R-R	6-2	200	5-19-86	1	2	3.57	9	7	0	0	35	41	14	14	1	8	36	.297	.444	.245	9.17	2.04
Flake, Stephen	R-R	5-10	170	11-13-83	2	1	1.71	12	0	0	0	21	17	7	4	1	5	22	.218	.136	.250	9.43	2.14
Gilliam, Chaz	R-R	6-3	210	7-8-88	0	0	4.00	7	0	0	0	9	12	5	4	0	3	8	.324	.286	.348	8.00	3.00
Ingoglia, Christopher	B-L	6-2	205	8-23-85	1	1	3.86	8	0	0	0	21	23	9	9	0	3	28	.267	.348	.238	12.00	1.29
Jackel, William	R-R	6-2	200	10-16-85	2	1	6.62	15	0	0	0	18	23	19	13	0	8	15	.303	.304	.302	7.64	4.08
Kaminska, Kyle	L-R	6-4	180	10-5-88	1	1	2.84	5	4	0	0	19	18	9	6	3	4	14	.254	.273	.245	6.63	1.89
Kensing, Logan	R-R	6-1	185	7-3-82	0	0	0.00	1	0	0	0	5	0	0	0	0	5	.000	.000	.000	15.00	0.00
Lamacchia, Marc	R-R	6-1	190	3-27-82	0	0	0.00	1	0	0	0	1	0	0	0	0	1	.000	.000	—	0.00	9.00
Linares, Kristhiam	L-L	6-1	175	5-17-86	2	1	2.21	10	6	0	0	41	30	15	10	0	17	45	.207	.172	.216	9.96	3.76
Mallory, Matthew	R-R	6-3	220	3-4-85	1	3	3.46	18	0	0	1	26	37	19	10	1	3	22	.319	.257	.346	7.62	1.04
Marinez, Jhan	R-R	6-2	165	8-12-88	0	0	10.80	3	0	0	0	3	5	5	4	0	4	4	.357	.250	.400	10.80	10.80
Martin, Kedrick	L-L	6-1	170	1-28-87	1	2	3.71	10	8	0	0	34	29	24	14	0	25	43	.228	.259	.220	11.38	6.62
Nolasco, Ricky	R-R	6-2	220	12-13-82	0	0	2.70	2	2	0	0	3	4	2	1	0	0	8	.286	.400	.222	21.60	0.00
Ortiz, Luis	R-R	6-1	186	10-28-86	0	0	0.00	1	0	0	0	1	0	0	0	0	0	.000	.000	.000	0.00	0.00
Paulauskas, Andrew	R-R	6-3	185	4-7-89	1	0	6.23	5	3	0	0	13	12	11	9	1	8	8	.245	.429	.171	5.54	5.54
Prieto, Daniel	L-R	6-0	195	4-22-88	0	1	6.00	8	0	0	0	12	14	13	8	1	8	13	.259	.125	.283	9.75	6.00
Roberts, Joshua	R-R	6-5	230	5-12-84	0	1	2.53	13	0	0	1	21	20	17	6	0	12	25	.230	.241	.224	10.55	5.06
Shafer, Christopher	R-R	6-2	245	5-16-89	1	2	4.15	13	2	0	1	17	21	15	8	2	5	13	.292	.276	.302	6.75	2.60
Tyler, Scott	R-R	6-5	265	8-20-82	2	0	2.16	5	1	0	0	8	7	2	2	1	3	16	.226	.357	.118	17.28	3.24
Van Looy, Jonathan	L-L	6-2	210	8-11-88	2	0	2.14	5	4	0	0	21	11	6	5	0	5	12	.159	.200	.153	5.14	2.14
Vargas, Elvin	R-R	6-4	210	5-29-84	0	0	6.00	2	0	0	0	3	4	2	2	0	2	4	.308	.000	.500	12.00	6.00
Zabala, Felix	R-R	5-10	150	7-1-84	0	0	0.00	3	0	0	0	3	1	0	0	0	0	1	.100	.333	.000	3.00	0.00

FIELDING

Catcher	PCT	G	PO	A	E	DP	PB
Arias	.934	14	64	7	5	0	2
Ceballos	.973	28	189	31	6	3	5
Escalona	1.000	16	110	18	0	0	3
Hoover	1.000	6	41	4	0	0	3
Lawler	.905	5	18	1	2	0	2
Pasek	1.000	1	10	0	0	0	0
Smith	1.000	5	31	5	0	0	0

First Base	PCT	G	PO	A	E	DP
Banks	.969	11	55	8	2	2
Escalona	.982	15	107	3	2	10
Lawler	1.000	3	17	0	0	1
MacDonald	1.000	10	88	3	0	5
Rojas	.995	24	183	7	1	12
Sears	.950	4	18	1	1	2

Second Base	PCT	G	PO	A	E	DP
Alcantara	1.000	4	5	9	0	1

	PCT	G	PO	A	E	DP
MacDonald	.933	4	7	7	1	1
Mercedes	.958	36	57	81	6	20
White	.936	19	37	36	5	12

Third Base	PCT	G	PO	A	E	DP
Alcantara	—	1	0	0	0	0
Dominguez	1.000	4	2	5	0	1
MacDonald	.714	2	1	4	2	1
Noel	.866	29	19	52	11	8
Rojas	.928	26	23	41	5	2

Shortstop	PCT	G	PO	A	E	DP
Alcantara	.913	7	5	16	2	1
Ceballos	1.000	1	1	0	0	0
Ontiveros	.872	7	6	28	5	3
Pasek	.913	41	43	103	14	18
Rojas	1.000	3	2	4	0	0
White	.846	5	6	5	2	0

Outfield	PCT	G	PO	A	E	DP
Arias	.857	11	5	1	1	1
Banks	.923	10	12	0	1	0
Crockett	1.000	27	47	0	0	0
De Aza	1.000	2	2	0	0	0
Dunn	.976	21	37	4	1	2
Lawler	1.000	12	12	1	0	0
Martinez	.964	28	22	5	1	1
Molina	1.000	8	7	1	0	0
Noel	1.000	5	10	0	0	0
Rojas	—	1	0	0	0	0
Short	.946	25	33	2	2	1
Stanton	1.000	8	14	1	0	0
Vargas	.943	20	32	1	2	1
White	.938	14	13	2	1	1

DOMINICAN SUMMER LEAGUE

BATTING	B-T	HT	WT	DOB	AVG	vLH	vRH	G	AB	R	H	2B	3B	HR	RBI	BB	HBP	SH	SF	SO	SB	CS	SLG	OBP
Alcantara, Milciades	R-R	6-0	176	10-16-89	.196	.111	.214	15	51	8	10	3	0	0	1	7	1	0	0	19	0	2	.255	.305
Arias, Pascual	R-R	6-1	165	9-3-88	.000	.000	.000	9	20	0	0	0	0	0	0	1	1	0	0	11	1	0	.000	.091
Asencio, Ramon	L-L	6-4	185	6-4-87	.216	.233	.212	57	148	26	32	6	1	3	21	42	6	0	2	52	13	5	.331	.404
Bonifacio, Joan	R-R	6-1	173	3-6-90	.170	.111	.188	54	153	23	26	6	1	1	18	32	5	0	0	71	8	3	.242	.332
Brito, Welington	R-R	6-5	200	5-13-89	.163	.107	.178	50	129	13	21	10	0	1	17	20	4	0	2	54	2	1	.264	.290
Calzado, Jose	R-R	5-11	135	3-2-88	.240	.375	.203	26	75	11	18	4	0	0	3	14	0	1	0	10	9	2	.293	.360
Castillo, Nestor	B-R	6-2	176	10-24-89	.266	.412	.222	64	222	38	59	6	2	1	12	49	3	0	0	68	24	9	.324	.405
Diaz, Aury	R-R	6-1	155	5-29-90	.234	.158	.253	57	192	26	45	4	5	0	19	34	2	1	1	32	10	4	.307	.354
Fermin, Miguel	R-R	6-0	180	2-11-85	.336	.261	.355	43	116	14	39	8	1	2	23	10	2	2	4	16	13	1	.474	.386
Garcia, Aneuris	R-R	6-0	150	12-30-89	.143	.130	.146	50	112	10	16	2	0	0	7	19	5	1	0	38	4	3	.161	.294
Geronimo, Jose	R-R	5-11	150	6-30-90	.156	.429	.105	17	45	4	7	1	0	0	3	2	3	0	0	15	0	0	.178	.240
Lima, Manuel	R-R	6-4	176	2-18-89	.000	.000	.000	2	3	1	0	0	0	0	0	2	1	0	0	3	0	0	.000	.500
Manzanillo, Ernesto	R-R	5-11	165	12-24-88	.250	.222	.257	41	136	31	34	5	3	2	10	24	2	1	0	35	13	0	.375	.370
Martes, Jean	L-L	5-11	170	10-18-88	.190	.150	.200	61	200	20	38	10	3	1	20	17	4	3	1	58	10	6	.285	.266
Mercedes, Luis	R-R	5-10	165	4-16-89	.206	.375	.154	10	34	5	7	0	0	1	3	8	0	1	0	8	5	0	.294	.357
Moronta, Rafael	R-R	6-1	173	1-16-89	.176	.231	.158	39	102	8	18	5	0	0	10	5	2	1	2	24	2	2	.225	.225
Perez, Juan Carlos	R-R	5-11	170	1-8-86	.148	.250	.130	9	27	2	4	0	0	0	0	0	0	0	0	4	0	0	.148	.148
Rodriguez, Jesus	R-R	6-1	175	1-11-90	.222	.222	.222	27	81	8	18	3	1	0	8	17	0	0	2	24	2	3	.284	.350
Salcedo, Richard	R-R	5-11	170	9-16-87	.236	.225	.239	62	216	35	51	11	3	0	27	24	7	2	2	23	13	7	.315	.329
Ugueto, Gabriel	B-R	5-10	135	5-23-88	.200	.235	.192	37	90	10	18	0	0	0	5	16	2	0	1	13	13	6	.200	.333

PITCHING	B-T	HT	WT	DOB	W	L	ERA	G	GS	CG	SV	IP	H	R	ER	HR	BB	SO	AVG	vLH	vRH	K/9	BB/9
Arias, Pascual	R-R	6-1	165	9-3-88	0	0	27.00	1	0	0	0	1	0	4	4	0	3	0	.000	.000	.000	0	20.25
Buret, Alfredo	R-R	6-1	160	8-22-87	3	2	3.86	12	8	0	0	56	51	29	24	2	16	40	.237	.269	.219	6.43	2.57
Caminero, Arquimedes	R-R	6-4	185	6-16-87	2	3	2.83	16	4	0	1	48	36	20	15	0	24	48	.209	.214	.207	9.06	4.53
Chirinos, Luis	R-R	6-2	170	4-22-90	0	4	5.08	11	9	1	0	39	49	23	22	1	12	34	.297	.304	.294	7.85	2.77
Encarnacion, Simon	R-R	6-3	202	3-2-88	0	0	11.12	5	0	0	0	6	3	7	7	1	7	7	.150	.000	.231	11.12	11.12
Estevez, Alvaro	R-R	6-2	180	3-15-89	2	2	5.66	14	4	0	0	35	44	27	22	1	22	25	.308	.295	.313	6.43	5.66
Franco, Juan	R-R	6-3	185	11-9-87	1	3	3.38	11	7	0	0	45	34	22	17	0	24	28	.202	.219	.192	5.56	4.76
German, Pedro	R-R	6-3	190	11-18-89	1	2	3.77	11	2	0	0	29	29	20	12	2	19	23	.252	.189	.282	7.22	5.97
Gil, Daniel	R-R	6-5	184	3-28-90	1	1	2.33	13	1	0	1	27	26	15	7	0	11	22	.250	.257	.246	7.33	3.67
Gonzalez, Saul	R-R	6-1	182	9-19-88	1	1	5.11	10	4	0	0	25	32	24	14	1	17	16	.299	.323	.289	5.84	6.20
Hernandez, Ricardo	L-L	5-10	152	1-23-88	1	5	5.89	19	0	0	0	5	18	21	15	12	0	9	15	.276	.222	.284	7.36	4.42
Jerez, Nelson	R-R	6-2	171	3-9-90	0	0	27.00	4	0	0	0	3	7	8	8	0	7	2	.538	.750	.444	6.75	23.62
Marinez, Jhan	R-R	6-1	165	8-12-88	2	3	4.70	5	5	0	0	23	14	17	12	1	19	25	.163	.179	.149	9.78	7.43
Martinez, Elias	L-L	6-2	175	12-1-88	0	0	36.00	1	0	0	0	1	2	4	4	1	1	3	.400	.000	.500	27.00	9.00
Martinez, Jose	R-R	6-2	185	2-14-89	3	1	3.49	11	3	0	2	28	26	11	11	0	14	28	.245	.282	.224	8.89	4.45
Matos, Wilson	R-R	6-2	180	4-10-88	1	4	1.46	24	0	0	3	37	27	11	6	0	18	29	.203	.224	.190	7.05	4.38
Mengoni, David	R-R	6-1	180	5-7-88	0	0	8.44	9	0	0	0	11	7	15	10	0	17	11	.175	.100	.200	9.28	14.34
Paniagua, Jose	R-R	6-2	190	8-20-73	0	0	1.74	2	2	0	0	10	8	2	2	0	6	8	.235	.273	.217	6.97	5.23
Ramirez, Andy	R-R	6-1	164	10-10-87	3	2	3.78	11	9	1	0	50	47	31	21	0	26	44	.257	.217	.276	7.92	4.68
Rojas, Wilfredo	R-R	6-2	150	8-31-89	1	4	3.69	13	5	0	0	39	53	40	16	3	14	28	.319	.241	.361	6.46	3.23
Rosario, Jose	R-R	6-0	170	2-16-86	2	4	4.26	8	6	0	0	38	39	23	18	0	19	33	.262	.300	.242	7.82	4.50
Solano, Aneurys	R-R	6-1	180	11-18-88	0	0	2.45	4	0	0	0	4	2	1	1	0	4	2	.267	.400	.200	9.82	2.45
Sulliven, Michael	R-R	6-2	185	9-7-88	1	1	8.68	10	0	0	0	9	11	9	9	0	21	7	.129	.250	.087	6.75	20.25
Ubiera, Ottoniel	L-L	6-4	190	7-5-89	0	1	8.44	4	1	0	0	5	6	7	5	0	6	3	.286	.143	.357	5.06	10.12

FIELDING

Catcher	PCT	G	PO	A	E	DP	PB
Fermin	.982	36	236	37	5	3	7
Geronimo	.967	15	75	14	3	0	6
Moronta	.972	37	172	36	6	2	13
Salcedo	1.000	1	1	0	0	0	0

First Base	PCT	G	PO	A	E	DP
Arias	.941	2	16	0	1	1
Asencio	.944	11	81	3	5	6
Brito	.974	42	274	20	8	22
Diaz	.964	19	149	12	6	13
Martinez	1.000	1	5	1	0	0
Moronta	.333	1	1	0	2	1
Perez	1.000	4	26	1	0	1
Salcedo	.976	6	36	4	1	6

Second Base	PCT	G	PO	A	E	DP
Alcantara	.833	8	16	9	5	3
Calzado	1.000	15	21	29	0	8
Diaz	.923	10	25	23	4	3

	PCT	G	PO	A	E	DP
Garcia	.875	9	11	10	3	2
Manzanillo	.857	5	14	10	4	4
Mercedes	.913	4	11	10	2	3
Salcedo	.909	8	12	18	3	3
Ugueto	.957	28	50	61	5	11

Third Base	PCT	G	PO	A	E	DP
Alcantara	1.000	2	0	3	0	0
Arias	.933	7	5	9	1	1
Calzado	.500	2	0	1	1	0
Diaz	.728	25	21	38	22	3
Manzanillo	.875	3	3	4	1	0
Mercedes	.900	5	8	10	2	0
Perez	.800	3	1	3	1	1
Salcedo	.913	31	20	74	9	4
Ugueto	.750	3	2	1	1	0

Shortstop	PCT	G	PO	A	E	DP
Alcantara	.950	4	9	10	1	3
Diaz	.818	4	2	7	2	1

	PCT	G	PO	A	E	DP
Garcia	.904	40	50	101	16	13
Manzanillo	.913	33	49	97	14	15
Mercedes	1.000	2	6	3	0	1
Salcedo	1.000	1	3	1	0	2
Ugueto	.857	1	3	3	1	1

Outfield	PCT	G	PO	A	E	DP
Asencio	.875	10	6	1	1	0
Bonifacio	.920	50	67	2	6	0
Calzado	.938	14	14	1	1	0
Castillo	.953	54	94	8	5	2
Diaz	—	1	0	0	0	0
Fermin	1.000	2	2	0	0	0
Martes	.911	57	66	6	7	0
Rodriguez	.889	26	41	7	6	1
Salcedo	.913	16	18	3	2	0
Ugueto	.667	2	2	0	1	0

Houston Astros

BRIAN MCTAGGART

The Astros underwent some huge transformations in 2007—on the field, in the clubhouse and in the front office.

Just two years removed from reaching the World Series, the Astros floundered early and spent most of the season near the bottom of the National League Central standings, finishing in fourth place at 73-89.

The poor season cost general manager Tim Purpura and manager Phil Garner their jobs. They were fired Aug. 27, and within a month Ed Wade had been named as a replacement for Purpura and interim manager Cecil Cooper had taken over for Garner permanently.

The end of the regular season brought an end to an era with the retirement of Craig Biggio after 20 seasons. The longest-tenured player in Astros history hit .251/.285/.381 with 31 doubles, 10 home runs and 50 RBIs in his final season and retired as the Astros' all-time leader in games, at-bats, hits, runs, walks, doubles and total bases.

The Astros also underwent a youth movement in 2007, with rookie catcher J.R. Towles playing in September after starting the year in high Class A Salem and rookie Josh Anderson starting in center field at year's end.

"They gave us something to hang our hat on," Cooper said of Towles and Anderson. "Those two guys, they've got a chance to be major league players for a long time. We just hope the progress continues and they continue to grow."

The Astros turned to youngsters in key roles with Towles, Anderson, NL rookie of the year candidate Hunter Pence and promising young pitchers like righthanders Felipe Paulino and Juan Gutierrez seeing action in the final weeks.

But the club still has a nucleus of established players that makes it reluctant to go into full rebuilding mode. Left fielder Carlos Lee, who signed a six-year, $100 million deal in the offseason, was as good as advertised, hitting .303/.354/.528 with 32 homers and 119 RBIs.

After coming off the best year of his career, first baseman Lance Berkman had a sub-par season, hitting .278/.386/.510 with 34 homers, 102 RBIs. The emergence of Pence (.322/.360/.539, 17 homers, 69 RBIs in 456 at-bats) helped carry the offense.

The Astros were counting on third baseman Morgan Ensberg and outfielder Jason Lane to have bounce-back seasons, but both struggled and were traded to San Diego late in the year.

Though Pence had a tremendous spring, Chris Burke began the year as the starter in center and struggled. Pence was back in May and held onto the job the rest of the year, though he missed a month with a broken wrist. Burke had been waiting for Biggio to retire since he came to the majors in 2004, and it appears the Astros will finally give him a chance to play second base full-time in 2008.

The Astros had breakdowns in their pitching staff and defense they couldn't overcome. The bullpen was inconsistent, with righthander Brad Lidge blowing eight saves while teetering in and out of the closer's role. He was traded to the Phillies in November.

The club traded righthanded set-up man Dan Wheeler to Tampa Bay in July in exchange for third baseman Ty Wigginton, a move that pushed infielder Mike Lamb out of the picture.

The rotation was a mess beyond righthander Roy Oswalt,

PLAYERS OF THE YEAR

MAJOR LEAGUE: CARLOS LEE, OF

The Astros' most expensive free agent acquisition played in all 162 games for the Astros. He hit .303/.354/.528, leading the team in average and slugging. Lee also led the Astros with 43 doubles, 190 hits, 331 total bases, 119 RBIs and 76 extra-base hits. His total bases ranked sixth in the National League, while his RBIs tied for third.

MINOR LEAGUE: TROY PATTON, LHP

Patton displayed excellent control, walking a combined 2.62 batters per nine innings in 151⅓ innings between Double-A and Triple-A. His 2.99 ERA for Double-A Corpus Christi would have led the league had he pitched enough innings to qualify. Patton had a 3.55 ERA in 12⅓ innings in the majors.

ORGANIZATIONAL LEADERS

BATTING ★Minimum 250 at-bats

★AVG	Raines, Tim, Corpus Christi/Round Rock		.313
R	Conrad, Brooks, Round Rock		85
H	Anderson, Josh, Round Rock		140
TB	Ransom, Cody, Round Rock		250
2B	Einertson, Mitch, Salem		40
3B	Flores, Josh, Salem/Corpus Christi		9
HR	Ransom, Cody, Round Rock		28
RBI	Sadler, Ray, Corpus Christi		93
BB	Self, Todd, Corpus Christi		71
SO	Conrad, Brooks, Round Rock		144
SB	Anderson, Josh, Round Rock		40
★OBP	Self, Todd, Corpus Christi		.396
★SLG	Ransom, Cody, Round Rock		.497

PITCHING ^Minimum 75 innings

W	Qualben, David, Lexington		11
L	Four players tied at		10
^ERA	James, Brad, Salem/Corpus Christi		3.03
G	Estrada, Paul, Round Rock		53
G	McKeller, Ryan, Salem/Corpus Christi		53
CG	Ventura, Ronnie, Corpus Christi		2
SV	Middleton, Kyle, Corpus Christi		23
IP	Trinidad, Polin, Lexington, Salem		157
BB	Gutierrez, Juan, Round Rock		63
	Qualben, David, Lexington		63
SO	Trinidad, Polin, Lexington/Salem		143
^AVG	James, Brad, Salem/Corpus Christi		.237

who have won 20 games with better run support and bullpen work. Righthander Woody Williams posted the highest ERA in his 15-year career in his first season in his hometown and the trade for righthander Jason Jennings proved disastrous after he underwent elbow surgery.

The defense took a hit when shortstop Adam Everett broke his leg in mid-June in a collision with Lee.

Cooper began reshaping his staff on the final day of the season, bringing Triple-A manager Jackie Moore as bench coach. Pitching coordinator Dewey Robinson replaces Dave Wallace as pitching coach. Wallace decided not to return for a second year, citing family reasons.

Meanwhile scouting director Paul Ricciarini was reassigned by Wade to a yet-to-be-determined role.

General Manager: Ed Wade. **Farm Director:** Ricky Bennett. **Scouting Director:** Pail Ricciarini

Class	Team	League	W	L	PCT	Finish*	Manager	Affiliate Since
Majors	Houston	National	73	89	.451	11th (16)	Phil Garner/Cecil Cooper	—
Triple-A	Round Rock Express	Pacific Coast	61	81	.430	14th (16)	Jackie Moore	2005
Double-A	Corpus Christi	Texas	67	73	.479	6th (8)	Dave Clark	2005
High A	Salem Avalanche	Carolina	79	60	.568	2nd (8)	Jim Pankovits	2003
Low A	Lexington Legends	South Atlantic	59	81	.421	13th (16)	Gregg Langbehn	2001
Short-season	Tri-City Valley Cats	New York-Penn	27	47	.365	14th (14)	Pete Rancont	2001
Rookie	Greeneville Astros	Appalachian	17	51	.250	9th (9)	Rodney Linares	2004
Overall 2007 Minor League Record			**310**	**393**	**.441**	**30th**		

* Finish in overall standings (No. of teams in league) ^League champion

ORGANIZATION STATISTICS

HOUSTON ASTROS
NATIONAL LEAGUE

BATTING	B-T	HT	WT	DOB	AVG	vLH	vRH	G	AB	R	H	2B	3B	HR	RBI	BB	HBP	SH	SF	SO	SB	CS	SLG	OBP
Anderson, Josh	L-R	6-2	195	8-10-82	.358	.389	.347	21	67	10	24	3	0	0	11	5	2	0	1	6	1	1	.403	.413
Ausmus, Brad	R-R	5-11	190	4-14-69	.235	.239	.234	117	349	38	82	16	3	3	25	37	6	4	1	74	6	1	.324	.318
Berkman, Lance	B-L	6-1	220	2-10-76	.278	.265	.282	153	561	95	156	24	2	34	102	94	8	0	5	125	7	3	.510	.386
Biggio, Craig	R-R	5-11	185	12-14-65	.251	.323	.227	141	517	68	130	31	3	10	50	23	3	7	5	112	4	3	.381	.285
Bruntlett, Eric	R-R	6-0	190	3-29-78	.246	.237	.253	80	138	16	34	5	0	0	14	20	1	6	0	27	6	3	.283	.346
Burke, Chris	R-R	5-11	180	3-11-80	.229	.292	.197	111	319	39	73	19	2	6	28	27	8	8	1	52	9	3	.357	.304
Ensberg, Morgan	R-R	6-2	220	8-26-75	.232	.259	.216	85	224	36	52	10	0	8	31	31	0	2	2	48	0	1	.384	.323
2-team (30 San Diego)					.230	—	—	115	282	47	65	13	0	12	39	38	0	2	2	67	0	1	.404	.320
Everett, Adam	R-R	6-0	170	2-5-77	.232	.214	.238	66	220	18	51	11	1	2	15	14	1	1	0	31	4	2	.318	.281
Lamb, Mike	L-R	6-1	200	8-9-75	.289	.362	.277	124	311	45	90	14	2	11	40	36	3	1	2	45	0	0	.453	.366
Lane, Jason	R-L	6-2	220	12-22-76	.178	.153	.196	68	169	18	30	5	0	8	27	16	3	1	3	30	1	1	.349	.257
2-team (3 San Diego)					.175	—	—	71	171	18	30	5	0	8	27	16	3	1	3	31	1	1	.345	.254
Lee, Carlos	R-R	6-2	240	6-20-76	.303	.338	.292	162	627	93	190	43	1	32	119	53	4	0	13	63	10	5	.528	.354
Loretta, Mark	R-R	6-0	185	8-14-71	.287	.317	.278	133	460	52	132	23	2	4	41	44	3	3	1	41	1	2	.372	.352
Munson, Eric	L-R	6-3	220	10-3-77	.235	.216	.242	50	132	14	31	4	0	4	15	16	0	0	2	15	0	0	.356	.313
Palmeiro, Orlando	L-L	5-11	185	1-19-69	.233	.200	.235	101	103	12	24	3	0	0	6	16	1	2	0	8	0	1	.262	.342
Pence, Hunter	R-R	6-4	210	4-13-83	.322	.354	.314	108	456	57	147	30	9	17	69	26	1	0	1	95	11	5	.539	.360
Quintero, Humberto	R-R	5-9	215	8-2-79	.226	.211	.235	29	53	2	12	2	0	0	1	2	2	0	0	13	0	0	.264	.281
Ransom, Cody	R-R	6-2	205	2-17-76	.229	.333	.192	19	35	9	8	2	0	1	3	9	2	0	0	9	0	0	.371	.413
Scott, Luke	L-R	6-0	210	6-25-78	.255	.271	.252	132	369	49	94	25	5	18	64	53	2	0	1	95	3	1	.504	.351
Towles, J.R.	R-R	6-2	190	2-11-84	.375	.333	.387	14	40	9	15	5	0	1	12	3	1	0	1	0	1	.575	.432
Wigginton, Ty	R-R	6-0	225	10-11-77	.284	.308	.277	50	169	24	48	12	0	6	18	13	3	0	2	40	2	0	.462	.342

PITCHING	B-T	HT	WT	DOB	W	L	ERA	G	GS	CG	SV	IP	H	R	ER	HR	BB	SO	AVG	vLH	vRH	K/9	BB/9
Albers, Matt	L-R	6-0	205	1-20-83	4	11	5.86	31	18	0	0	111	127	77	72	18	50	71	.291	.280	.298	5.77	4.07
Backe, Brandon	R-R	6-0	195	4-5-78	3	1	3.77	5	5	0	0	29	27	13	12	4	11	11	.248	.245	.250	3.45	3.45
Borkowski, Dave	R-R	6-1	230	2-7-77	5	3	5.15	64	0	0	1	72	76	46	41	8	34	63	.273	.300	.256	7.91	4.27
Driskill, Travis	R-R	6-0	215	8-1-71	0	1	4.50	2	0	0	0	6	10	6	3	1	1	4	.370	.250	.467	6.00	1.50
Gutierrez, Juan	R-R	6-3	200	7-14-83	1	1	5.91	7	3	0	0	21	25	14	14	3	6	16	.298	.216	.362	6.75	2.53
Jennings, Jason	L-R	6-2	235	7-17-78	2	9	6.45	19	18	0	0	99	119	73	71	19	34	71	.301	.309	.295	6.45	3.09
Lidge, Brad	R-R	6-5	210	12-23-76	5	3	3.36	66	0	0	19	67	54	29	25	9	30	88	.219	.184	.243	11.82	4.03
McLemore, Mark	L-L	6-2	220	10-9-80	3	0	3.86	29	0	0	0	35	38	17	15	5	18	35	.270	.419	.204	9.00	4.63
Miller, Trever	R-L	6-3	200	5-29-73	0	0	4.86	76	0	0	1	46	45	26	25	6	23	46	.249	.209	.289	8.94	4.47
Moehler, Brian	R-R	6-3	235	12-31-71	1	4	4.07	42	0	0	1	60	67	29	27	8	17	36	.282	.303	.268	5.43	2.56
Oswalt, Roy	R-R	6-0	185	8-29-77	14	7	3.18	33	32	1	0	212	221	80	75	14	60	154	.265	.272	.259	6.54	2.55
Patton, Troy	B-L	6-1	185	9-3-85	0	2	3.55	3	2	0	0	13	10	6	5	3	4	8	.213	.100	.243	5.68	2.84
Paulino, Felipe	R-R	6-2	180	10-5-83	2	1	7.11	5	3	0	0	19	22	15	15	5	7	11	.289	.310	.277	5.21	3.32
Qualls, Chad	R-R	6-5	225	8-17-78	6	5	3.05	79	0	0	5	83	84	29	28	10	25	78	.272	.248	.289	8.49	2.72
Randolph, Stephen	L-L	6-3	205	5-1-74	0	1	12.15	14	0	0	0	13	21	19	18	4	17	22	.362	.364	.361	14.85	11.48
Rodriguez, Wandy	B-L	5-11	160	1-18-79	9	13	4.58	31	31	1	0	183	179	102	93	22	62	158	.254	.252	.254	7.78	3.05
Sampson, Chris	R-R	6-1	190	5-23-78	7	8	4.59	24	19	0	0	122	138	64	62	20	30	51	.292	.291	.292	3.77	2.22
Sarfate, Dennis	R-R	6-4	225	4-9-81	1	0	1.08	7	0	0	0	8	5	1	1	0	1	14	.172	.182	.167	15.12	1.08
Wheeler, Dan	R-R	6-3	220	12-10-77	1	4	5.07	45	0	0	11	50	46	28	28	8	13	56	.245	.237	.250	10.15	2.36
White, Rick	R-R	6-4	245	12-23-68	1	0	7.67	23	0	0	0	29	36	25	25	4	14	15	.305	.289	.313	4.60	4.30
Williams, Woody	R-R	6-0	200	8-19-66	8	15	5.27	33	31	0	0	188	216	114	110	35	53	101	.286	.279	.292	4.84	2.54

FIELDING

Catcher	PCT	G	PO	A	E	DP	PB
Ausmus	.995	114	763	47	4	5	2
Biggio	1.000	1	1	0	0	0	0
Munson	.991	43	215	14	2	2	2
Quintero	.982	26	97	13	2	0	1
Towles	1.000	14	65	6	0	1	1

First Base	PCT	G	PO	A	E	DP
Ausmus	1.000	5	6	1	0	1
Berkman	.991	126	1015	103	10	86
Lamb	.987	43	198	29	3	25
Loretta	.994	24	148	15	1	8
Munson	1.000	5	11	0	0	0
Wigginton	1.000	1	3	0	0	0

Second Base	PCT	G	PO	A	E	DP
Ausmus	1.000	1	0	1	0	0

	PCT	G	PO	A	E	DP
Biggio	.979	114	191	267	10	54
Burke	.981	58	56	103	3	17
Loretta	1.000	49	47	50	0	14
Ransom	1.000	3	3	3	0	0

Third Base	PCT	G	PO	A	E	DP
Ausmus	—	2	0	0	0	0
Bruntlett	1.000	3	1	2	0	0
Ensberg	.929	68	36	107	11	12
Lamb	.936	58	29	88	8	8
Loretta	1.000	23	11	28	0	0
Ransom	1.000	2	1	1	0	0
Wigginton	.976	48	34	88	3	3

Shortstop	PCT	G	PO	A	E	DP
Bruntlett	.961	63	62	109	7	23
Burke	1.000	7	3	9	0	0

	PCT	G	PO	A	E	DP
Everett	.973	66	96	197	8	37
Loretta	.975	72	80	157	6	29
Ransom	.949	12	16	21	2	4

Outfield	PCT	G	PO	A	E	DP
Anderson	.970	19	32	0	1	0
Berkman	.962	31	49	1	2	1
Bruntlett	.909	7	10	0	1	0
Burke	.977	47	81	3	2	1
Lamb	—	1	0	0	0	0
Lane	1.000	55	123	2	0	1
Lee	.985	157	261	8	4	2
Palmeiro	1.000	25	20	2	0	0
Pence	.981	108	296	6	6	0
Scott	.986	107	204	8	3	2
Wigginton	—	2	0	0	0	0

ROUND ROCK EXPRESS

PACIFIC COAST LEAGUE

BATTING	B-T	HT	WT	DOB	AVG	vLH	vRH	G	AB	R	H	2B	3B	HR	RBI	BB	HBP	SH	SF	SO	SB	CS	SLG	OBP
Anderson, Josh	L-R	6-2	195	8-10-82	.273	.263	.277	132	513	64	140	17	6	2	43	32	8	10	1	75	40	8	.341	.325
Ardoin, Danny	R-R	6-0	220	7-8-74	.194	.184	.197	52	170	17	33	10	0	1	7	21	5	3	0	48	1	0	.271	.301
2-team (9 Memphis)					.208	—		61	197	24	41	13	0	2	11	27	5	3	0	52	1	0	.305	.319
Bruntlett, Eric	R-R	6-0	190	3-29-78	.278	.313	.264	61	227	31	63	10	4	1	21	31	1	2	1	36	13	4	.370	.365
Burke, Chris	R-R	5-11	180	3-11-80	.242	.250	.239	18	66	14	16	1	0	2	7	5	2	0	3	7	5	2	.348	.303
Conrad, Brooks	B-R	5-11	190	1-16-80	.218	.211	.221	139	533	85	116	36	3	22	70	63	5	1	3	144	12	3	.420	.305
Davidson, Kevin	R-R	5-9	185	7-21-80	.083	.000	.111	5	12	1	1	1	0	0	0	2	1	0	0	3	0	0	.167	.267
Fernando, Osvaldo	R-R	6-0	175	10-15-80	.231	.167	.286	9	13	0	3	0	0	0	0	0	0	0	0	0	0	0	.231	.231
Garcia, Jesse	R-R	5-10	170	9-24-73	.263	.337	.228	81	270	34	71	15	0	8	32	10	2	8	3	44	2	4	.407	.291
Klassen, Danny	R-R	6-0	190	9-22-75	.293	.293	.293	105	379	53	111	21	3	8	43	31	8	1	6	104	4	3	.427	.354
Lane, Jason	R-L	6-2	220	12-22-76	.319	.320	.319	50	185	37	59	15	0	9	41	23	2	0	4	26	2	1	.546	.393
Munson, Eric	L-R	6-3	220	10-3-77	.283	.283	.283	50	173	28	49	18	0	7	26	24	1	0	3	34	1	1	.509	.368
Pence, Hunter	R-R	6-4	210	4-13-83	.326	.276	.348	25	95	17	31	11	1	3	21	10	0	0	1	15	2	0	.558	.387
Quintero, Humberto	R-R	5-9	215	8-2-79	.333	.302	.347	53	177	22	59	12	1	5	22	4	2	5	0	21	0	2	.497	.355
Raines, Tim	B-R	5-10	195	8-31-79	.333	.318	.338	100	285	43	95	14	3	11	49	15	2	5	2	47	21	2	.519	.368
Ransom, Cody	R-R	6-2	205	2-17-76	.260	.255	.263	135	503	75	131	35	0	28	90	52	4	1	3	131	21	5	.497	.333
Rodriguez, Mike	L-L	5-10	180	10-15-80	.274	.259	.279	85	241	33	66	14	3	2	24	20	2	8	2	36	10	4	.382	.332
Saccomanno, Mark	R-R	6-3	210	4-30-80	.277	.243	.290	131	470	64	130	23	5	22	85	33	2	0	6	114	1	2	.487	.323
Torbert, Wallace	R-R	6-4	205	5-1-83	.237	.222	.250	32	76	9	18	4	1	0	8	9	0	2	0	21	1	1	.316	.318
Towles, J.R.	R-R	6-2	190	2-11-84	.279	.200	.321	13	43	5	12	0	0	0	2	4	1	2	0	7	2	4	.279	.354
Wesson, Barry	R-R	6-2	215	4-6-77	.243	.202	.268	90	222	21	54	8	1	3	17	28	0	3	1	55	9	3	.329	.327

PITCHING	B-T	HT	WT	DOB	W	L	ERA	G	GS	CG	SV	IP	H	R	ER	HR	BB	SO	AVG	vLH	vRH	K/9	BB/9
Albers, Matt	L-R	6-0	205	1-20-83	2	3	3.74	9	9	1	0	53	50	28	22	6	22	43	.256	.309	.188	7.30	3.74
Asencio, Miguel	R-R	6-2	240	9-29-80	1	3	7.43	28	0	0	3	40	57	34	33	8	17	18	.341	.343	.333	4.05	3.82
Backe, Brandon	R-R	6-0	195	4-5-78	3	2	4.32	5	5	0	0	25	27	12	12	4	11	25	.284	.278	.288	9.00	3.96
Barzilla, Philip	L-L	6-0	180	1-25-79	9	7	4.59	31	18	1	1	135	167	80	69	6	47	76	.306	.314	.301	5.05	3.13
Douglass, Chance	R-R	6-1	200	2-24-84	0	7	5.95	15	10	0	0	65	81	50	43	10	38	36	.318	.293	.341	4.98	5.26
Driskill, Travis	R-R	6-0	215	8-1-71	4	3	3.72	44	0	0	9	65	61	28	27	7	16	63	.256	.174	.326	8.68	2.20
Estrada, Paul	R-R	6-1	220	9-10-82	1	8	5.12	53	0	0	8	70	72	49	40	6	42	69	.264	.258	.268	8.83	5.37
Gordon, Brian	L-R	6-0	205	8-16-78	1	1	4.91	9	0	0	0	11	14	7	6	1	1	8	.341	.300	.381	6.55	0.82
Gothreaux, Jared	R-R	6-0	200	1-27-80	5	8	4.92	36	17	0	1	134	156	76	73	20	39	75	.296	.319	.275	5.05	2.63
Gutierrez, Juan	R-R	6-3	200	7-14-83	5	10	4.15	26	25	0	0	156	154	84	72	17	63	108	.261	.248	.273	6.23	3.63
Jennings, Jason	L-R	6-2	235	7-17-78	0	0	10.80	1	1	0	0	3	3	4	4	0	5	2	.250	.300	.000	5.40	13.50
McLemore, Mark	L-L	6-2	220	10-9-80	0	1	2.77	21	9	0	0	52	34	20	16	2	35	52	.185	.182	.187	9.00	6.06
Miller, Joshua	R-R	6-1	200	2-7-79	2	2	3.89	10	4	1	0	39	46	18	17	4	7	19	.303	.365	.258	4.35	1.60
Nieve, Fernando	R-R	6-0	195	7-15-82	1	3	6.23	5	5	0	0	22	30	19	15	1	15	13	.345	.404	.275	5.40	6.23
Park, Chan Ho	R-R	6-2	210	6-30-73	2	10	6.21	15	15	0	0	84	100	70	58	18	24	70	.292	.325	.261	7.50	2.57
2-team (9 New Orleans)					6	14	5.97	24	24	0	0	136	164	104	90	27	40	119	—	—	—	7.89	2.65
Patton, Troy	B-L	6-1	185	9-3-85	4	2	4.59	8	8	0	0	49	44	26	25	5	11	25	.247	.220	.255	4.59	2.02
Phelps, Travis	R-R	6-2	170	7-25-77	0	0	7.36	3	0	0	0	4	6	3	3	1	4	1	.429	.625	.167	2.45	9.82
Randolph, Stephen	L-L	6-3	205	5-1-74	10	2	1.90	31	0	0	4	52	23	14	11	5	22	78	.133	.153	.119	13.50	3.81
Reineke, Chad	R-R	6-6	210	4-9-82	5	5	4.68	32	16	0	0	100	99	61	52	7	52	95	.261	.255	.267	8.55	4.68
Rodriguez, Jose	R-R	6-0	170	1-15-82	4	4	5.00	52	0	0	4	72	77	42	40	10	33	57	.281	.265	.297	7.12	4.12
Sampson, Chris	R-R	6-1	190	5-23-78	1	0	0.00	2	0	0	0	3	3	0	0	0	2	0	.273	.333	.250	0.00	6.00
Sauerbeck, Scott	R-L	6-3	200	11-9-71	1	0	3.93	18	0	0	0	18	22	11	8	1	13	22	.286	.182	.364	10.80	6.3

FIELDING

Catcher	PCT	G	PO	A	E	DP	PB
Ardoin	.997	51	351	41	1	5	3
Conrad	1.000	2	4	0	0	0	0
Davidson	1.000	4	18	2	0	1	0
Munson	.980	35	223	25	5	5	3
Quintero	.983	47	312	45	6	5	4
Towles	1.000	15	80	5	0	0	0

First Base	PCT	G	PO	A	E	DP
Anderson	1.000	1	7	0	0	0
Ardoin	—	1	0	0	0	0
Bruntlett	1.000	3	20	3	0	2
Lane	.900	1	9	0	1	2
Munson	.992	15	121	9	1	14
Quintero	1.000	1	2	0	0	0
Ransom	.994	20	147	15	1	12
Saccomanno	.986	112	856	71	13	98

Second Base	PCT	G	PO	A	E	DP
Bruntlett	1.000	4	6	5	0	2
Burke	.971	10	14	19	1	3
Conrad	.974	123	239	313	15	85
Fernando	1.000	2	3	3	0	1
Garcia	.958	4	10	13	1	3
Klassen	.947	7	17	19	2	4

Third Base	PCT	G	PO	A	E	DP
Conrad	.935	13	9	20	2	4
Garcia	.833	2	2	3	1	2
Klassen	.947	35	17	73	5	9
Ransom	.981	91	56	149	4	13
Saccomanno	.946	16	7	28	2	1

Shortstop	PCT	G	PO	A	E	DP
Bruntlett	.963	14	16	36	2	7
Fernando	1.000	2	3	2	0	0

	PCT	G	PO	A	E	DP
Garcia	.965	68	96	182	10	33
Klassen	.969	45	80	107	6	33
Ransom	.992	27	43	83	1	17

Outfield	PCT	G	PO	A	E	DP
Anderson	.970	129	287	8	9	3
Bruntlett	1.000	44	115	2	0	0
Burke	1.000	7	14	0	0	0
Klassen	1.000	10	16	2	0	0
Lane	.957	47	87	1	4	0
Pence	1.000	25	62	4	0	2
Raines	.957	62	105	5	5	1
Ransom	1.000	2	2	0	0	0
Rodriguez	.975	47	75	4	2	0
Saccomanno	1.000	1	5	0	0	0
Torbert	.966	21	26	2	1	1
Wesson	.992	68	119	8	1	2

CORPUS CHRISTI HOOKS

TEXAS LEAGUE

BATTING	B-T	HT	WT	DOB	AVG	vLH	vRH	G	AB	R	H	2B	3B	HR	RBI	BB	HBP	SH	SF	SO	SB	CS	SLG	OBP
Ash, Jonathan	L-R	5-9	185	9-11-82	.300	.286	.304	79	280	33	84	16	2	3	33	26	7	9	0	17	2	3	.404	.374
Caraballo, Francisco	R-R	6-2	215	10-21-83	.256	.271	.252	124	390	45	100	27	1	13	57	27	5	2	3	110	5	2	.431	.311
Davidson, Kevin	R-R	5-9	185	7-21-80	.170	.286	.150	18	47	6	8	2	0	0	3	5	0	1	0	7	2	0	.213	.250
Fernando, Osvaldo	R-R	6-0	175	10-15-80	.250	.200	.269	41	92	10	23	5	0	0	3	1	0	3	1	13	6	2	.304	.255
Flores, Josh	R-R	6-0	200	11-18-85	.219	.235	.213	60	192	29	42	8	3	2	12	18	0	8	1	40	14	0	.323	.284
Goethals, James	R-R	5-11	195	7-12-82	.118	.000	.154	7	17	2	2	0	0	1	3	2	0	0	0	4	2	0	.294	.211
Johnson, Michael	L-L	6-3	225	6-25-80	.318	.294	.327	22	66	12	21	2	0	4	16	18	0	0	1	17	0	1	.530	.459
2-team (64 San Antonio)					.267	—		86	266	44	71	15	3	16	51	53	2	0	2	90	0	1	.526	.390
Mackor, Jeffrey	R-R	6-1	215	1-17-80	.219	.160	.250	26	73	9	16	1	0	3	9	6	1	0	1	17	0	0	.356	.284
Manzella, Tommy	R-R	6-2	190	4-16-83	.289	.323	.277	64	228	35	66	12	3	1	15	19	0	6	1	40	10	2	.382	.343
Maysonet, Edwin	R-R	6-1	180	10-17-81	.271	.267	.272	107	340	35	92	14	2	5	39	17	2	11	2	65	5	2	.368	.307

	B-T	HT	WT	DOB	AVG	vLH	vRH	G	AB	R	H	2B	3B	HR	RBI	BB	HBP	SH	SF	SO	SB	CS	SLG	OBP
Raines, Tim	B-R	5-10	195	8-31-79	.244	.278	.234	20	82	15	20	2	1	1	7	7	2	1	0	18	4	2	.329	.319
Sadler, Ray	R-R	6-1	200	9-19-80	.253	.268	.247	138	491	72	124	25	2	24	93	53	8	1	8	120	13	9	.458	.330
Santangelo, Lou	R-R	6-1	200	3-16-83	.243	.245	.242	58	206	30	50	9	2	5	17	23	0	1	1	57	2	0	.379	.317
Self, Todd	L-R	6-5	225	11-9-78	.294	.319	.286	124	428	72	126	24	1	13	69	71	5	0	6	96	4	2	.446	.396
Sellers, Neil	R-R	6-0	195	4-3-82	.282	.232	.300	111	358	49	101	23	1	7	43	19	6	1	2	61	0	2	.411	.327
Sutton, Drew	B-R	6-3	185	6-30-83	.269	.264	.270	128	480	81	129	28	1	9	53	57	7	8	6	86	24	5	.388	.351
Torbert, Wallace	R-R	6-4	205	5-1-83	.254	.300	.241	61	224	20	57	12	0	1	23	22	1	2	0	59	2	6	.321	.324
Towles, J.R.	R-R	6-2	190	2-11-84	.324	.291	.335	61	216	47	70	12	2	11	49	23	15	3	0	35	9	4	.551	.425
Varner, Noochie	R-R	6-0	210	12-7-80	.287	.300	.282	98	352	34	101	21	3	6	51	30	3	0	7	58	3	1	.415	.342

PITCHING	B-T	HT	WT	DOB	W	L	ERA	G	GS	CG	SV	IP	H	R	ER	HR	BB	SO	AVG	vLH	vRH	K/9	BB/9
Asencio, Miguel	R-R	6-2	240	9-29-80	1	3	4.70	10	9	0	0	44	53	24	23	4	16	27	.303	.304	.301	5.52	3.27
Backe, Brandon	R-R	6-0	195	4-5-78	1	0	5.40	1	1	0	0	5	5	3	3	1	2	4	.263	.200	.333	7.20	3.60
Barthmaier, Jimmy	R-R	6-5	230	1-6-84	2	9	6.20	24	16	0	0	90	116	73	62	11	44	73	.312	.304	.320	7.30	4.40
Bogusevic, Brian	L-L	6-3	215	2-18-84	1	1	7.40	6	6	0	0	24	29	21	20	1	14	17	.296	.393	.257	6.29	5.18
Douglass, Chance	R-R	6-1	200	2-24-84	6	2	3.12	12	11	1	0	81	70	31	28	5	21	65	.233	.221	.248	7.25	2.34
Englebrook, Evan	R-R	6-8	225	4-28-82	1	3	9.15	11	0	0	0	20	27	22	20	2	18	14	.329	.333	.327	6.41	8.24
Fairchild, Thomas	R-R	6-2	200	12-5-83	0	1	10.29	2	2	0	0	7	14	8	8	1	1	4	.424	.364	.455	5.14	1.29
Foli, Daniel	R-R	6-1	190	3-30-81	0	0	3.00	3	0	0	1	6	8	2	2	0	4	5	.364	.333	.385	7.50	6.00
Gervacio, Samuel	R-R	5-11	160	1-10-85	3	2	1.99	13	0	0	0	23	15	7	5	1	11	24	.197	.324	.095	9.53	4.37
Gordon, Brian	L-R	6-0	205	8-16-78	5	1	2.88	30	0	0	1	50	44	17	16	3	19	43	.230	.212	.253	7.74	3.42
James, Brad	R-R	6-2	210	6-19-84	1	5	5.17	9	9	0	0	47	53	27	27	2	20	22	.294	.343	.227	4.21	3.83
Jennings, Jason	L-R	6-2	235	7-17-78	0	0	0.00	1	1	0	0	5	3	0	0	0	1	2	.188	.182	.200	3.60	1.80
Lavigne, Tim	R-R	5-10	210	7-4-78	1	1	3.86	8	0	0	0	9	12	4	4	1	3	6	.343	.294	.389	5.79	2.89
Lidge, Brad	R-R	6-5	210	12-23-76	0	0	0.00	1	1	0	0	1	0	0	0	0	0	0	.000	.000	.000	0.00	0.00
McKeller, Ryan	R-R	6-5	220	7-8-83	0	0	9.00	5	0	0	0	8	13	8	8	1	4	5	.382	.467	.316	3.38	5.62
Melendez, German	R-R	6-0	195	9-13-80	6	5	4.18	44	4	0	4	80	67	39	37	13	33	69	.226	.250	.201	7.79	3.73
Middleton, Kyle	R-R	6-4	225	6-13-80	3	2	3.35	44	0	0	23	51	46	23	19	4	18	44	.238	.250	.227	7.76	3.18
Miller, Joshua	R-R	6-1	200	2-7-79	4	4	3.48	25	10	0	3	98	99	46	38	12	18	61	.261	.247	.280	5.58	1.65
Muecke, Josh	L-L	6-3	200	1-9-82	9	5	3.90	32	16	1	0	132	133	60	57	18	45	78	.263	.250	.271	5.33	3.08
Patton, Troy	B-L	6-1	185	9-3-85	6	6	2.99	16	16	0	0	102	96	38	34	10	33	69	.247	.193	.270	6.07	2.90
Paulino, Felipe	R-R	6-2	180	10-5-83	6	9	3.62	22	21	0	0	112	103	55	45	6	49	110	.238	.277	.193	8.84	3.94
Phelps, Travis	R-R	6-2	170	7-25-77	0	0	16.20	5	0	0	0	5	11	9	9	1	5	7	.440	.400	.467	12.60	9.00
Soto, Enyelbert	L-L	6-1	200	8-20-82	1	0	10.00	5	0	0	0	9	16	12	10	2	13	9	.372	.615	.267	9.00	13.00
Stiehl, Robert	R-R	6-3	215	12-9-80	0	0	7.47	10	0	0	0	16	19	14	13	1	11	10	.306	.429	.206	5.74	6.32
Thompson, Ryan	R-R	6-4	220	8-6-82	4	3	3.81	38	0	0	3	54	52	23	23	13	9	53	.246	.221	.271	8.78	1.49
Ventura, Ronnie	R-R	5-11	220	7-6-83	4	9	5.65	21	15	2	0	92	99	63	58	8	32	63	.273	.317	.227	6.14	3.12
White, Rick	R-R	6-4	245	12-23-68	0	0	3.00	2	2	0	0	3	3	1	1	0	0	3	.250	.000	.600	9.00	0.00
Wigdahl, Jeff	L-L	6-0	190	6-4-82	2	2	5.54	22	0	0	0	37	44	29	23	5	22	40	.293	.278	.302	9.64	5.30

FIELDING

Catcher	PCT	G	PO	A	E	DP	PB
Davidson	1.000	14	78	4	0	0	1
Goethals	1.000	5	37	2	0	0	0
Mackor	.975	23	153	5	4	1	1
Santangelo	.991	56	398	25	4	4	3
Towles	.987	47	286	21	4	4	0

First Base	PCT	G	PO	A	E	DP
Johnson	.965	15	101	8	4	14
Self	.991	100	798	66	8	75
Sellers	.980	36	235	14	5	19
Sutton	1.000	1	6	0	0	2

Second Base	PCT	G	PO	A	E	DP
Ash	.981	74	114	193	6	39
Fernando	1.000	14	19	27	0	4
Maysonet	.982	35	54	106	3	20
Sutton	.982	31	45	65	2	14

Third Base	PCT	G	PO	A	E	DP
Fernando	1.000	1	1	2	0	0
Maysonet	.778	2	2	5	2	2
Sellers	.974	57	47	64	3	5
Sutton	.950	96	56	136	10	12

Shortstop	PCT	G	PO	A	E	DP
Fernando	.952	18	24	36	3	7
Manzella	.975	59	89	142	6	40
Maysonet	.962	67	93	163	10	33
Sutton	.917	8	10	12	2	2

Outfield	PCT	G	PO	A	E	DP
Caraballo	.979	117	219	9	5	2
Flores	.973	57	139	4	4	0
Raines	1.000	20	44	0	0	0
Sadler	.991	136	324	9	3	2
Self	.955	12	20	1	1	0
Torbert	.975	59	110	6	3	2
Varner	.984	48	57	3	1	0

SALEM AVALANCHE   HIGH CLASS A

CAROLINA LEAGUE

BATTING	B-T	HT	WT	DOB	AVG	vLH	vRH	G	AB	R	H	2B	3B	HR	RBI	BB	HBP	SH	SF	SO	SB	CS	SLG	OBP
Einertson, Mitch	R-R	5-10	178	4-4-86	.305	.375	.281	122	446	68	136	40	3	11	87	35	10	0	5	75	5	4	.482	.365
Fernando, Osvaldo	R-R	6-0	175	10-15-80	.250	.333	.228	26	100	19	25	4	2	0	14	9	3	4	0	9	7	3	.330	.330
Flores, Josh	R-R	6-0	200	11-18-85	.325	.446	.282	63	246	49	80	16	6	5	30	23	4	3	0	47	25	5	.500	.392
Hart, Billy	R-R	6-2	215	11-2-82	.305	.300	.307	114	370	64	113	30	6	4	44	42	7	9	2	81	23	6	.451	.385
Iorg, Eli	R-R	6-3	200	3-14-83	.296	.298	.296	44	162	35	48	12	4	5	24	14	0	0	1	36	14	2	.512	.350
Johnson, Chris	R-R	6-3	220	10-1-84	.263	.167	.290	60	224	24	59	11	0	6	38	8	3	0	5	41	1	0	.393	.292
King, Ray	R-R	5-11	425	7-2-82	.229	.323	.197	87	258	38	59	13	0	1	21	26	5	14	3	41	5	3	.291	.308
Lopez, Jose	R-R	5-11	195	3-8-85	.241	.265	.236	71	237	23	57	13	0	0	35	16	8	3	1	57	0	1	.295	.309
Manzella, Tommy	R-R	6-2	190	4-16-83	.238	.302	.218	57	223	28	53	13	0	0	24	19	3	5	1	30	5	2	.296	.305
Ori, Mark	L-R	6-4	225	10-8-83	.272	.225	.282	115	415	58	113	22	1	9	56	45	6	0	2	64	2	1	.395	.350
Osborn, Pat	R-R	6-4	210	2-27-81	.261	.297	.250	48	157	23	41	9	2	1	21	12	4	1	5	26	3	1	.357	.320
Quintero, Cesar A	R-R	5-11	165	1-7-83	.247	.250	.246	69	243	35	60	11	3	5	38	9	4	2	3	56	15	1	.379	.282
Reed, Ryan	L-L	6-4	210	12-19-83	.233	.080	.248	87	279	48	65	11	7	10	39	17	7	3	0	78	9	3	.430	.294
Rosales, Orlando	R-R	5-8	180	4-9-84	.283	.385	.248	111	374	63	106	20	6	3	40	19	2	0	3	73	8	4	.393	.319
Sheldon, Ole	R-R	6-4	210	11-25-82	.298	.326	.289	56	178	31	53	8	0	6	25	34	4	0	5	24	1	1	.444	.412
Sutil, Wladimir	R-R	5-10	135	10-31-84	.272	.247	.279	112	393	61	107	15	0	0	41	36	17	9	5	47	36	10	.310	.355
Tellam, Justin	R-R	6-3	190	11-20-84	.272	.255	.280	44	147	18	40	11	0	1	22	20	4	0	3	30	0	0	.367	.368
Torres, Tim	B-R	6-2	180	11-12-83	.262	.241	.267	40	145	17	38	10	0	5	31	17	0	0	0	37	4	2	.434	.340
Towles, J.R.	R-R	6-2	190	2-11-84	.200	.130	.224	26	90	14	18	3	2	0	11	12	9	0	4	15	3	5	.278	.339

PITCHING	B-T	HT	WT	DOB	W	L	ERA	G	GS	CG	SV	IP	H	R	ER	HR	BB	SO	AVG	vLH	vRH	K/9	BB/9
Blazek, Christopher	L-L	6-0	195	3-2-84	4	2	4.07	50	0	0	8	66	61	33	30	5	28	62	.243	.219	.253	8.41	3.80
Bogusevic, Brian	L-L	6-3	215	2-18-84	7	4	4.01	21	21	1	0	114	133	57	51	7	39	91	.296	.269	.300	7.16	3.07
Cavanagh, Nick	R-R	6-2	210	3-14-82	0	2	5.54	18	0	0	0	26	32	21	16	4	6	21	.294	.302	.288	7.27	2.08

	B-T	HT	WT	DOB	W	L	ERA	G	GS	CG	SV	IP	H	R	ER	HR	BB	SO	AVG	vLH	vRH	K/9	BB/9
Diaz, Raymar	R-R	6-7	190	11-13-83	8	7	3.87	33	20	0	2	137	142	65	59	13	44	116	.266	.217	.300	7.60	2.88
Englebrook, Evan	R-R	6-8	225	4-28-82	4	3	1.90	21	3	0	1	52	47	16	11	1	14	40	.242	.218	.259	6.92	2.42
Escobar, Rodrigo	R-R	5-11	170	2-11-83	0	0	9.00	2	0	0	0	2	5	2	2	0	0	0	.625	1.000	.571	0.00	0.00
Gervacio, Samuel	R-R	5-11	160	1-10-85	1	3	2.44	39	0	0	18	55	42	16	15	1	15	80	.204	.210	.200	13.01	2.44
Hudspeth, Casey	R-R	6-0	165	10-1-84	2	1	3.89	7	7	1	0	42	41	19	18	3	10	25	.266	.260	.269	5.40	2.16
James, Brad	R-R	6-2	210	6-19-84	9	2	1.98	16	16	0	0	96	72	27	21	5	33	55	.207	.225	.194	5.17	3.10
McKeller, Ryan	R-R	6-5	220	7-8-83	7	4	2.84	48	0	0	7	76	64	27	24	7	25	54	.234	.213	.244	6.39	2.96
Norris, Bud	R-R	6-0	195	3-2-85	1	0	1.50	1	1	0	0	6	4	1	1	0	1	2	.190	.273	.100	3.00	1.50
Owens, Ryan	R-L	6-1	185	8-9-83	0	0	33.75	4	0	0	0	1	3	5	5	0	5	0	.500	.500	.500	0.00	33.75
Perez, Sergio	R-R	6-3	230	12-5-84	7	10	4.00	25	25	0	0	128	129	67	57	9	43	84	.265	.222	.294	5.89	3.02
Salamida, Christopher	L-L	6-0	180	5-7-84	8	8	5.85	27	25	0	0	131	155	91	85	16	51	101	.300	.301	.300	6.96	3.51
Shortell, Rory	R-R	6-3	205	6-3-81	7	4	3.95	45	7	0	2	100	95	49	44	8	27	66	.253	.224	.272	5.92	2.42
Soto, Enyelbert	L-L	6-1	200	8-20-82	3	2	2.75	22	0	0	1	36	35	14	11	2	13	24	.265	.233	.281	6.00	3.25
Sweeney, Matt	R-R	6-2	195	2-25-83	2	1	5.12	20	0	0	0	32	34	23	18	4	13	19	.276	.260	.288	5.40	3.69
Tellam, Justin	R-R	6-3	190	11-20-84	0	0	9.00	1	0	0	0	1	1	1	1	1	0	1	.250	.500	.000	9.00	0.00
Trinidad, Polin	L-L	6-2	170	11-19-84	2	1	2.81	4	4	0	0	26	23	9	8	4	3	23	.237	.357	.217	8.06	1.05
Walker, Sean	R-R	6-1	175	10-31-82	3	3	4.20	20	10	0	0	64	73	33	30	5	15	47	.284	.376	.232	6.58	2.10
Wigdahl, Jeff	L-L	6-0	190	6-4-82	2	0	2.54	18	0	0	2	28	24	8	8	1	8	33	.245	.367	.191	10.48	2.54

FIELDING

Catcher	PCT	G	PO	A	E	DP	PB
Lopez	.995	71	515	57	3	8	5
Tellam	.994	43	282	42	2	5	3
Towles	.995	26	173	20	1	3	1

First Base	PCT	G	PO	A	E	DP
Hart	1.000	6	39	1	0	2
Johnson	1.000	4	19	2	0	0
Ori	.985	79	640	33	10	62
Osborn	.987	34	281	21	4	18
Sheldon	.996	26	223	24	1	18

Second Base	PCT	G	PO	A	E	DP
King	.985	84	148	242	6	49

	PCT	G	PO	A	E	DP
Sutil	.967	40	65	82	5	19
Torres	.972	29	37	67	3	5

Third Base	PCT	G	PO	A	E	DP
Hart	.907	70	49	137	19	15
Johnson	.959	55	41	100	6	10
King	—	1	0	0	0	0
Osborn	.750	2	1	2	1	0
Sutil	.907	21	13	26	4	2

Shortstop	PCT	G	PO	A	E	DP
Fernando	.934	25	34	65	7	6
Manzella	.953	55	85	179	13	37
Sutil	.971	50	83	121	6	18

Torres	.915	10	9	34	4	9

Outfield	PCT	G	PO	A	E	DP
Einertson	.983	114	220	14	4	5
Flores	.977	58	118	8	3	1
Hart	1.000	22	35	2	0	0
Iorg	.959	37	69	1	3	0
Quintero	.979	69	126	13	3	1
Reed	.922	47	71	0	6	0
Rosales	.978	99	209	13	5	5

LEXINGTON LEGENDS

LOW CLASS A

SOUTH ATLANTIC LEAGUE

BATTING	B-T	HT	WT	DOB	AVG	vLH	vRH	G	AB	R	H	2B	3B	HR	RBI	BB	HBP	SH	SF	SO	SB	CS	SLG	OBP
Buchanan, Greg	B-R	5-11	180	11-16-83	.240	.266	.231	119	455	55	109	18	1	7	56	31	7	4	1	60	18	5	.330	.298
Caipen, Brandon	R-R	6-0	180	8-4-83	.219	.256	.205	43	160	27	35	3	4	3	8	9	2	5	0	30	8	3	.344	.269
Clemens, Koby	R-R	5-11	193	12-4-86	.252	.240	.256	115	413	65	104	21	0	15	56	53	8	4	6	112	8	2	.412	.344
Darnell, Andrew	R-R	6-1	215	7-15-86	.222	.500	.143	5	18	3	4	0	0	0	1	2	0	1	0	5	0	0	.222	.300
Evans, Tyler	R-R	6-2	180	5-2-84	.140	.125	.143	16	43	5	6	0	0	0	2	2	3	0	0	18	0	0	.140	.229
Florentino, Jhon	R-R	6-0	155	8-22-83	.257	.206	.270	87	315	42	81	16	3	4	44	33	0	2	3	67	5	4	.365	.325
Goethals, James	R-R	5-11	195	7-12-82	.073	.077	.071	14	41	1	3	0	0	1	1	6	1	0	0	19	0	0	.146	.208
Henriquez, Ralph	B-R	6-1	190	4-7-87	.185	.157	.194	103	372	30	69	12	1	7	36	21	0	0	4	86	2	0	.280	.227
Holder, Andrew	R-R	6-0	210	10-2-83	.252	.238	.258	69	226	26	57	8	0	6	28	14	6	1	4	49	3	3	.367	.308
Johnson, Chris	R-R	6-3	220	10-1-84	.259	.230	.268	64	255	37	66	14	0	8	44	17	1	1	3	38	1	4	.408	.304
Moresi, Nicholas	R-R	6-4	180	11-22-84	.235	.219	.241	111	387	63	91	17	7	10	39	39	10	3	1	111	15	2	.393	.320
Parraz, Jordan	R-R	6-3	220	10-8-84	.281	.227	.300	122	462	69	130	28	3	14	76	47	15	2	4	89	33	10	.446	.364
Quintero, Cesar A	R-R	5-11	165	1-7-83	.292	.255	.304	54	226	46	66	15	1	7	25	18	1	0	1	63	21	2	.460	.346
Ramirez, Ronald	R-R	5-11	165	1-30-86	.314	.333	.311	19	70	10	22	6	0	0	8	3	0	3	0	21	1	2	.400	.342
Sapp, Maxwell	L-R	6-2	220	2-21-88	.241	.209	.253	86	315	25	76	23	0	2	32	38	4	1	1	70	0	0	.333	.330
Taylor, Eric	R-R	6-3	195	7-29-85	.261	.337	.239	110	414	60	108	21	0	13	54	45	15	6	0	79	8	3	.406	.354
Torres, Tim	B-R	6-2	180	11-12-83	.291	.323	.278	68	223	44	65	11	1	9	30	48	1	3	0	58	22	3	.471	.419
Van Ostrand, James	R-R	6-4	210	8-7-84	.289	.322	.278	98	363	42	105	18	3	12	60	38	3	1	2	64	4	4	.455	.360

PITCHING	B-T	HT	WT	DOB	W	L	ERA	G	GS	CG	SV	IP	H	R	ER	HR	BB	SO	AVG	vLH	vRH	K/9	BB/9
Arguello, Douglas	L-L	6-3	190	11-21-84	6	10	5.24	29	27	0	0	139	152	100	81	13	59	100	.278	.283	.276	6.47	3.82
Bass, Corey	R-R	6-3	210	2-8-85	1	3	5.31	31	7	0	4	80	93	61	47	14	29	58	.284	.254	.305	6.55	3.28
Cavanagh, Nick	R-R	6-2	210	3-14-82	0	1	4.71	19	0	0	0	29	21	16	15	4	15	33	.196	.205	.191	10.36	4.71
Cespedes, Leandro	R-R	5-11	160	4-19-87	0	1	4.38	3	2	0	0	12	10	6	6	1	5	12	.213	.188	.226	8.76	3.65
DeYoung, Kyle	R-R	6-0	190	8-15-84	5	8	4.33	49	0	0	8	79	84	47	38	9	29	72	.273	.283	.267	8.20	3.30
Garate, Victor	L-L	6-1	160	9-25-84	3	1	6.43	26	0	0	1	42	47	32	30	3	35	41	.292	.259	.308	8.79	7.50
Hallberg, Bryan	R-R	6-0	185	4-23-85	2	5	8.42	21	6	0	1	57	79	57	53	11	36	40	.329	.316	.338	6.35	5.72
Hudspeth, Casey	R-R	6-0	165	10-1-84	5	5	4.83	21	21	0	0	110	126	77	59	11	42	63	.286	.294	.280	5.15	3.44
Kelly, Reid	R-R	6-1	182	10-31-86	1	3	5.16	28	0	0	6	45	46	27	26	6	28	48	.263	.273	.257	9.53	5.56
Luis, Santo	R-R	6-5	205	1-27-84	2	3	4.66	44	0	0	9	75	66	42	39	12	34	99	.228	.238	.100	11.83	4.06
Mayora, Cesar	R-R	6-2	185	1-1-84	2	1	7.36	10	0	0	0	15	20	14	12	3	4	16	.323	.444	.229	9.82	2.45
Norris, Bud	R-R	6-0	195	3-2-85	2	8	4.75	22	22	0	0	97	85	58	51	8	41	117	.233	.245	.225	10.89	3.82
Owens, Ryan	R-L	6-1	185	8-9-83	0	1	16.87	2	0	0	0	3	3	5	5	1	5	2	.250	.000	.500	10.12	6.75
Qualben, David	L-L	6-3	200	7-29-85	11	8	3.94	30	23	0	0	148	158	74	65	13	63	108	.284	.238	.303	6.55	3.82
Severino, Sergio	L-L	5-11	150	9-1-84	5	8	4.15	31	8	0	3	85	69	44	39	11	43	84	.218	.260	.198	8.93	4.57
Trinidad, Polin	L-L	6-2	170	11-19-84	6	8	4.18	23	23	1	0	131	118	62	61	16	35	120	.242	.241	.242	8.22	2.40
Wagler, Chad	R-R	6-1	185	9-11-83	8	7	5.08	45	1	0	5	90	97	56	51	11	33	58	.279	.239	.306	5.78	3.29

FIELDING

Catcher	PCT	G	PO	A	E	DP	PB
Caipen	1.000	3	18	1	0	0	1
Goethals	.983	14	103	11	2	0	2
Henriquez	.981	80	577	40	12	7	13
Sapp	1.000	51	368	30	0	2	18

First Base	PCT	G	PO	A	E	DP
Johnson	.992	12	115	12	1	18
Taylor	.991	105	949	69	9	78
Van Ostrand	1.000	25	213	22	0	15

Second Base	PCT	G	PO	A	E	DP
Buchanan	.983	117	191	326	9	64
Evans	.962	6	9	16	1	3

Ramirez	1.000	5	5	9	0	1
Taylor	1.000	2	1	6	0	0
Torres	.988	14	29	50	1	6

Third Base	PCT	G	PO	A	E	DP
Clemens	.891	99	48	190	29	20
Evans	1.000	1	1	0	0	0
Florentino	.950	13	4	15	1	0
Johnson	.926	29	20	68	7	6

Shortstop	PCT	G	PO	A	E	DP
Buchanan	.875	2	2	5	1	0
Evans	.950	4	6	13	1	3
Florentino	.917	67	116	170	26	38

Johnson	.941	19	22	58	5	7
Ramirez	.901	13	21	43	7	12
Torres	.967	38	66	112	6	26

Outfield	PCT	G	PO	A	E	DP
Caipen	.976	31	38	2	1	0
Darnell	1.000	1	1	0	0	0
Holder	.988	60	77	8	1	0
Moresi	.984	108	239	6	4	3
Parraz	.969	120	208	13	7	3
Quintero	.974	52	108	3	3	1
Torres	1.000	7	14	4	0	0
Van Ostrand	.985	50	64	3	1	0

TRI-CITY VALLEYCATS
SHORT-SEASON
NEW YORK-PENN LEAGUE

BATTING	B-T	HT	WT	DOB	AVG	vLH	vRH	G	AB	R	H	2B	3B	HR	RBI	BB	HBP	SH	SF	SO	SB	CS	SLG	OBP
Barnes, Brandon	R-R	6-2	210	5-15-86	.251	.311	.237	63	231	34	58	16	1	10	41	31	0	0	3	71	5	3	.459	.336
Brown, Steve	R-R	6-0	180	9-3-86	.276	.310	.270	51	181	23	50	7	0	1	21	7	5	1	0	36	6	2	.331	.321
Caipen, Brandon	R-R	6-0	180	8-4-83	.250	.250	.000	2	4	2	1	1	0	0	1	3	0	0	0	0	0	0	.500	.571
Carkeek, Kevin	R-R	6-3	200	10-20-84	.219	.130	.238	38	128	16	28	7	0	1	13	14	1	1	0	23	0	1	.297	.301
Corrado, Craig	R-R	6-2	185	9-10-84	.252	.261	.250	61	242	27	61	8	2	1	25	7	1	11	1	39	10	4	.314	.275
Cruz, Alberto	R-R	6-2	215	2-13-85	.206	.222	.201	56	175	21	36	6	1	6	20	21	5	0	0	60	1	0	.354	.308
Cusick, Matthew	L-R	5-10	190	5-5-86	.306	.235	.319	61	222	42	68	14	4	3	35	38	8	3	2	25	5	1	.446	.422
DeLome, Collin	L-R	6-2	195	12-18-85	.300	.324	.296	65	243	31	73	17	6	6	28	23	6	0	1	65	9	2	.494	.374
Dixon, Russell	L-R	6-2	205	8-28-85	.256	.229	.261	60	223	26	57	11	1	5	40	14	1	0	2	52	4	2	.381	.300
Everett, Catlin	B-R	6-1	190	10-5-85	.229	.154	.243	56	170	23	39	4	0	0	16	38	0	1	2	28	5	1	.253	.367
Fixler, Jonathan	R-R	6-1	205	6-13-86	.063	.000	.091	7	16	1	1	1	0	0	0	2	0	0	0	2	0	0	.125	.167
Frye, Chris	R-R	6-0	205	6-9-84	.226	.250	.222	18	53	3	12	4	0	0	1	5	1	0	0	17	4	1	.302	.305
Gamble, Charles	R-R	6-6	235	1-18-85	.237	.325	.211	49	173	27	41	7	0	4	17	16	1	1	0	39	0	0	.347	.305
Gonzalez, Axel	R-R	5-11	165	6-2-88	.200	.000	.217	10	25	6	5	1	0	1	3	4	3	0	0	7	1	1	.360	.375
Iacono, Sal	R-R	5-9	190	3-4-85	.180	.067	.200	33	100	7	18	5	0	0	6	16	2	0	0	19	0	1	.230	.305
Pellegrini, Brian	R-R	6-1	240	10-3-84	.071	.000	.091	5	14	0	1	0	0	0	1	1	0	0	0	6	0	0	.071	.188
Pestana, Reinaldo	R-R	6-1	180	5-24-87	.200	.500	.154	5	15	1	3	0	0	0	3	0	0	0	0	5	0	0	.200	.200
Pitts, Jared	R-R	6-3	225	9-11-85	.074	.167	.048	10	27	3	2	1	0	0	1	5	0	0	0	10	0	0	.111	.219
Ramirez, Ronald	R-R	5-11	165	1-30-86	.143	.000	.200	2	7	0	1	1	0	0	2	0	0	0	0	3	0	0	.286	.143
Stringer, Philip	R-R	5-9	170	12-27-84	.190	.500	.158	13	42	2	8	0	1	0	4	6	2	0	0	18	1	1	.238	.320
Sweet, Travis	R-R	6-0	190	4-17-86	.232	.259	.222	31	99	13	23	8	3	1	13	11	0	1	1	27	3	1	.404	.306

PITCHING	B-T	HT	WT	DOB	W	L	ERA	G	GS	CG	SV	IP	H	R	ER	HR	BB	SO	AVG	vLH	vRH	K/9	BB/9
Abad, Fernando	L-L	6-2	170	12-17-85	0	0	6.00	2	0	0	0	3	2	2	2	0	2	5	.182	.250	.143	15.00	6.00
Adams, Colt	R-R	6-5	220	5-23-85	2	3	6.51	7	6	0	0	28	38	22	20	2	8	10	.328	.308	.344	3.25	2.60
Bello, Anthony	L-L	6-2	200	10-9-85	4	5	4.69	14	14	0	0	71	81	41	37	5	23	56	.292	.281	.296	7.10	2.92
Dinelli, David	R-R	6-3	215	3-14-87	0	0	3.60	3	0	0	0	5	4	2	2	0	3	7	.211	.143	.250	12.60	5.40
Dominguez, Jason	R-R	6-2	193	10-24-85	2	0	1.35	21	0	0	10	33	13	6	5	0	8	26	.117	.220	.033	7.02	2.16
Espersen, Brian	R-R	6-2	235	5-18-86	0	2	9.00	12	4	0	0	22	34	25	22	3	19	15	.347	.313	.380	6.14	7.77
Fox, Kevin	L-L	6-1	180	8-24-85	1	0	7.77	17	0	0	0	24	41	23	21	4	10	14	.373	.351	.384	5.18	3.70
Garate, Victor	L-L	6-1	160	9-25-84	3	1	3.31	17	0	0	2	33	31	15	12	4	7	45	.242	.195	.264	12.40	1.93
Gil, Danny	R-R	6-3	195	3-28-85	2	2	10.94	15	0	0	1	26	39	34	32	4	13	27	.331	.302	.347	9.23	4.44
Hallberg, Bryan	R-R	6-0	185	4-23-85	3	3	4.54	10	2	0	0	34	35	20	17	0	11	31	.271	.316	.236	8.29	2.94
Icenogle, Jeff	L-L	6-2	205	5-30-84	3	4	2.36	15	10	1	0	61	57	20	16	2	26	68	.252	.343	.212	10.03	3.84
Koons, Mike	R-R	6-2	205	9-18-85	0	4	8.88	9	4	0	0	25	33	28	25	6	13	23	.314	.311	.317	8.17	4.62
Ladeuth, Carlos	R-R	5-11	180	6-13-84	2	4	2.41	20	4	0	2	52	50	20	14	4	8	39	.248	.264	.235	6.71	1.38
Leonhardt, Robert	R-R	6-5	220	9-27-84	1	3	6.55	15	6	0	0	44	74	50	32	1	24	22	.374	.385	.363	4.50	4.91
Miller, David	L-R	6-10	210	9-29-84	2	0	8.14	13	0	0	0	21	36	25	19	1	15	13	.371	.432	.321	5.57	6.43
Pardo, Luis	R-R	6-5	230	7-14-85	0	8	5.35	13	9	0	0	35	41	31	21	2	22	15	.299	.377	.250	3.82	5.60
Powell, Jordan	R-R	6-2	205	4-14-85	0	1	5.54	7	0	0	0	13	17	9	8	1	5	16	.333	.474	.250	11.08	3.46
Tucker, Cardoza	R-R	6-2	180	11-11-84	0	0	9.00	6	0	0	0	12	20	15	12	1	9	10	.370	.304	.419	7.50	6.75
Vessella, Thomas	R-L	6-6	205	10-12-85	2	7	4.63	15	15	0	0	72	80	46	37	2	23	52	.281	.276	.283	6.50	2.88

FIELDING

Catcher	PCT	G	PO	A	E	DP	PB
Caipen	1.000	1	4	1	0	0	0
Carkeek	.975	37	247	24	7	2	11
Iacono	.988	33	228	19	3	1	1
Pestana	.960	3	24	0	1	0	1

First Base	PCT	G	PO	A	E	DP
Cruz	.975	52	406	21	11	28
Fixler	.950	3	19	0	1	0
Gamble	.978	21	167	8	4	18
Pellegrini	1.000	3	19	0	0	0
Pestana	1.000	1	7	0	0	0

Second Base	PCT	G	PO	A	E	DP
Cusick	.985	57	98	159	4	33
Dixon	.855	12	20	39	10	3
Everett	1.000	1	1	0	0	0
Stringer	1.000	4	8	12	0	2

Third Base	PCT	G	PO	A	E	DP
Corrado	.824	42	32	52	18	3
Gamble	.873	26	10	45	8	4
Stringer	.920	9	7	16	2	0

Shortstop	PCT	G	PO	A	E	DP
Corrado	.871	20	28	46	11	8

Everett	.963	54	84	148	9	35
Ramirez	1.000	2	2	3	0	0

Outfield	PCT	G	PO	A	E	DP
Barnes	.990	53	103	1	1	0
Brown	.990	42	93	5	1	0
DeLome	.951	46	76	2	4	0
Dixon	.983	35	56	1	1	0
Frye	1.000	15	28	0	0	0
Gonzalez	.909	9	10	0	1	0
Pellegrini	1.000	1	2	0	0	0
Pitts	1.000	7	11	2	0	0
Sweet	1.000	24	35	5	0	1

GREENVILLE ASTROS
ROOKIE
APPALACHIAN LEAGUE

BATTING	B-T	HT	WT	DOB	AVG	vLH	vRH	G	AB	R	H	2B	3B	HR	RBI	BB	HBP	SH	SF	SO	SB	CS	SLG	OBP
Anderson, Drew	R-R	5-11	200	4-22-84	.222	.194	.236	33	108	11	24	4	2	3	15	11	0	1	0	38	2	2	.380	.294
Brown, Bryan	R-R	5-10	170	8-3-85	.237	.200	.253	37	131	20	31	7	1	1	16	15	0	1	2	24	3	1	.328	.311

BATTING	B-T	HT	WT	DOB	AVG	vLH	vRH	G	AB	R	H	2B	3B	HR	RBI	BB	HBP	SH	SF	SO	SB	CS	SLG	OBP
Cartwright, Albert	R-R	5-10	180	10-31-87	.224	.231	.222	18	49	7	11	2	0	0	6	8	1	0	2	12	4	1	.265	.333
Darnell, Andrew	R-R	6-1	215	7-15-86	.226	.268	.210	43	146	17	33	9	0	3	15	7	3	0	2	36	0	2	.349	.272
Frye, Chris	R-R	6-0	205	6-9-84	.299	.316	.292	18	67	11	20	6	1	1	10	5	2	0	1	16	5	3	.463	.360
Gonzalez, Axel	R-R	5-11	165	6-2-88	.215	.077	.275	39	130	14	28	5	1	2	16	9	2	0	2	21	3	2	.315	.273
Gonzalez, Pedro	L-R	5-11	182	10-29-86	.216	.143	.250	32	111	9	24	7	0	0	6	10	0	1	0	18	0	2	.279	.281
Johnson, Timothy	R-R	6-1	180	10-15-86	.186	.229	.165	47	145	13	27	7	1	0	9	14	4	2	2	45	5	1	.248	.273
Launier, Andrew	R-R	6-3	225	4-10-87	.256	.240	.262	48	176	19	45	14	0	3	24	10	1	0	0	52	1	1	.386	.299
Miller, Kyle	R-R	6-1	200	9-1-86	.234	.310	.201	56	197	22	46	7	0	7	23	13	3	0	0	53	1	1	.376	.291
Parks, Rafeal	R-R	6-2	180	2-15-88	.141	.100	.159	25	64	5	9	1	0	0	4	5	0	0	0	27	4	3	.156	.203
Pestana, Reinaldo	R-R	6-1	180	5-24-87	.266	.289	.257	44	139	12	37	6	0	1	14	8	1	1	1	33	0	1	.331	.309
Phipps, Cody	R-R	6-3	205	4-24-89	.200	1.000	.111	4	10	0	2	0	0	0	0	1	0	0	0	3	0	0	.200	.273
Pitts, Jared	R-R	6-3	205	9-11-85	.205	.129	.231	36	122	13	25	6	1	1	8	9	6	0	0	46	3	1	.295	.292
Rosario, Ebert	R-R	6-3	165	5-27-87	.273	.254	.280	59	220	25	60	14	3	2	26	4	4	1	1	25	4	1	.391	.297
Saylor, Drew	R-R	6-0	195	1-9-84	.286	.143	.357	6	21	3	6	2	0	0	2	1	2	0	0	4	0	1	.381	.375
Stringer, Philip	R-R	5-9	170	12-27-84	.156	.133	.165	32	109	9	17	2	1	0	3	8	0	1	0	28	4	2	.193	.214
Sweet, Travis	R-R	6-0	190	4-17-86	.270	.316	.250	18	63	11	17	4	3	2	8	12	2	0	1	19	2	0	.524	.397
Torrence, Devon	R-R	6-0	190	5-8-89	.149	.200	.134	30	87	8	13	2	0	0	3	3	0	1	0	48	5	2	.172	.330
Turner, Christopher	B-R	5-11	185	10-21-88	.134	.129	.136	33	97	7	13	2	0	0	4	7	1	1	0	40	3	1	.155	.200
Williams, Marques	R-R	6-0	185	10-24-85	.200	.000	.400	7	20	4	4	1	0	0	1	2	1	0	0	5	3	0	.250	.304

PITCHING	B-T	HT	WT	DOB	W	L	ERA	G	GS	CG	SV	IP	H	R	ER	HR	BB	SO	AVG	vLH	vRH	K/9	BB/9
Abad, Fernando	L-L	6-2	170	12-17-85	6	4	4.14	17	4	0	1	50	47	29	23	6	12	54	.246	.270	.240	9.72	2.16
Bono, Robert	R-R	6-2	175	12-12-88	0	4	7.34	11	8	0	0	34	39	31	28	6	20	18	.285	.357	.253	4.72	5.24
Cespedes, Leandro	R-R	5-11	160	4-19-87	4	5	3.15	11	10	0	0	54	48	23	19	2	12	52	.234	.237	.233	8.61	1.99
Ciriaco, Eduin	L-L	6-0	175	10-26-85	1	2	4.91	17	3	0	0	40	38	28	22	4	28	39	.241	.241	.240	8.70	6.25
Dinelli, David	R-R	6-3	215	3-14-87	0	3	8.83	7	5	0	0	17	22	19	17	1	10	22	.301	.320	.292	11.42	5.19
Duran, Jose	R-R	6-1	175	4-1-85	1	0	4.95	12	0	0	1	20	23	17	11	0	11	17	.284	.348	.259	7.65	4.95
Greenwalt, Kyle	R-R	6-0	200	9-29-88	0	7	7.53	12	8	0	0	35	55	40	29	1	12	28	.353	.396	.333	7.27	3.12
Lazu, Carlos	R-L	6-0	185	2-4-86	0	0	8.14	13	0	0	0	24	36	24	22	3	8	16	.340	.200	.372	5.92	2.96
Leon, Arcenio	R-R	6-1	162	9-22-86	0	7	4.67	15	9	0	0	54	56	37	28	1	27	43	.267	.263	.269	7.17	4.50
Noguera, Antonio	L-L	6-3	194	2-26-88	2	5	4.15	12	12	1	0	61	60	36	28	3	21	36	.259	.345	.246	5.34	3.12
Pinales, Agustin	R-R	6-2	185	8-28-85	1	4	8.24	16	5	0	0	39	64	45	36	6	16	35	.360	.415	.336	8.01	3.66
Pitkin, Colton	R-L	6-3	210	8-10-89	0	0	7.04	7	0	0	0	8	12	9	6	0	6	6	.333	.286	.345	7.04	7.04
Powell, Jordan	R-R	6-2	205	4-14-85	1	2	5.56	16	1	0	0	34	39	22	21	0	16	35	.283	.271	.289	9.26	4.24
Roberts, Mason	R-R	6-3	200	12-11-85	0	4	10.50	12	2	0	0	18	23	26	21	0	24	14	.311	.300	.315	7.00	12.00
Robinson, Brett	R-R	6-0	185	1-23-85	1	2	3.38	21	0	0	0	29	33	15	11	1	1	25	.270	.217	.303	7.67	0.31
Urbina, Guillermo	L-L	5-11	190	5-30-85	0	0	9.00	12	0	0	0	19	33	24	19	2	14	24	.355	.364	.352	11.37	6.63
Wabick, Brian	R-R	6-0	180	8-3-87	0	2	5.18	18	1	0	1	42	47	27	24	6	17	28	.276	.420	.217	6.05	3.67

FIELDING

Catcher	PCT	G	PO	A	E	DP	PB
Gonzalez	.981	31	235	22	5	2	4
Miller	1.000	1	1	0	0	0	0
Pestana	.977	43	267	30	7	1	10

First Base	PCT	G	PO	A	E	DP
Anderson	1.000	1	3	0	0	0
Launier	.993	34	288	10	2	24
Miller	.981	35	294	15	6	21
Pestana	1.000	1	2	0	0	1

Second Base	PCT	G	PO	A	E	DP
Anderson	.935	14	29	29	4	5
Cartwright	.930	13	24	29	4	5
Johnson	.915	19	35	40	7	7

	PCT	G	PO	A	E	DP
Saylor	1.000	6	5	12	0	1
Stringer	.945	22	44	59	6	11

Third Base	PCT	G	PO	A	E	DP
Miller	.778	6	4	10	4	0
Parks	—	1	0	0	0	0
Rosario	.849	56	46	112	28	6
Stringer	.862	9	6	19	4	0

Shortstop	PCT	G	PO	A	E	DP
Brown	.926	37	37	125	13	15
Cartwright	1.000	3	1	6	0	2
Johnson	.904	27	50	91	15	15
Stringer	.818	2	4	5	2	2

Outfield	PCT	G	PO	A	E	DP
Darnell	.960	40	67	5	3	2
Frye	.921	18	34	1	3	0
Gonzalez	.934	37	54	3	4	1
Parks	.970	21	29	3	1	0
Phipps	.889	4	8	0	1	0
Pitts	1.000	36	69	2	0	0
Rosario	1.000	1	1	0	0	0
Sweet	1.000	18	30	1	0	1
Torrence	.958	17	23	0	1	0
Turner	1.000	22	29	0	0	0
Williams	1.000	6	8	0	0	0

DSL ASTROS   ROOKIE

DOMINICAN SUMMER LEAGUE

BATTING	B-T	HT	WT	DOB	AVG	vLH	vRH	G	AB	R	H	2B	3B	HR	RBI	BB	HBP	SH	SF	SO	SB	CS	SLG	OBP
Almonte, Frank	R-R	6-2	190	1-24-89	.233	.147	.252	53	193	28	45	10	0	6	23	22	4	0	1	70	0	2	.378	.323
Arrendell, Miguel	R-L	6-0	175	3-26-88	.214	.360	.174	37	117	14	25	3	0	1	10	19	3	1	4	15	1	3	.265	.329
Beltre, Adrian	L-L	6-2	190	11-18-87	.136	.000	.176	7	22	0	3	0	0	0	0	1	1	0	0	2	0	1	.136	.174
Carela, Freidy	R-R	6-2	160	11-28-88	.240	.421	.198	31	100	7	24	7	0	1	9	3	4	1	0	26	4	2	.340	.290
Claxton, Randy	R-R	6-3	190	7-2-86	.237	.212	.243	56	169	20	40	10	0	0	18	39	11	0	1	32	2	1	.296	.409
Cuevas, Samuel	R-R	6-0	192	11-4-87	.259	.400	.227	43	158	24	41	7	1	0	16	19	6	2	2	35	10	3	.316	.357
De Leon, Jorge	R-R	6-0	168	8-15-87	.190	.167	.195	52	179	23	34	9	3	2	17	15	13	1	1	41	3	3	.307	.298
Domingo, Jose	R-R	6-2	170	10-18-86	.364	.000	.500	3	11	1	4	0	0	0	1	1	0	0	0	4	1	0	.364	.417
Henriquez, Victor	R-R	6-0	170	4-1-86	.205	.286	.194	37	117	14	24	4	0	0	14	15	2	3	2	21	5	4	.239	.301
Heredia, Ricardo	R-R	6-2	190	3-31-89	.122	.222	.094	15	41	1	5	1	0	0	1	4	3	0	0	12	0	2	.146	.250
Infante, Wilton	R-R	6-1	175	8-11-87	.309	.400	.294	36	139	23	43	6	1	2	11	8	3	2	1	23	16	5	.410	.358
King, Emilio	R-R	6-0	180	8-17-89	.161	.000	.196	21	62	9	10	1	2	1	6	4	3	1	0	16	0	2	.290	.246
Mejia, Jhoan	R-R	6-2	190	12-25-88	.246	.265	.243	56	203	29	50	11	0	0	28	24	7	0	8	29	0	1	.300	.335
Mojica, Carlos	R-R	6-0	190	6-7-88	.220	.056	.260	31	91	16	20	3	1	1	13	13	8	1	0	21	1	2	.308	.366
Ozuna, Yovanny	R-R	6-0	170	10-15-86	.175	.167	.175	22	63	4	11	1	0	0	4	4	1	0	1	30	0	0	.190	.232
Recio, Cristian	R-R	6-0	178	7-5-87	.233	.121	.265	45	150	18	35	9	1	1	10	5	3	0	4	47	9	1	.327	.272
Reyes, Carlos	R-R	6-0	178	12-5-87	.243	.243	.243	57	206	24	50	7	2	4	30	29	3	0	2	59	5	7	.354	.342
Rodriguez, Amilkin	B-R	6-2	190	3-13-88	.198	.133	.207	44	131	16	26	3	0	0	11	17	3	2	2	24	5	1	.221	.301

PITCHING	B-T	HT	WT	DOB	W	L	ERA	G	GS	CG	SV	IP	H	R	ER	HR	BB	SO	AVG	vLH	vRH	K/9	BB/9
Batista, Jose	R-R	6-2	155	5-24-88	0	1	2.79	11	1	0	0	10	7	12	3	0	16	5	.206	.250	.200	4.66	14.90
Belliard, Joan	R-R	6-2	185	3-3-89	0	0	8.35	9	0	0	1	18	29	21	17	3	7	15	.358	.333	.364	7.36	3.44
Espinal, Martin	R-R	6-0	190	11-3-86	5	5	3.76	14	14	0	0	69	62	39	29	5	16	63	.225	.222	.225	8.18	2.08
Gonzalez, Angel	L-L	6-0	158	8-12-88	4	2	3.35	14	5	0	1	43	35	23	16	1	30	45	.236	.100	.246	9.42	6.28

Name	B-T	HT	WT	DOB	W	L	ERA	G	GS	CG	SV	IP	H	R	ER	HR	BB	SO	AVG	vLH	vRH	K/9	BB/9
Lopez, Pedro	R-R	6-0	170	4-28-86	0	0	3.00	4	0	0	1	6	6	3	2	0	4	6	.261	.375	.200	9.00	6.00
Lopez, Wilfred	R-R	6-5	200	8-23-86	0	2	6.29	15	0	0	2	24	27	24	17	1	17	21	.278	.286	.275	7.77	6.29
Luna, Rafael	L-L	6-6	175	1-20-90	0	5	4.01	11	5	0	0	25	24	24	11	1	17	17	.226	.667	.214	6.20	6.20
Matulia, Dionisio	R-R	6-2	155	8-9-86	6	1	3.89	20	1	0	1	42	29	22	18	2	21	26	.199	.207	.197	5.62	4.54
Nina, Adan	R-R	6-0	165	1-24-87	1	1	1.91	11	0	0	1	28	22	9	6	0	10	14	.214	.160	.231	4.45	3.18
Ortiz, Wander	R-R	5-11	159	2-10-87	2	4	3.16	15	13	0	0	68	77	38	24	2	24	59	.277	.324	.260	7.77	3.16
Pio, Rafael	R-R	6-2	180	1-9-88	0	2	6.75	11	2	0	0	20	29	24	15	2	13	14	.341	.423	.305	6.30	5.85
Romero, Joel	R-R	6-0	180	7-25-88	2	6	2.07	13	12	0	0	61	48	26	14	3	21	67	.212	.164	.228	9.89	3.10
Trinidad, Jose	R-R	5-11	150	7-13-87	4	4	2.63	22	0	0	8	55	51	26	16	2	17	52	.260	.227	.270	8.56	2.80
Vargas, Radaulin	L-L	6-2	160	5-22-89	1	2	2.35	10	2	0	1	31	30	13	8	3	13	24	.268	.143	.276	7.04	3.82
Villar, Henry	R-R	5-11	150	5-24-87	4	4	2.45	13	13	0	0	73	64	26	20	4	12	69	.233	.271	.220	8.47	1.47

FIELDING

Catcher	PCT	G	PO	A	E	DP	PB
King	.965	20	122	16	5	0	2
Mojica	.971	31	241	24	8	3	10
Ozuna	.969	22	139	15	5	0	2

First Base	PCT	G	PO	A	E	DP
Claxton	.978	56	466	17	11	41
Mejia	.992	17	113	8	1	12
Rodriguez	1.000	1	7	0	0	0

Second Base	PCT	G	PO	A	E	DP
Arrendell	.949	37	76	93	9	19

Carela	.927	13	26	25	4	5
Henriquez	.888	21	35	60	12	11

Third Base	PCT	G	PO	A	E	DP
Mejia	.848	29	19	59	14	4
Rodriguez	.835	43	28	78	21	5

Shortstop	PCT	G	PO	A	E	DP
Carela	.879	17	21	37	8	8
De Leon	.922	52	90	170	22	30
Henriquez	.842	5	1	15	3	1

Outfield	PCT	G	PO	A	E	DP
Almonte	.902	34	37	0	4	0
Cuevas	.978	30	41	3	1	0
Domingo	1.000	2	4	0	0	0
Heredia	.926	14	24	1	2	0
Infante	.927	34	66	10	6	2
Recio	.958	41	43	3	2	0
Reyes	.960	57	91	4	4	0

VSL ASTROS　　　　　　　　　　　　　　　　　　ROOKIE

VENEZUELAN SUMMER LEAGUE

BATTING	B-T	HT	WT	DOB	AVG	vLH	vRH	G	AB	R	H	2B	3B	HR	RBI	BB	HBP	SH	SF	SO	SB	CS	SLG	OBP
Altuve, Jose	R-R	5-5	148	5-6-90	.343	.295	.364	64	204	40	70	12	4	0	36	28	5	3	3	16	15	5	.441	.429
Alvarez, Luis	R-R	5-11	198	2-28-90	.241	.286	.231	35	112	26	27	2	1	2	14	10	7	2	0	15	0	1	.330	.341
Armas, Herman	L-L	5-11	154	12-22-86	.300	.344	.286	70	250	51	75	9	3	9	48	40	9	5	1	48	10	3	.468	.413
Blanco, Robert	R-R	5-11	177	4-18-89	.273	.300	.265	40	132	19	36	11	0	0	13	10	8	3	3	23	4	2	.356	.353
Bonfante, Ricardo	R-R	5-9	140	10-21-88	.314	.345	.304	58	226	30	71	12	2	0	23	21	2	1	0	12	15	4	.385	.378
De Aguas, Jayson	L-R	6-2	210	1-28-87	.301	.320	.295	40	113	10	34	3	0	0	12	11	5	2	3	10	1	0	.327	.379
Figueroa, Oscar	R-R	5-11	154	1-10-88	.208	.217	.205	63	221	31	46	13	1	4	23	21	2	10	4	39	3	2	.330	.278
Garcia, Ricardo	R-R	5-9	142	1-20-89	.276	.263	.279	33	87	17	24	7	1	1	11	14	4	2	1	16	7	3	.414	.396
Hernandez, Federico	R-R	6-0	170	2-9-88	.299	.261	.314	48	167	24	50	10	2	1	23	11	1	3	1	20	2	1	.401	.344
Holder, Manuel	L-L	5-10	144	2-20-87	.240	.250	.236	64	192	24	46	4	5	0	17	12	1	4	3	34	3	2	.313	.284
Lopez, Yohender	L-L	6-0	145	9-4-86	.194	.000	.219	13	36	8	7	2	0	2	9	7	1	0	0	12	0	0	.417	.341
Medrano, Jhonny	R-R	6-1	156	9-12-87	.289	.220	.310	64	218	42	63	13	1	1	36	37	5	1	1	40	19	4	.372	.402
Nieves, Angel	R-R	5-11	175	7-11-90	.409	.600	.353	7	22	5	9	2	1	2	8	1	0	0	1	4	0	1	.864	.417
Paris, Juan	R-R	6-0	170	5-14-86	.287	.313	.277	50	167	18	48	7	0	3	23	13	3	4	3	16	3	1	.383	.344
Sumoza, Luis	R-R	5-10	186	6-9-89	.226	.067	.256	36	93	16	21	7	0	2	14	13	1	2	2	24	4	1	.366	.321
Tello, Renzo	R-R	6-1	156	6-30-87	.294	.333	.281	46	163	25	48	12	1	7	29	6	3	2	2	31	2	1	.509	.328
Valdes, Joseph	R-R	6-1	197	7-17-90	.269	.267	.270	18	52	9	14	4	0	0	8	6	2	1	1	10	2	0	.346	.361

PITCHING	B-T	HT	WT	DOB	W	L	ERA	G	GS	CG	SV	IP	H	R	ER	HR	BB	SO	AVG	vLH	vRH	K/9	BB/9
Berti, Danilo	L-L	5-9	215	3-11-89	2	3	4.24	13	10	0	0	57	60	33	27	2	17	41	.278	.167	.284	6.44	2.67
Betancourt, Luis	L-L	5-10	156	4-9-87	2	1	4.25	13	0	0	1	30	24	21	14	0	29	29	.220	.200	.221	8.80	8.80
Castellano, Julio	L-L	6-2	170	6-11-87	3	1	2.82	8	7	0	0	38	37	14	12	2	17	24	.261	.167	.265	5.63	3.99
Castillo, Jeiler	R-R	6-0	155	10-26-87	1	3	2.69	13	11	0	1	67	69	30	20	3	16	33	.270	.254	.275	4.43	2.15
Diaz, Dayan	R-R	5-10	156	2-10-89	1	1	2.05	13	0	0	0	22	12	5	5	1	15	17	.162	.143	.167	6.95	6.14
Garcia, Gabriel de Jesus	L-L	5-11	142	5-11-89	3	3	3.58	17	0	0	3	28	28	16	11	0	6	19	.259	.200	.262	6.18	1.95
Martinez, David	R-R	6-2	180	8-8-87	1	1	3.51	9	4	0	0	33	26	18	13	1	8	30	.203	.205	.202	8.10	2.16
Mendoza, Ricardo	R-R	6-0	162	6-28-89	5	0	3.68	13	10	0	0	51	50	28	21	4	19	31	.254	.289	.243	5.44	3.33
Moreno, Robert	R-R	5-11	169	9-20-89	2	0	2.76	12	0	0	4	16	12	6	5	2	5	9	.207	.214	.205	4.96	2.76
Palma, Wilfrido	L-L	6-1	194	6-12-87	3	1	3.32	13	7	0	0	43	24	17	16	1	24	27	.174	.167	.175	5.61	4.98
Paracuto, Erick	L-L	5-9	181	1-14-90	1	1	5.40	15	0	0	3	28	25	19	17	1	29	21	.238	.667	.225	6.67	9.21
Perez, German	L-L	5-11	147	9-21-89	7	1	2.07	14	13	0	0	70	58	19	16	1	19	54	.227	.278	.224	6.98	2.45
Perez, Yuri	R-R	5-11	148	8-8-90	1	3	4.32	18	0	0	2	33	39	20	16	2	16	13	.287	.308	.278	3.51	4.32
Pina, Wladimir	R-R	6-2	197	10-9-89	2	2	3.04	12	0	0	2	24	20	12	8	0	14	7	.241	.167	.271	2.66	5.32
Puentes, Julio	R-R	6-4	222	2-2-86	5	3	2.25	20	0	0	8	40	33	16	10	0	11	34	.234	.359	.186	7.65	2.48
Quevedo, Carlos	R-R	6-1	222	9-30-89	4	0	2.32	11	9	0	0	54	41	15	14	1	15	25	.217	.236	.209	4.14	2.48
Vegas, Hector	L-L	6-3	205	10-3-86	1	0	13.50	7	1	0	0	6	6	10	9	0	19	5	.273	.333	.263	7.50	28.50

FIELDING

Catcher	PCT	G	PO	A	E	DP	PB
Alvarez	.974	32	164	24	5	5	4
De Aguas	.976	16	70	13	2	1	0
Hernandez	.963	28	157	25	7	1	6
Valdes	1.000	8	29	5	0	1	4

First Base	PCT	G	PO	A	E	DP
De Aguas	.995	22	195	11	1	15
Figueroa	.985	33	243	12	4	15
Medrano	1.000	8	42	3	0	9
Paris	.996	28	222	23	1	16
Sumoza	.923	2	12	0	1	1
Tello	1.000	1	1	0	0	0

Second Base	PCT	G	PO	A	E	DP
Altuve	.960	51	112	125	10	25

Figueroa	.893	6	12	13	3	4
Garcia	.964	7	11	16	1	2
Sumoza	.975	19	38	40	2	7

Third Base	PCT	G	PO	A	E	DP
Figueroa	.875	8	3	11	2	2
Garcia	.840	14	10	32	8	2
Medrano	.919	45	42	139	16	13
Paris	.926	14	9	41	4	1
Sumoza	1.000	2	0	2	0	0

Shortstop	PCT	G	PO	A	E	DP
Bonfante	.933	56	77	161	17	29
Figueroa	.918	18	34	55	8	7
Nieves	.875	3	6	8	2	2
Sumoza	.889	3	6	2	1	0

Outfield	PCT	G	PO	A	E	DP
Armas	.943	68	112	4	7	0
Blanco	.947	38	65	7	4	4
Figueroa	—	1	0	0	0	0
Garcia	1.000	1	1	0	0	0
Holder	.984	60	115	11	2	4
Lopez	1.000	10	18	1	0	0
Medrano	1.000	10	8	1	0	0
Tello	.978	46	81	10	2	3

Kansas City Royals

BY ALAN ESKEW

Progress is sometimes painfully slow.

The Royals finished last in the American League Central for the fourth straight year, but after three straight seasons of losing 100 or more games the Royals went 69-93 in 2007.

"I'm disappointed in our won-loss record, but certainly not discouraged by any means because we do have a recognizable young talented core of players that we can build upon," Royals general manager Dayton Moore said.

The Royals had four rookies make significant contributions in 2007. Righthander Brian Bannister, who was acquired in a trade with the Mets at the 2006 Winter Meetings, led the staff in wins. At the same Winter Meetings, the Royals selected Joakim Soria in the Rule 5 draft from the Padres. Soria led all rookies with 17 saves in 21 opportunities and held opposing hitters to a .187 average.

Third baseman Alex Gordon, the second overall pick in the 2005 draft, was considered a primary rookie of the year candidate out of spring training, but got off to a slow start. He rebounded to hit 15 home runs and led the team with 36 doubles and topped AL rookies with 55 extra-base hits.

DH Billy Butler, the 14th overall pick in 2004 who won two minor league batting titles, hit .292 with 52 RBIs in 329 at-bats. While not a rookie, Tony Pena Jr., acquired in a trade with the Braves the final week of spring training, played steady shortstop in his first full year in the majors.

The Royals will have a rookie manager in 2008. Trey Hillman, who managed 11 seaons in the Yankees farm system and the past five years with the Nippon Ham Fighters in Japan, replaces Buddy Bell as manager. Hillman played three years in the Indians farm system, but never reached the majors. Bell announced he was stepping down as manager on Aug. 1.

The biggest improvement for the club came in pitching. Buoyed by the signing of free agent Gil Meche to a five-year, $55 million contract, the Royals had a 4.48 ERA, their best ERA since the strike-shortened 1994 season—a staff which included Cy Young Award winner David Cone and Kevin Appier. It was the first time since 2001 the Royals had an ERA less than 4.00.

Meche, who received the worst run support of any American League starter, went just 9-13 record, but could have had 15 to 17 wins if the Royals averaged more than 3.92 runs in his starts. Meche pitched a career-high 216 innings and his 156 strikeouts was the most by a Royal since Appier struck out 196 in 1997.

"What we need to do I think is to continue to build on our pitching, to build on our strengths," Moore said. "You've got to count on our young position players to improve and get better."

While the pitching was solid, the offense was lagging. The Royals finished last in the majors with 102 home runs and last in the American League with a .388 slugging percentage.

Outfielder Emil Brown led the team in RBIs for the third straight year, but his 62 RBIs was the lowest to top the Royals for a full-season in franchise history. John Buck's 18 home runs topped the club, but 13 were solo shots. Mark Teahen, who led the team with 18 home runs in 393 at-bats in 2006, hit just seven in 544 at-bats in 2007.

After hitting .297 in 2006, David DeJesus' average dropped to .260, but he did score a career-high 101 runs,

ORGANIZATIONAL LEADERS

BATTING		★Minimum 250 at-bats
★AVG	Padilla, Jorge, Omaha/Wichita	.316
R	Brazell, Craig, Wichita/Omaha	83
H	Brazell, Craig, Wichita/Omaha	171
TB	Brazell, Craig, Wichita/Omaha	326
2B	Brazell, Craig, Wichita/Omaha	38
3B	Greenberg, Adam, Wichita	11
HR	Brazell, Craig, Wichita/Omaha	39
RBI	Brazell, Craig, Wichita/Omaha	91
BB	Kaaihue, Kila, Wilmington/Wichita	76
SO	Vega, Miguel, Wilmington	137
SB	Robinson, Derrick, Burlington/Wilmington	35
★OBP	Stodolka, Mike, Wichita	.409
★SLG	Brazell, Craig, Wichita/Omaha	.601
PITCHING		^Minimum 75 innings
W	Hardy, Rowdy, Wilmington	15
L	Christensen, Daniel, Wichita	15
^ERA	Hardy, Rowdy, Wilmington	2.48
G	Plummer, Jarod, Wichita/Omaha	46
CG	Hardy, Rowdy, Wilmington	3
SV	Santos, Arthur, Wichita/Wilmington	12
IP	Hardy, Rowdy, Wilmington	167
BB	Lumsden, Tyler, Omaha	59
SO	Hochevar, Luke, Wichita/Omaha	138
^AVG	Cortes, Daniel, Wilmington	.226

the first Royal to cross the century mark since Carlos Beltran scored 102 runs in 2003.

The Royals have highly regarded pitching prospects, including righthanders Luke Hochevar, the first overall pick in the 2006 draft, and Billy Buckner, a 2004 second-round pick. Both who made their major league debuts in 2007 and will contend for rotation spots in 2008.

After picking no lower than second in the previous three drafts, the Royals will have the third overall pick in 2008. With Gordon and Butler debuting, the minor league system is bereft of potential impact bats. Shortstop Mike Moustakas, who was the second selection in the 2007 draft, set the California high school record with 24 home runs.

Lefthander Rowdy Hardy, a non-drafted free agent in 2006 out of Austin Peay, walked just 15 in 159 innings with high Class A Wilmington.

2007 PERFORMANCE

General Manager: Dayton Moore. **Farm Director:** J.J. Picollo. **Scouting Director:** Deric Ladnier

Class	Team	League	W	L	PCT	Finish*	Manager	Affiliate Since
Majors	Kansas City	American	69	93	.426	12th (14)	Buddy Bell	—
Triple-A	Omaha Royals	Pacific Coast	73	71	.507	8th (16)	Mike Jirschele	1969
Double-A	Wichita Wranglers	Texas	56	84	.400	8th (8)	Tony Tijerina	1995
High A	Wilmington Blue Rocks	Carolina	75	62	.547	3rd (8)	John Mizerock	2007
Low A	Burlington Bees	Midwest	61	77	.442	13th (16)	Jim Gabella	2001
Rookie	Idaho Falls Chukars	Pioneer	46	30	.605	3rd (8)	Brian Rupp	2001
Rookie	Burlington Royals	Appalachian	38	30	.559	3rd (9)	Darryl Kennedy	2007
Overall 2007 Minor League Record			**349**	**354**	**.496**	**14th**		

* Finish in overall standings (No. of teams in league) ^League champion

ORGANIZATION STATISTICS

KANSAS CITY ROYALS

AMERICAN LEAGUE

BATTING	B-T	HT	WT	DOB	AVG	vLH	vRH	G	AB	R	H	2B	3B	HR	RBI	BB	HBP	SH	SF	SO	SB	CS	SLG	OBP
Berroa, Angel	R-R	6-0	195	1-27-78	.091	.200	.000	9	11	0	1	0	0	0	0	1	0	1	1	4	0	1	.091	.167
Brazell, Craig	L-R	6-3	210	5-10-80	.250	1.000	.000	5	4	1	1	0	0	0	1	0	0	0	1	0	0	0	.250	.400
Brown, Emil	R-R	6-2	210	12-29-74	.257	.317	.217	113	366	44	94	13	1	6	62	24	1	0	6	71	12	2	.347	.300
Buck, John	R-R	6-3	220	7-7-80	.222	.189	.231	113	347	41	77	18	0	18	48	36	10	0	6	92	0	1	.429	.308
Butler, Billy	R-R	6-1	240	4-18-86	.292	.340	.272	92	329	38	96	23	2	8	52	27	2	0	2	55	0	0	.447	.347
Cortez, Fernando	L-R	6-1	190	8-10-81	.286	.500	.250	8	14	3	4	1	0	0	1	1	0	1	0	0	0	0	.357	.333
Costa, Shane	L-R	6-0	190	12-12-81	.223	.125	.232	55	103	13	23	6	1	0	12	5	0	0	1	23	0	1	.301	.257
DeJesus, David	L-L	6-0	190	12-20-79	.260	.240	.267	157	605	101	157	29	9	7	58	64	23	7	4	83	10	4	.372	.351
Gathright, Joey	L-R	5-10	185	4-27-81	.307	.282	.312	74	228	28	70	8	0	0	19	20	3	10	0	36	9	8	.342	.371
German, Esteban	R-R	5-9	195	1-26-78	.264	.277	.255	121	348	49	92	15	6	4	37	43	5	6	3	60	11	7	.376	.351
Gload, Ross	L-L	6-1	190	4-5-76	.288	.388	.269	102	320	37	92	22	3	7	51	16	2	0	8	39	2	2	.441	.318
Gordon, Alex	L-R	6-1	220	2-10-84	.247	.217	.258	151	543	60	134	36	4	15	60	41	13	1	2	137	14	4	.411	.314
Grudzielanek, Mark	R-R	6-1	200	6-30-70	.302	.321	.294	116	453	70	137	32	3	6	51	23	8	0	2	60	1	2	.426	.346
Huber, Justin	R-R	6-2	205	7-1-82	.100	.100	.000	8	10	2	1	0	0	0	0	0	0	0	0	2	0	0	.100	.100
LaRue, Jason	R-R	5-11	205	3-19-74	.148	.160	.143	66	169	14	25	9	0	4	13	17	4	3	2	66	1	0	.272	.240
Pena, Tony	R-R	6-2	180	3-23-81	.267	.271	.266	152	509	58	136	25	7	2	47	10	4	8	5	78	5	6	.356	.284
Phillips, Paul	R-R	5-11	205	4-15-77	.143	.000	.222	8	14	2	2	1	0	0	2	1	0	0	1	0	0	0	.214	.200
Sanders, Reggie	R-R	6-1	200	12-1-67	.315	.346	.298	24	73	12	23	7	0	2	11	11	1	0	0	15	0	1	.493	.412
Shealy, Ryan	R-R	6-5	240	8-29-79	.221	.125	.258	52	172	18	38	6	0	3	21	13	3	0	1	53	0	0	.308	.286
Smith, Jason	L-R	6-3	200	7-24-77	.188	.000	.203	40	85	9	16	2	1	6	14	3	0	0	1	29	0	0	.447	.213
2-team (27 Toronto)					.197	—	—	67	137	16	27	3	2	6	18	6	1	0	1	51	0	0	.380	.234
Sweeney, Mike	R-R	6-3	225	7-22-73	.260	.301	.242	74	265	26	69	15	1	7	38	17	5	0	2	29	0	0	.404	.315
Teahen, Mark	L-R	6-3	210	9-6-81	.285	.255	.297	144	544	78	155	31	8	7	60	55	3	4	2	127	13	5	.442	.353

PITCHING	B-T	HT	WT	DOB	W	L	ERA	G	GS	CG	SV	IP	H	R	ER	HR	BB	SO	AVG	vLH	vRH	K/9	BB/9
Bale, John	L-L	6-4	220	5-22-74	1	1	4.05	26	0	0	0	40	45	18	18	1	17	42	.290	.281	.297	9.45	3.82
Bannister, Brian	R-R	6-2	210	2-28-81	12	9	3.87	27	27	1	0	165	156	76	71	15	44	77	.249	.281	.219	4.20	2.40
Braun, Ryan	R-R	6-1	220	7-29-80	2	0	6.64	26	0	0	0	39	46	32	29	4	22	24	.299	.315	.284	5.49	5.03
Buckner, Billy	R-R	6-2	215	8-27-83	1	2	5.29	7	5	0	0	34	37	20	20	5	16	17	.294	.314	.268	4.50	4.24
Davies, Kyle	R-R	6-2	205	9-9-83	3	7	6.66	11	11	0	0	50	63	41	37	10	26	40	.304	.302	.308	7.20	4.68
De La Rosa, Jorge	L-L	6-1	210	4-5-81	8	12	5.82	26	23	0	0	130	160	88	84	20	53	82	.304	.234	.321	5.68	3.67
Dotel, Octavio	R-R	6-0	210	11-25-73	2	1	3.91	24	0	0	11	23	24	11	10	3	11	29	.264	.286	.245	11.35	4.30
Duckworth, Brandon	R-R	6-1	215	1-23-76	3	5	4.63	26	3	0	1	47	51	30	24	3	23	21	.276	.266	.283	4.05	4.44
Elarton, Scott	R-R	6-7	260	2-23-76	2	4	10.46	9	9	0	0	37	53	44	43	12	21	13	.338	.325	.351	3.16	5.11
Gobble, Jimmy	L-L	6-3	200	7-19-81	4	1	3.02	74	0	0	1	54	56	23	18	6	23	50	.277	.241	.319	8.39	3.86
Greinke, Zack	R-R	6-2	185	10-21-83	7	7	3.69	52	14	0	1	122	122	52	50	12	36	106	.265	.266	.263	7.82	2.66
Hochevar, Luke	R-R	6-5	205	9-15-83	0	1	2.13	4	1	0	0	13	11	4	3	1	4	5	.239	.273	.208	3.55	2.84
Hudson, Luke	R-R	6-3	205	5-2-77	0	1	18.00	1	1	0	0	2	2	5	4	1	4	0	.222	.143	.500	0.00	18.00
Meche, Gil	R-R	6-3	220	9-8-78	9	13	3.67	34	34	1	0	216	218	98	88	22	62	156	.263	.242	.284	6.50	2.58
Musser, Neal	L-L	6-1	235	8-25-80	0	1	4.38	17	0	0	0	25	32	13	12	5	14	19	.314	.395	.266	6.93	5.11
Nunez, Leo	R-R	6-1	175	8-14-83	2	4	3.92	13	6	0	0	44	44	21	19	8	10	37	.259	.275	.248	7.63	2.06
Peralta, Joel	R-R	5-11	190	3-23-76	1	3	3.80	62	0	0	1	88	93	39	37	9	19	66	.274	.248	.290	6.78	1.95
Perez, Odalis	L-L	6-0	225	6-11-77	8	11	5.57	26	26	0	0	137	178	90	85	14	50	64	.318	.301	.323	4.19	3.28
Riske, David	R-R	6-2	180	10-23-76	1	4	2.45	65	0	0	4	70	61	19	19	8	27	52	.240	.202	.265	6.72	3.49
Soria, Joakim	R-R	6-3	185	5-18-84	2	3	2.48	62	0	0	17	69	46	20	19	3	19	75	.187	.167	.200	9.78	2.48
Standridge, Jason	R-R	6-4	235	11-9-78	0	1	8.22	4	0	0	0	8	11	10	7	2	5	6	.314	.308	.318	7.04	5.87
Thomson, John	R-R	6-3	220	10-1-73	1	1	3.38	2	2	0	0	11	13	5	4	0	3	3	.317	.261	.389	2.53	2.53
Wellemeyer, Todd	R-R	6-3	225	8-30-78	0	1	10.34	12	0	0	0	16	25	19	18	4	11	9	.352	.444	.257	5.17	6.32

FIELDING

Catcher	PCT	G	PO	A	E	DP	PB
Buck	.989	112	697	29	8	6	3
LaRue	.985	65	311	24	5	3	2
Phillips	1.000	7	29	1	0	0	0

First Base	PCT	G	PO	A	E	DP
Brazell	1.000	1	7	0	0	2
Butler	.978	13	79	8	2	6
Gload	.996	89	633	45	3	78
Gordon	.993	32	132	8	1	16
Phillips	1.000	1	2	0	0	0
Shealy	1.000	52	402	29	0	37
Smith	1.000	3	12	0	0	1
Sweeney	.977	6	40	2	1	5
Teahen	1.000	9	45	0	0	4

Second Base	PCT	G	PO	A	E	DP
Berroa	—	1	0	0	0	0

	PCT	G	PO	A	E	DP
Cortez	.958	6	12	11	1	4
German	.984	56	83	105	3	27
Grudzielanek	.988	116	184	300	6	68
Pena	1.000	1	2	3	0	1
Smith	.947	7	9	9	1	5

Third Base	PCT	G	PO	A	E	DP
Berroa	—	1	0	0	0	0
German	.929	46	16	49	5	5
Gordon	.961	137	99	247	14	22
LaRue	1.000	1	0	1	0	0
Smith	.750	4	1	2	1	0

Shortstop	PCT	G	PO	A	E	DP
Berroa	1.000	4	4	11	0	6
German	.500	4	0	1	1	1
Gordon	1.000	1	2	1	0	0
Grudzielanek	1.000	3	1	2	0	0

	PCT	G	PO	A	E	DP
Pena	.966	150	208	438	23	98
Smith	.953	20	22	39	3	6

Outfield	PCT	G	PO	A	E	DP
Brown	.972	96	197	8	6	2
Butler	.800	6	4	0	1	0
Costa	.982	27	54	0	1	0
DeJesus	.990	156	401	5	4	0
Gathright	.977	72	170	3	4	0
German	1.000	8	6	2	0	0
Gload	1.000	8	10	1	0	0
Huber	1.000	3	2	0	0	0
Sanders	1.000	17	38	0	0	0
Teahen	.983	138	326	17	6	7

OMAHA ROYALS

TRIPLE-A

PACIFIC COAST LEAGUE

BATTING	B-T	HT	WT	DOB	AVG	vLH	vRH	G	AB	R	H	2B	3B	HR	RBI	BB	HBP	SH	SF	SO	SB	CS	SLG	OBP
Aviles, Mike	R-R	5-9	205	3-13-81	.296	.320	.286	133	538	78	159	27	6	17	77	30	2	5	6	59	5	5	.463	.332
Berroa, Angel	R-R	6-0	195	1-27-78	.300	.278	.310	81	307	47	92	17	0	8	40	25	9	6	5	44	2	2	.433	.364
Blanco, Andres	B-R	5-10	190	4-11-84	.196	.292	.164	28	97	8	19	2	0	0	8	5	0	3	2	12	0	0	.216	.231
Brazell, Craig	L-R	6-3	210	5-10-80	.307	.319	.302	105	433	68	133	33	0	32	76	20	0	1	1	83	0	1	.605	.337
Brewer, Jace	R-R	6-0	180	6-6-79	.275	.190	.333	16	51	7	14	3	0	0	6	7	1	0	1	7	1	1	.333	.367
Butler, Billy	R-R	6-1	240	4-18-86	.291	.302	.287	57	203	40	59	10	1	13	46	43	3	1	6	32	1	0	.542	.412
Clark, Cody	R-R	6-2	170	9-14-81	.286	.000	.286	3	7	1	2	1	0	1	2	0	0	1	0	0	0	0	.857	.286
Cortez, Fernando	L-R	6-1	190	8-10-81	.289	.325	.276	82	304	40	88	15	1	4	24	25	1	8	2	42	12	1	.385	.343
Costa, Shane	L-R	6-0	190	12-12-81	.326	.265	.352	59	233	46	76	20	3	5	14	26	5	1	2	20	8	2	.502	.402
Gathright, Joey	L-R	5-10	185	4-27-81	.341	.403	.314	60	223	44	76	10	4	0	25	43	7	1	3	24	25	8	.422	.457
Gload, Ross	L-L	6-1	190	4-5-76	.500	—	.500	1	4	1	2	0	0	1	1	0	0	0	0	0	0	0	1.250	.500
Huber, Justin	R-R	6-2	205	7-1-82	.276	.232	.294	77	286	39	79	13	1	18	68	20	8	0	4	48	1	0	.517	.336
Koonce, Graham	L-L	6-4	230	5-15-75	.243	.176	.264	20	70	10	17	6	0	4	14	14	0	0	1	22	0	1	.500	.365
LaRue, Jason	R-R	5-11	205	3-19-74	.083	.200	.000	4	12	2	1	1	0	0	0	0	0	2	1	0	3	0	0	.167	.214
Lewis, Richard	R-R	6-1	195	6-29-80	.233	.310	.202	84	292	42	68	12	1	5	32	19	4	9	4	62	3	1	.332	.285
Lubanski, Chris	L-L	6-3	206	3-24-85	.208	.257	.195	49	168	20	35	6	1	6	22	16	0	3	4	48	0	3	.363	.273
Maier, Mitch	L-R	6-2	210	6-30-82	.279	.287	.276	140	544	75	152	29	5	14	62	33	4	6	9	89	7	2	.428	.320
McCarthy, Bill	R-R	6-2	205	12-2-79	.276	.235	.296	27	105	13	29	3	0	5	13	5	4	1	1	20	3	0	.448	.330
Padilla, Jorge	R-R	6-2	200	8-11-79	.291	.317	.278	55	196	27	57	9	1	6	20	14	1	4	3	26	8	3	.439	.336
Phillips, Paul	R-R	5-11	205	4-15-77	.238	.289	.202	58	202	21	48	7	0	2	14	17	0	3	2	25	0	0	.302	.294
Shealy, Ryan	R-R	6-5	240	8-29-79	.262	.414	.215	34	122	14	32	7	0	7	24	15	1	0	1	28	0	0	.492	.345
Sweeney, Mike	R-R	6-3	225	7-22-73	.190	.200	.188	6	21	1	4	1	0	0	1	0	0	1	0	4	0	0	.238	.217
Tupman, Matt	L-R	5-11	190	11-25-79	.281	.266	.285	86	299	21	84	16	0	1	32	36	2	6	1	34	2	2	.344	.361
Wathan, Derek	B-R	6-3	190	12-13-76	.243	.259	.237	57	189	21	46	8	1	2	20	15	0	5	3	26	2	2	.328	.295

PITCHING	B-T	HT	WT	DOB	W	L	ERA	G	GS	CG	SV	IP	H	R	ER	HR	BB	SO	AVG	vLH	vRH	K/9	BB/9
Atencio, Greg	R-R	6-2	191	7-15-81	0	0	4.85	4	0	0	0	13	15	7	7	2	5	11	.278	.250	.294	7.62	3.46
Bale, John	L-L	6-4	220	5-22-74	0	1	2.84	8	4	0	0	13	13	5	4	0	1	12	.265	.263	.267	8.53	0.71
Bannister, Brian	R-R	6-2	210	2-28-81	1	1	2.61	4	4	0	0	21	16	11	6	4	4	14	.213	.130	.250	6.10	1.74
Bradley, Anthony	L-L	6-3	207	7-10-85	0	0	6.00	1	0	0	0	3	4	2	2	0	3	1	.333	.333	.333	3.00	9.00
Braun, Ryan	R-R	6-1	220	7-20-80	2	2	1.09	23	0	0	0	33	19	7	4	1	12	36	.173	.140	.194	9.82	3.27
Brazelton, Dewon	R-R	6-4	225	6-16-80	0	4	7.11	4	4	0	0	19	24	16	15	3	8	14	.320	.233	.378	6.63	3.79
Buckner, Billy	R-R	6-2	215	8-27-83	9	7	3.78	27	15	0	0	105	108	49	44	11	26	83	.271	.303	.241	7.14	2.24
Colon, Roman	R-R	6-6	225	8-13-79	0	0	0.00	1	0	0	0	2	3	0	0	0	1	0	.429	.500	.000	5.40	0.00
Day, Zach	R-R	6-4	215	6-15-78	1	1	3.93	11	9	0	0	37	34	25	16	2	26	11	.250	.274	.230	2.70	6.38
DeHoyos, Gabe	R-R	5-11	226	4-14-80	0	1	5.52	9	0	0	0	15	20	9	9	2	5	9	.333	.313	.357	5.52	3.07
Duckworth, Brandon	R-R	6-1	215	1-23-76	0	1	3.60	3	3	0	0	15	12	6	6	2	1	15	.214	.200	.226	9.00	0.60
Elarton, Scott	R-R	6-7	260	2-23-76	2	3	6.70	8	8	0	0	44	51	34	33	13	14	19	.288	.306	.276	3.86	2.84
Giron, Roberto	R-R	6-2	200	3-24-76	2	5	3.71	39	0	0	6	85	59	37	35	14	30	92	.193	.186	.198	9.74	3.18
Hendrickson, Ben	R-R	6-4	205	2-4-81	11	5	4.12	27	18	1	0	135	136	70	62	10	54	66	.267	.295	.245	4.39	3.59
Hochevar, Luke	R-R	6-5	205	9-15-83	1	3	5.12	10	10	0	0	58	53	34	33	11	21	44	.244	.252	.235	6.83	3.26
Hoelscher, Nate	L-L	6-2	205	11-11-79	5	3	5.18	35	5	0	3	80	87	48	46	10	21	43	.274	.212	.303	4.84	2.36
Hudson, Luke	R-R	6-3	205	5-27-77	0	1	5.00	2	2	0	0	9	11	7	5	2	4	14	.282	.176	.364	14.00	4.00
Lewis, Richard	R-R	6-1	195	6-29-80	0	0	6.00	2	0	0	0	3	2	2	2	1	1	1	.200	.286	.000	3.00	3.00
Lumsden, Tyler	L-L	6-4	215	5-9-83	9	6	5.88	25	24	0	0	119	141	89	78	11	59	74	.306	.245	.324	5.58	4.45
Markray, Thad	R-R	6-2	215	9-20-79	8	7	4.62	37	1	0	2	88	96	46	45	10	24	63	.283	.278	.287	6.47	2.46
Mildren, Paul	R-L	6-1	195	5-3-84	1	1	9.69	3	3	0	0	13	20	14	14	2	8	11	.345	.400	.333	7.62	5.54
2-team (21 Albuquerque)					6	8	6.28	24	24	0	0	119	135	92	83	18	60	76	—	—	—	5.75	4.54
Musser, Neal	L-L	6-1	235	8-25-80	4	1	0.49	32	0	0	8	55	32	5	3	1	11	47	.173	.281	.125	7.64	1.79
Nunez, Leo	R-R	6-1	175	8-14-83	1	2	2.74	5	4	0	0	23	16	7	7	3	4	19	.193	.219	.176	7.43	1.57
Plummer, Jarod	R-R	6-5	200	1-27-84	0	0	15.00	2	0	0	0	3	5	5	5	2	2	1	.357	.125	.667	3.00	6.00
Ray, Ken	R-R	6-3	215	11-27-74	3	4	4.15	35	0	0	2	61	64	29	28	8	32	58	.271	.275	.269	8.60	4.75
2-team (2 Nashville)					3	4	4.00	37	0	0	3	63	64	29	28	8	32	61	—	—	—	8.71	4.57
Shiell, Jason	R-R	6-0	215	10-19-76	1	4	4.66	27	7	0	3	77	90	46	40	10	27	39	.293	.265	.321	4.54	3.14
Standridge, Jason	R-R	6-4	235	11-9-78	2	1	3.86	5	0	0	0	5	6	2	2	0	5	3	.316	.500	.115	5.79	9.64
Tamayo, Danny	R-R	6-1	219	6-3-79	0	1	20.25	2	1	0	0	3	7	6	6	0	4	3	.538	.625	.400	10.12	13.50
Thompson, Sean	L-L	5-11	170	10-13-82	0	0	0.00	3	0	0	0	1	2	0	0	0	4	1	.400	.500	.333	0.00	18.00
Thomson, John	R-R	6-3	220	10-1-73	0	1	21.60	1	1	0	0	3	9	8	8	1	0	2	.500	.500	.500	5.40	0.00
Wright, Matt	R-R	6-4	250	3-13-82	10	5	4.06	28	21	0	0	137	142	68	62	21	40	98	.266	.270	.264	6.42	2.62

FIELDING

Catcher	PCT	G	PO	A	E	DP	PB
Clark	1.000	3	14	3	0	1	1
LaRue	1.000	1	6	0	0	0	0
Phillips	.995	57	381	35	2	3	6
Tupman	.991	86	515	43	5	4	10

First Base	PCT	G	PO	A	E	DP
Brazell	.983	57	504	26	9	64
Butler	.972	22	185	20	6	22
Cortez	1.000	5	34	3	0	4
Huber	.993	31	260	6	2	26
Koonce	1.000	10	90	4	0	15
Lewis	1.000	4	18	2	0	4
Shealy	.986	16	134	9	2	14
Wathan	1.000	4	30	1	0	2

Second Base	PCT	G	PO	A	E	DP
Aviles	.966	33	67	102	6	23
Berroa	1.000	6	8	11	0	2
Blanco	.968	7	12	18	1	8
Cortez	.979	46	94	142	5	38
Lewis	.994	37	70	110	1	27
Wathan	.988	19	32	53	1	17

Third Base	PCT	G	PO	A	E	DP
Aviles	.925	49	45	103	12	13
Berroa	.846	5	1	10	2	0
Brewer	1.000	12	6	23	0	1
Cortez	.957	25	20	46	3	7
Lewis	.915	31	15	60	7	9
Wathan	.932	28	25	57	6	6

Shortstop	PCT	G	PO	A	E	DP
Aviles	.980	53	88	153	5	40
Berroa	.987	70	92	207	4	52
Blanco	.957	21	40	70	5	19
Brewer	.900	4	6	12	2	2

Outfield	PCT	G	PO	A	E	DP
Butler	.975	26	37	2	1	0
Cortez	.950	7	19	0	1	0
Costa	.991	46	102	3	1	1
Gathright	.993	56	137	1	1	0
Huber	.989	41	87	2	1	0
Lewis	1.000	2	2	0	0	0
Lubanski	.973	48	103	5	3	0
Maier	.991	137	330	11	3	3
McCarthy	1.000	20	45	1	0	0
Padilla	.982	50	104	6	2	3
Phillips	1.000	1	2	1	0	0
Wathan	1.000	4	3	0	0	0

WICHITA WRANGLERS

TEXAS LEAGUE

DOUBLE-A

BATTING

BATTING	B-T	HT	WT	DOB	AVG	vLH	vRH	G	AB	R	H	2B	3B	HR	RBI	BB	HBP	SH	SF	SO	SB	CS	SLG	OBP
Arce, Valentino	R-R	5-11	167	6-7-85	.242	.417	.204	28	66	9	16	4	0	1	3	1	3	0	0	11	2	0	.348	.286
Blalock, Jake	R-R	6-4	205	8-6-83	.153	.136	.157	30	111	4	17	4	0	1	8	8	0	1	1	19	2	0	.216	.208
2-team (16 Frisco)					.158	—	—	46	158	7	25	5	1	1	17	12	1	1	3	30	2	0	.222	.218
Brazell, Craig	L-R	6-3	210	5-10-80	.349	.343	.351	30	109	15	38	5	0	7	15	11	0	0	0	19	0	0	.587	.408
Brewer, Jace	R-R	6-0	180	6-6-79	.250	.324	.229	47	168	22	42	10	1	2	12	5	2	5	0	32	2	2	.357	.280
Donachie, Adam	R-R	6-1	235	3-3-84	.207	.186	.212	84	271	34	56	12	0	9	35	31	2	3	0	76	0	0	.351	.293
Espino, Damaso	B-R	6-1	210	5-8-83	.260	.226	.265	72	231	17	60	11	0	2	21	22	3	1	0	29	1	2	.333	.332
Eure, Jeffrey	R-R	6-1	215	8-17-80	.209	.182	.213	24	91	9	19	4	1	2	11	6	3	0	0	29	2	1	.341	.280
Falu, Irving	B-R	6-0	173	6-6-83	.242	.265	.235	131	476	46	115	12	6	1	28	35	1	11	2	44	15	9	.298	.294
Gaffney, Michael	R-R	6-1	190	11-11-81	.243	.343	.224	67	218	20	53	10	0	3	17	17	3	3	1	33	2	0	.330	.305
Greenberg, Adam	L-R	5-9	180	2-21-81	.266	.276	.263	132	467	73	124	30	11	8	43	74	7	13	1	107	23	9	.428	.373
Howell, Jeffrey	R-R	6-0	200	4-1-83	.600	—	.600	2	5	3	1	0	0	0	0	0	0	0	0	1	0	0	.800	.600
Joseph, Onil	B-R	6-2	165	2-12-82	.254	.244	.257	105	347	39	88	12	4	3	30	20	2	7	2	73	11	12	.337	.296
Kaaihue, Kila	L-R	6-3	233	3-29-84	.246	.212	.255	70	244	37	60	13	0	12	40	41	2	1	0	40	0	0	.447	.359
Lewis, Richard	R-R	6-1	195	6-29-80	.260	.333	.229	15	50	2	13	1	0	0	6	3	0	1	1	6	0	1	.280	.296
Lubanski, Chris	L-L	6-3	206	3-24-85	.295	.216	.316	64	241	33	71	14	3	9	34	28	0	0	5	43	3	5	.490	.361
Lucas, Edward	R-R	6-4	205	5-21-82	.280	.219	.301	34	125	19	35	6	1	3	17	9	0	1	0	23	2	1	.416	.328
Nettles, Jeff	R-R	6-0	185	8-20-78	.267	.302	.258	58	221	24	59	14	0	8	41	16	0	0	4	52	1	0	.439	.311
Padilla, Jorge	R-R	6-2	200	8-11-79	.336	.302	.348	69	247	51	83	13	1	10	49	32	8	2	3	40	11	3	.518	.424
Sandberg, Jared	R-R	6-3	225	-3-2-78	.103	.214	.074	18	68	5	7	0	0	1	2	9	1	0	0	20	0	0	.147	.218
Stodolka, Mike	L-L	6-2	210	9-24-81	.291	.278	.296	110	381	69	111	27	1	12	59	73	4	0	2	91	4	0	.462	.409
Valentin, Geraldo	R-R	6-0	184	9-8-82	.288	.262	.295	112	437	48	126	19	3	2	54	25	3	11	4	46	5	11	.359	.328

PITCHING

PITCHING	B-T	HT	WT	DOB	W	L	ERA	G	GS	CG	SV	IP	H	R	ER	HR	BB	SO	AVG	vLH	vRH	K/9	BB/9
Atencio, Greg	R-R	6-2	191	7-15-81	4	7	5.29	32	11	1	0	100	110	67	59	11	41	77	.284	.313	.261	6.91	3.68
Bale, John	L-L	6-4	220	5-22-74	0	0	4.50	3	3	0	0	4	5	2	2	1	2	0	.313	.000	.417	0.00	4.50
Barnes, Justin	R-R	6-4	200	8-21-82	1	1	3.00	5	2	0	0	15	12	8	5	0	5	13	.214	.241	.185	7.80	3.00
Bausher, Tim	R-R	6-4	200	4-23-79	1	4	7.94	13	1	0	1	23	29	20	20	3	14	15	.315	.300	.327	5.96	5.56
Bernat, David	R-R	6-2	171	2-17-84	1	0	13.50	3	0	0	0	5	10	8	8	2	1	6	.417	.273	.538	10.12	1.69
Buckner, Billy	R-R	6-2	215	8-27-83	1	3	4.66	4	3	0	0	19	20	10	10	4	6	13	.253	.184	.317	6.05	2.79
Cedeno, Juan	L-L	6-1	165	8-19-83	3	2	6.33	35	1	0	0	70	89	50	49	10	27	47	.312	.316	.311	6.07	3.49
Christensen, Daniel	L-L	6-1	210	8-10-83	3	15	6.21	27	24	1	0	141	173	97	97	23	56	99	.312	.297	.317	6.33	3.58
Connolly, Michael	L-L	6-0	197	6-2-82	4	7	5.22	28	14	0	1	110	130	79	64	13	34	72	.288	.297	.283	5.87	2.77
Cromer, Jason	R-L	6-4	226	12-11-80	3	8	5.25	35	8	0	1	86	104	53	50	5	29	57	.301	.250	.322	5.99	3.05
De La Rosa, Jorge	L-L	6-1	210	4-5-81	0	1	11.12	3	2	0	0	6	10	8	7	3	4	7	.370	.500	.333	11.12	6.35
de la Vara, Gilbert	L-L	5-11	160	10-4-84	3	2	5.74	19	0	0	1	27	33	19	17	3	10	16	.306	.343	.288	5.40	3.38
DeHoyos, Gabe	R-R	5-11	226	4-14-80	6	0	1.64	29	2	0	4	55	38	11	10	2	19	44	.194	.159	.222	7.20	3.11
Dotel, Octavio	R-R	6-0	210	11-25-73	0	1	3.00	3	1	0	1	3	2	1	1	0	0	4	.200	.200	.200	12.00	0.00
Elarton, Scott	R-R	6-7	260	2-23-76	1	1	3.12	2	2	0	0	9	9	5	3	0	5	4	.243	.389	.105	4.15	5.19
Foster, John	L-L	6-0	200	5-17-78	1	0	3.48	8	0	0	0	10	8	4	4	1	5	11	.205	.267	.167	9.58	4.35
Hochevar, Luke	R-R	6-5	205	9-15-83	3	6	4.69	17	16	0	0	94	110	62	49	13	26	94	.286	.279	.294	9.00	2.49
Hudson, Luke	R-R	6-3	205	5-2-77	0	1	3.68	2	2	0	0	7	8	5	3	1	2	16	.258	.286	.235	14.73	2.45
Hughes, Dusty	L-L	5-10	187	6-29-82	6	2	3.08	25	16	1	1	108	98	44	37	5	45	77	.240	.198	.256	6.42	3.75
Lowery, Devon	L-R	6-1	195	3-24-83	0	1	11.05	6	0	0	0	7	12	11	9	2	10	7	.387	.500	.316	8.59	12.27
Mattox, D.J.	R-R	6-2	195	5-24-80	0	5	7.04	8	6	0	0	38	38	33	30	6	20	26	.252	.260	.244	6.10	4.70
Nunez, Leo	R-R	6-1	175	8-14-83	1	0	0.87	8	5	0	0	21	10	2	2	1	6	13	.147	.100	.184	5.66	2.61
Plummer, Jarod	R-R	6-5	200	1-27-81	5	6	3.08	44	0	0	11	79	65	32	27	13	16	90	.217	.218	.215	10.25	1.82
Rosa, Carlos	R-R	6-1	185	9-21-84	6	6	4.36	21	17	0	1	97	101	50	47	8	43	70	.272	.270	.275	6.49	3.99
Santos, Arthur	R-R	6-0	180	2-20-82	1	2	6.42	19	0	0	2	34	56	33	24	6	18	16	.373	.355	.386	4.28	4.81
Shiell, Jason	R-R	6-0	215	10-19-76	1	0	2.25	2	2	0	0	8	5	2	2	0	0	6	.167	.067	.267	6.75	0.00
Smith, Cody	R-R	6-3	200	4-20-82	1	0	6.43	10	0	0	0	14	25	16	10	0	8	6	.362	.355	.368	5.14	3.86
Tamayo, Danny	R-R	6-1	219	6-3-79	0	1	5.14	5	0	0	0	7	7	4	4	1	0	5	.250	.417	.125	6.43	0.00
Thomson, John	R-R	6-3	220	10-1-73	0	2	14.40	2	2	0	0	5	7	8	8	4	2	1	.318	.333	.300	7.20	3.60

ORGANIZATION STATISTICS

FIELDING

Catcher	PCT	G	PO	A	E	DP	PB
Donachie	.992	78	482	44	4	2	8
Espino	.992	69	437	43	4	4	6
Howell	1.000	2	7	2	0	0	0

First Base	PCT	G	PO	A	E	DP
Brazell	.988	9	71	10	1	7
Eure	.972	8	66	4	2	5
Gaffney	1.000	1	9	0	0	0
Kaaihue	.987	36	282	22	4	30
Lucas	1.000	1	9	1	0	1
Sandberg	1.000	1	13	0	0	0
Stodolka	.990	86	729	65	8	44
Valentin	—	1	0	0	0	0

Second Base	PCT	G	PO	A	E	DP
Arce	1.000	1	2	5	0	0

Brewer	1.000	9	18	25	0	5
Falu	1.000	45	71	110	0	17
Gaffney	.986	34	48	91	2	16
Lewis	1.000	5	11	12	0	3
Sandberg	1.000	1	1	0	0	0
Valentin	.977	52	87	126	5	20

Third Base	PCT	G	PO	A	E	DP
Espino	—	1	0	0	0	0
Eure	.967	13	6	23	1	1
Gaffney	.957	15	14	30	2	2
Lewis	.947	8	6	12	1	1
Lucas	.938	32	30	76	7	3
Nettles	.937	56	44	104	10	6
Sandberg	.902	15	7	30	4	1
Stodolka	1.000	1	0	1	0	0

Shortstop	PCT	G	PO	A	E	DP
Arce	.899	19	25	37	7	10
Brewer	.948	38	40	87	7	13
Falu	.948	88	136	232	20	48

Outfield	PCT	G	PO	A	E	DP
Blalock	1.000	25	56	2	0	0
Gaffney	1.000	4	5	0	0	0
Greenberg	.997	126	302	13	1	1
Joseph	.989	96	178	3	2	0
Lewis	—	1	0	0	0	0
Lubanski	.972	58	100	6	3	2
Padilla	.984	61	117	8	2	3
Stodolka	1.000	7	8	1	0	0
Valentin	.952	51	98	1	5	1

WILMINGTON BLUE ROCKS
HIGH CLASS A
CAROLINA LEAGUE

BATTING	B-T	HT	WT	DOB	AVG	vLH	vRH	G	AB	R	H	2B	3B	HR	RBI	BB	HBP	SH	SF	SO	SB	CS	SLG	OBP
Arce, Valentino	R-R	5-11	167	6-7-85	.232	.271	.214	48	151	19	35	9	0	0	10	6	3	0	1	19	7	2	.291	.273
Balduf, Todd	B-R	6-2	200	7-6-84	.150	.118	.10	20	1	3	0	0	1	4	1	2	0	3	0	0	.150	.320
Bigler, Brett	L-L	6-1	185	10-16-84	.259	.247	.263	109	328	44	85	13	2	0	29	74	3	2	1	68	15	11	.311	.399
Clark, Cody	R-R	6-2	170	9-14-81	.242	.196	.261	45	157	17	38	5	0	3	14	9	3	1	1	28	1	0	.331	.294
Cleveland, Jeremy	R-R	6-2	185	9-10-81	.274	.250	.284	43	146	16	40	10	0	2	16	22	1	2	2	30	0	0	.384	.368
Duarte, Jose	R-R	5-10	165	3-7-85	.290	.343	.269	128	493	82	143	26	5	1	42	48	3	7	1	77	34	13	.369	.356
Jirschele, Jeremy	R-R	5-9	195	11-14-82	.333	.100	.414	15	39	6	13	3	0	0	3	6	1	2	1	7	0	0	.410	.426
Johnson, Joshua	B-R	5-11	170	1-11-86	.252	.360	.209	83	262	28	66	11	2	1	31	41	1	2	1	49	4	7	.321	.354
Kaaihue, Kila	L-R	6-3	233	3-29-84	.251	.154	.284	60	207	28	52	8	0	9	42	35	4	0	7	38	1	0	.420	.360
Larsen, Andrew	R-R	6-0	200	12-14-82	.276	.333	.269	7	29	4	8	2	0	0	2	3	0	0	7	1	1	.345	.344
Lisson, Mario	R-R	6-2	193	5-31-84	.285	.331	.268	126	463	72	132	27	3	8	61	41	8	4	8	93	23	9	.408	.348
Maddox, Marc	R-R	5-11	185	9-16-83	.259	.297	.244	101	405	65	105	17	6	0	44	28	8	7	4	62	12	3	.331	.317
McCann, Brad	R-R	6-3	190	12-9-82	.277	.348	.245	58	220	30	61	18	0	6	30	19	6	0	3	55	1	1	.441	.347
McConnell, Chris	R-R	5-11	175	12-18-85	.236	.266	.222	66	208	20	49	9	2	3	20	16	4	3	0	43	6	4	.341	.303
McFall, Brian	R-R	6-3	215	3-17-84	.286	.236	.308	111	406	59	116	31	5	13	72	40	8	1	4	98	10	6	.483	.358
Peralta, Felix	R-R	6-0	175	9-30-85	.196	.292	.125	18	56	6	11	1	1	0	2	3	1	0	0	14	0	0	.250	.250
Perez, Wilver	R-R	5-11	165	8-28-83	.302	.265	.319	54	162	21	49	13	2	3	23	20	2	2	3	40	13	4	.463	.380
Robinson, Derrick	B-L	5-11	170	9-28-87	.385	.500	.200	3	13	1	5	0	0	0	1	0	0	0	0	1	0	0	.462	.429
Santana, Ethien	L-L	5-11	153	1-25-84	.100	.000	.129	13	40	2	4	1	0	0	0	1	0	1	0	14	3	0	.125	.122
Thibault, Kiel	R-R	6-0	200	3-2-84	.254	.300	.233	91	327	35	83	16	2	4	36	25	10	4	3	53	9	2	.352	.323
Vega, Miguel	R-R	6-3	224	7-31-85	.233	.232	.233	120	468	46	109	23	0	8	57	19	5	2	3	137	0	1	.333	.269

PITCHING	B-T	HT	WT	DOB	W	L	ERA	G	GS	CG	SV	IP	H	R	ER	HR	BB	SO	AVG	vLH	vRH	K/9	BB/9
Barnes, Justin	R-R	6-4	200	8-21-82	1	3	3.66	31	0	0	4	52	39	21	21	7	23	36	.212	.203	.219	6.27	4.01
Campbell, Matt	L-L	6-2	180	12-27-82	1	0	2.57	1	1	0	0	7	3	2	2	0	1	5	.130	.333	.100	6.43	1.29
Chambliss, Tyler	R-R	5-11	175	12-4-84	5	3	4.35	17	8	0	2	50	47	27	24	2	21	40	.255	.282	.236	7.25	3.81
Cortes, Daniel	R-R	6-5	205	3-4-87	8	8	3.07	24	24	0	0	123	102	50	42	7	45	120	.226	.177	.266	8.78	3.29
Crist, Kyle	R-R	6-3	194	6-27-83	0	1	9.00	1	0	0	0	2	3	2	2	1	1	1	.333	.333	.333	4.50	4.50
D'Amico, Yovany	R-R	5-11	223	8-18-84	5	2	4.53	27	0	0	1	50	47	26	25	7	14	31	.257	.211	.290	5.62	2.54
de la Vara, Gilbert	L-L	5-11	160	10-4-84	2	1	0.82	22	0	0	7	33	20	4	3	1	12	26	.180	.231	.153	7.09	3.27
Duckworth, Brandon	R-R	6-1	215	1-23-76	0	1	9.00	2	2	0	0	4	6	4	4	0	2	5	.333	.500	.200	11.25	4.50
Godin, Jason	R-R	6-5	170	9-9-83	0	3	6.75	5	4	1	0	23	32	18	17	1	6	10	.340	.400	.305	3.97	2.38
Green, Patrick	L-R	6-2	193	2-13-82	1	5	3.92	27	4	0	5	60	66	27	26	10	17	53	.281	.347	.231	7.99	2.56
Haltiwanger, Russell	R-R	6-2	180	4-21-84	5	3	3.92	37	0	0	5	60	53	28	26	5	29	41	.242	.260	.226	6.18	4.37
Hardy, Rowdy	L-L	6-4	170	10-26-82	15	5	2.48	26	22	3	1	167	144	52	46	6	16	91	.239	.226	.243	4.90	0.86
Humen, David	R-R	6-2	210	6-11-81	2	4	2.95	39	0	0	1	64	60	29	21	2	29	39	.252	.279	.231	5.48	4.08
Johnson, Blake	R-R	6-5	200	6-14-85	9	6	3.28	26	26	0	0	132	119	52	48	7	33	80	.244	.263	.230	5.47	2.26
Nicoll, Christopher	R-R	6-2	190	10-30-83	2	4	7.06	12	10	0	0	43	40	35	34	4	22	33	.255	.284	.229	6.85	4.57
Oliveros, Rayner	R-R	6-2	180	9-23-85	2	3	4.22	37	1	0	5	70	72	35	33	10	17	53	.276	.355	.207	6.78	2.18
Penn, Michael	R-R	6-4	205	4-21-82	3	2	4.04	13	11	0	0	62	67	30	28	8	12	41	.276	.257	.289	5.92	1.73
Pimentel, Julio Cesar	R-R	6-1	190	12-14-85	12	4	2.65	27	22	0	0	153	145	56	45	8	43	73	.250	.262	.241	4.30	2.53
Rosa, Carlos	R-R	6-1	185	9-21-84	2	1	0.39	4	4	0	0	23	15	2	1	0	3	15	.209	.224	.189	5.87	1.17
Santos, Arthur	R-R	6-0	180	2-20-82	0	2	3.16	22	0	0	10	31	35	12	11	3	7	19	.285	.333	.246	5.46	2.01
Wood, Blake	R-R	6-4	225	8-8-85	0	1	4.66	2	2	0	0	10	9	5	5	1	3	11	.257	.200	.300	10.24	2.79

FIELDING

Catcher	PCT	G	PO	A	E	DP	PB
Balduf	.961	9	44	5	2	0	1
Clark	.994	43	277	30	2	2	4
Thibault	.990	89	525	89	6	12	6

First Base	PCT	G	PO	A	E	DP
Kaaihue	.986	33	334	29	5	29
Lisson	.957	9	40	5	2	5
McCann	.988	32	299	19	4	24
Vega	.993	70	632	64	5	52

Second Base	PCT	G	PO	A	E	DP
Jirschele	1.000	5	7	10	0	2
Johnson	.958	50	78	129	9	24

Maddox	.985	86	150	244	6	46
Perez	.981	12	24	28	1	3

Third Base	PCT	G	PO	A	E	DP
Jirschele	1.000	1	0	1	0	0
Lisson	.958	117	92	230	14	28
Maddox	1.000	24	17	36	0	3
Perez	.938	14	5	25	2	3

Shortstop	PCT	G	PO	A	E	DP
Arce	.958	48	56	127	8	20
Johnson	.962	30	39	61	4	10
Lisson	.958	7	5	18	1	3
McConnell	.981	65	76	189	5	27

Outfield	PCT	G	PO	A	E	DP
Bigler	.975	107	182	11	5	2
Cleveland	.980	33	47	1	1	0
Duarte	.997	127	323	10	1	1
Jirschele	1.000	3	4	0	0	0
Larsen	1.000	5	9	0	0	0
McFall	.967	110	197	11	7	4
Peralta	.935	15	28	1	2	0
Perez	.974	19	33	4	1	0
Robinson	.900	3	9	0	1	0
Santana	1.000	11	17	0	0	0

BURLINGTON BEES

LOW CLASS A

MIDWEST LEAGUE

BATTING	B-T	HT	WT	DOB	AVG	vLH	vRH	G	AB	R	H	2B	3B	HR	RBI	BB	HBP	SH	SF	SO	SB	CS	SLG	OBP
Angel, Ryan	R-R	5-10	180	12-15-84	.500	—	.500	3	4	1	2	0	0	0	0	0	1	0	0	0	2	0	.500	.600
Bianchi, Jeff	R-R	6-0	175	10-5-86	.247	.272	.238	99	368	43	91	19	0	2	36	25	3	1	6	72	15	4	.315	.296
Boudreaux, Ross	R-R	5-11	197	4-30-82	.125	.000	.250	3	8	0	1	0	0	0	0	1	0	0	0	3	0	0	.125	.222
Castillo, Luis	R-R	6-3	175	1-18-84	.258	.321	.240	38	124	9	32	9	0	2	15	14	0	0	3	22	1	2	.379	.326
Craze, Ian	R-R	5-10	180	11-10-84	.167	—	.167	3	6	1	1	0	0	0	0	1	0	0	0	1	1	0	.167	.286
Dickerson, Joseph	L-L	6-1	190	10-3-86	.289	.291	.288	115	419	50	121	23	2	3	43	38	6	0	3	76	26	13	.375	.354
Dyson, Jarrod	L-R	5-10	160	8-15-84	.270	.364	.231	10	37	6	10	1	0	0	0	2	0	0	0	12	3	1	.297	.308
Everett, Brady	R-R	6-0	200	7-8-83	.266	.321	.243	107	384	50	102	30	2	10	46	29	5	3	2	69	3	5	.432	.324
Gonzalez, O.D.	R-R	6-1	190	9-12-84	.187	.154	.204	50	155	15	29	11	0	2	11	15	3	1	2	47	6	1	.297	.269
Howell, Jeffrey	R-R	6-0	200	4-1-83	.232	.183	.252	60	211	18	49	14	0	3	22	10	1	2	2	33	1	2	.341	.268
Jirschele, Jeremy	R-R	5-9	195	11-14-82	.250	.333	.195	23	68	8	17	4	0	2	7	5	1	1	0	9	0	0	.397	.311
Lucas, Scott	L-L	6-2	195	6-23-82	.194	.059	.244	25	62	8	12	0	1	0	9	12	2	1	2	19	0	0	.226	.333
Maddox, Marc	R-R	5-11	185	9-16-83	.301	.353	.286	21	73	14	22	3	0	2	17	9	1	0	2	12	2	0	.425	.376
McConnell, Chris	R-R	5-11	175	12-18-85	.231	.246	.225	57	212	25	49	12	1	1	14	20	5	2	1	36	14	2	.311	.311
Mertins, Kurt	R-R	6-0	175	4-22-86	.249	.250	.249	125	445	70	111	15	5	4	39	50	8	4	1	95	30	8	.333	.335
Morel, Alvi	L-L	6-0	153	8-28-84	.213	.103	.258	41	136	14	29	6	1	2	10	13	1	3	0	33	7	2	.316	.287
Morizio, Matthew	L-R	6-2	198	12-14-83	.250	.338	.215	71	228	20	57	9	0	5	27	28	4	3	3	56	1	4	.355	.338
Pennell, Vinny	L-R	6-0	188	7-21-85	.154	.000	.200	5	13	1	2	0	0	0	1	3	0	0	0	3	1	2	.154	.313
Peralta, Felix	R-R	6-0	175	9-30-85	.246	.250	.243	37	114	12	28	5	0	2	11	8	0	1	1	32	1	2	.342	.293
Robinson, Derrick	B-L	5-11	170	9-28-87	.243	.266	.233	102	407	42	99	11	3	2	26	32	2	4	4	100	34	7	.300	.299
Soto, Jesus	R-R	5-11	178	9-7-86	.226	.316	.198	57	164	18	37	4	0	3	13	7	3	3	3	21	1	1	.305	.266
Thompson, Michael	R-R	6-4	230	2-9-84	.217	.184	.228	108	387	35	84	22	0	19	54	15	13	0	0	89	1	0	.421	.270
Turner, Jase	L-R	6-3	230	2-22-83	.212	.123	.236	101	340	33	72	12	1	9	27	37	4	3	1	125	1	2	.332	.296
Walton, Jamar	L-R	6-4	195	1-5-86	.278	.275	.279	54	169	18	47	12	0	3	18	18	1	0	1	47	8	6	.402	.349

PITCHING	B-T	HT	WT	DOB	W	L	ERA	G	GS	CG	SV	IP	H	R	ER	HR	BB	SO	AVG	vLH	vRH	K/9	BB/9
Barrera, Henry	R-R	6-0	205	11-25-85	2	2	4.35	30	0	0	4	52	53	28	25	4	15	53	.261	.318	.220	9.23	2.61
Biddle, George	L-R	6-2	195	2-12-85	0	0	0.00	1	0	0	0	1	1	0	0	0	0	0	.250	.333	.000	0.00	0.00
Campbell, Matt	L-L	6-2	180	12-27-82	4	2	4.13	15	7	1	0	57	51	26	26	5	16	43	.238	.265	.226	6.83	2.54
Cegarra, Edward	R-R	5-11	174	2-27-89	1	6	5.12	16	9	0	1	58	61	37	33	6	16	37	.264	.292	.244	5.74	2.48
Chambliss, Tyler	R-R	5-11	175	12-4-84	3	0	2.12	19	2	0	3	47	32	16	11	1	18	54	.190	.209	.178	10.41	3.47
Cribb, Josh	R-R	5-10	190	2-24-83	3	8	5.40	32	8	0	3	93	107	58	56	7	27	94	.277	.261	.288	9.06	2.60
D'Amico, Yovany	R-R	5-11	223	8-18-84	0	0	1.32	6	0	0	1	14	9	3	2	1	2	14	.184	.056	.258	9.22	1.32
Di Pietro, Ryan	L-L	6-0	175	7-21-84	5	10	5.92	28	12	0	0	93	114	69	61	13	54	86	.302	.330	.291	8.35	5.24
Fisher, Brent	L-L	6-2	190	8-6-87	1	4	5.09	9	5	0	1	35	46	24	20	3	14	28	.322	.250	.342	7.13	3.57
Godin, Jason	R-R	6-5	170	9-23-84	5	6	3.46	19	16	0	1	96	79	40	37	0	36	60	.225	.255	.203	5.61	3.36
Gutierrez, Daniel	R-R	6-1	180	3-8-87	1	2	4.88	7	7	0	0	31	32	18	17	2	12	27	.264	.171	.313	7.76	3.45
Hartsock, Aaron	R-R	6-3	200	1-17-84	7	4	2.62	42	0	0	6	76	63	28	22	6	26	51	.226	.204	.238	6.07	3.09
Hayes, Chris	R-R	6-1	195	2-5-83	4	4	3.10	42	0	0	11	70	65	27	24	3	14	51	.252	.337	.209	6.59	1.81
Kniginyzky, Matthew	L-R	6-3	185	10-5-82	1	0	1.88	3	3	0	0	14	16	5	3	1	2	13	.296	.385	.214	8.16	1.26
Morales, Angelo	R-R	6-1	210	5-2-86	4	1	2.34	13	2	0	3	35	19	9	9	3	8	35	.160	.109	.192	9.09	2.08
Mozingo, Harold	R-R	6-1	175	3-29-85	7	8	4.75	19	18	1	0	95	98	58	50	8	26	82	.270	.279	.263	7.80	2.47
Santiago, Mario	R-R	6-2	210	12-16-84	5	10	3.74	26	20	1	1	132	125	64	55	13	39	70	.249	.222	.272	4.76	2.65
Teaford, Everett	L-L	6-0	155	5-15-84	6	8	4.68	27	21	0	0	135	147	83	70	11	36	84	.281	.375	.245	5.61	2.41
Thompson, Michael	R-R	6-4	230	2-9-84	0	0	0.00	1	0	0	0	1	0	0	0	0	0	0	1.000	—	.000	0.00	0.00
Wladyka, Jim	R-R	6-1	190	5-15-83	0	1	5.96	17	1	0	2	26	32	17	17	2	12	19	.305	.350	.277	6.66	4.21
Wood, Blake	R-R	6-4	225	8-8-85	2	1	3.03	7	7	0	0	36	32	12	12	3	14	26	.239	.353	.169	6.56	3.53

FIELDING

Catcher	PCT	G	PO	A	E	DP	PB
Boudreaux	1.000	3	15	3	0	1	1
Everett	.956	24	141	11	7	0	3
Howell	.989	49	322	44	4	4	6
Morizio	.987	71	453	61	7	7	12

First Base	PCT	G	PO	A	E	DP
Castillo	.990	22	179	17	2	15
Everett	.973	13	103	7	3	6
Jirschele	1.000	2	7	0	0	1
Lucas	.981	12	97	5	2	11
Mertins	1.000	1	2	0	0	0
Thompson	.972	15	101	4	3	8
Turner	.994	85	760	36	5	64

Second Base	PCT	G	PO	A	E	DP
Angel	1.000	2	3	3	0	0

	PCT	G	PO	A	E	DP
Bianchi	.909	6	9	11	2	5
Jirschele	1.000	2	5	2	0	2
Maddox	1.000	4	4	14	0	1
McConnell	.973	16	25	47	2	13
Mertins	.972	89	149	234	11	50
Soto	.986	28	54	85	2	18

Third Base	PCT	G	PO	A	E	DP
Howell	1.000	3	2	2	0	0
Jirschele	.943	16	11	22	2	1
Maddox	.925	16	6	31	3	3
Mertins	.885	21	10	36	6	4
Soto	.921	27	19	39	5	4
Thompson	.932	72	43	148	14	13

Shortstop	PCT	G	PO	A	E	DP
Bianchi	.972	82	134	243	11	53

	PCT	G	PO	A	E	DP
McConnell	.948	41	58	124	10	24
Mertins	.937	20	24	50	5	12

Outfield	PCT	G	PO	A	E	DP
Craze	1.000	2	3	0	0	0
Dickerson	.974	113	181	3	5	1
Dyson	1.000	9	13	0	0	0
Everett	.889	11	8	0	1	0
Gonzalez	.950	48	111	2	6	1
Jirschele	1.000	4	4	0	0	0
Lucas	1.000	1	2	0	0	0
Morel	.959	39	69	1	3	0
Pennell	1.000	4	6	0	0	0
Peralta	.988	36	81	4	1	1
Robinson	.970	101	222	4	7	3
Soto	1.000	7	7	0	0	0
Walton	.976	52	77	3	2	0

BURLINGTON ROYALS

ROOKIE

APPALACHIAN LEAGUE

BATTING	B-T	HT	WT	DOB	AVG	vLH	vRH	G	AB	R	H	2B	3B	HR	RBI	BB	HBP	SH	SF	SO	SB	CS	SLG	OBP
Amyx, Brett	R-R	6-6	230	3-17-85	.260	.216	.278	50	177	23	46	13	1	3	26	21	5	1	1	54	1	0	.395	.353
Beacham, Adam	R-R	5-8	170	10-14-83	.190	.000	.250	11	21	1	4	0	1	0	0	5	0	0	0	9	0	0	.286	.346
Doscher, Nicholas	R-R	6-2	205	5-20-87	.202	.108	.254	36	104	10	21	1	1	1	18	12	6	0	1	26	4	1	.260	.317
Graterol, Juan	R-R	6-1	170	2-14-89	.225	.238	.222	33	102	12	23	1	0	0	10	9	1	0	1	17	1	0	.235	.292
Hill, Thomas	R-R	5-11	200	9-12-85	.173	.167	.175	25	81	9	14	5	0	0	6	5	3	2	0	15	0	0	.235	.247
Jimenez, Antonio	B-R	6-2	157	4-20-87	.213	.111	.255	57	216	27	46	9	4	4	24	13	0	0	0	59	3	2	.347	.258
Lane, Jake	R-R	6-3	230	6-12-85	.315	.175	.378	53	184	45	58	16	4	6	41	30	17	0	1	50	9	6	.543	.453
Lough, David	L-L	6-0	180	1-20-86	.337	.208	.387	24	86	15	29	6	0	2	12	4	2	0	0	13	6	1	.477	.380

	B-T	HT	WT	DOB	AVG	vLH	vRH	G	AB	R	H	2B	3B	HR	RBI	BB	HBP	SH	SF	SO	SB	CS	SLG	OBP
Martin, Kyle	R-R	6-0	175	11-22-84	.242	.143	.283	58	215	33	52	17	0	10	35	13	5	2	5	46	3	1	.460	.294
Molina, Yeldrys	R-R	5-9	150	1-8-89	.209	.208	.210	49	153	17	32	6	1	1	10	6	1	2	1	32	2	1	.281	.242
Norris, Patrick	B-R	6-2	190	3-17-86	.294	.250	.316	60	228	55	67	6	2	0	11	39	0	2	0	59	30	5	.338	.397
Perez, Alwin	L-R	6-0	150	4-4-87	.282	.222	.294	56	206	34	58	7	1	6	34	19	4	5	3	40	7	6	.413	.349
Santos, Jose	R-R	6-0	165	10-7-84	.289	.222	.315	38	128	18	37	11	0	4	19	8	3	1	0	24	3	1	.469	.345
Severino, Neder	R-R	6-2	205	2-9-88	.237	.204	.250	54	186	22	44	7	2	3	17	12	2	2	1	42	4	4	.344	.289
Tucker, Wilson	R-R	6-1	205	1-14-85	.298	.343	.276	54	215	36	64	15	1	8	41	10	5	0	2	36	5	3	.488	.341

PITCHING	B-T	HT	WT	DOB	W	L	ERA	G	GS	CG	SV	IP	H	R	ER	HR	BB	SO	AVG	vLH	vRH	K/9	BB/9
Arias, Henry	R-R	6-3	201	1-6-85	2	3	6.26	13	9	0	0	46	60	38	32	4	18	29	.314	.333	.301	5.67	3.52
Augustine, Joe	R-R	6-2	219	1-18-85	4	1	2.36	11	6	0	0	46	31	17	12	5	9	27	.199	.162	.210	5.32	1.77
Belanger, Ryan	R-R	5-10	165	4-26-85	0	0	2.92	11	0	0	1	12	9	9	4	6	10	.200	.308	.156	7.30	4.38
Bernat, David	R-R	6-2	171	2-17-84	4	3	4.98	13	4	0	0	43	44	30	24	5	17	40	.265	.190	.306	8.31	3.53
Biddle, George	L-R	6-4	195	2-12-85	3	2	4.71	7	4	0	0	21	23	11	11	0	4	15	.299	.267	.319	6.43	1.71
Bradley, Anthony	L-L	6-3	207	7-10-85	2	2	2.09	12	7	0	3	52	34	15	12	3	13	51	.183	.091	.203	8.88	2.26
Caldera, Alexander	L-R	6-3	200	10-1-85	1	2	3.40	12	7	1	2	42	39	17	16	5	13	39	.239	.241	.239	8.29	2.76
Diaz, Jose	R-R	6-0	172	1-19-86	2	1	4.68	14	2	0	1	33	26	17	17	6	15	32	.220	.205	.228	8.82	4.13
Gausman, Brian	L-R	6-0	165	3-23-84	3	2	2.68	13	6	0	0	54	58	20	16	3	12	34	.280	.309	.266	5.70	2.01
Gjeldum, Ted	R-L	6-3	204	9-17-84	4	1	3.63	17	0	0	1	35	32	16	14	2	14	37	.237	.154	.257	9.61	3.63
Hastry, Bobby	R-R	6-1	200	5-8-85	2	3	3.65	14	0	0	1	25	31	15	10	2	7	13	.304	.343	.284	4.74	2.55
Lopez, Yensi	R-R	6-0	160	3-13-86	1	2	3.58	16	0	0	2	33	37	16	13	2	16	33	.285	.250	.298	9.09	4.41
Paukovits, Bryan	R-R	6-6	238	6-29-87	3	4	4.91	13	11	0	0	51	54	32	28	3	16	42	.271	.222	.294	7.36	2.81
Paulino, Eduardo	R-R	5-11	176	9-29-85	3	2	4.86	12	12	0	0	54	42	34	29	7	18	42	.212	.274	.176	7.04	3.02
Rollins, Jimmy	L-L	6-2	200	5-10-83	3	2	4.60	12	0	0	3	16	15	11	8	2	9	20	.246	.231	.250	11.49	5.17
Woods, Ryan	L-R	6-0	209	8-16-84	1	0	2.25	17	0	0	7	28	23	9	7	1	5	18	.217	.300	.167	5.79	1.61

FIELDING

Catcher	PCT	G	PO	A	E	DP	PB
Beacham	.978	10	41	4	1	0	3
Doscher	.979	30	169	22	4	2	9
Graterol	.991	27	190	24	2	1	6
Hill	.980	12	92	8	2	1	2

First Base	PCT	G	PO	A	E	DP
Amyx	.984	34	303	14	5	22
Jimenez	.958	4	18	5	1	2
Lane	.994	35	301	5	2	20

Second Base	PCT	G	PO	A	E	DP
Martin	.971	8	12	21	1	1

	PCT	G	PO	A	E	DP
Molina	.945	26	34	70	6	13
Perez	.915	30	38	59	9	8
Santos	.918	11	17	28	4	9
Third Base	PCT	G	PO	A	E	DP
Jimenez	.917	54	38	117	14	11
Santos	.927	19	13	38	4	3
Shortstop	PCT	G	PO	A	E	DP
Martin	.960	49	81	135	9	25
Molina	.988	19	23	56	1	5
Outfield	PCT	G	PO	A	E	DP
Doscher	1.000	1	3	0	0	0

	PCT	G	PO	A	E	DP
Lane	1.000	5	4	0	0	0
Lough	1.000	21	39	1	0	1
Norris	.978	60	130	5	3	2
Perez	.935	23	23	6	2	0
Santos	1.000	3	3	0	0	0
Severino	.987	50	70	5	1	1
Tucker	.964	54	97	9	4	2

IDAHO FALLS CHUKARS   ROOKIE

PIONEER LEAGUE

BATTING	B-T	HT	WT	DOB	AVG	vLH	vRH	G	AB	R	H	2B	3B	HR	RBI	BB	HBP	SH	SF	SO	SB	CS	SLG	OBP
Balduf, Todd	B-R	6-2	200	7-6-84	.308	.211	.329	35	104	11	32	2	0	2	17	15	2	0	0	21	1	1	.385	.405
Billick, Joe	R-R	6-2	230	5-30-85	.186	.208	.178	29	97	12	18	5	0	0	11	14	6	1	2	27	0	2	.237	.319
Bionde, Mike	R-R	5-9	180	4-30-84	.228	.250	.221	44	145	15	33	4	1	0	12	15	2	3	2	29	3	1	.269	.305
Eigsti, Ryan	R-R	6-2	195	8-24-85	.206	.111	.228	30	97	19	20	2	0	2	12	14	7	1	1	35	0	1	.289	.345
Evangelho, Zach	L-R	5-10	185	4-11-85	.271	.217	.279	53	170	20	46	5	1	0	14	12	11	2	2	29	3	3	.312	.354
Garcia, Fernando	B-R	6-0	160	7-28-88	.088	.000	.115	15	34	4	3	0	0	0	1	7	3	0	0	8	0	0	.088	.295
Gonzalez, O.D.	R-R	6-1	190	9-12-84	.297	.341	.288	69	266	56	79	15	2	9	38	32	2	4	4	74	17	6	.470	.372
Juan, Manni	R-R	5-11	170	2-5-86	.182	.163	.187	54	209	29	38	6	0	3	21	9	5	6	4	56	4	3	.254	.229
Koko, Rubi	R-R	6-3	195	3-25-86	.174	.156	.182	36	109	16	19	5	0	2	13	2	1	0	1	47	5	2	.275	.195
Martin, Kyle	R-R	6-0	175	11-22-84	.583	.500	.667	13	12	1	7	2	0	1	3	1	0	1	0	0	1	0	1.000	.615
Morel, Alvi	L-L	6-0	153	8-28-84	.229	.192	.237	41	144	16	33	7	1	1	15	10	1	2	2	39	6	0	.313	.280
Moustakas, Mike	L-R	6-0	195	9-11-88	.293	.125	.333	11	41	6	12	4	1	0	10	4	2	0	0	8	0	0	.439	.383
Norris, Patrick	B-R	6-2	190	3-17-86	.091	.500	.000	4	11	1	1	0	0	0	0	0	0	0	0	2	0	0	.091	.091
Ortiz, Adrian	L-R	6-0	172	1-14-87	.326	.333	.324	61	264	44	86	9	1	0	24	9	4	0	4	36	17	7	.367	.348
Robinson, Clint	L-L	6-4	225	2-16-85	.336	.422	.317	67	253	39	85	18	1	15	66	19	4	0	2	42	2	0	.593	.388
Seratelli, Anthony	B-R	6-0	205	2-27-83	.327	.305	.333	72	266	52	87	19	5	10	46	40	3	0	3	53	29	6	.549	.417
Tucker, Wilson	R-R	6-1	205	1-14-85	.328	.500	.311	15	67	12	22	10	2	1	10	2	1	0	1	10	1	2	.582	.348
Van De Keere, Devery	L-R	6-2	210	1-29-85	.284	.300	.280	70	268	37	76	15	2	3	30	34	3	1	1	47	5	2	.388	.386
Van Stratten, Nick	R-R	6-1	185	5-22-85	.316	.308	.318	24	98	21	31	4	4	2	14	13	2	1	0	9	7	2	.500	.407

PITCHING	B-T	HT	WT	DOB	W	L	ERA	G	GS	CG	SV	IP	H	R	ER	HR	BB	SO	AVG	vLH	vRH	K/9	BB/9
Baldwin, Burke	L-L	6-5	215	5-28-85	5	1	2.87	16	8	0	2	53	48	19	17	4	23	42	.244	.342	.220	7.09	3.88
Cassa, Pat	L-L	5-10	175	8-16-85	2	0	3.67	20	0	0	1	27	23	13	11	3	9	30	.228	.185	.243	10.00	3.00
Chavez, Chris	L-R	6-3	195	9-11-84	3	2	3.41	15	14	0	0	61	68	33	23	2	14	47	.291	.238	.331	6.97	2.08
Denton, Chris	R-L	6-1	195	11-15-83	1	2	4.15	16	1	0	0	39	42	24	18	6	15	29	.278	.289	.274	6.69	3.46
Evangelho, Zach	L-R	5-10	185	4-11-85	1	0	0.00	1	0	0	0	3	2	0	0	0	1	0	.200	.000	.286	3.00	0.00
Holland, Greg	R-R	5-11	180	11-20-85	6	1	3.48	22	0	0	6	34	28	16	13	1	15	37	.232	.255	.200	9.89	4.01
Hughes, Joseph	L-L	5-11	175	10-4-84	2	1	3.59	16	1	0	2	43	42	20	17	1	16	49	.258	.250	.261	10.34	3.38
Jensen, Matt	R-R	6-2	200	11-30-82	1	3	3.49	21	0	0	0	28	26	12	11	2	8	35	.241	.250	.234	11.12	2.54
Kniginyzky, Matthew	L-R	6-3	185	10-5-82	0	0	5.40	1	1	0	0	5	7	4	3	1	1	3	.350	.300	.400	5.40	1.80
Leonard, John	R-R	6-3	200	1-23-84	3	2	4.68	16	14	0	0	65	76	47	34	4	28	55	.293	.261	.318	7.58	3.86
Norton, Ben	R-R	6-2	210	10-12-84	1	6	3.95	16	14	0	0	57	65	32	25	3	22	56	.283	.327	.246	8.84	3.47
Peterson, Zach	B-R	6-1	165	11-6-84	5	3	2.89	15	8	0	1	56	49	25	18	5	8	67	.234	.235	.234	10.77	1.29
Phillips, Justin	L-L	6-3	220	7-20-84	3	1	3.97	15	1	0	0	48	52	26	21	2	17	39	.280	.333	.256	7.36	3.21
Roach, Jason	L-L	5-10	170	3-11-84	4	1	3.26	21	0	0	2	30	31	13	11	1	5	38	.270	.229	.288	11.27	1.48
Secott, Dane	R-R	6-0	180	12-14-84	5	1	0.79	15	1	0	0	34	20	5	3	0	14	31	.179	.231	.151	8.13	3.67
Snipes, Clegg	R-R	6-2	195	3-8-85	2	6	5.37	16	13	0	0	64	76	43	38	6	22	55	.305	.336	.281	7.77	3.11
Swaggerty, Ben	L-L	6-1	185	8-8-82	1	0	3.03	24	0	0	1	36	31	15	12	1	16	51	.225	.171	.243	12.87	4.04

FIELDING

Catcher	PCT	G	PO	A	E	DP	PB
Balduf	.981	27	234	27	5	2	2
Billick	.996	26	222	21	1	2	4
Eigsti	.984	24	209	30	4	2	6

First Base	PCT	G	PO	A	E	DP
Balduf	1.000	6	20	0	0	2
Billick	1.000	1	2	0	0	0
Eigsti	1.000	2	1	0	0	0
Robinson	.979	38	299	22	7	37
Seratelli	.993	35	286	19	2	23
Van De Keere	.984	8	59	1	1	7

Second Base	PCT	G	PO	A	E	DP
Bionde	.952	38	48	111	8	22
Evangelho	.975	28	40	75	3	16

Garcia	.952	14	22	18	2	2
Seratelli	.968	6	11	19	1	5

Third Base	PCT	G	PO	A	E	DP
Bionde	.714	6	0	5	2	0
Evangelho	1.000	6	4	8	0	1
Juan	1.000	5	3	11	0	4
Martin	1.000	1	1	1	0	0
Seratelli	.700	3	3	4	3	1
Van De Keere	.909	60	36	113	15	6

Shortstop	PCT	G	PO	A	E	DP
Bionde	.833	2	3	2	1	0
Evangelho	.943	13	9	24	2	5
Juan	.943	49	88	129	13	34
Martin	1.000	1	2	4	0	2

Moustakas	.976	8	18	23	1	6
Seratelli	.868	12	18	28	7	9

Outfield	PCT	G	PO	A	E	DP
Evangelho	—	1	0	0	0	0
Gonzalez	.967	66	109	9	4	1
Koko	.833	29	32	3	7	0
Morel	.969	38	60	3	2	2
Norris	1.000	4	4	0	0	0
Ortiz	.953	57	96	6	5	1
Seratelli	1.000	9	6	1	0	0
Tucker	1.000	15	17	0	0	0
Van Stratten	1.000	23	45	2	0	0

AZL ROYALS

ROOKIE

ARIZONA LEAGUE

BATTING

	B-T	HT	WT	DOB	AVG	vLH	vRH	G	AB	R	H	2B	3B	HR	RBI	BB	HBP	SH	SF	SO	SB	CS	SLG	OBP
Angel, Ryan	R-R	5-10	180	12-15-84	.260	.222	.268	47	150	25	39	9	1	3	25	13	0	4	2	27	3	1	.393	.315
Arias, Renny	R-R	6-0	183	11-13-87	.227	.400	.176	13	22	3	5	2	1	0	2	5	0	0	0	5	0	1	.409	.370
Blanco, Andres	B-R	6-0	190	4-11-84	.000	—	.000	2	2	0	0	0	0	0	0	0	0	0	0	0	0	0	.000	.000
Bonilla, Jose	R-R	5-10	188	8-4-88	.000	.000	.000	3	5	0	0	0	0	0	0	0	0	0	0	2	0	0	.000	.000
Craze, Ian	R-R	5-10	180	11-10-84	.254	.182	.275	45	142	21	36	5	1	2	20	15	4	1	1	31	12	7	.345	.340
Cruz, Diego	L-L	6-0	175	11-13-87	.276	.149	.316	54	199	34	55	9	4	1	32	14	8	0	0	35	4	5	.357	.348
Cruz, Fernando	B-R	6-2	184	3-28-90	.210	.114	.241	48	181	14	38	5	1	1	15	8	4	3	4	43	0	0	.265	.254
Donovan, Dennis	R-R	6-2	190	2-16-85	.248	.353	.220	46	161	18	40	10	0	2	18	11	6	0	1	24	0	2	.348	.318
Huber, Justin	R-R	6-2	205	7-1-82	.360	.500	.333	7	25	4	9	4	0	2	7	2	1	0	1	4	0	0	.760	.414
Jacobo, Astin	R-R	6-0	170	12-15-88	.126	.130	.125	38	95	9	12	4	2	0	4	10	4	0	0	54	1	0	.211	.239
Jose, Lifete	B-R	6-0	168	3-24-89	.235	.231	.236	47	183	27	43	5	1	0	20	23	4	2	2	36	6	1	.273	.330
McCauley, Sean	R-R	6-2	170	5-13-89	.286	.250	.297	31	84	15	24	10	0	2	13	10	2	0	0	19	0	1	.476	.375
Pennell, Vinny	L-R	6-0	188	7-21-85	.279	.152	.311	47	165	33	46	6	3	0	20	21	2	1	2	32	14	3	.352	.363
Perez, Salvador	R-R	6-3	175	5-10-90	.244	.368	.209	30	86	10	21	3	0	0	10	5	5	2	1	10	1	1	.279	.320
Reyes, Yenssi	R-R	5-10	182	10-23-87	.333	.500	.263	15	27	2	9	2	0	0	5	3	1	1	0	5	0	0	.407	.419
Richardson, Hilton	L-L	6-3	200	1-10-89	.199	.191	.201	48	191	36	38	2	3	4	15	20	6	1	0	66	12	7	.304	.295
Wood, David	L-L	6-2	185	12-21-84	.318	.259	.337	54	217	31	69	17	3	5	39	17	3	0	4	29	1	0	.493	.369

PITCHING

	B-T	HT	WT	DOB	W	L	ERA	G	GS	CG	SV	IP	H	R	ER	HR	BB	SO	AVG	vLH	vRH	K/9	BB/9
Belanger, Ryan	R-R	5-10	165	4-26-85	0	0	6.00	6	0	0	0	9	14	6	6	2	3	14	.359	.400	.333	14.00	3.00
Biddle, George	L-R	6-4	195	2-12-85	0	0	4.66	6	0	0	0	10	11	8	5	1	2	10	.250	.143	.300	9.31	1.86
Duffy, Daniel	L-L	6-2	185	12-21-88	2	3	1.45	11	9	0	0	37	24	14	6	0	17	63	.178	.103	.198	15.19	4.10
Farinas, Williams	R-R	6-0	175	1-5-87	2	3	3.55	14	8	0	1	51	47	21	20	4	16	36	.249	.222	.262	6.39	2.84
Feickert, Casey	R-R	6-3	180	8-5-88	1	1	9.20	11	0	0	0	15	19	15	15	2	8	17	.352	.143	.425	10.43	4.91
Foster, John	L-L	6-0	200	5-17-78	1	0	0.00	3	0	0	0	3	4	0	0	0	0	6	.286	.200	.333	16.20	0.00
Gutierrez, Daniel	R-R	6-1	180	3-8-87	0	0	0.00	1	1	0	0	3	1	0	0	0	1	3	.100	.000	.167	9.00	3.00
Hodge Nielsen, Peter	R-R	6-2	210	6-15-89	1	6	4.24	12	8	0	0	40	39	29	19	2	23	35	.252	.224	.268	7.81	5.13
Hodgson, Ivor	B-L	6-3	190	4-25-86	1	1	5.29	14	0	0	0	32	45	24	19	1	15	36	.328	.367	.307	10.02	4.18
Jorge, Victor	R-R	6-3	190	5-18-87	0	0	10.80	8	1	0	0	8	12	11	10	1	9	4	.333	.353	.316	4.32	9.72
Kniginyzky, Matthew	L-R	6-3	185	10-5-82	0	0	0.00	1	1	0	0	3	3	2	0	0	2	2	.250	.667	.111	6.00	6.00
Lehmann, Michael	B-R	6-2	190	5-3-89	5	1	2.64	14	1	0	1	44	36	23	13	4	23	40	.218	.185	.240	8.12	4.67
Lowery, Devon	L-R	6-1	195	3-24-83	0	0	2.25	2	2	0	0	4	4	1	1	0	0	9	.250	.167	.300	20.25	0.00
Mieles, Edwin	R-R	6-4	180	9-1-87	1	0	4.91	13	0	0	0	15	17	10	8	1	7	15	.288	.211	.325	9.20	4.30
Mitchell, Matthew	R-R	6-2	205	3-31-89	5	1	1.80	14	7	0	1	55	34	16	11	0	25	72	.183	.180	.184	11.78	4.09
Penn, Michael	R-R	6-4	205	4-21-82	0	1	5.63	4	4	0	0	8	8	5	5	0	1	11	.258	.273	.250	12.38	1.12
Rada, Orlando	L-L	5-11	165	12-20-85	0	1	3.15	10	0	0	0	20	29	11	7	0	4	21	.341	.300	.364	9.45	1.80
Runion, Sam	R-R	6-4	220	11-9-88	3	4	5.82	12	9	0	0	51	61	36	33	4	17	51	.310	.342	.290	9.00	3.00
Sanchez, Juan	R-R	5-11	153	2-8-89	1	0	11.05	7	0	0	0	7	10	11	9	0	5	7	.303	.333	.286	8.59	6.14
Santerre, Josh	L-L	6-1	185	4-19-84	3	1	1.96	12	1	0	1	18	16	4	4	0	6	25	.235	.208	.250	12.27	2.95
Sirrett, Onassis	R-R	5-11	170	12-15-88	1	2	8.53	8	0	0	0	19	24	20	18	2	12	21	.304	.308	.302	9.95	5.68
Thomson, John	R-R	6-3	220	10-1-73	0	0	6.75	1	1	0	0	1	3	1	1	0	0	2	.429	.667	.250	13.50	0.00
Toribio, Aneidy	L-L	6-1	172	5-21-88	0	0	5.79	3	0	0	0	5	4	3	3	1	5	5	.222	.500	.188	9.64	5.79
Van Slyke, Eric	R-R	6-1	220	5-11-84	1	1	0.83	18	0	0	9	22	14	3	2	0	5	29	.184	.154	.200	12.05	2.08
Vasquez, Alberto	R-R	6-3	158	7-22-88	0	0	7.84	8	0	0	0	10	21	9	9	1	4	13	.429	.647	.313	11.32	3.48
Wood, Blake	R-R	6-4	225	8-8-85	0	0	0.00	4	4	0	0	10	9	2	0	0	0	15	.250	.267	.238	13.97	0.00

FIELDING

Catcher	PCT	G	PO	A	E	DP	PB
Bonilla	1.000	3	9	2	0	0	2
McCauley	.985	29	235	34	4	2	3
Perez	.982	30	230	44	5	2	7
Reyes	.988	14	79	4	1	1	4

First Base	PCT	G	PO	A	E	DP
D. Cruz	.986	18	130	12	2	9
Huber	1.000	1	8	1	0	0
Wood	.973	38	273	20	8	28

Second Base	PCT	G	PO	A	E	DP
Angel	.968	40	74	78	5	14
Donovan	.961	25	43	56	4	13

Third Base	PCT	G	PO	A	E	DP
F. Cruz	.875	46	29	55	12	3
Donovan	.864	16	5	14	3	2

Shortstop	PCT	G	PO	A	E	DP
Blanco	1.000	2	0	1	0	0
F. Cruz	.900	3	3	6	1	2

Donovan	.892	10	14	19	4	8
Jose	.890	47	76	94	21	25

Outfield	PCT	G	PO	A	E	DP
Angel	.857	6	6	0	1	0
Arias	.778	12	6	1	2	0
Craze	.957	41	64	3	3	0
Huber	1.000	6	17	0	0	0
Jacobo	.981	37	42	10	1	0
Pennell	.913	47	69	4	7	0
Richardson	.958	48	69	0	3	0

DOMINICAN SUMMER LEAGUE

BATTING	B-T	HT	WT	DOB	AVG	vLH	vRH	G	AB	R	H	2B	3B	HR	RBI	BB	HBP	SH	SF	SO	SB	CS	SLG	OBP
Alvarez, Jhonson	R-R	5-11	160	1-2-90	.167	.063	.219	20	48	1	8	4	0	0	4	2	1	2	0	13	0	0	.250	.216
Aparicio, Julio	R-R	6-2	175	1-4-90	.216	.217	.216	53	185	22	40	8	3	2	24	15	2	0	2	40	2	6	.324	.279
Arias, Renny	R-R	6-0	183	11-13-87	.218	.238	.206	20	55	8	12	3	0	1	4	7	1	0	0	16	2	1	.327	.317
Batista, Deivy	R-R	5-11	150	5-7-88	.243	.203	.261	62	206	31	50	9	3	1	26	29	2	2	1	33	8	5	.330	.340
Cabrera, Santos	R-R	5-10	170	1-28-90	.098	.100	.097	13	41	4	4	2	0	0	1	2	0	0	0	12	0	0	.146	.140
Figueroa, Yunior	B-R	6-0	170	8-8-90	.176	.192	.169	33	91	10	16	2	4	1	11	21	1	2	2	29	3	1	.319	.330
Fortuna, Juan	R-R	5-11	185	1-12-89	.231	.333	.200	10	26	3	6	1	0	0	5	5	1	0	0	6	0	0	.269	.375
Franco, Angel	B-R	5-10	152	5-23-90	.282	.234	.303	59	209	38	59	10	2	1	18	23	1	4	1	34	14	7	.364	.355
Henriquez, Edwin	B-R	6-2	168	11-7-88	.250	.214	.264	61	204	26	51	11	4	0	24	16	4	2	3	58	3	8	.343	.313
Jacobs, Nestor	R-R	5-11	169	3-8-88	.210	.270	.175	39	100	12	21	5	2	0	16	16	5	1	3	23	2	1	.300	.339
Lake, Reymond	L-L	6-1	195	4-10-88	.230	.125	.270	41	87	12	20	4	1	0	7	15	1	1	0	22	4	4	.299	.350
Lantigua, Roberto	B-R	5-10	142	3-5-90	.207	.250	.187	51	135	14	28	4	1	0	15	32	4	2	1	33	15	4	.252	.372
Mariano, Miguel	L-R	6-0	170	10-11-88	.174	.214	.160	46	109	13	19	2	0	0	13	24	2	1	0	43	4	3	.193	.333
Marte, Alexis	R-R	6-2	197	6-13-85	.240	.192	.256	38	104	22	25	11	1	0	19	35	1	2	0	15	8	1	.365	.436
2-team (10 DSL)					.235	—	—	48	132	29	31	11	1	0	22	44	1	2	1	25	9	1	.333	.427
Peguero, Fausto	R-R	6-0	155	12-29-87	.238	.238	.238	48	122	24	29	2	4	1	9	8	5	3	1	43	14	3	.344	.309
Reyes, Yenssi	R-R	5-10	182	10-23-87	.217	.194	.231	29	83	10	18	5	0	0	9	17	5	0	2	13	1	1	.277	.374
Rosario, Luis	R-R	6-2	181	5-21-90	.228	.188	.238	23	79	11	18	4	0	0	7	6	0	0	0	12	1	2	.278	.282
Soto, Victor	R-R	5-11	150	10-16-88	.226	.136	.276	59	164	22	37	9	3	3	18	18	2	4	1	46	11	4	.372	.308
Ubri, Jhoan	R-R	6-3	202	1-1-90	.032	.000	.063	15	31	5	1	0	0	0	1	7	1	1	0	14	0	0	.032	.231

PITCHING	B-T	HT	WT	DOB	W	L	ERA	G	GS	CG	SV	IP	H	R	ER	HR	BB	SO	AVG	vLH	vRH	K/9	BB/9
Bonilla, Ariel	R-R	6-2	152	7-10-88	5	1	1.91	17	1	0	1	42	27	13	9	1	12	33	.173	.260	.132	7.02	2.55
Colon, Roque	R-R	5-10	152	4-23-88	0	2	12.66	12	0	0	1	11	18	16	15	2	16	10	.391	.455	.371	8.44	13.50
Cuevas, Gary	R-R	6-0	184	5-23-88	2	1	2.43	20	1	0	6	33	23	11	9	0	18	42	.193	.190	.195	11.34	4.86
De La Cruz, Deybi	R-R	5-11	158	3-25-90	2	1	2.18	14	7	0	4	33	30	12	8	1	10	34	.242	.214	.256	9.27	2.73
De La Cruz, Giancarlo	R-R	6-0	166	9-23-89	3	2	1.13	12	12	0	0	56	32	10	7	0	13	55	.169	.197	.154	8.84	2.09
De La Rosa, Starling	L-L	6-5	159	9-19-87	0	0	9.82	12	0	0	0	11	12	15	12	0	15	17	.293	.333	.289	13.91	12.27
Fortuna, Carlos	R-R	6-2	185	3-31-90	1	2	3.94	10	3	0	0	32	26	14	14	2	12	28	.234	.286	.217	7.88	3.38
Fortuna, Juan	R-R	5-11	185	1-12-89	0	0	2.45	1	0	0	0	4	1	2	1	0	2	0	.083	.500	.000	0.00	4.91
Garcia, Alberto	R-R	6-1	160	2-14-89	0	0	0.00	1	0	0	0	1	1	0	0	0	0	2	.250	.000	.500	18.00	0.00
Garcia, Angel	R-R	6-1	160	6-19-89	3	1	4.42	12	0	0	0	18	16	11	9	0	16	18	.235	.235	.235	8.84	7.85
Garrido, Santiago	R-R	6-0	178	10-4-89	1	4	3.35	14	9	0	1	43	34	22	16	0	28	34	.214	.204	.219	7.12	5.86
Herrera, Kelvin	R-R	5-10	162	12-31-89	4	1	0.84	11	5	0	1	43	30	6	4	1	15	50	.197	.157	.218	10.55	3.16
Marimon, Sugar Ray	R-R	6-1	168	9-30-88	1	2	2.05	14	10	0	0	44	28	14	10	2	18	40	.183	.102	.221	8.18	3.68
Mendoza, Rommel	R-R	5-11	150	9-26-88	1	0	1.00	6	0	0	0	9	4	1	1	0	8	8	.143	.100	.167	8.00	8.00
Ovando, Franklyn	R-R	6-1	178	11-4-88	0	1	7.20	2	0	0	0	5	5	4	4	1	4	3	.278	.400	.231	5.40	7.20
Perez, Leondy	R-R	6-1	175	6-19-90	4	1	2.88	16	5	0	1	41	31	14	13	2	23	40	.214	.149	.245	8.85	5.09
Rodriguez, Jonathan	R-R	6-1	165	12-13-88	3	2	4.76	10	1	0	0	17	10	11	9	0	12	9	.175	.118	.200	4.76	6.35
Sanchez, Gabriel	R-R	6-0	190	9-2-89	2	1	6.39	7	0	0	0	13	7	10	9	1	10	11	.149	.111	.172	7.82	7.11
Santiago, Leonel	R-R	6-0	178	12-23-89	2	2	2.80	12	5	0	0	35	30	14	11	2	8	30	.236	.245	.231	7.64	2.04
Santos, Darlyn	R-R	5-11	150	3-29-89	3	1	2.79	11	5	0	2	39	34	16	12	2	3	23	.236	.216	.247	5.35	0.70
Sirrett, Onassis	R-R	5-11	170	12-15-88	2	1	3.42	6	4	0	0	24	20	10	9	2	6	14	.230	.179	.254	5.32	2.28
Toribio, Luis	L-L	6-3	175	10-20-86	0	2	4.64	12	0	0	0	21	19	15	11	0	19	22	.232	.286	.227	9.28	8.02
Violi, Willer	R-R	6-1	165	5-29-90	0	0	21.60	5	0	0	0	3	5	8	8	1	9	4	.313	.400	.273	10.80	24.30
Zorrilla, Moises	L-L	6-2	206	11-20-86	0	0	15.26	7	0	0	0	8	11	14	13	1	13	8	.344	.000	.367	9.39	15.26

FIELDING

Catcher	PCT	G	PO	A	E	DP	PB
Alvarez	.982	15	98	10	2	0	6
Fortuna	1.000	4	19	1	0	0	0
Fortuna	1.000	10	72	16	0	1	1
Jacobs	.967	31	177	31	7	0	3
Lake	—	1	0	0	0	0	1
Reyes	.958	25	161	22	8	1	3

First Base	PCT	G	PO	A	E	DP
Batista	1.000	1	10	0	0	0
Henriquez	.993	41	256	9	2	20
Jacobs	.903	6	28	0	3	5
Marte	.996	29	215	15	1	16
Ubri	.987	11	73	2	1	4

Second Base	PCT	G	PO	A	E	DP
Batista	1.000	7	21	18	0	8

	PCT	G	PO	A	E	DP	PB
Figueroa	1.000	14	32	35	0	10	
Franco	.979	34	62	75	3	9	
Henriquez	.933	12	21	21	3	5	
Lantigua	1.000	2	4	1	0	0	
Soto	.943	22	27	56	5	9	

Third Base	PCT	G	PO	A	E	DP
Batista	.907	55	33	74	11	7
Batista	1.000	2	1	11	0	0
Franco	—	1	0	0	0	0
Henriquez	.860	21	9	34	7	5
Soto	.765	6	2	11	4	2

Shortstop	PCT	G	PO	A	E	DP
Batista	1.000	3	1	2	0	1
Figueroa	1.000	1	2	2	0	0
Franco	.938	31	31	74	7	12

	PCT	G	PO	A	E	DP
Lantigua	.950	49	51	121	9	18

Outfield	PCT	G	PO	A	E	DP
Aparicio	.919	45	54	3	5	0
Arias	.938	18	29	1	2	0
Batista	—	1	0	0	0	0
Cabrera	1.000	5	4	0	0	0
De La Rosa	1.000	2	1	0	0	0
Lake	.927	35	37	1	3	0
Mariano	.971	32	32	2	1	0
Marte	1.000	12	10	1	0	0
Peguero	.948	45	87	5	5	3
Rosario	.974	23	35	2	1	0
Soto	.903	28	25	3	3	1
Ubri	1.000	1	5	0	0	0

Los Angeles Angels

BY BILL SHAIKIN

If the standard for success is leaving an organization in better shape than the way you found it, Bill Stoneman did one of the best jobs in baseball history.

The Angels were a disaster when Stoneman arrived in the fall of 1999. Disney owned the team but didn't much care for it. The players threatened not to take the field one day unless the manager (Terry Collins) benched another player (Mo Vaughn). By the time the season ended, the Angels had lost 92 games, more than in their expansion season of 1961. Collins was out. So was general manager Bill Bavasi.

Tony Tavares, then the team president, wondered aloud why he could not fire all the players. He waved copies of Baseball America, which had rated the Angels' minor league system the worst in the game. He hired Stoneman as general manager and told him to feel free to blow everything up.

Stoneman took a deep breath, told Tavares the Angels had a pretty good nucleus that needed more resources in player development, then hired Mike Scioscia as manager. In Stoneman's third season, the Angels won a club-record 99 games and the first World Series in franchise history.

Arte Moreno bought the team in 2003, and with him came pockets deep enough to sign Vladimir Guerrero and Bartolo Colon in free agency, Jered Weaver and Nick Adenhart in the draft. The Angels won consecutive division championships for the first time, posted three consecutive winning seasons for the first time, sold three million tickets for the first time and continued to do so.

In 39 seasons before Stoneman, the Angels made three playoff appearances. In eight seasons under Stoneman, they made four playoff appearances, winning three division championships and one World Series title.

He so raised expectations that, when he retired as general manager after the 2007 season, local appreciation was tinged with encouragement. With the cautious Stoneman out, a fan base that now counts on October baseball wondered if the Angels might finally get that big bat.

The Angels won the American League West, then got swept by the Red Sox in the first round of the playoffs, out-scored 19-4 and out-homered 5-0. The Angels lost their entire outfield—Vladimir Guerrero, Gary Matthews Jr. and Garret Anderson— to injury for all or part of the series.

The lingering image: Curt Schilling brazenly walking Guerrero with runners on first and third, loading the bases in a scoreless game. Anderson was due up, but he had left the game because of injury. Reggie Willits, with no major league home runs, fouled out.

After the final game of a series in which slap-hitting infielder Maicer Izturis batted fifth, Scioscia publicly called for a big bat. Guerrero hit 27 home runs during the season—that's 25 or more for 10 consecutive seasons—but no teammate has hit 25 since the Angels exiled Jose Guillen to the Nationals in 2004.

Guerrero ranked among league leaders in all the Triple Crown categories, hitting .324 with 27 home runs and 125 RBIs. He walked more than he struck out, leading the AL with 28 intentional walks. Chone Figgins stole 41 bases and briefly contended for the AL batting title. Shortstop Orlando Cabrera posted career highs in batting average (.301), runs scored (101) and hits (192). Home-grown youngsters on the right side of the infield performed well—first baseman Casey Kotchman (.296/.372/.467) and second baseman

Howie Kendrick (.322/.347/.450).

John Lackey became the first Angel to lead the league in ERA since Frank Tanana in 1977. Lackey posted a 3.01 ERA, with Kelvim Escobar not far behind at 3.40. Righthanded closer Francisco Rodriguez recorded his third consecutive 40-save season.

In the minor leagues, three affiliates advanced to the playoffs—Salt Lake in the Triple-A Pacific Coast League, Cedar Rapids in the low Class A Midwest League and Orem in the Rookie-level Pioneer League.

The Angels selected outfielder Chris Pettit, 23, as minor league player of the year. Pettit hit .327/.411/.538 between high Class A Rancho Cucamonga and Cedar Rapids. They picked righthander Sean O'Sullivan, 20, as pitcher of the year. O'Sullivan went 10-7 at Cedar Rapids and led the league with a 2.22 ERA.

ORGANIZATION STATISTICS

General Manager: Bill Stoneman. **Farm Director:** Tony Reagins. **Scouting Director:** Eddie Bane

Class	Team	League	W	L	PCT	Finish*	Manager	Affiliate Since
Majors	Los Angeles	American	94	68	.580	3rd (14)	Mike Scioscia	—
Triple-A	Salt Lake Bees	Pacific Coast	74	69	.517	7th (16)	Brian Harper	2001
Double-A	Arkansas Travelers	Texas	65	75	.464	7th (8)	Bobby Magallanes	2001
High A	Rancho Cucamonga Quakes	California	69	71	.493	7th (10)	Bobby Mitchell	2001
Low A	Cedar Rapids Kernels	Midwest	78	61	.561	3rd (14)	Ever Magallanes	1993
Rookie	Orem Owlz	Pioneer	37	39	.487	4th (8)	Tom Kotchman	2001
Rookie	AZL Angels	Arizona	33	23	.589	2nd (9)	Ty Boykin	2001
Overall 2007 Minor League Record			**356**	**338**	**.513**	**9th**		

* Finish in overall standings (No. of teams in league) ^League champion

ORGANIZATION STATISTICS

LOS ANGELES ANGELS
AMERICAN LEAGUE

BATTING	B-T	HT	WT	DOB	AVG	vLH	vRH	G	AB	R	H	2B	3B	HR	RBI	BB	HBP	SH	SF	SO	SB	CS	SLG	OBP
Anderson, Garret	L-L	6-3	225	6-30-72	.297	.288	.300	108	417	67	124	31	1	16	80	27	0	0	6	54	1	0	.492	.336
Aybar, Erick	B-R	5-10	170	1-14-84	.237	.304	.216	79	194	18	46	5	1	1	19	10	2	3	2	32	4	4	.289	.279
Brown, Matthew	R-R	6-0	200	8-8-82	.000	.000	.000	4	5	0	0	0	0	0	0	0	0	0	0	1	1	0	.000	.286
Budde, Ryan	R-R	5-11	205	8-15-79	.167	.333	.133	12	18	0	3	1	0	0	1	0	0	0	0	6	0	0	.222	.167
Cabrera, Orlando	R-R	5-9	185	11-2-74	.301	.308	.299	155	638	101	192	35	1	8	86	44	5	3	11	64	20	4	.397	.345
Evans, Terry	R-R	6-3	205	1-19-82	.091	.167	.000	8	11	3	1	0	0	1	2	2	0	0	0	4	0	0	.364	.231
Figgins, Chone	B-R	5-8	180	1-22-78	.330	.326	.331	115	442	81	146	24	6	3	58	51	0	2	8	81	41	12	.432	.393
Gorneault, Nick	R-R	6-3	220	4-19-79	.000	.000	.000	2	4	1	0	0	0	0	0	1	0	0	0	1	0	0	.000	.200
Guerrero, Vladimir	R-R	6-3	235	2-9-76	.324	.321	.325	150	574	89	186	45	1	27	125	71	9	0	6	62	2	3	.547	.403
Haynes, Nathan	L-L	5-9	180	9-7-79	.267	.000	.279	40	45	10	12	0	1	0	1	3	0	0	0	11	1	2	.311	.313
Hillenbrand, Shea	R-R	6-1	210	7-27-75	.254	.260	.252	53	197	19	50	5	0	3	22	5	1	0	1	18	0	2	.325	.275
Izturis, Maicer	B-R	5-8	165	9-12-80	.289	.280	.291	102	336	47	97	17	2	6	51	33	0	1	4	39	7	1	.405	.349
Kendrick, Howie	R-R	5-10	200	7-12-83	.322	.325	.322	88	338	55	109	24	2	5	39	9	4	1	1	61	5	4	.450	.347
Kotchman, Casey	L-L	6-3	215	2-22-83	.296	.315	.292	137	443	64	131	37	3	11	68	53	4	3	5	43	2	4	.467	.372
Mathis, Jeff	R-R	6-0	200	3-31-83	.211	.242	.203	59	171	24	36	12	0	4	23	15	2	3	4	49	0	1	.351	.276
Matthews, Gary	B-R	6-3	225	8-25-74	.252	.175	.275	140	516	79	130	26	3	18	72	55	2	0	6	102	18	4	.419	.323
Molina, Jose	R-R	6-2	245	6-3-75	.224	.281	.204	40	125	9	28	8	0	0	10	3	0	3	0	30	2	1	.288	.242
2-team (29 New York)					.257	—	—	69	191	18	49	13	0	1	19	5	0	5	1	43	2	1	.340	.274
Morales, Kendry	B-R	6-1	225	6-20-83	.294	.241	.311	43	119	12	35	10	0	4	15	6	1	0	0	21	0	1	.479	.333
Murphy, Tommy	R-R	6-0	190	8-27-79	.184	.111	.207	20	38	2	7	1	0	0	2	0	1	0	0	9	0	0	.211	.205
Napoli, Mike	R-R	6-0	210	10-31-81	.247	.291	.232	75	219	40	54	11	1	10	34	33	5	1	5	63	5	2	.443	.351
Quinlan, Robb	R-R	6-1	215	3-17-77	.247	.269	.203	79	178	21	44	9	0	3	21	14	1	0	1	27	3	2	.348	.304
Rivera, Juan	R-R	6-2	225	7-3-78	.279	.276	.286	14	43	3	12	1	0	2	8	1	0	0	0	4	0	0	.442	.295
Willits, Reggie	B-R	5-11	185	5-30-81	.293	.333	.276	136	430	74	126	20	1	0	34	69	3	11	5	83	27	8	.344	.391
Wood, Brandon	R-R	6-3	185	3-2-85	.152	.200	.111	13	33	2	5	1	0	1	3	0	0	0	0	12	0	0	.273	.152

PITCHING	B-T	HT	WT	DOB	W	L	ERA	G	GS	CG	SV	IP	H	R	ER	HR	BB	SO	AVG	vLH	vRH	K/9	BB/9
Bootcheck, Chris	R-R	6-5	200	10-24-78	3	3	4.77	51	0	0	0	77	81	43	41	7	24	56	.274	.302	.253	6.52	2.79
Bulger, Jason	R-R	6-4	215	12-6-78	0	0	2.84	6	0	0	0	6	5	2	2	0	3	8	.227	.222	.231	11.37	4.26
Carrasco, Hector	R-R	6-2	235	10-22-69	2	1	6.57	29	1	0	0	38	44	34	28	8	23	33	.272	.188	.333	7.75	5.40
Colon, Bartolo	R-R	5-11	245	5-24-73	6	8	6.34	19	18	0	0	99	132	74	70	15	29	76	.320	.313	.325	6.89	2.63
Escobar, Kelvim	R-R	6-1	230	4-11-76	18	7	3.40	30	30	3	0	196	182	79	74	11	66	160	.248	.264	.233	7.36	3.04
Gwyn, Marcus	R-R	6-3	215	11-4-77	0	0	11.81	3	0	0	0	5	9	7	5	3	5	3	.360	.300	.400	5.06	8.44
Jones, Greg	R-R	6-2	205	11-15-76	0	0	6.23	9	0	0	0	9	10	6	6	2	5	5	.278	.250	.313	5.19	5.19
Lackey, John	R-R	6-6	245	10-23-78	19	9	3.01	33	33	2	0	224	219	87	75	18	52	179	.254	.280	.229	7.19	2.09
Moseley, Dustin	R-R	6-4	215	12-26-81	4	3	4.40	46	8	0	0	92	97	45	45	7	27	50	.277	.224	.323	4.89	2.64
Oliver, Darren	R-L	6-2	200	10-6-70	3	1	3.78	61	0	0	0	64	58	31	27	5	23	51	.239	.289	.209	7.13	3.22
Resop, Chris	R-R	6-3	215	11-4-82	0	0	4.15	4	0	0	0	4	4	2	2	1	1	2	.308	.286	.333	4.15	2.08
Rodriguez, Francisco	R-R	6-0	195	1-7-82	5	2	2.81	64	0	0	40	67	50	22	21	3	34	90	.204	.187	.217	12.03	4.54
Santana, Ervin	R-R	6-2	185	12-12-82	7	14	5.76	28	26	0	0	150	174	103	96	26	58	126	.288	.284	.292	7.56	3.48
Saunders, Joe	L-L	6-3	210	6-16-81	8	5	4.44	18	18	0	0	107	129	56	53	11	34	69	.298	.274	.304	5.79	2.85
Shields, Scot	R-R	6-1	180	7-22-75	4	5	3.86	71	0	0	2	77	62	36	33	7	33	77	.220	.214	.226	9.00	3.86
Speier, Justin	R-R	6-4	205	11-6-73	2	3	2.88	51	0	0	0	50	36	17	16	6	12	47	.202	.222	.186	8.46	2.16
Thompson, Rich	R-R	6-1	180	7-1-84	0	0	10.80	7	0	0	0	7	10	8	8	4	3	9	.345	.200	.421	12.15	4.05
Weaver, Jered	R-R	6-7	205	10-4-82	13	7	3.91	28	28	0	0	161	178	77	70	17	45	115	.280	.291	.269	6.43	2.52

FIELDING

Catcher	PCT	G	PO	A	E	DP	PB
Budde	.974	10	36	1	1	0	0
Mathis	.991	57	383	42	4	2	5
Molina	.987	40	283	17	4	2	2
Napoli	.986	75	460	32	7	2	1

First Base	PCT	G	PO	A	E	DP
Hillenbrand	.976	6	38	2	1	5
Kotchman	.997	130	978	68	3	103
Morales	1.000	19	119	9	0	11
Quinlan	.996	34	214	16	1	25

Second Base	PCT	G	PO	A	E	DP
Aybar	.976	43	60	106	4	25
Figgins	.960	9	9	15	1	1
Izturis	1.000	40	50	0	24	

Kendrick	.978	86	146	254	9	54

Third Base	PCT	G	PO	A	E	DP
Aybar	1.000	1	0	2	0	0
Brown	1.000	4	1	3	0	1
Figgins	.943	99	52	165	13	14
Izturis	.974	53	21	91	3	10
Quinlan	.917	10	4	7	1	0
Wood	.963	10	12	14	1	2

Shortstop	PCT	G	PO	A	E	DP
Aybar	.927	20	14	24	3	2
Cabrera	.983	153	239	415	11	104
Izturis	.917	3	8	3	1	1
Wood	1.000	3	0	2	0	0

Outfield	PCT	G	PO	A	E	DP
Anderson	.987	85	143	7	2	0
Aybar	1.000	8	5	0	0	0
Evans	1.000	7	4	0	0	0
Figgins	1.000	11	17	1	0	0
Gorneault	.857	2	5	1	1	0
Guerrero	.959	108	208	5	9	3
Haynes	1.000	33	26	1	0	0
Matthews	.987	135	362	7	5	2
Morales	1.000	6	4	0	0	0
Murphy	1.000	15	9	1	0	0
Quinlan	1.000	22	20	0	0	0
Rivera	1.000	9	9	1	0	0
Willits	.989	118	260	6	3	1

SALT LAKE BEES

TRIPLE-A

PACIFIC COAST LEAGUE

BATTING	B-T	HT	WT	DOB	AVG	vLH	vRH	G	AB	R	H	2B	3B	HR	RBI	BB	HBP	SH	SF	SO	SB	CS	SLG	OBP
Aybar, Erick	B-R	5-10	170	1-14-84	.333	.500	.250	3	12	2	4	0	0	0	2	0	0	0	0	2	2	1	.333	.333
Brown, Matthew	R-R	6-0	200	8-8-82	.276	.302	.265	110	391	69	108	30	2	19	60	45	5	1	0	106	5	9	.509	.358
Budde, Ryan	R-R	5-11	205	8-15-79	.295	.342	.280	47	156	21	46	12	0	4	28	18	1	0	2	27	2	2	.449	.367
Del Chiaro, Brent	R-R	6-3	240	6-26-79	.333	.167	.417	5	18	4	6	0	1	0	2	1	0	0	1	7	0	1	.444	.350
Duff, Tim	R-R	6-2	210	6-26-81	.243	.357	.174	10	37	5	9	1	0	2	7	1	0	0	0	12	0	0	.432	.263
Evans, Terry	R-R	6-3	205	1-19-82	.316	.327	.311	120	475	70	150	40	4	15	75	26	2	2	2	119	24	9	.512	.352
Eylward, Mike	R-R	6-2	210	9-28-79	.305	.341	.291	130	479	72	146	31	0	11	79	46	5	0	9	64	1	5	.438	.365
Figgins, Chone	B-R	5-8	180	1-22-78	.357	.750	.200	4	14	3	5	1	0	0	1	1	0	0	0	1	0	0	.429	.400
Gorneault, Nick	R-R	6-3	220	4-19-79	.261	.214	.279	128	471	82	123	24	1	19	59	58	3	1	0	108	17	8	.437	.346
Haynes, Nathan	L-L	5-9	180	9-7-79	.386	.233	.438	44	171	33	66	9	6	4	32	22	2	3	0	36	14	7	.579	.462
Izturis, Maicer	B-R	5-8	165	9-12-80	.353	—	.353	5	17	3	6	1	0	0	3	0	0	0	2	0	2	0	.412	.450
Johnson, Ben	B-R	5-11	205	10-17-81	.333	.333	.333	7	24	7	8	1	2	0	6	0	2	0	0	6	0	1	.542	.385
Kendrick, Howie	R-R	5-10	200	7-12-83	.300	.313	.294	13	50	9	15	1	0	3	11	1	2	0	1	9	1	0	.500	.333
Mathis, Jeff	R-R	6-0	200	3-31-83	.244	.253	.240	66	250	39	61	14	2	5	26	17	2	2	2	45	3	1	.376	.295
Morales, Kendry	B-R	6-1	225	6-20-83	.341	.354	.335	64	255	42	87	20	1	5	37	15	4	0	1	30	0	2	.486	.385
Murphy, Tommy	B-R	6-0	190	8-27-79	.270	.341	.241	80	307	36	83	18	6	4	32	23	2	3	2	67	15	10	.407	.323
Patchett, Gary	R-R	6-2	180	9-25-78	.253	.224	.262	77	221	33	56	2	0	0	18	17	3	5	1	49	1	1	.262	.314
Pavkovich, Adam	R-R	6-2	190	12-31-81	.267	.344	.229	88	281	43	75	25	1	2	32	29	4	1	2	57	3	7	.384	.342
Porter, Gregory	L-R	6-4	225	8-15-80	.345	.350	.344	56	200	38	69	12	0	7	33	18	2	0	1	44	4	0	.510	.403
Pride, Curtis	L-R	6-0	210	12-17-68	.196	.200	.196	20	56	9	11	6	0	0	4	5	2	0	1	17	4	0	.304	.281
Rivera, Juan	R-R	6-2	225	7-3-78	.262	.278	.256	15	61	4	16	8	0	0	7	3	0	0	1	6	0	0	.393	.292
Rosario, Anderson	R-R	6-0	170	3-2-85	.000	.000	.000	3	1	0	0	0	0	0	0	1	0	0	0	0	1	0	.000	.500
Smith, Casey	R-R	6-2	200	3-19-79	.290	.311	.281	109	393	49	114	24	5	2	53	28	2	7	3	54	13	3	.392	.338
Smith, Coby	R-R	6-0	200	9-21-80	.158	.250	.133	9	19	6	3	0	0	0	4	3	1	0	2	4	4	1	.158	.280
Wilson, Bobby	R-R	6-0	220	4-8-83	.295	.171	.352	40	132	15	39	13	1	3	22	8	0	1	0	18	1	0	.477	.336
Wood, Brandon	R-R	6-3	185	3-2-85	.272	.295	.265	111	437	73	119	27	1	23	77	45	1	0	5	120	10	1	.497	.338

PITCHING	B-T	HT	WT	DOB	W	L	ERA	G	GS	CG	SV	IP	H	R	ER	HR	BB	SO	AVG	vLH	vRH	K/9	BB/9
Arredondo, Jose	R-R	6-0	175	3-30-84	0	0	3.00	2	0	0	0	3	2	1	1	0	2	1	.222	.667	.000	3.00	6.00
Bonilla, Henry	R-R	6-0	195	8-16-78	12	8	5.78	29	29	1	0	165	203	114	106	22	50	90	.309	.310	.307	4.91	2.73
Brandt, Douglas	L-L	6-0	205	10-23-84	0	1	31.50	1	1	0	0	2	8	7	7	0	1	0	.571	—	.571	0.00	4.50
Bulger, Jason	R-R	6-4	215	12-6-78	5	2	3.76	49	0	0	10	53	51	24	22	4	24	81	.249	.250	.248	13.84	4.10
Colon, Bartolo	R-R	5-11	245	5-24-73	2	0	2.40	3	3	0	0	15	12	4	4	0	3	8	.214	.292	.156	4.80	1.80
Gwyn, Marcus	R-R	6-3	215	11-4-77	2	1	3.79	47	0	0	15	57	68	25	24	5	17	54	.302	.340	.273	8.53	2.68
Hensley, Matt	R-R	6-2	220	8-18-78	1	0	3.52	2	2	0	0	8	6	3	3	0	2	9	.214	.235	.182	10.57	2.35
Jones, Greg	R-R	6-2	205	11-15-76	4	2	4.86	36	0	0	3	54	68	34	29	7	14	39	.321	.333	.308	6.54	2.35
Liriano, Pedro	R-R	6-2	170	10-23-80	4	12	5.59	28	25	0	0	130	169	91	81	19	45	67	.321	.326	.316	4.63	3.11
Olenberger, Kasey	R-R	6-4	235	3-18-78	10	7	5.25	29	28	0	0	180	205	113	105	35	46	116	.289	.271	.310	5.80	2.30
Pullin, Aaron	R-R	6-3	200	2-17-81	1	1	5.50	12	0	0	0	18	22	11	11	3	7	10	.297	.192	.354	5.00	3.50
Resop, Chris	R-R	6-3	215	11-4-82	1	3	4.57	27	0	0	0	45	50	26	23	4	16	39	.276	.315	.236	7.74	3.18
Rouwenhorst, J.	L-L	6-1	180	9-25-79	10	10	4.96	33	26	1	0	158	197	101	87	16	44	83	.312	.211	.356	4.73	2.51
Santana, Ervin	R-R	6-2	185	12-12-82	2	1	5.01	5	5	0	0	32	39	19	18	4	10	32	.305	.290	.318	8.91	2.78
Saunders, Joe	L-L	6-3	210	6-16-81	4	7	5.11	14	14	0	0	86	89	53	49	10	20	84	.260	.205	.289	8.76	2.08
Seibel, Phil	L-L	6-1	200	1-28-79	0	1	11.25	2	2	0	0	8	17	13	10	4	4	5	.425	.500	.385	5.62	4.50
Serrano, Alex	R-R	6-1	200	2-18-81	3	5	5.04	47	0	0	4	70	93	44	39	8	10	46	.315	.343	.289	5.94	1.29
Shell, Steven	R-R	6-5	190	3-10-83	7	3	4.73	31	7	0	0	70	83	43	37	15	19	52	.306	.273	.341	6.65	2.43
Smith, Jesse	R-R	6-2	214	7-11-80	0	1	3.38	1	1	0	0	5	7	2	2	1	4	3	.318	.389	.000	5.06	6.75
Thompson, Rich	R-R	6-1	180	7-1-84	3	0	2.19	16	0	0	1	25	17	7	6	2	6	32	.193	.162	.216	11.68	2.19
Wilhite, Matt	R-R	6-1	185	7-3-81	3	4	4.70	49	0	0	3	75	89	48	39	8	20	40	.301	.303	.299	4.82	2.41

FIELDING

Catcher	PCT	G	PO	A	E	DP	PB
Budde	.977	33	225	28	6	3	1
Del Chiaro	1.000	10	53	15	0	1	2
Duff	1.000	10	53	15	0	1	2
Johnson	1.000	3	15	2	0	0	0
Mathis	.982	58	383	55	8	7	6
Wilson	.982	38	206	16	4	2	5

First Base	PCT	G	PO	A	E	DP
Brown	.988	8	75	4	1	7
Budde	.977	5	36	6	1	3
Eylward	.988	87	761	55	10	94
Morales	.986	43	385	24	6	46
Porter	1.000	1	6	1	0	2
Wilson	1.000	1	2	0	0	0

Second Base	PCT	G	PO	A	E	DP
Aybar	1.000	1	4	1	0	1

	PCT	G	PO	A	E	DP	PB
Brown	.943	13	23	27	3	7	
Izturis	1.000	4	4	11	0	2	
Kendrick	1.000	11	17	46	0	9	
Murphy	—	1	0	0	0	0	
Patchett	1.000	2	0	6	0	0	
Pavkovich	.982	55	109	159	5	43	
Ca. Smith	.969	69	115	198	10	58	

Third Base	PCT	G	PO	A	E	DP
Brown	.949	61	56	113	9	14
Eylward	.941	8	4	12	1	1
Figgins	.750	3	0	3	1	1
Pavkovich	.667	2	1	1	1	0
Wood	.920	74	48	137	16	17

Shortstop	PCT	G	PO	A	E	DP
Aybar	1.000	2	0	1	0	0
Izturis	1.000	1	3	1	0	0

	PCT	G	PO	A	E	DP
Patchett	.960	72	104	209	13	59
Pavkovich	1.000	1	1	4	0	1
Smith	.951	45	64	110	9	31
Wood	.962	34	54	98	6	23

Outfield	PCT	G	PO	A	E	DP
Brown	1.000	21	37	2	0	1
Evans	.996	112	237	12	1	3
Eylward	1.000	5	6	0	0	0
Gorneault	.963	109	231	5	9	2
Haynes	1.000	42	106	0	0	0
Murphy	.976	71	158	8	4	2
Pavkovich	1.000	27	40	2	0	0
Porter	.964	34	53	0	2	0
Pride	.909	10	20	0	2	0
Rivera	.957	12	20	2	1	1
Rosario	—	3	0	0	0	0
Co. Smith	.900	8	7	2	1	0

ARKANSAS TRAVELERS

DOUBLE-A

TEXAS LEAGUE

BATTING	B-T	HT	WT	DOB	AVG	vLH	vRH	G	AB	R	H	2B	3B	HR	RBI	BB	HBP	SH	SF	SO	SB	CS	SLG	OBP
Collet, Cody	R-R	6-0	195	1-22-85	.429	.750	.000	4	7	1	3	1	0	0	0	0	0	0	0	2	0	0	.571	.429
Collins, Michael	R-R	6-3	215	7-18-84	.242	.316	.208	119	429	43	104	18	3	5	45	12	15	5	2	70	5	4	.333	.286
Coon, Bradley	L-L	6-0	175	12-11-82	.301	.290	.305	58	226	37	68	8	4	1	17	23	3	5	1	36	25	12	.385	.372
Duff, Tim	R-R	6-2	210	6-26-81	.196	.192	.198	46	158	9	31	5	0	2	13	14	2	2	0	45	3	3	.266	.270
Fuller, Cody	R-R	6-0	190	9-19-82	.221	.254	.202	106	330	37	73	6	3	5	28	31	8	12	4	89	20	8	.288	.300
Johnson, Ben	B-R	5-11	205	10-17-81	.267	.289	.253	34	120	19	32	9	0	5	18	9	7	1	1	22	1	1	.467	.350

Name	B-T	HT	WT	DOB	AVG	vLH	vRH	G	AB	R	H	2B	3B	HR	RBI	BB	HBP	SH	SF	SO	SB	CS	SLG	OBP
Leahy, Ryan	R-R	5-10	180	7-8-81	.208	.163	.226	56	173	13	36	4	0	0	7	14	4	6	0	23	0	3	.231	.283
Morrissey, Adam	R-R	5-11	170	6-8-81	.263	.331	.227	134	486	85	128	27	2	9	50	92	15	5	1	131	12	7	.383	.396
Myers, Corey	R-R	6-1	225	6-5-80	.253	.217	.266	50	174	18	44	6	0	3	29	23	1	1	4	27	3	3	.339	.337
Pali, Matt	L-L	6-1	220	12-10-80	.242	.219	.249	96	322	28	78	10	1	7	35	23	8	2	2	61	5	6	.345	.307
Peel, Aaron	R-R	6-1	190	2-8-83	.255	.286	.241	83	310	34	79	20	2	7	38	6	8	2	3	43	2	0	.400	.284
Porter, Gregory	L-R	6-4	225	8-15-80	.294	.329	.278	73	272	30	80	15	3	4	45	16	6	0	3	53	13	6	.415	.343
Pride, Curtis	L-R	6-0	210	12-17-68	.239	.222	.244	44	159	18	38	8	1	3	23	23	1	0	2	48	5	4	.358	.335
Rodriguez, Sean	R-R	6-0	190	4-26-85	.254	.261	.251	136	508	84	129	31	2	17	73	54	19	2	4	132	15	8	.423	.345
Sandoval, Freddy	B-R	6-2	205	8-16-82	.305	.329	.293	127	472	84	144	32	6	11	72	67	5	12	7	78	21	11	.468	.392
Smith, Coby	R-R	6-0	200	9-21-80	.277	.323	.244	63	224	37	62	12	1	2	17	32	2	4	2	27	21	7	.366	.369
Wilson, Bobby	R-R	6-0	220	4-8-83	.271	.345	.238	50	181	24	49	9	0	6	27	22	0	0	1	26	5	3	.420	.348
Wipke, Flint	R-R	6-0	195	1-22-83	.313	.800	.091	5	16	4	5	0	0	0	1	3	0	0	0	2	1	0	.313	.421

PITCHING	B-T	HT	WT	DOB	W	L	ERA	G	GS	CG	SV	IP	H	R	ER	HR	BB	SO	AVG	vLH	vRH	K/9	BB/9
Adenhart, Nick	R-R	6-3	185	8-24-86	10	8	3.65	26	26	0	0	153	158	72	62	7	65	116	.273	.265	.281	6.82	3.82
Arredondo, Jose	R-R	6-0	175	3-30-84	0	1	2.52	23	0	0	10	25	16	10	7	2	12	28	.184	.200	.170	10.08	4.32
Austen, David	R-R	6-1	185	5-21-81	2	0	5.57	14	1	0	0	21	27	14	13	4	8	12	.307	.314	.302	5.14	3.43
Beck, Bradley	L-L	5-11	185	1-10-85	1	0	3.38	4	0	0	0	5	4	2	2	1	0	3	.211	.375	.091	5.06	0.00
Butcher, Brok	R-R	6-1	210	10-13-83	1	2	5.90	6	0	0	0	29	30	22	19	5	7	18	.254	.233	.276	5.59	2.17
Davidson, Daniel	L-L	6-4	225	1-8-81	2	4	2.06	7	7	0	0	44	34	14	10	4	8	25	.219	.208	.224	5.15	1.65
Diaz, Amalio	R-R	6-2	170	9-10-86	0	2	4.58	6	0	0	0	37	43	21	19	3	7	15	.293	.276	.303	3.62	1.69
Edens, Kyle	R-R	5-10	210	1-25-80	0	1	7.56	4	0	0	0	8	13	9	7	2	4	6	.351	.400	.318	6.48	4.32
Edwards, Bill	R-R	6-3	185	3-26-84	4	4	4.74	53	0	0	4	68	69	40	36	6	36	48	.263	.281	.248	6.32	4.74
Gonzalez, Miguel	R-R	6-1	165	5-27-84	8	4	3.37	30	19	1	1	131	128	53	49	13	42	81	.260	.234	.284	5.58	2.89
Green, Nick	R-R	6-4	200	8-20-84	10	8	3.68	28	28	2	0	178	164	80	73	17	32	107	.243	.264	.223	5.40	1.61
Holcomb, James	R-R	6-4	205	11-28-80	0	2	9.00	2	2	0	0	7	9	7	7	2	4	7	.333	.231	.429	5.14	9.00
Hunter, Christopher	R-R	6-4	200	12-12-80	3	4	9.24	22	3	0	1	38	57	41	39	8	23	23	.337	.353	.321	5.45	5.45
Kennard, Jeff	R-R	6-2	220	7-26-81	2	0	5.12	16	0	0	0	19	19	11	11	1	13	11	.264	.273	.256	5.12	6.05
Leahy, Ryan	R-R	5-10	180	7-8-81	0	0	0.00	1	0	0	0	1	0	0	0	0	0	0	.000	.000	—	0.00	0.00
Lynch, Kevin	R-R	6-2	200	1-2-83	1	2	3.75	9	0	0	0	12	14	7	5	0	5	7	.286	.294	.281	5.25	3.75
Mosebach, Robert	R-R	6-4	195	9-14-84	1	1	5.14	2	2	0	0	14	16	9	8	1	8	3	.302	.346	.259	1.93	5.14
O'Day, Darren	R-R	6-4	220	10-22-82	3	4	3.99	29	0	0	10	29	27	13	13	3	14	22	.252	.245	.259	6.75	4.30
Pullin, Aaron	R-R	6-3	200	2-17-81	4	4	3.77	39	0	0	1	43	36	19	18	2	21	33	.232	.292	.181	6.91	4.40
Rodriguez, Rafael	R-R	6-1	175	9-24-84	0	6	4.16	46	1	0	0	71	79	36	33	6	30	42	.287	.322	.260	5.30	3.79
Rodriguez Jr., F.	R-R	6-3	210	6-18-84	8	4	4.52	22	22	1	0	125	138	71	63	14	46	61	.285	.314	.255	4.38	3.30
Saenz, Chris	R-R	6-3	220	8-14-81	1	7	8.41	19	9	0	0	46	62	47	43	3	31	24	.341	.385	.297	4.70	6.07
Shell, Steven	R-R	6-5	190	3-10-83	0	0	0.68	5	0	0	0	13	10	1	1	1	1	19	.200	.190	.207	12.83	0.67
Smith, Jesse	R-R	6-2	214	7-11-80	1	2	2.14	4	4	0	0	21	23	5	5	1	3	17	.280	.234	.343	7.29	1.29
Stertzbach, Von	R-R	6-2	190	5-15-81	1	2	6.39	21	0	0	0	25	29	18	18	4	14	24	.293	.340	.245	8.53	4.97
Thompson, Rich	R-R	6-1	180	7-1-84	2	3	2.01	21	3	0	0	49	34	15	11	5	14	50	.193	.217	.172	9.12	2.55

FIELDING

Catcher	PCT	G	PO	A	E	DP	PB
Collet	1.000	2	3	0	0	0	0
Duff	.993	46	245	37	2	4	4
Johnson	.992	22	116	11	1	2	3
Myers	.986	25	134	11	2	4	5
Wilson	.991	43	289	33	3	4	3
Wipke	1.000	5	24	5	0	2	0

First Base	PCT	G	PO	A	E	DP
Collins	.992	111	964	58	8	94
Johnson	1.000	2	20	0	0	1
Myers	1.000	2	15	0	0	3
Pali	.990	24	175	24	2	17

Sandoval	1.000	1	1	0	0	0
Wilson	.977	4	41	2	1	3

Second Base	PCT	G	PO	A	E	DP
Leahy	.979	20	32	61	2	17
Morrissey	.985	121	201	338	8	79

Third Base	PCT	G	PO	A	E	DP
Collins	—	1	0	0	0	0
Leahy	.947	19	22	32	3	4
Myers	1.000	1	1	0	0	0
Sandoval	.939	122	96	211	20	26

Shortstop	PCT	G	PO	A	E	DP
Leahy	1.000	18	22	39	0	9

	PCT	G	PO	A	E	DP
Rodriguez	.970	125	211	370	18	82

Outfield	PCT	G	PO	A	E	DP
Coon	.981	58	153	4	3	2
Fuller	.993	106	258	10	2	4
Pali	1.000	44	95	2	0	0
Peel	.978	75	130	3	3	0
Porter	.992	54	112	8	1	2
Pride	1.000	25	50	1	0	0
Rodriguez	.938	5	13	2	1	0
Smith	.982	62	155	6	3	3

RANCHO CUCAMONGA QUAKES   HIGH CLASS A

CALIFORNIA LEAGUE

BATTING	B-T	HT	WT	DOB	AVG	vLH	vRH	G	AB	R	H	2B	3B	HR	RBI	BB	HBP	SH	SF	SO	SB	CS	SLG	OBP
Anderson, Garret	L-L	6-3	225	6-30-72	.222	.286	.182	6	18	3	4	1	0	0	2	1	0	0	0	3	0	0	.278	.263
Aybar, Erick	B-R	5-10	170	1-14-84	.400	—	.400	2	5	3	2	0	0	0	0	1	0	0	0	1	3	1	.400	.500
Brewer, Tadd	R-R	6-1	190	5-4-84	.208	.291	.157	46	144	19	30	5	2	0	14	12	4	5	1	37	3	2	.271	.286
Colmenares, Carlos	B-R	6-0	175	2-11-86	.333	.000	1.000	3	3	2	1	0	0	0	1	0	0	0	1	2	0	0	.333	.250
Coon, Bradley	L-L	6-0	175	12-11-82	.258	.222	.271	74	299	44	77	13	2	3	27	21	2	4	0	48	31	9	.344	.311
Davies, Josh	R-R	6-4	200	9-12-81	.071	.000	.250	6	14	1	1	0	0	0	0	0	0	0	0	9	0	0	.071	.133
Dini, Gregory	R-R	6-2	200	1-18-83	.216	.167	.226	12	37	3	8	2	0	0	5	2	0	0	0	7	0	0	.270	.256
Infante, Larry	B-R	5-10	160	4-4-85	.282	.143	.310	58	209	24	59	8	0	4	30	8	2	3	2	38	3	3	.378	.312
Izturis, Maicer	B-R	5-8	165	9-12-80	.318	.400	.250	7	22	5	7	1	0	0	3	0	0	0	1	3	0	0	.364	.444
Johnson, Ben	B-R	5-11	205	10-17-81	.277	.311	.259	71	260	39	72	12	2	14	48	21	10	3	5	48	13	0	.500	.348
Kendrick, Howie	R-R	5-10	200	7-12-83	.250	.333	.000	1	4	0	1	0	0	0	0	0	0	0	0	0	0	0	.250	.250
Knazek, Scott	R-R	6-1	215	11-4-84	.000	—	.000	5	2	0	0	0	0	0	0	0	0	0	0	4	0	0	.000	.077
Larue, Jeff	R-R	6-0	190	6-19-80	.255	.188	.290	29	94	16	24	5	0	4	15	5	1	2	1	31	1	1	.436	.297
Leblanc, Josh	L-R	6-1	190	9-15-81	.199	.167	.206	67	191	28	38	6	2	2	21	13	0	0	4	61	13	5	.283	.245
Martinez, Brett	R-R	6-0	200	10-14-83	.200	.111	.238	12	30	2	6	0	0	0	1	4	0	2	0	4	2	1	.200	.294
Morris, Dallas	R-R	6-2	210	7-13-82	.232	.313	.209	38	142	16	33	6	0	1	7	8	0	1	1	31	3	1	.296	.272
Nieves, Abel	R-R	5-11	175	8-14-85	.143	.167	.132	19	56	8	8	2	0	0	5	10	0	2	0	24	0	0	.179	.273
Peel, Aaron	R-R	6-1	190	2-8-83	.346	.330	.349	26	104	22	36	5	0	3	16	3	4	1	0	20	2	2	.481	.387
Pettit, Chris	R-R	6-0	193	8-15-84	.309	.293	.317	69	265	54	82	20	2	9	54	36	3	1	2	48	13	3	.502	.395
Reilly, Patrick	L-L	6-0	190	12-2-81	.225	.149	.237	96	325	35	73	10	3	12	49	26	3	1	6	99	4	5	.385	.283
Remole, Clifton	L-L	6-1	205	10-24-82	.278	.289	.289	91	332	45	95	19	0	6	54	24	3	1	3	37	3	1	.398	.330
Renz, Jordan	R-R	6-3	225	7-21-83	.227	.259	.215	109	401	56	91	19	1	20	62	29	3	1	6	144	4	2	.429	.280
Rivera, Juan	R-R	6-2	225	7-3-78	.400	.250	.500	3	10	3	4	1	0	0	2	0	0	0	0	2	0	0	.500	.400

Name	B-T	HT	WT	DOB	AVG	vLH	vRH	G	AB	R	H	2B	3B	HR	RBI	BB	HBP	SH	SF	SO	SB	CS	SLG	OBP
Rosario, Anderson	R-R	6-0	170	3-2-85	.122	.095	.132	28	74	5	9	0	1	1	3	2	0	2	0	41	3	0	.189	.145
Smith, Coby	R-R	6-0	200	9-21-80	.354	.350	.356	18	65	11	23	3	2	2	9	5	4	1	1	12	8	3	.554	.427
Statia, Hainley	B-R	5-10	160	1-19-86	.288	.268	.296	135	549	86	158	27	7	3	74	48	2	5	5	79	29	8	.379	.344
Sutton, Nate	L-R	6-0	190	9-1-82	.277	.290	.272	135	523	82	145	19	7	4	50	51	4	9	5	90	21	8	.363	.343
Toussaint, Drew	R-R	6-2	175	10-24-82	.272	.328	.246	114	394	55	107	24	4	9	47	35	5	1	2	102	7	4	.421	.337
Wipke, Flint	R-R	6-0	195	1-22-83	.176	.270	.137	65	216	21	38	11	0	2	18	25	2	1	0	77	5	2	.255	.267

PITCHING

Name	B-T	HT	WT	DOB	W	L	ERA	G	GS	CG	SV	IP	H	R	ER	HR	BB	SO	AVG	vLH	vRH	K/9	BB/9
Arredondo, Jose	R-R	6-0	175	3-30-84	2	4	6.43	28	0	0	4	35	46	31	25	5	11	34	.317	.340	.306	8.74	2.83
Austen, David	R-R	6-1	185	5-21-81	1	0	3.18	6	0	0	2	6	6	2	2	1	0	2	.240	.429	.167	3.18	0.00
Beck, Bradley	L-L	5-11	185	1-10-85	1	3	5.55	7	0	0	1	24	26	16	15	3	16	17	.277	.225	.315	6.29	5.92
Brandt, Douglas	L-L	6-0	205	10-23-84	2	0	2.70	22	2	0	2	43	34	14	13	3	15	51	.214	.267	.193	10.59	3.12
Butcher, Brok	R-R	6-1	210	10-13-83	5	7	2.69	18	15	3	1	110	105	36	33	4	28	59	.251	.269	.236	4.81	2.28
Colon, Bartolo	R-R	5-11	245	5-24-73	1	0	1.86	2	2	0	0	10	6	2	2	0	1	10	.162	.143	.174	9.31	0.93
Cook, Aaron	R-R	6-5	175	10-20-83	0	0	4.05	9	0	0	1	13	13	6	6	0	4	12	.271	.444	.167	8.10	2.70
Diaz, Amalio	R-R	6-2	170	9-10-86	0	0	6.27	4	0	0	0	37	57	31	26	3	14	21	.354	.435	.303	5.06	3.38
Fish, Robert	L-L	6-2	215	1-19-88	0	1	6.00	1	1	0	0	3	3	2	2	1	4	4	.273	.143	.500	12.00	12.00
Holler, Blake	L-L	6-4	165	1-22-85	0	0	1.38	2	0	0	0	13	11	3	2	1	2	8	.239	.333	.179	5.54	1.38
Hunter, Christopher	R-R	6-4	200	12-12-80	0	0	6.23	6	0	0	0	9	9	6	6	1	2	6	.257	.143	.333	6.23	2.08
Incinelli, Jared	R-R	6-4	200	4-12-83	3	2	4.09	32	1	0	0	51	48	26	23	6	29	35	.249	.242	.252	6.22	5.15
Jepsen, Kevin	R-R	6-3	215	7-26-84	1	5	4.19	44	0	0	3	54	61	29	25	2	38	50	.292	.290	.293	8.39	6.37
Lynch, Kevin	R-R	6-2	200	1-2-83	2	1	2.04	10	0	0	2	18	18	4	4	0	6	15	.269	.300	.255	7.64	3.06
Marek, Stephen	R-R	6-2	200	9-3-83	8	10	4.30	25	25	1	0	134	133	78	64	17	49	106	.257	.187	.296	7.12	3.29
Mattison, Tim	R-R	6-1	225	6-22-82	1	6	5.22	43	0	0	0	71	85	52	41	8	23	41	.299	.316	.291	5.22	2.93
McRobbie, Alex	R-R	6-2	185	1-16-83	6	1	3.43	10	10	1	0	60	61	27	23	6	16	48	.261	.224	.278	7.16	2.39
Moseubach, Robert	R-R	6-4	195	9-14-84	11	7	4.28	25	23	1	0	156	171	88	74	16	49	93	.285	.314	.265	5.38	2.83
O'Day, Darren	R-R	6-4	220	10-22-82	4	0	0.75	24	0	0	11	24	10	3	2	1	6	26	.120	.147	.102	9.75	2.25
Ortega, Anthony	R-R	6-0	170	8-24-85	7	11	4.02	28	28	1	0	163	157	84	73	17	68	127	.254	.264	.248	7.00	3.75
Rodriguez, Francisco	R-R	6-2	200	2-26-83	4	8	5.96	39	8	0	2	106	117	76	70	11	53	70	.285	.271	.296	5.96	4.51
Schoeninger, Tim	R-R	6-2	220	9-7-84	6	3	6.64	12	12	0	0	62	86	51	46	16	22	53	.326	.325	.327	7.65	3.18
Shearer, Kelly	L-L	6-3	200	4-8-85	0	0	3.86	3	0	0	0	2	2	1	1	0	1	2	.200	.000	.286	7.71	3.86
Speier, Justin	R-R	6-4	205	11-6-73	1	0	3.00	8	3	0	0	9	10	3	3	1	5	7	.294	.353	.235	7.00	5.00
Stertzbach, Von	R-R	6-2	190	5-15-81	1	0	9.22	14	0	0	3	14	17	14	14	3	12	16	.309	.300	.314	10.54	7.90
Thomas, Eric	R-R	6-9	230	3-21-81	1	2	12.71	7	2	0	0	11	13	17	16	3	13	17	.277	.400	.185	13.50	10.32
Thompson, Rich	R-R	6-1	180	7-1-84	0	0	0.00	1	0	0	0	2	1	0	0	0	0	3	.125	.167	.000	13.50	0.00
Weaver, Jered	R-R	6-7	205	10-4-82	1	0	0.82	2	2	0	0	11	5	1	1	1	3	12	.132	.200	.087	9.82	2.45

FIELDING

Catcher	PCT	G	PO	A	E	DP	PB
Dini	.989	12	85	3	1	0	2
Johnson	.987	54	353	35	5	2	2
Knazek	1.000	5	25	2	0	0	1
Martinez	.986	12	64	7	1	1	1
Wipke	.980	64	436	45	10	5	12

First Base	PCT	G	PO	A	E	DP
Davies	1.000	1	8	0	0	1
Johnson	.987	16	138	10	2	19
Larue	1.000	10	70	15	0	5
Nieves	1.000	3	28	3	0	1
Reilly	.982	58	546	41	11	59
Remole	.989	57	491	31	6	52

Second Base	PCT	G	PO	A	E	DP
Brewer	.949	8	18	19	2	7
Infante	1.000	4	6	12	0	1

	PCT	G	PO	A	E	DP
Nieves	1.000	2	4	4	0	2
Sutton	.982	129	279	392	12	94

Third Base	PCT	G	PO	A	E	DP
Brewer	.802	33	18	51	17	6
Colmenares	.500	1	0	2	2	0
Davies	.750	4	0	3	1	0
Infante	.923	48	27	93	10	14
Izturis	.933	6	3	11	1	1
Larue	.791	17	9	25	9	2
Morris	.975	37	38	80	3	13
Nieves	.882	5	3	12	2	0

Shortstop	PCT	G	PO	A	E	DP
Aybar	.900	2	6	3	1	2
Brewer	1.000	1	0	2	0	0
Colmenares	—	1	0	0	0	0
Infante	.920	8	8	15	2	4

	PCT	G	PO	A	E	DP
Nieves	1.000	1	0	1	0	0
Statia	.965	134	195	442	23	86

Outfield	PCT	G	PO	A	E	DP
Anderson	1.000	4	5	0	0	0
Coon	.989	74	176	3	2	0
Leblanc	.990	57	95	6	1	3
Peel	1.000	12	13	0	0	0
Pettit	1.000	69	116	7	0	0
Reilly	1.000	2	4	0	0	0
Remole	.960	97	179	15	8	3
Renz	1.000	2	4	0	0	0
Rivera	1.000	2	4	0	0	0
Rosario	.961	28	48	1	2	0
Smith	1.000	18	25	1	0	0
Toussaint	.955	69	99	7	5	0

CEDAR RAPIDS KERNELS   LOW CLASS A

MIDWEST LEAGUE

BATTING	B-T	HT	WT	DOB	AVG	vLH	vRH	G	AB	R	H	2B	3B	HR	RBI	BB	HBP	SH	SF	SO	SB	CS	SLG	OBP
Bourjos, Peter	R-R	6-1	175	3-31-87	.274	.250	.284	63	237	37	65	9	6	5	29	20	4	4	5	53	19	9	.426	.335
Brewer, Tadd	R-R	6-1	190	5-4-84	.286	.000	.333	10	28	4	8	3	1	0	3	7	1	0	0	6	2	0	.464	.444
Collet, Cody	R-R	6-0	195	1-22-85	.200	.250	.000	2	5	1	1	0	1	0	0	1	0	0	0	2	0	0	.400	.200
Conger, Hank	B-R	6-0	205	1-29-88	.290	.250	.304	84	290	33	84	20	0	11	48	21	2	2	5	48	9	4	.472	.336
Davies, Josh	R-R	6-4	200	9-12-85	.194	.167	.203	30	103	12	20	5	0	0	5	5	0	1	1	38	1	2	.243	.229
Dini, Gregory	R-R	6-2	200	1-18-83	.211	.500	.077	5	19	1	4	0	0	0	3	0	0	0	0	4	0	2	.211	.211
Infante, Larry	B-R	5-10	160	4-4-85	.000	—	.000	1	2	0	0	0	0	0	0	0	0	0	0	0	0	0	.000	.000
Johnson, Tyler	R-R	6-2	220	11-2-85	.244	.283	.234	80	291	43	71	19	5	11	34	18	6	1	1	105	18	7	.457	.301
Knazek, Scott	R-R	6-1	215	11-4-84	.250	.400	.217	9	28	3	7	0	0	0	1	5	0	0	0	7	1	0	.250	.364
Martinez, Brett	R-R	6-0	200	10-14-83	.192	.182	.200	8	26	4	5	0	1	0	6	3	0	0	0	9	0	0	.269	.276
Mount, Ryan	L-R	6-1	180	8-17-86	.251	.254	.250	85	303	47	76	11	3	7	36	29	3	0	2	70	19	6	.376	.320
Nieves, Abel	R-R	5-11	175	8-14-85	.258	.283	.253	70	236	33	61	8	5	1	25	33	0	2	4	45	6	6	.347	.344
Ortiz, Wilberto	R-R	5-10	180	11-30-85	.277	.235	.295	113	411	54	114	24	3	5	39	34	1	10	5	57	21	12	.387	.330
Perez, Julio	R-R	6-2	160	9-28-85	.216	.260	.195	67	227	20	49	9	2	11	34	17	3	2	0	68	3	2	.382	.279
Pettit, Chris	R-R	6-0	193	8-15-84	.346	.359	.341	64	228	47	79	24	1	9	41	23	12	0	3	41	17	4	.579	.429
Phillips, P.J.	R-R	6-3	170	9-23-86	.245	.230	.251	119	436	67	107	11	8	13	37	15	8	2	0	154	34	4	.397	.283
Rosario, Anderson	R-R	6-0	170	3-2-85	.202	.217	.202	50	152	20	33	9	1	6	19	10	5	2	0	60	2	3	.408	.287
Smith, Stantrel	R-R	6-4	211	10-21-83	.223	.224	.222	100	319	39	71	10	3	7	30	11	4	1	3	77	23	5	.339	.255
Sweeney, Matthew	L-R	6-3	210	4-4-88	.260	.272	.255	119	439	64	114	29	2	18	72	38	5	0	3	88	7	7	.458	.324
Trumbo, Mark	R-R	6-4	220	1-16-86	.272	.294	.264	128	471	57	128	27	2	14	76	34	6	0	5	98	10	8	.427	.326
Walker, Brian	L-R	6-0	215	7-17-85	.274	.300	.266	39	124	16	34	4	1	3	14	9	1	0	2	33	1	3	.395	.324

PITCHING	B-T	HT	WT	DOB	W	L	ERA	G	GS	CG	SV	IP	H	R	ER	HR	BB	SO	AVG	vLH	vRH	K/9	BB/9
Albano, Marco	R-R	5-11	215	8-26-83	0	0	0.00	5	0	0	0	5	3	0	0	0	2	6	.167	.400	.077	10.80	3.60
Arredondo, Felipe	R-R	6-4	225	10-4-86	1	1	3.26	41	0	0	1	58	49	24	21	4	14	59	.224	.278	.193	9.16	2.17
Bell, Trevor	L-R	6-2	180	10-12-86	8	4	4.14	21	21	0	0	115	136	64	53	8	23	90	.292	.342	.259	7.02	1.79
Brandt, Douglas	L-L	6-0	205	10-23-84	3	2	2.35	17	9	0	0	61	56	20	16	2	15	64	.239	.288	.220	9.39	2.20
Browning, Barret	L-L	6-1	170	12-28-84	9	4	2.80	48	0	0	8	74	54	25	23	2	26	74	.201	.132	.236	9.00	3.16
Cassevah, Bobby	R-R	6-3	195	9-11-85	2	1	2.32	18	0	0	1	31	25	9	8	0	13	25	.227	.200	.238	7.26	3.77
Connelly, P.J.	L-L	6-4	210	6-27-83	1	1	5.50	8	0	0	0	18	17	12	11	2	5	9	.254	.222	.275	4.50	2.50
Cook, Aaron	R-R	6-5	175	10-20-83	1	2	0.80	25	0	0	5	34	27	4	3	0	1	20	.220	.362	.132	5.35	0.27
Diaz, Amalio	R-R	6-2	170	9-10-86	3	6	4.47	16	6	0	1	52	75	28	26	5	12	31	.341	.304	.362	5.33	2.06
Haynes, Jeremy	R-R	6-2	180	5-28-86	5	6	3.06	19	19	0	0	94	98	40	32	3	41	75	.266	.217	.303	7.18	3.93
Herndon, David	R-R	6-3	230	9-4-85	13	8	4.02	25	24	2	0	152	175	80	68	10	20	83	.290	.293	.288	4.90	1.18
Herrera, Pedro	R-R	6-0	155	2-14-86	1	0	4.50	6	0	0	0	8	7	4	4	1	1	7	.233	.333	.167	7.88	1.12
Holler, Blake	L-L	6-4	165	1-22-85	3	3	3.41	23	7	0	0	66	76	35	25	8	15	63	.289	.283	.291	8.59	2.05
Leon, Sammy	R-R	6-0	160	5-19-85	1	0	5.68	6	0	0	0	6	7	4	4	0	6	6	.280	.333	.250	8.53	8.53
Madrigal, Warner A.	R-R	6-0	200	3-21-84	5	4	2.07	54	0	0	20	61	44	18	14	3	23	75	.202	.247	.168	11.07	3.39
Mendoza, Thomas	R-R	6-2	195	8-18-87	2	4	4.86	12	11	0	0	54	67	37	29	5	16	38	.307	.321	.299	6.37	2.68
O'Sullivan, Sean	R-R	6-1	220	9-1-87	10	7	2.22	25	25	0	0	158	136	58	39	6	40	125	.227	.211	.239	7.11	2.27
Romero, Robert	R-R	5-10	190	3-28-85	0	1	5.40	4	0	0	0	3	7	3	2	1	2	5	.389	.375	.400	13.50	5.40
Schoeninger, Tim	R-R	6-2	220	9-7-84	9	3	3.06	13	13	2	0	85	89	32	29	6	6	68	.269	.292	.251	7.17	0.63
Shearer, Kelly	L-L	6-3	200	4-8-85	1	2	1.86	15	1	0	1	29	23	11	6	3	12	18	.217	.219	.216	5.59	3.72
Sullivan, Anthony	R-R	5-11	185	7-2-84	0	0	1.80	3	0	0	0	5	2	1	1	0	0	5	.111	.000	.143	9.00	0.00
Veras, Vladimir	R-R	6-0	150	1-10-86	0	2	8.18	3	1	0	0	11	15	10	10	0	7	8	.333	.421	.269	6.55	5.73
West, Jim	R-R	6-2	175	12-21-84	0	0	0.00	5	0	0	0	7	8	2	0	0	3	3	.276	.111	.350	3.86	3.86

FIELDING

Catcher	PCT	G	PO	A	E	DP	PB
Albano	.900	1	7	2	1	0	0
Collet	1.000	2	12	2	0	0	0
Conger	.985	70	509	34	8	7	5
Dini	.975	5	36	3	1	0	2
Hodach	1.000	22	117	8	0	0	0
Knazek	.957	9	58	8	3	0	0
Martinez	.966	5	27	1	1	0	0
Walker	.996	36	218	29	1	1	2

First Base	PCT	G	PO	A	E	DP
Albano	1.000	1	3	0	0	1
Davies	.959	13	112	5	5	14
Nieves	.993	13	127	7	1	6
Trumbo	.989	114	1029	67	12	86

Second Base	PCT	G	PO	A	E	DP
Albano	.976	8	10	30	1	7
Brewer	1.000	6	15	19	0	4
Davies	1.000	1	0	1	0	0
Infante	1.000	1	0	3	0	0
Mount	.967	81	108	245	12	45
Nieves	.984	13	21	42	1	7
Ortiz	.982	35	40	121	3	12

Third Base	PCT	G	PO	A	E	DP
Albano	1.000	2	1	4	0	0
Brewer	1.000	1	0	1	0	0
Davies	.929	8	5	8	1	0
Nieves	.889	11	8	24	4	3
Ortiz	.975	34	22	55	2	2

Sweeney		.862	85	40	135	28	11

Shortstop	PCT	G	PO	A	E	DP
Ortiz	.930	27	35	84	9	14
Phillips	.926	117	181	319	40	64

Outfield	PCT	G	PO	A	E	DP
Albano	.947	12	16	2	1	0
Bourjos	.986	62	131	9	2	1
Davies	1.000	5	8	1	0	0
Johnson	.955	79	157	12	8	1
Perez	.959	66	114	3	5	0
Pettit	.968	60	80	11	3	2
Rosario	.989	50	88	2	1	1
Smith	.973	96	176	5	5	4

OREM OWLZ

ROOKIE

PIONEER LEAGUE

BATTING	B-T	HT	WT	DOB	AVG	vLH	vRH	G	AB	R	H	2B	3B	HR	RBI	BB	HBP	SH	SF	SO	SB	CS	SLG	OBP
Brossman, Jay	R-R	6-2	210	1-17-85	.346	.400	.329	65	272	46	94	14	0	7	44	19	1	2	2	48	4	0	.474	.388
De Los Santos, Anel	R-R	6-0	180	6-19-88	.255	.213	.276	50	188	19	48	8	4	6	37	4	0	0	2	44	0	0	.436	.268
Dini, Gregory	R-R	6-2	200	1-18-83	.250	.000	.300	7	24	2	6	1	1	1	8	2	0	0	0	3	0	0	.500	.308
Estrella, Hector	R-R	5-10	175	12-22-84	.300	.397	.263	61	230	40	69	11	3	4	35	23	6	1	2	37	5	1	.426	.375
Garcia, Christopher	L-R	6-2	225	11-25-87	.273	.188	.295	23	77	10	21	6	0	2	12	10	2	0	1	21	0	0	.429	.367
Giovanatto, Donato	R-R	6-1	195	10-20-84	.266	.192	.316	45	128	25	34	7	1	8	17	8	3	0	0	39	3	1	.523	.324
Gonzalez-Lopez, Jerry	R-R	5-9	175	10-30-85	.325	.268	.356	45	160	25	52	7	3	4	16	8	4	3	1	31	5	1	.481	.370
Gronkowski, Gordon	R-R	6-6	250	6-26-83	.344	.293	.360	66	244	44	84	19	0	8	50	27	4	0	2	63	0	0	.520	.415
Kennedy, Ryan	B-R	5-9	170	10-2-84	.188	.238	.175	33	101	13	19	2	0	0	9	17	2	3	0	12	2	3	.208	.317
Kiniry, Rian	L-R	5-10	160	12-12-86	.260	.211	.267	49	150	25	39	5	1	0	14	16	2	3	1	33	8	3	.307	.337
Miller, Deandre	B-R	5-9	175	5-18-85	.228	.204	.239	53	167	35	38	7	1	1	10	42	4	2	0	37	10	5	.299	.394
Moore, Jeremy	L-R	6-1	190	6-29-87	.272	.230	.289	68	254	50	69	13	6	14	54	19	3	4	1	68	17	5	.535	.329
Navarro, Efren	L-L	6-0	200	5-14-86	.212	.038	.264	40	113	16	24	4	0	1	11	11	2	2	1	21	1	1	.274	.291
Perez, Julio	R-R	6-0	160	9-28-85	.276	.289	.271	35	123	18	34	8	1	8	21	8	4	0	2	40	4	2	.553	.336
Pippin, Trevor	L-L	6-3	190	12-3-86	.188	.077	.214	48	138	17	26	2	0	0	16	16	0	2	2	51	3	1	.203	.269
Romine, Andrew	B-R	6-1	180	12-24-85	.286	.188	.323	56	231	38	66	6	6	5	35	16	2	0	0	38	12	4	.429	.337
Rosenbaum, Chris	R-R	6-1	205	4-2-84	.277	.417	.220	25	83	10	23	4	0	2	8	7	3	1	0	18	0	0	.398	.355
Thomas, Derrick	L-R	6-0	210	9-10-82	.571	—	.571	6	7	0	4	0	0	0	2	1	0	0	0	1	0	0	.571	.625
Walker, Brian	L-R	6-0	215	7-17-85	.125	.000	.250	3	8	1	1	1	0	0	1	0	0	0	1	0	0	.250	.222

PITCHING	B-T	HT	WT	DOB	W	L	ERA	G	GS	CG	SV	IP	H	R	ER	HR	BB	SO	AVG	vLH	vRH	K/9	BB/9
Anton, Michael	L-L	6-3	195	4-3-85	0	1	3.86	2	2	0	0	7	5	3	3	0	3	7	.200	.000	.278	9.00	3.86
Armstrong, C.	L-L	5-10	195	2-10-88	2	1	6.80	13	2	0	1	41	54	32	31	4	9	33	.316	.278	.333	7.24	1.98
Brasier, Ryan	R-R	6-0	190	8-26-87	1	2	2.08	26	0	0	9	30	22	9	7	2	7	26	.212	.279	.164	7.71	2.08
Cabrera, Francis	R-R	6-1	184	5-27-87	0	1	5.18	15	0	0	0	24	29	14	14	6	18	22	.305	.319	.292	8.14	6.66y
Calderon, Leonardo	L-L	5-11	170	7-31-86	0	1	12.27	8	0	0	0	7	9	12	10	1	11	6	.300	.167	.389	7.36	13.50
Cassevah, Bobby	R-R	6-3	195	9-11-85	0	0	4.32	6	0	0	0	8	6	4	4	0	5	9	.290	.417	.211	9.72	5.40
Chambers, Brian	R-R	6-3	202	8-14-85	3	1	1.85	18	0	0	0	24	20	7	5	2	9	22	.225	.219	.228	8.14	3.33
Davitt, Michael	R-R	6-5	205	9-8-86	0	3	5.67	13	8	0	0	33	39	21	21	2	16	30	.300	.313	.288	8.10	4.32
Dinga, Milan	R-R	6-2	205	12-27-84	0	0	0.35	4	0	0	0	7	6	2	1	0	1	6	.250	.231	.810	1.35
Fish, Robert	L-L	6-2	215	1-19-88	3	4	3.27	16	15	0	0	72	62	33	26	4	31	77	.239	.306	.224	9.67	3.89
Green, Lou	R-R	6-5	220	7-17-87	1	1	4.08	10	3	0	0	18	18	10	8	0	9	17	.269	.286	.261	8.66	4.58
Herrera, Pedro	R-R	6-0	155	2-14-86	0	0	0.00	1	0	0	0	1	3	1	0	0	0	1	.429	.400	.500	6.75	0.00
Holland, Tremayne	R-R	6-1	210	1-27-86	4	2	5.20	21	0	0	0	28	34	18	16	3	21	26	.298	.319	.284	8.46	6.83
Hurst, David	L-R	6-0	195	5-13-84	3	3	5.31	10	1	0	0	41	49	26	24	3	7	31	.302	.333	.288	6.86	1.55
Jimenez, Esmerlin	R-R	6-2	170	8-1-84	5	2	3.51	16	13	1	0	77	70	37	30	5	17	58	.244	.197	.287	6.78	1.99
Jung, Young-Il	R-R	6-2	190	11-16-88	0	1	9.00	3	3	0	0	9	10	12	9	1	6	9	.263	.182	.375	9.00	6.00

	B-T	HT	WT	DOB	W	L	ERA	G	GS	CG	SV	IP	H	R	ER	HR	BB	SO	AVG	vLH	vRH	K/9	BB/9
Lindsey, Dylan	R-R	6-3	205	7-13-85	0	1	7.04	6	0	0	0	8	6	8	6	1	11	2	.222	.267	.167	2.35	12.91
Schlecker, Derek	R-R	6-5	200	1-7-85	0	3	3.66	16	0	0	1	32	33	15	13	1	5	21	.264	.389	.169	5.91	1.41
Shearer, Kelly	L-L	6-3	200	4-8-85	0	0	1.93	1	0	0	0	5	4	1	1	1	3	1	.286	.333	.250	1.93	5.79
Tobin, Mason	R-R	6-3	210	7-8-87	2	1	3.21	6	6	0	0	28	23	10	10	0	7	23	.230	.216	.238	7.39	2.25
Towns, Jordan	R-R	6-2	220	9-21-85	6	3	3.46	19	0	0	0	42	38	17	16	2	21	38	.241	.286	.198	8.21	4.54
Veras, Vladimir	R-R	6-0	150	1-10-86	5	4	6.52	13	9	0	0	50	58	38	36	10	12	43	.287	.277	.296	7.79	2.17
Walden, Jordan	R-R	6-4	180	11-16-87	1	1	3.08	15	15	0	0	64	49	27	22	3	17	63	.209	.175	.248	8.81	2.38
West, Jim	R-R	6-2	175	12-21-84	1	2	3.91	16	0	0	0	25	32	13	11	2	12	33	.320	.400	.286	11.72	4.26

FIELDING

Catcher	PCT	G	PO	A	E	DP	PB
De Los Santos	.983	49	349	53	7	4	10
Dini	.979	6	37	9	1	0	3
Rosenbaum	.986	24	198	16	3	0	5
Thomas	1.000	3	14	0	0	0	0
Walker	1.000	1	1	0	0	0	0

First Base	PCT	G	PO	A	E	DP
Brossman	.909	1	8	2	1	1
Estrella	1.000	2	13	2	0	1
Garcia	1.000	12	94	3	0	7

	PCT	G	PO	A	E	DP
Gronkowski	.985	33	307	21	5	30
Navarro	.997	40	322	10	1	32
Second Base	**PCT**	**G**	**PO**	**A**	**E**	**DP**
Estrella	.968	37	62	119	6	21
Gonzalez-Lopez	.964	15	19	35	2	9
Kennedy	.986	32	56	86	2	21
Third Base	**PCT**	**G**	**PO**	**A**	**E**	**DP**
Brossman	.910	60	40	112	15	7
Estrella	.892	17	6	27	4	5
Gonzalez-Lopez	1.000	2	1	2	0	0

Shortstop	PCT	G	PO	A	E	DP
Gonzalez-Lopez	.918	26	42	70	10	19
Romine	.952	56	101	178	14	42
Outfield	**PCT**	**G**	**PO**	**A**	**E**	**DP**
Giovanatto	1.000	33	42	3	0	0
Kiniry	.986	43	70	3	1	0
Miller	.984	46	56	5	1	0
Moore	.970	60	93	3	3	1
Perez	.925	32	32	5	3	0
Pippin	.962	43	47	4	2	2

AZL ANGELS   ROOKIE

ARIZONA LEAGUE

BATTING	B-T	HT	WT	DOB	AVG	vLH	vRH	G	AB	R	H	2B	3B	HR	RBI	BB	HBP	SH	SF	SO	SB	CS	SLG	OBP
Bass, Justin	B-R	5-11	190	4-6-89	.275	.350	.245	20	69	8	19	2	1	0	7	6	1	0	0	13	4	1	.333	.342
Bohlken, Richard	R-R	5-11	185	11-22-88	.091	.000	.111	16	44	5	4	1	0	0	2	8	0	0	0	15	1	1	.114	.231
Bourjos, Peter	R-R	6-1	175	3-31-87	.313	.000	.313	4	16	3	5	0	1	0	2	1	0	0	0	2	0	0	.438	.353
Castillo, Angel	R-R	6-3	190	6-7-89	.252	.333	.235	31	119	19	30	4	1	4	23	19	2	0	0	39	5	0	.403	.364
Colmenares, Carlos	B-R	6-0	175	2-11-86	.300	.273	.306	18	60	13	18	2	0	1	6	9	0	1	1	13	2	1	.383	.386
Conger, Hank	B-R	6-0	205	1-29-88	.267	.000	.333	3	15	2	4	1	0	0	3	0	0	0	0	3	0	0	.333	.267
Contreras, Ivan	B-R	5-9	155	1-3-87	.311	.462	.265	49	222	41	69	8	8	1	32	14	1	3	1	42	21	8	.432	.353
Dicent, Raymi	R-R	6-1	180	11-15-87	.275	.211	.295	21	80	7	22	7	0	0	12	6	3	1	0	26	1	0	.363	.348
Fuller, Clayton	B-R	6-2	180	6-17-87	.301	.265	.313	45	183	55	55	10	4	5	30	24	7	2	2	52	21	6	.481	.398
Garcia, Christopher	L-R	6-2	225	11-25-87	.333	.500	.290	20	78	17	26	9	1	0	15	21	1	0	0	17	0	0	.474	.480
Gordon, Luke	R-R	5-10	205	10-1-84	.268	.200	.278	16	41	12	11	2	1	0	5	9	3	1	0	11	0	1	.366	.434
Knazek, Scott	R-R	6-1	215	11-4-84	.179	.211	.169	28	84	22	15	3	0	0	9	24	2	3	2	25	1	0	.214	.366
Loman, Seth	B-R	6-3	190	12-16-85	.323	.250	.345	45	155	33	50	15	1	9	34	29	13	0	2	69	0	0	.606	.462
Mann, Tyler	L-R	6-2	195	7-21-89	.274	.280	.271	27	95	16	26	5	0	0	12	14	2	1	0	27	2	1	.326	.378
Mount, Ryan	R-R	6-1	180	8-17-86	.333	.333	.333	3	12	0	4	0	0	0	0	1	1	0	0	1	0	0	.333	.429
Navarro, Efren	L-L	6-0	200	5-14-86	.353	.500	.333	5	17	4	6	3	0	0	3	3	0	0	1	2	0	1	.529	.429
Norman, Anthony	R-R	6-0	185	10-20-84	.362	.462	.333	44	174	40	63	4	10	0	33	19	6	2	1	19	12	1	.500	.440
Ortiz, Norberto	R-R	6-1	170	1-19-85	.296	.200	.311	17	71	12	21	6	0	2	11	6	0	2	1	17	5	2	.352	.346
Perez, Darwin	B-R	5-10	160	7-27-89	.253	.289	.242	47	162	24	41	7	2	0	22	25	3	4	1	43	4	1	.321	.361
Rosario, Alberto	R-R	6-0	165	1-10-87	.301	.214	.322	19	73	11	22	4	0	1	9	5	1	1	1	9	2	2	.397	.350
Villaescusa, Ivan	B-R	6-2	210	10-25-88	.161	.500	.111	10	31	7	5	3	0	0	4	6	0	1	0	5	0	0	.258	.297
Wing, Michael	R-R	6-1	180	10-25-88	.272	.265	.273	42	162	27	44	7	5	1	21	11	3	1	1	40	3	1	.395	.328

PITCHING	B-T	HT	WT	DOB	W	L	ERA	G	GS	CG	SV	IP	H	R	ER	HR	BB	SO	AVG	vLH	vRH	K/9	BB/9
Albano, Marco	R-R	5-11	215	8-26-83	0	0	0.00	5	0	0	0	5	1	0	0	0	1	12	.063	.000	.125	21.60	1.80
Anton, Michael	L-L	6-3	195	4-3-85	5	3	3.21	13	12	0	0	62	58	30	22	2	15	82	.241	.223	.252	11.97	2.19
Armstrong, C.	L-L	5-10	195	2-10-88	0	0	1.93	3	3	0	0	14	10	4	3	0	5	13	.208	.235	.194	8.36	3.21
Austen, David	R-R	6-1	185	5-21-81	1	1	3.60	3	0	0	0	5	4	2	2	1	1	3	.211	.286	.167	5.40	1.80
Cabrera, Francis	R-R	6-1	184	5-27-87	0	0	0.00	1	0	0	0	1	1	0	0	0	0	1	.250	1.000	.000	9.00	0.00
Calderon, Leonardo	L-L	5-11	170	7-31-86	1	0	2.92	10	0	0	0	12	9	8	4	0	8	21	.184	.125	.212	15.32	5.84
Chambers, Brian	R-R	6-3	202	8-14-85	0	0	3.60	3	0	0	0	5	5	2	2	0	0	3	.278	.200	.308	5.40	0.00
Coello, Robert	R-R	6-4	215	11-23-84	1	1	1.37	20	0	0	0	26	23	9	4	0	7	26	.232	.295	.182	8.89	2.39
Espinoza, Gustavo	L-L	6-0	170	9-9-86	0	0	6.75	2	0	0	0	1	1	1	1	0	3	0	.000	.000		20.25	6.75
Flores, Manuel	L-L	6-2	170	6-1-87	1	4	5.37	15	10	0	0	54	67	36	32	3	13	28	.307	.273	.326	4.70	2.18
Ford, A.J.	R-R	6-1	195	10-27-84	1	1	3.18	17	0	0	0	28	26	14	10	0	5	21	.236	.250	.226	6.67	1.59
Howard, Cephas	R-R	6-5	240	4-15-86	2	1	7.17	20	0	0	0	21	28	19	17	1	9	26	.308	.268	.340	10.97	3.80
Lindsey, Dylan	R-R	6-3	205	7-13-85	0	0	21.60	2	0	0	0	2	5	4	4	0	2	2	.625	1.000	.400	10.80	10.80
Manganaro, Nicholas	L-L	6-5	170	2-12-85	0	1	47.25	6	0	0	0	3	10	14	14	2	8	2	.588	.625	.556	6.75	27.00
McKiernan, Eddie	R-R	5-11	160	3-21-89	0	1	2.25	18	0	0	5	24	21	9	6	0	6	17	.241	.147	.302	6.38	2.25
Mendoza, Thomas	R-R	6-2	195	8-18-87	1	0	0.00	1	0	0	0	5	3	0	0	0	2	4	.250	.333	.182	7.20	3.60
Molina, Robin	R-R	6-3	185	6-29-87	7	3	3.34	13	12	0	0	62	55	30	23	1	39	24	.248	.274	.232	3.48	5.66
Page, Cory	R-R	6-3	190	10-18-89	3	0	5.83	19	0	0	1	29	27	25	19	2	16	22	.235	.209	.250	6.75	4.91
Perez, Jose	R-R	6-2	180	9-14-87	1	1	3.90	8	5	0	0	28	32	18	12	3	5	30	.278	.319	.250	9.76	1.63
Plefka, Jonathan	R-R	6-8	230	6-30-84	0	2	23.14	3	0	0	0	2	6	6	6	0	2	2	.500	.800	.286	7.71	7.71
Reckling, Trevor	L-L	6-1	195	5-22-89	3	1	2.75	9	5	0	2	36	33	13	11	2	7	55	.236	.167	.260	13.75	1.75
Rosario, Angel	R-R	6-2	160	4-30-86	2	2	5.57	17	0	0	3	21	17	15	13	2	9	26	.215	.211	.220	11.14	3.86
Short, Baron	R-R	6-5	230	8-2-86	1	1	7.71	8	0	0	0	9	12	11	8	0	4	11	.324	.250	.360	10.61	3.86
Speier, Justin	R-R	6-4	205	11-6-73	0	0	0.00	2	2	0	0	3	1	0	0	0	0	3	.111	.000	.143	9.00	0.00
Tobin, Mason	R-R	6-3	210	7-8-87	2	0	0.95	8	7	0	0	28	17	5	3	1	7	32	.177	.152	.190	10.16	2.22
Torres, Alexander	L-L	5-10	160	12-8-87	1	0	4.76	4	0	0	0	6	4	6	3	0	8	3	.190	.250	.176	4.76	12.71

ORGANIZATION STATISTICS

FIELDING

Catcher	PCT	G	PO	A	E	DP	PB
Conger	1.000	2	20	0	0	1	0
Knazek	.982	28	241	30	5	0	12
Rosario	.964	19	161	29	7	3	2
Villaescusa	.962	10	51	0	2	0	6

First Base	PCT	G	PO	A	E	DP
Colmenares	1.000	2	9	0	0	1
Garcia	.988	16	155	6	2	15
Gordon	1.000	2	2	0	0	0
Loman	.980	34	282	13	6	16
Navarro	1.000	4	40	2	0	4
Wing	1.000	1	12	0	0	0

Second Base	PCT	G	PO	A	E	DP
Contreras	.950	48	101	144	13	25
Gordon	.917	4	5	6	1	0
Mount	1.000	2	2	7	0	1
Wing	1.000	3	3	4	0	1

Third Base	PCT	G	PO	A	E	DP
Bohlken	.833	14	8	17	5	1
Colmenares	.898	15	12	32	5	2
Gordon	.727	6	1	7	3	1
Wing	.919	30	21	36	5	2

Shortstop	PCT	G	PO	A	E	DP
Bohlken	1.000	1	0	1	0	0

	PCT	G	PO	A	E	DP
Colmenares	1.000	1	1	2	0	0
Perez	.939	47	66	135	13	23
Wing	.871	9	10	17	4	4

Outfield	PCT	G	PO	A	E	DP
Bourjos	1.000	3	5	1	0	0
Castillo	.948	30	54	1	3	0
Dicent	.917	10	10	1	1	0
Fuller	.976	45	77	4	2	1
Gordon	1.000	1	1	0	0	0
Mann	.897	23	25	1	3	0
Norman	.956	44	62	3	3	0
Ortiz	.943	15	29	4	2	1

DSL ANGELS   ROOKIE

DOMINICAN SUMMER LEAGUE

BATTING

	B-T	HT	WT	DOB	AVG	vLH	vRH	G	AB	R	H	2B	3B	HR	RBI	BB	HBP	SH	SF	SO	SB	CS	SLG	OBP
Adames, Waskal	R-R	5-11	195	2-28-89	.262	.300	.255	19	65	8	17	0	0	0	6	4	3	1	1	19	1	0	.262	.329
Almanzar, Jean	B-R	5-7	150	2-7-89	.206	.207	.205	56	180	29	37	6	1	1	22	16	4	3	2	33	7	3	.267	.282
Amarista, Alexia	B-R	5-8	150	4-6-89	.340	.441	.324	65	241	52	82	14	4	5	39	25	4	1	2	23	16	6	.494	.408
Barrios, Emanuel	B-R	5-10	150	7-23-90	.179	.000	.217	19	28	8	5	0	0	0	4	6	2	0	2	8	1	1	.179	.342
Batista, Lay	R-R	6-2	180	8-4-89	.103	.000	.107	15	29	4	3	1	0	0	0	2	0	0	0	15	1	0	.138	.161
Beltre, Elvin	R-R	6-0	180	5-13-89	.219	.222	.218	31	96	9	21	3	0	0	8	4	1	0	1	21	1	2	.250	.255
Castano, Jeffrie	R-R	6-1	180	10-1-87	.236	.280	.228	51	174	20	41	9	1	1	25	13	5	1	1	31	7	2	.316	.306
Feliz, Erickson	R-R	6-1	190	3-6-88	.100	1.000	.077	15	40	2	4	0	0	0	4	1	2	2	0	15	0	0	.100	.163
Florian, Maximo	R-R	6-0	160	3-5-89	.222	.000	.233	23	63	6	14	2	0	1	8	9	0	0	2	21	2	2	.302	.311
Jimenez, Luis	R-R	6-1	170	1-18-88	.313	.205	.332	67	256	49	80	19	2	11	55	10	5	1	3	27	16	4	.531	.347
Lopez, Franklin	L-R	6-0	175	2-15-89	.183	.313	.162	37	115	16	21	4	1	0	7	6	2	3	0	22	2	1	.235	.236
Lugo, Carlos	R-R	6-0	190	11-20-89	.138	.000	.148	12	29	4	4	1	1	0	3	3	3	0	0	12	0	0	.241	.286
Martinez, Alejandro	R-R	6-3	180	2-24-88	.286	.371	.268	53	192	38	55	5	0	2	13	17	1	3	1	43	4	2	.344	.346
Martinez, Josue	R-R	6-3	210	11-14-88	.000	—	.000	1	2	0	0	0	0	0	0	0	0	0	0	2	0	0	.000	.000
Molina, Manuel	R-R	6-3	215	1-4-89	.235	.323	.220	64	217	37	51	12	0	4	34	29	8	3	3	71	4	4	.346	.342
Placencio, Francisco	R-R	6-2	175	9-7-87	.083	—	.083	6	12	1	1	1	0	0	1	2	0	1	0	7	0	0	.167	.214
Reynales, Andres	R-R	6-0	165	2-28-89	.152	.071	.169	27	79	10	12	3	0	0	8	5	1	4	0	33	1	0	.190	.212
Segura, Jean	R-L	5-11	155	3-17-90	.324	.450	.296	61	219	39	71	5	2	2	31	22	3	7	1	28	22	6	.393	.392
Sierra, Raddy	R-R	6-0	175	9-21-87	.317	.306	.319	65	240	61	76	16	1	9	31	29	13	2	1	67	26	7	.504	.417
Sumi, Ikko	R-R	5-9	200	10-20-87	.176	.385	.141	31	91	11	16	2	0	1	13	15	9	2	1	25	2	2	.231	.345

PITCHING

	B-T	HT	WT	DOB	W	L	ERA	G	GS	CG	SV	IP	H	R	ER	HR	BB	SO	AVG	vLH	vRH	K/9	BB/9
Alies, Crisaudy	R-R	5-10	175	1-14-89	4	3	2.00	16	1	1	3	45	36	13	10	2	4	28	.220	.218	.220	5.60	0.80
Almeida, Yeison	R-R	5-11	150	3-30-90	3	1	2.68	14	14	1	0	77	77	29	23	3	10	39	.262	.292	.252	4.54	1.16
Arenas, Orangel	R-R	6-0	165	3-31-89	1	3	2.45	10	4	0	1	33	31	14	9	1	6	21	.250	.190	.262	5.73	1.64
Baez, Suammy	R-R	6-4	200	9-28-88	5	3	3.18	18	0	0	0	40	34	20	14	2	11	32	.233	.355	.200	7.26	2.50
Camacho, Edgar	R-R	6-2	170	4-11-87	1	0	5.19	12	0	0	1	17	14	10	10	0	15	5	.226	.250	.217	2.60	7.79
Correa, Manuarys	R-R	6-3	170	1-5-89	8	1	2.16	14	14	0	0	88	71	27	21	3	27	68	.225	.275	.215	6.98	2.77
Done, Joaquin	R-R	6-3	200	10-30-88	3	0	1.44	6	6	0	0	31	23	9	5	0	14	25	.215	.222	.213	7.18	4.02
Duarte, Luis	R-R	6-1	180	8-7-87	4	0	1.76	11	2	0	1	31	21	6	6	1	7	28	.200	.182	.205	8.22	2.05
Feliz, Erickson	R-R	6-1	190	3-6-88	1	1	1.96	3	3	0	0	18	17	4	4	0	11	18	.279	.429	.234	8.84	5.40
Feliz, Starlin	L-L	6-0	200	6-28-88	4	3	2.16	10	10	0	0	58	47	28	14	2	27	33	.229	.273	.227	5.09	4.17
Lemus, Deivic	R-R	6-3	185	3-27-89	0	0	5.06	4	0	0	0	5	5	4	3	1	4	6	.250	.000	.278	10.12	6.75
Martinez Mesa, Fabio	R-R	6-3	190	10-29-89	1	2	6.75	13	3	0	1	25	27	22	19	0	26	30	.270	.353	.253	10.66	9.24
Pena, Ariel	R-R	6-3	186	5-20-89	10	2	2.26	14	14	2	0	80	62	27	20	1	32	54	.212	.213	.212	6.10	3.62
Pichardo, Pedro	R-R	6-1	190	7-16-88	2	0	0.57	17	0	0	8	32	20	4	2	0	11	25	.190	.077	.207	7.11	3.13
Porte, Carlos	R-R	6-2	180	9-18-86	2	1	2.37	10	0	0	0	19	13	6	5	0	5	12	.188	.125	.197	5.68	2.37
Santos, Jose	R-R	6-0	198	7-11-87	0	1	7.13	14	0	0	2	24	30	21	19	3	9	17	.300	.286	.302	6.38	3.38

FIELDING

Catcher	PCT	G	PO	A	E	DP	PB
Feliz	1.000	11	65	5	0	0	1
Lopez	.996	37	230	24	1	2	15
Lugo	.982	11	46	10	1	0	9
Sumi	.992	20	110	8	1	0	3

First Base	PCT	G	PO	A	E	DP
Barrios	1.000	1	3	1	0	0
Jimenez	—	1	0	0	0	0
A. Martinez	.958	9	65	3	3	9
Molina	.991	63	617	27	6	59
Placencio	1.000	3	25	0	0	1

Second Base	PCT	G	PO	A	E	DP
Almanzar	1.000	9	16	22	0	6

	PCT	G	PO	A	E	DP
Amarista	1.000	16	41	42	0	12
Barrios	.960	9	10	14	1	4
Segura	.957	44	101	121	10	32

Third Base	PCT	G	PO	A	E	DP
Almanzar	1.000	1	0	5	0	0
Barrios	.500	1	0	1	1	0
Batista	.941	11	3	13	1	1
Jimenez	.911	63	56	158	21	16
A. Martinez	1.000	5	8	13	0	2
Placencio	.833	2	2	3	1	0

Shortstop	PCT	G	PO	A	E	DP
Almanzar	.956	30	43	88	6	18
Amarista	.974	38	56	128	5	21

	PCT	G	PO	A	E	DP
Barrios	.900	2	4	5	1	4
A. Martinez	.972	6	4	31	1	2

Outfield	PCT	G	PO	A	E	DP
Adames	.964	19	26	1	1	1
Almanzar	.955	14	21	0	1	0
Barrios	—	2	0	0	0	0
Beltre	.923	30	43	5	4	2
Camacho	.833	1	4	1	1	0
Castano	.935	51	52	6	4	1
Florian	1.000	21	36	2	0	0
A. Martinez	1.000	4	10	0	0	0
Reynales	.973	27	31	5	1	0
Sierra	.984	64	122	5	2	0

Los Angeles Dodgers

BY TONY JACKSON

A season that began with stratospheric expectations came crashing to earth in late September when the Dodgers lost 11 of their final 14 games. Although they salvaged a winning season by taking two of three from San Francisco on the season's final weekend to finish 82-80, the Dodgers finished fourth in baseball's deepest division.

"If you're not going to the playoffs, you lost, and we all realize that," manager Grady Little said immediately after the season's final game. "People talk about being proud of the fact you're above .500 for the year, but we're not going to the postseason, so in my heart, we lost."

The Dodgers were coming off a wildcard berth last fall, and they had added a handful of key pieces over the winter in free agent signings, including righthander Jason Schmidt and lefthander Randy Wolf, catcher Mike Lieberthal and outfielders Luis Gonzalez and Juan Pierre. But Schmidt and Wolf each succumbed to shoulder injuries, with Schmidt missing the final four months and Wolf missing the entire second half. As a result, the Dodgers were forced to go with a patchwork rotation that at various times included Brett Tomko, Mark Hendrickson, Hong-Chih Kuo and Eric Stults—not one of whom was effective enough to stick around for long.

But there was no shortage of positives, and despite the fact it was a bad year, it wasn't necessarily a setback when it came to the overall organizational plan.

Several of the Dodgers' promising young players gained valuable experience, some of them a year ahead of time.

Righthander Chad Billingsley, a longtime prospect in his second big league season, finally broke a habit of walking too many batters and developed into a potential staff ace. Catcher Russell Martin joined righthanders Brad Penny and Takashi Saito at the All-Star Game.

First baseman James Loney returned to the majors on June 10 and played so well that he pushed veteran Nomar Garciaparra to third base. Loney batted .331 and hit 15 homers in just 344 at-bats after hitting only one homer in 233 at-bats at Triple-A Las Vegas. Five-tool outfield prospect Matt Kemp, another second-year big leaguer, overcame an early-season shoulder injury to hit .342 with 10 homers and 42 RBIs and also dramatically improved his baserunning late in the season after making a series of early-season mistakes.

Righthander Jonathan Broxton had a stellar season setting up for Saito, matching teammate Joe Beimer for the team high with 83 appearances.

Finally, outfielder Andre Ethier avoided the late-season collapse that plagued him as a rookie last year and finished strong, batting .284 with 32 doubles, 13 homers and 64 RBIs.

The Dodgers got productive seasons from veterans Pierre and Jeff Kent. Switch-hitting shortstop Rafael Furcal played in 138 games and was outstanding as always on defense but never seemed to recover from a severely sprained ankle he suffered late in spring training and batted a career-low .270.

Saito, meanwhile, posted 39 saves in 43 chances in his second season as the Dodgers' closer. Penny led the pitching staff and Derek Lowe was a frequent victim of poor run support.

At the minor league level, longtime fringe prospect Delwyn Young continued to play his way into a more prominent spot on the organizational radar at Triple-A Las Vegas. He hit .337 with 17 homers and led the Pacific Coast League with 54 doubles and 97 RBIs. He also had two major league stints, including a September callup, and hit .382.

ORGANIZATIONAL LEADERS

BATTING		★Minimum 250 at-bats
★AVG	Valdez, Wilson, Las Vegas	.343
R	Young, Delwyn, Las Vegas	107
H	Hu, Chin-Lung, Jacksonville/Las Vegas	168
TB	Young, Delwyn, Las Vegas	280
2B	Young, Delwyn, Las Vegas	54
3B	Rogowski, Ryan, Inland Empire	9
HR	Lindsey, John, Jacksonville/Las Vegas	30
RBI	Lindsey, John, Jacksonville/Las Vegas	121
BB	Raglani, Anthony, Jacksonville	85
SO	Raglani, Anthony, Jacksonville	139
SB	Rogowski, Ryan, Inland Empire	39
★OBP	Valdez, Wilson, Las Vegas	.413
★SLG	Lindsey, John, Jacksonville/Las Vegas	.59
PITCHING		^Minimum 75 innings
W	McDonald, James, Inland Empire/Jacksonville	13
L	Three players tied at	10
^ERA	Kershaw, Clayton, Great Lakes/Jacksonville	2.95
G	Hoorelbeke, Casey, Las Vegas	63
CG	Juarez, William, Jacksonville/Las Vegas	2
SV	Meloan, Jonathan, Jacksonville/Las Vegas	20
IP	Pinango, Miguel, Inland Empire/Las Vegas	154
BB	Miller, Greg, Las Vegas/Jacksonville	89
SO	McDonald, James, Inland Empire/Jacksonville	168
^AVG	Kershaw, Clayton, Great Lakes/Jacksonville	.201

Lefty Clayton Kershaw, last year's top draft pick, was so dominating at low Class A Midland (134 strikeouts in 97 innings) that he was promoted all the way to Double-A Jacksonville at midseason.

But the most notable seasons by any Dodgers minor leaguers were put up by righthander James McDonald and shortstop Chin-Lung Hu, the organization's pitcher and player of the year, respectively. McDonald went a combined 13-9, 3.07 at high Class A Inland Empire and Jacksonville, with 168 strikeouts and just 37 walks in 135 innings. He will be given a shot to make the major league staff in spring training. The formerly skinny Hu, who spent a lot of time in the weight room last winter, had a surprising power surge at Jacksonville and Las Vegas, hitting a combined 14 homers while batting .325. He made his big league debut in September.

2007 PERFORMANCE

General Manager: Ned Colletti. **Farm Director:** DeJon Watson. **Scouting Director:** Logan White

Class	Team	League	W	L	PCT	Finish*	Manager	Affiliate Since
Majors	Los Angeles	National	82	80	.506	9th (16)	Grady Little	—
Triple-A	Las Vegas 51s	Pacific Coast	67	77	.465	13th (16)	Lorenzo Bundy	2001
Double-A	Jacksonville Suns	Southern	80	60	.571	2nd (10)	John Shoemaker	2002
High A	Inland Empire 66ers	California	72	67	.518	6th (10)	Dave Collins	2007
Low A	Great Lakes Loons	Midwest	57	82	.410	12th (14)	Lance Parrish	2007
Rookie	Ogden Raptors	Pioneer	34	41	.453	6th (8)	Jeff Carter	2003
Rookie	GCL Dodgers	Gulf Coast	40	15	.727	1st (16)	Juan Bustabad	2001
Overall 2007 Minor League Record			**350**	**342**	**.506**	**11th**		

* Finish in overall standings (No. of teams in league) ^League champion

ORGANIZATION STATISTICS

LOS ANGELES DODGERS

NATIONAL LEAGUE

BATTING	B-T	HT	WT	DOB	AVG	vLH	vRH	G	AB	R	H	2B	3B	HR	RBI	BB	HBP	SH	SF	SO	SB	CS	SLG	OBP
Abreu, Tony	B-R	5-11	200	11-13-84	.271	.214	.290	59	166	19	45	14	1	2	17	7	3	0	2	21	0	0	.404	.309
Anderson, Marlon	L-R	5-11	200	1-6-74	.231	.000	.240	23	26	3	6	0	0	0	2	3	0	0	0	5	1	0	.231	.310
2-team (43 New York)					.295	—	—	66	95	17	28	7	0	3	27	8	0	1	2	17	4	1	.463	.343
Betemit, Wilson	B-R	6-3	230	11-2-81	.231	.250	.227	84	156	22	36	8	0	10	26	32	1	0	3	49	0	0	.474	.359
Clark, Brady	R-R	6-2	200	4-18-73	.224	.280	.182	47	58	7	13	4	0	0	5	6	1	1	0	11	1	2	.293	.308
2-team (21 San Diego)					.262	—	—	68	107	13	28	5	2	0	11	14	1	1	0	18	1	3	.346	.352
Ethier, Andre	L-L	6-2	210	4-10-82	.284	.279	.286	153	447	50	127	30	2	13	64	46	4	0	8	68	0	4	.452	.350
Furcal, Rafael	B-R	5-9	195	10-24-77	.270	.313	.254	138	581	87	157	23	4	6	47	55	1	2	3	68	25	6	.355	.333
Garciaparra, Nomar	R-R	6-0	190	7-23-73	.283	.213	.303	121	431	39	122	17	0	7	59	31	0	0	4	41	3	1	.371	.328
Gonzalez, Luis	L-R	6-2	210	9-3-67	.278	.317	.267	139	464	70	129	23	2	15	68	56	4	0	2	56	6	2	.433	.359
Hillenbrand, Shea	R-R	6-1	210	7-27-75	.243	.261	.234	20	70	6	17	0	2	1	9	2	0	0	2	12	0	1	.343	.257
Hu, Chin-Lung	R-R	5-11	190	2-2-84	.241	.200	.263	12	29	5	7	0	1	2	5	0	0	2	0	8	0	0	.517	.241
Kemp, Matt	R-R	6-2	230	9-23-84	.342	.390	.318	98	292	47	100	12	5	10	42	16	0	0	3	66	10	5	.521	.373
Kent, Jeff	R-R	6-2	210	3-7-68	.302	.299	.302	136	494	78	149	36	1	20	79	57	5	0	6	61	1	3	.500	.375
LaRoche, Andy	R-R	6-1	225	9-13-83	.226	.200	.235	35	93	16	21	5	0	1	10	20	1	0	1	24	2	1	.312	.365
Lieberthal, Mike	R-R	6-0	195	1-18-72	.234	.167	.254	38	77	6	18	2	0	1	4	1	0	0	11	0	0	.260	.280
Loney, James	L-L	6-3	220	5-7-84	.331	.319	.336	96	344	41	114	18	4	15	67	28	1	0	2	48	0	1	.538	.381
Martin, Russell	R-R	5-10	210	2-15-83	.293	.357	.273	151	540	87	158	32	3	19	87	67	7	0	6	89	21	9	.469	.374
Martinez, Ramon	R-R	6-0	190	10-10-72	.194	.200	.189	67	129	10	25	4	0	0	27	11	0	2	5	15	1	0	.225	.248
Moeller, Chad	R-R	6-3	215	2-18-75	.125	.000	.167	7	8	2	1	0	0	0	1	0	0	1	0	1	0	0	.125	.222
2-team (30 Cincinnati)					.161	—	—	37	56	8	9	1	0	1	2	0	1	1	0	18	0	0	.232	.175
Pierre, Juan	L-L	5-11	180	8-14-77	.293	.274	.301	162	668	96	196	24	8	0	41	33	6	20	2	37	64	15	.353	.331
Saenz, Olmedo	R-R	6-1	230	10-8-70	.191	.170	.206	92	110	9	21	5	0	4	18	16	2	0	4	25	0	0	.345	.295
Sweeney, Mark	L-L	6-1	215	10-26-69	.273	.250	.276	30	33	2	9	1	0	0	3	1	0	0	0	11	0	0	.303	.294
2-team (76 San Francisco)					.260	—	—	106	123	20	32	9	0	2	13	14	3	1	0	29	2	0	.382	.350
Valdez, Wilson	R-R	5-11	160	5-20-78	.216	.174	.235	41	74	12	16	2	1	0	7	4	1	0	1	12	1	0	.270	.263
Young, Delwyn	B-R	5-10	210	6-30-82	.382	.333	.421	19	34	4	13	1	1	2	3	2	0	0	0	5	1	0	.647	.417

PITCHING	B-T	HT	WT	DOB	W	L	ERA	G	GS	CG	SV	IP	H	R	ER	HR	BB	SO	AVG	vLH	vRH	K/9	BB/9
Beimel, Joe	L-L	6-3	215	4-19-77	4	2	3.88	83	0	0	1	67	63	30	29	1	24	39	.253	.188	.294	5.21	3.21
Billingsley, Chad	R-R	6-1	245	7-29-84	12	5	3.31	43	20	1	0	147	131	56	54	15	64	141	.241	.277	.210	8.63	3.92
Brazoban, Yhency	R-R	6-1	250	6-11-80	0	0	16.20	4	0	0	0	2	3	4	3	0	3	5	.333	.167	.667	27.00	16.20
Broxton, Jonathan	R-R	6-4	290	6-16-84	4	4	2.85	83	0	0	2	82	69	30	26	6	25	99	.220	.200	.247	10.87	2.74
Hendrickson, Mark	L-L	6-9	240	6-23-74	4	8	5.21	39	15	0	0	123	142	75	71	15	29	92	.292	.258	.300	6.75	2.13
Hernandez, Roberto	R-R	6-4	245	11-11-64	0	2	6.64	22	0	0	0	20	26	16	15	3	9	13	.317	.256	.372	5.75	3.98
Houlton, D.J.	R-R	6-4	225	8-12-79	0	2	4.18	18	0	0	0	28	28	14	13	5	7	21	.267	.255	.278	6.75	2.25
Hull, Eric	R-R	5-11	185	12-3-79	0	0	4.05	5	0	0	0	7	4	3	3	0	3	5	.174	.000	.267	6.75	4.05
Kuo, Hong-Chih	L-L	6-1	235	7-23-81	1	4	7.42	8	6	0	0	30	35	26	25	3	14	27	.285	.240	.296	8.01	4.15
Loaiza, Esteban	R-R	6-2	230	12-31-71	1	4	8.34	5	5	0	0	23	30	22	21	9	16	15	.299	.355	.268	5.96	6.35
Lowe, Derek	R-R	6-6	230	6-1-73	12	14	3.88	33	32	3	0	199	194	100	86	20	59	147	.254	.271	.239	6.64	2.66
Meloan, Jonathan	R-R	6-3	230	7-11-84	0	0	11.05	5	0	0	0	7	8	9	9	1	8	7	.286	.231	.333	8.59	9.82
Penny, Brad	R-R	6-4	260	5-24-78	16	4	3.03	33	33	0	0	208	199	75	70	9	73	135	.260	.229	.286	5.84	3.16
Proctor, Scott	R-R	6-1	195	1-2-77	3	0	3.38	31	0	0	0	32	25	14	12	4	15	27	.216	.196	.229	7.59	4.22
Saito, Takashi	R-R	6-2	200	2-14-70	2	1	1.40	63	0	0	39	64	33	10	10	5	13	78	.151	.186	.114	10.91	1.82
Schmidt, Jason	R-R	6-4	210	1-29-73	1	4	6.31	6	6	0	0	26	32	18	18	4	14	22	.296	.250	.333	7.71	4.91
Seanez, Rudy	R-R	6-0	225	10-20-68	6	3	3.79	73	0	0	1	76	78	33	32	10	27	73	.266	.269	.264	8.64	3.20
Stults, Eric	L-L	6-0	215	12-9-79	1	4	5.82	12	5	0	0	39	50	26	25	5	17	30	.314	.353	.304	6.98	3.96
Tomko, Brett	R-R	6-1	220	4-7-73	2	11	5.80	33	15	0	0	104	124	75	67	13	42	79	.295	.287	.302	6.84	3.63
2-team (7 San Diego)					4	12	5.55	40	19	0	0	131	149	89	81	18	48	105	—	—	—	7.20	3.29
Tsao, Chin-hui	R-R	6-1	210	6-2-81	0	1	4.38	21	0	0	0	25	18	12	12	3	8	16	.205	.195	.213	5.84	2.92
Wells, David	L-L	6-3	250	5-20-63	4	1	5.12	7	7	0	0	39	45	23	22	5	9	19	.296	.167	.320	4.42	2.09
2-team (22 San Diego)					9	9	5.43	29	29	0	0	157	201	97	95	22	42	82	—	—	—	4.69	2.40
Wolf, Randy	L-L	5-10	200	8-22-76	9	6	4.73	18	18	0	0	103	110	55	54	10	39	94	.273	.250	.278	8.24	3.42

FIELDING

Catcher

Catcher	PCT	G	PO	A	E	DP	PB
Lieberthal	.980	31	136	11	3	3	0
Martin	.988	145	1065	85	14	11	5
Moeller	1.000	7	25	1	0	0	0

First Base

First Base	PCT	G	PO	A	E	DP
Anderson	.909	2	9	1	1	1
Garciaparra	.993	68	556	27	4	52
Hillenbrand	1.000	2	6	0	0	1
Loney	.989	93	725	61	9	87
Martinez	1.000	1	2	0	0	0
Saenz	1.000	13	60	4	0	6
Sweeney	1.000	4	10	0	0	0

Second Base

Second Base	PCT	G	PO	A	E	DP
Abreu	1.000	25	19	48	0	10
Anderson	—	1	0	0	0	0
Betemit	1.000	1	1	0	0	1
Kent	.976	133	235	328	14	76
Martinez	.987	36	36	38	1	8
Valdez	1.000	12	16	25	0	5
Young	1.000	2	3	0	0	0

Third Base

Third Base	PCT	G	PO	A	E	DP
Abreu	.947	28	14	57	4	6
Betemit	.952	53	20	60	4	6
Garciaparra	.941	43	32	64	6	3
Hillenbrand	.925	18	14	35	4	5
LaRoche	.959	30	22	48	3	8
Martinez	.972	17	2	33	1	2
Saenz	1.000	3	0	1	0	0
Valdez	1.000	9	2	9	0	2

Shortstop

Shortstop	PCT	G	PO	A	E	DP
Abreu	.962	7	7	18	1	3
Betemit	1.000	2	0	1	0	0
Furcal	.972	138	241	426	19	99
Hu	.971	10	11	22	1	8
Martinez	1.000	8	8	15	0	4
Valdez	1.000	12	7	26	0	4

Outfield

Outfield	PCT	G	PO	A	E	DP
Betemit	—	1	0	0	0	0
Clark	.967	41	29	0	1	0
Ethier	.981	145	249	10	5	1
Gonzalez	.995	127	192	4	1	0
Kemp	.972	91	137	2	4	1
LaRoche	—	1	0	0	0	0
Loney	—	1	0	0	0	0
Pierre	.987	162	366	4	5	0
Valdez	1.000	3	2	0	0	0
Young	1.000	6	8	0	0	0

LAS VEGAS 51s   TRIPLE-A
PACIFIC COAST LEAGUE

BATTING

BATTING	B-T	HT	WT	DOB	AVG	vLH	vRH	G	AB	R	H	2B	3B	HR	RBI	BB	HBP	SH	SF	SO	SB	CS	SLG	OBP
Abreu, Tony	B-R	5-11	200	11-13-84	.355	.385	.343	54	234	48	83	22	5	2	18	14	4	0	1	34	5	0	.517	.399
Anderson, Marlon	L-R	5-11	200	1-6-74	.241	.333	.217	11	29	6	7	1	1	1	11	7	1	0	1	5	2	0	.483	.395
2-team (6 New Orleans)					.212	—		17	52	7	11	3	1	1	12	10	1	0	1	11	2	0	.365	.344
Barnes, Larry	L-L	6-1	195	7-23-74	.230	.317	.204	62	178	20	41	4	3	8	24	10	0	0	1	31	1	1	.421	.270
Becker, Joseph	R-R	5-11	175	11-8-85	.286	.333	.250	2	7	2	2	0	1	0	2	2	0	0	0	2	0	0	.571	.444
Bigbie, Larry	L-R	6-4	210	11-4-77	.349	.333	.352	34	126	22	44	12	1	3	14	18	0	2	0	24	1	0	.532	.431
Davis, Ben	B-R	6-4	215	3-10-77	.218	.176	.237	36	110	13	24	4	0	1	11	10	0	0	1	24	0	1	.282	.281
Erickson, Gorman	B-R	6-3	205	3-11-88	.000	—	.000	1	1	0	0	0	0	0	0	0	0	0	0	0	0	0	.000	.000
Freeman, Choo	R-R	6-2	200	10-20-79	.270	.288	.261	121	400	52	108	15	4	9	48	51	3	3	2	92	4	1	.395	.355
Garcia, Sergio	R-R	5-10	170	3-29-80	.292	.324	.280	66	250	44	73	15	0	8	33	25	1	7	3	39	6	1	.448	.355
Hillenbrand, Shea	R-R	6-1	210	7-27-75	.538	1.000	.500	3	13	3	7	1	0	1	4	0	0	0	0	3	0	0	.846	.538
2-team (9 Portland)					.255	—		12	47	5	12	2	0	1	5	1	0	0	0	7	0	0	.362	.271
Hu, Chin-Lung	R-R	5-11	190	2-2-84	.318	.381	.315	45	192	33	61	10	1	8	28	6	0	1	1	18	3	4	.505	.337
Huckaby, Ken	R-R	6-1	240	1-27-71	.274	.328	.254	68	237	14	65	5	0	1	29	10	2	2	0	52	0	0	.308	.309
Jones, Mitch	R-R	6-2	215	10-15-77	.303	.277	.312	52	185	42	56	14	1	19	60	29	3	0	2	60	2	0	.697	.402
Kemp, Matt	R-R	6-2	230	9-23-84	.329	.408	.295	39	161	32	53	16	3	4	20	12	0	2	0	26	9	2	.540	.374
LaRoche, Andy	R-R	6-1	225	9-13-83	.309	.370	.283	73	265	55	82	18	1	18	48	39	3	0	4	42	2	2	.589	.399
Lindsey, John	R-R	6-3	240	1-30-77	.333	.371	.315	77	300	51	100	26	1	19	88	21	10	0	2	56	0	0	.617	.393
Loney, James	L-L	6-3	220	5-7-84	.279	.264	.283	58	233	28	65	19	1	1	32	25	0	0	3	48	2	1	.382	.345
Martinez, Octavio	R-R	6-0	190	7-30-79	.324	.353	.315	23	71	12	23	1	1	0	6	3	1	0	1	9	0	0	.366	.355
Martinez, Ramon	R-R	6-0	190	10-10-72	.357	.667	.273	6	14	6	5	1	0	0	2	4	0	0	1	0	1	0	.429	.500
Maza, Luis	R-R	5-9	180	6-22-80	.330	.400	.311	68	227	31	75	21	0	3	34	17	4	4	4	36	2	0	.463	.381
McDougall, Marshall	R-R	6-1	200	12-19-78	.304	.338	.289	69	253	33	77	20	0	11	48	16	1	0	4	50	0	0	.514	.347
Moeller, Chad	R-R	6-3	215	2-18-75	.324	.300	.333	12	37	3	12	1	0	1	6	9	1	0	0	6	0	0	.432	.468
Perez, Antonio	B-R	5-11	185	12-29-79	.227	.313	.200	36	132	19	30	8	0	2	15	11	0	3	3	25	0	0	.333	.281
Rivera, Michael	R-R	6-0	186	5-13-85	.125	.091	.143	15	32	4	4	1	0	0	0	3	1	0	0	6	0	0	.156	.222
Ruan, Wilkin	R-R	6-0	180	9-18-78	.282	.195	.325	71	234	30	66	6	1	2	26	9	1	1	3	20	4	0	.376	.308
Stinnett, Kelly	R-R	5-11	235	2-4-70	.196	.208	.192	31	102	10	20	2	0	3	10	9	1	1	0	22	0	0	.304	.268
2-team (1 Memphis)					.204	—		32	103	10	21	2	0	3	11	9	1	1	0	22	0	0	.311	.274
Valdez, Wilson	R-R	5-11	160	5-20-78	.343	.341	.344	90	361	81	124	19	1	4	29	43	1	4	2	34	14	6	.435	.413
Young, Delwyn	B-R	5-10	210	6-30-82	.337	.365	.323	121	490	107	165	54	5	17	97	38	3	0	6	105	4	3	.571	.384

PITCHING

PITCHING	B-T	HT	WT	DOB	W	L	ERA	G	GS	CG	SV	IP	H	R	ER	HR	BB	SO	AVG	vLH	vRH	K/9	BB/9
Akin, Brian	R-R	6-3	185	10-13-81	2	2	5.02	7	1	0	0	14	15	8	8	1	8	19		.238	.313	11.93	5.02
Alexander, Mark	R-R	5-10	190	12-6-80	0	0	14.25	12	0	0	0	12	17	20	19	1	19	14	.327	.375	.306	10.50	14.25
Bauer, Rick	R-R	6-6	225	1-10-77	0	2	3.60	25	0	0	2	35	39	20	14	4	25	43	.285	.291	.280	11.06	6.43
Brazoban, Yhency	R-R	6-1	250	6-11-80	0	0	1.98	11	0	0	0	3	14	6	3	3	2	3	14	.133	.182	.087	9.22	1.98
Cyr, Eric	R-L	6-4	210	2-11-79	3	6	5.56	12	11	1	0	55	63	43	34	8	24	48	.286	.277	.290	7.85	3.93
Dasni, Chales	R-R	6-3	170	7-21-85	0	0	5.40	1	0	0	0	3	3	2	2	1	4	3	.273	.667	.125	8.10	10.80
Eckert, Harold	R-R	6-3	218	7-18-77	0	2	6.38	16	2	0	0	24	37	21	17	1	16	19	.356	.407	.300	7.12	6.00
Fussell, Chris	R-R	6-2	210	5-19-76	4	1	6.39	24	0	0	0	38	41	27	27	5	23	33	.277	.339	.233	7.82	5.45
Gonzalez, Luis	L-L	6-0	205	2-27-83	1	2	5.06	8	0	0	0	11	5	10	6	1	19	14	.139	.063	.200	11.81	16.03
Hamulack, Tim	R-L	6-2	220	11-14-76	0	1	4.00	7	0	0	1	9	6	4	4	1	1	13	.176	.125	.192	13.00	1.00
Hernandez, Roberto	R-R	6-4	245	11-11-64	0	0	0.00	1	0	0	0	1	0	0	0	0	0	2	.333	1.000	.000		
Hoorelbeke, Casey	R-R	6-8	245	4-4-80	4	4	5.55	50	0	2	9	94	114	64	58	8	31	49	.307	.295	.315	4.69	2.97
Houlton, D.J.	R-R	6-4	225	8-12-79	6	4	3.65	23	19	0	0	106	106	50	43	12	39	92	.258	.232	.281	7.81	3.31
Hull, Eric	R-R	5-11	185	12-3-79	4	3	2.74	49	0	0	11	66	59	22	20	3	26	81	.241	.262	.230	11.10	3.56
Juarez, William	R-R	6-2	203	4-27-81	6	6	5.78	21	18	1	0	95	118	63	61	12	42	77	.316	.328	.301	7.29	3.98
Kuo, Hong-Chih	L-L	6-1	235	7-23-81	0	1	3.60	7	5	0	0	20	18	9	8	2	8	28	.243	.276	.222	12.60	3.60
LaMura, B.J.	R-R	6-1	200	1-1-81	1	4	7.92	12	3	0	0	25	29	27	22	4	22	21	.296	.280	.313	7.56	7.92
Lundberg, Spike	B-R	6-1	185	5-4-77	7	7	6.94	33	20	0	0	121	176	93	93	22	36	80	.343	.344	.343	5.97	2.69
Mays, Joe	B-R	6-1	200	12-10-75	1	2	5.16	8	8	0	0	45	54	31	26	4	10	29	.290	.333	.259	5.76	1.99
Meloan, Jonathan	R-R	6-3	230	7-11-84	2	0	1.69	14	0	0	1	21	12	5	4	2	9	21	.158	.219	.114	8.86	3.80
Miller, Greg	L-L	6-6	220	11-3-84	1	1	7.85	14	7	0	0	29	19	31	25	1	46	32	.200	.206	.197	10.05	14.44
Perez, Tomas	B-R	5-11	185	12-29-73	0	0	0.00	1	0	0	0	2	3	0	0	0	1	2	.333	.750	.000	9.00	4.50
Pinango, Miguel	R-R	6-1	190	1-20-83	10	7	4.12	23	23	0	0	127	143	71	58	19	38	92	.291	.275	.303	6.54	2.70
Pollok, Dwayne	R-R	6-3	195	11-12-80	1	2	5.71	28	5	0	1	58	86	43	37	7	14	20	.350	.404	.313	3.09	2.16
Riley, Matt	L-L	6-1	225	8-2-79	5	4	6.53	36	0	0	2	51	52	40	37	8	38	54	.263	.278	.254	9.53	6.71
Smith, Travis	R-R	5-10	160	11-7-72	2	2	5.67	6	4	0	0	27	35	18	17	2	8	17	.313	.293	.324	5.67	2.67
Stults, Eric	L-L	6-0	215	12-9-79	5	7	7.56	21	17	0	0	89	134	76	75	12	36	81	.351	.340	.355	8.16	3.63
Tsao, Chin-hui	R-R	6-1	210	6-2-81	0	1	3.60	5	0	0	0	5	4	2	2	0	1	9	.211	.600	.071	16.20	1.80
White, Matt	R-L	5-11	200	8-19-77	2	4	3.83	40	0	0	0	52	51	24	22	6	17	44	.266	.260	.270	7.66	2.96
Wright, Wesley	R-L	5-11	160	1-28-85	1	2	9.18	14	1	0	0	17	28	23	17	4	18	18	.406	.500	.373	9.72	9.72

FIELDING

Catcher	PCT	G	PO	A	E	DP	PB
Davis	.991	30	218	6	2	1	3
Erickson	1.000	1	2	0	0	0	0
Huckaby	.987	62	427	38	6	4	5
O. Martinez	.979	20	127	11	3	2	2
Moeller	1.000	12	85	7	0	1	2
Stinnett	.992	30	231	10	2	1	3

First Base	PCT	G	PO	A	E	DP
Anderson	1.000	1	2	0	0	0
Barnes	.986	33	201	18	3	18
Hillenbrand	1.000	1	8	0	0	2
Huckaby	1.000	2	9	2	0	1
Jones	.987	20	142	10	2	13
Lindsey	.992	56	435	35	4	55
Loney	.997	36	270	26	1	31
McDougall	1.000	12	100	5	0	15

Second Base	PCT	G	PO	A	E	DP
Abreu	1.000	23	43	59	0	23
Anderson	1.000	2	5	1	0	0
Garcia	.990	47	82	120	2	25
Hu	.989	17	28	62	1	13

	PCT	G	PO	A	E	DP
R. Martinez	1.000	2	5	6	0	4
Maza	.963	19	29	49	3	12
McDougall	1.000	13	21	34	0	3
Perez	1.000	8	24	30	0	7
Rivera	.967	9	8	21	1	5
Valdez	.985	13	32	35	1	9

Third Base	PCT	G	PO	A	E	DP
Abreu	.946	12	11	24	2	5
Hillenbrand	1.000	1	1	0	0	0
Jones	.875	8	8	6	2	1
LaRoche	.949	64	47	121	9	12
R. Martinez	—	1	0	0	0	0
Maza	.941	23	11	37	3	5
McDougall	.939	35	29	64	6	8
Perez	1.000	6	3	11	0	1
Valdez	1.000	4	3	3	0	0

Shortstop	PCT	G	PO	A	E	DP
Abreu	.935	17	20	38	4	8
Becker	.867	2	5	8	2	1
Garcia	.958	20	21	47	3	13
Hu	.962	28	39	86	5	17

	PCT	G	PO	A	E	DP
R. Martinez	1.000	1	2	0	0	0
Perez	.930	22	42	65	8	16
Rivera	1.000	1	1	0	0	0
Valdez	.982	60	110	169	5	46

Outfield	PCT	G	PO	A	E	DP
Anderson	1.000	6	5	0	0	0
Barnes	.966	21	24	4	1	0
Bigbie	.978	22	45	0	1	0
Freeman	.981	114	248	5	5	2
Garcia	1.000	1	1	0	0	0
Jones	1.000	21	26	3	0	1
Kemp	.989	36	84	4	1	3
LaRoche	1.000	7	7	1	0	0
Loney	1.000	23	44	3	0	0
Maza	1.000	21	33	2	0	0
McDougall	1.000	8	8	0	0	0
Ruan	.964	67	113	20	5	1
Valdez	1.000	14	27	2	0	0
Young	.983	103	172	6	3	0

JACKSONVILLE SUNS   DOUBLE-A

SOUTHERN LEAGUE

BATTING	B-T	HT	WT	DOB	AVG	vLH	vRH	G	AB	R	H	2B	3B	HR	RBI	BB	HBP	SH	SF	SO	SB	CS	SLG	OBP
Allen, Luke	L-R	6-2	220	8-4-78	.236	.265	.222	33	106	14	25	4	0	1	9	13	1	0	0	17	2	3	.302	.325
Apodaca, Juan	R-R	5-11	188	7-15-86	.000	.000	.000	3	8	0	0	0	0	0	0	0	0	0	0	2	0	0	.000	.000
Concepcion Jr., Alberto	R-R	6-1	220	4-18-81	.239	.217	.249	82	289	46	69	14	2	12	60	22	11	0	3	68	0	2	.426	.314
Dewitt, Blake	L-R	5-11	175	8-20-85	.281	.379	.233	45	178	20	50	13	1	6	20	7	0	1	1	26	0	1	.466	.306
Dunlap, Cory	L-L	6-1	205	4-13-84	.226	.228	.224	121	399	46	90	18	0	7	60	68	2	0	6	76	0	0	.333	.337
Ellis, A.J.	R-R	6-3	240	4-9-81	.269	.275	.267	109	357	59	96	22	2	8	57	60	8	1	4	61	1	4	.409	.382
Giles, Thomas	L-L	6-0	190	8-28-83	.181	.286	.155	25	72	4	13	4	0	2	7	5	0	1	1	22	2	3	.319	.231
Gonzalez, Juan	R-R	6-0	165	2-23-82	.287	.326	.272	106	349	60	100	20	2	9	52	38	6	5	3	63	8	3	.433	.364
Howard, Kevin	L-R	6-2	190	6-25-81	.292	.329	.275	64	243	33	71	11	1	7	28	23	2	0	0	45	2	4	.432	.358
Hu, Chin-Lung	R-R	5-11	190	2-2-84	.329	.419	.293	82	325	56	107	30	5	6	34	26	1	3	1	33	12	4	.508	.380
Lindsey, John	R-R	6-3	240	1-30-77	.286	.372	.252	56	154	28	44	6	0	11	33	14	6	0	0	38	0	0	.539	.368
Martinez, Octavio	R-R	6-0	190	7-30-79	.364	.333	.375	4	11	4	4	0	0	2	6	3	0	0	1	3	0	0	.909	.467
Maza, Luis	R-R	5-9	180	6-22-80	.237	.296	.214	26	97	14	23	2	1	3	8	14	1	1	1	17	1	2	.371	.336
McDougall, Marshall	R-R	6-1	200	12-19-78	.263	.275	.258	70	262	39	69	16	1	11	47	16	1	0	5	48	3	2	.458	.303
Nicholson, David	R-R	6-0	175	10-22-82	.208	.231	.198	80	183	28	38	6	2	2	21	22	3	0	0	45	2	3	.295	.303
Paul, Xavier	L-R	6-0	200	2-25-85	.291	.267	.302	118	422	64	123	21	2	11	50	48	3	7	2	112	17	9	.429	.366
Raglani, Anthony	L-L	6-2	215	4-6-83	.248	.284	.233	136	456	76	113	24	5	21	68	85	3	1	0	139	9	7	.461	.369
Rohan, Jimmy	R-R	6-1	190	5-13-84	.238	.296	.209	67	164	16	39	7	1	0	22	16	1	1	2	28	0	0	.293	.306
Ruan, Wilkin	R-R	6-0	180	9-18-78	.289	.297	.286	45	135	22	39	7	1	0	14	3	0	1	0	20	7	2	.356	.304
Tomlin, James	R-R	6-0	183	8-12-82	.256	.310	.233	75	289	41	74	20	0	0	27	18	1	4	5	52	14	2	.325	.297

PITCHING	B-T	HT	WT	DOB	W	L	ERA	G	GS	CG	SV	IP	H	R	ER	HR	BB	SO	AVG	vLH	vRH	K/9	BB/9
Akin, Brian	R-R	6-3	185	10-13-81	1	2	4.37	37	0	0	2	68	64	37	33	3	42	91	.245	.229	.256	12.04	5.56
Alexander, Mark	R-R	5-10	190	12-6-80	5	1	4.41	36	0	0	5	67	54	34	33	11	35	81	.216	.263	.187	10.83	4.68
Alvarez, Carlos	L-L	5-9	160	3-31-85	3	0	3.86	7	0	0	0	14	15	7	6	0	11	10	.319	.467	.250	6.43	7.07
Cyr, Eric	R-L	6-4	210	2-11-79	6	3	3.18	16	16	0	0	91	97	39	32	7	17	57	.277	.235	.290	5.66	1.69
Elbert, Scott	L-L	6-1	210	8-13-85	0	1	3.86	3	3	0	0	14	6	6	6	0	10	24	.128	.200	.119	15.43	6.43
Ellis, A.J.	R-R	6-3	240	4-9-81	0	0	4.91	3	0	0	0	4	5	2	2	1	0	1	.313	.333	.308	2.45	0.00
Gonzalez, Luis	L-L	6-0	205	2-27-83	2	2	4.02	25	0	0	3	31	21	15	14	1	32	35	.193	.200	.190	10.05	9.19
Hammes, Zachary	R-R	6-6	240	5-15-84	5	8	5.23	26	15	0	0	95	110	60	55	11	30	76	.299	.320	.280	7.23	2.85
Juarez, William	R-R	6-2	203	4-22-81	4	2	4.79	8	8	1	0	47	54	29	25	6	20	36	.289	.299	.280	6.89	3.83
Kershaw, Clayton	L-L	6-3	210	3-19-88	1	2	3.65	5	5	0	0	25	17	13	10	4	17	29	.193	.188	.194	10.58	6.20
LaMura, B.J.	R-R	6-1	200	1-1-81	1	3	2.93	24	0	0	0	43	32	15	14	3	33	47	.208	.174	.235	9.84	6.91
McDonald, James	L-R	6-5	195	10-19-84	7	2	1.71	10	10	0	0	53	42	14	10	5	16	64	.218	.202	.229	10.94	2.73
Megrew, Michael	L-L	6-6	225	1-29-84	6	6	5.30	21	19	0	0	93	97	63	55	7	46	90	.269	.250	.273	8.68	4.44
Meloan, Jonathan	R-R	6-3	230	7-11-84	5	2	2.18	35	0	0	19	45	24	13	11	3	18	70	.155	.161	.151	13.90	3.57
Miller, Greg	L-L	6-6	220	11-3-84	1	2	4.69	20	7	0	1	48	46	31	25	2	43	65	.247	.200	.260	12.19	8.06
Norrito, Giuseppe	R-R	5-10	180	8-4-82	8	5	4.13	24	16	0	0	118	133	69	54	16	26	57	.285	.310	.263	4.36	1.99
Ojeda, Alvis	R-R	6-0	170	9-23-84	7	5	5.65	26	17	0	0	107	136	72	67	12	57	68	.312	.347	.289	5.74	4.81
Orenduff, Justin	R-R	6-2	205	5-27-83	8	5	4.21	27	23	0	0	109	112	58	51	16	45	113	.265	.282	.251	9.33	3.72
Quintana, Eduardo	R-R	6-2	175	6-30-85	0	0	7.71	1	0	0	0	2	2	2	2	0	3	1	.286	.500	.200	3.86	11.57
Riley, Matt	L-L	6-1	225	8-2-79	0	1	1.47	9	0	0	2	18	12	6	3	0	11	29	.188	.217	.171	14.24	5.40
Rohan, Jimmy	R-R	6-1	190	5-13-84	0	0	19.29	2	0	0	0	2	4	7	5	1	3	4	.333	.333	.333	15.43	11.57
Troncoso, Ramon	R-R	6-7	187	2-16-83	7	3	3.12	35	0	0	7	52	52	19	18	3	18	39	.263	.281	.248	6.75	3.12
Wade, Cory	R-R	6-2	180	5-28-83	0	1	1.36	14	0	0	0	33	22	5	5	2	11	33	.182	.173	.188	9.00	3.00
Wright, Wesley	R-L	5-11	160	1-28-85	6	2	2.49	30	1	0	2	61	45	19	17	4	31	68	.204	.179	.214	9.98	4.55

ORGANIZATION STATISTICS

FIELDING

Catcher	PCT	G	PO	A	E	DP	PB
Apodaca	1.000	3	16	1	0	0	0
Concepcion Jr.	.987	35	290	19	4	2	3
Ellis	.994	105	868	82	6	9	5
Martinez	1.000	3	11	3	0	0	0
Ruan	1.000	1	1	0	0	0	0

First Base	PCT	G	PO	A	E	DP
Allen	1.000	3	12	1	0	0
Concepcion Jr.	.972	28	193	17	6	16
Dunlap	.993	91	689	46	5	52
Ellis	1.000	1	3	0	0	0
Lindsey	.987	24	142	10	2	16
Nicholson	1.000	1	1	0	0	0
Rohan	.987	20	69	5	1	6

Second Base	PCT	G	PO	A	E	DP
Gonzalez	.975	57	99	135	6	34

Howard	.978	44	83	94	4	16
Maza	.971	26	45	57	3	14
Nicholson	.973	27	36	37	2	5
Rohan	.792	9	6	13	5	1

Third Base	PCT	G	PO	A	E	DP
Concepcion Jr.	.920	10	5	18	2	0
Dewitt	.993	44	42	91	1	5
Gonzalez	1.000	4	1	4	0	0
Howard	.952	16	7	33	2	4
Martinez	—	1	0	0	0	0
McDougall	.938	64	43	122	11	16
Nicholson	1.000	2	3	2	0	1
Rohan	.875	8	5	9	2	0

Shortstop	PCT	G	PO	A	E	DP
Gonzalez	.974	44	63	89	4	10
Hu	.971	81	113	218	10	48

McDougall	1.000	2	1	0	0	0
Nicholson	.913	16	15	27	4	5
Rohan	.889	13	9	15	3	1

Outfield	PCT	G	PO	A	E	DP
Allen	.966	28	54	2	2	0
Concepcion Jr.	1.000	12	15	2	0	1
Ellis	—	1	0	0	0	0
Giles	1.000	23	20	2	0	0
Howard	1.000	1	1	0	0	0
Lindsey	.667	5	2	0	1	0
Maza	1.000	1	1	0	0	0
Nicholson	.963	26	26	0	1	0
Paul	.974	105	214	9	6	4
Raglani	.969	135	241	5	8	0
Rohan	1.000	11	10	1	0	0
Ruan	1.000	41	58	5	0	0
Tomlin	.993	75	143	4	1	1

INLAND EMPIRE 66ers

HIGH CLASS A

CALIFORNIA LEAGUE

BATTING	B-T	HT	WT	DOB	AVG	vLH	vRH	G	AB	R	H	2B	3B	HR	RBI	BB	HBP	SH	SF	SO	SB	CS	SLG	OBP
Bell, Joshua	B-R	6-3	235	11-13-86	.173	.190	.167	20	75	4	13	2	1	2	9	3	0	0	1	19	0	0	.307	.203
Brooks, Parker	B-R	5-10	175	8-1-81	.000	.000	.000	2	5	1	0	0	0	0	0	0	0	0	1	0	0	0	.000	.000
De Jesus, Ivan	R-R	5-11	182	5-1-87	.287	.283	.289	121	428	69	123	23	3	4	52	57	3	9	5	64	11	6	.381	.371
Denker, Travis	R-R	5-9	170	8-5-85	.294	.347	.277	111	402	65	118	27	3	10	57	48	4	0	7	65	8	2	.450	.369
2-team (7 San Jose)					.300	—	—	118	427	72	128	30	3	11	66	55	4	0	7	67	9	2	.461	.379
Dewitt, Blake	L-R	5-11	175	8-20-85	.298	.278	.304	83	339	48	101	29	2	8	46	20	1	0	1	42	2	3	.466	.338
Furcal, Rafael	B-R	5-9	195	10-24-77	.167	—	.167	2	6	0	1	0	0	0	2	0	0	0	1	1	0	0	.167	.375
Godwin, Adam	R-R	5-11	170	12-13-82	.269	.242	.279	102	324	45	87	7	4	1	31	27	4	7	1	58	24	8	.324	.331
Gonzalez, Adolfo	R-R	5-11	160	6-13-85	.188	.000	.273	5	16	2	3	0	0	0	1	0	0	0	0	4	0	0	.188	.188
Gutierrez, Gabriel	R-R	5-11	175	11-24-83	.240	.283	.226	63	217	28	52	10	0	2	20	11	5	3	0	28	0	1	.313	.292
Harper, Anthony	L-R	6-0	200	10-15-84	.245	.308	.237	38	110	10	27	4	0	0	11	8	2	0	0	21	0	1	.282	.308
Herrera, Elian	B-R	5-11	169	2-1-85	.200	.364	.105	11	30	3	6	2	0	0	4	2	0	2	1	12	1	2	.267	.242
Hoffmann, Jamie	R-R	6-3	230	8-20-84	.309	.269	.321	116	433	67	134	22	7	9	81	47	4	5	6	70	19	7	.455	.378
Hunt, Bridger	R-R	6-0	185	7-24-85	.296	.283	.301	67	226	39	67	12	4	2	29	22	2	4	1	33	10	9	.412	.363
Justis, Shane	R-R	5-10	175	3-11-83	.297	.382	.267	95	293	55	87	15	4	6	45	31	7	5	4	44	12	1	.437	.373
Locke, Andrew	R-R	6-1	205	2-28-83	.280	.229	.296	79	286	30	80	11	3	7	30	17	3	2	2	47	4	6	.413	.325
Lopez, Esteban	R-R	6-1	210	6-20-84	.211	.000	.250	10	19	5	4	0	1	1	2	2	0	0	1	8	0	0	.474	.273
May, Lucas	R-R	6-0	190	10-24-84	.256	.347	.228	128	507	81	130	25	3	25	89	36	7	1	3	107	5	7	.465	.313
Mitchell, Russell	R-R	6-1	182	2-15-85	.270	.289	.264	126	488	81	132	32	4	22	82	31	10	3	5	126	5	5	.488	.324
Nicholson, David	R-R	6-0	175	10-22-82	.222	.462	.000	12	27	3	6	1	0	0	3	3	3	1	0	4	0	2	.259	.364
Pedroza, Jaime	B-R	5-10	175	9-12-86	.250	.250	.250	5	12	1	3	0	1	0	1	3	0	1	0	1	1	0	.250	.400
Rivera, Michael	R-R	6-0	186	5-13-85	.233	.357	.172	20	43	6	10	3	0	0	4	7	1	0	1	12	3	3	.302	.346
Rogowski, Ryan	L-L	6-0	204	1-26-84	.253	.307	.241	121	423	60	107	27	9	3	46	54	8	2	2	77	39	7	.381	.347
Tomlin, James	R-R	6-0	183	8-12-82	.283	.150	.314	31	106	15	30	10	1	0	15	14	1	1	0	9	7	3	.406	.372

PITCHING	B-T	HT	WT	DOB	W	L	ERA	G	GS	CG	SV	IP	H	R	ER	HR	BB	SO	AVG	vLH	vRH	K/9	BB/9
Alvarez, Carlos	L-L	5-9	160	3-31-85	1	2	6.56	15	0	0	1	23	28	17	17	3	10	24	.308	.258	.333	9.26	3.86
Alvarez, Mario	R-R	6-0	150	3-26-84	7	10	5.60	33	14	0	0	108	123	83	67	11	48	103	.291	.286	.296	8.61	4.01
Arias, Marlon	L-L	6-3	155	9-1-84	12	4	5.32	26	23	1	0	129	144	83	76	8	50	95	.283	.241	.300	6.65	3.50
Bastardo, Alberto	L-L	6-0	160	4-6-84	6	5	4.57	16	13	0	0	69	73	39	35	8	25	73	.274	.355	.242	9.52	3.26
Brazoban, Yhency	R-R	6-1	250	6-11-80	0	1	2.08	3	3	0	0	4	4	5	1	0	2	5	.222	.125	.300	10.38	4.15
Brooks, Parker	B-R	5-10	175	8-1-81	0	0	6.00	1	0	0	0	3	5	2	2	0	1	3	.417	.333	.444	9.00	3.00
Castillo, Jesus	R-R	6-1	190	5-31-84	6	9	4.78	28	22	0	0	130	144	84	69	9	40	97	.278	.290	.267	6.72	2.77
Felix, Francisco	R-R	5-11	191	7-28-83	2	3	5.51	29	4	0	2	67	73	43	41	9	26	58	.282	.382	.191	7.79	3.49
Gomez de Segura, M.	R-R	6-5	230	5-9-83	0	0	10.32	15	0	0	0	23	27	31	26	2	31	19	.293	.417	.214	7.54	12.31
Guerra, Javy	R-R	6-1	185	10-31-85	6	9	6.27	27	24	0	1	118	139	98	82	10	80	121	.296	.275	.316	9.25	6.12
Justis, Shane	R-R	5-10	175	3-11-83	0	0	0.00	1	0	0	0	1	0	0	0	0	0	0	.000	.000	.000	0.00	0.00
Leach, Brent	L-L	6-5	205	11-18-82	0	0	0.45	14	0	0	4	20	14	2	1	1	11	13	.203	.222	.196	10.35	4.95
McDonald, James	L-R	6-5	195	10-19-84	6	7	3.95	16	15	0	0	82	79	37	36	8	21	104	.253	.249	.259	11.41	2.30
Meque, Jacobo	L-L	6-2	175	10-1-83	5	2	4.72	55	0	0	4	55	47	39	29	5	42	78	.223	.267	.199	12.69	6.83
Pfeiffer, David	L-L	6-3	190	8-17-85	1	1	12.46	9	0	0	0	9	15	13	12	2	8	7	.375	.167	.412	7.27	8.31
Pinango, Miguel	R-R	6-1	190	1-20-83	1	3	4.61	5	5	0	0	27	26	16	14	6	6	21	.245	.262	.234	6.91	1.98
Pratt, Jordan	R-R	6-3	195	5-17-85	3	5	6.72	44	0	0	0	83	77	69	62	7	75	94	.249	.238	.259	10.19	8.13
Quintana, Eduardo	R-R	6-2	175	6-30-85	1	0	14.11	8	0	0	0	15	27	29	23	4	17	9	.397	.429	.364	5.52	10.43
Ramirez, Miguel	R-R	5-11	180	7-15-83	1	0	7.27	6	0	0	1	9	11	7	7	0	7	10	.289	.400	.217	10.38	7.27
Rodriguez, Jesus	R-R	6-0	180	9-13-85	1	2	3.45	26	0	0	3	60	62	25	23	6	15	49	.262	.256	.267	7.35	2.25
Schmidt, Jason	R-R	6-4	210	1-29-73	0	0	0.00	1	1	0	0	6	2	0	0	0	1	7	.105	.000	.333	10.50	1.50
Troncoso, Ramon	R-R	6-7	187	2-16-83	3	1	1.04	16	0	0	7	26	18	6	3	0	3	30	.194	.190	.196	10.38	1.04
Wade, Cory	R-R	6-2	180	5-28-83	7	0	2.45	25	2	0	6	66	50	19	18	6	17	67	.207	.170	.237	9.14	2.32
White, Cody	L-L	6-3	185	2-27-85	2	3	3.90	12	10	0	0	67	73	36	29	5	17	32	.277	.333	.256	4.30	2.28
White, Garrett	L-L	6-5	235	5-22-84	0	0	0.00	3	0	0	0	1	0	0	0	0	1	0	.000	.000	.000	6.00	0.00
Wilson, Kyle	R-R	6-2	200	4-21-83	1	0	1.09	25	0	0	14	33	26	6	4	1	5	30	.210	.203	.215	8.18	1.36
Wolf, Randy	L-L	5-10	200	8-22-76	0	0	6.75	1	1	0	0	4	6	3	3	2	1	4	.353	.333	.364	9.00	2.25

FIELDING

Catcher	PCT	G	PO	A	E	DP	PB
Gutierrez	.994	58	434	44	3	2	6
Harper	1.000	9	65	2	0	0	1
Lopez	1.000	8	30	7	0	0	0
May	.994	78	629	56	4	3	31
Herrera	.945	10	17	35	3	7	
Hunt	1.000	1	3	0	0	0	
Justis	.968	18	23	38	2	5	
Nicholson	1.000	1	3	3	0	0	
Pedroza	1.000	2	3	0	0	0	
Rivera	1.000	5	3	10	0	1	
Gonzalez	1.000	1	1	0	0	0	
Hunt	.897	7	11	15	3	4	
Justis	1.000	15	12	36	0	9	
Pedroza	.786	3	4	7	3	1	
Rivera	.923	4	2	10	1	1	

First Base	PCT	G	PO	A	E	DP
Brooks	1.000	1	2	1	0	0
Harper	.986	11	71	2	1	6
Hoffmann	—	1	0	0	0	0
Justis	.978	20	122	10	3	10
Locke	.987	12	69	6	1	14
Mitchell	.992	102	776	50	7	71
Nicholson	1.000	1	3	0	0	0

Second Base	PCT	G	PO	A	E	DP
Brooks	1.000	1	4	0	0	0
Denker	.974	110	210	268	13	58
Gonzalez	1.000	4	9	8	0	3

Third Base	PCT	G	PO	A	E	DP
Bell	.929	18	20	19	3	1
Dewitt	.932	81	65	139	15	13
Hunt	1.000	1	0	1	0	0
Justis	.881	18	10	27	5	4
Mitchell	1.000	19	17	38	0	2
Nicholson	1.000	2	1	3	0	2
Rivera	.875	7	5	9	2	1

Shortstop	PCT	G	PO	A	E	DP
De Jesus	.937	120	183	266	30	62
Furcal	1.000	1	1	0	0	0

Outfield	PCT	G	PO	A	E	DP
Godwin	.991	99	202	8	2	0
Hoffmann	.988	113	222	17	3	1
Hunt	.973	58	104	3	3	0
Justis	.833	6	5	0	1	0
Locke	.942	35	49	0	3	0
Rivera	—	1	0	0	0	0
Rogowski	.980	115	193	3	4	0
Tomlin	1.000	31	67	0	0	0

GREAT LAKES LOONS

LOW CLASS A

MIDWEST LEAGUE

BATTING	B-T	HT	WT	DOB	AVG	vLH	vRH	G	AB	R	H	2B	3B	HR	RBI	BB	HBP	SH	SF	SO	SB	CS	SLG	OBP
Apodaca, Juan	R-R	5-11	188	7-15-86	.259	.276	.252	58	205	23	53	6	1	8	27	16	4	1	1	39	2	0	.415	.323
Bell, Joshua	B-R	6-3	235	11-13-86	.289	.248	.303	108	398	65	115	21	3	15	62	39	1	0	0	109	5	1	.470	.354
Berezay, Matthew	B-R	5-11	175	11-15-83	.276	.263	.281	116	427	58	118	34	5	13	64	37	9	4	4	80	8	8	.471	.344
Brooks, Parker	B-R	5-10	175	8-1-81	.071	.000	.100	6	14	1	1	0	0	0	1	1	0	2	0	1	0	0	.071	.133
Fuller, Justin	B-R	6-1	175	7-10-83	.239	.200	.250	29	88	13	21	2	1	1	3	6	3	1	0	13	1	2	.318	.309
Giles, Thomas	L-L	6-0	190	8-28-83	.320	.300	.322	34	125	24	40	8	3	6	18	11	2	0	1	30	3	4	.576	.381
Gonzalez, Adolfo	R-R	5-11	160	6-13-85	.296	.366	.272	84	314	42	93	20	2	5	29	27	1	4	2	69	7	5	.420	.352
Herrera, Elian	B-R	5-11	169	2-1-85	.167	.400	.077	9	36	3	6	2	0	0	3	1	3	0	0	10	3	1	.222	.250
Hunt, Bridger	R-R	6-0	185	7-24-85	.296	.344	.270	46	179	29	53	7	1	1	19	15	2	2	2	30	6	5	.363	.354
Jansen, Kenley	B-R	6-2	178	9-30-87	.102	.077	.109	20	59	5	6	1	0	1	6	7	2	0	2	18	0	1	.169	.214
Lizarraga, Francisco	R-R	6-1	170	10-1-85	.261	.313	.239	79	284	35	74	17	0	6	29	11	2	11	0	76	11	5	.384	.293
Mathews, Brian	R-R	6-0	210	8-26-87	.319	.357	.302	23	91	8	29	6	0	1	2	5	0	0	0	18	3	0	.418	.354
Mattingly, Preston	R-R	6-3	205	8-28-87	.210	.254	.192	107	404	42	85	12	7	3	40	22	2	3	6	119	11	3	.297	.251
Perez, Eduardo	B-R	6-1	175	8-30-84	.311	.302	.315	116	447	56	139	20	2	14	60	34	3	0	2	91	8	5	.459	.362
Peterson, James	L-L	6-0	210	10-14-83	.271	.237	.279	60	210	20	57	11	0	3	28	24	0	1	0	67	1	4	.367	.346
Rivera, Juan	B-R	6-0	150	3-17-87	.252	.194	.268	39	143	20	36	5	1	4	16	8	0	2	0	28	3	4	.385	.291
Rivera, Michael	R-R	6-0	186	5-13-85	.211	.167	.231	6	19	2	4	0	0	0	2	1	1	0	0	3	1	0	.211	.286
Robinson, Trayvon	B-R	5-10	175	9-1-87	.253	.276	.242	110	396	50	100	9	4	2	31	32	4	10	1	119	22	9	.311	.314
Santana, Carlos	B-R	5-11	170	4-8-86	.223	.254	.213	86	292	32	65	20	1	7	36	40	1	0	0	45	5	3	.370	.318
Sutherland, David	L-L	6-6	175	2-4-84	.197	.217	.191	34	117	8	23	4	0	1	11	2	1	1	0	27	0	0	.256	.217
Taloa, Rick	R-R	6-4	250	12-14-84	.205	.190	.211	21	78	8	16	6	0	1	6	1	2	1	0	22	0	0	.321	.232
Van Slyke, Scott	R-R	6-5	195	7-24-86	.254	.304	.233	104	351	38	89	18	1	2	35	27	4	3	5	68	4	4	.328	.310

PITCHING	B-T	HT	WT	DOB	W	L	ERA	G	GS	CG	SV	IP	H	R	ER	HR	BB	SO	AVG	vLH	vRH	K/9	BB/9
Adkins, James	L-L	6-5	195	11-26-85	0	1	2.42	11	11	0	0	26	17	7	7	1	10	30	.181	.097	.222	10.38	3.46
Brannon, Blake	R-R	6-2	225	3-5-85	2	2	8.82	13	0	0	0	16	17	19	16	2	11	13	.258	.290	.229	7.16	6.06
Brooks, Douglas	R-R	6-4	210	8-12-82	1	2	5.67	13	0	0	2	27	31	19	17	0	11	20	.287	.326	.258	6.67	3.67
Castillo, Arismendy	R-R	6-3	190	12-10-84	3	8	5.36	23	11	0	0	92	115	76	55	4	61	67	.302	.321	.284	6.53	5.95
Coleman, Paul	L-L	6-4	195	5-11-84	2	5	5.10	11	9	0	0	55	72	35	31	3	21	29	.326	.295	.333	4.77	3.46
Diaz, Jose	R-R	6-4	300	2-27-84	0	0	6.75	2	0	0	0	1	2	1	1	1	3	0	.400	.333	.500	0.00	20.25
Felix, Francisco	R-R	5-11	191	7-28-83	1	1	0.76	10	3	0	1	35	19	10	3	0	9	35	.158	.158	.159	8.92	2.29
Figueroa, Jonathan	L-L	6-5	205	9-15-83	1	0	0.90	5	0	0	0	10	8	1	1	1	9	17	.216	.125	.286	15.30	8.10
Gardner, Michael	R-R	5-11	175	11-2-83	3	3	5.94	16	4	0	1	47	60	35	31	1	12	30	.300	.302	.298	5.74	2.30
German, Yulkin	L-L	6-2	180	8-27-83	0	0	17.44	12	0	0	0	16	37	34	31	1	21	12	.451	.500	.439	6.75	11.81
Gomez de Segura, M.	R-R	6-5	230	5-9-83	0	2	9.49	8	0	0	0	12	17	18	13	1	17	13	.333	.238	.400	9.49	12.41
Gonzalez, Adolfo	R-R	5-11	160	6-13-85	0	0	—	1	0	0	0	1	0	0	0	0	0	0	1.000	—	1.000	—	—
Johnson, Steve	R-R	6-1	200	8-31-87	3	6	4.85	18	16	0	0	82	90	57	44	2	40	65	.280	.290	.274	7.16	4.41
Jones, Joseph	R-R	6-5	210	11-16-82	1	3	5.40	26	0	0	1	58	63	40	35	0	32	42	.275	.261	.284	6.48	4.94
Kershaw, Clayton	L-L	6-3	210	3-19-88	7	5	2.77	20	20	0	0	97	72	39	30	5	50	134	.203	.151	.219	12.39	4.62
Malone, Christopher	R-R	6-4	230	6-28-83	1	3	5.77	14	3	0	1	39	42	37	25	4	23	41	.266	.241	.280	9.46	5.31
Melgarejo, Thomas	L-L	6-1	216	1-10-87	4	8	6.20	33	12	0	4	90	110	71	62	9	44	57	.302	.304	.302	5.70	4.40
Peterson, James	L-L	6-0	210	10-14-83	0	1	27.00	3	0	0	0	2	3	7	6	0	5	3	.375	.000	.500	13.50	22.50
Pfeiffer, David	L-L	6-3	190	8-17-85	4	2	3.19	12	3	0	1	37	32	18	13	0	24	19	.237	.351	.194	4.66	5.89
Ramirez, Miguel	R-R	5-11	180	7-15-83	2	1	1.57	41	0	0	15	52	44	12	9	1	30	56	.240	.282	.210	9.75	5.23
Rodriguez, Jesus	R-R	6-0	180	9-13-85	1	0	2.30	14	0	0	3	31	27	10	8	1	7	21	.227	.204	.243	6.03	2.01
Sanfler, Miguel	L-L	5-11	165	10-5-84	3	4	5.14	43	0	0	3	70	69	46	40	4	63	67	.259	.176	.292	8.61	8.10
Sexton, Timothy	R-R	6-6	185	6-30-87	3	1	3.57	5	0	0	0	23	24	11	9	2	9	5	.298	.259	.274	9.93	1.99
Smit, Kyle	R-R	6-3	165	10-14-87	5	5	8.34	5	5	0	0	23	26	26	21	2	12	26	.280	.316	.255	10.32	4.76
Wall, Joshua	R-R	6-6	190	1-21-87	6	10	4.18	26	24	1	1	129	136	71	60	8	48	103	.269	.300	.247	7.17	3.34
White, Cody	L-L	6-3	185	2-27-85	8	5	2.48	15	14	0	0	76	68	25	21	3	41	63	.236	.266	.225	7.43	4.83
White, Garrett	L-L	6-5	235	5-22-84	1	4	3.33	23	4	0	2	51	47	23	19	2	15	63	.242	.263	.234	11.05	2.63

FIELDING

Catcher	PCT	G	PO	A	E	DP	PB
Apodaca	.989	54	407	29	5	4	8
Brooks	1.000	2	12	3	0	0	0
Jansen	.995	19	173	14	1	0	7
Santana	.976	67	474	50	13	10	20

First Base	PCT	G	PO	A	E	DP
Gonzalez	1.000	4	28	1	0	3
Perez	.991	84	668	66	7	69
Peterson	.988	11	74	5	1	6
Sutherland	.990	28	175	19	2	19
Taloa	.977	15	122	7	3	7
Van Slyke	1.000	3	18	3	0	1

Second Base	PCT	G	PO	A	E	DP
Brooks	1.000	1	0	1	0	0
Fuller	.938	10	20	25	3	6
Gonzalez	.955	23	58	68	6	30

	PCT	G	PO	A	E	DP
Herrera	.979	9	19	28	1	6
Lizarraga	.905	5	7	12	2	1
Mattingly	.953	71	117	184	15	33
J. Rivera	.902	15	17	29	5	4
M. Rivera	.955	6	10	11	1	1

Third Base	PCT	G	PO	A	E	DP
Bell	.859	90	64	149	35	12
Fuller	.848	13	14	25	7	4
Gonzalez	.941	13	12	20	2	2
Mathews	.882	20	10	35	6	1
Perez	.875	2	5	2	1	1
J. Rivera	.333	2	0	1	2	0
Santana	.824	5	3	11	3	0

Shortstop	PCT	G	PO	A	E	DP
Fuller	.857	6	12	12	4	4
Gonzalez	.935	32	52	91	10	17

	PCT	G	PO	A	E	DP
Lizarraga	.948	71	99	190	16	50
Mattingly	.773	18	23	28	15	8
J. Rivera	.951	18	32	45	4	10

Outfield	PCT	G	PO	A	E	DP
Berezay	.968	94	143	6	5	1
Brooks	—	1	0	0	0	0
Giles	.962	32	47	4	2	0
Gonzalez	—	1	0	0	0	0
Hunt	.979	44	90	2	2	0
Mathews	.667	2	2	0	1	0
Peterson	.947	40	48	6	3	0
Robinson	.955	108	245	7	12	4
Santana	.750	4	9	0	3	0
Van Slyke	.982	101	205	11	4	3

OGDEN RAPTORS — ROOKIE

PIONEER LEAGUE

BATTING	B-T	HT	WT	DOB	AVG	vLH	vRH	G	AB	R	H	2B	3B	HR	RBI	BB	HBP	SH	SF	SO	SB	CS	SLG	OBP
Becker, Joseph	R-R	5-11	175	11-8-85	.286	.000	.500	2	7	3	2	0	0	0	0	2	0	0	0	1	1	0	.286	.444
Brown, Jeremy	R-R	6-1	195	4-2-84	.221	.130	.250	37	95	21	21	2	0	1	16	14	2	2	0	32	3	0	.274	.333
Dalton, Parker	R-R	6-1	185	7-7-83	.211	.238	.194	18	57	7	12	3	0	2	7	3	1	0	0	17	0	0	.368	.262
Fuller, Justin	B-R	6-1	175	7-10-83	.232	.375	.172	53	164	24	38	13	2	0	13	20	4	11	3	25	6	6	.335	.325
Gallagher, Austin	L-R	6-4	217	11-16-88	.284	.255	.296	55	197	28	56	11	0	4	17	19	0	1	1	33	1	1	.401	.346
Garabedian, Alex	R-R	6-2	210	8-26-85	.253	.265	.248	50	186	26	47	10	0	4	21	22	1	1	1	40	0	1	.371	.333
Gutierrez, Eloy	B-R	6-1	178	11-25-84	.167	.000	.167	4	6	1	1	0	0	0	1	1	0	0	0	3	0	0	.167	.286
Herrera, Elian	B-R	5-11	169	2-1-85	.282	.362	.244	50	181	28	51	10	3	1	27	25	4	1	1	39	3	3	.387	.379
Jansen, Kenley	B-R	6-2	178	9-30-87	.240	.220	.250	53	183	26	44	5	1	2	22	28	2	1	1	50	0	0	.311	.346
Kanaby, Erik	L-R	6-1	185	7-26-85	.338	.277	.356	58	207	25	70	5	0	1	21	30	2	1	0	35	8	10	.377	.427
Lopez, Esteban	R-R	6-1	210	6-20-84	.286	—	.286	2	7	1	2	1	0	0	1	1	0	0	0	2	0	0	.429	.375
Mathews, Brian	R-R	6-0	210	8-26-87	.287	.250	.298	37	136	21	39	6	0	5	24	9	3	0	2	31	4	1	.441	.340
Mier, Jessie	R-R	6-1	215	3-5-85	.194	.250	.185	8	31	4	6	1	0	0	3	4	0	0	0	4	0	0	.226	.286
Naccarata, Ivan	L-R	6-0	190	2-26-82	.167	.000	.222	4	12	3	2	0	0	0	1	0	0	0	4	0	0	.167	.231
Ortiz, Jaime	L-L	6-3	200	7-14-85	.274	.279	.273	59	226	30	62	10	1	11	35	13	7	0	0	62	0	0	.473	.333
Pedroza, Jaime	B-R	5-10	175	9-12-86	.360	.370	.357	56	211	33	76	18	1	8	40	14	7	4	3	44	4	4	.569	.413
Povey, Tycen	R-R	6-3	220	4-30-83	.241	.400	.158	11	29	4	7	2	1	0	0	1	1	0	0	9	0	0	.379	.290
Rosario, Jovanny	B-R	5-9	160	4-12-85	.331	.292	.344	70	281	47	93	11	4	5	34	21	1	4	3	50	22	8	.452	.376
Taloa, Rick	R-R	6-4	250	12-14-84	.221	.136	.255	21	77	8	17	2	1	3	10	2	1	0	0	20	0	0	.390	.250
Vetters, Travis	R-R	6-2	195	9-11-83	.315	.158	.379	57	197	45	62	13	5	14	41	14	9	1	3	49	1	2	.645	.381
Wallach, Matthew	L-R	6-2	190	2-17-86	.297	.364	.278	32	101	11	30	6	1	3	13	12	4	2	0	18	0	1	.465	.393

PITCHING	B-T	HT	WT	DOB	W	L	ERA	G	GS	CG	SV	IP	H	R	ER	HR	BB	SO	AVG	vLH	vRH	K/9	BB/9
Acheatel, Greg	R-R	6-4	205	9-29-83	0	0	2.25	2	0	0	0	8	12	6	2	1	2	4	.324	.278	.368	4.50	2.25
Blevins, Robert	R-R	6-0	200	1-16-85	3	2	3.49	12	9	0	0	57	57	29	22	6	9	51	.261	.261	.262	8.10	1.43
Brannon, Blake	R-R	6-2	225	3-5-85	0	1	6.00	7	1	0	0	15	12	11	10	2	6	16	.231	.190	.258	9.60	3.60
Brantley, Rodney	R-R	6-4	215	6-6-85	2	2	5.08	9	8	0	0	39	40	26	22	1	15	30	.272	.349	.214	6.92	3.46
Brooks, Douglas	R-R	6-4	210	8-12-82	3	4	5.90	17	6	0	1	50	64	40	33	4	27	61	.306	.268	.336	10.91	4.83
Caraballo, Jhonny	R-R	6-1	190	8-23-85	2	3	4.43	21	0	0	10	22	23	11	11	2	8	22	.271	.273	.269	8.87	3.22
Coleman, Paul	L-L	6-4	195	5-11-84	4	0	1.50	4	4	0	0	24	14	4	4	2	3	25	.171	.000	.197	9.38	1.12
Dasni, Chales	R-R	6-3	170	7-21-85	0	1	1.35	7	0	0	1	13	9	2	2	1	4	24	.196	.182	.208	16.20	2.70
Diaz, Wilfredo	L-L	5-11	180	1-22-87	3	3	4.58	17	8	0	0	55	62	33	28	5	23	61	.283	.311	.272	9.98	3.76
Gardner, Michael	R-R	5-11	175	11-2-83	6	5	3.93	15	15	1	0	85	96	54	37	7	26	49	.280	.281	.279	5.21	2.76
Gearhart, Kalen	R-R	6-2	210	8-12-85	1	0	3.54	17	0	0	0	28	37	11	11	3	6	22	.327	.326	.328	7.07	1.93
Gray, Tim	R-R	5-11	195	7-29-85	1	0	9.50	9	0	0	0	18	30	19	19	4	7	14	.375	.486	.289	7.00	3.50
Haldis, Jon	R-R	6-1	170	3-9-87	0	1	7.18	18	1	0	0	31	42	26	25	6	14	28	.328	.298	.352	8.04	4.02
Jones, Joseph	R-R	6-5	210	11-16-82	3	3	14.40	3	3	0	0	10	20	19	16	0	7	6	.400	.391	.407	5.40	6.30
Koss, Paul	R-R	6-4	215	6-17-85	3	1	5.12	18	0	0	2	32	39	21	18		9	33	.291	.269	.305	9.38	2.56
Krise, Kristopher	R-R	6-6	215	2-1-84	2	6	6.22	13	12	0	0	59	70	46	41	4	17	47	.295	.291	.299	7.13	2.58
Kutz, Given	R-R	6-3	215	11-5-84	1	0	3.00	18	0	0	1	30	25	11	10	3	7	24	.219	.157	.270	7.20	2.10
Quintana, Eduardo	R-R	6-2	175	6-30-87	1	0	8.38	6	0	0	0	10	14	9	9	1	8	9	.326	.412	.269	8.38	7.45
Sartor, Matthew	R-R	6-6	250	8-18-84	0	1	3.44	10	0	0	2	18	10	8	7	3	5	25	.161	.087	.205	12.27	2.45
Stanke, Cal	R-R	5-10	175	3-15-85	2	7	5.66	14	8	0	0	49	60	43	31	3	28	41	.306	.351	.279	7.48	5.11

FIELDING

Catcher	PCT	G	PO	A	E	DP	PB
Garabedian	.988	31	225	25	3	1	3
Jansen	.994	42	314	32	2	3	9
Mier	1.000	5	36	3	0	0	3
Wallach	1.000	5	25	3	0	0	3

First Base	PCT	G	PO	A	E	DP
Ortiz	.987	51	434	27	6	38
Taloa	.993	15	132	9	1	12
Wallach	.971	13	93	8	3	8

Second Base	PCT	G	PO	A	E	DP
Dalton	.969	14	20	42	2	11

	PCT	G	PO	A	E	DP
Fuller	.969	19	29	66	3	15
Herrera	.947	43	67	113	10	18
Mathews	1.000	1	3	6	0	1
Naccarata	.933	4	6	8	1	2

Third Base	PCT	G	PO	A	E	DP
Fuller	.870	9	8	12	3	0
Gallagher	.877	51	35	72	15	11
Mathews	.933	22	12	30	3	3

Shortstop	PCT	G	PO	A	E	DP
Becker	1.000	2	4	6	0	2
Dalton	1.000	2	1	5	0	0

	PCT	G	PO	A	E	DP
Fuller	.975	25	36	80	3	18
Pedroza	.917	50	54	134	17	28

Outfield	PCT	G	PO	A	E	DP
Brown	1.000	28	50	4	0	2
Gutierrez	.667	2	2	0	1	0
Herrera	1.000	7	4	1	0	0
Kanaby	.978	57	86	4	2	0
Mathews	.917	12	11	0	1	0
Povey	.933	10	12	2	1	0
Rosario	.945	68	116	4	7	0
Vetters	.974	57	107	5	3	1

GULF COAST LEAGUE

BATTING	B-T	HT	WT	DOB	AVG	vLH	vRH	G	AB	R	H	2B	3B	HR	RBI	BB	HBP	SH	SF	SO	SB	CS	SLG	OBP
Baez, Pedro	R-R	6-2	199	3-11-88	.274	.288	.268	53	201	35	55	14	2	3	39	17	6	0	5	40	3	1	.408	.341
Becker, Joseph	R-R	5-11	175	11-8-85	.284	.270	.290	51	201	39	57	13	1	1	20	28	5	1	0	41	10	4	.373	.385
Bert, Joris	L-L	5-10	165	5-16-87	.214	.143	.286	12	28	2	6	0	0	0	3	6	1	2	1	10	0	2	.214	.361
Bradley, Curt	B-R	5-9	150	6-29-85	.265	.231	.278	20	49	15	13	0	0	0	4	13	0	2	0	7	5	2	.265	.419
Casanova, Gabriel	R-R	6-1	190	7-29-84	.333	.375	.286	4	15	4	5	0	0	1	3	1	0	0	0	2	0	0	.533	.375
Collado, Keyter	R-R	5-11	178	6-8-86	.305	.303	.306	36	95	13	29	5	0	0	9	16	3	4	0	14	1	1	.358	.421
Dalton, Parker	R-R	6-1	185	7-7-83	.333	.000	.364	4	12	2	4	2	0	1	3	0	0	0	0	2	0	0	.750	.333
Erickson, Gorman	B-R	6-3	205	3-11-88	.163	.364	.105	18	49	10	8	0	0	0	5	8	3	0	1	16	0	1	.163	.311
Garcia, Johan	R-R	6-0	170	9-6-86	.295	.280	.302	27	78	20	23	5	0	0	10	10	1	4	1	20	6	1	.359	.378
Garcia, Yosanddy	R-R	6-0	170	10-20-87	.252	.184	.281	38	127	24	32	6	0	8	26	16	1	0	1	40	4	1	.488	.338
Gomez, Jesus	L-L	6-2	195	12-6-88	.000	.000	—	1	2	0	0	0	0	0	0	0	0	0	0	0	0	0	.000	.000
Guzman, Amauri	R-R	6-3	200	10-12-86	.310	.200	.394	20	58	12	18	1	1	2	13	7	2	0	1	20	0	1	.466	.397
Guzman, Johancy	B-R	5-10	155	4-20-87	.232	.333	.195	25	56	10	13	0	1	0	5	7	0	5	0	20	3	1	.268	.317
Jacobs, Franklin	R-R	6-5	260	11-25-88	.250	.273	.243	30	96	14	24	5	0	2	11	11	0	0	0	36	0	0	.365	.327
Lambo, Andrew	L-L	6-3	190	8-11-88	.343	.357	.336	54	181	38	62	15	1	5	32	29	5	0	3	34	1	2	.519	.440
Martin, John	R-R	6-3	205	12-13-83	.207	.125	.238	12	29	4	6	0	0	0	3	6	0	0	0	7	1	0	.207	.343
Orr, Kyle	L-R	6-5	205	9-29-88	.228	.302	.190	48	158	25	36	7	0	3	19	19	5	0	0	47	1	1	.329	.330
Poole, Lyndon	R-R	6-1	190	8-30-86	.205	.200	.206	36	88	17	18	7	1	0	17	15	8	4	2	22	4	3	.307	.363
Povey, Tycen	R-R	6-3	220	4-30-83	.133	.333	.083	7	15	0	2	0	0	0	1	3	0	0	1	2	0	0	.133	.263
Silverio, Alfredo	R-R	6-1	185	5-6-87	.373	.362	.378	51	193	38	72	9	3	6	46	11	3	0	5	32	5	3	.544	.406

PITCHING	B-T	HT	WT	DOB	W	L	ERA	G	GS	CG	SV	IP	H	R	ER	HR	BB	SO	AVG	vLH	vRH	K/9	BB/9
Alvarez, Carlos	L-L	5-9	160	3-31-85	1	0	2.08	4	2	0	0	9	3	2	2	1	2	14	.097	.000	.111	14.54	2.08
Contreras, Edwin	R-R	6-2	165	9-17-88	3	1	3.30	8	5	0	0	30	27	11	11	3	11	28	.245	.273	.234	8.40	3.30
Danielson, Danny	R-R	6-4	220	12-12-88	1	1	3.48	9	6	0	0	21	17	8	8	2	6	21	.224	.345	.149	9.15	2.61
Dominguez, Kelvin	L-L	6-2	180	4-4-85	3	2	3.06	9	0	0	0	18	17	8	6	0	12	28	.254	.300	.246	14.26	6.11
Dutton, Johnathan	L-L	6-1	155	9-30-87	5	2	3.28	13	4	0	1	60	61	22	22	8	23	58	.277	.273	.278	8.65	3.43
Garcia, Luis	R-R	6-2	175	1-30-87	3	0	3.55	12	0	0	0	25	29	11	10	0	17	17	.293	.323	.279	6.04	6.04
Gomez, Jesus	L-L	6-2	195	12-6-88	0	1	7.27	6	0	0	0	9	9	7	7	7	7	7	.182	.200	.179	7.27	7.27
Gracia, Mario	R-R	5-11	185	8-11-83	1	0	13.50	2	0	0	0	4	10	7	6	0	1	3	.455	.455	.455	6.75	2.25
Krise, Kristopher	R-R	6-6	215	2-1-84	1	0	0.00	1	0	0	0	6	4	0	0	0	2	6	.182	.286	.133	9.00	3.00
Malone, Christopher	R-R	6-4	230	6-28-83	0	0	3.38	4	0	0	0	8	4	4	3	1	5	12	.143	.000	.211	13.50	5.62
Miller, Justin	R-R	6-3	190	8-2-87	2	1	3.57	7	4	0	1	18	22	10	7	0	2	12	.306	.412	.273	6.11	1.02
Paredes, Ramon	L-L	6-3	192	11-28-84	2	0	4.50	10	0	0	1	16	19	12	8	1	5	18	.284	.200	.308	10.12	2.81
Perez, Eduardo	R-R	6-2	185	2-3-88	2	3	4.34	15	0	0	4	19	21	13	9	1	5	13	.276	.350	.250	6.27	2.41
Povey, Tycen	R-R	6-3	220	4-30-83	0	0	0.00	1	0	0	0	1	1	0	0	0	0	1	.250	.000	.500	9.00	0.00
Rondon, Daigoro	R-R	6-2	163	11-4-86	7	2	2.77	12	7	1	1	65	68	22	20	1	4	59	.275	.351	.243	8.17	0.55
Santiago, Andres	R-R	6-2	200	10-26-89	1	0	4.50	8	0	0	0	12	12	6	6	0	9	6	.273	.222	.286	4.50	6.75
Smit, Kyle	R-R	6-3	165	10-14-87	4	0	2.82	8	6	1	0	38	31	13	12	2	13	40	.217	.171	.231	9.39	3.05
Thompson, Eric	R-R	6-6	210	4-4-88	2	2	4.47	11	7	1	1	46	48	25	23	2	23	28	.267	.339	.229	5.44	4.47
Tuten, Brandon	R-R	6-2	185	10-1-85	2	0	2.08	8	0	0	2	9	8	3	2	1	3	12	.242	.083	.333	12.46	3.12
Vasquez, Luis	R-R	6-4	156	4-3-86	0	0	9.64	9	0	0	0	9	9	11	10	1	11	8	.250	.111	.296	7.71	10.61
Watt, Michael	L-L	6-1	185	2-24-89	0	0	3.00	10	6	0	0	21	18	8	7	0	6	18	.234	.214	.245	7.71	2.57
Withrow, Chris	R-R	6-3	195	4-1-89	0	0	5.00	6	4	0	0	9	5	5	5	0	4	13	.167	.333	.095	13.00	4.00

FIELDING

Catcher	PCT	G	PO	A	E	DP	PB
Collado	.996	34	243	26	1	3	5
Erickson	.992	18	116	12	1	2	3
Martin	1.000	10	67	7	0	2	3

First Base	PCT	G	PO	A	E	DP
Baez	1.000	1	1	0	0	0
Gomez	1.000	1	6	1	0	0
Jacobs	.977	5	42	1	1	7
Lambo	1.000	14	108	5	0	9
Martin	1.000	2	3	0	0	0
Orr	.990	38	284	17	3	24

Second Base	PCT	G	PO	A	E	DP
Casanova	.923	4	3	9	1	3
J. Garcia	.932	22	28	54	6	15
Y. Garcia	.964	31	65	67	5	21

Third Base	PCT	G	PO	A	E	DP
Baez	.931	53	27	94	9	5
Garcia	.778	3	1	6	2	0
Lambo	—	1	0	0	0	0

Shortstop	PCT	G	PO	A	E	DP
Becker	.968	51	68	141	7	31
Dalton	.913	4	5	16	2	4

	PCT	G	PO	A	E	DP
J. Garcia	—	2	0	0	0	0
Guzman	1.000	1	0	1	0	0

Outfield	PCT	G	PO	A	E	DP
Bert	1.000	11	15	2	0	0
Bradley	1.000	16	16	1	0	0
Guzman	.931	14	25	2	2	0
Guzman	.971	18	30	3	1	2
Lambo	.967	36	55	4	2	2
Poole	.984	29	61	1	1	1
Povey	1.000	4	5	0	0	0
Silverio	.958	48	62	7	3	1

DOMINICAN SUMMER LEAGUE

BATTING	B-T	HT	WT	DOB	AVG	vLH	vRH	G	AB	R	H	2B	3B	HR	RBI	BB	HBP	SH	SF	SO	SB	CS	SLG	OBP
Arias, Jose	R-R	6-3	200	10-15-88	.225	.359	.195	63	213	33	48	8	2	7	28	36	5	0	1	49	1	6	.380	.349
Aviles, Adrian	L-L	6-1	155	4-7-89	.244	.257	.240	51	164	16	40	1	1	0	14	23	2	3	1	32	8	8	.262	.342
Aybar, Rafael	B-R	6-0	160	5-14-90	.152	.167	.148	38	79	14	12	1	2	1	9	12	1	0	0	26	8	3	.253	.272
Bens, Edward	R-R	6-1	189	1-15-89	.191	.235	.176	26	68	10	13	3	0	0	9	10	1	0	0	16	0	1	.235	.304
Betegon, Adair	R-R	6-1	185	10-22-88	.235	1.000	.188	10	17	2	4	2	0	0	3	0	0	1	0	3	0	0	.353	.235
Brito, Pablo	L-L	6-1	195	8-16-85	.266	.273	.264	29	94	7	25	3	0	1	11	11	1	0	1	17	0	1	.330	.346
Castillo, Jerry	R-R	6-3	190	11-17-88	.206	.258	.189	49	126	24	26	4	0	0	11	5	9	4	2	40	13	5	.238	.282
Gonzalez, Cristian	B-R	6-1	169	6-6-88	.255	.296	.246	48	157	30	40	5	0	3	20	19	5	0	2	40	5	4	.344	.350
Guerrero, Pedro	R-R	6-3	181	12-3-88	.288	.289	.288	56	198	35	57	11	1	1	28	21	6	3	2	33	8	10	.369	.370
Jean, Ramon	R-R	6-0	160	10-10-87	.265	.317	.253	60	215	25	57	11	2	2	27	17	4	0	0	37	11	2	.363	.331
Marte, Alexis	L-L	6-2	197	6-13-85	.214	.200	.217	10	28	7	6	0	0	0	3	9	0	0	1	10	1	0	.214	.395
2-team (38 DSL)					.235	—	—	48	132	29	31	11	1	0	22	44	1	2	1	25	9	1	.333	.427
Mirabal, Charlie	R-L	5-11	164	4-2-87	.219	.194	.226	43	146	20	32	5	2	0	13	26	2	1	2	30	4	3	.281	.341
Ovando, Adolfo	R-R	6-0	176	6-1-86	.136	.000	.177	38	81	11	11	2	1	1	3	13	1	1	0	29	7	3	.222	.263
Sanchez, Jose	R-R	6-2	175	5-11-90	.143	.200	.125	22	42	1	6	1	0	0	2	9	1	2	0	15	0	2	.167	.308
Sucre, Marlon	R-R	6-2	160	3-12-90	.171	.125	.182	20	41	3	7	2	0	0	2	7	3	0	0	11	1	0	.220	.333
Tavarez, Pedro	R-R	5-10	172	6-28-87	.247	.314	.229	53	166	27	41	11	1	3	28	13	6	2	3	29	1	1	.380	.319
Turiano, Franklin	B-R	5-11	175	1-16-89	.059	.000	.077	12	17	1	1	0	0	0	1	2	0	0	0	6	0	0	.059	.158
Villalobos, Andrick	R-R	6-0	165	6-30-86	.276	.235	.284	46	105	12	29	5	0	0	13	9	7	0	0	9	1	1	.343	.372
Ynoa, Rafael	R-R	5-10	162	8-7-87	.206	.257	.193	51	170	38	35	8	2	1	24	42	3	3	3	19	9	3	.294	.367

PITCHING	B-T	HT	WT	DOB	W	L	ERA	G	GS	CG	SV	IP	H	R	ER	HR	BB	SO	AVG	vLH	vRH	K/9	BB/9
Aguasviva, Geison	L-L	6-2	166	8-3-87	8	2	1.50	12	12	0	0	66	43	14	11	0	14	69	.183	.130	.189	9.41	1.91
Castillo, Antonio	L-L	5-11	180	3-5-88	0	2	1.75	14	1	0	3	46	29	10	9	0	8	44	.178	.150	.182	8.55	1.55
De La Rosa, Rubby	R-R	6-1	170	3-4-89	0	0	13.50	6	1	0	0	6	11	10	9	0	10	6	.393	.429	.381	9.00	15.00
Dominguez, Kelvin	L-L	6-2	180	4-4-85	0	1	0.96	4	0	0	0	9	4	2	1	0	3	13	.125	.000	.143	12.54	2.89
Ferreras, Luis	R-R	6-0	151	12-28-89	2	0	0.99	23	0	0	12	27	17	3	3	0	17	27	.183	.152	.200	8.89	5.60
Frias, Carlos	R-R	6-4	170	11-13-89	6	2	1.81	13	11	0	0	50	30	17	10	0	25	39	.184	.224	.162	7.07	4.53
Lopez, Jhan	R-R	6-2	180	11-7-86	0	1	7.88	12	0	0	1	16	13	14	14	2	19	12	.228	.190	.250	6.75	10.69
Marte, Endy	L-L	5-11	160	8-9-88	1	0	7.07	11	0	0	0	14	20	13	11	1	8	17	.328	.182	.360	10.93	5.14
Medina, Bolivar	L-L	6-2	175	7-11-88	2	3	2.75	10	7	0	0	36	27	15	11	1	22	43	.206	.105	.223	10.75	5.50
Mirabal, Charlie	R-L	5-11	164	4-2-87	0	0	0.00	2	0	0	0	4	1	0	0	0	2	1	.077	.000	.091	2.25	4.50
Noboa, Pedro	R-R	6-1	170	8-10-86	3	3	1.40	11	3	1	1	39	18	9	6	0	10	56	.134	.130	.138	13.03	2.33
Ortega, Martires	R-R	6-2	180	1-8-88	1	1	2.57	7	1	0	0	14	8	4	4	0	17	9	.190	.286	.143	5.79	10.93
Pimentel, Elisaul	R-R	6-2	170	7-10-88	0	1	4.23	8	3	0	0	28	26	19	13	3	10	24	.241	.317	.194	7.81	3.25
Placencio, Alvin	R-R	6-0	190	9-20-86	1	0	8.53	3	0	0	0	6	12	7	6	0	2	6	.429	.500	.357	8.53	2.84
Prado, Marcel	R-R	6-4	226	11-22-87	1	0	1.24	13	4	0	0	36	23	9	5	0	23	41	.180	.225	.159	10.16	5.70
Rivas, Raul	R-R	5-11	170	1-18-85	3	0	1.49	18	0	0	3	36	24	7	6	0	15	24	.203	.288	.136	5.94	3.72
Santana, Juan	R-R	6-0	170	12-5-86	2	2	3.92	15	3	0	0	39	38	21	17	3	9	32	.252	.288	.224	7.38	2.08
Tamares, Daniel	R-R	6-3	170	12-20-89	1	1	4.70	8	3	0	0	15	18	14	8	1	5	11	.273	.333	.250	6.46	2.93
Tavarez, Gari	R-R	6-0	170	10-26-87	9	3	1.49	14	14	0	0	67	39	16	11	4	17	71	.167	.133	.189	9.58	2.30
Urriola, Marlon	R-R	6-2	165	7-1-88	3	3	3.62	11	5	0	0	27	26	15	11	3	16	13	.252	.206	.275	4.28	5.27

FIELDING

Catcher	PCT	G	PO	A	E	DP	PB
Bens	.989	16	77	12	1	0	3
Tavarez	.988	33	216	36	3	0	6
Turiano	.957	5	18	4	1	2	0
Villalobos	.989	37	222	42	3	0	6

First Base	PCT	G	PO	A	E	DP
Arias	.995	44	358	26	2	31
Betegon	.914	8	31	1	3	6
Gonzalez	1.000	12	89	4	0	4
Marte	1.000	5	22	3	0	3
Tavarez	.991	13	105	10	1	10

Second Base	PCT	G	PO	A	E	DP
Aybar	.969	21	38	57	3	16

	PCT	G	PO	A	E	DP
Jean	—	1	0	0	0	0
Mirabal	.978	19	44	47	2	15
Ynoa	.956	33	65	88	7	13

Third Base	PCT	G	PO	A	E	DP
Arias	.833	2	0	5	1	0
Aybar	—	1	0	0	0	0
Guerrero	.908	26	19	50	7	4
Jean	.854	36	18	64	14	3
Mirabal	.955	9	3	18	1	1

Shortstop	PCT	G	PO	A	E	DP
Aybar	.857	5	7	5	2	1
Guerrero	.954	28	61	84	7	19
Jean	.935	16	23	35	4	6

	PCT	G	PO	A	E	DP
Mirabal	.942	11	16	33	3	5
Ynoa	.873	14	25	37	9	10

Outfield	PCT	G	PO	A	E	DP
Arias	.938	17	14	1	1	0
Aviles	.937	51	69	5	5	2
Brito	1.000	16	15	0	0	0
Castillo	1.000	2	1	0	0	0
Castillo	.967	48	57	2	2	0
Gonzalez	.977	36	35	7	1	2
Marte	1.000	8	5	0	0	0
Ovando	.923	37	32	4	3	0
Sanchez	.882	19	13	2	2	0
Sucre	.833	12	14	1	3	0

Milwaukee Brewers

BY TOM HAUDRICOURT

It's impossible not to be disappointed when you don't win your division after leading it for 133 days of a baseball season, including 102 in a row during one stretch.

That scenario unfolded for the Brewers in 2007 when they were passed in the final days by their dreaded rivals, the Chicago Cubs, in the NL Central. Arriving perhaps a year ahead of schedule in the minds of some as a division contender, the Brewers followed the lead of their young core of players and bolted to a 24-10 start, best in franchise history.

The offense slipped into a malaise shortly afterward, prompting the Brewers to make a move on May 25 that would pay huge dividends for the remainder of the season. They called up third baseman Ryan Braun, a first-round draft pick in 2005 and offensive prodigy who was tearing up the Pacific Coast League.

The surprising first half led to national recognition, resulting in four players being selected for the All-Star Game for the first time since 1983. First baseman Prince Fielder became the first Brewer elected to start in fan balloting since Paul Molitor in 1988, and was joined on the NL squad by shortstop J.J. Hardy, closer Francisco Cordero and righthanded ace Ben Sheets.

The team began to slide in the second half, however, mostly associated with a starting rotation that didn't go deep in games, creating an onerous workload that eventually unraveled the bullpen. A key factor in that slippage was yet another injury to jinxed Sheets, who missed six weeks in the second half with an unusual injury to the middle finger on his pitching hand.

The Cubs finally caught the Brewers in late August, setting up a neck-and-neck battle between the clubs over the final five weeks. In large part because they couldn't win on the road (32-49) or hold onto leads (16 losses when leading by three runs or more), the Brewers were eliminated from playoff contention with two games remaining on their schedule.

There was no time to mourn, however. The Brewers had to at least split their final two games against San Diego—another club fighting for the playoffs—to assure a winning season for the first time in 15 years. With their fighting spirit and pride still intact, the Brewers won those last two games to finish 83-79 and finally give their fans a winning club.

"For anybody to think this year was a failure or that we didn't accomplish anything, they're dead wrong," manager Ned Yost said. "It's a step-by-step process. There's noting left for us to accomplish next year except winning the division."

Along the way, the entertaining Brewers set several club and individual records. With a major league-best 231 home runs, they shattered the club mark of 216 set by "Harvey's Wallbangers" in 1982. Fielder led the way by leading the league with 50 homers, becoming the youngest player in major league history to reach that plateau. Braun erased club rookie records set by Fielder the previous season by socking 34 homers and driving in 97 runs. Braun also set an all-time rookie record with a .634 slugging percentage.

Cordero smashed the team saves record by converting 44-of-51 opportunities, including 28-of-29 at home. The Brewers did everything better at home, going 51-30, the best mark in the NL.

In addition to the impact made by Braun, the Brewers called up their top pitching prospect, Yovani Gallardo, in mid-June. The 21-year-old righthander made immediate

PLAYERS OF THE YEAR

MAJOR LEAGUE: PRINCE FIELDER, 1B

Fielder had a breakout year in his second full season in the majors, leading the National League with 50 home runs. His .618 slugging average was also tops in the NL, and his 1.013 OPS ranked second. Fielder also led the Brewers with a .395 on-base percentage, 165 hits, 87 extra-base hits, 90 walks, 109 runs and 119 RBIs.

MINOR LEAGUE: MAT GAMEL, 3B

Gamel showed a balanced skill set this year in the high Class A Florida State League. Gamel hit .300/.378/.472, with 37 doubles (third-most in the FSL) and a 33-game hit streak that fell three short of the league record. He ranked in the FSL top 10 in average, on-base percentage and slugging.

ORGANIZATIONAL LEADERS

BATTING		*Minimum 250 at-bats
*AVG	Lefave, Andrew, West Virginia	.345
R	Caufield, Chuck, West Virginia	100
H	Escobar, Alcides, Brevard County/Huntsville	151
TB	Chapman, Stephen, West Virginia	228
2B	Gamel, Mat, Brevard County	37
3B	Iribarren, Hernan, Huntsville	12
HR	Nix, Laynce, Huntsville/Nashville	25
RBI	Katin, Brendan, Huntsville	94
BB	Gillespie, Cole, Brevard County	72
SO	Brewer, Brent, West Virginia	170
SB	Ford, Darren, West Virginia/Brevard County	67
*OBP	Lefave, Andrew, West Virginia	.432
*SLG	Dillon, Joe, Nashville	.605

PITCHING		^Minimum 75 innings
W	Pettyjohn, Adam, Huntsville/Nashville	16
L	Jackson, Zach, Nashville	10
	Lluberes, Rafael, Brevard County	10
^ERA	DiFelice, Mark, Huntsville/Nashville	2.31
G	Three players tied at	51
CG	Dickey, R.A., Nashville	3
SV	Shanks, E.J., West Virginia/Brevard Co./Huntsville	19
IP	Jackson, Zach, Nashville	170
BB	Lluberes, Rafael, Brevard County	69
SO	Inman, William, Brevard County/Huntsville	140
	Miller, Derek, Brevard County/Huntsville	140
^AVG	DiFelice, Mark, Huntsville/Nashville	.210

contributions, strengthening the rotation while stringing together 21 scoreless innings in September.

A thumb injury prevented the Brewers from taking a longer look at lefty Manny Parra, who bounced back from shoulder woes to re-establish himself as a top pitching prospect. During his brief stay at Triple-A Nashville before being summoned for good, Parra pitched a perfect game against Round Rock.

It was a banner year for the farm system, with Nashville, Double-A Huntsville, high Class A Brevard County, low Class A West Virginia and the Rookie-level Helena all advancing to post-season play. No championships were won but it was the best overall showing for the organization in many years.

2007 PERFORMANCE

General Manager: Doug Melvin. **Farm Director:** Reid Nichols. **Scouting Director:** Jack Zduriencik

Class	Team	League	W	L	PCT	Finish*	Manager	Affiliate Since
Majors	Milwaukee	Majors	83	79	.512	8th (16)	Ned Yost	—
Triple-A	Nashville Sounds	Pacific Coast	89	55	.618	1st (16)	Frank Kremblas	2005
Double-A	Huntsville Stars	Southern	75	62	.547	3rd (10)	Don Money	1999
High A	Brevard County Manatees	Florida State	74	62	.544	4th (12)	John Tamargo	2005
Low A	West Virginia Power	South Atlantic	82	54	.603	3rd	Mike Guerrero	2005
Rookie	Helena Brewers	Pioneer	48	28	.632	2nd (8)	Jeff Isom	2003
Rookie	AZL Brewers	Arizona	19	37	.339	9th (9)	Rene Gonzales	2001
Overall 2007 Minor League Record			**387**	**298**	**.565**	**2nd**		

* Finish in overall standings (No. of teams in league) ^League champion

ORGANIZATION STATISTICS

MILWAUKEE BREWERS

NATIONAL LEAGUE

BATTING

BATTING	B-T	HT	WT	DOB	AVG	vLH	vRH	G	AB	R	H	2B	3B	HR	RBI	BB	HBP	SH	SF	SO	SB	CS	SLG	OBP
Braun, Ryan	R-R	6-2	200	11-17-83	.324	.450	.282	113	451	91	146	26	6	34	97	29	7	0	5	112	15	5	.634	.370
Counsell, Craig	L-R	6-0	175	8-21-70	.220	.157	.234	122	282	31	62	12	2	3	24	41	3	6	2	47	4	2	.309	.323
Dillon, Joe	R-R	6-2	215	8-2-75	.342	.556	.276	39	76	12	26	8	2	0	10	5	1	0	0	14	0	0	.500	.390
Estrada, Johnny	B-R	5-11	210	6-27-76	.278	.313	.263	120	442	40	123	25	0	10	54	12	2	1	7	43	0	0	.403	.296
Fielder, Prince	L-R	6-0	260	5-9-84	.288	.261	.301	158	573	109	165	35	2	50	119	90	14	0	4	121	2	2	.618	.395
Graffanino, Tony	R-R	6-1	190	6-6-72	.238	.231	.243	86	231	34	55	8	0	9	30	24	3	0	2	44	0	1	.390	.315
Gross, Gabe	L-R	6-3	210	10-21-79	.235	.091	.244	93	183	28	43	12	2	7	24	25	1	0	1	37	3	1	.437	.329
Gwynn, Tony	L-R	6-0	190	10-4-82	.260	.316	.250	69	123	13	32	3	2	0	10	12	0	0	0	24	8	1	.317	.326
Hall, Bill	R-R	6-0	210	12-28-79	.254	.270	.247	136	452	59	115	35	0	14	63	40	3	1	7	128	4	5	.425	.315
Hardy, J.J.	R-R	6-2	190	8-19-82	.277	.316	.264	151	592	89	164	30	1	26	80	40	1	4	1	73	2	3	.463	.323
Hart, Corey	R-R	6-6	215	3-24-82	.295	.331	.278	140	505	86	149	33	9	24	81	36	13	5	7	99	23	7	.539	.353
Jenkins, Geoff	L-R	6-1	210	7-21-74	.255	.215	.262	132	420	45	107	24	2	21	64	32	9	0	3	116	2	2	.471	.319
Mench, Kevin	R-R	6-0	215	1-7-78	.267	.314	.212	101	288	39	77	20	3	8	37	16	1	0	3	21	3	1	.441	.305
Miller, Damian	R-R	6-3	220	10-13-69	.237	.235	.237	58	186	19	44	9	0	4	24	14	3	0	3	39	1	0	.349	.296
Nix, Laynce	L-L	6-0	205	10-30-80	.000	.000	.000	10	12	0	0	0	0	0	0	0	0	0	0	4	0	0	.000	.000
Rivera, Mike	R-R	6-0	220	9-8-76	.231	.500	.182	11	13	2	3	0	0	0	2	3	1	0	1	0	3	0	.692	.286
Rottino, Vinny	R-R	6-0	210	4-7-80	.222	.500	.000	8	9	0	2	1	0	0	3	0	0	0	0	1	0	0	.333	.222
Stocker, Mel	L-R	5-10	160	8-15-80	.000	.000	.000	8	0	4	0	0	0	0	0	0	0	0	0	0	0	0	.000	.000
Weeks, Rickie	R-R	6-0	205	9-13-82	.235	.258	.225	118	409	87	96	21	6	16	36	78	14	3	2	116	25	2	.433	.374

PITCHING

PITCHING	B-T	HT	WT	DOB	W	L	ERA	G	GS	CG	SV	IP	H	R	ER	HR	BB	SO	AVG	vLH	vRH	K/9	BB/9
Aquino, Greg	R-R	6-1	190	1-11-78	0	1	4.50	15	0	0	0	14	13	9	7	2	5	12	.245	.304	.200	7.71	3.21
Balfour, Grant	R-R	6-2	190	12-30-77	0	2	20.25	3	0	0	0	3	4	6	6	1	4	3	.333	.429	.200	10.12	13.50
Bush, Dave	R-R	6-2	210	11-9-79	12	10	5.12	33	31	0	0	186	217	110	106	27	44	134	.290	.246	.324	6.47	2.13
Capellan, Jose	R-R	6-4	235	1-13-81	0	2	4.50	7	0	0	0	12	13	6	6	2	6	8	.222	.143	.258	6.00	4.50
Capuano, Chris	L-L	6-2	220	8-19-78	5	12	5.10	29	25	0	0	150	170	93	85	20	54	132	.286	.259	.293	7.92	3.24
Cordero, Francisco	R-R	6-2	235	5-11-75	0	4	2.98	66	0	0	44	63	52	23	21	4	18	86	.218	.225	.212	12.22	2.56
Dessens, Elmer	R-R	5-11	200	1-13-71	1	1	6.60	12	0	0	0	15	24	16	11	3	3	12	.369	.448	.306	7.20	1.80
2-team (5 Colorado)					2	2	7.15	17	5	0	0	34	45	32	27	6	12	22	—	—	—	5.82	3.18
Gallardo, Yovani	R-R	6-1	210	2-27-86	9	5	3.67	20	17	0	0	110	103	48	45	8	37	101	.245	.247	.244	8.24	3.02
King, Ray	L-L	6-1	240	1-15-74	0	0	6.00	12	0	0	0	6	6	4	4	1	3	7	.261	.308	.200	10.50	4.50
2-team (55 Washington)					1	1	4.76	67	0	0	0	40	37	21	21	6	21	25	—	—	—	5.67	4.76
Linebrink, Scott	R-R	6-2	200	8-4-76	2	3	3.55	27	0	0	0	25	27	14	10	3	11	25	.276	.194	.313	8.88	3.91
2-team (44 San Diego)					5	6	3.71	71	0	0	1	70	68	33	29	12	25	50	—	—	—	6.40	3.20
McClung, Seth	L-R	6-6	260	2-7-81	0	1	3.75	14	0	0	0	12	11	9	5	0	5	11	.250	.313	.214	8.25	3.75
Parra, Manny	L-L	6-3	200	10-30-82	0	1	3.76	9	2	0	0	26	25	13	11	1	12	26	.255	.174	.280	8.89	4.10
Sheets, Ben	R-R	6-1	220	7-18-78	12	5	3.82	24	24	2	0	141	138	62	60	17	37	106	.253	.200	.300	6.75	2.36
Shouse, Brian	L-L	5-11	185	9-26-68	1	1	3.02	73	0	0	1	48	46	19	16	0	14	32	.257	.214	.295	6.04	2.64
Spurling, Chris	R-R	6-6	240	6-28-77	2	1	4.68	49	0	0	0	50	63	31	26	6	14	28	.303	.315	.294	5.04	2.52
Stetter, Mitch	L-L	6-4	195	1-16-81	1	0	3.60	6	0	0	0	5	2	2	2	0	2	4	.133	.222	.000	7.20	3.60
Suppan, Jeff	R-R	6-2	220	1-2-75	12	12	4.62	34	34	1	0	207	243	113	106	18	68	114	.298	.334	.271	4.96	2.96
Turnbow, Derrick	R-R	6-3	210	1-25-78	4	5	4.63	77	0	0	1	68	44	36	35	4	46	84	.183	.172	.189	11.12	6.09
Vargas, Claudio	R-R	6-3	220	6-19-78	11	6	5.09	29	23	0	1	134	153	80	76	23	54	107	.285	.320	.255	7.17	3.62
Villanueva, Carlos	R-R	6-3	215	11-28-83	8	5	3.94	59	6	0	1	114	101	52	50	16	53	99	.236	.250	.227	7.79	4.17
Wise, Matt	R-R	6-4	195	11-18-75	3	2	4.19	56	0	0	1	54	61	30	25	5	17	43	.285	.264	.296	7.21	2.85

FIELDING

Catcher	PCT	G	PO	A	E	DP	PB
Estrada	.993	113	803	37	6	6	5
Miller	.997	56	359	28	1	2	1
Rivera	1.000	11	33	2	0	0	0

First Base	PCT	G	PO	A	E	DP
Dillon	1.000	5	25	2	0	5
Fielder	.989	153	1163	99	14	115
Graffanino	1.000	9	64	6	0	7
Miller	.800	1	4	0	1	0
Rottino	1.000	1	4	0	0	1

Second Base	PCT	G	PO	A	E	DP
Counsell	.991	24	46	61	1	14
Dillon	1.000	3	10	6	0	2
Graffanino	.993	30	65	69	1	23
Weeks	.976	115	232	286	13	73

Third Base	PCT	G	PO	A	E	DP
Braun	.895	112	61	161	26	12
Counsell	1.000	50	21	73	0	10
Dillon	1.000	3	1	2	0	1
Graffanino	.973	23	28	43	2	3

Shortstop	PCT	G	PO	A	E	DP
Counsell	.987	27	20	55	1	14
Graffanino	—	1	0	0	0	0
Hardy	.978	149	168	397	13	83

Outfield	PCT	G	PO	A	E	DP
Dillon	1.000	9	13	1	0	0
Graffanino	1.000	3	7	0	0	0
Gross	.976	52	79	3	2	1
Gwynn	.980	39	49	1	1	0
Hall	.971	130	295	5	9	0
Hart	.991	128	324	4	3	0
Jenkins	.988	121	242	7	3	2
Mench	.983	78	111	6	2	2
Nix	1.000	5	1	0	0	0
Rottino	—	1	0	0	0	0
Stocker	1.000	6	3	0	0	0

PACIFIC COAST LEAGUE

BATTING	B-T	HT	WT	DOB	AVG	vLH	vRH	G	AB	R	H	2B	3B	HR	RBI	BB	HBP	SH	SF	SO	SB	CS	SLG	OBP
Abad, Andy	L-L	6-0	210	8-25-72	.316	.329	.312	83	269	49	85	12	0	12	59	24	1	1	5	35	6	2	.494	.368
Anderson, Drew	L-R	6-2	200	6-9-81	.273	.250	.280	108	377	57	103	28	3	4	36	28	2	5	3	89	16	5	.395	.324
Barnwell, Chris	R-R	5-10	180	3-1-79	.268	.345	.232	128	456	70	122	24	3	8	39	34	10	2	2	71	13	4	.386	.331
Braun, Ryan	R-R	6-2	200	11-17-83	.342	.516	.279	34	117	28	40	12	0	10	22	15	1	0	1	11	4	3	.701	.418
Chavez, Ozzie	B-R	6-1	160	7-13-83	.258	.258	.258	101	306	35	79	13	3	4	32	38	1	4	2	53	4	8	.359	.340
Closser, JD	B-R	5-10	200	1-15-80	.188	.167	.200	17	48	9	9	2	0	2	6	11	0	0	2	10	3	1	.354	.328
2-team (81 Sacramento)					.231	—	—	98	334	54	77	18	2	13	51	59	0	2	4	77	3	3	.413	.343
Crabbe, Callix	B-R	5-7	171	2-14-83	.287	.299	.281	130	457	84	131	23	9	9	38	67	3	8	6	70	17	14	.435	.377
Dillon, Joe	R-R	6-2	215	8-2-75	.317	.295	.325	94	319	69	101	28	2	20	73	50	2	0	7	34	6	1	.605	.405
Gross, Gabe	L-R	6-3	210	10-21-79	.355	.290	.400	20	76	13	27	3	2	4	10	14	0	0	0	14	2	0	.605	.456
Gwynn, Tony	L-R	6-0	190	10-4-82	.286	.353	.240	32	126	19	36	3	3	0	13	9	1	1	1	14	4	3	.357	.336
Hopf, J.R.	L-R	6-1	205	11-4-82	.273	.333	.250	7	22	3	6	0	0	2	2	1	0	0	0	6	0	0	.545	.304
Macias, Jose	B-R	5-8	190	1-25-72	.242	.196	.264	107	285	25	69	11	3	2	32	11	3	12	2	47	4	2	.323	.276
Nelson, Brad	L-R	6-2	220	12-23-82	.263	.225	.273	116	411	54	108	23	1	20	65	31	2	0	1	98	9	6	.470	.317
Nix, Laynce	L-L	6-0	205	10-30-80	.268	.267	.268	95	347	60	93	20	1	24	74	31	3	0	5	104	5	0	.539	.329
Rivera, Mike	R-R	6-2	220	9-8-76	.215	.236	.205	96	349	37	75	15	0	19	61	24	4	0	5	71	5	5	.421	.270
Rottino, Vinny	R-R	6-0	210	4-7-80	.289	.257	.303	107	377	59	109	17	3	12	53	37	9	3	4	58	15	9	.446	.363
Thomas, Charles	L-L	6-0	220	12-26-78	.233	.225	.235	69	189	25	44	10	0	3	20	18	0	3	2	44	6	1	.333	.297
2-team (22 Sacramento)					.232	—	—	91	263	32	61	12	0	3	25	24	1	3	2	59	8	1	.312	.297
Weeks, Rickie	R-R	6-0	205	9-13-82	.455	.500	.333	6	22	5	10	3	1	0	3	1	0	3	5	1	0	6	1	2	.682	.571

PITCHING	B-T	HT	WT	DOB	W	L	ERA	G	GS	CG	SV	IP	H	R	ER	HR	BB	SO	AVG	vLH	vRH	K/9	BB/9
Abad, Andy	L-L	6-0	210	8-25-72	0	0	0.00	1	0	0	0	1	1	0	0	0	0	1	.333	.000	.500	13.50	0.00
Aquino, Greg	R-R	6-1	190	1-11-78	3	2	2.33	35	0	0	7	39	26	12	10	2	19	45	.193	.161	.215	10.47	4.42
Balfour, Grant	R-R	6-2	190	12-30-77	1	1	1.69	24	0	0	5	32	17	6	6	2	11	47	.157	.186	.138	13.22	3.09
Barnwell, Chris	R-R	5-10	180	3-1-79	0	0	3.00	2	0	0	3	2	1	1	0	1	0	1	.182	.167	.200	3.00	3.00
Bray, Steve	R-R	6-1	193	12-22-80	5	2	1.62	42	3	0	1	78	59	15	14	4	26	73	.211	.211	.212	8.46	3.01
Capellan, Jose	R-R	6-4	235	1-13-81	3	2	3.86	17	3	0	1	28	23	15	12	1	14	22	.223	.238	.213	7.07	4.50
Dessens, Elmer	R-R	5-11	200	1-13-71	1	0	1.54	3	3	0	0	12	7	2	2	0	0	10	.167	.238	.095	7.71	0.00
2-team (1 Colorado Springs)					2	0	1.23	4	3	0	0	15	8	2	2	0	1	11	—	—	—	6.75	0.61
Dickey, R.A.	R-R	6-3	220	10-29-74	13	6	3.72	31	22	3	0	169	159	80	70	18	60	119	.252	.227	.271	6.32	3.19
DiFelice, Mark	R-R	6-2	190	8-23-76	4	2	3.10	10	10	0	0	58	45	21	20	6	9	63	.212	.222	.206	9.78	1.40
Dillard, Tim	B-R	6-4	215	7-19-83	8	4	4.74	34	16	1	0	133	167	72	70	13	37	62	.316	.323	.310	4.20	2.50
Gallardo, Yovani	R-R	6-1	210	2-27-86	8	3	2.90	13	13	0	0	78	53	26	25	4	28	110	.189	.189	.189	12.75	3.24
Ginter, Matt	R-R	6-1	220	12-24-77	0	0	40.50	1	0	0	0	1	2	3	3	0	2	0	.500	.500	.500	0.00	27.00
2-team (31 Memphis)					2	6	4.41	32	8	0	2	69	88	42	34	5	10	43	—	—	—	5.58	1.30
Gulin, Lindsay	L-L	6-2	175	11-2-76	0	0	5.68	3	1	0	0	6	9	4	4	1	3	4	.346	.545	.200	5.68	4.26
Hackman, Luther	R-R	6-4	195	10-6-74	1	2	3.61	41	0	0	18	42	33	17	17	4	22	37	.214	.232	.204	7.87	4.68
2-team (4 Oklahoma)					1	3	3.50	45	0	0	18	46	36	18	18	4	25	39	—	—	—	7.58	4.86
Jackson, Zach	L-L	6-5	220	5-13-83	11	10	4.46	29	28	1	0	170	184	95	84	13	64	123	.284	.234	.299	6.52	3.39
McClung, Seth	L-R	6-6	260	2-7-81	2	0	1.42	5	3	0	0	19	14	3	3	2	5	25	.206	.118	.294	11.84	2.37
Nunez, Franklin	R-R	6-0	175	1-18-77	0	0	4.50	2	0	0	1	2	3	1	1	0	2	2	.375	.500	.333	9.00	9.00
Oxspring, Chris	L-R	6-1	195	5-13-77	7	5	3.56	18	18	0	0	96	90	40	38	9	43	106	.248	.223	.267	9.94	4.03
Parra, Manny	L-L	6-3	200	10-30-82	3	1	1.73	4	4	1	0	26	15	6	5	1	7	25	.172	.273	.138	8.65	2.42
Pettyjohn, Adam	R-L	6-3	190	6-11-77	12	4	3.87	17	17	1	0	105	99	50	45	19	19	83	.243	.212	.256	7.14	1.63
Ray, Ken	R-R	6-3	215	11-27-74	0	0	0.00	2	0	0	1	2	0	0	0	0	0	3	.000	.000	.000	11.57	0.00
2-team (35 Omaha)					3	4	4.00	37	0	0	3	63	64	29	28	8	32	61	—	—	—	8.71	4.57
Salas, Marino	R-R	6-0	185	10-2-81	0	1	4.94	14	0	0	0	24	27	13	13	7	8	25	.278	.190	.345	9.51	3.04
Sarfate, Dennis	R-R	6-4	225	4-9-81	2	7	4.52	45	1	0	4	62	61	35	31	6	47	68	.270	.278	.265	9.92	6.86
Spurling, Chris	R-R	6-6	240	6-28-77	2	0	1.69	10	0	0	0	16	19	4	3	1	2	9	.292	.194	.382	5.06	1.12
Stetter, Mitch	L-L	6-4	195	1-16-81	1	0	4.30	24	0	0	1	15	8	7	7	1	5	19	.167	.108	.364	11.66	3.07
Thatcher, Joe	L-L	6-2	230	10-4-81	2	1	2.08	24	0	0	1	22	19	5	5	0	7	33	.226	.209	.244	13.71	2.91
2-team (8 Portland)					3	1	1.78	32	0	0	1	30	29	9	6	0	8	44	—	—	—	13.05	2.37
Villanueva, Carlos	R-R	6-3	215	11-28-83	0	0	3.24	2	2	0	0	8	3	3	3	1	1	9	.107	.077	.133	9.72	1.08
Villarreal, Luis	L-L	6-1	215	12-20-79	0	0	1.93	6	0	0	0	5	5	1	1	0	1	4	.313	.286	.333	7.71	1.93
Zumwalt, Alec	R-R	6-2	195	1-20-81	0	2	4.43	14	0	0	1	20	21	10	10	3	9	20	.280	.345	.239	8.85	3.98
2-team (20 Sacramento)					0	5	5.98	34	1	0	1	53	60	35	35	9	26	49	—	—	—	8.37	4.44

FIELDING

Catcher	PCT	G	PO	A	E	DP	PB
Closser	.991	13	102	4	1	1	4
Hopf	1.000	2	15	1	0	0	0
Rivera	.997	74	588	35	2	3	9
Rottino	.986	57	454	35	7	1	8

First Base	PCT	G	PO	A	E	DP
Abad	.996	56	440	35	2	41
Barnwell	—	1	0	0	0	0
Closser	1.000	1	9	2	0	0
Dillon	.989	10	81	6	1	6
Macias	1.000	2	2	0	0	0
Nelson	.996	56	445	33	2	53
Rivera	.993	17	140	11	1	14
Rottino	.990	13	93	5	1	5

Second Base	PCT	G	PO	A	E	DP
Barnwell	.967	16	26	62	3	15
Chavez	.993	38	56	93	1	20

	PCT	G	PO	A	E	DP
Crabbe	.992	83	158	227	3	50
Dillon	1.000	2	4	5	0	2
Macias	1.000	14	17	25	0	9
Weeks	1.000	3	7	7	0	1

Third Base	PCT	G	PO	A	E	DP
Barnwell	.923	13	11	13	2	3
Braun	.954	32	15	47	3	8
Chavez	1.000	11	9	20	0	2
Crabbe	1.000	2	3	4	0	0
Dillon	.962	54	39	113	6	8
Macias	.971	18	9	24	1	3
Nelson	.946	17	7	28	2	2
Rivera	.857	2	0	6	1	1
Rottino	.955	9	6	15	1	2

Shortstop	PCT	G	PO	A	E	DP
Barnwell	.978	96	136	256	9	53
Chavez	.950	49	58	132	10	28

Outfield	PCT	G	PO	A	E	DP
Abad	1.000	4	3	0	0	0
Anderson	.994	98	163	4	1	2
Crabbe	.988	38	80	2	1	0
Dillon	.960	17	24	0	1	0
Gross	.925	20	36	1	3	0
Gwynn	.986	32	73	0	1	0
Macias	.973	46	70	3	2	0
Nelson	1.000	29	36	0	0	0
Nix	.994	83	164	7	1	4
Rottino	.982	32	54	1	1	0
Thomas	.970	59	94	4	3	1

SOUTHERN LEAGUE

BATTING	B-T	HT	WT	DOB	AVG	vLH	vRH	G	AB	R	H	2B	3B	HR	RBI	BB	HBP	SH	SF	SO	SB	CS	SLG	OBP
Anderson, Drew	L-R	6-2	200	6-9-81	.444	.222	.500	12	45	12	20	7	2	1	11	0	0	1	0	10	1	3	.756	.444
Brantley, Michael	L-L	6-2	180	5-15-87	.251	.208	.258	59	187	28	47	6	1	0	21	29	1	5	1	25	17	3	.294	.353
Carlin, Michael	R-R	6-0	205	7-6-81	.215	.133	.286	24	65	9	14	5	0	1	7	13	2	0	3	17	1	0	.338	.349
Corporan, Carlos	B-R	6-3	210	1-7-84	.201	.176	.211	56	179	18	36	14	0	2	24	8	8	2	48	1	0	.313	.264
Crew, Ryan	R-R	6-0	175	8-31-83	.255	.279	.237	56	137	20	35	6	0	0	14	15	0	2	0	22	3	0	.299	.329
Davenport, Ron	L-R	6-2	190	10-16-81	.197	.235	.182	24	61	5	12	5	1	0	6	6	1	0	0	10	0	0	.311	.279
Escobar, Alcides	R-R	6-1	155	12-16-86	.283	.355	.256	62	226	27	64	5	4	1	28	11	0	6	2	36	4	3	.354	.314
Eure, Jeffrey	R-R	6-1	215	8-17-80	.181	.111	.222	23	72	5	13	2	1	0	7	6	3	0	0	25	0	0	.236	.272
Goetz, Mike	L-R	5-10	180	7-22-84	.000	.000	.000	1	4	0	0	0	0	0	0	0	0	0	0	0	0	0	.000	.000
Heether, Adam	R-R	6-0	190	1-14-82	.299	.355	.277	120	432	60	129	27	5	9	62	51	1	3	4	89	2	6	.447	.371
Iribarren, Hernan	L-R	6-1	180	6-29-84	.307	.208	.340	124	479	72	147	23	12	4	53	44	1	13	5	109	18	16	.430	.363
Katin, Brendan	R-R	6-1	235	1-28-83	.258	.250	.261	128	450	72	116	24	0	24	94	41	10	1	6	163	3	2	.471	.329
Mateo, Ruben	R-R	6-0	210	2-10-78	.241	.240	.241	24	83	14	20	2	0	5	15	13	6	0	1	26	1	1	.446	.379
Moss, Steve	R-R	6-2	185	1-12-84	.233	.287	.205	124	443	56	103	21	5	11	56	69	3	5	2	124	12	5	.377	.338
Nix, Laynce	L-L	6-0	205	10-30-80	.364	.000	.400	4	11	2	4	1	0	1	6	1	0	0	0	2	0	0	.727	.417
Palmisano, Lou	R-R	6-0	200	9-16-82	.256	.275	.248	103	351	49	90	22	1	11	63	57	8	0	5	80	8	2	.419	.368
Perez, Yohannis	R-R	6-0	190	10-11-82	.195	.197	.194	56	190	19	37	4	2	0	16	16	1	4	1	55	2	3	.237	.260
Rodriguez, Guilder	B-R	6-1	160	7-24-83	.303	.290	.310	59	175	28	53	1	0	0	16	23	0	7	1	27	8	5	.309	.382
Sollmann, Steve	R-R	5-11	195	4-1-82	.283	.303	.273	125	445	78	126	26	3	3	51	61	25	9	6	63	22	6	.375	.395
St. Pierre, Max	R-R	6-0	175	4-17-80	.156	.118	.200	10	32	3	5	0	0	0	3	4	0	0	1	3	0	0	.156	.243
Stocker, Mel	L-R	5-10	160	8-15-80	.255	.220	.264	112	267	56	68	8	10	3	23	27	6	6	2	50	35	6	.360	.334

PITCHING	B-T	HT	WT	DOB	W	L	ERA	G	GS	CG	SV	IP	H	R	ER	HR	BB	SO	AVG	vLH	vRH	K/9	BB/9
Balfour, Grant	R-R	6-2	190	12-30-77	0	0	2.38	8	0	0	2	11	8	3	3	0	4	21	.190	.250	.154	16.68	3.18
Crew, Ryan	R-R	6-0	175	8-31-83	0	0	0.00	3	0	0	0	3	1	0	0	0	2	5	.100	.000	.143	15.00	6.00
DiFelice, Mark	R-R	6-2	190	8-23-76	6	1	1.62	26	3	0	0	67	50	12	12	3	6	60	.207	.250	.179	8.10	0.81
Eure, Jeffrey	R-R	6-1	215	8-17-80	0	0	0.00	1	0	0	0	1	0	0	0	0	1	1	.000	.000	.000	9.00	9.00
Gulin, Lindsay	L-L	6-2	175	11-2-76	12	6	3.29	21	21	0	0	123	102	49	45	15	44	117	.226	.269	.213	8.56	3.22
Hall, Bo	R-R	6-0	187	9-5-80	5	2	3.46	34	0	0	1	55	41	22	21	6	36	56	.204	.174	.220	9.22	5.93
Hammond, Steve	R-L	6-2	205	4-30-82	7	9	4.69	29	26	2	1	142	163	85	74	19	43	109	.292	.304	.287	6.91	2.73
Hinton, Robert	R-R	6-2	190	8-13-84	2	3	5.94	39	0	0	2	53	50	36	35	4	27	44	.245	.224	.261	7.47	4.58
Housman, Jeff	L-L	6-3	180	8-4-81	3	2	5.36	32	0	0	0	40	48	24	24	3	29	28	.312	.222	.349	6.25	6.47
Inman, William	R-R	6-0	200	2-6-87	1	5	5.45	8	8	0	0	40	38	24	24	7	16	42	.259	.250	.265	9.53	3.63
Johnson, Dave	R-R	6-5	205	8-25-82	1	1	4.75	26	0	0	4	42	35	23	22	5	18	46	.236	.232	.239	9.94	3.89
Jones, Mike	R-R	6-4	220	4-23-83	2	2	5.08	6	6	0	0	28	34	21	16	2	12	16	.304	.316	.291	5.08	3.81
Miller, Derek	L-L	6-0	195	11-8-81	6	2	3.18	11	11	0	0	68	58	28	24	10	16	65	.233	.150	.259	8.60	2.12
Narron, Sam	L-L	6-7	200	7-12-81	7	9	4.21	27	26	1	0	152	176	78	71	11	26	95	.296	.264	.308	5.64	1.54
Parra, Manny	L-L	6-5	200	10-30-82	7	3	2.68	13	13	0	0	81	70	28	24	2	26	81	.234	.171	.256	9.04	2.90
Pena, Luis	R-R	6-5	200	1-10-83	0	4	2.89	35	0	0	12	47	36	15	15	1	14	42	.211	.246	.189	8.10	2.70
Perkins, Vince	L-R	6-5	240	9-27-81	1	2	9.39	12	0	0	0	15	23	19	16	2	16	21	.333	.393	.293	12.33	9.39
Pettyjohn, Adam	R-L	6-3	190	6-11-77	4	2	4.45	11	11	0	0	57	61	31	28	5	15	54	.271	.232	.284	8.58	2.38
Salas, Marino	R-R	6-0	185	10-2-81	0	0	1.42	37	0	0	17	38	25	7	6	2	14	29	.189	.216	.173	6.87	3.32
Shanks, E.J.	R-R	6-5	230	4-8-82	4	0	4.91	12	0	0	0	15	15	9	8	1	9	9	.288	.320	.259	5.52	5.52
Stetter, Mitch	L-L	6-4	195	1-16-81	0	0	0.00	2	0	0	0	1	0	0	0	0	2	4	.000	.000	.000	18.00	9.00
Thatcher, Joe	L-L	6-2	230	10-4-81	1	0	0.55	14	0	0	0	16	11	1	1	0	2	20	.193	.231	.161	11.02	1.10
Thurman, Corey	R-R	6-2	235	11-5-78	5	8	4.36	30	12	0	0	95	81	54	46	18	29	89	.231	.208	.250	8.43	2.75
Villarreal, Luis	L-L	6-1	215	12-20-79	1	1	6.75	8	0	0	0	11	12	8	5	1	5	10	.293	.273	.316	8.44	4.22

FIELDING

Catcher	PCT	G	PO	A	E	DP	PB
Corporan	.996	33	254	24	1	2	2
Palmisano	.995	98	744	50	4	7	2
St. Pierre	1.000	9	71	6	0	0	0

First Base	PCT	G	PO	A	E	DP
Brantley	1.000	2	11	0	0	1
Carlin	1.000	2	17	0	0	0
Corporan	.995	19	174	9	1	18
Crew	1.000	1	10	0	0	0
Eure	1.000	4	22	0	0	2
Rodriguez	1.000	2	21	0	0	1
Sollmann	.996	109	926	74	4	83

Second Base	PCT	G	PO	A	E	DP
Crew	1.000	1	4	3	0	0
Iribarren	.973	119	214	299	14	71

	PCT	G	PO	A	E	DP
Rodriguez	.964	18	33	47	3	11
Sollmann	1.000	1	2	2	0	0
Third Base	PCT	G	PO	A	E	DP
Eure	.886	16	9	22	4	1
Heether	.940	118	59	252	20	20
Rodriguez	.800	5	1	3	1	0
Sollmann	.857	5	1	11	2	1
Shortstop	PCT	G	PO	A	E	DP
Crew	1.000	1	1	1	0	0
Escobar	.981	61	106	155	5	35
Perez	.962	55	69	157	9	31
Rodriguez	.965	26	35	76	4	14
Outfield	PCT	G	PO	A	E	DP
Anderson	.909	10	10	0	1	0
Brantley	.988	51	81	2	1	1

	PCT	G	PO	A	E	DP
Carlin	1.000	12	18	2	0	2
Crew	1.000	21	26	1	0	0
Davenport	.929	14	12	1	1	0
Eure	1.000	1	1	0	0	0
Goetz	1.000	1	2	0	0	0
Iribarren	1.000	1	3	0	0	0
Katin	.941	111	187	4	12	0
Mateo	1.000	17	27	0	0	0
Moss	.992	120	244	1	2	0
Nix	.833	4	5	0	1	0
Rodriguez	—	1	0	0	0	0
Stocker	.987	90	148	4	2	0

FLORIDA STATE LEAGUE

BATTING	B-T	HT	WT	DOB	AVG	vLH	vRH	G	AB	R	H	2B	3B	HR	RBI	BB	HBP	SH	SF	SO	SB	CS	SLG	OBP
Barba, Ryan	R-R	6-0	190	12-6-84	.241	.167	.257	46	137	14	33	3	1	1	16	7	3	3	0	30	1	1	.299	.293
Bell, Mike	R-R	6-0	185	3-30-85	.257	.295	.247	120	436	67	112	17	2	13	71	26	12	4	9	74	8	4	.394	.311
Cain, Lorenzo	R-R	6-2	185	4-13-86	.276	.290	.272	126	482	67	133	21	3	2	44	37	9	4	1	97	24	9	.344	.338
Corporan, Carlos	B-R	6-3	210	1-7-84	.363	.304	.386	23	80	11	29	8	0	3	19	2	3	3	0	9	0	1	.575	.400
Corredor, Nestor	R-R	6-1	240	5-25-84	.169	.162	.171	60	177	12	30	4	0	1	15	8	0	6	1	29	0	0	.209	.204
Crew, Ryan	R-R	6-0	175	8-31-83	.250	.267	.244	33	108	12	27	7	0	1	11	12	0	3	3	18	3	1	.343	.317
De La Rosa, Anderson	R-R	6-0	190	8-1-84	.316	.200	.344	24	76	11	24	2	2	0	7	3	2	0	16	1	3	.395	.366
Errecart, Chris	R-L	6-1	210	2-11-85	.262	.306	.251	116	424	63	111	23	1	10	55	33	13	0	4	91	1	3	.392	.331
Escobar, Alcides	R-R	6-1	155	12-16-86	.325	.396	.309	63	268	37	87	8	3	0	25	7	3	2	3	35	18	10	.377	.345

	B-T	HT	WT	DOB	AVG	vLH	vRH	G	AB	R	H	2B	3B	HR	RBI	BB	HBP	SH	SF	SO	SB	CS	SLG	OBP
Fermaint, Charlie	R-R	5-9	180	10-11-85	.210	.225	.205	47	167	12	35	3	1	2	17	6	0	0	1	40	7	2	.275	.236
Ford, Darren	R-R	6-1	195	10-1-85	.231	.306	.214	72	273	46	63	7	1	4	27	35	1	5	3	67	36	6	.308	.317
Gamel, Mat	L-R	6-0	205	7-26-85	.300	.283	.305	128	466	78	140	37	8	9	60	58	3	2	5	98	14	7	.472	.378
Gillespie, Cole	R-R	6-1	205	6-20-84	.267	.253	.271	129	438	75	117	25	3	12	62	72	8	1	3	95	16	8	.420	.378
Hopf, J.R.	L-R	6-1	205	11-4-82	.219	.000	.238	50	137	14	30	5	2	3	15	17	0	0	0	43	1	0	.350	.305
Parejo, Freddy	R-R	6-2	175	10-16-84	.219	.195	.225	69	201	28	44	11	0	3	18	14	3	2	1	46	8	3	.318	.279
Perez, Yohannis	R-R	6-0	190	10-11-82	.287	.220	.302	62	223	26	64	7	1	1	33	14	4	1	2	34	6	2	.341	.337
Salome, Angel	R-R	5-7	195	6-8-86	.318	.365	.306	68	258	33	82	20	0	6	53	12	0	0	6	32	1	0	.465	.341
Yost IV, Ned	R-R	6-2	195	7-8-82	.248	.222	.260	47	145	12	36	5	0	0	17	23	0	2	0	54	1	0	.283	.351

PITCHING	B-T	HT	WT	DOB	W	L	ERA	G	GS	CG	SV	IP	H	R	ER	HR	BB	SO	AVG	vLH	vRH	K/9	BB/9
Baker, Joshua	R-R	6-5	220	4-2-82	0	2	15.19	4	1	0	0	5	7	9	9	0	10	4	.350	.333	.357	6.75	16.88
Cody, Christopher	L-L	6-0	180	1-7-84	2	1	3.60	5	5	0	0	20	18	8	8	2	6	23	.237	.333	.200	10.35	2.70
2-team (2 Lakeland)					2	2	4.15	7	7	0	0	26	26	12	12	2	8	26	—	—	—	9.00	2.77
Garrison, Steve	B-L	6-1	185	9-12-86	8	4	3.44	20	20	1	0	105	105	58	40	6	28	74	.253	.266	.249	6.36	2.41
Harper, Jesse	R-R	6-4	210	11-11-80	2	3	5.91	9	7	0	0	35	38	26	23	5	10	23	.277	.210	.333	5.91	2.57
Hinton, Robert	R-R	6-2	190	8-13-84	0	0	4.38	5	2	0	0	12	20	6	6	1	2	7	.377	.406	.333	5.11	1.46
Inman, William	R-R	6-0	200	2-6-87	4	3	1.72	13	13	0	0	79	56	17	15	4	23	98	.198	.164	.231	11.21	2.63
Johnson, Dave	R-R	6-5	205	8-25-82	2	0	2.36	19	0	0	4	27	17	7	7	3	6	26	.175	.171	.179	8.78	2.02
Lewis, Jeremy	R-L	6-4	180	9-12-80	0	1	6.45	16	0	0	1	22	27	18	16	1	9	16	.290	.206	.339	6.45	3.63
2-team (12 Lakeland)					0	3	4.50	28	0	0	1	40	37	22	20	2	14	32	—	—	—	7.20	3.15
Lluberes, Rafael	L-L	6-4	155	9-21-84	6	10	4.02	28	23	1	1	116	118	68	52	8	69	92	.263	.294	.250	7.12	5.34
Marksbury, Mike	R-R	6-2	210	2-26-82	2	0	9.88	13	0	0	0	14	18	15	15	1	12	16	.321	.227	.382	10.54	7.90
McClendon, Mike	R-R	6-5	215	4-3-85	5	6	4.23	16	14	2	1	89	108	52	42	6	19	46	.293	.326	.257	4.63	1.91
Miller, Derek	L-L	6-0	195	11-8-81	4	4	3.71	17	17	0	0	95	89	52	39	10	25	75	.240	.302	.221	7.13	2.38
Pena, Luis	R-R	6-5	200	1-10-83	5	0	2.08	16	0	0	6	22	14	5	5	1	7	27	.184	.139	.225	11.22	2.91
Perkins, Vince	L-R	6-5	240	9-27-81	1	2	7.32	23	2	0	1	39	39	34	32	3	27	34	.255	.221	.282	7.78	6.18
Roberts, Kevin	R-R	6-0	185	5-15-84	6	3	3.44	45	0	0	4	65	51	32	25	6	37	74	.207	.170	.233	10.19	5.10
Ryan, Patrick	R-R	6-0	200	5-31-83	3	3	1.75	34	0	0	5	51	37	10	10	2	14	45	.204	.193	.214	7.89	2.45
Shanks, E.J.	R-R	6-5	230	4-8-82	1	1	1.10	16	0	0	0	16	16	4	2	0	8	7	.237	.265	.200	3.86	4.41
Stanczyk, Ben	R-R	6-2	210	9-26-82	7	4	3.55	43	4	0	3	79	69	43	31	7	32	71	.234	.281	.204	8.12	3.66
Tucker, Rusty	R-L	6-1	190	7-15-80	0	0	3.52	12	0	0	1	15	17	7	6	0	8	10	.274	.182	.325	5.87	4.70
Wahpepah, Joshua	R-R	6-4	185	7-17-84	9	5	3.26	41	2	0	2	77	77	36	28	2	32	48	.263	.228	.285	5.59	3.72
Welch, David	R-L	6-4	215	6-2-87	6	7	3.43	29	20	1	0	121	141	55	46	13	21	87	.243	.273	.229	6.49	1.57
Wendte, Travis	R-R	6-2	195	11-17-82	1	1	2.70	11	0	0	0	23	23	11	7	2	9	13	.261	.250	.268	5.01	3.47
Wright, Brae	L-L	6-4	205	11-1-83	0	2	2.84	7	6	0	0	38	27	15	12	2	9	20	.194	.071	.225	4.74	2.13

FIELDING

Catcher	PCT	G	PO	A	E	DP	PB
Barba	1.000	1	1	0	0	0	0
Corporan	.978	13	77	12	2	0	0
Corredor	.994	59	417	50	3	1	11
De La Rosa	.987	24	137	19	2	1	6
Hopf	.959	14	64	6	3	1	0
Salome	.976	39	235	11	6	2	9

First Base	PCT	G	PO	A	E	DP
Corporan	.889	1	8	0	1	1
Crew	1.000	1	1	0	0	0
Errecart	.989	110	933	68	11	77
Hopf	1.000	7	40	1	0	8

	PCT	G	PO	A	E	DP
Yost IV	.964	23	180	7	7	8

Second Base	PCT	G	PO	A	E	DP
Barba	.972	5	16	19	1	6
Bell	.969	114	241	330	18	66
Crew	.974	16	37	38	2	6

Third Base	PCT	G	PO	A	E	DP
Barba	.968	15	7	23	1	0
Crew	.862	11	3	22	4	4
Gamel	.826	113	53	199	53	15

Shortstop	PCT	G	PO	A	E	DP
Barba	.877	15	15	35	7	5

	PCT	G	PO	A	E	DP
Crew	1.000	2	3	8	0	1
Escobar	.944	60	86	184	16	25
Perez	.969	62	73	205	9	37

Outfield	PCT	G	PO	A	E	DP
Cain	.976	119	274	10	7	5
Crew	1.000	2	3	0	0	0
Fermaint	.961	44	95	4	4	0
Ford	.950	70	151	2	8	0
Gillespie	.985	122	191	12	3	1
Parejo	.976	55	80	3	2	0

WEST VIRGINIA POWER　　　LOW CLASS A

SOUTH ATLANTIC LEAGUE

BATTING	B-T	HT	WT	DOB	AVG	vLH	vRH	G	AB	R	H	2B	3B	HR	RBI	BB	HBP	SH	SF	SO	SB	CS	SLG	OBP
Alonso, John	R-R	6-0	215	2-19-86	.280	.286	.277	74	261	38	73	27	1	6	59	17	4	0	0	52	2	1	.460	.333
Bouchie, Andy	R-R	6-1	205	8-6-85	.216	.225	.213	82	296	40	64	17	2	7	46	27	2	2	1	66	0	1	.358	.285
Brantley, Michael	L-L	6-2	180	5-15-87	.335	.329	.338	56	218	41	73	15	1	2	32	31	1	1	4	22	18	6	.440	.413
Brewer, Brent	R-R	6-2	190	12-19-87	.251	.211	.263	127	518	86	130	25	7	11	49	46	5	3	5	170	42	7	.390	.315
Caufield, Chuck	R-R	6-1	180	7-6-83	.285	.315	.276	132	522	100	149	32	6	7	84	41	18	1	10	80	17	5	.410	.352
Chapman, Stephen	L-L	6-0	180	10-12-85	.262	.175	.285	126	455	77	119	25	6	24	89	36	10	5	5	137	12	3	.501	.326
De La Rosa, Anderson	R-R	6-0	190	8-1-84	.208	.000	.263	10	24	3	5	1	1	0	7	1	0	0	1	7	3	0	.333	.231
Fermaint, Charlie	R-R	5-9	180	10-11-85	.248	.238	.250	75	294	43	73	10	1	3	20	26	3	3	3	68	20	10	.320	.313
Ford, Darren	R-R	6-1	195	10-1-85	.335	.356	.325	51	224	48	75	15	4	5	33	23	1	5	1	56	31	10	.504	.398
Green, Taylor	L-R	5-10	180	11-24-86	.327	.325	.328	111	397	68	130	29	2	14	86	51	5	2	5	65	0	5	.516	.406
Holmberg, Kenneth	R-R	5-9	175	2-21-83	.278	.228	.293	116	403	72	112	22	0	15	76	70	6	2	8	77	5	4	.444	.386
LaPorta, Matt	R-R	6-2	210	1-8-85	.318	.200	.342	23	88	18	28	8	0	10	27	7	5	0	2	22	0	1	.750	.392
Lefave, Andrew	L-L	5-10	205	4-24-86	.345	.313	.353	112	423	90	146	25	0	17	79	50	10	0	6	59	12	5	.525	.432
Maldonado, Martin	R-R	6-1	190	8-16-86	.221	.261	.210	66	208	20	46	8	0	2	22	14	13	6	1	36	2	0	.288	.309
Miller, Brad	R-R	6-0	185	12-11-85	.231	.231	.231	35	117	16	27	6	0	2	8	11	3	1	0	38	4	2	.333	.313
Mojica, Jimmy	R-R	5-11	170	11-3-83	.289	.239	.307	84	263	44	76	13	3	3	28	21	5	5	2	47	16	3	.395	.351
Wycklendt, Anthony	R-R	6-2	220	4-4-84	.000	.000	.000	2	6	0	0	0	0	0	1	0	0	0	3	0	0	.000	.143

PITCHING	B-T	HT	WT	DOB	W	L	ERA	G	GS	CG	SV	IP	H	R	ER	HR	BB	SO	AVG	vLH	vRH	K/9	BB/9
Aguilar, Omar	R-R	6-0	220	3-31-85	7	4	4.81	42	0	0	9	58	51	33	31	1	36	68	.241	.291	.206	10.55	5.59
Baron, Casey	L-L	6-2	185	11-29-84	0	0	1.80	3	0	0	0	5	4	1	1	1	0	3	.222	—	.222	5.40	0.00
Braddock, Zach	L-L	6-4	230	8-23-87	3	1	1.15	10	9	0	0	47	28	6	6	1	15	68	.168	.192	.163	13.02	2.87
Bramhall, Bobby	L-L	5-10	170	7-13-85	0	0	9.00	1	0	0	0	2	2	2	2	1	0	4	.250	.500	.167	18.00	0.00
Ferguson, Shawn	R-R	6-2	205	1-12-83	5	1	3.08	20	5	0	1	61	54	27	21	5	20	53	.234	.247	.224	7.78	2.93
Hand, Donovan	R-R	6-4	190	4-20-86	1	2	2.16	10	3	0	4	25	32	7	6	1	6	18	.311	.351	.288	6.12	0.00
Jeffress, Jeremy	R-R	6-0	175	9-21-87	9	5	3.13	18	18	0	0	86	62	43	30	8	44	95	.201	.205	.199	9.90	4.59
King, J.T.	R-R	6-2	210	1-25-85	8	2	4.67	31	2	0	3	62	64	34	32	6	26	34	.282	.253	.303	4.96	3.79
Kretzschmar, Matt	R-R	6-3	215	8-2-86	0	4	5.96	22	0	0	3	26	30	21	17	2	16	28	.291	.333	.266	9.82	5.61

Name	B-T	HT	WT	DOB			ERA	G	GS	CG	SV	IP	H	R	ER	HR	BB	SO	AVG	vLH	vRH	K/9	BB/9
Lawler, Patrick	R-R	6-3	225	12-19-84	0	0	4.50	1	1	0	0	2	2	1	1	0	0	3	.286	.333	.250	13.50	0.00
Lidyard, Dustin	R-R	6-2	220	9-29-85	3	2	4.83	34	0	0	0	69	68	38	37	4	32	70	.264	.239	.277	9.13	4.17
McClendon, Mike	R-R	6-5	215	4-3-85	5	2	2.87	11	11	0	0	63	46	22	20	6	12	47	.198	.213	.185	6.75	1.72
Mercedes, Roque	B-R	6-3	186	10-28-86	0	4	7.26	12	8	0	0	40	51	38	32	7	18	23	.313	.294	.326	5.22	4.08
Periard, Alexandre	L-R	6-1	180	6-15-87	7	7	3.55	23	18	0	2	109	115	49	43	8	21	55	.271	.284	.264	4.54	1.73
Ramirez, Luis	L-L	6-3	170	5-3-88	1	2	5.86	23	8	0	0	66	84	46	43	8	28	49	.312	.421	.269	6.68	3.82
Ramlow, Mike	L-L	6-6	185	3-2-86	5	5	6.11	27	20	0	1	105	130	77	71	16	35	80	.304	.260	.317	6.88	3.01
Romero, Jose	L-L	6-0	170	6-2-86	4	0	4.07	32	0	0	1	49	54	28	22	1	32	50	.278	.180	.313	9.25	5.92
Ryan, Patrick	R-R	6-0	200	5-31-83	2	0	3.23	16	0	0	0	31	23	13	11	3	12	30	.211	.225	.203	8.80	3.52
Shanks, E.J.	R-R	6-5	230	4-8-82	3	0	1.72	23	0	0	9	31	31	10	6	3	7	18	.250	.244	.253	5.17	2.01
Sutton, Jared	R-R	6-2	210	5-4-83	1	2	3.32	22	0	0	2	38	25	16	14	0	25	35	.188	.267	.148	8.29	5.92
Toneguzzi, Chris	B-R	6-4	260	2-6-83	6	5	6.20	15	12	0	0	65	82	48	45	8	20	39	.309	.321	.301	5.37	2.76
Wendte, Travis	R-R	6-2	195	11-17-82	6	0	2.50	28	0	0	5	58	43	20	16	4	16	49	.207	.192	.215	7.65	2.50
Wright, Brae	L-L	6-4	205	11-1-83	6	6	5.87	21	21	0	0	110	139	85	72	19	32	76	.307	.272	.320	6.20	2.61

FIELDING

Catcher	PCT	G	PO	A	E	DP	PB
Bouchie	.986	79	513	55	8	4	15
De La Rosa	1.000	1	8	0	0	0	1
Maldonado	.991	64	471	55	5	6	8

First Base	PCT	G	PO	A	E	DP
Alonso	.991	36	324	12	3	18
Brantley	.994	30	290	21	2	33
Chapman	1.000	1	10	0	0	2
De La Rosa	1.000	5	0	0	0	1
Green	1.000	3	19	0	0	2
Holmberg	1.000	1	8	1	0	0
Lefave	.992	68	611	36	5	60
Maldonado	1.000	2	6	1	0	0

Mojica	—	1	0	0	0	0

Second Base	PCT	G	PO	A	E	DP
Alonso	—	1	0	0	0	0
Green	1.000	1	6	0	2	
Holmberg	.975	80	129	223	9	58
Miller	.957	32	52	103	7	17
Mojica	.974	28	44	67	3	8

Third Base	PCT	G	PO	A	E	DP
Alonso	.800	2	2	2	1	1
Green	.925	104	69	213	23	17
Holmberg	.950	7	3	16	1	2
Maldonado	1.000	2	0	1	0	0
Mojica	.932	29	24	72	7	7

Shortstop	PCT	G	PO	A	E	DP
Brewer	.921	125	197	366	48	76
Mojica	.947	17	20	34	3	7

Outfield	PCT	G	PO	A	E	DP
Brantley	1.000	20	29	2	0	0
Caufield	.983	126	221	13	4	1
Chapman	.972	111	166	8	5	0
De La Rosa	.667	2	1	1	1	0
Fermaint	.959	73	181	5	8	1
Ford	.963	50	101	3	4	2
LaPorta	1.000	17	36	2	0	1
Lefave	.923	9	12	0	1	0
Mojica	1.000	7	10	0	0	0

ORGANIZATION STATISTICS

HELENA BREWERS   ROOKIE

PIONEER LEAGUE

BATTING	B-T	HT	WT	DOB	AVG	vLH	vRH	G	AB	R	H	2B	3B	HR	RBI	BB	HBP	SH	SF	SO	SB	CS	SLG	OBP
Cline, Matthew	R-R	5-10	155	10-18-85	.301	.395	.265	46	136	25	41	1	1	1	12	4	6	1	2	12	4	3	.346	.345
Crowell, Kurt	R-R	6-3	195	9-21-84	.289	.268	.295	49	190	34	55	17	2	5	30	15	2	1	0	41	1	0	.479	.348
Farris, Eric	R-R	5-10	170	3-3-86	.326	.418	.291	63	239	34	78	16	2	1	34	16	2	9	3	22	21	5	.423	.369
Fonseca, David	R-R	5-10	160	8-17-86	.213	.200	.217	40	127	13	27	4	0	2	12	8	3	5	0	25	3	3	.291	.273
Fryer, Eric	R-R	6-2	215	8-26-85	.209	.205	.210	43	139	25	29	7	0	3	19	14	2	1	1	28	4	3	.324	.288
Gindl, Caleb	L-L	5-9	185	8-31-88	.372	.344	.384	55	207	40	77	22	3	5	42	20	0	0	4	38	4	4	.580	.420
Goetz, Mike	L-R	5-10	180	7-22-84	.318	.219	.350	46	132	28	42	6	2	3	27	14	9	1	1	15	11	4	.462	.417
Haydel, Lee	L-R	5-11	175	7-15-87	.276	.278	.275	62	254	42	70	12	5	0	20	12	1	3	0	44	12	5	.362	.311
Houin, Scott	R-R	6-1	180	4-11-85	.182	.333	.158	9	22	4	4	2	0	0	2	2	0	0	0	7	1	1	.273	.250
LaPorta, Matt	R-R	6-2	210	1-8-85	.259	.154	.357	7	28	4	7	1	0	2	4	1	0	0	0	8	0	0	.519	.286
Lucroy, Jonathan	R-R	6-0	185	6-13-86	.342	.383	.332	61	234	35	80	18	2	4	39	16	1	0	2	37	0	3	.487	.383
McAngus, Zach	R-R	6-1	210	5-10-84	.253	.263	.250	31	79	11	20	2	0	2	10	6	1	0	1	15	0	0	.354	.310
McKnight, Scott	L-R	6-1	155	12-22-84	.138	.157	.130	30	65	5	9	1	1	0	2	3	1	2	0	16	1	2	.185	.182
Newton, Eric	R-R	6-1	200	6-17-84	.318	.286	.328	27	85	17	27	10	0	4	17	6	2	0	0	22	1	1	.576	.376
Neyens, D.J.	R-R	5-11	200	9-19-83	.111	.200	.077	8	18	0	2	1	0	0	2	1	0	0	0	6	0	0	.167	.158
Rindal, Curt	R-R	6-3	215	9-15-83	.324	.333	.320	49	142	19	46	7	1	2	18	12	4	1	1	21	1	2	.430	.390
Swaydan, Jordan	R-R	6-2	185	2-1-84	.200	.077	.250	18	45	2	9	1	0	1	6	1	0	1	1	5	1	0	.289	.213
Trejo, Edgar	R-R	6-3	200	7-28-89	.100	.000	.111	5	10	2	1	0	0	0	0	0	0	0	0	0	0	0	.100	.100
Wheeler, Zelous	R-R	5-10	200	1-16-87	.300	.288	.304	59	190	36	57	8	2	3	23	25	6	3	0	41	2	1	.411	.398
Wilson, Steffan	R-R	6-1	220	5-24-86	.328	.348	.321	50	183	31	60	12	2	12	40	18	2	1	1	50	0	1	.612	.392
Wycklendt, Anthony	R-R	6-2	220	4-4-84	.219	.154	.243	34	96	14	21	4	0	5	14	7	4	0	0	42	1	0	.417	.299

PITCHING	B-T	HT	WT	DOB	W	L	ERA	G	GS	CG	SV	IP	H	R	ER	HR	BB	SO	AVG	vLH	vRH	K/9	BB/9
Anundsen, Evan	R-R	6-3	210	5-17-88	7	5	4.77	15	15	0	0	77	81	50	41	6	20	59	.265	.296	.240	6.87	2.33
Baron, Casey	L-L	6-2	185	11-29-84	1	1	3.26	10	0	0	0	19	16	8	7	2	4	16	.225	.208	.234	7.45	1.86
Bramhall, Bobby	L-L	5-10	170	7-13-85	3	0	2.03	10	3	0	0	31	23	9	7	1	11	35	.202	.324	.150	10.16	3.19
Bryson, Robert	R-R	6-1	200	12-11-87	3	0	2.67	18	4	0	8	54	49	19	16	2	12	70	.245	.288	.217	11.67	2.00
De La Rosa, Dane	R-R	6-6	220	2-1-83	0	0	0.00	1	0	0	0	2	1	0	0	0	1	3	.143	.500	.000	13.50	4.50
Etheridge, Wes	R-R	6-1	185	8-12-84	0	3	15.43	5	0	0	0	5	10	9	8	2	4	5	.435	.400	.462	9.64	7.71
Frerichs, Corey	R-R	5-11	200	5-7-86	4	1	6.26	18	0	0	3	27	30	21	19	2	11	37	.283	.270	.290	12.18	3.62
Garcia, Jose	R-R	6-4	175	5-25-88	8	4	5.78	15	12	0	0	76	78	53	49	10	22	69	.268	.250	.283	8.14	2.59
Hand, Donovan	R-R	6-4	190	4-20-86	2	2	3.55	7	6	0	0	33	31	13	13	3	4	26	.250	.298	.209	7.09	1.09
Kjeldgaard, Brock	R-R	6-5	215	1-22-86	0	1	5.91	17	1	0	0	32	37	24	21	3	13	21	.287	.302	.276	5.91	3.66
Kretzschmar, Matt	R-R	6-3	215	8-2-86	0	0	0.00	2	0	0	2	2	3	0	0	0	1	0	.333	.500	.200	13.50	0.00
Lambertus, Pedro	R-R	6-3	215	6-4-88	0	0	12.00	3	0	0	1	3	3	4	4	1	3	1	.250	.000	.333	3.00	9.00
Langille, Craig	R-R	6-2	190	11-12-85	3	0	4.97	20	1	0	1	42	49	25	23	5	8	20	.283	.300	.274	4.32	1.73
Mercedes, Roque	B-R	6-3	186	10-28-86	7	4	3.75	15	15	0	0	84	88	45	35	7	20	70	.263	.292	.242	7.50	2.14
Merklinger, Daniel	L-L	6-1	195	11-19-85	1	0	3.95	13	0	0	1	27	26	17	12	1	16	40	.236	.346	.202	13.17	5.27
Nieves, Efrain	L-L	6-0	169	11-15-89	1	0	0.00	2	0	0	0	5	3	0	0	0	1	4	.188	.000	.250	7.71	1.93
Pasma, Curtis	L-L	6-0	206	9-19-85	0	1	3.60	10	0	0	4	43	48	22	19	3	5	49	.281	.283	.280	10.34	1.05
Robinson, Chad	R-R	6-5	210	11-13-87	0	5	8.48	10	8	0	0	29	40	29	27	6	23	29	.331	.233	.385	9.10	7.22
Seidel, Richard	R-R	6-5	200	9-3-87	4	0	3.07	12	8	0	0	41	30	20	14	2	16	36	.207	.200	.212	7.90	3.51
Tyson, Nicholas	R-R	6-3	185	1-13-88	4	1	2.48	17	3	0	2	40	29	14	11	3	7	36	.196	.218	.183	8.10	1.58

FIELDING

Catcher	PCT	G	PO	A	E	DP	PB
Fryer	.980	33	228	21	5	0	4
Lucroy	.987	35	263	44	4	4	5
Neyens	.975	8	33	6	1	0	1
Swaydan	.990	13	93	9	1	1	4

First Base	PCT	G	PO	A	E	DP
McAngus	.967	10	84	4	3	4
Newton	1.000	12	90	3	0	10
Rindal	.985	46	374	33	6	21
Swaydan	1.000	1	9	2	0	1
Wilson	.986	25	202	15	3	13

Second Base	PCT	G	PO	A	E	DP
Cline	.945	11	18	34	3	6

Farris	.975	62	93	177	7	28
McKnight	1.000	13	7	24	0	3

Third Base	PCT	G	PO	A	E	DP
McAngus	.879	15	7	22	4	0
McKnight	.875	2	3	4	1	0
Newton	1.000	1	0	1	0	0
Trejo	.800	5	0	8	2	0
Wheeler	.932	55	25	111	10	8
Wilson	.895	14	10	24	4	1

Shortstop	PCT	G	PO	A	E	DP
Cline	.957	28	29	83	5	10
Fonseca	.929	39	63	120	14	21
McKnight	.889	12	5	27	4	5

Wheeler	1.000	5	3	18	0	3

Outfield	PCT	G	PO	A	E	DP
Crowell	.974	46	72	3	2	2
Gindl	.988	52	74	6	1	0
Goetz	.984	41	59	3	1	1
Haydel	.968	61	88	3	3	0
Houin	1.000	9	5	0	0	0
LaPorta	1.000	4	5	0	0	0
McAngus	1.000	1	1	0	0	0
Wilson	1.000	1	1	0	0	0
Wycklendt	.960	30	23	1	1	0

AZL BREWERS
ARIZONA LEAGUE

ROOKIE

BATTING	B-T	HT	WT	DOB	AVG	vLH	vRH	G	AB	R	H	2B	3B	HR	RBI	BB	HBP	SH	SF	SO	SB	CS	SLG	OBP
Cequea, Allixon	R-R	6-1	175	6-16-90	.271	.172	.300	36	129	12	35	6	0	1	15	1	2	0	2	41	1	0	.341	.284
Crosby, Bryan	R-R	6-1	185	12-24-87	.179	.071	.214	23	56	4	10	0	0	0	9	9	1	1	0	26	0	1	.179	.303
Czimsky, Matthew	R-R	5-11	185	5-29-84	.314	.333	.309	26	70	16	22	6	0	0	11	13	2	1	0	17	1	1	.400	.435
D'Amico, Jesse	L-R	6-2	210	1-26-88	.200	.000	.250	3	5	1	1	0	0	0	0	1	0	0	0	2	0	0	.200	.333
Dennis, Christopher	L-R	6-1	205	9-15-88	.263	.185	.292	32	99	19	26	1	2	5	12	16	4	0	0	39	4	1	.465	.387
Felix, Jovanny	B-R	5-11	160	11-6-86	.186	.250	.171	34	129	11	24	3	0	0	12	8	1	5	0	48	1	7	.209	.239
Hall, Bill	R-R	6-0	210	12-28-79	.167	.000	.200	2	6	0	1	0	0	0	0	2	1	0	0	1	0	0	.167	.250
Hereaud, Carlos	R-R	6-1	195	2-20-86	.256	.257	.255	46	172	27	44	11	1	2	23	25	3	0	4	40	11	2	.366	.353
Houin, Scott	R-R	6-1	180	4-11-85	.326	.250	.333	12	46	13	15	1	1	3	11	3	0	0	0	14	7	0	.587	.367
Iacono, Charles	L-L	5-8	170	4-21-84	.225	.360	.198	47	151	38	34	2	3	0	10	45	4	3	1	31	30	6	.278	.413
Jensen, Ryan	R-R	5-10	180	9-21-88	.193	.143	.209	19	57	5	11	1	1	0	9	13	3	0	0	20	0	0	.246	.370
Medlin, CJ	R-R	6-2	235	3-3-82	.667	.000	1.000	3	3	0	2	0	0	0	1	1	1	0	0	1	0	0	.667	.800
Miller, Erik	R-R	6-3	200	8-23-87	.214	.273	.200	34	126	13	27	1	2	0	14	7	5	2	2	38	4	3	.254	.279
Neyens, D.J.	R-R	5-11	200	9-19-83	.269	.250	.273	13	26	3	7	1	1	0	3	3	0	0	0	8	2	0	.385	.345
Paciorek, Joseph	R-R	6-2	225	9-20-88	.281	.385	.253	40	121	20	34	3	2	2	13	23	5	3	0	38	5	3	.388	.416
Rangel, Jose	R-R	6-1	189	6-23-88	.151	.238	.115	24	73	6	11	0	0	3	5	1	0	34	1	1	.151	.235
Requena, Jonathan	R-R	5-11	215	3-25-89	.000	.000	—	2	2	0	0	0	0	0	0	0	0	0	0	0	0	0	.000	.000
Robulack, Cameron	L-R	6-3	220	11-2-88	.189	.000	.212	13	37	3	7	4	1	0	5	6	0	2	0	10	0	2	.351	.319
Sanchez, Luis	R-R	5-11	185	7-3-91	.288	.360	.266	32	104	20	30	3	2	1	7	6	5	0	0	36	3	3	.385	.357
Snijders, Ulrich	R-R	6-1	210	7-8-86	.226	.182	.239	27	93	14	21	4	2	4	9	10	1	0	0	39	1	0	.441	.308
Trejo, Edgar	R-R	6-3	200	7-28-89	.275	.263	.278	51	207	27	57	5	1	1	27	5	1	0	4	48	0	3	.324	.290
Vasquez, Miguel	B-R	6-1	185	11-25-86	.333	.400	.318	11	27	6	9	0	0	1	4	8	0	0	5	1	0	.444	.419
Whiteside, Brett	R-R	6-2	200	3-29-88	.228	.192	.236	39	136	22	31	7	1	2	19	19	3	0	1	54	3	5	.338	.333

PITCHING	B-T	HT	WT	DOB	W	L	ERA	G	GS	CG	SV	IP	H	R	ER	HR	BB	SO	AVG	vLH	vRH	K/9	BB/9
Arnold, Adam	R-R	6-0	185	5-15-86	0	2	8.79	7	3	0	0	14	19	19	14	1	13	12	.333	.375	.303	7.53	8.16
Bueno, Kristian	L-L	6-2	195	12-10-88	0	6	7.75	13	6	0	0	38	49	42	33	3	16	33	.301	.250	.327	7.75	3.76
Crespo, Jorge	R-R	6-2	195	2-3-87	0	1	9.20	12	2	0	0	29	34	34	30	3	25	24	.298	.280	.313	7.36	7.67
Cruz, Yeison	R-R	6-2	185	11-25-88	0	0	6.30	13	0	0	0	30	32	29	21	3	32	21	.258	.292	.237	6.30	9.60
Czimsky, Matthew	R-R	5-11	185	5-29-84	0	0	0.00	3	0	0	0	4	2	0	0	0	3	3	.118	.125	.111	6.23	6.23
Drinkard, Anthony	L-L	6-1	195	3-21-85	1	3	7.18	14	0	0	1	26	32	30	21	1	10	14	.286	.300	.280	4.78	3.42
Guerrero, Luis	R-R	6-0	170	6-20-90	3	0	3.64	13	4	0	0	42	35	23	17	0	39	27	.232	.279	.200	5.79	8.36
Hill, Shane	R-R	6-4	185	7-5-88	0	1	24.75	3	2	0	0	4	3	11	11	0	17	0	.250	.333	.222	0.00	38.25
Jimenez, Luis	R-R	6-7	207	9-18-88	2	2	6.55	14	0	0	0	34	34	32	25	3	33	39	.248	.286	.216	10.22	8.65
Lambertus, Pedro	R-R	6-3	215	6-4-88	1	4	7.12	14	6	0	0	43	53	41	34	0	31	28	.298	.343	.270	5.86	6.49
Lawler, Patrick	R-R	6-3	225	12-19-84	3	0	3.29	11	0	0	3	14	13	9	5	0	5	20	.245	.348	.167	13.17	3.29
Manzanillo, Santo	R-R	6-0	175	12-20-88	4	4	3.90	14	0	0	1	28	22	18	12	1	29	18	.214	.273	.186	5.86	9.43
Mejia, Harold	R-R	6-1	155	8-28-87	0	0	3.00	3	0	0	1	6	4	2	2	0	0	2	.182	.333	.125	3.00	0.00
Morales, Joel	R-R	6-3	206	3-12-89	0	5	8.05	12	7	0	0	35	56	34	31	3	15	29	.366	.420	.321	7.53	3.89
Nevakshonoff, Travis	R-R	6-0	180	7-2-88	0	1	11.78	10	3	0	0	18	29	31	24	1	26	6	.367	.308	.396	2.95	12.76
Nieves, Efrain	L-L	6-0	169	11-15-89	2	4	5.31	13	7	0	0	41	38	29	24	3	25	45	.244	.143	.312	9.96	5.53
Pascual, Rolando	B-R	6-6	218	2-8-89	0	1	9.00	3	3	0	0	5	6	6	5	0	7	6	.333	.400	.308	10.80	12.60
Rivas, Amaury	R-R	6-2	185	12-20-85	0	0	3.12	6	0	0	9	3	4	3	1	4	10	10	.107	.125	.083	10.38	4.15
Rosario, Adrian	R-R	6-4	180	9-30-89	3	3	6.75	14	2	0	0	37	50	40	28	2	32	23	.313	.236	.375	5.54	7.71
Salinas, Guillermo	R-R	6-1	180	10-28-88	0	0	4.85	15	0	0	1	26	33	19	14	4	21	23	.297	.304	.292	7.96	7.27
Stetter, Mitch	L-L	6-4	195	1-16-81	0	0	1.50	7	5	0	0	6	4	1	1	0	0	9	.190	.250	.154	13.50	0.00

FIELDING

Catcher	PCT	G	PO	A	E	DP	PB
Czimsky	.966	24	126	14	5	1	9
Medlin	1.000	3	8	1	0	0	1
Neyens	.964	10	47	7	2	0	4
Requena	1.000	2	5	0	0	0	1
Snijders	.945	16	94	10	6	0	8
Whiteside	.956	19	118	12	6	1	8

First Base	PCT	G	PO	A	E	DP
Cequea	1.000	3	19	1	0	2
Crosby	.900	3	7	2	1	0
Hereaud	.955	8	55	9	3	7
Paciorek	.967	27	212	22	8	17
Robulack	.964	8	50	3	2	1

Whiteside	.973	12	98	10	3	2

Second Base	PCT	G	PO	A	E	DP
Cequea	.943	15	33	33	4	9
Crosby	.905	9	4	15	2	1
Hereaud	.927	34	65	99	13	17
Vasquez	1.000	2	5	4	0	2

Third Base	PCT	G	PO	A	E	DP
Cequea	.941	12	10	22	2	0
Crosby	.667	5	0	2	1	0
Paciorek	.950	9	6	13	1	0
Trejo	.939	36	40	67	7	9

Shortstop	PCT	G	PO	A	E	DP
Crosby	.800	8	9	19	7	2

Sanchez	.865	32	48	87	21	15
Trejo	.955	14	27	36	3	6
Vasquez	.926	7	7	18	2	3

Outfield	PCT	G	PO	A	E	DP
Cequea	1.000	6	8	0	0	0
Dennis	.953	26	41	0	2	0
Felix	.968	34	57	4	2	2
Hall	1.000	2	5	0	0	0
Houin	1.000	12	25	2	0	0
Iacono	.987	42	73	1	1	0
Jensen	1.000	5	8	1	0	0
Miller	.945	34	86	0	5	0
Rangel	.902	24	35	2	4	0

Minnesota Twins

BY JOHN MILLEA

The transitions came at a steady pace as the 2007 season came to a close in Minnesota. The Twins had won four division titles in five years but fell off to a disappointing 79-83 third-place finish in the American League Central. It was the club's first losing season since 2000.

But the biggest news came not on the field but in the front office when general manager Terry Ryan, with no warning, announced he was stepping aside after 13 years. Assistant general manager Bill Smith took over, but Ryan's absence will take some getting used to.

The front office shake-up proved fitting since injuries and inconsistency also was a theme for the Twins' on-field play, which sheds some bright light on why the end result wasn't up to Minnesota's recent standards.

Catcher Joe Mauer, the 2006 American League batting champion, was hampered all year by leg injuries that caused him to miss more than 40 games. First baseman Justin Morneau, the reigning MVP, suffered a bruised lung in a home plate collision and sat for a stretch, and right fielder Michael Cuddyer was sidelined with back and thumb injuries.

An omen came in the first week of the season when Rondell White, who was expected to be the starting left fielder, went down with a calf strain that sidelined him until late-July.

"Sometimes the difference between great seasons and a season where you struggle is the health of your team," catcher Mike Redmond said. "It seems like we were battling from the start with guys' injuries, and we never had the lineup out there that we assumed was going to play all year."

Despite all those problems, the Twins were in the race for a playoff spot into late August. After a four-game sweep of the Orioles at the Metrodome, Minnesota was 5 1/2 games out of the division lead and hope was on the rise. But the Twins went into Cleveland, lost all three games, and were never a threat again.

That brand of inconsistency might be the best way to brand the Twins of 2007; they never put together a winning streak longer than five games. The lack of success was a surprise for a team that brought back its entire starting lineup and most of the pitching staff from a 2006 playoff team. But performance never matched expectations.

A prime example was infielder Nick Punto, who flirted with .300 in 2006 but finished the 2007 season hitting only .210.

Among the few positives, center fielder Torii Hunter set career highs in hits, doubles and RBIs and several young pitchers emerged as big league performers. The year began with heavy doubts about the rotation, and Ramon Ortiz and Sidney Ponson were gone after a few weeks and were replaced by rookie righthanders Matt Garza, Kevin Slowey and Scott Baker.

But injuries, drop-off performances and faltering fundamentals all contributed to the Twins' disappointing year.

The first offseason with Smith at the helm will be as important as any in recent years. Holes need to be filled—in particular, third base, designated hitter, left field and second base—and a list of free agents needs to be sorted out.

Hunter entered the offseason as the club's most high-profile free agent in years. Righthander Carlos Silva also is a free agent, and his departure would put another hole in an already young staff.

Two-time Cy Young winner Johan Santana has one year

MAJOR LEAGUE: JOHAN SANTANA, LHP

The game's most predictably dominant pitcher was again one of baseball's best. Santana finished third in baseball with 235 strikeouts. His 4.52-to-1 strikeout-to-walk ratio ranked fourth in the majors, while his 219 innings ranked 10th. His 3.33 ERA was a team-best for the fourth straight year, as were his 15 victories.

MINOR LEAGUE: KEVIN SLOWEY, RHP

Slowey showcased pinpoint control in 2007, walking 30 batters in 200 1/3 combined innings between Triple-A and the majors. Slowey led the International League with a 1.89 ERA, the second-lowest mark among pitchers in full-season leagues. His five complete games were the most in the minors.

BATTING		★Minimum 250 at-bats
★AVG	Guzman, Garrett, New Britain	.312
R	Dinkelman, Brian, Beloit/Fort Myers	104
H	Guzman, Garrett, New Britain	148
TB	Lis, Erik, Fort Myers	231
2B	Plouffe, Trevor, New Britain	37
3B	Dinkelman, Brian, Beloit/Fort Myers	10
HR	Lis, Erik, Fort Myers	18
RBI	Lis, Erik, Fort Myers	97
BB	Tolleson, Steven, Fort Myers	79
SO	Parmelee, Chris, Beloit	137
SB	Tolleson, Steven, Fort Myers	27
★OBP	Tolleson, Steven, Fort Myers	.388
★SLG	Buscher, Brian, New Britain/Rochester	.493
PITCHING		**^Minimum 75 innings**
W	Duensing, Brian, New Britain/Rochester	15
	Manship, Jeff, Beloit/Fort Myers	15
L	Ward, Zachary, Fort Myers	17
^ERA	Slowey, Kevin, Rochester	1.89
G	Korecky, Bobby, Rochester	66
CG	Slowey, Kevin, Rochester	5
SV	Delaney, Robert, Beloit/Fort Myers	35
SV	Korecky, Bobby, Rochester	35
IP	Duensing, Brian, New Britain/Rochester	167
BB	Sosa, Oswaldo, Fort Myers/New Britain	58
SO	Manship, Jeff, Beloit/Fort Myers	136
^AVG	Slowey, Kevin, Rochester	.223

remaining on his contract, leading to whispers that he might be traded if the front office fears he won't re-sign. Morneau and Cuddyer are arbitration-eligible, and Nathan has an option for 2008 season.

On the minor league level, the results from 2007 were similar to what took place with the Twins. For a couple years, the heir apparent to Hunter has been 2002 first-round pick Denard Span. But Span had a disappointing season at Triple-A and the front office doesn't relish the prospect of throwing Span into the major league mix.

First baseman Henry Sanchez played just 10 games for low Class A Elizabethton before being sidelined with a hand injury and outfielder Chris Parmelee hit just .239/.313/.414 for low Class A Beloit.

General Manager: Terry Ryan. **Farm Director:** Jim Rantz. **Scouting Director:** Mike Radcliff

Class	Team	League	W	L	PCT	Finish*	Manager	Affiliate Since
Majors	Minnesota	American	79	83	.488	8th (14)	Ron Gardenhire	—
Triple-A	Rochester Red Wings	International	77	67	.535	5th (14)	Stan Cliburn	2003
Double-A	New Britain Rock Cats	Eastern	69	72	.489	9th (12)	Riccardo Ingram	1995
High A	Fort Meyers Miracle	Florida State	70	70	.500	7th (12)	Kevin Boles	1993
Low A	Beloit Snappers	Midwest	79	61	.564	2nd (14)	Jeff Smith	2005
Rookie	Elizabethton Twins	Appalachian	50	18	.735	1st (9)^	Ray Smith	1974
Rookie	GCL Twins	Gulf Coast	37	19	.661	3rd (16)	Nelson Prada	1989
Overall 2007 Minor League Record			**382**	**307**	**.554**	**4th**		

* Finish in overall standings (No. of teams in league) ^League champion

ORGANIZATION STATISTICS

MINNESOTA TWINS

AMERICAN LEAGUE

BATTING

	B-T	HT	WT	DOB	AVG	vLH	vRH	G	AB	R	H	2B	3B	HR	RBI	BB	HBP	SH	SF	SO	SB	CS	SLG	OBP
Bartlett, Jason	R-R	6-0	185	10-30-79	.265	.319	.245	140	510	75	135	20	7	5	43	50	8	0	2	73	23	3	.361	.339
Buscher, Brian	L-R	6-0	200	4-18-81	.244	.200	.250	33	82	8	20	1	0	2	10	10	0	1	1	16	1	0	.329	.323
Casilla, Alexi	B-R	5-9	180	7-20-84	.222	.274	.181	56	189	15	42	5	1	0	9	9	0	5	1	29	11	1	.259	.256
Castillo, Luis	B-R	5-11	190	9-12-75	.304	.279	.312	85	349	54	106	11	3	0	18	29	0	5	1	28	9	4	.352	.356
Cirillo, Jeff	R-R	6-1	205	9-23-69	.261	.293	.242	50	153	18	40	9	2	2	21	15	1	3	2	13	2	0	.386	.327
Cuddyer, Michael	R-R	6-2	220	3-27-79	.276	.308	.263	144	547	87	151	28	5	16	81	64	7	0	5	107	5	0	.433	.356
Ford, Lew	R-R	6-0	200	8-12-76	.233	.256	.219	55	116	13	27	6	0	3	14	11	3	0	0	24	3	1	.362	.315
Heintz, Chris	R-R	6-1	205	8-6-74	.250	.313	.225	24	56	0	14	0	0	0	7	3	0	2	0	12	0	0	.250	.288
Hunter, Torii	R-R	6-2	225	7-18-75	.287	.314	.276	160	600	94	172	45	1	28	107	40	5	0	5	101	18	9	.505	.334
Jones, Garrett	L-L	6-4	225	6-21-81	.208	.077	.234	31	77	7	16	2	1	2	5	6	0	0	1	20	1	1	.338	.262
Kubel, Jason	L-R	6-0	210	5-25-82	.273	.236	.280	128	418	49	114	31	2	13	65	41	1	1	5	79	5	0	.450	.335
LeCroy, Matthew	R-R	6-2	230	12-13-75	.150	.125	.167	7	20	1	3	1	0	0	0	0	0	0	0	4	0	0	.200	.150
Mauer, Joe	L-R	6-5	215	4-19-83	.293	.283	.299	109	406	62	119	27	3	7	60	57	3	2	3	51	7	1	.426	.382
McDonald, Darnell	R-R	5-11	210	11-17-78	.100	.000	.143	4	10	0	1	0	0	0	0	1	0	0	0	3	0	0	.100	.182
Morales, Jose	B-R	5-11	190	2-20-83	1.000	—	1.000	1	3	1	3	1	0	0	0	0	0	0	0	0	0	0	1.333	1.000
Morneau, Justin	L-R	6-4	225	5-15-81	.271	.228	.294	157	590	84	160	31	3	31	111	64	5	0	9	91	1	1	.492	.343
Punto, Nick	B-R	5-9	185	11-8-77	.210	.175	.226	150	472	53	99	18	4	1	25	55	0	6	3	90	16	6	.271	.291
Rabe, Josh	R-R	6-3	215	10-15-78	.194	.200	.182	14	31	2	6	0	0	0	2	0	0	0	0	7	0	0	.194	.194
Redmond, Mike	R-R	5-11	200	5-5-71	.294	.330	.277	82	272	23	80	13	0	1	38	18	5	0	3	23	0	0	.353	.346
Rodriguez, Luis	B-R	5-9	190	6-27-80	.219	.226	.218	68	155	18	34	5	1	2	12	12	2	2	1	14	1	0	.303	.281
Tyner, Jason	L-L	6-1	180	4-23-77	.286	.233	.299	114	304	42	87	14	2	1	22	16	5	2	1	26	8	3	.355	.331
Watkins, Tommy	R-R	5-10	200	6-18-80	.357	.357	.357	9	28	2	10	0	0	0	6	3	0	0	0	4	1	0	.357	.438
White, Rondell	R-R	6-1	225	2-23-72	.174	.143	.194	38	109	8	19	4	0	4	20	6	3	0	1	19	0	0	.321	.235

PITCHING

	B-T	HT	WT	DOB	W	L	ERA	G	GS	CG	SV	IP	H	R	ER	HR	BB	SO	AVG	vLH	vRH	K/9	BB/9
Baker, Scott	R-R	6-4	210	9-19-81	9	9	4.26	24	23	2	0	144	162	70	68	15	29	102	.287	.323	.257	6.39	1.82
Blackburn, Nick	R-R	6-4	205	2-24-82	0	2	7.71	6	0	0	0	12	19	12	10	2	2	8	.365	.478	.276	6.17	1.54
Bonser, Boof	R-R	6-4	260	10-14-81	8	12	5.10	31	30	0	0	173	199	108	98	27	65	136	.286	.349	.214	7.08	3.38
Cali, Carmen	L-L	5-10	185	11-4-78	0	1	4.71	24	0	0	0	21	22	11	11	2	16	14	.265	.255	.278	6.00	6.86
Crain, Jesse	R-R	6-1	205	7-5-81	1	2	5.51	18	0	0	0	16	19	16	10	4	4	10	.292	.269	.308	5.51	2.20
DePaula, Julio	R-R	6-0	180	12-31-82	0	1	8.55	16	0	0	0	20	30	20	19	5	10	8	.357	.341	.372	3.60	4.50
Garza, Matt	R-R	6-4	205	11-26-83	5	7	3.69	16	15	0	0	83	96	44	34	8	32	67	.294	.314	.276	7.27	3.47
Guerrier, Matt	R-R	6-3	195	8-2-78	2	4	2.35	73	0	0	1	88	71	23	23	9	21	68	.220	.264	.187	6.95	2.15
Miller, Jason	L-L	6-1	195	7-20-82	0	0	18.00	4	0	0	0	4	7	8	8	2	3	2	.368	.200	.429	4.50	6.75
Nathan, Joe	R-R	6-4	220	11-22-74	4	2	1.88	68	0	0	37	72	54	15	15	4	19	77	.209	.221	.199	9.67	2.39
Neshek, Pat	B-R	6-3	205	9-4-80	7	2	2.94	74	0	0	0	70	44	25	23	7	27	74	.183	.181	.185	9.47	3.45
Ortiz, Ramon	R-R	6-0	175	5-23-73	4	4	5.14	28	10	0	0	91	112	54	52	12	15	44	.298	.311	.286	4.35	1.48
Perkins, Glen	L-L	5-11	200	3-2-83	0	0	3.14	19	0	0	0	29	23	10	10	2	12	20	.232	.250	.222	6.28	3.77
Ponson, Sidney	R-R	6-1	260	11-2-76	2	5	6.93	7	7	0	0	38	54	31	29	7	17	23	.335	.265	.410	5.50	4.06
Reyes, Dennys	R-L	6-3	245	4-19-77	2	1	3.99	50	0	0	0	29	34	14	13	1	21	21	.309	.273	.364	6.44	6.44
Rincon, Juan	R-R	5-11	210	1-23-79	3	3	5.13	63	0	0	0	60	65	38	34	9	28	49	.273	.313	.236	7.39	4.22
Santana, Johan	L-L	6-0	210	3-13-79	15	13	3.33	33	33	1	0	219	183	88	81	33	52	235	.225	.197	.234	9.66	2.14
Silva, Carlos	R-R	6-4	245	4-23-79	13	14	4.19	33	33	2	0	202	229	99	94	20	36	89	.287	.294	.280	3.97	1.60
Slowey, Kevin	R-R	6-3	195	5-4-84	4	1	4.73	13	11	0	0	67	82	39	35	16	11	47	.288	.267	.309	6.34	1.48

FIELDING

Catcher	PCT	G	PO	A	E	DP	PB
Heintz	1.000	21	106	5	0	0	1
LeCroy	.957	4	22	0	1	0	1
Mauer	.998	91	598	35	1	5	4
Morales	1.000	1	5	1	0	0	0
Redmond	1.000	56	385	24	0	4	0

First Base	PCT	G	PO	A	E	DP
Cirillo	.958	8	65	4	3	4
Cuddyer	1.000	4	30	4	0	4
Jones	1.000	8	57	4	0	5
LeCroy	1.000	1	3	0	0	0
Morneau	.996	143	1189	102	5	122
Rodriguez	1.000	3	3	1	0	1

Second Base	PCT	G	PO	A	E	DP
Casilla	.958	52	80	147	10	38
Castillo	.992	85	154	220	3	48
Punto	.973	25	46	63	3	11
Rodriguez	.984	21	24	38	1	10

Third Base	PCT	G	PO	A	E	DP
Buscher	.923	27	17	31	4	6
Cirillo	1.000	15	6	29	0	3
Punto	.973	108	83	171	7	11
Rodriguez	.958	38	25	43	3	7
Watkins	1.000	8	4	15	0	0

Shortstop	PCT	G	PO	A	E	DP
Bartlett	.960	138	205	415	26	97

	PCT	G	PO	A	E	DP
Casilla	1.000	5	4	8	0	2
Punto	.974	27	44	70	3	17
Watkins	1.000	1	1	0	0	0

Outfield	PCT	G	PO	A	E	DP
Cuddyer	.986	140	256	19	4	2
Ford	.984	49	59	1	1	1
Hunter	.995	155	387	5	2	0
Jones	.875	6	7	0	1	0
Kubel	.988	84	159	2	2	2
McDonald	1.000	3	2	1	0	1
Rabe	1.000	9	14	1	0	0
Tyner	.993	77	145	3	1	0
White	1.000	16	24	0	0	0

INTERNATIONAL LEAGUE

BATTING	B-T	HT	WT	DOB	AVG	vLH	vRH	G	AB	R	H	2B	3B	HR	RBI	BB	HBP	SH	SF	SO	SB	CS	SLG	OBP
Basak, Chris	R-R	6-2	190	12-6-78	.242	.500	.185	12	33	3	8	1	0	0	4	1	0	1	0	9	1	0	.273	.265
2-team (84 Scranton/Wilkes-Barre)					.252	—	—	96	341	50	86	20	1	7	42	22	4	4	4	64	14	3	.378	.302
Buscher, Brian	L-R	6-0	200	4-18-81	.311	.269	.321	40	132	21	41	7	0	7	22	13	1	0	1	11	1	0	.523	.374
Casilla, Alexi	B-R	5-9	180	7-20-84	.269	.337	.240	84	320	53	86	13	1	3	20	34	4	6	1	50	24	12	.344	.345
Deeds, Doug	L-L	6-2	190	6-2-81	.243	.205	.250	86	235	28	57	7	2	9	19	21	0	1	0	77	2	1	.404	.306
Feiner, Korey	R-R	5-11	210	9-25-81	.119	.136	.100	17	42	4	5	1	0	1	1	4	1	0	0	15	0	0	.214	.213
Ford, Lew	R-R	6-0	200	8-12-76	.262	.333	.242	35	122	14	32	12	0	2	17	17	0	0	0	30	2	1	.410	.353
Harvey, Ken	R-R	6-2	250	3-1-78	.235	.182	.333	5	17	3	4	1	0	1	5	0	0	0	0	4	0	0	.471	.235
Heintz, Chris	R-R	6-1	205	8-6-74	.275	.341	.252	48	167	18	46	8	0	1	15	11	4	1	1	32	0	0	.341	.333
Jones, Garrett	L-L	6-4	225	6-21-81	.280	.319	.263	107	400	57	112	32	3	13	70	32	5	0	9	83	2	2	.473	.334
LeCroy, Matthew	R-R	6-2	230	12-13-75	.194	.183	.200	80	247	12	48	12	0	3	25	26	5	3	0	48	0	0	.279	.281
Macri, Matt	R-R	6-2	200	5-29-82	.213	.250	.205	14	47	5	10	1	0	3	6	3	0	0	0	13	0	0	.426	.260
McDonald, Darnell	R-R	5-11	210	11-17-78	.277	.246	.287	61	224	32	62	12	2	5	32	19	4	1	4	35	19	2	.415	.339
2-team (73 Columbus)					.297	—	—	134	491	71	146	29	6	7	73	50	5	1	9	99	33	7	.424	.362
Morales, Jose	B-R	5-11	190	2-20-83	.311	.289	.318	108	376	42	117	25	1	2	37	30	3	1	1	44	1	4	.399	.366
Moses, Matt	L-R	6-0	210	2-20-85	.224	.171	.241	48	174	15	39	8	0	2	18	4	1	2	1	42	5	3	.305	.244
Oeltjen, Trent	L-L	6-1	190	2-28-83	.238	.264	.230	97	244	33	58	9	5	2	23	10	13	4	0	44	14	7	.340	.303
Rabe, Josh	R-R	6-3	215	10-15-78	.300	.500	.214	5	20	3	6	1	0	1	6	4	0	0	0	3	0	0	.500	.417
Rodriguez, Luis	B-R	5-9	190	6-27-80	.421	.500	.412	6	19	3	8	1	0	0	1	4	0	0	0	2	0	0	.474	.522
Span, Denard	L-L	6-0	195	2-27-84	.267	.244	.275	139	487	59	130	20	7	3	55	40	0	21	0	90	25	14	.355	.323
Tolbert, Matt	B-R	6-0	180	5-4-82	.293	.301	.289	121	417	65	122	24	7	6	53	37	5	12	6	56	11	3	.427	.353
Ugueto, Luis	B-R	6-0	195	2-15-79	.167	.000	.286	7	24	1	4	1	1	0	0	0	0	0	0	6	0	0	.292	.167
Velazquez, Gil	R-R	6-3	190	10-17-79	.240	.313	.198	69	183	26	44	9	1	1	16	13	3	5	2	35	3	0	.317	.299
Watkins, Tommy	R-R	5-10	200	6-18-80	.272	.303	.262	110	349	53	95	22	0	8	49	39	4	7	3	63	12	7	.404	.349
Williams, Glenn	R-R	6-2	195	7-18-77	.235	.175	.260	116	405	43	95	19	2	9	57	29	3	1	5	94	1	2	.358	.287

PITCHING	B-T	HT	WT	DOB	W	L	ERA	G	GS	CG	SV	IP	H	R	ER	HR	BB	SO	AVG	vLH	vRH	K/9	BB/9
Baker, Brad	R-R	6-2	180	11-6-80	0	2	7.56	12	0	0	0	17	23	15	14	3	6	20	.329	.300	.350	10.80	3.24
Baker, Scott	R-R	6-4	210	9-19-81	3	2	3.16	7	6	0	1	43	34	16	15	3	4	41	.219	.261	.186	8.65	0.84
Barrett, Ricky	L-L	6-0	190	3-9-81	2	1	4.11	22	1	0	1	31	30	14	14	3	14	34	.252	.231	.263	9.98	4.11
Bass, Brian	R-R	6-0	215	1-6-82	7	3	3.48	37	10	1	1	103	96	45	40	8	24	80	.246	.266	.227	6.97	2.09
Blackburn, Nick	R-R	6-4	205	2-24-82	7	3	2.11	17	17	3	0	111	96	32	26	7	12	57	.232	.222	.241	4.64	0.98
Cali, Carmen	L-L	5-10	185	11-4-78	5	1	2.45	31	0	0	1	48	42	17	13	1	14	28	.250	.273	.239	5.29	2.64
Crawford, Tristan	R-R	6-2	200	7-22-82	0	1	10.12	3	0	0	0	3	4	3	3	1	2	1	.364	.600	.167	3.38	6.75
Cummings, Jeremy	R-R	6-2	205	11-7-76	3	5	3.93	17	12	0	0	69	70	34	30	8	16	57	.263	.231	.295	7.47	2.10
2-team (12 Syracuse)					6	8	4.11	29	22	0	0	120	123	62	55	13	35	99	—	—	—	7.40	2.62
DePaula, Julio	R-R	6-0	180	12-31-82	12	5	2.90	49	0	0	2	84	66	33	27	8	27	63	.226	.194	.252	6.78	2.90
Duensing, Brian	L-L	5-11	195	2-22-83	11	5	3.24	19	19	3	0	117	115	54	42	13	30	86	.261	.250	.266	6.63	2.31
Garza, Matt	R-R	6-4	205	11-26-83	4	6	3.62	16	16	1	0	92	93	43	37	5	31	95	.260	.302	.230	9.29	3.03
Gassner, Dave	R-L	6-2	190	12-14-78	6	12	4.95	26	26	2	0	149	159	84	82	17	42	83	.276	.268	.278	5.01	2.54
Korecky, Bobby	R-R	5-11	180	9-16-79	5	6	3.71	66	0	0	35	85	80	42	35	5	34	71	.252	.297	.215	7.52	3.60
Lahey, Timothy	R-R	6-5	250	2-7-82	0	0	9.00	2	0	0	1	3	4	3	3	0	2	3	.308	.375	.200	9.00	6.00
Martinez, J.P	R-R	6-2	205	6-8-82	0	0	12.00	2	0	0	0	3	6	4	4	0	2	2	.462	.714	.167	6.00	6.00
Mijares, Jose	L-L	6-0	230	10-29-84	0	1	6.23	5	0	0	0	9	9	7	6	3	5	6	.265	.100	.333	6.23	5.19
Miller, Jason	L-L	6-1	195	7-20-82	1	5	3.94	31	10	0	0	75	84	35	33	10	24	37	.289	.326	.271	4.42	2.87
Mullins, Ryan	L-L	6-6	180	11-13-83	0	3	10.57	4	4	0	0	15	28	23	18	2	5	11	.400	.375	.413	6.46	2.93
Perkins, Glen	L-L	5-11	200	3-2-83	0	0	1.50	1	1	0	0	6	2	1	1	1	1	2	.105	.000	.118	3.00	1.50
Sawatski, Jay	L-L	6-2	195	5-7-82	0	0	4.87	11	1	0	0	20	25	11	11	1	4	16	.313	.323	.306	7.08	1.77
Slowey, Kevin	R-R	6-3	195	5-4-84	10	5	1.89	20	20	5	0	134	110	31	28	4	18	107	.223	.238	.207	7.20	1.21
Venafro, Mike	L-L	5-10	180	8-2-73	1	0	5.40	12	0	0	2	12	13	7	7	0	7	5	.277	.300	.259	3.86	5.40
2-team (31 Syracuse)					1	1	3.48	43	0	0	2	44	48	18	17	2	14	23	—	—	—	4.70	2.86
Williams, Jerome	R-R	6-3	240	12-4-81	0	1	9.00	8	1	0	1	11	18	11	11	0	7	6	.375	.273	.462	4.91	5.73
2-team (1 Columbus)					0	1	6.35	9	2	0	1	17	22	12	12	1	9	11	—	—	—	5.82	4.76

FIELDING

Catcher	PCT	G	PO	A	E	DP	PB
Feiner	.968	17	90	1	3	0	0
Heintz	.993	23	138	9	1	1	2
LeCroy	.993	23	129	9	1	1	2
Morales	.992	91	573	30	5	5	6
Williams	1.000	1	3	0	0	0	1

First Base	PCT	G	PO	A	E	DP
Deeds	1.000	3	6	0	0	1
Heintz	.990	13	93	11	1	10
Jones	.986	30	246	28	4	23
LeCroy	1.000	6	34	0	0	6
Velazquez	1.000	2	3	0	0	0
Williams	.992	104	869	71	8	93

Second Base	PCT	G	PO	A	E	DP
Casilla	.978	43	71	105	4	33
Macri	.857	2	4	2	1	1

Third Base	PCT	G	PO	A	E	DP
Basak	1.000	3	0	3	0	0
Buscher	.952	25	14	46	3	7
Heintz	.840	9	0	21	4	3
Macri	.950	10	4	15	1	0
Moses	.925	44	23	101	10	6
Tolbert	.977	10	10	33	1	4
Velazquez	.974	27	14	61	2	7
Watkins	.909	21	13	47	6	5
Williams	1.000	3	1	4	0	2

Shortstop	PCT	G	PO	A	E	DP
Basak	1.000	9	10	22	0	3
Casilla	.963	42	63	93	6	19

	.976	101	178	262	11	68
Tolbert	.976	101	178	262	11	68
Velazquez	1.000	1	1	0	0	0
Watkins	.933	4	7	7	1	2

Outfield	PCT	G	PO	A	E	DP
Rodriguez	1.000	6	9	23	0	4
Tolbert	.970	8	8	24	1	8
Ugueto	1.000	6	2	16	0	3
Velazquez	.965	55	91	133	8	33
Watkins	.981	49	78	131	4	33

Outfield	PCT	G	PO	A	E	DP
Deeds	1.000	35	41	1	0	1
Ford	1.000	35	60	1	0	1
Jones	.985	74	128	2	2	0
McDonald	.971	57	98	3	3	1
Oeltjen	.987	82	141	9	2	2
Rabe	1.000	2	2	0	0	0
Span	.984	136	359	4	6	1
Velazquez	1.000	1	2	0	0	0
Watkins	.920	33	40	6	4	0

NEW BRITAIN ROCK CATS — DOUBLE-A

EASTERN LEAGUE

BATTING	B-T	HT	WT	DOB	AVG	vLH	vRH	G	AB	R	H	2B	3B	HR	RBI	BB	HBP	SH	SF	SO	SB	CS	SLG	OBP
Allegra, Matthew	R-R	6-3	214	7-10-81	.241	.215	.250	106	373	57	90	30	2	13	57	32	5	1	2	94	2	2	.437	.308
Buscher, Brian	L-R	6-0	200	4-18-81	.308	.356	.293	63	247	37	76	19	1	7	37	31	4	0	2	30	2	2	.478	.391
Butera, Drew	R-R	6-1	205	8-9-83	.260	.429	.233	17	50	3	13	3	1	0	3	5	0	1	0	5	0	0	.360	.327
2-team (30 Binghamton)					.210	—	—	47	167	10	35	5	1	1	7	7	1	2	0	27	0	0	.269	.246
Christy, Jeff	R-R	6-1	205	4-13-84	.368	.143	.500	11	19	2	7	1	0	0	1	5	0	0	0	4	0	0	.421	.500
Eldridge, Rashad	B-R	6-1	185	10-16-81	.291	.326	.278	105	361	65	105	21	4	7	41	32	7	7	0	67	7	5	.429	.360
Feiner, Korey	R-R	5-11	210	9-25-81	.222	.200	.226	43	126	11	28	5	0	0	15	14	4	3	2	33	0	0	.262	.315
Geiger, Kyle	R-R	6-3	225	5-8-82	.250	.230	.257	85	276	37	69	17	1	4	35	17	5	1	4	44	0	0	.362	.301
Guzman, Garrett	L-L	5-10	180	2-7-83	.312	.333	.305	125	475	72	148	23	1	14	88	36	3	5	7	51	6	6	.453	.359
Hughes, Luke	R-R	6-0	190	8-2-84	.283	.309	.271	92	315	56	89	18	2	9	43	34	4	5	4	68	4	1	.438	.356
Molina, Felix	B-R	5-9	175	5-5-83	.272	.227	.284	117	426	51	116	20	3	8	45	35	3	4	4	70	7	6	.390	.329
Moses, Matt	L-R	6-0	210	2-20-85	.263	.153	.296	71	262	30	69	24	0	4	44	17	2	0	5	51	7	0	.401	.308
Peterson, Brock	R-R	6-3	215	11-20-83	.285	.283	.286	112	389	67	111	21	4	15	64	44	18	2	2	90	1	0	.476	.382
Plouffe, Trevor	R-R	6-1	175	6-15-86	.274	.300	.265	126	497	75	136	37	2	9	50	38	2	15	3	89	12	7	.410	.326
Roberts, Brandon	L-R	6-0	185	11-9-84	.293	.204	.308	110	369	50	108	13	4	3	39	32	5	12	2	56	14	7	.374	.355
Velazquez, Gil	R-R	6-3	190	10-17-79	.267	.250	.267	18	60	8	16	5	0	0	3	1	13	0	3	3	13	1	0	.511	.379
Winfree, David	R-R	6-3	215	5-5-85	.267	.336	.246	123	460	57	123	27	5	12	51	26	2	0	2	106	0	4	.426	.308

PITCHING	B-T	HT	WT	DOB	W	L	ERA	G	GS	CG	SV	IP	H	R	ER	HR	BB	SO	AVG	vLH	vRH	K/9	BB/9
Baker, Brad	R-R	6-2	180	11-6-80	2	5	5.33	17	13	0	0	78	85	51	46	11	25	56	.275	.295	.261	6.49	2.90
Blackburn, Nick	R-R	6-4	205	2-24-82	3	1	3.08	8	7	0	0	38	36	21	13	1	7	18	.240	.237	.243	4.26	1.66
Crawford, Tristan	R-R	6-2	200	7-22-82	8	5	5.16	27	11	0	0	82	100	59	47	12	29	66	.296	.275	.316	7.24	3.18
Duensing, Brian	L-L	5-11	195	2-22-83	4	1	2.66	9	9	0	0	51	47	19	15	2	7	38	.240	.205	.250	6.75	1.24
Floyd, Jesse	R-R	6-5	185	1-2-81	7	9	5.05	27	23	2	0	130	138	84	73	17	52	100	.271	.258	.281	6.92	3.60
Forystek, Brian	L-L	6-1	180	10-30-78	1	1	4.73	16	3	0	1	40	40	23	21	2	21	40	.267	.244	.276	9.00	4.73
Gabino, Armando	R-R	6-3	200	8-31-83	2	0	0.00	10	0	0	4	16	12	4	0	0	8	14	.207	.211	.205	7.88	4.50
Garcia, Angel	R-R	6-7	220	10-28-83	1	0	7.97	13	1	0	0	20	21	21	18	6	15	17	.259	.235	.277	7.52	6.64
Hill, Joshua	R-R	6-3	225	3-27-83	3	2	4.36	16	11	0	0	54	57	40	26	2	27	46	.260	.194	.310	7.71	4.53
Hughes, Luke	R-R	6-0	190	8-2-84	0	0	0.00	1	0	0	0	1	1	0	0	0	0	0	.250	—	.250	0.00	0.00
Lahey, Timothy	R-R	6-5	250	2-7-82	8	4	3.45	50	0	0	13	78	78	42	30	8	33	56	.255	.268	.246	6.43	3.79
Martinez, J.P	R-R	6-2	205	6-8-82	3	6	4.19	33	1	0	2	54	49	34	25	3	33	48	.247	.315	.208	8.05	5.53
Mata, Frank	R-R	6-0	168	3-11-84	0	4	5.36	32	0	0	3	49	66	29	29	4	22	28	.327	.357	.305	5.18	4.07
Mijares, Jose	L-L	6-0	230	10-29-84	5	3	3.54	46	0	0	9	61	40	26	24	7	48	75	.183	.247	.152	11.07	7.08
Morlan, Eduardo	R-R	6-2	178	3-1-86	1	0	2.25	2	0	0	0	4	3	1	1	0	3	7	.200	.400	.100	15.75	6.75
Mullins, Ryan	L-L	6-6	180	11-13-83	4	3	3.99	14	14	1	0	86	87	43	38	5	23	68	.264	.256	.267	7.14	2.42
Perkins, Glen	L-L	5-11	200	3-2-83	0	2	11.05	3	3	0	0	7	11	9	9	4	7	7	.344	.400	.318	8.59	8.59
Pino, Yohan	R-R	6-3	158	12-26-83	2	4	5.13	9	8	0	0	47	57	28	27	6	9	40	.302	.316	.292	7.61	1.71
Powers, Danny	R-R	6-1	195	7-24-82	2	5	5.28	34	0	0	1	60	76	37	35	4	23	43	.313	.367	.269	6.49	3.47
Sawatski, Jay	L-L	6-2	195	5-7-82	4	3	4.50	31	3	0	0	50	55	28	25	4	21	39	.274	.270	.275	7.02	3.78
Sosa, Oswaldo	R-R	6-4	225	9-19-85	1	4	4.50	9	9	0	0	48	45	28	24	4	23	35	.251	.218	.283	6.56	4.12
Swarzak, Anthony	R-R	6-3	195	9-10-85	5	4	3.23	15	14	1	0	86	78	34	31	6	23	76	.241	.191	.269	7.92	2.40
Waldrop, Kyle	R-R	6-5	215	10-27-85	3	6	5.34	11	11	0	0	59	74	42	35	7	19	33	.306	.362	.270	5.03	2.90

FIELDING

Catcher	PCT	G	PO	A	E	DP	PB
Butera	.986	17	129	7	2	1	4
Christy	1.000	11	48	1	0	1	1
Feiner	.997	42	262	31	1	2	3
Geiger	.988	81	549	32	7	10	13

First Base	PCT	G	PO	A	E	DP
Allegra	.946	8	47	6	3	7
Buscher	.917	1	11	0	1	2
Hughes	1.000	4	21	3	0	0
Peterson	.990	72	571	39	6	51
Velazquez	.984	8	52	9	1	8

| Winfree | .984 | 55 | 395 | 25 | 7 | 40 |

Second Base	PCT	G	PO	A	E	DP
Hughes	.986	46	81	125	3	30
Molina	.956	95	158	234	18	59
Moses	.944	7	4	13	1	3

Third Base	PCT	G	PO	A	E	DP
Buscher	.907	42	28	79	11	11
Hughes	1.000	9	5	14	0	1
Moses	.962	52	23	79	4	7
Velazquez	1.000	2	0	2	0	0
Winfree	.904	43	22	72	10	5

Shortstop	PCT	G	PO	A	E	DP
Molina	.918	16	30	37	6	15
Plouffe	.938	123	188	300	32	69
Velazquez	1.000	4	16	0	1	

Outfield	PCT	G	PO	A	E	DP
Allegra	.972	99	194	12	6	3
Eldridge	.991	96	230	2	2	0
Guzman	.990	114	197	6	2	1
Hughes	1.000	23	33	4	0	0
Roberts	.979	96	228	5	5	3
Velazquez	1.000	1	3	0	0	0

FORT MYERS MIRACLE — HIGH CLASS A

FLORIDA STATE LEAGUE

BATTING	B-T	HT	WT	DOB	AVG	vLH	vRH	G	AB	R	H	2B	3B	HR	RBI	BB	HBP	SH	SF	SO	SB	CS	SLG	OBP
Betsill, Matthew	B-R	6-5	190	8-16-84	.155	.216	.130	37	129	7	20	2	1	0	7	6	0	0	0	36	1	0	.186	.193
Christy, Jeff	R-R	6-1	205	4-13-84	.225	.236	.221	67	227	26	51	7	0	2	22	19	2	1	2	45	2	0	.282	.288
Cirillo, Jeff	R-R	6-1	205	9-23-69	.000	.000	.000	—	1	3	0	0	0	0	0	0	0	0	0	0	0	0	.000	.000
Dinkelman, Brian	L-R	5-11	195	11-10-83	.255	.218	.266	64	247	56	63	7	4	6	21	36	5	4	0	43	8	3	.389	.361
Feiner, Korey	R-R	5-11	210	9-25-81	.222	.000	.240	9	27	1	6	1	0	0	2	1	1	0	0	12	0	0	.259	.276
Gardenhire, Toby	R-R	6-0	170	11-28-82	.212	.234	.203	75	222	25	47	7	0	0	9	14	0	1	0	43	4	5	.243	.258
Lis, Erik	L-L	6-1	220	3-8-84	.274	.303	.265	132	492	58	135	34	4	18	97	41	4	1	2	109	15	4	.470	.334
Martin, Dustin	L-L	6-2	210	4-4-84	.294	.258	.307	32	119	23	35	8	0	3	19	11	3	1	1	25	5	2	.437	.366
2-team (93 St. Lucie)					.288	—	—	125	482	75	139	30	6	8	71	53	4	3	6	118	16	7	.425	.350
Mauer, Joe	R-R	6-5	215	4-19-83	.000		.000	1	3	0	0	0	0	0	0	1	0	0	0	0	0	0	.000	.250
Moore, Caleb	R-R	5-11	205	5-17-83	.196	.156	.212	49	163	15	32	4	1	1	10	9	2	0	2	23	0	0	.252	.244
Ovalle, Edward	R-R	5-11	178	6-15-85	.222	.259	.209	124	427	51	95	13	6	3	52	32	12	4	2	104	6	5	.337	.294
Portes, Juan	R-R	5-11	170	11-26-85	.269	.286	.263	132	495	71	133	24	5	12	62	43	8	4	2	89	7	3	.410	.336
Robbins, Whitney	L-R	6-0	205	9-25-84	.210	.153	.233	64	205	29	43	6	1	0	21	35	5	0	4	44	3	0	.249	.333
Sanchez, Javier	R-R	6-2	205	11-8-81	.191	.310	.138	31	94	11	18	2	0	0	10	13	5	0	0	15	0	0	.213	.321
Soto, Alexander	R-R	5-10	165	11-8-86	.250	.143	.294	7	24	2	6	1	0	0	4	2	0	0	1	5	0	0	.292	.296
Tintor, Eli	R-R	6-2	190	12-24-84	.178	.093	.204	55	185	9	33	6	2	0	16	16	1	1	2	63	2	1	.243	.245
Tolleson, Steven	R-R	5-10	180	11-1-83	.285	.315	.275	132	487	75	139	24	4	5	35	79	3	1	1	97	27	10	.382	.388

	B-R	6-0	195	DOB	AVG	vLH	vRH	G	AB	R	H	2B	3B	HR	RBI	BB	HBP	SH	SF	SO	SB	CS	SLG	OBP
Ugueto, Luis	B-R	6-0	195	2-15-79	.228	.164	.250	76	267	27	61	11	1	2	16	27	0	1	2	58	12	5	.300	.297
Valencia, Daniel	R-R	6-2	200	9-19-84	.291	.269	.298	61	230	28	67	8	2	6	31	16	0	0	4	48	1	0	.422	.332
White, Dwayne	L-L	6-1	195	4-7-83	.238	.192	.251	102	353	29	84	13	2	4	37	28	3	2	1	59	2	1	.320	.299
White, Rondell	R-R	6-1	225	2-23-72	.222	—	.222	4	9	2	2	1	0	0	1	1	1	0	0	0	0	0	.333	.364
Woodard, Johnny	L-R	6-4	208	9-15-84	.201	.175	.210	51	164	19	33	6	2	7	23	21	1	0	2	64	0	1	.390	.300

PITCHING	B-T	HT	WT	DOB	W	L	ERA	G	GS	CG	SV	IP	H	R	ER	HR	BB	SO	AVG	vLH	vRH	K/9	BB/9
Aselton, Kyle	R-L	6-5	215	2-28-83	0	3	3.79	39	4	0	0	71	59	37	30	4	49	81	.225	.167	.253	10.22	6.18
Delaney, Robert	L-R	6-3	225	9-8-84	2	0	1.54	17	0	0	7	23	19	4	4	1	10	27	.221	.194	.236	10.41	3.86
Gabino, Armando	R-R	6-3	200	8-31-83	2	2	3.16	26	0	0	4	37	27	17	13	1	15	25	.201	.222	.188	6.08	3.65
Garcia, Angel	R-R	6-7	220	10-28-83	0	2	3.38	25	0	0	4	45	33	22	17	1	26	44	.195	.189	.200	8.74	5.16
Gardenhire, Toby	B-R	6-0	170	9-11-82	0	0	0.00	1	0	0	0	1	1	0	0	0	0	0	.250	.333	.000	0.00	0.00
Hawes, Adam	L-R	6-4	190	4-25-83	2	1	6.34	19	0	0	1	33	49	29	23	1	13	15	.355	.434	.306	4.13	3.58
Hill, Joshua	R-R	6-3	225	3-27-83	3	2	3.00	17	4	0	0	39	45	17	13	1	13	36	.292	.273	.307	8.31	3.00
Manship, Jeff	R-R	6-0	165	1-16-85	8	5	3.15	13	13	0	0	71	77	38	25	5	25	59	.270	.241	.289	7.44	3.15
Marquez, Winston	L-L	6-1	160	8-19-87	0	0	27.00	1	0	0	0	1	3	3	3	0	1	0	.500	1.000	.400	0.00	9.00
Martinez, J.P	R-R	6-2	205	6-8-82	1	0	2.49	10	0	0	1	22	16	6	6	1	9	22	.200	.306	.114	9.14	3.74
Mata, Frank	R-R	6-0	168	3-11-84	2	0	1.33	13	0	0	1	20	19	4	3	0	7	14	.250	.194	.289	6.20	3.10
Morlan, Eduardo	R-R	6-2	178	3-1-86	4	3	3.15	41	0	0	18	66	55	25	23	7	17	92	.218	.186	.240	12.61	2.33
Mullins, Ryan	L-L	6-6	180	11-13-83	3	3	1.98	10	9	0	0	55	50	17	12	4	12	56	.238	.210	.250	9.22	1.98
Perkins, Glen	L-L	5-11	200	3-2-83	0	0	27.00	1	0	0	0	1	3	3	3	1	0	0	.500	.000	.600	0.00	9.00
Pino, Yohan	R-R	6-3	158	12-26-83	4	3	1.73	19	9	1	0	68	47	14	13	2	17	64	.192	.192	.191	8.51	2.26
Powers, Danny	R-R	6-1	195	7-24-82	0	0	1.29	8	0	0	0	14	10	3	2	0	13	14	.204	.227	.185	9.00	8.36
Rainville, Jay	R-R	6-3	230	10-16-85	9	11	3.29	27	26	0	0	142	145	67	52	9	31	110	.259	.276	.246	6.96	1.96
Shinskie, David	R-R	6-4	205	5-4-84	7	4	3.36	37	0	0	6	64	67	30	24	4	19	38	.269	.306	.245	5.32	2.66
Simonitsch, Errol	L-L	6-4	230	8-24-82	5	0	4.17	8	7	1	0	41	49	22	19	3	5	31	.301	.333	.291	6.80	1.10
Smit, Alexander	L-L	6-3	210	10-2-85	1	4	5.86	18	8	0	1	51	62	40	33	4	26	38	.297	.271	.309	6.75	4.62
2-team (4 Sarasota)					1	6	5.32	22	11	0	1	68	74	50	40	4	34	57	—	—	—	7.58	4.52
Sosa, Oswaldo	R-R	6-4	225	9-19-85	5	5	2.23	19	19	0	0	105	94	30	26	2	36	82	.238	.260	.225	7.03	3.09
Swarzak, Anthony	R-R	6-3	195	9-10-85	0	0	2.30	3	3	0	0	16	14	6	4	0	5	18	.241	.290	.185	10.34	2.87
Waldrop, Kyle	R-R	6-5	215	10-27-85	7	5	3.40	16	16	0	0	93	90	42	35	3	24	57	.260	.262	.259	5.54	2.33
Ward, Zachary	R-R	6-3	235	1-14-84	5	17	4.08	29	21	0	1	130	133	72	59	5	37	107	.260	.270	.253	7.41	2.56

FIELDING

Catcher	PCT	G	PO	A	E	DP	PB
Christy	.986	64	450	36	7	4	6
de San Miguel	1.000	1	13	1	0	0	0
Feiner	.984	9	60	3	1	1	2
Gardenhire	1.000	4	4	0	0	0	0
Mauer	1.000	1	10	1	0	0	0
Moore	.988	43	306	16	4	4	4
Sanchez	.981	18	143	8	3	1	4
Soto	1.000	7	39	6	0	0	3

First Base	PCT	G	PO	A	E	DP
Betsill	.981	19	150	9	3	14
Lis	.987	36	286	18	4	35
Robbins	.982	45	353	35	7	25
Woodard	.985	44	367	19	6	40

Second Base	PCT	G	PO	A	E	DP
Dinkelman	.973	44	84	131	6	34
Gardenhire	.977	24	53	76	3	20
Portes	.952	25	36	64	5	7
Tolleson	.953	47	98	143	12	32

Third Base	PCT	G	PO	A	E	DP
Betsill	.955	7	7	14	1	0
Cirillo	1.000	1	1	1	0	1
Gardenhire	.947	28	13	59	4	2
Portes	.919	42	29	50	7	9
Robbins	1.000	6	4	11	0	1
Valencia	.908	57	27	111	14	8

Shortstop	PCT	G	PO	A	E	DP
Betsill	.861	7	17	14	5	4

Shortstop (cont.)	PCT	G	PO	A	E	DP
Gardenhire	.930	15	26	40	5	9
Tolleson	.943	50	63	153	13	32
Ugueto	.948	68	105	203	17	46

Outfield	PCT	G	PO	A	E	DP
Dinkelman	1.000	15	23	1	0	0
Lis	.991	71	112	3	1	1
Martin	.986	27	70	1	0	0
Ovalle	.983	120	224	7	4	3
Portes	.967	55	113	6	4	2
Tintor	.966	55	108	4	4	0
Ugueto	1.000	1	2	0	0	0
R. White	.957	80	150	5	7	0
D. White	1.000	3	1	0	0	0

BELOIT SNAPPERS   LOW CLASS A

MIDWEST LEAGUE

BATTING	B-T	HT	WT	DOB	AVG	vLH	vRH	G	AB	R	H	2B	3B	HR	RBI	BB	HBP	SH	SF	SO	SB	CS	SLG	OBP
Benson, Joe	R-R	6-1	205	3-5-88	.255	.221	.266	122	432	73	110	18	8	5	38	49	15	6	5	124	18	16	.368	.347
Berg, Daniel	R-R	6-0	190	11-21-84	.214	.248	.198	101	323	29	69	14	1	3	36	32	8	2	3	98	3	1	.291	.298
Betsill, Matthew	B-R	6-5	190	8-16-84	.213	.204	.217	58	197	23	42	10	0	3	17	27	1	1	0	41	3	4	.310	.311
Cates, Chris	R-R	5-3	145	4-15-85	.202	.158	.220	42	129	12	26	3	0	0	13	10	1	3	1	10	1	2	.225	.262
de San Miguel, Allan	R-R	5-9	200	2-1-88	.190	.130	.207	34	105	10	20	3	0	4	20	9	2	2	2	33	1	3	.333	.263
Dinkelman, Brian	L-R	5-11	195	11-10-83	.283	.259	.291	67	240	48	68	16	6	7	21	30	5	2	1	34	10	0	.488	.373
Hernandez, David	R-R	5-11	195	5-6-85	.238	.000	.294	7	21	5	5	2	0	0	0	3	0	0	0	10	0	0	.333	.333
Luque, William	B-R	5-9	165	4-24-84	.125	.136	.119	24	64	4	8	2	0	0	3	3	1	0	1	12	1	0	.156	.174
Olson, Garrett	R-R	6-2	200	3-10-85	.219	.197	.228	123	416	48	91	20	0	6	50	20	17	1	3	76	10	4	.310	.281
Ortiz, Yancarlos	B-R	5-9	145	9-15-84	.212	.181	.222	97	288	28	61	8	1	0	23	23	2	5	3	59	4	8	.247	.272
Parmelee, Chris	L-L	6-1	200	2-24-88	.239	.190	.254	128	447	56	107	23	5	15	70	46	4	0	4	137	8	4	.414	.313
Petsch, Ben	R-R	6-2	205	9-3-84	.300	.500	.167	4	10	2	3	0	1	0	2	4	0	0	0	4	0	0	.500	.500
Ramos, Wilson	R-R	6-0	178	8-10-87	.291	.256	.304	73	292	40	85	17	1	8	42	19	5	0	6	61	1	1	.438	.345
Robinson, Mark	B-R	6-1	180	4-7-86	.132	.100	.107	12	38	2	5	1	0	0	5	1	0	1	2	12	0	1	.158	.146
Romero, Deibinson	R-R	6-1	170	9-24-86	.300	.000	.333	2	10	1	3	0	0	0	3	1	0	0	0	4	0	0	.400	.364
Santana, Ramon	R-R	5-9	152	6-20-86	.225	.333	.206	15	40	7	9	2	1	0	4	5	3	1	1	14	1	0	.325	.347
Santiesteban, Danny	R-R	6-2	170	2-17-85	.219	.125	.248	105	338	34	74	14	1	8	39	25	5	1	3	98	12	5	.337	.280
Singleton, Steven	B-R	5-11	160	9-14-84	.271	.222	.282	102	373	36	101	18	2	2	30	8	5	3	2	47	8	6	.346	.294
Tintor, Eli	R-R	6-2	190	12-24-84	.286	.328	.268	54	203	31	58	13	2	5	27	10	4	2	2	56	8	5	.443	.329
Tosoni, Rene	L-R	6-0	185	7-2-86	.273	.000	.300	2	11	3	3	1	0	0	1	0	0	0	0	2	0	0	.364	.273
Valencia, Daniel	R-R	6-2	200	9-19-84	.302	.268	.313	66	242	44	73	15	0	11	35	28	0	1	0	54	3	3	.500	.374
Woodard, Johnny	L-R	6-4	208	9-15-84	.276	.171	.298	66	203	37	56	11	0	10	31	37	5	0	1	64	1	2	.478	.398
Yersich, Gregory	R-R	6-0	205	10-7-86	.180	.171	.184	41	122	13	22	5	0	0	9	5	2	0	2	29	0	0	.221	.221

PITCHING	B-T	HT	WT	DOB	W	L	ERA	G	GS	CG	SV	IP	H	R	ER	HR	BB	SO	AVG	vLH	vRH	K/9	BB/9
Burnett, Alex	R-R	6-0	190	7-26-87	9	8	3.02	27	27	1	0	155	140	60	52	9	38	117	.239	.190	.275	6.79	2.21
Carnevales, Jesus	L-L	6-5	200	7-18-84	5	5	4.04	37	2	0	6	58	52	32	25	5	26	43	.272	.296	.261	6.95	4.20
Craig, Aaron	R-R	6-1	195	3-22-86	4	1	2.32	33	0	0	3	50	49	16	13	2	15	43	.255	.310	.213	7.69	2.68
Delaney, Robert	L-R	6-3	225	9-8-84	1	0	0.77	36	0	0	28	47	25	8	4	1	6	56	.152	.172	.140	10.80	1.16
Devries, Cole	R-R	6-1	190	2-12-85	9	5	3.41	27	25	0	0	148	161	73	56	17	36	108	.271	.285	.259	6.57	2.19

Name	B-T	HT	WT	DOB	W	L	ERA	G	GS	CG	SV	IP	H	R	ER	HR	BB	SO	AVG	vLH	vRH	K/9	BB/9
Fox, Matthew	R-R	6-3	192	12-4-82	7	2	3.50	22	13	0	0	82	75	35	32	7	23	66	.244	.221	.258	7.21	2.51
Gabino, Armando	R-R	6-3	200	8-31-83	1	0	0.82	12	0	0	0	22	18	2	2	1	4	16	.228	.321	.176	6.55	1.64
Hawes, Adam	L-R	6-4	190	4-25-83	3	7	4.37	13	13	0	0	70	77	49	34	4	22	39	.274	.328	.236	5.01	2.83
Hernandez, Danny	R-R	6-2	175	11-19-85	2	0	3.38	7	0	0	0	8	4	3	3	0	5	9	.143	.100	.167	10.12	5.62
Kirwan, Brian	R-R	6-4	205	6-9-87	2	8	5.30	19	18	1	0	90	100	63	53	8	37	67	.282	.289	.277	6.70	3.70
Land, Sean	L-L	6-5	230	9-27-84	1	1	2.57	5	0	0	1	7	6	4	2	0	5	4	.214	.143	.238	5.14	6.43
Leatherman, Dan	R-R	6-2	210	7-12-85	7	4	3.89	49	1	0	5	79	71	39	34	5	31	67	.245	.238	.249	7.67	3.55
Lugo, Jose	L-L	6-1	159	4-10-84	5	6	4.32	40	7	0	2	77	87	43	37	6	39	73	.285	.235	.309	8.53	4.56
Manship, Jeff	R-R	6-0	165	1-16-85	7	1	1.51	13	13	0	0	78	51	15	13	4	9	77	.185	.184	.185	8.92	1.04
Revelette, Adam	L-L	6-2	195	5-25-84	0	1	4.50	8	0	0	0	6	12	4	3	0	4	5	.400	.333	.429	7.50	6.00
Reyes, Henry	L-L	6-7	183	5-10-85	0	1	10.38	2	1	0	0	4	11	6	5	0	3	2	.500	.583	.400	4.15	6.23
Robertson, Tyler	L-L	6-5	220	12-23-87	9	5	2.29	18	16	2	1	102	87	33	26	3	33	123	.226	.200	.236	10.82	2.90
Slama, Anthony	R-R	6-3	180	1-6-84	1	1	1.48	21	0	0	10	24	15	4	4	0	9	39	.172	.179	.167	14.42	3.33
Vais, Danny	R-R	6-1	210	11-21-84	5	4	4.15	41	4	0	2	78	83	42	36	9	12	69	.271	.274	.269	7.96	1.38
Williams, Matthew	R-R	6-1	170	2-18-87	1	1	2.64	18	0	0	1	31	30	11	9	0	11	17	.248	.232	.262	4.99	3.23

FIELDING

Catcher	PCT	G	PO	A	E	DP	PB
Berg	.977	19	119	11	3	1	3
de San Miguel	.989	34	252	20	3	3	4
Hernandez	.971	5	28	5	1	0	0
Ramos	.995	51	363	75	2	5	7
Yersich	.976	40	265	17	7	3	4

First Base	PCT	G	PO	A	E	DP
Berg	.988	37	302	21	4	28
Betsill	.984	53	447	30	8	45
Olson	1.000	6	49	4	0	1
Parmelee	.800	1	4	0	1	0
Romero	1.000	1	2	0	0	0
Tintor	—	1	0	0	0	0
Valencia	1.000	2	5	0	0	1
Woodard	.979	52	438	25	10	40

Second Base	PCT	G	PO	A	E	DP
Cates	.951	9	11	28	2	5
Dinkelman	.982	50	90	133	4	36
Luque	1.000	13	19	24	0	6
Ortiz	1.000	1	1	0	0	0
Santana	.895	4	9	8	2	3
Singleton	.955	75	112	185	14	36

Third Base	PCT	G	PO	A	E	DP
Berg	.929	8	3	10	1	1
Betsill	.800	4	5	3	2	1
Cates	.960	12	8	16	1	1
Luque	1.000	3	0	2	0	0
Olson	.913	79	61	118	17	11
Romero	1.000	2	1	5	0	1
Valencia	.950	47	31	102	7	9

Shortstop	PCT	G	PO	A	E	DP
Cates	.968	24	27	65	3	12
Luque	.950	6	8	11	1	3
Olson	.857	9	5	13	3	1
Ortiz	.941	95	110	274	24	63
Santana	.923	5	4	8	1	1
Singleton	.878	22	26	46	10	11

Outfield	PCT	G	PO	A	E	DP
Benson	.975	109	230	7	6	3
Berg	1.000	5	4	0	0	0
Dinkelman	.962	18	25	0	1	0
Olson	.945	34	50	2	3	1
Parmelee	.968	112	176	8	6	6
Petsch	.750	2	3	0	1	0
Robinson	.952	12	19	1	1	0
Santana	1.000	2	2	0	0	0
Santiesteban	.928	102	184	9	15	1
Tintor	.986	47	64	4	1	0
Tosoni	1.000	2	3	0	0	0

ELIZABETHTON TWINS   ROOKIE

APPALACHIAN LEAGUE

BATTING	B-T	HT	WT	DOB	AVG	vLH	vRH	G	AB	R	H	2B	3B	HR	RBI	BB	HBP	SH	SF	SO	SB	CS	SLG	OBP
Cates, Chris	R-R	5-3	145	4-15-85	.429	.000	.429	2	7	4	3	0	0	0	1	1	0	0	0	0	0	0	.429	.500
Connor, Wesley	B-R	6-2	195	4-11-85	.293	.263	.304	40	140	22	41	11	1	3	18	12	5	0	1	31	8	0	.450	.367
De Los Santos, Estarlin	B-R	5-10	155	1-20-87	.264	.210	.286	67	284	60	75	13	6	1	41	26	8	2	2	66	27	7	.363	.341
Dolenc, Mark	R-R	6-3	215	11-8-84	.287	.333	.267	64	230	41	66	10	1	4	37	33	2	0	0	59	12	2	.391	.381
Hernandez, David	R-R	5-11	195	5-6-85	.192	.333	.150	10	26	2	5	1	0	1	3	2	0	0	0	6	1	0	.346	.250
Lawman, Matthew	R-R	6-0	170	6-26-87	.184	.281	.146	38	114	23	21	3	0	1	21	21	2	0	2	33	1	0	.237	.317
Lehmann, Daniel	R-R	5-11	190	9-5-85	.221	.174	.241	22	77	12	17	2	0	3	17	9	4	0	0	10	0	0	.364	.333
Leveret, Rene	R-R	6-2	224	11-19-85	.307	.338	.295	66	244	50	75	14	0	8	65	34	4	0	1	36	0	0	.463	.399
Lewis, Ozzie	R-R	6-4	193	3-21-86	.323	.364	.311	62	235	46	76	18	1	9	50	19	3	0	4	52	3	1	.523	.375
Palacios, Rodolfo	R-R	5-10	176	6-26-85	.346	.400	.313	8	26	7	9	3	0	0	3	8	0	0	0	5	0	0	.462	.500
Petsch, Ben	R-R	6-2	205	9-3-84	.311	.391	.275	23	74	19	23	4	1	2	16	21	0	0	0	15	2	0	.473	.463
Romero, Deibinson	R-R	6-1	170	9-24-86	.316	.375	.295	66	247	60	78	16	2	9	52	34	7	0	5	47	9	3	.506	.406
Sanchez, Henry	R-R	6-3	235	11-29-86	.258	.455	.150	10	31	10	8	2	0	1	8	11	1	0	0	7	0	0	.419	.465
Santiago, Eric	R-R	6-0	185	7-10-87	.240	.174	.278	39	125	17	30	7	0	0	16	13	6	1	0	20	3	1	.296	.340
Tosoni, Rene	L-R	6-0	185	7-2-86	.301	.255	.314	63	236	58	71	13	4	3	30	32	13	1	4	48	13	4	.428	.407
Yersich, Gregory	R-R	6-0	205	10-7-86	.312	.280	.324	50	186	35	58	12	0	2	30	15	5	0	3	23	0	0	.409	.373

PITCHING	B-T	HT	WT	DOB	W	L	ERA	G	GS	CG	SV	IP	H	R	ER	HR	BB	SO	AVG	vLH	vRH	K/9	BB/9
Alcala, Omar	L-L	5-11	145	12-24-86	1	1	7.83	15	0	0	0	23	28	22	20	0	16	22	.308	.000	.318	8.61	6.26
Allen, Michael	R-R	6-3	220	5-27-87	4	2	3.47	13	13	0	0	62	67	31	24	5	11	70	.277	.203	.303	10.11	1.59
Bromberg, David	L-R	6-5	230	9-14-87	9	0	2.78	13	11	0	0	58	45	19	18	4	32	81	.211	.249	.196	12.50	4.94
Castillo, Jose	R-R	6-1	175	12-23-84	5	1	2.25	8	5	0	0	36	27	9	9	3	9	25	.201	.167	.212	6.25	2.25
Erickson, Blair	R-R	6-1	210	10-28-84	0	0	1.53	18	0	0	11	18	14	6	3	1	3	17	.209	.250	.191	8.66	1.53
Hirschfeld, Steven	R-R	6-5	220	9-8-85	1	2	4.26	8	6	0	0	25	21	12	12	2	6	20	.221	.270	.190	7.11	2.13
Latham, Daniel	R-R	6-3	185	9-5-84	0	0	4.91	17	0	0	0	26	26	14	14	2	3	28	.255	.313	.229	9.82	1.05
Leavitt, Curtis	R-R	6-4	195	1-10-87	2	0	5.40	20	0	0	0	25	32	16	15	2	10	41	.320	.250	.342	14.76	3.60
McCardell, Michael	R-R	6-5	220	4-13-85	5	1	2.00	8	8	0	0	45	29	12	10	3	5	70	.179	.255	.144	14.00	1.00
Moore, Caleb	R-R	5-11	205	5-17-83	0	0	2.63	12	0	0	2	14	10	4	4	0	4	13	.222	.214	.226	8.56	2.63
Reyes, Henry	L-L	6-7	183	5-10-85	7	2	2.87	11	11	0	0	53	44	20	17	7	17	68	.218	.150	.225	11.48	2.87
Rogers, Michael	L-L	5-10	175	6-11-85	0	1	5.81	14	2	0	1	26	24	22	17	1	27	30	.247	.222	.250	10.25	9.23
Slama, Anthony	R-R	6-3	180	1-6-84	0	0	2.45	6	0	0	4	7	2	2	2	0	1	10	.091	.222	.000	12.27	1.23
Steedley, Spencer	L-L	6-2	195	5-31-85	2	3	2.92	18	1	0	1	37	28	14	12	1	12	51	.209	.138	.229	12.41	2.92
Tarsi, Michael	R-L	6-8	190	8-11-86	5	2	2.22	11	11	0	0	53	49	21	13	0	13	59	.238	.130	.251	10.08	2.22
Tippett, Bradley	R-R	6-2	176	2-11-88	7	1	0.93	21	0	0	3	39	20	4	4	1	4	51	.155	.000	.215	11.87	0.93
Van Mil, Loek	R-R	7-1	225	9-15-84	2	2	2.63	13	0	0	0	24	14	10	7	0	17	23	.171	.125	.190	8.62	6.38
Williams, Matthew	R-R	6-1	170	2-18-87	0	0	3.00	2	0	0	0	3	3	3	1	0	2	1	.250	.000	.429	3.00	6.00

FIELDING

Catcher	PCT	G	PO	A	E	DP	PB
Hernandez	1.000	3	8	1	0	0	0
Lehmann	.979	22	213	18	5	3	2
Palacios	.988	8	77	6	1	2	0
Petsch	1.000	1	2	0	0	0	0
Yersich	.995	40	368	48	2	4	4

First Base	PCT	G	PO	A	E	DP
Leveret	.986	65	483	18	7	42
Petsch	1.000	4	16	2	0	3
Sanchez	1.000	1	9	1	0	2
Yersich	1.000	2	13	1	0	1

Second Base	PCT	G	PO	A	E	DP
Lawman	.907	34	46	71	12	16
Santiago	.941	36	59	68	8	24
Tosoni	—	1	0	0	0	0

Third Base	PCT	G	PO	A	E	DP
Lawman	.900	4	2	7	1	0
Romero	.929	66	43	126	13	13
Santiago	1.000	1	0	3	0	0

Shortstop	PCT	G	PO	A	E	DP
Cates	1.000	2	1	4	0	0

De Los Santos	.926	67	81	168	20	34
Lawman	—	1	0	0	0	0
Santiago	1.000	1	0	1	0	0

Outfield	PCT	G	PO	A	E	DP
Connor	.970	30	30	2	1	1
Dolenc	.982	64	105	5	2	3
Lewis	.977	38	40	2	1	0
Petsch	1.000	12	12	1	0	1
Tosoni	.980	61	91	9	2	3

GCL TWINS　　　　　　　　　　　　　　　　　　ROOKIE

GULF COAST LEAGUE

BATTING	B-T	HT	WT	DOB	AVG	vLH	vRH	G	AB	R	H	2B	3B	HR	RBI	BB	HBP	SH	SF	SO	SB	CS	SLG	OBP
Beresford, James	L-R	6-1	155	1-19-89	.288	.262	.299	45	139	22	40	2	0	0	14	12	1	6	0	23	7	2	.302	.349
Biagini, Nick	L-L	6-1	230	1-9-85	.258	.261	.256	23	66	11	17	5	0	0	7	10	0	0	0	23	2	0	.333	.355
Brito, Jeanfred	R-R	5-8	150	12-21-87	.290	.259	.303	51	210	40	61	7	4	1	21	10	3	4	2	22	8	8	.376	.329
Diaz, Andres	R-R	6-1	195	7-22-88	.300	—	.300	4	10	0	3	1	0	0	0	1	0	0	0	2	0	0	.400	.364
Harrington, Kevin	L-R	6-6	185	4-8-88	.160	.000	.190	9	25	5	4	2	1	0	4	1	1	0	0	10	0	0	.320	.222
Harvey, Ken	R-R	6-2	250	3-1-78	.222	.143	.273	5	18	2	4	3	0	1	4	2	0	0	0	3	0	0	.556	.300
Hernandez, David	R-R	5-11	195	5-6-85	.323	.500	.211	11	31	4	10	4	0	0	2	3	1	0	0	7	1	0	.452	.400
Kelly, Paul	R-R	6-0	185	10-19-86	.200	—	.200	2	5	0	1	0	0	0	1	0	0	0	0	1	0	0	.200	.200
Lin, Wang-Wei	L-R	6-0	185	6-28-88	.194	.444	.151	24	62	10	12	4	1	0	4	6	0	2	0	25	4	3	.290	.265
Morales, Angel	R-R	6-1	180	11-24-89	.256	.214	.269	38	121	18	31	6	3	2	15	12	8	0	2	44	11	5	.405	.357
Papasan, Nicholas	R-R	5-9	170	3-14-88	.286	.600	.217	9	28	3	8	1	0	0	1	2	0	0	0	6	2	0	.321	.355
Rams, Daniel	R-R	6-2	205	12-19-88	.258	.130	.297	27	97	13	25	8	1	0	13	5	3	0	1	22	0	0	.361	.311
Revere, Ben	L-R	5-9	175	5-3-88	.325	.404	.299	50	191	46	62	6	10	0	29	13	8	2	2	20	21	9	.461	.388
Richardson, Juan	R-R	6-0	200	12-27-86	.317	.310	.319	54	202	33	64	10	2	1	33	13	3	0	2	16	14	10	.401	.364
Rohlfing, Daniel	R-R	6-0	185	2-12-89	.232	.200	.244	22	56	3	13	1	0	0	7	7	0	1	1	10	2	2	.250	.313
Santana, Ramon	R-R	5-9	152	6-20-86	.211	.308	.182	18	57	10	12	3	1	1	9	4	3	0	2	14	4	3	.351	.288
Schmiesing, Andrew	L-L	6-4	190	5-24-86	.321	.263	.352	35	109	19	35	4	0	0	13	18	3	1	3	17	5	2	.358	.421
Solarte, Yangervis	B-R	5-11	176	7-7-87	.303	.283	.311	52	175	25	53	4	3	1	33	11	2	10	5	18	7	3	.377	.342
Soto, Alexander	R-R	5-10	165	11-8-86	.273	.267	.275	22	66	9	18	5	0	2	10	4	3	1	1	20	1	0	.439	.338
Waltenbury, Jonathan	L-R	6-3	220	4-1-88	.244	.281	.231	41	123	19	30	6	0	3	16	18	2	0	1	31	1	1	.366	.347
White, Rondell	R-R	6-1	225	2-23-72	.435	.375	.467	7	23	1	10	4	0	0	3	3	0	0	0	2	0	0	.609	.500

PITCHING	B-T	HT	WT	DOB	W	L	ERA	G	GS	CG	SV	IP	H	R	ER	HR	BB	SO	AVG	vLH	vRH	K/9	BB/9
Acosta, Jose	R-R	6-2	186	11-11-86	2	0	3.18	14	0	0	0	23	24	11	8	0	14	4	.276	.281	.273	5.56	2.38
Arias, Santos	R-R	6-0	150	3-17-87	3	4	2.96	11	10	0	0	55	59	31	18	5	13	46	.280	.278	.280	7.57	2.14
Berlind, Daniel	R-R	6-7	210	12-3-87	6	2	1.93	11	9	0	0	56	37	16	12	4	20	52	.186	.176	.192	8.36	3.21
Eacott, Jarrad	L-L	5-11	190	8-2-88	3	0	2.28	15	1	0	0	28	24	9	7	0	10	19	.242	.368	.213	6.18	3.25
Fuentes, Nelvin	L-L	6-0	194	4-7-89	1	0	2.77	10	0	0	0	13	9	7	4	2	5	6	.205	.625	.111	4.15	3.46
Gessmann, Rodney	R-R	6-4	205	1-25-87	2	1	4.22	12	0	0	0	21	20	14	10	1	5	11	.244	.286	.222	4.64	2.11
Hamburger, Mark	R-R	6-4	195	2-5-87	2	1	1.20	8	0	0	0	15	12	4	2	0	4	12	.203	.227	.189	7.20	2.40
Hendriks, Liam	R-R	6-1	190	2-10-89	4	2	2.05	10	10	0	0	44	41	14	10	2	11	52	.241	.234	.245	10.64	2.25
Land, Sean	L-L	6-5	230	9-27-84	0	0	9.00	2	0	0	0	2	2	2	2	0	1	0	.250	.333	.200	0.00	4.50
Lobanov, Nick	R-L	6-0	195	3-26-89	0	0	0.00	3	0	0	0	3	4	0	0	0	1	2	.333	.333	.333	6.00	3.00
Marquez, Winston	L-L	6-1	160	8-19-87	3	3	3.04	11	10	0	0	47	38	21	16	0	30	35	.228	.167	.244	6.65	5.70
Martin, Lee	R-R	6-0	185	5-28-86	2	1	3.21	10	0	0	1	14	10	5	5	1	6	13	.208	.313	.156	8.36	3.86
McCardell, Michael	R-R	6-5	220	4-13-85	2	0	2.50	4	2	0	1	18	11	5	5	2	3	25	.177	.182	.175	12.50	1.50
Mopas, Michael	L-L	6-1	170	12-23-87	0	0	7.56	6	0	0	0	8	11	7	7	0	4	6	.314	.250	.323	6.48	4.32
Nolte, Charles	R-R	6-3	205	3-19-86	3	0	1.85	14	0	0	0	24	17	7	5	0	11	22	.193	.143	.226	8.14	4.07
Perkins, Glen	L-L	5-11	200	3-2-83	0	0	1.80	3	3	0	0	5	3	1	1	0	2	6	.167	.250	.143	10.80	3.60
Rodgers, Dominique	R-R	6-2	210	1-21-85	0	2	4.66	8	0	0	0	10	10	10	5	1	6	8	.263	.333	.231	8.38	5.59
Rondon, Danny	R-R	6-0	161	6-21-87	2	0	1.14	20	0	0	12	24	19	4	3	2	11	16	.218	.273	.185	6.08	4.18
Simonitsch, Errol	L-L	6-4	230	8-24-82	0	0	0.00	2	2	0	0	5	2	0	0	0	0	7	.118	.000	.154	12.60	0.00
Stuifbergen, Tom	R-R	6-3	200	9-26-88	0	0	2.19	7	0	0	0	12	6	4	3	0	3	9	.140	.143	.138	6.57	2.19
Toufar, Jakub	R-R	6-2	185	3-20-87	0	0	6.92	8	0	0	0	13	22	12	10	2	3	6	.373	.400	.353	4.15	2.08
Wright, Thomas	B-R	6-3	185	1-28-88	2	3	5.35	11	9	0	0	37	39	29	22	2	27	27	.264	.264	.263	6.57	6.57

FIELDING

Catcher	PCT	G	PO	A	E	DP	PB
Diaz	1.000	3	22	0	0	0	0
Hernandez	1.000	9	47	6	0	1	3
Rams	1.000	16	97	11	0	2	7
Rohlfing	1.000	18	102	9	0	0	6
Soto	.977	18	113	12	3	2	2

First Base	PCT	G	PO	A	E	DP
Biagini	1.000	14	100	7	0	9
Harvey	1.000	3	22	4	0	3
Rams	.950	4	35	3	2	3
Richardson	.923	4	24	0	2	5
Waltenbury	.976	38	302	19	8	40

Second Base	PCT	G	PO	A	E	DP
Beresford	1.000	4	13	12	0	6

Brito	.966	26	54	60	4	21
Papasan	.949	7	22	15	2	3
Santana	1.000	11	23	25	0	5
Solarte	1.000	10	14	18	0	7

Third Base	PCT	G	PO	A	E	DP
Richardson	.952	50	43	135	9	17
Santana	.667	1	1	1	1	0
Solarte	.870	4	4	16	3	3

Shortstop	PCT	G	PO	A	E	DP
Beresford	.935	40	55	117	12	26
Brito	.953	14	17	44	3	9
Kelly	1.000	2	4	5	0	1
Santana	.875	4	5	9	2	3
Solarte	—	1	0	0	0	0

Outfield	PCT	G	PO	A	E	DP
Biagini	1.000	7	4	0	0	0
Brito	.929	8	13	0	1	0
Harrington	1.000	9	10	1	0	1
Morales	.948	38	53	2	3	1
Revere	.982	49	106	4	2	0
Schmiesing	.955	31	41	1	2	0
Solarte	1.000	33	55	4	0	1
White	1.000	2	3	0	0	0

DOMINICAN SUMMER LEAGUE

BATTING	B-T	HT	WT	DOB	AVG	vLH	vRH	G	AB	R	H	2B	3B	HR	RBI	BB	HBP	SH	SF	SO	SB	CS	SLG	OBP
Arias, Emmanuel	R-R	6-0	173	3-13-87	.500	.500	.500	3	6	2	3	0	0	0	0	2	0	0	0	1	1	0	.500	.625
Arias, Jhonatan	R-R	5-10	180	2-18-89	.207	.333	.167	40	121	15	25	4	0	0	9	6	10	1	0	16	2	1	.240	.299
Caro, Felix	R-R	6-0	186	3-20-90	.212	.267	.193	65	212	20	45	8	1	0	24	14	9	0	2	57	3	5	.259	.287
Doran, Raynard	R-R	6-1	175	9-3-87	.160	.147	.165	53	131	13	21	3	1	1	14	14	6	9	2	36	7	5	.221	.268
Franco, Yancarlo	R-R	5-9	145	8-29-88	.193	.200	.193	52	135	20	26	4	4	1	12	18	1	5	0	32	8	1	.304	.292
Goncalves, Jonathan	R-R	5-11	159	5-13-89	.234	.250	.234	62	209	33	49	5	3	0	22	31	7	1	2	44	16	5	.287	.349
Hidalgo, Anderson	R-R	5-9	172	9-5-88	.305	.281	.318	55	190	27	58	13	3	2	28	27	3	5	1	28	8	8	.437	.398
Luciano, Manuel	R-R	6-0	184	1-19-88	.168	.235	.139	49	137	12	23	9	0	1	6	21	5	1	0	40	3	3	.255	.301
Mercedes, Jean Carlos	R-R	6-0	185	11-29-87	.056	.045	.063	27	71	6	4	0	1	0	2	12	0	0	1	22	1	3	.085	.190
Morillo, Domingo	R-R	6-1	163	8-13-87	.237	.224	.238	55	173	24	41	6	4	0	22	25	8	3	2	31	5	6	.318	.356
Parra, Leonardo	R-R	6-2	160	7-18-86	—	—	.000	1	0	0	0	0	0	0	0	0	0	0	0	0	0	0	—	—
Perez, Jairo	R-R	5-10	160	6-10-88	.091	.000	.130	10	33	2	3	0	0	0	6	1	4	0	0	1	0	1	.091	.211
Pinto, Josmil	R-R	5-11	184	3-31-89	.193	.174	.200	54	171	18	33	8	1	1	23	29	6	2	2	23	3	1	.269	.327
Sanchez, Juan	R-R	5-11	167	1-16-87	.263	.271	.258	64	224	34	59	9	1	1	21	32	10	6	7	27	20	6	.326	.370
Sierra, Eliel	R-R	5-10	162	1-21-86	.238	.211	.249	67	227	28	54	13	1	2	33	34	7	3	0	38	8	9	.330	.354
Soliman, Manuel	R-R	6-2	185	8-11-89	.189	.224	.180	63	201	22	38	4	0	4	16	26	8	3	1	46	5	3	.269	.305

PITCHING	B-T	HT	WT	DOB	W	L	ERA	G	GS	CG	SV	IP	H	R	ER	HR	BB	SO	AVG	vLH	vRH	K/9	BB/9
Acosta, Ramon	R-R	6-0	166	1-21-87	4	5	2.48	14	14	1	0	83	71	32	23	2	23	48	.233	.241	.229	5.18	2.48
Alvarez, Edison	L-R	6-3	163	8-4-88	5	1	0.78	26	2	0	7	58	41	10	5	0	11	48	.195	.235	.182	7.45	1.71
Arias, Emmanuel	R-R	6-0	173	3-13-87	0	2	6.00	6	0	0	0	6	5	4	4	0	4	5	.238	.600	.125	7.50	6.00
Caceres, Alvaro	L-L	6-0	165	5-4-86	3	1	1.08	22	0	0	0	42	28	10	5	0	11	32	.185	.125	.189	6.91	2.38
Cardenas, Eliecer	R-R	6-2	177	1-30-88	2	3	2.08	13	12	0	0	52	38	20	12	0	22	56	.201	.190	.204	9.69	3.81
De La Rosa, Rafael	R-R	6-1	165	10-19-86	0	3	2.72	29	0	0	8	40	40	14	12	1	21	28	.282	.351	.257	6.35	4.76
Garcia, Carlos	L-L	6-1	160	3-27-87	4	5	3.30	14	12	1	0	60	45	23	22	1	29	57	.206	.267	.202	8.55	4.35
Garcia, Martire	L-L	5-11	150	3-1-90	7	2	2.32	14	13	0	0	78	60	23	20	2	25	81	.217	.150	.223	9.39	2.90
Germosen, Deivi	R-R	6-0	155	8-1-89	0	1	21.60	9	4	0	0	10	14	26	24	1	25	10	.341	.364	.333	9.00	22.50
Mota, Kelvin	R-R	6-3	190	6-23-88	4	0	1.40	15	0	0	0	26	29	10	4	0	11	13	.287	.077	.360	4.56	3.86
Munoz, Miguel	R-R	6-2	182	8-4-88	5	3	2.04	14	14	1	0	71	45	22	16	2	34	43	.184	.209	.175	5.48	4.33
Parra, Leonardo	R-R	6-2	160	7-18-86	0	0	3.68	2	0	0	0	7	8	3	3	2	3	6	.286	.167	.318	7.36	3.68
Paulino, Francis	L-L	6-5	216	10-9-87	1	2	1.27	10	0	0	2	21	17	6	3	1	7	15	.224	.000	.230	6.33	2.95
2-team (5 DSL)					1	2	2.15	15	0	0	2	29	23	11	7	1	12	22	—	—	—	6.75	3.68
Portoreal, Rodolfo	R-R	6-4	200	5-10-86	2	4	6.84	14	0	0	0	26	35	24	20	0	16	8	.327	.265	.356	2.73	5.47
Santana, Eddy	R-R	6-1	165	9-21-87	2	0	2.27	24	0	0	2	48	45	19	12	1	12	30	.253	.317	.234	5.66	2.27

FIELDING

Catcher	PCT	G	PO	A	E	DP	PB
Arias	1.000	3	14	3	0	0	0
Arias	.990	37	237	52	3	1	3
Luciano	.955	11	56	7	3	0	2
Morillo	1.000	1	2	0	0	0	0
Pinto	.969	29	183	35	7	1	5

First Base	PCT	G	PO	A	E	DP
Caro	.967	22	164	10	6	9
Doran	.900	1	9	0	1	0
Luciano	.995	21	191	7	1	12
Morillo	.994	22	165	10	1	18
Perez	1.000	2	19	0	0	2
Soliman	.988	19	145	13	2	14

Second Base	PCT	G	PO	A	E	DP
Franco	1.000	21	28	41	0	7
Hidalgo	.995	52	97	122	1	25
Morillo	.950	3	9	10	1	4

Third Base	PCT	G	PO	A	E	DP
Caro	.822	32	26	71	21	8
Franco	1.000	2	1	3	0	0
Hidalgo	1.000	4	2	4	0	0
Morillo	.667	1	1	1	1	0
Sanchez	.900	2	1	8	1	0
Soliman	.843	45	27	91	22	5

Shortstop	PCT	G	PO	A	E	DP
Franco	.913	10	16	26	4	6

	PCT	G	PO	A	E	DP
Mercedes	1.000	1	3	1	0	0
Morillo	1.000	1	1	1	0	0
Sanchez	.940	63	110	220	21	35

Outfield	PCT	G	PO	A	E	DP
Caro	.900	11	9	0	1	0
Doran	.963	50	71	8	3	3
Franco	.909	19	20	0	2	0
Goncalves	.969	62	116	7	4	3
Mercedes	.895	16	17	0	2	0
Morillo	1.000	25	24	7	0	2
Pinto	.667	1	2	0	1	0
Sierra	.952	60	78	2	4	1

VENEZUELAN SUMMER LEAGUE (C=CHICAGO, M=MINNESOTA)

BATTING

BATTING	B-T	HT	WT	DOB	AVG	vLH	vRH	G	AB	R	H	2B	3B	HR	RBI	BB	HBP	SH	SF	SO	SB	CS	SLG	OBP
Andrades, Luis (C)	R-R	5-11	170	4-29-88	.175	.444	.130	28	63	9	11	0	0	0	4	14	2	2	0	21	3	2	.175	.342
Avila, Jose (C)	R-R	6-0	175	5-18-89	.188	.158	.200	26	64	11	12	0	1	0	4	19	4	2	1	22	1	1	.219	.398
Blanco, Juan (M)	R-R	5-10	152	4-24-89	.261	.200	.281	59	203	22	53	3	1	1	17	14	4	3	2	25	5	2	.300	.318
Bracho, Jose (C)	R-R	5-11	184	1-14-87	.236	.105	.283	27	72	8	17	5	0	0	7	6	8	0	1	12	0	0	.306	.356
Diaz, Julio (M)	R-R	5-11	210	1-19-89	.204	.087	.240	39	98	12	20	3	1	0	5	22	2	9	0	15	0	0	.255	.361
Galvan, Lesther (M)	R-R	5-10	178	4-10-90	.202	.231	.190	37	89	17	18	2	1	0	10	20	1	1	1	20	0	1	.247	.351
Gonzalez, Joelvis (M)	R-R	6-3	167	8-16-86	.274	.366	.244	56	168	17	46	4	0	0	13	20	0	3	2	20	8	2	.298	.347
Gonzalez, Xavier (M)	R-R	5-11	170	2-22-89	.184	.111	.211	37	98	13	18	2	0	0	8	11	3	2	2	16	0	2	.204	.281
Guevara, Jose (C)	R-R	6-1	180	3-17-88	.194	.143	.215	59	191	19	37	6	1	1	27	22	9	1	3	45	0	3	.251	.302
Lara, Herbert (M)	B-R	5-10	154	6-29-88	.300	.343	.282	66	240	34	72	5	4	0	32	36	9	1	0	25	16	4	.354	.411
Martin, Alfredo (L)	L-R	6-1	248	11-10-87	.225	.240	.218	22	80	9	18	1	0	2	10	12	2	0	0	28	0	0	.313	.340
Martinez, Yorby (M)	B-R	6-0	170	1-12-89	.219	.176	.239	47	160	20	35	2	0	0	14	19	7	3	1	28	3	4	.231	.326
Matheus, George (C)	R-R	6-0	170	7-20-88	.258	.233	.267	67	240	27	62	4	0	2	25	27	2	5	1	26	5	9	.300	.337
Requena, Jonathan (M)	R-R	5-11	178	1-18-86	.275	.324	.246	26	91	6	25	5	0	0	14	14	1	2	1	9	5	0	.330	.374
Rodriguez, Jairo (M)	R-R	5-11	180	8-24-88	.348	.323	.358	34	112	19	39	2	0	0	14	8	4	1	2	6	0	0	.366	.405
Romero, Carlos (C)	R-R	6-1	180	5-28-90	.153	.105	.170	30	72	11	11	0	0	0	7	5	5	3	0	8	0	0	.181	.256
Soto, Kevin (C)	R-R	6-1	170	10-12-88	.234	.262	.223	61	222	32	52	5	1	0	21	28	4	2	2	37	9	9	.266	.328

PITCHING

PITCHING	B-T	HT	WT	DOB	W	L	ERA	G	GS	CG	SV	IP	H	R	ER	HR	BB	SO	AVG	vLH	vRH	K/9	BB/9
Agudo, Juan (M)	L-L	6-2	196	4-26-87	2	2	2.84	17	5	0	0	38	29	15	12	2	20	27	.216	.455	.195	6.39	4.74
Bastidas, Pedro (M)	L-L	6-2	210	3-3-86	0	0	13.50	3	0	0	0	2	6	3	3	1	1	0	.600	—	.600	0.00	4.50
Carrillo, Carlos (M)	R-R	6-4	180	11-25-89	0	0	3.48	7	0	0	1	10	14	5	4	1	1	3	.326	.500	.308	2.61	0.87
Figueroa, Eduardo (C)	R-R	6-1	185	11-30-88	1	1	3.09	17	0	0	0	32	40	21	11	1	16	17	.305	.304	.306	4.78	4.50
Guerra, Pedro (M)	R-R	6-0	180	1-9-90	6	4	3.64	18	9	0	1	59	44	26	24	2	16	42	.200	.228	.190	6.37	2.43
Ibarra, Edgar (M)	L-L	5-11	165	5-31-89	2	4	3.19	16	15	0	0	73	79	35	26	1	21	53	.280	.217	.286	6.50	2.58
Infante, Edilmar (C)	R-R			12-19-87	2	4	4.00	14	14	1	0	79	88	48	35	7	13	37	.286	.324	.275	4.23	1.49
Marcano, Rafael (M)	R-R	6-3	200	5-24-87	2	0	1.93	14	0	0	0	19	19	8	4	0	5	4	.271	.238	.286	1.93	2.41
Mijares, Jean (M)	L-L	5-11	149	1-10-88	1	4	5.71	27	0	0	8	41	39	29	26	3	32	32	.248	.250	.248	7.02	7.02
Navarro, Reinaldo (C)	R-R	6-1	170	12-22-88	1	5	5.05	18	8	0	1	46	61	32	26	4	11	18	.318	.336	.306	3.50	2.14
Nunez, Manuel (M)	R-R	6-1		6-17-87	3	1	6.83	19	0	0	0	29	39	29	22	0	23	17	.339	.324	.346	5.28	7.14
Rodriguez, Gregorio (C)	R-R	6-2	184	9-11-88	3	3	3.21	15	5	0	0	42	58	25	15	0	8	19	.331	.286	.346	4.07	1.71
Rojas, Carlos (C)	R-R	6-1	170	5-22-90	3	3	4.08	24	2	0	4	46	55	22	21	0	16	19	.309	.345	.293	3.69	3.11
Sanchez, Angelo (M)	R-R	6-2	215	6-7-89	2	1	1.76	12	6	0	1	46	31	13	9	3	11	40	.191	.200	.189	7.83	2.15
Sanchez, Bruno (M)	R-R	6-6	170	11-8-86	4	3	3.11	10	6	0	0	46	57	25	16	0	5	20	.305	.365	.281	3.88	0.97

FIELDING

Catcher	PCT	G	PO	A	E	DP	PB
Bracho	.969	10	27	4	1	0	2
Diaz	.987	25	119	28	2	2	1
Guevara	.974	24	87	26	3	3	6
Rodriguez	.981	10	36	16	1	0	1
Romero	.935	20	79	21	7	5	3

First Base	PCT	G	PO	A	E	DP
Blanco	1.000	1	1	0	0	0
Diaz	1.000	12	99	3	0	10
Galvan	1.000	1	3	0	0	0
J. Gonzalez	1.000	7	32	1	0	2
Guevara	.984	14	117	11	2	11
Martin	.987	21	214	14	3	21
Martinez	1.000	1	1	0	0	0
Requena	—	1	0	1	0	0
Rodriguez	.990	11	94	4	1	10
Romero	.981	11	100	4	2	5

Second Base	PCT	G	PO	A	E	DP
Avila	.972	11	18	17	1	6
Blanco	.920	24	52	51	9	9
Galvan	1.000	1	2	4	0	0
J. Gonzalez	1.000	1	3	1	0	0
X. Gonzalez	.951	7	15	24	2	4
Martinez	.944	14	30	21	3	6
Matheus	1.000	11	28	29	0	5
Requena	.907	13	32	36	7	6

Third Base	PCT	G	PO	A	E	DP
Avila	.773	7	3	14	5	0
Blanco	1.000	9	9	22	0	3
Galvan	.840	7	3	18	4	0
J. Gonzalez	.881	11	13	24	5	2
X. Gonzalez	.911	20	11	40	5	4
Lara	1.000	1	1	2	0	0
Martinez	.946	13	10	25	2	0
Matheus	.963	10	8	18	1	2
Requena	.833	3	2	8	2	0

Shortstop	PCT	G	PO	A	E	DP
Avila	.846	3	3	8	2	0
Blanco	.846	4	10	12	4	3
J. Gonzalez	1.000	1	1	2	0	0
X. Gonzalez	1.000	1	1	2	0	0
Lara	.875	1	0	7	1	1
Martinez	.901	15	28	54	9	6
Matheus	.943	43	62	135	12	23
Requena	.880	5	6	16	3	0

Outfield	PCT	G	PO	A	E	DP
Andrades	.892	24	30	3	4	1
Avila	1.000	1	2	0	0	0
Blanco	.949	17	35	2	2	0
Galvan	.919	21	32	2	3	0
J. Gonzalez	.966	35	53	3	2	1
X. Gonzalez	1.000	3	4	0	0	0
Lara	.961	64	138	9	6	3
Martinez	1.000	1	1	0	0	0
Matheus	1.000	2	2	1	0	0
Requena	.889	4	8	0	1	0
Soto	.980	61	137	7	3	3

ORGANIZATION STATISTICS

New York Mets

BY ADAM RUBIN

The Mets set an unwelcome milestone in 2007: They became the first team in Major League Baseball history to squander a seven-game division lead with 17 games remaining and fail to reach the postseason.

The Mets, trying to earn the first back-to-back division titles in the franchise's history, had led the National League East from May 16 until the season's final weekend. On the last day of the regular season, which the Mets entered tied with the Phillies for first place, lefthander Tom Glavine had the second-shortest outing of his career, recording just one out in what became a seven-run first inning, and the Marlins beat the Mets 8-1.

The Phillies, whom shortstop Jimmy Rollins anointed "the team to beat" before spring training even began, finished off the Nationals at Citizens Bank Park, four minutes after the Mets' game ended, to claim the division title.

The downfall? The Mets went 5-12 in their final 17 games, beginning with a three-game sweep by the Phillies at Shea Stadium. They finished the season with a 1-6 homestand against Washington, St. Louis and Florida. The lone victory during that stretch came in Game No. 161 when John Maine came within four outs of the first no-hitter in franchise history in a 13-0 win against Florida.

Several milestones were achieved in '07 despite the bitterly disappointing ending. Most notably:

■ Glavine, at age 41, became the 23rd pitcher to record his 300th victory. In his second attempt, Glavine limited the Cubs to two runs in six innings at Wrigley Field on Aug. 5.

■ Third baseman David Wright became the fourth-youngest player to reach the 30-homer, 30-steal plateau when he went deep against Philadelphia's Geoff Geary on Sept. 16. Only Alex Rodriguez, Bobby Bonds and Jose Canseco were younger than Wright (24 years, 270 days) when they reached the milestone. Wright was the third Met to go 30-30, joining mentor Howard Johnson (1987, '89 and '91) and Darryl Strawberry ('87). Johnson, who began the season as the first-base coach, replaced the fired Rick Down as hitting coach at the all-star break.

■ Left fielder Moises Alou had the longest hitting streak in the majors at 30 games.

Righthander Pedro Martinez, in the third season of a four-year, $53 million contract, returned 11 months after rotator-cuff surgery and nearly stopped the team's late tailspin. He went 3-1, 2.57 in five September starts. Following team doctors' advice, Martinez was given extra rest between his starts.

Sidearm reliever Joe Smith and outfielder Carlos Gomez made their big league debuts in '07. Smith, the organization's third-round pick in 2006 from Wright State, earned a roster spot out of spring training. He began his career with $15\frac{1}{3}$ straight scoreless innings, setting a franchise rookie record to begin a career. But Smith hit a wall and was sent to the minors in late July.

Gomez, benefiting from injuries to Alou (a strained quadriceps muscle that sidelined him for $2\frac{1}{2}$ months), Lastings Milledge and Endy Chavez, hit .232/.288/.304 with two homers and 12 steals in 125 at-bats. Gomez required surgery to remove a portion of the hamate bone in his left hand after injuring it July 4 on a checked swing at Colorado.

The Mets suffered various injuries, with no position hit harder than second base. Jose Valentin had returned from a partial tear of the ACL in his right knee, only to fracture the

MAJOR LEAGUE: DAVID WRIGHT, 3B

Wright had an MVP-worthy 2007, hitting .325/.416/.546 with 30 homers and 34 steals, all career-best marks. His on-base percentage ranked fifth in the National League, and his 196 hits tied for fourth. Wright also was durable, playing in all but two games for the Mets. Wright's 92 walks and 42 doubles also led Mets hitters.

MINOR LEAGUE: KEVIN MULVEY, RHP

Mulvey opened his first full season with Double-A Binghamton, finishing fourth in the Eastern League with a 3.32 ERA. He kept the ball in the park, allowing just four home runs in 151⅔ innings. His strikeout rate wasn't overwhelming, but he accumulated 110 strikeouts, good for ninth in the EL.

BATTING		★Minimum 250 at-bats
★AVG	Wabick, D.J., Savannah	.306
R	Tatis, Fernando, New Orleans	90
H	Hernandez, Anderson, New Orleans	167
TB	Tatis, Fernando, New Orleans	241
2B	Murphy, Dan, St. Lucie	34
3B	Henry, Sean, St. Lucie	7
HR	Harper, Brett, Binghamton	24
RBI	Harper, Brett, Binghamton	88
BB	Tracy, Andy, New Orleans	89
SO	Harper, Brett, Binghamton	119
SB	Pellot, Hector, Savannah/St. Lucie	35
★OBP	Kiger, Mark, Binghamton/New Orleans	.420
★SLG	Harper, Brett, Binghamton	.500
PITCHING		^Minimum 75 innings
W	Mulvey, Kevin, Binghamton/New Orleans	12
L	Mizell, Jeremy, Savannah	15
^ERA	Mulvey, Kevin, Binghamton/New Orleans	3.2
G	Schmoll, Steve, New Orleans	54
CG	Aguilar, Salvador, Binghamton	2
CG	Niese, Jonathan, St. Lucie	2
SV	Muniz, Carlos, Binghamton/New Orleans	23
IP	Mulvey, Kevin, Binghamton/New Orleans	157.2
BB	Carvajal, Marcos, Binghamton	63
SO	Parnell, Robert, St. Lucie/Binghamton	136
^AVG	Humber, Philip, New Orleans	.244

tibia in his right shin fouling a ball off himself on July 20. Damion Easley then completely tore three ankle ligaments during an awkward slide at Washington on Aug. 18.

The Mets made two in-season trades—for Luis Castillo and Jeff Conine—to cover for injuries at second and first base, where Carlos Delgado slumped to .258/.333/.448 and then missed time with a hip injury. New York sent outfielder Dustin Martin and catcher Drew Butera to Minnesota for Castillo, and shortstop Jose Castro and outfielder Sean Henry to Cincinnati for Conine.

Triple-A New Orleans advanced to the Triple-A Pacific Coast League finals, where they were swept by a Sacramento team that would win the Bricktown Showdown. Short-season Brooklyn also made it to the New York-Penn League finals, where they faced Auburn, but also were swept.

General Manager: Omar Minaya. **Farm Director:** Adam Wogan. **Scouting Director:** Rudy Terrasas

Class	Team	League	W	L	PCT	Finish*	Manager	Affiliate Since
Majors	New York	National	88	74	.543	5th (16)	Willie Randolph	—
Triple-A	New Orleans Zephyrs	Pacific Coast	75	69	.521	6th (16)	Ken Oberkfell	2007
Double-A	Binghamton	Eastern	61	81	.430	11th (12)	Mako Oliveras	1992
High A	St. Lucie	Florida State	68	71	.489	8th (12)	Frank Cacciatore	1988
Low A	Savannah Sand Gnats	South Atlantic	41	94	.304	16th (16)	Tim Teufel	2007
Short-season	Brooklyn Cyclones	New York-Penn	49	25	.662	1st (14)	Edgar Alfonzo	2001
Rookie	Kingsport Mets	Appalachian	35	33	.515	3rd (9)	Donovan Mitchell	1980
Rookie	GCL Mets	Gulf Coast	20	35	.364	13th (16)	Juan Lopez	2004
Overall 2007 Minor League Record			**349**	**408**	**.461**	**27th**		

* Finish in overall standings (No. of teams in league) ^League champion

ORGANIZATION STATISTICS

NEW YORK METS

NATIONAL LEAGUE

BATTING	B-T	HT	WT	DOB	AVG	vLH	vRH	G	AB	R	H	2B	3B	HR	RBI	BB	HBP	SH	SF	SO	SB	CS	SLG	OBP
Alomar Jr., Sandy	R-R	6-3	235	6-18-66	.136	.200	.118	8	22	1	3	1	0	0	0	0	0	0	0	3	0	0	.182	.136
Alou, Moises	R-R	6-3	225	7-3-66	.341	.360	.335	87	328	51	112	19	1	13	49	27	2	0	3	30	3	0	.524	.392
Ambres, Chip	R-R	6-1	230	12-19-79	.333	—	.333	3	3	0	1	0	0	0	1	0	0	0	0	1	0	0	.333	.333
Anderson, Marlon	L-R	5-11	200	1-6-74	.319	.167	.333	43	69	14	22	7	0	3	25	5	0	1	2	12	3	1	.551	.355
2-team (23 Los Angeles)					.295	—	—	66	95	17	28	7	0	3	27	8	0	1	2	17	4	1	.463	.343
Beltran, Carlos	B-R	6-1	205	4-24-77	.276	.304	.265	144	554	93	153	33	3	33	112	69	2	1	10	111	23	2	.525	.353
Castillo, Luis	B-R	5-11	190	9-12-75	.296	.321	.287	50	199	37	59	8	2	1	20	24	0	7	1	17	10	2	.372	.371
Castro, Ramon	R-R	6-3	255	3-1-76	.285	.276	.287	52	144	24	41	6	0	11	31	10	1	0	2	39	0	0	.556	.331
Chavez, Endy	L-L	6-0	165	2-7-78	.287	.276	.289	71	150	20	43	7	2	1	17	9	0	5	1	16	5	2	.380	.325
Conine, Jeff	R-R	6-1	225	6-27-66	.195	.158	.227	21	41	2	8	2	0	0	5	7	0	1	1	8	0	0	.244	.306
2-team (80 Cincinnati)					.254	—	—	101	256	25	65	13	1	6	37	27	0	2	7	36	4	0	.383	.317
Delgado, Carlos	L-R	6-3	265	6-25-72	.258	.267	.254	139	538	71	139	30	0	24	87	52	11	0	6	118	4	0	.448	.333
DiFelice, Mike	R-R	6-2	225	5-28-69	.250	.200	.267	16	40	1	10	2	1	0	5	2	2	2	1	12	0	0	.350	.311
Easley, Damion	R-R	5-11	195	11-11-69	.280	.371	.202	76	193	24	54	6	0	10	26	19	5	0	1	35	0	1	.466	.358
Franco, Julio	R-R	6-1	210	8-23-58	.200	.250	.176	40	50	7	10	0	0	1	8	10	0	0	1	13	2	1	.260	.328
2-team (15 Atlanta)					.222	—	—	55	90	8	20	3	0	1	16	14	0	0	2	23	2	1	.289	.321
Gomez, Carlos	R-R	6-4	195	12-4-85	.232	.254	.212	58	125	14	29	3	0	2	12	8	3	0	3	27	12	3	.304	.288
Gotay, Ruben	B-R	5-11	190	12-25-82	.295	.194	.318	98	190	35	56	12	0	4	24	16	1	3	1	42	3	3	.421	.351
Green, Shawn	L-L	6-4	205	11-10-72	.291	.195	.326	130	446	62	130	30	1	10	46	37	5	1	1	62	11	1	.430	.352
Hernandez, Anderson	B-R	5-9	170	10-30-82	.333	.000	.500	4	3	1	1	0	0	0	0	0	0	0	0	1	0	0	.333	.333
Johnson, Ben	R-R	6-1	230	6-18-81	.185	.214	.154	9	27	2	5	1	0	0	1	2	0	0	1	11	0	0	.222	.233
Ledee, Ricky	L-L	6-1	225	11-22-73	.222	—	.222	17	36	6	8	3	0	1	6	5	0	1	1	10	1	0	.389	.310
Lo Duca, Paul	R-R	5-10	205	4-12-72	.272	.341	.245	119	445	46	121	18	1	9	54	24	6	3	10	33	2	0	.378	.311
Milledge, Lastings	R-R	6-0	205	4-5-85	.272	.317	.250	59	184	27	50	9	1	7	29	13	7	1	1	42	3	2	.446	.341
Newhan, David	L-R	5-10	185	9-7-73	.203	.000	.208	56	74	9	15	1	1	1	6	8	1	0	0	19	2	0	.284	.289
Reyes, Jose	B-R	6-1	200	6-11-83	.280	.318	.266	160	681	119	191	36	12	12	57	77	1	5	1	78	78	21	.421	.354
Valentin, Jose	B-R	5-10	190	10-12-69	.241	.275	.226	51	166	18	40	11	1	3	18	15	0	1	2	34	2	1	.373	.302
Wright, David	R-R	6-0	215	12-20-82	.325	.361	.311	160	604	113	196	42	1	30	107	94	6	0	7	115	34	5	.546	.416

PITCHING	B-T	HT	WT	DOB	W	L	ERA	G	GS	CG	SV	IP	H	R	ER	HR	BB	SO	AVG	vLH	vRH	K/9	BB/9
Adkins, Jon	L-R	6-0	220	8-30-77	0	0	0.00	1	0	0	0	1	0	0	0	0	0	0	.000	.000	.000	0.00	0.00
Burgos, Ambiorix	R-R	6-3	245	4-19-84	1	0	3.42	17	0	0	0	24	17	10	9	3	9	19	.200	.273	.122	7.23	3.42
Collazo, Willie	L-L	5-9	170	11-7-79	0	0	6.35	6	0	0	0	6	7	4	4	0	5	0	.318	.111	.462	0.00	7.94
Feliciano, Pedro	L-L	5-10	190	8-25-76	2	2	3.09	78	0	0	2	64	47	26	22	3	31	61	.200	.168	.221	8.58	4.36
Glavine, Tom	L-L	6-0	205	3-25-66	13	8	4.45	34	34	1	0	200	219	102	99	23	64	89	.281	.326	.266	4.00	2.88
Heilman, Aaron	R-R	6-5	225	11-12-78	7	7	3.03	81	0	0	1	86	72	36	29	8	20	63	.224	.234	.218	6.59	2.09
Hernandez, Orlando	R-R	6-2	220	10-11-69	9	5	3.72	27	24	0	0	148	109	64	61	23	64	128	.206	.245	.167	7.80	3.90
Humber, Philip	R-R	6-4	225	12-21-82	0	0	7.71	3	1	0	0	7	9	6	6	1	2	2	.300	.375	.214	2.57	2.57
Lawrence, Brian	R-R	6-0	195	5-14-76	1	2	6.83	6	6	0	0	29	43	22	22	4	13	18	.347	.401	.300	5.59	4.03
Maine, John	R-R	6-4	200	5-8-81	15	10	3.91	32	32	1	0	191	168	90	83	23	75	180	.235	.237	.234	8.48	3.53
Martinez, Pedro	R-R	5-11	195	10-25-71	3	1	2.57	5	5	0	0	28	33	11	8	0	7	32	.284	.319	.261	10.29	2.25
Mota, Guillermo	R-R	6-6	210	7-25-73	2	2	5.76	52	0	0	0	59	63	39	38	8	18	47	.264	.235	.284	7.13	2.73
Muniz, Carlos	R-R	6-1	180	3-12-81	0	0	7.71	2	0	0	0	2	1	2	2	0	2	2	.125	.000	.167	7.71	7.71
Park, Chan Ho	R-R	6-2	210	6-30-73	0	1	15.75	1	1	0	0	4	6	7	7	2	2	4	.333	.375	.300	9.00	4.50
Pelfrey, Mike	R-R	6-7	215	1-14-84	3	8	5.57	15	13	0	0	73	85	47	45	6	39	45	.298	.323	.277	5.57	4.83
Perez, Oliver	L-L	6-3	215	8-15-81	15	10	3.56	29	29	0	0	177	153	90	70	22	79	174	.229	.206	.235	8.85	4.02
Schoeneweis, Scott	L-L	6-0	190	10-2-73	0	2	5.03	70	0	0	2	59	62	36	33	8	28	41	.271	.204	.316	6.25	4.27
Sele, Aaron	R-R	6-3	220	6-25-70	3	2	5.37	34	0	0	0	54	78	34	32	5	21	29	.358	.420	.321	4.86	3.52
Smith, Joe	R-R	6-2	215	3-22-84	3	2	3.45	54	0	0	0	44	48	18	17	3	21	45	.274	.298	.266	9.14	4.26
Sosa, Jorge	R-R	6-2	220	4-28-77	9	8	4.47	42	14	0	0	113	109	58	56	10	41	69	.255	.326	.202	5.51	3.28
Urdaneta, Lino	R-R	6-1	220	11-20-79	0	0	9.00	2	0	0	0	1	2	1	1	1	0	0	.400	.000	.500	0.00	0.00
Vargas, Jason	L-L	6-0	215	2-2-83	0	1	12.19	2	2	0	0	10	17	14	14	4	2	4	.347	.000	.370	3.48	1.74
Wagner, Billy	L-L	5-11	205	7-25-71	2	2	2.63	66	0	0	34	68	55	22	20	6	22	80	.216	.241	.209	10.54	2.90
Williams, Dave	L-L	6-3	215	3-12-79	0	1	22.85	2	1	0	0	4	12	11	11	2	5	2	.522	.333	.550	4.15	10.38

FIELDING

Catcher	PCT	G	PO	A	E	DP	PB
Alomar Jr.	1.000	6	29	5	0	0	0
Castro	.987	50	303	12	4	1	1
DiFelice	.978	16	83	7	2	0	2
Lo Duca	.989	113	754	34	9	5	2

First Base	PCT	G	PO	A	E	DP
Anderson	1.000	7	0	0	0	0
Conine	.976	11	79	2	2	6
Delgado	.993	138	1133	74	8	101
Easley	1.000	2	20	0	0	2
Franco	1.000	6	22	3	0	3
Green	.989	17	81	5	1	3

Second Base	PCT	G	PO	A	E	DP
Castillo	.990	50	99	95	2	27

	PCT	G	PO	A	E	DP
Easley	.980	39	79	114	4	24
Gotay	.979	37	72	71	3	14
Newhan	.667	1	1	1	1	0
Valentin	.978	45	102	116	5	22

Third Base	PCT	G	PO	A	E	DP
Easley	.667	2	0	2	1	0
Franco	1.000	2	1	4	0	0
Gotay	1.000	2	0	5	0	0
Newhan	—	1	0	0	0	0
Wright	.954	159	107	324	21	24

Shortstop	PCT	G	PO	A	E	DP
Gotay	1.000	5	4	5	0	1
Hernandez	—	1	0	0	0	0
Reyes	.982	160	203	445	12	88

Outfield	PCT	G	PO	A	E	DP
Alou	.973	84	138	7	4	0
Ambres	—	1	0	0	0	0
Anderson	1.000	16	24	2	0	0
Beltran	.988	141	389	6	5	2
Chavez	1.000	67	101	1	0	0
Conine	1.000	3	1	0	0	0
Easley	1.000	9	13	0	0	0
Gomez	.967	52	85	3	3	1
Green	.986	110	203	2	3	0
Johnson	1.000	9	19	0	0	0
Ledee	1.000	11	22	0	0	0
Milledge	.983	52	112	2	2	0
Newhan	1.000	8	20	0	0	0

NEW ORLEANS ZEPHYRS   TRIPLE-A

PACIFIC COAST LEAGUE

BATTING	B-T	HT	WT	DOB	AVG	vLH	vRH	G	AB	R	H	2B	3B	HR	RBI	BB	HBP	SH	SF	SO	SB	CS	SLG	OBP
Alfaro, Jason	R-R	5-9	210	11-29-77	.283	.280	.284	99	311	42	88	15	0	13	51	16	0	3	5	44	1	1	.457	.313
Alomar Jr., Sandy	R-R	6-0	235	6-18-66	.292	.444	.256	45	144	15	42	8	1	4	29	8	0	1	3	24	1	0	.444	.323
Ambres, Chip	R-R	6-1	230	12-19-79	.274	.324	.256	120	427	80	117	23	0	21	71	71	3	0	3	107	7	0	.475	.379
Anderson, Marlon	L-R	5-11	200	1-6-74	.174	.167	.176	6	23	1	4	1	0	0	1	3	0	0	0	6	0	0	.217	.269
2-team (11 Las Vegas)					.212	—	—	17	52	7	11	3	1	1	12	10	1	0	1	11	2	0	.365	.344
Batista, Wilson	B-R	6-0	170	2-7-81	.231	.333	.167	12	39	5	9	0	0	1	2	2	0	0	0	6	0	0	.308	.268
Cancel, Robinson	R-R	6-0	195	5-4-76	.264	.178	.292	59	182	18	48	13	1	4	25	13	1	2	1	34	3	0	.412	.315
Coles, Corey	L-L	6-1	170	1-30-82	.200	.125	.227	9	30	5	6	1	0	0	1	2	1	2	0	3	1	0	.233	.273
DiFelice, Mike	R-R	6-2	225	5-28-69	.282	.307	.272	72	248	37	70	9	0	7	38	20	2	1	1	61	0	1	.403	.339
Feliciano, Jesus	L-L	6-0	174	6-6-79	.315	.303	.320	90	235	35	74	11	0	4	26	21	1	1	3	24	5	2	.413	.369
Gautreau, Jake	L-R	6-0	195	11-14-79	.226	.128	.251	62	226	18	51	13	0	6	30	5	3	0	2	36	0	0	.363	.250
Gomez, Carlos	R-R	6-4	195	12-4-85	.286	.316	.275	36	140	24	40	8	2	2	13	15	2	0	0	23	17	4	.414	.363
Gotay, Ruben	B-R	5-11	190	12-25-82	.256	.125	.288	23	82	12	21	7	1	2	13	14	1	0	1	14	1	1	.439	.367
Hermansen, Chad	R-R	6-2	190	9-10-77	.273	.182	.299	27	99	10	27	4	0	2	13	8	1	0	1	28	2	1	.374	.330
2-team (89 Albuquerque)					.281	—	—	116	392	56	110	19	3	11	57	38	4	1	4	112	11	3	.429	.347
Hernandez, Anderson	B-R	5-9	170	10-30-82	.301	.275	.311	128	554	84	167	28	5	5	42	31	3	4	5	82	16	9	.397	.339
Johnson, Ben	R-R	6-1	230	6-18-81	.271	.275	.270	53	188	26	51	10	0	2	12	25	3	1	1	36	3	1	.356	.364
Kiger, Mark	R-R	5-10	190	5-30-80	.121	.167	.111	14	33	5	4	1	0	1	2	7	0	0	0	16	0	0	.242	.275
Ledee, Ricky	L-L	6-1	225	11-22-73	.262	.272	.258	86	290	37	76	11	1	11	64	30	2	0	3	63	0	0	.421	.332
Matos, Luis	R-R	6-0	215	10-30-78	.204	.333	.162	14	49	4	10	3	0	0	4	6	1	0	0	10	1	1	.327	.304
Milledge, Lastings	R-R	6-0	205	4-5-85	.333	.375	.323	11	39	9	13	1	0	1	5	2	1	0	1	12	5	0	.436	.372
Negron, Miguel	L-L	6-2	195	8-22-82	.229	.286	.206	36	144	15	33	4	0	1	16	16	1	0	2	29	6	1	.278	.307
Newhan, David	L-R	5-10	185	9-7-73	.347	.271	.376	44	173	27	60	12	3	7	30	20	1	0	2	28	7	4	.572	.413
Tatis, Fernando	R-R	5-10	175	1-1-75	.276	.309	.265	131	497	90	137	31	5	21	67	62	6	1	6	103	8	6	.485	.359
Tracy, Andy	L-R	6-3	220	12-11-73	.271	.246	.280	135	472	88	128	24	1	23	87	89	5	0	8	110	2	3	.472	.387
Wooten, Shawn	R-R	5-10	230	7-24-72	.179	.000	.250	15	39	1	7	1	0	0	6	1	0	0	1	5	0	0	.205	.195

PITCHING	B-T	HT	WT	DOB	W	L	ERA	G	GS	CG	SV	IP	H	R	ER	HR	BB	SO	AVG	vLH	vRH	K/9	BB/9
Adkins, Jon	L-R	6-0	220	8-30-77	2	4	3.99	48	0	0	5	65	71	33	29	8	17	44	.282	.271	.287	6.06	2.34
Bostick, Adam	L-L	6-1	235	3-17-83	6	7	5.66	21	20	0	0	97	106	66	61	20	45	91	.283	.302	.276	8.44	4.18
Burgos, Ambiorix	R-R	6-3	245	4-19-84	0	0	6.75	8	0	0	0	9	10	7	7	2	4	13	.270	.238	.313	12.54	3.86
Camacho, Eddie	L-L	6-1	195	9-17-82	2	1	4.44	32	0	0	2	47	52	26	23	6	14	42	.277	.348	.235	8.10	2.70
Collazo, Willie	L-L	5-9	170	11-7-79	6	5	2.46	53	4	0	4	99	91	33	27	5	19	69	.252	.237	.261	6.29	1.73
Cullen, Ryan	L-L	6-2	204	1-20-80	2	4	3.06	40	0	0	0	68	68	28	23	8	16	50	.263	.257	.266	6.65	2.13
Humber, Philip	R-R	6-4	225	12-21-82	11	9	4.27	25	25	0	0	139	129	70	66	21	44	120	.244	.230	.256	7.77	2.85
Lawrence, Brian	R-R	6-0	195	5-14-76	8	3	3.81	13	13	1	0	85	88	38	36	6	9	57	.271	.317	.241	6.04	0.95
2-team (3 Colorado Springs)					8	5	4.73	16	16	2	0	105	120	57	55	9	14	67	—	—	—	5.76	1.20
Maldonado, Ivan	R-R	6-3	210	6-7-80	2	1	3.80	39	0	0	9	43	40	19	18	4	16	45	.247	.273	.229	9.49	3.38
McNab, Tim	R-R	6-0	175	6-4-80	1	1	3.63	11	0	0	0	17	14	7	7	1	7	9	.233	.333	.179	4.67	3.63
Mota, Guillermo	R-R	6-6	210	7-25-73	0	1	7.04	7	0	0	0	8	11	6	6	1	5	7	.344	.313	.375	8.22	5.87
Mulvey, Kevin	R-R	6-1	195	5-26-85	1	0	0.00	1	1	0	0	6	2	0	0	0	0	3	.095	.000	.143	4.50	0.00
Muniz, Carlos	R-R	6-1	180	3-12-81	0	0	0.00	3	0	0	0	6	4	0	0	0	1	4	.190	.200	.188	6.35	1.59
Nageotte, Clint	R-R	6-4	225	10-25-80	1	1	10.38	9	2	0	0	17	24	23	20	5	16	11	.348	.438	.270	5.71	8.31
Park, Chan Ho	R-R	6-2	210	6-30-73	4	4	5.57	9	9	0	0	52	64	34	32	9	16	49	.306	.330	.284	8.54	2.79
2-team (15 Round Rock)					6	14	5.97	24	24	0	0	136	164	104	90	27	40	119	—	—	—	7.89	2.65
Paulk, Robert	R-R	5-11	175	3-14-81	0	0	8.10	2	0	0	0	3	4	3	2	1	2	2	.267	.200	.300	5.40	2.70
Pelfrey, Mike	R-R	6-7	215	1-14-84	3	6	4.01	14	14	0	0	74	74	35	33	6	26	56	.261	.250	.269	6.81	3.16
Santiago, Jose	R-R	6-3	225	11-5-74	7	8	5.64	32	17	0	0	120	155	79	75	14	39	52	.318	.329	.308	3.91	2.93
Schmoll, Steve	R-R	6-2	215	2-24-80	2	3	3.76	54	0	0	4	77	84	39	32	5	18	47	.275	.292	.263	5.52	2.11
Smith, Joe	R-R	6-2	215	3-22-84	0	0	2.00	8	0	0	2	9	7	3	2	0	4	5	.233	.143	.261	5.00	4.00
Sosa, Jorge	R-R	6-2	220	4-28-77	4	0	1.13	5	5	0	0	32	29	6	4	1	4	29	.250	.222	.268	8.16	1.12
Urdaneta, Lino	R-R	6-1	220	11-20-79	1	0	5.84	10	0	0	0	6	12	12	8	8	3	2	2	.255	.235	.267	1.46	1.46
Vargas, Jason	L-L	6-0	215	2-2-83	9	7	4.97	24	24	0	0	125	141	77	69	14	44	108	.284	.301	.279	7.78	3.17
Williams, Dave	L-L	6-3	215	3-12-79	3	4	3.96	10	10	0	0	61	58	31	27	11	13	38	.250	.283	.224	5.58	1.91

FIELDING

Catcher	PCT	G	PO	A	E	DP	PB
Alomar Jr.	1.000	34	208	10	0	1	3
Cancel	.987	41	277	20	4	1	3
DiFelice	.994	67	442	38	3	12	8
Wooten	1.000	10	49	4	0	1	0

First Base	PCT	G	PO	A	E	DP
Alfaro	.967	7	51	8	2	4
Cancel	.984	7	58	5	1	6
DiFelice	1.000	1	8	1	0	0
Ledee	1.000	1	9	3	0	0
Newhan	1.000	4	28	3	0	4
Tracy	.995	124	1050	77	6	107
Wooten	1.000	1	15	0	0	0

Second Base	PCT	G	PO	A	E	DP
Alfaro	.921	17	33	49	7	12
Anderson	1.000	2	3	4	0	1
Batista	.979	10	19	27	1	6
Gautreau	.988	52	97	146	3	33
Gotay	.978	18	46	45	2	15
Hernandez	.968	20	51	71	4	15
Kiger	1.000	5	8	4	0	1
Newhan	.963	28	45	59	4	16

Third Base	PCT	G	PO	A	E	DP
Alfaro	.958	7	9	14	1	1
Gautreau	1.000	3	1	7	0	0
Gotay	1.000	2	3	6	0	0
Kiger	1.000	2	2	2	0	0
Newhan	1.000	4	1	7	0	0
Tatis	.937	122	85	256	23	22
Tracy	1.000	4	1	10	0	3
Wooten	1.000	1	0	1	0	1

Shortstop	PCT	G	PO	A	E	DP
Alfaro	.923	31	44	76	10	21
Gotay	1.000	3	3	6	0	0
Hernandez	.975	110	183	328	13	67
Kiger	.957	5	7	15	1	5

Outfield	PCT	G	PO	A	E	DP
Alfaro	.864	12	16	3	3	1
Ambres	.979	117	230	8	5	1
Anderson	1.000	4	9	0	0	0
Cancel	1.000	5	5	0	0	0
Coles	1.000	8	15	0	0	0
Feliciano	.969	65	120	6	4	1
Gomez	.981	36	105	1	2	0
Hermansen	.971	27	68	0	2	0
Johnson	.974	52	113	1	3	1
Ledee	.966	57	81	3	3	0
Matos	1.000	14	19	0	0	0
Milledge	.824	11	13	1	3	0
Negron	1.000	36	90	2	0	1
Newhan	1.000	10	16	2	0	0

BINGHAMTON METS

DOUBLE-A

EASTERN LEAGUE

BATTING	B-T	HT	WT	DOB	AVG	vLH	vRH	G	AB	R	H	2B	3B	HR	RBI	BB	HBP	SH	SF	SO	SB	CS	SLG	OBP
Alomar Jr., Sandy	R-R	6-3	235	6-18-66	.188	.167	.250	5	16	1	3	0	0	0	1	0	0	0	0	2	0	0	.188	.188
Arroyo, Rafael	R-R	5-9	170	10-26-82	.203	.188	.209	22	59	7	12	3	0	0	4	7	2	1	0	19	1	0	.254	.309
Batista, Wilson	B-R	6-0	170	2-7-81	.237	.268	.225	73	262	28	62	16	2	5	23	7	2	4	1	52	7	3	.370	.261
Butera, Drew	R-R	6-1	205	8-9-83	.188	.286	.157	30	117	7	22	2	0	1	4	2	1	1	0	22	0	0	.231	.208
2-team (17 New Britain)					.210	—	—	47	167	10	35	5	1	1	7	7	1	2	0	27	0	0	.269	.246
Cancel, Robinson	R-R	6-0	195	5-4-76	.259	.500	.158	20	54	5	14	3	0	2	6	2	0	1	2	12	1	2	.426	.276
Carp, Mike	L-R	6-2	215	6-30-86	.251	.173	.285	97	359	55	90	16	0	11	48	39	10	0	4	75	2	1	.387	.337
Chavez, Endy	L-L	6-0	165	2-7-78	.000	.000	.000	1	3	0	0	0	0	0	0	0	0	2	0	0	0	0	.000	.400
Coles, Corey	L-L	6-1	170	1-30-82	.296	.254	.308	66	274	36	81	10	2	1	22	24	1	3	2	44	9	4	.358	.352
Coronado, Jose	B-R	6-1	175	4-13-86	.212	.207	.213	81	307	31	65	7	2	1	15	31	1	5	2	84	7	3	.257	.284
Coultas, Ryan	R-R	6-3	180	4-24-82	.182	.250	.176	21	55	7	10	2	0	0	8	2	0	1	1	15	0	1	.218	.207
Cruz, J.E.	R-R	5-10	185	7-13-81	.208	.229	.201	94	264	24	55	14	3	4	28	35	9	7	5	66	5	3	.330	.316
Dziuba, Teddy	L-R	5-10	185	10-26-84	.000	—	.000	1	1	0	0	0	0	0	0	0	0	0	0	1	0	0	.000	.000
Guzman, Edwards	L-R	5-11	200	9-11-76	.226	.211	.233	17	62	3	14	2	0	0	8	5	0	0	0	10	0	0	.258	.284
Harper, Brett	L-R	6-4	185	7-31-81	.296	.288	.299	131	476	69	141	25	0	24	88	34	6	0	1	119	2	0	.500	.350
Harrison, Vince	R-R	5-11	222	11-29-79	.268	.178	.317	38	127	20	34	6	0	2	16	13	2	0	1	23	0	3	.362	.343
Hill, Jamar	R-R	6-3	200	9-20-82	.300	.340	.282	58	170	23	51	9	0	6	23	7	4	0	0	44	3	3	.459	.343
Jackson, Nic	L-R	6-3	200	9-25-79	.209	.190	.214	28	91	13	19	3	1	4	12	9	0	0	0	20	6	0	.396	.280
Kiger, Mark	R-R	5-10	190	5-30-80	.312	.356	.296	114	391	75	122	27	4	10	50	75	11	2	5	92	16	7	.478	.432
Martinez, Fernando	L-R	6-1	190	10-10-88	.271	.259	.275	60	236	32	64	11	1	4	21	20	3	0	1	51	3	4	.377	.336
Milledge, Lastings	R-R	6-0	205	4-5-85	.435	.750	.368	5	23	7	10	1	1	3	8	0	1	0	0	4	1	0	.957	.458
Negron, Miguel	L-L	6-2	195	8-22-82	.262	.226	.277	94	362	44	95	21	1	4	57	35	0	2	4	66	14	8	.359	.324
Nickeas, Mike	R-R	6-0	220	2-13-83	.217	.259	.201	65	212	26	46	10	0	1	15	18	2	2	3	37	2	3	.278	.281
Ragsdale, Corey	R-R	6-4	175	11-10-82	.192	.143	.211	43	99	14	19	3	1	1	10	20	4	6	1	32	9	2	.273	.347
Reyes, Jose A.	B-R	6-0	225	2-26-83	.214	.133	.240	42	126	12	27	5	0	3	21	13	0	1	2	26	2	0	.325	.284
Rivera, Luis	R-R	6-1	165	1-25-84	.316	.263	.342	18	57	11	18	2	0	4	7	2	2	2	0	10	1	0	.351	.409
Stewart, Caleb	R-R	6-2	230	6-11-82	.252	.250	.252	125	433	63	109	14	1	16	69	36	6	0	6	102	4	7	.400	.314
Wooten, Shawn	R-R	5-10	230	7-24-72	.250	.333	.000	0	0	0	0	0	0	0	0	0	0	0	0	0	0	0	.250	.250

PITCHING	B-T	HT	WT	DOB	W	L	ERA	G	GS	CG	SV	IP	H	R	ER	HR	BB	SO	AVG	vLH	vRH	K/9	BB/9
Aguilar, Salvador	R-R	6-0	190	1-9-82	7	9	5.81	28	20	2	0	119	164	88	77	4	41	64	.330	.324	.336	4.83	3.09
Camacho, Eddie	L-L	6-1	195	9-17-82	0	0	0.00	5	0	0	1	12	9	0	0	0	3	10	.214	.154	.241	7.71	2.31
Carvajal, Marcos	R-R	6-4	175	8-19-84	5	10	5.22	28	22	0	0	119	120	82	69	13	63	92	.259	.253	.263	6.96	4.76
Cullen, Ryan	L-L	6-2	204	1-20-80	0	1	4.38	8	0	0	0	12	18	6	6	3	0	12	.360	.313	.382	8.76	0.00
Devaney, Michael	R-R	6-4	220	7-31-82	6	9	4.85	22	20	1	0	104	105	60	56	11	43	71	.264	.257	.271	6.14	3.72
McNab, Tim	R-R	6-0	175	6-4-82	7	5	2.92	35	2	0	2	74	78	28	24	3	16	42	.277	.333	.224	5.11	1.95
Morales, Ricardo	L-L	6-1	170	12-9-83	3	2	5.28	13	4	1	0	44	46	26	26	7	11	27	.266	.277	.262	5.48	2.23
Mulvey, Kevin	R-R	6-1	195	5-26-85	11	10	3.32	26	26	0	0	152	145	74	56	4	43	110	.252	.285	.224	6.53	2.55
Muniz, Carlos	R-R	6-0	180	3-12-81	2	4	2.45	44	0	0	23	59	43	20	16	2	17	62	.197	.222	.180	9.51	2.61
Nall, Brandon	R-R	6-4	190	3-18-82	2	0	4.57	34	0	0	0	43	50	25	22	0	17	37	.278	.342	.234	7.68	3.53
Parnell, Robert	R-R	6-3	180	9-8-84	5	5	4.77	17	17	0	0	89	98	54	47	9	38	74	.276	.277	.275	7.51	3.86
Paulk, Robert	R-R	5-11	175	3-14-81	2	5	4.12	34	3	0	2	79	100	42	36	8	28	53	.306	.261	.341	6.06	3.20
Perez, Marcelo	R-R	6-1	166	10-10-80	1	5	5.53	47	0	0	0	70	85	45	43	6	33	69	.304	.328	.286	8.87	4.24
Sanchez, Jose	R-R	6-0	170	5-12-84	4	9	4.52	27	27	0	0	145	164	90	73	14	58	98	.281	.310	.254	6.07	3.59
Serfass, Joseph	R-R	6-3	215	5-6-81	3	3	5.83	32	0	0	0	46	54	31	30	8	9	31	.290	.287	.293	6.02	1.75
Simmons, Jeramy	R-R	6-0	200	9-30-82	0	0	0.00	2	0	0	0	5	4	0	0	1	1	1	.222	.250	.000	1.80	1.80
Swindell, Mike	R-R	6-1	190	9-26-81	0	1	15.00	1	1	0	0	3	5	5	5	0	4	3	.385	.500	.333	9.00	12.00
Tomasiewicz, Kevin	L-L	6-2	225	9-17-83	2	1	5.79	14	0	0	0	14	15	9	9	1	5	15	.263	.250	.273	9.64	3.21
Urdaneta, Lino	R-R	6-0	220	11-20-79	1	1	4.76	16	0	0	3	23	26	13	12	1	8	12	.289	.231	.333	4.76	3.18
Valdes, Raul	L-L	5-11	190	11-27-77	0	1	3.68	20	0	0	1	29	35	15	12	3	9	28	.299	.343	.280	8.59	2.76

FIELDING

Catcher	PCT	G	PO	A	E	DP	PB
Alomar Jr.	1.000	2	17	1	0	1	1
Arroyo	.978	18	126	6	3	2	3
Butera	.979	30	209	21	5	2	5
Cancel	.971	5	30	4	1	2	2
Guzman	.875	1	7	0	1	0	0
Lo Duca	1.000	1	5	0	0	0	0
Nickeas	.984	60	349	23	6	2	2
Reyes	1.000	32	202	10	0	3	1
Wooten	1.000	1	7	0	0	0	0

First Base	PCT	G	PO	A	E	DP
Cancel	.875	1	6	1	1	1
Carp	.988	92	793	59	10	71
Coultas	1.000	1	1	0	0	0
Cruz	1.000	1	2	0	0	0
Harper	.989	32	247	17	3	21
Kiger	.993	21	134	13	1	13
Negron	1.000	1	1	0	0	0
Reyes	—	1	0	0	0	0

Second Base	PCT	G	PO	A	E	DP
Batista	.969	45	89	133	7	28
Cruz	.980	79	153	193	7	39
Guzman	1.000	6	9	13	0	1
Harrison	1.000	1	3	5	0	2
Kiger	.956	20	44	43	4	11

Third Base	PCT	G	PO	A	E	DP
Coultas	1.000	4	4	9	0	1
Guzman	.955	9	7	14	1	4
Harrison	.905	31	16	51	7	4
Kiger	.946	74	39	136	10	16
Nickeas	.714	2	2	3	2	0
Ragsdale	.915	38	25	72	9	7

Shortstop	PCT	G	PO	A	E	DP
Batista	.903	17	26	39	7	11
Coronado	.946	81	131	222	20	47
Coultas	.905	14	17	40	6	5
Cruz	.917	3	4	7	1	2
Kiger	.927	13	7	31	3	3

	PCT	G	PO	A	E	DP
Rivera	.957	18	29	61	4	14

Outfield	PCT	G	PO	A	E	DP
Batista	.875	6	7	0	1	0
Cancel	.944	11	17	0	1	0
Chavez	1.000	1	3	0	0	0
Coles	1.000	63	135	7	0	2
Coultas	—	1	0	0	0	0
Cruz	1.000	3	3	0	0	0
Harper	.966	24	24	4	1	1
Harrison	1.000	3	4	0	0	0
Hill	.979	52	92	3	2	1
Jackson	.981	22	50	1	1	0
Kiger	—	1	0	0	0	0
Martinez	.975	58	116	3	3	1
Milledge	1.000	5	13	1	0	1
Negron	.985	84	190	8	3	3
Ragsdale	.500	1	1	0	1	0
Stewart	.985	119	248	11	4	4

ST. LUCIE METS　　　　　　　　　　　　　　　　　　　　HIGH CLASS A

FLORIDA STATE LEAGUE

BATTING	B-T	HT	WT	DOB	AVG	vLH	vRH	G	AB	R	H	2B	3B	HR	RBI	BB	HBP	SH	SF	SO	SB	CS	SLG	OBP
Arroyo, Rafael	R-R	5-9	170	10-26-82	.210	.231	.203	33	105	9	22	5	0	0	9	11	3	2	0	39	1	1	.257	.303
Batista, Wilson	B-R	6-0	170	2-7-81	.250	.500	.167	2	8	1	2	0	0	0	0	0	0	1	0	0	2	0	.250	.250
Bowman, Shawn	R-R	6-2	205	12-9-84	.150	.125	.167	6	20	3	3	0	0	1	2	1	0	0	1	8	1	0	.300	.182
Bucce, Yasmil	R-R	6-1	180	8-29-84	.186	.286	.161	21	70	7	13	1	0	0	7	5	0	1	0	12	0	0	.200	.240
Butera, Drew	R-R	6-1	205	8-9-83	.258	.364	.225	52	182	22	47	14	0	5	22	24	2	0	2	28	0	1	.418	.348
Carp, Mike	L-R	6-2	215	6-30-86	.250	—	.250	1	4	0	1	0	0	0	0	0	0	0	0	0	0	0	.250	.250
Castro, Jose	B-R	5-8	160	11-5-86	.318	.273	.333	77	308	47	98	12	1	2	25	11	11	13	1	21	7	10	.383	.363
Chavez, Endy	L-L	6-0	165	2-7-78	.500	.667	.462	4	16	3	8	1	0	0	2	0	0	0	0	0	0	1	.563	.500
Chavez, Ender	L-L	5-11	155	3-9-81	.279	.190	.300	40	111	15	31	4	1	0	9	23	3	4	1	16	5	5	.333	.413
Coles, Corey	L-L	6-1	170	1-30-82	.286	.261	.295	23	84	6	24	3	1	0	8	7	0	2	1	12	1	2	.345	.337
Concepcion, Ambiorix	R-R	6-2	180	3-19-82	.256	.220	.271	77	289	37	74	17	0	3	45	21	1	2	5	61	12	5	.346	.304
Coultas, Ryan	R-R	6-3	180	4-24-82	.257	.254	.258	59	183	25	47	5	4	3	27	12	1	1	1	40	2	1	.377	.305
Del Campo, Rogelio	L-R	5-10	195	7-25-86	.214	.200	.222	4	14	1	3	0	0	0	3	0	0	0	0	4	0	0	.214	.214
Dziuba, Teddy	L-R	5-10	185	10-26-84	.286	.400	.250	9	21	2	6	2	0	0	6	9	0	0	0	5	0	0	.381	.500
Evans, Nick	R-R	6-2	180	1-30-86	.286	.354	.262	103	378	65	108	25	1	15	54	53	3	2	4	64	3	0	.476	.374
Garcia, Emmanuel	L-R	6-2	188	3-4-86	.256	.258	.256	130	488	65	125	12	5	0	31	63	0	7	4	103	34	13	.301	.339
Gomez, Carlos	R-R	6-4	195	12-4-85	.154	.000	.286	5	13	1	2	0	0	0	0	1	1	0	0	4	2	0	.154	.267
Henry, Sean	R-R	5-10	154	8-18-85	.293	.278	.299	114	450	59	132	26	7	11	57	42	4	2	6	73	18	11	.456	.355
Hill, Jamar	R-R	6-3	200	9-20-82	.258	.205	.274	45	163	18	42	10	0	1	12	8	1	1	1	45	3	2	.337	.295
Malek, Bobby	L-R	6-1	205	7-6-81	.267	.333	.250	6	15	3	4	0	0	0	1	1	0	0	2	2	0		.267	.353
Malo, Jonathan	R-R	6-1	175	9-29-83	.255	.150	.292	78	231	29	59	10	0	6	40	23	1	4	3	37	2	4	.377	.322
Martin, Dustin	L-L	6-2	210	4-4-84	.287	.243	.304	93	363	52	104	22	6	5	52	42	1	2	5	93	11	5	.421	.358
2-team (32 Fort Myers)					.288	—	—	125	482	75	139	30	6	8	71	53	4	3	6	118	16	7	.425	.360
McCraw, Shane	L-R	6-0	185	3-11-86	.261	.167	.297	26	88	17	23	4	0	1	17	10	2	1	3	23	0	0	.341	.340
Medrano, Ignacio	R-R	6-2	160	7-17-86	.286	.375	.231	7	21	2	6	0	0	0	5	0	0	0	0	2	0	1	.286	.286
Mendez, Victor	B-R	5-11	205	6-28-80	.378	.353	.393	14	45	6	17	2	2	2	9	0	0	0	0	8	0	0	.644	.481
Milledge, Lastings	R-R	6-0	205	4-5-85	.250	.500	.000	1	4	1	1	0	0	0	0	0	0	0	0	1	0	0	.250	.400
Murphy, Dan	L-R	6-3	210	4-1-85	.285	.259	.295	135	502	68	143	34	3	11	78	42	4	0	11	61	6	3	.430	.338
Nickeas, Mike	R-R	6-0	220	2-13-83	.208	.292	.170	26	77	6	16	7	0	0	4	17	4	0	0	20	0	0	.299	.378
Pellot, Hector	R-R	5-11	184	2-8-87	.304	.444	.214	6	23	7	7	0	1	3	4	0	0	0	3	2	1		.522	.407
Petersen, Joshua	R-R	6-3	215	4-15-83	.277	.272	.279	89	307	40	85	16	3	7	34	12	7	3	1	57	3	2	.417	.318
Valentin, Jose	B-R	5-10	190	10-12-69	.125	.333	.000	3	8	4	1	0	0	1	4	2	0	0	1	2	0	0	.500	.273

PITCHING	B-T	HT	WT	DOB	W	L	ERA	G	GS	CG	SV	IP	H	R	ER	HR	BB	SO	AVG	vLH	vRH	K/9	BB/9
Abel, Nick	R-R	6-4	200	2-18-83	2	3	2.37	42	0	0	7	57	49	18	15	0	21	42	.234	.299	.197	6.63	3.32
Appell, Josh	L-L	6-1	195	6-23-83	0	0	0.00	1	0	0	0	1	0	0	0	0	0	0	.000	.000	.000	0.00	0.00
Beras, Alex	R-R	6-5	215	9-24-83	1	0	6.75	3	0	0	0	4	3	3	3	0	3	3	.214	.000	.250	6.75	6.75
Brown, Eric	R-R	6-6	225	2-23-84	10	8	4.13	26	25	0	0	144	168	79	66	9	30	68	.295	.257	.319	4.26	1.88
Camacho, Eddie	L-L	6-1	195	9-17-82	1	1	2.77	9	0	0	3	13	10	4	4	1	2	15	.213	.143	.225	10.38	1.38
Castillo, Jonathan	R-R	5-11	195	12-27-83	0	1	8.10	1	0	0	0	3	4	3	3	0	5	2	.308	.250	.333	5.40	13.50
Coultas, Ryan	R-R	6-3	180	4-24-82	1	0	0.00	1	0	0	0	2	0	0	0	1	0	0	.000	.000	.000	0.00	4.50
De La Torre, Jose	R-R	5-11	175	10-17-85	4	7	4.55	27	8	0	8	61	76	41	31	5	10	50	.302	.317	.291	7.34	1.47
Eager, Blake	R-R	6-3	205	5-19-82	1	0	6.34	15	6	0	0	38	54	34	27	7	11	23	.333	.257	.391	5.40	2.58
Guerra, Deolis	R-R	6-5	200	4-17-89	2	6	4.01	21	20	0	0	90	80	44	40	9	25	66	.240	.247	.234	6.62	2.51
Hietpas, Joe	R-R	6-3	230	5-1-79	4	3	2.47	27	0	0	1	44	41	14	12	0	9	22	.246	.257	.237	4.53	1.85
Hinchman, Grady	L-L	5-9	170	9-10-81	0	3	6.14	11	0	0	0	15	21	11	10	2	4	10	.323	.176	.375	6.14	2.45
Leaper, J.J.	R-R	6-1	160	3-12-87	0	1	8.25	4	3	0	0	12	21	15	11	5	6	4	.382	.464	.296	3.00	4.50
Marte, German	R-R	6-1	180	4-29-85	1	3	3.50	35	0	0	5	62	56	25	24	6	14	64	.235	.205	.253	9.34	2.04
Martinez, Pedro	R-R	5-11	195	10-25-71	1	1	3.21	3	3	0	0	14	13	8	5	2	3	13	.224	.286	.189	8.36	1.93
Mateo, Waner	R-R	6-5	175	2-5-85	0	1	7.36	5	0	0	0	11	14	12	9	1	5	8	.292	.200	.316	6.55	4.09
Meyers, Ryan	L-R	6-5	195	7-17-85	0	0	5.59	8	0	0	0	10	16	6	6	1	2	7	.390	.333	.423	6.52	1.86
Morales, Ricardo	L-L	6-1	170	12-9-83	2	0	4.60	11	1	0	1	29	37	21	15	6	12	18	.306	.194	.353	5.52	3.68
Murphy, Dan	L-R	6-3	210	4-1-85	0	0	—	0	0	0	0	0	0	0	0	0	1	0	0	—	—	.000	—	—
Nall, Brandon	R-R	6-4	190	3-18-82	3	2	2.21	11	0	0	4	20	15	8	5	1	3	21	.195	.258	.152	9.30	1.33
Niese, Jonathan	L-L	6-3	190	10-27-86	11	7	4.29	27	27	2	0	134	151	78	64	9	31	110	.285	.258	.291	7.37	2.08
Niesen, Eric	L-L	6-0	192	9-4-85	0	0	0.00	1	1	0	0	3	3	0	0	0	1	3	.273	.000	.300	9.00	3.00
Parnell, Robert	R-R	6-3	180	9-8-84	3	3	3.25	12	12	0	0	55	56	22	20	0	22	62	.259	.301	.238	10.08	3.58

	B-T	HT	WT	DOB	W	L	ERA	G	GS	CG	SV	IP	H	R	ER	HR	BB	SO	AVG	vLH	vRH	K/9	BB/9
Pelfrey, Mike	R-R	6-7	215	1-14-84	0	0	3.00	1	1	0	0	6	5	3	2	1	3	2	.250	.182	.333	3.00	4.50
Ruckle, Jacob	R-R	6-1	180	5-27-86	6	6	3.48	27	11	0	0	85	86	43	33	6	15	45	.263	.234	.284	4.75	1.58
Serfass, Joseph	R-R	6-3	215	5-6-81	1	2	7.30	11	1	0	0	25	33	24	20	4	5	13	.317	.229	.362	4.74	1.82
Simmons, Jeramy	R-R	6-0	200	9-30-82	0	2	5.77	18	0	0	0	39	56	28	25	6	13	28	.339	.333	.343	6.46	3.00
Stoner, Tobi	B-R	6-2	192	12-3-84	4	5	4.90	16	16	0	0	83	90	57	45	9	25	57	.280	.281	.278	6.21	2.72
Swindell, Mike	R-R	6-1	190	9-26-81	1	1	3.27	8	1	0	1	22	19	8	8	0	10	11	.244	.320	.208	4.50	4.09
Tomasiewicz, Kevin	L-L	6-2	225	9-17-83	5	1	3.60	37	0	0	3	65	55	26	26	3	19	44	.237	.215	.246	6.09	2.63
Urdaneta, Lino	R-R	6-1	220	11-20-79	0	0	0.00	2	0	0	0	2	0	0	0	0	1	0	.000	.000	.000	0.00	4.50
Valdes, Raul	L-L	5-11	190	11-27-77	0	1	6.14	3	1	0	0	7	8	5	5	0	6	5	.276	.286	.273	6.14	7.36
Waechter, Nicholas	R-R	6-3	200	11-30-84	0	0	15.00	1	1	0	0	3	7	5	5	1	1	1	.467	.500	.455	3.00	3.00
Williams, Dave	L-L	6-3	215	3-12-79	0	0	5.40	1	1	0	0	5	4	3	3	1	2	3	.222	.333	.167	5.40	3.60
Worthington, Tim	R-R	6-2	200	7-29-80	1	0	3.04	10	0	0	0	24	17	8	8	0	11	26	.198	.188	.204	9.89	4.18

FIELDING

Catcher	PCT	G	PO	A	E	DP	PB
Arroyo	.995	31	182	24	1	1	4
Bucce	1.000	4	18	4	0	0	0
Butera	.990	52	352	28	4	3	6
Dziuba	1.000	9	47	5	0	2	2
McCraw	.994	26	146	11	1	0	2
Nickeas	.963	20	116	14	5	0	0

First Base	PCT	G	PO	A	E	DP
Carp	1.000	1	12	0	0	0
Coultas	.993	15	136	10	1	17
Evans	.992	102	938	68	8	90
Malo	.982	8	52	3	1	5
Petersen	.988	18	155	9	2	16

Second Base	PCT	G	PO	A	E	DP
Batista	.917	2	2	9	1	2
Castro	1.000	1	1	1	0	0
Coultas	.980	10	22	26	1	7

Garcia	.957	69	147	229	17	54
Henry	1.000	1	3	6	0	0
Malo	.980	54	108	141	5	29
Medrano	—	1	0	0	0	0
Pellot	1.000	3	2	11	0	0
Valentin	1.000	3	7	7	0	4

Third Base	PCT	G	PO	A	E	DP
Bowman	1.000	2	3	4	0	1
Coultas	1.000	1	0	2	0	1
Malo	1.000	2	2	1	0	1
Murphy	.917	131	85	304	35	34
Petersen	.600	4	1	5	4	0

Shortstop	PCT	G	PO	A	E	DP
Castro	.957	76	111	268	17	48
Coultas	.891	8	15	34	6	7
Garcia	.929	56	81	153	18	31
Malo	1.000	1	2	1	0	0

Outfield	PCT	G	PO	A	E	DP
Arroyo	1.000	2	1	0	0	0
Ender Chavez	.972	29	32	3	1	0
Endy Chavez	1.000	4	6	2	0	1
Coles	1.000	17	20	2	0	0
Concepcion	.956	77	163	11	8	3
Coultas	1.000	6	5	1	0	0
Gomez	1.000	5	10	0	0	0
Henry	.966	114	192	5	7	1
Hill	.978	28	42	2	1	0
Malek	.889	6	6	2	1	1
Martin	.990	93	189	10	2	1
Medrano	1.000	5	6	0	0	0
Mendez	1.000	13	27	0	0	0
Milledge	1.000	1	1	0	0	0
Nickeas	1.000	2	6	0	0	0
Petersen	.977	33	41	1	1	0

SAVANNAH SAND GNATS   LOW CLASS A
SOUTH ATLANTIC LEAGUE

BATTING	B-T	HT	WT	DOB	AVG	vLH	vRH	G	AB	R	H	2B	3B	HR	RBI	BB	HBP	SH	SF	SO	SB	CS	SLG	OBP
Clark, Darren	L-L	6-0	188	7-21-84	.304	.348	.290	24	92	12	28	4	0	2	13	6	1	0	0	17	2	0	.413	.354
Cruz, Elvis	R-R	6-2	195	11-23-83	.208	.259	.179	53	149	15	31	5	0	5	12	7	2	0	3	46	3	0	.342	.248
Dziuba, Teddy	L-R	5-10	185	10-26-84	.000	—	.000	1	3	0	0	0	0	0	0	0	0	0	0	2	0	0	.000	.000
Eigsti, Jacob	R-R	6-0	185	6-13-84	.125	.333	.000	3	8	1	1	0	0	0	1	0	0	0	4	0	1	.125	.222
Holden, Joe	L-R	5-11	175	4-10-84	.260	.310	.248	88	304	54	79	14	3	6	29	28	3	5	2	66	19	3	.385	.326
Johnstone, Tyler	R-R	6-0	185	11-9-83	.071	.000	.100	7	14	0	1	0	0	0	0	0	0	0	0	3	0	0	.071	.071
Lagares, Juan	R-R	6-1	175	3-17-89	.210	.233	.204	83	281	26	59	12	6	2	16	18	2	3	0	64	11	7	.317	.262
Maccani, Tony	R-R	6-3	191	9-24-84	.048	.000	.059	9	21	0	1	0	0	0	1	3	1	1	0	5	0	0	.048	.200
Maldonado, Brahiam	R-R	6-0	185	9-18-85	.310	.222	.338	87	306	40	95	20	4	10	39	19	0	2	2	79	11	4	.500	.349
McCraw, Sam	L-R	6-0	185	3-11-86	.272	.200	.289	50	151	21	41	4	0	4	19	37	4	0	3	35	2	0	.377	.427
Pellot, Hector	R-R	5-11	184	2-8-87	.274	.313	.263	114	431	52	118	19	3	7	34	37	10	3	1	102	33	17	.381	.344
Pena, Francisco	R-R	6-2	230	10-12-89	.210	.230	.205	103	367	26	77	12	0	5	30	24	4	0	4	76	1	1	.283	.249
Pena, Richard	R-R	6-2	175	8-15-87	.205	.286	.188	11	39	9	8	1	1	1	2	10	0	0	0	10	2	0	.359	.367
Richey, Brandon	R-R	6-0	180	4-27-86	.167	.143	.172	11	36	5	6	1	0	0	1	4	0	1	0	9	0	0	.194	.250
Rivera, Luis	R-R	6-1	165	1-25-84	.254	.194	.271	47	138	7	35	5	1	0	11	5	2	0	3	15	1	2	.304	.290
Rodriguez, Joaquin	R-R	6-4	180	10-29-84	.333	.000	.412	9	21	3	7	0	0	0	1	2	2	0	0	3	0	1	.333	.440
Sanchez, Jonathan	L-L	6-2	175	9-3-85	.190	.200	.188	55	179	16	34	9	1	3	15	13	0	0	0	44	5	1	.302	.245
Santos, Jonathan	B-R	5-11	165	11-26-85	.188	.211	.178	21	64	10	12	2	0	0	6	10	0	1	0	17	3	0	.219	.297
Stegall, Daniel	L-R	6-3	180	9-24-87	.200	.173	.208	64	235	23	47	6	2	0	14	14	2	1	2	55	9	6	.243	.249
Thole, Josh	L-R	6-1	190	10-28-86	.267	.279	.265	117	389	46	104	17	0	3	36	61	4	4	0	57	4	4	.311	.372
Veloz, Greg	B-R	6-1	175	6-3-88	.171	.235	.153	66	234	20	40	7	1	2	14	23	0	3	2	73	15	4	.235	.243
Ventura, Leivi	R-R	6-1	185	7-19-83	.243	.319	.223	123	428	40	104	21	4	5	45	39	5	1	3	74	3	2	.346	.312
Wabick, D.J.	L-R	6-2	185	5-30-84	.306	.245	.323	118	428	38	131	32	1	8	64	27	2	1	3	86	1	2	.442	.348

PITCHING	B-T	HT	WT	DOB	W	L	ERA	G	GS	CG	SV	IP	H	R	ER	HR	BB	SO	AVG	vLH	vRH	K/9	BB/9
Beras, Alex	R-R	6-5	215	9-24-83	0	0	5.03	11	0	0	0	20	20	12	11	2	18	16	.263	.241	.277	7.32	8.24
Burns, Bradley	R-R	6-4	182	5-28-86	0	0	1.80	1	1	0	0	5	2	2	1	0	3	2	.111	.000	.118	3.60	5.40
Calero, Angel	L-L	6-3	170	9-25-86	2	0	1.54	2	2	0	0	12	8	2	2	2	5	8	.195	.000	.195	6.17	3.86
Carrillo, Matias	L-L	6-3	224	12-13-86	0	0	3.72	10	0	0	0	19	24	9	8	1	6	14	.300	.360	.273	6.52	2.79
Castillo, Jonathan	R-R	5-11	195	12-27-83	5	5	4.18	31	7	1	0	88	88	46	41	12	36	49	.257	.276	.249	4.99	3.67
Cruz, Elvis	R-R	6-2	195	11-23-83	0	0	4.50	2	0	0	0	2	2	1	1	0	2	3	.286	.000	.500	13.50	9.00
D'Alessandro, Joe	R-R	5-11	195	2-20-84	0	2	7.23	12	0	0	1	19	36	25	15	5	8	17	.391	.500	.353	8.20	3.86
Durkin, Matt	R-R	6-4	220	2-22-83	4	8	4.00	25	18	0	2	115	107	63	51	9	56	71	.244	.216	.259	5.57	4.40
Frederick, Emary	R-R	6-0	180	1-17-84	2	0	6.80	32	0	0	3	46	60	43	35	4	35	50	.308	.362	.285	9.71	6.80
Koons, David	R-R	6-1	180	3-13-84	1	6	4.29	29	0	0	5	42	44	27	20	1	9	35	.262	.273	.258	7.50	1.93
Mateo, Waner	R-R	6-5	175	2-5-85	0	1	5.26	18	1	0	0	38	37	22	22	4	10	30	.250	.244	.252	7.17	2.39
Meyers, Ryan	L-R	6-5	195	7-11-84	1	4	2.14	30	0	0	13	42	28	11	10	3	14	48	.185	.189	.184	10.29	3.00
Mizell, Jeremy	R-R	6-6	177	6-18-83	3	15	6.17	27	14	0	0	105	140	78	72	17	30	77	.318	.327	.314	6.60	2.57
Mullens, Greg	R-R	6-6	245	1-30-85	5	5	4.39	17	13	1	0	82	81	47	40	2	34	32	.256	.247	.259	3.51	3.73
Orta, Phillips	R-R	6-2	175	5-9-86	0	0	27.00	1	0	0	0	1	2	3	3	0	4	1	1.000	.000	1.000	13.50	67.50
Polanco, Julio	L-L	6-0	163	11-29-86	3	8	6.67	21	17	0	0	84	102	73	62	18	43	72	.293	.299	.292	7.75	4.63
Portillo, Nelson	R-R	6-0	180	9-8-85	3	12	5.31	30	12	0	0	97	110	72	57	12	37	67	.279	.333	.257	6.24	3.44
Privett, Todd	L-L	6-0	185	4-22-84	0	4	7.83	11	3	0	0	33	47	30	29	4	8	28	.326	.333	.326	7.56	2.16
Reyes, Jorge	R-R	6-4	170	5-15-84	1	0	0.00	1	1	0	0	5	4	0	0	0	4	5	.211	.250	.182	9.00	7.20
Simmons, Jeramy	R-R	6-0	200	9-30-82	3	0	4.91	18	0	0	3	26	31	21	14	4	11	23	.301	.333	.286	8.06	3.86
Sparks, Ricky	R-R	6-5	205	10-10-84	0	1	14.14	5	0	0	1	7	12	11	11	4	5	6	.364	.250	.400	7.71	6.43

ORGANIZATION STATISTICS

Stinson, Josh	R-R	6-4	195	3-14-88	3	11	4.86	26	21	0	0	109	131	77	59	13	33	52	.294	.367	.254	4.28 2.72
Stoner, Tobi	B-R	6-2	192	12-3-84	3	5	3.61	11	11	0	0	57	59	32	23	1	17	50	.259	.279	.246	7.85 2.67
Stronach, Tim	L-R	6-5	185	12-20-85	2	7	5.45	14	14	0	0	73	81	53	44	11	24	42	.280	.301	.272	5.20 2.97

FIELDING

Catcher	PCT	G	PO	A	E	DP	PB
Dziuba	1.000	1	7	1	0	0	0
Maccani	.982	9	49	7	1	0	1
McCraw	.976	37	206	33	6	0	9
Pena	.967	81	462	61	18	5	14
Thole	.971	11	60	6	2	0	2

First Base	PCT	G	PO	A	E	DP
Thole	.993	103	905	55	7	69
Ventura	1.000	5	31	1	0	2
Wabick	.981	31	238	16	5	26

Second Base	PCT	G	PO	A	E	DP
Eigsti	1.000	1	0	2	0	0
Johnstone	.941	4	6	10	1	4
Pellot	.971	83	166	203	11	40

	PCT	G	PO	A	E	DP	
Rivera	1.000	2	2	2	0	0	
Rodriguez	1.000	1	0	2	0	0	
Santos	.986	15	36	35	1	11	
Veloz	.940	33	63	79	9	20	

Third Base	PCT	G	PO	A	E	DP
Johnstone	—	1	0	0	0	0
Pellot	.800	2	0	4	1	0
Rivera	.923	4	3	9	1	0
Rodriguez	.905	8	2	17	2	1
Santos	1.000	3	2	3	0	0
Veloz	.615	5	1	7	5	0
Ventura	.940	119	95	267	23	28

Shortstop	PCT	G	PO	A	E	DP
Eigsti	.800	2	2	6	2	3

	PCT	G	PO	A	E	DP
Lagares	.911	82	118	291	40	43
Richey	.898	11	15	29	5	3
Rivera	.974	39	69	121	5	18
Santos	1.000	2	1	7	0	2

Outfield	PCT	G	PO	A	E	DP
Clark	1.000	23	31	0	0	0
Cruz	.971	45	96	4	3	2
Holden	.951	87	171	3	9	0
Maldonado	.952	86	152	6	8	1
McCraw	1.000	6	11	1	0	0
Pena	.964	11	27	0	1	0
Sanchez	.933	47	81	2	6	1
Stegall	.939	64	104	3	7	2
Wabick	.976	55	78	2	2	0

BROOKLYN CYCLONES   SHORT-SEASON

NEW YORK-PENN LEAGUE

BATTING	B-T	HT	WT	DOB	AVG	vLH	vRH	G	AB	R	H	2B	3B	HR	RBI	BB	HBP	SH	SF	SO	SB	CS	SLG	OBP
Abruzzo, Jordan	B-R	6-3	230	8-2-84	.250	—	.250	4	16	2	4	0	0	0	1	0	2	0	0	4	0	0	.250	.333
Alou, Moises	R-R	6-3	225	7-3-66	.250	1.000	.000	1	4	0	1	0	0	0	1	0	0	0	0	0	0	0	.250	.250
Bouchard, Matthew	R-R	6-0	185	12-12-86	.267	.091	.309	70	225	32	60	10	2	2	27	22	2	6	1	51	8	11	.356	.336
Bucce, Yasmil	R-R	6-1	180	8-29-84	.143	.200	.135	12	42	4	6	1	0	0	4	1	2	2	0	15	0	0	.167	.200
Carrera, Ezequiel	L-L	5-11	175	6-11-87	.300	.444	.279	20	70	11	21	2	0	0	6	4	1	2	0	13	6	1	.329	.347
Chavez, Ender	L-L	5-11	155	3-9-81	.170	.000	.174	16	47	6	8	0	0	0	3	6	0	1	0	13	2	1	.170	.264
Cordido, Cesar	R-R	5-10	175	9-10-85	.273	.200	.294	7	22	1	6	1	0	0	3	0	1	0	1	5	0	1	.318	.292
Duda, Lucas	L-R	6-4	225	2-3-86	.299	.302	.298	67	234	32	70	20	3	4	32	34	5	0	1	45	3	5	.462	.398
Eigsti, Jacob	R-R	6-0	185	6-13-84	.275	.295	.270	66	244	28	67	9	2	2	32	18	3	4	0	44	4	2	.352	.332
Fournier, Christopher	R-R	6-0	188	8-24-84	.224	.125	.250	21	76	12	17	2	0	1	9	8	1	0	1	24	6	2	.289	.302
Jacobs, Jason	R-R	6-0	210	12-9-83	.273	.225	.283	66	238	38	65	11	2	12	46	35	7	1	4	66	2	3	.487	.377
Jimenez, Jose	R-R	6-2	185	5-9-87	.000	.000	.000	1	2	0	0	0	0	0	1	1	0	0	0	0	0	0	.000	.333
Kawal, Brandon	R-R	6-3	215	10-29-84	.302	.286	.307	38	116	14	35	5	1	0	14	6	4	0	2	26	5	4	.362	.352
Lo Duca, Paul	R-R	5-10	205	4-12-72	.400	—	.400	2	5	1	2	0	0	1	2	1	1	0	0	2	0	0	01.000	.571
Lutz, Zachary	R-R	6-1	220	6-3-86	.000	—	.000	1	2	0	0	0	0	0	0	0	0	0	0	0	0	0	.000	.000
Malvagna, Steve	R-R	5-11	195	11-28-85	.333	.250	.400	6	9	1	3	0	0	0	0	0	0	0	0	4	0	0	.333	.333
Reyes, Raul	L-L	6-0	183	12-30-86	.233	.119	.256	71	253	42	59	13	4	9	33	27	6	5	1	94	9	6	.423	.321
Rodriguez, Joaquin	R-R	6-4	180	10-29-84	.273	.125	.320	28	66	11	18	3	0	0	11	12	0	0	3	18	2	0	.318	.370
Schilling, Micah	L-R	5-11	185	12-27-82	.283	.361	.269	71	244	49	69	17	0	1	15	60	2	4	1	58	13	7	.365	.427
Tatford, Jefferies	L-R	6-3	210	9-16-84	.169	.125	.174	28	77	6	13	4	0	1	7	5	1	1	0	22	0	0	.260	.229
Vogl, Will	R-R	5-9	175	12-10-83	.240	.209	.247	69	229	34	55	7	4	1	22	21	3	2	2	71	10	5	.319	.310
Voyles, J.R.	R-R	5-10	185	11-29-83	.254	.250	.255	49	169	24	43	11	1	3	29	17	7	5	3	30	4	2	.385	.342

PITCHING	B-T	HT	WT	DOB	W	L	ERA	G	GS	CG	SV	IP	H	R	ER	HR	BB	SO	AVG	vLH	vRH	K/9	BB/9
Antonini, Michael	R-L	6-0	190	8-6-85	0	0	0.46	7	2	0	0	20	13	1	1	0	5	12	.194	.208	.186	5.49	2.29
Appell, Josh	L-L	6-1	195	6-23-83	2	1	3.65	24	0	0	0	25	19	11	10	2	16	21	.218	.188	.236	7.66	5.84
Carr, Nicholas	R-R	6-1	195	4-19-87	5	2	3.80	14	14	0	0	66	55	31	28	4	27	74	.224	.265	.196	10.04	3.66
Cheney, Steven	R-R	6-5	200	7-3-86	4	4	2.70	18	0	0	0	40	33	15	12	2	12	39	.226	.241	.217	8.78	2.70
Clyne, Stephen	B-R	6-2	215	9-22-84	1	1	2.05	20	0	0	8	26	21	9	6	0	19	30	.214	.178	.177	10.25	6.49
Gee, Dillon	R-R	6-1	195	4-28-86	3	1	2.47	14	11	0	0	62	57	17	17	1	9	56	.249	.238	.258	8.13	1.31
Hinchman, Grady	L-L	5-9	170	9-10-81	1	1	3.71	21	0	0	1	27	25	12	11	1	10	30	.248	.212	.265	10.12	3.38
Koons, David	R-R	6-1	180	3-13-84	4	1	3.38	9	0	0	0	19	21	8	7	1	2	13	.284	.385	.229	6.27	0.96
Kunz, Eddie	R-R	6-5	250	4-8-86	1	1	6.75	12	0	0	5	12	8	9	9	0	8	9	.190	.105	.261	6.75	6.00
Leaper, J.J.	R-R	6-1	160	3-12-87	0	1	2.14	4	4	0	0	21	19	5	5	1	7	15	.250	.214	.271	6.43	3.00
McDonald, Daniel	L-R	5-11	195	4-17-86	1	2	3.16	20	0	0	3	26	10	10	9	0	20	30	.116	.167	.089	10.52	7.01
Morgan, William	R-R	6-1	205	11-3-85	3	0	2.02	22	0	0	2	36	22	8	8	2	8	39	.173	.200	.153	9.84	2.02
Mullens, Greg	R-R	6-6	245	1-30-85	1	0	4.91	4	0	0	0	7	8	5	4	0	3	3	.258	.438	.067	3.68	3.68
Niesen, Eric	L-L	6-0	192	9-4-85	0	3	3.30	9	9	0	0	30	30	19	11	1	25	27	.268	.258	.272	8.10	7.50
Olmsted, Michael	R-R	6-6	245	5-2-87	0	0	7.71	2	0	0	0	5	5	4	4	1	1	6	.278	.500	.100	11.57	1.93
Owen, Dylan	R-R	5-11	185	7-12-86	9	1	1.49	14	13	0	0	72	51	13	12	0	12	69	.197	.193	.200	8.59	1.49
Privett, Todd	L-L	6-0	185	4-22-86	0	0	0.00	1	1	0	0	3	3	0	0	0	0	2	.250	.000	.333	6.00	0.00
Ramirez, Edgar	R-R	6-4	215	11-30-83	4	0	3.07	19	1	0	1	29	21	14	10	1	18	23	.206	.114	.254	7.06	5.52
Rustich, Brant	R-R	6-6	225	1-23-85	2	0	2.13	10	0	0	2	13	4	3	3	2	1	11	.095	.222	.000	7.82	0.71
Stronach, Tim	L-R	6-5	185	12-20-85	4	2	3.41	11	4	0	0	32	36	15	12	1	19	14	.303	.286	.314	3.98	5.40
Waechter, Nicholas	R-R	6-3	200	11-30-84	5	4	3.89	15	15	1	0	69	62	31	30	3	17	60	.240	.267	.222	7.79	2.21

FIELDING

Catcher	PCT	G	PO	A	E	DP	PB
Abruzzo	1.000	4	31	5	0	1	0
Bucce	.977	11	72	13	2	0	2
Cordido	.984	7	51	9	1	1	0
Jacobs	.987	34	277	32	4	3	2
Lo Duca	1.000	1	6	1	0	0	0
Malvagna	1.000	1	3	1	0	0	0
Tatford	.981	19	143	10	3	1	4

First Base	PCT	G	PO	A	E	DP
Duda	.983	36	267	18	5	22
Eigsti	1.000	6	23	1	0	1
Jacobs	.991	21	202	12	2	18
Jimenez	1.000	1	1	0	0	0
Rodriguez	.994	20	152	10	1	7
Tatford	1.000	2	7	0	0	0

Second Base	PCT	G	PO	A	E	DP
Eigsti	1.000	2	3	11	0	0
Rodriguez	—	1	0	0	0	0
Schilling	.959	47	71	116	8	17
Vogl	—	1	0	0	0	0
Voyles	.992	27	45	80	1	17

Third Base	PCT	G	PO	A	E	DP
Eigsti	.938	54	44	93	9	8
Jimenez	—	1	0	0	0	0
Lutz	1.000	1	0	3	0	0
Rodriguez	.778	4	1	6	2	0
Voyles	.868	22	10	36	7	2

Shortstop	PCT	G	PO	A	E	DP
Bouchard	.972	68	91	184	8	33
Eigsti	1.000	7	8	13	0	3

Rodriguez	1.000	2	3	6	0	2

Outfield	PCT	G	PO	A	E	DP
Alou	—	1	0	0	0	0
Carrera	1.000	20	37	2	0	0
Chavez	1.000	16	23	2	0	0
Duda	.964	27	26	1	1	0
Eigsti	1.000	1	1	0	0	0
Kawal	1.000	36	46	2	0	0
Reyes	.991	71	112	1	1	0
Vogl	.993	69	126	9	1	2
Voyles	—	1	0	0	0	0

KINGSPORT METS   ROOKIE

APPALACHIAN LEAGUE

BATTING	B-T	HT	WT	DOB	AVG	vLH	vRH	G	AB	R	H	2B	3B	HR	RBI	BB	HBP	SH	SF	SO	SB	CS	SLG	OBP
Abruzzo, Jordan	B-R	6-3	230	8-2-84	.222	.000	.233	11	45	7	10	3	0	3	7	3	1	0	0	7	0	0	.489	.286
Bucce, Yasmil	R-R	6-1	180	8-29-84	.255	.250	.258	30	98	12	25	6	0	0	17	10	4	3	1	15	2	0	.316	.345
Clark, Darren	L-L	6-0	188	7-21-84	.277	.231	.288	36	130	23	36	8	1	5	19	13	3	0	0	27	3	1	.469	.356
Cordido, Cesar	R-R	5-10	175	9-10-85	.278	.269	.281	30	90	4	25	5	0	0	13	4	3	2	2	14	1	0	.333	.323
Del Campo, Rogelio	L-R	5-10	195	7-25-86	.091	.000	.125	5	11	1	1	0	0	1	1	0	0	1	0	2	0	0	.364	.091
Dziuba, Teddy	L-R	5-10	185	10-26-84	.167	—	.167	2	6	1	1	1	0	0	0	1	0	0	0	1	0	0	.333	.375
Giarraputo, Nicholas	R-R	6-3	200	5-29-88	.274	.237	.289	66	263	27	72	24	0	0	34	9	1	2	2	44	2	3	.365	.298
Gonzalez, Ernesto	R-R	5-10	165	1-16-87	.268	.060	.161	12	41	5	11	1	0	0	2	0	1	0	0	3	0	0	.293	.286
Green, Donald	R-R	6-1	200	7-29-85	.172	.182	.168	42	128	22	22	3	1	3	9	12	2	1	1	51	7	1	.281	.252
Hambrice, Jeremy	R-R	6-2	195	3-14-86	.252	.273	.241	41	127	17	32	4	1	3	13	19	2	1	0	41	5	4	.370	.358
Hubbert, B.J.	R-R	6-4	210	8-24-85	.264	.353	.222	14	53	5	14	4	1	1	3	4	0	0	0	18	1	0	.434	.316
Jimenez, Jose	R-R	6-2	185	5-9-87	.309	.316	.305	51	188	32	58	17	1	7	41	17	6	0	3	43	4	3	.521	.379
Johnson, Terry	R-R	6-2	180	2-20-85	1.000	1.000	—	2	1	1	0	1	0	0	0	0	0	0	0	0	0	0	1.000	1.000
Parker, Michael	R-R	5-10	180	2-28-85	.298	.304	.295	43	141	25	42	7	0	4	19	14	2	0	1	23	7	2	.433	.367
Pena, Richard	R-R	6-2	175	8-15-87	.227	.159	.255	47	154	33	35	5	3	3	14	28	6	1	1	46	7	0	.357	.365
Richey, Brandon	R-R	6-0	180	4-27-86	.243	.279	.226	41	136	19	33	9	0	3	22	12	3	7	2	38	5	2	.375	.314
Santos, Jonathan	B-R	5-11	165	1-4-86	.067	.000	.083	6	15	2	1	0	0	1	0	0	1	1	1	6	0	0	.133	.167
Stegall, Daniel	L-R	6-3	180	9-24-87	.226	.208	.234	66	248	32	56	10	6	0	27	33	3	6	1	67	11	3	.315	.323
Vaughn, Tyler	R-R	6-2	200	3-21-85	.284	.290	.281	25	88	20	25	9	0	3	14	4	5	0	0	18	1	1	.489	.351
Veloz, Greg	B-R	6-1	175	6-3-88	.271	.250	.281	66	258	43	70	13	9	5	28	26	3	7	1	62	18	7	.450	.344

PITCHING	B-T	HT	WT	DOB	W	L	ERA	G	GS	CG	SV	IP	H	R	ER	HR	BB	SO	AVG	vLH	vRH	K/9	BB/9
Antonini, Michael	R-L	6-0	190	8-6-85	1	1	3.71	5	3	0	0	17	16	8	7	3	2	18	.239	.143	.250	9.53	1.06
Arriechi, Nelson	L-L	6-2	185	11-28-85	0	0	10.13	3	0	0	0	5	4	7	6	0	6	4	.211	.500	.176	6.75	10.12
Bierd, Jose	R-R	6-2	155	5-8-85	2	0	6.49	14	1	0	1	26	24	20	19	2	16	24	.245	.206	.266	8.20	5.47
Burns, Bradley	R-R	6-4	182	5-28-86	3	1	3.51	12	6	0	1	41	41	18	16	1	11	34	.252	.306	.228	7.46	2.41
Calero, Angel	L-L	6-3	170	9-25-86	5	1	2.79	11	6	0	0	52	45	19	16	6	17	43	.234	.250	.232	7.49	2.96
Carrillo, Matias	L-L	6-3	224	12-13-86	0	0	1.23	5	0	0	2	7	5	4	1	0	2	4	.161	.250	.130	4.91	2.45
Cruz, Rhiner	R-R	6-2	165	11-1-86	1	1	0.71	11	0	0	4	13	7	1	1	0	14	13	.184	.111	.207	9.24	9.95
D'Alessandro, Joe	R-R	5-11	195	2-20-84	0	1	3.52	5	0	0	1	8	3	3	3	0	2	3	.120	.100	.133	3.52	2.35
Holdzkom, John	R-R	6-7	225	10-19-87	1	0	3.60	3	0	0	0	5	4	3	2	0	4	6	.235	.000	.286	10.80	7.20
Johnson, Kyle	R-R	6-3	225	1-21-85	2	1	5.96	16	0	0	0	23	24	22	15	3	17	13	.267	.310	.246	5.16	6.75
Lavorgna, Jason	R-R	5-9	190	3-4-86	0	4	8.72	14	0	0	0	22	38	25	21	3	6	20	.376	.333	.394	8.31	2.49
Martinez, Pedro P.	R-R	6-4	175	7-8-85	3	4	5.52	13	5	1	0	46	51	33	28	3	13	27	.271	.221	.300	5.32	2.56
Merritt, Roy	L-L	6-0	170	9-22-85	1	2	2.88	17	0	0	2	25	24	9	8	2	4	17	.255	.300	.243	6.12	1.44
Olivares, Manuel	R-R	6-0	170	5-22-86	3	3	4.56	13	0	0	1	49	54	37	25	6	14	30	.281	.278	.283	5.47	2.55
Olmsted, Michael	R-R	6-6	245	5-2-87	1	1	1.93	6	0	0	0	28	18	7	6	2	10	22	.182	.270	.129	7.07	3.21
Orta, Phillips	R-R	6-2	175	5-9-86	2	2	4.58	11	11	0	0	53	62	29	27	3	21	45	.297	.288	.300	7.64	3.57
Ramirez, Elvin	R-R	6-3	182	10-10-87	1	4	5.52	12	12	0	0	46	52	34	28	5	29	48	.280	.254	.293	9.46	5.72
Rodriguez, Jorge	R-R	6-3	182	5-10-87	4	4	4.60	13	5	0	0	47	48	36	24	4	26	47	.261	.203	.288	9.00	4.98
Rustich, Brant	R-R	6-6	225	1-23-85	1	0	0.87	5	2	0	0	10	6	1	1	0	1	10	.158	.286	.129	8.71	0.87
Sparks, Ricky	R-R	6-5	205	10-10-84	0	0	0.73	7	0	0	0	12	9	5	1	0	9	17	.205	.083	.250	12.41	6.57
Tabata, Marcos	R-R	5-10	175	6-12-86	3	3	7.49	13	5	0	2	40	51	36	33	2	16	41	.309	.415	.259	9.30	3.63
Valdez, Santiago	R-R	6-2	210	7-29-87	1	0	1.80	2	0	0	0	5	3	1	1	0	2	3	.188	.000	.231	5.40	3.60

FIELDING

Catcher	PCT	G	PO	A	E	DP	PB
Abruzzo	1.000	7	49	5	0	2	0
Bucce	.982	30	192	24	4	0	5
Cordido	.975	29	199	32	6	1	4
Del Campo	.971	4	31	2	1	0	1
Dziuba	.952	2	19	1	1	0	1

First Base	PCT	G	PO	A	E	DP
Giarraputo	1.000	12	82	0	0	9
Hambrice	.980	22	177	20	4	9
Jimenez	.991	37	309	16	3	28

Second Base	PCT	G	PO	A	E	DP
Gonzalez	.667	1	0	2	1	0

Johnson	1.000	2	1	1	0	1
Parker	1.000	6	8	12	0	0
Santos	1.000	1	4	0	0	1
Veloz	.942	61	141	150	18	41

Third Base	PCT	G	PO	A	E	DP
Giarraputo	.919	53	36	122	14	12
Jimenez	.878	13	12	24	5	3
Parker	1.000	4	3	11	0	2

Shortstop	PCT	G	PO	A	E	DP
Gonzalez	.917	10	7	26	3	2
Parker	.949	15	26	48	4	9
Richey	.888	39	52	107	20	19

Santos	.773	5	4	13	5	1

Outfield	PCT	G	PO	A	E	DP
Clark	.931	19	27	0	2	0
Green	.986	38	67	5	1	1
Hambrice	1.000	17	17	2	0	0
Hubbert	.952	13	20	0	1	0
Parker	1.000	17	28	0	0	0
Pena	.970	45	60	4	2	1
Stegall	.992	63	125	1	1	0

GULF COAST LEAGUE

BATTING	B-T	HT	WT	DOB	AVG	vLH	vRH	G	AB	R	H	2B	3B	HR	RBI	BB	HBP	SH	SF	SO	SB	CS	SLG	OBP
Aguayo, Luis	L-R	6-2	260	12-10-83	.165	.118	.177	25	79	6	13	1	0	0	7	7	2	0	1	34	0	1	.177	.247
Alou, Moises	R-R	6-3	225	7-3-66	.333	.500	.273	5	15	2	5	1	0	1	3	1	1	0	0	2	0	0	.600	.412
Bouchard, Maxime	L-R	6-2	210	5-10-85	.167	.167	.167	11	30	7	5	0	1	1	3	7	0	0	1	6	1	0	.333	.316
Carrera, Ezequiel	L-L	5-11	175	6-11-87	.341	.417	.313	45	179	41	61	8	3	1	26	26	2	2	0	29	16	5	.436	.430
Centeno, Juan	L-R	5-9	172	11-16-89	.146	.167	.138	12	41	4	6	0	0	0	2	3	1	0	0	6	0	0	.146	.222
Chavez, Endy	L-L	6-0	165	2-7-78	.625	1.000	.571	2	8	2	5	0	0	0	4	1	0	0	1	2	0	0	.625	.600
Del Campo, Rogelio	L-R	5-10	195	7-25-86	.300	.333	.292	14	30	7	9	3	0	2	7	4	0	0	5	1	0	.600	.382
Deluca, Sam	R-R	5-11	190	9-30-85	.282	.333	.267	14	39	6	11	2	0	1	7	4	1	0	2	1	0	.410	.364
Fernandez, Rafael	L-L	6-1	171	8-3-88	.625	.500	.667	3	8	4	5	0	0	0	2	2	0	0	0	0	0	0	.625	.700
Gonzalez, Ernesto	R-R	5-10	165	1-16-87	.262	.240	.269	26	103	12	27	5	0	0	9	5	4	1	0	11	5	1	.311	.321
Guzman, Carlos	L-R	6-2	190	5-24-86	.215	.278	.191	38	130	19	28	6	1	5	24	24	5	0	0	37	6	0	.392	.358
Hernandez, Dan	R-R	6-3	250	3-23-85	.182	.000	.250	3	11	2	2	0	0	1	4	0	0	0	4	0	0	.455	.182
Hubbert, B.J.	R-R	6-4	210	8-24-85	.203	.207	.202	35	128	19	26	5	0	3	12	9	7	0	1	52	4	3	.313	.290
Johnson, Terry	R-R	6-2	180	2-20-85	.192	.000	.270	19	52	6	10	1	0	1	5	5	2	0	6	0	0	.269	.288
Lucas, Richard	R-R	6-1	205	11-2-88	.264	.218	.280	52	212	27	56	8	2	2	30	15	3	0	1	66	2	1	.349	.320
Maat, Patrick	R-R	6-4	260	9-15-87	.190	.375	.147	19	42	4	8	2	0	0	3	10	1	0	1	12	0	0	.238	.352
Martin, Dustin	L-L	6-2	210	4-4-84	.500	.000	.667	2	4	1	2	0	0	0	0	0	0	0	0	0	0	0	.500	.500
Martinez, Fernando	L-R	6-1	190	10-10-88	.111	.333	.000	3	9	1	1	0	0	0	1	1	0	0	0	6	0	0	.333	.200
Martinez, Juan	R-R	5-11	200	2-28-89	.200	—	.200	3	10	0	2	1	0	0	1	0	0	0	3	0	0	.300	.273
Martinez, Samuel	R-R	5-11	175	7-6-87	.154	.118	.171	19	52	8	8	1	1	0	6	9	3	0	1	15	1	0	.212	.308
Medrano, Ignacio	R-R	6-2	160	7-17-86	.294	.276	.299	37	136	15	40	11	0	0	17	16	2	1	3	22	4	3	.375	.369
Mendez, Victor	B-R	5-11	205	6-28-80	.313	.429	.222	5	16	3	5	3	0	1	2	2	0	0	3	1	0	.688	.389
Milledge, Lastings	R-R	6-0	205	4-5-85	.143	.250	.000	2	7	1	1	1	0	0	1	1	0	0	2	0	1	.286	.333
Newman, James	R-R	5-10	178	10-23-83	.286	.500	.200	2	7	2	2	1	0	0	0	1	0	0	1	0	0	.429	.375
Ramos, Valentin	R-R	6-3	185	7-21-88	.250	.167	.265	13	40	12	10	1	0	0	3	12	1	0	0	17	1	0	.275	.434
Rivera, Luis	R-R	6-1	165	1-25-84	.207	.250	.190	7	29	4	6	0	1	0	3	1	0	0	1	1	1	.276	.233
Tejada, Ruben	R-R	5-11	165	9-1-89	.283	.323	.270	35	120	13	34	4	3	0	16	19	6	2	2	16	2	1	.367	.401
Welch, Stefan	L-R	6-3	175	8-12-88	.288	.061	.358	36	139	16	40	9	0	0	12	11	3	0	3	22	1	2	.353	.346
Wolff, John	L-R	6-0	180	11-3-83	.250	—	.250	2	4	0	1	0	0	0	0	0	0	0	1	0	0	.250	.250
Zavala, Gabriel	R-R	6-3	180	5-14-87	.285	.395	.252	49	165	22	47	8	3	6	30	10	11	0	1	54	3	0	.479	.364

PITCHING	B-T	HT	WT	DOB	W	L	ERA	G	GS	CG	SV	IP	H	R	ER	HR	BB	SO	AVG	vLH	vRH	K/9	BB/9
Abbott, Nicholas	R-R	6-2	170	7-17-88	0	3	7.31	10	2	0	0	16	18	17	13	0	12	10	.290	.133	.340	5.62	6.75
Arriechi, Nelson	L-L	6-2	185	11-28-85	0	0	2.65	12	0	0	0	17	12	6	5	1	11	15	.200	.143	.208	7.94	5.82
Batis, Raul	L-L	6-1	170	3-5-89	2	1	4.73	9	1	0	0	27	29	18	14	2	14	24	.279	.450	.238	8.10	4.73
Burgos, Ambiorix	R-R	6-3	245	4-19-84	0	0	0.00	3	1	0	1	4	0	1	0	0	0	1	.000	.000	.000	2.25	0.00
Carson, Robert	L-L	6-3	220	1-23-89	1	0	5.00	4	1	0	0	9	8	7	5	1	5	9	.216	.500	.161	9.00	5.00
Cleto, Maikel	R-R	6-1	210	5-1-89	1	2	5.03	11	4	0	1	34	34	21	19	2	25	28	.270	.241	.278	7.41	6.62
Cruz, Rhiner	R-R	6-2	165	11-1-86	2	0	0.00	4	0	0	0	6	1	0	0	0	5	4	.056	.000	.100	6.00	7.50
Dlouhy, Gavin	R-R	6-2	180	6-19-88	1	1	2.49	8	4	0	0	25	23	7	7	1	6	34	.258	.333	.214	12.08	2.13
Eager, Blake	R-R	6-3	205	5-19-82	0	0	0.00	1	0	0	0	1	0	0	0	0	1	0	.000	.000	.000	9.00	0.00
Figueroa, Rogers	R-R	6-2	185	10-19-87	1	1	2.95	10	4	0	1	37	27	16	12	1	18	28	.205	.267	.186	6.87	4.42
Hedrick, Nathan	R-R	6-10	220	9-13-86	1	3	7.94	17	0	0	1	23	25	22	20	2	27	13	.287	.250	.309	5.16	10.72
Holdzkom, John	R-R	6-7	225	10-19-87	0	1	6.00	4	0	0	0	6	6	5	4	1	3	4	.240	.286	.222	6.00	4.50
Leduc, Guillaume	R-R	6-4	192	7-28-87	1	1	2.21	6	3	0	0	20	18	12	5	0	10	14	.237	.154	.254	6.20	4.43
Martinez, Pedro	R-R	5-11	195	10-25-71	0	0	6.75	1	1	0	0	4	3	3	3	1	1	4	.200	.200	.200	9.00	2.25
Moviel, Scott	R-R	6-11	235	5-7-88	0	2	3.38	12	12	0	0	40	45	23	15	2	11	37	.281	.211	.320	8.33	2.48
Neguilis, Jacobo	R-R	6-3	180	4-25-84	0	4	6.75	8	8	0	0	27	29	23	20	3	12	11	.264	.250	.268	3.71	4.05
Olmsted, Michael	R-R	6-6	245	5-2-87	0	0	0.00	2	0	0	0	3	1	0	0	0	1	8	.100	.000	.111	24.00	3.00
Perez, Oliver	L-L	6-3	215	8-15-81	0	0	0.00	1	1	0	0	4	2	0	0	0	0	7	.143	.250	.100	15.75	0.00
Perez, Omar	L-L	6-2	178	7-31-86	0	4	8.28	9	3	0	0	25	26	25	23	3	21	25	.283	.091	.309	9.00	7.54
Puhl, Stephen	B-R	6-0	195	7-6-84	2	0	3.24	6	0	0	0	8	5	3	1	5	9	.161	.200	.143	9.72	5.40
Ragsdale, Corey	R-R	6-4	175	11-10-82	1	0	0.00	3	0	0	0	4	1	0	0	0	3	5	.083	.000	.125	11.25	6.75
Rojas, Luis	R-R	6-1	165	7-29-89	1	2	13.50	11	0	0	0	11	12	17	17	3	20	15	.293	.182	.333	11.91	15.88
Rosa, Wendy	R-R	6-0	170	8-26-86	2	1	2.70	12	3	0	0	30	21	11	9	0	24	36	.204	.259	.184	10.80	7.20
Santana, Yury	R-R	5-11	160	8-15-82	1	0	1.80	3	0	0	0	5	4	1	1	0	1	3	.222	.200	.231	5.40	1.80
Simeoli, Luis	R-R	6-3	194	6-28-88	2	1	6.04	12	0	0	0	25	28	20	17	1	20	18	.292	.200	.324	6.39	7.11
Sparks, Ricky	R-R	6-5	205	10-10-84	1	0	2.79	7	0	0	1	10	5	3	3	1	10	14	.143	.083	.174	13.03	9.31
Urdaneta, Lino	R-R	6-1	220	11-20-79	0	0	0.00	2	0	0	1	4	2	0	0	0	0	2	.143	.000	.154	4.50	0.00
Valdez, Santiago	R-R	6-2	210	7-29-87	0	5	5.09	14	0	0	3	18	15	11	10	0	12	15	.231	.316	.196	7.64	6.11
Vineyard, Nathan	L-L	6-2	200	10-3-88	0	3	5.27	9	7	0	0	27	30	18	16	4	9	33	.265	.333	.255	10.87	2.96

FIELDING

Catcher	PCT	G	PO	A	E	DP	PB
Centeno	.958	11	77	14	4	2	8
Del Campo	1.000	14	91	6	0	2	2
Maat	.992	19	113	6	1	0	13
F. Martinez	1.000	1	7	0	0	0	1
J. Martinez	1.000	3	22	6	0	0	0
S. Martinez	.992	19	108	10	1	1	22

First Base	PCT	G	PO	A	E	DP
Aguayo	.988	25	155	10	2	16
Bouchard	.975	5	36	3	1	4
Hernandez	.941	2	16	0	1	1
Welch	.992	26	234	13	2	33

Second Base	PCT	G	PO	A	E	DP
Deluca	1.000	1	6	0	0	0
Gonzalez	.953	13	26	35	3	12
Johnson	1.000	12	11	28	0	7

	PCT	G	PO	A	E	DP
Medrano	.966	25	64	76	5	20
Newman	.800	2	3	5	2	2
Tejada	.973	9	20	16	1	5

Third Base	PCT	G	PO	A	E	DP
Lucas	.924	49	25	96	10	11
Ramos	.000	1	0	0	1	0
Welch	.944	7	3	14	1	1

Shortstop	PCT	G	PO	A	E	DP
Gonzalez	1.000	12	12	30	0	8
Johnson	1.000	1	0	1	0	0
Ramos	.846	12	16	28	8	8
Rivera	.909	7	14	16	3	5
Tejada	.945	28	34	87	7	21
Wolff	1.000	2	3	4	0	1

Outfield	PCT	G	PO	A	E	DP
Alou	1.000	3	1	0	0	0

	PCT	G	PO	A	E	DP
Carrera	.962	44	100	0	4	0
Centeno	1.000	1	1	0	0	0
Chavez	1.000	1	1	0	0	0
Fernandez	1.000	3	3	0	0	0
Guzman	1.000	16	43	3	0	0
Hubbert	.984	35	54	8	1	2
Johnson	.889	7	8	0	1	0
Martin	—	1	0	0	0	0
F. Martinez	—	1	0	0	0	0
Medrano	1.000	14	25	2	0	0
Mendez	1.000	3	1	0	0	0
Milledge	1.000	1	3	0	0	0
Welch	1.000	2	3	0	0	0
Zavala	.875	47	48	1	7	0

DOMINICAN SUMMER LEAGUE

BATTING	B-T	HT	WT	DOB	AVG	vLH	vRH	G	AB	R	H	2B	3B	HR	RBI	BB	HBP	SH	SF	SO	SB	CS	SLG	OBP
Batista, Jose	R-R	6-2	223	1-6-89	.169	.095	.194	25	83	9	14	2	0	0	4	11	1	0	0	27	0	0	.193	.274
Campusano, Luis	R-R	6-0	165	3-6-86	.177	.108	.197	48	164	14	29	3	0	0	15	12	8	2	1	31	2	1	.195	.265
Castillo, Jairo	R-R	6-2	190	1-9-89	.173	.038	.225	53	191	17	33	7	0	2	11	19	2	1	0	68	0	0	.241	.255
Concepcion, Julio	R-R	6-4	194	9-5-89	.243	.255	.238	50	173	30	42	10	2	1	21	26	7	0	1	47	2	1	.341	.362
De Leon, Jeyckol	R-R	6-2	185	7-25-90	.194	.211	.188	22	67	8	13	3	0	0	6	4	3	1	2	17	0	0	.239	.263
Decuba, Quintin	L-R	6-3	180	9-9-87	.124	.111	.129	26	89	4	11	5	0	0	5	13	3	0	1	29	0	1	.180	.255
Eusebio, Ramon	R-R	6-3	178	8-31-88	.198	.222	.186	38	106	11	21	6	2	0	10	6	2	1	1	30	1	0	.292	.252
Francisco, Jose	R-R	6-0	173	8-29-87	.234	.130	.262	34	107	13	25	3	0	1	12	19	5	2	0	36	10	7	.290	.374
Guzman, Edward	R-R	6-4	184	9-13-89	.151	.088	.171	43	139	14	21	0	0	1	7	19	3	1	0	61	0	3	.173	.267
Hiraldo, Wily	B-R	5-11	153	8-9-88	.210	.210	.210	59	224	35	47	3	3	0	16	33	5	0	2	66	22	8	.250	.322
Lovera, Joel	R-R	6-0	180	12-9-86	.182	.048	.224	25	88	7	16	2	1	2	10	1	3	0	2	35	1	1	.295	.213
Martinez, Ruben	R-R	6-0	172	9-15-86	.248	.231	.255	63	214	44	53	4	6	1	19	48	7	0	3	66	33	7	.336	.397
Peralta, Manuelysis	R-R	6-3	205	4-6-87	.253	.205	.270	49	166	11	42	5	0	1	30	19	10	1	6	34	1	0	.301	.353
Valdespin, Jordany	L-R	5-10	150	12-23-87	.245	.237	.248	43	139	23	34	4	3	1	16	24	4	0	1	26	8	4	.338	.369
Zapata, Pedro	R-R	6-4	185	10-3-87	.325	.304	.333	41	160	27	52	6	5	0	20	12	4	2	2	30	23	6	.425	.382

PITCHING	B-T	HT	WT	DOB	W	L	ERA	G	GS	CG	SV	IP	H	R	ER	HR	BB	SO	AVG	vLH	vRH	K/9	BB/9
Abreu, Jose	R-R	6-4	195	9-1-89	0	0	24.55	6	0	0	0	4	3	10	10	0	15	5	.231	.143	.333	12.27	36.82
Bello, Julio	L-R	6-5	175	10-16-86	1	2	1.45	12	6	0	0	37	25	14	6	0	17	43	.189	.121	.212	10.37	4.10
Burgos, Jhoan	R-R	6-4	210	9-1-85	2	4	2.37	16	0	0	0	30	23	15	8	1	25	32	.235	.206	.250	9.49	7.42
Cabrera, Alan	R-R	6-3	205	3-9-87	0	3	4.64	13	4	0	0	33	27	23	17	0	23	18	.231	.261	.211	4.91	6.27
Cruz, Rhiner	R-R	6-2	165	11-1-86	0	1	2.70	4	1	0	1	13	8	9	4	0	10	18	.170	.125	.179	12.15	6.75
Feliz, Tony	R-R	6-4	205	11-3-85	0	2	13.50	8	2	0	0	10	16	17	15	0	18	11	.390	.471	.333	9.90	16.20
Guerrero, Rafael	R-R	5-11	180	3-23-89	0	4	5.18	17	3	0	0	40	31	25	23	0	28	41	.215	.224	.209	9.22	6.30
Guzman, Victor	R-R	6-2	170	7-15-87	4	3	3.42	12	6	0	0	47	41	24	18	0	23	37	.241	.280	.225	7.04	4.37
Guzman, Edward	R-R	6-4	184	9-13-89	0	0	4.50	1	1	0	0	4	5	2	2	0	2	5	.294	.143	.400	11.25	4.50
Hernandez, Jose	R-R	6-0	198	1-22-89	1	3	5.97	13	7	0	0	32	25	29	21	0	35	31	.217	.192	.225	8.81	9.95
Herrera, Roberto	L-L	6-2	170	5-18-88	2	1	3.68	10	5	0	2	29	26	18	12	1	21	32	.248	.125	.258	9.82	6.44
Marte, Eric	R-R	5-11	173	8-26-87	0	2	5.87	7	0	0	0	8	9	5	5	1	4	5	.310	.167	.412	5.87	4.70
Martinez, Pedro E.	R-R	5-11	173	6-20-87	0	1	1.96	10	0	0	1	18	17	5	4	0	6	17	.262	.111	.319	8.35	2.95
Mejia, Jenrry	R-R	6-0	162	10-11-89	2	3	2.47	14	7	0	1	44	24	17	12	0	27	47	.160	.136	.170	9.69	5.56
Mendez, Ismael	L-L	6-1	184	5-23-90	1	1	7.79	11	2	0	0	17	17	20	15	0	18	21	.258	.333	.241	10.90	9.35
Paredes, Thomas	R-R	6-3	170	6-3-88	1	3	1.43	13	3	0	0	44	39	11	7	0	6	41	.242	.281	.233	8.39	1.23
Paulino, Jhoan	R-R	6-2	175	4-25-88	0	2	8.25	9	1	0	1	12	8	12	11	0	16	14	.190	.375	.147	10.50	12.00
Pena, Victor	R-R	6-2	180	3-26-86	0	0	9.00	2	0	0	0	2	1	3	2	0	4	1	.125	.000	.125	4.50	18.00
Perez, Omar	L-L	6-2	178	7-31-86	0	0	2.70	5	3	0	0	13	8	9	4	0	12	13	.163	.500	.133	8.78	8.10
Rodriguez, Armando	R-R	6-2	185	1-28-88	2	2	3.46	11	2	0	0	26	17	14	10	1	21	29	.191	.071	.213	10.04	7.27
Taveras, Samuel	R-R	6-4	185	4-14-89	4	1	2.37	17	0	0	0	30	24	13	8	0	10	33	.212	.250	.200	9.79	2.97
Valentin, Jose	R-R	6-4	190	8-4-87	2	2	2.44	13	8	0	0	44	32	17	12	0	27	35	.203	.170	.216	7.11	5.48
Villalona, Carlos	R-R	6-1	177	8-19-85	2	1	4.15	15	4	0	1	35	24	20	16	4	33	37	.197	.250	.174	9.61	8.57

FIELDING

Catcher	PCT	G	PO	A	E	DP	PB
Campusano	.974	47	435	56	13	4	17
De Leon	.967	12	80	8	3	0	4
Decuba	.963	10	69	8	3	0	6

First Base	PCT	G	PO	A	E	DP
Batista	.909	1	8	2	1	1
Guzman	.989	24	172	16	2	14
Peralta	.965	44	335	24	13	35

Second Base	PCT	G	PO	A	E	DP
Eusebio	1.000	1	2	1	0	1

Third Base	PCT	G	PO	A	E	DP
Batista	.886	12	11	20	4	1
Castillo	.885	51	48	106	20	12
Eusebio	1.000	5	1	9	0	1

Shortstop	PCT	G	PO	A	E	DP
Eusebio	.908	24	39	40	8	5

Hiraldo	.953	12	18	23	2	6
Lovera	.937	16	27	32	4	8
Valdespin	.979	38	83	108	4	27
Valentin	.875	4	8	13	3	2

Hiraldo	.920	44	76	142	19	28

Outfield	PCT	G	PO	A	E	DP
Concepcion	.895	43	48	3	6	0
Decuba	1.000	4	3	0	0	0
Eusebio	—	1	0	0	0	0
Francisco	1.000	34	40	4	0	0
Guzman	.875	21	16	5	3	1
Martinez	.984	63	109	12	2	2
Peralta	1.000	1	1	0	0	0
Valdespin	—	1	0	0	0	0
Zapata	.968	38	57	3	2	0

VSL METS ROOKIE

VENEZUELAN SUMMER LEAGUE

BATTING	B-T	HT	WT	DOB	AVG	vLH	vRH	G	AB	R	H	2B	3B	HR	RBI	BB	HBP	SH	SF	SO	SB	CS	SLG	OBP
Alvarez, Imbewer	R-R	6-1	180	5-15-86	.323	.333	.320	57	201	39	65	10	2	4	22	37	5	2	1	35	27	8	.453	.439
Alvarez, Ricky	R-R	5-11	217	2-7-89	.206	.174	.216	26	97	11	20	5	1	1	8	4	4	0	2	20	3	1	.309	.262
Diaz, Cesar	R-R	6-2	160	12-7-88	.239	.286	.218	54	180	24	43	9	0	4	23	13	6	1	4	64	4	5	.356	.305
Diaz, Jose	B-R	6-0	172	7-26-89	.223	.163	.253	37	130	20	29	2	1	2	20	17	6	0	3	27	9	4	.300	.333
Hernandez, Luis	R-R	6-2	204	6-24-88	.224	.214	.229	46	147	16	33	5	1	1	19	15	9	1	0	29	2	2	.293	.333
Moreno, Nestor	B-R	5-11	195	6-21-88	.237	.167	.268	57	198	24	47	8	1	1	29	30	2	0	3	55	5	4	.303	.339
Nieves, Luis	R-R	5-11	160	12-15-88	.235	.291	.204	57	226	44	53	7	5	0	17	22	4	2	0	36	27	7	.310	.313
Nunez, Paulo	B-L	5-11	185	3-30-89	.178	.157	.189	51	146	11	26	5	0	0	15	27	3	0	1	36	0	1	.212	.316
Ortiz, Edgar	R-R	5-11	170	10-4-87	.173	.333	.152	17	52	4	9	1	0	0	2	6	2	1	0	17	2	3	.192	.283
Pirela, Adrian	R-R	6-0	205	12-19-88	.051	.000	.077	16	39	3	2	0	0	0	1	12	1	0	0	19	1	0	.051	.288
Rivas, David	B-R	6-0	170	1-11-88	.264	.267	.263	65	235	35	62	9	2	3	32	25	3	0	4	34	6	10	.357	.337
Rojas, Luis	R-R	5-11	176	1-24-89	.180	.203	.168	52	172	21	31	2	2	0	9	17	4	3	1	49	3	4	.215	.268
Soto, Breiner	R-R	6-2	147	2-23-90	.189	.235	.175	22	74	12	14	0	1	0	10	2	0	0	29	3	3	.216	.302
Tejada, Ruben	R-R	5-11	165	9-1-89	.364	.429	.329	32	121	32	44	5	0	3	25	19	6	1	2	19	16	5	.479	.466
Torres, Juan	R-R	6-1	180	10-7-88	.298	.232	.329	58	218	27	65	11	0	5	28	20	2	0	4	34	2	4	.417	.357
Van Gurp, Ray	R-R	5-11	165	1-2-89	.077	.000	.100	3	13	1	1	0	0	0	2	0	0	0	0	4	1	0	.077	.077

PITCHING	B-T	HT	WT	DOB	W	L	ERA	G	GS	CG	SV	IP	H	R	ER	HR	BB	SO	AVG	vLH	vRH	K/9	BB/9
Aguilar, Victor	R-R	6-2	175	3-18-89	0	0	9.00	5	0	0	0	6	7	6	6	1	4	2	.292	.286	.294	3.00	6.00
Aldama, Eduardo	R-R	6-1	175	12-23-89	2	1	2.81	10	4	0	2	26	28	13	8	0	6	20	.267	.250	.273	7.01	2.10
Alvarez, Manuel	R-R	5-11	200	12-18-85	1	4	4.29	13	11	0	0	57	56	38	27	1	25	42	.257	.271	.250	6.67	3.97

ORGANIZATION STATISTICS

Carreno, Josmar	R-R	5-11	180	8-13-87	0	0	3.00	5	1	0	0	12	9	4	4	0	5	5	.209	.308	.167	3.75	3.75
Casadilla, Yhonny	R-R	6-3	183	2-14-90	0	0	8.10	5	2	0	0	10	19	10	9	1	3	8	.388	.250	.455	7.20	2.70
Collado, Juan	R-R	6-3	170	8-22-87	1	3	6.75	10	5	0	1	28	30	21	21	1	18	17	.291	.280	.295	5.46	5.79
Diaz, Roberto	R-R	6-0	170	4-25-90	1	3	6.06	17	2	0	0	36	43	29	24	0	19	23	.297	.205	.330	5.80	4.79
Galarraga, Luis	R-R	6-2	180	12-5-87	1	4	4.50	10	5	0	0	32	35	21	16	1	13	16	.269	.375	.245	4.50	3.66
Guedez, Raul	R-R	5-11	180	9-27-84	2	3	5.72	15	4	0	1	50	66	41	32	2	19	34	.325	.286	.343	6.08	3.40
Hernandez, Oralbis	R-R	6-1	175	12-4-87	0	3	4.22	10	7	0	0	43	40	28	20	1	20	30	.242	.190	.260	6.33	4.22
Manaure, Edgar	R-R	6-1	165	5-20-89	0	0	3.00	3	0	0	0	3	4	2	1	0	3	4	.333	.167	.500	12.00	9.00
Mejias, Jose Angel	R-R	6-0	150	8-18-85	4	5	3.20	14	8	1	2	56	50	24	20	0	12	41	.230	.200	.241	6.55	1.92
Melendez, Oscar	R-R	6-0	170	9-15-86	2	5	5.51	14	6	0	0	49	55	43	30	2	25	37	.284	.226	.305	6.80	4.59
Montano, Elys	L-L	6-5	195	8-20-89	1	3	6.84	13	1	0	0	25	31	22	19	0	15	15	.310	.000	.323	5.40	5.40
Orta, Phillips	R-R	6-2	175	5-9-86	0	0	1.29	4	3	0	0	14	8	4	2	0	3	12	.167	.083	.194	7.71	1.93
Parra, Geofrank	R-R	6-1	175	11-28-87	1	2	4.14	17	0	0	1	46	60	32	21	1	6	21	.323	.271	.341	4.14	1.18
Peralta, Ramiro	R-R	6-3	180	9-8-89	1	5	5.79	13	4	0	0	23	19	21	15	0	25	15	.232	.227	.233	5.79	9.64
Romero, Johan	R-R	5-11	200	12-13-89	2	3	7.39	18	0	0	0	28	32	28	23	0	27	26	.291	.258	.304	8.36	8.68
Tovar, Orlando	L-L	6-3	213	3-26-88	1	3	4.07	13	6	0	1	49	61	26	22	1	15	42	.311	.368	.305	7.77	2.77

FIELDING

Catcher	PCT	G	PO	A	E	DP	PB
Hernandez	.981	20	88	15	2	1	8
Moreno	.966	28	161	39	7	1	14
Nunez	.989	28	157	24	2	0	5

First Base	PCT	G	PO	A	E	DP
Alvarez	1.000	3	22	1	0	1
Alvarez	1.000	1	10	0	0	2
Guedez	1.000	1	3	0	0	1
Hernandez	.975	14	109	6	3	5
Moreno	.958	20	176	6	8	12
Nunez	.974	16	109	4	3	17
Pirela	1.000	2	15	0	0	2
Rivas	.974	25	209	12	6	13

Second Base	PCT	G	PO	A	E	DP
Alvarez	.968	10	14	16	1	5

	PCT	G	PO	A	E	DP
Nieves	.991	19	45	60	1	17
Ortiz	.956	14	25	40	3	6
Rivas	.982	23	47	64	2	13
Tejada	.870	10	16	24	6	6

Third Base	PCT	G	PO	A	E	DP
Alvarez	.947	6	3	15	1	1
Alvarez	.846	7	4	18	4	0
Rivas	.800	7	2	6	2	1
Torres	.845	56	37	121	29	9

Shortstop	PCT	G	PO	A	E	DP
Nieves	.919	38	79	124	18	25
Ortiz	.800	1	2	2	1	0
Rivas	.923	6	17	19	3	5
Tejada	.940	22	32	78	7	10
Van Gurp	.882	3	6	9	2	1

Outfield	PCT	G	PO	A	E	DP
Alvarez	.903	36	54	2	6	1
Alvarez	—	1	0	0	0	0
Alvarez	.951	20	38	1	2	0
Diaz	.953	43	76	5	4	1
Diaz	.973	31	36	0	1	0
Ortiz	—	1	0	0	0	0
Pirela	.875	9	14	0	2	0
Rivas	1.000	8	14	0	0	0
Rojas	.956	47	85	1	4	0
Soto	.933	22	40	2	3	0

New York Yankees

BY GEORGE KING

The Yankees' 2007 season could be considered pedestrian compared to what happened immediately after it ended. Sure, Joe Torre almost got fired in May, GM Brian Cashman was threatened by George Steinbrenner later in the month and The Boss said Torre was managing for his job after the Yankees lost the first two AL Division Series games to the Indians in Cleveland.

Eventually, the Yankees were eliminated in the opening round for the third straight season. But that didn't completely erase the monster season Alex Rodriguez in which he carried the Yankees from April to the end of September before fading in the postseason.

The emergence of rookie righthanders Phil Hughes and Ian Kennedy in the starting rotation and Joba Chamberlain in the bullpen provided much-needed shots of adrenaline for a staff that had been stagnated by Carl Pavano, Kei Igawa and Kyle Farnsworth. After starting Tyler Clippard, Chase Wright, Jeff Karstens and Darrell Rasner in the first half, the Yankees found consistency late in the second half thanks to Andy Pettitte, Chien-Ming Wang and Hughes.

Yet, all of the drama involved in the first half—including Rodriguez' early 80 home run pace and the Yankees chase of the Red Sox, who opened a 14-game lead over them in the AL East—nothing compared to what happened in a two-week period in October.

Not only didn't Torre get fired, he rejected a one-year contract worth $5 million in base salary with a chance to make an additional $3 million in incentives. It was a deal the Yankees truly believed Torre would accept.

"It was the one year and the incentives were insulting," Torre said one day after turning the job down on Oct. 18. Three weeks later Torre accepted a job as manager of the Los Angeles Dodgers, bringing along hitting coach Don Mattingly and third-base coach Larry Bowa. Former Yankees catcher and bench coach Joe Girardi, the 2006 manager of the year with the Marlins, replaces Torre.

Losing a manager who won four World Series titles in 12 years and guided the Yankees into the postseason every year was enough to cripple most franchises. Then 10 days later, Rodriguez decided to opt out of the final three years of his contract, leaving $91 million on the table without even listening to what the Yankees were going to offer him to stay. The Yankees insisted they weren't going to offer the $30 million a year agent Scott Boras said Rodriguez was worth. However, with $30 million being subsidized by the Rangers for the next three seasons, the Yankees were prepared to make Rodriguez an offer that would raise his average annual salary above the $25.2 million a year he was making.

So, less than a month after being bounced from the playoffs, the Yankees watched Steinbrenner hand the organization to sons Hank and Hal, saw Torre walk out of a Legends Field meeting as the ex-manager and said goodbye to Rodriguez, who the team vowed wouldn't be chased as a free agent.

Hank Steinbrenner used the words "transition" and "patience" when talking about the dawn of a new era in The Bronx.

Cashman and his selected lieutenants were trusted with the chore of finding Torre's successor and even though George Steinbrenner wanted Mattingly to get the job,

Girardi was Cashman's choice and The Boss approved a three-year, $7.5 million deal.

Hank Steinbrenner showed he inherited his father's conviction gene when he announced shortly after taking over that Chamberlain will be in next year's rotation without checking with Cashman, and before Girardi was named manager and Dave Eiland was anointed pitching coach.

George's eldest son also developed a quick fondness for amateur scouting director Damon Oppenheimer.

"We have the best farm system in baseball, at least the best pitching," Hank Steinbrenner said.

The Yankees posted the best overall record in the minors, with their affiliates combining to go 484-351. However the team's brightest talent may be in the lower levels with outfielders Jose Tabata and Austin Jackson ranking among the high Class A Florida State League's Top 10 Prospects.

General Manager: Brian Cashman. **Farm Director:** Mark Newman. **Scouting Director:** Damon Oppenheimer

Class	Team	League	W	L	PCT	Finish*	Manager	Affiliate Since
Majors	New York	America	94	68	.580	3rd (14)	Joe Torre	—
Triple-A	Scranton/W-B Yankees	International	84	59	.587	1st (14)	Dave Miley	2007
Double-A	Trenton Thunder	Easter	83	59	.585	1st (12)^	Tony Franklin	2003
High A	Tampa Yankees	Florida State	83	56	.597	1st (12)	Luis Sojo	1994
Low A	Charleston RiverDogs	South Atlantic	78	62	.557	5th (16)	Torre Tyson	2005
Short-season	Staten Island Yankees	New York-Penn	47	28	.627	2nd (14)	Mike Gillespie	1999
Rookie	GCL Yankees	Gulf Coast	42	17	.712	1st (16)^	Jody Reed	1980
Overall 2007 Minor League Record			**417**	**281**	**.597**	**1st**		

* Finish in overall standings (No. of teams in league) ^League champion

ORGANIZATION STATISTICS

NEW YORK YANKEES

AMERICAN LEAGUE

BATTING	B-T	HT	WT	DOB	AVG	vLH	vRH	G	AB	R	H	2B	3B	HR	RBI	BB	HBP	SH	SF	SO	SB	CS	SLG	OBP
Abreu, Bobby	L-R	6-0	210	3-11-74	.283	.262	.289	158	605	123	171	40	5	16	101	84	3	0	7	115	25	8	.445	.369
Basak, Chris	R-R	6-0	190	12-6-78	.000	.000	.000	5	1	0	0	0	0	0	0	0	0	0	0	0	0	0	.000	.000
Betemit, Wilson	B-R	6-3	230	11-2-81	.226	.222	.227	37	84	11	19	4	0	4	24	6	0	2	0	33	0	0	.417	.278
Cabrera, Melky	B-L	5-11	200	8-11-84	.273	.250	.282	150	545	66	149	24	8	8	73	43	5	10	9	68	13	5	.391	.327
Cairo, Miguel	R-R	6-1	210	5-4-74	.252	.237	.261	54	107	12	27	7	0	0	10	8	1	4	1	19	8	1	.318	.308
Cano, Robinson	L-R	6-0	205	10-22-82	.306	.328	.296	160	617	93	189	41	7	19	97	39	8	1	4	85	4	5	.488	.353
Damon, Johnny	L-L	6-2	205	11-5-73	.270	.281	.266	141	533	93	144	27	2	12	63	66	2	1	3	79	27	3	.396	.351
Duncan, Shelley	R-R	6-5	215	9-29-79	.257	.303	.230	34	74	16	19	1	0	7	17	8	0	1	0	20	0	0	.554	.329
Giambi, Jason	L-R	6-3	235	1-8-71	.236	.239	.235	83	254	31	60	8	0	14	39	40	8	0	1	66	1	0	.433	.356
Gonzalez, Alberto	R-R	5-11	165	4-18-83	.071	.333	.000	12	14	3	1	0	0	0	1	1	0	0	0	1	0	0	.071	.133
Jeter, Derek	R-R	6-3	195	6-26-74	.322	.317	.324	156	639	102	206	39	4	12	73	56	14	3	2	100	15	8	.452	.388
Matsui, Hideki	L-R	6-2	210	6-12-74	.285	.274	.290	143	547	100	156	28	4	25	103	73	3	0	10	73	4	2	.488	.367
Mientkiewicz, Doug	L-R	6-2	205	6-19-74	.277	.231	.286	72	166	26	46	12	0	5	24	16	3	6	1	23	0	0	.440	.349
Molina, Jose	R-R	6-2	245	6-3-75	.318	.500	.250	29	66	9	21	5	0	1	9	2	0	2	1	13	0	0	.439	.333
2-team (40 Los Angeles)					.257	—		69	191	18	49	13	0	1	19	5	0	5	1	43	2	1	.340	.274
Nieves, Wil	R-R	5-11	190	9-25-77	.164	.200	.152	26	61	6	10	4	0	0	8	2	0	3	0	9	0	0	.230	.190
Phelps, Josh	R-R	6-3	225	5-12-78	.263	.264	.259	36	80	8	21	2	0	2	12	6	2	0	0	19	0	0	.363	.330
Phillips, Andy	R-R	6-0	210	4-6-77	.292	.280	.296	61	185	27	54	7	1	2	25	12	2	6	2	26	0	3	.373	.338
Posada, Jorge	B-R	6-2	205	8-17-71	.338	.331	.341	144	506	91	171	42	1	20	90	74	6	0	3	98	2	0	.543	.426
Rodriguez, Alex	R-R	6-3	225	7-27-75	.314	.272	.327	158	583	143	183	31	0	54	156	95	21	0	9	120	24	4	.645	.422
Sardinha, Bronson	L-R	6-1	220	4-6-83	.333	.500	.286	10	9	6	3	0	0	0	2	2	0	0	1	1	0	0	.333	.417
Thompson, Kevin	R-R	5-10	190	9-18-79	.190	.182	.200	13	21	2	4	3	0	0	2	2	0	0	0	10	0	0	.333	.261
2-team (9 Oakland)					.143	—		22	35	4	5	3	0	0	3	3	0	0	1	13	0	0	.229	.211

PITCHING	B-T	HT	WT	DOB	W	L	ERA	G	GS	CG	SV	IP	H	R	ER	HR	BB	SO	AVG	vLH	vRH	K/9	BB/9
Bean, Colter	R-R	6-6	255	1-16-77	0	1	12.00	3	0	0	0	3	5	4	4	0	5	2	.357	1.000	.308	6.00	15.00
Britton, Chris	R-R	6-3	280	12-16-82	0	1	3.55	11	0	0	0	13	9	5	5	2	4	5	.196	.118	.241	3.55	2.84
Brower, Jim	R-R	6-3	215	12-29-72	0	0	13.50	3	0	0	0	3	8	7	5	0	2	1	.500	.286	.667	2.70	5.40
Bruney, Brian	R-R	6-3	245	2-17-82	3	2	4.68	58	0	0	0	50	44	28	26	5	37	39	.243	.303	.209	7.02	6.66
Chamberlain, Joba	R-R	6-3	230	9-23-85	2	0	0.38	19	0	0	1	24	12	2	1	1	6	34	.145	.132	.156	12.75	2.25
Clemens, Roger	R-R	6-4	235	8-4-62	6	6	4.18	18	17	0	0	99	99	52	46	9	31	68	.261	.233	.282	6.18	2.82
Clippard, Tyler	R-R	6-4	170	2-14-85	1	1	6.33	6	6	0	0	27	29	19	19	6	17	18	.271	.208	.333	6.00	5.67
DeSalvo, Matt	R-R	6-0	180	9-11-80	1	3	6.18	7	6	0	0	28	34	20	19	2	18	10	.304	.359	.274	3.25	5.86
Farnsworth, Kyle	R-R	6-4	235	4-14-76	2	1	4.80	64	0	0	0	60	60	35	32	9	27	48	.256	.273	.242	7.20	4.05
Henn, Sean	R-L	6-4	225	4-23-81	2	2	7.12	29	1	0	0	37	44	32	29	6	27	28	.293	.288	.297	6.87	6.63
Hughes, Phil	R-R	6-5	220	6-24-86	5	3	4.46	13	13	0	0	73	64	39	36	8	29	58	.235	.264	.210	7.18	3.59
Igawa, Kei	L-L	6-1	210	7-13-79	2	3	6.25	14	12	0	0	68	76	48	47	15	37	53	.279	.320	.264	7.05	4.92
Karstens, Jeff	R-R	6-3	185	9-24-82	1	1	11.05	7	3	0	0	15	27	21	18	4	9	5	.397	.424	.371	3.07	5.52
Kennedy, Ian	R-R	6-0	190	12-19-84	1	0	1.89	3	3	0	0	19	13	6	4	1	9	15	.191	.161	.216	7.11	4.26
Mussina, Mike	L-R	6-2	190	12-8-68	11	10	5.15	28	27	0	0	152	188	90	87	14	35	91	.311	.315	.307	5.39	2.07
Myers, Mike	L-L	6-3	225	6-26-69	3	0	2.66	55	0	0	0	41	38	14	12	3	16	21	.247	.312	.182	4.65	3.54
2-team (17 Chicago)					4	0	4.80	72	0	0	0	54	59	33	29	6	23	27	—	—	—	4.47	3.81
Ohlendorf, Ross	R-R	6-4	235	8-8-82	0	0	2.84	6	0	0	0	6	5	2	2	1	2	9	.208	.267	.111	12.79	2.84
Pavano, Carl	R-R	6-5	240	1-8-76	1	0	4.76	2	2	0	0	11	12	7	6	1	2	4	.273	.208	.350	3.18	1.59
Pettitte, Andy	L-L	6-5	225	6-15-72	15	9	4.05	36	34	0	0	215	238	106	97	16	69	141	.286	.298	.282	5.89	2.88
Proctor, Scott	R-R	6-1	195	1-2-77	2	5	3.81	52	0	0	0	54	53	27	23	8	29	37	.257	.278	.241	6.13	4.80
Ramirez, Edwar	R-R	6-3	150	3-28-81	1	1	8.14	21	0	0	1	21	24	19	19	6	14	31	.286	.342	.239	13.29	6.00
Rasner, Darrell	R-R	6-3	210	1-13-81	1	3	4.01	6	6	0	0	25	29	14	11	4	8	11	.290	.375	.212	4.01	2.92
Rivera, Mariano	R-R	6-2	185	11-29-69	3	4	3.15	67	0	0	30	71	68	25	25	4	12	74	.248	.255	.241	9.34	1.51
Veras, Jose	R-R	6-5	235	10-20-80	0	0	5.79	9	0	0	2	9	6	6	6	0	7	7	.176	.154	.190	6.75	6.75
Villone, Ron	L-L	6-3	245	1-16-70	0	0	4.25	37	0	0	0	42	36	20	20	5	18	25	.234	.239	.230	5.31	3.83
Vizcaino, Luis	R-R	5-11	210	8-6-74	8	2	4.30	77	0	0	0	75	66	37	36	6	43	62	.235	.265	.213	7.41	5.14
Wang, Chien-Ming	R-R	6-3	225	3-31-80	19	7	3.70	30	30	1	0	199	199	84	82	9	59	104	.265	.286	.242	4.70	2.66
Wright, Chase	L-L	6-2	205	2-8-83	2	0	7.20	3	2	0	0	8	8	8	5	6	8	6	.293	.250	.310	7.20	5.40

FIELDING

Catcher

Catcher	PCT	G	PO	A	E	DP	PB
Molina	1.000	29	153	13	0	1	2
Nieves	.983	25	111	6	2	1	1
Phelps	—	1	0	0	0	0	0
Posada	.994	138	799	54	5	6	13

First Base

First Base	PCT	G	PO	A	E	DP
Betemit	1.000	14	67	4	0	9
Cairo	.977	22	162	9	4	16
Damon	.900	5	9	0	1	1
Duncan	1.000	9	24	3	0	6
Giambi	.991	18	108	6	1	10
Mientkiewicz	.996	70	482	23	2	59
Nieves	1.000	1	1	0	0	0
Phelps	.983	29	167	9	3	16
Phillips	1.000	57	380	28	0	44
Posada	1.000	1	6	0	0	1

Second Base

Second Base	PCT	G	PO	A	E	DP
Betemit	1.000	2	3	7	0	1
Cairo	1.000	3	6	7	0	0
Cano	.984	159	320	497	13	136
Phillips	1.000	1	0	1	0	0

Third Base

Third Base	PCT	G	PO	A	E	DP
Basak	1.000	3	0	1	0	0
Betemit	.882	14	1	14	2	3
Cairo	.909	7	1	9	1	2
Gonzalez	—	1	0	0	0	0
Phillips	1.000	9	1	2	0	0
Rodriguez	.965	154	106	251	13	30
Sardinha	—	1	0	0	0	0

Shortstop

Shortstop	PCT	G	PO	A	E	DP
Basak	—	1	0	0	0	0
Betemit	.947	8	9	9	1	2
Cairo	1.000	16	7	22	0	4
Gonzalez	.958	11	11	12	1	3
Jeter	.970	155	199	390	18	104

Outfield

Outfield	PCT	G	PO	A	E	DP
Abreu	.988	157	313	6	4	1
Betemit	1.000	1	1	0	0	0
Cabrera	.990	147	385	16	4	1
Cairo	1.000	3	2	0	0	0
Damon	.990	81	193	3	2	0
Duncan	1.000	12	14	2	0	1
Matsui	.986	112	213	6	3	0
Sardinha	.857	5	6	0	1	0
Thompson	1.000	11	14	0	0	0

SCRANTON/WILKES-BARRE YANKEES   TRIPLE-A
INTERNATIONAL LEAGUE

BATTING	B-T	HT	WT	DOB	AVG	vLH	vRH	G	AB	R	H	2B	3B	HR	RBI	BB	HBP	SH	SF	SO	SB	CS	SLG	OBP
Basak, Chris	R-R	6-2	190	12-6-78	.253	.207	.271	84	308	47	78	19	1	7	38	21	4	3	4	55	13	3	.390	.306
2-team (12 Rochester)					.252	—	—	96	341	50	86	20	1	7	42	22	4	4	4	64	14	3	.378	.302
Beattie, Andrew	B-R	5-8	175	2-28-78	.206	.167	.216	19	63	8	13	0	0	2	6	9	0	0	1	15	0	0	.302	.301
Cannizaro, Andy	R-R	5-10	170	12-19-78	.295	.318	.287	52	166	27	49	12	0	2	20	21	3	2	3	30	0	1	.404	.378
Chavez, Angel	R-R	6-1	180	7-22-81	.291	.254	.304	114	430	62	125	26	1	11	66	27	4	0	3	80	6	3	.433	.336
Chavez, Raul	R-R	5-11	210	3-18-73	.221	.254	.210	86	290	29	64	14	0	4	31	11	7	1	1	39	1	0	.310	.265
Christian, Justin	R-R	6-1	188	4-3-80	.325	.350	.312	40	169	32	55	8	4	1	16	10	2	2	0	19	17	2	.438	.370
Cruz Jr., Jose	B-R	6-0	210	4-19-74	.274	.308	.265	16	62	12	17	4	0	1	7	9	0	0	0	12	3	0	.387	.366
Duncan, Eric	L-R	6-3	195	12-7-84	.241	.211	.250	113	411	46	99	26	1	11	61	48	3	2	3	81	2	2	.389	.323
Duncan, Shelley	R-R	6-5	215	9-29-79	.295	.259	.307	91	336	58	99	18	1	25	79	45	3	0	3	82	2	2	.577	.380
Durazo, Erubiel	L-L	6-3	240	1-23-75	.263	.143	.313	29	95	17	25	5	0	3	12	18	0	0	1	19	0	0	.411	.377
Francia, Juan	B-R	5-9	145	1-4-82	.301	.226	.324	38	136	23	41	5	2	0	16	9	1	1	0	12	7	6	.368	.349
Gardner, Brett	L-L	5-10	180	8-24-83	.260	.217	.281	45	181	37	47	4	3	1	9	21	2	3	0	43	21	3	.331	.343
Giambi, Jason	L-R	6-3	235	1-8-71	.111	.000	.200	4	9	1	1	0	0	1	1	6	0	0	0	2	0	1	.444	.467
Gonzalez, Alberto	R-R	5-11	165	4-18-83	.247	.247	.247	106	384	44	95	21	10	1	35	24	6	9	3	49	11	5	.362	.300
Holmann, Mario	B-R	6-0	165	5-21-84	.000	.000	.000	3	3	0	0	0	0	0	0	0	0	0	0	2	0	0	.000	.000
Jackson, Austin	R-R	6-1	185	2-1-87	.333	.000	.500	1	3	2	1	1	0	0	0	2	0	0	0	2	1	0	.667	.600
Kinkade, Mike	R-R	6-1	210	5-6-73	.300	.500	.278	5	20	6	6	1	1	0	3	1	2	0	0	3	2	0	.450	.391
Mientkiewicz, Doug	L-R	6-2	205	6-19-74	.381	.500	.353	5	21	5	8	3	0	1	7	1	0	0	1	2	0	0	.667	.391
Nieves, Wil	R-R	5-11	190	9-25-77	.256	.182	.279	27	90	5	23	1	2	1	8	6	1	0	1	10	1	0	.344	.306
Phillips, Andy	R-R	6-0	210	4-6-77	.301	.361	.277	65	249	37	75	11	2	11	36	32	1	0	1	43	2	1	.494	.382
Plumley, Grant	R-R	6-0	185	12-21-81	.111	.000	.125	3	9	1	1	0	0	0	0	0	0	0	0	4	0	0	.111	.111
Reese, Kevin	L-L	5-11	195	3-11-78	.249	.279	.238	115	433	58	108	14	3	10	59	54	8	10	8	74	9	7	.365	.338
Santos, Omir	R-R	6-0	200	4-29-81	.234	.250	.227	51	167	13	39	8	0	3	19	10	1	2	2	35	1	1	.335	.278
Sardinha, Bronson	L-R	6-1	220	4-6-83	.222	.257	.209	109	388	48	86	21	5	11	56	46	2	1	2	77	10	3	.387	.306
Strong, Jamal	R-R	5-10	185	8-5-78	.286	.286	.286	40	91	23	26	3	2	0	6	16	3	0		16	3	1	.363	.425
Thompson, Kevin	R-R	5-10	190	9-18-79	.281	.262	.290	77	267	39	75	18	3	5	37	42	3	5	2	56	24	8	.427	.382

PITCHING	B-T	HT	WT	DOB	W	L	ERA	G	GS	CG	SV	IP	H	R	ER	HR	BB	SO	AVG	vLH	vRH	K/9	BB/9
Axford, John	R-R	6-5	195	4-1-83	0	0	13.50	1	0	0	0	1	2	1	1	0	1	1	.500	.667	.000	13.50	13.50
Beam, T.J.	R-R	6-7	215	8-28-80	4	3	3.59	29	0	0	3	48	51	20	19	6	10	45	.274	.326	.223	8.50	1.89
Bean, Colter	R-R	6-6	255	1-16-77	2	0	5.95	28	5	0	0	59	66	40	39	3	31	56	.291	.299	.283	8.54	4.73
Britton, Chris	R-R	6-3	280	12-16-82	4	2	2.51	37	0	0	8	57	51	19	16	3	14	58	.236	.237	.236	9.10	2.20
Brower, Jim	R-R	6-3	215	12-29-72	4	2	2.27	38	0	0	21	48	44	12	12	2	13	45	.254	.289	.227	8.50	2.45
2-team (6 Indianapolis)					5	2	2.45	44	0	0	22	55	53	15	15	2	15	49	—	—		8.02	2.45
Bruney, Brian	R-R	6-3	245	2-17-82	2	0	6.00	4	0	0	1	6	5	4	4	1	2	5	.217	.000	.417	7.50	3.00
Burke, Erick	L-L	6-4	230	8-14-77	0	0	18.90	3	0	0	0	3	7	7	7	0	4	1	.438	.400	.455	2.70	10.80
Chamberlain, Joba	R-R	6-2	230	9-23-85	1	0	0.00	3	1	0	0	8	5	0	0	0	1	18	.179	.154	.200	20.25	1.12
Claggett, Anthony	B-R	6-2	185	7-15-84	0	0	5.40	1	0	0	0	5	5	3	3	1	1	1	.250	.167	.375	1.80	1.80
Clemens, Roger	R-R	6-4	235	8-4-62	1	0	0.00	1	1	0	0	6	2	0	0	0	2	6	.100	.125	.083	9.00	3.00
Clippard, Tyler	R-R	6-4	170	2-14-85	4	4	4.15	14	14	0	0	69	82	40	32	7	35	55	.299	.324	.273	7.14	4.54
DeSalvo, Matt	R-R	6-0	180	9-11-80	9	5	2.70	20	20	0	0	113	92	39	34	4	56	102	.222	.273	.160	8.10	4.45
Farley, Chris	R-R	6-2	180	2-24-83	0	1	12.27	1	1	0	0	4	9	5	5	1	2	6	.450	.417	.500	14.73	4.91
Hacker, Eric	B-R	6-1	215	3-26-83	1	0	6.75	1	0	0	0	3	5	2	2	0	1	3	.417	.167	.667	10.12	3.38
Henn, Sean	R-L	6-4	225	4-23-81	1	3	3.24	16	3	0	0	33	29	12	12	1	9	30	.238	.190	.263	8.10	2.43
Hernandez, Runelvys	R-R	6-1	250	4-27-78	0	1	3.56	6	6	0	0	30	30	17	12	5	12	22	.248	.200	.276	6.53	3.56
3-team (7 Pawtucket, 4 Indianapolis)					1	7	4.35	17	17	0	0	83	98	61	40	14	29	51	—			5.55	3.16
Hughes, Phil	R-R	6-5	220	6-24-86	4	1	2.20	5	5	0	0	29	16	7	7	0	8	28	.167	.140	.196	8.79	2.51
Igawa, Kei	L-L	6-1	210	7-13-79	5	3	3.69	11	11	0	0	68	68	30	28	10	15	71	.260	.319	.238	9.35	1.98
Jackson, Steven	R-R	6-5	215	3-15-82	4	8	5.87	18	11	0	0	69	93	57	45	11	29	50	.317	.343	.293	6.52	3.78
Junge, Eric	R-R	6-5	215	1-5-77	3	1	5.16	8	4	0	0	30	26	20	17	3	14	19	.241	.191	.279	5.76	4.25
Karstens, Jeff	R-R	6-3	185	9-24-82	3	0	1.74	6	5	0	0	31	25	6	6	2	9	27	.219	.215	.224	7.84	2.61
Kennedy, Ian	R-R	6-0	190	12-19-84	1	1	2.08	6	6	0	0	35	25	8	8	2	11	34	.205	.210	.200	8.83	2.86
Kozlowski, Ben	L-L	6-6	210	8-16-80	5	7	3.00	42	6	0	1	81	71	32	27	8	31	80	.236	.178	.261	8.89	3.44
Lavigne, Tim	R-R	5-10	210	7-4-78	0	1	6.14	2	1	0	0	7	10	5	5	1	2	6	.345	.300	.368	2.45	2.45
Manning, Charlie	L-L	6-2	180	3-31-79	3	2	4.38	34	1	0	2	51	41	27	25	2	24	59	.210	.277	.177	10.34	4.21
Ohlendorf, Ross	R-R	6-4	235	8-8-82	3	3	5.02	21	9	0	0	66	86	39	37	7	24	48	.320	.318	.321	6.51	3.26
Patterson, Scott	R-R	6-7	227	6-20-79	0	0	0.00	1	0	0	0	3	0	0	0	0	0	0	1.000	.000	.000	0.00	0.00
Pope, Justin	B-R	6-0	190	11-8-79	2	1	6.00	13	2	0	0	24	27	17	16	6	5	10	.287	.288	.286	3.75	1.88
Ramirez, Edwar	R-R	6-3	150	3-28-81	1	0	0.90	25	0	0	6	40	20	4	4	0	14	69	.149	.170	.136	15.52	3.15
Rasner, Darrell	R-R	6-2	210	1-13-81	1	0	0.00	2	1	0	0	7	5	1	1	0	2	3	.172	.167	.176	3.38	2.25
Veras, Jose	R-R	6-5	195	10-20-80	1	0	4.50	12	0	0	4	16	17	8	8	1	7	17	.266	.270	.259	9.56	3.94

ORGANIZATION STATISTICS

	B-T	HT	WT	DOB			ERA	G	GS	CG	SV	IP	H	R	ER	HR	BB	SO	AVG	vLH	vRH	K/9	BB/9
Villone, Ron	L-L	6-3	245	1-16-70	0	1	1.90	17	0	0	1	24	21	6	5	0	10	27	.241	.250	.236	10.27	3.80
White, Steven	R-R	6-4	205	6-15-81	6	4	3.34	16	15	0	1	92	85	39	34	3	32	55	.251	.309	.190	5.40	3.14
Williamson, Scott	R-R	6-0	195	2-17-76	0	1	9.82	4	0	0	0	4	5	4	4	1	3	7	.313	.333	.286	17.18	7.36
Wright, Chase	L-L	6-2	205	2-8-83	8	3	4.01	15	14	0	1	85	79	44	38	7	42	40	.248	.265	.243	4.22	4.43

FIELDING

Catcher	PCT	G	PO	A	E	DP	PB
R. Chavez	.988	74	547	51	7	8	4
Nieves	1.000	26	220	20	0	0	1
Santos	.995	51	364	26	2	1	4

First Base	PCT	G	PO	A	E	DP
A. Chavez	1.000	2	10	0	0	2
R. Chavez	1.000	6	39	4	0	5
E. Duncan	.987	87	721	38	10	67
S. Duncan	.994	19	150	9	1	9
Durazo	1.000	8	54	6	0	6
Giambi	.909	2	9	1	1	0
Mientkiewicz	1.000	5	45	4	0	6
Phillips	.969	18	117	10	4	5

Second Base	PCT	G	PO	A	E	DP
Basak	1.000	4	5	13	0	2
Beattie	1.000	13	30	22	0	8
Cannizaro	.991	28	54	56	1	12
A. Chavez	.968	35	43	79	4	15

Francia	.985	36	53	81	2	18
Gonzalez	1.000	3	9	15	0	4
Holmann	1.000	2	1	0	0	0
Phillips	.985	31	62	67	2	19
Plumley	1.000	3	3	8	0	1

Third Base	PCT	G	PO	A	E	DP
Basak	.955	73	44	149	9	14
Beattie	1.000	3	0	8	0	0
Cannizaro	1.000	8	1	13	0	0
A. Chavez	.944	52	28	89	7	4
R. Chavez	.920	8	3	20	2	1
E. Duncan	.714	2	2	3	2	0
Kinkade	1.000	3	2	3	0	0

Shortstop	PCT	G	PO	A	E	DP
Basak	1.000	4	7	10	0	1
Cannizaro	.966	14	23	33	2	8
A. Chavez	.990	24	34	70	1	15
Francia	1.000	2	0	3	0	0

Gonzalez	.976	103	139	264	10	59
Holmann	1.000	1	0	1	0	0
Plumley	1.000	1	1	1	0	1

Outfield	PCT	G	PO	A	E	DP
Basak	1.000	5	4	0	0	0
Beattie	1.000	3	3	1	0	0
Christian	.962	40	100	1	4	0
Cruz Jr.	1.000	12	21	1	0	0
S. Duncan	.983	25	53	4	1	2
Francia	1.000	1	1	0	0	0
Gardner	.985	45	128	4	2	2
Jackson	1.000	1	1	0	0	0
Kinkade	—	1	0	0	0	0
Reese	1.000	105	176	6	0	0
Sardinha	.975	104	187	8	5	5
Strong	1.000	30	56	1	0	0
Thompson	.982	73	157	3	3	2

TRENTON THUNDER

DOUBLE-A

EASTERN LEAGUE

BATTING	B-T	HT	WT	DOB	AVG	vLH	vRH	G	AB	R	H	2B	3B	HR	RBI	BB	HBP	SH	SF	SO	SB	CS	SLG	OBP
Baldiris, Aarom	R-R	6-2	195	1-5-83	.240	.203	.250	87	287	35	69	8	1	8	34	28	6	3	2	48	1	0	.359	.319
Brown, Jason	R-R	6-2	200	5-22-74	.208	.500	.167	15	48	6	10	4	0	1	3	6	0	0	0	9	0	0	.354	.296
Cannizaro, Andy	R-R	5-10	170	12-19-78	.219	.250	.214	8	32	5	7	1	0	0	2	2	0	0	0	3	0	0	.250	.265
Carson, Matt	R-R	6-2	200	7-1-81	.248	.296	.234	129	471	72	117	24	3	16	76	33	9	2	6	109	19	4	.414	.306
Christian, Justin	R-R	6-1	188	4-3-80	.235	.250	.231	65	255	25	60	8	3	3	32	16	2	2	3	43	18	4	.325	.283
Conway, Dan	R-R	6-2	220	10-13-79	.207	.000	.231	8	29	3	6	1	0	1	6	1	1	0	0	10	0	0	.345	.258
Corona, Reegie	B-R	5-11	160	11-7-86	.221	.108	.262	35	140	19	31	6	0	0	18	2	1	2	30	7	2	.264	.315
Curtis, Colin	L-L	6-0	190	2-1-85	.242	.200	.250	61	240	32	58	10	1	3	15	17	3	0	2	47	1	1	.329	.298
Ehlers, Cody	L-L	5-11	190	4-16-82	.252	.244	.254	106	385	39	97	31	0	8	53	59	1	0	3	74	0	1	.395	.350
Francia, Juan	B-R	5-9	145	1-4-82	.198	.067	.224	31	91	9	18	0	0	0	5	7	0	0	1	16	5	5	.198	.253
Gardner, Brett	L-L	5-10	180	8-24-83	.300	.262	.311	54	203	43	61	14	5	0	17	33	0	1	4	32	18	4	.419	.392
Garrett, Shawn	B-R	6-3	220	11-2-78	.289	.250	.298	63	239	31	69	15	5	7	33	20	4	1	1	65	2	0	.481	.352
Gonzalez, Alberto	R-R	5-11	165	4-18-83	.330	.250	.358	28	109	18	36	5	0	3	16	10	1	3	2	14	1	1	.440	.385
Hall, Noah	R-R	5-11	200	6-9-77	.292	.394	.237	82	271	38	79	19	1	9	50	34	12	1	7	41	2	4	.469	.386
Kinkade, Mike	R-R	6-1	210	5-6-73	.349	.333	.355	22	83	14	29	6	0	2	15	6	4	0	1	13	0	0	.494	.415
Lafountain, J.T.	B-R	6-0	190	10-26-81	.158	.176	.150	20	57	4	9	3	0	0	4	6	0	0	1	17	0	0	.211	.234
Lopez, Gabriel	R-R	5-8	170	3-11-80	.249	.262	.246	124	409	39	102	21	1	1	47	37	7	5	6	53	3	3	.313	.318
Mendoza, Carlos	B-R	6-0	191	11-27-79	.210	.206	.211	84	267	27	56	13	0	0	17	40	2	3	1	54	4	1	.258	.316
Miranda, Juan	L-L	6-0	220	4-25-83	.265	.244	.272	55	196	29	52	17	2	7	46	23	5	0	3	46	0	1	.480	.352
Muich, Joseph	R-R	6-1	205	8-18-82	.118	.000	.125	5	17	0	2	0	0	0	1	0	0	0	0	3	1	0	.118	.167
Pena, Ramiro	B-R	5-11	165	7-18-85	.252	.302	.239	52	202	23	51	7	1	0	10	22	2	7	0	33	7	3	.297	.332
Pilittere, P.J.	R-R	6-0	215	11-23-81	.261	.299	.247	100	348	43	91	16	2	2	34	26	6	1	7	42	0	1	.336	.318
Raley, Russell	R-R	5-10	185	12-30-83	.000	—	.000	3	7	1	0	0	0	0	0	4	1	0	0	2	0	0	.000	.417
Santos, Omir	R-R	6-0	200	4-29-81	.211	.375	.167	10	38	4	8	2	0	0	1	0	0	0	0	8	0	0	.263	.231
Sardinha, Bronson	L-R	6-1	220	4-6-83	.429	.400	.439	15	56	14	24	3	1	4	18	7	0	0	1	10	3	0	.732	.484
Strong, Jamal	R-R	5-10	185	8-5-78	.229	.213	.234	58	201	25	46	3	1	0	14	37	4	3	0	29	12	2	.254	.360
Vechionacci, Marcos	B-R	6-2	170	8-7-86	.111	.000	.500	2	9	0	1	1	0	0	0	0	0	0	0	4	0	0	.222	.111

PITCHING	B-T	HT	WT	DOB	W	L	ERA	G	GS	CG	SV	IP	H	R	ER	HR	BB	SO	AVG	vLH	vRH	K/9	BB/9
Casadiego, Gerardo	R-R	6-0	180	12-19-80	3	3	3.86	35	0	0	9	42	42	21	18	6	21	45	.251	.208	.284	9.64	4.50
Chamberlain, Joba	R-R	6-2	230	9-23-85	4	2	3.35	8	7	0	0	40	32	15	15	4	15	66	.218	.153	.261	14.73	3.35
Clemens, Roger	R-R	6-4	235	8-4-62	0	0	5.06	1	1	0	0	5	3	3	3	0	4	5	.286	.364	.200	8.44	6.75
Clippard, Tyler	R-R	6-4	170	2-14-85	2	1	5.40	6	6	0	0	27	22	18	16	5	12	28	.227	.182	.250	9.45	4.05
Gardner, Michael	R-R	6-0	190	5-23-81	3	5	2.88	44	3	0	7	82	72	32	26	1	30	66	.235	.259	.215	7.30	3.32
Horne, Alan	R-R	6-4	195	1-5-83	12	4	3.11	27	27	0	0	153	149	68	53	10	57	165	.256	.253	.258	9.68	3.35
Hughes, Phil	R-R	6-5	220	6-24-86	0	0	1.29	2	2	0	0	7	5	1	1	0	2	11	.200	.100	.267	14.14	2.57
Jackson, Steven	R-R	6-5	215	3-15-82	0	1	3.86	10	0	0	1	21	20	11	9	1	9	16	.256	.417	.185	6.86	3.86
Jones, Jason	R-R	6-5	225	11-20-82	8	11	3.62	28	19	0	0	132	130	63	53	11	31	78	.258	.275	.245	5.33	2.12
Karstens, Jeff	R-R	6-3	185	9-24-82	1	0	1.80	1	1	0	0	5	4	1	1	0	2	5	.222	.286	.182	9.00	3.60
Kennard, Jeff	R-R	6-2	220	7-26-81	1	4	2.73	31	0	0	6	53	49	22	16	3	17	47	.247	.304	.198	8.03	2.91
Kennedy, Ian	R-R	6-0	190	12-19-84	5	1	2.59	9	9	0	0	49	27	14	14	2	17	57	.163	.154	.170	10.54	3.14
Kroenke, Zachary	R-L	6-3	210	4-21-84	0	1	9.42	15	0	0	2	14	21	16	15	5	12	12	.344	.522	.237	7.53	7.53
Lavigne, Tim	R-R	5-10	210	7-4-78	0	2	4.93	25	3	0	7	42	43	25	23	4	12	39	.262	.261	.263	8.36	2.57
Manning, Charlie	L-L	6-2	180	3-31-79	1	0	0.00	7	0	0	1	10	4	0	0	0	2	9	.118	.143	.100	8.38	1.86
Marquez, Jeffrey	R-R	6-2	175	8-10-84	15	9	3.65	27	27	2	0	155	166	80	63	11	44	94	.270	.292	.251	5.45	2.55
McCutchen, Daniel	R-R	6-2	195	9-26-82	3	2	2.41	7	7	0	0	41	30	11	11	2	12	36	.205	.196	.211	7.90	2.63
Patterson, Scott	R-R	6-7	227	6-20-79	4	2	1.09	43	3	0	2	74	45	13	9	1	15	91	.170	.151	.185	11.02	1.82
Pope, Justin	R-R	6-0	190	11-8-79	2	2	3.08	29	0	0	6	38	25	16	13	3	12	36	.181	.235	.149	8.53	2.84
Ramirez, Edwar	R-R	6-3	150	3-28-81	0	0	0.54	9	0	0	1	17	6	1	1	1	8	33	.103	.111	.097	17.82	4.32
Robertson, David	R-R	5-11	180	4-9-85	0	0	2.25	2	0	0	0	4	2	1	1	0	2	9	.143	.000	.200	20.25	4.50
Smith, Brett	R-R	6-5	220	8-12-83	7	4	2.97	17	16	1	0	91	61	32	30	7	47	80	.192	.157	.226	7.91	4.65
Thorp, Paul	R-R	6-0	200	9-23-80	0	1	2.40	15	0	0	1	30	26	10	8	1	19	21	.239	.252	.176	6.30	5.70
Whelan, Kevin	R-R	6-0	200	1-8-84	4	2	2.98	31	1	0	4	54	34	18	18	2	42	68	.180	.200	.167	11.26	6.96

Name	B-T	HT	WT	DOB	W	L	ERA	G	GS	CG	SV	IP	H	R	ER	HR	BB	SO	AVG	vLH	vRH	K/9	BB/9
Wordekemper, Eric	R-R	6-1	200	8-8-83	0	0	0.00	1	0	0	1	1	0	0	0	0	0	1	.000	—	.000	9.00	0.00
Wright, Chase	L-L	6-2	205	2-8-83	5	2	3.62	10	10	1	0	60	55	25	24	8	21	41	.249	.212	.265	6.18	3.17
Zimmermann, Rob	R-R	6-5	245	11-17-81	0	0	54.00	1	0	0	0	0	2	2	2	0	2	0	1.000	.000	1.000	0.00	54.00

FIELDING

Catcher	PCT	G	PO	A	E	DP	PB
Brown	.984	15	115	9	2	1	0
Conway	.972	8	65	4	2	0	1
Lafountain	.990	16	95	4	1	1	2
Muich	1.000	5	41	5	0	0	2
Pilittere	.995	97	780	60	4	5	7
Santos	1.000	9	61	8	0	0	0

First Base	PCT	G	PO	A	E	DP
Ehlers	.988	76	624	39	8	59
Garrett	.986	25	191	25	3	14
Kinkade	1.000	3	29	1	0	2
Mendoza	.987	12	71	3	1	10
Miranda	.982	29	204	13	4	16
Pilittere	1.000	2	18	1	0	1

Second Base	PCT	G	PO	A	E	DP
Francia	1.000	10	10	31	0	3

	PCT	G	PO	A	E	DP
Lopez	.981	124	217	345	11	70
Mendoza	1.000	9	16	31	0	4
Raley	1.000	1	1	1	0	0

Third Base	PCT	G	PO	A	E	DP
Baldiris	.894	85	67	118	22	6
Francia	.833	9	4	11	3	0
Kinkade	.860	18	9	34	7	2
Lafountain	1.000	2	1	2	0	0
Mendoza	.922	35	14	45	5	1
Vechionacci	1.000	2	2	4	0	0

Shortstop	PCT	G	PO	A	E	DP
Cannizaro	.909	8	6	14	2	2
Corona	.939	35	61	93	10	23
Francia	.941	7	14	18	2	5
Gonzalez	.975	28	28	88	3	14
Mendoza	.951	15	19	39	3	10

	PCT	G	PO	A	E	DP
Pena	.982	52	81	142	4	30

Outfield	PCT	G	PO	A	E	DP
Carson	.988	124	230	16	3	6
Christian	.974	59	109	4	3	0
Curtis	.991	59	109	2	1	0
Gardner	.992	53	115	3	1	3
Garrett	.943	18	31	2	2	0
Hall	.981	56	102	1	2	0
Lafountain	1.000	2	4	0	0	0
Mendoza	1.000	4	11	1	0	0
Sardinha	.962	14	24	1	1	0
Strong	.965	42	83	0	3	0

TAMPA YANKEES

HIGH CLASS A

FLORIDA STATE LEAGUE

BATTING	B-T	HT	WT	DOB	AVG	vLH	vRH	G	AB	R	H	2B	3B	HR	RBI	BB	HBP	SH	SF	SO	SB	CS	SLG	OBP
Battle, Tim	R-R	6-2	185	9-10-85	.218	.209	.221	130	491	67	107	16	7	9	52	31	3	5	1	149	20	8	.334	.268
Blumenthal, Ben	R-R	6-2	210	4-24-83	.200	.400	.133	7	20	1	4	0	0	0	1	4	0	0	0	6	0	0	.200	.333
Cervelli, Francisco	R-R	6-1	170	3-6-86	.279	.314	.265	89	290	34	81	24	2	2	32	36	16	4	2	59	4	3	.397	.387
Cooper, James	L-R	5-10	190	2-18-84	.259	.250	.262	32	108	11	28	4	2	3	10	7	2	0	0	17	0	1	.417	.316
Corona, Reegie	B-R	5-11	160	11-7-86	.271	.250	.277	100	395	56	107	17	3	3	37	51	4	5	5	65	22	6	.352	.356
Cuello, Prilys	B-R	5-11	168	11-17-88	.000	.000	.000	1	4	0	0	0	0	0	0	0	0	0	0	2	0	0	.000	.000
Curtis, Colin	L-L	6-0	190	2-1-85	.298	.279	.305	65	245	37	73	9	2	5	26	29	3	3	1	43	4	4	.412	.378
Giambi, Jason	L-R	6-3	235	1-8-71	.308	.000	.333	5	13	0	4	1	0	0	1	3	0	0	0	5	0	0	.385	.438
Gonzalez, Edwar	R-R	5-10	200	1-1-83	.259	.234	.266	131	518	64	134	27	5	9	68	27	5	0	3	89	13	8	.382	.300
Greenwood, Jared	L-R	5-10	210	3-29-84	.239	.250	.238	60	188	20	45	10	1	6	26	19	2	0	6	62	0	1	.399	.316
Holmann, Mario	B-R	6-0	165	5-21-84	.179	.333	.152	17	39	8	7	0	0	0	3	11	0	3	0	9	4	1	.179	.360
Ibarra, Walter	B-R	5-11	150	11-1-87	.179	.200	.174	10	28	5	5	1	0	0	0	2	0	0	0	9	1	0	.214	.233
Jackson, Austin	R-R	6-1	185	2-1-87	.345	.290	.362	67	258	53	89	15	6	10	34	22	2	0	2	48	13	5	.566	.398
Kunda, Chris	R-R	6-0	175	11-1-84	.250	.111	.296	15	36	3	9	0	0	0	2	4	0	0	0	10	2	1	.250	.325
Malec, Christopher	B-R	5-11	195	8-28-82	.323	.286	.335	67	229	31	74	17	1	5	41	27	6	0	1	21	4	4	.472	.407
Matsui, Hideki	L-R	6-2	210	6-12-74	.333	—	.333	2	6	1	2	0	0	0	0	0	0	0	0	0	0	0	.333	.333
Mientkiewicz, Doug	L-R	6-2	205	6-19-74	.429	.000	.462	5	14	4	6	3	0	0	8	3	0	0	0	1	0	0	.643	.529
Minor, Robbie	R-R	5-10	185	4-28-85	.208	.429	.118	10	24	6	5	2	0	0	2	2	0	0	0	7	0	0	.292	.269
Miranda, Juan	L-L	6-0	220	4-25-83	.264	.209	.284	67	250	35	66	17	3	9	50	29	7	0	7	60	1	0	.464	.348
Muich, Joseph	R-R	6-0	205	8-18-82	.286	.000	.286	3	7	1	2	0	0	0	0	1	0	0	0	0	0	0	.286	.375
Nunez, Eduardo	R-R	6-0	155	6-15-87	.285	.281	.286	30	123	16	35	5	0	1	13	7	3	0	1	18	9	0	.350	.336
Nunez, Luis	R-R	5-11	160	11-21-86	.267	.333	.262	12	45	5	12	3	0	0	2	0	0	1	0	8	1	0	.333	.267
O'Brien, Timothy	R-R	6-2	210	12-22-83	.174	.667	.100	10	23	4	4	1	0	0	2	3	4	0	0	4	0	0	.217	.367
Perez, Andres	R-R	6-0	185	5-23-84	.203	.250	.193	18	69	6	14	3	1	2	11	1	0	0	1	14	1	2	.362	.211
Plumley, Grant	R-R	6-0	185	12-21-81	.212	.333	.185	9	33	4	7	1	0	0	2	3	0	0	0	10	0	0	.242	.278
Raley, Russell	R-R	5-10	185	12-30-83	.209	.192	.220	21	67	6	14	4	0	0	6	3	0	0	0	16	0	0	.269	.243
Russo, Kevin	R-R	5-11	190	7-8-84	.281	.244	.292	109	385	47	108	22	3	2	45	15	5	3	6	66	19	6	.369	.311
Tabata, Jose	R-R	5-11	160	8-12-88	.307	.314	.304	103	411	56	126	16	2	5	54	33	10	1	1	70	15	7	.392	.371
Vechionacci, Marcos	B-R	6-2	170	8-7-86	.266	.261	.268	108	391	44	104	23	5	2	39	36	3	1	3	69	11	6	.366	.327

PITCHING	B-T	HT	WT	DOB	W	L	ERA	G	GS	CG	SV	IP	H	R	ER	HR	BB	SO	AVG	vLH	vRH	K/9	BB/9
Abreu, Erick	R-R	6-1	170	8-9-83	0	2	7.63	8	2	0	0	15	24	14	13	3	3	12	.364	.419	.314	7.04	1.76
Arias, Wilkins	L-L	6-1	150	11-4-80	6	3	4.59	41	0	0	0	69	70	37	35	4	29	60	.269	.299	.252	7.86	3.80
Axford, John	R-R	6-5	195	4-1-83	0	0	2.38	5	0	0	2	11	6	5	3	2	7	15	.162	.214	.130	11.91	5.56
Casadiego, Gerardo	R-R	6-0	180	12-19-80	0	0	1.50	4	0	0	0	6	2	1	1	0	3	5	.105	.000	.182	7.50	4.50
Castillo, Francisco	R-R	6-2	195	10-3-86	0	0	0.00	1	0	0	0	2	3	1	0	1	3	.375	1.000	.167	13.50	4.50
Chamberlain, Joba	R-R	6-2	230	9-23-85	4	0	2.03	7	7	0	0	40	25	10	9	0	11	51	.181	.143	.202	11.48	2.48
Claggett, Anthony	B-R	6-2	185	7-15-84	9	8	3.69	32	16	0	2	112	119	51	46	7	31	76	.274	.335	.224	6.09	2.48
Clemens, Roger	R-R	6-4	235	8-4-62	0	0	2.25	1	1	0	0	4	3	1	1	0	2	.200	.286	.125	4.50	0.00
Coke, Phil	L-L	6-1	210	7-9-82	7	3	3.09	17	16	1	0	99	93	36	34	4	37	76	.251	.239	.255	6.91	3.36
Gonell, Jacinto	R-R	6-1	165	9-9-83	1	1	4.63	7	0	0	0	12	10	6	6	3	6	7	.233	.188	.259	5.40	4.63
Hacker, Eric	B-R	6-1	215	3-26-83	3	3	6.10	9	7	0	0	38	52	28	26	3	14	22	.329	.381	.295	5.17	3.29
Hughes, Phil	R-R	6-5	220	6-24-86	0	0	0.00	1	1	0	0	2	0	1	0	0	2	3	.000	.000	.000	13.50	9.00
Igawa, Kei	L-L	6-1	210	7-13-79	1	1	2.00	2	2	0	0	9	7	4	2	0	3	6	.206	.000	.259	6.00	3.00
Karstens, Jeff	R-R	6-3	185	9-24-82	0	0	0.00	1	1	0	0	4	3	0	0	1	5	.200	.000	.273	11.25	2.25
Kennedy, Ian	R-R	6-0	190	12-19-84	6	1	1.29	11	10	1	0	63	39	9	9	2	22	72	.183	.176	.189	10.29	3.14
Kontos, George	R-R	6-3	215	6-12-85	4	6	4.02	19	17	0	0	94	95	51	42	15	30	101	.260	.308	.225	9.67	2.87
Kroenke, Zachary	R-L	6-3	205	4-21-84	2	2	2.27	29	0	0	0	44	34	16	11	2	19	33	.209	.228	.198	6.80	3.92
Kunda, Chris	R-R	6-0	175	11-1-84	0	0	0.00	1	0	0	0	1	0	0	0	1	0	.250	.000	.333	9.00	0.00
Martinez, Mike	R-R	6-2	190	4-12-81	4	4	3.20	29	3	0	0	79	85	29	28	8	22	48	.276	.248	.293	5.49	2.52
McCutchen, Daniel	R-R	6-2	195	9-26-82	11	2	2.50	17	16	0	0	101	86	29	28	7	21	67	.236	.224	.244	5.97	1.87
Ortiz, Jonathan	R-R	5-10	170	10-29-85	0	0	3.86	2	0	0	0	5	3	2	2	0	1	9	.188	.333	.100	17.36	1.93
Patterson, Garrett	L-L	6-2	220	5-11-82	1	0	4.50	1	0	0	0	2	2	1	1	1	0	.333	.000	.400	0.00	4.50
Quezada, Elvys	R-R	6-1	210	12-15-81	4	4	3.72	22	14	0	0	77	75	42	32	7	23	69	.246	.243	.247	8.03	2.68
Robertson, David	R-R	5-11	180	4-9-85	3	1	1.08	10	0	0	1	33	18	6	4	0	15	37	.159	.182	.145	9.99	4.05
Schmidt, Joshua	R-R	6-4	175	11-14-82	1	2	2.79	39	0	0	3	68	54	24	21	3	28	92	.214	.244	.198	12.24	3.70

ORGANIZATION STATISTICS

	B-T	HT	WT	DOB	W	L	ERA	G	GS	CG	SV	IP	H	R	ER	HR	BB	SO	AVG	vLH	vRH	K/9	BB/9
Smith, Brett	R-R	6-5	220	8-12-83	0	6	7.41	8	8	0	0	34	46	32	28	8	22	15	.331	.321	.337	3.97	5.82
Valdez, Jose	R-R	6-4	186	1-22-83	3	4	2.87	37	0	0	3	60	54	21	19	4	21	60	.240	.275	.221	9.05	3.17
Veras, Jose	R-R	6-5	235	10-20-80	0	0	0.00	2	1	0	0	3	0	0	0	0	2	5	.000	.000	.000	15.00	6.00
Villalona, Bryan	R-R	6-2	170	9-15-82	3	4	4.00	15	7	1	1	54	56	30	24	3	21	32	.263	.247	.274	5.33	3.50
Wang, Chien-Ming	R-R	6-3	225	3-31-80	0	0	5.40	1	1	0	0	5	5	3	3	0	1	4	.250	.500	.083	7.20	1.80
Whelan, Kevin	R-R	6-0	200	1-8-84	2	0	1.93	7	7	0	0	28	11	6	6	2	12	28	.117	.182	.060	9.00	3.86
White, Steven	R-R	6-4	205	6-15-81	1	0	3.65	2	2	0	0	12	13	6	5	2	2	11	.265	.154	.306	8.03	1.46
Wordekemper, Eric	R-R	6-1	200	8-8-83	2	0	0.57	43	0	0	33	47	39	5	3	0	11	34	.223	.213	.230	6.51	2.11

FIELDING

Catcher	PCT	G	PO	A	E	DP	PB
Blumenthal	1.000	7	46	4	0	0	2
Cervelli	.997	89	667	74	2	5	15
Greenwood	.992	46	335	33	3	4	10
Muich	1.000	2	17	1	0	1	0

Ibarra	.968	7	13	17	1	3
Kunda	.919	11	24	33	5	5
L. Nunez	1.000	2	5	6	0	1
Raley	.964	12	22	31	2	12
Russo	.977	104	207	339	13	81

Ibarra	1.000	3	2	6	0	2
Minor	1.000	7	4	17	0	3
E. Nunez	.955	30	38	89	6	20
L/ Nunez	.667	1	2	2	2	0
Raley	1.000	5	4	9	0	3

First Base	PCT	G	PO	A	E	DP
Greenwood	.968	10	84	6	3	13
Holmann	1.000	1	1	0	0	1
Kunda	1.000	3	10	2	0	2
Malec	.991	59	503	19	5	59
Mientkiewicz	1.000	3	14	0	0	1
Miranda	.991	65	532	29	5	56
O'Brien	1.000	2	21	2	0	1
Plumley	.941	3	15	1	1	4
Vechionacci	1.000	3	9	0	0	2

Third Base	PCT	G	PO	A	E	DP
Holmann	.900	7	4	5	1	2
Malec	1.000	2	1	4	0	1
Minor	.000	1	0	0	1	0
L. Nunez	.969	9	7	24	1	3
O'Brien	.909	8	0	10	1	0
Plumley	.900	8	3	6	1	0
Raley	1.000	5	4	5	0	0
Russo	.833	3	2	3	1	0
Vechionacci	.946	105	48	180	13	22

Outfield	PCT	G	PO	A	E	DP
Battle	.975	108	270	8	7	4
Cooper	.971	18	33	1	1	0
Curtis	.977	52	82	2	2	1
Gonzalez	.970	84	151	9	5	2
Jackson	.994	65	156	2	1	1
Matsui	1.000	2	2	0	0	0
L. Nunez	—	1	0	0	0	0
Perez	1.000	6	2	0	0	0
Tabata	.979	87	135	3	3	0

Second Base	PCT	G	PO	A	E	DP
Cuello	1.000	1	0	1	0	0
Holmann	.950	9	19	19	2	5

Shortstop	PCT	G	PO	A	E	DP
Corona	.942	98	152	287	27	77
Holmann	.750	1	0	3	1	0

CHARLESTON RIVERDOGS

LOW CLASS A

SOUTH ATLANTIC LEAGUE

BATTING	B-T	HT	WT	DOB	AVG	vLH	vRH	G	AB	R	H	2B	3B	HR	RBI	BB	HBP	SH	SF	SO	SB	CS	SLG	OBP
Anson, Kyle	B-R	6-0	200	4-21-83	.272	.211	.289	98	334	40	91	17	0	4	44	49	2	1	4	48	5	1	.359	.365
Aragon, Brian	L-L	6-1	190	1-24-84	.233	.273	.230	54	159	21	37	6	1	5	26	17	5	1	1	47	2	3	.377	.324
Baisley, Brian	R-R	6-3	223	12-19-82	.341	.286	.351	25	88	10	30	4	0	2	10	8	3	0	0	18	0	0	.455	.414
Calzado, Josue	R-R	6-1	160	11-6-85	.271	.278	.269	126	465	60	126	26	2	9	55	27	3	0	6	91	8	4	.394	.311
Carrara, Chris	R-R	5-10	185	5-11-85	.250	.333	.231	11	16	1	4	0	1	0	3	3	1	1	0	4	0	0	.375	.400
Cooper, James	L-R	5-10	190	2-18-84	.291	.125	.306	57	189	31	55	13	3	2	15	19	10	1	1	28	8	4	.423	.384
Cox, Daniel	L-R	6-1	180	7-10-86	.000	—	.000	2	5	0	0	0	0	0	0	0	0	0	0	0	0	0	.000	.000
Fortenberry, Seth	L-L	6-2	175	9-1-83	.255	.253	.256	140	505	97	129	23	4	18	87	73	11	0	6	137	25	8	.424	.358
Gil, Jose	R-R	6-0	170	9-4-86	.221	.160	.234	42	136	14	30	4	0	5	13	10	0	1	1	32	0	1	.360	.272
Hilligoss, Mitch	L-R	6-1	195	6-17-85	.310	.277	.317	128	520	83	161	35	4	4	53	33	2	2	2	65	35	7	.415	.352
Hollingsworth, Donald	L-L	5-9	175	5-15-85	.125	.000	.143	4	8	2	1	0	1	0	2	0	0	0	0	3	0	0	.375	.125
Jackson, Austin	R-R	6-1	185	2-1-87	.260	.250	.262	60	235	33	61	16	1	3	25	24	4	1	2	59	19	6	.374	.336
Ketron, Brandon	R-R	6-0	205	8-22-83	.500	.000	1.000	1	2	1	1	0	0	0	2	0	0	0	0	1	0	0	.500	.500
Kunda, Chris	R-R	6-1	175	11-1-84	.184	.176	.185	54	136	13	25	6	1	0	17	12	0	1	4	30	5	3	.243	.243
Malec, Christopher	B-R	5-11	195	8-28-82	.308	.289	.313	70	227	33	70	11	1	4	38	42	11	0	6	27	7	3	.419	.430
Muich, Joseph	R-R	6-1	205	8-18-82	.232	.200	.244	47	168	20	39	6	0	6	23	8	1	0	3	44	1	0	.375	.267
Nunez, Eduardo	R-R	6-0	155	6-15-87	.238	.270	.230	91	328	36	78	10	2	1	28	25	2	2	3	42	20	8	.290	.293
Nunez, Luis	R-R	5-11	160	11-21-86	.224	.313	.196	43	134	11	30	7	2	1	12	7	0	1	1	20	0	0	.328	.261
O'Brien, Timothy	R-R	6-2	210	12-22-83	.236	.207	.245	38	127	13	30	4	0	6	21	15	2	1	0	36	1	0	.409	.326
Odenreider, Chase	R-R	6-1	209	8-19-83	.291	.366	.258	46	134	22	39	4	2	4	19	12	11	1	1	21	4	1	.440	.392
Perez, Andres	R-R	6-0	185	5-23-84	.264	.273	.260	25	72	12	19	6	1	0	5	10	0	1	0	12	5	2	.375	.349
Pino, Wilmer	R-R	5-11	165	1-23-86	.239	.197	.250	108	347	49	83	13	1	5	31	18	4	2	4	45	21	1	.326	.282
Smith, Kevin	L-R	6-1	215	1-15-84	.297	.190	.315	83	296	43	88	25	0	1	58	35	5	0	1	58	1	1	.476	.380

PITCHING	B-T	HT	WT	DOB	W	L	ERA	G	GS	CG	SV	IP	H	R	ER	HR	BB	SO	AVG	vLH	vRH	K/9	BB/9
Artz, Stephen	R-R	6-2	200	4-23-84	2	1	2.91	12	0	0	1	22	10	8	7	1	6	27	.137	.056	.164	11.22	2.49
Axford, John	R-R	6-5	195	4-1-83	0	3	4.39	13	5	0	0	27	29	20	13	2	22	21	.276	.333	.238	7.09	7.42
Duff, Grant	R-R	6-6	210	12-19-82	14	8	3.82	27	27	0	0	139	135	71	59	15	80	82	.259	.227	.274	5.31	5.18
Dunn, Michael	L-L	6-1	185	5-23-85	12	5	3.42	27	27	0	0	145	136	69	55	14	45	138	.253	.190	.264	8.59	2.80
Hacker, Eric	R-R	6-1	215	3-26-83	9	2	2.56	17	17	0	0	95	89	34	27	5	18	54	.254	.292	.234	5.12	1.71
Hoover, Jesse	R-R	6-3	210	1-8-82	3	2	3.92	23	0	0	1	41	37	19	18	3	23	38	.239	.217	.253	8.27	5.01
Hovis, Jonathan	R-R	5-11	185	12-27-82	4	5	1.69	55	0	0	30	64	49	17	12	2	11	56	.208	.197	.212	7.88	1.55
Kunda, Chris	R-R	6-1	175	11-1-84	0	0	0.00	1	0	0	0	1	0	0	0	0	0	0	.167	.000	.500	0.00	0.00
Martinez, Brady	R-R	5-10	185	12-21-82	3	2	3.79	43	0	0	9	71	50	32	30	6	36	65	.198	.250	.180	8.20	4.54
Medina, Gabriel	R-R	6-5	235	2-17-84	3	2	3.83	15	5	0	1	42	32	20	18	5	11	40	.208	.196	.214	8.50	2.34
Noesi, Hector	R-R	6-2	174	1-26-87	1	1	4.50	5	5	0	0	20	25	10	10	2	8	11	.309	.222	.333	4.95	3.60
Norton, Timothy	R-R	6-5	230	5-23-83	1	3	3.71	5	5	0	0	27	28	14	11	0	8	32	.262	.273	.259	10.80	2.70
Nova, Ivan	R-R	6-4	210	1-12-87	6	8	4.98	21	21	0	0	99	121	64	55	8	31	54	.306	.293	.312	4.89	2.81
Patterson, Garrett	L-L	6-2	220	5-11-82	1	5	6.29	29	5	0	2	54	61	45	38	6	36	37	.280	.200	.314	6.13	5.96
Patterson, Paul	R-R	6-7	200	5-8-84	3	2	4.14	13	7	0	0	46	35	21	21	5	16	34	.207	.192	.214	6.70	3.15
Peterson, Nicholas	R-R	6-3	210	10-3-84	3	1	8.78	14	0	0	0	13	10	13	13	4	19	23	.192	.118	.229	15.52	12.83
Reyes, Angel	L-L	5-11	170	1-8-87	0	2	4.65	7	7	0	0	31	25	18	16	3	21	33	.217	.150	.232	9.58	6.10
Robertson, David	R-R	5-11	180	4-9-85	5	2	0.77	24	0	0	3	47	25	5	4	0	15	67	.151	.119	.168	12.83	2.87
Soto, Edgar	L-L	5-11	175	12-28-84	1	2	3.36	36	5	0	0	70	57	39	26	2	43	70	.223	.300	.204	9.04	5.56
Tejeda, Ferdin	R-R	6-0	185	9-15-82	2	2	2.55	31	1	0	1	60	43	18	17	5	13	45	.203	.206	.201	6.75	1.95
Trubee, Luke	R-R	6-3	195	11-20-83	5	1	3.61	47	0	0	2	72	64	32	29	4	15	56	.240	.241	.239	6.97	1.87
Villalona, Bryan	R-R	6-2	170	9-15-82	0	3	9.39	6	3	0	0	15	29	16	16	3	8	8	.397	.385	.400	4.70	1.76

FIELDING

Catcher	PCT	G	PO	A	E	DP	PB
Anson	.978	75	465	73	12	6	13
Baisley	1.000	8	42	6	0	1	1
Gil	.985	38	297	34	5	3	13
Ketron	1.000	1	3	0	0	0	0
Muich	.986	27	191	17	3	4	3
O'Brien	1.000	1	1	0	0	0	0

First Base	PCT	G	PO	A	E	DP
Aragon	1.000	6	43	2	0	4
Malec	.990	55	484	28	5	38
O'Brien	1.000	5	43	2	0	2
Odenreider	1.000	3	15	2	0	2
Smith	.997	78	653	42	2	65

Second Base	PCT	G	PO	A	E	DP
Carrara	1.000	7	6	11	0	0
Cox	1.000	2	1	0	0	0

	PCT	G	PO	A	E	DP
Kunda	.993	32	46	87	1	19
Malec	.978	9	25	20	1	11
L. Nunez	.981	14	18	33	1	7
Pino	.962	95	192	237	17	53

Third Base	PCT	G	PO	A	E	DP
Carrara	—	1	0	0	0	0
Cox	1.000	1	1	3	0	0
Hilligoss	.943	104	66	201	16	19
Kunda	.875	7	2	12	2	0
Malec	.900	6	2	7	1	1
L. Nunez	1.000	5	3	4	0	1
O'Brien	.971	23	14	52	2	4
Odenreider	.944	10	2	15	1	0
Smith	1.000	1	0	1	0	0

Shortstop	PCT	G	PO	A	E	DP
Carrara	—	1	0	0	0	0

	PCT	G	PO	A	E	DP
Hilligoss	.989	25	30	60	1	11
Kunda	.940	13	12	35	3	8
E. Nunez	.932	90	116	252	27	59
L. Nunez	.977	24	34	51	2	12

Outfield	PCT	G	PO	A	E	DP
Aragon	.951	27	35	4	2	0
Calzado	.968	126	228	12	8	2
Cooper	.977	54	83	3	2	1
Fortenberry	.996	133	240	5	1	1
Hilligoss	—	1	0	0	0	0
Hollingsworth	1.000	2	1	0	0	0
Jackson	.974	57	110	3	3	1
Kunda	—	1	0	0	0	0
L. Nunez	1.000	2	2	0	0	0
Odenreider	.966	26	26	2	1	0
Perez	.938	11	14	1	1	1

STATEN ISLAND YANKEES   SHORT-SEASON

NEW YORK-PENN LEAGUE

BATTING	B-T	HT	WT	DOB	AVG	vLH	vRH	G	AB	R	H	2B	3B	HR	RBI	BB	HBP	SH	SF	SO	SB	CS	SLG	OBP
Carrara, Chris	R-R	5-10	180	5-11-85	.000	.000	.000	12	12	2	0	0	0	0	0	2	0	0	1	3	0		.000	.143
Chavez, Brian	R-R	6-2	190	3-23-86	.121	.000	.149	27	58	4	7	3	0	0	3	2	1	4	1	17	1	1	.172	.161
Gil, Jose	R-R	6-0	170	9-4-86	.242	.238	.244	58	198	26	48	17	0	7	37	12	3	6	2	41	4	3	.434	.293
Holiday, Taylor	R-R	5-11	190	4-21-84	.290	.364	.271	66	262	41	76	12	1	3	27	21	8	5	2	48	16	7	.378	.358
Hollingsworth, Donald	L-L	5-9	175	5-28-85	.360	.381	.356	49	125	24	45	3	2	0	15	16	8	3	1	11	9	4	.416	.460
Howes, Isaiah	R-R	6-2	210	9-28-84	.193	.200	.190	39	114	14	22	6	0	2	10	11	3	1	0	37	1	1	.298	.281
Ketron, Brandon	R-R	6-0	205	8-22-83	.000	.000	.000	4	7	0	0	0	0	0	0	1	0	1	2	0	0		.000	.000
Krum, Austin	L-L	5-9	175	1-19-86	.238	.323	.222	60	202	32	48	14	4	1	22	16	4	2	1	44	11	5	.361	.305
Lasala, James	R-R	6-1	205	5-12-84	.200	.000	.211	15	20	3	4	0	0	0	0	1	0	0	3	0	0		.200	.238
Lonigro, Frank	B-R	6-2	220	5-18-85	.219	.176	.234	24	64	8	14	3	0	0	3	6	1	1	0	20	0	0	.266	.296
Morris, Matt	R-R	6-1	180	2-10-85	.216	.194	.223	46	139	13	30	5	1	2	12	6	4	3	0	31	3	1	.309	.268
Nunez, Luis	R-R	5-11	160	11-21-86	.236	.259	.229	34	123	19	29	7	2	1	13	10	1	3	2	8	5	2	.350	.294
O'Brien, Timothy	R-R	6-2	210	12-22-83	.143	.000	.167	2	7	0	1	0	0	0	0	1	0	0	0	0	0	0	.143	.250
Odenreider, Chase	R-R	6-1	209	8-19-83	.143	.250	.100	4	14	1	2	0	0	1	2	1	0	0	0	3	0	0	.357	.200
Perez, Andres	R-R	6-0	185	5-23-84	.077	.250	.045	7	26	2	2	0	0	0	2	2	0	1	8	0	0		.077	.138
Pruitt, Braedyn	L-R	6-2	175	3-23-85	.347	.414	.333	51	170	20	59	5	0	4	32	26	12	0	4	21	1	6	.447	.458
Raber, Christopher	L-R	6-3	225	6-3-85	.256	.182	.269	51	156	21	40	5	0	2	27	15	1	4	1	47	8	2	.327	.324
Snyder, Justin	L-R	5-9	190	4-8-86	.335	.389	.320	73	260	68	87	20	1	5	40	58	6	0	5	50	10	10	.477	.459
Sublett, Damon	L-R	6-1	190	9-22-85	.326	.378	.314	68	239	43	78	19	3	8	53	43	5	4	9	47	10	4	.531	.426
Wehrle, Ryan	R-R	6-3	200	5-31-85	.119	.250	.105	19	42	6	5	2	0	0	1	13	1	0	9	0	0		.167	.339
Williams, David	R-R	6-3	215	8-15-84	.276	.341	.260	64	221	25	61	12	0		19	21	6	2	1	49	7	2	.330	.353

PITCHING	B-T	HT	WT	DOB	W	L	ERA	G	GS	CG	SV	IP	H	R	ER	HR	BB	SO	AVG	vLH	vRH	K/9	BB/9
Axford, John	R-R	6-5	195	4-1-83	1	1	2.22	8	0	0	2	24	13	8	6	0	15	30	.153	.154	.152	11.10	5.55
Bartleski, Philip	R-R	6-7	240	4-22-83	1	1	4.03	13	0	0	1	22	22	14	10	0	8	19	.272	.256	.289	7.66	3.22
Betances, Dellin	R-R	6-7	185	3-23-88	1	2	3.60	6	6	0	0	25	24	11	10	0	17	29	.255	.233	.275	10.44	6.12
Chigges, Nicholas	R-R	6-0	195	9-23-84	3	4	2.29	19	4	0	2	55	43	15	14	3	21	62	.208	.244	.186	10.15	3.44
Farley, Chris	R-R	6-2	180	2-24-83	1	2	3.93	8	7	0	0	34	40	20	15	1	11	36	.292	.246	.329	9.44	2.88
Gonell, Jacinto	R-R	6-1	165	9-9-83	2	0	5.59	9	0	0	0	10	8	6	6	0	7	12	.229	.417	.130	11.17	6.52
Heyer, Craig	R-R	6-3	195	11-15-85	5	0	3.20	17	1	0	0	51	59	20	18	4	13	25	.301	.289	.308	4.44	2.31
Hollander, Kyle	R-R	5-9	185	11-6-84	1	0	3.27	14	0	0	0	22	23	9	8	1	8	10	.267	.237	.292	4.09	3.27
Jones, Fred	R-R	6-2	215	1-31-84	0	0	1.69	4	0	0	0	5	7	2	1	0	3	4	.292	.375	.250	6.75	5.06
Kapala, Daniel	R-R	6-5	220	9-6-85	0	0	3.94	10	0	0	0	16	16	10	7	1	6	10	.242	.300	.194	5.62	3.38
Karstens, Jeff	R-R	6-3	185	9-24-82	1	0	1.80	1	1	0	0	5	4	1	1	1	0	8	.211	.125	.273	14.40	0.00
Kiley, Jason	R-R	6-5	235	6-14-85	4	2	2.86	23	0	0	1	35	35	17	11	2	18	31	.267	.279	.257	8.05	4.67
Livek, Jeff	R-R	6-1	200	9-18-84	1	2	6.27	13	0	0	0	19	18	17	13	2	10	5	.261	.226	.289	2.41	4.82
McAllister, Zachary	R-R	6-5	230	12-8-87	4	6	5.17	16	15	0	0	71	80	42	41	3	28	75	.286	.302	.273	9.46	3.53
Medina, Gabriel	R-R	6-5	235	2-17-84	1	0	2.89	4	2	0	0	19	16	8	6	0	3	17	.219	.154	.255	8.20	1.45
Olbrychowski, Adam	R-R	6-3	180	9-7-86	3	5	4.47	13	13	0	0	58	51	34	29	4	33	51	.243	.260	.233	7.87	5.09
Ortiz, Jonathan	R-R	5-10	170	10-29-85	5	0	1.80	21	0	0	13	25	14	5	5	1	8	39	.173	.200	.152	14.04	2.88
Peterson, Nicholas	R-R	6-3	210	10-3-84	0	0	0.00	7	0	0	2	8	3	1	0	0	6	12	.115	.222	.059	13.50	6.75
Pope, Ryan	R-R	6-3	200	5-21-86	3	0	2.49	10	10	0	0	43	41	16	12	2	10	46	.256	.343	.189	9.55	2.08
Rasner, Darrell	R-R	6-3	210	1-13-81	0	0	5.14	2	2	0	0	7	8	4	4	1	3	3	.276	.182	.333	3.86	3.86
Reyes, Angel	L-L	5-11	110	1-8-87	0	0	14.54	3	2	0	0	4	10	9	7	0	12	3	.455	.500	.438	6.23	24.92
Segal, Justin	R-R	5-10	180	6-14-84	0	0	15.00	3	0	0	0	3	8	5	5	0	2	2	.471	.667	.429	6.00	6.00
Selene, Josue	R-R	6-0	180	10-8-85	0	0	4.50	2	0	0	0	2	3	1	1	0	2	2	.333	.000	.429	9.00	9.00
Stephens, Jason	R-R	6-4	190	10-10-84	4	1	1.88	9	7	0	0	43	33	11	9	1	10	39	.212	.250	.182	8.16	2.09
Zink, Ryan	R-R	6-4	210	4-1-85	6	1	3.23	15	5	0	0	47	45	19	17	2	22	39	.253	.286	.228	7.42	4.18

FIELDING

Catcher	PCT	G	PO	A	E	DP	PB
Gil	.981	55	420	47	9	3	12
Ketron	.967	4	28	1	1	0	0
Lasala	.929	12	35	4	3	0	2
Lonigro	.987	22	134	16	2	2	3

First Base	PCT	G	PO	A	E	DP
Holiday	.977	42	310	26	8	28
Odenreider	.976	4	37	4	1	3
Pruitt	.970	12	91	5	3	13
Raber	.995	27	192	15	1	17

Second Base	PCT	G	PO	A	E	DP
Carrara	1.000	1	1	0	0	0
Chavez	1.000	1	2	0	0	0

Snyder	1.000	13	26	31	0	9
Sublett	.970	65	87	169	8	40

Third Base	PCT	G	PO	A	E	DP
Carrara	—	1	0	0	0	0
Chavez	.941	14	5	11	1	1
O'Brien	1.000	2	0	3	0	1
Pruitt	.954	39	27	56	4	2
Snyder	.930	23	8	58	5	4
Wehrle	.889	13	4	20	3	3

Shortstop	PCT	G	PO	A	E	DP
Carrara	1.000	2	7	5	0	3
Chavez	.969	14	11	20	1	7
Nunez	.945	34	58	98	9	21

Snyder	.944	32	54	80	8	18
Wehrle	1.000	6	8	10	0	2

Outfield	PCT	G	PO	A	E	DP
Holiday	.984	32	60	2	1	0
Hollingsworth	.976	28	40	0	1	0
Howes	.889	15	15	1	2	0
Krum	.990	52	101	3	1	0
Morris	.980	46	48	2	1	0
Perez	1.000	7	7	0	0	0
Snyder	1.000	11	21	3	0	1
Williams	.989	61	82	4	1	0

GULF COAST LEAGUE

ORGANIZATION STATISTICS

BATTING	B-T	HT	WT	DOB	AVG	vLH	vRH	G	AB	R	H	2B	3B	HR	RBI	BB	HBP	SH	SF	SO	SB	CS	SLG	OBP
Almonte, Abraham	B-R	5-9	170	6-27-89	.288	.288	.287	49	160	29	46	4	3	3	16	21	1	2	1	34	8	9	.406	.372
Almonte, Zoilo	B-R	5-11	165	6-10-89	.268	.207	.295	50	190	25	51	11	2	3	24	9	2	3	1	35	2	2	.395	.307
Angelini, Carmen	R-R	6-1	185	9-22-88	.000	.000	.000	1	1	0	0	0	0	0	0	0	0	0	0	1	0	0	.000	.000
Blumenthal, Ben	R-R	6-2	210	4-24-83	.333	.261	.375	26	63	11	21	3	2	3	5	8	1	3	0	20	0	0	.587	.417
Castro, Kelvin	R-R	6-3	164	12-14-87	.277	.320	.260	49	177	25	49	10	3	1	22	6	2	3	0	42	6	1	.384	.308
Cox, Daniel	L-R	6-1	180	7-10-86	.167	.000	.200	5	6	1	1	0	0	0	0	0	0	0	0	0	0	0	.167	.167
Cuello, Prilys	B-R	5-11	168	11-17-88	.283	.316	.266	47	166	28	47	7	2	6	24	18	1	3	0	39	5	5	.458	.357
Day, Larry	R-R	5-11	210	3-22-85	.213	.133	.250	21	47	4	10	3	0	0	8	3	4	0	2	2	0	0	.277	.304
Dionicio, Andres	R-R	6-0	160	12-29-87	.121	.083	.143	10	33	2	4	0	1	0	4	1	1	0	0	11	0	1	.182	.171
Gattis, Gary	R-R	5-11	185	3-27-85	.286	.450	.172	16	49	7	14	4	0	1	6	5	3	0	1	8	3	1	.429	.379
Grote, Taylor	L-R	6-2	195	12-5-88	.000	—	.000	1	1	0	0	0	0	0	0	1	0	0	0	0	0	0	.000	.500
Ibarra, Walter	B-R	5-11	150	11-1-87	.205	.200	.207	16	39	6	8	2	0	0	4	4	2	0	1	8	0	1	.256	.304
Laird, Brandon	R-R	6-1	215	9-11-87	.339	.417	.308	45	168	27	57	14	1	8	29	6	2	1	1	26	0	0	.577	.367
Manzanillo, Gerson	L-R	5-11	155	5-7-86	.254	.150	.294	26	71	10	18	1	0	0	5	2	0	1	1	15	5	4	.268	.270
Mesa, Melky	R-R	6-1	165	1-31-87	.235	.244	.232	49	153	27	36	10	2	3	13	9	4	2	1	55	5	3	.386	.293
Minor, Robbie	R-R	5-10	185	4-28-85	.240	.143	.278	10	25	2	6	0	0	0	3	0	0	0	0	4	1	0	.240	.240
Montero, Jesus	R-R	6-4	225	11-28-89	.280	.333	.260	33	107	13	30	6	0	3	19	12	3	0	1	18	0	0	.421	.366
Parra, Freuny	R-R	5-11	195	11-2-87	.167	.500	.094	9	18	1	3	1	0	0	2	0	1	0	1	3	0	0	.222	.200
Perez, Andres	R-R	6-1	185	5-23-84	.280	.303	.270	32	107	15	30	5	0	5	11	13	2	1	1	17	4	2	.467	.366
Rodriguez, Gerardo	R-R	6-1	194	10-25-87	.233	.120	.279	32	86	15	20	6	0	2	12	7	8	0	0	31	1	2	.372	.347
Romine, Austin	R-R	6-1	195	11-22-88	.500	.000	.500	1	2	2	1	1	0	0	1	0	0	1	0	0	1	0	01.000	.667
Rufino, Wady	R-R	6-2	195	4-8-85	.345	.341	.347	38	116	25	40	8	1	6	24	13	4	0	2	19	0	1	.586	.422
Suttle, Brad	B-R	6-2	215	1-24-86	.125	—	.125	3	8	1	1	0	0	0	1	1	0	0	0	2	0	0	.125	.222
Wehrle, Ryan	R-R	6-3	200	5-31-85	.280	.382	.233	30	107	14	30	7	0	3	13	13	1	0	1	12	0	1	.430	.361

PITCHING	B-T	HT	WT	DOB	W	L	ERA	G	GS	CG	SV	IP	H	R	ER	HR	BB	SO	AVG	vLH	vRH	K/9	BB/9
Barreda, Manuel	R-R	5-11	165	10-8-88	5	0	3.00	11	3	0	1	39	30	20	13	3	15	44	.200	.219	.186	10.15	3.46
Beam, T.J.	R-R	6-7	215	8-28-80	0	0	2.57	4	3	0	0	7	6	2	2	0	1	7	.214	.200	.222	9.00	1.29
Castillo, Francisco	R-R	6-2	195	10-3-86	1	0	1.69	3	0	0	0	5	2	2	1	1	4	8	.111	.000	.182	13.50	6.75
Castillo, Noel	R-R	6-1	160	10-5-83	6	3	1.88	13	7	0	2	53	53	17	11	1	7	51	.261	.286	.244	8.72	1.20
De La Rosa, Wilkins	L-L	6-0	155	2-21-85	1	0	2.63	12	0	0	0	24	20	8	7	0	11	32	.235	.111	.269	12.00	4.12
Dennehy, Timothy	L-L	6-1	195	9-22-86	5	1	3.71	10	4	0	1	34	34	17	14	1	11	23	.258	.300	.245	6.09	2.91
Erickson, Casey	R-R	6-3	187	8-28-85	3	2	2.76	10	5	0	0	29	31	10	9	2	7	24	.267	.278	.263	7.36	2.15
Foard, Matt	L-L	6-3	210	3-10-85	1	1	5.73	9	0	0	0	11	20	7	7	1	3	10	.392	.250	.457	8.18	2.45
Gil, Daniel	R-R	6-3	187	4-24-89	2	1	6.00	5	1	0	0	15	18	12	10	0	4	12	.300	.290	.310	7.20	2.40
Gonell, Jacinto	R-R	6-1	165	9-9-83	1	0	0.48	11	0	0	2	19	8	2	1	0	8	23	.129	.103	.152	11.09	3.86
Guillen, Rudy	R-R	6-3	185	11-23-83	0	0	6.75	3	1	0	0	4	4	3	3	1	3	6	.250	.000	.364	13.50	6.75
Heredia, Jairo	R-R	6-1	189	10-8-89	2	2	2.72	11	6	0	0	46	39	15	14	4	11	52	.228	.229	.228	10.10	2.14
Hyde, Michael	R-R	6-1	192	6-28-84	3	0	3.46	9	0	0	0	13	7	5	5	0	3	11	.146	.190	.111	7.62	2.08
Karstens, Jeff	R-R	6-3	185	9-24-82	0	0	0.00	1	1	0	0	3	3	0	0	0	1	2	.214	.500	.167	5.40	2.70
Marquez, Dickson	R-R	6-2	170	4-19-86	2	3	2.66	11	4	0	2	44	37	18	13	3	11	45	.223	.254	.200	9.20	2.25
Ohlendorf, Ross	R-R	6-4	235	8-8-82	1	1	3.94	4	4	0	0	16	13	8	7	2	1	17	.206	.208	.205	9.56	0.56
Ortiz, Jonathan	R-R	5-10	170	10-29-85	0	0	0.00	3	0	0	2	3	0	0	0	0	0	5	.000	.000	.000	15.00	0.00
Pendleton, Lance	L-R	6-3	195	9-10-83	0	0	4.61	8	6	0	0	14	14	7	7	1	6	16	.255	.182	.303	10.54	3.95
Perez, Kelvin	R-R	6-1	140	10-16-85	5	3	2.84	11	5	0	0	38	32	15	12	2	9	32	.222	.222	.227	7.58	2.13
Reyes, Angel	L-L	5-11	170	1-8-87	0	0	3.38	6	2	0	0	11	9	4	4	0	11	13	.237	.222	.241	10.97	9.28
Saunders, Link	R-R	6-0	225	10-12-84	1	0	3.52	7	0	0	0	8	5	3	3	1	4	6	.192	.273	.133	7.04	4.70
Segal, Justin	R-R	5-10	180	6-14-84	1	0	3.12	8	0	0	0	9	7	3	3	0	6	10	.219	.300	.182	10.38	6.23
Selene, Josue	R-R	6-0	180	10-8-85	0	0	0.00	5	0	0	2	10	5	0	0	0	3	11	.156	.273	.095	10.24	2.79
Shafer, Jake	R-R	6-4	215	10-11-85	0	0	0.00	6	0	0	1	6	8	2	0	0	1	7	.267	.455	.158	9.95	1.42
Stephens, Jason	R-R	6-4	190	10-18-84	0	0	0.00	2	0	0	0	5	3	0	0	0	1	4	.188	.200	.182	7.71	1.93
Still, Alexi	R-R	6-3	195	12-15-83	0	0	10.80	3	0	0	0	2	2	2	2	0	8	1	.000	.000	.000	5.40	43.20
Thomas, Kyle	L-L	5-10	210	11-2-84	0	0	0.00	2	0	0	0	1	1	0	0	0	0	0	.250	.000	.333	0.00	0.00
Thomson, Brandon	L-L	5-11	175	8-17-85	2	0	1.02	15	0	0	7	18	9	10	2	1	8	14	.153	.091	.167	7.13	4.08
Veras, Jose	R-R	6-5	235	10-20-80	0	0	0.00	2	2	0	0	2	2	0	0	0	0	1	.250	.500	.167	4.50	0.00
Walker, Pete	R-R	6-2	195	4-8-69	0	0	0.00	4	3	0	1	6	5	1	0	0	0	9	.208	.100	.286	13.50	0.00

FIELDING

Catcher	PCT	G	PO	A	E	DP	PB
Blumenthal	.973	24	164	13	5	1	4
Day	.993	21	129	8	1	3	5
Montero	.995	23	172	9	1	0	4
Parra	1.000	5	26	1	0	0	1

First Base	PCT	G	PO	A	E	DP
Laird	.966	12	81	4	3	5
Rodriguez	.990	24	179	10	2	21
Rufino	.990	28	197	8	2	17

Second Base	PCT	G	PO	A	E	DP
A. Almonte	.957	18	31	36	3	13
Cuello	.893	39	56	78	16	17
Ibarra	1.000	4	4	9	0	3

Minor	1.000	5	6	8	0	2

Third Base	PCT	G	PO	A	E	DP
Castro	.889	24	19	45	8	3
Laird	.950	28	24	52	4	4
Minor	1.000	2	1	1	0	0
Suttle	.667	3	0	2	1	0
Wehrle	.952	6	7	13	1	2

Shortstop	PCT	G	PO	A	E	DP
Castro	.971	28	35	64	3	13
Cox	.833	4	2	3	1	0
Ibarra	.957	13	14	31	2	3
Minor	.833	2	1	4	1	2
Parra	1.000	1	1	3	0	2

Rodriguez	—	1	0	0	0	0
Wehrle	.949	21	18	57	4	7

Outfield	PCT	G	PO	A	E	DP
A. Almonte	1.000	22	39	2	0	0
Z. Almonte	.986	46	63	5	1	2
Dionicio	1.000	10	14	0	0	0
Gattis	1.000	12	21	1	0	0
Manzanillo	.968	23	29	1	1	0
Mesa	.957	47	84	5	4	1
Perez	1.000	29	37	2	0	0
Perez	1.000	1	3	0	0	0

DOMINICAN SUMMER LEAGUE

BATTING	B-T	HT	WT	DOB	AVG	vLH	vRH	G	AB	R	H	2B	3B	HR	RBI	BB	HBP	SH	SF	SO	SB	CS	SLG	OBP
Baez, Wangel	R-R	6-0	165	8-30-87	.133	.000	.154	10	15	5	2	1	0	0	4	0	0	0	2	3	0	.200	.316
2-team (32 DSL)					.246	—	—	42	118	23	29	4	3	2	9	18	0	1	0	26	10	2	.381	.346
Calderon, Ronny	L-R	5-9	155	12-6-87	.333	—	.333	2	6	0	2	1	0	0	1	0	0	0	0	0	0	0	.500	.333
Caro, Joel	R-R	6-0	185	2-8-86	.125	.000	.150	9	24	2	3	0	0	0	4	0	0	0	0	9	0	0	.125	.125
2-team (16 DSL)					.138	—	—	25	80	6	11	1	0	0	9	3	1	0	0	23	0	1	.150	.179
Chirinos, Yeider	R-R	5-9	150	2-9-89	.306	.270	.320	42	134	18	41	10	3	1	23	7	5	5	2	15	1	3	.448	.358
Classe, Luis	L-L	5-11	140	6-23-88	.187	.214	.183	37	107	14	20	3	2	0	12	16	2	1	0	22	2	1	.252	.304
Gomez, Roy	R-R	5-11	160	1-7-85	.328	.395	.306	53	177	31	58	11	0	4	23	16	3	2	2	23	7	1	.458	.389
Guerrero, Toribio	B-R	5-7	149	2-28-85	.273	.500	.222	9	11	2	3	0	0	0	1	1	0	0	0	2	1	0	.273	.333
2-team (14 DSL)					.216	—	—	23	37	8	8	1	1	0	1	4	0	0	0	11	2	0	.297	.293
Hernandez, Sandy	R-R	6-0	170	7-9-86	.214	.333	.182	8	14	1	3	1	0	0	2	1	0	0	0	3	1	1	.286	.267
Herrera, Julian	R-R	6-0	145	3-30-87	.244	.225	.248	49	193	20	47	15	1	0	17	9	2	1	0	33	0	4	.332	.284
Lapaix, Arielkis	R-R	5-11	186	10-14-88	.202	.200	.203	57	188	34	38	11	2	2	24	24	10	1	0	78	2	1	.314	.324
Paredes, Jimmy	B-R	6-1	178	11-25-88	.259	.292	.249	64	266	31	69	14	4	2	42	6	6	0	4	44	5	4	.365	.287
Perez, Nixton	R-R	5-11	165	7-16-88	.184	.143	.194	16	38	7	7	0	1	0	4	2	1	1	1	8	0	0	.237	.238
Pirela, Jose	B-R	5-10	191	11-21-89	.273	.308	.263	65	238	44	65	7	3	4	29	34	5	0	6	36	15	5	.378	.367
Ramirez, Alvaro	L-L	5-9	160	4-5-86	.316	.290	.324	66	250	58	79	13	8	3	31	39	13	1	3	38	26	16	.468	.430
Rijo, Juan	R-R	6-2	155	5-8-86	.291	.372	.265	55	175	24	51	9	1	0	24	16	2	3	2	16	4	2	.354	.354
Rodriguez, Reynaldo	B-R	6-0	165	2-7-86	.361	.240	.403	26	97	20	35	6	7	3	24	8	1	1	1	6	3	2	.660	.411
2-team (8 DSL)					.349	—	—	34	129	24	45	8	7	3	26	11	1	1	1	9	9	5	.589	.401
Rojas, Julio	L-R	5-11	160	7-22-88	.333	.000	.500	3	3	1	1	0	0	0	1	2	0	0	0	1	0	0	.333	.600
Santamaria, Jahdiel	R-R	6-3	170	4-5-87	.347	.286	.364	57	196	47	68	14	5	3	41	27	6	0	3	19	9	4	.515	.435
Saturria, Jonnathan	R-R	5-11	162	12-4-86	.273	.133	.301	32	88	13	24	7	0	0	7	10	2	1	0	11	1	3	.352	.360
Urena, Carlos	B-R	6-1	183	11-17-89	.225	.360	.182	28	102	18	23	6	0	4	15	8	3	0	5	34	1	0	.402	.288
2-team (24 DSL)					.237	—	—	52	190	29	45	9	2	8	32	11	8	0	5	59	3	0	.432	.299
Ventura, Nicolas	R-R	6-2	170	2-7-89	.188	.000	.200	9	16	4	3	0	0	0	2	5	0	0	0	2	2	1	.188	.381

PITCHING	B-T	HT	WT	DOB	W	L	ERA	G	GS	CG	SV	IP	H	R	ER	HR	BB	SO	AVG	vLH	vRH	K/9	BB/9
Atacho, Alan	R-R	6-1	171	3-21-88	2	2	1.13	6	4	0	0	24	17	5	3	2	5	16	.202	.222	.197	6.00	1.88
2-team (9 DSL)					3	5	2.97	15	8	0	0	58	50	24	19	2	18	42	—	—	—	6.55	2.81
Batista, Yoel	R-R	6-1	185	1-1-86	1	1	10.32	6	0	0	0	11	21	17	13	0	9	9	.382	.571	.354	7.15	7.15
2-team (9 DSL)					2	3	8.24	15	2	0	2	32	48	33	29	3	20	19	—	—	—	5.40	5.68
Conde, Jean	L-L	6-1	160	10-28-87	2	0	3.16	10	5	0	0	26	20	13	9	0	21	22	.230	.333	.226	7.71	7.36
Cordoba, Jonny	L-L	5-9	165	8-1-84	5	2	1.66	21	0	0	4	43	32	12	8	2	9	48	.203	.250	.201	9.97	1.87
Garcia, Charlyn	R-R	6-1	165	6-9-86	1	1	5.73	6	3	0	0	11	11	14	7	0	16	10	.239	.125	.263	8.18	13.09
Hernandez, Pablo	R-R	6-3	170	3-1-88	0	0	0.00	1	1	0	0	4	2	0	0	0	2	5	.167	.000	.182	12.27	4.91
Hernandez, Sandy	R-R	6-0	170	7-9-86	0	0	0.00	1	1	0	0	2	0	0	0	0	1	0	.000	.000	.000	0.00	4.50
Lozano, Luis	R-R	6-2	175	1-1-85	3	4	2.10	23	0	0	6	34	30	21	8	0	16	31	.229	.280	.217	8.13	4.19
Marcano, Pedro	R-R	5-11	165	10-8-86	1	0	8.00	4	1	0	0	9	8	10	8	2	14	8	.242	.500	.226	8.00	14.00
2-team (10 DSL)					2	3	5.52	14	7	0	0	29	26	21	18	4	28	36	—	—	—	11.05	8.59
Marte, Joel	R-R	5-11	195	1-18-88	5	2	4.04	14	6	0	0	49	39	27	22	1	23	58	.217	.244	.209	10.65	4.22
Marte, Ronny	R-R	6-1	173	2-26-86	2	1	4.24	12	8	0	0	47	48	30	22	2	12	36	.270	.235	.278	6.94	2.31
Martinez, Richard	R-R	6-1	194	7-19-88	2	3	4.67	13	8	0	0	44	42	31	23	4	25	41	.247	.237	.250	8.32	5.08
Mieses, Jose	R-R	5-11	162	9-18-85	2	0	0.73	8	0	0	1	12	5	1	1	0	5	9	.132	.100	.143	6.57	3.65
Orozco, Elvin	R-R	6-1	195	10-24-88	2	1	0.82	8	4	0	1	33	20	6	3	0	8	28	.180	.091	.202	7.64	2.18
2-team (6 DSL)					3	1	0.94	14	4	0	1	48	31	8	5	1	12	49	—	—	—	9.25	2.27
Paul, Dieudone	L-L	6-2	187	9-28-87	2	1	5.21	9	2	0	0	19	21	21	11	2	18	18	.269	.250	.270	8.53	8.53
2-team (5 DSL)					3	2	3.44	14	5	0	0	37	29	25	14	3	25	46	—	—	—	11.29	6.14
Rondon, Francisco	L-L	6-1	160	4-19-88	4	1	3.65	13	8	0	0	44	38	21	18	0	32	45	.235	.375	.227	9.14	6.50
Sanchez, Pedro	L-L	6-0	160	9-8-84	3	3	2.27	21	0	0	1	40	32	16	10	2	19	42	.216	.400	.210	9.53	4.31
Santana, Juan	R-R	6-1	174	2-12-89	0	1	4.61	4	3	0	0	14	11	8	7	1	5	10	.200	.278	.162	6.59	3.29
2-team (1 DSL)					1	1	4.80	5	3	0	0	15	11	9	8	1	7	11	—	—	—	6.60	4.20
Selene, Josue	R-R	6-0	180	10-8-85	2	0	2.65	10	4	0	0	34	22	14	10	1	7	28	.180	.107	.202	7.41	1.85
Suescun, Gustavo	R-R	6-0	187	11-21-85	2	0	1.26	19	2	0	3	43	26	10	6	3	9	50	.171	.091	.185	10.47	1.88
Tapia, Eric	L-L	6-1	193	9-6-87	1	2	5.06	11	7	0	0	32	39	25	18	0	28	21	.305	.000	.310	5.91	7.88
Tatis, Gabriel	R-R	6-0	180	5-18-85	1	0	2.04	12	0	0	1	18	19	5	4	0	9	16	.271	.412	.226	8.15	4.58
2-team (8 DSL)					2	1	2.53	20	0	0	1	32	29	11	9	0	12	33	—	—	—	9.28	3.38
Varillas, Andres	L-L	6-1	170	4-19-88	1	1	4.50	4	3	0	0	14	14	7	7	2	3	14	.259	.000	.259	9.00	1.93
2-team (7 DSL)					1	1	3.00	11	8	0	0	36	29	17	12	4	9	31	—	—	—	7.75	2.25

FIELDING

Catcher	PCT	G	PO	A	E	DP	PB
Calderon	1.000	2	17	1	0	0	0
Chirinos	.986	42	304	38	5	6	5
Saturria	.972	30	215	27	7	1	4
Ventura	.977	8	43	0	1	0	4

First Base	PCT	G	PO	A	E	DP
Classe	.990	17	88	13	1	2
Gomez	.987	40	290	19	4	27
Herrera	1.000	1	7	0	0	0
Rijo	.989	17	165	7	2	11
Saturria	.933	2	14	0	1	1

Second Base	PCT	G	PO	A	E	DP
Baez	.818	2	4	5	2	1
Gomez	.942	11	37	28	4	6
Guerrero	1.000	2	3	2	0	1

	PCT	G	PO	A	E	DP
Hernandez	1.000	6	6	6	0	1
Herrera	.870	9	19	21	6	4
Paredes	.852	10	24	22	8	2
Perez	1.000	1	2	1	0	0
Pirela	1.000	7	14	12	0	0
Rijo	.952	30	64	56	6	13

Third Base	PCT	G	PO	A	E	DP
Hernandez	1.000	1	0	1	0	0
Herrera	.800	20	17	35	13	0
Paredes	.865	43	28	100	20	13
Perez	.870	10	4	16	3	1
Rijo	.818	4	2	7	2	0

Shortstop	PCT	G	PO	A	E	DP
Baez	1.000	5	3	5	0	2
Guerrero	1.000	3	4	6	0	1

	PCT	G	PO	A	E	DP
Paredes	.918	15	29	38	6	3
Perez	—	1	0	0	0	0
Pirela	.874	55	72	130	29	23

Outfield	PCT	G	PO	A	E	DP
Caro	1.000	7	9	1	0	0
Classe	.889	22	24	0	3	0
Herrera	.867	15	11	2	2	0
Lapaix	.989	57	81	7	1	2
Ramirez	.949	63	104	7	6	2
Rojas	1.000	3	3	0	0	0
Santamaria	.961	36	47	2	2	1
Urena	.946	27	49	4	3	2
Ventura	1.000	1	1	0	0	0

ORGANIZATION STATISTICS

DOMINICAN SUMMER LEAGUE

ORGANIZATION STATISTICS

BATTING

BATTING	B-T	HT	WT	DOB	AVG	vLH	vRH	G	AB	R	H	2B	3B	HR	RBI	BB	HBP	SH	SF	SO	SB	CS	SLG	OBP
Acosta, Alberto	R-R	6-3	190	2-24-90	.234	.175	.258	45	137	17	32	7	1	2	17	17	3	0	0	36	0	1	.343	.331
Arcia, Francisco	B-R	6-0	155	9-14-89	.269	.295	.259	47	156	26	42	11	4	3	21	25	10	1	1	35	5	2	.449	.401
Arosemena, Alexis	R-R	6-4	185	9-30-86	.218	.264	.204	65	234	26	51	12	1	5	25	24	8	1	1	76	0	2	.342	.311
Baez, Luigi	L-L	6-0	160	6-11-89	.239	.149	.270	60	188	24	45	5	3	0	13	27	1	0	0	47	2	3	.298	.338
Baez, Wangel	R-R	6-0	165	8-30-87	.262	.158	.286	32	103	18	27	3	3	2	9	14	0	1	0	24	7	2	.408	.350
2-team (10 DSL)					.246	—	—	42	118	23	29	4	3	2	9	18	0	1	0	26	10	2	.381	.346
Caro, Joel	R-R	6-0	185	2-8-86	.143	.231	.116	16	56	4	8	1	0	0	5	3	1	0	0	14	0	1	.161	.200
2-team (9 DSL)					.138	—	—	25	80	6	11	1	0	0	9	3	1	0	0	23	0	1	.150	.179
De La Cruz, Aris	R-R	5-11	172	3-5-90	.077	.000	.098	24	52	4	4	0	0	0	1	3	2	0	0	22	0	0	.077	.158
Diaz, Israel	B-R	5-10	185	12-23-86	.138	.167	.130	20	29	6	4	2	0	0	3	6	2	1	0	5	2	1	.207	.324
Garcia, Jean	B-R	6-4	165	11-22-86	.173	.182	.169	27	81	11	14	1	0	1	13	18	0	1	0	14	2	0	.222	.323
Guerrero, Toribio	R-R	5-7	149	2-28-85	.192	.400	.143	14	26	6	5	1	1	0	3	0	0	0	9	1	0	.308	.276
2-team (9 DSL)					.216	—	—	23	37	8	8	1	1	0	1	4	0	0	11	2	0	.297	.293
Guillen, Luis	R-R	6-2	200	12-16-85	.333	.000	.400	5	18	6	6	0	0	2	5	3	1	0	0	7	0	0	.667	.455
Palomo, Jesus	R-R	5-11	170	12-15-89	.176	.111	.190	23	51	4	9	1	0	1	4	6	1	0	0	24	0	0	.255	.276
Parache, Luis	L-R	5-8	175	11-25-88	.246	.182	.271	45	118	15	29	8	1	1	9	13	0	1	3	21	1	1	.356	.313
Ramirez, Alcibiades	B-R	5-11	165	1-27-89	.111	.000	.125	5	9	1	1	0	0	0	1	1	0	0	0	4	0	0	.111	.200
Rodriguez, Reynaldo	R-R	6-0	165	2-7-86	.313	.167	.346	8	32	4	10	2	0	0	2	3	0	0	0	3	6	3	.375	.371
2-team (26 DSL)					.349	—	—	34	129	24	45	8	7	3	26	11	1	1	1	9	5	5	.589	.401
Romero, Yakensi	R-R	6-3	210	12-2-89	.144	.056	.161	40	111	9	16	1	1	3	8	30	2	0	0	35	0	0	.252	.336
Santana, Francisco	L-L	5-10	170	6-18-88	.264	.286	.258	51	197	29	52	11	7	3	25	14	2	2	1	38	6	2	.437	.318
Taveras, Damian	R-R	6-1	205	11-28-89	.207	.104	.241	55	193	22	40	6	1	1	16	22	6	0	1	50	0	2	.264	.306
Toussen, Jose	L-L	5-11	166	11-13-89	.235	.212	.243	62	255	23	60	12	4	3	31	17	4	0	0	72	2	4	.349	.293
Urena, Carlos	R-R	6-1	183	11-17-89	.250	.200	.276	24	88	11	22	3	2	4	17	3	5	0	0	25	2	0	.466	.313
2-team (28 DSL)					.237	—	—	52	190	29	45	8	3	8	32	11	8	0	5	59	3	0	.432	.299

PITCHING

PITCHING	B-T	HT	WT	DOB	W	L	ERA	G	GS	CG	SV	IP	H	R	ER	HR	BB	SO	AVG	vLH	vRH	K/9	BB/9
Arias, Justo	R-R	6-2	145	10-29-88	4	3	4.57	13	7	0	0	43	48	32	22	3	14	33	.281	.204	.311	6.85	2.91
Arias, Randy	R-R	6-0	160	11-13-89	1	0	7.31	7	0	0	0	16	18	15	13	1	9	5	.281	.238	.302	2.81	5.06
Atacho, Alan	R-R	6-1	171	3-21-88	1	3	4.28	9	4	0	0	34	33	19	16	0	13	26	.268	.405	.198	6.95	3.48
2-team (6 DSL)					3	5	2.97	15	8	0	0	58	50	24	19	2	18	42	—	—	—	6.55	2.81
Batista, Israel	R-R	6-1	172	11-5-87	4	4	4.21	22	6	0	2	62	54	41	29	3	29	36	.233	.265	.220	5.23	4.21
Batista, Yoel	R-R	6-1	185	1-1-86	1	2	7.08	9	2	0	0	20	27	16	16	3	11	10	.325	.320	.328	4.43	4.87
2-team (6 DSL)					2	3	8.24	15	2	0	2	32	48	33	29	3	20	19	—	—	—	5.40	5.68
Bravo, Wilfi	R-R	6-2	180	2-26-89	1	2	4.11	19	1	0	0	35	37	23	16	3	17	23	.264	.268	.263	5.91	4.37
Croussett, Melvin	L-R	6-1	168	12-28-88	2	2	1.42	17	0	0	2	38	22	10	6	0	25	55	.176	.182	.175	13.03	5.92
Delgado, Nerio	R-R	6-3	208	6-19-88	0	4	5.62	13	8	0	0	42	46	35	26	3	18	30	.279	.297	.267	6.48	3.89
Garcia, Jean	B-R	6-4	165	11-22-86	0	0	4.50	1	0	0	0	2	5	1	1	0	1	1	.500	.333	.571	4.50	4.50
Jimenez, Juan	R-R	6-1	170	10-26-88	0	4	3.92	8	5	0	0	21	20	15	9	1	13	18	.253	.167	.291	7.84	5.66
Lopez, Juan	R-R	6-1	170	6-23-90	0	3	4.18	11	8	0	0	24	28	18	11	1	10	22	.272	.118	.348	8.37	3.80
Marcano, Juan	L-L	6-1	160	8-24-90	0	2	1.37	7	5	0	0	20	10	6	3	0	6	23	.152	.000	.167	10.53	2.75
Marcano, Pedro	R-R	5-11	165	10-8-86	1	3	4.43	10	6	0	0	20	18	11	10	2	14	28	.240	.267	.222	12.39	6.20
2-team (4 DSL)					2	3	5.52	14	7	0	0	29	26	21	18	4	28	36	—	—	—	11.05	8.59
Martinez, Rafael	L-L	6-3	175	3-27-85	2	5	4.03	18	1	0	0	29	27	23	13	1	21	29	.241	.286	.238	9.00	6.52
Moreta, Francis	L-L	6-1	160	8-27-86	1	3	4.80	13	6	0	0	45	47	33	24	1	24	26	.280	.188	.289	5.20	4.80
Orozco, Elvin	R-R	6-1	195	10-24-88	1	0	1.23	6	0	0	0	15	11	2	2	1	4	21	.193	.238	.167	12.89	2.45
2-team (8 DSL)					3	1	0.94	14	0	0	1	48	31	8	5	1	12	49	—	—	—	9.25	2.27
Paul, Dieudone	L-L	6-2	187	9-28-87	1	1	1.53	5	3	0	0	18	8	4	3	1	7	28	.133	.167	.130	14.26	3.57
2-team (9 DSL)					3	2	3.44	14	5	0	0	37	29	25	14	3	25	46	—	—	—	11.29	6.14
Perez, Yang Carlos	B-R	6-2	160	6-23-85	1	2	4.00	5	0	0	1	9	10	6	4	1	4	9	.278	.154	.348	9.00	4.00
Ramirez, Adriano	R-R	6-1	170	11-20-86	0	0	6.75	7	0	0	0	11	11	8	8	0	8	11	.256	.143	.310	9.28	6.75
Ramirez, Alcibiades	B-R	5-11	165	1-27-89	0	0	9.00	1	0	0	0	2	3	2	2	0	0	3	.333	.333	.333	13.50	0.00
Ramirez, Jose	R-R	6-1	160	10-29-88	0	0	6.43	7	0	0	0	14	16	14	10	1	8	8	.267	.375	.227	5.14	5.14
Rodriguez, Reynaldo	R-R	6-0	165	2-7-86	0	0	4.50	1	0	0	0	2	3	4	1	0	2	1	.333	.250	.400	4.50	9.00
Santana, Juan	R-R	6-1	174	2-12-89	1	0	6.75	1	0	0	0	1	0	1	1	0	2	1	.000	.000	.000	6.75	13.50
2-team (4 DSL)					1	1	4.80	5	3	0	0	15	11	9	8	1	7	11	—	—	—	6.60	4.20
Tatis, Gabriel	R-R	6-0	180	5-18-85	1	1	3.14	8	0	0	0	14	10	6	5	0	3	17	.189	.286	.154	10.67	1.88
2-team (12 DSL)					2	1	2.53	20	0	0	1	32	29	11	9	0	12	33	—	—	—	9.28	3.38
Varillas, Andres	L-L	6-1	170	4-19-88	0	0	2.05	7	5	0	0	22	15	10	5	2	6	17	.185	.143	.189	6.95	2.45
2-team (4 DSL)					1	1	3.00	11	8	0	0	36	29	17	12	4	9	31	—	—	—	7.75	2.25

FIELDING

Catcher	PCT	G	PO	A	E	DP	PB
Arcia	.975	47	309	45	9	1	8
Diaz	1.000	10	61	3	0	0	0
Palomo	.955	22	116	11	6	0	6
Ramirez	1.000	3	7	1	0	0	1

First Base	PCT	G	PO	A	E	DP
Acosta	.964	21	152	11	6	11
Caro	1.000	2	7	1	0	0
De La Cruz	1.000	1	1	0	0	0
Diaz	1.000	4	3	0	0	1
Garcia	.969	19	136	18	5	10
Guerrero	1.000	2	5	1	0	2
Palomo	1.000	1	2	0	0	0
Romero	.960	30	228	15	10	20

Second Base	PCT	G	PO	A	E	DP
De La Cruz	.938	10	8	7	1	0
Guerrero	1.000	2	3	5	0	0
Parache	.953	32	65	56	6	15
Toussen	.911	31	54	90	14	19

Third Base	PCT	G	PO	A	E	DP
De La Cruz	.900	8	2	7	1	1
Garcia	1.000	4	0	5	0	0
Guerrero	1.000	3	0	1	0	0
Parache	.750	8	2	10	4	1
Taveras	.811	53	44	89	31	10

Shortstop	PCT	G	PO	A	E	DP
L. Baez	.900	2	7	2	1	1
W. Baez	.922	32	63	91	13	17

	PCT	G	PO	A	E	DP
Guerrero	.875	3	1	6	1	0
Parache	1.000	2	0	1	0	0
Toussen	.865	32	49	73	19	9

Outfield	PCT	G	PO	A	E	DP
Acosta	.875	7	7	0	1	0
Arosemena	.955	60	79	5	4	1
L. Baez	.962	41	46	4	2	0
Caro	1.000	11	8	4	0	0
Garcia	1.000	1	1	0	0	0
Guerrero	1.000	1	2	0	0	0
Guillen	1.000	5	6	0	0	0
Rojas		3	0	0	0	0
Romero	1.000	8	8	0	0	0
Santana	.966	49	108	5	4	0
Urena	.913	24	40	2	4	0

Oakland Athletics

BY CASEY TEFERTILLER

The A's had been winning for so long that it seemed the natural order of the universe that there would be a pennant race in Oakland in September.

For eight straight years, Oakland posted winning records. Five times the Athletics went to the playoffs, and in 2006 they reached the American League Divisional Series before the season ended in frigid Detroit.

That all came crashing down in 2007 when the team finished 76-85 for its first losing season since 1998.

There was no real mystery about the cause of Oakland's demise—the team fell apart with significant injuries. Oakland used 54 players, the most by the franchise since the 1915 Philadelphia A's used 56, and the most in the majors in 2007. The A's used the disabled list 22 times, with many of their top talents sidelined by injuries. Third baseman Eric Chavez, ace righthander Rich Harden, team leader Mark Kotsay and former rookies of the year Huston Street and Bobby Crosby all were among the contingent that missed extended time. Righthander Esteban Loaiza was down for the first five months, and the outfield became such a patchwork that players were constantly shuffled up and down from the minor leagues.

The season had begun with promise and expectations, with the addition of power source Mike Piazza and a pitching staff likely to rank among the best in baseball. The A's were actually seven games over .500 as late as June 20 before injuries in the bullpen became too much to overcome. By mid-July the breakdown was so complete that the A's began dealing away veterans for young talent, trading away catcher Jason Kendall in a move that would signal the organization was beginning to plan for the future.

Much of the last three months was spent in auditions, with young players receiving playing time to demonstrate where they fit in the 2008 Athletics. Several players earned further consideration, notably DH-outfielder Jack Cust, who led the team in homers (26) and RBIs (82) despite playing only 124 games after being acquired in a minor league deal with the Padres. Cust had been something of a legend through the years, a massive power hitter on the farm who never performed in the majors.

Rookie Kurt Suzuki took over for Kendall and likely earned the catching job for years to come, showing consistent improvement on defense and enough offense to play. Outfielder Travis Buck also made a big impression, hitting .288 with 34 extra-base hits in a half season of games, mostly while battling injuries. Mark Ellis put together the best season ever by an A's second baseman, matching his dazzling defense with 19 homers, 76 RBIs and a .276 average.

Righthander Dan Haren took over as the No. 1 starter and put together a dominant season. Chad Gaudin entered spring training as a reliever and joined the rotation when injuries created an opening. He put together an overpowering first half, but lost 10 times after the all-star break. His work was solid enough to earn a shot as a future starter. Joe Blanton completed the threesome of starters that gives the A's hope that they will have an effective rotation in 2008.

Perhaps the biggest excitement in the A's system was generated at Triple-A, where manager Tony DeFrancesco led the Sacramento Rivercats to the PCL championship, then beat the Richmond Braves, 7-1, at the Bricktown Showdown in Oklahoma City.

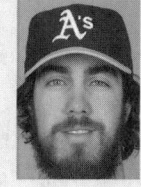

BATTING		★Minimum 250 at-bats
★AVG	Appert, Luke, Stockton/Midland	.304
R	Pennington, Cliff, Stockton/Midland	91
H	Barton, Daric, Sacramento	151
TB	Everidge, Tommy, Stockton/Midland	233
	Robnett, Richie, Midland/Sacramento	233
2B	Robnett, Richie, Midland/Sacramento	39
3B	Faison, Vince, Midland	9
HR	Everidge, Tommy, Stockton/Midland	26
RBI	Everidge, Tommy, Stockton/Midland	94
BB	Appert, Luke, Stockton/Midland	89
SO	Robnett, Richie, Midland/Sacramento	146
SB	Mitchell, Jermaine, Kane County	24
★OBP	Appert, Luke, Stockton/Midland	.424
★SLG	Perry, Jason, Midland/Sacramento	.525
PITCHING		**^Minimum 75 innings**
W	Ziegler, Brad, Midland/Sacramento	12
L	Komine, Shane, Sacramento	12
	Mazzaro, Vincent, Stockton	12
^ERA	Meyer, Dan, Midland/Sacramento	3.39
G	Gray, Jeff, Midland/Sacramento	54
G	Kilby, Brad, Stockton/Midland	54
CG	Braden, Dallas, Midland/Sacramento	2
CG	Heuser, James, Kane County	2
SV	Gray, Jeff, Midland/Sacramento	15
IP	Knox, Brad, Midland/Sacramento	164
BB	Rogers, Michael, Midland/Stockton	79
SO	Bailey, Andrew, Kane County/Stockton/Sacramento	150
^AVG	Bailey, Andrew, Kane County/Stockton/Sacramento	.223

What made the Cats' success so stunning is that the team endured 190 transactions during the season. Veteran infielder Lou Merloni served as captain and provided leadership to the ever-changing team. Top prospect Daric Barton hit .550 with four homers during the playoffs, then hit four more homers in 72 at-bats in his September callup.

The A's farm system has a well-deserved reputation for developing talent, but was left depleted after most of their top prospects reached the majors in recent years. When the season concluded, GM Billy Beane vowed to make rebuilding the farm system one of the organization's top priorities, saying he will increase scouting in Latin America, Asia and Australia.

General Manager: Billy Beane. **Farm Director:** Keith Lieppman. **Scouting Director:** Eric Kubota

Class	Team	League	W	L	PCT	Finish*	Manager	Affiliate Since
Majors	Oakland	American	76	86	.469	9th (14)	Bob Geren	—
Triple-A	Sacramento River Cats	Pacific Coast	84	60	.583	2nd (16)^	Tony DeFrancesco	2000
Double-A	Midland RockHounds	Texas	67	70	.489	5th (8)	Todd Steverson	1999
High A	Stockton Ports	California	64	76	.457	9th (10)	Darren Bush	2005
Low A	Kane County Cougars	Midwest	63	76	.453	10th (14)	Aaron Nieckula	2003
Short-season	Vancouver Canadians	Northwest	37	38	.493	2nd (8)	Rick Magnante	1979
Rookie	AZL Athletics	Arizona	25	31	.446	7th (9)	Ruben Escalera	1988
\Overall 2007 Minor League Record			340	351	.492	17th		

* Finish in overall standings (No. of teams in league) ^League champion

ORGANIZATION STATISTICS

OAKLAND ATHLETICS

AMERICAN LEAGUE

BATTING	B-T	HT	WT	DOB	AVG	vLH	vRH	G	AB	R	H	2B	3B	HR	RBI	BB	HBP	SH	SF	SO	SB	CS	SLG	OBP
Barton, Daric	L-R	6-0	225	8-16-85	.347	.296	.378	18	72	16	25	9	0	4	8	10	1	0	1	11	1	0	.639	.429
Bocachica, Hiram	R-R	5-11	195	3-4-76	.059	.000	.100	6	17	2	1	0	0	1	3	2	0	0	1	5	0	0	.235	.150
Bowen, Rob	B-R	6-3	225	2-24-81	.279	.308	.267	21	43	6	12	1	0	2	5	10	0	1	0	20	0	0	.442	.415
Bradley, Milton	B-R	6-0	225	4-15-78	.292	.375	.265	19	65	6	19	4	0	2	7	8	1	0	1	14	2	1	.446	.373
Brown, Dee	L-R	6-0	220	3-27-78	.000	.000	.000	8	3	0	0	0	0	0	0	0	0	0	0	2	0	0	.000	.000
Buck, Travis	L-R	6-2	225	11-18-83	.288	.323	.277	82	285	41	82	22	5	7	34	39	4	2	4	66	4	1	.474	.377
Chavez, Eric	L-R	6-1	230	12-7-77	.240	.234	.244	90	341	43	82	21	2	15	46	34	0	0	4	76	4	2	.446	.306
Crosby, Bobby	R-R	6-3	215	1-12-80	.226	.222	.228	93	349	40	79	15	0	8	31	23	2	0	6	62	10	2	.341	.278
Cust, Jack	L-R	6-1	230	1-16-79	.256	.218	.273	124	395	61	101	18	1	26	82	105	1	0	6	164	0	2	.504	.408
DaVanon, Jeff	B-R	6-0	200	12-8-73	.238	.600	.170	26	63	9	15	1	1	0	5	7	0	0	1	19	0	0	.286	.310
Ellis, Mark	R-R	5-11	190	6-6-77	.276	.313	.263	150	583	84	161	33	3	19	76	44	10	2	3	94	9	4	.441	.336
Furmaniak, J.J.	R-R	5-11	185	7-31-79	.176	.250	.154	16	17	5	3	1	0	0	1	3	2	0	0	8	0	0	.235	.364
Hannahan, Jack	L-R	6-2	205	3-4-80	.278	.400	.239	41	144	16	40	12	0	3	24	21	1	1	2	39	1	0	.424	.369
Johnson, Dan	L-R	6-2	225	8-10-79	.236	.234	.237	117	416	53	98	20	1	18	62	72	3	0	4	77	0	0	.418	.349
Kendall, Jason	R-R	6-0	195	6-26-74	.226	.176	.246	80	292	24	66	10	0	2	22	12	3	2	3	27	3	1	.281	.261
Kielty, Bobby	B-R	6-1	225	8-5-76	.200	.208	.182	13	35	4	7	1	0	0	3	3	1	0	1	9	0	0	.229	.275
2-team (20 Boston)					.218	—		33	87	10	19	3	0	1	12	8	2	0	4	26	0	0	.287	.287
Kotsay, Mark	L-L	6-0	205	12-2-75	.214	.130	.238	56	206	20	44	14	0	1	20	19	0	0	1	20	1	1	.296	.279
Langerhans, Ryan	L-L	6-3	205	2-20-80	.000	—	.000	2	4	0	0	0	0	0	0	1	0	0	0	2	0	0	.000	.000
Melhuse, Adam	B-R	6-2	210	3-27-72	.231	.000	.250	12	26	2	6	1	0	0	2	4	0	0	0	8	0	0	.269	.333
2-team (23 Texas)					.213	—		35	94	8	20	4	0	1	9	7	1	1	0	26	0	0	.287	.275
Melillo, Kevin	L-R	5-10	195	5-14-82	—	—	.000	1	0	0	0	0	0	0	0	1	0	0	0	0	0	0	—	1.000
Murphy, Donnie	R-R	5-10	185	3-10-83	.220	.279	.187	42	118	21	26	8	0	6	21	10	2	1	1	35	1	0	.441	.290
Piazza, Mike	R-R	6-3	215	9-4-68	.275	.292	.268	83	309	33	85	17	1	8	44	18	0	0	2	61	0	0	.414	.313
Putnam, Danny	L-L	5-10	200	9-17-82	.214	.222	.211	11	28	3	6	0	0	1	2	3	0	0	0	11	0	0	.321	.290
Scutaro, Marco	R-R	5-10	185	10-30-75	.260	.309	.245	104	338	49	88	13	0	7	41	35	2	2	2	40	2	1	.361	.332
Snelling, Chris	L-L	5-10	205	12-3-81	.350	.571	.231	6	20	4	7	0	0	0	0	5	0	0	0	4	0	0	.350	.480
Stewart, Shannon	R-R	5-11	210	2-25-74	.290	.269	.298	146	576	79	167	22	1	12	48	47	3	1	3	60	11	3	.394	.345
Suzuki, Kurt	R-R	6-0	205	10-4-83	.249	.151	.281	68	213	27	53	13	0	7	39	24	3	3	5	39	0	0	.408	.327
Swisher, Nick	B-L	6-0	215	11-25-80	.262	.291	.250	150	539	84	141	36	1	22	78	100	10	1	9	131	3	2	.455	.381
Thompson, Kevin	R-R	5-10	190	9-18-79	.071	.167	.000	9	14	2	1	0	0	0	1	1	0	0	0	3	0	0	.071	.133
2-team (13 New York)					.143	—		22	35	4	5	3	0	0	3	3	0	0	0	13	0	0	.229	.211
Walker, Todd	L-R	6-0	180	5-25-73	.271	.188	.313	18	48	5	13	1	0	0	4	2	0	0	2	4	0	0	.292	.288

PITCHING	B-T	HT	WT	DOB	W	L	ERA	G	GS	CG	SV	IP	H	R	ER	HR	BB	SO	AVG	vLH	vRH	K/9	BB/9
Blanton, Joe	R-R	6-3	250	12-11-80	14	10	3.95	34	34	3	0	230	240	106	101	16	40	140	.269	.291	.248	5.48	1.57
Blevins, Jerry	L-L	6-6	185	9-6-83	0	1	9.64	6	0	0	0	5	8	6	5	1	2	3	.348	.333	.357	5.79	3.86
Braden, Dallas	L-L	6-1	185	8-13-83	1	8	6.72	20	14	0	0	72	91	59	54	9	26	55	.303	.214	.324	6.84	3.24
Brown, Andrew	R-R	6-6	230	2-17-81	3	3	4.54	33	0	0	0	42	38	21	21	1	17	43	.245	.242	.247	9.29	3.67
Calero, Kiko	R-R	6-1	205	1-9-75	1	5	5.75	46	0	0	1	41	46	26	26	3	21	31	.293	.245	.315	6.86	4.65
Casilla, Santiago	R-R	6-0	200	7-25-80	3	1	4.44	46	0	0	2	51	43	25	25	6	22	44	.224	.212	.230	9.24	4.09
DiNardo, Lenny	L-L	6-4	190	9-19-79	8	10	4.11	35	20	0	0	131	136	74	60	13	50	59	.278	.304	.271	4.04	3.43
Duchscherer, Justin	R-R	6-3	205	11-19-77	3	3	4.96	17	0	0	0	16	18	9	9	3	8	13	.281	.400	.176	7.16	4.41
Embree, Alan	L-L	6-2	190	1-23-70	1	2	3.97	68	0	0	17	68	67	30	30	5	19	51	.258	.205	.278	6.75	2.51
Flores, Ron	L-L	5-10	195	8-9-79	0	2	3.57	17	0	0	0	18	16	8	7	2	12	15	.235	.095	.298	7.64	6.11
Gaudin, Chad	R-R	5-10	180	3-24-83	11	13	4.42	34	34	1	0	199	205	108	98	21	100	154	.267	.282	.250	6.95	4.52
Harden, Rich	L-R	6-1	190	11-30-81	1	2	2.45	7	4	0	0	26	18	7	7	3	11	27	.202	.292	.098	9.47	3.86
Haren, Dan	R-R	6-5	240	9-17-80	15	9	3.07	34	34	0	0	223	214	91	76	24	55	192	.247	.230	.264	7.76	2.22
Kennedy, Joe	R-L	6-4	250	5-24-79	3	9	4.37	27	16	0	0	101	109	53	49	9	48	42	.284	.203	.305	3.74	4.28
2-team (9 Toronto)					4	9	4.42	36	16	0	0	108	115	59	53	9	53	50	—	—	—	4.17	4.42
Komine, Shane	R-R	5-9	180	10-18-80	0	0	4.70	2	0	0	0	8	6	4	4	2	1	1	.214	.333	.158	1.17	1.17
Lewis, Colby	R-R	6-4	230	8-2-79	0	2	6.45	26	1	0	0	38	44	28	27	7	14	23	.293	.386	.255	5.50	3.35
Loaiza, Esteban	R-R	6-2	230	12-31-71	1	0	1.84	2	2	0	0	15	10	3	3	1	4	5	.192	.200	.188	3.07	2.45
Lugo, Ruddy	R-R	6-0	215	5-22-80	4	0	4.30	27	0	0	0	38	31	18	18	1	24	26	.226	.196	.244	6.21	5.73
2-team (11 Tampa Bay)					6	0	5.40	38	0	0	0	48	48	29	29	3	37	34	—	—	—	6.33	6.89
Marshall, Jay	L-L	6-5	185	2-25-83	1	2	6.43	51	0	0	0	42	50	33	30	3	22	18	.298	.296	.299	3.88	4.71
Meyer, Dan	R-L	6-3	210	7-3-81	0	2	8.82	6	3	0	0	16	20	19	16	2	9	11	.294	.400	.250	6.06	4.96
Ramirez, Erasmo	L-L	6-0	190	4-29-76	0	0	0.00	3	0	0	0	3	3	0	0	0	1	0	.273	.000	.429	0.00	3.00
Robertson, Connor	R-R	6-2	225	9-10-81	0	0	18.00	3	0	0	0	3	6	6	6	0	1	3	.545	1.000	.444	9.00	9.00
Street, Huston	R-R	6-0	195	8-2-83	5	2	2.88	48	0	0	16	50	35	20	16	5	12	63	.190	.224	.162	11.34	2.16
Witasick, Jay	R-R	6-4	250	8-28-72	1	0	3.60	16	0	0	0	15	14	6	6	1	9	10	.255	.250	.256	6.00	5.40
2-team (20 Tampa Bay)					1		05.17	36	0	0	0	31	31	19	18	2	27	18	—	—	—	5.17	7.76

FIELDING

Catcher	PCT	G	PO	A	E	DP	PB
Bowen	.990	21	92	4	1	0	1
Kendall	.992	80	485	34	4	4	7
Melhuse	1.000	10	42	5	0	1	1
Suzuki	.996	66	431	32	2	0	7

First Base	PCT	G	PO	A	E	DP
Barton	1.000	18	153	7	0	19
Johnson	.996	97	869	40	4	80
Swisher	.993	44	391	25	3	31
Walker	1.000	10	87	8	0	10

Second Base	PCT	G	PO	A	E	DP
Ellis	.994	150	302	499	5	104
Furmaniak	1.000	4	3	4	0	2
Murphy	1.000	2	1	1	0	1
Scutaro	1.000	13	19	44	0	10

Third Base	PCT	G	PO	A	E	DP
Chavez	.975	88	66	169	6	16
Furmaniak	1.000	2	0	2	0	0
Hannahan	.970	41	19	78	3	10
Melhuse	1.000	1	0	1	0	0
Murphy	1.000	1	0	1	0	0
Scutaro	.906	36	23	64	9	2

Shortstop	PCT	G	PO	A	E	DP
Crosby	.967	92	131	282	14	61
Furmaniak	.909	3	5	5	1	3
Murphy	.962	31	35	91	5	22
Scutaro	.970	43	52	111	5	22

Outfield	PCT	G	PO	A	E	DP
Bocachica	.909	6	10	0	1	0
Bradley	1.000	18	34	0	0	0
Brown	1.000	8	3	0	0	0
Buck	1.000	80	145	3	0	0
Cust	.959	60	93	1	4	0
DaVanon	1.000	25	40	1	0	0
Furmaniak	1.000	3	1	0	0	0
Kendall	1.000	2	1	0	0	0
Kielty	1.000	10	13	1	0	1
Kotsay	.986	56	141	5	2	3
Langerhans	.857	2	5	1	1	0
Putnam	.950	11	19	0	1	0
Scutaro	1.000	10	10	0	0	0
Snelling	1.000	6	9	1	0	0
Stewart	.987	142	289	4	4	2
Swisher	.992	105	246	3	2	0
Thompson	.800	8	4	0	1	0
Walker	—	1	0	0	0	0

SACRAMENTO RIVER CATS

TRIPLE-A

PACIFIC COAST LEAGUE

BATTING	B-T	HT	WT	DOB	AVG	vLH	vRH	G	AB	R	H	2B	3B	HR	RBI	BB	HBP	SH	SF	SO	SB	CS	SLG	OBP
Barton, Daric	L-R	6-0	225	8-16-85	.293	.268	.304	136	516	84	151	38	5	9	70	78	6	0	4	69	3	4	.438	.389
Blasi, Nicholas	R-R	5-10	200	9-23-81	.316	.389	.287	89	313	55	99	12	2	4	41	28	3	7	1	85	10	4	.406	.377
Bocachica, Hiram	R-R	5-11	195	3-4-76	.318	.300	.326	35	129	27	41	11	1	9	32	25	6	0	0	19	8	3	.628	.450
2-team (13 Portland)					.287	—		48	167	30	48	12	1	9	35	37	7	0	1	24	10	3	.533	.434
Bradley, Milton	B-R	6-0	225	4-15-78	.000		.000	2	1	0	0	0	0	0	0	0	0	0	0	0	0	0	.000	.000
Brown, Dee	L-R	6-0	220	3-27-78	.298	.308	.294	62	245	47	73	14	0	14	54	24	2	0	6	52	2	0	.527	.357
2-team (41 Tucson)					.293	—		103	376	72	110	21	0	16	78	37	3	0	6	76	3	1	.476	.355
Brown, Jeremy	R-R	5-10	220	10-25-79	.276	.265	.280	94	341	46	94	22	1	14	58	47	1	0	1	74	0	0	.469	.364
Buck, Travis	L-R	6-2	225	11-18-83	.143	1.000	.000	2	7	0	1	0	1	0	1	2	0	0	0	2	0	0	.429	.333
Castillo, David	R-R	5-9	185	9-15-81	.125	.000	.143	5	8	2	1	0	0	1	2	2	0	0	0	4	0	0	.300	.300
Closser, JD	B-R	5-10	200	1-15-80	.238	.191	.252	81	286	45	68	16	2	11	45	48	0	2	2	67	0	2	.423	.345
2-team (17 Nashville)					.231	—		98	334	54	77	18	2	13	51	59	0	2	4	77	3	3	.413	.343
Cornejo, Eduardo	L-R	5-10	175	11-19-81	.286	.000	.364	8	28	3	8	0	0	0	3	2	0	0	0	7	0	0	.286	.333
DaVanon, Jeff	B-R	6-0	200	12-8-73	.321	.500	.292	7	28	7	9	1	0	1	2	7	0	0	0	5	1	3	.464	.457
2-team (5 Tucson)					.326	—		12	43	10	14	1	0	1	2	8	1	0	0	7	1	3	.419	.442
Furmaniak, J.J.	R-R	5-11	185	7-31-79	.292	.275	.298	106	424	70	124	18	2	15	51	49	8	5	4	105	21	8	.450	.373
Johnson, Dan	L-R	6-2	225	8-10-79	.600	.000	.600	2	5	1	3	0	0	0	0	3	3	0	0	0	0	0	1.200	.750
Kielty, Bobby	B-R	6-1	225	8-5-76	.394	.429	.385	9	33	6	13	4	0	1	4	0	0	0	0	7	0	0	.515	.459
Kotsay, Mark	L-L	6-0	205	12-2-75	.270	.444	.214	10	37	2	10	1	0	0	2	7	0	0	1	2	0	0	.297	.386
Melhuse, Adam	B-R	6-2	210	3-27-72	.375	—	.375	2	8	0	3	2	0	0	0	0	0	0	0	3	0	0	.625	.375
Melillo, Kevin	L-R	5-10	195	5-14-82	.262	.230	.277	98	382	63	100	27	6	10	55	54	2	4	1	100	8	7	.442	.355
Merloni, Lou	R-R	5-10	200	4-6-71	.254	.261	.252	110	393	47	100	21	2	3	39	40	3	5	5	51	1	4	.341	.324
Murphy, Donnie	R-R	5-10	185	3-10-83	.326	.511	.258	45	175	31	57	19	2	3	22	17	2	3	2	44	4	2	.509	.388
Perez, Antonio	R-R	5-11	185	1-26-80	.218	.192	.230	26	87	9	19	3	1	2	6	6	4	1	1	21	1	2	.345	.343
Perry, Jason	L-R	6-0	200	8-18-80	.268	.208	.288	78	284	59	76	16	1	18	58	41	5	1	2	89	4	0	.521	.367
Petit, Gregorio	R-R	5-10	160	12-10-84	.277	.220	.295	67	235	20	65	12	0	2	28	16	3	3	3	48	1	2	.353	.327
Piazza, Mike	R-R	6-3	215	9-4-68	.412	.500	.385	3	17	1	7	2	0	0	1	0	0	0	0	3	0	0	.529	.412
Piedra, Jorge	L-L	6-0	200	4-17-79	.336	.288	.357	71	265	42	89	24	2	9	56	33	5	0	3	37	0	1	.543	.415
Powell, Landon	B-R	6-3	240	3-19-82	.294	1.000	.250	4	17	3	5	0	0	3	3	0	0	0	0	4	0	0	.824	.294
Putnam, Danny	L-L	5-10	200	9-17-82	.216	.182	.228	51	171	14	37	11	1	1	17	17	4	1	0	41	2	2	.310	.302
Robnett, Richie	L-L	5-10	200	9-17-83	.152	.000	.263	10	33	6	5	0	0	1	4	1	1	1	0	16	0	0	.152	.263
Snelling, Chris	L-L	5-10	205	12-3-81	.158	.333	.125	6	19	1	3	0	0	0	2	3	1	0	0	6	0	0	.158	.304
Stavisky, Brian	L-R	6-2	210	7-6-80	.238	.242	.235	22	84	8	20	6	0	1	12	3	0	1	0	20	1	1	.345	.264
Stokes, Jason	R-R	6-4	225	1-24-82	.186	.190	.184	18	59	10	11	0	0	5	11	9	0	0	2	23	0	0	.441	.294
Suzuki, Kurt	R-R	6-0	205	10-4-83	.280	.344	.252	55	211	32	59	9	0	3	27	21	4	1	3	41	0	0	.365	.351
Thomas, Charles	L-L	6-0	220	12-26-78	.230	.167	.260	22	74	7	17	2	0	0	5	6	1	0	0	15	2	0	.257	.296
2-team (69 Nashville)					.232	—		91	263	32	61	12	0	3	25	24	1	3	2	59	8	1	.312	.297
Turner, Lloyd	R-R	6-1	175	4-11-80	.203	.182	.213	36	69	16	14	2	2	0	5	8	1	3	1	16	2	0	.290	.291

PITCHING	B-T	HT	WT	DOB	W	L	ERA	G	GS	CG	SV	IP	H	R	ER	HR	BB	SO	AVG	vLH	vRH	K/9	BB/9
Alliston, Josh	R-R	6-5	232	2-29-80	0	0	0.00	2	0	0	0	4	2	0	0	0	0	4	.154	.500	.000	4.91	0.00
Bailey, Andrew	R-R	6-3	220	5-31-84	1	0	1.13	1	1	0	0	8	3	1	1	0	1	4	.115	.050	.333	4.50	1.12
Blevins, Jerry	L-L	6-6	185	9-6-83	1	0	0.00	1	0	0	0	3	1	0	0	0	0	4	.111	.000	.200	13.50	0.00
Bondurant, Steven	L-L	6-0	185	3-3-80	0	0	19.29	4	0	0	0	5	9	10	10	0	4	3	.429	.357	.571	5.79	7.71
Braden, Dallas	L-L	6-1	185	8-13-83	2	3	2.95	11	11	2	0	64	51	22	21	4	18	74	.213	.234	.204	10.41	2.53
Brown, Andrew	R-R	6-6	230	2-17-81	0	0	3.60	5	0	0	4	5	6	2	2	1	0	6	.300	.250	.333	10.80	0.00
2-team (32 Portland)					2	3	2.88	37	0	0	4	41	32	16	13	4	15	49	—			10.84	3.32
Casilla, Santiago	R-R	6-0	200	7-25-80	2	1	4.13	22	0	0	3	24	18	11	11	1	14	29	.209	.345	.140	10.88	5.25
Castillo, David	R-R	5-9	185	9-15-81	0	0	9.00	1	0	0	0	2	2	2	2	0	0	1	.250	.200	.333	4.50	0.00
Davis, Bradley	R-L	6-1	185	12-20-82	1	0	0.00	1	1	0	0	7	6	0	0	0	2	2	.240	.385	.083	2.57	2.57
Flores, Ron	L-L	5-10	195	8-9-79	1	2	2.72	40	0	0	1	36	38	22	11	4	17	26	.266	.240	.294	6.44	4.21
Foley, Charles	R-R	6-0	205	3-11-83	1	3	7.56	6	1	0	0	8	11	7	7	0	12	13	.306	.333	.278	12.96	7.56
Gray, Jeff	R-R	6-3	205	11-19-81	2	4	4.09	46	0	0	12	55	58	27	25	2	22	45	.274	.211	.300	7.36	3.60
Halsey, Brad	L-L	6-1	185	2-14-81	2	0	2.65	3	3	0	0	17	15	5	5	2	3	17	.238	.091	.317	9.00	1.59
Harden, Rich	L-R	6-1	190	11-30-81	0	0	0.00	1	0	0	0	1	0	0	0	0	0	2	.000	—	.000	18.00	0.00
Knox, Brad	R-R	6-2	230	5-27-82	9	7	4.79	23	22	1	0	139	151	89	74	14	43	67	.277	.280	.275	4.34	2.78
Kohn, Shawn	R-R	6-2	208	1-28-80	1	2	6.65	27	1	0	1	47	60	36	35	12	20	49	.316	.412	.262	9.32	3.80
Komine, Shane	R-R	5-9	180	10-18-80	5	12	4.87	23	23	0	0	133	143	76	72	21	46	99	.280	.298	.267	6.70	3.11
Landeros, Leonard	L-L	6-3	177	12-12-80	0	0	6.35	4	0	0	0	6	6	4	4	0	4	1	.300	.300	.300	1.59	6.35
Lewis, Colby	R-R	6-4	230	8-2-79	8	3	1.88	15	15	0	0	96	70	24	20	8	23	97	.202	.190	.210	9.13	2.16

Name	B-T	HT	WT	DOB	W	L	ERA	G	GS	CG	SV	IP	H	R	ER	HR	BB	SO	AVG	vLH	vRH	K/9	BB/9
Loaiza, Esteban	R-R	6-2	230	12-31-71	2	1	3.86	6	6	0	0	28	35	13	12	3	4	13	.313	.275	.333	4.18	1.29
Lugo, Ruddy	R-R	6-0	215	5-22-80	3	0	0.45	17	0	0	10	20	5	1	1	0	7	22	.081	.080	.081	9.90	3.15
Madsen, Michael	R-R	6-0	160	11-29-82	5	1	5.09	10	10	0	0	58	54	35	33	8	30	40	.245	.202	.281	6.17	4.63
Manon, Julio	R-R	6-0	200	6-10-73	1	1	3.44	15	0	0	1	18	10	9	7	3	8	29	.149	.080	.190	14.24	3.93
McBeth, Marcus	R-R	6-2	195	8-23-80	1	0	1.80	8	0	0	5	10	7	3	2	2	3	6	.200	.286	.143	5.40	2.70
Meaux, Ryan	L-L	5-11	170	10-5-78	0	0	1.98	13	0	0	0	14	12	4	3	0	4	14	.231	.269	.192	9.22	2.63
3-team (7 Fresno, 7 Memphis)					0	3	5.68	27	0	0	0	32	41	23	20	3	10	32	—	—	—	9.09	2.84
Meyer, Dan	R-L	6-3	210	7-3-81	8	2	3.28	21	21	0	0	115	103	44	42	12	51	105	.243	.310	.215	8.19	3.98
Montero, Agustin	R-R	6-3	210	8-26-77	0	0	27.00	1	0	0	0	1	1	2	2	1	3	1	.333	.500	.000	13.50	40.50
Olsen, Kevin	R-R	6-2	195	7-26-76	0	1	9.31	2	2	0	0	10	18	11	10	0	1	5	.409	.286	.522	4.66	0.93
Ramirez, Erasmo	L-L	6-0	190	4-29-76	3	0	1.27	19	0	0	2	21	18	3	3	0	2	11	.225	.211	.238	4.64	0.84
2-team (22 Albuquerque)					5	1	2.51	41	0	0	3	43	45	13	12	3	6	21	—	—	—	4.40	1.26
Ramirez, Luis	R-R	6-4	202	6-9-82	0	0	2.70	1	1	0	0	3	7	2	1	0	1	4	.389	.455	.286	10.80	2.70
Ramos, Mario	L-L	5-11	180	10-19-77	1	1	6.00	2	2	0	0	9	12	6	6	1	8	6	.308	.375	.290	6.00	8.00
Robertson, Connor	R-R	6-2	225	9-10-81	4	1	4.35	31	0	0	2	39	43	25	19	3	21	40	.283	.339	.247	9.15	4.81
Shafer, David	R-R	6-2	195	3-7-82	1	1	7.79	26	0	0	0	35	37	33	30	8	24	23	.276	.283	.272	5.97	6.23
Street, Huston	R-R	6-0	195	8-2-83	0	0	0.00	1	1	0	0	1	1	0	0	0	0	2	.250	.000	1.000	18.00	0.00
Tadano, Kazuhito	R-R	6-0	180	4-25-80	5	5	5.20	22	12	0	0	88	100	54	51	14	30	84	.281	.294	.269	8.56	3.06
Turner, Lloyd	R-R	6-1	175	4-11-80	0	0	0.00	1	0	0	0	1	1	0	0	0	0	1	.000	.000	—	0.00	9.00
Van Buren, Jermaine	R-R	6-2	200	7-2-80	1	0	2.25	21	0	0	2	24	20	6	6	1	11	26	.215	.263	.182	9.75	4.12
Windsor, Jason	R-R	6-2	235	7-16-82	5	3	5.40	10	10	0	0	57	67	36	34	3	25	41	.302	.315	.289	6.51	3.97
Ziegler, Brad	R-R	6-4	190	10-10-79	8	3	2.96	35	0	0	1	55	46	20	18	0	14	44	.231	.349	.176	7.24	2.30
Zumwalt, Alec	R-R	6-2	195	1-20-81	0	3	6.96	20	1	0	0	32	39	25	25	6	17	29	.312	.420	.240	8.07	4.73
2-team (14 Nashville)					0	5	5.98	34	1	0	1	53	60	35	35	9	26	49	—	—	—	8.37	4.44

FIELDING

Catcher	PCT	G	PO	A	E	DP	PB
J. Brown	.984	55	412	26	7	4	3
Castillo	1.000	2	8	0	0	0	0
Closser	.992	45	342	18	3	3	3
Melhuse	1.000	1	7	1	0	0	0
Powell	.969	4	27	4	1	0	0
Suzuki	.991	44	318	24	3	6	1

First Base	PCT	G	PO	A	E	DP
Barton	.992	115	964	72	8	103
J. Brown	.992	15	110	8	1	11
Closser	.970	8	58	6	2	6
Johnson	1.000	2	10	2	0	1
Merloni	.975	4	38	1	1	6
Piedra	1.000	1	3	0	0	0
Stokes	.984	7	54	6	1	5

Second Base	PCT	G	PO	A	E	DP
Cornejo	.972	7	15	20	1	8
Furmaniak	.970	25	57	73	4	17
Melillo	.977	88	167	263	10	61
Merloni	.983	15	23	36	1	9

	PCT	G	PO	A	E	DP
Murphy	1.000	4	7	4	0	2
Petit	.976	8	16	24	1	6
Turner	.900	2	2	7	1	0

Third Base	PCT	G	PO	A	E	DP
Barton	.816	18	8	32	9	4
J. Brown	.933	10	6	8	1	1
Furmaniak	.953	21	15	46	3	6
Melillo	.955	11	2	19	1	1
Merloni	.931	83	30	131	12	15
Murphy	1.000	1	1	1	0	0
Perez	1.000	4	4	4	0	1
Turner	.947	6	1	17	1	2

Shortstop	PCT	G	PO	A	E	DP
Furmaniak	.979	43	74	110	4	29
Merloni	1.000	8	12	15	0	4
Murphy	.983	39	64	107	3	26
Petit	.964	58	110	188	11	47

Outfield	PCT	G	PO	A	E	DP
Blasi	.995	88	210	6	1	1
Bocachica	.959	32	68	2	3	0
Bradley	1.000	2	1	0	0	0
D. Brown	1.000	25	41	2	0	0
Buck	1.000	2	2	0	0	0
DaVanon	.941	7	16	0	1	0
Furmaniak	.949	18	36	1	2	1
Kielty	1.000	6	7	1	0	0
Kotsay	1.000	7	6	0	0	0
Merloni	1.000	2	2	2	0	0
Murphy	—	1	0	1	0	1
Perez	1.000	20	39	1	0	1
Perry	.993	77	140	5	1	1
Piedra	.982	53	104	3	2	0
Putnam	1.000	47	87	2	0	2
Robnett	1.000	10	17	1	0	0
Snelling	1.000	3	3	0	0	0
Stavisky	.960	20	24	0	1	0
Thomas	.952	21	38	2	2	1
Turner	.917	21	22	0	2	0

MIDLAND ROCKHOUNDS

DOUBLE-A

TEXAS LEAGUE

BATTING	B-T	HT	WT	DOB	AVG	vLH	vRH	G	AB	R	H	2B	3B	HR	RBI	BB	HBP	SH	SF	SO	SB	CS	SLG	OBP
Appert, Luke	L-R	6-0	185	7-14-80	.276	.250	.284	79	275	36	76	17	1	5	45	48	4	3	6	49	1	0	.400	.384
Baisley, Jeff	R-R	6-3	210	12-19-82	.257	.220	.271	101	404	60	104	22	3	11	46	29	3	0	6	84	1	1	.408	.308
Blasi, Nicholas	R-R	5-10	200	9-23-81	.393	.364	.412	7	28	3	11	1	0	0	2	1	0	0	0	6	0	0	.429	.414
Castillo, David	R-R	5-9	185	9-15-81	.135	.000	.152	14	37	4	5	2	0	0	0	5	1	1	0	11	0	0	.189	.256
Colamarino, Brant	L-L	5-10	221	12-4-80	.241	.198	.259	101	361	40	87	22	0	9	44	32	10	1	1	78	1	1	.377	.319
Cornejo, Eduardo	L-R	5-10	175	11-19-81	.286	.231	.299	59	196	22	56	11	0	2	26	17	1	3	0	22	3	2	.372	.346
Everidge, Tommy	R-R	6-1	215	4-20-83	.361	.364	.361	10	36	7	13	4	0	0	4	2	0	0	0	5	0	0	.472	.395
Faison, Vince	L-R	5-11	195	1-22-81	.227	.266	.216	99	348	36	79	18	9	5	46	23	3	9	1	83	11	3	.374	.280
Herrera, Javier	R-R	5-10	205	4-9-85	.254	.294	.241	20	71	13	18	5	0	3	13	4	3	0	1	13	1	0	.451	.316
Leslie, Myron	B-R	6-3	220	5-2-82	.288	.311	.277	108	386	53	111	28	1	5	47	60	0	1	3	75	1	1	.404	.386
Myers, Casey	R-R	5-10	209	10-23-78	.303	.170	.406	35	122	21	37	3	1	3	13	15	3	2	2	18	0	0	.418	.387
Pennington, Cliff	B-R	5-11	185	6-15-84	.251	.162	.284	70	271	41	68	13	2	2	21	38	1	2	2	35	8	2	.336	.343
Perry, Jason	L-R	6-0	200	8-18-80	.256	.160	.302	21	78	15	20	7	0	5	17	11	6	0	0	20	0	0	.538	.389
Petit, Gregorio	R-R	5-10	160	12-10-84	.306	.300	.309	66	268	33	82	14	0	4	31	25	1	4	1	44	9	3	.403	.366
Powell, Landon	B-R	6-3	240	3-19-82	.292	.290	.293	60	219	46	64	9	2	11	39	36	0	0	1	40	1	0	.502	.391
Putnam, Danny	L-L	5-10	200	9-17-82	.327	.222	.349	13	52	9	17	1	2	1	15	5	0	0	0	4	1	2	.615	.386
Recker, Anthony	R-R	6-2	225	8-29-83	.204	.148	.229	58	201	16	41	12	0	4	20	17	1	0	0	63	0	1	.323	.269
Robnett, Richie	L-L	5-10	185	9-17-83	.267	.228	.284	120	490	73	131	39	2	18	74	34	3	0	4	130	4	3	.465	.316
Sellers, Justin	R-R	5-10	160	2-1-86	.156	.143	.158	14	45	2	7	1	0	0	3	3	1	2	0	10	2	0	.178	.224
Snyder, Brian	R-R	6-0	195	3-17-82	.254	.299	.236	111	370	63	94	31	1	8	48	75	2	2	4	100	1	1	.408	.379
Spanos, Vasili	R-R	6-1	225	2-25-81	.276	.270	.278	100	392	51	108	25	3	10	52	17	13	0	1	69	4	2	.431	.326

PITCHING	B-T	HT	WT	DOB	W	L	ERA	G	GS	CG	SV	IP	H	R	ER	HR	BB	SO	AVG	vLH	vRH	K/9	BB/9
Alliston, Josh	R-R	6-5	232	2-29-80	0	0	15.00	2	0	0	0	3	7	6	5	1	1	1	.467	.500	.444	3.00	3.00
Blevins, Jerry	L-L	6-6	185	9-6-83	1	3	3.32	17	0	0	1	22	18	10	8	2	5	29	.234	.240	.231	12.05	2.08
Bondurant, Steven	L-L	6-0	185	3-3-80	1	1	3.86	11	0	0	0	14	12	6	6	2	8	9	.240	.211	.258	5.79	5.14
Borrell, Danny	L-L	6-3	200	1-24-79	3	3	2.80	19	9	0	0	64	43	22	20	8	27	73	.185	.239	.163	10.21	3.78
Braden, Dallas	L-L	6-1	185	8-13-83	1	0	2.25	2	2	0	0	12	5	3	3	2	3	13	.128	.116	.136	9.75	2.25
Bumatay, Mike	L-L	6-0	170	10-9-79	3	1	5.54	27	0	0	1	26	28	20	16	4	22	31	.286	.290	.284	10.73	7.62
Coleman, Jeffrey	R-R	5-11	193	10-6-80	0	2	9.00	5	0	0	0	6	11	10	6	2	3	4	.367	.267	.467	6.00	4.50
Cramer, Bobby	L-L	6-1	193	10-28-79	5	1	1.89	12	7	0	0	52	45	17	11	3	10	50	.225	.149	.248	8.60	1.72
Deaton, Kevin	R-R	6-2	265	8-7-81	0	4	6.82	6	6	0	0	34	42	26	26	6	13	22	.307	.300	.312	5.79	3.41

Denham, Dan	R-R	6-2	195	12-24-82	1	1	4.86	12	0	0	0	17	21	11	9	3	7	7	.309	.361	.250	3.78	3.78
Faison, Vince	L-R	5-11	195	1-22-81	0	0	9.00	1	0	0	0	2	0	2	2	0	2	0	.000	.000	.000	0.00	9.00
Flannery, Mike	R-R	6-1	195	9-20-79	0	1	6.59	12	0	0	0	14	13	12	10	1	15	12	.250	.214	.292	7.90	9.88
Foley, Travis	R-R	6-0	205	3-11-83	4	1	4.14	39	0	0	0	4	46	42	22	21	3	16	44	.240	.356	.181	8.67	3.15
Fritz, Benjamin	R-R	6-4	238	3-29-81	11	11	5.67	28	28	0	0	149	173	99	94	8	68	88	.299	.295	.303	5.30	4.10
Glushon, Jason	R-R	6-2	195	5-26-85	0	1	3.00	2	1	0	0	6	8	4	2	1	1	9	.308	.250	.357	13.50	1.50
Gray, Jeff	R-R	6-3	205	11-19-81	2	0	0.00	8	0	0	3	12	7	1	0	0	2	12	.175	.111	.227	8.76	1.46
Kilby, Brad	L-L	6-2	225	2-19-83	3	3	2.88	47	0	0	0	66	63	24	21	6	22	69	.258	.237	.272	9.46	3.02
Knox, Brad	R-R	6-2	230	5-27-82	1	0	2.19	4	4	0	0	25	18	6	6	1	6	13	.202	.143	.255	4.74	2.19
Kohn, Shawn	R-R	6-2	208	1-28-80	0	4	3.23	23	1	0	0	39	25	14	14	4	15	44	.180	.123	.220	10.15	3.46
Leslie, Myron	B-R	6-3	220	5-2-82	0	0	0.00	1	0	0	0	2	2	0	0	0	1	0	.250	.250	.250	0.00	4.50
Madsen, Michael	R-R	6-0	160	11-29-82	5	2	2.76	11	11	1	0	65	51	21	20	2	26	69	.223	.270	.175	9.51	3.58
Meaux, Ryan	R-L	5-11	170	10-5-78	0	1	11.25	6	0	0	0	8	14	10	10	2	3	7	.389	.409	.357	7.88	3.38
2-team (4 Springfield)					0	1	9.26	10	0	0	0	12	18	12	12	2	3	9	—	—	—	6.94	2.31
Meyer, Dan	R-L	6-3	210	7-3-81	0	0	6.75	1	1	0	0	4	5	3	3	2	4	2	.357	.000	.385	4.50	9.00
Peterson, Trent	R-L	6-1	180	11-16-81	3	6	4.56	13	13	1	0	75	80	45	38	6	32	39	.272	.205	.294	4.68	3.84
Ramirez, Luis	R-R	6-4	202	6-9-82	4	6	5.21	13	13	0	0	67	68	39	39	6	23	50	.260	.289	.225	6.68	3.07
Ramos, Mario	L-L	5-11	180	10-19-77	1	2	5.32	15	7	0	1	46	58	30	27	4	13	36	.305	.323	.297	7.09	2.56
Rogers, Michael	R-R	6-1	205	10-24-82	2	0	7.30	11	2	0	0	25	29	20	20	5	23	13	.319	.350	.294	4.74	8.39
Shafer, David	R-R	6-2	190	3-7-82	0	0	2.28	24	0	0	8	24	19	6	6	1	8	21	.213	.194	.226	7.99	3.04
Sharpe, Steven	R-R	6-1	195	7-20-81	3	1	2.89	26	0	0	9	28	28	10	9	3	6	14	.252	.291	.214	4.50	1.93
Shipman, Andy	R-R	6-3	185	12-10-80	4	7	5.81	28	18	0	0	118	144	82	76	11	47	90	.306	.319	.295	6.88	3.59
Simmons, James	R-R	6-3	205	9-29-86	0	0	3.94	13	2	0	0	30	36	16	13	2	8	23	.308	.262	.333	6.98	2.43
Snyder, Brian	R-R	6-0	195	3-17-82	0	1	27.00	1	1	0	0	2	1	1	1	0	2	0	.667	1.000	.500	0.00	9.00
Tadano, Kazuhito	R-R	6-0	180	4-25-80	3	2	4.14	7	7	0	0	41	42	20	19	7	6	49	.259	.265	.253	10.67	1.31
Thomas, Adam	R-R	6-4	190	5-22-79	2	1	8.31	12	0	0	0	17	21	19	16	2	8	9	.300	.333	.279	4.67	4.15
Webb, Ryan	R-R	6-6	195	2-5-86	0	4	9.12	5	5	0	0	26	34	27	26	10	10	16	.324	.295	.344	5.61	3.51
Ziegler, Brad	R-R	6-4	190	10-10-79	4	0	1.14	15	0	0	1	24	19	6	3	0	4	18	.218	.282	.167	6.85	1.52

FIELDING

Catcher	PCT	G	PO	A	E	DP	PB
Castillo	.981	13	98	6	2	1	1
Myers	.976	13	80	3	2	0	0
Powell	.993	57	403	40	3	2	2
Recker	.976	56	425	21	11	2	8

First Base	PCT	G	PO	A	E	DP
Colamarino	.990	87	633	51	7	59
Everidge	1.000	5	38	3	0	2
Leslie	.969	10	83	10	3	6
Myers	1.000	3	12	2	0	0
Spanos	1.000	39	311	16	0	26

Second Base	PCT	G	PO	A	E	DP
Appert	1.000	2	5	3	0	1
Cornejo	.976	28	53	68	3	7

	PCT	G	PO	A	E	DP
Pennington	.944	6	7	10	1	2
Petit	.889	4	2	6	1	0
Sellers	1.000	8	14	20	0	8
Snyder	.971	96	157	243	12	53

Third Base	PCT	G	PO	A	E	DP
Baisley	.938	96	83	142	15	15
Cornejo	.892	16	10	23	4	0
Leslie	—	1	0	0	0	0
Snyder	.750	6	2	7	3	0
Spanos	.980	21	16	32	1	1

Shortstop	PCT	G	PO	A	E	DP
Baisley	—	1	0	0	0	0
Cornejo	.889	5	10	14	3	1
Pennington	.958	64	111	186	13	39

	PCT	G	PO	A	E	DP
Petit	.972	63	116	165	8	37
Sellers	.941	6	6	10	1	1

Outfield	PCT	G	PO	A	E	DP
Appert	.982	64	102	6	2	0
Blasi	1.000	7	13	0	0	0
Castillo	—	1	0	0	0	0
Colamarino	.900	6	9	0	1	0
Faison	.985	93	246	9	4	2
Herrera	.972	20	35	0	1	0
Leslie	.968	82	143	6	5	1
Perry	.970	18	31	1	1	0
Putnam	1.000	12	18	1	0	0
Robnett	.982	118	273	7	5	1

STOCKTON PORTS   HIGH CLASS A

CALIFORNIA LEAGUE

BATTING	B-T	HT	WT	DOB	AVG	vLH	vRH	G	AB	R	H	2B	3B	HR	RBI	BB	HBP	SH	SF	SO	SB	CS	SLG	OBP
Affronti, Michael	R-R	6-2	195	2-13-84	.321	.345	.313	26	109	18	35	5	2	2	12	7	2	1	3	20	2	1	.459	.364
Appert, Luke	L-R	6-0	185	7-14-80	.352	.265	.375	46	162	31	57	9	1	5	38	41	4	0	3	28	0	0	.512	.486
Arrieche, Carlos	R-R	6-1	177	3-30-85	.156	.000	.217	9	32	3	5	1	0	0	2	0	1	1	0	9	1	1	.188	.182
Blasi, Nicholas	R-R	5-10	200	9-23-81	.239	.211	.244	28	109	19	26	7	0	4	18	11	5	0	1	37	3	1	.413	.333
Boyd, Chad	L-L	5-10	190	3-21-85	.270	.244	.276	102	382	50	103	23	3	8	46	38	5	2	3	70	9	3	.408	.341
Brummett, John	R-R	6-1	205	12-7-83	.146	.267	.091	18	48	4	7	2	0	0	3	4	2	0	1	22	0	0	.188	.236
Castillo, David	R-R	5-9	185	9-15-81	.203	.333	.152	18	64	8	13	2	0	2	12	7	1	0	3	15	0	0	.328	.280
Everidge, Tommy	R-R	6-1	215	4-20-83	.258	.237	.264	124	461	75	119	13	3	26	90	66	6	0	6	103	2	2	.469	.354
Herrera, Javier	R-R	5-10	205	4-9-85	.274	.174	.296	62	252	45	69	17	0	9	39	19	6	0	2	60	11	7	.448	.327
Kleen, Steve	R-R	6-4	200	5-21-83	.272	.274	.272	118	430	75	117	24	2	5	45	49	8	0	2	92	2	1	.372	.356
Lawhorn, Darryl	L-R	6-2	180	12-18-82	.185	.231	.172	37	119	15	22	3	1	5	12	19	0	0	0	39	0	1	.353	.297
Martinez, Frank	B-R	6-0	164	7-19-85	.267	.250	.271	131	499	65	133	28	6	12	60	35	5	3	2	96	14	4	.419	.320
Omura, Isaac	L-R	5-10	175	1-21-84	.195	.176	.200	27	77	5	15	4	0	1	9	11	0	0	1	26	0	1	.286	.292
Padron, Raul	L-R	6-0	195	9-17-84	.223	.224	.223	96	345	48	77	25	0	13	52	22	1	3	4	87	2	2	.409	.269
Pennington, Cliff	B-R	5-11	185	6-15-84	.255	.224	.262	68	286	50	73	17	3	6	36	43	0	4	54	9	2		.399	.348
Piazza, Mike	R-R	6-3	215	9-4-68	.333	—	.333	3	9	2	3	0	0	2	4	2	0	0	3	0	1.000	.001	.455
Pineda, Jose	R-R	6-2	175	2-25-82	.271	.236	.280	112	414	66	112	25	2	10	64	35	5	0	4	112	3	5	.486	.332
Putnam, Danny	L-L	5-10	200	9-17-82	.286	.250	.300	3	14	3	4	1	0	1	5	0	0	0	0	0	.571	.286
Recker, Anthony	R-R	6-2	225	8-29-83	.319	.457	.291	56	207	39	66	17	2	13	47	27	5	0	5	48	2	0	.600	.402
Sellers, Justin	R-R	5-10	160	2-1-86	.274	.263	.277	114	434	72	119	25	4	4	37	46	8	1	6	69	11	4	.378	.350
Stavisky, Brian	L-R	6-2	210	7-6-80	.350	.375	.333	6	20	5	7	0	2	2	7	7	0	0	1	0	0	.850	.500
Turner, Lloyd	R-R	6-1	175	4-11-80	.230	.324	.200	43	152	26	35	7	1	5	16	10	5	1	2	31	5	6	.388	.296
Zeringue, Jon	R-R	6-2	215	3-29-83	.279	.283	.278	56	204	30	57	12	0	13	42	32	3	0	3	63	2	2	.529	.380

PITCHING	B-T	HT	WT	DOB	W	L	ERA	G	GS	CG	SV	IP	H	R	ER	HR	BB	SO	AVG	vLH	vRH	K/9	BB/9
Alliston, Josh	R-R	6-5	232	2-29-80	1	1	4.12	13	0	0	1	20	18	12	9	1	9	16	.243	.208	.260	7.32	4.12
Bailey, Andrew	R-R	6-3	220	5-31-84	3	4	3.82	11	11	0	0	66	56	31	28	8	31	72	.239	.286	.191	9.82	4.23
Bondurant, Steven	L-L	6-0	185	3-3-80	2	1	7.11	4	0	0	0	6	8	5	5	0	6	3	.296	.333	.278	4.26	8.53
Cramer, Bobby	L-L	6-1	193	10-28-79	4	1	3.80	9	8	0	0	45	45	23	19	1	10	41	.256	.237	.265	8.20	2.00
Currin, Patrick	R-R	6-0	190	5-12-84	4	7	4.80	43	1	0	12	66	65	39	35	5	22	73	.259	.316	.209	10.01	3.02
Davis, Bradley	R-L	6-1	185	12-20-82	6	6	5.17	30	15	0	1	111	110	66	64	15	36	80	.257	.267	.253	6.47	2.91
Deaton, Kevin	R-R	6-4	265	8-7-81	1	1	2.29	4	3	1	0	20	11	5	5	1	3	18	.167	.146	.200	8.24	1.37
Demel, Sam	R-R	6-0	210	10-23-85	0	0	7.07	11	0	0	0	14	16	16	11	2	15	13	.302	.296	.308	8.36	9.63

	B-T	HT	WT	DOB	W	L	ERA	G	GS	CG	SV	IP	H	R	ER	HR	BB	SO	AVG	vLH	vRH	K/9	BB/9
Denham, Dan	R-R	6-2	195	12-24-82	1	0	11.25	4	0	0	0	4	4	6	5	1	4	3	.222	.091	.429	6.75	9.00
Dewing, Branden	L-L	6-0	165	1-1-84	2	5	5.76	21	6	0	0	50	65	40	32	2	24	29	.307	.240	.343	5.22	4.32
Duchscherer, Justin	R-R	6-3	205	11-19-77	0	0	0.00	1	1	0	0	1	0	0	0	0	1	1	.000	.000	.000	9.00	0.00
Espinal, Leonardo	R-R	6-3	203	2-6-84	0	0	34.71	2	0	0	0	2	6	9	9	1	7	2	.462	.667	.400	7.71	27.00
Franco Jr., TJ	R-R	6-2	190	6-28-83	0	1	5.73	22	1	0	0	44	56	31	28	5	22	26	.309	.289	.330	5.32	4.50
Guzman, Jose	R-R	5-11	185	11-5-87	1	3	6.91	7	5	0	0	29	36	23	22	4	15	15	.313	.297	.333	4.71	4.71
Herrera, John	R-R	6-6	195	3-8-83	0	0	10.57	6	0	0	0	8	13	11	9	2	6	6	.382	.154	.524	7.04	7.04
Jukich, Ben	L-L	6-4	190	10-17-82	3	4	5.40	12	12	0	0	58	61	42	35	8	15	46	.261	.290	.248	7.10	2.31
Kilby, Brad	L-L	6-2	225	2-19-83	0	0	3.24	7	0	0	0	8	8	6	3	0	6	16	.176	.333	.091	17.28	6.48
Landeros, Leonard	L-L	6-3	177	12-12-80	0	2	9.20	12	0	0	0	15	17	15	15	3	12	17	.298	.273	.314	10.43	7.36
Lansford, Jared	R-R	6-2	190	10-22-86	0	1	9.00	1	1	0	0	5	4	4	4	0	3	2	.385	.400	.333	4.50	6.75
Madsen, Michael	R-R	6-0	160	11-29-82	1	2	3.75	4	4	0	0	24	21	10	10	1	9	20	.250	.256	.244	7.50	3.38
Mazzaro, Vincent	R-R	6-2	190	9-27-86	9	12	5.33	28	28	0	0	154	159	97	91	13	71	115	.271	.266	.277	6.74	4.16
Mitchell, Michael	R-R	6-2	200	10-27-81	0	0	3.24	5	0	0	0	8	7	5	3	1	6	6	.241	.333	.143	6.48	6.48
Muessig, Jeff	R-R	6-0	208	2-27-82	1	2	4.86	45	0	0	6	67	60	38	36	13	40	73	.238	.241	.236	9.86	5.40
Oakes, Earl	R-R	6-3	225	9-3-85	0	0	2.16	6	0	0	0	8	10	2	2	1	3	1	.313	.250	.350	1.08	3.24
Padron, Raul	L-R	6-0	195	9-17-84	0	0	9.00	1	0	0	0	1	1	1	1	0	2	0	.250	.000	.250	0.00	18.00
Peterson, Trent	R-L	6-1	180	11-16-81	5	3	4.01	17	8	0	1	61	61	35	27	4	27	41	.260	.241	.270	6.08	4.01
Ramirez, Luis	R-R	6-4	201	6-9-82	6	1	5.31	16	8	0	0	59	52	39	35	9	33	68	.228	.260	.190	10.31	5.01
Ray, Jason	R-R	5-11	195	7-14-84	1	1	2.53	8	0	0	0	11	5	4	3	0	9	14	.143	.222	.059	11.81	7.59
Rogers, Michael	R-R	6-1	205	10-24-82	2	6	8.95	19	12	0	0	64	73	71	64	14	56	65	.284	.303	.259	9.09	7.83
Semerano, Rob	R-R	6-1	185	7-18-81	6	1	6.04	15	0	0	3	22	23	15	15	3	12	18	.277	.333	.240	7.25	4.84
Sheridan, Eric	R-R	6-1	175	9-22-83	2	3	3.38	22	0	0	0	37	23	14	14	0	31	43	.177	.236	.133	10.37	7.47
Sullivan, Brad	R-R	6-0	195	9-12-81	0	0	6.43	5	0	0	0	7	11	6	5	0	3	4	.355	.300	.455	5.14	3.86
Tharpe, Derek	L-L	5-11	188	10-30-81	0	0	5.09	16	0	0	1	23	36	18	13	3	10	21	.356	.281	.391	8.22	3.91
Thomas, Adam	R-R	6-4	190	5-22-79	5	2	4.29	24	1	0	4	36	41	28	17	1	14	42	.270	.333	.213	10.60	3.53
Turner, Lloyd	R-R	6-1	175	4-11-80	0	0	9.00	1	0	0	0	1	2	1	1	0	0	0	.400	.000	.667	0.00	9.00
Walters, Nick	L-L	6-2	175	9-30-85	0	0	3.00	2	0	0	0	3	1	1	1	0	2	1	.111	.000	.143	3.00	6.00
Webb, Ryan	R-R	6-6	195	2-5-86	4	7	5.75	15	15	0	0	83	83	59	53	13	22	71	.255	.272	.234	7.70	2.39

FIELDING

Catcher	PCT	G	PO	A	E	DP	PB
Brummett	.979	10	45	2	1	1	2
Castillo	.981	17	138	15	3	3	4
Padron	.985	62	491	42	8	2	14
Recker	.989	53	414	39	5	2	15
Zeringue	1.000	2	10	1	0	0	0

First Base	PCT	G	PO	A	E	DP
Everidge	.984	98	750	86	14	80
Kleen	.992	32	237	27	2	25
Padron	.963	12	98	7	4	16

Second Base	PCT	G	PO	A	E	DP
Affronti	.964	19	29	51	3	6
Arrieche	.923	5	6	18	2	2
Martinez	.968	40	72	109	6	28
Omura	1.000	15	18	36	0	9
Pennington	1.000	2	1	4	0	1

	PCT	G	PO	A	E	DP
Sellers	.952	60	122	178	15	44
Turner	.889	7	12	12	3	2

Third Base	PCT	G	PO	A	E	DP
Appert	.964	12	13	14	1	1
Arrieche	1.000	3	3	4	0	0
Kleen	.826	8	8	11	4	3
Lawhorn	.921	15	7	28	3	5
Martinez	.897	92	65	143	24	13
Omura	.750	7	3	9	4	0
Turner	.920	9	5	18	2	4

Shortstop	PCT	G	PO	A	E	DP
Affronti	.926	9	7	18	2	4
Arrieche	.750	1	1	2	1	0
Martinez	.600	1	2	1	2	1
Omura	.875	1	3	4	1	0
Pennington	.956	66	117	187	14	40

	PCT	G	PO	A	E	DP
Sellers	.973	52	103	145	7	33
Turner	.960	14	22	26	2	7

Outfield	PCT	G	PO	A	E	DP
Appert	.974	22	37	1	1	0
Blasi	1.000	28	45	3	0	1
Boyd	.953	76	116	7	6	3
Dewing	1.000	1	1	0	0	0
Everidge	1.000	4	5	0	0	0
Herrera	.975	52	116	2	3	0
Kleen	.991	68	105	3	1	1
Lawhorn	1.000	7	8	0	0	0
Pineda	.956	110	214	5	10	1
Putnam	1.000	2	3	1	0	0
Sellers	—	1	0	0	0	0
Stavisky	1.000	1	3	0	0	0
Turner	1.000	13	23	0	0	0
Zeringue	.993	52	134	2	1	1

KANE COUNTY COUGARS   LOW CLASS A

MIDWEST LEAGUE

BATTING	B-T	HT	WT	DOB	AVG	vLH	vRH	G	AB	R	H	2B	3B	HR	RBI	BB	HBP	SH	SF	SO	SB	CS	SLG	OBP
Affronti, Michael	R-R	6-2	195	2-13-84	.264	.300	.249	78	295	38	78	15	0	5	29	18	4	6	2	48	8	2	.366	.313
Castillo, David	R-R	5-9	185	9-15-81	.304	.158	.400	13	46	3	14	1	0	0	3	9	1	0	0	9	0	0	.326	.429
Cobb, Larry	R-R	5-9	175	7-10-85	.211	.190	.224	80	275	46	58	10	1	4	31	41	4	1	2	53	10	5	.298	.320
Doolittle, Sean	L-L	6-3	190	9-26-86	.233	.267	.218	55	193	23	45	10	0	4	29	24	2	0	3	40	1	0	.347	.320
Dowling, Greg	L-L	6-3	240	11-15-83	.262	.277	.253	124	451	60	118	15	1	13	78	49	7	1	4	66	1	1	.386	.341
Hernandez, Samuel	R-R	5-10	162	9-9-84	.221	.222	.220	31	95	13	21	5	0	0	7	15	2	1	0	25	3	2	.274	.339
Horton, Joshua	L-R	6-1	195	2-19-86	.279	.205	.313	38	122	28	34	6	0	1	15	28	3	1	3	27	3	1	.352	.417
Johnson, Toddric	L-L	6-1	165	12-17-84	.242	.220	.252	104	372	45	90	16	1	6	48	35	5	1	3	85	3	1	.339	.313
Massaro, Michael	L-L	5-11	160	4-15-84	.286	.220	.315	129	490	62	140	17	1	5	35	58	2	2	2	81	13	11	.331	.362
Mendez, Ramiro	R-R	6-2	175	4-14-85	.200	.231	.185	37	120	15	24	7	0	2	15	11	0	0	1	33	0	0	.308	.265
Mitchell, Jermaine	L-L	6-0	205	11-2-84	.288	.368	.243	122	431	79	124	20	5	8	58	74	1	3	4	115	24	8	.413	.390
Omura, Isaac	L-R	5-10	175	1-21-84	.194	.276	.165	33	108	6	21	4	0	0	11	10	1	1	2	20	0	0	.231	.264
Pratt, Haas	R-R	6-3	215	9-17-81	.223	.256	.200	64	215	27	48	9	0	10	28	22	5	1	1	62	0	3	.405	.309
Rosendo, Gustavo	R-R	6-2	205	3-4-84	.216	.162	.243	68	222	11	48	8	0	1	18	14	1	2	2	32	2	2	.266	.264
Smith, Jacob	R-R	6-2	217	6-5-83	.293	.280	.301	37	133	14	39	10	0	1	6	16	3	1	0	23	0	1	.391	.382
Smith, Matt	R-R	5-11	210	1-30-86	.205	.194	.209	38	122	16	25	6	0	1	8	21	4	1	1	29	1	0	.279	.338
Sulentic, Matthew	L-R	5-10	170	10-6-87	.175	.161	.181	56	206	14	36	6	1	1	15	13	3	0	3	37	2	0	.218	.234
Valdez, Alex	B-R	6-1	180	9-2-84	.264	.266	.264	111	397	55	105	24	6	10	60	34	1	2	4	84	6	4	.431	.321
Vitters, Christian	L-R	6-2	205	6-26-85	.227	.228	.227	86	286	34	65	14	1	5	29	30	2	1	1	81	3	1	.336	.304

PITCHING	B-T	HT	WT	DOB	W	L	ERA	G	GS	CG	SV	IP	H	R	ER	HR	BB	SO	AVG	vLH	vRH	K/9	BB/9
Bailey, Andrew	R-R	6-3	220	5-31-84	1	4	3.35	11	10	1	0	51	42	25	19	6	22	74	.219	.271	.201	13.06	3.88
Banwart, Travis	R-R	6-3	200	2-14-86	2	1	2.60	12	6	0	1	45	36	21	13	2	10	41	.206	.231	.191	8.20	2.00
Cahill, Trevor	R-R	6-3	195	3-1-88	11	4	2.73	20	19	0	0	105	85	38	32	3	40	117	.220	.269	.191	10.00	3.42
Carignan, Andrew	R-R	5-11	200	7-23-86	1	1	2.03	12	0	0	4	13	6	7	3	0	11	19	.136	.176	.111	12.83	7.42
Currin, Patrick	R-R	6-0	190	5-12-84	0	0	3.14	8	0	0	0	14	11	5	5	1	7	21	.212	.222	.200	10.67	3.77
Deal, Scott	R-R	6-4	180	12-11-86	7	10	4.29	27	25	1	0	149	183	82	71	10	38	74	.304	.335	.283	4.47	2.30
Deaza, Inoel	R-R	6-2	180	5-10-86	0	6	6.65	13	5	0	0	43	57	32	32	8	13	36	.322	.338	.311	7.48	2.70
Demel, Sam	R-R	6-0	210	10-23-85	0	1	0.96	9	0	0	4	9	3	2	1	0	4	10	.107	.200	.056	9.64	3.86

Name	B-T	HT	WT	DOB	W	L	ERA	G	GS	CG	SV	IP	H	R	ER	HR	BB	SO	AVG	vLH	vRH	K/9	BB/9
Dewing, Branden	L-L	6-0	165	1-1-84	0	1	0.64	19	0	0	2	28	25	3	2	0	8	24	.227	.344	.179	7.71	2.57
Fernandez, Jason	R-R	6-2	175	1-8-85	8	2	2.77	31	11	1	2	111	82	39	34	5	46	99	.209	.267	.179	8.05	3.74
Franco Jr., TJ	R-R	6-2	190	6-28-83	2	2	2.67	17	0	0	2	34	33	12	10	1	7	24	.254	.289	.235	6.42	1.87
Gordon, Derrick	L-L	5-9	185	10-16-83	3	3	2.10	30	0	0	7	51	28	15	12	5	20	52	.157	.205	.142	9.12	3.51
Herrera, John	R-R	6-6	195	3-8-83	2	8	4.89	21	11	0	0	88	99	53	48	5	41	51	.283	.279	.285	5.20	4.18
Heuser, James	L-L	6-5	200	3-30-84	11	8	4.12	27	26	2	0	155	150	82	71	19	41	147	.253	.378	.221	8.54	2.38
Italiano, Thomas	R-R	6-3	190	7-22-86	0	3	12.71	6	6	0	0	17	32	25	24	3	16	24	.416	.346	.451	12.71	8.47
Madej, Ronald	L-L	6-1	200	5-23-83	0	2	4.50	10	0	0	0	16	18	9	8	1	12	15	.281	.273	.286	8.44	6.75
Moore, Scott	R-R	6-2	245	12-4-83	1	4	3.90	41	1	0	11	60	53	33	26	4	36	60	.236	.247	.230	9.00	5.40
Newby, Joey	R-R	6-2	205	3-8-82	0	3	8.59	9	0	0	0	15	23	16	14	1	8	12	.354	.429	.318	7.36	4.91
Piekarz, Joe	R-L	6-2	175	1-1-82	1	3	6.75	8	1	0	0	17	22	17	13	2	9	12	.314	.231	.364	6.23	4.67
Pratt, Haas	R-R	6-3	215	9-17-81	0	0	1.59	4	0	0	0	6	5	1	1	0	2	0	.227	.250	.214	0.00	3.18
Presutti, Shane	R-R	6-3	187	11-29-84	0	0	7.94	4	0	0	0	6	9	5	5	0	4	3	.346	.455	.267	4.76	6.35
Rodriguez, H.A.	R-R	6-1	175	2-25-87	6	8	3.07	20	18	1	0	100	75	38	34	2	58	106	.214	.180	.242	9.57	5.24
Sheridan, Eric	R-R	6-1	175	9-22-83	4	1	3.91	15	0	0	0	23	23	11	10	3	18	30	.261	.267	.259	11.74	7.04
Tharpe, Derek	L-L	5-11	188	10-30-81	0	0	6.35	6	0	0	0	11	14	10	8	1	2	8	.292	.308	.286	6.35	1.59
Walters, Nick	L-L	6-2	175	9-30-85	3	1	1.78	13	0	0	1	25	25	12	5	2	4	23	.253	.250	.253	8.17	1.42

FIELDING

Catcher	PCT	G	PO	A	E	DP	PB
Castillo	.991	11	104	7	1	2	0
Pratt	1.000	2	6	1	0	0	1
Rosendo	.977	62	482	37	12	4	12
J. Smith	.985	31	242	21	4	4	6
M. Smith	.986	38	278	14	4	1	2

First Base	PCT	G	PO	A	E	DP
Doolittle	.993	50	382	49	3	36
Dowling	.990	73	536	39	6	56
Pratt	.978	17	126	5	3	7
Rosendo	1.000	1	2	0	0	0
Vitters	.971	5	30	3	1	0

Second Base	PCT	G	PO	A	E	DP
Affronti	.971	6	12	22	1	9
Cobb	.956	71	141	164	14	42
Hernandez	1.000	11	14	19	0	4
Omura	.955	27	39	66	5	15
Valdez	.975	21	32	46	2	7
Vitters	.962	5	11	14	1	4

Third Base	PCT	G	PO	A	E	DP
Hernandez	.864	14	13	25	6	3
Omura	—	1	0	0	0	0
Valdez	.901	62	27	100	14	7
Vitters	.915	67	53	97	14	6

Shortstop	PCT	G	PO	A	E	DP
Affronti	.962	70	114	216	13	46
Hernandez	.714	5	3	7	4	1
Horton	.946	38	42	80	7	15
Valdez	.913	25	29	55	8	12
Vitters	.897	6	8	18	3	8

Outfield	PCT	G	PO	A	E	DP
Cobb	.889	4	8	0	1	0
Johnson	.981	91	145	8	3	3
Massaro	.996	124	257	10	1	4
Mendez	.974	35	71	5	2	0
Mitchell	.978	116	215	8	5	4
Sulentic	.966	53	83	1	3	0

VANCOUVER CANADIANS

SHORT-SEASON

NORTHWEST LEAGUE

BATTING	B-T	HT	WT	DOB	AVG	vLH	vRH	G	AB	R	H	2B	3B	HR	RBI	BB	HBP	SH	SF	SO	SB	CS	SLG	OBP
Arrieche, Carlos	R-R	6-1	177	3-30-85	.143	.200	.111	9	28	4	4	1	1	0	5	4	1	0	1	5	2	0	.250	.265
Brown, Corey	L-L	6-2	190	11-26-85	.268	.273	.265	59	213	31	57	18	4	11	48	37	3	0	3	77	5	3	.545	.379
Corporan, Angel	R-R	6-1	170	11-15-85	.250	—	.250	1	4	0	1	1	0	0	1	0	0	0	0	1	0	0	.500	.250
Correa, Walter	R-R	6-1	180	7-17-86	.209	.220	.204	60	206	31	43	9	1	3	30	18	10	4	4	60	5	3	.306	.298
Desme, Greg	R-R	6-2	205	4-4-86	.261	.667	.162	12	46	6	12	3	0	1	6	6	1	0	0	21	2	2	.391	.358
Doolittle, Sean	L-L	6-3	190	9-26-86	.283	.294	.276	13	46	6	13	3	0	0	4	9	2	0	0	10	0	0	.348	.421
Frash, Justin	L-R	5-9	190	4-4-86	.244	.375	.200	56	193	25	47	11	2	0	22	25	1	5	0	31	1	4	.321	.333
Hamblin, Daniel	R-R	6-1	210	2-10-85	.275	.239	.289	68	265	45	73	21	2	11	62	36	4	1	5	93	0	1	.494	.365
Horton, Joshua	L-R	6-1	195	2-19-86	.268	.273	.267	14	41	7	11	2	0	1	6	8	4	1	1	7	1	1	.390	.426
Keough, Shane	B-R	6-3	190	9-11-86	.214	.255	.199	54	187	33	40	6	2	2	15	19	4	0	1	68	15	8	.299	.299
Love, Dante	R-R	5-11	195	4-8-87	.220	.216	.222	36	118	13	26	10	0	0	9	5	3	2	1	34	0	0	.305	.321
Mendez, Ramiro	R-R	6-2	175	4-14-85	.600	.500	.625	3	10	3	6	0	0	0	2	0	0	0	0	0	0	0	.600	.667
Napoleon, Dusty	L-R	6-2	208	5-21-86	.235	.417	.196	42	136	14	32	5	0	1	16	19	8	1	1	32	1	1	.294	.360
Pruitt, J.D.	R-R	5-9	195	3-11-85	.211	.154	.234	61	180	44	38	7	1	3	15	50	34	1	1	64	4	2	.311	.460
Ray, Matthew	B-R	5-9	170	1-28-84	.206	.182	.216	51	155	17	32	8	0	1	11	24	1	2	1	58	10	1	.277	.315
Richard, Michael	R-R	5-11	180	8-20-84	.289	.267	.297	61	225	41	65	5	1	1	22	35	8	9	2	35	25	6	.333	.400
Rivera, Julio	R-R	5-11	178	7-20-87	.223	.200	.229	38	121	16	27	6	2	4	21	13	3	2	1	58	2	2	.405	.312
Sierra, Angel	B-R	6-0	172	8-2-88	.048	.000	.067	6	21	1	1	1	0	0	1	1	1	0	0	10	1	0	.095	.130
Sulentic, Matthew	L-R	5-10	170	10-6-87	.261	.229	.275	71	276	41	72	19	2	4	40	42	3	1	2	79	2	5	.388	.362

PITCHING	B-T	HT	WT	DOB	W	L	ERA	G	GS	CG	SV	IP	H	R	ER	HR	BB	SO	AVG	vLH	vRH	K/9	BB/9
Collins, Bryan	R-R	6-1	210	9-10-84	1	6	6.59	16	0	0	0	27	30	22	20	1	15	25	.283	.360	.214	8.23	4.94
Deaza, Inoel	R-R	6-2	180	5-10-86	5	7	3.90	12	12	0	0	60	66	33	26	6	15	40	.289	.296	.285	6.00	2.25
Espinal, Leonardo	R-R	6-3	203	2-6-84	0	2	3.43	20	0	0	12	21	15	10	8	1	13	21	.197	.200	.196	9.00	5.57
Eusebio, Keith	B-R	5-10	173	1-31-83	0	0	9.00	1	0	0	0	2	3	2	2	1	2	2	.333	.200	.500	4.50	9.00
Figueroa, Pedro	L-L	6-1	164	11-23-85	2	2	4.30	17	7	0	1	44	41	26	21	2	31	35	.252	.250	.252	7.16	6.34
Friend, Justin	R-R	6-1	205	6-21-86	0	2	3.25	17	1	0	1	28	26	11	10	0	19	31	.252	.189	.288	10.08	6.18
Gomez, Fabian	B-L	6-0	190	8-27-84	2	1	8.44	13	2	0	0	21	32	26	20	2	11	13	.352	.217	.397	5.48	4.64
Guzman, Jose	R-R	5-11	185	11-5-87	3	4	4.59	15	12	0	0	65	65	43	33	4	24	39	.262	.252	.271	5.43	3.34
Hernandez, Carlos	L-L	5-11	155	3-4-87	0	0	11.57	2	0	0	0	2	6	4	3	0	1	2	.500	.000	.500	7.71	3.86
Hertzler, Bradley	L-L	6-1	195	4-11-86	3	6	4.20	13	12	1	0	60	62	36	28	5	14	46	.270	.271	.269	6.90	2.10
Hodsdon, Scott	R-R	6-2	195	5-31-85	7	1	4.57	16	10	1	0	67	65	39	34	5	23	67	.256	.277	.239	9.00	3.09
Jenkins, Aaron	L-L	5-8	180	11-14-84	2	0	4.43	15	0	0	0	22	13	14	11	2	20	41	.160	.211	.145	16.52	8.06
Kerfoot, Charles	R-R	6-0	185	4-1-85	0	2	3.47	19	0	0	2	36	36	20	14	2	8	37	.263	.246	.275	9.17	1.98
Land, Lee	R-R	6-2	205	8-7-84	2	0	0.00	7	0	0	2	12	7	0	0	0	6	6	.163	.182	.143	4.38	4.38
Lysander, Brent	R-R	6-7	210	4-5-85	2	1	3.35	16	4	0	0	51	57	25	19	3	14	34	.297	.222	.342	6.00	2.47
Manzueta, Pascual	R-R	6-5	190	12-25-84	1	1	10.13	2	0	0	0	5	6	6	6	0	2	4	.381	.455	.300	6.75	3.38
Martinez, Leonardo	L-L	6-0	185	12-5-86	5	4	6.44	16	12	0	0	57	66	47	41	10	36	54	.282	.233	.293	8.48	5.65
Oakes, Earl	R-R	6-3	225	9-3-85	1	2	4.55	11	0	0	1	30	35	17	15	1	6	28	.302	.275	.316	8.49	1.82
Presutti, Shane	R-R	6-3	187	11-29-84	0	0	9.00	1	0	0	0	2	3	3	2	1	1	2	.375	.600	.000	9.00	4.50
Quine, John	R-R	6-0	180	10-8-83	0	0	4.43	10	2	0	0	22	17	12	11	0	20	15	.202	.214	.196	6.04	8.06
Sewell, Lance	L-L	6-3	205	6-17-86	0	1	4.05	9	0	0	0	7	5	3	3	1	5	10	.200	.111	.250	13.50	6.75
Tejeda, Edgar	R-R	6-0	180	3-4-87	0	0	7.20	1	1	0	0	5	8	4	4	1	3	2	.364	.455	.273	3.60	5.40
Walters, Nick	L-L	6-2	175	9-30-85	1	0	3.18	4	0	0	0	6	8	3	2	0	0	4	.320	.500	.304	6.35	0.00

FIELDING

Catcher	PCT	G	PO	A	E	DP	PB
Love	.975	30	207	26	6	1	4
Napoleon	1.000	14	100	9	0	1	4
Rivera	.986	37	236	41	4	1	5

First Base	PCT	G	PO	A	E	DP
Correa	1.000	2	1	1	0	0
Doolittle	.992	12	118	11	1	11
Hamblin	.994	51	439	28	3	49
Napoleon	.974	13	103	10	3	8

Second Base	PCT	G	PO	A	E	DP
Arrieche	.956	6	21	22	2	6
Corporan	1.000	1	1	7	0	0

	PCT	G	PO	A	E	DP
Correa	.976	24	52	68	3	15
Horton	—	1	0	0	0	0
Ray	.949	44	84	122	11	28
Richard	.925	7	18	19	3	3

Third Base	PCT	G	PO	A	E	DP
Arrieche	1.000	3	2	8	0	1
Correa	.944	19	17	34	3	2
Frash	.917	49	36	86	11	8
Hamblin	.889	7	8	8	2	1
Horton	1.000	1	0	2	0	0

Shortstop	PCT	G	PO	A	E	DP
Arrieche	.667	1	2	0	1	0

	PCT	G	PO	A	E	DP
Correa	.878	17	24	48	10	11
Horton	.884	12	15	23	5	6
Ray	1.000	1	2	2	0	1
Richard	.943	47	90	157	15	35

Outfield	PCT	G	PO	A	E	DP
Brown	.950	53	90	6	5	0
Correa	—	1	0	0	0	0
Desme	1.000	12	23	1	0	0
Keough	.965	50	80	2	3	0
Mendez	.800	3	4	0	1	0
Pruitt	.952	38	39	1	2	2
Sierra	1.000	4	5	3	0	0
Sulentic	.983	67	109	5	2	2

AZL ATHLETICS   ROOKIE

ARIZONA LEAGUE

BATTING	B-T	HT	WT	DOB	AVG	vLH	vRH	G	AB	R	H	2B	3B	HR	RBI	BB	HBP	SH	SF	SO	SB	CS	SLG	OBP
Arrieche, Carlos	R-R	6-1	177	3-30-85	.311	.343	.298	32	119	22	37	6	3	0	25	19	3	0	1	15	7	3	.412	.415
Barrone, Ben	R-R	6-2	210	11-7-84	.244	.353	.217	25	86	12	21	6	0	3	18	7	4	0	1	22	1	1	.419	.327
Corporan, Angel	R-R	6-1	170	11-15-85	.000	—	.000	1	3	0	0	0	0	0	0	1	0	0	0	0	0	1	.000	.250
Gil, Leonardo	R-R	6-1	160	8-18-87	.257	.256	.257	39	140	22	36	5	4	0	20	14	2	1	0	39	5	2	.350	.333
Hernandez, Franklin	R-R	6-3	165	4-19-87	.222	.077	.260	21	63	8	14	4	0	1	7	2	3	2	0	21	1	0	.333	.279
Hudson, Herbert	R-R	6-0	185	9-13-85	.231	.154	.253	31	117	14	27	3	1	0	12	12	2	3	0	30	5	4	.274	.313
James, Javier	R-R	6-0	172	3-1-85	.187	.160	.197	29	91	9	17	1	2	2	17	14	2	0	1	31	1	2	.308	.306
Klein, Adam	L-L	5-11	185	8-21-83	.263	.245	.272	45	152	51	40	5	2	0	11	58	5	0	1	37	33	7	.322	.477
Lissman, Michael	R-L	6-0	205	6-10-85	.295	.333	.278	36	129	24	38	14	2	3	26	17	7	1	3	18	1	2	.504	.397
Luis, Marcos	R-R	5-11	180	11-27-85	.292	.316	.292	44	168	25	50	14	1	1	31	9	4	2	2	22	3	1	.411	.344
Morales, Carlos	R-R	6-3	170	7-20-85	.252	.190	.268	29	103	13	26	5	1	2	17	16	1	2	0	23	1	1	.379	.358
Morris, Jed	L-R	5-11	200	3-4-80	.200	.000	.500	2	5	1	1	0	1	0	1	0	0	0	0	3	0	0	.600	.333
Nunez, Juan	R-R	6-2	191	8-27-87	.188	.056	.235	21	69	7	13	1	1	0	5	15	0	1	0	22	0	3	.232	.333
Ortiz, Gabriel	R-R	6-1	215	11-7-85	.147	.200	.125	23	68	7	10	3	1	1	6	6	0	1	0	23	2	0	.265	.216
Putnam, Danny	L-L	5-10	200	9-17-82	.316	.143	.417	6	19	2	6	0	0	1	2	2	0	0	0	3	0	0	.474	.381
Rodriguez, Raymond	R-R	6-2	191	8-11-89	.178	.286	.129	14	45	6	8	2	0	1	4	4	0	0	1	22	0	0	.289	.240
Rodriguez, Yunior	R-R	6-1	166	10-1-86	.218	.276	.200	37	124	16	27	8	0	0	13	7	1	2	1	24	1	2	.282	.263
Sierra, Angel	B-R	6-0	172	8-2-88	.186	.105	.216	25	70	12	13	2	1	0	5	16	1	1	0	29	4	4	.243	.345
Tirado, Francisco	B-R	6-0	175	7-30-87	.338	.400	.306	21	74	14	25	3	0	0	9	5	0	2	2	8	2	2	.378	.370
Wentzell, Daniel	L-L	6-3	200	5-16-85	.253	.167	.288	39	146	15	37	3	1	1	13	21	4	0	3	35	4	1	.308	.356
West, Jareck	R-R	5-10	210	4-30-85	.218	.308	.180	25	87	22	19	3	0	1	10	14	3	0	0	26	12	0	.287	.346

PITCHING	B-T	HT	WT	DOB	W	L	ERA	G	GS	CG	SV	IP	H	R	ER	HR	BB	SO	AVG	vLH	vRH	K/9	BB/9
Arrioja, Jorge	R-R	6-1	155	1-25-89	0	1	6.27	7	3	0	0	19	22	15	13	1	5	16	.286	.200	.340	7.71	2.41
Christensen, Kyle	R-R	6-3	225	9-18-88	2	3	4.36	14	13	0	0	66	74	39	32	1	25	71	.285	.290	.281	9.68	3.41
Cruz, Santiago	R-R	6-1	178	7-14-85	0	0	12.96	6	0	0	0	8	13	12	12	0	8	9	.342	.444	.250	9.72	8.64
Deaton, Kevin	R-R	6-4	265	8-7-81	0	0	0.00	5	0	0	0	7	3	0	0	0	4	7	.125	.111	.133	9.00	5.14
Dunn, Scott	R-R	6-3	200	5-23-78	0	0	10.12	3	2	0	0	3	1	3	3	0	3	6	.111	.000	.200	20.25	10.12
Eusebio, Keith	B-R	5-10	173	1-31-83	0	3	10.03	10	0	0	2	12	22	20	13	0	10	10	.379	.313	.405	7.71	7.71
Garcia, Hector	R-R	6-3	160	10-22-85	0	2	5.94	18	0	0	0	33	25	24	22	2	20	31	.214	.231	.200	8.37	5.40
Glushon, Jason	R-R	6-2	195	5-26-85	4	3	3.75	15	8	0	0	58	63	26	24	1	3	42	.273	.214	.316	6.55	0.47
Hernandez, Carlos	L-L	5-11	155	3-4-87	2	1	5.59	6	0	0	0	10	9	6	6	0	3	14	.237	.308	.200	13.03	2.79
Joseph, Jonathan	R-R	6-1	180	5-17-88	1	3	7.62	16	1	0	2	39	55	37	33	4	13	38	.327	.405	.266	8.77	3.00
Manzueta, Pascual	R-R	6-5	190	12-25-84	2	3	6.47	13	12	0	0	57	62	44	41	3	20	56	.273	.196	.331	8.84	3.16
Mitchell, Michael	R-R	6-2	200	10-27-81	0	1	14.73	4	0	0	0	4	8	7	6	0	4	4	.500	.667	.400	9.82	9.82
Morla, Ronny	R-R	6-4	180	5-19-88	4	2	3.70	15	8	0	0	58	53	29	24	3	17	52	.240	.240	.239	8.02	2.62
Pena, Francisco	R-R	6-1	188	1-22-85	1	1	4.70	14	0	0	2	15	16	8	8	0	11	13	.276	.375	.238	7.63	6.46
Ramos, Julio	L-L	6-1	158	2-13-88	0	1	5.40	2	2	0	0	8	9	6	5	2	3	5	.300	.375	.273	5.40	3.24
Reyes, Carmelo	R-R	6-2	165	9-9-85	2	2	7.62	15	0	0	1	26	31	23	22	6	17	11	.298	.333	.274	3.81	5.88
Robertson, Connor	R-R	6-2	225	9-10-81	1	0	0.00	1	0	0	0	2	0	0	0	0	0	4	.000	.000	.000	18.00	0.00
Tejeda, Edgar	R-R	6-0	180	3-4-87	3	2	6.00	11	2	0	2	24	30	19	16	1	11	28	.316	.235	.361	10.50	4.12
Villegas, Juan	R-R	6-0	170	1-20-87	3	3	3.50	13	5	0	1	46	43	22	18	2	23	43	.256	.237	.266	8.35	4.47

FIELDING

Catcher	PCT	G	PO	A	E	DP	PB
Barrone	.978	24	177	43	5	2	7
Morris	1.000	1	4	0	0	0	0
Nunez	.988	20	143	21	2	1	6
Ortiz	.985	20	121	9	2	1	9

First Base	PCT	G	PO	A	E	DP
Morales	.983	29	265	24	5	25
Wentzell	.996	27	230	33	1	20

Second Base	PCT	G	PO	A	E	DP
Arrieche	1.000	1	0	2	0	0
Gil	.943	9	13	20	2	5
Luis	.970	36	79	114	6	27

	PCT	G	PO	A	E	DP
Rodriguez	.975	13	15	24	1	6

Third Base	PCT	G	PO	A	E	DP
Arrieche	.916	31	22	65	8	7
Gil	.880	17	9	35	6	4
Luis	.875	6	4	10	2	1
Ortiz	.500	2	1	1	2	0
Y. Rodriguez	1.000	1	1	3	0	1

Shortstop	PCT	G	PO	A	E	DP
Corporan	1.000	1	0	3	0	1
Gil	.912	13	16	36	5	4
Luis	.800	2	2	2	1	0
R. Rodriguez	1.000	1	2	2	0	2

	PCT	G	PO	A	E	DP
Y. Rodriguez	.908	23	31	58	9	10
Tirado	.905	21	43	62	11	16

Outfield	PCT	G	PO	A	E	DP
Hernandez	1.000	14	15	0	0	0
Hudson	.898	24	43	1	5	0
James	.907	21	38	1	4	0
Klein	.960	35	45	3	2	0
Lissman	1.000	22	17	1	0	0
Putnam	1.000	4	7	1	0	0
R. Rodriguez	.857	12	16	2	3	0
Sierra	.969	22	30	1	1	0
Wentzell	1.000	8	15	1	0	1
West	1.000	21	32	0	0	0

DOMINICAN SUMMER LEAGUE

BATTING	B-T	HT	WT	DOB	AVG	vLH	vRH	G	AB	R	H	2B	3B	HR	RBI	BB	HBP	SH	SF	SO	SB	CS	SLG	OBP
Almanzar, Jose	R-R	6-1	172	8-20-86	.273	.500	.222	9	22	3	6	2	0	0	6	2	0	1	0	2	0	0	.364	.333
2-team (10 DSL)					.233	—	—	19	43	4	10	2	0	0	8	2	0	1	0	7	0	0	.279	.267
Benzant, Hector	R-R	6-1	171	1-25-87	.220	.150	.236	46	109	23	24	3	0	0	13	25	2	1	2	22	3	5	.248	.370
Castillo, Gernaldo	R-R	5-11	145	7-17-89	.273	.294	.265	57	183	34	50	6	1	0	19	45	4	1	0	21	12	6	.317	.427
Chevalier, Edward	R-R	6-1	215	5-13-88	.219	.226	.218	52	155	19	34	9	0	0	28	31	8	0	2	20	1	0	.277	.372
Crisostomo, Jose	L-R	6-1	181	4-20-89	.247	.140	.285	52	166	30	41	7	2	3	31	32	2	2	1	25	13	8	.367	.373
De La Cruz, Jonatan	R-R	6-0	160	5-28-88	.225	.241	.220	45	120	21	27	2	0	0	9	20	1	1	0	18	6	2	.242	.340
De Salas, Isidro	R-R	6-2	185	5-29-87	.222	.286	.207	49	108	21	24	5	0	0	17	13	4	0	1	35	9	2	.269	.325
Fernandez, Earving	L-L	6-0	175	6-9-88	.310	.000	.351	16	42	11	13	2	0	0	6	5	2	0	0	8	1	0	.357	.408
2-team (29 DSL)					.318	—	—	45	129	16	41	8	0	0	14	16	5	0	2	19	6	4	.380	.408
Garcia, Braulio	R-R	6-2	150	10-17-87	.257	.250	.259	40	113	17	29	7	0	2	18	20	4	2	1	17	5	0	.372	.384
Garcia, Elvis	R-R	6-2	178	11-8-89	.347	.400	.333	20	49	13	17	2	0	0	9	9	1	0	2	8	5	0	.388	.443
2-team (7 DSL)					.312	—	—	27	64	15	20	2	0	0	11	12	1	0	2	8	6	0	.344	.418
Garcia, Martire	R-R	6-0	180	11-22-86	.213	.205	.217	38	122	16	26	3	1	0	14	11	2	1	0	22	8	3	.254	.289
2-team (12 DSL)					.258	—	—	50	163	27	42	5	2	1	16	15	4	1	0	31	10	3	.331	.335
Landaeta, Douglas	R-R	6-1	170	11-25-88	.292	.160	.333	39	106	19	31	4	0	0	6	12	2	1	0	17	1	2	.330	.375
Made, Alcibiades	R-R	6-0	169	4-5-89	.298	.074	.388	28	94	16	28	3	2	1	16	14	4	0	0	23	4	1	.404	.411
2-team (15 DSL)					.306	—	—	43	147	23	45	6	2	2	27	23	5	0	0	31	7	2	.415	.417
Maduro, Richard	R-R	6-3	165	10-25-85	.179	.000	.200	13	28	6	5	0	0	0	1	3	2	0	0	7	1	1	.179	.303
2-team (41 DSL)					.207	—	—	54	164	32	34	2	1	0	9	16	5	2	0	33	11	5	.232	.297
Mateo, Kelvin	R-R	6-1	170	8-7-89	.333	.000	.333	1	3	0	1	0	0	0	1	2	0	0	0	0	0	0	.333	.600
2-team (11 DSL)					.148	—	—	12	27	0	4	0	0	0	3	5	0	0	1	3	0	0	.148	.273
Mercedes, Wilson	R-R	6-1	170	4-5-88	.244	.480	.186	43	127	22	31	7	0	1	14	24	5	1	0	21	9	4	.323	.385
Pena, Carlos	R-R	5-10	150	1-22-89	.375	.250	.417	8	16	2	6	1	0	0	5	3	0	0	0	2	0	0	.438	.474
2-team (16 DSL)					.241	—	—	24	54	5	13	1	0	0	8	7	0	1	0	12	1	1	.259	.328
Penaloza, Carmelo	R-R	6-0	165	3-1-87	.267	.000	.308	12	30	4	8	0	1	1	7	3	0	0	0	5	1	1	.433	.333
2-team (36 DSL)					.314	—	—	48	153	18	48	8	1	1	23	10	5	0	1	23	2	3	.399	.373
Rodriguez, Keyter	R-R	6-1	175	2-7-86	.277	.261	.282	56	195	33	54	12	3	3	30	15	8	2	4	40	6	1	.415	.350
Rodriguez, Yunior	R-R	6-1	166	10-1-86	.333	.500	.316	7	21	5	7	2	0	0	5	6	0	0	0	7	0	2	.429	.481
Santana, Lovesquis	L-L	5-10	180	10-21-87	.235	.000	.245	34	51	11	12	2	1	0	10	12	1	0	0	14	5	3	.314	.391
Soto, Ramon	R-R	6-2	190	11-3-87	.309	.393	.275	37	97	16	30	6	0	3	18	11	3	2	1	18	1	1	.464	.393
Taveras, Aneurys	R-R	6-1	180	5-5-89	—	—	.000	1	0	1	0	0	0	0	0	0	0	0	0	0	0	0	—	—
Toussaint, Franklin	R-R	6-1	174	9-16-89	.194	.176	.200	28	62	12	12	0	0	0	3	11	3	1	0	13	4	3	.194	.342
2-team (11 DSL)					.222	—	—	39	99	16	22	2	0	0	6	12	5	1	0	18	5	4	.242	.336

PITCHING	B-T	HT	WT	DOB	W	L	ERA	G	GS	CG	SV	IP	H	R	ER	HR	BB	SO	AVG	vLH	vRH	K/9	BB/9
Arrioja, Jorge	R-R	6-1	155	1-25-89	0	0	0.00	1	1	0	0	5	0	0	0	0	0	3	.000	.000	.000	5.79	0.00
Brujan, Mauricio	R-R	6-2	184	9-22-89	0	0	0.00	2	0	0	0	3	4	1	0	0	1	1	.333	.000	.333	3.00	3.00
2-team (10 DSL)					0	1	4.56	12	0	0	0	26	29	18	13	2	17	7	—	—	—	2.45	5.96
Castillo, Gernaldo	R-R	5-11	145	7-17-89	0	0	0.00	1	0	0	1	1	0	0	0	0	0	0	.000	—	.000	0.00	0.00
Castro, Mario	R-R	6-3	150	9-3-87	2	0	3.94	10	0	0	1	16	13	8	7	0	17	7	.224	.333	.218	3.94	9.56
Delgado, Richard	R-R	6-1	177	5-15-86	3	1	2.51	13	1	0	4	14	15	5	4	0	10	7	.300	.000	.363	4.40	6.28
Ferreras, Ronald	R-R	6-1	180	2-8-87	3	0	1.99	15	1	0	0	32	29	12	7	2	10	17	.246	.200	.255	4.83	2.84
German, Juan	R-R	6-5	170	12-25-85	2	0	3.63	9	1	0	1	17	15	8	7	0	13	14	.217	.250	.215	7.27	6.75
Joseph, Jonathan	R-R	6-1	180	5-17-88	1	0	1.23	2	1	0	0	7	3	1	1	0	3	5	.120	.000	.125	6.14	3.68
Juma, Alexis	R-R	6-1	180	5-23-88	0	0	22.50	3	0	0	0	2	3	5	5	0	6	1	.333	.000	.375	4.50	27.00
2-team (6 DSL)					0	0	7.82	9	0	0	0	13	12	13	11	1	12	10	—	—	—	7.11	8.53
Laureano, Melkin	R-R	6-3	185	8-26-85	4	2	2.89	12	6	0	0	44	33	18	14	1	19	26	.210	.182	.215	5.36	3.92
Morla, Ronny	R-R	6-4	180	5-19-88	1	0	2.08	2	2	0	0	9	8	2	2	0	1	6	.242	.000	.286	6.23	1.04
Mota, David	R-R	6-3	218	2-18-87	0	0	3.38	2	0	0	0	3	2	1	1	0	3	1	.182	1.000	.100	3.38	10.12
2-team (11 DSL)					1	2	7.11	13	0	0	0	19	20	19	15	0	23	19	—	—	—	9.00	10.89
Oliveros, Jose	R-R	6-0	170	9-29-87	7	3	3.24	14	6	1	0	56	38	16	14	2	13	43	.190	.235	.186	6.87	2.08
Penalba, Ricardo	R-R	5-11	170	1-6-89	0	3	4.91	13	0	0	6	15	12	8	8	0	8	16	.235	.000	.261	9.82	4.91
Penaloza, Carmelo	R-R	6-0	165	3-1-87	0	0	3.86	2	0	0	1	2	4	2	1	0	1	3	.364	.000	.400	11.57	3.86
Perez, Wilfredo	R-R	6-0	180	7-27-88	4	2	3.45	16	0	0	1	44	37	20	17	2	16	33	.230	.200	.235	6.70	3.25
Quinonez, Jose	R-R	6-1	186	3-12-88	5	3	4.20	13	10	0	0	41	35	21	19	1	22	38	.235	.087	.262	8.41	4.87
Ramirez, Anvioris	L-R	6-1	165	3-10-88	3	4	2.09	14	10	2	1	69	53	22	16	3	10	57	.218	.263	.214	7.43	1.30
Ramos, Julio	L-L	5-10	158	2-13-88	0	0	5.68	2	1	0	0	6	7	5	4	0	3	6	.292	.333	.286	8.53	4.26
Rey, Jose	R-R	6-1	176	3-17-90	0	0	10.12	3	0	0	0	3	7	3	3	0	0	2	.538	.000	.583	6.75	0.00
2-team (8 DSL)					0	2	6.08	11	1	0	0	24	26	18	16	2	10	32	—	—	—	12.17	3.80
Reyes, Carmelo	R-R	6-2	165	9-9-85	0	0	4.05	2	1	0	0	7	4	4	3	1	3	11	.174	.333	.118	14.85	4.05
Romero, Alvaro	R-R	6-2	160	4-6-87	2	2	3.16	14	9	0	0	37	34	14	13	0	16	28	.256	.346	.234	6.81	3.89
Samuel, David	R-R	6-1	174	3-8-87	1	0	2.45	3	1	0	0	7	6	2	2	0	5	2	.222	.500	.200	2.45	6.14
2-team (11 DSL)					1	0	4.70	14	1	0	1	23	19	13	12	2	17	14	—	—	—	5.48	6.65
Sanchez, Jose	R-R	6-2	170	10-24-89	0	0	12.46	3	1	0	0	4	5	7	6	1	5	2	.294	.000	.313	4.15	10.38
2-team (8 DSL)					0	1	12.27	11	1	0	0	11	17	20	15	1	14	11	—	—	—	9.00	11.45
Sentime, Carlos	R-R	6-2	195	12-6-87	3	2	3.83	13	7	1	0	45	44	25	19	3	19	27	.257	.300	.252	5.44	3.83
Taveras, Aneurys	R-R	6-1	180	5-5-89	0	0	3.00	4	1	0	0	6	1	2	2	0	7	6	.048	.000	.048	9.00	10.50
Vidal, Pedro	R-R	6-3	194	7-31-87	0	0	2.60	7	4	0	0	35	31	12	10	1	12	15	.246	.188	.255	3.89	3.12
2-team (9 DSL)					1	5	2.51	16	13	0	0	75	68	32	21	2	19	46	—	—	—	5.50	2.27

FIELDING

Catcher

Catcher	PCT	G	PO	A	E	DP	PB
Almanzar	.974	9	30	7	1	0	0
Chevalier	.979	8	41	6	1	0	1
M. Garcia	.978	32	156	25	4	0	1
Landaeta	—	1	0	0	0	0	0
Mateo	1.000	1	5	3	0	0	0
Penaloza	.962	10	49	1	2	0	2
Santana	—	1	0	0	0	0	0
Soto	.982	20	99	10	2	1	5

First Base

First Base	PCT	G	PO	A	E	DP
Chevalier	.995	43	350	14	2	30
De La Cruz	1.000	1	2	0	0	0
Fernandez	1.000	4	28	2	0	3
B. Garcia	1.000	4	33	1	0	1
Landaeta	1.000	1	1	0	0	0
Penaloza	1.000	2	19	0	0	3
Rodriguez	1.000	7	33	0	0	1
Soto	1.000	10	75	1	0	4
Toussaint	1.000	5	34	1	0	3

Second Base

Second Base	PCT	G	PO	A	E	DP
Benzant	.982	19	25	30	1	12
Castillo	1.000	27	41	60	0	13
De La Cruz	—	3	0	0	0	0
Fernandez	1.000	4	3	2	0	1
E. Garcia	1.000	1	2	0	0	0
Made	.929	8	22	17	3	6
Mercedes	1.000	13	24	29	0	6
Pena	.938	6	6	9	1	1
Toussaint	1.000	2	0	1	0	0

Third Base

Third Base	PCT	G	PO	A	E	DP
Almanzar	—	1	0	0	0	0
Benzant	.879	20	14	44	8	2
Castillo	.949	10	5	32	2	3
De La Cruz	.875	3	1	6	1	0
B. Garcia	.929	3	4	44	4	3
Made	.833	3	2	3	1	0
Mercedes	.962	17	12	39	2	5
Rodriguez	1.000	1	0	1	0	0
Rodriguez	.917	7	7	15	2	2

Shortstop

Shortstop	PCT	G	PO	A	E	DP
Benzant	.800	2	2	6	2	1
Castillo	.976	25	24	58	2	5
De La Cruz	.931	36	51	84	10	11
Mercedes	.956	13	10	33	2	8

Outfield

Outfield	PCT	G	PO	A	E	DP
Benzant	1.000	1	2	0	0	0
Castillo	1.000	2	1	0	0	0
Crisostomo	.978	51	86	5	2	1
De Salas	.940	48	74	4	5	1
Fernandez	1.000	1	1	0	0	0
E. Garcia	.962	19	25	0	1	0
Landaeta	.983	34	56	2	1	0
Maduro	1.000	11	11	1	0	0
Pena	1.000	1	1	0	0	0
Rodriguez	1.000	47	66	3	0	0
Santana	.971	23	33	1	1	0
Sentime	—	1	0	0	0	0
Toussaint	—	1	0	0	0	0

DSL ATHLETICS2 ROOKIE

DOMINICAN SUMMER LEAGUE

BATTING	B-T	HT	WT	DOB	AVG	vLH	vRH	G	AB	R	H	2B	3B	HR	RBI	BB	HBP	SH	SF	SO	SB	CS	SLG	OBP
Almanzar, Jose	R-R	6-1	172	8-20-86	.190	.000	.200	10	21	1	4	0	0	0	2	0	0	0	0	5	0	0	.190	.190
2-team (9 DSL)					.233	—	—	19	43	4	10	2	0	0	8	2	0	1	0	7	0	0	.279	.267
Andres, Graviel	R-R	6-2	165	8-26-87	.158	.000	.179	51	120	12	19	1	0	0	9	27	9	4	1	19	7	8	.167	.350
Brazoban, Yeudy	R-R	6-1	185	9-9-88	.201	.000	.209	44	144	11	29	2	0	1	11	9	1	1	1	27	5	1	.236	.252
Castillo, Alexander	L-L	6-2	215	9-24-87	.225	.308	.217	49	151	13	34	5	2	0	14	14	3	0	2	46	3	4	.285	.300
De Leon, Abraham	R-R	6-0	194	2-20-89	.285	.111	.295	48	158	25	45	8	0	0	16	18	7	3	1	29	10	6	.335	.380
Fernandez, Earving	L-L	6-0	175	6-9-88	.322	.100	.351	29	87	5	28	6	0	0	8	11	3	0	2	11	5	4	.391	.408
2-team (16 DSL)					.318	—	—	45	129	16	41	8	0	0	14	16	5	0	2	19	6	4	.380	.408
Garcia, Elvis	R-R	6-2	178	11-8-89	.200	.000	.214	7	15	2	3	0	0	0	2	3	0	0	0	1	0	0	.200	.333
2-team (20 DSL)					.312	—	—	27	64	15	20	2	0	0	11	12	1	0	2	8	6	0	.344	.418
Garcia, Martire	R-R	6-0	180	11-22-86	.390	.333	.395	12	41	11	16	2	1	1	2	4	2	0	0	9	2	0	.561	.468
2-team (38 DSL)					.258	—	—	50	163	27	42	5	2	1	16	15	4	1	0	31	10	3	.331	.335
Hernandez, Franklin	R-R	6-3	165	4-19-87	.273	.333	.263	5	22	2	6	1	0	0	2	3	0	0	1	4	1	0	.318	.346
Lopez, Diomes	R-R	6-2	195	1-30-89	.189	.000	.196	38	95	11	18	5	0	2	8	17	0	0	1	30	1	1	.305	.310
Made, Alcibiades	R-R	6-0	169	4-5-89	.321	.000	.347	15	53	7	17	3	0	1	11	9	1	0	0	8	3	1	.434	.429
2-team (28 DSL)					.306	—	—	43	147	23	45	6	2	2	27	23	5	0	0	31	7	2	.415	.417
Maduro, Richard	R-R	6-3	165	10-25-85	.213	.083	.226	41	136	26	29	2	1	0	8	13	3	2	0	26	10	4	.243	.296
2-team (13 DSL)					.207	—	—	46	164	32	34	2	1	0	9	16	5	2	0	33	11	5	.232	.297
Martinez, Juan	R-R	6-0	170	10-7-88	.227	.455	.202	45	110	18	25	6	0	0	5	9	1	2	1	24	4	4	.282	.289
Mateo, Kelvin	R-R	6-1	170	8-7-89	.125	.000	.130	11	24	0	3	0	0	0	3	0	0	0	1	3	0	0	.125	.214
2-team (1 DSL)					.148	—	—	12	27	0	4	0	0	0	3	5	0	0	1	3	0	0	.148	.273
Mota, Francis	R-R	6-2	187	10-26-88	.197	.000	.208	50	127	16	25	0	0	0	9	21	3	0	1	34	4	1	.197	.322
Pena, Carlos	R-R	5-10	150	1-22-89	.184	.000	.189	16	38	3	7	0	0	0	3	4	0	1	0	10	1	1	.184	.262
2-team (8 DSL)					.241	—	—	24	54	5	13	1	0	0	8	7	0	1	0	12	1	1	.259	.328
Penaloza, Carmelo	R-R	6-0	165	3-1-87	.325	.250	.333	36	123	14	40	8	0	0	16	7	5	0	1	18	1	2	.390	.382
2-team (12 DSL)					.314	—	—	48	153	18	48	8	1	1	23	10	5	0	1	23	2	3	.399	.373
Rodriguez, Jose	R-R	6-1	160	12-19-88	.190	.000	.208	29	58	2	11	2	0	0	9	18	0	1	0	17	0	0	.224	.382
Rojas, Kelvin	R-R	6-2	188	8-7-89	.201	.083	.211	53	159	16	32	3	1	2	13	17	3	1	2	42	5	3	.270	.287
Sosa, Wilfredo	R-R	6-2	175	10-24-88	.264	.286	.262	56	182	24	48	10	0	1	18	27	6	1	1	41	10	11	.335	.375
Torres, Lino	R-R	6-2	159	10-31-89	.143	.143	.143	37	105	7	15	3	1	0	7	15	3	2	1	22	8	4	.190	.266
Toussaint, Franklin	R-R	6-1	174	9-16-89	.270	.000	.313	11	37	4	10	2	0	0	3	1	2	0	0	5	1	1	.324	.325
2-team (28 DSL)					.222	—	—	39	99	16	22	2	0	0	6	12	5	1	0	18	5	4	.242	.336

PITCHING	B-T	HT	WT	DOB	W	L	ERA	G	GS	CG	SV	IP	H	R	ER	HR	BB	SO	AVG	vLH	vRH	K/9	BB/9
Abreu, Denny	R-R	6-0	180	8-24-86	1	2	1.47	14	2	0	0	31	22	9	5	0	25	23	.202	.125	.208	6.75	7.34
Adames, Joselito	R-R	6-3	190	10-26-88	1	4	5.11	15	12	0	0	37	42	28	21	3	38	44	.286	.348	.274	10.70	9.24
Brujan, Mauricio	R-R	6-2	184	9-22-89	0	1	5.16	10	0	0	0	23	25	17	13	2	16	6	.275	.667	.215	2.38	6.35
2-team (2 DSL)					0	1	4.56	12	0	0	0	26	29	18	13	2	17	7	—	—	—	2.45	5.96
Diaz, Ailin	R-R	6-3	168	11-14-87	0	1	24.75	9	1	0	0	8	17	25	22	1	13	8	.415	.500	.400	9.00	14.62
Diaz, Victor	R-R	6-1	220	10-26-89	1	5	7.85	19	2	0	0	29	29	32	25	0	40	24	.274	.400	.253	7.53	12.56
Francisco, Joanel	L-L	6-3	178	11-3-88	0	2	9.00	15	2	0	0	20	17	20	20	1	30	15	.236	.200	.239	6.75	13.50
Garcia, Hector	R-R	6-3	160	10-22-85	0	0	8.44	2	0	0	0	5	4	5	5	0	6	5	.200	.000	.211	8.44	10.12
German, Juan	R-R	6-1	160	12-2-89	0	0	8.44	5	0	0	0	5	2	5	5	0	8	4	.125	.000	.133	6.75	13.50
German, Johan	R-R	6-5	190	12-20-88	0	2	7.58	11	1	0	0	19	16	18	16	0	23	9	.215	.222	.214	4.26	10.89
Jose, Luis	R-R	6-4	195	9-26-87	1	2	2.83	15	2	0	1	29	20	14	9	0	16	16	.192	.417	.163	5.02	5.02
Juma, Alexis	R-R	6-1	180	5-23-88	0	0	5.06	6	0	0	0	11	9	8	6	1	6	9	.225	.500	.194	7.59	5.06
2-team (3 DSL)					0	0	7.82	9	0	0	0	13	12	13	11	1	12	10	—	—	—	7.11	8.53
Lezan, Pedro	R-R	6-2	185	10-10-87	0	1	11.05	10	2	0	0	15	21	22	18	0	23	6	.333	.500	.286	3.68	14.11
Medina, Jorge	L-L	6-1	185	12-21-89	0	2	9.45	6	0	0	0	7	8	7	7	1	3	6	.308	.333	.304	8.10	4.05
Mota, David	R-R	6-3	218	2-18-87	1	2	7.71	11	0	0	0	16	18	18	14	0	20	18	.269	.286	.267	9.92	11.02
2-team (2 DSL)					1	2	7.11	13	0	0	0	19	20	19	15	0	23	19	—	—	—	9.00	10.89
Mota, Francis	R-R	6-2	187	10-26-88	0	0	9.00	1	0	0	0	1	2	1	1	0	0	1	.400	1.000	.000	9.00	0.00
Pena, Jorge	R-R	6-1	226	12-31-88	1	3	5.54	15	3	0	1	26	17	19	16	2	26	27	.179	.125	.190	9.35	9.00
Peralta, Eiffer	R-R	6-3	186	5-30-88	0	1	5.68	2	2	0	0	6	7	6	4	0	3	2	.259	.333	.250	2.84	4.26
Rey, Jose	R-R	6-1	176	3-17-90	0	2	5.57	8	1	0	0	21	19	15	13	2	10	30	.238	.571	.205	12.86	4.29
2-team (3 DSL)					0	2	6.08	11	1	0	0	24	26	18	16	2	10	32	—	—	—	12.17	3.80
Reyes, Luis	R-R	6-2	160	2-4-88	1	3	6.91	12	3	0	0	27	36	29	21	2	19	24	.319	.214	.333	7.90	6.26
Samuel, David	R-R	6-1	174	3-8-87	0	0	5.74	11	0	0	1	16	13	11	10	2	12	12	.217	.333	.196	6.89	6.89
2-team (3 DSL)					1	0	4.70	14	1	0	1	23	19	13	12	2	17	14	—	—	—	5.48	6.65
Sanchez, Jose	R-R	6-2	170	10-24-89	0	1	12.15	8	0	0	0	7	12	13	9	0	9	9	.364	.286	.385	12.15	12.15
2-team (3 DSL)					0	1	12.27	11	1	0	0	11	17	20	15	1	14	11	—	—	—	9.00	11.45
Suero, Jose	R-R	6-2	170	11-3-87	1	4	7.58	19	4	0	0	38	52	35	32	1	22	17	.333	.357	.328	4.03	5.21
Vargas, Carlos	R-R	6-1	170	8-17-88	0	4	4.94	9	3	0	0	27	29	18	15	1	8	17	.269	.227	.279	5.60	2.63
Veliz, Leonardo	R-R	6-2	185	10-1-88	0	7	5.83	15	15	0	0	59	66	47	38	0	29	40	.280	.270	.281	6.14	4.45
Vidal, Pedro	R-R	6-3	194	7-31-87	1	5	2.43	9	9	0	0	41	37	20	11	1	7	31	.223	.250	.221	6.86	1.55
2-team (7 DSL)					1	5	2.51	16	13	0	0	75	68	32	21	2	19	46	—	—	—	5.50	2.27

FIELDING

Catcher	PCT	G	PO	A	E	DP	PB
Almanzar	.968	6	28	2	1	1	0
M. Garcia	.978	10	72	15	2	2	4
Lopez	.992	21	107	13	1	0	5
Mateo	.974	9	28	9	1	0	1
Penaloza	.978	19	119	16	3	1	3
Rodriguez	.935	18	60	12	5	0	3

First Base	PCT	G	PO	A	E	DP
Almanzar	1.000	1	1	0	0	0
Brazoban	.917	3	10	1	1	1
Castillo	.981	44	334	18	7	19
Fernandez	1.000	3	13	0	0	1
M. Garcia	1.000	2	13	0	0	1
Lopez	1.000	13	99	1	0	9
Mota	1.000	2	20	0	0	1

	PCT	G	PO	A	E	DP
Penaloza	.952	4	39	1	2	3
Rodriguez	.964	5	24	3	1	3
Toussaint	1.000	2	10	0	0	1

Second Base	PCT	G	PO	A	E	DP
Andres	1.000	15	20	24	0	3
Fernandez	.976	12	15	26	1	4
Made	1.000	1	0	2	0	0
Pena	1.000	13	16	23	0	4
Torres	.914	34	64	75	13	17
Toussaint	1.000	6	16	13	0	3

Third Base	PCT	G	PO	A	E	DP
Andres	.828	26	14	39	11	1
Fernandez	.833	7	1	9	2	0
Mota	.891	49	31	116	18	9
Sosa	1.000	2	3	4	0	0

	PCT	G	PO	A	E	DP
Toussaint	.000	2	0	0	5	0

Shortstop	PCT	G	PO	A	E	DP
Andres	.840	15	23	40	12	7
Made	.857	1	2	4	1	0
Sosa	.902	54	61	151	23	21
Torres	1.000	2	5	8	0	0

Outfield	PCT	G	PO	A	E	DP
Brazoban	.861	28	30	1	5	0
De Leon	.940	45	75	4	5	2
E. Garcia	.667	7	4	0	2	0
Hernandez	.800	5	8	0	2	0
Maduro	.956	37	80	6	4	0
Martinez	.974	35	33	4	1	0
Rojas	.899	50	71	0	8	0

Philadelphia Phillies

BY JIM SALISBURY

A month before spring training, Jimmy Rollins boldly proclaimed that the Phillies were the team to beat in the National League East. For much of the season, those words haunted the team, but in the end, they proved prophetic.

The Phillies, indeed were the team to beat in the NL East. Capitalizing on the Mets' historic collapse with an impressive late surge, the Phillies won the division on the final day of the season and made the playoffs for the first time in 14 years.

Their trip to the playoffs was short-lived, as they were swept in the division series by the Rockies. After leading the NL with 892 runs, the Phils hit just .172, struck out 26 times and scored just eight runs in the three-game series.

Manager Charlie Manuel sensed his hitters, most appearing in their first postseason, were tight in the series. General manager Pat Gillick added that the experience of playing in the postseason "would be beneficial" in the future. Rollins echoed that sentiment, saying the team would approach future playoff series, "A little better, a little easier. Let it happen, not try."

Despite their playoff failure, the Phillies provided long frustrated fans with much to feel good about. Resilience was the team's hallmark. It overcame a 4-11 start, a host of injuries to key players and a 4.76 team ERA (the second-highest ever for an NL playoff team) to win 89 games, the most since winning 97 in 1993.

While the Mets blew a seven-game lead by going 5-12 in the final 17 games, the Phillies went 13-4.

Entering the season, the Phillies had hopes of a formidable rotation. But offseason acquisition Freddy Garcia showed up hurt; the $10 million bust won just one game. Another offseason pickup, righthander Adam Eaton, proved unreliable, recording a 6.29 ERA in 162 innings.

Lefty Cole Hamels was everything advertised. He led the team with 15 wins and a 3.39 ERA, but once again raised health concerns by missing a month with a tender elbow late in the season. Hamels quieted some of those concerns by making three starts down the stretch and striking out 11 in his final regular season start.

Veteran reliever Tom Gordon battled shoulder issues early. In desperate need of a stabilizer at the back of the bullpen, the Phillies moved Opening Day starter Brett Myers to closer in May. Though he missed two months with a shoulder strain, Myers took to the role well.

Myers, Gordon and midseason acquisition J.C. Romero were brilliant late in the season. Cast aside by the Red Sox, Romero signed with the Phillies in June and had a 1.24 ERA in 51 games.

First baseman Ryan Howard, the 2006 NL MVP, missed time early and all-star second baseman Chase Utley was knocked out of the lineup for a month with a broken hand. Both players managed big seasons, though. Utley led all major league second basemen with 103 RBIs and Howard had 47 homers and 136 RBIs, despite setting the major league record for strikeouts in a season with 199. Center fielder Aaron Rowand made his first all-star team.

The key to the offense was Rollins, who backed up his big talk with an MVP-worthy season. He was the first player to ever reach 200 hits, 15 triples, 25 homers and 25 stolen bases. He was second in the league with 212 hits, and

Colorado's Matt Holliday (386) was the only player in the majors with more total bases. Rollins also played brilliant shortstop, making just 11 errors in 717 total chances.

A largely homegrown roster welcomed two solid additions in catcher Carlos Ruiz and righthander Kyle Kendrick.

In the minors, righthander Carlos Carrasco finished the season at Double-A and could pitch himself into the picture sometime in 2008. Third baseman Mike Costanzo appears ready for Triple-A next season and bulldog righthander Drew Carpenter led the minors in victories while leading high Class A Clearwater to the Florida State League championship.

2007 PERFORMANCE

General Manager: Pat Gillick. Farm Director: Steve Noworyta. Scouting Director: Marti Wolever

Class	Team	League	W	L	PCT	Finish*	Manager	Affiliate Since
Majors	Philadelphia	National	89	73	.549	3rd (16)	Charlie Manuel	—
Triple-A	Ottawa Lynx	International	55	88	.385	14th (14)	John Russell	2007
Double-A	Reading Phillies	Easter	70	71	.496	7th (12)	P.J. Forbes	1967
High A	Clearwater Threshers	Florida State	83	57	.593	2nd (12)^	Dave Huppert	1985
Low A	Lakewood BlueClaws	South Atlantic	69	65	.515	6th (16)	Steve Roadcap	2001
Short-season	Williamsport Crosscutters	New York-Penn	34	42	.447	9th	Gregg Legg	2007
Rookie	GCL Phillies	Gulf Coast	28	32	.467	9th (16)	Roly DeArmas	1999
Overall 2007 Minor League Record			**339**	**355**	**.488**	**19th**		

* Finish in overall standings (No. of teams in league) ^League champion

ORGANIZATION STATISTICS

PHILADELPHIA PHILLIES

NATIONAL LEAGUE

BATTING	B-T	HT	WT	DOB	AVG	vLH	vRH	G	AB	R	H	2B	3B	HR	RBI	BB	HBP	SH	SF	SO	SB	CS	SLG	OBP
Barajas, Rod	R-R	6-2	230	9-5-75	.230	.226	.231	48	122	16	28	8	0	4	10	21	2	1	0	24	0	1	.393	.352
Bourn, Michael	L-R	5-11	180	12-27-82	.277	.154	.312	105	119	29	33	3	3	1	6	13	0	1	0	21	18	1	.378	.348
Branyan, Russell	L-R	6-3	195	12-19-75	.222	.000	.286	7	9	2	2	0	0	2	5	0	0	0	0	6	0	0	.889	.222
3-team (61 San Diego, 21 St. Louis)					.196	—	—	89	163	22	32	5	1	10	26	28	2	0	1	69	1	0	.423	.320
Burrell, Pat	R-R	6-4	235	10-10-76	.256	.255	.257	155	472	77	121	26	0	30	97	114	4	0	8	120	0	0	.502	.400
Coste, Chris	R-R	6-1	215	2-4-73	.279	.405	.228	48	129	15	36	3	0	5	22	4	2	2	0	20	0	0	.419	.311
Dobbs, Greg	L-R	6-1	205	7-2-78	.272	.214	.277	142	324	45	88	20	4	10	55	29	1	0	4	67	3	0	.451	.330
Helms, Wes	R-R	6-4	220	5-12-76	.246	.282	.221	112	280	21	69	19	0	5	39	19	3	2	4	62	0	0	.368	.297
Howard, Ryan	L-L	6-4	255	11-19-79	.268	.225	.297	144	529	94	142	26	0	47	136	107	5	0	7	199	1	0	.584	.392
Iguchi, Tadahito	R-R	5-10	200	12-4-74	.304	.409	.255	45	138	22	42	10	0	3	12	13	1	1	3	23	6	1	.442	.361
Laforest, Pete	L-R	6-2	210	1-27-78	.091	.000	.100	14	11	2	1	0	0	1	2	0	0	0	4	0	0	.091	.231
2-team (10 San Diego)					.278	—	—	24	36	9	10	1	0	1	4	7	0	0	0	12	0	0	.389	.395
Nunez, Abraham	B-R	5-11	200	3-16-76	.234	.284	.213	136	252	24	59	10	1	0	16	30	1	4	0	48	2	0	.282	.318
Roberson, Chris	B-R	6-2	180	8-23-79	.286	.111	.368	28	28	6	8	0	0	0	1	1	0	0	4	2	0	.286	.310
Rollins, Jimmy	B-R	5-8	175	11-27-78	.296	.321	.286	162	716	139	212	38	20	30	94	49	7	0	6	85	41	6	.531	.344
Rowand, Aaron	R-R	6-0	200	8-29-77	.309	.315	.306	161	612	105	189	45	0	27	89	47	19	2	4	119	6	3	.515	.374
Ruiz, Carlos	R-R	5-10	200	1-22-79	.259	.189	.282	115	374	42	97	29	2	6	54	42	5	5	3	49	6	1	.396	.340
Utley, Chase	L-R	6-1	185	12-17-78	.332	.318	.340	132	530	104	176	48	5	22	103	50	25	1	7	89	9	1	.566	.410
Victorino, Shane	B-R	5-9	180	11-30-80	.281	.291	.276	131	456	78	128	23	3	12	46	37	10	5	2	62	37	4	.423	.347
Werth, Jayson	R-R	6-5	220	5-20-79	.298	.375	.257	94	255	43	76	11	3	8	49	44	2	2	1	73	7	1	.459	.404

PITCHING	B-T	HT	WT	DOB	W	L	ERA	G	GS	CG	SV	IP	H	R	ER	HR	BB	SO	AVG	vLH	vRH	K/9	BB/9
Alfonseca, Antonio	R-R	6-5	250	4-16-72	5	2	5.44	61	0	0	8	50	65	31	30	3	27	24	.314	.370	.278	4.35	4.89
Bisenius, Joe	R-R	6-4	205	9-18-82	0	0	0.00	2	0	0	0	2	2	0	0	0	2	3	.286	.200	.500	13.50	9.00
Castro, Fabio	L-L	5-7	185	1-20-85	0	0	6.00	10	1	0	0	12	9	8	8	2	13	14	.209	.063	.296	10.50	9.75
Condrey, Clay	R-R	6-3	215	11-19-75	5	0	5.04	39	0	0	2	50	61	30	28	4	16	27	.300	.299	.302	4.86	2.88
Davis, Kane	R-R	6-3	190	6-25-75	0	1	5.56	11	0	0	0	11	17	7	7	2	8	10	.340	.316	.355	7.94	6.35
Durbin, J.D.	R-R	6-0	210	2-24-82	6	5	5.15	18	10	1	1	65	71	42	37	6	36	39	.282	.286	.278	5.43	5.01
2-team (1 Arizona)					6	5	6.06	19	10	1	1	65	78	49	44	6	37	40	—	—	—	5.51	5.10
Eaton, Adam	R-R	6-2	200	11-23-77	10	10	6.29	30	30	0	0	162	192	117	113	30	71	97	.301	.322	.284	5.40	3.95
Ennis, John	R-R	6-5	220	10-17-79	0	0	8.22	3	1	0	1	8	12	7	7	1	3	8	.343	.400	.300	9.39	3.52
Garcia, Anderson	R-R	6-3	180	3-23-81	0	0	13.50	1	0	0	0	1	2	1	1	0	0	0	.500	1.000	.333	0.00	0.00
Garcia, Freddy	R-R	6-4	260	6-10-76	1	5	5.90	11	11	0	0	58	74	39	38	12	19	50	.318	.292	.339	7.76	2.95
Geary, Geoff	R-R	6-0	180	8-26-76	3	2	4.41	57	0	0	0	67	72	44	33	8	25	38	.283	.248	.309	5.08	3.34
Gordon, Tom	R-R	5-10	200	11-18-67	3	2	4.73	44	0	0	6	40	40	21	21	7	13	32	.263	.310	.222	7.20	2.93
Hamels, Cole	L-L	6-3	190	12-27-83	15	5	3.39	28	28	2	0	183	163	72	69	25	43	177	.237	.247	.236	8.69	2.11
Happ, J.A.	L-L	6-6	200	10-19-82	0	1	11.25	1	1	0	0	4	7	5	5	3	2	5	.368	.333	.375	11.25	4.50
Hernandez, Yoel	R-R	6-2	180	4-15-80	0	0	5.28	14	0	0	0	15	20	9	9	2	1	13	.303	.296	.308	7.63	0.59
Kendrick, Kyle	R-R	6-3	190	8-26-84	10	4	3.87	20	20	0	0	121	129	53	52	16	25	49	.280	.321	.241	3.64	1.86
Lieber, Jon	L-R	6-2	240	4-2-70	3	6	4.73	14	12	1	0	78	91	44	41	7	22	54	.293	.310	.278	6.23	2.54
Lohse, Kyle	R-R	6-2	210	10-4-78	3	0	4.72	13	11	0	0	61	64	33	32	6	24	42	.276	.270	.282	6.20	3.54
2-team (21 Cincinnati)					9	12	4.62	34	32	2	0	193	207	109	99	22	57	122	—	—	—	5.70	2.66
Madson, Ryan	R-R	6-6	200	8-28-80	2	2	3.05	38	0	0	1	56	48	19	19	5	23	43	.231	.170	.275	6.91	3.70
Mesa, Jose	R-R	6-3	235	5-22-66	1	2	5.54	40	0	0	1	39	34	32	24	6	19	20	.239	.233	.244	4.62	4.38
Moyer, Jamie	L-L	6-0	185	11-18-62	14	12	5.01	33	33	1	0	199	222	118	111	30	66	133	.285	.309	.279	6.01	2.98
Myers, Brett	R-R	6-4	220	8-17-80	5	7	4.33	51	3	0	21	69	61	33	33	9	27	83	.234	.183	.274	10.88	3.54
Romero, J.C.	B-L	5-11	205	6-4-76	1	2	1.24	51	0	0	0	36	15	5	5	1	25	31	.130	.125	.133	7.68	6.19
Rosario, Francisco	R-R	6-0	205	9-28-80	0	3	5.47	23	0	0	1	26	34	16	16	3	13	25	.321	.340	.304	8.54	4.44
Sanches, Brian	R-R	6-0	190	8-8-78	1	1	5.52	12	0	0	0	15	13	11	9	6	12	9	.241	.300	.206	5.52	7.36
Segovia, Zack	R-R	6-2	245	4-11-83	0	1	9.00	1	1	0	0	5	8	5	5	1	1	2	.400	.250	.500	3.60	1.80
Smith, Matt	L-L	6-4	215	6-15-79	0	0	11.25	9	0	0	0	4	4	5	5	0	11	1	.250	.400	.182	2.25	24.75
Zagurski, Michael	L-L	6-0	225	1-27-83	1	0	5.91	25	0	0	0	21	25	14	14	3	11	21	.287	.216	.340	8.86	4.64

FIELDING

Catcher	PCT	G	PO	A	E	DP	PB
Barajas	1.000	38	252	14	0	3	1
Coste	1.000	31	157	12	0	3	2
Ruiz	.997	111	688	54	2	4	5

First Base	PCT	G	PO	A	E	DP
Barajas	1.000	1	1	1	0	0
Coste	1.000	1	6	0	0	1
Dobbs	1.000	14	102	6	0	8
Helms	.990	18	93	4	1	12
Howard	.991	140	1191	103	12	124
Utley	1.000	1	6	0	0	2
Werth	1.000	1	1	0	0	0

Second Base	PCT	G	PO	A	E	DP
Dobbs	1.000	4	0	7	0	0
Iguchi	1.000	31	72	90	0	30
Nunez	1.000	4	11	4	0	2
Utley	.985	132	289	372	10	85

Third Base	PCT	G	PO	A	E	DP
Branyan	1.000	1	1	0	0	0
Dobbs	.945	68	44	77	7	7
Helms	.932	68	27	97	9	3
Nunez	.960	113	41	175	9	12

Shortstop	PCT	G	PO	A	E	DP
Nunez	1.000	8	0	3	0	1

Rollins	.985	162	227	479	11	110

Outfield	PCT	G	PO	A	E	DP
Bourn	1.000	90	76	0	0	0
Branyan	—	1	0	0	0	0
Burrell	.948	138	176	8	10	2
Dobbs	.955	17	21	0	1	0
Roberson	.950	18	18	1	1	1
Rowand	.995	161	392	11	2	2
Victorino	.988	117	232	10	3	4
Werth	.987	76	147	9	2	2

ORGANIZATION STATISTICS

OTTAWA LYNX   TRIPLE-A

INTERNATIONAL LEAGUE

BATTING	B-T	HT	WT	DOB	AVG	vLH	vRH	G	AB	R	H	2B	3B	HR	RBI	BB	HBP	SH	SF	SO	SB	CS	SLG	OBP
Abernathy, Brent	R-R	6-0	185	9-23-77	.286	1.000	.167	2	7	0	2	0	0	0	0	0	0	1	0	0			.286	.286
2-team (107 Columbus)					.266	—	—	109	357	38	95	17	1	2	36	35	1	5	3	37	15	6	.336	.331
Boyd, Shaun	R-R	5-11	188	8-15-81	.000	.000	—	1	2	0	0	0	0	0	0	1	0	0	0	1	0		.000	.333
Burnham, Gary	L-L	5-11	219	10-13-74	.292	.287	.295	137	493	59	144	35	0	12	84	70	13	0	5	73	0	1	.436	.391
Calloway, Ron	L-L	6-1	210	9-4-76	.200	.238	.188	31	90	11	18	3	0	0	3	8	0	0	0	13	1	0	.233	.265
Collier, Lou	R-R	5-10	195	8-21-73	.304	.383	.259	43	168	22	51	8	1	2	22	10	2	2	1	35	2	1	.399	.348
Coste, Chris	R-R	6-1	215	2-4-73	.233	.300	.200	26	90	8	21	5	0	0	10	1	1	0	1	14	0	0	.289	.317
Dawkins, Gookie	R-R	6-1	180	5-12-79	.274	.444	.221	31	113	12	31	7	0	1	7	11	2	2	1	31	1	2	.363	.346
Garciaparra, Michael	R-R	6-1	165	4-2-83	.154	.000	.200	4	13	1	2	0	0	0	1	4	1	0	0	4	0	0	.154	.389
Gradoville, Tim	R-R	6-3	195	1-30-80	.273	.000	.333	8	11	1	3	0	0	0	0	2	0	0	0	5	0	0	.273	.385
Hammond, Joey	R-R	6-1	190	10-27-77	.280	.400	.200	25	75	7	21	0	0	0	5	11	1	1	1	13	0	0	.293	.375
Jaramillo, Jason	B-R	6-0	200	10-9-82	.271	.293	.261	118	435	52	118	13	4	6	56	50	5	2	4	79	0	1	.361	.350
King, Brennan	R-R	6-2	220	1-20-81	.277	.219	.306	122	465	54	129	17	2	10	59	39	4	0	4	75	1	0	.387	.336
Leon, Carlos	B-R	5-10	181	8-31-79	.217	.217	.217	76	198	28	43	7	0	0	13	17	8	0	0	32	0	4	.253	.305
Merchan, Jesus	R-R	6-0	184	3-26-81	.385	.250	.444	3	13	5	5	0	1	1	2	1	0	1	0	2	0	0	.769	.421
Moran, Javon	R-R	5-10	170	9-30-82	.241	.292	.221	39	170	26	41	7	3	0	3	11	3	2	0	42	5	2	.318	.299
Padgett, Matt	L-R	6-2	215	7-22-77	.287	.262	.300	32	122	10	35	8	1	4	15	7	1	0	2	25	0	0	.467	.326
Roberson, Chris	B-R	6-2	180	4-8-79	.266	.280	.259	113	463	64	123	21	3	4	48	31	3	7	5	57	19	9	.350	.313
Ruiz, Randy	R-R	6-3	235	10-19-77	.215	.250	.191	22	79	11	17	4	0	4	11	9	0	0	0	23	0	0	.418	.295
Rushford, Jim	L-L	6-1	220	3-24-74	.266	.246	.274	120	413	27	110	24	0	2	47	30	7	3	4	31	1	0	.339	.324
Sandoval, Danny	B-R	5-11	205	4-7-79	.244	.241	.245	101	365	28	89	10	1	3	24	8	4	6	3	35	6	3	.301	.266
Swann, Pedro	L-R	6-0	205	10-27-70	.252	.149	.277	72	238	29	60	14	1	5	22	17	2	2	3	54	2	2	.382	.304
Thurston, Joe	L-R	5-11	190	9-29-79	.300	.277	.312	129	496	70	149	29	9	5	59	44	11	16	5	55	16	14	.425	.367
Wathan, Dusty	R-R	6-4	215	8-22-73	.272	.321	.234	75	243	24	66	14	1	0	23	18	12	2	2	39	3	1	.337	.349

PITCHING	B-T	HT	WT	DOB	W	L	ERA	G	GS	CG	SV	IP	H	R	ER	HR	BB	SO	AVG	vLH	vRH	K/9	BB/9
Anderson, Jason	L-R	6-0	190	6-9-79	2	2	5.32	23	2	0	1	44	50	27	26	4	11	32	.294	.273	.312	6.55	2.25
Bauer, Rick	R-R	6-6	225	1-10-77	2	4	7.36	16	4	0	0	33	48	33	27	8	22	21	.340	.421	.286	5.73	6.00
Bisenius, Joe	R-R	6-4	205	9-18-82	3	4	5.48	35	0	0	0	46	52	29	28	5	31	41	.301	.258	.327	8.02	6.07
Brito, Eude	L-L	5-11	190	8-19-78	1	6	6.17	20	10	0	0	58	74	42	40	9	34	31	.311	.315	.310	4.78	5.25
Cameron, Ryan	R-R	6-1	175	9-13-77	0	0	5.84	15	1	0	0	25	39	19	16	2	15	22	.368	.316	.397	8.03	5.47
Castro, Fabio	L-L	5-7	185	1-20-85	5	5	4.01	21	7	0	1	58	53	32	26	7	33	47	.249	.222	.258	7.25	5.09
Childers, Matt	R-R	6-5	190	12-3-78	7	4	5.17	19	19	1	0	103	138	63	59	11	26	73	.325	.291	.354	6.40	2.28
Condrey, Clay	R-R	6-3	215	11-19-75	1	0	2.45	10	0	0	1	22	19	7	6	0	5	10	.250	.267	.239	4.09	2.05
Crowell, Jim	R-L	6-4	225	5-14-74	0	0	15.19	2	2	0	0	5	12	9	9	0	5	4	.462	.500	.444	6.75	8.44
2-team (26 Syracuse)					1	4	7.44	28	8	0	0	56	75	49	46	3	27	23	—	—		4.37	4.37
Davis, Kane	R-R	6-3	190	6-25-75	3	3	3.06	41	0	0	4	53	46	21	18	2	26	60	.237	.230	.243	10.19	4.42
Durbin, J.D.	R-R	6-0	210	2-24-82	2	4	4.55	10	10	0	0	59	67	33	30	9	21	44	.288	.271	.302	6.67	3.19
Ennis, John	R-R	6-5	220	10-17-79	4	4	3.38	37	7	0	1	88	90	40	33	7	32	83	.269	.303	.239	8.49	3.27
Garcia, Anderson	R-R	6-2	180	3-23-81	1	5	5.13	37	1	0	4	60	63	35	34	7	20	42	.270	.261	.280	6.34	3.02
Geary, Geoff	R-R	6-0	180	8-26-76	2	1	2.52	14	0	0	0	25	28	9	7	0	1	21	.280	.280	.280	7.56	0.36
Happ, J.A.	L-L	6-6	200	10-19-82	4	6	5.02	24	24	0	0	118	118	74	66	12	62	117	.265	.291	.256	8.90	4.72
Hernandez, Yoel	R-R	6-2	210	4-15-80	1	3	3.94	22	0	0	5	30	33	14	13	0	14	16	.282	.241	.317	4.85	4.25
Jacobsen, Landon	R-R	6-3	220	5-4-79	2	7	4.80	13	12	1	0	69	89	48	37	5	31	38	.319	.301	.338	4.93	4.02
Knotts, Gary	R-R	6-4	225	2-12-77	1	2	5.89	3	3	2	0	18	21	12	12	4	8	11	.288	.273	.310	5.40	3.93
Mazone, Brian	L-L	6-4	200	7-26-76	3	2	2.21	6	6	0	0	37	30	14	9	4	8	20	.227	.243	.221	4.91	1.96
Miller, Justin	R-R	6-2	200	8-27-77	0	0	3.86	3	0	0	0	2	4	1	1	0	3	2	.400	.333	.429	7.71	11.57
Nelson, Bubba	R-R	6-1	195	8-26-81	3	7	5.19	12	11	1	0	69	68	42	40	10	27	40	.257	.272	.233	5.19	3.50
Rushford, Jim	L-L	6-1	220	3-24-74	0	0	9.00	1	0	0	0	1	2	1	1	0	0	1	.400	.000	.500	9.00	0.00
Sanches, Brian	R-R	6-0	190	8-8-78	2	3	4.75	36	1	0	16	47	57	29	25	5	8	52	.295	.304	.287	9.89	1.52
Segovia, Zack	R-R	6-2	245	4-11-83	1	9	6.05	13	13	1	0	77	99	55	52	8	28	22	.315	.331	.301	2.56	3.26
Smith, Matt	L-L	6-4	215	6-15-79	2	1	2.60	16	0	0	0	17	13	5	5	2	7	16	.210	.172	.242	8.31	3.63
Totten, Heath	R-R	6-3	210	9-30-78	1	5	7.09	6	6	0	0	33	49	28	26	2	8	11	.348	.391	.312	3.00	2.18
Weatherby III, Charles	R-R	6-0	208	12-23-78	2	1	3.16	9	4	0	0	31	26	13	11	2	8	16	.230	.190	.254	4.60	2.30
Zagurski, Michael	L-L	6-0	225	1-27-83	0	0	2.00	7	0	0	0	9	7	2	2	0	6	11	.212	.083	.286	11.00	6.00

FIELDING

Catcher	PCT	G	PO	A	E	DP	PB
Coste	1.000	6	45	5	0	0	0
Gradoville	1.000	2	10	2	0	0	0
Jaramillo	.978	109	708	75	18	9	10
Wathan	.995	29	176	20	1	1	1

First Base	PCT	G	PO	A	E	DP
Burnham	.990	44	361	24	4	40
Coste	1.000	16	125	14	0	14
Hammond	1.000	2	22	1	0	3
Padgett	.900	1	8	1	1	0
Ruiz	1.000	9	68	8	0	10
Rushford	.997	45	287	22	1	23
Wathan	.990	33	273	24	3	32

Second Base	PCT	G	PO	A	E	DP
Abernathy	.900	2	1	8	1	2
Dawkins	1.000	2	8	8	0	1

	PCT	G	PO	A	E	DP
Garciaparra	1.000	3	5	12	0	1
Hammond	.957	4	10	12	1	4
King	1.000	1	3	1	0	1
Leon	.983	13	29	29	1	6
Sandoval	1.000	16	32	50	0	16
Thurston	.985	104	229	296	8	66

Third Base	PCT	G	PO	A	E	DP
Coste	—	1	0	0	0	0
Dawkins	1.000	1	3	1	0	0
Hammond	.919	14	6	28	3	2
King	.973	120	88	201	8	22
Sandoval	.962	9	3	22	1	1
Wathan	—	1	0	0	0	0

Shortstop	PCT	G	PO	A	E	DP
Dawkins	.957	28	48	62	5	19
Garciaparra	1.000	1	0	2	0	0

	PCT	G	PO	A	E	DP
Leon	.950	40	69	101	9	21
Merchan	.905	3	8	11	2	2
Sandoval	.960	76	106	207	13	49

Outfield	PCT	G	PO	A	E	DP
Boyd	.667	1	2	0	1	0
Burnham	.962	15	25	0	1	0
Calloway	1.000	24	45	1	0	0
Collier	.967	33	55	3	2	0
Hammond	1.000	2	2	0	0	0
Leon	.842	15	16	0	3	0
Moran	.989	39	87	2	1	0
Padgett	1.000	31	61	3	0	0
Roberson	.961	112	287	11	12	2
Ruiz	1.000	5	12	0	0	0
Rushford	1.000	74	133	5	0	1
Swann	.969	68	123	1	4	0
Thurston	1.000	24	59	2	0	1

READING PHILLIES　　DOUBLE-A

EASTERN LEAGUE

BATTING	B-T	HT	WT	DOB	AVG	vLH	vRH	G	AB	R	H	2B	3B	HR	RBI	BB	HBP	SH	SF	SO	SB	CS	SLG	OBP
Barajas, Rod	R-R	6-2	230	9-5-75	.200	—	.200	2	5	0	1	0	0	0	0	0	0	0	0	0	0	0	.200	.200
Boyd, Shaun	R-R	5-11	188	8-15-81	.200	.333	.091	21	40	4	8	0	0	2	7	3	2	0	2	9	0	0	.350	.277
Burgamy, Brian	B-R	5-10	190	6-27-81	.191	.161	.205	56	183	20	35	7	0	3	11	26	2	1	1	47	4	2	.279	.297
Costanzo, Mike	L-R	6-3	215	9-9-83	.270	.262	.273	137	508	92	137	29	1	27	86	75	7	0	5	157	2	0	.490	.368
Coste, Chris	R-R	6-1	215	2-4-73	.287	.360	.265	27	108	14	31	5	0	5	31	5	1	0	2	13	0	0	.472	.319
Cuevas, Phillip	R-R	5-11	168	6-30-85	.000	—	.000	1	1	0	0	0	0	0	0	0	0	0	0	0	0	0	.000	.000
Florence, Branden	R-R	6-0	195	4-3-78	.350	.182	.556	10	9	3	7	2	1	0	4	4	1	0	0	3	0	0	.550	.480
Garciaparra, Michael	R-R	6-1	165	4-2-83	.240	.263	.231	84	271	32	65	4	3	3	26	34	9	4	1	54	6	2	.303	.343
Golson, Greg	R-R	6-0	190	9-17-85	.242	.186	.264	37	153	20	37	5	2	3	16	2	1	1	1	49	5	0	.359	.255
Gradoville, Tim	R-R	6-3	195	1-30-80	.152	.133	.161	46	138	12	21	4	0	0	5	11	4	3	1	43	4	1	.181	.234
Hammond, Joey	R-R	6-1	190	10-27-77	.300	.257	.319	92	333	62	100	12	2	6	51	38	1	1	3	43	4	3	.402	.371
Hill, Jason	R-R	6-3	210	3-17-77	.302	.300	.303	116	434	57	131	33	0	9	67	34	0	1	2	62	1	2	.440	.351
Jacobs, Greg	L-L	5-9	195	10-9-76	.310	.291	.315	133	462	75	143	39	2	21	83	43	8	0	2	64	2	5	.539	.377
Leon, Carlos	B-R	5-10	181	8-31-79	.167	.222	.133	7	24	1	4	1	0	0	2	0	0	0	0	4	0	1	.208	-.231
Made, Hector	R-R	6-1	155	12-18-84	.100	.000	.143	3	10	1	1	0	0	1	2	0	0	0	0	3	0	0	.400	.100
Merchan, Jesus	R-R	6-0	184	3-26-81	.330	.377	.314	81	276	53	91	16	2	7	44	23	14	5	4	17	10	3	.404	.404
Moran, Javon	R-R	5-10	170	9-30-82	.298	.259	.316	67	255	52	76	12	2	2	19	34	6	3	4	38	24	12	.384	.388
Padgett, Matt	L-R	6-2	215	7-22-77	.232	.284	.211	94	332	33	77	22	0	8	40	27	0	2	3	68	1	0	.370	.287
Ramos, Peeter	R-R	5-11	180	3-19-82	.305	.304	.305	80	282	41	86	9	0	8	37	32	5	1	4	39	5	5	.422	.381
Ruiz, Randy	R-R	6-3	235	10-19-77	.378	.364	.380	22	82	16	31	10	0	3	12	6	1	0	0	21	1	0	.610	.427
3-team (47 Altoona, 39 Connecticut)					.309	—	—	108	395	61	122	25	4	18	69	35	6	0	3	93	1	1	.529	.371
Shier, Peter	R-R	6-2	165	3-16-81	.077	.000	.091	6	13	1	1	0	0	0	0	0	1	0	0	2	0	0	.077	.143
Spidale, Mike	R-R	5-10	190	3-12-82	.314	.338	.306	68	264	44	83	5	6	2	21	19	6	1	2	19	11	3	.402	.371
Swann, Pedro	L-R	6-0	205	10-27-70	.243	.091	.313	21	70	6	17	4	0	2	13	9	0	0	1	17	2	3	.386	.325
Tejeda, Juan	R-R	6-2	195	1-26-82	.248	.254	.245	103	314	35	78	24	3	10	61	26	4	0	4	39	1	0	.439	.310
Thurston, Joe	L-R	5-11	190	9-29-79	.308	.167	.429	4	13	2	4	2	0	0	2	2	0	2	0	1	1	1	.462	.400
Utley, Chase	L-R	6-1	185	12-17-78	.100	.143	.000	3	10	1	1	0	0	0	0	1	0	0	0	2	0	0	.100	.182
Victorino, Shane	B-R	5-9	180	11-30-80	.333	—	.333	2	6	0	2	0	0	0	1	0	0	0	0	1	0	0	.333	.333
Wathan, Dusty	R-R	6-2	215	8-22-73	.400	—	.400	1	5	1	2	0	0	0	0	0	0	0	0	0	0	0	.400	.400

PITCHING	B-T	HT	WT	DOB	W	L	ERA	G	GS	CG	SV	IP	H	R	ER	HR	BB	SO	AVG	vLH	vRH	K/9	BB/9
Anderson, Jason	L-R	6-0	190	6-9-79	2	1	3.05	14	0	0	0	21	20	8	7	3	4	19	.253	.341	.143	8.27	1.74
Cameron, Ryan	R-R	6-1	175	9-13-77	0	1	5.61	30	2	0	1	43	46	27	27	6	30	49	.279	.259	.300	10.18	6.23
Carrasco, Carlos	R-R	6-3	180	3-21-87	6	4	4.86	14	13	1	0	70	65	42	38	9	46	49	.247	.237	.258	6.27	5.89
Castro, Fabio	L-L	5-7	185	1-20-85	2	0	2.70	11	0	0	1	17	12	5	5	0	6	24	.194	.231	.184	12.96	3.24
Davis, Allen	L-L	6-4	220	10-1-75	3	2	4.79	31	1	0	1	47	63	28	25	4	18	39	.321	.267	.346	7.47	3.45
De La Cruz, Julio	R-R	6-1	161	10-7-80	1	4	4.87	48	0	0	6	65	65	44	35	4	32	58	.256	.296	.217	8.07	4.45
Eaton, Adam	R-R	6-2	200	11-23-77	0	0	9.00	1	1	0	0	2	3	2	2	0	1	1	.429	.250	.667	4.50	0.00
Evangelista, Nicholas	R-R	6-4	215	3-17-82	0	0	7.36	9	0	0	0	11	15	10	9	2	6	7	.326	.435	.217	5.73	4.91
Garcia, Anderson	R-R	6-2	180	3-23-81	0	2	3.12	14	0	0	7	17	16	6	6	1	1	9	.239	.293	.154	9.87	0.52
Jacobsen, Landon	R-R	6-3	220	5-4-79	6	5	4.61	16	16	1	0	94	94	53	48	6	35	45	.264	.238	.291	4.32	3.36
Johnson, Nathan	R-R	6-1	210	1-13-82	0	0	6.08	11	0	0	0	13	17	9	9	2	4	10	.315	.407	.222	6.75	2.70
Kendrick, Kyle	R-R	6-3	190	8-26-84	4	7	3.21	12	12	1	0	81	82	38	29	3	18	50	.265	.270	.259	5.53	1.99
Key, Chris	R-L	6-3	210	10-30-77	5	2	2.65	58	0	0	18	75	76	28	22	4	12	28	.267	.214	.289	3.38	1.45
Knotts, Gary	R-R	6-4	225	2-12-77	1	2	0.86	3	3	1	0	21	12	6	2	0	9	16	.169	.237	.091	6.86	3.86
Madson, Ryan	L-R	6-6	200	8-28-80	0	0	0.00	2	0	0	0	3	3	0	0	0	4	3	.273	.286	.250	12.00	0.00
Maloney, Matthew	L-L	6-4	220	1-16-84	9	7	3.94	21	21	1	0	126	117	70	55	13	45	115	.246	.252	.245	8.24	3.22
Mateo, Julio	R-R	6-0	220	8-2-77	1	0	2.81	11	0	0	3	16	14	5	5	2	1	14	.237	.267	.207	7.88	0.56
Mathieson, Scott	R-R	6-3	190	2-27-84	0	0	9.00	2	0	0	0	2	3	3	2	1	2	1	.333	.250	.400	4.50	9.00
McClaskey, Tim	B-R	6-1	175	1-11-76	4	4	3.95	13	10	0	0	57	56	35	25	8	12	32	.249	.225	.268	5.05	1.89
Nelson, Bubba	R-R	6-1	195	8-26-81	2	1	1.67	24	3	0	1	43	23	8	8	2	16	44	.154	.141	.167	9.21	3.35
Outman, Josh	L-L	6-1	180	9-14-84	2	3	4.50	7	7	1	0	42	38	25	21	5	23	34	.242	.209	.254	7.29	4.93
Overholt, Pat	R-R	6-3	190	2-8-84	6	9	5.90	15	15	0	0	79	92	61	52	10	43	54	.294	.252	.331	6.13	4.88
Rojas, Chris	R-R	6-2	180	3-30-77	7	4	4.25	19	14	0	0	78	71	41	37	12	49	54	.247	.238	.255	6.24	5.63
Segovia, Zack	R-R	6-2	245	4-11-83	5	3	4.84	10	10	0	0	58	65	34	31	4	22	30	.290	.300	.279	4.68	3.43
Simpson, Allan	R-R	6-4	225	8-26-77	0	2	5.19	15	1	0	0	26	20	16	15	1	19	27	.220	.175	.255	9.35	6.57
Totten, Heath	R-R	6-3	210	9-30-78	2	5	3.38	14	11	0	0	56	61	23	21	3	13	31	.282	.323	.228	4.98	2.09
Trujillo, J.J.	R-R	6-0	180	10-9-75	0	1	4.67	12	0	0	0	17	15	9	9	0	8	18	.242	.231	.250	9.35	4.15
Weatherby III, Charles	R-R	6-0	208	12-23-78	0	1	11.85	8	1	0	0	14	25	24	18	4	11	10	.391	.457	.310	6.59	7.24
Willey, Cory	L-L	6-0	185	4-22-81	2	1	15.00	8	0	0	0	6	11	10	10	1	4	8	.367	.500	.318	12.00	6.00
Zagurski, Michael	L-L	6-0	225	1-27-83	0	0	1.29	6	0	0	0	7	2	1	1	0	2	8	.083	.333	.048	10.29	2.57

FIELDING

Catcher	PCT	G	PO	A	E	DP	PB
Barajas	1.000	2	11	0	0	0	0
Coste	.994	18	145	11	1	0	1
Gradoville	.989	42	235	29	3	6	4
Hill	.993	82	523	46	4	3	6
Wathan	1.000	1	3	1	0	0	0

First Base	PCT	G	PO	A	E	DP
Coste	1.000	7	50	7	0	5
Hammond	1.000	10	55	5	0	5
Hill	.967	30	185	19	7	22
Padgett	.985	49	371	22	6	35
Ruiz	1.000	4	27	4	0	2
Tejeda	.988	52	384	36	5	37

Second Base	PCT	G	PO	A	E	DP
Garciaparra	.909	5	6	14	2	2

	PCT	G	PO	A	E	DP
Hammond	1.000	32	60	86	0	18
Merchan	.981	25	48	56	2	13
Ramos	.983	78	162	178	6	44
Shier	1.000	1	1	0	0	0
Thurston	1.000	4	10	13	0	3
Utley	1.000	2	5	4	0	0

Third Base	PCT	G	PO	A	E	DP
Costanzo	.917	135	108	269	34	24
Hammond	1.000	3	2	4	0	0
Merchan	.778	5	3	4	2	2
Shier	1.000	1	0	2	0	0

Shortstop	PCT	G	PO	A	E	DP
Garciaparra	.957	78	112	176	13	36
Hammond	.946	20	27	43	4	11
Leon	1.000	7	5	19	0	3

	PCT	G	PO	A	E	DP
Made	.889	3	7	9	2	5
Merchan	.955	40	67	103	8	28
Shier	.818	3	8	10	4	3

Outfield	PCT	G	PO	A	E	DP
Boyd	.929	9	13	0	1	0
Burgamy	.992	51	114	3	1	2
Florence	1.000	3	8	0	0	0
Golson	1.000	36	95	4	0	2
Hammond	1.000	35	60	2	0	0
Jacobs	.989	126	248	14	3	4
Moran	.988	66	164	1	2	0
Padgett	1.000	42	68	1	0	0
Ruiz	1.000	14	17	2	0	0
Spidale	.992	55	118	2	1	2
Swann	.938	11	15	0	1	0
Victorino	1.000	1	1	0	0	0

CLEARWATER THRESHERS

HIGH CLASS A

FLORIDA STATE LEAGUE

BATTING	B-T	HT	WT	DOB	AVG	vLH	vRH	G	AB	R	H	2B	3B	HR	RBI	BB	HBP	SH	SF	SO	SB	CS	SLG	OBP
Antoniato, P.J.	R-R	5-9	185	7-2-83	.258	.242	.263	41	132	18	34	6	0	0	15	4	2	4	0	9	0	0	.303	.290
Baez, Welinson	R-R	6-3	190	7-7-84	.238	.175	.259	63	231	25	55	13	2	6	30	19	1	0	2	86	1	4	.390	.296
Blalock, Jake	R-R	6-4	205	8-6-83	.264	.225	.280	42	140	22	37	10	0	6	26	21	0	0	4	30	0	0	.464	.352
Boyd, Shaun	R-R	5-11	188	8-15-81	.231	.571	.156	10	39	4	9	2	0	1	4	5	0	0	5	1	0	.359	.318
Brown, Dominic	L-L	6-5	204	9-3-87	.444	.250	.600	3	9	2	4	1	0	1	7	2	0	0	0	0	0	0	.889	.545
Budde, Ryan	R-R	5-11	205	8-15-79	.200	—	.200	3	10	1	2	1	0	0	0	0	0	0	0	3	0	0	.300	.200
Burgamy, Brian	B-R	5-10	190	6-27-81	.262	.208	.282	68	260	43	68	14	3	10	38	44	0	1	3	52	7	5	.454	.365
Coste, Chris	R-R	6-1	215	2-4-73	.400	—	.400	3	10	3	4	1	0	0	1	0	0	0	0	1	0	0	.500	.400
Donald, Jason	R-R	6-1	190	9-4-84	.300	.323	.294	83	293	48	88	22	5	8	41	35	6	2	0	70	3	2	.491	.386
Garciaparra, Michael	R-R	6-1	165	4-2-83	.182	.400	.000	5	11	3	2	1	0	0	2	3	1	0	0	2	0	0	.273	.400
Golson, Greg	R-R	6-0	190	9-17-85	.285	.296	.281	99	418	66	119	27	3	12	52	21	4	2	4	124	25	8	.450	.322
Guevara, Orlando	B-R	6-1	175	9-13-83	.135	.100	.148	17	37	2	5	2	0	0	6	5	0	3	0	10	0	0	.189	.238
Hall, Victor	L-L	5-10	160	9-16-80	.239	.333	.224	18	67	8	16	1	2	0	2	5	0	2	0	19	3	0	.313	.292
Harman, Brad	R-R	6-1	175	11-19-85	.281	.267	.286	122	448	63	126	26	5	13	62	40	3	4	4	105	1	1	.449	.341
Harris, Clay	R-R	6-4	220	8-25-82	.255	.276	.248	103	364	43	93	23	0	10	64	40	4	1	3	61	0	0	.401	.333
Hernandez, Fidel	R-R	5-11	160	1-18-86	.247	.115	.302	27	89	4	22	2	0	0	8	1	0	3	0	6	1	2	.270	.256
Howard, Kevin	L-R	6-2	190	6-25-81	.174	.125	.184	15	46	6	8	0	0	0	2	6	1	0	0	11	1	1	.174	.283
Jackson, Nic	L-R	6-3	200	9-25-79	.273	.267	.274	20	77	13	21	6	1	0	6	5	1	0	0	12	6	3	.377	.325
Kennelly, Timothy	R-R	6-0	180	12-5-86	.167	.000	.200	5	6	0	1	0	0	0	1	1	0	0	0	0	0	0	.167	.286
Made, Hector	R-R	6-1	155	12-18-84	.247	.158	.278	42	146	21	36	8	0	0	6	13	1	0	0	28	2	2	.301	.313
Marson, Lou	R-R	6-1	200	6-26-86	.288	.319	.278	111	393	68	113	24	1	7	63	52	5	1	6	80	3	1	.407	.373
Miller, Jay	R-R	5-10	185	8-11-83	.278	.250	.286	5	18	4	5	1	0	0	2	1	0	0	0	4	0	0	.333	.350
Morales, Jaime	R-R	6-1	165	4-21-84	.000	.000	.000	1	3	0	0	0	0	0	0	1	0	0	0	1	0	0	.000	.000
Moran, Javon	R-R	5-10	170	9-30-82	.154	.000	.182	3	13	3	2	0	0	0	2	0	0	0	0	6	1	0	.154	.267
Quiroz, Arlon	R-R	6-0	170	11-13-86	.667	—	.667	2	3	1	2	1	0	0	1	0	0	0	0	1	0	0	1.000	.667
Sanchez, Jesus	R-R	5-11	160	9-24-87	1.000	1.000	—	1	1	0	1	0	0	0	0	0	0	0	0	0	0	0	1.000	1.000
Shier, Peter	R-R	6-2	165	3-16-81	.198	.333	.164	25	91	9	18	2	0	3	9	2	1	1	0	18	0	2	.319	.223
Slayden, Jeremy	L-R	6-0	185	7-28-82	.287	.345	.267	118	432	71	124	24	4	14	73	60	4	0	4	96	7	1	.458	.376
Spidale, Mike	R-R	6-1	190	3-12-82	.275	.292	.269	58	240	29	66	9	4	0	26	16	4	1	3	30	12	4	.346	.327
Suomi, John	L-R	5-11	199	10-5-80	.258	.111	.283	20	62	11	16	5	0	2	7	12	1	0	0	6	0	0	.435	.387
Thayer, Matt	R-L	5-10	173	2-21-82	.278	.346	.251	82	284	53	79	10	1	3	30	38	6	2	2	57	10	4	.331	.373
Urick, John	L-L	6-2	210	2-22-82	.240	.132	.268	77	262	35	63	14	1	10	55	35	3	2	6	78	0	1	.416	.330
Werth, Jayson	R-R	6-5	220	5-20-79	.077	.000	.125	4	13	3	1	0	0	0	0	0	0	0	0	4	0	0	.077	.077

PITCHING	B-T	HT	WT	DOB	W	L	ERA	G	GS	CG	SV	IP	H	R	ER	HR	BB	SO	AVG	vLH	vRH	K/9	BB/9
Austin, Richard	R-R	6-3	210	1-16-85	0	0	3.00	2	0	0	0	3	1	1	1	0	3	2	.111	.333	.000	6.00	9.00
Bastardo, Antonio	L-L	5-11	168	9-21-85	1	0	7.20	1	1	0	0	5	5	4	4	0	3	12	.250	.200	.267	21.60	5.40
Brauer, Daniel	L-L	6-0	210	10-14-83	4	3	6.00	8	8	0	0	36	33	24	24	2	28	35	.246	.345	.219	8.75	7.00
Brito, Eude	L-L	5-11	190	8-19-78	0	0	2.35	6	0	0	0	8	3	4	2	1	3	7	.111	.000	.200	8.22	3.52
Carpenter, Andrew	R-R	6-3	230	5-18-85	17	6	3.20	27	24	3	1	163	150	65	58	16	53	116	.242	.263	.228	6.40	2.93
Carrasco, Carlos	R-R	6-3	180	3-21-87	6	2	2.84	12	12	1	0	70	49	22	22	8	22	53	.199	.200	.198	6.85	2.84
Concepcion, Alexander	R-R	6-1	180	9-27-84	3	5	6.31	13	10	1	0	67	73	48	47	8	22	60	.279	.257	.294	8.06	2.96
Cruse, Andrew	R-R	6-1	200	5-31-84	6	4	4.64	6	4	0	0	33	32	21	17	3	13	22	.258	.333	.200	6.00	3.55
Davis, Allen	L-L	6-4	220	10-1-75	0	0	1.74	4	0	0	1	10	8	2	2	0	3	3	.222	.111	.259	2.61	2.61
Escalona, Sergio	L-L	6-0	178	8-3-84	0	0	2.25	1	1	0	0	4	8	1	1	0	2	4	.444	.500	.438	9.00	4.50
Garcia, Freddy	R-R	6-4	260	6-10-76	0	0	0.00	2	2	0	0	6	5	0	0	0	1	8	.217	.100	.308	11.37	1.42
Gordon, Tom	R-R	5-10	200	11-18-67	0	0	0.00	2	2	0	0	3	2	0	0	0	1	1	.111	.200	.000	3.38	3.38
Griffith, Derek	L-L	6-6	205	10-28-82	2	0	0.00	4	0	0	0	7	1	0	0	0	10	10	.042	.000	.059	12.27	12.27
Harker, Brett	R-R	6-3	185	7-9-84	2	2	6.69	32	1	0	13	39	46	29	29	5	15	24	.295	.375	.250	5.54	3.46
Hill, Ronald	R-R	6-3	225	11-29-82	5	4	2.23	27	0	0	5	40	30	11	10	3	13	30	.217	.186	.241	6.69	2.90
Johnson, Nathan	R-R	6-1	210	1-13-82	3	2	3.71	23	5	0	0	63	62	31	26	7	20	49	.264	.223	.291	7.00	2.86
Lieber, Jon	L-R	6-2	240	4-2-70	0	0	2.45	1	1	0	0	4	4	2	1	0	0	4	.250	.250	.250	9.82	0.00
Mathieson, Scott	R-R	6-3	190	2-27-84	0	0	4.50	3	2	0	0	4	3	2	2	0	3	5	.214	.000	.429	11.25	6.75
Myers, Brett	R-R	6-4	220	8-17-80	0	0	0.00	3	3	0	0	3	2	0	0	1	0	4	.182	.000	.286	10.80	2.70
Outman, Josh	L-L	6-1	180	9-14-84	10	4	2.45	20	18	0	0	117	104	35	32	7	54	117	.236	.210	.244	8.97	4.14
Overholt, Pat	R-R	6-3	190	2-8-84	4	6	3.82	13	12	0	0	73	67	36	31	10	30	56	.248	.260	.237	6.90	3.70
Pena, Carlos	R-R	6-4	165	5-15-84	0	0	54.00	1	0	0	0	1	4	4	4	0	1	0	.667	.000	.800	13.50	13.50
Pfinsgraff, Ben	R-R	6-0	180	11-13-83	0	0	8.35	4	4	0	0	18	31	19	17	2	1	12	.378	.364	.388	5.89	0.49
Rosario, Francisco	R-R	6-0	205	9-28-80	0	0	4.05	4	0	0	0	13	9	6	6	1	5	16	.188	.200	.174	10.80	3.38
Savage, William	R-R	6-3	205	4-3-83	4	3	3.63	42	0	0	3	62	61	29	25	2	17	48	.265	.227	.289	6.97	2.47
Stott, Zac	R-R	6-5	220	7-26-83	7	8	3.85	27	16	1	2	117	131	67	50	6	34	69	.282	.311	.263	5.31	2.62
Swindle, Robert	L-L	6-3	190	7-7-83	0	1	4.80	12	0	0	3	15	15	8	8	3	3	20	.254	.118	.310	12.00	1.80

Name	B-T	HT	WT	DOB	W	L	ERA	G	GS	CG	SV	IP	H	R	ER	HR	BB	SO	AVG	vLH	vRH	K/9	BB/9
Trujillo, J.J.	R-R	6-0	180	10-9-75	4	0	2.10	12	0	0	0	26	14	6	6	1	7	22	.161	.200	.128	7.71	2.45
Urick, John	L-L	6-2	210	2-22-82	0	0	0.00	1	0	0	0	1	0	0	0	0	0	1	.000	—	.000	9.00	0.00
Villarreal, Luis	L-L	6-1	215	12-20-79	0	4	5.21	15	0	0	0	47	59	36	27	2	15	44	.307	.364	.285	8.49	2.89
Weatherby III, Charles	R-R	6-0	208	12-23-78	0	0	4.88	15	1	0	2	31	34	17	17	3	8	35	.272	.260	.280	10.05	2.30
Willey, Cory	L-L	6-0	185	4-22-81	7	2	2.37	38	0	0	4	61	51	18	16	5	16	54	.232	.148	.281	8.01	2.37
Wylie, Jason	R-R	6-5	220	5-27-81	0	1	5.66	17	1	0	0	35	30	27	22	2	37	24	.227	.212	.238	6.17	9.51
Zagurski, Michael	L-L	6-0	225	1-27-83	0	0	1.10	12	0	0	5	16	6	2	2	0	4	30	.113	.211	.059	16.53	2.20

FIELDING

Catcher	PCT	G	PO	A	E	DP	PB
Budde	1.000	3	14	2	0	0	0
Coste	1.000	2	16	2	0	0	0
Guevara	1.000	16	88	8	0	1	3
Kennelly	1.000	5	15	1	0	0	1
Marson	.982	108	748	65	15	5	11
Sanchez	1.000	1	2	0	0	0	0
Suomi	.993	17	135	4	1	0	0

First Base	PCT	G	PO	A	E	DP
Coste	1.000	1	6	1	0	0
Harris	.990	81	636	46	7	56
Urick	.992	60	460	39	4	68

Second Base	PCT	G	PO	A	E	DP
Antoniato	.974	7	15	22	1	5
Harman	.973	110	202	308	14	87
Hernandez	.929	6	8	18	2	0
Howard	.985	13	26	39	1	9

Made	.955	4	9	12	1	3

Third Base	PCT	G	PO	A	E	DP
Antoniato	.971	31	21	46	2	3
Baez	.912	62	42	113	15	8
Coste	1.000	1	1	0	0	0
Harris	.800	11	4	16	5	3
Howard	1.000	1	1	0	0	0
Made	.946	36	26	61	5	5
Morales	1.000	1	1	0	0	0

Shortstop	PCT	G	PO	A	E	DP
Antoniato	1.000	3	1	7	0	0
Donald	.968	83	106	197	10	49
Garciaparra	1.000	3	2	9	0	0
Harman	.984	11	17	46	1	7
Hernandez	.897	18	33	45	9	12
Made	1.000	2	2	7	0	3
Shier	.972	25	29	74	3	20

Outfield	PCT	G	PO	A	E	DP
Blalock	1.000	8	11	0	0	0
Boyd	1.000	10	25	0	0	0
Brown	.857	3	6	0	1	0
Burgamy	.981	67	152	4	3	1
Golson	.971	96	227	4	7	0
Guevara	1.000	1	1	0	0	0
Hall	.957	13	21	1	1	0
Hernandez	1.000	1	1	0	0	0
Jackson	.909	9	10	0	1	1
Miller	1.000	4	5	0	0	0
Moran	1.000	3	6	0	0	0
Quiroz	.667	2	2	0	1	0
Slayden	.985	94	195	5	3	0
Spidale	.990	58	101	2	1	1
Thayer	.979	56	86	7	2	0
Werth	1.000	4	7	1	0	0

LAKEWOOD BLUECLAWS   LOW CLASS A
SOUTH ATLANTIC LEAGUE

BATTING	B-T	HT	WT	DOB	AVG	vLH	vRH	G	AB	R	H	2B	3B	HR	RBI	BB	HBP	SH	SF	SO	SB	CS	SLG	OBP
Antoniato, P.J.	R-R	5-9	185	7-2-83	.261	.270	.257	42	142	19	37	6	2	2	16	3	4	2	1	12	2	1	.373	.293
Baez, Welinson	R-R	6-3	190	7-7-84	.219	.254	.205	62	215	28	47	9	2	3	22	23	0	0	4	71	5	0	.321	.289
Barajas, Rod	R-R	6-2	230	9-5-75	.375	.000	.462	6	16	0	6	2	0	0	2	3	0	0	0	6	0	0	.500	.474
Berry, Quintin	L-L	6-1	165	11-21-84	.312	.288	.320	126	487	86	152	19	4	3	44	61	12	12	9	85	55	18	.386	.395
Cardenas, Adrian	L-R	6-0	185	10-10-87	.295	.301	.292	127	499	70	147	30	2	9	79	47	4	4	10	80	20	7	.417	.354
Demmink, Herman	L-R	5-11	190	9-21-83	.359	.500	.310	15	39	5	14	4	0	0	4	2	1	0	5	0	0	0	.462	.390
Donald, Jason	R-R	6-1	190	9-4-84	.310	.395	.289	51	197	41	61	9	3	4	30	29	6	3	3	39	2	5	.447	.409
Gosewisch, Tuffy	R-R	5-11	190	8-17-83	.224	.235	.219	92	339	52	76	24	2	5	45	29	7	2	4	69	0	3	.351	.296
Henry Jr., Carl	R-R	6-3	205	5-31-86	.184	.154	.195	102	342	46	63	12	4	9	38	18	7	4	3	139	13	3	.322	.238
Hernandez, Fidel	R-R	5-11	160	1-18-86	.276	.268	.279	72	275	26	76	8	1	0	29	13	1	3	4	32	20	6	.313	.307
Howard, Kevin	L-R	6-2	190	6-25-81	.317	.208	.343	32	126	19	40	8	2	0	25	10	0	0	2	21	2	0	.413	.362
Howard, Ryan	L-L	6-4	255	11-19-79	.333	.500	.250	2	6	1	2	1	0	1	4	2	0	0	0	0	0	0	1.000	.500
Kennelly, Timothy	R-R	6-0	180	12-5-86	.133	.200	.000	5	15	0	2	0	0	0	1	0	0	0	0	4	0	0	.133	.133
Key, Bradley	R-R	6-0	190	3-14-83	.121	.100	.130	10	33	1	4	2	0	0	2	2	0	0	1	12	0	0	.182	.167
Miller, Jay	R-R	5-10	185	8-11-83	.250	.275	.240	79	272	32	68	7	0	1	30	32	4	1	2	40	2	0	.287	.335
Milner, Gus	R-R	6-5	240	4-21-84	.286	.258	.296	131	458	71	131	29	3	10	66	63	4	0	8	102	19	9	.428	.371
Morales, Douglas	L-L	6-0	180	6-22-86	.250	.200	.259	104	240	25	60	13	0	0	26	15	5	1	1	45	3	1	.304	.307
Naughton, Joel	L-R	6-1	180	8-27-86	.259	.273	.257	56	193	19	50	10	1	2	17	19	1	5	2	36	2	3	.352	.326
Penprase, Zachary	R-B	6-2	180	2-16-85	.250	.273	.238	19	32	8	8	1	0	0	1	9	2	2	0	12	4	3	.281	.442
Reed, Matthew	R-R	6-2	225	8-24-82	.207	.286	.162	18	58	4	12	3	0	1	7	5	0	0	1	22	1	0	.310	.266
Robbins, Alan	L-R	6-0	205	7-7-83	.211	.000	.216	14	38	3	8	1	0	1	7	6	1	0	1	9	0	0	.316	.326
Victorino, Shane	B-R	5-9	180	11-30-80	.200	—	.200	1	5	1	1	0	0	0	0	0	1	0	0	0	0	0	.200	.200
Williams, Julian	R-R	5-11	175	7-27-83	.249	.304	.226	113	313	58	78	13	2	0	18	48	7	7	2	52	26	4	.304	.359
Yarbrough, Charlie	R-R	6-6	250	11-7-84	.215	.182	.227	66	242	16	52	19	2	2	30	11	2	3	0	70	1	0	.335	.262

PITCHING	B-T	HT	WT	DOB	W	L	ERA	G	GS	CG	SV	IP	H	R	ER	HR	BB	SO	AVG	vLH	vRH	K/9	BB/9
Bastardo, Antonio	L-L	5-11	168	9-21-85	9	0	1.87	15	15	0	0	92	63	23	19	3	42	98	.189	.162	.196	9.62	4.12
Blaine, Justin	L-L	6-4	188	3-12-84	1	0	4.53	28	0	0	1	44	27	28	22	1	50	37	.179	.213	.163	7.63	10.31
Byrd, Darren	R-R	6-3	170	10-24-86	9	11	4.04	26	25	1	0	156	149	85	70	10	65	112	.254	.285	.225	6.46	3.75
Concepcion, A.	R-R	6-2	180	9-27-84	3	1	3.83	20	1	0	0	40	38	19	17	2	17	44	.252	.282	.225	9.90	3.82
Cruse, Andrew	R-R	6-1	200	5-31-84	4	7	4.37	28	9	0	4	82	87	46	40	9	20	68	.270	.271	.270	7.43	2.19
Drabek, Kyle	R-R	6-0	185	12-8-87	5	1	4.33	11	10	0	0	54	50	29	26	9	23	46	.239	.257	.230	7.67	3.83
Dubee, Michael	R-R	6-2	177	1-12-86	4	4	3.88	30	0	0	1	56	52	25	24	2	22	54	.248	.253	.244	8.73	3.56
2-team (8 Kannapolis)					7	4	3.96	38	6	0	1	89	86	41	39	5	35	89	—	—	—	9.03	3.55
Dumont, Paige	R-R	6-8	240	11-26-84	0	2	3.65	10	0	0	2	12	11	6	5	0	4	9	.234	.238	.231	6.57	2.92
Escalona, Sergio	L-L	6-0	178	8-3-84	1	4	4.15	7	7	0	0	39	51	25	18	4	11	32	.321	.390	.297	7.38	2.54
Freeman, Jarrod	R-B	6-3	195	11-20-87	2	2	5.87	10	9	0	0	46	67	36	30	5	24	28	.349	.329	.362	5.48	4.70
Garcia, Edgar	R-R	6-2	190	9-20-86	4	9	4.12	20	20	0	0	114	119	61	52	10	32	83	.268	.277	.262	6.57	2.53
German, Matt	L-R	6-8	240	6-27-84	0	0	2.08	11	0	0	0	13	12	5	3	0	4	18	.240	.167	.263	12.46	2.77
Hill, Garet	R-R	6-5	217	5-24-84	6	4	2.18	39	2	0	7	70	61	21	17	3	15	60	.235	.245	.227	7.68	1.92
Hill, Ronald	R-R	6-3	225	11-29-82	0	2	2.63	17	0	0	10	24	18	7	7	1	9	22	.198	.219	.186	8.25	3.38
Mitchinson, Scott	R-R	6-3	185	12-28-84	3	3	4.12	8	8	0	0	44	34	23	20	5	14	50	.209	.138	.277	10.31	2.89
Monasterios, Carlos	R-R	6-2	175	3-21-86	11	11	4.62	26	26	1	0	156	155	93	80	13	55	114	.261	.271	.253	6.58	3.17
Morales, Douglas	L-L	6-0	180	6-22-86	0	0	0.00	1	0	0	0	1	0	0	0	0	3	0	.500	1.000	.000	27.00	0.00
Pfinsgraff, Ben	R-R	6-0	180	11-13-83	2	1	2.43	11	2	0	0	33	28	9	9	2	6	38	.222	.241	.208	10.26	1.62
Rhoads, Christopher	R-R	6-1	160	8-12-85	1	1	4.50	11	0	0	0	18	20	9	9	1	5	15	.274	.200	.313	7.50	2.50
Salmon, Kevin	R-R	6-2	220	11-9-83	1	0	4.26	9	0	0	0	19	22	9	9	1	7	9	.297	.281	.310	4.26	3.32
Schlitter, Brian	R-R	6-5	240	12-21-85	0	1	3.80	16	0	0	3	24	27	13	10	2	6	21	.287	.318	.260	7.99	2.28
Sterner, Zack	R-R	6-2	170	11-7-85	1	1	2.70	18	0	0	3	37	29	12	11	1	13	35	.209	.211	.206	8.59	3.19
Swindle, Robert	L-L	6-3	190	7-7-83	2	1	0.93	20	0	0	10	29	16	3	3	0	5	37	.168	.065	.219	11.48	1.55

FIELDING

Catcher	PCT	G	PO	A	E	DP	PB
Barajas	1.000	5	25	2	0	0	1
Gosewisch	.991	90	667	87	7	11	3
Kennelly	1.000	1	2	0	0	0	0
Naughton	.984	44	337	33	6	3	3
Robbins	—	1	0	0	0	0	0

First Base	PCT	G	PO	A	E	DP
K. Howard	.947	10	67	5	4	5
R. Howard	1.000	1	9	0	0	2
Kennelly	1.000	2	9	2	0	2
Key	.972	8	67	3	2	4
Morales	.993	104	642	49	5	55
Reed	.988	11	78	2	1	5
Yarbrough	.979	45	300	27	7	22

Second Base	PCT	G	PO	A	E	DP
Antoniato	1.000	5	10	19	0	6
Cardenas	.976	124	236	334	14	58
Demmink	.941	5	4	12	1	2
K. Howard	1.000	1	2	5	0	2
Penprase	1.000	3	4	3	0	1

Third Base	PCT	G	PO	A	E	DP
Antoniato	.949	27	14	61	4	7
Baez	.895	62	43	110	18	10
Demmink	.714	5	2	8	4	0
Henry Jr.	.860	31	24	56	13	4
K. Howard	.969	11	11	20	1	3
Penprase	.875	5	2	5	1	0

Shortstop	PCT	G	PO	A	E	DP
Antoniato	.958	7	6	17	1	2
Demmink	.947	4	7	11	1	1
Donald	.943	51	91	159	15	28
Hernandez	.921	72	115	189	26	30
Penprase	.929	5	4	9	1	1

Outfield	PCT	G	PO	A	E	DP
Berry	.989	126	255	5	3	2
Henry Jr.	.937	58	83	6	6	1
Miller	1.000	22	21	0	0	0
Milner	.969	127	214	7	7	1
Morales	1.000	1	1	0	0	0
Williams	.989	109	181	5	2	2

WILLIAMSPORT CROSSCUTTERS

SHORT-SEASON

NEW YORK-PENN LEAGUE

BATTING	B-T	HT	WT	DOB	AVG	vLH	vRH	G	AB	R	H	2B	3B	HR	RBI	BB	HBP	SH	SF	SO	SB	CS	SLG	OBP
Bacsu, Kirk	R-R	5-10	180	5-16-85	.152	.000	.192	14	33	3	5	1	0	0	3	1	1	1	0	8	0	0	.182	.200
Brown, Dominic	L-L	6-5	204	9-3-87	.295	.263	.312	74	285	43	84	11	5	3	32	27	2	0	3	49	14	7	.400	.356
Cuevas, Phillip	R-R	5-11	168	6-30-85	.250	.171	.292	40	100	12	25	2	1	0	8	5	0	2	1	31	4	3	.290	.283
Demmink, Herman	L-R	5-11	190	9-21-83	.182	.000	.400	6	11	0	2	1	0	0	0	1	0	0	0	4	0	0	.273	.250
Durant, Michael	R-R	6-5	230	1-2-87	.236	.208	.248	52	178	19	42	8	0	5	23	14	3	0	1	69	0	0	.365	.301
Galvis, Freddy	B-R	5-10	154	11-14-89	.203	.200	.204	38	143	20	29	5	1	0	7	10	0	3	0	20	9	4	.252	.255
Kennelly, Timothy	R-R	6-0	180	12-5-86	.235	.256	.224	39	115	6	27	7	0	2	8	9	1	2	0	23	2	1	.348	.296
Mach, Tyler	R-R	6-1	195	12-11-84	.287	.384	.247	65	247	33	71	19	2	5	38	21	9	0	2	33	1	2	.441	.362
Mangum, Caleb	R-R	5-11	185	1-3-85	.257	.235	.271	48	136	18	35	9	1	0	10	21	1	4	1	22	1	0	.346	.358
Mitchell, Derrick	R-R	6-2	170	1-5-87	.231	.276	.207	62	221	27	51	15	1	6	27	18	8	2	0	59	5	1	.389	.312
Morales, Jaime	R-R	6-1	165	4-21-84	.000	.000	.000	4	7	0	0	0	0	0	1	0	0	1	0	2	0	0	.000	.000
Myers, D'Arby	R-R	6-3	175	12-9-88	.240	.175	.276	46	179	28	43	7	0	1	17	11	1	2	1	34	11	6	.296	.286
Penprase, Zachary	R-R	6-2	180	2-16-85	.121	.000	.148	16	33	2	4	0	0	0	1	3	0	1	0	7	2	0	.121	.194
Prall, Rich	L-R	6-0	210	1-29-85	.222	.500	.000	3	9	3	2	1	0	0	1	0	0	0	0	3	0	0	.333	.222
Rizzotti, Matthew	L-L	6-5	235	12-24-85	.260	.211	.278	63	215	26	56	19	1	2	27	30	3	1	3	63	0	1	.386	.355
Robbins, Alan	L-R	6-0	205	7-7-83	.227	.250	.222	7	22	2	5	0	0	1	1	0	0	1	0	3	0	0	.364	.250
Sorgi, Adam	L-R	6-1	170	12-17-84	.198	.115	.231	35	91	10	18	3	0	0	5	8	3	4	0	17	2	0	.231	.284
Spencer, Matthew	L-L	6-4	225	1-27-86	.263	.261	.263	51	179	21	47	10	0	9	26	11	5	1	2	46	3	3	.469	.320
Taylor, Michael	R-R	6-6	250	12-19-85	.227	.250	.217	66	233	30	53	14	0	6	33	23	2	1	2	53	8	2	.365	.300
Williams, Jermaine	R-R	6-3	210	3-25-87	.088	.000	.111	26	68	6	6	0	0	1	5	4	0	0	2	22	1	0	.132	.139
Winn, Dennis	R-R	6-2	165	7-6-84	.091	.167	.000	4	11	0	1	1	0	0	0	0	0	0	0	4	0	0	.182	.091
Yarbrough, Charlie	R-R	6-6	250	11-7-84	.400	—	.400	2	5	0	2	1	0	0	1	0	0	0	0	0	0	0	.600	.400

PITCHING	B-T	HT	WT	DOB	W	L	ERA	G	GS	CG	SV	IP	H	R	ER	HR	BB	SO	AVG	vLH	vRH	K/9	BB/9
Austin, Richard	R-R	6-3	210	1-16-85	1	4	2.66	12	0	0	3	20	23	15	6	2	9	17	.277	.226	.308	7.52	3.98
Brummett, Tyson	R-R	6-0	150	8-15-84	5	5	3.40	15	12	1	0	77	71	34	29	2	14	55	.240	.219	.251	6.46	1.64
Chapman, Chance	R-R	6-4	200	2-27-84	5	3	2.09	14	14	0	0	78	70	31	18	1	20	67	.233	.277	.191	7.76	2.32
Diekman, Jacob	L-L	6-4	190	1-21-87	2	1	2.25	3	3	0	0	16	10	4	4	0	8	11	.189	.000	.204	6.19	4.50
Dumont, Paige	R-R	6-8	240	11-26-82	2	0	4.03	16	0	0	3	29	25	13	13	1	9	27	.225	.289	.192	8.38	2.79
Escalona, Sergio	L-L	6-0	178	8-3-84	2	2	7.57	7	7	0	0	27	32	26	23	2	19	26	.302	.296	.304	8.56	6.26
Freeman, Jarrod	R-R	6-3	195	11-20-87	0	3	4.15	9	4	0	1	30	33	15	14	1	11	21	.284	.360	.227	6.23	3.26
Garcia, Edgar	R-R	6-2	190	9-20-87	1	0	2.16	2	1	0	0	8	6	2	2	0	2	11	.200	.364	.105	11.88	2.16
German, Matt	L-L	6-8	240	6-27-84	0	1	1.23	15	0	0	7	22	12	3	3	1	9	28	.160	.048	.204	11.45	3.68
Gomez, Abel	L-L	6-0	170	11-29-84	0	0	29.08	4	0	0	0	4	12	14	14	2	6	3	.522	.714	.438	6.23	12.46
Harris, William	L-L	6-2	185	1-19-85	1	1	4.80	4	3	0	0	15	12	11	8	1	4	19	.203	.308	.174	11.40	2.40
Jeanes, Nate	L-L	6-3	190	6-29-84	0	0	8.10	2	0	0	0	3	7	3	3	0	1	2	.500	1.000	.462	5.40	2.70
Kissock, Christopher	R-R	6-4	195	5-2-85	2	3	3.74	13	2	0	2	34	37	17	14	2	9	26	.274	.286	.267	6.95	2.41
Lin, Yen-Feng	R-R	6-1	205	5-22-85	0	2	3.64	19	0	0	3	30	25	16	12	3	17	21	.227	.243	.219	6.37	5.16
Melendez, Moises	L-L	5-11	172	8-4-86	1	0	2.76	9	0	0	2	16	12	5	5	0	8	14	.211	.100	.234	7.71	4.41
Mitchinson, Scott	R-R	6-3	185	12-28-84	0	2	3.21	3	3	0	0	14	13	8	5	1	5	17	.241	.227	.250	10.93	3.21
Naylor, Drew	R-R	6-4	210	5-31-86	8	6	3.29	14	14	2	0	93	78	39	34	3	28	97	.228	.250	.209	9.35	2.70
Pena, Carlos	R-R	6-4	165	5-11-85	1	1	4.15	18	0	0	0	30	31	18	14	2	6	34	.258	.250	.263	10.09	1.78
Rhoads, Christopher	R-R	6-1	160	8-12-85	0	0	2.37	7	0	0	0	19	11	5	5	2	15	.177	.100	.214	7.11	0.95
Rocchio, Joseph	R-R	6-4	200	10-15-84	0	1	2.87	12	2	0	0	31	24	17	10	1	15	26	.212	.238	.197	7.47	4.31
Savery, Joe	L-L	6-3	215	11-4-85	2	3	2.73	7	7	0	0	26	22	9	8	0	13	22	.214	.381	.171	7.52	4.44
Schlitter, Brian	R-R	6-5	240	12-21-85	0	0	0.00	1	0	0	1	2	2	0	0	0	1	.222	.400	.000	4.50	0.00
Tejeda, Walter	L-L	6-3	187	9-28-85	0	4	6.65	8	3	0	0	22	30	20	16	2	5	10	.353	.143	.372	4.15	2.08
Wertz, Luke	R-R	6-1	175	9-20-85	1	0	0.00	3	1	0	1	8	6	0	0	0	2	9	.200	.250	.182	10.12	2.25

FIELDING

Catcher	PCT	G	PO	A	E	DP	PB
Bacsu	1.000	13	63	12	0	1	3
Demmink	—	1	0	0	0	0	0
Kennelly	.976	17	109	11	3	0	3
Mangum	.979	48	339	29	8	5	5
Prall	1.000	3	14	0	0	0	0
Robbins	1.000	7	53	3	0	0	0

First Base	PCT	G	PO	A	E	DP
Durant	.979	30	266	20	6	31
Kennelly	1.000	3	18	1	0	2
Rizzotti	.995	46	378	29	2	26

Second Base	PCT	G	PO	A	E	DP
Cuevas	1.000	5	6	7	0	3
Demmink	—	1	0	0	0	0

Mach	.956	56	103	155	12	36
Penprase	1.000	3	1	3	0	0
Sorgi	.985	18	21	45	1	12
Winn	.875	2	5	2	1	1

Third Base	PCT	G	PO	A	E	DP
Demmink	1.000	1	1	3	0	1
Kennelly	.900	16	10	17	3	5
Mitchell	.841	55	44	94	26	7
Morales	.857	4	2	4	1	2
Penprase	.857	4	3	3	1	1
Sorgi	1.000	3	0	4	0	0

Shortstop	PCT	G	PO	A	E	DP
Cuevas	.908	30	32	77	11	13
Galvis	.975	38	46	111	4	23

Penprase	.933	5	11	17	2	3
Sorgi	.905	10	13	25	4	7

Outfield	PCT	G	PO	A	E	DP
Brown	.954	74	136	9	7	0
Myers	.988	44	81	0	1	0
Penprase	—	1	0	0	0	0
Spencer	.940	45	76	3	5	1
Taylor	.943	55	77	5	5	2
Williams	1.000	22	19	2	0	0

GULF COAST LEAGUE

BATTING	B-T	HT	WT	DOB	AVG	vLH	vRH	G	AB	R	H	2B	3B	HR	RBI	BB	HBP	SH	SF	SO	SB	CS	SLG	OBP
Arzeno, Luis Ramon	R-R	5-11	190	8-9-84	.283	.333	.250	24	53	7	15	9	0	1	9	3	3	1	1	11	0	0	.509	.350
Binkoski, Tim	L-L	6-1	195	2-2-84	.219	.250	.200	30	96	10	21	4	2	1	16	12	1	1	2	23	4	1	.333	.306
Bolt, Karl	R-R	6-3	220	8-16-85	.256	.188	.290	57	207	28	53	10	4	8	31	18	7	1	0	34	1	1	.459	.336
D'Arnaud, Travis	R-R	6-2	195	2-10-89	.241	.275	.222	41	141	18	34	3	0	4	20	4	4	0	2	23	4	2	.348	.278
Jackson, Nic	L-R	6-3	200	9-25-79	.500	.500	—	1	2	1	1	0	0	0	1	0	0	0	0	0	0	0	.500	.667
Mattair, Travis	R-R	6-5	210	12-21-88	.235	.186	.262	54	200	19	47	10	1	3	21	12	6	0	1	58	1	1	.340	.297
McDonald, Darin	R-R	6-3	195	11-3-87	.187	.314	.141	42	134	16	25	2	0	2	12	12	1	0	1	38	2	5	.246	.257
McGill, Shawn	R-R	6-4	195	2-29-84	.273	.000	.300	6	11	1	3	1	0	0	1	1	0	0	0	1	0	0	.364	.333
Morales, Jaime	R-R	6-1	165	4-21-84	.255	.281	.243	31	102	13	26	5	0	0	2	9	2	3	0	13	2	3	.304	.327
Moran, Javon	R-R	5-10	170	9-30-82	.000	.000	.000	2	3	1	0	0	0	0	0	2	0	0	0	1	0	0	.000	.400
Murillo, Francisco	R-R	6-0	196	10-18-86	.242	.255	.236	51	178	22	43	16	0	7	36	21	2	0	3	57	2	1	.449	.324
Prall, Rich	L-R	6-0	210	1-29-85	.077	.200	.048	12	26	1	2	1	0	0	1	2	0	1	0	7	1	0	.115	.143
Quiroz, Arlon	R-R	6-0	170	11-13-86	.272	.338	.238	53	195	38	53	10	1	2	17	33	1	1	1	45	20	5	.364	.378
Rincon, Ambiorix	B-R	6-0	165	7-17-86	.258	.244	.263	43	159	20	41	15	1	0	21	14	3	1	2	27	7	3	.365	.326
Sanchez, Jesus	R-R	5-11	160	9-24-87	.208	.304	.178	34	96	12	20	4	0	0	3	15	0	0	0	29	3	1	.250	.315
Schoenberger, Alan	B-R	5-10	160	1-19-89	.167	.200	.154	6	18	8	3	1	0	0	0	6	0	0	0	5	0	1	.222	.375
Thayer, Matt	R-L	5-10	173	2-21-82	.333	.500	.250	2	6	4	2	1	0	0	0	2	0	0	2	0	0	0	.500	.500
Villegas Andino, Jesus	R-R	5-10	175	9-21-86	.184	.176	.188	32	98	9	18	4	2	0	8	6	7	1	0	18	3	1	.265	.279
Warren, T.J.	R-R	6-4	190	8-17-88	.211	.167	.228	36	109	8	23	3	0	1	4	9	1	1	0	42	4	1	.266	.277
Winn, Dennis	R-R	6-2	165	7-6-84	.371	.545	.292	29	105	13	39	9	2	2	13	4	1	0	0	21	1	2	.552	.400

PITCHING	B-T	HT	WT	DOB	W	L	ERA	G	GS	CG	SV	IP	H	R	ER	HR	BB	SO	AVG	vLH	vRH	K/9	BB/9
Austin, Richard	R-R	6-3	210	1-16-85	2	0	1.35	4	0	0	1	7	6	3	1	1	3	4	.222	.100	.294	5.40	4.05
Brauer, Daniel	L-L	6-0	210	10-14-83	0	1	0.00	1	1	0	0	2	2	1	0	0	1	3	.286	.000	.400	13.50	4.50
Breslin, Gerard	R-R	6-2	205	7-24-84	0	0	5.23	8	0	0	1	10	19	6	6	2	4	13	.396	.500	.292	11.32	3.48
Correa, Heitor	R-R	6-3	200	8-25-89	3	3	3.74	13	11	0	0	65	58	33	27	4	20	49	.230	.277	.241	6.78	2.77
De Fratus, Justin	B-R	6-4	215	10-21-87	2	3	4.30	10	8	0	0	46	51	25	22	1	3	34	.273	.278	.269	6.65	0.59
Diekman, Jacob	L-L	6-4	190	1-21-87	1	3	2.92	10	7	0	0	37	29	12	12	2	13	35	.209	.175	.222	8.51	3.16
Florentino, Antonio	R-R	6-4	180	6-5-87	1	3	4.68	14	5	0	0	50	43	28	26	4	20	31	.231	.292	.193	5.58	3.60
Forest, Jonathan	R-R	6-3	235	7-16-84	4	1	3.56	14	0	0	0	30	25	13	12	2	21	40	.229	.175	.261	11.87	6.23
Freeman, Jarrod	R-R	6-3	195	11-20-87	0	0	0.00	2	2	0	0	7	0	0	0	0	0	5	.000	.000	.000	6.43	0.00
Garcia, Freddy	R-R	6-4	260	6-10-76	0	0	4.50	1	1	0	0	2	1	1	1	0	0	2	.250	1.000	.000	9.00	0.00
Gordon, Tom	R-R	5-10	200	11-18-67	0	1	19.29	2	2	0	0	2	5	5	5	0	1	3	.417	.333	.500	11.57	3.86
James, Nathaniel	B-R	6-4	180	4-11-89	0	4	7.71	9	8	0	0	33	45	32	28	7	15	14	.321	.379	.270	3.86	4.13
Jeanes, Nate	L-L	6-3	190	6-29-84	1	1	4.22	14	0	0	2	21	19	10	10	1	6	18	.238	.500	.172	7.59	2.53
Mathieson, Scott	R-R	6-3	190	2-27-84	0	0	0.00	2	2	0	0	4	0	0	0	1	3	.000	.000	.000	13.50	4.50
Matos, Miguel	R-R	6-4	178	10-26-87	6	3	3.34	12	8	0	0	59	59	27	22	5	22	50	.260	.275	.252	7.58	3.34
Melendez, Moises	L-L	5-11	172	8-4-86	1	1	3.18	4	1	0	0	11	15	7	4	2	4	12	.306	.111	.350	9.53	3.18
Mitchinson, Scott	R-R	6-3	185	12-28-84	0	1	2.79	3	3	0	0	10	8	3	3	1	5	8	.216	.174	.286	7.45	4.66
Mulligan, Nolan	R-R	6-5	190	1-30-85	0	2	3.18	14	0	0	2	28	28	11	10	1	8	27	.264	.273	.258	8.58	2.54
Quiroz, Arlon	R-R	6-0	170	11-13-86	0	0	—	0	0	0	0	2	0	0	0	0	0	0	—	.000	.000	—	—
Rhoads, Christopher	R-R	6-1	160	8-12-85	0	1	2.57	3	0	0	2	7	5	2	2	0	3	9	.208	.286	.176	11.57	3.86
Romero, Mauricio	R-R	6-3	202	6-16-86	1	0	1.04	6	0	0	5	9	7	1	1	0	1	8	.233	.154	.294	8.31	1.04
Sampson, Julian	R-R	6-5	210	1-21-89	0	0	0.00	1	0	0	0	2	0	0	0	0	1	0	.000	.000	.000	4.50	0.00
Shanahan, Liam	R-R	6-1	190	11-1-84	1	3	6.04	13	0	0	0	22	33	19	15	2	5	19	.330	.279	.368	7.66	2.01
Slate, Kyle	R-R	6-5	200	4-23-89	0	0	4.50	1	1	0	0	2	4	2	1	0	1	4	.400	.000	.500	18.00	4.50
Smolin, Eric	R-R	6-3	180	1-31-85	1	1	7.59	9	0	0	0	11	16	10	9	0	4	6	.320	.261	.370	5.06	3.38
Sterner, Zack	R-R	6-2	170	11-7-85	1	0	1.69	2	0	0	0	5	3	1	1	1	2	2	.176	.250	.111	3.38	3.38
Tejeda, Walter	L-L	6-3	187	9-28-85	2	0	6.59	8	0	0	1	14	11	10	10	1	8	13	.216	.222	.214	8.56	5.27
Tilghman, Jack	R-R	6-2	205	5-19-87	1	0	2.63	7	0	0	0	14	9	4	4	0	7	6	.191	.105	.250	3.95	4.61

FIELDING

Catcher	PCT	G	PO	A	E	DP	PB
Arzeno	.968	14	54	7	2	0	0
D'Arnaud	.978	23	167	11	4	0	7
McGill	.900	6	24	3	3	0	1
Prall	.968	9	26	4	1	0	0
Sanchez	.966	30	148	21	6	0	2

First Base	PCT	G	PO	A	E	DP
Arzeno	1.000	2	4	0	0	0
Bolt	.984	47	406	23	7	26
Murillo	.982	13	100	7	2	6

Second Base	PCT	G	PO	A	E	DP
Morales	.978	11	17	28	1	4
Rincon	.961	41	59	115	7	17
Winn	.979	9	19	27	1	3

Third Base	PCT	G	PO	A	E	DP
Mattair	.958	48	39	97	6	9
Morales	.889	14	6	26	4	0

Shortstop	PCT	G	PO	A	E	DP
Morales	.900	5	4	14	2	2
Schoenberger	.742	6	9	14	8	0

	PCT	G	PO	A	E	DP
Villegas Andino	.922	31	61	80	12	11
Winn	.950	19	25	51	4	11

Outfield	PCT	G	PO	A	E	DP
Binkoski	.930	29	38	2	3	0
Jackson	1.000	1	3	0	0	0
McDonald	.973	41	69	2	2	0
Moran	1.000	2	1	0	0	0
Murillo	.946	29	34	1	2	0
Quiroz	.992	53	123	5	1	0
Thayer	1.000	2	6	0	0	0
Warren	1.000	36	52	3	0	1

DOMINICAN SUMMER LEAGUE

BATTING	B-T	HT	WT	DOB	AVG	vLH	vRH	G	AB	R	H	2B	3B	HR	RBI	BB	HBP	SH	SF	SO	SB	CS	SLG	OBP
Aguilar, Pedro	R-R	5-10	190	5-20-89	.288	.333	.285	43	132	18	38	7	0	4	22	13	2	1	3	17	1	2	.432	.353
Alvarez, Miguel	R-R	6-1	172	8-27-89	.242	.400	.236	41	153	18	37	4	0	0	12	11	1	1	2	27	12	1	.268	.293
Baez, Julio	R-R	6-1	180	5-12-87	.234	.167	.237	46	137	16	32	4	0	0	13	14	3	1	1	19	6	3	.263	.316
Balentien, Rudney	R-R	6-0	160	11-3-89	.236	.167	.239	40	123	15	29	6	0	0	13	15	2	2	0	34	12	3	.285	.329
Castillo, Lendy	R-R	6-1	170	4-8-89	.286	.250	.287	60	196	36	56	6	1	1	20	16	2	3	2	23	12	2	.342	.343
Castro, Leandro	R-R	5-11	175	6-15-89	.278	.167	.284	59	223	41	62	3	5	6	37	26	6	2	5	39	24	9	.417	.362
Checo, Emmanuel	R-R	6-0	190	12-18-87	.111	.000	.115	11	27	1	3	0	0	0	0	1	0	0	0	8	0	0	.111	.143
De Los Santos, Vladimir	R-R	6-1	176	8-6-86	.337	.500	.331	47	163	25	55	14	0	3	34	23	3	1	2	16	9	7	.479	.424
Gomez, Ferrel	R-R	5-11	170	10-17-86	.276	.571	.257	41	116	23	32	6	1	2	20	11	5	1	1	18	5	1	.397	.361
Martinez, Eduard	L-L	6-1	175	5-28-87	.261	.200	.263	46	142	26	37	4	2	2	19	31	1	3	1	26	8	8	.359	.394
Mejia, Juan	R-R	6-2	185	5-30-85	.258	.417	.247	57	198	37	51	4	1	2	20	24	9	1	1	41	19	3	.318	.362
Paulino, Luis	R-R	6-2	185	6-16-89	.129	.000	.133	13	31	8	4	1	1	0	1	4	3	0	0	16	2	0	.226	.289
Santa, Luis	R-R	5-11	166	9-24-87	.098	.000	.104	24	51	5	5	1	0	0	7	9	2	2	1	8	4	1	.118	.254
Soto, Jose	L-L	6-0	170	4-7-86	.128	.500	.111	20	47	5	6	1	0	0	2	6	1	0	0	11	1	0	.149	.241
Tejada, Cesar	B-R	6-1	170	11-11-88	.194	.000	.200	25	62	9	12	1	0	0	3	7	1	3	0	16	2	3	.210	.286
Valle, Sebastian	R-L	6-1	168	7-24-90	.284	.429	.278	54	176	29	50	13	1	2	25	29	5	3	1	26	4	4	.403	.398

PITCHING	B-T	HT	WT	DOB	W	L	ERA	G	GS	CG	SV	IP	H	R	ER	HR	BB	SO	AVG	vLH	vRH	K/9	BB/9
Alvarez, Dario	L-L	6-1	170	1-17-89	1	3	4.46	11	8	0	0	36	22	21	18	0	29	50	.173	.250	.162	12.39	7.18
Alvarez, Daurius	R-R	6-2	185	9-10-87	1	0	4.26	10	0	0	2	19	22	10	9	1	6	18	.282	.278	.283	8.53	2.84
Arias, Gabirel	R-R	6-2	185	12-6-89	2	0	0.00	4	1	0	1	8	4	1	0	0	1	9	.143	.000	.160	10.12	1.12
Bernabel, Edwin	R-R	6-2	170	2-4-86	0	2	3.57	23	0	0	12	23	19	12	9	0	14	27	.224	.154	.236	10.72	5.56
Carpio, Pedro	R-R	6-2	185	6-18-88	4	3	2.06	12	12	3	0	66	54	25	15	2	24	67	.227	.171	.236	9.18	3.29
Coats, Luis	R-R	6-2	195	1-4-85	0	0	4.50	2	0	0	0	2	4	1	1	0	0	2	.400	.000	.444	9.00	0.00
Feliciano, Pablo	R-R	6-4	174	12-23-86	0	1	41.73	5	0	0	0	4	7	17	17	0	12	6	.412	.000	.467	14.73	29.45
Fernandez, Kenny	R-R	6-2	167	2-19-87	7	0	1.53	12	0	0	1	29	19	6	5	0	6	31	.196	.200	.195	9.51	1.84
Flande, Yohan	L-L	6-2	170	1-27-86	3	2	2.36	13	12	1	0	72	61	27	19	2	27	62	.223	.100	.239	7.71	3.36
Gabot, Edgar	R-R	6-4	175	8-4-87	0	0	3.38	3	0	0	0	3	0	1	1	0	6	0	.000	.000	.000	0.00	20.25
Gil, Carlos	R-R	6-9	230	2-27-89	1	0	7.94	7	0	0	0	6	4	5	5	0	10	5	.211	.500	.176	7.94	15.88
Guillen, Jean	R-R	6-3	170	3-21-84	0	0	0.00	2	0	0	0	3	0	0	0	0	0	3	.000	.000	.000	9.00	0.00
Javier, Ramon	R-R	6-5	200	8-17-88	0	1	21.60	5	1	0	0	3	3	8	8	0	11	3	.273	.000	.273	8.10	29.70
Jimenez, Esmelvin	L-L	5-10	180	2-5-87	3	0	1.69	8	2	0	1	27	17	5	5	0	10	27	.193	.077	.213	9.11	3.38
Lebron, Siulman	R-R	6-1	170	6-11-87	3	1	3.10	10	0	0	0	20	21	12	7	0	7	8	.266	.167	.284	3.54	3.10
Lugo, Ebelin	R-R	6-2		4-23-90	6	1	2.79	10	10	1	0	58	46	22	18	3	25	32	.216	.080	.234	4.97	3.88
Luna, Daury	L-L	6-1	165	11-12-85	2	0	3.46	4	0	0	0	13	12	6	5	0	5	13	.261	.000	.293	9.00	3.46
Ramos, Efrain	R-R	6-0	180	11-28-85	0	1	4.50	7	0	0	1	10	9	5	5	0	1	8	.250	.333	.242	7.20	0.90
Roa, Carlos	R-R	6-2	189	9-2-87	0	0	0.00	2	0	0	0	3	1	0	0	0	1	2	.111	.000	.143	6.00	3.00
Santamaria, Joaquin	R-R	6-4	175	9-21-89	1	0	4.50	6	1	0	0	10	12	7	5	0	5	5	.308	.375	.290	4.50	4.50
Severino, Julio	L-L	6-2	168	11-7-88	0	0	0.00	2	0	0	0	2	0	0	0	0	4	1	.000	.000	.000	3.86	15.43
Simon, Reginal	R-R	6-3	177	12-28-89	5	1	1.69	12	10	1	0	64	46	16	12	1	33	38	.202	.171	.209	5.34	4.64
Sosa, Juan	R-R	6-2	165	10-11-89	6	2	2.49	11	6	1	0	47	37	15	13	0	28	28	.222	.273	.214	5.36	5.36

FIELDING

Catcher	PCT	G	PO	A	E	DP	PB
Aguilar	1.000	9	60	14	0	0	2
Checo	.967	11	46	12	2	1	0
Gomez	.969	31	157	30	6	1	4
Valle	.986	27	184	27	3	1	5

First Base	PCT	G	PO	A	E	DP
De Los Santos	.996	28	235	17	1	18
Gomez	1.000	9	48	3	0	5
Mejia	.957	10	60	6	3	7
Soto	.968	20	111	9	4	5
Valle	.938	5	29	1	2	3

Second Base	PCT	G	PO	A	E	DP
Baez	.981	29	55	49	2	7
Paulino	.800	1	3	1	1	0
Santa	.972	17	35	34	2	8
Tejada	.910	21	36	35	7	8

Third Base	PCT	G	PO	A	E	DP
Baez	.923	11	15	21	3	2
Mejia	.915	47	42	108	14	6
Paulino	.625	7	5	5	6	1
Santa	.667	3	1	3	2	0

Shortstop	PCT	G	PO	A	E	DP
Baez	1.000	5	1	7	0	2
Castillo	.932	60	97	136	17	22
Mejia	1.000	1	0	1	0	0
Santa	1.000	2	3	3	0	1

Outfield	PCT	G	PO	A	E	DP
Alvarez	.974	41	71	3	2	0
Balentien	.923	39	48	0	4	0
Castro	.968	59	111	10	4	2
De Los Santos	1.000	18	30	1	0	0
Martinez	.987	43	70	5	1	1

VENEZUELAN SUMMER LEAGUE

BATTING	B-T	HT	WT	DOB	AVG	vLH	vRH	G	AB	R	H	2B	3B	HR	RBI	BB	HBP	SH	SF	SO	SB	CS	SLG	OBP
Bravo, Daniel	R-R	6-1	165	5-1-87	.276	.146	.333	47	134	15	37	6	1	1	19	9	7	1	1	24	2	5	.358	.351
Diaz, Francisco	B-R	5-10	158	3-21-90	.234	.256	.227	54	158	13	37	8	1	0	14	6	1	0	3	25	3	1	.297	.262
Doi, Bruno	R-L	6-1	206	11-23-87	.248	.235	.252	56	141	23	35	10	0	3	19	20	2	0	3	36	6	2	.383	.343
Fuentes, Maruin	R-R	6-1	187	7-28-86	.271	.379	.240	50	133	11	36	3	2	1	18	9	1	2	1	20	1	0	.346	.319
Garcia, Harold	B-R	5-11	164	10-25-86	.296	.326	.285	49	169	35	50	10	1	2	28	12	12	3	0	26	9	2	.402	.383
Guerra, Jorge	R-R	6-1	170	9-12-87	.300	.265	.314	43	120	13	36	9	0	3	21	6	6	3	2	19	2	1	.450	.358
Hernandez, Cesar	B-R	5-10	166	5-23-90	.276	.237	.287	54	181	32	50	7	8	2	21	11	4	7	2	30	6	4	.436	.328
Lezcano, Norberto	B-R	6-3	166	12-5-88	.202	.105	.231	38	84	9	17	3	0	0	3	3	2	0	0	17	1	0	.238	.247
Martinez, Luis	R-R	6-5	183	12-22-89	.267	.209	.287	54	172	21	46	8	3	1	21	15	3	0	2	30	4	0	.366	.333
Murakami, Fabio	R-R	6-1	194	3-4-88	.276	.224	.293	67	232	35	64	13	1	2	35	18	5	1	3	25	7	8	.366	.337
Oviedo, Benjamin	R-R	5-10	160	2-23-85	.232	.256	.224	59	155	26	36	10	2	2	18	21	3	3	1	32	4	2	.361	.333
Reyes, Osmel	R-R	6-1	185	8-21-88	.268	.286	.257	22	56	3	15	0	0	1	8	4	0	0	0	12	1	1	.321	.317
Rodriguez, Yonderman	R-R	5-11	160	2-17-87	.361	.377	.354	64	230	41	83	13	1	1	36	24	4	0	1	20	19	8	.439	.429
Rossi, Levi	R-R	6-1	182	2-11-87	.305	.281	.317	57	177	29	54	6	5	1	12	8	7	3	1	35	10	6	.412	.358
Sosa, Nelson	R-R	5-11	148	9-30-89	.225	.226	.225	43	120	14	27	3	0	1	10	5	1	3	0	16	3	4	.275	.262
Torres, Winder	R-R	5-11	160	8-2-90	.292	.143	.337	37	120	25	35	5	1	2	11	18	2	3	1	25	4	3	.400	.390

PITCHING	B-T	HT	WT	DOB	W	L	ERA	G	GS	CG	SV	IP	H	R	ER	HR	BB	SO	AVG	vLH	vRH	K/9	BB/9
Ballestas, Freddy	R-R	6-3	170	10-4-86	9	3	1.26	16	15	1	0	100	62	28	14	2	19	98	.172	.189	.167	8.82	1.71
Bravo, Daniel	R-R	6-1	165	5-1-87	0	0	9.00	1	0	0	0	1	1	1	1	0	0	0	.500	.000	.667	0.00	9.00
Campo, Kirlian	B-L	6-0	180	5-17-90	1	5	6.87	20	2	0	1	38	34	33	29	2	30	43	.238	.444	.224	10.18	7.11
Cedeno, Howard	R-R	6-1	205	4-9-89	1	3	2.03	14	0	0	3	31	26	13	7	1	11	28	.220	.182	.235	8.13	3.19
Colmenarez, Juan	L-L	6-1	165	10-22-86	6	5	2.51	16	15	0	0	93	76	34	26	4	11	89	.222	.281	.215	8.58	1.06
Diaz, Francisco	B-R	5-10	158	3-21-90	0	0	0.00	1	0	0	0	2	0	0	0	0	2	2	.000	.000	.000	9.00	9.00
Diaz, Victor	R-R	6-6	229	5-19-89	0	2	9.68	12	8	0	0	18	10	21	19	0	31	26	.172	.105	.205	13.25	15.79
Espinoza, Berman	R-R	6-3	170	11-4-87	2	0	1.57	13	0	0	3	29	34	8	5	0	3	23	.293	.233	.314	7.22	0.94
Garcia, Harold	B-R	5-11	164	10-25-86	0	0	54.00	1	0	0	0	2	2	2	2	0	1	0	.667	—	.667	0.00	27.00
Jaspe, Williams	R-R	6-5	194	2-7-86	0	1	19.64	3	0	0	0	4	10	8	8	0	1	3	.500	.750	.438	7.36	2.45
Lara, Daniel	R-R	6-1	178	3-8-88	4	4	2.49	17	11	0	2	72	73	33	20	2	30	37	.261	.302	.242	4.60	3.73
Mata, Cristobal	R-R	5-11	155	6-19-86	3	1	1.88	12	0	0	2	24	23	7	5	0	12	25	.250	.182	.271	9.38	4.50
Medina, Darwin	R-R	6-1	188	9-5-86	1	1	4.70	9	2	0	2	23	23	16	12	0	10	26	.264	.217	.281	10.17	3.91
Medrano, Carlos	L-L	6-8	202	10-5-87	1	1	13.94	14	0	0	1	21	21	42	32	1	34	16	.259	.250	.260	6.97	14.81
Pirela, Jesus	R-R	6-0	152	3-13-89	0	2	5.63	13	0	0	1	24	21	17	15	1	18	17	.223	.192	.235	6.38	6.75
Rodriguez, Ricciard	L-L	6-0	170	1-21-88	0	0	1.47	8	0	0	0	18	18	3	3	1	5	12	.250	.444	.222	5.89	2.45
Romero, Raul	R-R	6-2	165	11-14-86	8	2	3.43	22	15	0	2	89	99	46	34	4	26	71	.285	.255	.297	7.15	2.62
Suarez, Jesus	R-R	6-3	200	12-5-88	0	1	7.58	12	2	0	0	30	41	35	25	2	26	17	.339	.452	.300	5.16	7.89

FIELDING

Catcher	PCT	G	PO	A	E	DP	PB
Diaz	.984	47	301	58	6	3	9
Fuentes	1.000	15	68	6	0	1	4
Guerra	.979	22	174	15	4	1	3

First Base	PCT	G	PO	A	E	DP
Bravo	1.000	11	79	3	0	9
Doi	.993	24	137	4	1	10
Fuentes	.978	28	204	14	5	13
Guerra	.978	16	84	5	2	7
Martinez	1.000	1	1	0	0	0
Reyes	1.000	19	120	8	0	14

Second Base	PCT	G	PO	A	E	DP
Diaz	—	1	0	0	0	0

		G	PO	A	E	DP
Garcia	.965	18	38	44	3	11
Hernandez	1.000	12	13	30	0	6
Oviedo	.946	18	27	26	3	7
Rodriguez	.981	21	40	62	2	15
Sosa	.827	17	18	25	9	4

Third Base	PCT	G	PO	A	E	DP
Diaz	1.000	1	0	2	0	0
Garcia	.810	32	26	68	22	5
Oviedo	.889	20	9	31	5	3
Rodriguez	.900	28	28	62	10	6

Shortstop	PCT	G	PO	A	E	DP
Hernandez	.920	43	63	110	15	19
Rodriguez	.929	17	27	38	5	6

		G	PO	A	E	DP
Sosa	.824	25	29	60	19	7

Outfield	PCT	G	PO	A	E	DP
Bravo	.913	33	41	1	4	0
Doi	1.000	20	15	1	0	0
Hernandez	—	1	0	0	0	0
Lezcano	.870	32	19	1	3	0
Martinez	.833	15	13	2	3	0
Murakami	.947	65	94	14	6	4
Oviedo	1.000	3	4	0	0	0
Rossi	.942	54	76	5	5	2
Torres	.953	36	58	3	3	1

Pittsburgh Pirates

BY JOHN PERROTTO

The Pittsburgh Pirates' 2007 season will be noted more for what happened off the field than on it.

That is a good thing because it was more of the same as the Pirates finished 68-94 and last in the National League Central. It was their 15th consecutive losing season, leaving the franchise just one short of the major league record set by the Philadelphia Phillies from 1933-48.

However, as the Pirates reached the cusp of some dubious history, they made major changes to the organization.

It started in January when Bob Nutting became controlling owner in place of Kevin McClatchy, who then resigned as CEO at the end of the season. McClatchy put together the ownership group that bought the Pirates in 1996 but the Nutting family had long had the biggest stake in the team.

Frank Coonelly was brought in as club president after serving as Major League Baseball's senior vice president and general counsel of labor.

General manager Dave Littlefield was fired after six futile seasons on the job that was punctuated by a curious deal at the trading deadline when he acquired veteran righthander Matt Morris and the $13.7 million remaining on his contract from the Giants. Morris went 3-4, 6.10 in 62 innings for the Pirates.

The Pirates hired Indians assistant GM Neal Huntington to replace Littlefield. Huntington then cleaned house as he fired manager Jim Tracy, who had a dismal 133-189 record in two seasons, along with the entire coaching staff, player development director Brian Graham and scouting director Ed Creech.

Huntington hired former Pirates third-base coach John Russell as manager and tabbed Tigers scout Greg Smith as scouting director. Kyle Smith takes over farm director and Bryan Minniti becomes the director of baseball operations.

Despite being 67-95 the previous two seasons, the Pirates came into 2007 optimistic after going 37-35 after the all-star break in 2006. The optimism grew with a season-opening sweep in Houston.

However Pittsburgh's season quickly went downhill before really hitting the skids in the second half. The Pirates lost 14-of-16 games to start the second half then 13-of-15 to end the season.

Despite posting three consecutive seasons of at least 90 losses for the first time since 1952-54, the season wasn't completely doom and gloom.

Lefthander Tom Gorzelanny and righthander Ian Snell proved a decent 1-2 punch at the top of the rotation. Gorzelanny was 14-10, 3.88 and Snell endured a five-game losing streak before finishing a respectable 9-12, 3.76. Righthander Matt Capps emerged as a star-caliber closer in his second full major league season after being promoted from set-up man on June 1.

Shortstop Jack Wilson and second baseman Freddy Sanchez formed an excellent double play combination and had decent years offensively. Wilson used a late-season rush to finish at .296/.350/.440 with 12 home runs and 56 RBIs while Sanchez, who converted from third base after winning the NL batting title in 2006, overcame early-season knee problems to hit .304/.343/.442 with 11 homers and 81 RBIs.

Right fielder Xavier Nady, who battled injuries all season, was solid and first baseman Adam LaRoche overcame a nightmarish first two months.

MAJOR LEAGUE: IAN SNELL, RHP

The Pirates ranked 26th in the majors in runs allowed, but Snell stood out as a bright spot in the rotation. The righthander had a team-low 3.76 ERA in a team-high 208 innings. Snell also led the Pirates with 177 strikeouts and a 2.6-to-1 strikeout-to-walk ratio. His innings, ERA and strikeout marks were each career bests.

MINOR LEAGUE: STEVEN PEARCE, 1B

Pearce went from high Class A to Triple-A in 2007, excelling at each level before earning a callup to Pittsburgh. He finished with a .333/.394/.622 line in the minors with 31 home runs and 40 doubles. Among all minor leaguers, Pearce tied for seventh in home runs and fifth in slugging.

ORGANIZATIONAL LEADERS

BATTING		★Minimum 250 at-bats
★AVG	Pearce, Steve, Lynchburg/Altoona/Indianapolis	.333
R	Pacheco, Jonel, Lynchburg/Hickory	98
H	Pearce, Steve, Lynchburg/Altoona/Indianapolis	162
TB	Pearce, Steve, Lynchburg/Altoona/Indianapolis	303
2B	Pearce, Steve, Lynchburg/Altoona/Indianapolis	40
3B	Bixler, Brian, Indianapolis	10
HR	Pearce, Steve, Lynchburg/Altoona/Indianapolis	31
RBI	Pearce, Steve, Lynchburg/Altoona/Indianapolis	113
BB	Delaney, Jason, Lynchburg/Altoona	76
SO	Bixler, Brian, Indianapolis	131
SB	Powell, Pedro, Lynchburg	67
★OBP	Delaney, Jason, Lynchburg/Altoona	.403
★SLG	Pearce, Steve, Lynchburg/Altoona/Indianapolis	.622
PITCHING		^Minimum 75 innings
W	Munoz, Luis, Indianapolis/Altoona	14
L	Three players tied at	13
^ERA	Munoz, Luis, Indianapolis/Altoona	3.57
G	Peterson, Matt, Indianapolis/Altoona	54
CG	Brazelton, Dewon, Altoona	3
SV	Peterson, Matt, Indianapolis/Altoona	29
IP	Redmond, Todd, Altoona/Lynchburg	160
BB	Bloom, Kyle, Lynchburg/Altoona	63
SO	Hughes, Jared, Hickory	109
^AVG	Tejera, Michael, Indianapolis	.248

However there were just as many negatives for a team that finished 26 games under .500, led by the collapse of left fielder Jason Bay. He hit .247/.327/.418 with 21 homers and 84 RBIs after posting a .292/.389/.547 average with 31 homers and 97 RBIs in his first three full major league seasons.

Lefthander Zach Duke, the Opening Day starter, missed nearly three months with elbow problems while center fielder and leadoff hitter Chris Duffy missed the final three months with ankle and shoulder injuries. Catcher Ronny Paulino slumped following a stellar rookie season.

The Pirates also had a losing season in the minor leagues as their six farm clubs went a combined 330-358.

However, first baseman/outfielder Steven Pearce had a breakout season, hitting .333/.394/.622 with 31 homers, 114 RBIs and 14 stolen bases between high Class A Lynchburg, Double-A Altoona and Triple-A Indianapolis.

General Manager: Neil Huntington. **Farm Director:** Brian Graham. **Scouting Director:** Ed Creech

Class	Team	League	W	L	PCT	Finish*	Manager	Affiliate Since
Majors	Pittsburgh	National	68	94	.420	16th (16)	Jim Tracy	—
Triple-A	Indianapolis Indians	International	70	73	.490	8th (14)	Trent Jewett	2005
Double-A	Altoona Curve	Eastern	73	68	.518	4th (12)	Tim Leiper	1999
High A	Lynchburg Hillcats	Carolina	55	82	.401	8th (8)	Jeff Branson	1995
Low A	Hickory Crawdads	South Atlantic	70	66	.515	6th (16)	Gary Green	1999
Short-season	State College Spikes	New York-Penn	36	39	.480	8th (14)	Turner Ward	1999
Rookie	GCL Pirates	Gulf Coast	26	30	.464	11th (16)	Tom Prince	1967
Overall 2007 Minor League Record			**330**	**358**	**.480**	**22nd**		

* Finish in overall standings (No. of teams in league) ^League champion

ORGANIZATION STATISTICS

PITTSBURGH PIRATES

NATIONAL LEAGUE

BATTING	B-T	HT	WT	DOB	AVG	vLH	vRH	G	AB	R	H	2B	3B	HR	RBI	BB	HBP	SH	SF	SO	SB	CS	SLG	OBP
Bautista, Jose	R-R	6-0	195	10-19-80	.254	.256	.253	142	532	75	135	36	2	15	63	68	4	4	6	101	6	3	.414	.339
Bay, Jason	R-R	6-2	205	9-20-78	.247	.227	.254	145	538	78	133	25	2	21	84	59	9	0	8	141	4	1	.418	.327
Castillo, Jose	R-R	6-1	220	3-19-81	.244	.246	.244	87	221	18	54	18	1	0	24	6	2	0	1	48	0	0	.335	.270
Cota, Humberto	R-R	6-0	220	2-7-79	.286	.000	.286	5	14	1	4	1	0	0	3	2	1	0	1	2	0	0	.357	.389
Davis, Rajai	R-R	5-11	195	10-19-80	.271	.294	.214	24	48	6	13	2	1	0	2	7	0	1	1	3	5	2	.354	.357
2-team (51 San Francisco)					.279	—	—	75	190	32	53	11	2	1	9	21	4	3	1	28	22	6	.374	.361
Doumit, Ryan	B-R	6-1	220	4-3-81	.274	.246	.282	83	252	33	69	19	2	9	32	22	4	0	1	59	1	2	.472	.341
Duffy, Chris	L-L	5-9	180	4-20-80	.249	.211	.261	70	241	31	60	11	3	3	22	21	3	2	3	43	13	4	.357	.313
Eldred, Brad	R-R	6-5	275	7-12-80	.109	.105	.111	19	46	3	5	1	0	2	3	1	0	0	0	16	0	0	.261	.128
Izturis, Cesar	B-R	5-9	190	2-10-80	.276	.195	.317	45	123	16	34	3	2	0	8	6	0	1	0	3	0	3	.333	.310
2-team (65 Chicago)					.258	—	—	110	314	31	81	14	2	0	16	19	1	3	0	19	3	3	.315	.302
Kata, Matt	B-R	6-1	185	3-14-78	.250	.136	.288	47	88	9	22	7	1	1	10	0	1	1	0	15	0	0	.386	.258
Kelly, Don	L-R	6-4	190	2-15-80	.148	.100	.160	25	27	2	4	0	0	0	3	2	0	0	3	0	0	.148	.281
LaRoche, Adam	L-L	6-3	205	11-6-79	.272	.299	.262	152	563	71	153	40	0	21	88	62	3	0	4	131	1	1	.458	.345
Maldonado, Carlos	R-R	6-1	240	1-3-79	.208	.250	.200	13	24	2	5	1	0	2	4	5	0	0	1	8	0	0	.500	.333
McLouth, Nate	L-R	5-11	185	10-28-81	.258	.269	.256	137	329	62	85	21	3	13	38	39	9	3	2	77	22	1	.459	.351
Morgan, Nyjer	L-L	6-0	170	7-2-80	.299	.259	.313	28	107	15	32	3	4	1	7	9	1	1	0	19	7	3	.430	.359
Nady, Xavier	R-R	6-2	210	11-14-78	.278	.295	.274	125	431	55	120	23	1	20	72	23	12	0	4	101	3	1	.476	.330
Paulino, Ronny	R-R	6-2	245	4-21-81	.263	.407	.218	133	457	56	120	25	0	11	55	33	2	0	2	79	2	2	.389	.314
Pearce, Steve	R-R	5-11	198	4-13-83	.294	.429	.259	23	68	13	20	5	1	0	6	5	0	0	0	12	2	1	.397	.342
Phelps, Josh	R-R	6-3	225	5-12-78	.351	.394	.318	58	77	13	27	4	2	5	19	14	3	0	1	23	0	0	.649	.463
Sanchez, Freddy	R-R	5-10	185	12-21-77	.304	.364	.282	147	602	77	183	42	4	11	81	32	8	2	9	76	0	1	.442	.343
Wilson, Jack	R-R	6-0	195	12-29-77	.296	.320	.289	135	477	67	141	29	2	12	56	38	6	7	7	46	2	5	.440	.350

PITCHING	B-T	HT	WT	DOB	W	L	ERA	G	GS	CG	SV	IP	H	R	ER	HR	BB	SO	AVG	vLH	vRH	K/9	BB/9
Armas, Tony	R-R	6-3	225	4-29-78	4	5	6.03	31	15	0	0	97	111	68	65	18	38	73	.287	.280	.294	6.77	3.53
Bayliss, Jonah	R-R	6-2	200	8-13-80	4	3	8.36	39	0	0	0	38	51	36	35	8	18	29	.323	.333	.319	6.93	4.30
Bullington, Bryan	R-R	6-4	220	9-30-80	0	3	5.29	5	3	0	0	17	24	11	10	3	5	7	.343	.481	.256	3.71	2.65
Capps, Matt	R-R	6-2	245	9-3-83	4	7	2.28	76	0	0	18	79	64	22	20	5	16	64	.220	.281	.181	7.29	1.82
Chacon, Shawn	R-R	6-3	220	12-23-77	5	4	3.94	64	4	0	1	96	95	42	42	9	48	79	.265	.317	.236	7.41	4.50
Davidson, David	L-L	6-1	195	4-23-84	0	0	22.50	2	0	0	0	2	6	6	5	1	2	0	.462	.500	.455	0.00	9.00
Duke, Zach	L-L	6-2	220	4-19-83	3	8	5.53	20	19	0	0	107	161	74	66	14	25	41	.359	.341	.363	3.44	2.10
Gorzelanny, Tom	L-L	6-2	220	7-12-82	14	10	3.88	32	32	1	0	202	214	90	87	18	68	135	.273	.217	.284	6.02	3.03
Grabow, John	L-L	6-2	205	11-4-78	3	2	4.53	63	0	0	1	52	56	27	26	6	19	42	.277	.238	.303	7.32	3.31
Kolb, Dan	R-R	6-4	210	3-29-75	0	0	9.00	3	0	0	0	3	6	3	3	1	2	2	.462	1.000	.364	6.00	6.00
Kuwata, Masumi	R-R	5-10	185	4-1-68	0	1	9.43	19	0	0	0	21	25	23	22	6	15	12	.301	.200	.345	5.14	6.43
Maholm, Paul	L-L	6-2	230	6-25-82	10	15	5.02	29	29	2	0	178	204	110	99	22	49	105	.295	.238	.305	5.32	2.48
Marte, Damaso	L-L	6-2	210	2-14-75	2	0	2.38	65	0	0	0	45	32	14	12	2	18	51	.200	.094	.271	10.12	3.57
McLeary, Marty	R-R	6-3	225	10-26-74	0	0	8.22	4	0	0	0	8	9	8	7	4	2	5	.281	.294	.267	5.87	2.35
Morris, Matt	R-R	6-5	215	8-9-74	3	4	6.10	11	11	0	0	62	78	44	42	6	22	29	.315	.257	.354	4.21	3.19
2-team (21 San Francisco)					10	11	4.89	32	32	3	0	199	240	123	108	18	61	102	—	—	—	4.62	2.76
Osoria, Franquelis	R-R	6-0	205	9-12-81	0	2	4.76	25	0	0	0	28	33	16	15	3	8	13	.289	.353	.263	4.13	2.54
Perez, Juan	R-L	6-0	175	9-3-78	0	0	4.38	17	0	0	0	12	14	7	6	2	8	10	.286	.313	.273	7.30	5.84
Rogers, Brian	R-R	6-4	190	7-17-82	0	0	13.50	3	0	0	0	2	3	3	3	2	1	1	.500	.500	.500	4.50	4.50
Sanchez, Romulo	R-R	6-5	245	4-28-84	1	0	5.00	16	0	0	0	18	16	10	10	2	8	11	.254	.353	.217	5.50	4.00
Sharpless, Josh	R-R	6-5	240	1-26-81	0	1	12.46	6	0	0	0	4	6	6	6	0	4	1	.368	.250	.455	2.08	2.08
Snell, Ian	R-R	5-11	190	10-30-81	9	12	3.76	32	32	1	0	208	209	94	87	22	68	177	.264	.284	.245	7.66	2.94
Torres, Salomon	R-R	5-11	210	3-11-72	2	4	5.47	56	0	0	12	53	57	34	32	7	17	45	.277	.275	.278	7.69	2.91
Van Benschoten, John	R-R	6-4	225	4-14-80	0	7	10.15	11	9	0	0	39	55	45	44	4	29	26	.335	.311	.350	6.00	6.69
Wasdin, John	R-R	6-2	190	8-5-72	1	1	5.95	12	0	0	0	20	32	13	13	1	8	10	.381	.296	.421	4.58	3.66
Youman, Shane	L-L	6-4	220	10-11-79	3	5	5.97	16	8	0	0	57	65	40	38	5	23	29	.298	.306	.297	4.55	3.61

FIELDING

Catcher	PCT	G	PO	A	E	DP	PB
Cota	1.000	5	30	2	0	0	0
Doumit	.987	28	149	7	2	2	5
Maldonado	1.000	13	64	2	0	0	0
Paulino	.992	129	784	58	7	9	8
Phelps	1.000	3	9	1	0	0	0

First Base	PCT	G	PO	A	E	DP
Doumit	1.000	3	12	0	0	1
Eldred	1.000	4	23	1	0	3
LaRoche	.996	151	1296	81	6	154
Pearce	1.000	2	12	0	0	5
Phelps	1.000	22	107	5	0	12

Second Base	PCT	G	PO	A	E	DP
Castillo	.946	20	45	25	4	11

Kata	1.000	10	14	14	0	6
Kelly	1.000	3	1	2	0	1
Sanchez	.987	146	313	379	9	121

Third Base	PCT	G	PO	A	E	DP
Bautista	.958	126	95	251	15	16
Castillo	.964	34	23	83	4	6
Izturis	1.000	11	3	11	0	0
Kata	.947	10	2	16	1	1

Shortstop	PCT	G	PO	A	E	DP
Castillo	.972	8	15	20	1	7
Izturis	.991	30	39	66	1	25
Kata	1.000	3	3	5	0	1
Kelly	1.000	5	5	6	0	1
Sanchez	—	1	0	0	0	0

Wilson	.983	131	177	452	11	112

Outfield	PCT	G	PO	A	E	DP
Bautista	.939	21	30	1	2	0
Bay	.972	142	265	13	8	3
Castillo	1.000	1	3	0	0	0
Davis	1.000	12	27	0	0	0
Doumit	.985	38	62	5	1	2
Duffy	.994	68	172	3	1	0
Eldred	1.000	8	8	0	0	0
Kata	1.000	3	2	0	0	0
Kelly	1.000	2	1	0	0	0
McLouth	.984	101	183	2	3	1
Morgan	.989	28	84	2	1	2
Nady	.995	109	192	4	1	0
Pearce	1.000	18	31	1	0	0

INDIANAPOLIS INDIANS TRIPLE-A

INTERNATIONAL LEAGUE

BATTING	B-T	HT	WT	DOB	AVG	vLH	vRH	G	AB	R	H	2B	3B	HR	RBI	BB	HBP	SH	SF	SO	SB	CS	SLG	OBP
Aguila, Chris	R-R	5-11	200	2-23-79	.250	.261	.246	55	172	23	43	5	1	4	22	9	1	1	0	41	2		.360	.291
Bixler, Brian	R-R	6-1	195	10-22-82	.274	.317	.259	129	475	77	130	23	10	5	51	54	17	10	0	131	28	4	.396	.368
Boeve, Adam	R-R	6-2	216	6-20-80	.277	.273	.279	29	83	13	23	1	1	4	6	14	4	2	0	23	6	3	.458	.406
Cota, Humberto	R-R	6-0	220	2-7-79	.284	.316	.276	30	95	9	27	6	0	0	9	7	0	1	1	8	2	0	.347	.330
Davis, Rajai	R-R	5-11	195	10-19-80	.318	.283	.329	53	211	31	67	12	4	4	30	21	3	2	2	25	27	9	.469	.384
de Caster, Yurendell	R-R	6-1	210	9-26-79	.280	.277	.281	120	407	55	114	25	1	9	54	58	9	1	2	95	13	8	.413	.380
Diaz, Einar	R-R	5-10	200	12-28-72	.254	.361	.207	38	118	15	30	8	0	2	13	8	6	0	0	8	5	1	.373	.333
Doumit, Ryan	B-R	6-1	220	4-3-81	.415	.444	.409	16	53	15	22	4	0	4	20	8	3	0	3	12	3	2	.717	.493
Edwards, Mike	R-R	6-1	200	11-24-76	.143	.000	.167	3	7	1	1	0	0	0	0	0	0	1	0	0	0	0	.143	.250
2-team (46 Louisville)					.251	—		49	167	26	42	12	0	2	21	14	1	6	2	26	5	0	.359	.310
Eldred, Brad	R-R	6-5	275	7-12-80	.209	.186	.218	86	311	37	65	10	2	15	45	20	9	0	2	90	9	3	.399	.275
Green, Nick	R-R	6-0	180	9-10-78	.245	.222	.253	26	102	9	25	6	0	5	20	2	1	0	1	28	1	2	.451	.264
Hernandez, Jose	R-R	6-1	190	7-14-69	.242	.278	.228	99	322	40	78	16	1	13	56	34	4	1	2	79	1	1	.419	.320
Johnson, Russ	R-R	5-10	185	2-22-73	.269	.253	.274	93	316	36	85	18	2	6	45	39	1	2	3	31	3	4	.396	.348
Kata, Matt	B-R	6-1	185	3-14-78	.278	.133	.316	19	72	12	20	5	1	2	5	7	0	1	1	8	2	1	.458	.338
Kelly, Don	L-R	6-0	190	2-15-80	.247	.278	.242	52	150	20	37	5	2	0	11	18	2	4	0	17	6	4	.307	.335
Maldonado, Carlos	R-R	6-1	240	1-3-79	.219	.258	.208	46	137	14	30	4	0	1	19	20	2	4	1	27	0	0	.270	.325
Matos, Luis	R-R	6-0	185	10-30-78	.257	.247	.260	98	343	46	88	23	1	3	30	18	18	1	2	54	9	7	.356	.325
McCutchen, Andrew	R-R	5-11	170	10-10-86	.313	.385	.296	17	67	7	21	4	0	1	5	4	0	0	1	11	4	3	.418	.347
Morgan, Nyjer	L-L	6-0	170	7-2-80	.305	.286	.310	44	164	30	50	4	2	0	10	15	3	2	0	28	26	7	.354	.374
Ordaz, Luis	R-R	5-11	170	8-12-75	.302	.267	.313	102	351	39	106	21	1	3	36	19	3	5	7	53	9	5	.393	.337
Parrish, David	R-R	6-3	220	6-13-78	.138	.150	.135	34	94	5	13	3	0	2	8	7	1	1	0	22	1	1	.234	.214
Pearce, Steve	R-R	5-11	198	4-13-83	.320	.391	.303	34	122	18	39	9	1	6	17	6	3	0	0	12	5	0	.557	.366
Reyes, Milver	R-R	5-11	200	9-3-82	.226	.300	.190	14	31	3	7	1	0	0	3	5	1	0	0	7	0	0	.258	.351
Ryan, Michael	L-R	6-0	190	7-6-77	.259	.244	.263	121	379	54	98	21	6	16	52	29	2	1	7	89	0	3	.472	.309
Sanchez, Freddy	R-R	5-10	185	12-21-77	.500	—	.500	1	2	1	1	0	0	0	2	0	0	0	0	0	0	0	01.000	.750
Truby, Chris	R-R	6-2	220	12-9-73	.316	.400	.286	6	19	2	6	1	0	1	4	1	0	0	0	8	1	0	.526	.350
Walker, Neil	B-R	6-2	210	9-10-85	.203	.333	.163	19	64	7	13	3	0	0	2	2	3	0	0	13	1	1	.250	.261

PITCHING	B-T	HT	WT	DOB	W	L	ERA	G	GS	CG	SV	IP	H	R	ER	HR	BB	SO	AVG	vLH	vRH	K/9	BB/9
Bayliss, Jonah	R-R	6-2	200	8-13-80	3	2	7.06	16	0	0	0	22	23	19	17	5	10	17	.277	.286	.271	7.06	4.15
Bouknight, Kip	R-R	6-0	190	11-16-78	1	1	4.50	3	3	0	0	18	19	10	9	3	8	12	.279	.281	.278	6.00	4.00
Brower, Jim	R-R	6-3	215	12-29-72	1	0	3.68	6	0	0	1	7	9	3	3	0	2	4	.300	.250	.333	4.91	2.45
2-team (38 Scranton/Wilkes-Barre)					5	2	2.45	44	0	0	2	55	53	15	15	2	15	49	—	—	—	8.02	2.45
Bullington, Bryan	R-R	6-4	220	9-30-80	11	9	4.00	26	26	0	0	151	146	70	67	10	59	89	.262	.270	.255	5.32	3.52
Burnett, Sean	L-L	6-1	195	9-17-82	4	5	4.48	15	15	0	0	70	83	39	35	4	39	31	.307	.276	.320	3.97	4.99
Chavez, Jesse	R-R	6-2	175	8-21-83	3	3	3.92	46	1	0	2	80	94	41	35	4	17	65	.290	.323	.267	7.28	1.90
Corey, Mark	R-R	6-3	220	11-16-74	1	1	4.13	23	1	0	0	33	36	18	15	1	26	23	.300	.385	.200	6.34	7.16
Davidson, David	L-L	6-1	195	4-23-84	1	0	1.17	6	0	0	0	8	6	2	1	0	3	9	.214	.333	.158	10.57	3.52
Duke, Zach	L-L	6-2	220	4-19-83	0	1	4.91	1	1	0	0	4	4	2	2	1	2	2	.438	.500	.417	2.45	4.91
Grabow, John	L-L	6-2	205	11-4-78	0	0	2.25	4	0	0	0	4	4	1	1	1	2	4	.286	.250	.300	9.00	4.50
Gryboski, Kevin	R-R	6-5	230	11-15-73	2	1	7.23	14	0	0	0	19	27	18	15	1	16	12	.346	.406	.304	5.79	7.71
Hernandez, Chris	R-R	6-0	204	8-3-80	0	3	5.54	10	0	0	3	13	11	9	8	2	4	9	.239	.053	.370	6.23	2.77
Hernandez, Runelvys	R-R	6-1	250	4-27-78	1	3	8.47	4	4	0	0	17	27	16	16	4	5	5	.446	.450	.442	2.65	2.65
3-team (7 Pawtucket, 6 Scranton/Wilkes-Barre)					1	7	4.35	17	17	0	0	83	98	61	40	14	29	51	—	—	—	5.55	3.16
Johnson, Russ	R-R	5-10	185	2-22-73	0	0	6.75	1	0	0	0	1	3	1	1	1	0	0	.500	.000	.600	0.00	0.00
Kolb, Dan	R-R	6-4	210	3-29-75	2	1	3.15	18	0	0	4	20	19	7	7	0	9	16	.247	.258	.239	7.20	4.05
Kuwata, Masumi	R-R	5-10	185	4-1-68	0	0	0.00	3	0	0	0	4	3	0	0	0	3	2	.200	.182	.250	6.23	0.00
McLeary, Marty	R-R	6-3	225	10-26-74	5	8	4.62	24	24	0	0	123	127	71	63	13	53	95	.268	.286	.252	6.97	3.89
Munoz, Luis	R-R	6-2	150	1-10-82	2	1	3.12	3	3	0	0	17	22	8	6	2	4	16	.319	.364	.278	8.31	2.08
Nannini, Mike	R-R	5-11	190	8-9-80	0	0	54.00	1	0	0	0	3	2	2	0	0	0	1	.750	1.000	.667	0.00	0.00
Osoria, Franquelis	R-R	6-0	205	9-12-81	2	5	2.63	39	0	0	11	55	51	22	16	3	19	33	.249	.286	.219	5.43	3.13
Perez, Juan	R-L	6-0	175	9-3-78	3	2	4.69	40	0	0	2	56	52	31	29	5	25	63	.243	.220	.258	10.19	4.04
Peterson, Matt	R-R	6-4	220	2-11-82	0	0	2.08	3	0	0	0	4	3	2	1	0	5	3	.200	.091	.500	6.23	10.38
Prinz, Bret	R-R	6-3	210	6-15-77	0	0	1.29	14	0	0	6	14	13	2	2	0	7	15	.255	.333	.167	9.64	4.50
2-team (15 Charlotte)					0	1	0.90	29	0	0	7	30	23	4	3	0	16	31	—	—	—	9.30	4.80
Rodriguez, Ricardo	L-R	6-3	190	5-21-78	0	2	11.12	2	1	0	0	6	12	8	7	2	2	4	.467	.579	.273	3.18	3.18
Rogers, Brian	R-R	6-4	190	7-17-82	2	1	3.05	48	0	0	2	65	50	23	22	5	32	65	.214	.204	.222	9.00	4.43
Sharpless, Josh	R-R	6-5	240	1-26-81	1	5	4.34	43	0	0	3	64	61	36	31	10	39	69	.249	.193	.294	9.65	5.46
Tejera, Michael	L-L	5-10	195	10-18-76	8	5	3.90	27	19	1	0	127	115	56	55	14	43	71	.248	.118	.303	5.03	3.05
Torres, Salomon	R-R	5-11	210	3-11-72	0	0	0.00	1	0	0	0	1	0	0	0	0	0	1	.000	.000	.000	20.25	0.00
Van Benschoten, John	R-R	6-4	225	4-14-80	10	7	2.56	19	19	1	0	109	98	35	31	8	51	79	.244	.240	.247	6.52	4.21
Wasdin, John	R-R	6-2	190	8-5-72	1	1	6.37	7	7	0	0	35	43	25	25	10	3	40	.297	.289	.304	10.19	0.76

	B-T	HT	WT	DOB	W	L	ERA	G	GS	CG	SV	IP	H	R	ER	HR	BB	SO	AVG	vLH	vRH	K/9	BB/9
Youman, Shane	L-L	6-4	220	10-11-79	4	6	4.70	15	15	0	0	82	94	45	43	3	36	61	.290	.290	.290	6.67	3.94
Zambrano, Victor	B-R	6-0	205	8-6-75	2	0	2.70	5	5	0	0	27	17	9	8	1	9	25	.185	.191	.178	8.44	3.04
2-team (8 Syracuse)					5	2	5.56	13	13	0	0	68	67	43	42	5	31	63	—	—	—	8.34	4.10

FIELDING

Catcher	PCT	G	PO	A	E	DP	PB
Cota	.994	25	158	13	1	1	1
Diaz	.988	35	217	25	3	5	0
Doumit	1.000	13	67	11	0	0	3
Maldonado	.986	45	268	20	4	2	1
Parrish	.984	29	168	14	3	3	3
Reyes	.976	12	78	4	2	0	0

First Base	PCT	G	PO	A	E	DP
de Caster	.997	60	512	58	2	48
Edwards	1.000	1	10	0	0	0
Eldred	.998	48	382	26	1	42
Hernandez	.994	19	166	8	1	19
Johnson	1.000	3	14	3	0	3
Pearce	.994	21	157	14	1	19
Truby	1.000	1	6	0	0	1

Second Base	PCT	G	PO	A	E	DP
Bixler	1.000	16	35	48	0	13
de Caster	1.000	11	18	25	0	8
Green	1.000	7	12	13	0	3

	PCT	G	PO	A	E	DP
Hernandez	.971	14	32	36	2	13
Johnson	1.000	1	3	4	0	2
Kata	1.000	1	1	5	0	0
Kelly	1.000	14	23	33	0	8
Ordaz	.993	91	161	264	3	63
Sanchez	1.000	1	3	3	0	1

Third Base	PCT	G	PO	A	E	DP
de Caster	.931	11	7	20	2	2
Edwards	1.000	1	1	1	0	0
Green	.667	4	1	7	4	2
Hernandez	.961	36	28	70	4	9
Johnson	.969	72	47	141	6	10
Kata	.800	1	1	3	1	0
Kelly	.895	6	8	9	2	1
Truby	.917	5	5	6	1	1
Walker	.953	17	14	27	2	2

Shortstop	PCT	G	PO	A	E	DP
Bixler	.967	113	142	327	16	80
Green	.938	5	7	8	1	1

	PCT	G	PO	A	E	DP
Hernandez	1.000	3	2	7	0	1
Kelly	.988	18	35	46	1	18
Ordaz	.971	9	12	22	1	3

Outfield	PCT	G	PO	A	E	DP
Aguila	.976	43	74	6	2	2
Boeve	.955	21	21	0	1	0
Davis	.976	52	117	7	3	2
de Caster	.898	25	41	3	5	0
Eldred	.977	29	40	2	1	0
Green	1.000	12	17	0	0	0
Kata	.974	16	37	0	1	0
Kelly	1.000	18	19	2	0	1
Matos	.981	92	208	4	4	2
McCutchen	1.000	17	36	0	0	0
Morgan	.972	42	101	4	3	0
Pearce	.941	10	15	1	1	0
Ryan	.977	94	163	7	4	1

ORGANIZATION STATISTICS

ALTOONA CURVE — DOUBLE-A

EASTERN LEAGUE

BATTING	B-T	HT	WT	DOB	AVG	vLH	vRH	G	AB	R	H	2B	3B	HR	RBI	BB	HBP	SH	SF	SO	SB	CS	SLG	OBP
Bergeron, Peter	L-R	6-0	190	11-9-77	.240	.211	.247	33	104	12	25	4	1	0	9	8	0	1	2	18	2	0	.298	.289
Boeve, Adam	R-R	6-2	216	6-20-80	.270	.263	.273	96	330	55	89	14	2	17	53	50	5	0	2	100	17	5	.479	.372
Bowers, Jason	R-R	5-10	183	1-27-78	.272	.258	.278	113	426	56	116	27	4	8	51	51	5	5	1	63	16	6	.411	.356
Buttler, Vic	L-L	6-0	175	8-12-80	.274	.307	.257	74	263	38	72	7	4	3	24	31	2	0	0	26	22	9	.365	.355
Chaves, Brandon	B-R	6-3	181	8-5-79	.265	.265	.265	105	336	41	89	17	2	0	40	39	6	4	2	79	19	6	.327	.350
Corley, Brad	R-R	6-2	198	12-28-83	.256	.357	.200	10	39	3	10	2	0	0	4	0	0	0	0	6	1	0	.308	.256
Delaney, Jason	R-R	6-3	215	11-9-82	.265	.262	.266	65	223	25	59	10	0	7	35	38	0	0	1	52	0	0	.404	.370
Elliott, Justin	R-R	5-11	195	4-27-82	.000	.000	.000	3	4	0	0	0	0	0	0	0	0	0	0	2	0	0	.000	.000
Falcon, Omar	B-R	6-1	210	9-1-82	.063	.000	.125	8	16	1	1	0	0	0	0	3	0	1	0	9	0	0	.063	.211
Fernandez, Alex	L-L	6-1	200	5-15-81	.219	.212	.221	82	215	22	47	11	0	2	23	12	0	1	2	30	1	0	.298	.258
Guzman, Javier	R-R	6-0	170	5-4-82	.310	.349	.287	52	171	19	53	13	0	2	25	5	2	3	2	20	7	0	.421	.333
Johnson, Russ	R-R	5-10	185	2-22-73	.205	.286	.189	13	44	8	9	2	0	3	5	7	1	0	1	6	2	0	.455	.321
Lee, Taber	B-R	6-1	185	10-18-80	.235	.244	.228	89	196	29	46	8	0	0	16	31	3	2	0	31	11	1	.276	.348
Maldonado, Carlos	R-R	6-1	240	1-3-79	.000	.000	.000	3	6	0	0	0	0	0	0	0	0	0	0	1	0	0	.000	.000
McCutchen, Andrew	R-R	5-11	170	10-10-86	.258	.299	.240	118	446	70	115	20	3	10	48	44	3	2	3	83	17	1	.383	.327
Meath, Matt	B-R	6-0	175	10-6-79	.273	.348	.100	17	33	6	9	2	0	0	0	6	1	0	0	9	1	0	.333	.400
Parrish, David	R-R	6-3	220	6-13-79	.244	.244	.243	46	156	18	38	9	0	3	19	10	1	2	1	32	0	0	.359	.292
Pearce, Steve	R-R	5-11	198	4-13-83	.334	.330	.337	81	290	57	97	27	2	14	72	33	4	0	8	45	7	2	.586	.400
Peterson, Brian	R-R	6-2	225	10-22-78	.272	.225	.291	83	250	30	68	14	1	3	30	27	2	9	3	38	0	2	.372	.344
Reyes, Milver	R-R	5-11	200	9-3-82	.230	.333	.159	27	74	2	17	4	0	0	6	5	0	0	1	19	0	0	.284	.275
Roneberg, Brett	L-L	6-2	205	2-5-79	.248	.218	.257	77	238	38	59	10	3	8	35	32	2	1	0	39	8	0	.416	.342
Ruiz, Randy	R-R	6-3	235	10-19-77	.290	.192	.336	47	162	20	47	9	1	7	30	18	2	0	3	32	0	1	.488	.362
3-team (22 Reading, 39 Connecticut)					.309	—	—	108	395	61	122	25	4	18	69	35	6	0	3	93	1	1	.529	.371
Truby, Chris	R-R	6-2	220	12-9-73	.333	.250	.368	7	24	9	1	0	2	9	1	0	0	0	4	0	1	.370	.357
Walker, Neil	B-R	6-3	210	9-10-85	.288	.285	.289	117	431	77	124	30	3	13	66	53	0	1	5	73	9	4	.462	.362

PITCHING	B-T	HT	WT	DOB	W	L	ERA	G	GS	CG	SV	IP	H	R	ER	HR	BB	SO	AVG	vLH	vRH	K/9	BB/9
Astacio, Olivo	R-R	6-5	190	7-28-84	0	0	0.00	1	0	0	0	2	0	0	0	0	2	1	.000	.000	.000	4.50	9.00
Belisario, Ronald	R-R	6-2	200	12-31-82	1	0	3.28	18	0	0	0	25	23	11	9	4	14	21	.245	.306	.207	7.66	5.11
Bloom, Kyle	R-L	6-3	185	2-21-83	1	1	0.90	2	2	0	0	10	5	3	1	1	6	10	.147	.091	.174	9.00	5.40
Bouknight, Kip	R-R	6-0	190	11-16-78	11	6	3.83	24	22	1	0	139	135	67	59	12	36	83	.259	.302	.226	5.39	2.34
Bowers, Jason	R-R	5-10	183	1-27-78	0	0	0.00	1	0	0	0	1	1	0	0	0	0	1	.250	.000	.333	9.00	0.00
Brazelton, Dewon	R-R	6-4	225	6-16-80	5	5	3.53	15	15	3	0	87	88	37	34	5	17	52	.274	.307	.244	5.40	1.77
Bresnehan, Patrick	R-R	6-1	195	4-23-85	1	0	4.50	3	0	0	0	6	5	3	3	0	2	3	.217	.556	.000	4.50	3.00
Crotta, Michael	R-R	6-6	210	9-24-84	0	1	10.12	1	1	0	0	3	6	7	3	0	2	0	.400	.286	.500	0.00	6.75
Davidson, David	L-L	6-1	195	4-23-84	3	1	4.22	39	0	0	2	60	44	30	28	3	30	55	.205	.213	.201	8.30	4.53
Hankins, Derek	R-R	6-4	190	7-1-83	0	1	12.27	1	1	0	0	4	4	6	5	1	5	2	.267	.300	.200	4.91	12.27
Hernandez, Chris	R-R	6-0	204	8-3-80	6	1	2.86	42	0	0	4	57	53	19	18	4	20	55	.250	.231	.264	8.74	3.18
Herrera, Yoslan	R-R	6-2	195	4-28-81	6	9	4.69	25	25	1	0	129	151	72	67	11	38	70	.296	.315	.279	4.90	2.66
Munoz, Luis	R-R	6-2	150	1-10-82	12	5	3.63	25	23	1	0	136	130	63	55	11	32	89	.250	.245	.255	5.88	2.11
Nannini, Mike	R-R	5-11	190	8-9-80	1	1	4.95	14	0	0	0	20	20	12	11	4	5	19	.247	.256	.238	8.55	2.25
Paniagua, Jose	R-R	6-2	190	8-20-73	0	0	3.00	5	0	0	0	9	10	3	3	1	3	4	.294	.222	.375	4.00	3.00
Peterson, Matt	R-R	6-4	220	2-11-82	4	2	1.98	51	0	0	29	64	50	14	14	4	27	56	.225	.231	.219	7.92	3.82
Redmond, Todd	R-R	6-3	185	5-17-85	1	1	3.12	3	3	0	0	17	15	6	6	2	3	12	.227	.324	.146	6.23	1.56
Reyes, Milver	R-R	5-11	200	9-3-82	0	0	0.00	1	0	0	0	1	0	0	0	0	1	0	.500	1.000	.000	0.00	9.00
Roach, Jason	R-R	6-4	205	4-20-76	4	3	5.00	32	0	0	1	63	76	44	35	4	28	39	.299	.287	.309	5.57	4.00
Sanchez, Romulo	R-R	6-5	245	4-28-84	6	3	2.81	40	0	0	1	58	43	24	18	8	17	52	.204	.263	.155	8.12	2.65
Shortslef, Josh	R-L	6-4	250	2-1-82	5	13	4.40	27	27	0	0	149	170	87	73	12	59	85	.295	.260	.308	5.12	3.56
Soler, Alay	R-R	6-1	240	10-9-79	1	1	6.00	14	5	0	1	39	48	30	26	3	19	24	.312	.257	.357	5.54	4.38
Starling, Wardell	R-R	6-4	205	3-14-83	3	8	6.48	32	12	1	0	85	96	64	61	5	32	51	.293	.292	.293	5.42	3.40
Vaclavik, Justin	R-R	6-1	185	5-27-84	2	6	8.39	24	3	0	0	34	50	37	32	3	21	28	.323	.313	.333	7.34	5.50
Williams, Brandon	R-R	6-6	230	9-6-84	0	0	10.80	2	0	0	0	3	6	4	4	0	1	2	.375	.444	.286	5.40	2.70

FIELDING

Catcher	PCT	G	PO	A	E	DP	PB
Elliott	1.000	1	1	0	0	0	0
Falcon	1.000	8	32	3	0	0	0
Maldonado	1.000	3	16	0	0	0	0
Parrish	.982	42	243	28	5	1	4
Peterson	.988	73	371	49	5	5	6
Reyes	.989	27	168	17	2	1	4

First Base	PCT	G	PO	A	E	DP
Chaves	—	1	0	0	0	0
Delaney	.987	31	222	14	3	20
Fernandez	1.000	1	0	0	0	0
Pearce	.991	77	681	57	7	85
Roneberg	1.000	25	145	15	0	9
Ruiz	.993	16	138	11	1	13
Truby	1.000	1	2	0	0	1

Second Base	PCT	G	PO	A	E	DP
Bowers	.991	92	195	267	4	68
Guzman	.886	8	13	18	4	5
Lee	.980	43	62	131	4	28
Truby	1.000	5	6	18	0	3

Third Base	PCT	G	PO	A	E	DP
Bowers	.967	5	5	14	1	2
Chaves	.909	5	3	7	1	2
Johnson	.947	13	8	28	2	3
Truby	—	1	0	0	0	0
Walker	.915	113	76	194	25	25

Shortstop	PCT	G	PO	A	E	DP
Bowers	.963	8	12	14	1	5
Chaves	.968	93	144	246	13	58
Guzman	.925	32	42	81	10	21

Lee	.908	22	26	53	8	12

Outfield	PCT	G	PO	A	E	DP
Bergeron	1.000	30	65	1	0	1
Boeve	.981	93	145	7	3	0
Buttler	.993	70	143	3	1	1
Chaves	1.000	6	8	0	0	0
Corley	1.000	10	27	0	0	0
Delaney	.978	20	45	0	1	0
Fernandez	.965	53	80	2	3	1
Guzman	1.000	3	3	1	0	0
Lee	—	1	0	0	0	0
McCutchen	.991	118	305	8	3	3
Meath	.944	14	17	0	1	0
Roneberg	.979	34	45	1	1	0
Ruiz	1.000	4	5	0	0	0

LYNCHBURG HILLCATS   HIGH CLASS A

CAROLINA LEAGUE

BATTING	B-T	HT	WT	DOB	AVG	vLH	vRH	G	AB	R	H	2B	3B	HR	RBI	BB	HBP	SH	SF	SO	SB	CS	SLG	OBP
Alvarez, Victor	B-R	5-11	185	6-17-83	.111	.000	.125	3	9	0	1	0	0	0	0	0	0	0	0	2	0	0	.111	.111
Blair, Cameron	R-R	5-11	175	10-27-82	.000	.000	.000	2	4	0	0	0	0	0	0	0	0	0	0	0	0	0	.000	.000
Boone, James	B-R	6-2	175	3-16-83	.255	.213	.275	50	192	31	49	12	0	6	34	17	8	0	2	35	8	4	.411	.338
Corley, Brad	R-R	6-2	198	12-28-83	.285	.339	.266	126	485	73	138	36	4	14	89	14	13	0	6	99	3	2	.462	.319
Davenport, Ron	R-R	6-2	190	10-16-81	.286	.333	.272	66	238	35	68	18	2	4	33	16	1	1	1	24	1	2	.429	.332
De Los Santos, Jose J.	R-R	5-11	160	8-10-84	.306	.200	.330	29	111	18	34	6	0	1	12	6	1	1	0	12	1	1	.387	.347
Delaney, Jason	R-R	6-3	215	11-9-82	.340	.424	.310	72	250	39	85	16	3	9	44	38	5	0	3	52	2	1	.536	.432
Diaz, Ricky	R-R	6-0	194	12-3-84	.000	.000	—	2	1	0	0	0	0	0	0	0	0	0	0	1	0	0	.000	.000
Diaz, Einar	R-R	5-10	200	12-28-72	.087	.250	.000	6	23	0	2	0	0	0	1	1	0	0	0	3	0	0	.087	.125
Falcon, Omar	B-R	6-1	210	9-1-82	.138	.130	.143	23	65	7	9	4	0	0	6	16	1	0	0	30	0	1	.200	.317
Ford, Shelby	B-R	6-3	190	12-15-84	.281	.250	.294	94	360	64	101	26	7	5	55	34	13	2	4	68	14	0	.433	.360
Gonzalez, Angel R.	B-R	5-11	165	12-28-85	.254	.293	.244	52	209	31	53	10	2	0	18	7	0	5	1	43	8	6	.321	.276
Johnson III, Tripper	R-R	6-1	199	4-28-82	.270	.280	.267	133	485	68	131	36	2	10	72	53	6	1	7	73	13	3	.414	.345
Kingsbury, Bobby	L-L	6-1	184	8-30-80	.233	.222	.235	13	43	3	10	4	0	0	6	3	0	0	0	10	0	0	.326	.283
Lerud, Steven	L-R	6-1	210	10-13-84	.202	.197	.204	84	287	27	58	17	1	4	31	31	9	0	1	63	3	2	.310	.299
Macia, Wanell	L-L	5-11	180	7-20-82	.206	.125	.218	21	63	6	13	2	0	0	5	0	1	0	1	10	0	0	.238	.206
Mansolino, Anthony	R-R	6-0	190	9-28-82	.222	.184	.236	93	333	26	74	8	0	3	23	18	4	2	3	66	1	4	.273	.268
Nino, Denny	R-R	6-1	211	6-4-83	.240	.238	.241	27	75	7	18	6	0	2	10	8	2	0	0	14	0	1	.400	.329
Pacheco, Jonel	R-R	5-9	170	10-3-82	.290	.400	.238	9	31	1	9	3	0	0	2	0	0	0	0	10	0	0	.387	.333
Pearce, Steve	R-R	5-11	198	4-13-83	.347	.365	.375	19	75	19	26	4	1	11	24	8	1	0	1	13	2	0	.867	.412
Peterson, Brian	R-R	6-2	225	10-22-78	.321	.200	.348	9	28	4	9	2	0	0	1	6	0	0	1	5	0	1	.393	.429
Picart, Greg	B-R	5-11	175	9-25-85	.236	.197	.251	80	258	27	61	14	4	5	35	13	5	1	6	41	1	4	.380	.280
Powell, Pedro	R-R	5-7	143	5-20-84	.241	.260	.235	124	485	71	117	16	7	0	29	56	6	11	3	94	67	17	.303	.325
Romak, Jamie	R-R	6-2	220	9-30-85	.252	.221	.261	85	294	49	74	21	1	15	45	55	6	0	0	90	2	2	.483	.380
Rosero, Ciro	R-R	6-1	160	7-25-86	.063	.000	.167	5	16	0	1	0	0	0	0	0	0	0	0	5	0	0	.063	.063
Schwartzbauer, Daniel	R-R	5-11	175	11-2-81	.252	.154	.287	47	147	20	37	10	0	0	12	18	1	2	1	36	4	0	.320	.335

PITCHING	B-T	HT	WT	DOB	W	L	ERA	G	GS	CG	SV	IP	H	R	ER	HR	BB	SO	AVG	vLH	vRH	K/9	BB/9
Amaro, Carlos	R-R	6-0	170	11-6-84	0	0	5.40	1	0	0	0	3	6	3	2	0	2	5	.400	.500	.286	13.50	5.40
Antelo, Derek	R-R	6-1	205	11-30-82	1	2	4.10	30	1	0	0	64	68	30	29	2	18	51	.271	.325	.244	7.21	2.54
Astacio, Olivo	R-R	6-5	190	7-28-84	0	1	8.22	7	0	0	1	15	14	16	14	3	12	19	.241	.278	.225	11.15	7.04
Belisario, Ronald	R-R	6-2	200	12-31-82	0	3	4.46	19	0	0	4	34	38	18	17	5	13	19	.281	.240	.306	4.98	3.41
Bloom, Kyle	R-L	6-3	185	2-21-83	9	12	5.51	25	25	1	0	129	144	83	79	14	57	90	.282	.184	.307	6.28	3.98
Bresnehan, Patrick	R-R	6-1	195	4-23-85	4	3	4.18	34	0	0	6	60	54	37	28	3	32	63	.232	.183	.264	9.40	4.77
Cabrera, Henry	R-R	6-4	190	12-17-83	0	1	12.00	1	1	0	0	3	6	4	4	0	1	3	.429	.000	.462	9.00	3.00
Craig, Dustin	R-R	6-4	240	4-9-82	0	0	5.94	8	0	0	0	17	22	11	11	1	5	10	.319	.292	.333	5.40	2.70
Cuffman, Jacob	R-R	6-4	200	3-3-85	0	0	0.00	1	0	0	0	1	0	0	0	0	0	1	.000	.000	.000	9.00	0.00
Diaz, Jose	R-R	6-1	164	3-20-87	3	3	6.16	8	4	0	1	38	52	35	26	5	12	21	.329	.300	.347	4.97	2.84
Garavito, Jean	R-R	5-11	186	1-11-85	5	5	4.25	34	13	2	1	112	116	62	53	7	43	65	.265	.253	.274	5.21	3.45
Hamilton, Clayton	R-R	6-5	200	6-15-82	3	7	6.36	15	15	0	0	69	85	51	49	6	25	33	.305	.317	.295	4.28	3.25
Hankins, Derek	R-R	6-4	190	7-1-83	8	6	5.24	22	22	1	0	113	129	72	66	13	37	77	.289	.266	.304	6.11	2.94
Holliday, Brian	L-L	6-2	202	6-1-84	3	2	5.74	28	3	0	0	69	99	57	44	6	37	35	.337	.380	.321	4.57	4.83
Johnson, Blair	R-R	6-4	218	3-25-84	1	4	6.82	8	8	0	0	32	40	25	24	3	15	21	.331	.372	.308	5.97	4.26
Linares, Serguey	R-R	6-4	225	2-1-83	6	7	4.35	16	16	0	0	83	79	49	40	9	47	38	.255	.279	.243	4.14	5.12
Macia, Wanell	L-L	5-11	180	7-20-82	0	0	0.00	1	0	0	0	1	2	0	0	0	0	0	.400	.333	.500	0.00	0.00
Moeves, Derrik	R-R	6-3	190	8-5-83	0	1	9.31	7	0	0	1	10	12	10	10	0	8	6	.300	.231	.333	5.59	7.45
Molleken, Dustin	L-R	6-4	228	8-21-84	0	0	5.79	2	0	0	0	5	7	3	3	0	1	8	.350	.600	.267	15.43	1.93
Pearson, Kyle	R-R	6-1	200	10-8-84	0	3	3.89	19	0	0	2	39	48	21	17	2	16	26	.304	.353	.280	5.95	3.66
Redmond, Todd	R-R	6-3	185	5-17-85	7	12	4.54	25	25	0	0	143	151	82	72	13	32	95	.275	.322	.251	5.99	2.02
Rodriguez, Dionis	R-R	6-2	181	2-8-86	0	0	3.60	1	1	0	0	5	4	2	2	0	1	2	.235	.222	.250	1.80	3.60
Swanson, Matt	R-R	6-8	240	10-17-82	2	6	4.50	41	0	0	15	50	45	30	25	3	39	35	.254	.231	.268	6.30	7.02
Uviedo, Ronald	R-R	6-2	150	10-7-86	0	0	4.09	4	0	0	0	11	9	5	5	2	3	7	.225	.200	.250	5.73	2.45
Valdez, Luis	R-R	6-2	180	5-5-84	3	4	4.79	36	1	0	5	73	87	44	39	4	26	78	.291	.250	.312	9.57	3.19

FIELDING

Catcher	PCT	G	PO	A	E	DP	PB
E. Diaz	.972	6	32	3	1	0	3
R. Diaz	1.000	1	3	0	0	0	0
Falcon	.985	21	124	11	2	0	1
Lerud	.980	81	465	72	11	6	25
Nino	.975	27	138	18	4	3	5
Peterson	1.000	9	72	6	0	0	0

First Base	PCT	G	PO	A	E	DP	
Davenport	.981	32	282	21	6	26	
De Los Santos	1.000	3	31	1	0	4	
Delaney	.981	47	392	28	8	40	
Mansolino	.984	40	353	16	6	31	
Pearce	.994	18	157	7	1	8	

Second Base	PCT	G	PO	A	E	DP	
Alvarez	1.000	2	5	6	0	3	

	PCT	G	PO	A	E	DP	
De Los Santos	.969	23	45	81	4	18	
Ford	.989	90	187	253	5	52	
Mansolino	.973	9	12	24	1	4	
Picart	1.000	21	47	41	0	12	

Third Base	PCT	G	PO	A	E	DP	
Alvarez	1.000	1	1	3	0	0	
Johnson III	.949	116	75	224	16	21	
Mansolino	.945	21	11	41	3	2	
Picart	1.000	1	0	1	0	0	
Schwartzbauer	—	1	0	0	0	0	

Shortstop	PCT	G	PO	A	E	DP	
Blair	.875	2	2	5	1	0	
Gonzalez	.891	35	46	109	19	23	
Picart	.962	55	84	197	11	38	
Schwartzbauer	.957	47	76	144	10	21	

Outfield	PCT	G	PO	A	E	DP
Boone	1.000	40	73	2	0	1
Corley	.991	110	215	4	2	1
Davenport	.944	18	33	1	2	0
Delaney	.975	21	38	1	1	0
Macia	1.000	19	36	1	0	0
Mansolino	1.000	2	3	0	0	0
Pacheco	1.000	9	19	0	0	0
Picart	1.000	3	4	0	0	0
Powell	.984	124	287	14	5	2
Romak	.946	73	119	3	7	1
Rosero	1.000	5	11	2	0	0

HICKORY CRAWDADS

SOUTH ATLANTIC LEAGUE

LOW CLASS A

BATTING	B-T	HT	WT	DOB	AVG	vLH	vRH	G	AB	R	H	2B	3B	HR	RBI	BB	HBP	SH	SF	SO	SB	CS	SLG	OBP
Alvarez, Victor	B-R	5-11	185	6-17-83	.000	.000	.000	3	1	1	0	0	0	0	0	1	0	0	0	0	0	0	.000	.500
Ambrose, Michael	R-R	6-0	180	11-28-83	.244	.250	.241	61	209	29	51	6	1	2	22	11	8	4	4	38	10	0	.311	.302
Blair, Cameron	R-R	5-11	175	10-27-82	.228	.154	.255	39	145	25	33	5	0	1	17	13	3	1	0	21	4	0	.283	.304
Boone, James	B-R	6-2	175	3-16-83	.327	.385	.309	27	107	18	35	6	0	4	17	8	5	0	0	20	0	2	.495	.400
De Los Santos, Jose J.	R-R	5-11	160	8-10-84	.326	.342	.314	25	89	13	29	6	0	0	7	8	0	2	0	11	2	2	.393	.381
De Los Santos, Jose L.	R-R	5-11	160	2-17-85	.224	.132	.264	36	125	10	28	2	0	0	7	4	1	6	0	20	3	5	.240	.254
Gonzalez, Angel R.	B-R	5-11	165	12-28-85	.282	.315	.266	53	216	31	61	9	2	1	25	13	2	8	0	45	5	10	.356	.329
Keel, Jared	R-R	6-1	190	8-3-84	.261	.293	.247	98	326	63	85	23	1	17	56	56	13	1	4	79	5	2	.494	.386
Kingsbury, Bobby	L-L	6-1	184	8-30-80	.275	.293	.267	91	335	50	92	21	4	10	62	42	5	2	5	67	19	3	.451	.359
Laboy, Albert	R-R	6-0	175	12-1-86	.287	.254	.302	63	230	32	66	6	1	6	26	16	2	6	4	49	6	3	.400	.333
Macia, Wanell	L-L	5-11	180	7-20-82	.233	.306	.203	59	215	22	50	10	1	1	18	2	1	3	1	29	8	2	.302	.242
Negrych, Jim	L-R	5-10	180	3-2-85	.282	.221	.300	86	340	57	96	14	4	2	48	27	4	3	2	48	4	1	.365	.340
Pacheco, Jonel	R-R	5-9	170	10-3-82	.315	.277	.330	119	463	97	146	25	5	27	99	41	4	0	6	71	18	7	.566	.372
Poni, Francis	R-R	6-0	223	8-1-83	.276	.200	.357	36	116	17	32	10	0	4	23	7	5	1	1	29	0	0	.466	.341
Prasch, Edward	L-R	6-0	180	1-25-86	.236	.143	.265	105	348	59	82	20	4	8	51	36	12	5	1	122	6	1	.385	.327
Presley, Alexander	L-L	5-9	180	7-25-85	.293	.297	.292	121	495	79	145	22	8	11	63	45	0	7	6	108	18	10	.436	.348
Romak, Jamie	R-R	6-2	220	9-30-85	.275	.143	.333	20	69	16	19	4	0	5	15	9	5	0	1	24	0	2	.551	.393
Sakamoto, Kent	R-R	6-0	215	11-3-83	.280	.344	.255	125	457	72	128	26	5	14	66	31	8	2	4	88	5	0	.451	.334
Sanchez, Danilo	R-R	5-11	230	10-25-80	.348	.375	.333	23	69	14	24	5	0	3	18	16	2	0	3	8	0	0	.551	.467
Walk, John	R-R	6-2	220	9-12-82	.000	.000	.000	2	5	0	0	0	0	0	1	1	0	0	0	2	0	0	.000	.286
Watts, Kristopher	L-R	6-1	200	7-15-84	.261	.226	.268	90	307	40	80	25	2	8	41	27	4	3	2	54	0	1	.433	.326

PITCHING	B-T	HT	WT	DOB	W	L	ERA	G	GS	CG	SV	IP	H	R	ER	HR	BB	SO	AVG	vLH	vRH	K/9	BB/9
Alvarez, Basilio	R-R	6-3	160	1-2-84	1	3	8.50	18	1	0	0	36	48	37	34	8	12	31	.324	.353	.309	7.75	3.00
Astacio, Olivo	R-R	6-5	190	7-28-84	1	1	3.54	30	0	0	11	48	39	22	19	0	28	71	.217	.188	.233	13.22	5.21
Benoit, Charles	L-L	6-2	215	9-24-84	9	3	2.71	50	0	0	4	80	73	28	24	4	29	83	.242	.280	.229	9.38	3.28
Cabrera, Henry	R-R	6-4	190	12-17-83	5	6	5.06	22	12	1	1	78	86	49	44	14	27	76	.277	.303	.261	8.73	3.10
Castorri, Christian	R-R	6-3	215	12-17-83	5	2	1.93	21	0	0	8	33	37	10	7	2	12	28	.287	.302	.279	7.71	3.31
Clapp, Bradley	R-R	6-3	215	5-19-86	6	10	6.41	24	20	0	0	105	131	84	75	14	39	67	.303	.352	.273	5.72	3.33
Craig, Dustin	R-R	6-4	240	4-9-82	3	3	3.07	11	8	0	0	44	46	20	15	3	19	34	.277	.210	.317	6.95	3.89
Crotta, Michael	R-R	6-6	210	9-24-84	10	5	4.39	26	25	1	0	137	169	82	67	10	28	74	.302	.347	.273	4.85	1.83
Cuffman, Jacob	R-R	6-4	200	3-3-85	0	0	24.55	9	0	0	0	7	13	21	20	2	14	7	.371	.294	.444	8.59	17.18
De Los Santos, Jose J.	R-R	5-11	160	8-10-84	0	1	54.00	1	0	0	0	1	4	6	6	1	6	1	.667	.667	.667	9.00	27.00
Delossantos, Rafael	R-R	6-3	160	12-10-86	2	2	3.46	7	4	0	0	26	18	10	10	0	22	25	.207	.235	.189	8.65	7.62
Diaz, Jose	R-R	6-1	164	3-20-87	0	0	3.00	1	1	0	0	6	4	2	2	0	0	6	.174	.333	.071	9.00	0.00
Felix, Michael	L-L	5-11	190	8-13-85	0	2	8.83	25	3	0	0	36	44	52	35	3	46	37	.289	.240	.299	9.34	11.61
Garcia, Felipe	R-R	5-11	165	9-20-82	1	1	5.14	15	0	0	2	21	17	12	12	5	11	16	.218	.265	.182	6.86	4.71
Hughes, Jared	R-R	6-7	220	7-4-85	8	9	4.64	27	27	0	0	145	162	94	75	11	54	109	.281	.295	.272	6.75	3.34
Krebs, Eric	R-R	6-3	185	5-16-85	2	2	4.82	15	5	0	1	37	34	22	20	1	22	48	.239	.231	.244	11.57	5.30
Linares, Serguey	R-R	6-4	225	2-1-83	1	1	1.61	4	4	0	0	22	14	7	4	0	9	10	.189	.087	.235	4.03	3.63
Lorenzo, Matt	L-R	6-3	205	6-21-82	1	0	6.10	14	0	0	0	31	30	22	21	4	11	26	.252	.184	.284	7.55	3.19
Macfarland, Stephen	R-R	6-2	185	11-17-85	3	2	4.80	39	1	0	0	66	58	37	35	5	48	69	.236	.240	.233	9.46	6.58
Martinez, Yoffri	R-R	6-3	170	12-3-85	0	1	18.36	5	1	0	0	8	14	17	17	2	15	4	.378	.300	.407	4.32	16.20
McSwain, Matt	R-R	6-2	185	8-15-85	3	1	5.59	15	9	0	0	58	64	37	36	8	25	50	.283	.289	.280	7.76	3.88
Moeves, Derrik	R-R	6-3	190	8-5-83	2	2	5.31	26	0	0	1	41	40	26	24	6	32	44	.245	.283	.223	9.74	7.08
Molleken, Dustin	L-R	6-4	228	8-21-84	3	1	4.50	13	0	0	0	26	32	15	13	3	8	31	.311	.294	.319	10.73	2.77
Pearson, Kyle	R-R	6-1	200	10-8-84	1	3	3.43	23	0	0	5	39	37	21	15	5	5	32	.242	.250	.238	7.32	1.14
Rodriguez, Dionis	R-R	6-2	181	2-8-86	0	2	10.80	5	4	0	0	15	24	19	18	3	13	4	.381	.308	.432	2.40	7.80
Sues, Jeffrey	R-R	6-4	228	6-8-83	5	8	7.18	8	8	0	0	31	37	26	25	9	19	26	.294	.302	.288	7.47	5.46
Uviedo, Ronald	R-R	6-2	150	10-7-86	0	0	9.00	3	0	0	0	3	3	3	3	1	2	7	.250	.143	.400	21.00	6.00
Watson, Anthony	L-L	6-4	210	5-30-85	1	1	3.86	3	3	0	0	14	14	6	6	2	1	18	.264	.444	.227	11.57	0.64

FIELDING

Catcher	PCT	G	PO	A	E	DP	PB
Poni	.976	33	229	18	6	1	9
Sanchez	.995	22	166	17	1	0	3
Walk	.938	2	13	2	1	0	0
Watts	.984	85	620	70	11	8	18

First Base	PCT	G	PO	A	E	DP
Keel	.984	22	173	9	3	12
Sakamoto	.992	122	1047	56	9	93

Second Base	PCT	G	PO	A	E	DP
Ambrose	.989	18	25	61	1	15
Blair	.993	27	65	76	1	18
J.J. De Los Santos	.983	14	24	33	1	10

	PCT	G	PO	A	E	DP
Negrych	.973	82	132	231	10	44

Third Base	PCT	G	PO	A	E	DP
Ambrose	1.000	3	1	5	0	0
J.J. De Los Santos	.933	3	2	12	1	1
Keel	.849	30	23	67	16	5
Prasch	.954	104	53	218	13	22

Shortstop	PCT	G	PO	A	E	DP
Alvarez	1.000	1	0	1	0	0
Ambrose	.942	33	38	93	8	10
Blair	.923	11	23	25	4	10
J.J. De Los Santos	.966	8	12	16	1	2
J.L. De Los Santos	.953	36	44	98	7	18

	PCT	G	PO	A	E	DP
Gonzalez	.903	53	77	165	26	34

Outfield	PCT	G	PO	A	E	DP
Ambrose	1.000	10	16	2	0	0
Boone	.979	23	44	2	1	0
Keel	.973	24	35	1	1	0
Kingsbury	.800	5	4	0	1	0
Laboy	.981	63	97	9	2	2
Macia	.980	55	93	5	2	1
Pacheco	.995	108	215	6	1	2
Presley	.974	116	220	2	6	0
Romak	1.000	18	39	1	0	0

STATE COLLEGE SPIKES   SHORT-SEASON

NEW YORK-PENN LEAGUE

BATTING	B-T	HT	WT	DOB	AVG	vLH	vRH	G	AB	R	H	2B	3B	HR	RBI	BB	HBP	SH	SF	SO	SB	CS	SLG	OBP
Ambrose, Michael	R-R	6-0	180	11-28-83	.286	.250	.298	22	77	14	22	6	2	1	8	5	6	1	1	17	2	1	.455	.371
Barksdale, James	L-L	5-10	175	5-7-85	.324	.182	.349	29	74	12	24	1	2	0	7	3	0	1	1	21	11	3	.392	.346
Byler, Justin	R-R	6-1	190	8-12-85	.312	.271	.331	69	263	41	82	18	2	8	43	17	6	0	4	68	1	0	.487	.362
Cavagnaro, Matt	B-R	5-11	185	8-11-85	.262	.267	.259	68	275	36	72	19	0	4	31	15	1	2	0	46	1	4	.375	.302
Clarkson, Matthew	L-R	6-3	200	2-24-84	.167	.250	.143	5	18	0	3	1	0	0	0	2	0	0	0	8	0	0	.222	.250
Davis, Marcus	R-R	6-3	200	11-11-84	.232	.315	.188	48	155	27	36	8	3	8	20	18	3	0	1	46	15	5	.477	.322
Diaz, Ricky	R-R	6-0	194	12-3-84	.222	.333	.167	6	9	0	2	1	0	0	3	0	0	0	1	2	0	0	.333	.200
Durham, Miles	R-R	6-4	205	3-21-83	.255	.279	.238	41	141	13	36	11	1	1	13	12	0	0	2	38	1	0	.369	.310
Fitzpatrick, John	R-R	6-3	225	7-26-84	.293	.381	.200	13	41	4	12	6	0	0	2	4	1	0	0	11	0	0	.439	.370
Friday, Brian	R-R	5-11	180	12-16-85	.295	.333	.275	40	156	31	46	10	1	2	13	10	9	1	0	33	6	4	.410	.371
Huber, Erik	R-R	6-6	230	3-6-85	.227	.250	.214	45	150	15	34	11	1	0	11	14	4	0	1	29	1	0	.313	.308
Igsema, Victor	R-R	6-2	172	11-16-85	.167	.250	.125	7	24	2	4	0	1	1	4	1	0	0	0	10	1	0	.375	.200
McClune, Austin	R-R	6-2	175	11-15-87	.260	.339	.224	59	196	20	51	3	3	0	19	5	1	7	1	32	15	3	.306	.281
Pena, Ronald	R-R	5-9	191	2-28-87	.000	.000	.000	1	2	0	0	0	0	0	0	0	0	0	0	2	0	0	.000	.000
Perez, Smelin	B-R	5-10	150	8-26-85	.252	.194	.281	57	206	22	52	12	4	1	20	9	1	4	0	32	11	7	.364	.287
Rios, Daniel	L-L	6-1	200	7-10-85	.208	.000	.241	33	96	6	20	3	0	2	6	7	1	0	1	27	1	1	.302	.267
Simon, Keanon	L-L	5-10	170	12-6-84	.335	.294	.344	54	185	28	62	14	1	1	27	17	3	2	1	28	9	3	.438	.398
Spain, Robert	L-R	6-4	205	5-7-85	.271	.158	.302	51	177	16	48	10	0	1	17	12	2	1	1	30	0	3	.345	.323
Stillwagon, Nicholas	R-R	6-0	190	11-21-82	.257	.344	.219	36	105	19	27	5	0	3	12	14	1	0	0	25	0	1	.390	.350
Walker, Andrew	R-R	6-0	210	1-22-86	.317	.357	.303	46	161	17	51	12	1	2	24	18	2	0	3	36	1	1	.441	.390

PITCHING	B-T	HT	WT	DOB	W	L	ERA	G	GS	CG	SV	IP	H	R	ER	HR	BB	SO	AVG	vLH	vRH	K/9	BB/9
Alvarez, Basilio	R-R	6-3	160	1-2-84	0	0	9.00	1	1	0	0	2	4	2	2	0	1	2	.400	.333	.429	9.00	4.50
Amato, Gary	R-R	6-1	200	2-5-86	0	0	2.70	3	0	0	0	7	2	2	2	1	2	7	.091	.091	.091	9.45	2.70
Bishop, Harrison	R-R	6-3	210	8-17-84	1	0	3.03	19	0	0	0	30	24	13	10	1	13	33	.224	.250	.211	10.01	3.94
Boleska, Thomas	R-R	6-0	190	7-30-86	0	0	1.35	4	0	0	1	7	8	2	1	0	3	9	.286	.308	.267	12.15	4.05
Cameron, Taylor	B-R	6-2	200	7-24-85	2	2	1.80	19	0	0	1	30	25	7	6	0	22	18	.236	.216	.246	5.40	6.60
Castorri, Christian	R-R	6-3	215	12-17-83	0	0	1.59	3	0	0	0	6	5	1	1	0	2	6	.238	.143	.286	9.53	3.18
Charry, Jorge	R-R	6-1	185	12-10-86	0	3	6.94	20	0	0	0	23	27	20	18	4	12	22	.281	.289	.276	8.49	4.63
Cuffman, Jacob	R-R	6-4	200	3-3-85	1	1	6.52	5	2	0	0	10	12	7	7	0	5	9	.293	.467	.192	8.38	4.66
Duke, Zach	L-L	6-2	220	4-19-83	1	0	1.59	1	1	0	0	6	3	1	1	0	2	3	.150	.000	.150	4.76	3.18
Felix, Michael	L-L	5-11	190	8-13-85	2	1	5.26	19	0	0	0	26	25	16	15	0	23	31	.263	.233	.277	10.87	8.06
Forrer, Daniel	R-L	6-3	195	11-1-83	0	0	27.00	3	0	0	0	3	6	8	8	0	6	1	.500	.250	.625	3.38	20.25
Foust, Matthew	R-R	6-2	225	10-8-84	3	6	4.47	14	13	0	0	50	45	38	25	0	34	42	.234	.274	.210	7.51	6.08
Martinez, Yoffri	R-R	6-3	170	12-3-85	0	1	5.95	15	2	0	0	20	23	14	13	2	15	19	.284	.286	.283	8.69	6.86
McPherson, Kyle	B-R	6-3	205	11-11-87	0	1	6.28	3	3	0	0	14	20	13	10	1	3	6	.323	.238	.366	3.77	1.88
Molleken, Dustin	L-R	6-4	228	8-21-84	1	0	1.08	4	0	0	0	8	6	2	1	1	1	5	.194	.500	.148	5.40	1.08
Moskos, Daniel	R-L	6-1	210	4-28-86	0	0	4.26	11	0	0	1	13	19	8	6	1	6	13	.328	.353	.317	9.24	4.26
Nunez, Eddy	L-L	6-1	149	10-2-84	0	0	3.60	2	0	0	0	5	7	3	2	0	3	4	.333	.333	.333	7.20	5.40
Robles, Moises	R-R	6-2	170	4-17-84	4	9	4.59	13	13	0	0	65	74	34	33	2	9	34	.287	.312	.273	4.73	1.25
Rodriguez, Dionis	R-R	6-2	181	2-8-86	3	1	3.73	12	6	0	1	41	45	18	17	7	16	25	.276	.245	.291	5.49	3.51
Simon, Adam	R-R	5-10	170	1-26-84	1	2	1.86	24	0	0	7	29	21	7	6	2	11	45	.200	.200	.200	13.97	3.41
Suero, Nicolas	R-R	6-2	160	12-10-84	3	5	3.86	15	13	1	0	82	102	44	35	2	3	47	.299	.272	.315	5.18	0.33
Tracy, Brian	R-R	6-4	220	12-22-83	3	2	4.37	14	0	0	0	28	26	13	11	4	14	14	.289	.333	.267	5.56	5.56
Uviedo, Ronald	R-R	6-2	150	10-7-86	2	0	3.92	21	0	0	12	21	16	9	9	4	3	26	.216	.261	.196	11.32	1.31
Watson, Anthony	L-L	6-4	210	5-30-85	6	1	2.52	10	10	0	0	54	47	17	15	4	7	40	.230	.245	.226	6.71	1.17
Welker, Duke	L-R	6-7	220	2-10-86	2	2	2.35	7	7	0	0	31	29	9	8	2	10	27	.259	.230	.294	7.92	2.93
Williams, Brandon	R-R	6-6	230	9-6-84	1	2	2.53	13	4	0	0	43	50	19	12	0	12	25	.298	.293	.300	5.27	2.53

FIELDING

Catcher	PCT	G	PO	A	E	DP	PB
Clarkson	1.000	5	27	6	0	0	1
Diaz	1.000	3	13	0	0	0	3
Pena	1.000	1	4	0	0	0	0
Stillwagon	.965	36	231	20	9	2	6
Walker	.988	39	230	26	3	2	3

First Base	PCT	G	PO	A	E	DP
Byler	.987	58	514	21	7	56
Fitzpatrick	1.000	5	35	2	0	2
Huber	—	1	0	0	0	0

	PCT	G	PO	A	E	DP
Rios	1.000	18	137	2	0	9

Second Base	PCT	G	PO	A	E	DP
Ambrose	1.000	1	2	0	0	0
Cavagnaro	.970	67	123	200	10	49
Perez	.892	7	16	17	4	5

Third Base	PCT	G	PO	A	E	DP
Perez	.898	35	20	77	11	7
Spain	.863	44	36	71	17	6

Shortstop	PCT	G	PO	A	E	DP
Ambrose	.956	21	23	63	4	14

	PCT	G	PO	A	E	DP
Friday	.958	39	53	129	8	24
Perez	.957	16	37	53	4	13

Outfield	PCT	G	PO	A	E	DP
Barksdale	.963	25	26	0	1	0
Davis	.970	45	61	3	2	3
Durham	1.000	28	66	0	0	0
Huber	1.000	25	35	1	0	0
Igsema	1.000	4	8	0	0	0
McClune	.985	59	124	8	2	0
Simon	.979	52	90	2	2	1

GULF COAST LEAGUE

BATTING	B-T	HT	WT	DOB	AVG	vLH	vRH	G	AB	R	H	2B	3B	HR	RBI	BB	HBP	SH	SF	SO	SB	CS	SLG	OBP
Acevedo, Andury	R-R	6-4	200	8-23-90	.444	.000	.571	8	18	2	8	2	1	0	1	0	1	0	0	5	0	0	.667	.474
Alvarez, Victor	B-R	5-11	185	6-17-83	.212	.233	.203	36	99	18	21	2	0	0	7	26	0	3	1	19	3	0	.232	.373
Bautista, Jose	R-R	6-0	195	10-19-80	.375	—	.375	2	8	1	3	2	0	0	1	0	0	0	0	1	0	0	.625	.375
Biela, Andrew	R-R	5-11	195	12-26-88	.302	.297	.304	34	106	18	32	6	3	0	17	13	6	1	0	24	2	3	.415	.408
Blair, Cameron	R-R	5-11	175	10-27-82	.500	.500	—	1	2	1	1	0	0	0	0	0	0	0	0	1	0	0	.500	.500
Bomback, Daniel	B-R	5-11	185	9-5-84	.255	.244	.261	43	137	20	35	10	1	1	19	19	4	1	1	13	0	4	.365	.360
Buttler, Vic	L-L	6-0	175	8-12-80	.273	.333	.263	6	22	6	6	1	1	0	1	3	0	0	0	1	1	0	.409	.360
Canal, Yonelvy	R-R	6-2	175	12-9-84	.267	.321	.241	28	86	12	23	6	1	5	22	7	0	0	1	32	4	3	.535	.319
Duffy, Chris	L-L	5-9	180	4-20-80	.308	.333	.300	4	13	1	4	1	0	0	1	1	1	0	0	0	0	0	.385	.400
Fields, Caleb	R-R	6-3	185	7-15-85	.270	.240	.283	43	163	30	44	8	3	2	18	17	0	2	1	25	6	5	.393	.337
Fitzpatrick, John	R-R	6-3	225	7-26-84	.236	.306	.209	42	127	30	30	6	1	9	31	29	4	0	5	21	1	1	.512	.382
Garcia, Juan	R-R	5-11	185	9-6-88	.109	.000	.146	22	64	6	7	0	0	0	4	6	0	2	1	20	2	1	.109	.183
Guzman, Javier	B-R	6-0	170	5-4-82	.095	.083	.111	6	21	2	2	1	0	0	1	0	0	0	1	3	0	0	.143	.091
Hagan, Thomas	L-R	6-2	195	9-22-83	.344	.289	.369	37	122	22	42	7	2	2	24	16	6	1	1	22	1	3	.484	.441
Latimore, Quincy	R-R	5-10	175	2-3-89	.257	.315	.231	45	171	29	44	9	2	3	17	16	9	0	0	25	13	4	.386	.352
Mayer, Michael	L-L	6-3	200	5-1-84	.212	.000	.304	15	33	4	7	0	0	0	5	5	0	0	0	11	1	0	.212	.316
Morgan, Nyjer	L-L	6-0	170	7-2-80	.308	.667	.200	4	13	3	4	0	0	0	1	2	1	0	0	3	0	0	.538	.438
Munoz, Joe	R-R	6-1	155	12-26-85	.202	.103	.238	34	109	15	22	8	1	1	11	9	4	1	2	18	2	1	.321	.282
Peley, Josue	R-R	6-0	177	12-24-87	.252	.316	.221	31	115	14	29	4	2	1	16	5	2	0	2	16	3	0	.348	.290
Pena, Ronald	R-R	5-9	191	2-28-87	.308	.429	.263	17	52	8	16	5	1	1	11	5	2	0	0	12	0	1	.500	.390
Rice, Chad	R-R	5-11	180	1-17-85	.159	.258	.122	41	113	22	18	2	0	0	11	20	11	1	0	21	3	1	.177	.340
Rosero, Ciro	R-R	6-1	160	7-25-86	.292	.357	.271	35	113	17	33	4	0	4	14	11	4	1	0	19	10	4	.434	.375
Silva, Carlos	R-R	6-2	165	5-31-87	.284	.250	.302	19	67	6	19	3	0	1	9	1	2	0	0	14	1	0	.373	.314
Vargas, Alex	L-L	6-2	202	6-5-86	.300	.400	.277	25	80	12	24	6	2	2	19	5	0	1	0	13	2	1	.500	.341

PITCHING	B-T	HT	WT	DOB	W	L	ERA	G	GS	CG	SV	IP	H	R	ER	HR	BB	SO	AVG	vLH	vRH	K/9	BB/9
Amaro, Carlos	R-R	6-0	170	11-6-84	2	1	3.97	12	3	0	1	48	39	24	21	4	12	36	.220	.207	.233	6.80	2.27
Amato, Gary	R-R	6-1	200	2-5-86	0	2	3.52	13	0	0	0	23	19	10	9	2	7	22	.221	.184	.250	8.61	2.74
Bankston, Maurice	R-R	6-4	205	6-17-87	0	2	3.38	2	0	0	0	3	3	3	1	0	0	3	.250	.200	.286	10.12	0.00
Boleska, Thomas	R-R	6-0	190	7-30-86	0	0	0.00	2	0	0	1	2	2	0	0	0	0	3	.250	.500	.167	13.50	0.00
Copley, Devin	R-R	6-3	220	10-28-86	0	1	4.50	2	0	0	0	4	5	3	2	0	1	4	.333	.167	.444	9.00	2.25
Cordero, Edward	R-R	5-10	162	3-28-85	1	0	6.32	15	0	0	0	16	17	11	11	2	4	11	.274	.200	.324	6.32	2.30
Delossantos, Rafael	R-R	6-3	160	12-10-86	1	5	4.29	8	8	0	0	36	44	27	17	0	4	38	.286	.297	.275	9.59	1.01
Diaz, Jose	R-R	6-1	164	3-20-87	1	0	1.13	3	3	0	0	16	13	2	2	0	7	6	.232	.231	.233	3.38	3.94
Duke, Zach	L-L	6-2	220	4-19-83	0	0	1.35	2	2	0	0	7	5	1	1	0	2	3	.217	.111	.286	4.05	2.70
Forrer, Daniel	R-L	6-3	195	11-1-83	0	0	4.15	3	0	0	0	4	1	2	2	0	2	3	.077	.000	.083	6.23	4.15
Garcia, Felipe	R-R	5-11	165	9-20-82	0	0	4.50	3	0	0	1	4	5	2	2	0	1	6	.294	.143	.400	13.50	2.25
Giblin, Sean	R-R	6-3	215	6-17-89	0	1	9.72	6	6	0	0	17	31	21	18	2	1	9	.383	.452	.340	4.86	0.54
Gryboski, Kevin	R-R	6-5	230	11-15-73	1	0	0.00	3	0	0	0	5	3	2	0	0	1	7	.143	.143	.143	11.81	1.69
Holden, Brandon	R-R	6-4	185	1-1-88	1	0	3.57	12	0	0	0	23	19	13	9	1	20	15	.244	.243	.244	5.96	7.94
Kelly, William	R-R	6-2	170	10-30-87	1	0	6.19	5	4	0	0	16	20	13	11	2	4	11	.317	.308	.324	6.19	2.25
Krebs, Eric	R-R	6-3	185	5-16-85	2	0	2.08	5	0	0	0	9	9	2	2	1	6	7	.265	.333	.211	7.27	6.23
Marte, Enmanuel	L-L	6-2	165	8-15-85	1	1	4.50	9	0	0	0	16	18	18	8	1	10	9	.277	.353	.250	5.06	5.62
McCullen, Matthew	R-R	6-1	205	1-22-83	1	2	3.65	10	0	0	0	25	22	12	10	1	3	16	.247	.189	.288	5.84	1.09
McPherson, Kyle	B-R	6-3	205	11-11-87	4	2	2.61	12	10	0	0	52	47	22	15	3	10	35	.246	.273	.223	6.10	1.74
McSwain, Matt	R-R	6-2	185	8-15-85	1	0	4.50	2	0	0	0	6	7	3	3	0	1	7	.280	.250	.308	10.50	1.50
Moskos, Daniel	R-L	6-1	210	4-28-86	0	0	0.00	2	0	0	0	3	4	0	0	0	0	3	.333	.000	.400	9.00	0.00
Nunez, Eddy	L-L	6-1	149	10-2-84	4	3	3.22	12	7	0	0	50	55	30	18	3	23	42	.278	.305	.266	7.51	4.11
Ortiz, Francisco	R-R	6-3	213	3-17-87	0	3	8.84	7	5	0	0	18	24	24	18	2	17	11	.300	.333	.283	5.40	8.35
Owens, Rudy	L-L	6-3	215	12-18-87	1	4	5.32	6	4	0	0	22	20	13	13	1	8	17	.238	.292	.217	6.95	3.27
Paniagua, Jose	R-R	6-2	190	8-20-73	0	0	0.00	2	0	0	0	4	5	3	0	0	6	7	.263	.429	.167	12.46	0.00
Paulino, Ricardo	R-R	6-1	182	8-8-86	3	1	4.28	10	2	0	2	27	26	13	13	1	8	21	.255	.340	.163	6.91	2.63
Torres, Salomon	R-R	5-11	210	3-11-72	0	0	0.00	2	2	0	0	3	2	0	0	0	4	4	.222	.000	.333	12.00	0.00
Vasquez, Malvin	R-R	6-3	165	5-10-86	1	1	6.85	13	0	0	0	22	26	18	17	1	8	21	.289	.205	.353	8.46	3.22

FIELDING

Catcher	PCT	G	PO	A	E	DP	PB
Garcia	.963	21	113	16	5	0	8
Peley	.970	26	168	25	6	3	9
Pena	.972	16	91	12	3	1	3

First Base	PCT	G	PO	A	E	DP
Fitzpatrick	.992	27	226	20	2	22
Hagan	.974	12	105	8	3	11
Mayer	1.000	1	14	1	0	1
Vargas	.985	21	182	12	3	22

Second Base	PCT	G	PO	A	E	DP
Acevedo	—	1	0	1	0	0
Alvarez	1.000	1	3	1	0	0
Blair	.000	1	0	0	1	0
Bomback	.947	10	8	28	2	5

	PCT	G	PO	A	E	DP
Fields	.964	42	84	103	7	21
Guzman	1.000	1	2	4	0	2
Rice	1.000	6	11	14	0	7

Third Base	PCT	G	PO	A	E	DP
Acevedo	.800	6	4	8	3	0
Alvarez	.909	10	7	23	3	3
Bautista	.833	2	1	4	1	1
Bomback	.918	29	14	53	6	6
Hagan	—	1	0	0	0	0
Silva	.766	19	10	26	11	2

Shortstop	PCT	G	PO	A	E	DP
Alvarez	.934	26	33	81	8	18
Guzman	.900	4	2	7	1	2
Rice	.957	35	43	133	8	21

Outfield	PCT	G	PO	A	E	DP
Biela	.955	30	39	3	2	0
Buttler	1.000	4	4	0	0	0
Canal	1.000	28	43	1	0	0
Duffy	1.000	1	3	0	0	0
Fitzpatrick	1.000	1	1	0	0	0
Hagan	1.000	14	19	0	0	0
Latimore	.986	36	64	4	1	1
Mayer	.857	12	6	0	1	0
Morgan	1.000	4	8	0	0	0
Munoz	.982	33	56	0	1	0
Rice	—	1	0	0	0	0
Rosero	1.000	29	44	1	0	0

DOMINICAN SUMMER LEAGUE

BATTING	B-T	HT	WT	DOB	AVG	vLH	vRH	G	AB	R	H	2B	3B	HR	RBI	BB	HBP	SH	SF	SO	SB	CS	SLG	OBP
Avila, Eric	R-R	6-1	168	6-9-90	.238	.400	.216	17	42	7	10	0	0	1	4	3	1	0	0	6	1	1	.310	.304
Belen, Ricardo	R-R	6-2	208	4-22-89	.571	1.000	.500	6	7	1	4	1	0	0	0	1	0	0	0	3	0	0	.714	.625
Cespedes, Starlin	B-R	6-1	164	2-15-88	.216	.300	.195	63	194	29	42	5	1	4	26	19	5	7	3	58	12	6	.314	.299
Chavez, Pedro	B-R	6-0	155	5-1-88	.258	.186	.277	57	209	26	54	12	1	7	37	15	4	1	2	42	8	4	.426	.317
De La Cruz, Melvin	R-R	5-11	179	3-5-90	.263	.294	.259	51	133	26	35	2	0	1	13	26	2	8	0	43	20	6	.301	.391
Encarnacion, Jairo	R-R	5-11	179	12-25-85	.311	.341	.304	65	212	36	66	7	2	4	29	30	11	2	3	27	4	2	.420	.418
Estanislao, Victor	R-R	5-11	170	3-6-87	.336	.524	.295	38	116	12	39	7	0	4	28	7	5	4	0	29	2	1	.500	.398
Feliz, Aneudy	R-R	6-1	190	7-20-87	.077	.000	.083	9	13	1	1	1	0	0	1	0	0	0	0	4	0	0	.154	.143
Fortuna, Maxel	R-R	6-2	185	8-3-88	.213	.156	.228	53	155	23	33	5	1	1	12	15	3	4	0	31	7	4	.277	.295
Frias, Francisco	R-R	6-0	170	5-30-87	.218	.250	.210	53	124	35	27	3	0	2	14	31	4	4	3	32	18	2	.290	.383
Garcia, Edward	B-R	6-1	152	8-21-87	.304	.149	.340	66	250	47	76	13	3	5	36	18	7	3	1	55	19	10	.440	.366
Guzman, Dagoberto	R-R	6-0	160	5-15-88	.224	.250	.212	20	49	5	11	0	1	1	8	3	1	1	1	14	0	2	.327	.278
Juan, Daniel	R-R	6-0	160	9-8-87	.250	.200	.269	18	36	10	9	2	1	0	5	8	1	1	0	14	3	1	.361	.400
Marte, Starling	R-R	6-1	168	10-9-88	.220	.286	.202	45	132	27	29	4	1	1	11	10	7	6	1	29	16	2	.288	.307
Morales, Jesus	R-R	5-11	163	3-2-87	.000	.000	.000	1	3	1	0	0	0	0	0	0	0	0	0	0	0	0	.000	.000
Moreta, Jose	L-L	6-3	181	10-6-88	.278	.500	.265	15	36	5	10	3	0	2	5	2	0	0	0	15	0	0	.528	.316
Pena, Silvio	R-R	6-0	175	8-9-87	.267	.200	.285	62	217	38	58	5	1	1	20	18	13	5	2	35	39	15	.313	.356
Rodriguez, Chris	R-R	5-11	183	1-22-90	.333	.000	.400	12	12	2	4	1	0	0	3	3	0	0	0	2	0	0	.417	.467
Rodriguez, Gerlis	B-R	6-1	175	5-29-88	.257	.269	.255	53	167	22	43	7	0	5	26	14	2	2	3	31	5	3	.389	.317
Rojas, Ariel	R-R	6-2	169	4-6-88	.179	.267	.146	23	56	7	10	4	0	1	7	4	2	0	0	16	0	0	.304	.258
Vasquez, Andy	R-R	6-1	168	10-8-87	.211	.200	.213	34	57	9	12	2	0	1	7	12	2	0	2	17	4	3	.298	.356

PITCHING	B-T	HT	WT	DOB	W	L	ERA	G	GS	CG	SV	IP	H	R	ER	HR	BB	SO	AVG	vLH	vRH	K/9	BB/9
Acosta, Richard	R-R	6-1	157	2-5-84	9	1	1.23	13	13	4	0	95	67	20	13	3	7	97	.194	.229	.185	9.19	0.66
Asencio, Ronney	R-R	6-0	216	5-20-88	0	1	6.23	9	0	0	1	9	7	6	1	2	8	8.31	12.46
Baez, Manuel	R-R	6-0	209	5-20-88	3	1	1.80	8	0	0	1	20	12	5	4	1	7	21	.164	.154	.167	9.45	3.15
Cedano, Rikelvin	R-R	5-10	150	10-22-89	6	2	3.51	17	2	0	4	51	47	24	20	2	15	60	.241	.250	.239	10.52	2.63
Devora, Meoli	R-R	6-2	157	11-27-87	3	0	2.25	13	13	0	0	52	35	17	13	3	29	63	.193	.250	.181	10.90	5.02
Figuereo, Freddy	R-R	6-1	155	10-11-87	3	3	3.07	12	12	0	0	67	69	27	23	4	11	34	.258	.238	.265	4.54	1.47
Garcia, Wilbin	R-R	6-4	175	3-15-89	0	1	6.14	11	0	0	2	22	20	19	15	1	18	15	.230	.182	.237	6.14	7.36
Guzman, Oliberto	R-R	5-10	167	8-5-90	6	0	2.87	14	2	0	0	38	37	20	12	0	10	23	.253	.231	.258	5.50	2.39
Juan, Papiro	R-R	5-10	175	5-13-88	0	0	6.08	9	0	0	0	13	11	16	9	0	15	15	.216	.200	.220	10.12	10.12
Navarro, Eliecer	L-L	5-9	177	10-26-87	8	2	2.83	14	13	0	1	70	64	24	22	3	17	85	.242	.333	.234	10.93	2.19
Rojas, Juan	R-R	5-11	148	2-11-83	6	2	1.81	18	1	0	6	50	37	12	10	2	10	57	.200	.282	.178	10.33	1.81
Sanchez, Daniel	R-R	5-11	165	4-27-86	3	1	1.53	16	0	0	7	29	23	7	5	0	12	15	.215	.333	.186	4.60	3.68
Septimo, Sandobal	R-R	6-0	165	11-24-89	0	1	6.75	4	0	0	0	7	11	9	5	0	2	5	.367	.500	.333	6.75	2.70
Vargas, Plasido	R-R	6-4	184	10-5-88	0	0	0.00	1	0	0	0	1	3	6	0	1	2	2	.429	.000	.500	18.00	18.00
Vasquez, Samuel	R-R	6-4	175	3-10-88	5	2	2.26	16	13	1	0	76	64	31	19	5	22	81	.222	.167	.237	9.63	2.62

FIELDING

Catcher	PCT	G	PO	A	E	DP	PB
Belen	1.000	3	11	0	0	0	0
Chavez	1.000	1	1	1	0	0	0
Encarnacion	.995	65	506	50	3	1	11
Feliz	1.000	8	34	3	0	0	0
C. Rodriguez	.966	12	26	2	1	0	2

First Base	PCT	G	PO	A	E	DP
Cespedes	1.000	1	1	0	0	0
Frias	.980	33	220	20	5	16
Morales	.875	7	0	1	1	0
Moreta	1.000	4	14	0	0	1
G. Rodriguez	.984	41	348	15	6	20
A. Vasquez	1.000	3	9	0	0	1
S. Vasquez	.889	1	8	0	1	0

Second Base	PCT	G	PO	A	E	DP
Avila	.853	11	17	12	5	1

Cespedes	.941	4	6	10	1	3
Chavez	.953	44	79	103	9	14
Frias	.981	12	28	23	1	5
Guzman	.971	11	9	24	1	3

Third Base	PCT	G	PO	A	E	DP
Avila	1.000	1	0	2	0	0
Cespedes	.876	57	31	103	19	4
Chavez	.958	9	4	19	1	1
Frias	—	1	0	0	0	0
A. Vasquez	.844	14	8	19	5	2

Shortstop	PCT	G	PO	A	E	DP
Avila	1.000	2	1	0	0	0
Cespedes	1.000	4	4	8	0	1
Frias	.824	4	6	8	3	1
Guzman	.931	12	9	18	2	1
Juan	.750	1	2	1	1	1

Pena	.930	61	84	170	19	24

Outfield	PCT	G	PO	A	E	DP
De La Cruz	.929	49	49	3	4	2
Estanislao	1.000	17	13	2	0	0
Fortuna	.967	45	57	2	2	1
Garcia	.991	65	100	7	1	2
Garcia	1.000	1	2	0	0	0
Juan	.857	10	11	1	2	0
Marte	.947	37	34	2	2	1
Rojas	.826	22	17	2	4	0
Rojas	1.000	1	3	0	0	0

VENEZUELAN SUMMER LEAGUE

BATTING	B-T	HT	WT	DOB	AVG	vLH	vRH	G	AB	R	H	2B	3B	HR	RBI	BB	HBP	SH	SF	SO	SB	CS	SLG	OBP
Aguilera, Jesus	R-R	6-1	190	8-9-87	.167	.176	.164	29	72	7	12	3	1	0	4	10	1	0	0	22	0	0	.236	.277
Alvarez, Emilio	B-R	6-1	169	5-3-89	.259	.300	.235	22	27	7	7	2	0	0	3	4	2	1	0	10	0	1	.333	.394
Cardona, Luis	B-R	5-10	152	7-29-88	.175	.188	.167	36	40	12	7	0	2	0	2	6	3	1	0	11	4	3	.275	.327
Chourio, Adenson	R-R	5-9	160	7-22-86	.319	.313	.321	68	229	61	73	8	3	1	19	48	11	6	0	31	44	16	.393	.458
Gonzalez, Gemmy	R-R	6-0	189	6-22-88	.226	.238	.222	61	186	27	42	7	0	9	31	19	7	0	3	71	6	4	.409	.316
Henry, Henry	R-R	5-9	164	5-29-87	.298	.375	.268	37	57	13	17	2	0	2	10	14	4	0	0	6	5	0	.439	.467
Leal, Carlos	R-R	5-10	170	2-10-90	.255	.387	.200	46	106	33	27	4	0	2	11	36	1	0	0	28	12	3	.349	.448
Lozada, Jonathan	R-R	5-10	150	12-17-88	.138	.000	.222	23	29	4	4	0	0	0	3	1	0	2	0	3	0	0	.138	.167
Marquez, Jairo	R-R	6-0	170	4-7-88	.339	.347	.336	54	189	38	64	10	1	4	46	20	7	1	1	15	2	2	.466	.419
Mavares, Dixon	R-R	5-11	165	7-8-86	.257	.300	.240	51	144	36	37	6	1	1	20	27	4	2	2	11	7	6	.333	.384
Negron, Antonio	R-R	5-10	150	9-17-85	.281	.311	.269	68	221	45	62	11	1	7	47	42	6	0	2	39	12	7	.434	.406
Neira, Anyelo	R-R	5-11	165	1-19-86	.286	.294	.282	52	119	14	34	4	1	3	18	10	8	0	0	40	1	2	.412	.380
Noris, Rogelios	R-R	6-2	192	3-12-89	.284	.259	.294	66	218	39	62	14	1	7	55	30	4	0	7	45	4	2	.468	.371
Pedron, Freizer	L-R	5-11	160	9-9-86	.337	.244	.362	61	190	38	64	15	1	1	36	23	9	10	1	35	25	9	.442	.430
Salazar, Carlos	R-R	5-11	165	11-2-87	.268	.333	.242	58	183	26	49	9	0	1	26	13	2	5	0	41	16	9	.333	.323
Sanchez, Victor	L-L	5-10	160	10-25-86	.325	.250	.341	54	157	36	51	7	3	0	28	23	2	4	0	23	21	11	.408	.418
Trinidad, Michaelangel	L-L	5-11	232	8-23-88	.246	.258	.243	51	142	24	35	11	0	4	24	25	12	0	4	38	1	0	.408	.393

PITCHING	B-T	HT	WT	DOB	W	L	ERA	G	GS	CG	SV	IP	H	R	ER	HR	BB	SO	AVG	vLH	vRH	K/9	BB/9
Alvarado, Gabriel	R-R	6-2	175	5-19-87	8	4	2.67	13	12	1	0	71	68	33	21	2	18	39	.250	.291	.231	4.97	2.29
Bandres, Berdis	R-R	5-9	150	6-10-89	0	0	4.22	9	0	0	0	11	8	5	5	1	6	8	.211	.000	.267	6.75	5.06
Barrios, Edison	R-R	6-1	152	10-11-88	1	1	1.59	5	4	0	1	23	20	5	4	1	1	14	.235	.294	.221	5.56	0.40
Bermudez, Elbis	R-R	6-1	179	11-11-88	1	2	3.48	12	9	0	0	44	37	24	17	1	17	25	.227	.195	.238	5.11	3.48
Bueno, Luis	L-L	6-1	160	11-17-87	5	0	1.83	11	7	0	0	39	32	14	8	1	14	23	.224	.200	.225	5.26	3.20
Canonez, Gabriel	R-R	6-5	245	3-12-87	0	1	2.00	7	0	0	1	9	6	3	2	1	9	6	.182	.125	.200	6.00	9.00
Carrasco, Roman	R-R	6-2	213	3-18-88	1	0	4.73	14	0	0	0	27	28	15	14	1	12	17	.272	.313	.254	5.74	4.05
Goatache, Deivis	L-L	6-0	139	6-23-88	1	1	2.25	7	0	0	0	12	11	4	3	1	5	6	.268	—	.268	4.50	3.75
Gutierrez, Edgar	R-R	6-0	170	4-16-88	1	2	2.51	18	0	0	3	29	18	9	8	1	14	21	.188	.174	.192	6.59	4.40
Gutierrez, Jorge	R-R	6-1	174	12-2-87	0	1	5.95	13	1	0	0	20	20	16	13	2	14	16	.270	.381	.226	7.32	6.41
Iriarte, Humberto	R-R	6-0	165	3-26-88	4	3	1.68	21	1	0	5	48	41	11	9	1	11	42	.227	.167	.248	7.82	2.05
Martinez, Jesus	L-L	5-11	165	12-4-86	2	1	5.03	14	0	0	2	34	44	20	19	5	4	24	.317	.500	.305	6.35	1.06
Moreno, Diego	R-R	6-1	177	7-21-86	1	0	2.42	13	0	0	2	22	17	6	6	1	5	16	.213	.348	.158	6.45	2.01
Ortiz, Wilson	R-R	5-11	181	11-6-85	6	1	1.27	14	12	1	0	71	35	14	10	1	20	72	.145	.143	.145	9.13	2.54
Pacheco, Alexis	R-R	6-0	194	10-21-87	2	0	2.45	13	0	0	1	18	14	5	5	1	6	6	.219	.208	.225	2.95	2.95
Paez, Ronald	R-R	6-0	167	12-18-88	0	0	0.00	2	0	0	0	2	3	3	0	0	3	1	.375	1.000	.286	5.40	16.20
Pereira, Nelson	L-L	5-11	180	2-12-89	10	1	2.33	14	12	0	1	66	54	23	17	2	18	59	.220	.313	.213	8.09	2.47
Ramos, Jhonatan	L-L	5-8	156	8-7-89	6	3	2.47	13	13	0	0	62	50	20	17	0	22	46	.227	.000	.231	6.68	3.19
Velasquez, Fidel	R-R	5-11	180	12-10-86	0	0	10.80	8	0	0	0	8	16	13	10	1	2	2	.390	.273	.433	2.16	2.16

FIELDING

Catcher	PCT	G	PO	A	E	DP	PB
Aguilera	.979	29	125	13	3	3	2
Marquez	.968	21	83	9	3	1	7
Neira	.992	51	236	23	2	2	3

First Base	PCT	G	PO	A	E	DP
Alvarez	.939	11	30	1	2	6
Marquez	1.000	17	108	8	0	12
Mavares	1.000	2	6	0	0	0
Negron	.991	27	221	12	2	17
Neira	1.000	3	5	1	0	1
Noris	1.000	3	12	0	0	2
Trinidad	.990	32	287	12	3	25

Second Base	PCT	G	PO	A	E	DP
Chourio	.933	19	24	32	4	5
Henry	.974	15	21	16	1	6

	PCT	G	PO	A	E	DP
Leal	1.000	2	1	0	0	0
Lozada	1.000	2	2	2	0	0
Mavares	.889	2	3	5	1	0
Pedron	.977	58	109	143	6	35

Third Base	PCT	G	PO	A	E	DP
Alvarez	.846	7	4	7	2	2
Chourio	.993	32	25	108	1	10
Henry	.818	14	4	23	6	1
Leal	1.000	4	0	1	0	0
Mavares	.926	25	19	44	5	5
Negron	.875	9	5	16	3	2

Shortstop	PCT	G	PO	A	E	DP
Chourio	.897	25	24	81	12	13
Leal	.902	36	60	88	16	18
Mavares	.903	23	28	56	9	10

Outfield	PCT	G	PO	A	E	DP
Cardona	.957	29	21	1	1	0
Gonzalez	.973	59	102	5	3	4
Lozada	1.000	19	11	0	0	0
Mavares	—	1	0	0	0	0
Noris	.934	57	65	6	5	1
Salazar	1.000	55	90	5	0	1
Sanchez	.939	53	74	3	5	2
Trinidad	1.000	4	2	0	0	0

St. Louis Cardinals

BY DERRICK GOOLD

The St. Louis Cardinals flirted briefly with contention, but a season laced with turmoil and tragedy ultimately swallowed them and left a proud franchise in an unusual situation—adrift and seeking a new identity.

Less than 12 months removed from their 10th World Series championship, the Cardinals finished their first losing season in the new millennium and fired general manager Walt Jocketty. Their roster was ragged as shortstop David Eckstein headed for free agency, lefthander Mark Mulder recovered from a second shoulder surgery and other stalwarts were lost or hampered by chronic injuries. Ownership had been creeping toward a more self-sustained organization—one with a replenished minor league system—and the erratic and disappointing play of the 78-84 Cardinals may have sped the changes.

"This is a very important time in this era of Cardinal history," said club chairman Bill DeWitt Jr., whose first move of October was to woo La Russa back for a 13th season with a two-year contract as the highest paid manager in the majors.

The Cardinals began defense of their 2006 title with ace righthander Chris Carpenter on the mound for Opening Day but didn't see him again for the rest of the season. Carpenter's year ended with Tommy John surgery, and his rehab will spill into 2008. The Cardinals were riddled by injuries all season. Third baseman Scott Rolen missed the final month of the year when he needed surgery on his left shoulder, the third surgery on the joint in the past three seasons.

First baseman Albert Pujols played most of the second half of the season with chronic hamstring pain, and coaches even refused to let him leg out groundballs for fear it would be the last base he'd run to in 2007. A furious finish kept his streak of 100-RBI seasons alive as he put together his seventh consecutive season of at least 30 homers, 100 RBIs and a .300 average.

The team had a significant injury at every position. Only Pujols had enough at-bats to qualify for the batting title.

And there was tragedy. In late April, the Cardinals lost reliever Josh Hancock was killed in an automobile accident. Hancock thrived as a versatile reliever for the World Series team. His was the second death of an active Cardinals pitcher in five years, stunning several members of the 2007 team that were Cardinals when Darryl Kile died in 2002.

Nailed at every turn by bruising blows, the Cardinals reached September and found themselves suddenly in contention. They got there mostly because of the stability provided by burgeoning star Adam Wainwright and reinvented righthander Braden Looper (12-12, 4.94), a career reliever until 2006. On Sept. 7, the Cardinals had a chance to move into first place with a victory. They lost their next seven, all on the road, for their first winless seven-game jaunt since 1972.

La Russa described himself as "tapped" and "toast" after the emotionally and mentally wearing season. Jocketty articulated the same feelings—even before he was fired. Seeing a widening rift in his front office between Jocketty's major league chamber and the Jeff Luhnow-directed farm system, DeWitt moved to eradicate the tension by removing Jocketty in early October. The team hired Jocketty's longtime assistant John Mozeliak as GM to integrate the front office, scouts and a group that specializes in statistical analysis.

The success story of the year was Rick Ankiel, who

returned to the majors as an outfielder on a power trip. Ankiel, the former pitching phenom, ripped 11 home runs and drove in 39 RBIs in 47 big league games. Combined with his numbers from his first turn as an every day player in Triple-A, Ankiel hit 43 homers and had 128 RBIs.

Double-A Springfield hosted most of the prospects the Cardinals are counting on, including center fielder Colby Rasmus and catcher Bryan Anderson (.298/.350/.388). The heft of the Cardinals' pitching prospects remain at Double-A or lower, a concern whose starting rotation set a franchise high with a 5.04 ERA and whose bullpen logged the most innings in club history.

"I don't think you can legitimately make this a transition club, where you bring in young guys who pitch and hit," La Russa said. "Help has to come through trade or free agency."

2007 PERFORMANCE

General Manager: Walt Jocketty. **Farm Director:** John Vuch. **Scouting Director:** Jeff Luhnow

Class	Team	League	W	L	PCT	Finish*	Manager	Affiliate Since
Majors	St. Louis	National	78	84	.481	10th (16)	Tony LaRussa	—
Triple-A	Memphis Redbirds	Pacific Coast	56	88	.389	16th (16)	Chris Maloney	1998
Double-A	Springfield Cardinals	Texas	73	63	.537	2nd (8)	Ron Warner	2005
High A	Palm Beach Cardinals	Florida State	71	69	.507	6th (12)	Gaylen Pitts	2003
Low A	Swing of the Quad Cities	Midwest	78	61	.561	3rd (14)	Keith Mitchell	2005
Short-season	Batavia Muckdogs	New York-Penn	31	43	.419	12th (14)	Mark DeJohn	2007
Rookie	Johnson City Cardinals	Appalachian	28	40	.412	7th (9)	Joe Almaraz	1974
Rookie	GCL Cardinals	Gulf Coast	24	30	.444	12th (16)	Enrique Brito	2007
Overall 2007 Minor League Record			**361**	**394**	**.478**	**23rd**		

* Finish in overall standings (No. of teams in league) ^League champion

ORGANIZATION STATISTICS

ST. LOUIS CARDINALS

NATIONAL LEAGUE

BATTING	B-T	HT	WT	DOB	AVG	vLH	vRH	G	AB	R	H	2B	3B	HR	RBI	BB	HBP	SH	SF	SO	SB	CS	SLG	OBP
Ankiel, Rick	L-L	6-1	210	7-19-79	.285	.391	.246	47	172	31	49	8	1	11	39	13	0	1	4	41	1	0	.535	.328
Barden, Brian	R-R	5-11	185	4-2-81	.217	.333	.200	15	23	6	5	1	0	0	2	0	0	0	4	5	0	0	.261	.280
2-team (8 Arizona)					.171	—	—	23	35	6	6	1	0	0	2	0	0	0	7	0	0	0	.200	.216
Bennett, Gary	R-R	6-0	210	4-17-72	.252	.227	.261	59	155	12	39	7	0	2	17	8	1	2	4	16	1	1	.335	.286
Branyan, Russell	L-R	6-3	195	12-19-75	.188	.000	.222	21	32	4	6	0	0	1	2	7	0	0	0	15	0	0	.281	.333
3-team (7 Philadelphia, 61 San Diego)					.196	—	—	89	163	22	32	5	1	10	26	28	2	0	1	69	1	0	.423	.320
Cairo, Miguel	R-R	6-1	210	5-4-74	.254	.286	.239	28	67	8	17	2	2	0	5	3	1	1	0	5	2	1	.343	.296
Duncan, Chris	L-R	6-5	230	5-5-81	.259	.213	.271	127	375	51	97	20	0	21	70	55	1	0	1	123	2	1	.480	.354
Eckstein, David	R-R	5-7	175	1-20-75	.309	.288	.314	117	434	58	134	23	0	3	31	24	12	7	7	22	10	1	.382	.356
Edmonds, Jim	L-L	6-1	210	6-27-70	.252	.198	.268	117	365	39	92	15	2	12	53	41	0	2	3	75	0	2	.403	.325
Encarnacion, Juan	R-R	6-3	215	3-8-76	.283	.290	.278	78	283	43	80	17	1	9	47	18	1	1	4	43	2	2	.445	.324
Esposito, Brian	R-R	6-1	205	2-24-79	—	—	—	1	0	0	0	0	0	0	0	0	0	0	0	0	0	0	—	—
Kennedy, Adam	L-R	6-1	195	1-10-76	.219	.122	.235	87	279	27	61	9	1	3	18	22	3	1	1	33	6	2	.290	.282
Ludwick, Ryan	R-L	6-3	220	7-13-78	.267	.221	.298	120	303	42	81	22	0	14	52	26	7	3	0	72	4	4	.479	.339
Miles, Aaron	B-R	5-8	185	12-15-76	.290	.286	.292	133	414	55	120	16	1	2	32	25	1	4	5	40	2	1	.348	.328
Molina, Yadier	R-R	5-11	220	7-13-82	.275	.288	.269	111	353	30	97	15	0	6	40	34	3	2	4	43	1	1	.368	.340
Pujols, Albert	R-R	6-3	230	1-16-80	.327	.367	.313	158	565	99	185	38	1	32	103	99	7	0	8	58	2	6	.568	.429
Rolen, Scott	R-R	6-4	240	4-4-75	.265	.204	.287	112	392	55	104	24	2	8	58	37	5	0	7	56	5	3	.398	.331
Ryan, Brendan	R-R	6-2	195	3-26-82	.289	.354	.238	67	180	30	52	9	0	4	12	15	1	3	0	19	7	0	.406	.347
Schumaker, Skip	L-R	5-10	195	2-3-80	.333	.375	.327	88	177	19	59	12	2	2	19	8	0	1	2	20	1	1	.458	.358
Spiezio, Scott	B-R	6-2	215	9-21-72	.260	.310	.250	81	223	31	60	14	0	4	31	27	4	0	3	40	0	1	.386	.354
Stinnett, Kelly	R-R	5-11	235	2-4-70	.159	.105	.175	26	82	7	13	3	0	1	5	5	0	0	0	22	0	0	.232	.207
Taguchi, So	R-R	5-10	170	7-2-69	.290	.314	.264	130	307	48	89	15	0	3	30	23	6	3	1	32	7	4	.368	.350
Wilson, Preston	R-R	6-2	220	7-19-74	.219	.208	.225	25	64	6	14	3	0	1	5	4	0	0	0	17	2	1	.313	.265

PITCHING	B-T	HT	WT	DOB	W	L	ERA	G	GS	CG	SV	IP	H	R	ER	HR	BB	SO	AVG	vLH	vRH	K/9	BB/9
Carpenter, Chris	R-R	6-6	230	4-27-75	0	1	7.50	1	1	0	0	6	9	5	5	0	1	3	.346	.375	.300	4.50	1.50
Cate, Troy	L-L	6-1	220	10-21-80	0	0	3.38	14	0	0	0	16	18	7	6	1	9	12	.290	.259	.314	6.75	5.06
Cavazos, Andy	R-R	6-3	225	1-5-81	0	0	10.35	17	0	0	0	20	27	27	23	5	16	15	.333	.357	.308	6.75	7.20
Dove, Dennis	R-R	6-4	205	8-31-81	0	0	15.00	3	0	0	0	3	5	5	5	2	1	1	.357	.200	.444	3.00	3.00
Falkenborg, Brian	R-R	6-6	230	1-18-78	0	1	4.82	16	0	0	0	19	22	10	10	2	8	16	.293	.321	.277	7.71	3.86
Flores, Randy	L-L	6-0	190	7-31-75	3	0	4.25	70	0	0	1	55	71	31	26	2	15	47	.310	.326	.299	7.69	2.45
Franklin, Ryan	R-R	6-3	190	3-5-73	4	4	3.04	69	0	0	1	80	70	28	27	8	11	44	.234	.238	.231	4.95	1.24
Hancock, Josh	R-R	6-3	220	4-11-78	0	1	3.55	8	0	0	0	13	14	6	5	2	5	9	.286	.389	.226	6.39	3.55
Isringhausen, Jason	R-R	6-3	230	9-7-72	4	0	2.48	63	0	0	32	65	42	21	18	4	28	54	.179	.196	.167	7.44	3.86
Jimenez, Kelvin	R-R	6-2	195	10-27-80	3	0	7.50	34	0	0	0	42	56	36	35	2	17	24	.320	.271	.345	5.14	3.64
Johnson, Tyler	B-L	6-2	200	6-7-81	1	1	4.03	55	0	0	0	38	31	18	17	4	16	24	.217	.224	.211	5.68	3.79
Keisler, Randy	L-L	6-2	200	2-24-76	0	0	5.19	4	3	0	0	17	21	12	10	3	5	5	.309	.154	.345	2.60	2.60
Looper, Braden	R-R	6-3	235	10-28-74	12	12	4.94	31	30	0	0	175	183	100	96	22	51	87	.269	.277	.262	4.47	2.62
Maroth, Mike	L-L	6-0	190	8-17-77	0	5	10.66	14	7	0	0	38	71	56	45	11	17	23	.394	.293	.424	5.45	4.03
Miles, Aaron	B-R	5-8	185	12-15-76	0	0	9.00	2	0	0	0	2	3	2	2	1	0	0	.375	.500	.333	0.00	0.00
Mulder, Mark	L-L	6-6	215	8-5-77	0	3	12.27	3	3	0	0	11	22	17	15	4	7	3	.440	.455	.436	2.45	5.73
Percival, Troy	R-R	6-3	240	8-9-69	3	0	1.80	34	1	0	0	40	24	8	8	3	10	36	.171	.220	.136	8.10	2.25
Pineiro, Joel	R-R	6-1	200	9-25-78	6	4	3.96	11	11	0	0	64	69	29	28	11	12	40	.279	.210	.327	5.65	1.70
Reyes, Anthony	R-R	6-2	230	10-16-81	2	14	6.04	22	20	1	0	107	108	77	72	16	43	74	.261	.290	.234	6.20	3.61
Spiezio, Scott	B-R	6-2	215	9-21-72	0	0	0.00	1	0	0	0	1	0	0	0	0	1	0	.000	.000	.000	0.00	9.00
Springer, Russ	R-R	6-4	225	11-7-68	8	1	2.18	76	0	0	0	66	41	18	16	3	19	66	.181	.235	.158	9.00	2.59
Thompson, Brad	R-R	6-1	190	1-31-82	8	6	4.73	44	17	0	0	129	157	76	68	23	40	53	.301	.343	.267	3.69	2.78
Wainwright, Adam	R-R	6-7	230	8-30-81	14	12	3.70	32	32	1	0	202	212	93	83	13	70	136	.269	.249	.283	6.06	3.12
Wellemeyer, Todd	R-R	6-3	225	8-30-78	3	2	3.11	20	11	0	0	64	52	31	22	7	29	51	.224	.268	.183	7.21	4.10
Wells, Kip	R-R	6-3	205	4-21-77	7	17	5.70	34	26	0	0	163	186	116	103	19	78	122	.287	.287	.287	6.75	4.32

FIELDING

Catcher	PCT	G	PO	A	E	DP	PB
Bennett	.996	52	244	9	1	1	2
Esposito	1.000	1	1	0	0	0	0
Molina	.991	107	582	63	6	8	7
Stinnett	.976	26	153	9	4	0	1

First Base	PCT	G	PO	A	E	DP
Bennett	1.000	1	1	0	0	1
Branyan	1.000	4	6	0	0	1
Cairo	1.000	2	11	1	0	2
Duncan	1.000	11	25	1	0	3
Edmonds	—	1	0	0	0	0
Molina	1.000	1	1	0	0	0
Pujols	.995	154	1325	124	8	132
Spiezio	1.000	9	72	2	0	6

Second Base	PCT	G	PO	A	E	DP
Barden	1.000	2	2	4	0	0

	PCT	G	PO	A	E	DP
Cairo	1.000	9	9	13	0	1
Kennedy	.981	79	156	211	7	46
Miles	.984	85	152	160	5	39
Ryan	.956	17	20	45	3	9
Spiezio	.941	5	8	8	1	3
Taguchi	.500	1	1	0	1	0

Third Base	PCT	G	PO	A	E	DP
Barden	1.000	1	2	0	0	1
Branyan	.963	9	6	20	1	5
Cairo	.964	15	4	23	1	4
Miles	1.000	3	0	8	0	0
Rolen	.969	112	85	226	10	22
Ryan	.938	24	19	41	4	7
Spiezio	.955	27	22	42	3	5

Shortstop	PCT	G	PO	A	E	DP
Barden	1.000	6	3	11	0	2

		G	PO	A	E	DP
Eckstein	.960	114	164	310	20	59
Kennedy	1.000	1	0	3	0	0
Miles	.948	40	73	91	9	24
Ryan	.970	28	31	65	3	15

Outfield	PCT	G	PO	A	E	DP
Ankiel	.979	44	91	3	2	0
Cairo	—	1	0	0	0	0
Duncan	.988	99	158	5	2	0
Edmonds	.981	103	244	8	5	4
Encarnacion	.941	74	125	2	8	0
Kennedy	—	1	0	0	0	0
Ludwick	.994	92	153	1	1	0
Miles	—	1	0	0	0	0
Schumaker	.970	57	64	1	2	0
Spiezio	.947	18	18	0	1	0
Taguchi	.983	109	172	3	3	2
Wilson	.931	16	27	0	2	0

MEMPHIS REDBIRDS   TRIPLE-A

PACIFIC COAST LEAGUE

BATTING	B-T	HT	WT	DOB	AVG	vLH	vRH	G	AB	R	H	2B	3B	HR	RBI	BB	HBP	SH	SF	SO	SB	CS	SLG	OBP
Ankiel, Rick	L-L	6-1	210	7-19-79	.267	.275	.264	102	389	62	104	15	3	32	89	25	4	0	5	90	4	3	.568	.314
Ardoin, Danny	R-R	6-0	220	7-8-74	.296	.375	.263	9	27	7	8	3	0	1	4	6	0	0	0	4	0	0	.519	.424
2-team (52 Round Rock)					.208	—		61	197	24	41	13	0	2	11	27	5	3	0	52	1	0	.305	.319
Barden, Brian	R-R	5-11	185	4-2-81	.235	.375	.192	20	68	7	16	3	0	2	12	5	1	0	3	13	0	0	.368	.286
					.263	—		103	354	43	93	12	2	4	37	36	8	5	3	69	2	3	.342	.342
Bozied, Tagg	R-R	6-3	215	7-24-79	.264	.336	.234	130	451	69	119	26	2	24	82	53	8	0	4	96	3	0	.490	.349
Cabrera, Jolbert	R-R	6-1	215	12-8-72	.231	.208	.244	45	130	10	30	5	1	2	8	7	4	5	2	23	0	2	.331	.287
2-team (19 Colorado Springs)					.265	—		64	200	21	53	14	1	4	21	8	6	5	3	28	0	2	.405	.309
Cairo, Miguel	R-R	6-1	210	5-4-74	.290	.222	.318	9	31	8	9	2	0	0	3	5	2	0	0	6	2	0	.355	.421
Christianson, Ryan	R-R	6-2	220	4-21-81	.211	.242	.198	42	114	17	24	5	0	5	13	11	0	1	0	35	0	1	.386	.280
Esposito, Brian	R-R	6-1	205	2-24-79	.178	.143	.194	77	242	11	43	6	0	4	16	11	1	0	0	52	0	2	.252	.217
Ferris, Michael	L-L	6-2	220	12-31-82	.216	.000	.220	22	51	5	11	3	0	2	5	6	0	0	0	12	1	1	.392	.298
Gonzalez, Edgar	R-R	6-0	180	6-14-78	.308	.328	.300	126	461	64	142	34	3	8	53	50	2	4	2	69	15	4	.447	.377
Hanson, Travis	L-R	6-2	205	1-24-81	.217	.164	.233	82	254	16	55	4	1	4	14	9	1	0	0	58	1	1	.287	.246
Hoffpauir, Jarrett	R-R	5-9	165	6-18-83	.300	.358	.277	55	190	27	57	10	0	4	24	29	1	4	1	21	2	3	.416	.394
Ludwick, Ryan	R-L	6-3	215	7-13-78	.340	.387	.320	29	106	27	36	8	0	8	36	10	0	0	5	20	1	1	.642	.380
Marrero, Eli	R-R	6-1	200	11-17-73	.500	—	.500	1	4	0	2	0	0	0	1	0	0	0	0	0	0	0	.500	.500
Mather, Joe	R-R	6-5	210	7-23-82	.241	.227	.246	70	253	32	61	10	1	13	31	23	10	2	0	51	6	0	.443	.329
McCoy, Mike	R-R	5-9	171	4-2-81	.247	.228	.253	90	239	31	59	8	0	3	16	45	1	11	0	43	12	4	.318	.368
Nelson, John	R-R	6-1	190	3-3-79	.162	.204	.125	47	105	11	17	3	0	5	11	7	1	0	2	41	0	0	.333	.237
2-team (54 Iowa)					.211	—		101	265	37	56	10	0	15	44	27	2	0	4	87	0	1	.419	.285
Pagnozzi, Matt	R-R	6-2	195	11-10-82	.220	.207	.223	47	141	10	31	6	0	2	9	7	4	2	1	36	1	0	.305	.275
Rodriguez, John	L-L	6-0	205	1-20-78	.263	.190	.288	55	160	35	42	12	1	8	27	23	7	0	2	35	1	0	.500	.375
Ryan, Brendan	R-R	6-2	195	3-26-82	.272	.298	.262	81	323	55	88	9	5	1	15	25	2	1	3	39	17	6	.341	.328
Schumaker, Skip	L-R	5-10	195	2-3-80	.306	.288	.314	59	232	34	71	16	0	7	31	27	2	2	1	37	2	3	.466	.382
Stavinoha, Nick	R-R	6-2	225	5-3-82	.261	.343	.230	139	501	50	131	17	0	13	49	31	4	1	2	81	7	1	.373	.309
Stinnett, Kelly	R-R	5-11	235	2-4-70	1.000	1.000	—	1	1	0	1	0	0	0	0	0	0	0	0	0	0	0	1.000	1.000
2-team (31 Las Vegas)					.204	—		32	103	10	21	2	0	3	11	9	1	1	0	22	0	0	.311	.274
Washington, Rico	L-R	5-9	195	5-30-78	.315	.297	.321	54	168	24	53	12	2	7	23	17	1	0	4	24	2	0	.536	.374

PITCHING	B-T	HT	WT	DOB	W	L	ERA	G	GS	CG	SV	IP	H	R	ER	HR	BB	SO	AVG	vLH	vRH	K/9	BB/9
Castellanos, Hugo	R-R	6-4	225	6-30-80	3	1	3.49	37	0	0	0	57	50	36	22	5	32	33	.243	.287	.210	5.24	5.08
Cate, Troy	L-L	6-1	220	10-21-80	2	5	6.81	33	9	0	0	71	88	61	54	14	30	60	.304	.303	.305	7.57	3.79
Cavazos, Andy	R-R	6-3	225	1-5-81	1	5	3.21	44	0	0	0	48	40	18	17	5	26	48	.231	.216	.242	9.06	4.91
Dove, Dennis	R-R	6-4	205	8-31-81	1	0	5.28	13	0	0	0	15	17	9	9	3	7	10	.293	.242	.360	5.87	4.11
Falkenborg, Brian	R-R	6-6	230	1-18-78	3	4	3.25	51	0	0	23	53	54	22	19	2	17	58	.260	.276	.243	9.91	2.91
Ginter, Matt	R-R	6-1	220	12-24-77	2	6	4.06	31	8	0	2	69	86	39	31	5	8	43	.310	.266	.346	5.64	1.05
2-team (1 Nashville)					2	6	4.41	32	8	0	2	69	88	42	34	5	10	43	—	—		5.58	1.30
Hawksworth, Blake	R-R	6-3	195	3-1-83	4	13	5.28	25	25	0	0	130	150	82	76	24	41	88	.295	.311	.282	6.11	2.85
Jimenez, Kelvin	R-R	6-2	195	10-27-80	2	3	2.72	30	0	0	1	40	46	16	12	2	11	34	.289	.235	.346	7.71	2.50
Johnson, Tyler	B-L	6-2	200	6-7-81	0	0	0.00	1	0	0	0	1	0	0	0	0	0	1	.000	.000	.000	9.00	0.00
Keisler, Randy	L-L	6-2	200	2-24-76	8	11	4.79	25	24	1	0	156	178	90	83	19	51	102	.292	.297	.291	5.88	2.94
Lambert, Chris	R-R	6-1	205	3-8-83	1	4	7.49	28	4	0	0	58	74	49	48	10	29	50	.319	.404	.261	7.80	4.53
Maroth, Mike	L-L	6-0	190	8-17-77	1	0	8.31	2	1	0	0	4	5	4	4	1	3	4	.294	.222	.375	8.31	6.23
Meaux, Ryan	R-L	5-11	170	10-5-78	0	0	9.00	7	0	0	0	6	10	7	6	3	2	9	.370	.417	.333	13.50	3.00
3-team (13 Sacramento, 7 Fresno)					0	3	5.68	27	0	0	0	32	41	23	20	3	10	32	—	—		9.09	2.84
Mulder, Mark	L-L	6-6	215	8-5-77	0	0	3.60	1	1	0	0	5	5	2	2	1	2	4	.278	.000	.417	7.20	3.60
Narveson, Chris	L-L	6-3	205	12-20-81	3	2	5.72	9	9	1	0	46	41	29	29	6	21	35	.244	.209	.256	6.90	4.14
Ohka, Tomo	B-R	6-1	200	3-18-76	0	2	6.87	3	3	0	0	18	27	15	14	2	3	7	.360	.415	.294	3.44	1.47
2-team (4 Tacoma)					0	5	8.78	7	7	0	0	41	65	41	40	8	12	16	—	—		3.51	2.63
Parisi, Mike	R-R	6-3	215	4-18-83	8	13	4.91	28	28	0	0	165	192	100	90	21	65	111	.298	.320	.279	6.05	3.55
Percival, Troy	R-R	6-3	240	8-9-69	0	0	1.35	6	0	0	0	7	4	1	1	0	5	9	.167	.182	.154	12.15	6.75
Perez, Chris	R-R	6-4	225	7-1-85	0	1	4.50	15	0	0	8	14	6	7	7	2	13	15	.143	.261	.000	9.64	8.36
Reyes, Anthony	R-R	6-2	230	10-16-81	1	1	2.79	6	6	0	0	39	27	12	12	4	11	33	.206	.159	.258	7.68	2.56
Russ, Chris	R-R	5-11	175	3-27-79	0	0	5.40	2	0	0	0	3	3	2	2	1	1	2	.231	.333	.200	5.40	2.70
Sillman, Mike	R-R	6-1	190	1-31-84	2	0	5.40	10	0	0	0	10	6	6	6	1	5	10	.179	.222	.154	8.10	9.00
Smith, Mike	R-R	5-11	205	9-19-77	11	13	5.19	31	25	0	0	160	182	95	92	17	49	127	.288	.301	.275	7.16	2.76
Thompson, Brad	R-R	6-1	190	1-31-82	0	0	4.32	2	1	0	0	8	8	4	4	1	2	4	.242	.150	.385	2.16	1.08
Venafro, Mike	L-L	5-10	180	8-2-73	0	1	12.79	8	0	0	0	13	19	9	9	6	5	4	.448	.455	.444	7.11	8.53
Worrell, Mark	R-R	6-1	190	3-8-83	3	2	3.09	50	0	0	4	67	58	25	23	6	25	66	.236	.283	.208	8.87	3.36

FIELDING

Catcher	PCT	G	PO	A	E	DP	PB
Ardoin	1.000	8	71	6	0	1	0
Christianson	.950	33	200	8	11	0	2
Esposito	.988	73	445	39	6	0	6
Marrero	1.000	1	9	0	0	0	0
Pagnozzi	.990	42	261	33	3	3	2

First Base	PCT	G	PO	A	E	DP
Bozied	.993	119	979	85	7	104
Cabrera	1.000	2	9	0	0	0
Cairo	1.000	1	7	2	0	4
Ferris	1.000	5	31	5	0	7
Mather	1.000	2	16	0	0	0
Washington	1.000	23	188	13	0	11

Second Base	PCT	G	PO	A	E	DP
Cabrera	1.000	2	1	5	0	0
Cairo	1.000	1	0	3	0	0
Gonzalez	.972	94	156	254	12	50
Hoffpauir	.980	42	89	109	4	36

	PCT	G	PO	A	E	DP	
McCoy	.966	12	22	35	2	9	
Washington	1.000	3	8	5	0	2	

Third Base	PCT	G	PO	A	E	DP
Barden	1.000	6	7	10	0	1
Cabrera	.944	20	12	22	2	2
Cairo	1.000	3	1	7	0	0
Esposito	—	1	0	0	0	0
Gonzalez	.957	22	11	34	2	5
Hanson	.980	69	36	110	3	6
Hoffpauir	.913	6	4	17	2	2
McCoy	—	1	0	0	0	0
Nelson	1.000	15	9	18	0	5
Washington	.923	19	12	36	4	3

Shortstop	PCT	G	PO	A	E	DP
Barden	.962	12	20	30	2	4
Cabrera	1.000	7	9	21	0	5
Cairo	1.000	2	4	4	0	2
Hoffpauir	1.000	4	6	8	0	3

	PCT	G	PO	A	E	DP
McCoy	.957	50	74	128	9	29
Nelson	1.000	1	1	0	0	0
Ryan	.981	77	130	233	7	51

Outfield	PCT	G	PO	A	E	DP
Ankiel	.971	98	223	8	7	3
Bozied	1.000	4	1	0	0	0
Cabrera	1.000	9	18	1	0	1
Cairo	1.000	2	2	1	0	0
Christianson	1.000	2	3	1	0	0
Gonzalez	1.000	3	6	0	0	0
Ludwick	1.000	24	47	0	0	0
Mather	.974	68	145	5	4	0
McCoy	1.000	12	18	0	0	0
Nelson	.941	11	14	2	1	0
Rodriguez	.981	36	52	1	1	0
Schumaker	.992	57	119	6	1	1
Stavinoha	.970	129	217	13	7	5

SPRINGFIELD CARDINALS — DOUBLE-A

TEXAS LEAGUE

BATTING	B-T	HT	WT	DOB	AVG	vLH	vRH	G	AB	R	H	2B	3B	HR	RBI	BB	HBP	SH	SF	SO	SB	CS	SLG	OBP
Anderson, Bryan	L-R	6-1	190	12-16-86	.298	.267	.308	103	389	51	116	15	1	6	53	32	2	2	6	77	0	1	.388	.350
Cazana Marti, Amaury	R-R	6-1	212	9-2-74	.308	.333	.302	30	107	24	33	5	0	6	20	9	2	0	1	23	1	0	.523	.370
Craig, Allen	R-R	6-2	190	7-18-84	.292	.167	.417	7	24	5	7	2	0	2	3	3	1	0	0	6	0	0	.750	.320
Danielson, Sean	B-R	5-8	165	8-6-82	.291	.247	.306	91	320	55	93	16	1	4	34	38	3	7	1	41	14	5	.384	.370
Encarnacion, Juan	R-R	6-3	215	3-8-76	.155	.143	.162	15	58	5	9	4	0	0	4	6	1	0	0	11	1	0	.224	.246
Ferris, Michael	L-L	6-2	220	12-31-82	.227	.133	.247	65	176	24	40	8	0	3	20	26	0	0	0	55	1	1	.324	.327
Gorecki, Reid	R-R	6-1	180	12-22-80	.237	.056	.293	24	76	9	18	1	0	0	8	11	0	0	0	20	3	2	.250	.333
Greene, Tyler	R-R	6-2	185	8-17-83	.244	.222	.251	65	221	41	54	17	2	8	25	16	5	4	1	62	10	2	.448	.309
Guerrero, Henry	R-R	6-0	189	4-4-82	.137	.143	.133	19	51	4	7	0	0	0	2	2	1	0	0	12	0	0	.255	.185
Haerther, Cody	L-R	6-1	205	7-14-83	.289	.222	.304	37	142	22	41	13	0	5	28	16	4	0	0	31	0	0	.486	.377
Hamilton, Mark	L-L	6-3	220	7-29-84	.250	.234	.255	68	248	32	62	15	0	6	41	24	1	2	1	54	1	1	.383	.318
Hoffpauir, Jarrett	R-R	5-9	165	6-18-83	.345	.229	.381	61	203	23	70	16	0	7	33	26	1	5	1	18	3	1	.527	.420
Jay, Jonathan	L-L	6-0	200	3-15-85	.235	.105	.265	26	102	17	24	4	2	2	11	11	4	0	0	19	4	1	.373	.333
Lucena, Juan	R-R	5-10	155	1-20-84	.257	.180	.290	92	303	36	78	13	2	2	33	17	5	3	4	20	1	1	.333	.304
Martinez, Jose	R-R	5-11	175	1-24-86	.300	.317	.295	66	250	37	75	13	0	10	46	14	3	3	4	24	0	0	.472	.339
Mather, Joe	R-R	6-5	210	7-23-82	.303	.400	.274	64	234	48	71	17	0	18	46	29	5	1	3	32	4	0	.607	.387
McCoy, Mike	R-R	5-9	171	4-2-81	.221	.200	.237	24	68	5	15	3	1	0	10	14	0	2	1	14	1	3	.294	.349
Pagnozzi, Matt	R-R	6-2	195	11-10-82	.209	.250	.185	13	43	5	9	3	0	0	3	2	1	1	0	11	0	0	.279	.261
Rasmus, Colby	L-L	6-2	195	8-11-86	.275	.241	.287	128	472	93	130	37	3	29	72	70	12	0	2	108	18	3	.551	.381
Richardson, Juan	R-R	6-1	215	1-27-79	.291	.327	.278	113	430	65	125	22	1	18	78	47	8	0	3	118	0	2	.472	.369
Rowlett, Casey	R-R	5-8	175	2-8-83	.244	.208	.259	77	246	36	60	11	4	2	20	19	2	4	2	41	6	0	.346	.301
Sanchez, Danilo	R-R	5-11	230	10-25-80	.161	.167	.160	11	31	3	5	1	0	1	4	7	0	0	1	10	0	0	.290	.308
Shorey, Mark	L-L	6-0	230	8-13-84	.263	.154	.291	61	190	25	50	11	0	11	33	14	0	1	0	45	0	0	.495	.325
Washington, Rico	R-R	5-9	195	5-30-78	.263	.214	.284	25	95	13	25	4	0	4	20	7	2	0	1	10	0	0	.432	.324

PITCHING	B-T	HT	WT	DOB	W	L	ERA	G	GS	CG	SV	IP	H	R	ER	HR	BB	SO	AVG	vLH	vRH	K/9	BB/9
Boggs, Mitch	R-R	6-3	195	2-15-84	11	7	3.84	26	26	0	0	152	167	86	65	15	62	117	.279	.281	.277	6.91	3.66
Castellanos, Hugo	R-R	6-4	225	6-30-80	1	2	2.45	9	0	0	0	11	11	5	3	2	7	11	.268	.462	.179	9.00	5.73
Cooper, Michael	R-R	6-2	205	2-2-84	1	2	7.71	21	0	0	0	28	36	26	24	6	20	21	.313	.283	.333	6.75	6.43
Daniels, Adam	L-L	6-2	190	8-16-82	5	7	5.94	15	15	0	0	73	84	53	48	5	34	43	.290	.348	.271	5.33	4.21
Garcia, Jaime	L-L	6-1	200	7-8-86	5	9	3.75	18	18	0	0	103	93	47	43	14	45	97	.245	.232	.249	8.45	3.92
Garcia, Jose	R-R	6-1	160	6-2-81	2	2	5.75	18	2	0	0	36	48	26	23	8	12	22	.336	.318	.343	5.50	3.00
Gregerson, Luke	L-R	6-3	200	5-14-84	0	0	0.00	1	0	0	0	1	1	0	0	0	1	3	.250	1.000	.000	27.00	9.00
Haberer, Eric	L-L	6-2	205	9-14-82	13	8	4.32	28	26	1	0	152	162	85	73	12	72	72	.284	.197	.308	4.26	4.26
Johnson, Tyler	B-L	6-2	200	6-7-81	0	0	3.00	3	1	0	0	3	2	1	1	0	2	3	.200	.000	.222	9.00	6.00
Lambert, Chris	R-R	6-1	205	3-8-83	0	2	3.42	5	5	0	0	26	24	11	10	5	8	17	.245	.245	.244	5.81	2.73
McClellan, Kyle	R-R	6-4	205	6-12-84	2	0	2.35	24	0	0	0	31	24	9	8	2	6	30	.214	.234	.200	8.80	1.76
Meaux, Ryan	R-R	5-11	170	10-5-78	0	0	4.91	4	0	0	0	4	4	2	2	0	2	2	.267	.286	.250	4.50	4.50
2-team (6 Midland)					0	1	9.26	10	0	0	0	12	18	12	12	2	3	9	—	—		6.94	2.31
Motte, Jason	R-R	6-0	200	6-22-82	3	3	2.20	44	0	0	8	49	36	13	12	3	22	63	.208	.222	.198	11.57	4.04
Ool, Kevin	L-L	5-11	185	1-4-81	4	2	5.08	21	8	0	0	57	80	43	32	4	17	35	.339	.284	.364	5.56	2.70
Perez, Chris	R-R	6-4	225	7-1-85	2	0	2.43	39	0	0	27	41	17	11	11	3	28	62	.126	.100	.141	13.72	6.20
Rauschenberger, Cory	R-R	6-1	185	7-31-84	11	8	4.68	28	26	1	0	144	148	85	75	16	53	79	.267	.325	.218	4.93	3.30
Rowlett, Casey	R-R	5-8	175	2-8-83	0	0	18.00	1	0	0	0	1	3	2	2	0	0	0	.500	1.000	.000	0.00	0.00
Russ, Chris	R-R	5-11	175	3-27-79	0	0	2.59	17	0	0	0	24	17	9	7	0	13	12	.198	.281	.148	4.44	4.81
Scherer, Matthew	R-R	6-5	230	1-20-83	4	3	3.60	55	0	0	1	70	70	31	28	6	24	69	.268	.345	.207	8.87	3.09
Sillman, Mike	R-R	6-1	190	12-3-81	1	1	6.52	9	0	0	2	10	14	7	7	1	10	11	.338	.250	.095	10.24	9.31
Stitt, Brian	R-R	5-11	201	8-26-82	1	0	4.67	10	0	0	0	17	19	9	9	3	4	11	.279	.391	.222	5.71	2.08
Walters, P.J.	R-R	6-4	200	3-12-85	3	4	2.37	8	8	1	0	49	42	13	13	4	15	37	.228	.290	.191	6.75	2.74
Webber, Nicholas	R-R	6-7	210	5-9-84	1	3	4.26	33	0	0	0	51	62	28	24	4	22	29	.308	.375	.271	5.15	3.91
Wellemeyer, Todd	R-R	6-3	225	8-30-78	0	0	0.00	1	1	0	0	1	3	0	0	0	1	2	.500	.333	.667	18.00	9.00
Zuercher, Zachary	L-L	6-2	215	4-10-84	3	0	2.68	37	0	0	1	44	37	15	13	3	22	28	.234	.167	.269	5.77	4.53

FIELDING

Catcher	PCT	G	PO	A	E	DP	PB
Anderson	.990	99	639	63	7	9	15
Guerrero	.981	17	92	11	2	1	2
Pagnozzi	.988	11	72	8	1	0	1
Sanchez	1.000	11	78	11	0	0	1

First Base	PCT	G	PO	A	E	DP
Ferris	.997	37	312	22	1	40
Hamilton	.987	62	562	27	8	59
Mather	.988	41	377	24	5	39
Washington	1.000	3	23	2	0	1

Second Base	PCT	G	PO	A	E	DP
Hoffpauir	.986	55	109	169	4	45
Lucena	.969	53	106	146	8	39

	PCT	G	PO	A	E	DP
McCoy	1.000	1	2	4	0	0
Rowlett	.965	37	72	92	6	26

Third Base	PCT	G	PO	A	E	DP
Craig	.833	4	1	9	2	1
Lucena	.940	24	19	60	5	3
McCoy	.833	6	0	5	1	1
Richardson	.933	90	46	191	17	20
Washington	.979	19	11	36	1	1

Shortstop	PCT	G	PO	A	E	DP
Greene	.962	62	113	213	13	55
Hoffpauir	1.000	1	2	3	0	2
Lucena	.889	5	6	10	2	1
Martinez	.972	66	97	218	9	53

	PCT	G	PO	A	E	DP
McCoy	1.000	4	0	8	0	0
Rowlett	.933	5	10	4	1	1

Outfield	PCT	G	PO	A	E	DP
Cazana Marti	.980	25	46	3	1	1
Danielson	.978	82	119	15	3	6
Encarnacion	1.000	13	21	1	0	0
Gorecki	.946	22	50	3	3	1
Haerther	1.000	31	40	0	0	0
Jay	1.000	24	41	1	0	0
Mather	1.000	28	34	4	0	2
McCoy	1.000	14	28	1	0	1
Rasmus	.978	123	261	11	6	3
Rowlett	.978	31	42	2	1	0
Shorey	.953	38	38	3	2	0

PALM BEACH CARDINALS　　　　　　　　　HIGH CLASS A

FLORIDA STATE LEAGUE

BATTING	B-T	HT	WT	DOB	AVG	vLH	vRH	G	AB	R	H	2B	3B	HR	RBI	BB	HBP	SH	SF	SO	SB	CS	SLG	OBP
Buckman, Brandon	L-L	6-6	205	2-14-84	.268	.283	.262	50	194	18	52	10	0	5	27	8	1	0	4	34	0	0	.397	.295
Cabrera, Jolbert	R-R	6-1	215	12-8-72	.000	—	.000	1	2	0	0	0	0	0	0	0	0	0	1	0	0	0	.000	.000
Church, Ian	R-R	5-10	181	2-28-81	.244	.220	.254	51	180	22	44	16	2	4	35	5	3	1	4	31	2	1	.422	.271
Contreras, Jose	B-R	6-0	170	4-26-85	.215	.174	.229	37	93	10	20	4	0	0	3	13	0	4	0	24	4	1	.258	.311
Craig, Allen	R-R	6-2	190	7-18-84	.312	.342	.301	112	423	77	132	25	2	21	77	35	6	0	4	79	8	3	.530	.370
Danielson, Sean	B-R	5-8	165	8-6-82	.355	.286	.375	12	31	9	11	1	0	0	2	1	0	1	0	5	5	0	.387	.375
Ferris, Michael	L-L	6-2	220	12-31-82	.212	.273	.182	9	33	3	7	2	0	1	9	2	0	0	2	4	0	0	.364	.243
Garcia, Isaias	R-R	5-10	180	8-20-84	.252	.225	.262	91	309	38	78	15	1	5	30	17	4	2	3	36	0	2	.356	.297
Gorsett, Luke	R-R	6-1	195	5-28-85	.310	.295	.315	47	171	15	53	12	2	5	33	7	4	1	1	25	6	5	.491	.350
Grossman, Chris	R-R	6-4	215	2-3-81	.319	.300	.327	21	69	11	22	5	0	4	7	2	0	1	0	11	0	0	.391	.382
Guerrero, Henry	R-R	6-0	189	4-4-82	.115	.000	.158	10	26	1	3	0	0	0	1	1	0	1	0	4	0	0	.115	.148
Hamilton, Mark	L-L	6-3	220	7-29-84	.290	.233	.311	60	221	31	64	12	0	13	49	20	1	0	2	48	1	0	.520	.348
Jay, Jonathan	L-L	6-0	200	3-15-85	.286	.250	.300	32	126	19	36	8	0	2	10	5	2	0	1	25	5	2	.397	.321
Martinez, Jose	R-R	5-11	175	1-24-86	.248	.215	.261	62	226	22	56	9	1	2	19	10	2	3	1	20	4	4	.323	.285
Nelson, Dan	B-R	5-11	180	2-12-84	.262	.235	.272	126	442	76	116	16	2	4	57	80	3	3	1	97	18	7	.335	.378
Rapoport, James	L-L	5-11	160	6-25-85	.236	.284	.218	89	347	43	82	6	5	0	23	33	3	5	1	71	21	7	.282	.307
Robinson, Shane	R-R	5-9	160	10-30-84	.253	.271	.246	43	166	22	42	6	1	3	13	16	2	3	3	16	14	4	.355	.321
Rowlett, Casey	R-R	5-8	175	2-8-83	.259	.268	.254	36	112	19	29	5	1	1	10	14	1	2	1	18	2	5	.348	.344
Sanchez, Danilo	R-R	5-11	230	10-25-80	.270	.174	.325	19	63	8	17	4	0	3	8	14	0	0	0	13	0	0	.476	.403
Shorey, Mark	L-L	6-0	200	8-13-84	.286	.316	.275	19	70	14	20	5	0	3	15	4	1	0	0	12	0	0	.486	.333
Solano, Donovan	R-R	5-10	165	12-17-87	.209	.216	.206	50	163	17	34	2	1	0	11	8	1	1	1	21	0	1	.233	.249
Southard, Nathan	R-R	5-10	185	10-27-83	.239	.315	.208	125	435	46	104	28	3	2	41	31	6	1	3	70	11	2	.331	.297
Van Slyke, A.J.	L-R	6-2	210	11-19-83	.283	.278	.284	109	371	40	105	26	1	3	31	29	1	0	3	78	18	4	.383	.334
Yarbrough, Brandon	L-R	6-2	180	11-9-84	.278	.241	.288	110	389	55	108	17	11	5	60	28	2	4	4	84	3	0	.416	.326

PITCHING	B-T	HT	WT	DOB	W	L	ERA	G	GS	CG	SV	IP	H	R	ER	HR	BB	SO	AVG	vLH	vRH	K/9	BB/9
Carpenter, Chris	R-R	6-6	230	4-27-75	0	1	6.23	2	2	0	0	4	7	5	3	0	1	4	.333	.333	.333	8.31	2.08
Cooper, Michael	R-R	6-2	205	2-2-84	1	1	5.02	25	0	0	0	38	49	25	21	2	20	23	.314	.316	.313	5.50	4.78
Daley, Gary	R-R	6-3	200	11-1-85	3	3	4.94	12	12	0	0	58	57	37	32	3	44	39	.273	.268	.277	6.02	6.79
Daniels, Adam	L-L	6-2	190	8-16-82	4	6	3.52	12	12	0	0	72	77	40	28	3	13	56	.272	.266	.274	7.03	1.63
Degerman, Eddie	R-R	6-4	205	9-14-83	4	4	5.93	11	10	0	0	55	50	41	36	3	36	57	.245	.217	.259	9.38	5.93
Furnish, Brad	B-L	6-1	185	1-19-85	3	3	4.91	8	5	0	0	37	33	22	20	3	22	24	.237	.263	.228	5.89	5.40
Gregerson, Luke	L-R	6-3	200	5-14-84	3	4	1.97	53	0	0	29	64	42	14	14	0	20	69	.188	.190	.187	9.70	2.81
Hearne, Trey	R-R	6-1	195	8-19-83	5	11	5.95	31	21	0	0	138	181	103	91	10	42	90	.323	.315	.329	5.88	2.75
McClellan, Kyle	R-R	6-4	205	6-12-84	4	1	1.24	16	1	0	0	29	22	4	4	0	4	24	.210	.238	.190	7.45	1.24
McCormick, Mark	R-R	6-2	195	10-15-83	0	0	0.00	1	1	0	0	3	2	0	0	0	0	2	.222	.500	.000	6.00	0.00
Mikrut, Jon	R-R	6-4	195	11-22-82	4	2	2.91	53	0	0	3	68	55	25	22	4	24	56	.218	.218	.219	7.41	3.18
Motte, Jason	R-R	6-0	200	6-22-82	1	0	0.90	9	0	0	3	10	7	2	1	0	1	6	.184	.188	.182	5.40	0.90
Mulder, Mark	L-L	6-6	215	8-5-77	0	2	1.93	3	3	0	0	9	7	6	2	0	3	5	.189	.125	.207	4.82	2.89
Narveson, Chris	L-L	6-3	205	12-20-81	0	0	2.70	3	3	0	0	10	10	4	3	1	3	6	.270	.375	.241	5.40	2.70
Norrick, Tyler	L-L	6-3	190	9-27-83	11	9	3.59	28	28	2	0	165	134	69	66	11	73	134	.221	.205	.227	7.29	3.97
Ottavino, Adam	R-R	6-5	215	11-22-85	12	8	3.08	27	27	1	0	143	130	63	49	10	63	128	.239	.253	.230	8.04	3.96
Pomeranz, Stuart	R-R	6-7	220	12-17-84	1	2	6.52	3	3	0	0	10	12	9	7	4	2	5	.300	.636	.172	4.66	1.86
Ransom, Robert	R-R	6-3	205	8-25-81	0	1	4.89	15	3	0	0	39	48	23	21	3	11	14	.320	.259	.354	3.26	2.56
Salas, Fernando	R-R	6-2	200	5-30-85	2	3	5.26	16	4	0	0	39	39	25	23	12	10	25	.260	.226	.284	5.72	2.29
Sanchez, Julio	R-R	6-1	158	7-11-85	0	0	13.50	2	0	0	0	3	3	4	4	0	2	1	.375	1.000	.286	3.38	6.75
Smith, Donnie	R-R	6-2	210	1-14-83	2	1	3.03	37	0	0	0	59	54	27	20	3	22	50	.242	.244	.241	7.58	3.34
Trent, Matthew	R-R	6-2	220	8-7-82	0	1	3.51	25	0	0	1	33	29	19	13	2	15	24	.228	.200	.244	6.48	4.05
Vander Weg, Scott	R-R	6-3	210	12-14-82	5	5	4.12	35	0	0	0	63	61	30	29	6	10	40	.245	.271	.229	5.68	1.42
Walters, P.J.	R-R	6-4	200	3-12-85	3	1	2.67	5	5	0	0	34	29	10	10	2	6	37	.225	.217	.229	9.89	1.60
Webber, Nicholas	R-R	6-7	210	5-9-84	2	0	4.63	8	0	0	0	12	9	7	6	0	7	11	.209	.304	.100	8.49	5.40
Zuercher, Zachary	L-L	6-2	215	4-10-84	1	0	2.84	5	0	0	0	6	4	2	2	0	2	4	.174	.000	.286	5.68	2.84

FIELDING

Catcher	PCT	G	PO	A	E	DP	PB
Grossman	.980	21	138	8	3	1	3
Guerrero	.983	10	55	4	1	2	1
Sanchez	.977	16	113	12	3	1	3
Yarbrough	.984	103	641	49	11	10	8

First Base	PCT	G	PO	A	E	DP
Buckman	.990	48	380	33	4	40
Craig	.992	16	113	7	1	16
Ferris	1.000	7	71	3	0	7
Hamilton	.991	36	324	21	3	26
Nelson	1.000	1	16	0	0	1
Van Slyke	.984	36	287	22	5	25

Second Base	PCT	G	PO	A	E	DP
Contreras	.914	9	11	21	3	8
Garcia	.970	82	143	218	11	55

	PCT	G	PO	A	E	DP
Martinez	1.000	3	2	5	0	0
Nelson	.965	32	59	79	5	16
Rowlett	.969	19	39	55	3	9
Solano	1.000	1	2	2	0	0

Third Base	PCT	G	PO	A	E	DP
Craig	.925	86	50	147	16	9
Garcia	.769	5	2	8	3	0
Nelson	.884	50	37	93	17	12
Rowlett	.900	3	2	7	1	0
Solano	1.000	2	2	5	0	0

Shortstop	PCT	G	PO	A	E	DP
Cabrera	—	1	0	0	0	0
Contreras	.927	27	34	81	9	16
Martinez	.969	58	82	164	8	30
Nelson	.875	14	10	25	5	3

	PCT	G	PO	A	E	DP
Solano	.938	47	72	138	14	33

Outfield	PCT	G	PO	A	E	DP
Church	1.000	48	79	2	0	0
Danielson	1.000	10	13	0	0	0
Gorsett	.988	47	75	5	1	1
Jay	1.000	8	12	0	0	0
Nelson	.967	27	29	0	1	0
Rapoport	.991	89	219	11	2	6
Robinson	.981	41	99	3	2	0
Rowlett	.917	13	22	0	2	0
Shorey	1.000	2	1	0	0	0
Southard	.996	125	249	10	1	1
Van Slyke	.979	28	44	2	1	0

SWING OF THE QUAD CITIES

LOW CLASS A

MIDWEST LEAGUE

BATTING	B-T	HT	WT	DOB	AVG	vLH	vRH	G	AB	R	H	2B	3B	HR	RBI	BB	HBP	SH	SF	SO	SB	CS	SLG	OBP
Alvarado, Wilmer	B-R	6-0	160	2-8-88	.200	.294	.179	27	95	7	19	6	0	0	7	7	2	0	1	25	1	0	.263	.267
Buckman, Brandon	L-L	6-6	205	2-14-84	.341	.308	.355	67	261	39	89	19	2	14	52	17	3	0	3	42	2	1	.590	.384
Cruz, Arnoldi	R-R	5-11	205	8-18-86	.282	.303	.271	49	195	26	55	10	1	5	34	17	1	0	3	25	3	1	.421	.338
DeJesus, Antonio	L-L	5-11	185	1-25-86	.262	.200	.289	42	130	30	34	4	0	1	17	22	3	1	3	29	9	4	.315	.373
Derba, Nicholas	R-R	5-10	190	9-9-85	.268	.240	.281	49	164	23	44	11	0	2	14	29	4	0	0	40	1	7	.372	.391
Dorn, Timothy	R-R	6-8	245	12-30-82	.196	.139	.232	28	92	11	18	5	1	2	9	16	2	0	1	33	1	1	.337	.324
Falcon, Omar	B-R	6-1	210	9-1-82	.253	.286	.242	24	83	11	21	3	0	3	11	11	2	0	0	38	0	0	.398	.354
Garcia, Jose	R-R	5-11	170	2-11-88	.202	.304	.164	33	84	10	17	4	0	0	5	7	1	2	1	18	3	4	.250	.269
Garcia, Isaias	R-R	5-10	180	8-20-84	.342	.000	.433	11	38	5	13	2	0	0	3	5	2	0	0	2	2	0	.395	.444
Gorsett, Luke	R-R	6-1	195	5-28-85	.286	.347	.263	77	266	40	76	21	2	4	18	12	10	0	3	44	1	0	.425	.337
Grossman, Chris	R-R	6-4	215	2-3-81	.277	.302	.268	65	231	25	64	14	0	6	42	20	3	0	3	36	0	0	.416	.339
Henley, Tyler	L-L	5-10	200	6-10-85	.156	.000	.172	12	32	4	5	2	0	2	5	1	1	1	1	9	0	0	.406	.200
Hill, Steve	R-R	5-11	190	3-14-85	.303	.304	.302	62	261	38	79	15	0	11	44	9	2	0	1	58	1	1	.487	.330
Jones, Daryl	L-L	5-11	180	6-25-87	.217	.222	.216	127	419	71	91	15	3	4	31	41	13	4	4	94	22	12	.296	.304
Landin, Jaime	R-R	5-10	175	4-19-84	.273	.352	.231	81	264	33	72	12	1	7	35	35	5	3	2	25	2	3	.405	.366
Lopez, Christian	R-R	6-0	162	1-23-87	.219	.250	.204	94	311	50	68	9	2	4	27	35	2	4	1	95	8	7	.299	.301
Marmol, Oliver	R-R	5-10	165	7-2-86	.209	.150	.227	31	86	12	18	3	1	0	7	7	4	2	1	13	4	2	.267	.296
Pham, Thomas	R-R	6-1	175	3-8-88	.063	.143	.040	14	32	3	2	0	0	1	3	2	0	0	9	3	0	.063	.189
Ramirez, Jose	R-R	5-11	175	3-12-85	.219	.196	.229	48	160	18	35	1	1	2	13	16	4	2	1	35	10	4	.275	.304
Rapoport, James	L-L	5-11	160	6-25-85	.219	.256	.205	43	160	22	35	6	1	1	8	13	0	1	1	35	10	2	.288	.267
Reyes, Christian	R-R	6-0	180	4-24-86	.273	.343	.245	100	374	39	102	14	0	12	63	20	3	0	4	93	0	1	.406	.312
Sandoval, Willian	B-R	5-10	170	12-27-85	.162	.106	.183	59	173	19	28	2	0	1	9	7	1	0	0	36	6	5	.191	.199
Schweitzer, Jared	R-R	6-1	185	10-13-83	.290	.350	.264	72	262	36	76	10	1	10	38	24	7	2	1	45	2	1	.450	.364
Shorey, Mark	L-L	6-0	180	8-13-84	.293	.286	.295	50	188	22	55	15	0	3	30	10	4	0	3	36	0	2	.420	.337
Solano, Donovan	R-R	5-10	165	12-17-87	.257	.244	.262	82	292	31	75	8	0	0	30	14	6	2	2	25	5	2	.284	.303

PITCHING	B-T	HT	WT	DOB	W	L	ERA	G	GS	CG	SV	IP	H	R	ER	HR	BB	SO	AVG	vLH	vRH	K/9	BB/9
Cairns, Jason	R-R	6-4	205	11-13-82	2	0	4.64	22	0	0	0	33	39	22	17	4	12	13	.293	.292	.294	3.55	3.27
Carrasco, Armando	R-R	6-1	205	7-1-85	6	2	2.19	41	0	0	0	53	52	18	13	4	26	49	.259	.253	.263	8.27	4.39
Degerman, Eddie	R-R	6-4	205	9-14-83	1	1	2.45	12	6	0	1	48	26	16	13	4	19	71	.160	.111	.192	13.41	3.59
Dickson, Brandon	R-R	6-5	190	11-3-84	11	7	3.50	31	23	0	1	144	148	74	56	9	41	84	.260	.217	.289	5.25	2.56
Dorn, Timothy	R-R	6-8	245	12-30-82	0	0	4.50	2	0	0	0	4	2	3	2	0	5	2	.154	.333	.000	4.50	11.25
Fick, Chuckie	R-R	6-5	187	11-11-85	1	0	2.16	9	0	0	0	25	27	10	6	1	5	13	.273	.400	.203	4.68	1.80
Furnish, Brad	B-L	6-1	185	1-19-85	3	3	2.42	21	12	0	2	82	56	31	22	7	27	76	.191	.183	.195	8.38	2.98
Garceau, Shaun	B-R	6-1	185	8-28-87	8	11	4.86	30	21	0	0	111	130	81	60	15	51	110	.293	.305	.284	8.92	4.14
Garcia, Jose	R-R	5-11	170	2-11-88	0	1	9.00	1	0	0	0	1	1	1	1	1	0	1	.250	.500	.000	9.00	0.00
Gonzalez, Marco	R-R	6-2	205	5-28-84	2	0	1.25	14	0	0	1	22	12	3	3	0	8	12	.162	.158	.167	4.98	3.32
Hernandez, Elvis	R-R	6-3	180	4-27-85	6	9	4.09	29	21	0	1	110	104	55	50	10	49	111	.246	.304	.203	9.08	4.01
Herron, Tyler	R-R	6-3	190	8-5-86	10	7	3.74	30	22	0	1	137	123	62	57	7	26	130	.240	.238	.242	8.52	1.70
King, Blake	R-R	6-1	195	4-11-87	2	3	5.21	19	9	0	0	57	44	36	33	3	44	62	.214	.224	.208	9.79	6.95
Lane, Matthew	R-R	6-8	225	8-17-84	2	0	4.50	7	0	0	0	8	10	4	4	1	5	5	.323	.389	.278	5.62	5.62
Maiques, Kenneth	R-R	6-1	185	6-25-85	1	5	1.53	52	0	0	31	53	34	16	9	3	20	57	.186	.171	.196	9.68	3.40
Mortensen, Clayton	R-R	6-4	180	4-10-85	0	2	3.12	10	10	0	0	40	44	17	14	2	8	45	.275	.278	.273	10.04	1.79
Mura, Kyle	R-R	6-4	215	11-24-84	7	0	1.66	45	0	0	3	60	44	12	11	2	13	63	.203	.194	.210	7.99	1.96
Sadlowski, Kyle	R-R	6-3	190	6-19-84	4	3	2.57	42	0	0	2	67	65	22	19	1	22	44	.261	.234	.277	5.94	2.97
Schellinger, Michael	R-R	6-2	190	12-2-82	6	4	3.62	33	5	0	1	75	74	36	30	4	23	64	.261	.200	.308	7.71	2.77
Schroeder, Brian	L-L	6-1	205	11-19-84	0	0	1.17	7	0	0	0	8	10	1	1	0	6	7	.333	.400	.300	8.22	7.04
Spade, Matt	L-L	5-11	180	4-26-87	0	2	11.25	3	1	0	0	4	9	7	5	1	2	4	.429	.250	.471	9.00	4.50
Walters, P.J.	R-R	6-4	200	3-12-85	6	1	2.62	17	10	0	1	69	59	25	20	2	12	73	.229	.215	.238	9.57	1.57

FIELDING

Catcher	PCT	G	PO	A	E	DP	PB
Alvarado	1.000	2	20	6	0	1	0
Derba	.994	39	280	44	2	6	4
Falcon	.987	17	141	13	2	2	4
Grossman	.985	52	414	53	7	3	6
Hill	1.000	13	76	10	0	1	4
Reyes	.994	19	158	19	1	2	2

First Base	PCT	G	PO	A	E	DP
Buckman	.994	57	478	52	3	39
Dorn	.973	21	201	12	6	17
Grossman	1.000	6	45	1	0	3
Hill	.995	27	209	9	1	19
Landin	1.000	1	9	2	0	0
Reyes	.988	20	160	6	2	15
Schweitzer	.992	13	111	12	1	8

Second Base	PCT	G	PO	A	E	DP
I. Garcia	.938	7	11	19	2	5

	PCT	G	PO	A	E	DP
J. Garcia	.954	19	32	51	4	10
Landin	.976	47	73	130	5	20
Lopez	.986	41	51	89	2	13
Schweitzer	.963	49	76	133	8	19

Third Base	PCT	G	PO	A	E	DP
Alvarado	.890	25	19	46	8	3
Cruz	.956	49	38	91	6	10
J. Garcia	1.000	3	1	3	0	1
Lopez	.800	3	2	2	1	0
Schweitzer	.750	1	0	3	1	0
Solano	.940	61	42	130	11	9

Shortstop	PCT	G	PO	A	E	DP
J. Garcia	.939	11	15	16	2	6
Lopez	.930	46	70	130	15	26
Marmol	.925	30	49	86	11	15
Sandoval	.956	47	60	115	8	15
Solano	.963	20	35	43	3	9

Outfield	PCT	G	PO	A	E	DP
DeJesus	.976	35	80	2	2	0
Gorsett	.981	71	94	7	2	1
Henley	.750	11	8	1	3	0
Hill	.927	26	34	4	3	0
Jones	.946	117	168	6	10	1
Landin	.964	22	23	4	1	1
Lopez	1.000	14	20	2	0	0
Pham	.923	12	11	1	1	0
Ramirez	.988	48	77	4	1	1
Rapoport	.935	38	71	1	5	0
Sandoval	.964	10	24	3	1	2
Shorey	.965	39	51	4	2	0

BATAVIA MUCKDOGS

SHORT-SEASON

NEW YORK-PENN LEAGUE

BATTING	B-T	HT	WT	DOB	AVG	vLH	vRH	G	AB	R	H	2B	3B	HR	RBI	BB	HBP	SH	SF	SO	SB	CS	SLG	OBP
Bolivar, Domnit	R-R	5-11	165	5-12-89	.181	.273	.120	24	83	9	15	1	1	0	2	5	2	1	0	26	2	1	.217	.244
Brown, Andrew	R-R	6-0	185	9-10-84	.238	.300	.208	66	239	34	57	14	7	7	40	31	3	0	3	52	1	2	.444	.330
Carpenter, David	R-R	6-2	200	7-15-85	.221	.237	.215	38	131	11	29	9	0	1	8	5	0	0	0	32	1	0	.313	.250
Cartie, Brian	R-R	6-0	190	4-2-85	.154	.333	.059	8	26	2	4	0	0	0	2	4	0	0	0	4	0	0	.154	.267
Cruz, Arnoldi	R-R	5-11	205	8-18-86	.375	—	.375	4	16	2	6	1	0	0	4	0	1	0	0	5	0	0	.438	.412
DeJesus, Antonio	L-L	5-11	185	1-25-86	.186	.214	.178	19	59	12	11	0	0	0	4	14	8	0	0	9	2	3	.186	.407
Derba, Nicholas	R-R	5-10	190	9-9-85	.267	.318	.237	19	60	7	16	7	0	1	8	12	3	0	0	15	0	1	.433	.413
Descalso, Daniel	L-R	5-10	190	10-19-86	.268	.250	.276	66	250	29	67	7	5	0	31	26	5	0	2	37	12	3	.336	.346
Edwards, Jonathan	R-R	6-5	230	1-8-88	.394	.385	.400	9	33	1	13	4	0	1	7	2	0	0	0	7	0	0	.606	.429
Fanning, Collin	R-R	6-2	180	9-21-85	.159	.192	.140	21	69	9	11	0	2	0	7	9	1	0	0	22	2	0	.217	.266
Folli, Mike	B-R	5-10	175	7-17-85	.222	.333	.167	6	27	3	6	1	1	0	3	1	0	0	0	6	2	0	.333	.250
Garcia, Jose	R-R	5-11	170	2-11-88	.375	.333	.389	6	24	4	9	1	0	0	4	2	0	0	0	2	1	2	.417	.423
Gonzalez, Steve	R-R	5-10	190	5-31-87	.176	.100	.204	23	74	4	13	1	0	0	4	5	2	1	0	20	0	1	.189	.247
Groff, William	R-R	5-11	180	11-17-84	.252	.300	.225	36	111	17	28	7	1	1	12	6	2	1	0	33	6	2	.360	.303
Henley, Tyler	L-L	5-10	200	6-10-85	.281	.250	.293	18	57	14	16	2	1	0	7	8	5	1	2	9	4	1	.351	.403
Hill, Steve	R-R	5-11	190	3-14-85	.436	.429	.440	10	39	4	17	5	1	1	11	5	1	0	0	5	0	0	.692	.511
Kozma, Peter	R-R	6-0	170	4-11-88	.148	.286	.100	8	27	1	4	0	1	0	2	1	0	0	0	7	1	1	.222	.179
Marmol, Oliver	R-R	5-10	165	7-2-86	.213	.184	.226	33	122	20	26	4	0	0	10	16	5	2	1	27	7	3	.246	.326
Marquez, Mateo	R-R	6-2	195	1-5-85	.191	.163	.204	44	136	8	26	8	2	1	17	9	6	1	1	49	2	2	.301	.270
Mitchell, Travis	R-R	6-3	185	9-27-87	.167	.182	.158	9	30	2	5	2	0	0	0	0	0	0	0	10	2	0	.233	.167
Oeder, Ross	R-R	5-8	165	4-19-85	.270	.298	.257	48	148	18	40	5	0	0	8	11	3	5	2	34	7	2	.304	.329
Pelt, Charlie	L-R	6-0	203	12-28-84	.212	.161	.228	40	132	10	28	8	2	1	13	4	0	0	4	44	0	1	.318	.302
Pham, Thomas	R-R	6-1	175	3-8-88	.205	.209	.203	67	239	33	49	8	5	2	16	25	1	1	0	60	14	6	.305	.283
Roberson, Justin	R-R	5-11	170	9-16-84	.255	.265	.250	55	196	26	50	12	3	2	22	15	2	3	0	44	6	2	.378	.315
Vasquez, Paul	R-R	5-10	160	3-7-85	.179	.071	.214	31	112	8	20	1	1	0	12	6	3	0	2	18	2	0	.205	.236

PITCHING	B-T	HT	WT	DOB	W	L	ERA	G	GS	CG	SV	IP	H	R	ER	HR	BB	SO	AVG	vLH	vRH	K/9	BB/9
Additon, Nicholas	L-L	6-3	170	12-16-87	1	0	0.00	5	2	0	0	5	2	0	0	0	1	5	.118	.167	.091	8.44	1.69
Andersen, Phillip	R-R	6-3	175	10-28-83	0	0	6.23	2	1	0	0	4	5	3	3	1	1	2	.294	.167	.364	4.15	2.08
Bilardello, Davis	L-L	6-3	190	12-3-84	3	2	4.15	26	0	0	1	30	30	18	14	1	16	18	.261	.179	.303	5.34	4.75
Broderick, Brian	R-R	6-6	205	9-1-86	1	1	3.48	8	4	0	0	31	31	13	12	5	3	30	.252	.280	.233	8.71	0.87
Collier, Logan	R-R	6-7	185	4-5-85	2	2	7.58	16	2	0	0	30	35	26	25	4	16	25	.297	.302	.292	7.58	4.85
Daman, Wayne	R-R	6-2	195	10-1-84	3	2	3.12	25	0	0	3	26	21	11	9	2	7	26	.221	.257	.200	9.00	2.42
Dew, Joshua	R-R	6-5	225	1-15-85	0	1	1.80	24	0	0	15	25	14	5	5	1	6	32	.159	.162	.157	11.52	2.16
Eager, Thomas	R-R	6-2	200	8-12-85	1	6	4.30	18	9	0	0	61	69	32	29	4	27	56	.291	.302	.284	8.31	4.01
Fiske, Justin	L-L	5-11	185	9-3-84	2	0	1.03	15	0	0	2	26	17	3	3	1	4	28	.187	.208	.179	9.57	1.37
Fritsche, Josh	R-L	6-1	225	11-22-84	0	4	6.00	12	1	0	0	18	25	14	12	2	8	19	.329	.308	.340	9.50	4.00
Garner, Brandon	R-R	6-0	165	8-27-86	3	5	4.37	18	9	0	1	58	66	35	28	6	19	32	.286	.347	.238	4.99	2.97
Gonzalez, Marco	R-R	6-2	205	5-28-84	0	0	2.70	4	0	0	0	3	8	3	1	0	0	3	.444	.571	.364	8.10	0.00
King, Blake	R-R	6-1	195	4-11-87	1	4	4.70	16	9	0	0	54	48	28	28	3	34	65	.240	.218	.257	10.90	5.70
Kopp, David	R-R	6-3	205	10-22-85	0	1	0.00	2	2	0	0	4	3	1	0	0	3	3	.200	.333	.111	6.75	6.75
Long, Clayton	R-R	6-0	195	9-19-85	0	6	4.66	19	8	0	1	58	64	36	30	6	33	47	.279	.364	.215	7.29	5.12
Maj, Jameson	R-R	6-4	225	10-22-85	0	0	0.00	2	0	0	0	1	2	0	0	0	2	1	.333	.667	.000	13.50	0.00
Mortensen, Clayton	R-R	6-4	180	4-10-85	1	1	1.77	6	4	0	0	20	13	4	4	0	11	23	.188	.195	.179	10.18	4.87
Parise, Pete	R-R	6-1	185	12-5-84	3	3	4.58	11	7	0	0	37	42	20	19	1	8	22	.288	.288	.288	5.30	1.93
Riddle, Ryan	L-L	6-2	180	6-10-85	2	1	5.48	15	0	0	0	21	28	17	13	1	11	19	.329	.320	.333	8.02	4.64
Stambaugh, Jonathan	L-L	6-2	200	10-25-84	3	2	3.15	17	9	0	0	66	72	26	23	3	8	53	.272	.328	.254	7.26	1.10
Todd, Jesse	R-R	5-11	210	4-20-86	4	1	2.78	16	7	0	0	58	48	23	18	2	14	69	.223	.297	.169	10.65	2.16
Wilson, Joshua	R-R	5-11	180	9-6-86	1	1	6.75	3	2	0	0	8	11	6	6	0	3	7	.306	.389	.222	7.88	3.38

FIELDING

Catcher	PCT	G	PO	A	E	DP	PB
Carpenter	.978	27	199	24	5	3	4
Derba	.976	14	107	13	3	1	1
Gonzalez	.980	18	127	19	3	2	5
Hill	1.000	2	10	2	0	0	1
Vasquez	.975	18	146	13	4	3	2

First Base	PCT	G	PO	A	E	DP
Brown	.993	51	410	31	3	34
Cruz	1.000	1	1	0	0	0
Hill	1.000	3	21	5	0	0
Pelt	.984	24	179	7	3	13

Second Base	PCT	G	PO	A	E	DP
Bolivar	1.000	2	2	4	0	0
Descalso	.961	22	36	63	4	17
Folli	.971	6	15	19	1	3

Garcia	.969	5	13	18	1	3
Groff	.923	16	19	29	4	5
Oeder	.944	28	23	61	5	10

Third Base	PCT	G	PO	A	E	DP
Bolivar	1.000	2	0	2	0	1
Brown	.966	14	13	15	1	0
Cartie	.875	8	5	16	3	1
Cruz	1.000	4	2	8	0	1
Descalso	.946	47	42	81	7	6
Oeder	1.000	4	3	8	0	1

Shortstop	PCT	G	PO	A	E	DP
Bolivar	.928	19	27	50	6	5
Garcia	1.000	1	1	2	0	1
Kozma	.727	8	5	19	9	1
Marmol	.931	32	54	95	11	20

Oeder	.908	15	26	33	6	8

Outfield	PCT	G	PO	A	E	DP
Brown	.833	2	5	0	1	0
DeJesus	.920	19	23	0	2	0
Edwards	1.000	5	10	1	0	0
Fanning	1.000	20	39	1	0	0
Groff	—	2	0	0	0	0
Henley	1.000	16	34	1	0	1
Hill	—	1	0	0	0	0
Marquez	.977	41	81	4	2	1
Mitchell	1.000	9	18	1	0	0
Pham	.992	64	110	11	1	2
Roberson	.981	51	99	4	2	1

JOHNSON CITY CARDINALS   ROOKIE

APPALACHIAN LEAGUE

BATTING	B-T	HT	WT	DOB	AVG	vLH	vRH	G	AB	R	H	2B	3B	HR	RBI	BB	HBP	SH	SF	SO	SB	CS	SLG	OBP
Alvarado, Wilmer	B-R	6-0	160	2-8-88	.146	.200	.132	16	48	8	7	3	0	0	5	7	3	0	0	13	1	0	.208	.293
Alvarez, Hector	B-R	6-0	175	1-25-87	.100	.250	.000	6	10	0	1	0	0	0	0	0	0	1	0	6	1	0	.100	.100
Arburr, Matthew	R-R	6-4	260	3-21-86	.207	.167	.226	44	135	17	28	8	2	5	20	14	0	0	1	56	0	0	.407	.280
Bolivar, Domnit	R-R	5-11	165	5-12-89	.240	.216	.250	39	129	11	31	6	1	1	17	4	2	4	3	26	3	1	.326	.268
Buck, Brian	R-R	6-1	190	2-3-86	.188	.250	.167	6	16	1	3	0	1	0	1	1	0	1	0	5	0	0	.313	.235
Castro, Ivan	R-R	6-0	185	11-17-87	.245	.267	.237	15	53	5	13	2	0	0	3	0	0	0	1	11	0	1	.283	.241
Chambers, Adron	L-L	5-10	185	10-8-86	.279	.242	.295	36	111	16	31	7	1	0	10	10	5	2	1	21	6	5	.360	.362
Cruz, Arnoldi	R-R	5-11	205	8-18-86	.280	.375	.235	6	25	2	7	2	0	2	2	2	0	0	0	2	1	0	.600	.333
Edwards, Jonathan	R-R	6-5	230	1-8-88	.245	.306	.223	55	188	27	46	12	1	7	33	28	2	0	2	68	0	3	.431	.345
Espinoza, Roberto	R-R	5-10	165	3-8-89	.145	.188	.130	23	62	6	9	1	0	1	1	6	1	1	0	23	1	1	.210	.232
Folli, Mike	B-R	5-10	175	7-17-85	.269	.141	.318	61	234	29	63	9	3	4	30	25	2	2	3	31	4	5	.385	.341
Garcia, Jose	R-R	5-11	170	2-11-88	.303	.263	.319	19	66	7	20	2	1	1	6	11	1	1	0	10	2	4	.409	.410
Hage, Joseph	R-R	6-0	180	2-17-89	.208	.154	.233	49	168	19	35	6	0	0	11	12	3	0	0	18	2	2	.244	.273
Kozma, Peter	R-R	6-0	170	4-11-88	.264	.176	.306	30	106	16	28	8	0	2	9	12	2	0	0	21	3	2	.396	.350
Mitchell, Travis	R-R	6-3	185	9-27-87	.293	.288	.295	54	191	19	56	10	2	1	16	8	1	6	1	48	10	5	.382	.323
Morales, Osvaldo	R-R	6-2	217	7-4-87	.213	.143	.242	17	47	8	10	5	0	3	6	7	0	0	0	21	0	0	.511	.315
Mulligan, Casey	R-R	6-2	190	10-5-87	.256	.186	.282	52	160	25	41	9	0	5	20	24	2	0	1	32	3	2	.406	.358
Pelt, Charlie	L-R	6-0	203	12-28-84	.406	.429	.400	9	32	4	13	3	0	1	9	6	0	0	0	10	0	0	.594	.500
Riportella , Beau	R-R	6-3	200	8-20-88	.315	.286	.325	48	168	31	53	4	1	2	15	13	1	1	1	31	10	2	.387	.366
Sanzillo, Robert	R-R	6-2	210	11-30-85	.136	.176	.122	24	66	9	9	2	0	0	5	9	3	0	0	22	2	1	.167	.269
Vasquez, Paul	R-R	5-10	160	3-7-85	.333	.538	.316	14	51	8	19	5	0	2	5	1	0	0	0	9	3	0	.588	.385
Vera, Nicholas	R-R	6-1	185	8-13-85	.286	.237	.307	58	199	27	57	11	0	4	29	17	1	0	3	35	4	3	.402	.341

PITCHING	B-T	HT	WT	DOB	W	L	ERA	G	GS	CG	SV	IP	H	R	ER	HR	BB	SO	AVG	vLH	vRH	K/9	BB/9
Additon, Nicholas	L-L	6-3	170	12-16-87	2	1	3.76	14	9	0	1	53	56	23	22	6	11	61	.267	.229	.274	10.42	1.88
Arredondo, Jose	R-R	6-1	166	9-3-87	5	5	3.04	15	8	0	1	56	44	27	19	4	14	41	.210	.200	.213	6.55	2.24
Broderick, Brian	R-R	6-6	205	9-1-86	2	2	1.75	8	5	0	0	36	31	12	7	3	4	23	.225	.288	.186	5.75	1.00
Diapoules, Mark	R-R	6-2	200	5-31-88	1	3	5.91	12	6	0	0	35	32	29	23	2	17	34	.234	.213	.244	8.74	4.37
Fick, Chuckie	R-R	6-5	187	11-11-85	1	0	1.29	8	0	0	2	14	9	3	2	0	6	12	.180	.250	.158	7.71	3.86
Gonzalez, Dylan	R-R	6-3	175	3-7-85	0	2	2.66	20	0	0	0	20	21	10	6	1	8	20	.273	.269	.275	8.85	3.54
Gonzalez, Reynier	R-R	6-3	180	11-5-88	1	1	5.06	3	2	0	0	11	12	7	6	1	7	9	.273	.313	.250	7.59	5.91
Hill, Steven	R-R	6-4	220	11-4-83	0	2	7.27	7	0	0	1	9	10	7	7	0	6	10	.303	.333	.296	10.38	6.23
Hodinka, Ryan	L-L	6-1	175	2-25-84	1	1	7.00	14	0	0	0	9	13	13	7	2	11	5	.325	.600	.286	5.00	11.00
Javier, Omar	R-R	6-3	165	10-4-87	0	8	6.66	14	8	0	1	51	61	44	38	6	30	30	.296	.280	.305	5.26	5.26
Leach, Tyler	R-R	6-3	200	9-8-86	2	3	5.30	13	8	0	1	36	36	24	21	2	21	22	.261	.259	.262	5.55	5.30
Mateo, Jose	R-R	6-2	180	8-31-86	4	2	3.41	15	10	0	0	61	57	35	23	2	24	44	.244	.250	.240	6.53	3.56
Mayes, LaCurtis	R-R	5-11	185	8-2-88	0	2	4.56	18	0	0	1	24	30	18	12	3	20	18	.323	.231	.358	6.85	7.61
Mendoza, Wladimir	L-L	6-0	160	5-20-86	1	0	6.97	10	0	0	0	10	4	10	8	1	17	12	.133	.000	.190	10.45	14.81
Parise, Pete	R-R	6-1	185	12-5-84	0	0	2.08	4	0	0	2	4	4	1	1	0	1	3	.250	.375	.125	6.23	2.08
Peralta, Senger	L-L	6-1	160	8-14-87	1	5	5.81	15	8	0	0	53	55	40	34	5	29	56	.270	.375	.250	9.57	4.96
Pichardo, Joel	R-R	5-11	160	2-20-88	2	1	1.64	15	0	0	0	22	22	8	4	3	5	11	.256	.333	.220	4.50	2.05
Rosales, Andres	R-R	6-0	140	6-13-88	1	0	2.79	7	4	0	0	29	23	9	9	0	5	38	.223	.098	.306	11.79	1.55
Sanchez, Eduardo	R-R	5-11	155	2-16-89	2	1	1.17	12	0	0	5	15	8	2	2	0	3	22	.154	.214	.132	12.91	1.76
Silva, Ray	R-R	6-4	250	2-21-84	2	1	6.14	21	0	0	1	22	23	19	15	1	13	16	.256	.240	.262	6.55	5.32
Spade, Matt	L-L	5-11	180	4-26-87	0	0	2.25	9	0	0	2	8	6	2	2	0	3	5	.207	.286	.182	5.62	3.38

FIELDING

Catcher	PCT	G	PO	A	E	DP	PB
Alvarado	1.000	1	1	0	0	0	1
Castro	.985	15	123	9	2	0	4
Espinoza	.968	22	104	18	4	0	4
Mitchell	.917	1	10	1	1	0	0
Mulligan	.985	29	180	15	3	2	8
Sanzillo	.900	3	9	0	1	0	0
Vasquez	.960	13	62	10	3	1	1

First Base	PCT	G	PO	A	E	DP
Arburr	.979	27	222	10	5	21
Morales	1.000	11	81	6	0	10
Mulligan	1.000	9	90	6	0	6
Pelt	.966	9	80	5	3	11
Vera	1.000	26	157	4	0	16

Second Base	PCT	G	PO	A	E	DP
Alvarez	1.000	2	0	2	0	0

	PCT	G	PO	A	E	DP
Bolivar	.920	3	13	10	2	2
Folli	.967	51	105	156	9	43
Garcia	.971	14	24	42	2	4
Vera	1.000	1	0	1	0	0

Third Base	PCT	G	PO	A	E	DP
Alvarado	.820	14	10	31	9	4
Alvarez	—	1	0	0	0	0
Arburr	—	1	0	0	0	0
Cruz	.958	6	4	19	1	3
Folli	.864	10	3	16	3	0
Garcia	—	1	0	0	0	0
Mulligan	.933	18	9	33	3	3
Vera	.864	28	21	55	12	7

Shortstop	PCT	G	PO	A	E	DP
Alvarez	1.000	3	0	6	0	1
Bolivar	.901	36	52	94	16	20

	PCT	G	PO	A	E	DP
Folli	1.000	1	0	1	0	0
Garcia	.960	4	12	12	1	5
Kozma	.906	30	28	87	12	16

Outfield	PCT	G	PO	A	E	DP
Buck	.600	5	3	0	2	0
Chambers	.926	30	47	3	4	0
Edwards	.930	43	49	4	4	2
Espinoza	1.000	1	3	1	0	0
Hage	.942	38	44	5	3	0
Mitchell	.962	53	94	6	4	2
Riportella	.969	43	61	2	2	0
Vera	1.000	8	10	1	0	1

GCL CARDINALS

ROOKIE

GULF COAST LEAGUE

BATTING	B-T	HT	WT	DOB	AVG	vLH	vRH	G	AB	R	H	2B	3B	HR	RBI	BB	HBP	SH	SF	SO	SB	CS	SLG	OBP
Alvarez, Hector	B-R	6-0	175	1-25-87	.125	.000	.250	12	24	2	3	0	0	0	3	2	0	0	0	10	2	0	.125	.192
Buck, Brian	R-R	6-1	190	2-3-86	.257	.235	.264	32	70	17	18	4	1	0	9	11	4	2	0	22	5	1	.343	.388
Cabrera, Juan	R-R	6-2	197	3-15-88	.227	.150	.261	27	66	6	15	3	0	0	4	4	2	0	0	29	1	1	.273	.292
Carpenter, David	R-R	6-2	200	7-15-85	.000	—	.000	2	1	0	0	0	0	0	0	0	0	0	0	1	0	0	.000	.000
Castro, Ivan	R-R	6-0	185	11-17-87	.203	.261	.167	20	59	1	12	2	0	0	2	1	0	0	2	8	1	2	.237	.210
Conde, Edwin	R-R	6-1	165	4-7-87	.173	.111	.193	28	75	7	13	4	1	1	11	7	1	0	1	32	1	1	.293	.250
Cruz, Arnoldi	R-R	5-11	205	8-18-86	.375	.500	.346	7	32	8	12	5	0	0	4	1	0	0	1	7	1	0	.531	.382
De La Cruz, Luis	R-R	5-10	164	5-6-89	.281	.200	.303	39	96	10	27	6	2	0	9	7	1	1	0	16	3	3	.385	.337
Espinoza, Roberto	R-R	5-10	165	3-8-89	.053	.000	.063	7	19	2	1	0	0	0	0	4	0	0	0	5	1	0	.053	.217
Gorecki, Reid	R-R	6-1	180	12-22-80	.313	.364	.286	10	32	7	10	5	0	0	5	4	0	0	0	4	0	0	.469	.389
Haerther, Cody	L-R	6-1	205	7-14-83	.333	.000	.444	4	12	1	4	1	1	0	1	1	0	0	0	1	0	0	.583	.385
Hage, Joseph	R-R	6-0	180	2-17-89	.393	.286	.429	7	28	8	11	1	1	2	6	2	1	0	0	1	0	0	.714	.452
Haran, Gerard	R-R	6-0	210	9-28-85	.194	.200	.192	12	31	3	6	2	0	1	3	7	0	0	0	6	0	0	.355	.342
Hiraldo, Braulio	B-R	5-11	179	7-18-88	.202	.182	.210	30	84	8	17	1	1	1	5	11	0	1	0	22	4	0	.274	.295
Ingram, D' Marcus	R-R	5-9	170	3-30-88	.325	.235	.360	39	120	22	39	4	0	0	10	19	3	1	0	15	17	5	.358	.430
Jay, Jonathan	L-L	6-0	200	3-15-85	.500	1.000	.000	1	2	0	1	0	0	0	0	0	0	0	0	0	0	0	.500	.500
Kingrey, Charles	L-L	6-2	210	1-19-85	.150	.200	.133	9	20	2	3	0	0	0	3	2	0	0	2	9	0	0	.150	.208
Kozma, Peter	R-R	6-0	170	4-11-88	.154	.286	.000	4	13	4	2	0	0	0	2	0	0	0	2	0	0	.154	.267
Lara, Edgar	R-R	6-3	210	3-2-89	.256	.222	.270	49	160	25	41	7	4	8	32	15	2	0	1	55	0	2	.500	.326
Martinez, Jairo	R-R	6-1	180	5-27-87	.272	.313	.250	31	92	10	25	4	1	1	17	6	5	0	0	34	3	0	.370	.350
Morales, Osvaldo	R-R	6-2	217	7-4-87	.290	.295	.287	39	131	17	38	9	0	8	29	20	0	1	0	43	2	1	.542	.384
Parejo, Frederick	R-R	6-0	165	7-5-90	.203	.182	.212	39	118	14	24	3	0	0	5	11	3	0	1	23	1	1	.229	.286
Robinson, Shane	R-R	5-9	160	10-30-84	.182	.000	.286	4	11	1	2	0	0	0	1	2	0	0	1	1	0	0	.182	.286
Rosario, Rainel	R-R	6-0	188	3-29-89	.096	.133	.067	28	52	4	5	1	1	0	2	6	1	0	0	26	1	0	.154	.203
Ruiz, Romulo	R-R	6-0	170	11-30-89	.190	.111	.218	43	137	13	26	3	2	0	13	9	2	4	2	26	4	2	.241	.247
Schonenberg, Carlos	R-R	6-1	168	8-14-86	.143	.000	.176	16	42	3	6	1	0	1	4	2	1	0	0	13	0	0	.238	.250
Thomas, Scott	L-R	5-11	202	3-5-87	.385	.167	.450	10	26	3	10	1	0	0	6	1	0	0	0	7	0	0	.423	.407
Toribio, Guillermo	B-R	6-0	160	3-3-87	.257	.227	.268	53	171	29	44	5	0	0	14	34	3	4	0	49	8	5	.287	.389
Washington, Rico	L-R	5-9	195	5-30-78	.429	.500	.400	6	14	6	6	0	1	1	5	5	0	0	0	1	0	0	.786	.579

PITCHING	B-T	HT	WT	DOB	W	L	ERA	G	GS	CG	SV	IP	H	R	ER	HR	BB	SO	AVG	vLH	vRH	K/9	BB/9
Andersen, Phillip	R-R	6-3	175	10-28-83	1	0	1.59	5	0	0	0	6	3	1	1	1	1	8	.150	.000	.214	12.71	1.59
Blazek, Michael	R-R	6-0	180	3-16-89	3	3	2.60	10	3	0	0	35	33	13	10	1	13	42	.254	.356	.200	10.90	3.38
Cardenas, Hector	L-L	6-3	180	12-14-86	1	5	4.98	13	2	0	0	34	28	24	19	3	21	31	.220	.280	.206	8.13	5.50
Conde, Edwin	R-R	6-1	165	4-7-87	0	0	6.75	1	0	0	0	1	3	1	1	0	1	0	.429	.500	.400	0.00	6.75
Daley, Gary	R-R	6-3	200	11-1-85	0	2	15.43	5	4	0	0	14	18	28	24	0	18	14	.305	.211	.350	9.00	11.57
Delgado, Ramon	R-R	6-3	195	9-3-86	0	0	4.50	10	0	0	0	10	9	5	5	0	5	11	.225	.182	.241	9.90	4.50
Gonzalez, Carlos	R-R	6-3	145	8-31-88	4	2	2.94	13	6	0	1	49	39	16	16	3	16	47	.217	.300	.185	8.63	2.94
Gonzalez, Reynier	R-R	6-3	180	11-5-88	2	0	1.01	10	3	0	0	36	31	6	4	0	14	34	.238	.162	.269	8.58	3.53
Hodinka, Ryan	L-L	6-1	175	2-25-84	0	0	9.00	1	0	0	0	1	2	1	1	0	0	2	.400	1.000	.250	18.00	0.00
Hooker, Deryk	R-R	6-4	185	6-21-89	1	1	2.32	10	3	0	0	31	28	13	8	1	11	47	.237	.071	.329	13.65	3.19
Lugo, Rigoberto	R-R	5-11	196	3-7-89	2	2	6.98	14	1	0	4	19	19	17	15	3	19	17	.250	.292	.231	7.91	8.84
Marquez, Fabian	R-R	6-1	170	11-12-86	2	2	5.01	12	7	0	0	32	35	24	18	2	25	22	.273	.282	.270	6.12	6.96
Martinez, Gustavo	R-R	6-2	172	4-30-88	0	2	9.39	8	1	0	0	15	23	18	16	0	13	5	.343	.579	.250	2.93	7.63
McCormick, Mark	R-R	6-2	195	10-31-83	0	0	1.93	3	3	0	0	5	1	2	1	0	2	4	.067	.000	.071	7.71	3.86
Mendoza, Wladimir	L-L	6-0	160	5-20-86	1	0	6.75	9	0	0	0	7	5	7	5	0	9	10	.217	.200	.231	13.50	12.15
North, Matthew	R-R	6-5	170	5-23-88	0	2	4.50	5	2	0	0	10	15	11	5	1	2	10	.341	.500	.316	9.00	1.80
Ortiz, Pablo	R-R	6-4	175	6-11-88	1	2	4.32	12	2	0	0	25	31	19	12	4	12	29	.304	.455	.232	10.44	4.32
Pichardo, Joel	R-R	5-11	160	2-20-88	0	0	0.00	6	0	0	0	3	2	0	0	0	6	9	.214	.333	.182	11.05	7.36
Pomeranz, Stuart	R-R	6-7	220	12-17-84	0	0	5.79	3	3	0	0	5	4	3	3	1	1	4	.250	.000	.400	7.71	1.93
Rada, Jose	R-R	6-1	180	4-13-88	1	2	5.51	8	1	0	0	16	23	10	10	0	5	20	.338	.300	.354	11.02	2.76
Rosales, Andres	R-R	6-0	140	6-13-88	1	0	0.43	6	4	1	0	21	15	2	1	1	3	26	.197	.348	.132	11.14	1.29
Russell, Ronald	R-R	6-2	185	7-27-89	0	0	3.86	8	0	0	0	7	7	3	3	0	12	8	.269	.333	.250	10.29	15.43
Samuel, Francisco	R-R	6-1	150	12-26-86	0	4	9.53	13	6	0	0	34	43	42	36	2	35	40	.309	.295	.316	10.59	9.26
Sanchez, Eduardo	R-R	5-11	155	2-16-89	0	1	1.50	7	0	0	0	6	2	2	1	0	1	6	.100	.500	.056	10.50	9.00
Sanchez, Julio	R-R	6-1	158	7-11-85	1	0	1.23	9	0	0	5	7	7	5	1	1	3	11	.241	.111	.300	13.50	3.68
Sillman, Mike	R-R	6-1	190	12-3-81	0	0	0.00	3	0	0	0	4	3	0	0	0	1	5	.250	.333	.222	11.25	2.25
Spade, Matt	L-L	5-11	180	4-26-87	3	0	0.75	12	0	0	0	12	9	1	1	1	3	14	.225	.333	.179	10.50	2.25
Zawacki, Brett	R-R	6-1	190	5-2-89	0	0	3.00	2	0	0	0	3	3	1	1	0	2	3	.250	.000	.333	9.00	6.00

FIELDING

Catcher	PCT	G	PO	A	E	DP	PB
Carpenter	1.000	2	7	1	0	0	1
Castro	.987	18	132	17	2	2	2
De La Cruz	.975	36	244	32	7	2	4
Espinoza	.980	7	47	1	1	1	3
Haran	1.000	5	26	0	0	0	2
Thomas	1.000	4	29	2	0	0	1

First Base	PCT	G	PO	A	E	DP
Conde	1.000	22	108	14	0	10
Haran	.939	7	28	3	2	6
Kingrey	1.000	1	1	0	0	0
Morales	.984	28	175	11	3	5
Rosario	1.000	1	2	0	0	0
Schonenberg	1.000	5	19	0	0	3
Thomas	.938	4	15	0	1	0

Second Base	PCT	G	PO	A	E	DP
Alvarez	.885	7	15	8	3	3
Castro	.500	1	1	0	1	0
Gorecki	—	1	0	0	0	0

Hiraldo	.968	18	33	28	2	6
Lara	1.000	1	2	1	0	1
Parejo	1.000	1	2	1	0	0
Toribio	.955	38	71	57	6	10

Third Base	PCT	G	PO	A	E	DP
Alvarez	—	2	0	0	0	0
Buck	—	1	0	0	0	0
Cabrera	.959	25	14	33	2	2
Cruz	.857	7	4	14	3	2
Hiraldo	1.000	5	0	2	0	0
Martinez	—	1	0	0	0	0
Morales	.795	14	8	23	8	4
Ruiz	.900	12	9	9	2	1
Schonenberg	1.000	1	0	2	0	0
Washington	1.000	4	2	4	0	0

Shortstop	PCT	G	PO	A	E	DP
Alvarez	1.000	3	3	2	0	1
Hiraldo	1.000	1	2	1	0	0
Kozma	.933	3	6	8	1	3

Ruiz	.921	35	45	71	10	12
Toribio	.880	20	14	52	9	4

Outfield	PCT	G	PO	A	E	DP
Buck	.978	27	43	2	1	0
Conde	—	1	0	0	0	0
Gorecki	1.000	6	8	0	0	0
Haerther	1.000	4	4	0	0	0
Hage	1.000	6	7	3	0	0
Hiraldo	1.000	1	1	0	0	0
Ingram	.985	36	62	4	1	1
Kingrey	1.000	3	4	0	0	0
Kozma	—	1	0	0	0	0
Lara	.951	32	36	3	2	0
Martinez	.938	10	14	1	1	0
Parejo	.943	36	62	4	4	1
Robinson	1.000	4	8	0	0	0
Rosario	1.000	22	12	0	0	0
Schonenberg	1.000	6	4	1	0	1

DSL CARDINALS

ROOKIE

DOMINICAN SUMMER LEAGUE

BATTING	B-T	HT	WT	DOB	AVG	vLH	vRH	G	AB	R	H	2B	3B	HR	RBI	BB	HBP	SH	SF	SO	SB	CS	SLG	OBP
Avila, Michael	R-R	6-0	160	9-7-89	.167	.111	.179	37	96	12	16	0	1	1	5	13	4	4	0	31	3	2	.219	.292
Cabrera, Juan	R-R	6-2	197	3-15-88	.165	.118	.177	22	79	3	13	1	0	0	8	4	2	1	0	25	0	0	.177	.224
Cabrera, Juan B	R-R	6-1	151	6-22-88	.220	.318	.200	47	127	19	28	4	0	1	9	17	2	2	1	31	4	2	.276	.320
Castillo, Juan	R-R	5-11	160	12-13-89	.292	.214	.305	57	192	24	56	8	0	2	36	28	4	1	3	21	3	0	.365	.388
Garay, Bernardo	R-L	6-4	190	4-30-87	.203	.286	.183	32	74	14	15	2	0	1	6	13	8	1	0	31	4	2	.270	.379
Gomez, Edwin	R-R	5-11	170	3-10-88	.298	.333	.292	50	168	38	50	13	0	4	32	39	4	0	1	35	13	4	.446	.439
Ito, Ramon	R-R	6-0	170	3-31-89	.098	.125	.094	27	61	10	6	1	2	0	3	17	1	1	0	29	1	0	.180	.304
Martina, Hayrich	R-R	6-0	170	8-3-90	.088	.000	.100	31	80	2	7	0	0	0	4	8	2	0	1	26	0	3	.088	.187
Martina, Quincy	B-R	6-0	155	2-14-87	.171	.429	.107	10	35	5	6	0	0	0	3	5	0	0	0	8	0	0	.171	.275
Martinez, Marcos	R-R	6-5	195	3-3-89	.094	.000	.107	34	85	6	8	2	0	1	5	9	0	0	2	46	0	0	.153	.177
Medina, David	L-L	6-3	162	1-1-89	.226	.146	.246	64	208	26	47	9	0	0	33	45	4	2	3	61	4	4	.269	.369
Montiel, Edgard	R-R	6-0	170	1-13-88	.244	.318	.233	53	168	19	41	9	0	1	24	27	8	3	2	19	3	2	.315	.371
Montilla, Jahir	R-R	6-1	191	12-24-88	.241	.217	.245	43	133	9	32	3	1	0	16	6	1	0	1	44	4	1	.278	.277
Mosquera, Juan	B-R	5-10	154	1-23-88	.299	.296	.300	49	157	42	47	4	1	0	13	51	6	4	1	39	18	10	.338	.484
Obregon, Ted	B-R	5-11	170	5-4-90	.229	.300	.217	23	70	14	16	2	0	0	7	16	2	4	0	16	7	4	.257	.386
Pasen, Jose	R-R	6-1	180	5-19-90	.165	.211	.157	51	127	8	21	1	0	0	6	26	1	1	2	45	4	3	.173	.308
Polanco, Jeudis	R-R	6-1	190	6-16-90	.273	.167	.291	44	128	14	35	4	1	0	14	15	2	0	1	9	0	0	.320	.356

PITCHING	B-T	HT	WT	DOB	W	L	ERA	G	GS	CG	SV	IP	H	R	ER	HR	BB	SO	AVG	vLH	vRH	K/9	BB/9
Corpas, Hector	R-R	6-3	170	1-5-90	0	1	6.49	9	1	0	1	26	32	20	19	3	11	15	.296	.357	.287	5.13	3.76
Cruz, Angel	R-R	6-4	200	4-25-88	4	4	3.76	13	4	0	0	41	43	23	17	2	16	41	.256	.167	.267	9.07	3.54
Grullion, Edwin	R-R	5-11	158	8-16-87	2	2	6.14	12	6	0	0	37	39	32	25	0	27	35	.265	.111	.287	8.59	6.63
Jaquez, Juan	R-R	6-0	172	11-7-86	1	2	6.59	17	1	0	2	27	22	24	20	0	34	30	.218	.083	.236	9.88	11.20
Maza, Julio	R-R	6-3	193	7-5-89	1	1	6.65	15	1	0	0	23	23	21	17	2	21	20	.267	.182	.280	7.83	8.22
Mejia, Carlos	R-R	6-2	180	11-28-88	5	2	4.28	20	2	0	4	48	33	28	23	5	38	42	.194	.095	.208	7.82	7.08
Nieto, Arquimedes	R-R	6-0	175	4-28-89	4	2	2.73	13	10	0	0	59	56	22	18	3	13	56	.247	.231	.249	8.49	1.97
Pinales, Alejandro	R-R	6-4	228	9-21-88	3	5	4.15	15	8	0	1	43	47	25	20	2	22	40	.267	.458	.237	8.31	4.57
Rosario, Jose	R-R	5-11	190	8-30-88	4	7	3.52	17	10	1	0	72	77	43	28	3	28	48	.278	.143	.298	6.03	3.52
Santos, Randy	R-R	6-2	190	8-21-88	2	4	3.92	14	10	2	1	64	52	36	28	0	27	66	.220	.423	.195	9.23	3.78
Santos, Walter	L-L	5-11	150	10-28-89	0	1	7.50	6	3	0	1	12	15	10	10	1	9	13	.326	.250	.342	9.75	6.75
Tapia, Angel	B-R	6-0	200	2-6-88	3	3	3.34	21	4	0	7	59	51	31	22	1	29	57	.233	.292	.226	8.65	4.40
Urena, Ramon	R-R	6-0	170	2-25-90	1	1	2.64	7	5	0	0	31	27	12	9	0	17	29	.235	.308	.225	8.51	4.99

FIELDING

Catcher	PCT	G	PO	A	E	DP	PB
Castillo	.971	35	250	55	9	1	9
Montiel	.971	12	77	24	3	2	1
Polanco	.978	24	144	38	4	2	3

First Base	PCT	G	PO	A	E	DP
J. Cabrera	.983	9	56	1	1	4
J.B. Cabrera	.950	2	19	0	1	1
Castillo	1.000	1	3	0	0	1
Garay	.961	9	47	2	2	6
Martinez	.989	27	167	13	2	17
Medina	.982	6	53	3	1	6
Montiel	.990	28	196	8	2	11

Second Base	PCT	G	PO	A	E	DP
Avila	.946	35	42	64	6	11

J. Cabrera	1.000	3	6	7	0	1
J.B. Cabrera	.968	23	45	47	3	5
H. Martina	1.000	6	10	7	0	1
Mosquera	.957	5	13	9	1	0
Obregon	1.000	11	24	15	0	5

Third Base	PCT	G	PO	A	E	DP
J. Cabrera	.811	13	5	25	7	4
J.B. Cabrera	1.000	1	0	1	0	0
Ito	.892	25	18	40	7	4
H. Martina	.794	20	16	38	14	2
Montiel	.929	16	10	29	3	3
Mosquera	.857	4	1	5	1	2

Shortstop	PCT	G	PO	A	E	DP
J. Cabrera	.667	1	0	4	2	0

J.B. Cabrera	.870	13	19	28	7	4
Mosquera	.948	41	83	119	11	24
Obregon	.922	14	19	40	5	6

Outfield	PCT	G	PO	A	E	DP
J. Cabrera	—	1	0	0	0	0
Garay	1.000	25	19	4	0	0
Gomez	.970	50	91	7	3	1
H. Martina	1.000	2	3	0	0	0
Q. Martina	.947	10	17	1	1	1
Martinez	—	3	0	0	0	0
Medina	.919	59	63	5	6	1
Montilla	.933	21	27	1	2	1
Pasen	.940	50	61	2	4	0
Polanco	—	1	0	0	0	0

VENEZUELAN SUMMER LEAGUE

BATTING	B-T	HT	WT	DOB	AVG	vLH	vRH	G	AB	R	H	2B	3B	HR	RBI	BB	HBP	SH	SF	SO	SB	CS	SLG	OBP
Alcala, Yorbel	B-R	6-0	160	1-17-90	.146	.125	.162	47	130	13	19	1	2	0	8	11	11	1	0	33	0	0	.185	.270
Bolivar, Billy	R-R	5-11	170	2-18-88	.215	.241	.204	56	195	20	42	8	0	0	23	17	6	1	3	32	8	2	.256	.294
Cardona, Ismael	R-R	5-10	175	4-22-89	.300	.388	.265	68	237	29	71	10	0	3	38	31	9	2	4	48	2	3	.380	.395
Chavez, Marcos	R-R	5-10	170	5-19-89	.065	.000	.087	13	31	1	2	0	0	0	2	3	1	2	0	11	0	0	.065	.171
Cortez, Jose	R-R	6-0	165	1-29-89	.246	.220	.256	54	167	10	41	11	1	1	18	12	7	0	2	34	2	2	.341	.319
Fonseca, Anthony	R-R	6-1	175	2-8-89	.222	.171	.250	41	99	10	22	1	0	0	4	9	4	3	0	17	5	5	.232	.313
Garcia, Hector	R-R	6-1	185	5-16-90	.174	.217	.159	25	92	8	16	3	0	2	9	8	0	0	0	18	1	0	.272	.240
Guzman, Francisco	R-R	6-0	180	2-20-88	.094	.000	.143	15	32	2	3	0	0	0	2	0	1	0	1	7	0	0	.094	.118
Jaspe, Peter	B-R	6-2	162	2-27-90	.186	.156	.198	52	161	24	30	3	0	1	9	18	11	2	1	52	3	0	.224	.309
Mannbel, Gerardo	R-R	5-11	165	5-16-90	.252	.290	.235	66	218	36	55	7	1	0	13	41	10	2	2	26	4	4	.294	.391
Obregon, Ted	B-R	5-9	170	5-4-90	.218	.300	.183	47	133	16	29	9	1	0	12	14	4	3	0	31	6	1	.301	.311
Perez, Roberto	R-R	6-0	185	8-31-88	.155	.150	.158	43	116	13	18	4	0	2	13	15	4	0	1	36	0	0	.241	.272
Perez, Wilson	R-R	6-2	180	5-30-89	.096	.000	.132	28	52	3	5	0	0	0	2	6	0	0	0	25	0	0	.096	.190
Rivero, Alberto	L-L	5-10	155	4-30-89	.264	.305	.243	53	174	26	46	5	3	1	16	28	6	3	1	34	1	3	.345	.383
Teran, Kleininger	L-R	6-1	175	7-23-89	.267	.243	.277	69	243	32	65	15	0	1	24	47	2	5	1	38	5	4	.342	.389
Vivas, Wilfred	R-R	5-11	160	11-8-89	.265	.303	.252	47	136	24	36	6	0	0	8	18	1	5	0	34	4	5	.309	.355

PITCHING	B-T	HT	WT	DOB	W	L	ERA	G	GS	CG	SV	IP	H	R	ER	HR	BB	SO	AVG	vLH	vRH	K/9	BB/9
Brito, David	R-R	6-1	175	11-12-88	1	3	6.20	20	0	0	1	25	39	21	17	2	9	12	.364	.286	.392	4.38	3.28
Calero, Jose	R-R	6-3	185	3-7-90	2	7	6.39	17	10	0	1	49	60	49	35	2	31	38	.302	.338	.282	6.93	5.66
Castillo, Richard	R-R	5-11	165	10-11-89	2	2	1.72	17	8	0	2	63	40	20	12	3	22	60	.183	.125	.206	8.62	3.16
Cedeno, Fernando	R-R	6-1	186	11-15-89	3	4	4.31	17	8	0	0	63	77	38	30	1	14	28	.300	.305	.298	4.02	2.01
Colorado, Moises	L-L	6-3	170	12-8-89	0	1	10.61	8	1	0	0	9	10	16	11	2	14	3	.278	.500	.265	2.89	13.50
Diaz, Omar	R-R	6-0	170	1-7-88	4	4	3.49	17	10	0	0	59	54	32	23	4	29	49	.249	.177	.277	7.43	4.40
Gonzalez, Yonathan	R-R	6-1	170	10-13-87	1	4	3.80	7	3	0	0	24	26	10	10	2	11	16	.280	.222	.303	6.08	4.18
Jimenez, Eleazar	R-R	5-11	150	3-4-88	4	1	3.56	21	0	0	2	30	32	16	12	2	14	20	.291	.407	.253	5.93	4.15
Lopez, Miguel	L-L	6-1	175	8-23-89	1	1	7.03	11	3	0	0	24	32	22	19	4	15	15	.323	.333	.323	5.55	5.55
Munoz, Orlando	R-R	6-1	165	2-22-90	1	3	3.34	21	1	0	2	30	29	15	11	1	21	20	.250	.194	.271	6.07	6.37
Noguera, Carlos	R-R	6-0	175	4-21-89	0	6	5.06	15	6	0	0	43	46	34	24	5	19	20	.272	.227	.288	4.22	4.01
Oraa, Carlos	R-R	6-3	170	10-5-89	0	1	3.44	14	0	0	1	18	13	8	7	0	9	8	.188	.250	.170	3.93	4.42
Penaloza, Jose	R-R	6-4	220	6-28-88	1	1	5.04	19	0	0	0	30	35	26	17	0	26	18	.285	.333	.267	5.34	7.71
Rios, Geney	R-R	5-11	175	2-12-88	2	2	3.92	16	10	1	0	60	49	36	26	4	36	47	.220	.148	.243	7.09	5.43
Rondon, Jorge	R-R	6-1	175	9-16-88	1	6	4.74	17	9	0	2	63	80	42	33	5	18	27	.321	.286	.332	3.88	2.59
Silva, Gustavo	R-R	6-1	170	8-21-90	0	0	108.00	1	0	0	0	0	4	5	4	0	1	0	.800	1.000	.500	0.00	27.00

FIELDING

Catcher	PCT	G	PO	A	E	DP	PB
Alcala	.971	46	219	45	8	4	15
Cardona	.984	27	149	33	3	2	7
Guzman	.929	7	21	5	2	0	4
R. Perez	1.000	2	1	0	0	0	0

First Base	PCT	G	PO	A	E	DP
Bolivar	—	1	0	0	0	0
Cardona	.983	16	115	4	2	11
Cortez	1.000	8	72	2	0	6
Garcia	.988	9	77	6	1	8
Guzman	1.000	4	15	1	0	2
Munoz	1.000	1	2	0	0	0
R. Perez	.986	34	258	17	4	22
Teran	1.000	8	83	6	0	8

Second Base	PCT	G	PO	A	E	DP
Bolivar	1.000	2	7	6	0	0
Chavez	.963	8	10	16	1	3
Cortez	1.000	1	2	0	0	0
Mannbel	.946	24	33	72	6	10
Obregon	.940	11	23	24	3	6
W. Perez	.800	1	3	1	1	1
Vivas	.918	36	78	91	15	30

Third Base	PCT	G	PO	A	E	DP
Bolivar	—	1	0	0	0	0
Cortez	.938	4	1	14	1	1
Garcia	.851	13	10	30	7	4
Mannbel	1.000	1	0	1	0	0
Teran	.835	55	28	109	27	5

Shortstop	PCT	G	PO	A	E	DP
Bolivar	.871	7	14	13	4	2
Mannbel	.954	43	89	140	11	29
Obregon	.912	28	44	80	12	16

Outfield	PCT	G	PO	A	E	DP
Bolivar	.973	49	99	8	3	3
Cortez	.943	33	45	5	3	1
Fonseca	.930	36	50	3	4	0
Jaspe	.895	42	48	3	6	0
Obregon	.667	4	2	0	1	0
R. Perez	1.000	2	2	0	0	0
W. Perez	.875	24	19	2	3	1
Rivero	.965	52	104	5	4	0
Teran	1.000	5	10	3	0	0

ORGANIZATION STATISTICS

San Diego Padres

JOHN MAFFEI

The Padres came within one win of the playoffs—which would have marked their third straight trip—but they lost a wild card play-in game to the Rockies in Denver. San Diego led by two runs going to the bottom of the 13th, but closer Trevor Hoffman uncharacteristically imploded for the second time in a week.

Despite the disappointment of being knocked out early, a lot went right for the Padres in 2007.

First baseman Adrian Gonzalez had another big year, hitting .282/.347/.502 with 30 home runs and 100 RBIs, all while playing Gold Glove-caliber defense. Likewise, shortstop Khalil Greene batted .254/.291/.468 with 27 homers and 97 RBIs and was again magnificent defensively.

After a miserable start during which he was hitting .107 in May, rookie third baseman Kevin Kouzmanoff finished the season at .275/.329/.457 with 18 home runs, had a bundle of big hits down the stretch and played solid defense.

This is the trio upon which the Padres will build.

Free-agent second baseman Marcus Giles (.229/.304/.317) was a bust, leaving open the possibility that Matt Antonelli, a first-round pick from Wake Forest in 2006, could be the man to fill the void in 2008.

Right fielder Brian Giles (.271/.361/.416 with 13 homers) finished the season as the team's leadoff man. Mike Cameron (.242/.328/.431 with 21 homers and 18 steals) provided power and leadership and excellent center-field defense, but he's a free agent and probably will move on.

Left fielder Milton Bradley, who hit .313/.413/.590 in 42 games after coming over from Oakland in a trade, was brilliant at times, but he tore the ACL in his right knee late in the season. He, too, is a free agent, though he will miss 2008.

On the farm, third baseman Chase Headley, a second-round pick in 2006 from Tennessee, won MVP honors in the Double-A Texas League. He could conceivably jump to the big leagues with Kouzmanoff moving to left field.

Catcher Josh Bard batted .285/.364/.404 but was the worst-throwing catcher in the big leagues. Michael Barrett, acquired from the Cubs in trade, hit just .226/.235/.286.

Righthanders Jake Peavy (19-6, 2.54) Chris Young (9-8, 3.12) and veteran Greg Maddux (14-11, 4.14) led a San Diego pitching staff that surrendered the fewest runs in the NL.

Four other righthanders helped flesh out the rotation. Brett Tomko was signed as a free agent late in the season and pitched well (2-1, 4.61). Clay Hensley, who suffered through an injury-plagued 2007 season after a solid year in 2006; Justin Germano, who was 7-10, 4.46; and Jack Cassel, who was 1-1, 3.97 in six September appearances, were the others.

Kevin Cameron, a major league Rule 5 pick from the Twins, posted a 2.79 ERA and did not allow a home run in 48 games. One year after Hoffman became the all-time saves leader, he set the bar even higher by surpassing 500 saves and finishing with 524.

Righthander Heath Bell, acquired in a trade with the Mets, was spectacular, going 6-4, 2.02 with 102 strikeouts and 30 walks in 93⅔ innings. He led all relievers in innings and strikeouts. Cla Meredith didn't equal his spectacular 2006 season, but he made 80 appearances and was 5-6, 3.50.

ORGANIZATIONAL LEADERS

BATTING		★Minimum 250 at-bats
★AVG	Myrow, Brian, Portland	.354
R	Antonelli, Matt, Lake Elsinore/San Antonio	123
H	Antonelli, Matt, Lake Elsinore/San Antonio	164
TB	Antonelli, Matt, Lake Elsinore/San Antonio	262
2B	Headley, Chase, San Antonio	38
3B	Baxter, Mike, Portland/Lake Elsinore	7
HR	Laforest, Pete, Portland	29
RBI	Huffman, Chad, Lake Elsinore/San Antonio	104
BB	Antonelli, Matt, Lake Elsinore/San Antonio	83
SO	Carter, Sam, Fort Wayne	124
SB	Diaz, Javis, Fort Wayne	31
★OBP	Myrow, Brian, Portland	.44
★SLG	Headley, Chase, San Antonio	.58
PITCHING		**^Minimum 75 innings**
W	Geer, Joshua, Portland/San Antonio	17
L	Cassel, Jack, Portland	14
^ERA	Buschmann, Matthew, Lake Elsinore	2.89
G	Rakers, Aaron, Portland	61
CG	Cassel, Jack, Portland	3
SV	Rodriguez, R.J., Fort Wayne/Lake Elsinore	18
IP	Geer, Joshua, Portland, San Antonio	177.1
BB	Delabar, Steve, Lake Elsinore/Fort Wayne	62
SO	LeBlanc, Wade, Lake Elsinore/San Antonio	145
^AVG	LeBlanc, Wade, Lake Elsinore/San Antonio	.217

A trade with the Brews at the deadline netted the Padres their most reliable lefthanded reliever in Joe Thatcher—not to mention righthander Will Inman and lefty Steve Garrison, two fine prospects. Thatcher went 2-2, 1.29 over 21 innings after the trade.

On the farm, Double-A San Antonio was named Baseball America's Minor League Team of the Year. Antonelli, Headley, catcher Nick Hundley and outfielder Will Venable headlined a prospect-laden offensive attack. The pitching was anchored by prospects Josh Geer, a 17-game winner, and lefties Cesar Ramos and Wade LeBlanc.

Lake Elsinore played for the high Class A California League championship, but lost in five games to San Jose. The Storm were led by first basemen Craig Cooper and Kyle Blanks, third baseman David Freese and righthander Matt Buschmann.

General Manager: Kevin Towers. **Farm Director:** Grady Fuson. **Scouting Director:** Bill Gayton

Class	Team	League	W	L	PCT	Finish*	Manager	Affiliate Since
Majors	San Diego	National	89	74	.546	4th (16)	Bud Black	—
Triple-A	Portland Beavers	Pacific Coast	58	86	.403	15th (16)	Rick Renteria	2001
Double-A	San Antonio Missions	Texas	73	66	.525	3rd (8)^	Randy Ready	2007
High A	Lake Elsinore Storm	California	74	54	.532	4th (10)	Carlos Lezcano	2001
Low A	Fort Wayne Wizards	Midwest	55	84	.396	13th (14)	Doug Dascenzo	1999
Short-season	Eugene Emeralds	Northwest	34	42	.447	6th (8)	Greg Riddoch	2001
Rookie	AZL Padres	Arizona	28	28	.500	4th (9)	Tony Muser	2004
Overall 2007 Minor League Record			**322**	**360**	**.472**	**25th**		

* Finish in overall standings (No. of teams in league) ^League champion

ORGANIZATION STATISTICS

SAN DIEGO PADRES

NATIONAL LEAGUE

BATTING	B-T	HT	WT	DOB	AVG	vLH	vRH	G	AB	R	H	2B	3B	HR	RBI	BB	HBP	SH	SF	SO	SB	CS	SLG	OBP
Bard, Josh	B-R	6-3	210	3-30-78	.285	.376	.250	118	389	42	111	27	2	5	51	50	0	1	3	58	0	1	.404	.364
Barrett, Michael	R-R	6-3	210	10-22-76	.226	.143	.241	44	133	6	30	8	0	0	12	2	0	0	1	21	0	0	.286	.235
2-team (57 Chicago)					.244	—	—	101	344	29	84	17	0	9	41	19	0	0	4	57	2	2	.372	.281
Blum, Geoff	B-R	6-3	205	4-26-73	.252	.238	.256	122	330	34	83	21	1	5	33	32	2	3	3	52	0	0	.367	.319
Bocachica, Hiram	R-R	5-11	195	3-4-76	.238	.226	.250	27	63	9	15	4	0	1	2	5	0	0	0	13	3	2	.349	.294
Bowen, Rob	B-R	6-3	225	2-24-81	.268	.350	.242	30	82	12	22	8	0	2	11	13	1	1	1	28	1	2	.439	.371
2-team (10 Chicago)					.212	—	—	40	113	15	24	9	0	2	13	17	1	1	2	41	1	2	.345	.316
Bradley, Milton	B-R	6-0	225	4-15-78	.313	.283	.330	42	144	31	45	5	1	11	30	23	2	0	0	27	3	1	.590	.414
Branyan, Russell	B-R	6-3	195	12-19-75	.197	.250	.191	61	122	16	24	5	1	7	19	21	2	0	1	48	1	0	.426	.322
3-team (7 Philadelphia, 21 St. Louis)					.196	—	—	89	163	22	32	5	1	10	26	28	2	0	1	69	1	0	.423	.320
Cameron, Mike	R-R	6-2	200	1-8-73	.242	.294	.222	151	571	88	138	33	6	21	78	67	8	2	3	160	18	5	.431	.328
Clark, Brady	R-R	6-2	200	4-18-73	.306	.357	.286	21	49	6	15	1	2	0	6	8	0	0	0	7	0	1	.408	.404
2-team (47 Los Angeles)					.262	—	—	68	107	13	28	5	2	0	11	14	1	1	0	18	1	3	.346	.352
Cruz Jr., Jose	B-R	6-0	210	4-19-74	.234	.221	.241	91	256	37	60	12	3	6	21	31	0	5	1	65	6	1	.375	.316
Ensberg, Morgan	R-R	6-2	220	8-26-75	.224	.250	.211	30	58	11	13	3	0	4	8	7	0	0	0	19	0	0	.483	.308
2-team (85 Houston)					.230	—	—	115	282	47	65	13	0	12	39	38	0	2	2	67	0	1	.404	.320
Giles, Brian	L-L	5-10	205	1-20-71	.271	.241	.286	121	483	72	131	27	2	13	51	64	4	0	1	61	4	6	.416	.361
Giles, Marcus	R-R	5-8	175	5-18-78	.229	.237	.225	116	420	52	96	19	3	4	39	44	3	6	3	82	10	3	.317	.304
Gonzalez, Adrian	L-L	6-2	220	5-8-82	.282	.263	.290	161	646	101	182	46	3	30	100	65	3	0	6	140	0	0	.502	.347
Greene, Khalil	R-R	5-11	195	10-21-79	.254	.268	.249	153	611	89	155	44	3	27	97	32	5	0	11	128	4	0	.468	.291
Hairston, Scott	R-R	6-0	200	5-25-80	.287	.250	.302	31	87	16	25	5	1	8	20	7	0	0	1	18	0	0	.644	.337
2-team (76 Arizona)					.243	—	—	107	263	37	64	18	2	11	36	26	1	3	1	55	2	0	.452	.313
Headley, Chase	B-R	6-2	195	5-9-84	.222	.167	.250	8	18	1	4	1	0	0	0	2	1	0	0	4	0	0	.278	.333
Kouzmanoff, Kevin	R-R	6-1	210	7-25-81	.275	.356	.240	145	546	67	150	30	2	18	74	32	10	2	6	94	1	0	.457	.329
Laforest, Pete	L-R	6-2	210	1-27-78	.360	.800	.250	10	25	7	9	1	0	1	3	5	0	0	0	8	0	0	.520	.467
2-team (14 Philadelphia)					.278	—	—	24	36	9	10	1	0	1	4	7	0	0	0	12	0	0	.389	.395
Lane, Jason	R-L	6-2	220	12-22-76	.000	.000	.000	3	2	0	0	0	0	0	0	0	0	0	0	1	0	0	.000	.000
2-team (68 Houston)					.175	—	—	71	171	18	30	5	0	8	27	16	3	1	3	31	1	1	.345	.254
Macias, Drew	L-L	6-3	175	3-7-83	—	.000	.000	1	0	1	0	0	0	0	0	0	0	0	0	0	0	0	—	—
Mackowiak, Rob	L-R	5-11	195	6-20-76	.196	.222	.191	28	56	6	11	3	0	0	2	3	2	0	0	18	1	0	.250	.262
McAnulty, Paul	L-R	5-10	220	2-24-81	.200	.286	.154	20	40	5	8	1	0	1	5	3	0	0	0	10	0	0	.300	.256
Morton, Colt	R-R	6-5	230	4-10-82	.000	—	.000	1	1	0	0	0	0	0	0	0	0	0	0	0	0	0	.000	.000
Myrow, Brian	L-R	5-11	190	9-4-76	.100	—	.100	12	10	0	1	1	0	0	1	1	0	0	4	0	0	.200	.250
Robles, Oscar	L-R	5-10	185	4-9-76	.231	.333	.217	24	26	0	6	0	0	0	2	2	0	5	0	4	0	0	.231	.286
Sledge, Terrmel	L-L	6-0	185	3-18-77	.210	.111	.225	100	200	22	42	9	0	7	23	27	3	1	2	60	1	2	.360	.310
Stansberry, Craig	R-R	6-0	185	3-8-82	.286	.333	.250	11	7	1	2	0	0	0	1	2	0	3	0	0	.286	.375

PITCHING	B-T	HT	WT	DOB	W	L	ERA	G	GS	CG	SV	IP	H	R	ER	HR	BB	SO	AVG	vLH	vRH	K/9	BB/9
Bell, Heath	R-R	6-3	225	9-29-77	6	4	2.02	81	0	0	2	94	60	21	21	3	30	102	.185	.216	.157	9.80	2.88
Brocail, Doug	L-R	6-5	250	5-16-67	5	1	3.05	67	0	0	0	77	66	33	26	8	24	43	.228	.182	.268	5.05	2.82
Cameron, Kevin	R-R	6-1	180	12-15-79	2	0	2.79	48	0	0	0	58	55	24	18	0	36	50	.249	.255	.243	7.76	5.59
Cassel, Jack	R-R	6-2	190	8-8-80	1	1	3.97	6	4	0	0	23	30	10	10	1	5	11	.326	.375	.300	4.37	1.99
Germano, Justin	R-R	6-3	205	8-6-82	7	10	4.46	26	23	0	0	133	133	72	66	14	40	78	.259	.244	.272	5.26	2.70
Hampson, Justin	L-L	6-1	200	5-24-80	2	3	2.70	39	0	0	0	53	48	17	16	1	16	34	.242	.213	.255	5.74	2.70
Hensley, Clay	R-R	5-11	190	8-31-79	2	3	6.84	13	9	0	0	50	62	40	38	5	32	30	.307	.287	.324	5.40	5.76
Hoffman, Trevor	R-R	6-0	215	10-13-67	4	5	2.98	61	0	0	42	57	49	21	19	2	15	44	.228	.299	.169	6.91	2.35
Ledezma, Wilfredo	L-L	6-4	210	1-21-81	0	0	6.28	9	1	0	0	14	20	11	10	2	8	16	.333	.286	.348	10.05	5.02
2-team (12 Atlanta)					0	2	6.85	21	1	0	0	24	32	21	18	3	12	23	—	—	—	8.75	4.56
Linebrink, Scott	R-R	6-2	200	8-4-76	3	3	3.80	44	0	0	1	45	41	19	19	9	14	25	.240	.222	.259	5.00	2.80
2-team (27 Milwaukee)					5	6	3.71	71	0	0	1	70	68	33	29	12	25	50	—	—	—	6.40	3.20
Maddux, Greg	R-R	6-0	180	4-14-66	14	11	4.14	34	34	1	0	198	221	92	91	14	25	104	.285	.280	.289	4.73	1.14
Meredith, Cla	R-R	6-0	180	6-4-83	5	6	3.50	80	0	0	0	80	94	38	31	6	17	59	.296	.286	.303	6.67	1.92
Peavy, Jake	R-R	6-1	180	5-31-81	19	6	2.54	34	34	0	0	223	169	67	63	13	68	240	.208	.242	.174	9.67	2.74
Rakers, Aaron	R-R	6-3	230	1-22-77	0	0	0.00	1	0	0	0	1	0	0	0	0	0	0	.250	.500	.000	0.00	0.00
Ring, Royce	L-L	6-0	220	12-21-80	1	0	3.60	15	0	0	0	15	11	8	6	1	14	17	.200	.250	.161	10.20	8.40
2-team (11 Atlanta)					1	0	2.70	26	0	0	0	20	13	8	6	1	17	21	—	—	—	9.45	7.65
Stauffer, Tim	R-R	6-1	205	6-2-82	0	1	21.13	2	2	0	0	8	15	18	18	5	6	6	.395	.467	.348	7.04	7.04
Thatcher, Joe	L-L	6-2	230	10-4-81	2	2	1.29	22	0	0	0	21	13	6	3	1	6	16	.167	.200	.151	6.86	2.57
Thompson, Mike	R-R	6-4	200	11-6-80	0	1	6.89	7	0	0	0	16	19	15	12	2	7	5	.317	.308	.324	2.87	4.02
Tomko, Brett	R-R	6-1	220	4-7-73	2	1	4.61	7	4	0	0	27	25	14	14	5	6	26	.240	.235	.245	8.56	1.98

					4	12	5.55	40	19	0	0	131	149	89	81	18	48	105	—	—	—	7.20	3.29
2-team (33 Los Angeles)																							
Wells, David	L-L	6-3	250	5-20-63	5	8	5.54	22	22	0	0	119	156	74	73	17	33	63	.322	.315	.324	4.78	2.50
2-team (7 Los Angeles)					9	9	5.43	29	29	0	0	157	201	97	95	22	42	82	—	—	—	4.69	2.40
Young, Chris	R-R	6-10	260	5-25-79	9	8	3.12	30	30	0	0	173	118	66	60	10	72	167	.192	.231	.155	8.69	3.75

FIELDING

Catcher	PCT	G	PO	A	E	DP	PB
Bard	.996	108	751	39	3	4	3
Barrett	.996	40	224	16	1	0	4
Bowen	.980	26	136	13	3	2	2
Laforest	.980	7	49	1	1	0	0

First Base	PCT	G	PO	A	E	DP
Blum	1.000	1	13	1	0	2
Ensberg	.889	1	7	1	1	1
Gonzalez	.994	161	1470	140	10	134
Laforest	.800	1	2	1	1	1

Second Base	PCT	G	PO	A	E	DP
Blum	.992	61	86	165	2	26
M. Giles	.987	112	203	332	7	75
Robles	1.000	8	4	15	0	1

Third Base	PCT	G	PO	A	E	DP
Stansberry	1.000	4	2	2	0	1
Blum	1.000	13	2	8	0	0
Branyan	1.000	24	10	40	0	9
Ensberg	.970	12	3	29	1	3
Headley	.833	5	2	3	1	0
Kouzmanoff	.932	136	91	209	22	12
Robles	1.000	4	2	3	0	0

Shortstop	PCT	G	PO	A	E	DP
Blum	.930	12	14	26	3	4
Greene	.984	153	218	461	11	98

Outfield	PCT	G	PO	A	E	DP
Blum	1.000	9	14	0	0	0

	PCT	G	PO	A	E	DP
Bocachica	1.000	22	35	2	0	1
Bradley	.974	40	73	3	2	1
Branyan	.933	12	14	0	1	0
Cameron	.987	150	365	7	5	2
Clark	1.000	19	31	0	0	0
Cruz Jr.	.993	70	147	5	1	2
B. Giles	.978	120	217	2	5	1
Hairston	1.000	27	25	1	0	0
Lane	1.000	2	1	0	0	0
Mackowiak	.962	14	24	1	1	0
McAnulty	1.000	9	16	0	0	0
Sledge	.989	57	88	2	1	0

PORTLAND BEAVERS — TRIPLE-A

PACIFIC COAST LEAGUE

BATTING	B-T	HT	WT	DOB	AVG	vLH	vRH	G	AB	R	H	2B	3B	HR	RBI	BB	HBP	SH	SF	SO	SB	CS	SLG	OBP
Alexander, Manny	R-R	5-10	180	3-20-71	.143	.000	.200	7	21	0	3	0	0	0	1	0	1	0	1	3	0	0	.143	.182
Alley, Josh	L-L	5-9	180	9-6-83	.167	.333	.000	5	12	1	2	1	0	0	1	0	0	0	0	5	0	0	.250	.167
Barrett, Michael	R-R	6-3	210	10-22-76	.182	.400	.000	3	11	2	2	1	0	0	1	0	0	0	0	2	0	0	.273	.182
Baxter, Mike	L-R	6-0	188	12-7-84	.207	.063	.385	10	29	1	6	2	1	0	7	1	0	0	0	8	1	0	.345	.233
Bocachica, Hiram	R-R	5-11	195	3-4-76	.184	.286	.125	13	38	3	7	1	0	0	3	12	1	0	1	5	2	0	.211	.385
2-team (35 Sacramento)					.287	—	—	48	167	30	48	12	1	9	35	37	7	0	1	24	10	3	.533	.434
Carlin, Luke	B-R	5-11	180	12-20-80	.220	.189	.233	98	300	35	66	20	2	0	17	47	0	6	0	77	0	3	.300	.326
Chang, Ray	R-R	6-0	204	8-24-83	.262	.226	.279	78	267	24	70	17	0	3	34	17	6	3	4	58	1	2	.360	.316
Ciofrone, Peter	L-R	5-10	201	9-28-83	.248	.280	.241	36	133	18	33	6	1	4	21	9	0	0	0	17	0	2	.398	.296
Clark, Brady	R-R	6-2	200	4-18-73	.339	.267	.364	14	59	12	20	3	0	3	6	8	5	3	0	11	1	0	.441	.418
Cruz, Luis	R-R	6-1	180	2-10-84	.168	.130	.188	45	155	15	26	10	1	5	17	9	1	0	2	24	0	0	.342	.216
Cust, Jack	L-R	6-1	230	1-16-79	.300	.286	.311	25	80	17	24	7	0	9	20	19	0	0	1	29	0	0	.725	.430
Dowdy, Brett	R-R	6-0	190	2-22-82	.241	.261	.229	38	116	19	28	5	1	0	5	8	1	0	1	19	4	1	.302	.294
Epping, Michael	L-L	5-11	190	8-28-83	.173	.182	.170	25	75	12	13	0	0	1	3	12	0	2	0	14	0	0	.213	.287
Gottier, Brandon	R-R	5-11	195	1-5-82	.118	.200	.083	8	17	2	2	0	0	0	0	1	0	0	0	4	0	0	.118	.167
Hatcher, Justin	R-R	5-9	195	5-12-80	.204	.154	.222	18	49	6	10	2	0	0	4	8	0	0	0	8	1	0	.245	.316
Hillenbrand, Shea	R-R	6-1	210	7-27-75	.147	.188	.111	9	34	2	5	1	0	0	1	1	0	0	0	4	0	0	.176	.171
2-team (3 Las Vegas)					.255	—	—	12	47	5	12	2	0	1	5	1	0	0	0	7	0	0	.362	.271
Howard, Joshua	L-L	5-11	180	4-6-83	.194	.286	.157	57	124	16	24	2	0	0	9	20	0	3	2	34	8	3	.210	.301
Huffman, Royce	R-R	6-0	200	1-11-77	.264	.305	.240	135	478	53	126	31	1	6	62	73	8	0	1	76	6	2	.370	.370
Hunter, Cedric	L-L	6-0	185	3-10-88	.500	.000	.667	3	4	1	2	0	0	1	3	1	0	0	1	0	0	0	.750	.600
Johnson, Michael	L-L	6-3	225	6-25-80	.133	.152	.119	27	75	9	10	2	0	2	8	11	0	0	1	26	0	0	.240	.241
King, Tom	R-R	5-11	170	8-3-84	.000	.000	.000	3	5	0	0	0	0	0	0	0	0	0	0	3	0	0	.000	.000
Laforest, Pete	L-R	6-2	210	1-27-78	.230	.194	.250	86	296	53	68	6	0	29	72	54	1	0	3	92	2	0	.544	.347
Macias, Drew	L-L	6-3	175	3-7-83	.282	.235	.303	31	110	14	31	6	1	2	11	21	0	0	0	25	3	1	.409	.397
McAnulty, Paul	L-R	5-10	220	2-24-81	.262	.233	.279	63	233	25	61	12	1	4	31	29	2	0	1	47	0	2	.373	.347
2-team (4 Colorado Springs)					.375	—	—	38	128	25	48	16	1	3	21	14	0	0	1	19	2	0	.586	.434
Menechino, Frank	R-R	5-8	200	1-7-71	.387	.366	.397	34	119	23	46	16	1	3	20	15	0	1	2	18	2	0	.613	.435
Myrow, Brian	L-R	5-11	190	9-4-76	.354	.357	.353	107	347	61	123	31	4	13	73	56	3	0	8	74	1	0	.579	.440
Ramirez, Yordany	R-R	6-1	187	7-31-84	.315	.256	.341	30	127	18	40	3	0	4	18	6	2	1	1	21	6	5	.433	.353
Robles, Oscar	L-R	5-10	185	4-9-76	.284	.290	.282	28	102	9	29	5	3	0	11	8	0	1	2	9	0	1	.392	.330
Ruth, Keoni	R-R	5-11	200	3-21-85	.226	.182	.238	17	53	7	12	2	0	0	5	9	2	1	0	11	1	0	.264	.359
Sansoe, Mike	R-R	6-0	185	11-6-82	.231	.250	.216	46	169	28	39	8	2	1	10	22	2	2	1	36	5	0	.320	.325
Schemmel, Jon	R-R	5-11	190	1-22-83	.256	.389	.160	13	43	7	11	2	0	2	8	5	2	3	2	9	1	0	.442	.346
Shabala, Adam	L-R	6-0	190	2-6-78	.167	.171	.165	50	144	19	24	4	2	1	8	21	0	2	0	40	4	2	.243	.273
Sinisi, Vince	L-L	6-0	195	11-7-81	.310	.250	.344	80	303	44	94	21	1	9	36	20	2	0	1	41	5	3	.475	.356
Sledge, Terrmel	L-L	6-0	185	3-18-77	.370	.286	.462	8	27	5	10	2	0	1	3	3	0	1	0	3	1	0	.556	.433
Sogard, Eric	L-R	5-10	180	5-22-86	.000	.000	—	1	3	0	0	0	0	0	0	0	1	0	0	3	0	0	.000	.250
Stansberry, Craig	R-R	6-0	185	3-8-82	.273	.253	.282	124	466	83	127	33	3	14	75	70	6	0	6	95	10	10	.446	.370

PITCHING	B-T	HT	WT	DOB	W	L	ERA	G	GS	CG	SV	IP	H	R	ER	HR	BB	SO	AVG	vLH	vRH	K/9	BB/9
Brooks, Frank	L-L	6-1	190	9-6-78	1	0	1.00	8	0	0	0	9	4	1	1	1	8	5	.143	.000	.182	5.00	8.00
Brown, Andrew	R-R	6-6	230	2-17-81	2	3	2.78	32	0	0	0	36	26	14	11	3	15	43	.200	.288	.141	10.85	3.79
2-team (5 Sacramento)					2	3	2.88	37	0	0	4	41	32	16	13	4	15	49	—	—	—	10.84	3.32
Burnside, Adrian	R-L	6-3	210	3-15-77	0	0	5.40	26	0	0	0	33	38	21	20	2	15	22	.284	.350	.255	5.94	4.05
Carrillo, Cesar	R-R	6-3	175	4-29-84	0	2	8.62	5	5	0	0	16	22	16	15	2	4	18	.338	.353	.323	4.60	8.04
Cassel, Jack	R-R	6-2	190	8-8-80	7	14	3.91	27	24	3	0	157	203	94	68	13	42	117	.315	.322	.309	6.72	2.41
Cassidy, Scott	R-R	6-2	180	10-3-75	4	4	6.53	40	0	0	10	40	56	31	29	5	14	49	.327	.380	.290	11.02	3.15
Daigle, Richie	R-R	6-0	197	9-9-82	1	0	1.69	5	0	0	0	5	5	1	1	0	2	3	.278	.500	.167	5.06	3.38
Deago, Roger	R-L	5-10	180	6-21-77	3	5	6.24	16	10	0	0	62	78	44	43	7	25	47	.311	.143	.351	6.82	3.63
Estes, Shawn	R-L	6-2	200	2-18-73	0	1	9.82	4	2	0	0	7	13	8	8	3	3	3	.382	.333	.409	3.68	3.68
Faris, Stephen	R-R	6-1	190	6-30-84	0	0	2.25	1	0	0	0	4	3	1	1	0	3	4	.214	.333	.000	9.00	6.75
Fossum, Casey	L-L	6-1	170	1-6-78	0	2	8.10	3	3	0	0	13	26	12	12	0	7	7	.448	.533	.419	4.73	4.73
Geer, Joshua	R-R	6-3	190	6-2-83	1	0	3.00	1	1	0	0	6	6	2	2	0	1	6	.286	.300	.273	9.00	1.50
Germano, Justin	R-R	6-3	205	8-6-82	4	0	1.69	5	5	0	0	32	23	7	6	0	3	20	.197	.236	.161	5.62	0.84
Hampson, Justin	L-L	6-1	200	5-24-80	1	1	3.55	10	0	0	0	13	12	6	5	3	8	12	.250	.133	.303	8.53	5.68
Hayhurst, Dirk	L-R	6-3	200	3-24-81	0	0	23.62	2	0	0	0	3	9	7	7	2	0	1	.600	.600	.600	3.38	0.00
Hensley, Clay	R-R	5-11	190	8-31-79	2	7	6.72	13	13	0	0	71	102	63	53	10	34	50	.333	.349	.322	6.34	4.31

Name	B-T	HT	WT	DOB	W	L	ERA	G	GS	CG	SV	IP	H	R	ER	HR	BB	SO	AVG	vLH	vRH	K/9	BB/9
Howard, Joshua	L-L	5-11	180	4-6-83	0	0	9.00	2	0	0	0	2	2	2	2	1	2	0	.250	.000	.333	0.00	9.00
Ketchner, Ryan	L-L	6-1	190	4-19-82	1	11	5.62	19	19	0	0	99	110	63	62	17	37	85	.281	.305	.272	7.70	3.35
Rakers, Aaron	R-R	6-3	230	1-22-77	4	5	5.70	61	0	0	0	79	101	50	50	17	20	58	.312	.347	.291	6.61	2.28
Ring, Royce	L-L	6-0	220	12-21-80	4	0	1.99	27	0	0	1	32	22	8	7	0	11	44	.188	.135	.231	12.51	3.13
Rosales, Leo	R-R	6-1	185	5-28-81	1	1	3.28	24	0	0	14	25	23	9	9	3	10	27	.245	.227	.260	9.85	3.65
Startup, Will	L-L	6-0	195	8-4-84	0	0	4.66	14	0	0	0	19	13	10	10	2	11	16	.183	.143	.200	7.45	5.12
Stauffer, Tim	R-R	6-1	205	6-2-82	8	5	4.34	25	20	0	0	131	147	73	63	12	36	96	.283	.319	.259	6.61	2.48
Strickland, Scott	R-R	5-10	215	4-26-76	4	1	4.58	15	0	0	0	20	18	10	10	2	11	23	.247	.207	.273	10.53	5.03
Stutes, Kyle	L-L	5-10	185	1-22-82	0	0	9.64	9	0	0	0	14	23	15	15	3	7	11	.365	.350	.372	7.07	4.50
Teague, Matt	R-L	6-3	210	12-14-84	0	0	0.00	2	2	0	0	9	5	0	0	0	4	9	.167	.000	.278	9.00	4.00
Thatcher, Joe	L-L	6-2	230	10-4-81	1	0	1.04	8	0	0	0	9	10	4	1	0	1	11	.278	.214	.318	11.42	1.04
2-team (24 Nashville)					3	1	1.78	32	0	0	1	30	29	9	6	0	8	44	—	—	—	13.05	2.37
Thompson, Mike	R-R	6-4	200	11-6-80	4	11	6.24	23	22	1	0	133	171	99	92	19	40	71	.312	.332	.294	4.82	2.71
Watkins, Steve	R-R	6-4	215	7-19-78	2	5	5.17	34	7	0	0	78	88	47	45	13	43	56	.287	.236	.321	6.43	4.94
Wells, Jared	R-R	6-4	200	10-31-81	3	7	5.24	47	10	0	9	93	107	59	54	9	48	87	.294	.269	.313	8.45	4.66
Woodard, Robert	R-R	6-1	205	1-10-85	0	1	15.00	2	0	0	0	3	4	5	5	1	2	3	.286	.222	.400	9.00	6.00

FIELDING

Catcher	PCT	G	PO	A	E	DP	PB
Barrett	1.000	3	8	1	0	1	0
Carlin	.994	82	600	50	4	10	6
Gottier	.947	6	30	6	2	1	1
Hatcher	.972	15	96	8	3	0	1
Laforest	.985	45	304	21	5	4	6
Menechino	.989	15	29	63	1	14	
Robles	1.000	3	3	9	0	2	
Ruth	.955	12	30	33	3	7	
Schemmel	1.000	2	2	7	0	2	
Stansberry	.982	85	152	220	7	41	
Huffman	1.000	4	7	9	0	3	
Robles	.984	13	19	42	1	7	
Stansberry	.949	28	40	72	6	16	

First Base	PCT	G	PO	A	E	DP
Ciofrone	1.000	1	8	0	0	1
Huffman	.996	32	262	20	1	25
Johnson	.970	15	123	6	4	13
Laforest	1.000	5	41	0	0	0
McAnulty	1.000	6	44	4	0	7
Myrow	.990	92	754	42	8	76
Robles	1.000	1	14	0	0	0
Sinisi	1.000	1	6	0	0	0

Second Base	PCT	G	PO	A	E	DP
Carlin	1.000	9	9	12	0	4
Chang	1.000	2	3	2	0	0
Cruz	.960	4	9	15	1	2
Dowdy	.963	13	24	28	2	10
Huffman	.901	16	25	39	7	8
King	1.000	1	2	1	0	0

Third Base	PCT	G	PO	A	E	DP
Alexander	1.000	3	1	4	0	0
Ciofrone	.833	2	3	2	1	1
Cruz	1.000	2	2	1	0	0
Dowdy	.786	6	2	9	3	0
Hillenbrand	.917	8	0	11	1	0
Huffman	.898	60	32	91	14	10
Laforest	.956	28	14	51	3	1
McAnulty	.875	6	4	10	2	0
Menechino	1.000	8	2	9	0	1
Robles	1.000	11	9	14	0	1
Schemmel	.900	10	11	16	3	3
Stansberry	.917	21	15	29	4	4

Shortstop	PCT	G	PO	A	E	DP
Alexander	1.000	2	1	4	0	0
Chang	.963	75	99	209	12	42
Cruz	.954	39	58	109	8	23

Outfield	PCT	G	PO	A	E	DP
Alley	1.000	3	7	0	0	0
Baxter	1.000	9	10	0	0	0
Bocachica	.955	11	19	2	1	1
Ciofrone	1.000	28	50	3	0	1
Clark	.963	13	24	2	1	1
Cust	.955	13	21	0	1	0
Dowdy	1.000	17	17	0	0	0
Epping	.923	21	60	6	5	0
Howard	.986	34	66	6	1	1
Huffman	.953	31	40	1	2	0
Hunter	1.000	1	2	0	0	0
Macias	1.000	31	59	2	0	0
McAnulty	.984	49	60	3	1	1
Myrow	—	1	0	0	0	0
Ramirez	.988	30	80	3	1	2
Sansoe	.976	45	82	1	2	0
Shabala	.953	41	78	4	4	0
Sinisi	.956	76	123	8	6	1
Sledge	1.000	7	6	1	0	0

SAN ANTONIO MISSIONS

DOUBLE-A

TEXAS LEAGUE

BATTING	B-T	HT	WT	DOB	AVG	vLH	vRH	G	AB	R	H	2B	3B	HR	RBI	BB	HBP	SH	SF	SO	SB	CS	SLG	OBP
Adams, Skip	R-R	6-0	200	10-18-79	.145	.143	.145	22	69	4	10	1	0	0	6	3	0	1	2	19	0	0	.159	.176
Antonelli, Matt	R-R	6-0	203	4-8-85	.294	.279	.299	49	187	34	55	11	1	7	24	30	3	0	3	36	10	3	.476	.395
Bonvechio, Brett	L-R	6-1	200	11-13-82	.266	.227	.274	40	128	23	34	9	0	9	27	22	1	0	3	28	0	0	.547	.370
Brown, Tim	L-L	6-3	228	2-21-83	.274	.218	.289	109	351	56	96	16	0	13	50	40	7	1	3	65	0	0	.430	.357
Ciofrone, Peter	L-R	5-10	201	9-28-83	.261	.303	.250	97	364	58	95	16	2	6	34	33	10	1	0	55	1	4	.365	.339
Ciriaco, Juan	R-R	6-0	159	8-15-83	.160	.222	.144	37	131	13	21	4	0	1	6	6	0	3	0	25	5	1	.214	.197
Cleveland, Jeremy	R-R	6-2	185	9-10-81	.250	.381	.196	28	72	6	18	4	1	0	8	7	0	1	0	16	0	0	.333	.313
Cruz, Luis	R-R	6-1	180	2-10-84	.252	.404	.210	69	238	24	60	10	0	4	19	13	2	0	3	20	3	0	.345	.293
Dowdy, Brett	R-R	6-0	190	2-22-82	.265	.246	.274	59	196	26	52	9	2	5	24	26	3	1	0	38	8	3	.408	.360
Hatcher, Justin	R-R	5-9	195	5-12-80	.100	.200	.000	4	10	2	1	0	0	0	1	2	1	0	0	1	0	0	.100	.308
Headley, Chase	B-R	6-2	195	5-9-84	.330	.364	.319	121	433	82	143	38	5	20	78	74	11	0	4	114	1	0	.580	.437
Howard, Joshua	L-L	5-11	180	4-6-83	.247	.188	.262	22	81	13	20	2	0	0	4	14	0	1	0	25	1	1	.272	.358
Huffman, Chad	R-R	6-1	217	4-29-85	.269	.281	.267	49	167	28	45	4	1	7	28	22	4	1	3	44	0	0	.431	.362
Hundley, Nick	R-R	6-1	210	9-8-83	.247	.282	.238	101	373	55	92	23	1	20	72	42	2	3	1	74	0	2	.475	.324
Johnson, Michael	L-L	6-3	225	6-25-80	.250	.273	.241	64	200	32	50	8	3	12	35	35	2	0	1	73	0	0	.525	.366
2-team (22 Corpus Christi)					.267	—	—	86	266	44	71	15	3	16	51	53	2	0	2	90	0	1	.526	.390
Kazmar, Sean	R-R	5-9	160	8-5-84	.208	.271	.190	78	269	30	56	10	2	6	33	24	3	0	3	46	6	1	.327	.278
Macias, Drew	L-L	6-3	175	3-7-83	.251	.242	.253	100	331	43	83	15	5	6	50	51	5	0	4	53	5	8	.399	.355
Morton, Colt	R-R	6-5	230	4-10-82	.266	.273	.264	29	94	17	25	3	0	6	19	15	4	1	2	34	0	0	.489	.383
Sansoe, Mike	R-R	6-0	185	11-6-82	.242	.286	.227	37	132	10	32	2	1	0	7	8	0	1	0	31	5	5	.273	.286
Valverde, Kody	R-R	6-0	205	3-14-83	.000	—	.000	1	4	0	0	0	0	0	0	0	0	0	0	2	0	0	.000	.000
Venable, Will	L-L	6-2	205	10-29-82	.278	.298	.272	134	515	66	143	19	3	8	68	38	10	5	4	84	21	2	.373	.337
Wagner, Michael	R-R	6-3	232	9-13-81	.167	.100	.192	15	36	2	6	1	0	1	5	2	0	0	1	14	0	0	.278	.205
Wooten, Shawn	R-R	5-10	230	7-24-72	.262	.172	.297	29	130	10	27	3	0	0	11	4	0	1		14	0	0	.291	.353

PITCHING	B-T	HT	WT	DOB	W	L	ERA	G	GS	CG	SV	IP	H	R	ER	HR	BB	SO	AVG	vLH	vRH	K/9	BB/9
Abraham, Paul	R-R	6-2	220	1-10-80	1	3	2.39	47	0	0	8	53	39	16	14	2	20	53	.204	.268	.156	9.06	3.42
Ayala, Manny	R-R	6-3	237	11-6-84	1	3	5.28	5	5	0	0	29	30	19	17	5	4	20	.278	.257	.316	6.21	1.24
Basham, Bobby	R-R	6-3	205	3-7-80	0	1	16.62	7	0	0	0	9	26	17	16	2	3	3	.520	.583	.462	3.12	3.12
Brooks, Frank	L-L	6-1	190	9-6-78	2	1	2.01	17	0	0	1	22	14	5	5	1	2	26	.179	.207	.163	10.48	0.81
Brown, Tim	L-L	6-3	228	2-21-83	0	0	9.00	1	0	0	0	1	1	1	1	1	0	1	.250	.000	.333	9.00	0.00
Burnside, Adrian	R-L	6-3	210	3-15-77	0	0	2.19	9	0	0	0	12	8	3	3	1	4	9	.178	.231	.156	6.57	2.92
Deago, Roger	R-L	5-10	180	6-21-77	3	3	4.16	19	11	0	0	71	61	34	33	9	25	76	.233	.257	.223	9.59	3.15
Ekstrom, Michael	R-R	6-0	185	8-30-83	7	10	4.76	27	27	0	0	144	183	85	76	6	47	98	.315	.316	.313	6.14	2.94
Ellis, Jonathan	R-R	6-0	190	10-3-82	3	4	4.29	55	0	0	2	50	45	26	24	5	32	40	.243	.247	.240	7.15	5.72
Geer, Joshua	R-R	6-3	190	6-2-83	16	6	3.20	26	26	2	0	171	163	67	61	9	27	102	.252	.269	.233	5.36	1.42
Hayhurst, Dirk	L-R	6-3	200	3-24-81	4	1	3.19	32	1	0	0	59	54	24	21	6	9	55	.236	.213	.252	8.34	1.37
Inman, William	R-R	6-0	200	2-6-87	3	3	4.17	7	7	0	0	41	33	19	19	6	19	40	.224	.268	.184	8.78	4.17

Player	B-T	HT	WT	DOB	W	L	ERA	G	GS	CG	SV	IP	H	R	ER	HR	BB	SO	AVG	vLH	vRH	K/9	BB/9
Jamison, Neil	R-R	6-3	185	8-4-83	3	5	4.32	53	0	0	12	58	65	36	28	7	26	45	.285	.269	.296	6.94	4.01
LeBlanc, Wade	L-L	6-3	202	8-7-84	7	3	3.45	12	11	0	0	57	48	22	22	8	19	55	.225	.213	.229	8.63	2.98
Lopez, Arturo	L-L	5-10	165	2-23-83	2	2	4.54	30	1	0	0	36	34	19	18	3	18	28	.262	.220	.288	7.07	4.54
Moreno, Edwin	R-R	6-1	170	7-30-80	0	0	1.62	16	0	0	9	17	10	3	3	2	8	18	.175	.147	.217	9.72	4.32
Oyervidez, Jose	R-R	5-11	195	2-18-82	0	1	5.65	6	6	0	0	29	32	19	18	2	12	19	.283	.274	.294	5.97	3.77
Ramos, Cesar	L-L	6-2	190	6-22-84	13	9	3.41	27	27	2	0	164	153	69	62	15	43	90	.249	.223	.258	4.95	2.36
Searles, Jonathan	R-R	6-3	200	1-18-81	4	3	3.62	38	1	0	0	70	59	32	28	5	36	52	.235	.272	.209	6.72	4.65
Stutes, Kyle	L-L	5-10	185	1-22-82	0	1	2.55	18	0	0	2	18	14	5	5	2	7	13	.222	.308	.162	6.62	3.57
Thompson, Sean	L-L	5-11	170	10-13-82	4	7	3.57	16	16	0	0	88	84	41	35	7	41	59	.258	.253	.261	6.01	4.18
2-team (8 Tulsa)					9	8	3.73	24	23	1	0	133	124	61	55	11	56	81	—	—	—	5.49	3.80

FIELDING

Catcher	PCT	G	PO	A	E	DP	PB
Hatcher	.969	3	30	1	1	1	0
Hundley	.987	94	619	45	9	8	9
Morton	1.000	20	148	12	0	4	2
Valverde	1.000	1	4	1	0	0	0
Wooten	.993	23	142	8	1	1	2

First Base	PCT	G	PO	A	E	DP
Adams	1.000	1	7	0	0	0
Bonvechio	1.000	12	109	3	0	5
Brown	.993	81	665	54	5	57
Ciofrone	1.000	1	8	1	0	0
Cleveland	1.000	1	1	0	0	0
Dowdy	1.000	1	2	1	0	1
Johnson	.997	35	268	30	1	32
Morton	.985	8	60	6	1	6
Wooten	1.000	5	48	4	0	5

Second Base	PCT	G	PO	A	E	DP
Adams	1.000	6	8	19	0	8
Antonelli	.975	49	83	111	5	23
Ciofrone	1.000	1	2	6	0	0
Dowdy	.983	26	50	69	2	14
Kazmar	.976	61	118	170	7	36

Third Base	PCT	G	PO	A	E	DP
Adams	—	1	0	0	0	0
Bonvechio	1.000	9	5	11	0	2
Ciofrone	.967	12	8	21	1	5
Cleveland	—	1	0	0	0	0
Dowdy	1.000	3	1	3	0	1
Headley	.963	119	74	212	11	22

Shortstop	PCT	G	PO	A	E	DP
Adams	.925	13	17	32	4	5

	PCT	G	PO	A	E	DP
Ciriaco	.940	37	64	107	11	22
Cruz	.952	68	107	193	15	39
Dowdy	.955	10	8	13	1	2
Kazmar	.917	16	18	48	6	9

Outfield	PCT	G	PO	A	E	DP
Adams	1.000	1	1	0	0	0
Ciofrone	.984	67	116	4	2	1
Cleveland	1.000	15	26	0	0	0
Dowdy	1.000	19	34	3	0	0
Howard	1.000	21	43	4	0	3
Huffman	.988	44	73	7	1	1
Macias	.991	97	191	18	2	2
Sansoe	.969	31	60	3	2	0
Venable	.993	129	285	7	2	2
Wagner	1.000	5	8	0	0	0

ORGANIZATION STATISTICS

LAKE ELSINORE STORM   HIGH CLASS A

CALIFORNIA LEAGUE

BATTING	B-T	HT	WT	DOB	AVG	vLH	vRH	G	AB	R	H	2B	3B	HR	RBI	BB	HBP	SH	SF	SO	SB	CS	SLG	OBP
Alley, Josh	L-L	5-9	180	9-6-83	.297	.357	.271	53	185	40	55	10	4	1	25	36	1	1	5	35	7	4	.411	.405
Antonelli, Matt	R-R	6-0	203	4-8-85	.314	.364	.302	82	347	89	109	14	4	14	54	53	4	0	2	58	18	6	.499	.409
Baxter, Mike	L-R	6-0	188	12-7-84	.276	.256	.281	111	417	74	115	21	6	7	44	44	3	2	4	75	12	6	.405	.346
Blanks, Kyle	R-R	6-6	281	9-11-86	.301	.370	.280	119	465	94	140	31	4	24	100	44	18	0	4	98	11	2	.540	.380
Bush, Matt	R-R	5-10	189	2-8-86	.204	.235	.198	29	98	8	20	2	1	1	17	16	0	0	2	21	1	0	.276	.310
Canham, Mitch	L-R	6-2	215	9-25-84	.000	.000	.000	2	7	0	0	0	0	0	1	0	0	0	1	2	0	0	.000	.000
Chang, Ray	R-R	6-0	204	8-24-83	.304	.545	.244	21	56	9	17	3	2	1	8	3	2	1	1	6	0	0	.482	.355
Ciriaco, Juan	R-R	6-0	159	8-15-83	.268	.106	.324	47	183	28	49	8	0	9	32	9	0	1	0	36	7	2	.459	.302
Cooper, Craig	R-L	6-2	223	10-27-84	.317	.356	.305	124	458	83	145	32	4	10	78	56	8	1	5	87	4	4	.469	.397
Crosta, Nic	R-R	6-1	214	11-17-82	.194	.169	.203	71	258	35	50	14	0	14	53	28	3	0	5	86	1	1	.411	.276
Epping, Michael	L-L	5-11	190	8-28-83	.167	.000	.200	2	6	0	1	0	0	0	0	0	0	0	0	0	0	0	.167	.167
Freese, David	R-R	6-2	217	4-28-83	.302	.298	.303	128	503	104	152	31	6	17	96	69	16	0	4	99	6	1	.489	.400
Giles, Brian	L-L	5-10	205	1-20-71	.400	.000	.500	3	5	2	2	0	0	1	3	4	0	0	0	2	0	0	.700	.571
Gottier, Brandon	R-R	5-11	195	1-5-82	.282	.346	.244	21	71	14	20	4	1	1	8	6	2	0	0	7	0	0	.408	.354
Hatcher, Justin	R-R	5-9	195	5-12-80	.231	.000	.300	4	13	2	3	1	0	0	2	1	0	0	0	1	1	0	.308	.286
Howard, Joshua	L-L	5-11	180	4-6-83	.265	.150	.313	20	68	8	18	4	1	0	5	8	0	3	1	18	2	1	.353	.338
Huffman, Chad	R-R	6-1	217	4-29-85	.307	.321	.304	84	316	63	97	19	2	15	76	42	10	0	3	56	0	1	.522	.402
Johnston, Seth	R-R	6-3	204	3-12-83	.292	.298	.290	95	363	56	106	19	4	8	51	36	2	2	2	82	1	2	.433	.357
Kazmar, Sean	R-R	5-9	160	8-5-84	.284	.301	.273	47	201	27	57	20	0	3	24	16	3	2	0	27	4	1	.428	.345
Lisk, Charles	R-R	6-3	219	1-3-83	.171	.333	.115	10	35	2	6	2	0	0	3	1	0	0	0	15	0	1	.229	.256
Lobaton, Jose	B-R	6-0	187	10-21-84	.260	.234	.267	90	304	50	79	15	3	10	47	41	3	2	7	79	0	0	.428	.346
McQueary, Aeden	R-R	5-11	180	9-19-84	.290	.364	.250	10	31	7	9	1	0	1	4	7	1	0	1	8	0	0	.419	.425
Morton, Colt	R-R	6-5	230	4-10-82	.500	.400	.526	6	24	5	12	7	0	3	8	4	2	0	0	3	0	0	1.167	.600
Perry, Robert	L-L	5-10	185	10-3-84	.259	.385	.235	19	81	14	21	4	2	1	2	9	0	2	2	14	3	1	.432	.326
Ramirez, Yordany	R-R	6-1	187	7-31-84	.269	.317	.256	82	286	45	77	17	2	4	43	9	3	4	1	43	22	6	.385	.298
Ruth, Keoni	R-R	5-11	200	3-21-85	.176	.333	.143	5	17	2	3	0	0	0	1	0	0	1	0	4	0	0	.176	.176
Schemmel, Jon	R-R	5-11	190	1-27-83	.309	.267	.325	15	55	11	17	0	0	0	5	4	0	0	0	11	1	0	.309	.415
Wagner, Michael	R-R	6-3	232	9-13-81	.250	.143	.294	8	24	3	6	0	1	2	6	3	0	0	0	1	0	0	.583	.333

PITCHING	B-T	HT	WT	DOB	W	L	ERA	G	GS	CG	SV	IP	H	R	ER	HR	BB	SO	AVG	vLH	vRH	K/9	BB/9
Ayala, Manny	R-R	6-3	237	11-6-84	11	3	2.22	17	17	0	0	101	95	30	25	7	19	74	.247	.233	.264	6.57	1.69
Brocail, Doug	L-R	6-5	250	5-16-67	0	0	0.00	1	1	0	0	2	2	0	0	0	0	3	.250	.333	.200	13.50	0.00
Burke, Greg	R-R	6-4	204	9-21-82	4	4	5.23	51	9	0	0	96	105	60	56	11	28	67	.272	.247	.295	6.26	2.62
Buschmann, Matthew	R-R	6-3	209	2-13-84	12	6	2.89	28	25	0	0	149	153	60	48	9	26	115	.270	.307	.233	6.93	1.57
Carter, Brent	R-L	6-3	210	10-10-82	9	6	6.77	31	16	0	0	104	149	82	78	15	18	66	.337	.335	.338	5.73	1.56
Culp, Nathan	L-L	6-2	180	10-9-84	5	4	4.81	12	10	0	0	64	90	44	34	5	11	39	.338	.212	.369	5.51	1.55
Daigle, Richie	R-R	6-0	197	9-9-82	5	8	5.95	29	22	0	0	118	156	89	78	12	38	78	.321	.366	.279	5.95	2.90
Delabar, Steve	R-R	6-5	227	7-17-83	2	6	5.59	20	0	0	0	29	26	21	18	5	16	33	.236	.235	.237	10.24	4.97
DeMark, Michael	R-R	6-0	198	5-20-83	2	1	3.74	44	0	0	0	53	45	34	22	7	30	70	.227	.224	.230	11.89	5.09
Dunn, Brooks	L-L	6-2	205	5-6-84	2	4	2.10	20	6	0	0	51	58	19	12	2	9	36	.286	.284	.287	6.31	1.58
Estes, Shawn	R-L	6-2	200	2-18-73	0	1	1.93	3	3	0	0	14	12	5	3	0	3	14	.240	.300	.200	9.00	1.93
Faris, Stephen	R-R	6-1	190	6-30-84	2	0	4.09	2	2	0	0	11	7	5	5	0	2	7	.189	.140	.233	5.73	1.64
Frieri, Ernesto	R-R	6-2	168	7-19-85	1	0	1.25	13	1	0	1	22	11	3	3	1	6	27	.155	.143	.158	11.22	2.49
Garrison, Steve	B-L	6-1	185	9-12-86	2	3	2.79	7	7	0	0	42	32	15	13	2	6	28	.205	.097	.232	6.00	1.29
Handley, Matt	L-L	6-1	205	6-7-83	1	0	0.77	10	0	0	0	12	3	1	1	1	9	11	.081	.100	.074	8.49	6.94
Hayhurst, Dirk	L-R	6-3	200	3-24-81	0	1	1.80	13	0	0	0	20	23	11	4	0	6	16	.288	.303	.277	7.20	2.70
Higelin, Brandon	L-L	6-1	195	4-8-83	0	3	5.22	41	0	0	0	50	61	34	29	4	22	41	.303	.239	.338	7.38	3.96
Lara, Orlando	L-L	5-10	185	5-20-85	2	1	5.40	3	3	0	0	15	14	9	9	3	10	14	.255	.563	.128	8.40	6.00
LeBlanc, Wade	L-L	6-3	202	8-7-84	6	5	2.64	16	16	0	0	92	72	32	27	5	17	90	.212	.175	.229	8.80	1.66
Link, Jon	R-R	6-2	205	3-23-84	2	1	3.07	41	0	0	13	41	32	16	14	5	11	45	.209	.224	.191	9.88	2.41

	B-T	HT	WT	DOB	W	L	ERA	G	GS	CG	SV	IP	H	R	ER	HR	BB	SO	AVG	vLH	vRH	K/9	BB/9
Lopez, Wilton	R-R	6-0	160	7-19-83	2	1	6.10	22	0	0	3	21	35	16	14	3	1	19	.372	.323	.397	8.27	0.44
Luebke, Cory	R-L	6-4	200	3-4-85	1	1	7.71	2	1	0	0	7	10	6	6	1	1	5	.357	.333	.360	6.43	1.29
Madden, John	R-R	6-4	229	12-2-82	1	4	5.74	43	0	0	5	42	56	31	27	2	21	44	.315	.360	.282	9.35	4.46
Rodriguez, R.J.	R-R	6-0	175	7-5-84	0	0	4.50	12	0	0	0	14	18	7	7	0	1	10	.305	.118	.381	6.43	0.64
Smith, Cody	R-R	6-3	200	4-20-82	0	0	12.00	4	0	0	0	6	10	8	8	0	3	6	.400	.231	.583	9.00	4.50
Stutes, Kyle	L-L	5-10	185	1-22-82	0	2	4.91	22	0	0	0	22	24	14	12	2	11	14	.276	.222	.314	5.73	4.50
Varnell, Grant	R-R	6-2	215	9-27-82	2	0	8.57	14	0	0	0	21	26	22	20	7	4	14	.289	.293	.286	6.00	1.71

FIELDING

Catcher	PCT	G	PO	A	E	DP	PB
Canham	.947	2	17	1	1	0	0
Gottier	.994	21	136	17	1	1	4
Hatcher	1.000	4	21	3	0	1	0
Lisk	.946	10	64	6	4	1	2
Lobaton	.983	90	661	72	13	3	11
McQueary	.971	10	62	6	2	2	1
Morton	.973	6	35	1	1	0	0

First Base	PCT	G	PO	A	E	DP
Blanks	.984	60	517	38	9	56
Cooper	.988	83	752	50	10	65
Johnston	1.000	1	9	0	0	2
Ramirez	—	1	0	0	0	0

Second Base	PCT	G	PO	A	E	DP
Antonelli	.967	76	134	218	12	40

	PCT	G	PO	A	E	DP
Chang	1.000	2	1	1	0	1
Ciriaco	1.000	10	24	23	0	7
Johnston	.968	26	39	81	4	19
Kazmar	.988	16	29	51	1	13
Ruth	.926	5	8	17	2	3
Schemmel	.955	9	19	23	2	8

Third Base	PCT	G	PO	A	E	DP
Antonelli	—	1	0	0	0	0
Freese	.958	126	59	238	13	15
Johnston	.889	14	5	19	3	3
Kazmar	1.000	1	1	1	0	0

Shortstop	PCT	G	PO	A	E	DP
Bush	.916	29	49	93	13	20
Chang	.966	19	18	39	2	11
Ciriaco	.934	37	52	104	11	22

	PCT	G	PO	A	E	DP
Johnston	.930	26	42	90	10	18
Kazmar	.963	29	45	84	5	22
Schemmel	1.000	6	11	11	0	2

Outfield	PCT	G	PO	A	E	DP
Alley	.988	50	80	2	1	0
Baxter	.983	103	167	10	3	1
Cooper	.953	24	40	1	2	1
Crosta	.945	48	50	2	3	0
Epping	1.000	1	3	0	0	0
Giles	1.000	2	4	1	0	0
Howard	.973	20	36	0	1	1
Huffman	.981	84	145	8	3	2
Perry	.962	19	50	1	2	0
Ramirez	.961	82	188	8	8	1
Wagner	1.000	7	15	0	0	0

FORT WAYNE WIZARDS — LOW CLASS A

MIDWEST LEAGUE

BATTING

	B-T	HT	WT	DOB	AVG	vLH	vRH	G	AB	R	H	2B	3B	HR	RBI	BB	HBP	SH	SF	SO	SB	CS	SLG	OBP
Baum, Justin	R-R	6-1	195	10-6-85	.286	.000	.345	22	70	8	20	7	0	2	5	10	2	0	0	20	0	0	.471	.390
Burke, Kyler	L-L	6-3	205	4-20-88	.211	.200	.217	62	213	24	45	7	1	1	21	26	3	0	1	73	3	1	.268	.305
Campbell, Michael	L-L	6-1	165	11-14-83	.235	.314	.216	62	183	24	43	7	1	3	19	12	4	0	2	31	1	1	.333	.294
Carter, Sam	R-R	6-4	210	6-5-83	.267	.315	.240	97	341	41	91	19	2	12	43	32	2	1	1	124	2	3	.440	.332
Conlon, Keith	R-R	6-3	210	3-14-83	.255	.231	.265	16	47	6	12	1	0	1	6	8	1	0	0	10	1	1	.340	.375
Contreras, Rayner	R-R	6-0	150	9-21-86	.276	.241	.293	73	268	26	74	12	2	7	37	22	2	0	5	53	7	6	.414	.330
Diaz, Javis	L-L	5-10	165	6-25-84	.277	.275	.278	117	460	67	130	14	6	7	36	46	4	5	0	103	31	14	.397	.347
Epping, Michael	L-L	5-11	190	8-28-83	.217	.053	.250	34	115	17	25	8	1	4	15	13	1	1	1	25	5	1	.409	.300
Gottier, Brandon	R-R	5-11	195	1-5-82	.250	.000	.333	2	8	2	2	2	0	0	1	0	1	0	0	2	0	0	.500	.333
Hernandez, Brian	R-R	6-1	180	11-3-83	.223	.189	.238	37	121	14	27	2	0	1	9	9	1	0	1	22	0	1	.264	.280
Hunt, Jeremy	R-R	6-2	210	12-22-83	.260	.266	.258	101	369	53	96	17	1	13	47	33	5	0	2	85	0	2	.417	.328
Hunter, Cedric	L-L	6-0	185	3-10-88	.282	.313	.267	129	496	53	140	20	2	7	58	47	2	0	4	78	8	9	.373	.344
Jones, Daryl	R-R	6-3	200	9-1-86	.266	.298	.250	69	244	35	65	16	6	12	42	31	3	0	2	65	2	0	.379	.328
King, Tom	R-R	5-11	170	8-3-84	.257	.276	.250	79	300	34	77	20	0	7	35	25	4	1	2	51	4	2	.393	.320
Lauderdale, Brian	R-R	5-10	170	6-29-83	.500	.500	.500	2	4	2	2	0	0	1	3	1	0	0	1	0	0	1.250	.600
Lopez, Jesus	R-R	5-11	165	9-19-87	.232	.245	.226	117	380	39	88	16	2	2	39	43	7	3	8	59	0	2	.300	.309
Martinez, Luis	R-R	6-0	210	4-3-85	.231	.222	.233	24	78	12	18	3	0	1	6	8	0	1	1	30	0	0	.308	.299
Payne, Danny	L-L	5-10	185	9-8-85	.000	.000	.000	2	7	2	0	0	0	0	0	1	2	0	0	6	0	0	.000	.222
Perry, Robert	L-L	5-10	185	10-3-84	.273	.083	.303	28	88	17	24	3	1	2	14	15	6	1	1	11	6	3	.398	.409
Pickett, Justin	R-R	6-1	205	6-16-85	.167	.000	.200	2	6	0	1	0	0	0	1	1	0	0	0	5	0	0	.167	.286
Rivera, Jodam	B-R	5-10	180	2-4-86	.225	.312	.193	91	284	34	64	14	0	5	26	43	2	4	2	43	2	1	.327	.329
Schemmel, Jon	R-R	5-11	190	1-27-83	.262	.324	.219	50	164	17	43	9	0	0	16	30	7	3	2	19	2	1	.311	.394
Sogard, Eric	L-R	5-10	180	5-22-86	.253	.133	.279	22	83	7	21	2	0	2	15	6	1	1	1	13	2	2	.349	.308
Stocco, Matt	R-R	6-1	210	8-16-83	.192	.206	.187	79	255	27	49	15	0	1	21	16	3	2	3	83	3	2	.263	.246
Stokes, Raymond	R-R	5-10	160	10-30-85	.000	.000	.000	1	3	0	0	0	0	0	1	0	0	0	0	1	0	0	.000	.000

PITCHING

	B-T	HT	WT	DOB	W	L	ERA	G	GS	CG	SV	IP	H	R	ER	HR	BB	SO	AVG	vLH	vRH	K/9	BB/9
Axelrod, Dylan	R-R	6-0	195	7-30-85	2	1	1.27	10	0	0	0	21	18	4	3	0	4	15	.237	.308	.200	6.33	1.69
Breit, Aaron	R-R	6-3	180	4-19-86	3	11	6.73	31	21	0	0	108	139	97	81	8	47	80	.310	.303	.315	6.65	3.90
Bush, Matt	R-R	5-10	189	2-8-86	0	0	0.00	1	0	0	0	0	0	0	0	0	0	0	.000	—	.000	0.00	0.00
Carter, Brian	R-L	6-3	210	10-10-82	1	0	3.97	2	2	0	0	11	15	7	5	0	6	6	.306	.333	.304	4.76	0.00
Culp, Nathan	L-L	6-2	180	10-9-84	3	3	3.16	14	14	0	0	80	75	35	28	4	13	54	.244	.203	.254	6.10	1.47
Davis, Tyler	R-R	6-3	195	5-15-85	0	0	1.13	6	0	0	1	8	8	1	1	0	0	7	.258	.286	.250	7.88	0.00
Delabar, Steve	R-R	6-5	227	7-17-83	2	5	5.96	21	12	0	0	68	63	49	45	8	46	48	.248	.233	.261	6.35	6.09
Dunn, Brooks	L-L	6-2	205	5-6-84	1	1	2.14	14	0	0	0	21	14	9	5	0	7	13	.179	.182	.179	5.57	3.00
Faris, Stephen	R-R	6-1	190	6-30-84	7	7	4.37	21	18	1	0	103	104	59	50	7	35	58	.263	.258	.269	5.07	3.06
Frieri, Ernesto	R-R	6-2	168	7-19-85	1	2	2.64	40	0	0	0	65	48	19	19	4	23	65	.209	.219	.201	9.05	3.20
Gomes, Brandon	R-R	5-11	175	7-15-84	1	0	4.68	14	11	0	0	60	65	41	31	3	11	44	.269	.295	.253	6.64	1.66
Handley, Matt	L-L	6-1	205	6-7-83	1	1	4.34	15	0	0	0	19	12	11	9	3	16	14	.188	.214	.180	6.75	7.71
Harrington, Allen	L-L	5-11	185	7-9-84	0	2	1.74	18	3	0	0	41	39	11	8	1	9	42	.239	.211	.248	9.15	1.96
Hussey, John	R-R	6-3	172	11-22-86	0	0	7.50	6	6	0	0	24	25	20	20	3	20	10	.272	.333	.237	3.75	7.50
Kirby, Jonathan	R-R	5-11	198	12-5-83	0	0	3.79	12	0	0	1	19	12	10	8	2	13	11	.179	.156	.200	5.21	6.16
Lara, Andrew	L-L	5-10	185	5-20-85	1	3	5.67	7	7	1	0	33	43	21	21	4	6	32	.314	.378	.290	8.64	1.62
Lopez, Wilton	R-R	6-0	160	7-19-83	0	0	3.30	22	0	0	0	30	34	11	11	2	2	17	.291	.260	.313	5.10	0.60
Luebke, Cory	R-L	6-4	200	3-4-85	1	2	3.33	5	5	0	0	27	29	13	10	2	5	30	.269	.400	.239	10.00	1.67
McDaid, Derek	R-R	6-3	220	9-27-83	3	3	4.91	52	1	0	0	81	93	52	44	11	23	42	.286	.326	.259	4.69	2.57
Menchaca, Pablo	R-R	6-4	225	11-28-87	1	0	7.36	4	0	0	0	7	12	8	6	1	1	6	.353	.286	.400	7.36	1.23
Miller, Drew	R-R	6-4	190	2-24-86	4	6	4.69	16	16	0	0	81	74	45	42	12	24	87	.244	.193	.286	9.71	2.68
Ociesa, Jacob	R-L	6-6	224	3-4-83	0	2	12.15	7	0	0	0	7	9	11	9	0	10	5	.321	.182	.412	6.75	13.50
Rivera, Jodam	B-R	5-10	180	2-4-86	0	1	6.00	2	0	0	0	3	3	2	2	0	0	0	.273	.400	.167	0.00	0.00
Rodriguez, R.J.	R-R	6-0	175	7-5-84	3	2	4.11	46	0	0	18	50	62	26	23	4	14	45	.302	.239	.354	8.05	2.50
Salazar, Yesid	R-R	6-1	175	11-2-86	2	0	2.38	6	0	0	0	11	12	3	3	1	4	7	.293	.538	.179	5.56	3.18
Schemmel, Jon	R-R	5-11	190	1-27-83	0	0	0.00	2	0	0	0	2	2	0	0	0	0	0	.222	.000	.400	0.00	0.00

	B-T	HT	WT	DOB	W	L	ERA	G	GS	CG	SV	IP	H	R	ER	HR	BB	SO	AVG	vLH	vRH	K/9	BB/9
Schmidt, Nick	L-L	6-5	220	10-10-85	0	1	6.43	3	1	0	0	7	8	5	5	0	6	6	.286	.308	.267	7.71	7.71
Underwood, Andrew	R-R	6-4	185	5-20-85	6	11	4.92	22	21	0	0	112	117	67	61	8	30	60	.273	.251	.292	4.84	2.42
Valdez, Rolando	R-R	6-1	191	1-8-86	2	7	4.11	58	0	0	9	57	61	28	26	1	17	53	.280	.236	.310	8.37	2.68
Vandel, Geoff	L-L	6-1	190	6-9-87	0	1	67.50	1	1	0	0	1	2	5	5	0	6	0	.667	.500	1.000	0.00	81.00
Varnell, Grant	R-R	6-2	215	9-27-82	0	3	2.12	22	0	0	0	34	27	10	8	0	11	19	.231	.250	.219	5.03	2.91

FIELDING

Catcher	PCT	G	PO	A	E	DP	PB
Gottier	1.000	2	17	0	0	0	1
Hernandez	.977	36	235	16	6	3	5
Martinez	.975	24	177	16	5	1	1
Pickett	1.000	2	17	0	0	0	0
Stocco	.973	78	442	60	14	7	5

First Base	PCT	G	PO	A	E	DP
Campbell	1.000	2	5	1	0	1
Carter	.833	2	3	2	1	1
Hunt	.992	74	604	27	5	62
Jones	.987	63	579	33	8	55
Rivera	.954	9	59	3	3	5

Second Base	PCT	G	PO	A	E	DP
Contreras	.900	11	13	23	4	6

	PCT	G	PO	A	E	DP
King	.967	67	108	185	10	42
Rivera	.975	38	58	100	4	26
Schemmel	.972	21	34	72	3	11
Sogard	.984	14	27	35	1	7
Stokes	1.000	1	2	2	0	1

Third Base	PCT	G	PO	A	E	DP
Baum	.859	20	11	44	9	3
Contreras	.859	61	36	128	27	12
Hunt	.920	16	5	18	2	0
Lauderdale	—	1	0	0	0	0
Rivera	.930	29	16	50	5	3
Schemmel	.864	23	20	31	8	2

Shortstop	PCT	G	PO	A	E	DP
Contreras	1.000	1	2	3	0	0

	PCT	G	PO	A	E	DP
King	.867	7	6	20	4	3
Lopez	.967	117	191	370	19	82
Rivera	.964	20	28	52	3	13
Schemmel	.889	2	3	5	1	2

Outfield	PCT	G	PO	A	E	DP
Burke	.978	60	84	5	2	3
Campbell	1.000	30	48	2	0	1
Carter	.993	79	134	13	1	6
Conlon	.913	10	19	2	2	0
Diaz	.957	92	174	3	8	1
Epping	1.000	19	34	0	0	0
Hunter	.982	113	263	5	5	1
Payne	1.000	1	4	0	0	0
Perry	.978	25	44	0	1	0
Stocco	1.000	1	1	0	0	0

EUGENE EMERALDS
NORTHWEST LEAGUE

SHORT-SEASON

BATTING	B-T	HT	WT	DOB	AVG	vLH	vRH	G	AB	R	H	2B	3B	HR	RBI	BB	HBP	SH	SF	SO	SB	CS	SLG	OBP
Baum, Justin	R-R	6-1	195	10-6-85	.269	.354	.232	41	160	27	43	11	0	8	33	18	4	0	2	41	1	0	.488	.353
Blauer, Robert	L-L	5-11	210	9-8-85	.276	.286	.273	58	192	26	53	8	0	1	27	36	4	0	2	32	0	1	.333	.397
Brown, Zachary	L-L	6-0	200	3-13-85	.133	.111	.143	7	30	2	4	0	0	2	4	1	0	0	1	7	0	0	.333	.156
Buschini, Shane	L-L	6-4	220	4-24-85	.159	.100	.176	12	44	2	7	1	0	1	3	3	0	0	0	15	2	0	.250	.213
Canham, Mitch	L-R	6-2	215	9-25-84	.293	.310	.287	28	116	20	34	4	1	2	18	11	5	1	0	35	5	2	.397	.379
Cannon, Luke	L-L	6-1	195	8-19-84	.167	.000	.250	2	6	3	1	1	0	0	0	2	1	1	0	5	0	0	.333	.444
Carrasco, Felix	B-R	6-1	220	2-14-87	.184	.182	.184	13	49	5	9	1	1	0	4	4	0	0	0	24	1	2	.245	.245
Carvajal, Yefri	R-R	5-11	190	1-22-89	.262	.300	.250	31	122	15	32	5	1	2	19	5	0	0	0	39	2	0	.369	.291
Chalk, Bradley	L-L	6-1	180	1-20-86	.229	.125	.254	22	83	14	19	2	2	0	6	10	0	0	2	22	0	2	.301	.312
Conlon, Keith	R-R	6-3	210	3-14-83	.324	.190	.383	21	68	16	22	6	1	2	15	4	5	1	0	13	3	1	.529	.403
Cumberland, Andrew	L-R	5-10	175	1-13-86	.333	.500	.286	4	18	6	6	1	0	0	2	1	0	0	2	0	0	0	.389	.429
Durango, Luis	B-R	5-9	145	4-23-86	.367	.347	.373	69	300	60	110	6	8	2	32	29	1	3	2	32	17	10	.460	.422
Garzon, Edgar	R-R	6-0	178	8-24-86	.200	.333	.167	4	15	0	3	0	0	0	2	0	0	1	0	1	0	0	.200	.200
Hernandez, Brian	R-R	6-1	180	11-4-83	.118	.000	.154	5	17	1	2	1	0	0	0	0	1	2	0	1	0	0	.176	.167
Joynt, Brian	R-R	6-4	205	3-14-85	.171	.125	.200	10	41	4	7	2	0	0	5	2	2	0	0	13	0	0	.220	.244
Kulbacki, Kellen	L-L	5-11	185	11-21-85	.301	.350	.283	61	226	33	68	13	3	8	39	27	5	0	4	56	1	1	.491	.382
Lauderdale, Brian	L-R	5-10	170	6-29-83	.270	.304	.261	33	115	26	31	8	1	5	13	9	3	1	0	37	5	0	.487	.339
Martinez, Luis	R-R	6-0	210	4-3-85	.278	.105	.340	21	72	9	20	7	0	1	11	19	1	0	1	22	0	1	.417	.430
McQueary, Aeden	R-R	5-10	180	9-19-84	.228	.353	.175	19	57	9	13	2	0	0	6	9	4	0	1	15	1	0	.263	.366
Parrino, Andrew	B-R	6-0	185	10-31-85	.271	.200	.296	69	251	32	68	20	1	3	38	30	7	1	0	73	2	2	.394	.365
Payne, Danny	L-L	5-10	185	9-8-85	.279	.245	.292	54	183	35	51	8	3	0	21	53	2	1	1	53	17	3	.355	.444
Pickett, Justin	R-R	6-1	205	6-16-85	.204	.122	.238	39	142	24	29	4	0	9	25	15	6	1	1	55	0	0	.423	.305
Ruth, Keoni	R-R	5-11	200	3-21-85	.222	.333	.167	9	36	3	8	3	0	1	9	2	0	0	1	4	0	1	.389	.256
Sogard, Eric	L-R	5-10	180	5-22-86	.256	.265	.253	31	125	20	32	9	0	2	18	19	0	1	0	16	4	2	.376	.354
Solis, Ali	R-R	6-0	176	9-29-87	.200	.000	.250	1	5	1	1	0	0	1	2	0	0	0	1	0	0	.800	.200
Stokes, Raymond	R-R	5-10	160	10-30-85	.255	.267	.250	18	55	17	14	3	2	0	9	15	7	1	0	14	9	3	.382	.468
Zawadzki, Lance	B-R	5-11	185	5-26-85	.267	.294	.262	25	101	13	27	4	1	2	14	10	1	0	0	24	1	0	.386	.339

PITCHING	B-T	HT	WT	DOB	W	L	ERA	G	GS	CG	SV	IP	H	R	ER	HR	BB	SO	AVG	vLH	vRH	K/9	BB/9
Florentino, Yoeli	R-R	6-0	170	10-3-85	0	0	11.25	2	0	0	0	4	8	5	5	0	1	0	.381	.364	.400	0.00	2.25
Garramone, Robert	R-R	6-2	175	8-22-87	5	6	5.48	19	10	0	0	64	72	49	39	7	25	36	.285	.289	.281	5.06	3.52
Gibbs, Dustin	R-R	6-5	190	5-12-84	1	2	5.14	24	0	0	0	35	33	23	20	3	27	43	.239	.277	.205	11.06	6.94
Gomes, Brandon	R-R	5-11	175	7-15-84	1	0	0.00	4	0	0	0	6	1	0	0	0	1	6	.053	.000	.077	8.53	1.42
Handley, Matt	L-L	6-4	205	6-7-83	0	1	10.71	20	0	0	0	21	29	30	25	2	21	19	.326	.182	.373	8.14	9.00
Harrington, Allen	L-L	5-11	185	7-3-86	0	1	3.48	6	0	0	0	10	14	5	4	0	5	10	.326	.100	.394	8.71	4.35
Hefner, Jeremy	R-R	6-4	215	3-11-86	2	5	3.90	17	11	0	0	62	51	33	27	3	20	74	.221	.250	.198	10.68	2.89
Higelin, Brandon	L-L	6-1	195	4-8-83	0	0	0.00	2	0	0	0	2	1	0	0	1	0	1	.167	—	.167	0.00	4.50
Huff, Matthew	R-R	6-2	185	2-18-84	0	3	7.50	23	0	0	2	24	29	24	20	3	25	23	.296	.255	.333	8.62	9.38
Hussey, John	R-R	6-3	172	11-22-86	4	5	6.66	22	7	0	0	53	59	46	39	5	44	56	.294	.200	.362	9.57	7.52
Hynes, Colt	L-L	5-11	200	6-28-85	3	2	1.54	30	0	0	4	41	31	9	7	1	6	50	.212	.152	.240	10.98	1.32
Kluber, Corey	R-R	6-4	215	4-10-86	1	1	3.51	10	7	0	0	33	28	16	13	1	15	33	.230	.276	.188	8.91	4.05
Latos, Matthew	R-R	6-5	210	12-9-87	1	4	3.83	16	13	0	0	56	58	30	24	1	22	74	.266	.279	.258	11.82	3.51
Luebke, Cory	R-L	6-4	200	3-4-85	3	0	1.46	8	3	0	0	25	18	6	4	2	2	26	.194	.174	.200	9.49	0.73
McBryde, Jeremy	R-R	6-2	195	5-1-87	1	6	5.31	17	12	0	1	59	67	39	35	6	18	56	.277	.283	.270	8.49	2.73
McDaniel, Adam	R-R	6-1	210	11-9-84	0	0	4.76	6	0	0	0	6	4	3	3	1	6	1	.190	.000	.267	1.59	9.53
McQueary, Aeden	R-R	5-10	180	9-19-84	0	0	4.50	2	0	0	0	2	3	2	1	0	1	3	.300	.333	.250	13.50	4.50
Menchaca, Pablo	R-R	6-4	225	11-28-87	1	0	3.60	1	1	0	0	5	6	2	2	0	1	3	.316	.500	.267	5.40	1.80
Perez, Chris	R-R	6-3	215	10-17-83	4	2	6.00	26	3	0	0	51	50	41	34	2	35	52	.246	.244	.248	9.18	6.18
Quezada, Jackson	R-R	6-4	170	8-26-84	3	2	3.75	21	0	0	7	24	22	12	10	0	4	29	.239	.279	.204	10.98	1.50
Salazar, Yesid	R-R	6-1	175	11-2-86	0	0	4.50	3	2	0	0	10	10	5	5	1	3	4	.256	.357	.200	3.60	2.70
Teague, Matt	R-L	6-3	210	12-14-84	1	0	4.38	11	7	0	0	39	39	21	19	6	6	32	.257	.289	.243	7.38	1.38
Woodard, Robert	R-R	6-1	205	1-10-85	3	2	3.89	23	0	0	2	35	33	17	15	2	11	40	.246	.279	.219	10.38	2.86

FIELDING

Catcher	PCT	G	PO	A	E	DP	PB
Canham	.991	21	219	13	2	2	8
Hernandez	1.000	5	34	2	0	0	1
Martinez	.993	15	138	7	1	2	2
McQueary	.993	18	124	16	1	0	1
Pickett	.984	18	164	18	3	0	4
Solis	1.000	1	2	2	0	1	0

First Base	PCT	G	PO	A	E	DP	
Blauer	.987	56	441	24	6	28	
Brown	.982	6	49	5	1	2	
Buschini	1.000	4	17	4	0	3	
Lauderdale	1.000	6	24	2	0	1	
Pickett	.971	13	95	7	3	10	

Second Base	PCT	G	PO	A	E	DP	
Lauderdale	.966	13	21	35	2	5	

	PCT	G	PO	A	E	DP
Parrino	.970	20	35	61	3	14
Ruth	.882	4	7	8	2	3
Sogard	.956	28	43	66	5	12
Stokes	.972	13	31	38	2	3

Third Base	PCT	G	PO	A	E	DP
Baum	.897	40	28	68	11	6
Carrasco	.824	13	11	17	6	2
Garzon	1.000	4	4	2	0	0
Joynt	.889	7	7	9	2	0
Lauderdale	.917	9	7	15	2	1
Ruth	.889	3	1	7	1	0

Shortstop	PCT	G	PO	A	E	DP
Cumberland	.917	3	5	6	1	1
Parrino	.965	47	60	132	7	16
Sogard	.889	4	4	12	2	0

	PCT	G	PO	A	E	DP
Stokes	1.000	4	6	10	0	3
Zawadzki	.885	20	26	59	11	11

Outfield	PCT	G	PO	A	E	DP
Buschini	1.000	6	8	2	0	0
Cannon	1.000	1	1	0	0	0
Carvajal	.923	20	35	1	3	0
Chalk	.962	21	24	1	1	0
Conlon	1.000	14	20	0	0	0
Durango	.942	64	105	8	7	4
Kulbacki	.988	55	77	4	1	0
Lauderdale	1.000	2	3	0	0	0
Payne	.968	50	88	3	3	2
Zawadzki	1.000	1	1	0	0	0

AZL PADRES

ARIZONA LEAGUE

BATTING	B-T	HT	WT	DOB	AVG	vLH	vRH	G	AB	R	H	2B	3B	HR	RBI	BB	HBP	SH	SF	SO	SB	CS	SLG	OBP
Brown, Zachary	L-L	6-0	200	3-13-85	.246	.189	.269	38	130	19	32	9	0	1	25	26	2	1	0	32	2	0	.338	.380
Buschini, Shane	L-L	6-4	220	4-24-85	.243	.182	.269	32	111	17	27	9	1	2	17	13	3	0	2	26	1	1	.396	.333
Carrasco, Felix	B-R	6-1	220	2-14-87	.288	.333	.270	15	52	5	15	0	1	0	6	9	0	0	0	16	0	2	.327	.393
Carvajal, Yefri	R-R	5-11	190	1-22-89	.340	.323	.348	25	100	27	34	13	0	1	22	10	2	0	2	22	5	0	.500	.404
Chalk, Bradley	L-L	6-1	180	1-20-86	.364	.500	.324	12	44	11	16	5	0	0	7	6	1	1	0	6	3	2	.477	.451
Ciriaco, Juan	R-R	6-0	159	8-15-83	.281	.250	.286	10	32	6	9	3	0	2	10	3	0	1	1	4	2	0	.563	.333
Cumberland, Andrew	L-R	5-10	175	1-13-89	.318	.450	.271	21	85	16	27	2	1	0	7	7	3	0	0	9	6	1	.365	.389
Florentino, Yoeli	R-R	6-0	170	10-3-85	.148	.200	.136	16	27	5	4	0	0	1	5	2	1	2	1	8	0	0	.259	.226
Garzon, Edgar	R-R	6-0	178	8-24-86	.305	.298	.307	50	187	31	57	13	2	2	24	24	3	0	1	39	2	2	.428	.391
Hernandez, Brian	R-R	6-1	180	11-4-83	.625	—	.625	2	8	1	5	1	0	0	4	1	0	0	0	0	0	0	.750	.667
Hill, Ryan	L-L	6-0	190	4-5-85	.213	.094	.248	49	141	16	30	4	1	1	19	31	2	0	0	32	4	0	.277	.362
Joynt, Brian	R-R	6-4	205	3-14-85	.207	.125	.238	31	87	15	18	5	0	0	10	17	1	1	1	29	3	0	.264	.340
Laurent, Phil	L-L	5-11	190	5-23-84	.129	.000	.143	11	31	3	4	0	1	0	0	6	0	0	0	14	0	1	.194	.270
Mayi, Jose	L-L	6-4	200	4-3-87	.211	.206	.212	38	133	29	28	4	2	4	21	27	1	0	0	35	0	1	.361	.348
McAnulty, Paul	L-R	5-10	220	2-24-81	.400	.250	.455	6	15	2	6	1	0	0	4	2	0	0	0	2	0	0	.467	.471
Mercado, Angel	R-R	6-0	205	8-19-85	.273	.333	.255	42	139	22	38	11	2	6	26	14	3	1	1	29	4	2	.511	.350
Morton, Colt	R-R	6-5	230	4-10-82	.290	.250	.316	11	31	9	9	4	0	0	3	4	0	4	0	11	0	0	.419	.366
Naylor, Clinton	L-R	6-0	176	8-3-88	.169	.067	.200	23	65	13	11	1	0	0	3	18	3	0	1	18	0	0	.185	.368
Perry, Robert	L-L	5-10	185	10-3-84	.391	.471	.362	16	64	22	25	6	3	2	9	10	5	0	0	6	9	3	.672	.506
Quiles, Emmanuel	R-R	5-11	186	10-26-89	.171	.250	.130	16	35	4	6	0	0	0	4	3	2	0	0	6	1	0	.171	.275
Rincon, Edinson	R-R	6-1	185	8-11-90	.178	.182	.176	15	45	6	8	1	0	0	7	1	0	0	1	11	0	0	.200	.302
Ruth, Keoni	R-R	5-11	200	3-21-85	.439	.556	.406	19	82	23	36	5	4	1	14	7	3	0	0	4	2	1	.634	.500
Solis, Ali	R-R	6-0	176	9-29-87	.253	.318	.228	27	79	11	20	4	0	0	14	11	3	1	1	21	0	0	.304	.362
Valdez, Jeudy	R-R	5-11	155	5-5-89	.281	.327	.264	47	192	31	54	7	4	3	30	15	5	1	2	44	11	3	.406	.346
Watson, Reggie	R-R	5-9	185	1-16-83	.281	.000	.360	10	32	6	9	0	1	1	4	8	1	0	1	11	3	2	.438	.429
Zawadzki, Lance	B-R	5-11	185	5-26-85	.433	.250	.500	10	30	8	13	3	0	1	5	3	0	0	0	8	0	0	.633	.485

PITCHING	B-T	HT	WT	DOB	W	L	ERA	G	GS	CG	SV	IP	H	R	ER	HR	BB	SO	AVG	vLH	vRH	K/9	BB/9
Axelrod, Dylan	R-R	6-0	195	7-30-85	0	2	5.40	11	0	0	2	12	15	11	7	0	4	15	.294	.316	.281	11.57	3.09
Basham, Bobby	R-R	6-3	205	3-7-80	0	0	1.80	1	1	0	0	5	7	3	1	0	1	0	.368	.500	.308	0.00	1.80
Brannan, Cooper	R-R	6-4	235	11-7-84	1	3	9.69	20	0	0	0	26	38	32	28	1	14	15	.336	.389	.312	5.19	4.85
Bush, Matt	R-R	5-10	189	2-8-86	1	0	1.23	6	0	0	0	7	5	1	1	0	2	16	.192	.111	.235	19.64	2.45
Castro, Simon	R-R	6-5	203	4-9-88	2	6	6.22	14	12	0	0	51	61	48	35	4	30	55	.298	.329	.279	9.77	5.33
Davis, Tyler	R-R	6-3	195	5-15-85	3	0	0.83	16	0	0	1	22	18	10	2	1	8	17	.214	.161	.245	7.06	3.32
Estes, Shawn	R-L	6-2	200	2-18-73	0	0	3.86	4	3	0	0	7	6	3	3	1	1	10	.214	.222	.211	12.86	1.29
Florentino, Yoeli	R-R	6-0	170	10-3-85	0	0	2.31	9	0	0	1	12	12	3	3	0	6	11	.267	.412	.179	8.49	4.63
Gribbin, Andrew	R-R	6-2	185	9-14-88	0	0	11.57	4	0	0	0	5	6	6	6	0	2	3	.286	.375	.231	3.86	3.86
Lara, Alexis	R-R	6-0	150	3-23-87	3	0	3.10	22	0	0	5	29	24	10	10	0	14	38	.226	.244	.215	11.79	4.34
Martinez, Jose	R-R	6-3	186	9-5-86	4	1	5.47	20	0	0	0	25	33	18	15	3	8	13	.317	.415	.254	4.74	2.92
McDaniel, Adam	R-R	6-1	210	11-9-84	1	1	4.15	13	0	0	1	13	15	8	6	1	8	14	.306	.381	.250	9.69	5.54
Mead, Tyler	L-R	6-1	180	8-15-87	2	4	4.34	14	12	0	0	58	64	45	28	7	23	39	.275	.257	.288	6.05	3.57
Medina, Vantroit	R-R	6-3	175	1-30-87	2	1	4.65	21	1	0	0	31	30	22	16	2	12	27	.238	.189	.258	7.84	3.48
Ociesa, Jacob	R-L	6-6	224	3-4-83	0	0	6.75	5	0	0	0	5	3	4	4	1	5	6	.176	.200	.167	10.12	8.44
Oland, Bryan	R-R	6-3	230	6-5-85	0	0	6.30	16	0	0	0	20	32	16	14	2	6	13	.360	.394	.339	5.85	2.70
Olsen, Shawn	R-R	6-1	190	6-5-84	0	1	33.75	3	0	0	0	1	7	5	5	1	2	0	.700	.750	.667	0.00	13.50
Pimentel, Jose	R-R	6-2	155	10-20-86	1	2	5.40	22	0	0	30	38	21	18	2	15	30	.304	.317	.298	9.00	4.50
Salazar, Yesid	R-R	6-1	175	11-2-86	1	0	1.17	10	0	0	2	15	10	2	2	4	11	.189	.320	.071	6.46	2.35
Underwood, Andrew	R-R	6-4	185	5-20-85	0	0	4.91	2	0	0	0	4	4	2	2	0	0	2	.286	.000	.364	4.91	0.00
Vandel, Geoff	L-L	6-1	190	6-9-87	5	4	4.29	13	13	0	0	65	82	39	31	4	12	48	.305	.345	.286	6.65	1.66
Viloria, Euclides	L-L	6-0	175	9-9-89	2	3	5.63	14	14	0	0	54	49	35	34	2	36	73	.238	.270	.231	12.09	5.96

FIELDING

Catcher	PCT	G	PO	A	E	DP	PB
Hernandez	1.000	2	20	1	0	0	0
Morton	1.000	5	14	2	0	0	0
Naylor	.990	23	177	18	2	2	9
Quiles	.966	13	75	9	3	0	2
Solis	.965	25	167	26	7	1	4

First Base	PCT	G	PO	A	E	DP
Brown	.988	29	227	14	3	20
Garzon	1.000	1	7	0	0	0
Mayi	.989	31	262	14	3	20
Morton	1.000	1	7	1	0	1

Second Base	PCT	G	PO	A	E	DP
Ciriaco	1.000	1	2	5	0	1
Garzon	.953	21	35	46	4	8

	PCT	G	PO	A	E	DP
Ruth	.977	19	35	51	2	13
Valdez	.938	21	36	54	6	12

Third Base	PCT	G	PO	A	E	DP
Carrasco	.813	13	9	30	9	3
Garzon	.905	26	22	73	10	3
Joynt	.800	6	4	8	3	1
Rincon	.742	14	7	16	8	0
Valdez	.000	1	0	0	1	0

Shortstop	PCT	G	PO	A	E	DP
Ciriaco	.889	9	11	21	4	5
Cumberland	.883	20	29	62	12	9
Garzon	1.000	1	2	2	0	1
Valdez	.940	27	47	78	8	13
Zawadzki	.895	4	5	12	2	1

Outfield	PCT	G	PO	A	E	DP
Buschini	.933	24	26	2	2	0
Carvajal	1.000	24	31	1	0	0
Chalk	1.000	7	14	1	0	0
Florentino	.769	14	9	1	3	1
Hill	.944	45	63	5	4	0
Joynt	.892	22	31	2	4	0
Laurent	1.000	8	7	0	0	0
McAnulty	—	2	0	0	0	0
Mercado	.972	28	33	2	1	1
Perry	1.000	16	34	0	0	0
Watson	.963	10	25	1	1	0

DSL PADRES   ROOKIE

DOMINICAN SUMMER LEAGUE

BATTING	B-T	HT	WT	DOB	AVG	vLH	vRH	G	AB	R	H	2B	3B	HR	RBI	BB	HBP	SH	SF	SO	SB	CS	SLG	OBP
Acosta, Kevin	R-R	5-9	150	4-15-89	.189	.222	.182	48	148	26	28	3	0	0	9	34	11	3	2	43	12	7	.209	.374
Andrade, Angel	R-R	6-2	205	1-6-90	.077	.200	.000	5	13	0	1	0	0	0	1	3	0	0	0	8	0	0	.077	.250
Armstrong, Joel	R-R	6-2	185	11-2-88	.158	.184	.151	54	184	18	29	8	0	2	26	21	17	0	3	66	3	1	.234	.298
Garce, Daniel	R-R	6-1	166	6-6-89	.260	.192	.277	39	127	23	33	3	0	0	6	22	4	0	1	41	3	1	.283	.383
Garcia, Carlos	R-R	6-3	165	3-29-89	.192	.290	.165	47	146	17	28	5	1	0	10	19	4	0	2	47	4	0	.240	.298
Gonzalez, Edisson	R-R	5-11	165	6-4-90	.208	.217	.207	46	144	14	30	6	0	2	19	27	7	0	1	43	7	3	.292	.358
Lopez, Jose	R-R	5-10	175	11-10-89	.221	.100	.263	35	77	15	17	3	0	0	7	19	5	1	1	24	1	4	.260	.402
Luna, Jansell	R-R	6-0	190	6-6-88	.229	.182	.241	36	105	6	24	5	0	0	17	11	0	0	2	29	1	0	.276	.297
Marte, Keisy	R-R	5-10	169	12-14-88	.228	.314	.203	47	158	20	36	12	1	2	15	36	0	2	2	39	7	4	.354	.367
Mato, Jose	L-L	5-11	155	12-14-88	.170	.250	.163	23	53	8	9	2	0	0	4	14	0	1	1	23	3	1	.208	.338
Nuno, Manuel	R-R	6-6	264	1-11-89	.167	.045	.200	36	102	12	17	4	0	0	4	17	2	0	0	38	0	1	.206	.298
Paulino, Jose	R-R	6-0	182	11-13-88	.194	.238	.184	43	124	10	24	1	0	0	4	16	5	1	0	37	5	1	.202	.310
Polanco, Wary	R-R	6-2	171	3-1-88	.171	.200	.167	37	105	14	18	4	0	0	9	23	4	0	2	34	2	4	.210	.336
Pozo, Jhonaldo	R-R	6-3	183	3-28-89	.140	.074	.153	53	164	6	23	7	1	1	12	21	1	1	0	74	0	0	.213	.242
Rincon, Edinson	R-R	6-1	185	8-11-90	.295	.318	.290	33	122	14	36	7	0	2	15	17	1	0	1	26	2	1	.402	.383
Sosa, Cesar	R-R	6-4	175	11-25-88	.152	.200	.140	58	171	12	26	5	0	0	11	28	4	0	1	62	1	2	.181	.284
Torres, Jose	R-R	6-2	180	8-21-88	.154	.333	.130	10	26	2	4	2	0	0	2	4	2	0	0	8	1	0	.231	.313

PITCHING	B-T	HT	WT	DOB	W	L	ERA	G	GS	CG	SV	IP	H	R	ER	HR	BB	SO	AVG	vLH	vRH	K/9	BB/9
Arias, Rafeal	R-R	6-0	165	1-3-89	0	3	7.84	23	0	0	2	21	27	23	18	0	16	12	.307	.258	.333	5.23	6.97
Berroa, Simon	R-R	6-4	165	10-28-87	0	9	4.42	13	13	0	0	59	63	41	29	1	22	42	.270	.309	.250	6.41	3.36
Carlin, Luis	R-R	6-3	200	2-28-89	1	1	7.23	13	0	0	0	24	38	30	19	0	14	14	.369	.400	.359	5.32	5.32
Chavez, Juan	R-R	6-0	200	12-25-89	3	2	5.56	11	9	0	0	45	47	33	28	4	23	20	.273	.235	.289	3.97	4.57
De La Cruz, Luis	R-R	6-6	195	6-15-89	1	5	7.77	9	8	0	0	22	18	21	19	1	22	13	.237	.471	.169	5.32	9.00
De Paula, Jose	L-L	6-2	165	3-4-90	2	5	2.44	14	13	0	0	66	52	27	18	0	21	78	.208	.095	.231	10.58	2.85
Hernandez, Pedro	L-L	5-10	200	4-12-89	0	1	2.03	9	0	0	1	13	12	6	3	1	4	13	.245	.333	.233	8.78	2.70
Ojeda, Erick	R-R	6-5	260	9-18-89	0	2	14.14	14	0	0	0	14	22	25	22	1	21	5	.349	.333	.357	3.21	13.50
Oramas, Juan	L-L	5-10	215	5-11-90	2	3	3.81	16	5	0	0	54	39	25	23	1	20	63	.196	.227	.192	10.44	3.31
Osuna, Steven	R-R	6-3	170	5-5-87	4	6	3.65	15	15	0	0	81	75	49	33	1	27	75	.247	.265	.235	8.30	2.99
Paredes, Enderson	R-R	6-2	135	8-23-86	1	2	4.86	16	0	0	1	17	22	25	9	1	14	12	.286	.400	.246	6.48	7.56
Rosario, Juan	R-R	6-1	178	12-12-89	3	2	4.41	20	0	0	1	33	30	24	16	1	18	35	.242	.240	.243	9.64	4.96
Sotelo, Victor	R-R	6-3	212	5-20-89	0	2	5.00	17	1	0	0	36	35	20	20	1	9	31	.246	.184	.280	7.75	2.25
Valdez, Stalyn	R-R	6-3	185	11-14-89	0	3	7.24	18	0	0	0	32	35	32	26	0	19	19	.267	.231	.291	5.29	5.29
Veras, Junior	R-R	6-1	215	1-16-87	1	0	1.99	19	0	0	4	23	12	9	5	0	8	22	.150	.120	.164	8.74	3.18

FIELDING

Catcher	PCT	G	PO	A	E	DP	PB
Luna	.949	28	172	16	10	3	5
Polanco	.989	36	237	41	3	2	10
Pozo	1.000	1	2	0	0	0	1
Torres	.982	7	51	5	1	2	0

First Base	PCT	G	PO	A	E	DP
Lopez	1.000	1	3	0	0	2
Luna	—	1	0	0	0	0
Nuno	.982	34	258	20	5	23
Paulino	1.000	1	3	0	0	1
Polanco	1.000	2	1	0	0	0
Pozo	.977	34	242	16	6	13
Torres	1.000	2	13	2	0	1

Second Base	PCT	G	PO	A	E	DP
Acosta	.932	37	70	66	10	18
Garce	1.000	2	2	2	0	1
Garcia	.969	12	9	22	1	3
Lopez	.943	19	37	46	5	8
Marte	.941	6	5	11	1	1

Third Base	PCT	G	PO	A	E	DP
Garcia	1.000	3	2	4	0	1
Lopez	1.000	0	1	0	0	0
Marte	.750	1	1	2	1	0
Paulino	.880	36	25	85	15	9
Pozo	.872	12	8	26	5	0
Rincon	.780	16	16	30	13	3

Shortstop	PCT	G	PO	A	E	DP
Garce	.899	28	44	63	12	14
Lopez	.810	5	8	9	4	0
Marte	.911	37	84	90	17	13

Outfield	PCT	G	PO	A	E	DP
Andrade	1.000	5	10	0	0	0
Armstrong	.924	54	67	6	6	2
Garcia	.925	26	37	0	3	0
Gonzalez	.922	42	66	5	6	2
Lopez	.667	2	2	0	1	0
Mato	.897	19	26	0	3	0
Paulino	—	1	0	0	0	0
Pozo	—	2	0	0	0	0
Sosa	1.000	58	79	4	0	2

San Francisco Giants

BY ANDY BAGGARLY

The Giants watched their franchise player break baseball's all-time home run record and they celebrated the All-Star Game at AT&T Park, but those were fleeting highs amid their third consecutive losing season.

Even as Barry Bonds hit 28 home runs to eclipse Hank Aaron's 33-year-old record, the 43-year-old slugger could not hold up a sagging lineup of veterans (Ray Durham, Dave Roberts, Rich Aurilia, Ryan Klesko) that GM Brian Sabean had signed over the winter for one more shot at the moon.

This time, Sabean missed wildly. The Giants finished 71-91 and in last place in the National League West—the team's first time in the cellar since 1996, the year before Sabean took control of the club.

A week before the season ended, owner Peter Magowan informed Bonds that he would not get his wish and return for a 16th and final season in a Giants uniform. That decision was all but made on July 13, when Magowan signed Sabean to a contract extension that runs through the 2009 season. While announcing the extension, Magowan talked about a philosophical shift away from short-term fixes and toward a healthier mix of home-grown talent and free agents. He compared the Giants' new model to clubs like the Braves, Dodgers and Padres.

"I don't want anyone to think we don't want to win in '08. We do," Magowan said. "But it will be a different philosophy, a different emphasis than has been the case the last several years."

The Giants still have hope of contending in the NL West, even though the Dodgers, Rockies and Diamondbacks are flush with young talent and the latter two clubs played for the NL pennant. Their hopes are pinned to young pitching, which appears to be among the most promising in baseball.

Tim Lincecum was so dominant at Triple-A Fresno that he forced the Giants to bump veteran Russ Ortiz from the rotation in May. The former Golden Spikes winner from Washington had thrown fewer than 63 minor league innings when promoted, but never gave the Giants a reason to think about sending him back. He had a sensational rookie season, striking out 150 in 146 ⅓ innings.

Matt Cain's 7-16 record was a product of bad luck and terrible run support. The 22-year-old's 3.65 ERA was the 10th best among NL starters, and his ERA against division rivals (2.63) was actually better than Cy Young favorite Jake Peavy (2.72) posted against the NL West. Cain's most impressive quality was his level-headed demeanor as he dealt with a difficult season.

Barry Zito was a disappointment as a $126 million acquisition, but his performance spiked in the second half. Righthander Kevin Correia came on strong in eight starts down the stretch.

Manager Bruce Bochy missed his old closer, Trevor Hoffman, and the strong bullpen he left behind in San Diego. The Giants played the most games in the majors decided by two or fewer, finishing with a 39-55 record in those games.

Sabean traded the unpopular Armando Benitez to Florida under duress in late May, and righthander Brad Hennessey spent most of the year in the closer role. But Brian Wilson showed electric stuff down the stretch, and Tyler Walker made a nice comeback from Tommy John surgery.

With the season lost, September became a time to showcase young players Second baseman Kevin Frandsen had a

PLAYERS OF THE YEAR

MAJOR LEAGUE: BARRY BONDS, OF

Bonds hit a team-high 28 home runs in 2007, breaking Hank Aaron's all-time record of 755 before setting a new record of 762. Bonds didn't have enough plate appearance to officially qualify, but his .480 on-base percentage would have easily been baseball's top mark. Bonds led the majors with 132 walks and 43 intentional walks.

MINOR LEAGUE: NATE SCHIERHOLTZ, OF

Schierholtz had a solid year for Triple-A Fresno, finishing with a .333/.363/.560 line. He ranked fifth in the Pacific Coast League in average, and was tied for third among all outfielders in full-season minor leagues. The 2003 second-rounder also collected 54 extra-base hits, including 16 homers.

ORGANIZATIONAL LEADERS

BATTING		★Minimum 250 at-bats
★AVG	Schierholtz, Nate, Fresno	.333
R	Burriss, Emmanuel, San Jose/Augusta	87
H	Bowker, John, Connecticut	160
TB	Bowker, John, Connecticut	273
2B	Pill, Brett, Augusta	47
3B	Velez, Eugenio, Connecticut/Fresno	9
HR	McClain, Scott, Fresno	31
RBI	McClain, Scott, Fresno	100
BB	Leone, Justin, Fresno	78
SO	Mooney, Michael, San Jose	132
SB	Burriss, Emmanuel, San Jose/Augusta	68
★OBP	Richardson, Antoan, San Jose	.399
★SLG	Schierholtz, Nate, Fresno	.56
PITCHING		^Minimum 75 innings
W	Snyder, Benjamin, Augusta	16
L	Broshuis, Garrett, Connecticut	17
^ERA	Pucetas, Kevin, Augusta	1.86
G	Wilding, Taylor, Connecticut/San Jose	51
CG	Broshuis, Garrett, Connecticut	2
SV	Anderson, Brian, Connecticut	29
IP	Cowart, Adam, Augusta	170
BB	Blackley, Travis, Fresno	68
SO	Martinez, Joseph, San Jose	151
^AVG	Sosa, Henry, Augusta/San Jose	.209

strong September to position himself for a starting job next year on a team that promises to have many new faces.

The Giants enjoyed tremendous success on the minor league level, where high Class A San Jose won the California League title, short-season Salem-Keizer won the Northwest League and low Class A Augusta (89-51) had the best winning percentage among full-season minor league affiliates. The Giants overall .575 winning percentage was second to the Yankees among major league organizations.

But other than the young players who matriculated to the big leagues, it was a mixed bag in terms of prospect development. Promising hitters like first baseman Travis Ishikawa and outfielder Eddy Martinez-Esteve had poor seasons that might have killed their long-term projectability, and as usual, the Giants won with overachievers and older players at the lower levels.

General Manager: Brian Sabean. **Farm Director:** Bobby Evans. **Scouting Director:** Matt Nerland

Class	Team	League	W	L	PCT	Finish*	Manager	Affiliate Since
Majors	San Francisco	National	71	91	.438	14th (16)	Bruce Bochy	—
Triple-A	Fresno Grizzlies	Pacific Coast	77	67	.535	4th (16)	Dan Rohn	1998
Double-A	Connecticut Defenders	Eastern	63	78	.447	10th (12)	Dave Machemer	2003
High A	San Jose Giants	California	73	67	.521	5th (10)^	Lenn Sakata	1988
Low A	Augusta GreenJackets	South Atlantic	89	51	.636	1st (16)	Roberto Kelly	2005
Short-season	Salem-Keizer	Northwest	57	19	.750	1st (8)^	Steve Decker	1997
Rookie	AZL Giants	Arizona	33	23	.589	2nd (9)	Bert Hunter	2000
Overall 2007 Minor League Record			**392**	**305**	**.562**	**3rd**		

* Finish in overall standings (No. of teams in league) ^League champion

ORGANIZATION STATISTICS

SAN FRANCISCO GIANTS

NATIONAL LEAGUE

BATTING	B-T	HT	WT	DOB	AVG	vLH	vRH	G	AB	R	H	2B	3B	HR	RBI	BB	HBP	SH	SF	SO	SB	CS	SLG	OBP
Alfonzo, Eliezer	R-R	5-11	210	2-7-79	.250	.150	.295	26	64	5	16	2	1	1	6	2	1	0	0	23	0	2	.359	.284
Aurilia, Rich	R-R	6-1	190	9-2-71	.252	.240	.260	99	329	40	83	19	2	5	33	22	4	0	3	45	0	0	.368	.304
Bonds, Barry	L-L	6-2	240	7-24-64	.276	.265	.283	126	340	75	94	14	0	28	66	132	3	0	2	54	5	0	.565	.480
Davis, Rajai	R-R	5-11	195	10-19-80	.282	.302	.266	51	142	26	40	9	1	1	7	14	4	2	0	25	17	4	.380	.363
2-team (24 Pittsburgh)					.279	—	—	75	190	32	53	11	2	1	9	21	4	3	1	28	22	6	.374	.361
Durham, Ray	B-R	5-8	190	11-30-71	.218	.200	.224	138	464	56	101	21	2	11	71	53	2	0	9	75	10	2	.343	.295
Feliz, Pedro	R-R	6-1	210	4-27-75	.253	.257	.252	150	557	61	141	28	2	20	72	29	1	0	3	70	2	2	.418	.290
Figueroa, Luis R.	B-R	5-9	165	2-16-74	.200	.000	.250	6	5	1	1	0	0	0	0	0	0	0	0	0	0	0	.200	.200
Frandsen, Kevin	R-R	6-0	180	5-24-82	.269	.262	.274	109	264	26	71	12	1	5	31	21	5	3	3	24	4	3	.379	.331
Klesko, Ryan	L-L	6-3	220	6-12-71	.260	.262	.259	116	362	51	94	27	3	6	44	46	1	1	1	68	5	1	.401	.344
Lewis, Fred	L-R	6-2	190	12-9-80	.287	.276	.289	58	157	34	45	6	2	3	19	19	3	1	0	32	5	1	.408	.374
Linden, Todd	B-R	6-3	220	6-30-80	.182	.240	.133	30	55	6	10	1	0	0	3	5	0	0	0	23	0	0	.200	.250
2-team (85 Florida)					.245	—	—	115	184	21	45	8	1	1	11	19	1	0	0	59	4	0	.315	.319
McClain, Scott	R-R	6-4	220	5-19-72	.182	.143	.250	8	11	1	2	0	0	0	0	0	0	0	0	2	0	0	.182	.182
Molina, Bengie	R-R	5-11	225	7-20-74	.276	.271	.277	134	497	38	137	19	1	19	81	15	2	1	2	53	0	0	.433	.298
Niekro, Lance	R-R	6-3	225	1-29-79	.176	.167	.200	11	17	0	3	0	0	0	0	1	0	0	0	5	0	0	.176	.222
Ortmeier, Dan	B-L	6-4	215	5-11-81	.287	.257	.310	62	157	20	45	7	4	6	16	7	1	0	2	41	2	1	.497	.317
Roberts, Dave	L-L	5-10	180	5-31-72	.260	.156	.285	114	396	61	103	17	9	2	23	42	0	4	0	66	31	5	.364	.331
Rodriguez, Guillermo	R-R	5-11	195	5-15-78	.253	.269	.246	39	87	10	22	6	0	1	14	10	0	0	1	17	0	1	.356	.327
Schierholtz, Nate	L-R	6-2	215	2-15-84	.304	.500	.266	39	112	9	34	5	3	0	10	2	1	0	2	19	3	1	.402	.316
Sweeney, Mark	L-L	6-1	215	10-26-69	.256	.250	.256	76	90	18	23	8	0	2	11	13	3	1	0	18	2	0	.411	.368
2-team (30 Los Angeles)					.260	—	—	106	123	20	32	9	0	2	13	14	3	1	0	29	2	0	.382	.350
Velez, Eugenio	B-R	6-1	160	5-16-82	.273	.000	.300	14	11	5	3	0	2	0	2	2	0	0	3	4	3	0	.636	.385
Vizquel, Omar	B-R	5-9	175	4-24-67	.246	.243	.247	145	513	54	126	18	3	4	51	44	1	14	3	48	14	6	.316	.305
Winn, Randy	B-R	6-2	195	6-9-74	.300	.351	.277	155	593	73	178	42	1	14	65	44	7	4	5	85	15	3	.445	.353

PITCHING	B-T	HT	WT	DOB	W	L	ERA	G	GS	CG	SV	IP	H	R	ER	HR	BB	SO	AVG	vLH	vRH	K/9	BB/9
Atchison, Scott	R-R	6-2	200	3-29-76	0	0	4.11	22	0	0	0	31	32	14	14	5	10	25	.274	.278	.272	7.34	2.93
Benitez, Armando	R-R	6-4	260	11-3-72	0	3	4.67	19	0	0	9	17	17	9	9	3	9	18	.254	.297	.200	9.35	4.67
2-team (36 Florida)					2	8	5.36	55	0	0	9	50	49	37	30	8	29	57	—	—	—	10.19	5.19
Blackley, Travis	L-L	6-3	200	11-4-82	0	0	7.27	2	2	0	0	9	10	7	7	2	5	5	.294	.111	.360	5.19	5.19
Cain, Matt	R-R	6-3	235	10-1-84	7	16	3.65	32	32	1	0	200	173	84	81	14	79	163	.235	.248	.224	7.33	3.56
Chulk, Vinnie	R-R	6-2	195	12-19-78	5	4	3.57	57	0	0	0	53	53	22	21	3	14	41	.264	.290	.250	6.96	2.38
Correia, Kevin	R-R	6-3	205	8-24-80	4	7	3.45	59	8	0	0	102	94	39	39	9	40	80	.242	.217	.257	7.08	3.54
Giese, Dan	R-R	6-3	200	5-19-77	0	2	4.82	8	0	0	0	9	8	5	5	4	2	7	.235	.143	.300	6.75	1.93
Hennessey, Brad	R-R	6-2	200	2-7-80	4	5	3.42	69	0	0	19	68	66	26	26	7	23	40	.257	.245	.265	5.27	3.03
Kline, Steve	R-L	6-1	230	8-22-72	1	2	4.70	68	0	0	2	46	58	25	24	2	18	17	.301	.318	.287	3.33	3.52
Lincecum, Tim	L-R	5-11	170	6-15-84	7	5	4.00	24	24	0	0	146	122	70	65	12	65	150	.226	.214	.238	9.23	4.00
Lowry, Noah	R-L	6-2	205	10-10-80	14	8	3.92	26	26	1	0	156	155	76	68	12	87	87	.265	.216	.278	5.02	5.02
Messenger, Randy	R-R	6-6	240	8-13-81	1	3	5.09	37	0	0	1	41	58	23	23	4	12	22	.343	.361	.330	4.87	2.66
2-team (23 Florida)					2	4	4.20	60	0	0	1	64	85	30	30	4	21	34	—	—	—	4.76	2.94
Misch, Pat	R-L	6-2	170	8-18-81	0	4	4.24	18	4	0	0	40	47	21	19	3	12	26	.296	.238	.316	5.80	2.68
Morris, Matt	R-R	6-5	215	8-9-74	7	7	4.35	21	21	0	0	137	162	79	66	12	39	73	.296	.307	.287	4.81	2.57
2-team (11 Pittsburgh)					10	11	4.89	32	32	3	0	199	240	123	108	18	61	102	—	—	—	4.62	2.76
Munter, Scott	R-R	6-6	260	3-7-80	1	1	4.22	12	0	0	0	11	14	5	5	0	4	4	.368	.273	.407	3.38	3.38
Ortiz, Russ	R-R	6-1	220	6-5-74	2	3	5.51	12	8	0	0	49	57	32	30	4	20	27	.295	.346	.259	4.96	3.67
Sanchez, Jonathan	L-L	6-2	180	11-19-82	1	5	5.88	33	4	0	0	52	57	34	34	8	28	62	.284	.197	.321	10.73	4.85
Taschner, Jack	L-L	6-3	210	4-21-78	3	1	5.40	63	0	0	0	50	44	31	30	4	29	51	.235	.316	.176	9.18	5.22
Threets, Erick	L-L	6-5	240	11-4-81	0	0	19.29	3	0	0	0	2	5	5	5	0	3	1	.417	.750	.250	3.86	11.57
Walker, Tyler	R-R	6-3	275	5-15-76	2	0	1.26	15	0	0	0	14	12	2	2	0	4	9	.250	.182	.308	5.65	2.51
Wilson, Brian	R-R	6-1	205	3-16-82	1	2	2.28	24	0	0	6	24	16	6	6	1	7	18	.188	.304	.145	6.85	2.66
Zito, Barry	L-L	6-4	210	5-13-78	11	13	4.53	34	33	0	0	197	182	105	99	24	83	131	.244	.242	.244	5.99	3.80

FIELDING

Catcher	PCT	G	PO	A	E	DP	PB
Alfonzo	.972	17	97	7	3	0	1
Feliz	—	1	0	0	0	0	0
Molina	.991	129	808	61	8	4	16
Rodriguez	.980	33	179	17	4	1	4

First Base	PCT	G	PO	A	E	DP
Aurilia	.995	55	375	18	2	42
Feliz	1.000	4	27	2	0	5
Klesko	.996	100	755	66	3	73
McClain	1.000	3	8	0	0	0
Niekro	1.000	3	24	2	0	4
Ortmeier	1.000	22	171	11	0	10
Sweeney	1.000	9	51	2	0	4

Second Base	PCT	G	PO	A	E	DP
Aurilia	.974	9	18	19	1	7
Durham	.978	124	244	300	12	86
Frandsen	.979	49	81	108	4	24
Velez	.900	4	5	4	1	2

Third Base	PCT	G	PO	A	E	DP
Aurilia	.931	22	15	39	4	6
Feliz	.973	143	93	302	11	28
Frandsen	1.000	9	2	11	0	2
Winn	1.000	1	1	0	0	0

Shortstop	PCT	G	PO	A	E	DP
Aurilia	.961	12	14	35	2	6
Figueroa	1.000	1	1	3	0	0
Frandsen	.985	22	28	38	1	7
Vizquel	.986	143	198	444	9	90

Outfield	PCT	G	PO	A	E	DP
Bonds	.976	110	162	2	4	0
Davis	1.000	50	104	3	0	0
Feliz	1.000	3	5	0	0	0
Figueroa	—	1	0	0	0	0
Frandsen	.933	13	13	1	1	0
Klesko	1.000	3	4	0	0	0
Lewis	.990	53	97	0	1	0
Linden	.930	27	38	2	3	0
Lowry	—	1	0	0	0	0
Ortmeier	1.000	34	46	0	0	0
Roberts	.988	102	247	6	3	0
Schierholtz	.980	30	48	0	1	0
Sweeney	1.000	10	7	0	0	0
Velez	—	2	0	0	0	0
Winn	.994	150	318	5	2	0

FRESNO GRIZZLIES

TRIPLE-A

PACIFIC COAST LEAGUE

BATTING	B-T	HT	WT	DOB	AVG	vLH	vRH	G	AB	R	H	2B	3B	HR	RBI	BB	HBP	SH	SF	SO	SB	CS	SLG	OBP
Alfonzo, Eliezer	R-R	5-11	210	2-7-79	.297	.318	.286	18	64	9	19	6	0	3	10	1	0	1	0	8	0	0	.531	.308
Aurilia, Rich	R-R	6-1	190	9-2-71	.333	—	.333	2	6	1	2	0	0	0	2	1	0	0	0	1	0	0	.333	.429
Bergolla, William	R-R	6-0	175	2-4-83	.306	.436	.260	99	356	63	109	22	1	7	37	31	3	3	4	47	12	3	.433	.363
Cordido, Julio	R-R	6-1	185	7-30-80	.250	.444	.158	19	28	4	7	3	0	1	3	3	0	0	0	4	0	0	.464	.323
De La Rosa, Tomas	R-R	5-10	180	1-28-78	.288	.344	.267	122	459	64	132	28	3	11	70	34	1	5	2	65	21	7	.434	.337
Figueroa,	B-R	5-9	165	2-16-74	.302	.370	.269	117	446	68	134	22	4	4	53	28	5	13	3	34	7	9	.397	.349
Frandsen, Kevin	R-R	6-0	180	5-24-82	.403	.350	.426	19	67	13	27	5	0	1	7	9	5	2	0	6	4	2	.522	.506
Gunther, Barry	B-R	6-0	190	3-18-82	.333	.000	.500	2	6	1	2	0	0	0	1	2	0	0	0	2	0	0	.333	.500
Horwitz, Brian	R-R	6-1	190	11-7-82	.326	.300	.337	84	264	32	86	21	2	1	21	21	4	0	1	22	2	0	.432	.383
Jennings, Todd	R-R	6-0	190	12-10-81	.206	.353	.152	22	63	4	13	3	0	1	3	1	2	0	0	16	0	0	.302	.242
Knoedler, Justin	R-R	6-2	215	7-17-80	.288	.284	.290	89	302	44	87	30	2	7	42	26	3	1	4	78	7	1	.470	.346
Leone, Justin	R-R	6-1	210	3-9-77	.269	.302	.253	128	428	83	115	30	4	20	60	78	4	0	5	109	26	1	.498	.383
Lewis, Fred	L-R	6-2	190	12-9-80	.292	.258	.312	42	171	31	50	8	6	8	32	19	1	0	0	36	9	1	.550	.366
Luster, Jeremiah	R-R	5-10	175	8-31-86	.333	.250	.500	2	6	0	2	0	0	0	0	2	0	0	0	1	0	0	.333	.500
McClain, Scott	R-R	6-4	220	5-19-72	.267	.283	.261	132	468	69	125	24	0	31	100	59	2	0	4	98	1	2	.517	.349
Niekro, Lance	R-R	6-3	225	1-29-79	.301	.356	.276	47	143	21	43	8	2	5	20	12	1	0	2	32	0	1	.490	.354
Ochoa, Ivan	R-R	5-9	160	12-16-82	.296	.377	.262	47	179	22	53	11	2	3	20	10	2	3	2	30	8	2	.430	.337
Ortmeier, Dan	B-L	6-4	215	5-11-81	.262	.310	.239	79	305	39	80	19	1	10	54	27	7	0	3	63	16	2	.430	.333
Roberts, Dave	L-L	5-10	180	5-31-72	.143	.333	.000	2	7	1	1	0	0	0	0	1	0	0	0	2	0	0	.143	.250
Rodriguez, Guillermo	R-R	5-11	195	5-15-78	.243	.333	.211	33	103	15	25	6	0	1	16	11	1	3	1	8	1	0	.330	.319
Santos, Chad	L-L	5-11	180	4-28-81	.243	.095	.280	33	103	22	25	7	0	4	15	16	1	0	0	30	0	1	.427	.350
Sarmiento, Elio	B-R	6-0	200	6-20-86	.222	—	.222	6	9	0	2	1	0	0	0	2	1	0	0	2	0	0	.333	.417
Schierholtz, Nate	L-R	6-2	215	2-15-84	.333	.279	.353	109	411	67	137	31	7	16	68	17	6	1	4	58	10	4	.560	.365
Thompson, William	L-L	6-1	180	11-20-82	.200	.286	.125	4	15	1	3	0	0	0	3	0	1	0	0	2	0	0	.267	.352
Timpner, Clay	L-L	6-2	195	5-13-83	.301	.202	.334	109	392	51	118	11	4	6	39	37	2	5	1	68	9	11	.395	.363
Velez, Eugenio	B-R	6-1	160	5-16-82	.278	.143	.364	4	18	5	5	0	0	0	0	2	1	0	0	3	5	0	.278	.381
Von Schell, Tyler	R-R	6-3	229	7-7-79	.261	.308	.200	6	23	2	6	2	0	0	2	1	0	0	0	5	0	0	.348	.292

PITCHING	B-T	HT	WT	DOB	W	L	ERA	G	GS	CG	SV	IP	H	R	ER	HR	BB	SO	AVG	vLH	vRH	K/9	BB/9
Atchison, Scott	R-R	6-2	200	3-29-76	3	2	2.01	38	1	0	4	54	44	17	12	1	8	51	.218	.221	.216	8.55	1.34
Begg, Chris	R-R	6-4	195	9-12-79	12	5	4.36	23	23	1	0	140	173	78	68	18	25	67	.309	.393	.244	4.30	1.60
Blackley, Travis	L-L	6-3	200	11-4-82	10	8	4.66	28	28	0	0	162	156	87	84	21	68	121	.259	.235	.269	6.71	3.77
Bowles, Brian	R-R	6-5	220	8-18-76	0	2	7.16	9	6	0	0	28	40	25	22	3	12	8	.351	.400	.296	2.60	3.90
De La Rosa, Carlos	L-L	6-2	190	7-15-84	0	0	0.00	1	0	0	0	1	0	0	0	0	0	1	.000	.000	.000	9.00	0.00
Giese, Dan	R-R	6-3	200	5-19-77	3	1	2.82	47	0	0	2	73	65	26	23	2	10	76	.236	.224	.245	9.33	1.23
Hines, Carlos	R-R	6-3	190	9-26-80	1	1	4.69	29	0	0	2	40	46	22	21	2	22	24	.297	.343	.261	5.36	4.91
Kim, Sun-Woo	R-R	6-2	180	9-4-77	8	8	4.87	25	18	1	0	118	131	77	64	11	35	88	.284	.306	.268	6.69	2.66
Kinney, Matt	R-R	6-5	230	12-16-76	12	10	4.02	27	26	1	0	157	164	84	70	25	36	141	.266	.289	.250	8.10	2.07
Lincecum, Tim	L-R	5-11	170	6-15-84	4	0	0.29	5	5	0	0	31	12	1	1	0	11	46	.119	.113	.125	13.35	3.19
Meaux, Ryan	R-L	5-11	170	10-5-78	0	3	8.25	7	0	0	0	12	19	12	11	0	4	9	.373	.304	.429	6.75	3.00
3-team (13 Sacramento, 7 Memphis)					0	3	5.68	27	0	0	0	32	41	23	20	3	10	32	—	—	—	9.09	2.84
Misch, Pat	R-L	6-2	190	8-18-81	2	5	2.30	34	3	0	1	67	54	24	17	4	19	74	.227	.252	.207	9.99	2.56
Munter, Scott	R-R	6-6	260	3-7-80	1	6	4.17	48	0	0	1	58	62	28	27	3	24	14	.279	.300	.265	2.16	3.70
Niekro, Lance	R-R	6-3	225	1-29-79	0	0	27.00	1	0	0	0	1	3	2	2	0	0	0	.600	.500	.667	0.00	0.00
Ortiz, Russ	R-R	6-1	220	6-5-74	1	1	3.24	5	3	0	0	17	16	7	6	0	6	9	.250	.348	.195	6.48	1.08
Palmer, Matt	R-R	6-2	200	3-21-79	11	8	4.32	29	25	1	0	150	155	80	72	17	51	98	.271	.286	.258	5.88	3.06
Rincon, Ricardo	L-L	5-9	210	4-13-70	1	0	1.69	7	0	0	0	5	7	1	1	0	1	3	.333	.375	.200	5.06	1.69
Rodriguez, Wilmin	L-L	6-2	175	5-13-85	0	0	0.00	1	0	0	0	1	0	0	0	0	0	0	.250	.000	.333	9.00	0.00
Sadler, Billy	R-R	6-0	200	9-21-81	3	2	5.95	40	0	0	6	42	36	31	28	5	35	59	.229	.288	.187	12.54	7.44
Sanchez, Jonathan	L-L	6-2	180	11-19-82	0	0	2.18	6	3	0	0	21	15	5	5	0	8	27	.197	.143	.218	11.76	3.48
Threets, Erick	L-L	6-5	240	11-4-81	3	1	3.46	40	3	0	1	55	46	26	21	4	35	40	.235	.143	.286	6.59	5.76
Walker, Tyler	R-R	6-3	275	5-15-76	1	2	4.70	20	0	0	7	23	25	12	12	5	10	23	.269	.349	.200	9.00	3.91
Wilson, Brian	R-R	6-1	205	3-16-82	1	2	2.10	31	0	0	11	34	24	13	8	0	24	37	.194	.250	.163	9.70	6.29

FIELDING

Catcher	PCT	G	PO	A	E	DP	PB
Alfonzo	.959	17	108	8	5	1	3
Gunther	1.000	2	5	2	0	0	0
Jennings	.993	20	125	8	1	1	1
Knoedler	.993	83	550	57	4	6	8
Rodriguez	.984	32	214	36	4	4	3
Sarmiento	1.000	2	12	0	0	0	1

First Base	PCT	G	PO	A	E	DP
Aurilia	1.000	1	7	0	0	0
Horwitz	1.000	4	18	2	0	1
Leone	1.000	2	10	0	0	0
McClain	.992	101	800	67	7	99
Niekro	.995	21	181	13	1	22
Ortmeier	1.000	6	50	4	0	5
Santos	.983	21	164	14	3	19
Thompson	.960	3	24	0	1	2

Second Base	PCT	G	PO	A	E	DP
Bergolla	.975	93	190	242	11	72

De La Rosa	1.000	33	50	86	0	28
Figueroa	.975	17	29	49	2	11
Frandsen	.980	10	19	31	1	7
Leone	1.000	4	4	15	0	1

Third Base	PCT	G	PO	A	E	DP
Aurilia	.500	1	0	1	1	0
De La Rosa	.938	79	46	119	11	13
Figueroa	1.000	2	2	2	0	0
Frandsen	.857	3	4	2	1	0
Leone	.943	58	35	98	8	9
McClain	.951	17	12	27	2	2

Shortstop	PCT	G	PO	A	E	DP
Aurilia	1.000	1	0	3	0	0
Cordido	.750	1	1	2	1	0
De La Rosa	.953	12	9	32	2	12
Figueroa	.965	87	147	272	15	85
Frandsen	.963	6	11	15	1	3
Leone	1.000	1	0	3	0	1

Ochoa	.944	46	62	122	11	26

Outfield	PCT	G	PO	A	E	DP
Cordido	1.000	4	6	0	0	0
Figueroa	1.000	5	5	0	0	0
Horwitz	.975	60	108	7	3	2
Knoedler	1.000	2	2	0	0	0
Leone	.978	63	129	4	3	1
Lewis	.953	41	81	1	4	1
Luster	1.000	2	6	0	0	0
Ortmeier	.993	69	134	3	1	0
Roberts	1.000	2	6	0	0	0
Santos	.667	5	4	0	2	0
Schierholtz	.981	101	198	9	4	2
Timpner	.986	102	213	6	3	0
Velez	.923	4	12	0	1	0

CONNECTICUT DEFENDERS

DOUBLE-A

EASTERN LEAGUE

BATTING

	B-T	HT	WT	DOB	AVG	vLH	vRH	G	AB	R	H	2B	3B	HR	RBI	BB	HBP	SH	SF	SO	SB	CS	SLG	OBP
Bowker, John	L-L	6-2	190	7-8-83	.307	.336	.296	139	522	79	160	35	6	22	90	41	12	0	12	103	3	7	.552	.363
Buller, Dayton	R-R	6-0	213	6-22-81	.195	.211	.190	23	77	8	15	1	2	0	10	5	1	0	1	23	0	0	.338	.250
Cordido, Julio	R-R	6-1	185	7-30-80	.224	.158	.253	35	125	14	28	8	0	2	19	14	1	0	2	22	2	1	.336	.303
Dobson, Pat	R-R	6-3	210	12-8-80	.223	.223	.223	104	305	38	68	21	1	5	27	33	7	1	4	76	9	3	.348	.309
Holm, Stephen	R-R	6-0	195	10-21-79	.272	.270	.272	84	254	35	69	14	0	9	28	42	6	3	0	39	3	1	.433	.387
Horwitz, Brian	R-R	6-1	190	11-7-82	.309	.273	.320	35	136	17	42	5	0	2	10	13	1	0	1	10	2	1	.390	.371
Ishikawa, Travis	L-L	6-3	225	9-24-83	.214	.286	.185	48	173	17	37	3	1	3	17	17	2	0	0	48	0	0	.295	.292
Jennings, Todd	R-R	6-0	190	12-10-81	.182	.204	.173	60	187	13	34	7	0	0	15	13	3	4	3	41	3	4	.219	.243
Klink, Simon	R-R	6-1	215	12-21-81	.262	.215	.279	117	408	40	107	18	3	11	45	37	2	3	3	110	1	1	.402	.324
Martinez-Esteve, Eddy	R-R	6-2	215	7-14-83	.239	.290	.223	37	134	10	32	2	1	1	10	12	1	0	0	33	2	1	.291	.306
McMains, Derin	R-R	6-0	180	11-3-79	.111	.333	.000	2	9	1	1	0	0	0	2	0	0	1	1	3	1	0	.111	.100
Minicozzi, Mark	R-R	6-1	210	2-11-83	.218	.145	.236	80	275	30	60	12	2	1	17	19	4	3	1	46	3	1	.287	.278
Requena, Alex	B-R	5-11	155	8-13-80	.222	.125	.247	45	117	14	26	6	1	0	12	15	1	2	0	28	14	5	.291	.316
Ruiz, Randy	R-R	6-3	235	10-19-77	.291	.304	.286	39	151	25	44	6	3	8	27	11	3	0	0	40	0	0	.530	.352
3-team (22 Reading, 47 Altoona)					.309	—		108	395	61	122	25	4	18	69	35	6	0	3	93	1	1	.529	.371
Sosa, Carlos	L-R	6-1	195	10-20-81	.271	.266	.273	112	376	55	102	24	2	9	54	47	2	0	4	91	3	4	.418	.352
Velez, Eugenio	B-R	6-1	160	5-16-82	.298	.233	.317	96	376	55	112	17	9	1	25	26	2	4	3	66	49	17	.399	.344
Von Schell, Tyler	R-R	6-3	229	7-7-79	.236	.194	.253	61	220	32	52	9	0	14	40	20	5	0	2	60	0	0	.468	.312
Wald, Jake	R-R	6-2	180	2-8-81	.241	.240	.242	115	361	45	87	21	4	7	38	31	14	8	0	94	11	3	.380	.325
Webb, Trey	R-R	6-0	170	2-11-82	.242	.310	.223	99	322	42	78	14	4	3	24	30	6	3	4	80	10	3	.339	.260

PITCHING

	B-T	HT	WT	DOB	W	L	ERA	G	GS	CG	SV	IP	H	R	ER	HR	BB	SO	AVG	vLH	vRH	K/9	BB/9
Anderson, Brian	R-R	6-3	210	5-25-83	1	5	3.93	47	0	0	29	50	55	27	22	4	20	46	.275	.293	.259	8.23	3.58
Bateman, Joe	R-R	6-2	170	5-6-80	4	1	2.88	29	0	0	0	56	52	21	18	5	21	47	.245	.235	.252	7.51	3.36
Begg, Chris	R-R	6-4	195	9-12-79	2	0	2.10	4	4	0	0	26	26	6	6	1	1	16	.274	.333	.213	5.61	0.35
Broshuis, Garrett	R-R	6-2	185	12-18-81	3	17	3.88	26	26	2	0	153	165	86	66	12	36	74	.277	.252	.299	4.35	2.12
Cox, Ben	R-R	6-2	220	9-20-81	0	8	4.50	17	11	0	0	54	57	28	27	4	28	37	.274	.260	.286	6.17	4.67
Espineli, Eugene	L-L	6-4	195	9-8-82	8	10	3.45	29	24	0	0	141	142	63	54	8	37	105	.264	.189	.286	6.70	2.36
Grace, Robert	R-R	6-1	165	2-2-83	0	0	0.00	2	0	0	0	2	1	0	0	0	0	2	.143	.500	.000	9.00	0.00
Hedrick, Justin	R-R	6-3	225	6-8-82	4	6	2.14	41	0	1	1	71	55	24	17	4	37	72	.215	.248	.187	9.08	4.67
Hinshaw, Alexander	L-L	6-4	190	10-31-82	3	1	1.96	17	5	0	0	41	22	13	9	2	19	50	.155	.119	.170	10.89	4.14
Ibanez, Yosandy	R-R	6-1	195	3-4-82	0	0	6.35	8	0	0	0	11	17	8	8	0	4	3	.354	.368	.345	2.38	3.18
Matos, Osiris	R-R	6-1	180	8-6-84	5	0	2.89	35	0	0	4	56	50	20	18	3	21	43	.239	.277	.209	6.91	3.38
McKae, Dave	R-R	6-2	190	11-24-81	4	4	4.24	17	17	1	0	104	95	52	49	9	17	66	.241	.239	.243	5.71	1.47
McNiven, Brooks	R-R	6-5	180	6-19-81	7	6	3.55	30	15	0	0	117	123	57	46	10	29	41	.272	.267	.275	3.16	2.24
Palmer, Matt	R-R	6-2	200	3-21-79	0	0	10.80	1	1	0	0	5	8	6	6	2	2	3	.381	.333	.444	5.40	3.60
Pereira, Nick	R-R	6-0	190	9-22-82	9	9	3.39	26	26	1	0	143	144	54	54	15	65	123	.231	.228	.234	7.72	4.08
Petersen, Jeff	R-R	6-4	225	10-16-81	2	2	5.09	16	0	0	0	23	32	18	13	3	12	10	.323	.395	.268	3.91	4.70
Pichardo, Kelvin	R-R	6-0	160	10-13-85	2	2	3.86	17	0	0	0	21	14	9	9	2	16	16	.194	.211	.176	6.86	6.86
Sack, Darren	R-R	6-4	190	7-19-82	2	5	8.39	9	9	0	0	40	56	40	37	7	22	25	.344	.343	.344	5.67	4.99
Sadler, Billy	R-R	6-0	200	9-21-81	0	0	0.73	9	0	0	0	12	3	1	1	1	6	18	.083	.048	.133	13.14	4.38
Sadowski, Ryan	R-R	6-4	185	10-4-82	4	3	3.04	35	3	0	1	68	56	29	23	3	27	50	.225	.244	.208	6.62	3.57
Sosa, Carlos	L-R	6-1	195	10-20-81	0	0	—	1	0	0	0	0	0	0	0	0	0	0	.000	—	.000	—	
Whitaker, Craig	R-R	6-4	170	11-19-84	0	0	36.00	1	0	0	0	1	4	4	4	0	3	1	.250	.000	.500	9.00	27.00
Wilding, Taylor	R-R	6-1	190	10-22-84	1	1	4.58	12	0	0	0	18	23	10	9	1	8	15	.333	.280	.364	7.64	4.08

FIELDING

Catcher	PCT	G	PO	A	E	DP	PB
Buller	.985	23	126	8	2	1	1
Holm	.991	69	423	37	4	2	6
Jennings	.987	56	334	42	5	4	7

First Base	PCT	G	PO	A	E	DP
Dobson	.984	28	227	14	4	19
Ishikawa	.985	47	434	35	7	45
Ruiz	1.000	9	68	5	0	5
Sosa	.983	8	55	2	1	2
Von Schell	.996	52	427	29	2	37

Second Base	PCT	G	PO	A	E	DP
Cordido	.962	31	54	99	6	15
Dobson	.932	13	21	20	3	3

McMains	1.000	2	5	8	0	0
Minicozzi	.968	21	34	58	3	12
Velez	.968	31	54	66	4	11
Wald	.972	16	28	41	2	12
Webb	.982	37	46	121	3	19

Third Base	PCT	G	PO	A	E	DP
Cordido	.923	5	5	7	1	0
Dobson	.667	3	1	5	3	1
Jennings	.500	1	1	0	1	0
Klink	.937	111	68	200	18	15
Minicozzi	.976	21	11	29	1	2
Wald	.800	4	2	6	2	0
Webb	1.000	5	2	7	0	4

Shortstop	PCT	G	PO	A	E	DP
Minicozzi	.975	36	47	107	4	26
Wald	.964	92	140	238	14	44
Webb	.978	25	39	52	2	14

Outfield	PCT	G	PO	A	E	DP
Bowker	.985	122	247	9	4	1
Dobson	.991	48	107	4	1	1
Horwitz	.985	32	65	0	1	0
Martinez-Esteve	1.000	25	41	1	0	0
Requena	.987	32	71	4	1	0
Ruiz	1.000	2	5	0	0	0
Sosa	.984	81	176	7	3	1
Velez	.965	62	137	0	5	0
Webb	.985	33	66	1	1	0

SAN JOSE GIANTS

CALIFORNIA LEAGUE

HIGH CLASS A

BATTING	B-T	HT	WT	DOB	AVG	vLH	vRH	G	AB	R	H	2B	3B	HR	RBI	BB	HBP	SH	SF	SO	SB	CS	SLG	OBP
Bocock, Brian	R-R	5-11	185	3-9-85	.220	.288	.200	87	345	42	76	19	3	4	37	35	3	9	6	105	15	10	.328	.293
Boyer, Bradley	L-R	6-0	185	10-4-83	.248	.266	.243	89	303	45	75	14	5	1	27	23	6	8	4	57	20	2	.337	.310
Burriss, Emmanuel	B-R	6-0	170	1-17-85	.165	.154	.168	36	139	23	23	2	0	0	8	12	2	4	3	20	17	3	.180	.237
Contreras, Anthony	L-R	5-11	185	9-26-83	.227	.233	.225	111	419	41	95	16	1	1	56	13	1	1	10	59	0	3	.277	.246
Copeland, Ben	L-L	6-1	195	12-17-83	.280	.159	.313	106	404	68	113	22	6	7	50	70	4	0	5	77	14	7	.416	.387
Denker, Travis	R-R	5-9	170	8-5-85	.400	.333	.409	7	25	7	10	3	0	1	9	7	0	0	0	2	1	0	.640	.531
2-team (111 Inland Empire)					.300	—	—	118	427	72	128	30	3	11	66	55	4	0	7	67	9	2	.461	.379
Dyche, Joseph	R-R	6-1	185	10-27-82	.000	.000	.000	2	4	0	0	0	0	0	0	0	0	0	0	2	0	0	.000	.000
Gunther, Barry	B-R	6-0	190	3-18-82	.197	.167	.212	25	76	6	15	2	1	0	7	12	0	0	0	14	0	1	.250	.307
Haines, Kyle	L-R	6-1	170	7-28-82	.250	.239	.257	60	172	31	43	8	0	3	17	32	3	2	2	30	6	2	.349	.373
Ishikawa, Travis	L-L	6-3	225	9-24-83	.268	.319	.252	56	198	35	53	15	1	13	34	19	4	0	1	78	0	0	.551	.342
Maroul, David	R-R	6-2	215	2-15-83	.221	.269	.203	118	420	61	93	30	2	20	50	25	5	1	3	112	2	0	.445	.272
Martinez-Esteve, Eddy	R-R	6-2	215	7-14-83	.207	.238	.197	23	82	5	17	5	0	0	8	9	0	0	1	13	0	0	.268	.286
Minicozzi, Mark	R-R	6-1	210	2-11-83	.328	.300	.354	16	58	8	19	4	2	2	19	7	1	0	1	12	0	0	.569	.403
Mooney, Michael	R-R	6-1	205	6-8-83	.245	.191	.262	127	482	60	118	24	4	12	56	29	9	3	7	132	21	4	.386	.296
Nunez, Ariel	R-R	6-3	190	8-3-85	.125	.091	.143	9	32	4	4	0	0	1	2	2	0	0	0	14	0	1	.219	.176
Requena, Alex	B-R	5-11	155	8-13-80	.296	.455	.256	19	54	9	16	3	0	0	7	10	0	2	1	12	3	3	.352	.400
Richardson, Antoan	R-R	5-8	165	10-8-83	.279	.355	.254	107	384	85	107	12	7	2	29	67	11	5	2	94	43	11	.362	.399
Sandoval, Pablo	B-R	5-11	180	8-11-86	.287	.269	.294	102	401	56	115	33	5	11	52	16	0	3	3	52	3	1	.476	.312
Simmons, James	R-R	6-3	190	9-3-85	.100	.250	.000	4	10	1	1	0	0	0	1	1	0	0	0	3	2	0	.100	.182
Thompson, William	L-L	6-1	180	11-20-82	.207	.125	.224	70	241	15	50	7	0	0	30	30	1	0	4	61	1	0	.237	.293
Von Schell, Tyler	R-R	6-3	229	7-7-79	.270	.429	.234	41	152	28	41	10	0	10	45	18	5	0	6	49	0	0	.533	.354
Witter, Adam	L-R	6-1	175	2-17-83	.260	.257	.260	102	362	55	94	24	1	18	74	44	3	0	3	93	2	1	.481	.342

PITCHING	B-T	HT	WT	DOB	W	L	ERA	G	GS	CG	SV	IP	H	R	ER	HR	BB	SO	AVG	vLH	vRH	K/9	BB/9
Cox, Ben	R-R	6-2	220	5-20-84	1	1	2.81	17	0	0	0	26	23	9	8	2	14	30	.232	.270	.210	10.52	4.91
English, Jesse	L-L	6-1	215	9-13-84	0	1	3.24	5	2	0	0	8	3	3	0	6	11	.258	.167	.316	11.88	6.48
Foltin, Wayne	R-R	6-2	200	12-11-82	1	1	7.14	29	0	0	5	29	35	25	23	3	22	27	.302	.310	.297	8.38	6.83
Ibanez, Yosandy	R-R	6-1	195	3-4-82	1	3	4.50	12	4	0	0	32	24	19	16	1	26	35	.207	.203	.211	9.84	7.31
Martinez, Gregorio	R-R	6-1	160	7-2-82	6	12	5.46	28	19	0	0	114	124	86	69	16	46	91	.239	.235	.313	7.21	3.64
Martinez, Joseph	L-R	6-3	185	2-26-83	10	10	4.26	28	28	0	0	163	172	85	77	11	36	151	.276	.271	.279	8.35	1.99
McKae, Dave	R-R	6-2	190	11-24-81	5	1	1.93	11	11	0	0	65	49	17	14	3	16	58	.213	.239	.186	7.99	2.20
Moreno, Anthony	R-R	5-11	198	5-4-83	4	3	4.32	31	0	0	1	50	50	30	24	3	18	41	.259	.213	.292	7.38	3.24
Newton, David	R-R	5-11	195	3-4-86	0	1	6.35	10	0	0	0	11	8	8	8	0	13	12	.216	.222	.211	9.53	10.32
Oakes, Jerry	L-R	6-5	191	4-4-82	0	0	5.79	9	0	0	0	9	4	10	6	2	15	11	.133	.077	.176	10.61	14.46
Ortiz, Russ	R-R	6-1	220	6-5-74	0	0	0.00	1	1	0	0	4	2	2	0	0	1	5	.143	.143	.143	11.25	2.25
Oseguera, Paul	L-L	6-0	180	1-6-84	10	6	3.54	27	26	1	0	158	145	72	62	10	35	132	.247	.276	.237	7.53	2.00
Paul, Ryan	L-L	6-4	205	8-10-84	4	2	2.72	34	1	0	0	46	31	15	14	2	20	40	.196	.208	.190	7.77	3.88
Pendley, Nathan	L-L	6-4	220	9-5-81	0	1	10.24	9	0	0	0	10	19	15	11	2	5	7	.413	.333	.441	6.52	4.66
Pichardo, Kelvin	R-R	6-0	160	10-13-85	2	3	3.09	29	0	0	3	47	37	24	16	2	17	71	.218	.232	.208	13.69	3.28
Quinowski, David	L-L	5-10	170	4-23-86	1	2	3.27	21	0	0	1	33	19	14	12	1	16	35	.160	.150	.165	9.55	4.36
Ray, Ronnie	R-R	6-3	195	5-11-84	11	8	4.62	30	24	0	0	148	160	89	76	15	48	112	.280	.285	.275	6.81	2.92
Romo, Sergio	R-R	5-11	185	3-4-83	6	2	1.36	41	0	0	9	66	35	12	10	4	15	106	.155	.143	.162	14.38	2.04
Sack, Darren	R-R	6-4	190	7-19-82	1	2	4.22	19	8	0	0	53	52	29	25	7	24	34	.260	.239	.271	5.74	4.05
Sanchez, Jonathan	L-L	6-2	180	11-19-82	0	0	0.00	2	2	0	0	3	0	0	0	0	1	5	.000	.000	.000	15.00	3.00
Sosa, Henry	R-R	6-2	185	7-28-85	5	5	4.38	14	14	0	0	64	66	36	31	8	36	78	.262	.302	.237	11.03	5.09
Waddell, Jason	R-L	6-2	206	6-11-81	1	1	1.84	30	0	0	1	44	48	14	9	0	12	50	.282	.338	.248	10.23	2.45
Walker, Tyler	R-R	6-3	275	5-15-76	0	0	1.74	10	0	0	3	10	9	2	2	0	2	15	.243	.222	.263	13.06	1.74
Wilding, Taylor	R-R	6-1	190	10-22-84	4	2	2.54	39	0	0	12	60	38	20	17	4	19	71	.178	.133	.210	10.59	2.83
Wilson, Brian	R-R	6-1	205	3-16-82	0	0	0.00	3	0	0	2	3	1	0	0	0	0	6	.091	.000	.333	18.00	0.00

FIELDING

Catcher	PCT	G	PO	A	E	DP	PB
Gunther	1.000	21	143	17	0	1	5
Sandoval	.993	59	520	52	4	7	12
Witter	.979	66	564	41	13	2	18

First Base	PCT	G	PO	A	E	DP
Ishikawa	.979	40	298	24	7	30
Maroul	1.000	2	7	0	0	1
Sandoval	1.000	42	325	28	0	26
Thompson	.993	45	375	31	3	28
Von Schell	.994	20	168	10	1	14

Second Base	PCT	G	PO	A	E	DP
Boyer	.980	73	99	193	6	34

	PCT	G	PO	A	E	DP
Contreras	.986	31	58	79	2	15
Denker	.920	7	10	13	2	3
Haines	.980	24	35	63	2	10
Minicozzi	.933	9	6	22	2	5

Third Base	PCT	G	PO	A	E	DP
Contreras	.897	25	10	25	4	2
Haines	.800	3	2	2	1	0
Maroul	.934	115	79	190	19	14
Minicozzi	1.000	6	3	11	0	1

Shortstop	PCT	G	PO	A	E	DP
Bocock	.947	87	152	255	23	56
Burriss	.940	35	38	103	9	15

	PCT	G	PO	A	E	DP
Haines	.968	20	33	57	3	16

Outfield	PCT	G	PO	A	E	DP
Contreras	.978	57	83	5	2	1
Copeland	.979	104	178	10	4	3
Dyche	1.000	2	2	0	0	0
Martinez-Esteve	1.000	18	25	1	0	0
Mooney	.979	124	220	17	5	2
Nunez	.813	8	13	0	3	0
Requena	.960	17	24	0	1	0
Richardson	.978	104	214	4	5	1
Simmons	.750	3	6	0	2	0

AUGUSTA GREEN JACKETS

SOUTH ATLANTIC LEAGUE

LOW CLASS A

BATTING	B-T	HT	WT	DOB	AVG	vLH	vRH	G	AB	R	H	2B	3B	HR	RBI	BB	HBP	SH	SF	SO	SB	CS	SLG	OBP
Bocock, Brian	R-R	5-11	185	3-9-85	.292	.167	.328	39	161	24	47	9	1	1	20	16	0	0	1	19	26	8	.379	.354
Boyer, Bradley	L-R	6-0	185	10-4-83	.255	1.000	.239	14	47	4	12	4	0	0	2	6	1	0	0	4	3	1	.340	.352
Buller, Dayton	R-R	6-0	213	6-6-83	.287	.359	.260	42	143	19	41	10	0	4	24	21	3	0	0	42	0	0	.441	.389
Burriss, Emmanuel	B-R	6-0	170	1-17-85	.321	.282	.332	89	365	64	117	14	4	0	38	28	5	4	3	49	51	15	.381	.374
Dyche, Joseph	R-R	6-1	185	10-27-82	.198	.138	.216	42	131	12	26	5	2	0	18	15	2	0	3	32	5	3	.267	.285
Felmy, Robert	L-L	5-10	168	4-29-84	.281	.279	.281	122	470	79	132	31	1	15	82	41	11	2	6	69	26	15	.447	.348
Graham, Tyler	R-R	6-0	180	1-25-84	.290	.269	.296	66	231	45	67	8	4	2	30	20	3	2	2	51	29	8	.385	.352
Gunther, Barry	B-R	6-0	190	3-18-82	.300	.200	.333	6	20	3	6	4	0	0	3	4	0	0	0	2	0	0	.500	.417
Gutierrez-Portalatin, H.	R-R	5-11	195	5-7-83	.247	.282	.237	85	295	41	73	10	1	5	34	25	9	1	3	40	1	0	.339	.322

	B-T	HT	WT	DOB	AVG	vLH	vRH	G	AB	R	H	2B	3B	HR	RBI	BB	HBP	SH	SF	SO	SB	CS	SLG	OBP
Hornostaj, Aaron	L-R	6-1	178	5-19-83	.125	1.000	.000	2	8	1	1	0	0	0	0	2	0	0	0	2	0	0	.125	.300
Jean, Juan	L-R	6-1	180	9-14-85	.314	.316	.314	38	121	13	38	4	0	0	20	8	2	1	0	17	2	1	.347	.366
McBryde, Michael	R-R	6-1	170	3-22-85	.276	.301	.269	119	417	71	115	17	4	7	61	27	7	3	3	100	14	11	.386	.328
Pill, Brett	R-R	6-4	200	9-9-84	.269	.281	.265	137	536	72	144	47	1	10	91	38	7	1	7	81	4	2	.416	.321
Ray, John	R-R	6-1	200	9-5-84	.167	.154	.174	16	36	2	6	0	0	1	3	0	0	1	0	11	0	0	.250	.167
Requena, Alex	B-R	5-11	155	8-13-80	.000	—	.000	5	9	0	0	0	0	0	0	0	0	1	0	2	0	1	.000	.000
Rohlinger, Ryan	R-R	6-1	185	10-7-83	.235	.209	.242	135	506	86	119	31	3	18	78	62	13	1	4	83	3	3	.415	.332
Rojas, Nestor	R-R	6-0	200	11-18-83	.210	.053	.258	24	81	11	17	3	0	0	9	8	0	0	0	23	0	0	.247	.281
Sanders, Marcus	R-R	6-0	160	8-25-85	.264	.271	.261	94	292	53	77	17	3	0	26	46	5	2	1	56	29	6	.342	.372
Sarmiento, Elio	B-R	6-0	200	6-20-86	.217	.353	.182	27	83	9	18	2	0	1	7	6	0	0	0	15	0	0	.277	.270
Schoop, Sharlon	R-R	6-0	160	4-15-87	.235	.207	.243	42	136	18	32	6	0	1	19	8	2	1	1	32	4	3	.301	.286
Simmons, James	R-R	6-3	190	9-3-85	.193	.213	.186	56	176	29	34	7	5	3	19	21	4	0	1	64	13	6	.341	.292
Webb, Trey	R-R	6-0	170	2-11-82	.000	—	.000	1	3	0	0	0	0	0	0	0	0	0	0	0	0	0	.000	.000
Weston, Matthew	L-L	6-3	215	5-20-84	.276	.200	.297	118	435	60	120	35	1	11	69	35	2	0	0	80	2	2	.437	.333

PITCHING	B-T	HT	WT	DOB	W	L	ERA	G	GS	CG	SV	IP	H	R	ER	HR	BB	SO	AVG	vLH	vRH	K/9	BB/9
Calicutt, Steven	L-L	6-2	190	2-7-84	6	5	3.88	33	16	0	2	104	106	55	45	8	35	67	.271	.247	.279	5.78	3.02
Cowart, Adam	R-R	6-2	190	8-18-83	14	7	2.39	28	28	0	0	170	152	59	45	4	28	95	.241	.249	.234	5.04	1.49
Cranston, Jared	B-L	6-2	195	4-18-85	0	0	9.00	9	0	0	0	10	13	12	10	0	3	13	.283	.400	.226	11.70	2.70
Foltin, Wayne	R-R	6-2	200	12-11-82	0	0	5.11	8	0	0	0	12	17	8	7	0	5	9	.327	.500	.200	6.57	3.65
Grace, Robert	R-R	6-1	165	2-2-83	2	3	2.98	18	4	0	2	45	37	15	15	4	7	39	.216	.135	.252	7.74	1.39
Griffin, Daniel	R-R	6-7	225	9-29-84	6	6	4.33	26	10	0	1	79	89	42	38	7	25	67	.284	.303	.275	7.63	2.85
King, Thomas	R-R	6-5	205	12-5-83	0	0	2.70	10	0	0	1	13	12	5	4	1	4	7	.250	.200	.273	4.73	2.70
Lussier, Paul	R-R	6-2	220	11-7-85	2	1	5.08	32	0	0	2	62	68	38	35	7	22	56	.276	.231	.303	8.13	3.19
Matos, Osiris	R-R	6-1	180	8-6-84	0	0	0.00	7	0	0	4	9	1	0	0	0	1	9	.036	.071	.000	9.00	1.00
Musgrave, Mike	R-R	6-2	185	4-10-84	0	1	3.86	14	1	0	1	23	26	13	10	1	6	21	.286	.286	.286	8.10	2.31
Newton, David	R-R	5-11	195	3-4-86	4	2	1.58	29	0	0	3	40	22	13	7	0	24	46	.164	.222	.135	10.35	5.40
Oakes, Jerry	L-R	6-5	191	4-29-82	0	0	216.00	2	0	0	0	0	4	8	8	1	3	0	.800	.667	1.000	0.00	81.00
Ortiz-Jusino, Adam	R-R	6-3	190	10-24-84	0	2	4.50	15	0	0	1	22	31	12	11	3	6	15	.330	.370	.313	6.14	2.45
Paul, Adam	R-R	6-6	214	2-17-84	0	0	4.15	6	0	0	0	9	4	2	2	1	2	3	.229	.000	.308	3.12	2.08
Pucetas, Kevin	R-R	6-4	225	11-27-84	15	4	1.86	27	23	0	1	145	124	40	30	7	21	104	.228	.240	.219	6.44	1.30
Shaver, Ryan	R-R	6-5	175	12-17-84	3	4	3.16	36	0	0	1	74	70	30	26	3	19	52	.258	.236	.273	6.32	2.31
Snyder, Benjamin	L-L	6-1	175	7-20-85	16	5	2.09	28	25	0	1	151	128	49	35	12	32	145	.225	.180	.239	8.64	1.91
Sosa, Henry	R-R	6-2	185	7-28-85	6	0	0.73	13	10	0	1	62	30	8	5	2	25	61	.144	.189	.119	8.85	3.63
Tanner, Clayton	R-L	6-1	180	12-5-87	12	8	3.59	27	23	1	0	135	147	61	54	5	44	104	.282	.311	.273	6.92	2.93
Trinidad, Juan	R-R	6-3	200	11-6-85	3	3	1.94	42	0	0	18	51	31	16	11	3	15	50	.172	.277	.113	8.82	2.65
Whitaker, Craig	R-R	6-4	170	11-19-84	0	0	7.08	13	0	0	1	20	24	18	16	1	12	17	.286	.258	.302	7.52	5.31

FIELDING

Catcher	PCT	G	PO	A	E	DP	PB
Buller	.992	32	237	24	2	1	4
Gunther	.973	4	35	1	1	0	1
Gutierrez	.991	62	412	36	4	1	11
Ray	.976	16	74	9	2	0	3
Rojas	.986	19	120	20	2	2	4
Sarmiento	.976	17	113	7	3	0	3

First Base	PCT	G	PO	A	E	DP
Jean	1.000	2	10	1	0	3
Pill	.988	125	1192	88	15	103
Rojas	1.000	1	7	0	0	2
Sarmiento	.875	2	7	0	1	0
Weston	.986	14	135	11	2	8

Second Base	PCT	G	PO	A	E	DP
Boyer	.927	12	24	27	4	11
Hornostaj	1.000	2	4	10	0	1
Jean	.976	19	32	50	2	11
Sanders	.958	82	147	219	16	49
Sarmiento	1.000	2	1	1	0	0
Schoop	.976	30	43	77	3	10

Third Base	PCT	G	PO	A	E	DP
Rohlinger	.966	133	81	321	14	27
Sarmiento	1.000	5	2	11	0	1
Schoop	.900	3	3	6	1	2
Webb	1.000	1	1	0	0	0

Shortstop	PCT	G	PO	A	E	DP
Bocock	.960	39	55	137	8	18

	PCT	G	PO	A	E	DP
Burriss	.951	88	122	284	21	48
Jean	.967	13	19	39	2	10
Sanders	1.000	1	2	0	0	0
Schoop	.971	7	16	18	1	5

Outfield	PCT	G	PO	A	E	DP
Dyche	.986	41	63	5	1	2
Felmy	.978	117	170	9	4	0
Graham	.982	63	101	6	2	1
McBryde	.949	118	269	10	15	2
Requena	1.000	4	4	0	0	0
Sarmiento	1.000	1	3	0	0	0
Schoop	1.000	1	2	0	0	0
Simmons	.964	52	76	5	3	0
Weston	1.000	32	55	1	0	0

SALEM-KEIZER VOLCANOES

SHORT-SEASON

NORTHWEST LEAGUE

BATTING	B-T	HT	WT	DOB	AVG	vLH	vRH	G	AB	R	H	2B	3B	HR	RBI	BB	HBP	SH	SF	SO	SB	CS	SLG	OBP
Ambort, Michael	B-R	6-1	215	4-23-85	.240	.357	.170	20	75	12	18	3	0	4	17	6	1	0	1	20	1	1	.440	.301
Baker, Garrett	R-R	6-2	180	11-16-83	.308	.365	.286	73	266	53	82	24	6	7	64	30	11	0	6	46	10	3	.523	.393
Bond, Brock	B-R	5-10	195	9-11-85	.342	.333	.345	42	158	41	54	10	2	0	19	26	6	6	0	21	7	2	.430	.453
D'alessio, Andrew	L-R	6-3	196	9-23-84	.556	.000	.667	4	18	8	10	4	1	2	8	2	0	0	0	3	0	0	1.222	.600
Davis, Andrew	B-R	5-11	195	2-11-84	.278	.256	.286	72	270	37	75	14	2	5	46	36	1	5	3	46	5	1	.400	.361
Downs, Matthew	R-R	6-2	190	3-19-84	.338	.337	.338	73	287	68	97	33	0	8	48	28	10	7	4	34	16	2	.537	.410
Edwards, Bruce	B-R	5-10	165	9-23-84	.241	.211	.257	53	170	30	41	3	3	0	20	34	4	3	0	36	7	3	.294	.380
Flores, Jose	B-R	5-11	175	8-17-87	.286	.308	.278	45	98	16	28	8	1	2	12	6	1	3	1	8	4	0	.449	.330
Gunther, Barry	B-R	6-0	190	3-18-82	.179	.250	.148	13	39	4	7	0	0	0	4	6	0	0	0	10	0	0	.179	.289
Jordan, Shane	L-L	5-7	170	11-26-84	.300	.289	.303	66	243	53	73	12	2	4	28	35	2	8	3	33	15	3	.416	.389
La Torre, Tyler	L-R	6-0	210	4-22-83	.316	.176	.346	31	95	19	30	4	2	1	11	14	0	4	0	19	1	1	.432	.404
Luster, Jeremiah	R-R	5-10	175	8-31-86	.243	.258	.231	40	70	19	17	3	1	1	6	13	2	1	1	14	4	1	.357	.372
Ray, John	R-R	6-1	200	9-5-84	.000	.000	.000	3	3	0	0	0	0	0	0	0	0	0	0	3	0	0	.000	.000
Rothford, Chad	B-R	6-5	250	4-27-85	.273	.228	.286	70	256	39	70	18	0	9	54	22	3	2	4	59	0	0	.449	.333
Schoop, Sharlon	R-R	6-0	160	4-15-87	.284	.239	.299	58	190	30	54	12	5	4	29	15	6	6	5	35	2	4	.463	.347
VanElderen, Sean	R-R	6-3	225	9-21-82	.290	.346	.263	65	248	47	72	27	3	5	37	16	3	2	2	56	9	4	.484	.338
Villalona, Angel	R-R	6-3	200	8-13-90	.167	.000	.222	5	12	1	2	0	0	0	1	0	1	0	0	2	1	0	.167	.231
Williams, Jackson	R-R	5-11	200	5-14-86	.231	.182	.256	42	130	20	30	3	0	5	20	16	7	4	4	27	0	0	.369	.338

PITCHING	B-T	HT	WT	DOB	W	L	ERA	G	GS	CG	SV	IP	H	R	ER	HR	BB	SO	AVG	vLH	vRH	K/9	BB/9
Bauer, Ricky	R-R	6-2	170	3-1-83	4	3	4.34	15	9	0	1	58	65	33	28	7	14	30	.285	.280	.291	4.66	2.17
Brewer, Thomas	R-R	6-2	200	8-30-84	9	1	3.05	14	14	0	0	65	67	22	22	5	16	52	.265	.250	.275	7.20	2.22
Bucardo, Wilber	R-R	6-2	175	11-20-87	0	0	3.60	1	1	0	0	5	7	3	2	0	1	3	.292	.316	.200	5.40	1.80
Clark, Craig	L-L	6-2	200	7-9-84	5	3	2.98	12	12	0	0	54	46	20	18	5	23	55	.232	.292	.213	9.11	3.81

	B-T	HT	WT	DOB	W	L	ERA	G	GS	CG	SV	IP	H	R	ER	HR	BB	SO	AVG	vLH	vRH	K/9	BB/9
Corgan, Chance	R-R	6-2	175	4-25-86	0	0	5.40	2	1	0	1	5	9	3	3	1	1	7	.375	.471	.143	12.60	1.80
Cranston, Jared	B-L	6-2	195	4-18-85	5	1	2.77	13	13	0	0	55	42	17	17	3	16	72	.215	.224	.212	11.71	2.60
De La Garza, Andrew	L-L	6-4	200	10-20-84	9	3	3.57	18	0	0	0	40	41	16	16	5	10	35	.272	.155	.344	7.81	2.23
De La Rosa, Carlos	L-L	6-2	190	7-15-84	1	0	2.55	15	0	0	0	18	14	6	5	2	8	13	.222	.222	.222	6.62	4.08
Edlefsen, Steven	B-R	6-2	175	6-27-85	2	0	1.62	18	0	0	2	33	14	8	6	0	16	26	.131	.139	.127	7.02	4.32
Egart, Timothy	R-R	6-4	205	3-13-85	3	0	2.94	20	1	0	2	34	32	12	11	3	7	44	.250	.316	.197	11.76	1.87
English, Jesse	L-L	6-2	215	9-13-84	5	0	0.69	10	1	0	0	26	14	2	2	0	5	46	.154	.241	.113	15.92	1.73
Joaquin, Waldis	R-R	6-2	190	12-25-86	3	0	2.84	15	5	0	0	38	24	13	12	2	16	30	.176	.196	.163	7.11	3.79
Macfarland, Stephen	R-R	6-2	185	11-17-85	0	0	18.00	4	0	0	4	5	8	8	1	5	2	.294	.300	.286	4.50	11.25
Maday, Daryl	R-R	6-2	225	8-12-85	5	2	2.32	14	3	0	1	43	41	12	11	4	10	28	.258	.270	.250	5.91	2.11
McGrath, Ryan	R-R	6-3	200	12-20-82	1	5	5.85	16	9	0	1	48	51	37	31	9	17	38	.271	.292	.260	7.17	3.21
Mixon, David	R-R	6-3	190	9-10-84	2	0	2.05	17	0	0	0	26	28	10	6	2	15	25	.264	.308	.239	8.54	5.13
Neitz, Jason	L-L	6-0	170	4-24-84	1	0	7.43	9	0	0	0	13	23	12	11	0	4	12	.371	.333	.386	8.10	2.70
Odle, Oliver	R-R	6-0	215	7-11-85	0	0	7.36	1	1	0	0	4	5	3	3	0	2	2	.294	.333	.200	4.91	4.91
Otero, Daniel	R-R	6-3	205	2-19-85	0	0	1.21	22	0	0	19	22	12	3	3	1	0	15	.152	.235	.089	6.04	0.00
Paterson, Joseph	R-L	6-1	210	5-19-86	1	0	5.59	9	0	0	0	10	15	6	6	0	2	13	.349	.267	.393	12.10	1.86
Paul, Adam	R-R	6-6	214	2-17-84	0	0	4.50	6	0	0	0	6	4	3	3	0	4	6	.250	.429	.176	9.00	6.00
Rodriguez, Wilmin	R-R	6-2	175	5-13-85	0	1	5.49	15	7	0	0	39	42	29	24	6	23	47	.275	.273	.275	10.75	5.26
Runzler, Daniel	L-L	6-4	215	3-30-85	0	0	9.00	1	0	0	0	1	2	1	1	0	2	1	.400	.000	.500	9.00	18.00
Rusova, Ivan	R-R	6-1	180	11-5-86	0	0	6.75	3	0	0	0	4	4	3	3	1	8	3	.267	.200	.300	6.75	18.00
Stolp, Eric	R-R	6-3	182	8-18-84	0	0	10.12	3	0	0	0	3	4	3	3	0	2	4	.333	.250	.375	13.50	6.75
Turpen, Daniel	R-R	6-4	215	8-17-86	0	0	1.86	10	0	0	0	19	15	6	4	1	7	18	.217	.286	.171	8.38	3.26
Wilshire, Richard	R-R	6-4	200	3-25-85	0	0	0.00	2	0	0	0	3	2	0	0	0	2	2	.182	.125	.333	5.40	5.40

FIELDING

Catcher	PCT	G	PO	A	E	DP	PB
Ambort	1.000	2	16	2	0	0	0
Gunther	.982	13	97	10	2	0	0
La Torre	.986	28	188	16	3	0	2
Ray	1.000	3	5	0	0	0	0
Williams	.980	42	312	38	7	3	8

First Base	PCT	G	PO	A	E	DP
Ambort	1.000	5	49	0	0	0
D'alessio	1.000	1	5	1	0	2
Downs	.997	45	308	24	1	24
Rothford	.992	44	342	26	3	35

VanElderen	1.000	1	2	0	0	0

Second Base	PCT	G	PO	A	E	DP
Bond	.960	40	65	129	8	25
Downs	.952	30	46	74	6	22
Flores	.932	23	19	22	3	3

Third Base	PCT	G	PO	A	E	DP
Davis	.967	66	52	150	7	12
Downs	.966	14	2	26	1	0
Flores	1.000	2	1	2	0	0
Luster	—	1	0	0	0	0
Villalona	1.000	2	3	3	0	0

Shortstop	PCT	G	PO	A	E	DP
Davis	.973	10	11	25	1	5
Flores	.934	18	23	34	4	7
Schoop	.967	58	95	171	9	38

Outfield	PCT	G	PO	A	E	DP
Baker	.984	52	59	2	1	0
Edwards	.956	46	65	0	3	0
Flores	1.000	1	1	0	0	0
Jordan	.981	61	100	4	2	1
Luster	1.000	28	30	0	0	0
VanElderen	.982	63	102	6	2	3

AZL GIANTS — ROOKIE

ARIZONA LEAGUE

BATTING	B-T	HT	WT	DOB	AVG	vLH	vRH	G	AB	R	H	2B	3B	HR	RBI	BB	HBP	SH	SF	SO	SB	CS	SLG	OBP
Alfonzo, Eliezer	R-R	5-11	210	2-7-79	.462	—	.462	5	13	2	6	0	0	0	5	0	1	0	1	1	0	0	.462	.467
Ambort, Michael	B-R	6-1	215	4-23-85	.500	.500	.500	4	12	5	6	0	0	0	3	0	2	0	0	3	0	0	.500	.571
Bond, Brock	B-R	5-10	195	9-11-85	.227	.222	.229	18	44	4	10	0	2	0	6	6	3	2	2	3	2	1	.318	.345
Bond, Casey	R-R	6-3	205	10-5-84	.262	.323	.250	52	191	28	50	6	4	3	25	16	3	1	1	58	11	8	.382	.327
Cividanes, Emmanuel	L-L	6-1	175	10-31-84	.200	.000	.500	2	5	0	1	1	0	0	1	0	0	0	0	1	0	0	.400	.200
Corona, Ramon	R-R	5-11	190	8-10-85	.295	.267	.302	20	78	16	23	8	2	1	8	6	3	0	1	15	5	2	.487	.364
Creswell, Tayler	R-R	6-0	170	2-11-87	.161	.200	.154	12	31	6	5	1	1	0	3	7	0	0	0	9	2	1	.258	.316
Culberson, Charlie	R-R	6-1	185	4-10-89	.286	.257	.294	46	161	32	46	8	5	1	16	19	5	0	2	38	19	1	.416	.374
D'alessio, Andrew	L-R	6-3	196	9-23-84	.306	.262	.319	49	186	41	57	15	1	14	51	21	1	0	2	43	0	2	.624	.376
Duggan, Dom	R-R	5-9	185	2-8-85	.292	.308	.288	49	171	36	50	7	6	2	17	28	6	5	0	36	14	4	.439	.410
Dyche, Joseph	R-R	6-0	185	10-27-82	.308	.375	.286	16	65	15	20	5	0	2	12	5	1	0	0	8	7	1	.477	.366
Gunther, Barry	B-R	6-0	190	3-18-82	.286	.000	.333	3	7	0	2	1	0	0	1	0	0	1	0	1	0	1	.429	.375
Jean, Juan	L-R	6-1	180	9-14-85	.333	—	.333	1	3	1	1	0	0	0	0	0	0	0	0	0	0	0	.333	.333
Klimas, Matthew	R-R	5-11	185	7-3-87	.309	.188	.346	25	68	11	21	1	1	1	9	8	1	0	0	14	0	2	.397	.390
Lara, Santiago	R-R	6-4	220	11-1-85	.179	.500	.154	13	28	5	5	0	0	2	4	2	2	1	0	14	0	0	.393	.281
Lopez, Josh	R-R	5-9	170	1-31-89	.175	.000	.189	18	40	4	7	0	1	0	3	2	0	0	0	10	2	0	.225	.214
Martinez-Esteve, Eddy	L-R	6-2	215	7-14-83	.310	.500	.278	15	42	2	13	1	0	3	11	1	0	0	9	0	0	.333	.463
Monell, Johnny	L-R	5-11	205	3-27-86	.240	.250	.237	28	75	11	18	3	1	3	19	15	2	0	1	16	3	4	.427	.376
Neal, Thomas	R-R	6-1	205	8-17-87	.308	.250	.323	10	39	7	12	3	0	1	4	5	2	0	0	7	0	0	.462	.413
Noonan, Nick	L-R	6-0	180	5-4-89	.316	.227	.340	52	206	33	65	11	4	3	40	12	2	3	1	20	18	3	.451	.357
Simmons, James	R-R	6-3	190	9-3-85	.187	.200	.183	27	91	14	17	1	4	1	13	11	1	0	1	35	1	0	.319	.279
Stromsmoe, Skyler	B-R	5-10	175	3-30-84	.290	.714	.236	28	62	16	18	3	5	0	11	11	4	1	9	7	1	.435	.449
Villalona, Angel	R-R	6-3	200	8-13-90	.285	.200	.310	52	200	40	57	12	3	5	37	15	5	0	4	42	1	1	.450	.344
White, John	L-L	6-3	220	2-27-84	.129	.083	.140	25	62	12	8	1	0	1	6	5	1	0	0	31	0	0	.194	.239
Zambrano, Eliezer	B-R	5-11	175	9-16-86	.254	.455	.208	20	59	10	15	2	0	1	5	5	3	0	0	6	3	0	.288	.343

PITCHING	B-T	HT	WT	DOB	W	L	ERA	G	GS	CG	SV	IP	H	R	ER	HR	BB	SO	AVG	vLH	vRH	K/9	BB/9
Alderson, Tim	R-R	6-6	217	11-3-88	0	0	0.00	3	2	0	0	5	4	0	0	0	0	12	.211	.500	.000	21.60	0.00
Brinson, Morgan	R-R	6-3	181	12-11-86	0	0	3.75	12	0	0	0	12	6	6	5	0	11	14	.143	.176	.120	10.50	8.25
Bucardo, Wilber	R-R	6-2	175	11-20-87	6	2	1.94	11	11	0	0	60	46	16	13	1	10	34	.213	.253	.184	5.07	1.49
Corgan, Chance	R-R	6-2	175	4-25-86	2	1	4.09	6	0	0	1	11	8	5	5	1	2	14	.200	.214	.192	11.45	1.64
Edens, Joseph	R-R	5-10	193	9-26-84	0	0	3.65	12	0	0	0	12	14	6	5	0	6	16	.286	.211	.333	11.68	4.38
Foppert, Jesse	R-R	6-6	220	7-10-80	0	0	45.00	3	0	0	0	1	5	5	5	0	4	1	.333	.500	.000	9.00	36.00
Geronimo, Gregorio	L-L	6-3	190	12-18-86	0	0	5.25	14	0	0	0	12	15	8	7	0	5	16	.306	.190	.393	12.00	3.75
Gomez, Josue	L-L	6-3	200	3-14-85	0	0	4.50	13	0	0	0	12	11	7	6	0	6	13	.229	.214	.235	9.75	4.50
Kerth, Andrew	R-R	6-4	210	5-6-85	1	1	3.91	15	1	0	0	23	23	13	10	1	11	16	.271	.212	.308	6.26	4.30
King, John	R-R	6-3	180	7-5-85	1	0	2.60	11	0	0	0	17	15	6	5	1	5	16	.234	.227	.238	8.31	2.60
Knepper, Lars	R-R	6-1	185	4-13-86	1	2	2.86	10	10	0	0	44	34	17	14	1	10	38	.215	.203	.226	7.77	2.05
Lamb, Cameron	R-R	6-3	195	5-29-88	1	1	9.00	11	2	0	0	14	14	14	14	3	4	10	.269	.231	.282	6.43	2.57
Loree, Mike	R-R	6-6	226	9-14-86	1	1	1.13	9	1	0	0	16	17	8	2	1	2	20	.270	.333	.231	11.25	0.56
Martinez, Roberto	L-L	6-1	175	5-5-86	3	2	3.22	11	11	0	0	45	38	21	16	2	23	54	.232	.182	.257	10.88	4.63
Musgrave, Mike	R-R	6-2	185	4-10-84	2	0	2.70	9	0	0	0	10	6	3	3	0	1	5	.200	.250	.150	4.50	0.90
Neitz, Jason	L-L	6-0	170	4-24-84	4	1	3.38	7	0	0	0	12	12	3	3	0	1	9	.375	.600	.273	9.00	1.12

Name	B-T	HT	WT	DOB	W	L	ERA	G	GS	CG	SV	IP	H	R	ER	HR	BB	SO	AVG	vLH	vRH	K/9	BB/9
Odle, Oliver	R-R	6-0	215	7-11-85	5	3	3.23	13	7	0	0	53	49	23	19	1	8	49	.237	.216	.255	8.32	1.36
Ortiz-Jusino, Adam	R-R	6-3	190	10-24-84	0	0	1.80	5	0	0	0	5	7	2	1	0	0	4	.333	.400	.313	7.20	0.00
Pannell, Jonathan	R-R	6-1	180	9-22-85	2	1	2.82	14	0	0	1	22	21	9	7	0	5	33	.253	.250	.255	13.30	2.01
Paterson, Joseph	R-L	6-1	210	5-19-86	1	0	0.00	4	0	0	0	5	1	1	0	0	0	8	.063	.000	.100	14.40	0.00
Patino, Geomar	R-R	6-3	180	1-21-87	2	0	9.00	11	0	0	0	10	15	10	10	1	7	9	.366	.455	.333	8.10	6.30
Reichard, Andrew	R-R	6-4	235	12-4-84	0	1	3.38	6	0	0	0	8	11	4	3	0	4	9	.333	.333	.333	10.12	4.50
Runzler, Daniel	L-L	6-4	215	3-30-85	1	2	3.44	15	0	0	4	18	15	8	7	1	6	24	.242	.214	.250	11.78	2.95
Rusova, Ivan	R-R	6-1	180	11-5-86	0	0	1.80	5	0	0	0	5	3	1	1	0	6	4	.188	.429	.000	7.20	10.80
Stolp, Eric	R-R	6-3	182	8-18-84	0	0	0.00	5	0	0	0	6	4	4	0	0	3	4	.200	.200	.200	6.00	4.50
Turpen, Daniel	R-R	6-4	215	8-17-86	0	0	0.00	4	0	0	1	9	10	1	0	0	3	5	.286	.231	.318	4.82	2.89
Valdez, Jose	R-R	6-7	190	8-1-88	0	4	6.95	11	11	0	0	34	34	28	26	1	33	43	.262	.219	.276	11.50	8.82
Whitaker, Craig	R-R	6-4	190	11-19-84	0	0	6.00	2	0	0	0	3	1	2	2	0	3	3	.100	.000	.125	9.00	9.00
Wilshire, Richard	R-R	6-4	200	3-25-85	0	1	2.51	13	0	0	4	14	15	5	4	0	7	15	.268	.261	.273	9.42	4.40

FIELDING

Catcher	PCT	G	PO	A	E	DP	PB
Alfonzo	1.000	3	16	4	0	0	2
Ambort	1.000	3	20	0	0	0	0
Gunther	.857	2	17	1	3	0	0
Klimas	.968	22	138	14	5	3	3
Monell	.974	24	168	18	5	1	6
Zambrano	.987	17	138	17	2	1	7

First Base	PCT	G	PO	A	E	DP
D'alessio	.985	43	350	33	6	28
Martinez-Esteve	1.000	3	18	3	0	3
White	.982	18	105	7	2	13

Second Base	PCT	G	PO	A	E	DP
B. Bond	.960	9	8	16	1	4

	PCT	G	PO	A	E	DP
Corona	1.000	14	24	39	0	9
Culberson	.810	6	8	9	4	1
Jean	1.000	1	2	2	0	0
Lopez	.974	12	19	18	1	3
Noonan	.958	22	34	57	4	11
Stromsmoe	.929	7	3	10	1	2

Third Base	PCT	G	PO	A	E	DP
B. Bond	1.000	8	3	7	0	0
Stromsmoe	1.000	6	2	2	0	0
Villalona	.864	52	25	89	18	9

Shortstop	PCT	G	PO	A	E	DP
Culberson	.937	38	45	103	10	16
Lopez	.962	6	8	17	1	5

Noonan	.935	21	35	65	7	13

Outfield	PCT	G	PO	A	E	DP
C. Bond	.950	52	68	8	4	2
Cividanes	1.000	2	2	0	0	0
Creswell	1.000	12	14	4	0	0
Duggan	.980	49	93	3	2	1
Dyche	.950	16	18	1	1	0
Lara	.941	12	16	0	1	0
Martinez-Esteve	1.000	8	8	1	0	1
Simmons	.956	26	38	5	2	1
Stromsmoe	1.000	14	9	1	0	0

DSL GIANTS
DOMINICAN SUMMER LEAGUE

ROOKIE

BATTING	B-T	HT	WT	DOB	AVG	vLH	vRH	G	AB	R	H	2B	3B	HR	RBI	BB	HBP	SH	SF	SO	SB	CS	SLG	OBP
Abad, Ramon	R-R	6-1	200	9-30-86	.264	.281	.259	55	148	27	39	3	1	6	25	22	5	0	2	60	8	5	.419	.373
Adrianza, Ehire	R-R	6-1	155	8-21-89	.241	.288	.228	66	249	44	60	17	2	0	30	41	4	3	5	31	23	6	.325	.351
Almonte, Gilberto	R-R	6-3	188	7-15-88	.200	.250	.188	25	60	6	12	1	0	0	8	1	0	0	1	12	1	1	.217	.304
Bautista, Jonathan	R-R	5-10	188	3-21-85	.270	.286	.267	19	37	6	10	1	0	0	6	2	2	0	5	3	0	.297	.400
Castillo, Luis	R-R	6-3	198	11-21-88	.172	.000	.196	24	58	7	10	1	0	0	3	10	1	0	1	12	1	0	.190	.300
Duran, Rey	R-R	6-0	200	7-31-89	.130	.200	.122	21	46	6	6	0	0	1	4	9	1	0	0	13	0	0	.196	.286
Fuentes, Robedluis	R-R	6-4	180	9-13-88	.220	.182	.229	55	59	15	13	3	0	0	8	12	3	0	0	10	5	1	.271	.378
Hernadez, Marcos	R-R	6-1	185	4-7-89	.048	.000	.063	16	21	0	1	0	0	0	2	3	1	0	0	9	0	0	.048	.200
Izturis, Julio	B-R	5-11	165	8-29-89	.246	.250	.244	67	232	43	57	5	0	0	30	30	12	2	2	30	36	7	.267	.359
Medina, Jose	R-R	6-0	180	11-29-86	.252	.178	.274	63	202	31	51	11	0	8	44	38	7	1	1	47	11	7	.426	.387
Navarro, Jesus	R-R	6-0	180	1-3-88	.179	.167	.183	60	145	20	26	2	2	3	20	24	2	7	1	29	1	0	.283	.302
Nunez, Juan	R-R	6-3	190	12-29-86	.077	.250	.000	13	13	3	1	0	0	0	3	5	3	0	1	7	0	0	.077	.409
Peguero, Francisco	R-R	6-0	175	6-1-88	.294	.298	.293	69	235	51	69	12	2	1	17	15	4	0	4	39	25	5	.374	.341
Quintana, Carlos	R-R	6-3	180	6-14-87	.276	.282	.274	68	214	35	59	8	5	3	36	32	8	0	2	45	3	7	.402	.387
Sanchez, Hector	B-R	6-0	185	11-17-89	.286	.429	.242	44	119	10	34	10	0	4	18	19	4	4	0	15	2	2	.471	.401
Santana, Victor	R-R	6-1	192	11-21-88	.247	.245	.247	65	223	38	55	13	0	4	27	32	14	1	2	49	3	0	.359	.373
Willoughby, Carlos	R-R	5-10	170	11-12-88	.291	.409	.250	50	86	23	25	2	1	0	11	13	6	1	0	11	12	3	.337	.419
Windster, Sundrendy	R-R	6-3	185	2-23-89	.237	.179	.252	46	135	18	32	7	0	1	12	15	5	0	0	46	3	2	.333	.335

PITCHING	B-T	HT	WT	DOB	W	L	ERA	G	GS	CG	SV	IP	H	R	ER	HR	BB	SO	AVG	vLH	vRH	K/9	BB/9
Azocar, Luis	L-L	5-11	180	9-6-86	2	0	3.45	21	0	0	0	29	19	13	11	2	20	29	.181	.333	.161	9.10	6.28
Bohorquez, Idelfonso	L-L	6-2	200	10-15-87	2	1	4.11	7	1	0	1	15	12	9	7	1	7	14	.218	.222	.217	8.22	4.11
Bucardo, Jorge	R-R	6-1	155	10-18-89	7	2	1.35	12	11	0	0	60	45	15	9	3	7	39	.200	.225	.188	5.85	1.05
Burgos, Raul	B-R	6-1	210	8-18-87	2	2	3.23	32	0	0	11	31	28	16	11	4	15	27	.237	.317	.195	7.92	4.40
Casilla, Jose	R-R	6-1	190	5-21-89	6	3	3.76	16	14	0	0	69	58	32	29	0	22	58	.223	.202	.236	7.53	2.86
Concepcion, Edward	R-R	6-3	190	10-3-88	1	2	5.91	26	0	0	0	32	36	22	21	5	20	26	.273	.292	.262	7.31	5.62
Geraldo, Walin	R-R	6-3	192	7-30-88	1	4	4.75	18	9	0	0	42	42	28	22	3	29	37	.269	.299	.247	7.99	6.26
Hernandez, Javier	R-R	6-4	180	9-27-87	7	1	2.63	18	9	0	0	72	52	29	21	3	24	44	.202	.235	.186	5.50	3.00
Marte, Kelvin	R-R	6-0	180	11-24-87	5	1	1.62	28	0	0	3	61	36	12	11	3	14	91	.167	.148	.178	13.43	2.07
Martinez, Rafael	R-R	6-3	185	7-9-88	1	1	2.57	3	2	0	0	7	4	2	2	0	2	6	.160	.000	.222	7.71	2.57
Noel, Franklin	L-L	6-1	175	12-20-88	4	2	2.45	26	3	1	9	59	47	23	16	0	26	57	.219	.219	.219	8.74	3.99
Nova, Meroly	L-L	6-6	165	4-16-86	2	0	3.38	7	1	0	2	16	13	8	6	1	8	13	.188	.048	.219	7.31	3.09
Prada, Marcos	R-R	6-0	180	8-31-90	1	0	3.38	18	2	0	1	29	21	11	11	2	20	22	.204	.231	.195	6.75	6.14
Rodriguez, Mario	L-L	6-2	190	8-21-88	8	2	3.16	16	13	0	0	77	71	33	27	3	21	62	.249	.189	.258	7.25	2.45

FIELDING

Catcher	PCT	G	PO	A	E	DP	PB
Bautista	.989	17	78	10	1	2	1
Duran	1.000	15	69	8	0	0	0
Izturis	1.000	1	1	0	0	0	0
Navarro	.998	60	361	50	1	1	9
Sanchez	1.000	8	29	3	0	0	2

First Base	PCT	G	PO	A	E	DP
Almonte	1.000	7	22	0	0	1
Bautista	1.000	1	1	0	0	0
Castillo	.962	18	122	4	5	12
Fuentes	1.000	1	2	0	0	1
Hernadez	.846	5	10	1	2	2
Nunez	1.000	1	2	0	0	0
Quintana	1.000	2	15	0	0	1
Sanchez	.988	29	238	10	3	14

	PCT	G	PO	A	E	DP
Santana	.988	29	241	5	3	16
Willoughby	—	1	0	0	0	0

Second Base	PCT	G	PO	A	E	DP
Almonte	.938	8	14	16	2	5
Izturis	.970	57	98	132	7	26
Medina	.972	16	34	35	2	5
Quintana	1.000	1	1	0	0	0
Willoughby	1.000	3	2	2	0	1

Third Base	PCT	G	PO	A	E	DP
Almonte	.875	3	2	5	1	1
Castillo	—	1	0	0	0	0
Hernadez	.667	2	0	2	1	0
Izturis	.909	1	9	1	1	0
Quintana	.894	67	47	155	24	7

Shortstop	PCT	G	PO	A	E	DP
Adrianza	.962	66	114	211	13	34
Almonte	1.000	1	2	4	0	0
Izturis	1.000	7	13	17	0	2

Outfield	PCT	G	PO	A	E	DP
Abad	.912	30	27	4	3	1
Almonte	—	2	0	0	0	0
Fuentes	1.000	51	19	0	0	0
Medina	1.000	23	2	1	0	0
Nunez	.667	4	2	0	1	0
Peguero	.962	69	120	5	5	1
Santana	.939	30	30	1	2	1
Willoughby	.979	41	44	3	1	1
Windster	.909	41	37	3	4	2

ORGANIZATION STATISTICS

Seattle Mariners

BY JOHN HICKEY

The Mariners had a season to remember in 2007.

It just wasn't quite the memory they were looking for.

Seattle started the season with a manager, Mike Hargrove, looking to get the team out of a three-year losing skid. While the Mariners won 88 games, the fifth-best total in the American League, Hargrove stunned the team seven games into what would become an eight-game winning streak by announcing he was leaving on July 1.

It took some time for the suitably shocked Mariners to pick up the pieces under new manager John McLaren, the former bench coach. But pick them up they did, and on the morning of Aug. 25, the Mariners were 20 games over .500, one game out of first place in the AL West and leading the AL wild-card race.

Then came something as completely unexpected as Hargrove's resignation. The team forgot how to win. The Mariners lost nine in a row and 13 out of 14, and by the time some equilibrium had been established, the postseason was simply a shattered dream.

The collapse was, as they say, a total team effort.

On the morning of Aug. 25, the team ERA was 4.59. But by season's end that figure had risen to 4.73.

The problems of 2007 began with the starting pitching, which was so inconsistent that even with Seattle finishing 14 games over .500, the team was outscored by 19 runs.

Much of Seattle's run differential problem can be put on the starting rotation, particularly righthander Jeff Weaver's terrible first six starts—opponents scored 54 runs in those six—and lefty Horacio Ramirez's amazingly consistent inconsistency.

Ramirez, who lost his spot in the rotation, was the best at winning without pitching well. He had a winning record (8-7) with a loser ERA (7.16).

Of all AL starting pitchers with 96 or more innings, Ramirez had the worst ERA. Weaver's 6.20 was second worst.

This is not to put all the blame on those two. Lefthander Jarrod Washburn was 8-6 at the all-star break and 2-9 after it. Righthander Felix Hernandez' return from an April injury probably came too soon. He gave up four hits in 17 innings before being hurt, and 205 hits in 173 innings afterward. Righthander Miguel Batista had a career-best 16 wins, but gave up six or more runs in a start six times.

Starting pitching troubles meant more was asked of the relievers. For most of the year, that was rewarded as inexperienced relievers Sean Green, Brandon Morrow, Ryan Rowland-Smith, Eric O'Flaherty and George Sherrill did a good job setting up closer J.J. Putz. Righthanders Green and Morrow and lefties Rowland-Smith and O'Flaherty essentially were untested minor leaguers before 2007, but all four proved their mettle.

The other minor league addition to make a splash was outfielder Adam Jones, who was called up in August, but played sparingly despite hitting 314/.382/.586 for Triple-A Tacoma.

The offense was one of just three in the AL with 1,600 or more hits. But because of the inability of hitters to work the count—Seattle was the only team in the league with fewer than 400 walks—the team's production suffered.

First baseman Richie Sexson had the worst year of his career, hitting .205/.295/.399 with 21 home runs and 63 RBIs before August hamstring troubles ended his season. McLaren stuck with Sexson and Raul Ibanez, another first-

MAJOR LEAGUE: ICHIRO SUZUKI, OF

Suzuki's combination of pure hitting ability and speed ranks among that of the all-time greats. As he made the transition from right field to his first year as a full-time center fielder, Suzuki led the majors with 238 hits and 203 singles. His .351 average ranked second in baseball, and his 37 stolen bases tied for fourth in the American League.

MINOR LEAGUE: ADAM JONES, OF

Widely praised for his five-tool ability, Jones put those tools to work as one of the Triple-A Pacific Coast League's best hitters. Jones finished third in the league in slugging percentage, hitting .314/.382/.586 for Tacoma. He hit 58 extra-base hits, including 25 home runs, six triples and 27 doubles.

BATTING		★Minimum 250 at-bats
★AVG	Jones, Adam, Tacoma	.314
R	Guzman, Jesus, High Desert	102
H	Reed, Jeremy, Tacoma	169
TB	Guzman, Jesus, High Desert	279
2B	LaHair, Bryan, Tacoma	46
3B	Limonta, Johan, High Desert	8
HR	Three players tied at	25
RBI	Guzman, Jesus, High Desert	112
BB	Tuiasosopo, Matt, West Tenn	76
SO	Jimerson, Charlton, West Tenn/Tacoma	139
SB	Jimerson, Charlton, West Tenn/Tacoma	35
★OBP	Saunders, Michael, High Desert/West Tenn	.39
★SLG	Jones, Adam, Tacoma	.586
PITCHING		^Minimum 75 innings
W	Rohrbaugh, Robert, West Tenn/Tacoma	13
L	Baldwin, Andrew, West Tenn	12
^ERA	Campillo, Jorge, Tacoma	3.07
G	Souza, Justin, Wisconsin	49
CG	Rohrbaugh, Robert, West Tenn/Tacoma	2
SV	Mateo, Julio, Tacoma	12
IP	Rohrbaugh, Robert, West Tenn/Tacoma	170
BB	Woerman, Joseph, West Tenn	68
SO	Tillman, Chris, Wisconsin/High Desert	139
^AVG	Woerman, Joseph, West Tenn	.226

half slumper. Ibanez justified the faith with a great final six weeks that put him atop the team's RBIs list with 107.

Ichiro Suzuki had one of the best years of his career, hitting .351/.396/.431 with 37 stolen bases and 111 runs. Imports Jose Vidro (.314/.381/.394) as the DH and right fielder Jose Guillen (.290/.353/.460) both met or exceeded expectations.

Catcher Kenji Johjima's offensive numbers all were down slightly from his 2006 debut, but overall had a better year, as his pitch calling, receiving and throwing all blossomed.

Both men up the middle, shortstop Yuniesky Betancourt and second baseman Jose Lopez, weren't up to expectations. Betancourt had 19 errors before turning his game around. Lopez had another good start to the season, but he was never the same player after his brother's June death. Such were Lopez' problems that McLaren put him on the bench multiple times to help him regain focus.

2007 PERFORMANCE

General Manager: Bill Bavasi. **Farm Director:** Benny Looper. **Scouting Director:** Bob Fontaine

Class	Team	League	W	L	PCT	Finish*	Manager	Affiliate Since
Majors	Seattle	American	88	74	.543	5th (14)	Mike Hargrove/John McLaren	—
Triple-A	Tacoma Rainiers	Pacific Coast	68	76	.472	12th (16)	Darren Brown	1995
Double-A	West Tennessee Diamond Jaxx	Southern	60	79	.432	9th (10)	Eddie Rodriguez	2007
High A	High Desert Mavericks	California	54	86	.386	10th (10)	Scott Steinmann	2007
Low A	Wisconsin Timber Rattlers	Midwest	53	85	.384	14th (14)	Jim Horner	1993
Short-season	Everett AquaSox	Northwest	35	41	.461	5th (8)	Mike Tosar	1995
Rookie	AZL Mariners	Arizona	37	19	.661	1st (9)^	Jose Moreno	2001
Overall 2007 Minor League Record			**307**	**386**	**.443**	**T-28th**		

* Finish in overall standings (No. of teams in league) ^League champion

ORGANIZATION STATISTICS

SEATTLE MARINERS

AMERICAN LEAGUE

BATTING	B-T	HT	WT	DOB	AVG	vLH	vRH	G	AB	R	H	2B	3B	HR	RBI	BB	HBP	SH	SF	SO	SB	CS	SLG	OBP
Balentien, Wladimir	R-R	6-2	190	7-2-84	.667	.000	1.000	3	3	1	2	1	0	1	4	0	0	0	1	0	0	0	2.000	.500
Beltre, Adrian	R-R	5-11	220	4-7-79	.276	.280	.274	149	595	87	164	41	2	26	99	38	2	0	4	104	14	2	.482	.319
Betancourt, Yuniesky	R-R	5-10	190	1-31-82	.289	.333	.277	155	536	72	155	38	2	9	67	15	1	3	4	48	5	4	.418	.308
Bloomquist, Willie	R-R	5-11	195	11-27-77	.277	.238	.290	91	173	28	48	3	0	2	13	10	1	4	0	35	7	5	.329	.321
Broussard, Ben	L-L	6-2	220	9-24-76	.275	.250	.277	99	240	27	66	10	0	7	29	17	4	0	3	50	2	0	.404	.330
Burke, Jamie	R-R	6-0	225	9-24-71	.301	.280	.307	50	113	19	34	8	0	1	12	7	4	5	0	17	0	1	.398	.363
Clement, Jeff	L-R	6-1	210	8-21-83	.375	.000	.400	9	16	4	6	1	0	2	3	3	0	0	0	3	0	0	.813	.474
Ellison, Jason	R-R	5-10	180	4-4-78	.283	.167	.357	63	46	9	13	0	0	0	0	1	0	1	0	12	3	3	.283	.298
Green, Nick	R-R	6-0	180	9-10-78	.000	.000	.000	6	7	0	0	0	0	0	0	0	0	0	0	3	0	0	.000	.000
Guillen, Jose	R-R	6-0	195	5-17-76	.290	.362	.268	153	593	84	172	28	2	23	99	41	19	0	5	118	5	1	.460	.353
Ibanez, Raul	L-R	6-2	220	6-2-72	.291	.256	.305	149	573	80	167	35	5	21	105	53	3	0	7	97	0	0	.480	.351
Jimerson, Charlton	R-R	6-3	210	9-22-79	1.000	—	1.000	11	2	5	2	0	0	1	1	0	0	0	0	2	0	2	2.500	1.000
Johjima, Kenji	R-R	6-0	200	6-8-76	.287	.327	.276	135	485	52	139	29	0	14	61	15	11	0	2	41	0	2	.433	.322
Johnson, Rob	R-R	6-1	200	7-22-83	.333	.000	.333	6	3	1	1	0	0	0	0	0	0	0	0	1	0	0	.333	.333
Jones, Adam	R-R	6-2	200	8-1-85	.246	.310	.194	41	65	16	16	2	1	2	4	4	1	1	0	21	2	1	.400	.300
Lopez, Jose	R-R	6-0	200	11-24-83	.252	.244	.254	149	524	58	132	17	2	11	62	20	5	9	3	64	2	3	.355	.284
Morse, Mike	R-R	6-4	225	3-22-82	.444	.571	.364	9	18	1	8	2	0	0	3	1	1	0	0	4	0	0	.556	.500
Reed, Jeremy	L-L	6-0	200	6-15-81	.176	—	.176	13	17	2	3	0	1	0	0	0	0	0	0	3	0	0	.294	.176
Sexson, Richie	R-R	6-8	235	12-29-74	.205	.238	.195	121	434	58	89	21	0	21	63	51	5	0	1	100	1	0	.399	.295
Suzuki, Ichiro	L-R	5-9	170	10-22-73	.351	.331	.358	161	678	111	238	22	7	6	68	49	3	4	2	77	37	8	.431	.396
Vidro, Jose	B-R	5-11	195	8-27-74	.314	.328	.309	147	548	78	172	26	0	6	59	63	1	5	8	57	0	0	.394	.381

PITCHING	B-T	HT	WT	DOB	W	L	ERA	G	GS	CG	SV	IP	H	R	ER	HR	BB	SO	AVG	vLH	vRH	K/9	BB/9
Baek, Cha Seung	R-R	6-4	220	5-29-80	4	3	5.15	14	12	1	0	73	87	45	42	6	14	49	.288	.267	.305	6.01	1.72
Batista, Miguel	R-R	6-1	195	2-19-71	16	11	4.29	33	32	0	0	193	209	101	92	18	85	133	.276	.295	.258	6.20	3.96
Campillo, Jorge	R-R	6-1	190	8-10-78	0	0	6.75	5	0	0	0	13	18	12	10	2	6	9	.333	.238	.394	6.07	4.05
Davis, Jason	R-R	6-6	225	5-8-80	2	0	6.31	16	0	0	0	26	29	21	18	4	16	14	.290	.343	.262	4.91	5.61
2-team (8 Cleveland)					2	0	5.84	24	0	0	0	37	42	27	24	4	25	19	—	—	—	4.62	6.08
Feierabend, Ryan	L-L	6-3	190	8-22-85	1	6	8.03	13	9	0	0	49	73	44	44	10	23	27	.353	.304	.366	4.93	4.20
Green, Sean	R-R	6-6	230	4-20-79	5	2	3.84	64	0	0	0	68	77	31	29	2	34	53	.298	.329	.286	7.01	4.50
Hernandez, Felix	R-R	6-3	230	4-8-86	14	7	3.92	30	30	1	0	190	209	88	83	20	53	165	.281	.300	.261	7.80	2.51
Huber, Jon	R-R	6-2	195	7-7-81	0	0	4.76	9	0	0	0	11	13	6	6	1	4	8	.302	.400	.250	6.35	3.18
Lowe, Mark	R-R	6-3	190	6-7-83	0	0	6.75	4	0	0	0	3	2	2	2	1	3	3	.200	.667	.000	10.12	10.12
Mateo, Julio	R-R	6-0	220	8-2-77	1	0	3.75	9	0	0	0	12	12	5	5	0	5	4	.255	.200	.281	3.00	3.75
Morrow, Brandon	R-R	6-3	190	7-26-84	3	4	4.12	60	0	0	0	63	56	29	29	3	50	66	.243	.278	.221	9.38	7.11
O'Flaherty, Eric	L-L	6-2	195	2-5-85	7	1	4.47	56	0	0	0	52	45	26	26	1	20	36	.232	.183	.277	6.19	3.44
Parrish, John	L-L	5-11	210	11-26-77	0	0	6.97	8	0	0	0	10	22	8	8	0	4	5	.440	.389	.469	4.35	3.48
2-team (45 Baltimore)					2	2	5.71	53	0	0	0	52	63	34	33	2	37	41	—	—	—	7.10	6.40
Putz, J.J.	R-R	6-5	250	2-22-77	6	1	1.38	68	0	0	40	72	37	11	11	6	13	82	.153	.148	.158	10.30	1.63
Ramirez, Horacio	L-L	6-1	210	11-24-79	8	7	7.16	20	20	0	0	98	139	86	78	13	42	40	.337	.330	.340	3.67	3.86
Reitsma, Chris	R-R	6-5	235	12-31-77	0	2	7.61	26	0	0	0	24	37	22	20	3	9	11	.359	.357	.361	4.18	3.42
Rowland-Smith, Ryan	L-L	6-3	205	1-26-83	1	0	3.96	26	0	0	0	39	39	19	17	4	15	42	.269	.275	.266	9.78	3.49
Sherrill, George	L-L	6-0	225	4-19-77	2	0	2.36	73	0	0	3	46	28	12	12	4	17	56	.179	.156	.212	11.04	3.35
Washburn, Jarrod	L-L	6-1	190	8-13-74	10	15	4.32	32	32	1	0	194	201	102	93	23	67	114	.268	.213	.288	5.30	3.11
Weaver, Jeff	R-R	6-5	200	8-22-76	7	13	6.20	27	27	3	0	147	190	105	101	23	35	80	.315	.324	.306	4.91	2.15
White, Rick	R-R	6-4	245	12-23-68	0	1	8.44	6	0	0	0	5	11	6	5	0	4	3	.458	.333	.533	5.06	6.75
White, Sean	R-R	6-4	215	4-25-81	1	1	5.60	15	0	0	0	35	35	24	22	2	20	16	.261	.250	.270	4.08	5.09
Woods, Jake	L-L	6-1	190	9-3-81	0	0	5.91	4	0	0	0	11	9	8	7	1	7	4	.220	.091	.267	3.38	5.91

Catcher	PCT	G	PO	A	E	DP	PB
Burke	.996	48	259	9	1	0	3
Johjima	.998	133	805	56	2	15	5
Johnson	1.000	4	2	0	0	0	0

First Base	PCT	G	PO	A	E	DP
Bloomquist	1.000	4	5	1	0	0
Broussard	.993	52	281	21	2	39
Morse	1.000	5	35	1	0	0
Sexson	.998	116	1000	72	2	102
Vidro	1.000	11	78	5	0	5

Second Base	PCT	G	PO	A	E	DP
Bloomquist	.938	20	23	38	4	9

Third Base	PCT	G	PO	A	E	DP
Green	1.000	2	2	2	0	1
Lopez	.989	146	280	423	8	105
Vidro	.969	10	19	12	1	2

Third Base	PCT	G	PO	A	E	DP
Beltre	.958	147	121	287	18	24
Bloomquist	1.000	20	11	29	0	2
Lopez	.875	3	2	5	1	1
Morse	1.000	3	0	5	0	2

Shortstop	PCT	G	PO	A	E	DP
Betancourt	.967	152	239	435	23	110
Bloomquist	.984	20	23	39	1	5
Green	1.000	3	0	2	0	0

Outfield	PCT	G	PO	A	E	DP
Morse	—	1	0	0	0	0
Balentien	—	3	0	0	0	0
Bloomquist	1.000	24	22	0	0	0
Broussard	1.000	22	35	0	0	0
Ellison	.967	52	29	0	1	0
Guillen	.972	150	268	9	8	3
Ibanez	.975	131	224	10	6	2
Jimerson	1.000	3	1	0	0	0
Jones	.953	38	39	2	2	1
Morse	—	1	0	0	0	0
Reed	1.000	4	3	0	0	0
Suzuki	.998	155	424	8	1	3

TACOMA RAINERS
TRIPLE-A

PACIFIC COAST LEAGUE

BATTING	B-T	HT	WT	DOB	AVG	vLH	vRH	G	AB	R	H	2B	3B	HR	RBI	BB	HBP	SH	SF	SO	SB	CS	SLG	OBP
Balentien, Wladimir	R-R	6-2	190	7-2-84	.291	.252	.304	124	477	77	139	24	4	24	84	54	3	2	8	105	15	4	.509	.362
Boucher, Sebastien	L-R	6-0	190	10-19-81	.298	.091	.329	28	84	16	25	4	0	1	12	14	0	1	0	15	3	3	.381	.398
Burroughs, Sean	L-R	6-2	180	9-12-80	.167	.125	.250	4	12	2	2	1	0	0	0	3	1	0	0	3	0	0	.250	.375
Chen, Yung Chi	R-R	5-11	170	7-13-83	.333	.333	.333	5	15	2	5	2	0	0	3	0	0	1	2	3	1	1	.467	.294
Clement, Jeff	L-R	6-1	210	8-21-83	.275	.315	.259	125	455	76	125	35	3	20	80	61	10	4	0	88	0	0	.497	.370
Dawkins, Gookie	R-R	6-1	180	5-12-79	.250	.218	.262	81	308	36	77	12	2	4	32	19	0	3	1	55	11	3	.341	.293
Green, Nick	R-R	6-0	180	9-10-78	.337	.250	.366	66	285	52	96	15	6	16	46	21	2	1	3	60	4	3	.600	.385
Jimerson, Charlton	R-R	6-3	210	9-22-79	.308	.450	.244	17	65	7	20	4	1	2	7	5	0	1	0	22	5	1	.492	.372
Johnson, Rob	R-R	6-1	200	7-22-83	.268	.296	.258	112	422	57	113	26	0	6	40	39	1	3	0	62	7	7	.372	.331
Jones, Adam	R-R	6-2	200	8-1-85	.314	.318	.313	101	420	75	132	27	6	25	84	36	11	0	2	106	8	7	.586	.382
LaHair, Bryan	L-R	6-5	215	11-5-82	.275	.193	.303	138	552	79	152	46	2	12	81	49	0	1	4	126	0	1	.431	.332
Meneses, Alex	R-R	5-10	185	12-21-83	—	—	.000	1	1	0	0	0	0	0	0	1	0	0	0	0	0	0	.000	1.000
Morse, Mike	R-R	6-4	225	3-22-82	.309	.257	.326	76	291	48	90	26	0	6	39	26	3	1	3	47	5	3	.460	.368
Navarro, Oswaldo	R-R	6-0	155	10-2-84	.249	.250	.249	128	446	51	111	21	0	4	45	33	7	5	2	86	4	3	.323	.304
Nelson, Jon	R-R	6-5	235	1-16-79	.214	.222	.210	49	173	19	37	12	3	3	19	4	2	1	0	58	4	1	.370	.240
Nunez, Israel	R-R	6-1	200	9-1-85	.143	.333	.000	2	7	0	1	1	0	0	0	0	0	0	0	1	0	0	.286	.143
Nunez, Luis	R-R	6-0	170	12-31-86	.167	—	.167	2	6	0	1	1	0	0	0	0	0	0	0	1	0	0	.333	.167
Prettyman, Ronnie	L-R	6-2	190	1-6-81	.274	.222	.286	69	241	36	66	13	1	7	34	13	2	6	2	45	2	1	.423	.314
Redman, Prentice	R-R	6-3	185	8-23-79	.304	.278	.314	20	69	15	21	5	0	2	5	6	1	0	0	15	0	4	.464	.368
Reed, Jeremy	L-L	6-0	185	6-15-81	.300	.230	.322	135	564	92	169	37	5	13	64	47	3	9	5	73	14	9	.452	.354
Reynolds, Kevin	L-L	6-1	185	7-1-82	.263	.200	.286	8	19	1	5	0	0	0	2	1	0	4	0	4	0	0	.263	.300
Santin, Daniel	L-L	6-2	205	11-7-84	.000	—	.000	1	1	0	0	0	0	0	0	0	0	0	0	0	0	0	.000	.000
Ust, Brant	R-R	6-2	200	7-17-78	.245	.298	.221	49	151	11	37	9	0	3	17	10	3	2	3	37	0	0	.364	.299

PITCHING	B-T	HT	WT	DOB	W	L	ERA	G	GS	CG	SV	IP	H	R	ER	HR	BB	SO	AVG	vLH	vRH	K/9	BB/9
Baek, Cha Seung	R-R	6-4	220	5-29-80	1	1	3.19	6	6	0	0	31	33	13	11	1	10	18	.273	.294	.257	5.23	2.90
Campillo, Jorge	R-R	6-1	190	8-10-78	9	6	3.07	24	22	0	0	149	151	55	51	11	39	99	.264	.254	.273	5.97	2.35
Cerda, Jaime	L-L	6-0	200	10-26-78	0	3	8.87	17	0	0	0	23	29	28	23	3	20	15	.290	.306	.275	5.79	7.71
Chick, Travis	R-R	6-3	215	6-10-84	0	1	22.09	3	0	0	0	4	9	10	9	2	4	3	.474	.200	.571	7.36	9.82
Cortez, Renee	R-R	6-2	180	12-9-82	1	1	5.54	9	0	0	0	13	14	8	8	1	9	8	.264	.316	.235	5.54	6.23
Cotter, Aaron	R-R	6-4	250	1-2-84	0	0	13.50	1	0	0	0	1	1	1	1	0	1	0	.500	.000	1.000	0.00	13.50
Davis, Jason	R-R	6-6	225	5-8-80	0	2	7.11	5	5	0	0	25	37	21	20	2	14	16	.346	.413	.295	5.68	4.97
De La Cruz, Jose	R-R	6-6	206	9-23-83	0	0	11.32	8	0	0	3	10	18	13	13	2	5	6	.375	.368	.379	5.23	4.35
Done, Juan	R-R	6-2	220	10-2-80	2	8	5.15	21	6	0	1	65	75	42	37	6	25	32	.295	.291	.299	4.45	3.48
Downs, Brodie	R-R	6-4	240	7-19-79	1	0	3.60	4	0	0	0	5	3	7	2	0	7	6	.167	.250	.100	10.80	12.60
Embry, Byron	R-R	6-2	240	9-5-76	0	6	5.70	25	0	0	4	36	38	25	23	4	30	41	.286	.359	.217	10.16	7.43
Feierabend, Ryan	L-L	6-3	190	8-22-85	6	4	3.99	19	19	1	0	108	131	57	48	9	33	70	.305	.287	.311	5.82	2.74
Fiorenza, Andrew	R-R	6-2	210	6-24-84	0	1	24.00	1	0	0	0	3	8	8	8	1	3	4	.500	.500	.500	12.00	9.00
Green, Sean	R-R	6-6	230	4-20-79	2	1	2.04	10	0	0	1	18	13	5	4	0	8	10	.210	.179	.235	5.09	4.08
Harmon, Robert	R-R	6-7	239	9-28-83	0	1	12.27	1	1	0	0	4	6	5	5	0	4	2	.400	.250	.571	4.91	9.82
Hrynio, Michael	R-R	6-2	213	11-18-82	0	0	0.00	1	0	0	0	1	1	0	0	0	2	2	.250	.500	.000	18.00	0.00
Huber, Jon	R-R	6-2	195	7-7-81	1	4	7.56	24	1	0	5	33	43	33	28	5	9	28	.309	.296	.318	7.56	2.43
Jimenez, Cesar	L-L	5-11	180	11-12-84	2	1	3.51	16	0	0	2	26	28	15	10	2	12	23	.269	.235	.286	8.06	4.21
Johannesen-Ellis, T.	R-R	6-4	230	2-23-88	0	0	9.00	1	0	0	0	1	3	1	1	0	0	1	.500	—	—	9.00	0.00
Lehr, Justin	R-R	6-2	215	8-3-77	7	1	3.99	27	17	0	1	120	132	62	53	8	41	61	.286	.282	.289	4.59	3.08
Lowe, Mark	R-R	6-3	190	6-7-83	0	0	5.68	7	3	0	0	6	12	4	4	1	5	5	.387	.375	.400	7.11	4.26
Mackintosh, Jason	R-L	6-0	205	7-2-80	2	1	4.69	28	1	0	1	48	61	25	25	7	13	38	.303	.338	.281	7.12	2.44
Mateo, Julio	R-R	6-2	220	8-2-77	3	1	0.79	24	0	0	12	34	25	4	3	3	2	29	.200	.234	.164	7.60	0.52
Mickolio, Kameron	R-R	6-9	256	5-10-84	3	3	3.75	14	0	0	1	24	19	12	10	3	10	28	.213	.167	.255	10.50	3.75
Mortimore, Travis	L-L	6-5	225	8-1-84	0	0	6.75	1	0	0	0	1	2	1	1	0	2	0	.333	.667	.000	0.00	13.50
O'Flaherty, Eric	L-L	6-2	195	2-5-85	0	0	1.13	6	0	0	3	8	5	1	1	0	4	6	.179	.167	.188	9.00	4.50
Ohka, Tomo	B-R	6-1	200	3-18-76	0	3	10.32	4	4	0	0	23	38	26	26	6	9	9	.384	.250	.448	3.57	3.57
2-team (3 Memphis)					t	0	5	8.78	7	7	0	0	41	65	41	40	8	12	16	—	—	3.51	2.63
Paredes, Edward	L-L	6-0	175	9-30-86	0	0	0.00	1	0	0	0	5	0	0	0	0	1	5	.000	.000	—	9.00	1.80
Parque, Jim	L-L	5-11	170	2-8-76	1	3	7.80	11	7	0	0	45	73	45	39	6	19	24	.372	.310	.399	4.80	3.80
Parrish, John	L-L	5-11	210	11-26-77	1	0	14.54	3	0	0	0	4	8	7	7	1	4	4	.421	.500	.412	8.31	8.31
Ramirez, Horacio	L-L	6-1	210	11-24-79	1	0	6.30	2	2	0	0	10	7	7	7	3	3	5	.194	.200	.192	4.50	2.70
Reitsma, Chris	R-R	6-5	235	12-31-77	0	0	0.00	2	1	0	0	3	1	0	0	0	1	2	.100	.333	.000	6.00	3.00
Rohrbaugh, Robert	R-L	6-2	195	12-28-83	6	3	2.95	13	13	2	0	85	84	31	28	10	26	49	.258	.170	.291	5.17	2.74
Rowland-Smith, Ryan	L-L	6-3	205	1-26-83	3	4	3.67	25	0	0	1	42	35	20	17	2	22	50	.226	.311	.170	10.80	4.75
Sandoval, Juan	R-R	6-1	170	1-13-81	1	2	10.06	14	1	0	0	17	35	20	19	5	11	5	.427	.308	.535	2.65	5.82
Thomas, Brad	L-L	6-4	235	10-12-77	8	6	4.87	34	15	1	2	116	138	68	63	8	42	100	.296	.261	.313	7.74	3.25
Ust, Brant	R-R	6-2	200	7-17-78	0	0	36.00	1	0	0	0	1	3	4	4	2	1	1	.500	.500	9.00	9.00
Wagner, Michael	L-L	6-2	225	3-28-85	0	0	9.00	1	0	0	0	2	2	2	2	0	1	1	.400	—	.400	9.00	4.50
White, Rick	R-R	6-4	245	12-23-68	1	1	1.00	7	0	0	0	9	4	1	1	1	5	6	.133	.143	.125	6.00	5.00

ORGANIZATION STATISTICS

	B-T	HT	WT	DOB	W	L	ERA	G	GS	CG	SV	IP	H	R	ER	HR	BB	SO	AVG	vLH	vRH	K/9	BB/9
White, Sean	R-R	6-4	215	4-25-81	1	1	2.53	2	2	0	0	11	11	4	3	0	2	7	.262	.308	.241	5.91	1.69
Woods, Jake	L-L	6-1	190	9-3-81	5	7	6.91	25	18	0	1	115	151	88	88	17	42	79	.325	.312	.333	6.20	3.30

FIELDING

Catcher	PCT	G	PO	A	E	DP	PB
Clement	.994	74	484	29	3	4	13
Johnson	.987	69	430	34	6	5	8
I. Nunez	1.000	2	15	0	0	0	0
Ust	1.000	2	2	0	0	0	0

First Base	PCT	G	PO	A	E	DP
LaHair	.994	133	1189	70	7	122
Nelson	.978	5	44	1	1	6
Prettyman		1	0	0	0	0
Ust	1.000	9	45	4	0	5

Second Base	PCT	G	PO	A	E	DP
Chen	.967	5	14	15	1	5
Dawkins	.984	48	111	141	4	35
Green	.982	23	47	63	2	13

	PCT	G	PO	A	E	DP
Meneses	1.000	1	0	1	0	0
Navarro	.979	50	93	144	5	30
L. Nunez	1.000	1	2	1	0	0
Ust	1.000	23	34	68	0	16

Third Base	PCT	G	PO	A	E	DP
Burroughs	.000	2	0	0	1	0
Dawkins	.973	12	15	21	1	3
Green	.889	4	1	7	1	1
Morse	.971	55	21	113	4	11
Prettyman	.953	64	50	134	9	12
Ust	.935	16	14	29	3	3

Shortstop	PCT	G	PO	A	E	DP
Dawkins	.974	20	32	43	2	13
Green	.983	31	36	77	2	16

	PCT	G	PO	A	E	DP
Morse	.957	21	23	44	3	12
Navarro	.956	80	110	240	16	56

Outfield	PCT	G	PO	A	E	DP
Balentien	.972	117	230	15	7	1
Boucher	.954	23	62	0	3	0
Green	1.000	12	12	0	0	0
Jimerson	.957	16	44	1	2	0
Jones	.986	101	280	12	4	3
Morse	1.000	3	5	0	0	0
Nelson	.927	27	37	1	3	0
Prettyman	1.000	1	1	0	0	0
Redman	1.000	18	47	2	0	1
Reed	.992	120	253	10	2	0
Reynolds	1.000	6	11	0	0	0

WEST TENN DIAMOND JAXX

DOUBLE-A

SOUTHERN LEAGUE

BATTING	B-T	HT	WT	DOB	AVG	vLH	vRH	G	AB	R	H	2B	3B	HR	RBI	BB	HBP	SH	SF	SO	SB	CS	SLG	OBP
Boucher, Sebastien	L-R	6-0	190	10-19-81	.219	.218	.220	59	228	37	50	9	2	1	11	34	2	4	1	53	13	7	.289	.325
Craig, Casey	L-R	6-1	185	1-12-85	.216	.179	.232	30	97	10	21	3	2	0	7	14	0	4	0	23	3	2	.289	.315
Frazier, Jeff	R-R	6-3	195	8-10-82	.245	.237	.250	78	302	29	74	12	1	4	30	21	2	1	2	54	0	2	.331	.297
Garth, Ronald	R-R	5-11	165	11-5-84	.250	.333	.000	1	4	1	1	0	0	0	1	0	0	0	1	0	0	0	.250	.400
Hubbard, Thomas	L-R	6-2	215	4-16-82	.270	.259	.277	131	488	73	132	31	5	15	78	65	8	0	7	135	1	1	.447	.361
Jimerson, Charlton	R-R	6-3	210	9-22-79	.276	.248	.296	82	322	54	89	18	3	23	73	29	6	3	1	117	30	9	.565	.336
Johnson, Brent	R-R	6-2	185	5-21-82	.291	.316	.272	117	453	68	132	30	1	7	50	55	11	4	2	55	8	7	.408	.380
Meneses, Alex	R-R	5-10	185	12-21-83	.205	.261	.143	13	44	13	9	2	0	0	4	10	1	0	1	11	2	0	.250	.357
Merchan, Jesus	R-R	6-0	184	3-26-81	.247	.276	.233	24	89	11	22	5	0	2	7	4	3	3	0	9	2	1	.371	.302
Minaker, Christopher	R-R	6-0	195	3-24-84	.227	.224	.228	101	353	38	80	10	1	3	27	26	4	3	4	65	2	7	.286	.284
Monzon, Erick	R-R	6-0	190	11-30-81	.222	.194	.242	68	230	20	51	11	2	6	30	26	0	5	2	52	4	3	.365	.298
Nelson, Jon	R-R	6-5	235	1-16-80	.222	.000	.222	5	18	5	4	2	0	2	4	2	1	0	0	6	0	0	.667	.333
Oliveros, Luis	R-R	6-1	205	6-18-83	.286	.288	.285	50	175	20	50	12	0	3	19	12	3	6	1	26	0	0	.406	.340
Prettyman, Ronnie	L-R	6-2	190	8-4-81	.200	.300	.175	16	50	4	10	2	0	0	3	7	0	3	0	16	1	1	.240	.298
Redman, Prentice	R-R	6-3	185	8-23-79	.245	.292	.214	93	343	44	84	16	3	13	49	48	8	2	5	77	4	4	.423	.347
Rivera, Rene	R-R	5-10	210	7-31-83	.214	.244	.191	91	323	29	69	16	0	5	40	24	4	3	2	86	1	2	.310	.275
Saunders, Michael	L-R	6-4	205	11-19-86	.288	.333	.270	15	52	8	15	1	2	1	7	7	0	1	0	20	2	1	.442	.373
Tuiasosopo, Matt	R-R	6-2	210	5-10-86	.260	.265	.257	129	446	74	116	27	5	9	57	76	11	1	14	113	4	8	.404	.371
Valbuena, Luis	L-R	5-10	160	11-30-85	.239	.191	.266	122	444	55	106	23	3	11	44	48	1	6	6	83	10	6	.378	.311
Wilson, Michael	B-R	6-2	215	6-29-83	.188	.200	.182	55	208	30	39	7	2	10	28	17	8	0	2	89	3	0	.385	.272

PITCHING	B-T	HT	WT	DOB	W	L	ERA	G	GS	CG	SV	IP	H	R	ER	HR	BB	SO	AVG	vLH	vRH	K/9	BB/9
Asher, David	R-L	6-1	195	2-18-83	0	0	6.16	23	0	0	2	19	23	15	13	1	9	14	.291	.294	.289	6.63	4.26
Baldwin, Andrew	R-R	6-5	215	10-20-82	5	12	4.23	27	26	1	0	166	193	88	78	12	19	115	.292	.369	.228	6.23	1.03
Chick, Travis	R-R	6-3	215	6-10-84	6	6	4.62	17	15	0	0	88	84	47	45	10	37	70	.256	.279	.236	7.19	3.80
De La Cruz, Jose	R-R	6-6	206	9-23-83	1	2	3.18	34	0	0	2	51	44	19	18	2	27	41	.238	.214	.257	7.24	4.76
Done, Juan	R-R	6-2	220	10-2-80	2	3	4.19	11	3	0	0	43	41	23	20	3	21	21	.253	.237	.267	4.40	4.40
Downs, Brodie	R-R	6-4	240	7-19-79	1	1	1.96	11	0	0	2	18	17	4	4	0	7	11	.246	.212	.278	5.40	3.44
Fillinger, Chad	R-R	6-4	210	10-26-82	1	2	5.13	20	0	0	1	33	35	20	19	3	13	32	.280	.347	.237	8.64	3.51
Fister, Douglas	L-R	6-8	200	2-4-84	7	8	4.60	24	24	1	0	131	156	78	67	14	32	85	.302	.313	.293	5.84	2.20
Hrynio, Michael	R-R	6-2	213	11-18-82	3	1	3.89	20	0	0	2	35	28	15	15	0	19	27	.222	.263	.188	7.01	4.93
Jakubauskas, Chris	R-R	6-2	210	12-22-78	0	4	4.94	16	3	1	0	51	53	30	28	3	21	39	.273	.283	.265	6.88	3.71
James, Craig	R-R	6-1	175	3-10-83	5	4	6.14	44	0	0	10	59	71	41	40	5	26	46	.300	.268	.321	7.06	3.99
Johannesen-Ellis, T.	R-R	6-4	230	2-23-88	0	0	0.00	1	0	0	0	4	3	0	0	0	2	2	.273	—	4.91	0.00
Lowe, Mark	R-R	6-3	190	6-7-83	0	0	3.38	3	1	0	0	3	2	1	1	0	2	1	.222	.200	.250	3.38	6.75
Mackintosh, Jason	R-L	6-0	205	7-2-80	0	1	7.94	2	2	0	0	6	7	5	5	2	3	7	.292	.375	.250	11.12	4.76
Mickolio, Kameron	R-R	6-9	256	5-10-84	3	1	1.82	18	0	0	2	30	24	9	6	0	12	27	.224	.348	.131	8.19	3.64
Rivera, Mumba	R-R	6-5	205	12-10-80	4	7	5.27	42	0	0	6	56	54	40	33	13	38	71	.250	.224	.271	11.34	6.07
Rohrbaugh, Robert	R-L	6-2	195	12-28-83	7	5	3.28	15	15	0	0	85	84	35	31	5	21	62	.257	.358	.216	6.56	2.22
Sandoval, Juan	R-R	6-1	170	1-13-81	1	4	4.29	26	0	0	3	50	49	24	24	5	13	29	.263	.266	.262	5.19	2.32
Thomas, Justin	L-L	6-3	220	1-18-84	4	9	5.51	24	24	0	0	119	147	82	73	11	61	100	.308	.327	.303	7.54	4.60
Trolia, Aaron	R-R	6-2	210	5-10-81	3	2	6.91	21	1	0	1	43	53	36	33	5	18	39	.303	.384	.245	8.16	3.77
Wagner, Michael	L-L	6-4	225	3-28-85	0	0	11.12	4	0	0	0	6	7	7	7	3	2	3	.292	.273	.308	6.35	4.76
Woerman, Joseph	R-R	6-3	200	12-12-82	7	7	3.74	27	25	0	0	144	119	69	60	8	68	124	.226	.237	.217	7.73	4.24

FIELDING

Catcher	PCT	G	PO	A	E	DP	PB
Oliveros	.990	50	364	23	4	3	4
Rivera	.991	91	615	70	6	9	15

First Base	PCT	G	PO	A	E	DP
Hubbard	.988	113	922	86	12	85
Johnson	.984	8	59	3	1	6
Monzon	.976	15	111	9	3	8
Prettyman	.971	7	57	11	2	9

Second Base	PCT	G	PO	A	E	DP
Garth	.857	1	4	2	1	0
Meneses	1.000	5	17	11	0	3
Minaker	1.000	1	1	0	0	0

	PCT	G	PO	A	E	DP
Monzon	.980	12	16	32	1	8
Valbuena	.978	122	236	351	13	76

Third Base	PCT	G	PO	A	E	DP
Monzon	.900	11	9	18	3	2
Prettyman	.800	1	2	2	1	0
Tuiasosopo	.952	127	99	236	17	21

Shortstop	PCT	G	PO	A	E	DP
Meneses	1.000	3	3	3	0	3
Merchan	.909	24	29	61	9	11
Minaker	.972	174	144	244	11	58
Monzon	.963	19	32	45	3	12
Prettyman	.500	1	0	1	1	1

Outfield	PCT	G	PO	A	E	DP
Boucher	1.000	50	122	6	0	4
Craig	.972	22	32	3	1	0
Frazier	.991	60	108	8	1	2
Jimerson	.995	73	202	5	1	1
Johnson	.994	85	173	5	1	0
Monzon	1.000	1	0	1	0	0
Nelson	.889	4	7	1	1	0
Redman	1.000	70	132	3	0	2
Saunders	.946	12	34	1	2	0
Wilson	.989	46	89	5	1	0

HIGH DESERT MAVERICKS

HIGH CLASS A

CALIFORNIA LEAGUE

BATTING	B-T	HT	WT	DOB	AVG	vLH	vRH	G	AB	R	H	2B	3B	HR	RBI	BB	HBP	SH	SF	SO	SB	CS	SLG	OBP
Colina, Edilio	R-R	6-2	175	10-10-88	.213	.313	.178	17	61	8	13	2	0	0	5	4	2	0	0	1	0	1	.246	.284
Colton, Chris	R-R	6-1	198	9-21-82	.284	.320	.265	53	148	31	42	9	4	7	18	20	0	1	3	29	2	2	.541	.363
Craig, Casey	L-R	6-1	185	1-12-85	.304	.330	.294	93	378	83	115	23	4	11	49	52	5	7	5	67	20	4	.474	.391
Diaz, Juan	B-R	6-3	180	12-12-88	.150	.500	.000	6	20	1	3	0	1	0	2	2	0	0	0	8	0	0	.250	.227
Dominguez, Jeffrey	B-R	6-2	153	7-31-86	.261	.276	.255	130	494	66	129	28	4	5	55	37	1	8	5	96	18	8	.364	.311
Dotel, Welington	R-R	6-1	180	10-2-85	.250	.000	.333	1	4	0	1	0	0	0	0	0	0	0	0	2	0	0	.250	.250
Eastley, Reed	L-L	6-2	210	7-24-83	.265	.250	.270	45	166	20	44	9	0	1	19	17	3	1	2	41	1	0	.337	.340
Flaig, Jeffrey	R-R	6-2	170	3-3-85	.253	.296	.236	78	293	40	74	15	0	4	34	14	6	3	2	49	2	3	.345	.298
Frazier, Jeff	R-R	6-3	195	8-10-82	.329	.404	.294	44	173	20	57	19	1	4	27	12	2	0	0	14	0	2	.520	.380
Garth, Ronald	R-R	5-11	165	11-5-84	.159	.174	.154	27	88	5	14	3	0	0	8	7	3	1	1	17	0	0	.193	.242
Guzman, Jesus	R-R	6-1	165	6-14-84	.301	.329	.290	130	518	102	156	38	5	25	112	50	8	6	3	85	3	3	.539	.370
Hargrove, Andy	R-L	6-1	240	10-31-81	.174	.089	.218	40	132	14	23	2	0	6	13	14	2	0	2	47	0	1	.326	.260
Hernandez, Eddy	L-L	6-3	170	8-4-84	.190	.170	.197	53	184	23	35	7	0	4	22	14	0	0	0	79	0	0	.293	.247
Hurba, Craig	R-R	6-2	225	8-25-81	.125	.250	.000	2	8	0	1	0	0	0	0	0	0	0	0	3	0	0	.125	.125
Limonta, Johan	L-L	6-0	205	8-4-83	.300	.290	.304	129	474	72	142	21	8	12	72	49	5	1	7	91	2	5	.454	.366
Mangini, Matt	L-R	6-4	220	12-21-85	.226	.267	.213	17	62	7	14	1	2	2	8	6	1	0	0	21	1	0	.403	.304
McConnell, Brandon	R-R	6-4	205	2-8-85	.200	.000	.222	3	10	1	2	0	0	0	1	0	0	0	0	5	0	0	.200	.273
Meneses, Alex	R-R	5-10	185	12-21-83	.176	.222	.167	22	51	9	9	2	0	0	4	10	1	2	1	15	1	0	.216	.317
Moore, Adam	R-R	6-3	215	5-8-84	.307	.320	.302	115	433	74	133	30	3	22	102	41	8	0	9	84	1	0	.543	.371
Pena, Omar	R-R	5-11	175	3-2-82	.239	.313	.216	21	67	10	16	5	0	0	3	3	0	1	1	11	1	1	.313	.268
Reynolds, Kevin	L-L	6-1	185	7-1-82	.400	.350	.415	26	85	18	34	4	0	1	14	3	3	1	2	16	6	2	.482	.430
Saunders, Michael	L-R	6-4	205	11-19-86	.299	.324	.288	108	431	91	129	25	4	14	77	60	8	5	3	116	27	10	.473	.392
Scott, Travis	L-R	6-3	220	4-24-85	.276	.342	.261	62	214	40	59	6	2	13	48	33	0	2	0	48	0	1	.505	.372
Triunfel, Carlos	R-R	5-11	175	2-27-90	.288	.211	.318	50	208	32	60	10	2	0	22	12	2	3	0	31	3	4	.356	.333
Tucker, J.B.	R-R	6-0	200	2-20-82	.200	.333	.000	4	10	1	2	1	0	0	4	1	0	0	1	3	0	0	.300	.250
Womack, Josh	L-L	6-0	194	1-5-84	.207	.226	.200	57	188	34	39	6	4	2	16	17	2	3	2	45	8	6	.314	.278

PITCHING	B-T	HT	WT	DOB	W	L	ERA	G	GS	CG	SV	IP	H	R	ER	HR	BB	SO	AVG	vLH	vRH	K/9	BB/9
Adcock, Nathan	R-R	6-5	190	2-25-88	1	3	8.84	5	5	0	0	18	20	26	18	0	22	11	.278	.303	.256	5.40	10.80
Allen, Nicholas	R-R	6-1	210	6-15-83	4	3	6.40	43	3	0	9	97	136	84	69	18	23	43	.326	.353	.308	3.99	2.13
Asher, David	R-L	6-1	195	2-18-83	0	2	5.87	25	0	0	0	23	21	19	15	4	7	23	.231	.207	.242	9.00	2.74
Bello, Cibney	L-R	6-5	209	9-10-82	6	10	6.91	22	21	0	0	116	153	106	89	28	54	91	.317	.291	.338	7.06	4.19
Bibens-Dirkx, Austin	R-R	6-2	190	4-29-85	3	1	4.42	31	0	0	8	39	40	25	19	2	20	26	.258	.297	.231	6.05	4.66
Blanco, Ivan	R-R	6-1	190	9-24-83	1	1	10.72	17	0	0	2	23	38	39	27	5	19	23	.349	.390	.324	9.13	7.54
Cotter, Aaron	R-R	6-4	250	1-2-84	3	5	6.42	40	10	0	2	102	131	85	73	10	42	62	.303	.288	.311	5.45	3.69
Escalona, Jose	L-L	5-11	165	1-7-86	4	10	7.41	36	15	0	0	98	129	94	81	21	52	77	.316	.252	.341	7.05	4.76
Fagan, Paul	L-L	6-5	195	4-13-85	6	9	6.68	43	7	0	1	90	110	74	67	9	44	58	.299	.276	.307	5.78	4.38
Flores, Ruben	R-R	6-4	165	5-19-84	2	4	7.62	16	8	0	0	52	62	48	44	10	35	64	.292	.228	.351	11.08	6.06
Jensen, Aaron	R-R	6-2	180	6-11-84	2	6	6.88	26	12	0	5	69	102	67	53	10	19	43	.343	.287	.376	5.58	2.47
Kappel, Brian	R-R	6-0	215	1-7-83	2	1	5.06	12	0	0	0	16	17	12	9	3	5	14	.274	.250	.294	7.88	2.81
Lockwood, Jon	R-R	6-2	210	12-12-81	0	3	6.58	6	6	0	0	26	33	19	19	5	11	21	.308	.255	.365	7.27	3.81
Marquez, Miguel	R-R	6-3	180	10-28-87	0	0	4.91	1	0	0	0	4	6	2	2	1	3	3	.353	.364	.333	7.36	7.36
Martinez, Roman	R-R	6-3	160	8-9-84	6	3	3.48	46	0	0	1	88	85	56	44	8	26	85	.244	.311	.201	8.66	2.65
Snyder, Jason	R-R	6-6	205	4-6-83	0	0	8.80	10	0	0	0	15	26	19	15	2	14	12	.394	.361	.433	7.04	8.22
Sullivan, John	R-R	6-3	220	2-22-82	0	2	9.56	10	0	0	0	16	23	17	17	3	14	14	.343	.304	.364	7.88	1.69
Tillman, Chris	R-R	6-5	195	4-15-88	6	7	5.26	20	20	0	0	103	107	79	60	12	48	105	.266	.268	.264	9.20	4.21
Uhlmansiek, Steven	L-L	6-3	185	2-10-83	2	0	8.92	26	0	0	0	36	52	44	36	12	28	26	.333	.300	.349	6.44	6.94
Vega, Marwin	R-R	6-0	175	10-27-86	5	10	4.90	24	24	1	0	129	149	88	70	14	43	82	.296	.342	.268	5.74	3.01
Venegas, Alfredo	R-R	6-1	180	5-11-86	0	2	8.68	2	2	0	0	9	12	9	9	2	5	6	.324	.556	.250	4.82	4.82
Wagner, Michael	L-L	6-4	225	3-28-85	0	0	81.00	1	0	0	0	0	2	3	3	0	2	0	.667	.667	.000	0.00	54.00
Zapata, Juan	R-R	6-3	180	8-6-84	1	4	6.33	36	7	0	3	81	104	68	57	19	34	75	.308	.281	.324	8.33	3.78

FIELDING

Catcher	PCT	G	PO	A	E	DP	PB
Eastley	—	1	0	0	0	0	0
Hurba	1.000	1	6	0	0	0	0
Moore	.989	101	683	64	8	5	21
Scott	.973	38	270	22	8	5	10
Tucker	1.000	4	19	9	0	0	0

First Base	PCT	G	PO	A	E	DP
Eastley	.995	25	187	15	1	13
Flaig	1.000	4	28	1	0	1
Guzman	1.000	5	26	3	0	5
Hargrove	.967	22	166	11	6	22
Limonta	.981	84	679	29	14	62
Moore	.977	5	42	0	1	7
Scott	1.000	9	58	9	0	8

Second Base	PCT	G	PO	A	E	DP
Colina	.833	2	1	4	1	0
Dominguez	.979	49	93	135	5	44

	PCT	G	PO	A	E	DP	PB
Flaig	1.000	1	1	0	0	0	
Garth	.976	26	47	76	3	5	
Guzman	.959	49	107	126	10	32	
Meneses	.971	9	13	21	1	3	
Pena	.915	8	15	28	4	8	

Third Base	PCT	G	PO	A	E	DP
Colina	.950	13	12	26	2	2
Dominguez	.800	1	1	3	1	0
Eastley	1.000	3	1	5	0	0
Flaig	.878	71	51	151	28	17
Guzman	.851	31	17	40	10	4
Mangini	.893	17	14	36	6	5
Meneses	1.000	9	6	14	0	1
Pena	.923	8	7	17	2	1
Scott	.500	1	0	1	1	0

Shortstop	PCT	G	PO	A	E	DP
Colina	.900	3	6	3	1	0

	PCT	G	PO	A	E	DP
Diaz	.923	6	6	18	2	4
Dominguez	.929	80	151	214	28	45
Flaig	1.000	1	2	3	0	0
Guzman	.500	2	1	1	2	1
Pena	.667	4	2	0	1	0
Triunfel	.926	50	96	154	20	37

Outfield	PCT	G	PO	A	E	DP
Colton	.967	56	56	3	2	0
Craig	.982	91	212	9	4	1
Dotel	1.000	1	3	0	0	0
Frazier	.948	43	89	2	5	0
Guzman	.955	29	41	1	2	0
Hernandez	.933	46	79	5	6	1
Limonta	.850	26	31	3	6	1
McConnell	.833	2	5	0	1	0
Reynolds	1.000	23	40	0	0	0
Saunders	.983	91	227	4	4	1
Womack	.972	52	102	1	3	0

WISCONSIN TIMBER RATTLERS

LOW CLASS A

MIDWEST LEAGUE

BATTING	B-T	HT	WT	DOB	AVG	vLH	vRH	G	AB	R	H	2B	3B	HR	RBI	BB	HBP	SH	SF	SO	SB	CS	SLG	OBP
Avila, Gerardo	L-L	6-2	185	7-15-86	.253	.143	.293	25	79	5	20	4	1	1	6	7	0	0	0	24	0	2	.367	.314
Beamon, Calvin	L-L	6-0	190	5-8-84	.247	.296	.233	63	243	37	60	8	1	3	21	25	6	3	1	59	14	6	.325	.331
Beltran, Juan	R-R	6-0	165	6-26-86	.241	.200	.252	67	199	19	48	9	0	2	17	15	7	3	1	46	10	6	.317	.315

ORGANIZATION STATISTICS

Name	B-T	HT	WT	DOB	AVG	vLH	vRH	G	AB	R	H	2B	3B	HR	RBI	BB	HBP	SH	SF	SO	SB	CS	SLG	OBP
Bonilla, Leury	R-R	6-3	170	2-8-85	.258	.258	.259	96	325	38	84	22	2	4	31	12	1	10	5	97	11	9	.375	.283
Diaz, Juan	B-R	6-3	180	12-12-88	.228	.119	.260	75	259	22	59	12	0	1	18	19	3	6	0	53	2	10	.286	.288
Diaz, Ogui	R-R	6-2	170	12-1-85	.186	.184	.187	39	129	3	24	3	1	0	10	1	0	2	1	36	9	4	.225	.191
Dickey, Gavin	R-R	5-11	200	9-29-83	.230	.219	.235	77	243	32	56	12	2	7	31	14	6	5	3	67	12	8	.383	.286
Eastley, Reed	L-L	6-2	210	7-24-83	.265	.215	.284	67	234	36	62	16	1	4	21	40	4	1	1	47	3	1	.393	.380
Fernandez, Jair	R-R	6-1	210	12-10-86	.260	.275	.255	52	146	15	38	11	0	2	13	16	3	4	1	29	2	0	.377	.343
Garth, Ronald	R-R	5-11	165	11-5-84	.277	.273	.278	48	188	35	52	9	1	8	23	14	5	2	1	43	3	1	.463	.341
Halman, Gregory	R-R	6-4	192	8-26-87	.182	.163	.188	52	187	26	34	5	0	4	15	8	5	1	1	77	15	7	.273	.234
Hargrove, Andy	R-L	6-1	240	10-31-81	.220	.200	.228	30	82	10	18	4	0	4	16	9	0	0	0	30	0	1	.415	.297
Henson, Julian	R-R	5-10	190	4-10-87	.267	.200	.300	5	15	1	4	1	0	0	0	3	1	0	0	6	0	0	.333	.421
Lawhorn, Trevor	R-R	6-2	180	12-18-82	.252	.167	.271	29	103	15	26	4	0	3	20	13	1	0	1	24	1	1	.379	.339
Liddi, Alex	R-R	6-4	176	8-14-88	.240	.265	.230	113	400	41	96	28	3	8	52	36	5	6	4	123	5	4	.385	.308
Lo, Kuo Hui	R-R	6-2	188	9-26-85	.288	.257	.300	104	358	65	103	21	7	4	37	45	3	0	4	86	32	9	.419	.368
McOwen, James	L-R	6-0	200	9-26-85	.269	.290	.260	56	208	17	56	11	0	0	33	9	0	3	2	55	5	4	.322	.297
Meneses, Alex	R-R	5-10	185	12-21-83	.188	.105	.212	28	85	14	16	2	1	0	7	24	1	2	1	22	7	1	.235	.369
Nunez, Israel	R-R	6-1	200	9-1-85	.214	.167	.250	4	14	0	3	0	0	0	0	1	1	0	0	6	0	0	.214	.313
Nunez, Luis	R-R	6-0	170	12-31-85	.195	.421	.121	23	77	6	15	0	1	0	6	4	1	2	0	18	2	3	.221	.244
Ochoa, Blake	R-R	6-0	180	9-5-85	.346	.000	.450	7	26	3	9	3	0	0	4	0	0	0	0	4	0	0	.462	.346
Peguero, Carlos	L-L	6-5	210	2-22-87	.263	.292	.253	79	297	35	78	21	6	9	50	16	7	0	1	97	4	3	.465	.315
Reynolds, Kevin	L-L	6-1	185	7-1-82	.095	.000	.111	6	21	1	2	0	0	0	0	1	0	0	0	6	1	0	.095	.136
Sams, Kalian	R-R	6-3	220	8-25-86	.205	.143	.228	48	156	18	32	7	2	4	8	15	3	0	0	73	1	1	.353	.287
Santin, Daniel	L-L	6-3	205	11-7-84	.203	.292	.150	19	64	3	13	3	0	0	3	1	0	1	1	9	0	1	.250	.212
Triunfel, Carlos	R-R	5-11	175	2-27-90	.309	.243	.330	43	152	18	47	8	2	0	14	5	3	1		23	4	8	.388	.342
Welsh, Guy	R-R	6-2	205	5-15-85	.304	.500	.235	7	23	4	7	2	0	0	4	4	0	2	1	5	2	2	.391	.393
White, Joseph	L-R	6-3	210	1-14-86	.291	.283	.294	57	189	27	55	10	0	3	35	28	3	1	1	51	0	1	.392	.389

PITCHING	B-T	HT	WT	DOB	W	L	ERA	G	GS	CG	SV	IP	H	R	ER	HR	BB	SO	AVG	vLH	vRH	K/9	BB/9
Adcock, Nathan	R-R	6-5	190	2-25-88	2	8	3.70	17	16	0	0	88	85	60	36	7	38	66	.247	.289	.220	6.78	3.90
Baek, Cha Seung	R-R	6-4	220	5-29-80	0	0	4.91	1	1	0	0	4	5	2	2	1	0	6	.313	.200	.364	14.73	0.00
Barb, Andrew	R-R	6-3	190	10-6-84	3	1	2.33	32	0	0	10	39	25	12	10	4	14	55	.179	.210	.154	12.80	3.26
Bonilla, Leury	R-R	6-3	170	2-8-85	0	0	0.00	2	0	0	0	1	1	0	0	0	0	0	.000	—	.000	13.50	0.00
Butler, Tony	L-L	6-7	205	11-18-87	4	7	4.75	20	18	1	0	85	78	52	45	10	46	73	.247	.369	.215	7.70	4.85
Dilone, Natividad	R-R	6-0	160	9-8-82	1	2	3.00	11	0	0	1	18	19	8	6	0	14	18	.275	.346	.233	9.00	7.00
DuRocher, John	R-R	6-4	215	6-21-84	0	1	63.00	1	1	0	0	1	7	7	7	1	3	1	.778	.833	.667	9.00	27.00
Fernandez, Eddy	L-L	6-2	175	11-22-86	0	2	7.98	8	2	0	0	15	22	14	13	4	2	13	.361	.385	.354	7.98	1.23
Fiorenza, Andrew	R-R	6-2	210	6-24-84	0	2	4.50	17	0	0	2	26	24	19	13	3	11	20	.238	.211	.254	6.92	3.81
Gallagher, Nolan	R-R	6-3	190	12-20-85	0	2	4.58	4	4	0	0	20	23	13	10	3	14	15	.303	.406	.227	6.86	6.41
Gibson, Rollie	L-L	6-2	220	12-30-83	2	5	6.99	45	0	0	0	57	72	51	44	7	29	59	.301	.310	.297	9.37	4.61
Harmon, Robert	R-R	6-7	239	9-28-83	1	4	5.88	17	3	0	0	34	29	33	22	2	30	24	.236	.383	.145	6.42	8.02
Johannesen-Ellis, T.	R-R	6-4	230	2-23-88	1	0	3.63	9	1	0	0	17	21	7	7	4	4	8	.304	.200	.385	4.15	2.08
Kantakevich, Joseph	R-R	6-2	195	5-9-84	3	4	2.55	48	0	0	6	78	60	28	22	3	18	69	.211	.322	.136	8.00	2.09
Kappel, Brian	R-R	6-0	215	1-7-83	1	0	3.33	20	0	0	1	24	20	9	9	3	7	20	.225	.227	.224	7.40	2.59
Kelley, Shawn	R-R	6-2	215	4-26-84	1	1	2.25	9	0	0	0	12	16	4	3	1	4	14	.308	.563	.194	10.50	3.00
Orta, Ricky	R-R	6-2	195	11-6-84	4	6	4.74	22	19	1	0	93	84	55	49	12	43	102	.242	.230	.249	9.87	4.16
Parker, Kyle	R-R	6-3	205	4-8-85	5	10	3.66	22	19	1	0	112	108	53	43	4	42	99	.255	.269	.246	7.96	3.38
Renaud, Keith	R-R	6-1	215	2-7-86	2	0	3.50	18	2	0	1	36	27	16	14	2	18	30	.213	.220	.209	7.50	4.50
Renfree, Matthew	R-R	6-8	220	1-16-85	0	1	9.00	1	1	0	0	4	4	4	4	0	1	3	.450	.438	.500	6.75	2.25
Richard, Steven	R-R	6-3	240	3-7-85	7	4	3.21	24	16	0	1	95	86	45	34	8	41	82	.238	.267	.221	7.74	3.87
Souza, Justin	R-R	6-1	185	10-22-85	5	7	4.73	49	3	0	2	91	119	65	48	12	8	58	.304	.302	.305	5.72	0.79
Tillman, Chris	R-R	6-5	195	4-15-88	1	4	3.55	8	8	0	0	33	31	21	13	1	13	34	.238	.217	.262	9.27	3.55
Uhlmansiek, Steven	L-L	6-3	185	2-10-83	1	3	4.34	12	0	0	0	26	25	17	14	1	11	22	.260	.136	.297	7.71	3.86
Varvaro, Anthony	R-R	6-0	180	10-31-84	4	11	4.69	22	21	0	1	104	94	67	54	7	51	112	.233	.193	.265	9.72	4.43
Wagner, Michael	L-L	6-4	225	3-28-85	4	2	3.12	33	0	0	2	43	35	17	15	2	11	39	.217	.196	.227	8.10	2.28
White, Sean	R-R	6-4	215	4-25-81	1	0	0.00	1	1	0	0	5	2	0	0		1	4	.143	.400	.000	7.20	1.80
White, Joseph	L-R	6-3	210	1-14-86	0	0	0.00	2	0	0	0	2	3	1	0	0	0	0	.375	.500	.250	0.00	0.00
Williams, Harold	L-L	6-4	190	9-23-84	0	0	1.93	11	1	0	0	19	12	4	4	0	21	16	.200	.176	.209	7.71	10.12
Williamson, Fabian	R-L	6-2	175	10-20-88	0	0	0.00	1	1	0	0	6	3	0	0	0	2	4	.143	.222	.083	6.00	3.00

FIELDING

Catcher	PCT	G	PO	A	E	DP	PB
Beltran	.982	64	430	75	9	10	23
Bonilla	1.000	3	6	0	0	0	1
Eastley	1.000	4	3	0	0	0	0
Fernandez	.982	52	389	36	8	5	8
Henson	.976	5	35	5	1	0	1
Nunez	1.000	4	37	3	0	0	1
Ochoa	1.000	6	51	3	0	1	1
Santin	.984	18	120	4	2	1	1

First Base	PCT	G	PO	A	E	DP
Avila	.988	23	156	14	2	14
Bonilla	.985	21	126	7	2	9
Eastley	.993	50	427	31	3	33
Hargrove	.971	29	191	11	6	15
Liddi	.984	7	55	8	1	6
White	.981	26	200	12	4	24

Second Base	PCT	G	PO	A	E	DP
Bonilla	.950	10	19	19	2	5
O. Diaz	.933	16	29	41	5	6
Garth	.960	48	75	116	8	24
Lawhorn	.976	24	42	78	3	21
Meneses	.965	23	25	58	3	11
Nunez	.914	21	39	46	8	5

Third Base	PCT	G	PO	A	E	DP
Bonilla	.927	24	18	33	4	3
O. Diaz	.750	4	2	4	2	0
Eastley	1.000	3	6	2	0	0
Lawhorn	.857	2	2	4	1	0
Liddi	.899	106	55	186	27	11
Welsh	.944	6	4	13	1	1

Shortstop	PCT	G	PO	A	E	DP
Bonilla	.975	8	15	24	1	8

	PCT	G	PO	A	E	DP
J. Diaz	.939	75	125	226	23	47
O. Diaz	.889	16	25	39	8	7
Meneses	.667	2	1	3	2	1
Triunfel	.917	43	67	109	16	25

Outfield	PCT	G	PO	A	E	DP
Avila	1.000	5	1	0	0	0
Beamon	.967	58	110	6	4	2
Bonilla	.925	30	33	4	3	0
Dickey	.986	70	138	4	2	1
Halman	.979	51	89	3	2	0
Lo	.954	100	154	12	8	4
McOwen	.966	55	79	6	3	1
Meneses	1.000	1	1	0	0	0
Peguero	.957	11	21	1	1	0
Reynolds	1.000	5	10	0	0	0
Sams	.949	44	71	4	4	1

EVERETT AQUASOX

SHORT-SEASON

NORTHWEST LEAGUE

BATTING	B-T	HT	WT	DOB	AVG	vLH	vRH	G	AB	R	H	2B	3B	HR	RBI	BB	HBP	SH	SF	SO	SB	CS	SLG	OBP
Almonte, Denny	B-R	6-2	187	9-24-88	.100	.143	.077	5	20	0	2	0	0	0	0	1	1	0	0	11	1	0	.100	.143
Benitez, Deybis	R-R	6-2	170	4-23-87	.184	.182	.184	47	136	11	25	3	0	1	13	16	1	4	1	44	2	0	.228	.300
Brock, Jermaine	L-L	6-2	175	1-29-87	.230	.282	.214	51	165	13	38	7	1	0	12	16	0	4	0	69	11	7	.285	.298

	B-T	HT	WT	DOB	AVG	vLH	vRH	G	AB	R	H	2B	3B	HR	RBI	BB	HBP	SH	SF	SO	SB	CS	SLG	OBP
Carroll, Daniel	R-R	6-1	175	1-6-89	.176	.250	.154	4	17	0	3	0	0	0	0	0	0	0	0	6	2	1	.176	.176
Colina, Edilio	R-R	6-2	175	10-10-88	.277	.200	.297	51	188	27	52	6	2	2	15	7	9	5	2	32	4	2	.362	.330
Davenport, James	R-R	6-4	190	6-1-85	.236	.269	.225	30	106	14	25	8	1	0	11	6	6	4	1	33	5	0	.330	.311
Diaz, Ogui	R-R	6-2	170	12-1-85	.225	.191	.239	63	244	24	55	12	1	3	14	7	2	2	1	64	13	9	.320	.252
Dotel, Welington	R-R	6-1	180	10-2-85	.250	.172	.270	40	140	14	35	9	2	2	17	7	1	1	1	60	3	4	.386	.289
Dunbar, Jeffrey	R-R	6-4	220	6-8-85	.247	.162	.274	51	154	16	38	9	1	4	21	19	5	2	5	47	2	2	.396	.339
Dunigan, Joseph	L-L	6-1	215	3-29-86	.231	.300	.211	62	225	28	52	6	1	4	23	18	3	2	0	75	12	5	.320	.297
Gillies, Tyson	L-R	6-1	185	10-31-88	.625	.500	.750	4	8	3	5	0	0	0	2	0	0	0	0	1	2	0	.625	.625
Halman, Gregory	R-R	6-4	192	8-26-87	.307	.352	.293	62	238	37	73	19	1	16	37	21	4	1	1	85	16	8	.597	.371
Henson, Julian	R-R	5-10	190	4-10-87	.143	.333	.000	5	7	0	1	1	0	0	1	0	0	0	0	2	0	0	.286	.250
Hernandez, Jairo	R-R	6-3	185	5-8-85	.160	.125	.176	10	25	1	4	1	0	0	0	1	0	0	0	7	1	1	.200	.192
Hurba, Craig	R-R	6-2	225	8-25-81	.280	.077	.351	16	50	8	14	5	0	3	10	8	0	0	1	17	0	0	.560	.373
Liverpool, Marquise	R-R	5-11	191	4-16-86	.222	.000	.250	7	9	5	2	0	0	1	1	0	0	0	0	3	2	0	.222	.300
Mangini, Matt	L-R	6-4	220	12-21-85	.291	.115	.377	22	79	12	23	4	0	2	9	13	1	0	0	18	3	0	.418	.398
Mena, Roberto	R-R	6-0	185	1-17-85	.205	.200	.207	43	122	11	25	3	1	0	3	4	2	1	0	21	6	1	.246	.242
Ochoa, Blake	R-R	6-0	180	9-5-85	.250	.200	.265	17	44	2	11	2	0	2	8	4	3	0	0	15	0	0	.432	.353
Pimentel, Manelik	R-R	6-2	185	10-19-84	.268	.267	.269	57	194	22	52	12	0	4	24	22	4	0	1	55	0	0	.392	.353
Sams, Kalian	R-R	6-3	220	8-25-86	.225	.188	.238	56	191	32	43	13	1	7	22	32	1	1	2	72	9	4	.414	.318
Sanchez, Kris	L-L	6-3	220	1-9-84	.227	.381	.202	48	150	22	34	8	0	1	16	18	3	0	1	51	0	1	.300	.320
Santin, Daniel	L-L	6-3	205	11-7-84	.217	.000	.250	8	23	2	5	1	0	0	2	3	0	0	0	3	0	0	.261	.308

PITCHING	B-T	HT	WT	DOB	W	L	ERA	G	GS	CG	SV	IP	H	R	ER	HR	BB	SO	AVG	vLH	vRH	K/9	BB/9
Brown, Aaron	R-R	6-6	200	5-25-86	2	1	1.95	20	0	0	6	37	25	8	8	3	15	49	.187	.194	.177	11.92	3.65
Brown, Will	L-L	6-3	215	10-9-87	1	0	5.01	17	0	0	0	23	23	14	13	4	16	19	.264	.387	.196	7.33	6.17
Deaver, Craig	L-L	6-5	190	1-17-85	0	0	6.10	11	0	0	0	10	12	8	7	0	8	10	.286	.154	.345	8.71	6.97
Gallagher, Nolan	R-R	6-3	190	12-20-85	1	1	0.84	6	6	0	0	32	19	5	3	2	6	24	.167	.194	.135	6.75	1.69
Harmon, Robert	R-R	6-7	239	9-28-83	4	6	5.37	14	14	0	0	69	79	51	41	6	41	57	.290	.276	.304	7.47	5.37
Harris, Bryan	R-R	6-2	200	9-15-83	1	1	1.16	18	0	0	8	23	20	8	3	1	3	22	.233	.286	.182	8.49	1.16
Hill, Nicholas	L-L	6-0	190	1-30-85	1	3	0.51	18	0	0	2	35	24	6	2	0	9	45	.197	.219	.189	11.57	2.31
Kelley, Shawn	R-R	6-2	215	4-26-84	1	0	3.00	3	0	0	0	3	2	1	1	1	0	4	.200	.250	.167	12.00	0.00
Lowe, Mark	R-R	6-3	190	6-7-83	0	0	0.00	1	1	0	0	1	0	0	0	0	0	0	.000	.000	.000	0.00	0.00
McKerney, Brandon	R-R	6-4	195	8-3-86	1	3	6.29	21	0	0	2	34	39	28	24	2	12	20	.291	.297	.286	5.24	3.15
Meyer, Keith	L-R	6-4	180	2-10-86	1	0	2.62	18	1	0	1	34	19	10	10	4	23	34	.165	.080	.231	8.91	6.03
Moorer, Ryan	R-R	6-3	205	3-2-86	2	2	4.96	20	0	0	0	33	35	19	18	2	13	32	.278	.228	.319	8.82	3.58
Paredes, Edward	L-L	6-0	175	9-30-86	7	6	3.99	16	15	0	0	86	75	47	38	2	48	61	.235	.254	.231	6.41	5.04
Pettis, Marquis	R-R	6-2	180	9-9-82	2	0	2.36	16	0	0	0	27	23	7	7	0	11	29	.225	.174	.268	9.79	3.71
Ramirez, Juan	R-R	6-3	175	8-16-88	3	7	4.30	15	15	0	0	75	61	49	36	3	43	73	.211	.234	.185	8.72	5.14
Renaud, Keith	R-R	6-1	215	2-7-86	0	0	16.20	1	0	0	0	2	3	3	3	0	2	3	.286	.000	.333	16.20	10.80
Roy, Philip	R-R	6-4	175	7-29-87	3	0	6.21	16	0	0	0	29	35	22	20	3	14	30	.297	.351	.246	9.31	4.34
Salinas, Doug	R-R	6-4	195	12-5-88	2	8	5.91	15	15	0	0	70	89	53	46	6	31	70	.306	.301	.312	9.00	3.99
Solomon, Aaron	R-R	6-2	205	8-6-85	0	0	10.13	6	0	0	0	5	4	6	6	0	15	6	.235	.222	.250	10.12	25.31
Venegas, Alfredo	R-R	6-1	180	5-11-86	3	3	5.36	10	9	0	0	45	56	30	27	3	18	42	.303	.283	.326	8.34	3.57

FIELDING

Catcher	PCT	G	PO	A	E	DP	PB
Dunbar	.988	49	382	36	5	1	7
Henson	.960	4	19	5	1	0	1
Hurba	1.000	12	67	1	0	0	3
Ochoa	.984	15	122	5	2	0	2
Santin	1.000	6	42	1	0	0	0

First Base	PCT	G	PO	A	E	DP
Pimentel	.995	38	344	19	2	22
Sanchez	.995	44	347	27	2	38
Santin	1.000	1	6	0	0	0

Second Base	PCT	G	PO	A	E	DP
Benitez	.953	16	19	42	3	7
Colina	.956	45	67	130	9	23

Mena	.988	24	30	52	1	13	

Third Base	PCT	G	PO	A	E	DP
Benitez	.860	23	14	29	7	0
Davenport	.892	30	22	44	8	4
Diaz	1.000	1	0	1	0	0
Mangini	.895	21	16	35	6	3
Mena	1.000	1	1	0	0	0
Pimentel	1.000	3	2	1	0	0

Shortstop	PCT	G	PO	A	E	DP
Benitez	1.000	4	4	13	0	2
Colina	.920	4	8	15	2	5
Diaz	.936	61	87	176	18	34
Mena	.945	14	18	34	3	6

Outfield	PCT	G	PO	A	E	DP
Almonte	1.000	5	5	0	0	0
Benitez	1.000	2	2	1	0	1
Brock	.936	42	70	3	5	0
Carroll	.714	4	5	0	2	0
Dotel	.967	34	55	4	2	1
Dunigan	.961	53	69	4	3	0
Gillies	1.000	2	4	0	0	0
Halman	.990	59	94	3	1	0
Hernandez	1.000	6	5	1	0	0
Liverpool	1.000	3	1	0	0	0
Mena	1.000	2	1	0	0	0
Sams	.979	27	44	3	1	0

AZL MARINERS   ROOKIE

ARIZONA LEAGUE

BATTING	B-T	HT	WT	DOB	AVG	vLH	vRH	G	AB	R	H	2B	3B	HR	RBI	BB	HBP	SH	SF	SO	SB	CS	SLG	OBP
Almonte, Denny	B-R	6-2	187	9-24-88	.161	.333	.114	18	56	11	9	2	1	0	5	6	1	0	0	26	3	0	.232	.254
Arias, Jonathan	R-R	6-3	190	2-8-88	.196	.333	.180	22	56	7	11	3	0	0	5	13	1	4	1	19	0	0	.250	.352
Britton, Dwight	B-R	6-0	170	7-17-87	.263	.333	.242	30	80	16	21	2	0	0	8	5	1	1	1	25	9	0	.288	.318
Carroll, Daniel	R-R	6-1	175	1-6-89	.323	.314	.325	53	201	39	65	9	6	0	24	27	5	4	1	56	27	11	.428	.415
Davenport, James	R-R	6-4	190	6-1-85	.267	.333	.259	11	30	2	8	1	1	0	3	2	2	1	0	7	1	1	.367	.353
Dotel, Welington	R-R	6-1	180	10-2-85	.375	—	.375	7	16	4	6	2	0	1	3	4	0	0	0	5	0	0	.688	.500
Fromm, Brandon	L-L	6-2	220	3-4-85	.241	.226	.244	45	158	20	38	13	2	3	26	13	2	2	5	44	1	0	.405	.298
Fuentes, Juan	R-R	6-1	170	1-28-86	.313	.480	.264	31	112	20	35	9	0	0	18	12	0	3	3	12	1	1	.393	.370
Garth, Ronald	R-R	5-11	165	11-5-84	.100	.200	.000	5	10	3	1	1	0	0	1	2	1	0	0	0	0	0	.200	.308
Gillies, Tyson	L-R	6-1	185	10-31-88	.221	.357	.194	35	86	20	19	3	2	0	6	6	9	0	0	23	9	6	.302	.337
Henson, Julian	R-R	5-10	190	4-10-87	.000	.000	.000	4	5	0	0	0	0	0	0	0	0	0	0	2	0	0	.000	.286
Hurba, Craig	R-R	6-2	225	8-25-81	.125	.000	.143	4	8	1	1	0	0	0	1	0	0	0	0	3	0	0	.125	.125
Mangini, Matt	L-R	6-4	220	12-21-85	.000	.000	.000	2	6	0	0	0	0	0	0	0	0	0	0	1	0	0	.000	.250
Martinez, Mario	R-R	6-2	175	11-13-89	.281	.281	.280	52	196	36	55	9	1	1	26	6	3	3	1	31	3	2	.352	.311
Mateo, Alfredo	R-L	6-3	200	9-12-87	.290	.435	.261	40	138	16	40	8	1	1	24	14	1	0	2	42	0	1	.384	.359
McConnell, Brandon	R-R	6-4	205	2-8-85	.282	.154	.300	32	103	14	29	7	1	3	14	9	3	0	0	19	2	4	.456	.357
McOwen, James	L-R	6-0	200	9-26-85	.333	.000	.500	1	3	1	1	0	0	0	1	0	0	0	0	0	0	0	.667	.333
Mendez, Maximo	L-L	6-2	150	11-24-86	.252	.333	.237	47	159	33	40	5	7	3	27	28	3	5	1	69	13	5	.428	.372
Meneses, Alex	R-R	5-10	185	12-21-83	.300	1.000	.222	3	10	5	3	0	1	0	4	1	0	0	0	4	0	0	.300	.533
Morse, Mike	R-R	6-4	225	3-22-82	.200	.000	.231	5	15	2	3	1	0	0	3	0	0	0	0	3	0	0	.267	.333
Nelson, Jon	R-R	6-5	235	1-16-80	.250	.000	.333	4	12	0	3	0	0	0	3	1	0	0	0	3	0	0	.333	.375

BATTING	B-T	HT	WT	DOB	AVG	vLH	vRH	G	AB	R	H	2B	3B	HR	RBI	BB	HBP	SH	SF	SO	SB	CS	SLG	OBP
Nunez, Israel	R-R	6-1	200	9-1-85	.279	.429	.259	25	61	8	17	0	0	0	7	6	2	1	1	14	1	2	.279	.357
Nunez, Luis	R-R	6-0	170	12-31-86	.261	.200	.277	45	165	17	43	11	1	0	26	8	3	5	4	32	5	6	.339	.300
Phillips, Anthony	R-R	5-9	160	4-11-90	.279	.333	.267	45	122	24	34	1	0	0	9	19	0	2	1	43	5	7	.287	.373
Triunfel, Carlos	R-R	5-11	175	2-27-90	.273	.500	.222	3	11	1	3	0	0	0	3	0	0	0	2	1	0	0	.273	.231
Welsh, Guy	R-R	6-2	220	5-15-85	.228	.091	.250	28	79	11	18	2	0	0	7	11	0	1	1	17	1	1	.253	.319
Wilson, Michael	B-R	6-2	215	6-29-83	.600	.500	.667	2	10	4	6	3	0	1	5	2	0	0	0	1	1	0	1.200	.667

PITCHING	B-T	HT	WT	DOB	W	L	ERA	G	GS	CG	SV	IP	H	R	ER	HR	BB	SO	AVG	vLH	vRH	K/9	BB/9
Baek, Cha Seung	R-R	6-4	220	5-29-80	0	0	0.00	1	0	0	0	3	1	0	0	0	0	6	.091	.000	.167	18.00	0.00
Barb, Andrew	R-R	6-3	190	10-6-84	0	0	12.00	2	0	0	0	3	6	4	4	0	0	5	.400	.750	.273	15.00	0.00
Bills, S. Taylor	R-R	6-5	245	1-2-85	3	0	3.00	12	0	0	0	15	18	7	5	0	5	11	.327	.154	.381	6.60	3.00
Blanco, Ivan	R-R	6-1	190	9-24-83	0	0	0.00	2	2	0	0	3	2	0	0	0	0	3	.182	.200	.167	9.00	0.00
Cortez, Renee	R-R	6-4	180	12-9-82	0	0	0.00	1	1	0	0	1	1	1	0	0	0	2	.250	.000	.333	18.00	0.00
Dominguez, Robbie	R-R	6-3	190	10-26-85	3	1	2.01	14	8	0	0	45	26	17	10	1	15	37	.168	.176	.163	7.46	3.02
Downs, Brodie	R-R	6-4	240	7-19-79	1	0	4.50	1	0	0	0	2	3	1	1	0	0	1	.333	.333	.333	4.50	0.00
DuRocher, John	R-R	6-4	215	6-21-84	3	2	5.03	18	7	0	0	48	54	30	27	3	27	37	.293	.354	.261	6.89	5.03
Fernandez, Eddy	L-L	6-2	175	11-22-86	3	1	2.01	13	0	0	0	22	25	11	5	1	5	13	.275	.280	.273	5.24	2.01
Javier, Carlos	R-R	6-3	170	5-28-87	1	0	5.68	5	0	0	0	6	7	6	4	1	3	3	.292	.222	.333	4.26	4.26
Jimenez, Cesar	L-L	5-11	180	11-12-84	0	0	0.00	3	2	0	0	6	4	0	0	0	0	6	.190	.000	.308	9.00	0.00
Johannesen-Ellis, T.	R-R	6-4	230	2-23-88	0	1	3.91	12	2	0	0	25	28	21	11	1	11	19	.272	.154	.344	6.75	3.91
Marquez, Miguel	R-R	6-3	180	10-28-87	3	0	2.10	8	6	0	0	30	26	8	7	2	14	23	.241	.229	.247	6.90	4.20
Martinez, Javier	L-R	6-3	225	5-26-85	0	0	5.40	3	0	0	0	5	4	3	3	1	2	5	.211	.167	.231	9.00	3.60
Mortimore, Travis	L-L	6-5	225	8-1-84	3	1	1.91	27	0	0	10	38	29	14	8	0	16	43	.210	.179	.222	10.27	3.82
Moviel, Gregory	L-L	6-6	220	12-19-84	0	3	24.00	1	1	0	0	6	11	17	16	0	14	7	.393	.556	.316	10.50	21.00
Ortiz, Richard	L-L	6-2	185	11-26-87	1	3	3.95	16	5	0	0	41	39	24	18	3	15	38	.253	.225	.263	8.34	3.29
Ramirez, Horacio	L-L	6-1	210	11-24-79	1	0	0.00	1	1	0	0	7	9	1	0	0	0	4	.310	.000	.391	5.14	0.00
Renfree, Matthew	R-R	6-8	220	1-16-85	3	1	2.57	19	2	0	1	35	38	16	10	1	6	31	.286	.264	.300	7.97	1.54
Romeijn, Ramon	R-R	6-0	180	8-12-90	0	0	7.04	6	0	0	0	8	9	7	6	0	5	9	.290	.400	.238	10.57	5.87
Roy, Philip	R-R	6-4	175	7-29-87	2	0	1.29	2	0	0	0	7	4	1	1	0	3	3	.167	.429	.059	3.86	3.86
Santiago, Julio	L-L	6-0	155	12-8-85	0	0	2.57	3	0	0	1	7	9	3	2	0	0	10	.290	.200	.333	12.86	0.00
Snyder, Jason	R-R	6-6	205	4-6-83	0	1	14.54	5	0	0	0	4	8	8	7	0	3	4	.444	.444	.444	8.31	6.23
Venegas, Alfredo	R-R	6-1	180	5-11-86	1	0	0.87	2	1	0	0	10	7	3	1	0	3	12	.194	.125	.250	10.45	2.61
White, Sean	R-R	6-4	215	4-25-81	0	2	7.84	3	3	0	0	10	19	10	9	0	4	11	.413	.467	.387	9.58	3.48
Wild, Jacob	R-R	6-5	195	8-18-84	3	1	1.88	17	4	0	0	48	33	11	10	2	14	62	.199	.185	.208	11.62	2.62
Williams, Harold	L-L	6-4	190	9-23-84	0	0	0.00	0	0	0	0	2	0	0	0	0	0	2	.000	.000	.000	0.00	9.00
Williamson, Fabian	R-L	6-2	175	10-20-88	6	2	3.43	14	12	0	0	66	68	32	25	3	25	73	.278	.243	.292	10.01	3.43

FIELDING

Catcher	PCT	G	PO	A	E	DP	PB
Arias	.981	18	140	18	3	2	6
Fuentes	1.000	19	147	16	0	1	4
Henson	1.000	4	19	1	0	0	0
Hurba	1.000	4	11	1	0	0	1
I. Nunez	.973	24	143	37	5	5	2
L. Nunez	1.000	2	17	1	0	0	3
Phillips	1.000	1	1	0	0	0	0

First Base	PCT	G	PO	A	E	DP
Davenport	—	1	0	0	0	0
Fromm	.992	43	346	20	3	27
Martinez	1.000	1	11	2	0	2
Mateo	.989	14	84	4	1	12
McConnell	1.000	4	24	1	0	4
Nelson	1.000	1	1	0	0	0
Welsh	1.000	3	22	0	0	2

Second Base	PCT	G	PO	A	E	DP
Arias	1.000	1	1	4	0	1
Garth	1.000	2	3	4	0	1
I. Nunez	1.000	1	2	2	0	0
L. Nunez	.958	42	78	106	8	26
Phillips	.969	14	19	43	2	11

Third Base	PCT	G	PO	A	E	DP
Davenport	1.000	7	4	10	0	1
Garth	1.000	2	0	3	0	0
Mangini	.400	2	2	0	3	0
Martinez	.925	19	18	19	3	4
Mateo	.891	26	14	43	7	1
Meneses	1.000	2	0	1	0	0
Morse	1.000	1	2	2	0	0
Welsh	.793	13	9	14	6	3

Shortstop	PCT	G	PO	A	E	DP
Fromm	1.000	1	5	3	0	2

(Shortstop cont.)	PCT	G	PO	A	E	DP
Martinez	.938	32	54	82	9	19
Meneses	.667	1	1	1	1	0
Morse	1.000	1	3	3	0	1
Phillips	.955	29	36	71	5	14
Triunfel	.778	2	1	6	2	2

Outfield	PCT	G	PO	A	E	DP
Almonte	.952	17	19	1	1	0
Britton	.970	29	30	2	1	0
Carroll	.946	52	82	6	5	1
Dotel	1.000	7	11	0	0	0
Gillies	.955	31	41	1	2	1
McConnell	1.000	13	7	0	0	0
McOwen	—	1	0	0	0	0
Mendez	.958	46	85	6	4	2
Nelson	1.000	2	2	0	0	0
Wilson	1.000	1	2	0	0	0

DSL MARINERS

ROOKIE

DOMINICAN SUMMER LEAGUE

BATTING	B-T	HT	WT	DOB	AVG	vLH	vRH	G	AB	R	H	2B	3B	HR	RBI	BB	HBP	SH	SF	SO	SB	CS	SLG	OBP
Carvajal, Ameilis	R-R	6-2	170	3-6-89	.213	.200	.216	48	141	21	30	5	0	3	15	35	3	3	0	53	10	3	.312	.380
Familia, Emmanuel	R-R	6-2	190	2-5-87	.229	.208	.233	49	153	21	35	4	0	5	24	17	5	0	2	39	4	5	.340	.322
Flores, Mario	R-R	6-3	195	10-9-87	.228	.208	.234	39	101	12	23	7	1	4	15	15	1	0	1	30	0	1	.436	.331
Lebron, Rey	R-R	6-3	185	11-26-89	.133	.095	.143	41	98	15	13	1	0	2	14	22	5	0	1	37	3	5	.204	.317
Lora, McyQuin	R-R	6-5	180	9-22-87	.170	.000	.192	33	88	12	15	4	0	0	7	12	1	1	0	32	3	1	.216	.277
Marte, Augusto	R-R	6-2	190	8-17-89	.236	.182	.246	30	72	16	17	5	2	0	11	11	3	0	1	36	2	2	.361	.356
Martinez, Fray	R-R	6-3	170	5-20-89	.083	.000	.093	26	48	8	4	1	0	0	1	4	1	0	0	29	0	1	.104	.170
Mendez, Joel	R-R	6-3	175	5-7-88	.303	.176	.338	51	185	32	56	9	1	1	19	14	3	5	0	39	17	4	.378	.361
Mercedes, Hector	R-R	6-1	200	11-10-87	.282	.304	.278	49	156	23	44	5	0	5	25	14	8	0	0	24	0	0	.410	.371
Morla, Ramon	R-R	6-1	175	11-20-89	.233	.323	.200	34	116	23	27	7	0	2	13	18	7	1	2	35	4	7	.345	.364
Ozuna, Victor	R-R	6-2	180	12-2-86	.210	.250	.207	30	62	14	13	0	0	0	7	8	5	1	1	25	6	4	.210	.342
Peguero, Luis	R-R	6-2	160	11-17-86	.259	.125	.292	34	81	13	21	2	1	0	6	13	4	1	3	19	8	1	.309	.376
Rijo, Cristian	L-R	6-6	180	11-25-88	.203	.207	.202	53	143	13	29	4	2	2	21	9	0	0	0	24	0	2	.301	.250
Rodriguez, Robert	R-R	6-4	180	7-22-90	.265	.108	.314	50	155	17	41	5	1	2	14	10	4	2	1	29	3	4	.348	.324
Soto, George	R-R	6-2	190	11-19-89	.259	.200	.275	57	216	25	56	18	3	1	30	19	2	1	2	33	7	3	.384	.322
van Heydoorn, Rudy	R-R	6-3	180	4-17-89	.194	.077	.222	45	134	15	26	6	2	2	15	16	2	2	1	43	7	5	.313	.288
Zapata, Angel	R-R	6-2	185	11-25-87	.304	.364	.281	24	79	17	24	1	0	0	8	14	3	2	0	19	8	6	.316	.427

PITCHING	B-T	HT	WT	DOB	W	L	ERA	G	GS	CG	SV	IP	H	R	ER	HR	BB	SO	AVG	vLH	vRH	K/9	BB/9
Alcantara, Ariel	R-R	6-3	190	5-13-89	4	3	2.10	14	11	0	0	51	33	18	12	1	15	44	.181	.211	.178	7.71	2.63
Bautista, Felix	R-R	6-3	180	10-10-87	0	1	3.51	17	0	0	2	33	42	19	13	1	11	30	.307	.350	.299	8.10	2.97
Bremon, Tony	R-R	6-1	165	12-5-87	2	4	4.53	18	0	0	2	46	47	31	23	1	14	39	.263	.115	.288	7.69	2.76
Celestino, Miguel	R-R	6-5	170	10-10-89	4	2	3.38	14	1	0	0	29	25	12	11	1	17	14	.234	.235	.233	4.30	5.22

Name	B-T	HT	WT	DOB	W	L	ERA	G	GS	CG	SV	IP	H	R	ER	HR	BB	SO	AVG	vLH	vRH	K/9	BB/9
Duarte, Victor	R-R	6-2	155	10-21-86	1	1	0.90	12	0	0	3	20	13	5	2	0	5	24	.191	.111	.203	10.80	2.25
Echavarria, Angel	R-R	6-3	190	4-22-86	1	3	4.28	14	4	0	0	27	30	17	13	2	11	14	.278	.211	.292	4.61	3.62
Fernandez, Anthony	L-L	6-4	180	6-8-90	1	2	3.80	18	0	0	2	24	13	14	10	3	24	22	.163	.200	.160	8.37	9.13
Franco, Juan	L-L	6-3	170	8-8-86	2	1	1.63	17	1	0	2	39	31	9	7	1	13	36	.215	.063	.234	8.38	3.03
Garcia, Francisco	L-L	6-1	180	8-14-89	2	0	2.08	10	0	0	0	13	6	4	3	0	12	18	.136	.250	.111	12.46	8.31
Germocen, Nelson	R-R	6-5	200	9-16-88	0	2	2.49	17	0	0	2	25	17	9	7	0	19	37	.189	.111	.208	13.14	6.75
Mercedes, Bruno	R-R	6-3	170	10-6-88	1	0	2.27	10	3	0	3	32	26	9	8	1	10	20	.230	.154	.240	5.68	2.84
Perdomo, Jose	R-R	6-4	200	4-12-90	1	1	4.43	12	5	0	0	20	19	14	10	0	14	17	.247	.455	.212	7.52	6.20
Perez, Henry	L-L	6-3	170	10-18-89	5	4	2.82	16	14	1	0	54	44	21	17	1	20	60	.220	.167	.225	9.94	3.31
Pineda, Michael	R-R	6-5	180	1-18-89	6	1	2.29	15	12	0	0	59	70	25	15	2	11	48	.286	.282	.286	7.32	1.68
Suriel, Walter	R-R	6-2	190	7-21-86	4	4	2.62	14	12	0	0	65	63	26	19	2	13	64	.255	.327	.237	8.82	1.79
Vizcaino, Joan	R-R	6-6	195	4-25-89	0	1	9.39	8	1	0	0	8	10	9	8	0	7	4	.294	.333	.290	4.70	8.22
Yan, Fello	R-R	6-2	180	9-8-90	0	0	27.00	1	0	0	0	0	0	2	1	0	2	1	.000	.000	.000	27.00	54.00

FIELDING

Catcher	PCT	G	PO	A	E	DP	PB
Familia	.993	42	257	39	2	2	10
Flores	.954	22	145	20	8	0	4
Mercedes	.979	12	81	11	4	0	1

First Base	PCT	G	PO	A	E	DP
Mercedes	.990	30	193	8	2	15
Peguero	1.000	2	12	0	0	0
Rijo	.994	51	337	19	2	29
van Heydoorn	—	1	0	0	0	0

Second Base	PCT	G	PO	A	E	DP
Carvajal	.974	36	64	85	4	14
Martinez	1.000	7	15	14	0	2
Morla	.949	20	46	28	4	9
Ozuna	.800	3	3	1	1	1

	PCT	G	PO	A	E	DP
Peguero	.938	6	8	7	1	3
Zapata	1.000	5	4	15	0	2

Third Base	PCT	G	PO	A	E	DP
Martinez	.926	8	7	18	2	0
Morla	.808	7	9	12	5	1
Ozuna	.857	3	2	4	1	0
Peguero	.921	13	11	24	3	1
van Heydoorn	.935	43	28	87	8	8
Zapata	.889	2	0	8	1	0

Shortstop	PCT	G	PO	A	E	DP
Martinez	.875	6	7	7	2	2
Morla	1.000	1	1	3	0	0
Ozuna	.906	7	12	17	3	2
Peguero	.944	5	4	13	1	2

	PCT	G	PO	A	E	DP
Soto	.902	50	89	140	25	27

Outfield	PCT	G	PO	A	E	DP
Familia	1.000	1	2	0	0	0
Lebron	.915	40	49	5	5	1
Lora	.960	30	24	0	1	0
Marte	.935	27	28	1	2	0
Mendez	.950	50	88	7	5	1
Morla	1.000	1	1	0	0	0
Ozuna	1.000	1	1	0	0	0
Peguero	1.000	5	2	0	0	0
Rijo	1.000	3	1	0	0	0
Rodriguez	.940	49	75	3	5	0
Zapata	.875	13	12	2	2	1

VSL MARINERS

ROOKIE

VENEZUELAN SUMMER LEAGUE

BATTING	B-T	HT	WT	DOB	AVG	vLH	vRH	G	AB	R	H	2B	3B	HR	RBI	BB	HBP	SH	SF	SO	SB	CS	SLG	OBP
Agudelo, Jorge	R-R	6-0	175	5-30-89	.231	.073	.286	51	160	31	37	5	2	0	17	23	14	3	1	34	3	6	.288	.374
Batista, Yidid	R-R	6-0	175	10-13-89	.284	.320	.268	54	162	33	46	5	1	0	19	15	9	5	0	23	5	4	.327	.376
Del Rio, Cesar	R-R	6-1	180	11-11-87	.287	.226	.317	37	94	12	27	3	2	4	16	13	5	0	1	23	0	1	.489	.398
Espinoza, Humberto	R-R	6-1	175	11-1-86	.310	.267	.322	56	145	31	45	10	1	1	32	24	5	5	1	5	1	0	.414	.423
Fuentes, Cesar	R-R	6-0	180	4-12-87	.314	.281	.326	69	242	54	76	12	1	2	47	28	11	4	3	38	9	8	.397	.405
Garcia, Alejandro	R-R	6-2	190	9-16-89	.141	.160	.130	33	71	3	10	2	0	0	3	4	1	0	0	27	0	1	.169	.197
Garcia, Eduardo	R-R	6-2	190	9-16-89	.191	.138	.215	40	94	8	18	4	1	0	9	16	0	0	1	42	0	2	.255	.306
Gonzalez, Larry	R-R	5-11	170	2-1-88	.265	.273	.263	39	102	12	27	4	1	0	10	7	5	0	0	15	1	1	.324	.342
Hernandez, Jose	R-R	6-1	165	1-12-88	.297	.286	.302	30	74	6	22	4	0	0	10	7	0	3	1	12	0	0	.351	.354
Loaisiga, Jonathan	R-R	6-0	185	6-12-89	.307	.241	.339	35	88	19	27	7	0	1	16	11	1	2	0	17	3	0	.420	.390
Ramirez, Carlos	B-R	5-11	145	12-2-88	.266	.211	.291	55	184	33	49	14	2	0	20	25	5	6	2	30	2	3	.364	.366
Rangel, Rigoberto	R-R	6-1	167	6-21-89	.280	.308	.269	68	232	43	65	14	6	4	46	33	8	1	2	54	4	2	.444	.385
Rivero, Jose	R-R	6-2	180	5-30-86	.300	.339	.287	70	240	42	72	12	2	11	61	25	21	0	2	74	4	3	.504	.410
Serrano, Terry	B-R	6-1	165	2-6-87	.239	.200	.253	66	222	40	53	8	1	1	25	41	3	11	6	40	10	8	.297	.357
Torrealba, Rafael	R-R	6-2	175	9-5-89	.182	.083	.204	36	66	10	12	3	0	1	10	10	1	4	1	8	1	0	.227	.295
Velasquez, Roberto	B-R	5-11	160	2-14-90	.244	.234	.248	59	172	22	42	3	2	1	10	17	6	9	0	27	5	5	.302	.333

PITCHING	B-T	HT	WT	DOB	W	L	ERA	G	GS	CG	SV	IP	H	R	ER	HR	BB	SO	AVG	vLH	vRH	K/9	BB/9
Acosta, Rhonny	R-R	6-3	188	12-4-88	6	3	0.67	12	0	0	1	40	21	8	3	1	15	39	.154	.093	.183	8.70	3.35
Campos, Manuel	R-R	6-2	175	1-12-90	1	0	5.75	11	0	0	0	20	29	17	13	1	6	17	.333	.421	.309	7.52	2.66
Chourio, Johalbi	R-R	6-2	158	11-24-88	1	2	5.76	13	5	0	0	30	39	21	19	1	19	20	.325	.351	.313	6.07	5.76
Cruz Ayala, Danny	R-R	6-0	180	4-20-89	5	5	3.13	13	10	0	0	46	34	22	16	0	32	43	.210	.182	.224	8.41	6.26
Guaipe, Maykol	R-R	6-3	175	8-11-90	1	0	1.67	15	1	0	0	27	29	7	5	1	9	13	.282	.200	.315	4.33	3.00
Guanire, Oberth	R-R	6-6	190	6-21-90	4	0	2.84	14	2	0	0	38	40	16	12	0	8	27	.272	.318	.252	6.39	1.89
Jimenez, Jose	L-L	6-0	180	3-23-87	1	1	1.57	20	0	0	15	29	16	7	5	1	12	23	.172	.429	.151	7.22	3.77
Medina, Yoervis	R-R	6-3	210	7-27-88	4	2	3.42	16	6	1	2	50	64	23	19	1	19	36	.320	.435	.286	6.48	3.42
Montbrum, Kervin	R-L	5-11	175	6-3-88	3	2	3.96	15	2	0	2	36	31	21	16	1	22	31	.244	.091	.259	7.68	5.45
Nava, Jessie	R-R	6-3	165	9-18-87	2	0	1.13	11	0	0	0	32	18	5	4	0	19	22	.168	.071	.203	6.19	5.34
Rios, Jose	L-L	5-10	178	3-2-90	7	1	3.09	14	10	0	0	64	66	30	22	0	24	45	.274	.318	.269	6.33	3.38
Rodriguez, Leonardo	R-R	6-2	185	4-15-88	5	0	1.82	15	0	0	0	69	50	20	14	1	24	34	.206	.190	.211	4.41	3.12
Sabala, Reynaldo	R-R	6-3	187	8-16-90	3	1	1.48	13	4	0	0	30	26	8	5	0	13	24	.232	.261	.225	7.12	3.86
Sanchez, Carlos	R-R	6-2	185	7-14-87	0	1	2.42	16	0	0	0	1	22	20	13	6	1	20	14	.250	.292	.232	5.64	8.06
Seco, Edlando	L-L	6-2	178	7-23-88	1	3	2.31	15	0	0	2	47	26	19	12	0	29	37	.164	.111	.167	7.14	5.59
Tome, Jean	R-R	6-2	200	9-5-89	3	2	3.42	14	10	0	0	47	35	20	18	1	23	36	.201	.204	.200	6.85	4.37

FIELDING

Catcher	PCT	G	PO	A	E	DP	PB
Del Rio	.968	32	158	25	6	2	10
Espinoza	1.000	6	24	3	0	0	2
Gonzalez	.985	37	167	30	3	1	4
Hernandez	.985	23	106	23	2	1	7

First Base	PCT	G	PO	A	E	DP
Del Rio	.947	5	17	1	1	0
Espinoza	.994	43	342	19	2	40
A. Garcia	.978	20	122	9	3	13
Hernandez	1.000	4	31	0	0	2
Loaisiga	1.000	23	173	6	0	14

Second Base	PCT	G	PO	A	E	DP
Agudelo	.960	36	93	99	8	20

	PCT	G	PO	A	E	DP
Batista	1.000	2	3	2	0	0
Ramirez	.983	41	108	124	4	39
Velasquez	1.000	1	1	5	0	0

Third Base	PCT	G	PO	A	E	DP
Agudelo	.778	14	8	13	6	0
Fuentes	.917	62	37	128	15	14
Ramirez	.947	5	13	1	0	0
Serrano	—	2	0	0	0	0

Shortstop	PCT	G	PO	A	E	DP
Batista	.917	7	10	23	3	5
Fuentes	.952	10	17	23	2	2
Ramirez	.667	1	0	2	1	1
Serrano	.952	12	21	38	3	6

	PCT	G	PO	A	E	DP
Velasquez	.923	59	88	188	23	46

Outfield	PCT	G	PO	A	E	DP
A. Garcia	.800	6	4	0	1	0
E. Garcia	.967	30	27	2	1	0
Loaisiga	1.000	1	1	0	0	0
Rangel	.956	61	83	4	4	1
Rivero	.963	68	98	7	4	1
Serrano	.990	59	88	10	1	0
Torrealba	.958	27	23	0	1	0

Tampa Bay Devil Rays

BY MARC TOPKIN

The Devil Rays won only five more games in 2007 than they did they season before. But they felt they got a whole lot better.

The Rays considered the season a huge step forward in terms of performance by their young major leaguers, progress by their minor league prospects, talent level throughout the organization and integration of philosophies and processes.

"We should make a good charge at being a 50-50 team next year. And the year after that is the year I really expect us to move forward," manager Joe Maddon said

Though the Rays finished last in the AL East for the ninth time in 10 seasons, and lost 90-plus games for the 10th straight time, they truly believe they are in position to make a quantum leap because of the talent they have and the ability to keep the team intact.

"I think we need fewer players than ever before," executive vice president Andrew Friedman said. "Where we stand today is much better than where we've been in the past."

The Rays had some big stories during their 66-96 season despite having the lowest payroll in the majors. First baseman Carlos Pena swept the three comeback player of the year awards after making the roster due to a late spring training injury to Greg Norton. Pena hit a team-record 46 homers (fourth most in the majors) and 121 RBIs (sixth most) at the bargain price of $800,000, which should make ensuing negotiations with agent Scott Boras, and a potential arbitration hearing, almost as interesting as his season.

Right fielder Delmon Young made a solid bid for the AL rookie of the year after playing in all 162 games and leading all rookies with 186 hits. Lefthander Scott Kazmir led the AL with 239 strikeouts and had a third-straight winning season on a team that was a cumulative 97 games under .500 during that span. B.J. Upton became the first 20-20 man in team history, and could have made a run at 30-30 had he not missed five weeks, while emerging as a silky smooth center fielder. Left fielder Carl Crawford finished tied for the AL stolen base title at 50 despite missing the final two weeks with a groin strain and righthander James Shields established himself as a legitimate frontline starter in his first full major league season.

The Rays were also quite a fan club. Tampa Bay hitters set an AL record by striking out 1,324 times (the fifth-highest total in major league history) while Devil Rays pitchers had 1,194 strikeouts (the sixth most in AL history), making Tampa the sixth team in the last 50 years to lead their league in both categories and the first to do so in the AL while having the highest ERA (5.53).

Tampa Bay scored a team-record 782 runs, but gave up too many late. Despite mixing and matching relievers throughout the season, the bullpen posted a 6.16 ERA and converted only 28-of-49 save opportunities.

How bad was the bullpen? The Devil Rays lost seven games they led in the ninth inning and 15 when leading in the seventh. Tampa Bay blew leads of 8-1 once and 7-1 twice and they were outscored 467-323 after the fifth inning. And they lost 13 times on the final at-bat.

On Nov. 8, the team announced it was officially shortening its first name to Rays by exorcising the Devil, changing its primary colors to blue and adopting new logos and trademarks.

Though the core of young players could stay intact for awhile, the Rays made some significant on-field changes.

ORGANIZATION STATISTICS

Bill Evers, the former Triple-A manager who was longest-tenured uniformed employee in the organization, was let go after two seasons as the major league bench coach, replaced by former Rays outfielder Dave Martinez.

They considered another change when pitching coach Jim Hickey was arrested on DUI and other charges after returning home from the Sept. 30 finale, but team officials decided to keep him after a month of investigation and deliberation.

Double-A Montgomery repeated as Southern League champions and low Class A Columbus won the South Atlantic League title. Outfielder Ryan Royster and righthander Wade Davis were the organization's minor league players of the year. Third baseman Evan Longoria will go to spring training with a chance to join the big league Opening Day lineup.

General Manager: Andrew Friedman. **Farm Director:** Mitch Lukevics. **Scouting Director:** R.J. Harrison

Class	Team	League	W	L	PCT	Finish*	Manager	Affiliate Since
Majors	Tampa Bay	American	66	96	.407	14th (14)	Joe Maddon	—
Triple-A	Durham Bulls	International	80	63	.559	3rd (14)	Charlie Montoyo	1998
Double-A	Montgomery Biscuits	Southern	81	59	.579	1st (10)^	Billy Gardner Jr.	2004
High A	Vero Beach Devil Rays	Florida State	59	79	.428	10th (12)	Joe Szekely	2007
Low A	Columbus Catfish	South Atlantic	82	53	.607	2nd (16)^	Jim Morrison	2007
Short-season	Hudson Valley Renegades	New York-Penn	34	42	.447	9th (14)	Matt Quatraro	1996
Rookie	Princeton Devil Rays	Appalachian	33	35	.485	5th (9)	Jamie Nelson	1997
Overall 2007 Minor League Record			**369**	**331**	**.527**	**7th**		

* Finish in overall standings (No. of teams in league) ^League champion

ORGANIZATION STATISTICS

TAMPA BAY DEVIL RAYS

AMERICAN LEAGUE

BATTING	B-T	HT	WT	DOB	AVG	vLH	vRH	G	AB	R	H	2B	3B	HR	RBI	BB	HBP	SH	SF	SO	SB	CS	SLG	OBP
Baldelli, Rocco	R-R	6-4	200	9-25-81	.204	.156	.219	35	137	16	28	6	0	5	12	9	3	1	0	35	4	1	.358	.268
Cantu, Jorge	R-R	6-3	200	1-30-82	.207	.225	.167	25	58	4	12	1	0	0	4	5	1	0	1	16	0	0	.224	.277
Casanova, Raul	B-R	6-0	235	8-23-72	.253	.250	.254	29	79	12	20	1	1	6	11	7	1	0	2	17	0	0	.519	.315
Crawford, Carl	L-L	6-2	215	8-5-81	.315	.318	.314	143	584	93	184	37	9	11	80	32	5	1	2	112	50	10	.466	.355
Dukes, Elijah	R-R	6-2	250	6-26-84	.190	.260	.164	52	184	27	35	3	2	10	21	33	2	0	1	44	2	4	.391	.318
Gomes, Jonny	R-R	6-1	225	11-22-80	.244	.313	.218	107	348	48	85	20	2	17	49	35	7	0	4	126	12	4	.460	.322
Guzman, Joel	R-R	6-6	250	11-24-84	.243	.125	.276	16	37	5	9	1	2	0	4	2	0	0	0	10	0	0	.378	.282
Harris, Brendan	R-R	6-1	200	8-26-80	.286	.345	.264	137	521	72	149	35	3	12	59	42	4	8	1	96	4	1	.434	.343
Iwamura, Akinori	L-R	5-9	175	2-9-79	.285	.323	.268	123	491	82	140	21	10	7	34	58	1	4	5	114	12	8	.411	.359
Mohr, Dustan	R-R	6-1	210	6-19-76	.125	.250	.000	7	16	1	2	0	0	1	2	0	0	0	0	6	0	1	.313	.125
Navarro, Dioner	B-R	5-9	205	2-9-84	.227	.226	.227	119	388	46	88	19	2	9	44	33	1	7	5	67	3	1	.356	.286
Norton, Greg	B-R	6-1	205	7-6-72	.243	.174	.251	75	202	25	49	9	0	4	23	37	0	0	1	55	1	1	.347	.358
Paul, Josh	R-R	6-1	210	5-19-75	.190	.242	.167	35	105	8	20	3	0	1	9	6	0	4	0	30	1	0	.248	.234
Pena, Carlos	L-L	6-2	215	5-17-78	.282	.271	.286	148	490	99	138	29	1	46	121	103	10	1	8	142	1	0	.627	.411
Riggans, Shawn	R-R	6-2	210	7-25-80	.100	1.000	.000	3	10	1	1	0	0	0	2	0	0	0	0	1	0	0	.100	.100
Ruggiano, Justin	R-R	6-2	205	4-12-82	.214	.000	.214	7	14	2	3	0	0	0	3	1	0	0	0	5	0	0	.214	.267
Upton, B.J.	R-R	6-3	185	8-21-84	.300	.281	.306	129	474	86	142	25	1	24	82	65	4	1	4	154	22	8	.508	.386
Velandia, Jorge	R-R	5-9	190	1-12-75	.320	.000	.372	14	50	7	16	4	0	2	11	8	1	1	0	17	0	0	.520	.424
Wigginton, Ty	R-R	6-0	225	10-11-77	.275	.275	.275	98	378	47	104	21	0	16	49	28	5	0	6	73	1	4	.458	.329
Wilson, Josh	R-R	6-1	175	3-26-81	.251	.284	.238	90	263	25	66	15	3	2	24	12	4	3	3	51	6	2	.354	.291
Young, Delmon	R-R	6-3	215	9-14-85	.288	.299	.285	162	645	65	186	38	0	13	93	26	3	0	7	127	10	3	.408	.316
Zobrist, Ben	B-R	6-3	200	5-26-81	.155	.182	.147	31	97	8	15	2	0	1	9	3	1	2	2	21	2	0	.206	.184

PITCHING	B-T	HT	WT	DOB	W	L	ERA	G	GS	CG	SV	IP	H	R	ER	HR	BB	SO	AVG	vLH	vRH	K/9	BB/9
Balfour, Grant	R-R	6-2	190	12-30-77	1	0	6.14	22	0	0	0	22	26	15	15	1	16	27	.313	.359	.273	11.05	6.55
Camp, Shawn	R-R	6-1	200	11-18-75	0	3	7.20	50	0	0	0	40	63	33	32	7	18	36	.368	.370	.368	8.10	4.05
Corcoran, Tim	R-R	6-2	210	4-15-78	0	0	6.75	9	0	0	0	17	17	14	13	2	12	6	.258	.316	.234	3.12	6.23
Dohmann, Scott	R-R	6-1	200	2-13-78	3	0	3.31	31	0	0	0	33	29	13	12	3	18	26	.257	.241	.271	7.16	4.96
Fossum, Casey	L-L	6-1	170	1-6-78	5	8	7.70	40	10	0	0	76	109	71	65	15	27	53	.339	.369	.322	6.28	3.20
Glover, Gary	R-R	6-5	225	12-3-76	6	5	4.89	67	0	0	2	77	87	44	42	12	27	51	.288	.286	.290	5.94	3.14
Hammel, Jason	R-R	6-6	220	9-2-82	3	5	6.14	24	14	0	0	85	100	58	58	12	40	64	.294	.310	.277	6.78	4.24
Howell, J.P.	L-L	6-0	180	4-25-83	1	6	7.59	10	10	0	0	51	69	45	43	8	21	49	.318	.296	.325	8.65	3.71
Jackson, Edwin	R-R	6-3	210	9-9-83	5	15	5.76	32	31	1	0	161	195	116	103	19	88	128	.299	.313	.285	7.16	4.92
Kazmir, Scott	L-L	6-0	190	1-24-84	13	9	3.48	34	34	0	0	207	196	91	80	18	89	239	.251	.217	.263	10.41	3.88
Lugo, Ruddy	R-R	6-0	215	5-22-80	2	0	9.28	11	0	0	0	11	17	11	11	2	13	8	.362	.333	.400	6.75	10.97
	2-team (27 Oakland)				6	0	5.40	38	0	0	0	48	48	29	29	3	37	34	—	—	—	6.33	6.89
Orvella, Chad	R-R	5-11	195	10-1-80	0	2	14.63	10	0	0	0	8	13	13	13	3	10	6	.400	.500	.345	6.75	11.25
Reyes, Al	R-R	6-1	230	4-10-70	2	4	4.90	61	0	0	26	61	49	35	33	13	21	70	.215	.240	.187	10.38	3.12
Ridgway, Jeff	R-L	6-3	210	8-17-80	0	0	189.00	3	0	0	0	0	7	7	7	1	1	0	.875	1.000	.750	0.00	27.00
Ryu, Jae Kuk	R-R	6-3	220	5-30-83	1	2	7.33	17	0	0	0	23	31	19	19	2	11	14	.326	.354	.298	5.40	4.24
Salas, Juan	R-R	6-2	230	11-7-78	1	1	3.72	34	0	0	0	36	36	19	15	7	17	26	.248	.260	.235	6.44	4.21
Seo, Jae	R-R	6-0	225	5-24-77	3	4	8.13	11	10	0	0	52	84	53	47	11	16	28	.372	.375	.368	4.85	2.77
Shields, Jamie	R-R	6-4	215	12-20-81	12	8	3.85	31	31	1	0	215	202	98	92	28	36	184	.247	.243	.250	7.70	1.51
Sonnanstine, Andy	L-R	6-3	185	3-18-83	6	10	5.85	22	22	0	0	131	151	87	85	24	26	97	.293	.318	.266	6.68	1.79
Stokes, Brian	R-R	6-1	210	9-7-79	2	7	7.07	59	0	0	0	62	90	49	49	11	25	35	.344	.346	.341	5.05	3.61
Switzer, Jon	L-L	6-3	210	8-13-79	0	2	8.05	21	0	0	0	19	27	17	17	2	7	13	.338	.242	.404	6.16	3.32
Wheeler, Dan	R-R	6-3	220	12-10-77	0	5	5.76	25	0	0	0	25	28	20	16	3	10	26	.277	.294	.260	9.36	3.60
Wilson, Josh	R-R	6-1	175	3-26-81	0	0	0.00	1	0	0	0	1	1	0	0	0	1	0	.250	.000	.333	0.00	9.00
Witasick, Jay	R-R	6-4	250	8-28-72	0	0	6.61	20	0	0	0	16	17	13	12	1	18	8	.279	.346	.229	4.41	9.92
	2-team (16 Oakland)				1	0	5.17	36	0	0	0	31	31	19	18	2	27	18	—	—	—	5.17	7.76

FIELDING

Catcher	PCT	G	PO	A	E	DP	PB
Casanova	.980	23	138	9	3	3	4
Navarro	.984	112	814	67	14	11	6
Paul	.992	35	228	21	2	3	4
Riggans	.941	3	31	1	2	0	0

First Base	PCT	G	PO	A	E	DP
Cantu	1.000	7	49	3	0	5
Guzman	.923	2	11	1	1	2
Norton	1.000	3	5	1	0	0
Pena	.993	144	1054	130	8	116
Wigginton	1.000	17	116	15	0	14

Second Base	PCT	G	PO	A	E	DP
Cantu	1.000	1	2	2	0	2
Harris	.994	47	75	96	1	26

	1.000	1	2	2	0	1
Iwamura	1.000	1	2	2	0	1
Upton	.952	48	106	133	12	26
Velandia	1.000	11	17	29	0	7
Wigginton	.982	39	74	89	3	24
Wilson	.949	27	44	68	6	19

Third Base	PCT	G	PO	A	E	DP
Guzman	1.000	8	3	7	0	1
Harris	.750	4	2	1	1	0
Iwamura	.975	120	79	197	7	17
Wigginton	.938	32	23	52	5	3
Wilson	.880	3	8	19	3	4

Shortstop	PCT	G	PO	A	E	DP
Guzman	—	3	0	0	0	0
Harris	.968	87	111	221	11	54

	PCT	G	PO	A	E	DP
Velandia	1.000	4	7	12	0	4
Wilson	.959	50	67	118	8	30
Zobrist	.943	30	37	63	6	17

Outfield	PCT	G	PO	A	E	DP
Baldelli	1.000	20	62	3	0	1
Crawford	.986	139	286	3	4	1
Dukes	1.000	40	87	3	0	1
Gomes	1.000	57	95	5	0	2
Mohr	1.000	5	9	0	0	0
Norton	1.000	9	4	1	0	0
Ruggiano	1.000	4	6	0	0	0
Upton	.991	78	204	11	2	2
Young	.979	160	314	16	7	7

DURHAM BULLS   TRIPLE-A

INTERNATIONAL LEAGUE

BATTING	B-T	HT	WT	DOB	AVG	vLH	vRH	G	AB	R	H	2B	3B	HR	RBI	BB	HBP	SH	SF	SO	SB	CS	SLG	OBP
Baldelli, Rocco	R-R	6-4	200	9-25-81	.125	.000	.125	2	8	2	1	0	0	1	1	1	0	0	0	2	0	0	.500	.222
Bankston, Wes	R-R	6-4	215	11-23-83	.238	.164	.256	104	390	46	93	23	1	15	59	25	2	0	9	88	2	0	.418	.282
Butler, Brent	R-R	6-0	180	2-11-78	.268	.260	.272	78	284	27	76	19	0	4	26	14	1	1	3	42	1	1	.377	.301
Cantu, Jorge	R-R	6-3	200	1-30-82	.242	.143	.271	24	91	12	22	5	1	1	10	8	0	0	1	21	0	0	.352	.300
2-team (24 Louisville)					.276	—	—	48	185	24	51	14	1	3	23	13	3	0	1	36	0	0	.411	.332
Casanova, Raul	B-R	6-0	235	8-23-72	.291	.219	.312	44	141	14	41	9	0	5	21	12	0	0	3	32	0	0	.461	.346
Gomes, Jonny	R-R	6-1	225	11-22-80	.302	.100	.364	13	43	6	13	2	0	1	7	11	2	0	0	15	4	1	.419	.464
Guzman, Joel	R-R	6-6	250	11-24-84	.242	.214	.251	110	414	44	100	17	2	16	64	23	2	0	6	117	9	2	.408	.281
Hernandez, Michel	R-R	6-0	210	8-12-78	.276	.235	.421	51	170	22	47	4	0	4	19	16	1	2	0	13	0	1	.371	.342
Johnson, Elliot	B-R	6-0	185	3-9-84	.207	.225	.202	129	463	56	96	17	6	11	45	43	8	9	1	139	16	6	.341	.285
Johnson, Joshua	R-R	6-0	205	11-3-82	.276	.216	.311	31	98	14	27	5	0	3	8	4	3	1	0	32	0	0	.418	.324
Longoria, Evan	R-R	6-2	210	10-7-85	.269	.182	.293	31	104	19	28	8	0	5	19	22	1	0	1	29	0	0	.490	.398
Lopez, Christian	R-R	6-1	185	10-10-84	.167	—	.167	2	6	0	1	0	0	0	0	0	0	0	0	0	0	0	.167	.167
Maniscalco, Matthew	R-R	5-10	180	2-18-81	.171	.211	.158	25	76	4	13	2	0	0	4	5	0	0		19	1	1	.197	.222
Mohr, Dustan	R-R	6-1	210	6-19-76	.229	.255	.221	58	201	25	46	15	0	9	24	18	2	0	0	79	1	1	.438	.299
Owens, Jeremy	R-R	6-0	200	12-9-76	.261	.302	.243	111	341	42	89	16	6	7	32	19	0	2	3	123	15	3	.405	.298
Pridie, Jason	L-R	6-1	190	10-9-83	.318	.292	.325	63	245	47	78	16	4	10	39	22	2	2	3	47	12	3	.539	.375
Richard, Chris	L-L	6-2	210	6-7-74	.284	.210	.300	102	342	63	97	24	2	14	57	42	16	0	4	85	9	3	.488	.384
Riggans, Shawn	R-R	6-2	210	7-25-80	.281	.500	.232	33	121	10	34	9	1	4	16	4	6	1	1	30	0	1	.471	.333
Ruggiano, Justin	R-R	6-2	205	4-12-82	.309	.248	.329	127	482	78	149	29	2	20	73	53	8	2	1	151	26	11	.502	.386
Upton, B.J.	R-R	6-3	185	8-21-84	.429	—	.429	2	7	1	3	0	0	1	0	0	1	0	0	0	0	0	.857	.429
Velandia, Jorge	R-R	5-9	190	1-12-75	.249	.270	.242	120	433	44	108	24	4	5	32	28	3	7	6	95	6	6	.358	.296
Weber, Jon	L-L	5-10	190	1-20-78	.265	.250	.267	39	136	20	36	5	2	3	21	21	1	0	3	24	0	0	.397	.360
Zobrist, Ben	B-R	6-3	200	5-26-81	.279	.258	.288	61	222	42	62	14	2	7	22	43	5	3	3	38	8	3	.455	.403

PITCHING	B-T	HT	WT	DOB	W	L	ERA	G	GS	CG	SV	IP	H	R	ER	HR	BB	SO	AVG	vLH	vRH	K/9	BB/9
Andrade, Steve	R-R	6-1	260	2-6-78	3	2	4.55	38	0	0	0	59	53	31	30	4	31	50	.228	.242	.218	7.58	4.70
Butler, Brent	R-R	6-0	180	2-11-78	0	0	0.00	1	0	0	0	1	0	0	0	0	0	1	.333	.000	.500	9.00	0.00
Camp, Shawn	R-R	6-1	200	11-18-75	0	1	1.17	12	0	0	4	15	13	2	2	0	2	16	.232	.182	.304	9.39	1.17
Corcoran, Tim	R-R	6-2	210	4-15-78	1	1	2.51	10	0	0	0	14	13	4	4	1	6	13	.245	.217	.267	8.16	3.77
De Los Santos, R.	R-R	6-1	175	6-1-84	1	1	7.20	6	0	0	0	15	21	12	12	3	3	5	.344	.290	.400	3.00	1.80
Dohmann, Scott	R-R	6-1	200	2-13-78	4	1	2.03	37	0	0	5	49	37	12	11	2	13	48	.213	.261	.181	8.88	2.40
Hammel, Jason	R-R	6-6	220	9-2-82	4	5	3.42	13	13	2	0	76	61	29	29	3	28	75	.216	.243	.187	8.84	3.30
Howell, J.P.	L-L	6-0	180	4-25-83	7	8	3.38	21	21	1	0	128	110	63	48	16	34	145	.229	.212	.235	10.20	2.39
Johnson, Joshua	R-R	6-0	205	11-3-82	0	0	0.00	2	0	0	0	2	3	0	0	0	1	1	.333	.400	.250	4.50	4.50
Lugo, Ruddy	R-R	6-0	215	5-22-80	2	1	1.84	11	0	0	0	15	12	5	3	0	12	7	.231	.286	.167	4.30	7.36
McClung, Seth	L-R	6-6	260	2-7-81	1	5	1.99	40	0	0	5	59	38	18	13	3	43	68	.184	.230	.151	10.43	6.60
Medlock, Calvin	R-R	5-10	195	11-8-82	2	0	3.45	9	0	0	0	16	9	7	6	2	9	8	.173	.167	.179	4.60	5.17
2-team (13 Louisville)					4	1	4.55	22	0	0	0	32	26	17	16	2	23	25	—	—	—	7.11	6.54
Niemann, Jeff	R-R	6-9	280	2-28-83	12	6	3.98	25	25	0	0	131	144	69	58	13	46	123	.277	.297	.260	8.45	3.16
Orvella, Chad	R-R	5-11	195	10-1-80	3	3	3.12	42	0	0	20	52	39	20	18	6	19	53	.204	.221	.193	9.17	3.29
Peguero, Tony	R-R	6-3	190	2-17-81	2	4	7.35	22	9	0	0	64	79	54	52	15	40	29	.315	.338	.289	4.10	5.65
Prochaska, Mike	L-L	6-1	210	5-23-80	1	1	2.55	5	5	0	0	25	16	7	7	3	13	14	.195	.235	.185	5.11	4.74
Ridgway, Jeff	R-L	6-3	210	8-17-80	2	3	3.06	54	0	0	4	65	54	25	22	8	30	67	.228	.163	.269	9.32	4.18
Ryu, Jae Kuk	R-R	6-3	220	5-30-83	5	4	4.04	14	14	1	0	71	67	36	32	5	21	67	.244	.246	.241	8.45	2.65
Salas, Juan	R-R	6-2	230	11-7-78	1	0	2.08	7	0	0	1	9	5	2	2	0	3	12	.161	.231	.111	12.46	3.12
Seo, Jae	R-R	6-0	225	5-24-77	9	4	3.69	17	16	0	0	98	98	42	40	8	14	64	.266	.291	.241	5.90	1.29
Shackelford, Brian	L-L	6-1	205	8-30-76	0	0	3.09	11	0	0	0	12	11	4	4	3	4	7	.262	.222	.292	5.40	3.09
2-team (41 Louisville)					0	5	4.47	52	0	0	1	44	45	24	22	3	17	21	—	—	—	4.26	3.45
Sonnanstine, Andy	L-R	6-3	185	3-18-83	6	4	2.66	11	11	0	0	71	60	24	21	8	13	66	.228	.252	.203	8.37	1.65
Switzer, Jon	L-L	6-3	210	8-13-79	0	0	0.82	23	0	0	1	33	26	4	3	0	8	23	.226	.229	.225	6.27	2.18
Talbot, Mitch	R-R	6-2	200	10-17-83	13	9	4.53	29	29	1	0	161	169	89	81	13	59	124	.274	.249	.298	6.93	3.30
Thayer, Dale	R-R	6-0	190	12-17-80	0	0	2.89	8	0	0	0	9	5	3	3	0	4	9	.167	.100	.200	8.68	3.86
Witasick, Jay	R-R	6-4	250	8-28-72	1	0	0.00	6	0	0	1	7	2	0	0	0	2	8	.077	.000	.167	9.82	2.45

FIELDING

Catcher	PCT	G	PO	A	E	DP	PB
Casanova	.985	41	302	17	5	1	6
Hernandez	1.000	49	355	50	0	1	2
J. Johnson	.981	30	195	11	4	3	2
Lopez	.909	2	9	1	1	1	1
Riggans	.993	30	257	20	2	1	2

First Base	PCT	G	PO	A	E	DP
Bankston	.988	78	677	45	9	75
Butler	.980	18	137	10	3	17
Cantu	.989	9	81	5	1	7
Casanova	1.000	1	2	0	0	0
Guzman	1.000	12	100	7	0	10
Richard	.990	33	273	15	3	31

Second Base	PCT	G	PO	A	E	DP
Butler	.974	8	11	27	1	4

	PCT	G	PO	A	E	DP
Cantu	1.000	3	4	6	0	1
E. Johnson	.960	123	191	335	22	95
Maniscalco	1.000	5	7	12	0	4
Upton	1.000	2	3	3	0	0
Velandia	1.000	9	10	36	0	4

Third Base	PCT	G	PO	A	E	DP
Butler	.972	18	4	31	1	0
Cantu	—	1	0	0	0	0
Guzman	.945	74	45	128	10	17
Longoria	.968	28	15	45	2	1
Maniscalco	.917	12	10	23	3	3
Velandia	.955	16	10	32	2	7

Shortstop	PCT	G	PO	A	E	DP
Butler	.958	8	10	13	1	3
Guzman	1.000	1	0	1	0	0

	PCT	G	PO	A	E	DP
Maniscalco	.920	6	3	20	2	2
Velandia	.977	83	83	219	7	55
Zobrist	.953	52	71	154	11	39

Outfield	PCT	G	PO	A	E	DP
Baldelli	1.000	1	2	0	0	0
Butler	1.000	16	30	0	0	0
Gomes	1.000	7	10	0	0	0
Mohr	.992	56	116	1	1	0
Owens	.979	104	182	3	4	1
Pridie	.982	63	156	6	3	2
Richard	.989	59	84	3	1	0
Ruggiano	.971	119	192	9	6	5
Weber	.963	29	46	6	2	0

MONTGOMERY BISCUITS

DOUBLE-A

SOUTHERN LEAGUE

BATTING	B-T	HT	WT	DOB	AVG	vLH	vRH	G	AB	R	H	2B	3B	HR	RBI	BB	HBP	SH	SF	SO	SB	CS	SLG	OBP
Andrus, Erold	B-L	6-2	170	7-16-84	.238	.239	.237	54	206	27	49	14	0	2	14	11	1	4	0	42	2	1	.335	.280
Arhart, Josh	R-R	6-1	240	9-13-79	.216	.211	.219	50	167	18	36	10	0	2	17	17	5	1	3	34	0	0	.311	.302
Asanovich, Josh	R-R	6-2	185	1-31-83	.242	.257	.233	121	401	45	97	19	1	5	34	39	7	8	2	70	7	5	.332	.318
Badeaux, Brooks	B-R	5-10	177	10-20-76	.275	.323	.240	103	396	53	109	20	2	1	49	35	3	8	3	51	1	4	.343	.336
Breen, Patrick	L-L	6-3	215	6-23-82	.194	.176	.200	86	279	34	54	11	5	7	38	36	1	0	4	104	4	6	.344	.284
Brignac, Reid	L-R	6-3	180	1-16-86	.260	.286	.243	133	527	91	137	30	5	17	81	55	3	1	10	94	15	5	.433	.328
Cottrell, Patrick	R-R	5-11	179	3-16-82	.292	.250	.313	6	24	3	7	1	0	1	4	2	0	0	1	5	0	0	.458	.333
Cumberland, Shaun	L-R	6-2	185	8-1-84	.246	.244	.247	99	354	33	87	14	2	6	34	29	1	2	2	71	3	8	.347	.303
2-team (31 Chattanooga)					.259	—	—	130	467	44	121	23	2	7	51	36	4	2	3	91	4	9	.362	.316
Hughes, Rhyne	L-L	6-2	175	9-9-83	.295	.222	.333	21	78	12	23	4	1	2	15	9	2	1	1	23	0	1	.449	.378
Jaso, John	L-R	6-2	205	9-19-83	.316	.308	.320	109	380	62	120	24	2	12	71	59	4	2	5	49	2	2	.484	.408
Longoria, Evan	R-R	6-2	210	10-7-85	.307	.340	.285	105	381	78	117	21	0	21	76	51	12	0	3	81	4	0	.528	.403
Martinez, Gabriel	L-R	6-2	180	5-17-83	.272	.297	.258	105	386	43	105	15	1	15	82	31	4	2	5	100	1	1	.433	.329
Norton, Greg	B-R	6-1	205	7-6-72	.280	.125	.353	7	25	2	7	2	0	0	4	5	1	0	0	4	0	0	.360	.419
Nowak, Chris	R-R	6-5	225	2-21-83	.304	.349	.274	104	368	54	112	21	4	7	55	54	5	0	5	73	18	3	.440	.396
Paul, Josh	R-R	6-1	210	5-19-75	.400	—	.400	3	10	2	4	0	0	0	2	4	0	0	0	2	0	0	.458	.571
Perez, Fernando	B-R	6-1	195	4-28-83	.308	.308	.308	102	393	84	121	24	10	8	33	76	2	5	0	104	32	18	.481	.423
Pridie, Jason	L-R	6-1	190	10-9-83	.290	.248	.319	71	279	42	81	16	7	4	27	14	4	1	2	45	14	7	.441	.331
Sisk, Aaron	R-R	6-0	190	9-17-78	.143	.000	.200	5	14	1	2	1	0	0	2	0	0	0	0	2	0	0	.214	.143
Spring, Matthew	R-R	6-2	215	11-7-84	.165	.088	.206	29	97	11	16	4	0	4	11	5	0	3	2	32	0	0	.330	.202

PITCHING	B-T	HT	WT	DOB	W	L	ERA	G	GS	CG	SV	IP	H	R	ER	HR	BB	SO	AVG	vLH	vRH	K/9	BB/9
Barratt, Jonathan	R-L	5-9	165	3-19-85	4	10	5.46	20	18	0	0	91	94	60	55	9	59	48	.280	.264	.284	4.76	5.86
Corcoran, Tim	R-R	6-2	210	4-15-78	2	1	3.44	14	0	0	3	18	12	7	7	1	9	20	.188	.207	.171	9.82	4.42
Davis, Wade	R-R	6-5	220	9-7-85	7	3	3.15	14	14	0	0	80	74	37	28	3	30	81	.249	.228	.274	9.11	3.38
De Los Santos, R.	R-R	6-1	175	6-1-84	5	4	2.75	40	3	0	0	72	67	29	22	3	15	38	.250	.258	.246	4.75	1.88
DeBarr, Nick	R-R	6-4	220	8-24-83	3	4	3.47	53	0	0	4	83	78	37	32	5	33	52	.254	.298	.226	5.64	3.38
Feldkamp, Derek	R-R	6-4	210	5-9-83	2	7	6.52	22	14	0	0	77	98	61	56	16	28	52	.301	.293	.306	6.05	3.26
Flanagan, Jeremy	R-R	6-3	215	4-14-81	5	3	5.23	40	2	0	1	76	87	51	44	8	35	40	.286	.318	.268	4.76	4.16
Henderson, Brian	L-L	5-11	195	5-19-82	6	3	2.97	59	0	0	1	67	62	25	22	5	25	45	.249	.222	.267	6.07	3.38
Houser, James	L-L	6-4	185	12-15-84	5	4	3.65	20	20	0	0	104	88	51	42	10	39	90	.230	.125	.257	7.81	3.39
Lynn, Kevin	R-R	5-11	185	11-12-78	0	0	2.25	3	0	0	0	4	4	1	1	1	0	4	.250	.167	.300	9.00	0.00
Mason, Christopher	R-R	6-0	185	7-1-84	15	4	2.57	28	28	1	0	161	147	52	46	7	44	136	.241	.279	.207	7.59	2.45
Matthews, Jarod	R-R	6-2	212	11-10-82	0	1	24.92	5	0	0	0	4	5	12	12	0	10	3	.294	.400	.250	6.23	20.77
McGee, Jacob	L-L	6-3	190	8-6-86	3	2	4.24	5	5	0	0	23	19	11	11	2	13	30	.224	.167	.246	11.57	5.01
Meek, Evan	R-R	6-1	190	5-12-83	2	1	4.30	44	0	0	1	67	74	36	32	2	34	69	.287	.268	.298	9.27	4.57
Peguero, Tony	R-R	6-3	190	2-17-81	1	1	4.50	7	4	0	0	30	34	18	15	4	15	20	.291	.367	.211	6.90	4.50
Prochaska, Mike	L-R	6-1	210	5-23-80	7	7	3.89	21	20	2	0	113	106	56	49	13	35	77	.248	.213	.260	6.11	2.78
Salas, Juan	R-R	6-2	230	11-7-78	0	0	27.00	2	0	0	0	1	4	4	4	0	2	2	.500	.500	.500	13.50	13.50
Seddon, Chris	L-L	6-3	220	10-13-83	3	4	4.94	12	12	0	0	71	71	40	39	7	23	40	.274	.136	.315	5.07	2.92
2-team (14 Carolina)					6	10	4.64	26	26	0	0	140	136	77	72	13	48	98	—	—	—	6.32	3.09
Thayer, Dale	R-R	6-0	190	12-17-80	9	0	2.26	47	0	0	21	60	40	16	15	4	20	54	.187	.176	.194	8.15	3.02
Wayne, Brett	R-R	6-0	185	4-28-80	2	0	4.79	29	0	0	0	47	56	34	25	6	33	35	.292	.274	.306	6.70	6.32

FIELDING

Catcher	PCT	G	PO	A	E	DP	PB
Arhart	.997	45	327	18	1	1	3
Jaso	.989	70	475	44	6	4	9
Paul	1.000	2	11	2	0	0	0
Spring	.972	27	154	21	5	2	3

First Base	PCT	G	PO	A	E	DP
Hughes	.985	20	180	11	3	16
Martinez	.993	44	386	27	3	29
Norton	1.000	2	27	2	0	1
Nowak	.988	76	667	45	9	69
Spring	1.000	1	5	1	0	0

Second Base	PCT	G	PO	A	E	DP
Asanovich	.976	121	193	329	13	77
Badeaux	.990	26	31	67	1	12
Sisk	.833	2	3	2	1	1

Third Base	PCT	G	PO	A	E	DP
Badeaux	1.000	10	4	17	0	2
Cottrell	.944	6	2	15	1	1
Longoria	.963	98	86	200	11	15
Martinez	.972	13	11	24	1	1
Nowak	.972	16	10	25	1	2
Sisk	.571	2	1	3	3	0

Shortstop	PCT	G	PO	A	E	DP
Badeaux	.918	14	23	33	5	8
Brignac	.963	127	179	394	22	76

Outfield	PCT	G	PO	A	E	DP
Andrus	1.000	52	95	7	0	0
Badeaux	.974	48	73	3	2	0
Breen	.972	63	102	2	3	0
Cumberland	.974	99	218	5	6	0
Martinez	1.000	5	2	1	0	0
Nowak	—	3	0	0	0	0
Perez	.985	101	257	8	4	2
Pridie	.988	69	161	6	2	0

VERO BEACH DEVIL RAYS

HIGH CLASS A

FLORIDA STATE LEAGUE

BATTING	B-T	HT	WT	DOB	AVG	vLH	vRH	G	AB	R	H	2B	3B	HR	RBI	BB	HBP	SH	SF	SO	SB	CS	SLG	OBP
Andrus, Erold	B-L	6-2	170	7-16-84	.267	.238	.278	63	243	38	65	7	2	8	28	21	1	0	1	43	1	4	.412	.327
Baldelli, Rocco	R-R	6-4	200	9-25-81	.000	.000	.000	2	5	1	0	0	0	0	0	1	0	0	0	1	0	0	.000	.167
Brennan, Jackson	R-R	6-0	185	8-28-82	.240	.229	.243	117	409	75	98	22	1	9	44	55	20	2	5	93	13	4	.364	.354
Cottrell, Patrick	R-R	5-11	179	3-16-82	.258	.254	.260	117	449	62	116	23	4	10	60	21	6	4	5	55	3	7	.394	.297
Cunningham, Christopher	R-R	6-0	200	8-24-82	.250	.315	.224	55	188	29	47	8	0	3	22	12	5	1	1	45	2	3	.340	.311
Devins, Matthew	R-R	6-2	200	5-23-83	.261	.353	.215	64	203	26	53	8	1	4	30	28	1	4	3	31	1	2	.369	.349
Groce, Garrett	R-R	6-1	190	4-24-83	.232	.279	.212	78	298	33	69	12	1	6	21	19	2	2	1	68	7	5	.339	.281
Hall, James	L-R	6-3	210	5-19-84	.272	.135	.307	103	357	47	97	18	2	11	40	28	2	2	0	89	5	0	.426	.328
Hughes, Rhyne	L-L	6-2	175	9-9-83	.329	.280	.345	94	334	65	110	24	1	12	57	35	1	1	2	62	1	1	.515	.392
Jamieson, Alex	L-R	5-11	205	4-7-83	.219	.143	.238	36	105	10	23	4	0	1	17	10	2	1	3	16	0	0	.286	.292
Johnson, Joshua	R-R	6-0	205	10-13-84	.000	.000	.000	5	13	1	0	0	0	0	0	0	0	1	0	3	0	0	.000	.000
Lopez, Christian	R-R	6-1	185	10-10-84	.230	.174	.252	94	318	30	73	13	2	3	24	14	6	4	1	46	2	2	.311	.274
Paul, Josh	R-R	6-1	210	5-19-75	.160	.333	.136	7	25	3	4	0	0	1	0	1	0	0	1	2	0	0	.160	.154
Pedroza, Sergio	L-R	6-1	180	2-23-84	.286	.261	.293	116	399	59	114	27	4	22	70	43	13	3	7	95	1	2	.539	.368
Riggans, Shawn	R-R	6-2	210	7-25-80	.300	.500	.269	8	30	3	9	2	0	0	5	1	0	0	0	5	0	0	.367	.323
Sisk, Aaron	R-R	6-0	190	9-17-78	.276	.367	.247	72	246	41	68	9	1	12	49	24	3	0	5	51	2	4	.467	.342
St. Clair, Jason	R-R	5-10	173	9-27-82	.153	.000	.188	18	59	6	9	0	0	0	1	4	1	4	0	8	5	0	.153	.219
Upton, B.J.	R-R	6-3	185	8-21-84	.235	.143	.300	7	17	4	4	0	0	1	3	5	0	0	2	2	0	0	.412	.375
Vick, Hunter	B-R	5-9	165	4-12-82	.214	.258	.199	113	384	34	82	9	2	1	31	32	6	7	5	72	4	4	.255	.281
Walton, Neil	R-R	6-5	180	2-23-84	.232	.189	.248	89	280	26	65	14	5	2	30	18	2	4	2	75	12	7	.339	.281
Williams, Shawn	R-R	6-2	190	9-18-83	.194	.111	.222	24	72	8	14	3	0	0	8	7	0	1	3	14	0	0	.236	.256

PITCHING	B-T	HT	WT	DOB	W	L	ERA	G	GS	CG	SV	IP	H	R	ER	HR	BB	SO	AVG	vLH	vRH	K/9	BB/9
Beltre, Jonathan	L-L	5-10	175	7-1-80	5	2	5.51	37	2	0	1	67	75	47	41	5	25	69	.276	.283	.274	9.27	3.36
Butler, Joshua	R-R	6-5	195	12-11-84	4	3	4.93	10	9	1	0	49	51	31	27	9	21	34	.273	.211	.315	6.20	3.83
Davis, Wade	R-R	6-5	220	9-7-85	3	0	1.84	13	13	1	0	78	54	20	16	5	21	88	.196	.275	.124	10.11	2.41
De La Cruz, Eddie	R-R	6-3	161	10-6-81	5	6	3.98	45	0	0	8	54	53	29	24	1	36	52	.262	.246	.270	8.61	5.96
Dupas, Greg	R-R	6-6	230	1-31-84	4	8	5.33	39	6	0	6	74	88	58	44	7	36	60	.298	.281	.311	7.26	4.36
Feldkamp, Derek	R-R	6-4	210	5-9-83	1	2	7.17	5	4	0	0	21	29	21	17	4	8	14	.322	.333	.313	5.91	3.38
Gonzalez, Jino	L-L	6-2	210	9-5-82	5	6	2.86	43	1	0	1	91	81	40	29	6	34	93	.238	.280	.220	9.16	3.35
Kamrath, Jeff	R-R	6-3	210	4-6-82	3	10	4.59	27	18	2	0	112	105	64	57	10	49	122	.249	.224	.268	9.83	3.95
Kelly, Chris	R-R	6-3	200	7-14-82	4	5	4.15	26	0	0	1	43	60	25	20	2	18	19	.328	.371	.301	3.95	3.74
Lockwood, Brian	R-R	6-2	180	2-20-81	0	1	54.00	2	0	0	0	1	6	6	6	2	4	0	.857	1.000	.833	0.00	36.00
Lynn, Kevin	R-R	5-11	185	11-12-78	1	6	4.52	42	2	0	8	70	80	40	35	10	14	68	.283	.328	.251	8.78	1.81
McGee, Jacob	L-L	6-3	190	8-6-86	5	4	2.93	21	21	0	0	117	86	45	38	8	39	145	.203	.141	.219	11.19	3.01
Moviel, Paul	R-R	6-6	220	9-28-82	2	7	6.69	24	9	1	0	70	92	60	52	9	31	52	.323	.380	.288	6.69	3.99
Reyes, Al	R-R	6-1	230	4-10-70	0	0	9.00	1	0	0	0	1	2	1	1	1	0	1	.400	.500	.333	9.00	0.00
Rodriguez, Claudio	R-R	6-5	244	6-29-83	0	0	9.00	1	0	0	0	3	3	3	3	0	2	0	.273	.167	.400	0.00	9.00
Waechter, Doug	R-R	6-4	225	1-28-81	4	4	4.74	9	9	1	0	44	53	23	23	6	5	34	.308	.333	.291	7.01	1.03
Walker, Aaron	L-L	6-3	210	2-4-82	0	0	2.82	17	0	0	1	22	21	9	7	3	7	21	.244	.241	.246	8.46	2.82
Walker, Matthew	R-R	6-3	195	8-16-86	4	9	5.55	31	15	0	0	96	96	75	59	8	82	76	.264	.255	.270	7.15	7.71
Witasick, Jay	R-R	6-4	250	8-28-72	0	0	0.00	2	2	0	0	2	1	0	0	0	1	1	.167	.000	.250	4.50	4.50
Wlodarczyk, Michael	L-L	6-5	230	12-2-82	9	6	3.85	27	26	3	0	138	130	62	59	10	68	102	.248	.270	.242	6.65	4.43

FIELDING

Catcher	PCT	G	PO	A	E	DP	PB
Jamieson	.992	32	242	14	2	3	3
Johnson	1.000	2	9	1	0	0	0
Lopez	.980	89	659	113	16	18	13
Paul	1.000	4	18	4	0	0	0
Pedroza	.948	14	66	6	5	1	4
Riggans	.972	5	33	2	1	0	0

First Base	PCT	G	PO	A	E	DP
Devins	.993	35	270	14	2	34
Hughes	.988	87	675	42	9	58
Johnson	1.000	1	3	0	0	1
Williams	.993	18	131	11	1	10

Second Base	PCT	G	PO	A	E	DP
Cottrell	.909	2	5	5	1	2

Devins	1.000	8	14	23	0	2
Sisk	.976	10	25	16	1	7
St. Clair	.932	18	28	40	5	4
Upton	1.000	3	2	4	0	0
Vick	.980	105	165	223	8	61
Williams	.909	2	5	5	1	4

Third Base	PCT	G	PO	A	E	DP
Cottrell	.952	109	80	216	15	34
Devins	.878	16	9	27	5	5
Sisk	.971	12	7	26	1	1
Vick	.750	1	0	3	1	0
Williams	.833	2	1	4	1	0

Shortstop	PCT	G	PO	A	E	DP
Sisk	.953	46	57	105	8	24

Vick	1.000	11	10	23	0	3
Walton	.920	88	105	184	25	20

Outfield	PCT	G	PO	A	E	DP
Andrus	1.000	60	128	10	0	6
Brennan	.991	116	222	5	2	0
Cottrell	—	1	0	0	0	0
Cunningham	.975	41	75	3	2	1
Groce	.980	70	141	5	3	3
Hall	.993	95	144	7	1	1
Pedroza	.947	37	54	0	3	0
Upton	1.000	3	11	0	0	0

COLUMBUS CATFISH

LOW CLASS A

SOUTH ATLANTIC LEAGUE

BATTING	B-T	HT	WT	DOB	AVG	vLH	vRH	G	AB	R	H	2B	3B	HR	RBI	BB	HBP	SH	SF	SO	SB	CS	SLG	OBP
Albernaz, Craig	R-R	5-8	177	10-30-82	.170	.200	.154	39	100	11	17	3	0	0	3	10	3	2	1	22	0	1	.200	.263
Ashley, Nevin	R-R	6-2	210	8-14-84	.280	.241	.289	119	429	76	120	13	8	12	60	49	4	1	7	92	20	8	.431	.354
Callender, Joey	R-R	5-11	165	11-25-83	.238	.293	.221	91	328	37	78	11	0	1	34	21	2	5	4	49	7	8	.280	.285
De La Rosa, Jairo	R-R	6-2	170	9-8-85	.211	.208	.212	122	398	44	84	20	1	6	37	21	3	8	5	124	8	7	.312	.253
Dhaenens, Seth	L-R	6-2	175	5-20-84	.282	.250	.288	65	188	18	53	10	1	0	26	18	2	0	2	45	1	6	.346	.348
Fields, Matthew	R-R	6-4	255	7-8-85	.247	.197	.261	100	360	44	89	23	0	19	71	19	2	0	0	120	4	1	.469	.289
Grandstrand, Brett	R-R	6-0	175	11-13-82	.211	.262	.201	76	246	21	52	13	2	1	23	13	5	9	3	33	8	5	.293	.262
Jennings, Desmond	R-R	6-2	180	10-30-86	.315	.387	.298	99	387	75	122	21	5	9	37	45	12	2	2	53	45	15	.465	.401
Loyola, Maiko	R-R	5-11	174	7-19-85	.248	.261	.246	67	206	40	51	14	1	4	18	39	1	1	0	41	19	8	.383	.370
Matulia, John	L-L	6-0	175	8-16-86	.257	.230	.263	113	443	57	114	16	7	4	39	31	5	7	2	90	19	10	.352	.312
Pickerell, Steven	R-R	6-3	215	2-5-82	.091	.000	.100	6	11	1	1	0	0	0	0	1	0	0	0	6	0	0	.091	.231
Royster, Ryan	R-R	6-2	210	7-25-86	.329	.364	.320	125	474	90	156	31	4	30	98	36	5	0	3	121	17	5	.601	.380
Spring, Matthew	R-R	6-2	215	11-7-84	.209	.200	.211	30	91	9	19	4	1	3	18	10	0	0	0	37	0	0	.374	.287
Stewart, Quinn	R-R	6-0	190	8-28-83	.251	.253	.250	112	386	62	97	18	1	21	63	41	8	1	2	122	21	5	.466	.334
Suarez, Cesar	R-R	5-11	170	8-17-83	.306	.290	.310	133	520	79	159	42	1	11	87	38	11	0	7	69	31	11	.454	.361

PITCHING

PITCHING	B-T	HT	WT	DOB	W	L	ERA	G	GS	CG	SV	IP	H	R	ER	HR	BB	SO	AVG	vLH	vRH	K/9	BB/9
Baker, Brian	R-R	6-5	190	1-10-83	4	3	2.40	39	0	0	7	79	60	29	21	3	29	68	.208	.266	.173	7.78	3.32
Butler, Joshua	R-R	6-5	195	12-11-84	5	1	2.33	13	13	0	0	77	63	25	20	3	20	54	.224	.282	.183	6.28	2.33
Callender, Joey	R-R	5-11	165	11-25-83	0	0	4.50	1	0	0	0	2	2	1	1	1	1	1	.286	.000	.667	4.50	4.50
Davis, Hunter	R-R	6-1	175	7-25-81	1	0	6.00	8	0	0	1	15	14	11	10	1	9	13	.237	.318	.189	7.80	5.40
Falk, Matt	L-R	6-3	190	8-25-84	3	0	5.92	29	0	0	0	52	57	35	34	7	24	35	.281	.264	.290	6.10	4.18
Fines, Woods	R-R	6-4	180	8-14-85	7	7	4.41	24	24	0	0	118	139	68	58	8	45	67	.297	.292	.301	5.10	3.42
Frontz, Neal	R-R	6-3	190	4-6-84	4	6	2.75	40	0	0	18	75	68	28	23	4	16	70	.231	.262	.214	8.36	1.91
Hall, Jeremy	R-R	6-3	200	9-16-83	1	0	1.50	1	1	0	0	6	4	1	1	0	4	4	.200	.200	.200	6.00	6.00
Hellickson, Jeremy	R-R	6-1	185	4-8-87	13	3	2.67	21	21	1	0	111	87	36	33	7	34	106	.214	.206	.220	8.57	2.75
Kelly, Chris	R-R	6-3	200	7-14-82	1	0	2.19	10	0	0	0	25	26	10	6	1	8	15	.277	.333	.250	5.47	2.92
Kline, Will	R-R	6-2	215	9-10-84	0	4	4.97	9	9	0	0	29	38	19	16	4	11	27	.309	.345	.277	8.38	3.41
Morse, Ryan	L-L	6-3	200	5-21-84	5	6	3.99	30	16	0	0	124	127	62	55	9	49	95	.268	.303	.257	6.90	3.56
Noel, Wilton	R-R	6-5	180	1-1-83	5	1	4.79	34	2	0	1	77	75	47	41	11	44	50	.251	.315	.215	5.84	5.14
Owen, Ryan	L-L	6-4	200	7-26-84	4	3	4.22	36	1	0	7	70	72	41	33	4	24	58	.263	.245	.272	7.42	3.07
Reid, Ryan	L-R	5-11	215	4-24-85	6	5	2.97	39	0	0	10	73	56	26	24	2	24	93	.216	.208	.222	11.52	2.97
Rollins, Heath	R-R	6-1	190	5-25-85	17	4	2.54	27	27	1	0	159	132	57	45	11	38	149	.223	.272	.188	8.42	2.15
Townsend, Wade	R-R	6-4	230	2-22-83	6	10	5.08	21	21	0	0	103	91	65	58	16	53	92	.238	.280	.205	8.06	4.65

FIELDING

Catcher	PCT	G	PO	A	E	DP	PB
Albernaz	.988	39	201	43	3	6	3
Ashley	.992	88	632	82	6	6	16
Pickerell	1.000	3	4	0	0	0	0
Spring	.994	22	144	18	1	0	2

First Base	PCT	G	PO	A	E	DP
Dhaenens	.995	50	397	21	2	39
Fields	.983	94	842	46	15	81
Grandstrand	1.000	1	2	0	0	0
Stewart	1.000	1	13	1	0	2

Second Base	PCT	G	PO	A	E	DP
Callender	.972	85	145	238	11	49

	PCT	G	PO	A	E	DP
Dhaenens	.962	8	10	15	1	2
Grandstrand	.978	50	112	153	6	35

Third Base	PCT	G	PO	A	E	DP
Callender	1.000	5	3	12	0	1
Dhaenens	1.000	2	1	1	0	0
Grandstrand	1.000	6	1	13	0	1
Spring	—	1	0	0	0	0
Suarez	.925	129	83	248	27	26

Shortstop	PCT	G	PO	A	E	DP
De La Rosa	.940	122	185	334	33	72
Dhaenens	.000	1	0	0	1	0
Grandstrand	.982	18	30	81	2	13

Outfield	PCT	G	PO	A	E	DP
Dhaenens	1.000	1	2	0	0	0
Grandstrand	—	1	0	0	0	0
Jennings	.990	88	188	5	2	4
Loyola	1.000	54	79	6	0	3
Matulia	.964	97	182	4	7	1
Royster	.982	105	156	5	3	0
Stewart	.974	74	106	6	3	0

HUDSON VALLEY RENEGADES

SHORT-SEASON

NEW YORK-PENN LEAGUE

BATTING	B-T	HT	WT	DOB	AVG	vLH	vRH	G	AB	R	H	2B	3B	HR	RBI	BB	HBP	SH	SF	SO	SB	CS	SLG	OBP
Carroll, Jeff	R-R	6-2	192	8-14-84	.250	.500	.200	3	12	1	3	1	0	0	1	2	0	0	1	2	0	0	.333	.333
Cipriano, Cody	R-R	6-0	200	1-7-85	.271	.250	.278	59	214	43	58	8	4	6	29	35	5	1	3	63	10	2	.430	.381
Colon, Kevin	R-R	5-11	165	7-6-84	.227	.192	.236	43	132	17	30	1	0	0	8	6	1	2	0	23	1	1	.235	.266
De Leon, Epifanio	R-R	6-5	205	1-5-86	.094	.167	.077	9	32	3	3	0	0	1	4	1	0	0	0	19	0	0	.188	.121
Fermin, Angel	R-R	6-2	190	10-30-85	.194	.216	.187	53	160	22	31	8	2	1	21	20	5	2	3	53	3	2	.288	.298
Fronk, Reid	L-R	6-1	185	7-21-86	.311	.324	.307	37	122	28	38	14	1	5	27	15	2	1	0	30	5	1	.566	.396
Humphrey, Ben	R-R	6-4	225	4-15-84	.238	.200	.250	5	21	5	5	1	1	1	3	1	0	0	0	8	0	1	.524	.273
Loyola, Maiko	R-R	5-11	174	7-19-85	.307	.348	.292	44	176	37	54	8	6	4	29	21	0	2	0	38	19	3	.489	.381
Luna, Omar	R-R	5-11	165	12-13-86	.265	.125	.293	13	49	5	13	1	0	0	3	2	0	0	0	7	2	2	.286	.294
Matthews, Brad	B-R	6-0	175	6-8-83	.154	.000	.190	11	26	5	4	1	0	1	4	2	1	0	1	5	1	0	.308	.233
Mayer, James	R-R	5-11	165	3-8-84	.287	.438	.256	36	94	12	27	4	1	0	8	5	3	4	2	10	2	3	.351	.337
McCormick, Michael	R-R	6-2	200	9-6-86	.276	.321	.262	67	239	35	66	20	1	8	44	27	2	0	2	66	3	5	.469	.352
O'Malley, Shawn	R-R	5-10	155	12-28-87	.242	.298	.219	48	161	21	39	6	4	0	10	20	5	7	0	40	12	3	.329	.344
Paxton, Ian	R-R	6-1	210	9-4-83	.210	.125	.222	20	62	6	13	5	0	0	5	5	1	0	0	11	0	0	.290	.279
Pickerell, Steven	R-R	6-3	215	2-5-82	.130	.400	.056	7	23	2	3	0	0	0	1	4	1	0	0	9	1	0	.130	.286
Salem, Emeel	L-L	6-0	180	2-11-85	.311	.400	.282	58	225	41	70	11	7	1	23	24	4	2	2	27	28	4	.436	.384
Sexton, Gregory	R-R	6-2	205	2-8-85	.256	.277	.250	57	215	28	55	6	2	4	27	15	6	0	3	27	3	3	.358	.318
Vogt, Stephen	L-R	6-0	215	11-1-84	.300	.333	.288	70	240	40	72	8	0	4	48	31	0	1	7	31	6	1	.383	.371
Williams, Shawn	R-R	6-2	190	9-18-83	.239	.143	.256	17	46	4	11	5	0	0	8	6	0	1	1	11	0	1	.348	.321
Wrigley, Henry	R-R	6-3	180	8-9-86	.235	.264	.226	67	243	28	57	10	3	3	33	20	4	0	2	37	10	3	.337	.301

PITCHING	B-T	HT	WT	DOB	W	L	ERA	G	GS	CG	SV	IP	H	R	ER	HR	BB	SO	AVG	vLH	vRH	K/9	BB/9
Baird, John	R-R	6-4	220	5-16-86	1	1	5.50	7	2	0	1	18	24	15	11	1	8	15	.320	.371	.275	7.50	4.00
Barnett, Travis	R-R	6-7	215	10-2-83	1	0	4.33	19	0	0	0	27	27	15	13	2	12	31	.257	.268	.250	10.33	4.00
Boggan, Kevin	R-R	6-2	195	5-2-85	0	0	1.33	14	1	0	7	27	16	6	4	0	9	28	.162	.222	.111	9.33	3.00
Booth, Noah	L-L	6-1	240	8-1-84	0	3	4.76	18	0	0	4	23	22	13	12	5	6	26	.256	.346	.217	10.32	2.38
Cobb, Alexander	R-R	6-1	180	10-7-87	5	6	3.54	16	16	0	0	81	78	36	32	4	31	62	.259	.265	.253	6.86	3.45
Cuevas, Aneudi	R-R	6-1	182	10-6-81	0	0	0.00	6	0	0	0	6	5	4	0	0	3	3	.208	.143	.235	4.50	4.50
Darcy, Jesse	R-R	6-4	205	6-13-85	6	5	4.35	14	12	0	0	62	63	38	30	4	15	50	.260	.259	.262	7.26	2.18
Della Grotta, Robert	R-R	6-2	220	9-18-84	0	2	6.30	19	0	0	0	30	28	26	21	2	16	21	.248	.240	.254	6.30	4.80
Echeverria, Diego	R-R	5-11	190	1-1-85	4	8	7.10	14	14	0	0	65	76	58	51	5	32	24	.309	.333	.287	3.34	4.45
Florentino, Bladimir	R-R	6-2	187	9-20-84	1	0	5.40	19	0	0	0	22	18	13	13	0	14	31	.220	.222	.217	12.88	5.82
Flores, Brian	L-L	5-10	190	1-1-85	2	3	5.57	15	3	0	1	32	34	24	20	1	12	31	.262	.159	.314	8.63	3.34
Garcia, Justin	R-R	6-1	195	12-14-86	0	0	2.25	4	0	0	0	8	5	2	2	0	1	8	.172	.167	.176	9.00	1.12
Johnson, Joshua	R-R	6-0	180	10-6-84	5	2	3.38	14	12	0	0	64	53	25	24	10	18	45	.221	.265	.188	6.33	2.53
Ragan, Jason	B-R	6-0	175	12-12-82	5	4	2.80	11	11	0	0	64	53	25	20	4	22	36	.224	.272	.193	5.04	3.08
Rodriguez, Claudio	R-R	6-5	244	6-29-83	0	2	6.03	19	1	0	0	31	37	22	21	2	10	26	.291	.286	.297	7.47	2.87
Suchowiecki, Mark	R-L	6-1	195	2-22-83	1	3	4.82	20	0	0	0	28	26	19	15	2	17	22	.248	.324	.206	7.07	5.46
Waechter, Doug	R-R	6-4	225	1-28-81	2	1	1.42	4	4	1	0	19	16	5	3	1	0	12	.216	.172	.244	5.68	0.00
Zimmerman, Ryan	R-R	6-0	185	9-19-84	1	0	2.23	19	0	0	1	32	36	14	8	2	8	16	.290	.353	.247	4.45	2.23

FIELDING

Catcher	PCT	G	PO	A	E	DP	PB
McCormick	.984	58	385	44	7	5	11
Paxton	.983	17	95	18	2	1	2
Pickerell	1.000	1	5	1	0	0	0
Vogt	1.000	4	19	3	0	0	1
Williams	1.000	1	2	0	0	0	0

First Base	PCT	G	PO	A	E	DP
Humphrey	.952	2	19	1	1	0
Vogt	1.000	7	59	7	0	7
Williams	.968	6	56	4	2	2
Wrigley	.982	62	512	35	10	37

Second Base	PCT	G	PO	A	E	DP
Cipriano	.972	53	95	116	6	29

	PCT	G	PO	A	E	DP
Colon	.946	11	22	31	3	3
Matthews	1.000	8	10	16	0	1
Mayer	1.000	7	16	20	0	2

Third Base	PCT	G	PO	A	E	DP
Carroll	1.000	3	0	11	0	0
Colon	.947	9	4	14	1	2
Matthews	1.000	1	0	1	0	0
Mayer	.923	5	3	9	1	1
Sexton	.926	52	40	111	12	7
Williams	1.000	3	2	7	0	1
Wrigley	.846	6	3	8	2	0

Shortstop	PCT	G	PO	A	E	DP
Colon	.871	20	29	52	12	7

	PCT	G	PO	A	E	DP
Luna	.984	13	19	41	1	8
Mayer	1.000	1	3	1	0	0
O'Malley	.954	44	70	118	9	21

Outfield	PCT	G	PO	A	E	DP
De Leon	.900	9	17	1	2	0
Fermin	.830	38	37	2	8	0
Fronk	1.000	33	51	2	0	1
Loyola	.964	43	77	3	3	1
Mayer	1.000	7	12	0	0	0
Salem	.975	58	114	2	3	2
Vogt	.990	55	97	4	1	0
Williams	—	1	0	0	0	0

PRINCETON DEVIL RAYS   *ROOKIE*

APPALACHIAN LEAGUE

BATTING	B-T	HT	WT	DOB	AVG	vLH	vRH	G	AB	R	H	2B	3B	HR	RBI	BB	HBP	SH	SF	SO	SB	CS	SLG	OBP
Acosta, Mayobanex	R-R	6-1	205	11-20-87	.234	.211	.244	38	124	12	29	10	0	1	11	12	2	2	0	33	2	2	.339	.312
Arhart, Josh	R-R	6-1	240	9-13-79	.333	.500	.250	3	6	3	2	1	0	0	2	3	0	0	0	0	0	0	.500	.556
Biell, Dustin	L-R	6-0	175	3-19-89	.218	.231	.213	49	179	26	39	7	2	0	20	13	3	1	2	56	7	5	.279	.279
Carroll, Jeff	R-R	6-2	192	8-14-84	.251	.305	.230	59	211	27	53	13	2	0	27	20	4	1	2	37	2	2	.332	.325
Edwards, Jared	R-R	6-3	210	12-11-86	.216	.195	.224	41	139	14	30	8	2	2	17	12	2	1	2	53	11	3	.345	.284
Estrada, Robi	B-R	5-10	170	10-8-88	.232	.262	.221	44	155	20	36	6	0	1	11	16	0	1	1	31	5	3	.290	.302
Humphrey, Ben	R-R	6-4	225	4-15-84	.236	.213	.246	56	195	22	46	13	3	4	28	25	6	0	3	61	7	3	.395	.336
Kang, Kyeong	L-L	6-2	200	2-6-88	.276	.277	.276	55	203	25	56	14	4	3	22	20	0	1	0	44	3	3	.429	.341
Luna, Omar	R-R	5-11	165	12-13-86	.289	.258	.301	58	232	30	67	13	3	2	26	12	2	2	1	36	10	5	.397	.328
Mollicone, John	R-R	6-1	220	9-9-85	.256	.250	.259	17	39	5	10	1	0	1	4	6	0	0	0	8	0	1	.359	.356
Reynolds, Justin	R-R	6-2	195	11-13-86	.270	.309	.256	64	215	32	58	11	2	4	16	23	2	3	2	51	16	6	.395	.343
Ross, Michael	B-R	5-8	180	8-11-86	.258	.209	.278	57	225	39	58	6	5	1	17	25	4	2	0	48	36	6	.342	.343
Rousseve, Brandon	R-R	6-1	175	8-4-84	.000	—	.000	1	3	0	0	0	0	0	0	0	0	0	0	2	0	0	.000	.000
Scholzen, Jimmy	R-R	6-2	165	8-2-85	.162	.128	.179	43	142	14	23	4	1	1	17	15	2	2	2	34	6	1	.225	.248
Sonoqui, Eli	L-L	6-2	195	1-20-88	.333	.471	.286	19	66	10	22	5	2	1	14	6	0	0	1	20	3	0	.515	.384
Thomas, Mark	R-R	6-1	180	5-5-88	.276	.344	.247	33	105	16	29	12	0	5	24	7	3	1	2	28	2	3	.533	.333

PITCHING	B-T	HT	WT	DOB	W	L	ERA	G	GS	CG	SV	IP	H	R	ER	HR	BB	SO	AVG	vLH	vRH	K/9	BB/9
Andujar, Chris	R-R	6-2	180	8-24-87	0	4	6.56	12	11	0	0	47	64	41	34	0	22	27	.335	.315	.343	5.21	4.24
Ayers, Kyle	R-R	6-4	220	9-6-89	3	3	3.86	13	2	0	2	37	32	17	16	3	10	26	.224	.268	.206	6.27	2.41
Barnese, Nick	R-R	6-2	170	1-11-89	2	2	3.22	9	8	0	0	36	30	19	13	1	4	37	.216	.250	.198	9.17	0.99
Boggan, Kevin	R-R	6-2	195	5-2-85	0	0	0.00	3	0	0	0	8	5	0	0	1	7		.185	.222	.167	8.22	1.17
Brophy, Kevin	R-R	5-11	190	2-27-85	0	0	4.60	12	0	0	0	16	12	10	8	0	17	8	.226	.095	.313	4.60	9.77
Chapa, Angel	R-R	6-2	170	6-14-87	0	2	3.52	17	0	0	2	31	33	12	12	2	11	29	.277	.275	.278	8.51	3.23
Chavez, Kevin	R-R	6-3	206	6-24-89	2	1	8.38	5	0	0	0	10	8	10	9	1	9	7	.216	.071	.304	6.52	8.38
Cruz, Joseph	R-R	6-4	190	7-20-88	2	0	0.00	3	0	0	0	9	5	0	0	3	13		.161	.000	.192	13.00	3.00
De La Cruz, Jose	L-L	5-11	173	8-16-87	0	2	8.66	8	4	0	0	18	21	21	17	3	25	21	.309	.400	.283	10.70	12.74
De Los Santos, Frank	L-L	6-0	165	11-17-87	4	5	3.64	13	13	0	0	64	64	30	26	5	16	43	.257	.324	.245	6.02	2.24
Dettrich, Julius	L-L	6-4	175	9-23-88	0	0	27.00	2	0	0	0	2	4	5	5	1	0	1	.500	1.000	.429	5.40	0.00
Fessler, Christopher	R-R	6-3	200	11-21-84	4	0	2.63	18	0	0	4	27	18	11	8	2	9	20	.189	.294	.131	6.59	2.96
Fisher, Matthew	R-R	6-2	195	9-6-83	0	1	8.10	4	0	0	0	7	10	10	6	2	8	8	.323	.556	.227	10.80	10.80
Garcia, Justin	R-R	6-1	195	12-14-86	1	1	2.84	17	0	0	4	25	20	10	8	1	6	24	.208	.259	.188	8.53	2.13
Hall, Jeremy	R-R	6-3	200	9-16-83	4	1	1.56	12	12	0	0	69	62	15	12	4	11	59	.242	.226	.250	7.66	1.43
Hayes, Tyree	R-R	6-0	175	8-8-88	4	7	4.64	13	13	0	0	66	73	43	34	4	24	41	.278	.273	.280	5.59	3.27
Hinkle, Austin	R-R	6-1	200	5-24-86	4	2	1.64	10	2	0	1	33	22	8	6	0	8	27	.186	.185	.188	7.36	2.18
Humphrey, Ben	R-R	6-4	225	4-15-84	0	0	36.00	1	0	0	0	1	4	4	4	1	1	0	.667	.000	.667	0.00	9.00
Luck, Chris	R-R	6-3	175	7-10-89	3	1	2.17	13	0	0	0	37	30	15	9	1	12	43	.217	.229	.214	10.37	2.89
Mollicone, John	R-R	6-1	220	9-9-85	0	0	0.00	1	0	0	0	1	1	0	0	0	0	0	.250	.000	.250	0.00	0.00
Moore, Matthew	L-L	6-2	205	6-18-89	0	0	2.66	8	3	0	0	20	12	6	6	1	16	29	.160	.154	.161	12.84	7.08
Southern, Michael	R-R	6-1	190	1-8-87	0	3	2.45	19	0	0	6	22	25	16	6	1	9	26	.269	.280	.265	10.64	3.68

FIELDING

Catcher	PCT	G	PO	A	E	DP	PB
Acosta	.983	38	256	27	5	0	8
Arhart	1.000	3	13	2	0	0	0
Mollicone	1.000	13	63	3	0	0	0
Thomas	.956	24	169	26	9	1	7

First Base	PCT	G	PO	A	E	DP
Carroll	.985	14	122	6	2	4
Humphrey	.983	33	328	12	6	17
Mollicone	1.000	1	2	0	0	1
Scholzen	1.000	6	38	4	0	4

	PCT	G	PO	A	E	DP
Sonoqui	.994	19	162	5	1	19

Second Base	PCT	G	PO	A	E	DP
Luna	1.000	7	12	15	0	2
Ross	.940	46	84	121	13	21
Rousseve	1.000	1	1	0	0	0
Scholzen	.949	17	20	54	4	10

Third Base	PCT	G	PO	A	E	DP
Carroll	.911	46	28	105	13	10
Luna	.956	17	7	36	2	0
Scholzen	.882	10	10	20	4	0

Shortstop	PCT	G	PO	A	E	DP
Estrada	.899	38	38	104	16	14
Luna	.918	32	55	101	14	20

Outfield	PCT	G	PO	A	E	DP
Biell	.962	49	93	7	4	2
Edwards	.988	41	76	4	1	2
Humphrey	1.000	10	12	1	0	0
Kang	.843	43	42	1	8	0
Reynolds	.946	64	105	1	6	0

DSL DEVIL RAYS

DOMINICAN SUMMER LEAGUE

BATTING	B-T	HT	WT	DOB	AVG	vLH	vRH	G	AB	R	H	2B	3B	HR	RBI	BB	HBP	SH	SF	SO	SB	CS	SLG	OBP
Cipriota, Jacinto	R-R	5-11	180	3-23-90	.223	.156	.243	43	139	14	31	5	1	1	11	14	6	0	2	27	5	2	.295	.317
Contreras, Ruben	B-R	6-2	190	8-18-87	.177	.140	.188	53	181	17	32	6	1	1	15	26	2	1	2	50	9	5	.238	.284
Cuello, Juan	R-R	5-11	170	5-9-89	.247	.286	.235	50	178	31	44	7	2	0	15	13	5	4	1	23	10	6	.309	.315
Dorville, Edward	B-R	6-1	185	11-5-88	.200	.200	.200	34	60	10	12	2	1	0	4	7	4	1	0	28	5	1	.267	.324
Echavarria, Nelson	B-R	6-1	160	9-26-88	.111	.200	.097	12	36	3	4	0	1	0	1	3	1	1	0	18	0	0	.167	.200
Francisco, Tomas	R-R	6-0	210	4-4-88	.233	.237	.232	44	150	16	35	6	1	1	14	10	6	1	0	23	0	0	.307	.307
Gomez, Hector	L-L	5-2	187	2-13-88	.251	.190	.272	62	231	34	58	10	2	8	40	22	0	2	2	60	7	7	.416	.314
Gomez, Jhonatan	R-R	6-1	180	11-13-88	.171	.133	.184	39	117	10	20	3	0	0	10	14	1	1	1	37	3	0	.197	.263
Guerrero, Jorge	R-R	6-0	170	9-12-88	.243	.302	.216	39	140	16	34	6	0	0	7	13	3	0	1	38	4	2	.286	.321
Guillen, Cesar	R-R	6-1	185	3-15-89	.215	.109	.248	57	195	27	42	7	0	1	19	35	3	1	1	38	11	8	.267	.342
Isenia, Ludson	B-R	6-1	206	11-24-89	.183	.111	.207	39	109	7	20	5	0	1	10	14	0	1	1	45	2	2	.257	.274
Luis, Diogenes	B-R	5-10	169	5-7-87	.258	.261	.257	29	97	17	25	3	2	1	8	12	4	5	1	20	8	2	.361	.360
Montero, Juan	R-R	6-2	165	10-5-85	.118	.000	.133	9	17	1	2	1	0	0	2	3	0	0	0	6	2	0	.176	.250
Novas, Ramon	R-R	6-2	170	10-14-87	.313	.327	.309	65	233	33	73	11	1	6	33	15	2	1	2	47	10	2	.446	.357
Olivares, Gerardo	R-R	6-0	187	8-14-88	.260	.245	.265	56	196	27	51	10	1	1	21	14	6	1	2	27	3	1	.337	.326
Paredes, Salvador	R-R	6-1	170	6-16-84	.208	.286	.188	55	168	35	35	13	0	7	34	29	7	3	0	56	12	3	.411	.348

PITCHING	B-T	HT	WT	DOB	W	L	ERA	G	GS	CG	SV	IP	H	R	ER	HR	BB	SO	AVG	vLH	vRH	K/9	BB/9
Almonte, Wilmer	R-R	5-11	164	8-19-89	0	1	4.91	3	2	0	0	7	6	4	4	1	2	9	.207	.182	.222	11.05	2.45
Amargos, Jordi	R-R	5-11	165	2-5-86	0	2	3.65	16	4	0	0	37	27	19	15	3	21	28	.201	.154	.221	6.81	5.11
Blanco, Juan	R-R	6-1	170	4-27-87	1	1	4.08	12	0	0	0	18	16	9	8	1	9	19	.232	.190	.250	9.68	4.58
Colome, Alexander	R-R	6-2	184	12-31-88	1	6	2.97	14	11	0	0	39	30	18	13	1	31	50	.208	.265	.179	11.44	7.09
De La Cruz, Jose	L-L	5-11	173	8-16-87	0	0	6.43	3	3	0	0	7	13	9	5	0	0	10	.361	.500	.353	12.86	0.00
Duenas, Carlos	L-L	5-11	165	12-28-87	3	2	4.27	16	3	0	0	53	40	31	25	2	37	48	.211	.158	.216	8.20	6.32
Galan, Genaro	L-L	6-2	196	1-20-88	0	3	7.62	13	8	0	0	28	26	31	24	0	34	43	.234	.238	.233	13.66	10.80
Hernandez, Alexis	R-R	6-3	167	3-14-89	1	0	10.50	7	0	0	0	6	10	8	7	0	4	2	.385	.400	.375	3.00	6.00
Jasco, Joselo	R-R	6-0	170	10-12-88	1	0	5.40	15	0	0	0	20	13	17	12	0	26	17	.186	.185	.186	7.65	11.70
Marte, Luis	R-R	6-1	163	12-15-86	2	1	1.17	28	0	0	12	31	21	6	4	0	6	28	.193	.083	.247	8.22	1.76
Martinez, Carlos	R-R	5-11	160	7-15-89	1	2	6.43	6	5	0	0	14	12	11	10	0	16	6	.240	.333	.172	3.86	10.29
Mateo, Victor	R-R	6-5	180	7-27-89	0	2	6.39	15	1	0	0	38	44	45	27	3	25	27	.295	.382	.245	6.39	5.92
Mavares, Deivis	R-R	5-11	156	9-19-86	3	1	4.65	19	0	0	0	31	20	23	16	2	31	41	.187	.132	.217	11.90	9.00
Mercedes, Aneuris	R-R	6-0	180	5-1-87	1	1	3.97	8	1	0	0	23	17	14	10	0	17	18	.213	.125	.271	7.15	6.75
Monegro, Jose	R-R	6-2	180	3-22-90	1	2	4.06	16	6	0	0	51	55	36	23	6	13	35	.270	.268	.271	6.18	2.29
Montero, Juan	R-R	6-2	165	10-5-85	0	0	3.48	6	0	0	0	10	7	4	4	0	7	8	.194	.143	.227	6.97	6.10
Mujica, Juan	L-L	5-10	185	3-21-90	1	3	7.04	7	3	0	0	15	5	14	12	0	22	14	.106	.000	.135	8.22	12.91
Ozoria, Ronny	R-R	6-3	185	6-5-89	3	5	9.51	20	0	0	0	24	20	32	25	0	38	18	.227	.240	.222	6.85	14.45
Paredes, Salvador	R-R	6-1	170	6-16-84	1	0	9.53	3	0	0	0	6	9	6	6	1	1	9	.333	.222	.389	14.29	1.59
Reyes, Robinson	L-L	6-4	200	11-15-88	0	6	9.33	14	11	0	0	27	20	36	28	1	45	22	.200	.231	.195	7.33	15.00
Santana, Juan	R-R	6-0	180	3-5-86	3	4	1.05	15	3	0	0	43	25	10	5	1	13	57	.169	.182	.161	12.02	2.74
Silfa, Raymond	L-L	6-0	170	5-1-88	0	1	1.69	3	2	0	0	11	6	5	2	0	4	6	.162	.200	.156	5.06	3.38
Wilsino, Juan	R-R	6-3	190	3-22-89	1	3	3.47	15	7	0	0	49	44	23	19	2	16	35	.237	.212	.250	6.39	2.92

FIELDING

Catcher	PCT	G	PO	A	E	DP	PB
Francisco	.979	33	241	37	6	2	8
J. Gomez	.975	22	137	16	4	2	13
Olivares	.968	22	156	27	6	1	3

First Base	PCT	G	PO	A	E	DP
Dorville	1.000	1	1	0	0	0
H. Gomez	.971	21	155	11	5	17
J. Gomez	.980	11	85	12	2	5
Guillen	.980	41	329	14	7	32
Paredes	.818	1	8	1	2	2

Second Base	PCT	G	PO	A	E	DP
Cipriota	.974	39	66	82	4	19

	PCT	G	PO	A	E	DP
Cuello	.955	6	11	10	1	0
Guerrero	.945	28	60	78	8	18
Paredes	1.000	2	3	1	0	0

Third Base	PCT	G	PO	A	E	DP
Cuello	.846	8	5	6	2	2
Francisco	.960	8	6	18	1	2
Guerrero	.957	8	5	17	1	3
Paredes	.955	52	62	129	9	13

Shortstop	PCT	G	PO	A	E	DP
Cuello	.883	33	53	75	17	14
Echavarria	.818	11	14	22	8	4
Guerrero	.909	2	7	3	1	1

	PCT	G	PO	A	E	DP
Luis	.938	29	44	77	8	18

Outfield	PCT	G	PO	A	E	DP
Contreras	.976	53	80	3	2	0
Dorville	.926	24	23	2	2	0
H. Gomez	.904	42	44	3	5	1
Guillen	.917	8	11	0	1	0
Isenia	.833	28	29	1	6	1
Luis	—	1	0	0	0	0
Montero	1.000	9	9	1	0	0
Novas	.969	64	85	8	3	1

VSL REDS/DEVIL RAYS

VENEZUELAN SUMMER LEAGUE (STATISTICS FOR THIS TEAM ARE ON PAGE 103)

Texas Rangers

BY EVAN GRANT

Saddled with starting pitching problems, the Rangers straggled to a losing record and a second-division finish in the AL West in 2007.

Despite the presence of a new manager and promises of new approaches, the Rangers still failed to get quality starting pitching. The rotation helped the Rangers' dig a hole that had them 19 games under .500 by mid June. Though the second half was modestly better, the Rangers' rotation posted an AL-worst 5.50 ERA (it ranked 29th of 30 teams in the majors).

Texas' 2007 showing was on par with the team's performance this century. Since 2000, the Rangers have the worst rotation in baseball at 5.48. Texas has averaged 76 victories and finished third or last in the four-team AL West in each of the past eight seasons.

Every member of manager Ron Washington's Opening Day rotation either spent time on the DL or was demoted to the minors. Righthanders Kevin Millwood and Vincente Padilla, who each pitched 200 innings in 2006, failed to combine for 300 innings in 2007. Righthander Brandon McCarthy, acquired from the Chicago White Sox in an offseason deal, failed to have the breakout season the Rangers had hoped for, due largely to a number of health issues. Righthander Robinson Tejeda, whose 1.70 ERA over September and October in 2006 gave hope for a strong 2007, was banished to the minors by the all-star break and never did return.

The poor start led the Rangers to bid farewell to first baseman Mark Teixeira, perhaps the club's most successful first-round draft selection of all-time. Teixeira, who can be a free agent after the 2008 season, turned down an eight-year, $140 million contract offer and was dealt to Atlanta in a seven-player deal at the trading deadline.

The Rangers did seem to respond better to Washington's ministrations after the Teixeira deal. Despite an offense lacking in typical Texas punch, they climbed as close as five games of .500 in early September. That was one of the few highlights of the season. The others included: Sammy Sosa's 600th home run; the performance of a bullpen that featured a number of homegrown contributors, including righthander Joaquin Benoit and lefty C.J. Wilson; and the continued strong performance of shortstop Michael Young. Young, who was hitting .192 in early May, finished the season with a team-best .315 average and piled up 200 hits. It was his fifth consecutive .300 average, 200-hit season, joining Ichiro Suzuki as the only active players to have five consecutive 200-hit seasons.

The real highlight of the season for the Rangers, however, was not about performance, but rather about talent acquisition, particularly young talent.

In addition to trading Teixeira, the Rangers also dealt veteran outfielder Kenny Lofton and righthander Eric Gagne and brought back nine players, all 25-years-old or younger. The majority of the acquisitions were under the age of 21. The Rangers also had their biggest draft class since the draft was reduced to 50 rounds. Texas had two first-round selections, which it used on righthanders Blake Beavan and Michael Main. The Rangers had three more selections in the sandwich round, getting center fielder Julio Borbon, righthander Neil Ramirez and righthander Tommy Hunter. And the Latin American scouting program, headed up A.J. Preller produced a highly-regarded class.

By the time the Rangers reported to Instructional League, the sting of another losing season had worn off. There was excitement over the new acquisitions, including 17-year-old outfielder Engel Beltre (via the Red Sox), who slugged .583 in the Arizona League; 20 year-old Venezuelan shortstop Elvis Andrus (Braves), considered among the top shortstop prospects in the high Class A California League; 20-year-old Dominican lefthander Neftali Feliz (Braves), who struck out 27 in 15 innings with short-season Spokane; and 23-year-old Venezuelan catcher Max Ramirez (Indians), who hit in 12 of his first 13 games with high Class A Bakersfield.

All of them were at instructional league. Under the Arizona sun, they wore camp-issued T-shirts that proclaimed "The Future is Here."

2007 PERFORMANCE

General Manager: Jon Daniels. **Farm Director:** Jon Lombardo. **Scouting Director:** Ron Hopkins

Class	Team	League	W	L	PCT	Finish*	Manager	Affiliate Since
Majors	Texas	American	75	87	.463	10th (14)	Ron Washington	—
Triple-A	Oklahoma RedHawks	Pacific Coast	71	72	.497	10th (16)	Bobby Jones	1983
Double-A	Frisco RoughRiders	Texas	85	55	.607	1st (8)	Dave Anderson	2003
High A	Bakersfield Blaze	California	57	83	.407	9th (10)	Carlos Subero	2005
Low A	Clinton LumberKings	Midwest	70	67	.511	7th (14)	Mike Micucci	2003
Short-season	Spokane Indians	Northwest	33	42	.440	7th (8)	Andy Fox	2003
Rookie	AZL Rangers	Arizona	22	34	.393	8th (9)	Pedro Lopez	2003
Overall 2007 Minor League Record			**338**	**353**	**.489**	**18th**		

* Finish in overall standings (No. of teams in league) ^League champion

ORGANIZATION STATISTICS

TEXAS RANGERS

AMERICAN LEAGUE

BATTING	B-T	HT	WT	DOB	AVG	vLH	vRH	G	AB	R	H	2B	3B	HR	RBI	BB	HBP	SH	SF	SO	SB	CS	SLG	OBP
Blalock, Hank	L-R	6-1	200	11-21-80	.293	.298	.292	58	208	32	61	16	3	10	33	21	1	0	2	38	4	1	.543	.358
Botts, Jason	B-R	6-5	250	7-26-80	.240	.333	.208	48	167	19	40	8	1	2	14	19	3	0	1	59	1	0	.335	.326
Byrd, Marlon	R-R	6-0	235	8-30-77	.307	.327	.300	109	414	60	127	17	8	10	70	29	5	0	6	88	5	3	.459	.355
Catalanotto, Frank	L-R	6-0	195	4-27-74	.260	.231	.261	103	331	52	86	20	4	11	44	28	11	6	1	37	2	1	.444	.337
Cruz, Nelson	R-R	6-3	230	7-1-80	.235	.212	.245	96	307	35	72	15	2	9	34	21	2	1	1	87	2	4	.384	.287
Diaz, Victor	R-R	6-0	200	12-10-81	.240	.212	.269	37	104	13	25	4	0	9	25	1	2	0	1	33	0	0	.538	.259
Guzman, Freddy	B-R	5-10	165	1-20-81	.167	1.000	.000	8	6	2	1	0	0	1	1	0	0	0	0	2	0	1	.667	.167
Hairston Jr., Jerry	R-R	5-10	185	5-29-76	.189	.288	.150	73	159	22	30	7	0	3	16	11	3	7	4	24	5	1	.289	.249
Kata, Matt	B-R	6-1	185	3-14-78	.186	.097	.256	31	70	12	13	2	0	2	6	5	1	1	0	18	1	0	.300	.250
Kinsler, Ian	R-R	6-0	200	6-22-82	.263	.339	.239	130	483	96	127	22	2	20	61	62	9	8	4	83	23	2	.441	.355
Laird, Gerald	R-R	6-1	225	11-13-79	.224	.239	.218	120	407	48	91	18	3	9	47	30	2	5	4	103	6	2	.349	.278
Lofton, Kenny	L-L	5-11	190	5-31-67	.303	.221	.325	84	317	62	96	16	3	7	23	39	2	2	3	28	21	4	.438	.380
2-team (52 Cleveland)					.296	—		136	490	86	145	26	4	7	38	56	2	6	5	51	23	7	.414	.367
Mahar, Kevin	R-R	6-5	220	6-8-81	.167	.222	.111	7	18	2	3	1	0	0	1	0	0	0	0	7	0	0	.222	.167
Melhuse, Adam	B-R	6-2	210	3-27-72	.206	.240	.186	23	68	6	14	3	0	1	7	3	1	1	0	18	0	0	.294	.250
2-team (12 Oakland)					.213	—		35	94	8	20	4	0	1	9	7	1	1	0	26	0	0	.287	.275
Metcalf, Travis	R-R	6-3	215	8-17-82	.255	.237	.265	57	161	25	41	12	1	5	21	13	0	5	2	41	0	1	.435	.307
Murphy, David	L-L	6-4	215	10-18-81	.340	.400	.325	43	103	16	35	12	1	2	14	7	0	0	0	19	0	0	.534	.382
2-team (3 Boston)					.343	—		46	105	17	36	12	2	2	14	7	0	0	0	20	0	0	.552	.384
Quiroz, Guillermo	R-R	6-1	200	11-29-81	.400	.500	.375	9	10	1	4	1	0	0	2	1	0	0	0	2	0	0	.500	.455
Relaford, Desi	B-R	5-9	185	9-16-73	.115	.100	.125	14	26	2	3	0	0	0	2	0	0	0	0	6	0	1	.115	.179
Saltalamacchia, Jarrod	B-R	6-4	195	5-2-85	.251	.130	.298	46	167	28	42	7	1	7	21	9	0	0	4	47	0	0	.431	.290
Sosa, Sammy	R-R	6-0	225	11-12-68	.252	.328	.222	114	412	53	104	24	1	21	92	34	3	0	5	112	0	0	.468	.311
Stewart, Chris	R-R	6-4	210	2-19-82	.243	.400	.219	17	37	4	9	2	0	0	3	3	0	3	0	6	0	0	.297	.300
Teixeira, Mark	B-R	6-3	220	4-11-80	.297	.372	.269	78	286	48	85	24	1	13	49	45	3	0	1	66	0	0	.524	.397
Vazquez, Ramon	L-R	5-11	170	8-21-76	.230	.184	.246	104	300	42	69	13	3	8	28	29	2	12	2	72	1	0	.373	.300
Wilkerson, Brad	L-L	6-0	205	6-1-77	.234	.258	.224	119	338	54	79	17	1	20	62	43	1	3	4	107	4	1	.467	.319
Young, Michael	R-R	6-1	200	10-19-76	.315	.309	.316	156	639	80	201	37	1	9	94	47	5	0	1	107	13	3	.418	.366

PITCHING	B-T	HT	WT	DOB	W	L	ERA	G	GS	CG	SV	IP	H	R	ER	HR	BB	SO	AVG	vLH	vRH	K/9	BB/9
Benoit, Joaquin	R-R	6-3	220	7-26-77	7	4	2.85	70	0	0	6	82	68	28	26	6	28	87	.225	.172	.268	9.55	3.07
Chen, Bruce	L-L	6-1	215	6-19-77	0	0	7.20	5	0	0	0	10	11	11	8	3	6	7	.275	.400	.233	6.30	5.40
Eyre, Willie	R-R	6-2	205	7-21-78	4	6	5.16	33	2	0	1	68	78	42	39	8	32	42	.291	.248	.323	5.56	4.24
Feldman, Scott	L-R	6-5	210	2-7-83	1	2	5.77	29	0	0	0	39	44	26	25	3	32	19	.284	.316	.265	4.38	7.38
Francisco, Frank	R-R	6-2	235	9-11-79	1	1	4.55	59	0	0	0	59	57	33	30	3	38	49	.258	.221	.286	7.43	5.76
Gabbard, Kason	L-L	6-3	205	4-8-82	2	1	5.58	8	8	0	0	40	40	25	25	5	23	26	.265	.316	.248	5.80	5.13
2-team (7 Boston)					6	4	4.65	15	15	1	0	81	68	42	42	8	41	55	—	—	—	6.09	4.54
Gagne, Eric	R-R	6-0	240	1-7-76	2	0	2.16	34	0	0	16	33	23	8	8	2	12	29	.192	.155	.226	7.83	3.24
2-team (20 Boston)					4	2	3.81	54	0	0	16	52	49	22	22	3	21	51	—	—	—	8.83	3.63
Galarraga, Armando	R-R	6-4	180	1-15-82	0	0	6.23	3	1	0	0	9	8	6	6	2	7	6	.250	.263	.231	6.23	7.27
Koronka, John	L-L	6-1	180	7-3-80	0	2	7.84	2	2	0	0	10	16	9	9	0	5	2	.372	.250	.400	1.74	4.35
Littleton, Wes	R-R	6-2	210	9-2-82	3	2	4.31	35	0	0	2	48	48	23	23	6	16	24	.262	.236	.279	4.50	3.00
Loe, Kameron	R-R	6-7	240	9-10-81	6	11	5.36	28	23	0	0	136	162	96	81	13	56	78	.295	.328	.262	5.16	3.71
Mahay, Ron	L-L	6-2	190	6-28-71	2	0	2.77	28	0	0	1	39	33	12	12	3	21	32	.236	.250	.224	7.38	4.85
McCarthy, Brandon	R-R	6-7	200	7-7-83	5	10	4.87	23	22	0	0	102	111	62	55	9	48	59	.278	.292	.263	5.22	4.25
Mendoza, Luis	L-R	6-3	180	10-31-83	1	0	2.25	6	3	0	0	16	13	4	4	1	4	7	.232	.281	.167	3.94	2.25
Millwood, Kevin	R-R	6-4	230	12-24-74	10	14	5.16	31	31	0	0	173	213	111	99	19	67	123	.301	.288	.311	6.41	3.49
Murray, A.J.	B-L	6-3	220	3-17-82	1	2	4.50	14	2	0	0	28	25	15	14	6	15	18	.238	.308	.215	5.79	4.82
Otsuka, Akinori	R-R	6-0	210	1-13-72	2	1	2.51	34	0	0	4	32	26	10	9	1	6	21	.218	.172	.262	6.40	2.51
Padilla, Vicente	R-R	6-2	220	9-27-77	6	10	5.76	23	23	0	0	120	146	88	77	16	50	71	.299	.329	.271	5.31	3.74
Rheinecker, John	L-L	6-2	230	5-29-79	4	3	5.36	23	7	0	0	50	61	38	30	9	28	40	.295	.229	.328	7.15	5.01
Tejeda, Robinson	R-R	6-3	230	3-24-82	5	9	6.61	19	19	0	0	95	110	78	70	17	60	69	.290	.317	.264	6.51	5.66
Volquez, Edinson	R-R	6-0	200	7-3-83	2	1	4.50	6	6	0	0	34	34	18	17	4	15	29	.262	.222	.299	7.68	3.97
White, Bill	L-L	6-3	215	11-20-78	2	0	4.82	9	0	0	0	9	8	5	5	1	7	9	.242	.286	.211	8.68	6.75
Wilson, C.J.	L-L	6-1	215	11-18-80	2	1	3.03	66	0	0	12	68	50	25	23	4	33	63	.208	.112	.275	8.30	4.35
Wood, Mike	R-R	6-3	220	4-26-80	3	2	5.33	21	4	0	0	51	68	36	30	9	15	25	.321	.342	.296	4.44	2.66
Wright, Jamey	R-R	6-5	205	12-24-74	4	5	3.62	20	9	0	0	77	72	35	31	6	41	39	.259	.268	.253	4.56	4.79

FIELDING

Catcher	PCT	G	PO	A	E	DP	PB
Laird	.984	119	675	75	12	13	9
Melhuse	1.000	15	80	5	0	0	2
Quiroz	.926	8	25	0	2	0	0
Saltalamacchia	.985	22	127	5	2	1	0
Stewart	.981	17	99	5	2	3	3

First Base	PCT	G	PO	A	E	DP
Catalanotto	1.000	14	94	6	0	8
Kata	1.000	4	25	0	0	2
Saltalamacchia	.960	24	204	12	9	21
Teixeira	.998	74	614	47	1	74
Vazquez	1.000	7	31	0	0	3
Wilkerson	.994	68	497	19	3	51

Second Base	PCT	G	PO	A	E	DP
Hairston Jr.	1.000	16	25	41	0	12
Kata	.800	2	3	1	1	2

	PCT	G	PO	A	E	DP
Kinsler	.977	130	283	436	17	98
Relaford	1.000	12	11	27	0	6
Vazquez	1.000	13	18	32	0	9

Third Base	PCT	G	PO	A	E	DP
Blalock	.935	39	18	69	6	9
Hairston Jr.	.941	10	3	13	1	1
Kata	.833	7	3	7	2	0
Melhuse	1.000	5	0	12	0	1
Metcalf	.947	55	35	89	7	14
Vazquez	.960	71	46	123	7	17

Shortstop	PCT	G	PO	A	E	DP
Hairston Jr.	1.000	2	1	0	0	0
Kata	1.000	6	7	6	0	2
Vazquez	1.000	19	16	42	0	8
Young	.972	150	211	446	19	107

Outfield	PCT	G	PO	A	E	DP
Botts	1.000	28	62	1	0	0
Byrd	.987	109	223	9	3	5
Catalanotto	1.000	64	98	2	0	0
Cruz	.972	94	167	6	5	1
Diaz	.972	26	35	0	1	0
Guzman	1.000	4	5	0	0	0
Hairston Jr.	.974	49	73	3	2	0
Kata	1.000	10	12	2	0	1
Laird	—	1	0	0	0	0
Lofton	.985	80	186	5	3	3
Mahar	1.000	7	10	0	0	0
Murphy	.985	43	61	4	1	1
Relaford	—	2	0	0	0	0
Sosa	1.000	16	32	1	0	0
Wilkerson	.981	51	101	2	2	0

OKLAHOMA REDHAWKS   TRIPLE-A
PACIFIC COAST LEAGUE

ORGANIZATION STATISTICS

BATTING	B-T	HT	WT	DOB	AVG	vLH	vRH	G	AB	R	H	2B	3B	HR	RBI	BB	HBP	SH	SF	SO	SB	CS	SLG	OBP
Arias, Joaquin	R-R	6-1	165	9-21-84	.182	.000	.200	3	11	3	2	0	0	0	1	0	0	0	0	2	1	0	.182	.182
Botts, Jason	B-R	6-5	250	7-26-80	.320	.353	.304	102	369	69	118	36	4	13	78	81	1	0	8	102	0	1	.545	.436
Byrd, Marlon	R-R	6-0	235	8-30-77	.358	.364	.355	44	176	29	63	15	2	6	32	13	5	0	1	30	3	2	.568	.415
Catalanotto, Frank	L-R	6-0	195	4-27-74	.385	.429	.333	4	13	5	5	2	0	0	2	1	0	0	1	0	0	.538	.500
Cruz, Nelson	R-R	6-3	230	7-1-80	.352	.347	.354	44	162	32	57	9	1	15	45	21	2	0	2	34	1	2	.698	.428
Diaz, Victor	R-R	6-0	200	12-10-81	.321	.329	.318	69	271	39	87	15	2	14	65	21	3	0	4	81	3	0	.546	.371
Fox, Adam	R-R	5-11	200	11-23-81	.269	.179	.320	21	78	10	21	5	1	2	14	5	0	1	1	9	0	0	.436	.310
Gold, Nate	R-R	6-3	230	6-12-80	.292	.245	.312	122	469	74	137	25	1	26	103	40	4	0	9	104	0	0	.516	.347
Guzman, Freddy	B-R	5-10	165	1-20-81	.269	.304	.254	133	535	92	144	22	8	4	34	62	6	1	6	88	56	14	.363	.348
Hairston Jr., Jerry	R-R	5-10	185	5-29-76	.133	.250	.091	4	15	2	2	0	0	1	1	2	0	0	0	1	0	0	.333	.235
Hulett, Tug	L-R	5-10	185	2-28-83	.275	.257	.283	132	517	95	142	31	2	11	67	64	7	1	6	114	20	4	.406	.359
Kinsler, Ian	R-R	6-0	200	6-22-82	.385	.400	.375	3	13	1	5	0	0	0	3	0	0	0	1	2	0	.385	.357
Mahar, Kevin	R-R	6-5	220	6-8-81	.276	.350	.243	99	391	53	108	22	2	6	37	14	2	1	2	98	4	1	.389	.303
Matranga, Dave	R-R	6-0	185	1-8-77	.266	.291	.248	77	248	36	66	9	2	10	30	31	6	8	2	62	10	1	.440	.359
Metcalf, Travis	R-R	6-3	215	8-17-82	.148	.133	.152	18	61	2	9	3	0	0	6	7	0	1	1	17	0	0	.197	.232
Meyer, Drew	L-R	5-10	200	8-29-81	.213	.216	.213	72	225	28	48	11	0	1	10	27	1	1	0	44	2	3	.276	.300
Morban, Jose	B-R	6-1	170	10-2-79	.231	.200	.250	4	13	1	3	0	0	0	0	1	0	0	0	7	1	2	.231	.286
Murphy, David	L-L	6-4	215	10-18-81	.286	.500	.200	2	7	0	2	0	0	0	0	0	0	0	0	3	0	0	.286	.286
Ojeda, Miguel	R-R	6-1	230	1-29-75	.216	.300	.195	28	97	11	21	5	0	2	9	7	1	0	1	23	0	0	.330	.274
Quiroz, Guillermo	R-R	6-1	200	11-29-81	.266	.273	.264	71	259	22	69	16	0	6	33	15	1	1	2	52	0	0	.398	.307
Relaford, Desi	B-S	5-9	185	9-16-73	.266	.301	.249	88	316	45	84	17	2	6	52	41	3	2	2	54	6	0	.389	.354
Roth, Tony	R-R	6-0	175	10-20-82	.056	.000	.067	6	18	1	1	1	0	0	0	0	0	0	0	8	0	0	.111	.056
Stewart, Chris	R-R	6-4	210	2-19-82	.242	.255	.235	45	153	18	37	8	0	2	21	12	1	2	4	19	0	2	.333	.294
Trzesniak, Nick	R-R	6-0	210	11-19-80	.313	.333	.308	5	16	2	5	1	0	0	4	0	0	0	0	3	0	0	.375	.450
Vazquez, Ramon	L-R	5-11	170	8-21-76	.258	.158	.298	35	132	27	34	10	2	2	13	24	2	1	2	27	3	1	.409	.375
West, Kevin	R-R	6-2	225	1-1-80	.272	.271	.273	89	334	41	91	19	0	12	47	30	4	0	4	82	0	1	.437	.336

PITCHING	B-T	HT	WT	DOB	W	L	ERA	G	GS	CG	SV	IP	H	R	ER	HR	BB	SO	AVG	vLH	vRH	K/9	BB/9
Astacio, Ezequiel	R-R	6-3	200	11-4-79	3	5	5.50	31	2	0	2	52	48	39	32	5	12	56	.236	.322	.172	9.63	4.30
Baker, Chris	R-R	6-1	195	8-24-77	4	4	6.64	15	11	0	0	61	87	48	45	11	19	32	.340	.347	.333	4.72	2.68
Bumstead, Michael	R-R	6-4	210	7-8-77	0	2	11.47	14	0	0	0	24	42	33	31	6	17	18	.382	.400	.364	6.66	6.29
Chen, Bruce	L-L	6-1	215	6-19-77	1	1	5.63	4	4	0	0	16	17	11	10	3	3	12	.270	.192	.324	6.75	1.69
Cruceta, Francisco	R-R	6-2	215	7-4-81	3	0	3.02	25	5	0	1	66	38	25	22	2	40	70	.164	.161	.166	9.59	5.48
Eyre, Willie	R-R	6-2	205	7-21-78	1	0	0.00	5	0	0	1	7	2	0	0	0	1	8	.083	.000	.154	9.82	1.23
Feldman, Scott	L-R	6-5	210	2-7-83	1	1	4.50	21	0	0	2	30	28	18	15	1	12	24	.246	.255	.239	7.20	3.60
Francisco, Frank	R-R	6-2	235	9-11-79	1	0	0.00	5	0	0	2	6	0	0	0	0	3	14	.000	.000	.000	21.00	4.50
Galarraga, Armando	R-R	6-4	180	1-15-82	2	2	4.74	4	4	1	0	25	23	13	13	1	11	21	.237	.313	.163	7.66	4.01
German, Franklyn	R-R	6-7	260	1-20-80	2	2	3.49	47	0	0	7	59	44	28	23	5	46	72	.206	.179	.227	10.92	6.98
Hackman, Luther	R-R	6-4	195	10-6-74	0	1	2.25	4	0	0	0	4	3	1	1	0	3	2	.250	.250	.250	4.50	6.75
2-team (41 Nashville)					1	3	3.50	45	0	0	18	46	36	18	18	4	25	39	—	—	—	7.58	4.86
Hurley, Eric	R-R	6-4	195	9-17-85	4	7	4.91	13	13	0	0	73	65	45	40	13	28	59	.236	.164	.283	7.24	3.44
Koronka, John	L-L	6-1	180	7-3-80	6	4	4.41	14	14	0	0	84	88	45	41	9	37	53	.274	.260	.280	5.70	3.98
Lee, Derek	L-L	6-3	215	8-20-74	1	3	4.70	8	4	0	0	31	39	18	16	2	12	19	.315	.206	.356	5.58	3.52
Littleton, Wes	R-R	6-2	210	9-2-82	0	1	5.01	23	0	0	2	32	31	19	18	5	8	21	.258	.235	.275	5.85	2.23
Mahay, Ron	L-L	6-2	190	6-28-71	0	1	11.12	4	0	0	0	6	10	8	7	1	4	5	.370	.300	.412	7.94	6.35
Mathis, Douglas	R-R	6-3	220	6-7-83	0	3	10.66	3	2	0	0	13	21	16	15	2	6	8	.375	.385	.367	5.68	4.26
Matranga, Dave	R-R	6-0	185	1-8-77	0	0	9.00	1	0	0	0	1	2	1	1	1	0	0	.500	.000	.667	0.00	0.00
McCarthy, Brandon	R-R	6-7	200	7-7-83	0	0	0.00	1	1	0	0	4	3	0	0	0	0	6	.188	.143	.222	12.46	0.00
Murray, A.J.	B-L	6-3	220	3-17-82	3	3	3.08	41	1	0	5	53	42	19	18	2	25	51	.221	.253	.200	8.72	4.27
Redman, Mark	L-L	6-5	245	1-5-74	2	4	5.34	9	9	1	0	56	70	34	33	3	21	28	.315	.276	.329	4.53	3.40
2-team (2 Colorado Springs)					2	4	4.90	11	11	1	0	68	87	38	37	4	25	33	—	—	—	4.37	3.31
Relaford, Desi	B-R	5-9	185	9-16-73	0	0	0.00	1	0	0	0	2	1	1	0	0	1	0	.143	.143	.000	0.00	4.50
Rheinecker, John	L-L	6-2	230	5-29-79	4	2	3.57	9	9	0	0	58	59	26	23	4	12	30	.271	.239	.286	4.66	1.86
Rowe, Steven	R-R	6-4	210	7-17-80	6	4	6.78	35	4	0	0	72	88	54	54	13	26	46	.301	.256	.335	5.78	3.27
Rupe, Josh	R-R	6-2	210	8-18-82	2	2	4.62	7	7	0	0	37	39	20	19	4	14	20	.279	.316	.253	4.86	3.41
Shoemaker, Scott	R-R	6-4	210	9-21-81	0	1	5.87	7	1	0	0	15	17	11	10	3	1	8	.270	.243	.308	4.70	0.59
Simon, Alfredo	R-R	6-4	230	5-8-81	5	10	6.43	22	22	1	0	119	152	92	85	19	46	73	.315	.355	.274	5.52	3.48
Tejeda, Robinson	R-R	6-3	230	3-24-82	1	3	8.20	5	4	0	0	19	27	18	17	0	15	20	.346	.302	.400	9.64	7.23
Touchet, Danny	R-R	6-2	202	1-12-82	0	0	0.00	1	0	0	0	1	2	0	0	0	0	0	.400	.500	.000	0.00	0.00
Vasquez, Jorge	R-R	6-1	210	7-16-78	0	0	2.35	7	0	0	0	8	4	2	2	0	8	12	.160	.333	.105	14.09	9.39
Volquez, Edinson	R-R	6-0	200	7-3-83	6	1	1.41	8	8	0	0	51	25	8	8	0	21	66	.146	.139	.152	11.65	3.71

Name	B-T	HT	WT	DOB	W	L	ERA	G	GS	CG	SV	IP	H	R	ER	HR	BB	SO	AVG	vLH	vRH	K/9	BB/9
Wagner, Michael	R-R	6-1	190	12-17-84	0	0	0.00	1	0	0	0	1	1	0	0	0	1	2	.250	.250	.000	18.00	9.00
White, Bill	L-L	6-3	215	11-20-78	0	0	0.00	1	0	0	0	2	2	0	0	0	2	2	.250	.000	.400	10.80	10.80
Williams, Randy	L-L	6-3	195	9-18-75	2	1	3.98	34	0	0	0	43	40	20	19	6	13	39	.241	.277	.218	8.16	2.72
Wood, Mike	R-R	6-3	220	4-26-80	9	3	3.23	16	15	1	0	98	83	40	35	7	21	73	.232	.242	.220	6.73	1.94
Wright, Jamey	R-R	6-5	205	12-24-74	2	1	4.41	3	3	0	0	16	21	11	8	2	3	11	.304	.385	.256	6.06	1.65

FIELDING

Catcher	PCT	G	PO	A	E	DP	PB
Ojeda	1.000	27	167	9	0	0	4
Quiroz	.990	71	486	26	5	1	12
Stewart	.989	45	325	35	4	3	10
Trzesniak	.974	5	34	4	1	0	0

First Base	PCT	G	PO	A	E	DP
Gold	.987	122	1042	83	15	102
Matranga	1.000	3	23	1	0	2
Morban	1.000	1	6	0	0	0
Ojeda	1.000	1	11	0	0	1
West	1.000	20	169	9	0	19

Second Base	PCT	G	PO	A	E	DP
Hulett	.979	104	210	306	11	73
Kinsler	1.000	3	14	7	0	2
Matranga	1.000	8	19	21	0	7
Relaford	.959	16	31	39	3	9

	PCT	G	PO	A	E	DP
Vazquez	1.000	13	15	42	0	7

Third Base	PCT	G	PO	A	E	DP
Fox	.945	21	19	33	3	0
Hulett	1.000	9	7	15	0	1
Matranga	.979	16	16	31	1	4
Metcalf	1.000	18	12	46	0	7
Meyer	1.000	4	2	7	0	0
Morban	.750	3	1	2	1	0
Relaford	.910	66	33	119	15	9
Roth	1.000	1	1	0	0	0
Vazquez	1.000	1	1	0	0	0
West	.900	10	3	15	2	3

Shortstop	PCT	G	PO	A	E	DP
Arias	1.000	2	1	8	0	2
Hairston Jr.	.950	3	7	12	1	1
Hulett	.984	18	21	41	1	10

	PCT	G	PO	A	E	DP
Matranga	.969	41	43	115	5	27
Meyer	.977	62	64	188	6	32
Roth	1.000	5	3	8	0	2
Vazquez	.975	21	40	78	3	22

Outfield	PCT	G	PO	A	E	DP
Botts	.950	51	94	2	5	1
Byrd	.976	36	82	1	2	0
Cruz	.989	44	91	3	1	1
Diaz	1.000	43	52	2	0	0
Guzman	.993	129	300	5	2	1
Hairston Jr.	1.000	1	1	0	0	0
Mahar	.988	96	158	9	2	2
Meyer	1.000	2	1	0	0	0
Murphy	1.000	2	3	0	0	0
West	.979	34	44	2	1	0

FRISCO ROUGHRIDERS

DOUBLE-A

TEXAS LEAGUE

BATTING	B-T	HT	WT	DOB	AVG	vLH	vRH	G	AB	R	H	2B	3B	HR	RBI	BB	HBP	SH	SF	SO	SB	CS	SLG	OBP
Benjamin, Casey	L-R	6-2	190	8-1-80	.243	.289	.225	131	469	73	114	25	5	10	54	72	3	12	2	72	8	1	.382	.346
Berkery, Thomas	R-R	6-1	180	9-29-82	.167	.000	.211	7	24	1	4	0	0	0	1	1	0	1	1	6	0	0	.167	.192
Blalock, Jake	R-R	6-4	205	8-6-83	.170	.208	.130	16	47	3	8	1	1	0	9	4	1	0	2	11	0	0	.234	.241
2-team (30 Wichita)					.158	—	—	46	158	7	25	5	1	1	17	12	1	1	3	30	2	0	.222	.218
Boggs, Brandon	B-R	5-11	205	1-9-83	.266	.304	.247	104	354	69	94	21	4	19	55	70	1	0	4	103	10	4	.508	.385
Catalanotto, Frank	L-R	6-0	195	4-27-74	.000	—	.000	1	4	1	0	0	0	0	0	1	0	0	0	0	0	0	.000	.200
Davis, Chris	L-R	6-3	210	3-17-86	.294	.229	.324	30	109	21	32	7	0	12	25	13	1	0	1	27	0	0	.688	.371
Donovan, Todd	R-R	6-1	180	8-12-78	.254	.200	.271	16	63	11	16	1	2	0	5	9	1	0	0	10	6	3	.333	.356
Duran, German	R-R	5-10	185	8-3-84	.300	.338	.284	130	480	81	144	32	5	22	84	34	7	4	4	77	11	2	.525	.352
Fasano, Jim	L-R	6-5	230	7-20-83	.284	.167	.305	69	236	27	67	14	1	9	39	18	1	1	4	38	0	0	.466	.332
Fox, Adam	R-R	5-11	200	11-23-81	.277	.337	.241	80	274	38	76	12	3	6	28	19	5	5	2	54	5	4	.409	.333
Frostad, Emerson	L-R	6-1	210	1-13-83	.241	.226	.248	90	307	39	74	13	1	13	44	33	4	0	3	83	3	1	.417	.320
Furtado, Micah	L-R	5-7	170	6-9-82	.484	.273	.600	10	31	5	15	3	0	1	5	2	1	0	1	1	1	1	.677	.529
Hairston Jr., Jerry	R-R	5-10	185	5-29-76	.167	.000	.167	3	12	2	2	1	0	1	2	0	0	0	3	3	0	0	.500	.167
Harrison, Ben	R-R	6-4	203	9-18-81	.160	.167	.154	8	25	3	4	0	0	1	1	4	1	0	0	8	0	0	.280	.300
Mahar, Kevin	R-R	6-5	220	6-8-81	.242	.174	.265	25	91	14	22	2	1	3	14	11	6	0	0	23	3	0	.385	.361
Manriquez, Salomon	R-R	6-1	190	9-15-82	.275	.311	.255	71	247	34	68	12	0	16	53	25	1	0	3	56	0	1	.518	.341
Mayberry, John	R-R	6-6	230	12-21-83	.241	.225	.247	69	245	35	59	10	0	14	38	20	4	1	1	62	7	1	.453	.307
Metcalf, Travis	R-R	6-3	215	8-17-82	.280	.277	.281	55	200	38	56	18	0	7	34	21	1	0	4	44	2	1	.475	.345
Murphy, Steven	L-R	6-2	210	4-22-84	.277	.276	.277	130	488	70	135	33	3	11	66	28	5	2	6	103	5	4	.424	.319
Richardson, Kevin	R-R	6-3	230	9-12-80	.222	.212	.226	91	320	42	71	8	0	14	45	25	8	3	1	85	0	2	.378	.294
Roth, Tony	R-R	6-0	175	10-20-82	.139	.118	.158	22	36	5	5	2	0	1	3	0	0	0	9	0	0	.194	.205
Teagarden, Taylor	R-R	6-1	200	12-21-83	.294	.296	.293	29	102	19	30	3	0	7	16	10	1	0	2	39	0	0	.529	.357
Teixeira, Mark	B-R	6-3	220	4-11-80	.000	—	.000	1	2	0	0	0	0	0	0	2	0	0	0	0	0	0	.000	.500
Webster, Anthony	L-R	6-0	197	4-10-83	.277	.215	.296	105	411	66	114	25	3	8	39	21	6	3	3	55	30	11	.411	.320
West, Kevin	R-R	6-2	225	1-1-80	.297	.300	.296	11	37	5	11	1	0	2	6	4	1	0	1	8	0	0	.486	.372
Wilkerson, Brad	L-L	6-0	205	6-1-77	.300	.333	.000	3	10	3	3	2	1	0	0	4	0	0	1	0	0	0	.300	.429

PITCHING	B-T	HT	WT	DOB	W	L	ERA	G	GS	CG	SV	IP	H	R	ER	HR	BB	SO	AVG	vLH	vRH	K/9	BB/9
Baker, Chris	R-R	6-1	195	8-24-77	0	2	4.61	3	3	0	0	14	10	7	7	3	6	9	.200	.161	.263	5.93	3.95
Batista, Kendy	R-R	6-2	165	7-5-81	0	1	7.20	1	1	0	0	5	5	5	4	0	3	5	.278	.300	.250	9.00	5.40
Bumstead, Michael	R-R	6-4	210	7-8-77	1	0	8.10	6	0	0	0	7	6	6	6	4	6	8	.240	.250	.235	10.80	5.40
Chenard, Ken	R-R	6-3	195	8-30-78	3	8	6.42	34	8	0	2	69	78	50	49	10	44	90	.283	.267	.295	11.80	5.77
Farnum, Matt	R-R	6-2	195	6-1-81	3	2	4.50	15	0	0	0	20	18	11	10	1	12	15	.247	.324	.179	6.75	5.40
Fox, Adam	R-R	5-11	200	11-23-81	0	0	0.00	1	0	0	0	1	0	0	0	0	0	0	.000	.000	.000	0.00	0.00
Frostad, Emerson	L-R	6-1	210	1-13-83	0	0	9.00	2	0	0	0	2	2	2	2	1	0	0	.250	.250	.250	0.00	0.00
Gagne, Eric	R-R	6-0	240	1-7-76	0	1	3.38	3	2	0	0	3	2	1	1	1	1	3	.200	.333	.143	10.12	3.38
Galarraga, Armando	R-R	6-4	180	1-15-82	9	6	4.02	23	22	2	0	128	122	58	57	14	47	114	.255	.243	.264	8.04	3.31
Garr, Brennan	R-R	6-2	190	2-22-84	0	0	2.57	6	0	0	0	7	8	4	2	0	5	5	.267	.286	.250	6.43	12.86
Herrera, Daniel	L-L	5-8	145	10-21-84	5	2	3.78	34	0	0	0	52	43	24	22	3	20	64	.232	.246	.226	11.01	3.44
Hurley, Eric	R-R	6-4	195	9-17-85	7	2	3.25	15	14	1	0	89	71	39	32	13	27	76	.219	.217	.221	7.71	2.74
Ingram, Jesse	R-R	6-1	200	4-27-82	3	1	4.21	56	0	0	26	62	43	31	29	10	28	70	.191	.185	.195	10.16	4.06
Knippschild, Ryan	L-R	6-1	195	9-24-82	0	1	3.38	1	0	0	0	3	4	2	1	0	2	1	.308	.167	.429	3.38	6.75
Kometani, Paul	R-R	6-4	200	12-24-82	3	4	4.27	39	6	0	8	78	82	41	37	3	29	70	.268	.272	.264	8.08	3.35
Loe, Kameron	R-R	6-7	240	9-10-81	0	0	6.00	1	1	0	0	3	1	3	2	0	5	1	.100	.000	.167	3.00	15.00
Mahay, Ron	L-L	6-2	190	6-28-71	0	0	0.00	3	0	0	0	5	5	2	0	0	1	4	.263	.125	.364	7.71	1.93
Mathis, Douglas	R-R	6-3	200	6-7-83	11	7	3.76	22	22	1	0	132	140	59	55	7	40	93	.276	.279	.273	6.29	2.73
Mendoza, Luis	L-R	6-3	180	10-31-83	15	4	3.93	26	25	3	0	149	145	75	65	11	48	93	.255	.278	.235	5.63	2.91
Millwood, Kevin	R-R	6-4	230	12-24-74	0	0	0.00	1	1	0	0	5	1	0	0	0	1	3	.063	.000	.091	5.40	1.80
Padilla, Vicente	R-R	6-2	220	9-27-77	0	1	5.73	5	5	0	0	11	11	7	7	1	8	11	.262	.214	.286	9.00	6.55
Puffer, Brandon	R-R	6-3	190	10-5-75	3	3	3.20	51	0	0	1	65	61	27	23	6	21	48	.245	.289	.223	6.68	2.92
Rice, Scott	L-L	6-6	220	9-21-81	0	0	0.00	1	0	0	0	2	4	0	0	0	0	4	.444	.333	.500	0.00	0.00
Rowe, Steven	R-R	6-4	210	7-17-80	0	0	2.61	4	2	0	0	10	6	3	3	0	2	5	.167	.286	.091	4.35	1.74
Schlact, Michael	R-R	6-7	205	12-9-85	3	3	5.08	6	6	1	0	34	36	21	19	6	8	23	.267	.222	.306	6.13	2.13
Shoemaker, Scott	R-R	6-4	210	9-21-81	6	2	4.27	20	9	0	0	78	71	38	37	12	32	47	.245	.232	.255	5.42	3.69

Name	B-T	HT	WT	DOB	W	L	ERA	G	GS	CG	SV	IP	H	R	ER	HR	BB	SO	AVG	vLH	vRH	K/9	BB/9
Touchet, Danny	R-R	6-2	202	1-12-82	0	0	3.86	4	0	0	0	5	8	3	2	0	2	2	.364	.444	.308	3.86	3.86
Vasquez, Jorge	R-R	6-1	215	7-16-78	2	3	4.20	27	1	0	0	45	36	25	21	6	32	57	.218	.281	.185	11.40	6.40
Volquez, Edinson	R-R	6-0	200	7-3-83	8	1	3.55	11	11	0	0	58	46	23	23	9	19	62	.212	.208	.216	9.57	2.93
White, Bill	L-L	6-3	215	11-20-78	2	0	4.44	43	0	0	2	49	48	26	24	4	26	64	.253	.275	.236	11.84	4.81
Williams, Randy	L-L	6-3	195	9-18-75	1	1	7.89	16	0	0	1	22	32	20	19	5	7	12	.348	.300	.385	4.98	2.91
Wright, Jamey	R-R	6-5	205	12-24-74	0	0	4.50	1	1	0	0	4	6	2	2	0	0	2	.353	.429	.300	4.50	0.00

FIELDING

Catcher	PCT	G	PO	A	E	DP	PB
Manriquez	.981	48	317	41	7	3	8
Richardson	.994	80	638	56	4	7	4
Teagarden	1.000	14	107	4	0	0	0

First Base	PCT	G	PO	A	E	DP
Fasano	.991	39	302	12	3	33
Fox	.988	23	154	4	2	18
Frostad	.987	79	591	70	4	54
Richardson	1.000	4	28	5	0	1
Roth	1.000	3	11	1	0	0
Teixeira	1.000	1	6	1	0	1

Second Base	PCT	G	PO	A	E	DP
Berkery	1.000	4	4	3	0	0
Duran	.974	126	224	345	15	69

Catcher (cont.)	PCT	G	PO	A	E	DP
Fox	1.000	8	11	30	0	7
Frostad	—	1	0	0	0	0
Roth	.967	9	10	19	1	3

Third Base	PCT	G	PO	A	E	DP
Berkery	.833	3	1	4	1	0
Davis	.892	29	14	44	7	1
Fox	.962	41	11	65	3	6
Frostad	.571	3	1	3	3	0
Furtado	1.000	10	7	20	0	4
Metcalf	.965	54	50	87	5	13
Roth	.917	7	3	8	1	1

Shortstop	PCT	G	PO	A	E	DP
Benjamin	.968	130	221	318	18	74
Berkery	1.000	2	5	3	0	2

	PCT	G	PO	A	E	DP
Duran	.818	3	4	5	2	0
Fox	.914	9	16	16	3	3

Outfield	PCT	G	PO	A	E	DP
Blalock	1.000	13	23	0	0	0
Boggs	.987	99	227	6	3	1
Donovan	.977	16	41	1	1	0
Fox	1.000	1	1	0	0	0
Harrison	.941	7	15	1	1	0
Mahar	1.000	24	52	1	0	0
Mayberry	.985	68	126	3	2	0
Murphy	.982	121	216	6	4	1
Webster	.977	74	122	4	3	1
West	.750	3	3	0	1	0
Wilkerson	1.000	1	1	0	0	0

BAKERSFIELD BLAZE

HIGH CLASS A

CALIFORNIA LEAGUE

BATTING	B-T	HT	WT	DOB	AVG	vLH	vRH	G	AB	R	H	2B	3B	HR	RBI	BB	HBP	SH	SF	SO	SB	CS	SLG	OBP
Abreu, Johany	B-R	6-0	165	4-3-84	.208	.160	.225	27	96	17	20	1	1	0	3	8	3	0	0	23	1	2	.240	.290
Andrus, Elvis	R-R	6-0	185	8-26-88	.300	.273	.307	27	110	19	33	2	0	2	12	10	2	1	0	19	15	8	.373	.369
Berkery, Thomas	R-R	6-1	180	9-29-82	.252	.259	.249	97	313	58	80	12	0	5	32	58	6	5	8	75	4	8	.336	.369
Blalock, Jake	R-R	6-4	205	8-6-83	.283	.250	.293	14	53	5	15	6	0	1	11	5	0	0	0	12	0	0	.453	.345
Blunt, Terrance	B-R	6-1	185	8-14-82	.159	.286	.113	41	132	18	21	2	1	0	6	23	0	1	0	27	9	3	.189	.284
Boggs, Brandon	B-R	5-11	205	1-9-83	.250	.286	.239	26	92	17	23	9	1	4	17	14	2	0	0	28	5	1	.500	.361
Bradbury, Josh	R-R	6-2	210	3-2-85	.412	.250	.462	5	17	3	7	1	0	0	5	1	0	0	0	2	0	0	.471	.444
Cadena, Nickolas	R-R	6-1	185	11-17-82	.217	.196	.225	48	157	15	34	5	1	6	22	11	3	0	1	54	0	1	.376	.293
Creswell, Reece	L-R	6-3	205	7-5-85	.190	.250	.176	8	21	2	4	0	0	1	2	2	0	0	0	11	0	0	.333	.261
Davis, Chris	L-R	6-3	210	3-17-86	.298	.351	.281	99	386	69	115	28	3	24	93	22	5	0	5	123	3	3	.573	.340
Fasano, Jim	L-R	6-5	230	7-20-83	.271	.182	.288	18	70	11	19	4	0	4	12	5	0	0	0	11	0	0	.500	.320
Furtado, Micah	L-R	5-7	170	6-9-82	.246	.164	.272	80	297	42	73	11	3	4	45	24	3	9	5	39	7	1	.343	.304
Gentry, Craig	R-R	6-2	190	11-29-83	.272	.229	.285	51	213	31	58	16	1	1	18	12	6	1	3	46	16	7	.371	.325
Harrigan, Hunter	R-R	6-1	210	4-17-83	.202	.238	.190	28	84	10	17	5	0	2	9	4	4	0	2	42	0	0	.333	.266
Harrison, Ben	R-R	6-4	203	9-18-81	.240	.269	.231	61	221	26	53	10	0	6	29	17	5	0	3	75	4	1	.367	.305
Kemp, Chris	L-R	6-4	210	8-24-83	.194	.250	.185	12	31	2	6	1	0	0	4	4	0	0	0	7	0	0	.226	.286
Mayberry, John	R-R	6-6	230	12-21-83	.230	.203	.238	63	244	47	56	15	1	16	45	28	3	0	2	64	9	1	.496	.314
Mehl, Truan	L-R	6-2	200	3-20-83	.268	.283	.263	105	410	59	110	21	4	6	45	26	2	6	5	61	16	10	.383	.312
Peterson, David	R-R	5-10	170	8-22-83	.259	.280	.253	36	112	17	29	1	0	1	4	5	3	2	0	31	4	0	.295	.308
Ramirez, Max	R-R	5-11	170	10-11-84	.307	.333	.302	32	114	16	35	10	0	4	20	21	2	0	1	39	1	0	.500	.420
Roth, Tony	R-R	6-0	175	10-20-82	.236	.143	.268	20	55	1	13	5	0	0	4	13	0	0	0	10	1	1	.327	.382
Smith, Matt	L-R	5-10	172	6-12-83	.229	.241	.225	99	345	47	79	12	1	1	31	37	2	11	4	88	4	6	.278	.304
Teagarden, Taylor	R-R	6-1	200	12-21-83	.315	.397	.290	81	292	75	92	25	0	20	67	65	6	0	1	89	2	1	.606	.448
Thon, Freddie	L-L	6-2	215	4-9-84	.284	.299	.280	113	429	42	122	27	1	11	66	9	1	1	0	73	2	5	.429	.300
Valichka, Brian	B-R	6-3	200	8-21-83	.274	.283	.271	71	230	26	63	17	2	1	27	14	1	7	2	50	4	3	.378	.316
Weber, Jon	L-L	5-10	190	1-20-78	.356	.293	.380	37	149	34	53	14	0	5	25	15	1	0	1	15	9	5	.550	.416
Whittleman, John	L-R	6-2	195	2-11-87	.240	.292	.225	29	104	18	25	9	0	3	15	23	0	0	2	33	0	3	.413	.372

PITCHING	B-T	HT	WT	DOB	W	L	ERA	G	GS	CG	SV	IP	H	R	ER	HR	BB	SO	AVG	vLH	vRH	K/9	BB/9
Altman, Kevin	R-R	6-2	170	12-24-84	0	3	5.13	34	3	0	0	47	62	36	27	0	37	42	.312	.327	.296	7.99	7.04
Ballard, Michael	R-L	6-2	180	2-6-84	5	3	4.99	14	14	0	0	88	96	52	49	12	22	72	.274	.217	.298	7.34	2.24
Batista, Kendy	R-R	6-2	165	7-5-81	6	2	3.97	20	18	0	1	95	86	44	42	5	27	94	.241	.247	.234	8.87	2.55
Bay, Ronald	R-R	6-3	155	8-7-83	3	7	5.21	15	15	0	0	74	78	48	43	12	37	71	.275	.243	.304	8.60	4.48
Bumstead, Michael	R-R	6-4	210	7-8-77	1	1	7.62	3	3	0	0	13	15	12	11	3	6	15	.278	.233	.333	10.38	4.15
Crow, Craig	R-R	6-2	200	11-25-83	0	0	7.94	3	0	0	0	6	5	5	5	1	8	3	.278	.273	.286	4.76	12.71
Diaz, J.B.	R-R	6-2	185	6-9-83	4	3	7.08	38	12	0	1	102	146	87	80	23	30	60	.340	.385	.302	5.31	2.66
Donovan, Patrick	L-L	6-1	185	2-22-84	0	0	17.47	4	0	0	0	6	13	14	11	4	5	0	.433	.375	.455	0.00	7.94
Farnum, Matt	R-R	6-2	195	6-1-81	1	2	8.44	13	0	0	1	16	25	19	15	3	6	21	.338	.370	.319	11.81	3.38
Garr, Brennan	R-R	6-2	190	2-22-84	0	0	1.10	10	0	0	0	16	9	2	2	1	6	20	.158	.241	.071	11.02	3.31
Giles, Josh	R-R	6-1	175	8-3-84	6	7	4.25	56	0	0	1	72	58	39	34	10	45	92	.218	.230	.205	11.50	5.62
Herrera, Daniel	L-L	5-8	145	10-21-84	2	0	3.27	7	1	0	1	11	14	4	4	1	5	11	.298	.167	.343	9.00	4.09
Hyatt, Jared	R-R	6-5	205	1-15-84	0	0	3.00	9	0	0	0	9	5	4	3	2	6	12	.156	.200	.118	12.00	6.00
Izquierdo, Ivan	R-R	6-1	205	10-14-83	0	2	8.31	7	0	0	0	9	11	11	8	0	8	7	.314	.444	.176	7.27	8.31
Knippschild, Ryan	L-L	6-1	195	9-24-82	3	6	5.32	44	0	0	3	64	77	42	38	7	24	45	.307	.232	.355	6.30	3.36
Marte, Jose	R-R	6-5	185	9-4-83	2	4	5.91	40	0	0	11	46	48	37	30	5	36	58	.271	.250	.287	11.43	7.09
Pluta III, Anthony	R-R	6-2	225	10-28-82	2	0	8.68	15	0	0	0	19	22	18	18	0	30	20	.314	.371	.257	9.64	14.46
Poveda, Omar	R-R	6-4	200	9-28-87	1	2	5.14	5	5	0	0	28	27	18	16	4	13	33	.250	.210	.304	10.61	4.18
Quintero, Jorge	R-R	6-1	175	4-17-87	0	1	2.89	3	2	0	0	9	6	4	3	1	7	5	.194	.071	.294	4.82	6.75
Ramsey, Keith	B-L	6-1	175	3-5-80	0	2	15.63	3	2	0	0	6	17	15	11	4	4	3	.486	.818	.333	4.26	5.68
Schlact, Michael	R-R	6-7	205	12-9-85	5	7	5.77	21	21	0	0	115	133	86	74	14	42	59	.286	.338	.239	4.60	3.28
Shoemaker, Scott	R-R	6-4	210	9-21-81	1	0	1.80	5	1	0	3	15	9	3	3	1	3	10	.173	.250	.107	6.00	1.80
Swanson, Glenn	L-L	6-1	175	5-15-83	1	4	4.87	7	7	0	0	41	48	25	22	3	16	41	.291	.176	.321	9.07	3.54
Touchet, Danny	R-R	6-2	202	1-12-82	4	5	2.81	34	1	0	2	67	54	26	21	4	27	50	.222	.177	.262	6.68	3.61
Vasquez, Jorge	R-R	6-2	215	7-16-78	0	0	0.00	1	0	0	0	1	0	0	0	1	0	1	.000	.000	.000	13.50	0.00
Volquez, Edinson	R-R	6-0	200	7-3-83	0	4	7.13	7	7	0	0	35	27	28	28	4	20	38	.211	.190	.209	9.68	5.09
Wagner, Michael	R-R	6-1	190	12-17-84	1	3	7.28	29	0	0	0	47	59	39	38	5	34	47	.312	.345	.284	9.00	6.51

Walker, Andrew	R-R	6-1	175	4-20-83	9	13	4.99	28	28	1	0	168	196	113	93	31	30	107	.290	.291	.290	5.74	1.61
Wilson, Jon	R-R	6-1	200	4-28-83	0	2	6.39	11	0	0	2	13	18	9	9	2	4	10	.333	.313	.364	7.11	2.84

FIELDING

Catcher	PCT	G	PO	A	E	DP	PB
Creswell	1.000	3	5	0	0	0	1
Harrigan	.994	25	163	11	1	4	3
Ramirez	.995	24	196	20	1	1	3
Teagarden	.976	30	222	21	6	4	0
Valichka	.985	68	489	48	8	6	13

First Base	PCT	G	PO	A	E	DP
Berkery	.990	16	93	10	1	6
Blunt	1.000	4	23	4	0	4
Cadena	.979	14	88	4	2	9
Fasano	1.000	4	38	1	0	1
Kemp	.986	8	66	5	1	7
Roth	.988	9	75	4	1	9
Thon	.985	97	779	47	13	81

Second Base	PCT	G	PO	A	E	DP
Abreu	.939	10	21	25	3	5
Berkery	.982	21	45	65	2	15

	PCT	G	PO	A	E	DP
Cadena	.889	5	3	5	1	0
Furtado	.971	73	133	200	10	48
Peterson	.980	24	30	66	2	7
Smith	.986	17	28	41	1	6

Third Base	PCT	G	PO	A	E	DP
Abreu	—	1	0	0	0	0
Berkery	1.000	7	7	14	0	1
Cadena	.833	8	2	8	2	0
Davis	.897	91	69	167	27	21
Peterson	1.000	1	0	1	0	0
Roth	.944	8	6	11	1	0
Whittleman	.930	29	20	46	5	4

Shortstop	PCT	G	PO	A	E	DP
Abreu	1.000	1	4	0	0	0
Andrus	.949	27	42	70	6	14
Berkery	.946	22	29	58	5	12
Peterson	.936	10	7	37	3	5

	PCT	G	PO	A	E	DP
Roth	1.000	1	0	4	0	1
Smith	.967	82	130	225	12	59

Outfield	PCT	G	PO	A	E	DP
Abreu	.941	14	30	2	2	0
Berkery	.978	31	40	5	1	0
Blalock	1.000	10	16	2	0	0
Blunt	1.000	38	88	3	0	2
Boggs	.980	22	46	3	1	0
Bradbury	1.000	4	8	0	0	0
Cadena	1.000	12	12	0	0	0
Furtado	—	1	0	0	0	0
Gentry	.979	51	134	5	3	1
Harrison	.949	50	73	1	4	0
Mayberry	1.000	59	103	4	0	1
Mehl	.983	103	210	16	4	5
Weber	.987	37	76	0	1	0

CLINTON LUMBERKINGS   LOW CLASS A

MIDWEST LEAGUE

BATTING	B-T	HT	WT	DOB	AVG	vLH	vRH	G	AB	R	H	2B	3B	HR	RBI	BB	HBP	SH	SF	SO	SB	CS	SLG	OBP
Backman II, Wally	L-R	6-2	215	1-7-86	.211	.167	.218	44	128	8	27	3	0	1	9	10	1	4	0	60	2	4	.258	.273
Berkery, Thomas	R-R	6-1	180	9-29-82	.250	.000	.333	2	4	0	1	0	0	0	0	2	0	0	0	1	0	1	.250	.500
Bradbury, Josh	R-R	6-2	210	3-2-85	.164	.059	.200	23	61	2	10	2	0	0	4	1	3	0	1	16	0	0	.197	.212
Gac, Ian	R-R	6-3	240	8-10-85	.091	1.000	.000	3	11	1	1	0	0	0	0	1	1	0	0	6	0	0	.091	.231
Gentry, Craig	R-R	6-2	190	11-29-83	.274	.262	.278	55	223	40	61	15	0	3	12	15	7	0	3	37	24	3	.381	.335
Gerrard, Grant	L-L	6-4	220	5-1-84	.231	.179	.256	32	117	11	27	6	0	1	13	12	0	0	1	34	3	1	.308	.300
Gomez, Mauro	R-R	6-2	190	9-7-84	.262	.250	.266	132	497	72	130	28	0	21	74	23	18	0	3	115	2	3	.445	.316
Gossage, Kevin	R-R	6-4	190	2-16-87	.145	.300	.089	24	76	5	11	4	0	0	3	5	2	2	0	30	1	0	.197	.217
Harrigan, Hunter	R-R	6-1	210	4-17-83	.140	.059	.158	30	93	9	13	5	0	1	8	2	6	0	0	40	0	0	.226	.208
Heafner, Jay	R-R	5-10	175	1-1-84	.250	.204	.269	58	188	20	47	9	1	2	27	21	3	0	3	48	3	1	.340	.330
Herren, K.C.	L-R	6-2	200	8-21-85	.276	.260	.282	128	453	68	125	30	12	6	49	61	3	0	2	80	12	10	.435	.364
Kemp, Chris	L-R	6-4	210	8-24-83	.291	.179	.321	43	134	19	39	5	0	4	19	16	2	0	0	23	1	2	.418	.375
Lemon, Marcus	L-R	5-11	173	6-3-88	.261	.302	.249	128	460	62	120	26	6	3	38	56	11	3	5	100	14	14	.363	.352
Mehl, Truan	L-R	6-2	200	3-20-83	.429	.000	.429	7	21	5	9	2	1	0	6	0	1	1	0	4	1	0	.619	.455
Ogden, Chad	R-R	5-10	180	5-1-85	.174	.167	.176	19	46	6	8	1	1	1	3	4	3	2	0	10	0	0	.304	.283
Paisano, David	R-R	6-1	165	11-26-87	.203	.235	.193	88	306	43	62	11	1	3	20	20	10	1	1	85	20	2	.275	.273
Peterson, David	R-R	5-10	170	8-22-83	.207	.237	.184	23	87	10	18	3	0	1	9	4	1	1	1	26	2	2	.276	.247
Pina, Manuel	R-R	5-11	165	6-5-87	.228	.213	.233	86	281	20	64	13	0	1	23	15	6	0	4	28	0	0	.285	.278
Smith, Kenneth	R-R	5-10	185	5-18-84	.143	.250	.100	7	14	1	2	0	0	0	1	0	0	0	0	7	0	0	.143	.200
Tracy, Chad	R-R	6-3	205	7-4-85	.250	.244	.251	134	509	64	127	35	2	14	84	50	5	0	5	93	9	1	.400	.320
Vallejo, Jose	R-R	6-0	172	9-11-86	.269	.294	.260	129	513	68	138	17	5	1	46	44	1	5	4	102	47	3	.327	.326
Whittleman, John	L-R	6-2	195	2-11-87	.271	.227	.286	95	336	56	91	25	1	14	57	63	1	0	6	91	5	3	.476	.382

PITCHING	B-T	HT	WT	DOB	W	L	ERA	G	GS	CG	SV	IP	H	R	ER	HR	BB	SO	AVG	vLH	vRH	K/9	BB/9
Ballard, Michael	R-L	6-2	180	2-6-84	9	4	3.93	14	14	1	0	76	87	41	33	5	14	59	.283	.228	.303	7.02	1.67
Coffman, Broc	L-L	6-2	215	3-28-85	5	6	4.22	20	20	0	0	102	103	55	48	9	40	70	.259	.217	.271	6.16	3.52
Crow, Craig	R-R	6-2	200	11-25-83	0	0	15.00	4	0	0	0	6	12	10	10	2	4	1	.414	.000	.600	1.50	6.00
Dennis, Christopher	L-R	6-2	205	1-3-84	0	0	4.94	22	0	0	7	24	27	18	13	2	8	21	.281	.258	.292	7.99	3.04
Fogle, Nathan	R-R	6-4	225	12-27-83	0	0	6.75	3	0	0	0	4	5	5	3	0	3	3	.313	.333	.300	6.75	6.75
Garr, Brennan	R-R	6-2	190	2-22-84	0	3	2.31	25	0	0	5	39	25	13	10	2	16	50	.177	.184	.174	11.54	3.69
Gudex, Timothy	L-L	6-0	165	9-23-82	2	4	3.98	30	1	0	4	54	61	25	24	4	13	55	.280	.319	.269	9.11	2.15
Haar, Jeremiah	L-R	6-2	190	12-29-84	6	5	4.02	35	15	0	7	112	128	60	50	13	28	63	.288	.263	.306	5.06	2.25
Hollis, Jonathan	R-R	6-3	240	9-17-83	2	6	4.43	39	0	0	2	69	63	41	34	9	29	42	.240	.247	.237	5.48	3.78
Hyatt, Jared	R-R	6-5	205	5-15-84	0	1	2.57	4	0	0	0	7	5	2	2	0	1	10	.192	.143	.211	12.86	1.29
Izquierdo, Ivan	R-R	6-1	205	10-14-83	3	3	2.59	30	0	0	1	49	41	17	14	3	18	31	.225	.221	.228	5.73	3.33
Jones, Beau	L-L	6-1	195	8-25-86	4	1	2.70	7	6	0	0	27	23	10	8	3	12	29	.228	.250	.213	9.79	4.05
Kiker, Kasey	L-L	5-10	170	11-19-87	7	4	2.90	20	20	0	0	96	84	35	31	10	41	112	.237	.212	.244	10.46	3.83
Kirkman, Michael	L-L	6-3	185	9-18-86	0	1	7.43	5	2	0	0	13	17	12	11	1	12	12	.304	.316	.297	8.10	8.10
Locke, Jared	L-L	6-6	225	8-14-84	0	2	7.71	7	0	0	0	9	11	12	8	2	8	8	.289	.222	.310	8.68	7.71
Lueke, Joshua	R-R	6-5	220	12-5-84	0	3	3.34	20	0	0	6	35	29	19	13	4	10	31	.225	.256	.209	7.97	2.57
Marte, Jose	R-R	6-5	185	9-4-83	2	0	2.45	5	0	0	3	7	5	3	2	1	2	9	.192	.154	.231	11.05	2.45
Maxwell, Anton	L-L	5-9	180	6-23-85	0	0	4.91	5	0	0	1	7	5	4	4	0	2	4	.208	.400	.158	4.91	2.45
Phillips, Zachary	L-L	6-1	178	9-21-86	11	7	2.91	27	27	0	0	152	139	56	49	6	43	157	.247	.255	.244	9.32	2.55
Poveda, Omar	R-R	6-4	200	9-28-87	11	4	2.79	21	21	0	0	126	94	44	39	10	32	120	.208	.205	.211	8.59	2.29
Reed, Evan	R-R	6-2	225	12-31-85	1	1	1.80	4	0	0	0	20	9	5	4	0	7	11	.136	.100	.152	4.95	3.15
Rice, Scott	L-L	6-6	220	9-21-81	0	0	0.00	3	0	0	0	4	1	0	0	3	4		.077	.000	.100	9.00	6.75
Santana, Julio	B-R	6-1	175	12-26-85	0	0	0.00	6	0	0	0	10	4	1	0	0	4	5	.125	.000	.182	4.66	3.72
Slusarz, John	R-R	6-3	170	7-19-84	1	7	2.88	41	0	0	2	66	60	29	21	6	27	62	.248	.253	.245	8.50	3.70
Swanson, Glenn	L-L	6-1	175	5-15-83	6	1	2.93	7	7	0	0	43	36	15	14	4	6	42	.229	.265	.220	8.79	1.26
Zamzow, Brett	R-R	6-5	200	12-19-84	0	2	4.79	30	0	0	1	41	47	25	22	3	17	32	.283	.217	.321	6.97	3.70

FIELDING

Catcher	PCT	G	PO	A	E	DP	PB
Gossage	.994	23	159	20	1	1	4
Harrigan	.985	30	175	22	3	2	2
Pina	.983	84	599	82	12	3	6
Tracy	1.000	11	88	8	0	0	2

First Base	PCT	G	PO	A	E	DP
Backman II	.947	4	32	4	2	3
Gomez	.983	110	942	58	17	101
Kemp	.983	21	169	8	3	16
Tracy	1.000	7	43	4	0	2
Whittleman	1.000	2	1	1	0	0

Second Base	PCT	G	PO	A	E	DP
Heafner	1.000	2	2	2	0	1
Ogden	.952	5	8	12	1	3

| Peterson | .941 | 6 | 16 | 16 | 2 | 5 |
| Vallejo | .963 | 127 | 280 | 373 | 25 | 89 |

Third Base	PCT	G	PO	A	E	DP
Backman II	1.000	1	0	1	0	0
Berkery	.833	1	1	4	1	0
Gomez	.778	4	4	3	2	0
Heafner	.922	35	21	62	7	5
Ogden	.947	6	6	12	1	1
Peterson	1.000	5	1	10	0	2
Smith	1.000	6	6	11	0	3
Whittleman	.880	85	48	164	29	16

Shortstop	PCT	G	PO	A	E	DP
Heafner	.750	1	1	2	1	1
Lemon	.946	122	196	351	31	82

| Ogden | 1.000 | 5 | 6 | 11 | 0 | 3 |
| Peterson | .974 | 11 | 14 | 24 | 1 | 6 |

Outfield	PCT	G	PO	A	E	DP
Backman II	1.000	23	26	0	0	0
Bradbury	1.000	20	33	0	0	0
Gentry	.990	54	92	4	1	1
Gerrard	1.000	28	45	3	0	1
Herren	.973	121	205	8	6	2
Kemp	1.000	1	1	0	0	0
Mehl	1.000	7	9	0	0	0
Paisano	.963	88	202	7	8	4
Tracy	.972	86	105	1	3	0

SPOKANE INDIANS   SHORT-SEASON

NORTHWEST LEAGUE

BATTING	B-T	HT	WT	DOB	AVG	vLH	vRH	G	AB	R	H	2B	3B	HR	RBI	BB	HBP	SH	SF	SO	SB	CS	SLG	OBP
Anderson, Ronnie	R-R	5-11	162	11-1-86	.154	.250	.111	4	13	0	2	0	0	0	0	1	0	1	0	3	0	0	.154	.214
Barrios, Victor	R-R	5-11	175	9-29-86	.219	.192	.230	50	178	19	39	8	1	5	16	16	2	0	0	31	3	1	.360	.291
Beltre, Engel	L-L	6-1	169	11-1-89	.211	.357	.125	9	38	3	8	0	0	0	1	2	1	0	0	10	2	1	.211	.250
Borbon, Julio	L-L	6-1	190	2-20-86	.172	.250	.160	7	29	1	5	0	0	0	2	2	0	0	0	3	3	1	.172	.226
Creswell, Reece	L-R	6-3	205	7-5-85	.000	—	.000	1	1	0	0	0	0	0	0	0	0	0	0	1	0	0	.000	.000
Fry, Eric	L-R	5-10	190	8-9-87	.247	.357	.229	28	97	5	24	4	1	2	10	11	2	0	0	27	0	2	.371	.336
Gac, Ian	R-R	6-3	240	8-10-85	.237	.333	.202	70	257	41	61	18	0	17	45	24	5	0	2	80	2	1	.506	.313
Gossage, Kevin	R-R	6-4	190	2-16-87	.208	.250	.167	7	24	3	5	1	1	0	1	1	0	0	0	7	0	0	.333	.240
Gradoville, Chris	R-R	6-1	220	7-10-84	.229	.300	.211	15	48	3	11	2	1	1	13	3	0	3	0	9	0	0	.375	.298
Greene, Jonathan	R-R	6-0	200	9-16-85	.248	.264	.242	58	206	30	51	12	1	11	44	24	13	0	3	55	0	0	.476	.358
James, Andres	B-R	5-9	150	11-25-87	.195	.207	.190	57	195	19	38	2	0	0	13	6	3	2	4	44	10	3	.205	.224
Killian, Billy	L-R	6-1	190	6-12-86	.258	.000	.333	12	31	4	8	1	0	0	3	1	0	0	0	4	0	0	.355	.343
Lawson, Matthew	R-R	6-0	195	11-18-85	.295	.328	.283	56	224	32	66	10	4	2	27	16	8	4	2	48	11	8	.402	.360
Marquardt, Steven	R-R	6-2	210	6-11-86	.227	.294	.206	43	141	19	32	8	0	1	9	29	3	0	0	43	1	0	.305	.370
Moreland, Mitchell	L-L	6-2	230	9-6-85	.259	.286	.250	27	108	10	28	7	1	2	15	8	0	1	1	25	1	0	.398	.308
Murphy, Kyle	R-R	6-0	184	9-6-84	.177	.176	.178	16	62	7	11	4	2	0	4	6	4	0	0	16	2	1	.306	.292
Osuna, Renny	R-R	6-0	172	4-24-85	.274	.317	.259	62	252	42	69	12	2	1	25	21	3	3	1	33	6	6	.349	.336
Rodriguez, Timothy	R-R	6-2	210	1-24-87	.265	.275	.260	41	136	19	36	6	1	0	14	7	3	0	3	23	1	2	.324	.309
Salas, Luke	L-L	5-11	185	11-10-84	.238	.143	.286	23	63	9	15	1	2	0	7	13	0	1	1	17	1	2	.317	.364
Santana, Cristian	R-R	6-0	175	6-18-89	.320	.571	.222	6	25	1	8	2	0	1	4	1	0	0	6	6	0	0	.520	.346
Smith, Kenneth	R-R	5-10	185	5-18-84	.240	.286	.226	36	121	16	29	5	0	2	12	13	1	0	0	22	3	0	.331	.319
Smith, Timothy	L-L	6-3	225	6-14-86	.284	.368	.258	23	81	18	23	5	0	1	9	11	4	0	0	16	1	2	.383	.396
Stoneburner, Davis	R-R	6-0	175	1-14-85	.235	.235	.235	29	85	12	20	4	1	0	4	1	1	1	1	16	0	1	.306	.313
Yan, Johan	R-R	6-3	185	9-27-88	.156	.037	.203	28	96	7	15	3	0	2	11	7	1	0	1	44	0	0	.250	.219

PITCHING	B-T	HT	WT	DOB	W	L	ERA	G	GS	CG	SV	IP	H	R	ER	HR	BB	SO	AVG	vLH	vRH	K/9	BB/9
Brigham, Jacob	R-R	6-3	190	2-10-88	5	4	3.16	15	15	0	0	77	69	43	27	9	34	65	.248	.246	.250	7.60	3.97
Castillo, Fabio	R-R	6-1	190	2-19-89	3	5	5.92	14	14	0	0	62	73	46	41	4	27	46	.289	.293	.285	6.64	3.90
Crow, Craig	R-R	6-2	200	11-25-83	0	0	8.10	4	0	0	0	3	6	3	3	0	2	6	.400	.200	.500	16.20	5.40
Dennis, Christopher	L-R	6-2	205	1-3-84	0	0	0.93	7	0	0	5	10	2	1	1	1	3	12	.065	.091	.050	11.17	2.79
Falcon, Ryan	R-L	6-0	195	8-27-84	5	2	2.68	26	0	0	1	47	39	16	14	2	6	62	.223	.175	.246	11.87	1.15
Feliz, Neftali	R-R	6-3	180	5-2-88	0	2	3.60	8	1	0	0	15	13	8	6	2	12	27	.228	.231	.226	16.20	7.20
Hoben, Daniel	L-L	5-11	185	6-29-87	0	0	8.31	4	1	0	0	9	12	10	8	1	7	7	.343	.556	.269	7.27	7.27
Holland, Derek	B-L	6-2	185	10-9-86	4	5	3.22	16	14	0	0	67	57	33	24	7	21	83	.224	.245	.218	11.15	2.82
Hunter, Tommy	R-R	6-3	255	7-3-86	2	3	2.55	10	0	0	1	18	15	7	5	0	1	13	.221	.200	.242	6.62	0.51
Jaimes, Jose	R-R	6-2	180	6-26-84	3	1	4.35	22	2	0	0	39	41	24	19	2	16	40	.259	.267	.253	9.15	3.66
Kirkman, Michael	L-L	6-3	185	9-18-86	1	4	7.00	9	6	0	0	27	33	30	21	2	25	24	.306	.231	.316	8.00	8.33
Laughter, Andrew	R-R	6-4	227	2-24-85	0	1	2.03	26	0	0	11	31	32	9	7	0	4	32	.267	.286	.250	9.29	1.16
Lueke, Joshua	R-R	6-5	220	12-5-84	0	0	0.00	2	0	0	0	3	2	0	0	0	0	6	.200	.400	.000	20.25	0.00
Main, Michael	R-R	6-2	170	12-14-88	2	0	4.70	5	5	0	0	15	14	11	8	1	7	18	.237	.174	.278	10.57	4.11
Maxwell, Anton	L-L	5-9	180	6-23-85	1	0	3.77	13	0	0	0	14	13	7	6	0	6	11	.241	.280	.207	10.05	3.77
Nelo, Hector	R-R	6-1	200	11-5-86	1	2	6.55	15	0	0	0	22	20	20	16	1	21	21	.244	.359	.140	8.59	8.59
Reed, Evan	R-R	6-4	225	12-31-85	0	0	2.04	7	4	0	1	18	9	7	4	0	9	23	.150	.118	.192	11.72	4.58
Sattler, Daniel	R-R	6-3	190	11-11-83	1	2	4.35	22	0	0	0	39	33	21	19	2	11	48	.231	.246	.221	10.98	2.52
Stewart, Jordan	R-R	6-1	210	8-29-83	2	2	3.02	24	0	0	0	45	38	20	15	3	17	42	.225	.280	.181	8.46	3.43
Tatusko, Ryan	R-R	6-5	200	3-27-85	3	7	4.13	16	13	0	0	65	66	41	30	4	22	50	.262	.210	.308	6.89	3.03
Ueno, Keisuke	R-R	6-4	205	3-6-86	0	2	3.79	21	0	0	0	36	26	18	15	3	21	39	.200	.231	.179	9.84	5.30

FIELDING

Catcher	PCT	G	PO	A	E	DP	PB
Gossage	.985	7	60	5	1	0	2
Gradoville	1.000	12	120	15	0	0	5
Greene	.980	45	394	54	9	5	16
Killian	.964	11	72	8	3	0	2
Santana	1.000	4	24	0	0	0	1

First Base	PCT	G	PO	A	E	DP
Gac	.990	43	365	25	4	24
Moreland	.990	21	171	19	2	12
Osuna	.990	12	95	6	1	9

Second Base	PCT	G	PO	A	E	DP
Lawson	.956	45	78	117	9	20

| Osuna | .945 | 31 | 65 | 73 | 8 | 14 |

Third Base	PCT	G	PO	A	E	DP
Osuna	1.000	16	11	33	0	1
Smith	.918	26	8	37	4	1
Stoneburner	.789	6	3	12	4	0
Yan	.905	28	13	54	7	6

Shortstop	PCT	G	PO	A	E	DP
James	.922	56	91	147	20	28
Stoneburner	.906	21	30	47	8	8

Outfield	PCT	G	PO	A	E	DP
Anderson	1.000	4	5	0	0	0

Barrios	.987	48	69	6	1	2
Beltre	.857	9	12	0	2	0
Borbon	1.000	7	10	0	0	0
Fry	.952	26	38	2	2	0
Marquardt	.955	40	56	7	3	0
Moreland	1.000	1	1	0	0	0
Murphy	1.000	16	29	1	0	0
Rodriguez	.952	38	59	0	3	0
Salas	.973	20	33	3	1	1
T. Smith	.938	23	29	1	2	0
Stoneburner	—	1	0	0	0	0

ARIZONA LEAGUE

BATTING	B-T	HT	WT	DOB	AVG	vLH	vRH	G	AB	R	H	2B	3B	HR	RBI	BB	HBP	SH	SF	SO	SB	CS	SLG	OBP
Abreu, Johany	B-R	6-0	165	4-3-84	.200	.000	.286	3	10	3	2	0	0	0	1	2	0	0	0	3	1	1	.200	.333
Alfonzo, Miguel	R-R	6-3	190	4-21-88	.310	.378	.276	31	113	12	35	7	1	1	16	12	6	2	0	31	9	5	.416	.405
Anderson, Ronnie	R-R	5-11	162	11-1-86	.245	.297	.217	31	106	19	26	7	1	0	10	12	0	3	0	25	11	3	.330	.322
Arias, Joaquin	R-R	6-1	165	9-21-84	.286	.333	.250	2	7	1	2	1	0	0	1	0	0	0	1	2	0	0	.429	.250
Beltre, Engel	L-L	6-1	169	11-1-89	.310	.385	.276	22	84	19	26	3	4	4	15	8	4	1	2	21	3	2	.583	.388
Borbon, Julio	L-L	6-1	190	2-20-86	.250	.000	.286	2	8	0	2	1	0	0	0	1	0	0	0	1	0	1	.375	.333
Bubalo, Ty	R-R	6-3	214	8-8-83	.105	.000	.167	8	19	2	2	0	0	1	3	2	0	0	0	9	1	0	.263	.190
Creswell, Reece	R-R	6-3	205	7-5-85	.286	.154	.364	11	35	6	10	3	0	1	6	4	3	0	1	10	1	1	.457	.395
De Los Santos, Leonel	R-R	5-10	170	10-2-89	.286	.143	.429	4	14	1	4	0	0	0	3	1	0	0	0	2	0	1	.286	.333
Dominguez, Carlos	R-R	6-1	177	6-8-86	.000	.000	.000	2	4	0	0	0	0	0	0	0	0	0	0	2	0	0	.000	.000
Donovan, Todd	R-R	6-1	180	8-12-78	.167	.000	.200	2	6	1	1	1	0	0	0	1	1	0	0	1	0	0	.333	.286
Ecker, Donnie	L-R	6-4	190	3-9-86	.267	.296	.254	34	90	21	24	1	1	2	11	8	6	1	2	17	11	2	.367	.358
Fry, Eric	L-R	5-10	190	8-9-87	.288	.150	.348	19	66	16	19	3	3	1	13	8	1	0	0	12	3	0	.470	.373
Gentry, Craig	R-R	6-2	190	11-29-83	.273	.333	.250	3	11	4	3	0	0	0	1	1	1	0	0	3	2	0	.273	.385
Gonzalez, Julio	R-R	6-1	160	12-27-87	.253	.240	.259	27	79	10	20	4	0	0	3	9	1	1	0	15	6	4	.304	.337
Gossage, Kevin	R-R	6-4	190	2-16-87	.156	.077	.188	15	45	4	7	2	0	1	4	5	0	1	1	17	0	0	.267	.235
Kaase, Jacob	L-R	6-1	185	4-14-86	.237	.286	.216	41	139	14	33	7	0	1	18	11	2	3	0	20	5	2	.309	.303
Murphy, Kyle	R-R	6-0	184	9-6-84	.156	.111	.169	23	77	13	12	1	0	0	6	10	1	0	0	26	4	1	.169	.261
Ogden, Chad	R-R	5-10	180	5-1-85	.364	.357	.366	15	55	9	20	4	1	1	8	5	2	1	0	9	4	0	.527	.435
Ortiz, Michael	L-L	6-2	200	5-2-89	.302	.241	.331	46	172	27	52	8	2	3	29	14	5	0	1	34	1	2	.424	.370
Podraza, Cody	R-R	5-8	185	11-6-87	.294	.375	.269	11	34	8	10	0	0	0	3	7	0	0	1	4	6	2	.294	.405
Salas, Luke	L-L	5-11	185	11-10-84	.383	.500	.310	13	47	8	18	2	1	1	6	3	0	1	0	9	0	2	.532	.431
Santana, Cristian	R-R	6-0	175	6-18-89	.302	.259	.319	27	96	20	29	7	3	3	15	12	9	0	0	27	3	3	.531	.427
Solis, Emmanuel	R-R	6-3	195	6-29-89	.205	.300	.162	45	166	19	34	12	1	0	18	14	0	0	2	57	5	0	.289	.264
Sowers, Jason	L-R	6-0	195	12-26-86	.082	.000	.114	17	49	5	4	0	0	1	5	9	0	0	0	15	2	0	.143	.224
Story, Bret	R-R	6-1	215	2-13-85	.170	.231	.150	20	53	6	9	2	0	0	2	3	0	0	0	23	0	0	.208	.190
Velazquez, Miguel	R-R	6-2	205	5-15-88	.330	.290	.349	24	94	18	31	5	2	2	21	7	2	0	2	27	7	1	.489	.381
West, Matthew	R-R	6-1	200	11-21-88	.301	.364	.284	29	103	21	31	1	4	0	17	9	8	0	1	21	1	3	.388	.397
Yan, Johan	R-R	6-3	185	9-27-88	.200	.308	.170	16	60	6	12	4	0	1	9	5	0	0	1	26	1	0	.317	.258

PITCHING	B-T	HT	WT	DOB	W	L	ERA	G	GS	CG	SV	IP	H	R	ER	HR	BB	SO	AVG	vLH	vRH	K/9	BB/9
Batista, Kendy	R-R	6-2	165	7-5-81	0	0	0.00	2	0	0	0	2	1	0	0	0	1	4	.143	.000	.250	18.00	4.50
Bryan, Melvin	R-R	6-6	190	9-30-86	0	0	9.17	13	0	0	0	18	19	20	18	3	13	12	.268	.304	.250	6.11	6.62
Bumstead, Michael	R-R	6-4	210	7-8-77	1	1	2.31	5	2	0	0	12	13	7	3	0	8	13	.283	.318	.250	10.03	6.17
De Los Santos, M.	L-L	6-1	170	7-10-88	0	1	6.35	3	0	0	0	6	7	4	4	0	3	6	.292	.286	.294	9.53	4.76
Font, Wilmer	R-R	6-4	210	5-24-90	2	3	4.53	14	10	0	0	46	41	33	23	2	24	61	.238	.277	.215	12.02	4.73
Gomez, Kennil	R-R	6-3	170	4-8-88	2	1	3.15	17	1	0	1	34	30	15	12	0	10	38	.231	.170	.265	9.96	2.62
Grullon, Geuris	L-L	6-5	185	12-20-89	1	2	8.14	13	4	0	0	21	23	29	19	0	16	25	.256	.391	.209	10.71	6.86
Hall, Jesse	L-L	6-1	180	9-24-85	0	1	8.84	14	0	0	0	19	30	24	19	0	11	16	.341	.429	.313	7.45	5.12
Henry, Benjamin	R-R	6-1	190	4-9-89	0	4	7.07	10	6	0	0	28	27	27	22	1	17	29	.245	.283	.219	9.32	5.46
Hoben, Daniel	L-L	5-11	185	6-29-87	2	2	6.08	10	1	0	1	24	27	18	16	1	15	22	.281	.174	.315	8.37	5.70
Hyatt, Jared	R-R	6-5	205	5-15-84	0	2	3.68	5	0	0	0	7	7	5	3	1	3	12	.233	.273	.211	14.73	3.68
Indriago, Luis	R-R	6-4	178	5-6-88	1	0	10.34	12	0	0	0	16	24	21	18	1	12	14	.343	.393	.310	8.04	6.89
Main, Michael	R-R	6-2	170	12-14-88	0	1	1.42	5	5	0	0	13	9	2	2	1	6	16	.196	.250	.167	11.37	4.26
Mathis, Douglas	R-R	6-3	220	6-7-83	0	0	16.87	1	1	0	0	3	7	5	5	0	1	2	.500	.556	.400	6.75	3.38
Nam, Yoon-Hee	L-L	6-2	165	8-4-87	4	1	3.62	16	0	0	2	32	32	15	13	1	4	35	.256	.200	.274	9.74	1.11
Peralta, Juan	R-R	5-11	180	4-26-86	1	1	6.59	16	0	0	1	27	29	26	20	1	12	30	.250	.222	.268	9.88	3.95
Pimentel, Carlos	R-R	6-3	180	12-1-89	0	5	5.53	13	12	0	0	42	44	31	26	3	17	59	.270	.358	.227	12.54	3.61
Quintero, Jorge	R-R	6-1	175	4-17-87	0	0	0.96	12	3	0	0	28	17	4	3	0	7	22	.168	.032	.229	7.07	2.25
Rice, Scott	L-L	6-6	220	9-21-81	0	0	0.00	4	0	0	0	4	2	0	0	0	1	7	.154	.143	.167	15.75	2.25
Rupe, Josh	R-R	6-2	210	8-18-82	0	0	0.00	2	2	0	0	3	1	0	0	0	1	3	.100	.250	.000	9.00	3.00
Santana, Julio	B-R	6-1	175	12-26-85	2	1	2.16	13	0	0	1	17	13	5	4	0	2	11	.203	.095	.256	5.94	1.08
Soto, Eleno	R-R	6-3	185	12-28-87	4	2	3.77	15	0	0	0	31	34	21	13	1	5	13	.270	.386	.207	3.77	1.45
Turner, Ryan	R-L	6-1	175	2-8-85	2	2	1.67	16	0	0	1	27	36	13	5	1	1	30	.310	.296	.315	10.00	0.33
Wilkins, Robert	R-R	6-4	225	8-20-89	0	4	5.25	10	6	0	0	24	29	22	14	1	8	14	.287	.256	.306	5.25	3.00

FIELDING

Catcher	PCT	G	PO	A	E	DP	PB
Bubalo	.971	5	32	1	1	0	3
De Los Santos	.906	4	42	6	5	1	0
Gossage	.970	13	91	7	3	0	6
Santana	.973	24	190	30	6	1	12
Story	.955	17	120	7	6	0	3

First Base	PCT	G	PO	A	E	DP
Bubalo	1.000	1	1	0	0	0
Ecker	.917	8	31	2	3	3
Ortiz	.962	43	333	22	14	33
Solis	1.000	2	22	0	0	1
Sowers	.983	7	54	3	1	4
Yan	1.000	2	16	0	0	1

Second Base	PCT	G	PO	A	E	DP
Abreu	1.000	3	4	6	0	0

	PCT	G	PO	A	E	DP	PB
Ecker	.923	12	18	30	4	5	
Gonzalez	.930	26	29	51	6	11	
Murphy	.900	2	3	6	1	0	
Ogden	1.000	8	12	19	0	4	
West	.970	14	31	33	2	9	

Third Base	PCT	G	PO	A	E	DP
Ecker	1.000	3	1	3	0	1
Solis	.812	37	17	52	16	3
West	.955	10	10	11	1	2
Yan	.741	10	3	17	7	2

Shortstop	PCT	G	PO	A	E	DP
Arias	.750	2	2	1	1	0
Ecker	.750	3	3	6	3	1
Kaase	.943	40	62	119	11	23
Ogden	.933	8	8	20	2	2

	PCT	G	PO	A	E	DP
West	.931	6	12	15	2	3

Outfield	PCT	G	PO	A	E	DP
Alfonzo	.968	27	30	0	1	0
Anderson	.981	28	48	3	1	0
Beltre	.894	21	42	0	5	0
Borbon	1.000	2	3	0	0	0
Donovan	1.000	2	3	0	0	0
Ecker	1.000	6	4	0	0	0
Fry	.818	17	17	1	4	0
Gentry	1.000	3	5	0	0	0
Murphy	.975	21	37	2	1	1
Podraza	1.000	10	23	0	0	0
Salas	.947	11	18	0	1	0
Sowers	1.000	2	4	0	0	0
Velazquez	.939	24	44	2	3	0

DOMINICAN SUMMER LEAGUE

BATTING	B-T	HT	WT	DOB	AVG	vLH	vRH	G	AB	R	H	2B	3B	HR	RBI	BB	HBP	SH	SF	SO	SB	CS	SLG	OBP
Alfonzo, Edward	R-R	6-1	175	10-29-89	.218	.250	.208	44	142	34	31	5	1	0	11	20	7	4	0	63	13	4	.268	.343
Alfonzo, Miguel	R-R	6-3	190	4-21-88	.186	.200	.182	14	43	7	8	1	0	2	6	8	6	0	1	15	1	3	.349	.379
De Jesus, Junior	B-R	6-2	160	2-2-89	.186	.241	.158	32	86	21	16	1	1	1	10	22	0	3	0	37	4	1	.256	.352
De Los Santos, Leonel	R-R	5-10	170	10-2-89	.263	.300	.250	35	114	13	30	7	1	2	7	8	4	1	0	19	4	1	.395	.333
Gomez, Jhonny	R-R	6-2	186	12-21-89	.170	.100	.188	37	100	13	17	4	0	1	11	17	1	2	1	32	7	4	.240	.294
Gonzalez, Julio	R-R	6-1	160	12-27-87	.176	.200	.167	6	17	2	3	1	0	0	1	1	1	0	0	2	0	0	.235	.263
Gonzalez, Mervin	R-R	6-2	190	3-16-89	.157	.091	.175	33	102	19	16	0	1	5	16	15	15	3	0	32	2	1	.324	.348
Inirio, Jorge	B-R	5-11	170	5-8-87	.213	.300	.183	34	80	12	17	3	0	2	13	12	3	0	2	22	4	3	.325	.330
Lara, Juvenal	R-R	6-1	190	3-19-90	.228	.182	.239	25	57	3	13	2	1	0	10	7	3	0	0	13	0	0	.298	.343
Martinez, Edward	R-R	5-9	160	3-28-88	.238	.440	.195	49	143	22	34	2	1	0	13	18	0	4	1	35	12	4	.266	.321
Moreno, Miguel	R-R	6-0	170	1-9-90	.148	.233	.120	39	122	10	18	2	0	2	7	15	3	2	2	48	2	3	.213	.254
Mota, Ramon	B-R	6-2	180	7-20-90	.124	.040	.148	39	113	15	14	3	0	0	9	21	5	2	1	60	9	3	.150	.286
Perez, Alison	R-R	6-0	190	9-3-89	.243	.222	.250	15	37	5	9	3	0	0	4	9	2	1	0	11	0	0	.324	.417
Pimentel, Guillermo	R-R	6-2	175	11-12-89	.219	.125	.244	54	151	31	33	6	0	2	17	20	8	2	2	46	6	4	.298	.337
Puello, Alberto	R-R	6-2	180	10-20-87	.292	.333	.284	56	195	35	57	10	2	2	34	26	4	0	4	27	4	0	.395	.380
Salas, Roan	R-R	5-10	175	8-9-90	.290	.310	.284	44	124	15	36	6	0	0	23	10	2	2	2	13	3	3	.339	.348
Selen, Alejandro	R-R	5-11	148	3-20-89	.277	.333	.267	48	155	25	43	8	1	1	23	18	6	2	1	22	2	3	.361	.372
Valdez, Jairo	R-R	6-2	190	11-6-88	.305	.303	.306	46	177	29	54	12	0	4	23	9	0	0	1	28	2	1	.441	.337
Ventura, Ariel	L-R	6-1	177	12-4-88	.279	.229	.292	59	179	24	50	6	3	1	22	20	5	2	3	56	8	5	.363	.362
Vizcaino, Stanly	R-R	6-2	165	10-9-88	.264	.217	.274	38	129	20	34	8	1	0	14	9	6	1	3	32	6	4	.341	.333

PITCHING	B-T	HT	WT	DOB	W	L	ERA	G	GS	CG	SV	IP	H	R	ER	HR	BB	SO	AVG	vLH	vRH	K/9	BB/9
Beltre, Omar	R-R	6-3	190	8-24-81	2	0	1.17	7	4	0	1	31	22	7	4	0	6	38	.198	.105	.217	11.15	1.76
Borjas, Kelvin	L-L	6-1	175	6-30-89	3	3	3.55	12	11	0	0	63	64	32	25	2	18	44	.266	.400	.263	6.25	2.56
Boscan, Wilfredo	R-R	6-2	160	10-26-89	2	1	1.75	13	8	0	0	57	42	14	11	1	13	61	.210	.419	.153	9.69	2.06
Bryan, Melvin	R-R	6-6	190	9-30-86	0	0	4.50	1	0	0	0	2	2	1	1	0	1	2	.286	.000	.400	9.00	4.50
De Jesus, Juan	L-L	6-2	165	2-8-88	0	0	4.50	3	0	0	0	2	2	3	1	0	2	4	.250	.000	.250	18.00	9.00
De Jesus, Junior	B-R	6-2	160	2-2-89	0	0	6.75	1	0	0	0	1	1	1	1	0	1	0	.250	—	.250	0.00	6.75
De La Cruz, Michael	R-R	6-3	180	11-28-89	1	0	5.49	10	0	0	0	20	13	14	12	2	24	19	.197	.111	.229	8.69	10.98
De Leon, Kelvin	R-R	6-6	180	1-5-89	0	2	7.20	13	3	0	0	25	28	22	20	1	27	19	.301	.278	.307	6.84	9.72
De Los Santos, Miguel	L-L	6-1	170	7-10-88	0	0	0.00	1	0	0	0	3	0	0	0	0	2	2	.000	—	.000	6.75	0.00
De Los Santos, Ovispo	R-R	6-1	180	11-19-87	4	2	2.01	12	12	0	0	63	49	30	14	1	14	53	.210	.333	.176	7.61	2.01
Fabian, Gedron	L-L	6-4	220	5-3-89	0	2	15.43	8	1	0	0	14	27	25	24	1	7	13	.403	.167	.426	8.36	4.50
Gomez, Kennil	R-R	6-3	170	4-8-88	0	0	0.00	2	0	0	0	3	0	0	0	0	4	0	.000	.000	.000	12.00	0.00
Grullon, Juan	L-L	6-2	180	3-4-90	1	0	3.12	11	9	0	0	43	46	17	15	2	18	40	.282	.143	.288	8.31	3.74
Marinez, Yeyser	R-R	6-3	180	11-7-84	0	0	13.50	3	0	0	0	2	2	3	3	0	6	5	.222	1.000	.125	22.50	27.00
Medina, Emiliano	R-R	6-3	175	7-18-90	1	2	2.31	4	0	0	1	12	6	3	3	0	3	10	.140	.000	.176	7.71	2.31
Mendoza, Anyenil	R-R	6-3	170	12-9-89	3	4	3.91	13	9	0	1	48	44	33	21	3	19	44	.233	.257	.227	8.19	3.54
Ogando, Alexi	R-R	6-4	185	10-5-83	6	1	0.96	15	0	0	3	28	25	4	3	1	7	35	.248	.286	.241	11.25	2.25
Ortiz, Joseph	L-L	5-7	175	8-13-90	1	2	2.70	18	0	0	7	27	21	12	8	0	8	38	.212	.333	.208	12.83	2.70
Peralta, Juan	R-R	5-11	180	4-26-86	0	0	2.45	2	0	0	0	4	3	1	1	0	0	5	.250	—	.250	12.27	0.00
Quintero, Jhoan	R-R	6-4	200	12-11-89	0	1	3.78	11	1	0	1	17	16	9	7	0	4	16	.239	.250	.236	8.64	2.16
Quintero, Jorge	R-R	6-1	175	4-17-87	0	0	—	1	0	0	0	0	0	0	0	0	2	0	.000	.000	—	—	—
Rojas, Jonathan	R-R	6-1	185	3-22-88	1	3	7.91	12	5	0	0	33	39	32	29	4	20	31	.307	.250	.323	8.45	5.45
Rosendo, Ender	R-R	6-4	195	9-15-89	5	2	2.60	15	0	0	1	28	22	12	8	0	10	17	.214	.182	.222	5.53	3.25
Sepulveda, Amaury	R-R	6-0	163	10-10-88	2	5	4.20	13	6	0	0	41	23	18	10	2	21	41	.164	.204	.143	9.00	4.61
Sibid, Pepe	R-R	6-1	186	2-2-88	2	4	4.28	15	0	0	0	27	22	22	13	1	17	30	.216	.111	.238	9.88	5.60
Urbina, Jose	R-R	6-3	190	9-8-88	1	0	3.86	5	0	0	0	9	6	4	4	0	5	4	.182	.333	.125	3.86	4.82
Zapata, Cristian	R-R	6-2	175	11-23-88	0	0	3.18	7	0	0	1	6	6	8	2	0	10	2	.273	.000	.300	3.18	15.88

FIELDING

Catcher	PCT	G	PO	A	E	DP	PB
De Los Santos	.961	33	265	28	12	2	9
De Los Santos	1.000	2	11	1	0	0	2
Gonzalez	.982	12	97	14	2	0	6
Lara	.982	20	89	19	2	1	8
Perez	1.000	4	25	0	0	0	0
Puello	.975	13	100	16	3	1	3

First Base	PCT	G	PO	A	E	DP
E. Alfonzo	—	1	0	0	0	0
Gonzalez	1.000	1	10	1	0	1
Gonzalez	1.000	1	1	0	0	1
Inirio	.875	2	6	1	1	0
Lara	1.000	2	12	2	0	2
Martinez	1.000	2	3	0	0	0
Moreno	1.000	1	1	0	0	0
Puello	.977	33	272	26	7	23

	PCT	G	PO	A	E	DP
Salas	1.000	5	37	1	0	2
Valdez	.984	20	164	15	3	16
Vizcaino	.982	14	106	6	2	6
Second Base	PCT	G	PO	A	E	DP
De Jesus	1.000	2	2	2	0	3
Gonzalez	1.000	4	4	4	0	0
Inirio	.878	10	18	18	5	2
Martinez	.960	6	6	18	1	4
Salas	.951	13	19	20	2	5
Selen	.947	41	89	89	10	19
Vizcaino	.962	5	11	14	1	3
Third Base	PCT	G	PO	A	E	DP
Inirio	.813	8	3	10	3	0
Martinez	1.000	1	0	1	0	0
Moreno	.926	38	29	83	9	6
Salas	.900	16	16	29	5	5

	PCT	G	PO	A	E	DP
Vizcaino	.811	17	12	18	7	3
Shortstop	PCT	G	PO	A	E	DP
De Jesus	.881	29	40	78	16	8
Inirio	.870	10	16	31	7	7
Martinez	.910	40	50	122	17	21
Puello	1.000	1	0	1	0	0
Salas	.000	1	0	0	1	0
Vizcaino	1.000	1	0	1	0	0
Outfield	PCT	G	PO	A	E	DP
E. Alfonzo	.939	40	53	9	4	2
M. Alfonzo	.800	12	12	0	3	0
Gomez	.935	33	29	0	2	0
Mota	.956	39	37	6	2	1
Pimentel	.973	49	64	9	2	3
Valdez	1.000	14	17	0	0	0
Ventura	.944	47	48	3	3	0

Toronto Blue Jays

BY LARRY MILLSON

It was supposed to be a season in which the Blue Jays hit well and then hoped they had enough pitching beyond righthanders Roy Halladay and A.J. Burnett and closer B.J. Ryan to contend.

It was supposed to be a year to build on a second-place finish in the AL East in 2006. Instead, it worked the other way around. The pitching was better than expected, but the hitting was missing, partly because of several key injuries.

After winning 87 games in 2006 to finish second behind the Yankees, the Blue Jays won 83 games in 2007 to finish in their more familiar third position behind the Red Sox and Yankees. The disappointing season was in the words of general manager J.P. Ricciardi, "Due to circumstances beyond our control."

Those circumstances mostly were injuries, which handicapped the club all season long. When it was over, Ricciardi talked about keeping the team basically intact.

Ryan, Reed Johnson, Halladay, Burnett, Lyle Overbay, Gregg Zaun, Troy Glaus, Vernon Wells, John McDonald, Brandon League, Gustavo Chacin and Shaun Marcum were among those who missed time to injury or illness. Halladay who led the majors with seven complete games had an appendectomy in May. In all, there were 13 surgeries performed on 12 players.

"We ended up finishing over .500," Ricciardi said. "I'm really proud of the guys because they could have limped to the finish line, but they sprinted to the finish line. I was proud of that, proud of the fact that we finished with back-to-back winning years."

Injuries to the pitching staff could develop into a long-term benefit as it created opportunities for righthanders Marcum, Jesse Litsch and Dustin McGowan, who emerged as starters and Casey Janssen, another righthander, who was strong in a set-up role. Jeremy Accardo thrived after being promoted to closer when Ryan's season ended early with Tommy John surgery.

The team ERA of 4.00 ranked second in the AL.

But the gaps in the hitting weren't overcome, even though 39-year-old Matt Stairs came through with a .289/.368/.549 season when injuries provided him with more playing time than expected, particularly in left field and at first base.

Key members of the batting order like Wells, Glaus and Overbay had injuries and underachieved at the plate. Johnson came back from back surgery three months into the season but did not provide the same leadoff spark as the year before.

One highlight was DH Frank Thomas' 500th home run, hit on June 28 at the Metrodome. He finished the season at 513, 18th on the all-time list.

Right fielder Alex Rios continued to develop as a hitter with some power, and Aaron Hill established himself at second base.

There were not enough of those positives—the .259 team average was 12th in the AL and the 753 runs was 10th—to save the job of hitting coach Mickey Brantley. He was replaced by Gary Denbo, who was hired from the Yankees organization. Denbo was the Yankees' major league hitting coach in 2001.

Other shuffling ensued. Bench coach Ernie Whitt was moved to first base coach, third base coach Brian Butterfield

moved to bench coach and Marty Pevey moved from first base coach to third.

Brad Arnsberg, Bruce Walton and Alex Andreopoulos continue as pitching coach, bullpen coach and bullpen catcher respectively.

In the minors, the Auburn Doubledays won their first short-season New York-Penn League championship since 1998 and the Lansing Lugnuts were eliminated in the first round of the low Class A Midwest League playoffs. Outfielder Travis Snider led the MWL in RBIs (93), doubles (35) and slugging percentage (.525).

First baseman Josh Kreuzer batted .309/.431/.542 with 20 homers for Dunedin to win the MVP Award in the high Class A Florida State League. He led the FSL in on-base percentage (.431), slugging percentage (.542) and runs (92).

2007 PERFORMANCE

General Manager: J.P. Ricciardi. **Farm Director:** Dick Scott. **Scouting Director:** Jon Lalonde

Class	Team	League	W	L	PCT	Finish*	Manager	Affiliate Since
Majors	Toronto	American	83	79	.512	7th (14)	John Gibbons	—
Triple-A	Syracuse Chiefs	International	64	80	.444	11th (14)	Doug Davis	1978
Double-A	New Hampshire Fisher Cats	Eastern	70	73	.490	8th (12)	Bill Masse	2003
High A	Dunedin Blue Jays	Florida State	72	68	.514	5th (12)	Omar Malave	1987
Low A	Lansing Lugnuts	Midwest	78	61	.561	3rd (14)	Gary Cathcart	2005
Short-season	Auburn Doubledays	New York-Penn	47	29	.618	3rd (14)^	Dennis Holmberg	2001
Rookie	GCL Blue Jays	Gulf Coast	36	24	.600	4th (16)	Clayton McCullough	2007
Overall 2007 Minor League Record			**367**	**335**	**.523**	**8th**		

* Finish in overall standings (No. of teams in league) ^League champion

ORGANIZATION STATISTICS

TORONTO BLUE JAYS

AMERICAN LEAGUE

BATTING	B-T	HT	WT	DOB	AVG	vLH	vRH	G	AB	R	H	2B	3B	HR	RBI	BB	HBP	SO	SH	SF	SB	CS	SLG	OBP
Adams, Russ	L-R	6-1	195	8-30-80	.233	.000	.259	27	60	14	14	3	0	2	12	7	0	2	0	14	2	1	.383	.313
Clark, Howie	L-R	5-10	195	2-13-74	.204	.000	.213	31	49	6	10	2	0	0	2	7	0	0	1	5	1	0	.245	.298
Clayton, Royce	R-R	6-0	200	1-2-70	.254	.246	.258	69	189	23	48	14	0	1	12	14	1	3	3	50	2	1	.344	.304
2-team (8 Boston)					.246			77	195	24	48	14	0	1	12	14	1	3	3	53	2	1	.333	.296
Fasano, Sal	R-R	6-2	225	8-10-71	.178	.125	.189	16	45	5	8	3	0	1	4	2	1	1	0	19	0	0	.311	.229
Glaus, Troy	R-R	6-5	240	8-3-76	.262	.361	.235	115	385	60	101	19	1	20	62	61	5	0	5	102	0	1	.473	.366
Griffin, John-Ford	L-L	6-2	215	11-19-79	.300	—	.300	6	10	4	3	1	0	1	3	3	0	0	1	5	0	0	.700	.429
Hill, Aaron	R-R	5-11	195	3-21-82	.291	.317	.283	160	608	87	177	47	2	17	78	41	0	3	5	102	4	3	.459	.333
Inglett, Joe	L-R	5-10	180	6-29-78	.600	.000	.750	2	5	0	3	0	1	0	2	0	0	0	0	0	0	1	01.000	.600
Johnson, Reed	R-R	5-10	180	12-8-76	.236	.325	.202	79	275	31	65	13	2	2	14	16	11	5	0	56	4	2	.320	.305
Lind, Adam	L-L	6-2	195	7-17-83	.238	.194	.251	89	290	34	69	14	0	11	46	16	1	2	2	65	1	2	.400	.278
Luna, Hector	R-R	6-1	190	2-1-80	.167	.278	.083	22	42	5	7	0	0	1	4	2	1	0	1	10	2	0	.238	.217
McDonald, John	R-R	5-11	185	9-24-74	.251	.329	.223	123	327	32	82	20	2	1	31	11	2	12	1	48	7	2	.333	.279
Olmedo, Ray	B-R	5-11	170	5-31-81	.216	.000	.244	27	51	6	11	4	0	0	1	2	0	1	0	9	0	0	.294	.245
Overbay, Lyle	L-L	6-2	235	1-28-77	.240	.287	.224	122	425	49	102	30	2	10	44	47	1	0	3	78	2	0	.391	.315
Phillips, Jason	R-R	6-1	220	9-27-76	.208	.191	.216	55	144	11	30	7	0	1	12	10	2	2	0	21	0	1	.278	.269
Rios, Alex	R-R	6-5	195	2-18-81	.297	.345	.283	161	643	114	191	43	7	24	85	55	6	0	7	103	17	4	.498	.354
Roberts, Ryan	R-R	5-11	190	9-19-80	.077	.000	.100	8	13	2	1	0	0	0	0	2	1	0	0	7	0	0	.077	.250
Smith, Jason	L-R	6-3	200	7-24-77	.212	.111	.233	27	52	7	11	1	1	0	4	3	1	0	0	22	0	0	.269	.268
2-team (40 Kansas City)					.197	—		67	137	16	27	3	2	6	18	6	1	0	1	51	0	0	.380	.234
Stairs, Matt	L-R	5-9	215	2-27-68	.289	.289	.288	125	357	58	103	28	1	21	64	44	2	0	2	66	2	1	.549	.368
Thigpen, Curtis	R-R	5-11	190	4-19-83	.238	.256	.224	47	101	13	24	5	0	0	11	8	0	1	0	17	2	0	.287	.294
Thomas, Frank	R-R	6-5	275	5-27-68	.277	.336	.259	155	531	63	147	30	0	26	95	81	7	0	5	94	0	0	.480	.377
Wells, Vernon	R-R	6-1	225	12-8-78	.245	.311	.226	149	584	85	143	36	4	16	80	49	3	0	6	89	10	4	.402	.304
Zaun, Gregg	B-R	5-10	190	4-14-71	.242	.290	.229	110	331	43	80	24	1	10	52	51	2	1	6	55	0	0	.411	.341

PITCHING	B-T	HT	WT	DOB	W	L	ERA	G	GS	CG	SV	IP	H	R	ER	HR	BB	SO	AVG	vLH	vRH	K/9	BB/9
Accardo, Jeremy	R-R	6-2	190	12-8-81	4	4	2.14	64	0	0	30	67	51	19	16	4	24	57	.206	.161	.250	7.62	3.21
Banks, Josh	R-R	6-3	195	7-18-82	0	0	7.36	3	1	0	0	7	11	6	6	1	2	2	.344	.273	.500	2.45	2.45
Burnett, A.J.	R-R	6-4	230	1-3-77	10	8	3.75	25	25	2	0	166	131	74	69	23	66	176	.214	.200	.231	9.56	3.59
Chacin, Gustavo	L-L	5-11	195	11-4-80	2	1	5.60	5	5	0	0	27	29	17	17	6	7	11	.266	.269	.265	3.62	2.30
De Jong, Jordan	R-R	6-2	180	4-12-79	0	0	8.00	6	0	0	0	9	11	9	8	0	5	7	.297	.391	.143	7.00	5.00
Downs, Scott	L-L	6-2	190	3-17-76	4	2	2.17	81	0	0	1	58	47	15	14	3	24	57	.223	.209	.238	8.84	3.72
Frasor, Jason	R-R	5-10	170	8-9-77	1	5	4.58	51	0	0	3	57	47	29	29	3	23	59	.220	.245	.200	9.32	3.63
Gronkiewicz, Lee	R-R	5-11	185	8-21-78	0	0	2.25	1	0	0	0	4	2	1	1	1	2	2	.154	.143	.167	4.50	4.50
Halladay, Roy	R-R	6-6	225	5-14-77	16	7	3.71	31	31	7	0	225	232	101	93	15	48	139	.268	.265	.270	5.55	1.92
Janssen, Casey	R-R	6-4	205	9-17-81	2	3	2.35	70	0	0	6	73	67	22	19	4	20	39	.247	.257	.241	4.83	2.48
Kennedy, Joe	R-L	6-4	250	5-24-79	1	0	5.14	9	0	0	0	7	6	6	4	0	5	8	.231	.188	.300	10.29	6.43
2-team (27 Oakland)					4	9	4.42	36	16	0	0	108	115	59	53	9	53	50	—	—	—	4.17	4.42
League, Brandon	R-R	6-3	190	3-16-83	0	0	6.17	14	0	0	0	12	19	8	8	1	7	7	.380	.458	.308	5.40	5.40
Litsch, Jesse	R-R	6-1	195	3-9-85	7	9	3.81	20	20	0	0	111	116	56	47	14	36	50	.270	.308	.229	4.05	2.92
Marcum, Shaun	R-R	6-0	185	12-14-81	12	6	4.13	38	25	0	1	159	149	76	73	27	49	122	.249	.259	.237	6.91	2.77
McGowan, Dustin	R-R	6-3	220	3-24-82	12	10	4.08	27	27	2	0	170	146	80	77	14	61	144	.230	.237	.198	7.64	3.24
Ohka, Tomo	B-R	6-1	200	3-18-76	2	5	5.79	10	10	0	0	56	68	39	36	10	22	21	.300	.299	.300	3.38	3.54
Ryan, B.J.	L-L	6-6	260	12-28-75	0	2	12.46	5	0	0	3	4	7	7	6	1	4	3	.333	.333	.333	6.23	8.31
Tallet, Brian	L-L	6-7	220	9-21-77	2	4	3.47	48	0	0	0	62	49	26	24	1	28	54	.215	.247	.194	7.80	4.04
Taubenheim, Ty	R-R	6-6	220	11-17-82	0	0	9.00	1	1	0	0	5	5	5	5	1	4	4	.278	.286	.273	7.20	7.20
Towers, Josh	R-R	6-1	190	2-26-77	5	10	5.38	25	15	0	0	107	129	73	64	18	22	76	.297	.305	.290	6.39	1.85
Vermilyea, Jamie	R-R	6-4	195	2-10-82	0	0	0.00	2	0	0	0	6	5	0	0	0	2	2	.227	.125	.286	3.00	0.00
Wolfe, Brian	R-R	6-3	220	11-29-80	3	1	2.98	38	0	0	0	45	36	17	15	5	9	22	.224	.348	.130	4.37	1.79
Zambrano, Victor	B-R	6-0	205	8-6-75	0	2	10.97	8	2	0	0	11	20	13	13	5	11	5	.417	.400	.429	4.22	9.28
2-team (5 Baltimore)					0	3	10.17	13	4	0	0	23	32	26	26	6	22	16	—	—	—	6.26	8.61

FIELDING

Catcher	PCT	G	PO	A	E	DP	PB
Fasano	.970	16	93	5	3	0	1
Phillips	.991	49	308	14	3	2	2
Thigpen	1.000	22	103	11	0	1	1
Zaun	.987	103	590	41	8	4	2

First Base	PCT	G	PO	A	E	DP
Clark	1.000	3	17	1	0	3
Luna	1.000	2	7	1	0	0
Overbay	.996	119	1060	101	5	107
Phillips	1.000	4	22	2	0	2
Stairs	.986	45	377	31	6	32
Thigpen	.991	14	99	10	1	11

Second Base	PCT	G	PO	A	E	DP
Adams	1.000	2	4	3	0	0
Clark	1.000	3	2	4	0	0

Hill	.983	160	244	560	14	114
Roberts	1.000	1	0	1	0	0

Third Base	PCT	G	PO	A	E	DP
Adams	.850	16	6	11	3	0
Clark	1.000	10	4	17	0	2
Glaus	.967	114	63	197	9	24
Inglett	—	1	0	0	0	0
Luna	.935	15	6	23	2	3
McDonald	.975	15	10	29	1	5
Olmedo	1.000	2	2	2	0	0
Roberts	.667	3	0	2	1	0
Smith	1.000	15	12	28	0	5

Shortstop	PCT	G	PO	A	E	DP
Clark	—	2	0	0	0	0
Clayton	.973	68	73	176	7	30

McDonald	.982	102	148	294	8	66
Olmedo	.988	24	24	60	1	15
Smith	.875	3	1	6	1	2

Outfield	PCT	G	PO	A	E	DP
Griffin	1.000	3	5	0	0	0
Johnson	1.000	78	122	3	0	0
Lind	1.000	80	137	5	0	0
Luna	—	1	0	0	0	0
Rios	.977	161	287	11	7	1
Roberts	1.000	1	3	0	0	0
Stairs	1.000	57	66	3	0	0
Wells	.991	148	321	5	3	0

SYRACUSE CHIEFS   TRIPLE-A

INTERNATIONAL LEAGUE

BATTING	B-T	HT	WT	DOB	AVG	vLH	vRH	G	AB	R	H	2B	3B	HR	RBI	BB	HBP	SO	SH	SF	SB	CS	SLG	OBP
Adams, Russ	L-R	6-1	195	8-30-80	.262	.182	.290	113	431	62	113	23	2	11	54	41	5	6	1	57	3	3	.401	.333
Barker, Kevin	L-L	6-1	200	7-26-75	.260	.267	.257	130	470	68	122	22	1	18	76	74	2	0	7	119	2	0	.426	.358
Bormaster, Brian	R-R	5-9	205	10-19-81	.000	—	.000	1	1	0	0	0	0	0	0	0	0	0	0	0	0	0	.000	.000
Clark, Howie	L-R	5-10	195	2-13-74	.272	.238	.283	22	81	8	22	3	0	3	15	6	0	0	0	6	1	0	.420	.322
Corrente, David	R-R	6-2	210	10-13-83	.323	.194	.360	12	31	8	10	2	0	3	7	2	1	1	0	9	0	0	.677	.382
Cota, Carlo	R-R	5-9	185	9-18-80	.000	.000	.000	1	4	0	0	0	0	0	0	0	0	0	0	0	0	0	.000	.000
Diaz, Robinzon	R-R	5-11	220	9-19-83	.338	.304	.357	19	65	4	22	3	0	1	10	1	1	2	0	6	0	0	.431	.358
Duncan, Jeff	L-L	6-2	190	12-9-78	.213	.194	.218	43	141	23	30	1	0	0	6	21	1	4	1	33	6	2	.220	.317
Fasano, Sal	R-R	6-2	225	8-10-71	.262	.327	.226	47	145	18	38	4	0	8	14	6	11	0	1	33	1	0	.455	.337
Griffin, John-Ford	L-L	6-2	215	11-19-79	.252	.252	.252	133	484	69	122	28	4	26	83	59	1	0	7	144	4	0	.488	.330
Hassey, Brad	R-R	5-10	180	11-28-79	.176	.083	.213	30	85	10	15	1	0	0	3	6	0	2	0	13	0	0	.188	.231
Hattig, John	B-R	6-2	215	2-27-80	.268	.313	.242	100	347	38	93	18	1	11	52	39	1	1	3	107	0	2	.421	.341
Johnson, Reed	R-R	5-10	180	12-8-76	.375	—	.375	2	8	1	3	0	0	0	1	0	1	0	1	0	0	0	.375	.444
Kratz, Erik	R-R	6-4	245	6-15-80	.214	.200	.220	35	112	10	24	2	0	5	19	8	1	3	0	28	0	1	.366	.273
Lind, Adam	L-L	6-2	195	7-17-83	.299	.294	.302	46	174	20	52	8	2	6	28	14	1	0	1	42	0	0	.471	.353
Luna, Hector	R-R	6-1	190	2-1-80	.343	.294	.360	18	67	15	23	7	1	2	8	9	3	0	0	14	0	0	.567	.443
2-team (83 Buffalo)					.267	—	—	101	390	54	104	25	1	8	43	30	5	0	4	62	4	4	.397	.324
Lydon, Wayne	B-R	6-2	190	4-17-81	.254	.291	.237	126	493	80	125	21	5	5	39	50	1	12	2	102	26	8	.347	.322
Mottola, Chad	R-R	6-3	230	10-15-71	.267	.239	.278	106	405	71	108	24	3	17	56	33	3	0	3	78	6	1	.467	.324
Olmedo, Ray	B-R	5-11	170	5-31-81	.290	.323	.277	97	328	32	95	12	1	1	26	28	1	14	2	53	7	5	.341	.345
Quintana, Al	R-R	6-0	220	11-9-82	.375	—	.375	5	16	3	6	2	0	0	2	0	0	1	0	2	0	0	.500	.375
Roberts, Ryan	R-R	5-11	190	9-19-80	.249	.272	.241	100	337	46	84	16	1	12	47	55	2	2	3	85	1	2	.409	.355
Santos, Sergio	R-R	6-2	240	7-4-83	.191	.083	.229	13	47	4	9	2	0	0	4	1	0	1	1	10	2	0	.234	.204
Schneider, John	R-R	6-3	250	2-14-80	.104	.143	.088	17	48	4	5	2	0	1	2	4	0	0	0	18	0	0	.208	.173
Thigpen, Curtis	R-R	5-11	190	4-19-83	.285	.271	.292	50	179	20	51	10	0	3	20	17	2	1	3	23	1	0	.391	.348
Vento, Mike	R-R	6-0	195	5-25-78	.261	.310	.242	84	295	38	77	21	0	7	41	25	6	0	4	66	0	0	.403	.327
Zaun, Gregg	B-R	5-10	190	4-14-71	.091	.000	.125	3	11	1	1	0	0	0	1	0	0	0	2	0	0	.091	.167

PITCHING	B-T	HT	WT	DOB	W	L	ERA	G	GS	CG	SV	IP	H	R	ER	HR	BB	SO	AVG	vLH	vRH	K/9	BB/9
Banks, Josh	R-R	6-3	195	7-18-82	12	10	4.63	27	27	3	0	169	192	89	87	22	24	101	.284	.286	.281	5.38	1.28
Burnett, A.J.	R-R	6-4	230	1-3-77	0	0	1.80	1	1	0	0	5	3	1	1	0	1	7	.167	.091	.286	12.60	1.80
Chacin, Gustavo	L-L	5-11	195	11-4-80	0	2	7.45	3	3	0	0	10	13	8	8	1	3	5	.333	.167	.407	4.66	2.79
Crowell, Jim	R-L	6-4	225	5-14-74	1	4	6.62	26	6	0	0	50	63	40	37	3	22	19	.312	.219	.355	3.40	3.93
2-team (2 Ottawa)					1	4	7.44	28	8	0	0	56	75	49	46	3	27	23	—	—	—	3.72	4.37
Cummings, Jeremy	R-R	6-2	205	11-7-76	3	3	4.35	12	10	0	0	52	53	28	25	5	19	42	.266	.228	.318	7.32	3.31
2-team (17 Rochester)					6	8	4.11	29	22	0	0	120	123	62	55	13	35	99	—	—	—	7.40	2.62
De Jong, Jordan	R-R	6-2	180	4-12-79	6	5	3.91	30	0	0	2	53	49	28	23	4	20	61	.237	.179	.286	10.36	3.40
Gonzalez, Geremi	R-R	6-0	220	1-8-75	2	1	2.78	5	5	0	0	23	18	7	7	1	11	25	.217	.147	.265	9.93	4.37
Good, Andrew	R-R	6-1	210	9-19-79	0	0	4.26	3	1	0	0	6	10	4	3	2	5	5	.333	.286	.348	7.11	2.84
Gronkiewicz, Lee	R-R	5-11	185	8-21-78	3	1	2.82	23	1	0	2	45	38	19	14	4	6	46	.217	.165	.267	9.27	1.21
Houston, Ryan	R-R	6-4	230	9-22-79	2	2	4.30	50	0	0	5	61	55	34	29	6	29	62	.241	.292	.185	9.20	4.30
Iriki, Yusaku	R-R	5-10	180	8-13-72	0	1	9.39	3	2	0	0	8	10	9	8	1	8	8	.294	.263	.333	7.04	8.22
James, Justin	R-R	6-3	215	9-13-81	3	3	3.68	36	4	0	2	71	66	35	29	7	20	43	.243	.277	.206	5.45	2.54
Kemp, Beau	R-R	6-0	190	10-31-80	0	3	5.50	10	0	0	0	18	19	16	11	2	9	10	.271	.233	.300	5.00	4.50
Kennedy, Joe	R-L	6-4	250	5-24-79	0	0	0.00	2	0	0	0	3	2	0	0	0	1	3	.200	.250	.167	10.12	3.38
League, Brandon	R-R	6-3	190	3-16-83	0	0	3.00	11	0	0	0	12	12	9	4	0	6	10	.267	.240	.300	7.50	4.50
Leek, Randy	L-L	6-0	175	4-18-77	0	0	10.80	2	0	0	0	8	19	11	10	2	3	6	.452	.538	.414	6.48	3.24
Litsch, Jesse	R-R	6-1	195	3-9-85	1	0	1.80	2	2	0	0	15	12	3	3	0	3	10	.226	.286	.188	6.00	1.80
MacDonald, Mike	R-R	6-1	195	10-29-81	6	8	4.88	23	23	1	0	135	161	83	73	10	34	83	.297	.342	.250	5.55	2.27
Mahomes, Pat	R-R	6-4	200	8-9-70	1	1	7.04	3	0	0	0	15	24	12	12	2	3	6	.364	.389	.333	3.52	1.76
McGowan, Dustin	R-R	6-3	220	3-24-82	0	2	1.64	5	5	0	0	22	16	6	4	0	9	29	.208	.242	.182	11.86	3.68
Neal, Blaine	L-R	6-5	240	4-6-78	5	7	4.15	47	0	0	11	56	58	29	26	8	27	50	.262	.264	.261	7.99	4.31
Ramirez, Ismael	R-R	6-3	200	3-3-81	1	4	5.88	14	10	0	0	49	76	36	32	6	19	25	.349	.419	.283	4.59	3.49
Redman, Mark	L-L	6-5	245	1-5-74	0	2	5.12	4	4	0	0	19	26	18	11	3	12	10	.321	.276	.346	4.66	5.59
2-team (1 Richmond)					1	2	3.96	5	5	0	0	25	31	18	11	3	14	16	—	—	—	5.76	5.04
Roney, Matt	R-R	6-3	245	1-10-80	2	2	1.83	12	0	0	3	20	11	4	4	1	7	20	.155	.167	.146	9.15	3.20
Sauerbeck, Scott	R-L	6-3	200	11-9-71	1	1	4.18	23	0	0	1	24	30	13	11	0	7	22	.309	.350	.281	10.27	2.66
Scobie, Jason	R-R	6-1	195	9-1-79	1	2	3.18	7	3	0	0	17	13	6	6	0	7	6	.224	.231	.219	3.18	3.71
Tallet, Brian	L-L	6-7	220	9-21-77	0	0	1.35	7	0	0	0	7	4	2	1	1	3	11	.174	.167	.182	14.85	4.05
Taubenheim, Ty	R-R	6-6	215	11-17-82	4	7	6.37	19	16	1	0	89	107	64	63	12	33	73	.296	.326	.269	7.38	3.34
Thomson, John	R-R	6-3	220	10-1-73	2	4	4.58	7	7	0	0	39	43	24	20	3	15	30	.285	.233	.333	6.86	3.43
Tressler, Aaron	R-R	6-1	185	3-28-82	1	0	5.40	1	0	0	0	2	3	1	1	0	1	0	.375	.400	.333	0.00	5.40

	B-T	HT	WT	DOB	W	L	ERA	G	GS	CG	SV	IP	H	R	ER	HR	BB	SO	AVG	vLH	vRH	K/9	BB/9
Venafro, Mike	L-L	5-10	180	8-2-73	0	1	2.78	31	0	0	0	32	35	11	10	2	7	18	.287	.196	.342	5.01	1.95
2-team (12 Rochester)					1	1	3.48	43	0	0	2	44	48	18	17	2	14	23	—	—	—	4.70	2.86
Vermilyea, Jamie	R-R	6-4	195	2-10-82	2	2	4.15	25	1	0	1	43	39	22	20	4	20	32	.242	.293	.198	6.65	4.15
Wolfe, Brian	R-R	6-3	220	11-29-80	2	0	1.04	17	0	0	0	26	18	4	3	1	6	23	.191	.214	.173	7.96	2.08
Zambrano, Victor	B-R	6-0	205	8-6-75	3	2	7.40	8	8	0	0	41	50	34	34	4	22	38	.301	.326	.270	8.27	4.79
2-team (5 Indianapolis)					5	2	5.56	13	13	0	0	68	67	43	42	5	31	63	—	—	—	8.34	4.10

FIELDING

Catcher	PCT	G	PO	A	E	DP	PB
Bormaster	1.000	1	2	0	0	0	0
Corrente	.970	12	63	2	2	0	0
Diaz	.990	17	97	7	1	0	2
Fasano	.983	41	276	22	5	3	2
Kratz	.986	30	188	17	3	1	2
Roberts	1.000	2	1	0	0	0	0
Schneider	.990	17	95	5	1	0	0
Thigpen	.981	41	250	15	5	2	4
Zaun	1.000	1	5	0	0	0	0

First Base	PCT	G	PO	A	E	DP
Barker	.987	126	1045	95	15	93
Clark	1.000	2	16	1	0	1
Hattig	1.000	7	52	2	0	0
Kratz	—	1	0	0	0	0
Mottola	.906	7	42	6	5	5
Roberts	.977	9	72	13	2	4
Thigpen	1.000	1	3	1	0	0

Second Base	PCT	G	PO	A	E	DP
Adams	.962	102	157	278	17	48
Clark	1.000	8	15	36	0	5
Diaz	1.000	1	0	1	0	0
Hassey	1.000	3	6	4	0	1
Olmedo	—	1	0	0	0	0
Quintana	1.000	1	3	6	0	0
Roberts	.961	32	54	93	6	18
Thigpen	.900	3	6	3	1	0

Third Base	PCT	G	PO	A	E	DP
Adams	.889	5	3	5	1	0
Hassey	.981	20	10	43	1	3
Hattig	.919	87	55	160	19	14
Quintana	1.000	3	4	1	0	0
Roberts	.918	35	22	45	6	5

Shortstop	PCT	G	PO	A	E	DP
Adams	1.000	1	1	3	0	0

	PCT	G	PO	A	E	DP
Clark	1.000	6	12	19	0	5
Hassey	.842	6	5	11	3	3
Luna	.953	18	23	38	3	7
Olmedo	.963	93	144	269	16	53
Roberts	1.000	13	17	34	0	5
Santos	.903	13	20	45	7	10

Outfield	PCT	G	PO	A	E	DP
Clark	1.000	3	5	0	0	0
Duncan	.989	42	92	1	1	1
Griffin	.967	105	168	6	6	2
Johnson	1.000	2	4	0	0	0
Lind	.985	39	63	4	1	0
Lydon	.978	125	303	10	7	3
Mottola	.970	66	124	6	4	2
Roberts	.889	9	24	0	3	0
Thigpen	—	1	0	0	0	0
Vento	.944	50	82	2	5	0

NEW HAMPSHIRE FISHER CATS

DOUBLE-A

EASTERN LEAGUE

BATTING	B-T	HT	WT	DOB	AVG	vLH	vRH	G	AB	R	H	2B	3B	HR	RBI	BB	HBP	SO	SH	SF	SB	CS	SLG	OBP
Bormaster, Brian	R-R	5-9	205	10-19-81	.211	.154	.240	17	38	4	8	1	0	1	3	6	0	3	0	6	0	0	.316	.318
Cannon, Chip	L-R	6-5	225	11-30-81	.241	.214	.248	109	394	57	95	23	1	17	53	54	3	0	155	1	0	4	2	.434	.334
Clark, Howie	L-R	5-10	195	2-13-74	.333	.000	.500	1	3	0	1	0	0	0	0	0	1	0	0	0	0	0	0	.333	.500
Cosby, Rob	R-R	6-2	215	4-2-81	.291	.238	.303	110	437	50	127	34	1	16	70	25	6	0	79	0	1	4	3	.483	.338
Diaz, Robinzon	R-R	5-11	220	9-19-83	.316	.364	.302	74	301	33	95	17	1	3	30	11	3	2	16	5	0	4	9	.409	.344
Hassey, Brad	R-R	5-10	180	11-28-79	.200	.000	.222	3	10	1	2	0	0	0	3	0	0	0	1	2	0	0	0	.200	.182
Klosterman, Ryan	R-R	5-11	185	5-28-82	.205	.200	.207	103	341	43	70	17	1	3	29	37	7	6	1	68	22	4	.287	.295
Kratz, Erik	R-R	6-4	245	6-15-80	.250	.435	.219	49	160	22	40	15	1	8	30	12	5	2	33	0	0	.506	.317
Lydon, Wayne	B-R	6-2	190	4-17-81	.323	.333	.321	8	31	5	10	1	0	2	8	4	0	0	7	3	1	.548	.400
Majewski, Dustin	L-L	5-11	205	8-16-81	.245	.265	.239	130	466	61	114	30	3	14	59	55	3	3	1	108	1	4	.412	.352
Mathews, Aaron	R-R	5-10	185	5-10-82	.293	.343	.279	119	471	64	138	34	4	8	48	27	4	1	4	79	5	2	.433	.334
Mayorson, Manuel	R-R	5-10	185	3-10-83	.274	.304	.266	116	452	55	124	25	2	1	28	40	3	5	1	36	7	7	.345	.337
Overbay, Lyle	L-L	6-2	235	1-28-77	.267	.400	.200	4	15	2	4	1	0	1	5	3	0	0	0	3	0	0	.533	.389
Patterson, Ryan	R-R	5-11	205	5-2-83	.267	.340	.246	111	446	53	119	27	0	18	68	23	1	1	4	102	1	4	.448	.302
Peralta, Juan	B-R	6-0	170	6-24-83	.283	.309	.275	79	272	29	77	8	1	3	28	26	0	8	0	57	2	1	.353	.346
Santos, Sergio	R-R	6-2	240	7-4-83	.250	.271	.245	113	432	63	108	34	2	20	62	43	6	0	2	97	2	0	.477	.324
Schneider, John	R-R	6-3	250	2-14-80	.186	.188	.186	47	145	18	27	7	0	5	19	25	3	0	42	0	0	.338	.318
Smith, David	R-R	6-2	190	1-12-81	.276	.299	.270	129	463	85	128	35	1	24	70	53	9	1	4	105	4	5	.512	.359

PITCHING	B-T	HT	WT	DOB	W	L	ERA	G	GS	CG	SV	IP	H	R	ER	HR	BB	SO	AVG	vLH	vRH	K/9	BB/9
Bormaster, Brian	R-R	5-9	205	10-19-81	0	0	9.00	2	0	0	0	3	6	3	3	1	1	1	.500	.556	.333	3.00	3.00
Carlson, Jesse	L-L	6-1	160	12-31-80	8	2	4.86	58	0	0	6	70	77	39	38	4	18	81	.282	.242	.305	10.36	2.30
De Jong, Jordan	R-R	6-2	180	4-12-79	0	0	0.64	9	0	0	0	14	6	1	1	0	6	18	.128	.074	.200	11.57	3.86
Falkenbach, Connor	R-R	6-0	185	2-22-82	0	0	10.38	7	0	0	0	9	17	10	10	1	0	8	.415	.444	.391	8.31	0.00
Fowler, Eric	L-L	6-3	220	3-18-83	4	4	7.14	9	9	0	0	40	63	33	32	7	18	21	.366	.286	.392	4.69	4.02
Gronkiewicz, Lee	R-R	5-11	185	8-21-78	3	2	1.80	24	0	0	11	30	31	7	6	3	4	37	.279	.310	.245	11.10	1.20
Iriki, Yusaku	R-R	5-10	180	8-13-72	3	5	4.35	16	13	0	0	81	88	43	39	7	30	55	.276	.285	.268	6.14	3.35
Isenberg, Kurt	R-L	6-0	190	1-15-82	4	11	5.53	23	23	1	0	124	163	81	76	8	39	90	.317	.301	.321	6.55	2.84
James, Justin	R-R	6-3	215	9-13-81	0	2	4.76	7	1	0	0	17	20	10	9	0	6	15	.286	.297	.273	7.94	3.18
League, Brandon	R-R	6-3	190	3-16-83	1	1	3.52	6	0	0	0	8	5	3	3	0	7	7	.185	.250	.133	8.22	8.22
Litsch, Jesse	R-R	6-1	195	3-9-85	7	2	2.35	10	10	1	0	61	51	24	16	5	14	46	.219	.199	.247	6.75	2.05
MacDonald, Mike	R-R	6-1	195	10-29-81	3	1	2.51	5	5	0	0	29	31	14	8	1	9	10	.274	.328	.204	3.14	2.83
Machi, Jean	R-R	6-0	170	2-1-82	2	4	3.53	48	0	0	2	82	68	35	32	8	24	56	.224	.271	.184	6.17	2.64
Matumoto, Jo	L-L	5-10	170	2-5-71	3	4	3.54	45	5	0	1	86	74	37	34	4	43	77	.235	.204	.249	8.03	4.48
Overbey, Seth	L-R	6-2	165	4-30-84	2	4	4.26	30	0	0	2	51	55	26	24	3	15	32	.284	.338	.246	5.68	2.66
Purcey, David	L-L	6-5	235	4-22-82	3	5	5.37	11	11	1	0	62	67	41	37	4	16	55	.277	.333	.250	7.98	2.32
Ramirez, Ismael	R-R	6-3	200	3-3-81	1	1	5.70	6	4	0	0	24	33	15	15	3	2	18	.330	.389	.261	6.85	0.76
Rogers, Adam	R-R	6-4	235	10-2-84	0	0	0.00	1	0	0	0	1	0	0	0	0	0	0	.000	—	.000	0.00	0.00
Romero, Ricky	R-L	6-1	200	11-6-84	3	6	4.89	18	18	1	0	88	98	57	48	9	51	80	.279	.293	.275	8.15	5.20
Roney, Matt	R-R	6-3	245	1-10-80	2	1	6.92	17	0	0	1	26	42	25	20	1	9	20	.353	.393	.317	10.38	3.12
Savickas, Russ	R-R	6-4	190	7-30-83	3	8	8.10	8	8	0	0	33	52	34	30	7	23	13	.354	.429	.254	3.51	6.21
Schneider, John	R-R	6-3	250	2-14-80	0	0	0.00	1	1	0	0	1	1	0	0	0	0	1	.250	.500	.000	9.00	0.00
Stidfole, Sean	R-R	6-3	195	3-24-83	1	0	2.60	30	0	0	0	52	45	19	15	3	29	39	.233	.240	.229	6.75	5.02
Taubenheim, Ty	R-R	6-6	250	11-17-82	2	1	2.01	5	5	0	0	31	21	7	7	2	11	29	.193	.214	.170	8.33	3.16
Thorpe, Tracy	R-R	6-4	250	12-15-80	5	4	4.61	46	0	0	10	57	46	29	29	5	29	55	.220	.206	.235	8.74	4.61
Tressler, Aaron	R-R	6-1	185	3-28-82	0	0	27.00	1	1	0	0	1	2	3	3	1	1	1	.400	.667	.000	9.00	9.00
Trias, Orlando	R-R	6-3	215	3-16-84	1	1	5.79	4	3	0	0	14	21	15	9	3	7	4	.350	.382	.308	2.57	4.50
Yates, Kyle	R-R	5-10	190	1-8-83	9	9	4.53	27	27	0	0	151	184	83	76	22	43	98	.306	.300	.312	5.84	2.56
Zambrano, Victor	B-R	6-0	205	8-6-75	0	0	5.68	1	1	0	0	6	10	5	4	1	0	4	.357	.385	.333	5.68	0.00

FIELDING

Catcher	PCT	G	PO	A	E	DP	PB
Bormaster	.979	17	86	6	2	0	1
Diaz	.992	52	330	28	3	4	10
Kratz	.997	45	318	29	1	4	4
Schneider	.983	40	266	27	5	2	4

First Base	PCT	G	PO	A	E	DP
Cannon	.989	103	806	96	10	80
Cosby	.991	34	298	19	3	34
Kratz	1.000	1	7	1	0	1
Overbay	.974	4	35	2	1	3
Schneider	1.000	1	5	0	0	1

Second Base	PCT	G	PO	A	E	DP
Klosterman	.963	21	49	55	4	10
Mayorson	.975	60	105	132	6	40
Peralta	.974	68	130	164	8	40

Third Base	PCT	G	PO	A	E	DP
Clark	—	1	0	0	0	0
Cosby	.944	67	54	114	10	11
Diaz	.850	8	4	13	3	0
Hassey	1.000	3	1	3	0	0
Klosterman	.907	47	35	101	14	6
Mayorson	.920	24	14	32	4	0

Shortstop	PCT	G	PO	A	E	DP
Klosterman	.931	19	32	49	6	10
Mayorson	.921	19	22	36	5	11
Santos	.965	111	144	331	17	71

Outfield	PCT	G	PO	A	E	DP
Klosterman	1.000	9	19	0	0	0
Lydon	.905	8	17	2	2	2
Majewski	.974	121	295	7	8	3
Mathews	.980	111	230	12	5	1
Patterson	.979	98	185	6	4	2
Smith	.976	84	154	9	4	1

DUNEDIN BLUE JAYS   HIGH CLASS A

FLORIDA STATE LEAGUE

BATTING	B-T	HT	WT	DOB	AVG	vLH	vRH	G	AB	R	H	2B	3B	HR	RBI	BB	HBP	SO	SH	SF	SB	CS	SLG	OBP
Butler, Jacob	R-R	6-1	200	2-9-83	.273	.304	.264	124	428	80	117	27	0	23	85	65	4	0	8	95	1	3	.498	.368
Calderone, Adam	L-R	6-2	195	3-17-84	.276	.333	.261	17	58	5	16	1	0	0	3	11	0	0	1	11	1	3	.293	.386
Collins, Joel	R-R	6-1	195	4-24-86	.000	.000	.000	1	1	0	0	0	0	0	0	1	1	0	0	0	0	0	.000	.500
Corrente, David	R-R	6-2	210	10-13-83	.220	.250	.200	39	123	18	27	7	0	7	25	12	5	1	2	40	0	0	.447	.310
Cota, Carlo	R-R	5-9	185	9-18-80	.279	.324	.264	114	427	70	119	32	0	6	48	53	8	1	6	84	7	4	.396	.364
Garibaldi, Anthony	R-R	6-1	200	12-19-80	.200	.387	.149	47	145	16	29	4	2	3	20	12	4	1	0	50	2	0	.317	.280
Gonzalez, Jesus	R-R	6-4	200	7-9-84	.267	.315	.248	51	187	23	50	15	0	6	34	6	2	1	0	32	1	1	.444	.297
Gutierrez, Chris	R-R	5-10	170	3-12-84	.248	.235	.251	68	242	34	60	9	1	2	26	29	5	1	1	30	0	2	.318	.339
Hatch, Anthony	L-R	6-4	195	8-30-83	.249	.206	.261	116	481	67	120	24	6	15	53	32	7	1	2	86	5	4	.418	.305
Hetherington, Luke	R-R	6-0	210	4-13-83	.280	.268	.284	70	254	41	71	9	4	6	32	25	13	0	5	74	18	4	.417	.367
Jeroloman, Brian	L-R	6-0	195	5-10-85	.259	.265	.257	100	290	32	75	14	0	3	39	85	1	0	6	57	0	0	.338	.421
Johnson, Reed	R-R	5-10	180	12-8-76	.333	1.000	.273	4	12	1	4	1	0	1	1	2	0	0	4	0	0	0	.667	.429
Kreuzer, Josh	R-R	6-5	235	9-28-82	.309	.286	.317	117	404	92	125	34	0	20	71	62	25	0	1	82	1	2	.542	.431
Nielsen, Eric	R-R	6-0	225	11-14-81	.325	.322	.325	117	453	75	147	41	0	7	67	33	8	0	5	52	4	3	.461	.377
Patterson, Ryan	R-R	5-11	205	5-2-83	.190	.429	.071	5	21	1	4	2	0	0	1	2	0	0	3	0	0	.286	.261
Patton, Cory	L-L	5-8	215	6-18-82	.269	.250	.275	122	457	69	123	34	3	10	54	50	4	1	6	98	4	3	.422	.342
Peralta, Juan	B-R	6-0	170	6-24-83	.224	.375	.167	15	58	5	13	1	1	0	2	0	0	1	0	11	0	0	.276	.224
Phillips, Kyle	L-R	6-3	235	4-3-84	.306	.203	.328	104	389	44	119	19	0	10	62	35	0	0	4	51	0	0	.432	.360
Quintana, Al	R-R	6-0	220	11-9-82	.243	.326	.202	41	140	18	34	6	1	1	12	12	2	2	1	28	0	0	.321	.310
Rodriguez, Yuber	B-R	6-0	200	11-17-83	.083	.000	.091	5	12	1	1	0	0	0	0	2	0	0	1	5	0	0	.333	.077
Sanchez, Luis	B-R	6-0	150	5-27-87	.082	.083	.081	20	49	5	4	0	0	0	2	9	1	1	0	14	0	1	.082	.237

PITCHING	B-T	HT	WT	DOB	W	L	ERA	G	GS	CG	SV	IP	H	R	ER	HR	BB	SO	AVG	vLH	vRH	K/9	BB/9
Barbara, Michael	R-R	6-3	170	4-27-85	0	0	1.80	3	0	0	0	5	3	1	1	0	2	8	.167	.111	.222	14.40	3.60
Bell, Kristian	R-R	6-1	190	1-11-84	3	7	5.33	22	11	0	0	78	89	47	46	9	28	46	.289	.304	.280	5.33	3.24
Berroa, Yesson	R-R	6-5	230	7-30-82	1	3	5.13	18	0	0	0	26	31	20	15	4	13	29	.304	.300	.306	9.91	4.44
Blackwell, Chad	R-R	6-1	145	1-7-83	2	1	2.28	15	0	0	1	24	22	7	6	3	4	19	.244	.263	.231	7.23	1.52
Carnline, Billy	R-R	6-3	205	1-3-84	2	1	3.89	26	0	0	0	39	44	20	17	6	12	20	.282	.258	.298	4.58	2.75
Core, Danny	R-R	6-1	205	7-17-81	2	1	6.91	22	1	0	0	27	42	30	21	1	18	16	.344	.410	.313	5.27	5.93
Estanga, Edgar	L-L	5-10	230	10-18-85	0	1	16.20	4	0	0	0	5	14	10	9	1	1	5	.483	.583	.412	9.00	1.80
Falkenbach, Connor	R-R	6-0	185	2-22-82	2	4	4.21	49	0	0	30	51	63	29	24	2	13	44	.299	.362	.248	7.71	2.28
Fowler, Eric	L-L	6-3	220	3-18-83	1	2	5.40	7	5	0	0	30	39	25	18	2	6	18	.302	.250	.317	5.40	1.80
Harang, Daryl	L-L	6-2	195	11-19-82	1	2	2.73	34	0	0	2	30	21	10	9	0	8	23	.202	.125	.268	6.98	2.43
Iriki, Yusaku	R-R	5-10	180	8-13-72	1	0	3.09	2	2	0	0	12	8	4	4	0	3	9	.186	.176	.192	6.94	2.31
Isenberg, Kurt	R-L	6-0	190	1-15-82	2	3	3.81	5	5	0	0	26	28	13	11	1	6	27	.275	.160	.312	9.35	2.08
League, Brandon	R-R	6-3	190	3-16-83	0	0	4.50	4	0	0	0	6	5	3	3	1	2	6	.208	.333	.133	9.00	3.00
Magee, Brandon	R-R	6-5	205	7-26-83	9	8	3.91	28	27	1	0	157	161	77	68	14	54	76	.267	.228	.297	4.37	3.10
Martin, Adrian	R-R	6-1	175	9-2-84	5	3	2.56	13	5	0	0	46	34	13	13	3	4	40	.201	.195	.207	7.88	0.79
McGuigan, Patrick	R-R	6-1	185	9-8-84	0	0	1.50	5	0	0	0	6	4	1	1	0	4	.182	.000	.308	6.00	0.00
Overbey, Seth	L-R	6-2	165	4-30-84	0	1	0.90	9	0	0	2	10	8	1	1	0	3	8	.242	.182	.273	7.20	2.70
Phillips, Paul	R-R	6-2	225	1-26-84	4	1	6.26	26	0	0	1	27	30	20	19	7	10	25	.270	.262	.275	8.23	3.29
Ray, Robert	R-R	6-5	185	1-21-84	3	3	4.86	18	15	1	1	67	83	40	36	3	24	57	.304	.358	.268	7.70	3.24
Rogers, Adam	R-R	6-4	235	10-2-84	0	0	2.25	3	0	0	0	4	3	1	1	0	0	3	.200	.000	.333	6.75	0.00
Romero, Ricky	R-L	6-1	200	11-6-84	0	0	3.86	1	1	0	0	5	4	2	2	0	1	2	.250	.333	.200	3.86	1.93
Sauerbeck, Scott	R-L	6-3	200	11-9-71	1	0	5.14	5	0	0	0	7	6	5	4	0	4	5	.222	.500	.200	6.43	5.14
Savickas, Russ	R-R	6-4	190	7-30-83	6	8	4.09	21	17	1	0	99	102	54	45	5	31	52	.263	.236	.282	4.73	2.82
Serro, Ted	R-R	6-4	205	10-2-84	2	1	3.72	23	0	0	0	29	28	15	12	1	18	19	.252	.273	.239	5.90	5.59
Stidfole, Sean	R-R	6-3	195	3-12-84	1	0	1.76	26	0	0	0	31	23	9	6	1	14	22	.205	.234	.185	6.46	4.11
Thomson, John	R-R	6-3	220	10-1-73	1	0	4.09	2	2	0	0	11	13	8	5	2	1	11	.289	.353	.250	9.00	0.82
Tressler, Aaron	R-R	6-1	185	3-28-82	5	5	3.72	33	10	0	0	85	86	35	35	4	48	75	.270	.217	.300	7.97	5.10
Trias, Orlando	R-R	6-3	215	3-16-84	6	7	4.03	23	14	0	0	89	98	50	40	10	26	55	.282	.315	.256	5.54	2.62
Wideman, A.J.	R-L	5-11	190	6-8-85	11	5	3.61	22	22	1	0	135	136	57	54	18	25	84	.268	.333	.252	5.61	1.67
Zambrano, Victor	B-R	6-0	205	8-6-75	0	0	4.50	1	1	0	0	4	1	2	2	0	7	3	.077	.111	.000	6.75	15.75
Zick, Jeremy	R-R	6-1	210	8-25-82	0	1	3.29	5	2	0	0	14	12	10	5	2	5	8	.218	.167	.258	5.27	3.29
Zinnicker, John	R-L	6-2	180	7-10-84	1	0	4.15	8	0	0	0	9	8	4	4	0	9	8	.267	.308	.235	8.31	9.35

FIELDING

Catcher	PCT	G	PO	A	E	DP	PB
Collins	1.000	1	1	0	0	0	0
Corrente	.982	36	200	21	4	2	1
Jeroloman	.993	92	542	52	4	4	11
Phillips	.990	18	89	8	1	0	2

First Base	PCT	G	PO	A	E	DP
Kreuzer	.988	104	972	49	12	95
Patton	1.000	3	23	1	0	1
Phillips	.992	36	336	22	3	30

Second Base	PCT	G	PO	A	E	DP
Cota	.980	113	223	376	12	78
Gutierrez	.983	14	25	32	1	6
Hatch	.951	13	26	51	4	12

Peralta	1.000	3	3	5	0	1
Quintana	1.000	1	0	4	0	1

Third Base	PCT	G	PO	A	E	DP
Garibaldi	.882	6	3	12	2	0
Gutierrez	.900	4	1	8	1	0
Hatch	.953	95	71	230	15	27
Quintana	.913	36	27	78	10	4

Shortstop	PCT	G	PO	A	E	DP
Garibaldi	.923	34	37	106	12	19
Gonzalez	.927	32	43	110	12	21
Gutierrez	.967	51	78	155	8	35
Hatch	1.000	1	2	2	0	0
Peralta	.981	11	19	34	1	11

Sanchez	.936	19	27	46	5	9

Outfield	PCT	G	PO	A	E	DP
Butler	.968	104	145	6	5	0
Calderone	1.000	17	29	2	0	0
Garibaldi	1.000	1	2	0	0	0
Hetherington	.974	65	148	3	4	0
Johnson	1.000	2	1	0	0	0
Kreuzer	—	1	0	0	0	0
Nielsen	.966	113	188	12	7	2
Patterson	1.000	5	7	1	0	0
Patton	.996	115	215	7	1	0
Rodriguez	1.000	5	5	0	0	0

LANSING LUGNUTS   LOW CLASS A
MIDWEST LEAGUE

BATTING	B-T	HT	WT	DOB	AVG	vLH	vRH	G	AB	R	H	2B	3B	HR	RBI	BB	HBP	SO	SH	SF	SB	CS	SLG	OBP
Baksh, Jonathan	L-R	6-1	205	3-1-85	.244	.148	.261	63	180	20	44	5	0	1	18	15	1	0	2	37	8	4	.289	.303
Barron, Raul	B-R	6-0	170	4-4-86	.226	.219	.230	65	208	32	47	7	3	2	25	16	3	6	3	32	5	2	.317	.287
Bell, Josh	R-R	6-0	220	7-3-84	.189	.244	.159	60	227	18	43	12	2	7	29	16	1	0	0	88	0	1	.352	.246
Bormaster, Brian	R-R	5-9	205	10-19-81	.265	.333	.227	11	34	6	9	2	0	1	3	2	0	0	0	7	1	0	.412	.306
Campbell, Scott	R-R	5-11	190	9-25-84	.279	.242	.292	107	390	68	109	17	4	7	43	68	5	1	4	56	4	5	.397	.390
Diaz, Jonathan	B-R	5-8	160	4-10-85	.246	.336	.205	120	357	65	88	19	6	1	51	82	15	17	2	55	8	2	.342	.406
Emanuele, Chris	R-R	6-0	180	2-17-84	.266	.299	.244	100	368	54	98	22	6	6	51	39	4	1	3	91	9	3	.408	.341
Franko, Paul	R-R	6-1	200	6-7-84	.300	.400	.236	29	90	12	27	7	0	3	20	17	2	1	2	25	0	0	.478	.414
Gutierrez, Chris	R-R	5-10	170	3-12-84	.244	.152	.306	24	82	15	20	8	0	0	10	14	3	0	1	16	3	0	.341	.370
Jaspe, Jonathan	B-R	5-11	205	4-11-85	.281	.306	.268	95	317	52	89	23	1	3	52	42	4	1	4	48	0	0	.388	.368
Lane, Matthew	L-R	6-2	225	5-23-84	.255	.194	.272	99	337	44	86	27	2	8	53	30	5	0	4	93	0	2	.418	.322
Liuzza, Matthew	R-R	6-0	215	2-3-84	.259	.314	.232	86	309	45	80	17	3	14	42	41	3	2	0	90	2	1	.469	.351
Metropoulos, Joey	R-R	6-2	265	10-23-84	.198	.273	.159	27	96	14	19	8	0	4	13	8	3	0	1	33	0	0	.406	.278
Nelson, Kevin	R-R	6-3	215	4-8-81	.272	.333	.241	26	81	18	22	5	1	3	19	12	3	0	0	25	0	0	.469	.385
Pettway, Brian	R-R	6-1	225	7-29-83	.250	.263	.244	87	300	44	75	20	1	13	47	43	1	1	3	101	0	1	.453	.343
Rodriguez, Yuber	B-R	6-0	200	11-17-83	.240	.252	.234	98	359	61	86	17	4	7	36	29	4	2	1	108	11	8	.368	.303
Shoffit, Sean	L-R	6-2	195	6-9-85	.253	.243	.256	125	415	78	105	21	13	8	52	78	1	1	4	133	23	3	.424	.369
Snider, Travis	L-L	5-11	245	2-2-88	.313	.311	.314	118	457	72	143	35	7	16	93	49	3	0	8	129	3	10	.525	.377
Stone, Wesley	R-R	5-10	195	4-16-87	.444	.000	.571	2	9	0	4	1	0	0	1	1	0	0	0	1	0	0	.556	.500

PITCHING	B-T	HT	WT	DOB	W	L	ERA	G	GS	CG	SV	IP	H	R	ER	HR	BB	SO	AVG	vLH	vRH	K/9	BB/9
Dials, Zachary	R-R	6-1	205	7-22-85	4	6	4.87	22	15	0	2	85	91	55	46	5	23	43	.266	.270	.263	4.55	2.44
Dougher, James	R-R	6-7	225	7-3-85	0	0	—	1	1	0	0	0	0	0	0	0	1	0	—	.000	—	—	—
Estanga, Edgar	L-L	5-10	230	10-18-85	1	1	2.20	10	0	0	4	16	9	5	4	0	4	17	.161	.300	.083	9.37	2.20
Fowler, Eric	L-L	6-3	220	3-18-83	0	0	0.00	1	1	0	0	5	3	1	0	0	1	6	.188	.143	.222	9.64	1.93
Ginley, Kyle	R-R	6-2	225	9-1-86	7	6	4.73	26	26	0	0	122	142	81	64	11	41	129	.292	.271	.309	9.54	3.03
Godfrey, Graham	R-R	6-3	205	8-9-84	6	7	3.98	21	21	0	0	111	132	63	49	8	36	74	.302	.321	.285	6.02	2.93
Gonzalez, Reidier	R-R	5-11	215	11-1-86	9	7	3.53	20	20	1	0	115	121	55	45	4	30	71	.271	.318	.240	5.57	2.35
Harrison, Benjamin	L-L	6-1	190	4-14-84	6	3	3.55	44	0	0	2	71	68	28	28	3	23	68	.245	.236	.249	8.62	2.92
Keng, Po-Hsuan	R-R	6-1	235	10-15-84	1	5	4.50	34	0	0	6	54	56	31	27	4	21	51	.253	.300	.221	8.50	3.50
Lirette, Chase	R-R	6-3	210	6-9-85	5	5	4.42	10	10	0	0	59	59	38	29	6	19	41	.261	.245	.276	6.25	2.90
Lowe, Ron	R-L	6-0	210	9-6-83	3	1	3.90	18	0	0	2	32	37	14	14	1	15	28	.301	.250	.325	7.79	4.18
Martin, Adrian	R-R	6-1	175	9-2-84	2	2	0.83	19	4	0	4	43	35	9	4	1	5	33	.216	.217	.215	6.85	1.04
McGuigan, Patrick	R-R	6-1	185	9-8-84	0	0	9.00	1	0	0	0	3	5	3	3	1	3	2	.385	.400	.375	6.00	9.00
Overbey, Seth	L-R	6-2	165	4-30-84	1	0	0.00	16	0	0	7	25	12	0	0	0	4	21	.146	.129	.157	7.66	1.46
Phillips, Paul	R-R	6-2	225	1-26-84	1	1	2.45	25	0	0	11	29	25	10	8	1	7	34	.223	.245	.206	10.43	2.15
Pinto, Julio	R-R	6-0	170	10-23-84	3	4	4.21	38	7	0	1	83	77	46	39	5	22	85	.238	.217	.254	9.18	2.38
Reddout, Chris	L-L	6-6	215	12-15-82	9	1	3.13	41	1	0	0	83	89	39	29	5	25	47	.274	.290	.267	5.08	2.70
Rodriguez, Edward	R-R	6-4	185	10-6-84	3	2	3.72	47	1	0	5	73	67	35	30	2	33	68	.240	.282	.216	8.42	4.09
Rogers, Adam	R-R	6-4	235	10-2-84	0	0	7.90	7	0	0	0	14	21	15	12	3	2	11	.350	.303	.407	7.24	1.32
Serro, Ted	R-R	6-4	205	10-2-84	2	0	9.95	13	0	0	0	13	13	16	14	1	19	12	.260	.238	.276	8.53	13.50
Starner, Nathan	L-L	6-2	190	5-29-84	12	9	4.43	28	28	1	0	140	161	82	69	15	40	143	.288	.273	.293	9.17	2.57
Tritz, Noah	R-R	5-10	220	2-19-84	0	0	4.91	1	0	0	0	4	6	2	2	0	1	1	.375	.000	.462	2.45	2.45
Wideman, A.J.	R-L	5-11	190	6-8-85	3	0	3.74	4	0	0	0	22	25	11	9	1	9	17	.301	.286	.306	7.06	3.74
Zick, Jeremy	R-R	6-1	210	8-25-82	0	1	10.38	3	0	0	0	4	9	5	5	2	1	3	.429	.400	.438	6.23	2.08

FIELDING

Catcher	PCT	G	PO	A	E	DP	PB
Bormaster	.976	7	36	5	1	0	0
Jaspe	.992	70	472	46	4	4	13
Liuzza	.989	58	418	45	5	8	7
Nelson	.972	15	102	1	3	0	4

First Base	PCT	G	PO	A	E	DP
Franko	.982	22	160	4	3	17
Lane	.986	59	472	39	7	45
Liuzza	1.000	11	79	9	0	4
Metropoulos	1.000	21	177	11	0	18
Nelson	1.000	10	73	6	0	10
Pettway	1.000	2	16	0	0	0
Shoffit	.976	32	252	28	7	18

Second Base	PCT	G	PO	A	E	DP
Barron	1.000	24	60	63	0	16
Campbell	.979	105	204	316	11	61
Gutierrez	.985	15	25	40	1	7
Shoffit	.947	5	4	14	1	2
Stone	1.000	2	4	3	0	1

Third Base	PCT	G	PO	A	E	DP
Barron	.886	24	12	58	9	2
Bell	.843	52	26	81	20	4
Campbell	.800	3	3	1	1	0
Gutierrez	1.000	2	0	7	0	0
Lane	.880	14	9	13	3	2
Shoffit	.889	55	32	104	17	8

Shortstop	PCT	G	PO	A	E	DP
Barron	.932	18	18	51	5	11
Campbell	1.000	1	0	1	0	0
Diaz	.955	120	211	383	28	69
Gutierrez	.951	7	19	20	2	4
Stone	1.000	1	1	3	0	1

Outfield	PCT	G	PO	A	E	DP
Baksh	.959	56	91	3	4	1
Emanuele	.974	85	142	9	4	2
Pettway	.959	76	87	6	4	0
Rodriguez	.964	93	158	3	6	0
Shoffit	.933	21	27	1	2	0
Snider	.911	110	149	14	16	3

NEW YORK-PENN LEAGUE

BATTING	B-T	HT	WT	DOB	AVG	vLH	vRH	G	AB	R	H	2B	3B	HR	RBI	BB	HBP	SO	SH	SF	SB	CS	SLG	OBP
Arencibia, J.P.	R-R	6-1	210	1-5-86	.254	.296	.241	63	228	31	58	17	1	3	25	14	5	0	2	56	0	0	.377	.309
Calderone, Adam	L-R	6-2	195	3-17-84	.259	.370	.234	72	247	39	64	13	4	8	35	36	3	1	7	46	7	2	.441	.352
Condotta, Steven	R-R	5-11	175	3-18-85	.231	.000	.231	10	13	3	3	0	0	0	0	0	0	1	0	3	0	2	.231	.231
Ebarb, C.J.	L-R	5-11	215	6-11-83	.257	.000	.279	44	113	15	29	4	0	4	18	21	2	0	1	30	0	0	.398	.380
Emaus, Bradley	R-R	6-0	190	3-28-86	.228	.242	.223	39	136	21	31	6	0	2	14	12	2	1	1	26	2	0	.316	.298
Franko, Paul	R-R	6-1	200	6-7-84	.255	.333	.231	20	51	7	13	4	1	1	9	6	4	0	0	10	0	0	.431	.377
Frost, Baron	R-R	6-0	190	2-19-84	.214	.121	.243	42	140	13	30	5	0	2	20	14	0	0	2	23	2	0	.293	.282
Haupt, Christopher	R-R	6-0	200	5-18-87	.075	.083	.071	16	40	3	3	1	0	0	4	1	1	0	18	0	0	.100	.119
Mastroianni, Darin	R-R	5-11	190	8-26-85	.287	.353	.268	68	230	50	66	11	4	3	26	36	5	0	3	42	20	10	.409	.391
Rodriguez, Manuel	L-L	6-3	190	1-6-85	.291	.281	.293	73	282	40	82	16	3	10	49	12	1	0	2	64	0	0	.475	.320
Sanchez, Luis	B-R	6-0	150	5-27-87	.253	.265	.248	60	186	20	47	3	1	0	17	19	0	3	1	55	2	1	.280	.320
Santana, Victor	R-R	6-4	210	2-25-84	.232	.224	.235	69	211	36	49	8	2	9	35	19	4	2	0	89	3	3	.417	.308
Scobee, Shawn	R-R	6-1	210	10-11-84	.202	.207	.200	41	109	15	22	4	0	6	17	13	6	1	1	63	1	0	.404	.318
Soto, Leance	R-R	6-2	220	6-13-85	.224	.143	.247	29	98	7	22	5	1	0	14	7	0	0	0	37	2	0	.296	.276
Stone, Wesley	R-R	5-10	195	4-16-87	.291	.500	.233	26	55	9	16	3	1	0	2	3	0	0	0	15	1	0	.382	.328
Sweppenhiser, Kelly	R-R	6-0	185	11-25-83	.154	.143	.156	24	39	8	6	1	0	1	3	3	1	0	0	8	0	0	.256	.233
Vasquez, Carlos	R-R	6-0	150	5-15-86	.246	.226	.253	50	118	20	29	5	2	1	13	9	3	6	2	35	5	6	.347	.311
Zeskind, Benjamin	B-R	6-0	180	1-19-83	.300	.322	.293	68	233	45	70	12	3	8	33	31	4	2	2	56	2	2	.481	.389

PITCHING	B-T	HT	WT	DOB	W	L	ERA	G	GS	CG	SV	IP	H	R	ER	HR	BB	SO	AVG	vLH	vRH	K/9	BB/9
Aguirre, Wilfreddy	L-L	6-1	210	11-8-86	0	5	4.60	8	8	0	0	43	48	23	22	4	13	30	.286	.405	.252	6.28	2.72
Barbara, Michael	R-R	6-3	170	4-27-85	2	0	1.64	9	0	0	2	11	9	2	2	0	2	7	.237	.400	.179	5.73	1.64
Benson, Shane	R-R	6-4	210	12-15-86	1	2	6.00	6	6	0	0	24	30	21	16	3	7	18	.297	.350	.262	6.75	2.62
Bird, Ryan	R-R	5-11	185	8-18-84	3	2	1.71	11	0	0	0	21	12	10	4	3	7	28	.156	.107	.184	12.00	3.00
Cecil, Brett	R-L	6-3	220	7-2-86	1	0	1.27	14	13	0	0	50	36	10	7	1	11	56	.197	.233	.186	10.15	1.99
Cheng, Chi-Hung	L-L	6-0	200	6-20-85	1	1	2.77	3	3	0	0	13	8	5	4	0	7	13	.178	.200	.175	9.00	4.85
Crowell, Cody	L-L	6-3	215	8-23-85	6	2	3.02	26	0	0	4	45	38	17	15	3	22	53	.224	.306	.201	10.68	4.43
Estanga, Edgar	L-L	5-10	230	10-18-85	5	0	1.27	13	0	0	2	21	15	4	3	0	8	31	.185	.182	.186	13.08	3.38
Farina, Alan	R-R	5-11	195	8-9-86	0	2	4.91	6	3	0	0	11	10	7	6	1	10	14	.233	.182	.250	11.45	8.18
Leffler, Robert	R-R	6-2	210	8-7-84	0	0	0.00	4	0	0	0	5	1	0	0	0	3	6	.071	.167	.000	11.57	5.79
Lowe, Ron	R-L	6-0	210	9-6-83	1	0	2.19	8	0	0	6	12	7	3	3	0	2	10	.171	.100	.194	7.30	1.46
McGuigan, Patrick	R-R	6-1	185	9-8-84	0	1	2.35	5	0	0	0	8	7	4	2	0	4	7	.226	.286	.208	8.22	4.70
Melek, Nathan	R-R	5-11	170	2-2-84	4	2	3.98	15	0	0	0	32	29	16	14	0	7	28	.246	.353	.202	7.96	1.99
Mills, Bradley	L-L	6-0	185	3-5-85	2	0	2.00	6	2	0	0	18	9	4	4	0	6	21	.143	.111	.156	10.50	3.00
Nieves, Javier	R-R	5-10	190	2-5-84	3	1	2.66	24	1	0	0	44	35	15	13	3	20	44	.217	.271	.195	9.00	4.09
Perez, Luis	L-L	6-0	160	1-20-85	3	3	3.70	16	16	0	0	75	73	37	31	1	38	71	.252	.172	.274	8.48	4.54
Rogers, Adam	R-R	6-4	235	10-2-84	3	1	2.27	17	0	0	2	32	35	13	8	0	6	31	.276	.310	.259	8.81	1.71
Rzepczynski, Marc	L-L	6-3	205	8-29-85	5	0	2.76	11	7	0	0	46	33	21	14	2	17	49	.201	.178	.210	9.66	3.35
Taylor, Drew	L-L	6-5	225	8-2-82	1	0	4.55	16	1	0	0	28	31	14	14	2	11	20	.274	.286	.271	6.51	3.58
Tritz, Noah	R-R	5-10	220	2-19-84	1	2	7.13	17	0	0	0	24	34	23	19	2	9	14	.340	.452	.290	5.25	3.38
Walter, Kyle	R-L	6-3	195	7-16-84	1	5	6.00	15	15	0	0	63	74	53	42	5	34	49	.290	.254	.301	7.00	4.86
Wice, Joe	L-L	6-6	230	9-1-85	4	0	3.12	23	1	0	6	40	41	18	14	1	3	51	.263	.282	.256	11.38	0.67

FIELDING

Catcher	PCT	G	PO	A	E	DP	PB
Arencibia	.985	56	466	46	8	5	18
Ebarb	1.000	14	89	9	0	3	2
Haupt	.979	16	85	8	2	1	3

First Base	PCT	G	PO	A	E	DP
Emaus	1.000	2	12	1	0	0
Franko	.985	10	64	2	1	3
Rodriguez	.984	68	569	43	10	35
Santana	.966	4	25	3	1	2

Second Base	PCT	G	PO	A	E	DP
Condotta	1.000	1	0	2	0	0
Emaus	.952	6	6	14	1	3

	PCT	G	PO	A	E	DP
Mastroianni	.962	61	106	148	10	21
Stone	.893	10	10	15	3	1
Vasquez	.844	14	13	14	5	0

Third Base	PCT	G	PO	A	E	DP
Emaus	.916	27	18	58	7	4
Soto	.937	29	13	46	4	5
Stone	.962	11	5	20	1	1
Sweppenhiser	.900	14	4	23	3	1
Vasquez	.889	5	3	5	1	1

Shortstop	PCT	G	PO	A	E	DP
Condotta	1.000	4	3	5	0	1
Sanchez	.959	59	87	192	12	22

	PCT	G	PO	A	E	DP
Stone	.800	2	1	7	2	1
Vasquez	.886	21	20	42	8	6

Outfield	PCT	G	PO	A	E	DP
Calderone	.983	72	112	4	2	1
Frost	1.000	35	50	2	0	0
Mastroianni	.750	3	3	0	1	0
Santana	.975	66	114	1	3	0
Scobee	.903	26	27	1	3	0
Zeskind	.933	56	56	0	4	0

GULF COAST LEAGUE

BATTING	B-T	HT	WT	DOB	AVG	vLH	vRH	G	AB	R	H	2B	3B	HR	RBI	BB	HBP	SO	SH	SF	SB	CS	SLG	OBP
Ahrens, Kevin	B-R	6-1	190	4-26-89	.230	.302	.205	48	165	19	38	6	0	3	21	25	2	0	47	3	0	.321	.339
Chavez, Yohermyn	R-R	6-3	200	1-26-89	.301	.281	.311	50	176	29	53	12	2	6	21	20	6	0	50	7	2	.494	.389
Collins, Joel	R-R	6-1	195	4-24-86	.257	.211	.275	22	70	13	18	4	0	7	16	9	5	0	17	0	0	.614	.376
Condotta, Steven	R-R	5-11	175	3-18-85	.176	.111	.250	6	17	1	3	1	0	0	1	2	1	0	1	0	0	.235	.300
Del Campo, Jonathan	B-R	6-2	185	5-18-88	.337	.240	.371	27	95	19	32	11	1	1	17	12	0	1	28	2	0	.505	.407
Denis-Fortier, Kevin	L-R	6-3	205	9-22-87	.240	.263	.232	23	75	9	18	3	2	1	5	9	3	1	20	1	0	.373	.341
Ebarb, C.J.	L-R	5-11	215	6-11-83	.333	1.000	.250	3	9	2	3	1	0	0	0	3	0	0	4	0	0	.444	.500
Eiland, Eric	L-L	6-2	190	9-16-88	.216	.135	.250	51	176	22	38	7	1	1	14	22	4	0	62	16	1	.284	.315
Fernandez, Luis	R-R	6-0	150	11-16-87	.269	.316	.250	27	67	7	18	3	0	0	4	6	0	0	4	0	1	.313	.329
Fuenmayor, Balbino	R-R	6-3	195	11-26-89	.174	.205	.165	48	178	13	31	5	2	1	12	12	5	0	68	0	0	.242	.244
House, Chris	R-R	5-9	170	2-3-88	.179	.083	.205	23	56	9	10	1	1	1	10	15	1	0	26	3	0	.286	.351
Jackson, Justin	R-R	6-2	175	12-11-88	.187	.143	.202	42	166	20	31	1	1	2	13	20	0	2	44	7	4	.241	.274
McDade, Michael	B-R	6-2	230	5-8-89	.221	.216	.222	39	136	11	30	6	0	1	17	13	1	0	29	0	0	.287	.291
Nicolas, Bartolo	L-L	6-2	170	8-25-84	.269	.243	.277	40	156	17	42	7	0	2	12	11	1	0	28	4	2	.353	.321
Paquette, Jeff	R-R	6-4	243	6-11-85	.136	.143	.133	10	22	0	3	0	0	0	2	1	1	0	7	0	0	.136	.240
Sierra, Moises	R-R	6-1	185	9-24-88	.203	.156	.224	43	143	17	29	5	1	5	15	5	4	1	39	2	2	.357	.248
Talley, Jonathan	L-R	6-4	220	2-18-89	.227	.148	.271	25	75	3	17	3	0	1	10	4	1	0	21	0	1	.307	.275
Tolisano, John	B-R	5-11	179	10-7-88	.246	.213	.257	49	183	35	45	5	0	10	33	26	0	2	40	7	1	.437	.336

PITCHING	B-T	HT	WT	DOB	W	L	ERA	G	GS	CG	SV	IP	H	R	ER	HR	BB	SO	AVG	vLH	vRH	K/9	BB/9
Ashman, Chris	R-R	6-0	180	3-7-83	1	1	1.65	9	0	0	0	16	11	9	3	2	2	9	.175	.167	.178	4.96	1.10
Bird, Ryan	R-R	5-11	185	8-18-84	2	1	1.93	11	0	0	2	14	10	3	3	1	4	15	.196	.077	.237	9.64	2.57
Buckwalter, Ross	L-R	6-0	195	1-27-85	4	1	3.54	17	0	0	3	28	28	13	11	1	5	11	.267	.194	.297	3.54	1.61
Carreno, Joel	R-R	6-0	190	3-7-87	6	4	2.62	12	12	0	0	65	60	27	19	4	13	64	.243	.262	.233	8.82	1.79
Cheng, Chi-Hung	L-L	6-1	200	6-20-85	0	2	6.52	4	4	0	0	10	9	10	7	3	7	11	.225	.000	.250	10.24	6.52
Collins, Tim	L-L	5-7	155	8-29-89	0	0	4.50	7	0	0	0	6	6	3	3	0	2	7	.273	.143	.333	10.50	3.00
Cook, Jacob	R-L	6-1	195	3-15-85	3	1	3.28	16	0	0	1	25	29	14	9	1	7	18	.293	.158	.325	6.57	2.55
Cuthbertson, Brad	R-R	5-10	175	1-7-85	2	2	3.66	12	11	0	0	47	44	21	19	5	18	59	.251	.241	.256	11.38	3.47
Dougher, James	R-R	6-7	225	7-3-85	2	1	1.56	12	11	0	0	52	36	10	9	1	10	51	.189	.176	.197	8.83	1.73
Gailey, Frank	L-L	5-11	185	11-18-85	4	2	2.45	18	0	0	1	33	30	9	9	2	6	28	.240	.217	.245	7.64	1.64
Jennings, Nathan	R-R	6-0	180	12-24-84	0	0	5.68	7	0	0	1	6	10	6	4	1	2	6	.333	.111	.429	8.53	2.84
League, Brandon	R-R	6-3	190	3-16-83	0	0	0.00	1	1	0	0	1	1	0	0	0	0	1	.333	1.000	.000	0.00	0.00
Leffler, Robert	R-R	6-2	210	8-7-84	1	0	1.25	20	0	0	8	22	20	4	3	2	5	24	.247	.321	.208	9.97	2.08
Letko, Brian	L-L	6-5	195	1-23-85	2	4	1.50	12	10	0	0	48	41	12	8	3	6	47	.228	.200	.229	8.81	1.12
Lynch, Mike	L-L	6-2	195	1-15-87	1	1	9.62	13	0	0	0	24	35	30	26	4	11	16	.340	.115	.416	5.92	4.07
McGuigan, Patrick	R-R	6-1	185	9-8-84	0	0	5.40	4	0	0	1	3	4	2	2	0	2	0	.267	.500	.182	0.00	5.40
Melek, Nathan	R-R	5-11	170	2-2-84	1	0	3.78	7	0	0	0	17	20	11	7	1	2	15	.299	.238	.326	8.10	1.08
Monti, Jason	R-R	6-1	210	3-15-85	5	0	3.65	19	0	0	0	37	35	18	15	1	5	35	.240	.271	.224	8.51	1.22
Serro, Ted	R-R	6-4	205	10-2-84	0	0	6.23	8	0	0	0	9	11	6	6	0	4	6	.355	.500	.304	6.23	4.15
Walden, Marcus	R-R	6-0	195	9-13-88	2	4	3.05	12	10	0	0	44	45	21	15	3	12	32	.265	.269	.262	6.50	2.44
Walter, Kyle	R-L	6-3	195	7-16-84	0	0	1.93	1	1	0	0	5	4	1	1	0	2	6	.235	.000	.235	11.57	3.86
Zinnicker, John	R-L	6-2	180	7-10-84	0	0	1.98	12	0	0	2	14	17	4	3	0	4	14	.298	.286	.300	9.22	2.63

FIELDING

Catcher	PCT	G	PO	A	E	DP	PB
Collins	.992	18	119	11	1	0	3
Ebarb	1.000	3	23	2	0	0	0
House	.987	21	134	13	2	0	0
Paquette	.984	8	59	2	1	1	4
Talley	.993	22	138	11	1	1	5

First Base	PCT	G	PO	A	E	DP
Condotta	1.000	1	7	0	0	0
Denis-Fortier	.979	22	172	13	4	18
McDade	.994	38	331	14	2	27
Talley	1.000	2	8	0	0	0

Second Base	PCT	G	PO	A	E	DP
Condotta	1.000	1	1	2	0	0
Del Campo	1.000	7	7	18	0	1
Fernandez	.923	7	11	25	3	2
Tolisano	.935	46	85	131	15	28

Third Base	PCT	G	PO	A	E	DP
Ahrens	.932	24	10	45	4	3
Del Campo	1.000	4	2	11	0	0
Fuenmayor	.871	34	25	63	13	10

Shortstop	PCT	G	PO	A	E	DP
Ahrens	.961	12	17	32	2	6
Condotta	.923	3	4	8	1	2
Fernandez	.929	13	16	36	4	8
Jackson	.951	36	45	111	8	18

Outfield	PCT	G	PO	A	E	DP
Chavez	.985	48	60	5	1	0
Del Campo	1.000	9	12	1	0	0
Eiland	.972	48	102	1	3	1
Nicolas	.976	38	79	4	2	1
Sierra	.958	43	86	6	4	3

DSL BLUE JAYS1   ROOKIE

DOMINICAN SUMMER LEAGUE

BATTING	B-T	HT	WT	DOB	AVG	vLH	vRH	G	AB	R	H	2B	3B	HR	RBI	BB	HBP	SO	SH	SF	SB	CS	SLG	OBP
Aponte, Yeico	L-L	6-2	190	12-17-88	.203	.130	.230	59	207	17	42	5	2	0	12	12	9	0	1	72	5	3	.246	.275
Arcila, Daniel	R-L	6-1	152	7-4-90	.167	.182	.161	54	162	12	27	5	2	0	11	21	0	4	1	56	2	2	.222	.261
Chirinos, Enyer	R-R	5-11	176	9-10-88	.253	.232	.260	59	225	33	57	8	3	0	12	26	1	0	2	42	5	5	.316	.331
Escalante, Alesone	B-R	6-4	180	8-29-88	.225	.229	.224	56	182	19	41	4	0	0	20	28	3	1	1	46	5	3	.247	.336
Falcon, Manuel	R-R	5-11	165	1-31-90	.231	.136	.255	37	117	10	27	3	0	0	14	13	3	3	0	27	4	1	.256	.323
Gonzalez, Gonzalo	R-R	5-10	162	7-10-89	.204	.229	.196	43	142	17	29	5	0	0	15	19	4	2	2	27	3	4	.239	.311
Hernandez, Leonardo	R-R	5-11	182	2-22-90	.261	.304	.242	46	176	16	46	4	0	0	18	14	3	2	0	34	1	1	.284	.326
Mata, Argenis	R-R	5-11	165	6-12-86	.276	.259	.283	56	210	31	58	6	4	0	17	16	7	2	1	40	9	1	.343	.346
Monge, Manuel	R-R	6-1	184	2-10-90	.139	.184	.115	45	137	14	19	4	0	0	3	9	6	2	0	64	6	3	.168	.224
Ortega, Carlos	R-R	6-1	155	3-20-89	.169	.182	.165	45	130	12	22	1	0	0	3	11	4	7	0	43	1	2	.177	.255
Ramirez, Welinton	R-R	6-2	175	4-13-87	.270	.297	.262	68	237	37	64	11	3	3	30	29	8	0	5	48	26	8	.380	.362
Rodriguez, Henry	R-L	5-11	182	10-19-87	.249	.184	.265	50	189	18	47	11	0	3	19	6	10	4	1	58	1	1	.354	.306
Silva, Wilfredo	R-R	6-1	160	10-8-88	.000	.000	.000	3	7	0	0	0	0	0	0	1	0	1	0	3	0	0	.000	.125
Vasquez, Simon	R-R	5-11	201	6-18-88	.259	.265	.257	43	147	17	38	6	0	0	17	17	4	1	2	28	1	1	.299	.347

PITCHING	B-T	HT	WT	DOB	W	L	ERA	G	GS	CG	SV	IP	H	R	ER	HR	BB	SO	AVG	vLH	vRH	K/9	BB/9
Alvarez, Henderson	R-R	6-1	175	4-18-90	1	2	5.61	8	7	0	0	26	36	18	16	0	8	20	.324	.192	.365	7.01	2.81
Belliard, Maximiliano	L-L	6-2	162	4-11-86	3	4	2.22	14	12	2	1	81	79	26	20	1	15	59	.259	.273	.258	6.56	1.67
Bustamante, Juan	R-R	6-0	170	7-13-86	5	3	2.88	13	13	0	0	78	77	30	25	5	23	67	.257	.258	.256	7.73	2.65
Cardie, Jose	R-R	6-4	175	1-8-88	1	4	3.51	16	2	1	0	41	47	31	16	2	17	31	.280	.303	.274	6.80	3.73
Castillo, Joel	L-L	6-1	170	8-22-87	4	5	2.91	12	11	0	0	59	48	30	19	2	20	56	.231	.400	.222	8.59	3.07
Manchego, Ronald	R-L	6-1	170	5-2-89	0	0	4.50	2	0	0	0	2	1	1	1	0	4	3	.143	.000	.167	13.50	18.00
Martinez, Cristian	R-R	6-1	172	3-24-89	0	1	18.47	6	1	0	0	6	11	13	13	0	14	1	.407	.333	.417	1.42	19.89
Mendez, Willi	L-L	6-2	187	8-11-86	2	3	3.32	20	0	0	7	43	40	19	16	0	24	60	.248	.714	.227	12.46	4.98
Pimentel, Sandy	R-R	6-2	165	9-17-85	2	5	3.86	23	3	0	3	51	59	30	22	0	15	32	.294	.283	.297	5.61	2.63
Quero, Jhomar	R-R	6-2	170	3-19-86	1	1	5.06	13	0	0	0	32	36	22	18	3	12	22	.290	.208	.310	6.19	3.38
Ramirez, Alex	R-R	6-2	188	2-11-90	0	8	8.86	13	6	0	0	42	53	42	41	4	27	20	.306	.514	.250	4.32	5.83
Rojas, Carlos	L-L	5-11	176	12-18-87	0	3	3.38	15	1	0	0	35	36	19	13	2	10	33	.259	.400	.248	8.57	2.60
Severino, Wascar	R-R	6-1	165	8-1-86	3	5	5.15	15	6	1	0	58	66	43	33	6	23	31	.283	.317	.272	4.84	3.59
Zarate, Robert	L-L	6-2	165	2-1-87	1	3	2.54	8	8	0	0	46	51	23	13	0	11	58	.273	.250	.273	11.35	2.15

ORGANIZATION STATISTICS

FIELDING

Catcher	PCT	G	PO	A	E	DP	PB
Hernandez	.982	24	148	15	3	1	9
Rodriguez	.982	35	279	42	6	1	10
Vasquez	.976	12	65	15	2	2	1

First Base	PCT	G	PO	A	E	DP
Hernandez	.984	15	119	4	2	6
Mata	.987	16	142	6	2	9
Rodriguez	.978	14	127	6	3	13
Vasquez	.995	25	205	12	1	8

Second Base	PCT	G	PO	A	E	DP
Chirinos	.955	31	69	80	7	14

Falcon	.976	19	43	39	2	7
Gonzalez	.958	8	23	23	2	5
Mata	.986	14	30	38	1	4
Silva	1.000	2	2	2	0	0

Third Base	PCT	G	PO	A	E	DP
Escalante	.907	48	32	124	16	6
Falcon	1.000	7	8	10	0	0
Mata	.946	17	17	53	4	5

Shortstop	PCT	G	PO	A	E	DP
Arcila	.906	53	101	139	25	23
Chirinos	.932	18	27	41	5	5

Gonzalez	1.000	1	0	2	0	0
Mata	.000	1	0	0	1	0

Outfield	PCT	G	PO	A	E	DP
Aponte	.947	57	84	6	5	2
Falcon	.000	1	0	0	1	0
Gonzalez	.947	27	33	3	2	0
Monge	.895	43	50	1	6	0
Ortega	.971	29	31	3	1	1
Ramirez	.980	64	134	12	3	2

DSL BLUE JAYS2 — ROOKIE

DOMINICAN SUMMER LEAGUE

BATTING

	B-T	HT	WT	DOB	AVG	vLH	vRH	G	AB	R	H	2B	3B	HR	RBI	BB	HBP	SO	SH	SF	SB	CS	SLG	OBP
Bejas, Emilio	L-L	5-11	170	8-30-89	.102	.132	.086	49	108	22	11	1	2	0	9	24	2	0	1	37	6	3	.148	.274
Carmona, Victor	R-R	6-1	201	7-26-86	.213	.200	.220	26	80	3	17	1	0	0	6	7	0	1	0	21	0	0	.225	.276
De La Cruz, Tony	B-R	6-1	150	3-29-87	.191	.167	.200	57	188	31	36	12	3	0	14	25	5	3	0	30	18	10	.287	.303
Diaz, Joel	R-R	6-5	192	1-6-85	.259	.288	.249	67	228	25	59	10	0	5	40	25	7	0	3	50	2	1	.368	.346
Diaz, Manuel	R-R	6-1	175	2-20-87	.057	.087	.043	33	70	5	4	1	0	0	2	13	1	1	0	29	1	0	.071	.214
Farias, Dany	B-R	6-0	180	9-27-85	.275	.182	.313	54	189	27	52	7	2	2	24	13	11	0	4	27	8	4	.365	.350
Ferrini, Leonardo	B-R	6-0	147	4-17-89	.240	.226	.245	46	125	13	30	3	0	0	9	10	1	2	0	30	3	5	.264	.301
Gonzalez, Arvin	R-L	6-1	160	2-25-88	.237	.313	.213	60	198	22	47	8	0	0	18	13	3	2	3	37	16	8	.278	.290
Hurtado, Luis	R-R	5-11	175	11-4-88	.234	.176	.252	46	137	8	32	5	0	1	19	7	2	3	0	16	0	0	.292	.281
Molina, Nestor	R-R	6-1	179	1-9-89	.208	.212	.207	52	144	23	30	4	3	0	13	26	7	5	1	32	11	3	.278	.354
Natera, Fausto	B-R	6-1	168	8-15-88	.213	.207	.216	64	197	45	42	6	4	0	11	40	8	0	1	48	10	4	.284	.366
Perez, Yensy	R-R	5-11	160	7-21-87	.298	.324	.287	65	235	42	70	14	4	0	27	17	23	0	0	33	28	6	.391	.400
Suero, Edward	R-R	6-2	200	9-30-89	.160	.167	.158	64	200	24	32	4	0	5	28	22	12	2	1	66	4	4	.255	.281
Vega, Hermino	R-R	5-10	160	5-21-88	.173	.179	.171	40	110	8	19	3	1	0	10	10	1	3	3	14	1	1	.218	.242

PITCHING

	B-T	HT	WT	DOB	W	L	ERA	G	GS	CG	SV	IP	H	R	ER	HR	BB	SO	AVG	vLH	vRH	K/9	BB/9
Bello, Fernando	R-R	6-1	180	4-27-89	2	5	3.28	18	1	0	5	49	49	20	18	2	15	38	.259	.148	.313	6.93	2.74
Christie, Dane	L-L	6-7	226	3-7-86	2	2	5.54	15	0	0	0	26	22	29	16	1	24	24	.237	.273	.225	8.31	8.31
Cuotto, Jonas	R-R	—		9-21-86	5	3	2.45	13	13	0	0	66	56	25	18	1	21	50	.231	.165	.272	6.82	2.86
Estevez, Francisco	R-R	6-1	170	12-5-85	0	1	4.74	6	2	0	2	19	17	10	10	1	7	16	.246	.222	.258	7.58	3.32
Farias, Dany	B-R	6-0	180	9-27-85	0	0	9.00	1	0	0	0	1	2	1	1	0	0	1	.400	—	.400	9.00	0.00
Fuenmayor, Kevin	R-R	6-3	150	4-5-90	1	1	4.99	10	6	0	0	31	33	21	17	3	15	26	.273	.237	.289	7.63	4.40
Hernandez, Juan	L-L	6-0	178	10-25-87	4	6	4.30	14	13	0	0	75	76	43	36	4	21	60	.258	.314	.250	7.17	2.51
Jimenez, Jose	R-R	6-3	200	9-22-86	2	2	5.76	19	1	0	2	30	27	19	19	2	23	21	.243	.341	.186	6.37	6.98
Mayora, Yorman	R-R	6-1	175	4-20-87	2	2	4.33	12	7	0	1	35	45	25	17	1	12	25	.302	.314	.296	6.37	3.06
Mendez, Pedro	R-R	6-1	208	10-5-87	2	3	7.20	14	1	0	0	30	30	28	24	2	21	19	.259	.194	.288	5.70	6.30
Molina, Nestor	R-R	6-1	179	1-9-89	0	0	0.00	1	0	0	0	1	0	0	0	0	1	0	.000	.000	.000	0.00	9.00
Peraza, Juan	L-L	5-11	180	7-23-85	2	2	1.97	12	0	0	3	32	20	10	7	0	17	37	.179	.000	.192	10.41	4.78
Perez, Castillo	R-R	6-3	185	8-20-87	3	3	1.87	14	14	1	0	82	75	35	17	3	18	65	.237	.246	.232	7.13	1.98
Rodriguez, Carlos	L-L	6-0	175	5-24-86	4	1	1.36	15	3	0	4	40	31	7	6	1	7	43	.217	.269	.205	9.76	1.59
Sifontes, Kennett	R-R	6-0	185	5-26-85	4	2	3.19	23	0	0	4	42	30	22	15	1	17	38	.190	.148	.212	8.08	3.61
Vargas, Jose	L-L	6-0	166	7-19-90	1	3	3.10	10	9	0	0	41	47	16	14	1	10	38	.288	.259	.294	8.41	2.21

FIELDING

Catcher	PCT	G	PO	A	E	DP	PB
Bejas	1.000	1	4	1	0	0	0
Carmona	.983	9	48	9	1	1	1
Hurtado	.976	38	229	20	6	2	2
Vega	.967	38	226	34	9	4	5

First Base	PCT	G	PO	A	E	DP
Bejas	1.000	1	1	0	0	0
J. Diaz	.984	59	480	24	8	26
Gonzalez	.981	17	100	4	2	8
Molina	1.000	1	4	0	0	0
Suero	.500	1	1	0	1	0

Second Base	PCT	G	PO	A	E	DP
De La Cruz	.944	10	32	19	3	2
Ferrini	.979	25	44	50	2	4
Gonzalez	.957	42	75	105	8	14

Third Base	PCT	G	PO	A	E	DP
De La Cruz	.786	4	4	7	3	0
Farias	.949	49	53	116	9	7
Gonzalez	.833	3	2	3	1	0
Molina	.959	17	10	37	2	0

Shortstop	PCT	G	PO	A	E	DP
Ferrini	.909	19	14	36	5	4

Natera	.940	60	100	135	15	12

Outfield	PCT	G	PO	A	E	DP
Bejas	.972	42	65	5	2	4
De La Cruz	.928	40	59	5	5	1
M. Diaz	.906	30	24	5	3	2
Farias	1.000	2	1	0	0	0
Molina	.980	31	43	5	1	1
Perez	.946	65	132	7	8	1
Suero	.964	24	26	1	1	1

Washington Nationals

BY LACY LUSK

The Nationals were on the field for two of baseball's biggest celebrations in 2007, a year in which they believe they took key steps toward their own joyous occasions.

After a 9-25 start, first-year manager Manny Acta and Washington won half of their final 128 games to finish 73-89, two games ahead of the Marlins for fourth place in the National League East. It was a respectable finish for a franchise that focused on improving its player development program in its first full year with the Lerner family as owners and Stan Kasten as team president.

As the building process was taking place, the Nationals' season intersected with history on Aug. 7, when lefthander Mike Bacsik allowed Barry Bonds' record-breaking 756th career home run in San Francisco. Bacsik, signed in the off-season as a minor league free agent, was one of 13 starting pitchers for the Nationals during the season.

In the final two weeks, Washington affected the National League East race by taking five of six games from the Mets and losing five of seven to the Phillies. On Sept. 30, the final day of the season, Philadelphia beat the visiting Nationals 6-1, and won the division to finish one game ahead of New York, which lost its finale to Florida.

One of Washington's two late wins against Philadelphia was a 5-3 decision on Sept. 23 in the final baseball game played at RFK Stadium. The Nationals will move into a park on the banks of the Anacostia River in 2008.

During the Nationals' final weekend, the club announced that it had picked up the 2009 option of Acta's contract

"Manny's ability to lead, as well as his infectious optimism and attention to detail is impressive," general manager Jim Bowden said. "I feel the Nationals' future is in good hands with one of the best young managers in baseball."

Pitching coach Randy St. Claire had a staff that accomplished a first for a full major league season: The Nationals finished the season without a 10-game winner or a 10-game loser. Opening Day starter John Patterson went 1-5, 7.47 in 31 innings before eventually having surgery on a nerve in his pitching arm, but young starters like Jason Bergmann, Matt Chico and Shawn Hill showed promise along with John Lannan, the Nationals minor league pitcher of the year.

On the hitting side, first baseman Dmitri Young won the NL comeback player of the year award, filling in for Nick Johnson, who missed the entire season with a fractured femur. Coming back from substance abuse and medical problems, Young started the spring with Nationals minor leaguers in accelerated development camp. But he beat out the likes of Travis Lee and Larry Broadway for the big league job by Opening Day and eventually played in the All-Star Game.

Young tied for eighth in the NL with a career-best .320 batting average. He and second baseman Ronnie Belliard signed multi-year extensions with the club during the season.

While 2005 first-round pick Ryan Zimmerman followed his runner-up rookie of the year season with team highs of 24 home runs and 91 RBIs, 2006 first-rounder Chris Marrero was named the best batting prospect in the Class A South Atlantic and Carolina leagues. As for the 2007 draft, the organization spent the second-most money on its picks from the first 10 rounds in all of baseball.

Lefthanders Ross Detwiler, Josh Smoker and Jack McGeary all received seven-figure bonuses. Detwiler, the

MAJOR LEAGUE: RYAN ZIMMERMAN, 3B

In his second full season, Zimmerman couldn't match his rookie year, when he finished second in the NL rookie of the year voting. However, Zimmerman played in all 162 games and flashed above-average defense at third base. Zimmerman hit .266/.330/.458 and led the Nationals with 24 home runs, 174 hits and 99 runs.

MINOR LEAGUE: CHRIS MARRERO, OF

Marrero turned 19 years old on July 2, but that didn't stop him from crushing low Class A pitching and then holding his own against older competition in high Class A. Marrero hit .293/.337/.545 with low Class A Hagerstown, before going .259/.338/.431 following a promotion to high Class A Potomac.

ORGANIZATIONAL LEADERS

BATTING		★Minimum 250 at-bats
★AVG	Watson, Brandon, Columbus	.313
R	Maxwell, Justin, Hagerstown/Potomac	86
H	Daniel, Michael, Hagerstown/Potomac	143
TB	Maxwell, Justin, Hagerstown/Potomac	233
2B	Daniel, Michael, Hagerstown/Potomac	35
3B	Three players tied at	6
HR	Maxwell, Justin, Hagerstown/Potomac	27
RBI	Marrero, Christopher, Hagerstown/Potomac	88
BB	Whitesell, Josh, Harrisburg	87
SO	Mortimer, Steve, Potomac/Harrisburg	154
SB	Bernadina, Rogearvin, Columbus/Harrisburg	40
★OBP	Whitesell, Josh, Harrisburg	.425
★SLG	Maxwell, Justin, Hagerstown/Potomac	.533
PITCHING		^Minimum 75 innings
W	Martis, Shairon, Potomac	14
L	Novoa, Yunior, Hagerstown	12
^ERA	Lannan, John, Potomac/Harrisburg/Columbus	2.31
G	Booker, Chris, Columbus	55
CG	Jones, Justin, Hagerstown/Potomac/Harrisburg	2
	Novoa, Yunior, Hagerstown	2
SV	Booker, Chris, Columbus	30
IP	Martis, Shairon, Potomac	151
BB	Fruto, Emiliano, Columbus	59
	Hinckley, Michael, Harrisburg	59
SO	Balester, Collin, Harrisburg/Columbus	117
^AVG	Lannan, John, Potomac/Harrisburg/Columbus	.206

sixth overall pick, got $2.15 million and pitched his first major league inning. Smoker, a supplemental first-rounder, received $1 million, while the sixth-rounder McGeary signed for a $1.8 million bonus instead of playing at Stanford but will still attend the university at the Nationals' expense for at least two years.

Marrero, Lannan and center fielder Justin Maxwell, a fourth-round pick in 2005, had the breakout seasons. Maxwell stole 35 bases and hit 27 homers between low Class A Hagerstown and high Class A Potomac, earning a big league callup. In his third career at-bat, he hit a grand slam for his first major league hit—the first player in franchise history to do that since pitcher Scott Sanderson in 1982.

General Manager: Jim Bowden. **Farm Director:** Andy Dunn. **Scouting Director:** Dana Brown

Class	Team	League	W	L	PCT	Finish*	Manager	Affiliate Since
Majors	Washington	National	73	89	.451	11th (16)	Manny Acta	—
Triple-A	Columbus Clippers	International	64	80	.444	11th (14)	John Stearns	2007
Double-A	Harrisburg Senators	Eastern	55	86	.390	12th (12)	Scott Little	1991
High A	Potomac Nationals	Carolina	69	68	.504	4th (8)	Rany Knorr	2005
Low A	Hagerstown Suns	South Atlantic	55	81	.404	15th (16)	Tommy Herr	2007
Short-season	Vermont Lake Monsters	New York-Penn	38	37	.507	6th (14)	Darnell Coles	1994
Rookie	GCL Nationals	Gulf Coast	23	31	.426	13th (16)	Bobby Henley	1998

Overall 2007 Minor League Record   304   383   .443   T-28th

* Finish in overall standings (No. of teams in league) ^League champion

ORGANIZATION STATISTICS

WASHINGTON NATIONALS

NATIONAL LEAGUE

BATTING	B-T	HT	WT	DOB	AVG	vLH	vRH	G	AB	R	H	2B	3B	HR	RBI	BB	HBP	SO	SH	SF	SB	CS	SLG	OBP
Batista, Tony	R-R	6-0	225	12-9-73	.257	.234	.278	80	101	10	26	3	0	2	16	12	3	0	2	14	0	0	.347	.347
Belliard, Ronnie	R-R	5-8	195	4-7-75	.290	.329	.275	147	511	57	148	35	1	11	58	34	1	6	5	72	3	0	.427	.332
Casto, Kory	L-R	6-1	195	12-8-81	.130	.071	.150	16	54	1	7	2	0	0	3	2	0	0	1	17	0	0	.167	.158
Church, Ryan	L-L	6-1	190	10-14-78	.272	.229	.287	144	470	57	128	43	1	15	70	49	8	0	3	107	3	2	.464	.349
Fick, Robert	L-R	6-1	200	3-15-74	.234	.143	.258	118	197	24	46	6	1	2	16	19	3	1	1	42	0	1	.305	.309
Flores, Jesus	R-R	6-1	185	10-26-84	.244	.270	.220	79	180	21	44	9	0	4	25	14	3	0	0	48	0	1	.361	.310
Guzman, Cristian	B-R	6-0	195	3-21-78	.328	.357	.318	46	174	31	57	6	6	2	14	15	1	0	2	21	2	0	.466	.380
Jimenez, D'Angelo	B-R	6-0	190	12-21-77	.245	.200	.264	73	102	14	25	7	0	2	10	21	1	4	0	22	2	1	.373	.379
Kearns, Austin	R-R	6-4	225	5-20-80	.266	.292	.258	161	587	84	156	35	1	16	74	71	12	0	4	106	2	2	.411	.355
Langerhans, Ryan	L-L	6-3	205	2-20-80	.198	.269	.184	103	162	24	32	6	2	6	22	22	1	1	1	63	3	0	.370	.296
2-team (20 Atlanta)					.170	—	—	123	206	27	35	7	2	6	23	28	2	1	2	79	3	1	.311	.273
Logan, Nook	R-R	6-2	180	11-28-79	.265	.305	.237	118	325	39	86	18	4	0	21	19	0	5	1	86	23	5	.345	.304
Lopez, Felipe	B-R	6-1	185	5-12-80	.245	.269	.235	154	603	70	148	26	9	6	50	53	4	5	6	109	24	9	.352	.308
Maxwell, Justin	R-R	6-5	225	11-6-83	.269	.375	.100	15	26	5	7	0	0	2	5	1	0	0	0	8	1	0	.500	.296
Pena, Wily Mo	R-R	6-3	245	1-23-82	.293	.415	.239	37	133	24	39	4	0	8	22	8	4	0	0	36	2	0	.504	.352
Restovich, Michael	R-R	6-4	250	1-3-79	.143	.045	.500	15	28	0	4	1	0	0	1	1	0	0	0	8	0	0	.179	.172
Schneider, Brian	L-R	6-1	195	11-26-76	.235	.212	.244	129	408	33	96	21	1	6	54	56	2	4	7	56	0	0	.336	.326
Snelling, Chris	L-L	5-10	205	12-3-81	.204	.000	.256	24	49	6	10	1	1	1	7	9	3	0	0	11	0	1	.327	.361
Watson, Brandon	L-R	6-1	170	9-30-81	.278	.000	.313	5	18	2	5	1	0	0	2	1	0	0	1	1	0	.333	.316
Wilson, Josh	R-R	6-1	175	3-26-81	.053	.000	.091	15	19	3	1	0	0	0	0	5	1	0	0	6	0	0	.053	.280
Young, Dmitri	B-R	6-2	220	10-11-73	.320	.301	.327	136	460	57	147	38	1	13	74	44	1	0	3	74	0	0	.491	.378
Zimmerman, Ryan	R-R	6-2	210	9-28-84	.266	.374	.235	162	653	99	174	43	5	24	91	61	3	0	5	125	4	1	.458	.330

PITCHING	B-T	HT	WT	DOB	W	L	ERA	G	GS	CG	SV	IP	H	R	ER	HR	BB	SO	AVG	vLH	vRH	K/9	BB/9
Abreu, Winston	R-R	6-2	170	4-5-77	0	1	5.93	26	0	0	0	30	37	21	20	7	9	26	.303	.222	.351	7.71	2.67
Albaladejo, Jonathan	R-R	6-5	250	10-30-82	1	1	1.88	14	0	0	0	14	7	3	3	1	2	12	.149	.182	.120	7.53	1.26
Ayala, Luis	R-R	6-2	175	1-12-78	2	2	3.19	44	0	0	1	42	43	16	15	5	12	38	.267	.243	.286	5.95	2.55
Bacsik, Mike	L-L	6-3	190	11-11-77	5	8	5.11	29	20	0	0	118	141	73	67	26	29	45	.295	.287	.297	3.43	2.21
Bergmann, Jason	R-R	6-4	205	9-25-81	6	6	4.45	21	21	0	0	115	99	59	57	18	42	86	.231	.263	.200	6.71	3.28
Booker, Chris	R-R	6-3	235	12-9-76	1	0	18.00	3	0	0	0	1	2	2	2	1	1	1	.333	.500	.000	9.00	9.00
Bowie, Micah	L-L	6-4	220	11-10-74	4	3	4.55	30	8	0	0	57	55	30	29	7	27	42	.261	.250	.266	6.59	4.24
Chico, Matt	L-L	6-0	205	6-10-83	7	9	4.63	31	31	0	0	167	183	96	86	26	74	94	.281	.273	.283	5.07	3.99
Colome, Jesus	R-R	6-2	200	12-23-77	5	1	3.82	61	0	0	1	66	64	30	28	6	27	43	.258	.311	.218	5.86	3.68
Cordero, Chad	R-R	6-0	195	3-18-82	3	3	3.36	76	0	0	37	75	75	31	28	8	29	62	.260	.221	.295	7.44	3.48
Detwiler, Ross	R-L	6-5	185	3-6-86	0	0	0.00	1	0	0	0	1	0	0	0	0	0	1	.000	.000	.000	9.00	0.00
Hanrahan, Joel	R-R	6-3	215	10-6-81	5	3	6.00	12	11	0	0	51	59	35	34	9	38	43	.286	.267	.305	7.59	6.71
Hill, Shawn	R-R	6-2	180	4-28-81	4	5	3.42	16	16	0	0	97	86	42	37	9	25	65	.235	.288	.189	6.01	2.31
King, Ray	L-L	6-1	240	1-15-74	1	1	4.54	55	0	0	0	34	31	17	17	5	18	18	.246	.161	.328	4.81	4.81
2-team (12 Milwaukee)					1	1	4.76	67	0	0	0	40	37	21	21	6	21	25	—	—	—	5.67	4.76
Lannan, John	L-L	6-5	200	9-27-84	2	2	4.15	6	6	0	0	35	36	17	16	3	17	10	.273	.273	.273	2.60	4.41
Munoz, Arnie	L-L	5-9	170	6-21-82	0	0	6.75	13	0	0	0	5	6	4	4	2	7	3	.273	.286	.267	5.06	11.81
Patterson, John	R-R	6-6	210	1-30-78	1	5	7.47	7	7	0	0	31	39	26	26	5	22	15	.310	.328	.294	4.31	6.32
Rauch, Jon	R-R	6-11	285	9-27-78	8	4	3.61	88	0	0	4	87	75	37	35	7	21	71	.230	.208	.249	7.32	2.16
Redding, Tim	R-R	6-0	195	2-12-78	3	6	3.64	15	15	0	0	84	84	35	34	10	38	47	.265	.245	.282	5.04	4.07
Rivera, Saul	B-R	5-11	155	12-7-77	4	6	3.68	85	0	0	3	93	88	39	38	1	42	64	.255	.271	.244	6.19	4.06
Schroder, Chris	R-R	6-3	210	8-20-78	2	3	3.18	37	0	0	0	45	36	19	16	2	15	43	.208	.250	.183	8.54	2.98
Simontacchi, Jason	R-R	6-2	190	11-13-73	6	7	6.37	13	13	0	0	71	95	53	50	13	23	42	.330	.307	.351	5.35	2.93
Speigner, Levale	R-R	5-11	175	9-24-80	2	3	8.78	19	6	0	0	40	58	39	39	4	23	19	.341	.324	.354	4.27	5.18
Traber, Billy	L-L	6-5	200	9-18-79	2	2	4.76	28	2	0	0	40	50	22	21	4	13	27	.314	.176	.380	6.13	2.95
Wagner, Ryan	R-R	6-4	210	7-15-82	0	2	5.74	14	0	0	0	16	20	11	10	2	8	9	.313	.269	.342	5.17	4.60
Williams, Jerome	R-R	6-3	240	12-4-81	0	5	7.20	6	6	0	0	30	34	26	24	6	18	15	.283	.281	.286	4.50	5.40

FIELDING

Catcher	PCT	G	PO	A	E	DP	PB
Flores	.986	55	262	30	4	1	4
Schneider	.992	122	702	53	6	4	5

First Base	PCT	G	PO	A	E	DP
Batista	.992	27	121	3	1	16
Belliard	.975	9	39	0	1	5
Casto	1.000	2	13	0	0	1
Fick	.989	84	344	22	4	32
Schneider	—	1	0	0	0	0
Young	.990	116	788	61	9	90

Second Base	PCT	G	PO	A	E	DP
Belliard	.989	115	277	286	6	80
Jimenez	1.000	10	13	22	0	3

	PCT	G	PO	A	E	DP
Lopez	.995	43	90	113	1	34

Third Base	PCT	G	PO	A	E	DP
Batista	1.000	2	0	1	0	0
Belliard	1.000	2	1	3	0	0
Jimenez	—	1	0	0	0	0
Zimmerman	.955	161	140	348	23	39

Shortstop	PCT	G	PO	A	E	DP
Belliard	1.000	4	6	9	0	1
Guzman	.956	44	67	105	8	33
Jimenez	.923	11	17	19	3	4
Lopez	.957	111	154	289	20	56
Wilson	.800	7	5	15	5	2

Outfield	PCT	G	PO	A	E	DP
Casto	1.000	12	18	0	0	0
Church	.991	128	314	4	3	1
Fick	.950	19	18	1	1	0
Kearns	.995	159	380	9	2	4
Langerhans	.992	78	128	0	1	0
Logan	.992	111	248	2	2	0
Maxwell	1.000	6	17	0	0	0
Pena	1.000	34	57	0	0	0
Restovich	1.000	8	11	0	0	0
Snelling	1.000	20	28	1	0	0
Watson	1.000	5	9	0	0	0

COLUMBUS CLIPPERS

TRIPLE-A

INTERNATIONAL LEAGUE

BATTING	B-T	HT	WT	DOB	AVG	vLH	vRH	G	AB	R	H	2B	3B	HR	RBI	BB	HBP	SO	SH	SF	SB	CS	SLG	OBP
Abernathy, Brent	R-R	6-0	185	9-23-77	.266	.325	.237	107	350	38	93	17	1	2	36	35	1	4	3	37	15	6	.337	.332
2-team (2 Ottawa)					.266	—		109	357	38	95	17	1	2	36	35	1	4	3	37	15	6	.336	.331
Alexander, Manny	R-R	5-10	180	3-20-71	.235	.235	.235	95	272	33	64	13	3	2	23	17	1	3	2	51	3	3	.327	.281
Batista, Tony	R-R	6-0	225	12-9-73	.290	.156	.347	30	107	14	31	7	1	6	22	8	3	0	2	16	1	0	.542	.350
Bernadina, Rogearvin	L-L	6-0	175	6-12-84	.167	.083	.200	13	42	6	7	3	0	0	1	9	1	1	0	11	0	1	.238	.327
Brito, Juan	R-R	5-11	205	11-7-77	.240	.175	.271	62	196	13	47	14	0	3	24	15	1	4	2	48	0	0	.357	.294
Broadway, Larry	L-L	6-4	230	12-17-80	.249	.220	.259	105	338	45	84	22	2	13	49	60	1	0	5	86	1	0	.441	.359
Casto, Kory	L-R	6-1	195	12-8-81	.246	.210	.257	114	411	56	101	20	2	11	55	54	2	2	3	106	4	4	.384	.334
Castro, Bernie	B-R	5-10	170	7-14-79	.280	.280	.281	118	428	63	120	20	6	1	32	37	1	10	5	64	34	8	.362	.335
Dorta, Melvin	R-R	5-11	160	1-15-82	.271	.375	.243	69	188	21	51	12	3	0	18	15	1	5	4	26	7	6	.367	.322
Escobar, Alex	R-R	6-1	190	9-6-78	.148	.000	.167	7	27	3	4	1	0	0	1	4	0	0	0	9	0	0	.185	.258
Godwin, Tyrell	L-R	6-0	200	7-10-79	.216	.333	.194	15	37	2	8	1	0	0	1	2	0	0	0	6	1	1	.243	.256
2-team (26 Louisville)					.234	—		41	145	14	34	8	1	0	11	9	0	0	0	24	4	3	.303	.279
Gonzalez, Alex	R-R	6-0	200	4-8-73	.167	.200	.125	5	18	0	3	1	0	0	0	0	0	0	0	5	0	0	.222	.167
Guerrero, Cristian	R-R	6-7	175	7-12-80	.167	.250	.000	6	6	1	1	1	0	0	1	3	0	0	0	4	0	0	.333	.444
Harper, Brandon	R-R	6-4	200	4-29-76	.185	.234	.170	84	276	29	51	13	0	2	27	25	3	2	0	50	2	0	.254	.260
Jennings, Robin	L-L	6-2	210	4-11-72	.250	.167	.267	31	104	14	26	9	0	4	14	7	0	0	1	14	0	0	.452	.295
Jimenez, D'Angelo	B-R	6-0	190	12-21-77	.368	.340	.379	50	171	28	63	13	2	7	25	31	0	0	2	19	2	2	.591	.461
Langerhans, Ryan	L-L	6-3	205	2-20-80	.275	.125	.343	14	51	11	14	3	0	1	2	6	0	2	0	15	1	0	.392	.351
Lombard, George	L-R	6-0	210	9-14-75	.244	.242	.245	49	127	13	31	6	0	4	11	16	1	2	1	42	10	3	.386	.331
McDonald, Darnell	R-R	5-11	210	11-17-78	.315	.355	.298	73	267	39	84	17	4	2	41	31	1	0	5	64	14	5	.431	.382
2-team (61 Rochester)					.297	—		134	491	71	146	29	6	7	73	50	5	1	9	99	33	7	.424	.362
Nunez, Abraham	B-R	6-3	210	2-5-77	.278	.245	.288	124	414	46	115	25	0	17	68	33	3	1	4	110	3	5	.461	.333
Restovich, Michael	R-R	6-4	250	1-3-79	.270	.386	.224	97	356	42	96	19	2	20	58	33	1	1	2	108	3	2	.503	.332
San Pedro, Erick	R-R	6-0	205	10-5-83	.200	.200	.200	9	20	2	4	0	0	0	1	2	0	0	0	10	0	0	.200	.238
Suomi, John	L-R	5-11	199	10-5-80	.176	.200	.167	5	17	3	3	0	1	0	1	2	0	0	1	4	0	0	.294	.250
Thissen, Greg	R-R	6-4	185	6-1-81	.154	.000	.182	8	13	0	2	0	0	0	0	3	0	0	0	3	0	0	.154	.313
Watson, Brandon	L-R	6-1	170	9-30-81	.313	.212	.341	103	399	47	125	11	6	2	29	21	2	14	4	51	17	8	.386	.347
Yepez, Marcos	B-R	5-10	160	12-29-81	.250	.333	.000	4	4	0	1	0	0	0	1	0	0	0	0	4	0	0	.250	.400

PITCHING	B-T	HT	WT	DOB	W	L	ERA	G	GS	CG	SV	IP	H	R	ER	HR	BB	SO	AVG	vLH	vRH	K/9	BB/9
Abernathy, Brent	R-R	6-0	185	9-23-77	0	0	4.50	2	0	0	0	2	1	1	1	1	2	0	.143	.000	.250	0.00	9.00
Abreu, Winston	R-R	6-2	170	4-5-77	3	0	1.20	37	0	0	5	52	24	7	7	2	20	82	.133	.153	.119	14.10	3.44
Albaladejo, Jonathan	R-R	6-5	250	10-30-82	3	0	1.13	15	0	0	0	24	14	3	3	2	7	21	.165	.200	.145	7.88	2.62
Ayala, Luis	R-R	6-2	175	1-12-78	0	0	1.29	5	0	0	0	7	4	1	1	1	2	5	.174	.222	.000	6.43	2.57
Bacsik, Mike	L-L	6-3	190	11-11-77	1	3	4.00	9	5	0	0	36	40	18	16	6	6	28	.290	.275	.296	7.00	1.50
Balester, Collin	R-R	6-5	190	6-6-86	2	3	4.18	10	10	0	0	52	49	27	24	3	23	40	.255	.272	.240	6.97	4.01
Bergmann, Jason	R-R	6-4	205	9-25-81	2	1	1.50	5	5	0	0	24	20	4	4	0	6	22	.233	.228	.241	8.25	2.25
Booker, Chris	R-R	6-3	235	12-9-76	2	5	2.95	55	0	0	30	58	37	19	19	4	39	83	.184	.207	.165	12.88	6.05
Bowie, Micah	L-L	6-4	230	11-10-74	0	2	3.95	3	3	0	0	14	12	6	6	1	5	8	.255	.214	.273	5.27	3.29
Carrasco, Hector	R-R	6-2	235	10-22-69	1	2	8.84	15	0	0	0	18	23	22	18	4	15	10	.315	.290	.333	4.91	7.36
Chico, Matt	L-L	6-0	205	6-10-83	1	1	3.27	2	2	0	0	11	9	4	4	1	5	7	.231	.222	.233	5.73	4.09
Claussen, Brandon	R-L	6-2	200	5-1-79	1	1	6.98	4	4	0	0	19	29	19	15	2	7	13	.337	.250	.364	6.05	3.26
Colome, Jesus	R-R	6-2	200	12-23-77	0	0	0.00	1	0	0	0	1	0	0	0	0	3	2	.000	—	.000	18.00	0.00
Diaz, Felix	R-R	6-1	190	7-27-80	5	4	5.66	21	14	0	0	83	92	55	52	14	32	54	.288	.297	.282	5.88	3.48
Foli, Daniel	R-R	6-1	190	3-30-81	0	0	3.14	10	0	0	0	14	12	5	5	1	10	15	.235	.250	.226	9.42	6.28
Fruto, Emiliano	R-R	6-3	230	6-6-84	3	9	5.26	18	16	0	0	87	78	52	51	6	59	68	.249	.233	.266	7.01	6.08
Hall, Josh	R-R	6-2	190	12-16-80	1	1	7.20	3	0	0	0	10	14	8	8	0	5	5	.333	.286	.381	4.50	4.50
Hanrahan, Joel	R-R	6-3	215	10-6-81	5	4	3.70	15	15	0	0	75	65	36	31	10	36	71	.226	.252	.197	8.48	4.30
Hill, Shawn	R-R	6-2	190	4-28-81	0	1	1.80	1	1	0	0	5	4	1	1	0	0	5	.222	.375	.100	9.00	0.00
Jennings, Robin	L-L	6-2	210	4-11-72	0	0	0.00	2	0	0	0	1	2	0	0	0	1	0	.333	.000	.333	0.00	0.00
Kolb, Dan	R-R	6-1	190	6-5-80	0	0	9.00	8	0	0	0	15	18	15	15	3	12	12	.295	.323	.267	7.20	7.20
Lannan, John	L-L	6-5	200	9-27-84	3	1	1.66	7	6	0	0	38	30	8	7	1	12	19	.213	.175	.228	4.50	2.84
Magrane, Jim	R-R	6-2	205	7-23-78	1	2	4.15	4	3	0	0	17	17	9	8	2	5	10	.254	.250	.263	5.19	2.60
Martinez, Anastacio	R-R	6-2	180	11-3-78	2	3	4.73	9	5	0	0	32	31	25	17	3	21	28	.248	.267	.231	7.79	5.85
2-team (14 Toledo)					6	7	4.46	23	11	1	0	73	67	46	36	5	43	61	—	—	—	7.56	5.33
Michalak, Chris	L-L	6-2	195	1-4-71	5	3	3.33	20	16	0	0	100	99	44	37	10	26	46	.268	.222	.286	4.14	2.34
Morales, Alexis	R-R	5-11	170	12-20-82	1	1	6.91	12	0	0	0	14	15	12	11	2	17	17	.273	.294	.238	10.67	10.67
Munoz, Arnie	L-L	5-9	170	6-21-82	3	1	2.56	54	0	0	0	53	46	17	15	5	18	46	.229	.198	.250	7.86	3.08
Nall, T.J.	R-R	6-1	175	11-4-80	0	1	9.45	4	3	0	0	13	24	14	14	5	9	12	.387	.267	.500	8.10	6.07
Perez, Beltran	R-R	6-2	180	10-24-81	1	1	7.27	2	2	0	0	9	17	7	7	1	1	8	.415	.438	.400	8.31	1.04
Redding, Tim	R-R	6-0	195	2-12-78	9	5	5.32	17	16	0	0	90	110	58	53	9	24	63	.304	.303	.305	6.32	2.41
Rivera, Saul	B-R	5-11	155	12-7-77	0	1	13.50	1	0	0	0	1	2	1	1	0	0	2	.667	—	.667	0.00	

Player	B-T	HT	WT	DOB	W	L	ERA	G	GS	CG	SV	IP	H	R	ER	HR	BB	SO	AVG	vLH	vRH	K/9	BB/9
Rueckel, Danny	R-R	6-0	175	9-25-79	0	0	16.62	4	0	0	0	4	1	8	8	0	6	0	.071	.200	.000	0.00	12.46
Schroder, Chris	R-R	6-3	210	8-20-78	2	2	1.64	26	0	0	1	33	23	8	6	0	18	45	.202	.208	.197	12.27	4.91
Simontacchi, Jason	R-R	6-2	190	11-13-73	0	1	5.91	2	2	0	0	11	17	7	7	0	1	3	.386	.304	.476	2.53	0.84
Speigner, Levale	R-R	5-11	175	9-24-80	3	4	4.96	17	6	0	0	49	63	30	27	1	20	33	.310	.278	.331	6.06	3.67
Stammen, Craig	R-R	6-3	215	3-9-84	0	1	12.27	1	1	0	0	4	4	5	5	1	3	2	.267	.444	.000	4.91	7.36
Traber, Billy	L-L	6-5	200	9-18-79	2	3	2.90	14	4	0	0	40	40	21	13	2	7	29	.260	.167	.302	6.47	1.56
Valdez, Edward	R-R	6-2	190	2-8-80	2	5	4.74	43	1	0	2	80	99	45	42	8	37	60	.307	.303	.310	6.78	4.18
Van Buren, Jermaine	R-R	6-2	200	7-2-80	0	3	4.50	26	0	0	1	40	36	24	20	8	21	32	.242	.183	.281	7.20	4.73
Williams, Jerome	R-R	6-3	240	12-4-81	0	0	1.50	1	1	0	0	6	4	1	1	1	2	5	.190	.222	.167	7.50	3.00
2-team (8 Rochester)					0	1	6.35	9	2	0	1	17	22	12	12	1	9	11	—	—	—	5.82	4.76
Yepez, Marcos	B-R	5-10	160	12-29-81	0	0	13.50	1	0	0	0	1	1	2	2	1	1	0	.200	—	.200	0.00	6.75

FIELDING

Catcher

Catcher	PCT	G	PO	A	E	DP	PB
Brito	.995	57	395	32	2	2	3
Harper	.988	81	556	39	7	7	7
San Pedro	.957	6	39	5	2	1	0
Suomi	.974	5	37	1	1	0	0
Dorta	.935	11	12	17	2		6
Jimenez	1.000	8	13	11	0		3
Yepez	1.000	2	1	0	0		0
Jimenez	.938	24	36	55	6		15

First Base

First Base	PCT	G	PO	A	E	DP
Abernathy	1.000	24	104	9	0	8
Broadway	.991	102	800	66	8	78
Casto	.909	1	7	3	1	2
Jennings	.991	30	214	18	2	24
Restovich	1.000	1	2	0	0	0
Thissen	1.000	2	6	2	0	2

Second Base

Second Base	PCT	G	PO	A	E	DP
Abernathy	.965	38	52	85	5	26
Castro	.975	105	202	266	12	58

Third Base

Third Base	PCT	G	PO	A	E	DP
Abernathy	.938	48	25	51	5	5
Batista	1.000	25	15	48	0	7
Casto	.902	62	29	90	13	9
Dorta	1.000	12	2	11	0	1
Jimenez	.920	15	9	14	2	1
Thissen	1.000	4	1	4	0	0
Yepez	.667	1	0	4	2	2

Shortstop

Shortstop	PCT	G	PO	A	E	DP
Alexander	.964	90	127	198	12	49
Dorta	.955	44	48	99	7	23
Gonzalez	1.000	5	9	12	0	3

Outfield

Outfield	PCT	G	PO	A	E	DP
Abernathy	1.000	3	2	0	0	0
Bernadina	1.000	13	30	0	0	0
Casto	.988	50	78	2	1	1
Dorta	1.000	2	2	0	0	0
Escobar	.929	6	13	0	1	0
Godwin	1.000	13	25	1	0	0
Guerrero	1.000	5	2	1	0	0
Langerhans	1.000	14	25	0	0	0
Lombard	1.000	34	68	2	0	0
McDonald	.968	70	144	5	5	0
Nunez	.978	106	214	4	5	2
Restovich	.981	57	102	3	2	1
Watson	.981	94	207	5	4	1

HARRISBURG SENATORS　　DOUBLE-A

EASTERN LEAGUE

BATTING

Player	B-T	HT	WT	DOB	AVG	vLH	vRH	G	AB	R	H	2B	3B	HR	RBI	BB	HBP	SO	SH	SF	SB	CS	SLG	OBP
Bernadina, Rogearvin	L-L	6-0	175	6-12-84	.270	.244	.278	97	371	58	100	15	2	6	36	38	2	80	3	1	40	13	.369	.340
Blanco, Tony	R-R	6-1	175	11-10-81	.237	.260	.227	71	253	30	60	12	1	10	43	15	5	59	0	2	5	0	.411	.291
Brown, Dee	R-R	6-0	230	10-21-82	.251	.382	.192	58	175	20	44	7	0	4	16	9	7	42	2	0	2	0	.360	.314
Bynum, Seth	R-R	6-0	185	12-19-80	.231	.313	.207	66	212	21	49	5	1	6	34	19	5	44	2	3	4	2	.349	.305
Castro, Ofilio	R-R	6-0	160	8-18-83	.254	.254	.254	57	197	24	50	8	1	0	22	24	1	43	6	1	1	3	.305	.336
DeMent, Dan	R-R	5-10		6-17-78	.280	.330	.260	121	407	66	114	29	2	10	67	44	5	99	3	4	2	0	.435	.354
Diaz, Frank	R-R	6-2	180	10-6-83	.255	.288	.244	115	416	55	106	20	2	14	56	26	3	68	2	5	9	3	.413	.300
Dorta, Melvin	R-R	5-11	160	1-15-82	.196	.250	.170	45	168	21	33	6	1	1	11	11	1	22	2	1	6	5	.262	.249
Escobar, Alex	R-R	6-1	190	6-9-78	.188	.000	.214	5	16	0	3	2	0	0	1	0	0	2	0	1	1	0	.313	.176
Fulse, Sheldon	B-R	6-1	200	11-10-81	.281	.375	.238	59	178	40	50	9	1	4	16	35	0	53	2	0	14	3	.410	.399
Guerrero, Cristian	R-R	6-7	175	7-12-80	.248	.167	.278	49	133	19	33	5	2	7	24	19	0	47	1	1	3	1	.474	.340
Herrera, Javi	R-R	6-1	200	10-8-81	.257	.250	.258	39	113	17	29	4	0	4	17	23	3	16	0	2	1	2	.398	.390
2-team (18 Akron)					.228	—		57	167	19	38	5	0	4	23	25	5	26	0	5	1	2	.329	.337
Ivany, Devin	R-R	6-2	185	7-27-82	.178	.300	.093	22	73	8	13	4	0	0	7	7	0	21	2	1	1	1	.233	.244
Jennings, Robin	L-L	6-2	210	4-11-72	.282	.333	.267	22	78	9	22	4	0	3	7	7	0	14	0	0	1	0	.449	.341
Larson, Brandon	R-R	6-2	210	5-24-76	.238	.234	.239	52	189	31	45	9	0	8	18	13	1	38	0	1	2	1	.413	.289
Logan, Brett	R-R	6-2	215	12-31-82	.102	.227	.000	20	49	2	5	1	0	0	1	3	1	15	1	0	2	0	.122	.170
Melo, Juan	B-R	6-1	160	10-11-76	.239	.176	.263	54	188	13	45	8	0	6	23	16	3	28	2	3	1	4	.346	.305
Montz, Luke	R-R	6-2	205	7-7-83	.233	.213	.242	40	146	22	34	5	1	5	19	8	1	50	1	2	0	0	.384	.274
Mortimer, Steve	L-L	6-3	215	6-10-81	.232	.278	.224	70	228	32	53	13	1	9	33	35	2	94	0	0	1	2	.417	.340
Powell, Brandon	L-R	6-0	191	8-15-80	.305	.143	.330	39	115	25	35	4	0	2	25	6	3	22	2	3	4	1	.427	.362
Robinson, Wade	L-R	6-2	165	1-12-81	.209	.125	.223	39	110	9	23	3	0	0	6	12	0	17	1	0	2	1	.236	.287
Rogelstad, Matt	L-R	6-3	185	9-13-82	.000	—	.000	1	3	0	0	0	0	0	0	0	0	3	0	0	0	0	.000	.000
Suomi, John	L-R	5-11	199	10-5-80	.223	.200	.225	36	112	11	25	7	1	2	14	7	2	19	1	0	0	0	.357	.281
Thissen, Greg	R-R	6-4	185	6-1-81	1.000	—	1.000	1	1	0	1	0	0	0	1	0	0	0	0	0	0	0	1.000	1.000
Whitesell, Josh	L-L	6-0	220	4-14-82	.284	.243	.300	119	387	78	110	23	1	21	74	87	10	107	0	3	6	2	.512	.425
Yepez, Marcos	B-R	5-10	160	12-29-81	.291	.380	.265	63	220	35	64	8	1	3	20	12	4	52	2	4	4	2	.350	.360

PITCHING

Player	B-T	HT	WT	DOB	W	L	ERA	G	GS	CG	SV	IP	H	R	ER	HR	BB	SO	AVG	vLH	vRH	K/9	BB/9
Albaladejo, Jonathan	R-R	6-5	250	10-30-82	4	3	4.17	21	0	0	2	37	30	20	17	3	15	35	.222	.197	.243	8.59	3.68
Balester, Collin	R-R	6-6	190	6-6-86	2	7	3.74	17	17	0	0	99	103	47	41	9	25	77	.268	.297	.235	7.02	2.28
Campbell, Brett	R-R	6-0	170	10-17-81	3	5	4.91	47	0	0	9	59	54	39	32	5	34	60	.235	.239	.232	9.20	5.22
Carr, Adam	R-R	6-1	185	4-1-84	1	0	1.64	7	0	0	2	11	7	2	2	1	9	13	.189	.250	.143	10.64	7.36
DeMent, Dan	R-R	5-10	191	6-17-78	0	0	9.00	1	0	0	0	1	2	1	1	0	0	0	.500	.333	1.000	0.00	0.00
Foli, Daniel	R-R	6-1	190	3-30-81	0	2	8.39	11	3	0	0	25	34	28	23	3	17	27	.327	.283	.373	9.85	6.20
Hall, Josh	R-R	6-2	190	12-16-80	2	3	3.95	28	1	0	1	57	48	26	25	3	29	43	.230	.211	.244	6.79	4.58
Hinckley, Michael	R-L	6-3	170	10-5-82	9	10	5.83	25	23	0	0	117	145	85	76	15	59	70	.304	.294	.307	5.37	4.53
Jones, Justin	L-L	6-3	215	9-25-84	2	0	5.19	3	3	0	0	17	20	11	10	2	4	9	.317	.200	.340	4.67	2.08
King, Ray	L-L	6-1	240	1-15-74	0	0	0.00	1	1	0	0	1	0	0	0	1	1	1	.000	.000	.000	6.75	6.75
Kolb, Dan	R-R	6-1	190	6-5-80	2	2	3.79	23	0	0	2	40	30	21	17	4	28	32	.213	.205	.221	7.14	6.25
Lannan, John	L-L	6-5	200	9-27-84	3	2	3.25	6	5	0	0	36	31	14	13	2	15	20	.233	.194	.247	5.00	3.75
Magrane, Jim	R-R	6-2	205	7-23-78	6	8	3.99	26	18	0	0	131	147	67	58	9	36	83	.282	.288	.277	5.72	2.48
Martinez, Anastacio	R-R	6-2	180	11-3-78	0	2	4.88	6	5	0	0	24	26	18	13	1	15	17	.277	.220	.341	6.38	5.62
Martinez, Carlos	R-R	6-4	177	3-30-84	2	0	6.56	9	0	0	0	23	24	20	17	1	14	15	.273	.425	.146	5.79	5.40
Mock, Garrett	R-R	6-4	215	4-25-83	1	5	5.79	11	11	0	0	51	66	41	33	5	28	41	.311	.358	.264	7.19	4.91
Morales, Alexis	R-R	5-11	170	12-20-82	3	2	3.04	16	0	0	2	24	12	8	8	0	26	34	.152	.229	.091	12.93	9.89
Mortimer, Steve	L-L	6-3	215	6-10-81	0	0	0.00	1	0	0	1	0	0	0	0	0	0	2	.000	.000	.000	18.00	0.00
Nall, T.J.	R-R	6-2	175	11-4-80	3	9	4.85	12	12	0	0	69	88	46	37	10	22	44	.311	.280	.343	5.77	2.88
2-team (2 Portland)					3	11	5.18	14	13	0	0	75	96	53	43	12	28	48	—	—	—	5.79	3.38

Name	B-T	HT	WT	DOB	W	L	ERA	G	GS	CG	SV	IP	H	R	ER	HR	BB	SO	AVG	vLH	vRH	K/9	BB/9
O'Connor, Michael	L-L	6-3	170	8-17-80	3	7	7.07	15	15	1	0	71	86	59	56	21	19	46	.290	.329	.276	5.80	2.40
Perez, Beltran	R-R	6-2	180	10-24-81	6	6	4.37	22	20	0	0	115	126	62	56	17	36	62	.275	.297	.255	4.84	2.81
Perrault, Josh	R-R	6-3	205	6-11-82	0	0	6.75	4	0	0	0	3	7	6	2	0	1	1	.467	.167	.667	3.38	3.38
Perrin, Devin	R-R	6-7	225	5-14-81	1	0	2.57	5	0	0	0	7	4	2	2	1	3	7	.160	.154	.167	9.00	3.86
Plexico, Gerald	L-L	6-4	210	2-24-80	2	5	4.07	43	3	0	1	66	65	32	30	11	33	37	.263	.244	.272	5.02	4.48
Robinson, Wade	L-R	6-2	165	1-12-81	0	0	0.00	1	0	0	0	1	0	0	0	0	0	0	.000	.000	.000	0.00	0.00
Rueckel, Danny	R-R	6-0	175	9-25-79	0	1	4.66	8	0	0	0	10	11	5	5	0	10	7	.282	.190	.389	6.52	9.31
Trahan, David	R-R	6-3	185	2-27-81	0	0	2.89	15	0	0	1	19	20	10	6	1	9	14	.278	.355	.220	6.75	4.34
Valdez, Edward	R-R	6-2	190	2-8-80	0	0	0.00	3	0	0	1	5	2	0	0	0	2	4	.111	.222	.000	7.20	3.60
Williams, Jerome	R-R	6-3	240	12-4-81	0	3	9.08	14	4	0	0	36	53	47	36	8	16	26	.349	.329	.371	6.56	4.04
Zinicola, Zechry	R-R	6-1	220	3-2-85	0	4	5.46	42	0	0	6	58	53	35	35	3	36	45	.248	.281	.220	7.02	5.62

FIELDING

Catcher	PCT	G	PO	A	E	DP	PB
Herrera	.985	37	238	19	4	4	4
Ivany	.970	22	150	11	5	4	3
Logan	.992	19	107	13	1	2	0
Montz	.967	38	215	20	8	4	4
Suomi	.995	32	192	11	1	0	6

	PCT	G	PO	A	E	DP
Dorta	.941	8	10	22	2	4
Melo	.973	12	18	18	1	4
Powell	.984	15	21	39	1	8
Robinson	.967	18	33	54	3	13
Thissen	1.000	1	1	2	0	1
Yepez	.938	19	36	40	5	7

	PCT	G	PO	A	E	DP
Dorta	.962	35	57	96	6	27
Robinson	.962	13	14	36	2	3
Yepez	.957	47	66	111	8	19

First Base	PCT	G	PO	A	E	DP
DeMent	.979	6	40	7	1	4
Jennings	1.000	6	47	2	0	4
Larson	1.000	2	6	0	0	1
Melo	1.000	11	54	5	0	8
Mortimer	.994	37	280	38	2	36
Whitesell	.986	92	730	69	11	51

Second Base	PCT	G	PO	A	E	DP
Bynum	1.000	11	22	29	0	7
Castro	.987	19	30	47	1	8
DeMent	.980	58	93	151	5	34

Third Base	PCT	G	PO	A	E	DP
Castro	.937	38	16	73	6	5
DeMent	.865	38	20	70	14	6
Larson	.958	42	27	65	4	5
Melo	.981	23	14	37	1	2
Powell	.625	4	2	3	3	0
Robinson	.778	7	2	12	4	3
Rogelstad	1.000	1	1	1	0	0

Shortstop	PCT	G	PO	A	E	DP
Bynum	.928	54	71	135	16	34
Castro	.833	1	3	2	1	1

Outfield	PCT	G	PO	A	E	DP
Bernadina	.989	95	252	11	3	3
Blanco	.987	44	73	2	1	0
Brown	.964	44	80	0	3	0
DeMent	1.000	20	34	1	0	0
Diaz	.983	114	226	8	4	1
Escobar	1.000	4	5	0	0	0
Fulse	1.000	54	89	3	0	1
Guerrero	1.000	40	60	2	0	0
Jennings	1.000	15	26	1	0	0
Mortimer	.984	31	61	2	1	1

POTOMAC NATIONALS   HIGH CLASS A

CAROLINA LEAGUE

BATTING	B-T	HT	WT	DOB	AVG	vLH	vRH	G	AB	R	H	2B	3B	HR	RBI	BB	HBP	SO	SH	SF	SB	CS	SLG	OBP
Baez, Edgardo	R-R	6-2	190	7-12-85	.278	.361	.247	76	270	37	75	11	1	10	50	39	1	74	1	4	10	7	.437	.366
Brown, Dee	R-R	6-0	230	10-21-82	.284	.333	.269	58	225	38	64	14	2	3	29	18	12	52	0	0	8	2	.404	.369
Bynum, Seth	R-R	6-2	185	12-19-80	.316	.385	.280	9	38	2	12	6	0	0	5	0	0	7	0	0	0	0	.474	.316
Castro, Ofilio	R-R	6-0	160	8-18-83	.304	.391	.280	55	214	27	65	14	0	0	21	19	1	27	6	3	7	4	.369	.359
Daniel, Michael	L-R	6-3	180	8-17-84	.296	.382	.276	71	280	37	83	20	5	4	41	29	2	62	4	5	16	6	.446	.361
Davis, Leonard	L-R	5-10	195	12-24-83	.262	.143	.286	23	84	8	22	4	0	1	10	1	0	22	1	1	0	2	.452	.267
Desmond, Ian	R-R	6-2	185	9-20-85	.264	.268	.263	129	458	69	121	30	4	13	45	57	11	99	6	4	27	11	.432	.357
Escobar, Alex	R-R	6-1	190	9-6-78	.125	.000	.250	2	8	1	1	0	0	0	1	1	0	1	0	0	0	0	.125	.222
Ivany, Devin	R-R	6-2	185	7-27-82	.275	.286	.273	36	131	18	36	5	0	5	19	7	2	26	0	4	4	2	.427	.313
Lowrance, Marvin	L-L	6-0	215	7-16-84	.256	.231	.261	98	348	57	89	22	1	16	51	61	4	87	1	2	2	2	.463	.371
Marrero, Christopher	R-R	6-3	210	7-2-88	.259	.275	.255	68	255	40	66	11	3	9	35	32	0	63	0	3	0	0	.431	.338
Maxwell, Justin	R-R	6-5	225	11-6-83	.263	.310	.253	58	228	35	60	10	0	13	43	24	4	65	0	4	21	5	.491	.338
McMillan, Brett	L-R	6-5	215	11-18-83	.257	.311	.245	69	237	33	61	14	0	4	36	40	0	59	1	0	1	3	.367	.365
Montz, Luke	R-R	6-2	205	7-7-83	.269	.345	.240	60	201	43	54	15	1	7	39	45	3	54	2	2	3	2	.458	.406
Mortimer, Steve	L-L	6-3	215	6-10-81	.253	.250	.254	52	170	23	43	8	1	12	40	17	6	60	0	2	8	4	.524	.338
Nunez, Alex	L-R	5-11	170	4-30-81	.364	1.000	.300	3	11	2	4	1	0	0	2	1	0	3	0	0	1	0	.455	.462
Peacock, Brian	R-R	6-1	185	8-26-84	.212	.289	.192	60	217	27	46	9	0	6	19	15	5	50	3	1	2	3	.336	.277
Plasencia, Francisco	L-L	6-1	192	6-19-84	.209	.160	.218	47	158	19	33	13	0	1	11	15	2	33	1	3	2	4	.310	.281
Powell, Brandon	L-R	6-0	191	8-15-80	.293	.222	.309	55	198	35	58	8	5	8	31	21	4	57	2	1	11	6	.505	.371
Rogelstad, Matt	R-R	6-3	185	9-13-82	.302	.360	.289	113	404	52	122	27	3	4	50	35	12	50	3	7	9	11	.446	.369
Rooney, Sean	B-R	5-10	205	4-12-86	.333	—	.333	2	3	1	1	0	0	0	1	0	0	0	0	1	0	0	.333	.400
Sandora, Robert	L-R	6-0	200	8-5-81	.261	.143	.282	23	46	4	12	5	0	0	2	5	0	7	0	0	0	0	.370	.320
Sorensen, Logan	L-L	6-1	195	8-12-81	.273	.000	.429	3	11	1	3	1	0	0	3	0	0	6	0	0	0	0	.364	.273
Thissen, Greg	R-R	6-4	185	6-1-81	.259	.296	.242	75	228	43	59	14	2	4	27	43	3	59	6		6	4	.390	.375
Yepez, Marcos	B-R	5-10	160	12-29-81	.307	.345	.289	44	179	30	55	10	1	1	20	22	1	36	3	0	9	10	.391	.386

PITCHING	B-T	HT	WT	DOB	W	L	ERA	G	GS	CG	SV	IP	H	R	ER	HR	BB	SO	AVG	vLH	vRH	K/9	BB/9
Ayala, Luis	R-R	6-2	175	1-12-78	0	0	0.00	3	0	0	0	3	1	0	0	0	1	1	.111	.167	.000	3.38	3.38
Baeza, Eddy	R-R	6-1	190	10-19-84	0	3	4.88	40	0	0	6	52	45	29	28	4	26	44	.239	.194	.264	7.66	4.53
Bunn, Greg	R-R	6-1	210	2-3-83	2	0	5.40	22	0	0	0	32	32	23	19	3	26	35	.267	.212	.287	9.95	7.39
Carr, Adam	R-R	6-1	185	4-1-84	3	1	1.81	41	0	0	10	50	30	12	10	4	38	65	.171	.116	.208	11.78	6.89
Detwiler, Ross	R-L	6-5	185	3-6-86	2	2	4.22	5	4	0	0	21	27	11	10	1	9	13	.310	.188	.338	5.48	3.80
Estrada, Marco	R-R	6-0	180	7-5-83	5	3	4.94	11	11	0	0	58	67	32	32	7	17	54	.291	.256	.313	8.33	2.62
Everts, Clint	B-R	6-2	170	8-10-84	4	10	4.81	38	12	0	2	97	102	62	52	8	56	78	.272	.269	.274	7.21	5.18
Foli, Daniel	R-R	6-1	190	3-30-81	0	0	9.00	5	0	0	0	6	7	6	6	1	6	6	.280	.273	.286	9.00	9.00
Hill, Shawn	R-R	6-2	180	4-28-81	0	0	1.29	2	2	0	0	7	3	1	1	0	1	4	.125	.500	.091	5.14	1.29
Jones, Justin	L-L	6-3	215	9-25-84	7	8	3.96	17	16	2	0	91	103	53	40	4	36	70	.293	.286	.294	6.92	3.56
Kolb, Dan	R-R	6-1	190	6-5-80	0	0	3.00	2	0	0	1	3	2	1	1	1	2	5	.182	.333	.125	15.00	6.00
Lambert, Bryan	R-R	6-9	240	10-19-81	0	0	16.20	3	0	0	0	5	10	9	9	0	6	1	.500	.556	.455	1.80	10.80
Lannan, John	L-L	6-5	200	9-27-84	6	0	2.13	8	8	0	0	51	31	13	12	3	15	35	.179	.083	.204	6.22	2.66
Martinez, Carlos	R-R	6-4	177	3-30-84	1	4	4.95	14	8	0	1	56	66	39	31	2	16	23	.295	.323	.275	3.67	2.56
Martis, Shairon	R-R	6-1	175	3-30-87	14	8	4.23	27	26	1	0	151	150	83	71	9	52	108	.258	.286	.239	6.44	3.10
Meyers, Bradley	R-R	6-6	195	9-13-85	0	0	5.06	3	3	0	0	11	15	6	6	1	6	9	.357	.438	.308	5.91	7.59
Mock, Garrett	R-R	6-4	195	4-25-83	1	0	0.00	1	1	0	0	6	3	0	0	0	1	5	.143	.200	.091	7.50	1.50
Morales, Alexis	R-R	5-11	170	12-20-82	1	0	0.00	10	0	0	3	13	3	1	0	0	7	19	.075	.154	.037	12.83	4.73
Patterson, John	R-R	6-6	210	1-30-78	0	0	6.75	2	2	0	0	5	6	4	4	2	5	2	.300	.375	.250	3.38	8.44
Pearson, Anthony	R-R	6-3	190	8-14-81	0	2	5.88	21	0	0	0	26	23	18	17	3	25	19	.242	.212	.258	6.58	8.65
Peralta, Yader	R-R	6-1	170	2-22-86	1	0	6.52	7	0	0	0	10	8	7	7	1	4	14	.229	.333	.174	13.03	3.72

ORGANIZATION STATISTICS

	B-T	HT	WT	DOB	W	L	ERA	G	GS	CG	SV	IP	H	R	ER	HR	BB	SO	AVG	vLH	vRH	K/9	BB/9
Perrault, Josh	R-R	6-3	205	6-11-82	5	3	3.51	46	0	0	5	67	56	27	26	8	25	73	.232	.310	.191	9.86	3.38
Pfau, Dan	R-L	6-0	190	6-12-84	1	0	2.08	3	0	0	0	4	2	1	1	1	5	2	.154	.143	.167	4.15	10.38
Spradlin, Jack	R-L	6-2	170	9-23-84	3	6	3.92	45	8	0	1	87	85	39	38	8	31	75	.254	.207	.272	7.73	3.19
Stammen, Craig	R-R	6-3	215	3-9-84	8	6	4.18	28	22	0	0	125	156	79	58	9	54	96	.311	.330	.299	6.91	3.89
Thissen, Greg	R-R	6-4	185	6-1-81	0	0	3.00	3	0	0	0	3	1	1	1	0	2	0	.111	.000	.167	0.00	6.00
Trahan, David	R-R	6-3	185	2-27-81	1	2	2.66	29	0	0	1	44	32	15	13	1	17	23	.211	.135	.250	4.70	3.48
VanAllen, Cory	L-L	6-3	180	12-24-84	3	7	5.49	13	13	0	0	59	78	43	36	3	23	54	.325	.309	.330	8.24	3.51
Yost, Gene	R-L	6-3	185	6-23-81	1	3	5.33	32	0	0	1	49	58	33	29	6	21	27	.299	.232	.326	4.96	3.86

FIELDING

Catcher	PCT	G	PO	A	E	DP	PB
Ivany	.995	28	186	16	1	0	2
Montz	.994	47	282	46	2	5	1
Peacock	.987	53	408	48	6	2	4
Rooney	1.000	1	9	0	0	0	0
Sandora	.991	20	95	14	1	2	1

First Base	PCT	G	PO	A	E	DP
McMillan	.990	68	571	38	6	53
Montz	1.000	9	83	9	0	8
Mortimer	.994	52	443	43	3	50
Powell	1.000	1	12	1	0	3
Rogelstad	.991	14	97	9	1	9
Sorensen	1.000	2	17	1	0	1
Thissen	1.000	1	7	2	0	1

Second Base	PCT	G	PO	A	E	DP
Bynum	1.000	4	7	8	0	1

	PCT	G	PO	A	E	DP
Castro	.978	42	77	101	4	28
Nunez	1.000	1	2	3	0	0
Powell	.955	15	30	34	3	8
Rogelstad	.970	33	56	74	4	19
Thissen	.992	24	49	80	1	17
Yepez	.913	25	32	73	10	19

Third Base	PCT	G	PO	A	E	DP
Castro	.960	10	6	18	1	2
Davis	.905	22	10	28	4	2
Nunez	1.000	1	2	1	0	0
Powell	.897	22	11	41	6	5
Rogelstad	.912	49	36	78	11	8
Thissen	.954	45	23	102	6	9

Shortstop	PCT	G	PO	A	E	DP
Bynum	1.000	3	3	13	0	1
Desmond	.949	127	194	399	32	80

	PCT	G	PO	A	E	DP
Rogelstad	.833	3	3	2	1	0
Yepez	.970	5	10	22	1	7

Outfield	PCT	G	PO	A	E	DP
Baez	.958	74	124	13	6	2
Brown	.973	52	105	2	3	0
Daniel	.956	60	107	2	5	0
Lowrance	.991	64	103	5	1	2
Marrero	.953	57	76	6	4	0
Maxwell	.984	55	123	2	2	1
Mortimer	—	1	0	0	0	0
Plasencia	.989	46	88	2	1	0
Powell	.000	2	0	0	1	0
Rogelstad	1.000	3	3	0	0	0
Sorensen	—	1	0	0	0	0
Thissen	1.000	1	1	0	0	0
Yepez	1.000	5	5	0	0	0

HAGERSTOWN SUNS
LOW CLASS A

SOUTH ATLANTIC LEAGUE

BATTING	B-T	HT	WT	DOB	AVG	vLH	vRH	G	AB	R	H	2B	3B	HR	RBI	BB	HBP	SO	SH	SF	SB	CS	SLG	OBP
Blanco, Tony	R-R	6-1	175	11-10-81	.000	.000	.000	1	4	0	0	0	0	0	0	0	0	3	0	0	0	0	.000	.000
Bond, Lindon	R-R	6-0	170	11-17-84	.200	.286	.167	27	75	9	15	4	0	2	3	4	1	2	0	34	0	1	.333	.250
Cabral, Marcos	R-R	6-0	180	4-4-84	.289	.306	.284	105	388	47	112	25	2	5	45	49	7	5	5	68	7	4	.402	.374
Castro, Jonathan	B-R	6-1	160	11-29-83	.164	.179	.159	35	110	12	18	1	0	0	7	11	2	4	0	29	1	2	.173	.252
Daniel, Michael	L-R	6-3	180	8-17-84	.290	.278	.292	54	207	38	60	15	1	7	37	19	6	3	1	50	9	5	.473	.365
Davis, Leonard	L-R	5-10	195	12-24-83	.290	.302	.288	96	348	47	101	29	4	16	56	25	5	4	3	86	7	6	.534	.344
Fulse, Sheldon	B-R	6-1	200	11-10-81	.196	.077	.242	13	46	4	9	3	1	0	4	4	1	0	0	16	4	1	.304	.275
Guzman, Francisco	R-R	6-4	195	12-21-83	.241	.299	.224	88	295	34	71	12	0	7	40	20	8	4	3	50	6	4	.353	.304
Ivany, Devin	R-R	6-2	185	7-27-82	.167	.000	.200	4	12	1	2	1	0	0	0	3	0	1	0	1	1	0	.250	.333
Jacobsen, Robert	R-R	6-1	205	8-30-84	.222	.190	.232	70	243	29	54	11	0	2	24	33	5	3	0	75	11	7	.292	.327
King, Stephen	R-R	6-2	195	10-2-87	.180	.167	.184	35	128	16	23	4	0	2	9	13	1	0	0	51	5	4	.258	.261
Lawhorn, Trevor	R-R	6-2	180	12-18-82	.267	.296	.256	115	105	11	28	13	1	2	18	3	1	1	0	28	0	2	.467	.294
Logan, Brett	R-R	6-2	215	12-31-82	.083	.000	.100	4	12	1	1	0	0	0	1	3	2	0	1	5	0	1	.167	.333
Lowrance, Marvin	L-L	6-3	215	7-16-84	.326	.421	.300	24	89	12	29	5	0	4	11	18	1	1	0	13	0	3	.517	.444
Marrero, Christopher	R-R	6-3	210	7-2-88	.293	.357	.278	57	222	31	65	14	0	14	53	14	3	0	4	39	0	4	.545	.337
Martinez, Michael	B-R	5-9	145	9-16-82	.250	.228	.257	115	404	54	101	21	5	0	32	27	4	11	4	68	13	3	.327	.301
Maxwell, Justin	R-R	6-5	225	11-6-83	.301	.205	.324	56	209	51	63	12	2	14	40	26	6	0	3	57	14	3	.579	.389
McMillan, Brett	L-R	6-5	215	11-18-83	.266	.217	.274	51	169	27	45	12	0	5	21	33	4	1	1	38	1	1	.426	.396
Napoli, Joe	R-R	6-4	230	10-4-82	.255	.196	.275	106	364	59	94	22	4	11	46	28	20	3	3	93	9	6	.427	.339
Nichols, Patrick	R-R	6-2	210	9-12-84	.200	.341	.144	41	145	12	29	8	1	3	18	11	3	1	0	55	1	0	.331	.270
Nunez, Alex	L-R	5-11	170	4-30-81	.271	.263	.272	70	170	33	46	6	0	6	23	17	2	29	1	0	6	4	.412	.342
Plasencia, Francisco	L-L	6-1	192	6-19-84	.260	.217	.273	70	269	47	70	11	0	14	38	34	2	1	4	57	4	3	.457	.343
Poppert, John	R-L	6-0	185	4-14-82	.214	.133	.232	26	84	9	18	4	0	0	5	6	0	0	2	24	0	1	.262	.261
Reininger, Jarrett	R-R	5-10	190	12-3-82	.077	.222	.000	9	26	1	2	0	0	1	2	8	0	1	0	11	0	0	.077	.107
San Pedro, Erick	R-R	6-0	205	10-5-83	.231	.105	.271	25	78	10	18	6	1	0	9	8	2	1	2	20	0	1	.333	.311
Solano, Jhonatan	R-R	6-0	180	8-12-85	.248	.286	.240	83	298	39	74	15	0	3	38	42	4	3	1	53	0	3	.329	.348
Tolan, Robert	B-R	6-0	200	7-15-85	.229	.182	.250	10	35	6	8	3	0	0	1	3	1	0	0	14	1	0	.314	.308

PITCHING	B-T	HT	WT	DOB	W	L	ERA	G	GS	CG	SV	IP	H	R	ER	HR	BB	SO	AVG	vLH	vRH	K/9	BB/9
Abreu, Edulin	R-R	6-3	160	8-8-84	0	2	7.52	5	5	0	0	20	22	21	17	0	8	12	.268	.290	.255	5.31	3.54
Arnesen, Erik	R-R	6-3	260	10-19-84	6	7	4.61	24	15	0	0	94	119	65	48	13	19	51	.304	.301	.306	4.90	1.83
Baeza, Eddy	R-R	6-1	190	10-19-84	1	0	1.08	5	0	0	0	8	8	1	1	0	4	8	.267	.000	.400	8.64	4.32
Baldwin, Zachary	R-L	6-5	225	5-21-83	4	6	4.15	25	12	0	2	98	116	59	45	9	27	68	.289	.277	.293	6.27	2.49
Bunn, Greg	R-R	6-1	210	2-23-83	1	0	2.36	14	0	0	0	27	19	7	7	1	10	29	.209	.294	.158	9.79	3.38
De Los Santos, Juan	R-L	6-0	184	1-15-83	1	0	13.86	11	0	0	2	12	25	20	19	0	16	10	.439	.353	.475	7.30	11.68
Drag, Devin	L-R	6-3	230	9-29-83	0	0	4.91	5	0	0	0	7	7	4	4	1	2	3	.233	.250	.227	3.68	2.45
Estrada, Marco	R-R	6-0	180	7-5-83	1	5	5.25	8	8	0	0	36	39	24	21	4	17	35	.279	.288	.272	8.75	4.25
Jackson, Aaron	B-R	6-0	175	3-28-86	6	5	5.04	45	1	0	4	89	95	63	50	9	34	62	.276	.304	.258	6.25	3.43
Jones, Justin	L-L	6-3	215	9-25-84	2	0	0.00	2	2	0	0	13	6	0	0	0	0	8	.143	.250	.132	5.68	0.00
Levinski, Don	R-R	6-4	200	10-20-82	2	7	5.37	13	13	0	0	62	64	41	37	5	37	59	.264	.281	.248	8.56	5.37
Lugo, Chris	R-R	6-1	185	11-10-86	2	5	5.38	41	5	0	4	87	100	60	52	8	32	60	.286	.308	.272	6.21	3.31
Mandel, Jeff	B-R	6-3	190	4-30-85	4	7	6.71	14	13	0	0	62	87	49	46	6	17	49	.333	.315	.346	7.15	2.48
Martinez, Michael	B-R	5-9	145	9-16-82	0	0	0.00	2	0	0	0	2	0	0	0	0	2	0	.000	.000	.000	0.00	10.80
Mavroulis, Coby	L-L	6-3	180	2-7-83	2	1	6.34	39	0	0	0	44	61	35	31	5	22	30	.337	.238	.390	6.14	4.50
Meyers, Bradley	R-R	6-6	195	9-13-85	1	1	0.44	4	4	0	0	21	13	4	1	1	8	9	.178	.133	.209	3.92	3.48
Nichols, Patrick	R-R	6-2	210	9-12-84	0	0	22.50	2	0	0	0	2	7	5	5	0	1	1	.583	.750	.500	4.50	4.50
Novoa, Yunior	L-L	6-4	180	9-11-84	5	12	4.22	25	23	2	0	117	129	66	55	12	35	94	.277	.340	.258	7.21	2.68
Nunez, Jhonny	R-R	6-3	185	11-26-85	4	6	4.05	23	22	0	0	107	97	59	48	10	48	86	.239	.261	.222	7.26	4.05
Peralta, Yader	R-R	6-1	170	2-22-86	4	1	3.19	24	1	0	3	48	29	20	17	4	22	54	.177	.134	.206	10.12	4.12
Perks, Matthew	R-R	6-7	200	8-20-85	1	3	6.38	7	2	0	1	18	21	19	13	0	14	12	.280	.281	.279	5.89	6.87
Pfau, Dan	R-L	6-0	190	6-12-84	0	0	11.17	7	0	0	0	10	17	12	12	1	7	8	.378	.462	.344	7.45	6.52

VanAllen, Cory	L-L	6-3	180	12-24-84	1	3	3.62	11	11	0	0	55	67	37	22	5	6	51	.291	.286	.292	8.40	0.99
Vargas, Buzz	R-R	6-6	220	10-21-83	0	1	12.91	8	0	0	1	8	16	13	11	2	4	7	.432	.278	.579	8.22	4.70
Welsh, Joseph	L-L	6-4	180	9-29-84	3	2	4.53	30	0	0	0	46	55	31	23	2	25	32	.297	.211	.336	6.31	4.93
Wilkie, Josh	R-R	6-2	190	7-22-84	3	6	3.49	47	0	0	11	80	86	42	31	7	34	70	.278	.287	.273	7.88	3.82
Yost, Gene	R-L	6-3	185	6-23-81	1	1	12.46	4	0	0	0	4	8	7	6	2	2	4	.364	.250	.429	8.31	4.15

FIELDING

Catcher	PCT	G	PO	A	E	DP	PB
Ivany	1.000	3	25	2	0	0	1
Logan	.971	4	30	3	1	0	1
Nichols	.982	21	154	11	3	0	4
Poppert	.986	21	124	13	2	1	0
San Pedro	.983	24	151	21	3	4	4
Solano	.980	67	443	55	10	4	9

First Base	PCT	G	PO	A	E	DP
Jacobsen	.991	68	592	39	6	42
McMillan	.989	51	423	21	5	44
Napoli	.961	22	160	12	7	22
Poppert	1.000	2	16	0	0	2

Second Base	PCT	G	PO	A	E	DP
Cabral	.960	74	131	206	14	30
Castro	.990	24	43	53	1	14
Davis	.934	20	37	48	6	11

Martinez	.990	17	41	54	1	15
Nunez	.963	6	13	13	1	5
Solano	1.000	2	2	1	0	1

Third Base	PCT	G	PO	A	E	DP
Cabral	.824	8	3	11	3	0
Castro	.545	7	1	5	5	0
Davis	.891	56	52	104	19	9
Lawhorn	.902	26	18	56	8	3
Martinez	1.000	7	4	12	0	2
McMillan	1.000	2	0	1	0	0
Nunez	.884	29	20	56	10	12
Reininger	.826	9	5	14	4	2

Shortstop	PCT	G	PO	A	E	DP
Cabral	.894	15	25	51	9	13
Castro	.833	2	2	3	1	0
King	.907	34	40	96	14	16

Martinez	.916	90	160	268	39	46

Outfield	PCT	G	PO	A	E	DP
Bond	-	.914	25	32	0	3	0
Castro	—	1	0	0	0	0
Daniel	.957	50	84	5	4	3
Davis	.889	4	8	0	1	0
Fulse	.905	11	19	0	2	0
Guzman	.956	68	99	9	5	0
Jacobsen	1.000	2	4	1	0	0
Lowrance	.956	22	41	2	2	0
Marrero	.953	47	58	3	3	1
Mavroulis	1.000	1	1	0	0	0
Maxwell	.992	54	127	2	1	1
Napoli	.952	62	116	4	6	1
Plasencia	.972	69	160	11	5	1
Tolan	.929	9	13	0	1	0

VERMONT LAKE MONSTERS   SHORT-SEASON
NEW YORK-PENN LEAGUE

BATTING	B-T	HT	WT	DOB	AVG	vLH	vRH	G	AB	R	H	2B	3B	HR	RBI	BB	HBP	SO	SH	SF	SB	CS	SLG	OBP
Alvarez, Jean	R-R	6-2	185	2-15-87	.168	.147	.180	34	95	9	16	2	1	0	6	10	1	5	0	35	0	3	.211	.255
Bass, Garrett	L-R	6-2	225	8-27-84	.293	.296	.292	59	198	28	58	13	4	6	42	10	1	3	39	16	4	.490	.325
Benner, Anthony	L-R	5-11	175	3-4-87	.256	.200	.264	58	160	20	41	7	0	1	14	21	5	1	0	27	1	1	.319	.360
Burgess, Michael	L-L	5-11	195	10-20-88	.286	.250	.293	19	70	10	20	1	1	3	10	10	1	0	23	1	1	.457	.383
Caputo, Richard	R-R	6-1	185	10-3-84	.143	.000	.250	6	14	3	2	0	0	1	2	2	0	1	0	3	0	0	.357	.250
De la Cruz, Jorge	R-R	6-3	210	10-2-85	.119	.158	.087	15	42	4	5	2	0	0	5	3	0	0	14	0	0	.167	.178
DeLaughter, Ryan	R-R	6-3	210	12-31-86	.150	.182	.138	17	40	4	6	0	1	0	1	3	0	0	23	1	0	.200	.209
Englund, Stephen	R-R	6-3	190	6-6-88	.220	.364	.188	17	59	10	13	4	0	1	7	8	1	0	22	0	3	.339	.319
Gildea, Mark	B-R	6-2	190	1-11-86	.247	.222	.256	52	178	29	44	6	3	2	11	28	4	2	0	46	16	7	.348	.362
King, Stephen	R-R	6-2	195	10-2-87	.333	.500	.318	6	24	3	8	2	0	0	2	1	0	0	7	0	0	.417	.360
Lyons, Daniel	R-R	5-10	185	8-21-84	.208	.241	.198	72	236	39	49	7	3	0	21	32	18	7	3	59	17	3	.263	.343
Martinez, Jonathan	B-R	6-0	170	9-23-84	.134	.063	.157	32	67	6	9	0	0	0	5	9	1	0	20	4	2	.134	.247
Rhinehart, Bill	L-L	6-0	202	11-22-84	.299	.280	.305	60	214	36	64	18	0	5	43	22	7	0	4	32	5	1	.453	.377
Rogers, Jake	R-R	6-1	180	3-16-84	.232	.213	.238	59	198	20	46	7	1	2	17	14	4	2	1	40	5	2	.308	.295
Rooney, Sean	R-R	5-10	205	4-12-86	.281	.295	.276	52	167	20	47	9	3	1	20	16	2	2	0	22	1	0	.389	.351
Seuss, Aaron	R-R	6-1	195	3-5-85	.293	.222	.316	69	256	25	75	11	2	4	37	19	4	1	2	46	1	5	.398	.349
Stinson, Craig	R-R	6-2	205	8-22-83	.160	.208	.145	34	100	8	16	1	0	1	14	17	5	2	2	32	1	1	.200	.306
Tolan, Robert	B-R	6-0	200	7-15-85	.208	.250	.188	11	24	5	5	0	0	1	5	1	0	2	0	6	1	0	.333	.240
Whiting, Brandon	R-R	5-10	170	5-11-83	.250	.226	.257	62	232	47	58	7	2	2	23	26	9	5	1	53	37	5	.323	.347

PITCHING	B-T	HT	WT	DOB	W	L	ERA	G	GS	CG	SV	IP	H	R	ER	HR	BB	SO	AVG	vLH	vRH	K/9	BB/9
Abreu, Edulin	R-R	6-3	160	8-8-84	4	3	3.75	19	2	0	3	50	49	31	21	5	24	36	.257	.321	.206	6.44	4.29
Alaniz, Adrian	R-R	6-2	200	3-12-84	8	2	2.39	13	8	0	0	60	42	18	16	2	8	62	.187	.221	.157	9.25	1.19
Alvarez, Jean	R-R	6-2	185	2-15-87	0	0	0.00	1	0	0	1	1	1	0	0	0	1	2	.250	.500	.000	18.00	9.00
Beno, Martin	R-R	6-0	180	8-24-86	2	1	4.15	16	0	0	2	22	9	12	10	0	16	38	.118	.182	.070	15.78	6.65
Buchter, Ryan	L-L	6-3	185	2-13-87	1	2	6.82	20	0	0	2	32	41	29	24	3	19	34	.313	.342	.301	9.66	5.40
Drag, Devin	L-R	6-3	230	9-29-83	1	0	6.43	10	0	0	0	14	17	10	10	1	7	5	.315	.250	.367	3.21	4.50
Gibson, Glenn	L-L	6-4	195	9-21-87	4	3	3.10	12	12	0	0	58	47	23	20	3	15	58	.223	.283	.203	9.00	2.33
Harrison, Ryan	R-R	6-2	190	7-12-86	1	4	3.86	22	0	0	3	28	27	14	12	1	17	24	.250	.268	.239	7.71	5.46
Kimball, Cole	R-R	6-3	225	8-1-85	3	6	4.20	14	13	0	1	64	52	35	30	4	40	72	.223	.320	.154	10.07	5.60
Mandel, Jeff	B-R	6-3	190	4-30-85	0	0	4.50	1	0	0	0	2	2	1	1	0	1	1	.286	.333	.250	4.50	4.50
Matias, Randy	R-R	6-0	160	9-19-86	0	1	5.56	6	0	0	1	11	13	9	7	0	5	17	.271	.261	.280	13.50	3.97
McGeary, Jack	L-L	6-3	195	3-19-89	0	1	13.50	2	1	0	0	3	3	5	4	0	5	4	.273	.750	.000	13.50	16.88
Pena, Hassan	R-R	6-2	210	3-25-85	4	5	4.25	13	13	0	0	59	55	36	28	3	33	36	.256	.345	.198	5.46	5.01
Peralta, Yader	R-R	6-1	170	2-22-86	0	0	6.75	1	1	0	0	4	2	3	3	0	4	6	.154	.167	.143	13.50	9.00
Perks, Matthew	R-R	6-7	200	8-20-85	1	0	5.67	15	0	0	2	27	37	17	17	1	14	12	.333	.333	.333	4.00	4.67
Pisker, Luke	R-R	6-4	210	7-16-85	0	2	3.54	17	0	0	1	20	14	9	8	1	5	30	.192	.188	.195	13.28	2.21
Smoker, Josh	L-L	6-2	195	11-26-88	0	0	4.50	2	2	0	0	4	2	2	2	0	3	5	.167	.333	.111	11.25	6.75
Staudt, Caleb	R-R	6-5	210	8-18-84	1	0	2.19	20	0	0	2	37	21	11	9	3	19	24	.171	.115	.226	5.84	4.62
Tavarez, Alberto	R-R	5-11	175	3-31-84	0	2	7.48	23	0	0	6	22	21	21	18	0	33	36	.253	.282	.227	14.95	13.71
Vargas, Buzz	R-R	6-6	220	10-21-83	0	1	7.20	3	0	0	1	5	6	4	4	1	4	1	.300	.273	.333	1.80	7.20
Willems, Colton	R-R	6-3	175	7-30-88	3	2	1.84	12	12	0	0	59	55	25	12	2	26	31	.251	.276	.228	4.76	3.99
Zimmermann, Jordan	R-R	6-2	200	5-23-86	5	2	2.38	13	11	0	0	53	45	14	14	2	18	71	.228	.234	.225	12.06	3.06

FIELDING

Catcher	PCT	G	PO	A	E	DP	PB
German	.979	9	44	2	1	0	0
Rooney	.984	45	337	35	6	4	14
Stinson	.992	32	219	23	2	2	4

First Base	PCT	G	PO	A	E	DP
Alvarez	1.000	6	30	2	0	2
De la Cruz	1.000	1	9	0	0	1
Rhinehart	.993	60	490	48	4	47
Rogers	—	1	0	0	0	0
Rooney	1.000	1	2	0	0	0
Seuss	.987	10	73	3	1	6

Second Base	PCT	G	PO	A	E	DP
Alvarez	1.000	10	14	16	0	5
King	1.000	6	9	18	0	5

	PCT	G	PO	A	E	DP	PB
Martinez	.958	6	13	10	1	0	
Rogers	.969	55	91	127	7	31	

Third Base	PCT	G	PO	A	E	DP
Alvarez	.889	8	4	12	2	2
Benner	.951	56	29	68	5	8
Caputo	.941	6	5	11	1	4
Martinez	.950	11	4	15	1	1
Rogers	.900	4	3	6	1	0

Shortstop	PCT	G	PO	A	E	DP
Lyons	.944	72	104	197	18	40
Martinez	.909	8	5	15	2	2

Outfield	PCT	G	PO	A	E	DP
Alvarez	.909	9	9	1	1	0

	PCT	G	PO	A	E	DP
Bass	1.000	1	1	0	0	0
Burgess	.933	18	24	4	2	2
De la Cruz	.944	11	17	0	1	0
DeLaughter	1.000	12	6	2	0	1
Englund	.885	16	23	0	3	0
Gildea	.990	51	97	2	1	1
Seuss	.990	57	92	8	1	2
Tolan	1.000	8	9	1	0	0
Whiting	1.000	55	90	0	0	1

GCL NATIONALS   ROOKIE

GULF COAST LEAGUE

BATTING	B-T	HT	WT	DOB	AVG	vLH	vRH	G	AB	R	H	2B	3B	HR	RBI	BB	HBP	SO	SH	SF	SB	CS	SLG	OBP
Blackwood, Christopher	L-R	6-2	165	11-23-87	.225	.143	.257	35	102	18	23	0	0	0	10	11	3	2	0	34	5	4	.225	.319
Blanco, Tony	R-R	6-1	175	11-10-81	.296	.250	.304	10	27	4	8	3	0	2	4	3	2	0	9	0	0	.630	.406
Bond, Lindon	R-R	6-0	170	11-17-84	.000	.000	.000	1	4	0	0	0	0	0	0	0	0	2	0	0	0	.000	.000
Booker, Zach	R-R	6-0	220	4-24-85	.298	.364	.298	17	47	9	14	2	0	0	8	9	4	0	14	1	2	.340	.450
Burgess, Michael	L-L	5-11	195	10-20-88	.336	.214	.370	36	128	22	43	6	3	8	32	25	0	0	1	37	1	2	.617	.442
Castillo, Luis	B-R	6-1	175	11-28-89	.120	.200	.100	10	25	3	3	0	0	0	1	4	1	0	9	0	1	.120	.267
Cruz, Frank	B-R	6-0	156	1-8-89	.111	.000	.136	24	54	7	6	1	0	0	1	16	0	1	24	3	1	.130	.314
De Castro, Angel	R-R	6-1	177	1-22-85	.237	.263	.230	50	177	27	42	6	1	1	24	29	4	1	42	5	1	.299	.354
Englund, Stephen	R-R	6-3	190	6-6-88	.253	.474	.183	24	79	18	20	3	0	0	2	28	1	0	24	13	4	.291	.454
Gonzalez, Esmailyn	B-R	5-11	175	9-21-89	.245	.333	.215	33	106	13	26	3	2	0	11	19	5	0	18	4	2	.311	.382
Hidalgo, Richard	R-R	6-2	180	7-24-87	.169	.250	.145	31	89	8	15	3	0	0	5	2	0	0	41	0	0	.202	.229
Ivany, Devin	R-R	6-2	185	7-27-82	.333	1.000	.333	1	3	0	1	0	0	0	2	1	0	1	2	0	0	.333	.400
King, Stephen	R-R	6-2	195	10-27-87	.248	.318	.222	42	161	20	40	6	1	9	30	12	4	1	47	1	2	.466	.315
Leon, Sandy	B-R	5-11	175	3-13-89	.202	.125	.229	31	94	10	19	0	0	0	11	17	0	4	15	0	0	.202	.324
Lombard, George	L-R	6-0	210	9-14-75	.467	.500	.462	5	15	3	7	2	0	0	1	4	0	1	0	2	1	1	.600	.579
Lopez, Yhonson	L-L	6-1	160	10-27-88	.286	.407	.247	36	112	16	32	5	0	2	18	17	0	1	28	4	4	.384	.377
Nolan, Rick	R-R	6-0	180	4-23-86	.255	.143	.271	17	55	9	14	2	0	2	5	1	0	1	17	1	2	.291	.311
Norris, Derek	R-R	6-0	210	2-14-89	.203	.231	.196	37	123	16	25	6	2	4	15	25	2	0	38	2	1	.382	.344
Poppert, John	R-R	6-0	185	4-14-82	.250	1.000	.100	4	12	4	3	0	1	0	2	0	0	0	5	1	0	.417	.250
Powell, Brandon	L-R	6-0	191	8-15-80	.250	.111	.364	5	20	2	5	2	0	1	2	1	0	0	7	0	0	.500	.286
Pridmore, Clint	R-R	6-3	230	9-8-86	.156	.167	.153	32	77	10	12	1	0	1	9	8	6	0	29	1	0	.208	.283
Smolinski, Jake	R-R	5-11	185	2-9-89	.305	.360	.288	28	105	18	32	8	0	1	16	13	1	0	24	7	2	.410	.387
Souza, Steven	R-R	6-3	205	4-24-89	.194	.200	.193	44	144	17	28	9	0	4	19	18	4	0	46	4	1	.340	.299
Tolan, Robert	B-R	6-0	180	7-15-85	.182	.200	.176	6	22	4	4	1	0	0	4	3	0	0	8	0	1	.227	.269

PITCHING	B-T	HT	WT	DOB	W	L	ERA	G	GS	CG	SV	IP	H	R	ER	HR	BB	SO	AVG	vLH	vRH	K/9	BB/9
Almonte, Robert	R-R	6-1	195	5-10-86	1	0	7.45	13	0	0	0	19	22	16	16	0	21	16	.306	.300	.308	7.45	9.78
Arnold, Patrick	R-R	6-1	190	10-31-88	0	5	8.78	10	6	0	0	27	43	27	26	4	10	25	.364	.421	.338	8.44	3.38
Atilano, Luis	R-R	6-3	215	5-10-85	0	0	6.75	1	0	0	0	1	1	1	1	0	1	2	.200	.000	.333	13.50	6.75
Beno, Martin	R-R	6-0	180	8-24-86	0	0	0.00	1	0	0	0	1	0	0	0	0	0	2	.000	—	.000	18.00	0.00
Bergmann, Jason	R-R	6-4	205	9-25-81	0	0	0.00	1	1	0	0	3	2	0	0	0	2	4	.167	.000	.200	12.00	6.00
Bowie, Micah	L-L	6-4	220	11-10-74	0	0	3.60	2	1	0	0	5	6	3	2	0	1	7	.300	.125	.417	12.60	1.80
Bravo, Wuillys	L-L	6-0	160	7-9-87	2	3	7.76	13	3	0	0	31	45	31	27	6	9	28	.321	.320	.322	8.04	2.59
Clark, Bradley	R-R	6-6	200	10-11-86	1	0	3.38	2	0	0	0	5	3	2	2	0	1	10	.167	.250	.100	16.88	1.69
Claussen, Brandon	R-L	6-2	200	5-1-79	0	0	3.00	3	0	0	0	15	14	6	5	2	1	18	.250	.091	.289	10.80	0.60
Colome, Jesus	R-R	6-2	200	12-23-77	1	0	0.00	2	1	0	0	3	2	0	0	0	0	2	.182	.400	.000	6.00	0.00
Corporan, Moises	R-R	6-4	200	10-25-85	0	0	0.00	1	1	0	0	3	1	0	0	0	0	1	.111	.250	.000	0.00	4.05
De Leon, Noel	R-R	6-5	176	7-6-88	2	2	8.10	10	0	0	0	13	26	20	12	2	6	9	.377	.318	.404	6.07	4.05
De Los Santos, Juan	R-L	6-0	184	1-15-83	1	1	13.50	2	0	0	0	1	2	1	1	0	2	1	.667	.000	.667	13.50	27.00
Dean, Philip	R-R	6-3	175	10-27-88	3	1	4.06	9	5	0	0	31	27	16	14	1	11	26	.225	.333	.184	7.55	3.19
DeLaughter, Ryan	R-R	6-3	210	12-31-86	0	0	54.00	2	0	0	0	1	2	6	6	0	3	2	.400	.667	.000	18.00	27.00
Detwiler, Ross	R-L	6-5	185	3-6-86	0	0	2.25	4	4	0	0	12	11	3	3	1	3	15	.234	.300	.216	11.25	2.25
Erb, Shane	R-R	6-5	180	5-3-87	0	0	37.80	2	0	0	0	2	8	7	7	1	1	0	.615	1.000	.545	0.00	5.40
Estrada, Marco	R-R	6-0	180	7-5-83	0	0	3.18	4	4	0	0	11	19	6	4	1	3	13	.365	.333	.387	10.32	2.38
Figuereo, Johan	R-R	6-2	195	3-2-86	0	0	18.00	1	0	0	0	1	3	2	2	0	0	1	.500	1.000	.400	9.00	0.00
Funk, Shane	R-R	6-6	235	5-9-87	0	0	54.00	1	0	0	0	1	0	4	4	0	5	0	.000	.000	.000	0.00	67.50
Gunderson, Kyle	R-R	6-3	215	1-31-85	0	1	0.48	10	0	0	4	19	14	2	1	1	6	9	.209	.045	.289	4.34	2.89
Jones, Desmond	R-R	6-2	195	3-16-86	0	0	27.00	3	0	0	0	2	6	9	5	1	2	5	.545	.600	.500	5.40	10.80
Martinez, Carlos	R-R	6-4	177	3-30-84	1	1	4.50	3	0	0	0	4	4	2	2	1	1	3	.286	.500	.200	6.75	2.25
Matias, Randy	R-R	6-0	160	9-19-86	4	1	1.64	10	4	0	0	38	32	8	7	1	9	43	.225	.231	.223	10.10	2.11
McCollum, Jeffery	R-R	6-3	230	9-25-85	0	1	7.50	10	0	0	0	12	14	10	10	2	7	9	.298	.143	.364	6.75	5.25
McCoy, Patrick	L-L	6-4	200	8-3-88	1	2	3.81	10	5	0	0	28	28	18	12	3	13	24	.248	.280	.239	7.62	4.13
Meyers, Bradley	R-R	6-6	195	9-13-85	0	0	0.00	3	3	0	0	9	2	0	0	0	0	8	.067	.000	.083	9.00	0.00
Mock, Garrett	R-R	6-4	215	4-25-83	0	2	4.70	3	2	0	0	8	11	7	4	3	1	8	.333	.444	.292	9.39	1.17
Morales, Alexis	R-R	5-11	170	12-20-82	0	0	9.00	1	0	0	0	1	1	2	1	0	1	2	.250	.000	.333	18.00	9.00
Peacock, Bradley	R-R	6-1	175	2-2-88	1	1	3.89	13	7	0	0	39	38	23	17	1	15	34	.242	.279	.228	7.78	3.43
Perrin, Devin	R-R	6-7	225	5-14-81	2	0	0.00	5	0	0	0	8	1	0	0	0	2	11	.042	.000	.063	12.91	2.35
Phillabaum, Justin	R-R	6-2	180	4-18-86	0	6	4.26	17	0	0	1	25	30	22	12	1	14	26	.294	.348	.278	9.24	4.97
Pinales, Jose	R-R	6-2	175	9-1-85	0	3	3.21	18	0	0	2	28	21	15	10	1	25	41	.206	.192	.211	13.18	8.04
Severino, Atahualpa	L-L	5-9	170	11-6-84	1	0	2.94	13	5	0	0	34	25	12	11	3	10	28	.208	.227	.204	7.49	2.67
Shepard, Steven	R-R	6-4	230	8-9-86	1	0	8.68	10	0	0	0	9	5	12	9	1	15	10	.152	.000	.200	9.64	14.46
Tuomi, Kai	L-L	6-1	190	7-26-85	1	1	7.50	15	0	0	3	18	28	16	15	1	6	17	.350	.538	.313	8.50	3.00

FIELDING

Catcher	PCT	G	PO	A	E	DP	PB
Booker	1.000	2	5	0	0	0	1
Leon	.989	30	239	24	3	2	4
Nolan	.990	12	87	10	1	0	4
Norris	.953	14	116	7	6	0	8
Poppert	1.000	4	19	1	0	0	0
Smolinski	1.000	3	21	1	0		2

First Base	PCT	G	PO	A	E	DP
Blanco	1.000	3	19	2	0	1
Booker	.966	9	54	2	2	5
De Castro	.983	16	110	5	2	5
Hidalgo	.979	9	44	2	1	4
Lopez	—	1	0	0	0	0
Nolan	1.000	1	3	0	0	0
Norris	1.000	1	6	0	0	0
Powell	1.000	2	16	2	0	0
Pridmore	.961	28	137	11	6	15

Second Base	PCT	G	PO	A	E	DP
Castillo	.867	14	12	14	4	2
Cruz	.872	14	20	14	5	2
De Castro	.972	18	36	34	2	15
King	.929	22	25	53	6	8
Lopez	—	1	0	0	0	0

Third Base	PCT	G	PO	A	E	DP
De Castro	.720	11	11	7	7	0
Hidalgo	.000	1	0	0	1	0
King	1.000	2	0	2	0	0
Powell	1.000	3	1	7	0	0
Pridmore	.833	4	0	5	1	0
Souza	.875	44	26	72	14	5

Shortstop	PCT	G	PO	A	E	DP
Cruz	1.000	10	6	18	0	3

	PCT	G	PO	A	E	DP
De Castro	1.000	1	1	0	0	0
Gonzalez	.943	32	39	76	7	13
King	.905	18	18	49	7	6

Outfield	PCT	G	PO	A	E	DP
Blackwood	.969	30	60	3	2	0
Blanco	1.000	3	1	0	0	0
Bond	1.000	1	4	0	0	0
Burgess	.983	34	55	4	1	0
Englund	.977	23	43	0	1	0
Hidalgo	.897	23	24	2	3	0
Lombard	1.000	5	11	0	0	0
Lopez	.966	33	55	1	2	0
Pridmore	1.000	3	7	0	0	0
Smolinski	.974	24	37	1	1	1
Tolan	1.000	4	9	0	0	0

DSL NATIONALS2 — ROOKIE

DOMINICAN SUMMER LEAGUE

BATTING	B-T	HT	WT	DOB	AVG	vLH	vRH	G	AB	R	H	2B	3B	HR	RBI	BB	HBP	SO	SH	SF	SB	CS	SLG	OBP
Altuve, Jose	R-R	6-1	185	2-20-88	.174	.316	.147	37	121	7	21	5	0	0	14	8	5	3	1	23	0	1	.215	.252
Arias, Dani	B-R	5-11	175	8-24-87	.294	.429	.259	9	34	2	10	1	0	0	5	1	2	1	1	9	2	2	.324	.342
2-team (43 DSL)					.311	—	—	52	190	30	59	7	0	1	34	24	4	6	2	34	18	9	.363	.395
Castillo, Luis	B-R	6-1	175	11-28-89	.096	.000	.111	19	52	2	5	1	0	0	3	8	1	1	0	25	0	0	.115	.230
Cuevas, Eleazar	R-R	6-0	175	4-6-87	.228	.276	.220	55	193	23	44	9	0	0	17	15	2	2	3	57	14	5	.275	.286
De La Cruz, Manuel	R-R	6-4	195	10-31-86	.207	.000	.273	10	29	2	6	1	2	0	3	2	0	0	0	12	0	1	.379	.258
Fermin Jr., Felix	R-R	5-11	155	11-27-84	.257	.250	.258	35	109	11	28	2	0	0	8	16	6	1	0	17	2	2	.275	.382
Gomez, Samuel	R-R	6-2	160	9-26-86	.235	.250	.232	34	102	24	24	2	7	1	11	18	3	4	2	36	8	3	.422	.360
Hernandez, Weesley	L-L	6-3	192	9-21-88	.180	.167	.182	18	50	5	9	2	0	1	4	5	0	0	0	20	0	1	.280	.255
2-team (8 DSL)					.159	—	—	26	69	6	11	2	0	1	4	6	0	0	0	31	1	1	.232	.227
Hodge, Alejandro	R-R	6-0	160	11-15-89	.264	.240	.269	60	159	43	42	3	1	0	13	35	12	0	1	38	22	7	.296	.430
Jimenez, Hendry	B-R	5-10	160	12-30-89	.290	.167	.307	41	145	27	42	6	3	0	22	13	1	1	5	27	7	3	.332	.341
Martinez, Ricardo	R-R	6-0	175	11-27-88	.259	.333	.250	12	27	5	7	2	0	0	4	4	5	0	0	6	1	0	.333	.444
2-team (15 DSL)					.264	—	—	27	72	11	19	6	1	0	8	9	9	0	0	16	2	0	.375	.411
Molina, Dionis	R-R	6-0	180	4-15-87	.083	.000	.100	9	24	1	2	0	0	0	1	0	1	0	1	0	7	0	1	.083	.120
Montilla, Angelberth	R-R	6-1	180	4-11-89	.230	.364	.200	16	61	8	14	5	1	0	6	13	5	1	0	26	3	4	.344	.319
2-team (18 DSL)					.200	—	—	34	115	17	23	9	2	0	16	18	5	1	0	26	5	6	.313	.333
Pena, Jose	R-R	6-2	180	12-16-86	.085	.000	.103	24	47	3	4	1	0	0	2	9	3	0	0	28	1	0	.106	.271
2-team (2 DSL)					.111	—	—	26	54	3	6	3	0	0	4	10	3	0	0	31	1	0	.167	.284
Pena, Wilfri	R-R	6-0	180	5-2-87	.254	.130	.278	41	138	17	35	7	0	1	14	15	1	1	2	28	5	2	.326	.327
Soriano, Francisco	B-R	5-11	169	6-16-87	.324	.333	.323	35	111	6	36	3	5	0	16	44	0	0	2	22	10	12	.441	.516
Tejeda, Yeurys	R-R	6-1	150	2-24-88	.202	.200	.203	26	84	7	17	2	0	0	8	9	3	2	2	25	5	0	.226	.296
2-team (31 DSL)					.257	—	—	57	191	29	49	9	1	4	30	22	7	3	5	55	13	1	.377	.347
Urdaneta, Juan	L-L	6-4	185	5-20-89	.168	.140	.168	53	167	20	28	2	0	1	10	22	4	1	1	43	3	3	.198	.278
Vargas, Miguel	R-R	6-2	195	6-20-86	.183	.267	.167	33	93	16	17	3	1	0	9	14	1	1	0	27	4	2	.237	.296
2-team (7 DSL)					.180	—	—	40	111	17	20	3	1	0	9	14	2	1	0	34	4	2	.225	.283
Vinicio, Daniel	R-R	6-2	187	10-7-85	.216	.278	.204	36	111	12	24	8	0	1	18	9	3	0	1	35	4	3	.315	.290
Vizcaino, Victor	R-R	6-1	200	7-6-87	.179	.250	.173	20	56	5	10	2	0	0	5	10	1	0	0	24	1	0	.214	.313

PITCHING	B-T	HT	WT	DOB	W	L	ERA	G	GS	CG	SV	IP	H	R	ER	HR	BB	SO	AVG	vLH	vRH	K/9	BB/9
Acosta, Eduar	R-R	6-3	188	3-8-85	0	0	0.00	9	0	0	4	13	6	0	0	0	3	15	.146	.000	.171	10.38	2.08
2-team (13 DSL)					1	3	4.23	22	0	0	5	28	29	17	13	0	11	36	—	—	—	11.71	3.58
Almonte, Raudy	L-L	6-6	190	2-27-89	2	7	8.10	13	7	0	0	33	28	35	30	1	34	25	.231	.125	.239	6.75	9.18
Aracena, Miguel	L-L	6-2	165	3-30-87	3	2	6.46	10	6	0	0	31	26	22	22	1	21	38	.234	.190	.244	11.15	6.16
2-team (6 DSL)					3	3	6.15	16	9	0	0	45	49	39	31	1	28	57	—	—	—	11.32	5.56
Arana, Juan	R-R	6-4	170	4-25-87	2	1	5.40	11	2	0	0	17	18	11	10	0	22	12	.316	.250	.327	6.48	11.88
Arias, Yael	R-R	6-1	170	12-17-85	1	3	3.23	19	0	0	0	53	38	26	19	3	28	40	.191	.250	.180	6.79	4.75
Campana, Joel	L-L	6-3	180	5-28-90	0	0	2.45	5	2	0	0	11	8	3	3	0	5	12	.205	.333	.194	9.82	4.09
Castillo, Alberto	R-R	6-3	180	9-3-85	0	0	4.91	12	1	0	0	22	27	21	12	0	18	27	.310	.367	.281	11.05	7.36
2-team (2 DSL)					0	0	5.47	14	1	0	0	29	29	25	15	0	22	30	—	—	—	10.95	8.03
Castillo, Rafael	R-R	6-2	165	3-8-88	0	1	9.00	3	1	0	0	5	7	6	5	0	6	3	.318	.167	.375	5.40	10.80
2-team (5 DSL)					0	1	6.75	8	1	0	0	9	14	16	7	0	10	6	—	—	—	5.79	9.64
De La Rosa, Ruben	R-R	5-9	165	4-2-87	4	3	4.38	18	1	0	1	37	40	29	18	3	20	58	.270	.219	.284	14.11	4.86
2-team (9 DSL)					6	3	2.18	15	11	0	0	66	45	25	16	1	24	64	—	—	—	8.73	3.27
Frias, Marcos	R-R	6-2	190	12-19-88	4	1	0.38	6	3	0	0	24	9	2	1	0	6	28	.115	.111	.116	10.50	2.25
Guzman, Antonio	R-R	6-1	145	12-15-87	0	1	4.58	9	1	0	0	20	19	12	10	2	11	17	.264	.333	.241	7.78	5.03
Ollarves, Johan	R-R	6-4	175	2-1-88	2	1	7.43	14	2	0	0	13	7	12	11	0	15	7	.163	.143	.167	4.73	10.12
2-team (5 DSL)					2	1	4.72	11	5	0	0	27	18	19	14	0	31	21	—	—	—	7.09	10.46
Ozuna, Crucito	R-R	6-0	160	1-12-85	0	2	4.60	14	4	0	0	31	25	23	16	1	22	34	.217	.350	.189	9.77	6.32
Paez, Ironel	R-R	6-1	165	7-28-90	0	0	3.60	7	0	0	0	10	7	4	4	0	13	8	.212	.182	.227	7.20	11.70
Rivera, Manuel	R-R	6-2	170	7-2-87	1	4	4.32	13	6	0	0	33	33	19	16	1	24	32	.280	.250	.288	8.64	6.48
Sabala, Miguel	R-R	6-4	195	10-13-86	2	2	3.86	15	1	0	0	26	20	18	11	2	22	43	.208	.226	.200	15.08	7.71
Silverio, Roddi	R-R	6-2	204	8-21-86	1	3	3.78	15	0	0	2	17	16	11	7	1	12	16	.258	.231	.265	8.64	6.48
Tanco, Federico	R-R	5-11	180	4-15-86	0	1	3.60	2	2	0	0	10	8	7	4	0	2	12	.200	.125	.250	15.30	1.80
2-team (12 DSL)					6	2	1.80	14	13	0	0	75	66	23	15	2	11	106	—	—	—	12.72	1.33
Taveras, Jose	L-L	6-5	190	11-10-87	1	2	3.99	11	5	0	1	29	37	21	13	1	10	30	.308	.294	.311	9.20	3.07
2-team (3 DSL)					1	2	4.36	14	5	0	1	33	44	26	16	2	13	32	—	—	—	8.73	3.55
Tejada, Derlyn	R-R	6-1	178	9-11-87	0	2	6.04	9	3	0	0	22	29	20	15	0	8	16	.319	.316	.319	6.45	3.22
Urena, Jorge	R-R	5-11	190	10-3-86	0	1	0.79	2	2	0	0	11	7	2	1	0	1	15	.175	.200	.160	11.91	0.79
2-team (11 DSL)					6	3	1.87	13	13	0	0	72	54	23	15	1	17	90	—	—	—	11.20	2.12
Vargas, Rafael	R-R	6-5	190	2-9-88	0	0	4.12	10	0	0	0	20	19	17	9	0	11	13	.253	.250	.255	5.95	7.78

2-team (3 DSL)				0	0	5.48	13	0 0 0	21	21	22	13	0	23	14	—	—	—	5.91	9.70
Vizcaino, Francisco	L-L	6-0	160	7-26-88	2	2	5.15	14	7 0 0	37	32	26	21	1	30	34	.227	.105	.246	8.35	7.36

FIELDING

Catcher	PCT	G	PO	A	E	DP	PB
Altuve	.982	27	200	24	4	0	5
Martinez	1.000	11	82	6	0	1	3
Pena	.955	30	258	37	14	1	2

First Base	PCT	G	PO	A	E	DP
Altuve	.957	4	21	1	1	2
Fermin Jr.	1.000	1	2	0	0	0
Hodge	1.000	1	2	0	0	0
Pena	.667	1	2	0	1	0
Urdaneta	.975	49	334	12	9	32
Vizcaino	.917	5	31	2	3	5
Vizcaino	.935	13	65	7	5	6

Second Base	PCT	G	PO	A	E	DP
Arias	1.000	2	2	5	0	0
Fermin Jr.	.949	23	33	41	4	8
Gomez	1.000	1	2	0	0	0

	PCT	G	PO	A	E	DP
Jimenez	.955	41	89	80	8	21
Molina	1.000	1	3	4	0	1
Tejeda	1.000	1	4	3	0	2
Vargas	.900	2	6	3	1	1
Vinicio	1.000	1	0	1	0	0

Third Base	PCT	G	PO	A	E	DP
Castillo	.200	1	1	4	0	0
Castillo	.769	18	19	21	12	1
Fermin Jr.	.979	14	19	28	1	1
Molina	1.000	7	2	12	0	2
Tejeda	1.000	6	4	9	0	2
Vargas	.892	29	14	52	8	2
Vinicio	1.000	1	1	3	0	2

Shortstop	PCT	G	PO	A	E	DP
Arias	.944	7	11	23	2	4
Arias	.667	1	1	1	1	0

	PCT	G	PO	A	E	DP
Fermin Jr.	.889	1	4	4	1	1
Soriano	.931	35	65	97	12	26
Tejeda	.925	19	25	49	6	2
Vargas	1.000	2	1	5	0	0

Outfield	PCT	G	PO	A	E	DP
Cuevas	.929	55	71	8	6	1
De La Cruz	1.000	9	5	1	0	0
Gomez	.891	30	36	5	5	1
Hernandez	.929	17	11	2	1	1
Hodge	.989	58	91	3	1	1
Montilla	1.000	16	19	2	0	1
Pena	1.000	23	19	3	0	3
Pena	1.000	1	1	0	0	0
Urdaneta	1.000	3	2	0	0	0

DSL NATIONALS1 ROOKIE

DOMINICAN SUMMER LEAGUE

BATTING	B-T	HT	WT	DOB	AVG	vLH	vRH	G	AB	R	H	2B	3B	HR	RBI	BB	HBP	SO	SH	SF	SB	CS	SLG	OBP
Arias, Dani	B-R	5-11	175	8-24-87	.314	.313	.315	43	156	28	49	6	0	1	29	23	2	5	1	25	16	7	.372	.407
2-team (9 DSL)					.311	—	—	52	190	30	59	7	0	1	34	24	4	6	2	34	18	9	.363	.395
Beltre, Juan	R-R	5-11	185	12-20-85	.310	.278	.317	57	203	49	63	11	0	1	40	27	12	2	1	36	29	3	.379	.420
Bompart, Alfredo	R-R	6-2	200	4-2-87	.167	.000	.167	5	12	1	2	0	0	0	0	2	0	0	0	7	0	0	.167	.286
Cabral, Carlos	B-R	6-3	185	8-19-85	.212	.200	.215	35	99	22	21	4	1	1	9	18	3	2	1	30	8	1	.303	.347
Fukunaga, Claudio	B-R	5-10	165	11-5-87	.226	.143	.239	23	53	11	12	3	1	0	5	12	3	0	0	14	1	2	.321	.397
Heredia, Valerio	B-R	5-10	150	3-14-86	.324	.364	.317	29	74	24	24	2	0	0	15	13	3	4	3	17	10	6	.351	.430
Hernandez, Weesley	L-L	6-3	192	9-21-88	.167	.000	.111	8	19	1	2	0	0	0	0	1	0	0	0	11	1	0	.105	.150
2-team (18 DSL)					.159	—	—	26	69	6	11	2	0	1	4	6	0	0	0	31	1	1	.232	.227
Hiciano, Yan Carlos	R-R	5-8	174	11-28-86	.243	.250	.242	38	115	21	28	10	0	0	18	11	10	1	0	19	2	1	.330	.360
Martinez, Ricardo	R-R	6-0	175	11-27-88	.267	1.000	.250	15	45	6	12	4	1	0	4	5	4	0	0	10	1	0	.400	.389
2-team (12 DSL)					.264	—	—	27	72	11	19	6	1	0	8	9	9	0	0	16	2	0	.375	.411
Mojica, Francisco	R-R	6-0	190	1-7-87	.141	.188	.130	30	85	14	12	2	1	1	14	13	5	0	2	31	3	2	.224	.286
Montilla, Angelberth	R-R	6-1	180	4-11-89	.167	.125	.174	18	54	9	9	4	1	0	10	13	2	1	0	17	2	2	.278	.348
2-team (16 DSL)					.200	—	—	34	115	17	23	9	2	0	16	18	5	1	0	26	5	6	.313	.333
Morales, Jesus	R-R	6-1	165	12-4-89	.221	.231	.220	31	95	25	21	3	0	0	12	22	1	2	2	14	7	3	.253	.367
Pena, Jose	R-R	6-2	180	12-16-86	.286	—	.286	2	7	0	2	2	0	0	2	1	0	0	0	3	0	0	.571	.375
2-team (24 DSL)					.111	—	—	26	54	3	6	3	0	0	4	10	3	0	0	31	1	0	.167	.284
Perez, Eury	R-R	6-0	180	5-30-90	.253	.250	.254	51	158	41	40	5	1	0	14	32	7	2	1	39	15	5	.297	.399
Sanchez, Adrian	B-R	6-0	160	8-16-90	.269	.310	.259	42	145	21	39	11	1	1	19	12	7	4	0	25	4	3	.379	.354
Solorzano, Luis	R-R	6-3	165	3-4-87	.222	.200	.224	20	54	9	12	1	1	0	8	9	1	2	0	14	2	2	.278	.344
Taveras, Danny	R-R	5-9	175	8-2-86	.248	.219	.257	42	137	34	34	4	0	0	23	35	5	5	0	20	30	3	.277	.418
Tejeda, Yeurys	R-R	6-1	150	2-24-88	.299	.455	.281	31	107	22	32	7	1	4	22	13	4	1	3	30	8	1	.495	.386
2-team (26 DSL)					.257	—	—	57	191	29	49	9	1	4	30	22	7	3	5	55	13	1	.377	.347
Urbina, Eduardo	R-R	6-2	200	9-24-87	.282	.237	.291	64	227	43	64	9	3	3	39	33	7	0	5	51	10	7	.388	.382
Vargas, Miguel	R-R	6-2	195	6-20-86	.167	—	.167	7	18	1	3	0	0	0	0	0	1	0	0	7	0	0	.167	.211
2-team (33 DSL)					.180	—	—	40	111	17	20	3	1	0	9	14	2	1	0	34	4	2	.225	.283
Willians, Ferdinand	R-R	6-2	185	3-4-87	.234	.069	.271	52	158	27	37	7	0	1	25	35	9	0	3	44	1	1	.297	.395

PITCHING	B-T	HT	WT	DOB	W	L	ERA	G	GS	CG	SV	IP	H	R	ER	HR	BB	SO	AVG	vLH	vRH	K/9	BB/9
Acosta, Eduar	R-R	6-3	188	3-8-85	1	3	7.98	13	0	0	1	15	23	17	13	0	8	21	.354	.500	.268	12.89	4.91
2-team (9 DSL)					1	3	4.23	22	0	0	5	28	29	17	13	0	11	36	—	—	—	11.71	3.58
Aracena, Miguel	L-L	6-2	165	3-30-87	0	1	5.52	6	3	0	0	15	23	17	9	0	7	19	.343	.333	.344	11.66	4.30
2-team (10 DSL)					3	3	6.15	16	9	0	0	45	49	39	31	1	28	57	—	—	—	11.32	5.56
Blanco, Wilmer	R-R	6-0	160	2-12-86	4	1	2.87	13	8	0	0	47	28	19	15	1	28	49	.169	.204	.152	9.38	5.36
Castillo, Alberto	R-R	6-3	180	9-3-85	0	0	10.12	2	0	0	0	3	2	4	3	0	4	3	.200	.667	.000	10.12	13.50
2-team (12 DSL)					0	0	5.47	14	1	0	0	25	29	25	15	0	22	30	—	—	—	10.95	8.03
Castillo, Rafael	R-R	6-2	165	3-8-88	0	0	4.15	5	0	0	0	4	7	10	2	0	4	3	.318	.375	.286	6.23	8.31
2-team (3 DSL)					0	1	6.75	8	1	0	0	9	14	16	7	0	10	6	—	—	—	5.79	9.64
Corporan, Moises	R-R	6-4	200	10-25-85	1	0	7.56	3	3	0	0	8	6	7	7	0	6	12	.214	.200	.217	12.96	6.48
De Los Santos, Amado	R-R	6-1	167	10-29-85	5	1	1.70	17	7	1	0	64	58	25	12	1	26	55	.247	.350	.211	7.77	3.68
Frias, Marcos	R-R	6-2	190	12-19-88	2	2	3.21	9	8	0	0	42	36	23	15	1	18	36	.237	.190	.255	7.71	3.86
2-team (6 DSL)					6	3	2.18	15	11	0	0	66	45	25	16	1	24	64	—	—	—	8.73	3.27
Jaime, Juan	R-R	6-1	180	8-2-87	3	0	1.35	14	0	0	0	27	11	7	4	0	14	34	.121	.167	.104	11.48	4.73
Martinez, Juan	R-R	6-0	182	8-16-85	1	2	1.30	10	7	0	0	42	29	7	6	0	14	38	.203	.212	.198	8.21	3.02
Molina, Santiago	R-R	6-1	195	5-23-87	2	1	2.79	14	0	0	1	19	15	8	6	1	17	26	.211	.296	.159	12.10	7.91
Mota, Victor	R-R	6-2	200	10-21-88	0	0	5.79	3	0	0	0	5	3	3	3	0	5	7	.176	.000	.250	13.50	9.64
Ollarves, Johan	R-R	6-4	175	2-1-88	0	0	2.03	5	3	0	0	13	11	7	3	0	16	14	.239	.200	.250	9.45	10.80
2-team (6 DSL)					2	1	4.72	11	5	0	0	27	18	19	14	0	31	21	—	—	—	7.09	10.46
Peralta, Carlos	R-R	6-1	185	7-29-85	4	1	1.73	28	0	0	15	36	21	10	7	1	15	42	.167	.222	.144	10.40	3.72
Perez, Julio	R-R	5-11	165	10-26-87	3	0	2.33	11	0	0	0	19	7	5	5	0	12	27	.092	.053	.109	12.57	5.59
Pinales, Jose	R-R	6-2	175	9-1-85	1	0	0.00	4	0	0	1	7	2	3	0	0	9	14	.083	.167	.056	18.00	11.57
Severino, Atahualpa	L-L	5-9	170	11-6-84	3	0	0.48	3	3	0	0	19	14	2	1	0	2	31	.212	.000	.222	14.95	0.96
Silva, Damian	R-R	5-11	172	11-23-86	6	0	1.14	19	0	0	0	32	16	7	4	0	22	25	.157	.125	.171	7.11	6.25
Tanco, Federico	R-R	5-11	180	4-15-86	6	1	1.52	12	11	2	0	65	58	16	11	2	9	89	.232	.266	.206	12.32	1.25
2-team (2 DSL)					6	2	1.80	14	13	2	0	75	66	23	15	2	11	106	—	—	—	12.72	1.32
Taveras, Jose	L-L	6-5	190	11-10-87	0	0	7.36	3	0	0	0	4	7	5	3	1	3	2	.389	1.000	.353	4.91	7.36
2-team (11 DSL)					1	2	4.36	14	5	0	1	33	44	26	16	2	13	32	—	—	—	8.73	3.55
Urena, Jorge	R-R	5-11	190	10-3-86	6	2	2.07	11	11	2	0	61	47	21	14	1	16	75	.210	.306	.173	11.07	2.36
2-team (2 DSL)					6	3	1.87	13	13	3	0	72	54	23	15	1	17	90	—	—	—	11.20	2.12
Vallejo, Radhames	R-R	6-2	185	1-3-87	1	0	3.18	3	0	0	0	6	5	2	2	0	5	6	.238	.125	.308	9.53	7.94
Vargas, Rafael	R-R	6-5	190	2-9-88	0	0	21.60	3	0	0	0	2	2	5	4	0	6	1	.333	.000	.400	5.40	32.40
2-team (10 DSL)					0	0	5.48	13	0	0	0	21	21	22	13	0	23	14	—	—	—	5.91	9.70
Vasquez, Wanel	R-R	6-3	190	1-15-87	0	0	0.00	1	0	0	1	1	0	0	0	0	0	2	.250	.000	1.000	18.00	0.00

FIELDING

Catcher	PCT	G	PO	A	E	DP	PB
Bompart	.875	1	5	2	1	0	0
Hiciano	.983	36	312	42	6	2	10
Martinez	.984	15	114	10	2	1	0
Taveras	.964	20	201	12	8	1	3

First Base	PCT	G	PO	A	E	DP
Bompart	—	1	0	0	0	0
Urbina	.984	63	442	41	8	42
Willians	.929	4	24	2	2	1

Second Base	PCT	G	PO	A	E	DP
Arias	1.000	1	0	1	0	0
Fukunaga	.968	21	30	31	2	7
Heredia	.944	8	5	12	1	2

	PCT	G	PO	A	E	DP
Sanchez	.906	39	58	68	13	16
Tejeda	1.000	7	10	12	0	6

Third Base	PCT	G	PO	A	E	DP
Sanchez	1.000	2	1	0	0	0
Solorzano	.667	3	3	3	3	0
Tejeda	.949	20	15	22	2	4
Vargas	.600	3	1	2	2	0
Willians	.846	47	41	85	23	13

Shortstop	PCT	G	PO	A	E	DP
Arias	.951	43	70	124	10	16
Solorzano	.897	12	14	21	4	4
Taveras	1.000	2	3	6	0	1
Tejeda	.898	10	24	20	5	5

	PCT	G	PO	A	E	DP
Vargas	.667	4	0	4	2	1

Outfield	PCT	G	PO	A	E	DP
Beltre	.930	39	38	2	3	0
Cabral	.950	33	37	1	2	0
Heredia	.905	21	18	1	2	0
Hernandez	.750	6	3	0	1	0
Mojica	1.000	27	23	3	0	0
Molina	—	1	0	0	0	0
Montilla	.967	18	28	1	1	0
Morales	.968	24	28	2	1	1
Pena	1.000	2	2	0	0	0
Perez	.975	46	73	5	2	1

MINOR
LEAGUES

Hitting streaks highlight record-breaking season

BY JOSH LEVENTHAL

Hit streaks made headlines in minor league baseball at a historical rate in 2007. Like a busy hurricane season, as soon as one streak came to an end another one seemed to be bearing down a record.

Only four times since 2000 had a player hit in 30 consecutive games, yet four players accomplished the feat in 2007 (including the minors' longest hit streak since Eisenhower was in office) and three league records either fell or were matched.

Triple-A Columbus outfielder Brandon Watson broke a 95-year-old International League record by hitting in 43 consecutive games. Low Class A Charleston's Mitch Hilligoss toppled the South Atlantic League mark by hitting in 38 straight games and high Class A Bakersfield third baseman Chris Davis' 35-game hit streak matched the California League mark. High Class A Brevard County third baseman Mat Gamel hit in 33 straight games, falling three hits shy of the Florida State League record.

Watson made national headlines with his 43-game run that broke Jack Lelivelt's mark from 1912. It was the longest streak in the minors since 1954, and the sixth-longest of all time, and earned Watson a big league promotion the day after it ended.

The 25-year-old Watson, who entered the season with just 68 major league at-bats but a .304 career minor league average in 797 at-bats, insisted he didn't do anything differently at the plate during the streak.

"I'm the same player, as far as putting the ball in play and hoping it falls," Watson said. "My greatest strength is just to put the ball in play and see what happens. It takes a lot of things to go your way for something like this to happen."

Watson fell short of the longest minor league hitting streak, held by Joe Wilhoit of Wichita, who in 1919 recorded a base hit in 69 consecutive games. Hall of Famer Joe DiMaggio, whose 56-game hitting streak is the longest in major league history, is second on the minor league list with a 61-game hitting streak for San Francisco of the Pacific Coast League in 1933. Third on the list is Roman Mejias, whose 55-game hitting streak for Waco in 1954 is the longest of the post-World War II era.

Hilligoss began the hit-streak season in late April and used a bit of theatrics to reach 38. He matched the league record of 35 despite grounding out to second base to end the sixth inning of a game against Columbus, leaving him hitless and his teammates to figure out a way to get the third baseman one more chance. Thanks to their patience—the players successfully got three of the next eight batters to reach so Hilligoss could get one more shot--Hilligoss made the most of another opportunity, doubling in the bottom of the eighth.

"Everyone got together," Charleston manager Torre Tyson said. "I told everyone they were taking a strike. Some guys took up to two strikes. They did everything they could to get on base."

Hilligoss set the record the following night by laying

Brandon Watson's 43-game hitting streak broke a 95-year-old Triple-A International League record

a bunt down the third-base line in the bottom of the seventh inning for his only hit in five at-bats.

Davis matched former Athletics farmhand Brent Gates' league record 35-game hit streak in unusual fashion: by hitting for power. Davis boosted his average from .257/.303/.505 at the start of his streak to .312/.354/.592 at its end. He had 23 one-hit games during the streak and his contact percentage (68 percent) was in stark contrast to that of Watson (87 percent) and Hilligos (85 percent).

Tragedy Strikes Tulsa

One of the darkest days in minor league history occurred on July 22 when Tulsa Drillers coach Mike Coolbaugh was killed during a game after being struck in the back of the neck by a line drive while coaching first base.

Coolbaugh, 35, was the first player to be killed in an on-field incident during a professional game in over 30 years. Coolbaugh is survived by his wife Mandy (who was pregnant with their third child) and two sons.

Coolbaugh, a native of San Antonio, enjoyed a 17-year playing career with nine organizations and innumerable minor league teams. He reached the big leagues for just 82 at-bats, 70 with the Brewers in 2001 and 12 with the Cardinals in 2002. Coolbaugh was also one of the last players cut from the 2000 Olympic team that won a gold medal in Sydney, getting beat out by veteran Mike Kinkade.

Coolbaugh had 258 career minor league home runs, and five seasons when he hit at least 23. He played in

Proper Name: Michael Robert Coolbaugh. **Born:** June 5, 1972 in Binghamton, N.Y. **Ht.:** 6-1. **Wt.:** 190. **Bats:** R. **Throws:** R. **School:** Theodore Roosevelt HS, San Antonio, Texas. Career Transactions: Selected by Blue Jays in 16th round of 1990 draft; signed June 12, 1990; Selected by Rangers from Blue Jays in Rule 5 minor league draft, Dec. 4, 1995; Granted free agency, Oct. 15, 1996; Signed by Athletics, Nov. 4, 1996; Granted free agency, Oct. 17, 1997; Signed by Rockies, March 12, 1998; Granted free agency, Oct. 16, 1998; Signed by Yankees, Nov. 17, 1998; Granted free agency, Oct. 15, 1999; re-signed by Yankees, Oct. 22, 1999; Granted free agency, Oct. 15, 2000; Signed by Brewers, Nov. 13, 2000; Granted free agency, Oct. 15, 2001; Signed by Cardinals, Dec. 11, 2001; Granted free agency, Sep. 30, 2002; Signed by Phillies, Dec. 5, 2002; Released by Phillies, Feb. 5, 2003; Signed by Astros, July 9, 2003; Granted free agency, Oct. 15, 2003; re-signed by Astros, Nov. 7, 2003; Granted free agency, Oct. 15, 2004; Signed by Astros, Nov. 5, 2004; Granted free agency, Oct. 15, 2005; Signed by Royals, Nov. 3, 2005; Granted free agency, Oct. 15, 2006.

CAREER RECORD

Yr	Club (League)	Class	AVG	G	AB	R	H	2B	3B	HR	RBI	BB	SO	SB	OBP	SLG
90	Medicine Hat (Pio)	R	.190	58	211	21	40	9	0	2	16	13	47	3	.238	.261
91	St. Catherines (NYP)	A	.230	71	256	28	59	13	2	3	25	17	40	4	.283	.332
92	St. Catherines (NYP)	A	.286	15	49	3	14	1	1	0	2	3	12	0	.327	.347
93	Hagerstown (SAL)	A	.244	112	389	58	95	23	1	16	62	32	94	4	.304	.432
94	Dunedin (FSL)	A	.263	122	456	53	120	33	3	16	66	28	94	3	.313	.454
95	Knoxville (SL)	AA	.240	142	500	71	120	32	2	9	56	37	110	7	.305	.366
96	Charlotte (FSL)	A	.287	124	449	76	129	33	4	15	75	42	80	8	.357	.479
	Tulsa (TL)	AA	.348	7	23	6	8	3	0	2	9	2	3	1	.444	.739
97	Huntsville (SL)	AA	.308	139	559	100	172	37	2	30	132	52	105	8	.369	.542
98	Colorado Springs (PCL)	AAA	.277	108	386	62	107	35	2	16	75	32	93	0	.331	.503
99	Columbus (IL)	AAA	.276	114	391	65	108	31	2	15	66	38	112	5	.340	.481
00	Columbus (IL)	AAA	.271	117	387	63	105	28	0	23	61	67	96	6	.380	.522
01	Indianapolis (IL)	AAA	.268	94	347	49	93	24	3	10	50	39	92	3	.347	.441
	Milwaukee (NL)	MAJ	.200	39	70	10	14	6	0	2	7	5	16	0	.273	.371
02	St. Louis (NL)	MAJ	.083	5	12	0	1	0	0	0	0	1	3	0	.154	.083
	Memphis (PCL)	AAA	.243	116	411	62	100	20	1	29	75	51	126	9	.338	.509
03	Round Rock (TL)	AA	.259	42	147	24	38	6	0	7	29	22	43	1	.349	.442
04	New Orleans (PCL)	AAA	.295	123	404	74	119	30	0	30	82	47	96	2	.368	.592
05	Round Rock (PCL)	AAA	.281	123	488	88	137	30	1	27	101	47	111	10	.344	.512
06	Royals (AZL)	R	.333	6	21	6	7	1	0	0	0	6	4	2	.517	.381
	Omaha (PCL)	AAA	.223	57	197	19	44	9	0	8	25	31	48	1	.336	.391
MAJOR LEAGUE TOTALS			**.183**	**44**	**82**	**10**	**15**	**6**	**0**	**2**	**7**	**6**	**19**	**0**	**.256**	**.329**
MINOR LEAGUE TOTALS			**.266**	**1690**	**6071**	**928**	**1615**	**398**	**24**	**258**	**1007**	**606**	**1406**	**77**	**.337**	**.467**

the Royals organization in 2006 and went through spring training with Tabasco of the Mexican League in 2007, though he came home before the season started.

Coolbaugh joined the Drillers on July 3 as interim hitting coach. His older brother Scott is the hitting coach for the league's Frisco team, and their jobs as coaches indicated just how much they loved the game and how much they wanted to stay involved.

Coolbaugh is believed to be the first professional player or coach to die as a result of an on-field accident since Salem outfielder Francisco Alfredo Edmead died in 1974 after colliding with second baseman Pablo Cruz in a Carolina League game. In 2000, Kelsey Osburn, a 20-year-old playing in the Northeastern summer collegiate league, died after being struck by a line drive during batting practice.

The baseball community has rallied to help provide for Coolbaugh's family since his passing. The Rockies agreed to give Coolbaugh a full postseason share. A golf tournament and auction was held to benefit Coolbaugh. And the Drillers and a Tulsa bank established a fund in his memory to benefit his family. All of the proceeds will go directly to the family, and a donation can be made to: Mike Coolbaugh Memorial Fund c/o Spirit Bank, 1800 S. Baltimore Ave., Tulsa, OK 74119.

Moore, Moss Step Down

Last season marked the finale for two longtime baseball officials: Minor League Baseball president Mike Moore and South Atlantic League president John Henry Moss.

Moore oversaw the largest growth period in minor league history during his 16-year tenure as president while Moss retired as the only president of the SAL after spending 50 years in charge of the league (formerly known as the Western Carolina League).

Moore announced in May that he planned to retire from the position he has held without opposition since 1991, with his longtime assistant Pat O'Conner garnering the sole nomination to replace him (the vote was to be held at the Winter Meetings in December). He rose to prominence during a tumultuous time in minor league history. As chief administration officer under then-president Sal Artiaga, Moore negotiated a renewal of the Professional Baseball Agreement with the major leagues in 1990. It initially drew the ire of many minor league owners, but ultimately changed the landscape of minor league baseball.

Among the key components of the PBA were facilities standards that necessitated upgrades at most ballparks. What the standards created was a surge of renovated and new ballparks that has drove minor league baseball's awakening into full-blown prosperity.

Moore advocated changing the structure of the National Association when he ran for president—winning a hotly contested election—and he considers it his most significant accomplishment. The change increased the involvement of owners by creating a board of trustees with one owner from every league.

"Prior to 1992, we operated for 100 years on a system of an executive committee and there was not enough direct input from the owners," he said. "In the 1980s I felt there was more interest and involvement from owners, and that owners should be more involved in the direction of the industry . . . From that point on, we were able to make progress to fit with the modern times."

Moss became the youngest person elected president of a professional baseball league when he took the Western Carolina League from semipro to professional status in 1948. That league operated until 1952.

In 1960, Moss reorganized the circuit as the Western Carolinas League, and it became known as the South Atlantic League in 1980. He has served as the league's president in every season of its existence and was honored with a lifetime contract in 1990, becoming the only person in baseball with that type of job security.

"It has indeed been a privilege for me to serve as president of the South Atlantic League," Moss said. "The league has a storied history that has brought the great game of baseball to many of the finest cities this country has to offer throughout the Southeast and the Eastern Seaboard. I consider it a tremendous lifetime reward to meet and work with so many wonderful people who have worked so hard for the good of their communities."

Under Moss' direction, the South Atlantic League has played in 43 cities, represented by 114 different ownership groups. He has stressed the importance of providing quality, family entertainment at an affordable price, which allowed the league to grow to 16 clubs in eight states.

Small Town, Big History

Opening Day of the Appalachian League held special meaning for Bluefield in June as the team celebrated an accomplishment that makes this quaint mountain town particularly unique from a baseball perspective.

Bluefield, which on its Website boasts being Virginia's tallest town, now has another distinction: It hosts the first team in the history of minor league baseball to be continuously affiliated with the same major league club for 50 years.

With a handshake, the Baltimore Orioles adopted the minor league outpost on the border of West Virginia and Virginia in 1957, and the agreement has been renewed by a handshake ever since. Bowen Field, the picturesque ballpark surrounded by forested hills, had previously housed teams affiliated with the Boston Braves, Washington Senators, Boston Red Sox and Brooklyn Dodgers.

But since 1957, the Orioles have sent fresh-faced rookies straight out of high school or college to Bluefield. The Florida State League's Lakeland Flying Tigers and the Eastern League's Reading Phillies are the next longest in tenure of affiliation, but they both began their current affiliations in 1967, a full 10 years after Bluefield.

"Kids from all walks of life can come in here and feel (as though) they can play baseball as opposed to putting up with a lot of outside (social) pressures," Orioles farm director David Stockstill said.

Another Year, Another Record

The annual reminder that minor league baseball is in the midst of a golden era came with the news at the end of the season that the affiliated minors had once again set an attendance record.

Even with franchise values increasing seemingly with each team sold and marketing and sponsorship deals on the rise, there is no better indication of the sport's health than the sound of clicking turnstiles—which in 2007

ORGANIZATION STANDINGS

Cumulative farm club records for the 30 major organizations, with winning percentages going back five years. Most organizations have six affiliates.

	2007						
	W	L	PCT	2006	2005	2004	2003
1. N.Y. Yankees	417	281	.597	.551	.541	.514	.501
2. Milwaukee	387	298	.565	.495	.473	.453	.469
3. San Francisco	392	305	.562	.557	.555	.471	.454
4. Minnesota	382	307	.554	.534	.535	.502	.503
5. Cleveland	371	322	.535	.537	.525	.540	.576
6. Detroit	371	328	.531	.537	.555	.467	.481
7. Tampa Bay	369	331	.527	.483	.464	.472	.497
8. Toronto	367	335	.523	.499	.523	.572	.531
9. L.A. Angels	356	338	.513	.490	.489	.455	.510
10. Cincinnati	352	343	.506	.519	.454	.470	.480
11. L.A. Dodgers	350	342	.506	.504	.490	.502	.485
12. Boston	349	347	.501	.506	.512	.503	.496
13. Chi. Cubs	344	346	.499	.524	.492	.538	.474
14. Kansas City	377	382	.497	.496	.500	.501	.527
15. Colorado	353	358	.496	.487	.501	.482	.508
16. Arizona	351	360	.494	.525	.496	.489	.513
17. Oakland	340	351	.492	.530	.545	.576	.532
18. Baltimore	371	386	.490	.481	.498	.458	.486
19. Texas	338	353	.489	.423	.491	.549	.547
20. Philadelphia	339	355	.488	.526	.429	.467	.462
21. Atlanta	334	353	.486	.474	.482	.514	.497
22. Pittsburgh	330	358	.480	.491	.519	.511	.581
23. St. Louis	361	394	.478	.499	.492	.520	.451
24. Chi. White Sox	334	369	.475	.426	.504	.504	.494
25. Florida	323	367	.468	.465	.501	.455	.502
26. San Diego	322	371	.465	.513	.472	.501	.476
27. N.Y. Mets	349	408	.461	.477	.509	.547	.503
28. Seattle	307	386	.443	.456	.517	.508	.527
29. Washington	304	383	.443	.440	.438	.424	.437
30. Houston	310	393	.441	.557	.494	.533	.500

POSTSEASON PLAYOFFS

League	Champion	Runner-Up
International	Richmmond (Braves)	Durham (Devil Rays)
Pacific Coast	Sacramento (Athletics)	New Orleans (Mets)
Eastern	Trenton (Yankees)	Akron (Indians)
Southern	Montgomery (Devil Rays)	Huntsville (Brewers)
Texas	San Antonio (Padres)	Springfield (Cardinals)
California	San Jose (Giants)	Lake Elsinore (Padres)
Carolina	Frederick (Orioles)	Salem (Astros)
Florida State	Clearwater (Phillies)	Brevard County (Brewers)
Midwest	West Michigan (Tigers)	Beloit (Twins)
South Atlantic	Columbus (Devil Rays)	West Virginia (Brewers)
New York-Penn	Auburn (Blue Jays)	Brooklyn (Mets)
Northwest	Salem-Keizer (Giants)	Tri-City (Rockies)
Appalachian	Elizabethton (Twins)	Danville (Braves)
Pioneer	Orem (Angels)	Idaho Falls (Royals)
Arizona	Mariners	Giants
Gulf Coast	Yankees	Dodgers

MINOR LEAGUES

turned 42,812,812 times.

The attendance mark—which includes the Mexican League—topped last year's record by over 1.1 million and marked the fourth straight season a new record had been established.

Every league saw an increase in attendance in 2007 except the Texas League, which was coming off a record 2006 season, and the Appalachian League, which operated with one fewer team. Four leagues set attendance records: Pacific Coast, Midwest, South Atlantic and Pioneer.

CONTINUED ON PAGE 319

Hard work helps Bruce rise to the top

On a brutally hot day late in the season, only a handful of Louisville players were out for optional batting practice, but that didn't matter to the Reds' top prospect. As a matter of fact, nothing about the game is optional to Jay Bruce.

"I don't care what it is, if I can learn something and it makes me a better player, I'm there," the 20-year-old outfielder said. "I don't care if it's a thousand degrees outside. I'm going to get better with more experience.

"I'm not a guy to blow off early work no matter what level I'm at. I could be a first-rounder or an undrafted free agent—I'm going to play the game the same way."

No one in the Reds organization would ask Bruce to change a thing about the way he plays the game. The 2005 first-round pick not only has as much talent as any prospect, but he also brings leadership skills that set him apart.

"That's the one thing about him everyone says," Reds farm director Terry Reynolds said. "He's a great leader. He's a fun player to watch because of his skills, but he's a fun player to be around off the field as well.

"There isn't too much to do until he's the complete package, but the complete person is already there. It's been pre-assembled. He had that when he got here."

Bruce started 2007 at high Class A Sarasota, hitting .325/.379/.586 with 11 homers and 49 RBIs in 286 at-bats before being promoted to Double-A Chattanooga. Bruce spent just 16 games with the Lookouts before hitting the road for Triple-A Louisville in what was to be a temporary move because of injuries.

"That was the plan the whole time," Reynolds said. "We called him up as a matter of circumstance and a matter of need at the time. Jay got the chance to prove himself."

And prove himself Bruce did. The 6-foot-2 lefthanded-hitter took on more advanced pitching at a .305/.358/.567 clip and stuck himself in the middle of Louisville's lineup. For the season, he finished going a combined .319/.375/.567 with 26 home runs, 46 doubles and 89 RBIs. He also had one of the season's signature moments when he lashed a ball off the wall at San Francisco's AT&T Park in the Futures Game, then turned on the jets and legged out a triple.

Krivsky made a visit to Louisville near the end of the regular season, in part to tell Bruce he wasn't in the organization's plans for a September callup, but raved about his ability and makeup—calling both off the charts. At the same time, the Reds GM said it was premature to think Bruce would debut in Cincinnati as a 21-year-old in 2008.

"He's got a nice package of skills and ability to go along with that makeup," Krivsky said. "He's 20 years old and having success in Triple-A. We're certainly pleased with what he's done this year and extremely excited to have him in our organization. But for as much talent as he has, his family deserves all the credit for the quality person he is. Something like that cannot be quantified."

PLAYER OF THE YEAR

STAN DENNY

Jay Bruce played at three levels and finished 2007 batting in the middle of Triple-A Louisville's lineup

PREVIOUS WINNERS

1981—Mike Marshall, 1b, Albuquerque (Dodgers)
1982—Ron Kittle, of, Edmonton (White Sox)
1983—Dwight Gooden, rhp, Lynchburg (Mets)
1984—Mike Bielecki, rhp, Hawaii (Pirates)
1985—Jose Canseco, of, Huntsville/ Tacoma (Athletics)
1986—Gregg Jefferies, ss, Columbia/Lynchburg/Jackson (Mets)
1987—Gregg Jefferies, ss, Jackson/Tidewater (Mets)
1988—Tom Gordon, rhp, Appleton/Memphis/Omaha (Royals)
1989—Sandy Alomar, c, Las Vegas (Padres)
1990—Frank Thomas, 1b, Birmingham (White Sox)
1991—Derek Bell, of, Syracuse (Blue Jays)
1992—Tim Salmon, of, Edmonton (Angels)
1993—Manny Ramirez, of, Canton/Charlotte (Indians)
1994—Derek Jeter, ss, Tampa/Albany/Columbus (Yankees)
1995—Andruw Jones, of, Macon (Braves)
1996—Andruw Jones, of, Durham/Greenville/Richmond (Braves)
1997—Paul Konerko, 1b, Albuquerque (Dodgers)
1998—Eric Chavez, 3b, Huntsville/Edmonton (Athletics)
1999—Rick Ankiel, lhp, Arkansas/Memphis (Cardinals)
2000—Jon Rauch, rhp, Winston-Salem/Birmingham (White Sox)
2001—Josh Beckett, rhp, Brevard County/Portland (Marlins)
2002—Rocco Baldelli, of, Bakersfield/Orlando/Durham (Devil Rays)
2003—Joe Mauer, c, Fort Myers/New Britain (Twins)
2004—Jeff Francis, lhp, Tulsa/Colorado Springs(Rockies)
2005—Delmon Young, of, Montgomery/Durham (Devil Rays)
2006—Alex Gordon, 3b, Wichita (Royals)

Moore led minors through golden era

After overseeing the largest growth period in minor league history as president of Minor League Baseball for the past 16 years, Mike Moore had much simpler goals for his immediate future.

"I would like some time to enjoy my grandkids and do a little bass fishing," Moore said.

Perhaps no single person has had a bigger influence on the direction of minor league baseball in recent years, as the sport has grown from a mom-and-operation to a big business where franchise values seem to increase annually.

Moore, who held his position as president without opposition since 1991, rose to prominence during a tumultuous time in minor league history. As chief administration officer under then-president Sal Artiaga, Moore negotiated a renewal of the Professional Baseball Agreement with the major leagues in 1990. It initially drew the ire of many minor league owners, but ultimately changed the landscape of minor league baseball.

Among the key components of the PBA were facilities standards that necessitated upgrades at most ballparks. What the standards created was a surge of renovated and new ballparks that drove minor league baseball's awakening into full-blown prosperity.

Moore advocated changing the structure of the

EXECUTIVE OF THE YEAR

National Association when he ran for president—winning a hotly contested election—and he considers it his most significant accomplishment. The change increased the involvement of owners by creating a board of trustees with one owner from every league.

Moore recognizes the minors' growth has pushed the game out of many smaller communities that once typified the sport. He said now the minors must focus on remaining affordable

"I think our biggest challenge now is to be able to keep our costs under control—the cost of running a ballpark and hiring employees and the cost of running a franchise is going up like everything else," he said. "Those costs we've been able to keep under control pretty well and not pass onto the fans."

MINOR LEAGUES

CONTINUED FROM PAGE 317

The 16-team PCL paced the minors by 7,420,095, edging the 14-team International League (6,721,465). Sacramento topped the PCL and all domestic teams for the eighth straight season by drawing 710,253 to Raley Field.

Sacramento was hardly alone in its success at the gate. Triple-A Scranton-Wilkes Barre certainly reaped the benefits of being a first-year Yankees affiliate. After selling the equivalent of 47,000 tickets in its first day of sales after announcing the Yankees were coming to town, the team increased its overall attendance by over 200,000 and drew a total of 580,908 in 66 openings—fifth-best in the IL.

"We were used to one or two sellouts a year (as a Phillies affiliate)," said Scranton GM Jeremy Ruby, adding that he did not expect the northeastern Pennsylvania

city's Yankees following to translate so strongly at the ticket booth. "It's been a whirlwind."

In fact, becoming a Yankees affiliate and being purchased by Mandalay Baseball—arguably the most successful multi-team ownership group in the minors—turned out to be a perfect storm of sorts for Scranton, as the most marketable team in professional sports joined forces with owners experienced in the art of fan entertainment and willing to commit resources.

The team boosted merchandise sales significantly, added gameday staff and worked out a ballpark naming rights deal with PNC Financial Services.

Blasts From The Past

A trio of minor league veterans had resurgent seasons that ended with two completing the year in the major leagues.

Triple-A Omaha first baseman Craig Brazell topped the minors in home runs with 39, an honor he likely would have had more competition for if Cardinals pither-turned-slugger Rick Ankiel had not been called up to the big leagues after belting 32 homers in just 102 games with Triple-A Memphis.

Triple-A Portland third baseman Brian Myrow, who was originally signed by the Yankees out of the independent Northern League in 1999, won the minors batting title with a .354 average. The 31-year-old Myrow edged the Cubs' 24-year-old catching prospect Geovany Soto, who finished the season hitting .353 with Triple-A Omaha.

Brazell was a fifth-round pick of the Mets in 1998 who finished second in the minors in 1998 with a .385 average with Rookie-level Kingsport. He drove in 101 runs in 2002 and played in 24 big league games in 2004. He suf-

MINOR LEAGUE AVERAGES

League	Level	AVG	OBP	SLG	R/G	ERA	K/9	BB/9	HR/9
International	AAA	.262	.332	.395	4.36	3.97	7.07	3.36	0.79
Pacific Coast	AAA	.279	.346	.437	5.13	4.68	6.89	3.40	1.01
Eastern	AA	.263	.335	.399	4.62	4.18	7.03	3.49	0.81
Southern	AA	.259	.334	.392	4.57	4.07	7.60	3.55	0.76
Texas	AA	.264	.338	.407	4.64	4.30	6.90	3.47	0.90
California	Hi A	.271	.344	.426	5.59	4.85	7.51	3.58	0.96
Carolina	Hi A	.262	.338	.394	4.69	4.13	6.97	3.55	0.72
Florida State	Hi A	.261	.330	.383	4.48	3.95	7.08	3.26	0.67
Midwest	Lo A	.255	.324	.372	4.34	3.76	7.66	3.19	0.64
South Atlantic	Lo A	.263	.336	.399	4.99	4.32	7.53	3.45	0.79
New York-Penn	SS	.253	.332	.365	4.52	3.88	7.87	3.52	0.52
Northwest	SS	.259	.344	.386	5.13	4.30	8.41	3.84	0.66
Appalachian	R	.257	.333	.379	4.90	4.16	8.33	3.47	0.60
Pioneer	R	.274	.345	.415	5.47	4.57	8.09	3.28	0.82
Arizona	R	.263	.335	.399	4.62	4.18	7.03	3.49	0.81
Gulf Coast	R	.263	.335	.399	4.62	4.18	7.03	3.49	0.81

Walbeck builds a winner for Tigers

O n any given day during early work, most minor league managers are relatively easy to find.

But Double-A Erie manager Matt Walbeck isn't most minor league managers. In fact, in some ways he hasn't been able to let go of the catching gear that helped him carve out a 17-year professional playing career—11 of which were spent in the big leagues.

Before batting practice, Walbeck often likes to don the mask and get behind the plate to catch bullpen sessions for his pitching staff.

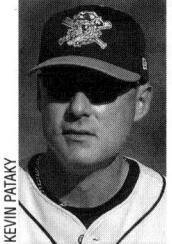

Matt Walbeck

"Now, I don't do it all the time," Walbeck said. "But I think having the opportunity to catch a guy's side session really gives you a feel for what their stuff is like. You see things from there you wouldn't normally see."

Walbeck still spends the bulk of his pregame time poring over scouting reports, meeting with players and staff, building relationships—not only within the clubhouse, but also between the organization and its affiliate—hitting fungoes and throwing a mean BP.

An eighth-round pick of the Cubs in 1987 out of Sacramento High, Walbeck is new to managing. But that doesn't detract from his style, his communication skills, or the fact that he's a winner.

"Wally's done a tremendous job in our organization in terms of developing players with a winning attitude," Tigers general manager Dave Dombrowski said. "He has a unique style and his players always play hard for him. He's strict enough to let them know where the line is, but he also likes to keep things loose. He's just been outstanding in that role."

In 2003, Walbeck was about to turn 34 and weighing his options at Triple-A Toledo when he approached Tigers farm director Glenn Ezell about the possibility of managing.

"We talked about it in the dugout for a while, and then he came back the next day to ask more questions," Ezell said. "That told me a lot about him. The thoughtfulness and the amount of respect he had for that kind of position . . . I look back to that conversation, just a few years ago and he's always had a great atmosphere in every clubhouse. He's old-school and I really liked his juice. Wally has tremendous energy and a tireless work ethic—two things that have carried over from his playing days."

That juice, combined with his ability to balance personalities and get the most out of his players,

MANAGER OF THE YEAR

PREVIOUS WINNERS

1989—Buck Showalter, Albany (Yankees)
1990—Kevin Kennedy, Albuquerque (Dodgers)
1991—Butch Hobson, Pawtucket (Red Sox)
1992—Grady Little, Greenville (Braves)
1993—Terry Francona, Birmingham (White Sox)
1994—Tim Ireland, El Paso (Brewers)
1995—Marc Bombard, Indianapolis (Reds)
1996—Carlos Tosca, Portland (Marlins)
1997—Gary Jones, Edmonton (Athletics)
1998—Terry Kennedy, Iowa (Cubs)
1999—John Mizerock, Wichita (Royals)
2000—Joel Skinner, Buffalo (Indians)
2001—Jackie Moore, Round Rock (Astros)
2002—John Russell, Edmonton (Twins)
2003—Dave Brundage, San Antonio (Mariners)
2004—Marty Brown, Buffalo (Indians)
2005—Ken Oberkfell, Norfolk (Mets)
2006—Todd Claus, Portland (Red Sox)

helped him fulfill his daily duties, but also made his clubs perennial playoff contenders. Walbeck won the Midwest League title in his first season as skipper in 2004 at low Class A West Michigan, made another playoff appearance with the Whitecaps a year later, and then won the MWL again in 2006.

Walbeck, 38, moved up to Erie this year, guiding the Seawolves to the Eastern League Southern Division title with an 81-59 record. Erie lost in the playoffs, but accomplished one of Ezell's goals for 2007, "bring back respectability" to an Erie club that finished last the two previous two seasons and hadn't won 80 games since 2004.

One of the biggest reasons for Erie's success was first baseman Jeff Larish, a 2005 fifth-rounder who batted .267/.390/.515 with 28 homers. In his final regular season at-bat, Larish hit a grand slam to hit the 100-RBI plateau.

"It was a tremendous experience playing for Wally," Larish said. "He was able to keep all our guys focused and relaxed and came out with a positive attitude every day . . . He can keep everybody loose whether they just got to Double-A or have big league experience"

Erie's closer this season was 40-year-old right-hander Alan Mills, who had 12 years of big league experience and wound up recording 23 saves.

"All the players were constantly asking him questions," Walbeck said. "And if they weren't, I was. Before you know it, having Alan there was just like having another coach."

fered a broken finger in 2005, limiting him to 52 games with Triple-A Norfolk and signed with the Dodgers after the season. He hit .247 with 21 home runs and 91 RBIs for Double-A Jacksonville while playing with a hand not completely healed.

The Royals signed Brazell—who had never hit more than 24 homers in a season—as a minor league free agent before the 2007 season and he began with Double-A Wichita, hitting .349 with seven home runs in 30 games

before earning a promotion to Omaha.

"I've been able to hit home runs in the past, but this year they're coming in bunches," Brazell said.

Brazell earned a brief big league promotion following the season and was added to the Royals 40-man roster.

Ankiel led the minors in home runs at the time of his promotion in early August and hit a three-run shot in his first big league game in three years. It had been over two years since Ankiel nearly walked away from baseball

TRIPLE-A

Pos.	Player, Team (Organization)	AVG	OBP	SLG	AB	R	H	2B	3B	HR	RBI	BB	SO	SB
1B	Joey Votto, Louisville (Reds)	.294	.381	.478	496	74	146	21	2	22	92	70	110	17
2B	Eric Patterson, Iowa (Cubs)	.297	.362	.455	516	94	153	28	6	14	65	54	85	24
3B	Ian Stewart, Colo. Springs (Rockies)	.304	.379	.478	414	72	126	23	2	15	65	49	92	11
SS	Brian Bixler, Indianapolis (Pirates)	.274	.368	.436	475	77	130	23	10	5	51	54	131	28
OF	Justin Ruggiano, Durham (Devil Rays)	.309	.386	.502	482	78	149	29	2	20	73	53	151	26
OF	Adam Jones, Tacoma (Mariners)	.314	.382	.586	420	75	132	27	6	25	84	36	106	8
OF	Brandon Moss, Pawtucket (Red Sox)	.282	.363	.471	493	66	139	41	2	16	78	61	148	3
DH	Shelley Duncan, Scranton/WB (Yankees)	.295	.380	.577	336	58	99	18	1	25	79	45	82	2

Pos	Pitcher, Team (Organization)	W	L	ERA	G	GS	SV	IP	H	HR	BB	SO	GO/AO	AVG
SP	Kevin Slowey, Rochester (Twins)	10	5	1.89	20	20	0	134	110	4	18	107	0.86	.223
SP	Nick Blackburn, Rochester (Twins)	7	3	2.11	17	17	0	111	96	7	12	57	1.53	.232
SP	Aaron Laffey, Buffalo (Indians)	9	3	3.08	16	15	0	96	89	5	23	75	2.83	.243
SP	Garrett Olson, Norfolk (Orioles)	9	7	3.16	22	22	0	128	95	13	39	120	1.11	.208
RP	Edwar Ramirez, Scranton/WB (Yankees)	1	0	0.90	25	0	6	40	20	0	14	69	1.04	.149

Player of the Year: Adam Jones, Tacoma (Mariners), **Manager of the Year:** Charlie Montoyo, Durham (Devil Rays), **Team of the Year:** Durham (Devil Rays)

DOUBLE-A

Pos.	Player, Team (Organization)	AVG	OBP	SLG	AB	R	H	2B	3B	HR	RBI	BB	SO	SB
C	John Jaso, Montgomery (Devil Rays)	.316	.408	.484	380	62	120	24	2	12	71	59	49	2
1B	Jordan Brown, Akron (Indians)	.333	.421	.484	483	85	161	36	2	11	76	63	56	11
2B	Mike Hollimon, Erie (Tigers)	.282	.371	.478	471	91	133	34	8	14	76	64	121	17
3B	Evan Longoria, Montgomery (D-Rays)	.307	.403	.528	381	78	117	21	0	21	76	51	81	4
SS	Jed Lowrie, Portland (Red Sox) .297	.410	.501	337	61	100	31	7	8	49	65	58	5	
OF	Colby Rasmus, Springfield (Cardinals)	.275	.381	.551	472	93	130	37	3	29	72	70	108	18
OF	Fernando Perez, Montgomery (D-Rays)	.308	.423	.481	393	84	121	24	10	8	33	76	104	32
OF	Justin Upton, Mobile (Diamondbacks)	.309	.399	.556	259	48	80	17	4	13	53	37	51	10
DH	Chase Headley, San Antonio (Padres)	.330	.437	.580	433	82	143	38	5	20	78	74	114	1

Pos	Pitcher, Team (Organization)	W	L	ERA	G	GS	SV	IP	H	HR	BB	SO	GO/AO	AVG
SP	Chris Mason, Montgomery (Devil Rays)	15	4	2.57	28	28	0	161	147	7	44	136	1.53	.241
SP	Clay Buchholz, Portland (Red Sox)	7	2	1.77	16	15	0	87	55	4	22	116	0.95	.180
SP	Gio Gonzalez, Birmingham (White Sox)	9	7	3.18	27	27	0	150	116	10	57	185	1.46	.216
SP	Radhames Liz, Bowie (Orioles)	11	4	3.22	25	25	0	137	101	13	70	161	0.71	.204
RP	Jonathan Meloan, Jacksonville (Dodgers)	5	2	2.18	35	0	19	45	24	3	18	70	1.10	.155

Player of the Year: Evan Longoria, Montgomery (Devil Rays), **Manager of the Year:** Pop Warner, Springfield (Cardinals), **Team of the Year:** San Antonio (Padres)

HIGH CLASS A

Pos.	Player, Team (Organization)	AVG	OBP	SLG	AB	R	H	2B	3B	HR	RBI	BB	SO	SB
C	Taylor Teagarden, Bakersfield (Rangers)	.315	.448	.606	292	75	92	25	0	20	67	65	89	2
1B	Kyle Blanks, Lake Elsinore (Padres)	.301	.380	.540	465	94	140	31	4	24	100	44	98	11
2B	Matt Antonelli, Lake Elsinore (Padres)	.314	.409	.499	347	89	109	14	4	14	54	53	58	18
3B	Allen Craig, Palm Beach (Cardinals)	.312	.370	.530	423	77	132	25	2	21	77	35	79	8
SS	Chris Nelson, Modesto (Rockies)	.289	.358	.503	529	97	153	42	7	19	99	55	92	27
OF	Cameron Maybin, Lakeland (Tigers)	.304	.393	.486	296	58	90	14	5	10	44	43	83	25
OF	Jordan Schafer, Myrtle Beach (Braves)	.294	.354	.477	436	70	128	34	8	10	43	40	95	19
OF	Jay Bruce, Sarasota (Reds)	.325	.379	.589	268	49	87	27	5	11	49	24	67	4
DH	Chris Davis, Bakersfield (Rangers)	.298	.340	.573	386	69	115	28	3	24	93	22	123	3

Pos	Pitcher, Team (Organization)	W	L	ERA	G	GS	SV	IP	H	HR	BB	SO	GO/AO	AVG
SP	Brandon Hynick, Modesto (Rockies)	16	5	2.52	28	28	0	182	170	13	31	136	1.08	.243
SP	Josh Outman, Clearwater (Phillies)	10	4	2.45	20	18	0	117	104	7	54	117	1.24	.236
SP	Ian Kennedy, Tampa (Yankees)	6	1	1.29	11	10	0	63	39	2	22	72	0.69	.183
SP	Jake McGee, Vero Beach (Devil Rays)	5	4	2.93	21	21	0	117	86	8	39	145	0.85	.203
RP	Eric Wordekemper, Tampa (Yankees)	2	0	0.57	43	0	33	47	39	0	11	34	2.05	.223

Player of the Year: Brandon Hynick, Modesto (Rockies), **Manager of the Year:** Tommy Thompson, Frederick (Orioles), **Team of the Year:** Clearwater (Phillies)

after his career unraveled following a well-documented meltdown on the pitching mound.

Ankiel's comeback began in a Redbirds jersey, where any skepticism about his transformation into a position player was erased when he hit seven home runs in April, five in May and 19 in a 52-game stretch in June and July. The comeback began to make headlines following a three-homer performance against Iowa on June 16 and gathered even more steam when he homered in four con-secutive games in early July and hit three in a four-game span later that month.

Two weeks later Ankiel was in the big leagues and hit three home runs in his first weekend back.

"You can't put it into words," he said. "It's almost . . . euphoric."

Myrow has never been considered much of a prospect during a nine-year career with three organizations. He hit .306 with Double-A Trenton in 2003 and led the minors

MINOR LEAGUES

LOW CLASS A

Pos.	Player, Team (Organization)	AVG	OBP	SLG	AB	R	H	2B	3B	HR	RBI	BB	SO	SB
C	James Skelton, W. Michigan (Tigers)	.309	.402	.448	353	60	109	24	2	7	52	55	53	18
1B	Chris Carter, Kannapolis (White Sox)	.291	.383	.522	467	84	136	27	3	25	93	67	112	3
2B	Chris Coghlan, Greensboro (Marlins)	.325	.419	.534	305	60	99	26	4	10	64	47	43	19
3B	Taylor Green, West Virginia (Brewers)	.327	.406	.516	397	68	130	29	2	14	86	51	65	0
SS	Hector Gomez, Asheville (Rockies)	.266	.309	.421	534	89	142	34	8	11	61	29	120	20
OF	John Raynor, Greensboro (Marlins)	.333	.429	.519	445	110	148	28	8	13	57	66	98	54
OF	Travis Snider, Lansing (Blue Jays)	.313	.377	.525	457	72	143	35	7	16	93	49	129	3
OF	Desmond Jennings, Columbus (D-Rays)	.315	.401	.465	387	75	122	21	5	9	37	45	53	45
DH	Ryan Royster, Columbus (Devil Rays)	.329	.380	.601	474	90	156	31	4	30	98	36	121	17

Pos	Pitcher, Team (Organization)	W	L	ERA	G	GS	SV	IP	H	HR	BB	SO	GO/AO	AVG
SP	Fautino de los Santos, Kan. (White Sox)	9	4	2.40	21	15	0	98	49	5	36	121	1.03	.148
SP	Tyler Robertson, Beloit (Twins)	9	5	2.29	18	16	1	102	87	3	33	123	2.00	.226
SP	Trevor Cahill, Kane County (Athletics)	11	4	2.73	20	19	0	105	85	3	40	117	1.83	.220
SP	Brett Anderson, South Bend (D'backs)	8	4	2.21	14	14	0	81	76	3	10	85	1.96	.248
RP	Jon Hovis, Charleston (Yankees)	4	5	1.69	55	0	30	64	49	2	11	56	2.83	.208

Player of the Year: Travis Snider, Lansing (Blue Jays), **Manager of the Year:** Jeff Smith, Beloit (Twins), **Team of the Year:** Columbus (Devil Rays)

SHORT-SEASON

Pos.	Player, Team (Organization)	AVG	OBP	SLG	AB	R	H	2B	3B	HR	RBI	BB	SO	SB
C	Josh Donaldson, Boise (Cubs)	.346	.470	.605	162	37	56	11	2	9	35	37	34	6
1B	Justin Byler, State College (Pirates)	.312	.362	.487	263	41	82	18	2	8	43	17	68	1
2B	Tony Thomas, Boise (Cubs)	.308	.404	.544	182	44	56	12	8	5	33	25	41	28
3B	Clayton Conner, Yakima (Diamondbacks)	.351	.400	.626	171	35	60	12	4	9	45	11	44	0
SS	Justin Snyder, Staten Island (Yankees)	.335	.459	.477	260	68	87	20	1	5	40	58	50	10
OF	Luis Durango, Eugene (Padres)	.367	.422	.460	300	60	110	6	8	2	32	29	32	17
OF	Greg Halman, Everett (Mariners)	.307	.371	.597	238	37	73	19	1	16	37	21	85	16
OF	Corey Brown, Vancouver (Athletics)	.268	.379	.545	213	31	57	18	4	11	48	37	77	5
DH	Kellen Kulbacki, Eugene (Padres)	.301	.382	.491	226	33	68	13	3	8	39	27	56	1

Pos	Pitcher, Team (Organization)	W	L	ERA	G	GS	SV	IP	H	HR	BB	SO	GO/AO	AVG
SP	Jordan Zimmermann, Vermont (Nats)	5	2	2.38	13	11	0	53	45	2	18	71	1.39	.228
SP	Hector Correa, Jamestown (Marlins)	6	2	3.22	11	11	0	59	61	5	13	83	0.94	.261
SP	Brett Cecil, Auburn (Blue Jays)	1	0	1.27	14	13	0	50	36	1	11	56	2.18	.197
SP	Matt Latos, Eugene (Padres)	1	4	3.83	16	13	0	56	58	1	22	74	1.11	.266
RP	Josh Dew, Batavia (Cardinals)	0	1	1.80	24	0	15	25	14	1	6	32	1.37	.159

Player of the Year: Greg Halman, Everett (Mariners), **Manager of the Year:** Steve Decker, Salem-Keizer (Giants), **Team of the Year:** Salem-Keizer (Giants)

ROOKIE

Pos.	Player, Team (Organization)	AVG	OBP	SLG	AB	R	H	2B	3B	HR	RBI	BB	SO	SB
C	Jonathan Lucroy, Helena (Brewers)	.342	.383	.487	234	35	80	18	2	4	39	16	37	0
1B	Christian Marrero, Great Falls (White Sox)	.305	.383	.561	269	53	82	21	6	12	63	36	43	3
2B	Nick Noonan, AZL Giants (Giants)	.316	.357	.451	206	33	65	11	4	3	40	12	20	18
3B	Brandon Waring, Billings (Reds)	.311	.369	.614	267	63	83	17	2	20	61	21	83	1
SS	Todd Frazier, Billings (Reds)	.319	.409	.513	160	29	51	6	5	5	25	18	22	3
OF	Cody Johnson, Danville (Braves)	.305	.374	.630	243	51	74	18	5	17	57	26	72	7
OF	Salvador Sanchez, Great Falls (White Sox)	.343	.394	.544	283	57	97	16	10	7	51	18	59	18
OF	Michael Burgess, GCL Nats (Nationals)	.336	.442	.617	128	22	43	6	3	8	32	25	37	1
DH	Caleb Gindl, Helena (Brewers)	.372	.420	.580	207	40	77	22	3	5	42	20	38	4

Pos	Pitcher, Team (Organization)	W	L	ERA	G	GS	SV	IP	H	HR	BB	SO	GO/AO	AVG
SP	Cole Rohrbough, Danville (Braves)	3	2	1.08	8	7	0	33	20	1	8	58	1.69	.167
SP	David Bromberg, Elizabethton (Twins)	9	0	2.78	13	11	0	58	45	4	32	81	1.54	.211
SP	Jeff Locke, Danville (Braves)	7	1	2.66	13	11	0	61	48	2	8	74	1.85	.213
SP	Mike McCardell, Elizabethton (Twins)	5	1	2.00	8	8	0	45	29	3	5	70	1.25	.179
RP	Brad Tippett, Elizabethton (Twins)	7	1	0.93	21	0	3	39	20	1	4	51	0.91	.155

Player of the Year: Brandon Waring, Billings (Reds), **Manager of the Year:** Ray Smith, Elizabethton (Twins), **Team of the Year:** Elizabethton (Twins)

in runs and extra-base hits while finishing second in on-base percentage and slugging.

The performance earned Myrow his second big league promotion—the Dodgers called him up in 2005 during a rash of injuries—and he went 1-for-10 with the Padres.

■ Three organizations had two affiliates win league titles: the Yankees (Double-A Trenton, Rookie-level Gulf Coast), Devil Rays (Double-A Montgomery, low Class A Coumbus) and Giants (high Class A San Jose, short-season Salem-Keizer.) Yet there wasn't a bigger surprise than Frederick (Orioles) winning the high Class A Carolina League. In fact, the Keys simply reaching the playoffs was remarkable considering they posted a negative-154 run differential and finished 32-37 in each half of the split-season schedule—good for first place one time and third another.

KEVIN PATAKY

ROBERT GURGANUS

Steven Pearce socked 31 home runs at three levels of the Pirates farm system

James McDonald struck out 168 batters and reached Double-A with the Dodgers

MINOR LEAGUES

FIRST TEAM

Pos.	Player, Team (Organization)	AVG	OBP	SLG	AB	R	H	2B	3B	HR	RBI	BB	SO	SB
C	Geovany Soto, Iowa (Cubs)	.353	.424	.652	385	75	136	31	3	26	109	53	94	0
1B	Steven Pearce, Lynch./Alt./Ind. (Pirates)	.333	.394	.622	487	94	162	40	4	31	113	47	70	14
2B	Matt Antonelli, L.E./San Antonio (Padres)	.307	.404	.491	534	123	164	25	5	21	78	83	94	28
3B	Evan Longoria, Mont./Durham (Devil Rays)	.299	.402	.520	485	97	145	29	0	26	95	73	110	4
SS	Jed Lowrie, Portland/Pawtucket (Red Sox)	.298	.393	.503	497	82	148	47	8	13	70	77	91	5
OF	Jay Bruce, Sara./Chat./Louisville (Reds)	.319	.375	.587	521	87	166	46	8	26	89	47	135	8
OF	Colby Rasmus, Springfield (Cardinals)	.275	.381	.551	472	93	130	37	3	29	72	70	108	18
OF	Justin Upton, Visalia/Mobile (D'backs)	.319	.410	.551	385	75	123	23	6	18	70	56	79	19
DH	Travis Snider, Lansing (Blue Jays)	.313	.377	.525	457	72	143	35	7	16	93	49	129	3

Pos.	Pitcher, Team (Organization)	W	L	ERA	G	GS	SV	IP	H	HR	BB	SO	G/F	AVG
SP	Clay Buchholz, Portland/Pawtucket (Red Sox)	8	5	2.44	24	23	0	125	87	9	35	171	1.09	.193
SP	Ian Kennedy, Tampa/Trenton/SWB (Yankees)	12	3	1.91	26	25	0	146	91	6	50	163	0.88	.182
SP	Joba Chamberlain, Tampa/Tren./SWB (Yankees)	9	2	2.45	18	15	0	88	62	4	27	135	1.57	.198
SP	James McDonald, I.E./Jacksonville (Dodgers)	13	9	3.07	26	25	0	135	121	13	37	168	0.79	.240
RP	Edwar Ramirez, Trenton/SWB (Yankees)	4	0	0.79	34	0	7	57	26	1	22	102	1.06	.135

SECOND TEAM

Pos.	Player, Team (Organization)	AVG	OBP	SLG	AB	R	H	2B	3B	HR	RBI	BB	SO	SB
C	Taylor Teagarden, Baker./Frisco (Rangers)	.310	.426	.586	394	94	122	28	0	27	83	75	128	2
1B	Jordan Brown, Akron (Indians)	.333	.421	.484	483	85	161	36	2	11	76	63	56	11
2B	Adrian Cardenas, Lakewood (Phillies)	.295	.354	.417	499	70	147	30	2	9	79	47	80	20
3B	Chase Headley, San Antonio (Padres)	.330	.437	.580	433	82	143	38	5	20	78	74	114	1
SS	Chin-Lung Hu, Jack./Las Vegas (Dodgers)	.325	.364	.507	517	89	168	40	6	14	62	32	51	15
OF	Desmond Jennings, Columbus (Devil Rays)	.315	.401	.465	387	75	122	21	5	9	37	45	53	45
OF	Adam Jones, Tacoma (Mariners)	.314	.382	.586	420	75	132	27	6	25	84	36	106	8
OF	Cameron Maybin, GCL/Lake./Erie (Tigers)	.316	.409	.523	323	68	102	15	5	14	53	51	91	25
DH	Ryan Royster, Columbus (Devil Rays)	.329	.380	.601	474	90	156	31	4	30	98	36	121	17

Pos.	Pitcher, Team (Organization)	W	L	ERA	G	GS	SV	IP	H	HR	BB	SO	G/F	AVG
SP	Wade Davis, Vero Beach/Montgomery (Devil Rays)	10	3	2.50	27	27	0	158	128	8	51	169	1.30	.223
SP	Gio Gonzalez, Birmingham (White Sox)	9	7	3.18	27	27	0	150	116	10	57	185	1.46	.216
SP	Brandon Hynick, Modesto (Rockies)	16	5	2.52	28	28	0	182	170	13	31	136	1.08	.243
SP	Jake McGee, Vero Beach/Montgomery (Devil Rays)	8	6	3.15	26	26	0	140	105	10	52	175	0.85	.207
RP	Jonathan Meloan, Jack./Las Vegas (Dodgers)	7	2	2.03	49	0	20	67	36	5	27	91	1.10	.156

Ready takes Missions from worst to first

Randy Ready knew he had some work ahead of him when he returned to the Double-A Texas League in April.

The San Antonio Missions first-year manager didn't have a roster filled with high-powered prospects in the Padres farm system. He didn't have a proven cleanup hitter, or a leadoff guy, or a closer, and the pitching rotation was a work in progress. Not surprisingly, the Missions finished last in the first half in the league's Southern Division, 16 games behind Frisco.

Then the Padres made a few roster moves, and a handful of players who showed potential in the first half began to emerge as leaders. The team clinched a playoff berth during the last homestand of the year, swept Frisco in the divisional series and beat Springfield three-games-to-one for its first Texas League pennant since 2003 and 11th overall.

"Going from worst to first is a quite a tribute to everybody on this team," said Ready, who won the Texas League batting title in 1982 for the El Paso Diablos. "We had guys on this team who did their jobs and got things done."

Two of those players earned the league's top individual honors in 2007: Third baseman Chase Headley and righthander Josh Geer were voted the league's player and pitcher of the year, respectively.

Headley won the batting title and was a threat to win the league's triple crown for much of the year. The switch-hitter wound up at .330 in a season when just four players in the league topped .300, and he finished with 20 home runs and 78 RBIs.

"There were no weaknesses in his game," Ready said. "He adjusted to all pitching, right- and lefthanded, cut down on his errors and played a solid third base all year long."

Geer, a changeup specialist who barely made the Missions as their No. 5 starter, emerged as the ace of the staff. He had the league's lowest ERA at 3.20 and won a league-high 16 games, as well as one in the playoffs.

"He was our go-to-guy," Ready said of Geer, who was drafted by the Padres out of Rice in 2005. "The club was confident when he took to the mound that we were going to win that night. That's the greatest compliment that you can give any pitcher."

Two other players who were with San Antonio all season made the league's postseason all-star team: outfielder Will Venable, who returned to his forte of slash-and-run hitting in the second half and hit a team-best .387 in the playoffs, and catcher Nick Hundley, who handled a pitching staff that finished the season with the league's best team ERA.

But it was the newcomers who were able to make the difference, thanks in part to a midseason visit

Matt Antonelli's midseason promotion keyed San Antonio's run to the Southern League championship

from Padres general manager Kevin Towers.

"The last thing he said to me before he left was, 'Grady'll get you fixed up,'" Missions president Burl Yarbrough said, referring to farm director Grady Fuson. "They made a couple of moves, and we were the best team in the league the second half."

Among the biggest was the promotion of three players from high Class A Lake Elsinore: second baseman Matt Antonelli, outfielder Chad Huffman and lefthander Wade LeBlanc.

Antonelli gave the Missions a spark in the batting order, and Huffman gave Ready more flexibility in the outfield. LeBlanc, a second-round draft pick in 2006, might have been the best second-half pitcher in the league. He went 7-3, 3.45 in 12 starts, and gave up a total of five earned runs in his last six appearances, including the playoffs.

The bullpen got its closer when the Padres signed righthander Edwin Moreno in July. He was 8-3, 2.71 in the Mexican League—mostly as a starter—and in San Antonio he was even better, going 9-for-10 in save opportunities and giving up three earned runs in 17 innings.

The Missions' hottest hitter in the postseason, Brett Dowdy, joined the team from Triple-A Portland in June and was the everyday second baseman until Antonelli arrived. He served in a utility role after that, and finished hitting .265/.360/.408, then went 11-for-29 with three homers in the playoffs.

"He was the MVP of the whole postseason," Ready said. "He got an opportunity to make something happen, and he slugged his way through the playoffs."

As did the Missions.

PREVIOUS WINNERS

1993—Harrisburg/Eastern (Expos)	1998—Mobile/Southern (Padres)	2003—Sacramento/Pacific Coast (Athletics)
1994—Wilmington/Carolina (Royals)	1999—Trenton/Eastern (Red Sox)	2004—Lancaster/California (Diamondbacks)
1995—Norfolk/International (Mets)	2000—Round Rock/Texas (Astros)	2005—Jacksonville/Southern (Dodgers)
1996—Edmonton/Pacific Coast (Athletics)	2001—Lake Elsinore/California (Padres)	2006—Tucson/Pacific Coast (Diamondbacks)
1997—West Michigan/Midwest (Tigers)	2002—Akron/Eastern (Indians)	

BILL NICHOLS

John Whittleman

BILL NICHOLS

Rick Vanden Hurk

When the World team has won in the All-Star Futures Game, it has usually done so with dominant pitching, and its 2007 victory at San Francisco's AT&T Park was no exception. But this year's squad added potent offense as well, scoring in five of seven innings to come away with a 7-2 win.

The World pitching staff struck out 10 in seven innings and allowed six hits to keep the U.S. offense in check most of the day. The only bright spots for the U.S. were solo home runs by Diamondbacks outfielder Justin Upton in the third (off the White Sox' Fautino de los Santos) and Rangers third baseman John Whittleman in the fifth (off the Mets' Deolis Guerra).

The U.S. lineup had plenty of strong hitters, but they didn't get many good swings off World pitchers. Jacoby Ellsbury, who led off and played the entire game in left field for the U.S., and Ian Stewart, who batted cleanup as the DH, both finished the game 0-for-4.

"Where the World pitching was real disappointing last year, it was completely different this year," one veteran scout said. "We didn't really see anything spectacular defensively on that side because the pitching was so dominant."

Ellsbury, who just returned from his first big league stint with the Red Sox, didn't hit a ball out of the infield and struck out twice. He said the pitchers he saw on the World staff compared favorably to the big league pitching he just faced.

"They were solid," he said. "I faced four different guys leading off innings, and I didn't know what they were going to throw. They all threw very well. They all have big league stuff."

Cardinals catcher Bryan Anderson saw several good pitchers on the U.S. staff while behind the plate, and struck out and hit a ball to first base in his two at-bats. He echoed Ellsbury's thoughts.

"My first at-bat, the guy (Carlos Carrasco) threw a bunch of changeups," Anderson said. "You're up there thinking this is an all-star type of game and he's going to come after you, and he doubled up on changeups, then threw a fastball away, and then threw me a changeup away (for the strikeout).

"All the pitchers I saw were pretty impressive. (U.S. starter) Jeff Niemann was pretty good, really good stuff, but everyone I caught today was really impressive, and the World team guys obviously were too. I'm surprised there were four home runs with all the good pitching there was."

World batters provided plenty of offense to back up the pitching. Their seven runs tied the all-time high for the World squad, matching the total the Alfonso Soriano-led group scored in the first Futures Game.

Mariners outfielder Michael Saunders led the game off with a single, then stole second for a go-go offense under manager Juan Marichal. The World team stole four bases on five attempts in the first three innings.

Saunders scored the game's first run on a double by Dodgers shortstop Chin-Lung Hu, who won the Larry Doby Award as the game's MVP. Hu also scored a run in the first on a sacrifice fly from Mariners outfielder Wladimir Balentien, staking the World team to a 2-0 lead. Hu said he will send the trophy back to his family in Taiwan.

UNITED STATES ROSTER

Pitchers: Collin Balester (Nationals), Clay Buchholz (Red Sox), Joba Chamberlain (Yankees), Matt Garza (Twins), Luke Hocheaver (Royals), Clayton Kershaw (Dodgers), Chuck Lofgren (Indians), Michael Madsen (Athletics), Jeff Niemann (Devil Rays), Garrett Olson (Orioles). **Catchers:** Bryan Anderson (Cardinals), J.R. Towles (Astros). **Infielders:** Brian Bocock (Giants), Adrian Cardenas (Phillies), Chris Coghlan (Marlins), Brent Lillibridge (Braves), Evan Longoria (Devil Rays), Steven Pearce (Pirates), Ian Stewart (Rockies), John Whittleman (Indians). **Outfielders:** Jay Bruce (Reds), Jacoby Ellsbury (Red Sox), Cameron Maybin (Tigers), Colby Rasmus (Cardinals), Justin Upton (Diamondbacks).

WORLD ROSTER

Pitchers: Pedro Beato (Orioles), Carlos Carrasco (Phillies), Fautino De Los Santos (White Sox), Emiliano Fruto (Nationals), Deolis Guerra (Mets), Serguey Linares (Pirates), Franklin Morales (Rockies), Henry Sosa (Giants), Rich Thompson (Angels), Rick Vanden Hurk (Marlins). **Catchers:** Robinzon Diaz (Blue Jays), Max Ramirez (Indians). Infielders: Elvis Andrus (Braves), German Duran (Rangers), Alcides Escobar (Brewers), Chin-Lung Hu (Dodgers), Freddy Sandoval (Angels), Geovany Soto (Cubs), Craig Stansberry (Padres), Joey Votto (Reds). **Outfielders:** Wladimir Balentien (Mariners), Carlos Gonzalez (Diamondbacks), Gorkys Hernandez (Tigers), Fernando Martinez (Mets), Michael Saunders (Mariners).

FUTURES GAME, JULY 8, 2007,
WORLD 7, UNITED STATES 2

WORLD	AB	R	H	BI	BB	SO	U.S.	AB	R	H	BI	BB	SO
Saunders cf	1	2	0	0	1	0	Ellsbury lf	4	0	0	0	0	2
Hernandez ph-cf	1	1	0	0	1	0	Upton cf	2	1	1	1	0	1
Hu ss	2	1	2	2	0	0	Rasmus cf	2	0	0	0	0	0
Andrus ph-ss	2	0	0	0	0	1	Longoria 3b	1	0	1	0	0	0
Balentien rf	3	0	1	2	0	1	Whittleman 3b	1	1	1	1	1	0
Votto 1b	4	1	1	1	0	2	Stewart dh	4	0	0	0	0	1
Ramirez dh	3	1	1	0	0	1	Pearce 1b	1	0	0	1	0	0
Duran 2b	2	0	0	0	0	1	Tolbert 1b	1	0	0	0	0	1
Stansberry 2b	1	0	0	0	0	0	Lillibridge ss	2	0	0	0	0	2
Diaz c	2	0	2	0	0	0	Bocock ss	0	0	0	1	0	0
Soto c	1	0	0	0	0	1	Bruce rf	3	0	1	0	0	1
Gonzalez lf	1	0	0	1	0	0	Coghlan 2b	1	0	0	0	1	0
Van Ostrand lf	1	1	1	1	0	0	Cardenas 2b	1	0	1	0	0	0
Sandoval 3b	2	0	0	0	0	1	Anderson c	2	0	0	0	0	1
Escobar 3b	1	0	0	0	0	0	Towles c	1	0	0	0	0	1
TOTALS	27	7	8	7	2	8	TOTALS	26	2	5	2	4	10

World	201 101	2—7
U.S.	001 010	0—2

E: Coghlan. **LOB:** World 3, United States 8. **2B:** Hu, Longoria, Ramirez, Balentien. **3B:** Bruce. **HR:** Upton, Votto, Whittleman, Van Ostrand. **SB:** Saunders 2, Hu, Diaz. **CS:** Hu. **SF:** Balentien, Gonzalez.

WORLD	IP	H	R	ER	BB	SO	HR	U.S.	IP	H	R	ER	BB	SO	HR
Vanden Hurk W	1.0	1	0	0	0	1	0	Niemann L	1.0	1	2	1	0	1	0
Carrasco	1.0	1	0	0	1	2	0	Lofgren	1.0	1	0	0	1	0	0
de los Santos	1.0	1	1	1	1	2	1	Chamberlain	1.0	1	1	1	1	1	0
Sosa	1.0	0	0	0	0	0	0	Mulvey	1.0	2	1	1	0	1	0
Guerra	0.2	1	1	1	0	0	1	Hochevar	1.0	0	0	0	0	0	0
Morales	1.0	0	0	0	1	3	0	Buchholz	1.0	1	1	1	0	2	1
Beato	0.1	1	0	0	1	0	0	Kershaw	0.2	1	2	2	1	1	1
Thompson	0.2	0	0	0	1	0	0	Balester	0.1	1	0	0	1	0	0
Fruto	0.1	0	0	0	1	0	0								

MINOR LEAGUES

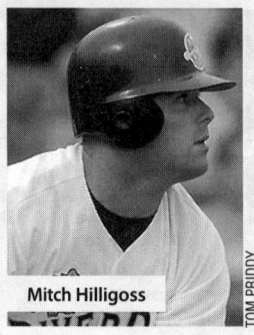

Mitch Hilligoss

TOM PRIDDY

Lee Mitchell

TOM PRIDDY

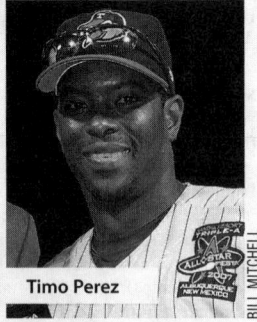

Timo Perez

BILL MITCHELL

MINOR LEAGUES

The International League opened with a show of offensive firepower, then closed with a display of pitching power to take a 7-5 win over the Pacific Coast League in the 20th annual Triple-A all-star game.

Albuquerque has long had a reputation as a hitter's haven, and it took the all-star pitchers no time to find out why. All the runs were scored in the first four innings, which featured four home runs and five doubles.

When the starters gave way to the relievers, however, the hitters were suddenly silent. The International League went down in order in four of the last five innings, but its pitchers were good enough to hold the Pacific Coast League in check over the same stretch and preserve the win.

Richmond righthander Manny Acosta (Braves) won the pitcher of the game award for his impressive seventh inning, when he struck out Iowa second baseman Eric Patterson (Cubs) and Tacoma outfielder Adam Jones (Mariners) and retired Las Vegas outfielder Delwyn Young (Dodgers) on a comebacker. He pitched consistently in the mid-90s and touched 96 mph.

The pitchers who followed Acosta may have been even more impressive--or at least more dramatic. Rochester righthander Bobby Korecky (Twins) pitched the eighth and worked into a bases-loaded jam when Albuquerque shortstop Robert Andino (Marlins) came to the plate.

The 12,367 Albuquerque fans who turned out at Isotopes Park were energized by the rally and raised one of the loudest cheers of the night for Andino, who worked the count full.

"He's a righthanded hitter, so the first thing I tried was to get him with my slider," he said. When Andino laid off, Korecky switched gears for the payoff pitch. "I just decided to throw it a little harder and elevate the fastball, and fortunately he swung through it."

Andino's swing and miss on a 93 mph fastball ended the eighth, but the PCL had one more challenge before the game ended. This time another hometown hero, DH Valentino Pascucci--who hit a two-run home run in the first off IL starter Bryan Bullington--came to the plate after Jones had reached on a single. The Albuquerque fans sent up an even bigger cheer for the matchup against Norfolk righthander Cory Doyne.

Doyne, who already has a Norfolk franchise-record 26 saves on the season, quickly got Pascucci down two strikes and appeared to have struck him out with a curveball on the outside corner. But it was called a ball and Pascucci had one more chance.

ALL-STAR ROUNDUP

EASTERN LEAGUE: The North and South divisions were tied at two in the third inning when the game was canceled because fog had engulfed Norwich's Dodd Stadium. Managers Dave Machemer (North) and Tim Bogar (South), along with the umpiring crew and EL president Joe McEacharn, moved to call the game after routine fly balls began falling for hits because of a lack of visibility.

SOUTHERN LEAGUE: Mississippi's J.C. Holt and Carl Loadenthal (Braves) each had three hits at the top of the order, but it wasn't enough for the Southern League's South all-stars, which lost 7-4 to the North at Trustman Park in Pearl, Miss. The victory was the third in a row for the North squad. Carolina's Lee Mitchell (Marlins) won MVP honors for singling home two runs.

TEXAS LEAGUE: Astros farmhand Jonny Ash earned MVP honors by ending a 10th-inning tie with a game-winning RBI single, giving the South a 5-4 victory against the North at at his home ballpark, Corpus Christi's Whataburger Stadium. Ash's heroics followed a game-tying home run to lead off the inning by San Antonio outfielder Will Venable (Padres), who earlier had singled, stolen a base and scored a run.

CAROLINA-CALIFORNIA LEAGUE: Just hours after Lancaster's Bubba Bell (Red Sox) was shut out in the home run derby, the California League's second-leading home run hitter saved face by keying a 10-5 Cal League rout over the Carolina League and took home MVP honors in the two leagues' 11th annual all-star game at Stockton's Banner Island Ballpark. Bell, whose 16 homers are second only to Lancaster teammate Aaron Bates' 17, went 3-for-5 with two RBIs and a run scored and helped key a three-run second inning with a two-run, two-out single.

FLORIDA STATE LEAGUE: Palm Beach's Allen Craig (Cardinals) and Vero Beach's Rhyne Hughes (Devil Rays) hit back-to-back home runs during a five-run fifth inning to lift the East to an 8-4 win at Daytona's Jackie Robinson Ballpark. Craig went 2-for-4 with two runs scored and two RBIs to take home MVP honors. Palm Beach lefthander Tyler Norrick earned the victory, pitching one shutout inning. Sarasota righthander Logan Ondrusek gave up five runs on five hits and a walk to take the loss.

MIDWEST LEAGUE: The East had 13 different players collect at least one hit in an 8-2 victory at Kane County's Elfstrom Stadium.. In turn, the West sent 15 pitchers to the mound. The East broke a 1-1 tie in the third when West Michigan outfielder and MVP Deik Scram (Tigers) walked and scored on a double by Dayton second baseman Justin Turner (Reds).

SOUTH ATLANTIC LEAGUE: The North needed just four hits to secure a 3-1 victory, with their runs coming in the fourth inning at Rome's State Mutual Stadium. Greensboro second baseman Chris Coghlan (Marlins) had an RBI double and scored on Lake County first baseman Matt Whitney's (Indians) double. Despite the loss, Charleston third baseman Mitch Hilligoss (Yankees) took home the MVP trophy for his 3-for-5 performance, which included a double and the team's lone RBI.

TEAM

WINS
Nashville (Pacific Coast)	89
Augusta (South Atlantic)	89
Kinston (Carolina)	87
Frisco (Texas)	85
Sacramento (Pacific Coast)	84
Scranton/WB (International)	84

LONGEST WINNING STREAK
Augusta (South Atlantic)	14
West Virginia (South Atlantic)	14
Lake Elsinore (California)	13
Fort Myers (Florida State)	12
Huntsville (Southern)	12
Jacksonville (Southern)	12
Montgomery (Southern)	12
Salem (Carolina)	12

LOSSES
Savannah (South Atlantic)	94
Memphis (Pacific Coast)	88
Ottawa (International)	88
Lakeland (Florida State)	87
Harrisburg (Eastern)	86
High Desert (California)	86
Portland (Pacific Coast)	86

LONGEST LOSING STREAK
Wisconsin (Midwest)	14
Vero Beach (Florida State)	12
Eugene (Northwest)	11
Frederick (Carolina)	11
Lynchburg (Carolina)	11

BATTING AVERAGE*
Tucson (Pacific Coast)	.297
Lancaster (California)	.296
Las Vegas (Pacific Coast)	.296
Colorado Springs (Pacific Coast)	.292
Salt Lake (Pacific Coast)	.289

RUNS
Lancaster (California)	1081
Lake Elsinore (California)	875
Iowa (Pacific Coast)	822
Las Vegas (Pacific Coast)	817
West Virginia (South Atlantic)	804

HOME RUNS
Lancaster (California)	217
Albuquerque (Pacific Coast)	180
Frisco (Texas)	176
Iowa (Pacific Coast)	172
Nashville (Pacific Coast)	159

STOLEN BASES
Augusta (South Atlantic)	212
Columbus (South Atlantic)	200
Lakeland (Florida State)	200
Cedar Rapids (Midwest)	196
Asheville (South Atlantic)	186

EARNED RUN AVERAGE*
Augusta (South Atlantic)	3.02
Trenton (Eastern)	3.20
Cedar Rapids (Midwest)	3.21
Tampa (Florida State)	3.23
Beloit (Midwest)	3.28

STRIKEOUTS
San Jose (California)	1234
Jacksonville (Southern)	1188
Inland Empire (California)	1165
Trenton (Eastern)	1159
Nashville (Pacific Coast)	1148

INDIVIDUAL BATTING

BATTING AVERAGE*
Brian Myrow (Portland)	.354
Geovany Soto (Iowa)	.353
Andrew Lefave (West Virginia)	.345
Wilson Valdez (Las Vegas)	.343
Bubba Bell (Lancaster, Portland)	.337

Craig Brazell led the minor leagues with 39 home runs

Delwyn Young (Las Vegas)	.337
Nate Schierholtz (Fresno)	.333
Jordan Brown (Akron)	.333
Steve Pearce (Lynchburg, Altoona, Indianapolis)	.333
John Raynor (Greensboro)	.333

RUNS
Zachary Daeges (Lancaster)	124
Matt Antonelli (Lake Elsinore, San Antonio)	123
Bubba Bell (Lancaster, Portland)	118
Eric Young Jr. (Modesto)	113
John Raynor (Greensboro)	110

HITS
Jordan Schafer (Rome, Myrtle Beach)	176
Chris Carter (Tucson, Pawtucket)	174
Craig Brazell (Wichita, Omaha)	171
Michael Griffin (Sarasota, Chattanooga)	171
Gerardo Parra (South Bend, Visalia)	171

TOP HITTING STREAKS
Brandon Watson (Columbus)	43
Mitch Hilligoss (Charleston)	38
Chris Davis (Bakersfield, Frisco)	35
Mat Gamel (Brevard County)	33
Jeff Kindel (Modesto)	26
Terrmel Sledge (Portland)	26

MOST HITS (ONE GAME)
Matt Antonelli (Lake Elsinore)	6
Kyle Blanks (Lake Elsinore)	6
Jake Gautreau (New Orleans)	6
Ernesto Mejia (Danville)	6
Manuel Rodriguez (Auburn)	6
Carlos Triunfel (High Desert)	6

TOTAL BASES
Craig Brazell (Wichita, Omaha)	326
Jay Bruce (Sarasota, Chattanooga, Louisville)	306
Steve Pearce (Lynchburg, Altoona, Indianapolis)	303
Zachary Daeges (Lancaster)	298
Chris Davis (Bakersfield, Frisco)	296

EXTRA-BASE HITS
Zachary Daeges (Lancaster)	81
Jay Bruce (Sarasota, Chattanooga, Louisville)	80
Craig Brazell (Wichita, Omaha)	77
Delwyn Young (Las Vegas)	76
Steve Pearce (Lynchburg, Altoona, Indianapolis)	75

DOUBLES
Zachary Daeges (Lancaster)	55
Delwyn Young (Las Vegas)	54
Jordan Schafer (Rome, Myrtle Beach)	49
Christian Colonel (Tulsa)	47
Jed Lowrie (Portland, Pawtucket)	47
Brett Pill (Augusta)	47

TRIPLES
Andres Torres (Erie, Toledo)	20
Robert Andino (Albuquerque)	13
Sean Shoffit (Lansing)	13
K.C. Herren (Clinton)	12
Hernan Iribarren (Huntsville)	12
Anthony Jackson (Asheville)	12
Eric Reed (Albuquerque)	12

HOME RUNS
Craig Brazell (Wichita, Omaha)	39
Chris Davis (Bakersfield, Frisco)	36
Valentino Pascucci (Albuquerque)	34
Rick Ankiel (Memphis)	32
Scott Seabol (Albuquerque)	32
Matthew Whitney (Lake County, Kinston)	32

RUNS BATTED IN
John Lindsey (Jacksonville, Las Vegas)	121
Chris Davis (Bakersfield, Frisco)	118
Zachary Daeges (Lancaster)	113
Steve Pearce (Lynchburg, Altoona, Indianapolis)	113
Matthew Whitney (Lake County, Kinston)	113

MOST RBIS, ONE GAME
Deibinson Romero (Elizabethton)	10
Scott Cousins (Greensboro)	9
Joshua Rodriguez (Kinston)	9
7 players tied	8

STOLEN BASES
Ovandy Suero (Lakeland)	75
Eric Young Jr. (Modesto)	73
Emmanuel Burriss (San Jose, Augusta)	68
Darren Ford (West Virginia, Brevard County)	67
Pedro Powell (Lynchburg)	67

CAUGHT STEALING
Diory Hernandez (Myrtle Beach, Mississippi)	22
Bradley Coon (Rancho Cucamonga, Arkansas)	21
Quentin Davis (Myrtle Beach)	21
Ovandy Suero (Lakeland)	21
5 players tied	18

HIT BY PITCH
J.D. Pruitt (Vancouver)	34
Brian Barton (Akron, Buffalo)	30
Josh Kreuzer (Dunedin, Tennessee, Iowa)	25
Steve Sollmann (Huntsville)	25
J.R. Towles (Salem, Corpus Christi, Round Rock)	25

WALKS
Jon Still (Greenville, Lancaster)	105
Adam Morrissey (Arkansas)	92
Luke Appert (Stockton, Midland)	89
Andy Tracy (New Orleans)	89
Jeff Natale (Portland)	88

STRIKEOUTS
Greg Golson (Clearwater, Reading)	173
Brent Brewer (West Virigina)	170
Brendan Katin (Huntsville)	163
Chris Dickerson (Chattanooga, Louisville)	162
Gregory Halman (Wisconsin, Everett)	162

SACRIFICE FLIES
Matt Tuiasosopo (West Tenn)	14
John Bowker (Connecticut)	12
Dan Murphy (St. Lucie)	11
9 players tied	10

SACRIFICE HITS
Denard Span (Rochester)	21
Nate Spears (Daytona, Tennessee)	19
Quentin Davis (Myrtle Beach)	18
William Rhymes (Lakeland, Erie)	18
Joe Thurston (Reading, Ottawa)	18

SLUGGING PERCENTAGE*
Geovany Soto (Iowa)	.652
Steve Pearce (Lynchburg, Altoona, Indianapolis)	.622
Craig Brazell (Wichita, Omaha)	.601
Ryan Royster (Columbus)	.601
Chris Davis (Bakersfield, Frisco)	.598

BILL MITCHELL

MINOR LEAGUES

ON-BASE PERCENTAGE*

Brian Myrow (Portland)	.440
Chase Headley (San Antonio)	.437
Jason Botts (Oklahoma)	.436
Aaron Bates (Lancaster, Portland)	.435
Javier Brito (Mobile)	.433

ON BASE PLUS SLUGGING (OPS)*

Geovany Soto (Iowa)	1.076
Brian Myrow (Portland)	1.019
Chase Headley (San Antonio)	1.016
Steve Pearce (Lynchburg, Altoona, Indianapolis)	1.016
Taylor Teagarden (Bakersfield, Frisco)	1.012

BATTING AVERAGE* BY POSITION
CATCHERS

Geovany Soto (Iowa)	.353
Mark Wagner (Lancaster)	.318
John Jaso (Montgomery)	.316
Jose Morales (Rochester)	.311
Taylor Teagarden (Bakersfield, Frisco)	.310

FIRST BASEMEN

Brian Myrow (Portland)	.354
Andrew Lefave (West Virginia)	.345
Jordan Brown (Akron)	.333
Steve Pearce (Lynchburg, Altoona, Indianapolis)	.333
Javier Brito (Mobile)	.327

SECOND BASEMEN

Tony Granadillo (Lancaster, Portland)	.326
Jarrett Hoffpauir (Memphis, Springfield)	.323
Omar Quintanilla (Colorado Springs)	.319
Martin Prado (Richmond)	.316
Daniel Mayora (Asheville)	.312

THIRD BASEMEN

Chase Headley (San Antonio)	.330
Taylor Green (West Virginia)	.327
Allen Craig (Palm Beach, Springfield)	.311
Matt Craig (Tennessee, Iowa)	.311
Michael Griffin (Sarasota, Chattanooga)	.310

SHORTSTOPS

Wilson Valdez (Las Vegas)	.343
Chin-Lung Hu (Jacksonville, Las Vegas)	.325
Jesus Merchan (West Tenn, Reading, Ottawa)	.312
Jose Castro (St. Lucie, Chattanooga)	.312
Asdrubal Cabrera (Akron, Buffalo)	.310

OUTFIELDERS

Bubba Bell (Lancaster, Portland)	.337
Delwyn Young (Las Vegas)	.337
Nate Schierholtz (Fresno)	.333
John Raynor (Greensboro)	.333
Josh Kroeger (Tennessee, Iowa)	.330

DESIGNATED HITTERS

Zachary Daeges (Lancaster)	.330
Kyle Phillips (Dunedin)	.306
Kyle Blanks (Lake Elsinore)	.301
Noochie Varner (Corpus Christi)	.287
Sergio Pedroza (Vero Beach)	.286

INDIVIDUAL PITCHING

EARNED RUN AVERAGE*

Kevin Pucetas (Augusta)	1.86
Kevin Slowey (Rochester)	1.89
Ian Kennedy (Tampa, Trenton, Scranton/WB)	1.91
Benjamin Snyder (Augusta)	2.09
Sean O'Sullivan (Cedar Rapids)	2.22
Jeff Manship (Beloit, Fort Myers)	2.30
Christopher Cody (W. Mich., Lakeland, Brevard Cty)	2.30
Mark DiFelice (Huntsville, Nashville)	2.31
John Lannan (Potomac, Harrisburg, Columbus)	2.31
Nick Blackburn (New Britain, Rochester)	2.36

WORST ERA*

Evan MacLane (Tucson)	7.70
Spike Lundberg (Las Vegas)	6.94
Jake Woods (Tacoma)	6.91
Cibney Bello (High Desert)	6.91
Ryan O'Malley (Tennessee, Iowa)	6.90

WINS

Andrew Carpenter (Clearwater)	17
Joshua Geer (Portland, San Antonio)	17
Heath Rollins (Columbus)	17
Keith Weiser (Asheville)	17
Brandon Hynick (Modesto)	16
Alan Johnson (Tulsa, Modesto)	16
Adam Pettyjohn (Huntsville, Nashville)	16
Benjamin Snyder (Augusta)	16

LOSSES

Garrett Broshuis (Connecticut)	17
Zachary Ward (Fort Myers)	17
Charlie Haeger (Charlotte)	16
T.J. Nall (Columbus, Harrisburg, Portland, Lancaster)	16
Daniel Christensen (Wichita)	15
Jeremy Mizell (Savannah)	15
Pat Overholt (Clearwater, Reading)	15

GAMES

Bobby Korecky (Rochester)	66
Casey Hoorelbeke (Las Vegas)	63
Josh Papelbon (Greenville)	62
Derrik Lutz (Chattanooga, Sarasota)	61
Aaron Rakers (Portland)	61

CARL KLINE

Gio Gonzalez led the minor leagues with 185 strikeouts

COMPLETE GAMES

Kevin Slowey (Rochester)	5
22 players tied	3

SAVES

Steven Register (Tulsa)	37
Robert Delaney (Beloit, Fort Myers)	35
Bobby Korecky (Rochester)	35
Chris Perez (Eugene, Springfield, Memphis)	35
Eric Wordekemper (Tampa, Trenton)	34

SHUTOUTS

Armando Galarraga (Oklahoma, Frisco)	3
Nick Blackburn (New Britain, Rochester)	2
Andrew Carpenter (Clearwater)	2
Carlos Carrasco (Clearwater, Reading)	2
Gary Knotts (Reading, Ottawa)	2
Cesar Ramos (San Antonio)	2
Robert Rohrbaugh (West Tenn, Tacoma)	2
Virgil Vasquez (Toledo)	2
Ronnie Ventura (Corpus Christi)	2

INNINGS PITCHED

Brandon Hynick (Modesto)	182.1
Alan Johnson (Tulsa, Modesto)	181.2
Kasey Olenberger (Salt Lake)	180.0
Nick Green (Arkansas)	178.1
Joshua Geer (Portland, San Antonio)	177.1

WALKS

Greg Miller (Las Vegas, Jacksonville)	89
Chris Waters (Norfolk, Bowie)	89
John Barnes (Lancaster, Portland, Pawtucket)	88
Matthew Walker (Vero Beach)	82
Grant Duff (Charleston)	80
Javy Guerra (Inland Empire)	80

STRIKEOUTS

Gio Gonzalez (Birmingham)	185
William Inman (Brevard Cty., Huntsville, San Antonio)	180
Matthew Maloney (Reading, Chattanooga, Louisville)	177
Jacob McGee (Vero Beach, Montgomery)	175
Clay Buchholz (Portland, Pawtucket)	171

HITS ALLOWED

Kasey Olenberger (Salt Lake)	205
J.R. Mathes (Iowa)	204
Henry Bonilla (Salt Lake)	203
Jack Cassel (Portland)	203
Simon Ferrer (Asheville)	203

STRIKEOUTS PER NINE INNINGS
(STARTERS)*

Clayton Kershaw (Great Lakes, Jacksonville)	12.02
James McDonald (Inland Empire, Jacksonville)	11.24
William Inman (Brevard Cty., Huntsville, San Antonio)	10.17
Johnny Cueto (Sarasota, Chattanooga, Louisville)	9.48
Aneury Rodriguez (Asheville)	9.47

STRIKEOUTS PER NINE INNINGS
(RELIEVERS)*

Chris Booker (Columbus)	12.88
Carlos Guevara (Chattanooga)	12.63
Jonathan Meloan (Jacksonville, Las Vegas)	12.29
Brian Akin (Jacksonville, Las Vegas)	12.18
Jose A. Rojas (Dayton, Sarasota)	12.03

BATTING AVERAGE AGAINST
(STARTERS)*

Clayton Kershaw (Great Lakes, Jacksonville)	.201
John Lannan (Potomac, Harrisburg, Columbus)	.205
Wade LeBlanc (Lake Elsinore, San Antonio)	.216
Esmerling Vasquez (Mobile)	.217
William Inman (Brevard Cty., Huntsville, San Antonio)	.220

BATTING AVERAGE AGAINST
(RELIEVERS)*

Jonathan Meloan (Jacksonville , Las Vegas)	.156
Adam Carr (Potomac, Harrisburg)	.175
Chris Booker (Columbus)	.184
Pedro Viola (Dayton, Sarasota, Chattanooga)	.186
Seth McClung (Durham, Nashville)	.186

MOST STRIKEOUTS, ONE GAME

David Hernandez (Frederick)	18
Dallas Braden (Sacramento)	17
Michael Ballard (Clinton)	14
Duane Below (West Michigan)	14
Fautino De Los Santos (Kannapolis)	14
Tim Lincecum (Fresno)	14
Radhames Liz (Bowie)	14

WILD PITCHES

Olivo Astacio (Hickory, Lynchburg, Altoona)	29
Eddie Degerman (Quad Cities, Palm Beach)	28
Daniel Bard (Lancaster, Greenville)	27
Jared Hughes (Hickory)	27
Michael Felix (Hickory, State College)	25

BALKS

Juan Ramirez (Everett)	7
Jonathan Barratt (Montgomery)	6
Jordan Latham (Boise)	6
Michael Rozier (GCL Red Sox, Lancaster)	6
5 players tied	5

HIT BATTERS

Bryant Thompson (Yakima)	22
Darren Byrd (Lakewood)	19
Michael Eisenberg (Lake Co., Mahoning Valley)	19
Kyle Waldrop (New Britain, Fort Myers)	19
5 players tied	17

INDIVIDUAL FIELDING

MOST ERRORS

Mat Gamel (Brevard County)	53
Brent Brewer (West Virginia)	48
Dylan Johnston (Boise, Peoria)	46
Daniel Garcia (Greensboro)	46
Angel R. Gonzalez (Hickory, Lynchburg)	45

MINOR LEAGUES

	INTERNATIONAL LEAGUE	PACIFIC COAST LEAGUE	EASTERN LEAGUE	SOUTHERN LEAGUE	TEXAS LEAGUE	CALIFORNIA LEAGUE	CAROLINA LEAGUE	FLORIDA STATE LEAGUE	MIDWEST LEAGUE	SOUTH ATLANTIC LEAGUE
Best Batting Prospect	Joey Votto, Louisville	Ryan Braun, Nashville	Jordan Brown, Akron	Justin Upton, Mobile	Chase Headley, San Antonio	Bubba Bell, Lancaster	Chris Marrero, Potomac	Jay Bruce, Sarasota	Gerardo Parra, South Bend	Chris Marrero, Hagerstown
Best Power Prospect	Shelley Duncan, Scranton/Wilkes-Barre	Rick Ankiel, Memphis	Jeff Larish, Erie	Evan Longoria, Montgomery	Joe Mather, Springfield	Chris Davis, Bakersfield	Wes Hodges, Kinston	Jay Bruce, Sarasota	Juan Francisco, Dayton	Chris Carter, Kannapolis
Best Strike-Zone Judgment	Joey Votto, Louisville	Daric Barton, Sacramento	Jordan Brown, Akron	Justin Upton, Montgomery	Jonny Ash, Corpus Christi	Aaron Bates, Lancaster	Max Ramirez, Kinston	Mat Gamel, Brevard County	John Whittleman, Clinton	Chris Coghlan, Greensboro
Best Baserunner	Jacoby Ellsbury, Pawtucket	Freddy Guzman, Oklahoma	Eugenio Velez, Connecticut	Carl Loadenthal, Mississippi	Anthony Webster, Frisco	Eric Young Jr., Modesto	Josh Flores, Salem	Cameron Maybin, Lakeland	Matt Camp, Peoria	John Raynor, Greensboro
Fastest Baserunner	Jacoby Ellsbury, Pawtucket	Felix Pie, Iowa	Eugenio Velez, Connecticut	Emilio Bonifacio, Mobile	Corey Wimberly, Tulsa	Eric Young Jr., Modesto	Pedro Powell, Lynchburg	Ovandy Suero, Lakeland	Gorkys Hernandez, West Michigan	John Raynor, Greensboro
Best Pitching Prospect	Kevin Slowey, Rochester	Yovani Gallardo, Nashville	Clay Buchholz, Portland	Manny Parra, Huntsville	Franklin Morales, Tulsa	Brandon Hynick, Modesto	Brad James, Salem	Joba Chamberlain, Tampa	Clayton Kershaw, Great Lakes	Tommy Hanson, Rome
Best Fastball	Matt Garza, Rochester	Tim Lincecum, Fresno	Radhames Liz, Bowie	Kam Mickolio, West Tenn	Juan Morillo, Tulsa	Pedro Strop, Modesto	Bob McCrory, Frederick	Jake McGee, Vero Beach	Clayton Kershaw, Great Lakes	Henry Sosa, Augusta
Best Breaking Pitch	Andy Sonnanstine, Durham	Yovani Gallardo, Nashville	Clay Buchholz, Portland	Gio Gonzalez, Birmingham	Franklin Morales, Tulsa	Jams McDonald, Inland Empire	Chorye Spoone, Frederick	Will Inman, Brevard County	Jeff Manship, Beloit	Wilfrido Perez, Delmarva
Best Changeup	Edwar Ramirez, Scranton/Wilkes-Barre	Dallas Braden, Sacramento	Clay Buchholz, Portland	Gio Gonzalez, Birmingham	Danny Ray Herrera, Frisco	Wade Leblanc, Lake Elsinore	Julio Pimentel, Wilmington	Carlos Carrasco, Clearwater	Brett Anderson, South Bend	Josh Wilkie, Hagerstown
Best Control	Kevin Slowey, Rochester	Yovani Gallardo, Nashville	Eddie Bonine, Erie	Chris Mason, Montgomery	Chance Douglass, Corpus Christi	Brandon Hynick, Modesto	Rowdy Hardy, Wilmington	Daniel McCutchen, Tampa	Jeff Manship, Beloit	Kevin Pucetas, Augusta
Best Reliever	Cory Doyne, Norfolk	Ryan Speier, Colorado Springs	James Hoey, Bowie	Jon Meloan, Jacksonville	Chris Perez, Springfield	Daniel Stange, Visalia	Bob McCrory, Frederick	Josh Roenicke, Sarasota	Robert Delaney, Beloit	Jonathan Hovis, Charleston
Best Defensive Catcher	Jason Jaramillo, Ottawa	Kurt Suzuki, Sacramento	Wyatt Toregas, Akron	Clint Sammons, Mississippi	Nick Hundley, San Antonio	Neil Wilson, Modesto	Cole Armstrong, Winston-Salem	Lou Marson, Clearwater	Wellington Castillo, Peoria	Tuffy Gosewich, Lakewood
Best Defensive First Baseman	Casey Rogowski, Charlotte	Micah Hoffpauir, Iowa	Josh Whitesell, New Hampshire	Steve Sollmann, Huntsville	Mike Stodolka, Wichita	Aaron Bates, Lancaster	Kala Kaaihue, Myrtle Beach	Rhyne Hughes, Vero Beach	Brandon Buckman, Quad Cities	Lars Anderson, Greeneville
Best Defensive Second Baseman	Matt Tolbert, Rochester	Tony Abreu, Las Vegas	Mark Hollimon, Erie	Emilio Bonifacio, Mobile	German Duran, Frisco	Matt Antonelli, Lake Elsinore	Shelby Ford, Lynchburg	Kevin Russo, Tampa	Scott Sizemore, West Michigan	Chris Coghlan, Greensboro
Best Defensive Third Baseman	Mike Hessman, Toledo	Brian Barden, Tucson	Mark Kiger, Binghamton	Van Pope, Mississippi	Chase Headley, San Antonio	David Freese, Lake Elsinore	Wes Hodges, Kinston	Michael Griffin, Sarasota	Josh Lansford, Peoria	Jared Goedert, Lake County
Best Defensive Shortstop	Yunel Escobar, Richmond	Anderson Hernandez, New Orleans	Asdrubal Cabrera, Akron	Chin-Lung Hu, Jacksonville	Gregorio Petit, Midland	Brian Bocock, San Jose	Elvis Andrus, Myrtle Beach	Alcides Escobar, Brevard County	Jesus Lopez, Fort Wayne	Hector Gomez, Asheville
Best Infield Arm	Yunel Escobar, Richmond	Tony Abreu, Las Vegas	Sergio Santos, New Hampshire	Van Pope, Mississippi	Gregorio Petit, Midland	Hainley Statia, Rancho Cucamonga	Ian Desmond, Potomac	Alcides Escobar, Brevard County	Jesus Lopez, Fort Wayne	Hector Gomez, Asheville
Best Defensive Outfielder	Jacoby Ellsbury, Pawtucket	Adam Jones, Tacoma	Matt Joyce, Erie	Carl Loadenthal, Mississippi	Colby Rasmus, Springfield	Dexter Fowler, Modesto	Jordan Schafer, Myrtle Beach	Greg Golson, Clearwater	Drew Stubbs, Dayton	Desmond Jennings, Columbus
Best Outfield Arm	Ryan Raburn, Toledo	Ryan Braun, Nashville	Clete Thomas, Erie	Carlos Gonzalez, Mobile	Colby Rasmus, Springfield	Leyson Septimo, Visalia	Jordan Schafer, Myrtle Beach	Nate Southard, Palm Beach	Gerardo Parra, South Bend	Jordan Parraz, Lexington
Most Exciting Player	Ben Francisco, Buffalo		Andrew McCutchen, Altoona	Justin Upton, Mobile	Colby Rasmus, Springfield	Eric Young Jr., Modesto	Elvis Andrus, Myrtle Beach	Cameron Maybin, Lakeland	Gorkys Hernandez, West Michigan	John Raynor, Greensboro
Best Manager Prospect	Trent Jewett, Indianapolis	Tony DeFrancesco, Sacramento	Tim Bogar, Akron	John Shoemaker, Jacksonville	Pop Warner, Springfield	Dave Collins, Inland Empire	Mike Sarbaugh, Kinston	Luis Sojo, Tampa	Tom Brookens, West Michigan	Mike Guerrero, West Virginia

MINOR LEAGUES

Honoring excellence

Baseball America's annual Bob Freitas Awards are presented to franchises that show sustained excellence in the business of minor league baseball.

They were first presented in 1989, shortly after the death of Freitas, a longtime minor league operator, promoter and ambassador. Franchises must be in operation for at least five seasons before they're eligible to win.

Triple A: Albuquerque

Ken Young faced a series of difficult decisions when he and his partners moved the Calgary Cannons to Albuquerque to begin play in 2003.

Albuquerque had a rich minor league baseball history but had been without a baseball team since 2000, when the Albuquerque Dukes (a longtime Dodgers affiliate) moved to Portland.

This new franchise, however, was a Marlins' affiliate. Young and general manager Dave Traub knew they had to find a way to respect the history of baseball in Albuquerque while building their own unique brand that differentiated themselves from the Dukes. To create a new identity, the new franchise let fans vote on a team name. Fifty seven percent of voters wanted the team to be named the Isotopes, a reference to an episode of "The Simpsons" in which Homer Simpson tries to stop the local baseball team—the Springfield Isotopes—from moving to Albuquerque.

Some long-time Dukes fans were not thrilled with the Isotopes moniker, but the team realized that it would be a boon to merchandising revenue, both at the park and online. To acknowledge the historical importance of the Dukes to Albuquerque, Isotopes jerseys emulated the Dukes' red and yellow color configuration.

"We realized the merchandising was going to be key to our success," Traub said. "There was a certain percentage of the traditionalists that wanted to keep the Dukes name, but the Isotopes name caught on so quickly. The amount of merchandise sales we were able to make was very good."

Both Traub and Young are quick to note that the Isotopes were also the beneficiaries of some serendipity. Florida won the World Series and the Isotopes won their division in their first year as a Marlins' affiliate.

"The big thing is that Albuquerque has a great history of baseball," Young said. "We were fortunate to be able to bring a franchise here, and the city did a great job of building a first-rate facility for a reasonable price."

Double-A: Frisco

The Frisco RoughRiders debuted in suburban Dallas-Fort Worth in 2003, and have dominated attendance standings from the first time the gates opened.

No matter the team's record, fans just keep coming out to Dr Pepper Ballpark. And 2007 was no different, as the RoughRiders averaged better than 8,000 fans a game for the third straight year.

Aside from a beautiful facility, the RoughRiders attract fans by focusing on providing a premium family atmosphere, quality control and quirky, innovative ideas. "We can't control how the team plays," Sonju said, "but we can control our customer service. That starts with parking the car. We have friendly parking attendants, a balloon or piece of candy for the kids. And when they get to the ballpark we have a free game program. We want everyone to have something in their hand."

One attraction so popular that it has its own heading on the RoughRiders Website is the women's restrooms. The front office hired a professional interior decorator to design the women's bathrooms and the usual line is worth the wait as these bathrooms have benches, plants and other decorations.

While Frisco can't take credit for the pool pavilion—the Diamondbacks opened their ballpark with one in 1998—the RoughRiders have a distinct advantage. Their pool is about $5,000 cheaper in nightly rent and is the ideal solution to the brutal Texas summer weather.

MINOR LEAGUES

In an effort to build a relationship with a new fan base, Albuquerque ownership allowed fans to vote for the team name in 2003. The Isotopes, a reference to The Simpsons television show, has been a marketing success

Class A: Lake Elsinore

Lake Elsinore's commitment to the community turned into an unexpected marketing tool and revenue source five years when the team decided to sponsor 15 or 20 local baseball teams—a roughly $150 investment per team that included paying for uniforms, donating some equipment, offering reduced-price tickets and even providing pins that the players would swap with other teams at tournaments.

The Storm's unique logo, which features a pair of piercing eyes, was such a hit that opposing teams' parents and coaches responded with inquires about sponsoring their teams.

So the Storm added another 15 or 20 local teams the following season. And then another 15 or 20. Out-of-state teams sought Lake Elsinore's sponsorship, and soon the Storm was sponsoring entire leagues. The club now sponsors 350 teams. The team has set up its own press in-house and takes care of most of the Storm gear worn by youngsters around the country.

While their hearts were in the right place—"It turned it into a big success story, sort of by accident," Oster said—the venture has also been pretty good for the team's bottom line. Coaches and parents wanting to join the Storm Mania buy matching pullovers, caps and a variety of gear from the club.

"This was a good way to get our name out there," Oster said. "Some of the financial benefit is when coaches and family members want to buy their own stuff. That is where you see some of the money coming back."

Short-Season: Missoula

Stable and committed are two adjectives that aptly describe the Missoula Osprey franchise and its ownership, the Ellis family. But they're more than just words, they're qualities that have been put to the test since the franchise came to Montana eight years ago.

The Ellis familybought the team in 1992, when it was in Lethbridge, Alberta, and at least one member of the family has been involved in minor league baseball since 1984, when Judy Ellis, whose married to team president Mike Ellis, took a job cooking burgers for the Lodi Crushers of the California League. She is the Osprey's executive vice president. Their son Matt is the team's vice president and general manager, and his wife Shelly is the vice president of finance and merchandising.

So wherever they have been, the Ellises have become known for fostering a family atmosphere among their employees, resulting in uncommon front-office stability.

"We are a family organization," Mike Ellis said. "We treat the entire organization as family. We really believe in running it like a business, but focusing on family."

The Elisses had to wait two years for its ballpark to be built after moving to Missoula in 1999. In the meantime, the Osprey built a complete roster of entertainment for fans. One promotion they've become known for is their dubbing the sixth inning "the peanut inning." If the Osprey score a run in the sixth, the team throws bags of peanuts to the crowd.

"We focus on the whole product," Matt Ellis said. "The experience is more than a baseball game."

BY MATT EDDY

Toledo seemed primed to three-peat as International League champions, but that was before the Mud Hens' roster was ravaged by a series of big league callups to Detroit just before the playoffs.

After weathering the recall of outfielder Ryan Raburn in July, Toledo rolled to its third straight Western Division title. The losses of their two other hitting stars, however, proved insurmountable. Outfielder Timo Perez and third baseman Mike Hessman both were added to the Tigers major league roster on the eve of the IL playoffs. Hessman was especially missed, as he won league MVP honors for hitting .254/.256/.540 with 31 home runs and 101 RBIs in 117 games.

Guided by league manager of the year Dave Miley, Scranton/Wilkes-Barre cruised to its second straight Northern Division crown in its first season as an affiliate of the Yankees. Like Toledo, Scranton went down quietly in the first round of the playoffs.

Things were much more exciting in the Southern Division, where Durham edged Richmond by just two games, after a late-season Bulls surge fueled by the additions of third baseman Evan Longoria and outfielder Jason Pridie to the offense. Outfielder Justin Ruggiano also got hot in the second half and finished at .309/.386/.502 with 20 homers and 26 steals, making him the IL's only 20-20 player in 2007.

The Braves jumped off to a 15-5 start in April, but played .500 ball through the end of the season, three times going 15-15 during a month. The Bulls took the opposite course, trudging along near .500 through June before going 38-22 to close the year.

Naturally, the two teams, who had gone 8-8 in head-to-head play during the season, locked horns again in the Governors' Cup finals. Durham held a two-games-to-one advantage going into the fourth game of the finals, but rain postponed the contest, forcing the teams to meet the next day for a doubleheader, which was necessary because the Triple-A championship game, the Bricktown Showdown, was just three days away.

Richmond won both ends of the doubleheader handily to secure their first IL title since 1994 and their fifth overall. The Braves' offense, led by shortstops Yunel Escoar and

TOP 20 PROSPECTS

1. Jay Bruce, of, Louisville Bats (Reds)
2. Homer Bailey, rhp, Louisville Bats (Reds)
3. Matt Garza, rhp, Rochester Red Wings (Twins)
4. Josh Fields, 3b, Charlotte Knights (White Sox)
5. Jed Lowrie, ss, Pawtucket Red Sox
6. Jacoby Ellsbury, of, Pawtucket Red Sox
7. Brent Lillibridge, ss, Richmond Braves
8. Yunel Escobar, ss, Richmond Braves
9. Jeff Niemann, rhp, Durham Bulls (Devil Rays)
10. Joey Votto, 1b/of, Louisville Bats (Reds)
11. Adam Miller, rhp, Buffalo Bisons (Indians)
12. Garrett Olson, lhp, Norfolk Tides (Orioles)
13. Brandon Moss, of, Pawtucket Red Sox
14. Brandon Jones, of, Richmond Braves
15. Adam Lind, of, Syracuse Chiefs (Blue Jays)
16. Collin Balester, rhp, Columbus Clippers (Nationals)
17. Jason Hammel, rhp, Durham Bulls (Devil Rays)
18. Kevin Slowey, rhp, Rochester Red Wings (Twins)
19. Aaron Laffey, lhp, Buffalo Bisons (Indians)
20. Jason Pridie, of, Durham Bulls (Devil Rays)

CARL KLINE

Brent Lillibridge, who each played about half the season in Richmond, and outfielder Brandon Jones, ranked first in the league with a .271 average during the regular season. The pitching staff gave up just 554 runs, the lowest figure in the league, though they lacked the star power of the offense. Righthander Kevin Barry, Trey Hodges and Blaine Boyer paced the Braves in games started.

Columbus outfielder Brandon Watson broke a 95-year-old league record with a 43-game hitting streak that ended in June. The streak was the longest in the minors in 53 years, and tied for the eighth longest in history. Joe Wilhoit hit in 69 straight for Wichita in 1919, which remains the record.

Buffalo outfielder Ben Francisco won the IL batting title with a .318/.382/.496 season, while Rochester righthander Kevin Slowey won the ERA title by more than a run. For going 10-5, 1.89 in 134 innings, Slowey was named the league's most valuable pitcher.

Ottawa played its final season in Canada. The franchise will move to Allentown, Pa., for the 2008 season.

STANDINGS

Page	Northern Division	W	L	PCT	GB	Manager	Attendance	Average	Last Penn.
201	Scranton/W-B Yankees (Yankees)	84	59	.587	—	Dave Miley	580,908	8,802	None
181	Rochester Red Wings (Twins)	77	67	.535	7½	Stan Cliburn	473,288	7,064	1997
106	Buffalo Bisons (Indians)	75	67	.528	8½	Torey Lovullo	572,635	8,947	2004
72	Pawtucket Red Sox (Red Sox)	67	75	.472	16½	Ron Johnson	611,379	8,861	1984
296	Syracuse Chiefs (Blue Jays)	64	80	.444	20½	Doug Davis	380,152	5,760	1976
222	Ottawa Lynx (Phillies)	55	88	.385	29	John Russell	126,894	1,923	1995

Page	Southern Division	W	L	PCT	GB	Manager	Attendance	Average	Last Penn.
279	Durham Bulls (Devil Rays)	80	63	.559	—	Charlie Montoyo	520,952	7,235	2003
54	Richmond Braves (Braves)	77	64	.546	2	Dave Brundage	342,090	5,031	2007
63	Norfolk Tides (Orioles)	69	74	.483	11	Gary Allenson	464,034	6,725	1985
89	Charlotte Knights (White Sox)	63	80	.441	17	Marc Bombard	311,119	4,382	1999

Page	Western Division	W	L	PCT	GB	Manager	Attendance	Average	Last Penn.
122	Toledo Mud Hens (Tigers)	82	61	.573	—	Mike Rojas	590,159	8,431	2006
97	Louisville Bats (Reds)	74	70	.514	8½	Rick Sweet	653,915	9,210	2001
232	Indianapolis Indians (Pirates)	70	73	.490	12	Trent Jewett	586,785	8,383	2000
305	Columbus Clippers (Nationals)	64	80	.444	18½	John Stearns	507,155	7,245	1996

PLAYOFFS—Semifinals: Richmond defeated Scranton/Wilkes-Barre 3-1 and Durham defeated Toledo 3-0 in best-of-five series.
Finals: Richmond defeated Durham 3-2 in best-of-five series.

CLUB BATTING

	AVG	G	AB	R	H	2B	3B	HR	RBI	BB	SO	SB	CS	OBP	SLG
Richmond	.271	141	4659	650	1262	249	32	87	606	443	830	144	65	.340	.394
Ottawa	.267	143	4821	553	1287	231	27	59	517	412	760	57	41	.332	.363
Buffalo	.266	142	4686	664	1248	244	36	129	622	500	1002	112	60	.341	.416
Louisville	.264	144	4857	656	1282	247	34	129	627	511	1117	102	33	.337	.408
Scranton/WB	.263	143	4781	679	1256	243	41	112	628	489	862	136	49	.336	.401
Columbus	.262	144	4738	575	1239	250	33	97	541	478	999	118	54	.329	.390
Durham	.262	143	4818	638	1260	263	33	146	600	434	1222	110	45	.328	.421
Indianapolis	.262	144	4767	629	1251	240	36	107	578	434	965	163	71	.334	.395
Rochester	.262	144	4684	593	1229	246	32	82	551	391	886	123	58	.324	.381
Norfolk	.261	144	4771	568	1247	224	32	92	533	418	880	112	52	.322	.380
Syracuse	.260	144	4805	653	1250	232	21	140	613	500	1051	60	24	.333	.405
Toledo	.258	143	4786	671	1233	257	38	126	633	554	1152	115	68	.339	.406
Charlotte	.254	143	4835	608	1229	217	15	131	559	475	1015	120	53	.324	.387

CLUB PITCHING

	ERA	G	CG	SHO	SV	IP	H	R	ER	HR	BB	SO	AVG
Durham	3.59	143	5	13	41	1256	1146	563	501	117	458	1103	.243
Toledo	3.62	143	6	7	38	1282	1249	574	516	106	422	908	.26
Rochester	3.64	144	15	12	45	1237	1207	565	500	103	331	911	.258
Richmond	3.65	141	2	13	32	1229	1195	554	498	95	504	980	.26
Scranton/WB	3.67	143	0	13	49	1256	1205	574	508	98	476	1101	.253
Louisville	3.75	144	2	8	40	1275	1272	591	528	95	430	960	.262
Norfolk	3.83	144	3	9	50	1262	1230	603	534	100	425	1024	.256
Pawtucket	4.05	142	4	3	35	1248	1230	659	561	121	477	1040	.257
Indianapolis	4.10	144	2	8	34	1256	1291	641	570	108	530	940	.27
Charlotte	4.12	143	6	3	36	1259	1233	647	577	127	560	989	.258
Buffalo	4.18	142	8	10	35	1234	1260	662	573	113	464	954	.265
Columbus	4.21	144	0	15	39	1244	1226	649	579	121	540	1004	.259
Syracuse	4.56	144	5	4	27	1244	1348	709	627	116	418	942	.275
Ottawa	4.78	143	6	3	34	1240	1395	737	657	125	500	903	.288

CLUB FIELDING

	PCT	PO	A	E	DP		PCT	PO	A	E	DP
Scranton/WB	.983	3768	1348	90	119	Ottawa	.978	3719	1422	117	131
Indianapolis	.982	3769	1530	98	149	Rochester	.978	3712	1499	119	145
Toledo	.982	3846	1634	100	178	Columbus	.977	3733	1357	121	127
Richmond	.981	3687	1355	100	138	Pawtucket	.976	3744	1452	126	112
Norfolk	.980	3785	1490	108	115	Buffalo	.975	3703	1411	133	134
Charlotte	.979	3777	1465	111	137	Louisville	.975	3826	1584	137	157
Durham	.978	3768	1476	118	146	Syracuse	.971	3733	1475	156	117

INDIVIDUAL BATTING LEADERS (Minimum 446 Plate Appearances)

	AVG	G	AB	R	H	2B	3B	HR	RBI	BB	SO	SB
Francisco, Ben, Buffalo	.318	95	377	60	120	27	2	12	51	36	66	22
Prado, Martin, Richmond	.316	103	395	61	125	23	3	4	41	34	41	5
Watson, Brandon, Columbus	.313	103	399	47	125	11	6	2	29	21	51	17
Morales, Jose, Rochester	.311	108	376	42	117	25	1	2	37	30	44	1
Ruggiano, Justin, Durham	.309	127	482	78	149	29	2	20	73	53	151	26
Perez, Timo, Toledo	.309	122	489	76	151	39	1	13	69	35	47	13
Thurston, Joe, Ottawa	.300	129	496	70	149	29	9	5	59	44	55	16
House, J.R., Norfolk	.298	110	419	52	125	32	2	11	66	43	59	1
Ellsbury, Jacoby, Pawtucket	.298	87	363	66	108	14	5	2	28	32	47	33
McDonald, Darnell, Columbus-Rochester	.297	134	491	71	146	29	6	7	73	50	99	33

INDIVIDUAL PITCHING LEADERS (Minimum 115 Innings)

	W	L	ERA	G	GS	CG	SV	IP	H	R	ER	BB	SO
Slowey, Kevin, Rochester	10	5	1.89	20	20	5	0	134	110	31	28	18	107
Olson, Garrett, Norfolk	9	7	3.16	22	22	1	0	128	95	49	45	39	120
Duensing, Brian, Rochester	11	5	3.24	19	19	3	0	117	115	54	42	30	86
Howell, J.P., Durham	7	8	3.38	21	21	1	0	128	110	63	48	34	145
Chiavacci, Ron, Toledo	12	6	3.39	26	23	0	0	151	148	64	57	43	126
Vasquez, Virgil, Toledo	12	5	3.48	25	25	2	0	155	139	64	60	33	127
Dumatrait, Phil, Louisville	10	6	3.53	22	22	0	0	125	114	57	49	49	76
Hansack, Devern, Pawtucket	10	7	3.61	25	23	0	0	140	126	62	56	40	131
Bazardo, Yorman, Toledo	10	6	3.75	23	21	2	0	137	134	66	57	43	69
Tejera, Michael, Indianapolis	8	5	3.90	27	19	1	0	127	115	55	55	43	71

ALL-STAR TEAM

C: Jose Morales, Rochester. **1B:** Joey Votto, Louisville. **2B:** Martin Prado, Richmond. **3B:** Mike Hessman, Toledo. **SS:** Brian Bixler, Indianapolis. **OF:** Ben Francisco, Buffalo; Timo Perez, Toledo; Justin Ruggiano, Durham. **DH:** Shelley Duncan, Scranton/Wilkes-Barre. **Utility:** Aaron Herr, Louisville. **SP:** Kevin Slowey, Rochester. **RP:** Cory Doyne, Norfolk. **Most Valuable Player:** Mike Hessman, Toledo. **Most Valuable Pitcher:** Kevin Slowey, Rochester. **Rookie of the Year:** Joey Votto, Louisville. **Manager of the Year:** Dave Miley, Scranton/Wilkes-Barre.

DEPARTMENT LEADERS

BATTING

OBP	Hannahan, Jack, Toledo	.422
SLG	Duncan, Shelley, Scranton/W-B	.577
R	Blanco, Gregor, Richmond	81
H	Cervenak, Mike, Norfolk	157
TB	Ruggiano, Justin, Durham	242
XBH	Moss, Brandon, Pawtucket	59
2B	Moss, Brandon, Pawtucket	41
3B	Bixler, Brian, Indianapolis	10
	Gonzalez, Alberto, Scranton/W-B	10
HR	Hessman, Mike, Toledo	31
RBI	Hessman, Mike, Toledo	101
SAC	Span, Denard, Rochester	21
SF	Four tied at	9
BB	Shelton, Chris, Toledo	83
IBB	Burnham, Gary, Ottawa	9
HBP	Timmons, Wes, Richmond	19
SO	Hessman, Mike, Toledo	153
SB	Castro, Bernie, Columbus	34
CS	Blanco, Gregor, Richmond	18
GIDP	Tiffee, Terry, Norfolk	23
AB/SO	Rushford, Jim, Ottawa	13.32

PITCHING

G	Korecky, Bobby, Rochester	66
GS	Talbot, Mitch, Durham	29
CG	Slowey, Kevin, Rochester	5
SHO	Blackburn, Nick, Rochester	2
SHO	Vasquez, Virgil, Toledo	2
GF	Korecky, Bobby, Rochester	59
SV	Korecky, Bobby, Rochester	35
W	Phillips, Heath, Charlotte	13
W	Talbot, Mitch, Durham	13
L	Haeger, Charlie, Charlotte	16
IP	Phillips, Heath, Charlotte	173.2
H	Phillips, Heath, Charlotte	198
R	Phillips, Heath, Charlotte	90
R	Pauley, David, Pawtucket	90
ER	Banks, Josh, Syracuse	87
HB	Bean, Colter, Scranton/W-B	14
BB	Broadway, Lance, Charlotte	78
SO	Howell, J.P., Durham	145
SO/9-S	Howell, J.P., Durham	10.2
SO/9-R	Booker, Chris, Columbus	12.88
WP	Broadway, Lance, Charlotte	12
WP	Larrison, Preston, Toledo	12
BK	Phillips, Heath, Charlotte	4
AVG	Olson, Garrett, Norfolk	.208

FIELDING

C	PCT	Rose, Mike, Buffalo	.993
	PO	Sardinha, Dane, Toledo	732
	A	Jaramillo, Jason, Ottawa	75
	E	Jaramillo, Jason, Ottawa	18
	DP	Rose, Mike, Buffalo	10
	PB	Smith, Ryan, Charlotte	12
	CS%	Harper, Brandon, Columbus	.41
1B	PCT	Rogowski, Casey, Charlotte	.995
	PO	Shelton, Chris, Toledo	1202
	A	Barker, Kevin, Syracuse	95
	E	Barker, Kevin, Syracuse	15
	DP	Shelton, Chris, Toledo	144
2B	PCT	Thurston, Joe, Ottawa	.985
	PO	Thurston, Joe, Ottawa	229
	A	Johnson, Elliot, Durham	335
	E	Johnson, Elliot, Durham	22
	DP	Johnson, Elliot, Durham	95
3B	PCT	Hessman, Mike, Toledo	.975
	PO	King, Brennan, Ottawa	88
	A	Hessman, Mike, Toledo	264
	E	Hattig, John, Syracuse	19
	DP	Hessman, Mike, Toledo	34
SS	PCT	Gonzalez, Alberto, Scranton/W-B	.976
	PO	Olmedo, Ray, Syracuse	144
	A	Bixler, Brian, Indianapolis	327
	E	Bixler, Brian, Indianapolis	16
		Luna, Hector, Syracuse	16
		Olmedo, Ray, Syracuse	16
	DP	Bixler, Brian, Indianapolis	80
OF	PCT	Sweeney, Ryan, Charlotte	1.000
		Reese, Kevin, Scranton/W-B	1.000
	PO	Span, Denard, Rochester	359
	A	Sweeney, Ryan, Charlotte	13
	E	Roberson, Chris, Ottawa	12
	DP	Ruggiano, Justin, Durham	5
		Sardinha, Bronson, Scranton/W-B	5

MINOR LEAGUES

BY MATT EDDY

N othing could prevent the Sacramento River Cats from winning their third Pacific Coast League title since moving to the city in 2000. Not playing three consecutive elimination games in the first round of the playoffs, or a roster poked full of holes by major league defections.

The River Cats took it a step further by defeating the International League's Richmond Braves 7-1 for Triple-A supremacy in the Bricktown Showdown, thus extending the PCL's winning streak in the event. Tucson defeated Toledo in the inaugural Triple-A championship game in 2006.

Led by outfielder Jorge Piedra, shortstop J.J. Furmaniak and 21-year-old first baseman Daric Barton, Sacramento led the league only in batter walks and strikeouts, on its way to a 84-60 record and seven-game cushion over Fresno in the Pacific Conference's Southern Division. Lefties Dan Meyer and Dallas Braden and righthander Colby Lewis paced the pitching staff.

Down two-games-to-none and facing elimination in the first round of the playoffs, Sacramento rattled off three consecutive wins against Salt Lake to advance to the second round. Barton clubbed a deciding three-run homer in game five, and his four longballs (in five games) led all PCL postseason batters. The River Cats had a much easier time with New Orleans in the finals, sweeping them in three games, though they had to make due without Barton, who had been called to the big leagues immediately after the first round.

During the course of the 2007 season, Sacramento also lost its starting catcher (Kurt Suzuki), second baseman (Donnie Murphy), shortstop (Furmaniak) and one of its best pitchers (Braden) for large blocks of the season.

New Orleans advanced to finals after dispatching with Nashville, owners of the league's best regular-season record. The Sounds, led by PCL manager of the year Frank Kremblas, held nearly a half-run advantage in team ERA, 3.57 to 4.00, despite losing righthanders Yovani Gallardo and Chris Oxspring, at midseason (Gallardo to the major leagues, Oxspring to a contract in Korea). Nashville also boasted the league's pitcher of the year, righthander R.A.

TOP 20 PROSPECTS

1. **Yovani Gallardo, rhp, Nashville Sounds (Brewers)**
2. Adam Jones, of, Tacoma Rainiers (Mariners)
3. Billy Butler, of/1b, Omaha Royals
4. Andy LaRoche, 3b, Las Vegas 51s (Dodgers)
5. Ian Stewart, 3b, Colorado Springs Sky Sox (Rockies)
6. Felix Pie, of, Iowa Cubs
7. Carlos Gomez, of, New Orleans Zephyrs (Mets)
8. James Loney, 1b/of, Las Vegas 51s (Dodgers)
9. Brandon Wood, 3b/ss, Salt Lake Bees (Angels)
10. Luke Hochevar, rhp, Omaha Royals
11. Jeff Clement, c, Tacoma Rainiers (Mariners
12. Mike Pelfrey, rhp, New Orleans Zephyrs (Mets)
13. Edinson Volquez, rhp, Oklahoma RedHawks (Rangers)
14. Wladimir Balentien, of, Tacoma Rainiers (Mariners)
15. Troy Patton, lhp, Round Rock Express (Astros)
16. Eric Hurley, rhp, Oklahoma RedHawks (Rangers)
17. Billy Buckner, rhp, Omaha Royals
18. Chin-Lung Hu, ss, Las Vegas 51s (Dodgers)
19. Daric Barton, 1b, Sacramento River Cats (Athletics)
20. Geovany Soto, c/1b, Iowa Cubs

Dickey, who went 13-6, 3.72 in 169 innings.

Another Nashville pitcher, lefthander Manny Parra, tossed the season's only perfect game in his second Triple-A start. He struck out 11 Round Rock batters in the June 25 start and threw 77 of his 107 pitches for strikes. It was the eighth perfect game in PCL history, but only the third in a nine-inning game.

Iowa's Geovany Soto became the first catcher since Sandy Alomar Jr. in 1989 to win the league's MVP award. Soto hit .353/.424/.652 with 26 home runs and 109 RBIs in just 110 games. He paced all full-season minor leaguers in slugging, but missed out on the batting title when he and eventual-winner Brian Myrow, of Portland, were called to the majors with three games remaining on the PCL schedule.

STANDINGS

AMERICAN CONFERENCE

Page	Northern Division	W	L	PCT	GB	Manager	Attendance	Average	Last Penn.
174	Nashville Sounds (Brewers)	89	55	.618	—	Frank Kremblas	411,959	5,885	2005
80	Iowa Cubs (Cubs)	79	65	.549	10	Buddy Bailey	576,310	8,233	None
148	Omaha Royals (Royals)	73	71	.507	16	Mike Jirschele	326,627	4,803	None
242	Memphis Redbirds (Cardinals)	56	88	.389	33	Chris Maloney	633,129	8,793	2000
Page	Southern Division	W	L	PCT	GB	Manager	Attendance	Average	Last Penn.
190	New Orleans Zephyrs (Mets)	75	69	.521	—	Ken Oberkfell	368,210	5,260	2001
131	Albuquerque Isotopes (Marlins)	72	70	.507	2	Dean Treanor	563,686	8,053	1994
287	Oklahoma RedHawks (Rangers)	71	72	.497	3½	Bob Jones	529,690	7,567	1965
140	Round Rock Express (Astros)	61	81	.430	13	Jackie Moore	662,595	9,466	None

PACIFIC CONFERENCE

Page	Northern Division	W	L	PCT	GB	Manager	Attendance	Average	Last Penn.
157	Salt Lake Bees (Angels)	74	69	.517	—	Brian Harper	466,123	6,565	1979
114	Colorado Springs Sky Sox (Rockies)	69	75	.479	5½	Tom Runnells	274,408	4,158	1995
270	Tacoma Rainiers (Mariners)	68	76	.472	6½	Darren Brown	345,538	4,867	2001
253	Portland Beavers (Padres)	58	86	.403	16½	Rick Renteria	388,963	5,478	1983
Page	Southern Division	W	L	PCT	GB	Manager	Attendance	Average	Last Penn.
211	Sacramento River Cats (Athletics)	84	60	.583	—	Tony DeFrancesco	710,235	10,003	2007
262	Fresno Grizzlies (Giants)	77	67	.535	7	Dan Rohn	520,093	7,430	None
46	Tucson Sidewinders (Diamondbacks)	75	67	.528	8	Bill Plummer	270,853	3,983	2006
165	Las Vegas 51s (Dodgers)	67	77	.465	17	Lorenzo Bundy	371,676	5,162	1988

PLAYOFFS—Semifinals: Sacramento defeated Salt Lake 3-2 and New Orleans defeated Nashville 3-1 in best-of-five series. **Finals:** Sacramento defeated New Orleans 3-0 in best-of-five series.

CLUB BATTING

	AVG	G	AB	R	H	2B	3B	HR	RBI	BB	SO	SB	CS	OBP	SLG
Tucson	.297	142	4897	780	1453	311	49	92	714	517	729	76	42	.367	.437
Las Vegas	.296	144	5076	817	1502	319	36	147	753	450	952	61	22	.355	.460
Colorado Springs	.292	144	4943	748	1444	320	38	131	696	416	1026	98	46	.353	.452
Salt Lake	.289	143	4928	767	1425	320	33	128	717	434	1009	125	72	.350	.445
Albuquerque	.287	142	4799	784	1377	256	60	180	741	466	1062	139	53	.353	.478
Iowa	.287	144	4983	822	1430	279	37	172	778	464	969	91	37	.350	.461
Fresno	.286	144	5049	747	1442	307	39	140	690	460	894	138	47	.350	.445
Tacoma	.281	144	5063	747	1424	321	33	148	694	441	1019	83	47	.343	.445
Omaha	.280	144	4906	686	1372	256	25	151	641	428	758	80	34	.340	.434
Oklahoma	.278	143	4899	738	1361	282	29	139	701	524	1066	112	35	.350	.432
Sacramento	.277	144	4988	765	1382	293	31	139	716	613	1079	73	45	.361	.432
New Orleans	.269	144	4899	703	1320	245	21	139	657	499	987	86	35	.339	.413
Nashville	.268	144	4764	718	1277	257	34	159	661	460	903	121	67	.335	.436
Round Rock	.265	142	4836	659	1280	268	33	134	621	427	1046	147	49	.328	.417
Memphis	.258	144	4841	630	1248	228	19	156	587	443	960	77	32	.325	.409
Portland	.254	144	4808	662	1221	271	26	115	617	601	1019	65	38	.340	.393

CLUB PITCHING

	ERA	G	CG	SHO	SV	IP	H	R	ER	HR	BB	SO	AVG
Nashville	3.57	144	7	11	41	1270	1171	547	503	118	452	1148	.247
Fresno	4.01	144	4	9	36	1290	1294	658	574	122	440	1020	.263
Sacramento	4.19	144	3	9	44	1299	1286	670	605	134	489	1084	.259
New Orleans	4.31	144	1	7	32	1270	1338	671	608	152	380	953	.272
Omaha	4.42	144	1	9	33	1277	1297	694	624	157	454	904	.266
Round Rock	4.64	142	3	10	30	1253	1326	736	646	139	519	955	.276
Iowa	4.66	144	2	7	37	1274	1436	742	660	146	463	995	.288
Tucson	4.73	142	2	5	42	1250	1423	765	657	123	486	979	.287
Oklahoma	4.78	143	4	5	22	1244	1264	724	660	134	505	981	.264
Memphis	4.82	144	2	5	38	1255	1370	740	671	156	469	965	.282
Tacoma	4.92	144	4	7	40	1285	1487	778	701	132	495	900	.292
Salt Lake	5.03	143	2	2	36	1259	1495	783	699	167	364	891	.298
Portland	5.08	144	4	5	34	1251	1470	782	707	150	477	994	.293
Colorado Springs	5.12	144	4	3	43	1246	1418	798	709	124	552	807	.292
Albuquerque	5.34	142	1	3	40	1233	1409	832	728	163	516	835	.288
Las Vegas	5.40	144	2	3	29	1265	1474	853	758	153	582	1067	.295

CLUB FIELDING

	PCT	PO	A	E	DP		PCT	PO	A	E	DP
Nashville	.984	3810	1457	86	133	Fresno	.978	3871	1541	122	168
Oklahoma	.981	3731	1484	103	131	New Orleans	.978	3811	1513	122	137
Tacoma	.981	3854	1494	106	145	Iowa	.977	3821	1530	124	159
Colorado Springs	.980	3739	1743	113	203	Memphis	.977	3764	1510	124	135
Las Vegas	.980	3796	1478	106	148	Tucson	.975	3750	1509	137	147
Omaha	.980	3831	1529	108	164	Portland	.974	3754	1465	142	136
Round Rock	.979	3759	1437	111	141	Albuquerque	.973	3698	1489	144	143
Sacramento	.979	3897	1462	117	148	Salt Lake	.973	3777	1528	148	172

INDIVIDUAL BATTING LEADERS (Minimum 446 Plate Appearances)

	AVG	G	AB	R	H	2B	3B	HR	RBI	BB	SO	SB
Myrow, Brian, Portland	.354	107	347	61	123	31	4	13	73	56	74	1
Soto, Geovany, Iowa	.353	110	385	75	136	31	3	26	109	53	94	0
Valdez, Wilson, Las Vegas	.343	90	361	81	124	19	1	4	29	43	34	14
Young, Delwyn, Las Vegas	.337	121	490	107	165	54	5	17	97	38	105	4
Schierholtz, Nate, Fresno	.333	109	411	67	137	31	7	16	68	17	58	10
Carter, Chris, Tucson	.324	126	503	74	163	39	4	18	84	50	68	2
Botts, Jason, Oklahoma	.320	102	369	69	118	36	4	13	78	81	102	0
Quintanilla, Omar, Colorado Springs	.319	98	348	54	111	30	4	3	43	31	65	3
Smith, Seth, Colorado Springs	.317	129	451	68	143	32	6	17	82	39	73	7
Evans, Terry, Salt Lake	.316	120	475	70	150	40	4	15	75	26	119	24

INDIVIDUAL PITCHING LEADERS (Minimum 115 Innings)

	W	L	ERA	G	GS	CG	SV	IP	H	R	ER	BB	SO
Campillo, Jorge, Tacoma	9	6	3.07	24	22	0	0	149	151	55	51	39	99
Meyer, Dan, Sacramento	8	2	3.28	21	21	0	0	115	103	44	42	51	105
Dickey, R.A., Nashville	13	6	3.72	31	22	3	0	169	159	80	70	60	119
Cassel, Jack, Portland	7	14	3.91	27	24	3	0	157	203	94	68	42	117
Lehr, Justin, Tacoma	7	1	3.99	27	17	0	1	120	132	62	53	41	61
Kinney, Matt, Fresno	12	10	4.02	27	26	1	0	157	164	84	70	36	141
Wright, Matt, Omaha	10	5	4.06	28	21	0	0	137	142	68	62	40	98
Pinango, Miguel, Las Vegas	10	7	4.12	23	23	0	0	127	143	71	58	38	92
Hendrickson, Ben, Omaha	11	5	4.12	27	18	1	0	135	136	70	62	54	66
Gutierrez, Juan, Round Rock	5	10	4.15	26	25	0	0	156	154	84	72	63	108

DEPARTMENT LEADERS

BATTING

OBP	Myrow, Brian, Portland	.44
SLG	Soto, Geovany, Iowa	.652
R	Young, Delwyn, Las Vegas	107
H	Reed, Jeremy, Tacoma	169
TB	Seabol, Scott, Albuquerque	290
XBH	Young, Delwyn, Las Vegas	76
2B	Young, Delwyn, Las Vegas	54
3B	Andino, Robert, Albuquerque	13
HR	Pascucci, Valentino, Albuquerque	34
RBI	Soto, Geovany, Iowa	109
SAC	Figueroa, Luis R., Fresno	13
SF	Seabol, Scott, Albuquerque	10
BB	Tracy, Andy, New Orleans	89
IBB	Tracy, Andy, New Orleans	8
HBP	Barmes, Clint, Colorado Springs	22
SO	Conrad, Brooks, Round Rock	144
SB	Guzman, Freddy, Oklahoma	56
CS	Crabbe, Callix, Nashville	14
CS	Guzman, Freddy, Oklahoma	14
GIDP	Aviles, Mike, Omaha	24
AB/SO	Figueroa, Luis R., Fresno	13.03

PITCHING

G	Hoorelbeke, Casey, Las Vegas	63
GS	Bonilla, Henry, Salt Lake	29
CG	Dickey, R.A., Nashville	3
	Cassel, Jack, Portland	3
SHO	Rohrbaugh, Robert, Tacoma	2
GF	Speier, Ryan, Colorado Springs	47
SV	Speier, Ryan, Colorado Springs	33
W	Dickey, R.A., Nashville	13
L	Three players tied at	14
IP	Olenberger, Kasey, Salt Lake	180
H	Olenberger, Kasey, Salt Lake	205
R	Carrasco, D.J., Tucson	121
ER	Bonilla, Henry, Salt Lake	106
HB	Kaiser, Marc, Colorado Springs	14
BB	Kaiser, Marc, Colorado Springs	79
SO	Kinney, Matt, Fresno	141
SO/9-S	Oxspring, Chris, Nashville	9.94
SO/9-R	Hull, Eric, Las Vegas	11.1
WP	Three players tied at	14
BK	10 players tied at	2
AVG	Meyer, Dan, Sacramento	.243

FIELDING

C	PCT	Rivera, Mike, Nashville	.997
	PO	Carlin, Luke, Portland	600
	A	Knoedler, Justin, Fresno	57
	E	Christianson, Ryan, Memphis	11
	DP	DiFelice, Mike, New Orleans	12
	PB	Clement, Jeff, Tacoma	13
	CS%	Knoedler, Justin, Fresno	.4
1B	PCT	Tracy, Andy, New Orleans	.995
	PO	Koshansky, Joe, Colorado Springs	1267
	A	Koshansky, Joe, Colorado Springs	86
	E	Koshansky, Joe, Colorado Springs	17
	DP	Koshansky, Joe, Colorado Springs	166
2B	PCT	Nix, Jayson, Colorado Springs	.986
	PO	Conrad, Brooks, Round Rock	239
	A	Nix, Jayson, Colorado Springs	404
	E	Conrad, Brooks, Round Rock	15
	DP	Nix, Jayson, Colorado Springs	124
3B	PCT	Seabol, Scott, Albuquerque	.957
	PO	Seabol, Scott, Albuquerque	105
	A	Tatis, Fernando, New Orleans	256
	E	Stewart, Ian, Colorado Springs	26
	DP	Seabol, Scott, Albuquerque	31
SS	PCT	Hernandez, Anderson, New Orleans	.975
	PO	Andino, Robert, Albuquerque	226
	A	Andino, Robert, Albuquerque	402
	E	Andino, Robert, Albuquerque	33
	DP	Barmes, Clint, Colorado Springs	90
OF	PCT	Coats, Buck, Iowa	.997
	PO	Maier, Mitch, Omaha	330
	A	Ruan, Wilkin, Las Vegas	20
	E	Abercrombie, Reggie, Albuquerque	9
		Anderson, Josh, Round Rock	9
		Gorneault, Nick, Salt Lake	9
	DP	Smith, Seth, Colorado Springs	7

MINOR LEAGUES

ALL-STAR TEAM

C: Geovany Soto, Iowa. **1B:** Joe Koshansky, Colorado Springs. **2B:** Eric Patterson, Iowa. **3B:** Scott Seabol, Albuquerque. **SS:** Robert Andino, Albuquerque. **OF:** Rick Ankiel, Memphis; Adam Jones, Tacoma; Delwyn Young, Las Vegas. **DH:** Valentino Pascucci, Albuquerque. **RHP:** R.A. Dickey, Nashville. **LHP:** Adam Pettyjohn, Nashville. **RP:** Ryan Speier, Colorado Springs. **Most Valuable Player:** Geovany Soto, Iowa. **Pitcher of the Year:** R.A. Dickey, Oklahoma. **Rookie of the Year:** Wladimir Balentien, Tacoma. **Manager of the Year:** Frank Kremblas, Nashville.

EASTERN LEAGUE DOUBLE-A

BY BEN BADLER

The 2007 season was one few in Trenton will ever forget. The Thunder, once known mostly for having the minor leagues' ugliest logo, were known this year for having one of the best (and most talented) teams in the minors.

The Thunder not only finished with the best overall record in the Eastern League—with a team loaded with prospects, not veterans—but also finished the job with a playoff run that carried the franchise to its first EL title in 14 seasons in the league. To top it all off, the league unveiled a spiffy new logo after the season as part of a celebration of the franchise's 15th anniversary in New Jersey.

Trenton got off to a blistering 17-2 start thanks to a standout pitching staff. Trenton's arms carried the team throughout the season, posting a 3.18 team ERA that ranked second behind only low Class A Augusta (3.02) among full-season minor league teams.

Trenton's pitching made up for its mediocre offense, which finished eighth out of 12 teams in the EL with a .331 team on-base percentage and last with a .363 slugging average. The Thunder's 598 runs were the second-lowest total in the league.

The Thunder were the only team in the EL's Northern Division to finish with a winning record. In the Southern Division, Erie—which allowed the second-fewest runs in the league behind Trenton—edged out Akron by one and a half games for divisional supremacy. Erie manager Matt Walbeck also earned recognition as Baseball America's Minor League Manager of the Year, in addition to winning the league's manager of the year honor.

In the postseason, however, Akron got revenge against Erie with a semifinal series victory. Trenton got past Portland in the semifinals, then went on to beat Akron for the EL championship.

The playoff title was all the more impressive considering that righthanders Joba Chamberlain and Ian Kennedy already had graduated to the Yankees, while the Indians sent top arms Adam Miller and Jeremy Sowers down from Triple-A to bolster the Akron pitching staff for the EL postseason.

When it came to pro potential, though, no pitcher in the league could match the total package of Portland righthander Clay Buchholz, the league's No. 1 prospect.

TOP 20 PROSPECTS

1. Clay Buchholz, rhp, Portland Sea Dogs (Boston)
2. **Andrew McCutchen, of, Altoona Curve (Pirates)**
3. Fernando Martinez, of, Binghamton (Mets)
4. Asdrubal Cabrera, ss, Akron Aeros (Indians)
5. Ian Kennedy, rhp, Trenton Thunder (Yankees)
6. Jair Jurrjens, rhp, Erie SeaWolves (Tigers)
7. Alan Horne, rhp, Trenton Thunder (Yankees)
8. Jed Lowrie, ss, Portland Sea Dogs (Red Sox)
9. Neil Walker, 3b, Altoona Curve (Pirates)
10. Collin Balester, rhp, Harrisburg Senators (Nationals)
11. Jordan Brown, 1b/of, Akron Aeros (Indians)
12. Radhames Liz, rhp, Bowie Baysox (Orioles)
13. Justin Masterson, rhp, Portland Sea Dogs (Red Sox)
14. Kyle Kendrick, rhp, Reading Phillies
15. Chuck Lofgren, lhp, Akron Aeros (Indians)
16. Jeff Larish, 1b, Erie SeaWolves (Tigers)
17. Brian Barton, of, Akron Aeros (Indians)
18. Brian Duensing, lhp, New Britain Rock Cats (Twins)
19. Mike Costanzo, 3b, Reading Phillies
20. Nolan Reimold, of, Bowie Baysox (Orioles)

RODGER WOOD

He showed what he could do with a no-hitter against the Orioles in his second big league start. The Sea Dogs, who finished in the middle of the pack in runs allowed, led the league with 718 runs scored.

Kennedy and EL pitcher of the year Alan Horne represented Trenton as two of the top 10 prospects in the EL, and Chamberlain would have joined them had he not fallen just short of qualifying. Horne led the league with a 3.11 ERA. His 165 strikeouts also led the EL. Erie righthander Jair Jurrjens finished second in ERA at 3.20 before helping the Tigers down the stretch in a late-season callup.

Akron first baseman Jordan Brown led the league in hitting at .333, while his .421 on-base percentage ranked third in the league, and he was selected as the league MVP at season's end.

Binghamton third baseman Mark Kiger led the EL in OBP at .432. Erie first baseman Jeffrey Larish hit 28 home runs and drove in 101 runs, both of which were tops in the league.

STANDINGS

Page	Northern Division	W	L	PCT	GB	Manager(s)	Attendance	Average	Last Penn.
202	Trenton Thunder (Yankees)	83	59	.585	—	Tony Franklin	412,312	5,890	2007
73	Portland Sea Dogs (Red Sox)	71	72	.497	12½	Arnie Beyeler	421,368	6,483	2006
297	New Hampshire Fisher Cats (Blue Jays)	70	73	.490	13½	Bill Masse	371,710	5,310	2004
182	New Britain Rock Cats (Twins)	69	72	.489	13½	Riccardo Ingram	341,816	5,341	2001
263	Connecticut Defenders (Giants)	63	78	.447	19½	D. Machemer/S. Turner	195,235	3,004	2002
191	Binghamton Mets (Mets)	61	81	.430	22	Mako Oliveras	230,078	3,486	1994

Page	Southern Division	W	L	PCT	GB	Manager	Attendance	Average	Last Penn.
123	Erie SeaWolves (Tigers)	81	59	.579	—	Matt Walbeck	220,401	3,613	None
106	Akron Aeros (Indians)	80	61	.567	1½	Tim Bogar	355,376	5,553	2005
233	Altoona Curve (Pirates)	73	68	.518	8½	Tim Leiper	356,339	5,318	None
64	Bowie Baysox (Orioles)	72	68	.514	9	Bien Figueroa	287,098	4,222	None
223	Reading Phillies (Phillies)	70	71	.496	11½	P.J. Forbes	466,385	6,663	2001
306	Harrisburg Senators (Nationals)	55	86	.390	26½	Scott Little	229,241	3,527	1999

PLAYOFFS—Semifinals: Akron defeated Erie 3-1 and Trenton defeated Portland 3-1 in best-of-five series. **Finals:** Trenton defeated Akron 3-1 in best-of-five series. **NOTE:** Teams' individual batting and pitching statistics can be found on page indicated in lefthand column.

CLUB BATTING

	AVG	G	AB	R	H	2B	3B	HR	RBI	BB	SO	SB	CS	OBP	SLG
Akron	.277	141	4699	684	1300	247	32	96	625	498	798	147	62	.352	.404
New Britain	.277	141	4690	676	1300	281	33	106	626	408	871	63	36	.341	.419
Reading	.273	141	4745	686	1295	252	23	124	651	468	865	85	43	.344	.414
Altoona	.265	141	4582	636	1214	243	26	100	598	508	857	141	38	.341	.395
Bowie	.265	140	4705	653	1249	250	29	119	599	395	954	78	56	.324	.407
New Hampshire	.264	143	4877	645	1287	309	18	144	613	465	995	53	29	.333	.423
Portland	.263	143	4695	718	1235	283	41	94	657	590	945	75	32	.351	.401
Erie	.261	140	4538	699	1184	237	43	133	653	489	1063	103	51	.337	.420
Trenton	.254	142	4690	598	1189	243	28	72	553	494	855	94	33	.331	.363
Connecticut	.253	141	4610	576	1168	225	39	100	520	405	1042	116	52	.320	.384
Binghamton	.252	142	4739	618	1196	212	19	103	564	448	1070	95	54	.323	.370
Harrisburg	.249	141	4622	645	1149	212	18	121	594	492	1088	112	46	.326	.381

CLUB PITCHING

ERA		G	CGSHO	SV	IP	H	R	ER	HR	BB	SO	AVG
Trenton	3.20	142	4	18	43 1247	1078	519	440	90	467	1159	.232
Connecticut	3.68	141	4	10	38 1214	1177	586	496	96	431	863	.255
Erie	3.77	140	12	7	38 1194	1172	580	499	107	348	874	.257
Akron	4.02	141	1	6	38 1218	1202	611	538	103	463	990	.259
Altoona	4.24	141	7	9	39 1198	1230	643	565	98	419	814	.268
Reading	4.28	141	6	3	38 1207	1202	670	569	110	491	898	.261
Portland	4.37	143	4	6	34 1208	1203	666	587	120	553	1053	.261
Bowie	4.45	140	2	7	37 1219	1211	692	601	128	567	1038	.260
New Britain	4.45	141	4	4	33 1198	1256	703	590	115	477	950	.268
Binghamton	4.49	142	4	7	32 1241	1364	713	619	97	447	911	.278
New Hampshire	4.49	143	4	6	33 1251	1377	699	624	113	455	981	.280
Harrisburg	4.83	141	1	4	27 1213	1294	752	650	135	542	872	.273

CLUB FIELDING

	PCT	PO	A	E	DP		PCT	PO	A	E	DP
Akron	.978	3654	1335	114	133	New Hampshire	.974	3754	1463	138	133
Portland	.978	3624	1321	112	138	Bowie	.973	3656	1295	139	123
Altoona	.976	3595	1442	122	139	Erie	.973	3581	1564	141	128
Connecticut	.976	3642	1417	125	117	Harrisburg	.973	3639	1424	139	124
Trenton	.976	3740	1366	127	114	New Britain	.971	3595	1306	144	127
Reading	.975	3621	1343	128	126	Binghamton	.969	3724	1416	162	131

INDIVIDUAL BATTING LEADERS (Minimum 440 Plate Appearances)

	AVG	G	AB	R	H	2B	3B	HR	RBI	BB	SO	SB
Brown, Jordan, Akron	.333	127	483	85	161	36	2	11	76	63	56	11
Barton, Brian, Akron	.314	106	389	56	122	18	2	9	59	41	99	20
Kiger, Mark, Binghamton	.312	114	391	75	122	27	4	10	50	75	92	16
Guzman, Garrett, New Britain	.312	125	475	72	148	23	1	14	88	36	51	6
Cabrera, Asdrubal, Akron	.310	96	368	78	114	23	3	8	54	45	42	23
Jacobs, Greg, Reading	.310	133	462	75	143	39	2	21	83	43	64	2
Ruiz, Randy, Altoona-Reading-Connecticut	.309	108	395	61	122	25	4	18	69	35	93	1
Bowker, John, Connecticut	.307	139	522	79	160	35	6	22	90	41	103	3
Hill, Jason, Reading	.302	116	434	57	131	33	0	9	67	34	62	1
Velez, Eugenio, Connecticut	.298	96	376	55	112	17	9	1	25	26	66	49

INDIVIDUAL PITCHING LEADERS (Minimum 114 Innings)

	W	L	ERA	G	GS	CG	SV	IP	H	R	ER	BB	SO
Horne, Alan, Trenton	12	4	3.11	27	27	0	0	153	149	68	53	57	165
Liz, Radhames, Bowie	11	4	3.22	25	25	2	0	137	101	60	49	70	161
Mulvey, Kevin, Binghamton	11	10	3.32	26	26	0	0	152	145	74	56	43	110
Pereira, Nick, Connecticut	9	9	3.39	26	26	1	0	143	124	64	54	65	123
Espineli, Eugene, Connecticut	8	10	3.45	29	24	0	0	141	142	63	54	37	105
McNiven, Brooks, Connecticut	7	6	3.55	30	15	0	0	117	123	57	46	29	41
Jones, Jason, Trenton	8	11	3.62	28	19	0	0	132	130	63	53	31	78
Munoz, Luis, Altoona	12	5	3.63	25	23	1	0	136	130	63	55	32	89
Marquez, Jeffrey, Trenton	15	9	3.65	27	27	2	0	155	166	80	63	44	94
Lewis, Scott, Akron	7	9	3.68	27	25	0	0	135	135	58	55	34	121

ALL-STAR TEAM

C: Jason Hill, Reading. **1B:** Jordan Brown, Akron. **2B:** Michael Hollimon, Erie. **3B:** Oscar Salazar, Bowie. **SS:** Asdrubal Cabrera, Akron. **OF:** John Bowker, Connecticut; Garrett Guzman, New Britain; Greg Jacobs, Reading. **DH:** Brett Harper, Binghamton. **Utility:** Mark Kiger, Binghamton. **RHP:** Alan Horne, Trenton. **LHP:** Matt Maloney, Reading. **RP:** Matt Peterson, Altoona.

Most Valuable Player: Jordan Brown, Akron. **Pitcher of the Year:** Alan Horne, Trenton. **Rookie of the Year:** Jordan Brown, Akron. **Manager of the Year:** Matt Walbeck, Erie.

DEPARTMENT LEADERS

BATTING

OBP	Kiger, Mark, Binghamton	.432
SLG	Jimenez, Luis Antonio, Bowie	.591
R	Thomas, Clete, Erie	97
H	Brown, Jordan, Akron	161
TB	Bowker, John, Connecticut	273
XBH	Salazar, Oscar, Bowie	63
	Bowker, John, Connecticut	63
2B	Salazar, Oscar, Bowie	39
	Jacobs, Greg, Reading	39
3B	Torres, Andres, Erie	11
HR	Larish, Jeff, Erie	28
RBI	Larish, Jeff, Erie	101
SAC	Plouffe, Trevor, New Britain	15
SF	Bowker, John, Connecticut	12
BB	Natale, Jeff, Portland	88
IBB	Larish, Jeff, Erie	9
	Jacobs, Greg, Reading	9
HBP	Barton, Brian, Akron	28
SO	Costanzo, Mike, Reading	157
SB	Velez, Eugenio, Connecticut	49
CS	Velez, Eugenio, Connecticut	17
GIDP	Bowker, John, Connecticut	17
AB/SO	Mayorson, Manuel, New Hamp.	12.56

PITCHING

G	Carlson, Jesse, New Hampshire	58
	Key, Chris, Reading	58
GS	Six players tied at	27
CG	Brazelton, Dewon, Altoona	3
	Trahern, Dallas, Erie	3
SHO	13 players tied at	1
GF	James, Michael, Portland	50
SV	Peterson, Matt, Altoona	29
	Anderson, Brian, Connecticut	29
W	Marquez, Jeffrey, Trenton	15
L	Broshuis, Garrett, Connecticut	17
IP	Trahern, Dallas, Erie	162.2
H	Yates, Kyle, New Hampshire	184
R	Sanchez, Jose, Binghamton	90
ER	Nottingham, Shawn, Akron	79
HB	Nall, Brandon, Binghamton	13
BB	Waters, Chris, Bowie	86
SO	Horne, Alan, Trenton	165
SO/9-S	Buchholz, Clay, Portland	12.13
SO/9-R	Patterson, Scott, Trenton	11.61
WP	Gardner, Michael, Trenton	17
BK	Herrera, Yoslan, Altoona	4
AVG	Liz, Radhames, Bowie	.204

FIELDING

C	PCT	Pilittere, P.J., Trenton	.995
	PO	Pilittere, P.J., Trenton	780
	A	Pilittere, P.J., Trenton	60
	E	Torrealba, Steve, Erie	12
	DP	Geiger, Kyle, New Britain	10
	PB	Brown, Dusty, Portland	15
	CS%	Toregas, Wyatt, Akron	.52
1B	PCT	Larish, Jeff, Erie	.994
	PO	Larish, Jeff, Erie	1113
	A	Cannon, Chip, New Hampshire	96
	E	Jimenez, Luis Antonio, Bowie	11
		Whitesell, Josh, Harrisburg	11
	DP	Larish, Jeff, Erie	94
2B	PCT	Reyes, Argenis, Akron	.983
	PO	Reyes, Argenis, Akron	244
	A	Lopez, Gabriel, Trenton	345
	E	Molina, Felix, New Britain	18
	DP	Reyes, Argenis, Akron	82
3B	PCT	Klink, Simon, Connecticut	.937
	PO	Costanzo, Mike, Reading	108
	A	Costanzo, Mike, Reading	269
	E	Costanzo, Mike, Reading	34
	DP	Pinckney, Andrew, Portland	26
SS	PCT	Santos, Sergio, New Britain	.965
	PO	Plouffe, Trevor, New Britain	188
	A	Santos, Sergio, New Hampshire	331
	E	Plouffe, Trevor, New Britain	32
	DP	Santos, Sergio, New Hampshire	71
OF	PCT	Fiorentino, Jeff, Bowie	.993
	PO	Crowe, Trevor, Akron	317
	A	Joyce, Matthew, Erie	20
	E	Thomas, Clete, Erie	11
	DP	Carson, Matt, Trenton	6

BY ALAN MATTHEWS

The Montgomery Biscuits didn't appear to be in need of reinforcements, but the team that parlayed one of the minors' most impressive late-season stretches into a playoff berth received their biggest hit of the year from a player who didn't spend a single day in Montgomery prior to the postseason.

With Montgomery trailing 3-1 with one out, outfielder Sergio Pedroza hit a three-run home run in the top of the ninth inning of the decisive game of the Southern League championship series to lead the Biscuits to their second straight title with a 4-3 win over Huntsville.

It was also the second year in a row that Montgomery defeated the Stars, who came from behind to defeat Tennessee in the first round and sent their closer to the mound with a two-run lead against the Biscuits.

Luis Pena, who had dialed his fastball up to 99 mph during the postseason, surrendered a hit and a walk before giving up Pedroza's home run. Pedroza, who batted .286 with a team-leading 22 homers at high Class A Vero Beach during the regular season, had also faced Pena in the Florida State League.

The Biscuits defeated the Stars in four games to claim the crown in 2006, and were the first Southern League team to capture back-to-back titles since the Montgomery Rebels won three straight championships from 1975-77.

Biscuits outfielder Chris Nowak was MVP of the SL championship series, batting .611 (11-for-18) with three homers and six RBIs in the five games. Lefthander Jake McGee went 1-0, 2.45 in 11 innings during the series.

It was McGee's promotion from the FSL in August that keyed the Biscuits' surge. Montgomery won 15 of its last 16 games to claim the Southern Division's second-half title, then knocked off first-half champion Mississippi in the first round.

Despite an 80-60 overall record, the Jacksonville Suns failed to advance to the playoffs for the first time in three years. They fell one game short to the Braves, losing out on the last day of the first half, then blew a lead that was as large as five games in late July in the second half. Jacksonville managed just 10 wins in its final 27 games.

Third baseman Evan Longoria was the Biscuits' regular season catalyst, and the league's MVP, despite spending the final month of the season in Triple-A. Longoria batted .307 and ranked among the league leaders in home runs (21) and RBIs (76). He ranked second on the league's postseason Top 20 Prospects list, behind Justin Upton, who was one of three players who spent time in Mobile before contributing in Arizona during the Diamondbacks' National League West title run.

TOP 20 PROSPECTS

1. **Justin Upton, of, Mobile BayBears (Diamondbacks)**
2. Evan Longoria, 3b, Montgomery Biscuits (Devil Rays)
3. Wade Davis, rhp, Montgomery Biscuits (Devil Rays)
4. Johnny Cueto, rhp, Chattanooga Lookouts (Reds)
5. Brandon Jones, of, Mississippi Braves
6. Reid Brignac, ss, Montgomery Biscuits (Devil Rays)
7. Tyler Colvin, of, Tennessee Smokies (Cubs)
8. Manny Parra, lhp, Huntsville Stars (Brewers)
9. Gio Gonzalez, lhp, Birmingham Barons (White Sox)
10. Carlos Gonzalez, of, Mobile BayBears (Diamondbacks)
11. Mark Reynolds, 3b, Mobile BayBears (Diamondbacks)
12. Chin-Lung Hu, ss, Jacksonville Suns (Dodgers)
13. Brent Lillibridge, ss, Mississippi Braves
14. Jonathan Meloan, rhp, Jacksonville Suns (Dodgers)
15. Max Scherzer, rhp, Mobile BayBears (Diamondbacks)
16. Jo Jo Reyes, lhp, Mississippi Braves
17. Diory Hernandez, ss, Mississippi Braves
18. James McDonald, rhp, Jacksonville Suns (Dodgers)
19. Gaby Hernandez, rhp, Carolina Mudcats (Marlins)
20. Alcides Escobar, ss, Huntsville Stars (Brewers)

STANDINGS: SPLIT SEASON

FIRST HALF

NORTH	W	L	PCT	GB
Huntsville	37	31	.544	—
Tennessee	36	32	.529	1
West Tenn	31	39	.443	7
Chattanooga	29	41	.414	9
Carolina	28	42	.400	10

SOUTH	W	L	PCT	GB
Mississippi	42	28	.600	—
Jacksonville	41	29	.586	1
Mobile	37	33	.529	5
Montgomery	35	35	.500	7
Birmingham	32	38	.457	10

SECOND HALF

NORTH	W	L	PCT	GB
Huntsville	38	31	.551	—
Chattanooga	38	32	.543	½
Tennessee	37	33	.529	1½
Carolina	32	38	.457	6½
West Tenn	29	40	.420	9

SOUTH	W	L	PCT	GB
Montgomery	46	24	.657	—
Jacksonville	39	31	.557	7
Mobile	34	35	.493	11½
Birmingham	30	40	.429	16
Mississippi	25	44	.362	20½

PLAYOFFS—Semifinals: Huntsville defeated Tennessee 3-2 and Montgomery defeated Mississippi 3-1 in best-of-five series. **Final:** Montgomery defeated Huntsville 3-2 in best-of-five series.

Upton arrived in the SL on May 14 and hit a home run in his first Double-A at-bat, then made a quick ascent to Arizona, where he was joined by third baseman Mark Reynolds and second baseman Emilio Bonifacio.

Mobile's Javier Brito won the SL batting title with a .327 mark, and Montgomery righthander Chris Mason was named the league's most valuable pitcher after pacing the circuit in ERA (2.57), backing a 15-4 record.

STANDINGS

Page	Team	W	L	PCT	GB	Manager	Attendance	Average	Last Penn.
280	Montgomery Biscuits (Devil Rays)	81	59	.579	—	Billy Gardner	311,872	4,586	2007
166	Jacksonville Suns (Dodgers)	80	60	.571	1	John Shoemaker	396,012	5,739	2005
175	Huntsville Stars (Brewers)	75	62	.547	4½	Don Money	164,079	2,449	2001
81	Tennessee Smokies (Cubs)	73	65	.529	7	Pat Listach	258,121	3,971	2004
47	Mobile BayBears (Diamondbacks)	71	68	.511	9½	Brett Butler/Matt Williams	232,235	3,466	2004
55	Mississippi Braves (Braves)	67	72	.482	13½	Phillip Wellman	246,674	3,575	1997
98	Chattanooga Lookouts (Reds)	67	73	.479	14	Jayhawk Owens	242,104	3,459	1988
90	Birmingham Barons (White Sox)	62	78	.443	19	Rafael Santana	280,171	4,002	2002
271	West Tenn Diamond Jaxx (Mariners)	60	79	.432	20½	Eddie Rodriguez	113,351	1,643	2000
132	Carolina Mudcats (Marlins)	60	80	.429	21	Brandon Hyde	273,198	3,903	2003

NOTE: Teams' individual batting and pitching statistics can be found on page indicated in lefthand column.

CLUB BATTING

	AVG	G	AB	R	H	2B	3B	HR	RBI	BB	SO	SB	CS	OBP	SLG
Mobile	.271	139	4633	664	1255	255	35	102	599	440	970	134	68	.339	.407
Tennessee	.271	138	4681	636	1270	237	25	104	580	428	879	85	34	.335	.399
Montgomery	.269	140	4765	695	1284	251	40	114	649	532	986	102	61	.346	.411
Mississippi	.262	139	4702	617	1232	236	35	84	554	484	1065	159	83	.336	.381
Chattanooga	.259	140	4803	628	1244	276	44	113	589	496	1215	115	42	.332	.405
Huntsville	.259	137	4500	647	1165	215	47	73	587	507	1036	142	61	.341	.376
Jacksonville	.257	140	4681	679	1201	247	26	119	626	508	972	86	49	.334	.397
Birmingham	.252	140	4735	566	1191	227	21	81	517	430	970	114	64	.317	.360
Carolina	.248	140	4638	603	1149	263	30	129	558	504	1219	86	46	.328	.401
West Tenn	.247	139	4669	623	1154	237	32	115	568	526	1091	90	61	.330	.386

CLUB PITCHING

	ERA	G	CG	SHO	SV	IP	H	R	ER	HR	BB	SO	AVG
Mississippi	3.82	139	0	8	39	1235	1234	602	523	78	448	986	.264
Mobile	3.88	139	2	7	34	1210	1198	613	521	97	479	1036	.261
Huntsville	3.92	137	3	9	39	1199	1138	577	520	117	410	1062	.252
Birmingham	3.98	140	0	8	34	1257	1257	644	553	74	484	1125	.261
Jacksonville	4.01	140	1	10	41	1240	1202	635	552	118	575	1188	.255
Montgomery	4.01	140	3	12	31	1250	1220	638	556	106	502	939	.258
Chattanooga	4.15	140	0	9	36	1248	1242	656	575	108	473	1146	.262
Tennessee	4.17	138	2	8	37	1217	1185	631	561	131	497	968	.256
Carolina	4.30	140	1	6	28	1222	1175	674	584	101	517	986	.254
West Tenn	4.50	139	3	6	31	1239	1294	688	619	104	470	967	.272

CLUB FIELDING

	PCT	PO	A	E	DP		PCT	PO	A	E	DP
Huntsville	.980	3598	1372	103	116	Carolina	.976	3667	1412	124	112
West Tenn	.980	3718	1400	105	127	Chattanooga	.976	3744	1400	129	117
Jacksonville	.978	3721	1328	116	104	Tennessee	.976	3652	1380	123	114
Montgomery	.978	3749	1478	119	123	Birmingham	.972	3771	1550	151	136
Mississippi	.977	3705	1360	118	126	Mobile	.972	3630	1420	144	120

INDIVIDUAL BATTING LEADERS (Minimum 443 Plate Appearances)

	AVG	G	AB	R	H	2B	3B	HR	RBI	BB	SO	SB
Brito, Javier, Mobile	.327	127	440	72	144	29	2	11	72	78	90	1
Jaso, John, Montgomery	.316	109	380	62	120	24	2	12	71	59	49	2
Holt, J.C., Mississippi	.312	94	385	47	120	17	5	0	22	40	77	20
Perez, Fernando, Montgomery	.308	102	393	84	121	24	10	8	33	76	104	32
Hernandez, Diory, Mississippi	.307	115	433	50	133	25	1	7	59	29	68	22
Longoria, Evan, Montgomery	.307	105	381	78	117	21	0	21	76	51	81	4
Iribarren, Hernan, Huntsville	.307	124	479	72	147	23	12	4	53	44	109	18
Nowak, Chris, Montgomery	.304	104	368	54	112	21	4	7	55	54	73	18
Castillo, Wilkin, Mobile	.302	109	410	50	124	31	3	6	46	17	62	18
Loadenthal, Carl, Mississippi	.3	129	476	72	143	17	5	0	31	62	80	40

INDIVIDUAL PITCHING LEADERS (Minimum 115 Innings)

	W	L	ERA	G	GS	CG	SV	IP	H	R	ER	BB	SO
Mason, Chris, Montgomery	15	4	2.57	28	28	1	1	0	161.1	147	52	46	44	136
Vasquez, Esmerling, Mobile	10	6	2.99	29	29	0	0	0	165.1	125	61	55	60	151
Egbert, Jack, Birmingham	12	8	3.06	28	28	0	0	0	161.2	138	63	55	44	165
Gonzalez, Gio, Birmingham	9	7	3.18	27	27	0	0	0	150	116	57	53	57	185
Wing, Ryan, Birmingham	6	6	3.24	35	17	0	0	0	114	89	44	41	46	93
Gulin, Lindsay, Huntsville	12	6	3.29	21	21	0	0	0	123	102	49	45	44	117
Harrison, Matt, Mississippi	5	7	3.39	20	20	0	0	0	116.2	118	51	44	34	78
Holliman, Mark, Tennessee	10	11	3.57	27	26	2	1	0	161.1	157	68	64	57	108
Bueno, Francisley, Mississippi	4	6	3.67	22	19	0	0	0	112.2	132	55	46	26	77
Woerman, Joseph, West Tenn	7	7	3.74	27	25	0	0	0	144.1	119	69	60	68	124

ALL-STAR TEAM

C: John Jaso, Montgomery. **1B:** Javier Brito, Mobile. **2B:** Emilio Bonifacio, Mobile. **3B:** Evan Longoria, Montgomery. **SS:** Chin-Lung Hu, Jacksonville. **OF:** Charlton Jimerson, West Tenn; Brendan Katin, Huntsville; Fernando Perez, Montgomery; Justin Upton, Mobile. **DH:** Lee Mitchell, Carolina. **Utility:** Wilkin Castillo, Mobile. **RHP:** Chris Mason, Montgomery. **LHP:** Gio Gonzalez, Birmingham. **RP:** Dale Thayer, Montgomery. **Most Valuable Player:** Evan Longoria, Montgomery. Most Outstanding Pitcher: Chris Mason, **Montgomery. Manager of the Year:** Don Money, Huntsville.

DEPARTMENT LEADERS

BATTING

OBP	Brito, Javier, Mobile	.433
SLG	Jimerson, Charlton, West Tenn	.565
R	Brignac, Reid, Montgomery	91
H	Bonifacio, Emilio, Mobile	157
TB	Brignac, Reid, Montgomery	228
XBH	Three players tied at	52
2B	Aldridge, Cory, Birmingham	33
	Gonzalez, Carlos, Mobile	33
3B	Iribarren, Hernan, Huntsville	12
HR	Katin, Brendan, Huntsville	24
RBI	Katin, Brendan, Huntsville	94
SAC	Castillo, Wilkin, Mobile	16
SF	Tuiasosopo, Matt, West Tenn	14
BB	Raglani, Anthony, Jacksonville	85
IBB	Loadenthal, Carl, Mississippi	6
HBP	Sollmann, Steve, Huntsville	25
SO	Katin, Brendan, Huntsville	163
SB	Bonifacio, Emilio, Mobile	41
CS	Hernandez, Diory, Mississippi	20
GIDP	Johnson, Brent, West Tenn	17
AB/SO	Salas, Issmael, Tennessee	9.56

PITCHING

G	Hernandez Jr., Fernando, Birmingham	60
GS	Vasquez, Esmerling, Mobile	29
CG	Four players tied at	2
SHO	Five players tied at	1
GF	Thayer, Dale, Montgomery	43
SV	Thayer, Dale, Montgomery	21
W	Mason, Christopher, Montgomery	15
L	Whisler, Wes, Birmingham	13
IP	Baldwin, Andrew, West Tenn	166
H	Whisler, Wes, Birmingham	195
R	Whisler, Wes, Birmingham	107
ER	Whisler, Wes, Birmingham	87
HB	Woerman, Joseph, West Tenn	15
BB	Veal, Donald, Tennessee	73
SO	Gonzalez, Gio, Birmingham	185
SO/9-S	Gonzalez, Gio, Birmingham	11.1
SO/9-R	Guevara, Carlos, Chattanooga	12.63
WP	Gulin, Lindsay, Huntsville	16
BK	Barratt, Jonathan, Montgomery	6
AVG	Wing, Ryan, Birmingham	.211

FIELDING

C	PCT	Palmisano, Lou, Huntsville	.995
		Sammons, Clint, Mississippi	.995
	PO	Ellis, A.J., Jacksonville	868
	A	Ellis, A.J., Jacksonville	82
	E	Castillo, Wilkin, Mobile	9
	DP	Ellis, A.J., Jacksonville	9
		Rivera, Rene, West Tenn	9
	PB	Rivera, Rene, West Tenn	15
	CS%	Sammons, Clint, Mississippi	.48
1B	PCT	Sollmann, Steve, Huntsville	.996
	PO	Psomas, Grant, Carolina	927
	A	Psomas, Grant, Carolina	91
	E	Hubbard, Thomas, West Tenn	12
	DP	Hubbard, Thomas, West Tenn	85
2B	PCT	Holt, J.C., Mississippi	.985
	PO	Valbuena, Luis, West Tenn	236
	A	Valbuena, Luis, West Tenn	351
	E	Iribarren, Hernan, Huntsville	14
	DP	Asanovich, Josh, Montgomery	77
3B	PCT	Mitchell, Lee, Carolina	.97
	PO	Tuiasosopo, Matt, West Tenn	99
	A	Heether, Adam, Huntsville	252
	E	Kelly, Christopher, Birmingham	26
	DP	Kelly, Christopher, Birmingham	24
SS	PCT	Minaker, Christopher, West Tenn	.972
	PO	Brignac, Reid, Montgomery	179
	A	Brignac, Reid, Montgomery	394
	E	Brignac, Reid, Montgomery	22
	DP	Brignac, Reid, Montgomery	76
OF	PCT	Collaro, Thomas, Birmingham	.994
	PO	Cumberland, Shaun, Chattanooga	286
	A	Fuld, Sam, Tennessee	13
	E	Katin, Brendan, Huntsville	12
		Gonzalez, Carlos, Mobile	12
	DP	Four players tied at	4

MINOR LEAGUES

BY WILL LINGO

B y the end of the 2007 season, the Texas League had two teams that stood out above the rest of the league: the San Antonio Missions and Springfield Cardinals.

It was appropriate, then, that those two teams swept to the league finals, with the Missions then outdueling the Cardinals to take their first league title since 2003. San Antonio's success on the field also led to its selection as Baseball America's Minor League Team of the Year.

The Cardinals were the most consistent team in the league, winning both halves in the Northern Division with a talented team that placed five players among the league's Top 20 Prospects, including No. 1 prospect Colby Rasmus. Rasmus showed his all-around talent by hitting a league-leading 29 home runs as well as stealing 18 bases and playing a strong center field.

But San Antonio was the better team in the finals, dominating Springfield to win the title in four games in a best-of-five series. Utilityman Brett Dowdy was the star of the playoffs, batting .379 with three home runs in 29 postseason at-bats.

San Antonio was in its first season as a Padres affiliate after being a Mariners farm team from 2001-06, and the Padres sent a wealth of reinforcements to boost the team at midseason after the Missions finished in last place in their division in the first half. The most notable additions were second baseman Matt Antonelli, who sparked the lineup, and lefthander Wade LeBlanc, who bolstered the rotation, after they were promoted from Class A.

But the Missions' two best players were third baseman Chase Headley and righthander Josh Geer, both of whom were with the team all season long. Headley was selected as the league MVP after the season after threatening to win the league triple crown, while Geer won pitcher of the year honors after winning a league-high 16 games as well as leading the league with a 3.20 ERA. Headley established himself as one of the best prospects in the Padres organization by batting .330 with 20 home runs and 78 RBIs.

The Texas League is traditionally one of the more offensive circuits in the minors, but it wasn't loaded with can't-miss hitters this season. True, the top two prospects were position players, and they were a clear cut above the rest of the talent in the league. But most of the hitters who followed them have limitations or obvious holes in their games. A notable example was Rangers outfielder John Mayberry Jr., a 2005 first-round pick who has a great body and light-tower power when he connects, but also a long swing and gets himself out most of the time.

That wasn't true for Rasmus or Headley, who showed complete skills in the field and at the plate.

TOP 20 PROSPECTS

1. **Colby Rasmus, of, Springfield Cardinals**
2. Chase Headley, 3b, San Antonio Missions (Padres)
3. Nick Adenhart, rhp, Arkansas Travelers (Angels)
4. Greg Reynolds, rhp, Tulsa Drillers (Rockies)
5. Luke Hochevar, rhp, Wichita Wranglers (Royals)
6. Matt Antonelli, 2b, San Antonio Missions (Padres)
7. Franklin Morales, lhp, Tulsa Drillers (Rockies)
8. Eric Hurley, rhp, Frisco RoughRiders (Rangers)
9. Troy Patton, lhp, Corpus Christi Hooks (Astros)
10. J.R. Towles, c, Corpus Christi Hooks (Astros)
11. Chris Perez, rhp, Springfield Cardinals
12. Jaime Garcia, lhp, Springfield Cardinals
13. Juan Morillo, rhp, Tulsa Drillers (Rockies)
14. German Duran, 2b, Frisco RoughRiders (Rangers)
15. Sean Rodriguez, ss, Arkansas (Angels)
16. Felipe Paulino, rhp, Corpus Christi (Astros)
17. Bryan Anderson, c, Springfield Cardinals
18. Richie Robnett, of, Midland RockHounds (Athletics)
19. Josh Geer, rhp, San Antonio Missions (Padres)
20. Joe Mather, of, Springfield Cardinals

STEVE MOORE

STANDINGS: SPLIT SEASON

FIRST HALF					SECOND HALF				
NORTH	**W**	**L**	**PCT**	**GB**	**NORTH**	**W**	**L**	**PCT**	**GB**
Springfield	36	31	.537	—	Springfield	37	32	.536	—
Tulsa	35	35	.500	2½	Tulsa	34	34	.500	2½
Arkansas	31	39	.443	6½	Arkansas	34	36	.486	3½
Wichita	25	45	.357	12½	Wichita	31	39	.443	6½
SOUTH	**W**	**L**	**PCT**	**GB**	**SOUTH**	**W**	**L**	**PCT**	**GB**
Frisco	47	23	.671	—	San Antonio	42	27	.609	—
Midland	41	26	.612	4½	Frisco	38	32	.543	4½
Corpus Christi	31	39	.443	16	Corpus Christi	36	34	.514	4½
San Antonio	31	39	.443	16	Midland	26	44	.371	16½

PLAYOFFS—Semifinals: Springfield defeated Tulsa 3-0 and San Antonio defeated Frisco 3-0 in best-of-five series. **Finals:** San Antonio defeated Springfield 3-1 in a best-of-five series.

The pitching crop was deeper than usual. Righthanders Nick Adenhart (Arkansas) and Luke Hochevar (Wichita) may not have dominated as much as expected, but their potential was obvious. Tulsa righty Greg Reynolds did carve up TL hitters before getting shut down with shoulder soreness in mid-June.

The Texas League is one of the most stable in the minor leagues, but it will see a franchise move for 2008, with the Wichita Wranglers leaving after 20 years in Kansas for a new ballpark in Springdale, Ark. The team will be known as the Northwest Arkansas Naturals.

STANDINGS

Page	Team	W	L	PCT	GB	Manager	Attendance	Average	Last Penn.
288	Frisco RoughRiders (Rangers)	85	55	.607	—	Dave Anderson	545,421	8,264	2004
243	Springfield Cardinals (Cardinals)	73	63	.537	10	Ron Warner	460,063	7,078	1994
254	San Antonio Missions (Padres)	73	66	.525	11½	Randy Ready	277,150	4,264	2007
115	Tulsa Drillers (Rockies)	69	69	.500	15	Stu Cole	296,017	4,485	1998
212	Midland RockHounds (Athletics)	67	70	.489	16½	Todd Steverson	270,331	4,096	2005
140	Corpus Christi Hooks (Astros)	67	73	.479	18	Dave Clark	479,289	7,048	2006
157	Arkansas Travelers (Angels)	65	75	.464	20	Bobby Magallanes	372,475	5,644	2001
149	Wichita Wranglers (Royals)	56	84	.400	29	Tony Tijerina	113,368	1,829	1999

NOTE: Teams' individual batting and pitching statistics can be found on page indicated in lefthand column.

CLUB BATTING

	AVG	G	AB	R	H	2B	3B	HR	RBI	BB	SO	SB	CS	OBP	SLG
Springfield	.271	136	4587	692	1243	256	17	148	659	465	886	68	23	.345	.431
Corpus Christi	.267	140	4648	644	1242	244	24	109	600	455	943	107	43	.338	.400
Tulsa	.267	138	4658	637	1242	285	15	112	588	384	916	106	50	.331	.406
Frisco	.264	140	4624	705	1223	245	29	176	664	454	980	91	36	.335	.444
Midland	.264	137	4650	644	1229	291	26	107	606	501	959	52	22	.341	.407
Wichita	.261	140	4574	576	1196	222	32	96	525	466	834	86	56	.334	.387
Arkansas	.259	140	4567	605	1183	225	28	84	538	464	915	157	86	.339	.376
San Antonio	.256	139	4591	642	1176	214	27	133	612	524	950	67	30	.339	.401

CLUB PITCHING

	ERA	G	CG	SHO	SV	IP	H	R	ER	HR	BB	SO	AVG
San Antonio	3.82	139	4	11	36	1199	1156	562	508	104	402	902	.256
Springfield	4.07	136	3	9	39	1178	1194	619	532	116	499	876	.267
Frisco	4.19	140	9	14	41	1214	1154	614	560	126	486	1057	.250
Arkansas	4.24	140	4	7	27	1215	1239	639	569	113	451	799	.267
Tulsa	4.29	138	6	9	39	1207	1187	638	576	118	489	926	.260
Corpus Christi	4.41	140	4	10	35	1211	1250	659	593	125	467	925	.266
Midland	4.51	137	2	5	28	1208	1233	670	604	120	468	986	.266
Wichita	4.93	140	3	4	25	1202	1324	744	658	143	452	913	.279

CLUB FIELDING

	PCT	PO	A	E	DP		PCT	PO	A	E	DP
Arkansas	.981	3646	1407	96	141	Corpus Christi	.978	3634	1255	112	120
San Antonio	.981	3597	1393	95	124	Wichita	.978	3605	1115	96	
Tulsa	.980	3622	1538	104	150	Springfield	.976	3533	1552	127	160
Frisco	.979	3639	1302	104	117	Midland	.975	3624	1280	126	107

INDIVIDUAL BATTING LEADERS *(Minimum 434 Plate Appearances)*

	AVG	G	AB	R	H	2B	3B	HR	RBI	BB	SO	SB
Headley, Chase, San Antonio	.330	121	433	82	143	38	5	20	78	74	114	1
Colonel, Christian, Tulsa	.309	134	527	78	163	47	0	17	84	46	80	6
Sandoval, Freddy, Arkansas	.305	127	472	84	144	32	6	11	72	67	78	21
Duran, German, Frisco	.300	130	480	81	144	32	5	22	84	34	77	11
Anderson, Bryan, Springfield	.298	103	389	51	116	15	1	6	53	32	77	0
Frey, Christopher, Tulsa	.295	132	474	65	140	30	6	1	34	36	61	12
Self, Todd, Corpus Christi	.294	124	428	72	126	24	1	13	69	71	96	4
Stodolka, Mike, Wichita	.291	110	381	69	111	27	1	12	59	73	91	4
Richardson, Juan, Springfield	.291	113	430	65	125	22	1	18	78	47	118	0
Valentin, Geraldo, Wichita	.288	112	437	48	126	19	3	2	54	25	46	5

INDIVIDUAL PITCHING LEADERS *(Minimum 112 Innings)*

	W	L	ERA	G	GS	CG	SV	IP	H	R	ER	BB	SO
Geer, Joshua, San Antonio	16	6	3.20	26	26	2	0	171	163	67	61	27	102
Gonzalez, Miguel, Arkansas	8	4	3.38	30	19	1	1	131	128	53	49	42	81
Ramos, Cesar, San Antonio	13	9	3.41	27	27	2	0	164	153	69	62	43	90
Adenhart, Nick, Arkansas	10	8	3.65	26	26	0	0	153	158	72	62	65	116
Green, Nick, Arkansas	10	8	3.68	28	28	2	0	178	164	80	73	32	107
Thompson, Sean, San Antonio-Tulsa	9	8	3.73	24	23	1	0	133	124	61	55	56	81
Mathis, Douglas, Tulsa	11	7	3.76	22	22	1	0	132	140	59	55	40	92

ALL-STAR TEAM

C:Bryan Anderson, Springfield; Nick Hundley, San Antonio. **1B:**Mike Stodolka, Wichita. **2B:**German Duran, Frisco. **3B:**Chase Headley, San Antonio. **SS:**Sean Rodriguez, Arkansas. **OF:**Colby Rasmus, Springfield; Richie Robnett, Athletics; Ray Sadler, Corpus Christi; Will Venable, San Antonio. **DH:** Christian Colonel, Tulsa. Utility:Freddy Sandoval, Arkansas. **P:**Josh Geer, San Antonio; Miguel Gonzalez, Arkansas; Nick Green, Arkansas; Luis Mendoza, Frisco; Troy Patton, Corpus Christi. **RP:**Chris Perez, Springfield; Steven Register, Tulsa. **Player of the Year:** Chase Headley, San Antonio. Pitcher of the Year: Josh Geer, San Antonio. **Manager of the Year:** Dave Anderson, Frisco.

DEPARTMENT LEADERS

BATTING

OBP	Headley, Chase, San Antonio	.437
SLG	Headley, Chase, San Antonio	.580
R	Rasmus, Colby, Springfield	93
H	Colonel, Christian, Tulsa	163
TB	Colonel, Christian, Tulsa	261
XBH	Rasmus, Colby, Springfield	69
2B	Colonel, Christian, Tulsa	47
3B	Greenberg, Adam, Wichita	11
HR	Rasmus, Colby, Springfield	29
RBI	Sadler, Ray, Corpus Christi	93
SAC	Herrera, Jonathan, Tulsa	17
SF	Sadler, Ray, Corpus Christi	8
BB	Morrissey, Adam, Arkansas	92
IBB	Headley, Chase, San Antonio	7
HBP	Rodriguez, Sean, Arkansas	19
SO	Rodriguez, Sean, Arkansas	132
SB	Wimberly, Corey, Tulsa	36
CS	Three players tied at	12
GIDP	Valentin, Geraldo, Wichita	23
AB/SO	Falu, Irving, Wichita	10.82

PITCHING

G	Register, Steven, Tulsa	60
GS	Green, Nick, Arkansas	28
	Fritz, Ben, Midland	28
CG	Mendoza, Luis, Frisco	3
SHO	Three players tied at	2
GF	Register, Steven, Tulsa	54
SV	Register, Steven, Tulsa	37
W	Geer, Joshua, San Antonio	16
L	Christensen, Daniel, Wichita	15
IP	Green, Nick, Arkansas	178.1
H	Ekstrom, Michael, San Antonio	183
R	Mattheus, Ryan, Tulsa	100
ER	Mattheus, Ryan, Tulsa	98
HB	Adenhart, Nick, Arkansas	17
BB	Haberer, Eric, Springfield	72
SO	Deduno, Samuel, Tulsa	121
SO/9-S	Hochevar, Luke, Wichita	8.86
SO/9-R	Plummer, Jarod, Wichita	10.25
WP	Three players tied at	13
BK	Thompson, Sean, Tulsa	3
AVG	Paulino, Felipe, Corpus Christi	.238

FIELDING

C	PCT	Richardson, Kevin, Frisco	.994
	PO	Anderson, Bryan, Springfield	639
	A	Anderson, Bryan, Springfield	63
	E	Recker, Anthony, Midland	11
	DP	Anderson, Bryan, Springfield	9
	PB	Anderson, Bryan, Springfield	15
CS%		Richardson, Kevin, Frisco	.41
1B	PCT	Rifkin, Aaron, Tulsa	.996
	PO	Collins, Michael, Arkansas	964
	A	Frostad, Emerson, Frisco	70
	E	Frostad, Emerson, Frisco	9
	DP	Rifkin, Aaron, Tulsa	102
2B	PCT	Morrissey, Adam, Arkansas	.985
	PO	Duran, German, Frisco	224
	A	Duran, German, Frisco	345
	E	Wimberly, Corey, Tulsa	17
	DP	Morrissey, Adam, Arkansas	79
3B	PCT	Headley, Chase, San Antonio	.963
	PO	Sandoval, Freddy, Arkansas	96
	A	Colonel, Christian, Tulsa	219
	E	Sandoval, Freddy, Arkansas	20
	DP	Sandoval, Freddy, Arkansas	26
SS	PCT	Rodriguez, Sean, Arkansas	.97
	PO	Benjamin, Casey, Frisco	221
	A	Herrera, Jonathan, Tulsa	400
	E	Herrera, Jonathan, Tulsa	22
	DP	Herrera, Jonathan, Tulsa	99
OF	PCT	Czarniecki, Jordan, Tulsa	1
	PO	Sadler, Ray, Corpus Christi	324
	A	Macias, Drew, San Antonio	18
	E	Rasmus, Colby, Springfield	6
	DP	Danielson, Sean, Springfield	6

BY JOSH LEVENTHAL

The California League is known as a hitter's league, and rightfully so considering the minors' top two scoring teams resided in Lancaster and Lake Elsinore. Yet San Jose rode the league's best pitching staff to overcome the league's worst offense for its second title in three years.

The league's mound of talent was obvious, as four of the top seven prospects were pitchers.

The Giants' championship outlook seemed bleak after they fell into a two-game hole against Lake Elsinore in the best-of-five championship. But the Giants limited the Storm—which had averaged 6.3 runs a game during the regular season—to just two over the final three games.

Giants righthander Henry Sosa, who had struggled down the season's stretch run, started Game Five and yielded one run on two hits over four innings before Adam Cowart, Jason Waddell and Sergio Romo combined to pitch no-hit ball over the final five innings.

The Storm's sudden power outage was not without precedent, as it proved to be one of the league's streakiest teams. At the time of the promotion of its best hitter, Matt Antonelli, Lake Elsinore began a franchise-record 13-game win streak that boosted its overall record to 58-43. The wins quickly led to losses, as the Storm dropped nine of its next 10 games.

Lancaster boasted the league's most prolific offense but made national headlines for coming out on the wrong side of a record-setting rout. The JetHawks scored 1,081 runs—over 200 more than Lake Elsinore—in 2007, but fell to the Storm 30-0 at their blustery home, Clear Channel Stadium. The next night Lancaster first baseman Aaron Bates hit four home runs, a California League record that would be matched later in the season by teammate, and former indy leaguer, Brad Correll.

"I've never seen a minor league curtain call," said Lancaster manager Chad Epperson, which is exactly what Bates took after his fourth blast in the eighth inning.

Diamondbacks outfielder Justin Upton finished as the league's top-rated prospect after making quite an impression in a brief stay in Visalia. Upton hit just .152 in his first nine Cal League games but didn't look back, homering in five consecutive games during a late-April stretch that included a 13-game hit streak.

Unlike in years past—when the Cal League produced slam-dunk prospects like Reid Brignac and Franklin Morales in 2006 and Brandon Wood, Howie Kendrick, Stephen Drew and Billy Butler in 2005—the league had few sure things after Upton. There was young talent like High Desert's 19-year-old righthander Chris Tillman (who was rated third after going 4-1, 1.82 in August) and 17-

year-old shortstop Carlos Triunfel (who rated sixth after hovering around .300 following a midseason promotion). Inland Empire righthander James McDonald revived his career with a dominating three months in the league, and Lancaster's 24-year-old center fielder Bubba Bell put up the most impressive statistics in the minors and led the league in all three triple crown categories at the time of his promotion on July 4.

TOP 20 PROSPECTS

1. Justin Upton, of, Visalia Oaks (Diamondbacks)
2. **Henry Sosa, rhp, San Jose Giants**
3. Chris Tillman, rhp, High Desert Mavericks (Mariners)
4. Matt Antonelli, 2b, Lake Elsinore Storm (Padres)
5. Justin Masterson, rhp, Lancaster JetHawks (Red Sox)
6. Carlos Triunfel, ss, High Desert Mavericks (Mariners)
7. James McDonald, rhp, Inland Empire 66ers (Dodgers)
8. Chris Nelson, ss, Modesto Nuts (Rockies)
9. Chris Davis, 3b, Bakersfield Blaze (Rangers)
10. Dexter Fowler, of, Modesto Nuts (Rockies)
11. Brandon Hynick, rhp, Modesto Nuts (Rockies)
12. Wade LeBlanc, lhp, Lake Elsinore Storm (Padres)
13. Taylor Teagarden, c, Bakersfield Blaze (Rangers)
14. Eric Young Jr., 2b, Modesto Nuts (Rockies)
15. Hainley Statia, ss, Rancho Cucamonga Quakes (Angels)
16. Michael Saunders, of, High Desert Mavericks (Mariners)
17. Andrew Bailey, rhp, Stockton Ports (Athletics)
18. Kelvin Pichardo, rhp, San Jose Giants
19. Brooks Brown, rhp, Visalia Oaks (Diamondbacks)
20. Bubba Bell, of, Lancaster JetHawks (Red Sox)

BILL MITCHELL

STANDINGS: SPLIT SEASON

FIRST HALF

NORTH	W	L	PCT	GB
San Jose	39	31	.557	—
Stockton	35	35	.500	4
Modesto	34	36	.486	5
Visalia	34	36	.486	5
Bakersfield	29	41	.414	10

SOUTH	W	L	PCT	GB
Lancaster	39	31	.557	—
Inland Empire	39	31	.557	—
Lake Elsinore	37	33	.529	2
R. Cucamonga	33	37	.471	6
High Desert	31	39	.443	8

SECOND HALF

NORTH	W	L	PCT	GB
Visalia	43	27	.614	—
Modesto	42	28	.600	1
San Jose	34	36	.486	9
Stockton	29	41	.414	14
Bakersfield	28	42	.400	15

NORTH	W	L	PCT	GB
Lancaster	44	26	.629	—
Lake Elsinore	37	32	.536	6½
R. Cucamonga	36	34	.514	8
Inland Empire	33	36	.478	10½
High Desert	23	47	.329	21

PLAYOFFS—Division Series: Lake Elsinore defeated Inland Empire 2-1 and Visalia defeated Modesto 2-0 in best-of-three series. **Semifinals:** Lake Elsinore defeated Lancaster 3-1 and San Jose defeated Visalia 3-1 in best-of-five series. **Finals:** San Jose defeated Lake Elsinore 3-2 in a best-of-five series.

STANDINGS

Page	Team	W	L	PCT	GB	Manager	Attendance	Average	Last Penn.
73	Lancaster Jethawks (Red Sox)	83	57	.593	—	Chad Epperson	125,353	1,817	None
48	Visalia Oaks (Diamondbacks)	77	63	.550	6	Hector De La Cruz	83,452	1,192	1978
116	Modesto Nuts (Rockies)	76	64	.543	7	Jerry Weinstein	158,936	2,271	2004
255	Lake Elsinore Storm (Padres)	74	65	.532	8½	Carlos Lezcano	231,069	3,398	2001
264	San Jose Giants (Giants)	73	67	.521	10	Lenn Sakata	171,028	2,479	2007
167	Inland Empire 66ers (Dodgers)	72	67	.518	10½	Dave Collins	174,152	2,488	2006
158	Rancho Cucamonga Quakes (Angels)	69	71	.493	14	Bobby Mitchell	290,843	4,155	1994
213	Stockton Ports (Athletics)	64	76	.457	19	Darren Bush	218,497	3,121	2002
289	Bakersfield Blaze (Rangers)	57	83	.407	26	Carlos Subero	78,888	1,160	1989
272	High Desert Mavericks (Mariners)	54	86	.386	29	Scott Steinmann	117,262	1,675	1997

NOTE: Teams' individual batting and pitching statistics can be found on page indicated in lefthand column.

CLUB BATTING

	AVG	G	AB	R	H	2B	3B	HR	RBI	BB	SO	SB	CS	OBP	SLG
Lancaster	.296	140	5039	1081	1493	352	42	217	1008	672	1060	34	22	.385	.512
Lake Elsinore	.284	139	4882	875	1388	279	47	148	803	551	981	101	40	.364	.452
Visalia	.284	140	4812	711	1365	255	45	112	653	439	893	111	73	.352	.425
High Desert	.275	140	4900	802	1346	266	44	133	734	479	1024	96	53	.344	.428
Inland Empire	.274	139	4817	718	1321	261	48	103	658	445	856	152	74	.341	.412
Modesto	.267	140	4783	763	1279	286	58	114	701	469	1109	173	73	.340	.423
Stockton	.264	140	4829	755	1274	267	32	158	696	531	1087	78	43	.342	.431
Bakersfield	.262	140	4782	732	1255	269	20	128	669	476	1147	116	70	.334	.407
Rancho Cucamonga	.257	140	4798	688	1232	219	35	99	617	397	1102	171	61	.318	.379
San Jose	.247	140	4763	685	1178	253	38	106	618	481	1091	150	49	.320	.383

CLUB PITCHING

	ERA	G	CG	SHO	SV	IP	H	R	ER	HR	BB	SO	AVG
San Jose	3.82	140	1	5	37	1257	1159	636	532	96	463	1234	.246
Lake Elsinore	4.23	139	0	10	22	1219	1325	674	572	109	329	986	.277
Visalia	4.29	140	3	5	45	1232	1231	693	586	117	419	1047	.259
Modesto	4.34	140	6	8	32	1239	1231	689	593	100	478	945	.258
Rancho Cucamonga	4.40	140	7	6	32	1251	1311	703	611	130	490	945	.27
Inland Empire	4.94	139	1	6	43	1239	1294	792	678	108	559	1165	.269
Stockton	5.29	140	1	2	32	1240	1267	827	726	136	596	1082	.264
Bakersfield	5.36	140	1	8	26	1238	1364	840	735	162	538	1047	.28
Lancaster	5.49	140	0	4	34	1239	1391	871	755	162	509	936	.284
High Desert	6.44	140	1	1	22	1252	1558	1085	891	198	559	963	.302

CLUB FIELDING

	PCT	PO	A	E	DP		PCT	PO	A	E	DP
Inland Empire	.974	3717	1268	133	107	Rancho Cucamonga	.971	3753	1543	157	148
San Jose	.973	3770	1403	141	115	Lake Elsinore	.970	3657	1478	157	133
Bakersfield	.972	3715	1406	146	134	Visalia	.970	3696	1400	160	97
Lancaster	.971	3716	1526	158	148	Stockton	.968	3720	1375	169	129
Modesto	.971	3718	1465	157	127	High Desert	.959	3755	1414	223	133

INDIVIDUAL BATTING LEADERS (Minimum 434 Plate Appearances)

	AVG	G	AB	R	H	2B	3B	HR	RBI	BB	SO	SB
Bates, Aaron, Lancaster	.332	98	373	89	124	21	2	24	88	69	83	0
Daeges, Zachary, Lancaster	.330	127	515	124	170	55	5	21	113	82	97	4
Granadillo, Tony, Lancaster	.326	109	445	104	145	36	7	8	63	54	65	2
Wagner, Mark, Lancaster	.318	95	368	71	117	35	1	14	82	55	46	0
Cooper, Craig, Lake Elsinore	.317	124	458	83	145	32	4	10	78	56	87	4
Kindel, Jeff, Modesto	.317	126	477	79	151	34	7	14	83	41	81	3
Antonelli, Matt, Lake Elsinore	.314	82	347	89	109	14	4	14	54	53	58	18
Byrne, Bryan, Visalia	.310	128	478	75	148	25	5	13	74	66	78	4
Hoffmann, Jamie, Inland Empire	.309	116	433	67	134	22	7	9	81	47	70	19
Moore, Adam, High Desert	.307	115	433	74	133	30	3	22	102	41	84	1

INDIVIDUAL PITCHING LEADERS (Minimum 112 Innings)

	W	L	ERA	G	GS	CG	SV	IP	H	R	ER	BB	SO
Hynick, Brandon, Modesto	16	5	2.52	28	28	3	0	182	170	64	51	31	136
Buschmann, Matthew, Lake Elsinore	12	6	2.89	28	25	0	0	149	153	60	48	26	115
Johnson, Alan, Modesto	14	7	2.99	26	26	1	0	169	162	69	56	47	119
Oseguera, Paul, San Jose	10	6	3.54	27	26	1	0	158	145	72	62	35	132
Ortega, Anthony, Rancho Cucamonga	7	11	4.02	28	28	1	0	163	157	84	73	68	127
Ambriz, Hector, Visalia	10	8	4.08	28	26	2	0	150	137	79	68	50	133
Martinez, Joseph, San Jose	10	10	4.26	28	28	0	0	163	172	85	77	36	151
Mosebach, Robert, Rancho Cucamonga	11	7	4.28	25	23	1	0	156	171	88	74	49	93
Marek, Stephen, Rancho Cucamonga	8	10	4.30	25	25	1	0	134	133	78	64	49	106
Roe, Chaz, Modesto	7	11	4.33	29	29	2	0	170	148	93	82	73	131

ALL-STAR TEAM

C: Adam Moore, High Desert; 1B: Aaron Bates, Lancaster; 2B: Eric Young, Modesto; 3B: Chris Davis, Bakersfield/David Freese, Lake Elsinore; SS: Chris Nelson, Modesto; OF: Bubba Bell, Lancaster; Zach Daeges, Lancaster; Michael Saunders, High Desert; DH: Kyle Blanks, Lake Elsinore. Utility: Jesus Guzman, High Desert. SP: Manny Ayala, Lake Elsinore; Matt Buschmann, Lake Elsinore; Brandon Hynick, Modesto. RP: Taylor Wilding, San Jose. Most Valuable Player: Bubba Bell, Lancaster. Pitcher of the Year: Brandon Hynick, Modesto. Rookie of the Year: Bubba Bell, Lancaster. Manager of the Year: Chad Epperson, Lancaster.

DEPARTMENT LEADERS

BATTING

OBP	Bates, Aaron, Lancaster	.456
SLG	Bell, Bubba, Lancaster	.665
R	Daeges, Zach, Lancaster	124
H	Daeges, Zach, Lancaster	170
TB	Daeges, Zach, Lancaster	298
XBH	Daeges, Zach, Lancaster	81
2B	Daeges, Zach, Lancaster	55
3B	Young Jr., Eric, Modesto	11
HR	Everidge, Tommy, Stockton	26
RBI	Daeges, Zachary, Lancaster	113
SAC	Young Jr., Eric, Modesto	12
SF	Contreras, Anthony, San Jose	10
BB	Daeges, Zachary, Lancaster	82
IBB	Limonta, Johan, High Desert	7
HBP	Bates, Aaron, Lancaster	19
	Hankerd, Cyle, Visalia	19
SO	Renz, Jordan, Rancho Cucamonga	144
SB	Young Jr., Eric, Modesto	73
CS	Young Jr., Eric, Modesto	18
GIDP	De Jesus, Ivan, Inland Empire	20
AB/SO	Bell, Bubba, Lancaster	8.26

PITCHING

G	Giles, Josh, Bakersfield	56
GS	Roe, Chaz, Modesto	29
CG	Hynick, Brandon, Modesto	3
	Butcher, Brok, Rancho Cucamonga	3
SHO	Seven players tied at	1
GF	Rhoades, Chad, Lancaster	40
SV	Rhoades, Chad, Lancaster	16
	Stange, Daniel, Visalia	16
W	Hynick, Brandon, Modesto	16
L	Walker, Andrew, Bakersfield	13
	Cupps, Anthony, Visalia	13
IP	Hynick, Brandon, Modesto	182.1
H	Walker, Andrew, Bakersfield	196
R	Torra, Matthew, Visalia	115
ER	Torra, Matthew, Visalia	106
HB	Bello, Cibney, High Desert	16
BB	Guerra, Javy, Inland Empire	80
SO	Martinez, Joseph, San Jose	151
SO/9-S	Tillman, Chris, High Desert	9.2
SO/9-R	Romo, Sergio, San Jose	14.38
WP	Pratt, Jordan, Inland Empire	24
BK	Rozier, Michael, Lancaster	6
AVG	Roe, Chaz, Modesto	.235

FIELDING

C	PCT	May, Lucas, Inland Empire	.994
	PO	Moore, Adam, High Desert	683
	A	Lobaton, Jose, Lake Elsinore	72
	E	Lobaton, Jose, Lake Elsinore	13
		Witter, Adam, San Jose	13
	DP	Sandoval, Pablo, San Jose	7
	PB	May, Lucas, Inland Empire	31
	CS%	Wagner, Mark, Lancaster	.35
1B	PCT	Mitchell, Russell, Inland Empire	.992
	PO	Kindel, Jeff, Modesto	1046
	A	Byrne, Bryan, Visalia	91
	E	Kindel, Jeff, Modesto	18
	DP	Kindel, Jeff, Modesto	107
2B	PCT	Sutton, Nate, Rancho Cucamonga	.982
	PO	Sutton, Nate, Rancho Cucamonga	279
	A	Sutton, Nate, Rancho Cucamonga	392
	E	Young Jr., Eric, Modesto	25
	DP	Sutton, Nate, Rancho Cucamonga	94
3B	PCT	Freese, David, Lake Elsinore	.958
	PO	Maroul, David, San Jose	79
	A	Freese, David, Lake Elsinore	238
	E	Flaig, Jeffrey, High Desert	28
	DP	Davis, Chris, Bakersfield	21
SS	PCT	Statia, Hainley, Rancho Cucamonga	.965
	PO	Nelson, Christopher, Modesto	201
	A	Statia, Hainley, Rancho Cucamonga	442
	E	Ciriaco, Pedro, Visalia	32
	DP	Statia, Hainley, Rancho Cucamonga	86
OF	PCT	Becktel, Travis, Modesto	1
	PO	Thomson, Gregory, Visalia	246
	A	Hoffmann, Jamie, Inland Empire	17
		Mooney, Michael, San Jose	17
	E	Pineda, Jose, Stockton	10
	DP	Mehl, Truan, Bakersfield	5

MINOR LEAGUES

BY CHRIS KLINE

The Frederick Keys went from a sub-.500 club during the regular season to the hottest team in the Carolina League in the postseason, losing just once to claim their second Mills Cup championship in three seasons.

Frederick went 32-37 in the first half of the season but still won the Northern Division, as the league's powerhouse teams were concentrated in the South. The Keys finished with an identical record in the second half but finished third this time, as Wilmington and Potomac both bounced back with winning records.

But Frederick got it all together when it mattered most. Righthanders Chorye Spoone and Brad Bergesen were dominant on the mound for the Keys in the playoffs, going a combined 3-0, and the club got production out of a well-balanced offensive attack under first-year skipper Tommy Thompson.

"There might have been clubs with better overall talent than what we had, but our players gave it everything they had every night," Thompson said. "They played with a lot of heart."

Third baseman Ryan Finan, center fielder Kenard Jones, catcher Zach Dillon, first baseman Mark Fleisher and right fielder Brent Krause all ranked among the top hitters in the CL playoffs, with Finan driving in seven runs and slugging .818 in the postseason.

But it was Spoone who brought home the playoff MVP award. A 2005 eighth-round pick, Spoone went 2-0, 1.00 with a 17-1 strikeout-walk ratio in 18 innings in the playoffs for Frederick.

The CL title was just Frederick's third championship in its 26-year history, as the Keys swept past Wilmington in the divisional playoffs then beat Salem 3-1 in the five-game championship series.

Kinston, seeking to become the first club to win back-to-back CL titles since Myrtle Beach in 1999-2000, claimed the best regular season record at 87-52, but was swept in the first round of the Southern Division series against Salem.

Salem was nearly as dominant during the regular season, finishing with an overall record of 79-60, while Frederick sat 10 games under the .500 mark at 64-74. But it was the Keys who performed better in the finals.

The league MVP award went to Salem outfielder Mitch Einertson, who was also named the MVP in the Rookie-level Appalachian League in 2004, but had struggled for two years in low Class A.

The prospect who made the biggest strides in 2007 was Myrtle Beach center fielder Jordan Schafer, who ranked No. 1 in the league's Top 20 Prospects list. Schafer

began the year at low Class A Rome, and wound up finishing the season leading the minors in hits.

The Carolina-California League all-star game shifted to the West Coast in 2007, and the California League cruised to a 10-5 win at Stockton's Banner Island Ballpark. The 2008 game will be back in the Carolina League, hosted at Myrtle Beach's Coastal Federal Field.

After changing affiliates from the Royals to the Red Sox for the 2005 season, Wilmington got back together with Kansas City for 2007. The team has been successful on the field no matter who its affiliate has been, as the Blue Rocks made the postseason for the 12th time since they entered the league in 1993.

TOP 20 PROSPECTS

RODGER WOOD

1. Jordan Schafer, of, Myrtle Beach Pelicans (Braves)
2. Chris Marrero, of, Potomac Nationals
3. Elvis Andrus, ss, Myrtle Beach Pelicans (Braves)
4. Max Ramirez, c, Kinston Indians
5. Wes Hodges, 3b, Kinston Indians
6. Chorye Spoone, rhp, Frederick Keys (Orioles)
7. Brandon Erbe, rhp, Frederick Keys (Orioles)
8. Tommy Hanson, rhp, Myrtle Beach Pelicans (Braves)
9. Adam Carr, rhp, Potomac Nationals
10. Matt Whitney, 1b, Kinston Indians
11. Mitch Einertson, of, Salem Avalanche (Astros)
12. Daniel Cortes, rhp, Wilmington Blue Rocks (Royals)
13. Josh Rodriguez, ss, Kinston Indians
14. Sergio Perez, rhp, Salem Avalanche (Astros)
15. Brad James, rhp, Salem Avalanche (Astros)
16. Brad Bergesen, rhp, Frederick Keys (Orioles)
17. Shelby Ford, 2b, Lynchburg Hillcats (Pirates)
18. Jairo Cuevas, rhp, Myrtle Beach Pelicans (Braves)
19. Julio Pimentel, rhp, Wilmington Blue Rockies (Royals)
20. Kyle McCulloch, rhp, Winston-Salem Warthogs (White Sox)

STANDINGS: SPLIT SEASON

FIRST HALF

NORTH	W	L	PCT	GB
Frederick	32	37	.464	—
Wilmington	30	38	.441	1½
Lynchburg	29	38	.433	2
Potomac	29	39	.426	2½

SOUTH	W	L	PCT	GB
Kinston	45	24	.652	—
Salem	41	28	.594	4
Winston-Salem	38	31	.551	7
Myrtle Beach	30	39	.435	15

SECOND HALF

NORTH	W	L	PCT	GB
Wilmington	45	24	.652	—
Potomac	40	29	.580	5
Frederick	32	37	.464	13
Lynchburg	26	44	.371	19½

SOUTH	W	L	PCT	GB
Kinston	42	28	.600	—
Salem	38	32	.543	4
Myrtle Beach	29	41	.414	13
Winston-Salem	26	43	.377	15½

PLAYOFFS—Semifinals: Salem defeated Kinston 2-1 and Frederick defeated Wilmington 2-0 in best-of-three series. **Finals:** Frederick defeated Salem 3-1 in a best-of-five series.

STANDINGS

Page	Team	W	L	PCT	GB	Manager	Attendance	Average	Last Penn.
107	Kinston Indians (Indians)	87	52	.626	—	Mike Sarbaugh	115,195	1,745	2006
141	Salem Avalanche (Astros)	79	60	.568	8	Jim Pankovits	258,469	3,916	2001
150	Wilmington Blue Rocks (Royals)	75	62	.547	11	John Mizerock	306,430	4,574	1999
307	Potomac Nationals (Nationals)	69	68	.504	17	Randy Knorr	165,000	2,463	1989
65	Frederick Keys (Orioles)	64	74	.464	22½	Tommy Thompson	283,065	4,423	2007
90	Winston-Salem Warthogs (White Sox)	64	74	.464	22½	Tim Blackwell	161,180	2,442	2003
56	Myrtle Beach Pelicans (Braves)	59	80	.424	28	Rocket Wheeler	215,059	3,117	2000
234	Lynchburg Hillcats (Pirates)	55	82	.401	31	Jeff Branson	164,413	2,529	2002

NOTE: Teams' individual batting and pitching statistics can be found on pagdice inated in lefthand column.

CLUB BATTING

	AVG	G	AB	R	H	2B	3B	HR	RBI	BB	SO	SB	CS	OBP	SLG
Kinston	.271	139	4657	782	1262	264	25	152	713	605	947	104	38	.362	.436
Potomac	.271	137	4602	682	1245	275	29	124	629	546	1054	147	88	.354	.424
Salem	.271	139	4690	716	1271	272	40	73	641	413	871	166	54	.340	.393
Wilmington	.262	137	4600	602	1207	244	30	61	535	461	935	141	64	.336	.368
Winston-Salem	.262	138	4569	607	1195	247	32	108	540	391	945	170	80	.324	.401
Lynchburg	.258	137	4567	626	1178	271	34	89	579	420	899	130	51	.329	.391
Myrtle Beach	.255	139	4616	583	1178	214	35	82	538	449	970	144	79	.326	.370
Frederick	.249	138	4556	582	1133	255	21	80	530	519	847	110	83	.330	.367

CLUB PITCHING

	ERA	G	CG	SHO	SV	IP	H	R	ER	HR	BB	SO	AVG
Wilmington	3.43	137	5	10	42	1217	1127	517	464	90	356	823	.249
Kinston	3.56	139	3	9	41	1213	1194	569	476	89	390	907	.256
Salem	3.80	139	2	8	41	1220	1215	584	515	96	393	944	.262
Winston-Salem	3.93	138	3	4	33	1192	1158	647	517	83	510	996	.255
Potomac	4.21	137	3	10	31	1192	1202	649	558	90	536	958	.265
Myrtle Beach	4.47	139	1	6	37	1215	1212	728	599	106	652	1005	.261
Frederick	4.77	138	6	7	31	1215	1244	736	644	114	484	1028	.266
Lynchburg	5.03	137	5	9	35	1180	1317	750	657	101	483	807	.284

CLUB FIELDING

	PCT	PO	A	E	DP		PCT	PO	A	E	DP
Wilmington	.980	3652	1557	108	119	Lynchburg	.972	3539	1514	143	123
Kinston	.975	3638	1430	131	99	Myrtle Beach	.971	3646	1395	148	116
Salem	.974	3661	1475	137	119	Frederick	.969	3645	1509	165	129
Potomac	.973	3576	1506	141	134	Winston-Salem	.966	3577	1611	181	139

INDIVIDUAL BATTING LEADERS (Minimum 434 Plate Appearances)

	AVG	G	AB	R	H	2B	3B	HR	RBI	BB	SO	SB
Hart, Billy, Salem	.305	114	370	64	113	30	6	4	44	42	81	23
Einertson, Mitch, Salem	.305	122	446	68	136	40	3	11	87	35	75	5
Rogelstad, Matt, Potomac	.302	113	404	52	122	27	3	4	50	35	50	9
Schafer, Jordan, Myrtle Beach	.294	106	436	70	128	34	8	10	43	40	95	19
Davis, Blake, Frederick	.291	93	357	49	104	24	3	4	28	35	71	11
Alvarez, Roberto, Myrtle Beach	.291	101	385	49	112	20	3	6	50	24	80	6
Duarte, Jose, Wilmington	.290	128	493	82	143	26	5	1	42	48	77	34
Castillo, Javier, Winston-Salem	.288	116	403	41	116	28	2	9	62	35	82	9
Hodges, Wes, Kinston	.288	104	393	60	113	22	3	15	71	44	90	0
McFall, Brian, Wilmington	.286	111	406	59	116	31	5	13	72	40	98	10

INDIVIDUAL PITCHING LEADERS (Minimum 112 Innings)

	W	L	ERA	G	GS	CG	SV	IP	H	R	ER	BB	SO
Deters, James, Kinston	12	4	2.24	33	10	0	1	112	101	36	28	21	66
Hardy, Rowdy, Wilmington	15	5	2.48	26	22	3	1	167	144	52	46	16	91
Pimentel, Julio Cesar, Wilmington	12	4	2.65	27	22	0	0	153	145	56	45	43	73
Cortes, Daniel, Wilmington	8	8	3.07	24	24	0	0	123	102	50	42	45	120
Spoone, Chorye, Frederick	10	9	3.26	26	25	3	0	152	108	65	55	67	133
Johnson, Blake, Wilmington	9	6	3.28	26	22	1	1	132	119	52	48	33	80
Cuevas, Jairo, Myrtle Beach	6	12	3.55	25	25	0	0	132	113	74	52	71	116
Richard, Clayton, Winston-Salem	8	12	3.63	28	27	1	0	161	159	86	65	59	99
McCulloch, Kyle, Winston-Salem	7	7	3.64	22	22	0	0	121	116	62	49	42	88
Rodriguez, Derek, Winston-Salem	14	5	3.69	28	28	1	0	161	164	80	66	55	124

ALL-STAR TEAM

C: Max Ramirez, Kinston. **1B:** Micah Schnurstein, Winston-Salem. **2B:** Shelby Ford, Lynchburg. **3B:** Wes Hodges, Kinston. **SS:** Josh Rodriguez, Kinston. **OF:** Brad Corley, Lynchburg; Jose Duarte, Wilmington; Mitch Einertson, Salem; Jordan Schafer, Myrtle Beach. **DH:** Kala Kaaihue, Myrtle Beach. **Utility:** Ryan Finan, Frederick; Mario Lisson, Wilmington. **SP:** Rowdy Hardy, Wilmington. **RP:** Scott Roehl, Kinston. **Most Valuable Player:** Mitch Einertson, Salem. **Most Valuable Pitcher:** Rowdy Hardy, Wilmington. **Manager of the Year:** Mike Sarbaugh, Kinston.

DEPARTMENT LEADERS

BATTING

OBP	Kaaihue, Kala, Myrtle Beach	.41
SLG	Kaaihue, Kala, Myrtle Beach	.583
R	Rodriguez, Joshua, Kinston	84
H	Duarte, Jose, Wilmington	143
TB	Schnurstein, Micah, Winston-Salem	258
XBH	Schnurstein, Micah, Winston-Salem	65
2B	Einertson, Mitch, Salem	40
3B	Davis, Quentin, Myrtle Beach	11
HR	Schnurstein, Micah, Winston-Salem	25
RBI	Corley, Brad, Lynchburg	89
SAC	Davis, Quentin, Myrtle Beach	18
SF	Lisson, Mario, Wilmington	8
	Cunningham, Aaron, Winston-Salem	8
BB	Bigler, Brett, Wilmington	74
IBB	Schnurstein, Micah, Winston-Salem	6
HBP	Head, Jerad, Kinston	17
	Sutil, Wladimir, Salem	17
SO	Vega, Miguel, Wilmington	137
SB	Powell, Pedro, Lynchburg	67
CS	Davis, Quentin, Myrtle Beach	21
GIDP	Lisson, Mario, Wilmington	16
AB/SO	Tucker, Jonathan, Frederick	9.91

PITCHING

G	Blazek, Christopher, Salem	50
GS	Rodriguez, Derek, Winston-Salem	28
CG	Three players tied at	3
SHO	Six players tied at	1
GF	Roehl, Scott, Kinston	38
SV	Roehl, Scott, Kinston	24
W	Hardy, Rowdy, Wilmington	15
L	Four players tied at	12
IP	Hardy, Rowdy, Wilmington	167
H	Rodriguez, Derek, Winston-Salem	164
R	Erbe, Brandon, Frederick	95
ER	Salamida, Christopher, Salem	85
HB	Shortell, Rory, Salem	15
	Hardy, Rowdy, Wilmington	15
BB	Cuevas, Jairo, Myrtle Beach	71
SO	Hernandez, David, Frederick	168
SO/9-S	Hernandez, David, Frederick	10.48
SO/9-R	Payano, Nelson, Myrtle Beach	12.1
WP	Stammen, Craig, Potomac	16
BK	Cuevas, Jairo, Myrtle Beach	3
AVG	Spoone, Chorye, Frederick	.2

FIELDING

C	PCT	Lopez, Jose, Salem	.995
	PO	Camarena, Jose, Myrtle Beach	544
	A	Thibault, Kiel, Wilmington	89
	E	Lerud, Steven, Lynchburg	11
		Armstrong, Cole, Winston-Salem	11
	DP	Thibault, Kiel, Wilmington	12
	PB	Lerud, Steven, Lynchburg	25
	CS%	Lerud, Steven, Lynchburg	.4
1B	PCT	Schnurstein, Micah, Winston-Salem	.986
	PO	Schnurstein, Micah, Winston-Salem	1148
	A	Schnurstein, Micah, Winston-Salem	92
	E	Schnurstein, Micah, Winston-Salem	17
	DP	Schnurstein, Micah, Winston-Salem	111
2B	PCT	—	—
	PO	Ford, Shelby, Lynchburg	187
	A	Ford, Shelby, Lynchburg	253
	E	Johnson, Brandon, Winston-Salem	12
	DP	Ford, Shelby, Lynchburg	52
3B	PCT	Lisson, Mario, Wilmington	.958
	PO	Lisson, Mario, Wilmington	92
	A	Lisson, Mario, Wilmington	230
	E	Castillo, Javier, Winston-Salem	29
	DP	Lisson, Mario, Wilmington	28
SS	PCT	Andrus, Elvis, Myrtle Beach	.949
		Desmond, Ian, Potomac	.949
	PO	Desmond, Ian, Potomac	194
	A	Desmond, Ian, Potomac	399
	E	Rodriguez, Joshua, Kinston	32
		Desmond, Ian, Potomac	32
	DP	Desmond, Ian, Potomac	80
OF	PCT	Duarte, Jose, Wilmington	.997
	PO	Duarte, Jose, Wilmington	323
	A	Three players tied at	14
	E	Romak, Jamie, Lynchburg	7
		McFall, Brian, Wilmington	7
	DP	Einertson, Mitch, Salem	5
		Rosales, Orlando, Salem	5

MINOR LEAGUES

BY J.J. COOPER

Brad Harman seems to perform best in pressure situations.

The Australian second baseman first got noticed by showing a better than expected bat as one of the younger players involved in the World Baseball Classic. After a solid but unspectacular 2007 season with Clearwater, Harman took over come playoff time.

Harman homered, doubles and singled with two runs scored and two RBIs as Clearwater beat Brevard County 5-2 in the deciding game of the Florida State League championship series. He also drove in the winning run as part of a 3-for-6 night in Clearwater's 6-4 win in Game Two of the best of five series.

The title was Clearwater's first since 1993 and their first since being renamed the Threshers. Clearwater got plenty of pitching help to compliment Harman--Will Savage threw four scoreless innings of relief to win Game Two while Andrew Carpenter allowed two runs in 6⅓ innings to win the clincher.

Thanks to its warm weather and close location to teams' spring training complexes, the Florida State League is always home to a number of baseball's best prospects. But even by Florida State League standards the league was overflowing with talent for prospect watchers to dream about thanks to outfielders Jay Bruce and Cameron Maybin.

Both were quickly promoted to higher levels with Bruce finishing the season in Triple-A while Maybin made it to Detroit, but both left lasting impressions among the rest of the Florida State League before leaving. Bruce's .325/.379/.586 stint with Sarasota outshone Maybin's .304/.393/.486 numbers with Lakeland, but both were clearly the class of the league.

Bruce and Maybin each went 2-for-3 with a double in the Florida State League all-star game, but their West team fell to the West 8-4. Palm Beach's Allen Craig, Vero Beach's Rhyne Hughes and Brevard County's Cole Gillespie all homered for the East. Craig was named the game's MVP with a 2-for-4, 2 RBI night.

While Bruce and Maybin may have been the league's top stars, the Tampa Yankees and Vero Beach Devil Rays each had rotations worthy of envy. Before he helped solidify the Yankees big league bullpen, Joba Chamberlain (4-0, 2.03) combined with Ian Kennedy (6-1, 1.29) to baffle FSL hitters. Vero Beach's pairing of Wade Davis (3-0, 1.84) and Jacob McGee (5-4, 2.93) was nearly as impressive.

Dunedin's Josh Kreuzer finished second in the league in home runs with 20 to earn league MVP honors. Tampa closer Eric Wordekemper was named the league's pitcher of the year as he went 2-0, 0.57 with 33 saves in 43 appearances.

TOP 20 PROSPECTS

1. Jay Bruce, of, Sarasota Reds
2. **Cameron Maybin, of, Lakeland Flying Tigers (Tigers)**
3. Jake McGee, lhp, Vero Beach Devil Rays
4. Wade Davis, rhp, Vero Beach Devil Rays
5. Johnny Cueto, rhp, Sarasota Reds
6. Carlos Carrasco, rhp, Clearwater Threshers (Phillies)
7. Ian Kennedy, rhp, Tampa Yankees
8. Deolis Guerra, rhp, St. Lucie (Mets)
9. Jose Tabata, of, Tampa Yankees
10. Austin Jackson, of, Tampa Yankees
11. Chris Volstad, rhp, Jupiter Hammerheads (Marlins)
12. Alcides Escobar, ss, Brevard County Manatees (Brewers)
13. Tyler Colvin, of, Daytona Cubs
14. Josh Outman, lhp, Clearwater Threshers (Phillies)
15. Adam Ottavino, rhp, Palm Beach Cardinals
16. Brett Sinkbeil, rhp, Jupiter Hammerheads (Marlins)
17. Frank Cervelli, c, Tampa Yankees
18. Eduardo Morlan, rhp, Fort Myers Miracle (Twins)
19. Jeff Samardzija, rhp, Daytona Cubs
20. Rhyne Hughes, 1b, Vero Beach Devil Rays

STANDINGS: SPLIT SEASON

FIRST HALF

NORTH	W	L	PCT	GB
Brevard Cty.	41	28	.594	—
Palm Beach	36	34	.514	5½
Vero Beach	34	35	.493	7
Daytona	32	37	.464	9
Jupiter	31	39	.443	10½
St. Lucie	31	39	.571	10½

WEST	W	L	PCT	GB
Sarasota	43	27	.614	—
Tampa	41	28	.594	1½
Clearwater	39	31	.557	4
Dunedin	31	39	.443	12
Fort Myers	30	40	.429	13
Lakeland	29	41	.414	14

SECOND HALF

EAST	W	L	PCT	GB
St. Lucie	37	32	.536	—
Palm Beach	35	35	.500	2½
Brevard Cty.	33	34	.493	3
Jupiter	32	39	.464	5
Daytona	25	43	.368	11½
Vero Beach	25	44	.362	12

WEST	W	L	PCT	GB
Clearwater	44	26	.629	—
Tampa	42	28	.600	2
Dunedin	41	29	.586	3
Fort Myers	40	30	.571	4
Sarasota	38	32	.543	6
Lakeland	24	46	.343	20

PLAYOFFS—Semifinals: Brevard County defeated St. Lucie 2-1 and Clearwater defeated Sarasota 2-1 in best-of-three series. **Finals:** Clearwater defeated Brevard County 3-1 in a best-of-five series.

STANDINGS

Page	Team	W	L	PCT	GB	Manager	Attendance	Average	Last Penn.
203	Tampa Yankees (Yankees)	83	56	.597	—	Luis Sojo	123,829	1,848	2004
224	Clearwater Threshers (Phillies)	83	57	.593	0½	Dave Huppert	166,359	2,483	2007
99	Sarasota Reds (Reds)	81	59	.579	2½	Pat Kelly/Joe Ayrault	38,313	599	1963
175	Brevard County Manatees (Brewers)	74	62	.544	7½	John Tamargo	83,954	1,333	2001
298	Dunedin Blue Jays (Blue Jays)	72	68	.514	11½	Omar Malave	48,326	721	None
244	Palm Beach Cardinals (Cardinals)	71	69	.507	12½	Gaylen Pitts	77,805	1,179	2005
182	Fort Myers Miracle (Twins)	70	70	.500	13½	Kevin Boles	115,647	1,807	1985
192	St. Lucie Mets (Mets)	68	71	.489	15	Frank Cacciatore	100,646	1,548	2006
133	Jupiter Hammerheads (Marlins)	63	76	.453	20	Luis Dorante	82,386	1,248	1991
281	Vero Beach Devil Rays (Devil Rays)	59	79	.428	23½	Joe Szekely	46,989	770	1990
82	Daytona Cubs (Cubs)	57	80	.416	25	Jody Davis	146,195	2,284	2004
123	Lakeland Flying Tigers (Tigers)	53	87	.379	30½	Kevin Bradshaw	48,326	785	1992

NOTE: Teams' individual batting and pitching statistics can be found on page indicated in lefthand column.

CLUB BATTING

	AVG	G	AB	R	H	2B	3B	HR	RBI	BB	SO	SB	CS	OBP	SLG
St. Lucie	.273	139	4594	618	1254	232	35	75	566	454	844	117	68	.341	.388
Dunedin	.272	140	4631	698	1258	280	18	121	640	536	907	44	30	.355	.418
Sarasota	.270	140	4711	679	1272	259	38	102	616	420	957	80	48	.335	.406
Tampa	.270	139	4710	625	1272	241	43	73	567	409	940	144	63	.336	.386
Clearwater	.267	140	4649	683	1240	256	32	104	639	490	1009	84	41	.340	.403
Brevard County	.266	136	4496	618	1197	213	28	71	565	386	908	146	60	.330	.373
Palm Beach	.265	140	4662	616	1235	234	33	82	568	388	827	122	48	.325	.382
Daytona	.254	137	4510	596	1144	214	39	89	550	360	950	105	56	.316	.378
Vero Beach	.253	138	4434	601	1120	203	26	105	541	378	876	59	45	.318	.381
Jupiter	.252	139	4562	614	1148	217	32	84	549	467	969	123	57	.325	.368
Lakeland	.252	140	4529	563	1140	189	37	84	500	439	1079	200	54	.320	.365
Fort Myers	.241	140	4575	564	1104	185	33	76	495	451	983	86	37	.316	.346

CLUB PITCHING

	ERA	G	CG	SHO	SV	IP	H	R	ER	HR	BB	SO	AVG
Tampa	3.23	139	3	12	45	1233	1133	507	442	91	422	1061	.244
Fort Myers	3.29	140	2	8	38	1209	1167	548	442	59	410	1030	.251
Brevard County	3.67	136	5	6	39	1166	1100	589	474	85	423	936	.246
Clearwater	3.81	140	6	12	39	1202	1132	578	509	97	447	998	.250
Sarasota	3.81	140	3	10	48	1215	1156	603	514	76	486	1121	.251
Palm Beach	3.95	140	3	13	36	1201	1151	616	526	82	456	934	.252
Jupiter	3.97	139	6	12	32	1195	1262	647	526	67	408	865	.270
Dunedin	4.06	140	4	6	37	1192	1249	623	534	101	400	827	.269
St. Lucie	4.17	139	2	9	33	1188	1268	656	548	95	331	846	.273
Vero Beach	4.35	138	8	10	27	1154	1166	659	557	106	502	1051	.263
Daytona	4.53	137	6	6	32	1166	1279	696	583	125	428	800	.280
Lakeland	4.75	140	4	5	30	1176	1321	753	613	82	465	780	.284

CLUB FIELDING

	PCT	PO	A	E	DP		PCT	PO	A	E	DP
Tampa	.976	3699	1416	125	153	St. Lucie	.970	3564	1568	158	144
Clearwater	.974	3605	1345	131	134	Daytona	.969	3499	1381	157	107
Dunedin	.974	3575	1594	138	134	Fort Myers	.969	3626	1390	162	129
Sarasota	.974	3645	1281	133	118	Jupiter	.967	3586	1596	177	122
Vero Beach	.971	3462	1253	141	120	Brevard County	.965	3499	1413	180	102
Palm Beach	.970	3602	1379	154	130	Lakeland	.964	3527	1501	186	164

INDIVIDUAL BATTING LEADERS (Minimum 434 Plate Appearances)

	AVG	G	AB	R	H	2B	3B	HR	RBI	BB	SO	SB
Nielsen, Eric, Dunedin	.325	117	453	75	147	41	0	7	67	33	52	4
Craig, Allen, Palm Beach	.312	112	423	77	132	25	2	21	77	35	79	8
Kreuzer, Josh, Dunedin	.309	117	404	92	125	34	0	20	71	62	82	1
Tabata, Jose, Tampa	.307	103	411	56	126	16	2	5	54	33	70	15
Phillips, Kyle, Dunedin	.306	104	389	44	119	19	0	10	62	35	51	0
Rhymes, William, Lakeland	.304	88	326	43	99	12	2	4	45	34	38	24
Griffin, Michael, Sarasota	.303	90	386	65	117	24	2	7	45	21	47	12
Gamel, Mat, Brevard County	.300	128	466	78	140	37	8	9	60	58	98	14
Henry, Sean, St. Lucie	.293	114	450	59	132	26	7	11	57	42	73	18
Jenkins, Andrew, Jupiter	.289	112	425	51	123	20	3	4	54	24	74	1

INDIVIDUAL PITCHING LEADERS (Minimum 112 Innings)

	W	L	ERA	G	GS	CG	SV	IP	H	R	ER	BB	SO
Outman, Josh, Clearwater	10	4	2.45	20	18	0	0	117	104	35	32	54	117
McGee, Jacob, Vero Beach	5	4	2.93	21	21	0	0	117	86	45	38	39	145
Ottavino, Adam, Palm Beach	12	8	3.08	27	27	1	0	143	130	63	49	63	128
Badenhop, Burke, Lakeland	10	6	3.13	23	23	1	0	135	130	61	47	34	78
Atkins, Mitch, Daytona	8	7	3.13	20	20	1	0	115	99	51	40	31	88
Carpenter, Andrew, Clearwater	17	6	3.20	27	24	3	1	163	150	65	58	53	116
Rainville, Jay, Fort Myers	9	11	3.29	27	26	0	0	142	145	67	52	31	110
Thompson, Aaron, Jupiter	4	6	3.37	20	19	0	0	115	121	64	43	35	84
Welch, David, Brevard County	6	7	3.43	29	20	1	0	121	111	55	46	21	87
Norrick, Tyler, Palm Beach	11	9	3.59	28	28	2	0	165	134	69	66	73	134

ALL-STAR TEAM

C: Lou Marson, Clearwater/Francisco Cervelli, Tampa. **1B:** Josh Kreuzer, Dunedin. **2B:** Will Rhymes, Lakeland. **3B:** Allen Craig, Palm Beach/Mat Gamel, Brevard County. **SS:** Jose Castro, St. Lucie. **OF:** Jacob Butler, Dunedin; Erik Lis, Fort Myers; Cameron Maybin, Lakeland; Jose Tabata, Tampa. **DH:** Sergio Pedroza, Vero Beach. **P:** Luke Gregerson, Palm Beach; Daniel McCutchen, Tampa; Jacob McGee, Vero Beach; Adam Ottavino, Palm Beach; Josh Outman, Clearwater; Eric Wordekemper, Tampa (Cardinals). **Most Valuable Player:** Josh Kreuzer, Dunedin. **Pitcher of the Year:** Eric Wordekemper, Tampa. **Manager of the Year:** John Tamargo, Brevard County.

DEPARTMENT LEADERS

BATTING

SLG	Kreuzer, Josh, Dunedin	.542
R	Kreuzer, Josh, Dunedin	92
H	Nielsen, Eric, Dunedin	147
TB	Lis, Erik, Fort Myers	231
XBH	Lis, Erik, Fort Myers	56
2B	Nielsen, Eric, Dunedin	41
3B	Yarbrough, Brandon, Palm Beach	11
HR	Butler, Jacob, Dunedin	23
RBI	Lis, Erik, Fort Myers	97
SAC	Spears, Nate, Daytona	15
	Septimo, Agustin, Jupiter	15
SF	Murphy, Dan, St. Lucie	11
BB	Jeroloman, Brian, Dunedin	85
IBB	Gamel, Mat, Brevard County	9
HBP	Kreuzer, Josh, Dunedin	25
SO	Szymanski, Brandon, Sarasota	153
SB	Suero, Ovandy, Lakeland	75
CS	Suero, Ovandy, Lakeland	21
GIDP	Ovalle, Edward, Fort Myers	19
	Concepcion, Ambiorix, St. Lucie	19
AB/SO	Nielsen, Eric, Dunedin	8.71

PITCHING

G	Lutz, Derrik, Sarasota	54
GS	Norrick, Tyler, Palm Beach	28
CG	Carpenter, Andrew, Clearwater	3
	Wlodarczyk, Michael, Vero Beach	3
SHO	Carpenter, Andrew, Clearwater	2
GF	Doolittle, Todd, Jupiter	47
SV	Wordekemper, Eric, Tampa	33
W	Carpenter, Andrew, Clearwater	17
L	Ward, Zachary, Fort Myers	17
IP	Norrick, Tyler, Palm Beach	165.1
H	Hearne, Trey, Palm Beach	181
R	Hearne, Trey, Palm Beach	103
ER	Hearne, Trey, Palm Beach	91
HB	Ward, Zachary, Fort Myers	14
BB	Walker, Matthew, Vero Beach	82
SO	McGee, Jacob, Vero Beach	145
SO/9-S	McGee, Jacob, Vero Beach	11.19
SO/9-R	Morlan, Eduardo, Fort Myers	12.61
WP	Degerman, Eddie, Palm Beach	16
BK	Thompson, Daryl, Sarasota	3
	De La Cruz, Eddie, Vero Beach	3
AVG	McGee, Jacob, Vero Beach	.203

FIELDING

C	PCT	Cervelli, Francisco, Tampa	.997
	PO	Marson, Lou, Clearwater	748
	A	Lopez, Christian, Vero Beach	113
	E	Lopez, Christian, Vero Beach	16
	DP	Lopez, Christian, Vero Beach	18
	PB	Cervelli, Francisco, Tampa	15
	CS%	Cervelli, Francisco, Tampa	.41
1B	PCT	Evans, Nick, St. Lucie	.992
	PO	Kreuzer, Josh, Dunedin	972
	A	Errecart, Chris, Brevard County	68
		Evans, Nick, St. Lucie	68
	E	Roberson, Ryan, Lakeland	14
	DP	Roberson, Ryan, Lakeland	107
2B	PCT	Cota, Carlo, Dunedin	.98
		Vick, Hunter, Vero Beach	.98
	PO	Bell, Mike, Brevard County	241
	A	Cota, Carlo, Dunedin	376
	E	Bell, Mike, Brevard County	18
	DP	Harman, Brad, Clearwater	87
3B	PCT	Hatch, Anthony, Dunedin	.953
	PO	Murphy, Dan, St. Lucie	85
	A	Murphy, Dan, St. Lucie	304
	E	Gamel, Mat, Brevard County	53
	DP	Murphy, Dan, St. Lucie	34
		Cottrell, Patrick, Vero Beach	34
SS	PCT	Corona, Reegie, Tampa	.942
	PO	Septimo, Agustin, Jupiter	176
	A	Septimo, Agustin, Jupiter	329
	E	Septimo, Agustin, Jupiter	34
	DP	Corona, Reegie, Tampa	77
OF	PCT	Patton, Cory, Dunedin	.996
		Southard, Nathan, Palm Beach	.996
	PO	Cain, Lorenzo, Brevard County	274
	A	Gillespie, Cole, Brevard County	12
		Nielsen, Eric, Dunedin	12
	E	Szymanski, Brandon, Sarasota	13
	DP	Rapoport, James, Palm Beach	6
		Andrus, Erold, Vero Beach	6

MINOR LEAGUES

BY NATHAN RODE

With the coming and going of prospects at all levels, it's difficult for any minor league team to be repeat champions. The West Michigan Whitecaps didn't seem bothered.

After sweeping each of the first two rounds against Lansing and South Bend, the Whitecaps met the Beloit Snappers in the finals for a riveting five-game series.Beloit had also swept through its preliminary series, handling Quad Cities in the first round and Clinton in the second.

West Michigan quickly went up 2-0 in the series before Beloit battled back and forced a decisive Game Five. The Whitecaps capitalized on six Snapper errors to capture the title in an 11-5 win.

Catcher James Skelton and second baseman Scott Sizemore led West Michigan's offense in nine postseason games. Skelton hit .306/.390/.361 in 36 at-bats with four RBIs while Scott Sizemore hit .303/.439/.485 in 33 at-bats and added two home runs. Lefthander Duane Below struck out 17 and went 2-0, 2.63 in 13⅔ innings.

Outfielder Gorkys Hernandez—who was traded by the Tigers to the Braves in the Edgar Renteria deal following the season—received player of the year honors after hitting .293/.344/.391 in 481 at-bats with 54 stolen bases.

Great Lakes lefthander Clayton Kershaw was tabbed the league's prospect of the year and finished at the top of Baseball America's prospect rankings for the league as well. He went 7-5, 2.77 in 97 innings and struck out 134 before being called up to Double-A Jacksonville.

Travis Snider was the youngest player in the league at 19, but his bat seemed to be the most advanced. In 457 at-bats he hit .313/.377/.525 with 16 home runs. His season was highlighted by July 7 when he hit the cycle against Fort Wayne. His 5-for-5 performance helped him break out of a slump in which he was hitting .121/.355/.152 in 33 at-bats.

The Swing of the Quad Cities used an interesting approach with its pitching staff, having tandem starters for a majority of the season. Rather than max out a starter each game, the Swing would throw two starters for 4-5 innings each. The most notable tandem was made up by lefthander Brad Furnish and righthander Tyler Herron. They combined to go 11-8, 3.13 with three saves.

Outfielder Gerardo Parra led the league in hitting with a .320 clip while righthander Sean O'Sullivan held the ERA mark at 2.22. Juan Francisco popped 25 home runs for Dayton to lead the league. Scram (Tigers) walked and

scored on a double by Dayton second baseman Justin Turner (Reds).

TOP 20 PROSPECTS

1. Clayton Kershaw, lhp, Great Lakes (Dodgers)
2. Travis Snider, of, Lansing Lugnuts (Blue Jays)
3. Brett Anderson, lhp, South Bend (Diamondbacks)
4. Gorkys Hernandez, of, West Michigan (Tigers)
5. Hank Conger, c, Cedar Rapids (Angels)
6. Carlos Triunfel, ss, Wisconsin (Mariners)
7. Jose Ceda, rhp, Peoria (Cubs)
8. Gerardo Parra, of, South Bend (Diamondbacks)
9. Josh Bell, 3b, Great Lakes (Dodgers)
10. Drew Stubbs, of, Dayton (Reds)
11. Tyler Herron, rhp, Quad Cities (Cardinals)
12. Omar Poveda, rhp, Clinton (Rangers)
13. Jeff Manship, rhp, Beloit (Twins)
14. John Whittleman, 3b, Clinton (Rangers)
15. Juan Francisco, 3b, Dayton (Reds)
16. Drew Miller, rhp, Fort Wayne (Padres)
17. Kasey Kiker, lhp, Clinton (Rangers)
18. Sean O'Sullivan, rhp, Cedar Rapids (Angels)
19. Trevor Cahill, rhp, Kane County (Athletics)
20. Tyler Robertson, lhp, Beloit (Twins)

PAUL GIERHART

STANDINGS: SPLIT SEASON

FIRST HALF

NORTH	W	L	PCT	GB
Dayton	44	26	.629	—
West Michigan	38	32	.543	6
Lansing	35	34	.507	8½
Great Lakes	34	36	.486	10
South Bend	34	36	.486	10
Fort Wayne	31	38	.449	12½

WEST	W	L	PCT	GB
Beloit	44	26	.629	—
Clinton	41	26	.612	1½
Cedar Rapids	38	31	.551	5½
Quad Cities	38	31	.551	5½
Peoria	31	38	.449	12½
Burlington	30	39	.435	13½
Kane County	24	45	.348	19½
Wisconsin	22	46	.324	21

SECOND HALF

EAST	W	L	PCT	GB
West Michigan	45	25	.643	—
Lansing	43	27	.614	2
South Bend	34	34	.500	10
Dayton	34	36	.486	11
Fort Wayne	24	46	.343	21
Great Lakes	23	46	.333	21½

WEST	W	L	PCT	GB
Cedar Rapids	40	30	.571	—
Quad Cities	40	30	.571	—
Peoria	40	30	.571	—
Kane County	39	31	.557	1
Beloit	35	35	.500	5
Burlington	31	38	.449	8½
Wisconsin	31	39	.443	9
Clinton	29	41	.414	11

PLAYOFFS—Division Series: Clinton defeated Cedar Rapids 2-1, South Bend defeated Dayton 2-1, Beloit defeated Quad Cities 2-0 and West Michigan defeated Lansing 2-0 in best-of-three series. Semifinals: Beloit defeated Clinton 2-0 and West Michigan defeated South Bend 2-0 in best-of-three series. Finals: West Michigan defeated Beloit 3-2 in a best-of-five series.

STANDINGS

Page	Team	W	L	PCT	GB	Manager	Attendance	Average	Last Penn.
124	West Michigan Whitecaps (Tigers)	83	57	.593	—	Tom Brookens	377,412	5,470	2007
183	Beloit Snappers (Twins)	79	61	.564	4	Jeff Smith	82,819	1,255	1995
299	Lansing Lugnuts (Blue Jays)	78	61	.561	4½	Gary Cathcart	341,746	5,178	2003
159	Cedar Rapids Kernels (Angels)	78	61	.561	4½	Ever Magallanes	173,219	2,707	1994
245	Swing of the Quad Cities (Cardinals)	78	61	.561	4½	Keith Mitchell	148,773	2,254	1990
100	Dayton Dragons (Reds)	78	62	.557	5	Donnie Scott	585,348	8,608	None
290	Clinton LumberKings (Rangers)	70	67	.511	11½	Mike Micucci	116,261	1,735	1991
83	Peoria Chiefs (Cubs)	71	68	.511	11½	Ryne Sandberg	259,784	3,820	2002
48	South Bend Silver Hawks (D'backs)	68	70	.493	14	Mark Haley	149,281	2,333	2005
214	Kane County Cougars (Athletics)	63	76	.453	19½	Aaron Nieckula	468,869	7,213	2001
151	Burlington Bees (Royals)	61	77	.442	21	Jim Gabella	66,857	998	1999
168	Great Lakes Loons (Dodgers)	57	82	.410	25½	Lance Parrish	324,564	4,773	2000
256	Fort Wayne Wizards (Padres)	55	84	.396	27½	Doug Dascenzo	237,966	3,606	None
272	Wisconsin Timber Rattlers (Mariners)	53	85	.384	29	Jim Horner	197,511	3,238	1984

NOTE: Teams' individual batting and pitching statistics can be found on page indicated in lefthand column.

CLUB BATTING

	AVG	G	AB	R	H	2B	3B	HR	RBI	BB	SO	SB	CS	OBP	SLG
West Michigan	.268	140	4726	648	1268	243	43	74	590	437	893	181	70	.335	.385
South Bend	.265	138	4597	618	1217	224	35	81	546	501	864	67	51	.344	.382
Dayton	.263	140	4762	669	1254	233	28	106	594	379	1061	122	57	.325	.391
Great Lakes	.261	139	4677	582	1223	229	32	94	528	367	1082	104	64	.320	.384
Lansing	.259	139	4616	718	1194	273	53	104	658	602	1168	77	42	.349	.408
Quad Cities	.256	139	4653	625	1191	211	16	94	553	396	940	95	54	.323	.369
Cedar Rapids	.255	139	4519	611	1154	231	42	112	540	339	1108	196	89	.314	.399
Peoria	.254	139	4597	581	1166	196	23	61	513	364	925	136	69	.313	.346
Fort Wayne	.252	139	4600	557	1158	210	21	83	506	469	1006	79	52	.326	.361
Clinton	.248	137	4558	590	1131	240	30	77	504	426	1036	144	50	.321	.365
Wisconsin	.248	138	4502	546	1117	236	31	71	495	385	1216	145	94	.315	.362
Kane County	.247	139	4579	589	1133	203	16	73	524	522	950	80	42	.329	.347
Burlington	.243	138	4534	511	1104	222	16	76	446	393	1014	157	64	.310	.350
Beloit	.242	140	4547	585	1099	217	29	87	523	395	1075	93	65	.312	.360

CLUB PITCHING

	ERA	G	CG	SHO	SV	IP	H	R	ER	HR	BB	SO	AVG
Cedar Rapids	3.21	139	4	11	38	1189	1196	521	424	69	303	957	.260
Beloit	3.28	140	4	11	53	1214	1160	542	443	81	368	1040	.250
West Michigan	3.31	140	3	7	42	1237	1166	535	455	76	359	1081	.249
Quad Cities	3.32	139	0	11	45	1209	1113	552	446	81	424	1086	.244
Dayton	3.44	140	1	10	37	1225	1131	545	464	96	479	1109	.246
Clinton	3.51	137	1	11	39	1198	1121	557	467	99	400	1044	.247
Kane County	3.78	139	6	11	35	1193	1139	593	494	83	476	1078	.251
South Bend	3.84	138	3	7	31	1194	1215	590	508	92	367	985	.264
Lansing	3.96	139	2	8	44	1205	1263	644	525	79	385	1004	.268
Peoria	4.03	139	1	13	36	1206	1105	618	539	96	503	1031	.242
Wisconsin	4.10	138	3	4	28	1187	1144	684	537	102	497	1068	.251
Burlington	4.14	138	3	12	37	1195	1182	622	548	92	387	928	.258
Fort Wayne	4.45	139	2	9	29	1191	1225	680	589	89	403	876	.266
Great Lakes	4.57	139	1	5	35	1199	1249	747	603	58	624	1051	.267

CLUB FIELDING

	PCT	PO	A	E	DP		PCT	PO	A	E	DP
West Michigan	.975	3711	1412	133	121	Clinton	.966	3594	1448	179	135
Dayton	.973	3675	1399	141	112	Fort Wayne	.966	3574	1468	177	142
Burlington	.972	3585	1443	146	124	Beloit	.965	3642	1436	183	134
South Bend	.972	3583	1465	147	127	Cedar Rapids	.965	3567	1486	182	117
Peoria	.969	3618	1337	161	106	Lansing	.965	3616	1582	187	123
Quad Cities	.968	3628	1535	172	112	Wisconsin	.960	3560	1423	209	119
Kane County	.967	3580	1316	167	120	Great Lakes	.957	3596	1399	227	125

INDIVIDUAL BATTING LEADERS (Minimum 434 Plate Appearances)

	AVG	G	AB	R	H	2B	3B	HR	RBI	BB	SO	SB
Parra, Gerardo, South Bend	.320	110	444	64	142	25	4	6	57	30	51	24
Snider, Travis, Lansing	.313	118	457	72	143	35	7	16	93	49	129	3
Turner, Justin, Dayton	.311	117	466	70	145	25	4	10	59	39	72	12
Perez, Eduardo, Great Lakes	.311	116	447	56	139	20	2	14	60	34	91	8
Skelton, James, West Michigan	.309	101	353	60	109	24	2	7	52	55	53	18
Hernandez, Gorkys, West Michigan	.293	124	481	84	141	25	5	4	50	36	69	54
Adduci, James, Peoria	.292	107	401	54	117	18	2	2	48	30	98	20
Side, Joey, South Bend	.291	129	478	76	139	25	7	1	51	53	72	5
Bell, Joshua, Great Lakes	.289	108	398	65	115	21	3	15	62	39	109	5
Dickerson, Joseph, Burlington	.289	115	419	50	121	23	2	3	43	38	76	26

INDIVIDUAL PITCHING LEADERS (Minimum 112 Innings)

	W	L	ERA	G	GS	CG	SV	IP	H	R	ER	BB	SO
O'Sullivan, Sean, Cedar Rapids	10	7	2.22	25	25	0	0	158	136	58	39	40	125
Poveda, Omar, Clinton	11	4	2.79	21	21	0	0	126	94	44	39	32	120
Phillips, Zachary, Clinton	11	7	2.91	27	27	0	0	152	139	56	49	43	157
Below, Duane, West Michigan	13	5	2.97	26	26	0	0	146	128	54	48	58	160
Burnett, Alex, Beloit	9	8	3.02	27	27	1	0	155	140	60	52	38	117
Devries, Cole, Beloit	9	5	3.41	27	25	0	0	148	161	73	56	36	108
Valdez, Cesar, South Bend	7	10	3.41	25	25	2	0	148	130	63	56	32	106
Webb, Travis, Dayton	7	5	3.45	28	21	0	0	115	105	50	44	62	114
Dickson, Brandon, Quad Cities	11	7	3.50	31	23	0	1	144	148	74	56	41	84
Gonzalez, Reidier, Lansing	9	7	3.53	20	20	1	0	115	121	55	45	30	71

ALL-STAR TEAM

C: James Skelton, West Michigan. **1B:** Brad Miller, South Bend. **2B:** Justin Turner, Dayton. **SS:** Chris Valaika, South Bend. **3B:** Juan Francisco, Dayton. **OF:** Gerardo Parra, South Bend; Travis Snider, Lansing; Gorkys Hernandez, West Michigan. **DH:** Michael Thompson, Burlington. **RHP:** Jeff Manship, Beloit. **LHP:** Clayton Kershaw, Great Lakes. **RP:** Rob Delaney, Beloit; Barret Browning, Cedar Rapids. **Most Valuable Player:** Gorkys Hernandez, West Michigan. **Prospect of the Year:** Clayton Kershaw, Great Lakes. **Manager of the Year:** Tom Brookens, West Michigan.

DEPARTMENT LEADERS

BATTING

OBP	Diaz, Jonathan, Lansing	.406
SLG	Snider, Travis, Lansing	.525
R	Stubbs, Drew, Dayton	93
H	Perales, Daniel, South Bend	156
TB	Perales, Daniel, South Bend	256
XBH	Snider, Travis, Lansing	58
	Perales, Daniel, South Bend	58
2B	Tracy, Chad, Clinton	35
	Snider, Travis, Lansing	35
3B	Shoffit, Sean, Lansing	13
HR	Francisco, Juan, Dayton	25
RBI	Snider, Travis, Lansing	93
SAC	Diaz, Jonathan, Lansing	17
SF	Three players tied at	8
BB	Diaz, Jonathan, Lansing	82
IBB	Whittleman, John, Clinton	6
	Francisco, Juan, Dayton	6
HBP	Gomez, Mauro, Clinton	18
SO	Francisco, Juan, Dayton	161
SB	Hernandez, Gorkys, West Michigan	54
CS	Benson, Joe, Beloit	16
GIDP	Gomez, Mauro, Clinton	18
AB/SO	Sanchez, Yunesky, South Bend	11.33

PITCHING

G	Valdez, Rolando, Fort Wayne	58
GS	Starner, Nathan, Lansing	28
CG	Six players tied at	2
SHO	11 players tied at	1
GF	Jensen, Brett, West Michigan	50
SV	Maiques, Kenneth, Quad Cities	31
W	Herndon, David, Cedar Rapids	13
	Gonzalez, Rafael, Dayton	13
	Below, Duane, West Michigan	13
L	Five players tied at	11
IP	Barnette, Tony, South Bend	160
H	Deal, Scott, Kane County	183
R	Breit, Aaron, Fort Wayne	97
ER	Breit, Aaron, Fort Wayne	81
HB	Delabar, Steve, Fort Wayne	13
BB	Sanfler, Miguel, Great Lakes	63
SO	Below, Duane, West Michigan	160
SO/9-S	Kershaw, Clayton, Great Lakes	12.39
SO/9-R	Fien, Casey, West Michigan	11.36
WP	Herrera, John, Kane County	21
BK	Gordon, Derrick, Kane County	5
	Heuser, James, Kane County	5
AVG	Poveda, Omar, Clinton	.208

FIELDING

C	PCT	Brashear, Justin, South Bend	.995
	PO	Skelton, James, West Michigan	615
	A	Rodriguez, Eddy, Dayton	84
	E	Castillo, Wellington, Peoria	15
	DP	Santana, Carlos, Great Lakes	10
		Beltran, Juan, Wisconsin	10
	PB	Beltran, Juan, Wisconsin	23
	CS%	Rodriguez, Eddy, Dayton	.45
		Jaspe, Jonathan, Lansing	.45
1B	PCT	Strieby, Ryan, West Michigan	.993
	PO	Miller, Brad, South Bend	1116
	A	Miller, Brad, South Bend	103
	E	Miller, Brad, South Bend	18
	DP	Miller, Brad, South Bend	104
2B	PCT	Campbell, Scott, Lansing	.979
	PO	Vallejo, Jose, Clinton	280
	A	Vallejo, Jose, Clinton	373
	E	Vallejo, Jose, Clinton	25
	DP	Vallejo, Jose, Clinton	89
3B	PCT	De Leon, Santo, West Michigan	.929
	PO	Francisco, Juan, Dayton	86
	A	De Leon, Santo, West Michigan	190
	E	Bell, Joshua, Great Lakes	35
	DP	Mena, Steve, South Bend	20
SS	PCT	Lopez, Jesus, Fort Wayne	.967
	PO	Diaz, Jonathan, Lansing	211
	A	Diaz, Jonathan, Lansing	383
	E	Phillips, P.J., Cedar Rapids	40
	DP	Lemon, Marcus, Clinton	82
		Lopez, Jesus, Fort Wayne	82
OF	PCT	Massaro, Michael, Kane County	.996
	PO	Hernandez, Gorkys, W. Michigan	277
	A	Stubbs, Drew, Dayton	15
	E	Snider, Travis, Lansing	16
	DP	Parmelee, Chris, Beloit	6
		Carter, Sam, Fort Wayne	6

BY NATHAN RODE

They say pitching is the key to playoff success and based on that formula, the Augusta GreenJackets seemed poised for an easy championship in the South Atlantic League. For the first two months the rotation was led by Henry Sosa, who went 6-0, 0.73 in 62 innings before he was summoned to help high Class A San Jose. Despite his departure, the GreenJackets didn't falter. The team had an overall ERA of 3.02 and four starters that reached double-digits in victories.

Righthander Kevin Pucetas garnered pitcher of the year accolades and a 15-4, 1.86 line in 145 innings. Adam Cowart, Benjamin Snyder and Clayton Tanner combined to go 42-20, 2.59 and lead the GreenJackets to a first-place finish in the Southern Division and the league's best overall record.

Unfortunately for Augusta, the Columbus Catfish were their first-round playoff opponent and before the GreenJackets knew it, they were out in two games. The Catfish outscored Augusta 18-3 and got strong outings from Jeremy Hellickson and Heath Rollins.

The Catfish continued their playoff cleaning with a sweep of the West Virginia Power in three games to capture the Sally League title in John Henry Moss' final season as South Atlantic League president. Moss founded the league as the Western Carolinas League and had been its only president before deciding to retire. He will be replaced by Eric Krupa in 2008.

Coaches and scouts were underwhelmed with the star talent, but that be attributed to the struggles and injuries of potential impact players.

A couple of youngsters, Kyle Drabek and Billy Rowell ,were hit with injuries early that had effects on their seasons. Drabek had Tommy John surgery after going 5-1, 4.33 in 54 innings and Rowell didn't debut until May 23 because of a strained oblique. His power was a little weaker than the Orioles would have hoped as he hit .273/.335/.426 in 352 at-bats, but the injury and fact that he was only 19 made those numbers easier to swallow.

On a brighter note for Baltimore's system, Brandon Snyder bounced back after a dreadful 2006 campaign. He settled in nicely at a new position (first base) and took a more positive attitude and approach with each game.

The Greensboro Grasshoppers left fielder John Raynor took the MVP honors when he hit .333/.429/.519 in 445 at-bats and was among league leaders in hitting, stolen bases, runs scored and on-base percentage.

TOP 20 PROSPECTS

1. Desmond Jennings, of, Columbus (Devil Rays)
2. Hector Gomez, ss, Asheville (Rockies)
3. Fautino de los Santos, rhp, Kannapolis (White Sox)
4. Lars Anderson, 1b, Greenville (Red Sox)
5. Chris Marrero, of, Hagerstown (Nationals)
6. Jordan Schafer, of, Rome (Braves)
7. Henry Sosa, rhp, Augusta (Giants)
8. Jeremy Hellickson, rhp, Columbus (Devil Rays)
9. Ryan Royster, of, Columbus (Devil Rays)
10. Chris Carter, 1b, Kannapolis (White Sox)
11. Chris Coghlan, 2b, Greensboro (Marlins)
12. John Raynor, of, Greensboro (Marlins)
13. Adrian Cardenas, ss, Lakewood (Phillies)
14. Tommy Hanson, rhp, Rome (Braves)
15. Brandon Snyder, 1b, Delmarva (Orioles)
16. Jared Goedert, 3b, Lake County (Indians)
17. Daniel Mayora, ss, Asheville (Rockies)
18. Justin Maxwell, of, Hagerstown (Nationals)
19. Josh Reddick, of, Greenville (Red Sox)
20. Billy Rowell, 3b, Delmarva (Orioles)

SPORTS ON FILM

STANDINGS: SPLIT SEASON

FIRST HALF

NORTH	W	L	PCT	GB
West Virginia	48	20	.706	—
Greensboro	38	32	.543	11
Lakewood	33	32	.508	13½
Delmarva	34	33	.507	13½
Lake County	31	39	.443	18
Lexington	31	39	.443	18
Hagerstown	29	38	.433	18½
Hickory	27	40	.403	20½
SOUTH	**W**	**L**	**PCT**	**GB**
Augusta	50	20	.714	—
Asheville	42	27	.609	7½
Columbus	41	29	.586	9
Charleston	37	33	.529	13
Kannapolis	32	38	.457	18
Greenville	29	40	.420	20½
Rome	29	41	.414	21
Savannah	20	50	.286	30

SECOND HALF

NORTH	W	L	PCT	GB
Hickory	43	26	.623	—
Lakewood	36	33	.522	7
West Virginia	34	34	.500	8½
Delmarva	34	35	.493	9
Lake County	33	35	.485	9½
Greensboro	33	37	.471	10½
Lexington	28	42	.400	15½
Hagerstown	26	43	.377	17
SOUTH	**W**	**L**	**PCT**	**GB**
Columbus	41	24	.631	—
Charleston	41	29	.586	2½
Augusta	39	31	.557	4½
Asheville	38	31	.551	5
Kannapolis	37	32	.536	6
Rome	37	33	.529	6½
Greenville	29	41	.414	14½
Savannah	21	44	.323	20

PLAYOFFS—Semifinals: Columbus defeated Augusta 2-0 and West Virginia defeated Hickory 2-1 in best-of-three series. **Finals:** Columbus defeated West Virginia 3-0 in a best-of-five series.

STANDINGS

Page	Team	W	L	PCT	GB	Manager	Attendance	Average	Last Penn.
264	Augusta GreenJackets (Giants)	89	51	.636	—	Roberto Kelly	177,780	2,614	1999
281	Columbus Catfish (Devil Rays)	82	53	.607	4½	Jim Morrison	71,809	1,041	2007
176	West Virginia Power (Brewers)	82	54	.603	5	Mike Guerrero	248,766	3,713	1990
117	Asheville Tourists (Rockies)	80	58	.580	8	Joe Mikulik	164,910	2,461	1984
204	Charleston RiverDogs (Yankees)	78	62	.557	11	Torre Tyson	284,718	4,126	None
225	Lakewood BlueClaws (Phillies)	69	65	.515	17	Steve Roadcap	442,256	6,410	2006
235	Hickory Crawdads (Pirates)	70	66	.515	17	Gary Green	170,000	2,537	2004
134	Greensboro Grasshoppers (Marlins)	71	69	.507	18	Edwin Rodriguez	441,106	6,487	1982
66	Delmarva Shorebirds (Orioles)	68	68	.500	19	Gary Kendall	220,219	3,441	2000
91	Kannapolis Intimidators (White Sox)	69	70	.496	19½	Chris Jones	114,140	1,812	2005
57	Rome Braves (Braves)	66	74	.471	23	Randy Ingle	232,674	3,372	2003
108	Lake County Captains (Indians)	64	74	.464	24	Chris Tremie	330,352	5,082	None
142	Lexington Legends (Astros)	59	81	.421	30	Gregory Langbehn	385,506	5,754	2001
74	Greenville Drive (Red Sox)	58	81	.417	30½	Gabe Kapler	339,356	4,991	1998
308	Hagerstown Suns (Nationals)	55	81	.404	32	Tom Herr	146,763	2,258	None
193	Savannah Sand Gnats (Mets)	41	94	.304	40½	Tim Teufel	91,722	1,555	1996

NOTE: Teams' individual batting and pitching statistics can be found on page indicated in lefthand column.

CLUB BATTING

	AVG	G	AB	R	H	2B	3B	HR	RBI	BB	SO	SB	CS	OBP	SLG
West Virginia	.281	136	4717	804	1326	278	34	128	745	482	1005	184	63	.355	.436
Hickory	.275	136	4667	745	1282	245	38	124	684	414	913	113	51	.342	.423
Kannapolis	.274	139	4708	770	1291	277	41	112	676	441	868	120	53	.341	.422
Asheville	.270	138	4673	779	1260	328	54	124	724	511	1167	186	90	.347	.443
Charleston	.265	140	4631	645	1227	235	30	87	581	447	867	167	53	.337	.385
Columbus	.265	135	4567	664	1212	239	32	121	613	393	1010	200	90	.330	.411
Augusta	.264	140	4702	716	1242	264	30	79	653	437	874	212	85	.334	.383
Greensboro	.264	140	4774	753	1259	266	25	156	695	482	1125	185	51	.338	.428
Greenville	.261	139	4758	686	1244	252	43	107	611	517	1119	92	44	.340	.400
Lakewood	.261	134	4582	631	1195	230	30	53	543	452	966	177	63	.332	.359
Lake County	.260	138	4713	737	1224	236	29	113	665	609	1052	84	41	.351	.394
Delmarva	.259	137	4670	662	1210	245	31	88	587	433	1094	145	56	.329	.381
Hagerstown	.255	137	4541	636	1156	258	22	117	580	455	1068	100	69	.332	.398
Rome	.255	140	4748	646	1211	264	26	101	581	461	994	83	63	.327	.385
Lexington	.252	140	4758	650	1197	231	24	118	600	464	1039	151	47	.326	.385
Savannah	.245	135	4318	463	1059	191	27	60	402	388	942	125	55	.312	.344

CLUB PITCHING

	ERA	G	CG	SHO	SV	IP	H	R	ER	HR	BB	SO	AVG
Augusta	3.02	140	1	18	40	1238	1140	506	416	70	339	980	.244
Columbus	3.61	135	2	8	44	1195	1111	561	479	92	433	997	.246
Charleston	3.70	140	0	10	41	1203	1091	590	494	95	480	991	.242
Lakewood	3.75	134	2	7	41	1201	1137	586	498	84	449	1031	.249
Rome	3.90	140	1	7	33	1229	1217	651	531	66	472	1088	.258
Delmarva	3.91	137	2	3	36	1221	1126	655	530	73	590	1074	.245
Asheville	4.08	138	5	7	32	1204	1290	646	545	111	386	1045	.275
Greensboro	4.30	140	5	7	26	1223	1283	706	582	136	335	1046	.267
West Virginia	4.32	136	0	4	40	1207	1220	665	579	113	447	994	.263
Lake County	4.55	138	1	10	26	1207	1211	709	611	126	407	1059	.258
Hagerstown	4.76	137	2	7	31	1176	1313	766	616	107	453	912	.281
Lexington	4.93	140	1	2	37	1237	1274	778	673	147	533	1072	.266
Savannah	5.04	135	2	6	28	1126	1254	759	625	129	453	798	.278
Hickory	5.13	136	2	6	33	1196	1292	787	680	126	554	1034	.275
Kannapolis	5.13	139	2	2	32	1190	1302	805	677	102	543	1031	.277
Greenville	5.32	139	1	2	29	1204	1334	818	709	111	512	951	.282

CLUB FIELDING

	PCT	PO	A	E	DP		PCT	PO	A	E	DP
Augusta	.974	3715	1630	144	122	Asheville	.967	3611	1414	173	131
Charleston	.973	3608	1478	140	131	Greenville	.966	3611	1507	179	124
Columbus	.973	3585	1495	142	135	Greensboro	.964	3669	1517	191	112
Lexington	.971	3710	1559	160	127	Rome	.964	3687	1418	190	110
Hickory	.970	3588	1450	157	119	Kannapolis	.963	3571	1318	186	110
West Virginia	.969	3621	1482	163	129	Delmarva	.961	3664	1399	208	118
Lake County	.968	3623	1399	168	109	Savannah	.961	3377	1425	196	107
Lakewood	.968	3604	1412	166	112	Hagerstown	.956	3527	1462	230	124

INDIVIDUAL BATTING LEADERS (Minimum 434 Plate Appearances)

	AVG	G	AB	R	H	2B	3B	HR	RBI	BB	SO	SB
Lefave, Andrew, West Virginia	.345	112	423	90	146	25	0	17	79	59	59	12
Raynor, John, Greensboro	.333	116	445	110	148	28	8	13	57	66	98	54
Royster, Ryan, Columbus	.329	125	474	90	156	31	4	30	98	36	121	17
Green, Taylor, West Virginia	.327	111	397	68	130	29	2	14	86	51	65	0
Burriss, Emmanuel, Augusta	.321	89	365	64	117	14	4	0	38	28	49	51
Pacheco, Jonel, Hickory	.315	119	463	97	146	25	5	27	99	41	71	18
Jennings, Desmond, Columbus	.315	99	387	75	122	21	5	9	37	45	53	45
Berry, Quintin, Lakewood	.312	126	487	86	152	19	4	3	44	61	85	55
Mayora, Daniel, Asheville	.312	127	516	88	161	42	1	14	78	41	124	26
Hilligoss, Mitch, Charleston	.310	128	520	83	161	35	4	4	53	33	65	35

INDIVIDUAL PITCHING LEADERS (Minimum 112 Innings)

	W	L	ERA	G	GS	CG	SV	IP	H	R	ER	BB	SO
Pucetas, Kevin, Augusta	15	4	1.86	27	23	0	1	145	124	40	30	21	104
Snyder, Ben, Augusta	16	5	2.09	28	28	0	1	151	128	49	35	32	145
Cowart, Adam, Augusta	14	7	2.39	28	28	0	0	170	152	59	45	28	95
Rollins, Heath, Columbus	17	4	2.54	27	27	1	0	159	132	57	45	38	149
Taylor, Graham, Greensboro	11	3	2.68	25	25	3	0	164	135	59	49	18	135
Richmond, Jamie, Rome	7	6	3.05	25	24	0	0	139	141	71	47	25	98
Schmidt, Kyle, Delmarva	6	8	3.37	23	23	0	0	131	125	60	49	38	145
Dunn, Michael, Charleston	12	5	3.42	27	27	0	0	145	136	69	55	45	138
Tanner, Clayton, Augusta	12	8	3.59	27	23	1	0	135	147	61	54	44	104
Weiser, Keith, Asheville	17	7	3.75	28	28	1	0	175	195	86	73	30	126

ALL-STAR TEAM

C: Michael McKenry, Asheville. **1B:** Michael Paulk, Asheville. **2B:** Daniel Mayora, Asheville. **SS:** Hector Gomez, Asheville; Emmanuel Burriss, Augusta. **3B:** Taylor Green, West Virginia. **OF:** John Raynor, Greensboro; Ryan Royster, Columbus; Desmond Jennings, Columbus. **DH:** Chris Carter, Kannapolis. **RHP:** Kevin Pucetas, Augusta. **LHP:** Ben Snyder, Augusta **Most Valuable Player:** John Raynor, Greensboro. **Most Outstanding Pitcher:** Kevin Pucetas, Augusta. **Most Outstanding Prospect:** Fautino De Los Santos, Kannapolis. **Manager of the Year:** Joe Mikulik, Asheville.

DEPARTMENT LEADERS

BATTING

OBP	Still, Jon, Greenville	.432
	Lefave, Andrew, West Virginia	.432
SLG	Royster, Ryan, Columbus	.601
R	Raynor, John, Greensboro	110
H	Mayora, Daniel, Asheville	161
	Hilligoss, Mitch, Charleston	161
TB	Royster, Ryan, Columbus	285
XBH	Royster, Ryan, Columbus	65
2B	Pill, Brett, Augusta	47
3B	Jackson, Anthony, Asheville	12
HR	Royster, Ryan, Columbus	30
RBI	Pacheco, Jonel, Hickory	99
SAC	Florimon Jr., Pedro, Delmarva	13
SF	Three players tied at	10
BB	Still, Jon, Greenville	87
IBB	Paulk, Mike, Asheville	8
HBP	Napoli, Joe, Hagerstown	20
SO	Brewer, Brent, West Virginia	170
SB	Berry, Quintin, Lakewood	55
CS	Berry, Quintin, Lakewood	18
GIDP	Pill, Brett, Augusta	17
	Cardenas, Adrian, Lakewood	17
AB/SO	Blackwood, Jacob, Greensboro	9.25

PITCHING

G	Papelbon, Josh, Greenville	62
GS	Four players tied at	28
CG	Taylor, Graham, Greensboro	3
SHO	Five players tied at	1
GF	Papelbon, Josh, Greenville	56
SV	Hovis, Jonathan, Charleston	30
W	Weiser, Keith, Asheville	17
	Rollins, Heath, Columbus	17
L	Mizell, Jeremy, Savannah	15
IP	Weiser, Keith, Asheville	175.1
H	Ferrer, Simon, Asheville	203
R	Rasner, Jacob, Kannapolis	118
ER	Rasner, Jacob, Kannapolis	106
HB	Byrd, Darren, Lakewood	19
BB	Duff, Grant, Charleston	80
SO	Rodriguez, Aneury, Asheville	160
SO/9-S	Norris, Bud, Lexington	10.89
SO/9-R	Luis, Santo, Lexington	11.83
WP	Hughes, Jared, Hickory	27
BK	Jeffress, Jeremy, West Virginia	5
AVG	Taylor, Graham, Greensboro	.222

FIELDING

C	PCT	Ashley, Nevin, Columbus	.992
	PO	Gosewisch, Tuffy, Lakewood	667
	A	Gosewisch, Tuffy, Lakewood	87
	E	Pena, Francisco, Savannah	18
	DP	Gosewisch, Tuffy, Lakewood	11
	PB	Three players tied at	18
	CS%	Hatcher, Chris, Greensboro	.45
1B	PCT	Morales, Douglas, Lakewood	.993
		Thole, Josh, Savannah	.993
	PO	Pill, Brett, Augusta	1192
	A	Anderson, Lars, Greenville	93
	E	Whitney, Matthew, Lake County	16
	DP	Pill, Brett, Augusta	103
2B	PCT	Buchanan, Greg, Lexington	.983
	PO	Abreu, Miguel, Delmarva	238
	A	Abreu, Miguel, Delmarva	368
	E	Abreu, Miguel, Delmarva	25
	DP	Mayora, Daniel, Asheville	80
3B	PCT	Rohlinger, Ryan, Augusta	.966
	PO	Ventura, Leivi, Savannah	95
	A	Rohlinger, Ryan, Augusta	321
	E	Blackwood, Jacob, Greensboro	35
	DP	Ventura, Leivi, Savannah	28
SS	PCT	Diaz, Argenis, Greenville	.952
	PO	Brewer, Brent, West Virginia	197
	A	Brewer, Brent, West Virginia	366
	E	Brewer, Brent, West Virginia	48
	DP	Brewer, Brent, West Virginia	76
OF	PCT	Fortenberry, Seth, Charleston	.996
	PO	Jackson, Anthony, Asheville	271
	A	Reddick, Josh, Greenville	19
	E	McBryde, Michael, Augusta	15
	DP	Place, Jason, Greenville	6

BY BEN BADLER

Auburn lefthander Brett Cecil picked a perfect time to turn in the longest outing of his young pro career. Cecil, the Blue Jays' supplemental round pick out of Maryland in June, held Brooklyn to one run on four hits while striking out eight over seven innings of work to lead the Doubledays to their first New York-Penn League title in 30 years. Catcher J.P. Arencibia gave the Doubledays the lead in the fifth with a two-run homer, and Auburn went on to a 4-1 win to sweep the best-of-three championship series.

The Doubledays had reached the playoffs in each of the previous five seasons under manager Dennis Holmberg, but they finally broke through to win it all with a team loaded with quality lefthanded pitching. Cecil was the No. 1 prospect in the league, and fellow lefthanders Marc Rzepczynski and Luis Perez also proved to be key members of the rotation.

Brooklyn fell just short of its second league title despite posting the best record in the league. League ERA champion Dylan Owen (9-1, 1.49) anchored a stellar Cyclones staff that posted a league-best 2.93 ERA. Owen threw five shutout innings to propel Brooklyn past defending champion Staten Island and into the finals, and he was scheduled to pitch the third game of the championship series. But he never got a chance to take the mound against Auburn because Brooklyn's offense was held to just a pair of runs over the first two games.

The Cyclones and Doubledays weren't the only talented teams in the NY-P in 2007. The league was teeming with quality prospects, and the talent wasn't limited to the usual group of college draftees making their pro debuts. Sure, the influx of college talent was impressive—three lefthanders taken in the first or supplemental first round graced the top four spots on the league's top prospects list—but so was the collection of 2006 high school draftees. In fact, five of the league's 10 best prospects and nine of the top 20 played the season as teenagers, led by Marlins righty Hector Correa.

Of course, two other supplemental first-round picks out of Pacific Northwest colleges would have cracked the top 10 had they not fallen just short of qualifying. Lowell

TOP 20 PROSPECTS

1. Brett Cecil, lhp, Auburn (Blue Jays)
2. Joe Savery, lhp, Williamsport (Phillies)
3. Hector Correa, rhp, Jamestown (Marlins)
4. Daniel Moskos, lhp, State College (Pirates)
5. Jordan Zimmerman, rhp, Vermont (Nationals)
6. Ryan Kalish, of, Lowell (Red Sox)
7. J.P. Arencibia, c, Auburn (Blue Jays)
8. Oscar Tejeda, ss, Lowell (Red Sox)
9. Glenn Gibson, lhp, Vermont (Nationals)
10. Dellin Betances, rhp, Staten Island (Yankees)
11. Colton Willems, rhp, Vermont Lake Monsters (Nationals)
12. Yamaico Navarro, ss/3b, Lowell Spinners (Red Sox)
13. Jess Todd, rhp, Batavia Muckdogs (Cardinals)
14. Duke Welker, rhp, State College Spikes (Pirates)
15. Dominic Brown, of, Williamsport Crosscutters (Phillies)
16. Nick Carr, rhp, Brooklyn Cyclones (Mets)
17. Damon Sublett, 2b, Staten Island Yankees
18. Zach McAllister, rhp, Staten Island Yankees
19. Michael McCormick, c, Hudson Valley Renegades (Devil Rays)
20. Brant Rustich, rhp, Brooklyn Cyclones (Mets)

RODGER WOOD

lefty Nick Hagadone missed by just one inning. Batavia righty Clayton Mortensen, out of Gonzaga, fell five innings short before earning a callup to low Class A.

The NY-P also featured an impressive collection of young, slick-fielding shortstops. Lowell teenagers Oscar Tejeda and Yamaico Navarro cracked the Top 20. Williamsport's Freddy Galvis (who was just 17), Auburn's Luis Sanchez and Hudson Valley's Shawn O'Malley all garnered plaudits for their superb glovework--though all have a long way to go offensively and didn't make the list. State College's Brian Friday was another quality shortstop and had a more polished bat, thanks to three strong years at Rice.

Friday had a strong case for breaking into the Top 20, but competition in 2007 was thick. Other players who would have been worthy of spots in most years include Williamsport righthander Drew Naylor, Aberdeen lefty Zach Britton, Rzepczynski, Tri-City outfielder Collin DeLome and State College outfielder Austin McClune.

STANDINGS

Page	McNamara Division	W	L	PCT	GB	Manager	Attendance	Average	Last Penn.
194	Brooklyn Cyclones (Mets)	49	25	.662	—	Edgar Alfonzo	294,972	8,194	2001
205	Staten Island Yankees (Yankees)	47	28	.627	2½	Mike Gillespie	164,207	4,321	2006
67	Aberdeen IronBirds (Orioles)	34	42	.447	16	Andy Etchebarren	241,215	6,519	1983
282	Hudson Valley Renegades (Devil Rays)	34	42	.447	16	Matt Quatraro	153,697	4,391	1999

Page	Pinckney Division	W	L	PCT	GB	Manager	Attendance	Average	Last Penn.
300	Auburn Doubledays (Blue Jays)	47	29	.618	—	Dennis Holmberg	66,222	1,790	2007
109	Mahoning Valley Scrappers (Indians)	37	37	.500	9	Tim Laker	129,601	3,703	2004
236	State College Spikes (Pirates)	36	39	.480	10½	Turner Ward	151,394	4,205	1994
226	Williamsport Crosscutters (Phillies)	34	42	.447	13	Greg Legg	70,884	1,916	2003
246	Batavia Muckdogs (Cardinals)	31	43	.419	15	Mark Dejohn	44,270	1,230	1963
135	Jamestown Jammers (Marlins)	28	47	.373	18½	Darin Everson	48,305	1,421	1991

Page	Stedler Division	W	L	PCT	GB	Manager	Attendance	Average	Last Penn.
125	Oneonta Tigers (Tigers)	44	32	.579	—	Andy Barkett	49,118	1,403	1998
75	Lowell Spinners (Red Sox)	40	36	.526	4	Gary DiSarcina	198,453	5,364	None
309	Vermont Lake Monsters (Nationals)	38	37	.507	5½	Darnell Coles	90,311	2,737	1996
143	Tri-City ValleyCats (Astros)	27	47	.365	16	Pete Rancont	136,809	3,800	1997

PLAYOFFS— Semifinals: Auburn defeated Oneonta 2-1 and Brooklyn defeated Staten Island 2-0 in best-of-three series. **Finals:** Auburn defeated Brooklyn 2-0 in a best-of-three series. **NOTE:** Teams' individual batting and pitching statistics can be found on page indicated in lefthand column.

CLUB BATTING

	AVG	G	AB	R	H	2B	3B	HR	RBI	BB	SO	SB	CS	OBP	SLG
State College	.272	75	2511	323	684	151	22	35	280	183	541	76	36	.330	.392
Staten Island	.268	75	2459	372	658	133	14	36	319	283	497	89	48	.354	.377
Oneonta	.265	76	2517	389	666	131	31	41	347	282	520	77	33	.348	.390
Hudson Valley	.262	76	2492	383	652	118	32	39	336	262	517	106	39	.338	.382
Brooklyn	.260	74	2390	348	622	116	19	37	298	278	605	74	50	.346	.371
Lowell	.257	76	2530	366	651	127	16	33	314	289	584	87	39	.345	.359
Mahoning Valley	.257	74	2478	324	638	101	21	21	285	249	529	78	24	.336	.341
Aberdeen	.255	76	2502	364	638	105	26	43	329	247	572	74	21	.329	.369
Auburn	.253	76	2529	382	640	118	23	58	334	256	676	47	26	.329	.387
Tri-City	.245	74	2390	308	586	119	19	39	290	262	552	54	17	.328	.360
Vermont	.245	73	2396	330	588	97	22	31	287	257	558	107	39	.332	.343
Williamsport	.241	76	2521	309	608	137	11	41	274	218	574	63	30	.309	.353
Batavia	.232	74	2440	288	566	108	31	19	252	231	579	72	34	.312	.325
Jamestown	.229	75	2391	268	548	123	15	50	235	239	596	65	37	.309	.356

CLUB PITCHING

	ERA	G	CG	SHO	SV	IP	H	R	ER	HR	BB	SO	AVG
Brooklyn	2.94	74	1	10	22	639	523	240	208	23	239	583	.224
Auburn	3.48	76	0	4	22	665	615	320	254	31	247	651	.242
Staten Island	3.52	75	0	5	22	654	624	305	256	29	274	609	.253
Mahoning Valley	3.56	74	0	2	20	638	605	304	252	44	217	485	.253
Williamsport	3.57	76	3	6	23	656	604	325	259	30	222	579	.243
Vermont	3.82	75	0	9	24	635	561	329	269	32	317	605	.237
Lowell	3.83	76	0	6	20	666	613	344	283	43	255	632	.242
State College	3.83	75	1	3	23	645	671	327	273	38	238	513	.266
Oneonta	3.85	76	2	3	24	653	614	341	279	33	291	546	.247
Batavia	3.93	74	0	4	24	646	654	324	282	43	233	586	.262
Hudson Valley	4.22	76	1	2	14	640	617	360	300	45	234	487	.253
Aberdeen	4.33	76	0	4	18	653	666	422	314	39	269	556	.261
Jamestown	4.45	75	1	5	18	633	652	379	312	51	251	574	.264
Tri-City	5.18	74	1	2	15	615	726	434	350	42	249	494	.294

CLUB FIELDING

	PCT	PO	A	E	DP		PCT	PO	A	E	DP
Brooklyn	.977	1917	767	64	55	Auburn	.965	1994	809	101	49
Vermont	.973	1906	723	74	66	Hudson Valley	.965	1919	783	98	54
Staten Island	.970	1963	769	85	68	Lowell	.965	1997	769	99	63
Mahoning Valley	.968	1913	773	90	79	Batavia	.963	1937	736	104	56
Oneonta	.968	1958	800	91	58	Williamsport	.962	1968	782	110	68
Jamestown	.967	1899	736	90	55	Tri-City	.959	1845	726	109	53
State College	.967	1934	793	92	71	Aberdeen	.955	1958	829	131	61

INDIVIDUAL BATTING LEADERS *(Minimum 236 Plate Appearances)*

	AVG	G	AB	R	H	2B	3B	HR	RBI	BB	SO	SB
Martin, Todd, Mahoning Valley	.360	54	197	27	71	8	1	8	40	23	40	0
Pruitt, Braedyn, Staten Island	.347	51	170	20	59	5	0	4	32	26	21	1
Henry, Justin, Oneonta	.340	67	250	49	85	11	2	1	31	33	22	14
Simon, Keanon, State College	.335	54	185	28	62	14	1	1	27	17	28	9
Snyder, Justin, Staten Island	.335	73	260	68	87	20	1	5	40	58	50	10
Sublett, Damon, Staten Island	.326	68	239	43	78	19	3	8	53	43	47	10
Bourquin, Ron, Oneonta	.325	57	194	31	63	13	3	2	28	31	35	2
Byler, Justin, State College	.312	69	263	41	82	18	2	8	43	17	68	1
Salem, Emeel, Hudson Valley	.311	58	225	41	70	11	7	1	23	24	27	28
Curry, Ryan, Jamestown	.308	62	224	38	69	13	0	8	27	17	33	2

INDIVIDUAL PITCHING LEADERS *(Minimum 61 Innings)*

	W	L	ERA	G	GS	CG	SV	IP	H	R	ER	BB	SO
Owen, Dylan, Brooklyn	9	1	1.49	14	13	0	0	72	51	13	12	12	69
Chapman, Chance, Williamsport	5	3	2.09	14	14	0	0	78	70	31	18	20	67
Icenogle, Jeff, Tri-City	3	4	2.36	15	10	1	0	61	57	20	16	26	68
Moscoso, Guillermo, Oneonta	8	2	2.37	14	14	2	0	80	75	25	21	15	68
Alaniz, Adrian, Vermont	8	2	2.39	13	8	0	0	60	42	18	16	8	62
Gee, Dillon, Brooklyn	3	1	2.47	14	11	0	0	62	57	17	17	9	56
Ragan, Jason, Hudson Valley	5	6	2.80	11	11	0	0	64	53	25	20	22	36
Stambaugh, Jonathan, Batavia	3	2	3.15	17	9	0	1	66	72	26	23	8	53
Naylor, Drew, Williamsport	8	6	3.28	14	14	2	0	93	78	39	34	28	97
Craft, Jordan, Lowell	7	3	3.31	15	10	0	0	65	43	28	24	28	64

DEPARTMENT LEADERS

BATTING

OBP	Snyder, Justin, Staten Island	.459
SLG	Martin, Todd, Mahoning Valley	.533
R	Snyder, Justin, Staten Island	68
H	Snyder, Justin, Staten Island	87
TB	Wells, Casper, Oneonta	136
XBH	Wells, Casper, Oneonta	38
2B	Jimenez, Jorge, Lowell	23
3B	Wells, Casper, Oneonta	11
HR	Jacobs, Jason, Brooklyn	12
RBI	Sublett, Damon, Staten Island	53
SAC	Corrado, Craig, Tri-City	11
SF	Sublett, Damon, Staten Island	9
BB	Schilling, Micah, Brooklyn	60
IBB	Carlson, Christopher, Oneonta	4
HBP	Lyons, Daniel, Vermont	18
SO	Reyes, Raul, Brooklyn	94
SB	Whiting, Brandon, Vermont	37
CS	Bouchard, Matthew, Brooklyn	11
GIDP	Taylor, Michael, Williamsport	10
AB/SO	Jimenez, Jorge, Lowell	13.22

PITCHING

G	Ventura, Felix, Lowell	28
	Krol, Noah, Oneonta	28
GS	Perez, Luis, Auburn	16
	Cobb, Alexander, Hudson Valley	16
CG	Moscoso, Guillermo, Oneonta	2
	Naylor, Drew, Williamsport	2
SHO	Waechter, Nicholas, Brooklyn	1
	Moscoso, Guillermo, Oneonta	1
GF	Krol, Noah, Oneonta	24
SV	Krol, Noah, Oneonta	17
W	Owen, Dylan, Brooklyn	9
L	Robles, Moises, State College	9
IP	Naylor, Drew, Williamsport	93.1
H	Suero, Nicolas, State College	102
R	Echeverria, Diego, Hudson Valley	58
ER	Echeverria, Diego, Hudson Valley	51
HB	Eisenberg, Michael, Mahoning Valley	16
SO	Naylor, Drew, Williamsport	97
BB	Vasquez, Sendy, Oneonta	48
SO/9-S	Correa, Hector, Jamestown	12.73
SO/9-R	Blackley, Adam, Lowell	15.5
WP	Beattie, Eric, Lowell	14
BK	Collier, Logan, Batavia	3
	Pena, Hassan, Vermont	3
AVG	Craft, Jordan, Lowell	.187

FIELDING

C	PCT	Weeden, Tyler, Lowell	.997
	PO	Arencibia, J.P., Auburn	466
	A	Gil, Jose, Staten Island	47
	E	Stillwagon, Nicholas, State College	9
		Gil, Jose, Staten Island	9
	DP	Four players tied at	5
	PB	Arencibia, J.P., Auburn	18
	CS%	Langley, Torre, Jamestown	.37
1B	PCT	Brown, Andrew, Batavia	.993
		Rhinehart, Bill, Vermont	.993
	PO	Carlson, Christopher, Oneonta	599
	A	Rhinehart, Bill, Vermont	48
	E	Cruz, Alberto, Tri-City	11
	DP	Byler, Justin, State College	56
2B	PCT	Cusick, Matthew, Tri-City	.985
	PO	Cavagnaro, Matt, State College	123
	A	Cavagnaro, Matt, State College	200
	E	Adams, Ryan, Aberdeen	15
	DP	Cavagnaro, Matt, State College	49
3B	PCT	Jimenez, Jorge, Lowell	.958
	PO	Eigsti, Jacob, Brooklyn	44
		Mitchell, Derrick, Williamsport	44
	A	Sexton, Gregory, Hudson Valley	111
	E	Mitchell, Derrick, Williamsport	26
	DP	Jimenez, Jorge, Lowell	14
SS	PCT	Bouchard, Matthew, Brooklyn	.972
		Patino, Jorge, Oneonta	.972
	PO	Thompson, Mark, Mahon. Valley	113
	A	Thompson, Mark, Mahon. Valley	222
	E	Henson, Tyler, Aberdeen	28
	DP	Thompson, Mark, Mahon. Valley	49
OF	PCT	White, Adam, Mahoning Valley	1
		Whiting, Brandon, Vermont	1
	PO	Brown, Dominic, Williamsport	136
	A	Brown, Dominic, Williamsport	12
	E	Fermin, Angel, Hudson Valley	8
	DP	White, Adam, Mahoning Valley	4

MINOR LEAGUES

MINOR LEAGUES

BY ALAN MATTHEWS

Manager Steve Decker has become an institution in Oregon, and part of his reputation is putting consistent winners on the field. The 2007 season was no exception, as the Giants affiliate in Salem-Keizer won its second straight Northwest League title and fourth in eight years.

With a remarkable 57-19 regular season record, Salem-Keizer was the only team in the league to finish with a record above .500, as the Volcanoes manhandled the league from the outset of the season.

With a lineup loaded with sluggers who cut their teeth in college, such as infielders Matt Downs and Bond Brock and outfielders Garrett Baker and Sean Van Elderen, Salem-Keizer had a blend of power and patience that's rare for a short-season league.

Leads came early and often for the Volcanoes, and they were secure, thanks to a seasoned pitching staff that didn't blow away hitters with velocity, but rather mixed multiple pitches and hit its spots every time out. Salem-Keizer was an amazing 48-0 when leading after six innings.

"Last year was Apollo Creed and this year was Rocky Balboa," Decker said. "We did not have a lot of those tools guys on this year's team, but we had a group of guys that really know how to play the game and when we got a lead late, we weren't losing."

Danny Otero led the NWL with 19 saves and Steve Edlefson and Jesse English helped bridge the gap in setup and middle-relief roles. Edlefson, a converted shortstop and English, who returned from Tommy John surgery to go 5-0, 0.69 with 46 strikeouts and five walks in 26 innings, epitomized the Volcanoes' selfless approach.

When the Giants sent first baseman/DH Andy D'Alessio from the Rookie-level Arizona League to Salem-Keizer for the final week of the regular season and the playoffs, the former Clemson product fortified a Volcanoes lineup that proved to be too much for Tri-City in the playoffs.

After winning the opening game of the best-of-five series, the Dust Devils sent three of the league's best pitchers to the mound in Games Two (Connor Graham), Three (Bruce Billings) and Four (Cory Riordan), and yet they still came away with losses each night, as Salem-Keizer celebrated a three-games-to-one victory.

The Volcanoes became the first team in the Northwest League in more than a decade to win back-to-back championships.

Downs, a 23-year-old from Alabama who split time

TOP 20 PROSPECTS

1. Matt Latos, rhp, Eugene (Padres)
2. Josh Donaldson, c, Boise (Cubs
3. Juan Ramirez, rhp, Everett (Mariners)
4. Tony Thomas, 2b, Boise (Cubs)
5. Fabio Castillo, rhp, Spokane (Rangers)
6. Kellen Kulbacki, of, Eugene (Padres)
7. Tommy Hunter, rhp, Spokane (Rangers)
8. Greg Halman, of, Everett (Mariners)
9. Helder Velazquez, ss, Tri City (Rockies)
10. Matt Mangini, 3b, Everett (Mariners)
11. Corey Brown, of, Vancouver (Athletics)
12. Bruce Billings, rhp, Tri City (Rockies)
13. Cory Riordan, rhp, Tri City (Rockies)
14. Mitch Canham, c, Eugene (Padres)
15. Robinson Fabian, rhp, Tri City (Rockies)
16. Kyler Burke, of, Boise (Cubs)
17. Edward Paredes, lhp, Everett (Mariners)
18. Chris Huseby, rhp, Boise (Cubs)
19. Brian Rike, of, Tri City (Rockies)
20. Jake Brigham, rhp, Spokane (Rangers)

BILL MITCHELL

between first, third and second base in 2007, was named the NWL co-MVP after leading the league's best offense with a .338 average. Downs' 41 extra-base hits were tops in the league, and he also led the league in runs with 68. He batted .357 in the championship series against Tri-City with three runs and drove in three more.

Downs finished well behind the league's batting champ, and shared MVP honors with fleet-footed center fielder Luis Durango, who posted a league-best .367 average for Eugene.

With its reliance on older players with more limited ceilings, Salem-Keizer did not dominate the league's prospect list as it dominated on the field.

Because while the pride of the NWL was loaded with polished players, the league's best prospects were mostly unfinished projects. Even the No. 1 player on the league prospect list, Eugene righthander Matt Latos, still has a ways to go with his consistency and command. Latos signed with the Padres as a draft-and-follow just before the 2007 draft and went 1-4, 3.83 in 56 innings.

"It was very comparable to what it was last year," Vancouver manager Rick Magnante said. "Overall, the talent pool might have been a little stronger last year, but this is an advanced first-year league with predominantly college players and Latin players who have two or three years of service. We saw a good combination of those Latin players and a lot of the same players who were in Alaska, Cape Cod and some of the other top college summer leagues a year ago."

STANDINGS

Page	Eastern Division	W	L	PCT	GB	Manager	Attendance	Average	Last Penn.
117	Tri-City Dust Devils (Rockies)	37	39	.487	—	Freddie Ocasio	75,308	1,982	None
84	Boise Hawks (Cubs)	37	39	.487	—	Tom Beyers	102,878	2,707	2004
291	Spokane Indians (Rangers)	33	42	.440	3½	Tim Hulett	192,021	5,053	2005
49	Yakima Bears (Diamondbacks)	33	43	.434	4	Mike Bell	70,117	1,895	2000
Page	Western Division	W	L	PCT	GB	Manager	Attendance	Average	Last Penn.
265	Salem-Keizer Volcanoes (Giants)	57	19	.750	—	Steve Decker	118,722	3,124	2007
215	Vancouver Canadians (Athletics)	37	38	.493	19½	Rick Magnante	126,491	3,419	None
273	Everett AquaSox (Mariners)	35	41	.461	22	Mike Tosar	106,683	2,883	1985
257	Eugene Emeralds (Padres)	34	42	.447	23	Greg Riddoch	134,949	3,551	1980

PLAYOFFS: Salem-Keizer defeated Tri-City 3-1 in a best-of-five series. **NOTE:** Teams' individual batting and pitching statistics can be found on page indicated in lefthand column.

CLUB BATTING

	AVG	G	AB	R	H	2B	3B	HR	RBI	BB	SO	SB	CS	OBP	SLG
Salem-Keizer	.289	76	2628	497	760	178	28	57	424	305	472	82	25	.371	.443
Eugene	.272	76	2629	423	714	130	25	52	373	335	652	71	31	.365	.399
Yakima	.264	76	2603	385	687	128	22	40	325	246	577	74	31	.337	.376
Boise	.262	76	2542	426	667	147	27	51	385	316	587	77	33	.351	.402
Tri-City	.254	76	2559	378	651	135	23	46	346	256	575	97	48	.334	.379
Everett	.243	76	2535	304	617	129	12	51	261	219	791	94	45	.314	.364
Vancouver	.243	75	2471	378	600	136	18	43	334	363	743	76	39	.357	.365
Spokane	.241	75	2511	320	604	115	19	48	284	233	583	47	31	.317	.359

CLUB PITCHING

	ERA	G	CG	SHO	SV	IP	H	R	ER	HR	BB	SO	AVG
Salem-Keizer	3.44	76	0	8	27	677	630	291	256	58	236	629	.246
Spokane	3.93	75	0	2	19	662	613	375	289	44	272	680	.244
Everett	4.18	76	0	2	20	674	642	375	313	42	328	630	.250
Tri-City	4.37	76	0	4	21	674	691	379	324	47	209	643	.266
Vancouver	4.59	75	2	19	653	674	405	332	46	289	557	.269
Boise	4.63	76	0	2	16	660	670	426	334	60	335	588	.263
Eugene	4.73	76	0	1	16	668	666	418	350	46	300	670	.257
Yakima	4.77	76	0	3	16	660	714	442	349	45	304	583	.275

CLUB FIELDING

	PCT	PO	A	E	DP		PCT	PO	A	E	DP
Salem-Keizer	.974	2031	868	78	73	Boise	.962	1981	810	109	69
Tri-City	.970	2021	754	86	61	Spokane	.962	1986	755	107	53
Everett	.968	2022	796	94	62	Vancouver	.961	1960	860	115	74
Eugene	.964	2003	754	102	53	Yakima	.957	1979	806	126	57

INDIVIDUAL BATTING LEADERS (Minimum 236 Plate Appearances)

	AVG	G	AB	R	H	2B	3B	HR	RBI	BB	SO	SB
Durango, Luis, Eugene	.367	69	300	60	110	6	8	2	32	29	32	17
Downs, Matthew, Salem-Keizer	.338	73	287	68	97	33	0	8	48	28	34	16
Wright, Ty, Boise	.317	52	189	40	60	12	2	8	44	23	22	6
Hallberg, Mark, Yakima	.313	58	233	44	73	15	1	6	32	22	21	12
Frey, Evan, Yakima	.309	58	246	48	76	8	6	0	21	27	42	13
Baker, Garrett, Salem-Keizer	.308	73	266	53	82	24	6	7	64	30	46	10
Thomas, Tony, Boise	.308	46	182	44	56	12	8	5	33	25	41	28
Halman, Gregory, Everett	.307	62	238	37	73	19	1	16	37	21	85	16
Wyatt, Jonathan, Boise	.306	66	245	61	75	18	4	4	41	42	47	12
Mee, Michael, Yakima	.304	54	191	30	58	10	1	0	27	28	28	3

INDIVIDUAL PITCHING LEADERS (Minimum 61 Innings)

	W	L	ERA	G	GS	CG	SV	IP	H	R	ER	BB	SO
Collmenter, Joshua, Yakima	6	3	2.71	14	12	0	0	66	60	22	20	21	57
Billings, Bruce, Tri-City	4	2	2.97	15	15	0	0	79	59	30	26	16	89
Brewer, Thomas, Salem-Keizer	9	1	3.05	14	14	0	0	65	67	22	22	16	52
Brigham, Jacob, Spokane	5	4	3.16	15	15	0	0	77	69	43	27	34	65
Holland, Derek, Spokane	4	5	3.22	16	14	0	0	67	57	33	24	21	83
Huseby, Christopher, Boise	2	5	3.39	15	15	0	0	66	61	39	25	31	53
Christianson, Chase, Yakima	4	5	3.77	16	11	0	1	72	81	40	30	29	67
Hefner, Jeremy, Eugene	2	5	3.90	17	11	0	0	62	51	33	27	20	74
Fabian, Robinson, Tri-City	4	6	3.96	15	15	0	0	77	85	42	34	26	67
Paredes, Edward, Everett	7	6	3.99	16	15	0	0	86	75	47	38	48	61

ALL-STAR TEAM

C: Jonathan Greene, Spokane. **1B:** Danny Hamblin, Vancouver. **2B:** Matt Downs, Salem-Keizer. **3B:** Clayton Connor, Yakima. **SS:** Mark Hallberg, Yakima. **OF:** Luis Durango, Eugene; Greg Halman, Everett; Jonathan Wyatt, Boise. **DH:** Garrett Baker, Salem-Keizer. **LHP:** Edward Paredes, Everett. **RHP:** Thomas Brewer, Salem-Keizer. **LHRP:** Ryan Falcon, Spokane. **RHRP:** Danny Otero, Salem-Keizer.

Most Valuable Player: (tie) Matt Downs, Salem-Keizer/Luis Durango, Eugene. **Manager of the Year:** (tie) Steve Decker, Salem-Keizer/Greg Riddoch, Eugene.

DEPARTMENT LEADERS

BATTING

OBP	Donaldson, Joshua, Boise	.47
SLG	Halman, Gregory, Everett	.597
R	Downs, Matthew, Salem-Keizer	68
H	Durango, Luis, Eugene	110
TB	Downs, Matthew, Salem-Keizer	154
XBH	Downs, Matthew, Salem-Keizer	41
2B	Downs, Matthew, Salem-Keizer	33
3B	Thomas, Tony, Boise	8
	Durango, Luis, Eugene	8
HR	Gac, Ian, Indians	17
RBI	Baker, Garrett, Salem-Keizer	64
SAC	Mitchell, Michael, Tri-City	9
	Richard, Michael, Vancouver	9
SF	Smith, Marquez, Boise	6
	Baker, Garrett, Salem-Keizer	6
BB	Payne, Danny, Eugene	53
IBB	Halman, Gregory, Everett	4
	Holcomb, Darin, Tri-City	4
HBP	Pruitt, J.D., Vancouver	34
SO	Hamblin, Daniel, Vancouver	93
SB	Mitchell, Michael, Tri-City	32
CS	Mitchell, Michael, Tri-City	11
GIDP	Velazquez, Helder, Tri-City	10
AB/SO	Hallberg, Mark, Yakima	11.1

PITCHING

G	Pena, Riquy, Tri-City	31
GS	Eight players tied at	15
CG	Hertzler, Bradley, Vancouver	1
	Hodsdon, Scott, Vancouver	1
SHO	Hertzler, Bradley, Vancouver	1
GF	Pena, Riquy, Tri-City	26
SV	Otero, Daniel, Salem-Keizer	19
W	Brewer, Thomas, Salem-Keizer	9
	De La Garza, Andrew, Salem-Keizer	9
L	Salinas, Doug, Everett	8
IP	Paredes, Edward, Everett	85.2
H	Salinas, Doug, Everett	89
	Fournier, Daniel, Yakima	89
R	Thompson, Bryant, Yakima	58
ER	Thompson, Bryant, Yakima	49
HB	Thompson, Bryant, Yakima	22
BB	Paredes, Edward, Everett	48
SO	Billings, Bruce, Tri-City	89
SO/9-S	Cranston, Jared, Salem-Keizer	11.71
SO/9-R	Brown, Aaron, Everett	11.92
WP	Fabian, Robinson, Tri-City	15
BK	Ramirez, Juan, Everett	7
AVG	Billings, Bruce, Tri-City	.208

FIELDING

C	PCT	Donaldson, Joshua, Boise	.99
	PO	Greene, Jonathan, Spokane	394
	A	Greene, Jonathan, Spokane	54
	E	Greene, Jonathan, Spokane	9
		Schmidt, Konrad, Yakima	9
	DP	Donaldson, Joshua, Boise	5
		Greene, Jonathan, Spokane	5
	PB	Greene, Jonathan, Spokane	16
	CS%	Williams, Jackson, Salem-Keizer	.43
1B	PCT	Hamblin, Daniel, Vancouver	.994
	PO	Sawyer, Marc, Boise	491
	A	Sawyer, Marc, Boise	30
	E	Sawyer, Marc, Boise	8
	DP	Hamblin, Daniel, Vancouver	49
2B	PCT	—	—
	PO	Thomas, Tony, Boise	91
	A	Colina, Edilio, Everett	130
	E	Batten, Joseph, Yakima	12
	DP	Ray, Matthew, Vancouver	28
3B	PCT	Davis, Andrew, Salem-Keizer	.967
	PO	Davis, Andrew, Salem-Keizer	52
	A	Davis, Andrew, Salem-Keizer	150
	E	Ramirez, Ramon, Yakima	13
	DP	Davis, Andrew, Salem-Keizer	12
SS	PCT	Schoop, Sharlon, Salem-Keizer	.967
	PO	Hallberg, Mark, Yakima	107
	A	Diaz, Ogui, Everett	176
	E	Johnston, Dylan, Boise	28
	DP	Schoop, Sharlon, Salem-Keizer	38
OF	PCT	Halman, Gregory, Everett	.99
	PO	Mitchell, Michael, Tri-City	156
	A	Wyatt, Jonathan, Boise	9
	E	Durango, Luis, Eugene	7
		Rike, Brian, Tri-City	7
	DP	Wyatt, Jonathan, Boise	4
		Durango, Luis, Eugene	4

BY NATHAN RODE

To no one's surprise, Danville and Elizabethton dominated the Rookie-level Appalachian League again. They met for the third straight year in the championship series, claimed 11 of 14 spots on the postseason all-star team and accounted for 14 of the players on Baseball America's Top 20 Prospects list.

Elizabethton swept the D-Braves in the playoffs with two straight victories in the best-of-three championship series, and the Twins also claimed both of the league's major awards.

Righthander David Bromberg was named pitcher of the year after going 9-0, 2.78, while outfielder Ozzie Lewis grabbed the MVP award after finishing fourth or better in all three triple-crown categories at .323-9-50. Danville, meanwhile, boasted the Appy's two best prospects in lefty Cole Rohrbough and outfielder Cody Johnson, a pair of 2006 draft picks.

It was a year for emerging pitchers as the Twins and Braves relied on quality arms to top their respective divisions. Elizabethton had Bromberg and fellow righthander Mike McCardell, who joined the team in July after being taken in the sixth-round out of Division II Kutztown and a short stint in the Gulf Coast League. The Bromberg-McCardell punch delivered a 14-1, 2.45 line in 103 innings.

The Braves seem to have found a couple of lefthanders with potential in Cole Rohrbough, a draft-and-follow out of Western Nevada Community College and Jeffrey Locke, a second-round pick out of a New Hampshire high school in 2006.

Rohrbough went 3-2, 1.08 in 33 innings before being moved to low Class A Rome. During his time with Danville he used a fastball-curveball combination that helped him average almost 16 strikeouts per nine innings.

Locke was a hard-luck loser in the championship, but was dominant for most of the summer. He went 7-1, 2.66 in 61 innings and held opponents to a .213 average. On paper, the Danville staff seemed unstoppable with Rohrbough, Locke, Steve Evarts (4-0, 1.95), Edgar Osuna (5-3, 2.47) and Jose Ortegano (6-1, 1.48), but the Twins had just enough offense in the end.

Though Lewis won the MVP honors, the Braves' Johnson was impressive offensively, leading the league with 17 home runs. He also answered some questions about his defense after playing most of the season in left field and committing just four errors.

The Royals made their debut in Burlington as the

TOP 20 PROSPECTS

1. Cole Rohrbough, lhp, Danville (Braves)
2. Cody Johnson, of, Danville (Braves)
3. David Bromberg, rhp, Elizabethton (Twins)
4. Neftali Feliz, rhp, Danville (Braves)
5. Jeffrey Locke, lhp, Danville (Braves)
6. Nick Barnese, rhp, Princeton (Devil Rays)
7. Pete Kozma, ss, Johnson City (Cardinals)
8. Brandon Hicks, ss, Danville (Braves)
9. Steve Evarts, lhp, Danville (Braves)
10. Mike McCardell, rhp, Elizabethton (Twins)
11. Michael Fisher, ss, Danville (Braves)
12. Jose Martinez, of, Bristol (White Sox)
13. Estarlin De Los Santos, ss, Elizabethton (Twins)
14. Loek Van Mil, rhp, Elizabethton (Twins)
15. Deibinson Romero, 3b, Elizabethton (Twins)
16. Ozzie Lewis, of, Elizabethton (Twins)
17. Ebert Rosario, 3b, Greeneville (Astros)
18. Bradley Tippett, rhp, Elizabethton (Twins)
19. Kraig Binick, of, Bluefield (Orioles)
20. Kyle Greenwalt, rhp, Greeneville (Astros)

BILL SETLIFF

team's major league affiliate, after the Indians left town following the 2006 season, and they were successful considering the competition, going 38-30 to finish in second place behind Danville in the Appy League East. They didn't have anyone crack the top 20 prospects list, but outfielders David Lough and Patrick Norris drew some attention. Lough battled injuries, but showed some pop for his 5-foot-10 frame and Norris was second in the league with 30 stolen bases.

The league also had to function with just nine teams in 2007, when the Blue Jays announced in the offseason that they were leaving Pulaski and Appalachian League president Lee Landers was unable to find an acceptable replacement. He not only looked for a new major league affiliate for Pulaski, but also considered creative solutions such as a team of prospects from the Mexican League or a co-op team, but none of the ideas won acceptance from the major league farm directors who serve as the league's board of directors.

The nine-team structure forced the league to play an odd schedule that featured mostly two-game series, more time on the road and increased travel costs. Pulaski was left with an empty stadium that the small Virginia city had paid thousands of dollars to renovate. Landers had several candidates to move into Pulaski for the 2008 season, however, and was optimistic the league would return to 10 teams.

STANDINGS

Page	Eastern Division	W	L	PCT	GB	Manager	Attendance	Average	Last Penn.
58	Danville Braves	48	20	.706	—	Paul Runge	42,016	1,236	2007
151	Burlington Royals	38	30	.559	10	Darryl Kennedy	33,060	1,002	1993
283	Princeton Devil Rays	33	35	.485	15	Jamie Nelson	26,882	867	1994
68	Bluefield Orioles	32	36	.471	16	Alex Arias	28,995	932	2001
Page	Western Division	W	L	PCT	GB	Manager	Attendance	Average	Last Penn.
184	Elizabethton Twins	50	18	.735	—	Ray Smith	30,134	972	2005
195	Kingsport Mets	35	33	.515	15	Donovan Mitchell	34,301	1,183	1995
247	Johnson City Cardinals	28	40	.412	22	Joe Almaraz	21,101	703	1976
92	Bristol White Sox	25	43	.368	25	Bobby Thigpen	20,768	692	2002
143	Greeneville Astros	17	51	.250	33	Rodney Linares	51,425	1,558	2004

PLAYOFFS: Danville defeated Elizabethton 2-1 in best-of-three series. **NOTE:** Teams' individual batting and pitching statistics can be found on page indicated in lefthand column.

MINOR LEAGUES

CLUB BATTING

	AVG	G	AB	R	H	2B	3B	HR	RBI	BB	SO	SB	CS	OBP	SLG
Elizabethton	.287	68	2282	466	656	129	16	47	409	291	458	79	18	.379	.420
Danville	.280	68	2343	386	655	146	17	55	345	207	567	45	25	.350	.427
Burlington	.258	68	2302	357	595	120	18	48	304	206	522	78	31	.332	.389
Kingsport	.257	68	2221	330	570	130	23	41	284	210	526	74	27	.332	.391
Johnson City	.256	68	2265	295	580	115	13	41	253	217	519	58	37	.327	.373
Bluefield	.249	68	2238	346	557	118	27	30	300	283	567	47	16	.342	.366
Bristol	.249	68	2163	285	539	92	20	33	244	199	537	67	34	.322	.356
Princeton	.249	68	2239	295	558	124	26	26	256	215	542	110	43	.321	.363
Greeneville	.222	68	2212	240	492	108	14	26	213	182	593	52	28	.290	.319

CLUB PITCHING

	ERA	G	CG	SHO	SV	IP	H	R	ER	HR	BB	SO	AVG
Danville	3.10	68	0	7	28	599	526	257	205	29	192	653	.232
Elizabethton	3.17	68	0	5	22	574	483	241	202	32	192	680	.226
Princeton	3.67	68	0	6	19	586	555	303	239	33	222	496	.248
Burlington	3.86	68	1	4	21	589	558	307	253	50	192	482	.249
Johnson City	4.18	68	0	8	18	578	557	343	267	42	255	492	.251
Kingsport	4.49	68	1	1	14	579	589	358	289	45	242	489	.261
Bluefield	4.66	68	1	2	17	579	647	365	298	31	226	496	.279
Bristol	4.77	68	0	5	15	557	612	374	295	43	234	551	.275
Greeneville	5.67	68	1	1	9	579	675	452	363	42	255	492	.286

CLUB FIELDING

	PCT	PO	A	E	DP		PCT	PO	A	E	DP
Danville	.970	1796	719	79	49	Princeton	.953	1758	751	125	51
Burlington	.968	1768	718	83	53	Bristol	.951	1670	669	120	56
Elizabethton	.966	1723	625	82	61	Johnson City	.951	1733	750	127	70
Bluefield	.962	1737	778	99	49	Greeneville	.947	1737	711	138	50
Kingsport	.957	1738	717	109	63						

INDIVIDUAL BATTING LEADERS (Minimum 236 Plate Appearances)

	AVG	G	AB	R	H	2B	3B	HR	RBI	BB	SO	SB
Miles, Cole, Danville	.333	60	234	40	78	6	4	2	27	23	28	11
Lewis, Ozzie, Elizabethton	.323	62	235	46	76	18	1	9	50	19	52	3
Romero, Deibinson, Elizabethton	.316	66	247	60	78	16	2	9	52	34	47	9
Riportella , Beau, Johnson City	.315	48	168	31	53	4	1	2	15	13	31	10
Lane, Jake, Burlington	.315	53	184	45	58	16	4	6	41	30	50	9
Yersich, Gregory, Elizabethton	.312	50	186	35	58	12	0	2	30	15	23	0
Jimenez, Jose, Kingsport	.309	51	188	32	58	17	1	7	41	17	43	4
Leveret, Rene, Elizabethton	.307	66	244	50	75	14	0	8	65	34	36	0
Johnson, Cody, Danville	.305	63	243	51	74	18	5	17	57	26	72	7
Tosoni, Rene, Elizabethton	.301	63	236	58	71	13	4	3	31	32	48	13

INDIVIDUAL PITCHING LEADERS (Minimum 61 Innings)

	W	L	ERA	G	GS	CG	SV	IP	H	R	ER	BB	SO
Ortegano, Jose, Danville	6	1	1.48	13	9	0	0	61	44	14	10	11	55
Hall, Jeremy, Princeton	4	1	1.56	12	12	0	0	69	62	15	12	11	59
Osuna, Edgar, Danville	5	3	2.47	13	6	0	2	55	55	19	15	11	66
Locke, Jeffrey, Danville	7	1	2.66	13	11	0	1	61	48	23	18	8	74
Bromberg, David, Elizabethton	9	0	2.78	13	11	0	0	58	45	19	18	32	81
Gleason, Sean, Bluefield	5	4	2.93	14	10	0	0	68	78	28	22	14	61
Arredondo, Jose, Johnson City	5	5	3.04	15	8	0	1	56	44	27	19	14	41
Cespedes, Leandro, Greeneville	4	5	3.15	11	10	0	0	54	48	23	19	12	52
Lin, Po-Yu, Bristol	6	5	3.30	14	11	0	0	63	71	33	23	17	65
Mateo, Jose, Johnson City	4	2	3.41	15	10	0	0	61	57	35	23	24	44

ALL-STAR TEAM

C: Gregory Yersich, Elizabethton. **1B:** Rene Leveret, Elizabethton. **2B:** Cole Miles, Danville. **3B:** Deibinson Romero, Elizabethton. **SS:** Estarlin De Los Santos, Elizabethton. **Utility IF:** Matt Tucker, Bluefield. **OF:** Kraig Binick, Bluefield; Cody Johnson, Danville; Ozzie Lewis, Elizabethton. Utility **OF:** Rene Tosoni, Elizabethton. **DH:** Jake Lane, Burlington. **RHP:** David Bromberg, Elizabethton. **LHP:** Jeff Locke, Danville. **RP:** Nick Fellman, Danville. **Player of the Year:** Ozzie Lewis, Elizabethton. **Pitcher of the Year:** David Bromberg, Elizabethton. **Manager of the Year:** Paul Runge, Danville.

DEPARTMENT LEADERS

BATTING

OBP	Lane, Jake, Burlington	.453
SLG	Johnson, Cody, Danville	.63
R	De Los Santos, Estarlin, Elizabethton	60
	Romero, Deibinson, Elizabethton	60
H	Miles, Cole, Danville	78
	Romero, Deibinson, Elizabethton	78
TB	Johnson, Cody, Danville	153
XBH	Johnson, Cody, Danville	40
2B	White, Jason, Bluefield	24
	Giarraputo, Nicholas, Kingsport	24
3B	Veloz, Greg, Kingsport	9
HR	Johnson, Cody, Danville	17
RBI	Leveret, Rene, Elizabethton	65
SAC	Richey, Brandon, Kingsport	7
	Veloz, Greg, Kingsport	7
SF	Martin, Kyle, Burlington	5
	Romero, Deibinson, Elizabethton	5
BB	Julius, Jacob, Bluefield	49
IBB	White, Jason, Bluefield	2
	Humphrey, Ben, Princeton	2
HBP	Lane, Jake, Burlington	17
SO	White, Jason, Bluefield	73
SB	Ross, Michael, Princeton	36
CS	Gerst, Kent, Bristol Sox	9
GIDP	Coe, Adam, Danville	9
	Leveret, Rene, Elizabethton	9
AB/SO	Rosario, Ebert, Greeneville	8.8

PITCHING

G	Fellman, Nicholas, Danville	22
GS	Four players tied at	13
CG	Four players tied at	1
SHO	Caldera, Alexander, Burlington	1
GF	Fellman, Nicholas, Danville	20
SV	Fellman, Nicholas, Danville	16
W	Bromberg, David, Elizabethton	9
L	Paniagua, Onarkys, Bristol	10
IP	Hall, Jeremy, Princeton	69.1
H	Egan, Pat, Bluefield	78
	Gleason, Sean, Bluefield	78
R	Paniagua, Onarkys, Bristol	61
ER	Paniagua, Onarkys, Bristol	44
HB	Diapoules, Mark, Johnson City	11
BB	Lee, Bryan, Bluefield	38
SO	Bromberg, David, Elizabethton	81
SO/9-S	McCardell, Michael, Elizabethton	14
SO/9-R	Fellman, Nicholas, Danville	14.79
WP	Orta, Phillips, Kingsport	12
BK	Five players tied at	4
AVG	Ortegano, Jose, Danville	.199

FIELDING

C	PCT	Monaghan, Brendan, Bluefield	1
	PO	Yersich, Gregory, Elizabethton	368
	A	Yersich, Gregory, Elizabethton	48
	E	Thomas, Mark, Princeton	9
	DP	Yersich, Gregory, Elizabethton	4
	PB	Pestana, Reinaldo, Greeneville	10
	CS%	Acosta, Mayobanex, Princeton	.31
1B	PCT	Morris, Joshua, Danville	.99
	PO	Leveret, Rene, Elizabethton	483
	A	Morris, Joshua, Danville	24
	E	Andrade, Jorge, Bristol Sox	7
		Leveret, Rene, Elizabethton	7
	DP	Leveret, Rene, Elizabethton	42
2B	PCT	Folli, Mike, Johnson City	.967
	PO	Veloz, Greg, Kingsport	141
	A	Folli, Mike, Johnson City	156
	E	Veloz, Greg, Kingsport	18
	DP	Folli, Mike, Johnson City	43
3B	PCT	Romero, Deibinson, Elizabethton	.929
	PO	Rosario, Ebert, Greeneville	46
	A	Romero, Deibinson, Elizabethton	126
	E	Rosario, Ebert, Greeneville	28
	DP	Romero, Deibinson, Elizabethton	13
SS	PCT	Martin, Kyle, Burlington	.96
	PO	White, Jason, Bluefield	93
	A	White, Jason, Bluefield	206
	E	Vargas, Hancer, Bristol	24
	DP	White, Jason, Bluefield	35
OF	PCT	Stegall, Daniel, Kingsport	.992
	PO	Norris, Patrick, Burlington	130
	A	Tucker, Wilson, Burlington	9
	A	Tosoni, Rene, Elizabethton	9
	E	Kang, Kyeong, Princeton	8
	DP	Three players tied at	3

BY BEN BADLER

The Orem Owlz squeaked into the Pioneer League playoffs, finishing with a 37-39 overall record in the regular season. They finished with a blast, as third baseman Jay Brossman hit the game-winning home run in the 16th inning to give the Owlz a 3-2 victory over Great Falls to win the PL championship.

Despite a mediocre regular season, the Owlz went 4-0 in the playoffs to sweep through both rounds, getting key postseason contributions from righthander Jordan Walden and lefthander Robert Fish. The championship is the Owlz' third title in four years.

Great Falls dominated the league during the regular season, finishing with a league-best 51-24 overall record during the regular season. Idaho Falls won both halves in the Southern Division, but fell to Orem in the semifinals of the playoffs. Helena, with the second-best overall record in the league, got swept by Great Falls in the other semifinal matchup.

Perhaps the most impressive about the White Sox was that they won not with older players but with prospects, as six players from the team ranked among the league's top 20 prospects.

The highest draft picks from the 2007 draft to play in the Pioneer League were Idaho Falls shortstop Mike Moustakas (second overall) and Helena outfielder Matt LaPorta (seventh overall), although neither amassed significant playing time in the league.

Great Falla lefthander Aaron Poreda, a first-rounder, and Billings shortstop Todd Frazier, a supplemental first-rounder, were the two other highest picks from the 2007 draft to play in the Pioneer League this season.

Frazier and Poreda dominated the league as expected, and the two ranked first and fourth, respectively, among the PL's top 20 prospects. Frazier hit .319/.409/.513 in 160 at-bats for the Mustangs, while Poreda held down a 1.17 regular-season ERA and did not allow an earned run in two playoff starts.

Just as notable, however, were the performances put forth by some of the players who fell to some of the later rounds in the draft and boosted their prospect status with impressive showings this year.

Helena outfielder Caleb Gindl, a fifth-rounder, took the league by storm, winning the batting title at .372. Gindl's .420 on-base percentage also ranked second in the league behind the .427 mark posted by Ogden's Eric Kanaby.

Billings third baseman Brandon Waring, a seventh-rounder, nearly broke the league record with 20 homers, giving him a total of 47 for the year between pro ball and Wofford. Waring had a stretch of 10 games in which he

TOP 20 PROSPECTS

R. DEAN HENDRICKSON

1. Todd Frazier, ss, Billings (Reds)
2. Caleb Gindl, of, Helena (Brewers)
3. Jordan Walden, rhp, Orem (Angels)
4. Aaron Poreda, lhp, Great Falls (White Sox)
5. Brandon Waring, 3b, Billings (Reds)
6. Jonathan Lucroy, c, Helena (Brewers)
7. Austin Gallagher, 3b, Ogden (Brewers)
8. Robert Bryson, rhp, Helena (Brewers)
9. Reynaldo Navarro, ss, Missoula (Diamondbacks)
10. Christian Marrero, 1b, Great Falls (White Sox)
11. Salvador Sanchez, of, Great Falls (White Sox)
12. Jaime Ortiz, 1b, Ogden (Dodgers)
13. Jhoulys Chacin, rhp, Casper (Rockies)
14. Robert Fish, lhp, Orem (Angels)
15. John Ely, rhp, Great Falls (White Sox)
16. Justin Reed, of, Billings (Reds)
17. Andrew Romine, ss, Orem (Angels)
18. Jimmy Gallagher, of, Great Falls (White Sox)
19. Adrian Ortiz, of, Idaho Falls (Royals)
20. Lyndon Estill, of, Great Falls (White Sox)

STANDINGS: SPLIT SEASON

FIRST HALF				SECOND HALF			
NORTH	**W**	**L**	**PCT**	**GB**	**NORTH**	**W**	**L**	**PCT**	**GB**
Helena	26	12	.684	—	Great Falls	27	10	.730	—
Great Falls	24	14	.632	2	Helena	22	16	.579	5½
Billings	20	17	.541	5½	Billings	17	21	.447	10½
Missoula	14	24	.368	12	Missoula	13	25	.342	14½
SOUTH	**W**	**L**	**PCT**	**GB**	**SOUTH**	**W**	**L**	**PCT**	**GB**
Idaho Falls	23	15	.605	—	Idaho Falls	23	15	.605	—
Ogden	17	20	.459	5½	Orem	20	18	.526	3
Orem	17	21	.447	6	Ogden	17	21	.447	6
Casper	10	28	.263	13	Casper	12	25	.324	10½

PLAYOFFS—Semifinals: Orem defeated Idaho Falls 2-0 and Great Falls defeated Helena 2-1 in best-of-three series. **Finals:** Orem defeated Great Falls 2-0 in a best-of-three series.

hit 10 home runs.

Idaho Falls first baseman Clint Robinson grabbed league MVP honors, as the 22-year-old first baseman led the Chukars to double first-place finishes in the PL South with a 46-30 overall record. The lefthanded-hitting Robinson hit .333/.388/.593 in 253 at-bats, clubbing 15 home runs and 18 doubles.

White Sox righthander Juan Moreno led the league with a 2.39 ERA. Moreno, who relied on control and deception, walked just 11 batters in 90 innings. His 77 strikeouts also tied for a league-high, and his innings pitched were the second-most in the PL.

The Casper Rockies announced after the season that they will change their name to the Casper Ghosts.

STANDINGS

Page	Team	W	L	PCT	GB	Manager(s)	Attendance	Average	Last Penn.
92	Great Falls White Sox (White Sox)	51	24	.680	—	Chris Cron	107,045	2,816	2002
177	Helena Brewers (Brewers)	48	28	.632	3½	Jeffrey Isom	39,396	1,064	1984
153	Idaho Falls Chukars (Royals)	46	30	.526	5½	Brian Rupp	104,960	2,762	2000
101	Billings Mustangs (Reds)	37	38	.493	14	J. Kruzel/F. Benavides	95,309	2,575	2001
160	Orem Owlz (Angels)	37	39	.487	14½	Tom Kotchman	109,125	2,871	2007
170	Ogden Raptors (Dodgers)	34	41	.453	17	Jeff Carter	130,266	3,520	None
50	Missoula Osprey (Diamondbacks)	27	49	.355	24½	Damon Mashore	86,881	2,286	2006
118	Casper Rockies (Rockies)	22	53	.293	29	Tony Diaz	45,354	1,259	None

NOTE: Teams' individual batting and pitching statistics can be found on page indicated in lefthand column.

MINOR LEAGUES

CLUB BATTING

	AVG	G	AB	R	H	2B	3B	HR	RBI	BB	SO	SB	CS	OBP	SLG
Great Falls	.297	75	2661	496	790	186	40	67	440	284	556	82	45	.372	.472
Helena	.291	76	2620	421	762	152	23	55	373	201	495	68	40	.350	.429
Ogden	.285	75	2591	396	738	129	20	64	346	256	566	53	37	.358	.424
Orem	.278	76	2698	434	751	125	27	71	399	255	607	74	27	.348	.424
Billings	.275	75	2647	460	727	142	34	74	408	235	622	55	29	.342	.438
Idaho Falls	.274	76	2655	411	728	132	21	51	357	252	572	101	38	.346	.397
Missoula	.248	76	2586	373	642	133	14	58	333	245	618	48	34	.322	.378
Casper	.241	75	2495	312	601	106	17	46	278	221	767	64	45	.316	.352

CLUB PITCHING

	ERA	G	CG	SHO	SV	IP	H	R	ER	HR	BB	SO	AVG
Idaho Falls	3.63	76	0	5	15	683	686	347	275	42	233	665	.263
Great Falls	3.75	75	0	5	21	672	684	334	280	44	215	636	.264
Orem	4.28	76	1	2	15	681	682	372	324	53	258	604	.263
Helena	4.35	76	0	4	22	675	675	386	324	58	201	629	.259
Billings	4.90	75	0	5	14	663	722	434	358	60	294	604	.278
Ogden	4.93	75	1	2	17	654	736	429	353	61	231	592	.284
Casper	5.14	75	0	2	10	654	764	474	372	74	240	552	.289
Missoula	5.86	76	0	2	11	666	790	527	425	94	277	521	.291

CLUB FIELDING

	PCT	PO	A	E	DP		PCT	PO	A	E	DP
Orem	.970	2043	882	90	80	Billings	.964	1988	800	105	73
Helena	.969	2016	918	93	57	Idaho Falls	.962	2049	834	113	76
Great Falls	.966	2014	881	102	70	Missoula	.953	1998	835	140	73
Ogden	.965	1962	797	99	66	Casper	.952	1961	818	141	72

INDIVIDUAL BATTING LEADERS (Minimum 236 Plate Appearances)

	AVG	G	AB	R	H	2B	3B	HR	RBI	BB	SO	SB
Gindl, Caleb, Helena	.372	55	207	40	77	22	3	5	42	20	38	4
Pedroza, Jaime, Ogden	.360	56	211	33	76	18	1	8	40	14	44	4
Brossman, Jay, Orem	.346	65	272	46	94	14	0	7	44	19	48	4
Gronkowski, Gordon, Orem	.344	66	244	44	84	19	0	8	50	27	63	0
Sanchez, Salvador, Great Falls	.343	70	283	57	97	16	10	7	51	18	59	18
Lucroy, Jonathan, Helena	.342	61	234	35	80	18	2	4	39	16	37	0
Kanaby, Erik, Ogden	.338	58	207	25	70	5	0	1	21	30	35	8
Robinson, Clint, Idaho Falls	.336	67	253	39	85	18	1	15	66	19	42	2
Gallagher, Jim, Great Falls	.332	67	247	52	82	21	1	9	44	35	38	7
Rosario, Jovanny, Ogden	.331	70	281	47	93	11	4	5	34	21	50	22

INDIVIDUAL PITCHING LEADERS (Minimum 61 Innings)

	W	L	ERA	G	GS	CG	SV	IP	H	R	ER	BB	SO
Moreno, Juan, Great Falls	6	4	2.39	16	16	0	0	90	83	29	24	11	77
Walden, Jordan, Orem	1	1	3.08	15	15	0	0	64	49	27	22	17	63
Chacin, Jhoulys, Casper	6	5	3.13	16	16	0	0	92	85	45	32	26	77
Fish, Robert, Orem	3	4	3.27	16	15	0	0	72	62	33	26	31	77
Jimenez, Esmerlin, Orem	5	2	3.51	16	13	1	0	77	70	37	30	17	58
Montano, Luis, Billings	8	4	3.62	15	13	0	0	82	81	37	33	20	64
Mercedes, Roque, Helena	7	4	3.75	15	15	0	0	84	88	49	35	20	70
Carter, Anthony, Great Falls	5	3	3.93	15	15	0	0	71	78	34	31	17	62
Gardner, Michael, Ogden	6	5	3.93	15	15	1	0	85	96	54	37	26	49
Del Rosario, Enerio, Billings	5	4	3.97	15	15	0	0	70	77	40	31	30	40

ALL-STAR TEAM

C: Jonathan Lucroy, Helena. **1B:** Clint Robinson, Idaho Falls. **2B:** Eric Farris, Helena. **3B:** Jay Brossman, Orem. **SS:** Jaime Pedroza, Ogden. **OF:** Caleb Gindl, Helena; Jovanny Rosario, Ogden; Salvador Sanchez, Great Falls. **DH:** Michael McKennon, Billings. **P:** Roque Mercedes, Helena; Jhoulys Chacin, Casper; Luis Montano, Billings; Robert Fish, Orem; Juan Moreno, Great Falls. **Most Valuable Player:** Clint Robinson, Idaho Falls. **Pitcher of the Year:** Juan Moreno, Great Falls. **Manager of the Year:** Chris Cron, Great Falls.

DEPARTMENT LEADERS

BATTING

OBP	Kanaby, Erik, Ogden	.427
SLG	Vetters, Travis, Ogden	.645
R	Waring, Brandon, Billings	63
H	Sanchez, Salvador, Great Falls W. Sox	97
TB	Waring, Brandon, Billings	164
XBH	Retherford, C.J., Great Falls W. Sox	47
2B	Retherford, C.J., Great Falls W. Sox	30
3B	Sanchez, Salvador, Great Falls W. Sox	10
HR	Waring, Brandon, Billings	20
RBI	Robinson, Clint, Idaho Falls	66
SAC	Fuller, Justin, Ogden	11
SF	Gallagher, Jim, Great Falls	6
	Marrero, Christian, Great Falls	6
BB	Miller, Deandre, Orem	42
IBB	Robinson, Clint, Idaho Falls	3
HBP	Rumler, Elijah, Missoula	13
SO	Christensen, David, Casper	95
SB	Seratelli, Anthony, Idaho Falls	29
CS	Sanchez, Salvador, Great Falls	13
GIDP	Gallagher, Austin, Ogden	11
AB/SO	Farris, Eric, Helena	10.86

PITCHING

G	Perez, Wander, Great Falls	28
GS	Three players tied at	16
CG	Gardner, Michael, Ogden	1
	Jimenez, Esmerlin, Orem	1
SHO	Gardner, Michael, Ogden	1
GF	Brasier, Ryan, Orem	22
SV	Caraballo, Jhonny, Ogden	10
W	Montano, Luis, Billings	8
	Garcia, Jose, Helena	8
L	Fischer, Jeff, Casper	10
IP	Chacin, Jhoulys, Casper	92
H	Gardner, Michael, Ogden	96
R	Durst, Jason, Missoula	66
ER	Durst, Jason, Missoula	57
HB	Sena, Giornale, Missoula	11
BB	Ravin, Joshua, Billings	41
SO	Three players tied at	77
SO/9-S	Fish, Robert, Orem	9.85
SO/9-R	Bryson, Robert, Helena	13.1
WP	Molina, Jonathan, Casper	14
BK	Four players tied at	3
AVG	Walden, Jordan, Orem	.209

FIELDING

C	PCT	Jansen, Kenley, Ogden	.994
	PO	De Los Santos, Anel, Orem	349
	A	De Los Santos, Anel, Orem	53
	E	De Los Santos, Anel, Orem	7
	DP	Lucroy, Jonathan, Helena	4
		De Los Santos, Anel, Orem	4
	PB	Rosario, Wilin, Casper	12
	CS%	De Los Santos, Anel, Orem	.35
1B	PCT	McKennon, Michael, Billings	.992
	PO	McKennon, Michael, Billings	579
	A	McKennon, Michael, Billings	46
	E	Cunningham, Jeffrey, Casper	12
	DP	McKennon, Michael, Billings	57
2B	PCT	Farris, Eric, Helena	.975
	PO	Harbin, Taylor, Missoula	121
	A	Farris, Eric, Helena	177
	E	Murry, Zack, Casper	15
		Harbin, Taylor, Missoula	15
	DP	Mollenhauer, Dale, Great Falls	45
3B	PCT	Wheeler, Zelous, Helena	.932
	PO	Waring, Brandon, Billings	46
	A	Waring, Brandon, Billings	130
	E	Lowe, Shane, Casper	19
	DP	Waring, Brandon, Billings	13
		Retherford, C.J., Great Falls	13
SS	PCT	Romine, Andrew, Orem	.952
	PO	Navarro, Reynaldo, Missoula	114
	A	Paiml, Greg, Great Falls	205
	E	Navarro, Reynaldo, Missoula	28
	DP	Romine, Andrew, Orem	42
OF	PCT	Gallagher, Jim, Great Falls	1
	PO	Menchaca, Brandon, Billings	125
	A	Sanchez, Salvador, Great Falls	9
		Gonzalez, O.D., Idaho Falls	9
	E	Walker, Derrick, Missoula	8
	DP	Sanchez, Salvador, Great Falls	3
		Urena, Ariel, Missoula	3

MINOR LEAGUES

BY WILL LINGO

The Mariners were the best team in the Arizona League in the first half of the season. The Giants were the best team in the second half.

And in the end, it was the overall prowess of the Mariners, who finished with the best overall record in the league, that allowed them to win the league title in a one-game playoff.

Righthander Jake Wild struck out 14 in eight innings and surrendered only four hits to help the Mariners beat the Giants 8-5 in the championship game. Third baseman Mario Martinez was 2-for-4 with an RBI and two runs scored.

Wild capped off a season when he went 3-1, 1.88 to finish second in the league ERA race. It was his teammate, righthander Robbie Dominguez, who made the league all-star team, however, after he went 3-1, 2.01. With that one-two punch in the rotation—not to mention closer Travis Mortimore, who had 10 saves and a 1.91 ERA—it was no surprise that the Mariners led the league in team ERA at 3.39. The team also played solid defense behind the strong arms and led the league in fielding percentage.

The league's offensive standout was Angels outfielder Anthony Norman, who led the AZL in batting at .362 and won the league MVP award. He was old for the league at 22, however.

When 22-year-olds are considered too aged, it's obvious that the Arizona League has only a few veterans: the managers and coaches who return to the league year after year. Ruben Escalera was in his sixth season as Athletics manager, as was Bert Hunter with the Giants. Cubs coaches Carmelo Martinez and Rick Tronerud have combined for nearly 20 years of AZL experience.

These veteran AZL observers and others say the league has gotten younger as more organizations emphasize Latin American scouting and send those players to complex leagues for their first U.S. pro experience. The two best prospects in the league were Latins: Giants third baseman Angel Villalona and Rangers outfielder Engel Beltre.

The most important number regarding Villalona isn't $2.1 million (the bonus he got when he signed out of the Dominican Republic in 2006) but rather 1990 (the year he was born). He played most of the season at 16 and batted .285 with five home runs.

Beltre, who signed with the Red Sox for $600,000 out of the Dominican in the summer of 2006, hit much better following his inclusion in the Eric Gagne trade with the Rangers. He batted just .208 in the Gulf Coast League

while with Boston, but he hit .310 in 22 games in the AZL to earn a promotion to the Northwest League at the end of the season.

Baseball's new Aug. 15 signing deadline for draft picks led to extended negotiations that precluded many first-rounders from the 2007 draft from arriving in the AZL early enough to qualify for Baseball America's prospect list.

That's why the likes of Cubs third baseman Josh Vitters (who went just 2-for-30 with nine strikeouts) and righthanders Tim Alderson (Giants) and Michael Main (Rangers) weren't on the Top 20 Prospects list, even though their talent would dictate inclusion.

Several of the league's stats leaders didn't make the list mostly because of their advanced age, such as Giants first baseman Andy D'Alessio (14 homers) and Norman.

TOP 20 PROSPECTS

1. Angel Villalona, 3b, Giants
2. Engel Beltre, of, Rangers
3. Nick Noonan, 2b, Giants
4. Danny Duffy, lhp, Royals
5. Wilmer Font, rhp, Rangers
6. Wilber Bucardo, rhp, Giants
7. Drew Cumberland, ss, Padres
8. Danny Carroll, of, Mariners
9. Cristian Santana, c, Rangers
10. Mario Martinez, ss/3b, Mariners
11. Mason Tobin, rhp, Angels
12. Michael Anton, lhp, Angels
13. Matt Mitchell, rhp, Royals
14. Yefri Carvajal, of, Padres
15. Charlie Culberson, 2b/ss, Giants
16. Larry Suarez, rhp, Cubs
17. Clay Fuller, of, Angels
18. Sam Runion, rhp, Royals
19. Ivan Contreras, 2b, Angels
20. Jacob Wild, rhp, Mariners

STANDINGS: SPLIT SEASON

FIRST HALF	W	L	PCT	GB		SECOND HALF	W	L	PCT	GB
Mariners	20	8	.714	—		Giants	19	9	.679	—
Angels	19	9	.679	1		Mariners	17	11	.607	2
Padres	18	10	.643	2		Royals	16	12	.571	3
Cubs	14	14	.500	6		Angels	14	14	.500	5
Giants	14	14	.500	6		Athletics	13	15	.464	6
Athletics	12	16	.429	8		Cubs	13	15	.464	6
Royals	12	16	.429	8		Brewers	12	16	.429	7
Rangers	10	18	.357	10		Rangers	12	16	.429	7
Brewers	7	21	.250	13		Padres	10	18	.357	9

PLAYOFFS: The Mariners defeated the Giants in a one-game championship.

STANDINGS

Page	Team	Complex	W	L	PCT	GB	Manager	Last Penn.
274	Mariners	Peoria	37	19	.661	—	Jose Moreno	2007
161	Angels	Tempe	33	23	.589	4	Tyrone Boykin	None
266	Giants	Scottsdale	33	23	.589	4	Bert Hunter	2005
258	Padres	Peoria	28	28	.500	9	Tony Muser	2006
152	Royals	Surprise	28	28	.500	9	Lloyd Simmons	2003
85	Cubs	Mesa	27	29	.482	10	Ricardo Medina	2002
216	Athletics	Phoenix	25	31	.446	12	Ruben Escalera	2001
292	Rangers	Surprise	22	34	.393	15	Pedro Lopez	None
178	Brewers	Phoenix	19	37	.339	18	Charlie Greene	1990

NOTE: Teams' individual batting and pitching statistics can be found on page indicated in lefthand column.

CLUB BATTING

	AVG	G	AB	R	H	2B	3B	HR	RBI	BB	SO	SB	CS	OBP	SLG
Angels	.285	56	1963	378	560	101	35	22	295	260	490	84	27	.380	.406
Cubs	.275	56	1978	285	544	99	44	20	252	152	448	52	37	.334	.400
Giants	.275	56	1939	351	533	91	35	42	301	215	429	95	32	.359	.423
Padres	.274	56	1977	358	541	111	23	28	298	285	443	56	25	.375	.396
Mariners	.267	56	1908	317	509	94	23	13	253	205	498	82	48	.347	.361
Rangers	.260	56	1872	299	486	87	24	24	250	193	475	90	37	.342	.370
Royals	.251	56	1940	283	486	94	20	22	245	177	422	54	29	.326	.354
Athletics	.248	56	1878	302	465	88	21	17	250	260	454	83	36	.349	.344
Brewers	.245	56	1875	280	459	59	20	22	223	224	592	75	38	.337	.333

CLUB PITCHING

	ERA	G	CG	SHO	SV	IP	H	R	ER	HR	BB	SO	AVG
Mariners	3.39	56	0	4	14	504	488	256	190	19	192	478	.258
Giants	3.50	56	0	5	11	496	452	239	193	15	185	497	.244
Angels	4.00	56	1	4	11	493	477	284	219	20	180	472	.252
Royals	4.02	56	0	4	13	501	509	285	223	26	208	562	.264
Cubs	4.16	56	0	3	14	505	506	301	233	23	212	443	.263
Rangers	4.88	56	0	1	8	483	502	350	260	18	198	494	.260
Padres	4.91	56	0	2	8	496	559	344	271	34	213	455	.280
Athletics	5.43	56	0	3	10	494	539	340	292	26	200	458	.278
Brewers	6.52	56	0	0	7	490	551	454	351	29	383	392	.280

CLUB FIELDING

	PCT	PO	A	E	DP		PCT	PO	A	E	DP
Mariners	.965	1511	616	78	58	Cubs	.951	1514	657	112	68
Giants	.958	1487	609	91	51	Padres	.949	1489	610	112	46
Athletics	.957	1482	651	95	49	Brewers	.939	1470	573	132	39
Angels	.955	1479	587	97	41	Rangers	.939	1449	546	130	46
Royals	.953	1503	518	100	44						

INDIVIDUAL BATTING LEADERS (Minimum 174 Plate Appearances)

	AVG	G	AB	R	H	2B	3B	HR	RBI	BB	SO	SB
Norman, Anthony, Angels	.362	44	174	40	63	4	10	0	33	19	19	12
Rosa, Jovan, Cubs	.340	39	144	25	49	7	1	3	26	10	34	0
Perez, Carlos, Cubs	.338	43	145	20	49	10	3	2	31	14	28	1
Carroll, Daniel, Mariners	.323	53	201	39	65	9	6	0	24	27	56	27
Loman, Seth, Angels	.323	45	155	33	50	15	1	9	34	29	69	0
Wood, David, Royals	.318	54	217	31	69	17	3	5	39	17	43	1
Noonan, Nick, Giants	.316	52	206	33	65	11	4	3	40	12	20	18
Contreras, Ivan, Angels	.311	49	222	41	69	8	8	1	32	14	42	21
D'alessio, Andrew, Giants	.306	49	186	41	57	15	1	14	51	21	43	0
Garzon, Edgar, Padres	.305	50	187	31	57	13	2	2	24	24	39	2

INDIVIDUAL PITCHING LEADERS (Minimum 45 Innings)

	W	L	ERA	G	GS	CG	SV	IP	H	R	ER	BB	SO
Mitchell, Matthew, Royals	5	1	1.80	14	7	0	1	55	34	16	11	25	72
Wild, Jacob, Mariners	3	1	1.88	17	4	0	2	48	33	11	10	14	62
Bucardo, Wilber, Giants	6	2	1.94	11	11	0	0	60	46	16	13	10	34
Dominguez, Robbie, Mariners	3	1	2.01	14	8	0	0	45	26	17	10	15	37
Lehmann, Michael, Royals	5	1	2.64	14	1	0	1	44	36	23	13	23	40
Anton, Michael, Angels	5	3	3.21	13	12	0	0	62	58	30	22	15	82
Martinez, Roberto, Giants	3	2	3.22	11	11	0	0	45	38	21	16	23	54
Odle, Oliver, Giants	5	3	3.23	13	7	0	0	53	49	23	19	8	49
Molina, Robin, Angels	7	3	3.34	13	12	1	0	62	55	30	23	39	24
Williamson, Fabian, Mariners	6	2	3.43	14	12	0	0	66	68	32	25	25	73

ALL-STAR TEAM

C: Carlos Perez, Cubs. **1B:** Andrew D'alessio, Giants. **2B:** Ivan Contreras, Angels. **3B:** Edgar Trejo, Brewers. **SS:** Nick Noonan, Giants. **OF:** Daniel Carroll, Mariners; Antony Norman, Angels; Vinny Pennell, Royals. **DH:** David Wood, Royals. **LHP:** Mike Anton, Angels. **RHP:** Robbie Dominguez, Mariners. **LHRP:** Travis Mortimore, Mariners. **RHRP:** Eric Van Slyke, Royals. **Most Valuable Player:** Anthony Norman, Angels. **Manager of the Year:** Jose Moreno, Mariners.

DEPARTMENT LEADERS

BATTING

OBP	Klein, Adam, Athletics		.477
SLG	D'alessio, Andrew, Giants		.624
R	Fuller, Clayton, Angels		55
H	Contreras, Ivan, Angels		69
	Wood, David, Royals		69
TB	D'alessio, Andrew, Giants		116
XBH	D'alessio, Andrew, Giants		30
2B	Wood, David, Royals		17
3B	Norman, Anthony, Angels		10
HR	D'alessio, Andrew, Giants		14
RBI	D'alessio, Andrew, Giants		51
SAC	Four players tied at		5
SF	Fromm, Brandon, Mariners		5
BB	Klein, Adam, Athletics		58
IBB	26 players tied at		1
HBP	Loman, Seth, Angels		13
SO	Loman, Seth, Angels		69
	Mendez, Maximo, Mariners		69
SB	Klein, Adam, Athletics		33
CS	Carroll, Daniel, Mariners		11
GIDP	Bond, Casey, Giants		8
AB/SO	Noonan, Nick, Giants		10.3

PITCHING

G	Mortimore, Travis, Mariners		27
GS	Viloria, Euclides, Padres		14
CG	Molina, Robin, Angels		1
SHO	Molina, Robin, Angels		1
GF	Mortimore, Travis, Mariners		25
SV	Mortimore, Travis, Mariners		10
W	Molina, Robin, Angels		7
L	Three players tied at		6
IP	Christensen, Kyle, Athletics		66
H	Vandel, Geoff, Padres		82
R	Castro, Simon, Padres		48
ER	Manzueta, Pascual, Athletics		41
HB	Castro, Simon, Padres		9
BB	Molina, Robin, Angels		39
	Guerrero, Luis, Brewers		39
SO	Anton, Michael, Angels		82
SO/9-S	Pimentel, Carlos, Rangers		12.68
SO/9-R	Lara, Alexis, Padres		11.79
WP	Grullon, Geuris, Rangers		17
BK	Flores, Manuel, Angels		4
AVG	Mitchell, Matthew, Royals		.183

FIELDING

C	PCT	Perez, Carlos, Cubs		.993
	PO	Knazek, Scott, Angels		241
	A	Perez, Salvador, Royals		44
	E	Sabates, Roberto , Cubs		8
	DP	Nunez, Israel, Mariners		5
	PB	Knazek, Scott, Angels		12
		Santana, Cristian, Rangers		12
	CS%	Perez, Carlos, Cubs		.49
1B	PCT	Fromm, Brandon, Mariners		.992
	PO	D'alessio, Andrew, Giants		350
	A	Wentzell, Daniel, Athletics		33
		D'alessio, Andrew, Giants		33
	E	Ortiz, Michael, Rangers		14
	DP	Ortiz, Michael, Rangers		33
2B	PCT	Angel, Ryan, Royals		.968
	PO	Contreras, Ivan, Angels		101
	A	Contreras, Ivan, Angels		144
	E	Contreras, Ivan, Angels		13
		Hereaud, Carlos, Brewers		13
	DP	Luis, Marcos, Athletics		27
3B	PCT	Cruz, Fernando, Royals		.875
	PO	Trejo, Edgar, Brewers		40
	A	Villalona, Angel, Giants		89
	E	Villalona, Angel, Giants		18
	DP	Rosa, Jovan, Cubs		11
SS	PCT	Kaase, Jacob, Rangers		.943
	PO	Jose, Lifete, Royals		76
	A	Perez, Darwin, Angels		135
	E	Sanchez, Luis, Brewers		21
		Jose, Lifete, Royals		21
	DP	Guzman, Gian, Cubs		26
OF	PCT	Iacono, Charles, Brewers		.987
	PO	Duggan, Dom, Giants		93
	A	Perez, Nelson, Cubs		11
	E	Pennell, Vinny, Royals		7
	DP	Perez, Nelson, Cubs		5

BY CHRIS KLINE

The way the Gulf Coast League Dodgers cruised through the regular season, winning the Eastern Division by 10½ games, the club was considered the frontrunner to win the league title.

With a roster heavily loaded with prospects, the Dodgers went 40-15 in 2007. Their 322 runs were by far the most scored in the league, and they also led the GCL in fielding percentage. But they weren't able to come through in the playoffs, ultimately folding to the GCL Yankees in the three-game championship series.

The Yankees were nearly as dominant as the Dodgers during the regular season, going 42-17 during the regular season.

They were more reliant on pitching, leading the league with a 2.73 team ERA, but their bats also came alive during the GCL's brief playoffs, when they hit .299 as a team to defeat the Twins in a one-game playoff before disposing of the Dodgers 2-1.

"It's one of the hottest leagues temperature-wise in professional baseball," Yankees manager Jody Reed said. "It's very easy for these kids to wear down and drop their level of competition. But to their credit, our kids really stepped up—they wanted to win the whole thing.

"Maybe some people think winning a title in the GCL isn't a big deal, but they're dead wrong. Yes, you're developing players, but being able to develop them while establishing a winning environment—that's something you can't put a price tag on. And winning the championship meant the world to these kids. I mean, they really went bananas. I couldn't believe it."

Reed, who took home GCL manager of the year honors, also had a lot of talent to work with. Catcher Jesus Montero belted two homers in the championship series. Righthander Jairo Heredia earned comparisons to Pedro Martinez and went 2-2, 2.72 in 46 innings.

And Abraham and Zoilo Almonte set the tone for the club every day—Abraham for his scrappy play as a leadoff hitter, and Zoilo for his presence in the middle of the lineup.

"Our coaches did an outstanding job with a lot of our guys, and you could see the improvement from the end

TOP 20 PROSPECTS

ED WOLFSTEIN

1. Michael Burgess, of, Nationals
2. Jesus Montero, c, Yankees
3. Ben Revere, of, Twins
4. Che-Husan Lin, of, Red Sox
5. John Tolisano, 2b, Blue Jays
6. Pedro Baez, 3b, Dodgers
7. Oscar Tejeda, ss, Red Sox
8. Neftali Soto, ss, Reds
9. Luis de la Cruz, c, Cardinals
10. Andrew Lambo, 1b/of, Dodgers
11. Devin Mesoraco, c, Reds
12. Kevin Aherns, 3b/ss, Blue Jays
13. Kyle Lotzkar, rhp, Reds
14. Scott Moviel, rhp, Mets
15. Jairo Heredia, rhp, Yankees
16. D'Marcus Ingram, of, Cardinals
17. Deryk Hooker, rhp, Cardinals
18. Daniel Berlind, rhp, Twins
19. Angel Morales, of, Twins
20. Tyler Kolodny, 3b, Orioles

of extended spring training to the end of the season," Reed said. "But it starts with a credit to the scouting department for giving us all those raw tools to work with."

The Dodgers also had their fair share of tools, with 2007 first-round pick Chris Withrow, lefthander Michael Watt and righthander Justin Miller on the mound, and the polished bats of Andrew Lambo, Pedro Baez and Alfredo Silverio.

Silverio won the league batting title by batting .373 with six home runs, while Lambo finished third at .343 with five home runs.

Withrow touched 98 mph several times during his start against the Yankees in the championship series, and Miller might wind up being remembers as the biggest sleeper in the GCL in 2007.

It was the second straight year the Dodgers lost in the GCL finals, and marked the fourth time the club lost in the finals since 2001.

It also might have been the Dodgers' final season in the GCL at the Vero Beach complex, as the club will move its spring training facilities to Arizona.

STANDINGS

Page	Eastern Division	Complex Site	W	L	PCT	GB	Manager	Last Penn.
169	Dodgers	Vero Beach	40	15	.727	—	Juan Bustabad	1990
136	Marlins	Jupiter	29	25	.537	10 ½	Tim Cossins	None
248	Cardinals	Jupiter	24	30	.444	15 ½	Enrique Brito	None
310	Nationals	Melbourne	23	31	.426	16 ½	Bobby Henley	1991
196	Mets	St. Lucie	20	35	.364	20	Juan Lopez	None
Page	**Northern Division**	**Complex Site**	**W**	**L**	**PCT**	**GB**	**Manager**	**Last Penn.**
206	Yankees	Tampa	42	17	.712	—	Jody Reed	2007
300	Blue Jays	Dunedin	36	24	.600	6 ½	Clayton McCullough	None
110	Indians	Winter Haven	28	31	.475	14	Rouglas, Odor	None
227	Phillies	Clearwater	28	32	.467	14 ½	Roly de Armas	2002
126	Tigers	Lakeland	28	32	.467	14 ½	Benigno Castillo	None
59	Braves	Lake Buena Vista	17	43	.283	25 ½	Luis Ortiz	2003
Page	**Southern Division**	**Complex Site**	**W**	**L**	**PCT**	**GB**	**Manager**	**Last Penn.**
185	Twins	Fort Myers	37	19	.661	—	Nelson Prada	None
68	Orioles	Sarasota	32	24	.571	5	Ramon Sambo	None
76	Red Sox	Fort Myers	30	26	.536	7	Dave Tomlin	2006
237	Pirates	Bradenton	26	30	.464	11	Tom Prince	None
101	Reds	Sarasota	15	41	.268	22	P. Kelly/R. Ortegon/R. Burleson	None

PLAYOFFS— Semifinals: The Yankees defeated the Twins in a one-game playoff. **Finals:** The Yankees defeated the Dodgers 2-1 in a best-of-three series. **NOTE:** Teams' individual batting and pitching statistics can be found on page indicated in lefthand column.

CLUB BATTING

	AVG	G	AB	R	H	2B	3B	HR	RBI	BB	SO	SB	CS	OBP	SLG
Twins	.283	56	1814	293	513	86	26	12	238	154	337	88	48	.349	.379
Dodgers	.279	55	1731	322	483	89	10	32	269	223	412	44	24	.371	.397
Yankees	.275	59	1904	290	523	103	17	47	246	153	403	40	33	.340	.421
Mets	.258	55	1845	266	476	82	16	25	238	206	437	50	19	.348	.360
Pirates	.256	56	1854	299	474	93	21	33	261	216	339	55	32	.349	.382
Orioles	.253	56	1879	281	476	106	14	23	235	205	423	65	26	.339	.361
Indians	.251	59	1935	273	486	95	4	25	241	179	468	94	20	.327	.343
Red Sox	.250	56	1843	255	460	101	19	32	218	171	431	70	36	.321	.377
Marlins	.249	55	1776	253	443	102	4	19	213	201	427	38	25	.339	.343
Tigers	.249	60	1920	260	479	68	13	33	228	179	454	52	23	.322	.350
Reds	.245	56	1837	229	450	75	17	22	185	153	402	31	23	.312	.340
Cardinals	.243	54	1740	233	422	72	16	24	201	199	470	62	24	.329	.344
Phillies	.242	60	1939	249	469	108	13	31	215	186	454	58	28	.319	.359
Nationals	.237	55	1781	258	422	69	10	33	226	273	522	54	31	.349	.343
Blue Jays	.234	60	1965	246	459	81	11	42	221	216	535	53	14	.319	.350
Braves	.225	60	1942	208	436	68	3	24	187	120	425	56	24	.278	.300

CLUB PITCHING

	ERA	G	CG	SHO	SV	IP	H	R	ER	HR	BB	SO	AVG
Yankees	2.73	59	0	9	21	494	425	194	149	24	158	496	.228
Twins	2.92	56	0	6	15	477	420	213	155	24	182	395	.236
Blue Jays	3.12	60	0	7	19	525	506	234	182	35	129	475	.251
Marlins	3.23	55	0	3	16	470	434	246	168	16	178	483	.242
Tigers	3.38	60	3	4	16	497	455	246	186	27	163	429	.243
Red Sox	3.50	56	0	2	18	486	495	265	189	21	138	385	.261
Dodgers	3.66	55	3	5	11	452	440	210	181	25	171	422	.256
Indians	3.70	59	1	4	8	496	441	259	204	24	176	450	.233
Orioles	3.70	56	1	2	16	492	483	250	202	22	186	392	.259
Phillies	4.10	60	0	3	14	509	502	266	232	37	178	419	.254
Pirates	4.18	56	0	2	12	480	491	292	223	27	160	376	.263
Cardinals	4.33	54	1	4	13	453	445	275	218	25	259	480	.256
Mets	4.61	55	0	0	9	470	430	292	241	30	286	427	.244
Braves	4.70	60	0	1	8	505	523	327	260	55	229	470	.264
Nationals	4.77	55	0	3	10	468	497	309	247	37	208	456	.267
Reds	4.85	56	0	1	7	466	484	337	251	28	233	384	.265

CLUB FIELDING

	PCT	PO	A	E	DP		PCT	PO	A	E	DP
Dodgers	.973	1356	546	53	51	Pirates	.961	1441	644	84	58
Blue Jays	.967	1576	656	76	50	Mets	.959	1409	571	85	59
Twins	.967	1431	598	70	65	Cardinals	.957	1358	483	83	32
Yankees	.967	1481	526	69	48	Indians	.957	1487	562	93	44
Tigers	.965	1492	576	74	47	Marlins	.955	1412	558	92	43
Braves	.962	1515	560	81	59	Nationals	.952	1405	494	95	34
Orioles	.962	1476	636	83	61	Red Sox	.951	1458	609	106	44
Phillies	.962	1526	610	84	36	Reds	.944	1397	548	115	35

INDIVIDUAL BATTING LEADERS (Minimum 174 Plate Appearances)

	AVG	G	AB	R	H	2B	3B	HR	RBI	BB	SO	SB
Silverio, Alfredo, Dodgers	.373	51	193	38	72	9	3	6	46	11	32	5
Rojas, Jesus, Marlins	.348	52	181	33	63	14	0	4	30	27	32	1
Lambo, Andrew, Dodgers	.343	54	181	38	62	15	1	5	32	29	34	1
Carrera, Ezequiel, Mets	.341	45	179	41	61	8	3	1	26	26	29	15
Laird, Brandon, Yankees	.339	45	168	27	57	14	1	8	29	6	26	0
Burgess, Michael, Nationals	.336	36	128	22	43	6	3	8	32	25	37	1
Revere, Ben, Twins	.325	50	191	46	62	6	10	0	29	13	20	21
Polanco, Elvin, Orioles	.318	54	217	35	69	18	0	5	37	14	39	3
Kolodny, Tyler, Orioles	.318	43	151	33	48	10	2	6	30	15	30	6
Richardson, Juan, Twins	.317	54	202	33	64	10	2	1	33	13	16	14

INDIVIDUAL PITCHING LEADERS (Minimum 45 Innings)

	W	L	ERA	G	GS	CG	SV	IP	H	R	ER	BB	SO
Letko, Brian, Blue Jays	2	4	1.50	12	10	0	0	48	41	12	8	6	47
Dougher, James, Blue Jays	2	1	1.56	12	11	0	0	52	36	10	9	10	51
Alvarez, Jose, Red Sox	4	1	1.84	11	9	0	0	49	36	24	10	14	38
Frias, Santo, Indians	2	3	1.88	9	9	0	0	48	36	17	10	8	47
Castillo, Noel, Yankees	6	3	1.88	13	7	0	2	53	53	17	11	7	51
Berlind, Daniel, Twins	6	2	1.93	11	9	0	0	56	37	16	12	20	52
Miller, Ryan, Indians	4	2	2.40	9	9	1	0	45	26	15	12	12	44
Johnson, Brandon, Tigers	4	5	2.58	12	11	0	0	59	59	31	17	11	45
McPherson, Kyle, Pirates	4	2	2.61	12	10	0	0	52	47	22	15	10	35
Carreno, Joel, Blue Jays	6	4	2.62	12	12	0	0	65	60	27	19	13	64

ALL-STAR TEAM

C: Keyter Collado, Dodgers. **1B:** Elvin Polanco, Orioles. **2B:** John Tolisano, Blue Jays. **3B:** Brandon Laird, Yankees. **SS:** Joseph Becker, Dodgers. **OF:** Michael Burgess, Nationals; Ben Revere, Twins; Alfredo Silverio, Dodgers. **DH:** Jesus Rojas, Marlins. **SP:** Daniel Berlind, Twins. **RP:** Danny Rondon, Twins. **Manager of the Year:** Jody Reed, Yankees.

DEPARTMENT LEADERS

BATTING

OBP	Burgess, Michael, Nationals	.442
SLG	Burgess, Michael, Nationals	.617
R	Revere, Ben, Twins	46
H	Silverio, Alfredo, Dodgers	72
TB	Silverio, Alfredo, Dodgers	105
XBH	Sumoza, Luis, Red Sox	24
2B	Polanco, Elvin, Orioles	18
3B	Revere, Ben, Twins	10
HR	Tolisano, John, Blue Jays	10
RBI	Silverio, Alfredo, Dodgers	46
SAC	Solarte, Yangervis, Twins	10
SF	Six players tied at	5
BB	Lester, Calvin, Orioles	43
IBB	21 players tied at	1
HBP	Zavala, Gabriel, Mets	11
	Rice, Chad, Pirates	11
SO	Fuenmayor, Balbino, Blue Jays	68
SB	Velasquez, Isaias, Indians	22
CS	Richardson, Juan, Twins	10
GIDP	Baez, Pedro, Dodgers	10
	Polanco, Elvin, Orioles	10
AB/SO	Richardson, Juan, Twins	12.63

PITCHING

G	Mieses, Santo, Tigers	25
GS	Carreno, Joel, Blue Jays	12
	Moviel, Scott, Mets	12
CG	Nine players tied at	1
SHO	Four players tied at	1
GF	Franco, Santo, Tigers	22
SV	Franco, Santo, Tigers	12
	Rondon, Danny, Twins	12
W	Orman, Conrad, Orioles	8
L	Three players tied at	7
IP	McCurry, Cole, Orioles	67
H	Rivero, Raul, Orioles	77
R	Samuel, Francisco, Cardinals	42
ER	Samuel, Francisco, Cardinals	36
HB	Orman, Conrad, Orioles	12
BB	Samuel, Francisco, Cardinals	35
SO	Carreno, Joel, Blue Jays	64
SO/9-S	Cuthbertson, Brad, Blue Jays	11.18
SO/9-R	Pinales, Jose, Nationals	13.18
WP	Samuel, Francisco, Cardinals	15
BK	Noel, Luis, Orioles	4
AVG	Miller, Ryan, Indians	.160

FIELDING

C	PCT	Kennelly, Mathew, Braves	.996
		Collado, Keyter, Dodgers	.996
	PO	Bowen, Joseph, Tigers	262
	A	Bernardo, Luis, Orioles	42
	E	De La Cruz, Luis, Cardinals	7
		Gilardo, Peter, Red Sox	7
	DP	Tarnow, Joshua, Orioles	5
	PB	Martinez, Samuel, Mets	22
	CS%	De La Cruz, Luis, Cardinals	.51
1B	PCT	Freeman, Frederick, Braves	.995
	PO	Polanco, Elvin, Orioles	472
	A	Polanco, Elvin, Orioles	27
	E	Waltenbury, Jonathan, Twins	8
	DP	Freeman, Frederick, Braves	52
2B	PCT	Fields, Caleb, Pirates	.964
	PO	Tolisano, John, Blue Jays	85
	A	Tolisano, John, Blue Jays	131
	E	Cuello, Prilys, Yankees	16
	DP	Tolisano, John, Blue Jays	28
3B	PCT	Mattair, Travis, Phillies	.958
	PO	Richardson, Juan, Twins	43
	A	Richardson, Juan, Twins	135
	E	Parrott, Hayden, Tigers	22
	DP	Richardson, Juan, Twins	17
SS	PCT	Becker, Joseph, Dodgers	.968
	PO	Tejeda, Oscar, Red Sox	83
	A	Becker, Joseph, Dodgers	141
	E	Sime, Samuel, Braves	18
	DP	Becker, Joseph, Dodgers	31
OF	PCT	Ray, Nicholas, Orioles	1
		McBratney, Marc, Tigers	1
	PO	Quiroz, Arlon, Phillies	123
	A	Hubbert, B.J., Mets	8
	A	Zavala, Gabriel, Mets	7
	DP	Ellis, Lee, Orioles	4
		Lin, Che-Hsuan, Red Sox	4

MINOR LEAGUES

Complete team-by-team numbers for all DSL and VSL teams can be found in the Organization Statistics section, beginning on Page 43.

DOMINICAN SUMMER LEAGUE

BY CHRIS KLINE

For an extended stretch of the season, no team in baseball was hotter than the DSL Phillies, who strung together an unprecedented 22-game win streak at the tail end of the 2007 season.

The Phillies finished the season with a 45-18 record. The scary thing is that was the third-best record in the DSL—a league which featured two teams with fewer than 20 wins, and one—the DSL Athletics 2—who finished with nine victories.

The DSL Nationals went 49-15, and the Pirates finished 52-17.

But it was the Yankees who made it to the finals against the Nats, with Washington's club winning 3-2 in the best-of-five series. The DSL Nationals got quality outings from 20-year-old righthander Juan Jaime and 21-year-old righthander Federico Tanco, who combined for 23 strikeouts in 16 postseason innings.

Tigers' lefty Edward Reynoso led the regular season in strikeouts, fanning 110 in just 71 innings. The strikeouts were just one staggering statistic during Reynoso's season—the 18-year-old went 9-0, 0.76, allowed just 36 hits, walked 23 and held opponents to a .150 average.

STANDINGS

BOCA CHICA SOUTH	W	L	PCT	GB
Yankees1	44	26	.629	—
Cubs	41	30	.577	3½
Reds	39	30	.565	4½
Twins	39	32	.549	5½
Rockies	37	33	.529	7
Diamondbacks	30	40	.429	14
Indians	27	42	.391	16½
Blue Jays1	23	47	.329	21

BOCA CHICA NORTH	W	L	PCT	GB
Giants	49	21	.700	—
Dodgers	43	24	.642	4½
Royals	39	29	.574	9
Red Sox	38	31	.551	10½
Blue Jays2	34	36	.486	15
Marlins	25	44	.362	23½
Devil Rays	24	46	.343	25
Yankees2	23	44	.343	24½

SANTO DOMINGO NORTH	W	L	PCT	GB
Phillies	45	18	.714	—
Athletics1	41	22	.651	4
Mariners	34	30	.531	11½
Cardinals	30	35	.462	16
Athletics2	9	54	.143	36

SANTO DOMINGO WEST	W	L	PCT	GB
Nationals1	49	15	.766	—
Tigers	45	20	.692	4½
Nationals2	25	39	.391	24
Mets	24	41	.369	25½
Padres	18	46	.281	31

SAN PEDRO DE MACORIS	W	L	PCT	GB
Pirates	52	17	.754	—
Angels	49	21	.700	3½
Braves	37	31	.544	14½
Rangers	35	34	.507	17
White Sox2	31	37	.456	20½
Astros	29	39	.426	22½
Orioles	26	44	.371	26½
White Sox1	17	53	.243	35½

PLAYOFFS—Division Series: Angels defeated Phillies 2-1 and Yankees1 defeated Giants 2-0 in best-of-three series. Semifinals: Yankees1 defeated Pirates 2-1 and Nationals1 defeated Angels 2-0 in best-of-three series. Finals: Nationals1 defeated Yankees1 3-2 in a best-of-five series.

INDIVIDUAL BATTING LEADERS
(MINIMUM 194 PLATE APPEARANCES)

	AVG	AB	R	H	2B	3B	HR	RBI	SB
Bermudez, Ronald, Red Sox	.349	229	37	80	19	3	3	39	12
Santamaria, Jahdiel, Yankees1	.347	196	47	68	14	5	3	41	9
Casamayor, Omar, Orioles	.344	215	40	74	12	4	1	29	18
Amarista, Alexia, Angels	.340	241	52	82	14	4	5	39	16
Marte, Alfredo, Diamondbacks	.328	265	30	87	19	4	4	45	3
Gomez, Roy, Yankees1	.328	177	31	58	11	0	4	23	7
Buckridge, Shaydron, White Sox2	.325	160	26	52	8	0	0	25	7
Segura, Jean, Angels	.324	219	39	71	5	2	2	31	22
Nina, Angelys, Rockies	.323	254	33	82	19	3	3	43	24
Sierra, Raddy, Angels	.317	240	61	76	16	1	9	31	26

INDIVIDUAL PITCHING LEADERS
(MINIMUM 58 INNINGS)

	W	L	ERA	G	SV	IP	H	BB	SO
Reynoso, Edward, Tigers	9	0	0.76	13	0	70.2	36	23	110
Alvarez, Edison, Twins	5	1	0.78	26	7	58	41	11	48
Charagua, Wilmer, Rockies	4	3	1.08	28	0	66.2	57	8	53
Acosta, Richard, Pirates	9	1	1.23	13	0	95	67	7	97
Bucardo, Jorge, Giants	7	2	1.35	12	0	60	45	7	39
Mendez, Alejandro, Tigers	5	4	1.37	15	0	78.2	52	30	103
Tavarez, Gari, Dodgers	9	3	1.49	14	0	66.2	39	17	71
Aguasviva, Geison, Dodgers	8	2	1.50	12	0	66	43	14	69
Marte, Kelvin, Giants	5	1	1.62	28	3	61	36	14	91
Simon, Reginal, Phillies	5	1	1.69	12	0	64	46	33	38

VENEZUELAN SUMMER LEAGUE

BY CHRIS KLINE

The Pirates' work in Latin America is beginning to reap dividends, as the DSL Pirates advanced to the postseason, while the VSL Pirates won the regular season title.

The VSL Pirates took the first game of the league championship series, but then stumbled in the final two, as the Astros claimed the VSL title.

Much of the reason for the Pirates' success began on the mound, as righthanders Wilson Ortiz and Gabriel Alvarado and lefthanders Nelson Pereira and Jhonatan Ramos all ranked among the league's top pitchers in ERA. Perhaps the most intriguing is Pereira, an 18-year-old El Salvador native who finished the year 10-1, 2.33 in 66 innings.

Tigers' 18-year-old outfielder Alexis Espinoza led the league with 12 homers, while Phillies righthander Freddy Ballestas finished tops on the circuit in strikeouts with 98 in 100 innings. The 20-year-old righthander's fastball sits in the 90-93 mph range, touching 94 with an above-average breaking ball.

STANDINGS

	W	L	PCT	GB		W	L	PCT	GB
Pirates	49	21	.700	—	Cubs/Twins	32	35	.478	15½
Astros	48	22	.686	1	Cardinals	23	46	.333	25½
Mariners	47	24	.662	2½	Mets	20	48	.294	28
Tigers	38	32	.543	11	Devil Rays/Reds	17	51	.250	31
Phillies	36	31	.537	11½					

PLAYOFFS—Astros defeated Pirates 2-1 in a best-of-three series.

INDIVIDUAL BATTING LEADERS
(MINIMUM 194 PLATE APPEARANCES)

	AVG	AB	R	H	2B	3B	HR	RBI	SB
Rodriguez, Yonderman, Phillies	.361	230	41	83	13	1	1	36	19
Hernandez, David, Devil Rays/Reds	.344	209	38	72	13	1	3	27	4
Altuve, Jose, Astros	.343	204	40	70	12	4	0	36	15
Marquez, Jairo, Pirates	.339	189	38	64	10	1	4	46	2
Pedron, Freizer, Pirates	.337	190	38	64	15	1	1	36	25
Alvarez, Imbewer, Mets	.323	201	39	65	10	2	4	22	27
Omana, Gustavo, Devil Rays/Reds	.321	193	29	62	10	0	2	37	0
Chourio, Adenson, Pirates	.319	229	61	73	8	3	1	19	44
Gonzalez, Orlando, Tigers	.319	251	32	80	9	1	5	48	3
Contreras, Efrain, Devil Rays/Reds	.315	241	54	76	14	0	11	36	25

INDIVIDUAL PITCHING LEADERS
(MINIMUM 58 INNINGS)

	W	L	ERA	G	SV	IP	H	BB	SO
Ballestas, Freddy, Phillies	9	3	1.26	16	0	100	62	19	98
Ortiz, Wilson, Pirates	6	1	1.27	14	0	71	35	20	72
Castillo, Richard, Cardinals	2	2	1.72	17	2	62.2	40	22	60
Rodriguez, Leonardo, Mariners	5	0	1.82	15	0	69.1	50	24	34
Perez, German, Astros	7	2	2.07	14	0	69.2	58	19	54
Pereira, Nelson, Pirates	10	1	2.33	14	1	65.2	54	18	59
Ramos, Jhonatan, Pirates	6	3	2.47	13	0	62	50	22	46
Lara, Daniel, Phillies	4	4	2.49	17	2	72.1	73	30	37
Colmenarez, Juan, Phillies	6	5	2.51	16	0	93.1	76	11	89
Alvarado, Gabriel, Pirates	8	4	2.67	13	0	70.2	68	18	39

Phoenix righthander Nick Blackburn didn't earn the victory in the 2007 Arizona Fall League championship game, but the Twins prospect was the key to the Desert Dogs winning their fourth straight championship with a 7-2 win over the Surprise Rafters in front of nearly 1,500 fans at Scottsdale Stadium. Blackburn yielded only one run on five hits in six innings, striking out two and walking one.

"He has been effective the whole season," Phoenix manager Rafael Santana said. "There's no difference between today and the regular season. He's a great pitcher."

Blackburn, who made his big league debut with the Twins this year, credited a change in his pitching philosophy—throwing more offspeed pitches—for his AFL success. It paid off for him, as he posted a 4-0 record with a 1.64 ERA and 20/2 K/BB rate during the AFL season. Along the way, Blackburn ran off a string of 19 consecutive scoreless innings.

"In my last two outings of the regular season, I was just being too stubborn," Blackburn said. "I knew I needed to slow my pitchers down, but I was never doing it. Even my first start out here, I ran into the same problem . . . everything was hard . . . I was staying with my hard fastball, cutter and sinker. Guys were sitting on it and getting their timing down, and I was just getting punished.

"Once I was able to finally quit being stubborn and commit myself, everything settled in real well and I was throwing all of my off speed for strikes."

Blackburn's only mistake in the championship game was a curveball in the third inning to Surprise third baseman Sean Rodriguez (Angels), who sent the pitch over the left-field fence to tie the game at one.

"I had just told my catcher (fellow Twin farmhand Drew Butera) the inning before that any time I get a good pitch to start off a hitter, I like to double it up," Blackburn said. "After that, I was punished . . . it's almost like he knew it was coming."

Surprise starter Fernando Rodriguez Jr. (Angels) wasn't nearly as effective as Blackburn, lasting only 1 2/3 innings, giving up five Phoenix hits and walking one.

Phoenix' initial tally came in the first inning as Cliff Pennington (Athletics) scored from second on Ryan Sweeney's (White Sox) two-out opposite field double. It was the first of three hits for Pennington, who led the Desert Dogs' 15-hit attack. Five other Phoenix players tallied two hits each.

Rodriguez was lucky to escape with a 1-0 deficit. The Desert Dogs stranded four runners in the first two innings and a fifth, Nyjer Morgan (Pirates), was thrown out at third base attempting to stretch a double in the game's first at-bat.

After Sean Rodriguez tied the game in the bottom of the third, Phoenix regained the lead in the next inning when Morgan singled with two outs, scoring Matt Macri (Twins) from second base.

The Rafters tied the game a second time in the bottom of the seventh after Blackburn was replaced by reliever Chris Hernandez (Pirates). Brad Snyder (Indians) singled to open the inning and advanced to third on Elvis Andrus' (Rangers) line-drive double. Craig Tatum (Reds) flied out to center field for the first out, scoring Snyder

TOP 20 PROSPECTS

1. Cameron Maybin, of, Peoria Saguaros (Tigers)
2. Evan Longoria, 3b, Scottsdale (Devil Rays)
3. Travis Snider, of, Scottsdale (Blue Jays)
4. Matt LaPorta, of, Mesa (Brewers)
5. Adam Miller, rhp, Surprise (Indians)
6. Andrew McCutchen, of, Phoenix (Pirates)
7. Reid Brignac, ss, Scottsdale (Devil Rays)
8. Jordan Schafer, of, Peoria Javelinas (Braves)
9. Dexter Fowler, of, Peoria Javelinas (Rockies)
10. Taylor Teagarden, c, Surprise (Rangers)
11. Matt Antonelli, 2b, Peoria Saguaros (Padres)
12. Anthony Swarzak, rhp, Phoenix (Twins)
13. Jeff Clement, c, Peoria Javelinas (Mariners)
14. Jake Arrieta, rhp, Phoenix (Orioles)
15. Eugenio Velez, 2b/of, Scottsdale (Giants)
16. Joe Savery, lhp, Peoria Saguaros (Phillies)
17. Max Scherzer, rhp, Scottsdale (Diamondbacks)
18. Sean Gallagher, rhp, Surprise (Cubs)
19. John Mayberry, of, Surprise (Rangers)
20. David Huff, lhp, Surprise (Indians)

and advancing Andrus to third. Sean Rodriguez was hit by a pitch, putting runners on the corners with one out. Jose Duarte (Royals) then popped out to first base for the second out.

With two outs, Marc Maddox (Royals) hit a sinking liner to center field. The ball was snared just above the ground by a sliding Andrew McCutchen (Pirates), preventing the Rafters from taking the lead.

The Desert Dogs took the lead for good in the top of the eighth. After Sweeney drew a walk off reliever Rich Rundles (Indians), the Rafters called Mike Finocchi (Indians) from the bullpen. The righthander induced Jason Delaney (Pirates) to hit a sharp grounder to shortstop, but Andrus' errant throw pulled Maddox off the bag at second base and both runners were safe.

After a passed ball and a ground out to shortstop, Macri gave the Desert Dogs the lead for good with a sacrifice fly to right field. Phoenix added an insurance run when Chris Getz (White Sox) narrowly beat out an infield hit, driving in Delaney to make the score 4-2.

Phoenix scored three more times in the top half of the ninth off Rafter relievers Tyler Pelland (Reds) and Paul Kometani (Rangers).

The Desert Dogs called on closer Bob McCrory (Orioles) for the bottom of the ninth. The frustrated Rafter bench erupted after leadoff batter Andrus was called out on strikes, resulting in the ejection of coaches Jon Nunnally and Steve Luebber. After play was resumed, Tatum grounded out to second base and Sean Rodriguez singled for this second hit of the game. McCrory then fanned pinch hitter Chris Lubanski (Royals) to give the Desert Dogs the win. Hernandez earned the win in relief of Blackburn. Rundles was the losing pitcher.

"Pitching was a big key for the ballgame today," Santana said after the game. "We took advantage of the mistakes they made and were able to capitalize on them."

Team USA and Team China each played six games in the AFL in 2007 as a warm-up for the World Cup in Taiwan, which the United States eventually won over Cuba.

STANDINGS

EASTERN DIVISION	W	L	PCT	GB
Phoenix Desert Dogs	20	11	.645	—
Scottsdale Scorpions	16	16	.500	4½
Mesa Solar Sox	14	17	.452	6

WESTERN DIVISION	W	L	PCT	GB
Surprise Rafters	19	13	.594	—
Peoria Javelinas	17	15	.531	2
Peoria Saguaros	10	22	.313	9

INTERNATIONAL DIVISION	W	L	PCT	GB
Team USA	4	2	.667	—
Team China	1	5	.167	3

INDIVIDUAL BATTING LEADERS

(MINIMUM 2 PLATE APPEARANCES/TEAM GAME)

PLAYER, TEAM	AVG	G	AB	R	H	HR	RBI
Young, Delwyn, USA	.524	6	21	5	11	1	4
Wimberly, Corey, Jav	.407	18	59	13	24	0	9
Fuld, Sam, Mesa	.402	29	107	20	43	3	14
Jin, Limin, China	.357	6	14	1	5	0	0
Sizemore, Scott, Sag	.356	21	90	18	32	2	18
Schierholtz, Nate, Scott	.348	23	89	15	31	4	10
Gardner, Brett, Jav	.343	26	108	27	37	0	16
Chen, Yung Chi, Jav	.339	17	59	11	20	1	12
LaRoche, Andy, USA	.333	5	18	2	6	1	4
Coghlan, Chris, Sag	.329	20	73	7	24	0	9

INDIVIDUAL PITCHING LEADERS

(MINIMUM .4 INNINGS/TEAM GAME)

PITCHER, TEAM	W	L	ERA	IP	H	BB	SO
Arrieta, Jake, Phx	1	0	0.00	16	8	7	16
Hernandez, Chris, Phx	1	0	0.00	13	9	2	7
Hernandez Jr., Fernando, Phx	0	0	0.00	13	5	4	11
Morlan, Eduardo, Phx	1	0	0.00	13	8	6	7
Stetter, Mitch, Mesa	1	0	0.00	13	8	3	20
Stevens, Jeff, USA	0	0	0.00	6	2	1	6
Yu, Lei, China	1	0	0.00	5	2	3	2
Gronkiewicz, Lee, USA	1	0	0.00	4	4	0	6
Booker, Chris, USA	0	0	0.00	3	1	2	3
Xu, Zheng, China	0	0	0.00	3	0	1	1

MESA SOLAR SOX

BATTING	AVG	AB	R	H	2B	3B	HR	RBI	BB	SO	SB
Brown, Dusty	.273	55	1	15	1	0	0	1	6	12	0
Clevenger, Steve	.200	15	3	3	1	0	0	0	1	3	0
Einertson, Mitch	.260	73	9	19	3	0	4	12	6	17	0
Fuld, Sam	.402	107	20	43	11	2	3	14	17	15	10
Hamilton, Mark	.171	41	3	7	2	0	4	13	9	0	
Heether, Adam	.259	54	9	14	3	1	1	4	9	17	1
Hoffpauir, Jarrett	.236	55	9	13	1	0	0	9	12	4	3
Lansford, Josh	.257	74	4	19	5	0	0	8	5	11	0
LaPorta, Matt	.241	112	12	27	9	1	6	22	17	28	1
Lowrie, Jed	.163	98	12	16	5	0	1	14	10	14	3
Manzella, Tommy	.302	53	9	16	4	0	0	4	4	12	1
Marti, Amaury	.220	41	6	9	1	0	1	8	5	13	1
Palmisano, Lou	.214	42	5	9	1	0	0	4	10	8	1
Simokaitis, Joe	.172	64	8	11	1	1	1	7	7	15	1
Still, Jon	.146	82	10	12	3	0	2	8	15	22	0

PITCHING	W	L	ERA	G	GS	SV	IP	H	BB	SO
Avery, Matt	0	0	5.23	8	0	0	10	11	8	9
Barthmaier, Jimmy	2	1	9.69	11	0	0	13	19	7	12
Berg, Justin	1	1	7.07	10	0	0	14	19	6	8
Boggs, Mitch	0	2	5.21	6	6	0	19	19	8	14
Dillard, Tim	1	0	6.52	11	0	1	10	15	7	5
Gallagher, Sean	0	0	1.13	8	2	0	16	12	4	13
Gregerson, Luke	0	1	7.04	6	0	0	8	13	4	10
Haigwood, Daniel	1	2	4.87	7	7	0	20	24	12	17
Hammond, Steve	1	3	5.87	7	7	0	23	24	7	16
Holdzkom, Lincoln	0	0	3.86	7	0	0	7	2	4	10
James, Brad	1	2	7.00	6	5	0	18	20	7	9
Johnson, Dave	1	0	2.45	9	0	0	11	10	3	14
Jones, Hunter	0	1	8.78	10	0	0	13	23	4	10
Motte, Jason	2	0	3.00	11	0	1	12	10	5	10
Muecke, Josh	0	0	1.56	13	0	0	17	11	6	9
Pomeranz, Stuart	2	0	0.64	5	5	0	14	9	5	3

	W	L	ERA	G	GS	SV	IP	H	BB	SO
Reineke, Chad	0	2	3.86	11	0	1	14	7	5	14
Stetter, Mitch	1	0	0.00	11	0	1	13	8	3	20
Vaquedano, Jose	0	1	4.61	11	0	0	14	16	6	11

PEORIA JAVELINAS

BATTING	AVG	AB	R	H	2B	3B	HR	RBI	BB	SO	SB
Casto, Kory	.281	64	14	18	6	1	1	9	12	13	1
Chen, Yung Chi	.339	59	11	20	2	0	1	12	12	10	2
Clement, Jeff	.269	52	11	14	2	0	3	12	7	13	0
Colonel, Christian	.258	31	5	8	0	0	1	9	5	5	0
Fowler, Dexter	.224	107	9	24	3	3	0	17	14	28	4
Gardner, Brett	.343	108	27	37	0	2	0	10	17	17	16
Hicks, Brandon	.188	69	7	13	3	0	2	7	8	24	0
Holt, J.C.	.244	45	8	11	1	1	0	4	4	12	2
Ivany, Devin	.233	43	9	10	2	0	3	8	3	8	1
Maxwell, Justin	.207	111	19	23	7	0	2	15	16	33	15
Sammons, Clint	.219	32	4	7	1	0	1	10	3	8	0
Schafer, Jordan	.324	105	20	34	6	1	1	16	12	25	10
Tuiasosopo, Matt	.293	82	17	24	5	0	1	15	12	22	0
Wimberly, Corey	.407	59	13	24	2	2	0	9	5	5	7

PITCHING	W	L	ERA	G	GS	SV	IP	H	BB	SO
Carr, Adam	0	0	3.18	7	1	0	11	8	4	10
Clarke, Darren	0	0	4.70	7	0	1	8	7	4	12
Downs, Brodie	1	1	5.94	10	0	0	17	17	9	12
Grube, Jarrett	0	0	6.00	7	0	0	9	14	3	14
Jackson, Steven	0	1	5.63	9	0	0	16	21	7	19
Jung, Sung Ki	0	0	3.97	10	0	2	11	13	7	15
Lo, Ching Lung	0	2	6.75	5	4	0	15	13	8	14
Mock, Garrett	1	2	4.78	8	7	0	26	26	11	21
Morales, Alexis	0	0	11.74	7	0	0	8	14	6	
Morton, Charlie	4	1	2.57	6	5	0	21	15	8	20
Nelson, Brad	0	0	3.55	8	0	0	13	17	4	5
Nix, Michael	3	0	4.73	10	0	0	13	20	9	15
Ohlendorf, Ross	0	0	3.52	6	0	0	8	4	3	
Rivera, Mumba	0	1	6.97	7	0	0	10	7	9	11
Thomas, Justin	0	1	5.40	4	0	0	5	5	4	4
Thompson, Sean	2	2	4.43	7	5	0	20	17	10	20
White, Steven	0	1	6.23	7	3	0	17	19	6	11
Woerman, Joseph	2	2	6.86	7	7	0	20	22	17	17
Wordekemper, Eric	1	0	2.89	8	0	1	9	8	2	8
Zinicola, Zechry	1	1	3.48	10	0	1	10	10	6	5

PEORIA SAGUAROS

BATTING	AVG	AB	R	H	2B	3B	HR	RBI	BB	SO	SB
Antonelli, Matt	.214	56	9	12	3	0	0	5	10	9	0
Coghlan, Chris	.329	73	7	24	5	1	0	9	10	8	0
Costanzo, Mike	.189	90	6	17	1	0	2	10	11	32	0
Dewitt, Blake	.281	57	12	16	3	2	0	6	6	7	0
Golson, Greg	.266	109	17	29	6	3	2	16	8	23	8
Gosewisch, Tuffy	.250	48	4	12	0	0	1	6	2	11	0
Hayes, Brett	.188	64	8	12	5	1	0	2	4	12	0
Hundley, Nick	.244	41	7	10	2	0	1	14	6	10	0
Larish, Jeff	.264	87	16	23	7	0	1	14	16	26	0
Miller, Jai	.233	86	8	20	3	1	1	9	6	33	1
Paul, Xavier	.248	105	15	26	4	0	0	8	9	28	2
Sizemore, Scott	.356	90	18	32	6	4	2	18	10	14	3
Venable, Will	.228	92	12	21	6	0	3	13	3	21	0

PITCHING	W	L	ERA	G	GS	SV	IP	H	BB	SO
Anderson, Jason	0	3	4.50	8	0	0	10	10	4	8
Badenhop, Burke	2	2	3.24	10	0	0	17	19	3	14
Ellis, Jonathan	0	1	5.56	11	0	0	11	9	8	11
Gerbe, Jeff	0	1	9.42	9	0	1	14	27	10	13
Hammes, Zachary	0	0	6.43	11	0	0	14	14	9	7
Hudgins, John	0	1	8.76	5	4	0	12	17	8	8
Jamison, Neil	0	0	10.13	12	0	2	5	9	2	5
Krol, Noah	0	0	6.30	7	0	0	10	9	9	13
Miller, Greg	0	3	12.79	6	6	0	13	23	16	15
Molldrem, Craig	0	0	12.27	10	0	0	11	15	8	12
Nestor, Scott	0	1	4.35	10	0	0	10	10	9	11
Nolasco, Ricky	1	2	5.57	7	7	0	24	22	7	19
Orenduff, Justin	0	1	4.41	11	0	0	16	18	10	14
Overholt, Pat	3	2	5.23	9	4	0	21	18	3	11
Savery, Joe	1	1	0.64	5	5	0	14	4	11	5
Startup, Will	1	0	0.71	12	0	0	13	9	2	9
Wade, Cory	0	0	1.74	9	0	0	10	9	1	10
Wright, Wesley	0	1	5.06	12	0	1	21	27	11	18

PHOENIX DESERT DOGS

BATTING	AVG	AB	R	H	2B	3B	HR	RBI	BB	SO	SB
Baisley, Jeff	.203	79	7	16	4	0	3	15	6	20	0
Butera, Drew	.250	32	4	8	2	0	0	6	3	5	0
Davis, Blake	.240	50	10	12	1	0	0	9	5	10	6
Delaney, Jason	.234	107	10	25	4	1	0	14	21	25	2
Getz, Chris	.278	79	13	22	3	0	0	8	10	5	2
Macri, Matt	.257	101	13	26	9	0	2	9	9	22	2
McCutchen, Andrew	.286	98	13	28	5	2	0	4	14	12	8
Morgan, Nyjer	.258	93	18	24	2	2	1	9	12	14	10
Padron, Raul	.320	50	3	16	4	0	1	3	5	10	0
Pennington, Cliff	.241	58	14	14	4	0	1	10	18	19	9
Plouffe, Trevor	.280	50	7	14	4	0	0	8	7	13	1
Reimold, Nolan	.245	106	16	26	4	0	6	23	11	33	2
Sweeney, Ryan	.286	84	13	24	2	0	1	13	9	18	5

PITCHING	W	L	ERA	G	GS	SV	IP	H	BB	SO
Arrieta, Jake	1	0	0.00	14	0	0	16	8	7	16
Blackburn, Nick	4	0	1.64	6	6	0	22	13	2	20
Chavez, Jesse	1	2	6.00	11	0	0	12	20	4	9
Davidson, David	0	1	0.96	10	0	0	9	7	3	6
Day, Dewon	0	1	1.38	11	0	0	13	9	4	17
Dowdy, Justin	0	0	0.00	3	0	0	3	1	2	4
Egbert, Jack	1	0	3.26	6	6	0	19	14	11	17
Gray, Jeff	0	2	5.68	11	0	0	13	16	7	9
Haehnel, David	2	2	8.25	11	0	0	12	16	12	8
Hernandez, Fernando	0	0	0.00	12	0	2	13	5	4	11
Hernandez, Chris	1	0	0.00	13	0	0	13	9	2	7
Kilby, Brad	0	1	1.59	11	0	0	11	10	7	6
McCrory, Bob	2	1	1.50	12	0	5	12	4	4	11
Morlan, Eduardo	1	0	0.00	12	0	1	13	8	6	7
Mullins, Ryan	1	0	2.84	6	5	0	19	15	6	20
Penn, Hayden	1	0	6.45	7	7	0	22	27	10	27
Russell, Adam	2	0	2.81	11	0	0	16	16	8	16
Simmons, James	0	0	2.89	9	0	0	9	7	3	8
Swarzak, Anthony	1	1	2.05	7	7	0	22	20	4	12

SCOTTSDALE SCORPIONS

BATTING	AVG	AB	R	H	2B	3B	HR	RBI	BB	SO	SB
Brignac, Reid	.177	113	9	20	2	0	2	6	3	16	1
Burriss, Manny	.365	52	9	19	1	1	0	6	3	8	8
Carp, Mike	.243	107	12	26	9	0	0	16	8	17	0
Castillo, Wilkin	.196	56	6	11	5	0	0	2	3	15	2
Cunningham, Aaron	.267	86	12	23	2	0	2	15	11	20	3
Jaso, John	.256	39	6	10	1	0	3	6	7	6	0
Nickeas, Mike	.196	46	3	9	2	0	1	6	3	11	0
Patterson, Ryan	.275	80	10	22	3	1	3	7	9	14	1
Santos, Sergio	.319	94	12	30	10	0	5	20	3	15	1
Schierholtz, Nate	.348	89	15	31	8	1	4	10	1	12	1
Snider, Travis	.316	98	23	31	6	2	4	11	15	29	1
Sollmann, Steve	.308	26	7	8	2	0	0	3	2	4	1
Sollmann, Steve	.231	52	9	12	4	0	0	3	2	8	2
Stewart, Caleb	.318	44	10	14	2	0	6	11	6	12	0

PITCHING	W	L	ERA	G	GS	SV	IP	H	BB	SO
Anderson, Brian	0	1	0.00	12	0	4	12	8	1	9
Bostick, Chris	2	0	2.74	6	6	0	23	20	13	23
Camacho, Eddie	0	2	2.31	10	0	0	12	15	2	9
DeBarr, Nick	0	1	2.45	9	0	0	11	7	1	6
James, Justin	0	0	4.80	9	0	0	15	17	4	9
Kunz, Eddie	0	1	10.13	9	0	0	11	15	8	11
Medlock, Calvin	0	0	1.62	10	0	0	17	7	2	19
Meek, Evan	1	0	0.93	9	0	0	10	3	5	9
Muniz, Carlos	0	1	3.27	8	0	1	11	13	5	9
Munter, Scott	1	0	2.00	10	0	0	9	13	3	6
Pereira, Nick	4	1	3.38	7	7	0	29	29	14	26
Prochaska, Mike	3	2	6.55	6	6	0	22	27	4	13
Purcey, David	1	2	1.23	6	6	0	22	13	9	25
Romero, Ricky	1	1	3.86	9	1	0	12	8	5	12
Romo, Sergio	0	0	0.64	9	0	0	14	12	4	16
Rosen, Mark	0	0	12.38	10	0	0	8	9	9	7
Scherzer, Max	1	1	2.13	8	0	0	13	6	5	18
Smith, Greg	2	2	2.61	6	6	0	21	19	8	17
Vasquez, Esmerling	0	0	2.35	8	0	0	8	4	7	7

SURPRISE RAFTERS

BATTING	AVG	AB	R	H	2B	3B	HR	RBI	BB	SO	SB
Andrus, Elvis	.353	51	10	18	4	1	0	3	5	10	5
Aubrey, Michael	.275	91	14	25	6	0	5	11	10	10	1
Dickerson, Chris	.259	81	16	21	2	2	4	15	10	21	5
Duarte, Jose	.156	45	8	7	1	0	0	5	7	12	2
Gimenez, Chris	.239	46	8	11	3	0	2	6	6	11	0
Gimenez, Chris	.220	50	9	11	3	0	2	6	6	12	0
Johnson, Ben	.196	46	6	9	1	1	1	5	4	12	0
Kaaihue, Kila	.203	69	10	14	3	0	3	15	17	18	0
Lubanski, Chris	.200	85	12	17	3	3	3	15	8	22	0
Maddox, Marc	.321	81	12	26	5	1	2	13	11	14	2
Mayberry, John	.214	84	12	18	1	0	5	13	11	17	1
Rodriguez, Sean	.217	83	12	18	6	0	3	10	8	29	1
Rosales, Adam	.292	48	7	14	3	1	1	10	4	9	2
Snyder, Brad	.250	28	1	7	0	0	1	4	2	6	0
Tatum, Craig	.255	47	6	12	2	0	1	4	4	8	0
Teagarden, Taylor	.271	48	7	13	1	0	3	10	6	18	0

PITCHING	W	L	ERA	G	GS	SV	IP	H	BB	SO
Austen, David	1	0	2.13	10	0	0	13	10	2	4
Feldman, Scott	1	1	4.24	8	0	0	17	16	8	16
Finocchi, Mike	3	0	0.00	9	0	0	10	7	4	5
Harrison, Matt	5	0	2.00	7	7	0	27	16	7	19
Herrera, Daniel	0	0	2.53	10	0	0	11	7	6	5
Hoelscher, Nate	1	0	1.50	10	0	1	12	11	2	10
Huff, David	1	1	6.06	7	2	0	16	16	3	15
Hughes, Dusty	1	0	2.45	6	6	0	22	16	8	17
Jukich, Ben	0	3	8.20	6	6	0	19	26	10	13
Kometani, Paul	0	0	1.80	9	0	3	10	5	2	17
Lecure, Sam	1	2	4.85	7	0	0	13	15	4	12
Lowery, Devon	0	0	2.70	6	0	0	7	4	5	7
Lumsden, Tyler	1	0	6.00	7	0	0	12	14	5	11
Miller, Adam	0	2	9.00	5	5	0	13	18	3	11
Newsom, Randy	0	0	0.00	5	0	0	5	5	1	3
O'Day, Darren	1	1	2.38	10	0	2	11	8	0	6
Pelland, Tyler	1	1	1.08	9	0	2	8	7	6	10
Rodriguez, Fernando	2	1	3.97	6	6	0	23	31	8	13
Rundles, Rich	0	0	1.04	8	0	0	9	2	6	5
Stertzbach, Von	0	0	5.00	9	0	0	9	7	9	7
Viola, Pedro	0	0	13.50	8	0	0	7	15	2	7

TEAM USA

BATTING	AVG	AB	R	H	2B	3B	HR	RBI	BB	SO	SB
Anderson, Bryan	.300	10	0	3	0	0	0	1	0	3	0
Bixler, Brian	.174	23	1	4	0	0	1	5	0	8	1
Colvin, Tyler	.263	19	1	5	1	0	0	5	1	3	2
Hollimon, Mike	.100	10	1	1	0	0	0	0	1	3	0
Hollimon, Mike	.200	30	5	6	1	0	2	4	3	10	1
Jaramillo, Jason	.250	12	3	3	0	0	1	3	2	0	0
LaRoche, Andy	.333	18	2	6	1	0	1	4	1	2	1
Longoria, Evan	.286	21	5	6	2	0	0	1	2	8	0
Longoria, Evan	.308	65	14	20	6	0	4	9	6	21	0
Nix, Jayson	.316	19	4	6	2	0	0	2	1	3	2
Pearce, Steve	.308	26	6	8	3	0	2	3	1	2	1
Rasmus, Colby	.286	21	4	6	4	0	0	1	4	4	0
Ruggiano, Justin	.176	17	1	3	0	1	0	2	2	5	1
Young, Delwyn	.524	21	5	11	3	0	1	4	0	4	0

PITCHING	W	L	ERA	G	GS	SV	IP	H	BB	SO
Blevins, Jerry	0	0	2.45	3	0	0	4	2	2	5
Booker, Chris	0	0	0.00	2	0	1	3	1	2	3
Duensing, Brian	0	0	1.50	2	1	0	6	6	0	3
Gronkiewicz, Lee	1	0	0.00	3	0	0	4	4	0	6
Karstens, Jeff	0	0	2.70	2	2	0	7	4	0	8
Musser, Neal	1	0	2.45	4	0	1	4	1	1	3
Outman, Josh	1	0	1.50	2	0	0	6	5	1	5
Outman, Josh	1	1	3.95	5	3	0	14	16	3	13
Perez, Chris	0	1	22.50	3	0	0	2	5	2	2
Shell, Steven	0	0	13.50	3	0	0	3	4	1	3
Stevens, Jeff	0	0	0.00	3	0	1	3	1	0	4
Stevens, Jeff	0	0	0.00	6	0	1	6	2	1	6
Trahern, Dallas	1	1	5.40	2	1	0	5	6	3	3
Wright, Matt	0	0	3.86	2	2	0	7	8	1	2

MINOR LEAGUES

WAIPAHU, Hawaii

North Shore manager Kevin Bradshaw got the obligatory water cooler treatment after his Honu were declared champions of the 2007 Hawaii Winter Baseball season, but he wasn't the only one to get wet.

The championship game between the Honu and Waikiki BeachBoys was canceled because of rain. Although the rain stopped shortly after the game was scheduled to start, the field conditions were considered unsafe. Also, the players and coaching staff had flights home later that night and the next day, so the game could not be rescheduled.

The Honu (26-12), who won the West by 12 1/2 games, were awarded the overall title by virtue of having the best record. In fact, they posted the only winning record in the four-team league. The BeachBoys (19-19), who clinched the East title on the last day of the regular season, were runners-up.

"It was kind of the downer for the fans and a downer for us because we didn't get to play it out to see who really would've won," said Honu third baseman Mat Gamel (Brewers). "But I understand the field was kind of unsafe, so it's really not worth getting anybody hurt to the point where it might be a career-ending injury."

Obviously, Bradshaw (Tigers) was pleased with this team's performance for the season.

"Unfortunately, you never want to settle it with a rainout, but at the same time, I'm very proud of these guys," Bradshaw said. "The record we had, the way we went about our business, the way we played the game. Our win-loss record speaks for itself."

Although the Honu had the best record, BeachBoys manager Donovan Mitchell (Mets) liked his team's chances.

"I'm very disappointed," Mitchell said. "It would've been a good championship game. We had our best pitcher (Kyohei Muranaka) going against one of their best pitchers (Shinya Nakayama). You just never would've known in a one-game playoff. But you can't do anything about Mother Nature."

Muranaka (Yakult Swallows) was 3-1 with a 2.00 ERA, which was sixth-best in the league. Nakayama (Orix Buffaloes) won the most games in the league at 6-2, 3.12.

For their title, the Honu received Sony Walkmans, while the BeachBoys were given Sony noise-canceling headphones.

The 200 or so fans who showed up were rewarded with free food and drinks, compliments of the league chairman Duane Kurisu. Prizes that were to be given out via drawings during the game were still handed out to those who hung around. Fans were able to score autographs from the players as they waited for their buses. Players also dished out equipment, such as bats, that they didn't want to lug on the plane.

This was the second year of the revived developmental league that originally ran from 1993-97. Les Murakami Stadium at the University of Hawaii was unavailable because its turf was being replaced; it is the only true baseball stadium on the island of Oahu.

TOP 20 PROSPECTS

1. Matt Wieters, c, Honolulu (Orioles)
2. Austin Jackson, of, Honolulu (Yankees)
3. Brandon Snyder, 1b/3b, Honolulu (Orioles)
4. Brett Sinkbeil, rhp, North Shore (Marlins)
5. Daniel Bard, rhp, Honolulu (Red Sox)
6. Bud Norris, rhp, North Shore (Astros)
7. George Kontos, rhp, Honolulu (Yankees)
8. Mat Gamel, 3b, North Shore (Brewers)
9. Kris Medlen, rhp, Honolulu (Braves)
10. Josh Bell, 3b, West Oahu (Dodgers)
11. Blake Wood, rhp, West Oahu (Royals)
12. Chris Valaika, ss/2b, North Shore (Reds)
13. Argenis Diaz, ss, Honolulu (Red Sox)
14. Mike McKenry, c, Waikiki (Rockies)
15. Jermaine Mitchell, of, Waikiki (Athletics)
16. Stephen Chapman, 1b, North Shore (Brewers)
17. Jason Place, of, Honolulu (Red Sox)
18. Lucas Duda, 1b, Waikiki (Mets)
19. Jonathan Lucroy, c, North Shore (Brewers)
20. Dan Murphy, 3b, Waikiki (Mets)

Most of this season's games were held at Hans L'Orange, which is a municipal recreation park that required major upgrades to satisfy Major League Baseball. Kurisu said MLB threatened to cancel the season but his brother, Hervy Kurisu, the league president, convinced MLB that Hans L'Orange would meet its standards. Six games were played on Big Island and six more on Maui.

Kurisu said games will return to Murakami Stadium next season, but there will be fewer there because the Rainbows hold fall workouts during the same time.

Gamel was voted the Hawaii Winter Baseball MVP in a voting by the media and league officials. Gamel led or was near the lead in most of the offensive categories. He batted .333 with a league-leading eight home runs and tied for second with 25 RBIs.

"I was really trying to focus on defense," he said. "I feel that I made a lot of improvements over there and that was the main thing I tried to take out of this."

Gamel showed that his defense at third base is still a work in progress. He committed a league high 10 errors in 30 games for an .880 fielding percentage.

HWB was about more than just sharpening their baseball skills, though. It was an educational experience.

"It was a good learning experience, playing with all the Japanese players," Gamel said. "To learn their culture, to learn what they think about the game, their philosophies because their philosophies are different from ours. I enjoyed it. I had a real good time."

Besides tours to the volcanic craters on Maui and the Big Island, the players also were given a private tour of the USS Arizona Memorial at Pearl Harbor.

While the Japanese dominated five of the six pitchers' spots on the all-star team, Honu pitcher Brett Sinkbeil (Marlins) also had good season, finishing 3-1, 1.64. He had 24 strikeouts and 16 walks in 33 innings.

—STACY KANESHIRO

ALYSON BOYER

Orioles prospect Brandon Snyder was Hawaii Winter Baseball's leading hitter, finishing with a .378 average

MINOR LEAGUES

STANDINGS

EASTERN DIVISION

	W	L	PCT	GB
Waikiki BeachBoys	19	19	.500	—
Honolulu Sharks	17	20	.459	1½

WESTERN DIVISION

	W	L	PCT	GB
North Shore Honu	26	12	.684	—
West Oahu CaneFires	13	24	.351	12½

INDIVIDUAL BATTING LEADERS

(MINIMUM 76 PLATE APPEARANCES)

PLAYER, TEAM	AVG	G	AB	R	H	HR	RBI
Snyder, Brandon, Hon	.378	26	90	13	34	2	15
Diaz, Argenis, Hon	.358	32	106	17	38	0	16
Burke, Kyler, Hon	.333	26	87	13	29	1	10
Gamel, Mat, NS	.333	33	120	25	40	8	25
Yokogawa, Fuminori, Hon	.313	31	96	18	30	1	13
Santangelo, Lou, NS	.304	25	79	16	24	1	12
Gac, Ian, WO	.303	31	109	19	33	7	19
Wilson, Michael, Wai	.303	35	119	21	36	7	30
Lucroy, Jonathan, NS	.299	23	77	9	23	0	8
Abreu, Miguel, Hon	.297	35	118	21	35	2	12

INDIVIDUAL PITCHING LEADERS

(MINIMUM 15 INNINGS)

PITCHER, TEAM	W	L	ERA	IP	H	BB	SO
Matsuoka, Ken, Wai	2	0	0.00	24	16	1	24
Miyamoto, Ken, WO	0	0	0.31	29	17	11	26
Kamoshida, Takashi, NS	0	0	0.98	28	11	13	45
Bard, Daniel, Hon	0	0	1.08	17	8	15	15
Sinkbeil, Brett, NS	3	1	1.64	33	21	16	24
Muranaka, Kyohei, Wai	3	1	2.00	36	32	17	44
Johnson, Steve, WO	2	2	2.05	31	20	7	23
Tamaki, Yutaka, Wai	4	0	2.22	49	35	10	47

Thall, Chad, Hon		1	3	2.55	25	19	10	23
Wilson, Tyler, Hon		0	0	2.57	21	18	8	29

HONOLULU SHARKS

BATTING	AVG	AB	R	H	2B	3B	HR	RBI	BB	SO	SB
Abreu, Miguel	.297	118	21	35	10	1	2	12	1	12	8
Britton, Phillip	.080	50	4	4	1	0	0	1	4	19	1
Burke, Kyler	.333	87	13	29	8	1	1	10	9	37	1
Diaz, Argenis	.358	106	17	38	5	2	0	16	10	18	2
Flowers, Tyler	.192	99	18	19	4	0	3	18	18	33	3
Jackson, Austin	.271	133	25	36	10	5	3	22	18	38	8
Kobe, Takumi	.222	81	8	18	5	2	0	12	13	23	1
Ohiro, Shoji	.191	68	10	13	2	0	1	6	10	29	3
Place, Jason	.213	80	16	17	6	0	4	8	13	39	2
Samson, Nate	.225	71	12	16	2	0	0	4	8	18	1
Snyder, Brandon	.378	90	13	34	5	2	2	15	5	23	0
Suttle, Brad	.100	80	7	8	3	0	1	6	15	30	0
Wieters, Matt	.283	106	13	30	9	1	1	17	12	15	0
Yokogawa, Fuminori	.313	96	18	30	6	2	1	13	10	25	11

PITCHING	W	L	ERA	G	GS	SV	IP	H	BB	SO
Aihara, Katsuyuki	1	1	8.31	12	0	1	13	20	3	9
Bard, Daniel	0	0	1.08	16	0	0	17	8	15	15
Britton, Phillip	0	0	9.00	1	0	0	1	1	2	0
Claggett, Anthony	1	1	6.04	14	0	0	22	29	9	14
Furuya, Takuya	3	2	4.97	9	8	0	38	40	11	31
James, Jimmy	2	3	3.31	8	8	0	35	32	15	43
Kontos, George	3	4	3.71	8	7	0	34	34	10	42
Matsuzaki, Shingo	1	3	4.87	9	8	0	41	33	16	59
Medlen, Kris	0	1	1.88	11	0	1	14	10	4	27
Ouellette, Ryan	1	1	9.31	15	0	0	19	31	9	16
Tanaka, Ryohei	4	1	3.02	8	8	0	42	39	7	40
Texeira, Kanekoa	0	0	8.31	8	0	0	9	12	3	4
Thall, Chad	1	3	2.55	16	0	2	25	19	10	23
Wilson, Tyler	0	0	2.57	16	0	2	21	18	8	29

NORTH SHORE HONU

BATTING	AVG	AB	R	H	2B	3B	HR	RBI	BB	SO	SB
Chapman, Stephen	.294	126	19	37	9	1	1	13	9	42	4
Corley, Brad	.265	117	19	31	9	0	4	25	5	29	1
Gamel, Mat	.333	120	25	40	9	0	8	25	17	30	3
Griffin, Michael	.270	141	20	38	4	2	2	10	1	22	4
Hart, Billy	.171	35	6	6	1	0	0	2	2	11	3
Laster, Jeramy	.268	82	11	22	6	1	6	19	3	36	2
Lucroy, Jonathan	.299	77	9	23	6	0	0	8	7	16	0
Nagata, Masahiro	.272	92	16	25	7	0	0	7	15	21	2
Presley, Alex	.306	36	8	11	0	0	0	5	1	7	1
Ryan, Dusty	.182	55	5	10	6	0	1	5	17	20	1
Santangelo, Lou	.304	79	16	24	7	0	1	12	14	24	0
Valaika, Chris	.269	108	14	29	5	0	3	17	7	31	2
Worth, Daniel	.292	65	11	19	4	1	0	6	5	15	2
Yoshida, Shintaro	.243	74	14	18	1	1	0	9	15	12	2

PITCHING	W	L	ERA	G	GS	SV	IP	H	BB	SO
Aguilar, Omar	1	0	3.74	16	0	1	22	16	14	20
Benoit, Charles	4	0	3.32	14	0	2	22	17	9	13
Cruse, Andy	1	2	4.00	10	3	0	27	31	8	22
Johnson, Blair	3	1	3.26	8	6	0	30	29	8	28
Kamoshida, Takashi	0	0	0.98	16	0	5	28	11	13	45
Marceaux, Jacob	0	0	4.67	14	0	2	17	20	12	13
Nakayama, Shinya	6	2	3.12	9	8	0	40	20	11	55
Naylor, Drew	0	1	7.30	8	0	1	12	12	7	19
Norris, Bud	2	1	3.65	7	6	0	25	16	12	33
Ondrusek, Logan	2	2	5.72	8	6	0	28	38	12	23
Roberts, Kevin	1	1	4.82	15	0	2	19	15	13	20
Sinkbeil, Brett	3	1	1.64	8	7	1	33	21	16	24
Walker, Sean	2	0	3.20	6	2	1	20	17	10	15

WAIKIKI BEACH BOYS

BATTING	AVG	AB	R	H	2B	3B	HR	RBI	BB	SO	SB
Coronado, Jose	.118	34	7	4	1	0	0	3	4	12	1
Duda, Lucas	.340	53	12	18	6	1	3	13	5	7	0
Garcia, Emmanuel	.348	66	13	23	5	2	0	1	8	7	8
Garner, Cole	.145	62	7	9	1	0	1	3	2	22	1
Inouye, Matt	.229	35	4	8	2	0	0	3	1	9	0
Kindel, Jeff	.272	103	16	28	8	1	3	17	16	24	0
Maroul, David	.194	72	12	14	4	0	4	9	10	25	1
McCraw, Sean	.143	35	5	5	1	0	1	5	8	13	0
McKenry, Michael	.281	96	17	27	9	0	5	15	12	27	2
Mitchell, Jermaine	.250	88	10	22	3	1	0	8	17	24	2
Murphy, Dan	.274	95	17	26	9	0	4	21	11	22	1
Pellot, Hector	.275	109	10	30	1	0	3	12	8	29	4
Richardson, Antoan	.255	110	18	28	3	5	0	12	23	34	14
Sellers, Justin	.281	89	13	25	7	1	1	15	9	22	6
Wilson, Michael	.303	119	21	36	11	2	7	30	18	41	4
Womack, Josh	.191	110	16	21	1	2	1	10	15	36	6

PITCHING	W	L	ERA	G	GS	SV	IP	H	BB	SO
Carr, Nicholas	1	0	3.65	5	1	0	12	11	10	10
Griffin, Daniel	0	1	16.62	3	0	1	4	0	0	
Jensen, Aaron	1	1	5.73	12	1	0	22	26	4	19
Lansford, Jared	0	3	5.87	9	8	1	31	35	6	20
Lindsay, Shane	0	2	5.50	9	4	3	18	11	16	19
Matsuoka, Ken	2	0	0.00	5	3	0	24	16	1	24
Muranaka, Kyohei	3	1	2.00	10	4	2	36	32	17	44
Newton, David	2	0	6.75	12	0	3	13	16	5	19
Patton, David	0	1	4.76	12	0	0	17	23	9	24
Rustich, Brant	3	1	5.82	12	0	1	17	19	11	17
Simons, Zach	0	0	8.22	5	0	1	8	11	1	8
Sullivan, Josh	1	4	6.17	9	5	1	23	25	14	24
Tamaki, Yutaka	4	0	2.22	10	8	0	49	35	10	47
Tsujimoto, Kent	1	1	5.30	11	0	0	19	17	18	14
Williams, Harold	1	0	8.31	11	0	0	13	19	13	15

WEST OAHU CANEFIRES

BATTING	AVG	AB	R	H	2B	3B	HR	RBI	BB	SO	SB
Bell, Joshua	.213	94	15	20	5	1	3	17	11	26	0
Bianchi, Jeff	.284	74	13	21	4	1	0	3	6	20	5
Gac, Ian	.303	109	19	33	7	0	7	19	9	35	0
Gentry, Craig	.184	98	14	18	5	0	0	7	7	32	1
Hatch, Anthony	.273	121	19	33	7	1	4	20	11	21	1
Herren, K.C.	.211	95	9	20	4	2	0	7	6	17	0
Hoffmann, Jamie	.278	97	12	27	2	2	0	7	10	23	7
Hoshi, Hidekazu	.170	94	7	16	0	2	0	4	4	31	2
Jansen, Kenley	.206	63	9	13	3	0	0	2	11	13	0
Jeroloman, Brian	.237	59	8	14	4	0	1	9	14	9	0
Martin, Todd	.217	46	6	10	3	0	1	6	4	8	0
Mitchell, Russell	.270	111	11	30	11	0	3	19	6	28	2
Rogowski, Ryan	.237	93	17	22	3	0	3	18	21	20	6
Tracy, Chad	.232	95	15	22	5	0	7	20	8	25	3

PITCHING	W	L	ERA	G	GS	SV	IP	H	BB	SO
Chambliss, Tyler	1	1	7.50	9	0	1	18	23	10	18
Cooper, Michael	1	3	8.49	9	4	1	23	34	11	28
Gonzalez, Marco	0	2	11.17	7	0	2	10	0	0	
Itokazu, Keisaku	1	1	2.76	9	7	0	42	43	10	39
Johnson, Steve	2	2	2.05	7	7	0	31	20	7	23
Kimura, Fumikazu	1	3	4.23	8	4	0	28	27	21	25
Miyamoto, Ken	0	0	0.31	16	0	3	29	17	11	26
Santos, Reid	0	1	5.24	13	0	2	22	21	13	26
Stiller, Erik	1	4	5.06	8	8	0	32	38	8	36
Wagner, Neil	0	0	9.68	12	0	0	18	27	12	16
Wilson, Kyle	0	3	7.84	13	0	0	21	29	10	26
Wood, Blake	2	1	3.55	8	8	0	33	33	19	57

INDEPENDENT LEAGUES

Trio of new leagues join fold

BY J.J. COOPER

The old saying about weather in Florida applies just as well to independent baseball. If you aren't happy with who is playing where, just wait a couple of minutes and things will change.

That was true again in 2007. Three new leagues popped up, but only two survived the season. The Can-Am League saw the two teams in its championship series both announce they might not return for 2008. The Northern League had a public feud where two Canadian teams complained about unfair treatment before bolting the league to join the Golden Baseball League.

In other words, it was just another normal year in the independent leagues. While there was plenty of turnover, that didn't detract from another very solid years for the indy leagues overall. Just a couple of years ago it was noteworthy when independent baseball topped five million in attendance. This year more than eight million fans came out to watch independent baseball, and where independent baseball was once focused in the Northeast and Midwest, independent leagues dotted parks in every region of the country and Canada in 2007.

A Trio Of Neophytes

Three new leagues, the Continental, New York State and South Coast Leagues, all debuted in 2007 although only the Continental and South Coast Leagues were still around when the season ended.

Of the new leagues, the South Coast League had the strongest debut. After hiring independent leagues veteran Kash Beauchamp as its director of player personnel the league was able to acquire above-average talent for a first-year league and the league's decision to hire managers like Wally Backman, Phil Plantier and Cecil Fielder gave the league some name recognition among fans. Attendance figures were not overwhelming by any stretch, but the league did draw more than 1,000 fans at five of its six venues and is aiming to expand in 2008.

The New York State League's debut didn't go nearly as smoothly. With only one city on board, the league's idea was to open a four-team league in one city. The citizens of Utica, N.Y., weren't exactly caught up in the drama of watching four teams without any geographical ties battle it out game after game. The league pulled the plug in the middle of the season.

The New York State League's quick decision to fold left officials of some of the more established independent leagues mulling the idea of creating a minimum list of criteria that must be reached to be called an official independent league. Their worry is that any time an independent league folds it damages the brand of independent baseball as a whole. The idea would be that a league must have teams in multiple cities, play an extensive schedule (not just games on the weekends), keep official statistics and reach other criteria before being allowed to be called a true independent league, as opposed to the semipro leagues that dot the nation.

While the idea may have some merit, it also faces a large stumbling block: it seems entirely against the spirit of independent baseball. The indy leagues formed because the National Association's rules on territories restricted many cities from any hope of having minor league baseball

Anderson's Scott Houin proved to be one of the stars of the new South Coast League

which leaves many team owners opposed to too many regulations.

Unlike the New York State League, the Continental Baseball League had no problem completing its first season. The league, composed of a travel team and three teams in Houston and Dallas suburbs, managed to dodge rain drops that plagued the entire season to crown Tarrant County as the league's first champion.

Plenty Of Turnover

If the new leagues were trying to establish themselves, that doesn't mean that the long-time leagues were any more static. In the past decade most available attractive markets have been snapped up by one league or another, which has left the existing leagues to battle over fewer and fewer markets to expand into.

Most leagues have announced plans for expansion in the upcoming years, but the constant churn of poor performing teams usually means that expansion ends up just replacing existing teams that shut down or move on.

For instance the American Association, itself a combination of surviving Central Baseball League franchises and teams that split off from the Northern League, announced as soon as the season ended that it was adding teams in Wichita and Grand Prairie, Texas. The new teams were originally expected to allow the league to expand to 12 teams, which would have allowed the league to split into two geographically cohesive divisions. But soon thereafter the league announced that Coastal Bend and St. Joe's were considering going dark which would keep the league at 10 teams.

That's four more teams than the Northern League will have. The eight-team league lost Calagry and Edmonton after the season when the two teams announced they were leaving to join the Golden Baseball League.

Well-traveled Brinkley makes history

BY J.J. COOPER

If he wanted to, Darryl Brinkley could play the role of the bitter veteran to perfection.

It took him five years to simply prove he was worthy of being signed to a minor league deal--even though he hit .529 as a college senior and was named the Caribbean Series MVP while playing against big leaguers. He then hit .355 for Nashville in his first taste of Triple-A baseball, followed it up by hitting .323 the next year and still found himself watching other players get the call to the big leagues.

Two years later he saw his only shot at a big league call-up squashed when he was stuck in Australia during the flight groundings that followed 9/11. His spot on the Orioles roster was gone by the time he made it back.

But Brinkley doesn't lament what happened. He simply grabs his bat, goes back out and keeps on hitting.

This year he became the first Northern Leaguer to hit .400, going 9-for-13 in his final three games to reach the mark, shattering the league batting average record by 24 points. He also led the league hits, on-base percentage and runs scored while carrying Calgary to its first every playoff appearance—the Vipers lost in the Northern League championship series to Gary. And he did all of this as a 38-year-old, at a time when many of his former teammates have long ago hung up their spikes.

For all of that, Brinkley has been named Baseball America's 2007 Independent Leagues Player of the Year. It's Brinkley's second honor from Baseball America, as he was BA's Winter Player of the Year in 1996, a year after Carlos Delgado won that award and a year before Bartolo Colon won it. Both of them were just beginning outstanding big league careers at the time of their awards, Brinkley was just looking for a team to give him a chance to play in affiliated ball for the first time.

That's been the story wherever Brinkley has played. It seems that he had to set himself on fire to get noticed. Coming out of Sacred Heart in 1991, his high average wasn't enough to attract the attention of any scouts. With no independent leagues to turn to (the Northern League didn't begin playing until 1993), Brinkley signed with the Dutch Major Leagues. He spent three years in Europe before getting his first chance at playing in the U.S in independent ball. That trip was part of a world tour that has seen him play in The Netherlands, Italy, Canada, Mexico, Korea, the Dominican Republic and Venezuela in addition to the U.S.

"I'm not a prospect no more, so you've got to do good to keep playing," Brinkley said. "My motto was

Darryl Brinkley became the first Northern Leaguer to hit .400 for an entire season

always if you hit for a high average you'll keep a job."

It's a motto that's worked out well for Brinkley for nearly two decades now. He's always hit, and he's always found a team willing to give him a job.

It's not that easy to explain why Brinkley never ended up in the majors. He can hit, he can run and he has a solid arm. But he never had that combination of luck and opportunity that would give him a line in the Baseball Encyclopedia. His late start (he didn't reach Triple-A until he was 29-years-old) didn't help either. Despite having plenty of opportunities to play what-if, Brinkley is more focused on what-is. "It hurt at first (to not make the majors), but what are you going to do?" Brinkley said. "I'm not the biggest religious guy you're going to find, but the man upstairs gave me longevity. I'm still playing. I've gotten the chance to see the world, and my family has gotten a chance to see the world."

As the offseason began, Brinkley wasn't sure if he wanted to hang the cleats up after hitting .400 and go out on top, or if he'll come back for another year. But he does know its been a heck of a ride for the past 15 years.

PREVIOUS WINNERS

1996 — Darryl Motley, of, Fargo-Moorhead (Northern)	**2002** — Bobby Madritsch, lhp, Winnipeg (Nortnern)
1997 — Mike Meggers, of, Winnipeg/Duluth (Northern)	**2003** — Jason Shelley, rhp, Rockford (Frontier)
1998 — Morgan Burkhart, 1b, Richmond (Frontier)	**2004** — Victor Rodriguez, ss, Somerset (Atlantic)
1999 — Camrine Cappucio, of, New Jersey (Northern)	**2005** — Eddie Lantigua, 3b, Quebec (Can-Am)
2000 — Anthony Lewis, 1b, Duluth-Superior (Northern)	**2006** — Ian Church, Kalamazoo (Frontier)
2001 — Mike Warner, of, Somerset (Atlantic)	

AMERICAN ASSOCIATION

It's hard to find a Fort Worth Cat who remembers what it's like to go home unhappy at the end of a season.

After two years, the American Association has had one champion as the Cats repeated as league champs, rallying to beat St. Paul three games to two in the best-of-five championship series. Fort Worth also won the final Central League title of the now-defunct league.

When it came to the deciding game, Fort Worth turned to Joel Kirsten, the same ace who had pitched them to titles in 2005 and 2006. Kirsten allowed fix hits and one run while Jordan Foster homered and Kelley Gulledge hit a two-run single as part of a three-run seventh that led Fort Worth to a 4-1 win in the deciding game.

Foster was named the series MVP. He had 19 hits in the postseason.

FIRST HALF

NORTH DIVISION	W	L	PCT	GB
Lincoln	34	13	.723	
Sioux Falls	31	17	.646	3½
St. Paul	28	20	.583	6½
Sioux City	15	33	.313	19½
St. Joe	15	33	.313	19½

SOUTH DIVISION	W	L	PCT	GB
El Paso	28	20	.583	
Shreveport	23	24	.489	4½
Fort Worth	21	24	.467	5½
Coastal Bend	21	25	.457	6½
Pensacola	20	27	.426	7½

SECOND HALF

NORTH DIVISION	W	L	PCT	GB
St. Paul	29	19	.604	
Sioux City	25	23	.521	4
Lincoln	23	23	.500	5
Sioux Falls	22	26	.458	7
St. Joe	19	29	.396	10

SOUTH DIVISION	W	L	PCT	GB
Fort Worth	32	16	.667	
El Paso	28	20	.583	4
Shreveport	24	24	.500	8
Pensacola	19	29	.396	13
Coastal Bend	17	29	.370	14

PLAYOFFS: Semifinals—St. Paul defeated Lincoln 3-0 and Fort Worth defeated El Paso 3-2 in best-of-five series. **Finals:** Fort Worth defeated St. Paul 3-2 in best-of-five series.

MANAGERS: Coastal Bend—John Harris; **El Paso**—Butch Henry; **Fort Worth**—Stan Hough; **Lincoln**—Tim Johnson; **Pensacola**—Mac Seibert; **Shreveport**—Bob Flori; **Sioux City**—Ed Nottle; **Sioux Falls**—Steve Shirley; **St. Joe**—Al Gallagher; **St. Paul**—George Tsamis.

ATTENDANCE: St. Paul 297,834; El Paso 211,316; Fort Worth; 141,330; Lincoln 193,040; Sioux Falls 144,025; Sioux City 92,786; Pensacola 92,466; Coastal Bend 58,715; Shreveport 57,085; St. Joe 30,244.

ALL-STAR TEAM: C—Marcel Longmire, St. Paul; **1B**—Walter Olmstead, El Paso; **2B**—Josh Patton, Lincoln; **3B**—Trino Aguilar, Pensacola; **SS**—Albenis Machado, El Paso; **OF**—Brian Fryer, Coastal Bend/Fort Worth; Jorge Moreno, Sioux City; Seth Pietsch, Lincoln; **DH**—Jorge Alvarez, El Paso Diablos. **LHP**—Joel Kirsten, Fort Worth; **RHP**—Pat Mahomes, Sioux Falls; **RP**—Jerrod Fuell, Sioux Falls.

Player of the Year: Jorge Alvarez, El Paso. **Rookie Player of the Year:** Cesar Aranguren, Pensacola. **Rookie Pitcher of the Year:** Matt Clayman, Shreveport. **Manager of the Year:** Butch Henry, El Paso.

INDIVIDUAL BATTING LEADERS

BATTER, CLUB	AVG	G	AB	R	H	HR	RBI
Smith, Will, Sioux Falls	.367	61	259	42	95	9	36
Bourassa, Adam, St. Paul	.353	65	224	56	79	1	33
Alvarez, Jorge, El Paso	.352	95	420	75	148	8	91
Pietsch, Seth, Lincoln	.349	93	370	68	129	9	60
Olmstead, Walter, El Paso	.341	93	370	79	126	12	66
Cordova, Ricardo, Pensacola	.336	72	298	36	100	3	39
Patton, Josh, Lincoln	.335	88	316	52	106	5	63
Balet, Pichi, Lincoln	.330	85	345	63	114	7	61
Llanos, Alex, Sioux City	.329	87	325	58	107	5	53
Lofton, James, Coastal Bend	.326	83	337	43	110	2	50

INDIVIDUAL PITCHING LEADERS

PITCHER, CLUB	W	L	ERA	IP	H	BB	SO
Bays, Leonard, Sioux Falls	8	1	2.90	84	66	32	85
Gardner, Jarrett, Lincoln	10	4	2.97	130	132	18	95
Gwaltney, Lee, Fort Worth	6	2	3.16	105	95	30	59
Miller, Colby, Shreveport	6	9	3.18	127	120	37	83
Walters, Cory, Fort Worth	10	5	3.18	122	117	24	103
Whinnery, Brian, St. Paul	6	5	3.19	116	120	35	70
Mahomes, Pat, Sioux Falls	12	3	3.21	135	140	44	109
Kirsten, Joel, Fort Worth	6	5	3.32	117	109	21	68
Scheafer, Carl, Pensacola	8	4	3.32	84	73	20	46
Wiltshire, Greg, El Paso	11	7	3.35	129	109	42	103

COASTAL BEND AVIATORS

BATTER	AVG	AB	R	H	2B	3B	HR	RBI	SB
Apodaca, Luis, of	.316	19	2	6	0	1	0	3	0
Arrowood, Jason, c	.304	23	1	7	1	0	0	1	0
★Figueroa, Juan, of	.290	169	23	49	10	1	1	22	1
Flores, Pedro, of	.167	6	3	1	0	0	0	0	0
Foust, J.D., 3b	.298	215	30	64	13	0	1	26	10
★Fryer, Brian, of	.295	322	56	95	14	3	4	34	30
Gerdes, Chase, of	.175	80	8	14	5	0	0	7	3
Grau, Philip, of	.221	217	25	48	12	0	1	24	4
Ketter, Steve, c	.183	115	15	21	2	1	0	7	0
Lewis, Will, 2b	.273	260	34	71	16	0	5	32	8
Lofton, James, ss	.326	337	43	110	23	1	2	50	12
Morales, Steve, c	.293	215	32	63	10	0	7	32	1
Rachal, Ryan, of	.250	60	10	15	1	0	0	2	0
Richardson, Grant, 3b	.301	322	52	97	23	3	8	55	3
Smith, Bryon, 1b	.286	339	51	97	13	0	10	54	0
Smith, Ryan, ss	.117	77	8	9	0	2	0	4	2
★Spencer, Matt, of	.250	236	20	59	16	2	2	30	3
Tully, Travis, of	.327	55	7	18	1	1	0	4	1
Van Dusen, Derrick, of	.200	15	2	3	2	0	0	2	0

PITCHERS	W	L	ERA	G	SV	IP	H	BB	SO
Atlee, Thomas	2	1	3.16	36	17	37	30	8	53
Domangue, Eric	1	1	9.64	2	0	9	13	4	8
Flores, Pedro	5	6	3.79	19	0	102	104	29	80
Grau, Philip	0	0	18.00	1	0	1	2	2	0
Haines, Timothy	5	5	5.47	46	1	82	95	43	85
Heaston, Bryan	0	4	10.38	5	0	22	30	13	12
★Hendricks, T.J.	1	7	5.27	10	0	56	79	8	13
Hull, Kevin	6	10	5.43	19	0	111	154	58	64
Hunton, Jon	1	2	2.23	36	2	40	29	16	54
Jimenez, Juan	0	1	8.31	3	0	4	9	3	4
Lee, Kevin	1	3	8.19	7	0	30	46	14	11
Lopez, Jose	0	1	4.50	2	0	10	14	4	10
Martin, Brian	2	1	2.14	2	0	21	9	13	21
Martinez, Miguel	2	3	5.45	39	0	71	61	39	63
Pickens, J.R.	4	2	4.08	8	0	46	60	8	33
Pudewell, Nathaniel	0	0	7.71	3	0	2	4	3	2
Richardson, Grant	0	0	36.00	1	0	1	5	1	0
Van Dusen, Derrick	6	7	4.37	18	0	107	117	39	78
★Wilkinson, Matt	2	0	4.57	16	1	22	24	9	21

EL PASO DIABLOS

BATTER	AVG	AB	R	H	2B	3B	HR	RBI	SB
Alvarez, Jorge, 2b	.352	420	75	148	43	1	8	91	6
Belcher, Jordan, of	.312	346	47	108	19	0	1	48	7
Camacho, Juan, 3b	.295	410	63	121	30	1	11	75	0
Cervera, Michael	.000	2	0	0	0	0	0	0	0
Clary, Casey, of	.195	87	10	17	2	1	2	8	1
Conley, Evan, 2b	.256	336	43	86	13	0	1	43	3
Drew, Kory, of	.309	372	78	115	23	4	6	70	7
Grupp, Brian, of	.091	22	1	2	0	0	0	0	0
Izquierdo, Joel, 2b	.188	64	8	12	0	0	0	6	3
Jaquez, Reyes, c	.500	2	1	1	0	0	0	1	0
Kent, Mat, c	.285	330	38	94	30	0	6	49	0
Machado, Albenis, ss	.317	344	73	109	21	3	0	30	28
Olmstead, Walter, 1b	.341	370	79	126	33	8	12	66	16
★Reininger, J.D., of	.328	67	11	22	6	0	2	4	3
Strankman, Dallas, 2b	.000	2	0	0	0	0	0	1	0
Wood, Logan, of	.240	338	59	81	17	3	13	42	8

PITCHERS	W	L	ERA	G	SV	IP	H	BB	SO
★Androsko, Todd	0	0	1.13	5	0	8	5	2	5
Cameron, Dustin	5	2	2.56	38	0	56	54	15	43
Cervera, Michael	4	1	3.63	26	0	84	85	34	75
Darley, Ned	3	6	3.07	35	18	41	42	19	25

INDEPENDENT LEAGUES

	W	L	ERA	G	SV	IP	H	BB	SO
Freites, Julio.	0	2	3.94	21	0	30	34	13	17
Knoff, Justin.	6	2	3.92	20	0	57	65	17	40
Marshall, Jacoby.	0	0	10.38	4	0	4	7	6	2
Montoya, Eric.	0	0	6.17	3	0	12	19	4	9
Neiser, Evan.	0	0	3.38	10	0	11	8	8	7
Neitz, Josh.	9	4	3.92	20	0	110	138	33	66
ONeal, Charles.	3	3	9.30	7	0	30	43	19	21
Romero, Garvis.	0	6	2.29	32	1	59	52	12	37
Salini, Robert.	0	0	16.88	3	0	3	3	5	3
Strankman, Dallas.	0	0	5.77	29	0	48	48	29	30
Torres, Andy.	6	3	6.58	16	0	90	133	28	32
Trolia, Aaron.	2	0	1.64	5	0	22	18	9	14
Wachman, Robert.	4	4	6.35	16	0	74	109	23	52
Wiltshire, Greg.	11	7	3.35	22	1	129	109	42	103

FORT WORTH CATS

BATTER	AVG	AB	R	H	2B	3B	HR	RBI	SB
Adolfo, Carlos, of.	.279	233	55	65	15	0	8	45	5
Allen, John, of.	.248	125	10	31	7	0	2	21	2
Carter, Charles, 1b.	.307	358	58	110	16	3	6	47	21
Christison, Dallas, 2b.	.234	141	15	33	8	0	0	16	17
Dubarry, B.J., c.	.172	29	4	5	1	0	0	1	1
Foster, Jordan, of.	.304	309	49	94	19	1	3	32	3
★Fryer, Brian, of.	.458	24	5	11	4	0	0	4	4
Green, Terence, 3b.	.314	363	71	114	21	4	1	27	26
Gulledge, Kelley, c.	.302	268	52	81	22	1	12	51	0
Harkrider, Kip, 2b.	.185	92	7	17	2	0	0	12	1
Hendricks, K.J., 2b.	.250	108	16	27	4	1	0	11	12
Maitland, Ben, of.	.114	44	6	5	0	0	0	4	0
Miller, Adam, c.	.245	151	18	37	7	0	0	18	0
Mirizzi, Marc, ss.	.301	359	61	108	21	0	9	64	5
Molyneux, John, of.	.271	59	5	16	1	0	0	5	1
Moye, Alan, of.	.233	249	32	58	11	1	6	50	7
Roberson, Trey, of.	.229	70	7	16	2	1	0	9	2
Shankle, Brooks, dh.	.000	8	0	0	0	0	0	0	0
★Spencer, Matt, of.	.186	59	5	11	5	0	1	10	0
Trout, Steven, 2b.	.265	34	4	9	2	1	0	5	0
Wojcik, Tim, 2b.	.270	37	5	10	2	0	0	5	1

PITCHERS	W	L	ERA	G	SV	IP	H	BB	SO
Beaver, Bryant.	1	0	8.46	15	1	22	37	13	12
Blasko, Chadd.	1	1	7.94	2	0	6	8	3	6
Burnau, Ryan.	0	1	0.66	7	1	14	10	3	18
Figueroa, Juan.	1	3	4.73	24	4	32	41	17	47
Gwaltney, Lee.	6	2	3.16	23	1	105	95	30	59
Hintz, Beau.	2	2	3.03	15	0	33	29	15	27
Kirsten, Joel.	6	5	3.32	19	1	117	109	21	68
Layfield, Scotty.	1	0	7.71	5	2	5	7	2	5
★Marsden, Aaron.	6	4	3.83	23	3	52	62	17	45
Martin, Nick.	7	5	5.23	18	0	95	104	39	67
Ramos, Mario.	2	2	8.27	6	0	33	50	10	25
Scherzer, Max.	1	0	0.56	3	0	16	9	4	25
★Trytten, Ryan.	3	2	1.98	15	0	50	43	15	34
Valentin, Dan.	5	5	4.00	21	1	70	80	20	52
Varnell, Grant.	2	0	0.96	9	2	19	12	3	8
★Vasquez, Tim.	0	2	1.38	8	3	13	8	3	19
Walters, Cory.	10	5	3.18	20	0	122	117	24	103
Weems, Ryan.	0	1	14.29	5	0	6	18	4	7

LINCOLN SALTDOGS

BATTER	AVG	AB	R	H	2B	3B	HR	RBI	SB
Balet, Pichi, of.	.330	345	63	114	22	2	7	61	3
Cooley, Brett, 1b.	.315	359	62	113	19	0	13	65	1
Dempsey, Joe, c.	.309	55	10	17	1	0	0	5	2
Duchek, Matt, c.	.156	77	6	12	1	0	2	9	0
Gallardo, Carlos, of.	.188	48	6	9	2	0	0	3	1
Garcia, Tony, ss.	.325	317	45	103	13	0	4	34	2
★Gordon, Casey, 3b.	.000	2	0	0	0	0	0	0	0
Harrington, Corey, of.	.267	251	41	67	10	1	5	26	29
Harris, Gary, of.	.222	27	3	6	3	0	0	3	2
Lusero, Cody, 2b.	.250	56	8	14	2	0	0	6	2
McCoy, Ross, of.	.302	96	11	29	7	0	1	12	0
Mendoza, Aaron, c.	.232	246	29	57	4	0	2	28	0
Patton, Josh, 2b.	.335	316	52	106	23	1	5	63	8
Pedroza, Chris, c.	.286	7	1	2	0	0	0	0	0
Pietsch, Seth, of.	.349	370	68	129	31	2	9	60	24
Warner, Bryan, of.	.311	370	68	115	13	0	9	49	2
Yaconetti, Jay, 3b.	.278	349	45	97	17	0	5	47	1

PITCHERS	W	L	ERA	G	SV	IP	H	BB	SO
Blitstein, Jeffrey.	2	2	7.17	4	0	21	27	7	14
Brown, Joe.	1	2	4.19	33	0	39	35	19	46
Campbell, Brian.	2	3	4.41	6	0	35	32	14	19
Cannon, Jon.	1	0	0.56	3	0	16	11	3	7
Eichelberger, Jared.	0	0	5.28	4	0	15	14	12	5

	W	L	ERA	G	SV	IP	H	BB	SO
Gardner, Jarrett	10	4	2.97	21	0	130	132	18	95
Greenhouse, Michael	0	0	7.71	3	0	7	17	4	5
★Howerton, Jason	0	1	11.88	6	0	8	19	1	2
Jakubauskas, Chris	6	0	2.42	7	0	45	28	18	44
Kaminski, John	0	0	4.00	5	0	18	17	19	7
Kauten, Joshua	7	4	3.67	17	1	98	108	21	88
Nowlin, Chris	0	0	0.00	1	0	0	2	2	0
Reichert, Dan	7	5	4.50	17	0	114	114	27	100
Roberts, Mark	6	4	3.08	45	0	53	48	9	64
Ruwe, Kyle	10	3	4.57	30	0	100	120	15	60
Staggs, Nathan.	2	3	4.79	18	1	41	38	16	37
Thompson, Johnny	1	1	3.64	13	0	30	29	15	25
★Trytten, Ryan	0	1	6.23	6	0	4	7	3	3
Varner, Matthew.	2	3	3.80	45	20	45	45	15	37
Warner, Bryan	0	0	0.00	2	0	3	2	4	4

PENSACOLA PELICANS

BATTER	AVG	AB	R	H	2B	3B	HR	RBI	SB
Aguilar, Trino, 3b.	.291	364	56	106	17	2	16	47	23
Aranguren, Cesar, 2b.	.302	324	49	98	11	0	4	30	7
Bethea, Larry, dh.	.265	34	2	9	2	0	0	3	1
Brown, Bo, ss.	.223	184	22	41	7	0	2	19	8
Calzado, Napoleon, of.	.324	204	33	66	13	3	8	43	3
Cordova, Ricardo, ss.	.336	298	36	100	16	8	3	39	14
Decarlo, Michael, c.	.258	155	10	40	6	0	3	17	2
Hulett, Joe, c.	.274	106	10	29	5	0	2	9	1
Koenig, Lance, 2b.	.171	35	1	6	0	0	0	0	2
Land, Joshua, of.	.073	41	3	3	1	1	0	4	1
Lytle, Chaz, of.	.222	45	2	10	0	0	0	2	4
★Merle, Jesen, of.	.000	1	0	0	0	0	0	0	0
Miller, Jamie, of.	.424	33	5	14	2	0	0	3	1
Ragar, Joshua, c.	.183	71	9	13	3	0	0	8	1
★Reininger, J.D., of.	.206	218	25	45	12	0	4	29	3
Revall, Andrew, of.	.205	44	5	9	0	0	1	4	1
Reynolds, Chris, of.	.224	254	29	57	8	1	0	20	7
Rodriguez, Jeff, 1b.	.333	3	1	1	0	0	0	0	0
Rodriguez, Marcos, 1b.	.321	327	52	105	15	2	3	45	7
Tablado, Raul, 3b.	.217	60	6	13	5	0	0	5	0
Warrick, Nathan, of.	.261	203	28	53	7	1	0	10	20
Williams, Bo, 1b.	.261	238	23	62	19	0	4	33	2
Younghanz, Michael, dh.	.000	10	0	0	0	0	0	0	0

PITCHERS	W	L	ERA	G	SV	IP	H	BB	SO
★Androsko, Todd.	5	6	6.16	14	0	69	95	27	37
Baca, Noel.	2	1	5.16	10	0	45	43	23	35
Creighton, Matthew.	0	4	6.30	7	0	30	25	25	19
Davis, Hunter.	2	1	1.00	23	6	27	20	7	17
★Edwards, Andrew.	2	2	4.25	7	0	36	40	16	34
Hall, Darryl.	0	3	7.06	7	0	22	23	11	10
Kling, Brandon.	0	0	5.40	18	0	25	28	10	21
Matthews, Jarod.	0	1	7.20	1	0	5	5	3	3
★Merle, Jesen.	3	4	6.46	12	0	61	90	12	49
Montero, Oscar.	1	2	3.72	27	1	36	34	20	55
Orgovan, Joe.	0	0	1.23	4	0	7	8	2	2
Pawelczyk, Kyle.	0	1	9.69	6	0	13	24	8	6
Pinkston, Friedel.	0	2	27.00	2	0	3	13	2	1
Rodriguez, Jeff.	1	2	4.20	33	0	75	108	22	40
Scheafer, Carl.	8	4	3.32	50	2	84	73	20	46
Thompson, Chris.	6	6	3.88	43	11	56	61	26	57
Vandermeer, Scott.	2	3	5.95	7	0	35	45	10	19
Williamson, Logan.	4	6	5.25	34	1	86	85	52	61
Young, Colin.	3	8	3.79	20	0	119	125	36	79

SHREVEPORT SPORTS

BATTER	AVG	AB	R	H	2B	3B	HR	RBI	SB
Albert, Jeff, 2b-3B.	.000	4	0	0	0	0	0	1	0
Benes, Richie, ss.	.125	16	2	2	1	0	0	0	0
Bryant, Tommy, of.	.285	355	44	101	20	1	6	52	0
Burns, Deacon, of.	.298	379	64	113	20	3	5	37	29
Cooksey, Bryan, ss.	.216	208	27	45	9	2	2	18	2
Entrekin, Alex, c.	.224	67	4	15	4	0	0	9	0
Falu, Melvin, 3b.	.322	152	17	49	6	1	1	28	1
Gambill, Chad, of.	.291	333	58	97	18	1	12	64	1
Hamilton, Ryan, 3b.	.141	78	9	11	2	1	0	3	0
Hudson, Brandon, of.	.266	94	12	25	4	0	0	6	1
Humphries, Justin, c.	.285	354	56	101	30	4	11	61	0
Joffrion, Jack, 2b.	.280	200	29	56	10	1	7	29	1
Maddox, Dusty, of.	.203	74	12	15	4	2	2	10	3
Pride, Austin, of.	.233	120	16	28	6	0	2	16	0
Robinson, Wade, ss.	.314	194	25	61	10	4	0	22	0
Schmidt, J.P., of.	.294	374	61	110	26	3	2	43	41
Ventura, Juan, 3b.	.308	263	29	81	12	4	2	28	4

PITCHERS	W	L	ERA	G	SV	IP	H	BB	SO
Clayman, Matt.	2	5	2.73	30	4	56	48	27	58

INDEPENDENT LEAGUES

	W	L	ERA	G	SV	IP	H	BB	SO
Cunningham, Aaron	3	0	3.12	29	4	40	34	17	29
Cunningham, Derek	4	6	4.40	19	1	92	106	38	60
★Hendricks, T.J.	2	5	9.26	8	0	35	61	16	20
Hudson, Brandon	2	2	3.60	15	2	20	20	5	17
Lawrence, Matt	0	0	1.80	6	0	5	9	5	6
Lewis, Fielding	0	0	0.00	1	0	0	2	0	0
Miller, Colby	6	9	3.18	20	0	127	120	37	83
Snow, Bert	4	8	3.79	19	0	126	115	53	85
Tarbutton, Donnie	3	0	6.75	9	0	12	19	3	5
Tyson, Leo	1	2	9.88	19	0	27	31	21	17
Welch, Daniel	1	1	4.28	8	0	48	44	14	28
Williams, Cody	1	0	7.41	10	0	17	24	7	12
Wilson, Grant	4	1	3.78	32	1	52	55	16	27
Winters, Mal.	8	3	3.78	25	2	79	98	19	54
Yeatman, Matt	6	5	4.88	19	2	90	116	44	61

SIOUX CITY EXPLORERS

BATTER	AVG	AB	R	H	2B	3B	HR	RBI	SB
Benavidez, Julian, 1b	.261	268	32	70	15	1	8	44	0
★Cox, Billy, c	.253	95	16	24	8	0	2	10	0
Daubert, Jake, 3b	.281	392	56	110	20	2	9	63	2
Francisco, Alexander, ph	.000	2	0	0	0	0	0	0	0
Goldberg, Zach, c	.333	9	2	3	0	0	1	2	0
Harris, Shea, c	.158	57	7	9	1	0	1	4	0
James, Willie, 2b	.273	55	7	15	0	1	0	6	1
Jones, Brandon, 3b	.266	218	32	58	10	1	8	35	0
Jones, Dustin, of	.324	102	22	33	1	0	0	14	5
Llanos, Alex, 2b	.329	325	58	107	19	1	5	53	11
McCoola, Nick, ss	.306	268	37	82	9	2	1	29	2
Moreno, Jorge, of	.294	378	76	111	28	2	14	60	27
Navarro, Ramon, ss	.163	92	12	15	1	0	0	4	2
O'Donnell, Brendon, of	.000	1	0	0	0	0	0	0	0
Pirman, Pete, of	.273	366	41	100	20	2	4	42	8
Quarberg, Erik, 1b	.129	31	2	4	1	0	0	0	0
Radwan, Jason, c	.161	56	5	9	0	0	3	7	0
Richardson, Mike, c	.208	106	20	22	5	0	4	13	0
Tonkin, Shea, c	.143	28	4	4	1	0	0	1	0
Tuttle, Jason, of	.291	378	51	110	13	1	1	40	23
★Weichard, Paul, of	.204	98	13	20	7	1	2	12	1

PITCHERS	W	L	ERA	G	SV	IP	H	BB	SO
★Buchanan, Brian	4	6	4.50	13	0	74	91	18	41
Cebula, Nick	0	2	4.80	4	1	15	21	3	13
Cheek, Cameron	5	1	3.38	14	1	59	71	7	23
Cordero, Jose.	0	2	5.87	3	0	15	18	7	8
Daniels, Isaac	0	1	6.39	14	0	31	38	13	19
Dupic, Ryan	0	0	15.43	3	0	5	11	6	3
Fiallo, Javier	0	0	7.56	4	0	8	9	1	5
Francisco, Alexander	10	6	5.32	21	0	117	134	35	77
Gross, Rafael	2	1	5.67	7	0	27	41	2	14
Guy, Brad	2	7	3.49	15	0	116	126	16	54
Hewitt, Brian	0	0	0.00	2	0	1	1	0	2
Hoffman, Eric.	0	0	0.00	1	0	0	2	0	0
James, Rory.	1	6	6.70	23	4	50	57	25	47
Koch, Jon.	3	4	7.21	17	0	44	51	18	28
Marotz, Ty	2	5	4.00	8	0	54	64	11	41
★Marsden, Aaron	0	2	18.78	2	0	8	17	3	3
Martinez, Lenny	0	4	4.50	1	0	2	0	3	2
Nunes, Mike.	0	4	4.79	15	0	21	26	13	14
O'Loughlin, Luke	0	4	4.50	1	0	2	3	0	2
Reid, Brett	2	2	4.64	24	1	33	32	14	35
Schmal, Joel	2	2	4.01	33	1	49	60	17	23
Scholten, J.D.	0	2	8.25	10	1	12	17	5	6
Simpson, Allan	0	0	3.86	2	0	2	4	1	2
★Weichard, Paul	0	0	0.00	1	0	1	0	0	0
★Wilkinson, Matt	2	2	2.51	29	12	33	33	12	29
Wilson, Aaron	2	3	5.79	7	0	37	51	21	17
Wooley, Robert	3	1	6.92	9	0	26	35	12	25

SIOUX FALLS CANARIES

BATTER	AVG	AB	R	H	2B	3B	HR	RBI	SB
Arriaga, Rene, dh	.250	4	1	1	0	0	0	0	0
Arroyo, Abner, 1b	.314	290	40	91	14	1	6	46	1
Coughlan, Cameron, of	.300	233	45	70	8	1	1	16	30
Fermin, Angelo, ss	.225	120	24	27	4	3	1	13	7
★Figueroa, Juan, 1b	.269	160	20	43	15	1	2	20	0
★Gordon, Casey	.296	71	17	21	4	1	2	11	3
Imwalle, Matt, 3b	.263	353	56	93	25	2	15	49	1
Keesee, David, 2b	.214	117	10	25	2	0	0	6	2
Lawhorn, Trevor, of	.305	128	23	39	5	2	8	24	1
Lessler, Damon, 2b	.211	114	15	24	1	0	3	16	2
Lydy, Scott, of	.258	62	6	16	5	0	0	7	2
Marks, Tim, c	.305	298	39	91	8	0	3	36	1
Miller, Orlando, ss	.306	183	29	56	7	2	8	41	6
Quintana, Wil, of	.232	241	41	56	7	2	12	40	5

	AVG	AB	R	H	2B	3B	HR	RBI	SB
Shanks, James, of	.276	283	43	78	20	2	6	44	16
Smith, Jake, c	.157	83	8	13	2	0	0	1	0
Smith, Will, of	.367	259	42	95	20	1	9	36	1
Van Iderstine, Ben, of	.315	384	57	121	24	3	7	63	5

PITCHERS	W	L	ERA	G	SV	IP	H	BB	SO
Bays, Leonard	8	1	2.90	31	0	84	66	32	85
Casares, Kelly	3	3	2.23	30	0	40	43	13	37
Cheppenko, Kevin	6	6	4.63	16	0	93	106	35	65
Donlin, Sean.	2	3	4.25	24	0	49	51	22	49
Ford, Ryan	7	5	3.54	17	0	104	103	32	67
Fuell, Jerrod	1	2	5.52	32	23	31	39	12	35
Garrison, Aaron	1	2	4.59	33	1	49	50	25	39
Hoegh, Owen	0	0	13.50	1	0	2	4	2	3
Keoppel, Trey	1	1	7.77	7	0	24	28	15	24
Landing, Jeffrey	6	5	4.85	18	0	102	116	30	71
Mahomes, Pat	12	3	3.21	19	0	135	140	44	109
Posey, Micah	4	10	5.45	18	0	101	136	40	67
Regas, Kris.	2	2	1.45	35	1	43	40	9	52

ST·JOE BLACKSNAKES

BATTER	AVG	AB	R	H	2B	3B	HR	RBI	SB
Balkan, Adam, of	.274	62	8	17	1	0	0	2	0
Beever, James, c	.092	65	6	6	0	0	0	2	0
Burgos, Victor, of	.262	61	5	16	4	0	0	8	1
Fowler, David, of	.253	380	62	96	15	8	7	55	31
★Gordon, Casey, ss	.296	253	34	75	12	3	1	25	10
Jennings, Josh, of	.263	38	3	10	1	0	0	1	0
Johnson, Carl, 1b	.186	43	4	8	1	1	1	4	2
Lane, Andy, 3b	.000	9	0	0	0	0	0	0	1
McQuigg, Carter, 3b	.195	128	20	25	8	1	1	9	0
Miaso, Curt, of	.251	342	47	86	12	2	8	39	9
Misenhelter, Jeryn, 1b	.300	10	0	3	0	1	0	2	0
Padilla, Eric, 2b	.151	53	5	8	0	0	0	5	4
Palmer, Cody, c	.154	26	1	4	0	0	0	2	0
Parzyk, Dylan, c	.298	161	16	48	5	0	2	24	0
Rios, Brian, 3b	.207	29	4	6	1	0	1	3	0
Robles, Terry, 2b	.267	176	28	47	10	2	0	14	3
Sosebee, Chad, 3b	.234	346	36	81	22	3	4	45	4
Wallis, Jacob, c	.181	127	7	23	5	0	1	14	0
★Weichard, Paul, of	.313	134	20	42	4	1	3	23	7
Whitesides, Jake, 1b-2B	.279	247	35	69	18	7	2	24	3
Wilson, Andy, of	.270	378	39	102	11	1	2	36	15
Yount, Dustin, 1b	.280	304	45	85	16	2	6	50	0

PITCHERS	W	L	ERA	G	SV	IP	H	BB	SO
Alvarez, Mark.	0	0	3.97	5	0	11	12	3	4
Balbuena, Caleb	2	2	2.17	24	4	29	21	9	35
Beever, James	1	1	4.36	10	0	33	38	12	13
Bicknell, Greg.	4	2	4.91	8	0	55	62	9	45
★Bolton, Dustin	2	8	4.48	18	0	94	101	17	52
★Buchanan, Brian	1	6	6.46	10	0	61	73	22	33
Burger, Nick	0	0	0.00	1	0	1	2	1	0
Dechristofaro, Vinnie	5	8	4.96	43	0	62	64	36	53
Dehart, Rick	2	2	3.44	5	0	34	36	8	21
★Edwards, Andrew	1	8	5.18	15	0	75	95	34	53
Freeborn, Brandon	0	0	0.00	1	0	1	1	1	2
Gett, Alex	0	0	1.13	3	0	16	14	1	18
Glick, David	0	4	6.59	6	0	29	41	18	16
Goodman, Mark	2	5	3.52	43	1	64	76	23	26
Gowey, Jeremiah	0	0	10.80	3	0	7	14	5	1
★Howerton, Jason	1	0	3.55	5	0	13	14	6	4
Marchildon, Chris.	0	2	4.34	8	1	19	23	13	4
★Merle, Jesen	0	2	9.00	4	0	14	31	1	5
Raab, Kellen	6	8	4.58	22	0	120	146	34	81
★Shepherd, Alec	5	1	3.20	12	0	65	67	22	41
Sosebee, Chad	0	0	0.00	1	0	2	1	0	2
★Vasquez, Tim	1	2	4.86	34	4	37	41	23	44
Williams, Ryan	1	1	3.94	4	0	16	19	4	7
Wilson, Andy	0	0	0.00	1	0	0	0	0	0

ST·PAUL SAINTS

BATTER	AVG	AB	R	H	2B	3B	HR	RBI	SB
Adams, Skip, 1b	.225	204	32	46	13	1	2	39	10
Bourassa, Adam, of	.353	224	56	79	11	3	1	33	16
Brunson, Matt, 2b	.261	165	31	43	5	1	0	10	17
Carlson, Kevin, c	.116	43	3	5	2	0	0	2	0
★Cox, Billy, c	.268	56	6	15	4	1	0	5	0
Davis, Jay, of	.289	45	9	13	0	0	0	9	1
Fonseca, Alex, 2b	.221	163	28	36	5	0	4	28	15
Gripp, Ryan, 3b	.261	23	5	6	0	0	2	4	0
Heath, Demetrius, 2b	.377	61	14	23	5	1	0	5	8
Jordan, Scooter, of	.297	317	71	94	8	2	3	34	36
Kramer, Sean, ph	.000	1	0	0	0	0	0	0	0
Krause, Brent, of	.379	227	36	86	20	3	4	41	11

Longmire, Marcel, c	.324	370	74	120	21	1	16	79	15
Lopez, Josue, 1b	.248	105	14	26	4	0	6	28	1
Olow, Adam, of	.269	212	38	57	14	1	5	42	1
Priddy, Ryan, ss.	.224	219	19	49	3	1	1	18	4
Sprout, Brian, of	.304	365	64	111	22	1	7	52	6
Sullivan, Kevin, c	.283	60	5	17	1	0	1	5	0
Thomas, Ben, 3b	.260	327	47	85	15	0	3	40	6
Valenzuela, Fernando, 1b .	.338	77	5	26	4	0	0	12	1
White, Derrick, of.	.391	64	12	25	7	0	3	21	2
Wooten, Shawn, c	.385	13	1	5	1	0	0	2	0

PITCHERS	W	L	ERA	G	SV	IP	H	BB	SO
★Bolton, Dustin	1	1	4.50	2	0	14	13	4	4
Brandenburg, Adam	6	4	4.22	16	0	92	84	42	67
Cierlik, Jason	1	3	6.00	16	0	18	19	13	16
Embry, Byron	3	1	2.73	19	3	30	30	12	39
Fitzgerald, Kevin	0	0	1.93	4	0	5	5	0	2
Foster, Kyle	0	1	4.78	21	0	43	45	16	39
Harrington, Matt.	0	1	3.86	4	0	12	15	6	5
Howerton, John	1	0	6.43	6	0	14	23	8	7
Huguet, J.C.	2	0	3.00	2	0	12	13	6	7
Huizinga, Jon	5	1	3.83	36	1	52	58	20	33
Kramer, Sean	1	0	5.52	11	0	15	19	6	16
Lord, Justin	4	4	4.24	11	0	68	81	9	42
McKenzie, Marcus	0	1	9.00	2	0	6	8	5	4
Pierce, Tony	4	2	3.10	37	12	41	30	21	57
Postlewait, Jacob	6	7	4.12	14	0	83	96	32	43
Priddy, Ryan.	0	0	0.00	3	0	3	2	2	2
Ruud, Charlie	11	3	3.63	20	0	139	144	23	110
★Shepherd, Alec	3	2	4.91	5	0	33	33	13	11
Tricoglou, Jamie.	0	1	6.41	16	3	20	21	12	22
Urban, Jeff	0	2	13.94	3	0	10	24	4	9
Villarreal, Luis	3	0	2.52	4	0	25	23	6	28
Whinnery, Brian	6	5	3.19	21	0	116	120	35	70

ATLANTIC LEAGUE

Jose Herrera picked a perfect time for a once-in-a-lifetime game.

The former Athletics prospect hit three home runs in the deciding game of the Atlantic League championship series as Newark beat Somerset 13-7. Herrera hit a two-run home run in the first to cut a Somerset lead to one, 3-2, followed it up with a solo home run in the third to even the game 3-3, then hit a three-run home run was a big part of an eight-run eighth inning that lead the Bears to the seemingly easy win.

It was Newark's first title since 2002 while Somerset was denied its fourth title in seven years.

Somerset's Brian Adams was named the league's pitcher of the year thanks to his 15-2, 3.68 season. Newark's Victor Rodriguez and Bridgeport's Jesse Hoorelbeke shared the player of the year honors. Rodriguez led the league with a .367 batting average while Hoorelbeke hit a league and independent leagues' best 33 home runs.

FIRST HALF

NORTH DIVISION	W	L	PCT	GB
Newark	36	27	.571	
Long Island	35	28	.556	1
Bridgeport	35	28	.556	1
Road Warriors	16	46	.258	19½

SOUTH DIVISION	W	L	PCT	GB
Camden	39	24	.619	
Somerset	35	28	.556	4
Lancaster	29	34	.460	10
York	26	36	.419	12½

SECOND HALF

NORTH DIVISION	W	L	PCT	GB
Long Island	37	26	.587	
Newark	36	27	.571	1
Road Warriors	26	37	.413	11
Bridgeport	25	38	.397	12

SOUTH DIVISION	W	L	PCT	GB
Somerset	40	23	.635	
York	32	31	.508	8
Lancaster	28	35	.444	12
Camden	28	35	.444	12

PLAYOFFS: Semifinals—Newark defeated Long Island 2-0 and Somerset defeated Camden 2-1 in best-of-three series. Finals: Newark defeated Somerset 3-1 in best-of-five series.

Managers: Bridgeport—Tommy John; **Camden**—Joe Ferguson;

Lancaster—Rick Wise; **Long Island**—Dave LaPoint; **Newark**—Wayne Krenchicki; **Road Warriors**—Jeff Scott; **Somerset**—Sparky Lyle; **York**—Chris Hoiles.

ATTENDANCE: Long Island 427,536; Somerset 371,520; Lancaster 346,875; York 218,826; Camden 258,177; Newark 186,807; Bridgeport 167,372.

ALL-STAR TEAM: C—Randy McGarvey, Camden; **1B**—Jesse Hoorelbeke, Bridgeport; **2B**—Javier Colina, Newark; **3B**—Jay Caligiuri, Bridgeport; **SS**—Ramon Castro, Newark; **Utility**—P.J. Rose, Long Island; Nate Espy,York; **OF**—Carl Everett, Long Island; Mike Lockwood, Somerset; Steven Doetsch, Road Warriors; Ray Navarrete Long Island; **DH**—Victor Rodriguez Newark. **RHP**—Gary Knotts, Newark; **LHS**—Brian Adams, Somerset; **RP**—Danny Graves, Long Island; Derrick DePriest, Lancaster.

Pitcher of the Year: Brian Adams, Somerset; **Players of the Year:** Victor Rodriguez, Newark; Jesse Hoorelbeke, Bridgeport. **Manager of the Year:** Jeff Scott, Road Warriors.

BATTER, CLUB	AVG	G	AB	R	H	HR	RBI
Rodriguez, Victor, Newark	.365	115	436	70	159	16	98
McGarvey, Randy, Camden	.355	89	287	48	102	5	36
Castro, Ramon, Newark	.343	88	327	61	112	9	49
Rose, P.J., Long Island.	.342	117	453	71	155	14	95
Caligiuri, Jay, Bridgeport	.320	111	394	79	126	14	78
Gomes, Joey, Newark.	.320	89	316	41	101	11	43
Demarco, Matt, Camden	.317	95	312	44	99	5	52
Espy, Nate, York	.316	119	433	82	137	22	90
Ambrosini, Dominick, Lancaster	.316	100	380	62	120	19	70
Hoorelbeke, Jesse, Bridgeport	.313	117	432	86	135	33	96

PITCHER, CLUB	W	L	ERA	IP	H	BB	SO
Knotts, Gary, Newark	7	5	2.65	109	85	40	86
Van Hekken, Andy, Somerset	9	3	3.12	115	112	35	83
Castillo, Carlos, R. Warriors	8	9	3.34	121	112	24	94
Adams, Brian, Somerset	15	2	3.68	156	160	35	117
Castillo, Frank, York	8	4	3.75	110	100	32	52
Porzio, Mike, Bridgeport	11	8	3.94	155	162	53	121
Stevens, Josh, Lancaster	10	10	4.08	159	196	34	91
Halama, John, Long Island	8	10	4.14	167	201	44	93
Martinez, Gustavo, Lancaster.	8	8	4.30	126	138	50	88
Sturge, Justin, Bridgeport	6	9	4.32	117	129	44	84

BRIDGEPORT BLUEFISH

BATTER	AVG	AB	R	H	2B	3B	HR	RBI	SB
★Aracena, Sandy, c	.245	49	7	12	2	0	0	4	0
★Baez, Fleming, c	.105	19	0	2	0	0	0	1	0
★Blue, Vince, of	.234	64	7	15	6	1	0	7	2
Boyd, Shaun, of	.345	113	29	39	2	2	4	24	3
Caligiuri, Jay, 3b.	.320	394	79	126	33	1	14	78	2
Darula, Bobby, of	.265	117	14	31	6	2	1	20	6
Deleon, Sandy, c	.194	67	3	13	0	0	1	12	1
Espada, Angel, 2b	.309	181	37	56	4	0	2	12	11
Figueroa, Luis, 3b	.317	202	20	64	12	0	2	45	0
Frazier, Alex, of	.233	30	4	7	2	0	1	6	0
Hernandez, Johnny, of	.299	147	27	44	9	4	2	18	5
Hine, Steve, 2b.	.275	153	28	42	7	2	1	19	6
Hoorelbeke, Jesse, 1b	.313	432	86	135	19	0	33	96	0
Lucca, Lou, 3b	.226	159	18	36	4	0	4	12	0
Made, Kelington, 3b.	.300	20	3	6	1	0	0	4	0
Malek, Bobby, of	.282	475	81	134	19	6	7	65	19
McCracken, Quinton, of . . .	.271	414	59	112	16	1	8	66	10
Nathans, John, c	.200	165	26	33	5	1	2	24	1
Ortiz, Nick, ss.	.297	471	93	140	28	4	9	65	20
Otanez, Willis, 1b.	.315	54	4	17	4	1	0	7	0
Rojas, Tommy, c	.243	136	23	33	10	1	4	21	0
Sanchez, Marcos, c	.305	213	31	65	10	7	4	29	0
Spivey, Junior, 2b.	.333	249	60	83	18	0	5	39	8
Vroman, Doug of	.176	17	0	3	0	0	0	1	1

PITCHERS	W	L	ERA	G	SV	IP	H	BB	SO
★Ahearne, Pat	0	0	13.50	1	0	4	9	0	2
Beech, Matt	12	8	5.15	25	0	156	171	59	110
Bentz, Chad	1	1	12.41	9	0	12	20	11	15
Berger, Garrett	0	5	6.72	28	0	74	89	74	42
Bergstrom, Rafael	0	4	5.90	6	0	29	37	6	18
Bierbrodt, Nick	2	4	12.25	11	0	32	33	48	28
Boehringer, Brian	2	3	6.04	5	0	25	33	4	11
★Dicken, Randy	1	0	8.22	2	0	8	10	6	8
★Edwards, Bryan	2	3	7.25	10	0	45	56	26	17
Fahrner, Evan	1	2	5.08	34	0	51	63	22	42
Fesh, Sean	1	1	3.42	16	0	26	22	18	15
★Ford, Matt	0	0	21.60	2	0	2	6	4	1
Henggeler, Keith	0	0	18.00	1	0	1	2	0	0
Hoorelbeke, Jesse	0	0	0.00	1	0	1	0	1	1
Junge, Eric.	2	2	3.69	9	0	46	52	8	42
Kent, Steven.	4	5	5.02	30	0	75	84	48	56

	W	L	ERA	G	SV	IP	H	BB	SO
Mercado, Hector	2	3	4.53	33	1	44	51	19	36
Pals, Jordan	0	1	10.13	1	0	3	7	0	2
Perez, Franklin	2	2	2.40	52	6	60	52	27	52
Perisho, Matt	2	1	6.66	23	1	26	40	15	15
Porzio, Mike	8	8	3.94	25	0	155	162	53	121
Ramos, Eddy	4	4	1.56	44	16	58	45	19	51
Rueckel, Danny	0	2	17.47	15	0	17	24	21	12
Sturge, Justin	6	9	4.32	24	0	117	129	44	84
★Ulloa, Enmanuel	4	2	4.41	6	0	33	35	11	26

CAMDEN RIVERSHARKS

BATTER	AVG	AB	R	H	2B	3B	HR	RBI	SB
Abreu, Dennis, of	.303	512	85	155	27	9	13	62	14
★Aqueron, Rene, 2b	.270	137	21	37	7	1	1	25	1
★Baez, Fleming, c	.286	14	0	4	0	0	0	1	0
★Bautista, Danny, of	.313	16	3	5	1	0	0	3	0
Berroa, Christian, ss	.118	17	0	2	0	0	0	2	0
Biernbaum, L.J., of	.292	411	70	120	28	1	22	82	13
Davis, Ben, c	.331	133	18	44	6	3	3	19	1
Demarco, Matt, 2b	.317	312	44	99	22	2	5	52	7
★Garcia, Omar, 1b	.333	6	1	2	0	0	0	0	0
Guerrero, Christian, of	.290	145	24	42	6	0	7	23	6
Jaramillo, Milko, ss	.244	275	31	67	15	1	4	36	4
Lehr, Ryan, 1b	.232	125	14	29	6	0	2	14	0
★Lopez, Luis, 3b	.333	3	2	1	0	0	0	1	0
Maness, Dwight, ss	.279	416	75	116	21	5	21	62	21
Marval, Raul, 2b	.338	65	12	22	3	0	2	10	1
McGarvey, Randy, c	.355	287	48	102	11	2	5	36	4
Metheny, Brent, 3b	.133	15	2	2	1	0	0	1	0
★Nivar, Ramon, ss	.256	39	5	10	1	1	0	1	1
Noviskey, Josh, c	.221	77	9	17	6	0	2	7	1
Paquette, Craig, 3b	.229	397	41	91	17	1	12	48	3
Pena, Angel, 1b	.261	211	33	55	12	0	7	24	1
Shier, Pete, 2b	.271	229	30	62	7	2	3	20	5
★Singleton, Justin, of	.207	150	17	31	4	2	4	15	5
Strauss, Brad, 1b	.269	297	44	80	17	2	6	42	6

PITCHERS	W	L	ERA	G	SV	IP	H	BB	SO
Balbuena, Caleb	0	0	8.31	7	0	9	10	8	7
Burke, Erick	2	2	5.80	37	0	76	101	35	65
Buttenfield, Nate	3	1	4.56	18	0	51	59	29	31
★Cain, Tim	4	3	6.31	24	0	46	55	17	21
★Castillo, Alberto	2	0	2.31	28	4	35	24	7	31
Costello, Ryan	7	10	4.97	21	0	112	145	26	63
★Davis, Brendon	0	1	5.17	13	0	16	17	21	16
★Dicken, Randy	0	2	5.68	23	0	32	36	27	27
★Edwards, Bryan	0	0	22.50	2	0	4	10	1	2
Ferrari, Anthony	13	5	4.82	25	0	125	133	53	69
Fussell, Chris	0	1	1.23	22	17	22	19	7	22
Ion, Mark	9	3	4.94	31	1	78	91	40	55
★Leclair, Aric	4	4	3.76	34	1	53	44	29	56
Linares, Ramon	3	2	2.11	47	11	55	37	23	58
Lockwood, Luke	1	4	6.75	10	0	47	62	16	18
Noviskey, Josh	0	0	0.00	1	0	1	1	0	0
Pote, Lou	0	0	0.00	4	2	6	2	4	7
Powell, Greg	6	12	4.56	25	0	160	196	38	59
Schurman, Ryan	7	8	4.70	22	0	134	158	35	66
Shier, Pete	0	0	9.00	1	0	1	1	1	0
Viera, Rolando	1	0	4.50	1	0	6	4	3	7
Walker, Kevin, 2b	4.000	0.8	1.74	7	0	0	0	0	1

LANCASTER BARNSTORMERS

BATTER	AVG	AB	R	H	2B	3B	HR	RBI	SB
Ambrosini, Dominick, of	.316	380	62	120	20	2	19	70	4
★Blue, Vince, of	.233	43	2	10	2	0	0	6	0
Booker, Steve, of	.250	28	1	7	0	0	0	1	1
Burkhart, Lance, c	.275	295	46	81	21	1	17	50	1
★Cesar, Dionys, 3b	.314	70	8	22	4	0	1	5	3
★Cleveland, Russ, c	.230	226	25	52	13	0	6	27	2
Crozier, Eric, 1b	.240	125	30	30	6	1	8	20	2
Deitrick, Jeremy, c	.241	83	8	20	4	0	1	13	1
Delgado, Dario, 3b	.185	27	4	5	2	0	0	0	0
Foster, Quincy, of	.261	203	28	53	6	2	2	15	19
Gonzalez, Danny, ss	.292	479	77	140	29	2	16	67	13
★Hake, Travis, 2b	.216	102	19	22	6	0	1	9	1
Hart, Bo, 2b	.245	98	16	24	11	0	2	12	3
Hileman, Jutt, of	.287	463	72	133	26	0	17	82	8
Jose, Felix, dh	.167	18	0	3	1	0	0	3	0
Martinez, Felix, 3b	.255	110	11	28	6	0	0	7	6
★Santana, Manny, 1b	.152	33	4	5	0	0	0	2	0
Todd, Jeremy, of	.262	404	66	106	27	0	24	79	0
Van Note, Steve, 3b	.232	293	39	68	14	2	7	39	4
Van Rossum, Chris, of	.254	355	56	90	11	4	13	57	14
Williams, Clyde, of	.222	9	1	2	1	0	1	2	0

Wolff, John, 2b	.077	13	0	1	0	0	0	0	0
Woods, Michael, 2b	.294	361	71	106	21	6	11	41	13

PITCHERS	W	L	ERA	G	SV	IP	H	BB	SO
Ackerman, Eric	5	2	4.35	47	3	70	78	17	43
Andrews, Clayton	1	4	8.26	6	0	28	48	16	15
★Armitage, Barry	2	4	5.06	23	0	53	68	32	33
Benson,	1	0	1.59	1	0	6	4	5	3
Brock, Chris	0	1	5.40	21	1	40	44	12	46
★Cleveland, Russ	0	0	0.00	2	0	2	0	3	1
★Davis, Brendon	0	1	11.57	2	0	2	2	2	2
DePriest, Derrick	0	2	1.06	51	20	59	37	13	64
Evert, Brett	4	8	5.98	19	0	84	89	53	67
Griffith, Derek	0	2	15.00	2	0	6	11	9	2
Harris, Ryan	2	1	7.66	28	1	45	68	14	22
Henkel, Rob	7	9	5.40	22	0	120	143	47	74
Hutton, Jon	0	0	0.00	3	0	4	2	4	2
Lira, James	7	8	6.37	27	2	88	105	54	57
Martinez, Gustavo	8	8	4.30	22	0	126	138	50	88
Norderum, Jason	0	0	7.48	16	0	22	27	18	16
★Norton, Phil	0	0	10.80	2	0	3	6	3	2
Odom, Lance	0	1	13.50	2	0	2	4	2	0
Parker, Zach	6	1	2.49	9	0	51	49	16	24
Peeples, Ross	4	3	4.27	49	0	72	73	14	45
Pennington, Todd	0	1	8.18	8	0	11	19	3	7
Sobkowiak, Scott	0	3	7.20	11	0	30	45	13	17
Stevens, Josh	10	10	4.08	24	0	159	196	34	91
Vazquez, Santiago	0	0	10.80	2	0	2	3	3	0

LONG ISLAND DUCKS

BATTER	AVG	AB	R	H	2B	3B	HR	RBI	SB
Acuna, Ron, of	.222	27	6	6	0	0	0	2	0
Alfonzo, Edgardo, ss	.266	384	53	102	23	0	5	56	1
Cafiero, Rob, 1b	.161	124	10	20	2	0	1	6	1
★Cesar, Dionys, 3b	.355	93	11	33	8	0	0	8	4
Everett, Carl, of	.312	391	77	122	24	0	25	97	4
★Harris, Estee, of	.267	146	19	39	7	0	5	18	2
★Hutchins, Norm, of	.309	298	38	92	20	1	6	47	10
Leon, Jose, 3b	.000	7	0	0	0	0	0	0	0
Lewis, Mark, 2b	.000	2	0	0	0	0	0	0	0
Navarrete, Ray, of	.308	468	104	144	42	2	18	67	11
Nelson, Bryant, 3b	.268	317	49	85	11	0	8	39	7
Offerman, Jose, 2b	.335	263	52	88	18	1	8	46	5
Piedra, Jorge, of	.336	116	19	39	7	1	4	20	0
Pogue, Jamie, c	.248	222	40	55	13	0	5	21	2
Price, Jared, c	.212	226	34	48	11	0	11	35	0
Rolls, Damian, 3b	.247	235	27	58	6	4	2	30	8
Rose, P.J., 1b	.342	453	71	155	24	0	14	95	1
★Suarez, Gabriel, ss	.394	33	4	13	0	1	0	3	3
Taylor, Reggie, of	.333	75	15	25	3	0	3	5	5
Wathan, Derek, ss	.264	129	20	34	7	2	3	13	1

PITCHERS	W	L	ERA	G	SV	IP	H	BB	SO
★Ahearne, Pat	1	3	8.85	4	0	20	32	4	11
★Cain, Tim	0	2	5.65	6	0	14	14	6	9
Crudale, Mike	1	1	6.35	17	0	17	14	11	17
Davis, Lance	9	4	4.79	18	0	113	128	14	88
Erdos, Todd	2	1	9.72	30	1	25	37	18	23
Espinal, Jose	3	2	4.44	5	0	24	29	13	14
Garcia, James	4	2	6.32	18	0	74	95	44	41
Graves, Danny	4	5	3.90	62	33	65	71	13	27
Grezlovski, Ben	7	2	3.39	58	0	61	63	22	41
Halama, John	8	10	4.14	26	0	167	201	44	93
Leek, Randy	5	1	2.23	13	0	85	66	17	62
★Mannix, Kevin	0	0	0.00	3	0	2	3	1	1
Osborne, Donovan	6	5	5.43	17	0	104	128	22	49
Pulsipher, Bill	2	0	3.60	4	0	25	31	5	15
Riedling, John	5	3	6.32	17	0	68	83	32	44
Tolar, Kevin	0	1	5.73	15	0	11	11	7	8
Valentine, Joe	4	2	1.54	37	2	35	26	9	37
Wade, Travis	5	1	4.08	46	0	64	71	19	36
Watson, Mark	1	4	8.87	44	0	46	66	19	37
Yarnall, Ed	5	5	3.93	21	0	87	93	24	69

NEWARK BEARS

BATTER	AVG	AB	R	H	2B	3B	HR	RBI	SB
★Arteaga, Josh, ss	.214	56	9	12	2	0	1	5	1
Castro, Ramon, ss	.343	327	61	112	22	0	9	49	4
Colina, Javier, 2b	.309	466	92	144	27	6	26	101	4
Gomes, Joey, of	.320	316	41	101	17	3	11	43	3
★Gutierrez, Vic, ss	.329	140	24	46	8	2	1	14	0
Headley, Jack, of	.301	103	18	31	4	1	1	15	3
Herrera, Jose, of	.357	308	48	110	22	0	12	48	1
★Jiannetti, Joe, of	.227	194	24	44	10	0	3	19	3
Mateo, Ruben, of	.288	66	14	19	4	0	5	10	1

BATTER	AVG	AB	R	H	2B	3B	HR	RBI	SB
Mendez, Donaldo, ss	.315	108	22	34	8	0	2	7	8
Nettles, Marcus, of	.297	306	56	91	10	6	0	24	49
Pachot, John, c	.258	325	32	84	20	0	6	48	2
Peavey, Pat, 3b	.280	150	25	42	9	0	6	27	1
Reed, Keith, of	.286	497	97	142	26	1	21	78	22
Rodriguez, Victor, 1b	.365	436	70	159	31	1	16	98	0
Smith, Corey, 3b	.274	446	78	122	37	3	18	72	6
Torres, Jason, c	.209	139	15	29	7	0	4	17	0

PITCHERS	W	L	ERA	G	SV	IP	H	BB	SO
Allen, Blake	0	0	10.64	9	0	11	19	9	5
Almonte, Ed	2	5	2.62	44	9	58	47	24	52
★Armitage, Barry	1	0	4.38	7	0	12	12	5	7
Babula, Shaun	1	0	4.05	6	1	7	8	3	8
Bergman, Dusty	1	0	1.00	3	0	18	16	8	13
Brownlie, Bobby	8	4	3.41	14	0	90	93	26	79
Crampton, Steve	1	0	12.15	5	0	7	11	6	7
★Davis, Brendon	0	4	9.13	15	0	23	31	23	11
Diangelo, Jason	3	9	5.90	49	14	61	83	18	58
Eckert, Harold	5	0	2.59	10	0	59	48	22	71
Garcia, Jose	5	0	5.27	13	0	70	77	28	57
Hill, Jeremy	3	0	1.96	11	2	23	20	9	21
Huisman, Justin	3	1	1.79	25	4	40	29	7	40
Kimbell, Matt	0	0	12.27	5	0	11	19	9	8
Knotts, Gary	7	5	2.65	16	0	109	85	40	86
Kramer, Sean	0	0	8.53	4	0	6	8	7	5
Miller, Jeff	1	0	9.64	4	0	5	9	3	4
Mirabal, Carlos	8	8	4.78	21	0	134	177	33	83
Pacheco, Delvis	7	3	5.76	21	1	100	110	34	61
Phelps, Travis	0	2	5.24	10	2	22	22	7	17
Phillips, Mark	1	3	6.89	7	0	33	32	28	33
Robertson, Jeriome	5	5	4.89	14	0	81	95	23	61
Rodriguez, Joe	0	0	13.50	3	0	3	2	3	0
Smith, Corey	1	0	3.00	3	0	3	2	3	2
Smith, Matt	1	0	7.08	10	0	20	27	20	28
Sweeney, Matt	5	3	4.35	10	0	52	53	18	33
Swindle, Robert	0	1	1.93	9	0	9	8	3	9
Trujillo, J.J.	1	0	0.00	11	1	16	7	3	12
Woodyard, Mark	2	1	3.60	3	0	20	15	9	11

ROAD WARRIORS

BATTER	AVG	AB	R	H	2B	3B	HR	RBI	SB
★Aqueron, Rene, 2b	.309	97	19	30	3	1	0	10	5
★Aracena, Sandy, c	.293	167	18	49	7	0	2	15	0
★Arteaga, Josh, ss	.258	256	28	66	17	1	3	38	3
★Baez, Fleming, c	.255	47	5	12	3	0	0	8	0
Bladergroen, Ian, 1b	.275	265	39	73	21	0	9	51	1
Bryan, Jason, of	.270	330	44	89	16	0	13	38	0
Cardona, David, of	.000	4	0	0	0	0	0	0	0
Chiaravolloti, Vito, 1b	.296	392	69	116	32	4	19	81	0
Doetsch, Steve, of	.284	405	76	115	21	7	22	65	9
★Ezi, Travis, of	.275	403	74	111	18	7	10	47	28
Fenwick, Ron, 3b	.204	284	30	58	10	0	1	21	0
★Garcia, Omar, 1b	.259	228	19	59	11	0	3	26	0
★Harris, Estee, of	.227	163	19	37	8	1	6	27	2
Housel, David, 3b	.250	380	60	95	18	3	9	42	10
★Hutchins, Norm, of	.278	108	16	30	5	3	3	16	2
Mejia, Jorge, 2b	.221	149	18	33	5	0	2	17	5
Mejia, Manuel, c	.287	328	31	94	21	1	5	41	1
★Suarez, Gabriel, ss	.252	305	38	77	13	0	2	24	10
Turay, Alhaji, of	.200	5	2	1	0	0	1	4	0
Valdez, Nick, c	.182	11	1	2	0	0	1	2	0

PITCHERS	W	L	ERA	G	SV	IP	H	BB	SO
Baez, Benito	2	3	2.08	40	9	43	38	15	45
★Baez, Fleming	0	0	0.00	2	1	1	0	0	1
★Cahill, Casey	0	1	3.53	23	2	36	29	13	22
★Castillo, Alberto	3	2	3.00	18	0	33	28	8	38
Castillo, Carlos	0	3	9.34	20	0	121	112	24	94
★Dicken, Randy	1	4	6.79	13	0	52	51	47	45
Eickhorst, Chris	1	4	5.62	48	2	82	98	45	43
Fenwick, Ron	0	0	0.00	3	0	2	0	1	2
Flinn, Chris	0	2	15.88	5	0	6	9	14	5
Garcia, Mike	0	0	0.00	1	0	0	1	1	0
Gonzalez, Bernie	1	0	3.07	14	0	15	12	12	14
Guerrero, Julio	0	6	4.80	50	4	60	80	12	42
Harkcom, James	1	7	7.65	13	0	58	71	35	28
★Hesseltine, Charlie	2	7	6.89	13	0	63	74	31	42
★Leclair, Aric	0	2	7.43	10	0	13	21	3	10
★Mannix, Kevin	0	3	3.13	17	0	32	31	18	11
Marcotte, Trevor	4	4	7.67	20	1	56	75	35	33
Martinez, Miguel	1	1	3.00	9	0	15	5	12	19
Mattison, Kieran	3	1	6.59	9	0	29	39	20	26
Myers, Damien	6	13	4.93	28	0	146	172	70	77
Skrmetta, Matt	0	0	5.06	4	0	5	8	6	5
Soto, Darwin	7	8	5.49	34	2	98	131	56	59

Tam, Jeff	0	1	7.07	13	0	14	23	1	12
★Ulloa, Enmanuel	3	5	4.80	12	0	69	75	24	55

SOMERSET PATRIOTS

BATTER	AVG	AB	R	H	2B	3B	HR	RBI	SB
Allen, Luke, of	.260	96	19	25	2	0	5	9	2
Anderson, Travis, c	.295	251	41	74	15	0	10	45	9
Ayala, Elliott, ss	.305	403	58	123	22	4	4	58	15
Belcher, Jay, c	.304	112	20	34	7	0	5	19	1
Boran, Patrick, of	.192	234	38	45	6	1	3	27	13
French, Anton, of	.258	62	8	16	2	1	2	6	5
Garcia, Daniel, 2b	.273	264	67	72	18	1	6	26	39
Goelz, Bryan, of	.164	67	6	11	0	0	1	6	1
Hall, Noah, of	.500	4	0	2	0	0	0	0	0
Hernandez, Michel, c	.342	76	11	26	6	0	3	16	1
Kinkade, Mike, 1b	.350	20	4	7	1	0	0	2	1
Larson, Brandon, 3b	.339	127	23	43	6	0	6	25	0
Leathers, Todd, 1b	.312	231	34	72	11	0	10	46	2
Lockwood, Mike, of	.278	464	90	129	14	4	23	92	22
Morban, Jose, 3b	.291	278	46	81	20	3	12	45	13
Nettles, Jeff, 3b	.316	209	50	66	17	1	19	60	0
Olivares, Teuris, 2b	.300	417	79	125	20	3	10	56	15
Pressley, Josh, 1b	.281	327	37	92	18	0	13	55	5
Romano, Jason, of	.281	288	46	81	21	0	7	45	6
★Santana, Manny, c	.040	25	1	1	0	0	0	0	0
Zinter, Alan, of	.261	299	51	78	18	0	13	43	0

PITCHERS	W	L	ERA	G	SV	IP	H	BB	SO
Adams, Brian	15	2	3.68	26	0	156	160	35	117
Allen, Luke	0	0	13.50	1	0	1	2	1	1
Almonte, Hector	2	0	5.34	30	1	30	29	18	36
Anderson, Jason	0	0	0.00	1	1	1	0	1	1
★Cahill, Casey	4	0	3.65	31	1	44	46	19	26
Cannon, Jon	2	3	4.02	11	0	56	52	24	41
Elder, Dave	0	0	0.82	2	0	11	6	2	4
Knight, Brandon	12	5	4.03	29	0	92	86	23	111
Marsonek, Sam	6	8	5.03	35	0	93	100	50	59
Mikkelsen, Lincoln	2	1	4.24	3	0	17	20	7	13
★Norton, Phil	0	0	7.11	8	0	6	5	11	4
Peralta, Tony	2	3	7.34	34	1	38	55	12	31
Ramsey, Keith	6	9	4.63	21	0	122	137	37	75
Reith, Brian	2	3	2.70	8	0	40	26	17	30
Richardson, Jason	2	4	4.37	40	0	58	57	28	74
Rojas, Chris	2	2	3.14	5	0	29	26	14	19
Solveson, Saul	3	1	3.79	50	4	57	54	25	43
Spiehs, R.D.	2	3	3.17	55	23	60	55	13	35
Thorp, Paul	2	4	2.68	35	1	37	44	17	29
Urban, Jeff	0	0	7.82	8	0	13	18	5	9
Van Hekken, Andy	9	3	3.12	18	0	115	112	35	83
Wiggins, Scott	2	2	3.89	8	0	39	53	8	34

YORK REVOLUTION

BATTER	AVG	AB	R	H	2B	3B	HR	RBI	SB
★Aracena, Sandy, c	.368	57	10	21	2	0	2	10	0
Aspito, Jason, of	.307	199	36	61	9	1	11	32	3
★Bautista, Danny, of	.329	79	9	26	5	0	0	10	1
Bautista, Rayner, ss	.299	421	53	126	36	0	7	64	2
Bergeron, Peter, of	.273	264	46	72	13	5	3	20	5
Brown, Greg, c	.273	154	13	42	6	0	2	19	0
★Cleveland, Russ, 3b	.222	27	1	6	1	0	0	1	0
Cotto, Luis, 3b	.244	246	34	60	8	1	4	22	6
De Renne, Keoni, 2b	.302	331	57	100	23	2	5	36	19
Dryer, Matt, 1b	.255	341	51	87	16	2	17	69	0
Espy, Nate, 1b	.316	433	82	137	22	6	22	90	3
★Ezi, Travis, of	.170	47	5	8	1	0	0	1	4
★Gutierrez, Vic, 3b	.284	95	12	27	3	1	0	5	1
★Hake, Travis, 2b	.253	87	13	22	3	0	0	7	3
Hunt, Kelly, 3b	.212	52	6	11	1	0	3	9	0
★Jiannetti, Joe, of	.333	108	23	36	9	1	2	19	4
★Lopez, Luis, 3b	.276	29	3	8	0	0	1	4	0
Matos, Willie, 1b	.202	114	8	23	2	0	2	10	0
★Nivar, Ramon, 2b	.306	252	36	77	14	0	3	28	21
Redman, Tike, of	.464	28	6	13	2	0	0	5	1
★Singleton, Justin, of	.282	305	50	86	19	2	12	54	9
Tanaka, Kazunori, of	.251	319	44	80	11	4	0	31	18
Taveras, Luis, c	.250	256	26	64	8	0	7	30	0

PITCHERS	W	L	ERA	G	SV	IP	H	BB	SO
Aspito, Jason	0	0	0.00	1	0	1	0	1	1
Baerlocher, Ryan	2	1	3.00	5	0	36	32	5	41
Batson, Byron	2	2	5.16	26	3	75	85	18	44
Brown, Greg	0	1	9.00	1	0	1	2	1	1
Castillo, Frank	8	4	3.75	19	0	110	100	32	52
Cline, Zachary	0	0	18.00	3	0	4	12	2	3
Cooper, Chris	2	3	5.02	26	0	38	51	10	27

★Edwards, Bryan	5	4	4.96	15	0	98	110	31	42
Farnsworth, Jeff	3	2	4.50	34	1	40	42	22	45
★Ford, Matt	2	4	6.97	14	0	41	52	33	27
Franklin, Wayne	8	3	4.19	16	0	86	94	50	70
Gil, Dave	2	4	3.43	9	0	63	61	14	46
Hartmann, Pete	1	2	6.46	5	0	31	42	16	19
★Hesseltine, Charlie	1	0	8.22	14	0	31	40	20	14
Hirsh, Matthew	1	8	8.05	14	0	38	46	29	20
Kleine, Victor	0	0	2.67	19	0	27	30	11	22
Maust, David	5	8	4.70	27	0	88	89	35	57
Nunez, Franklin	1	0	2.76	30	12	33	31	12	51
Olson, Jason	6	5	4.03	42	1	67	56	26	57
Smyth, Steve	1	3	6.39	16	1	31	38	19	28
Steinborn, Chris	8	14	6.13	24	0	148	187	58	52
Thomas, Adam	0	0	1.50	11	5	12	10	0	11
★Ulloa, Enmanuel	0	0	0.00	1	0	1	1	1	2

Rios, Brian, Sussex	.331	75	299	40	99	4	50
Granato, Anthony, Atlantic City	.329	86	316	77	104	7	50
Torres, Mike, North Shore	.326	91	350	47	114	6	63
Berry, Boomer, Quebec	.325	91	345	74	112	3	39
Naccarata, Ivan, Quebec	.321	51	215	52	69	4	29
Lantigua, Eddie, Quebec	.319	90	351	60	112	21	82
Beauregard, Keith, Worcester	.317	71	227	42	72	5	31

INDIVIDUAL PITCHING LEADERS

PITCHER, CLUB	W	L	ERA	IP	H	BB	SO
Kelly, John, New Jersey	7	3	2.34	146	125	42	130
Viera, Rolando, Brockton	11	6	2.50	126	133	53	106
Bicondoa, Ryan, North Shore	10	2	2.82	124	102	27	105
Okamoto, Akira, Nashua	9	2	2.88	131	111	21	115
Whitworth, Brad, New Haven	7	4	2.93	108	96	24	54
Nagasaka, Hideki, Nashua	10	1	2.94	113	92	61	69
Kosyk, Bucky, New Haven	4	2	3.08	79	80	23	35
Bishop, Matt, North Shore	9	5	3.16	105	129	23	55
Rodaway, Brian, Atlantic City	15	3	3.23	136	123	45	90
McTamney, Mike, Brockton	6	10	3.28	148	150	40	100

CAN-AM LEAGUE

If this was farewell at least they went out to a standing ovation. The Can-Am League's championship series featured a matchup of the North Shore Spirit, a team that had already announced it wouldn't return in 2008, against the Nashua Pride, a team whose ownership was weighing the option of folding after struggling to draw for several years.

In the battle of teams heading to the gallows the Pride proved a little more sprightly. Nashua swept North Shore in three games as league most valuable player Olmo Rosario hit a two-run homer in the deciding Game 3. After the series a season-ticket drive saved the Pride from extinction.

FIRST HALF

	W	L	PCT	GB
New Jersey	31	15	.674	
Nashua	27	19	.587	4
Quebec	27	20	.574	4½
North Shore	25	21	.543	6
Worcester	24	23	.511	7½
Atlantic City	22	24	.478	9
New Haven County	21	26	.447	10½
Brockton	20	26	.435	11
Grays	20	27	.426	11½
Sussex	15	31	.326	16

SECOND HALF

	W	L	PCT	GB
North Shore	32	15	.681	
Atlantic City	29	17	.630	2½
New Haven County	26	20	.565	5½
Grays	24	23	.511	8
Nashua	23	24	.489	9
Quebec	22	25	.468	10
Brockton	22	25	.468	10
Worcester	19	28	.404	13
Sussex	19	28	.404	13
New Jersey	18	29	.383	14

PLAYOFFS: Semifinals—North Shore defeated Atlantic City 3-1 and Nashua defeated New Jersey 3-2 in best-of-five series. **Finals**—Nashua defeated North Shore 3-0 in best-of-three series.

MANAGERS: Atlantic City—Chris Carminucci; **Brockton**—Chris Miyake; **Grays**—Dan Shwam; **Nashua**—Butch Hobson; **New Haven County**—Mike Church; **New Jersey**—Joe Calfapietra; **North Shore**—Vic Davilla; **Quebec**—Michel Laplante; **Sussex**—Brian Drahman; **Worcester**—Rich Gedman.

ATTENDANCE: Nashua 169,999; Quebec 161,789; North Shore 110,336; Worcester 120,145; New Jersey 107,663; Atlantic City 105,149; Sussex 101,638; New Haven County 82,651; Nashua 80,737.

ALL-STAR TEAM: C—Patrick Perry, Worcester; **1B**—Eddie Lantigua, Quebec; **2B**—Boomer Berry, Quebec; **3B**—Anthony Granato, Atlantic City; **SS**—Olmo Rosario, Nashua; **OF**—Ervin Alcantara, New Haven County; Jeremy Pickrel, New Haven County/ New Jersey; Mike Torres, North Shore; **DH**—Sandy Madera, New Jersey; **LHP**—Brian Rodaway, Atlantic City; **RHP**—John Kelly, Brockton/ New Jersey; **RP**—Matt Pike, Atlantic City.

Player of the Year: Olmo Rosario, Nashua. **Pitcher of the year:** . Rookie Player of the year: Tony Gonzalez, Brockton.rsey Jackals RHP Ryan Pacyna

INDIVIDUAL BATTING LEADERS

BATTER, CLUB	AVG	G	AB	R	H	HR	RBI
Madera, Sandy, New Jersey	.364	86	343	69	125	21	75
Rosario, Olmo, Nashua	.362	88	367	57	133	12	59
Burke, Joe, Atlantic City	.333	72	270	44	90	2	41

ATLANTIC CITY SURF

BATTER	AVG	AB	R	H	2B	3B	HR	RBI	SB
Burke, Joe, 1b	.333	270	44	90	13	6	2	41	9
Burke, Mark, 1b	.261	161	26	42	8	0	2	26	0
★Crescenzi, Chris, 3b	.239	46	3	11	2	0	0	3	1
Daly, Rich, 1b	.048	42	3	2	0	0	1	3	0
★Dworken, Mikaela, c	.143	14	2	2	1	0	0	1	0
★Fischer, Rob, of	.279	229	31	64	15	1	7	48	5
Granato, Anthony, 3b	.329	316	77	104	25	4	7	50	29
Harris, Shea, c	.214	28	6	6	1	0	0	1	0
Keesee, David, ss	.250	148	20	37	1	1	4	18	2
Kitch, Denver, ss	.206	97	12	20	3	0	1	9	3
Lytle, Chaz, of	.250	8	0	2	0	0	0	0	0
Mears, Magic, 2b	.250	16	3	4	2	0	0	0	3
Montague, Ed, of	.302	368	56	111	32	3	6	69	6
Quintana, Wil, of	.267	187	31	50	12	0	5	41	1
Renick, Josh, 2b	.220	296	40	65	12	0	0	24	7
Rosa, Wally, c	.257	230	24	59	13	0	2	34	3
Sanchez, Angel, c	.143	21	3	3	1	0	0	2	0
★Santana, Rico, of	.257	148	22	38	13	0	4	20	10
Taylor, Lucas, of	.267	348	72	93	6	4	0	28	39
Walker, Ryan, of	.281	57	8	16	1	0	1	9	0
Warfle, Patrick, 2b	.360	25	6	9	0	0	0	2	2
★Williams, Clyde, 1b	.383	47	8	18	1	0	4	12	2

PITCHERS	W	L	ERA	G	SV	IP	H	BB	SO
Brower, Kevin	1	1	6.16	25	1	31	34	22	26
Freedman, Coogie	4	4	5.14	29	0	75	93	43	60
Graves, Donovan	0	4	8.53	5	0	25	38	8	8
★Hendricks, Donavon	1	0	5.59	16	0	19	23	12	9
Huguet, J.C.	9	5	4.15	22	0	115	6	35	74
Mansfield, Monte	6	10	5.81	23	0	110	14	35	88
Martinez, Mario	0	1	12.27	4	0	7	11	2	4
Mitsumori, Shingo	1	2	6.60	11	0	30	44	18	11
Pike, Matthew	2	1	3.04	47	24	50	59	15	44
Rafferty, Ryan	1	2	5.57	38	1	42	59	17	38
Rodaway, Brian	15	3	3.23	20	0	136	7	45	90
Runser, Greg	0	0	10.29	13	1	14	26	6	2
Scheuing, Matt	0	3	8.20	4	0	19	25	6	10
Staggs, Nathan	1	0	0.93	8	0	10	4	4	9
★Thurmond, Ben	5	3	4.81	12	0	67	86	18	44
Tricoglou, Jamie	5	1	1.37	41	0	53	32	18	69
Wladyka, James	0	1	2.25	1	0	4	5	4	3

BROCKTON ROX

BATTER	AVG	AB	R	H	2B	3B	HR	RBI	SB
Allen, John of	.275	200	31	55	13	1	5	29	4
Alvarado, Andre, ss	.219	64	11	14	0	1	0	6	2
Coronado, Jeremy, of	.291	327	54	95	10	1	2	32	21
De La Cruz, Fredy, ss	.261	207	20	54	13	2	0	28	2
Douglas, Charlie, 3b	.214	14	2	3	0	0	0	0	0
★Edmondson, Jerod, of	.373	67	15	25	2	0	2	14	2
Falu, Melvin, 3b	.318	110	24	35	12	1	3	34	2
Gonzalez, Tony, of	.298	215	36	64	14	2	8	38	6
★Hough, Joe, of	.240	167	28	40	6	3	3	12	8
Julien, Eugene, 2b	.209	191	22	40	5	2	1	13	11
Lebron, Francisco, 1b	.302	321	51	97	15	1	14	57	0
Maloney, Matt, of	.309	188	33	58	11	1	3	24	16
Mariot, Ian	.217	92	14	20	1	0	0	4	11
McGhee, Joe, c	.318	22	1	7	3	0	0	7	0
★Mejia, Jorge, ss	.329	70	11	23	5	0	1	10	5
Nunez, Alex, 2b	.257	191	24	49	6	3	1	16	7
Radwan, Jason, c	.246	224	22	55	7	0	5	29	3

	AVG	AB	R	H	2B	3B	HR	RBI	SB
Rubin, Lee, c	.221	122	15	27	5	0	1	18	0
Scarola, Chris, of	.000	8	1	0	0	0	0	0	0
Senjem, Guye, of	.203	148	17	30	11	1	2	18	2
Sickles, Ryan, of	.177	79	8	14	0	0	0	4	1
Smucker, Justin, 2b	.000	2	0	0	0	0	0	0	0
★Welch, John, 1b	.231	13	2	3	1	0	0	0	0
Wyland, Stevem 3b	.167	6	0	1	0	0	0	0	0

PITCHERS	W	L	ERA	G	SV	IP	H	BB	SO
Burnau, Ryan	1	2	6.86	21	2	21	25	7	17
Carreras, Luis	5	4	6.12	27	0	60	75	30	38
Falu, Melvin	0	0	0.00	1	0	0	0	0	0
Foeman, Kevin	0	1	12.33	10	0	15	22	15	9
★Galvez, Gary	2	6	3.88	9	0	53	55	18	43
★George, Kyle	1	2	5.13	25	3	33	42	17	29
Gonzalez, Tony	0	0	0.00	1	0	0	0	2	0
★Hendricks, Donavon	1	4	4.02	11	0	31	31	14	19
Kafka, Ari	0	1	7.20	21	0	30	31	19	30
★Kelly, John	7	2	2.27	18	0	127	109	34	114
Koch, Jon	0	3	9.00	9	0	16	18	12	12
Martin, Chris	1	2	8.84	6	0	18	23	10	8
McTamney, Mike	6	10	3.28	22	0	148	150	40	100
★Morse, Bryan	3	4	4.31	10	0	63	65	25	36
Reilly, Matthew	3	2	1.87	28	0	43	41	25	27
★Rispoli, Tom	0	0	13.50	2	0	2	3	2	3
Stephens, Amad	1	1	6.75	17	9	16	23	5	16
Stokley, Billy	0	1	11.25	4	0	4	6	4	2
Tanguy, Brian	0	0	5.14	4	0	7	6	3	5
Viera, Rolando	11	6	2.50	19	0	126	133	53	106

	AVG	AB	R	H	2B	3B	HR	RBI	SB
Rodriguez, Luis, c	.281	263	38	74	7	0	3	39	4
Rojas, Tommy, 3b	.321	78	13	25	4	0	2	16	1
Rosario, Olmo, ss	.362	367	57	133	25	4	12	59	25
★Torres, Chris, c	.193	114	9	22	4	0	0	7	1
★Velasquez, Jose, 1b	.167	60	10	10	3	0	0	6	1
Wasserman, Austin, of	.257	218	32	56	11	1	4	17	4

PITCHERS	W	L	ERA	G	SV	IP	H	BB	SO
Bausher, Tim	4	5	3.09	10	0	58	43	37	40
Burrows, Angelo	2	2	5.16	32	2	52	48	22	47
Creighton, Matt	0	0	0.00	1	0	0	0	0	1
Duplissie, Bryan	0	0	9.00	1	0	1	2	1	1
★Feliz, Rainer	0	0	0.00	1	0	2	1	0	0
Fisher, Matt	0	1	27.00	2	0	1	2	5	0
Gannon, Joe	1	1	3.30	9	1	30	23	19	18
Garces, Rich	6	4	4.42	36	17	39	39	15	35
Gomez, Abel	0	0	22.09	4	0	4	4	5	4
Hintz, Beau	1	2	6.59	8	0	29	38	13	17
Kosow, Jason	2	5	3.36	23	0	72	71	40	48
Mann, Jim	1	2	5.49	20	0	20	20	6	24
Nagasaka, Hideki	10	1	2.94	19	0	113	92	61	89
Okamoto, Akira	9	2	2.88	19	0	131	111	21	115
Palazzolo, Steve	7	4	2.14	43	0	55	41	22	63
Paul, Jason	0	5	7.99	11	0	33	51	12	24
Rodriguez, Luis	0	0	10.80	2	0	2	3	2	1
Stevens, Lance	3	6	3.78	22	0	95	89	41	56
Thornton, Tom	0	1	6.91	14	0	29	44	10	23
★Torres, Chris	0	0	9.00	2	0	2	4	1	1
Yano, Eiji	2	2	5.72	14	0	50	48	27	19

GRAYS

BATTER	AVG	AB	R	H	2B	3B	HR	RBI	SB
Baker, Brian, of	.156	141	14	22	6	1	2	16	3
Bennett, Anthony, of	.247	231	26	57	5	1	1	27	5
Cabrera, Mayke, 1b	.189	74	7	14	5	0	0	5	1
Catchot, Sheldon, of	.176	17	3	3	0	1	0	1	1
Colafemina, Josh, 2b	.262	328	59	86	13	1	0	23	32
Gabriel, Chad, of	.293	369	49	108	16	2	13	54	8
Gamble, Sean, of	.273	304	48	83	15	0	6	49	6
Gonzalez, Josue, c	.198	96	10	19	3	0	0	5	0
James, Willie, ss	.189	90	12	17	5	0	0	4	6
Jeroloman, Charles, ss	.290	162	22	47	9	3	7	37	5
Lewis, Marcus, of	.173	133	24	23	1	3	0	5	10
Monjaras, Gavin, ss	.229	96	9	22	1	1	0	9	3
Pendergrass, Tyrone, of	.238	63	8	15	4	0	0	4	5
Pierre, Mike, of	.285	137	12	39	4	3	1	25	8
Tinius, Ben, 3b	.275	335	49	92	24	1	7	50	3
Tucker, J.B., c	.270	289	51	78	20	1	12	42	8
Van Allen, Larry, of	.077	13	2	1	0	0	0	2	1
★Velasquez, Jose, 1b	.285	295	39	84	11	0	7	42	0

PITCHERS	W	L	ERA	G	SV	IP	H	BB	SO
Bartlett, Richard	4	8	5.10	18	0	101	114	51	55
Catchot, Sheldon	1	0	7.13	11	0	18	21	18	7
Dannemiller, Beau	9	6	3.67	20	0	125	118	51	59
Dunn, Jerry	0	0	0.92	36	18	39	33	13	37
Hanson, Adam	1	2	9.68	6	0	18	19	16	9
Jones, Fontella	5	5	4.43	11	0	67	62	39	33
Monjaras, Gavin	0	0	9.00	1	0	1	2	0	0
Nielsen, Dustin	5	4	5.23	32	0	64	76	19	47
O'Donnell, Tony	5	1	4.11	35	1	50	40	23	31
Ramirez, Froilan	0	0	3.86	8	1	16	12	14	6
Sausville, Dan	1	0	3.78	6	0	17	18	5	10
Shaw, Elliott	7	8	5.78	18	0	100	90	93	58
Snipp, Craig	2	2	4.02	25	0	54	52	24	38
Stull, Everett	3	11	6.42	18	0	104	135	48	53
Zachary, Matt	1	3	3.02	36	1	45	46	17	21

NASHUA PRIDE

BATTER	AVG	AB	R	H	2B	3B	HR	RBI	SB
Acey, Jermy, 2b	.305	262	43	80	11	2	6	39	11
★Colabello, Chris, 1b	.318	154	33	49	12	0	8	34	0
Creighton, Matt, 3b	.231	186	19	43	11	0	0	20	4
Creighton, Tom, 2b	.300	230	36	69	5	1	1	16	10
Crosland, Jason, 3b	.273	33	2	9	2	0	1	6	0
Dillard, Andy, 3b	.190	42	3	8	1	0	2	8	0
Duplissie, Bryan, 1b	.256	313	43	80	20	0	17	59	0
★Edmondson, Jerod, of	.328	67	7	22	3	1	0	7	1
Funaro, Jeff, c	.087	23	3	2	1	0	0	1	0
Giannotti, Rich, of	.238	307	45	73	14	2	3	30	8
Joffrion, Jack, 2b	.265	34	3	9	0	0	1	4	1
★Laplante, Adam, c	.000	21	2	0	0	0	0	0	0
Miller, Bode, of	.000	2	0	0	0	0	0	0	0
★Mottram, Allen, c	.220	41	7	9	2	0	2	6	0
Ramistella, John, of	.272	349	58	95	21	2	11	45	13

NEW HAVEN COUNTY CUTTERS

BATTER	AVG	AB	R	H	2B	3B	HR	RBI	SB
Alcantara, Ervin, of	.300	357	62	107	21	3	10	44	31
★Dworken, Mikaela, c	.171	35	3	6	2	0	1	3	0
Encarnacion, Orlando, of	.227	269	31	61	15	2	7	30	1
Gaskin, Chris, 1b	.270	330	38	89	22	0	8	60	6
Gullen, Eddie, of	.000	4	0	0	0	0	0	0	0
Hackney, Matt, c	.213	202	31	43	4	1	1	13	6
Koch, Thomas, 2b	.132	68	10	9	0	1	0	3	1
Leonard, Mike, c	.204	54	4	11	0	0	0	5	0
Mayo, Jeff, c	.103	39	5	4	0	0	0	0	1
Mercurio, Matt, 2b	.226	328	54	74	14	3	4	31	11
★Pickrel, Jeremy, of	.299	261	59	78	17	9	11	51	23
Stanley, Henri, of	.272	294	52	80	15	5	7	40	7
Terni, Chas, ss	.259	332	36	86	23	0	5	44	0
Vroman, Doug, of	.261	23	3	6	0	0	0	2	2
Whiteside, Kevin, of	.233	180	23	42	15	1	0	14	4
Zamora, Junior, 3b	.247	344	45	85	20	1	11	66	6

PITCHERS	W	L	ERA	G	SV	IP	H	BB	SO
Bonesio, Ryan	7	5	4.15	18	0	108	115	42	60
Brainer, Bryan	2	2	6.27	17	0	37	38	22	19
Culpepper, Kevin	2	4	3.86	14	0	63	77	25	21
Davis, John	0	0	4.15	4	0	4	5	6	4
Dicso, Greg	0	1	7.07	11	0	14	12	18	11
Farrell, Jeff	0	2	9.28	6	0	21	28	19	6
Joyce, Mike	2	4	3.29	42	1	52	51	13	29
Kalb, Aaron	0	1	9.00	3	0	7	14	3	4
Kosyk, Bucky	4	2	3.08	15	0	79	80	23	35
Marcotte, Trevor	1	1	7.88	3	0	16	25	6	14
Piechowski, Adam	6	2	2.31	38	0	47	39	18	55
Ramirez, Joslin	2	1	9.95	4	0	19	30	12	13
★Rispoli, Tom	1	2	12.60	11	0	15	17	29	6
★Salvato, Matt	2	2	2.25	11	0	24	24	14	14
★Spitaleri, Stephen	0	0	2.25	3	0	4	2	1	2
Stawarz, Jarrett	1	2	5.51	7	0	33	36	11	21
Valles, Rolando	5	5	3.56	21	0	104	114	24	60
Vroman, Doug	0	0	40.50	1	0	1	1	3	2
Weimer, Andy	5	6	3.19	48	20	59	53	26	29
Whigham, David	0	0	37.80	3	0	2	2	6	2
Whitworth, Brad	7	4	2.93	16	0	108	96	24	54

NEW JERSEY JACKALS

BATTER	AVG	AB	R	H	2B	3B	HR	RBI	SB
Anderson, Doug, 3b	.000	2	0	0	0	0	0	0	0
Calzado, Napoleon, of	.308	13	1	4	0	0	0	1	0
★Frazier, Alex, of	.246	65	8	16	2	0	2	12	3
Kuklick, Clay, c	.259	189	22	49	4	2	0	19	1
Lauderdale, Matt, c	.295	183	36	54	12	1	8	34	0
Leandro, Francisco, of	.261	349	72	91	20	3	2	43	12
Madera, Sandy, 1b	.364	343	69	125	23	0	21	75	2
Miaso, Curt, of	.211	19	0	4	0	0	0	1	0
Mihalics, Joe, 2b	.245	314	49	77	11	1	2	38	9
★Pickrel, Jeremy, 1b	.143	21	1	3	1	0	0	3	2
Raniere, Chris, ss	.143	7	2	1	0	0	0	1	0

INDEPENDENT LEAGUES

BATTER	AVG	AB	R	H	2B	3B	HR	RBI	SB
Reyes, Guillermo, ss	.314	239	39	75	10	2	3	38	9
Rodriguez, Marcos, 1b	.304	69	9	21	5	0	2	9	2
Smithlin, Zach, of	.294	347	63	102	10	2	0	47	33
Thigpen, Jud, of	.256	297	43	76	15	1	9	42	4
Turner, Tim, of	.238	105	18	25	7	0	1	11	22
Veras, Wilton, 3b	.283	343	53	97	15	2	5	48	1
★Williams, Clyde, 1b	.288	267	41	77	18	1	10	50	7
Yount, Dustin, dh	.259	27	2	7	1	0	0	2	0

PITCHERS	W	L	ERA	G	SV	IP	H	BB	SO
Atlee, Thomas	0	1	11.57	3	1	2	2	1	5
Banks, Demetrius	2	0	5.37	23	0	59	67	35	55
Bennett, Joel	3	2	3.24	12	0	72	71	17	53
Brey, Josh	5	6	4.26	19	0	106	107	44	46
Davis, Hunter	1	1	1.15	11	1	16	7	4	13
★Fitzgerald, Kevin	3	4	3.55	27	1	33	32	15	25
Garza, Justin	2	5	3.33	41	1	51	47	20	39
★George, Kyle	1	3	4.70	12	0	15	10	9	9
Hunton, Jon	0	1	8.10	3	0	3	7	3	1
★Kelly, John	0	1	2.79	3	0	19	16	8	16
Kramer, Sean	1	0	12.00	8	0	9	15	9	6
Looper, Aaron	0	1	9.00	1	0	5	7	2	7
Murphey, Tim	0	0	2.70	4	0	3	4	5	3
Ool, Kevin	3	3	5.36	12	0	44	48	13	27
Pacyna, Ryan	6	2	3.35	29	0	81	82	23	45
Pavlik, Isaac	8	5	3.97	26	0	113	129	29	93
Sabo, Tim	0	0	7.50	14	0	18	27	9	14
★Spitaleri, Stephen	0	1	9.95	4	0	6	11	3	2
Thigpen, Jud	0	0	0.00	1	0	0	0	0	1
★Thurmond, Ben	5	2	6.17	9	0	42	54	16	34
Tucker, Rusty	0	1	1.48	25	14	24	11	17	37
Turner, Tim	0	0	0.00	1	0	1	1	0	1
Van Gorder, Mike	0	0	16.88	3	0	3	7	2	0
Vicaro, Michael	8	5	3.55	17	0	89	62	34	81

NORTH SHORE SPIRIT

BATTER	AVG	AB	R	H	2B	3B	HR	RBI	SB
Balkan, Adam, of	.143	35	2	5	0	0	0	2	0
Blakely, Darren, of	.219	128	18	28	2	4	7	23	1
Cordova, Ricardo, 2b	.208	24	4	5	2	0	0	1	1
Davilla, Vic, 1b	.329	79	14	26	4	0	5	22	1
★Fischer, Rob, of	.237	59	11	14	4	0	1	6	5
French, Anton, of	.375	24	3	9	1	0	0	3	5
Gil, Gilbert, 2b	.284	134	21	38	8	0	1	11	4
Gutierrez, Juan, c	.000	7	1	0	0	0	0	0	0
★Hough, Joe, of	.121	58	9	7	4	0	0	2	1
Lopez, Josue, 1b	.313	233	30	73	10	1	8	42	1
Lopez, Luis, 3b	.266	203	29	54	11	0	4	34	2
McGuire, Jared, of	.136	22	3	3	0	0	0	0	2
★Mottram, Allen, c	.268	71	9	19	4	0	0	6	1
Perez, Jerson, ss	.312	276	45	86	16	1	7	41	12
Rea, Brad, 1b	.284	109	11	31	5	0	3	17	0
Roche, Gary, 2b	.291	309	40	90	15	2	1	27	6
Rodriguez, Carlos, of	.224	210	29	47	11	3	6	28	3
Rosa, Wally, c	.259	58	7	15	2	0	0	7	1
Teilon, Nelson, 3b	.360	50	9	18	5	0	4	8	0
★Tewksbary, Bob, ss	.000	6	0	0	0	0	0	0	0
★Torres, Chris, 1b	.364	11	0	4	1	0	0	0	0
Torres, Mike, of	.326	350	47	114	20	1	6	63	7
Trezza, Alex, c	.250	260	46	65	16	2	10	33	0
Weed, B.J., of	.268	336	66	90	15	2	1	27	35
★Welch, John, of	.288	59	8	17	2	0	3	12	2
Wood, Chris, 1b	.000	1	0	0	0	0	0	1	0

PITCHERS	W	L	ERA	G	SV	IP	H	BB	SO
Arroyo, Luis	1	0	1.38	2	0	13	13	2	5
Baker, Jamie	4	1	1.38	37	1	52	36	13	40
Bicondoa, Ryan	10	2	2.82	18	0	124	102	27	105
Bishop, Matt	9	5	3.16	18	0	105	129	23	55
Drage, Derek	3	4	1.83	43	13	54	39	24	47
Farley, Chris	8	2	1.41	10	0	64	50	15	71
★Fitzgerald, Kevin	0	0	5.79	10	4	9	11	6	7
★Galvez, Gary	5	3	3.50	10	0	64	55	24	41
Langdon, Donny	2	1	3.45	41	2	31	33	11	30
Martin, Brandon	2	0	2.21	9	0	20	11	8	15
Matos, Josue	0	2	5.74	3	0	16	18	7	10
★McNamara, Shaun	1	4	6.07	13	0	30	46	16	29
★Morse, Bryan	1	2	3.79	4	0	19	21	3	11
★Mottram, Allen	0	0	0.00	2	0	2	1	1	1
Robinson, Dennis	4	3	3.48	28	1	78	81	11	31
Scheafer, Carl	1	1	2.84	5	0	6	5	0	4
Siak, Joey	6	4	5.30	20	0	112	150	16	49
Simon, Billy	0	0	9.00	5	1	5	6	6	7
Soriano, Julio	0	1	7.20	8	1	10	7	11	10

QUEBEC CAPITALES

BATTER	AVG	AB	R	H	2B	3B	HR	RBI	SB
Benes, Richie, of	.000	8	0	0	0	0	0	0	0
Berry, Boomer, 2b	.325	345	74	112	21	4	3	39	17
Curkovic, Tommy, 1b	.267	30	5	8	1	0	0	1	1
Deschenes, Patrick, 3b	.357	98	11	35	4	0	3	19	0
Dunn, Keith, of	.000	3	1	0	0	0	0	0	0
Emond, Benoit, of	.267	165	18	44	6	0	0	15	5
Galloway, Mike, of	.329	161	26	53	7	3	10	34	0
Lantigua, Eddie, 1b	.319	351	60	112	17	1	21	82	12
LaPlante, Michel, of	.143	7	1	1	0	0	0	1	0
Lehr, Ryan, 3b	.255	94	13	24	4	0	5	18	0
Martin, Scott, of	.232	233	36	54	8	0	6	30	6
★Mejia, Jorge, ss	.294	17	1	5	1	0	1	1	0
Naccarata, Ivan, ss	.321	215	52	69	19	0	4	29	4
Rojas, Ivan, of	.242	99	15	24	7	0	5	21	1
Sandoval, Jjallil, ss	.279	68	11	19	4	0	0	6	4
Scalabrini, Pat	.325	160	25	52	9	0	5	41	1
Stang, Corey, of	.309	178	26	55	12	4	3	26	3
Stevens, Greg, c	.295	329	50	97	17	2	14	45	7
Tomlinson, Goef, of	.270	204	53	55	11	2	4	26	9
Trainor, Nick, of	.229	166	18	38	11	1	4	19	6
Turay, Alhaji, of	.217	23	4	5	1	0	1	8	0
Uchida, Takayoshi, ss	.165	230	29	38	2	0	4	17	15

PITCHERS	W	L	ERA	G	SV	IP	H	BB	SO
Beavers, Kevin	5	4	4.02	19	0	110	127	44	53
Burke, John	1	0	3.86	11	1	14	16	5	8
DeMontigny, Mathieu	0	0	4.22	6	0	11	18	7	5
Dumesnil, Brian	2	0	0.57	17	5	16	12	4	16
Dunn, Keith	9	5	4.22	20	0	119	133	30	68
Gelinas, Karl	4	4	1.91	11	0	61	60	8	35
Hernandez, Santos	1	0	2.57	1	0	7	6	0	5
LaPlante, Michel	0	0	5.14	1	0	7	9	4	3
Major, Marc	2	0	3.50	13	0	18	18	6	12
McLaughlin, Brad	2	1	4.15	13	0	35	33	24	15
Mendoza, Cristian	1	3	1.55	27	7	29	22	16	31
Moore, Chris	0	1	1.50	1	0	6	4	2	2
Pello, Brandon	1	3	5.74	19	0	27	36	14	22
Perez, Jorge	4	8	5.68	14	0	82	84	45	61
Ribas, Gabe	2	0	6.85	4	0	24	27	5	24
Rodriguez, Raul	0	0	4.70	2	0	8	9	2	5
Ryan, Shawn	1	1	6.16	24	0	61	58	46	38
Simard, Michel	9	8	3.53	20	0	127	137	34	84
Stanton, TJ	5	7	5.30	37	6	53	54	25	60
Uchida, Takayoshi	0	0	0.00	1	0	1	0	2	0

SUSSEX SKYHAWKS

BATTER	AVG	AB	R	H	2B	3B	HR	RBI	SB
Alcott, Jason, c	.159	63	7	10	3	0	1	10	0
Bergeron, Jabe, 1b	.304	336	51	102	17	2	5	49	0
Bethea, Larry, dh	.272	320	41	87	17	0	7	46	0
Booth, Jeremy, c	.500	10	2	5	1	0	0	1	0
Ceriani, Matt, c	.215	181	15	39	8	0	0	17	0
★Crescenzi, Chris, c	.351	57	8	20	3	3	1	10	0
★Frazier, Alex, of	.298	252	47	75	19	0	10	48	8
Friend, Steve, ss	.107	84	8	9	2	0	3	6	1
Gandolfo, Rob, 2b	.273	337	40	92	17	0	0	46	7
Grimes, Scott, of	.261	314	49	82	19	2	5	45	7
Lemieux, Jon, c	.269	78	16	21	3	1	0	9	4
Mungle, Jon, dh	.111	27	2	3	1	0	0	0	0
Perodin, Ron, of	.282	380	58	107	7	5	0	20	31
Richmond, B.J., of	.195	77	4	15	1	1	0	7	2
Rios, Brian, 3b	.331	299	40	99	24	3	4	50	1
Rios, Kevin, ss	.275	258	27	71	15	1	1	39	1
Scanzano, Mike, 3b	.130	23	4	3	1	0	0	0	0
★Solano, Euvi, 3b	.300	60	9	18	2	0	0	5	0
Terrill, Tom, c	.250	32	4	8	0	0	0	1	0

PITCHERS	W	L	ERA	G	SV	IP	H	BB	SO
Barreras, Rene	1	3	8.76	10	0	25	34	20	12
Beltran, Saydel	0	0	4.05	4	0	7	12	4	3
Benitez, Edisbel	6	6	4.48	24	2	90	95	35	74
Braun, Bart	4	4	4.47	36	0	52	40	32	41
Brooks, Jay	0	1	19.29	1	0	2	5	5	3
Campbell, Dayle	0	3	6.21	26	0	42	53	28	33
Colletto, N	0	0	4.50	1	0	2	2	1	2
Davis, Vince	6	8	4.28	18	1	109	108	58	62
Dittfurth, Ryan	5	3	3.73	21	0	140	129	42	121
★Feliz, Rainer	0	0	7.36	5	1	7	11	4	5
Forbes, Keith	0	1	8.10	2	0	7	6	11	5
Ford, Brian	1	4	6.41	8	0	27	43	15	8
Hartung, Mike	0	0	11.57	3	0	2	5	1	2

	W	L	ERA	G	SV	IP	H	BB	SO
Hirsh, Matthew	1	4	7.09	9	0	47	56	37	30
Lipson, David	1	1	6.75	11	1	13	12	18	11
Lobban, Ryan	1	5	7.17	20	0	54	74	27	44
★Merchant, Jamie	3	2	3.38	20	6	56	53	22	52
Norderum, Jason	0	2	7.45	3	0	10	9	11	6
Orgovan, Joe	0	1	0.00	1	0	0	2	0	0
Rijo, Fernando	0	0	6.00	3	0	3	3	1	1
★Solano, Euvi	0	0	9.00	1	0	1	3	0	0
Stephens, Trey	1	2	3.86	22	1	77	75	46	40
Steward, Spencer	0	1	10.13	3	0	3	6	4	3
Tisch, Tim	0	6	7.50	6	0	30	37	24	17

WORCESTER TORNADOES

BATTER	AVG	AB	R	H	2B	3B	HR	RBI	SB
Beauregard, Josh, of	.241	311	34	75	11	4	6	42	10
Beauregard, Keith, of	.317	227	42	72	12	1	5	31	15
★Colabello, Chris, 1b	.288	177	31	51	17	1	5	28	6
Decarlo, Michael, 1b	.296	71	10	21	6	0	4	15	0
Farkes, Josh, of	.176	34	3	6	4	0	0	0	0
Lahair, Jeff, 2b	.233	159	21	37	9	0	1	18	2
MacMillan, Michael, 3b	.260	262	34	68	10	1	3	25	2
Pena, Omar, ss	.267	172	27	46	10	0	5	25	7
Perry, Patrick, c	.305	331	51	101	17	0	7	50	2
Ramos, Dom, 2b	.311	354	58	110	15	6	5	43	21
Sabino, Luism of	.333	30	4	10	2	1	0	3	0
★Santana, Rico, of	.271	133	20	36	3	0	3	19	7
Simek, Matt, 2b	.222	9	2	2	0	0	0	0	0
Smith, Greg, of	.213	94	5	20	5	0	0	9	3
★Solano, Euvi, 3b	.257	136	26	35	6	2	1	14	6
★Tewksbary, Bob, ss	.238	42	7	10	1	0	1	8	1
Valera, Yohanny, c	.263	369	54	97	25	1	7	53	1
Wishy, Andrew, of	.238	315	51	75	16	6	10	52	6
PITCHERS	W	L	ERA	G	SV	IP	H	BB	SO
Beras, Alexis	0	1	10.38	8	0	9	15	5	6
Bevis, P.J.	3	5	4.62	25	4	39	52	8	35
Birtwell, John	4	3	4.12	31	12	44	44	13	51
Guerrero, Junior	7	5	3.76	21	0	122	119	52	93
Mattox, D.J.	2	2	1.47	6	0	31	19	13	30
★McNamara, Shaun	2	1	4.40	15	0	31	39	23	16
Meagher, Michael	3	6	6.37	20	0	78	88	57	70
★Merchant, Jamie	0	0	0.00	5	0	10	4	6	15
Mitchell, Ryan	3	4	2.35	20	0	57	42	19	37
Pena, Alex	5	5	5.94	21	1	106	149	33	68
Pena, Eduardo	5	3	5.56	29	0	45	43	25	36
★Salvato, Matt	0	1	3.38	13	0	21	28	10	7
Shank, Chris	5	0	2.23	34	3	65	70	18	58
Weagle, Matt	2	7	4.70	19	0	100	115	30	54
Willett, Reid	2	8	7.90	21	0	76	114	34	50

CONTINENTAL LEAGUE

Tarrant County finished the regular season with the league's best record and fittingly rolled through a round-robin tournament to win the first-ever Continental League title. Surprisingly their toughest competition came from the Texas Heat, a travel team that spent the entire season playing road games.

While most travel teams are the weak sisters of their league, the Heat finished eight games above .500, led by league MVP Robby Winn. Winn hit 21 home runs in only 42 games.

The Blue Thunder's Justin Blackstock hit .373 to lead the league in hitting while pitcher of the year Zach Duncan was the league's wins (5) and ERA (3.14) leader.

OVERALL

Tarrant County Blue Thunder	30	17	.638	—
Texas Heat	25	17	.595	2½
Lewisville Lizards	19	25	.432	9½
Bay Area Toros	13	28	.317	14

PLAYOFFS: Tarrant County defeated Texas and Bay Area in a round-robin championship tournament.

MANAGERS: Bay Area—Jim Bolt; **Lewisville**—Tom Goodwin; **Tarrant County**—Curtis Wilkerson; **Texas**—Royce Holder.

Most Valuable Player: Robby Winn, Texas. **Pitcher of the Year:** Zach Duncan, Tarrant County. **Mangaer of the Year:** Curtis Wilkerson, Tarrant County.

BAY AREA TOROS

BATTER	AVG	AB	R	H	2B	3B	HR	RBI	SB
Aragon, Koko	.267	30	6	8	1	1	0	4	0

	AVG	AB	R	H	2B	3B	HR	RBI	SB
Caraway, Drew	.223	103	16	23	5	0	3	11	5
Chandler, Marcus	.294	102	17	30	6	1	0	10	10
Colvin, Michael	.225	71	12	16	2	0	0	6	4
Cooper, K.C.	.300	10	2	3	0	0	0	0	0
Cox, Daniel	.304	115	28	35	6	0	9	30	0
Crossland, Brett	.288	59	9	17	2	0	1	12	0
Dresch, Cassidy	.309	94	20	29	3	1	1	10	11
Espinoza, David	.288	52	3	15	2	0	0	14	0
Guzman, Freddy	.271	59	5	16	3	0	1	9	1
Holmes, Danny	.167	48	7	8	1	0	2	5	0
Hyatt, Chris	.257	35	3	9	0	0	0	4	0
Lay, Coy	.297	37	14	11	1	0	0	2	8
Mandile, Joseph	.258	31	4	8	1	0	0	4	3
Medrano, Mike	.282	124	22	35	12	0	2	16	2
Odell, Josh	.261	134	31	35	7	0	12	35	3
Scott, Noah	.094	32	1	3	1	0	0	1	0
Sencion, Sergio	.154	13	1	2	1	0	0	1	0
Smeltzer, Smeltzer	.143	7	1	1	0	0	0	0	0
Stuart, Wayne	.000	1	0	0	0	0	0	0	0
Truitt, Steven	.222	9	1	2	1	0	0	2	0
Wade, Kyle	.269	134	19	36	8	1	2	13	10
Wharton, Ben	.200	25	5	5	0	0	0	4	8
Williams, Zach	.261	69	5	18	1	2	1	6	2
PITCHERS	W	L	ERA	G	SV	IP	H	BB	SO
Bleeker, Jason	2	5	5.68	9	0	52	55	42	35
Cantrell, James	0	1	6.43	2	0	7	12	5	2
Chandler, Marcus	0	0	4.50	5	0	10	12	7	0
Crosby, Bobby	0	1	10.00	14	0	18	16	22	17
Fulcher, Brian	1	0	3.38	2	0	3	2	6	2
Gowey, Jeremiah	0	0	99.00	3	0	0	3	6	0
Guzman, Freddy	0	0	81.00	1	0	0	2	1	0
Hecker, Steve	0	0	12.00	1	0	3	4	2	6
Kelly, Sean	0	0	19.06	4	0	6	12	4	5
Laycock, Keegan	3	3	5.94	18	3	33	32	24	34
Lehrman, Hunter	0	1	18.00	1	0	2	2	3	0
Lewis, Fielding	0	0	60.75	2	0	1	7	3	0
Pudewell, Nate	0	0	99.00	1	0	0	2	1	0
Sandridge, Jerrett	1	2	7.59	15	0	21	25	24	17
Schoenholtz, John	0	0	12.60	3	0	5	6	5	5
Sencion, Mario	0	0	12.00	2	0	3	8	2	5
Sisk, Brandon	0	6	7.93	10	0	48	61	45	55
Smeltzer, Will	5	2	4.45	10	0	61	57	35	48
Ward, Dugan	0	1	6.28	8	0	14	16	12	11
Ward, Gabe	0	1	5.87	5	0	23	24	12	15
Whitman, Kevin	0	0	10.80	9	0	17	21	24	14
Williams, Zach	1	4	7.36	11	0	29	37	17	13

LEWISVILLE LIZARDS

BATTER	AVG	AB	R	H	2B	3B	HR	RBI	SB
Allen, Ryan	.269	104	22	28	3	0	7	19	4
Carattini, Carlos	.188	16	1	3	0	0	0	1	1
Dennis, Jace	.442	77	16	34	7	0	2	12	3
Doyle, Andrew	.091	33	2	3	0	0	0	5	1
Elwis, John	.176	17	0	3	0	0	0	1	0
Grooms, Ryan	.156	32	3	5	1	0	0	2	3
Hastings, Ray	.172	87	10	15	1	0	0	10	2
Howard, Ryan	.340	53	13	18	3	0	3	15	1
Jennings, Josh	.260	169	31	44	7	0	7	31	19
Lewis, Mark	.301	93	29	28	2	0	3	13	12
Longoria, Jesse	.325	169	35	55	9	0	13	46	3
Melendez, Luis	.156	32	4	5	0	0	0	1	1
Patterson, Kyle	.111	27	1	3	0	0	0	1	2
Smith, Robert	.188	32	4	6	0	0	1	4	1
Spann, Mario	.301	143	18	43	7	0	4	20	7
White, Earl	.235	98	26	23	6	0	4	12	6
Wood, Jody	.203	64	9	13	1	0	2	6	0
Wright, Aaron	.286	147	32	42	5	0	9	23	6
Yates, Adam	.286	105	18	30	6	0	3	15	11
PITCHERS	W	L	ERA	G	SV	IP	H	BB	SO
Anderson, Jerry	2	3	4.97	6	0	38	41	22	33
Buchan, Paul	1	4	7.98	7	0	38	42	26	38
Garza, Rudy	0	0	0.00	3	1	3	4	2	3
Gomez, Joseph	0	0	9.00	8	0	17	29	9	3
Green, Glenn	2	1	7.30	17	1	25	32	11	24
Mattison, Kieran	2	4	5.59	11	0	56	61	34	79
Monte, Philip	4	1	5.23	9	0	53	58	33	34
Parker, Ben	1	3	5.30	12	3	19	12	13	18
Press, Cody	1	1	6.17	11	0	42	57	15	26
Reeves, Mike	3	4	5.08	15	0	39	37	27	42
Sartor, Matt	1	0	5.28	8	0	15	14	10	23
Strann, Randy	2	0	3.31	12	3	16	11	10	25
Wilcher, Justin	0	2	7.31	3	0	16	20	8	10

INDEPENDENT LEAGUES

TARRANT BLUE THUNDER

BATTER	AVG	AB	R	H	2B	3B	HR	RBI	SB
Anderson, Jonathan	.209	91	18	19	1	0	4	15	18
Arias, Garvi	.224	49	11	11	3	0	0	5	3
Betourne, Alan	.262	84	21	22	3	0	8	17	2
Belt, James	.222	99	21	22	3	0	2	10	5
Blackstock, Josh	.373	142	47	53	12	2	3	28	10
Cogbill, Bo	.248	113	25	28	4	0	7	22	6
Cruz, Kenny	.188	32	8	6	0	0	0	5	1
Esquivel, Lale	.336	119	35	40	2	0	13	39	2
Fiallo. Adriell	.263	38	8	10	0	1	0	6	2
Hamilton, Mike	.059	17	2	1	0	0	0	0	1
Jordan, Lamont	.303	155	44	47	7	0	5	32	11
Krailo, Karl	.474	90	40	45	7	0	18	43	1
McGinty, Bryan	.100	20	2	2	1	0	0	2	0
Narvaez, Carlos	.083	24	5	2	2	0	0	2	1
Pagan, Joseph	.357	154	45	55	9	0	20	44	3
Pena, Hanssel	.283	53	12	15	1	0	3	15	2
Quintana, Estevan	.308	104	23	32	6	0	9	34	2
Schmitt, Billy	.431	65	26	28	2	0	9	26	5
Sencion, Sergio	.158	19	2	3	0	0	0	5	0
Smith, Austin	.200	10	2	2	0	0	1	3	0
Washington, Stephen	.298	94	18	28	2	0	7	28	4
Watson, Adam	.250	8	3	2	0	0	0	0	0

PITCHERS	W	L	ERA	G	SV	IP	H	BB	SO
Aguirre, Jason	4	1	5.74	13	1	47	60	24	46
Belt, James	0	0	0.00	1	0	0	0	1	0
Betounre, Alan	0	0	0.00	1	0	1	2	1	1
Blackstock, Josh	0	0	54.00	1	0	0	1	1	1
Blankenship, Scott	2	2	10.23	13	1	22	36	20	25
Burger, Brent	4	2	5.94	11	1	47	49	29	28
Bryant, JB	0	2	12.41	8	1	12	20	4	10
Castellano, Ruben	0	0	18.90	4	0	3	9	8	1
Castillo, George	2	1	6.26	17	7	23	25	9	23
Cogbill, Bo	0	2	2.93	9	2	15	15	12	29
Cruz, Kenny	0	0	0.00	1	0	1	1	0	0
Diaz, Eric	3	0	5.53	6	0	28	31	8	20
Duncan, Zach	5	2	3.14	10	0	57	57	17	52
Esquivel, Lale	0	0	36.00	1	0	1	3	0	1
Frias, Hector	2	1	3.22	12	1	22	15	19	27
Garcia, Geivy	0	0	2.25	2	1	4	2	1	7
Hamilton, Mark	1	1	19.64	2	0	4	13	1	1
Kelne, Andrew	1	0	3.27	2	0	11	9	3	10
Kirsch, Brad	0	0	12.00	2	0	3	1	3	2
O'Brien, Joe	1	0	12.00	17	1	21	32	18	17
Pagan, Joseph	0	1	9.00	1	0	1	2	1	1
Servais. Allen	0	0	4.91	2	0	4	4	4	4
Smith, Austin	0	0	2.08	2	0	4	1	4	4
Thornton, Marcus	3	0	3.48	8	0	34	33	8	28
Weems, Ryan	4	0	5.19	8	0	43	52	13	47

TEXAS HEAT

BATTER	AVG	AB	R	H	2B	3B	HR	RBI	SB
Brown, Ryan	.283	53	10	15	0	0	2	8	0
Elliott, Mitch.	.326	172	48	56	12	1	10	32	45
Elmore,Ross	.284	116	37	33	8	0	6	22	3
Enciso, Nick	.329	143	22	47	7	1	8	29	2
Estrada, Michael	.200	30	4	6	1	0	0	3	1
Gaston, Kevin	.333	75	21	25	7	0	1	13	6
Hicks, Billie	.221	122	24	27	4	1	4	20	7
Jackson, Jake.	.205	44	8	9	0	0	1	6	1
January, Javerro.	.236	72	17	17	5	0	2	11	13
Matusik, Jon	.263	152	20	40	7	0	2	19	2
McLin, A.	.088	34	2	3	0	0	0	0	2
Meagher, Justin	.361	144	41	52	12	0	9	37	9
Oldenburg,Samson	.250	36	4	9	2	0	1	8	1
Poles, Donnie	.254	63	17	16	2	1	3	12	7
Reynolds,J.	.276	76	13	21	4	0	2	9	0
Winn, Robby	.341	179	46	61	4	0	21	64	0

PITCHERS	W	L	ERA	G	SV	IP	H	BB	SO
Beseda, Adam	1	1	3.75	9	0	12	9	4	6
Blaylock, Don	2	1	4.91	11	1	18	23	12	16
Cumbie, Beau	4	3	6.40	9	0	45	50	29	20
French, Tyler.	3	2	5.29	11	0	48	53	16	49
Furrow, Donald	1	0	3.65	10	2	12	9	7	13
Furrow, Jason	0	1	4.50	6	0	10	6	8	12
Greanead, Matt	0	1	13.86	10	0	12	16	14	20
Klassen, Trevor	2	5	6.61	9	0	49	49	29	39
Knittel, Bobby	1	0	11.74	3	0	8	18	2	6
Leger, Ryan	5	1	3.71	11	0	51	45	14	49
Pello, Brandon	0	0	1.12	8	4	8	5	4	18
Pierzchala,Eric	0	0	10.12	3	0	5	12	5	3
Russo, Brody	1	0	6.23	11	0	13	14	8	13

	W	L	ERA	G	SV	IP	H	BB	SO
Stapleton, A.	0	0	15.43	2	0	2	5	2	0
Stapleton, Chilion	0	0	3.38	2	0	3	2	3	3
Steinkamp, Matt.	0	0	0.00	3	0	2	4	0	2
Wollscheid,Joe.	4	0	6.16	7	0	31	38	18	24
Young, Robert	1	2	4.35	14	1	21	20	7	29

FRONTIER LEAGUE

After winning nearly 71 percent of their games during the regular season, there was some thought that the Frontier League playoffs would just be the coronation to acknowledge the Thunderbolts' dominance.

It didn't end up being nearly that easy, but in the end Windy City did earn its first title, winning three consecutive do-or-die games to beat Washington for its first Frontier League title.

It was a disheartening end for Washington. The Wild Things have made it to the Frontier League playoffs in each of the past six years, but Washington manager John Massarelli is still looking for his first title.

EAST DIVISION	W	L	PCT	GB
Washington	55	40	.579	
Chillicothe	47	49	.490	8½
Florence	42	54	.438	13½
Slippery Rock	29	66	.305	26

CENTRAL DIVISION	W	L	PCT	GB
Windy City	68	28	.708	
Rockford	52	43	.547	15½
Kalamazoo	51	45	.531	17
Traverse City	46	50	.479	22

WEST DIVISION	W	L	PCT	GB
Gateway	64	29	.688	
Southern Illinois	49	47	.510	16½
River City	36	60	.375	29½
Evansville	34	62	.354	31½

PLAYOFFS: Semifinals—Washington defeated Gateway 3-0 and Windy City defeated Rockford 3-0 in best-of-five series. **Finals**—Windy City defeated Washington 3-2 in best-of-five series.

MANAGERS: Chillicothe—Mark Mason; **Evansville**—Jeff Pohl; **Florence**—Jamie Keefe; **Gateway**—Phil Warren; **Kalamazoo**—Fran Riordan; **River City**—Toby Rumfield; **Rockford**—J.D. Arndt; **Slippery Rock**—Greg Jelks; **Southern Illinois**—Mike Pinto; **Traverse City**—Jon Cahill; **Washington**—John Massarelli; **Windy City**—Andy Haines.

ATTENDANCE: Southern Illinois 259,392; Traverse City 206,102; Gateway 196,134; Washington 155,894; Evansville 131,707; Rockford 113,930; River City 100,556; Florence 99,333; Chillicothe 84,383; Windy City 81,586; Kalamazoo 54,950; Slippery Rock 19,253.

ALL-STAR TEAM:C—Mike Russell, Kalamazoo; **1B**—Mike Breyman, Gateway; **2B**—Ralph Santana, Southern Illinois; **3B**—Joe Ramos, Kalamazoo; **SS**—Travis Garcia, Chillicothe; **OF**—Jon Armitage, Gateway; Mike Coles, Windy City; Jason James, Rockford; **DH**—Dustin Roberts, Gateway; **SP**—Aaron Ledbetter, Washington; **RP**—Matt Petty, Windy City.

Most Valuable Player: Travis Garcia, Chillicothe; **Most Valuable Pitcher:** Aaron Ledbetter, Washington. **Manager of the Year:** Andy Haines, Windy City. **Rookie of the Year:** Ryan Basham, Florence.

INDIVIDUAL BATTING LEADERS

BATTER, CLUB	AVG	G	AB	R	H	HR	RBI
Watson, Reggie, Florence	.357	54	221	45	79	2	28
James, Jason, Rockford.	.345	84	322	44	111	7	61
Santana, Ralph, Southern Illinois	.342	91	368	67	126	3	47
Armitage, Jon, Gateway	.336	81	304	56	102	18	59
Hagen, Matt, Rockford	.335	93	352	59	118	13	62
Long, Wesley, Windy City.	.334	95	353	74	118	7	67
Breyman, Mike, Gateway	.331	91	335	70	111	22	70
Coles, Mike, Windy City	.330	89	342	68	113	9	69
Hall, Chris, Southern Illinois	.318	91	349	62	111	13	55
Sauls, Matt, Rockford	.318	60	233	50	74	7	44

INDIVIDUAL PITCHING LEADERS

PITCHER, CLUB	W	L	ERA	IP	H	BB	SO
Flanigan, Ryan, Chillicothe	9	2	1.28	77	41	9	56
Watson, Tanner, Rockford	11	3	2.17	104	64	31	77
McCullough, Brian, Chillicothe	5	3	2.20	78	65	32	51
Phillips, Shawn, Windy City	8	4	2.45	121	107	12	100
Ledbetter, Aaron, Washington	14	2	2.71	130	108	25	103
Nathanson, David, Traverse City.	5	2	2.95	76	70	11	42
Hunton, Brock, Windy City	10	6	2.96	100	74	36	66
Phillips, Billy, Windy City	8	5	3.09	116	120	33	80
Cline, Zachary, Slippery Rock	10	6	3.10	110	98	42	85
Dessau, Erik, Gateway	14	2	3.13	138	140	31	91

CHILLICOTHE PAINTS

BATTER	AVG	AB	R	H	2B	3B	HR	RBI	SB
Baywal, Tim. dh	.000	9	0	0	0	0	0	0	0
Busson, Blake, of	.176	17	0	3	0	0	0	0	0
Butler, Kevin, of	.206	34	3	7	2	0	0	1	0
Cantu, Adrian, 3b	.303	330	60	100	18	1	13	61	1
Cummins, Daniel, c	.289	232	29	67	15	1	8	42	8
Derhak, Alex, c	.226	53	6	12	3	0	1	7	2
Garcia, Travis, ss	.307	391	73	120	27	2	19	70	12
★Koenig, Lance, of	.270	211	29	57	15	2	3	23	14
Mendoza, Jaziel, of	.295	78	15	23	2	0	5	8	1
Miller, Josh, of	.262	84	4	22	6	0	1	9	1
Ng, Gavin, of	.265	313	58	83	11	4	0	24	19
Parrish, Jeff, c	.140	43	6	6	4	0	1	2	0
Poterson, Jonathan, 1b	.231	373	47	86	27	0	7	65	3
Richardson, Dustin, of	.171	35	4	6	1	0	0	2	0
Rutgers, Paul, of	.254	346	58	88	22	3	6	41	3
Saterlee, Erin, 2b	.000	2	0	0	0	0	0	0	0
Sobel, Evan, 2b	.147	136	15	20	3	0	0	5	2
Storrer, Travis, of	.262	275	32	72	18	3	5	46	1
★Thomas, J.T., of	.258	209	33	54	8	1	4	23	13
Torres, John, of	.200	85	8	17	3	1	0	2	9

PITCHERS	W	L	ERA	G	SV	IP	H	BB	SO
Arreola, Daryl	3	4	3.19	24	5	73	69	20	52
Cunningham, Perry	11	5	3.98	21	0	127	141	31	76
Diaz, Eli	0	0	1.69	5	0	5	5	7	3
Drabek, Justin	3	4	5.62	28	0	74	92	20	41
Flanigan, Ryan	9	2	1.28	40	4	77	41	9	56
Gamboa, Aaron	1	3	5.10	8	0	30	28	15	16
Gray, Tim	1	0	2.45	5	0	18	11	10	7
★Hartfelder, Kurt	1	4	7.98	6	0	29	43	15	9
Johnson, Bryan	6	7	6.05	18	0	86	74	67	65
Johnson, Zachary	0	2	5.89	6	0	18	25	16	10
Marshall, Brian	2	4	5.94	16	0	47	44	37	27
Marshall, Jesse	0	3	11.00	3	0	9	15	5	6
★McCullough, Brian	4	2	2.01	15	0	58	42	20	36
★Meigs, Tyler	1	1	1.42	14	0	19	11	10	14
Palmer, Lucas	3	2	7.14	5	0	29	36	13	26
Quarles, Jason	0	0	7.02	11	0	17	17	14	14
Santiago, Manny	0	0	27.00	1	0	1	3	1	0
Schmieder, Bill	0	1	4.01	7	0	34	36	6	22
Sinclair, Landon	0	0	6.75	8	0	13	14	9	8
Teall, Eric	2	5	3.22	34	16	64	42	23	77
Wiesler, Marty	0	0	4.02	11	0	16	13	7	9

EVANSVILLE OTTERS

BATTER	AVG	AB	R	H	2B	3B	HR	RBI	SB
Auty, Timothy, of	.239	109	16	26	6	0	2	8	1
★Bethel, Ryan, ss	.249	253	30	63	12	1	2	35	3
Bradley, Brandon, of	.179	39	2	7	2	0	0	0	0
Burton, Daniel, of	.244	160	23	39	5	0	6	17	9
Carr, Justin, of	.256	195	20	50	7	1	0	19	2
Chinn, Steve, 3b	.235	51	9	12	1	0	0	3	1
Edwards, Matt, 1b	.275	131	18	36	9	0	4	25	0
Field, J.C., c	.216	134	19	29	3	0	3	15	2
Haas, Keith, 3b	.100	10	0	1	0	0	0	1	3
Harper, Grant, of	.174	23	0	4	1	0	0	2	0
Heffron, Adam, of	.195	82	8	16	5	1	1	8	0
Hurst, Jason, of	.107	28	1	3	0	0	0	1	0
Lehmann, Shaun, of	.200	40	9	8	3	0	0	5	1
Miller, Chad, 3b	.118	17	2	2	0	0	0	0	0
Miller, Josh, of	.100	10	1	1	0	0	0	0	0
Montgomery, Cody, 3b	.204	108	11	22	8	0	1	17	1
O'Donnell, Brendon, of	.208	24	4	5	0	1	0	2	1
Owen, J.J., 1b	.295	105	13	31	4	0	3	11	0
Pace, Zack, of	.254	291	53	74	12	3	1	28	24
Pennino, Tom, c	.223	188	18	42	6	0	2	19	3
Popp, Nick, of	.125	8	0	1	0	0	0	0	0
Rachal, Ryan, of	.257	109	17	28	5	0	0	14	7
Reynolds, Matt, 3b	.232	233	27	54	10	2	2	15	11
Roth, Tony, ss	.378	37	7	14	1	0	0	2	1
Sickles, Ryan, 3b	.274	95	11	26	6	2	0	15	1
Smith, Kyle, 2b	.222	315	50	70	12	1	5	43	29
Spry, Michael, 2b	.295	173	22	51	6	1	9	28	2
Teller, Rhett, 1b	.200	45	3	9	3	0	1	6	0
Wahl, Kasey, 1b	.257	101	11	26	5	0	1	14	2

PITCHERS	W	L	ERA	G	SV	IP	H	BB	SO
Baitinger, Jordan	0	1	9.00	1	0	5	9	1	1
Bille, Michael	1	3	1.70	38	15	48	42	14	39
Conroy, James	8	9	4.43	19	0	112	110	39	97
Del Prete, Anthony	1	1	8.04	14	0	16	23	11	10
Greenhouse, Michael	0	3	6.35	7	0	34	39	18	24
Haggerty, Jake	5	8	5.02	21	0	104	104	42	105

BATTER	AVG	AB	R	H	2B	3B	HR	RBI	SB
Jordan, Justin	6	8	3.13	19	0	124	126	23	96
Lewis, Jonathan	2	4	2.76	33	1	49	47	12	38
★Michael, Jeff	0	1	1.42	4	0	6	7	1	4
Murray, Mark	3	4	3.34	18	0	57	60	26	33
O'Brien, Kyle	2	0	9.49	9	0	12	26	6	5
Obenchain, Steve	1	1	4.63	4	0	23	28	5	20
Paduch, Jim	0	3	4.37	5	0	23	33	9	20
Pawelczyk, Kyle	0	3	4.19	31	1	39	40	17	40
Restivo, Matt	2	4	6.42	8	0	41	45	18	34
Shaffer, Eric	0	1	5.19	6	0	9	10	5	12
Souther, Scott	1	4	4.33	10	1	35	38	12	26
Trout, Jared	1	4	4.30	27	1	67	87	16	54
Wilson, Thomas	1	0	5.75	4	0	20	21	12	15
Woods, Andy	0	0	11.25	3	0	4	7	5	4

FLORENCE FREEDOM

BATTER	AVG	AB	R	H	2B	3B	HR	RBI	SB
★Acosta, Jesse, 2b	.409	22	3	9	1	0	0	4	0
Basham, Ryan, of	.298	362	56	108	21	1	17	74	2
Billingslea, Courtne, of	.125	8	0	1	1	0	0	0	0
Blacken, Beau, 1b	.316	361	76	114	26	2	15	73	3
Evans, Tyler, ss	.192	52	7	10	1	1	0	6	3
Foust, J.D., of	.277	159	23	44	6	0	2	18	4
Gonzalez, Eddie, of	.199	136	13	27	6	2	0	10	2
Grogan, Timothy, 3b	.239	306	44	73	20	0	9	45	3
Guttridge, Dan, of	.208	48	4	10	1	1	1	5	1
Haas, Keith, 2b	.083	24	1	2	0	0	0	1	0
Holland, Joe, 2b	.306	196	33	60	13	0	2	34	1
Leon, Chad, of	.143	21	1	3	0	0	0	1	0
Lex, Joshua, c	.270	274	39	74	14	1	6	44	5
Marek, Truman, of	.242	33	5	8	2	0	0	2	1
Martin, Collin, 1b	.171	70	7	12	2	0	0	5	0
Neal, Joe, c	.286	14	3	4	1	0	0	1	0
Perez, Tony, ss	.254	67	12	17	0	1	0	7	1
Salotti, Nick, c	.315	178	28	56	15	0	6	29	0
★Smith, Andrew, 2b	.260	100	16	26	3	0	0	9	0
Steinbach, Ryan, ss	.300	20	3	6	1	0	0	2	0
Stone, Greg, ss	.271	402	67	109	7	3	3	43	8
Wadowski, Mike, of	.253	150	21	38	6	0	2	18	2
Watson, Reggie, of	.357	221	45	79	14	3	2	28	20
★Yoho, Nathan, of	.293	92	11	27	7	2	0	14	3

PITCHERS	W	L	ERA	G	SV	IP	H	BB	SO
Acosta, Domingo	1	4	4.26	20	3	44	55	16	38
Bennion, Jason	1	2	1.86	19	1	29	24	12	24
Bowlin, Jason	5	5	5.86	27	1	101	139	36	75
Brown, Luke	5	2	7.12	10	0	54	70	23	38
Bruns, Josh	5	2	3.65	15	0	91	85	34	86
Castle, Cody	3	2	4.41	37	1	51	53	23	53
Dunning, Nick	2	0	3.30	10	0	46	31	27	37
★Fogelson, Scott	1	1	2.73	5	0	33	30	14	31
Furrow, Jason	0	0	5.40	2	0	3	6	2	1
Gonzalez, Eddie	0	0	4.91	5	0	7	9	1	4
Gray, Zack	1	3	5.00	15	0	27	34	12	23
Honce, Mike	1	1	3.72	17	0	19	25	13	21
Janszen, Mark	2	5	6.38	15	0	24	22	22	23
Konecny, Bill	0	1	8.44	3	0	5	9	2	3
Marksbury, Matt	2	1	4.09	6	0	11	9	6	9
Martin, Collin	0	0	9.00	1	0	1	2	0	0
Mason, Dane	2	3	5.18	7	0	33	41	10	18
★McCullough, Brian	1	1	2.79	16	0	19	23	12	15
Morrison, Ryan	0	0	9.82	4	0	4	7	6	1
Ochiai, Yon	0	0	16.88	1	0	3	9	1	3
Payton, Jason	0	2	7.88	2	0	8	15	1	9
Quijano, Alain	5	7	4.35	31	0	112	116	44	75
★Rainey, Matthew	0	0	7.84	9	0	10	14	13	4
Trent, Craig	3	3	6.27	9	0	47	51	34	46
★Troop, Jon	1	0	3.15	31	0	40	38	19	34
Watkins, Dave	2	2	4.62	14	1	25	27	19	27
Webb, Chris	2	1	11.45	5	0	11	23	7	6

GATEWAY GRIZZLIES

BATTER	AVG	AB	R	H	2B	3B	HR	RBI	SB
★Acosta, Jesse, ss	.221	181	21	40	7	0	1	22	3
Andrews, Greg, 2b	.242	124	18	30	4	1	7	26	1
Armitage, Jon, of	.336	304	56	102	22	2	18	59	11
★Arrowood, Jason, c	.281	32	7	9	1	0	1	1	0
Beck, Eric, c	.293	92	20	27	5	1	4	20	0
★Bradburry, Kyle, 3b	.220	59	4	13	1	0	2	6	0
Breyman, Michael, 1b	.331	335	70	111	22	0	22	70	1
Dietz, Josh, 1b	.270	74	12	20	2	0	2	11	0
Gibson, Chris, of	.260	181	19	47	5	0	1	15	2
Holdren, Stephen, of	.311	341	72	103	16	8	23	73	0
Lisk, Charlie, c	.201	229	37	46	7	2	15	41	2
Marshall, Dan, 2b	.100	10	2	1	0	0	0	1	0

BATTER	AVG	AB	R	H	2B	3B	HR	RBI	SB
★McCarthy, Joey, ss	.000	6	2	0	0	0	0	0	0
Paula, Manny, 3b	.299	274	53	82	23	1	15	47	10
Roberts, Dustin, of	.301	356	88	107	19	0	29	73	6
Saltzgaber, Ryan, ss	.320	222	35	71	11	2	7	28	4
Sullivan, Ryan, 3b	.281	270	48	76	15	1	11	45	0
★Vincent, Jeff, of	.262	164	34	43	7	2	6	28	9

PITCHERS	W	L	ERA	G	SV	IP	H	BB	SO
Chambers, Scott	1	0	1.69	3	0	5	5	5	1
Dessau, Erik	14	2	3.13	20	0	138	140	31	91
★Dow, Jeremy	1	1	6.00	14	0	42	46	28	43
Herman, Jason	5	1	4.79	17	1	73	87	19	43
Hertel, James	7	1	1.83	27	1	44	33	9	27
★Himes, Drew	0	2	8.56	3	0	14	26	0	7
Kellbach, Brandon	7	1	3.96	34	0	52	56	19	41
★Little, Chris	4	3	3.20	13	0	56	54	18	48
★Logan, Brian	0	0	14.40	6	0	5	7	12	4
McKinney, Billy	1	2	4.34	15	0	37	48	8	28
★Rainey, Matthew	1	0	7.11	5	1	6	3	6	4
Ridener, Eric.	2	1	2.11	39	20	38	26	18	52
Roelle, Justin	0	2	7.96	6	0	26	26	19	16
Roush, Nathan	8	4	4.01	16	0	101	117	29	75
Russo, Noah	0	0	1.80	4	0	5	3	4	8
★Staatz, Justin	1	2	2.73	23	1	26	16	26	29
Sullivan, Ryan	0	0	6.00	1	0	3	8	0	1
Trevino, Toro	11	5	5.09	19	0	117	130	40	83
Warren, Kyle	1	0	14.73	4	0	4	8	4	1
Wasylak, David.	0	2	5.90	10	0	29	26	29	16

KALAMAZOO KINGS

BATTER	AVG	AB	R	H	2B	3B	HR	RBI	SB
Anderson, Brandon, of	.000	16	2	0	0	0	0	0	0
Brachold, Keith, of	.261	352	54	92	22	3	12	62	7
Brady, Mike, ss.	.215	93	12	20	2	0	1	10	2
Bulkley, Aaron, of.	.136	59	6	8	3	1	1	6	3
Carter, Josh, of.	.311	351	65	109	21	1	12	75	6
Eastman, Trevor, c	.183	120	12	22	5	0	1	10	0
Goldberg, Zack, c.	.261	23	3	6	2	0	1	5	0
Gonzalez, Orestes, c.	.200	15	1	3	1	0	0	0	0
Grose, Jeff, of	.314	344	65	108	14	3	5	45	13
Johnson, A.J., of	.263	114	17	30	7	0	5	21	1
Kmiecik, Kyle, 2b	.281	342	47	96	21	2	10	49	7
Mader, Josh, ss	.239	46	9	11	0	0	0	4	4
Moron, Robert, 1b	.239	188	23	45	9	0	6	34	7
Ramos, Joseph, 3b	.302	378	70	114	34	7	5	52	32
Russell, Mike, c	.255	278	52	71	18	0	17	61	1
★Smith, Andrew, ss	.277	119	17	33	4	0	0	10	5
Williams, Simon, of	.274	329	66	90	18	3	9	38	13
Young, Jeff, ss	.225	80	14	18	4	1	2	7	3

PITCHERS	W	L	ERA	G	SV	IP	H	BB	SO
Brown, Tyler.	0	1	15.19	2	0	5	11	3	5
★Brownell, John	4	4	3.38	34	0	56	49	20	45
Caldwell, Daniel	2	0	3.69	40	1	61	46	42	51
Cicatello, Justin	0	2	6.97	11	0	10	12	11	11
Davis, Chris	0	0	16.20	3	0	5	11	4	4
Devalk, Dane	5	6	5.59	18	0	58	67	27	41
Dipietro, Joe.	0	2	10.93	7	0	14	20	6	6
Eddy, Cooper	2	1	5.74	6	0	27	34	8	15
★Fogelson, Scott	5	6	4.55	14	0	59	72	33	38
Fyvie, Dan	2	2	6.87	4	0	18	27	12	9
Grose, Jeff	0	0	4.50	1	0	2	3	1	1
Hinkle, Paul	0	1	13.50	3	0	4	6	6	4
Jenkins, Clay	0	0	15.43	1	0	2	5	3	0
Kearcher, Kyle	0	1	9.49	6	0	12	19	4	9
Kelly, Mark	1	1	3.41	36	9	37	33	25	44
Kemp, Matt	0	0	7.50	4	0	6	8	6	1
Koch, Jon.	0	0	6.75	6	0	7	7	3	7
Lare, Trenton	5	4	3.17	12	0	65	65	20	62
Lewis, James	0	0	9.00	5	0	10	12	5	7
Long, Jeff.	11	5	3.85	20	0	140	140	40	78
Lovelady, Matt	0	0	121.50	2	0	1	7	3	1
Mann, Sam.	3	2	3.65	15	0	86	88	26	55
Ritsche, Keith.	1	0	7.36	3	0	4	6	2	2
★Shippey, Steve.	5	3	2.76	12	0	85	68	27	62
Sullivan, John	0	1	5.52	26	12	31	34	28	35
★Troop, Jon.	2	2	1.59	12	0	17	10	6	19
Waters, Mitch.	0	1	7.71	9	0	8	7	5	

RIVER CITY RASCALS

BATTER	AVG	AB	R	H	2B	3B	HR	RBI	SB
★Albano, Anthony, of	.310	100	12	31	4	0	0	13	0
Bettis, Andy, 1b	.274	234	36	64	16	1	9	38	0
Bielski, Chris, of.	.167	60	3	10	0	0	0	5	4
Brown, Collin, of	.250	16	3	4	1	0	0	3	0

	AVG	AB	R	H	2B	3B	HR	RBI	SB
Bunn, Jared, of.	.242	62	8	15	3	3	0	5	3
Christison, Dallas, ss	.270	37	3	10	0	0	0	2	2
Clemons, Chris, c	.250	4	0	1	0	0	0	0	0
Colon, Angel, 3b.	.245	273	39	67	14	0	7	38	1
Czyz, Ryan, of	.231	229	46	53	9	1	2	18	11
Hendricks, Trey, of	.258	360	43	93	10	0	10	44	1
Hough, Brad, ss	.285	355	57	101	25	1	10	53	18
Landry, Jeff, 2b	.291	265	43	77	18	2	4	28	4
Laurent, Phillip, of	.341	217	41	74	14	4	12	46	5
Leake, Matthew, of	.100	20	3	2	0	0	0	0	0
Lup, Ken, c.	.269	268	33	72	12	1	1	27	10
Miller, Jeff, of	.307	140	26	43	11	1	7	26	1
Mosby, Bobby, 1b	.273	242	41	66	13	0	19	53	0
Newman, Joseph, of	.136	22	3	3	0	0	0	3	1
Quintana, Estevan, of	.125	16	1	2	0	0	0	0	0
Rowe, Tim, of.	.188	32	8	6	2	0	0	4	2
Rzepka, Brian, of	.176	17	2	3	0	0	1	4	1
★Sweet, Andrew, c.	.289	228	34	66	14	0	3	32	5
Wong, Andrew, 2b	.000	2	2	0	0	0	0	0	1

PITCHERS	W	L	ERA	G	SV	IP	H	BB	SO
Antonides, Chris.	0	0	14.54	2	0	4	11	3	3
Ayala, Albert.	5	5	6.46	16	0	70	79	42	46
Benacka, Mike	2	5	5.01	36	20	41	32	35	60
Bretl, Adam	0	1	14.29	6	0	11	20	8	9
★Brockman, Ben	0	0	3.07	8	0	15	26	0	11
Brook, Steven.	11	7	5.24	20	0	122	147	35	86
Cahoon, Gary	0	2	12.27	6	0	4	10	5	4
Catalano, Chad	0	0	5.40	7	0	8	13	9	10
Cheek, Cameron	0	1	0.00	3	0	4	4	4	1
Cherry, Brad	1	0	5.87	4	0	8	12	3	9
Clem, Chris	2	9	5.13	19	0	126	154	39	92
Doherty, Ryan	1	1	2.42	20	0	26	27	12	20
★Dugan, Tim	1	2	5.89	6	0	37	33	20	28
Evosevich, Scott.	0	0	7.94	5	0	11	23	3	9
Fowler, Taylor	0	2	9.69	9	0	13	20	13	10
Hansen, Bryan	1	6	5.23	28	0	65	71	37	42
★Hartfelder, Kurt	0	1	9.00	2	0	9	15	5	2
★Hummel, Rick	2	0	2.70	5	0	3	4	1	1
★Keller, Matt	0	0	20.25	3	0	1	4	0	0
Linder, Chad.	3	3	5.03	25	0	34	34	23	27
Martinez, Mario	0	0	9.00	1	0	1	2	0	2
Miller, Jonathan	5	4	3.89	18	1	72	69	22	57
Muldoon, Patrick	0	0	9.00	3	0	2	1	3	2
Newman, Joseph	0	1	4.50	12	0	10	4	7	12
O'Loughlin, Luke	0	1	5.93	7	0	14	18	9	9
Pacella, J.J.	1	2	7.36	3	0	15	18	10	7
Taylor, Brody	0	2	7.24	4	0	14	22	7	8
Thomson, Jordan.	0	0	8.10	16	1	20	35	10	12
Ursin, Damian	1	3	5.34	15	0	32	32	29	19
Walker, Collin	0	2	5.40	10	0	12	11	3	10
★Young, Justin	0	0	5.91	7	0	11	14	6	14

ROCKFORD RIVERHAWKS

BATTER	AVG	AB	R	H	2B	3B	HR	RBI	SB
Anthonsen, Joe, 2b	.232	327	46	76	13	1	0	28	16
Brooks, Jonathan, ss	.299	117	23	35	7	3	1	16	3
Cohen, Brandon, of	.273	139	22	38	10	0	9	29	0
Day, Johnny, 2b	.300	30	3	9	2	0	1	8	1
Dutton, Brad, ss	.288	281	54	81	11	5	2	24	20
Hagen, Matt, 3b	.335	352	59	118	23	1	13	62	27
Henderson, Will, 1b	.265	257	31	68	16	0	9	40	2
Huskins, Joey, of	.224	201	25	45	13	0	0	22	1
James, Jason, of	.345	322	44	111	23	1	7	61	5
Kimbrough, Justus, c.	.252	127	10	32	6	0	0	13	1
McArdle, Ryan, of	.167	18	2	3	0	0	1	3	0
McFadden, Sean, of	.191	89	15	17	3	2	0	11	2
Perkins, Robert, c	.244	45	2	11	4	0	0	3	0
Roldan, Victor, 3b	.200	90	8	18	1	0	0	6	0
Sauls, Matt, of	.318	233	50	74	10	3	7	44	14
Sweet, Andrew, c	.260	77	12	20	3	1	2	11	0
Turay, Alhaji, of	.352	145	30	51	18	0	4	21	6
Valiente, Roberto, of	.257	304	47	78	15	1	3	36	21
Vanderhook, Cory, c.	.059	17	1	1	0	0	0	0	0

PITCHERS	W	L	ERA	G	SV	IP	H	BB	SO
Baca, Jason	4	2	2.03	30	8	31	22	19	25
Bauer, Garrett.	7	5	4.15	19	0	100	86	65	81
Behning, Luke	0	0	0.00	5	0	4	1	5	4
Bringelson, Roy	0	5	3.34	35	1	32	32	18	27
Brnardic, Ryan	3	1	3.15	26	0	34	34	17	20
Brockman, Ben.	0	0	11.42	7	0	9	15	7	8
★Brownell, John	0	1	5.63	9	0	8	16	1	7
Bryan, Gerad	0	0	27.00	3	0	2	3	5	2
Catalano, Chad	0	0	11.00	5	0	9	8	9	9
Cramphin, James	4	4	3.69	12	0	68	65	28	57

	W	L	ERA	G	SV	IP	H	BB	SO
D'aversa, Frank	0	0	4.15	2	0	4	4	3	1
Darling, Bobby	0	0	5.87	5	0	8	10	4	8
Dickert, Reed	1	0	0.82	2	0	11	6	3	18
Dowling, Dave	6	7	4.22	30	2	75	77	27	61
★Gragg, John	2	3	4.97	7	0	38	38	16	26
Hagerty, Luke	0	1	33.75	3	0	1	2	8	2
★Himes, Drew	0	0	12.27	3	0	7	11	3	4
James, Jason	0	2	10.38	7	0	9	11	6	9
Mack, Bobby	1	2	5.58	17	1	31	31	6	24
Marksbury, Mike	0	0	1.33	20	14	20	8	10	32
Mehne, Matt	0	1	6.75	6	0	4	4	5	0
Parker, Shaun	6	2	2.76	10	0	59	40	31	33
Rizzi, Vinnie	0	0	10.38	2	0	4	5	3	2
Salter, Brady	7	5	4.86	19	0	109	129	30	70
Towery, Dane	3	0	1.77	15	1	20	23	6	17
Watson, Tanner	11	3	2.17	15	0	104	64	31	77
Young, Justin	0	0	5.68	4	0	6	9	3	0
Ziegler, Dan	0	2	12.00	2	0	6	9	4	2

SLIPPERY ROCK SLIDERS

BATTER	AVG	AB	R	H	2B	3B	HR	RBI	SB
★Acosta, Jesse, 3b	.246	69	7	17	3	0	0	5	0
★Albano, Anthony, of	.268	205	28	55	11	0	4	29	1
Armenio, John, 1b	.429	7	1	3	1	0	0	0	0
Arndt, Gary, ss	.130	69	6	9	1	0	0	1	1
Bowling, Casey, of	.267	360	47	96	12	1	9	34	6
Butch, Phil, 2b	.299	274	33	82	6	1	1	11	11
Chapman, Travis, c	.207	29	2	6	2	0	0	3	0
Curry, Jason, of	.198	197	22	39	10	0	5	20	3
Dandridge, Jon, of	.202	168	15	34	9	1	4	15	2
Darrah, Mike, c	.125	8	0	1	0	0	0	2	0
Dennis, Bernie, 1b	.253	186	19	47	7	0	1	20	0
Dixon, Dorian, c	.286	168	9	48	10	0	4	19	0
Donald, Cy, 2b	.249	257	24	64	6	3	0	15	3
Georgion, Steve, 1b	.143	35	3	5	1	0	0	1	1
Hickey, Jon, ss	.049	41	2	2	1	0	0	1	1
Hine, Robbie, ss	.202	114	12	23	3	0	0	12	0
Holley, Kevin, 1b	.208	106	8	22	5	0	3	8	0
Hudson, Steve, 2b	.239	46	1	11	1	0	0	1	0
Klausman, Jarrod, 1b	.219	96	11	21	2	1	1	9	2
Lonergan, Kory, 3b	.180	61	3	11	3	0	0	5	3
Macleod, John, c	.000	7	0	0	0	0	0	0	0
★McCarthy, Joey, ss	.111	9	1	1	0	0	0	0	0
Richardson, Michael, 3b	.091	22	2	2	0	0	0	2	0
Vickers, Bryan, c	.254	177	24	45	14	1	9	44	0
Von Behren, Jason, 1b	.200	45	3	9	1	0	0	6	0
Westman, Ryley, c	.253	83	8	21	5	0	0	5	1
★Yoho, Nathan, of	.247	231	29	57	15	3	6	22	8

PITCHERS	W	L	ERA	G	SV	IP	H	BB	SO
Armenio, John	0	0	7.71	4	0	9	9	5	5
Bachman, John	1	2	7.48	7	0	22	27	15	22
Baxter, Brian	3	1	3.15	21	0	40	34	18	24
Bucklew, Kory	3	5	4.28	23	0	74	97	22	36
Button, Seth	0	0	2.25	2	0	4	4	2	0
Cline, Jason	1	3	6.61	16	0	33	39	26	18
Cline, Zachary	10	6	3.10	19	0	110	98	42	85
Dandridge, Jon	0	0	0.00	4	0	4	2	2	4
Duclos, Derek	0	6	6.69	10	0	39	42	14	20
Griffith, Derek	2	4	9.82	7	0	22	18	35	17
Hollister, Billye	0	1	23.14	1	0	2	6	1	3
★Keller, Matt	0	1	1.50	7	0	12	9	8	8
Lasinski, Greg	0	4	4.70	30	10	44	53	17	20
Less, Steve	0	0	7.88	4	0	8	12	2	2
Liogghio, Justin	0	0	10.80	3	0	3	3	1	3
McConnell, Caleb	0	2	1.80	2	0	10	8	2	8
McEnaney, Alex	0	2	5.59	4	0	19	21	8	12
Parise, Pete	0	1	4.35	6	0	10	11	1	13
Parker, Rhett	0	1	11.20	9	0	14	20	15	5
Robinson, Justin	0	1	6.75	6	0	12	14	4	12
Rubio, Chris	2	3	4.40	25	1	43	39	22	40
Schwartz, Dan	2	5	4.17	12	0	69	66	37	41
Simon, Jared	1	1	1.46	22	6	37	26	5	28
Smith, Judson	0	4	4.84	8	0	35	40	20	17
★Tapper, Jon	0	1	9.53	6	0	6	6	9	10
Tracy, Nick	3	12	5.91	19	0	105	130	54	54
Vickers, Bryan	0	0	18.00	2	0	3	7	1	1

SOUTHERN ILLINOIS MINERS

BATTER	AVG	AB	R	H	2B	3B	HR	RBI	SB
★Arrowood, Jason, c	.303	119	17	36	6	1	1	20	0
Beason, Seth, 1b	.197	61	9	12	3	0	1	5	0
Dorn, Tim, 1b	.349	129	33	45	4	0	12	35	0
Hall, Chris, 3b	.318	349	62	111	20	3	13	55	1
Hanson, Ryan, c	.206	34	6	7	2	0	0	2	0

BATTER	AVG	AB	R	H	2B	3B	HR	RBI	SB
Harryman, Eric, ss	.125	40	2	5	1	0	0	0	0
Kane, Ryan, of	.278	245	40	68	12	0	1	14	14
Keene, Willie, of	.263	209	29	55	12	3	4	31	1
Koski, Kevin, of	.297	91	20	27	5	2	1	14	7
Marshall, Andre, of	.301	93	17	28	6	4	5	21	3
Metropoulos, Joey, 1b	.326	144	20	47	11	0	9	32	0
Moffitt, Andrew, of	.288	59	13	17	5	0	3	8	0
Navarro, Ramon, ss	.000	12	0	0	0	0	0	0	0
Patrick, Sean, c	.083	12	1	1	0	0	0	2	0
Perdomo, Bryant, c	.218	55	9	12	3	0	1	4	1
Santana, Ralph, 2b	.342	368	67	126	21	2	3	47	25
Scanzano, Mike, ss	.309	291	45	90	7	0	1	21	3
Simon, Scott, 1b	.264	201	24	53	11	1	1	36	0
Smith, Casey, 1b	.119	42	3	5	1	0	2	5	0
Suttle, Eric, of	.252	218	22	55	10	0	2	18	3
Torres, Jose, of	.209	91	15	19	2	0	2	8	0
Vega, Eric, of	.204	103	6	21	4	0	0	10	2
Victor, Mike, 1b	.243	144	16	35	5	0	7	27	2
Wirth, Robert, c	.298	205	30	61	11	1	4	31	0

PITCHERS	W	L	ERA	G	SV	IP	H	BB	SO
Adams, Jason	0	0	12.27	3	0	4	7	1	4
Almonte, Danny	0	1	5.28	6	0	31	30	19	17
Bailey, Griffin	2	4	6.27	15	0	56	67	23	45
Beason, Seth	0	0	0.00	1	0	0	1	0	1
Blomquist, Brian	4	8	4.36	19	0	97	113	28	47
Hahn, Charlie	4	3	4.70	16	0	61	81	20	28
Holcomb, Scott	1	0	13.50	4	0	6	4	9	6
Hope, Travis	5	3	1.61	33	14	45	39	10	25
★Hummel, Rick	1	1	1.84	23	1	29	25	12	18
Irle, Roy	2	0	17.05	7	3	6	12	9	4
★Little, Chris	4	5	4.44	9	0	53	52	18	34
★Logan, Brian	2	1	3.26	28	1	30	30	25	35
Lovell, Benjamin	2	2	5.79	9	1	28	28	8	12
McGraw, Chris	2	2	6.23	13	0	17	16	13	13
McKenzie, Marcus	3	3	6.03	7	0	37	44	20	15
Pridgeon, Kipp	2	0	6.05	15	0	19	21	14	14
Qualls, Jon	3	3	5.65	23	0	72	95	11	37
Quigley, Ryan	0	1	4.76	4	0	17	21	12	16
Romero, Wilfredo	0	0	6.75	2	0	1	3	2	1
★Tapper, Jon	0	0	2.08	4	0	4	8	4	4
Tierney, Chris	1	1	3.71	3	0	17	16	4	6
Tisone, Nick	8	3	3.82	19	0	127	121	36	79
★Ward, Josh	0	0	9.39	6	0	8	15	4	3
Wilburn, Brian	1	1	5.03	26	0	34	27	16	23
Wooley, Robert	2	4	3.51	10	0	51	45	33	42

TRAVERSE CITY BEACH BUMS

BATTER	AVG	AB	R	H	2B	3B	HR	RBI	SB
★Bradbury, Kyle, 3b	.183	71	6	13	4	1	1	11	0
Brown, Jeff, of	.207	299	38	62	8	0	5	37	4
Carter, Justin	.118	17	1	2	1	0	0	3	1
Dickerson, R.C., of	.160	50	12	8	3	0	0	4	4
Garza, Aaron, of	.279	165	20	46	7	0	10	33	4
Holmes, Justin, ss	.268	362	51	97	17	2	5	39	11
Kalter, Zack, of	.304	368	49	112	21	4	3	51	8
★Koenig, Lance, 2b	.237	114	23	27	11	0	0	19	7
Lawson, Eric, 2b	.045	22	1	1	0	0	0	1	1
Ledbetter, Curtis, c	.306	304	46	93	19	1	6	44	1
Orr, Sam, 3b	.309	288	58	89	20	0	6	44	5
Rademacher, Matt, c	.176	136	10	24	6	0	0	14	1
★Ramsey, Ben, 3b	.228	57	8	13	2	0	1	5	0
Roblin, Brad, of	.333	159	28	53	2	3	0	15	9
Smith, Nick, c	.083	12	0	1	0	0	0	0	0
★Thomas, J.T., of	.279	104	21	29	7	2	0	20	6
★Vincent, Jeff, of	.295	173	39	51	9	4	2	33	12
Yamamoto, Takeshi, 3b	.292	24	4	7	0	0	0	2	0
Young, Steve, 2b	.219	183	29	40	4	0	0	13	15

PITCHERS	W	L	ERA	G	SV	IP	H	BB	SO
Beigh, David	0	0	0.00	1	0	0	0	0	0
Bell, Derek	0	0	8.10	3	0	3	2	4	1
Bostelman, Brett	3	2	2.34	42	3	50	46	31	37
Brookes, Craig	0	0	0.00	2	0	3	1	1	3
Casoli, Tony	3	8	6.33	15	0	87	111	25	55
Dillard, Matt	2	1	2.04	14	0	18	12	3	8
★Dow, Jeremy	2	2	5.91	8	0	11	11	5	9
★Dugan, Tim	0	1	18.00	1	0	4	8	4	2
Gehring, Ryan	7	8	4.50	20	0	124	148	25	76
Hawkins, Dan	0	4	7.71	8	0	14	17	15	10
Kalter, Zack	1	0	2.25	3	0	4	5	3	4
Klovstad, Buddy	0	3	6.48	6	0	33	46	8	23
Locke, Jared	1	1	3.42	21	2	24	19	17	25
McClellan, Robbie	4	5	4.22	12	0	60	65	22	51
★Meigs, Tyler	1	2	2.66	20	11	24	14	6	26

	W	L	ERA	G	SV	IP	H	BB	SO
Nathanson, David	5	2	2.95	12	0	76	70	11	42
Nelson, Jack	1	0	1.82	18	0	25	18	8	16
Pepper, Nick	2	0	3.28	33	4	36	33	16	29
Rembisz, Bryan	7	0	1.87	19	0	63	52	21	51
★Shippey, Steve	0	4	11.79	8	0	24	37	15	26
Thornton, Tom	2	4	4.86	7	0	37	41	6	31
Tognetti, Phil	2	3	4.16	21	0	71	72	36	48
★Ward, Josh	0	0	13.50	2	0	3	5	1	3
Williams, Jeff	4	2	4.61	38	0	57	53	23	52
Phillips, Shawn	8	4	2.45	19	0	121	107	12	100
Ramon, Amos	5	2	2.35	18	0	46	28	12	32
Rebyanski, Anthony	3	0	3.50	41	1	44	38	32	60
Smolar, Jordan	0	0	2.65	14	0	17	10	11	21
Taylor, Brody	2	3	5.29	6	0	32	46	12	17
Taylor, Scott	1	1	8.44	6	0	11	12	3	7
Ziegler, Josiah	0	0	3.72	5	0	10	10	8	5

WASHINGTON WILD THINGS

BATTER	AVG	AB	R	H	2B	3B	HR	RBI	SB
★Bethel, Ryan, ss	.234	47	7	11	0	2	2	10	1
Earnhart, Eric, 3b	.254	173	21	44	7	4	1	22	7
Garza, Mario, c	.237	245	31	58	9	1	12	45	2
Gregula, Justin, 3b	.250	32	4	8	2	0	2	8	0
Knapp, Robbie, 1b	.306	310	54	95	24	1	13	66	5
Messner, Nathan, 1b	.306	324	62	99	19	0	10	51	3
Newman, J.J., 2b	.198	91	13	18	3	0	0	6	3
O'Brien, Pat, c	.219	196	29	43	9	3	8	24	4
Padgett, Kyle, ss	.199	226	31	45	8	4	6	30	5
Quintana, Rene, 2b	.294	204	26	60	13	1	3	30	6
★Ramsey, Ben, 3b	.326	46	9	15	6	0	1	9	3
Rine, Jarod, of	.275	302	49	83	10	6	3	32	33
Sidick, Chris, of	.244	324	71	79	14	6	13	42	22
Sutton, Matt, of	.295	339	61	100	15	6	12	58	26
Vernon, Rob, of	.258	124	15	32	4	0	2	12	15
Werman, Kyle, 2b	.237	93	13	22	1	1	1	8	1

PITCHERS	W	L	ERA	G	SV	IP	H	BB	SO
Cochran, Tom	6	8	3.90	20	0	115	99	51	93
Davis, Ryan	2	0	7.33	21	1	27	41	12	25
Foeman, Kevin	0	2	8.79	4	0	14	17	12	11
Gett, Alex	1	0	2.57	2	0	7	5	1	7
Hahn, Cory	0	0	6.43	4	0	7	7	3	6
Hauff, Michael	1	1	6.65	7	0	22	20	18	20
Heisel, Ian	1	1	2.14	18	6	34	26	7	34
Hlebovy, Gus	3	5	2.47	35	11	44	29	15	52
Hollenbeck, J.J.	6	4	3.41	22	0	95	83	20	74
Ledbetter, Aaron	14	2	2.71	21	0	130	108	25	103
Mattison, Justin	6	1	2.37	34	2	57	43	37	61
★Michael, Jeff	0	0	6.75	17	0	28	40	22	17
Ogrodnik, Matt	0	0	11.25	3	0	4	9	2	6
Revelette, Adam	1	0	20.25	1	0	1	5	1	2
Risser, Travis	4	2	1.09	25	6	50	46	17	42
Rivera, Chris	1	0	3.00	2	0	9	7	4	5
Sadler, Patrick	3	1	7.43	8	0	27	28	21	18
Schon, Andy	2	2	5.84	7	0	25	29	6	18
Sharick, Alex	0	1	3.38	12	1	19	19	9	18
★Staatz, Justin	0	3	5.59	6	1	19	20	18	19
Stanley, Pat	1	2	9.19	4	0	16	16	16	15
Stidfole, Alan	4	3	4.36	12	0	64	65	20	58
Werman, Kyle	0	0	5.40	3	0	5	4	5	1

WINDY CITY THUNDERBOLTS

BATTER	AVG	AB	R	H	2B	3B	HR	RBI	SB
Balster, Scott, of	.269	175	23	47	8	0	3	23	4
Billak, Scott, of	.265	272	48	72	16	2	4	40	12
Check, Travis, 3b	.308	13	2	4	1	0	0	0	0
Coles, Mike, of	.330	342	68	113	16	5	9	69	27
Concepcion, Gavin, c	.207	121	14	25	6	0	2	19	1
Graham, Ryan, 2b	.204	98	11	20	1	0	0	7	3
Hawke, Matthew, 1b	.290	324	47	94	26	0	10	78	2
Horn, Josh, 3b	.302	301	64	91	19	0	7	53	9
Long, Wesley, ss	.334	353	74	118	36	3	7	67	31
Lowen, John, c	.257	272	27	70	9	0	6	37	1
Marconi, Rob, of	.263	346	55	91	19	4	9	38	24
McCarthy, John, of	.233	270	53	63	9	1	1	25	20
Mejia, Gilberto, 3b	.264	212	37	56	8	3	3	25	3
Ramon, Amos, 3b	.277	148	22	41	8	1	0	13	3

PITCHERS	W	L	ERA	G	SV	IP	H	BB	SO
Borne, Danny	0	0	9.00	28	0	29	36	29	21
Causey, Mike	4	0	3.75	38	4	50	41	18	40
Clousner, Josh	0	0	10.38	5	0	4	7	5	1
Fussell, Eric	12	2	3.26	19	0	113	108	26	66
★Gragg, John	0	1	8.59	7	0	15	21	7	7
Hess, Isaac	10	2	3.28	32	1	58	43	40	60
Hunton, Brock	10	6	2.96	21	0	100	74	36	98
Madej, Ronald	0	0	10.80	4	0	2	1	5	1
Mault, Jeff	3	0	3.70	11	1	24	19	17	21
Mazzone, Nick	0	0	30.00	2	0	3	12	3	4
Petty, Matt	2	2	2.66	43	26	47	34	21	61
Phillips, Billy	8	5	3.09	20	0	116	120	33	80

Normally a championship team is built around a steady core of veterans who get some help from a couple of new faces.

Chico had a different formula. Rookie Daniel Nava stepped into the cleanup spot from day one and led the Outlaws for their first title, hitting .371/.425/.625 while earning the league MVP honors. He was helped by league pitcher of the year Todd Gelatka, who picked up 18 saves, The Outlaws knocked off Long Beach three games to one in the best-of-five championship series.

FIRST HALF

	W	L	PCT	GB
Chico	25	13	.658	—
Long Beach	23	15	.605	2
Yuma	21	17	.553	4
Orange County	19	19	.500	6
Reno	18	19	.486	6½
St. George	7	30	.189	17½

SECOND HALF

	W	L	PCT	GB
Long Beach	25	13	.658	—
Yuma	21	17	.553	4
Chico	19	19	.500	6
Orange County	18	20	.474	7
St. George	16	22	.421	9
Reno	15	23	.395	10

PLAYOFFS: Chico defeated Long Beach 3-1 in best-of-5 series.

MANAGERS: Chico—Mark Parent; **Long Beach**—Darrell Evans; **Orange County**—Garry Templeton; **Reno**—Les Lancaster; **St. George**—Cory Snyder; **Yuma**—Mike Marshall.

ATTENDANCE: Chico 69,330; Yuma 54,818; Long Beach 50,791; Reno 50,330; Orange County 36,526; St. George 23,870.

ALL-STAR TEAM: C—Buddy Morales, Orange County; **1B**—Jaime Martinez, Long Beach; **2B**—David Bacani, Orange County; **SS**—Jesse Kovacs, Chico; **3B**—Henry Calderon, Yuma; **Utility**—Ryan Stevenson, St. George; **OF**—Daniel Nava, Chico; Kane Simmons, Reno; Johnny Kaplan, Long Beach; Yosvanny Almario, Yuma. **DH**—Peanut Williams, Orange County; **SPs**—Ben Fox, Orange County; Derek Loop, Chico; Ryan Claypool, Long Beach; Roger Luque, Yuma; Dusty Bergman, Reno; **RPs**—Todd Gelatka, Chico; Dane De La Rosa, Long Beach; Anthony Pluta, St. George; Neil Hayes, Yuma.

Most Valuable Player: Daniel Nava, Chico.; **Pitcher of the Year:** Todd Gelatka, Chico. **Rookie of the Year:** Kane Simmons, Reno.

Rookie Pitcher of the Year: Dustin Gober, Long Beach.

INDIVIDUAL BATTING LEADERS

BATTER, CLUB	AVG	G	AB	R	H	HR	RBI
Nava, Daniel, Chico	.371	72	256	70	95	12	59
Goss, Mike, Yuma	.367	52	188	59	69	2	27
Almario, Yosvanny, Yuma	.357	72	280	56	100	7	58
Williams, Peanut, Orange County	.344	69	259	50	89	13	56
Flowers, Brett, St. George	.341	62	229	37	78	3	42
Pohle, Richard, Orange County	.338	67	263	43	89	8	58
Senreiso, Juan, Reno	.328	56	229	49	75	7	54
Stevenson, Ryan, St. George	.326	73	291	68	95	10	44
Simmons, Kane, Reno	.326	55	215	47	70	18	54
Kaplan, John, Long Beach	.320	70	306	75	98	7	45

INDIVIDUAL PITCHING LEADERS

PITCHER, CLUB	W	L	ERA	IP	H	BB	SO
Luque, Roger, Yuma	5	6	2.57	88	80	25	70
Fox, Ben, Orange County	5	3	2.99	69	55	15	74
Bergman, Dusty, Reno	6	3	3.40	101	101	45	64
Loop, Derrick, Chico	8	5	3.82	92	94	47	58
Natale, Mike, Orange County	4	4	3.93	94	93	22	116
Jefferson, John, Chico	6	2	4.06	64	57	23	44
Gober, Dustin, Long Beach	5	1	4.25	66	63	27	57
Woodyard, Mark, St. George	3	10	4.44	105	115	35	85
Claypool, Ryan, Long Beach	7	3	4.46	85	92	40	52
Singleton, Nick, Chico	2	4	4.59	84	91	21	94

CHICO OUTLAWS

BATTER	AVG	AB	R	H	2B	3B	HR	RBI	SB
Alcott, Jason, c	.097	31	2	3	0	0	0	1	0
Bambino, Richard, c	.203	59	6	12	1	0	1	8	1
Boggs, Steve, of	.296	335	53	99	17	0	3	45	17
Compo, James, of	.000	6	0	0	0	0	0	0	0
Dean, Tyler, of	.238	21	5	5	0	0	0	5	2
Dragicevich, Scott, 3b	.291	282	51	82	16	2	4	40	7
Ferris, Jacob, of	.247	73	14	18	1	0	4	14	1
Gibson, Dave, ph	.000	1	0	0	0	0	0	0	0
Gossage, Todd, 3b	.276	199	43	55	12	1	5	42	4
Kovacs, Jesse, ss	.284	264	51	75	18	3	6	46	4
Kuzmic, Craig, c	.265	68	20	18	4	0	3	10	1
Matteucci, Jason, of	.292	219	38	64	11	3	3	28	11
McLintock, Jake, of	.000	9	1	0	0	0	0	0	0
Nava, Daniel, of	.371	256	70	95	23	3	12	59	18
Oster, Jesse, 3b	.175	40	5	7	2	0	0	2	1
Pierson, David, 2b	.252	107	15	27	4	0	0	8	9
Pringle, Eric, 2b	.281	221	49	62	7	3	2	36	21
Ungricht, Brock, c	.299	147	15	44	13	0	1	32	1
Van Meetren, Jason, 1b	.244	250	48	61	8	1	4	42	7

PITCHERS	W	L	ERA	G	SV	IP	H	BB	SO
Bicknell, Greg	2	1	4.50	3	0	18	20	4	23
Campbell, Matt	4	0	2.70	5	0	27	24	10	10
Gelatka, Todd	2	2	3.10	30	18	29	30	11	29
Howard, Daniel	1	2	6.45	7	0	22	27	8	10
Jefferson, John	6	2	4.06	24	0	64	57	23	44
Jones, Steven	0	1	5.63	3	0	16	18	9	15
Loop, Derrick	8	5	3.82	17	0	92	94	47	58
McKinley, Jacob	3	3	6.43	18	1	77	86	41	56
Mclintock, Jake	2	2	5.63	17	2	32	43	20	19
Oster, Jesse	4	2	3.74	27	2	34	29	20	30
Pearson, Tyler	5	6	6.92	15	0	65	91	13	42
★Segovia, John	2	0	5.49	22	0	41	46	16	34
Singleton, Nick	2	4	4.59	15	0	84	91	21	94
Springman, Phil	3	2	6.83	15	0	57	68	23	36
Wilson, Paul	0	0	5.40	8	0	8	7	13	3

LONG BEACH ARMADA

BATTER	AVG	AB	R	H	2B	3B	HR	RBI	SB
Araiza, Jorge, ss	.289	256	40	74	18	0	7	32	5
Cicatelli, Cole, c	.282	181	22	51	12	0	3	29	2
Gross, Kirk, 3b	.257	241	45	62	7	3	1	27	5
Ikenaga, Daisuke, ss	.174	69	8	12	0	1	0	6	0
Kaplan, John, of	.320	306	75	98	26	5	7	45	51
Klemm, Chris, of	.270	293	68	79	14	3	5	32	19
Larue, Jeff, 3b	.342	111	30	38	7	0	6	24	5
Martinez, Jaime, 1b	.298	275	57	82	18	2	14	63	5
★Mayorga, Gabriel, ss	.239	142	24	34	7	0	2	18	1
Mooneyham, Jason, 1b	.204	113	22	23	3	3	1	15	0
Myers, Corey, c	.125	16	1	2	1	0	0	1	0
Ramirez, David, c	.273	154	19	42	6	1	3	20	1
Trumble, Dan, of	.263	236	50	62	11	2	13	66	10
Wakeland, Chris, of	.294	228	39	67	20	0	10	52	2

PITCHERS	W	L	ERA	G	SV	IP	H	BB	SO
Araiza, Jorge	0	0	22.50	1	0	2	6	0	2
Buller, Sean	2	2	3.21	26	3	28	24	9	19
Claypool, Ryan	7	3	4.46	16	0	85	92	40	52
Currier, Rik	4	1	1.58	6	0	40	23	11	44
De La Rosa, Dane	2	4	3.69	39	16	46	42	16	53
Fischer, Rich	4	1	3.89	12	1	44	41	5	49
George, Taylor	3	4	4.72	28	1	34	32	16	26
Gober, Dustin	5	1	4.25	15	0	66	63	27	57
Gross, Kirk	0	0	3.00	1	0	3	3	1	4
Heaverlo, Jeff	7	5	5.32	16	0	107	105	42	106
Layfield, Andrew	3	1	4.96	16	0	49	50	23	22
Mooneyham, Jason	0	0	6.00	6	0	9	13	1	2
★Nikolic, Adam	1	0	0.84	7	0	11	11	2	10
Ramirez, David	0	0	0.00	1	0	1	1	1	1
Ramsey, Justin	3	4	5.19	9	0	43	48	24	23
Smith, Bud	2	1	5.04	5	0	25	33	5	12
Thompson, Brandon	0	0	5.84	9	0	12	16	8	9
Vianna, Marcel	2	6	6.48	17	0	25	30	15	18
Zick, Jeremy	4	0	1.61	10	0	45	22	15	42

ORANGE COUNTY FLYERS

BATTER	AVG	AB	R	H	2B	3B	HR	RBI	SB
Bacani, David, 2b	.320	297	66	95	19	7	4	33	22
★Coit, Johnny, of	.246	61	9	15	4	1	1	10	0
Davis, Aaron, of	.310	142	31	44	7	3	0	24	8
Douglas, Charlie, 1b	.261	23	3	6	1	0	1	2	0
★Douglas, James, 3b	.250	4	3	1	0	0	0	0	0
Entrekin, Alex, c	.182	11	2	2	0	0	0	3	0
★Farina, Peter, c	.179	28	3	5	2	0	0	2	0
Goodman, Scott, 1b	.259	251	43	65	13	0	13	53	0
Levier, Bret, ss	.261	291	42	76	13	3	4	45	4
Marshall, Jon, c	.188	32	5	6	2	0	0	3	0
★Mayorga, Gabriel, 3b	.233	43	4	10	2	0	1	6	0
Morales, Buddy, c	.310	229	43	71	12	2	2	33	3
Okano, Mark, of	.263	232	44	61	13	2	5	33	9
Pohle, Richard, of	.338	263	43	89	23	1	8	58	5
Templeton, Garry, of	.279	258	57	72	5	3	3	39	13
Thomas, Brett, 3b	.289	97	11	28	2	1	1	12	1
Williams, Peanut, 1b	.344	259	50	89	15	0	13	56	4
Wong, Andrew, 3b	.182	11	1	2	0	1	0	1	0
Zamora, Hector, 3b	.281	57	6	16	2	1	0	5	0

PITCHERS	W	L	ERA	G	SV	IP	H	BB	SO
Arizmendi, Daniel	3	4	4.40	11	0	29	33	21	32
Casanova, Nicholas	2	0	3.48	23	3	34	23	11	24
Caughey, Trevor	0	0	3.86	12	0	16	16	4	24
Coggin, Dave	0	2	6.94	12	6	12	16	7	6
Dickert, Reed	6	3	4.62	17	0	86	75	46	112
★Douglas, James	2	2	6.58	9	0	40	54	21	29
Evangelista, Antonio	0	0	9.00	2	0	4	5	0	4
Fox, Ben	5	3	2.99	11	0	69	55	15	74
Fulcher, Brian	0	1	5.06	3	0	5	6	4	1
Gallegos, Gary	1	2	14.73	5	0	7	11	9	9
Grijalva, Jon	2	2	27.00	2	0	5	15	6	5
Holguin, Nathan	2	2	7.29	12	0	42	55	16	33
Howerton, Jason	2	2	4.97	13	1	29	38	5	18
McRobbie, Alex	3	0	2.70	6	0	40	35	9	43
Natale, Mike	4	5	3.93	15	0	94	93	22	116
Okano, Mark	0	0	0.00	2	0	2	0	1	0
Ruvalcaba, Ezequiel	0	2	3.52	18	0	23	19	19	23
★Salini, Robert	3	3	8.71	11	0	41	59	23	29
Soto, Andrew	3	3	4.50	12	0	24	27	10	25
Terrebonne, Jared	0	0	5.40	11	0	13	11	14	11
Thompson, Brandon	0	0	8.71	8	1	10	13	11	9
Woolery, Mike	1	3	10.08	6	0	25	37	7	20

RENO SILVER SOX

BATTER	AVG	AB	R	H	2B	3B	HR	RBI	SB
Amar, Adam, 1b	.354	96	22	34	11	0	5	19	1
Brown, Ryan, 1b	.327	55	17	18	2	0	4	15	1
Chikazawa, Masashi, c	.260	123	20	32	5	1	4	18	3
Cole, Maurice, 2b	.277	119	23	33	5	1	6	20	4
Devoir, Jordan, ss	.241	58	7	14	1	0	1	8	0
Done, Mike, of	.282	248	48	70	22	1	8	42	11
Hahn, Dustin, 3b	.152	33	3	5	0	0	0	2	1
Hall, Victor, of	.306	301	75	92	10	7	9	37	46
Johnson, J.J., of	.136	22	2	3	0	0	1	5	0
Kowalski, Ryan, of	.285	200	34	57	12	0	1	25	19
Madrid, Carlos, 3b	.315	143	23	45	9	0	5	29	5
McLeod, Josh, c	.245	49	12	12	2	0	0	6	0
Melton, Joe, c	.278	18	1	5	2	0	0	0	0
Nash, David, c	.000	9	1	0	0	0	0	1	0
★Nowlin, Cody, 1b	.247	81	17	20	5	1	1	7	1
★Rodrigues, Jose, c	.274	215	38	59	17	1	8	42	3
Senreiso, Juan, of	.328	229	49	75	19	1	7	54	20
Sherrill, J.J., of	.133	15	2	2	1	0	1	4	2
Simmons, Kane, of	.326	215	47	70	9	1	18	54	1
Sindlinger, Chuck, 3b	.262	172	25	45	8	1	0	20	5
Snyder, Gary, of	.222	9	0	2	0	0	0	1	0
Tully, Travis, of	.232	69	10	16	3	0	0	5	5
Walker, Sam, ss	.259	170	18	44	10	1	1	25	3

PITCHERS	W	L	ERA	G	SV	IP	H	BB	SO
Balteff, Shawn	2	4	5.45	21	1	35	30	23	37
Bergman, Dusty	6	4	3.40	15	0	101	101	45	64
Brock, Eric	0	0	19.50	4	0	6	15	6	5
Evans, Josh	4	0	5.68	28	0	44	60	25	33
Everitt, Keaton	1	0	6.00	2	0	9	11	4	5
Harendza, Adam	1	3	6.68	8	0	32	39	22	26
Johnson, James	1	5	5.19	15	0	95	121	25	75
Johnston, Kelly	0	1	18.00	1	0	3	7	3	1
Martinez, Jason	2	4	7.99	24	0	47	54	35	27
Moran, Nick	5	3	4.95	14	0	87	87	33	63
★Nikolic, Adam	3	1	5.19	20	2	26	28	14	19
Parris, Matt	5	8	5.79	18	0	73	83	45	53
★Peck, Mike	0	0	12.71	8	1	6	8	10	3
Plouffe, Marshall	0	1	12.71	9	1	11	23	7	12
Saenz, Chris	4	8	8.10	5	0	27	41	16	22
Scott, Matt	0	0	9.00	2	0	7	8	6	6
Soriano, Julio	0	0	2.70	3	0	3	4	4	4
Testa, Chris	1	2	6.23	11	1	13	13	10	12
Thomas, Eric	1	1	4.12	16	7	20	15	12	19
Walentin, Joe	1	1	5.79	6	0	9	13	7	9

INDEPENDENT LEAGUES

ST·GEORGE ROADRUNNERS

BATTER	AVG	AB	R	H	2B	3B	HR	RBI	SB
Alcott, Jason, c	.152	33	2	5	1	0	0	2	0
Burrows, Greg, of	.305	59	8	18	6	0	1	14	5
★Coit, Johnny, c	.266	94	14	25	6	0	1	12	4
Daguio, Brandon, ss	.111	27	2	3	0	0	0	1	0
Edwards, Madison, 3b	.200	10	1	2	0	0	0	1	0
Flowers, Brett, 1b	.341	229	37	78	10	0	3	42	2
Guerrero, Santiago, of	.257	171	28	44	11	0	5	17	6
Haran, Gerard, c	.238	21	1	5	0	0	0	5	0
Harris, Gary, of	.270	304	43	82	17	4	6	44	11
Hicks, Dustin, c	.239	113	18	27	6	0	5	22	3
Jones, Albert, ss	.059	17	1	1	0	0	1	2	0
Lemon, Greg, 2b	.380	71	16	27	2	0	0	12	5
Made, Kelington, c	.077	13	1	1	0	0	0	1	0
Melo, Juan, 3b	.330	94	22	31	11	0	7	18	2
★Nowlin, Cody, 1b	.339	171	32	58	13	2	6	27	3
Rivkin, Matt, 3b	.204	49	7	10	2	0	2	11	0
Rogers, Tanner, 2b	.185	27	6	5	0	1	0	2	1
Rust, Jason, of	.167	12	2	2	0	0	0	0	0
Sands, Geron, 2b	.191	136	14	26	7	0	3	13	4
Shankle, Brooks, 3b	.192	26	4	5	1	0	0	4	1
Stevenson, Ryan, of	.326	291	68	95	25	9	10	44	11
Vargo, Paul, c	.000	10	0	0	0	0	0	0	0
Villezcas, Marcos, ss	.223	224	32	50	7	2	1	22	3
Wagner, Geoff, of	.304	224	51	68	14	0	10	38	3
Wong, Andrew, 3b	.000	7	0	0	0	0	0	0	0
Wright, Steven, of	.297	175	26	52	11	0	2	28	2

PITCHERS	W	L	ERA	G	SV	IP	H	BB	SO
Baca, Anthony	0	0	3.60	7	0	10	11	4	12
Baysinger, Trent	0	0	10.57	5	0	8	14	5	6
Buker, Ben	1	1	6.82	6	0	32	43	12	28
Collis, Devin	1	1	9.36	15	0	25	33	18	25
Correa, Jose	1	1	6.06	3	0	16	22	6	10
Dotel, Melido	0	1	7.36	4	0	7	6	9	6
★Douglas, James	0	1	11.45	6	0	11	18	6	11
Fraser, Loren	0	0	27.00	1	0	1	2	0	1
★Graves, Donovan	3	3	6.16	15	1	50	77	12	20
Hall, Danny	3	4	5.21	10	0	47	46	30	25
Joyce, Michael	0	1	11.57	4	0	7	10	4	10
Kalb, Aaron	0	1	9.00	2	0	3	7	4	1
Krout, Will	0	0	22.50	1	0	2	6	1	0
Martinson, Joe	1	2	9.87	10	0	17	33	13	12
Mattison, Eric	1	2	7.47	3	0	16	22	8	10
Muro, Joey	0	2	7.23	10	0	19	18	30	25
Norderum, Jason	1	0	2.16	5	0	8	4	9	11
★Peck, Mike	0	2	20.25	2	0	4	6	8	4
Pena, Matthew	0	3	7.57	10	2	27	46	13	23
Pluta, Tony	2	1	5.56	21	10	23	23	22	19
Reed, Cole	0	1	23.63	2	0	3	10	2	3
Renery, Mike	0	2	6.61	15	0	31	43	24	23
★Salini, Robert	0	0	22.95	3	0	7	14	9	5
★Segovia, John	2	0	2.19	6	1	12	12	10	8
Silvas, Danny	1	0	8.80	3	0	15	18	6	12
Sprouse, Shannon	3	6	7.29	18	0	63	80	57	50
Storey, Mike	0	6	9.21	23	0	57	87	34	43
Wells, Pat	0	1	11.42	5	0	9	16	9	8
Winter, Haley	1	0	8.76	8	0	12	21	5	13
Woodyard, Mark	3	10	4.44	16	0	105	115	35	85

YUMA SCORPIONS

BATTER	AVG	AB	R	H	2B	3B	HR	RBI	SB
Almario, Yosvany, of	.357	280	56	100	20	1	7	58	21
Bernal, Hector, 2b	.250	240	37	60	15	2	0	27	4
Calderon, Henry, 3b	.306	297	53	91	21	0	6	59	12
Crouch, Nikolaus, 1b	.239	222	38	53	11	0	10	38	1
★Farina, Peter, of	.246	69	10	17	1	0	0	10	1
French, Christopher, of	.077	13	3	1	0	0	0	0	0
Gipson, Ryan, 2b	.000	6	1	0	0	0	0	0	1
Goss, Mike, of	.367	188	59	69	16	1	2	27	26
Janeway, Richard, of	.304	214	53	65	11	4	6	33	8
Jova, Maikel, of	.318	305	49	97	19	4	4	67	6
LaChapelle, Alex, of	.000	2	0	0	0	0	0	0	0
Matos, Pascual, c	.261	203	29	53	11	0	6	28	3
★Mayorga, Gabriel, 2b	.317	41	4	13	0	0	1	6	0
Peterson, Robert, c	.292	89	22	26	2	0	1	13	2
Prado, Jordan, ss	.310	229	50	71	16	2	4	36	2
★Rodriguez, Jose, of	.263	38	7	10	1	0	4	14	0
Swanson, Brian, 1b	.000	4	0	0	0	0	0	0	0
Valentine, A.J., 1b	.264	174	35	46	11	3	7	34	7
Wilson, Aaron, of	.000	0	0	0	0	0	0	0	0

PITCHERS	W	L	ERA	G	SV	IP	H	BB	SO
Bunyan, Brian	0	0	17.47	2	0	6	8	2	8

	W	L	ERA	G	SV	IP	H	BB	SO
Devaul, Ray	0	0	6.43	5	0	7	10	3	4
★Graves, Donovan	0	2	8.64	4	0	17	29	1	16
Hayes, Neil	4	1	3.92	26	10	39	35	19	49
Langlois, Chris	2	1	2.91	3	0	22	16	7	17
Luque, Roger	5	6	2.57	13	0	88	80	25	70
Maydew, Eric	4	3	5.31	15	0	59	81	11	48
Merricks, Charles	6	3	5.87	15	0	84	102	43	58
Mills, Aaron	0	1	5.40	3	0	10	15	5	9
Perez, Jorge	2	0	3.28	4	0	25	24	10	26
Saucedo, Matthew	1	4	8.45	22	2	38	60	18	26
Sikora, Marc	0	0	108.00	2	0	0	1	1	0
Soja, Steve	6	5	4.91	16	0	92	104	24	60
Solis, Marcos	1	2	3.52	9	0	23	22	11	14
Stephens, Amad	1	1	9.35	10	4	9	10	8	14
Swanson, Brian	0	0	10.80	2	0	2	2	1	0
Thorne, Aaron	0	0	2.84	5	1	6	5	4	1
White, Evan	7	3	4.70	15	0	92	102	25	60
Wilson, Aaron	3	2	7.36	15	1	33	40	11	21

NORTHERN LEAGUE

Willie Glen is the winningest pitcher in Gary Railcats history. He's also proven to be their money man come playoff time.

Glen improved to 8-0 in the postseason as he held the Calgary Vipers to three hits for a complete-game win in the deciding Game 5 of the championship series. Glen went 4-0 during the playoffs as he allowed Glen allowed three runs in 33 innings this year in the postseason after throwing 17 scoreless innings in the playoffs in 2006.

He also set a Northern League record with 162 strikeouts, topping Bobby Madritsch's previous record of 153 on his way to being named the league's pitcher of the year and outstanding player of the championship series.

While Fargo-Moorhead didn't make it to the championship series, manager Doug Simunic did continue his impressive run of success. Simunic picked up his 800th Northern League win while taking a team to the playoffs for the 14 times in 15 seasons in the league.

FIRST HALF

NORTH DIVISION	W	L	PCT	GB
Calgary	29	19	.604	
Winnipeg	27	20	.574	1½
Fargo-Moorhead	26	21	.553	2½
Edmonton	19	29	.396	10

SOUTH DIVISION	W	L	PCT	GB
Gary	30	18	.625	
Joliet	22	26	.458	8
Schaumburg	20	28	.417	10
Kansas City	18	30	.375	12

SECOND HALF

NORTH DIVISION	W	L	PCT	GB
Fargo-Moorhead	31	17	.646	
Winnipeg	25	23	.521	6
Calgary	21	27	.438	10
Edmonton	19	29	.396	12

SOUTH DIVISION	W	L	PCT	GB
Gary	28	20	.583	
Kansas City	26	22	.542	2
Joliet	23	25	.479	5
Schaumburg	19	29	.396	9

PLAYOFFS: Semifinals—Gary defeated Winnipeg 3-2 and Calgary defeated Fargo-Moorhead 3-0 in best-of-five series. **Finals**—Gary defeated Calgary 3-2 in best-of-five series.

MANAGERS: Calgary—Mike Busch; **Edmonton**—Frank Reberger; **Fargo-Moorhead**—Doug Simunic; **Gary**—Greg Tagert; **Joliet**—Hal Lanier; **Kansas City**—Andy McCauley; **Schaumburg**—Steve Maddock; **Winnipeg**—Rick Forney.

ATTENDANCE: Winnipeg 300,938; Kansas City 289,162; Schaumburg 206,749; Joliet 184,611; Fargo-Moorhead 170,122; Gary 166,338; Edmonton 82,414; Calgary 71,363.

ALL-STAR TEAM: C—Luis Alen, Winnipeg; **1B**—Jason Colson, Calgary; **2B**—Rob Watson, Kansas City; **3B**—Carlos Duncan, Calgary; **SS**—Nelson Castro, Calgary; **OF**—Darryl Brinkley, Calgary; Fehlandt Lentini, Winnipeg; Joe Mathis, Fargo-Moorhead; **DH**—Juan Diaz, Joliet; **RHP**—Willie Glen, Gary SouthShore; **LHP**—Josh Habel, Gary.

Most Valuable Player: Darryl Brinkley, Calgary. **Pitcher of the Year:** Willie Glen, Gary. **Rookie of the Year:** Mike Just, Fargo-Moorhead. **Manager of the Year:** Greg Tagert, Gary.

INDIVIDUAL BATTING LEADERS

BATTER, CLUB	AVG	G	AB	R	H	HR	RBI
Brinkley, Darryl, Calgary	.399	87	376	88	150	14	82
Diaz, Juan, Joliet	.358	96	383	74	137	28	80
Duncan, Carlos, Calgary	.350	93	397	77	139	13	82
Watson, Rob, Kansas City	.343	95	385	80	132	8	72
Johnston, Clint, Edmonton	.342	75	269	44	92	5	42
Delgado, Mario, Kansas City	.341	94	399	57	136	15	81
Just, Mike, Fargo-Moorhead	.336	94	330	56	111	4	55
Alen, Luis, Winnipeg	.333	82	285	43	95	3	44
Castro, Nelson, Calgary	.323	84	384	56	124	4	43
Eggleston, Aharon, Kansas City	.321	91	336	66	108	1	62

INDIVIDUAL PITCHING LEADERS

PITCHER, CLUB	W	L	ERA	IP	H	BB	SO
Forystek, Brian, Joliet	4	4	2.73	82	72	33	70
Habel, Josh, Gary	12	7	2.96	155	130	46	105
Glen, Willie, Gary	12	1	3.03	140	111	36	162
Grybash, Dan, Schaumburg	9	5	3.39	135	123	46	100
Renkert, Dane, Fargo-Moorhead	13	1	3.94	121	108	47	92
Kintzler, Brand, Winnipeg	5	2	4.07	77	78	13	41
Keppinger, Bill, Schaumburg	5	7	4.10	112	118	32	77
Kusiewicz, Mike, Winnipeg	7	4	4.20	84	106	20	52
Pote, Lou, Edmonton	8	8	4.21	105	127	44	75
Richmond, Scott, Edmonton	10	9	4.26	146	147	47	110

Recuenco, Rob, 3b	.269	219	38	59	12	1	2	35	2
Ryan, Tim, of	.253	166	30	42	7	1	2	26	1
Sandel, George, ss	.293	389	69	114	17	5	2	50	11
★Shorsher, Adam, c	.303	132	24	40	9	0	3	20	1
Teller, Rhett, 1b	.212	104	17	22	4	0	1	22	0
Wallis, Scott, 3b	.188	32	2	6	0	0	1	3	0
Webster, Rob, of	.167	24	4	4	0	0	0	3	0

PITCHERS	W	L	ERA	G	SV	IP	H	BB	SO
★Alexander, Jordy	1	1	7.00	4	0	18	28	6	11
Castro, Dorian	5	9	5.92	26	0	128	166	29	70
Hall, Danny	0	0	10.59	10	0	17	32	11	8
Henry, Mike	2	7	7.13	29	0	88	131	45	40
Johnson, Mike	2	7	4.90	27	4	94	113	37	73
★Johnston, Clint	0	0	0.00	2	0	2	0	1	1
Kemlo, Chris	0	5	10.38	16	0	39	75	22	25
Landeros, Leonard	0	1	11.12	13	0	11	25	9	5
★Moenter, Curtis	2	1	8.22	22	1	31	49	13	34
Monsma, Quinn	0	0	11.68	10	0	12	19	8	10
Pote, Lou	8	8	4.21	38	5	105	127	44	75
Richmond, Scott	10	9	4.26	23	0	146	147	47	110
Rivard, Reggie	1	7	8.29	24	0	51	89	22	40
Sikaras, Pete	2	1	10.43	17	5	15	20	15	10
★Sobkow, Phil	1	1	5.88	17	0	34	42	16	29
Teller, Rhett	0	0	9.00	2	0	2	2	1	0
★Waite, Randy	4	1	4.85	24	2	26	26	22	17

CALGARY VIPERS

BATTER	AVG	AB	R	H	2B	3B	HR	RBI	SB
Ashman, Shaun, of	.222	135	18	30	3	1	0	15	0
Brinkley, Darryl, of	.399	376	88	150	32	1	14	82	18
Castro, Nelson, ss	.323	384	56	124	38	2	4	43	15
Colson, Jason, 1b	.290	390	67	113	25	2	16	89	0
Duncan, Carlos, 3b	.350	397	77	139	25	3	13	82	20
Evans, Mitch, c	.286	245	40	70	10	1	3	41	0
Kuramochi, Manabu, 2b	.286	308	65	88	5	5	0	39	31
Lyons, Tom, of	.333	3	0	1	0	0	0	1	0
★McEachran, Aaron, 3b	.311	45	6	14	2	0	1	7	0
Miller, Drew, of	.299	355	74	106	17	2	10	69	6
★Moenter, Curtis, of	.000	2	0	0	0	0	0	0	0
★Nichols, Kyle, of	.302	225	38	68	10	0	9	43	0
Ouellette, Maxim, of	.000	6	0	0	0	0	0	0	0
Price, Kevin, c	.243	177	32	43	16	0	2	26	0
Tang, Jorge, of	.277	336	57	93	14	3	1	40	4
Wyland, Ryan	.143	7	0	1	0	0	0	1	0

PITCHERS	W	L	ERA	G	SV	IP	H	BB	SO
★Alexander, Jordy	3	2	4.31	11	0	48	50	18	35
Brown, Matt	0	0	0.00	2	0	2	0	2	0
Burguillos, Daivis	0	0	11.12	7	1	11	22	9	6
Freeborn, Geoff	6	2	4.25	42	2	42	44	25	36
Greusel, Evan	7	3	4.50	19	2	88	100	27	65
Groeger, Jeff	3	3	5.84	18	1	86	92	32	66
Klatt, Ryan	3	7	7.44	37	2	75	99	20	48
Lyons, Tom	3	6	6.25	39	2	59	75	33	35
Manning, David	1	0	6.30	11	4	10	10	8	7
Minami, Kazuaki	10	5	5.52	24	0	122	173	38	74
★Moenter, Curtis	0	3	9.89	19	4	24	42	8	21
★Nichols, Kyle	0	0	0.00	1	0	1	0	1	1
Olson, Ryan	3	2	3.80	34	5	47	57	14	48
Price, Kevin	0	0	9.00	1	0	1	2	1	1
Sarver, Scott	1	3	3.86	7	0	28	23	16	14
Schutt, Chris	9	5	7.75	21	1	106	150	48	43
★Sobkow, Phil	0	2	8.22	6	0	23	38	5	17
Stein, Mike	0	0	18.00	1	0	1	2	1	1
★Waite, Randy	0	3	4.22	24	3	32	28	20	13
Wyland, Ryan	0	2	11.10	15	1	36	52	30	12

EDMONTON CRACKER CATS

BATTER	AVG	AB	R	H	2B	3B	HR	RBI	SB
Aspito, Jason, 3b	.252	151	22	38	5	2	3	22	1
Becker, Chris, 2b	.252	318	53	80	19	0	2	38	3
Betts, Todd, 1b	.275	120	16	33	5	0	1	13	0
★Chappell, Dan. dh	.667	3	1	2	0	0	0	0	0
★House, Kevin, of	.301	166	28	50	7	4	2	20	16
Johnson, Mike, of	.364	11	1	4	0	0	0	3	1
★Johnston, Clint, 1b	.374	171	23	64	14	0	3	29	0
★Lundberg, Jordan, 3b	.156	32	5	5	1	0	0	3	1
Martinez, Dave, c	.255	55	9	14	2	1	0	11	0
McClain, Terrence, of	.304	372	69	113	15	6	11	59	9
★McEachran, Aaron, 1b	.242	95	9	23	5	0	2	17	0
★Munhall, Brian, c	.244	201	29	49	7	2	4	23	7
Ndungidi, Sambu, of	.287	108	15	31	9	0	3	15	0
★Nichols, Kyle, 1b	.331	154	26	51	8	0	7	29	0
Radmanovich, Ryan, of	.286	227	38	65	10	1	13	45	0

FARGO-MOORHEAD REDHAWKS

BATTER	AVG	AB	R	H	2B	3B	HR	RBI	SB
Arneson, Justin, of	.333	21	4	7	1	0	0	2	2
Austin, Richard, of	.304	365	69	111	22	2	15	67	12
Haugen, Casey, c	.206	102	27	21	3	0	0	11	4
★Johnston, Clint, 1b	.286	98	21	28	10	0	2	13	0
Just, Mike, 2b	.336	330	56	111	24	4	4	55	20
Lawhorn, Darryl, 3b	.280	186	33	52	11	2	10	38	1
Lopez, Robbie, c	.000	1	0	0	0	0	0	0	0
Mathis, Joe, of	.305	380	77	116	21	8	17	70	16
★Maxwell, Keith, 1b	.313	16	2	5	0	0	1	1	0
Maycock, Dan, of	.299	107	19	32	11	1	0	17	0
Meadows, Tydus, of	.301	332	74	100	19	0	17	59	4
Melo, Juan, 1b	.262	84	13	22	6	0	1	8	3
★Munhall, Brian, c	.289	128	20	37	6	1	0	15	3
Munoz, Billy, 1b	.294	170	30	50	10	0	9	35	0
Salazar, Ruben, 3b	.317	312	51	99	15	0	10	61	1
★Shorsher, Adam, c	.216	199	32	43	15	0	4	25	0
Sullivan, Jared, of	.150	20	1	3	0	0	0	2	0
Wayment, Kory, ss	.285	383	56	109	20	4	5	55	12
Weber, Jon, of	.283	60	10	17	5	0	1	10	2

PITCHERS	W	L	ERA	G	SV	IP	H	BB	SO
Cotton, Nate	3	3	2.44	42	22	44	33	19	39
★Culp, Brandon	0	0	7.71	4	0	9	14	4	4
George, Todd	3	4	5.09	10	0	58	62	33	27
Goltz, Brandon	2	1	7.01	9	0	26	37	17	17
Harmsen, Brandon	0	2	2.65	12	0	17	16	6	13
Hewitt, Brian	0	0	0.00	1	0	0	1	0	1
★Howerton, John	0	0	11.57	2	0	5	12	1	3
★Lawson, Brett	1	1	4.15	14	0	26	22	25	24
Maycock, Dan	0	0	9.00	2	0	3	4	2	0
Michael, Mark	4	6	5.00	18	0	94	95	50	59
Peschel, Mike	7	4	4.58	13	0	71	78	36	48
Renkert, Dane	13	1	3.94	19	0	121	108	47	92
Rowe, Adam	5	6	1.94	46	1	70	63	25	44
Schutt, Jason	5	3	3.29	39	0	66	56	17	28
Sergent, Joe	7	1	3.80	13	0	71	65	35	57
Shaw, Joshua	0	0	10.13	1	0	3	8	1	0
Simpson, Gerrit	4	7	5.24	22	0	93	96	43	53
Young, Doug	3	1	4.20	41	0	60	70	21	41

GARY SOUTHSHORE RAILCATS

BATTER	AVG	AB	R	H	2B	3B	HR	RBI	SB
Allensworth, Jermaine, of	.278	309	46	86	12	0	2	35	12
Blakeley, Eric, 1b	.238	160	21	38	3	2	1	13	1
Detienne, Dave, 1b	.286	332	40	95	12	6	2	46	12
Haake, Steve, of	.282	348	59	98	25	4	4	49	21
McNamee, Eric, 2b	.263	361	50	95	10	1	0	36	7
Mueller, Dale, of	.258	209	20	54	3	1	1	22	15
Pecci, Jay, ss	.266	364	54	97	11	7	5	43	10
Price, Nate, of	.254	248	44	63	14	4	6	39	13
Reese, Mike, of	.280	164	30	46	6	4	5	31	5
Senjem, Jose, of	.158	19	1	3	0	0	0	1	0
Townsend, Tanner, 3b	.267	374	47	100	27	2	4	44	10
Wallace, Brett, c	.210	62	8	13	0	0	1	4	1
Yepez, Jose, c	.272	294	43	80	22	1	6	56	1

PITCHERS	W	L	ERA	G	SV	IP	H	BB	SO
Blackwell, Chad	4	0	1.09	29	4	41	25	14	38
Brinkmann, Matt	1	0	1.40	15	0	19	14	6	17
Brown, Jared	1	0	10.13	10	0	13	20	11	6
Byard, David	3	0	2.47	36	0	44	36	24	40
Cogan, Tony	1	6	2.77	46	25	49	45	13	31
Crowell, Jim	0	1	4.02	12	1	16	20	2	5
Edsall, Steve	2	3	5.24	31	0	34	40	29	15
Glen, Willie	12	1	3.03	23	0	140	111	36	162
Habel, Josh	12	7	2.96	24	0	155	130	46	105
Kerber, Travis	8	7	4.75	18	0	108	123	29	50
McElwain, Logan	0	0	0.00	1	0	1	1	0	0
Mueller, Dale	0	0	3.00	3	0	3	4	1	1
Mumma, Brad	1	3	4.66	35	0	37	40	17	20
Obenchain, Steve	2	1	3.31	20	0	35	29	13	28
Paduch, Jim	3	5	5.23	12	0	64	67	34	29
Panozzo, Joe	1	0	13.50	5	0	5	8	5	2
Shelley, Jason	7	4	4.85	17	0	95	90	44	56
Stipovich, Cole	0	0	16.20	5	0	3	10	2	2
Wallace, Brett	0	0	0.00	1	0	1	0	1	1

PITCHERS	W	L	ERA	G	SV	IP	H	BB	SO
Boughner, Anthony	8	5	5.50	20	0	129	152	33	58
Braxton, Larkin	1	3	12.23	5	0	18	34	13	11
Caughey, Trevor	0	4	5.85	12	0	40	49	23	31
Core, Danny	4	1	3.57	33	0	40	39	14	53
Costi, Justin	2	1	5.94	9	0	17	20	8	6
Dehart, Rick	2	4	4.62	6	0	37	38	21	14
Delgado, Mario	0	0	3.00	2	1	3	5	0	2
Durost, Kenny	6	5	6.14	19	0	92	99	69	60
Gord, Nelson	0	0	4.50	2	0	2	3	1	0
Hummel, Rick	0	0	9.00	5	0	12	19	5	6
Jackson, Dan	1	6	8.69	35	7	79	106	45	55
★Jenkins, Raymond	1	1	6.26	15	0	23	23	13	11
Kramer, Sean	0	0	4.26	6	0	6	5	5	5
Krawczyk, Christopher	7	5	5.35	27	0	116	136	43	57
Krysa, Jonathan	1	6	9.42	9	0	43	57	44	21
Lewis, Lavon	3	3	5.93	17	0	58	70	21	35
Reid, Brett	3	4	5.40	17	0	20	21	12	17
Schlichting, Travis	1	2	5.29	41	0	51	72	29	47
Schweitzer, Matt	4	2	1.84	46	7	54	39	19	68
Watson, Rob	0	0	0.00	4	0	5	3	0	4

JOLIET JACKHAMMERS

BATTER	AVG	AB	R	H	2B	3B	HR	RBI	SB
Blackmon, Dennis, c	.289	284	37	82	10	1	9	40	0
Brown, Chris, 2b	.263	338	54	89	21	3	10	47	14
Diaz, Juan, 1b	.358	383	74	137	19	1	28	80	1
Ehrnsberger, Chad, 3b	.283	315	49	89	24	2	11	63	0
Harris, Cory, of	.297	374	76	111	23	3	16	57	8
Hutting, Tim, ss	.281	391	65	110	17	2	4	48	1
Lopez, Javier, of	.174	86	6	15	4	1	0	10	2
Mazurek, Matt, of	.333	39	7	13	4	0	0	6	3
★Monegan, Anthony, of	.251	235	34	59	6	3	2	18	9
Mosby, Bobby, 1b	.342	38	4	13	1	0	1	6	0
Nicholson, Derek, 1b	.294	313	51	92	15	3	14	54	1
Scriven, Eric, of	.270	248	29	67	7	0	1	20	6
Sullivan, Kevin, of	.226	159	18	36	8	0	3	24	1
Wayne, Nicholas, c	.286	14	2	4	0	0	0	1	0
Whitesides, Jake, of	.284	141	21	40	4	4	1	17	9
Zeedyk, Eric, c	.000	4	0	0	0	0	0	0	0

PITCHERS	W	L	ERA	G	SV	IP	H	BB	SO
Bunyan, Brian	0	0	19.29	2	0	2	6	4	5
Cierlik, Jason	1	0	1.15	9	0	16	8	14	13
Eddy, Cooper	0	0	45.00	2	0	1	5	1	1
Ellison, Derrick	5	2	3.35	44	3	54	37	32	59
Fiske, Justin	0	0	4.50	4	0	6	6	2	0
Forystek, Brian	4	4	2.73	16	0	82	72	33	70
Garcia, James	0	3	7.20	5	0	25	38	10	15
Harmelink, Michael	0	0	36.00	1	0	1	1	3	0
Harris, Mark	1	0	9.00	1	0	1	1	3	0
Jenkins, Raymond	2	8	6.64	13	0	64	88	42	52
Kleine, Victor	0	1	4.50	2	0	10	15	4	9
Patterson, Lonnie	0	0	5.11	9	0	12	10	7	16
Petrusek, Matt	1	2	3.46	41	11	52	54	10	42
Regits, Josh	2	4	6.10	8	0	41	45	25	16
Renault, Nick	5	6	5.08	12	0	73	72	47	51
★Russell, Steve	0	1	6.88	13	0	17	16	14	18
Sevier, Nate	13	4	4.66	20	0	126	126	37	91
Smith, Matt	6	8	5.25	20	0	123	149	35	43
Tucker, Glenn	0	1	6.14	11	0	15	20	5	9
Williams, Aaron	4	4	3.16	47	4	63	64	21	41
Zaleski, Kyle	1	2	4.02	23	0	40	40	23	42
★Ziegler, Dan	1	0	5.31	6	0	20	18	15	13

KANSAS CITY T-BONES

BATTER	AVG	AB	R	H	2B	3B	HR	RBI	SB
Arlis, Patrick, c	.262	168	22	44	10	0	1	19	2
Belcher, Jason, c	.243	136	20	33	4	0	1	12	0
Benjamin, Al, of	.285	260	49	74	23	3	12	50	1
Brown, Neb, 3b	.314	366	68	115	22	3	8	62	22
Correll, Brad, of	.333	96	22	32	6	1	6	17	2
Delgado, Mario, 1b	.341	399	57	136	32	2	15	81	1
Easley, Austin, of	.263	224	45	59	12	1	4	30	8
Eggleston, Aharon, of	.321	336	66	108	20	5	1	62	22
Gord, Nelson, of	.269	227	41	61	13	1	5	27	6
Jaros, Nick, of	.299	67	14	20	5	0	2	10	5
Jones, J.J., of	.118	17	2	2	0	0	0	0	0
Jones, Josiah, dh	.000	2	0	0	0	0	0	0	0
McCallum, Geoff, ss	.275	265	48	73	12	0	1	28	7
McIntire, Jeremy, c	.111	9	0	1	0	0	0	0	0
Mendez, Donaldo, ss	.235	81	14	19	3	2	0	12	1
Parzyk, Dylan, c	.150	20	1	3	0	0	1	2	0
Pickering, Calvin	.310	316	59	98	20	1	18	83	7
Schlichting, Travis, 3b	.200	15	1	3	1	0	0	1	0
Watson, Rob, 2b	.343	385	80	132	29	2	8	72	5

SCHAUMBURG FLYERS

BATTER	AVG	AB	R	H	2B	3B	HR	RBI	SB
Almonte, Sandy, ss	.317	186	28	59	12	3	3	24	20
Bass, Kevin, 1b	.217	83	7	18	4	0	2	12	0
Burgos, Victor, of	.182	22	3	4	1	0	1	1	0
★Chappell, Dan, 1b	.200	5	0	1	1	0	0	2	0
Delgado, Dario, 3b	.253	257	32	65	9	1	6	39	11
Derhak, Alex, c	.236	157	17	37	5	0	4	21	0
Fonseca, Alex, ss	.280	75	12	21	4	0	2	14	4
Heath, Demetrius, 2b	.318	283	57	90	10	2	3	22	26
Hoffman, David, c	.286	70	12	20	3	0	1	9	2
★House, Kevin, of	.230	135	17	31	3	0	2	7	8
★Hurst, Jimmy, of	.374	147	21	55	6	0	7	31	4
Landry, Mike, c	.111	18	0	2	0	0	0	0	0
Leon, Kyle, of	.256	160	16	41	5	0	6	25	4
Malone, Billy, of	.234	342	47	80	15	1	7	32	19
Matlock, Robert, of	.299	67	8	20	1	0	0	8	6
★Maxwell, Keith, 1b	.232	99	7	23	6	0	1	11	1
★Monegan, Anthony, of	.235	136	26	32	5	3	3	12	7
Morrison, Bryce, of	.214	42	7	9	2	1	1	4	1
Noviskey, Josh, c	.234	111	13	26	1	0	1	17	0
O'Sullivan, Patrick, 1b	.309	272	47	84	21	0	14	53	3
Riggs, Eric, ss	.444	9	4	4	1	0	0	1	1
Rohde, Mike, 2b	.318	245	42	78	15	4	2	32	6
Snavely, Christian, of	.265	351	62	93	18	1	11	63	6

PITCHERS	W	L	ERA	G	SV	IP	H	BB	SO
Adamczyk, Tyler	0	2	11.63	11	0	22	37	22	10
Bryant, John	1	23.63	2	0	3	5	3	2	
★Culp, Brandon	0	4	6.00	27	0	51	62	23	32
Davis, Vince	0	1	13.50	2	0	3	6	0	1
Dickinson, Drew	7	12	6.42	21	0	116	167	48	62
Dunnett, Randy	0	1	7.71	7	0	16	16	10	5
Fontana, Rob	0	0	3.60	7	0	10	9	5	6
Grybash, Dan	9	5	3.39	22	0	135	123	46	100
Harris, Nat	9	7	4.90	22	0	121	137	45	58
Harris, Ryan	1	5	6.30	7	0	40	54	15	28
★Howerton, John	0	0	10.13	3	0	3	7	6	0
Keppinger, Billy	5	7	4.10	18	0	112	118	32	77
Litchfield, B.J.	0	0	10.13	3	0	3	5	4	1
Madej, Ronald	0	0	21.60	2	0	2	1	5	0
Martin, Brian	0	1	14.00	9	0	9	12	12	6
Morrison, James	6	5	3.77	52	16	60	58	28	60
Pence, Howard	0	0	8.10	2	0	3	5	3	1
Piekarz, Joe	0	0	14.54	4	0	4	8	4	3
Popp, Jim	0	0	9.00	3	0	2	6	1	2
Robinson, Justin	0	0	5.79	12	0	19	19	10	11
Toohey, John	0	3	6.95	31	0	45	49	27	48
Villafuerte, Brandon	1	1	1.08	39	1	50	37	17	50
Wieda, Michael	0	0	0.00	1	0	0	2	0	0
Yano, Eiji	1	2	11.91	8	0	11	23	8	6
★Ziegler, Dan	0	0	0.00	1	0	1	1	2	0

WINNIPEG GOLDEYES

BATTER	AVG	AB	R	H	2B	3B	HR	RBI	SB
Alen, Luis, c	.333	285	43	95	23	1	3	44	2
Coughlan, Cameron, of	.225	89	14	20	2	0	1	10	10
French, Antoin, of	.275	138	25	38	4	3	5	20	10
Gray, Antoin, 2b	.285	344	59	98	20	1	12	53	8
★Hurst, Jimmy, of	.236	123	23	29	6	2	4	20	2
Latham, Chris, of	.300	237	51	71	16	0	13	46	16
Lentini, Fehlandt, of	.321	405	86	130	36	7	10	54	42
★Lundberg, Jordan, c	.232	69	12	16	1	0	3	9	0

BATTER	AVG	AB	R	H	2B	3B	HR	RBI	SB
★McEachran, Aaron, 1b....	.250	92	11	23	5	0	1	11	0
Metheny, Brent, 3b........	.304	326	68	99	21	0	21	70	17
Poulin, Max, ss	.283	325	53	92	14	7	6	48	6
Schade, Scott, 1b........	.244	221	24	54	11	0	3	31	2
Smith, Demond, of.......	.391	87	23	34	5	2	4	20	7
Stang, Corey, of........	.295	105	18	31	7	2	0	10	3
Young, Walter, 1b.......	.313	383	54	120	13	0	21	78	2
★Ziegler, Dan, of	.250	12	4	3	2	0	0	2	0

PITCHERS	W	L	ERA	G	SV	IP	H	BB	SO
Acosta, Nibaldo	1	0	3.07	9	0	15	16	5	4
Ariail, Ryan..............	2	1	5.13	42	1	47	49	29	46
Basilio, Manny	0	3	13.97	6	0	10	16	9	9
Beuning, Brian	0	2	3.95	36	0	41	43	25	43
Bicknell, Greg...........	0	3	4.91	5	0	29	35	9	15
Blitstein, Jeffrey	4	1	4.11	7	0	46	49	12	13
Bott, Glenn..............	3	3	5.51	12	0	64	75	25	44
Davis, Matt..............	6	2	2.98	44	18	45	43	26	41
Herman, Jason...........	0	1	8.31	6	0	13	22	5	4
Kintzler, Brandon	5	2	4.07	29	1	77	78	13	41
Kusiewicz, Mike	7	4	4.20	14	0	84	106	20	52
★Lawson, Brett	4	3	4.43	9	0	43	36	35	42
★Lundberg, Jordan	0	0	0.00	1	0	1	1	0	0
Moore, Benjamin	8	7	5.06	20	0	116	135	39	101
Pease, Dustin	1	2	3.26	29	0	30	23	18	21
Pendarvis, Chad..........	0	0	20.25	2	0	1	2	1	1
Posey, Joel..............	8	6	4.81	21	0	116	134	65	89
Poulin, Max	0	0	0.00	1	0	1	0	0	0
Rapp, Randy	1	2	5.70	22	0	30	39	18	23
★Russell, Steve	1	1	8.00	9	0	9	13	9	9
Velazquez, Juan	0	0	17.47	5	0	6	18	2	4
★Ziegler, Dan	0	0	9.35	6	0	9	10	6	7

UNITED LEAGUE

The Alexandria Aces are still the only champ in United League history after winning their second straight title. Alexandria was the league's dominant team and headed into the playoffs in fine fashion, going 33-13 over the second half. They were so dominant that no other team in the league finished above .500 during the second half. Aces manager Ricky VanAsselberg had told the local paper before the series began that he knew he would be branded as a choke artist if his team didn't win the title, but he didn't need to worry. They wrapped up the title by sweeping Rio Grande Valley in the championship series outscoring the WhiteWings 33-11.

FIRST HALF	W	L	PCT	GB
Rio Grande	29	21	.569	
Alexandria	27	22	.560	1½
Amarillo	26	24	.510	3
Edinburg	25	25	.510	4
San Angelo	22	28	.431	7
Laredo	20	29	.420	8½

SECOND HALF	W	L	PCT	GB
Alexandria	33	13	.717	
San Angelo	22	23	.489	10½
Rio Grande	21	24	.467	11½
Amarillo	21	24	.467	11½
Laredo	21	25	.457	12
Edinburg	18	27	.400	14½

PLAYOFFS: Alexandria swept Rio Grande Valley 4-0 in best-of-seven series. **MANAGERS: Alexandria**—Ricky VanAsselberg; **Amarillo**—Buddy Biancalana; **Edinburg**—Vince Moore; **Laredo**—Angel Davilla; **San Angelo**—Doc Edwards; **Rio Grande Valley**—Eddie Dennis.
ATTENDANCE: Amarillo 153,262; **San Angelo** 106,411; **Edinburg** 85,566; Rio Grande 74,663; Alexandria 71,204; Laredo 57,908
Most Valuable Player: Nelson Teilon, Edinburg. **Pitcher of the Year:** Adam Cox, Alexandria. **Rookie of the Year:** Ronnie Gaines, San Angelo. **Manager of the Year:** Ricky VanAsselberg, Alexandria.

BATTER, CLUB	AVG	G	AB	R	H	HR	RBI
Teilon, Nilson, Edinburg	.364	91	374	62	136	21	95
Langague, Selwyn , Alexandria	.353	93	382	72	135	9	80
Bravo, Danny, Amarillo............	.344	95	384	73	132	13	83
Medina, Rodney., Edinburg	.340	85	338	53	115	0	29
Gaines, Ronny, San Angelo	.334	94	404	77	135	19	53
Schneidmiller, Gary., Amarillo......	.332	86	316	60	105	7	65
Wenger, Justin, Amarillo..........	.329	80	307	65	101	4	44
Paz, Richard, Alexandria	.323	93	325	82	105	10	60
Tranum, Josh, Alexandria..........	.321	88	312	53	100	4	65
Rodriguez, Andres, San Angelo	.320	95	362	57	116	12	53

PITCHER, CLUB	W	L	ERA	IP	H	BB	SO
★Cox, Adam, Alexandria	12	2	2.38	106	87	46	117

BATTER	AVG	AB	R	H	2B	3B	HR	RBI	SB
Massetti, Luke, San Angelo	.8	4	2.51	100	98	15	102		
★Rogers, Joseph, Rio Grande Valley .11	3	3.25	122	118	23	95			
Hernandez, Santos, Laredo	.9	4	3.28	110	100	39	123		
Montoya, Eric, Edinburg..........	.6	4	3.54	89	75	42	83		
★Arroyo, Luis, Laredo	.8	4	3.55	124	126	63	128		
Guerra, Aaron, Edinburg	.9	3	3.68	103	114	23	95		
Duff, Matthew, San Angelo.........	.8	6	3.69	105	94	32	95		
★Williams, Julian, Rio Grande Valley . .6	5	3.73	82	86	45	59			
★James, Frank, Alexandria	.9	5	3.95	96	110	43	82		

AMARILLO DILLAS

BATTER	AVG	AB	R	H	2B	3B	HR	RBI	SB
Ashton, Josh, ss	.280	325	49	91	13	5	2	46	8
★Bonner, Adam, 1b	.229	48	4	11	3	0	0	9	0
Bravo, Danny, of.........	.344	384	73	132	27	3	13	83	14
Chapman, Jack, 1b.......	.258	252	33	65	15	1	5	48	4
Cleary, Dan, of	.000	5	1	0	0	0	0	0	0
Crespi, Ryan, of	.333	54	10	18	1	2	0	5	2
★Donahoo, Brett, of......	.283	272	54	77	21	6	7	54	13
Figueroa, Carlos, 2b......	.314	370	74	116	12	1	5	54	16
Hitchcock, Brendon, 1b ...	.329	82	24	27	5	0	0	15	1
Jackson, Drew	.000	1	0	0	0	0	0	0	0
Knippling, Cole, 1b.......	.000	2	0	0	0	0	0	0	0
Marshall, Jonathan, c.....	.194	31	3	6	1	0	0	3	0
Moore, Kevin, of.........	.172	29	5	5	2	0	0	4	0
Owens, Ricky, 3b	.298	151	34	45	14	0	4	32	1
★Padilla, Ericnardo, ss....	.500	2	0	1	1	0	0	0	0
Parker, Carnell, of	.231	13	2	3	0	1	0	0	0
Ramos, Jordan, 2b.......	.283	290	60	82	13	3	4	34	11
Reynoso, Jonathan, of....	.271	332	58	90	19	2	9	58	17
Schneidmiller, Gary, 3b ...	.332	316	60	105	23	3	7	65	23
Shay, Nick, 1b	.253	83	12	21	2	1	1	10	4
Wenger, Justin, c	.329	307	65	101	15	2	4	44	8

PITCHERS	W	L	ERA	G	SV	IP	H	BB	SO
Allen, Kyle	6	7	5.60	20	0	100	140	47	88
Allen, Taylor.............	9	8	4.26	21	0	133	148	61	101
Bogart, Brady	0	0	0.00	1	0	1	2	0	0
Bravo, Danny	0	0	9.00	1	0	1	2	0	1
Burger, Nick	3	2	5.47	31	5	53	72	24	37
★Cassidy, Kevin	0	1	7.84	11	0	10	18	13	7
Caughey, Trevor	0	1	5.87	3	0	15	21	6	16
★Chitwood, Josh	0	0	10.80	4	0	5	10	0	2
★Donahoo, Brett	0	0	3.00	2	0	3	3	4	4
★Ferrand, Dario	1	2	6.31	6	0	26	32	13	18
Funk, Shane	0	0	0.00	1	0	0	0	2	0
Green, Glenn	0	0	2.08	3	0	4	4	2	4
Griffin, Charles	6	3	4.42	9	0	59	70	13	40
Irby, Mike...............	1	2	5.34	21	0	29	44	8	21
Jackson, Drew	5	5	2.45	42	5	66	60	18	76
Jessee, Clay	0	0	36.00	2	0	1	2	3	0
★Jordan, Robert	1	1	3.46	2	0	13	16	5	7
Kirsch, Brad	0	0	0.00	2	0	1	0	2	1
Lawrence, Matt	1	0	10.29	4	0	7	8	4	6
Lugo, Jorge	5	5	3.97	14	0	82	84	32	67
Morrison, Shawn	4	4	4.53	17	0	52	64	25	30
Myers, Josh	1	0	1.56	2	0	17	14	6	12
Nieto, Jose..............	1	2	5.65	20	0	43	54	16	29
Pearson, Craig	1	0	6.07	3	0	13	16	13	13
Pierzchala, Eric	0	1	10.50	2	0	6	6	7	1
Switala, Stan	0	0	0.00	1	0	0	0	2	0
Vazquez, John	0	0	1.42	7	0	13	12	4	11
Waters, Christopher	2	5	5.25	27	2	72	66	43	43

ALEXANDRIA ACES

BATTER	AVG	AB	R	H	2B	3B	HR	RBI	SB
Burwell, Wilson, 3b	.253	194	28	49	11	0	5	29	2
Cherry, Evan, of	.234	239	31	56	17	1	1	24	3
Fitzpatrick, Edward, c......	.200	120	13	24	4	1	0	13	1
Guance, Walkill, 2b	.293	341	66	100	16	1	11	48	39
Karr, Palmer, of	.276	381	59	105	23	0	18	86	11
Langague, Selwyn, of	.353	382	72	135	25	1	9	80	11
★Lewis, Marcus, of	.161	56	8	9	0	0	1	4	6
Macilvane, Kevin, c	.202	104	15	21	3	0	2	15	1
Paz, Richard, ss	.323	325	82	105	28	2	10	60	2
Pendergrass, Tyrone, of...	.286	196	44	56	5	2	3	14	19
Rivero, Sergio, of	.250	16	2	4	1	0	1	3	0
Sabatella, Bryan, 3b......	.313	352	59	110	20	4	5	53	32
Tranum, Josh, of	.321	312	53	100	24	0	4	65	4
Turney, Brad, 1b.........	.200	70	10	14	3	0	0	8	1
Umbria, Jose, c	.246	134	22	33	4	0	0	12	0

PITCHERS	W	L	ERA	G	SV	IP	H	BB	SO
Bengel, Buddy	5	4	5.13	19	0	107	121	35	96
★Bonilla, Danny...........	0	1	11.45	5	0	11	19	8	12

INDEPENDENT LEAGUES

	W	L	ERA	G	SV	IP	H	BB	SO
Bridges, Donnie	1	2	7.23	12	0	24	26	21	32
Bunyan, Brian	3	2	5.59	13	0	37	42	16	30
★Cassidy, Kevin	0	1	6.23	7	0	9	12	8	4
★Chitwood, Josh	0	0	5.00	7	0	9	6	4	3
Cox, Adam	12	2	2.38	17	0	106	87	46	117
Dowdy, Justin	2	3	1.37	48	24	53	21	22	102
Foster, Charles	3	0	2.60	22	0	35	33	13	39
Frey, Adam	6	3	5.18	21	1	89	114	36	66
Galarraga, Luis	7	4	4.53	24	0	95	111	40	70
Hopes, Justin	0	0	16.20	3	0	2	7	1	1
James, Frank	9	5	3.95	17	0	96	110	43	82
Matos, Josue	0	1	7.56	2	0	8	10	4	9
Moody, Jason	1	2	5.40	10	0	12	15	5	7
Nolen, Walt	4	2	5.50	35	0	52	65	29	61
Ovalles, Juan	6	2	4.06	55	5	69	52	27	115
Pendarvis, Chad	0	0	21.60	2	0	3	6	5	5
Tranum, Josh	0	0	9.00	1	0	1	2	0	2
Turney, Brad	1	0	3.86	6	0	7	7	5	4
Valera, Yuery	0	1	7.36	3	0	4	5	4	2

LAREDO BRONCOS

BATTER	AVG	AB	R	H	2B	3B	HR	RBI	SB
Cepeda, Benigro, of	.125	8	0	1	0	0	0	2	0
Clemente, Edgard, of	.309	152	25	47	11	0	8	27	0
Cruz, Orlando, of	.353	136	12	48	8	0	1	17	5
★Devarie, Jm, ss	.227	203	35	46	6	1	1	17	10
Judkins, Chris, of	.195	169	26	33	5	1	1	13	15
★Kealy, Greg, 2b	.105	19	1	2	1	0	0	1	0
★Kottke, Ryan, c	.277	65	8	18	2	1	0	8	0
Lebron, Hector, 1b	.266	184	23	49	11	0	2	27	3
Lebron, Juan, of	.291	330	46	96	21	1	15	62	10
Lopez, Javier, of	.314	220	35	69	13	2	3	28	7
Lopez, Paul, 3b	.000	6	1	0	0	0	0	0	0
Lopez, Pedro, ss	.280	254	52	71	12	1	1	17	20
Maldonado, Edwin, 2b	.312	349	66	109	27	4	10	68	10
Marrero, Jonathan, c	.163	43	5	7	1	0	0	6	1
★McGuire, Cameron, c	.260	208	36	54	15	0	7	40	3
★Nichols, Brian, 1b	.197	76	7	15	1	0	1	8	1
Ponce, Arnoldo, ss	.296	27	3	8	1	0	0	3	0
Ramos, Luis, of	.257	175	32	45	6	1	1	17	8
Reyes, Ivan, 3b	.225	329	44	74	8	1	13	42	13
Rosa, Randy, c	.218	110	14	24	3	0	2	14	1
Sanders, Nick, 2b	.263	19	1	5	1	0	0	0	0
★Senreiso, Juan, of	.325	83	19	27	5	0	3	17	10

PITCHERS	W	L	ERA	G	SV	IP	H	BB	SO
Alvarez, Mark	1	2	8.59	12	0	15	25	9	8
Arroyo, Luis	8	4	3.55	18	0	124	126	63	128
Cepeda, Benigno	3	4	6.35	11	1	45	65	18	39
Cordero, Jose	6	6	5.74	19	0	107	121	67	121
Cotto, Giovanni	0	0	0.00	1	0	0	2		1
Daly, Brian	4	7	5.00	22	4	94	113	41	55
★Gibson, Kyle	1	2	4.50	29	0	36	46	16	43
Hernandez, Santos	9	4	3.28	17	0	109.2	100	39	123
Jimenez, Juan	2	3	7.58	10	0	38	55	26	32
Johnson, Brian	0	3	12.51	3	0	14	30	11	6
★Jones, Rustin	0	2	3.45	30	1	29	28	11	30
Laurel, Albert	0	2	6.89	15	0	31	44	10	23
Lozado, Henry	4	5	5.37	32	10	54	52	21	64
Martin, Brandon	0	0	5.06	11	0	16	20	11	12
Parfett, Rob	0	5	7.16	9	0	33	53	12	18
Ramos, Luis	0	0	8.10	3	0	3	10	3	1
Rosa, Ramesis	1	2	6.46	7	0	24	34	12	12
Rosa, Randy	0	0	5.63	6	0	8	9	3	3
Smith, John	2	3	5.57	23	2	21	18	14	34

RIO GRANDE VALLEY WHITEWINGS

BATTER	AVG	AB	R	H	2B	3B	HR	RBI	SB
Acey, Jermy, 2b	.327	101	16	33	9	0	4	20	2
★Beal, John, 2b	.275	40	8	11	1	0	0	2	4
Bergstrom, Bub, of	.263	338	80	89	10	4	0	33	37
Bramasco, Omar, ss	.294	327	59	96	27	3	11	53	13
Cardona, David, of	.308	104	18	32	6	0	4	18	6
★Devarie, Jim, 1b	.000	0	1	0	0	0	0	0	0
Encarnacion, Teodoro, of	.161	93	9	15	4	0	2	3	2
Fox, Ryan, 3b	.275	338	69	93	29	0	23	83	6
Griffin, Kevin, c	.291	182	34	53	11	0	3	20	12
★Kottke, Ryan, c	.200	70	7	14	3	0	1	11	0
Martinez, Alejandro, 1b	.296	199	16	59	14	1	2	24	3
McLain, Sam, of	.250	280	34	70	15	4	4	36	3

	AVG	AB	R	H	2B	3B	HR	RBI	SB
★Nichols, Brian, 1b	.330	182	30	60	6	5	6	34	5
★Padilla, Ericnardo, ss	.308	52	12	16	2	0	0	8	7
Peguero, Miguel, 3b	.271	343	50	93	14	2	8	60	2
Piper Jordan, Andre, of	.287	216	43	62	16	3	3	23	16
Revall, Andrew, of	.000	7	1	0	0	0	0	0	0
Reynoso, Danilo, c	.215	107	13	23	4	1	5	17	1
Rosario, Samuel, 2b	.242	33	4	8	1	0	0	4	3
Sanchez, Luany, of	.250	96	8	24	5	0	3	9	1
Valdez, Jesus, of	.000	6	0	0	0	0	0	0	0

PITCHERS	W	L	ERA	G	SV	IP	H	BB	SO
★Ahrendt, Bryce	0	0	11.25	6	0	8	18	7	12
Bennett, Derek	4	2	0.71	35	22	38	21	13	31
Bergstrom, Bub	0	0	0.00	1	0	1	2	0	0
★Bonilla, Danny	2	7	6.72	14	0	71	79	43	44
Corchado, Jose	1	0	8.59	6	0	7	4	14	8
Cordero, Angel	1	2	7.76	6	0	27	37	19	14
Cress, Joseph	4	7	7.12	17	0	86	120	41	48
Darling, Bobby	4	1	7.29	18	0	42	54	27	19
Delacruz, Maximino	6	7	4.36	18	0	105	112	36	89
Evangelista, Antonio	0	0	5.73	4	0	11	11	11	8
Evoniuk, Kenny	3	3	4.97	16	0	42	34	36	40
Frias, Jusef	0	0	8.00	7	1	9	10	16	8
Fulcher, Brian	1	1	9.90	5	0	10	20	4	8
Gale, Chris	6	3	4.81	24	1	58	75	14	54
Giron, Ysabel	0	2	15.43	3	0	7	16	5	5
Lutz, Todd	1	2	3.95	26	1	57	64	26	47
Matta, Felix	0	0	7.80	11	0	15	17	12	8
★Nichols, Brian	0	0	0.00	1	0	0	3	2	0
Peguero, Miguel	0	0	0.00	1	0	1	1	0	1
Rogers, Joseph	11	3	3.25	18	0	122	118	23	95
Williams, Julian	6	5	3.73	20	0	82	86	45	59

SAN ANGELO COLTS

BATTER	AVG	AB	R	H	2B	3B	HR	RBI	SB
Allan, Josh, c	.271	188	28	51	15	1	7	30	0
★Allen, Eric, 1b	.322	143	18	46	10	1	2	20	0
Anderson, John, 2b	.292	137	18	40	8	1	0	25	7
★Beal, John, 2b	.230	200	34	46	8	1	0	11	19
Crosland, Jason, 1b	.305	334	61	102	15	1	17	73	1
Dennis, Bernard, c	.136	22	2	3	1	0	0	1	0
Diaz, Jason, 2b	.290	124	23	36	5	1	0	12	5
Diggs, Wyn, c	.234	64	7	15	4	0	0	9	0
★Donahoo, Brett, of	.306	72	10	22	4	0	3	9	2
Edwards, Madison, of	.297	148	17	44	14	0	3	22	3
Gaines, Ronny, of	.334	404	77	135	26	10	19	53	29
Harryman, Eric, ss	.198	121	17	24	7	1	1	9	2
Hicks, Billie, ss	.270	37	8	10	1	1	0	3	1
Hollingsworth, Josh, 3b	.246	126	20	31	7	0	4	13	0
★Kealy, Greg, ss	.310	29	4	9	3	0	0	2	1
Landry, Michael, c	.202	109	8	22	5	2	0	16	0
★Lewis, Marcus, of	.245	98	16	24	4	0	0	10	4
Miller, Jamie, 3b	.100	20	0	2	0	0	0	0	0
Mongiardo, Chris, c	.000	5	0	0	0	0	0	1	0
Morrison, Bryce, of	.275	280	42	77	15	3	6	39	10
Rhomberg, Joe, 2b	.288	52	3	15	5	0	0	11	0
Roberson, Trey, of	.291	86	17	25	5	0	3	11	2
Rodriguez, Andres, 1b	.320	362	57	116	16	2	12	53	1
Ryan, Tim, of	.176	17	2	3	1	0	0	1	0
Torres, Jose, 3b	.257	74	16	19	4	1	2	6	3

PITCHERS	W	L	ERA	G	SV	IP	H	BB	SO
★Ahrendt, Bryce	0	1	4.24	6	0	17	16	9	13
Artz, Stephen	1	4	2.86	25	10	28	26	3	46
Boutwell, Brad	0	0	4.15	3	0	4	2	3	1
★Chitwood, Josh	1	0	3.18	4	0	6	6	4	5
Duff, Matthew	8	6	3.69	18	0	105	94	32	95
Fleming, Taylor	3	1	1.93	25	1	47	32	16	45
★Flores, Neomar	0	1	8.22	5	0	8	9	4	10
Gaines, Ronny	0	1	5.40	1	0	2	2	1	1
★Gibson, Kyle	0	0	2.45	3	0	7	6	6	5
Greanead, Matt	0	0	1.80	5	0	5	8	7	4
Green, Brian	0	0	6.75	4	0	4	4	4	2
Henschel, Brian	8	7	4.62	20	0	129	158	17	88
★Jordan, Robert	1	8	4.31	14	0	79	95	21	85
Massetti, Luke	8	4	2.51	18	0	100	98	15	102
Monsma, Quinn	2	0	7.27	9	0	17	18	14	15
Mulle, Ryan	5	4	4.38	28	1	72	80	24	58
Rodgers, Caleb	3	1	5.58	9	0	40	51	10	23
Roque, Darryl	3	8	5.90	19	0	90	108	28	70
Vacek, Chase	1	5	2.25	39	9	48	46	10	48

INTERNATIONAL
BASEBALL

Cubans continue their dominance in Pan Ams

I n a relatively quiet year on the international front, Cuba still got an opportunity to flex its muscle.

Team USA's run through the Pan American Games ended in a manner that was all too familiar. Cuba, winner of all nine Pan Am baseball tournaments since 1967, made it 10 straight with a 3-1 win over the United States in Rio de Janeiro, Brazil.

It was deja vu all over again for Team USA, which also suffered a 3-1 loss to Cuba in the 2003 gold-medal game, when Jered Weaver was outdueled by 31-year-old Norge Vera. This time around, it was 36-year-old Cuban stalwart Adiel Palma beating 20-year-old Jacob Thompson, as Cuba's best faced a team of college players.

Professional players are eligible to play internationally—and indeed most other countries did send teams made up of pros—but the U.S. sends its college national team because the Pan Am Games no longer serve as an Olympic qualifier.

Palma limited the U.S. to a run on four hits over 7⅔ innings while striking out nine, before handing off to fellow veteran Pedro Luis Lazo, who struck out three in recording the last four outs. The U.S. has gotten to Lazo in other forums, including last fall in the Olympic qualifier and in the 2000 Olympic gold medal game, but this time he got the last laugh.

Team USA had its best chance to tie the game in the ninth when Pedro Alvarez (Vanderbilt) singled off Lazo with two outs. Justin Smoak (South Carolina), who was tied for the team lead with three home runs, flied out to center field to end the game.

"It was a tough loss, but I thought we played well," U.S. coach Mike Weathers (Long Beach State) said. "We couldn't solve their pitching. Both teams played very well. We should be very proud to win a silver medal. We overcame a lot and accomplished many things. These guys will take home a lot of memories."

The Cubans got to Thompson for two runs in the third inning on Alexander Mayeta's two-run double, and they tacked on another in the fourth, chasing Thompson. Team USA answered with its only run in the bottom of the fourth, when Jordan Danks led off with a double and Smoak singled him home.

The USA bullpen kept it close for the rest of the game, as Tyson Ross, Josh Romanski, Brett Hunter and Cody Satterwhite combined to pitch five shutout innings of relief, allowing just three hits while striking out five. Palma and Lazo were too much for Team USA's offense, which struck out 12 times without drawing a walk and managed just one hit after the fifth inning.

Palma has been Cuba's best lefthanded pitcher internationally for the last five years, and he was tailor-made to face a lefthanded-heavy American lineup.

The game started early on a Friday morning, after being delayed a day by rain, which is just one of many factors that plagued the tournament. If the delay had stretched much longer, the U.S. had considered forfeiting because of its commitments to play exhibition games in minor league

Vanderbilt's Pedro Alvarez was one of the offensive standouts for USA Baseball's college team

ROBERT GURGANUS

parks. Because of poor lighting, Team USA played all of its games during the day.

The U.S. won a doubleheader to advance to the championship round, beating host Brazil 7-5 and then edging past Mexico 2-1. Satterwhite (Mississippi) saved both ends of the doubleheader as the Americans moved to 4-0 in the event, with earlier victories against the Dominican Republic and Nicaragua.

Team USA Wraps Modest Season

USA Baseball's College national team then wrapped up its 37-game, 57-day schedule with a third-place finish in the World Port Tournament in the Netherlands. Team USA wore down toward the end of the summer, as power arms Lance Lynn, Brian Matusz and Jacob Thompson left the team prior to the trip to Rotterdam because of heavy workloads, and key offensive contributors Pedro Alvarez (arm) and Logan Forsythe (stress fracture in foot) were slowed by injuries at the end of the tournament. Consecutive losses to eventual champion Cuba and second-place Taiwan ended Team USA's run short of the finals.

Eric Campbell, USA Baseball's general manager of national teams, said the team's schedule was the toughest it had faced since 2004. As a result, the Americans lost their annual Japan Series for the first time ever on U.S. soil, then finished with a silver medal at the Pan American Games in Brazil en route to a 25-12 record on the summer. It was the first time since 1999 that Team USA reached double

INTERNATIONAL BASEBALL

digits in losses.

"We played a really good schedule, but it says that you're not just going to show up with Team USA and go 28-2, that's just not going to happen," Campbell said, referencing the team's record from 2006. "From my standpoint, I just wanted more. I'm not disappointed in them, I just wanted more from them on the field."

Rosters for the Pan Am games had to be submitted by June 11, so the team was selected without the benefit of trials, as in most years. Campbell said not having the trials made it difficult to determine which players were fresh and which were worn out, plus it eliminated a crucial aspect of competition vital to the national team experience. He said if a similar early roster deadline causes future issues, the national team will institute a fall trial.

New Leader For IBAF

The International Baseball Federation elected former U.S. Air Force general and Yankees executive Harvey Schiller as its new president. IBAF delegates chose Schiller, an American, over Cuba's Reynaldo Gonzalez Lopez and Netherlands broadcaster Theo Reitsma, who withdrew from the election prior to the balloting.

Schiller, whose 58 votes doubled the total of Lopez, replaces the late Aldo Notari, who died in July 2006.

In a statement released by USA Baseball, the new IBAF president said his main objective will be to get baseball back in the official Olympic program, and that the international baseball community must work together to achieve that goal.

Baseball will be in the 2008 Games (the U.S., Cuba and China are already in the eight-nation field), but is not scheduled to be in the Games thereafter—the sport was voted out of the Games in July 2005 (along with softball). USA Baseball executive director Paul Seiler said having Schiller on board makes the Olympic goal possible.

"Over the past six months our federation has had the pleasure of working with Harvey Schiller with the common goal of his election," Seiler said. "We have long believed Harvey is the right person to lead the IBAF during this exciting time for the sport of baseball internationally, and thus we are very pleased with the outcome of today's vote."

Schiller's primary task will be to lobby nations in anticipation of the next vote regarding the Olympic program, scheduled for October 2009 in Copenhagen, Denmark. At that time, the host city of the 2016 Games will be decided as well.

"It's probably unrealistic to try to get on the program for 2012 (in London)," Seiler said. "But what the game plan would be for 2016 is to support cities that are baseball friendly as hosts, such as the American bid (likely Chicago or Los Angeles) or Tokyo, and then to educate the voters about baseball to get it back in the games."

A former member of the NCAA Executive Committee, Schiller also worked with the United States Olympic Committee and has extensive experience with Olympic politics. In 1990 he was elected USOC executive director and secretary general, in which capacity he was involved with baseball's first appearance in the Olympic Games, in Barcelona in 1992. Schiller also has worked for YankeeNets (as chairman and CEO), the corporate parent of the Yankees, and in 2003 he was appointed to the independent commission studying the reorganization of the United States Olympic Committee.

"Harvey is an accomplished professional whose multifaceted career, Olympic experience and passion for our sport make him an outstanding choice to lead the IBAF," MLB commissioner Bud Selig said in a statement. "We share his desire to return baseball to the 2016 Olympic Games."

USA Baseball Opens Training Center

A shared vision of USA Baseball, Major League Baseball and the town of Cary, N.C., became reality. The ceremonial ribbon cutting by USA Baseball president Mike Gaski and Cary mayor Ernie McAlister marked the opening of the $11 million USA Baseball National Training Complex, which includes three training field and a main stadium with a full

COLLEGE NATIONAL TEAM STATISTICS

Player, Pos.	Year	School	AVG	AB	R	H	2B	3B	HR	RBI	SB
Josh Romanski, of/lhp	So.	San Diego	.333	54	10	18	6	0	0	8	3
Pedro Alvarez, 3b	So.	Vanderbilt	.315	127	23	40	9	0	7	30	5
Brett Wallace, of/1b	So.	Arizona State	.312	109	13	34	4	0	2	26	0
Logan Forsythe, of	So.	Arkansas	.309	94	19	29	6	0	1	16	6
Tommy Medica, c	Fr.	Santa Clara	.308	65	16	20	2	0	1	12	1
Jordan Danks, of	So.	Texas	.287	115	37	33	4	2	2	12	5
Ryan Flaherty, 2b	So.	Vanderbilt	.270	115	13	31	7	0	2	14	8
Kieschnick, Roger	So.	Texas Tech	.255	102	14	26	2	1	7	26	1
Jordy Mercer, ss/rhp	So.	Oklahoma State	.250	68	15	17	3	0	1	6	4
Justin Smoak, 1b	So.	South Carolina	.223	121	18	27	10	0	3	19	0
Danny Espinosa, ss	So.	Long Beach State	.215	79	11	17	2	0	0	8	3
Jeremy Hamilton, of	So.	Wright State	.209	43	8	9	1	0	0	5	3
Petey Paramore, c	So.	Arizona State	.111	63	9	7	1	0	0	3	1

Pitcher	Year	School	W	L	ERA	APP	SV	IP	H	BB	SO
Brett Hunter, rhp	So.	Pepperdine	3	0	0.66	14	1	27	10	13	31
Tyson Ross, rhp	So.	California	4	1	0.82	8	0	44	31	7	39
Scott Gorgen, rhp	So.	UC Irvine	1	1	0.84	2	0	11	9	1	18
Jordy Mercer, rhp	So.	Oklahoma State	1	0	1.12	10	0	16	10	1	18
Eric Surkamp, lhp	So.	North Carolina State	1	0	1.15	4	0	16	7	7	15
Jacob Thompson, rhp	So.	Virginia	1	2	1.27	5	0	21	13	8	13
Brian Matusz, lhp	So.	San Diego	3	1	1.33	4	0	20	11	7	21
Mike Minor, lhp	Fr.	Vanderbilt	5	2	1.64	9	0	33	30	4	37
Lance Lynn, rhp	So.	Mississippi	2	1	1.80	5	0	25	12	9	26
Ryan Berry, rhp	Fr.	Rice	2	1	1.88	7	0	38	26	15	26
Cody Satterwhite, rhp	So.	Mississippi	1	0	2.55	14	4	18	14	11	16
Joe Kelly, rhp	Fr.	UC Riverside	1	0	4.50	10	0	12	13	7	9
Seth Frankoff, rhp	Fr.	UNC Wilmington	0	1	7.50	3	0	6	7	2	8
Josh Romanski, lhp	So.	San Diego	0	1	7.71	8	0	16	24	3	20

Mike Minor

NATHAN RODE

INTERNATIONAL BASEBALL

press box and separate suites for scoring, radio and other press members.

During the opening speeches, several involved with the development expressed their gratitude for the hours of planning and construction to get the job done.

"When somebody does something for you that you didn't expect, you're taken aback," Paul Seiler, executive director of USA Baseball said as he addressed the fans, players and scouts. "Thank you falls short. Thank you really doesn't scratch the surface with how we feel with this community."

The complex sits on 221 acres in Thomas Brooks Park, off a state highway less than 10 miles from Interstate 40 near Raleigh and Durham. The main stadium has a capacity of 1,754 and more than 250 can sit on the grass hills down the lines.

Gaski turned his words into a baseball friendly language, saying that the day was a victory. "So many of us here have been involved in baseball our entire lives," he said. "We have an understanding of what it takes to win. And that's teamwork, cooperation, help, communication, and various people at various times making significant contributions to create the outcome. This event, this structure probably encapsulates that better than anything I have ever seen before."

Aside from local fans and scouts, there were 144 high school players and members of 72 host families in attendance for the Tournament of Stars, which moved from Joplin, Mo.

The Tournament of Stars made its Cary debut after the opening ceremonies, providing just a hint of the top-notch competition that will take place there in coming years. Jimmy Lee Solomon, Major League Baseball's executive vice president of operations, was there to represent MLB and expressed the importance of amateur baseball, stating that it is the lifeblood of Major League Baseball.

"This has been a fantastic endeavor to watch this stadium come out of the ground," Solomon added.

USA Baseball has been based in North Carolina (specifically Durham Bulls Athletic Park) since 2003 but hasn't had a permanent home for its teams until the construction of the National Training Complex. Its new home is Cary, a growing Raleigh suburb with more than 120,000 residents, and that suburban sprawl is evident with all the construction surrounding Thomas Brooks Park.

McAlister was excited over the opening and is looking forward to the growth of the baseball programs and relationship with his town. "It's an opportunity for us to develop more of a relationship with USA Baseball and with Major League Baseball," McAlister said. "The economic development opportunity for us is huge. As you can see today, people from all over the nation came in here for this tournament."

McAlister also noted the importance of having a community that knows the benefits the complex will bring and also enjoys baseball. "What you have in Cary is a committed council that understands the value of having first class facilities and is willing to make that investment," he said. "It's an exciting time for us. It brings a national spotlight to Cary."

World Cup Provides Olympic Appetizer

■ Team USA played in the World Cup in November in Taiwan, featuring a beefed up roster compared to the 2005 team that finished in ninth place in the Netherlands.

Cuba has had a stranglehold on the international competition since 1984, when the Cubans began a streak of nine straight World Cup gold medals. They will try to make it 10 in a row this year, but Team USA has an improved roster that features some of the top prospects in baseball, mixed in with a number of other minor leaguers on the cusp of breaking into the major leagues. For many of these players, success with this year's Team USA could lead to placement on next year's Olympic roster—unless, of course, those players are in the big leagues.

The Americans have not defeated Cuba in World Cup play since 1970, and Team USA's last gold medal in the competition came in 1974. Team USA did have success in the World Cup in 2001, when the team won the silver medal. The 2001 team, which was managed by current Red Sox manager Terry Francona, featured outfielder Carl Crawford and second baseman Orlando Hudson, as well as other future big leaguers such as lefthander Chris Capuano and first baseman Ben Broussard.

■ The United States had already qualified for the 2008 Olympics in Beijing (along with Cuba) after advancing to the finals of a 2006 qualifying tournament. The Netherlands had also earned a spot in the eight-team field, as had China as the host country. Asia had yet to play its qualifying tournament, which was for one berth in the games. Eight nations that failed to qualify in their initial tournaments, including Canada, were scheduled to play in a second-chance tournament in Taiwan in March 2008 that would fill the final three spots in the Olympic baseball field.

■ As part of its efforts to raise the level of baseball skill in the run-up to the Olympics, the Chinese national team came to Arizona during spring training for workouts and exhibition games against minor league players, as it has for each of the last four springs.

"This is a great opportunity for our guys to elevate their game against tough, professional competition," said former major league manager and player Jim Lefebvre, who has managed Team China since 2003 and will lead the squad in Beijing.

Lefebvre and pitching coach Bruce Hurst were hired by Major League Baseball to work with the team. In four years, Lefebvre and Hurst have done an impressive job. Team China was eliminated quickly in the 2006 World Baseball Classic, but the Chinese were competitive in every game until their frontline pitchers had to leave because of pitch-count restrictions.

■ The World Baseball Classic will make its second appearance in 2009, Major League Baseball announced. "Timing and format still have to be discussed, but we're going to go ahead with it," MLB chief operating officer Bob Dupuy said.

MLB hopes to run the event every four years following 2009 and plans to keep it out of the Olympic cycle. Japan won the inaugural event in March 2006, beating Cuba 10-6 in the final. The United States was eliminated in the second round.

Monterrey returns to pinnacle

The Monterrey Sultans won their ninth Mexican League title—but their first in more than a decade—with a seven-game series win over Yucatan.

Monterrey had not won the league championship since going back to back in 1995-96, but it completed a dominant season with sluggers Karim Garcia and Luis Garcia providing most of the firepower. Karim Garcia hit 20 home runs during the regular season while Luis Garcia hit 11, and both players added five more during the playoffs. Veteran Mendy Lopez also had five home runs in the playoffs for the Sultans, who won their division in both half-seasons and finished the regular season with a 68-38 record overall.

Monterrey took a 1-0 lead in the first when Karim Garcia singled and scored on Lopez' two-out base hit, and Garcia also led off the third with a solo home run. Walter Silva shut out Yucatan over 5⅓ innings, and Maximo De La Rosa got the final out after giving up a two-out solo homer in the ninth, sealing the championship in front of 27,000 fans.

Garcia, who spent parts of 11 seasons in the major leagues, ranked fifth in the Mexican League with a .374 average during the season.

Luis Garcia was the hero in the semifinals, hitting two home runs to lead Monterrey past Saltillo in a 6-2 win as the Sultans won the series in five games. Garcia went a perfect 3-for-3 with a pair of walks and hit his first home run off Jose Lima in the first inning. He added a solo shot in the ninth. Karim Garcia hit a solo homer in the third off Lima and Mendy Lopez added an RBI single in the fifth.

The Lions reached the finals when Oscar Rivera pitched eight strong innings and Izzy Alcantara homered in a 1-0 victory over the Mexico Red Devils. Like Monterrey, Yucatan won its series in five games. Yucatan won the chance to defend its title by winning the second-half title in the Southern Division, after finishing below .500 in first half.

Puebla's Donny Leon was selected as the league's MVP after leading the league with 31 home runs and finishing third in the league batting race at .384 as he helped the team reach the playoffs. Leon, a Puerto Rico native in his third season in Mexico, beat out Yucatan's Willie Romero and Karim Garcia for the award.

Former major league Nerio Rodriguez was the league's pitcher of the year, after he went 13-3, 2.64 for Monclova in his second season in Mexico. He beat out Paul Ortega of Quintana Roo. Mexico Red Devils lefthander Orlando Lara was the league's rookie of the year, going 6-2, 4.43 in 61 innings.

STANDINGS

FIRST HALF

NORTH

	W	L	PCT	GB
Monterrey	36	18	.667	—
Saltillo	35	21	.625	2
Puebla	29	27	.518	8
Laguna	28	28	.500	9
Tijuana	26	29	.473	10½
Monclova	25	31	.446	12
Aguascalientes	25	31	.446	12
Chihuahua	19	37	.339	18

SOUTH

	W	L	PCT	GB
Mexico	37	19	.661	—
Quintana Roo	36	20	.643	1
Tabasco	29	27	.518	8
Oaxaca	27	28	.491	9½
Yucatan	26	30	.464	11
Campeche	25	31	.446	12
Minatitlan	22	34	.393	15
Veracruz	21	35	.375	16

SECOND HALF

NORTH

	W	L	PCT	GB
Saltillo	33	19	.635	—
Monterrey	33	20	.623	½
Monclova	32	21	.604	1½
Puebla	30	24	.556	4
Chihuahua	26	26	.500	7
Laguna	24	28	.462	9
Tijuana	22	30	.423	11
Aguascalientes	15	36	.294	17½

SOUTH

	W	L	PCT	GB
Yucatan	35	19	.648	—
Mexico	32	22	.593	3
Quintana Roo	28	26	.519	7
Tabasco	27	27	.500	8
Oaxaca	25	29	.463	10
Veracruz	24	29	.453	10½
Campeche	21	31	.404	13
Minatitlan	17	37	.315	18

PLAYOFFS—Division Series: Saltillo defeated Puebla 4-1, Mexico defeated Tabasco 4-3, Monterrey defeated Monclova 4-3 and Yucatan defeated Quintana Roo 4-1 in best-of-seven series. **Semifinals:** Yucatan defeated Mexico 4-1 and Monterrey defeated Saltillo 4-1 in best-of-seven series. **Finals:** Monterrey defeated Yucatan 4-3 in a best-of-seven series.

ATTENDANCE—Saltillo 502,992; Monterrey 491,628; Tijuana 451,522; Laguna 335,931; Monclova 247,497; Yucatan 234,469; Quintana Roo 214,556; Mexico 192,352; Oaxaca 187,493; Veracruz 181,716; Chihuahua 159,565; Aguascalientes 158,307; Tabasco 157,320; Minatitlan 134,948; Puebla 124,601; Campeche 113,700.

INDIVIDUAL BATTING LEADERS
(MINIMUM 300 PLATE APPEARANCES)

	AVG	AB	R	H	2B	3B	HR	RBI	SB
Rivera, Carlos, Oaxaca	.410	361	75	148	26	0	16	73	3
Gil, Geronimo, Mexico	.396	265	60	105	21	0	12	44	1
Leon, Donny, Puebla	.384	346	74	133	16	0	31	104	1
Rodriguez, Fernando, Aguascalientes	.378	307	51	116	19	1	11	58	3
Garcia, Karim, Monterrey	.374	294	73	110	22	4	20	63	8
Valdez, Mario, Laguna	.372	266	54	99	23	0	7	45	1
Romero, Willie, Yucatan	.366	410	79	150	24	15	13	101	19
Otanez, Willis, Veracruz	.362	367	73	133	21	1	21	89	2
White, Derrick, Tijuana	.358	363	73	130	25	1	19	75	6
Bojorquez, Victor, Mexico	.357	401	79	143	39	6	11	74	4

INDIVIDUAL PITCHING LEADERS
(MINIMUM 88 INNINGS)

	W	L	ERA	G	SV	IP	H	BB	SO
Ortega, Pablo, Quintana Roo	12	3	2.38	20	0	113	91	28	56
Rodriguez, Nerio, Monclova	13	3	2.64	22	0	146	135	44	93
Moreno, Edwin, Minatitlan	8	3	2.71	17	2	103	76	17	80
Lara, Mauricio, Monterrey	8	3	2.73	21	0	102	88	34	65
Campos, Francisco, Campeche	9	4	2.89	21	0	128	131	28	108
Rodriguez, Raul, Monclova	6	6	3.12	20	0	121	134	24	51
Elvira, Abraham, Veracruz	8	7	3.16	21	0	120	112	48	61
Verdugo, Oswaldo, Yucatan	9	4	3.27	23	0	96	84	30	68
Lima, Jose , Saltillo	13	4	3.60	22	0	160	170	33	76
Aceves, Alfredo, Monterrey	11	5	3.64	18	0	106	96	33	70

INTERNATIONAL BASEBALL

Chunichi wins first title in 53 years

BY WAYNE GRACZYK

The Central League's Chunichi Dragons defeated the Pacific League's Hokkaido Nippon Ham Fighters four games to one to win the best-of-seven Japan Series and reign as Japanese baseball champions for 2007. The same two teams played in the 2006 Japan Series with the Fighters winning, also in five games.

The Dragons, managed by Hiromitsu Ochiai, won their first title in 53 years, and Chunichi's victory broke a four-year winning streak by Pacific League clubs. The final contest, played at the Dragons' home Nagoya Dome, featured a combined perfect game by two Chunichi pitchers.

Righthander Daisuke Yamai did not allow a Nippon Ham baserunner through eight innings while protecting a 1-0 lead, but he pulled out after developing a blister. Ochiai called on ace lefty closer Hitoki Iwase to work the ninth, and he retired the three Fighters hitters he faced to preserve the perfect game.

Chunichi finished second to the Tokyo Yomiuri Giants in the regular season but earned the right to represent the Central League in the Japan Series by sweeping the Giants in the best-of-five second round of the league's first-ever Climax Series of playoffs.

The Dragons also swept the Hanshin Tigers, who finished in third place, in the best-of-three first round of the Climax Series.

Nippon Ham, under American manager Trey Hillman, won its second consecutive Pacific League regular season title and went to the Japan Series again after defeating the second-place Chiba Lotte Marines, managed by Bobby Valentine, three games to two in the second round of the Pacific playoffs.

The Marines had beaten the Fukuoka SoftBank Hawks, managed by all-time home run king Sadaharu Oh, two games to one in the first round.

Hillman's club finished first despite lagging in almost every major offensive category, and his managerial skills did not go unnoticed. After leading the Fighters for five seasons, the Texas native was hired to manage the Kansas City Royals in 2008.

Two other U.S. managers did not fare so well. Marty Brown's Hiroshima Carp finished in fifth place in the six-team Central League, and the Orix Buffaloes were last in the Pacific League under Terry Collins, in his first year in Japan.

Fifty-seven foreigners played in Japan in 2007, and among the individual statistical leaders were Yakult Swallows outfielders Alex Ramirez and Aaron Guiel and pitcher Seth Greisinger. The Venezuelan-born Ramirez led both leagues with 122 RBIs and slammed 29 home runs.

Ramirez' .343 average was good for runner-up in the Central batting race behind teammate Norichika Aoki, who won his second hitting title while batting .346.

Canadian Guiel belted 35 homers to tie for second in the home run derby, along with American first baseman Tyrone Woods of Chunichi. Yokohama BayStars third baseman Shuichi Murata had 36 to win the league home run crown. Greisinger topped the Central League with 16 wins and posted a league second-best 2.84 ERA.

Other noteworthy foreign pitchers in the Central League

were Yokohama closer Marc Kroon, who saved 31 games with a .2.76 ERA, and Hanshin Australian lefty set-up man Jeff Williams, who had a 0.96 ERA in 60 appearances.

In the Pacific League, Orix slugger Tuffy Rhodes had 42 homers in a comeback after sitting out the 2006 season. The 39-year-old Rhodes missed his fifth home run title in Japan, however, as first baseman/DH Takeshi Yamasaki of the Tohoku Rakuten Golden Eagles socked 43 and also led with 108 RBIs.

Eagles utility player Rick Short hit .330, good for second in the Pacific batting race behind veteran Atsunori Inaba of the Fighters, who batted .334. Nippon Ham righthander Ryan Glynn (9-8) compiled the league's third-best ERA at 2.21.

A pair of popular 21-year-young pitchers provided excitement in the Pacific League. Lotte southpaw Yoshihisa Naruse went 16-1, 1.817, and just behind him was Nippon Ham righty Yu Darvish, son of a Japanese mother and Iranian father. He went 15-5, 1.82 and led both leagues with 210 strikeouts.

Righthander Hideaki Wakui, who assumed the title of ace of the Seibu Lions after the departure of Daisuke Matsuzaka to the Boston Red Sox, was the PL's leading winner with a 17-10 record.

Three Japanese stars eligible for free agency could be looking to continue their careers in the major leagues in 2008: Chunichi lefthanded-hitting outfielder Kosuke Fukudome, Hiroshima righthanded starting pitcher Hiroki Kuroda, and Lotte closer Masahide Kobayashi, also a righty.

Fukudome, 30, led the Central League in batting in 2002 (.342) and 2006 (.351) and was the league MVP in 2006. He was hampered by bone chips in his right (throwing) elbow in 2007, though, and saw no action after the all-star break in July. His 2007 stats include a .294 average, 13 homers and 48 RBIs.

Kuroda, 32, went 12-8, 3.56, and Kobayashi, 33, saved 27 while posting a 3.61 ERA in 49 appearances.

STANDINGS

CENTRAL LEAGUE

	W	L	T	PCT.	GB
Yomiuri Giants	80	63	1	.559	—
Chunichi Dragons	78	64	2	.549	1 ½
Hanshin Tigers	74	66	4	.529	4 ½
Yokohama BayStars	71	72	1	.497	9
Hiroshima Carp	60	82	2	.423	19 ½
Yakult Swallows	60	84	0	.417	20 ½

CLIMAX SERIES PLAYOFFS—Chunichi defeated Hanshin 2-0 in best-of-three series; Chunichi defeated Yomiuri 3-0 in best-of-five series for league championship.

INDIVIDUAL BATTING LEADERS
(MINIMUM 446 PLATE APPEARANCES)

	AVG	AB	R	H	2B	3B	HR	RBI	SB
Aoki, Norichika, Swallows	.346	557	114	193	26	2	20	58	17
Ramirez, Alex, Swallows	.343	594	80	204	41	3	29	122	0
Tani, Yoshitomo, Giants	.318	541	63	172	31	0	10	53	10
Ogasawara, Michihiro, Giants	.313	566	95	177	33	1	31	88	4
Kurihara, Kenta, Carp	.310	565	77	175	37	1	25	92	3
Takahashi, Yoshinobu, Giants	.308	503	76	155	29	1	35	88	1

	AVG.	AB	R	H	2B	3B	HR	RBI	SB
Saeki, Takahiro, BayStars	.302	404	49	122	25	3	16	67	0
Aikawa, Ryoji, BayStars	.302	391	37	118	12	1	2	33	0
Akahoshi, Norihiro, Tigers	.300	400	61	120	12	1	0	19	24
Miyamoto, Shinya, Swallows	.300	464	42	139	18	3	5	39	3
Ibata, Hirozaku, Dragons	.296	588	87	174	34	4	5	45	23
Nioka, Tomohiro, Giants	.295	508	68	150	22	0	20	83	1
Tanaka, Hiroyasu, Swallows	.295	451	58	133	23	8	5	51	8
Morino, Masahiko, Dragons	.294	530	75	156	29	2	18	97	1
Nakamura, Norihiro, Dragons	.293	457	64	134	24	0	20	79	2
Arai, Takahiro, Carp	.290	556	84	161	22	0	28	102	1
Murata, Shuichi, BayStars	.287	526	94	151	30	1	36	101	1
Maeda, Tomonori, Carp	.285	414	41	118	17	0	15	71	1
Kinjo, Tatsuhiko, BayStars	.284	511	66	145	27	2	14	66	2
Abe, Shinnosuke, Giants	.275	499	72	137	20	0	33	101	1
Yoshikawa, Yuuki, BayStars	.274	519	69	142	21	4	24	85	5
Lee, Seung Yeop, Giants	.274	541	84	148	29	2	30	74	4
Toritani, Takashi, Tigers	.273	565	67	154	19	4	10	43	7
Woods, Tyrone, Dragons	.270	466	85	126	16	0	35	102	3
Nishi, Toshihisa, BayStars	.270	556	68	150	27	2	10	45	3
Higashide, Akihiro, Carp	.269	458	57	123	12	0	0	15	13
Kanemoto, Tomoaki, Tigers	.265	533	74	141	17	3	31	95	1
Araki, Masahiro, Dragons	.263	457	66	120	15	0	1	25	31
Lee, Byung Kyu, Dragons	.262	478	43	125	23	1	9	46	0
Soyogi, Eishin, Carp	.260	519	69	135	20	4	18	56	20
Iihara, Yasushi, Swallows	.246	418	56	103	19	4	8	32	23
Guiel, Aaron, Swallows	.245	497	78	122	18	0	35	79	2
Sheets, Andy, Tigers	.243	498	60	121	20	0	9	54	0
Tanishige, Motonobu, Dragons	.236	382	33	90	15	0	6	44	0

REMAINING U.S. AND LATIN PLAYERS

	AVG.	AB	R	H	2B	3B	HR	RBI	SB
Ochoa, Alex, Carp	.300	290	36	87	18	1	7	31	2
Hollins, Damon, Giants	.257	370	43	95	23	1	12	45	2
Gonzalez, Luis, Giants	.247	73	9	18	4	0	3	12	0
Riggs, Adam, Swallows	.217	138	11	30	5	0	3	19	0

INDIVIDUAL PITCHING LEADERS
(MINIMUM 144 INNINGS)

	W	L	ERA	G	SV	IP	H	BB	SO
Takahashi, Hisanori, Giants	14	4	2.75	28	0	187	168	50	141
Greisinger, Seth, Swallows	16	8	2.84	30	0	209	185	31	159
Utsumi, Tetsuya, Giants	14	7	3.02	28	0	188	183	48	180
Miura, Daisuke, BayStars	11	13	3.06	28	0	185	184	51	159
Kisanuki, Hiroshi, Giants	12	9	3.09	26	0	149	144	35	131
Asakura, Kenta, Dragons	12	7	3.36	29	0	172	173	50	105
Terahara, Hayato, BayStars	12	12	3.36	27	0	185	171	46	163
Kawakami, Kenshin, Dragons	12	8	3.55	26	0	167	175	23	145
Kuroda, Hiroki, Carp	12	8	3.56	26	0	180	176	42	123
Nakata, Kenichi, Dragons	14	8	3.59	28	0	170	158	81	177
Otake, Kan, Carp	9	10	3.77	27	0	146	137	59	104
Ishii, Kazuhisa, Swallows	9	10	4.16	28	0	167	156	49	163

REMAINING U.S., AUSTRALIAN AND LATIN PLAYERS

	W	L	ERA	G	SV	IP	H	BB	SO
Obispo, Wirfin, Giants	0	0	0.00	2	0	1	1	1	1
Caridad, Esmailin, Carp	0	0	0.00	2	0	1	2	1	0
Williams, Jeff, Tigers	1	2	0.96	60	0	65	42	16	66
Sikorski, Brian, Swallows	1	2	2.29	29	1	39	30	12	38
Gracesqui, Franklin, Dragons	3	0	2.35	17	0	23	12	18	13
Cruz, Rafael, Dragons	1	3	2.66	17	0	20	13	6	18
Kroon, Marc, BayStars	3	1	2.76	43	31	42	35	15	65
Cubillan, Darwin, Tigers	2	2	3.36	35	0	62	60	20	34
Vogelsong, Ryan, Tigers	7	6	4.13	20	0	107	113	41	91
Yan, Esteban, Tigers	6	5	4.46	21	0	104	110	31	52
Diaz, Joselo, BayStars	3	4	4.59	45	2	67	47	58	61
White, Matt, BayStars	0	3	4.96	24	0	33	35	11	26
Ramirez, Santiago, Dragons	1	0	5.47	27	0	26	27	12	11
Powell, Jeremy, Giants	0	2	5.80	7	0	40	52	12	20
Fernandez, Jared, Carp	3	8	6.04	30	0	92	117	34	33
Gonzalez, Geremi, Giants	1	2	6.52	5	0	19	22	6	17
Marte, Victor, Carp	0	1	8.31	17	0	17	28	10	13

PACIFIC LEAGUE

	W	L	T	PCT.	GB
Hokkaido Nippon Ham Fighters	79	60	5	.568	—
Chiba Lotte Marines	76	61	7	.555	2
Fukuoka SoftBank Hawks	73	66	5	.525	6
Tohoku Rakuten Golden Eagles	67	75	2	.472	13 ½
Seibu Lions	66	76	2	.465	14 ½
Orix Buffaloes	62	77	5	.446	17

CLIMAX SERIES PLAYOFFS—Lotte defeated SoftBank 2-1 in best-of-three series; Nippon Ham defeated Lotte 3-2 in best-of-five series for league championship.

INDIVIDUAL BATTING LEADERS
(MINIMUM 446 PLATE APPEARANCES)

	AVG.	AB	R	H	2B	3B	HR	RBI	SB
Inaba, Atsunori, Fighters	.334	527	61	176	39	0	17	87	6
Short, Rick, Eagles	.330	418	31	138	31	0	4	53	2
Omura, Naoyuki, Hawks	.319	455	44	145	20	0	1	31	11
Wada, Kazuhiro, Lions	.315	501	77	158	23	1	18	49	7
Nakajima, Hiroyuki, Lions	.300	533	68	160	28	5	12	74	9
Morimoto, Hichori, Fighters	.300	584	91	175	27	3	3	44	31
Nishioka, Tsuyoshi, Marines	.300	494	76	148	31	3	3	40	27
Cabrera, Alex, Lions	.295	541	51	130	15	0	27	81	0
Rhodes, Tuffy, Buffaloes	.291	464	75	135	19	0	42	96	0
Muramatsu, Arihito, Buffaloes	.289	453	56	131	11	3	0	28	9
LaRocca, Greg, Buffaloes	.286	503	79	144	29	0	27	79	2
Hayakawa, Daisuke, Marines	.283	459	72	130	17	8	5	44	16
Takasu, Yosuke, Eagles	.283	481	54	136	26	1	1	44	15
Kitagawa, Hirotoshi, Buffaloes	.280	557	60	156	31	1	9	61	4
Sato, G.G., Lions	.280	486	65	136	31	3	25	69	7
Kokubo, Hiroki, Hawks	.277	466	70	129	26	0	25	82	2
Isobe, Koichi, Eagles	.277	441	43	122	20	2	5	48	5
Honda, Yuichi, Hawks	.275	550	62	151	25	5	2	42	34
Shibahara, Hiroshi, Hawks	.273	429	46	117	28	3	6	40	1
Agbayani, Benny, Marines	.272	390	45	106	21	0	13	51	7
Tamura, Hitoshi, Hawks	.271	509	61	138	28	3	13	68	3
Satozaki, Tomoya, Marines	.270	477	56	129	27	3	14	75	1
Fernandez, Jose, Eagles	.270	444	52	120	15	1	22	79	8
Omura, Saburo, Marines	.269	472	67	127	28	4	7	68	13
Watanabe, Naoto, Eagles	.268	410	60	110	17	1	2	26	25
Matsunaka, Nobuhiko, Hawks	.266	440	60	117	26	1	15	68	1
Yamasaki, Takeshi, Eagles	.261	506	86	132	27	2	43	108	1
Kataoka, Yasuyuki, Lions	.256	422	40	108	19	2	3	34	38
Tanaka, Kensuke, Fighters	.255	526	66	134	24	7	3	31	27
Tsuchiya, Teppei, Eagles	.254	472	57	120	18	2	10	48	8
Seguignol, Fernando, Fighters	.249	470	50	117	21	0	21	68	0
Kaneko, Makoto, Fighters	.243	419	34	102	15	4	4	53	9
Hosokawa, Toru, Lions	.239	393	39	94	24	0	10	43	2

REMAINING U.S. AND LATIN PLAYERS

	AVG.	AB	R	H	2B	3B	HR	RBI	SB
Allen, Chad, Buffaloes	.286	290	28	83	14	1	4	34	2
Buchanan, Brian, Hawks	.285	288	25	82	19	0	11	48	1
Ortiz, Jose, Marines	.284	250	33	71	18	0	7	39	2
Hyzdu, Adam, Hawks	.272	136	13	37	8	0	7	14	0
Zuleta, Julio, Marines	.267	277	36	74	10	1	15	51	2
Liefer, Jeff, Lions	.261	138	19	36	9	0	8	28	1
Watson, Matt, Marines	.203	138	12	28	7	0	4	13	2
Green, Andy, Fighters	.197	61	2	12	5	0	0	3	0
Witt, Kevin, Eagles	.174	115	12	20	0	1	6	15	0
Jones, Mitch, Fighters	.160	94	3	15	6	1	1	7	1

INDIVIDUAL PITCHING LEADERS
(MINIMUM 144 INNINGS)

	W	L	ERA	G	SV	IP	H	BB	SO
Naruse, Yoshihisa, Marines	16	1	1.82	24	0	173	132	27	138
Darvish, Yu, Fighters	15	5	1.82	26	0	208	123	49	210
Glynn, Ryan, Fighters	9	8	2.21	24	0	155	129	33	111
Watanabe, Shunsuke, Marines	9	6	2.44	25	0	177	154	34	93
Sugiuchi, Toshiya, Hawks	15	3	2.46	28	0	198	166	46	187
Takeda, Masaru, Fighters	9	4	2.54	35	0	149	113	17	101
Kobayashi, Hiroyuki, Marines	13	3	2.69	25	0	171	157	38	163
Wakui, Hideaki, Lions	17	10	2.79	28	0	213	199	50	141
Wada, Tsuyoshi, Hawks	12	10	2.82	26	0	182	168	42	169
Asai, Hideki, Eagles	8	3	3.12	31	0	144	146	40	107
Davey, Tom, Buffaloes	8	11	3.21	26	0	163	180	44	116
Kishi, Takayuki, Lions	11	7	3.40	24	0	156	131	55	142
Hirano, Yoshihisa, Buffaloes	8	13	3.72	27	0	172	172	28	124
Tanaka, Masahiro, Eagles	11	7	3.82	28	0	186	183	68	196
Nishiguchi, Fumiya, Lions	9	11	4.23	25	0	154	149	44	103
Shimizu, Naoyuki, Marines	6	10	4.78	25	0	145	189	39	101

REMAINING U.S. AND LATIN PLAYERS

	W	L	ERA	G	SV	IP	H	BB	SO
Standridge, Jason, Hawks	7	1	3.00	17	0	54	51	23	35
Nitkowski, C.J., Hawks	1	1	3.18	46	0	34	25	21	24
Guttormson, Rick, Hawks	5	7	3.52	22	0	143	138	28	89
Sweeney, Brian, Fighters	6	8	3.70	21	0	109	109	36	56
Graman, Alex, Lions	4	6	4.08	40	17	79	84	34	61
Johnson, Jason, Lions	1	4	4.35	7	0	41	44	10	19
Carter, Lance, Buffaloes	3	5	4.48	34	6	86	102	22	50
Guzman, Domingo, Eagles	2	4	5.01	11	0	56	56	22	40
Gissell, Chris, Lions	1	9	5.21	14	0	74	92	24	56
Serafini, Dan, Buffaloes	2	5	5.40	9	0	45	57	20	23
Bass, Adam, Eagles	0	2	7.63	5	0	15	30	3	13

Former star leads Wyverns to first title

BY THOMAS ST. JOHN

The 2007 season saw the return of many of Korea's baseball heroes back home, as Choi Hee-seop and Bong Jung-keun both joined the Korean team that had originally drafted them and Lee Man-soo, voted Korea's most popular player of all time, took over as manager of the SK Wyverns.

Choi and Bong both signed lucrative contracts in Korea but failed to do anything special, while Lee was instrumental in helping the Wyverns secure first place in the eight-team league and ultimately win their first championship. Lee had spent many years in the White Sox organization as a bullpen catcher but was never forgotten in Korea, even after his retirement 10 seasons before.

The 2007 season saw a slight increase in attendance over previous seasons, but many in Korea think the numbers could take a hit as many popular, older players were released by teams in order to save money and make room for younger players.

The SK Wyverns turned on the juice late in the Korean Series to overcome the Doosan Bears, who had won the first two games, to take their first ever Korean Series 4-2.

It was no surprise to anyone that the series was all about pitching, and foreign pitchers at that. The Bears got some R&R this season, with a combined 36 wins from their two imports, Daniel Rios and Matt Randle. Rios was nothing short of outstanding with a 22-5 record, and his 2.05 ERA was by far the best in the league.

Rios and Randle started the first two games of the series and won both on the road before coming back to Seoul. It was almost a given that the Bears would have some luck at home, but a shaky bullpen and spotty hitting was the team's undoing.

SK, led by Lee, won the next four games to pull off one of the biggest upsets in Korean Series history.

Among individual standouts, Hanwha pitcher Ryu Hyun-jin showed he was not a one-season wonder by posting similar marks to his stellar rookie season, when he went 18-6-1, 2.23 with 204 strikeouts in 202 innings. In 2007 he went 17-7, 2.94 with 178 strikeouts. The Eagles rode into the playoffs on his pitching and are expecting the same and more next season from the solidly built 20 year-old.

On the Olympic front, many of Korea's top stars have declined to take part in the games citing personal reasons, leaving the country with a big hole in many places going into the event in 2008. A medal would likely keep the sport's popularity high, while anything short of that could leave a sour taste in the mouths of the fans.

STANDINGS

	W	L	T	PCT	GB
SK Wyverns	72	48	5	.600	—
Doosan Bears	70	54	2	.565	4
Hanwha Eagles	66	56	2	.541	7
Samsung Lions	62	60	4	.508	11
LG Twins	58	62	6	.483	14
Hyun. Unicorns	56	69	1	.448	18 ½
Lotte Giants	55	68	3	.447	18 ½
KIA Tigers	51	73	1	.411	23

INDIVIDUAL BATTING LEADERS

	AVG	H	HR	RBI	R
Lee Hyun-kon, Kia	.338	153	2	48	63
Yang Joon-hyuk, Samsung	.337	149	22	72	78
Lee Dae-ho, Lotte	.335	139	29	87	79
Chong Kun-woo, SK	.323	110	9	44	62
Kim Dong-joo, Doosan	.322	123	19	78	61
Jacob Crews, Hanwha	.321	134	22	85	68
Lee Jong-uk, Doosan	.316	147	1	46	84
Lee Ho-joon, SK	.313	110	14	71	56
Lee Taek-kun, Hyundai	.313	137	11	56	74
Park Jin-man, Samsung	.312	104	7	56	34

OTHER FOREIGN PLAYERS

	AVG	AB	H	HR	RBI	R
Jacob Crews, Hanwha	.321	418	134	22	85	68
Cliff Brumbaugh, Hyundai	.308	438	135	29	87	75
Larry Sutton, Kia	.274	106	29	2	10	14
Pedro Valdez, LG	.283	435	123	13	72	50
Felix Jose, Lotte	.256	86	22	1	12	5
Robert Perez, Lotte	.273	176	48	8	28	21

INDIVIDUAL PITCHING LEADERS

	ERA	W	L	S	IP	SO
Daniel Rios, Doosan	2.07	22	5	0	—	147
Chae Byung-rong, SK	2.84	11	8	0	—	84
Chong Min-chul, Hanwha	2.90	12	5	0	—	66
Ryu hyun-jin, Hanwha	2.94	17	7	0	—	178
Matt Randle, Doosan	3.12	12	8	0	—	113
Park Myung-hwan, LG	3.19	10	6	0	—	117
Kenny Rayburn, SK	3.27	17	8	0	—	98
Jamie Brown, Samsung	3.33	12	8	0	—	68
Sohn Min-han, Lotte	3.34	13	10	0	—	95
Jang Won-sam, Hyundai	3.63	9	10	0	—	132

OTHER FOREIGN PLAYERS

	ERA	W	L	S	IP	SO
Mickey Calloway, Hyundai	4.18	2	6	0	56	24
Mike Romano, SK	3.69	12	4	0	147	81
Brian Mazone, Samsung	4.18	7	11	0	125	76
Chris Wilson, Samsung	3.79	1	6	0	38	9
Cedrick Bowers, Hanwha	4.15	11	13	0	158	140
Seth Etherton, Kia	4.22	2	2	0	32	24
Jason Scobey, Kia	3.92	8	10	0	126	58
Chris Okspring, LG	3.24	4	5	0	80	41
Tim Harikkala, LG	5.21	6	8	0	86	24

Lions take crown in rematch with Bears

BY BEN CHEN

While the Chinese Professional Baseball League in Taiwan remained in flux, one thing remained constant: the La New Bears and the President Lions were the two most consistent and talented teams in the league, and their records reflected that. The Lions then cruised to another league championship in the playoffs.

The CPBL splits its season into two 50-game halves. The Macoto Cobras won the first half-season title, while the La New Bears won the second half. In the past, the two half-season winners played each other for the league title, but the playoff format was revised this year, with the Bears automatically winning a spot in the Taiwan Series because they had a better record than the Cobras.

The Cobras were forced to play the President Lions, who won the wild card playoff spot, in a best-of-five series to determine who would advance to meet the Bears. The Lions won the wild card by having the best overall record in the league. In the playoff series, the Lions swept the Cobras in three games, winning by a combined margin of 36-6.

This set up a rematch of the 2006 Taiwan Series, when the Bears swept the Lions in four games. This time, however, the President Lions were favored because they had the best offense in the league (scoring 625 runs in the regular season) and two of the best pitchers in Pete Munro and Wei-Lun Pan.

The Bears had already lost their top two pitchers from 2006, after Si-Yo Wu went to play in Japan and Kenny Rayborn moved on to Korea. Then Gary Rath, their ace for 2007, went down with an injury late in September and was

a scratch for the Taiwan Series.

The Bears' fortunes rested on the shoulders of former major leaguer Chin-Feng Chen. Despite missing part of the season with an injury, Chen hit 26 home runs in 301 at-bats, and his .382 average was the second-highest in league history—trailing only Jay Kirkpatrick's .387 in 1998 with the Sinon Bulls.

The Lions lived up to their billing by defeating the Bears in seven games. A big reason for their success was righthander Nelson Figueroa, a former major leaguer who was signed in August. He started and won games one, four and seven—getting the win in the last two—and won the Taiwan Series MVP award.

The series was a slugfest, as the teams combined to hit 22 home runs (11 each) to set a new series record. The Bears, led by Chen's four home runs in the series, hit homers in all seven games.

The Lions set a team record for most runs scored (48) in a championship series and won the team's first championship since the 2000 season and fifth overall. It capped off a tremendous year when several individuals also broke long-standing league records. Lions third baseman Tilson Brito set the record for most home runs in a season with 33, and first baseman Kuo-Ching Kao broke the league record for most hits in a season with 152.

Despite an exciting season, the league did receive a black eye when five Chinatrust players were banned from the league on charges of fixing games. Team captain Han-Chou Tseng, star shortstop Chang-Ming Cheng, Chun-Lin Chi, Chien-Wei Chen and Kwei-Yu Huang all had their contracts terminated.

STANDINGS

FIRST HALF

	W	L	T	GB
Macoto Cobras	28	21	1	—
President Lions	27	23	0	1 ½
La New Bears	26	24	0	2 ½
Brother Elephants	24	25	1	4
Sinon Bulls	24	25	1	4
Chinatrust Whales	19	30	1	9

SECOND HALF

	W	L	T	GB
La New Bears	32	18	0	—
President Lions	31	18	1	½
Chinatrust Whales	27	22	1	4 ½
Brother Elephants	25	25	0	7
Sinon Bulls	18	32	0	14
Macoto Cobras	16	34	0	16

INDIVIDUAL BATTING LEADERS

	AVG	AB	2B	3B	HR	RBI
Chin-Feng Chen, Bears	.382	301	13	3	26	66
Cheng-Min Peng, Elephants	.362	345	17	0	21	64
Kuo-Ching Kao, Lions	.358	425	24	1	20	89
Chia-Hsien Hsieh, Cobras	.352	372	32	2	19	79
Fu-Hao Liu, Lions	.338	328	25	1	9	58
Jui-Chen Chen, Elephants	.322	283	11	1	1	39
Wu-Hsiung Pan, Lions	.319	360	14	4	6	44
Tai-Shan Chang, Bulls	.318	402	19	0	19	80
Da-Hung Cheng, Bulls	.315	311	15	5	3	35
Tilson Brito, Lions	.313	399	21	0	33	107

INDIVIDUAL PITCHING LEADERS

	W	L	ERA	IP	SO	BB
Pete Munro, Lions	14	7	2.03	190	107	28
Wei-Lun Pan, Lions	16	2	2.26	123	79	24
Iba Tomokazu, Bulls	9	9	2.67	138	97	39
Yu-Wei Hsu, Bears	9	3	2.70	113	81	32
Lorenzo Barcelo, Whales	8	9	3.10	194	143	40
Yu-Cheng Liao, Elephants	4	7	3.32	119	68	58
Gary Rath, Bears	12	5	3.52	143	117	40
Fu-Te Ni, Whales	7	12	3.53	122	125	42
Chien-Fu Yang, Bulls	7	11	3.68	132	94	47
Joey Dawley, Elephants	10	7	3.75	144	153	74

INTERNATIONAL BASEBALL

Pitchers' paradise

ITALY

BY HARVEY SAHKER

Serie A/1 operated with only eight clubs in 2007. It was the smallest complement of teams in Italy's top league since 1982.

Grosseto defeated Nettuno four games to three in the Italy Series to win its its second national championship in the last four years and the fourth in its history. The series featured three shutouts, appropriate after a regular season in which the losing team failed to score in almost twenty percent of all games.

It was the third Italian title in five years for Grosseto manager Mauro Mazzotti, who piloted Bologna to Serie A/1 titles in 2003 and 2005.

Venezuelan righthander Junior Oberto was ineffective for Grosseto in the Italy Series (0-2, 7.59), losing as many games as he did in the entire regular season (8-2, 1.44). Longtime minor and independent leaguer Linc Mikkelsen took up the slack. The 40-year old righty posted a shutout in Game One and was the winner in Game Seven. He also notched a pair of victories in Grosseto's best-of-seven semifinal against Bologna. It was his first season in Italy.

Game Seven of the Italy Series was a real nailbiter for an estimated 7,000 fans at the Stadio Roberto Jannella in Grosseto. The home team went into the top of the ninth with a comfortable 5-0 lead, but Nettuno fought back. The visitors scored four times and had a pair of runners aboard with two out when Mikkelsen was lifted in favour of reliever Emiliano Ginanneschi, 36, who made his Grosseto debut back in 1991. Mikkelsen had thrown 141 pitches when he was yanked. Ginanneschi (4-1, 2.47 with 6 saves in the regular season) retired the next batter to end the game.

Oberto threw a perfect game on the second day of the regular season as Grosseto beat San Marino 6-0. Oberto, 26, struck out the last two batters of the game and ended up with 9 K's.

Just over one month later, in mid-May, former major leaguer Andrew Lorraine pitched a no-hitter for Godo in a 4-0 win Avigliana. Lorraine had eight strikeouts in the contest and walked three batters.

Lorraine's gem was a rare highlight for Godo. The club finished in seventh despite the presence of Lorraine (4-7, 3.53) and long-time Pirates farm hand Shaun Skrehot, who batted just .239 but finished the season in a second place tie with 7 homers.

STANDINGS

	W	L	PCT	GB
Parma	28	14	.667	—
Bologna	27	15	.643	1
Grosseto	26	16	.619	2
Nettuno	25	17	.595	3
San Marino	21	21	.500	7
Rimini	21	21	.500	7
Godo	12	30	.286	16
Avigliana	8	34	.190	20

PLAYOFFS—Semifinals: Grosetto defeated Bologna 4-1 and Nettuno defeneated Parma 4-3 in best-of-seven series. **Finals:** Grosetto defeated Nettuno 4-3 in best-of-seven series.

Growth continues

CHINA

As the 2008 Olympics in Beijing draw ever closer, baseball in China continues to grow and develop, with professional teams from other nations taking an interest in the nation and Chinese players getting better training at an earlier age.

In the meantime, China's own professional league continues to grow, splitting into two divisions for the 2007 season. One thing remains constant, however: the Tianjin Lions are the league's dominant team. The Lions defeated the Guangdong Leopards three games to one in the Chinese Baseball League finals for the second year in a row, as the rivalry between the league's two best franchises continued to grow.

The series began in Guangzhou, home of the Leopards, and the teams split the first two games. In the first game in Tianjin, Tianjin sent ace Su Changlong to the mound, and Guangdong countered with its ace, Chen Junyi. Tianjin also moved middle-of-the order batter Wang Chao to the leadoff spot, and he got on base several times.

After seven innings, the score was tied 1-1. Guangdong surged ahead in the eighth with three runs, but Tianjin answered with five in the bottom of the inning to win 8-4. The top hitter in the game was Tianjin's Meng Zhaopeng, who had two doubles and a triple, with three RBIs.

In a must-win situation in Game Four, Guangdong scored first with two runs in the second inning, and Guangdong pitcher Liu Kai kept Tianjin off the board for the first four innings.

But the Lions tied it at 2-2 in the fifth inning, and in the sixth, Tianjin cleanup hitter Luo Yubin walked, and Liu Zhicheng knocked him home with a triple, which was the only extra-base hit on the day. The Lions added one more run to make the score 4-2.

With that, Tianjin closer Lu Jiangang came in and shut the door on the Leopard to clinch the championship, pitching a flawless final two innings.

After the game, the league handed out its individual awards in an on-field ceremony. Guangdong's Liu Kai won the best rookie awards, and Tianjin's Wang Chao won the best hitter and RBI award. Lu Jiangang was voted best pitcher (as well as best righthander) and MVP of the series. To close out the awards, Guangdong's Chen Junyi won the best lefty award, and Liu Guangbiao won the best defense award.

STANDINGS

NORTH	W	L	PCT	GB
Tianjin Lions	16	5	.761	—
Beijing Tigers	15	6	.714	1
Sichuan Dragons	8	13	.380	8
SOUTH	**W**	**L**	**PCT**	**GB**
Guangdong Leopards	14	7	.667	—
Shanghai Eagles	7	14	.333	7
Jiangsu Hopestars	3	18	.142	11

PLAYOFFS—Semifinals: Tianjin defeated Shanghai 3-0 and Guangdong defeated Beijing 3-1 in best-of-five series. **Finals:** Tianjin defeated Guangdong 3-1 in best-of-five series.

Santiago wins rematch with Industriales

While Cuba continued as one of the dominant players on the international baseball scene, winning another Pan American Games title in anticipation of the 2008 Olympics, spirited play in the nation's Serie Nacional continued to highlight its passion for baseball.

Santiago de Cuba won its seventh national title in the 46th edition of Cuba's national baseball series, exacting revenge with a 4-2 series win over Industriales. A year earlier, Industriales had taken the championship with a 4-2 series win over Santiago.

The Wasps and Industriales have dominated the national series over the last decade, with one of the two teams winning every title except one since 1999. This was Santiago's fifth in that time, while the Blue Lions have three. The other was won by Holguin in 2002.

Pinar del Rio and Santiago had the best regular season records, but Pinar was upset in the first round of the playoffs by La Habana.

Santiago won the clinching game of the finals 8-2, led by the bats of Julio Ruiz and Alberto Bicet in front of a full house at its home park, and coming back to win against Industriales' ace, Deinys Suarez.

Industriales opened with two quick runs against Santiago lefthander Albert Carrion, who was pulled after just 11 pitches to the first three batters and did not record an out. But that was all the Lions would score as Alberto Bicet and Felix Rivera came in to shut the door, with Bicet pitching 7⅔ innings and Rivera getting the final four outs.

Suarez made it into the fifth inning before giving up two runs that broke a 2-2 tie and turned the tide of the game. Santiago plated four more runs to clinch the title, with Jose Ruiz keying a three-run eighth (to go with his third-inning solo home run) that started the celebration for the Wasps.

STANDINGS

WEST

GROUP A	W	L	PCT	GB
Pinar del Río	56	34	.622	—
Isla de la Juventud	43	47	.478	13
Metropolitanos	29	61	.322	27
Matanzas	26	64	.289	30
GROUP B	W	L	PCT	GB
Industriales	53	36	.596	—
Sancti Spiritus	51	38	.573	2
Havana Province	46	44	.511	7½
Cienfuegos	42	48	.473	11½

WEST

GROUP C	W	L	PCT	GB
Villa Clara	52	38	.578	—
Las Tunas	50	40	.556	2
Camagüey	50	40	.556	2
Ciego de Ávila	48	42	.533	4
GROUP D	W	L	PCT	GB
Santiago de Cuba	57	32	.640	—
Granma	45	45	.500	12½
Holguin	39	50	.438	18
Guantánamo	31	59	.344	26½

PLAYOFFS—Quarterfinals: Havana Province defeated Pinar del Rio 3-2, Industriales defeated Sancti Spiritus 3-1, Villa Clara defeated Las Tunas 3-2, and Santiago de Cuba defeated Camaguey 3-1 to win best-of-five series. **Semifinals:** Industriales defeated Havana Province 4-0 and Santiago de Cuba defeated Villa Clara 4-3 to win best-of-seven series. **Finals:** Santiago de Cuba defeated Industriales 4-2 to win best-of-seven series.

INDIVIDUAL BATTING LEADERS
(MINIMUM 238 PLATE APPEARANCES)

PLAYER, TEAM	AVE	AB	R	H	2B	3B	HR	RBI
Osmani Urrutia, Las Tunas	.371	326	46	121	15	1	8	54
Isaac Martinez, Ciego de Avila	.370	200	28	74	18	1	2	31
Michel Enriquez, Juventud	.368	239	45	88	19	1	4	37
Roberqui Videaux, Guantanamo	.359	290	50	104	27	1	5	37
Giorvis Duvergel, Guantanamo	.356	298	72	106	15	0	8	28
Alexei Bell, Santiago	.355	296	75	105	22	5	8	60
Jorge Padron, Pinar del Rio	.355	369	67	131	15	7	1	44
Yoandry Urgelles, Industriales	.351	322	65	113	27	2	8	54
Juan Linares, Havana	.345	319	62	110	23	3	16	65
Yuliesky Gourriel, Sancti Spiritus	.345	348	65	120	28	0	13	46
Yordanis Samon, Granma	.342	310	46	106	21	0	2	43
Frederich Cepeda, Sancti Spiritus	.337	273	48	92	10	4	5	41
Eriel Sanchez, Sancti Spiritus	.336	298	46	100	21	1	8	62
Alexei Ramirez, Pinar del Rio	.335	340	65	114	13	4	20	68
Rolando Meriño, Santiago	.335	245	51	82	17	1	11	60
Yunior Paumier, Holguin	.331	326	35	108	22	2	1	31
Yasser Gomez, Industriales	.330	309	43	102	12	3	0	31
Yoilan Cerce, Guantanamo	.325	305	51	99	16	5	6	39
Luis F. Rivera, Juventud	.325	348	63	113	22	5	4	33
Luis E. Gavilan, Pinar del Rio	.325	255	27	83	12	0	1	28

INDIVIDUAL PITCHING LEADERS
(MINIMUM 88 INNINGS)

PLAYER, TEAM	W	L	ERA	G	IP	SO	BB
Ciro Licea, Granma	9	3	1.15	18	133	77	20
Jonder Martinez, Havana	10	3	1.40	18	122	79	32
Yunieski Maya, Pinar del Rio	6	3	1.40	29	90	71	24
Angel Peña, Sancti Spiritus	9	3	1.45	18	118	55	32
Elier Sanchez, Camaguey	13	3	1.90	22	128	72	51
Norge Vera, Santiago	9	4	1.92	15	108	56	22
Robelio Carrillo, Villa Clara	7	3	1.96	18	101	66	48
Arleys Sanchez, Industriales	10	4	2.01	16	99	62	40
Vladimir Baños, Pinar del Rio	9	3	2.04	19	128	49	25
Ismel Jimenez, Sancti Spiritus	7	3	2.10	21	111	58	39
Frank Montieth, Industriales	6	4	2.27	15	91	61	30
Deynis Suarez, Industriales	8	5	2.32	16	101	71	28

INTERNATIONAL BASEBALL

Repeat for Kinheim

BY HARVEY SAHKER

Kinheim defeated the Hoofddorp Pioniers three games to none in the Holland Series to win their second straight Dutch Major League title.

Right-handed reliever Michiel van Kampen was voted MVP of the series. The 31-year old Haarlem native and Albertson College alumnus pitched in all three games and did not allow a run in five and two-thirds innings. He saved Game One and Game Three, and was the winning pitcher in Game Two, a 4-3 decision that went a Holland Series record 13 innings.

Vaughan Harris, the winner of Game Three, was pitching in his second national championship of 2007. Harris, 26, had played for the New South Wales Patriots in Australia's Claxton Shield in January. He was 9-0 in the DML regular season.

Kinheim had a league leading team batting average of .331 and had five hitters in the top ten. Danny Rombley, 26, who spent six years in the Montreal Expos organization, hit .462 in the Holland Series after winning the DML batting crown.

Hoofddorp advanced to the Holland Series after sweeping heavily favoured Neptunus in the semi-finals. The Pioniers batted .260 as a team, good enough for fourth in the league. The fences at Hoofddorp had been moved in prior to the beginning of the season. Before 2007, the Pioniers played home games in a field that was a perfect quarter-circle. From foul pole to foul pole, the fence was 120 meters (approximately 400 feet) from the plate. The shrunken outfield did little to improve Hoofdorp's collective power, however. The Pioniers hit only five home runs in the regular season.

Kinheim also won the European Cup. The continental club championship took place in San Marino in mid-June. Kinheim eked out a 3-1 victory in the final against the Rouen Huskies, France's entry in the tournament.

The Dutch national team won the European Championships in September, thus earning a berth at the 2008 Olympics in Beijing. It was their fifth straight triumph in the biennial tournament. The Netherlands went undefeated in the competition. Earlier in the season, Kinheim's Dirk van 't Klooster broke the record for games played as a member of the national team.

Long-time Neptunus and national team hurler Rob Cordemans began the season playing pro ball in Taiwan. Cordemans was cut in late May and joined ADO of The Hague shortly thereafter (1-3, 3.88).

STANDINGS

	W	L	PCT	GB
Kinheim	33	7	.825	—
Neptunus	32	7	.821	½
Hoofddorp Pioniers	22	17	.564	10 ½
Amsterdam Pirates	21	18	.538	11 ½
HCAW	17	22	.436	15 ½
ADO	15	24	.385	17 ½
Sparta/Feyenoord	13	25	.342	19
RCH	12	27	.308	20 ½
Almere Magpies	11	29	.275	22

PLAYOFFS—Semifinals: Kinheim defeated Amsterdam 3-2 and Hoofddorp defeated Neptunus 3-0 in best-of-five series. **Finals:** Kinheim defeated Hoofddorp 3-0 in best-of-five series.

INDIVIDUAL BATTING LEADERS
(MINIMUM 105 PLATE APPEARANCES)

PLAYER, TEAM	AVG	G	AB	R	H	HR	RBI	BB	SO	SB
Danny Rombley, Kin	.392	40	176	44	69	0	19	18	19	11
Roel Koolen, Kin	.386	26	88	22	34	0	26	21	8	1
Vince Rooi, Kin	.368	40	144	43	53	3	34	36	16	2
Fausto Alvarez, Amst	.365	38	126	28	46	12	35	29	15	1
Ryan Murphy, RCH	.365	35	126	19	46	3	20	13	25	4
Dirk van 't Klooster, Kin	.360	40	172	44	62	1	32	18	11	2
Harvey Monte, ADO	.357	37	140	24	50	3	24	11	10	2
Johnny Balentina, Nep	.350	29	120	22	42	0	18	16	3	16
Petr Baroch, RCH	.336	35	140	19	47	1	16	9	17	7
René Cremer, Kin	.335	40	155	33	52	0	18	12	12	7

INDIVIDUAL PITCHING LEADERS
(MINIMUM 31 INNINGS)

PITCHER, TEAM	W	L	ERA	G	SV	IP	H	BB	SO
Duko Jansen, Kin	2	1	0.78	20	1	34.2	18	15	36
Chris Ryan, Nep	1	1	0.99	20	4	36.1	30	13	46
Leon Boyd, Nep	9	0	1.22	12	0	66.2	42	17	61
Dave Draijer, Hoof	3	3	1.29	23	8	35.0	27	6	21
Diegomar Markwell, Nep	9	1	1.45	13	0	87.0	68	16	62
Stephen Spragg, HCAW	4	3	1.93	24	6	65.1	49	24	45
David Bergman, Kin	12	2	2.06	15	0	96.0	69	28	75
Kenny Berkenbosch, Amst	6	4	2.11	15	1	85.1	79	17	55
Vaughan Harris, Kin	9	0	2.12	13	0	63.2	46	16	38
Erik-Jan Lind, Hoof	1	0	2.18	16	1	41.1	31	25	19

Tejada leads Dominicans to Caribbean title

BY CHRIS KLINE

CAROLINA, P.R.

With his theatrics on the mound and flamboyant style, righthander Jose Lima embodies a number of characteristics of Latin American baseball. Of course, it didn't hurt that he was at the center of most 2007 Caribbean Series storylines.

It was shortstop Miguel Tejada (Orioles), however, whose play contributed most heavily to the Dominican Republic's Caribbean Series championship, reinforcing his stature as the heart and soul of Dominican baseball.

Tejada did not win Series MVP—that honor went to third baseman Tony Batista—but he set the tone for the Dominicans with his all-out play, defensive wizardry and a star power unmatched by any other player. He hit .304/.448/.522 in 23 at-bats with six runs and five RBIs.

And he did it all despite flu-like symptoms that plagued him throughout the tournament.

"I love to play and I love to play for my country," Tejada said. "I play hard because this means something to me. It means something to the fans and all the people in my home that helped me when I was coming up. To win a Caribbean Series is very special to me."

The Dominicans were simply outstanding, establishing themselves as the team to beat in the tournament after defeating Venezuela 4-3 in an 18-inning game that lasted 6½ hours in the Series opener. The Dominicans' thrashing of Mexico and Puerto Rico by a combined score of 21-0 didn't hurt either, and they won their first five games of the round-robin tournament on their way to a 5-1 record.

Things could have gone either way for the Dominican Republic in the game following their draining tournament-opening win, especially as they were matched up in the early game against a scrappy Mexico team the next day.

But righthander Jose Acevedo (Orioles) pitched eight shutout innings before turning it over to righthander Jose Capellan (Brewers), who whiffed two in the final inning of work. The Dominicans rocked Mexico, 9-0, and the road to the Caribbean Series title was smoothly paved.

In the Dominican Republic's first showdown with Puerto Rico--attended equally by fans of each club in sold-out Roberto Clemente Walker Stadium--the visiting fans were especially eager to rush the field in celebration of the Dominican's 12-0 blasting of the home team.

In a scene reminiscent of vintage World Series fan celebrations, the Dominican faithful ran around the entire field, waving flags, playing salsa music, celebrating in the parking lot and honking their car horns all the way home.

The Dominicans had a much easier time with Venezuela the second time around, moving to a perfect 4-0 with a 7-1 victory. They stretched their winning streak to five, and all but wrapped up the series, with a 5-3 win over Mexico.

Pitching set the tone for the Dominicans, as Lima, Acevedo, lefthander Fabio Castro (Phillies) and righthander Julian Tavarez (Red Sox) all were brilliant. So was righthander Jose Vargas, a castoff by the Indians who played the last two seasons in Taiwan. The 29-year-old Vargas pitched four scoreless innings in the Series, topped out at 93 mph,

WINTER BASEBALL

Miguel Tejada set the tone for the Dominican Republic with his all-out play

ED WOLFSTEIN

and earned a one-year deal with the Rangers. In the Series, the Dominicans allowed just eight runs and posted a 1.01 ERA, but credit is due to more than just the arms.

Veteran catcher Alberto Castillo caught every inning of every game in the Series, including the marathon win over Venezuela. The 37-year-old backstop batted .261 with three doubles.

"Castillo was very, very important to our pitching staff throughout the Series, but all season as well," Dominican manager Felix Fermin said. "Without him, we are not the same club, we don't have the same confidence, and we definitely don't have the same experience. Alberto Castillo was a very big reason we won this Series."

The Dominicans were so balanced, so team-oriented, that second baseman Anderson Hernandez (Mets) was the only player to rank in the top 10 in hitting in the Series--and he barely made it at No. 10.

"This team, it means so much for us to win a championship for the Dominican Republic," Lima said. "You see them out there. They're crazy about us and we're crazy about them. We just came into this Series very loose and relaxed. I wasn't very relaxed in my first game, but as a team, we won. As a team, we kept it together. Whenever we needed something from somebody we seemed to get it. That's the sign of a good team."

Puerto Rico (4-2)

Outfielder Armando Rios hit .545 to lead all tournament

INTERNATIONAL BASEBALL

batters, edging Mexico outfielder Luis Garcia who hit .458. Puerto Rico placed four players in the top 10 in hitting.

It was the 12-0 loss to the Dominican Republic that stung them, and Venezuela finished any title hopes for Puerto Rico with a 3-1 win in Game Five.

"We kept hearing how we didn't stand a chance in this series, but this is very disappointing," Puerto Rico manager Lino Rivera said. "The Dominicans are king, and we're not happy with second place. We were hoping to bring Puerto Rico back to the top, but that didn't happen. We are all very sad, but you can be sure we'll come out and play hard tomorrow regardless of not bringing a title back to Puerto Rico."

Slugger Juan Gonzalez, who returned to play for Puerto Rico as the team's designated hitter, batted .385 (10-for-26) but was not a deep threat in the Series.

Venezuela (2-4)

It was a disappointing Series for Venezuela, a team that came in figuring to match up with the Dominicans. But Miguel Cabrera (Marlins) pulled out of the tournament before the club even left Caracas, and manager Buddy Bailey was forced to use Randall Simon (Phillies) in his cleanup hole.

Simon, though, was declared ineligible for the final game because the Caribbean Baseball Federation had suspended him for three seasons after he violated his contract with Aguilas (Dominican Republic) to sign with Aragua (Venezuela). He will not be able to return to any league in Mexico, Venezuela, the Dominican Republic or Puerto Rico until 2010.

"I'm not going to lie to you, that changed things a little bit for us," Bailey said. "It put pressure on other guys, but you've got to stand up to that pressure. But, really, we never stopped making all these errors. I thought we pitched well. We just didn't execute when we really needed to."

The lack of a marquee star proved no detriment to Venezuela's pitching throughout the tournament. Righthanders Cory Bailey (Cubs) and Tim McClaskey (Phillies) pitched well when they needed to, but the dynamic duo of relievers Francisco Butto (Yankees) and Yorman Bazardo (Tigers) were the most impressive of the bunch.

"Bazardo to me was one of our best relievers all year and he's got a great changeup," Buddy Bailey said. "But he's not a starter. I don't understand that mentality at all. This guy can light you up with short stints out of the pen, but doesn't sustain it. He's showed us some guts in certain situations too. They both have."

Mexico (1-5)

After getting off to a poor start, the popular storyline with team Mexico was Vinny Castilla's retirement, and how the veteran third baseman would walk off into the sunset after accepting a job with the Rockies as a special assistant to the general manager.

And even though his final plate appearance turned out to be an intentional walk in a game in which Castilla went 1-for-3 with a double, it was the only game Mexico won in the Series.

"It's great to go finish my career like this," Castilla said. "To have my country go out of this tournament a winner is special."

The area that hurt Mexico most throughout the Series was its outfield defense. Center fielder and catalyst Chris Roberson (Phillies) opted out of the Caribbean Series after his Mexican Pacific League team (Hermosillo) won its title.

So the club was forced to use a combination of Derrick White, Jon Weber (Diamondbacks) and Luis Garcia on the outfield corners, leaving manager Lorenzo Bundy with Alfredo Amezaga (Marlins) and Karim Garcia (Phillies) in center field.

"He decided to go home and prepare for spring training," Bundy said of Roberson. "It was his decision and I'll leave it at that."

And even though the Mexico team won only one game, it still showed character.

After getting outscored 33-4 over its first three games, Mexico lost two close ones--4-2 to Puerto Rico and 5-3 to the Dominican Republic.

"We played hard, but really, not one break went our way until the last day," Bundy said. "Our guys could have thrown in the towel, but I could have told you they'd never do that. They haven't done that all year--and not that we ran up against teams like these every day--but they always want to win. We're proud to wear these red, white and green uniforms and represent this country."

WINTER BASEBALL

DOMINICAN LEAGUE

REGULAR SEASON	W	L	PCT	GB
Tigres del Licey	26	16	.619	—
Aguilas Cibaenas	11	7	.611	3
Gigantes del Cibao	9	7	.563	4
Leones del Escogido	8	9	.471	5 ½
Estrellas de Oriente	7	11	.389	7
Azucareros del Este	3	14	.176	10 ½
PLAYOFFS	W	L	PCT	GB
Aguilas Cibaenas	12	5	.706	—
Tigres del Licey	12	6	.667	½
Gigantes del Cibao	10	8	.556	2 ½
Azucareros del Este	1	16	.059	11

PLAYOFFS—Aguilas defeated Licey 5-2 in best-of-nine series for league championship.

INDIVIDUAL BATTING LEADERS
(MINIMUM 2.7 PA/TEAM GAME)

BATTER, CLUB	AVG	G	AB	R	H	HR	RBI
Mendez, Victor, Gigantes	.409	13	44	8	18	5	13
Abreu, Tony, Aguilas	.365	15	52	9	19	1	5
Guzman, Joel, Estrellas	.357	14	56	6	20	1	4
Gorneault, Nick, Gigantes	.333	14	45	15	15	2	11
Moss, Brandon, Aguilas	.327	14	55	5	18	3	10
Aybar, Erick, Licey	.321	27	109	13	35	0	12
Toregas, Wyatt, Azucareros	.320	16	50	7	16	1	5
Aybar, Willy, Licey	.303	33	122	23	37	2	16
Lopez, Mendy, Aguilas	.299	16	67	10	20	1	7
Hernandez, Anderson, Licey	.287	25	101	16	29	0	9

INDIVIDUAL PITCHING LEADERS
(MINIMUM 0.8 PA/TEAM GAME)

PITCHER, CLUB	W	L	ERA	IP	H	BB	SO
Simon, Alfredo, Gigantes	0	1	1.35	13	8	6	8
Lee, Derek, Aguilas	4	0	1.50	30	29	6	13
Heredia, Felix, Azucareros	2	2	1.69	27	19	7	17
Smith, Mike, Azucareros	0	2	1.80	15	14	3	7
Tankersley, Dennis, Licey	3	2	2.38	34	23	10	18
Martinez, Anastacio, Estrellas	0	1	2.45	15	14	8	14
Lima, Jose , Aguilas	0	1	2.55	18	15	6	11
Rodriguez, Nerio, Escogido	1	0	2.83	29	31	3	17
Gulin, Lindsay, Licey	2	2	3.74	34	27	12	24
Giron, Roberto, Estrellas	1	2	4.30	15	12	3	13

MEXICAN PACIFIC LEAGUE

	W	L	PCT	GB
★#Naranjeros de Hermosillo	41	26	.612	—
Venados de Mazatlan	38	27	.585	2
Yaquis de Obregon	39	29	.574	2 ½
Tomateros de Culiacan	32	33	.492	8

Mayos de Navojoa	31	36	.463	10
Caneros de los Mochis	30	38	.441	11 ½
Aguilas de Mexicali	28	39	.418	13
Algodoneros de Guasave	28	39	.418	13

★First-half champion. #Second-half champion.

PLAYOFFS—First Round: Hermosillo defeated Mochis 4-1, Mazatlan defeated Navojoa 4-1, and Culiacan defeated Obregon 4-3 in best-of-seven series. **Semifinals:** Hermosillo defeated Obregon 4-3, and Mazatlan defeated Culiacan 4-3 in best-of-seven series. **Championship:** Hermosillo defeated Mazatlan 4-0 in best-of-seven series.

INDIVIDUAL BATTING LEADERS
(MINIMUM 3.1 PA/TEAM GAME)

BATTER, CLUB	AVG	G	AB	R	H	HR	RBI
Orantes, Ramon, Mochis	.365	61	211	24	77	7	19
Canizalez, Juan, Hermosillo	.353	61	235	33	83	7	40
White, Derrick, Mexicali	.346	63	231	43	80	12	43
Durazo, Erubiel, Hermosillo	.344	63	227	52	78	18	56
Gastelum, Carlos Alberto, Hermosillo	.338	63	216	40	73	0	16
Sievers, Carlos, Mexicali	.320	66	241	34	77	11	49
Ortiz, Jose, Mochis	.316	67	256	35	81	17	55
Castillo, Jesus, Mexicali	.306	65	209	31	64	3	24
Clark, Doug, Navojoa	.303	58	198	47	60	11	41
Amador, Jose, Navojoa	.302	66	248	42	75	10	47

INDIVIDUAL PITCHING LEADERS
(MINIMUM 0.8 PA/TEAM GAME)

PITCHER, CLUB	W	L	ERA	IP	H	BB	SO
Rivera, Oscar, Navojoa	8	2	1.51	77	50	21	67
Soria, Joakim, Obregon	9	1	2.41	78	60	20	79
Shearn, Tom, Navojoa	6	3	2.76	72	61	27	61
Campillo, Jorge, Culiacan	5	4	3.07	76	55	18	67
Bustillos, Oscar, Mazatlan	6	2	3.17	71	56	32	60
Ortega, Pablo, Mazatlan	7	6	3.29	93	97	24	40
Arellano, Salvador, Hermosillo	4	2	3.99	68	60	24	37
Mendoza, Mario, Navojoa	4	5	4.30	92	97	30	30
Diaz, Rafael, Mochis	4	4	4.55	85	77	22	64
Rodriguez, Francisco, Mochis	4	7	4.68	73	78	31	35

PUERTO RICAN LEAGUE

	W	L	PCT	GB
Indios de Mayaguez	27	17	.614	—
Criollos de Caguas	23	21	.523	4
Lobos de Arecibo	22	22	.500	5
Gigantes de Carolina	22	23	.489	5 ½
Leones de Ponce	21	24	.467	6 ½
Atenienses de Manatí	18	26	.409	9

PLAYOFFS—Semifinals: Ponce defeated Manati 4-0 and Carolina defeated Caguas 4-1 in best-of-seven series. **Final:** Carolina defeated Ponce 5-3 in best-of-nine series.

INDIVIDUAL BATTING LEADERS
(MINIMUM 119 PLATE APPEARANCES)

BATTER, CLUB	AVG	G	AB	R	H	HR	RBI
Negron, Mickey, Caguas	.381	39	126	24	48	3	21
Feliciano, Jesus, Arecibo	.331	44	175	24	58	1	9
Ortiz, Nick, Caguas	.318	31	110	12	35	0	15
Matos, Julius, Mayaguez	.318	34	129	12	41	2	13
Nieves, Raul, Ponce	.309	38	136	15	42	0	6
Casanova, Raul, Caguas	.294	39	143	17	42	5	31
Clemente, Edgar, Carolina	.291	38	134	16	39	3	16
Botts, Jason, Caguas	.288	32	118	19	34	4	15
Padilla, Jorge, Arecibo	.285	44	151	15	43	4	23
Navarrete, Rey, Carolina	.283	32	99	15	28	3	15

INDIVIDUAL PITCHING LEADERS
(MINIMUM 0.8 PA/TEAM GAME)

PITCHER, CLUB	W	L	ERA	IP	H	BB	SO
Chen, Bruce, Caguas	5	0	0.72	50	19	8	59
Pulsipher, Bill, Arecibo	4	3	1.68	70	52	14	44
Albaladejo, Jonathan, Mayaguez	6	2	2.12	59	49	12	54
Román, Orlando, Caguas	5	1	2.13	63	47	20	26
Kershner, Jason, Arecibo	1	5	2.30	5	51	7	31
Alvarado, Giancarlo, Ponce	5	3	2.47	69	53	25	56
Rojas, Chris, Mayaguez	3	2	2.60	55	50	28	32
Edwards, Brian, Ponce	3	4	3.57	58	47	24	22
Moss, Damian, Mayaguez	3	3	4.09	51	53	28	33
Waters, Chris, Caguas	0	8	4.53	50	45	25	30

VENEZUELAN LEAGUE

OCCIDENTAL DIVISION

	W	L	PCT	GB
Tigres de Aragua	41	21	.661	—
Aguilas del Zulia	35	27	.565	6
Cardenales de Lara	29	33	.468	12
Pastora de los Llanos	25	37	.403	16

ORIENTAL DIVISION

	W	L	PCT	GB
Navegantes del Magallanes	36	26	.581	—
Leones del Caracas	29	33	.468	7
Tiburones de La Guaira	27	35	.435	9
Caribes de Oriente	26	36	.419	10

PLAYOFFS

	W	L	PCT	GB
Navegantes del Magallanes	12	4	.750	—
Tigres de Aragua	11	5	.688	1
Aguilas del Zulia	8	8	.500	4
Cardenales de Lara	6	10	.375	6
Leones del Caracas	3	13	.188	9

CHAMPIONSHIP SERIES—Aragua defeated Magallanes 4-1 in best-of-seven series for league championship.

INDIVIDUAL BATTING LEADERS
(MINIMUM 2.7 PA/TEAM GAME)

BATTER, CLUB	AVG	G	AB	R	H	HR	RBI
Scutaro, Marco, Caracas	.367	41	150	31	55	1	18
Romero, Alex, Aragua	.345	59	203	32	70	2	34
Bergolla, William, Caracas	.335	52	212	32	71	1	17
Simon, Randall, La Guaira	.331	44	166	27	55	4	27
Mendez, Carlos, Caracas	.330	50	191	23	63	4	26
Hernandez, Luis, La Guaira	.323	49	161	24	52	1	22
Romero, Wilfredo, Aragua	.323	52	164	29	53	1	19
Camacho, Juan, Zulia	.321	45	162	22	52	6	29
Gonzalez, Carlos, Zulia	.318	53	198	33	63	9	41
Blanco, Gregor, La Guaira	.317	55	183	36	58	1	12

INDIVIDUAL PITCHING LEADERS
(MINIMUM 0.8 PA/TEAM GAME)

PITCHER, CLUB	W	L	ERA	IP	H	BB	SO
Begg, Chris, Zulia	4	1	1.08	50	45	9	24
Estrada, Horacio, Aragua	5	1	1.96	69	55	11	50
Bailey, Cory, Aragua	3	3	2.24	68	63	4	45
Garcia, Rosman, Aragua	2	1	2.47	51	50	11	32
Harris, Jeff, Lara	4	3	2.51	61	45	9	26
Connolly, Michael, Llanos	4	1	2.61	52	38	17	39
Duarte, Renny, Caracas	3	2	2.72	50	50	12	28
Totten, Heath, Zulia	6	2	2.74	62	72	8	31
Bonilla, Henr, Aragua	3	2	2.80	61	58	13	32
Thurman, Corey, Oriente	3	2	2.84	57	54	14	45

COLLEGE BASEBALL

Barney, Canham lead Beavers to another title

BY AARON FITT

OMAHA

Darwin Barney emerged from the gaggle of Oregon State players draped in white "National Champions" T-shirts, took a few steps toward home plate, then wheeled around and yelled, "Mitch! Mitch! Let's go!"

A moment later, Mitch Canham forced his way through the throng. Barney put his left arm around Canham's shoulders, and the duo approached the makeshift platform set up near the plate. Together the two juniors hoisted the massive national championship trophy over their heads and posed for pictures. Then they turned to their teammates, calling, "Hey everybody, get in here!"

It wasn't the first time Barney and Canham have led their teammates during the past three years, but it was the last. The pair put the finishing touches on one of the great three-year runs in college baseball history, leading the Beavers to a 9-3 win against North Carolina and their second consecutive national title, capping off their third straight trip to the College World Series. Appropriately, Barney's two-run homer in the second inning–with Canham on first base–gave Oregon State the lead for good.

But Barney and Canham weren't thinking about the last three years. They were thinking about the 2007 Beavers, whose improbable run through the postseason made them the first team ever to finish with a sub-.500 record in its conference and go on to win the national title.

"All I can think about right now is what just happened between those lines," Barney said. "The men that we brought together and that I've been with since September, that's what's most special to me right now. The past three years of my career, it's been fun, but right now it's all about the team, and it's about every single one of these guys contributing today. Even the guys that didn't get into the game, they're right there on the top step feeding us in as we come in from the field."

That team-first attitude has defined the Beavers during their remarkable run, and they proved to be the best, most complete team in the nation by simply dominating the 2007 College World Series. Oregon State won its final 10 games in the postseason and became the first team ever to win four consecutive CWS games by six or more runs.

"What an unbelievable accomplishment that is to win back-to-back national championships," North Carolina coach Mike Fox said. "I'm not sure–you can't ever say never–but I'm not sure that's going to be done here too many times at this level, as many good teams are there are here at this level."

Strong Start, Soft Middle

For a while, it was uncertain Oregon State would even make it into the NCAA tournament to have a chance to defend its title. The Beavers started the season with a bang, as four pitchers combined to throw a no-hitter against Hawaii-Hilo on Jan. 25. OSU kept rolling from there, despite playing its first 17 games away from home, and the Beavers were sitting pretty at 23-3, ranked fourth in the nation head-

Darwin Barney's second-inning home run gave Oregon State the lead for good against UNC

DENNIS HUBBARD

ing into Pacific-10 Conference play.

But Oregon State's quest for a third consecutive Pac-10 title hit a road block in its first conference series at Arizona, where OSU was unceremoniously swept. The Beavers battled back to a .500 conference record by winning their next three Pac-10 series, but their bats went cold down the stretch. Oregon State dropped three consecutive series—to Washington, Washington State and Arizona State—averaging fewer than three runs per game in the seven losses. OSU needed to win its final regular-season series at UCLA just to have a shot at an at-large NCAA tournament bid.

"I think the defining moment was we had a little meeting Wednesday before we headed to UCLA, and we said, 'This is what we've got to do. There's no easy way to tell you, but we win two out of three, or we're going home,'" Oregon State coach Pat Casey said. "I think that was something they all realized, and people like Mitch and Barney, other people that have been around, they got the grasp of what we needed to do, and they decided themselves in the locker room that we've got to go down and get that thing turned around. We did it, and since then I feel like they've gotten into a pretty good rhythm of playing the game."

Still, the Beavers finished just 10-14 in conference, good enough for sixth place, and they were shipped to the Charlottesville regional as a No. 3 seed. After winning their opener against Rutgers, the Beavers dropped a 13-inning classic to host Virginia, putting them in the familiar posi-

School	New Coach (Previous School/Job)	Former Coach (Reason for Departure)
UC Irvine	Mike Gillespie (Yankees, short-season)	Dave Serrano (Cal State Fullerton)
Cal State Fullerton	Dave Serrano (UC Irvine head coach)	George Horton (Oregon)
Campbell	Greg Goff (Montevallo, Ala., head coach)	Chris Wiley (interim)
Dallas Baptist	Dan Heefner (Dallas Baptist assistant)	Eric Newman (Nebraska assistant)
Florida	Kevin O'Sullivan (Clemson assistant)	Pat McMahon (fired)
Florida International	Turtle Thomas (Arizona State assistant)	Danny Price (fired)
La Salle	Mike Lake (La Salle assistant)	Lee Saverio (fired)
Liberty	Jim Toman (South Carolina assistant)	Matt Royer (resigned)
McNeese State	Terry Burrows (St. Louis High, Lake Charles, La., head coach)	Chris Fackler (interim)
Morehead State	Jay Sorg (Reds, Triple-A)	John Jarnagin (fired)
New Mexico	Ray Birmingham (New Mexico JC head coach)	Rich Alday (resigned)
North Dakota State	Tod Brown (Bowling Green State assistant)	Mitch McLeod (resigned)
Northwestern State	J.P. Davis (Northwestern State assistant)	Mitch Gaspard (Alabama assistant)
Oakland	John Musachio (Oakland assistant)	Dylan Putnam (resigned)
Oregon	George Horton (Cal State Fullerton)	none
Radford	Joe Raccuia (Alabama assistant)	Lew Kent (resigned)
Richmond	Mark McQueen (associate head coach)	Ron Atkins (retired)
Saint Louis	Darin Hendrickson (Central Mo. State head coach)	Bob Hughes (resigned)
Tennessee	Todd Raleigh (Western Carolina head coach)	Rod Delmonico (fired)
Texas A&M-Corpus Christi	Scott Malone (UNLV assistant coach)	Hector Salinas (interim)
Western Carolina	Bobby Moranda (Georgia Tech assistant)	Todd Raleigh (Tennessee)
Wofford	Todd Interdonato (Wofford assistant)	Steve Traylor (retired)

tion of having to win three consecutive elimination games to prolong their season. That was what Oregon State did in the 2006 College World Series, when it won six consecutive elimination games. Rain forced OSU to play two games on Monday during regionals, and after winning the first against Rutgers, Oregon State trailed the Cavaliers 3-1 heading into the eighth inning of the nightcap. That's when everything clicked into place.

"About the seventh or eighth inning at Virginia, we were getting beat, and something happened in our dugout," Casey said. "I'm not sure why or how, but we got pretty energized and inspired. From that time on, there was never a time I didn't think we were going to be very, very tough to handle. And I don't know why, I've never had that feeling. I've always been confident, but this was different. It was magic. We felt it in the hotel, we felt it in the bus, we felt it in practice.

"We were getting no-hit in the super-regional game (by Michigan's Zach Putnam), we're just sitting there as a team talking about how we're going to get this one down, tomorrow we're going to throw (Mike) Stutes. It was something strange that happened, and our club felt it, it was some type of energy. And it never went away."

The Beavers wouldn't lose again in 2007, coming back to beat Virginia with three runs in the eighth inning, then taking the decisive game of the regional the next day, then sweeping Michigan in two games at the Corvallis super-regional before vanquishing Cal State Fullerton, Arizona State and UC Irvine to earn a rematch with the Tar Heels in the CWS finals. Oregon State cruised to an 11-4 win in the first game against UNC, then sent Stutes to the mound in Game Two.

North Carolina actually grabbed a 1-0 lead in the first inning, the first time OSU had trailed in its last 61 innings. But Stutes minimized the damage by getting Seth Williams to fly out to center with runners on the corners. Stutes–who also started Game Two of the CWS finals a year earlier, when he allowed four runs over three innings–settled down after that, holding the Tar Heels to three runs on seven hits over 5⅓ innings.

Oregon State seemed energized after escaping the rocky

UNC first inning with just one run on the board, and Barney's two-run homer to left keyed a three-run inning that chased North Carolina starter Luke Putkonen. Closer Andrew Carignan replaced Putkonen and kept the Tar Heels in the game by allowing two runs over 3⅓ innings, as the two teams traded solitary runs in the third and the fifth. But UNC had no answer for Oregon State's two-run seventh and ninth innings. The Beavers got much of their production from the No. 6 and No. 7 spots in the lineup, where outfielders John Wallace and Scott Santschi combined to go 6-for-7 with three runs and three RBIs.

New Faces Contribute

The Tar Heels, on the other hand, continued to struggle with men on base. They had plenty of chances in Game Two, but they were just 1-for-10 with runners in scoring position. In the two CWS finals losses, UNC was 2-for-20 with men in scoring position. UNC appeared to have something going in the seventh, when Williams doubled down the left-field line with one out and Tim Fedroff on first base. But Fox waved Fedroff around third, and Barney made a perfect relay throw to Canham, who blocked the plate and tagged Fedroff out to take the wind out of UNC's sails.

"That might have been the first extra-base hit we've had with somebody on base, so I guess I got caught up in trying to score a run there," Fox said. "In hindsight, I should have put the stop sign up, but that's the way it goes."

One key to that play for Oregon State was something subtle, but it should give the Beavers hope they can extend their dynasty even without Barney, Canham and co. A huge reason OSU is so good is its superior feel for the game, something intangible that is personified in players like Barney. Freshman second baseman Joey Wong demonstrated that same savvy on Williams' double.

"You always try to read the game when the ball's hit like that, and I knew there was a pretty good runner on base," Barney said. "Myself, I didn't think they were going to send him in that situation–if I'm the manager, that's not what you want to do, I was pretty surprised. So I made sure Joey was following me, and something me and Joey try to do is always give each other information. He let me know

Rosenblatt Stadium, Omaha, June 15-June 24

BRACKET ONE	W	L	RS	RA
North Carolina	4	1	28	25
Rice	2	2	34	27
Louisville	1	2	23	20
Mississippi State	0	2	9	20

Bracket One Final: North Carolina 7, Rice 4.

BRACKET TWO	W	L	RS	RA
Oregon State	3	0	22	9
UC Irvine	2	2	18	23
Arizona State	1	2	18	24
Cal State Fullerton	0	2	6	8

Bracket Two Final: Oregon State 7, UC Irvine 1

CWS FINALS
(BEST OF THREE)

June 23: Oregon State 11, North Carolina 4
June 24: Oregon State 9, North Carolina 3

INDIVIDUAL BATTING LEADERS
(MINIMUM 10 AT-BATS)

Player, Team	AVG	AB	R	H	2B	3B	HR	RBI	BB
Scott Santschi, Oregon State	.538	13	3	7	0	0	1	5	4
Bryan Petersen, UC Irvine	.533	15	1	8	1	1	0	3	3
Eric Sogard, Arizona State	.500	14	0	7	0	0	0	4	0
Mitch Canham, Oregon State	.400	20	4	8	0	0	1	5	2
Tyler Henley, Rice	.400	.15	5	6	1	0	0	2	2
Petey Paramore, Arizona State	.400	10	3	4	2	0	1	2	3
Boomer Whiting, Louisville	.400	10	4	4	1	0	0	2	4
Danny Lehmann, Rice	.389	18	5	7	3	0	0	4	0
Logan Johnson, Louisville	.385	13	5	5	0	0	4	6	0
Jorge Castillo, Louisville	.385	13	2	5	1	0	0	1	1

INDIVIDUAL PITCHING LEADERS
(MINIMUM 6 INNINGS)

Pitcher, Team	W	L	ERA	G	SV	IP	H	BB	SO
Cole St. Clair, Rice	0	0	0.00	2	1	7	6	1	4
Daniel Turpen, Oregon State	1	0	1.12	1	0	8	5	3	5
Brian Harris, Cal State Fullerton	0	1	1.50	2	0	6	5	3	5
Joe Paterson, Oregon State	0	0	1.74	5	1	10	8	1	10
Andrew Carignan, North Carolina	0	0	1.80	5	3	10	5	4	9
Wes Roemer, Cal State Fullerton	0	1	2.25	1	0	8	7	0	7
Dylan Axelrod, UC Irvine	1	0	2.45	3	0	7	6	3	9
Adam Warren, North Carolina	2	0	2.61	2	0	10	6	4	6
Jorge Reyes, Oregon State	2	0	2.92	2	0	12	11	3	6
Luke Putkonen, North Carolina	1	1	3.12	2	0	9	6	3	8

ALL-TOURNAMENT TEAM

C—Mitch Canham, Oregon State. **1B**—Dustin Ackley, North Carolina. **2B**—Joey Wong, Oregon State. **SS**—Darwin Barney, Oregon State. **3B**—Diego Seastrunk, Rice. **OF**—Bryan Petersen, UC Irvine; Tim Fedroff, North Carolina; Scott Santschi, Oregon State. **DH**—Mike Lissman, Oregon State. **P**—Jorge Reyes, Oregon State; Andrew Carignan, North Carolina.

Most Outstanding Player—Jorge Reyes, rhp, Oregon State.

the guy was running, he said, 'Relay, relay!' I just turned and threw it."

Another freshman, righthander Jorge Reyes, was named the CWS Most Outstanding Player after starting and winning Oregon State's opener against Cal State Fullerton and its CWS finals opener against North Carolina. Reyes has already etched his name alongside former Beaver greats–and he has at least two more years remaining in Corvallis.

"Jorge is lights out. You can see it in his eyes, you can see it in his mannerisms," Barney said. "That's what it takes to be a pitcher, that's what Jonah Nickerson had, that's what Kevin Gunderson had, and I think Jorge Reyes can do a lot of good things in his future."

For Barney, Canham, lefthander Joe Paterson and the other OSU players who headed to the professional ranks after the CWS, their legacy is already secure, and they leave the program in capable hands. There can be no doubting that Oregon State—which didn't even make the NCAA tournament field from 1987 through 2004—is now a college baseball superpower, and not just because the Beavers joined elite programs Louisiana State, Stanford,

Southern California and Texas as the only schools to repeat as national champions.

"I don't have to convince these guys that they're Texas or USC, because they're Oregon State," Casey said. "We don't need to be anybody but who we are, and tonight in Omaha, Nebraska, we're the best club in the country."

Hit Men

When UC Irvine first baseman Taylor Holiday was hit by a pitch to lead off the 13th inning of the Anteaters' epic 5-4 win against Cal State Fullerton, an issue that had been simmering under the surface of the 2007 CWS boiled over.

Titans coach George Horton was ejected for arguing that Holiday got hit by the pitch intentionally, and Irvine turned the leadoff baserunner into the game-winning rally. Holiday later admitted that he was indeed trying to get hit by the pitch.

Partly because of the presence of Irvine and Fullerton, who emphasize getting on base using any means necessary, the 2007 CWS shattered the record for most hit batsmen. In all, 53 batters were hit, obliterating the old mark of 36 set in 2003. At least two batters were hit in all 15 games of the 2007 CWS.

Some coaches were calling for a re-examination of the hit batsmen rules, where players would be required to make a better effort to get out of the way of pitches. But the larger sentiment seemed to be that this was just a fluke year.

"It's part of the game, especially in college," UNC righthander Robert Woodard said. "Hitters stand on top of the plate. As a pitcher you have to pitch inside to put pressure on the batters. Also, when it's hot outside your hand sweats and sometimes you just lose your grip on the ball. I think in a lot of situations this year that has been the case with a lot of pitchers."

APR Spurs Sweeping Changes

RPI (Ratings Percentage Index) used to be the most important acronym in college baseball, and for the first time in 2007, the NCAA released its RPI rankings during the season (see chart, page 418).

But the NCAA's APR (Academic Progress Rate) has usurped the RPI in importance. Using the APR—a measurement that has replaced graduation rates and grade-point averages as the most important measure of how athletic departments handle student-athletes—the NCAA is reshaping the college baseball landscape.

As April ended, the NCAA approved a legislative reform package put forward by the Baseball Academic Enhancement Working Group, which had been formed to help baseball improve its APR. The sport has consistently ranked near the bottom of the NCAA's APR rankings, bunched with football and men's basketball as the worst three sports. Coaches who opposed the new legislation drummed up enough protests to force an override vote at the August meeting of the NCAA board of directors, but the package was approved with just one alteration.

To improve baseball's APR, the Working Group came up with a series of changes, starting with the elimination of the one-time transfer exemption. Starting in the summer of 2008, players will have to sit out a season after switching schools before gaining eligibility to play.

Baseball players now will have to be academically certified at the start of the fall semester, which will eliminate mid-year transfers and prevent players from taking too few spring courses and catching up in the fall.

The most controversial provision approved by the NCAA

was added to make the transfer elimination more palatable to players. All scholarship players will have to receive at least a 25 percent aid package, and the number of players who can receive scholarships will be limited to 27. Also, squad sizes will be capped at 35. The original proposal called for a minimum scholarship of 33 percent, but that threshold was lowered to 25 percent as a compromise in August.

Coaches contacted about the changes since they were first proposed consistently complained about the roster caps and the lack of flexibility engendered by the minimum scholarship aid. The common refrain: Why should the NCAA tell 280-plus Division I college baseball coaches how to spend their scholarship money? As Mississippi State coach Ron Polk put it, "They gave us chump change—that's what I call 11.7 scholarships. Now they are telling us how to spend our chump change."

Dave Keilitz, executive director of the American Baseball Coaches Association and a guiding force on the Working Group, said the Working Group was concerned that schools

COLLEGE WORLD SERIES CHAMPIONS 1947-2007

Year	Champion	Coach	Record	Runner-Up	MVP
1947	California★	Clint Evans	31-10	Yale	None selected
1948	Southern California	Sam Barry	40-12	Yale	None selected
1949	Texas★	Bibb Falk	23-7	Wake Forest	Charles Teague, 2b, Wake Forest
1950	Texas	Bibb Falk	27-6	Washington State	Ray VanCleef, of, Rutgers
1951	Oklahoma★	Jack Baer	19-9	Tennessee	Sid Hatfield, 1b-p, Tennessee
1952	Holy Cross	Jack Baer	21-3	Missouri	Jim O'Neill, p, Holy Cross
1953	Michigan	Ray Fisher	21-9	Texas	J.L. Smith, p, Texas
1954	Missouri	Hi Simmons	22-4	Rollins	Tom Yewcic, c, Michigan State
1955	Wake Forest	Taylor Sanford	29-7	Western Michigan	Tom Borland, p, Oklahoma State
1956	Minnesota	Dick Siebert	33-9	Arizona	Jerry Thomas, p, Minnesota
1957	California★	George Wolfman	35-10	Penn State	Cal Emery, 1b-p, Penn State
1958	Southern California	Rod Dedeaux	35-7	Missouri	Bill Thom, p, Southern California
1959	Oklahoma State	Toby Greene	27-5	Arizona	Jim Dobson, 3b, Oklahoma State
1960	Minnesota	Dick Siebert	34-7	Southern California	John Erickson, 2b, Minnesota
1961	Southern California★	Rod Dedeaux	43-9	Oklahoma State	Littleton Fowler, p, Oklahoma State
1962	Michigan	Don Lund	31-13	Santa Clara	Bob Garibaldi, p, Santa Clara
1963	Southern California	Rod Dedeaux	37-16	Arizona	Bud Hollowell, c, Southern California
1964	Minnesota	Dick Siebert	31-12	Missouri	Joe Ferris, p, Maine
1965	Arizona State	Bobby Winkles	54-8	Ohio State	Sal Bando, 3b, Arizona State
1966	Ohio State	Marty Karow	27-6	Oklahoma State	Steve Arlin, p, Ohio State
1967	Arizona State	Bobby Winkles	53-12	Houston	Ron Davini, c, Arizona State
1968	Southern California★	Rod Dedeaux	45-14	Southern Illinois	Bill Seinsoth, 1b, Southern California
1969	Arizona State	Bobby Winkles	56-11	Tulsa	John Dolinsek, of, Arizona State
1970	Southern California	Rod Dedeaux	51-13	Florida State	Gene Ammann, p, Florida State
1971	Southern California	Rod Dedeaux	53-13	Southern Illinois	Jerry Tabb, 1b, Tulsa
1972	Southern California	Rod Dedeaux	50-13	Arizona State	Russ McQueen, p, Southern California
1973	Southern California★	Rod Dedeaux	51-11	Arizona State	Dave Winfield, of-p, Minnesota
1974	Southern California	Rod Dedeaux	50-20	Miami	George Milke, p, Southern California
1975	Texas	Cliff Gustafson	56-6	South Carolina	Mickey Reichenbach, 1b, Texas
1976	Arizona	Jerry Kindall	56-17	Eastern Michigan	Steve Powers, dh-p, Arizona
1977	Arizona State	Jim Brock	57-12	South Carolina	Bob Horner, 3b, Arizona State
1978	Southern California★	Rod Dedeaux	54-9	Arizona State	Rod Boxberger, p, Southern California
1979	Cal State Fullerton	Augie Garrido	60-14	Arkansas	Tony Hudson, p, Cal State Fullerton
1980	Arizona	Jerry Kindall	45-21	Hawaii	Terry Francona, of, Arizona
1981	Arizona State	Jim Brock	55-13	Oklahoma State	Stan Holmes, of, Arizona State
1982	Miami★	Ron Fraser	57-18	Wichita State	Dan Smith, p, Miami (Fla.)
1983	Texas★	Cliff Gustafson	66-14	Alabama	Calvin Schiraldi, p, Texas
1984	Cal State Fullerton	Augie Garrido	66-20	Texas	John Fishel, of, Cal State Fullerton
1985	Miami (Fla.)★	Ron Fraser	64-16	Texas	Greg Ellena, dh, Miami (Fla.)
1986	Arizona	Jerry Kindall	49-19	Florida State	Mike Senne, of, Arizona
1987	Stanford	Mark Marquess	53-17	Oklahoma State	Paul Carey, of, Stanford
1988	Stanford	Mark Marquess	46-23	Arizona State	Lee Plemel, p, Stanford
1989	Wichita State	Gene Stephenson	68-16	Texas	Greg Brummett, p, Wichita State
1990	Georgia	Steve Webber	52-19	Oklahoma State	Mike Rebhan, p, Georgia
1991	Louisiana State★	Skip Bertman	55-18	Wichita State	Gary Hymel, c, Louisiana State
1992	Pepperdine★	Andy Lopez	48-11	Cal State Fullerton	Phil Nevin, 3b, Cal State Fullerton
1993	Louisiana State	Skip Bertman	53-17	Wichita State	Todd Walker, 2b, Louisiana State
1994	Oklahoma★	Larry Cochell	50-17	Georgia Tech	Chip Glass, of, Oklahoma
1995	Cal State Fullerton★	Augie Garrido	57-9	Southern California	Mark Kotsay, of-p, Cal State Fullerton
1996	Louisiana State★	Skip Bertman	52-15	Miami	Pat Burrell, 3b, Miami
1997	Louisiana State★	Skip Bertman	57-13	Alabama	Brandon Larson, ss, Louisiana State
1998	Southern California	Mike Gillespie	49-17	Arizona State	Wes Rachels, 2b, Southern California
1999	Miami★	Jim Morris	50-13	Florida State	Marshall McDougall, 2b, Florida State
2000	Louisiana State★	Skip Bertman	52-17	Stanford	Trey Hodges, rhp, Louisiana State
2001	Miami★	Jim Morris	53-12	Stanford	Charlton Jimerson, of, Miami
2002	Texas★	Augie Garrido	57-15	South Carolina	Huston Street, rhp, Texas
2003	Rice	Wayne Graham	58-12	Stanford	John Hudgins, rhp, Stanford
2004	Cal State Fullerton	George Horton	47-22	Texas	Jason Windsor, rhp, Cal State Fullerton
2005	Texas★	Augie Garrido	56-16	Florida	David Maroul, 3b, Texas
2006	Oregon State	Pat Casey	50-16	North Carolina	Jonah Nickerson, rhp, Oregon State
2007	Oregon State★	Pat Casey	49-18	North Carolina	Jorge Reyes, rhp, Oregon State

★Undefeated

that offer just a few scholarships—say, three to five—would be affected most, with perhaps as few as nine out of 35 players receiving scholarship aid in a worst-case scenario. He understands the complaints but explained that college baseball had few alternatives.

"There's no doubt you do not have as much flexibility as what you've had in the past," Keilitz said. "But the data shows that the flexibility that we've had in the past is also one of the reasons for the huge number of transfers . . . The smaller the scholarship, the greater the chance of the kid leaving.

"In the whole APR component, the biggest problem was the transfer, so the committee felt a bottom had to be created."

Coaches have long feared roster caps, which many schools had instituted on their programs as a way of complying with Title IX gender-equity legislation. Keilitz explained, "The cap of 27 was established because the data shows the larger number of players on the team also cre-

ated greater turnover, because all players are looking for playing time. So the cap was established at 27, that was based on the average number of players on scholarship Division I teams have had in recent years."

Penalties Assessed

The NCAA released its latest APR report just days after the sweeping legislation was first approved in April, and the report showed baseball was making progress before making the significant changes. Baseball still performs on par with football and basketball, with a 934 three-year APR score (on a scale of 1-1,000), ranking third-worst in the NCAA ahead of just football (931) and men's basketball (927).

"We have realized improvement in some of the areas that needed it," NCAA president Myles Brand said in an official statement. "Football is up—that's good. Perhaps the most pleasant surprise, though, is in baseball, which is up significantly."

Programs that grade below 900 are penalized 10 percent of their 11.7 scholarships.

This year, six baseball programs were penalized the full 10 percent—Fresno State, New Mexico, Temple, Texas-Arlington, Texas A&M-Corpus Christi and Texas Tech. Several other schools have to cough up more than one scholarship, including Oral Roberts (1.06), Lipscomb (1.10) and Florida International (1.12). In all, 27 schools either saw scholarships reduced (20 in all, some by as little as .05 scholarships) or were publicly reprimanded (seven).

However, the news was better for baseball than expected. The sport made progress, as last year 10 programs, including Texas, were penalized the full 1.17 scholarships, and 71 schools fell below the cut line, compared to 27 this year. Also, last year's baseball-wide average was 931, and that score was 922 in 2005.

So baseball has shown modest progress. The sport presents challenges unique among college sports, from the baseball draft to summer leagues, which the NCAA has failed to recognize or appreciate when meting out APR penalties. But on its own, college baseball has improved in this measure of academic progress.

"We would solve the APR problem ourselves if given the time," Polk said. "If the NCAA would have given us a couple of years, we would have fixed it ourselves."

As The Carousel Turns

The coaching carousel had a wild ride in June and literally came full circle when Alabama coach Jim Wells, who announced his retirement June 21, was announced as the Crimson Tide's new coach six days later.

Wells, 52, completed his 13th season as Alabama's head coach, compiling a 553-272 career record. He became the school's all-time winningest coach in 2006 and guided the Tide to the College World Series in 1996, '97 and '99. The Tide was national runner-up in 1997, losing to Louisiana State, and Wells was BA's Coach of the Year. However, Alabama missed regionals in 2001, 2004 and 2007, with a 31-26 record this spring that left the Tide on the outside looking in during the 64-team NCAA tournament. Former Wells assistant Mitch Gaspard later left his head coaching job at Northwestern State to become the associate head coach and heir apparent to Wells at Alabama.

The Crimson Tide had company searching for a new coach in the Southeastern Conference, as Tennessee fired Rod Delmonico and replaced him with Western Carolina's Todd Raleigh. Notably, Western Carolina—which eventually hired Georgia Tech assistant Bobby

RPI RANKINGS

The Ratings Percentage Index is an important tool used by the NCAA in selecting at-large teams for the 64-team Division I regional tournament. The NCAA now releases its RPI rankings during the season, and these were the top 100 finishers for 2007. A team's rank in the final Baseball America Top 25 is indicated in parentheses, and College World Series teams are in boldface.

1. Rice (3)	56-14	51. St. John's	41-19
2. Vanderbilt (6)	54-13	52. LSU	29-26
3. **North Carolina** (2)	57-16	53. Memphis	36-27
4. **Arizona State** (5)	49-15	54. Kentucky	34-19
5. Texas (11)	46-17	55. South Florida	34-26
6. Texas A&M (12)	48-19	56. Tennessee	34-25
7. South Carolina (10)	46-20	57. Troy	34-27
8. Coastal Carolina (20)	50-13	58. Southern California	27-29
9. **Oregon State** (1)	49-18	59. Evansville	35-23
10. Long Beach State	39-20	60. Cal Poly	32-24
11. Florida State (14)	49-13	61. Alabama	31-26
12. **UC Irvine** (4)	47-17	62. California	29-26
13. Virginia (16)	45-16	63. Liberty	36-25
14. La.-Lafayette	45-17	64. Houston	28-28
15. Mississippi (17)	40-25	65. Sam Houston State	40-24
16. San Diego (18)	43-18	66. Penn St.	31-26
17. **Mississippi State** (8)	38-22	67. UT San Antonio	36-22
18. Clemson (15)	41-23	68. Central Florida	27-32
19. Arkansas (21)	43-21	69. Ohio State	38-24
20. Missouri (24)	42-18	70. Florida Atlantic	36-22
21. Arizona	42-17	71. Virginia Tech	23-31
22. Wichita State (13)	53-22	72. Southern Illinois	34-22
23. Miami (Fla.)	37-24	73. Va. Commonwealth	37-23
24. North Carolina State	38-23	74. South Alabama	31-26
25. **Cal State Fullerton** (9)	38-25	75. Washington State	28-26
26. **Louisville** (7)	47-24	76. Brigham Young	37-20
27. Wake Forest	34-29	77. Winthrop	33-27
28. Oklahoma	34-24	78. Austin Peay	40-22
29. East Carolina	40-23	79. Georgia	23-33
30. Baylor	35-27	80. Gonzaga	33-25
31. Nebraska	32-27	81. Stanford	28-28
32. Texas Christian (25)	48-14	82. New Orleans	38-26
33. Southern Miss.	39-23	83. Duke	29-25
34. Georgia Tech	32-25	84. Texas Tech	28-27
35. Michigan (19)	42-19	85. Fresno State	38-29
36. Creighton	45-16	86. Texas State	37-23
37. UCLA (22)	33-28	87. Elon	32-29
38. Oklahoma State (23)	42-21	88. Middle Tenn.	32-28
39. Western Carolina	42-20	89. Washington	29-27
40. Kansas State	34-24	90. Georgia Southern	34-28
41. Charlotte	49-12	91. Central Michigan	35-21
42. Stetson	42-21	92. Connecticut	34-27
43. Rutgers	42-21	93. Southeastern La.	34-21
44. College of Charleston	39-19	94. UNC Wilmington	29-27
45. Florida	29-30	95. Boston College	24-27
46. Oral Roberts	40-17	96. Citadel	34-27
47. Pepperdine	35-22	97. Eastern Michigan	32-24
48. Auburn	31-25	98. Kennesaw St.	32-23
49. UC Riverside	38-21	99. Ill.-Chicago	35-21
50. Minnesota	41-18	100. Mercer	33-25

FIRST TEAM

Pos.	Name	Year	AVG	OBP	SLG	AB	R	H	HR	RBI	SB
C	Matt Wieters, Georgia Tech	Jr.	.358	.480	.592	218	42	78	10	59	2
1B	Brett Wallace, Arizona State	So.	.415	.495	.702	248	73	103	15	75	11
2B	Tony Thomas, Florida State	Jr.	.430	.522	.733	258	91	111	11	43	31
3B	Pedro Alvarez, Vanderbilt	So.	.386	.463	.684	272	76	105	18	68	6
SS	Todd Frazier, Rutgers	Jr.	.377	.502	.757	247	87	93	22	65	25
OF	Grant Desme, Cal Poly	Jr.	.405	.494	.733	195	54	79	15	53	12
OF	Kellen Kulbacki, James Madison	Jr.	.398	.538	.785	191	56	76	19	49	9
OF	Kyle Russell, Texas	So.	.336	.456	.807	223	68	75	28	71	10
DH	Matt LaPorta, Florida	Sr.	.402	.582	.817	169	60	68	20	52	2
UT	Joe Savery, Rice	Jr.	.360	.441	.504	258	55	93	5	57	4

		Year	W	L	ERA	SV	IP	H	BB	K	AVG
SP	Preston Guilmet, Arizona	So.	12	2	1.87	0	135	100	34	146	.205
SP	Adam Mills, Charlotte	Sr.	14	2	1.01	0	143	93	27	141	.188
SP	David Price, Vanderbilt	Jr.	11	1	2.63	0	133	95	31	194	.199
SP	Jacob Thompson, Virginia	So.	11	0	1.50	0	114	79	32	101	.198
RP	Casey Weathers, Vanderbilt	Sr.	12	2	2.37	7	49	25	21	75	.154
UT	Joe Savery, Rice	Jr.	10	1	2.78	0	87	75	38	57	.239

SECOND TEAM

Pos.	Name	Year	AVG	OBP	SLG	AB	R	H	HR	RBI	SB
C	Buster Posey, Florida State	So.	.382	.453	.520	246	66	94	3	65	4
1B	Yonder Alonso, Miami	So.	.376	.519	.705	210	57	79	18	74	13
2B	Eric Sogard, Arizona State	Jr.	.394	.489	.623	231	74	91	11	57	17
3B	Brandon Waring, Wofford	Jr.	.401	.518	.851	222	73	89	27	74	12
SS	Jaime Pedroza, UC Riverside	Jr.	.325	.394	.570	237	55	77	13	55	5
OF	Corey Brown, Oklahoma State	Jr.	.335	.493	.741	224	82	75	22	71	23
OF	Dominic de la Osa, Vanderbilt	Jr.	.378	.452	.727	249	65	94	20	62	20
OF	Brian Rike, Louisiana Tech	Jr.	.346	.471	.705	217	74	75	20	66	16
DH	Blake Stouffer, Texas A&M	Jr.	.398	.487	.668	256	58	102	12	85	22
UT	Zach Putnam, Michigan	So.	.341	.408	.535	217	38	74	8	59	1

		Year	W	L	ERA	SV	IP	H	BB	K	AVG
SP	Bryan Henry, Florida State	Sr.	14	2	2.60	0	118	103	22	117	.238
SP	Brian Matusz, San Diego	So.	10	3	2.85	0	123	98	37	163	.214
SP	Nick Schmidt, Arkansas	Jr.	11	3	2.69	0	124	84	51	111	.196
SP	James Simmons, UC Riverside	Jr.	11	3	2.40	0	124	103	15	116	.220
RP	Pat Venditte, Creighton	Jr.	8	2	1.88	4	96	62	22	99	.189
UT	Zach Putnam, Michigan	So.	8	4	4.13	0	94	93	35	79	.263

Moranda—has proven a launching pad for its last four coaches: Jack Leggett (who left for Clemson), Keith LeClair (East Carolina), Rodney Hennon (Georgia Southern) and Raleigh (Tennessee).

Meanwhile, those Clemson-South Carolina recruiting battles might not be quite as intense from now on. About a week after Florida hired Clemson recruiting coordinator Kevin O'Sullivan as its head coach, Liberty hired South Carolina recruiting coordinator Jim Toman as its new coach. Toman and O'Sullivan are regarded as two of the nation's hardest-working recruiters, and both have demonstrated a keen eye for talent.

Toman was the third high-profile recruiting coordinator to land a head coaching job in June, following O'Sullivan and former Arizona State assistant Turtle Thomas, who was hired away by Florida International.

Duck Dominoes

But the coaching merry-go-round was just getting started, as August and September proved uncharacteristically busy.

Oregon got everything started by announcing in mid-July that it was reinstating its baseball program for the 2008-09 academic year after a 28-year hibernation.

Determined to make a major splash with his coaching hire, Ducks athletic director Pat Kilkenny unsuccessfully wooed big names like Vanderbilt's Tim Corbin and UC Irvine's Dave Serrano, but wound up netting an even bigger fish. Oregon hired George Horton away from Cal State Fullerton in late-August, signing him to a five-year contract worth at least a guaranteed $400,000 annually. Horton had led the Titans to six College World Series appearances and one national title in 11 years.

Horton's departure created a void at Fullerton, and Serrano eventually stepped into it after originally declaring he would not be leaving Irvine for Fullerton, out of deference for longtime Horton assistant Rick Vanderhook. But when it became apparent that Vanderhook was not going to get the job, Serrano—the 2007 Baseball America coach of the year—had a change of heart.

The final domino fell in late September when the Anteaters hired former Southern California coach Mike Gillespie to replace Serrano. Gillespie, who was forced to retire from the Trojans in 2006 after guiding them to four CWS appearances and one national championship in 20 years, will now coach less than an hour from his former employers, who replaced him a year earlier with his son-in-law, Chad Kreuter.

REGIONALS

May 30—June 2
64 teams, 16 four-team, double-elimination tournaments. Winners advance to super-regionals.

CHAPEL HILL, N.C., REGIONAL
NORTH CAROLINA
Participants: No. 1 North Carolina (48-12), No. 2 East Carolina (39-21), No. 3 Western Carolina (40-18), No. 4 Jacksonville (34-26).
Champion: North Carolina (3-0).
Runner-Up: Western Carolina (2-2).
Outstanding Player: Josh Horton, ss, North Carolina.

CHARLOTTESVILLE, VA., REGIONAL VIRGINIA
Participants: No. 1 Virginia (43-14), No. 2 Rutgers (41-19), No. 3 Oregon State (38-17), No. 4 Lafayette (33-18).
Champion: Oregon State (4-1).
Runner-Up: Virginia (2-2).
Outstanding Player: Joe Paterson, lhp, Oregon State

COLLEGE STATION, TEXAS, REGIONAL TEXAS A&M
Participants: No. 1 Texas A&M (44-16), No. 2 Louisiana-Lafayette (43-15), No. 3 Ohio State (37-22), No. 4 Le Moyne (34-17).
Champion: Texas A&M (4-1).
Runner-Up: Louisiana-Lafayette (2-2).
Outstanding Player: Blake Stouffer, of, Texas A&M.

COLUMBIA, MO., REGIONAL
MISSOURI
Participants: No. 1 Missouri (40-16), No. 2 Miami (36-22), No. 3 Louisville (40-20), No. 4 Kent State (33-24).
Champion: Louisville (4-1).
Runner-Up: Missouri (2-2).
Outstanding Player: Chris Dominguez, 3b, Louisville.

COLUMBIA, S.C., REGIONAL
SOUTH CAROLINA
Participants: No. 1 South Carolina (42-18), No. 2 N.C. State (37-21), No. 3 Charlotte (47-10), No. 4 Wofford (30-31).
Champion: South Carolina (3-0).
Runner-Up: Charlotte (2-2).
Outstanding Player: Justin Smoak, 1b, South Carolina.

FAYETTEVILLE, ARK., REGIONAL
ARKANSAS
Participants: No. 1 Arkansas (41-19), No. 2 Creighton (44-14), No. 3 Oklahoma State (38-19), No. 4 Albany (29-27).
Champion: Oklahoma State (3-0).
Runner-Up: Arkansas (2-2).
Outstanding Player: Rebel Ridling, 1b, Oklahoma State

HOUSTON REGIONAL RICE
Participants: No. 1 Rice (49-12), No. 2 Texas Christian (46-12), No. 3 Baylor (34-25), No. 4 Prairie View (34-23).
Champion: Rice (3-0).
Runner-Up: TCU (2-2).
Outstanding Player: Joe Savery, lb/lhp, Rice

LONG BEACH REGIONAL
LONG BEACH STATE
Participants: No. 1 Long Beach State (37-18), No. 2 UCLA (30-26), No. 3 Pepperdine (35-20), No. 4 Illinois-Chicago (34-19).
Champion: UCLA (3-0).
Runner-Up: Long Beach State (2-2).
Outstanding Player: Jermaine Curtis, 3b, UCLA

MYRTLE BEACH, S.C., REGIONAL
COASTAL CAROLINA
Participants: No. 1 Coastal Carolina (48-11), No. 2 Clemson (38-21), No. 3 Stetson (41-19), No. 4 Virginia Commonwealth (37-21).
Champion: Clemson (3-0).
Runner-Up: Coastal Carolina (2-2).
Outstanding Player: Andy D'Alessio, 1b, Clemson

NASHVILLE REGIONAL
VANDERBILT
Participants: No. 1 Vanderbilt (51-11), No. 2 Michigan (39-16), No. 3 Memphis (36-25), No. 4 Austin Peay (39-20).
Champion: Michigan (3-1).
Runner-Up: Vanderbilt (3-2).
Outstanding Player: Nate Recknagel, 1b, Michigan.

OXFORD, MISS., REGIONAL
MISSISSIPPI
Participants: No. 1 Mississippi (37-23), No. 2 Southern Mississippi (38-21), No. 3 Troy (34-25), No. 4 Sam Houston State (38-22).
Champion: Mississippi (3-0).
Runner-Up: Sam Houston St. (2-2).
Outstanding Player: Lance Lynn, rhp, Mississippi.

ROUND ROCK, TEXAS, REGIONAL
TEXAS
Participants: No. 1 Texas (44-15), No. 2 UC Irvine (40-15), No. 3 Wake Forest (33-27), No. 4 Brown (27-19).
Champion: UC Irvine (3-0).
Runner-Up: Texas (2-2).
Outstanding Player: Taylor Holliday, util, UC Irvine.

SAN DIEGO REGIONAL
SAN DIEGO
Participants: No. 1 San Diego (43-16), No. 2 Cal State Fullerton (33-23), No. 3 Minnesota (40-16), No. 4 Fresno State (36-27).
Champion: Cal State Fullerton (3-0).
Runner-Up: San Diego (2-2).
Outstanding Player: Clark Hardman, of, Cal State Fullerton.

TALLAHASSEE, FLA., REGIONAL
FLORIDA STATE
Participants: No. 1 Florida State (47-11), No. 2 Mississippi State (33-20), No. 3 Stetson (41-19), No. 4 Bethune-Cookman (33-25).
Champion: Mississippi State (3-0).
Runner-Up: Florida State (2-2).
Outstanding Player: Justin Pigott, lhp, Mississippi State

TEMPE, ARIZ., REGIONAL
ARIZONA STATE
Participants: No. 1 Arizona State (43-13), No. 2 UC Riverside (37-19), No. 3 Nebraska (30-25), No. 4 Monmouth (36-22-1).
Champion: Arizona State (3-0).
Runner-Up: Nebraska (2-2).
Outstanding Player: Mike Leake, rhp, Arizona State.

WICHITA, KAN., REGIONAL
WICHITA STATE
Participants: No. 1 Wichita State (49-19), No. 2 Arizona (40-15), No. 3 Oral Roberts (40-15), No. 4 New Orleans (37-24).
Champion: Wichita State (4-1).
Runner-Up: Arizona (2-2).
Outstanding Player: Derek Schermerhorn, 1b, Wichita State.

SUPER-REGIONALS

June 6—10
16 teams, eight best-of-three series. Winners advance to College World Series.

CLEMSON (41-21) AT MISSISSIPPI STATE (36-20)
Super-Regional Site: Starkville, Miss.
Mississippi State wins 2-0, advances to College World Series.

MICHIGAN (42-17) AT OREGON STATE (42-18)
Super-Regional Site: Corvallis, Ore.
Oregon State wins 2-0, advances to College World Series.

MISSISSIPPI (40-23) AT ARIZONA STATE (46-13)
Site: Tempe, Ariz.
Arizona State wins 2-0, advances to College World Series.

OKLAHOMA STATE (41-19) AT LOUISVILLE (44-21)
Super-Regional Site: Louisville.
Louisville wins 2-1, advances to College World Series.

SOUTH CAROLINA (45-18) AT NORTH CAROLINA (51-12)
Super-Regional Site: Chapel Hill, N.C.
North Carolina wins 2-1, advances to College World Series.

TEXAS A&M (48-17) AT RICE (52-12)
Super-Regional Site: Houston.
Rice wins 2-0, advances to College World Series.

UC IRVINE (43-15) AT WICHITA STATE (53-20)
Super-Regional Site: Wichita, Kan.
UC Irvine wins 2-0, advances to College World Series.

UCLA (33-26) AT CAL STATE FULLERTON (36-23)
Super-Regional Site: Fullerton, Calif.
Cal State Fullerton wins 2-0, advances to College World Series.

David Price, straight from the source

PLAYER OF THE YEAR

W hat more can we say about David Price? We featured the Vanderbilt lefthander in 2006 when he won our Summer Player of the Year award; we ranked him No. 1 on our preseason draft prospects list and kept him there all year long; we chronicled his amazing weekly exploits for the Commodores this spring, when he went 11-1, 2.63 with 194 strikeouts and 31 walks in 133 innings; and we detailed his inevitable selection as the No. 1 pick in the 2007 draft by the Devil Rays.

Now that Price can add the label of Baseball America's 2007 College Player of the Year to his impressive resume, we'll let other people do the talking. We asked those who have coached Price, those who have coached against him, and even Price himself to try to put his season and his talent into historical context. Here's what they said.

Vanderbilt coach Tim Corbin: "As good as he is for your team when he's pitching, he drives the level of energy for your team up three or four notches when he's not playing because he's an active participant. I've never seen a kid who sits on the bench—he doesn't sit, he leans over the railing with a fungo bat in his hand—and he doesn't miss a pitch. He's far beyond a cheerleader, cheerleader is almost mocking what kind of a kid he is. He's like an extension of a coach, he's into every single pitch. He's the first one off the bench every single time, not second or third, he's first. He's so competitive, he doesn't want to finish second in anything. It's not a put-on, it's just what he does."

Texas Christian coach Jim Schlossnagle, who was Price's pitching coach with Team USA last summer: "It seems like every third year there's a guy that is supposed to be 'can't-miss,' but here's the thing about David Price that can't miss is makeup. And I am talking about absolutely off the charts makeup, from work ethic to team orientation to selflessness. On days he's not pitching, he's literally the bat boy. He was that all summer long for Team USA. That kid is team before self, more so than any other player I've ever been around. He's amazing."

South Carolina coach Ray Tanner: "You talk about his arm, who is it, Sandy Koufax? Vida Blue? I don't know. I used to tell everybody we're facing Vida Blue today when we had to face Vandy. But I'm really impressed with the complete player that David Price is."

Louisiana State coach Paul Mainieri: "He was a very fierce, fierce competitor. He's very emotional out there, but he competed in a way that wasn't offensive to the other team. He did it with class. I watched the kid the next two days, he was in the dugout leading the cheering for his

As dominant as David Price was, his otherworldly numbers just scratch the surface of his value

DANNY PARKER

teammates, the first guy out of the dugout to congratulate his teammates. To me it was very refreshing to see a superstar like that. I think he's going to do some real special things like that. There's no way this kid can miss being a superstar in the big leagues in my opinion."

Arkansas coach Dave Van Horn: "Really what I saw in David Price and what made him so tough is every Friday night, Vanderbilt knew they were going to win. That's such a positive when you're practicing during the week, going on the road to someone else's ballpark, you know you have David Price on the mound, he's going to give you eight quality innings, and you're going to be 1-0 going into Saturday."

David Price: "This has been hands down the greatest year of my life. I give all the credit to my teammates and my coaches and my family, they've been there for me all year. I guess I've been on top of the draft boards all year, but my teammates just treated me like I'm a normal teammate. They helped me out a lot this year. This could have been a very, very stressful year, but there was no stress at all thanks to them."

PREVIOUS WINNERS

1981 — Mike Sodders, 3b, Arizona State	1990 — Mike Kelly, of, Arizona State	1999 — Jason Jennings, rhp, Baylor
1982 — Jeff Ledbetter, of/lhp, Florida State	1991 — David McCarthy, 1b, Stanford	2000 — Mark Teixeira, 3b, Georgia Tech
1983 — Dave Magadan, 1b, Alabama	1992 — Phil Nevin, 3b, Cal State Fullerton	2001 — Mark Prior, rhp, Southern California
1984 — Oddibe McDowell, of, Arizona State	1993 — Brooks Kieschnick, dh/rhp, Texas	2002 — Khalil Greene, ss, Clemson
1985 — Pete Incaviglia, of, Oklahoma State	1994 — Jason Varitek, c, Georgia Tech	2003 — Rickie Weeks, 2b, Southern
1986 — Casey Close, of, Michigan	1995 — Todd Helton, 1b/lhp, Tennessee	2004 — Jered Weaver, rhp, Long Beach State
1987 — Robin Ventura, 3b, Oklahoma State	1996 — Kris Benson, rhp, Clemson	2005 — Alex Gordon, 3b, Nebraska
1988 — John Olerud, 1b/lhp, Washington State	1997 — J.D. Drew, of, Florida State	2006 — Andrew Miller, lhp, North Carolina
1989 — Ben McDonald, rhp, Louisiana State	1998 — Jeff Austin, rhp, Stanford	

Serrano shows UC Irvine how to win

BY AARON FITT

OMAHA

COACH OF THE YEAR

UC Irvine coach Dave Serrano knew he had a special group of players way back in September. By February, he was privately but confidently telling people his team was capable of not only making a regional, but winning one. Deep down, he thought his team was capable of doing far more than that, but something held him back from saying so.

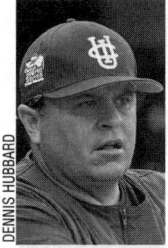

DENNIS HUBBARD

Dave Serrano

"We had the right guys coming back, we had the right mix of guys coming in, and everybody thinks they can win in September when everybody's coming in," Serrano said. "But these guys just did things right—the way they dressed, they showed up to practice on time, they showed up in the weight room, they did things right. If I was at a place like Cal State Fullerton with the same team, a program that knew how to get to Omaha, I would have said this team's going to Omaha. But the reason I hesitated to say that was because this program had never even won a single regional game, let alone a regional."

But Serrano knew something about getting to Omaha. He had done it five times as an assistant coach with Tennessee and Fullerton, even winning a national championship with the Titans in 2004, when he earned Assistant Coach of the Year honors. So when the Anteaters were shipped to the Round Rock regional as a No. 2 seed and pitted against No. 4 national seed Texas, Serrano wasn't daunted. Instead, he simply turned Irvine into a program that can now say it knows how to get to Omaha.

The Anteaters swept through the regional, then went on the road and swept Wichita State in a super-regional to earn a trip to the College World Series in just the sixth season since the program was reinstated after a 10-year hibernation. UCI wasn't satisfied just reaching the CWS, winning a pair of thrilling extra-inning games against two more traditional powerhouses, Cal State Fullerton and Arizona State.

By always demanding excellence, Serrano raised the bar at Irvine. For that, he is Baseball America's 2007 Coach of the Year.

Serrano's high expectations for his club aren't just reserved for games. The Anteaters are held to the highest standards even in practice. When the players are playing catch at the start of practice, they are required to run hills for every ball that touches the ground. Serrano credits assistant coach Greg Bergeron for that idea.

"The first day they started, they didn't know (Bergeron) was counting, they had to run 10 to 12 hills," Serrano said. "But by the end we had it down to one to two. It's about playing catch. We want to do everything at the highest level of competitiveness—it's about quality repetition, quality in everything they do."

The Anteaters don't walk nonchalantly onto the practice field—they jog. They are required to maintain their concentration through batting practice, infield practice, even setting up and clearing the field. UCI has turned clearing the field into a own game, timing how fast they can take down the batting cage, screens and tarps. By season's end, the 'Eaters could do it in 27 seconds.

Of course, practice isn't all business for Irvine. The coaching staff has fostered an atmosphere where players can stay loose by goofing around, performing skits and executing elaborate handshakes.

"We like to have fun," Serrano said. "That probably starts a little bit with my personality—I like to have fun, joke around, it keeps them looser. I try to emphasize in them there's a bigger skill than this game. When you start looking at this game bigger than that, you're setting yourself up to fail. They say play baseball, they don't say work baseball."

Serrano is quick to share the credit for his team's success with assistant coaches Bergeron, Sergio Brown and Nathan Choate, as well as his supportive family (wife Tracy and three sons Kyle, Zachary and Parker). He learned from his apprenticeship under Fullerton coach George Horton the value of delegating responsibility, and he says he could not have become the head coach he is today if Horton had not trusted him to handle the Titans' pitchers and recruiting duties.

"He wasn't the most talented player, but at his level, he played above his capabilities," Horton said of Serrano, who played for two years at Cerritos (Calif.) Junior College and another season at Fullerton. "His work ethic, tenacity, intelligence, and as you can tell, he has a great rapport with everyone. He understood the science of pitching, but most of all, I think it is his people skills."

Horton left Fullerton to lead the reinstitution of Oregon's program after the season, and Serrano replaced his mentor at Fullerton.

PREVIOUS WINNERS

1981 — Ron Fraser, Miami
1982 — Gene Stephenson, Wichita State
1983 — Barry Shollenberger, Alabama
1984 — Augie Garrido, Cal State Fullerton
1985 — Ron Polk, Mississippi State
1986 — Skip Bertman, Louisiana State
Dave Snow, Loyola Marymount
1987 — Mark Marquess, Stanford
1988 — Jim Brock, Arizona State

1989 — Dave Snow, Long Beach State
1990 — Steve Webber, Georgia
1991 — Jim Hendry, Creighton
1992 — Andy Lopez, Pepperdine
1993 — Gene Stephenson, Wichita State
1994 — Jim Morris, Miami
1995 — Pat Murphy, Arizona State
1996 — Skip Bertman, Louisiana State
1997 — Jim Wells, Alabama

1998 — Pat Murphy, Arizona State
1999 — Wayne Graham, Rice
2000 — Ray Tanner, South Carolina
2001 — Dave Van Horn, Nebraska
2002 — Augie Garrido, Texas
2003 — George Horton, Cal State Fullerton
2004 — David Perno, Georgia
2005 — Rick Jones, Tulane
2006 — Pat Casey, Oregon State

UNC's Ackley lets his bat do his talking

There aren't a lot of goofy Dustin Ackley stories floating around. When Ackley showed up for a television pre-production meeting with three older North Carolina players before the Chapel Hill super-regional, he just sat quietly in the corner while his teammates prattled on. Eventually, one of the producers started to apologize to Ackley for not asking him more questions, but shortstop Josh Horton interrupted to say that's just the way Ackley likes it.

When pressed a couple of weeks later at the College World Series for an offbeat Ackley anecdote, Horton came up empty.

"There's nothing I can throw him under the bus for, I wish I could," Horton said. "He's just that type of kid. He's all smiles, and real shy, but when it comes down to being at the ballpark, he is all business. He's good at what he does, and he's definitely been a crucial part of our success."

What Ackley does is hit. In fact, UNC's freshman first baseman led the nation and set a new single-season school record with 119 hits. He finished the season batting .402/.448/.591 with 10 home runs and 74 RBIs in 296 at-bats, helping to power UNC back to the CWS finals for a second straight season. His season to remember earned Ackley Baseball America's Freshman of the Year honors.

But most of those memories were created on the field, apparently.

"There really aren't any Dustin Ackley stories, not really," UNC closer Andrew Carignan said. "He's pretty much all business. He may not be the loudest guy, but in our lineup he might be the loudest guy."

Ackley led the nation in batting average for much of the season, and he carried a .442 average into the championship game of the ACC tournament. But Ackley fell into a deep slump for the first few weeks of the postseason, and his average actually dipped below .400 for the first time since March 9 during a June 20 game in Omaha.

"I don't think I was pressing at all; I've been doing the

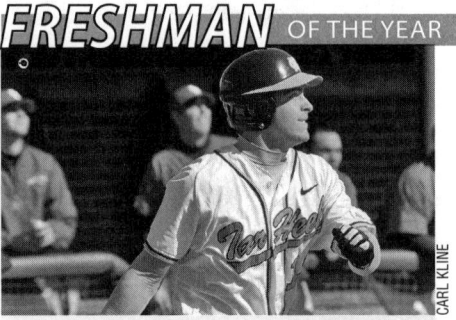

Dustin Ackley's 119 hits were a UNC record

same things I was always doing," Ackley said. "I haven't tried to do too much with a ball or a pitch or anything, so I don't think pressing's the right word for it."

Finally, in that June 20 game against Rice, Fox dropped Ackley from his No. 3 hole to the No. 7 spot. Ackley responded with two hits, including a huge three-run homer in the seventh inning that broke open a close game and propelled the Tar Heels to a 6-1 victory. It was his first home run since May 11, but it wouldn't be his last; Ackley went deep again in a 7-4 win against the Owls the next day, helping put the Tar Heels into the CWS Finals.

Fox knew Ackley's talent meant it was only a matter of time before he snapped out of his slump. Appropriately, Fox' favorite Ackley story describes some on-field exploits.

"He hit a home run, it's been reported, he cracked the bat when he hit it," Fox said. "Against UNC Wilmington, he hit a three-run homer, it sounded funny when it came off the bat, but it went out there at (UNC's) Boshamer (Stadium).

"He's not much of a jokester, he's all business. Dusty, he's a neat kid. He's very quiet, and very unassuming, doesn't say a whole lot, and I think people like that."

FRESHMAN ALL-AMERICA TEAM

Pos.	Name	AVG	OBP	SLG	AB	R	H	HR	RBI	SB
C	Richard Jones, The Citadel	.335	.390	.645	200	41	67	15	61	2
1B	Dustin Ackley, North Carolina	.402	.448	.591	296	70	119	10	74	11
2B	Brandon Turner, Mississippi St.	.399	.443	.514	208	46	83	3	48	4
3B	Matt Prokopowicz, Hofstra	.416	.491	.574	197	41	82	6	52	8
SS	Cole Figueroa, Florida	.332	.383	.504	262	48	87	11	50	7
OF	Jordan Henry, Mississippi	.376	.435	.542	263	60	99	1	17	12
OF	Mark Sobolewski, Miami	.345	.395	.510	255	47	88	8	54	14
OF	Gabe Cohen, UCLA	.345	.404	.549	206	35	71	10	36	4
DH	Chris Dominguez, Louisville	.266	.327	.528	267	47	71	15	61	9
UT	Jeff Lockwood, Tennessee	.315	.407	.424	184	29	58	4	34	1

		W	L	ERA	SV	IP	H	BB	K	AVG
SP	Mike Leake, Arizona State	13	2	3.69	1	127	129	29	94	.258
SP	Eric Erickson, Miami	10	4	2.50	1	90	84	16	63	.243
SP	Mike Minor, Vanderbilt	9	1	3.09	2	90	76	19	88	.226
RP	A.J. Griffin, San Diego	6	2	2.70	11	63	49	23	65	.224
UT	Jeff Lockwood, Tennessee	2	2	4.44	8	47	58	16	42	.302

SECOND TEAM

C-Tommy Medica, Santa Clara (.373-1-23). **1B**- Shaun Kort, Nevada (.392-6-50). **2B**-Dallas Poulk, N.C. State (.394-1-26). **3B**-Jason Stidham, Florida State (.366-6-48). **SS**-Grant Green, Southern California (.316-2-24). **OF**-Tim Fedroff (.344-5-41), Anthony Gallas, Kent State (.332-10-46), Brian Kemp, St. John's (.348-1-33). **DH**-Zach Miller, Mississippi (.364-4-31). **UT**-Anthony Aliotti, St. Mary's (.320-1-37). SP-Jorge Reyes, Oregon State (7-3, 3.10), Justin Marks, Louisville (9-2, 2.67), Wes Musick, Houston (6-5, 3.00), Brad Boxberger, Southern California (3-5, 3.20). **RP**-Jason Stoffel, Arizona (5-0, 1.87). **UT**-Anthony Aliotti, St. Mary's (6-4, 4.44).

PREVIOUS WINNERS

1982 — Cory Snyder, 3b, Brigham Young
1983 — Rafael Palmeiro, of, Mississippi State
1984 — Greg Swindell, lhp, Texas
1985 — Jack McDowell, rhp, Stanford
1986 — Robin Ventura, 3b, Oklahoma State
1987 — Paul Carey, of, Stanford
1988 — Kirk Dressendorfer, rhp, Texas
1989 — Alex Fernandez, rhp, Miami
1990 — Jeffrey Hammonds, of, Stanford
1991 — Brooks Kieschnick, rhp-dh, Texas
1992 — Todd Walker, 2b, Louisiana State
1993 — Brett Laxton, rhp, Louisiana State
1994 — R.A. Dickey, rhp, Tennessee
1995 — Kyle Peterson, rhp, Stanford
1996 — Pat Burrell, 3b, Miami
1997 — Brian Roberts, ss, North Carolina
1998 — Xavier Nady, 2b, California
1999 — James Jurries, 2b, Tulane
2000 — Kevin Howard, 3b, Miami
2001 — Michael Aubrey, of/lhp, Texas
2002 — Stephen Drew, ss, Florida State
2003 — Ryan Braun, ss, Miami
2004 — Wade LeBlanc, lhp, Alabama
2005 — Joe Savery, lhp, Rice
2006 — Pedro Alvarez, 3b, Vanderbilt

Batting Average Through Games 06/24/2007 Minimum 2.5 At-Bats Per Game Min 100 AB

BATTING

BATTING AVERAGE	YEAR	POS	G	AB	H	AVG
Ryan Lavarnway, Yale	So.	OF	43	150	70	0.467
Greg Sexton, William & Mary	Sr.	INF	54	209	95	0.455
Ryne White, Purdue	So.	OF	53	199	90	0.452
John Koehniein, Youngstown State	So.	INF	56	249	108	0.434
Robbie Widlansky, Fla. Atlantic	Jr.	3B	58	240	104	0.433
Alex Gregory, Radford	So.	INF	40	158	68	0.430
Tony Thomas Jr., Florida State	Jr.	2B	62	258	111	0.430
Tim Binkoski, Quinnipiac	Sr.	OF	48	191	81	0.424
Ryan Curry, Bradley	Sr.	INF	53	209	87	0.416
Matt Prokopowicz, Hofstra	Fr.	INF	54	197	82	0.416
James McOwen, Florida Int'l	Jr.	OF	54	220	91	0.414
Sal Iacono, Princeton	Sr.	3B	39	150	62	0.413
Mike McKenna, Fla. Atlantic	Jr.	OF	56	218	90	0.413
Travis Sweet, Iowa	Jr.	INF	54	206	85	0.413
David Williams, Rutgers	Sr.	OF	60	228	94	0.412
Ryan Murphy, Brown	Jr.	OF	45	139	57	0.410
Charlie Gamble, N.C. A&T	Sr.	INF	59	225	92	0.409
Erik Huber, Eastern Ill.	Sr.	1B	45	159	65	0.409
Ross Oeder, Wright State	Sr.	2B	57	228	93	0.408
Cole White, Army	Jr.	OF	48	179	73	0.408
Erik Kanaby, Lamar	Sr.	OF	57	224	91	0.406
Kraig Binick, NYIT	Sr.	OF	52	207	84	0.406
Grant Desme, Cal Poly	Jr.	OF	50	195	79	0.405
Wayne Kendrick, Middle Tenn.	Sr.	INF	60	247	100	0.405
Ty Wright, Oklahoma State	Sr.	OF	53	215	87	0.405
Angel Mercado, Bethune-Cookman	Sr.	OF	54	203	82	0.404
Keith Stein, Sam Houston State	Jr.	OF	64	255	103	0.404
Brett Wallace, Arizona State	So.	1B	63	265	107	0.404
Kris Rochelle, Charlotte	Sr.	C	61	228	92	0.404
Matt LaPorta, Florida	Sr.	1B	52	169	68	0.402
Dustin Ackley, North Carolina	Fr.	1B	73	296	119	0.402
Andy Parrino, Le Moyne	Jr.	SS	51	199	80	0.402
Brandon Waring, Wofford	Jr.	SS	63	222	89	0.401
Brad McElroy, Charlotte	Jr.	OF	61	242	97	0.401
Lars Davis, Illinois	Jr.	C	58	225	90	0.400
Jason Graham, A&M-Corpus Christi	Sr.	INF	54	210	84	0.400
Selmon Pearson, Alabama State	Sr.	3B	38	140	56	0.400
Eric Sogard, Arizona State	Jr.	INF	64	250	100	0.400
Brandon Turner, Mississippi State	So.	INF	55	208	83	0.399
Keith Conlon, TCU	Sr.	OF	49	173	69	0.399
Blake Stouffer, Texas A&M	Jr.	3B	67	256	102	0.398
Robbie Blauer, UC Santa Barb.	Sr.	1B	54	211	84	0.398
Kellen Kulbacki, James Madison	Jr.	OF	53	191	76	0.398
Jordan Pacheco, New Mexico	Jr.	2B	55	219	87	0.397
Josh Groves, Wis.-Milwaukee	So.	C	45	139	55	0.396
Nick Santomauro, Dartmouth	Fr.	OF	37	124	49	0.395
Andrew Meyers, Monmouth	Jr.	INF	60	223	88	0.395
Rob Vernon, UNC Asheville	Sr.	OF	60	246	97	0.394
Dallas Poulk, North Carolina State	Fr.	INF	56	170	67	0.394
Chris Dunn, Florida Int'l	Sr.	OF	46	155	61	0.394
Marc Sawyer, Yale	Sr.	1B	43	155	61	0.394
Marcus Davis, Alcorn State	Sr.	OF	45	145	57	0.393
Matt Browning, James Madison	Fr.	3B	41	107	42	0.393
Shaun Kort, Nevada	Fr.	INF	60	222	87	0.392
Mike Mee, Minnesota	Sr.	1B	58	217	85	0.392
Tyler Stovall, Central Mich.	Jr.	C	54	225	88	0.391
Tim Park, William & Mary	Jr.	C	54	220	86	0.391
Brian Pellegrini, St. Bonaventure	Sr.	1B	46	174	68	0.391
Clay Whittemore, Jacksonville State	Jr.	OF	60	238	93	0.391
Isaiah Howes, Louisville	Sr.	OF	71	279	109	0.391
Kenny Smith, Western Caro.	Jr.	2B	62	249	97	0.390
Garrett Young, Liberty	Jr.	OF	50	198	77	0.389
Larry Gempp Jr., Ill.-Chicago	Sr.	OF	55	206	80	0.388
Michael Richard, Prairie View	Sr.	SS	59	201	78	0.388
Steve Wyland, Albany (N.Y.)	Sr.	INF	56	196	76	0.388
Rob Wilson, Davidson	Sr.	P	53	199	77	0.387
Andrew Franco, Appalachian State	Jr.	C	56	212	82	0.387
Steven Hill, Stephen F. Austin	Sr.	1B	59	225	87	0.387
Alex Buchholz, Delaware	So.	INF	55	238	92	0.387
Tyler Mach, Oklahoma State	Sr.	2B	63	259	100	0.386
Pedro Alvarez, Vanderbilt	So.	3B	66	272	105	0.386
John Rickards, La Salle	Jr.	2B	46	161	62	0.385

Junior second-baseman Tony Thomas batted .430 for Florida State

Graham Maiden, Col. of Charleston	Sr.	1B	56	187	72	0.385
Chris Campbell, Col. of Charleston	Sr.	2B	58	265	102	0.385
Johnny Giavotella, New Orleans	So.	INF	64	247	95	0.385
Jake Owens, Northwestern	Jr.	2B	54	221	85	0.385
Derek VanBuskirk, Michigan	Jr.	INF	46	146	56	0.384
Tommy Baldridge, Coastal Caro.	Jr.	OF	63	240	92	0.383
Jared Bolden, VCU	So.	1B	55	227	87	0.383
David Cooper, California	So.	INF	54	204	78	0.382
Buster Posey, Florida State	So.	SS	62	246	94	0.382
Ryan Flaherty, Vanderbilt	So.	INF	67	273	104	0.381
Justin Henry, Mississippi	Jr.	2B	65	260	99	0.381
David Wood, Texas State	Sr.	INF	60	255	97	0.380
Peter Allen, Fairfield	Jr.	OF	45	163	62	0.380
Clark Hardman, Cal State Fullerton	Jr.	OF	62	271	103	0.380
Preston Paramore, Arizona State	So.	C	64	224	85	0.379
Tim Alberts, Niagara	Jr.	OF	47	174	66	0.379
Mark Kelly, Southern Ill.	So.	C	56	232	88	0.379
Justin Parker, Wright State	So.	INF	53	190	72	0.379
Sonny Meade, Citadel	So.	OF	57	227	86	0.379
Trent Lockwood, UTSA	Fr.	C	57	230	87	0.378
Joel Gonzalez, Md.-East. Shore	Jr.	OF	54	180	68	0.378
Dominic de la Osa, Vanderbilt	Jr.	SS	66	249	94	0.378
Todd Frazier, Rutgers	Jr.	SS	63	247	93	0.377
Daniel Bomback, Fla. Atlantic	Jr.	INF	58	255	96	0.376
Barrett Shaft, Western Caro.	Jr.	OF	60	255	96	0.376
Jordan Henry, Mississippi	Fr.	OF	65	263	99	0.376
Yonder Alonso, Miami (Fla.)	So.	1B	61	210	79	0.376
Ben Lasater, Col. of Charleston	Sr.	INF	50	210	79	0.376

HOME RUNS		CL	POS	G	HR
Kyle Russell, Texas		So.	OF	63	28
Brandon Waring, Wofford		Jr.	SS	63	27
Steven Hill, Stephen F. Austin		Sr.	1B	59	24
Corey Brown, Oklahoma State		Jr.	OF	63	22
Jeff Cunningham, South Ala.		Jr.	1B	55	22
Todd Frazier, Rutgers		Jr.	SS	63	22
Danny Hamblin, Arkansas		Sr.	1B	64	22
Justin Smoak, South Carolina		So.	1B	66	22
Scott Krieger, George Mason		So.	OF	54	20
Matt LaPorta, Florida		Sr.	1B	52	20

CARL KLINE

	CL	POS	G	
n Rike, Louisiana Tech	Jr.	OF	59	20
nny Smith, Western Caro.	Sr.	2B	62	20
Dominic de la Osa, Vanderbilt	Jr.	SS	66	20
James Darnell, South Carolina	So.	INF	64	19
Kellen Kulbacki, James Madison	Jr.	OF	53	19
Yonder Alonso, Miami (Fla.)	So.	1B	61	18
Pedro Alvarez, Vanderbilt	So.	3B	66	18
William Block, Fla. Atlantic	So.	INF	57	18
Allan Dykstra, Wake Forest	So.	1B	63	18
Isaiah Howes, Louisville	Sr.	OF	71	18
Travis Jones, South Carolina	Jr.	INF	66	18
Jonathan Lucroy, La.-Lafayette	Jr.	C	62	18
Rawley Bishop, Middle Tenn.	So.	INF	58	17
Andy D'Alessio, Clemson	Sr.	1B	59	17
Bryan Hagerich, Delaware	Sr.	OF	55	17
Logan Johnson, Louisville	Sr.	INF	71	17
Joe Mahoney, Richmond	Jr.	1B	60	17
Brian Pellegrini, St. Bonaventure	Sr.	1B	46	17
Chris Raber, Coastal Caro.	Sr.	OF	63	17
Clint Robinson, Troy	Sr.	1B	59	17
Garrett Baker, Dallas Baptist	Sr.	OF	56	16
Daniel Bomback, Fla. Atlantic	Jr.	INF	58	16
Marcus Davis, Alcorn State	Sr.	OF	45	16
Scott Hawkins, La.-Lafayette	So.	C	59	16
Shane Kirkley, Wofford	Jr.	INF	62	16
Tyler Mach, Oklahoma State	Sr.	2B	63	16
Mike McKenna, Fla. Atlantic	Jr.	OF	56	16
Blake Murphy, Western Caro.	Jr.	C	61	16
Devin Thomas, Brown	Sr.	C	48	16
Brett Wallace, Arizona State	So.	1B	63	16
Drew Anderson, New Orleans	Sr.	OF	62	15
John Brandt, Wofford	Sr.	DH	63	15
Grant Desme, Cal Poly	Jr.	OF	50	15
Phil Disher, South Carolina	Jr.	C	64	15
Chris Dominguez, Louisville	So.	3B	67	15
Johnny Giavotella, New Orleans	So.	INF	64	15
Richard Jones, Citadel	Fr.	C	57	15
Charlie Kingrey, McNeese State	Sr.	OF	48	15
Ben Lasater, Col. of Charleston	Sr.	INF	50	15
Kiel Roling, Arizona State	So.	C	58	15
Kane Simmons, Belmont	Sr.	OF	60	15
Chris Swauger, Citadel	Jr.	OF	61	15
Robbie Widlansky, Fla. Atlantic	Jr.	3B	58	15
Austin Adams, TCU	Sr.	OF	61	14
Alex Avila, Alabama	So.	INF	57	14
Mike Bianucci, Auburn	So.	INF	47	14
Justin Bour, George Mason	Fr.	1B	51	14
Cody Cipriano, UC Irvine	Sr.	INF	63	14
Pete Clifford, Jacksonville	Sr.	OF	62	14
Robert Crumpler, VMI	Sr.	1B	55	14
Cody Decker, UCLA	So.	C	54	14
Chris Fournier, George Mason	Jr.	C	54	14
Mike Gilmartin, Wofford	Fr.	SS	63	14
Albie Goulder, Louisiana Tech	Jr.	1B	58	14
Jonathan Greene, Western Caro.	Jr.	OF	62	14
Gabe Jacobo, Sacramento State	So.	1B	56	14
Ryan Lavarnway, Yale	So.	OF	43	14
Joey Lieberman, Memphis	Sr.	DH	62	14
Trent Lockwood, UTSA	Fr.	C	57	14
Bill Moss, Memphis	Sr.	2B	63	14
Cody Overbeck, Mississippi	So.	OF	62	14
Rebel Ridling, Oklahoma State	Jr.	1B	63	14
Bobby Verbick, Sam Houston State	Jr.	OF	64	14
David Wood, Texas State	Sr.	INF	60	14

HOME RUNS PER GAME

	CL	POS	G	HR	PG
Kyle Russell, Texas	So.	OF	63	28	0.44
Brandon Waring, Wofford	Jr.	SS	63	27	0.43
Steven Hill, Stephen F. Austin	Sr.	1B	59	24	0.41
Jeff Cunningham, South Ala.	Jr.	1B	55	22	0.40
Matt LaPorta, Florida	Sr.	1B	52	20	0.38
Scott Krieger, George Mason	So.	OF	54	20	0.37
Brian Pellegrini, St. Bonaventure	Sr.	1B	46	17	0.37
Kellen Kulbacki, James Madison	Jr.	OF	53	19	0.36
Marcus Davis, Alcorn State	Sr.	OF	45	16	0.36
Corey Brown, Oklahoma State	Jr.	OF	63	22	0.35
Todd Frazier, Rutgers	Jr.	SS	63	22	0.35
Danny Hamblin, Arkansas	Sr.	1B	64	22	0.34
Brian Rike, Louisiana Tech	Jr.	OF	59	20	0.34
Justin Smoak, South Carolina	So.	1B	66	22	0.33
Devin Thomas, Brown	Sr.	C	48	16	0.33
Kenny Smith, Western Caro.	Sr.	2B	62	20	0.32
William Block, Fla. Atlantic	So.	INF	57	18	0.32
Charlie Kingrey, McNeese State	Sr.	OF	48	15	0.31
Bryan Hagerich, Delaware	Sr.	OF	55	17	0.31
Dominic de la Osa, Vanderbilt	Jr.	SS	66	20	0.30
Grant Desme, Cal Poly	Jr.	OF	50	15	0.30
Ben Lasater, Col. of Charleston	Sr.	INF	50	15	0.30
James Darnell, South Carolina	So.	INF	64	19	0.30
Yonder Alonso, Miami (Fla.)	So.	1B	61	18	0.30
Rawley Bishop, Middle Tenn.	So.	INF	58	17	0.29

Sophmore outfielder Kyle Russell led the NCAA with 28 home runs for Texas

JOHN WILLIAMSON

RUNS BATTED IN PER GAME

	CL	Pos	G	RBI	PG
Chris Campbell, Col. of Charleston	Sr.	2B	58	82	1.41
Marcus Davis, Alcorn State	Sr.	OF	45	62	1.38
Kenny Smith, Western Caro.	Sr.	2B	62	84	1.35
Sean Coughlin, Kentucky	Sr.	C	54	73	1.35
Devin Thomas, Brown	Sr.	C	48	64	1.33
Tyler Mach, Oklahoma State	Sr.	2B	63	81	1.29
David Wood, Texas State	Sr.	INF	60	77	1.28
Brian Pellegrini, St. Bonaventure	Sr.	1B	46	59	1.28
Ryan Lavarnway, Yale	So.	OF	43	55	1.28
Blake Stouffer, Texas A&M	Jr.	3B	67	85	1.27
Scott Krieger, George Mason	So.	OF	54	68	1.26
Anthony McLin, Jackson State	Sr.	OF	55	69	1.25
Bobby Verbick, Sam Houston State	Jr.	OF	64	80	1.25
Brett Wallace, Arizona State	So.	1B	63	78	1.24
Steven Hill, Stephen F. Austin	Sr.	1B	59	73	1.24
Garrett Baker, Dallas Baptist	Sr.	OF	56	69	1.23
Yonder Alonso, Miami (Fla.)	So.	1B	61	74	1.21
Clint Robinson, Troy	Sr.	1B	59	71	1.20
Robbie Widlansky, Fla. Atlantic	Jr.	3B	58	69	1.19
Neall French, Cincinnati	Sr.	INF	55	65	1.18
Bill Rhinehart, Arizona	Sr.	OF	56	66	1.18
Brandon Waring, Wofford	Jr.	SS	63	74	1.17
Jared Davis, IPFW	Jr.	OF	46	54	1.17
Evan Bigley, Dallas Baptist	So.	INF	52	61	1.17
Austin Adams, TCU	Sr.	OF	61	71	1.16

DOUBLES PER GAME

	Cl	Pos	G	2B	PG
Tony Thomas Jr., Florida State	Jr.	2B	62	33	0.53
Brian Pellegrini, St. Bonaventure	Sr.	1B	46	24	0.52
Peter Allen, Fairfield	Jr.	OF	45	23	0.51
David Rubinstein, Appalachian State	So.	OF	59	30	0.51
Alex Buchholz, Delaware	So.	INF	55	27	0.49
Justin Parker, Wright State	So.	INF	53	26	0.49
Josh Groves, Wis.-Milwaukee	So.	C	45	21	0.47

Roger Kieschnick, Texas Tech	So.	OF	55	25	0.45
Caleb Joseph, Lipscomb	So.	C	56	25	0.45
Tyler Belcher, Old Dominion	Sr.	C	55	24	0.44
Mitch Moreland, Mississippi State	Jr.	INF	60	26	0.43
Brian Friday, Rice	Jr.	SS	68	29	0.43
Brad McElroy, Charlotte	Jr.	OF	61	26	0.43
Sawyer Carroll, Kentucky	Jr.	INF	54	23	0.43
Ryan Curry, Bradley	Sr.	INF	53	22	0.42
Kevin Carkeek, Oakland	Sr.	INF	41	17	0.41
Robbie Widlansky, Fla. Atlantic	Jr.	3B	58	24	0.41
Justin Jenkins, West Virginia	Sr.	3B	51	21	0.41
Chris Taylor, Charlotte	Jr.	C	61	25	0.41
John Keene, Savannah State	Sr.	C	54	22	0.41
James McOwen, Florida Int'l	Jr.	OF	54	22	0.41
Nate Toth, Radford	Jr.	C	42	17	0.40
Brandon Douglas, UNI	So.	INF	47	19	0.40
Trent Lockwood, UTSA	Fr.	C	57	23	0.40
Ross Oeder, Wright State	Sr.	2B	57	23	0.40

TRIPLES PER GAME

	Cl	Pos	G	3B	PG
LaDale Hayes, Alabama A&M	So.	OF	39	8	0.21
Brandon Menchaca, Delaware	Jr.	OF	55	11	0.20
Corey Shimada, Utah	So.	INF	55	10	0.18
Cory Lane, Charlotte	Sr.	2B	61	11	0.18
Grant Green, Southern California	Fr.	INF	56	10	0.18
Jeff Davis, Eastern Mich.	Jr.	OF	44	7	0.16
Matt Stiffler, Ohio	Jr.	OF	52	8	0.15
Mike Massa, Dayton	Sr.	INF	53	8	0.15
Kevin Mattison, UNC Asheville	Jr.	OF	53	8	0.15
Steve Daniels, Brown	So.	OF	48	7	0.15
Chris Dove, Elon	So.	OF	55	8	0.15
Jon Gaston, Arizona	So.	OF	56	8	0.14
Austin Krum, Dallas Baptist	Jr.	OF	56	8	0.14
Taylor Holiday, UC Irvine	Jr.	INF	64	9	0.14
Ollie Linton, UC Irvine	So.	OF	57	8	0.14
Chris Campbell, Col. of Charleston	Sr.	2B	58	8	0.14
Drew Hoisington, Toledo	Jr.	OF	54	7	0.13
James Sims, Jackson State	Jr.	OF	55	7	0.13
Evan Armitage, Miami (Ohio)	Jr.SP/RP		56	7	0.13
Justin Henry, Mississippi	Jr.	2B	65	8	0.12
Jemile Weeks, Miami (Fla.)	So.	2B	50	6	0.12
Collin Delome, Lamar	Jr.	OF	59	7	0.12
Joseph DiGeronimo, Wagner	Sr.	INF	51	6	0.12
Brint Hardy, UAB	So.	OF	51	6	0.12
Chris Jackson, VCU	So.	INF	60	7	0.12

STOLEN BASES

	CL	POS	G	SB	CS	PG
Tony Campana, Cincinnati	Jr.	OF	56	60	14	1.07
Boomer Whiting, Louisville	Sr.	OF	71	73	14	1.03
James Conrad, Lafayette	Sr.	OF	52	49	6	0.94
Justin Kelly, Grambling	So.	INF	41	33	5	0.80
Nate Parks, Virginia Tech	Sr.	OF	54	39	9	0.72
Michael Richard, Prairie View	Sr.	SS	59	42	8	0.71
Kyle Messineo, Monmouth	Sr.	OF	60	42	4	0.70
Shawn Roof, Illinois	Sr.	INF	58	40	8	0.69
Mark McLaughlin, Georgetown	Sr.	OF	54	37	7	0.69
Marcus Davis, Alcorn State	Sr.	OF	45	29	4	0.64
Kraig Binick, NYIT	Sr.	OF	52	32	4	0.62
Mickey Shupin, George Washington	Sr.	2B	54	33	7	0.61
Kyle Latiolais, Mississippi Val.	Sr.	INF	51	31	9	0.61
Deric Manrique, UNI	So.	OF	50	30	2	0.60
Eric Cattoni, St. Mary's (Cal.)	Sr.	OF	47	28	4	0.60
Eric Farris, Loyola Marymount	Jr.	INF	56	33	9	0.59
Steve Daniels, Brown	So.	OF	48	28	5	0.58
Eric Rose, Michigan	Sr.	OF	59	34	6	0.58
Chris Dove, Elon	So.	OF	55	31	9	0.56
Joseph DiGeronimo, Wagner	Sr.	INF	51	28	4	0.55
K.K. Chalmers, Memphis	Jr.	OF	61	33	5	0.54
Bruce Edwards, Auburn	Sr.	OF	52	28	5	0.54
Leon Johnson, Brigham Young	So.	OF	54	29	8	0.54
Wilford White, Prairie View	Jr.	INF	47	25	2	0.53
Matt Foote, New Mexico	Sr.	OF	53	28	6	0.53

TOUGHEST TO STRIKE OUT

	Cl	Pos	G	AB	KK	Avg.
Mike Sheridan, William & Mary	So.	1B	54	209	5	41.8
J.B. Shuck, Ohio State	So.	P	50	187	6	31.2
Sam DeLuca, St. John's (N.Y.)	Sr.	INF	60	231	9	25.7
Bradley Boyer, Washington	So.	INF	47	182	8	22.8
John Koehnlein, Youngstown State	So.	INF	56	249	11	22.6
Turner Washington, Alabama A&M	Jr.	C	38	118	6	19.7

Rutger's shortstop Todd Frazier scored 1.38 runs a game last season

Robbie Blauer, UC Santa Barb.	Sr.	1B	54	211	11	19.2
Daniel Webb, Illinois	Jr.	OF	57	202	11	18.4
Johnathan Stevens, Alabama State	Sr.	INF	38	145	8	18.1
Ryne White, Purdue	So.	OF	53	199	11	18.1
Shawn Roof, Illinois	Sr.	INF	58	198	11	18.0
Jesse Hart, Wis.-Milwaukee	Jr.	2B	47	197	11	17.9
Chris Campbell, Col. of Charleston	Sr.	2B	58	265	15	17.7
Wayne Kendrick, Middle Tenn.	Sr.	INF	60	247	14	17.6
Drew Davis, Elon	Sr.	C	57	189	11	17.2
Billy Alvino, High Point	So.	C	48	171	10	17.1
Wes Dorrell, Cal Poly	Fr.	C	54	188	11	17.1
Eric Farris, Loyola Marymount	Jr.	INF	56	232	14	16.6
Kasey Wahl, Evansville	Sr.	1B	58	229	14	16.4
Ryan Dew, Ohio State	Fr.	INF	51	130	8	16.3
Robert Perry, Long Beach State	Sr.	OF	59	242	15	16.1
Errol Hollinger, Liberty	So.	C	53	175	11	15.9
Erik Huber, Eastern Ill.	Sr.	1B	45	159	10	15.9
Brett Pendell, Western Ill.	Jr.	OF	57	222	14	15.9
Chris Luick, Lafayette	So.	1B	52	189	12	15.8

RUNS PER GAME

	Cl	Pos	G	R	PG
Oliver Marmol, Col. of Charleston	Jr.	INF	56	84	1.50
Tony Thomas Jr., Florida State	Jr.	2B	62	91	1.47
Ross Oeder, Wright State	Sr.	2B	57	79	1.39
Todd Frazier, Rutgers	Jr.	SS	63	87	1.38
James Sims, Jackson State	Jr.	OF	55	73	1.33
Jason White, Iowa	Sr.	SS	53	70	1.32
Corey Brown, Oklahoma State	Jr.	OF	63	82	1.30
James Conrad, Lafayette	Sr.	OF	52	67	1.29
Mike Brown, Kentucky	Sr.	INF	53	68	1.28
Brian Rike, Louisiana Tech	Jr.	OF	59	74	1.25
Brian Pellegrini, St. Bonaventure	Sr.	1B	46	57	1.24
Danny Payne, Georgia Tech	Jr.	OF	56	68	1.21
Trey Sutton, Southern Miss.	Jr.	2B	57	69	1.21
Steven Hill, Stephen F. Austin	Sr.	1B	59	71	1.20
Blake Murphy, Western Caro.	Jr.	C	61	73	1.20
Chris Dunn, Florida Int'l	Sr.	OF	46	55	1.20
Brett Wallace, Arizona State	So.	1B	63	75	1.19
Tim Park, William & Mary	Jr.	C	54	64	1.19
Travis Sweet, Iowa	Jr.	INF	54	63	1.17
Anthony McLin, Jackson State	Sr.	OF	55	64	1.16
Kenny Smith, Western Caro.	Sr.	2B	62	72	1.16
Brandon Waring, Wofford	Jr.	SS	63	73	1.16

	CI		G			
Eric Sogard, Arizona State	Jr.	INF	64	74		1.16
Marcus Davis, Alcorn State	Sr.	OF	45	52		1.16
Daniel Bomback, Fla. Atlantic	Jr.	INF	58	67		1.16

SLUGGING PERCENTAGE

	CI	Pos	G	AB	TB	SLG PCT
Ryan Lavarnway, Yale	So.	OF	43	150	131	0.873
Brandon Waring, Wofford	Jr.	SS	63	222	189	0.851
Marcus Davis, Alcorn State	Sr.	OF	45	145	122	0.841
Brian Pellegrini, St. Bonaventure	Sr.	1B	46	174	145	0.833
Steven Hill, Stephen F. Austin	Sr.	1B	59	225	184	0.818
Matt LaPorta, Florida	Sr.	1B	52	169	138	0.817
Kyle Russell, Texas	So.	OF	63	223	180	0.807
Kellen Kulbacki, James Madison	Jr.	OF	53	191	150	0.785
Kenny Smith, Western Caro.	Sr.	2B	62	249	189	0.759
Todd Frazier, Rutgers	Jr.	SS	63	247	187	0.757
Corey Brown, Oklahoma State	Jr.	OF	63	227	167	0.736
Grant Desme, Cal Poly	Jr.	OF	50	195	143	0.733
Tony Thomas Jr., Florida State	Jr.	2B	62	258	189	0.733
Robbie Widlansky, Fla. Atlantic	Jr.	3B	58	240	175	0.729
Devin Thomas, Brown	Sr.	C	48	188	137	0.729
Dominic de la Osa, Vanderbilt	Jr.	SS	66	249	181	0.727
Jeff Cunningham, South Ala.	Jr.	1B	55	198	142	0.717
Mike McKenna, Fla. Atlantic	Jr.	OF	56	218	156	0.716
Greg Sexton, William & Mary	Sr.	INF	54	209	149	0.713
Scott Krieger, George Mason	So.	OF	54	219	156	0.712
Brian Rike, Louisiana Tech	Jr.	OF	59	217	153	0.705
Yonder Alonso, Miami (Fla.)	So.	1B	61	210	148	0.705
Alex Buchholz, Delaware	So.	INF	55	238	164	0.689
Trent Lockwood, UTSA	Fr.	C	57	230	158	0.687
Brett Wallace, Arizona State	So.	1B	63	265	182	0.687
26 Pedro Alvarez, Vanderbilt	So.	3B	66	272	186	0.684

WALKS PER GAME

	CI	Pos	G	BB		PG
Danny Payne, Georgia Tech	Jr.	OF	56	62		1.11
Matt Webb, Centenary (La.)	Sr.	OF	59	64		1.08
Matt LaPorta, Florida	Sr.	1B	52	55		1.06
Kellen Kulbacki, James Madison	Jr.	OF	53	56		1.06
Yonder Alonso, Miami (Fla.)	So.	1B	61	64		1.05
Corey Brown, Oklahoma State	Jr.	OF	63	66		1.05
Matt Rizzotti, Manhattan	Jr.	1B	54	56		1.04
Todd Frazier, Rutgers	Jr.	SS	63	62		0.98
Brian Spear, Kentucky	Jr.	INF	54	53		0.98
Dusty Napoleon, Iowa	Jr.	C	53	50		0.94
Austin Knight, Dallas Baptist	So.	INF	56	51		0.91
Allan Dykstra, Wake Forest	So.	1B	63	57		0.90
Matt Wieters, Georgia Tech	Jr.	C	57	51		0.89
Ben Price, UC Riverside	Jr.	INF	52	46		0.88
Matt Stiffler, Ohio	Jr.	OF	52	45		0.87
Ryan Hill, Rutgers	Jr.	OF	63	54		0.86
Blake Murphy, Western Caro.	Jr.	C	61	52		0.85
Richard Stout, New Mexico State	Jr.	INF	52	44		0.85
Johnny Giavotella, New Orleans	So.	INF	64	54		0.84
Preston Paramore, Arizona State	So.	C	64	53		0.83
Vince Riggi, Richmond	Sr.	OF	57	47		0.82
Justin Smoak, South Carolina	So.	1B	66	54		0.82
Justin Frash, Hawaii	Sr.	3B	59	48		0.81
James Darnell, South Carolina	So.	INF	64	51		0.80
Ryan Pond, North Carolina State	Jr.	OF	58	46		0.79

SACRIFICE HITS PER GAME

	CL	POS	G	SH		PG
Ben Orloff, UC Irvine	So.	2B	65	34		0.52
Dom Duggan, Coastal Caro.	Sr.	OF	63	27		0.43
Ryan James, Binghamton	Jr.	3B	44	17		0.39
Matt Rademacher, Coastal Caro.	Sr.	C	52	20		0.38
Jonathan Anderson, Duke	Sr.	OF	54	20		0.37
Cooper Stewart, Western Ill.	So.	C	51	18		0.35
Dan Biedenharn, Wright State	Sr.	INF	57	20		0.35
Scott Gaffney, Penn State	Jr.	INF	49	17		0.35
Brad Jones, Bradley	Sr.	OF	47	16		0.34
Dillon Sudduth, Southeastern La.	Sr.	1B	55	18		0.33
Derek Martin, Coastal Caro.	Jr.	INF	63	20		0.32
Jason Pape, West Virginia	Sr.	1B	51	16		0.31
Matt Cline, Long Beach State	Sr.	2B	58	18		0.31
Ross Sinclair, Creighton	Sr.	OF	55	17		0.31
Tom Zebroski, George Washington	Fr.	INF	52	16		0.31
Roger Tomas, Miami (Fla.)	Sr.	INF	59	18		0.31
Mike Bionde, Rutgers	Sr.	2B	63	19		0.30
Eric Skinner, Auburn	So.	INF	45	13		0.29
Matt Hall, Arizona State	So.	3B	52	15		0.29
Drew Robertson, Middle Tenn.	Fr.	C	56	16		0.29

Charlotte righthander Adam Mills led the nation with a 1.01 ERA

Moriba George, Norfolk State	Sr.	INF	47	13	0.28
Josh Sanders, Jacksonville State	Fr.	SS	58	16	0.28
Nate Santiago, Centenary (La.)	Sr.	INF	48	13	0.27
Scott Viator, Southeastern La.	Sr.	INF	45	12	0.27
Adam Weaver, Elon	Sr.	INF	60	16	0.27

HIT BY PITCH PER GAME

	CL	POS	G	HBP	PG
Brendan Akashian, Holy Cross	Jr.	C	35	23	0.66
Robbie Knight, Creighton	Fr.	OF	60	35	0.58
Sean Osborne, Indiana State	Jr.	C	49	26	0.53
Graham Maiden, Col. of Charleston	Sr.	1B	56	29	0.52
Ben Terry, Wake Forest	Jr.	OF	51	26	0.51
Chad Schroeder, Ill.-Chicago	Sr.	SS	51	25	0.49
Brett Lilley, Notre Dame	Jr.	3B	56	27	0.48
Michael Stephan, Stony Brook	So.	P	48	23	0.48
Benji Marshall, Richmond	Sr.	INF	54	25	0.46
Logan Johnson, Louisville	Sr.	INF	71	32	0.45
Justin Handler, La Salle	So.	3B	48	21	0.44
John Rickards, La Salle	Jr.	2B	46	19	0.41
Joel Collins, South Ala.	Jr.	C	55	22	0.40
Oliver Marmol, Col. of Charleston	Jr.	INF	56	22	0.39
Christian Winstanley, Morehead State	Jr.	C	51	20	0.39
Brock Bond, Missouri	Jr.	INF	59	23	0.39
John McKee, Missouri	Sr.	INF	60	23	0.38
A.J. Yoder, VMI	So.	INF	55	21	0.38
Shawn Roof, Illinois	Sr.	INF	58	22	0.38
Juan Mendoza, Southern U.	Jr.	INF	43	16	0.37
Antone DeJesus, Kentucky	Jr.	OF	54	20	0.37
Charlie Lenhard, Akron	Sr.	OF	46	17	0.37
Justin Pierce, Portland	Sr.	OF	49	18	0.37
Matt LaPorta, Florida	Sr.	1B	52	19	0.37
Jonathan Greene, Western Caro.	Jr.	OF	62	22	0.35

PITCHING

EARNED RUN AVERAGE

	CL	POS	APP	IP	R	ER	ERA
Adam Mills, Charlotte	Sr.	P	18	142.7	27	16	1.01
Chance Chapman, Oral Roberts	Sr.	RP	22	94.0	17	14	1.34
Ryan Woods, Le Moyne	Sr.	P	30	60.3	14	9	1.34
Jay Monti, Sacred Heart	Sr.	SP	12	80.3	26	12	1.34
Jacob Thompson, Virginia	So.	SP	17	114.0	23	19	1.50
Luke Prihoda, Sam Houston State	Sr.	P	35	72.7	20	13	1.61
Anthony Capra, Wichita State	So.	P	24	76.7	27	15	1.76
Matthew Wilson, Bucknell	Jr.	P	9	60.7	17	12	1.78
Luke Pisker, VCU	Jr.	P	31	68.0	16	14	1.85
Preston Guilmet, Arizona	So.	P	18	135.0	34	28	1.87

Name	CL	POS	APP	IP			ERA
David Phelps, Notre Dame	So.	RP	15	110.3	35	23	1.88
Pat Venditte, Creighton	Jr.	RP	38	95.7	21	20	1.88
Nick Hill, Army	Sr.	P	13	84.7	22	18	1.91
Justin Fiske, Texas State	Jr.	P	19	111.7	34	24	1.93
Josh Collmenter, Central Mich.	Jr.	P	15	116.3	27	25	1.93
Todd Roth, Penn	Fr.	P	13	68.3	18	15	1.98
Barry Enright, Pepperdine	Jr.	SP/RP	18	131.3	38	29	1.99
Bryan Rembisz, Vermont	Sr.	SP/RP	13	70.3	25	16	2.05
Corey Kluber, Stetson	Jr.	P	17	114.0	37	26	2.05
Cory Luebke, Ohio State	Jr.	P	16	117.7	45	27	2.06
Christian Friedrich, Eastern Ky.	So.	P	14	81.7	29	19	2.09
Justin Friend, Oklahoma State	Jr.	P	28	76.7	28	18	2.11
Mitch Harris, Navy	Jr.	P	14	88.3	34	21	2.14
Jesse Darcy, Manhattan	Sr.	P	14	107.0	33	26	2.19
Anthony Shawler, Old Dominion	So.	OF	15	114.7	33	28	2.20
Ross Detwiler, Missouri State	Jr.	SP/RP	14	89.0	30	22	2.22
Aaron Shafer, Wichita State	Sr.	P	15	84.7	28	21	2.23
Kyle Nicholson, Texas A&M	Sr.	P	25	124.0	34	31	2.25
Luke Foss, Norfolk State	Sr.	P	16	86.7	29	22	2.28
Ben Mancuso, Creighton	Jr.	SP/RP	14	77.0	22	20	2.34
Matt Langwell, Rice	Jr.	P	23	84.3	29	22	2.35
Steve Crnkovich, Ill.-Chicago	Fr.	P	14	94.0	30	25	2.39
Shawn Kelley, Austin Peay	Sr.	P	17	127.7	39	34	2.40
James Simmons, UC Riverside	Jr.	P	17	123.7	48	33	2.40
Sean Doolittle, Virginia	Jr.	1B	16	82.3	28	22	2.41
George Biddle, Eastern Mich.	Sr.	P	15	93.0	41	25	2.42
Ryan Buch, Monmouth	Fr.	P	14	81.0	27	22	2.44
Dustin Renfrow, Southeast Mo. State	Jr.	P	15	95.0	36	26	2.46
Josh Dew, Troy	Sr.	1B	27	65.3	19	18	2.48
Tyson Ross, California	So.	P	17	115.7	37	32	2.49
T.J. Brewer, Arkansas State	Sr.	SP	14	90.3	37	25	2.49
Eric Erickson, Miami (Fla.)	Fr.	P	16	90.0	33	25	2.50
Alex Wilson, Winthrop	So.	P	17	111.3	43	31	2.51
Matt Gorgen, California	So.	P	31	61.0	20	17	2.51
Zack Pitts, Louisville	Jr.	RP	20	121.7	47	34	2.51
Randy Boone, Texas	Sr.	P	41	71.3	30	20	2.52
Ryan Belanger, Southern Miss.	Sr.	P	17	106.3	38	30	2.54
Tim Erickson, Lamar	Jr.	SP/RP	25	63.7	25	18	2.54
Ben Norton, Evansville	Sr.	SP/RP	17	98.7	37	28	2.55
Ethan Hollingswort, Western Mich.	Jr.	P	11	74.0	30	21	2.55

WINS	CL	POS	APP	IP	W	L	PCT
Bryan Henry, Florida State	Sr.	3B	18	117.7	14	2	0.875
Adam Mills, Charlotte	Sr.	P	18	142.7	14	2	0.875
Mike Leake, Arizona State	Fr.	P	25	127.0	13	2	0.867
Scott Gorgen, UC Irvine	So.	P	22	136.7	13	3	0.813
Josh Satow, Arizona State	Jr.	RP	20	133.7	13	3	0.813
Caleb Glafenhein, E. Tenn. State	Sr.	SP/RP	28	115.3	13	7	0.650
Adam Warren, North Carolina	So.	P	15	70.7	12	0	1.000
Bobby Gagg, Coastal Caro.	So.	SP	17	112.0	12	2	0.857
Preston Guilmet, Arizona	So.	P	18	135.0	12	2	0.857
Corey Kluber, Stetson	Jr.	P	17	114.0	12	2	0.857
Casey Weathers, Vanderbilt	Sr.	RP	31	49.3	12	2	0.857
Adrian Alaniz, Texas	Jr.	P	19	104.3	12	3	0.800
Wes Etheridge, UC Irvine	Jr.	P	29	132.7	12	4	0.750
Mike Stutes, Oregon State	Jr.	P	22	132.7	12	4	0.750
Barry Enright, Pepperdine	Jr.	SP/RP	18	131.3	12	5	0.706
Jacob Thompson, Virginia	So.	SP	17	114.0	11	0	1.000
Nick Chigges, Col. of Charleston	Sr.	P	16	107.3	11	1	0.917
David Newmann, Texas A&M	Jr.	P	18	105.7	11	1	0.917
David Price, Vanderbilt	Jr.	SP/RP	18	133.3	11	1	0.917
Joe Savery, Rice	Jr.	SP/RP	18	93.3	11	1	0.917
Brian Flores, Arizona State	Jr.	P	24	125.0	11	2	0.846
Anthony Shawler, Old Dominion	So.	OF	15	114.7	11	2	0.846
Robert Woodard, North Carolina	Sr.	P	19	114.7	11	2	0.846
Ryan Berry, Rice	Fr.	P	23	122.7	11	3	0.786
Thomas Eager, Cal Poly	So.	P	18	126.0	11	3	0.786
Chris Johnson, TCU	Jr.	P	17	93.0	11	3	0.786
Jeff Kaplan, Cal State Fullerton	Jr.	P	20	122.7	11	3	0.786
Shawn Kelley, Austin Peay	Sr.	P	17	127.7	11	3	0.786
Kyle Nicholson, Texas A&M	Sr.	P	25	124.0	11	3	0.786
Nick Schmidt, Arkansas	Jr.	SP	18	124.0	11	3	0.786
James Simmons, UC Riverside	Jr.	P	17	123.7	11	3	0.786
Brian Sisk, Lamar	Jr.	P	17	100.7	11	3	0.786
Cody Adams, Southern Ill.	So.	P	16	107.7	11	5	0.688
Ben Austin, Wofford	Jr.	OF	19	107.7	11	6	0.647
Jacob Howard, Sam Houston St.	So.	SP/RP	19	110.0	11	6	0.647
Wes Roemer, Cal State Fullerton	Jr.	P	20	144.0	11	7	0.611

SAVES	CL	POS	APP	IP	SV
Luke Prihoda, Sam Houston State	Sr.	P	35	72.7	18
Andrew Carignan, North Carolina	Jr.	P	40	63.0	18
Paul Koss, Southern California	Sr.	RP	29	29.0	16
Andy Masten, Creighton	Sr.	P	34	49.0	16
Kevin Crum, VMI	So.	RP	24	34.0	14

Name	CL	POS	APP	IP		ERA
Matt Shoemaker, Eastern Mich.	Jr.	P	25	34.0	14	
Jordan Flasher, George Mason	So.	C	27	38.0	14	
Ryan Woods, Le Moyne	Sr.	P	30	60.3	14	
Brian Alas, Richmond	Jr.	SP/RP	36	66.0	14	
Shane Matthews, East Caro.	Sr.	SP/RP	39	48.0	14	
Randy Boone, Texas	Sr.	P	41	71.3	14	
David Cales, Ill.-Chicago	So.	INF	24	36.3	13	
Blair Erickson, UC Irvine	Sr.	P	26	23.0	13	
Cory Gearrin, Mercer	Jr.	P	26	44.3	13	
Sam Demel, TCU	Jr.	SP	32	49.3	13	
Matt German, Northern Ill.	Sr.	P	34	46.0	13	
Ross Humes, Washington State	So.	SP/RP	25	44.0	12	
Noah Krol, Wichita State	Sr.	INF	26	34.3	12	
Jason Dominguez, Pepperdine	Jr.	RP	29	39.0	12	
Robbie Elsemiller, Stetson	Jr.	P	30	45.7	12	
Eddie Kunz, Oregon State	Jr.	SP/RP	31	46.3	12	
David Slovak, Delaware	Jr.	P	35	47.7	12	
James Hayes, Rider	So.	INF	19	22.0	11	
Jason Jarvis, Arizona State	Fr.	P	21	30.0	11	
Josh Oslin, Minnesota	Sr.	P	21	21.3	11	
Matt Karl, Connecticut	Jr.	INF	22	28.3	11	
Daniel Edwards, Kansas State	Jr.	P	23	35.7	11	
Drew O'Neil, Penn State	Jr.	P	23	33.7	11	
Chris Manning, Belmont	Jr.	RP	24	27.0	11	
Nick Hagadone, Washington	Jr.	RP	25	68.3	11	
Joseph Edens, Samford	Sr.	RP	26	37.7	11	
Colin Lynch, St. John's (N.Y.)	So.	SP/RP	26	34.7	11	
Bryant George, Southern Ill.	Fr.	P	27	34.3	11	
Casey Lambert, Virginia	Sr.	SP/RP	28	43.7	11	
Eryk McConnell, North Carolina State	Jr.	P	28	52.3	11	
Nick Cassavechia, Baylor	Jr.	P	30	52.0	11	
Luke Pisker, VCU	Jr.	P	31	68.0	11	
Bryan Shaw, Long Beach State	So.	P	31	49.0	11	
Evan Reed, Cal Poly	Jr.	P	32	42.3	11	
Shawn Sanford, South Fla.	Fr.	P	32	72.7	11	
A.J. Griffin, San Diego	Fr.	P	34	63.3	11	

STRIKEOUTS PER NINE INNINGS	CL	Pos	App	IP	SO	K/9
Josh Dew, Troy	Sr.	1B	27	65.3	97	13.4
David Price, Vanderbilt	Jr.	SP/RP	18	133.3	194	13.1
Jess Todd, Arkansas	Jr.	P	23	93.3	128	12.3
Chance Chapman, Oral Roberts	Sr.	RP	22	94.0	127	12.2
Mitch Harris, Navy	Jr.	P	14	88.3	119	12.1
Nich Conaway, Oklahoma	So.	P	29	63.3	85	12.1
Aaron Jenkins, UNI	Jr.	SP/RP	14	94.7	126	12.0
Brian Matusz, San Diego	So.	SP	18	123.0	163	11.9
Danny Farquhar, La.-Lafayette	So.	SP/RP	30	87.7	115	11.8
Tim Murphy, UCLA	So.	OF	19	76.0	96	11.4
Luke Burnett, Louisiana Tech	So.	P	19	91.3	115	11.3
Jeremy Hefner, Oral Roberts	Jr.	P	16	86.0	107	11.2
Chris Salberg, Fla. Atlantic	Sr.	P	25	100.3	124	11.1
Christian Friedrich, Eastern Ky.	So.	P	14	81.7	101	11.1
Ross Detwiler, Missouri State	Jr.	SP/RP	14	89.0	110	11.1
Matt Gorgen, California	So.	P	31	61.0	75	11.1
Zachary Groh, Binghamton	Jr.	P	12	71.3	86	10.9
Josh Moffitt, Belmont	Jr.	SP	18	73.3	87	10.7
Sean Morgan, Tulane	Jr.	SP/RP	17	103.0	122	10.7
Lance Lynn, Mississippi	So.	SP	18	123.3	146	10.7
Nick Hill, Army	Sr.	P	13	84.7	100	10.6
Kyle Thebeau, Texas A&M	So.	P	29	79.0	92	10.5
Marc Rzepczynski, UC Riverside	Sr.	P	12	72.7	84	10.4
Rhett Ballard, Virginia Tech	So.	P	34	64.3	74	10.4
Kyle Gibson, Missouri	Fr.	P	28	67.3	77	10.3

STRIKEOUTS	CL	POS	APP	IP	SO
David Price, Vanderbilt	Jr.	SP/RP	18	133.3	194
Brian Matusz, San Diego	So.	SP	18	123.0	163
Wes Roemer, Cal State Fullerton	Jr.	P	20	144.0	150
Preston Guilmet, Arizona	So.	P	18	135.0	146
Lance Lynn, Mississippi	So.	SP	18	123.3	146
Adam Mills, Charlotte	Sr.	P	18	142.7	141
Will Kline, Mississippi	Jr.	RP	18	124.7	134
James Adkins, Tennessee	Jr.	SP	17	122.0	133
Anthony Shawler, Old Dominion	So.	OF	15	114.7	130
Mike Stutes, Oregon State	Jr.	P	22	132.7	129
Jess Todd, Arkansas	Jr.	P	23	93.3	128
Chance Chapman, Oral Roberts	Sr.	RP	22	94.0	127
Aaron Jenkins, UNI	Jr.	SP/RP	14	94.7	126
Ryan Berry, Rice	Fr.	P	23	122.7	125
Chris Salberg, Fla. Atlantic	Sr.	P	25	100.3	124
Sean Morgan, Tulane	Jr.	SP/RP	17	103.0	122
Clayton Mortensen, Gonzaga	Sr.	SP	16	119.3	122
Eammon Portice, High Point	Jr.	P	17	105.0	120
Tyson Ross, California	So.	P	17	115.7	120

BATTING

BATTING AVERAGE	G	AB	H	BA
Col. of Charleston	58	2170	760	.350
Florida State	62	2256	789	.350
Arizona State	64	2294	791	.345
Florida Atlantic	58	2119	723	.341
Appalachian State	59	2148	707	.329
Michigan	61	2059	674	.327
St. John's (N.Y.)	60	2186	713	.326
Jackson State	56	1772	575	.324
Iowa	54	1746	566	.324
Vanderbilt	67	2417	782	.324
Western Carolina	62	2242	725	.323
Coastal Carolina	63	2116	679	.321
Charlotte	61	2194	704	.321
Illinois	58	1989	638	.321
Sam Houston State	64	2203	706	.320
Kentucky	54	1854	594	.320
Oklahoma State	63	2232	713	.319
William & Mary	54	1856	592	.319
Florida International	55	1973	629	.319
Brown	48	1599	508	.318
UC Irvine	65	2197	697	.317
George Mason	54	1927	611	.317
Wright State	58	2045	647	.316
West Virginia	51	1719	543	.316
Texas	63	2118	669	.316

RUNS PER GAME	G	R	PG
Col. of Charleston	58	552	9.5
Arizona State	64	599	9.4
Florida State	62	562	9.1
Kentucky	54	461	8.5
Jackson State	56	470	8.4
Western Carolina	62	520	8.4
Appalachian State	59	483	8.2
Florida Atlantic	58	469	8.1
South Carolina	66	520	7.9
Central Michigan	56	432	7.7

HOME RUNS PER GAME	G	HR	PG
Wofford	63	108	1.71
South Carolina	66	113	1.71
Florida Atlantic	58	93	1.60
Col. of Charleston	58	92	1.59
New Orleans	64	90	1.41
Western Carolina	62	87	1.40
Oklahoma State	63	86	1.37
Florida	59	74	1.25
Dallas Baptist	56	70	1.25
Stephen F. Austin	59	73	1.24

TRIPLES PER GAME	G	3B	PG
Brigham Young	57	34	0.60
Jackson State	56	33	0.59
Arizona	59	33	0.56
Charlotte	61	33	0.54
UC Irvine	65	32	0.49
Southern	44	21	0.48
Oklahoma	58	27	0.47
Delaware	55	25	0.45
Col. of Charleston	58	26	0.45
UAB	58	25	0.43

DOUBLES PER GAME	G	2B	PG
Appalachian State	59	168	2.85
Florida State	62	172	2.77
Wright State	58	152	2.62
Col. of Charleston	58	149	2.57
UNC Wilmington	56	142	2.54
Arizona State	64	155	2.42
Western Carolina	62	148	2.39

South Carolina led the nation with 113 home runs in 2007, paced by Justin Smoak

NATHAN RODE

	G			
Charlotte	61		144	2.36
Vanderbilt	67		158	2.36
St. Bonaventure	52		121	2.33

SLUGGING PCT.	G	AB	TB	SLG
Col. of Charleston	58	2170	1237	.570
Florida Atlantic	58	2119	1164	.549
Arizona State	64	2294	1219	.531
Wofford	63	2179	1131	.519
Oklahoma State	63	2232	1157	.518
Western Carolina	62	2242	1158	.517
Florida State	62	2256	1162	.515
South Carolina	66	2347	1192	.508
Texas	63	2118	1058	.500
Coastal Carolina	63	2116	1048	.495

STOLEN BASES PER GAME	G	SB	CS	PG
Prairie View	59	156	28	2.64
Lafayette	53	140	29	2.64
Jackson State	56	132	18	2.36
Cincinnati	56	130	34	2.32
Alcorn State	45	102	13	2.27
Texas A&M	67	151	40	2.25
Louisville	71	153	47	2.15
UC Irvine	65	140	51	2.15
Savannah State	54	115	33	2.13
Morehead State	52	110	46	2.12

PITCHING

EARNED RUN AVERAGE	G	IP	R	ER	ERA
Charlotte	61	549.3	208	161	2.64
Wichita State	75	669.0	249	199	2.68
Virginia	61	553.7	207	173	2.81
Rice	70	625.7	260	211	3.04
Louisville	71	636.7	282	222	3.14
Pepperdine	57	508.7	230	188	3.33
San Diego	61	545.0	247	204	3.37

COLLEGE BASEBALL

Oral Roberts	57	498.0	221	191	3.45
Texas	63	561.3	254	216	3.46
St. John's (N.Y.)	60	528.3	247	204	3.48
Oregon State	67	600.7	253	232	3.48
North Carolina	73	657.0	302	257	3.52
Vanderbilt	67	606.7	266	239	3.55
Creighton	61	540.3	244	214	3.56
Florida State	62	552.0	259	219	3.57
Long Beach State	59	546.3	272	217	3.57
Mississippi	65	587.7	280	234	3.58
Coastal Carolina	63	562.7	279	227	3.63
Kent State	59	526.0	285	214	3.66
UC Riverside	59	523.3	291	214	3.68
Austin Peay	62	542.3	265	223	3.70
Central Michigan	56	497.0	271	205	3.71
Cal St. Fullerton	63	563.0	280	233	3.72
Evansville	58	505.0	259	209	3.72
Clemson	64	572.3	292	237	3.73

WINNING PCT	W	L	T	PCT
Vanderbilt	54	13	0	.806
Charlotte	49	12	0	.803
Rice	56	14	0	.800
Coastal Carolina	50	13	0	.794
Florida State	49	13	0	.790
North Carolina	57	16	0	.781
TCU	48	14	0	.774
Arizona State	49	15	0	.766
Virginia	45	16	0	.738
Creighton	45	16	0	.738

STRIKEOUTS/9 IP	G	IP	SO	K/9
Vanderbilt	67	606.7	632	9.4
Arizona	59	526.7	541	9.2
South Carolina	66	597.3	606	9.1
Wichita State	75	669.0	670	9.0
Arkansas	64	569.0	565	8.9
Oral Roberts	57	498.0	488	8.8
Troy	61	550.3	538	8.8
Florida Atlantic	58	513.7	496	8.7
Mississippi	65	587.7	560	8.6
Tulane	60	528.0	486	8.3

FIELDING

FIELDING PCT	G	PO	A	E	PCT
Arizona State	64	1708	732	53	.979
Oregon State	67	1802	752	59	.977
Rutgers	63	1676	669	58	.976
Mississippi	65	1763	629	60	.976
Texas	63	1684	618	58	.975
Oral Roberts	57	1494	602	54	.975
Florida State	62	1656	644	60	.975
Creighton	61	1621	706	61	.974
TCU	62	1656	705	62	.974
Wichita State	75	2007	772	73	.974
San Francisco	55	1445	635	55	.974
North Carolina	73	1971	765	73	.974
Tulane	60	1584	609	59	.974

Arizona State's defense, featuring Andrew Romine, led the nation in fielding percentage

BILL MITCHELL

UC Irvine	65	1736	714	66	.974
South Carolina	66	1792	609	65	.974
California	55	1454	641	57	.974
Vanderbilt	67	1820	695	69	.973
Manhattan	54	1347	600	54	.973
Miami (Ohio)	56	1477	649	59	.973
Southern Miss.	62	1632	707	65	.973
Southern California	56	1493	574	58	.973
Missouri	60	1608	657	64	.973
Pepperdine	57	1526	632	61	.973
Austin Peay	62	1627	747	68	.972
Texas State	60	1565	588	62	.972

DOUBLE PLAYS PER GAME	G	DP	PG
Southeastern La.	55	73	1.33
Creighton	61	77	1.26
Illinois	58	73	1.26
Rice	70	84	1.20
Towson	51	60	1.18
Pepperdine	57	67	1.18
Massachusetts	47	55	1.17
California	55	61	1.11
UNC Wilmington	56	62	1.11
Kent State	59	64	1.08

Batters: 10 or more at-bats. **Pitchers:** 5 or more innings

1. OREGON STATE

Coach: Pat Casey; **Record:** 49-18

Player, Pos., Year	AVG	AB	R	H	2B	3B	HR	RBI	SB
Mitch Canham, if/c, Jr.	.326	227	52	74	13	1	10	59	3
Mike Lissman, of/dh, Sr.	.317	246	52	78	12	0	10	61	5
Jordan Lennerton, 1b, Jr.	.313	217	42	68	17	1	10	51	0
Scott Santschi, of, Sr.	.309	81	13	25	4	0	1	13	1
Darwin Barney, ss, Jr.	.302	278	53	84	20	2	5	56	14
Jason Ogata, if, So.	.294	187	31	55	11	0	4	42	3
Joey Wong, 2b, Fr.	.288	205	41	59	5	2	0	19	2
John Wallace, of, So.	.282	110	19	31	5	3	1	26	3
Braden Wells, of, Jr.	.277	112	21	31	4	0	0	3	11
Brett Casey, if, Fr.	.273	11	4	3	1	0	0	0	0
Chris Hopkins, cf, Jr.	.266	203	57	54	11	3	2	27	17
Drew George, if, Jr.	.259	135	26	35	10	1	1	16	4
Koa Kahalehoe, of, So.	.244	78	17	19	4	0	0	9	4
Lonnie Lechelt, if, Jr.	.227	119	18	27	7	1	2	11	9
Scotty Berke, of, Fr.	.222	18	2	4	2	0	0	0	0
Dale Solomon, c/if, Fr.	.200	35	3	7	2	0	0	5	0
Erik Ammon, c, Jr.	.160	25	4	4	0	0	0	4	0

Player, Pos., Year	W	L	ERA	G	SV	IP	H	BB	SO
Mark Grbavac, rhp, So.	0	1	2.25	28	3	36	30	17	36
Anton Maxwell, lhp, Sr.	3	1	2.36	19	0	27	22	11	24
Eddie Kunz, rhp, Jr.	3	1	2.91	31	12	46	31	18	37
Jorge Reyes, rhp, Fr.	7	3	3.10	24	0	81	73	18	64
Daniel Turpen, rhp, Jr.	10	1	3.44	23	2	97	94	25	62
Joe Paterson, lhp, Jr.	10	6	3.61	26	2	130	129	26	85
Mike Stutes, rhp, Jr.	12	4	4.07	22	0	133	111	60	129
Blake Keitzman, lhp, Fr.	1	0	4.40	23	1	31	31	11	25
Greg Keim, rhp, Sr.	2	1	5.59	9	0	10	8	4	4

2. NORTH CAROLINA

Coach: Mike Fox; **Record:** 57-16

Player, Pos., Year	AVG	AB	R	H	2B	3B	HR	RBI	SB
Dustin Ackley, of/1b, Fr.	.402	296	70	119	20	3	10	74	11
Tim Fedroff, of, Fr.	.344	209	48	72	7	5	5	41	5
Josh Horton, ss, Jr.	.335	269	66	90	18	6	9	53	6
Tim Federowicz, c, So.	.333	291	46	97	19	1	4	65	2
Garrett Gore, 2b, So.	.324	170	31	55	8	0	2	27	2
Reid Fronk, of, Jr.	.318	283	73	90	21	5	11	58	1
Kyle Seager, if, Fr.	.308	201	34	62	10	1	2	30	4
Seth Williams, of, Jr.	.293	232	46	68	10	0	9	42	6
Chad Flack, 3b, Jr.	.247	283	47	70	15	0	7	46	6
Bryan Steed, if, Sr.	.318	22	2	7	0	2	0	5	0
Drew Poulk, of, Fr.	.275	80	20	22	3	1	4	11	3
Benji Johnson, c, Jr.	.264	129	26	34	6	1	7	29	0
Kyle Shelton, if, Jr.	.262	61	6	16	5	0	0	10	0
Mike Cavasinni, of, Fr.	.231	39	17	9	0	0	0	3	0
Ryan Graepel, ss, Fr.	.231	13	0	3	1	0	0	3	0

Player, Pos., Year	W	L	ERA	G	SV	IP	H	BB	SO
Robert Woodard, rhp, Sr.	11	2	3.30	19	0	115	119	28	84
Luke Putkonen, rhp, So.	8	2	4.57	17	0	83	90	24	60
Alex White, rhp, Fr.	6	7	4.94	19	0	98	100	48	83
B.J. Dail, rhp, Fr.	0	0	0.00	10	0	12	7	6	9
Andrew Carignan, rhp, Jr.	2	1	1.43	40	18	63	39	28	69
Adam Warren, rhp, So.	12	0	2.17	15	0	71	56	28	49
Rob Wooten, rhp, Jr.	6	1	2.35	47	0	54	51	23	58
Matt Danford, rhp, Sr.	5	0	3.22	31	1	50	45	25	34
Brian Moran, lhp, Fr.	0	0	3.38	13	0	8	6	1	7
Mike Facchinei, rhp, Jr.	1	0	4.09	10	0	22	19	14	14
Rob Catapano, lhp, Fr.	1	1	4.50	27	1	14	9	9	10
Tim Federowicz, rhp, So.	2	2	4.55	19	3	28	29	8	26
Tyler Trice, rhp, Jr.	1	0	5.03	20	0	20	21	9	11
Matt Cox, lhp, So.	2	0	5.56	22	0	11	11	11	10
Jared Bard, rhp, Fr.	0	0	6.75	5	0	5	8	4	5

3. RICE

Coach: Wayne Graham; **Record:** 56-14

Player, Pos., Year	AVG	AB	R	H	2B	3B	HR	RBI	SB
Joe Savery, 1b, Jr.	.356	275	58	98	19	2	6	60	4
Brian Friday, if, Jr.	.336	280	62	94	29	2	3	30	14
Aaron Luna, if, So.	.315	235	57	74	15	3	13	66	7
Tyler Henley, of, Jr.	.313	262	59	82	12	4	6	32	8
Danny Lehmann, c, Jr.	.313	95	37	61	16	1	4	40	2
Jess Buenger, if, So.	.306	216	44	66	12	1	7	47	2
Diego Seastrunk, 3b, Fr.	.304	214	31	65	11	2	1	42	0
Jordan Dodson, ut, Jr.	.302	212	43	64	13	0	8	55	6

Player, Pos., Year	AVG	AB	R	H	2B	3B	HR	RBI	SB
Jared Gayhart, of, So.	.339	165	45	56	9	5	4	42	2
J.P. Padron, if, Jr.	.310	71	17	22	7	0	1	10	2
Derek Myers, if, Jr.	.300	20	12	6	1	0	0	4	3
Jimmy Comerota, if, Fr.	.294	17	5	5	1	0	0	0	0
Chad Lembeck, of, Jr.	.2541	42	25	36	5	1	1	20	3
Adam Zornes, c, So.	.203	59	6	12	2	0	4	9	0
Travis Reagan, c/if, Sr.	.163	49	10	8	0	0	2	3	0

Player, Pos., Year	W	L	ERA	G	SV	IP	H	BB	SO
Matt Langwell, rhp, Jr.	8	2	2.35	23		184.1	63	32	57
Joe Savery, lhp, Jr.	11	1	2.99	18	0	93	93	41	61
Ryan Berry, rhp, Fr.	11	3	3.01	23	0	123	112	34	125
Ryne Tacker, rhp, Sr.	9	1	3.01	22	3	71.2	61	21	67
Chris Kelley, rhp, Jr.	3	3	3.43	16	0	76	79	28	58
Cole St. Clair, rhp, Jr.	0	0	1.91	16	9	28	22	8	26
Jared Gayhart, rhp, So.	0	1	2.16	6	1	8	7	4	5
Bobby Bramhall, lhp, Jr.	7	2	2.35	28	6	61	36	33	80
Scott Lonergan, rhp, Jr.	4	0	3.16	20	0	31	28	7	28
Kyle Gunderson, rhp, Sr.	1	0	3.46	12	0	13	13	4	11
Mike Ojala, rhp, So.	2	0	4.38	9	0	12	11	7	9
Bryan Price, rhp, So.	0	0	7.84	8	0	10	17	7	12
Will McDaniel, rhp, Jr.	0	0	8.22	6	0	7	8	4	10

4. UC IRVINE

Coach: Dave Serrano; **Record:** 47-17-1

Player, Pos., Year	AVG	AB	R	H	2B	3B	HR	RBI	SB
Taylor Holiday, ut, Jr.	.348	267	69	93	24	9	5	43	19
Ollie Linton, of, So.	.342	152	30	52	4	8	0	15	18
Matt Morris, of, Sr.	.339	230	48	78	9	3	6	54	18
Cody Cipriano, if, Sr.	.339	233	62	79	14	3	14	60	10
Sean Madigan, of, Fr.	.333	126	24	42	8	1	1	26	3
Ben Orloff, if, So.	.324	244	46	79	10	0	0	33	20
Bryan Petersen, of, Jr.	.323	226	42	73	8	4	5	38	27
Jeff Cusick, if, Fr.	.319	91	14	29	2	1	3	20	5
Tyler Vaughn, if, Jr.	.305	200	34	61	10	2	1	36	7
Aaron Lowenstein, c, Jr.	.296	152	23	45	3	1	0	21	10
Zach Robinson, if, Sr.	.276	58	6	16	4	0	0	6	3
Tony Asaro, ut, So.	.255	51	11	13	2	0	1	6	3
Francis Larson, c, Fr.	.233	73	9	17	7	0	1	11	0
Luis Tovar, if, Fr.	.231	26	5	6	0	0	0	3	1
Josh Tavelli, if, Sr.	.222	18	3	4	0	0	0	1	1
Nick Baligod, of, Fr.	.190	21	1	4	0	0	1	2	0
Dillon Bell, of, Fr.	.143	14	4	2	1	0	0	2	1

Player, Pos., Year	W	L	ERA	G	SV	IP	H	BB	SO
Tom Calahan, lhp, Jr.	2	0	1.61	22	0	22	17	7	24
Cory Hamilton, rhp, Fr.	4	1	2.25	11	0	24	27	12	15
Reid Suitor, rhp, Fr.	3	0	2.35	6	0	15	14	7	10
Wes Etheridge, rhp, Jr.	12	4	2.65	29	1	133	128	31	112
Scott Gorgen, rhp, So.	13	3	2.83	22	0	137	118	41	117
Blair Erickson, rhp, Sr.	0	0	3.91	26	13	23	19	15	32
Dylan Axelrod, rhp, Sr.	6	4	3.96	34	4	73	68	23	79
Eric Pettis, rhp, Fr.	4	0	4.53	25	0	60	58	21	37
Christian Bergman, rhp, Fr.	0	4	4.98	14	0	22	33	5	10
Chris Lopez, rhp, Jr.	1	0	6.23	8	0	9	11	6	11
Gary Nakashima, rhp, Sr.	1	0	6.75	10	0	20	25	4	12
Daniel Bibona, lhp, Fr.	1	1	6.84	16	0	26	35	10	25
Cole Hathcock, rhp, Fr.	0	0	12.75	9	0	12	26	5	10

5. ARIZONA STATE

Coach: Pat Murphy; **Record:** 49-15

Player, Pos., Year	AVG	AB	R	H	2B	3B	HR	RBI	SB
Brett Wallace, 1b/3b, Jr.	.404	265	75	107	17	5	16	78	12
Eric Sogard, 2b, Jr.	.400	250	74	100	12	4	11	62	18
Petey Paramore, c, So.	.379	224	64	85	18	1	6	52	4
Jason Jarvis, rhp/of, Jr.	.375	16	3	6	4	0	0	5	0
Matt Spencer, of/lhp, Jr.	.369	195	46	72	16	2	9	52	8
Kiel Roling, c, So.	.356	194	57	69	10	0	15	63	0
Ike Davis, of, So.	.349	238	56	83	23	0	8	61	6
Ryan Sontag, of, Jr.	.345	58	13	20	2	2	0	11	2
Tim Smith, of, Jr.	.333	186	52	62	12	0	3	27	8
Mike Jones, of, So.	.316	19	8	6	1	1	0	0	2
Matt Hall, 3b, So.	.313	112	27	35	10	0	4	24	1
Greg Bordes, c, So.	.308	13	2	4	1	0	0	1	0
Andrew Romine, ss, Jr.	.300	213	55	64	13	2	0	41	21
CJ Retherford, if, Jr.	.298	57	12	17	5	0	4	23	1
Rocky Laguna, of, Jr.	.295	61	20	18	3	0	1	10	2
Joe Persichina, util, Sr.	.254	71	16	18	3	0	0	10	1
Raoul Torrez, util, Fr.	.233	43	8	10	1	0	0	3	1
Jarred Bogany, of, So.	.190	58	10	11	2	1	2	15	0
Mike Leake, rhp/of, Fr.	.176	17	1	3	1	0	0	5	0

Player, Pos., Year	W	L	ERA	G	SV	IP	H	BB	SO
Ike Davis, of/lhp, So.	1	1	1.35	7	0	7	3	5	8
Scott Mueller, rhp, Jr.	1	0	2.65	14	0	17	15	6	13
Josh Satow, lhp, Jr.	13	3	2.76	20	0	134	119	53	119
Mike Leake, rhp/of, Fr.	13	2	3.69	25	1	127	126	29	94
Brian Flores, lhp, Jr.	11	2	3.89	24	0	125	115	47	95
Matt Spencer, of/lhp, Jr.	1	0	4.35	11	1	10	9	17	10
CJ Retherford, c/rhp, Sr.	2	2	4.38	5	1	12	9	7	4
Jason Jarvis, rhp/of, Fr.	2	2	4.50	21	11	30	31	8	22
Ted Aust, rhp, Jr.	0	0	6.10	8	1	10	12	3	6
Jason Mitchell, rhp, Fr.	0	1	6.30	11	0	10	11	5	10
Joey Parigi, lhp, So.	3	1	6.57	17	2	38	43	32	31
Matt Trink, rhp, Sr.	0	1	8.10	6	0	7	12	4	7
Dustin Brader, rhp, Jr.	2	0	9.47	13	0	19	28	12	11
Joe Hatasaki, lhp, Fr.	0	0	10.50	4	0	6	11	3	2
Adam Bailey, lhp, Fr.	0	0	10.97	10	0	11	16	4	13

6. VANDERBILT
Coach: Tim Corbin; Record: 54-13

Player, Pos., Year	AVG	AB	R	H	2B	3B	HR	RBI	SB
Pedro Alvarez, 3b, Jr.	.386	272	76	105	21	3	18	68	6
Ryan Flaherty, ss, So.	.381	273	59	104	23	3	4	57	12
Dominic de la Osa, ss, Jr.	.378	249	65	94	23	2	20	62	20
Matt Meingasner, of, Sr.	.321	184	39	59	8	4	7	37	4
Alex Feinberg, ss, Jr.	.317	252	50	80	17	1	4	44	1
Andrew Giobbi, c, Jr.	.312	125	19	39	10	1	1	25	1
Ryan Davis, of, Jr.	.309	123	19	38	7	0	1	26	5
David Macias, of, Jr.	.300	260	55	78	16	1	0	26	10
Jonathan White, of, So.	.289	90	15	26	7	1	3	14	6
Kurt Lipton, of, So.	.289	45	6	13	2	0	0	3	2
Shea Robin, c, Jr.	.286	234	34	67	9	0	2	35	2
Brian Harris, ss, Fr.	.283	46	12	13	1	0	0	5	1
Brad French, 1b, Jr.	.267	165	27	44	8	0	2	23	5
Parker Hanks, of, Jr.	.265	68	11	18	5	0	3	14	0
Carter Hawkins, c, Sr.	.143	14	1	2	0	0		1	0
Adam Cronk, 1b, Jr.	.091	11	1	1	0	0	1	3	0

Player, Pos., Year	W	L	ERA	G	SV	IP	H	BB	SO
Jason Cunningham, lhp, Fr.	0	0	1.23	4	0	7	7	3	3
Casey Weathers, rhp, Sr.	12	2	2.37	31	7	49	25	21	75
David Price, lhp, Jr.	11	1	2.63	18	0	133	95	31	194
Mike Minor, lhp, Fr.	9	1	3.09	19	2	90	76	19	88
Ty Davis, rhp, Jr.	3	0	3.12	19	1	49	33	19	41
Brett Jacobson, rhp, So.	6	3	3.15	21	1	74	83	15	58
Cody Crowell, lhp, Jr.	4	1	4.05	22	2	67	58	59	14
Nick Christiani, rhp, Jr.	5	3	4.11	17	0	70	71	36	57
Tyler Rhoden, rhp, Jr.	4	0	5.84	12	0	25	35	5	24
Stephen Shao, lhp, Sr.	0	2	7.07	18	0	28	37	8	24

7. LOUISVILLE
Coach: Dan McDonnell; Record: 47-24

Player, Pos., Year	AVG	AB	R	H	2B	3B	HR	RBI	SB
Isaiah Howes, of, Sr.	.391	279	65	109	20	3	18	69	9
Boomer Whiting, of, Sr.	.368	258	80	95	9	1	1	27	73
Logan Johnson, ut, Sr.	.365	266	78	97	27	2	17	65	9
Jorge Castillo, 1b, Jr.	.311	244	25	76	15	0	7	62	1
Daniel Burton, 1b/of, Sr.	.309	282	57	87	10	1	8	57	21
Alec Lowrey, of, So.	.300	50	5	15	1	0	0	7	1
Chris Cates, ss, Sr.	.299	251	50	75	14	2	0	23	17
Pete Rodriguez, of, Sr.	.289	190	34	55	15	1	2	24	5
Derrick Alfonso, c, Jr.	.274	234	32	64	9	3	5	31	4
Chris Dominguez, 3b/rhp, Fr.	.262	271	47	71	19	3	15	61	9
Justin McClanahan, 3b, Jr.	.250	104	16	26	6	1	5	24	3
Greg Del George, 2b, Sr.	.250	20	4	5	0	0	0	3	0
Jeff Arnold, c, Fr.	.211	19	3	4	2	0	0	3	0
Chris Pelaez, of, Fr.	.143	35	5	5	1	0	0	4	0

Player, Pos., Year	W	L	ERA	G	SV	IP	H	BB	SO
Zack Pitts, rhp, Jr.	10	3	2.52	20	0	122	105	24	91
Justin Marks, lhp, Fr.	9	2	2.67	19	0	105	71	38	87
Trystan Magnuson, rhp, Sr.	3	3	1.77	37	9	61	43	11	59
Gavin Logsdon, lhp, So.	2	0	1.92	32	0	52	34	15	33
Kyle Hollander, rhp, Sr.	4	1	2.40	29	2	45	31	18	46
Colby Wark, rhp, Jr.	3	4	3.56	25	1	66	51	45	75
Tyler Mathis, rhp, Jr.	3	0	3.60	7	0	35	30	13	26
James Belanger, rhp, Jr.	1	4	3.94	19	0	59	53	28	29
Skylar Meade, rhp, Sr.	9	4	4.24	23	0	47	42	15	29
Andrew Salguiero, rhp, So.	2	0	4.50	16	0	18	13	13	20
Kyle Thornton, rhp, Jr.	1	1	7.53	13	0	14	16	12	10
Chris Dominguez, 3b/rhp, Fr.	0	1	9.64	11	0	9	14	6	7

8. MISSISSIPPI STATE
Coach: Ron Polk; Record: 38-22

Player, Pos., Year	AVG	AB	R	H	2B	3B	HR	RBI	SB
Brandon Turner, 2b, Fr.	.399	208	46	83	13	1	3	48	4
Edward Easley, c, Jr.	.358	243	59	87	16	0	12	63	1
Mitch Moreland, 1b/lhp, Jr.	.343	239	43	82	26	0	10	62	1
Jeffrey Rea, 2b, Sr.	.343	245	57	84	10	2	1	22	13
Russ Sneed, 3b, Fr.	.315	54	7	17	2	0	1	9	1
Wyn Digs, c, Sr.	.316	19	2	6	0	0	0	2	0
Joseph McCaskill, of, Sr.	.312	189	40	59	14	0	1	23	0
Jeff Flagg, 1b, So.	.312	93	15	29	5	2	5	23	0
Connor Powers, ss, Fr.	.306	209	38	64	12	2	8	37	0
Brian LaNinfa, 1b, Sr.	.301	216	34	65	14	0	5	43	1
Mark Goforth, of, So.	.282	170	34	48	3	0	0	16	12
Cade Hoggard, of, Fr.	.276	29	2	8	2	0	0	1	1
Michael Rutledge, 3b, Jr.	.250	12	4	3	0	0	0	0	0
Jet Butler, ss, Fr.	.245	102	11	25	3	1	2	12	3
Nick Hardy, of, Jr.	.216	37	10	8	0	1	1	5	4
Andy Rice, of, Jr.	.209	110	17	23	6	1	2	18	1
Matt Richardson, of, Sr.	.000	10	0	0	0	0	0	0	0

Player, Pos., Year	W	L	ERA	G	SV	IP	H	BB	SO
Ricky Bowen, rhp, Fr.	5	2	3.00	27	5	36	36	13	37
Mitch Moreland, 1b/lhp, Jr.	3	0	3.20	16	2	20	18	3	28
Aaron Weatherford, rhp, So.	3	2	3.53	20	5	66	58	25	72
John Lalor, rhp, Jr.	3	1	4.17	21	3	50	43	20	54
Justin Pigott, lhp, Jr.	7	7	4.51	17	0	114	133	24	76
Chad Crosswhite, rhp, So.	8	5	4.69	22	2	79	106	27	66
Greg Houston, rhp, Fr.	1	1	5.33	16	1	25	43	7	24
Tyler Whitney, lhp, Fr.	5	1	5.72	10	0	46	57	8	43
Josh Johnson, rhp, Jr.	3	3	6.02	14	0	64	74	20	62
Jesse Carver, rhp, Jr.	0	0	8.87	10	0	22	39	14	18
Jared Koon, rhp, So.	0	0	9.69	5	0	13	23	4	12

9. CAL STATE FULLERTON
Coach: George Horton; Record: 38-25

Player, Pos., Year	AVG	AB	R	H	2B	3B	HR	RBI	SB
Clark Hardman, of, Jr.	.380	271	53	103	14	4	5	47	9
Josh Fellhauer, of, Fr.	.304	161	34	49	5	3	3	28	6
Nick Mahin, of, Jr.	.294	187	41	55	8	3	10	48	6
John Curtis, c, Sr.	.286	206	42	59	17	0	6	45	1
Chris Jones, of, So.	.272	180	33	49	15	1	1	33	7
Matt Wallach, c, Jr.	.255	141	32	36	6	1	5	28	1
Evan McArthur, 3b, Sr.	.247	174	30	43	10	1	4	31	5
Joe Scott, inf, Jr.	.246	203	34	50	10	2	0	24	8
Joel Weeks, inf, Jr.	.297	74	19	22	2	0	0	10	2
Jake Vasquez, inf, Sr.	.267	101	19	27	4	0	2	13	1
Khris Davis, of, Fr.	.256	125	25	32	4	0	0	15	4
Billy Pinkerton, inf, Fr.	.239	46	5	11	0	0	0	7	1
Corey Jones, inf, Fr.	.238	122	9	29	4	1	2	24	0
Bryan Harris, rhp/inf, Sr.	.220	50	9	11	4	0	1	9	1
Jon Wilhite, inf, Jr.	.200	35	2	7	0	0	0	2	0
Dustin Garneau, c, So.	.194	36	4	7	1	0	1	6	0
Matthew Fahey, of, So.	.067	15	2	1	0	0	0	2	0

Player, Pos., Year	W	L	ERA	G	SV	IP	H	BB	SO
Justin Klipp, rhp, Sr.	2	0	2.15	19	1	38	29	13	28
Nolan Bruyninckx, rhp, Jr.	0	2	2.55	16	1	18	16	4	14
Bryan Harris, rhp/inf, Sr.	2	3	2.65	18	3	34	24	7	25
Dustin Birosak, lhp, Jr.	0	0	2.89	19	2	19	17	6	15
Wes Roemer, rhp, Jr.	11	7	3.19	20	0	144	144	22	150
Jeff Kaplan, rhp, Jr.	11	3	3.30	20	0	123	115	43	83
Travis Kelly, rhp, Fr.	0	0	3.68	5	0	7	6	6	7
Adam Jorgenseon, rhp, Jr.	4	2	4.29	28	8	63	64	19	57
Sean Urena, rhp, Fr.	3	3	4.50	12	0	56	56	21	35
Paul Canedo, lhp, Jr.	0	1	6.00	15	0	12	17	4	9
Michael Morrison, rhp, Fr.	5	3	6.08	15	1	37	43	23	26
Ryan Ackland, rhp, Jr.	0	0	10.80	5	0	8	13	4	6

10. SOUTH CAROLINA
Coach: Ray Tanner; Record: 46-20

Player, Pos., Year	AVG	AB	R	H	2B	3B	HR	RBI	SB
Kyle Enders, c, Fr.	.417	12	3	5	1	0	0	3	0
James Darnell, inf, So.	.331	239	61	79	7	7	19	63	4
Phil Disher, c, Jr.	.328	235	40	77	16	1	15	63	0
Travis Jones, inf, Jr.	.318	261	68	83	14	2	18	68	13
Trent Kline, c, Jr.	.317	227	48	72	19	1	6	42	4
Justin Smoak, 1b, So.	.315	260	64	82	16	0	22	72	0
Harley Lail, inf, Jr.	.291	172	46	50	9	2	4	25	10
Andrew Crisp, inf, So.	.283	226	44	64	3	0	8	28	3
Drew Martin, 1b, Sr.	.279	43	8	12	3	0	3	9	0
Steven Reinhold, of, Jr.	.275	80	22	22	6	0	1	9	5
Reese Havens, inf, So.	.274	234	38	64	12	0	5	43	3
Cheyne Hurst, of, Sr.	.265	117	33	31	6	1	1	14	9
Robbie Grinestaff, of, Sr.	.259	54	8	14	4	0	3	15	0
Jon Willard, of, Sr.	.213	94	17	20	5	1	6	12	0

Player, Pos., Year	W	L	ERA	G	SV	IP	H	BB	SO
Jordan Costner, rhp, Jr.	3	0	0.73	10	0	12	9	3	10
Craig Thomas, lhp, So.	0	0	2.45	5	0	7	8	2	10
Jeff Jeffords, rhp, Sr.	6	1	3.12	24	6	49	31	21	60
Curtis Johnson, rhp, Jr.	1	3	3.38	31	3	43	31	17	54
Harris Honeycutt, rhp, Jr.	8	5	3.47	17	1	96	81	45	105
Arik Hempy, lhp, Jr.	7	3	3.58	13	0	65	56	32	64
Mike Cisco, rhp, So.	6	2	3.84	16	0	87	88	18	74
Alex Farotto, lhp, So.	1	0	4.06	18	0	31	26	14	45
Blake Cooper, rhp, Fr.	7	2	4.48	17	0	60	65	23	44
Forrest Beverly, lhp, Sr.	1	0	4.50	4	0	8	10	4	6
Jay Brown, rhp, Jr.	2	0	4.66	4	0	19	19	6	20
Will Atwood, lhp, So.	2	2	4.91	25	1	55	64	19	41
Wynn Pelzer, rhp, Jr.	2	2	5.22	25	1	40	42	18	47
Sean Wideberg, rhp, Jr.	0	0	6.97	9	0	10	12	15	14

11. TEXAS
Coach: Augie Garrido; **Record:** 46-17

Player, Pos., Year	AVG	AB	R	H	2B	3B	HR	RBI	SB
Chance Wheeless, 1b, Sr.	.376	237	57	89	16	4	4	42	7
Josh Prince, rhp/inf, Jr.	.371	89	14	33	7	0	0	16	2
Bradley Suttle, inf, So.	.359	234	49	84	17	2	12	68	2
Kyle Russell, of, So.	.336	223	68	75	11	5	28	71	10
Jordan Danks, of, So.	.332	238	63	79	17	3	4	38	19
Nick Peoples, of, Sr.	.329	213	46	70	14	4	4	38	18
Chais Fuller, ss/2b, Sr.	.324	102	17	33	6	2	2	19	2
Travis Tucker, inf, So.	.307	228	45	70	5	1	1	34	21
Preston Clark, c, So.	.286	213	36	61	17	2	8	45	2
Russ Moldenhauer, c. Fr.	.278	144	19	40	9	1	6	32	0
Kyle Lusson, of, Fr.	.240	25	3	6	2	0	0	0	1
Clay Van Hook, inf, Sr.	.235	17	2	4	0	0	0	2	0
Jeff Boes, inf, So.	.200	15	3	3	1	1	0	3	0
Brett Lewis, c/inf, Sr.	.170	53	6	9	3	0	0	4	0
Michael Demperio, inf, Fr.	.156	45	10	7	1	0	0	4	4
Pat McCrory, ss/rhp, So.	.067	30	3	2	1	0	0	1	0

Player, Pos., Year	W	L	ERA	G	SV	IP	H	BB	SO
Randy Boone, rhp, Sr.	5	6	2.52	41	14	71	64	12	70
Adrian Alaniz, rhp, Jr.	12	3	2.59	19	0	104	81	31	91
Joseph Krebs, lhp, Sr.	9	1	2.60	35	0	93	84	19	86
Austin Wood, lhp, So.	8	1	3.15	25	1	86	81	21	45
James Russell, lhp, Jr.	8	4	3.86	21	0	110	108	28	91
Alex Posey, lhp, Fr.	0	0	3.52	6	0	8	10	3	2
Pat McCrory, rhp/ss, So.	1	0	3.65	19	0	25	21	16	19
Hunter Harris, rhp, Fr.	2	0	5.89	10	0	18	24	7	14
Keith Shinaberry, lhp, Sr.	0	2	5.96	22	0	26	25	6	15
Kyle Walker, lhp, So.	1	0	10.80	7	0	13	16	19	9

12. TEXAS A&M
Coach: Rob Childress; **Record:** 48-19

Player, Pos., Year	AVG	AB	R	H	2B	3B	HR	RBI	SB
Blake Stouffer, of, Jr.	.398	256	58	102	23	5	12	85	22
Parker Dalton, inf, Sr.	.356	208	54	74	8	3	5	37	18
Brandon Hicks, inf, Jr.	.338	278	75	94	21	2	10	59	28
Luke Anders, 1b, So.	.336	211	35	71	11	1	11	46	2
Craig Stinson, c, Sr.	.332	223	39	74	15	2	12	50	1
Darby Brown, 1b, Jr.	.322	118	19	38	4	1	1	27	2
Brodie Greene, inf, Fr.	.312	93	18	29	2	0	0	8	7
Josh Stinson, c, Sr.	.308	91	18	28	6	0	1	15	2
Ben Feltner, of, Jr.	.303	251	48	76	9	2	1	24	34
Kyle Collignan, of, So.	.284	218	42	62	9	3	10	37	17
Brian Ruggiano, inf, So.	.255	102	25	26	9	1	1	14	9
Daman Aaron, of, Jr.	.205	44	7	9	3	0	0	5	1
Dane Carter, inf, So.	.203	74	14	15	2	0	1	11	7
Kirkland Rivers, of/lhp, Jr.	.200	30	3	6	0	0	0	1	0
Spencer Jackson, 1b/of, Jr.	.190	58	10	11	1	0	1	6	1
Josey Parker, inf, Jr.	.130	23	0	3	1	0	0	2	0
Jeff Hulett, inf, Fr.	.000	11	0	0	0	0	0	0	0

Player, Pos., Year	W	L	ERA	G	SV	IP	H	BB	SO
Travis Starling, rhp, Fr.	1	0	1.33	15	2	20	18	7	15
Jordan Chambless, rhp, Jr.	2	0	1.86	4	0	10	3	2	17
Kyle Nicholson, rhp, Sr.	11	3	2.25	25	4	124	96	21	99
Gary Campfield, rhp, Jr.	3	0	2.63	21	3	27	21	22	27
David Newmann, lhp, Jr.	11	1	2.81	18	0	106	79	50	102
Scott Migl, rhp, Fr.	7	3	3.77	20	0	74	82	18	33
Kyle Thebeau, rhp, So.	3	6	4.67	29	6	79	74	36	92
Clayton Ehlert, of/rhp, Fr.	1	1	4.70	8	0	23	24	10	18
Kirkland Rivers, of/lhp, Jr.	2	3	5.21	24	2	38	41	20	25
Kiel Renfro, rhp, So.	2	0	5.23	20	0	31	41	16	21
Matt Ueckert, lhp, Jr.	1	1	5.40	13	0	18	29	5	9
Jason Meyer, lhp, Sr.	4	1	8.10	18	0	43	52	26	42

13. WICHITA STATE
Coach: Gene Stephenson; **Record:** 53-22

Player, Pos., Year	AVG	AB	R	H	2B	3B	HR	RBI	SB
Damon Sublett, inf, Jr.	.354	268	57	95	15	4	5	45	14
Derek Schermerhorn, ut, Sr.	.347	245	54	85	8	1	7	38	23
Clinton McKeever, ut, Fr.	.333	18	2	6	0	0	0	1	0
Conor Gillaspie, 3b, So.	.325	295	55	96	24	4	6	63	12
Andy Dirks, of/lhp, Jr.	.320	250	51	80	11	0	3	31	19
Matt Brown, of, Jr.	.303	284	49	86	15	4	8	61	18
Tyler Weber, c, Jr.	.297	236	31	70	13	0	11	49	0
Josh Workman, ss/2b, So.	.289	201	38	58	10	1	4	30	18
Tyler Hill, ut, Jr.	.288	156	26	45	6	0	2	29	5
Danny Jackson, 1b, Sr.	.283	138	19	39	6	0	4	24	1
Cody Lassley, ut, Fr.	.275	40	10	11	2	0	0	6	4
Harrison Dreiling, ss/2b, Fr.	.269	26	5	7	1	1	0	5	1
Dusty Coleman, inf, Fr.	.264	201	32	53	10	1	2	19	7
Bret Bascue, of, Fr.	.256	39	7	10	2	1	1	5	3
Blake Hurlbutt, of, Jr.	.205	88	17	18	3	0	2	12	4
Noah Krol, inf/rhp, Sr.	.163	49	5	8	0	0	0	2	0
Ryan Jones, of, Fr.	.155	58	18	9	1	1	1	5	4

Player, Pos., Year	W	L	ERA	G	SV	IP	H	BB	SO
Anthony Capra, lhp, So.	7	1	1.76	24	1	77	57	24	77
Noah Booth, lhp, Sr.	6	1	1.23	30	6	51	43	11	48
Noah Krol, inf/rhp, Sr.	2	2	2.10	26	12	34	23	7	49
Kyle Touchatt, rhp, Sr.	2	1	2.22	23	2	49	38	13	58
Aaron Shafer, rhp, So.	8	2	2.23	15	0	85	69	23	90
Andy Womack, rhp, Jr.	3	2	2.54	14	0	28	17	8	31
Rob Musgrave, lhp, Jr.	10	2	2.59	18	0	111	96	17	85
Travis Banwart, rhp, Jr.	10	5	2.68	18	0	111	95	33	111
Tyson Fugett, lhp, Fr.	1	1	3.00	9	0	21	21	8	20
Khol Nanney, rhp, Jr.	1	1	3.14	10	0	14	11	7	9
Max Hutson, lhp, Jr.	1	2	4.26	11	0	32	34	11	33
Jared Simon, rhp, Sr.	0	2	4.28	20	0	27	29	2	23
Matt Smith, rhp, So.	2	0	7.41	8	0	17	20	4	19

14. FLORIDA STATE
Coach: Mike Martin; **Record:** 49-13

Player, Pos., Year	AVG	AB	R	H	2B	3B	HR	RBI	SB
Tony Thomas, 2b, Jr.	.430	258	91	111	33	6	11	50	31
Buster Posey, c, So.	.382	246	66	94	21	2	3	65	4
Jack Rye, of, Jr.	.372	234	53	87	12	0	10	61	6
Jason Stidham, inf, Fr.	.366	235	59	86	17	3	6	48	5
Mark Gildea, of, So.	.362	127	35	46	10	1	2	28	9
Mark Hallberg, ss, Jr.	.360	250	68	90	14	3	3	56	11
D'Vontrey Richard, of, Jr.	.351	131	41	46	5	3	2	20	2
Ohmed Danesh, of, Fr.	.321	84	16	27	6	1	2	20	2
Brandon Reichert, inf, Sr.	.311	225	43	70	16	0	3	51	1
Ruairi O'Connor, of, So.	.296	98	18	29	10	0	1	22	4
Dennis Guinn, of, Jr.	.286	154	29	44	13	1	5	37	0
Travis Anderson, of, Sr.	.281	89	19	25	7	1	3	11	0
Tommy Oravetz, 2b, So.	.297	74	15	22	5	0	1	17	0
Brady Thomas, c, So.	.294	17	2	5	3	0	0	3	0
Stephen Cardullo, inf, Fr.	.273	11	2	3	0	0	1	5	0
Devin Gonzalez, inf, Fr.	.133	15	3	2	0	0	0	3	0

Player, Pos., Year	W	L	ERA	G	SV	IP	H	BB	SO
Bryan Henry, rhp, Sr.	14	2	2.60	18	0	118	103	27	117
Michael Hyde, rhp, Sr.	10	2	3.35	19	0	83	76	30	63
Ryan Strauss, rhp, Jr.	10	3	3.40	17	0	87	86	35	56
Jimmy Marshall, rhp, So.	2	0	1.39	23	0	32	23	16	27
Matt Fairel, lhp, Fr.	2	0	2.94	21	1	34	28	12	26
Caleb Graham, rhp, So.	1	2	4.00	13	1	27	21	15	23
Brian Chambers, rhp, Jr.	3	0	4.02	31	1	40	41	16	26
Travis Burge, lhp, So.	1	0	4.34	27	1	29	25	10	27
Casey Whitmer, rhp, Fr.	1	0	4.40	12	0	14	13	10	17
Bo O'Dell, rhp, So.	3	1	5.06	13	0	32	32	12	24
Danny Rosen, rhp, Jr.	2	2	5.52	26	8	46	45	19	64
Luke Tucker, rhp, Sr.	0	1	9.00	8	1	6	6	5	8

15. CLEMSON
Coach: Jack Leggett; **Record:** 41-23

Player, Pos., Year	AVG	AB	R	H	2B	3B	HR	RBI	SB
Stan Widmann, ss, Jr.	.409	22	5	9	1	1	1	6	3
Brad Chalk, of, Jr.	.366	161	26	59	10	2	0	18	9
Doug Hogan, c, Jr.	.350	234	44	82	15	3	13	46	9
Marquez Smith, inf, Sr.	.336	250	54	84	13	2	13	56	6
Andy D'Alessio, 1b, Sr.	.319	213	49	68	12	2	17	50	1
Taylor Harbin, 2b/ss, Jr.	.296	253	42	75	19	1	11	62	14
Alex Lee, of, Fr.	.288	52	12	15	2	0	0	6	1

Player	AVG	AB	R	H	2B	3B	HR	RBI	SB
Addison Johnson, of, Fr.	.286	217	35	62	8	5	1	23	8
Wilson Boyd, of, Fr.	.285	193	39	55	7	3	2	30	1
Ben Paulsen, 1b/3b, Fr.	.258	178	27	46	9	0	5	20	0
J.D. Burgess, inf, Fr.	.236	140	21	33	3	1	1	16	1
David Bunnell, inf, Sr.	.234	47	7	11	3	0	0	6	0
D.J. Mitchell, of/rhp, So.	.208	130	19	27	5	0	2	12	8
Alex Burg, c/of, So.	.196	97	12	19	3	0	0	9	1
Tim Morris, 1b/of, Fr.	.059	17	2	1	0	0	0	0	0

Player, Pos., Year	W	L	ERA	G	SV	IP	H	BB	SO
Ryan Hinson, lhp, So.	6	2	2.74	19	0	82	72	39	60
Daniel Moskos, lhp, Jr.	3	6	3.29	27	6	79	80	33	78
David Kopp, rhp, Jr.	6	3	3.79	18	0	100	108	29	75
Stephen Clyne, rhp, Sr.	5	2	2.58	31	3	45	44	18	48
Matt Vaughn, rhp, So.	4	0	2.75	16	1	39	41	14	37
D.J. Mitchell, of/rhp, So.	5	0	3.27	15	0	52	48	16	49
Chris Fidrych, lhp, So.	0	0	3.38	10	0	5	3	2	3
Alan Farina, rhp, Jr.	6	3	3.77	25	1	57	41	27	72
Justin Sarratt, rhp, Fr.	0	1	4.85	13	0	13	21	5	13
P.J. Zocchi, rhp, Jr.	4	2	5.09	17	1	58	67	26	56
Matt Zoltak, rhp, Fr.	1	3	5.66	17	0	21	23	12	16
Alex Martin, lhp, So.	0	0	6.00	9	0	6	3	5	5
Josh Thrailkill, rhp, Fr.	0	0	9.00	3	0	5	9	0	5

16. VIRGINIA
Coach: Brian O'Connor; **Record:** 45-16

Player, Pos., Year	AVG	AB	R	H	2B	3B	HR	RBI	SB
Greg Miclat, inf, Jr.	.376	170	51	64	11	4	0	34	32
David Adams, inf, Jr.	.372	226	45	84	11	4	5	43	10
Brandon Guyer, of, Jr.	.370	227	51	84	19	0	8	50	18
Jeremy Farrell, inf, So.	.349	86	17	30	7	0	2	16	2
Ryan Hudson, c, Sr.	.302	43	9	13	3	1	1	8	0
Sean Doolittle, lhp/1b, Jr.	.301	226	41	68	14	1	7	53	5
Mike Mitchell, of, Sr.	.299	147	31	44	1	1	0	22	19
Patrick Wingfield, inf, Jr.	.297	195	40	58	10	0	3	30	9
Brandon Marsh, of, Jr.	.294	221	45	65	9	3	3	44	14
Tyler Cannon, inf, Fr.	.279	226	42	63	10	3	2	32	8
Beau Seabury, c, Sr.	.269	193	24	52	9	0	2	22	2
Tim Henry, c, Sr.	.268	123	21	33	8	0	0	31	7
John Scaglione, inf, Sr.	.273	66	16	18	3	0	0	10	2

Player, Pos., Year	W	L	ERA	G	SV	IP	H	BB	SO
Jacob Thompson, rhp, So.	11	0	1.50	17	0	114	79	32	101
Alex Smith, lhp, Sr.	0	0	2.04	26	0	18	14	5	14
Casey Lambert, lhp, Sr.	3	3	2.06	28	11	44	34	12	54
Sean Doolittle, lhp/1b, Jr.	8	3	2.40	16	0	82	76	21	69
Robert Poutier, Jr.	0	0	2.61	7	0	10	7	4	4
Jake Rule, rhp, Jr.	6	4	2.63	29	0	41	41	19	43
Michael Schwimer, rhp, Jr.	3	1	2.77	23	2	39	32	12	48
Pat McAnaney, lhp, Jr.	2	0	3.34	12	0	35	40	6	28
Andrew Carraway, rhp, So.	5	0	3.60	22	0	45	45	16	43
Jeff Lorick, lhp, Fr.	2	1	4.13	13	1	33	36	14	24
Matt Packer, lhp, Fr.	3	3	4.22	16	0	64	89	20	59
Neal Davis, lhp, Fr.	2	1	5.40	13	1	25	31	6	22

17. MISSISSIPPI
Coach: Mike Bianco; **Record:** 40-25

Player, Pos., Year	AVG	AB	R	H	2B	3B	HR	RBI	SB
Justin Henry, inf, Jr.	.381	260	52	99	14	8	0	38	22
Jordan Henry, of, Fr.	.376	263	60	99	4	2	1	17	12
Zach Miller, inf, Fr.	.368	144	30	53	7	3	4	31	5
Zack Cozart, inf, Jr.	.311	257	49	80	12	1	5	47	16
Logan Power, of, So.	.292	260	44	76	11	0	11	51	6
Cody Overbeck, inf, So.	.288	236	45	68	16	0	14	58	5
Evan Button, inf, So.	.278	108	22	30	5	1	3	15	6
C.J. Ketchum, c/inf, Jr.	.267	150	12	40	3	0	1	17	0
Fuller Smith, of, Jr.	.254	126	17	32	2	1	1	17	2
Brett Basham, c, So.	.206	155	16	32	4	2	1	24	0
Alex Kliman, c, Jr.	.321	78	13	25	8	0	2	17	0
Cullan Kight, 1b, Fr.	.316	19	5	6	1	0	0	2	0
JoJo Tann, of, So.	.308	13	14	4	2	0	0	1	0
Kyle Mills, dh, Jr.	.270	74	8	20	2	0	4	9	0
Peyton Farr, inf, Jr.	.200	40	7	8	4	0	0	4	0

Player, Pos., Year	W	L	ERA	G	SV	IP	H	BB	SO
Lance Lynn, rhp, So.	8	5	2.85	18	0	123	94	44	146
Will Kline, rhp, Jr.	7	3	3.75	18	0	125	112	45	134
Brett Bukvich, lhp, Jr.	7	3	4.10	17	1	68	66	28	52
Scott Bittle, rhp, So.	2	5	2.79	28	7	42	42	17	59
Phillip Irwin, rhp, Fr.	2	0	3.07	9	0	15	15	10	11
Cody Satterwhite, rhp, So.	4	4	3.31	27	4	54	49	28	44
Nathan Baker, lhp, Fr.	6	2	3.92	16	0	64	63	20	40
Craig Rodriguez, lhp, Sr.	2	2	4.10	21	1	37	43	16	28
Jesse Simpson, rhp, So.	1	1	4.44	12	0	24	25	4	10
Justin Cryer, rhp, Fr.	1	0	4.55	15	1	28	16	16	32

18. SAN DIEGO
Coach: Rich Hill; **Record:** 43-18

Player, Pos., Year	AVG	AB	R	H	2B	3B	HR	RBI	SB
Justin Snyder, inf, Jr.	.352	253	50	89	21	0	4	36	8
Shane Buschini, of, Sr.	.348	227	57	79	20	2	13	58	10
Josh Romanski, lhp/of, So.	.335	224	43	75	10	2	3	30	8
Jordan Abruzzo, c, Sr.	.332	256	56	85	15	1	8	59	3
Logan Gelbrich, c, Jr.	.316	212	35	67	16	0	4	38	5
Kevin Hansen, inf, Jr.	.316	225	32	71	11	2	0	34	3
Sean Nicol, inf, So.	.300	237	42	71	10	2	5	30	9
Daniel Magness, 1b, Jr.	.286	220	24	63	7	0	0	35	3
Mike Metzger, of, Jr.	.282	131	26	37	8	1	0	15	4
Kevin Muno, inf, Fr.	.243	70	15	17	3	1	0	4	5
James Meador, ut, Fr.	.215	65	7	14	1	0	0	8	2

Player, Pos., Year	W	L	ERA	G	SV	IP	H	BB	SO
A.J. Griffin, rhp, Fr.	6	2	2.70	34	11	63	49	23	65
Brian Matusz, lhp, So.	10	3	2.85	18	0	123	98	37	163
Josh Romanski, lhp/of, So.	9	1	3.05	18	0	112	90	24	92
Anthony Slama, rhp, So.	2	3	3.18	24	2	51	58	20	40
Matt Couch, rhp, Jr.	9	2	3.60	19	1	100	99	21	69
Ricardo Pecina, lhp, So.	5	4	3.86	19	0	61	63	26	41
Russel Holzhauer, rhp, Jr.	2	2	3.42	18	1	26	33	4	11

19. MICHIGAN
Coach: Rich Maloney; **Record:** 42-19

Player, Pos., Year	G	AB	R	H	2B	3B	HR	RBI	SB
Anthony Toth, inf, Fr.	.440	25	6	11	0	1	0	5	0
Derek VanBuskirk, of, Jr.	.384	146	17	56	11	2	3	32	5
Kevin Cislo, 2b, So.	.364	162	40	59	5	1	1	23	7
Nate Recknagel, 1b, Jr.	.352	227	60	80	19	2	12	61	4
Doug Pickens, ut, Jr.	.338	231	37	78	12	2	5	41	3
Zach Putnam, rhp, Jr.	.330	224	38	74	14	2	8	59	1
Jason Christian, ss, So.	.328	244	64	80	22	2	7	44	14
Adam Abraham, rhp/3b, So.	.320	231	46	74	15	0	5	45	0
Brad Roblin, of, Jr.	.320	175	44	56	12	0	1	24	22
Eric Rose, of, Sr.	.309	204	48	63	4	3	4	37	34
Chris Berset, c, Fr.	.301	83	19	25	6	0	2	18	0
Alan Oaks, inf, So.	.204	49	9	10	5	1	2	9	0
Kenny Fellows, of, So.	.150	20	2	3	1	0	0	1	2
Mike Dufek, rhp/1b, Fr.	.095	21	0	2	1	0	0	2	0

Player, Pos., Year	W	L	ERA	G	SV	IP	H	BB	SO
Sam Yashinsky, lhp, Fr.	0	0	0.00	5	0	6	3	3	4
Adam Abraham, rhp/3b, So.	5	1	2.97	15	2	33	33	11	24
Mike Wilson, lhp, So.	7	1	3.52	15	0	72	57	45	64
Zach Putnam, rhp, Jr.	8	5	3.87	16	0	102	94	38	97
Ben Jenzen, rhp, So.	2	1	4.39	25	5	41	33	18	32
Andrew Hess, rhp, Sr.	7	2	4.52	13	0	66	74	33	36
Chris Fetter, rhp, So.	6	3	4.71	16	1	71	85	21	48
Michael Powers, rhp, So.	3	3	4.76	30	4	57	62	15	52
Eric Katzman, lhp, Fr.	3	2	5.92	13	0	24	27	22	20
Jeff DeCarlo, rhp, Fr.	1	1	6.10	4	0	10	9	8	10
Mike Dufek, rhp/1b, Fr.	0	0	7.59	9	0	11	13	4	6
Brad Seddon, lhp, Fr.	0	0	8.56	11	0	14	19	13	12

20. COASTAL CAROLINA
Coach: Gary Gilmore; **Record:** 50-13

Player, Pos., Year	AVG	AB	R	H	2B	3B	HR	RBI	SB
Ricky Grice, inf, Fr.	.563	16	4	9	1	0	1	4	0
Tommy Baldridge, of, Jr.	.383	240	62	92	15	3	13	58	9
David Sappelt, of, So.	.359	276	62	99	17	7	10	50	7
Matt Rademacher, c, Sr.	.340	162	38	55	9	0	7	40	2
Dom Duggan, of, Jr.	.325	240	63	78	20	1	9	34	11
Chris Raber, inf, Sr.	.317	230	60	73	11	1	17	58	13
Dock Doyle, c, So.	.310	142	29	44	8	0	2	18	2
Derek Martin, inf, Sr.	.304	217	31	66	14	1	2	45	0
David Anderson, rhp/inf, So.	.301	136	22	41	5	0	6	23	1
Adam Vrable, inf, Jr.	.296	199	41	59	13	1	1	29	16
Tyler Bortnick, inf, So.	.269	208	32	56	6	0	6	39	4
Dustin Koca, lhp/of, Jr.	.138	29	6	4	0	0	0	3	0
Eric Godsy, inf, Fr.	.000	1	2	0	0	0	0	0	0

Player, Pos., Year	W	L	ERA	G	SV	IP	H	BB	SO
Bobby Gagg, rhp, So.	12	2	2.57	17	0	112	102	27	84
David Anderson, inf/rhp, So.	5	4	3.36	29	10	67	64	16	45
Andy DeLaGarza, lhp, Sr.	9	2	3.51	17	0	103	111	22	53
Dustin Koca, lhp/of, Jr.	2	0	2.13	10	0	13	12	5	8
Kent Altman, rhp, So.	2	0	2.64	17	1	31	36	3	20
Nick McCully, rhp, Fr.	7	3	3.48	23	4	54	47	18	43
Joey Haug, rhp, Jr.	1	0	3.66	19	0	20	20	8	10
Pete Andrelczyk, rhp, So.	2	1	4.33	23	1	27	25	10	24
John Mariotti, rhp, Sr.	8	0	4.35	17	0	91	103	19	65
Dan Lombardozzi, rhp, Fr.	0	0	4.70	6	0	8	5	4	6
Travis Risser, rhp, Sr.	2	1	5.25	20	3	24	32	9	16

21. ARKANSAS
Coach: Dave Van Horn; Record: 43-21

Player, Pos., Year	AVG	AB	R	H	2B	3B	HR	RBI	SB
Logan Forsythe, inf/of, So.	.347	225	55	78	16	2	9	55	18
Brad Secrist, of, Fr.	.313	64	14	20	4	2	1	8	1
Casey Coon, inf, Sr.	.312	231	43	72	13	0	9	71	7
Jacob Julius, of, Jr.	.309	68	13	21	4	0	5	21	1
Wayne Hrozek, of, Jr.	.298	84	17	25	4	0	3	20	2
Matt Willard, inf, So.	.293	140	41	41	9	1	0	16	8
Tim Smalling. rhp/ss, Fr.	.288	146	33	42	8	1	2	24	1
Sean Jones, of, Jr.	.282	149	38	42	8	0	2	17	6
Ben Tschepikow, inf, Jr.	.279	179	34	50	9	1	1	29	3
Danny Hamblin, 1b, Sr.	.276	232	59	64	13	0	22	60	4
Jeff Nutt, c, Jr.	.274	186	21	51	16	0	3	41	1
Jake Dugger, of, Sr.	.268	220	54	59	14	0	6	26	10
Brian Walker, c, Jr.	.268	183	36	49	12	0	11	36	1
Aaron Murphree, of, Jr.	.243	37	6	9	3	0	0	1	2
Stephen Robison, of, Sr.	.176	34	12	6	2	0	1	5	3
Jerrod Carroll, inf/of, Fr.	.167	12	2	2	0	0	0	1	1

Player, Pos., Year	W	L	ERA	G	SV	IP	H	BB	SO
Nick Schmidt, lhp, Jr.	11	3	2.69	18	0	124	84	51	111
Jess Todd, rhp, Jr.	9	3	2.89	23	2	93	83	26	128
James Gilbert, lhp, Sr.	1	0	3.31	7	0	16	17	8	11
Duke Welker, rhp, Jr.	7	5	3.59	18	0	98	81	39	80
Shaun Seibert, rhp, Jr.	0	1	3.79	6	1	19	15	12	18
Chris Rhoads, rhp, Sr.	3	1	4.75	24	1	42	47	20	41
Brian McLelland, rhp, Sr.	1	1	4.81	20	1	34	41	7	36
Travis Hill, rhp, Jr.	3	2	4.84	29	3	45	49	12	44
Chad Pierce, c, Fr.	1	0	5.40	5	0	7	9	5	7
Stephen Richards, lhp, Fr.	1	2	5.64	15	1	22	22	11	20
Dallas Keuchel, lhp, Fr.	6	3	5.88	24	1	52	65	19	49
Evan Cox, rhp, Fr.	0	0	6.57	9	2	12	13	4	16
Scott Limbocker, lhp, Fr.	0	0	6.75	3	0	5	6	5	4

22. UCLA
Coach: John Savage; Record: 33-28

Player, Pos., Year	AVG	AB	R	H	2B	3B	HR	RBI	SB
Alden Carrithers, inf, Sr.	.352	233	53	82	16	0	2	32	9
Gabe Cohen, of, So.	.345	206	35	71	12	0	10	36	4
Brandon Crawford, inf, Jr.	.335	248	50	83	17	2	7	55	11
Jermaine Curtis, inf, Jr.	.329	152	31	50	8	0	4	33	5
Cody Decker, inf, Jr.	.307	192	33	59	11	0	14	57	1
Will Penniall, of, Sr.	.297	148	26	44	8	0	2	16	7
Justin Uribe, of/lhp, Jr.	.285	123	21	35	7	2	2	18	0
Brady Dolan, c, Jr.	.280	75	16	21	2	1	1	7	1
Ryan Babineau, c, Jr.	.272	206	34	56	7	2	5	37	6
Casey Haerther, inf, So.	.263	114	12	30	4	0	1	15	4
Mickey Weisser, of/1b, Sr.	.253	91	12	23	1	1	0	10	4
Tim Murphy, lhp/of, Jr.	.244	82	14	20	7	0	0	5	4
Eddie Murray, inf, Jr.	.244	41	9	10	0	0	0	1	0
Tim Stewart, inf, So.	.205	112	13	23	6	0	3	17	1
Corey Ashner, inf, So.	.071	14	0	1	0	0	0	0	0

Player, Pos., Year	W	L	ERA	G	SV	IP	H	BB	SO
Kevin Brophy, rhp, Sr.	0	1	3.50	16	0	18	10	15	15
Garett Claypool, rhp, So.	3	1	3.54	24	4	53	44	18	35
Tyson Brummett, rhp, Sr.	10	6	4.04	20	0	138	146	33	111
Gavin Brooks, lhp, So.	6	7	4.47	18	0	111	111	30	98
Jason Novak, rhp, Jr.	3	0	4.83	24	0	41	40	20	38
Charles Brewer, rhp, So.	0	1	5.40	4	0	7	9	4	5
Tim Murphy, lhp/of, Jr.	5	4	5.68	19	2	76	84	33	96
Brant Rustich, rhp, Jr.	3	2	6.67	20	6	30	31	20	28
Brendan Lafferty, lhp, Jr.	3	2	7.62	25	0	28	38	8	13
Paul Schmidt, lhp, Sr.	0	2	7.98	11		15	17	10	9
Matthew Drummond, lhp, So.	0	1	8.49	8	0	12	12	8	9

23. OKLAHOMA STATE
Coach: Frank Anderson; Record: 42-21

Player, Pos., Year	AVG	AB	R	H	2B	3B	HR	RBI	SB
Ty Wright, of, Sr.	.405	215	54	87	14	3	8	42	5
Tyler Mach, 2b, Sr.	.386	259	60	100	24	1	16	81	1
Keanon Simon, of, Sr.	.338	240	51	81	16	4	3	27	12
Rebel Ridling, 1b, Jr.	.336	268	42	90	16	2	14	68	1
Corey Brown, of, Jr.	.335	227	82	76	15	5	22	71	23
Matt Mangini, 3b, Jr.	.332	241	59	80	17	2	9	49	6
Jordy Mercer, ss, So.	.299	154	26	46	11	1	5	24	5
Matt Lopez, 3b, Fr.	.289	90	25	26	7	0	3	18	0
Kevin David, inf, Fr.	.278	36	6	10	1	0	0	9	0
Steve Ptak, of, Jr.	.256	78	14	20	4	1	0	7	5
Donnie Webb, of, So.	.256	43	8	11	2	0	1	7	1
Dusty Harvard, of, Fr.	.250	44	12	11	2	1	0	2	1
Ryan Pittman, c, Fr.	.242	33	6	8	2	0	1	3	1
Ryan Flavell, c, Sr.	.236	144	19	34	6	1	3	17	0
Kendall Horner, inf, So.	.232	56	7	13	4	0	0	9	0
Dylan Brown, of, Fr.	.227	75	12	17	3	0	1	7	2
John Schindler, c, Sr.	.111	27	1	3	0	0	0	4	0

Player, Pos., Year	W	L	ERA	G	SV	IP	H	BB	SO
Justin Friend, rhp, Jr.	6	3	2.11	28	7	77	69	15	81
Aerik Taylor, rhp, Fr.	0	0	2.16	5	0	8	4	3	5
Brandon Adams, rhp, Sr.	2	0	3.00	13	0	15	13	5	14
Josh Fritsche, lhp, Sr.	2	0	3.47	18	1	23	25	6	24
Tyler Blandford, rhp, Fr.	2	0	3.52	11	0	23	21	10	21
Jordy Mercer, ss, So.	3	1	3.81	11	3	26	26	11	25
Martin Beno, rhp, Jr.	1	3	3.86	21	1	44	39	17	29
Joe Kent, lhp, So.	4	3	3.88	13	0	51	46	18	48
Robbie Weinhardt, rhp, Jr.	3	1	4.39	21	0	41	45	9	47
Oliver Odle, rhp, Sr.	7	5	4.81	20	0	97	125	12	65
Jeff Breedlove, rhp, So.	0	4	5.36	20	1	49	69	15	39
Andrew Oliver, lhp, Fr.	6	1	5.52	13	0	44	45	26	42
Matt Gardner, rhp, Jr.	4	0	5.70	8	0	30	21	5	18
Tyler Lyons, lhp, Fr.	0	0	5.71	20	1	17	22	5	17
Matt Willis, rhp, Fr.	1	0	5.87	6	0	8	12	3	5

24. MISSOURI
Coach: Tim Jamieson; Record: 42-18

Player, Pos., Year	AVG	AB	R	H	2B	3B	HR	RBI	SB
Evan Frey, of, Jr.	.348	224	65	78	11	5	4	35	10
Brock Bond, inf, Jr.	.316	209	53	66	12	2	1	44	12
Jacob Priday, of/c, Jr.	.297	219	45	65	14	4	13	59	4
Kyle Mach, inf, So.	.294	194	35	57	8	0	2	25	2
Ryan Lollis, of, So.	.294	235	35	69	11	2	3	52	14
Aaron Senne, c, Jr.	.289	218	35	63	17	2	7	43	4
Trevor Coleman, c, Fr.	.282	170	35	48	11	0	9	42	0
Cary Arndt, inf, Sr.	.259	170	28	44	5	1	0	11	3
John McKee, inf, Sr.	.251	207	40	52	9	1	8	40	2
Dan Pietroburgo, c, Jr.	.227	66	9	15	1	0	0	6	0
Kurt Calvert, of, Jr.	.214	28	8	6	2	0	0	3	4
Lee Fischer, inf, Jr.	.169	71	9	12	0	0	0	7	4
Dan Quinn, c, Sr.	.158	19	2	3	0	0	0	1	0
Greg Folgia, inf/rhp, Fr.	.111	18	3	2	1	0	0	0	0

Player, Pos., Year	W	L	ERA	G	SV	IP	H	BB	SO
Ryan Gargano, lhp, So.	0	0	1.73	19	0	26	15	8	13
Scooter Hicks, lhp, So.	4	0	2.73	23	6	26	23	5	16
Aaron Crow, rhp, So.	9	4	3.59	18	0	118	109	33	90
Ian Berger, rhp, So.	5	1	3.96	15	0	52	58	17	32
Kyle Gibson, rhp, Fr.	8	3	4.12	28	7	68	62	19	77
Greg Folgia, inf/rhp, Fr.	5	4	4.50	26	2	60	62	16	41
Brant Combs, lhp, So.	1	1	4.67	20	0	17	22	9	8
Stephan Holst, rhp, Sr.	2	2	4.72	14	0	40	55	17	24
Rick Zagone, lhp, So.	7	2	5.03	17	0	102	122	28	77
Ryan Allen, rhp, Fr.	0	0	7.53	11	1	14	22	4	15

25. TEXAS CHRISTIAN
Coach: Jim Schlossnagle; Record: 48-14

Player, Pos., Year	AVG	AB	R	H	2B	3B	HR	RBI	SB
Keith Conlon, of, Sr.	.399	173	52	69	11	5	9	41	12
Austin Adams, of, Sr.	.328	238	57	78	16	3	14	71	3
Andrew Walker, c, Jr.	.328	229	51	75	21	1	12	58	2
Steven Trout, inf, Jr.	.326	233	55	75	18	0	4	44	6
Clint Arnold, of, Jr.	.326	215	43	70	16	0	4	39	13
Matt Vern, c, Jr.	.319	210	42	67	17	5	5	36	8
Corey Steglich, inf, So.	.314	105	21	33	7	0	1	20	2
Ben Carruthers, inf, So.	.303	201	35	61	6	1	4	31	9
Bryan Kervin, ss, Jr.	.290	162	50	76	12	1	4	32	6
Hunt Woodruff, c/of, Jr.	.273	77	12	21	4	0	2	12	0
Teddy Kreder, ut, Jr.	.267	15	4	4	2	0	0	2	0
Matt McGuirk, of, Sr.	.205	117	19	24	2	1	5	18	2
Steve Ellington, inf, Jr.	.200	65	10	13	2	0	0	4	1
Matt Carpenter, inf, Jr.	.185	27	6	5	1	0	0	3	1

Player, Pos., Year	W	L	ERA	G	SV	IP	H	BB	SO
Seth Garrison, rhp, Jr.	1	0	1.96	6	1	23	21	3	23
Sam Demel, rhp, Jr.	7	1	2.17	32	13	50	36	17	71
Taylor Cragin, rhp, So.	2	0	2.42	13	1	22	21	8	21
Jake Arrieta, rhp, Jr.	9	3	3.01	17	0	99	90	50	93
Steven Maxwell, rhp, Fr.	1	0	3.86	15	0	21	24	6	22
Tyler Lockwood, rhp, Fr.	5	2	4.09	26	0	55	65	17	43
Chris Johnson, rhp, Jr.	11	3	4.16	17	0	93	91	48	54
Derek VerHagen, lhp, Fr.	1	0	4.24	13	1	17	16	9	21
Chance Corgan, rhp, Jr.	7	1	4.48	18	0	86	92	34	64
Chase Perry, rhp, Sr.	0	2	4.78	10	0	26	35	6	16
Cody Dunbar, rhp, Jr.	1	1	5.79	17	0	19	26	12	17
Donald Furrow, lhp, Fr.	3	1	7.03	19	1	40	50	15	39

★Won Conference Tournament   **Boldface:** NCAA regional participant/conference department leader

AMERICA EAST CONFERENCE

	Conference		Overall	
	W	L	W	L
Binghamton	17	5	28	19
Stony Brook	16	7	31	24
★Albany	13	11	29	29
Maine	12	11	22	31
Vermont	10	13	21	29
Hartford	9	14	15	34
Maryland-Baltimore County	4	20	13	40

ALL-CONFERENCE TEAM: C–Tom Hill, Sr., Albany. **1B**–Brendon Hitchcock, Sr., Binghamton. **2B**–Matt Simek, Sr., Binghamton. **3B**–Steve Wyland, Sr., Albany. **SS**–Justin Smucker, Sr., Binghamton. **OF**–Dave West, So., Albany. **OF**–Matt McGraw, Sr., Maine. **OF**–Rob Leonard, So., Stony Brook. **DH**–Will Delawter, Jr., UMBC. **SP**–Zach Groh, Jr., Binghamton. **SP**–Gary Novakowski, Jr., Stony Brook. **RP**–Alexander Beaulieu, Jr., Albany.

Player of the Year: Brendon Hitchcock, Binghamton. **Pitcher of the Year:** Gary Novakowski, Stony Brook. **Rookie of the Year:** Myckie Lugbauer, Fr., Maine. **Coach of the Year:** Tim Sinicki, Binghamton.

INDIVIDUAL BATTING LEADERS
(MINIMUM 125 AT-BATS)

	AVG	AB	R	H	2B	3B	HR	RBI	SB
Wyland, Steve, Albany	.388	196	45	**76**	14	4	5	45	9
Barrett, Joel, Maine	.372	196	40	73	18	0	**8**	44	2
Delawter, Will, UMBC	.365	170	26	62	14	0	6	38	0
Hitchcock, Brendon, Binghamton	.364	165	32	60	13	1	5	39	5
Simek, Matt, Binghamton	.361	158	31	57	17	0	5	46	12
Smith, Curt, Maine	.351	205	**46**	72	12	5	**8**	**48**	9
Leonard, Robert, Stony Brook	.344	186	35	64	8	2	**8**	45	0
Sobocinski, Ben, Hartford	.333	186	32	62	14	1	1	24	12
Perry, Bill, Hartford	.327	168	28	55	16	2	4	25	8
Donovan, Sean, Albany	.322	174	34	56	9	0	2	37	3
Cather, Billy, Maine	.321	184	35	59	12	0	4	26	17
Smucker, Justin, Binghamton	.320	181	44	58	18	1	2	24	3
Rembisz, Bryan, Vermont	.317	186	26	59	10	5	1	27	12
Witkowski, Brian, Stony Brook	.317	205	**46**	65	14	3	3	21	**22**
Bowen, Steve, UMBC	.315	162	21	51	12	0	5	17	1
Hill, Tom, Albany	.311	196	34	61	**22**	0	6	34	5
James, Ryan, Binghamton	.311	148	33	46	10	1	2	24	4
Chapman, Jim, Vermont	.305	187	28	57	7	0	1	24	6
Lugbauer, Myckie, Maine	.301	153	20	46	9	1	5	27	1
Sipp, Chris, Stony Brook	.299	201	33	60	6	1	0	29	2
Henry, Kyle, Vermont	.298	178	24	53	13	1	5	28	0
Hackett, Brian, Maine	.296	135	16	40	1	0	0	18	0
Huntington, Will, Vermont	.294	143	29	42	13	1	0	15	12
Massie, Kyle, UMBC	.292	178	29	52	12	0	0	17	12
McGraw, Matt, Maine	.288	212	43	61	5	**6**	4	28	19
Echevarria, Justin, Stony Brook	.287	164	16	47	6	0	2	21	2
Stouffer, Brady, Hartford	.286	185	39	53	13	2	5	13	15
Lemon, Mark, UMBC	.279	136	12	38	6	2	0	14	3
Dunn, Henry, Binghamton	.277	119	22	33	3	1	1	20	6
Menendez, Danny, Maine	.276	163	33	45	9	1	2	25	6

INDIVIDUAL PITCHING LEADERS
(MINIMUM 50 INNINGS)

	W	L	ERA	G	SV	IP	H	BB	SO
Rembisz, Bryan, Vermont	5	3	**2.05**	13	1	70.1	62	17	79
Albert, Justin, Vermont	4	3	2.21	10	0	53.0	**39**	24	32
Dennis, Jeff, Binghamton	4	2	2.62	12	0	55.0	45	25	54
Van Gorder, Mike, Binghamton	5	3	2.95	12	0	64.0	72	**14**	34
Szymanski, Weston, Hartford	6	5	2.99	14	0	78.1	73	15	41
Groh, Zach, Binghamton	**8**	1	3.28	12	0	71.1	53	24	86
Diamond, Scott, Binghamton	5	3	3.45	12	0	62.2	77	16	42
Hertzler, Brad, Maine	4	5	3.58	14	1	73.0	68	17	71
Naples, John, Albany	**8**	3	3.71	14	0	80.0	73	34	49
Jung, Kurt, Stony Brook	6	5	4.17	13	0	77.2	92	21	44
Henry, Kyle, Vermont	4	**8**	4.22	13	0	74.2	85	22	47
Novakowski, Gary, Stony Brook	5	2	4.28	15	0	67.1	77	14	47
Balsinde, Alejandro, Maine	3	5	4.40	20	3	71.2	95	**14**	33
Moraski, Pete, Hartford	2	4	4.53	13	0	49.2	47	20	36
Evans, Steve, UMBC	3	5	4.66	12	0	75.1	90	19	43

ATLANTIC COAST CONFERENCE

ATLANTIC	Conference		Overall	
	W	L	W	L
Florida State	24	6	49	13
Clemson	18	12	41	23
NC State	16	14	38	23
Wake Forest	14	16	34	29
Boston College	12	17	24	27
Maryland	7	23	26	30

COASTAL	W	L	W	L
★North Carolina	21	9	57	16
Virginia	19	9	45	16
Miami	17	13	37	24
Georgia **Tech**	15	14	32	25
Duke	8	22	29	25
Virginia Tech	7	23	23	31

ALL-CONFERENCE TEAM: C–Matt Wieters, Jr., Georgia Tech; Buster Posey, So., Florida State. **1B**–Dustin Ackley, Fr., North Carolina. **2B**–Tony Thomas, Jr., Florida State. **3B**–Marquez Smith, Sr., Clemson; Jason Stidham, Fr., Florida State. **SS**–Mark Hallberg, Jr., Florida State; Josh Horton, Jr., North Carolina. **OF**–Brandon Guyer, Jr., Virginia; Danny Payne, Jr., Georgia Tech; Jack Rye, Jr., Florida State. **UT**–Sean Doolittle, Jr., Virginia. **SP**–Erick Erickson, Fr., Miami; Bryan Henry, Sr., Florida State; Jacob Thompson, So., Virginia. **RP**–Andrew Carignan, Jr., North Carolina.

Player of the Year: Tony Thomas, Florida State. **Pitcher of the Year:** Bryan Henry, Florida State. **Freshman of the Year:** Dustin Ackley, North Carolina. **Coach of the Year:** Mike Martin, Florida State.

INDIVIDUAL BATTING LEADERS
(MINIMUM 125 AT-BATS)

	AVG	AB	R	H	2B	3B	HR	RBI	SB
Thomas Jr., Tony, Florida State	.430	258	**91**	111	**33**	**6**	11	50	31
Ackley, Dustin, North Carolina	.402	**296**	70	119	20	3	10	**74**	10
Poulk, Dallas, NC State	.394	170	33	67	8	4	1	26	7
Posey, Buster, Florida State	.382	246	66	94	21	2	3	65	4
Alonso, Yonder, Miami	.376	210	57	79	13	1	**18**	**74**	13
Rye, Jack, Florida State	.372	234	53	87	12	0	10	61	6
Adams, David, Virginia	.372	226	45	84	11	4	5	43	10
Guyer, Brandon, Virginia	.370	227	51	84	19	0	8	50	18
Payne, Danny, Georgia Tech	.370	219	68	81	20	3	4	36	20
Freiman, Nate, Duke	.369	217	36	80	19	0	7	48	3
Stidham, Jason, Florida State	.366	235	59	86	17	3	6	48	5
Crancer, Wally, Georgia Tech	.363	215	40	78	11	0	8	52	1
Gallagher, Jimmy, Duke	.360	211	58	76	20	2	6	43	16
Hallberg, Mark, Florida State	.360	250	68	90	14	3	3	56	11
Wieters, Matt, Georgia Tech	.358	218	42	78	17	2	10	59	2
Hogan, Doug, Clemson	.350	234	44	82	15	3	13	46	9
Campbell, Eric, Boston College	.350	200	35	70	20	0	4	41	3
Sobolewski, Mark, Miami	.345	255	47	88	16	1	8	54	14
Fedroff, Tim, North Carolina	.344	209	48	72	7	5	5	41	5
Anderson, Jonathan, Duke	.337	190	40	64	5	1	0	16	14
Tomas, Roger, Miami	.337	208	45	70	15	1	1	29	11
Smith, Marquez, Clemson	.336	250	54	84	13	2	13	56	6
Horton, Josh, North Carolina	.335	269	66	90	18	**6**	9	53	6
Federowicz, Tim, North Carolina	.333	291	46	97	19	1	4	65	2
Tekotte, Blake, Miami	.333	219	50	73	19	2	3	25	15
Fox, Willy, Wake Forest	.332	193	31	64	15	3	5	42	9
Casario, AJ, Maryland	.331	166	31	55	10	3	3	28	14
Fisher, Michael, Georgia Tech	.330	206	33	68	14	2	3	38	7
O'Brien, Sean, Virginia Tech	.327	208	44	68	20	2	1	32	5
Pond, Ryan, NC State	.326	193	52	63	13	3	7	41	4
Jones, Marcus, NC State	.321	184	29	59	8	2	4	33	6
Thomas, Brian, Virginia Tech	.319	216	28	69	17	0	3	47	8
Ferguson, Pat, NC State	.319	166	39	53	13	1	3	23	1
D'Alessio, Andy, Clemson	.319	213	49	68	12	2	17	50	1
Parks, Nate, Virginia Tech	.319	210	47	67	9	1	3	22	**39**

INDIVIDUAL PITCHING LEADERS
(MINIMUM 50 INNINGS)

	W	L	ERA	G	SV	IP	H	BB	SO
Thompson, Jacob, Virginia	11	0	**1.50**	17	0	114.0	79	32	101
Doolittle, Sean, Virginia	8	3	2.40	16	0	82.1	76	21	69

	W	L	ERA	G	SV	IP	H	BB	SO
Erickson, Eric, Miami	10	4	2.50	16	1	90.0	84	16	63
Henry, Bryan, Florida State	14	2	2.60	18	0	117.2	103	27	117
Hinson, Ryan, Clemson	6	2	2.74	19	0	82.0	72	39	60
Niesen, Eric, Wake Forest	6	5	3.00	30	0	84.0	66	38	83
Bajoczky, Tony, Duke	9	3	3.22	14	0	92.1	76	23	57
Maine, Scott, Miami	5	5	3.28	17	0	96.0	97	24	74
Moskos, Daniel, Clemson	3	6	3.29	27	6	79.1	80	33	78
Woodard, Robert, North Carolina	11	2	3.30	19	0	114.2	119	28	84
Hyde, Michael, Florida State	10	2	3.35	19	0	83.1	76	30	63
Strauss, Ryan, Florida State	10	3	3.40	17	0	87.1	86	35	56
Cecil, Brett, Maryland	5	6	3.47	30	8	62.1	62	19	62
Surkamp, Eric, NC State	4	5	3.47	16	0	96.0	92	27	84
Burns, Eddie, Georgia Tech	3	3	3.58	18	0	70.1	69	17	66
Duncan, David, Georgia Tech	7	4	3.72	16	0	104.0	106	30	86
Boggan, Kevin, Boston College	5	5	3.73	13	0	79.2	81	34	78
Kopp, David, Clemson	6	3	3.79	18	0	99.2	108	29	75
Brackman, Andrew, NC State	6	4	3.81	13	0	78.0	78	37	74
Garcia, Enrique, Miami	8	4	3.82	22	1	92.0	84	31	80
Ratliff, Ted, Boston College	6	3	3.96	17	0	72.2	70	20	65
Baron, Casey, Maryland	4	5	4.06	16	0	93.0	111	16	60
Hunter, Ben, Wake Forest	8	6	4.07	28	2	77.1	83	29	79
Packer, Matt, Virginia	3	3	4.22	16	0	64.0	89	20	59
Redd, Adam, Virginia Tech	3	6	4.41	16	1	67.1	75	32	57
Ballard, Rhett, Virginia Tech	6	2	4.48	34	1	64.1	51	27	74
Putkonen, Luke, North Carolina	8	2	4.57	17	0	82.2	90	24	60
Wells, Andrew, Virginia Tech	4	4	4.62	14	0	78.0	91	27	36
Jeanes, Nate, Boston College	2	4	4.66	13	0	73.1	80	18	65
White, Alex, North Carolina	6	7	4.94	19	0	98.1	100	48	83

ATLANTIC SUN CONFERENCE

	Conference		Overall	
	W	L	W	L
Stetson	21	6	42	21
Mercer	17	10	33	25
Belmont	16	11	34	26
★Jacksonville	15	12	34	28
Kennesaw State	13	14	32	23
North Florida	13	14	24	32
Gardner-Webb	12	15	26	32
Lipscomb	12	15	28	30
East Tennessee State	11	16	26	29
Campbell	5	22	11	45

ALL-CONFERENCE TEAM: C–Caleb Joseph, So., Lipscomb. **1B**–Jeremy Cruz, So., Stetson. **2B**–T.J. Thompson, Fr., North Florida. **3B**–Braedyn Pruitt, Sr., Stetson. **SS**–Billy Shaughnessy, Jr., Mercer. **OF**–Justin Bass, Jr., Stetson; Pete Clifford, Sr., Jacksonville State; Shane Jordan, Sr., Stetson. **DH**–Brian Pruitt, So., Stetson. **SP**–Chris Ingoglia, Sr., Stetson; Corey Kluber, Jr., Stetson; Charles Lee, Sr., Belmont. **RP**–Cory Gearrin, Jr., Mercer.

Player of the Year: Pete Clifford, Jacksonville. **Pitcher of the Year:** Cory Kluber, Stetson. **Freshman of the Year:** Rex Brothers, Lipscomb. **Coach of the Year:** Pete Dunn, Stetson.

INDIVIDUAL BATTING LEADERS
(MINIMUM 125 AT-BATS)

	AVG	AB	R	H	2B	3B	HR	RBI	SB
Robbins, Jacob, Kennesaw State	.383	188	42	72	4	2	0	22	24
Bass, Justin, Stetson	.362	235	56	85	17	5	5	54	6
Jordan, Shane, Stetson	.354	257	65	91	17	2	2	28	17
Clifford, Pete, Jacksonville	.351	231	55	81	17	2	14	59	21
Dandridge, Jon, North Florida	.348	204	37	71	10	3	5	40	5
Tucker, Wilson, Belmont	.346	234	52	81	20	2	9	42	4
Pruitt, Braedyn, Stetson	.345	223	49	77	14	0	8	46	1
Baker, Martin, Kennesaw State	.344	215	58	74	10	1	1	24	20
Smith, Daniel, Campbell	.342	152	32	52	3	1	1	14	2
Joseph, Caleb, Lipscomb	.339	221	45	75	25	1	8	48	11
Floyd, Carlton, Campbell	.339	230	30	78	13	2	2	27	7
Cooke, Daniel, Gardner-Webb	.338	198	31	67	5	3	4	38	22
Wagner, Daniel, Belmont	.338	157	23	53	7	1	0	23	4
Russell, Anthony, East Tenn.	.335	218	39	73	19	0	10	44	3
Shaughnessy, Billy, Mercer	.333	210	37	70	13	1	2	27	11
Aughey, Justin, East Tenn.	.332	205	35	68	13	1	8	38	4
Tindle, Adam, Stetson	.329	164	24	54	13	2	0	32	4
Petsch, Ben, Belmont	.329	231	53	76	15	2	8	43	11
Cruz, Jeremy, Stetson	.328	244	35	80	17	3	3	44	0
Opachich, Chuck, Jacksonville	.327	214	39	70	11	1	0	27	16
Bond, Casey, Lipscomb	.326	230	47	75	9	4	5	24	24
McArdle, Ryan, Jacksonville	.324	238	30	77	20	0	6	51	2
Wilkins, Ryan, Lipscomb	.322	205	33	66	8	3	4	35	6
Simmons, Kane, Belmont	.321	218	47	70	21	4	15	56	5

	AVG	AB	R	H	2B	3B	HR	RBI	SB
Renfroe, Eric, Mercer	.320	200	46	64	12	1	9	31	12
Thompson, Josh, Mercer	.317	221	33	70	16	1	10	51	1
Armstrong, Mike, Mercer	.316	234	51	74	16	0	5	39	3
Wiley, Derek, Belmont	.314	242	47	76	15	0	10	48	3
Reynolds, Matt, Belmont	.313	243	55	76	11	2	7	24	15
Crawford, Matt, Mercer	.310	155	37	48	7	1	1	21	13

INDIVIDUAL PITCHING LEADERS
(MINIMUM 50 INNINGS)

	W	L	ERA	G	SV	IP	H	BB	SO
Kluber, Corey, Stetson	12	2	2.05	17	0	114.0	90	36	117
Ingoglia, Chris, Stetson	9	6	3.16	24	0	111.0	98	36	95
McClurg, Brandon, Lipscomb	4	4	3.25	18	3	72.0	62	26	57
Young, Justin, Jacksonville	5	5	3.29	21	2	93.0	91	35	65
Heckathorn, Kyle, Kennesaw State	4	2	3.31	11	0	68.0	60	24	77
Dale, Dan, Kennesaw State	5	3	3.37	19	0	69.1	69	24	55
Brothers, Rex, Lipscomb	7	4	3.51	16	0	95.0	68	57	93
Blalock, Bubba, Kennesaw State	2	6	3.60	19	1	55.0	64	19	48
Rogers, Casey, Kennesaw State	5	2	3.71	18	1	68.0	72	20	65
Smithson, Rob, Lipscomb	7	6	3.73	18	1	91.2	81	39	73
Brantley, New, Mercer	6	3	3.81	17	0	106.1	101	30	91
Lee, Charles, Belmont	8	2	3.84	17	0	98.1	91	42	72
Hitchcock, Jake, Stetson	5	2	3.89	17	0	78.2	70	22	42
Langston, Brandon, East Tenn.	6	7	3.93	17	0	105.1	115	25	69
Gardner, Matt, Jacksonville	7	6	3.95	22	2	98.0	99	35	50
Meador, Ben, Belmont	5	4	4.00	26	1	72.0	81	24	46
Bell, Derek, Kennesaw State	4	2	4.11	17	1	70.0	81	16	44
Webster, Boone, Mercer	7	5	4.15	19	0	86.2	95	41	56
Atteo, John, North Florida	6	4	4.25	15	1	82.2	92	19	49
Campbell, Ben, Gardner-Webb	7	6	4.44	17	0	95.1	111	22	46
Merry, Taylor, Lipscomb	4	2	4.53	17	4	59.2	58	29	40
Johnson, Brad, North Florida	4	7	4.53	16	0	91.1	95	24	80
Scott, Brandon, Campbell	1	5	4.57	17	0	63.0	65	31	47
Testa, Carlo, Belmont	3	7	4.60	16	0	76.1	87	25	58
Dechert, Justin, Stetson	6	3	4.65	27	4	69.2	67	29	45
Boyette, Justin, Mercer	4	4	4.84	15	0	70.2	85	14	55
Glafenhein, Caleb, East Tenn.	13	7	4.99	28	6	115.1	160	24	50

ATLANTIC 10 CONFERENCE

	Conference		Overall		
	W	L	W	L	T
★Charlotte	23	4	49	12	0
Fordham	19	8	36	21	0
Richmond	18	9	32	28	0
Xavier	17	10	29	31	0
Rhode Island	16	11	23	29	0
St. Bonaventure	14	12	25	27	0
George Washington	14	13	23	30	1
Massachusetts	13	14	25	25	0
Saint Louis	12	14	16	37	0
Duquesne	10	17	23	28	0
Dayton	9	18	21	33	0
Temple	9	18	18	37	0
La Salle	8	19	17	32	0
Saint Joseph's	6	21	10	39	0

ALL-CONFERENCE TEAM: C–Kris Rochelle, Sr., Charlotte. **1B**–Brian Pellegrini, Sr., St. Bonaventure. **2B**–Eric Reese, Jr., Fordham. **3B**–Aaron Bray, So., Charlotte. **SS**–Michael Parker, Sr., George Washington. **OF**–Sean Barksdale, So., Temple; Charlie Kruer, Jr., George Washington; Brad McElroy, Jr., Charlotte. **DH**–Eric Larson, Sr., Rhode Island. **SP**–Adam Mills, Sr., Charlotte; Spencer Steedley, Sr., Charlotte. **RP**–Gerard Breslin, Sr., La Salle.

Player of the Year: Brian Pellegrini, St. Bonaventure. **Pitch of the Year:** Adam Mills, Charlotte. **Rookie of the Year:** Matt Zielinksi, Richmond. **Coach of the Year:** Loren Hibbs, Charlotte.

INDIVIDUAL BATTING LEADERS
(MINIMUM 125 AT-BATS)

	AVG	AB	R	H	2B	3B	HR	RBI	SB
Rochelle, Kris, Charlotte	.404	228	64	92	18	2	6	50	9
McElroy, Brad, Charlotte	.401	242	65	97	26	2	11	68	14
Pellegrini, Brian, St. Bonaventure	.391	174	68	68	24	1	17	59	5
Rickards, John, La Salle	.385	161	31	62	11	5	7	31	6
Parker, Michael, George Washington	.373	225	59	84	22	0	10	60	13
Weber, James, Temple	.368	234	50	86	11	1	3	34	2
Reese, Eric, Fordham	.362	224	58	81	9	1	4	35	14
Barksdale, Sean, Temple	.359	217	36	78	13	3	7	59	14
Wotring, Alex, Richmond	.356	208	42	74	14	3	6	44	7
Orzechowski, Stan, Temple	.349	235	52	82	20	3	6	32	8

INDIVIDUAL PITCHING LEADERS
(MINIMUM 50 INNINGS)

	W	L	ERA	G	SV	IP	H	BB	SO
Mills, Adam, Charlotte	14	2	1.01	18	0	142.2	93	27	141
Muschko, La Salle	1	1	2.95	12	0	58.0	54	18	40
Burge, Dennis, La Salle	4	4	3.00	22	1	54.0	52	14	40
Steedley, Spencer, Charlotte	8	2	3.05	18	0	112.2	86	37	92
Sever, Dave, Saint Louis	4	7	3.18	15	0	90.2	92	35	73
Eilenberg, Mitchell, Massachusetts	3	0	3.25	19	1	52.2	59	22	28
Rohr, Eric, Saint Louis	6	4	3.25	14	0	97.0	105	14	54
Zielinski, Matt, Richmond	6	5	3.30	15	0	90.0	94	29	70
Bird, Ryan, Saint Louis	0	5	3.33	13	1	78.1	84	22	59
Rosenbaum, Zach, Charlotte	9	1	3.33	16	0	81.0	70	23	60
Konecny, Bill, Xavier	3	6	3.53	15	0	89.1	86	42	48
Haselhorst, Quinn, Dayton	2	5	3.80	14	0	92.1	100	23	60
Comiskey, Tim, Massachusetts	3	4	3.83	12	0	47.0	44	30	21
Riordan, Cory, Fordham	7	4	3.95	14	0	100.1	111	29	100
Norcott, James, Rhode Island	5	9	3.95	16	0	84.1	102	18	52

BIG EAST CONFERENCE

	Conference		Overall	
	W	L	W	L
St. John's	20	7	41	19
★Rutgers	20	7	42	21
Louisville	19	8	47	24
Pittsburgh	15	11	27	27
South Florida	13	14	34	26
Villanova	12	15	29	25
Notre Dame	11	15	28	28
Connecticut	10	14	34	27
West Virginia	10	16	29	22
Cincinnati	10	16	28	28
Seton Hall	9	15	25	25
Georgetown	8	19	21	34

ALL-CONFERENCE TEAM: C–Brendan Monaghan, Sr., St. John's. **1B**–Ryan Mahoney, Sr., St. John's. **2B**–Logan Johnson, Sr., Louisville. **3B**–Gil Zayas, Jr., St. John's. **SS**–Todd Frazier, Jr., Rutgers. **OF**–Boomer Whiting, Sr., Louisville; Justin Jenkins, Sr., West Virginia; David Williams, Sr., Rutgers. **DH**–Jonathan Gossard, Jr., Rutgers. **P**–Dan Osterbrock, So. Cincinnati; Zack Pitts, Jr., Louisville; David Phelps, So., Notre Dame; Scott Barnes, So., St. John's.

Player of the Year: Todd Frazier, Rutgers. **Pitcher of the Year:** Zack Pitts, Louisville. **Freshman of the Year:** Justin Marks, Louisville. **Coach of the Year:** Ed Blankmeyer, Louisville.

INDIVIDUAL BATTING LEADERS
(MINIMUM 125 AT-BATS)

	AVG	AB	R	H	2B	3B	HR	RBI	SB
Williams, Dave, Rutgers	.412	228	59	94	19	0	5	52	10
Howes, Isaiah, Louisville	.391	279	65	109	20	3	18	69	9
Frazier, Todd, Rutgers	.377	247	87	93	24	2	22	65	25
Pollock, A.J., Notre Dame	.372	196	39	73	7	2	3	28	11
Jenkins, Justin, West Virginia	.372	215	46	80	21	3	11	47	10
Lilley, Brett, Notre Dame	.371	197	55	73	7	3	1	14	5
Whiting, Boomer, Louisville	.368	258	80	95	9	1	1	29	73
White, Adam, West Virginia	.365	211	45	77	9	1	0	32	11
Johnson, Logan, Louisville	.365	266	78	97	27	2	17	65	9
McLaughlin, Mark, Georgetown	.360	211	37	76	17	1	4	26	37
Shunk, Derek, Villanova	.357	210	49	75	12	3	2	34	7
Zayas, Gil, St. John's	.353	238	40	84	21	0	4	53	0
Deluca, Sam, St. John's	.351	231	48	81	18	1	2	46	9
Hill, Ryan, Rutgers	.350	237	60	83	12	1	11	59	8
Kemp, Brian, St. John's	.348	230	53	80	10	2	1	34	25
French, Neall, Cincinnati	.343	201	36	69	14	3	11	65	2
Grantham, Jeff, St. John's	.342	155	30	53	8	4	0	30	3
Edwards, Tom, Rutgers	.340	238	44	81	10	0	7	48	7
Diaz, Walter, South Florida	.339	236	56	80	11	1	1	29	15
Donovan, Dennis, Connecticut	.333	249	34	83	10	0	9	46	2
Kuhn, Tyler, West Virginia	.332	211	43	70	15	1	5	52	6
Campana, Tony, Cincinnati	.329	237	51	78	5	1	1	18	60
Bouchard, Matthew, Georgetown	.329	219	33	72	12	1	6	41	16
Maruszak, Addison, South Florida	.329	210	45	69	13	0	4	44	6
Harrison, Josh, Cincinnati	.327	220	59	72	17	2	9	56	21
Anninos, Chris, St. John's	.325	200	47	65	9	0	8	37	5
Butler, Dexter, South Florida	.324	213	33	69	11	0	1	44	2
Markel, Austin, West Virginia	.322	183	34	59	12	0	4	36	11
Gossard, Jon, Rutgers	.322	199	38	64	11	3	6	35	1
Monaghan, Brendan, St. John's	.321	190	44	61	9	0	0	34	9
Button, Seth, Pittsburgh	.318	198	28	63	16	1	8	32	3
Pape, Jason, West Virginia	.317	164	37	52	13	2	4	32	6

Dolbier, James, Villanova	.315	168	31	53	11	3	3	25	12
Pappas, Mark, Seton Hall	.314	140	18	44	9	1	3	16	1
Smith, Anthony, St. John's	.313	233	45	73	16	1	11	48	5
Miller, Greg, Seton Hall	.312	189	43	59	9	4	5	19	2
Castillo, Jorge, Louisville	.311	244	25	76	15	0	7	62	1
Burton, Daniel, Louisville	.309	282	57	87	10	1	8	57	21
Walsh, John, Seton Hall	.308	201	31	62	11	2	8	42	3
Terpak, Dan, Villanova	.307	205	41	63	10	6	8	48	7

INDIVIDUAL PITCHING LEADERS
(MINIMUM 50 INNINGS)

	W	L	ERA	G	SV	IP	H	BB	SO
Phelps, David, Notre Dame	8	5	1.88	15	0	110.1	96	30	102
Pitts, Zack, Louisville	10	3	2.52	20	0	121.2	105	24	91
Marks, Justin, Louisville	9	2	2.67	19	0	104.2	71	38	87
Osterbrock, Dan, Cincinnati	9	1	2.67	14	0	94.1	77	25	82
Gaggioli, Michael, Georgetown	2	5	2.86	14	0	85.0	84	20	48
Barnes, Scott, St. John's	7	2	2.93	15	0	95.1	92	34	99
Cantwell, Keith, Seton Hall	4	1	2.95	14	0	73.1	72	23	64
Brown, George, St. John's	6	2	3.09	14	0	78.2	85	23	46
McGinn, Brendan, Connecticut	8	1	3.15	12	0	71.1	72	16	48
Sanford, Shawn, South Florida	3	4	3.22	32	11	72.2	53	29	63
Saris, Jimmy, Georgetown	4	6	3.25	14	0	91.1	87	32	78
Yecker, Jared, St. John's	7	4	3.27	17	1	77.0	70	21	43
Otero, Danny, South Florida	9	7	3.32	18	0	122.0	132	23	87
Nappo, Greg, Connecticut	4	3	3.50	12	0	69.1	57	32	45
Whitlock, Josh, West Virginia	7	5	3.51	13	0	74.1	58	40	69
Nardozzi, Paul, Pittsburgh	5	6	3.68	15	0	93.0	82	21	90
Tarsi, Mike, Connecticut	6	4	3.70	14	0	87.2	87	26	64
Tosoni, Matt, St. John's	5	3	3.71	13	0	63.0	74	10	42
Ellis, Jordon, Villanova	6	1	3.75	15	0	69.2	59	35	40
Healing, Steve, Rutgers	10	4	3.81	17	0	108.2	122	21	63

BIG SOUTH CONFERENCE

	Conference		Overall	
	W	L	W	L
★Coastal Carolina	17	4	50	13
Winthrop	15	6	33	27
Liberty	14	7	36	25
Virginia Military Institute	10	11	34	21
High Point	10	11	27	30
UNC Asheville	9	12	22	38
Charleston Southern	7	14	22	34
Radford	2	19	10	36

ALL-CONFERENCE TEAM: C–Matt Rademacher, Sr., Coastal Carolina. **1B**–Chris Raber, Sr., Coastal Carolina. **2B**–Kenneth Negron, So., Liberty. **3B**–Alex Gregory, So., Radford. **SS**–Chad Rice, Sr., VMI. **OF**–David Sappelt, Soph., Coastal Carolina; Rob Vernon, Sr., UNC Asheville; Tommy Baldridge, Jr., Coastal Carolina. **DH**– Tim Nanry, Sr., Liberty. **SP**–Bobby Gagg, So., Coastal Carolina; Alex Wilson, So., Winthrop; Jason Franzblau, So., Winthrop. **RP**–David Anderson, So., Coastal Carolina.

Player of the Year: David Sappelt, Coastal Carolina. **Pitcher of the Year:** Bobby Gagg, Coastal Carolina. **Freshman of the Year:** Robby Kuzdale, High Point. **Coach of the Year:** Gary Gilmore, Coastal Carolina.

INDIVIDUAL BATTING LEADERS
(MINIMUM 125 AT-BATS)

	AVG	AB	R	H	2B	3B	HR	RBI	SB
Gregory, Alex, Radford	.430	158	22	68	13	0	5	33	2
Vernon, Rob, UNC Asheville	.394	246	51	97	20	6	8	57	18
Young, Garrett, Liberty	.389	198	53	77	12	2	8	46	6
Baldridge, Tommy, Coastal Carolina	.383	240	62	92	15	3	13	58	9
Negron, Kenneth, Liberty	.364	206	50	75	12	4	1	24	15
Sappelt, David, Coastal Carolina	.359	276	62	99	17	7	10	50	7
John, Phil, Liberty	.348	184	64	64	9	3	1	29	7
Rademacher, Matt, Coastal Carolina	.340	162	38	55	9	0	7	40	2
Cowan, Jeff, High Point	.339	218	49	74	8	1	1	29	11
Schwartz, Randy, High Point	.338	225	34	76	16	0	9	57	1
Manion, Bill, High Point	.337	175	31	59	11	1	1	30	8
Kuzdale, Robby, High Point	.330	227	51	75	14	3	4	38	18
Fyle, Justin, Charleston Southern	.330	212	37	70	14	0	5	36	3
Crumpler, Robert, VMI	.330	197	55	65	22	0	14	52	0
Tisdale, Eddie, Winthrop	.330	180	27	59	9	1	2	27	4
Keller, P.K., Liberty	.328	177	31	58	6	1	3	42	2
Carey, Phil, Winthrop	.325	206	30	67	11	2	4	37	3
Duggan, Dom, Coastal	.325	240	63	78	20	1	9	34	11
Van Es, Eddie, VMI	.320	206	41	66	14	1	7	42	5
Wheeler, Alfie, High Point	.320	203	33	65	4	1	0	24	5
Raber, Chris, Coastal Carolina	.317	230	60	73	11	1	17	58	13

	AVG	AB	R	H	2B	3B	HR	RBI	SB
Mignogna, Steve, Radford	.316	155	25	49	5	2	2	23	5
Brundridge, Wes, Charleston Southern	.312	221	41	69	16	0	5	26	2
Greene, Corey, Radford	.312	141	23	44	6	0	7	21	5
Williams, David, UNC Asheville	.310	232	31	72	18	0	1	31	4
Giammaresi, David, Liberty	.308	201	38	62	17	2	4	40	0
Hayes, Anthony, Charleston Southern	.307	202	30	62	10	0	5	33	3
Froehlich, Billy, Winthrop	.307	199	36	61	15	3	6	36	5
Gaillard, Patrick, Liberty	.306	183	37	56	10	1	2	28	6
Martin, Derek, Coastal Carolina	.304	217	31	66	14	1	2	45	0
Lentz, Tommy, Winthrop	.302	222	47	67	15	0	8	41	3
Vrable, Adam, Coastal Carolina	.296	199	41	59	13	1	1	29	16
Nanry, Tim, Liberty	.296	216	36	64	16	1	6	42	1
Yoder, A.J., VMI	.296	189	39	56	13	4	2	28	6
Krogmeier, Chris, Charleston Southern	.295	207	25	61	6	0	1	23	6

INDIVIDUAL PITCHING LEADERS
(MINIMUM 50 INNINGS)

	W	L	ERA	G	SV	IP	H	BB	SO
Wilson, Alex, Winthrop	6	4	2.51	17	0	111.1	83	39	97
Gagg, Bobby, Coastal Carolina	12	2	2.57	17	0	112.0	102	27	84
Bowman, Michael, VMI	6	3	2.73	17	0	99.0	85	26	110
Barham, Trey, VMI	9	5	3.09	19	0	87.1	93	32	79
Franzblau, Jason, Winthrop	8	4	3.13	19	1	112.0	109	28	90
Anderson, David, Coastal Carolina	5	4	3.36	29	10	67.0	64	16	45
Solbach, Michael, Liberty	7	2	3.46	14	0	80.2	79	27	54
DeLaGarza, Andy, Coastal Carolina	9	2	3.51	17	0	102.2	111	22	53
Henderson, Chris, VMI	6	3	3.70	20	0	82.2	85	16	61
Portice, Eammon, High Point	6	8	4.11	17	0	105.0	89	55	120
Mariotti, John, Coastal Carolina	8	0	4.35	17	0	91.0	103	19	65
Higgins, Cody, Charleston Southern	6	4	4.37	16	0	68.0	70	24	30
DeRatt, Alan, UNC Asheville	5	4	4.54	20	0	101.0	106	29	69
Page, Ryan, Liberty	3	3	4.57	25	4	63.0	79	13	44
Baughn, Graham, UNC Asheville	7	5	4.74	21	0	104.1	121	36	48
Stokes, David, Liberty	8	6	4.82	17	0	93.1	114	18	61
Umberger, Dustin, Liberty	5	4	4.83	18	0	95.0	112	34	54
O'Donnell, Bubba, High Point	3	7	5.15	17	2	85.2	106	28	70
Duty, Chris, VMI	5	3	5.43	15	0	59.2	62	21	60
Light, Tyler, Liberty	5	5	5.56	17	1	69.2	95	22	43

BIG 10 CONFERENCE

	Conference		Overall	
	W	L	W	L
Michigan	21	7	42	19
Minnesota	18	9	41	18
Penn State	20	10	31	26
Iowa	17	13	31	23
Illinois	16	14	31	27
★Ohio State	15	15	38	24
Michigan State	15	16	25	26
Purdue	11	20	22	32
Northwestern	9	23	18	36
Indiana	8	23	19	35

ALL-CONFERENCE TEAM: C–Lars Davis, Illinois. 1B–Ryne White, So., Purdue. 2B–Kevin Cislo, So., Michigan. 3B–Nate Hanson, So., Minnesota. SS–Jason White, Sr., Iowa. OF–Travis Street, Jr., Iowa; Mike Mee, Sr., Minnesota; Matt Nohelty, So., Minnesota. DH–Zach Putnam, So., Michigan. SP–Zach Putnam, So., Michigan; Mike Wilsom, So., Michigan; Cory Luebke, Jr., Ohio State; Craig Clark, Sr., Penn State. RP–Drew O'Neil, So., Penn State.

Player of the Year: Lars Davis, Illinois. Pitcher of the Year: Cory Luebke, Ohio State. Freshman of the Year: Matt Bischoff, Purdue. Coach of the Year: Rich Maloney, Michigan.

INDIVIDUAL BATTING LEADERS
(MINIMUM 125 AT-BATS)

	AVG	AB	R	H	2B	3B	HR	RBI	SB
White, Ryne, Purdue	.452	199	48	90	16	1	8	47	9
Sweet, Travis, Iowa	.413	206	63	85	13	4	8	52	25
Davis, Lars, Illinois	.400	225	55	90	10	3	13	56	8
Mee, Mike, Minnesota	.392	217	45	85	12	2	5	49	7
Owens, Jake, Northwestern	.385	221	48	85	12	1	1	39	18
VanBuskirk, Derek, Michigan	.384	146	17	56	11	2	3	32	5
Means, Andrew, Indiana	.369	195	32	72	10	3	1	30	27
Gerstenberger, Steve, Michigan State	.368	209	37	77	14	0	3	31	11
Toole, Justin, Iowa	.367	147	40	54	11	2	1	34	4
Nohelty, Matt, Minnesota	.367	207	48	76	2	0	2	26	24
Angle, Matt, Ohio State	.366	216	53	79	11	4	0	34	22
Cislo, Kevin, Michigan	.364	162	40	59	5	1	1	23	7
Napoleon, Dusty, Iowa	.354	175	44	62	12	0	4	56	5
Curry, Caleb, Iowa	.354	164	36	58	9	3	2	41	11
Mule, Antonio, Northwestern	.353	201	41	71	10	2	8	41	4

	AVG	AB	R	H	2B	3B	HR	RBI	SB
Recknagel, Nate, Michigan	.352	227	60	80	19	2	12	61	4
Hudson, Kyle, Illinois	.351	171	35	60	5	4	0	28	16
Blackburn, Joe, Penn State	.347	219	40	76	15	5	0	35	7
Miller, Justin, Ohio State	.346	234	27	81	15	1	1	51	0
Zoeller, Jason, Ohio State	.345	194	37	67	11	1	9	41	1
Shuck, J.B., Ohio State	.342	187	32	64	4	2	1	37	8
Snowden, Ryan, Illinois	.341	229	45	78	21	1	2	31	11
McCallum, Derek, Minnesota	.340	144	24	49	7	1	2	34	1
Hanson, Nate, Minnesota	.338	225	50	76	14	0	10	51	3
Pickens, Doug, Michigan	.338	231	37	78	12	2	5	41	3
Mojzik, Jeff, Purdue	.336	125	18	42	9	2	1	21	5
Goebbert, Jake, Northwestern	.335	194	34	65	14	2	1	37	2
Cavagnaro, Matt, Penn State	.335	233	43	78	8	2	2	23	8
White, Jason, Iowa	.333	207	70	69	11	3	10	38	17
Crawford, Evan, Indiana	.333	183	30	61	13	1	1	30	18
Webb, Daniel, Illinois	.332	202	29	67	12	1	1	37	1
Roberts, Chris, Michigan State	.331	145	23	48	6	1	2	27	3
Putnam, Zach, Michigan	.330	224	38	74	14	2	8	59	1
Baran, Kyle, Minnesota	.330	197	36	65	15	0	1	34	7
Hastings, Ryan, Illinois	.330	191	38	63	10	1	6	33	6
Christian, Jason, Michigan	.328	244	64	80	22	2	7	44	14
Wooldrik, Matt, Iowa	.323	158	22	51	10	0	0	22	3
Jones, Dennis, Michigan State	.322	180	33	58	12	2	1	36	15
Fields, Caleb, Northwestern	.322	208	35	67	12	0	1	31	5
Kennedy, Tony, Ohio State	.322	177	42	57	5	2	1	30	15

INDIVIDUAL PITCHING LEADERS
(MINIMUM 50 INNINGS)

	W	L	ERA	G	SV	IP	H	BB	SO
Luebke, Cory, Ohio State	9	1	2.07	16	0	117.2	93	28	98
Clark, Craig, Penn State	6	4	2.77	14	0	91.1	85	32	63
Bischoff, Matt, Purdue	3	2	2.85	14	2	60.0	55	8	61
Buske, Tom, Minnesota	5	2	3.43	14	0	60.1	68	17	36
Wilson, Mike, Michigan	7	1	3.52	15	0	71.2	57	45	64
Brookes, Craig, Michigan State	4	6	3.65	14	0	81.1	89	21	57
Putnam, Zach, Michigan	8	5	3.87	16	0	102.1	94	38	87
Lindblom, Josh, Purdue	3	4	4.13	17	1	56.2	66	10	51
Tufts, Tyler, Indiana	3	9	4.21	13	0	87.2	116	17	42
Hale, Jake, Ohio State	4	3	4.25	26	10	65.2	71	26	48
Bashore, Matt, Indiana	4	7	4.33	13	0	70.2	70	29	50
Sedlmeyer, Tony, Purdue	6	4	4.34	13	0	56.0	68	25	27
Kibler, Jon, Michigan State	5	5	4.34	12	0	66.1	71	31	41
Brabender, Dustin, Minnesota	5	1	4.40	15	0	77.2	81	31	39
Hess, Andrew, Michigan	7	2	4.52	13	0	65.2	74	33	36
Roark, Tanner, Illinois	8	2	4.55	13	0	83.0	102	33	46
Fetter, Chris, Michigan	6	3	4.71	16	1	70.2	85	21	48
Powers, Michael, Michigan	3	3	4.76	30	4	56.2	62	15	52
Shuck, J.B., Ohio State	4	4	4.88	15	0	79.1	92	33	59
Stobart, Ryan, Penn State	2	4	5.04	17	0	50.0	67	14	25
Erdman, Nick, Iowa	7	3	5.15	13	0	71.2	81	23	24
Myers, Ryan, Northwestern	4	5	5.15	14	1	71.2	88	36	58
Heines, Ricky, Purdue	6	7	5.23	14	0	75.2	93	22	55
Schwartz, Dan, Northwestern	4	4	5.24	12	0	68.2	89	30	53
Turnbull, Steve, Iowa	2	4	5.26	13	0	65.0	81	27	44

BIG 12 CONFERENCE

	Conference		Overall	
	W	L	W	L
Texas	21	6	46	17
Missouri	19	8	42	18
Oklahoma State	16	11	42	21
Nebraska	14	13	32	27
★**Texas A&M**	13	13	48	19
Baylor	12	15	35	27
Oklahoma	11	16	34	24
Kansas State	10	16	34	24
Kansas	9	17	28	30
Texas Tech	8	18	28	27

ALL-CONFERENCE TEAM: C–Preston Clark, So., Texas. 1B–Chance Wheeless, Jr., Texas. 2B–Tyler Mach, Sr., Oklahoma State. 3B–Bradley Suttle, So., Texas. SS–Beamer Weems, So., Baylor. OF–Corey Brown, Jr., Oklahoma State; Ty Wright, Sr., Oklahoma State; Kyle Russell, So., Texas. DH–Jacob Priday, Jr., Missouri; Luke Anders, So., Texas A&M. UT–Blake Stouffer, Jr., Texas A&M. SP–Aaron Crow, So., Missouri; Adiran Alaniz, Jr., Texas; Kyle Nicholson, Sr., Texas A&M. RP–Daniel Edwards, Jr., Kansas State.

Player of the Year: Kyle Russell, Texas. Pitcher of the Year: Adrian Alaniz, Texas. Freshman of the Year: Trevor Coleman, Missouri. Newcomer of the Year (tie): David Newmann, Texas A&M; Brandon Hicks, Texas A&M. Coach of the Year (tie): Tim Jamieson, Missouri; Augie Garrido, Texas.

INDIVIDUAL BATTING LEADERS
(MINIMUM 125 AT-BATS)

	AVG	AB	R	H	2B	3B	HR	RBI	SB
Wright, Ty, Oklahoma State	.405	215	54	87	14	3	8	42	5
Stouffer, Blake, Texas A&M	.398	256	58	102	23	5	12	85	22
Mach, Tyler, Oklahoma State	.386	259	60	100	24	1	16	81	1
Wheeless, Chance, Texas	.376	237	57	89	16	4	4	42	7
Wiley, Byron, Kansas State	.366	194	42	71	8	1	7	44	14
Suttle, Bradley, Texas	.359	234	49	84	17	2	12	68	2
Dalton, Parker, Texas A&M	.356	208	54	74	8	3	5	37	18
Dunigan, Joe, Oklahoma	.352	219	44	77	10	4	11	54	0
Ivey, Aaron, Oklahoma	.351	151	35	53	2	1	0	13	23
Frey, Evan, Missouri	.348	224	65	78	11	5	4	35	10
Williams, Jackson, Oklahoma	.344	183	33	63	15	3	4	44	2
Simon, Keanon, Oklahoma State	.339	239	51	81	16	4	3	27	12
Hicks, Brandon, Texas A&M	.338	278	75	94	21	2	10	59	28
Anders, Luke, Texas A&M	.336	211	35	71	11	1	11	46	2
Russell, Kyle, Texas	.336	223	68	75	11	5	28	71	10
Ridling, Rebel, Oklahoma State	.336	268	42	90	16	2	14	68	1
Tezak, Jeff, Nebraska	.335	197	31	66	14	3	3	37	6
Brown, Corey, Oklahoma State	.335	227	82	76	15	5	22	71	23
Allman, John, Kansas	.333	198	41	66	15	3	4	44	3
Mangini, Matt, Oklahoma State	.332	241	59	80	17	2	9	49	6

INDIVIDUAL PITCHING LEADERS
(MINIMUM 50 INNINGS)

	W	L	ERA	G	SV	IP	H	BB	SO
Friend, Justin, Oklahoma State	6	3	2.11	28	7	76.2	69	15	81
Nicholson, Kyle, Texas A&M	11	3	2.25	25	4	124.0	96	21	99
Boone, Randy, Texas	5	6	2.52	41	14	71.1	64	12	70
Alaniz, Adrian, Texas	9	3	2.59	19	0	104.1	81	31	91
Krebs, Joseph, Texas	9	1	2.60	35	0	93.1	84	19	86
Newmann, David, Texas A&M	11	1	2.81	18	0	105.2	79	50	102
Wertz, Luke, Nebraska	4	1	2.98	16	0	60.1	51	18	66
Hutt, Brad, Kansas State	9	4	3.07	15	0	99.2	95	29	56
Wood, Austin, Texas	8	1	3.15	25	1	85.2	81	21	45
Taylor, Heath, Oklahoma	9	3	3.57	20	0	90.2	76	53	80
Crow, Aaron, Missouri	9	4	3.59	18	0	117.2	109	34	90
Migl, Scott, Texas A&M	7	3	3.77	20	0	74.0	82	18	33
Russell, James, Texas	8	4	3.86	21	0	109.2	108	28	91
Marciel, Wally, Kansas	5	3	3.94	19	0	59.1	60	18	47
Foust, Matt, Nebraska	2	4	4.02	27	7	65.0	61	32	53
Watson, Tony, Nebraska	6	4	4.09	15	0	99.0	96	30	81
Gibson, Kyle, Missouri	8	3	4.14	28	7	67.1	62	19	77
Porlier, Stephen, Oklahoma	7	5	4.18	16	0	90.0	89	33	99
Folgia, Greg, Missouri	5	4	4.50	26	2	60.0	62	16	41
Mandel, Jeff, Baylor	7	8	4.55	17	0	97.0	106	26	77

BIG WEST CONFERENCE

	Conference		Overall		
	W	L	W	L	T
★UC Riverside	16	5	38	21	0
UC Irvine	15	6	47	17	1
Long Beach State	15	6	39	20	0
Cal Poly	13	8	32	24	0
Cal State Fullerton	10	11	38	25	0
UC Santa Barbara	9	12	23	31	0
Pacific	3	18	16	43	0
Cal State Northridge	3	18	15	41	0

ALL-CONFERENCE TEAM: C—Travis Howell, Jr., Long Beach State; Joe Olivera, So., Pacific. **1B**—Robbie Blauer, Sr., UC Santa Barbara. **2B**—Cody Cipriano, Sr., UC Irvine. **3B**—Justin Baum, Jr., Pacific. **SS**—Jaime Pedroza, Jr., UC Riverside. **OF**—Grant Desme, Jr., Cal Poly; Clark Hardman, Jr., Cal State Fullerton; Robert Perry, Sr., Long Beach State. **DH**—Shane Peterson, So., Long Beach State. **UT**—Taylor Holiday, Jr., UC Irvine. **SP**—Scott Gorgen, Jr., UC Irvine; Thomas Eager, So., Cal Poly; James Simmons, Jr., UC Riverside. **RP**—Joe Kelly, Fr., UC Riverside.

Player of the Year: Grant Desme, Cal Poly. **Pitcher of the Year:** James Simmons, UC Riverside. Freshman **Player of the Year:** Joey Gonzales, UC Riverside. **Freshman Pitcher of the Year:** Joe Kelly, UC Riverside. **Coach of the Year:** Doug Smith, UC Riverside.

INDIVIDUAL BATTING LEADERS
(MINIMUM 125 AT-BATS)

	AVG	AB	R	H	2B	3B	HR	RBI	SB
Desme, Grant, Cal Poly	.405	195	54	79	17	1	15	53	12
Blauer, Robbie, UC Santa Barbara	.398	211	36	84	17	2	4	43	1
Hardman, Clark, Cal State Fullerton	.380	271	53	103	14	4	5	47	9
Baum, Justin, Pacific	.367	226	44	83	16	1	8	43	3
Andrade Jr., Jorge, Cal State Northridge	.364	209	37	76	15	3	7	40	1

	AVG	AB	R	H	2B	3B	HR	RBI	SB
Gonzales, Joey, UC Riverside	.356	180	41	64	14	0	2	19	9
Holiday, Taylor, UC Irvine	.348	267	69	93	24	9	5	43	19
Linton, Ollie, UC Irvine	.342	152	30	52	8	4	0	21	15
Morris, Matthew, UC Irvine	.339	230	48	78	9	3	6	54	18
Cipriano, Cody, UC Irvine	.339	233	62	79	14	3	14	60	10
Schafer, Logan, Cal Poly	.335	176	36	59	8	4	4	34	2
Perry, Robert, Long Beach State	.335	242	50	81	13	4	6	50	1
Morel, Brent, Cal Poly	.333	192	40	64	17	3	5	32	5
Godfrey, Brandon, Long Beach State	.333	144	27	48	8	1	0	20	2
Madigan, Sean, UC Irvine	.333	126	24	42	8	1	1	26	3
Fox, Chris, UC Santa Barbara	.328	204	40	67	11	0	3	30	14
Oliveira, Joe, Pacific	.327	257	45	84	12	4	3	24	5
Peterson, Shane, Long Beach State	.327	199	40	65	11	3	4	40	12
Pedroza, Jaime, UC Riverside	.325	237	55	77	17	1	13	55	5
Orloff, Ben, UC Irvine	.324	244	46	79	10	0	0	33	20
Peterson, Bryan, UC Irvine	.323	226	42	73	8	4	5	38	27
Espinosa, Danny, Long Beach State	.319	210	44	67	13	4	7	38	2
Wible, Aaron, UC Riverside	.313	224	36	70	14	1	10	51	2
Cline, Matt, Long Beach State	.312	205	37	64	6	2	0	24	9
Rose, Patrick, UC Santa Barbara	.312	170	28	53	8	1	2	20	5

INDIVIDUAL PITCHING LEADERS
(MINIMUM 50 INNINGS)

	W	L	ERA	G	SV	IP	H	BB	SO
Simmons, James, UC Riverside	11	3	2.40	17	0	123.2	103	15	116
Etheridge, Wes, UC Irvine	12	4	2.65	29	1	132.2	128	31	112
Rzepczynski, Marc, UC Riverside	6	2	2.72	12	0	72.2	63	25	84
Gorgen, Scott, UC Irvine	13	3	2.83	22	0	136.2	118	41	117
Liebel, Andrew, Long Beach State	9	3	2.84	25	1	101.1	98	19	59
Arif, Omar, Long Beach State	6	5	2.99	19	0	78.1	83	23	40
Roemer, Wes, Cal State Fullerton	11	7	3.19	20	0	144.0	144	22	150
Kaplan, Jeff, Cal State Fullerton	11	3	3.30	20	0	122.2	115	43	83
Eager, Thomas, Cal Poly	11	3	3.43	18	0	126.0	111	59	99
Worley, Vance, Long Beach State	1	2	3.64	11	0	54.1	58	12	38
Axelrod, Dylan, UC Irvine	6	4	3.96	34	4	72.2	68	23	79
McElroy, Manny, Long Beach State	5	3	4.25	12	0	59.1	59	15	30
Jorgenson, Adam, Cal State Fullerton	4	2	4.29	29	8	63.0	64	19	57
Pasma, Curtis, Pacific	3	6	4.50	24	1	84.0	97	28	65
Urena, Sean, Cal State Fullerton	3	3	4.50	12	0	56.0	56	21	35
Cassa, Pat, UC Riverside	2	5	4.52	18	1	83.2	98	27	55
Pettis, Eric, UC Irvine	4	0	4.53	25	0	59.2	58	21	36
Jolicour, Jimmy, Cal State Northridge	5	3	4.65	11	0	69.2	86	20	44
Peterson, Shane, Long Beach State	2	2	4.85	15	0	55.2	56	16	42
Tracy, Brian, UC Santa Barbara	1	3	5.03	19	1	53.2	61	38	26
Ford, Mike, UC Santa Barbara	2	2	5.05	17	0	82.0	91	34	68
Runzler, Dan, UC Riverside	4	6	5.06	22	0	69.1	77	44	73
Haar, Jason, Pacific	3	3	5.06	18	0	58.2	74	19	30
Morlock, Steve, UC Santa Barbara	3	7	5.13	15	3	54.1	79	18	31
Rocchio, Joe, Cal State Northridge	2	8	5.25	18	3	85.2	99	44	60

COLONIAL ATHLETIC ASSOCIATION

	Conference		Overall	
	W	L	W	L
Old Dominion	18	11	35	24
Delaware	18	11	32	23
★Virginia Commonwealth	18	11	37	23
UNC Wilmington	18	11	29	27
George Mason	14	14	27	27
Georgia State	15	15	26	32
William & Mary	13	16	29	25
Northeastern	12	17	24	22
James Madison	11	17	22	31
Towson	11	18	21	30
Hofstra	11	18	18	20	34

ALL-CONFERENCE TEAM: C—Jason Bour, Jr., Jason Bour. **1B**—Jared Bolden, So., Virginia Commonwealth. **2B**—Chris Fournier, Jr., George Mason. **3B**—Greg Sexton, Sr., William & Mary. **SS**—Sergio Miranda, Jr., Virginia Commonwealth. **OF**—Kellen Kulbacki, Jr., James Madison; Scott Krieger, So., George Mason; Ryan Hagerich, Sr., Delaware. **DH**—Luke Gordon, Jr., Georgia State. **UT**—Tim Park, Jr., William & Mary. **UT**—Tim Park, Jr., William & Mary. **SP**—Anthony Shawler, So., Old Dominion; Dan Hudson, So., Old Dominion. **RP**—Luke Pisker, Jr., Virginia Commonwealth.

Player of the Year (tie): Kellen Kulbacki, James Madison; Greg Sexton, William & Mary. **Freshman of the Year:** Matt Prokopowicz, Hofstra. **Coach of the Year:** Jim Sherman, Delaware.

INDIVIDUAL BATTING LEADERS
(MINIMUM 125 AT-BATS)

	AVG	AB	R	H	2B	3B	HR	RBI	SB
Sexton, Greg, William & Mary	.455	209	52	95	18	3	10	61	8

	AVG	AB	R	H	2B	3B	HR	RBI	SB
Prokopowicz, Matt, Hofstra	.416	197	41	82	11	1	6	52	8
Kulbacki, Kellen, James Madison	.398	191	56	76	15	1	19	49	9
Park, Tim, William & Mary	.391	220	64	86	16	0	10	47	5
Buchholz, Alex, Delaware	.387	238	46	92	27	6	11	63	5
Bolden, Jared, VCU	.383	227	50	87	18	5	5	49	17
Zahm, Mike, Old Dominion	.371	229	60	85	23	4	7	61	10
Miranda, Sergio, VCU	.370	262	51	97	17	0	2	36	9
Fournier, Chris, George Mason	.369	214	60	79	20	1	14	53	13
Pelt, Charlie, Georgia State	.369	198	40	73	13	0	10	40	2
Bour, Jason, George Mason	.366	202	40	74	17	3	13	50	0
Tamsin, Mike, Northeastern	.366	172	39	63	10	1	8	40	2
Krieger, Scott, George Mason	.365	219	59	80	12	2	20	68	6
Schreiter, Ryan, Towson	.358	176	26	63	13	1	2	34	2
McWhorter, Brent, William & Mary	.356	219	58	78	19	3	6	36	11
Campana, Andrew, Hofstra	.356	180	47	64	9	1	0	26	19
Jablonski, Ryan, Delaware	.354	246	60	87	20	1	6	34	4
Halford, Steve, UNC Wilmington	.352	236	54	83	21	1	1	47	3
Henderson, Chris, George Mason	.351	194	38	68	16	1	1	27	0
Gordon, Luke, Georgia State	.350	220	43	77	16	1	10	53	2
Skellchock, Kyle, Towson	.350	200	48	70	16	3	9	39	4
Moses, Mitchell, James Madison	.347	150	36	52	12	0	4	34	18
Suttle, Eric, Georgia State	.343	181	35	62	12	4	3	24	6
Porter, Josh, Northeastern	.342	149	17	51	9	0	4	18	1
Jackson, Chris, VCU	.341	246	46	84	14	7	4	57	15
Rochon-Salvas, J-M, Georgia State	.341	220	47	75	9	5	4	27	11
Sheridan, Mike, William & Mary	.340	209	43	71	14	0	4	39	3
Milano, Dan, Northeastern	.337	172	39	58	10	2	13	48	3
Appel, Jason, UNC Wilmington	.336	146	24	49	9	2	3	24	12
Conley, Brian, Towson	.335	176	39	59	7	3	11	37	5
Tsakonas, Adam, Delaware	.335	182	33	61	14	3	7	35	4
Batts, Jonathan, UNC Wilmington	.330	182	38	60	15	0	9	60	4
Hagerich, Bryan, Delaware	.329	216	46	71	9	1	17	52	13
Stoneburner, Davis, James Madison	.324	204	45	66	12	1	7	40	9
Lyon, Mike, Northeastern	.321	190	33	61	13	3	10	33	3

INDIVIDUAL PITCHING LEADERS
(MINIMUM 50 INNINGS)

	W	L	ERA	G	SV	IP	H	BB	SO
Mattaliano, Mick, VCU	4	2	1.78	33	2	55.2	51	12	36
Pisker, Luke, VCU	9	2	1.85	31	11	68.0	44	22	56
Shawler, Anthony, Old Dominion	11	2	2.20	15	0	114.2	95	29	130
Bowling, Adam, Georgia State	6	2	2.93	26	0	58.1	51	25	46
Lasko, Bobby, James Madison	1	2	3.03	26	8	62.1	68	14	45
Kerfoot, Chad, Delaware	5	2	3.24	15	1	75.0	68	14	59
Hudson, Dan, Old Dominion	8	5	3.46	15	0	106.2	93	44	109
Harris, Billy, Delaware	7	1	3.59	16	0	87.2	79	29	98
Dabrowiecki, Kris, Northeastern	7	4	3.60	12	0	75.0	78	26	59
Dooley, Kevin, Georgia State	3	2	3.60	27	4	50.0	50	19	43
Frago, Charlie, Hofstra	3	2	3.61	14	0	72.1	87	20	34
Hatcher, Jeff, UNC Wilmington	5	6	3.70	17	0	82.2	91	24	63
Cropper, Daniel, UNC Wilmington	5	5	3.75	15	0	84.0	80	22	54
Deane, Phillip, VCU	3	5	4.02	16	0	65.0	66	16	47
Dupski, Jon, Towson	4	3	4.23	21	3	55.1	59	15	33
Jaycox, Dan, George Mason	3	2	4.23	12	0	61.2	65	18	49
Thomson, Jeff, Northeastern	5	5	4.38	12	0	74.0	87	9	50
Curd, Nate, Towson	3	5	4.43	16	0	63.0	66	29	34
Carter, Dexter, Old Dominion	2	5	4.50	14	0	70.0	74	28	65
Eppley, Cody, VCU	7	5	4.66	18	0	85.0	105	13	68
Bergh, Ryan, Old Dominion	5	6	4.84	18	0	89.1	116	31	63
Palmer, Will, Georgia State	7	6	4.90	17	0	90.0	96	42	51
Cook, Jacob, James Madison	6	5	4.98	26	0	77.2	86	27	62
Leonard, John, VCU	5	2	5.01	17	1	93.1	105	40	69
Wieland, Bill, VCU	5	2	5.16	21	1	52.1	59	18	30

CONFERENCE USA

	Conference		Overall	
	W	L	W	L
★Rice	22	2	56	14
East Carolina	14	9	40	23
Southern Mississippi	14	10	39	23
Houston	12	12	28	28
Memphis	12	12	36	27
Alabama-Birmingham	12	12	25	33
Tulane	9	15	34	26
Central Florida	7	17	27	32
Marshall	5	18	21	32

ALL-CONFERENCE TEAM: C–Danny Sawyer, Sr., UAB. **IF**–Brian Friday, Sr., Rice. **IF**–Joe Savery, Jr., Rice. **IF**–Trey Sutton, Sr., Southern Miss. **IF**–Kiko Vazquez, So., UCF. **OF**–J.R. Bond, Sr., UAB. **OF**–Jimmy Cesario, So., Houston. **OF**–Harrison Eldridge, Jr., East Carolina. **DH/UT**–Joey Lieberman, Sr., Memphis. **P**–Ryan Berry, Fr., Rice. **P**–Shooter Hunt, So., Tulane. **P**–Wes Musick, Fr., Houston. **P**–Ryne Tacker, Sr., Rice. **RP**–Shane Mathews, Jr., East Carolina.

Player of the Year: Joe Savery, Rice. **Pitcher of the Year:** Ryne Tacker, Rice. **Freshman of the Year:** Ryan Berry, Rice. Newcomer of the Year: Jimmy Cesario, Houston. Keith LeClair. **Coach of the Year:** Wayne Graham, Rice.

INDIVIDUAL BATTING LEADERS
(MINIMUM 125 AT-BATS)

	AVG	AB	R	H	2B	3B	HR	RBI	SB
Murray, Michael, Memphis	.375	240	58	90	21	0	4	37	6
Sutton, Trey, Southern Mississippi	.368	239	69	88	18	3	8	38	12
Vazquez, Kiko, Central Florida	.364	206	36	75	17	1	9	57	1
Amar, Adam, Memphis	.358	240	52	86	12	2	9	51	4
Bond, J.R., Alabama-Birmingham	.358	218	48	78	14	5	4	47	7
Savery, Joe, Rice	.356	275	58	98	19	2	6	60	4
Auer, Tyson, Central Florida	.356	233	46	83	12	2	0	31	27
Cesario, Jimmy, Houston	.352	219	35	77	13	1	3	35	5
Dozier, Brian, Southern Mississippi	.339	248	57	84	17	0	4	28	5
Lovdahl, Ryne, Alabama-Birmingham	.338	219	50	74	13	2	5	47	0
Moss, Bill, Memphis	.338	234	54	79	16	1	14	54	2
Bell, Phil, Alabama-Birmingham	.336	226	44	76	8	2	3	37	7
Friday, Brian, Rice	.336	280	62	94	29	2	3	30	14
Keedy, Ryan, Alabama-Birmingham	.333	198	40	66	8	2	4	33	3
Valle, Josh, Marshall	.331	139	18	46	7	0	1	24	2
Mollenhauer, Dale, East Carolina	.329	170	40	56	11	3	3	26	9
Emaus, Brad, Tulane	.329	219	43	72	6	2	5	35	3
Blount, Jody, Southern Mississippi	.326	184	35	60	10	2	6	36	4
Irvin, Josh, Memphis	.325	163	28	53	18	1	4	45	1
Guidry, Tim, Tulane	.325	237	42	77	11	0	5	38	4
Batts, Stephen, East Carolina	.323	226	43	73	15	4	5	56	12
Stirneman, Josh, Houston	.323	223	39	72	12	1	7	40	1
Rowley, Jeff, Marshall	.319	141	29	45	7	0	3	21	1
Wood, Ryan, East Carolina	.318	198	41	63	9	0	5	23	14
Luna, Aaron, Rice	.315	235	57	74	15	3	13	66	7
Richardson, Ryan, Central Florida	.313	201	30	63	9	1	1	19	12
Henley, Tyler, Rice	.313	262	59	82	12	4	6	32	8
Lehmann, Danny, Rice	.313	195	37	61	16	1	4	40	2
Everett, Cat, Tulane	.307	228	25	70	5	0	0	32	9
Presley, Zak, Houston	.306	173	35	53	4	1	2	28	13
Buenger, Jess, Rice	.306	216	44	66	12	1	7	47	2
Seastrunk, Diego, Rice	.304	214	31	65	11	2	1	42	0
Dodson, Jordan, Rice	.302	212	43	64	13	0	8	55	6
Dyer, Jared, Tulane	.300	160	25	48	4	1	2	17	1
Lormand, Ryan, Houston	.298	235	49	70	12	1	4	39	23

INDIVIDUAL PITCHING LEADERS
(MINIMUM 50 INNINGS)

	W	L	ERA	G	SV	IP	H	BB	SO
Langwell, Matt, Rice	8	2	2.35	23	1	84.1	63	32	57
Belanger, Ryan, Southern Mississippi	8	4	2.54	17	0	106.1	97	18	86
Hunt, Shooter, Tulane	6	6	2.62	16	0	99.2	85	30	104
Savery, Joe, Rice	11	1	2.99	18	0	93.1	82	41	61
Musick, Wes, Houston	6	5	3.00	15	0	93.0	87	34	73
Berry, Ryan, Rice	11	3	3.01	23	0	122.2	112	34	125
Tacker, Ryne, Rice	9	1	3.01	22	3	71.2	61	21	67
Bowden, Barry, Southern Mississippi	7	4	3.11	16	0	98.1	93	28	86
Kelley, Chris, Rice	3	3	3.43	16	0	76.0	79	28	58
Sasser, Dustin, East Carolina	5	4	3.52	17	0	94.2	106	48	68
Dowdy, Josh, East Carolina	5	2	3.62	14	0	74.2	71	15	38
Kloskowski, Mitch, Ala.-Birmingham	5	5	3.84	16	1	86.2	77	40	52
Good, Jaager, Central Florida	5	5	3.89	16	0	88.0	90	32	62
Gomes, Brandon, Tulane	7	6	3.92	16	0	96.1	103	18	74
Hose, T.J., East Carolina	6	5	3.97	18	0	95.1	97	45	70
Morgan, Sean, Tulane	8	4	4.11	17	1	103.0	89	49	122
Wallace, Brian, Ala.-Birmingham	2	4	4.71	21	4	63.0	81	31	24
Clark, David, Southern Mississippi	8	5	4.85	17	0	94.2	85	38	73
Brown, Aaron, Houston	6	6	4.98	20	2	86.2	91	46	54
Chrisman, Brian, Marshall	3	6	5.55	11	0	58.1	70	25	53
Sweat, Kyle, Central Florida	4	5	5.62	17	1	65.2	79	16	38
Slone, Jeremy, Marshall	3	4	6.22	13	0	85.1	105	33	45
Grisham, Ben, Memphis	4	4	6.34	13	1	65.1	91	25	36
Dobies, Adam, Marshall	3	5	6.39	17	0	76.0	97	26	45
McGregor, Scott, Memphis	5	4	6.63	15	1	73.1	99	24	35

HORIZON LEAGUE

	Conference		Overall	
	W	L	W	L
★Illinois-Chicago	21	7	34	19
Wright State	21	9	36	22
Wisconsin-Milwaukee	16	14	25	32
Cleveland State	10	17	14	44
Butler	10	20	22	33
Youngstown State	9	21	19	37

ALL-CONFERENCE TEAM: C–Joe Dempsey, Sr., Butler. **1B**–Jeremy Hamilton, So., Wright State. **2B**–Jesse Hart, Jr., UW-Milwaukee. **3B**–John Koehnlein, So., Youngstown State. **SS**–Ross Oeder, Sr., Wright State. **OF**–Dustin Bucalo, Sr., Butler. **OF**–Larry Gempp Jr., Sr., UIC. **OF**–Micky Pingree, Jr., UIC. **DH**–Justin Parker, So., Wright State. **UT**–Josh Groves, So., UW-Milwaukee. **P**–Zach Peterson, Sr., UIC. **P**– Erich Schanz, Sr., Wright State. UIC.

Player of the Year: Ross Oeder, Sr., Wright State. **Pitcher of the Year:** Zach Peterson, UIC. Newcomer of the Year: Micky Pingree, UIC. **Relief Pitcher of the Year:** David Cales, So., UIC. **Coach of the Year:** Mike Dee, UIC.

INDIVIDUAL BATTING LEADERS
(MINIMUM 125 AT-BATS)

	AVG	AB	R	H	2B	3B	HR	RBI	SB
Koehnlein, John, Youngstown State	.434	249	51	108	9	2	0	33	8
Oeder, Ross, Wright State	.408	228	79	93	23	4	8	36	25
Gempp Jr., Larry, Illinois-Chicago	.397	194	37	77	10	4	7	54	6
Groves, Josh, Wisconsin-Milwaukee	.396	139	24	55	21	0	1	29	3
Parker, Justin, Wright State	.379	190	49	72	26	0	5	38	8
Hamilton, Jeremy, Wright State	.374	222	48	83	22	6	9	62	1
Diedrich, Erich, Youngstown State	.362	207	42	75	12	2	8	44	2
Hart, Jesse, Wisconsin-Milwaukee	.360	197	30	71	14	0	3	20	4
Rainwater, Nick, Illinois-Chicago	.358	193	41	69	4	0	2	27	8
Bucalo, Dustin, Butler	.339	177	23	60	10	2	2	18	7
Berkovitz, Grant, Wisconsin-Milwaukee	.335	209	39	70	13	2	5	37	1
Pingree, Micky, Illinois-Chicago	.333	159	24	53	18	0	4	45	3
Biedenharn, Dan, Wright State	.332	232	50	77	11	1	2	46	7
Pauley, Joe, Butler	.324	210	41	68	11	1	5	31	5
Carr, Jake, Illinois-Chicago	.322	171	40	55	9	2	5	28	2

INDIVIDUAL PITCHING LEADERS
(MINIMUM 50 INNINGS)

	W	L	ERA	G	SV	IP	H	BB	SO
Crnkovich, Steve, Illinois-Chicago	4	3	2.27	17	0	91.0	85	17	50
Kruszka, Ryan, Butler	2	5	2.96	14	1	54.2	59	17	37
Dages, Jon, Butler	6	7	3.40	17	0	98.0	112	20	62
Peterson, Zach, Illinois-Chicago	3	5	3.59	16	0	100.1	108	23	62
Hungerman, Josh, Cleveland State	2	9	3.82	13	0	77.2	85	34	61
Kearcher, Kyle, Wright State	10	4	3.83	14	0	89.1	99	18	48
Schanz, Erich, Wright State	6	5	3.86	14	0	79.1	77	26	41
Michalkiewicz, Robert, Wis.-Milwaukee	6	4	4.03	14	0	98.1	120	17	53
Procner, Stephen, Cleveland State	4	9	4.31	15	0	100.1	102	44	75
Bokowy, Brian, Butler	3	6	4.36	16	0	76.1	97	19	51
Zink, Ryan, Illinois-Chicago	6	3	4.79	12	0	62.0	62	20	37
Holleran, Garret, Wright State	4	6	5.06	15	0	89.0	109	24	45
Hewitt, Brandon, Cleveland State	2	8	5.17	15	0	76.2	105	31	45
Engle, Lucas, Youngstown State	4	6	5.24	14	0	91.0	109	24	56
Luczak, Dan, Wisconsin-Milwaukee	4	7	5.42	15	0	83.0	91	43	59

IVY LEAGUE

	Conference		Overall	
GEHRIG	W	L	W	L
Pennsylvania	12	8	20	19
Princeton	11	9	15	24
Columbia	10	10	16	28
Cornell	8	12	15	23

ROLFE				
★Brown	14	6	27	21
Harvard	12	8	18	18
Yale	8	12	16	27
Dartmouth	5	15	8	29

ALL CONFERENCE TEAM: C–Devin Thomas, Sr., Brown. **1B**–Marc Sawyer, Sr., Yale. **2B**–Bryan Tews, Jr., Brown. **3B**–Sal Iacono, Sr., Princeton. **SS**–Matt Nuzzo, So., Brown. **OF**–Ryan Murphy, Jr., Brown. **OF**–Nick Santomauro, Fr., Dartmouth. **OF**–Matt Vance, Jr., Harvard. **UT**–Ryan Lavarnway, So., Yale. **DH**–Justin Milo, Fr., Cornell. **P**–Jeff Dietz, Jr., Brown. **P**–Todd Roth, Fr., Penn. **RP**–Blake Hamilton, Sr., Cornell.

Player of the Year: Devin Thomas, Brown. **Pitcher of the Year:** Jeff Dietz, Brown. **Rookie of the Year:** Todd Roth, Penn.

INDIVIDUAL BATTING LEADERS
(MINIMUM 125 AT-BATS)

	AVG	AB	R	H	2B	3B	HR	RBI	SB
Lavarnway, Ryan, Yale	.467	150	33	70	17	1	14	55	4
Iacono, Sal, Princeton	.413	150	27	62	12	1	5	55	2
Murphy, Ryan, Brown	.410	139	42	57	6	1	2	24	11
Sawyer, Marc, Yale	.394	155	40	61	16	0	3	21	8
Williams, Ron, Columbia	.374	179	28	67	9	1	3	36	6
Thomas, Devin, Brown	.372	188	51	70	11	4	16	64	12
Nuzzo, Matt, Brown	.371	186	33	69	14	2	2	28	7
Vance, Matt, Harvard	.341	135	21	46	9	3	3	30	12
Ford, Nathan, Cornell	.338	142	16	48	6	0	2	27	1
Lucian, Spencer, Princeton	.331	130	16	43	6	0	1	18	2
Dietz, Jeff, Brown	.328	174	33	57	15	0	9	53	1
Armeny, Kyle, Pennsylvania	.326	141	35	46	14	0	8	33	0
Nwaka, Alex, Pennsylvania	.324	142	32	46	4	1	2	16	9
Cox, Josh, Yale	.324	173	37	56	12	4	0	16	24
Van Horn, Greg, Princeton	.323	133	30	43	11	2	4	20	8
DiRicco, Domenic, Cornell	.319	141	31	45	9	2	0	13	8
Boaen, Joey, Pennsylvania	.310	158	31	49	9	4	4	26	9
Wright, Damon, Dartmouth	.303	132	24	40	5	0	1	22	8
Papenhause, Robert, Brown	.302	159	29	48	10	0	5	39	8
Tews, Bryan, Brown	.301	176	35	53	6	3	6	30	8
DeGeorge, Dan, Princeton	.298	141	26	42	11	0	0	13	0
Gordon, William, Pennsylvania	.291	151	29	44	8	0	4	28	2
Corn, Josh, Pennsylvania	.288	132	22	38	7	0	2	23	2
Ward, Andrew, Columbia	.285	165	19	47	10	2	3	30	3
Heinz, Jimmy, Cornell	.285	151	28	43	7	3	4	22	5

INDIVIDUAL PITCHING LEADERS
(MINIMUM 50 INNINGS)

	W	L	ERA	G	SV	IP	H	BB	SO
Roth, Todd, Pennsylvania	6	2	1.98	13	0	68.1	57	14	62
Dietz, Jeff, Brown	9	4	2.81	14	0	96.0	89	22	84
Hyland, Jim, Cornell	4	5	3.98	9	0	54.1	55	11	31
Young, Russell, Dartmouth	2	5	4.03	9	0	51.1	66	12	33
Walz, Eric, Princeton	3	1	4.11	9	0	57.0	60	24	36
Baumann, John, Columbia	5	2	4.11	12	0	65.2	60	18	36
Haviland, Shawn, Harvard	3	3	4.26	10	0	57.0	57	23	36
Birmingham, Jim, Pennsylvania	4	2	4.48	14	0	64.1	55	38	44
Cramphin, James, Brown	6	4	4.80	13	0	80.2	77	42	86
Josselyn, Brandon, Yale	3	4	4.83	11	1	54.0	68	15	39
Purdy, Bill, Columbia	5	4	4.89	12	0	70.0	86	25	34
Perkins, Henry, Columbia	1	6	5.50	9	0	52.1	71	15	29
Miller, Steven, Princeton	3	6	5.57	9	0	53.1	55	27	48
Schropp, Stefan, Yale	3	4	5.76	11	0	50.0	66	18	41
Wilkerson, Jeff, Dartmouth	3	4	6.75	11	0	57.1	85	13	37

METRO ATLANTIC ATHLETIC CONFERENCE

	Conference		Overall	
	W	L	W	L
★LeMoyne	22	3	34	19
Manhattan	21	5	35	19
Marist	14	12	21	32
Canisius	13	12	20	35
Saint Peter's	13	13	23	29
Fairfield	12	14	18	28
Siena	10	13	12	33
Rider	11	15	20	29
Iona	8	18	16	35
Niagara	3	21	15	32

ALL-CONFERENCE TEAM: C–Nick Derba, Manhattan. **1B**–Matt Rizzotti. Manhattan, **2B**–Patrick Freeney, Marist. **3B**–Steve Crawford, Le Moyne. **SS**–Andy Parrino, Le Moyne. **OF**–Ian Choy, Canisius. **OF**–Tim Alberts, Niagara. **OF**–Kevin Kallert, Saint Peter's. **DH**–Peter Allen, Fairfield. **UT**–Sean Olson, Rider. **SP**–Bobby Blevins, Le Moyne. **SP**–Jesse Darcy, Manhattan.

Player of the Year: Andy Parrino, Le Moyne. **Co-Pitchers of the Year:** Bobby Blevins, Le Moyne.; Jesse Darcy, Manhattan. **Relief Pitcher of the Year:** Ryan Woods, Le Moyne. **Rookie of the Year:** Ian Choy, Canisius. **Coach of the Year:** Derek England, Saint Peter's.

INDIVIDUAL BATTING LEADERS
(MINIMUM 125 AT-BATS)

	AVG	AB	R	H	2B	3B	HR	RBI	SB
Parrino, Andy, LeMoyne	.402	199	46	80	17	2	9	44	5
Allen, Peter, Fairfield	.380	163	35	62	23	1	5	35	5
Alberts, Tim, Niagara	.379	174	39	66	11	2	8	42	9
Kallert, Kevin, Saint Peter's	.376	157	35	59	8	2	6	29	12
Reimer, Kevin, Canisius	.358	173	40	62	11	1	4	38	5
Choy, Ian, Canisius	.358	173	15	62	12	1	1	26	2
Rizzotti, Matt, Manhattan	.352	182	41	64	10	0	11	43	0
Willis, Jake, Siena	.339	165	25	56	12	1	3	19	7
Alexander, Dennis, Saint Peter's	.337	166	33	56	10	1	0	15	8
Feeney, Pat, Marist	.337	205	39	69	11	0	1	39	1
Klepps, Chris, Siena	.331	142	23	47	7	1	3	17	7
Brown, Mike, LeMoyne	.329	140	28	46	11	3	3	23	13
Crawford, Stephen, LeMoyne	.327	217	44	71	13	0	3	26	17
Most, Max, Marist	.325	203	39	66	6	2	1	31	7
Olson, Sean, Rider	.315	184	27	58	12	1	6	42	5
O'Neill, Corey, LeMoyne	.312	154	23	48	14	3	4	32	4
Anderson, Kenny, Marist	.306	193	36	59	14	1	4	35	0
Curylo, Richard, Marist	.306	144	27	44	3	1	0	14	9
St. Amant, Phil, LeMoyne	.305	197	22	60	18	0	5	41	0
Cramer, Jason, Niagara	.302	139	23	42	3	1	0	13	16
McGuire, Mike, Saint Peter's	.301	183	29	55	13	0	7	32	1
Ruiz, Rene, Manhattan	.299	194	41	58	12	1	2	26	2
Abbatiello, Allie, Iona	.297	195	24	58	10	1	7	29	10
Hayes, David, Rider	.296	179	33	53	9	1	6	34	7
McCollum, Matt, Rider	.288	146	16	42	11	0	1	21	5
Rago, Jason, Fairfield	.287	157	25	45	3	2	5	25	4
Asis, Ryan, Canisius	.286	161	21	46	9	3	3	18	8
Mahoney, Kevin, Canisius	.284	197	42	56	13	4	6	34	5
Musolf, Travis, Marist	.284	208	48	59	11	1	3	36	19
Maertz, Santo, Saint Peter's	.284	134	22	38	8	1	2	24	3

INDIVIDUAL PITCHING LEADERS
(MINIMUM 50 INNINGS)

	W	L	ERA	G	SV	IP	H	BB	SO
Woods, Ryan, LeMoyne	7	2	1.34	30	14	60.1	42	13	41
Darcy, Jesse, Manhattan	9	3	2.19	14	0	107.0	100	22	60
Beaulac, Eric, LeMoyne	8	1	2.94	15	0	82.2	56	56	81
Pendergast, Brian, Manhattan	8	1	3.05	21	5	56.0	49	17	43
Blevins, Bobby, LeMoyne	9	3	3.07	15	0	111.1	95	37	104
Santerre, Josh, Manhattan	7	5	3.10	13	0	87.0	68	22	76
Supplee, Erik, Marist	5	3	3.35	16	2	86.0	96	17	54
Miksitz, Eric, Saint Peter's	4	3	3.40	14	0	84.2	70	27	75
Moberg, Matt, Siena	3	6	3.51	10	0	56.1	52	21	42
Ciallella, Doug, Fairfield	2	2	3.74	15	0	53.0	57	16	28
Costigan, Tom, Manhattan	8	3	3.84	15	1	89.0	94	16	64
DiNuzzo, Bobby, Iona	2	5	3.92	13	0	57.1	60	23	35
Kamintzky, Ed, Fairfield	5	4	4.03	11	0	60.1	64	30	53
Petrowski, Mike, Rider	5	6	4.03	14	0	80.1	81	25	57
Gariano, Robert, Fairfield	3	7	4.04	12	0	64.2	54	16	46

MID-AMERICAN CONFERENCE

	Conference		Overall	
EAST	W	L	W	L
★Kent State	19	8	33	26
Miami (Ohio)	16	9	32	24
Buffalo	11	16	16	35
Akron	8	16	23	24
Ohio	8	19	23	31
Bowling Green	7	20	22	32
WEST				
Eastern Michigan	21	4	32	24
Central Michigan	21	6	35	21
Northern Illinois	16	11	34	24
Toledo	14	13	26	28
Western Michigan	8	16	16	33
Ball State	8	19	20	34

ALL-CONFERENCE TEAM: C–Kurt Davidson, Jr., Akron. **1B**–Ben Humphrey, Sr., Central Michigan. **1B**–Marc Krauss, Fr., Ohio. **2B**–Mike Folli, Jr., Buffalo. **3B**–Andrew Davis, Jr., Kent State. **SS**–Jordan Petratis, So., Miami. **OF**–Tyler Stovall, Jr., Central Michigan. **OF**–Steve Bradshaw, Jr., Eastern Michigan. **OF**–Anthony Gallas, Fr., Kent State. **DH**–Greg Rohan, So., Kent State. **SP**–Josh Collmenter, Jr., Central Michigan. **SP**–George Biddle, Sr., Eastern Michigan. **SP**–Jeff Fischer, Jr., Eastern Michigan. **SP**–John Ely, Jr., Miami. **RP**–Matt German, Sr., Northern Illinois.

Player of the Year: Tyler Stovall, Central Michigan. **Pitcher of the Year:** Josh Collmenter, Central Michigan. **Freshman of the Year:** Marc Krauss, Ohio. **Coach of the Year:** Roger Coryell, Eastern Michigan.

INDIVIDUAL BATTING LEADERS
(MINIMUM 125 AT-BATS)

	AVG	AB	R	H	2B	3B	HR	RBI	SB
Stovall, Tyler, Central Michigan	.391	225	58	88	15	3	6	59	20
Krauss, Marc, Ohio	.369	187	41	69	19	1	8	42	6
Humphrey, Ben, Central Michigan	.362	229	58	83	18	1	10	48	12
Walker, Willie, Ohio	.362	188	34	68	12	0	3	45	3
Stiffler, Matt, Ohio	.359	209	58	75	10	8	3	40	9
McNulty, Doug, Akron	.356	180	35	64	13	4	4	36	11
Carroll, Jeff, Miami (Ohio)	.348	184	36	64	14	2	1	37	0
Folli, Mike, Buffalo	.346	188	35	65	13	1	0	15	12
Johnson, Josh, Toledo	.345	148	27	51	12	0	2	21	2
Savage, Brett, Akron	.344	131	25	45	9	0	2	19	1
Hillier, Brandon, Miami (Ohio)	.338	231	48	78	12	3	3	26	9
Wells, Kurt, Bowling Green	.333	168	40	56	7	0	3	29	12
Gallas, Anthony, Kent State	.332	211	44	70	14	1	10	46	4
Simon, Scott, Northern Illinois	.329	222	40	73	15	0	3	37	1
Davis, Andrew, Kent State	.328	241	42	79	16	1	7	54	2
Davidson, Kurt, Akron	.325	197	40	64	15	0	10	44	0
Besl, Brandon, Ohio	.323	229	45	74	17	0	5	41	1
Oester, Jake, Toledo	.323	186	38	60	12	2	3	24	3
Davis, Jeff, Eastern Michigan	.321	165	27	53	10	7	2	18	9
Tremblay, Chris, Kent State	.321	209	43	67	8	3	0	23	14
Seykora, Jesse, Northern Illinois	.320	222	50	71	18	3	8	42	5
Reed, Danny, Northern Illinois	.319	188	35	60	9	0	6	31	7
Gentile, Zach, Western Michigan	.319	185	38	59	7	1	1	20	5
Petraitis, Jordan, Miami (Ohio)	.318	217	44	69	11	4	4	33	8
Turk, John, Akron	.318	129	18	41	6	3	1	22	0
Hoorelbeke, Sean, Central Michigan	.317	161	33	51	7	2	7	51	3
Dager, Pedro, Western Michigan	.316	133	24	42	3	1	1	16	6
Pizzuto, Bobby, Buffalo	.314	172	25	54	4	2	1	26	12
Stoeklen, Matt, Ball State	.311	193	29	60	16	0	8	39	1
Bond, Wayne, Ball State	.309	207	38	64	8	2	5	23	15
Nadeau, Chris, Miami (Ohio)	.308	195	47	60	10	2	0	41	1
Helps, Jeff, Central Michigan	.307	202	46	62	10	3	2	32	8
Earnhart, Eric, Ball State	.307	150	32	46	9	1	2	17	9
Boley, Scott, Toledo	.306	222	36	68	11	1	7	39	6
Haas, Kevin, Akron	.306	160	27	49	7	1	0	16	7

INDIVIDUAL PITCHING LEADERS
(MINIMUM 50 INNINGS)

	W	L	ERA	G	SV	IP	H	BB	SO
Collmenter, Josh, Central Michigan	9	4	1.93	15	0	116.1	84	26	117
Biddle, George, Eastern Michigan	8	4	2.42	15	0	93.0	91	25	59
Hollingsworth, Ethan, Western Michigan	4	4	2.55	11	0	74.0	74	18	54
Ely, John, Miami (Ohio)	8	3	2.89	14	0	102.2	95	23	96
Fischer, Jeff, Eastern Michigan	8	5	3.00	15	0	102.0	87	44	95
Johnson, Tyler, Bowling Green	6	5	3.31	14	0	89.2	84	14	52
Smith, Evan, Kent State	4	5	3.39	15	0	79.2	82	27	31
Taylor, Dan, Central Michigan	7	2	3.49	19	0	85.0	79	42	51
Radanovic, Mike, Buffalo	3	2	3.68	12	0	80.2	78	35	62
Smith, Kyle, Kent State	4	2	3.84	15	0	70.1	63	44	44
Hoffman, Sean, Eastern Michigan	7	2	3.97	17	0	81.2	80	32	54
Morrison, Billy, Western Michigan	3	6	4.01	11	0	74.0	81	11	34
Rigo, Chris, Ohio	2	4	4.18	17	2	71.0	71	30	42
Stines, Brenden, Ball State	2	8	4.20	15	0	75.0	84	30	68
Mementowski, Kevin, Ohio	3	3	4.21	13	0	62.0	81	18	36
Graham, Connor, Miami (Ohio)	5	4	4.24	13	0	80.2	80	34	76
Badgley, Mark, Northern Illinois	4	4	4.27	23	0	84.1	82	30	83
Feeney, Trevor, Northern Illinois	6	7	4.30	14	0	98.1	108	18	61
Jernstad, Matt, Northern Illinois	4	2	4.39	14	0	80.0	83	33	66
Gumpf, Adam, Bowling Green	1	3	4.58	22	3	57.0	49	23	41
Cantrell, Nick, Bowling Green	4	8	5.01	18	0	70.0	97	22	30
Schlarb, Matt, Ohio	7	3	5.07	20	0	55.0	68	32	35
Copp, Brandon, Northern Illinois	5	3	5.22	18	0	58.2	70	23	44
Tourangeau, Mark, Buffalo	3	4	5.30	13	0	56.0	58	35	42
Inselmann, Mike, Toledo	4	5	5.38	13	0	77.0	89	29	48

MID-EASTERN ATHLETIC CONFERENCE

	Conference		Overall	
	W	L	W	L
★Bethune-Cookman	16	1	33	27
Florida A&M	11	7	16	36
North Carolina A&T	11	7	28	31
Delaware State	10	8	22	27
Norfolk State	9	8	25	25
Maryland-Eastern Shore	5	13	10	45
Coppin State	0	18	0	44

ALL-CONFERENCE TEAM: C–Lyall Foran, Sr., Norfolk State. INF–Charlie Gamble, Sr., North Carolina A&T. INF–Chris Henault, Sr., Bethune-Cookman. INF–Tom Shelley, Jr., Delaware State. INF–Alejandro Jimenez, So., Bethune-Cookman. INF–Ernie Banks, Jr., Norfolk State. INF–Juan Serrano, Sr., Norfolk State. OF–Angel Mercado, Sr., Bethune-Cookman. OF–Darryl Evans, Fr., Florida A&M. OF–Christian Beatty, Fr., North Carolina A&T. DH–Angel Negron, Sr., Bethune-Cookman. SP–Francisco Rodriguez, Sr., Bethune-Cookman. SP–Luke Foss, Sr., Norfolk State. RP–Joseph Gautier, So., Bethune-Cookman.

Player of the Year: Charlie Gamble, North Carolina A&T. Pitcher of the Year: Francisco Rodriguez, Bethune-Cookman. Rookie of the Year: Christian Beatty, North Carolina A&T. Coach of the Year: Mervyl Melendez, Bethune-Cookman.

INDIVIDUAL BATTING LEADERS
(MINIMUM 125 AT-BATS)

	AVG	AB	R	H	2B	3B	HR	RBI	SB
Gamble, Charlie, NC A&T	.409	225	56	92	19	3	10	57	17
Mercado, Angel, Bethune-Cookman	.404	203	43	82	8	4	8	37	10
Gonzalez, Joel, Maryland-Eastern Shore	.378	180	35	68	14	1	1	34	13
Shelley, Tom, Delaware State	.378	135	29	51	11	0	0	17	9
Foran, Lyall, Norfolk State	.368	155	33	57	15	1	4	38	1
Evans, Darryl, Florida A&M	.366	213	42	78	11	2	4	42	18
Banks, Ernie, Norfolk State	.362	160	34	58	13	2	2	34	2
Serrano, Juan, Norfolk State	.362	160	28	58	13	0	6	34	0
Negron, Angel, Bethune-Cookman	.339	221	39	75	10	0	9	49	1
McIntyre, Joe, NC A&T	.339	224	43	76	22	1	7	65	4
Kinnear, Kory, NC A&T	.337	190	31	64	12	0	6	41	3
Lalane, Charles, Norfolk State	.335	185	41	62	6	0	0	22	5
Jimenez, Alejandro, Bethune-Cookman	.331	160	35	53	9	2	6	30	19
Gravely, Brandon, Delaware State	.329	164	38	54	11	2	6	38	10
Jones, Jeremy, NC A&T	.323	229	62	74	18	3	7	45	13
Bittner, Justin, Delaware State	.317	145	34	46	5	2	2	25	1
Millan, Elvin, Florida A&M	.313	134	26	42	6	0	2	18	2
Beatty, CJ, NC A&T	.313	195	34	61	11	2	10	38	1
James, David, Florida A&M	.312	154	31	48	9	4	3	27	10
Henault, Chris, Bethune-Cookman	.305	210	37	64	15	0	10	42	2
Gordon, Adam, Florida A&M	.299	154	30	46	4	3	1	20	11
Mayo, Nick, NC A&T	.294	238	54	70	15	2	3	27	14
Allen, Eric, Delaware State	.292	144	37	42	10	4	8	33	11
Wade, Joe, NC A&T	.288	139	21	40	9	0	3	17	4
McFadden, Corey, Florida A&M	.284	190	42	54	9	2	4	24	8

INDIVIDUAL PITCHING LEADERS
(MINIMUM 50 INNINGS)

	W	L	ERA	G	SV	IP	H	BB	SO
Foss, Luke, Norfolk State	10	2	2.28	16	0	86.2	81	16	62
Blackwell, Dustin, Bethune-Cookman	8	6	3.10	18	1	107.1	88	23	72
Gautier, Joseph, Bethune-Cookman	5	2	3.26	17	1	66.1	74	17	53
Rodriguez, Francisco, Beth.-Cookman	10	4	3.33	19	1	110.2	118	24	88
Burgos, Hiram, Bethune-Cookman	6	7	3.40	20	0	84.2	88	31	75
Schabacker, Leon, Norfolk State	4	7	3.87	18	0	88.1	83	24	65
Williams, De'Mece, Norfolk State	5	3	4.14	17	0	67.1	73	28	42
Baylor, Ben, Florida A&M	0	5	4.25	9	0	53.0	61	12	31
Longchamps, Dustin, Md.-ES	4	11	4.26	19	0	112.0	112	66	101
Seal, Joey, Norfolk State	3	6	4.29	26	4	84.0	91	31	75
Primus, John, NC A&T	4	4	5.16	18	0	89.0	87	38	80
McAllister, JR, Delaware State	7	4	5.25	17	0	85.2	99	38	93
Dill, Austin, Florida A&M	5	3	5.37	17	0	57.0	60	33	28
Manego, Cirilo, Florida A&M	5	6	5.46	15	0	97.1	115	51	88
Friel, Jamie, Delaware State	3	5	5.46	18	1	61.0	73	26	39

MID-CONTINENT CONFERENCE

	Conference		Overall	
	W	L	W	L
★Oral Roberts	19	1	40	17
Western Illinois	11	9	31	26
Valparaiso	10	10	22	34
Centenary	9	11	28	31
Southern Utah	6	14	11	45
Oakland	5	15	20	34

ALL-CONFERENCE TEAM: C–Kevin Carkeek, Sr., Oakland. 1B–Chad Rothford, Sr., Oral Roberts. 2B–Jake Kahaulelio, Sr., Oral Roberts. 3B–Chester Wilson, So., Southern Utah. SS–Adam Younger, Jr., Oral Roberts. OF–Travis Check, Sr., Western Illinois. OF–Brendan Duffy, Jr., Oral Roberts. OF–Justin Wilson, So., Oakland. DH–Brian Van Kirk, Jr., Oral Roberts. UT–Joe Wright, Jr., Southern Utah. SP–Chance Chapman, Sr., Oral Roberts. SP–Brandon Fulenchek, Sr., Centenary. SP–Jeremy Hefner, Jr., Oral Roberts. RP–Eric Crichton, Sr., Oral Roberts.

Co-Players of the Year: Travis Check, Western Illinois; Brendan Duffy, Oral Roberts. Pitcher of the Year: Chance Chapman, Oral Roberts. Newcomer of the Year: Jeremy Hefner, Oral Roberts. Coach of the Year: Stan Hyman, Western Illinois.

INDIVIDUAL BATTING LEADERS
(MINIMUM 125 AT-BATS)

	AVG	AB	R	H	2B	3B	HR	RBI	SB
Pendell, Brett, Western Illinois	.357	221	61	79	19	0	3	31	17
Duffy, Brendan, Oral Roberts	.356	216	62	77	10	3	1	29	21
Stafford, Andrew, Oakland	.354	189	42	67	9	0	3	40	10
Wilson, Justin, Oakland	.348	201	44	70	9	2	4	29	11
Arensdorff, Michael, Valparaiso	.344	221	43	76	17	1	1	19	1
Aona, Bucky, Southern Utah	.337	172	16	58	4	0	4	25	3
Rickert, Jeff, Valparaiso	.335	212	45	71	7	2	2	24	2
Check, Travis, Western Illinois	.329	213	59	70	11	2	8	49	18
Carkeek, Kevin, Oakland	.324	145	29	47	17	0	9	42	1
Warfle, Pat, Oral Roberts	.324	204	51	66	7	5	4	36	20
Ryan, Dan, Oakland	.321	165	37	53	11	1	3	25	4
Nelson, Carmeron, Southern Utah	.318	192	30	61	15	0	8	33	6
Minissale, Kelly, Oral Roberts	.316	196	39	62	6	4	6	43	4
Pearson, Stephen, Oral Roberts	.316	136	21	43	5	0	5	31	1
Kahaulelio, Jake, Oral Roberts	.314	210	46	66	11	2	6	46	8
Heath, Ryan, Oakland	.311	132	30	41	10	1	4	32	7
Penney, Cameron, Centenary	.311	219	38	68	10	1	0	34	12
Wright, Joe, Southern Utah	.309	139	17	43	11	0	1	19	3
Saenz, Teddy, Centenary	.308	208	41	64	16	1	1	33	10
Webb, Matt, Centenary	.306	183	56	56	16	2	9	30	24

INDIVIDUAL PITCHING LEADERS
(MINIMUM 50 INNINGS)

	W	L	ERA	G	SV	IP	H	BB	SO
Chapman, Chance, Oral Roberts	8	1	1.34	22	5	94.0	66	28	127
Sullivan, Jerry, Oral Roberts	5	0	2.04	12	0	53.0	44	8	45
Hefner, Jeremy, Oral Roberts	9	2	3.03	16	0	86.0	67	29	107
Crichton, Erik, Oral Roberts	4	5	3.07	25	5	58.2	55	21	48
Robinson, Dakota, Centenary	2	5	3.41	31	4	58.0	61	7	37
Mazzone, Nick, Valparaiso	4	7	3.55	12	0	71.0	71	22	36
Fulenchek, Brandon, Centenary	8	5	3.66	18	0	108.1	125	35	62
Yergin, Harvey, Valparaiso	4	6	4.18	15	0	97.0	130	20	56
Sheehan, Jeremy, Centenary	8	5	4.55	17	0	89.0	108	19	41
Tolsma, Travis, Western Illinois	4	5	4.84	15	0	74.1	93	20	42
Trausch, Matt, Oakland	5	4	5.01	16	1	64.2	74	16	42
DiBernardo, Mark, Western Illinois	4	1	5.13	14	0	59.2	79	8	48
Leath, Quinn, Western Illinois	2	5	5.17	14	0	71.1	89	26	39
Ashman, Chris, Oral Roberts	5	3	5.18	18	0	74.2	88	24	51
Noland, Johnny, Centenary	2	7	5.76	21	0	75.0	84	37	51
Gibbs, Elliott, Valparaiso	2	7	5.81	13	0	52.2	67	17	40
Kaage, Will, Centenary	4	6	6.48	16	0	66.2	93	21	24
Wittwer, Dustin, Southern Utah	1	6	6.87	15	0	73.1	102	30	46

MISSOURI VALLEY CONFERENCE

	Conference		Overall	
	W	L	W	L
Wichita State	20	4	53	22
★Creighton	19	5	45	16
Southern Illinois	13	11	34	22
Bradley	13	11	32	21
Evansville	13	11	35	23
Northern Iowa	8	16	23	28
Illinois State	8	16	20	32
Indiana State	7	17	26	26
Missouri State	7	17	23	34

ALL-CONFERENCE TEAM: C–Mark Kelly, So., Southern Illinois. 1B–Darin Ruf, So., Creighton. 2B–Ryan Curry, Sr., Bradley. 3B–Conor Gillaspie, So., Wichita State. SS–Brandon Douglas, So., UNI. OF–Matt Brown, Jr., Wichita State. OF–Deric Manrique, So., UNI. OF–Jim Viscomi, Jr., Evansville. DH–Kevin Dubler, So., Illinois State. UT–Adam Hills, Jr., Southern Illinois. SP–Travis Banwart, Jr., Wichita State. SP–Ben Mancuso, Jr., Creighton. SP–Kai Tuomi, Sr., Evansville. RP–Andy Masten, Sr., Creighton. RP–Pat Venditte, Jr., Creighton. Joe Carter

Player of the Year: Darin Ruf, Creighton. Pitcher of the Year: Ben Mancuso, Creighton. Newcomer of the Year: Andy Masten, Creighton. Freshman of the Year: Brad Altbach, Bradley. Coach of the Year: Ed Servais, Creighton.

INDIVIDUAL BATTING LEADERS
(MINIMUM 125 AT-BATS)

	AVG	AB	R	H	2B	3B	HR	RBI	SB
Curry, Ryan, Bradley	.416	209	51	87	22	2	5	45	7
Kelly, Mark, Southern Illinois	.379	232	28	88	13	0	2	63	1
Ruf, Darin, Creighton	.374	230	53	86	19	3	8	57	1
Viscomi, Jim, Evansville	.374	222	59	83	15	4	0	17	22
Schmidt, Chris, Indiana State	.363	204	43	74	10	2	3	30	13
Sublett, Damon, Wichita State	.354	268	57	95	15	4	5	45	14
Wahl, Kasey, Evansville	.354	229	44	81	16	0	8	61	1
Manrique, Deric, Northern Iowa	.351	202	49	71	16	2	3	36	30
Robets, Aaron, Southern Illinois	.349	218	52	76	5	1	0	17	13
Carr, Justin, Bradley	.348	158	31	55	12	1	5	36	3
Schermerhorn, Derek, Wichita State	.347	245	54	85	8	1	7	38	23
Hoffmann, Eric, Northern Iowa	.342	161	28	55	4	2	1	31	3
Gradoville, Chris, Creighton	.339	239	45	81	15	2	5	56	2
Douglas, Brandon, Northern Iowa	.339	186	40	63	19	1	3	29	5
Brumagin, Dave, Indiana State	.339	192	29	65	10	1	3	33	6
Tumilty, Pat, Evansville	.338	210	33	71	15	3	3	47	10
Anetsberger, Ryan, Illinois State	.328	186	32	61	12	1	5	30	8
Gillaspie, Conor, Wichita State	.325	295	55	96	24	4	6	63	12
Paul, Kyle, Missouri State	.323	198	32	64	14	3	4	37	3
Dirks, Andy, Wichita State	.320	250	51	80	11	0	3	31	19
Hills, Adam, Southern Illinois	.319	207	37	66	14	0	3	49	2
Dubler, Kevin, Illinois State	.317	199	36	63	20	2	4	37	11
Keane, Nolan, Missouri State	.314	207	45	65	9	2	9	32	9
Brewer, Dan, Bradley	.313	211	49	66	12	3	10	30	20
Sinclair, Ross, Creighton	.310	168	37	52	4	1	0	16	7

INDIVIDUAL PITCHING LEADERS
(MINIMUM 50 INNINGS)

	W	L	ERA	G	SV	IP	H	BB	SO
Capra, Anthony, Wichita State	7	1	1.76	24	1	76.2	57	24	77
Venditte, Pat, Creighton	8	2	1.88	38	4	95.2	62	22	99
Detwiler, Ross, Missouri State	4	5	2.22	14	0	89.0	64	38	110
Shafer, Aaron, Wichita State	8	2	2.23	15	0	84.2	69	23	90
Mancuso, Ben, Creighton	10	3	2.34	14	0	77.0	77	20	60
Norton, Ben, Evansville	9	4	2.55	17	0	98.2	66	39	87
Musgrave, Rob, Wichita State	10	2	2.59	18	0	111.1	96	17	85
Banwart, Travis, Wichita State	10	5	2.68	18	0	110.2	95	32	111
Tuomi, Kai, Evansville	10	4	2.76	16	0	97.2	111	25	43
Wright, Chris, Bradley	4	2	2.77	18	3	81.1	67	36	51
Sajewich, Jim, Illinois State	3	2	2.89	27	2	53.0	47	20	32
Caroll, Scott, Missouri State	4	5	2.93	13	0	89.0	98	25	81
Adams, Cody, Southern Illinois	11	5	3.01	16	0	107.2	103	22	89
Jenkins, Aaron, Northern Iowa	4	4	3.04	14	0	94.2	76	56	126
Kirk, Nick, Northern Iowa	4	3	3.38	15	0	72.0	74	39	62

MOUNTAIN WEST CONFERENCE

	Conference		Overall	
	W	L	W	L
★Texas Christian	20	3	48	14
Brigham Young	17	7	37	20
San Diego State	12	12	29	30
New Mexico	12	12	28	30
Utah	12	12	24	31
Nevada-Las Vegas	10	14	24	36
Air Force	0	23	9	44

ALL-CONFERENCE TEAM: C–Andrew Walker, Jr., TCU. 1B–Jay Brossman., Sr., Utah. 2B–Jordan Pacheco, Jr., New Mexico. 3B–Nick Romero, So., San Diego State. SS–Bryan Kervin, Jr., TCU. OF–Austin Adams, Sr., TCU. OF–Clint Arnold, Jr., TCU. OF–Ryan Kowalski, Sr., UNLV. DH–Karl Bolt, Sr., Air Force. P–Jesse Craig, Jr., BYU. P–Bobby LaFromboise, Jr., New Mexico. P–Jake Arrieta, Jr., TCU. RP–Sam Demel, Jr., TCU.

Player of the Year: Jordan Pacheco, New Mexico. **Pitcher of the Year:** Jesse Craig, BYU. **Co-Freshman of the Year:** Steve Parker, BYU; Stephen Strasburg, San Diego State. **Coach of the Year:** Jim Schlossnagle, TCU.

INDIVIDUAL BATTING LEADERS
(MINIMUM 125 AT-BATS)

	AVG	AB	R	H	2B	3B	HR	RBI	SB
Conlon, Keith, Texas Christian	.399	173	52	69	11	5	9	41	12
Pacheco, Jordan, New Mexico	.397	219	63	87	21	2	5	50	7
Wells, Stephen, Brigham Young	.371	178	30	66	9	5	3	32	11
Stovall, Daniel, New Mexico	.365	249	51	91	18	2	11	59	2
Ko, Kasey, Brigham Young	.358	187	29	67	16	1	2	45	0
Bolt, Karl, Air Force	.354	192	34	68	16	3	8	47	9
Walton, Kent, Brigham Young	.350	223	53	78	17	6	8	45	12

Parker, Steve, Brigham Young	.347	196	40	68	13	4	6	38	6
Shimada, Corey, Utah	.346	211	60	73	10	10	6	45	12
Smith, Keith, Nevada-Las Vegas	.345	252	49	87	14	0	9	48	5
Hibbitts, Matt, New Mexico	.341	208	37	71	10	1	7	44	1
Brossman, Jay, Utah	.341	226	45	77	18	4	10	49	13
Kowalski, Ryan, Nevada-Las Vegas	.336	220	36	74	14	2	1	41	17
Adams, Austin, Texas Christian	.328	238	57	78	16	3	14	71	3
Walker, Andrew, Texas Christian	.328	229	51	75	21	1	12	59	2
Burnham, Nate, Utah	.326	233	58	76	13	1	5	32	21
Trout, Steven, Texas Christian	.326	233	55	76	18	0	4	44	6
Arnold, Clint, Texas Christian	.326	215	43	70	16	0	4	39	12
Navarro Jr., Efren, Nevada-Las Vegas	.325	194	34	63	14	0	2	31	1
Green, Garett, San Diego State	.324	210	31	68	12	0	1	35	6
Vern, Matt, Texas Christian	.319	210	42	67	17	5	5	36	8
Romero, Nick, San Diego State	.319	226	35	72	13	5	6	47	5
Nakayama, Apana, Brigham Young	.318	223	44	71	12	2	11	42	6
Hollick, Ian, New Mexico	.312	218	39	68	6	1	2	31	0
Hennis, Dustin, Utah	.312	186	26	58	11	1	7	48	2

INDIVIDUAL PITCHING LEADERS
(MINIMUM 50 INNINGS)

	W	L	ERA	G	SV	IP	H	BB	SO
Craig, Jesse, Brigham Young	10	2	2.94	20	0	125.1	137	21	86
Arrieta, Jake, Texas Christian	9	3	3.01	17	0	98.2	90	50	93
Sewell, Lance, San Diego State	5	6	3.16	17	0	77.0	67	33	74
Lafromboise, Bobby, New Mexico	7	3	3.35	15	1	88.2	82	31	74
Johnson, Chris, Texas Christian	11	3	4.16	17	0	93.0	91	48	54
King, Eric, Utah	6	3	4.36	15	0	76.1	95	30	54
Hirschfeld, Steven, San Diego State	5	4	4.41	15	0	79.2	78	25	68
Wortham, Jake, Brigham Young	8	4	4.43	15	0	83.1	93	21	54
Fife, Stephen, Utah	6	2	4.43	17	0	63.0	77	31	53
Billings, Bruce, San Diego State	4	4	4.48	17	0	84.1	92	35	59
Corgan, Chance, Texas Christian	7	1	4.48	18	0	86.1	92	34	64
Cullers, Chad, Utah	4	5	4.70	18	0	61.1	73	11	30
Muir, Jordan, Brigham Young	6	4	5.65	14	0	73.1	96	28	40
Heyer, Craig, Nevada-Las Vegas	6	8	5.69	21	0	110.2	137	43	79
Norton, Jacob, New Mexico	5	7	5.85	17	0	92.1	110	31	50

NORTHEAST CONFERENCE

	Conference		Overall		
	W	L	W	L	T
Quinnipiac	21	7	29	18	1
Mount St. Mary's	21	7	35	22	0
★Monmouth	17	10	36	24	1
Central Connecticut State	14	14	26	26	0
Sacred Heart	12	15	22	31	0
Wagner	11	17	17	34	0
Long Island	10	17	16	35	0
Fairleigh Dickinson	4	23	9	45	0

ALL-CONFERENCE TEAM: C–Adam Taha, Sr., CCSU. **1B–**Andy Meyers, Jr., Monmouth. **2B–**Randy Gress, Sr., Quinnipiac. **3B–**John Delaney, Jr., Quinnipiac. **SS–**Joe DiGeronimo, Sr., Wagner. **OF–**Tim Binkoski, Sr., Quinnipiac. **OF–**Kyle Messineo, Sr., Monmouth. **OF–**Ryan Murray, Jr., Mount St. Mary's. **DH–**Jeff Hanson, Jr., Sacred Heart. **UT–**Rob Tencza, Sr., Sacred Heart. **SP–**Brad Brach, Jr., Monmouth. **SP–**Jay Monti, Sr., Sacred Heart. **Player of the Year:** Tim Binkoski, Quinnipiac.

Pitcher of the Year: Brad Brach, Monmouth. **Rookie of the Year:** Ryan Buch, Monmouth. **Coach of the Year:** Scott Thomson, Mount St. Mary's.

INDIVIDUAL BATTING LEADERS
(MINIMUM 125 AT-BATS)

	AVG	AB	R	H	2B	3B	HR	RBI	SB
Binkoski, Tim, Quinnipiac	.424	191	41	81	15	2	3	39	10
Meyers, Andy, Monmouth	.395	223	49	88	18	0	9	65	9
Murray, Ryan, Mount St. Mary's	.385	135	35	52	4	0	10	31	2
Hanson, Jeff, Sacred Heart	.376	173	33	65	19	0	7	46	0
Cruz, Orlando, Long Island	.367	139	15	51	10	0	5	29	1
Digeronimo, Joseph, Wagner	.347	199	42	69	10	6	3	37	28
Higgins, Kyle, Monmouth	.344	247	59	85	21	2	1	38	9
Smith, Eric, Mount St. Mary's	.343	201	45	69	18	2	7	61	5
Messineo, Kyle, Monmouth	.340	197	69	67	8	4	8	36	42
Delleani, Peter, Wagner	.339	168	27	57	10	1	8	38	3
Taha, Adam, Central Connecticut State	.339	180	41	61	6	1	1	25	12
Eiden, Matt, Mount St. Mary's	.338	160	28	54	7	0	1	22	0
Vincent, Jeff, Fairleigh Dickinson	.335	161	36	54	10	1	1	21	13
Medina, Vincente, Fairleigh Dickinson	.333	135	22	45	9	1	5	33	3
Grabowski, Chris, Fairleigh Dickinson	.329	167	29	55	11	5	1	22	19
Rizzo, Ryan, Quinnipiac	.325	209	33	68	19	1	3	32	7

	AVG	AB	R	H	2B	3B	HR	RBI	SB
Collazo, Chris, Monmouth	.318	220	35	70	3	0	1	33	2
Mainetti, Jeff, Quinnipiac	.314	194	32	61	8	1	12	50	2
Hodgson, Ivor, Mount St. Mary's	.311	219	49	68	11	4	6	30	15
Sand, Zachary, Fairleigh Dickinson	.308	169	21	52	10	2	1	27	4
Rodriguez, Jovan, Sacred Heart	.307	166	36	51	7	2	0	22	16
Paganotti, John, Fairleigh Dickinson	.307	163	18	50	4	0	0	18	5
Teters, Shawn, Monmouth	.306	180	31	55	7	0	1	29	6
Mastrianni, Matt, Wagner	.304	194	25	59	9	1	4	28	5
McKee, Bobby, Sacred Heart	.302	162	29	49	6	1	1	27	2

INDIVIDUAL PITCHING LEADERS
(MINIMUM 50 INNINGS)

	W	L	ERA	G	SV	IP	H	BB	SO
Monti, Jay, Sacred Heart	8	4	1.34	12	0	80.1	60	14	63
Buch, Ryan, Monmouth	9	2	2.44	14	0	81.0	67	37	76
Scribner, Evan, Central Conn. State	6	6	2.78	21	7	77.2	65	15	84
Tesseyman, John, Central Conn. State	6	4	2.79	14	0	61.1	58	7	36
Brach, Brad, Monmouth	9	3	2.89	15	0	99.2	94	21	84
Gianini, Matt, Central Connecticut State	3	6	3.00	12	0	69.0	72	16	69
Testa, Joe, Wagner	4	6	3.01	14	1	80.2	76	22	82
Mayer, Andy, Quinnipiac	8	2	3.20	12	0	78.2	72	15	44
Kerski, Ken, Central Connecticut State	7	2	3.36	12	0	69.2	62	29	48
Maynard, Mike, Long Island	4	3	3.88	11	0	60.1	71	29	52
Egan, Pat, Quinnipiac	4	3	4.09	13	0	66.0	58	25	46
Gloor, Chris, Quinnipiac	4	2	4.22	13	0	59.2	54	23	68
Tencza, Rob, Sacred Heart	5	6	4.32	12	0	66.2	77	14	39
Duffy, Joe, Quinnipiac	3	1	4.42	11	1	55.0	72	20	40
Germuth, Andrew, Mount St. Mary's	8	5	4.59	14	0	84.1	104	16	53

OHIO VALLEY CONFERENCE

	Conference		Overall		
	W	L	W	L	T
★Austin Peay State	19	8	40	22	0
Jacksonville State	18	9	33	27	0
Southeast Missouri	16	10	32	24	0
Samford	14	13	32	28	0
Eastern Kentucky	12	12	24	29	1
Murray State	12	13	18	35	0
Eastern Illinois	12	14	23	28	0
Tennessee Tech	12	15	26	28	0
Morehead State	9	18	16	36	0
Tennessee-Martin	7	19	19	36	0

ALL-CONFERENCE TEAM: C–Steve Soper, Tennessee Tech. **1B**–Jake Lane, Austin Peay State. **2B**–Bert Smith, Jacksonville State. **SS**–Michael Marseco, Samford. **3B**–Jake Ball, Jacksonville State. **OF**–Clay Whittemore, Jacksonville State; Mark Chagnon, Eastern Illinois; Tyler Pittman, Murray State. **UT**–Asif Shah, Southeast Missouri. **SP**–Shawn Kelley, Austin Peay State; Christian Friedrich. **RP**–Joseph Edens, Samford. **P**

layer of the Year: Clay Whittemore, Jacksonville State. **Pitcher of the Year:** Shawn Kelley, Austin Peay State. **Freshman of the Year:** Jim Klocke, Southeast Missouri. **Coach of the Year:** Gary McClure, Austin Peay State.

INDIVIDUAL BATTING LEADERS
(MINIMUM 125 AT-BATS)

	AVG	AB	R	H	2B	3B	HR	RBI	SB
Huber, Erik, Eastern Illinois	.409	159	41	65	14	1	9	42	4
Whittemore, Clay, Jacksonville State	.391	238	53	93	20	0	3	69	6
Soper, Steve, Tennessee Tech	.373	201	41	75	18	1	10	59	0
Chagnon, Mark, Eastern Illinois	.365	178	31	65	9	3	0	32	9
Hudson, Seth, Murray State	.359	217	43	78	8	6	0	32	5
Smith, Bert, Jacksonville State	.359	234	65	84	12	2	2	35	31
Owen, Tyler, Murray State	.353	167	23	59	8	0	5	41	0
Kinder, Ryan, Morehead State	.353	190	34	67	15	0	7	49	1
Marseco, Michael, Samford	.350	240	47	84	13	2	3	33	7
Winstanley, Christian, Morehead State	.350	180	37	63	9	1	5	27	7
Hanna, Trent, Morehead State	.345	148	32	51	10	1	1	27	9
Farrar, Tyler, Austin Peay State	.341	255	53	87	16	2	7	44	17
Sprowl, Brian, Tennessee Tech	.340	200	48	68	13	0	4	27	1
Reilly, Sean, Tennessee Tech	.331	160	40	53	10	3	1	30	3
Carden, Bryce, Tennessee-Martin	.329	149	29	49	6	4	0	22	5
Dudley, Kyle, Tennessee-Martin	.328	189	40	62	11	2	4	31	9
Lane, Jake, Austin Peay State	.328	177	34	58	10	5	8	40	10
Padilla, Omar, Southeast Missouri	.325	212	54	69	12	2	8	36	10
Klocke, Jim, Southeast Missouri	.324	179	38	58	10	0	4	38	3
Ball, Jake, Jacksonville State	.323	232	40	75	13	1	5	57	1
Smith, Matt, Austin Peay State	.321	156	26	50	12	1	2	28	4
Gargis, Parker, Samford	.319	232	40	74	11	1	12	47	15
Wagner, Matt, Southeast Missouri	.318	198	29	63	7	1	7	42	1
Davis, Matt, Eastern Kentucky	.317	189	31	60	13	1	5	47	4
Cleckler, Nick, Jacksonville State	.316	187	48	59	8	2	2	32	11

INDIVIDUAL PITCHING LEADERS
(MINIMUM 50 INNINGS)

	W	L	ERA	G	SV	IP	H	BB	SO
Friedrich, Christian, Eastern Kentucky	5	4	2.09	14	0	81.2	44	36	101
Kelley, Shawn, Austin Peay State	11	3	2.40	17	0	127.2	112	11	82
Renfrow, Dustin, Southeast Missouri	5	1	2.46	15	0	95.0	86	22	48
Shah, Asif, Southeast Missouri	7	3	3.22	17	1	89.1	83	35	72
Reynolds, Matt, Austin Peay State	10	3	3.26	19	0	102.0	96	26	77
Hand, Donovan, Jacksonville State	7	8	3.78	15	0	104.2	94	22	88
Tidwell, Chandler, Samford	3	5	3.91	16	0	92.0	91	26	61
Mantooth, Ryne, Austin Peay State	8	4	3.91	16	0	92.0	92	28	52
Drinkard, Tony, Jacksonville State	7	3	4.05	16	0	93.1	107	31	60
Dobbs, Jared, Tennessee Tech	5	4	4.18	18	1	64.2	70	18	38
Mabee, Henry, Morehead State	5	4	4.19	16	1	88.0	106	28	82
Syberg, Josh, Southeast Missouri	4	4	4.32	15	0	81.1	88	23	69
Hill, Trent, Samford	6	6	4.35	17	0	70.1	75	33	51
Knapp, David, Samford	3	4	4.42	16	0	71.1	63	24	59
Smith, Matt, Tennessee Tech	5	3	4.50	14	0	78.0	89	29	63
Willoughby, McKenzie, Eastern Ky	4	4	4.71	23	5	63.0	70	31	53
Ehmke, Josh, Samford	6	4	4.79	14	0	67.2	68	33	60
Bess, Tyler, Morehead State	2	7	5.08	18	1	78.0	96	38	54
Vaculik, Chris, Eastern Illinois	4	8	5.53	20	1	68.1	76	28	56
Buckholt, Ryan, Tennessee-Martin	4	3	5.57	19	0	64.2	80	40	59

PACIFIC-10 CONFERENCE

	Conference		Overall	
	W	L	W	L
★Arizona State	19	5	49	15
Arizona	15	9	42	17
UCLA	14	10	33	28
California	12	12	29	26
Washington	11	13	29	27
Oregon State	10	14	49	18
Washington State	10	14	28	26
Stanford	9	15	28	28
Southern California	8	16	27	29

ALL-CONFERENCE TEAM: C–Mitch Canham, Jr., Oregon State; Petey Paramore, So., Arizona State. **1B**–David Cooper, So., California; Cody Decker, So., UCLA; Brett Wallace, So., Arizona State. **2B**–Eric Sogard, Jr., Arizona State. **3B**–Jermaine Curtis, So., UCLA. **SS**–Brandon Crawford, So., UCLA. **INF**–Adam Sorgi, Jr., Stanford. **OF**–Gabe Cohen, Fr., UCLA; Ike Davis, So., Arizona State; Sean Ratliff, So., Stanford; Michael Taylor, Jr., Stanford; Bill Rhinehart, Sr., Arizona. **DH**–Kiel Roling, So., Arizona State. **SP**–Tyson Brummett, Sr., UCLA; Preston Guilmet, So., Arizona; Nick Hagadone, Jr., Washington; Mike Leake, Fr., Arizona State; Tyson Ross, So., California; Josh Satow, Jr., Arizona State.

Player of the Year: Brett Wallace, Arizona State. **Pitcher of the Year:** Preston Guilmet, Arizona. **Freshman of the Year (tie):** Gabe Cohen, UCLA; Grant Green, Southern California. **Coach of the Year:** Pat Murphy, Arizona State.

INDIVIDUAL BATTING LEADERS
(MINIMUM 125 AT-BATS)

	AVG	AB	R	H	2B	3B	HR	RBI	SB
Wallace, Brett, Arizona State	.404	265	75	107	17	5	16	78	12
Sogard, Eric, Arizona State	.400	250	74	100	12	4	11	62	18
Cooper, David, California	.382	204	39	78	14	0	12	55	2
Paramore, Petey, Arizona State	.379	224	64	85	18	1	6	52	4
Sorgi, Adam, Stanford	.375	160	27	60	11	1	0	27	0
Rhinehart, Bill, Arizona	.372	223	54	83	16	5	13	66	5
Spencer, Matt, Arizona State	.369	195	46	72	16	2	9	52	8
Boyer, Bradley, Washington	.363	182	33	66	16	1	3	29	0
Roling, Kiel, Arizona State	.356	194	57	69	10	0	15	63	0
Ziegler, C.J., Arizona	.355	228	59	81	23	2	13	63	1
Hague, Matt, Washington	.353	221	51	78	15	1	13	49	3
Carrithers, Alden, UCLA	.352	233	53	82	16	0	2	32	9
Davis, Ike, Arizona State	.349	238	56	83	23	0	8	61	6
Rindal, Curt, Washington	.348	224	42	78	21	1	10	50	0
Cohen, Gabe, UCLA	.345	206	35	71	12	0	10	36	4
August, Joey, Stanford	.343	172	28	59	7	1	2	27	3
Ratliff, Sean, Stanford	.339	233	61	79	13	4	12	45	10
Suttmeier, Scott, Washington State	.336	137	29	46	3	1	2	21	5
Sedbrook, Colt, Arizona	.335	188	52	63	12	1	1	24	7
Taylor, Michael, Stanford	.335	233	44	78	16	3	12	59	1
Crawford, Brandon, UCLA	.335	248	50	83	17	2	7	55	11
Glenn, Brad, Arizona	.333	213	44	71	17	2	10	62	9
Smith, Tim, Arizona State	.333	186	52	62	12	0	3	27	8
Kobernus, Jeff, California	.331	181	31	60	5	1	1	22	13
Munster, Brett, California	.327	165	27	54	12	1	1	22	5
Canham, Mitch, Oregon State	.326	227	52	74	13	1	10	59	3
Cusick, Matt, Southern California	.324	204	26	66	11	2	1	39	10

	AVG	AB	R	H	2B	3B	HR	RBI	SB
Steele, T.J., Arizona	.323	223	41	72	14	4	7	47	**21**
Smith, Blake, California	.320	178	31	57	12	1	6	30	3
Gaston, Jon, Arizona	.319	188	40	60	14	8	6	33	12
Lissman, Mike, Oregon State	.317	246	52	78	12	0	10	61	5
Green, Grant, Southern California	.316	228	42	72	14	**10**	2	24	6
Gran, Paul, Washington State	.314	204	37	64	11	4	6	34	11
Lennerton, Jordan, Oregon State	.313	217	42	68	17	1	10	51	0
Cutler, Charlie, California	.310	155	24	48	6	0	2	27	9

INDIVIDUAL PITCHING LEADERS
(MINIMUM 50 INNINGS)

	W	L	ERA	G	SV	IP	H	BB	SO
Guilmet, Preston, Arizona	12	2	**1.87**	18	0	135.0	100	34	**146**
Ross Tyson, California	6	6	2.49	17	0	115.2	103	39	120
Gorgen, Matt, California	3	5	2.51	31	9	61.0	**54**	22	75
Satow, Josh, Arizona State	**13**	3	2.76	20	0	133.2	119	53	119
Hagadone, Nick, Washington	6	1	2.77	25	11	68.1	62	**17**	72
Reyes, Jorge, Oregon State	7	3	3.10	24	0	81.1	73	18	64
Boxberger, Brad, Southern California	3	5	3.20	14	0	90.0	78	34	72
Daman Jr., Wayne, Washington State	5	4	3.28	14	0	85.0	84	32	55
Bennigson, Craig, California	5	3	3.34	26	0	70.0	75	30	50
Turpen, Daniel, Oregon State	10	1	3.44	23	2	96.2	94	25	62
Paterson, Joe, Oregon State	10	6	3.61	26	2	129.2	129	26	85
Leake, Mike, Arizona State	**13**	3	3.69	25	1	127.0	126	29	94
Flores, Brian, Arizona State	11	2	3.89	24	0	125.0	115	47	95
Brummett, Tyson, UCLA	10	6	4.04	20	0	**138.0**	146	33	111
Stutes, Mike, Oregon State	12	4	4.07	22	0	132.2	111	60	129

PATRIOT LEAGUE

	Conference		Overall		
	W	L	W	L	T
★Lafayette	17	7	33	20	0
Army	12	7	25	23	1
Navy	12	8	35	20	0
Holy Cross	8	11	12	23	0
Bucknell	8	12	16	24	0
Lehigh	2	18	13	30	1

ALL-CONFERENCE TEAM: C–Brendan Akashian, Jr., Holy Cross. **1B**–Thomas Hamilton, Jr., Navy. **2B**–Michael Garcia, Sr., Navy. **3B**–Jeff Butler, So., Lafayette. **SS**– Tyler Stampone, So., Holy Cross. Liam O'Connor, Jr., Lehigh. **OF**–Cole White, Jr., Army; Ryan Gryskevicz, Sr., Bucknell; James Conrad, Sr., Lafayette; Mike Raible, Sr., Lafayette. **DH**–Kevin Leasure, Sr., Lafayette. **SP**–Nick Hill, Sr., Army; Matt Kamine, Sr., Lafayette. **RP**–Jason Buursma, Jr., Bucknell.

Player of the Year: Cole White, Army. **Pitcher of the Year:** Nick Hill, Army. **Freshman of the Year:** Ben Yoder, Bucknell. **Coach of the Year:** Joe Kinney, Lafayette

INDIVIDUAL BATTING LEADERS
(MINIMUM 125 AT-BATS)

	AVG	AB	R	H	2B	3B	HR	RBI	SB
White, Cole, Army	.408	179	27	73	12	3	4	29	16
Conrad, James, Lafayette	.369	203	**67**	**75**	7	4	0	11	**49**
Butler, Jeff, Lafayette	.349	166	33	58	10	0	0	22	8
Garcia, Michael, Navy	.346	182	41	63	4	2	1	24	8
Hamilton, Thomas, Navy	.345	148	21	51	9	1	1	31	0
Luick, Chris, Lafayette	.344	189	37	65	8	3	4	29	15
O'Connor, Liam, Lehigh	.342	152	35	52	11	0	0	23	10
Gryskevicz, Ryan, Bucknell	.338	148	21	50	11	1	2	25	3
Raible, Mike, Lafayette	.327	171	27	56	5	1	1	40	14
Bet, Nick, Lehigh	.307	163	25	50	11	3	2	34	9
Perron, Matt, Holy Cross	.305	131	21	40	5	1	2	19	7
Grandizio, Dane, Bucknell	.304	135	22	41	14	0	0	17	8
Buursma, Jason, Bucknell	.299	134	22	40	9	3	2	19	1
Harris, Mitch, Navy	.293	174	36	51	10	**4**	8	47	2
Roth, Norm, Holy Cross	.293	140	35	41	8	2	3	22	5
Stampone, Tyler, Holy Cross	.291	134	17	39	4	0	2	21	3
Hayes, Tom, Lafayette	.291	172	15	50	6	0	1	29	14
Leasure, Kevin, Lafayette	.289	204	26	59	**16**	0	5	**51**	3
Capozzi, Tony, Army	.288	153	20	44	2	1	0	14	6
Polchinski, J.P., Army	.281	167	25	47	5	2	2	24	3

INDIVIDUAL PITCHING LEADERS
(MINIMUM 50 INNINGS)

	W	L	ERA	G	SV	IP	H	BB	SO
Wilson, Mathew, Bucknell	4	4	**1.78**	9	0	60.2	45	24	42
Hill, Nick, Army	7	3	1.91	13	0	84.2	69	18	100
Harris, Mitch, Navy	**8**	5	2.14	14	0	88.1	58	36	**119**
Reese, Kevin, Lafayette	7	1	2.96	14	1	67.0	66	14	50

	W	L	ERA	G	SV	IP	H	BB	SO
Kamine, Matt, Lafayette	7	5	2.97	13	0	**94.0**	98	13	72
Gjeldum, Ted, Lafayette	3	3	3.09	13	0	78.2	77	24	41
Drake, Oliver, Navy	3	3	3.22	14	0	67.0	63	21	52
Clothier, Drew, Army	4	4	3.31	21	1	73.1	89	23	68
White, Cole, Army	7	3	3.49	14	0	67.0	59	19	54
Atkins, Jeremy, Lafayette	6	2	3.50	11	0	61.2	66	20	29
McCoy, Mark, Navy	**8**	4	4.35	14	0	80.2	87	22	62
Curry, Matt, Bucknell	4	6	4.37	10	0	57.2	66	18	44
Mittag, Nathan, Bucknell	0	5	5.34	10	0	55.2	66	14	31
Hockman, Joel, Lehigh	1	6	5.40	13	0	53.1	70	24	33
Mayhew, Ben, Army	1	**7**	5.48	16	0	67.1	80	12	49

SOUTHEASTERN CONFERENCE

	Conference			Overall		
EAST	W	L	T	W	L	T
★Vanderbilt	22	8	0	54	13	0
South Carolina	17	13	0	46	20	0
Florida	15	15	0	29	30	0
Tennessee	13	15	0	34	25	0
Kentucky	13	16	1	34	19	1
Georgia	11	19	0	23	33	0
WEST						
Arkansas	18	12	0	43	21	0
Mississippi State	15	13	0	38	22	0
Mississippi	16	14	0	40	25	0
Alabama	15	15	0	31	26	0
Louisiana State	12	17	1	29	26	1
Auburn	10	20	0	31	25	0

ALL-CONFERENCE TEAM: C–Edward Easley, Jr., Mississippi State. **1B**–Matt LaPorta, Sr., Florida. **2B**–Travis Jones, Jr., South Carolina. **3B**–Pedro Alvarez, So., Vanderbilt. **SS**–Zack Cozart, Jr., Mississippi. **OF**–Emeel Salem, Sr., Alabama; Dominic de la Osa, Jr., Vanderbilt; Brian Leclerc, Jr., Florida. **SP**–David Price, Jr., Vanderbilt; Nick Schmidt, Jr., Arkansas; Jess Todd, Jr., Arkansas. **RP**–Casey Weathers, Sr., Vanderbilt.

Player of the Year: Matt LaPorta, Florida. **Pitcher of the Year:** David Price, Vanderbilt. **Freshman of the Year:** Jordan Henry, Mississippi. **Coach of the Year:** Tim Corbin, Vanderbilt.

INDIVIDUAL BATTING LEADERS
(MINIMUM 125 AT-BATS)

	AVG	AB	R	H	2B	3B	HR	RBI	SB
LaPorta, Matt, Florida	**.402**	169	60	68	10	0	20	52	2
Turner, Brandon, Mississippi State	.399	208	46	83	13	1	3	48	4
Alvarez, Pedro, Vanderbilt	.386	272	**76**	**105**	21	3	18	68	6
Flaherty, Ryan, Vanderbilt	.381	**273**	59	104	23	3	4	57	12
Henry, Justin, Mississippi	.381	260	52	99	14	**8**	0	38	12
de la Osa, Dominic, Vanderbilt	.378	249	65	94	23	2	20	62	20
Henry, Jordan, Mississippi	.376	263	60	99	4	2	1	17	12
Brown, Mike, Kentucky	.369	195	68	72	19	1	3	38	14
Easley, Edward, Mississippi State	.358	243	59	87	16	0	12	63	1
Spear, Brian, Kentucky	.358	176	56	63	14	1	5	49	2
Salem, Emeel, Alabama	.351	231	61	81	7	3	7	32	23
Carroll, Sawyer, Kentucky	.350	214	48	75	23	2	3	56	4
Donaldson, Josh, Auburn	.349	215	63	75	19	0	11	54	17
Forsythe, Logan, Arkansas	.347	225	55	78	16	2	9	55	18
Coughlin, Sean, Kentucky	.344	221	53	76	16	3	13	**73**	0
Moreland, Mitch, Mississippi State	.343	239	43	82	**26**	0	10	62	1
Rea, Jeffrey, Mississippi State	.343	245	57	84	10	2	1	22	13
Simunic, Andy, Tennessee	.333	225	44	75	12	3	1	27	**29**
Figueroa, Cole, Florida	.332	262	48	87	12	0	11	50	7
Darnell, James, South Carolina	.331	239	61	79	7	2	19	63	4
Arencibia, J.P., Tennessee	.330	191	47	63	15	1	8	42	2
Edwards, Bruce, Auburn	.328	201	53	66	5	2	0	19	28
Disher, Phil, South Carolina	.326	236	40	77	16	1	15	63	0
Bianucci, Mike, Auburn	.326	175	46	57	11	1	14	51	8
Wilkes, Ryan, Kentucky	.324	185	36	60	13	1	2	41	4
Delmonico, Tony, Tennessee	.323	229	53	74	11	0	9	49	10
Wyatt, Jonathan, Georgia	.323	223	47	72	10	1	6	37	16
Meingasner, Matt, Vanderbilt	.321	184	39	59	8	4	7	37	4
DeJesus, Antone, Kentucky	.318	201	52	64	8	3	1	36	16
Jones, Travis, South Carolina	.318	261	68	83	14	2	18	68	13
Feinberg, Alex, Vanderbilt	.317	252	50	80	17	1	4	44	1
Belcher, Brandon, Alabama	.317	145	17	46	3	1	2	17	5
Kline, Trent, South Carolina	.317	227	48	72	19	1	6	42	4
Olson, Matt, Georgia	.317	221	25	70	13	2	5	43	4
Dean, Blake, Louisiana State	.316	206	30	65	12	3	7	47	1
Smoak, Justin, South Carolina	.315	260	64	82	16	0	**22**	72	0
Lockwood, Jeff, Tennessee	.315	184	29	58	8	0	4	34	1
Greinke, Luke, Auburn	.314	210	41	66	6	0	1	36	9
Leclerc, Brian, Florida	.313	179	32	56	12	1	3	32	2

	AVG	AB	R	H	2B	3B	HR	RBI	SB
McCaskill, Joseph, Mississippi State	.312	189	40	59	14	0	1	23	0
Coon, Casey, Arkansas	.312	231	43	72	13	0	9	71	7
Cozart, Zack, Mississippi	.311	257	49	80	14	1	5	46	16
Gomes, Yan, Tennessee	.310	226	48	70	11	0	8	47	4
Beckham, Gordon, Georgia	.307	228	43	70	19	1	13	51	7
Powers, Connor, Mississippi State	.306	209	38	64	12	2	8	37	0
Matthes, Kent, Alabama	.305	200	31	61	9	2	8	45	7
LaNinfa, Brian, Mississippi State	.301	216	34	65	14	0	5	43	1
Macias, David, Vanderbilt	.300	260	55	78	16	1	0	26	10
Bentley, Matt, Alabama	.299	194	33	58	9	0	12	36	4
Avila, Alex, Alabama	.296	223	38	66	15	2	14	61	3

INDIVIDUAL PITCHING LEADERS
(MINIMUM 50 INNINGS)

	W	L	ERA	G	SV	IP	H	BB	SO
Price, David, Vanderbilt	11	1	2.63	18	0	133.1	95	31	194
Schmidt, James, Arkansas	11	3	2.69	18	0	124.0	84	51	111
Adkins, James, Tennessee	7	7	2.80	17	0	122.0	104	43	133
Butts, Brett, Auburn	2	2	2.83	26	6	54.0	47	23	54
Lynn, Lance, Mississippi	8	5	2.85	18	0	123.1	94	44	146
Todd, Jess, Arkansas	9	3	2.89	23	2	93.1	83	26	128
Burnside, Paul, Auburn	7	1	3.06	11	0	67.2	56	22	54
Minor, Mike, Vanderbilt	9	1	3.09	19	2	90.1	76	19	88
Jacobson, Brett, Vanderbilt	6	3	3.15	21	1	74.1	83	15	58
Satterwhite, Cody, Mississippi	4	4	3.31	27	4	54.1	49	28	44
Hurst, David, Florida	2	2	3.44	27	6	52.1	54	15	30
Honeycutt, Harris, South Carolina	8	5	3.47	17	1	96.0	81	45	105
Weatherford, Aaron, Mississippi State	3	2	3.53	20	5	66.1	58	25	72
Dodson, Stephen, Georgia	4	6	3.56	19	0	81.0	71	20	49
Hempy, Arik, South Carolina	7	3	3.58	13	0	65.1	56	32	64
Welker, Duke, Arkansas	7	5	3.59	18	0	97.2	81	39	80
Robert, Bernard, Alabama	4	5	3.64	12	0	64.1	59	26	46
Kline, Will, Mississippi	7	3	3.75	18	0	124.2	112	45	134
Edmondson, Josh, Florida	2	1	3.83	31	0	51.2	76	11	30
Cisco, Mike, South Carolina	6	2	3.84	16	0	86.2	88	18	74
Hunter, Tommy, Alabama	5	3	3.87	26	5	107.0	100	35	96
Baker, Nathan, Mississippi	6	2	3.92	16	0	64.1	63	20	40
Crowell, Cody, Vanderbilt	4	1	4.05	22	2	66.2	58	17	59
Bukvich, Brett, Mississippi	7	3	4.10	17	1	68.0	66	28	52
Christiani, Nick, Vanderbilt	5	3	4.11	17	0	70.0	71	36	57
Mullaney, Kyle, Florida	4	2	4.25	18	0	55.0	63	22	24
Bradford, Jared, Louisiana State	10	4	4.41	23	5	96.0	95	16	81
Cooper, Blake, South Carolina	7	2	4.48	17	0	60.1	65	23	44
Holder, Trevor, Georgia	2	3	4.50	20	0	64.0	73	26	60
Pigott, Justin, Mississippi State	7	7	4.51	17	0	113.2	133	24	76
McClain, Lance, Tennessee	6	5	4.64	20	0	83.1	94	40	39
Stroup, Will, Alabama	3	1	4.65	24	2	71.2	77	24	46
Moreau, Nathan, Georgia	6	2	4.65	15	0	71.2	73	24	48
Crosswhite, Chad, Mississippi State	8	5	4.69	22	2	78.2	106	27	66

SOUTHERN CONFERENCE

	Conference		Overall	
	W	L	W	L
Western Carolina	20	7	42	20
College of Charleston	20	7	39	19
Elon	15	12	32	29
Appalachian State	14	13	33	26
UNC Greensboro	14	13	30	30
Georgia Southern	13	14	34	28
The Citadel	12	15	34	27
Furman	11	16	19	36
★Wofford	8	19	30	33
Davidson	8	19	19	34

ALL-CONFERENCE TEAM: C–Blake Murphy, Sr., Western Carolina. **1B**–Zach Brown, Sr., Citadel. **2B**–Kenny Smith, Sr., Western Carolina. **3B**–Brandon Waring, Jr., Wofford. **SS**–Oliver Marmol, Jr., College of Charleston. **OF**–Jonathan Greene, Sr., Western Carolina; Michael Harrington, Jr., College of Charleston; David Rubinstein, So., Appalachian State. **DH**–Richard Jones, Fr., Citadel. **SP**–Nick Chigges, Sr., College of Charleston; Drew Saberhagen, Jr., Western Carolina. **RP**–Greg Holland, Jr., Western Carolina.

Player of the Year: Kenny Smith, Western Carolina. **Pitcher of the Year:** Nick Chigges, College of Charleston. **Freshman of the Year:** Richard Jones, Citadel. **Coach of the Year (tie):** John Pawlowski, College of Charleston; Todd Raleigh, Western Carolina.

INDIVIDUAL BATTING LEADERS
(MINIMUM 125 AT-BATS)

	AVG	AB	R	H	2B	3B	HR	RBI	SB
Waring, Brandon, Wofford	.401	222	73	89	13	3	27	74	12
Smith, Kenny, Western Carolina	.390	249	72	97	24	4	20	84	14

	AVG	AB	R	H	2B	3B	HR	RBI	SB
Wilson, Rob, Davidson	.387	199	41	77	14	0	7	33	0
Franco, Andrew, Appalachian State	.387	212	45	82	19	2	8	63	1
Maiden, Graham, College of Charleston	.385	187	46	72	13	1	10	42	3
Campbell, Chris, College of Charleston	.385	265	59	102	21	8	12	82	4
Meade, Sonny, The Citadel	.379	227	47	86	13	2	5	44	1
Shaft, Barrett, Western Carolina	.376	255	55	96	17	1	3	29	7
Lasater, Ben, College of Charleston	.376	210	57	79	14	2	15	54	2
Murphy, Blake, Western Carolina	.367	221	73	81	20	1	16	66	7
Harrington, Michael, Charleston	.364	261	62	95	19	2	13	66	4
Rubinstein, David, Appalachian State	.361	252	67	91	30	4	3	43	12
Feltes, Greg, UNC Greensboro	.360	197	42	71	13	3	5	45	6
Davis, Drew, Elon	.360	189	42	68	14	0	1	35	6
Garabedian, Alex, Charleston	.353	232	51	82	16	0	13	58	1
Brown, Zach, The Citadel	.353	238	69	84	21	2	13	45	1
Carrier, Tim, UNC Greensboro	.350	260	55	91	12	2	6	31	17
Prosser, Tom, Appalachian State	.346	179	46	62	10	6	0	32	5
Welsh, Guy, UNC Greensboro	.345	229	39	79	20	2	5	49	1
Marmol, Oliver, College of Charleston	.345	229	84	79	20	3	7	45	28
Harrow, Isaac, Western Carolina	.342	228	47	78	22	3	7	56	4
Ingram, John, Western Carolina	.341	246	60	84	16	2	13	65	6
Shehan, Chris, Georgia Southern	.341	249	59	85	21	1	10	50	12
Osborn, Blake, Davidson	.338	198	38	67	17	1	3	30	1
Austin, Chase, Elon	.337	175	33	59	14	1	3	42	0
Jones, Richard, The Citadel	.335	200	41	67	11	3	15	61	2
Liles, Nick, Western Carolina	.335	227	43	76	11	1	2	41	5
Dove, Chris, Elon	.333	201	40	67	9	8	2	30	31
Arnold, Matt, The Citadel	.332	220	39	73	6	1	5	31	6
Crissey, Alden, Davidson	.331	236	41	78	15	1	6	41	1
Greene, Jonathan, Western Carolina	.331	236	61	78	13	0	14	57	11
Orton, Ricky, UNC Greensboro	.330	176	37	58	17	0	6	42	0
Altenhof, Jason, Appalachian State	.327	251	52	82	15	3	0	35	15
Parker, Jeremiah, Georgia Southern	.324	179	44	58	17	0	13	44	2
Kirkley, Shane, Wofford	.323	248	57	80	14	3	16	55	1

INDIVIDUAL PITCHING LEADERS
(MINIMUM 50 INNINGS)

	W	L	ERA	G	SV	IP	H	BB	SO
Saberhagen, Drew, Western Carolina	9	1	2.87	16	0	106.2	114	18	42
Falcon, Ryan, UNC Greensboro	8	7	2.93	16	0	104.1	94	16	84
Chigges, Nick, College of Charleston	11	1	3.52	16	0	107.1	98	38	112
Goldberg, Jake, College of Charleston	6	1	3.72	17	0	82.1	88	26	49
Hensley, Steven, Elon	8	5	3.93	17	1	100.2	95	42	107
Eubanks, Aaron, Georgia Southern	3	5	4.32	17	0	66.2	72	26	51
Austin, Ben, Wofford	11	6	4.35	19	1	107.2	109	59	96
Sexton, Tyler, Western Carolina	8	3	4.45	18	0	99.0	110	34	83
Beliveau, Jeff, College of Charleston	3	2	4.56	17	0	73.0	61	50	74
Klinker, Matt, Furman	5	6	4.57	16	0	86.2	85	26	70
Jackson, Jay, Furman	1	4	4.59	13	0	68.2	74	32	41
Wrenn, Wes, The Citadel	6	6	4.64	17	0	104.2	129	23	61
Reifsnider, Matt, The Citadel	3	5	5.11	21	2	68.2	93	22	39
Booker, Zach, Elon	5	4	5.16	17	1	82.0	86	50	42
Crim, Matt, The Citadel	7	3	5.18	17	0	90.1	118	21	58
Sherrill, Garrett, Appalachian State	10	5	5.21	28	6	76.0	90	28	75
Edens, Aubrey, Appalachian State	2	3	5.31	16	1	62.2	78	28	42
Romanowicz, Will, Elon	6	3	5.36	17	1	92.1	123	28	56
Gibbs, Matt, UNC Greensboro	4	4	5.42	18	0	88.0	92	28	42
Rook, Jason, Appalachian State	6	7	5.44	17	0	81.0	85	48	81
Smith, Justin, The Citadel	7	4	5.63	29	0	84.2	99	45	80
Murray, Drew, Georgia Southern	4	7	5.66	18	0	76.1	94	32	64
Wilson, Rob, Davidson	2	10	5.71	18	0	97.2	128	28	66
Lewter, Jesse, Elon	4	4	5.79	22	1	65.1	94	24	45
Andress, Matt, Appalachian State	6	5	5.83	18	0	83.1	96	36	55

SOUTHLAND CONFERENCE

	Conference		Overall	
EAST	W	L	W	L
Lamar	20	10	34	25
McNeese State	17	12	21	34
Southeastern Louisiana	16	14	34	21
Northwestern State	15	14	25	28
Central Arkansas	10	20	21	32
Nicholls State	6	24	10	45
WEST				
Texas-San Antonio	24	6	36	22
Texas State	20	10	37	23
★Sam Houston State	18	12	40	24
Stephen F. Austin	17	13	31	28
Texas A&M-Corpus Christi	12	18	27	29
Texas-Arlington	4	26	13	40

ALL-CONFERENCE TEAM: C–Michael Ambort, Jr., Lamar. **1B**–Steven Hill, Sr., Stephen F. Austin. **2B**–Ryan Baker, Sr., Lamar. **3B**–Bryan Cartie, Jr.,

McNeese State. **SS**–Brandon Richey, Jr., Northwestern State. **OF**–Charlie Kingrey, Sr., McNeese State; Eric Kanaby, Sr., Lamar; Bobby Verbick, Jr., Sam Houston State. **DH**–Karl Krailo, Sr., Sam Houston State. **SP**–Luke Prihoda, Sr., Sam Houston State; Justin Fiske, Sr., Texas State; Brian Sisk, Jr., Lamar.

Player of the Year: Steven Hill, Stephen F. Austin. **Pitcher of the Year:** Luke Prihoda, Sam Houston State. **Freshman of the Year:** Tim Palincsar, Texas-San Antonio. Newcomer of the Year: Trent Lockwood, Texas-San Antonio. **Coach of the Year:** Sherman Corbett, Texas-San Antonio.

DH–Doyle Harrington, Jr., Jackson State. **OF**–Marcus Davis, Sr., Alcorn State; LaDale Hayes, So., Alabama A&M; Anthony McLin, Sr., Jackson State. **SP**–Matthew Chase, Sr., Prairie View A&M; Josh Froneberger, Jr., Alabama State; Wrandal Taylor, Jr., Prairie View A&M.

Freshman of the Year: Kyle Smith, Texas Southern. **Newcomer of the Year:** James Sims, Jackson State. **Outstanding Hitter of the Year:**Michael Richard, Prairie View A&M. **Pitcher of the Year:** Matthew Chase, Prairie View A&M. **Player of the Year:** Michael Richard, Prairie View A&M

INDIVIDUAL BATTING LEADERS
(MINIMUM 125 AT-BATS)

	AVG	AB	R	H	2B	3B	HR	RBI	SB
Kenaby, Erick, Lamar	.406	224	62	91	16	1	2	23	11
Stein, Keith, Sam Houston State	.404	255	53	103	7	4	0	39	11
Graham, Jason, Texas A&M-CC	.400	210	37	84	17	0	2	49	1
Hill, Steven, Stephen F. Austin	.387	225	71	87	17	4	24	73	10
Wood, David, Texas State	.380	255	43	97	20	1	14	77	2
Lockwood, Trent, Texas-San Antonio	.378	230	49	87	23	3	14	57	3
Williams, Chase, Texas A&M-CC	.375	152	41	57	8	2	6	27	7
Rudy, Kyle, Texas-Arlington	.374	190	29	71	13	0	1	21	0
Verbick, Bobby, Sam Houston State	.370	254	53	94	23	5	14	80	10
Ambort, Michael, Lamar	.368	220	46	81	22	0	11	63	5
Richey, Brandon, Northwestern State	.365	200	31	73	10	3	7	32	18
Krailo, Karl, Sam Houston State	.362	246	44	89	17	1	6	50	1
Burch, Chase, Southeastern Louisiana	.361	202	41	73	11	0	5	53	5
Cartie, Bryan, McNeese State	.361	191	35	69	19	0	3	41	24
Kingrey, Charlie, McNeese State	.360	189	43	68	14	0	15	47	6
Summerlin, Ty, Southeastern Louisiana	.356	191	40	68	11	1	2	28	12
Saltzgaber, Ryan, Texas-San Antonio	.343	230	45	79	12	2	9	40	7
Gardner, Zach, Stephen F. Austin	.342	190	38	65	6	4	2	20	7
Nyborg, Craig, Central Arkansas	.341	182	30	62	13	0	8	35	0
Garza, Aaron, Texas State	.341	232	51	79	15	0	5	40	16
Warren, Matt, Central Arkansas	.333	201	45	67	15	0	11	32	1
Slinkman, Danny, Texas-Arlington	.333	144	27	48	13	3	1	28	3
DeLeon, Collin, Lamar	.329	234	60	77	15	7	10	57	8
Rockett, Michael, Texas-San Antonio	.325	246	45	80	15	1	8	52	7
Randell, Laurn, Texas State	.323	186	48	60	15	0	1	22	11

INDIVIDUAL BATTING LEADERS
(MINIMUM 125 AT-BATS)

	AVG	AB	R	H	2B	3B	HR	RBI	SB
Pearson, Selmon, Alabama State	.400	140	32	56	13	1	7	31	4
Davis, Marcus, Alcorn State	.393	145	52	57	11	3	16	62	29
Richard, Michael, Prairie View A&M	.388	201	63	78	20	1	2	37	42
Stamps, Chris, Jackson State	.376	210	52	79	17	2	7	64	8
Bard, Sean, Mississippi Valley State	.376	189	44	71	21	1	9	52	6
Mclin, Anthony, Jackson State	.376	205	64	77	18	1	11	69	18
Anderson, Calvin, Southern	.362	141	29	51	9	1	6	32	1
Stevens, Johnathan, Alabama State	.359	145	44	52	14	4	5	31	19
Rivera, Jose, Arkansas-Pine Bluff	.355	152	33	54	9	2	2	23	18
Taylor, Shawn, Alcorn State	.355	155	49	55	16	4	7	40	17
Brown, Julian, Grambling State	.353	156	38	55	7	2	2	18	6
Pearce, Brandon, Alcorn State	.351	151	26	53	15	0	1	28	3
Barker, Reggie, Arkansas-Pine Bluff	.344	160	38	55	9	1	0	19	11
Dennis, Spenser, Prairie View A&M	.339	168	39	57	15	1	5	45	8
Richard, Myrio, Prairie View A&M	.331	157	45	52	10	2	4	35	23
Mendoza, Juan, Southern	.329	155	42	51	9	3	6	38	3
Camper, LaDerek, Jackson State	.325	191	54	62	5	3	3	28	18
Sims, James, Jackson State	.322	211	73	68	7	7	5	40	26
Pearson, Dars, Grambling State	.307	137	17	42	7	1	1	25	5
Kelly, Justin, Grambling State	.305	141	34	43	2	4	1	26	33
Varnell, Zac, Arkansas-Pine Bluff	.304	135	24	41	8	4	1	26	8
Hayes, LaDale, Alabama A&M	.302	129	30	39	9	8	3	22	4
McCollum, Jerome, Ark.-Pine Bluff	.302	169	31	51	8	1	3	26	9
Suncar, Jose, Grambling State	.300	130	27	39	13	4	3	23	5
Marshall, Ron, Grambling State	.298	131	20	39	1	1	2	33	3

INDIVIDUAL PITCHING LEADERS
(MINIMUM 50 INNINGS)

	W	L	ERA	G	SV	IP	H	BB	SO
Prihoda, Luke, Sam Houston State	7	3	1.61	35	18	72.2	53	11	65
Fiske, Justin, Texas State	9	3	1.93	19	1	111.2	78	39	110
Erickson, Tim, Lamar	3	3	2.54	25	7	63.2	55	16	42
Blakley, Josh, Texas-San Antonio	4	2	2.60	29	1	69.1	68	13	59
Howard, Jacob, Sam Houston State	11	6	2.70	19	0	110.0	117	30	78
Hart, Mike, Texas State	8	5	3.25	16	0	91.1	78	37	87
Baca, Jason, Texas State	4	2	3.30	30	3	71.0	55	29	74
Proudfoot, Ryan, Texas-San Antonio	4	2	3.30	14	0	62.2	45	38	51
Siers, Steven, Texas State	6	2	3.32	19	0	76.0	73	28	33
Denton, Chris, McNeese State	6	6	3.58	17	0	103.0	97	39	63
Harrington, Allen, Lamar	9	4	3.72	16	0	109.0	104	39	103
Marshall, Jesse, Sam Houston State	8	3	3.72	18	0	101.2	108	36	52
Sisk, Brian, Lamar	11	3	3.75	17	0	100.2	119	25	74
Miley, Wade, Southeastern Louisiana	7	3	3.86	15	0	95.2	106	40	77
Black, Josh, Southeastern Louisiana	8	3	3.97	15	0	90.2	95	26	90
Luetge, Lance, Stephen F. Austin	7	5	4.22	18	0	85.1	96	25	52
Lehmann, Erich, Stephen F. Austin	9	2	4.38	18	0	109.0	126	17	82
Ruffin, Josh, Texas-San Antonio	6	4	4.48	16	0	98.1	105	42	71
Schrom, Jared, Stephen F. Austin	5	3	4.64	19	0	95.0	101	38	75
Gee, Dillon, Texas-Arlington	4	8	4.67	16	0	111.2	138	22	96

SOUTHWESTERN ATHLETIC CONFERENCE

EAST	Conference		Overall	
	W	L	W	L
Jackson State	17	7	33	23
Alcorn State	15	9	25	20
Mississippi Valley State	14	10	19	36
Alabama State	7	14	12	25
Alabama A&M	4	17	10	29

WEST				
★Prairie View A&M	17	7	34	25
Southern	15	9	26	18
Arkansas-Pine Bluff	10	14	14	30
Grambling State	9	15	18	29
Texas Southern	9	15	13	28

ALL-CONFERENCE TEAM: C–Cortez Cole, Fr., JSU. **1B**–Sean Bard, Jr., Mississippi Valley State. **2B**–Shawn Taylor, Sr., Alcorn State. **3B**–Chris Stamps, Jr., Jackson State. **SS**–Michael Richard, Sr., Prairie View A&M.

INDIVIDUAL PITCHING LEADERS
(MINIMUM 50 INNINGS)

	W	L	ERA	G	SV	IP	H	BB	SO
Maloy, Jarrett, Southern	4	1	2.68	11	1	53.2	55	10	33
Merritt, Roydrick, Southern	7	1	2.91	12	0	68.0	50	24	52
Gonzalez, Joseph, Alcorn State	8	3	3.40	15	1	82.0	78	31	50
Chase, Matthew, Prairie View A&M	10	2	3.55	18	1	88.2	81	28	67
Taylor, Wrandal, Prairie View A&M	9	6	4.11	19	1	92.0	90	28	89
Garth, Antonio, Southern	4	3	4.70	11	0	51.2	43	20	34
Moring, Justin, Arkansas-Pine Bluff	6	6	5.00	18	0	75.2	63	45	64
Garcia, Francisco, Alcorn State	5	3	5.03	18	1	62.2	57	38	46
Froneberger, Josh, Alabama State	5	4	5.12	12	1	72.0	70	34	81
De La Calle, David, Jackson State	5	3	5.51	18	1	85.0	118	20	45
Adams, John, Jackson State	7	3	5.71	18	1	63.0	60	41	50
Moss, Andy, Mississippi Valley State	6	4	5.79	25	0	56.0	62	26	36
Jordan, Darryl, Alcorn State	5	4	6.08	13	0	63.2	60	42	41
Hilburn, Zeb, Alabama State	4	5	6.23	12	0	60.2	69	20	32
Reid, Scott, Mississippi Valley State	2	9	6.26	18	3	83.1	108	13	69

SUN BELT CONFERENCE

	Conference		Overall	
	W	L	W	L
Louisiana-Lafayette	23	7	45	17
★New Orleans	16	14	38	26
Middle Tennessee	16	14	32	28
Troy	16	14	34	27
Louisiana-Monroe	15	14	29	28
Florida Atlantic	15	15	36	22
Western Kentucky	15	15	25	30
South Alabama	13	16	31	26
Arkansas State	13	17	23	32
Florida International	12	17	26	29
Arkansas-Little Rock	9	20	21	31

ALL-CONFWEERENCE TEAM: C–Jonathan Lucroy, Jr., Louisiana-Laffay-ette. **1B**–Jeff Cunningham, Jr., South Alabama. **2B**–Johnny Giavotella, So., New Orleans. **3B**–William Block, So., Florida Atlantic. **SS**–Matt Ray, Sr., Middle Tennessee. **OF**–Robbie Widlansky, Jr., Florida Atlantic; James McOwen, Jr., Florida International; Clint Robinson, Sr., Troy. **DH**–Scott Hawkins, So., Louisiana-Lafayette. **SP**–T.J. Brewer, Sr., Arkansas State; Buddy Glass, Jr., Louisiana-Lafayette. **RP**–Josh Dew, Sr., Troy.

Player of the Year: Robbie Widlansky, Florida Atlantic. **Pitcher of the Year:** Josh Dew, Troy. **Freshman of the Year:** Bart Carter, Western Kentucky. Newcomer of the Year: Nolan Gisclair, Louisiana-Lafayette. **Coach of the Year:** Tony Robichaux, Lousiana-Lafayette.

INDIVIDUAL BATTING LEADERS
(MINIMUM 125 AT-BATS)

	AVG	AB	R	H	2B	3B	HR	RBI	SB
Widlansky, Robbie, Florida Atlantic	.433	240	61	104	24	1	15	69	9
McOwen, James, Florida International	.414	220	54	91	22	3	2	44	10
McKenna, Mike, Florida Atlantic	.413	218	46	90	14	2	16	60	8
Kendrick, Wayne, Middle Tennessee	.405	247	62	100	22	3	5	45	8
Dunn, Chris, Florida International	.394	155	55	61	13	2	6	32	17
Giavotella, John, New Orleans	.385	247	65	95	19	4	15	65	17
Bomback, Daniel, Florida Atlantic	.376	255	67	96	14	1	16	60	7
Baxter, T.J., New Orleans	.374	235	68	88	12	6	11	60	11
Doss, David, South Alabama	.365	233	52	85	18	5	8	52	1
Robinson, Clint, Troy	.364	239	62	87	18	1	17	71	1
Pullin, Bryan, Florida International	.362	213	53	77	15	0	7	46	10
Lucroy, Jonathan, La.-Lafayette	.360	264	56	95	19	3	18	68	1
Toomey, Clint, South Alabama	.356	208	48	74	5	6	2	46	11
Schwaner, Nick, New Orleans	.353	133	25	47	3	3	4	23	3
Tatford, Jefferie, La.-Lafayette	.351	222	62	78	18	2	10	46	4
Weidlich, Kevin, Troy	.350	237	42	83	13	0	11	55	1
Cook, Daniel, Florida Atlantic	.349	235	57	82	14	3	6	39	15
Gisclair, Nolan, La.-Lafayette	.348	224	43	78	10	4	13	54	11
Eller, Brandon, Arkansas State	.347	219	42	76	12	1	4	26	7
Hawkins, Scott, La.-Lafayette	.344	209	54	72	11	2	16	49	6

INDIVIDUAL PITCHING LEADERS
(MINIMUM 50 INNINGS)

	W	L	ERA	G	SV	IP	H	BB	SO
Dew, Josh, Troy	7	2	2.48	27	10	65.1	49	27	97
Brewer, T.J., Arkansas State	5	4	2.49	15	0	90.1	78	38	98
Salberg, Chris, Florida Atlantic	7	3	3.05	25	2	100.1	85	47	124
Farquhar, Danny, La.-Lafayette	6	3	3.08	30	6	87.2	79	22	115
Solich, Brent, La.-Lafayette	5	2	3.21	17	0	73.0	78	17	63
Mixon, David, Louisiana-Monroe	5	1	3.28	23	8	74.0	58	29	63
Glass, Buddy, La.-Lafayette	7	5	3.42	16	0	81.2	95	21	65
Reilley, Brett, Middle Tennessee	4	3	3.50	32	5	54.0	42	14	41
Whalen, Stephen, New Orleans	9	5	3.61	30	4	67.1	67	35	56
Robinson, Brad, Middle Tennessee	8	2	4.00	16	0	83.1	82	33	74
Carter, Bart, Western Kentucky	6	5	4.13	19	0	85.0	82	37	64
Moody, Hunter, La.-Lafayette	8	3	4.13	15	0	85.0	97	21	75
Scott, Matt, Middle Tennessee	5	5	4.19	13	0	81.2	83	25	48
Christensen, Keith, La.-Monroe	4	5	4.27	16	0	78.0	79	29	52
Gates, Nathan, Arkansas State	4	7	4.40	16	0	92.0	107	29	47
Tolliver, Ashur, Ark.-Little Rock	6	5	4.45	19	0	89.0	98	36	77
Klumpp, David, Ark.-Little Rock	4	6	4.65	16	0	100.2	126	21	92
Doan, Joey, South Alabama	5	6	4.82	15	0	97.0	116	24	59
Ridings, Matt, Western Kentucky	7	3	4.83	15	0	91.0	93	38	73
Baxter, Lance, South Alabama	4	3	4.84	14	0	61.1	71	27	39
Ramos, Jorge, Florida International	4	4	4.97	14	1	58.0	67	30	46

WEST COAST CONFERENCE

	Conference		Overall		
	W	L	W	L	T
★San Diego	18	3	43	18	0
Gonzaga	15	6	33	25	0
Pepperdine	14	7	35	22	0
San Francisco	9	12	27	28	0
Santa Clara	9	12	27	29	0
Loyola Marymount	9	12	22	33	1
Portland	7	14	21	30	0
Saint Mary's College	3	18	21	29	1

ALL-CONFERENCE TEAM: C–Jordan Abruzzo, Sr., San Diego; Tommy Medica, Fr., Santa Clara; Jon Norfolk, Sr., San Francisco. **1B**–Mitchell Bialosky, Jr., San Francisco; Ryan Wiegand, So., Gonzaga. **2B**–Justin Snyder, Jr., San Diego. **3B**–Darin Holcomb, Jr., Gonzaga. **SS**–Danny Worth, Jr., Pepperdine. **OF**–Donald Brown, Jr., Pepperdine; Shane Buschini, Sr.; San Diego; Jonnie Knoble, Sr., San Francisco; Adrian Ortiz, Jr., Pepperdine; Angelo Songco, Fr., Loyola Marymount; Shawn Wayt, Jr., Gonzaga. **DH**–James Allan, Sr., Portland; Logan Gelbrich, Jr., San Diego. **UT**–Josh Romanski, So., San Diego. **SP**–Matt Couch, Jr., San Diego; Barry Enright, Jr., Pepperdine; A.J. Griffin, Fr., San Diego; Brian Matusz, So., San Diego; Brad Meyers, Jr., Loyola Marymount; Clayton Mortensen, Sr., Gonzaga; Adam Olbrychowski, Jr., Pepperdine; Aaron Poreda, Jr., San Francisco.

Player of the Year: Shane Buschini, San Diego. **Pitcher of the Year:** Clayton Morensen, Gonzaga. **Freshman of the Year:** Angelo Songco, Loyola Marymount. **Coach of the Year:** Rich Hill, San Diego.

INDIVIDUAL BATTING LEADERS
(MINIMUM 125 AT-BATS)

	AVG	AB	R	H	2B	3B	HR	RBI	SB
Medica, Tommy, Santa Clara	.373	161	32	60	9	4	1	23	5
Holcomb, Darin, Gonzaga	.369	233	49	86	17	0	6	40	5
Wells, Randy, Saint Mary's	.354	178	26	63	11	3	1	37	5
Snyder, Justin, San Diego	.352	253	50	89	21	0	4	36	8
Farris, Eric, Loyola Marymount	.349	232	46	81	12	3	3	28	33
Worth, Danny, Pepperdine	.344	241	43	83	19	2	3	36	11
Buschini, Shane, San Diego	.344	227	57	78	20	2	13	58	10
Alcantar, Gabe, Santa Clara	.343	207	37	71	15	1	3	33	5
Ortiz, Adrian, Pepperdine	.342	243	51	83	5	4	1	20	16
Wayt, Shawn, Gonzaga	.341	129	10	44	9	1	1	22	3
Bialosky, Mitchell, San Francisco	.339	177	24	60	11	0	5	39	0
Wiegand, Ryan, Gonzaga	.338	216	38	73	14	0	6	45	3
Romanski, Josh, San Diego	.335	224	43	75	10	2	3	30	8
Abruzzo, Jordan, San Diego	.332	256	56	85	15	1	8	59	3
Bacon, Carl, Santa Clara	.332	211	19	70	14	0	1	33	0
d'Arnaud, Chase, Pepperdine	.331	175	34	58	9	1	3	28	4
Brown, Donald, Pepperdine	.328	195	34	64	13	0	3	25	6
Railey, Joey, San Francisco	.327	220	42	72	11	2	1	31	22
Winston, Bryan, Gonzaga	.324	188	37	61	8	0	2	26	4
Chavez, Brian, San Francisco	.324	188	27	61	16	1	1	28	2
Songco, Angelo, Loyola Marymount	.321	193	36	62	22	3	4	33	5
Powell, Chase, Portland	.321	159	22	51	12	1	2	20	2
Thames, Eric, Pepperdine	.320	200	33	64	9	5	0	44	5
Aliotti, Anthony, Saint Mary's	.320	172	23	55	2	0	1	37	2
Norfolk, Jonathan, San Francisco	.316	158	18	50	9	0	3	26	2

INDIVIDUAL PITCHING LEADERS
(MINIMUM 50 INNINGS)

	W	L	ERA	G	SV	IP	H	BB	SO
Enright, Barry, Pepperdine	12	5	1.99	18	0	131.1	117	14	91
Griffin, A.J., San Diego	6	2	2.70	34	11	63.1	49	23	65
Matusz, Brian, San Diego	10	3	2.85	18	0	123.0	98	37	163
Poreda, Aaron, San Francisco	7	6	2.89	14	0	99.2	92	18	66
Olbrychowski, Adam, Pepperdine	5	3	2.90	22	1	68.1	60	20	41
Romanski, Josh, San Diego	9	1	3.05	18	0	112.0	90	24	92
Kalush, Steve, Santa Clara	1	2	3.13	28	4	54.2	50	15	53
Slama, Anthony, San Diego	2	3	3.18	24	2	51.0	58	20	40
Dufloth, Jason, San Francisco	5	4	3.35	15	0	88.2	92	12	43
Wickswat, Matt, Santa Clara	7	5	3.41	16	0	97.2	107	32	88
Meyers, Brad, Loyola Marymount	4	4	3.46	16	0	109.1	116	23	85
Gruener, David, Portland	3	5	3.51	14	0	89.2	101	17	58
Couch, Matt, San Diego	9	2	3.60	19	1	100.0	99	21	69
Kutz, Given, Portland	6	6	3.77	16	0	105.0	108	31	93
Jensen, Alex, Saint Mary's	1	2	3.84	20	1	61.0	65	14	30
Pecina, Ricardo, San Diego	5	4	3.86	19	0	60.2	63	26	41
Mortensen, Clayton, Gonzaga	9	2	3.92	16	0	119.1	116	42	122
Hunter, Brett, Pepperdine	6	5	3.94	19	2	82.1	69	47	76
Dickmann, Robert, Pepperdine	6	4	3.96	17	0	84.0	98	26	48
Brandt, Donald, Santa Clara	4	2	4.28	11	0	54.2	60	22	32

WESTERN ATHLETIC CONFERENCE

	Conference		Overall	
	W	L	W	L
★Fresno State	17	7	38	29
Nevada	15	9	35	26
Louisiana Tech	14	10	35	24
Hawaii	11	13	34	25
San Jose State	11	13	34	26
Sacramento State	10	14	17	40
New Mexico State	6	18	22	34

ALL-CONFERENCE TEAM: C–Danny Grubb, So., Fresno State. **1B**–Albie Goulder, Sr., Louisiana Tech. **2B**–Erik Wetzel, So., Fresno State. **3B**–David Flores, Jr., Sacramento State. **SS**–Dennis Winn, Sr., Louisiana Tech. **OF**–Loren Storey, Sr., Fresno State; Steve Susdorf, Jr., Fresno State; Brian Rike, Jr., Louisiana Tech; Terry Walsh, Jr., Nevada. **UT**–Brandon Hudson, Sr., Louisiana Tech. **DH**–Baker Kurkow, Sr., Nevada. **SP**–Tanner Scheppers, So., Fresno State; Justin Wilson, So., Fresno State; Ryan Rodriguez, Sr., Nevada. **RP**–Matt Renfree, Sr., Nevada.

Player of the Year: Brian Rike, Louisiana Tech. **Pitcher of the Year:** Ryan Rodriguez, Nevada. **Freshman of the Year:** Shaun Kort, Nevada. **Coach of the Year:** Wade Simoneaux, Louisiana Tech.

INDIVIDUAL BATTING LEADERS
(MINIMUM 125 AT-BATS)

	AVG	AB	R	H	2B	3B	HR	RBI	SB
Kort, Shaun, Nevada	.392	222	44	87	17	4	6	50	5
Walsh, Terry, Nevada	.368	171	37	63	11	2	5	30	1
Jacobo, Gabe, Sacramento State	.363	223	44	81	12	2	14	44	10
Sanchez, Kris, Hawaii	.362	218	42	79	23	3	10	66	2
Winn, Dennis, Louisiana Tech	.351	185	30	65	11	1	8	26	3
Giovanatto, Donato, San Jose State	.351	231	49	81	22	5	6	54	10
Balatico, Chris, San Jose State	.350	200	36	70	14	4	1	31	6
Schmidt, Konrad, Nevada	.349	209	42	73	15	2	8	47	5
Frash, Justin, Hawaii	.346	208	50	72	19	3	3	35	0
Wetzel, Erik, Fresno State	.346	266	58	92	10	5	1	36	7
McKimmy, Marcus, San Jose State	.346	214	58	74	14	1	7	45	11
Rike, Brian, Louisiana Tech	.346	217	74	75	14	2	20	66	16
Hee, Jonathan, Hawaii	.345	206	46	71	14	1	0	21	3
Bellows, Kyle, San Jose State	.343	236	48	81	14	0	6	47	3
Hudson, Brandon, Louisiana Tech	.343	207	48	71	15	1	4	44	4
Scaperotta, Joseph, New Mexico State	.341	217	47	74	19	3	10	59	7
Susdorf, Steve, Fresno State	.340	259	53	88	14	2	12	68	12
Quade, Marcus, New Mexico State	.339	227	36	77	13	0	8	53	1
Haislet, Brandon, Hawaii	.335	215	51	72	18	2	4	39	13
Christensen, Eli, Hawaii	.331	166	30	55	6	2	2	26	3
Storey, Loren, Fresno State	.329	249	55	82	7	5	7	38	22
Lapin, Brian, Fresno State	.328	262	44	86	17	3	10	61	5
Aguirre, Leo, New Mexico State	.324	170	25	55	9	0	2	31	0
Goulder, Albie, Louisiana Tech	.323	201	46	65	8	1	14	51	3
Jones, Courtney, Louisiana Tech	.322	149	26	48	13	0	10	40	2
Angel, Ryan, San Jose State	.321	243	47	78	13	2	8	46	15
Blair, Ryan, Sacramento State	.316	206	30	65	3	5	3	26	18
Dye, Montana, Sacramento State	.316	187	28	59	11	3	8	38	1
Krukow, Baker, Nevada	.314	156	22	49	6	0	3	26	0
Rodriguez, Jason, Nevada	.313	198	42	62	13	1	4	38	1

INDIVIDUAL PITCHING LEADERS
(MINIMUM 50 INNINGS)

	W	L	ERA	G	SV	IP	H	BB	SO
Wilson, Justin, Fresno State	9	5	3.19	25	0	101.2	103	58	105
Daly, Matt, Hawaii	5	2	3.38	25	1	74.2	53	33	80
Schneider, Joshua, Hawaii	3	2	3.58	16	0	78.0	84	19	35
Rodrigues, Mark, Hawaii	9	3	3.75	18	0	98.1	111	10	39
Sobczak, Scott, San Jose State	6	2	3.86	22	5	72.1	78	14	42
Rodriguez, Ryan, Nevada	9	7	3.92	18	0	119.1	121	36	106
Moseley, Dylan, Louisiana Tech	7	4	4.07	14	0	84.0	91	28	41
Harrington, Ian, Hawaii	7	8	4.35	18	0	97.1	116	21	79
Allison, Clayton, Fresno State	10	4	4.50	23	0	108.0	123	37	68
Burke, Brandon, Fresno State	4	7	4.65	28	5	81.1	104	25	47
Gausman, Brian, New Mexico State	6	4	4.70	22	1	90.0	114	35	84
Scheppers, Tanner, Fresno State	6	6	4.74	25	0	93.0	106	32	94
Vidal, Steven, San Jose State	6	4	4.82	25	1	89.2	112	22	63
Howe, Kyle, Nevada	4	3	4.84	16	0	70.2	87	28	52
Burnett, Luke, Louisiana Tech	5	8	4.93	19	1	91.1	72	65	115

INDEPENDENTS

	Overall	
	W	L
Longwood	34	19
South Dakota State	34	19
Savannah State	31	23
Dallas Baptist	30	26
New York Tech	25	27
Utah Valley State	25	30
UC Davis	24	32
New Jersey Tech	15	28
North Dakota State	16	31
Northern Colorado	16	35
Texas-Pan American	17	39
Hawaii-Hilo	12	35
Indiana-Purdue-Fort Wayne	9	37
Chicago State	4	53

ALL-INDEPENDENT TEAM: C–Derrick Thomas, Sr., Utah Valley State. **1B**–Tyson Fisher, Jr.,South Dakota State. **2B**–Adam Symons, Jr., Northern Colorado. **3B**–Daniel Descalso, Sr., UC Davis. **SS**–Eli Slesk, Sr,, Utah Valley State. **OF**–Kraig Binick, Jr., New York Institute of Technology; Jared Davis, Jr., IPFW; Austin Krum, Jr., Dallas Baptist; Kwesi Mitchell, Sr., New Jersey Institute of Technology. **UT**–Scott Kimble, Fr., Longwood. **DH**–Garrett Baker, Sr., Dallas Baptist. **SP**–Matt Bowman, Sr., South Dakota State; Joe Esposito, Jr., New York Institute of Technology; Brian McCullough, Sr., Longwood; Marcus Moore, Jr., Utah Valley State. **RP**–Isaac Johnson, So., South Dakota State; Mike Roth, Sr., New York Institute of Technology

Player of the Year: Kraig Binick, New York Institute of Technology. **Pitcher of the Year:** Brian McCullough, Longwood. **Newcomer of the Year:** Jared Davis, IPFW. **Coach of the Year:** Reggie Christiansen, South Dakota State

INDIVIDUAL BATTING LEADERS
(MINIMUM 125 AT-BATS)

	AVG	AB	R	H	2B	3B	HR	RBI	SB
Binick, Kraig, New York Tech	.406	207	58	84	17	5	8	35	31
Thomas, Derrick, Utah Valley State	.401	197	54	79	19	1	15	66	2
Descalso, Daniel, UC Davis	.397	232	53	92	22	3	4	43	6
Bailey, Robbie, Longwood	.392	171	37	67	10	2	6	23	20
Fisher, Tyson, South Dakota State	.387	173	49	67	10	2	4	34	1
Davis, Jared, IU-PU-Fort Wayne	.376	173	37	65	18	0	9	54	6
Brinkerhoff, Jace, Utah Valley State	.371	167	37	62	12	1	4	26	2
Mitchell, Kwesi, New Jersey Tech	.371	151	42	56	10	0	13	44	12
Ross, Jonathan, Savannah State	.368	163	32	60	9	0	3	26	13
Childress, Tyler, Longwood	.366	142	31	52	10	0	8	37	3
Dempsey, Matt, UC Davis	.362	196	30	71	6	0	4	27	3
Slesk, Eli, Utah Valley State	.359	217	61	78	21	3	4	43	3
Hanigan, Tim, South Dakota State	.356	177	35	63	7	1	1	31	4
Langlais, Ryan, North Dakota State	.355	155	31	55	12	2	10	38	1
Ray, John, Northern Colorado	.351	188	51	66	18	1	14	38	0

INDIVIDUAL PITCHING LEADERS
(MINIMUM 50 INNINGS)

	W	L	ERA	G	SV	IP	H	BB	SO
McCullough, Brian, Longwood	6	4	2.57	16	1	105.0	98	28	73
Esposito, Joe, New York Tech	7	5	2.95	13	0	94.2	70	58	91
Taylor, Randall, Dallas Baptist	7	4	3.13	25	3	92.0	94	27	97
Light, Kevin, Longwood	5	3	3.30	13	0	62.2	57	21	49
Bowman, Matt, South Dakota State	8	3	3.53	15	0	104.2	104	15	66
Farrell, John, Longwood	5	3	3.63	13	0	69.1	78	15	39
Keene, John, Savannah State	5	2	3.64	15	1	54.1	60	16	30
Wymer, Josh, Texas-Pan American	5	7	3.66	16	0	110.2	106	44	65
McAtee, Brad, UC Davis	4	4	3.76	15	0	93.1	99	43	57
Laber, Jake, North Dakota State	6	6	3.89	15	0	83.1	81	47	68
Moore, Marcus, Utah Valley State	6	4	3.92	18	3	87.1	98	35	96
Meaker, Jordan, Dallas Baptist	6	3	3.93	18	0	94.0	96	30	76
Reeker, Jeff, UC Davis	6	5	4.14	14	0	78.1	88	13	22
Thielbar, Caleb, South Dakota State	7	3	4.15	15	0	78.0	89	21	44
Ballew, Patrick, Savannah State	8	6	4.52	18	1	97.2	115	29	77

NCAA DIVISION II

The Tampa Spartans have done it again. The top-ranked Spartans (53-10) defeated Columbus State (Ga.) 7-2 to win their fifth Division II national championship. Tampa also became the first school to win back-to-back titles since it accomplished the same feat in 1992-93, back when current head coach Joe Urso played second base.

All-America reliever Jonathan Holt (4-2), who went on to be drafted in the fifth round by the Indians, made the surprise start in the title game and threw a complete game six-hitter, giving up only one earned run and striking out eight without yielding a walk. Holt had thrown 57 innings in 30 previous games this season and picked up his second win of Tampa's four victories in the World Series.

The combination of stellar hitting and good pitching propelled the Spartans. The Spartans' batting average was a tournament-field best (.368), and they scored 37 runs and collected 56 hits during the four-game series. The Spartans pitching was equally impressive, as they only allowed nine earned runs (2.25 team ERA).

World Series
Site: Montgomery, Ala.
Participants: Tampa (53-10), Columbus State, Ga. (51-19), Southern Indiana (43-23), Cal State-Los Angeles (45-17-1), Angelo State (Texas) (51-20), Franklin Pierce, N.H. (49-11), Nebraska-Omaha (37-24), Kutztown, Pa. (49-7).
Champion: Tampa
Runner-Up: Columbus State
Outstanding Player: Jonathan Holt, Tampa
FIRST ROUND
Nebraska-Omaha 5, Kutztown 4 (10 innings)
Tampa 13, Cal State-L.A. 5
Angelo State 12, Franklin Pierce 3 (10 innings)
Columbus State 11, Southern Indiana 2
SECOND ROUND
Cal State-L.A. 4, Kutztown 1 (Kutztown eliminated)
Tampa 9, Nebraska-Omaha 2
Southern Indiana 3, Franklin Pierce 0 (Franklin Pierce eliminated)
Columbus State 5, Angelo State 4
THIRD ROUND
Southern Indiana 12, Angelo State 10 (Angelo State eliminated)
Cal State-L.A. 4, Nebraska-Omaha 2 (Nebraska-Omaha eliminated)
SEMIFINALS
Columbus State 9, Cal State-L.A. 4 (Cal State-L.A. eliminated)
Tampa 8, Southern Indiana 1 (Southern Indiana eliminated)
CHAMPIONSHIP
Tampa 7, Columbus State 2

DIVISION III

Kean (N.J.) completed an undefeated run through the D-III World Series, beating Emory (Ga.), 5-4 in 10 innings to earn its first Division III national championship. The Cougars won two games in extra innings and held opponents to a combined 10 runs in an event that saw 24,872 spectators, the second-largest paid attendance in its 32-year history.

Through four games the Eagles (43-10) had scored 45 runs, including games with 16 and 18 runs. But against Kean (43-8) the Eagles' bats went stagnant, and Emory registered four runs on eight hits. Cougars righthander Andrew Cupido came on in the fifth inning with the scored tied at four and pitched 5 2/3 scoreless innings for the victory. Cupido allowed seven batters to reach base on three hits and four walks, while managing to squeeze out of multiple jams to keep his team alive.

The first extra-innings title game since 1989 was tied until the bottom of the 10th when the Eagles' carelessness in the field finally got the best of them. In that inning, Emory committed two of its four errors, allowing the first two runners to reach base. After an intentional walk, senior shortstop Perry Schatzow singled up the middle to bring home the winning run.

World Series
Site: Appleton, Wis.
Participants: Wisconsin-Stevens Point (34-17), Emory Ga. (43-10), Eastern Connecticut State, (38-12), Carthage College Wis. (37-13), Chapman, Calif. (41-8), Kean N.J. (43-8), Marietta College Ohio. (32-17), SUNY-Cortland (42-7).
Champion: Kean
Runner-Up: Emory
Outstanding Player: Jordan Zimmermann, Wisconsin-Stevens Point
FIRST ROUND
Wisconsin-Stevens Point 2, Emory 0
Carthage College 15, Eastern Connecticut State 4
Chapman 8, Marietta 4
Kean 4, SUNY-Cortland 1
SECOND ROUND
Emory 5, Eastern Connecticut State 4 (Eastern Connecticut State eliminated)
SUNY-Cortland 9, Marietta 3 (Marietta eliminated)
Wisconsin-Stevens Point 12, Carthage College 8
Kean 3, Chapman 1
THIRD ROUND
SUNY-Cortland 5, Carthage College 2 (Carthage College eliminated)
Emory 16, Chapman 7 (Chapman eliminated)
Kean 7, Wisconsin-Stevens Point 4
SEMIFINALS
Emory 6, SUNY-Cortland 3 (SUNY-Cortland eliminated)
Emory 18, Wisconsin-Stevens Point 7 (Wisconsin-Stevens Point eliminated)
CHAMPIONSHIP
Kean 5, Emory 4

NAIA

Host Lewis-Clark (Idaho) State cruised to its 15th NAIA national championship (and second consecutive title), and third baseman Beau Mills led the way.

A first-round pick (13th overall) of the Indians in the June draft, Mills capped his college career in style, belting three home runs in a 9-2 victory against Spring Arbor (Mich.) in the championship game. Mills, the tournament MVP and NAIA player of the year, set a new NAIA record with 38 home runs. He belted a three-run shot in the first inning, a grand slam in the fourth and a solo homer in the sixth.

Spring Arbor had five losses all year—two to LCSC in the World Series.

World Series
Site: Lewiston, Idaho
Participants: Lindenwood, Mo. (47-20), Houston Baptist, Texas. (43-21), Cumberland,Tenn. (48-20-1), Bellevue, Neb. (47-15), Lewis-Clark State, Idaho. (58-5), Lee, Tenn. (51-15), St. Thomas, Fla. (46-16-1), Walsh, Ohio. (29-30), Spring Arbor, Mich. (48-5), Azusa Pacific, Calif. (51-10).
Champion: Lewis-Clark State College
Runner-Up: Spring Arbor
Outstanding Player: Beau Mills, Lewis-Clark State College

SMALL COLLEGES

FIRST ROUND
Walsh 3, St. Thomas 2
Lindenwood 18, Houston Baptist 4
Bellevue 12, Cumberland 10
Lewis-Clark State 11, Lee 7

SECOND ROUND
Houston Baptist 5, Cumberland 2 (Cumberland eliminated)
Lee 5, St. Thomas 4 (St. Thomas eliminated)
Spring Arbor 8, Walsh 5
Lindenwood 14, Azusa Pacific 9

THIRD ROUND
Houston Baptist 10, Walsh 5 (Walsh eliminated)
Azusa Pacific 7, Lee 4 (Lee eliminated)
Bellevue 9, Lindenwood 7
Lewis-Clark State 7, Spring Arbor 0

FOURTH ROUND
Houston Baptist 5, Azusa Pacific 1 (Azusa Pacific eliminated)
Spring Arbor 14, Lindenwood 6 (Lindenwood eliminated)
Lewis-Clark State 8, Bellevue 1

SEMIFINALS
Spring Arbor 7, Bellevue 5 (Bellevue eliminated)
Lewis-Clark State 8, Houston Baptist 7 (Houston Baptist eliminated)

CHAMPIONSHIP
Lewis-Clark State 9, Spring Arbor 2

JUNIOR COLLEGES

Chipola (Fla.) became the first Florida team since 1988 to win the NJCAA Division I World Series, defeating top-ranked New Mexico JC 7-3 in front of 9,593 at Suplizio Field in the national championship in Grand Junction, Colo. It was the first national baseball title for Chipola, alma mater of big leaguers such as Adam Loewen and Russell Martin.

Chipola's Ryan Chaffee pitched a complete-game five-hitter while striking out eight against a New Mexico team that was averaging nearly 10 runs a game in tournament play. Chipola's Logan Pierce, Paul Gatchel and Tom Hatcher led the Indians' offensive attack as they each collected three hits in the championship game. Trey Manz added a home run in the fourth. Chipola freshman righthander Drew Parker was tabbed the tournament MVP as he earned two of the Indians' four wins on the mound and got the save in the other two.

No team in the tournament was able to cool off the Chipola's bats. The Indians, who scored 27 runs in a semifinal victory against Spartanburg (S.C.) Methodist, batted a tournament-best .392 and collected 96 hits, including 27 extra-base hits.

Division I
Site: Grand Junction, Colo.
Participants: Chipola, Fla. (41-18), Iowa Western, (42-18), Shelton State, Ala. (46-17), Spartanburg Methodist, S.C. (54-14), Young Harris, Ga. (46-22), New Mexico, (55-8-1), Western Nevada, (41-24-2), Delgado, La. (31-22), Cowley County, Kan. (47-18), San Jacinto-North, Texas. (46-15).
Champion: Chipola
Runner-Up: New Mexico
Outstanding Player: Drew Parker, Chipola

Division II
Site: Millington, Tenn.
Participants: Longview, Mo. (41-18), Elgin, Ill. (45-11), Miles, Mont. (39-18), Northwest Mississippi (40-17), Frederick, MD. (33-12), Scottsdale, Ariz. (45-22), Monroe, N.Y. (36-13), Kellogg, Mich. (44-15).
Champion: Longview
Runner-Up: Kellogg
Outstanding Player: Chris Matlock, Longview

Longview won 10 of its finall 11 games this season and beat Kellogg twice in a best-of-three showdown to win the national championship.

Division III
Site: Tyler, Texas
Participants: Herkimer County, N.Y. (), Joliet, Ill. (), Tyler, Texas. (), Montgomery Co-Germantown, MD. (), Ridgewater, Minn. (), Suffolk West, N.Y. (), Brookdale, N.J. (), Massasoit, Mass. ().
Champion: Tyler. **Runner-Up:** Joliet
Outstanding Player: Brock LeMire, Tyler

Tyler (Texas) Junior College claimed its first-ever national champoinship, beating Joliet (Ill.) JC 13-5 in the final game of the NJCAA Division III World Series. The Apaches pounded out 15 hits and took advantage of 10 walks. Tyler hit a tournament-best .374 and scored 41 runs in five games while also posting an event-best 3.21 ERA.

California Community College
Site: Fresno
Participants: Fresno City (43-8), Sacramento City (35-15), Riverside (37-18), Cypress (31-22)
Champion: Riverside
Runner-Up: Cypress
Outstanding Player: Matt Clark, Riverside

Freshman Bryant Hollingsworth allowed one run in a complete-game victory for Riverside Community College, which defeated Cypress 6-1 to win the California Community Colleges championship. Hollingsworth (7-1) did not allow a run until the ninth inning, recording six strikeouts, one walk and allowing six hits in the process. The complete game was the fifth of Hollingsworth's 14 starts this season. Third baseman Matt Clark, the tournament's MVP, added a two-run double in the fifth that gave Riverside a 3-0 lead. For the Tigers, the championship is their first since they won three straight titles from 2000 to 2002.

Northwest Athletic Association of Community Colleges
Site: Longview, Wash.
Participants: Green River (34-18), Columbia Basin (36-17), Bellevue (37-11), Mt. Hood (36-9), Lower Columbia (36-7), Linn-Benton (21-25), Walla Walla (32-18), Skagit Valley (35-15)
Champion: Bellevue
Runner-Up: Skagit Valley
Outstanding Player: Kyle Decater, Bellevue

Bellevue CC freshman Kyle Decater hit a solo home run in the third inning that proved to be all the run support that starting pitcher Mike Lee would need in the championship game. Lee, a 2006 27th-round pick of the Yankees, held Skagit Valley scoreless through seven innings and picked up the win as the Bulldogs beat the Cardinals 3-0 to win their first championship since 1979.

CAPE COD LEAGUE

EAST	W	L	T	PCT	PTS
Yarmouth-Dennis	31	12	1	.721	63
Chatham	25	16	3	.610	53
Brewster	22	19	3	.537	47
Orleans	23	20	1	.535	47
Harwich	14	28	2	.333	30
WEST	**W**	**L**	**T**	**PCT**	**PTS**
Bourne	25	17	2	.595	52
Falmouth	22	22	0	.500	44
Hyannis	20	21	3	.488	43
Wareham	15	29	0	.341	30
Cotuit	14	27	3	.341	31

PLAYOFFS—Semifinals: Falmouth defeated Bourne 2-0 and Yarmouth-Dennis defeated Chatham 2-0 in best-of-three series.
Finals: Yarmouth-Dennis defeated Falmouth 2-0 in best-of-three series.

INDIVIDUAL BATTING LEADERS
(MINIMUM 119 PLATE APPEARANCES)

	AVG	G	AB	R	H	HR	RBI
Gillaspie, Conor, Falmouth	.345	32	113	20	39	7	22
Castro, Jason, Yarmouth-Dennis	.341	39	129	31	44	4	24
Alonso, Yonder, Brewster	.338	44	151	24	51	4	25
Peterson, Shane, Hyannis	.338	42	154	24	52	1	19
Hoef, Kevin, Bourne	.317	34	120	20	38	1	9
Ochinko, Sean, Yarmouth-Dennis	.315	38	124	24	39	8	23
Havens, Reese, Cotuit	.314	41	156	22	49	5	25
Dykstra, Allan, Chatham	.308	40	133	24	41	5	31
Adams, David, Falmouth	.302	42	169	26	51	0	18
Hague, Matthew, Falmouth	.299	42	154	20	46	2	19

INDIVIDUAL PITCHING LEADERS
(MINIMUM 35 INNINGS)

	W	L	ERA	IP	H	BB	SO
Crow, Aaron, Falmouth	3	1	0.67	40	19	9	36
Gibson, Kyle, Falmouth	2	0	1.17	46	34	11	51
Oliver, Andy, Wareham	1	1	1.41	45	22	24	54
Mitchell, D.J., Bourne	1	2	1.47	49	34	23	58
Green, Scott, Yarmouth-Dennis	3	1	1.56	40	31	9	35
Colla, Mike, Brewster	3	1	1.67	43	35	13	40
Brewer, Charles, Chatham	2	2	1.94	42	30	12	29
Zagone, Rick, Bourne	4	1	2.09	47	35	13	40
Couch, Matt, Brewster	2	1	2.29	51	45	15	46
Doyle, Terry, Yarmouth-Dennis	6	3	2.35	54	42	30	41

BOURNE

BATTING	AVG	AB	R	H	2B	3B	HR	RBI	SB
Baehl, Jared	.000	7	0	0	0	0	0	1	0
Basham, Brett	.309	68	5	21	1	1	0	9	0
*Clark, Andrew	.200	25	5	5	1	0	0	1	0
*Criaris, Nick	.250	4	0	1	0	0	0	0	0
Dinatale, Dave	.087	23	3	2	0	0	0	1	1
Drechsel, Chris	.280	25	7	7	0	0	0	2	0
Guez, Ben	.282	156	24	44	7	2	3	24	9
Hall, Matt	.277	83	10	23	7	1	1	14	3
Haney, Jesse	.063	16	0	1	0	0	0	1	0
Hoef, Kevin	.317	120	20	38	3	2	1	9	9
2*Karl, Matt	.000	7	0	0	0	0	0	0	0
T*Karl, Matt	.000	7	0	0	0	0	0	0	0
Maruszak, Addison	.278	108	14	30	4	0	1	17	4
Mitchell, D.J.	.200	15	2	3	1	0	0	3	0
*Moreland, Mitch	.268	82	8	22	2	0	3	12	0
Perry, Bill	.222	126	17	28	4	0	2	10	2
Pruitt, Brian	.241	133	15	32	7	1	3	27	1
Richard, Jeff	.333	3	0	1	1	0	0	0	0
Satin, Josh	.255	149	19	38	10	0	4	22	3
Smith, Kyle	.224	67	8	15	2	0	1	8	0
Soares, Ryan	.400	5	2	2	0	0	0	1	0
Steele, T.J.	.311	45	6	14	2	1	0	4	3
*Workman, Josh	.267	101	19	27	1	0	1	9	9
Zornes, Adam	.242	66	10	16	3	0	2	10	1
PITCHING	**W**	**L**	**ERA**	**G**	**SV**	**IP**	**H**	**BB**	**SO**
Farmer, Tom	0	0	16.20	1	0	1.2	2	2	0
Flasher, Jordan	2	0	1.35	18	9	20.0	12	8	25
Folino, John	0	0	2.84	2	0	6.1	4	2	8
2 Gemberling, Brad	1	0	0.00	1	0	4.0	1	0	2
T Gemberling, Brad	1	0	2.61	4	0	10.1	3	0	5

Gorgen, Matt	2	1	2.25	15	1	24.0	23	8	24
Haney, Jesse	1	1	5.68	18	0	25.1	29	11	20
Harris, Mitch	1	3	3.94	8	0	29.2	27	10	25
Hensley, Steven	4	2	3.89	9	0	37.0	35	10	35
Hose, TJ	4	3	2.58	10	1	38.1	28	15	35
Kapteyn, Wade	1	0	5.74	6	0	15.2	17	14	12
2*Karl, Matt	0	0	4.60	13	0	15.2	13	9	14
T*Karl, Matt	0	0	4.67	15	0	17.1	14	12	16
*Kent, Joe	2	1	2.91	6	0	21.2	19	12	14
Mather, Arric	0	0	0.00	1	0	5.2	1	1	4
Mitchell, D.J.	1	2	1.47	8	0	49.0	34	23	58
*Moreland, Mitch	0	1	3.86	7	0	7.0	5	4	9
Richard, Jeff	2	1	2.86	20	3	28.1	25	14	30
Storey, Mickey	0	1	7.71	3	0	4.2	9	0	4
Wojnar, Jeff	0	0	0.00	1	0	1.1	3	1	0
*Zagone, Rick	4	1	2.09	9	0	47.1	35	13	40

BREWSTER

BATTING	AVG	AB	R	H	2B	3B	HR	RBI	SB
*Alonso, Yonder	.338	151	24	51	12	0	4	25	6
Babineau, Ryan	.223	112	16	25	6	2	1	13	2
Cook, Ryan	.000	1	0	0	0	0	0	0	0
*Cooper, David	.284	67	15	19	6	0	2	15	0
*Cutler, Charlie	.271	118	13	32	3	1	1	16	4
Doss, David	.231	117	17	27	4	2	1	12	5
Fox, Willy	.250	12	1	3	1	0	0	3	0
Glenn, Brad	.197	61	10	12	4	0	3	13	2
Hall, Tavo	.233	90	12	21	4	1	0	11	8
Hamilton, Cory	.000	1	0	0	0	0	0	0	0
Hanlon, Ryan	.246	57	6	14	2	0	0	6	1
Kemp, Brian	.273	22	4	6	0	1	0	3	3
Land, Lee	.000	1	0	0	0	0	0	0	0
Lima, Danny	.270	126	15	34	3	0	0	10	3
#Marseco, Michael	.228	101	14	23	1	2	0	9	4
Priday, Jacob	.211	95	9	20	7	0	2	11	0
*Rodriguez, Victor	.000	1	0	0	0	0	0	0	0
*Tekotte, Blake	.256	156	30	40	6	1	1	16	22
*Wiley, Byron	.217	60	12	13	2	0	2	9	4
*Yount, Austin	.192	78	9	15	2	0	0	6	3
PITCHING	**W**	**L**	**ERA**	**G**	**SV**	**IP**	**H**	**BB**	**SO**
Colla, Mike	3	1	1.67	7	0	43.0	35	13	40
Cook, Ryan	4	1	2.87	8	0	47.0	38	18	43
Couch, Matt	2	1	2.29	9	0	51.0	45	15	46
Crabtree, Adam	0	1	15.00	7	0	6.0	9	6	8
Davis, Erik	4	1	4.78	7	0	32.0	29	18	25
Doss, David	0	0	9.00	1	0	1.0	2	1	0
Hamilton, Cory	0	1	7.47	13	0	15.2	23	9	15
*Hornbeck, Ben	1	1	1.93	15	1	28.0	20	14	35
Kledzick, Brad	1	4	5.97	7	0	34.2	40	16	22
Kupillas, Chris	2	2	5.11	13	0	24.2	28	15	19
Land, Lee	1	2	2.78	19	8	22.2	16	8	25
Porlier, Stephen	1	1	4.91	2	0	11.0	9	5	5
*Shinaberry, Keith	3	0	1.47	20	1	18.1	19	0	10
Warren, Adam	0	3	7.71	8	0	23.1	29	14	22
Yount, Austin	0	0	5.87	8	2	15.1	21	4	6

CHATHAM

BATTING	AVG	AB	R	H	2B	3B	HR	RBI	SB
*Beausoleil,Travis	.118	17	2	2	0	0	0	2	0
Crisp, Andrew	.280	107	10	30	4	0	0	7	3
Curtis, Jermaine	.295	122	22	36	8	1	3	24	4
*Dykstra, Allan	.308	133	24	41	8	0	5	31	0
Federowicz, Tim	.297	91	15	27	7	0	1	14	0
#Glime, Gregg	.150	60	5	9	3	0	1	8	0
*Johnson, Addison	.276	174	32	48	5	2	1	11	8
Lyons, Scott	.246	126	14	31	1	3	1	13	2
McAvoy, Kevin	.257	105	6	27	6	1	1	15	0
*O'Brien, Sean	.248	117	15	29	6	1	1	15	2
Ostrander, Mark	.143	7	0	1	0	0	0	0	1
Papenhause, Robert	.222	9	0	2	0	0	0	1	0
Pietroforte, Robert	.091	11	1	1	0	0	0	1	0
Putnam, Dan	.256	90	18	23	1	1	4	13	0
*Seager, Kyle	.274	106	17	29	4	1	1	9	1
Surina, Michael	.429	7	0	3	1	0	0	1	0
*Synan, Jeremy	.388	49	6	19	2	0	0	6	1
*Tri, Rich	.189	37	5	7	2	0	0	6	0
Watten, Trey	.246	61	10	15	1	0	0	6	1
White, Alex	.000	2	0	0	0	0	0	0	0
Zaneski, Zach	.300	20	1	6	2	0	0	1	0

PITCHING	W	L	ERA	G	SV	IP	H	BB	SO
Brewer, Charles	2	2	1.94	7	0	41.2	30	12	29
*Brooks, Gavin	0	0	2.61	2	0	10.1	9	4	14
Carpenter, Chris	0	1	2.00	2	0	9.0	7	4	13
Couture, Kevin	2	1	0.90	15	0	30.0	16	7	26
Federowicz, Tim	0	0	18.00	1	0	1.0	3	1	2
Forrest, Ryan	0	0	9.00	2	0	2.0	2	1	1
Giannini, Matt	1	1	7.24	5	0	13.2	17	6	17
*Hinson, Ryan	3	3	4.58	7	0	35.1	38	12	35
*Houck, Mitch	2	0	5.50	13	0	18.0	19	12	19
*Lorick, Jeff	0	1	6.91	13	0	27.1	31	12	27
McAvoy, Kevin	0	0	0.00	1	0	0.2	1	1	1
McHugh, Collin	1	1	3.00	2	0	6.0	2	3	4
*Milone, Tom	6	1	2.91	8	0	52.1	44	7	46
*Moreau, Nathan	0	1	10.80	4	0	15.0	24	10	15
Putnam, Zach	2	0	0.75	4	0	12.0	7	2	16
Shannon, Greg	0	0	4.91	5	3	7.1	9	6	11
Shaw, Bryan	2	0	3.15	17	7	20.0	11	7	34
*Springston, Cliff	1	2	2.88	5	0	25.0	20	11	19
Watten, Trey	0	1	3.18	6	0	11.1	8	6	9
White, Alex	2	1	2.10	7	1	25.2	18	8	31
Wooten, Rob	1	0	1.77	13	1	20.1	15	9	32

COTUIT

BATTING	AVG	AB	R	H	2B	3B	HR	RBI	SB
*Baker, Aaron	.224	152	15	34	8	0	3	15	6
*Barham, Trey	.500	2	0	1	1	0	0	3	0
Bianucci, Mike	.228	57	16	13	0	0	3	10	9
Brach, Brad	1.000	1	0	1	0	0	0	0	0
*Clark, Matt	.297	37	7	11	3	0	2	5	1
Delmonico, Tony	.267	116	20	31	6	0	3	18	4
Dupart, Curtis	.220	82	12	18	2	2	1	7	6
*Figueroa, Correy	.194	72	14	14	1	0	0	8	4
Gomes, Yan	.231	13	1	3	1	0	0	2	0
Harrison, Josh	.264	148	20	39	7	1	2	13	14
*Havens, Reese	.314	156	22	49	12	0	5	25	7
2 Joseph, Caleb	.254	118	15	30	8	0	1	13	6
T Joseph, Caleb	.256	121	15	31	8	0	1	14	6
*Lollis, Ryan	.182	66	9	12	2	0	1	12	13
Pigott, Jonathan	.182	55	2	10	1	0	0	2	4
*Rook, Jason	.333	30	7	10	1	0	0	6	3
*Shuck, J.B.	.086	35	3	3	1	0	0	1	0
*Stock, Robert	.228	123	13	28	5	0	4	20	1
#Ussery, Jeff	.000	7	0	0	0	0	0	0	0
*White, Ryne	.269	134	18	36	4	0	2	12	2
*Wilson, Brian	.240	25	2	6	0	0	1	2	1

PITCHER	W	L	ERA	G	SV	IP	H	BB	SO
*Barham, Trey	0	0	6.75	2	0	4.0	4	4	2
*Birmingham, Jim	1	1	7.53	9	0	14.1	17	11	14
Brach, Brad	0	1	1.93	1	0	4.2	8	1	4
*Brothers, Rex	0	4	6.30	7	0	20.0	26	11	20
*Calez, Adam	1	0	3.86	4	0	4.2	3	2	6
Cisco, Michael	1	5	3.74	8	0	45.2	59	8	29
*Costello, Matt	0	1	4.50	5	0	10.0	13	3	8
Fetter, Chris	0	1	4.54	8	0	35.2	37	18	27
Lindblom, Josh	4	1	4.46	17	2	38.1	38	20	47
Meaker, Jordan	1	0	7.86	14	0	26.1	39	14	27
Richards, Garrett	1	1	4.76	15	0	28.1	27	16	21
Rook, Jason	0	0	2.61	5	0	10.1	9	9	11
*Shuck, J.B.	3	2	3.30	8	0	43.2	41	20	38
Staehely, Christian	1	2	6.35	5	0	17.0	23	12	10
Stock, Robert	0	1	7.88	9	3	8.0	13	8	9
Strauss, Ryan	0	3	6.35	3	0	11.1	13	7	10
Wilson, Brian	1	2	3.76	11	1	38.1	35	19	36
*Wright, Matt	0	2	5.01	12	0	23.1	29	19	23

FALMOUTH

BATTING	AVG	AB	R	H	2B	3B	HR	RBI	SB
Adams, David	.302	169	26	51	14	3	0	18	9
Barto, Aja	.277	42	24	41	4	0	2	11	15
*Carey, Phil	.225	35	12	27	8	1	0	11	2
*Caseres, Stephen	.000	2	0	0	0	0	0	0	0
Claiborne, Preston	.107	22	3	3	1	0	0	2	0
*Dubler, Kevin	.219	35	12	25	4	0	1	14	4
Farrell, Jeremy	.191	39	19	27	7	0	2	23	5
*Gillaspie, Conor	.345	32	20	39	12	2	7	22	6
Giobbi, Andrew	.196	32	15	21	3	0	2	10	0
Hague, Matthew	.299	42	20	46	8	3	2	19	3
Hopkins, Chris	.265	23	9	18	0	0	0	7	7
1 Joseph, Caleb	.333	2	0	1	0	0	0	1	0
Ladow, Kelly	.000	1	0	0	0	0	0	0	0
Miller, Greg	.333	1	0	1	0	0	0	0	0

BATTING	AVG	AB	R	H	2B	3B	HR	RBI	SB
Nuzzo, Matt	.158	12	1	6	2	0	0	3	0
*Ochletree, Evan	.171	10	4	6	1	0	1	2	0
Stevens, Bobby	.200	2	2	1	0	0	0	0	0
*Wallace, John	.182	22	7	14	3	0	0	4	0
*Wong, Joey	.252	29	17	29	2	0	0	10	5

PITCHING	W	L	ERA	G	SV	IP	H	BB	SO
Bird, Erik	2	1	2.96	16	3	24.1	24	0	18
Burnett, Luke	2	1	4.18	18	6	23.2	20	7	41
Cantwell, Keith	0	0	0.00	1	0	3.2	4	1	6
Claiborne, Preston	3	2	3.32	11	0	19.0	16	12	22
*Copp, Brandon	0	2	5.87	2	0	7.2	10	1	8
Crow, Aaron	3	1	0.67	8	0	40.1	19	9	36
*Elam, Sam	0	0	14.79	9	0	14.0	8	26	17
*Friedrich, Christain	4	1	2.68	7	0	37.0	28	24	52
Gibson, Kyle	2	0	1.17	8	0	46.0	34	11	51
Graffy, Brett	0	2	0.87	17	2	20.2	14	12	24
Hague, Matthew	0	0	27.00	1	0	0.1	3	0	0
Hunt, Shooter	2	2	4.71	8	0	36.1	32	20	48
Moseley, Dylan	0	4	8.86	13	0	21.1	33	10	18
Phelps, David	0	0	7.27	2	0	8.2	12	5	5
Shafer, Aaron	2	2	4.26	8	0	38.0	35	19	30
Thebeau, Kyle	1	1	3.79	11	0	19.0	21	10	29
Weiland, Kyle	1	2	2.38	14	0	22.2	16	13	27
Wilson, Alex	0	1	13.50	2	0	4.0	9	5	3

HARWICH

BATTING	AVG	AB	R	H	2B	3B	HR	RBI	SB
*Avila, Alex	.241	137	15	33	11	1	2	13	1
*Bolden, Jared	.189	106	7	20	5	0	0	8	7
Crawford, Evan	.000	1	0	0	0	0	0	0	0
*Day, Kyle	.243	144	21	35	6	2	3	11	9
Dayleg, Terrence	.121	58	8	7	2	0	0	2	0
*DiCesare, Anthony	.429	14	1	6	0	0	0	2	1
Dominguez, Chris	.216	97	14	21	4	1	3	8	3
*Figueroa, Cole	.281	146	14	41	5	0	1	13	7
Giavotella, Johnny	.255	137	19	35	5	0	1	16	7
Jacobson, Brett	.000	1	0	0	0	0	0	0	0
Lanning, Jeff	.250	8	0	2	0	0	0	0	0
*Lockwood, Ryan	.400	5	0	2	0	0	0	0	1
Matthes, Kent	.200	75	8	15	5	1	1	9	1
*Miller, Matt	.172	64	7	11	3	0	0	3	2
*Opitz, Jake	.219	64	9	14	3	0	2	5	2
Paxson, JB	.093	75	4	7	1	0	1	3	0
Strausbaugh, Steve	.239	142	13	34	6	0	2	22	2
Willinsky, Mark	1.000	1	0	1	0	0	0	0	0
Wise, J.T.	.261	92	8	24	7	0	2	15	0
Zeid, Josh	1.000	1	0	1	0	0	0	0	0

PITCHING	W	L	ERA	G	SV	IP	H	BB	SO
Avila, Alex	0	0	0.00	1	0	1.0	0	0	0
*Barnes, Scott	0	1	8.00	2	0	9.0	9	6	12
Black, Sean	0	1	4.32	3	0	8.1	13	3	9
Boleska, Tom	0	1	2.25	3	0	4.0	5	1	2
*Crawford, Evan	1	0	0.67	16	5	27.0	17	12	41
Dabrowiecki, Kris	1	3	4.02	8	0	31.1	37	15	13
Dayleg, Terrence	0	0	0.00	1	0	1.2	0	0	1
Farquhar, Danny	2	4	3.38	15	0	37.1	36	18	49
Frevert, Matt	0	1	6.50	16	2	18.0	15	10	24
Hudson, Dan	3	4	3.33	8	0	46.0	40	22	55
Jacobson, Brett	2	3	4.15	10	1	43.1	49	18	52
2*Kulik, Ryan	1	3	5.47	6	0	24.2	31	10	15
T*Kulik, Ryan	1	3	6.26	9	0	27.1	38	12	16
*Quigley, Miers	0	2	9.53	3	0	5.2	8	1	8
Willinsky, Mark	1	0	9.20	13	0	14.2	20	18	15
Wise, J.T.	0	0	0.00	1	0	1.1	0	0	1
*Young, Corey	2	2	4.05	7	0	46.2	41	15	39
Zeid, Josh	0	2	4.12	13	0	43.2	45	12	34
Zocchi, PJ	1	1	6.35	5	0	11.1	12	10	8

HYANNIS

BATTING	AVG	AB	R	H	2B	3B	HR	RBI	SB
Bell, Phil	.271	118	16	32	2	0	1	15	8
Brewer, Dan	.297	158	23	47	11	0	7	30	7
Cornstubble, Dale	.224	49	1	11	2	0	0	6	0
Darnell, James	.250	128	23	32	5	1	8	27	0
Elmendorf, Scott	.238	101	17	24	2	0	0	8	0
*Gonzales, Joey	.255	94	15	24	5	1	1	9	3
Jackson, Ryan	.215	149	9	32	6	0	0	15	0
Larson, Francis	.069	29	3	2	0	0	0	0	0
*Long, Patrick	.198	111	15	22	2	0	0	3	6
#Macias, David	.215	149	16	32	2	1	0	7	2
*Peterson, Shane	.338	154	24	52	8	2	1	19	4
Robin, Shea	.229	109	11	25	3	0	1	8	1

	AVG	AB	R	H	2B	3B	HR	RBI	SB
Vazquez, Kiko	.208	120	10	25	3	0	3	14	1

PITCHING	W	L	ERA	G	SV	IP	H	BB	SO
Daly, Matt	1	4	4.25	8	0	42.1	39	24	47
Doyle, Andrew	4	1	2.83	7	0	47.2	46	14	28
Franzblau, Jason	4	3	3.50	7	0	46.1	37	17	41
Harris, Hunter	2	1	2.55	14	1	24.2	17	8	27
Hudson, Austin	2	2	3.59	8	0	47.2	40	16	36
Jolicoeur, James	0	1	4.41	11	0	32.2	28	11	32
*Pecina, Ricardo	1	0	5.60	9	1	17.2	22	8	23
Penney, Stephen	2	0	0.93	13	0	29.0	26	7	33
Sherrill, Garrett	3	2	1.84	16	2	29.1	21	7	31
Stohr, Tyler	0	0	2.08	10	5	13.0	12	7	14
Stowell, Bryce	1	5	3.72	8	0	38.2	32	13	44
*Wood, Austin	0	2	4.67	4	0	17.1	24	9	11

ORLEANS

BATTING	AVG	AB	R	H	2B	3B	HR	RBI	SB
*Atwood, Will	.000	1	0	0	0	0	0	0	0
*Carrithers, Alden	.198	111	29	22	9	0	1	7	5
Cordoso, Josh	.000	3	0	0	0	0	0	0	0
*Crawford, Brandon	.189	132	15	25	4	1	4	14	8
D'Arnaud, Chase	.185	130	12	24	6	0	3	16	2
Freiman, Nate	.286	147	17	42	5	1	2	28	2
*Gaston, Jon	.256	86	16	22	3	2	0	5	7
*Jimenez, Jose	.197	132	9	26	2	1	2	18	0
Jones, Jericho	.000	1	0	0	0	0	0	0	0
Jones, Marcus	.219	32	4	7	1	0	0	2	2
*Linton, Ollie	.271	96	13	26	1	0	0	10	15
Muno, Kevin	.182	22	4	4	0	0	0	1	1
*Raben, Dennis	.298	151	28	45	10	2	6	35	3
#Reese, Eric	.216	97	11	21	1	2	0	4	4
Shunick, Clayton	.000	0	1	0	0	0	0	0	0
Sobolewski, Mark	.189	132	9	25	8	0	0	10	5
Tartamella, Travis	.200	75	4	15	2	2	0	5	0
Tignor, Hampton	.139	79	8	11	1	0	0	4	0

PITCHING	W	L	ERA	G	SV	IP	H	BB	SO
*Atwood, Will	4	0	2.25	14	0	32.0	29	12	27
*Bennigson, Craig	1	1	3.14	8	0	43.0	31	24	48
Boxberger, Brad	1	0	1.24	7	0	29.0	15	11	26
Brown, Sam	0	3	2.86	17	0	22.0	16	12	26
*Catapano, Rob	3	1	0.92	14	0	19.2	14	3	17
Christiani, Nick	3	3	1.88	19	4	28.2	23	6	22
1 Gemberling, Brad	0	0	4.26	3	0	6.1	5	0	3
Kamppi, Kyle	1	0	1.50	12	0	18.0	10	7	15
1 *Karl, Matt	0	0	5.40	2	1	1.2	1	3	2
Maertz, Santo	0	0	0.00	1	0	1.0	0	1	0
*McAnaney, Pat	2	3	3.32	8	0	40.2	35	14	40
Novak, Jason	1	1	4.60	13	0	15.2	17	10	15
Pelzer, Wynn	1	2	5.68	3	0	12.2	12	11	11
Perry, Ryan	1	2	4.15	18	4	21.2	21	10	30
Schwimer, Michael	2	2	3.51	7	0	33.1	27	16	28
Shunick, Clayton	1	2	2.89	9	0	37.1	30	13	41
*Surkamp, Eric	2	0	1.85	5	0	24.1	20	8	26

WAREHAM

BATTING	AVG	AB	R	H	2B	3B	HR	RBI	SB
*Booker, Ben	.250	84	12	21	2	2	0	3	5
*Cavasinni, Mike	.159	44	4	7	0	0	0	0	2
*Davis, Ike	.246	57	4	14	3	0	0	6	1
de la Osa, Dominic	.119	101	6	12	1	1	1	9	7
*Dean, Blake	.250	124	13	31	3	0	4	15	3
Demperio, Michael	.173	75	9	13	0	0	0	4	5
*Dickerson, Dustin	.215	107	8	23	2	0	1	8	1
Dietz, Jeff	.000	5	0	0	0	0	0	0	0
*Fon, Diallo	.340	47	4	16	2	0	0	5	5
Garrity, Bryan	.167	78	2	13	0	0	0	3	3
Henry, Seth	.196	92	10	18	3	0	0	2	3
Hollander, Mike	.071	14	1	1	1	0	0	1	0
*Moldenhauer, Russ	.218	124	8	27	4	1	0	6	4
Murton, Luke	.189	127	7	24	5	0	2	9	1
Ogata, Jason	.222	81	8	18	5	0	3	9	1
Phegley, Josh	.269	67	5	18	5	0	0	6	0
Savastano, Scott	.000	5	0	0	0	0	0	0	0
#Weems, Beamer	.257	144	13	37	9	0	0	11	5

PITCHING	W	L	ERA	G	SV	IP	H	BB	SO
*Bashore, Matt	0	0	0.00	1	0	1.0	0	0	1
*Bleich, Jeremy	4	2	2.44	8	0	44.1	39	12	47
*Davis, Ike	1	0	0.00	3	1	2.2	0	5	1
Dietz, Jeff	1	1	0.73	19	0	24.2	21	8	28
Hicks, Chris	0	1	1.19	18	8	22.2	15	5	25

		W	L	ERA	G	SV	IP	H	BB	SO
Hollander, Mike		0	0	6.75	3	0	2.2	2	1	2
*Keuchel, Dallas		2	4	3.20	10	0	59.0	63	16	45
Langwell, Matt		0	0	5.40	4	0	6.2	9	2	6
2 McHugh, Collin		0	0	2.65	8	0	17.0	14	13	19
T McHugh, Collin		1	1	2.74	10	0	23.0	16	16	23
*Miley, Wade		1	6	2.61	9	0	58.2	44	34	53
Moldenhauer, Russ		0	0	0.00	1	0	1.0	1	0	1
*Moore, Josh		1	1	3.72	7	0	9.2	9	2	7
*Oliver, Andy		1	1	1.41	9	0	44.2	22	24	54
*Parker, Nathan		1	1	6.75	4	0	6.2	10	4	5
*Petiton, Matt		0	0	10.38	2	0	4.1	8	0	3
Purdy, Bill		0	0	0.00	1	0	1.0	1	0	0
*Sewell, Lance		1	1	10.13	2	0	2.2	4	2	4
Tufts, Tyler		1	2	4.05	4	0	13.1	20	4	6
Volz, Kendal		1	7	4.83	8	0	50.1	49	14	50
Whelan, Sam		0	2	3.86	9	0	9.1	16	3	8

YARMOUTH-DENNIS

BATTING	AVG	AB	R	H	2B	3B	HR	RBI	SB
Anderson, David	.222	9	1	2	0	0	0	0	0
#Ayers, Johnny	.259	54	9	14	1	1	0	6	5
Barnes, Jeremy	.125	8	1	1	1	0	0	0	0
Beckham, Gordon	.284	155	25	44	9	1	9	35	6
*Castro, Jason	.341	129	31	44	7	0	4	24	6
Coon, Casey	.462	13	1	6	1	0	0	2	0
Cowgill, Collin	.290	138	24	40	4	4	2	20	10
Green, Grant	.291	127	27	37	8	0	4	12	11
*Long, Matt	.214	84	13	18	6	0	1	13	4
Luna, Aaron	.299	67	14	20	2	0	5	12	1
Mauldin, D.J.	.000	0	1	0	0	0	0	0	0
Ochinko, Sean	.315	124	24	39	9	0	8	23	0
Posey, Buster	.281	128	13	36	3	0	3	19	4
*Railey, Joey	.245	106	20	26	6	0	1	15	7
#Romero, Nick	.259	139	22	36	7	0	1	17	2
#Seastrunk, Diego	.243	37	4	9	2	0	0	3	0
*Stewart, Luke	.192	26	4	5	1	0	2	3	0
*Tamsin, Mike	.241	87	7	21	3	0	1	5	0

PITCHING	W	L	ERA	G	SV	IP	H	BB	SO
Anderson, David	1	0	8.62	8	0	15.2	28	7	7
Burns, Eddie	5	1	2.56	8	0	52.2	41	9	41
Carlucci, Nick	0	0	0.00	2	0	2.0	1	0	1
Cassavechia, Nick	1	1	1.07	16	11	25.1	18	3	24
Dodson, Steve	1	1	4.15	3	0	17.1	14	4	13
Doyle, Terry	6	3	2.35	9	0	53.2	42	30	41
Gagg, Bobby	3	0	2.64	7	1	30.2	30	8	17
Green, Scott	3	1	1.56	9	1	40.1	31	9	35
*Haughian, Nick	0	0	0.00	2	1	4.0	2	1	2
Haviland, Shawn	0	0	0.00	2	0	1.0	2	0	0
Holder, Trevor	4	1	0.89	8	0	30.1	21	8	28
1 *Kulik, Ryan	0	0	13.50	3	0	2.2	7	2	1
Lynch, Colin	0	1	3.52	14	0	15.1	8	13	17
Mauldin, D.J.	1	0	3.00	11	0	18.0	12	6	18
Sanford, Shawn	1	1	4.44	9	0	24.1	22	10	22
Seastrunk, Diego	0	0	27.00	2	0	1.1	4	3	1
Sullivan, Jerry	3	0	0.56	4	0	16.0	13	5	10
*Wickswat, Matt	2	2	3.66	11	1	32.0	30	9	30

ALASKA LEAGUE

	W	L	PCT	GB
Fairbanks AIA Fire	24	11	.686	—
Mat-Su Miners	24	11	.686	—
Kenai Peninsula Oilers	17	18	.486	7
Alaska Goldpanners of Fairbanks	17	18	.486	7
Anchorage Bucs	13	22	.371	11
Anchorage Glacier Pilots	10	25	.286	14

INDIVIDUAL BATTING LEADERS
(MINIMUM 100 PLATE APPEARANCES)

	AVG	AB	R	H	2B	3B	HR	RBI	SB
Buss, Nick, Oilers	.369	157	29	58	6	5	2	23	29
Sebek, Todd, Pilots	.362	149	23	54	7	1	3	28	23
Morgan, Kyle, Bucs	.354	127	22	45	11	3	2	13	4
Tremblay, Chris, Panners	.352	165	29	58	5	1	0	14	10
Nieuwenhuis, Kirk, AIA	.333	156	35	52	8	4	4	30	3
Keller, Paul, AIA	.331	160	29	53	9	0	6	25	19
Wyatt, Brent, Panners	.327	162	34	53	9	4	1	27	15
Skinner, Justin, AIA	.324	136	10	44	5	0	2	20	4
Diaz, Mike, Pilots	.324	145	21	47	8	4	1	18	9
Martin, Paul, Panners	.318	151	30	48	2	0	3	26	4

INDIVIDUAL PITCHING LEADERS
(MINIMUM 30 INNINGS)

	W	L	ERA	G	SV	IP	BB	SO
Peterson, Max, Miners	5	0	1.31	13	1	34.1	17	37
Erickson, Jason, Miners	3	3	1.56	10	1	52.0	8	35
Eskew, Jared, Miners	2	1	1.57	7	0	34.1	11	28
Millard, Ryan, AIA	3	2	1.83	11	0	64.0	17	49
Vicini, David, Pilots	1	3	1.93	18	2	51.1	15	33
Brown, George, Miners	1	1	2.13	7	0	38.0	13	21
Rivers, Alex, Miners	5	1	2.16	8	0	41.2	11	29
Bennett, Bobby, AIA	3	2	2.17	13	0	37.1	12	22
Thomson, Matt, Oilers	4	4	2.37	9	0	41.2	7	33
Wood, Justin, AIA	7	2	2.49	12	0	65.0	16	36

ATLANTIC COLLEGIATE LEAGUE

WOLFF	W	L	PCT	GB
Kutztown Rockies	33	6	.846	—
Lehigh Valley Catz	25	15	.625	8½
Quakertown Blazers	18	20	.474	14½
Jersey Pilots	18	22	.450	15½
KAISER	W	L	PCT	GB
Metro New York Cadets	21	14	.600	—
Stamford Robins	15	23	.395	7½
Long Island Stars	11	26	.297	11
New York Generals	11	26	.297	11

PLAYOFFS—First Round: Lehigh Valley defeated Jersey and Long Island Island defeated Stamford in one-game playoffs.
Semifinals: Kutztown defeated Lehigh Valley 2-0 and Long Island defeated Metro New York 2-0 in best-of-three series.
Finals: Kutztown defeated Long Island in a one-game championship.

INDIVIDUAL BATTING LEADERS
(MINIMUM 100 PLATE APPEARANCES)

	AVG	AB	R	H	2B	3B	HR	RBI	SB
Greig, TJ, Long Island	.403	129	19	52	4	0	1	15	8
Matos, Adam, Kutztown	.385	104	20	40	5	2	0	11	16
Shapiro, Dan, Jersey	.374	115	21	43	4	0	1	14	16
Matera, Paddy, Jersey	.374	107	22	40	3	0	0	10	3
Kahn, John, Metro New York	.368	114	25	42	6	1	0	15	15
Mare, Joseph, Stamford	.368	76	13	28	4	1	0	11	0
Gaffney, Ryan, New York	.356	118	18	42	5	1	0	20	3
Kidd, James, Stamford	.355	121	30	43	8	8	1	25	1
Maher, Matt, New York	.344	122	23	42	4	2	0	17	14
Walsh, Patrick, Long Island	.343	99	14	34	3	0	1	13	4
Santomauro, Nicholas, Jersey	.333	93	8	31	5	2	0	20	7
Eiden, Matt, Lehigh Valley	.326	89	16	29	3	1	0	13	5
Valdez, Effrey, Long Island	.324	105	12	34	4	0	1	16	1
Romano, Joseph, Metro New York	.324	102	17	33	1	0	0	16	4
Reed, Michael, Lehigh Valley	.324	68	15	22	2	2	0	8	8

INDIVIDUAL PITCHING LEADERS
(MINIMUM 30 INNINGS)

	W	L	ERA	G	SV	IP	H	BB	SO
Page, Ryan, Lehigh Valley	6	1	0.92	9	0	49.0	39	5	61
Roth, Todd, Lehigh Valley	6	1	1.57	9	0	46.0	39	4	44
Mendez, Jairo, Jersey	5	1	1.96	9	0	55.0	41	10	33
Gardo, Dan, Kutztown	7	0	2.04	9	0	53.0	36	15	42
Green, Ben, Long Island	4	2	2.08	12	3	47.2	39	13	50
Proudfoot, Ryan, Lehigh Valley	2	3	2.21	8	0	40.2	36	19	48
Gorski, Darin, Quakertown	2	4	2.45	11	0	47.2	36	17	49
Barry, Richard, Metro New York	3	2	2.76	9	0	42.1	37	8	17
Angelo, Greg, Quakertown	4	0	3.02	11	0	41.2	40	20	42
Costigan, Tom, New York	4	4	3.23	9	0	53.0	48	22	42

CAL RIPKEN SR. LEAGUE

	W	L	PCT	GB
Youse's Maryland Orioles	26	14	.650	—
Rockville Express	27	15	.643	—
Bethesda Big Train	24	18	.571	3
Silver Spring-Tacoma Thunderbirds	19	19	.500	6
Herndon Braves	19	22	.463	7½
College Park Bombers	15	24	.385	10½
Maryland Redbirds	12	30	.286	14

PLAYOFFS– Rockville defeated Bethesda in the championship of a six-team, double-elimination tournament.

INDIVIDUAL BATTING LEADERS
(MINIMUM 100 PLATE APPEARANCES)

	AVG	AB	R	H	2B	3B	HR	RBI	SB
Celenza, Mike, College Park	.357	112	13	40	9	0	2	18	0
Jusino, Tony, Maryland	.322	121	11	39	2	0	0	9	1
Fowler, Joe, Silver Spring-Tacoma	.317	145	22	46	13	2	2	28	1
Park, Tim, Silver Spring-Tacoma	.312	109	21	34	10	1	0	10	0
Parker, Jarrett, Herndon	.311	119	19	37	3	3	3	22	5
Warden, KC, College Park	.310	116	12	36	7	1	1	21	3
Jackson, Chris, Youse's Maryland	.304	161	38	49	6	7	1	21	9
Smith, Bert, Bethesda	.301	163	39	49	6	1	0	17	20
Allen, Eric, Rockville	.299	127	29	38	10	3	3	28	8
Whittemore, Clay, Bethesda	.290	138	19	40	9	0	0	19	5
Karcich, Jon, Bethesda	.289	114	23	33	8	0	3	16	4
Zuanich, Mike, Rockville	.283	99	18	28	7	2	2	14	3
Jakubowski, Jeremy, College Park	.275	102	20	28	4	1	1	13	20
Foster, Andrew, Bethesda	.270	137	31	37	6	1	1	25	2
Buchholz, Alex, Youse's Maryland	.270	115	27	31	6	2	1	21	9

INDIVIDUAL PITCHING LEADERS
(MINIMUM 30 INNINGS)

	W	L	ERA	G	SV	IP	H	BB	SO
Kuhn, Jason, Herndon	1	0	0.81	15	0	33.1	17	12	38
Francis, Dan, Rockville	3	2	1.57	8	0	34.1	27	10	24
Whitley, Rob, Youse's Maryland	1	0	1.85	12	1	34.0	25	14	28
Swinson, Scott, Youse's Maryland	4	1	2.03	7	0	48.2	37	5	33
Umberger, Zach, Youse's Maryland	4	0	2.35	9	0	38.1	32	6	29
Laber, Jake, Silver Spring-Tacoma	3	4	2.49	9	0	51.2	44	25	56
Joseph, Josh, Silver Spring-Tacoma	1	3	2.49	9	0	47.0	40	18	20
Anderson, Zach, Maryland	3	2	2.55	10	1	42.1	33	19	42
Stangroom, Mike, Maryland	0	4	2.58	11	0	45.1	35	16	36
Gerjets, Dan, Silver Spring-Tacoma	4	0	2.59	9	0	48.2	44	10	25

CENTRAL ILLINOIS COLLEGIATE LEAGUE

	W	L	PCT	GB
Dubois County Bombers	25	23	.521	—
Quincy Gems	24	24	.500	1
DuPage County Dragons	24	24	.500	1
Danville Dans	23	25	.479	2

PLAYOFFS– Dubois defeated DuPage in the championship of a four-team tournament.

INDIVIDUAL BATTING LEADERS
(MINIMUM 100 PLATE APPEARANCES)

	AVG	AB	R	H	2B	3B	HR	RBI	SB
McCormick, Thomas, Quincy	.337	190	41	64	10	1	9	40	7
Wolgamot, Ben, Danville	.329	161	29	53	9	0	0	14	18
Goldsmith, Bradley, Dubois	.313	192	38	60	11	2	2	31	28
Gorman, Rich, Dubois	.304	148	34	45	9	2	4	23	16
Powers, Connor, DuPage	.302	129	27	39	5	1	5	19	4
Wille, Matt, Quincy	.299	187	28	56	9	0	0	23	23
Martin, Casey, Dubois	.299	194	25	58	10	2	0	33	2
Melton, Derek, Dubois	.299	134	18	40	11	0	2	17	0
Melker, Adam, DuPage	.293	147	28	43	8	0	0	15	8
Myers, Jon, Quincy	.291	165	27	48	9	0	4	24	6
Duffy, Ryan, DuPage	.288	125	21	36	11	0	6	35	2
Tyrell, Cole, DuPage	.287	157	34	45	6	0	3	19	22
Meador, James, Danville	.281	153	22	43	5	3	3	23	9
Blaser, Tyson, Quincy	.276	152	26	42	8	1	1	26	3
Nappi, Jason, Danville	.271	129	18	35	7	0	0	15	6

INDIVIDUAL PITCHING LEADERS
(MINIMUM 30 INNINGS)

	W	L	ERA	G	SV	IP	H	BB	SO
Manns, Mike, DuPage	3	2	2.75	13	0	52.1	49	35	49
Sims, Dallas, Dubois	4	1	2.86	12	0	66.0	58	32	49
Filip, Tom, DuPage	4	3	3.09	19	0	46.2	48	15	47
Harmon, Marc, Dubois	4	0	3.43	13	0	60.1	56	15	33
Doyle, Patrick, Quincy	2	5	3.54	10	0	53.1	59	27	32
Walsh, Jake, Danville	2	5	3.65	12	0	61.2	63	24	49
Jernstad, Matt, DuPage	5	3	3.76	13	1	55.0	54	22	47
Beatty, Andrew, DuPage	4	2	3.98	10	0	52.0	59	34	22
Sestak, Connor, Danville	3	3	4.14	9	0	45.2	41	34	33
Hellhake, Greg, Quincy	1	3	4.20	16	0	45.0	45	21	31

INDIVIDUAL BATTING LEADERS
(MINIMUM 100 PLATE APPEARANCES)

COASTAL PLAIN LEAGUE

NORTH	W	L	PCT	GB
+*Edenton Steamers	39	16	.709	—
Peninsula Pilots	32	23	.582	7
Wilson Tobs	27	29	.482	12 ½
Petersburg Generals	22	31	.415	16
Outer Banks Daredevils	21	30	.412	16 ½

SOUTH	W	L	PCT	GB
+*Fayetteville Swampdogs	42	14	.750	—
Florence RedWolves	27	27	.500	14
Columbia Blowfish	23	31	.426	18
New Bern River Rats	21	31	.404	19
Wilmington Sharks	22	33	.400	19 ½

WEST	W	L	PCT	GB
+*Thomasville HiToms	39	16	.709	—
Spartanburg Stingers	31	24	.564	8
Martinsville Mustangs	28	26	.519	10 ½
Asheboro Copperheads	17	38	.309	22
Gastonia Grizzlies	16	38	.296	22 ½

+First-half champion   *Second-half champion
PETITT CUP TOURNAMENT: Thomasville defeated Peninsula in the championship game of an eight-team tournament.

INDIVIDUAL BATTING LEADERS
(MINIMUM 100 PLATE APPEARANCES)

	AVG	AB	R	H	2B	3B	HR	RBI	SB
Conley, Brian, Edenton	.372	196	40	73	7	2	5	33	17
Kruml, Ray, Fayetteville	.355	169	38	60	7	1	0	31	22
Roller, Kyle, Thomasville	.351	188	38	55	9	0	9	38	1
Alberts, Tim, Spartanburg	.348	210	39	73	18	1	5	35	19
Batts, Stephen, Wilmington	.341	173	35	59	12	1	4	23	5
Pecora, Chris, Fayetteville	.340	191	25	65	9	1	2	42	23
Smith, Matt, Fayetteville	.338	145	25	49	2	1	0	26	9
Scott, Brandon, Wilson	.336	229	38	77	15	2	2	31	28
Campbell, Eric, Martinsville	.335	191	32	64	12	0	5	38	11
Thomas, David, Thomasville	.335	194	49	65	17	0	9	35	15

INDIVIDUAL PITCHING LEADERS
(MINIMUM 30 INNINGS)

	W	L	ERA	G	SV	IP	H	BB	SO
Broyles, Wade, Thomasville	6	0	0.24	24	0	37.2	17	17	57
McKellar, Coleman, Edenton	4	0	0.56	6	0	32.0	22	3	13
Michon, Brandon, Edenton	3	1	0.84	24	1	32.0	16	13	26
Primus, Jon, Edenton	6	0	1.22	9	0	59.0	42	10	42
Gloor, Chris, New Bern	3	2	1.30	9	0	48.1	21	18	78
Koehler, Tom, New Bern	5	1	1.44	9	0	50.0	34	22	55
Walker, Brett, Peninsula	4	3	1.59	9	0	56.2	46	13	31
Reeser, Ben, Fayetteville	8	0	1.61	12	1	61.1	45	13	29
McLean, Tio, Petersburg	3	1	1.62	20	5	55.2	40	28	80
Groh, Zach, Edenton	7	0	1.75	8	0	51.1	27	20	57

FLORIDA COLLEGIATE SUMMER LEAGUE

	W	L	PCT	GB
Winter Springs Barracudas	24	13	.649	—
Leesburg Lightning	20	12	.625	1 ½
Altamonte Springs Snappers	15	18	.455	7
Winter Park Diamond Dawgs	12	19	.387	9
Sanford River Rats	12	21	.364	10

PLAYOFFS– Leesburg defeated Altamonte Springs in the championship of a five-team tournament.

INDIVIDUAL BATTING LEADERS
(MINIMUM 80 PLATE APPEARANCES)

	AVG	AB	R	H	2B	3B	HR	RBI	SB
Prano, John, Sanford	.344	96	11	33	3	0	0	13	10
Simonelli, Matt, Leesburg	.326	95	16	31	3	0	1	16	6
Danesh, Ohmed, Winter Springs	.316	117	20	37	9	0	3	21	5
Russell, Tim, Winter Springs	.316	95	8	30	6	0	1	17	1
Peacock, Jason, Leesburg	.310	113	17	35	7	1	1	19	1
Braaten, B., Altamonte Springs	.308	78	8	24	6	0	1	18	1
Hubbard, Austin, Leesburg	.304	79	12	24	5	0	0	7	0
McCarty, Tyler, Winter Springs	.303	142	24	43	8	0	0	25	12
Duarte, Mario, Leesburg,	.302	96	21	29	2	3	0	12	6
Whiting, Corey, Winter Springs	.299	87	18	26	3	0	1	6	11
Cauley, Tommy, Winter Park	.289	90	13	26	3	0	0	10	13
Compagnone, Frank, Sanford	.276	98	10	27	6	0	1	9	14
Lopez, Matt, Winter Springs	.276	98	21	27	4	0	0	6	11
Arnold, Colin, Winter Park	.274	106	21	29	8	0	0	12	12
Bailey, Dwayne, Sanford	.270	122	16	33	4	0	0	12	17

INDIVIDUAL PITCHING LEADERS
(MINIMUM 20 INNINGS)

	W	L	ERA	G	SV	IP	H	BB	SO
Durham, John, Altamonte Springs	2	2	0.72	8	1	37.1	22	8	36
Novikoff, Chris, Winter Springs	3	0	0.89	8	0	40.2	18	24	25
Buonanni, Drew, Leesburg	2	0	0.90	9	1	30.0	15	14	30
Walters, Jeff, Winter Springs	2	2	1.01	9	0	44.2	26	22	30
Turner, Jonathan, Leesburg	2	0	1.17	9	0	38.1	31	17	26
Barbot, Michael, Winter Park	2	0	1.42	8	0	31.2	26	12	15
Marsocci, Blake, Leesburg	2	1	1.78	20	11	30.1	23	6	44
Eckard, Scott, Sanford	1	1	1.80	5	0	25.0	17	8	33
Sweat, Kyle, Winter Springs	2	0	1.82	7	0	29.2	21	15	30
Burns, David, Winter Springs	5	2	1.83	19	2	34.1	30	13	30

GREAT LAKES LEAGUE

W		L	PCT	GB
Lima Locos		26	12	.684	—
Columbus All-Americans		25	13	.658	1
Delaware Cows		25	14	.641	1 ½
Cincinnati Steam		23	14	.622	2 ½
Grand Lake Mariners		23	15	.605	3
Southern Ohio Copperheads		23	15	.605	3
Stark County Terriers		20	20	.500	7
Lake Erie Monarchs		18	19	.486	7 ½
Licking County Settlers		17	22	.436	9
Xenia Athletes in Action		7	32	.179	19 ½
Anderson Servants		4	35	.103	23 ½

PLAYOFFS: Columbus defeated Delaware in the championship of a six-team, double-elimination tournament

INDIVIDUAL BATTING LEADERS
(MINIMUM 80 PLATE APPEARANCES)

	AVG	AB	R	H	2B	3B	HR	RBI	SB
Oester, Jake, Cincinnati	.376	117	24	44	12	2	3	16	0
Betsch, Rick, Cincinnati	.373	75	15	28	3	0	0	11	2
Holloway, B.J., Lima	.371	89	21	33	6	1	1	17	5
Nurre, Tommy, Cincinnati	.363	91	14	33	7	2	2	16	0
Stiffler, Matt, Southern Ohio	.357	84	24	30	7	1	2	15	6
Mercer, Jeff, Anderson	.356	101	10	36	10	0	1	15	0
Krauss, Marc, Grand Lake	.352	128	20	45	7	2	2	30	3
Diedrich, Eric, Columbus	.350	120	26	42	8	1	4	27	2
Campana, Tony, Southern Ohio	.349	126	27	44	5	2	0	11	24
Bonner, Bryan, Lima	.347	95	15	33	3	0	1	13	8

INDIVIDUAL PITCHING LEADERS
(MINIMUM 30 INNINGS)

	W	L	ERA	G	SV	IP	H	BB	SO
Bischoff, Matt, Lima	5	0	1.02	9	0	44.0	32	10	41
Janke, Lance, Anderson	0	2	1.35	7	1	33.1	26	10	31
Hale, Jake, Columbus	3	2	1.39	5	0	32.1	24	14	26
Haselhorst, Quinn, Columbus	4	0	1.62	6	0	39.0	31	1	28
Leady, Kevin, Lake Erie	5	2	1.73	10	0	52.0	30	17	36
Winterhalter, Matt, Cincinnati	3	2	1.91	7	0	33.0	25	12	20
Campitella, Sam, Xenia	1	3	1.95	10	0	55.1	45	27	33
Jackson, Jay, Delaware	5	0	1.96	8	1	36.2	26	6	38
Jacobs, Michael, Grand Lake	2	0	2.17	9	0	37.1	31	10	22
Jackson, Matt, Delaware	2	2	2.23	8	1	36.1	23	12	20

JAYHAWK LEAGUE

	W	L	PCT	GB
Derby Twins	33	13	.717	—
Hays Larks	29	15	.659	3
El Dorado Broncos	27	19	.587	6
Nevada Griffons	25	21	.543	8
Liberal BeeJays	22	24	.478	11
Joplin Splashers	14	30	.318	18
Dodge City A's	8	36	.182	24

INDIVIDUAL BATTING LEADERS
(MINIMUM 100 PLATE APPEARANCES)

	AVG	AB	R	H	2B	3B	HR	RBI	SB
Lagreid, Greg, Nevada	.397	156	28	62	18	2	8	50	5
Morrison, Erick, Hays	.376	125	21	47	7	0	0	11	15
Jones, Jeffrey, Liberal	.356	160	27	57	7	1	4	23	3
Adams, Nick, Nevada	.348	155	39	54	7	3	3	28	19
Ferreira, Kevin, Derby	.333	129	19	43	4	0	0	14	11
Michalek, Rich, Hays	.331	139	22	46	5	2	0	22	22
Douglas, Brandon, Derby	.328	134	27	44	9	0	2	16	9
Nipp, Jordan, El Dorado	.323	130	26	42	5	4	1	17	1

	AVG	AB	R	H	2B	3B	HR	RBI	SB
Angel, Rickey, Hays	.308	130	24	40	10	0	3	22	2
Scavuzzo, Andrew, Joplin	.308	130	14	40	10	0	3	22	4
Maxie, Kyle, Liberal	.307	114	13	35	2	0	1	18	5
Fitzgerald, Tommy, Nevada	.306	147	20	45	7	0	0	21	3
Ottrando, Anthony, Nevada	.298	124	27	37	3	1	3	20	5
McConnell, Matt, Liberal	.290	138	26	40	6	0	0	11	2
Embury, Dane, Derby	.289	135	28	39	10	0	7	30	5

INDIVIDUAL PITCHING LEADERS
(MINIMUM 30 INNINGS)

	W	L	ERA	G	SV	IP	H	BB	SO
Musgrave, Rob, El Dorado	3	0	0.68	7	0	40.0	28	6	41
Nehls, Brock, Hays	6	1	1.24	8	0	51.0	37	7	52
Young, Cameron, Derby	4	0	1.80	8	0	35.0	17	9	30
Sintes, Jonathan, Derby	3	1	2.34	8	0	42.3	27	18	39
Pierpoint, Gary, Hays	4	2	2.47	7	0	43.7	38	17	26
Gawron, John, Joplin	1	1	2.52	8	0	39.3	36	8	36
Whitaker, Matt, Derby	4	2	2.59	8	1	41.7	29	24	44
Braeckel, Eric, Derby	3	1	2.70	6	0	30.0	22	4	32
Larsen, Garret, Liberal	5	0	2.88	8	0	50.0	42	20	39
Morgal, Matt, Joplin	1	4	2.91	7	0	46.3	45	9	33

NEW ENGLAND COLLEGIATE LEAGUE

NORTH	W	L	PCT	GB
Holyoke Giants	26	16	.619	—
Vermont Mountaineers	24	18	.571	2
Keene Swamp Bats	22	20	.524	4
Lowell All-Americans	21	23	.477	6
Concord Quarry Dogs	19	24	.442	7 ½
Sanford Mainers	19	24	.442	7 ½
SOUTH	W	L	PCT	GB
Torrington Twisters	24	16	.600	—
Newport Gulls	25	17	.595	—
North Adams SteepleCats	23	19	.548	2
Manchester Silkworms	19	22	.463	5 ½
Danbury Westerners	16	24	.400	8
Pittsfield Dukes	13	28	.317	11 ½

PLAYOFFS–Quarterfinals: Torrington defeated Manchester 2-0, Newport defeated North Adams 2-1, Holyoke defeated Lowell 2-1, and Vermont defeated Keene 2-0 in best-of-three series.
Semifinals: Newport defeated Torrington 2-0 and Vermont defeated Holyoke 2-0 in best-of-three series.
Finals: Vermont defeated Newport 2-0 in a best-of-three series.

INDIVIDUAL BATTING LEADERS
(MINIMUM 100 PLATE APPEARANCES)

	AVG	AB	R	H	2B	3B	HR	RBI	SB
Kemp, Brian Michael, Sanford	.398	181	38	72	5	5	0	19	32
Poulk, Drew, Newport	.354	99	16	35	12	0	2	16	4
Akashian, Brendan, Lowell	.352	145	28	51	7	1	8	27	9
Reynolds, Simi, Concord	.348	112	10	39	2	1	0	8	2
Pollock, A.J., Vermont	.348	135	29	47	15	0	1	20	13
Savastano, Scott, Pittsfield	.348	92	12	32	6	1	1	17	3
Underhill, Cory, Danbury	.342	152	28	52	6	0	2	20	21
Pinto, Max, North Adams	.342	114	19	39	6	2	3	13	3
Bellows, Kyle, Holyoke	.341	135	21	46	12	1	3	19	1
Green, Garett, Torrington	.335	161	19	54	11	0	0	25	9
Lieneck, Jeff, Pittsfield	.333	75	8	25	7	1	0	8	1
Gran, Paul, Keene	.328	116	21	38	11	0	3	19	14
Hightower, Kody, Holyoke	.322	149	32	48	7	0	3	22	7
Sheridan, Mike, Vermont	.320	128	15	41	8	3	1	23	5
Paulsen, Ben, Keene	.318	66	10	21	4	0	2	11	0

INDIVIDUAL PITCHING LEADERS
(MINIMUM 30 INNINGS)

	W	L	ERA	G	SV	IP	H	BB	SO
Wilk, Adam, Newport	3	2	1.12	8	0	48.1	25	10	26
Gilblair, Shawn, Holyoke	4	1	1.17	9	0	53.2	46	15	42
Houck, Kurt, Torrington	4	2	1.60	8	0	39.1	32	9	29
Bignall, Drew, Lowell	3	4	1.65	9	0	54.2	48	18	41
Perlman, Max, Vermont	4	3	1.73	9	0	52.0	49	8	44
Novakowski, Gary,Torrington	3	2	1.81	8	0	49.2	43	12	44
Gaggioli, Mike, Vermont	3	3	1.82	9	0	49.1	47	13	45
Thompson, Mike, Holyoke	6	1	1.86	9	0	58.0	45	26	53
Germane, Robert, North Adams	4	3	1.95	13	2	37.0	30	9	30
Landry, Kevin, Sanford	4	2	2.05	9	0	52.2	40	30	42

NORTHWOODS LEAGUE

NORTH	W	L	PCT	GB
*Duluth Huskies	41	27	.603	—
+St. Cloud River Bats	35	31	.530	5
Mankato MoonDogs	35	32	.522	5 ½
Alexandria Beetles	33	35	.485	8
Rochester Honkers	32	34	.485	8
Thunder Bay Border Cats	28	40	.412	13
Brainerd Blue Thunder	26	41	.388	14 ½
SOUTH	W	L	PCT	GB
+Green Bay Bullfrogs	43	25	.632	—
*Eau Claire Express	42	26	.618	1
Madison Mallards	38	29	.567	4 ½
Wisconsin Woodchucks	36	31	.537	6 ½
Waterloo Bucks	29	38	.433	13 ½
La Crosse Loggers	27	41	.397	16
Battle Creek Bombers	26	41	.388	16 ½

+First-half champion   *Second-half champion
PLAYOFFS–Semifinals: St. Cloud defeated Duluth 2-0 and Eau Claire defeated Green Bay 2-1 in best-of-three series.
Finals: St. Cloud defeated Eau Claire 2-0 in a best-of-three series.

INDIVIDUAL BATTING LEADERS
(MINIMUM 184 PLATE APPEARANCES)

	AVG	AB	R	H	2B	3B	HR	RBI	SB
Hanson, Nate, Mankato	.363	204	27	74	16	0	5	28	3
Ruf, Darin, Wisconsin	.347	199	40	69	16	1	8	34	0
Dirks, Andy, Brainerd	.347	202	48	70	13	7	3	22	29
Molina, Randy, Madison	.342	193	34	66	15	1	4	39	4
Sappelt, David, Battle Creek	.329	173	26	57	13	1	0	18	10
Robertson, David, Green Bay	.328	268	53	88	15	0	3	32	45
Wikoff, Brandon, Madison	.323	167	42	54	2	0	0	14	8
Hubbard, Bobby, Madison	.315	216	36	68	12	5	3	46	12
Delaney, John, Battle Creek	.313	201	31	63	11	0	2	17	2
Upchurch, Josh, Alexandria	.313	256	46	80	7	3	5	32	40
Dellwo, Tim, Alexandria	.307	251	36	77	13	1	4	43	15
White, Cole, La Crosse	.305	164	15	50	6	0	4	23	5
Fanelli, Matt, St. Cloud	.301	209	25	63	10	2	0	28	3
Thames, Eric, La Crosse	.301	209	32	63	13	5	3	43	15
Wheeler, Tim, St. Cloud	.300	223	29	67	11	1	2	27	20

INDIVIDUAL PITCHING LEADERS
(MINIMUM 54 INNINGS)

	W	L	ERA	G	SV	IP	H	BB	SO
Walker, Justin, La Crosse	4	3	1.60	9	0	56.1	46	11	56
Morales, Isaac, St. Cloud	5	3	1.61	10	0	56.0	50	15	58
Fields, Matt, Thunder Bay	5	5	1.70	11	0	74.1	46	15	86
Trausch, Matt, Wisconsin	6	2	1.77	12	0	86.1	69	10	32
Marks, Andy, Duluth	7	3	1.83	13	0	83.2	53	37	83
Close, Tom, Waterloo	3	4	1.86	29	6	63.0	43	14	50
Jennings, Dan, Waterloo	4	3	2.01	11	0	67.0	54	31	64
Martin, Greg, Rochester	8	2	2.09	12	0	73.1	57	31	50
Fritsch, Craig, Rochester	5	1	2.21	12	0	69.1	49	21	52
Worthington, Adam, Eau Claire	5	3	2.25	9	0	64.0	41	30	68

TEXAS COLLEGIATE LEAGUE

ROGERS HORNSBY	W	L	PCT	GB
Wichita Falls Roughnecks	25	18	.581	—
McKinney Marshals	23	17	.575	0 ½
Denton Outlaws	24	21	.533	2
Weatherford Wranglers	20	23	.465	5
Mineral Wells Steam	14	30	.318	11 ½
TRIS SPEAKER	W	L	PCT	GB
Coppell Copperheads	26	18	.591	—
Brazos Valley Bombers	23	20	.535	2 ½
Duncanville Deputies	20	23	.465	5 ½
Colleyville LoneStars	17	22	.436	6 ½

PLAYOFFS–Semifinals: McKinney defeated Wichita Falls 2-0 and Coppell defeated Brazos Valley 2-0 in best-of-three series.
Finals: Coppell defeated McKinney 2-1 in a best-of-three series.

INDIVIDUAL BATTING LEADERS
(MINIMUM 100 PLATE APPEARANCES)

	AVG	AB	R	H	2B	3B	HR	RBI	SB
Dao, John, Wichita Falls	.365	104	13	38	10	0	2	16	10
Slinkman, Danny, Wichita Falls	.363	102	24	37	6	1	1	13	2
Butler, Joey, Weatherford	.347	124	18	43	7	2	0	20	15
Richburg, Chris, Wichita Falls	.346	127	25	44	15	5	2	33	0
Nommensen, Brett, McKinney	.333	117	23	39	9	3	2	15	14
Belt, Brandon, Coppell	.333	93	22	31	7	2	4	22	3
Harris, R.J., Wichita Falls	.327	101	24	33	5	4	0	18	4
Blackmon, Charlie, Colleyville	.316	95	11	30	4	1	1	6	2
Kendricks, Brandon, Duncanville	.314	105	19	33	4	1	0	11	10
Fester, Jonas, Coppell	.314	121	32	38	6	0	2	14	8
Coffman, Bo, Mineral Wells	.312	125	18	39	9	2	4	24	2
Seefeld, Jason, Wichita Falls	.306	134	22	41	6	0	4	23	6
Hernandez, Jose, Denton	.297	138	25	41	4	2	4	30	3
Jones, Sean, Coppell	.295	112	23	33	5	2	0	13	13
Ladendorf, Tyler, Denton	.295	149	23	44	10	3	0	15	18

INDIVIDUAL PITCHING LEADERS
(MINIMUM 30 INNINGS)

	W	L	ERA	G	SV	IP	H	BB	SO
Murray, Justin, McKinney	5	2	0.54	8	0	50.0	31	8	48
Maxwell, Steven, Denton	4	0	0.56	7	0	32.0	13	7	39
Anderson, Chase, Wichita Falls	4	0	1.24	8	0	36.1	21	22	44
Kibler, Jon, Weatherford	5	0	1.36	5	0	33.0	18	12	29
Whitmer, Case, Brazos Valley	2	2	1.54	9	1	46.2	27	18	51
McCain, Mark, McKinney	5	1	1.57	13	0	34.1	28	15	21
Richards, Stephen, McKinney	2	2	1.57	7	0	34.1	23	10	45
Bronson, Evan, Colleyville	3	3	1.72	8	0	47.0	34	6	39
Davis, Tyler, Brazos Valley	2	1	1.72	21	6	31.1	27	10	31
Hicks, Scooter, Brazos Valley	4	2	2.01	7	0	31.1	28	10	24

VALLEY LEAGUE

	W	L	T	PCT	GB
Waynesboro Generals	30	13	1	.693	—
Harrisonburg Turks	28	16	0	.636	2 ½
Luray Wranglers	26	18	0	.591	4 ½
Winchester Royals	25	19	0	.568	5 ½
Staunton Braves	24	20	0	.545	6 ½
Covington Lumberjacks	22	22	0	.500	8 ½
Front Royal Cardinals	22	22	0	.500	8 ½
Woodstock River Bandits	21	23	0	.477	9 ½
New Market Rebels	18	26	0	.409	12 ½
Fauquier Gators	14	30	0	.318	16 ½
Haymarket Senators	11	32	1	.261	19

PLAYOFFS—Quarterfinals: Waynesboro defeated Woodstock 2-1, Covington defeated Harrisonburg 2-0, Luray defeated Front Royal 2-1, and Staunton defeated Winchester 2-1 in best-of-three series.
Semifinals: Waynesboro defeated Covington 2-1 and Luray defeated Staunton 2-0 in best-of-three series.
Finals: Waynesboro defeated Luray 3-1 in a best-of-five series.

INDIVIDUAL BATTING LEADERS
(MINIMUM 100 PLATE APPEARANCES)

	AVG	AB	R	H	2B	3B	HR	RBI	SB
Greinke, Luke, Winchester	.417	120	25	50	12	0	5	32	5
Sontag, Ryan, Winchester	.361	119	27	43	5	1	5	32	6
Taylor, Rober, Harrisonburg	.352	122	22	43	6	0	4	14	2
Cueto, Jose, Winchester	.328	134	22	44	8	1	6	24	11
Stanley, Nick, New Market	.325	154	23	50	15	0	2	20	0
O'Neill, Corey, Haymarket	.323	130	13	42	7	2	0	26	4
Brannon, Nolan, New Market	.323	127	14	41	6	0	0	17	1
Kipnis, Jason, Covington	.318	154	46	49	11	2	9	41	24
Kuhn, Tyler, Luray	.318	170	35	54	9	2	3	22	11
Barrett, Zach, Staunton	.312	173	23	54	8	1	2	32	9
Adams, Ryan, Waynesboro	.309	152	21	47	8	1	1	23	2
Davidson, Kurt, Waynesboro	.307	215	36	66	14	1	5	54	5
Lambert, Scott, Fauquier	.303	89	14	27	2	0	0	8	3
McDonough, Brian, Fauquier	.303	142	13	43	5	2	1	19	3
Semeniuk, Ryan, Winchester	.303	152	28	46	13	1	3	29	4

INDIVIDUAL PITCHING LEADERS
(MINIMUM 30 INNINGS)

	W	L	ERA	G	SV	IP	H	BB	SO
Gilliam, Robert, Luray	7	1	1.26	12	1	57.0	37	18	81
Umberger, Dustin, Luray	9	0	1.29	11	0	63.0	38	19	88
Wheeler, Tim, Harrisonburg	3	4	1.76	9	0	51.0	43	9	48
Blakney, Zac, Fauquier	5	1	1.78	11	0	55.2	38	21	62
Brantley, Rod, Harrisonburg	2	2	2.12	7	0	46.2	28	23	40
Brewer, Russ, Waynesboro	4	2	2.15	11	0	54.1	46	10	54
Sherman, Chad, Staunton	5	2	2.47	10	0	51.0	33	23	56
Tolliver, Ashur, Harrisonburg	4	0	2.52	9	0	50.0	38	20	61
Dages, Jon, Waynesboro	7	2	2.62	13	0	68.2	72	5	47
Greinke, Luke, Winchester	3	1	2.66	8	0	50.2	48	20	48

WEST COAST COLLEGIATE

EAST	W	L	PCT	GB
Moses Lake Pirates	29	13	.690	—
Wenatchee AppleSox	23	18	.561	5 ½
Spokane RiverHawks	13	29	.310	16
Kelowna Falcons	12	30	.286	17

WEST	W	L	PCT	GB
Corvallis Knights	27	15	.643	—
Kitsap BlueJackets	24	18	.571	3
Bend Elks	23	19	.548	4
Bellingham Bells	16	25	.390	10 ½

PLAYOFFS— Semifinals: Moses Lake defeated Wenatchee 2-1 and Corvallis defeated Kitsap 2-1 in best-of-three series.
Finals: Moses Lake defeated Corvallis 2-0 in a best-of-three series.

INDIVIDUAL BATTING LEADERS
(MINIMUM 80 PLATE APPEARANCES)

	AVG	AB	R	H	2B	3B	HR	RBI	SB
Van Wyck, Curtis, Wenatchee	.352	108	14	38	3	0	0	11	1
Van Winkle, Tyson, Spokane	.336	107	15	36	5	0	0	3	9
Mandelblatt, Zach, Wenatchee	.331	154	28	51	14	4	0	15	12
Tinoco, Steve, Moses Lake	.331	151	23	50	6	2	0	18	12
Gebbers, Hawkins, Wenatchee	.328	116	20	38	9	1	0	14	7
Kim, Zach, Moses Lake	.327	171	32	56	5	1	0	13	16
George, Drew, Bend	.326	86	21	28	5	1	1	14	7
Lind, Joey, Kitsap	.325	160	21	52	3	0	0	26	4
Poppert, Derek, Bend	.321	131	20	42	2	2	0	18	6
Murphy, Jim, Corvallis	.319	94	13	30	4	0	4	20	0
Kuykendall, Brandon, Kitsap	.315	146	20	46	10	0	2	18	13
Wyckoff, Matt, Corvallis	.313	134	17	42	5	0	0	13	7
Horst, Bryan, Spokane	.306	98	17	30	7	1	0	12	7
Lee, Ryan, Kelowna	.303	155	21	47	3	1	0	9	27
Baird, Dillon, Wenatchee	.299	144	17	43	7	0	3	19	1

INDIVIDUAL PITCHING LEADERS
(MINIMUM 30 INNINGS)

	W	L	ERA	G	SV	IP	H	BB	SO
Applebee, Paul, Bellingham	4	1	0.60	7	0	45.1	34	12	39
Todd, Austin, Kelowna	0	3	1.04	8	0	34.2	25	18	26
Murphy, J.R., Corvallis	2	1	1.14	8	0	47.1	30	13	42
Reneau, Dale, Moses Lake	5	2	1.40	9	0	58.0	42	12	62
Fife, Stephen, Bellingham	3	0	1.59	8	0	34.0	22	11	30
Triolo, Mark, Bellingham	2	4	1.60	10	0	62.0	52	25	44
Rogers, Tyler, Moses Lake	4	1	1.62	9	0	55.2	52	17	37
Rossman, Matt, Kitsap	3	0	1.70	12	1	37.0	27	2	35
Sokolowski, Matt, Kelowna	3	3	1.80	11	0	70.0	66	17	39
Proszek, A.J., Spokane	2	1	2.15	8	1	46.0	43	9	27
Nunley, Kyle, Kitsap	0	2	2.21	8	0	40.2	38	14	20
Howe, Kyle, Kitsap	5	2	2.24	9	0	60.1	40	21	39
Guinn, Aaron, Spokane	3	3	2.37	10	0	38.0	37	22	29
Pullen, Brandon, Bellingham	0	5	2.38	6	0	34.0	35	14	17
Guidos, Ben, Moses Lake	3	2	2.43	8	0	37.0	34	16	34

HIGH SCHOOL BASEBALL

Wilson High dresses up to take down national title

BY ALAN MATTHEWS

If high school seniors prepared for exams the way they do the prom, we'd all have brought home straight A's. For generations, it's been the school year's most anticipated occasion, but for 11 seniors on the Wilson High baseball team, prom night carried significance for a much different reason.

On the night when their peers reveled in their last hurrah together, Elliot Glynn and his teammates sat around a table at senior first baseman Chase Kaesman's house, dressed in tuxedos, and rather than soaking in the celebration of the evening, turned discussion to the task ahead.

"It was a pretty passionate conversation," said Glynn, the team's co-captain who delivered an emotional speech that night. "The day before, we had won our first-round (play-off) game. I had never been part of a team that actually won a playoff game, and we ended up talking about how much we wanted to keep it alive, just win."

Which is precisely what the Bruins went out and did, earning a pair of come-from-behind victories the following week before polishing off the season with a 5-1 win over Anaheim's Canyon High at Dodger Stadium to claim the California Interscholastic Federation Southern Section Division I championship.

Wilson (Long Beach, Calif.) entered the final week of the season as the No. 1 team in the country, and thus secured the top spot in the Baseball America/National High School Baseball Coaches Association Top 50 poll, becoming just the second California school in the 15-year history of the poll to finish No. 1.

"Senior leadership was the backbone of this team," said Andy Hall, a 20-year coaching veteran, including seven years as the head coach at Wilson. "When you hear stories like that, for those guys to be thinking about our season rather than the prom, that's pretty special.

"This was the finest team I've coached."

With an enrollment of approximately 4,400 students and an athletic department that has produced former major leaguers Bobby Grich, Jeff and Sean Burroughs as well as a summer Olympian in every Olympics since 1956, including a handful of record-setting swimmers, Wilson has long been a hotbed for standout prep teams. The 2006 season was no exception, as the Bruins got off to an 11-3 start before losing eight of their final 16 games that year.

The tailspin was underscored by selfishness and dissension, not a lack of talent, and it left Hall with a sour taste.

"I remember telling them that, 'if we have another season with all of the non-baseball related stuff, next year will be my last as your coach,'" Hall said. "After the meeting, Glynn

Wilson High celebrates its national title after a win in the CIF playoffs at Dodger Stadium

came up to me, put his arm around me, and assured me that next year would be different.

"Those (seniors) did a great job on that level. We were a great team because we had great players who cared about each other."

With the 2006 implosion behind them, the Bruins opened the '07 season ranked No. 6 in the Preseason BA/NHSBCA poll, and again got off to a strong start, advancing to the championship game of the season-opening Loara Tournament in Orange County.

There, they squared off against another nationally-ranked team in Cypress (Calif.) High, which boasted the nation's best high school hitter in senior third baseman Josh Vitters. Cypress won 9-6, but the tone for the season had been set.

"It set us back a little, we were pretty down about it," Glynn said. "And we said, 'we're never going to be the bridesmaid anymore.'"

Wilson rolled off an 11-game winning streak before dropping its second game of the season, this time to nation-

PREVIOUS WINNERS

Previous final No. 1 teams in the Baseball America/National High School Baseball Coaches Association Top 50 poll:

1992—Westminster Christian HS, Miami
1993—Greenway HS, Phoenix
1994—Sarasota (Fla.) HS

1995—Germantown (Tenn.) HS
1996—Westminster Christian HS, Miami
1997—Jesuit HS, Tampa
1998—Vestavia Hills (Ala.) HS
1999—Lassiter HS, Marietta, Ga.
2000—Gloucester Catholic HS, Gloucester City, N.J.

2001—Seminole (Fla.) HS
2002—Elkins HS, Missouri City, Texas
2003—Chatsworth (Calif.) HS
2004—Chatsworth (Calif.) HS
2005—Russell County HS, Seale, Ala.
2006—The Woodlands (Texas) HS

Wilson High of Long Beach finished its season 32-3 and won the California Interscholastic Federation Southern Section Division I championship. The staff of Baseball America and the National High School Baseball Coaches Association unanimously voted Wilson High as the final No. 1 team in the 2007 Top 50 rankings. Records do not include ties.

Rank	School	Record	Accomplishment
1	Wilson HS, Long Beach	32-3	CIF DI Southern Section champion
2	Seton Hall Prep, West Orange, N.J.	32-1	State Non-Public A champion
3	Horizon HS, Scottsdale, Ariz.	31-3	State 5-A champion
4	Bishop Moore HS, Orlando	31-1	State 4-A champion
5	West Lauderdale HS, Collinsville, Miss.	38-2	State 4-A champion
6	Brophy Prep, Phoenix	30-4	State 5-A runner up
7	Lakewood (Calif.) HS	28-5	CIF DI Southern Section second round
8	Chatsworth (Calif.) HS	30-4	CIF DI L.A. City Section champion
9	James River HS, Midlothian, Va.	25-2	State 3-A champion
10	Palm Beach Gardens (Fla.) HS	25-4	State 6-A regional semifinalist
11	Moody HS, Corpus Christi, Texas	39-3	State 4-A champion
12	Winter Springs (Fla.) HS	26-2	State 6-A regional quarterfinalist
13	Cypress-Fairbanks HS, Cypress, Texas	32-7	State 5-A champion
14	Klein-Collins HS, Spring, Texas	36-6	State 5-A semifinalists
15	East Rutherford HS, Forest City, N.C.	31-2	State 2-A champion
16	Katy (Texas) HS	32-5	State 5-A regional quarterfinalist
17	South Caldwell HS, Hudson, N.C.	31-3	State 4-A champion
18	Barbe HS, Lake Charles, La.	35-5	State 5-A quarterfinalist
19	Sarasota (Fla.) HS	28-3	State 6-A champion
20	Monroe HS, Bronx	48-2	State public school Class A runner up
21	Cullman (Ala.) HS	48-7	State 5-A champion
22	Owasso (Okla.) HS	35-3	State 6-A champion
23	Auburn (Wash.) HS	24-3	State 3-A runner-up
24	Langham Creek HS, Houston	35-5	State 5-A regional semifinalist
25	Madison HS, Vienna, Va.	21-3	State 3-A regional semifinalist
26	Cartersville (Ga.) HS	26-4	Region 6 3-A champion
27	Pace (Fla.) HS	27-4	State 5-A semifinalist
28	Lexington (Ky.) Catholic HS	30-4	11th region finalist
29	Valley Christian HS, San Jose	33-4	CIF DI Central Coast Section champion
30	Dunwoody (Ga.) HS	34-4	State 3-A champion
31	Oakland HS, Murfreesboro, Tenn.	42-2	State 3-A sectional
32	Calvert Hall HS, Baltimore	33-0	MIAA A conference champion
33	Thousand Oaks (Calif.) HS	25-5	CIF DI Southern Section quarterfinalist
34	Calhoun (Ga.) HS	34-4	State 2-A runner-up
35	Bishop Gorman HS, Las Vegas	35-6	State 4-A champion
36	Chino (Calif.) HS	25-4	CIF Southern Section second round
37	Palm Beach Central HS, Wellington, Fla.	24-7	State 6-A regional finalist
38	Captain Shreve HS, Shreveport, La.	37-4	State 4-A runner-up
39	The Woodlands (Texas) HS	31-6	State 5-A region quarterfinalist
40	Greenbrier HS, Evans, Ga.	32-4	State 4-A champion
41	Bellaire (Texas) HS	31-3	State 5-A second round
42	Jordan HS, Sandy, Utah	23-4	State 5-A champion
43	Blue Springs (Mo.) HS	25-2	State 4-A champion
44	Cretin-Derham Hall HS, St. Paul, Minn.	26-4	State 3-A champion
45	Norwell HS, Ossian, Ind.	35-0	State 3-A champion
46	Notre Dame Academy, Middleburg, Va.	32-4	State D-I champion
47	New Trier HS, Winnetka, Ill.	30-4	State 2-A runner-up
48	Seaman HS, Topeka, Kan.	22-1	State 5-A runner-up
49	Connetquot HS, Bohemia, N.Y.	25-1	State public school AA quarterfinalist
50	Moeller HS, Cincinnati	27-4	District champion

ally-ranked Thousand Oaks (Calif.) High 7-4 in the Lions Easter Tournament, which featured five games in three days. But after a late-April setback in a rematch against conference rival and defending CIF Southern Section champion Lakewood (Calif.) High, which was ranked No. 4 at the time, Wilson never stumbled again, winning its last nine games and marching to the top of the CIF's most competitive section (California doesn't have a state playoff).

Along the way, the Bruins defeated a third-round draft pick in Simi Valley High senior righthander Nicholas Barnese, and then held a second-rounder, El Modena High first baseman Freddie Freeman, to 0-for-3 with a walk.

Traditional power Esperanza High was the hottest team in the region entering the postseason, and after knocking off Lakewood, Esperanza drew Wilson, with a date at Dodger Stadium on the line.

The Bruins found themselves on the ropes once again, falling behind 1-0 and again 3-1 before rallying in the bottom of the seventh to pull out a 5-4 win that Hall likened to, "one of those football games where whoever had the ball last was going to win."

Hall knew his team was built for success, and during its rigorous schedule, watched it develop the resolve it needed to match its ability. With Glynn stepping to the front of the rotation, as well as the clubhouse, all the other pieces fell in place. Junior Ray Hanson was the perfect complement to Glynn—a righthander with power stuff to go with Glynn's feel and command from the left side. Hanson went 9-0, 2.16

and led the team in innings (71) and strikeouts (77) while Glynn added nine wins and 72 strikeouts with 19 walks in 68 innings.

Kaesman and senior catcher Tyler Albright provided the heart of the order with thump, and senior second baseman Pat Radford reinvented himself, improving his approach at the plate tenfold from his junior season, to provide the lineup with balance.

But when the Bruins weren't out-executing their opponents, they could rely on superior talent with senior shortstop Ryan Dent and junior center fielder Aaron Hicks, who doubled as the team's closer.

Dent was one of the nation's best middle infield prospects who, before being drafted in the supplemental first-round by the Red Sox, capped his four-year varsity career with a .468 average, seven triples, 28 stolen bases and a mind-blowing 30-7 walk-strikeout ratio.

Hicks might be drafted higher than Dent in 2008. He was 44-for-45 in stolen bases, posted a .370 average and went 3-0 with three saves and 27 strikeouts in 19 innings on the mound, running his fastball up to 94 mph.

Junior third baseman Zach Wilson (.379-3-33) had committed to Arizona State before his junior season had ended, and Albright (.346-1-24) headed to Harvard to play in the Ivy League.

Glynn was also bound for the East Coast, and opted not to sign with the Devil Rays, who drafted him in the 46th round, choosing instead to pitch and play outfield for Connecticut beginning in the spring of 2008.

As news spread about Wilson's national ranking, the buzz in the community heightened. Each of Wilson's playoff games were packed with hundreds of fans, and eventually the team brought home Wilson's fourth CIF sectional title, the first since 1957. Four times in the last nine years, Wilson played for the section title, but came away empty each time.

But this year's edition would not be deterred from the task at hand, and can now make up for celebration time lost along the way.

Tumultuous Conclusion

The series of events that led to Wilson landing in the No. 1 spot in the poll was as unpredictable as it was intriguing, and made the 2007 high school season one of the more entertaining finishes in recent memory. The preseason No. 1 team, Seton Hall Prep (West Orange, N.J.), held the top spot in the poll until stumbling in a mid-May game against Roxbury High (Succasunna, N.J.), and the loss proved to be costly. Behind the powerful right arm of Rick Porcello, the Pirates went on to win their third consecutive Non-Public Class A state championship and finished the season with a 32-1 record and a No. 2 ranking.

Seton Hall Prep defeated St. Joseph's High (Metuchen) 10-1 behind Porcello's complete-game five-hitter, just two days after he was drafted in the first round by the Tigers.

A first-team All-American in the pre- and postseason and Gatorade's national player of the year, Porcello finished his senior season 10-0, 1.18 with 112 strikeouts and 15 walks in 71 innings. Seton Hall Prep's No. 2 starter, senior righthander Evan Danieli, went 11-0, 0.45, tying the school record for wins in a season. He went on to Notre Dame after graduating. The Pirates had a 1.53 team ERA and a .353 team average.

Seton Hall's lone loss came one day before Arizona's 5-A championship game was played, opening the door for Phoenix power Brophy Prep to claim the top spot with a win against its archrival, Horizon High (Scottsdale, Ariz.),

East snaps three-game losing streak in fifth-annual Aflac Classic

On a field full of the most talented rising senior high school players in the country, the most fundamental skill escaped them.

The East scored two runs on three walks, a wild pitch and a passed ball in the ninth inning, then took the lead on a sacrifice fly to claim a 5-4 victory over the West in the fifth annual Aflac Classic at Tony Gwynn Field in San Diego Aug. 12, 2007.

Tim Beckham's sac fly was his second of the game, and the shortstop from Griffin (Ga.) High also walked and drove in a third run with an eighth-inning triple on his way to MVP honors.

Nine of the 14 pitchers to appear in the matchup between the nation's top rising high school seniors hit 90 mph or better, and showed good command in what was generally a well played contest in front of a sellout crowd on the campus of San Diego State.

West righthander Gerrit Cole (Lutheran High, Orange, Calif.) touched 96 mph in an 11-pitch third inning that included two strikeouts, and fellow righthanders Tim Melville (Holt High, Wentzville, Mo.), Ryan O'Sullivan (Valhalla High, El Cajon, Calif.), B.J. Hermsen (West Delaware High, Manchester, Iowa) and Bubba Meyer (Greensburg, Ind., High) were among the West pitchers to show an impressive combination of stuff and feel for pitching.

An East hitter didn't make hard contact until the sixth inning, and West pitchers allowed just three baserunners the first three trips through the order.

Thanks to the late East rally, Beckham stole MVP honors from West catcher Kyle Skipworth (Patriot High, Riverside, Calif.), who drove a ball deep to right field for a sacrifice fly in his first at-bat before ripping a two-run home run over the right-center field fence that gave the West a 3-0 lead in the third inning.

It all unraveled in the top of the ninth when West righthander/outfielder Aaron Hicks (Wilson High, Long Beach) struggled with his command in his first pitching appearance in almost two months.

Hicks, who had been slowed by a sore shoulder, touched 93 mph and flashed a nasty split-finger fastball, as well as an 82-83 mph breaking ball—some of the best raw stuff on display—but 20 of his 32 pitches were balls, including the two wild pitches and passed ball that allowed the East to tie it.

Beckham ended the drama when he sliced a 93 mph Hicks fastball to right field, to push across the go-ahead run with his second sac fly.

"I battled him to a full count and had seen everything he had, so there was no way he was striking me out at that point," Beckham said. "This is so much more than a showcase. It's an event where you face off against the best players from all over the country."

which entered the showdown ranked seventh. Instead, Brophy (30-4) lost 9-6 and fell to No. 6. Horizon, which finished its season 31-3, was ranked No. 3.

It was the Huskies' second state title in three years, and avenged the 2006 state title game loss, an 11-1 whitewashing that Brophy Prep celebrated over Horizon.

Horizon coach Eric Kibler said the '06 championship game, as well as losses in two of three meetings against Brophy Prep during the regular season this year, served as additional incentive. "They were ready to go," Kibler said. "The crowd was huge and it was a lot of fun."

So with Seton Hall and Brophy stubbing their toes, the door was ajar for one of a handful of Texas teams to climb to the top of the polls. The Lone Star State featured at least three teams that had a shot at a national title at the outset of the playoffs, but the picture quickly blew up.

Katy (Texas) High took the No. 1 ranking into the regional quarterfinals, only to lose 1-0 and 6-0 in a best-of-three series against then-No. 11 Langham Creek High of Houston.

Langham Creek's rise was thwarted a week later when it lost a 9-8 heartbreaker in the decisive game of a best-of-three series against Kingwood (Texas) High.

With junior outfielder Robbie Grossman setting the table and a trio of pitchers carrying the workload on the mound, Cy-Fair High (Cypress, Texas) won its final 27 games of the season, culminating with a 6-1 victory against South High (Harlingen) to prevail as Texas' 5-A champs. The state title was the first in the school's history, snapping a 27-year dry spell for Cy-Fair coach Woody Champagne and earning the Bobcats a No. 13 ranking in the BA/NHSBCA Top 50 poll, the highest ranking of any Texas school this year.

Titlists Arise From All Classifications

■ A pair of precocious juniors led their team to a state title in a lower class of the topsy-turvy Texas playoffs. Rogers High junior righthander Taylor Jungmann tossed six innings of one-hit, shutout ball in the 2-A semifinals in a 9-2 victory against Blanco High in 95-degree temperatures at Dell Diamond in Round Rock. Jungmann improved his record to 13-0, 0.40 on the season, including a perfect 5-0 mark in the playoffs.

Because of an ankle injury to Rogers' No. 2 pitcher Alan Valenzuela, Rogers was forced to go to its bullpen, trailing 4-1 in the title tilt against Hooks High. State tournament MVP Ricky Brenek answered the call by throwing five shutout innings of relief, and Rogers came from behind for an 8-4 victory to claim the state title.

"We know we're going to win when (Jungmann) pitches, but we didn't always use him every chance we could throughout the season," Rogers coach Craig Coheley said. "Having sat Taylor out during the year and using the other kids paid big dividends, because those guys were ready. It saved us."

With an enrollment of about 225 students, Rogers (36-2) is one of the state's smallest 2-A schools, yet it has racked up 109 wins in the past four years. Jungmann transferred to Georgetown (Texas) High for his senior season, however.

■ Two Corpus Christi prep baseball powerhouses, Moody and Calallen High, met in a much-anticipated three-game series in the area (second) round of the Texas 4-A playoffs. Moody, which appeared in the 5-A final three times in the last five years, leaving victorious in 2005, moved down to the 4-A classification because of enrollment qualifications in 2007.

That meant Calallen, one of the state's 4-A juggernauts

Prep prospects battle in Cape Classic

WAREHAM, Mass.

Spillane Field hosted the Baseball Express Cape Cod High School Classic, giving scouts and college coaches a look at some of the marquee players in the prep class of 2008. Fans who couldn't make it to Wareham could also get a look, as the game was broadcast live on MLB.com.

MIKE JANES

L.J. Hoes

The Baseball Factory team scored four times in a sloppy seventh inning to secure a 6-5 win over the Team One squad, but much of the intrigue happened early in the action. Team One's Pablo Bermudez (Miami Springs, Fla., High) took Baseball Factory starter Quinton Miller (Shawnee High, Medford, N.J.) deep to left field to lead off the ballgame, but Miller showed impressive poise, bouncing back to retire the next six batters to end his outing—four of them via the strikeout.

Two-way star Jordan Swagerty (Prestonwood Christian Academy, Plano, Texas) earned most outstanding player honors for Team One after getting the start on the mound, allowing just an unearned run and a hit in two innings of work, then adding a pair of singles later in the game. And athletic outfielder L.J. Hoes (St. John's College High, Washington, D.C.) took home most outstanding player honors for the victorious Baseball Factory team after reaching base three times and showing off speed and arm strength in the outfield.

"This is a tremendous thing for me, just to build more confidence and know that I can go out with these players and compete real well," Hoes said. "The players here are just tremendous—some of the top players in the country, possibly pro guys or all-Americans next year."

—AARON FITT

for years, had a new kid on the block, and although it was just the area round, for one weekend in May, Southeast Texas was bedlam.

More than 6,900 fans packed Whataburger Field, the home of the Double-A Corpus Christi Hooks for the series finale, and the three-game total attendance was 18,037.

Calallen, which was ranked No. 43 in the preseason Top 50, struck first to win the series opener 4-3, but Moody had the last laugh.

"We told them we weren't ready to go (home)," Moody coach Corky Gallegos said. "We weren't ready to let go of their hard work and investment. They're a special, coachable group."

Game Two went to Moody—a 4-3 victory in 10 dramatic innings. Moody's nine-hole hitter, Andrew Perez, belted a home run to tie the game 2-2, then Ronnie Flores extended his 29-game hitting streak with the game-winning single in the 10th.

"The atmosphere was electric," Gallegos said. "It's a dream to have as a player. Everybody was out to watch it."

Moody polished off Calallen 8-1 the following day to advance, and went on to win the 4-A championship.

■ John Lowery has coached Jefferson High (Shenandoah Junction, W.Va.) to each of the baseball program's 998 wins since it was started in 1973. Over the years, it'd be understandable if Lowery's nine state titles started running together, but the veteran coach was savoring his latest one in 2007 just as much as the previous eight.

"They all have their own things you remember," Lowery said. "The first one (in 1979) always stands out, and the one in '88 because my sons were on the team."

After losing five starters off the 2006 state quarterfinalist squad, 2007 didn't figure to mark another title run. But the new-look lineup that was anchored by senior third baseman Drew Stevens developed quicker than Lowery anticipated.

Stevens drove in six runs to spark a nine-run first inning that paced the Cougars' 11-4 win over Wilson High (Beckley, W.Va.) in the 3-A title game.

Lowery's 998 wins rank him sixth among active coaches and 10th all-time. His career record is 998-262-3.

■ A three-run homer from junior outfielder Seth Baldwin proved to be plenty to lead East Rutherford High (Forest City, N.C.) to North Carolina's 2-A title and a final No. 15 ranking in the BA/NHSBCA Top 50. The Cavaliers (31-2) defeated two-time defending 2-A champion North Lenoir High (La Grange, N.C.) 8-1 in the decisive game of the best-of-three championship series.

■ Utah's second-largest classification championship turned out to be a fitting end to the prolific high school career of well-decorated senior lefthander Tanner Robles. Robles, who committed to Oregon State, put a wrap on his perfect prep career when he scored the game-winning run in Cottonwood High's (Salt Lake City) 8-7 win in the 4-A championship game. The title was the third straight for the Colts.

Robles tossed a complete-game in a 7-3 victory against Mountain Crest High (East Hyrum) in the semifinals, his final pitching appearance, capping his career with a 33-0 record in four seasons on the varsity squad.

■ After a lengthy career as a head high school coach in Georgia, Allan Dyer quickly constructed a state power in Colorado. Cherokee Trail High (Aurora) defeated Denver's Jefferson High 10-4 to capture the state 4-A title in just the school's third season with a varsity team. The Cougars (24-3) battled back after falling to West High (Greeley) 7-4 in the second round of the double elimination state tournament.

Heart Of The Country

On Jan. 8, 2007, Brent Warren celebrated his 17th birthday as most teenagers do when it falls on a school day. He woke up, got dressed and went to class. But unlike most 17-year-olds, Warren was overjoyed to have the chance to go to school, even if it was his birthday.

It was his first day back at Xavier High in Cedar Rapids, Iowa, in almost a month, and the first time in nine weeks his life seemed back to normal.

On Nov. 1 a routine physical before the start of basketball season revealed that Warren had a congenital heart condition. An exceptional athlete and one of the nation's top baseball prospects, Warren was told he could no longer

Iowa prep outfielder Brent Warren overcame open-heart surgery during his junior year

play sports. He would require open-heart surgery.

"Here I was, a high school kid living in the high school world, just going to school and enjoying life. And a bomb is dropped like this," Warren said.

Warren and his parents spent the next month going from one doctor to the next, gathering information and opinions on the best way to treat his heart condition. He had a bicuspid aortic valve, meaning the valve had not developed normally and was restricting blood flow to his body.

They discovered his heart had a second flaw—coarctation of his aorta, a more serious, less common condition that, in combination with the other ailment, would likely lead to an aneurism.

The Warrens flew to the Mayo Clinic in Minnesota, where Dr. Thoralf Sundt performed an aortic bypass. The surgery went well, and Warren's aortic valve was repaired rather than replaced.

But as Warren lay in his hospital bed the day after Christmas, he prepared himself for the long-term prognosis, expecting to hear that his dream of playing major league baseball would have to remain just that, and that his heart would never be stable enough to allow for significant cardiovascular activity.

"The doctor came in to go over the data with him and the first thing Brent said was, 'Doctor, please, you have to tell me, am I going to play again?,' " said Brent's father Chris Warren. "When the doctor looked him straight in the face and said he thought there remained a chance he would (play again), he literally almost fainted.

"He sat and cried for 15 minutes. Amazingly, it was the first time he had cried throughout the entire process."

Warren lost 20 pounds from his 6-foot-2 frame, but made it back to the field for his junior season, and led Xavier High to a second 3-A state-championship game appearance, only this time losing an 8-0 decision to West Delaware High (Manchester, Iowa).

Moustakas makes history

If you weren't there, all you need to do is listen as Jason Hisey tells the story. The head coach of USA Baseball's 2006 junior national team and a former Team USA player himself, Hisey was in the third-base dugout during an elimination game of last year's World Junior Championships against Cuba at Huelga Stadium in Sancti Spiritus, Cuba, when Mike Moustakas made "the catch."

With Cuba's best hitter up and Team USA grasping for confidence after an unconvincing showing in the tournament's pool play, Moustakas, an infielder by trade, tracked a deep fly ball to the warning track in left field, gathered himself, and leaped to reach over the wall and steal a three-run home run from Cuban phenom Dayan Viciedo.

"You should have seen him," Hisey likes to recall of Viciedo, the slugger who stopped in the midst of his home run trot when Moustakas made the catch. "It was one of those moments you don't forget."

The play shifted momentum of the game, which Team USA went on to win, and exemplifies the type of player Moustakas has always known he is, but some were reluctant to acknowledge during most of his unprecedented high school career.

The senior from Chatsworth (Calif.) High carried the momentum of his performance in Cuba into his senior season, belting a California single-season record 24 home runs, which amounted to 52 for his career, also a state record.

"Moose," as he's known around the field, was the first high school player drafted in 2007 when he was taken with the second pick by the Royals. Moustakas was selected as the L.A. City Section player of the year for the second straight year, and trumped that honor by becoming just the second player from the Golden State to be named Baseball America's High School Player of the Year.

"One of his last games I saw, he hit two long home runs," Royals scouting director Deric Ladnier said. "It was almost as if you expected it to happen, and it did."

Expecting The Best

Despite Moustakas' track record of performance as an underclassman in high school, the expectations of his professional potential were relatively modest as he prepared for his final campaign. Although he's manned the middle of the diamond as the Chancellors' shortstop since he was a freshman in 2004, somewhere in just about every scouting report on the 5-foot-11, 175-pounder was a line about his pudgy body and lack of a true position.

The summer prior to his senior season when he appeared in the Area Code Games in Long Beach, Moustakas moved from shortstop to third base to catcher, and even first base. While he showed some promise at the plate, there was not a consensus he'd hit enough to profile as an everyday player at a corner infield position. He was even considered his team's second-best player, behind third baseman Matt Dominguez.

All along, Moustakas was quietly confident, and this spring the masses began to concur.

"It was one of the few times that (the scouting staff) sat around the room and we felt this guy was going to hit, and he was going to hit big, and everyone in the room felt strongly about that," Ladnier said.

Hitting big became a specialty of Moustakas' as soon as he stepped onto the field for Chatsworth's varsity squad his freshman season. He quickly carved out a spot in the Chancellors' starting lineup and batted .321-2-19 with 23 walks, 10 strikeouts and nine doubles while starting all 35 games for Chatsworth's second of back-to-back national championship teams that went 35-0.

He worked diligently on his conditioning and when he came out for his final high school season, weighed in at 6-feet, 190 pounds and matched his uncanny knack for hitting with the physical tools—including an outstanding arm that allowed him to throw high-90s fastballs as Chatsworth's closer—to dominate his competition.

On May 8 against El Camino Real High (Woodland Hills, Calif.), Moustakas slammed a first-inning home run over the right-field fence for the 48th of his career, breaking the state record set by John Drennen, a first-team All-American in 2005 out of San Diego's Rancho Bernardo High and now an Indians farmhand.

A week later, Chris Walston's (El Capitan High, Lakeside) single-season state record came tumbling down when Moustakas drilled his 22nd home run, another tape-measure shot that sailed over two chain-link fences and landed on the windshield of the opposing team's right fielder's Toyota Corolla.

Moustakas would add two more down the stretch, helping Chatsworth win another City Section championship and finish ranked No. 8 nationally. He finished his senior season 56-for-97 (.577) with seven doubles, four triples and 59 RBIs. He walked 28 times and was called out on strikes just twice.

You might not have been there to see it, but his story is one you don't forget.

PREVIOUS WINNERS

1992—Preston Wilson, of-rhp, Bamberg-Ehrhardt (S.C.) HS
1993—Trot Nixon, of/lhp, New Hanover HS, Wilmington, N.C.
1994—Doug Million, lhp, Sarasota (Fla.) HS
1995—Ben Davis, c, Malvern (Pa.) Prep
1996—Matt White, rhp, Waynesboro Area (Pa.) HS
1997—Darnell McDonald, of, Cherry Creek HS, Englewood, Colo.
1998—Drew Henson, 3b/rhp, Brighton (Mich.) HS
1999—Josh Hamilton, of/lhp, Athens Drive HS, Raleigh
2000—Matt Harrington, rhp, Palmdale (Calif.) HS
2001—Joe Mauer, c, Cretin-Derham Hall, St. Paul, Minn.
2002—Scott Kazmir, lhp, Cypress Falls HS, Houston
2003—Jeff Allison, rhp, Veterans Memorial HS, Peabody, Mass.
2004—Homer Bailey, rhp, LaGrange (Texas) HS
2005—Justin Upton, ss, Great Bridge HS, Chesapeake, Va.
2006—Adrian Cardenas, ss/2b, Monsignor Pace HS, Opa Locka, Fla.

BILL MITCHELL TONY FARLOW LARRY GOREN DAVID STONER

Tim Alderson **Justin Jackson** **Matt Dominguez** **Matt Harvey** **Jake Smolinski**

FIRST TEAM

POS., PLAYER, SCHOOL	CLASS	B-T	HT.	WT.	AVG	AB	R	H	2B	3B	HR	RBI	SB	DRAFTED/COLLEGE
C Yasmani Grandal, Miami Springs (Fla.) HS	Sr.	B-R	6-2	205	.433	90	31	39	8	0	13	46	0	Red Sox (27)/Miami
IF Kevin Ahrens, Memorial HS, Houston	Sr.	B-R	6-2	180	.426	108	47	46	10	1	11	43	7	Blue Jays (1)
IF Matt Dominguez, Chatsworth (Calif.) HS	Sr.	R-R	6-2	185	.443	106	46	47	9	2	13	42	1	Marlins (1)
IF Mike Moustakas, Chatsworth (Calif.) HS	Sr.	L-R	6-0	190	.577	97	49	56	7	4	24	59	4	Royals (1)
IF Josh Vitters, Cypress (Calif.) HS	Sr.	R-R	6-3	195	.390	77	30	30	6	2	9	29	8	Cubs (1)
OF Wendell Fairley, George County-Lucedale (Miss.) HS	Sr.	L-R	6-0	190	.538	91	26	49	13	3	9	36	13	Giants (1)
OF Jason Heyward, Henry County HS, McDonough, Ga.	Sr.	L-L	6-2	198	.520	50	42	29	7	3	8	29	17	Braves (1)
OF Ben Revere, Lexington (Ky.) Catholic HS	Sr.	L-R	5-9	152	.516	91	47	47	10	5	9	41	24	Twins (1)
UT Michael Main, Deland (Fla.) HS	Sr.	R-R	6-1	171	.457	105	38	48	8	6	3	22	24	Rangers (1)

	CLASS	B-T	HT.	WT.	W	L	ERA	G	SV	IP	H	BB	SO	DRAFTED
P Tim Alderson, Horizon HS, Scottsdale, Ariz.	Sr.	R-R	6-7	208	12	0	1.07	14	2	72	46	5	111	Giants (1)
P Blake Beavan, Irving (Texas) HS	Sr.	R-R	6-7	210	9	2	0.19	11	0	73	23	4	139	Rangers (1)
P Madison Bumgarner, South Caldwell HS, Hudson, N.C.	Sr.	R-L	6-5	220	11	2	1.05	14	1	86	45	11	143	Giants (1)
P Jarrod Parker, Norwell HS, Ossian, Ind.	Sr.	R-R	6-1	175	12	0	0.10	12	0	70	25	11	116	Diamondbacks (1)
P Rick Porcello, Seton Hall Prep, West Orange, N.J.	Sr.	R-R	6-5	188	10	0	1.18	14	2	71	48	15	112	Tigers (1)
UT Michael Main, Deland (Fla.) HS	Sr.	R-R	6-1	171	12	1	1.02	13	0	82	51	13	121	Rangers (1)

SECOND TEAM

POS., PLAYER, SCHOOL	CLASS	B-T	HT.	WT.	AVG	AB	R	H	2B	3B	HR	RBI	SB	DRAFTED
C Devin Mesoraco, Punxsutawney (Pa.) HS	Sr.	R-R	6-1	195	.429	56	32	24	7	1	5	17	6	Reds (1)
IF Drew Cumberland, Pace HS, Milton, Fla.	Sr.	L-R	5-10	170	.518	81	35	42	9	1	3	24	17	Padres (1S)
IF Justin Jackson, Roberson HS, Asheville, N.C.	Sr.	R-R	6-2	175	.520	98	53	51	12	5	12	39	21	Blue Jays (1S)
IF Pete Kozma, Owasso (Okla.) HS	Sr.	R-R	6-1	180	.522	113	56	59	21	6	11	55	14	Cardinals (1)
IF Nick Noonan, Parker HS, San Diego	Sr.	L-R	6-1	175	.540	124	64	67	15	10	15	55	42	Giants (1S)
OF Gary Brown, Diamond Bar HS, Walnut, Calif.	Sr.	R-R	6-0	170	.612	80	44	49	9	2	4	21	15	A's(12)/Cal State Full.
OF Kentrail Davis, Theodore (Ala.) HS	Sr.	L-R	5-9	195	.410	78	38	32	3	6	6	22	29	Rockies (14)/Tenn.
OF Garret Nash, Jordan HS, Sandy, Utah	Sr.	B-R	6-0	180	.520	77	53	40	15	4	8	33	46	Rangers (4)/Ore.State
UT Will Middlebrooks, Liberty-Eylau HS, Texarkana, Texas	Sr.	R-R	6-4	215	.555	110	52	6	22	2	7	48	22	Red Sox (5)

	CLASS	B-T	HT.	WT.	W	L	ERA	G	SV	IP	H	BB	SO	DRAFTED
P Kyle Blair, Los Gatos (Calif.) HS	Sr.	R-R	6-3	200	9	2	0.31	14	0	90	38	13	147	Dodgers (5)/San Diego
P Matt Harvey, Fitch HS, Groton, Conn.	Sr.	R-R	6-4	190	6	1	0.68	8	0	51	25	16	106	Angles (3)/N.C.
P Neil Ramirez, Kempsville (Va.) HS	Sr.	R-R	6-3	190	7	2	1.12	14	1	69	44	29	94	Rangers (1S)
P Josh Smoker, Calhoun (Ga.) HS	Sr.	L-L	6-2	190	13	0	0.95	14	0	74	32	30	154	Nationals (1S)
P Chris Withrow, Midland (Texas) Christian HS	Sr.	R-R	6-3	195	8	1	1.32	8	3	58	40	8	90	Dodgers (1)
UT Will Middlebrooks, Liberty-Eylau HS, Texarkana, Texas	Sr.	R-R	6-4	215	13	0	0.86	15	0	81	44	12	147	Red Sox (5)

THIRD TEAM

POS., PLAYER, SCHOOL	CLASS	B-T	HT.	WT.	AVG	AB	R	H	2B	3B	HR	RBI	SB	DRAFTED
C Travis D'Arnaud, Lakewood (Calif.) HS	Sr.	R-R	6-0	180	.433	104	42	45	11	4	7	52	8	Phillies (1S)
IF Ryan Dent, Wilson HS, Long Beach	Sr.	R-R	5-10	180	.468	94	44	44	7	7	0	29	28	Red Sox (1S)
IF Hunter Morris, Grissom HS, Huntsville, Ala.	Sr.	L-R	6-4	200	.476	107	67	51	8	3	13	44	19	Red Sox (2)/Auburn
IF Jake Smolinski, Boylan Catholic HS, Rockford, Ill.	Sr.	R-R	6-0	185	.562	89	53	50	14	0	9	43	15	Nationals (2)
IF John Tolisano, Estero (Fla.) HS	Sr.	B-R	6-0	190	.518	83	43	43	10	3	8	42	19	Blue Jays (2)
OF Denny Almonte, Florida Christian HS, Miami	Sr.	B-R	6-1	173	.418	67	34	28	6	0	10	31	24	Mariners (2)
OF Chad Jones, Southern Lab HS, Baton Rouge, La.	Sr.	L-L	6-3	222	.577	52	26	30	4	6	6	24	15	Astros (13)/Lou.State
OF David Mailman, Providence HS, Charlotte	Sr.	L-L	6-1	170	.541	61	41	33	6	1	14	33	14	Red Sox (7)
UT Derek Dietrich, Saint Ignatius HS, Cleveland	Sr.	L-R	6-2	195	.486	72	29	35	9	0	10	43	9	Astros (3)/Ga. Tech

	CLASS	B-T	HT.	WT.	W	L	ERA	G	SV	IP	H	BB	SO	DRAFTED
P Jonathan Bachanov, University HS, Orlando	Sr.	R-R	6-5	220	9	2	0.37	11	0	65	28	19	103	Angels (1S)
P Jack McGeary, Roxbury Latin HS, West Roxbury, Mass.	Sr.	L-L	6-3	200	5	1	0.88	7	0	40	11	21	80	Nationals (6)
P Scott Moviel, St. Edward HS, Berea, Ohio	Sr.	R-R	6-10	245	6	2	1.26	11	1	50	40	9	102	Mets (2)
P Rob Rasmussen, Poly HS, Pasadena	Sr.	L-L	5-11	160	12	0	0.33	18	1	86	26	33	200	Dodgers (27)/UCLA
P Nathan Vineyard, Woodland HS, Cartersville, Ga.	Sr.	L-L	6-3	200	9	3	1.19	12	0	71	12	12	130	Mets (1S)
UT Derek Dietrich, Saint Ignatius HS, Cleveland	Sr.	L-R	6-2	195	0	0	0.12	7	4	8	1	4	17	Astros (3)/Ga. Tech

★college listed for players choosing to attend

HIGH SCHOOL BASEBALL

Youth Team USA finishes first; juniors take bronze

Catcher Luke Bailey's two-run home run capped a four-run first inning in the youth national team's 8-2 defeat of Brazil in the championship game of its annual international tournament, which was held this year in Barquisimeto, Venezuela.

The youth team, made up of 16-and-under players, went undefeated in six games at the event, capturing a gold medal in international play for the second year in a row.

Bailey, a sophomore from Troup County High in LaGrange, Ga., was one of six Team USA regulars to bat at least .400, outscoring Mexico, Brazil, Cuba and Colombia 75-13. Second baseman Justin Charles (Elk Grove, Calif., High) led the team with a .688 average (11-for-16) and 10 RBIs on his way to tournament MVP honors. Center fielder Andrew Aplin (Vanden High, Fairfield, Calif.) was another offensive catalyst.

Zach Lee, one of three sophomores named to the youth roster, picked up his second win of the tournament by holding Brazil to one earned run on six hits in five innings of the title tilt. The righthander from McKinney (Texas) High struck out eight in the victory, including the first four batters he faced, and was 2-0, 0.90 with seven hits allowed and 14 strikeouts in 10 innings overall.

The event originally included teams from 10 countries and was scheduled as a World Youth Championship event. However, the International Baseball Federation rescinded its affiliation because of political differences between the governments of Taiwan and the host country, Venezuela. Taiwan's youth team did not receive visas from Venezuela and therefore could not participate in the event, leading to IBAF's decision.

USA Baseball's junior national team, a group of 18-and-under players, fell short in its bid for a gold medal at the Pan American Junior Championship in Ixtapa, Mexico.

In a battle of unbeaten teams, Cuba blanked host Mexico 7-0 to capture the gold medal and defend its 2005 title.

The U.S. junior national team (4-2) capitalized on six errors to defeat Canada 6-2 in the bronze-medal game, qualifying for the 2008 World Junior Championship in Edmonton, Alberta.

Team USA rolled to wins over Panama, Puerto Rico and Aruba in its first three games of the tournament by a combined score of 39-5 before dropping successive one-run decisions to Mexico and Cuba.

Team USA was two outs away from clinching a spot in the gold-medal game when Cuba rallied for three runs in the bottom of the ninth inning to defeat the U.S. 3-2 in the semifinals. Shortstop Adenis Echeverria drove in the game-winning run with a double to left field off U.S. lefty Nick Maronde (Lexington, Ky., Catholic High).

Senior righthander Ryan Weber (Clearwater, Fla., Central Catholic High) struck out 14 and walked one in 16 innings, and carried a shutout into the ninth against Cuba.

"We flirted with trouble the whole game and were able to make a pitch or make a play to get out of it," junior national team general manager Ray Darwin said. "They're eight and nine-hole hitters were very good, and when those guys got on in the ninth, it set them up, and finally they got the hits to go ahead.

"It's sickening to think about it."

Senior outfielder Robbie Grossman (Cy-Fair High, Cypress, Texas) paced the U.S. offense with eight hits.

AMATEUR/YOUTH CHAMPIONS 2007

USA BASEBALL HEADQUARTERS: Durham, N.C.

JUNIOR TEAM (18-and-Under)

Event	Site	Champion	Runner-up
Tournament of Stars	Cary, N.C.	USA Stars	AABC
COPABE Junior Pan-Am Championship	Ixtapa, Mexico	Cuba	Mexico

YOUTH TEAM (16-and-Under)

Event	Site	Champion	Runner-up
IBAF World Youth Championship^	Barquisimeto, Venez.	USA	Brazil
USA Junior Olympics—East	Palm Beach County, Fla.	*Palm Beach (PAL)	Florida Pokers
USA Junior Olympics—West	Peoria/Sunrise, Ariz.	ABD Bulldogs 16	Norcal Black Sox 16

^Event not sanctioned by IBAF as World Championship
*Co-champions declared

ALL-AMERICAN AMATEUR BASEBALL ASSOCIATION (AAABA) HEADQUARTERS: Zanesville, Ohio

Event	Site	Champion	Runner-up
World Series (21-and-Under)	Johnstown, Penn.	Youse's Maryland Orioles	McLean (Va.) Raiders

AMATEUR ATHLETIC UNION (AAU) HEADQUARTERS: LAKE BUENA VISTA, FLA.

Event	Site	Champion	Runner-up
10-and-Under (65-foot)	Charlotte	Virginia Storm	Raleigh Wildcats
11-and-Under (70-foot)	Lake Buena Vista, Fla.	Blue Springs (Mo.) Classics	Norwalk (Calif.) Stingrays
12-and-Under	Newport News, Va.	Mt. Juliet (Tenn.) Bearcats	Tidewater (Va.) Drillers
13-and-Under (90-foot)	Myrtle Beach, S.C.	Carolina Angels	Virginia Diamonds
14-and-Under (90-foot)	Sarasota, Fla.	Tampa Smokers	Southwest Florida Dirtbags
15-and-Under	Kingsport, Tenn.	Tri State Arsenal Blue	Carolina Avalanche
16-and-Under	Knoxville, Tenn.	East Cobb (Ga.) Astros	Palm Beach County (Fla.) PAL
18-and-Under	Orlando	Chet Lemon's Juice	Homeplate Yankees

AMERICAN AMATEUR BASEBALL CONGRESS (AABC) HEADQUARTERS: Farmington, N.M.

Event	Site	Champion	Runner-up
Gil Hodges	Brooklyn, N.Y	.Maryland Orioles	Georgia Heat
Pee Wee Reese (12 & U)	Toa Baja, Puerto Rico	Puerto Rico Arevica	Maryland Harford Sox
Sandy Koufax (13 & U)	Battle Creek, Mich.	Spring Creek (N.Y.) Black Sox	Utica (N.Y.) Falcons
Sandy Koufax (14 & U)	Douglasville, Ga.	Southern California Bombers	Dallas Texas Mustangs
Mickey Mantle (15 & U)	Owasso, Okla.	Nortex (Texas)	Texas Hurricanes
Mickey Mantle (16 & U)	McKinney, Texas	Midland (Ohio) Braves	California Rockies
Connie Mack (18 & U)	Farmington, N.M.	Midland (Ohio) Braves	East Cobb (Ga.) Yankees
Stan Musial (open)	Huntsville, Texas	Lombard (Ill.) Orioles	Northwest Wildcats

AMERICAN LEGION BASEBALL HEADQUARTERS: Indianapolis

Event	Site	Champion	Runner-up
World Series (19 & U)	Bartlesville, Okla.	Columbia, Tenn.	Eden Prairie, Minn.

BABE RUTH BASEBALL HEADQUARTERS: Trenton, N.J.

Event	Site	Champion	Runner-up
Cal Ripken (10 & U)	Vincennes, Ind.	Elk Grove, Calif.	Tillmans Corner, Ala.
Cal Ripken (11-12)	Van Buren, Ark.	South Lexington, Ky.	Scottsdale, Ariz.
13-year-old	Loudoun County, Va.	Tallahassee, Fla.	NW Bakersfield, Calif.
14-year-old	Glen Allen, Va.	Hamilton, Ariz.	Tallahassee, Fla.
13-15-year-olds	Andalusia, Ala.	Merrick, NY	Henderson County, Ky.
16-year-old	Bentonville, Ark.	Mobile, Ala.	Mid County, Texas
16-18-year-old	Newark, Ohio	San Gabriel Valley, Calif.	Denham Springs, La.

CONTINENTAL AMATEUR BASEBALL ASSOCIATION (CABA) HEADQUARTERS: Westerville, Ohio

Event	Site	Champion	Runner-up
9-and-Under	Crystal Lake, Ill.	Cincinnati Flames	Plainfield (Ill.) Diamond Kings
10-and-Under	Lynwood, Ill.	Region (Ind.) Redbirds	The Future , Ill.
11-and-Under	Crystal Lake, Ill.	Orlando Sparks National	Elk Grove Travelers, Ill.
12-and-Under	Cincinnati	Huntsville (Ala.) Gameday A's	Illinois Lightning
12-and-Under (wood)	Tulsa	Tulsa Hurricanes	Oilfield (Okla.) Heat
13-and-Under	Marion, Ohio	Naperville (Ill.) Renegades	Carolina Puerto Rico Angels
14-and-under (60-foot)	Lebanon, Tenn.	Columbus (Ohio) Cobras	Johnson City (Tenn.) Jr. Toppers
14-and-Under (54-foot)	Mentor/Painesville, Ohio	Mentor (Ohio) Vipers	Pennsylvania Golden Triangle
15-and-Under	Crystal Lake, Ill.	East Cobb (Ga.) Astros	Jefferson Parish , La.
16-and-Under	Marietta, Ga.	Columbus (Ohio) Cobras	Georgia Roadrunners
High school age	Euclid, Ohio	Brooklyn Bergen Beach	Hamlin Park (Ill.) Top Tier
18-and-Under (wood)	Charleston, S.C.	Columbus (Ohio) Sharks	Richmond Braves

LITTLE LEAGUE BASEBALL HEADQUARTERS: Williamsport, Pa.

Event	Site	Champion	Runner-up
Little League (11-12)	Williamsport, Pa.	Warner Robins, Ga.	Japan
Junior League (13-14)	Taylor, Mich.	Pearl City, Hi.	Makati City, Phillipines
Senior League (15-16)	Bangor, Me.	Cartersville, Ga.	Falcon, Venez.
Big League (17-18)	Easley, S.C.	Easley, S.C.	San Juan, P.R.

NATIONAL AMATEUR BASEBALL FEDERATION (NABF) HEADQUARTERS: Bowie, Md.

Event	Site	Champion	Runner-up
Freshman (12 & U)	Hopkinsville, Ky.	East Cobb (Ga.) Astros	Cincinnati Flames
Sophomore (14 & U)	Springboro, Oh.	Glen Cove (N.Y.) Cardinals	Home Lending Solutions (Ind.) Gators
Junior (16 & U)	Northville, Mich.	Greenbush-Schodack (N.Y.) Devilcats	Independence (Mo.) Hammers
High School (17 & U)	Northville, Mich.	Kinect (Ohio) Nationals	Chesapeke (Va.) Clippers
Senior (18 & U)	Jackson, Miss.	Houston Heat	Evansville (Ind.) Razorbacks
College (22 & U)	Rising Sun, Md.	Long Island (N.Y.) Astros	Lower Bucks (Pa.) Indians
Major (open)			

PERFECT GAME/WORLD WOOD BAT ASSOCIATION SUMMER CHAMPIONSHIPS HEADQUARTERS: Cedar Rapids, Iowa

Event	Site	Champion	Runner-up
14-and-Under	Marietta, Ga.	East Cobb (Ga.) Astros	NorCal Baseball
15-and-Under	Marietta, Ga.	East Cobb (Ga.) Astros	NorCal Black Sox
16-and-Under	Marietta, Ga.	Knoxville Yard	Rockdale (Ga.) Rhinos
17-and-Under	Marietta, Ga.	East Cobb (Ga.) Braves	Richmond (Va.) Braves
18-and-Under	Marietta, Ga.	Chet Lemon's Juice	South Charlotte Panthers

PONY BASEBALL HEADQUARTERS: Washington, Pa.

Event	Site	Champion	Runner-up
Mustang (9-10)	Irving, Texas	Santa Clarita, Calif.	Guasave, Mexico
Bronco (11-12)	Monterey, Calif.	Tamiami, Fla.	Walnut Valley, Calif.
Pony (13)	Chino Hills, Calif.	Simi, Calif.	Jefferson Parish, La.
Pony (13-14)	Washington, Pa.	Trujillo Alta, P.R.	Long Beach, Calif.
Colt (15-16)	Lafayette, Ind.	Levittown (Toa Boja) P.R.	Jurupa, Calif.
Palomino (17-18)	Rancho Cucamonga, Calif.	Levittown (Toa Boja) P.R.	Taiwan

REVIVING BASEBALL IN INNER CITIES (RBI) HEADQUARTERS: New York

Event	Site	Champion	Runner-up
Junior (13-15)	Los Angeles	Detroit	St. Petersburg, Fla.
Senior (16-18)	Los Angeles	Philadelphia	Los Angeles

DRAFT

New draft signing deadline pushes bonuses higher

BY JOHN MANUEL

In several ways, Major League Baseball's 2007 draft went exactly as scripted.

As expected, Vanderbilt lefthander David Price went No. 1 overall to the Devil Rays. He was one of a record-tying seven lefthanders drafted in first round, as the strongest position of the draft class was in full evidence.

And as predicted, the strongest high school draft class in years reversed a recent trend, as more prep players (17) were picked in the first round than collegians (13).

It all went down for the first time on television, as the draft's first round as well as most of the supplemental round was shown live on ESPN2.

It was a significant change from earlier drafts, which had been held with little or no fanfare with a conference call—and, in recent years, with the call streamed over the Internet. In this case, the draft actually became an event, held in an auditorium at Walt Disney World in Florida,

DAVID STONER

Vanderbilt lefthander David Price was no surprise as the No. 1 selection by the Devil Rays

YEAR-BY-YEAR BONUS PROGRESSION

Signing bonuses have grown exponentially since 1965, when the draft was instituted—to curtail the growth of signing bonuses. From a first-round average of less than $50,000 in the first several years of the draft, that average grew to more than $2 million by 2001. But Major League Baseball's efforts to curb bonuses in recent years—chiefly through setting recommended payments for each pick in the first 10 rounds—have slowed growth and even led to a decline in some years.

Following is a year-by-year breakdown of average first-round signing bonuses and the annual percentage change:

Year	Average	Change	Year	Average	Change
1965	$42,516	—	1987	$128,480	+10.5%
1966	$44,430	+4.5%	1988	$142,540	+10.9%
1967	$42,898	-3.4%	1989	$176,008	+23.5%
1968	$43,850	+2.2%	1990	$252,577	+43.5%
1969	$43,504	-0.8%	1991	$365,396	+44.7%
1970	$45,230	+3.9%	1992	$481,893	+31.9%
1971	$45,197	-0.1%	1993	$613,037	+27.2%
1972	$44,952	-0.5%	1994	$790,357	+28.9%
1973	$48,832	+8.6%	1995	$918,019	+16.1%
1974	$53,333	+9.2%	1996@	$944,400	+2.9%
1975	$49,333	-7.5%	1997	$1,325,536	+40.4%
1976	$49,631	+0.6%	1998	$1,637,667	+23.1%
1977	$48,813	-1.6%	1999	$1,809,767	+10.5%
1978	$67,892	+39.1%	2000	$1,872,586	+3.5%
1979	$68,094	+0.2%	2001	$2,154,280	+15.0%
1980	$74,025	+8.7%	2002	$2,106,793	-2.2%
1981	$78,573	+6.1%	2003	$1,765,667	-16.2%
1982	$82,615	+5.1%	2004	$1,958,448	+10.9%
1983	$87,236	+5.6%	2005	$2,018,000	+3.0%
1984	$105,392	+20.8%	2006	$1,933,333	-4.2%
1985	$118,115	+12.1%	2007	$2,098,083	+8.5%
1986	$116,300	-1.6%			

@ Does not include four loophole free agents.

NOTE: The signing bonus average for first-round picks from 1965-82 includes the value of college scholarship plans and incentive bonus plans, in addition to the cash bonus paid. From 1983 on, the amount represents only the cash bonus paid.

with the full complement of ESPN baseball personalities on hand, as well as some of the players who were considered likely first-round picks.

"It's a great day for us and this is such an important day," commissioner Bud Selig said. "This is a special event and we want to communicate that as best as possible to all of our fans. This is really a dramatic manifestation of how the sport has improved. This will get bigger and bigger."

Selig could have said the same thing about signing bonuses a little more than two months later. Despite MLB's determined (if not best) efforts, signing bonuses went up for first-round picks, as agents, players and even clubs used the new Aug. 15 signing deadline to get around the slot bonuses the commissioner's office recommended.

The new deadline, the most significant of several draft changes implemented as part of baseball's new Collective Bargaining Agreement, created a drop-dead date for draft negotiations for the first time, as anyone who hadn't signed by the deadline went back into the draft pool. It made for great media and fan commentary and great theater in mid-August, as most of the premium picks in the draft waited until the last minute to sign (or not). What's debatable is whether it made the draft process any better.

"I think the deadline helped, but it's also natural that things would gravitate toward the deadline," said Devil Rays general manager Andrew Friedman, whose Rays had the worst record in the majors again in 2007, and again hold the No. 1 overall pick in 2008. "We knew it was going to be expensive. And we knew it was going to wind up close to the deadline."

Price agreed to terms about six hours before the cutoff, signing a six-year major league contract that included a $5.6 million bonus and $8.25 million in guaranteed money, with incentives that could drive the total value to $11.25 million. The Baseball America College Player of the Year, Price led the nation with 194 strikeouts and just 31 walks in 133 innings while going 11-1, 2.63.

When Price signed, the Royals were still negotiating with the No. 2 overall pick, BA High School Player of the Year Mike Moustakas. No. 3 pick Josh Vitters (Cubs) and No. 5 pick Matt Wieters (Orioles), like Moustakas, cut their deals far closer to the deadline.

After holding out for a reported $7 million, Moustakas agreed to a $4 million bonus, about 10 minutes before the 11:59 p.m. deadline. The Royals were reluctant to go above a $3.15 million offer that they believed Moustakas' camp had agreed to on draft day, but in the end, GM Dayton Moore decided the Royals could pay California's all-time prep home run record holder what they paid Alex Gordon with the second overall pick in 2005.

No one in draft history has received quite the kind of bonus the Orioles gave to Wieters. Three minutes before the deadline, the Orioles still were uncertain whether the Georgia Tech All-American catcher would accept their $6 million offer, the second-largest bonus in draft history. He did, after reportedly seeking a major league deal worth more than $10 million.

But while Wieters' offer ranks second to Justin Upton's (Diamondbacks, 2005) on the all-time record ledger, Upton's $6.1 million bonus was payable over five years due to MLB's two-sport rules. Wieters' bonus actually is the largest in draft history in terms of present value. He made his pro debut in Hawaii Winter Baseball.

Leverage Lost

MLB designed the deadline to theoretically give some leverage to clubs by limiting extended holdouts. The commissioner's office also reduced its bonus recommendations for each slot in the first five rounds by 10 percent, with the anticipated effect of reducing bonuses across the board.

The opposite occurred, however. There were 184 picks in the first five rounds in 2007, and 171 of them signed, receiving an average bonus of $685,328. In 2006, 179 of the first 184 picks agreed to terms, getting an average bonus of $662,531. So despite the 10 percent reduction in slots, the bonuses rose 3 percent.

The increase was even more pronounced in the first round. This year's top 30 picks signed for an average of $2,098,083, up 9 percent from 2006 ($1,933,333). The 2007 average was the third-highest ever, trailing 2001 ($2,154,280) and 2002 ($2,106,793).

Several of the above-slot deals were done weeks before the deadline, but teams were reluctant to make them official. MLB can't officially punish any that don't toe the line, but no club wanted to be the first to draw the ire of the commissioner's office.

"We all knew there would be a lot of last-minute signings," Royals scouting director Deric Ladnier said. "I think we all knew there could be some sort of frenzy on the final day, but it's better to not have all the signings spread out through the fall and spring."

The deal that got the ball rolling belonged to New Jersey prep righthander Rick Porcello, a client of agent Scott Boras, who was rated the second-best pitcher in the draft behind Price. While Boras represented Moustakas

RECORD BREAKING BONUSES

Rick Monday, the No. 1 overall pick in baseball's first-ever draft in 1965, signed with the Athletics for $100,000—a bonus record that lasted for a decade. The mark has been broken several times since, most recently in 2005, when No. 1 overall choice Justin Upton received $6.1 million from the Diamondbacks.

The figures below represent cash bonuses and don't include guaranteed money from major league contracts, college scholarship plans or incentives. They also don't factor in discount rates for bonuses spread over multiple years for two-sport athletes, such as Upton. The list considers only players who signed with the clubs that drafted them and does not include the four loophole free agents from 1996. Among that group is former Devil Rays righthander Matt White, who established a bonus standard that still stands when he signed for $10.2 million.

Year	Player, Pos., Club (Round)	Bonus
1965	Rick Monday, of, Athletics (1)	$100,000
1975	Danny Goodwin, c, Angels (1)	$125,000
1978	Kirk Gibson, of, Tigers (1)	$150,000
	*Bob Horner, 3b, Braves (1)	$162,000
1979	Bill Bordley, lhp, Giants (1#)	$200,000
	Todd Demeter, 1b, Yankees (2)	$208,000
1988	Andy Benes, rhp, Padres (1)	$235,000
1989	Tyler Houston, c, Braves (1)	$241,500
	*Ben McDonald, rhp, Orioles (1)	$350,000
	*John Olerud, 1b, Blue Jays (3)	$575,000
1991	Mike Kelly, of, Braves (1)	$575,000
	Brien Taylor, lhp, Yankees (1)	$1,550,000
1994	Paul Wilson, rhp, Mets (1)	$1,550,000
	Josh Booty, 3b, Marlins (1)	$1,600,000
1996	Kris Benson, rhp, Pirates (1)	$2,000,000
1997	Rick Ankiel, lhp, Cardinals (2)	$2,500,000
	Matt Anderson, rhp, Tigers (1)	$2,505,000
1998	*J.D. Drew, of, Cardinals (1)	$3,000,000
	*Pat Burrell, 3b, Phillies (1)	$3,150,000
	Mark Mulder, lhp, Athletics (1)	$3,200,000
	Corey Patterson, of, Cubs (1)	$3,700,000
1999	Josh Hamilton, of, Devil Rays (1)	$3,960,000
2000	Joe Borchard, of, White Sox (1)	$5,300,000
2005	Justin Upton, ss, Diamondbacks (1)	$6,100,000

*Major league contract. #January draft.

FIRST ROUND TRENDS

Year	College	HS	Hitters	Pitchers	Average Bonus	Change
1999	15	15	10	*20	$1,809,767	+10.5%
2000	12	18	13	17	$1,872,586	+3.5%
2001	18	12	10	*20	*$2,154,280	+15.0%
2002	14	16	14	16	$2,106,793	-2.2%
2003	18	12	*20	10	$1,765,667	*-16.2%
2004	17	13	11	19	$1,958,448	+10.9%
2005	19	10	17	13	#$1,817,500	-7.2%
2006	16	13	12	18	$1,933,333	-4.2%
2007	13	17	13	17	$2,098,083	+8.5%

*Draft record.

NOTE: College includes junior college selections.

and Wieters (among others), Porcello was the player who fell the furthest in the first round, going No. 27 overall to the Tigers because of signability concerns that proved well-founded.

On Aug. 13, word came out that Porcello would get a $7 million major league deal (including a $3.58 million bonus), matching the record for the biggest guarantee ever given a high school draftee, set by Josh Beckett in 1999. Boras had set Beckett as his target for the Porcello contract and proved that even with the deadline and MLB's focus on reducing bonuses, he could deliver.

Before Porcello's deal, the most anyone had gone above slot in the first round was $170,000 by Georgia high school outfielder Jason Heyward, who the Braves drafted at No. 14. Heyward signed for $1.7 million, getting the 2006 value for his draft slot in what became a trend for late-signing mid-first-round picks.

"It's like with the price of gas," one agent grumbled during the process. "People see the price go up to $3 and get all whiny, and then the price comes down to $2.65 and everyone gets so excited. That's what signing for last year's slot is like."

Those deals became an afterthought in a way, as four of the top five picks grappled with the repercussions of Porcello's deal with the Tigers. So did the final choice in the first round.

North Carolina State righthander Andrew Brackman entered 2007 as the second-rated college pitcher behind Price, but an elbow injury and signability concerns (he was also represented by Boras) caused him to drop to the Yankees at No. 30.

Nevertheless, on the afternoon of Aug. 15, Brackman signed a deal that stunned industry insiders. While his $3.35 million bonus wasn't a surprise, he got a major league contract that guaranteed him $4.55 million. Most shocking of all for a former college basketball player who pitched just 149 innings for the Wolfpack and who the Yankees knew needed Tommy John surgery shortly after signing, his deal includes roster bonuses and club options that could drive its total value over seven years to $13 million—making it potentially the most lucrative contract in draft history. Brackman had surgery after the draft and most likely will not pitch in a professional game until 2009.

"This is my 32nd draft," Boras said on draft day. "It's about credibility . . . We want to have a quality business decision for the club, and we try to be selective about the players we represent, and we try to do everything we can to help the player be as good as they can be."

Both the Yankees and Tigers continued to splurge beyond the first round. New York followed the Brackman announcement by signing five more picks for a combined $3.5 million, including Texas third baseman Bradley Suttle for $1.3 million—a record for the fourth round—and Louisiana prep shortstop Carmen Angelini for $1 million, the second-largest bonus ever in the 10th round.

Detroit set a short-lived sixth-round record with a

DRAFT ORDER 2008

With another stumble to the finish, Tampa Bay clinched the first overall pick in the 2008 draft, the Devil Rays' second consecutive year with the first pick in the draft. They are the first team to have back-to-back No. 1 picks, and it's also the ninth consecutive season they'll have a top 10 pick. One more year would tie the Expos (1970-1979) and Mariners (1978-1987) for the longest stretches of top 10 picks.

The 2008 draft will be the fourth time since the Devil Rays' inaugural draft in 1999 that the franchise will have the No. 1 pick. No team has ever had the top pick in consecutive seasons. Only the Mets and Padres have had more No. 1 picks (five) than the Devil Rays.

The following is a list of the raw draft order for 2008, but keep in mind that picks in the second half of the draft could change based on free-agent signings and compensation picks.

1. Tampa Bay Devil Rays	16. Milwaukee Brewers
2. Pittsburgh Pirates	17. Toronto Blue Jays
3. Kansas City Royals	18. Atlanta Braves
4. Baltimore Orioles	19. Chicago Cubs
5. San Francisco Giants	20. Seattle Mariners
6. Florida Marlins	21. Detroit Tigers
7. Cincinnati Reds	22. New York Mets
8. Chicago White Sox	23. San Diego Padres
9. Washington Nationals	24. Philadelphia Phillies
10. Houston Astros	25. Colorado Rockies
11. Texas Rangers	26. Arizona Diamondbacks
12. Oakland Athletics	27. Los Angeles Angels
13. St. Louis Cardinals	28. New York Yankees
14. Minnesota Twins	29. Cleveland Indians
15. Los Angeles Dodgers	30. Boston Red Sox

$1.4975 bonus to Alabama shortstop Cale Iorg, and also gave Illinois prep lefty Casey Crosby $748,500 in the fifth round. Crosby's bonus was spread out over five years under MLB provisions for two-sport athletes, as he was a star high school football wide receiver.

Sneaking somewhat under the radar were the Nationals, who signed Georgia high school lefty Josh Smoker for an above-slot $1 million as the first pick in the supplemental first round. Washington then stunned the industry with a last-minute deal with Massachusetts prep lefty Jack McGeary. McGeary eclipsed Iorg's sixth-round record with a $1.8 million bonus, and the Nationals agreed to pay for him to attend Stanford as a full-time student and play baseball only in the summer until he graduates, if he chooses.

The Orioles set one more bonus record by round, giving fifth-rounder Jake Arrieta, a righthander out of Texas Christian and a preseason All-American, $1.1 million. And the Red Sox gave lefthander Zach Britton $700,000 in the 23rd round, another record.

At the other end of the spectrum, the Astros would not go over slot for any of their early draft picks. So after losing their first- and second-round picks for signing free agents Carlos Lee and Woody Williams following the 2006 season, the Astros failed to sign their first choice of the '07 draft, third-rounder Derek Dietrich, an Ohio prep infielder, as well as fourth-rounder Brett Eibner, a righthander from The Woodlands (Texas) High. The organization also failed to sign another Texas prep righty, Chad Bettis of Lubbock, and one of the draft's best athletes, 13th-rounder Chad Jones. An outfielder/lefthander, Jones attended Louisiana State, where he played defensive back for the football team and was also expected to play baseball.

DRAFT

The last time a team failed to sign any of its first four picks was the Yankees in 1980, when they gave up two picks for free agents (Rudy May and Bob Watson) and had their contract with third-rounder Billy Cannon voided.

The Astros' top selection who signed was Lamar outfielder Collin Delome. They spent just $536,000 for their draft picks in the first 10 rounds, by far the least of any club, less than half as much as the Angels, who checked in at No. 29 with $1.29 million. The Angels signed only one player, supplemental first-rounder Jonathan Bachanov, a Florida prep righthander, for more than $150,000.

First-Round Trends

The first round revolved around lefties, as the seven who went in the first 30 picks tied the record set in 2004. Of the lefties who went in 2004, only Jeremy Sowers had made much of a big league impact three years later, so clubs are hoping for more of a return from the '07 class.

Three college southpaws—Price, Clemson's Daniel Moskos (Pirates, fourth overall) and Missouri State's Ross Detwiler (Nationals, sixth)—went off the board quickly. Three more followed in No. 19 Joe Savery of Rice (Phillies), No. 23 Nick Schmidt of Arkansas (Padres) and the 25th overall pick Aaron Poreda of San Francisco, who went to the White Sox. One prep lefty, North Carolina's Madison Bumgarner, was taken No. 10 by the Giants.

Bumgarner was the second high school pitcher drafted, after the Diamondbacks took Indiana righty Jarrod Parker ninth overall. The Rangers snagged a pair of prep righties in Michael Main (23) and Metroplex native Blake Beavan (17), who where teammates in 2006 with USA Baseball's junior national team.

The biggest surprises of the first round included Florida senior Matt LaPorta, whom the Brewers took seventh overall, and Twins pick Ben Revere, the smallest first-rounder at 5-foot-9, 152 pounds. Revere, an outfielder out of Lexington (Ky.) Catholic High, ranked No. 135 on BA's predraft list and was among the draft's fastest players, having been timed at 6.28 seconds over 60 yards. He also had a fine debut, hitting .325 with 10 triples and 21 stolen bases in the Rookie-level Gulf Coast League, ranking as

Florida slugger Matt LaPorta signed quickly with the Brewers for $2 million

the No. 3 prospect in the league.

LaPorta, the 2005 Division I home run champion with the Gators, played first base throughout his college career, and had played some catcher as well, but the Brewers took him as a left fielder. LaPorta had one of the best debuts of any 2007 first-rounder, signing quickly for a $2 million bonus, then hitting 13 home runs in 138 at-bats, including the South Atlantic League playoffs.

While LaPorta signed quickly and other Boras clients signed for lucrative contracts, four Boras clients didn't sign and instead went to college—righthanders Josh Fields (back to Georgia as a senior), the Angels' Harvey (North Carolina) and Greg Peavey (Oregon State), and Alabama prep outfielder Kentrail Davis (Tennessee).

What's Next

When scouting directors met in August in Denver at the annual scouting directors meetings, there was more speculation about how the complexion of the draft had changed, as opposed to substantive discussion regarding its flaws.

"Until there's a hard-line slotting system, the bottom line is it's not going to work," said an American League scouting director who wished to remain anonymous.

Instead of quibbling over how the draft did or didn't work, discussion turned to what the residual effects would be moving forward.

"Next year, does every agent in the world tell the small-market teams, 'We don't want you picking our players,' or does everyone sign on August 14th?" a National League scouting director said. "You'd like to think that there are enough kids who want to get their professional careers started (who believe) signing for X amount is a pretty good way to do it . . . But we'll find out next June."

HISTORICAL SIGNIFICANCE

Fifteen players in draft history have signed for bonuses of $4 million or more, including three in 2007. Matt Wieters, taken fifth overall by the Orioles, led the way with $6 million, the largest up-front bonus and second-highest overall in draft history. For players who signed major league contracts, only the bonus is included.

Player, Pos.	Club, Year (Round)	Bonus
Justin Upton, ss	Diamondbacks '05 (1)	$6,100,000
Matt Wieters, c	Orioles '07 (1)	$6,000,000
*David Price, lhp	Devil Rays '07 (1)	$5,600,000
Joe Borchard, of	White Sox '00 (1)	$5,300,000
Joe Mauer, c	Twins '01 (1)	$5,150,000
B.J. Upton, ss	Devil Rays '02 (1)	$4,600,000
*Mark Teixeira, 3b	Rangers '01 (1)	$4,500,000
*Dewon Brazelton, rhp	Devil Rays '01 (1)	$4,200,000
Gavin Floyd, rhp	Phillies '01 (1)	$4,200,000
*Mark Prior, rhp	Cubs '01 (1)	$4,000,000
Bryan Bullington, rhp	Pirates '02 (1)	$4,000,000
Jered Weaver, rhp	Angels '04 (1)	$4,000,000
*Stephen Drew, ss	Diamondbacks '04 (1)	$4,000,000
Alex Gordon, 3b	Royals '05 (1)	$4,000,000
Mike Moustakas, ss	Royals '07 (1)	$4,000,000

*Received major league contract.

DAVID STONER

In the first 20 years of the draft, no player received a major league contract. Bo Jackson got the first big league deal in 1986, as the Royals gave him a $1.066 million package to lure him away from the NFL. Major league contracts for draftees are becoming much more commonplace, as there have been at least two in every draft since 1998 and a total of 36 overall.

Four players received big league deals in 2007, tying the record established in 2000 and matched in 2004. The Tigers gave Rick Porcello a $7 million contract, equaling the largest guarantee ever handed to a high school draftee (Josh Beckett, Marlins, 1999). Here's the complete list:

Year	Club (Round)	Player, Pos.	Bonus	Guarantee
1986	Royals (4)	Bo Jackson, of	$100,000	$1,066,000
1989	Orioles (1)	Ben McDonald, rhp	350,000	824,000
	Blue Jays (3)	John Olerud, 1b	575,000	800,000
1990	Athletics (1)	*Todd Van Poppel, rhp	500,000	1,200,000
1992	Angels (1)	Pete Janicki, rhp	90,000	215,000
1993	Mariners (1)	*Alex Rodriguez, ss	1,000,000	1,300,000
1998	Phillies (1)	Pat Burrell, 1b/of	3,150,000	8,000,000
	Cardinals (1)	J.D. Drew, of	3,000,000	7,000,000
	Cardinals (2)	Chad Hutchinson, rhp	2,300,000	3,400,000
1999	Marlins (1)	*Josh Beckett, rhp	3,625,000	7,000,000
	Tigers (1)	Eric Munson, c	3,500,000	6,750,000
2000	Reds (1)	*David Espinosa, ss	None	2,950,000
	Reds (2)	Dane Sardinha, c	None	1,950,000
	Padres (2)	Xavier Nady, 3b	1,100,000	2,850,000
	Devil Rays (5)	Jace Brewer, ss	450,000	1,200,000
2001	Cubs (1)	Mark Prior, rhp	4,000,000	10,500,000
	Devil Rays (1)	Dewon Brazelton, rhp	4,200,000	4,800,000
	Rangers (1)	Mark Teixeira, 3b	4,500,000	9,500,000
2002	Orioles (1)	†Adam Loewen, lhp	3,200,000	4,020,000
	Indians (1)	Jeremy Guthrie, rhp	3,000,000	4,000,000
	Rockies (4)	Jeff Baker, 3b	200,000	2,000,000
2003	Devil Rays (1)	*Delmon Young, of	3,700,000	5,800,000
	Brewers (1)	Rickie Weeks, 2b	3,600,000	4,790,000
2004	Tigers (1)	Justin Verlander, rhp	3,120,000	4,500,000
	Mets (1)	Philip Humber, rhp	3,000,000	4,200,000
	Devil Rays (1)	Jeff Niemann, rhp	3,200,000	5,200,000
	Diamondbacks (1)	Stephen Drew, ss	4,000,000	5,500,000
2005	Mets (1)	Mike Pelfrey, rhp	3,550,000	5,250,000
	Red Sox (1)	Craig Hansen, rhp	1,300,000	4,000,000
2006	Royals (1)	Luke Hochevar, rhp	3,500,000	5,250,000
	Tigers (1)	Andrew Miller, lhp	3,550,000	5,450,000
	Diamondbacks (1)	Max Scherzer, rhp	$3,000,000	$4,300,000
2007	Devil Rays (1)	David Price, lhp	$5,600,000	$8,500,000
	Rick Porcello, rhp	Tigers (1)	$3,580,000	$7,000,000
	Andrew Brackman, rhp	Yankees (1)	$3,350,000	$4,550,000
	Julio Borbon, of	Rangers (1s)	$800,000	$1,300,000

*High school signee. †Draft-and-follow, signed the following year.

Jeremy Guthrie   Mark Prior

Justin Verlander   Rickie Weeks

Delmon Young   Mike Pelfrey

School And Family Ties

■ Rice had 14 players drafted, tying the record for most selected players off one roster. The record originally was set in 1982 by Arizona State, and Cal State Fullerton matched it in 2005. Other big draft contributors included the Puerto Rico Baseball Academy, a high school that had 12 players selected. That actually was two fewer players than the Academy had drafted in 2004 and 2005, but there were still calls from Puerto Rico to ask MLB to exclude Puerto Rico from the draft, as it had been prior to 1989.

Other colleges that also made strong contributions to the draft were Clemson, Oklahoma State and Texas (11), Cal State Fullerton and Georgia Tech (10), and Arkansas, Nebraska, Pepperdine and Texas A&M (nine).

■ Moustakas and Marlins first-round pick Matt Dominguez became the sixth pair of high school team-mates drafted in the first round of the same draft. The feat has happened four times in the last seven drafts: 2000, Rancho Bernardo High in San Diego (Scott Heard, Matt Wheatland); 2002, Cypress Falls High, Houston (Clint Everts, Scott Kazmir); 2004, Wolfson High, Jacksonville, Fla. (Billy Butler, Eric Hurley) and now 2007.

Among the prominent players with family ties who were drafted in 2007:

■ Indians first-round pick Beau Mills, drafted 13th overall, is the son of Red Sox bench coach and former big league infielder Brad Mills. The younger Mills led NAIA Lewis-Clark (Idaho) State to its 14th national championship and set a school record with 38 home runs.

■ Reds supplemental first-rounder Todd Frazier, the 34th overall pick out of Rutgers, was the third Frazier brother to be drafted, joining Charles (1999, Marlins) and Jeff (2004, Tigers). Mets second-rounder Scott Moviel also was the third Moviel brother drafted, joining Paul (2003, White Sox) and Greg (2006, Mariners).

■ Iorg is the second son of ex-big leaguer Garth Iorg drafted, joining Astros farmhand Eli (2005).

■ Two Romines were picked in 2007: Austin, a California prep catcher, went in the second round to the Yankees, while Andrew, a shortstop out of Arizona State, went in the fifth round to the Angels. Their father Kevin played in the big leagues. Padres supplemental first-rounder Drew Cumberland (46th overall) is the younger brother of outfielder Shaun Cumberland (Reds). Texas lefthander James Russell, son of ex-big league righty Jeff Russell, went in the 14th round to the Cubs, signing for $350,000.

■ The White Sox drafted first baseman Devon Shines, son of their first-base coach and longtime minor league manager Razor Shines, in the 41st round. Also in the 41st round, the Angels selected manager Mike Scioscia's son Matt out of Southern California's Crespi High; Matt decided to attend Notre Dame.

Draft Trivia

■ This was the first year of several new draft rules, with the draft shortened to five rounds on the first day (and held on a Thursday, rather than the usual Tuesday), mostly to accommodate the longer, made-for-TV first round. Another new rule awarded teams a compensatory selection in the first three rounds for unsigned draft picks, theoretically giving the teams more leverage to sign players. Accordingly, the Braves received pick 69A (between picks 69 and 70) in the 2008 draft after failing to sign Fields, the Georgia closer, with the 69th overall selection in '07, and the Red Sox got pick 84A for failing to land Alabama prep first baseman Hunter Morris, who attended Auburn.

■ Four teams received 2008 supplemental third-round picks after failing to sign their third-rounders in '07: Philadelphia (Brandon Workman, who opted to attend Texas), Houston (Dietrich, to Georgia Tech), San Diego (Tommy Toledo, Florida) and the L.A. Angels (Harvey, North Carolina).

■ Rangers second-round pick Matt West, who signed for $405,000, was suspended in late August for 50 games for violating the commissioner's office policy against performance-enhancing drugs. West hit .301/.397/.388 in 103 at-bats in the Rookie-level Arizona League in his debut and set a dubious record for the highest-drafted player suspended for PEDs in his debut season. A surprising power surge during his senior season at Bellaire (Texas) High in 2007 helped him climb draft boards.

■ U.S. Military Academies were in draft news, led by lefthander Nick Hill out of Army. Hill led the nation in ERA in 2005 and pitched for USA Baseball's college national team in 2006, posting a career 33-12, 2.20 mark for the Cadets. He signed with the Mariners as a seventh-round pick for $70,000. His former closer at Army, Milan Dinga, signed for $20,000 as the Angels' 10th-rounder. The top military prospect, Navy righthander Mitch Harris, went to the Braves in the 24th round but didn't sign, as Naval Academy students are required to serve five years in active duty once they begin classes their junior year.

■ The U.S. Defense Department ruled that Karl Bolt, the Phillies' 15th-round pick out of Air Force, must serve at least two years before he can pursue his baseball career. Bolt, a second lieutenant in the Air Force, had

Bonus slotting not only has resulted in a big slowdown in bonus inflation, but it also has allowed major league teams to continue to sign premium draft picks in record numbers. Teams signed all but 22 of their picks from the first 10 rounds in 2006, and the great majority of those players were in the ninth and 10th rounds.

First-round pick Max Scherzer was likely to sign rather than going back into the 2007 draft, and there are several draft-and-follows who will be eligible to sign until a week before the '07 draft. This will be the last year of the draft-and-follow process, as draft rules changes will end the practice.

Listed below are all the unsigned players from the first 10 rounds, with the number of their overall selection, as well as the colleges they're attending:

FIRST ROUND

11. Diamondbacks. Max Scherzer, rhp	not in school

SECOND ROUND

59. Nationals. Sean Black, rhp	Seton Hall

THIRD ROUND

79. Devil Rays. Nick Fuller, rhp	South Carolina
102. Angels. Russ Moldenhauer, of	Texas

FIFTH ROUND

156. Twins. Devin Shepherd, of	Oklahoma

SIXTH ROUND

183. Padres. Tim Bascom, rhp	Central Florida

SEVENTH ROUND

211. Nationals. Sam Brown, rhp	North Carolina State
218. Athletics. Michael Leake, rhp	Arizona State
222. #Angels. Jarrad Page, of	NFL

NINTH ROUND

270. Blue Jays. Cole Figueroa, ss	Florida
271. *Nationals. Joey Rosas, lhp	Yavapai (Ariz.) CC
274. *Mets. Jeremy Barfield, of	San Jacinto (Texas) JC
278. Athletics. Danny Hamblin, 1b	Arkansas
285. White Sox. Chris Duffy, 3b	Central Florida

10TH ROUND

293. Dodgers. Andy D'Alessio, 1b	Clemson
295. Orioles. Emeel Salem, of	Alabama
301. *Nationals. Marcus Salmon, c	Miami-Dade CC
304. Mets. Phillips Orta, rhp	Western Nebraska CC
306. Twins. Jared Mitchell, of	Louisiana State
309. Astros. Nathan Karns, rhp	North Carolina State
313. Red Sox. Kyle Snyder, rhp	Indian River (Fla.) JC
316. Cardinals. Blair Erickson, rhp	UC Irvine

#Still eligible to sign
*Draft-and-follow; eligible to sign prior to 2006 draft

applied for a waiver that would allow him to fulfill his military commitment in the offseasons, after his baseball career or with an extended term in the reserves. Bolt was assigned to MacDill Air Force Base in Florida and was not allowed to attend instructional league. Bolt hit .256/.336/.459 in the Rookie-level Gulf Coast League with eight home runs.

■ Two Top 25 college football programs had their quarterbacks drafted. West Virginia's Pat White went in the 27th round, three years after they failed to sign him out of high school in the fourth round. White remained in school and didn't sign, returning to lead the Mountaineers on the football field. However, the Braves signed fifth-rounder Dennis Dixon, Oregon's starting signal caller, for a $137,700 bonus. Dixon had not played baseball since 2003, his senior year in high school, and struggled in two Rookie-ball stops (12-for-74, .162) before returning to Oregon for football in August.

FIRST OVERALL PICKS: THROUGH THE YEARS

Rick Monday

Chipper Jones

Joe Mauer

Following is a year-by-year breakdown of the first overall pick in the June regular phase and his cash bonus, his highest level attained and his 2006 status. If a different player earned the largest bonus in that year, that player is noted along with the order he was picked and his bonus.

Year	No. 1 Pick	School	Hometown	Highest Level	Bonus	Largest Bonus (Pick Number)	Amount
1965	Rick Monday, of, Athletics	Arizona State U.	Santa Monica, Calif.	Majors	$100,000	same	
1966	Steve Chilcott, c, Mets	Antelope Valley HS	Lancaster, Calif.	Triple-A	75,000	Reggie Jackson, of, Athletics (2)	$80,000
1967	Ron Blomberg, 1b, Yankees	Druid Hills HS	Atlanta	Majors	65,000	#Mike Adamson, rhp, Orioles	75,000
1968	Tim Foli, ss, Mets	Notre Dame HS	Sherman Oaks, Calif.	Majors	74,000	Lloyd Allen, rhp, Angels (12)	75,000
1969	Jeff Burroughs, of, Senators	Wilson HS	Long Beach, Calif.	Majors	88,000	same	
1970	Mike Ivie, c, Padres	Walker HS	Decatur, Ga.	Majors	75,000	#Dave Kingman, 1b, Giants	80,000
1971	Danny Goodwin, c, White Sox	Central HS	Peoria, Ill.	DNS	DNS	Ed Kurpiel, 1b, Cardinals (8)	83,750
1972	Dave Roberts, 3b, Padres	U. of Oregon	Corvallis, Ore.	Majors	70,000	Jamie Quirk, ss, Royals (18)	78,000
1973	*David Clyde, lhp, Rangers	Westchester HS	Houston	Majors	65,000	^Alan Bannister, ss, Phillies	85,000
1974	*Bill Almon, ss, Padres	Brown U.	Warwick, R.I.	Majors	90,000	Willie Wilson, of, Royals (18)	90,000
1975	*Danny Goodwin, c, Angels	Southern U.	Peoria, Ill.	Majors	125,000	same	
1976	Floyd Bannister, lhp, Astros	Arizona State U.	Seattle	Majors	100,000	Paul Molitor, ss, Twins (3)	77,500
1977	Harold Baines, of, White Sox	St. Michaels HS	St. Michaels, Md.	Majors	32,000	same	
1978	*Bob Horner, 3b, Braves	Arizona State U.	Glendale, Ariz.	Majors	162,000	Todd Demeter, 1b, Yankees (51)	208,000
1979	Al Chambers, 1b, Mariners	Harris HS	Harrisburg, Pa.	Majors	60,000	same	
1980	Darryl Strawberry, of, Mets	Crenshaw HS	Los Angeles	Majors	152,500	Terry Blocker, of, Mets (4)	127,500
1981	Mike Moore, rhp, Mariners	Oral Roberts U.	Eakly, Okla.	Majors	100,000	Kenny Williams, of, Wh. Sox (78)	160,000
1982	Shawon Dunston, ss, Cubs	Jefferson HS	New York	Majors	135,000	Kurt Stillwell, ss, Reds (2)	135,000
1983	Tim Belcher, rhp, Twins	Mt. Vernon Nazarene Coll.	Sparta, Ohio	Majors	DNS	same	
1984	Shawn Abner, of, Mets	Mechanicsburg HS	Mechanicsburg, Pa.	Majors	150,500	Bobby Witt, rhp, Rangers (3)	179,000
1985	B.J. Surhoff, c, Brewers	U. of North Carolina	Rye, N.Y.	Majors	150,000	same	
1986	Jeff King, 3b, Pirates	U. of Arkansas	Colorado Springs	Majors	180,000	Mark Merchant, of, Pirates (2)	165,000
1987	Ken Griffey Jr., of, Mariners	Moeller HS	Cincinnati	Majors	160,000	Jack McDowell, rhp, Wh. Sox (5)	165,000
1988	Andy Benes, rhp, Padres	U. of Evansville	Evansville, Ind.	Majors	235,000	same	
1989	*Ben McDonald, rhp, Orioles	Louisiana State U.	Denham Springs, La.	Majors	350,000	*John Olerud, 1b, Blue Jays (79)	575,000
1990	Chipper Jones, ss, Braves	The Bolles School	Jacksonville	Majors	275,000	*Todd Van Poppel, rhp, A's (14)	500,000
						Tony Clark, 1b, Tigers (2)	500,000
1991	Brien Taylor, lhp, Yankees	East Carteret HS	Beaufort, N.C.	Double-A	1,550,000	same	
1992	Phil Nevin, 3b, Astros	Cal State Fullerton	Placentia, Calif.	Majors	700,000	Jeffrey Hammonds, of, Orioles (4)	975,000
1993	*Alex Rodriguez, ss, Mariners	Westminster Christian HS	Miami	Majors	1,000,000	Darren Dreifort, rhp, Dodgers (2)	1,300,000
1994	Paul Wilson, rhp, Mets	Florida State U.	Orlando, Fla.	Majors	1,550,000	Josh Booty, ss, Marlins (5)	1,600,000
1995	Darin Erstad, of, Angels	U. of Nebraska	Jamestown, N.D.	Majors	1,575,000	same	
1996	@Kris Benson, rhp, Pirates	Clemson U.	Kennesaw, Ga.	Majors	2,000,000	Matt White, rhp, Giants (7)	10,200,000
1997	Matt Anderson, rhp, Tigers	Rice U.	Louisville	Majors	2,505,000	same	
1998	*Pat Burrell, 3b, Phillies	U. of Miami	Boulder Creek, Calif.	Majors	3,150,000	Corey Patterson, of, Cubs (3)	3,700,000
1999	Josh Hamilton, of, Devil Rays	Athens Drive HS	Raleigh, N.C.	Majors	3,960,000	same	
2000	Adrian Gonzalez, 1b, Marlins	Eastside HS	Chula Vista, Calif.	Majors	3,000,000	Joe Borchard, of, White Sox (12)	5,300,000
2001	Joe Mauer, c, Twins	Cretin-Derham Hall	St. Paul, Minn.	Majors	5,150,000	same	
2002	Bryan Bullington, rhp, Pirates	Ball State U.	Fishers, Ind.	Majors	4,000,000	B.J. Upton, ss, Devil Rays (2)	4,600,000
2003	*Delmon Young, of, Devil Rays	Camarillo HS	Camarillo, Calif.	Majors	3,700,000	Jered Weaver, rhp, Angels	4,000,000
2004	Matt Bush, ss, Padres	Mission Bay HS	El Cajon, Calif.	Class A	3,150,000	Stephen Drew, ss, D-backs	4,000,000
2005	Justin Upton, ss, D'backs	Great Bridge HS	Chesapeake, Va.	Majors	6,100,000	same	
2006	Luke Hochevar, rhp, Royals	No School		Majors	3,500,000	Andrew Miller, lhp	3,550,000
2007	David Price, lhp, Devil Rays	Vanderbilt		Majors		same	

* Signed major league contract; cash bonus only reported. # Selected in June secondary phase.
^ Selected in January draft. @ Includes four loophole free agents; White signed with Devil Rays.

DRAFT

Rick Porcello

Matt Wieters

David Price

Selection, Team: Player, Pos.	School	Bonus
1. Royals: Luke Hochevar, rhp	Fort Worth	$3,500,000
2. Rockies: Greg Reynolds, rhp	Stanford	$3,250,000
3. Devil Rays: Evan Longoria, 3b	Long Beach State	$3,000,000
4. Pirates: Brad Lincoln, rhp	Houston	$2,750,000
5. Mariners: Brandon Morrow, rhp	California	$2,450,000
6. Tigers: Andrew Miller, lhp	North Carolina	$3,550,000
7. Dodgers: Clayton Kershaw, lhp	HS-Dallas	$2,300,000
8. Reds: Drew Stubbs, of	Texas	$2,000,000
9. Orioles: Bill Rowell, 3b	HS-Pennsauken, N.J.	$2,100,000
10. Giants: Tim Lincecum, rhp	Washington	$2,025,000
11. Diamondbacks: Max Scherzer, rhp	Missouri	Unsigned
12. Rangers: Kasey Kiker, lhp	HS-Seale, Ala.	$1,600,000
13. Cubs: Tyler Colvin, of	Clemson	$1,475,000
14. Blue Jays: Travis Snider, of	HS-Everett, Wash.	$1,700,000
15. Nationals: Chris Marrero, of	HS-Opa Locka, Fla.	$1,625,000
16. Brewers: Jeremy Jeffress, rhp	HS-South Boston, Va.	$1,550,000
17. Padres: Matt Antonelli, 3b	Wake Forest	$1,575,000
18. Phillies: Kyle Drabek, rhp/ss	HS-The Woodlands, Texas	$1,550,000
19. Marlins: Brett Sinkbeil, rhp	Missouri State	$1,525,000
20. Twins: Chris Parmelee, of/1b	HS-Chino Hills, Calif.	$1,500,000
21. Yankees: Ian Kennedy, rhp	Southern California	$2,250,000
22. Nationals: Colton Willems, rhp	HS-Fort Pierce, Fla.	$1,425,000
23. Astros: Max Sapp, c	HS-Orlando	$1,400,000
24. Braves: Cody Johnson, 1b	HS-Lynn Haven, Fla.	$1,375,000
25. Angels: Hank Conger, c	HS-Huntington Beach, Calif	$1,350,000
26. Dodgers: Bryan Morris, rhp	Motlow State (Tenn.) CC	$1,325,000
27. Red Sox: Jason Place, of	HS-Piedmont, S.C.	$1,300,000
28. Red Sox: Daniel Bard, rhp	North Carolina	$1,550,000
29. White Sox: Kyle McCulloch, rhp	Texas	$1,050,000
30. Cardinals: Adam Ottavino, rhp	Northeastern	$950,000
31. Dodgers: Preston Mattingly, ss	HS-Evansville, Ind.	$1,000,000
32. Orioles: Pedro Beato, rhp	St. Petersburg (Fla.) JC	$1,000,000
33. Giants: Emmanuel Burriss, ss	Kent State	$1,000,000
34. Diamondbacks: Brooks Brown, rhp	Georgia	$900,000
35. Padres: Kyler Burke, of	HS-Ooltewah, Tenn.	$950,000
36. Marlins: Chris Coghlan, 3b	Mississippi	$950,000
37. Phillies: Adrian Cardenas, ss	HS-Opa Locka, Fla.	$925,000
38. Braves: Cory Rasmus, rhp	HS-Seale, Ala.	$900,000
39. Indians: David Huff, lhp	UCLA	$900,000
40. Red Sox: Kris Johnson, lhp	Wichita State	$850,000
41. Yankees: Joba Chamberlain, rhp	Nebraska	$1,100,000
42. Cardinals: Chris Perez, rhp	Miami	$800,000
43. Braves: Steve Evarts, lhp	HS-Tampa	$800,000
44. Red Sox: Caleb Clay, rhp	HS-Cullman, Ala.	$775,000
45. Royals: Jason Taylor, of	HS-Virginia Beach	$762,500
46. Rockies: David Christensen, of	HS-Parkland, Fla.	$750,000
47. Devil Rays: Josh Butler, rhp	San Diego	$725,000
48. Pirates: Mike Felix, lhp	Troy	$725,000
49. Mariners: Chris Tillman, rhp	HS-Fountain Valley, Calif.	$680,000
50. Tigers: Ronnie Bourquin, 3b	Ohio State	$690,000

Selection, Team: Player, Pos.	School	Bonus
51. Braves: Jeff Locke, lhp	HS-Conway, N.H.	$675,000
52. Reds: Sean Watson, rhp	Tennessee	$670,000
53. Padres: Chad Huffman, of	Texas Christian	$660,000
54. Cardinals: Brad Furnish, lhp	Texas Christian	$600,000
55. Diamondbacks: Brett Anderson, lhp	HS-Stillwater, Okla.	$950,000
56. Indians: Steven Wright, rhp	Hawaii	$630,000
57. Indians: Josh Rodriguez, ss	Rice	$625,000
58. Orioles: Ryan Adams, 2b	HS-New Orleans	$675,000
59. Nationals: Sean Black, rhp	HS-Medford, N.J.	Did Not Sign
60. Brewers: Brent Brewer, ss	HS-Tyrone, Ga.	$600,000
61. Padres: Wade LeBlanc, lhp	Alabama	$590,000
62. Mets: Kevin Mulvey, rhp	Villanova	$585,000
63. Marlins: Tom Hickman, of	HS-Lindale, Ga.	$575,000
64. Twins: Joe Benson, of	HS-Joliet, Ill.	$575,000
65. Phillies: Drew Carpenter, rhp	Long Beach State	$570,000
66. Athletics: Trevor Cahill, rhp	HS-Vista, Calif.	$560,000
67. Astros: Sergio Perez, rhp	Tampa	$550,000
68. Braves: Dustin Evans, rhp	Georgia Southern	$530,000
69. Indians: Wes Hodges, 3b	Georgia Tech	$1,000,000
70. Nationals: Stephen Englund, of	HS-Bellevue, Wash.	$515,000
71. Red Sox: Justin Masterson, rhp	San Diego State	$510,000
72. Braves: Chase Fontaine, ss	Daytona Beach (Fla.) CC	$500,000
73. White Sox: Matt Long, rhp	Miami (Ohio)	$330,000
74. Cardinals: Jon Jay, of	Miami	$480,000
75. Indians: Matt McBride, c	Lehigh	$445,000
76. Cardinals: Mark Hamilton, 1b	Tulane	$465,000
77. Royals: Blake Wood, rhp	Georgia Tech	$460,000
78. Rockies: Keith Weiser, lhp	Miami (Ohio)	$455,000
79. Devil Rays: Nick Fuller, rhp	HS-Marietta, Ga.	Did Not Sign
80. Pirates: Shelby Ford, 2b	Oklahoma State	$450,000
81. Mariners: Tony Butler, lhp	HS-Oak Creek, Wis.	$445,000
82. Tigers: Brennan Boesch, of	California	$445,000
83. Red Sox: Aaron Bates, 1b	North Carolina State	$440,000
84. Reds: Chris Valaika, ss	UC Santa Barbara	$437,500
85. Orioles: Zach Britton, lhp	HS-Weatherford, Texas	$435,000
86. Diamondbacks: Dallas Buck, rhp	Oregon State	$250,000
87. Diamondbacks: Cyle Hankerd, of	Southern California	$430,000
88. Rangers: Chad Tracy, c	Pepperdine	$427,500
89. Giants: Clayton Tanner, lhp	HS-Concord, Calif.	$425,000
90. Marlins: Torre Langley, c	HS-Douglasville, Ga.	$422,500
91. Nationals: Stephen King, ss	HS-Winter Park, Fla.	$750,000
92. Brewers: Cole Gillespie, of	Oregon State	$417,500
93. Padres: Cedric Hunter, of	HS-Decatur, Ga.	$415,000
94. Mets: Joe Smith, rhp	Wright State	$410,000
95. Marlins: Scott Cousins, of	San Francisco	$407,500
96. Twins: Tyler Robertson, lhp	HS-Fair Oaks, Calif.	$405,000
97. Phillies: Jason Donald, ss	Arizona	$400,000
98. Athletics: Matt Sulentic, of	HS-Dallas	$395,000
99. Astros: Nick Moresi, of	Fresno State	$390,000
100. Braves: Chad Rodgers, lhp	HS-Stow, Ohio	$385,000

Number represents order of selection • **Boldface** indicates player signed

ARIZONA DIAMONDBACKS (9)

1. **Jarrod Parker, rhp, Norwell HS, Ossian, Ind.**
1s. **Wes Roemer, rhp, Cal State Fullerton** (Supplemental choice—50th overall—for loss of Type B free agent Craig Counsell)
1s. **Ed Easley, c, Mississippi State** (Supplemental choice—61st over-all—for loss of Type B free agent Miguel Batista)
2. **Barry Enright, rhp, Pepperdine**
3. **Reynaldo Navarro, ss, Puerto Rico Baseball Academy, Guaynabo, P.R.**
4. **Sean Morgan, rhp, Tulane**
5. **Tyrell Worthington, of, South Central HS, Winterville, N.C.**
6. **Scott Maine, lhp, Miami**
7. **Bryan Augenstein, rhp, Florida**
8. **Taylor Harbin, 2b, Clemson**
9. **Mark Hallberg, ss, Florida State**
10. **Evan Frey, of, Missouri**
11. **Josh Ellis, rhp, Wake Forest**
12. **Bryan Henry, rhp, Florida State**
13. **Sean Coughlin, c, Kentucky**
14. Bobby LaFromboise, lhp, New Mexico
15. **Josh Collmenter, rhp, Central Michigan**
16. **Mike Mee, of, Minnesota**
17. **Chance Wheeless, 1b, Texas**
18. Sammy Solis, lhp, Agua Fria HS, Litchfield Park, Ariz.
19. Michael Solbach, rhp, Liberty
20. **Pete Clifford, of, Jacksonville**
21. **Anthony Smith, of, St. John's**
22. **Ty Davis, rhp, Vanderbilt**
23. **Ian Harrington, lhp, Hawaii**
24. **Luke Prihoda, rhp, Sam Houston State**
25. **Billy Spottiswood, rhp, Chico State (Calif.)**
26. **Tom Layne, lhp, Mount Olive (N.C.)**
27. Austin Garrett, lhp, Pensacola (Fla.) JC
28. **Evan Scribner, rhp, Central Connecticut State**
29. **Omar Arif, lhp, Long Beach State**
30. **Bill Musselman, c, Saint Louis**
31. Gary Bulman, rhp, Greenbrier Christian Academy, Chesapeake, Va.
32. Joey Stevens, c, Pensacola (Fla.) JC
33. Chuck Huggins, lhp, UC Santa Barbara
34. Chris Kelley, rhp, Rice
35. **Josh Blake, lhp, Auburn**
36. Tyler Conn, lhp, Southern Mississippi
37. **Jimmy Principe, of, Brookdale (N.J.) CC**
38. **Aaron Hanke, of, UC Davis**
39. **Eli Rumler, ss, Kansas State**
40. Torrey Jacoby, 2b, Notre Dame Prep, Scottsdale, Ariz.
41. **Danny Rosen, rhp, Florida State**
42. Golden Tate, of, Pope John Paul II HS, Hendersonville, Tenn.
43. Andrew Allen, 1b, Desert Vista HS, Phoenix
44. Nick Ewing, rhp, Oakmont HS, Roseville, Calif.
45. Garrett Bullock, lhp, Wake Forest
46. Josh Garcia, 1b, Brophy Prep, Phoenix
47. Mike Greco, 3b, Notre Dame Prep, Scottsdale, Ariz.
48. **Joe Ayers, ss, Boston College**
49. Matt Newman, of, Brophy Prep, Phoenix
50. Dylan Moseley, rhp, Louisiana Tech

ATLANTA BRAVES (14)

1. **Jason Heyward, of, Henry County HS, McDonough, Ga.**
1s. **Jon Gilmore, 3b, Iowa City (Iowa) HS** (Supplemental choice—33rd overall—for loss of Type A free agent Danys Baez)
2. **Joshua Fields, rhp, Georgia** (Choice from Orioles as compensation for Baez)
2. **Freddie Freeman, 1b/rhp, El Modena HS, Orange, Calif.**
3. **Brandon Hicks, ss, Texas A&M**
4. **Cory Gearrin, rhp, Mercer**
5. **Dennis Dixon, of, Oregon**
6. **Michael Fisher, ss, Georgia Tech**
7. **Travis Jones, 2b, South Carolina**
8. Colby Shreve, rhp, CC of Southern Nevada
9. **Tim Ladd, lhp, Georgia Tech**
10. **Tommy Palica, lhp, Golden West (Calif.) JC**
11. Brandon Belt, lhp, San Jacinto (Texas) JC
12. **Nick Fellman, rhp, Minnesota State-Mankato**
13. **Chad Maddox, of, Tennessee**
14. **Caleb Brewer, rhp, Harris County HS, Hamilton, Ga.**
15. Paul Demny, rhp, East Bernard (Texas) HS
16. Eddie Burns, rhp, Georgia Tech
17. **Benji Johnson, c, North Carolina**
18. **Randy Gress, ss, Quinnipiac**

19. Brett Butts, rhp, Auburn
20. **C.J. Lee, of, East Tennessee State**
21. **Kuyaunnis Miles, of, Chattahoochee Valley (Ala.) CC**
22. Lyle Allen, of, Cartersville (Ga.) HS
23. Edmond Sparks, c, Lovejoy HS, Hampton, Ga.
24. Mitch Harris, rhp, Navy
25. **Rico Reid, rhp, East Coweta HS, Sharpsburg, Ga.**
26. **Daniel Elorriaga-Matra, c, Douglas HS, Parkland, Fla.**
27. Adam Milligan, of, Walters State (Tenn.) CC
28. **Rashod Henry, of, Lumberton (Miss.) HS**
29. Gary Gillheeney, rhp, Bishop Hendricken HS, Warwick, R.I.
30. Rene Escobar, 1b, Riverside (Calif.) CC
31. **Benino Pruneda, rhp, San Jacinto (Texas) JC**
32. **T.J. Wohlever, lhp, Western Nevada CC**
33. Craig Kimbrel, rhp, Wallace State (Ala.) CC
34. Robert Maddox, 1b, Villa Angela-St. Joseph HS, Cleveland
35. Chris Moon, of, Tucson (Ariz.) HS
36. Vernell Warren, 2b, Grant HS, Portland, Ore.
37. Randy Yard, rhp, Palm Desert (Calif.) HS
38. Will Casey, lhp, Kennesaw Mountain HS, Kennesaw, Ga.
39. Elliott Armstrong, of, Harlan Community HS, Chicago
40. Anthony Whitenton, ss, Heritage HS, Conyers, Ga.
41. Sheldon Johnson, rhp, Deptford (N.J.) HS
42. Bryson Rahler, c, Cajon HS, San Bernardino, Calif.
43. Ryan Chaffee, rhp, Chipola (Fla.) JC
44. Dock Doyle, c, Coastal Carolina
45. Tarus Thomas, of, St. Dominic HS, Oyster Bay, N.Y.
46. Brett Krill, of, Aliso Niguel HS, Aliso Viejo, Calif.
47. Goldy Simmons, rhp, San Diego CC
48. Joe Lincoln, c, Tipton (Mo.) HS
49. Tyreace House, of, JC of the Canyons (Calif.)
50. Andrew Armstrong, lhp, Ashby HS, Bridgewater, Va.

BALTIMORE ORIOLES (5)

1. **Matt Wieters, c, Georgia Tech**
2. (Choice to Braves as compensation for Type A free agent Danys Baez)
3. (Choice to Mets as compensation for Type A free agent Chad Bradford)
4. **Tim Bascom, rhp, Bradenton (South Coast)**
5. **Jake Arrieta, rhp, Texas Christian**
6. **Joe Mahoney, 1b, Richmond**
7. **Matt Angle, of, Ohio State**
8. **Shane Mathews, rhp, East Carolina**
9. **Malcolm Crowley, ss, Galveston (Texas) JC**
10. Eryk McConnell, rhp, North Carolina State
11. **Robbie Widlansky, of, Florida Atlantic**
12. **Wally Crancer, of, Georgia Tech**
13. **Jordan Wolf, c, Xavier**
14. **Hank Williamson, rhp, San Jacinto (Texas) JC**
15. Tyrone Hambly, 3b, Grayson County (Texas) CC
16. **Tyler Kolodny, 3b, El Camino Real HS, Woodland Hills, Calif.**
17. **Jason White, ss, Iowa**
18. **John Mariotti, rhp, Coastal Carolina**
19. **Brian Parker, rhp, Lewis-Clark State (Idaho)**
20. **Sean Gleason, rhp, St. Mary's**
21. **Scott Mueller, rhp, Arizona State**
22. **Collin Allen, rhp, Lamar (Colo.) CC**
23. **Tony Kirbis, rhp, Point Loma Nazarene (Calif.)**
24. Dan Klein, rhp, Servite (Calif.) HS
25. **Cliff Flagello, rhp, Shorter (Ga.)**
26. **Justin Moore, rhp, Chancellor HS, Fredericksburg, Va.**
27. **Kraig Binick, of, New York Tech**
28. **Stephen Procner, lhp, Cleveland State**
29. **Danny Heller, of, Pierce (Calif.) JC**
30. **Brandon Cooney, rhp, Florida Atlantic**
31. **Matt Tucker, 3b, Dallas Baptist**
32. Pete Andrelczyk, rhp, Coastal Carolina
33. **Jacob Julius, of, Arkansas**
34. **Kyle Touchatt, rhp, Wichita State**
35. **Eric Perlozzo, 2b, Shippensburg (Pa.)**
36. **Calvin Lester, of, Prairie View A&M**
37. Merrill Kelly, rhp, Desert Mountain HS, Scottsdale, Ariz.
38. Michael Harrington, c, Charleston
39. Joe Yermal, rhp, McDonogh HS, Bel Air, Md.
40. **Aaron Odom, rhp, Texas Tech**
41. Russell Wilson, 2b/ss, Collegiate HS, Richmond, Va.
42. **Joe DiGeronimo, ss, Wagner**
43. **Cole McCurry, lhp, Tennessee Wesleyan**
44. Travis Dirk, rhp, Navarro (Texas) JC
45. **Jacob Smith, lhp, Brescia (Ky.)**
46. **Lee Ellis, of, California Lutheran**

47. Preston Pehrson, c, Towson
48. Nick Ray, of, Northwest Nazarene (Idaho)
49. Tyler Newsome, of, Marist HS, Chicago
50. Mike Gioioso, ss, Mount St. Mary's

BOSTON RED SOX (20)

1. (Choice to Dodgers as compensation for Type A free agent Julio Lugo)
1s. Nick Hagadone, lhp, Washington (Supplemental choice—55th overall—for loss of Type B free agent Alex Gonzalez)
1s. Ryan Dent, ss/2b, Wilson HS, Long Beach (Supplemental choice—62nd overall—for loss of Type B free agent Keith Foulke)
2. Hunter Morris, 1b, Grissom HS, Huntsville, Ala.
3. Brock Huntzinger, rhp, Pendleton Heights HS, Pendleton, Ind.
4. Chris Province, rhp, Southeastern Louisiana
5. Will Middlebrooks, 3b/rhp, Liberty-Eylau HS, Texarkana, Texas
6. Anthony Rizzo, 1b/lhp, Douglas HS, Parkland, Fla.
7. David Mailman, 1b, Providence HS, Charlotte, N.C.
8. Adam Mills, rhp, UNC Charlotte
9. Kade Keowen, of, Louisiana State-Eunice JC
10. Kenneth Roque, ss, Puerto Rico Baseball Academy, Guaynabo, P.R.
11. Thomas Pressly, rhp, Marcus HS, Flower Mound, Texas
12. Eammon Portice, rhp, High Point
13. Justin Grimm, rhp, Virginia HS, Bristol, Va.
14. Jake Cowan, rhp, Roswell (Ga.) HS
15. Scott Green, rhp, Kentucky
16. Austin Bailey, rhp, Prattville (Ala.) HS
17. Jaren Matthews, 1b/of, Don Bosco Prep, Teaneck, N.J.
18. Hunter Strickland, rhp, Pike County HS, Zebulon, Ga.
19. David Marks, of, Edmonds (Wash.) CC
20. Dan Milano, c, Northeastern
21. Aaron Reza, ss, Oklahoma
22. Will Latimer, lhp, Trinidad State (Colo.) JC
23. Drake Britton, lhp, Tomball (Texas) HS
24. Matt Presley, 3b, Cheyenne Mountain HS, Colorado Springs
25. Seth Garrison, rhp, Texas Christian
26. Deshaun Brooks, 3b, Benedict (S.C.)
27. Yasmani Grandal, c, Miami Springs (Fla.) HS
28. Nick Tepesch, rhp, Blue Springs (Mo.) HS
29. Juan Carlin, lhp, Riverview HS, Sarasota, Fla.
30. Will Vazquez, c, Kent State
31. Daniel Buller, lhp, Fresno (Calif.) CC
32. Ridge Carpenter, of, Kalani HS, Honolulu, Hawaii
33. Garrett Larsen, rhp, Navarro (Texas) JC
34. Tony Bajoczky, rhp, Duke
35. Sean Tierney, lhp, Clover Hill HS, Midlothian, Va.
36. Scott Lyons, ss, Mount San Antonio (Calif.) JC
37. Scott Lonergan, rhp, Rice
38. Derrick Stultz, rhp, Wharton HS, Tampa
39. Jonathan Roof, ss, St. Mary's HS, Paducah, Ky.
40. Ryan Fischer, rhp, Lodi (Calif.) HS
41. Mike Bourdon, c, Northwest Catholic HS, West Hartford, Conn.
42. Chad Povich, rhp, Dixie State (Utah) College
43. Scott Cure, lhp, Idalia (Colo.) HS
44. Emmanuel Solano, ss, Miami-Dade (Fla.) CC
45. Peter Gilardo, c, Dominican (N.Y.)
46. Garrett Young, of, Liberty

CHICAGO CUBS (3)

1. Josh Vitters, 3b, Cypress (Calif.) HS
1s. Josh Donaldson, c, Auburn (Supplemental choice—48th overall—for loss of Type B free agent Juan Pierre)
2. (Choice to Nationals as compensation for Type A free agent Alfonso Soriano)
3. Tony Thomas, 2b, Florida State
4. Darwin Barney, ss, Oregon State
5. Brandon Guyer, of, Virginia
6. Casey Lambert, lhp, Virginia
7. Ty Wright, of, Oklahoma State
8. Marquez Smith, 3b, Clemson
9. Clark Hardman, of, Cal State Fullerton
10. Leon Johnson, of, Brigham Young
11. Chris Siegfried, lhp, Portland
12. Ryan Acosta, rhp/ss, Clearwater (Fla.) Central Catholic HS
13. Jonathan Wyatt, of, Georgia
14. James Russell, lhp, Texas
15. Marc Sawyer, 1b, Yale
16. Zach Ashwood, lhp, Kansas
17. Arik Hempy, lhp, South Carolina
18. Jeffrey Rea, 2b, Mississippi State
19. Kyle Day, c, Michigan State
20. Jose Made, ss, Dominican (N.Y.)
21. Dustin Sasser, lhp, East Carolina
22. Craig Muschko, rhp, La Salle
23. Stephen Vento, rhp, Palm Beach (Fla.) CC

24. Scott Meyer, rhp, Lamar
25. Victor Sanchez, 3b/c, Gahr HS, Norwalk, Calif.
26. Michael Bunton, lhp, Charleston
27. Clayton Suss, rhp, Cooper City (Fla.) HS
28. Bill Moss, 2b, Memphis
29. Andrew Cashner, rhp, Angelina (Texas) JC
30. Luke Sommer, of, San Francisco
31. Brian Leclerc, of, Florida
32. Luis Bautista, c, Florida International
33. Preston Clark, c, Texas
34. Enrique Garcia, rhp, Miami
35. J.C. Casey, rhp, Kickapoo HS, Springfield, Mo.
36. Billy Mottran, 3b, Dowling (N.Y.)
37. Mike McGee, rhp, Port St. Lucie (Fla.) HS
38. Yuri Higgins, rhp, South Florida
39. Roberto Sabates, c, No school (Miami)
40. Corey Bachman, rhp, Virginia Military Institute
41. Jordan Herr, of, Pittsburgh
42. Colt Sedbrook, inf, Arizona
43. Garrett Clyde, rhp, San Jacinto (Texas) JC
44. Bryan Jost, 1b, Minnesota
45. Ryan Lewis, of, Yakima Valley (Wash.) CC
46. Tyler Clark, rhp, Springfield (Mo.) Catholic HS
47. Josh Walter, rhp, Texas State
48. Carlos Rivera, of, East Aurora (Ill.) HS
49. Jordan Rogers, rhp, San Jacinto (Texas) JC
50. Blake Murphy, c, Western Carolina

CHICAGO WHITE SOX (25)

1. Aaron Poreda, lhp, San Francisco
2. Nevin Griffith, rhp, Middleton HS, Tampa
3. John Ely, rhp, Miami (Ohio)
4. Leroy Hunt, rhp, Sacramento (Calif.) CC
5. Nathan Jones, rhp, Northern Kentucky
6. Johnnie Lowe, rhp, Point Loma Nazarene (Calif.)
7. Jimmy Gallagher, of, Duke
8. Lyndon Estill, of, Lower Columbia (Wash.) CC
9. Kenny Gilbert, of, DeSoto (Texas) HS
10. Brian Guinn, ss, Berkeley (Calif.) HS
11. Jordan Kendall, of, Contra Costa (Calif.) JC
12. Kevin Skogley, lhp, Nevada-Las Vegas
13. Sergio Miranda, ss, Virginia Commonwealth
14. John Curtis, c, Cal State Fullerton
15. Greg Paiml, ss, Alabama
16. Nick Mahin, of, Cal State Fullerton
17. Dale Mollenhauer, ss, East Carolina
18. Levi Maxwell, rhp, West Virginia
19. Henry Mabee, rhp, Morehead State
20. Logan Johnson, 2b, Louisville
21. Mitchell Delaney, 1b, St. Thomas of Villanova HS, LaSalle, Ontario
22. Justin Klipp, rhp, Cal State Fullerton
23. Charlie Shirek, rhp, Nebraska
24. Kevin Patterson, 1b/c, Oak Mountain HS, Birmingham
25. Dan Albritton, rhp, Florida Southern
26. Mike Bolsenbroek, rhp, Santa Ana (Calif.) JC
27. Caleb Hurst, rhp, Beyer HS, Modesto, Calif.
28. Chris Epps, of/rhp, Dunwoody (Ga.) HS
29. Jabari Blash, of, Amalie HS, St. Thomas, V.I.
30. John Flanagan, lhp, Belleville (Ill.) HS
31. Eduardo Orozco, rhp, Rubidoux HS, Riverside, Calif.
32. Andre Lamontagne, rhp, Long Beach State
33. Mitch Levier, of, Fullerton (Calif.) JC
34. Ryan Sharpley, rhp, Marshall (Mich.) HS
35. Zach Babbit, 2b, Albany HS, Richmond, Calif.
36. Oney Guillen, 2b, North Park (Ill.) JC
37. Alex Rodriguez, 3b, La Salle HS, Miami
38. Grant Monroe, rhp, Schaumburg (Ill.) HS
39. Roddy Jones, of, Chamblee (Ga.) HS
40. Austin King, 2b, Gallia Academy HS, Gallipolis, Ohio
41. Devon Shines, 1b, Westwood (Texas) HS
42. Mike Jones, of, Arizona State
43. Baldwin Vargas, rhp, New Jersey City
44. John Grim, 1b, John Hersey HS, Arlington Heights, Ill.
45. Ronnie Morales, lhp, Wichita State

CINCINNATI REDS (15)

1. Devin Mesoraco, c, Punxsutawney (Pa.) HS
1s. Todd Frazier, 3b, Rutgers (Supplemental choice—34th overall—for loss of Type A free agent Rich Aurilia)
1s. Kyle Lotzkar, rhp, South Delta (B.C.) SS (Supplemental choice—53rd overall—for loss of Type B free agent Scott Schoeneweis)
2. Zack Cozart, ss, Mississippi
3. Scott Carroll, rhp, Missouri State (Choice from Giants as compensation for Aurilia)

3. Neftali Soto, 3b, Colegio Marista HS, Manati, P.R.
4. Blake Stouffer, 3b/of, Texas A&M
5. Drew Bowman, lhp, Nebraska
6. Evan Hildenbrandt, rhp, Mennonite Educational Institute SS, Abbotsford, B.C.
7. Brandon Waring, 3b, Wofford
8. Drew O'Neill, rhp, Penn State
9. Alexis Oliveras, of, Puerto Rico Baseball Academy, Guaynabo, P.R.
10. Harris Honeycutt, rhp, South Carolina
11. Jordan Wideman, c, Streetsville SS, Mississauga, Ont.
12. Scott Gaffney, rhp/ss, Penn State
13. Brandon Menchaca, of, Delaware
14. Joseph Krebs, lhp, Texas
15. Matt Klinker, rhp, Furman
16. Shea Snowden, lhp, Brandon (Miss.) HS
17. Jesse Craig, rhp, Brigham Young
18. Taylor Jordan, rhp, Merritt Island (Fla.) HS
19. Jeff Jeffords, rhp, South Carolina
20. Jake Kahaulelio, ss, Oral Roberts
21. Jeremy Horst, lhp, Armstrong Atlantic State (Ga.)
22. Tyler Rhoden, rhp, Vanderbilt
23. Jason Bour, c, George Mason
24. Frank Meade, c, Rutgers
25. Eli Rimes, 1b, Sonoma State (Calif.)
26. Curtis Partch, rhp, Merced (Calif.) JC
27. Jason Roenicke, rhp, Cuesta (Calif.) JC
28. Derrick Conaster, rhp, Tallahassee (Fla.) CC
29. Steven Otterness, lhp, Embry-Riddle (Fla.)
30. Brett Bartles, 3b, Duke
31. Jordan Hotchkiss, rhp, Brevard (N.C.)
32. Brandon Douglas, ss, Northern Iowa
33. Brodie Pullen, 3b, Calhoun (Ga.) HS
34. Jeremy Vinyard, rhp, Boaz (Ala.) HS
35. Thad Weber, rhp, Nebraska
36. Leon Landry, 3b, Baker (La.) HS
37. Scott Alexander, lhp, Cardinal Newman HS, Santa Rosa, Calif.
38. Ari Ronick, lhp, Portland
39. Jimmy Nelson, rhp, Niceville (Fla.) HS
40. Ross Hopkins, c, Tyee HS, Seatac, Wash.
41. Kevin Hickey, of, Concordia (N.Y.)
42. Sean Bierman, lhp, Kinnelon (N.J.) HS
43. Austin Taylor, 3b, Thomas County Central HS, Thomasville, Ga.
44. Josh Beal, rhp, Independence (Kan.) CC
45. Jordan Brown, rhp, Meridian (Miss.) CC
46. Mike McGuire, rhp, Delaware
47. Drew Benes, 3b, Westminster Christian Academy, St. Louis
48. Michael Henry, rhp, St. Patrick's HS, Ottawa, Ont.
49. Cameron Gray, rhp, Silverthorn Collegiate HS, Toronto
50. Jordan Chambless, rhp, Texas A&M

CLEVELAND INDIANS (13)

1. Beau Mills, 1b/3b, Lewis-Clark State (Idaho)
2. (Choice to Mets as compensation for Type A free agent Roberto Hernandez)
3. (Choice to Phillies as compensation for Type A free agent David Dellucci)
4. T.J. McFarland, lhp, Stagg HS, Palos Heights, Ill.
5. Jonathan Holt, rhp, Tampa
6. Bo Greenwell, of, Riverdale HS, Fort Myers, Fla.
7. Cole St. Clair, lhp, Rice
8. Mark Thompson, ss, Lewis-Clark State (Idaho)
9. Adam White, of, West Virginia
10. Heath Taylor, lhp, Oklahoma
11. Matt Hague, of/rhp, Washington
12. Gary Campfield, rhp, Texas A&M
13. Matt Brown, rhp, Wichita State
14. Daniel Morales, rhp, San Francisco
15. Chris Jones, lhp, Gaither HS, Tampa
16. Doug Hogan, c, Clemson
17. Miles Morgan, rhp, Texas Tech
18. Kyle Landis, rhp, Pittsburgh
19. Bobby Coyle, of, Chatsworth (Calif.) HS
20. Jeff Hehr, ss, Eastern Michigan
21. Jared Clark, of/rhp, Cal State Fullerton
22. Stihl Sowers, rhp, North Lenoir HS, Wheat Swamp, N.C.
23. Shaeffer Hall, lhp, Jefferson County (Mo.) CC
24. Adam Zornes, c, Rice
25. Kyle Leiendecker, lhp, Homestead HS, Fort Wayne, Ind.
26. Michael Valadez, c, Lee (Tenn.)
27. Daniel Edwards, rhp, Kansas State
28. Scott Savastano, 3b/ss, Franklin Pierce (N.H.)
29. Garrett Rieck, rhp, Chico State (Calif.)
30. Bryce Brentz, rhp, South-Doyle HS, Knoxville, Tenn.
31. Jason Hessler, rhp, St. Joseph's
32. Joey Mahalic, rhp/3b, Wilson HS, Portland, Ore.

33. Tyler Kuhn, 3b/ss, West Virginia
34. Josh Judy, rhp, Indiana Tech
35. Brian Juhl, c, Stanford
36. P.J. Zocchi, rhp, Clemson
37. Dean Kiekhefer, lhp, Oldham County HS, Buckner, Ky.
38. Johnny Williams, rhp, Tampa
39. Eric Jokisch, lhp, Virginia (Ill.) HS
40. Dallas Cawiezell, rhp, Valparaiso
41. Tommy Luce, rhp, Seminole State (Okla.) JC
42. Bryce Tafelski, c, Santa Ynez (Calif.) HS
43. Travis Howell, c, Long Beach State
44. Ryan Royster, of, UC Davis
45. Dan Evatt, of, Grapevine (Texas) HS
46. Brock Simpson, of, Kansas
47. Kevin Rucker, of, Pioneer Valley HS, Santa Maria, Calif.
48. Walter Diaz, ss, Miami
49. Matt Willard, ss, Arkansas
50. Doug Pickens, c, Michigan

COLORADO ROCKIES (8)

1. Casey Weathers, rhp, Vanderbilt
2. Brian Rike, of, Louisiana Tech
3. Lars Davis, c, Illinois
4. Isaiah Froneberger, lhp, Forest Park HS, McDonough, Ga.
5. Connor Graham, rhp, Miami (Ohio)
6. Cory Riordan, rhp, Fordham
7. Jeff Cunningham, 1b, South Alabama
8. Parker Frazier, rhp, Bishop Kelley HS, Tulsa, Okla.
9. Jordan Pacheco, 2b, New Mexico
10. Jeff Fischer, rhp, Eastern Michigan
11. Andy Groves, rhp, Purdue
12. Darin Holcomb, 3b, Gonzaga
13. Beau Seabury, c, Virginia
14. Kentrail Davis, of, Theodore (Ala.) HS
15. Kenny Durst, lhp, West Virginia
16. Mitch Lively, rhp, Cal State Sacramento
17. Austin Chambliss, rhp, Middle Georgia JC
18. Brian Lapin, of, Fresno State
19. Evan Chambers, of, Lakeland (Fla.) HS
20. Matt Reynolds, lhp, Austin Peay
21. Chris Sale, lhp, Lakeland (Fla.) HS
22. Brent Bowman, 1b, Louisiana-Monroe
23. Don Taylor, rhp, Dallas Baptist
24. Brandon Miller, lhp, Fresno State
25. Mike Mitchell, of, Virginia
26. Stephen Shao, lhp, Vanderbilt
27. James Sims, of, Jackson State
28. John Rodriguez, lhp, Mississippi
29. Andres Marrero, rhp, Puerto Rico Baseball Academy, Guaynabo, P.R.
30. Bruce Billings, rhp, San Diego State
31. Israel Troupe, of, Tift County HS, Tifton, Ga.
32. Kenny Williams Jr., of, Wichita State
33. Wayman Gooch, rhp, Ohlone (Calif.) JC
34. Travis Lawler, rhp, A&M Consolidated HS, College Station, Texas
35. Dan Renken, rhp, Orange (Calif.) Lutheran HS
36. Joey Williamson, rhp, Notre Dame
37. Nick Gallego, 2b, Esperanza HS, Anaheim
38. Warren Schaeffer, ss, Virginia Tech
39. Chris Vasami, 1B, Elon
40. Richie Rowland, c, Cloverdale (Calif.) HS
41. Johnny Bowden, c, Southern California
42. David Coulon, lhp, Arizona
43. Devin Lohman, ss, Righetti HS, Santa Maria, Calif.
44. Chad Lembeck, of, Rice
45. Zach Jones, c, Jordan HS, Sandy, Utah
46. Kyle Saukko, rhp, Granite Bay (Calif.) HS
47. Logan Schafer, of, Cal Poly
48. Chris Morton, 3b, Bellevue (Wash.) HS
49. Brandon Reichert, inf, Florida State
50. Billy McHenry, 2b, Cheyenne (Wyo.) East HS

DETROIT TIGERS (27)

1. Rick Porcello, rhp, Seton Hall Prep, West Orange, N.J.
1s. Brandon Hamilton, rhp, Stanhope Elmore HS, Millbrook, Ala. (Supplemental choice—60th overall—for loss of Type B free agent Jamie Walker)
2. Danny Worth, ss, Pepperdine
3. Luke Putkonen, rhp, North Carolina
4. Charlie Furbush, lhp, Louisiana State
5. Casey Crosby, lhp, Kaneland HS, Maple Park, Ill.
6. Cale Iorg, ss, Alabama
7. Devin Thomas, c, Brown
8. Manny Miguelez, lhp, Miami

9. Justin Henry, 2b, Mississippi
10. Dominic De la Osa, of, Vanderbilt
11. Gary Perinar, rhp, Minnesota
12. Chris White, of, Sacramento (Calif.) CC
13. Londell Taylor, of, Vian (Okla.) HS
14. Chris Hernandez, lhp, Monsignor Pace HS, Opa Locka, Fla.
15. Kody Kaiser, of, Oklahoma City
16. Mark Brackman, rhp, William Jewell (Mo.)
17. Noah Krol, rhp, Wichita State
18. Kevin Rhoderick, rhp, Horizon HS, Scottsdale, Ariz.
19. Andrew Hess, rhp, Michigan
20. Erik Crichton, rhp, Oral Roberts
21. Kyle Brule, rhp, Marcos de Niza HS, Tempe, Ariz.
22. Kris Rochelle, c, UNC Charlotte
23. Brandon Harrigan, c, Oklahoma City
24. Barret Loux, rhp, Stratford (Texas) HS
25. Colin Kaline, 2b, Groves HS, Beverly Hills, Mich.
26. Matt Hoffman, lhp, Owasso (Okla.) HS
27. Steve Susdorf, of, Fresno State
28. Warren McFadden, of, Tulane
29. Wade Lamont, 1b, Flagler (Fla.)
30. Jon Kibler, lhp, Michigan State
31. Paul Nardozzi, rhp, Pittsburgh
32. Forrest Moore, lhp, Parkview Baptist HS, Baton Rouge, La.
33. Shawn Roof, ss, Illinois
34. Kyle Peter, c, Washburn (Kan.)
35. Sean Finefrock, rhp, Butler County (Kan.) CC
36. Tanner Rindels, of, Seward County (Kan.) CC
37. Toby Matchulat, rhp, Redford Union HS, Redford, Mich.
38. Austin Woodard, lhp, Bishop Carroll HS, Wichita, Kan.
39. Jake Oberlechner, ss, Arkansas City (Kan.) HS
40. D'Andrea Vaughn, of, Tavares (Fla.) HS
41. D.J. LeMahieu, 3b, Brother Rice HS, Bloomfield Hills, Mich.
42. Matt Robertson, rhp, Valley Center (Kan.) HS
43. Richard Zumaya, rhp, Bonita Vista HS, Chula Vista, Calif.
44. Kolby Wood, rhp, Berrien Springs (Mich.) HS

FLORIDA MARLINS (12)

1. Matt Dominguez, 3b, Chatsworth (Calif.) HS
2. Mike Stanton, 1b/of, Notre Dame HS, Sherman Oaks, Calif.
3. Jameson Smith, c, Fresno (Calif.) CC
4. Bryan Petersen, of, UC Irvine
5. Steven Cishek, rhp, Carson-Newman (Tenn.)
6. Taiwan Easterling, of, Oak Grove HS, Hattiesburg, Miss.
7. Andrew Paulauskas, rhp, Tremper HS, Kenosha, Wis.
8. Jay Voss, lhp, Kaskaskia (Ill.) JC
9. Marcus Crockett, of, Compton (Calif.) CC
10. Brandon Barrow, lhp, Zachary (La.) HS
11. Brett Durand, rhp, Delta State (Miss.)
12. Garrett Parcell, rhp, San Diego State
13. Chris Shafer, rhp, Cajon HS, San Bernardino, Calif.
14. Lucas Waters, 3b, Eastern Kentucky
15. Ryan Anetsberger, 3b, Illinois State
16. Adam Campbell, rhp, New Orleans
17. Mike Pasek, ss, Apple Valley (Calif.) HS
18. Chris Ingoglia, lhp, Stetson
19. Charley Williams, of, Itawamba (Miss.) CC
20. Marc Lewis, lhp, Creighton
21. Ryan Curry, 2b, Bradley
22. Chaz Gilliam, rhp, Cyril (Okla.) HS
23. Daniel Prieto, lhp, Long Beach (Calif.) CC
24. Kevin Hammons, lhp, Tusculum (Tenn.)
25. Kyle Kaminska, rhp, Naperville (Ill.) Central HS
26. Bryan Hagerich, of, Delaware
27. Ray White, ss, Compton (Calif.) CC
28. Virgil Hill, ss, Valencia (Calif.) HS
29. Ben Lasater, 3b, Charleston
30. A.J. Battisto, rhp, Georgia Southern
31. Justin Harper, rhp, Yavapai (Ariz.) JC
32. Josh Thompson, c, Mercer
33. Derek Blacksher, rhp, McNeese State
34. Stephen Flake, rhp, Southern Poly State (Ga.)
35. Josh Roberts, rhp, Portland
36. Matt Mallory, rhp, Science and Arts of Oklahoma
37. Kellen St. Luce, lhp, All Saints Cathedral HS, St. Thomas, V.I.
38. Tyler Waldron, rhp, Golden Sierra HS, Garden Valley, Calif.
39. Ricky Rossman, of, Claremont (Calif.) HS
40. Mike McCravey, lhp, JC of the Canyons (Calif.)
41. Skyler Crawford, rhp, Hartnell (Calif.) JC
42. Jim Lawler, c, Arkansas-Little Rock
43. Stephen Kohlscheen, rhp, Norman (Okla.) North HS
44. Ernie Banks, 1b, Norfolk State
45. Kevin Stanley, c, Las Lomas HS, Walnut Creek, Calif.
46. John Hellweg, rhp, St. Dominic HS, O'Fallon, Mo.

47. Mitch Rider, c, North Gwinnett HS, Suwanee, Ga.
48. Jacob Elmore, 2b, Wallace State (Ala.) CC
49. Kyle Rose, of, Lee HS, Huntsville, Ala.
50. Rafael Carlot, 3b, Southeastern (N.C.) CC

HOUSTON ASTROS (17)

1. (Choice to Rangers as compensation for Type A free agent Carlos Lee)
2. (Choice to Padres as compensation for Type A free agent Woody Williams)
3. Derek Dietrich, 3b, St. Ignatius HS, Cleveland
4. Brett Eibner, rhp, The Woodlands (Texas) HS
5. Collin DeLome, of, Lamar
6. David Dinelli, rhp, Sierra (Calif.) JC
7. Russell Dixon, 2b, Auburn
8. Chad Bettis, rhp, Monterey HS, Lubbock, Texas
9. Luis Pardo, rhp, Florida Gulf Coast
10. Matt Cusick, 2b/3b, Southern California
11. Robert Bono, c/rhp, Waterford (Conn.) HS
12. Brian Pellegrini, 1b, St. Bonaventure
13. Chad Jones, of/lhp, Southern Lab HS, Baton Rouge, La.
14. Craig Corrado, 3b, Tampa
15. Matt Fitts, rhp, Lewis-Clark State (Idaho)
16. Devon Torrence, of, Canton (Ohio) South HS
17. Mason Renders, rhp, Cisco (Texas) JC
18. Brian Esperson, rhp, Mercyhurst (Pa.)
19. Jon Fixler, c, Indiana
20. Kyle Greenwalt, rhp, Souderton (Pa.) HS
21. Kyle Miller, c, Central Florida CC
22. Drew Anderson, of, New Orleans
23. Charlie Gamble, 3b, North Carolina A&T
24. Philip Stringer, ss, Auburn
25. Kevin Carkeek, c, Oakland
26. Sal Iacono, c, Princeton
27. Brett Robinson, rhp, Florida Southern
28. Jared Pitts, of, Stephen F. Austin State
29. Travis Sweet, 3b, Iowa
30. Danny Gil, rhp, Miami
31. Jason Dominguez, rhp, Pepperdine
32. David Miller, rhp, Stephen F. Austin State
33. Cody Phipps, of, Vauxhall HS, Crows Nest Pass, Alb.
34. Brian Wabick, rhp, Oakton (Ill.) CC
35. Jordan Powell, rhp, Southern Illinois
36. Albert Cartwright, of, Polk (Fla.) CC
37. Jacob Leonhardt, rhp, Stephen F. Austin State
38. Robbie Weinhardt, rhp, Oklahoma State
39. Brian Fletcher, 3b/of, Starr's Mill HS, Fayetteville, Ga.
40. Kyle Erdman, lhp, Oakton (Ill.) CC
41. Jim Pitkin, lhp, Sterling HS, Baytown, Texas
42. Chris Turner, of, Brandon (Fla.) HS
43. Marques Williams, of, Compton (Calif.) CC
44. Cat Everett, ss, Tulane

KANSAS CITY ROYALS (2)

1. Mike Moustakas, 3b, Chatsworth (Calif.) HS
2. Sam Runion, rhp, Reynolds HS, Asheville, N.C.
3. Danny Duffy, lhp, Cabrillo HS, Lompoc, Calif.
4. Mitch Hodge, rhp, Prince of Wales SS, Vancouver, B.C.
5. Adrian Ortiz, of, Pepperdine
6. Fernando Cruz, ss, Dorado, P.R.
7. Hilton Richardson, of, Lake Washington HS, Kirkland, Wash.
8. Casey Feickert, rhp, Antelope Valley (Calif.) JC
9. Zach Kenyon, rhp, Davenport (Iowa) Central HS
10. Greg Holland, rhp, Western Carolina
11. David Lough, of, Mercyhurst (Pa.)
12. Sean McCauley, c, Osbourn HS, Manassas, Va.
13. Alex Caldera, rhp, Chaffey (Calif.) JC
14. Matt Mitchell, rhp, Barstow (Calif.) HS
15. Ryan Eigsti, c, Bradley
16. Patrick Norris, of, Oklahoma City
17. Ivor Hodgson, of, Mount St. Mary's
18. Stephen Dodson, rhp, Georgia
19. Joe Billick, c, Southern Poly State (Ga.)
20. Mike Lehmann, rhp, Pearl River Central HS, Carriere, Miss.
21. Josh Billeaud, rhp, Louisiana State-Eunice JC
22. Jacob Rodriguez, rhp, East Los Angeles JC
23. Geoff Brown, lhp, Jackson HS, Mill Creek, Wash.
24. Ben Norton, rhp, Evansville
25. Clint Robinson, 1b, Troy
26. Nat Lovell, rhp, Fresno (Calif.) JC
27. Dane Secott, rhp, Minnesota State-Mankato
28. Fernando Garcia, 2b, Manatee (Fla.) CC
29. Kyle Martin, ss, Texas Tech
30. Brett Amyx, 1b, Texas-Tyler
31. Keaton Hayenga, rhp, Eastlake (Wash.) HS

32. Jake Lane, 1b, Austin Peay State
33. Will Tucker, of, Belmont
34. Tom Hill, c, Albany
35. Garrett Weber, ss, Clovis (Calif.) HS
36. Mike Bionde, 2b, Rutgers
37. Derek Rodriguez, of, Ignacio (Colo.) HS
38. Brian Leach, rhp, Northwest Mississippi CC
39. Trevor Feeney, rhp, Northern Illinois
40. Clegg Snipes, rhp, Troy
41. Tyler Topp, rhp, Riverside (Calif.) CC
42. Doug Antilla, rhp, MidAmerica Nazarene (Kan.)
43. Chris Snipes, lhp, Middle Georgia JC
44. Chris Hopkins, of, Oregon State
45. Brandon Fowler, c, Westview HS, San Diego
46. Scott Boley, 3b, Toledo
47. John Anderson, rhp, Bossier Parish (La.) CC
48. Devery Van De Keere, 3b, Louisiana-Lafayette
49. Joe Vierra, 3b, Quartz Hill (Calif.) HS
50. Brandon Van Riper, c, Farmington (N.M.) HS

LOS ANGELES ANGELS (24)

1. (Choice to Rangers as compensation for Type A free agent Gary Matthews Jr.)
1s. Jonathan Bachanov, rhp, University HS, Orlando, Fla. (Supplemental choice—58th overall—for loss of Type B free agent Adam Kennedy)
2. (Choice to Blue Jays as compensation for Type A free agent Justin Speier)
3. Matt Harvey, rhp, Fitch HS, Groton, Conn.
4. Trevor Pippin, of, Middle Georgia JC
5. Andrew Romine, ss, Arizona State
6. Ryan Brasier, rhp, Weatherford (Texas) JC
7. Baron Short, rhp, Southern
8. Trevor Reckling, lhp, St. Benedict's Prep, Newark, N.J.
9. Tyler Mann, of, Princess Anne HS, Virginia Beach, Va.
10. Milan Dinga, rhp, Army
11. Martin Viramontes, rhp, Bullard HS, Fresno, Calif.
12. Mike Anton, lhp, Virginia Military Institute
13. David Clark, rhp, Southern Mississippi
14. Tanner Robles, lhp, Cottonwood HS, Salt Lake City
15. Chris Garcia, 3b, St. Petersburg (Fla.) JC
16. Mason Tobin, rhp, Everett (Wash.) CC
17. Eddie McKiernan, rhp, Monrovia (Calif.) HS
18. Zack Martin, 3b, Andrew (Ga.) JC
19. Ryan Kennedy, 2b, Tampa
20. Tremayne Holland, rhp, Brewton-Parker (Ga.) College
21. Justin Bass, 2b, Clements HS, Sugar Land, Texas
22. Steven Salas, rhp, Chandler-Gilbert (Ariz.) CC
23. Mike Bianucci, 3b/of, Auburn
24. DeAndre Miller, of, Loyola Marymount
25. Jordan Towns, rhp, West Georgia
26. Michael Wing, ss, Upland (Calif.) HS
27. Patrick White, of, West Virginia
28. Ty Pryor, rhp, North Florida
29. Brian Walker, c, Arkansas
30. Matt Davis, rhp, Jacksonville
31. Derek Schlecker, rhp, Western Michigan
32. Rich Bohlken, 2b, La Cueva HS, Albuquerque
33. Donato Giovanatto, of, San Jose State
34. Carlos Ramirez, c, Chandler-Gilbert (Ariz.) CC
35. Luke Gordon, of, Georgia State
36. Jay Brossman, 3b, Utah
37. Cephas Howard, rhp, None
38. Cory Page, rhp, Huntingtown (Md.) HS
39. Jayson Brown, rhp, Barry (Fla.)
40. Hector Estrella, 2b, Southern California
41. Matt Scioscia, 1b, Crespi HS, Encino, Calif.
42. Jeremy Thorne, rhp, Florida Southern
43. Terrell Alliman, of, Bluevale Collegiate Institute, Waterloo, Ont.
44. Alex Hale, rhp, Richmond
45. Chris Bullard, of, Harris County HS, Hamilton, Ga.
46. Brandon Lodge, ss, Tesoro HS, Las Flores, Calif.
47. Billy Falasco, rhp, Seminole (Fla.) HS
48. Sean Loggins, c, McCluer North HS, Florissant, Mo.
49. Chris Vitus, rhp, Sheldon HS, Sacramento
50. Efren Navarro, 1b/lhp, Nevada-Las Vegas

LOS ANGELES DODGERS (22)

1. Chris Withrow, rhp, Midland (Texas) Christian HS (Choice from Red Sox as compensation for Type A free agent Julio Lugo)
1. (Choice to Giants as compensation for Type A free agent Jason Schmidt)
1s. James Adkins, lhp, Tennessee (Supplemental choice—39th overall—for loss of Lugo)
2. Michael Watt, lhp, Capistrano Valley HS, Mission Viejo, Calif.
3. Austin Gallagher, 3b, Manheim Township HS, Lancaster, Pa.

4. Andrew Lambo, 1b/of, Newbury Park (Calif.) HS
5. Kyle Blair, rhp, Los Gatos (Calif.) HS
6. Justin Miller, rhp, Johnson County (Kan.) CC
7. Danny Danielson, rhp, Russell County HS, Seale, Ala.
8. Alex Garabedian, c, College of Charleston
9. Jaime Pedroza, ss, UC Riverside
10. Erik Kanaby, of, Lamar
11. Paul Koss, rhp, Southern California
12. Jessie Mier, c, Lewis-Clark State (Idaho)
13. Bobby Blevins, rhp, Le Moyne
14. Devin Fuller, rhp, Gilbert (Ariz.) HS
15. Cal Stanke, rhp, Wisconsin-Oshkosh
16. Andres Santiago, rhp, Colegio Carmen Sol, Bayamon, P.R.
17. Chris Jacobs, 1b, Glenn HS, Kernersville, N.C.
18. Given Kutz, rhp, Portland
19. Joris Bert, of, Frank Phillips (Texas) JC
20. Sean Koecheler, rhp, Palm Beach Gardens (Fla.) HS
21. Terry Doyle, rhp, Boston College
22. Matt Wallach, c, Cal State Fullerton
23. Nathan Carter, ss, De La Salle HS, Concord, Calif.
24. Parker Dalton, ss, Texas A&M
25. Timothy Sexton, rhp, Miami-Dade CC
26. Taylor Cole, rhp, Bishop Gorman HS, Las Vegas
27. Rob Rasmussen, lhp, Poly HS, Pasadena, Calif.
28. Nathan Woods, of, Xavier HS, Cedar Rapids, Iowa
29. Chad Keefer, 1b, North Central Texas CC
30. Justin Coats, ss, Seminole State (Okla.) JC
31. Rafael Thomas, of, Lufkin (Texas) HS
32. Matt Gardner, rhp, Oklahoma State
33. Jonathan Gonzalez, rhp, Cardinal Hayes HS, Bronx, N.Y.
34. Garrett Poe, 1b, Silver City (N.M.) HS
35. Ryan Christenson, lhp, Arnett (Okla.) HS
36. Tim Jones, rhp, Redan HS, Stone Mountain, Ga.
37. Gabriel Casanova, 2b, Barry (Fla.)
38. Matt Szczur, c, Lower Cape May (N.J.) HS
39. John Hay, of, JC of the Canyons (Calif.)

MILWAUKEE BREWERS (7)

1. Matt LaPorta, 1b, Florida
2. (Choice to Cardinals as compensation for Type A free agent Jeff Suppan)
3. Jonathan Lucroy, c, Louisiana-Lafayette
4. Eric Farris, 2b/ss, Loyola Marymount
5. Caleb Gindl, of/lhp, Pace HS, Milton, Fla.
6. Dan Merklinger, lhp, Seton Hall
7. Efrain Nieves, lhp, Puerto Rico Baseball Academy, Guaynabo, P.R.
8. David Fonseca, ss, Pierce (Calif.) JC
9. Kristian Bueno, lhp, Calallen HS, Corpus Christi, Texas
10. Eric Fryer, c, Ohio State
11. Cody Scarpetta, rhp, Guilford HS, Rockford, Ill.
12. Wes Etheridge, rhp, UC Irvine
13. Chris Dennis, of, St. Thomas of Villanova SS, LaSalle, Ont.
14. Donovan Hand, rhp, Jacksonville State
15. Joey Paciorek, 3b, Blaine (Wash.) HS
16. Joel Morales, rhp, Puerto Rico Baseball Academy, Guaynabo, P.R.
17. Erik Miller, of, Scottsdale (Ariz.) CC
18. Bobby Bramhall, lhp, Rice
19. Zealous Wheeler, 3b, Wallace State (Ala.) CC
20. Cameron Robulack, 1b, Silverthorn Collegiate Institute, Toronto
21. Connor Hoehn, rhp, St. John's HS, Washington, D.C.
22. Matt Cline, ss, Long Beach State
23. Cody Hawn, 3b, South-Doyle HS, Knoxville, Tenn.
24. Jonathan White, of, Vanderbilt
25. Chad Bell, lhp, South-Doyle HS, Knoxville, Tenn.
26. Ben Feltner, of, Texas A&M
27. Josh Trejo, lhp, Logan HS, Union City, Calif.
28. Steffan Wilson, 3b, Harvard
29. Travis Nevakshonoff, of, Humphries SS, Castlegar, B.C.
30. Corey Frerichs, rhp, Temple (Texas) JC
31. Jon Clarence, lhp, Columbus North (Ind.) HS
32. Miguel Vasquez, ss, Seminole (Fla.) CC
33. Ryan Jensen, of, None
34. Casey Baron, lhp, Maryland
35. Curtis Rindal, 1b, Washington
36. Curtis Pasma, lhp, Pacific
37. Rick Hague, ss, Klein Collins HS, Spring, Texas
38. Kurt Crowell, of, Cal State Los Angeles
39. Joe Scott, ss, Cal State Fullerton
40. Jordan Tanner, rhp, Neshannock (Pa.) HS
41. Adam Arnold, rhp, Thompson Rivers (B.C.)
42. Chase Reid, rhp, Carroll HS, Southlake, Texas
43. Cullen Sexton, rhp, Stevens Point (Wis.) HS
44. Shawn Zarraga, c/3b, Trinity Christian HS, Boynton Beach, Fla.
45. Matt Sergey, rhp, South Plantation HS, Plantation, Fla.
46. Stewart Ijames, of, Owensboro (Ky.) Catholic HS
47. Aaron Tullo, rhp, St. Petersburg JC

DRAFT

MINNESOTA TWINS (28)

1. **Ben Revere, of, Lexington (Ky.) Catholic HS**
2. **Danny Rams, c/1b, Gulliver Prep, Miami**
3. **Angel Morales, of, Puerto Rico Baseball Academy, Guaynabo, P.R.**
4. **Reggie Williams, 3b, Bellflower (Calif.) HS**
5. Nate Striz, rhp, Santa Fe Catholic HS, Lakeland, Fla.
6. **Mike McCardell, rhp, Kutztown (Pa.)**
7. **Dan Berlind, rhp, Pierce (Calif.) JC**
8. **Danny Lehmann, c, Rice**
9. **Steven Hirschfeld, rhp, San Diego State**
10. **Blair Erickson, rhp, UC Irvine**
11. **Andrew Schmiesing, of, St. Olaf (Minn.)**
12. **Mike Tarsi, lhp, Connecticut**
13. Elliot Soto, ss, Dundee-Crown HS, Carpentersville, Ill.
14. **Dan Rohlfing, c, Oakville HS, St. Louis**
15. **Daniel Latham, rhp, Tulane**
16. **Nelvin Fuentes, lhp, Puerto Rico Baseball Academy, Guaynabo, P.R.**
17. Jose Rodriguez, of/1b, Hialeah (Fla.) HS
18. **Lee Martin, rhp, Southern Arkansas**
19. **Ben Petsch, c, Belmont**
20. Tom Farmer, rhp, Akron
21. **Ozzie Lewis, of, Fresno State**
22. Mickey Storey, rhp, Florida Atlantic
23. Josh Workman, 2b, Wichita State
24. **Charles Nolte, rhp, San Diego State**
25. **Spencer Steedley, of/lhp, UNC Charlotte**
26. Kyle Witten, rhp, Bakersfield (Calif.) JC
27. Kyle Heyne, rhp, Ball State
28. Seth Rosin, rhp, Mounds View HS
29. Fred Atkins, of, JC of Marin (Calif.)
30. Josh Adams, ss, Eagle's View Academy, Jacksonville, Fla.
31. Mike Kvasnicka, of, North HS, Lakeville, Minn.
32. Johnny Bromberg, rhp, Palisades HS, Mission Viejo, Calif.
33. Evan Danieli, rhp, Seton Hall Prep, West Orange, N.J.
34. Stephen Branca, ss, Newsome HS, Lithia, Fla.
35. Ryan Strauss, rhp, Florida State
36. **Dominique Rodgers, rhp, Kent State**
37. Julien Pollard, 2b, Washington HS, Tacoma, Wash.
38. **Chris Cates, ss, Louisville**
39. Joe Leftridge, of, Duncanville (Texas) HS
40. Chase Anderson, rhp, North Central Texas CC
41. Jon Griffin, rhp, Lakewood Ranch HS, Bradenton, Fla.
42. Troy Scott, 1b, Auburn (Ala.) HS
43. **Andres Diaz, c, Palm Beach (Fla.) CC**
44. Zach Barger, of, Long Beach State
45. Kevin Arico, rhp, Hunterdon Central HS, Flemington, N.J.
46. John Williams, 3b, Niles North HS, Skokie, Ill.
47. Chris Heston, rhp, Seminole (Fla.) CC
48. Ken Smalley, rhp, Logan (Ill.) JC
49. Nick Cobler, lhp, Butler (Kan.) CC
50. Chris Freshcorn, c, Alonso HS, Tampa

NEW YORK METS (29)

1. (Choice to Giants as compensation for Type A free agent Moises Alou)
1s. **Eddie Kunz, rhp, Oregon State** (Supplemental choice—42nd overall—for loss of Type A free agent Roberto Hernandez)
1s. **Nathan Vineyard, lhp, Woodland HS, Cartersville, Ga.** (Supplemental choice—47th overall—for loss of Type A free agent Chad Bradford)
2. **Scott Moviel, rhp, St. Edward HS, Berea, Ohio** (Choice from Indians as compensation for Hernandez)
2. **Brant Rustich, rhp, UCLA**
3. **Eric Niesen, lhp, Wake Forest** (Choice from Orioles as compensation for Bradford)
3. **Stephen Clyne, rhp, Clemson**
4. **Richard Lucas, 3b, Wolfson HS, Jacksonville, Fla.**
5. **Zach Lutz, 3b, Alvernia (Pa.)**
6. **Guillaume Leduc, rhp, Montpetit HS, Montreal**
7. **Lucas Duda, 1b, Southern California**
8. **Dan McDonald, rhp, Seton Hall**
9. **Michael Olmstead, rhp, Cypress (Calif.) JC**
10. **Brandon Richey, ss, Northwestern State**
11. **Matt Bouchard, ss, Georgetown**
12. **Will Morgan, rhp, Lewis-Clark State (Idaho)**
13. **Jordan Abruzzo, c, San Diego**
14. **Robert Carson, lhp, Hattiesburg (Miss.) HS**
15. **Jefferies Tatford, c, Louisiana-Lafayette**
16. **Chris Fournier, of, George Mason**
17. Brandon Efferson, rhp, Zachary (La.) HS
18. **Michael Antonini, lhp, Georgia College**
19. **Ernesto Gonzalez, ss, George Wallace (Ala.) CC**
20. **Dylan Owen, rhp, Francis Marion (S.C.)**
21. **Dillon Gee, rhp, Texas-Arlington**
22. **Tyler Vaughn, 3b, UC Irvine**

---

23. Norberto Navarro, c, Pasco-Hernando (Fla.) CC
24. **Michael Parker, 2b, George Washington**
25. **Cole Abbott, rhp, Weber HS, Ogden, Utah**
26. **Brad Burns, rhp, Oklahoma**
27. **Kyle Catto, rhp, Southern Illinois**
28. Kyle Maxie, c, Pearl River (Miss.) CC
29. **Roydrick Merritt, lhp, Southern**
30. Rylan Sandoval, 2b, Chabot (Calif.) JC
31. Tony Peraza, lhp, La Mirada (Calif.) HS
32. **Juan Centeno, c, Antonio Lucchetti HS, Arecibo, P.R.**
33. Nicholas Abshire, ss, None
34. **Terry Johnson, ss, William Carey (Miss.)**
35. **Jason Lavorgna, rhp, Eastern Connecticut State**
36. Glen Johnson, ss/3b, South Fork HS, Hobe Sound, Fla.
37. **Jose Alvarez, 3b, Otay Ranch HS, Chula Vista, Calif.**
38. **Brandon Kawal, of, Concordia (Calif.)**
39. **Alonzo Harris, ss, McComb (Miss.) HS**

NEW YORK YANKEES (30)

1. **Andrew Brackman, rhp, North Carolina State**
2. **Austin Romine, c, El Toro HS, Lake Forest, Calif.**
3. **Ryan Pope, rhp, Savannah College of Art & Design (Ga.)**
4. **Brad Suttle, 3b, Texas**
5. **Adam Olbrychowski, rhp, Pepperdine**
6. **Chase Weems, c, Columbus (Ga.) HS**
7. **Damon Sublett, 2b/rhp, Wichita State**
8. **Taylor Grote, of, The Woodlands (Texas) HS**
9. **Austin Krum, of, Dallas Baptist**
10. **Carmen Angelini, ss, Barbe HS, Lake Charles, La.**
11. **Isaiah Howes, of, Louisville**
12. **Manuel Barreda, rhp, Sahuarita (Ariz.) HS**
13. **Nick Chigges, rhp, Charleston**
14. **Braedyn Pruitt, 3b, Stetson**
15. **Dave Williams, of, Rutgers**
16. Daniel Mahoney, rhp, Cushing Academy, Ashburnham, Mass.
17. **Ryan Zink, rhp, Illinois-Chicago**
18. Chris Carpenter, rhp, Kent State
19. **Taylor Holiday, of, UC Irvine**
20. **Ryan Wehrle, ss, Nebraska**
21. **Justin Snyder, 2b, San Diego**
22. **Craig Heyer, rhp, Nevada-Las Vegas**
23. **Matt Morris, of, UC Irvine**
24. Greg Peavey, rhp, Hudson's Bay HS, Vancouver, Wash.
25. **Jason Kiley, rhp, Florida Gulf Coast**
26. **Gary Gattis, of, Yavapai (Ariz.) JC**
27. **Brandon Laird, 3b, Cypress (Calif.) JC**
28. **Jeff Livek, rhp, Carthage (Wis.)**
29. **Matt Pilgreen, rhp, Louisiana-Lafayette**
30. **Chris Carrara, 2b, Winthrop**
31. Chad Dawson, rhp, Indiana State
32. **Brian Chavez, ss, San Francisco**
33. **Fred Jones, rhp, Evansville**
34. Drew Storen, rhp, Brownsburg (Ind.) HS
35. Greg Holle, rhp, Christian Brothers HS, Loudonville, N.Y.
36. **Danny Cox, ss, Washington**
37. **Steven Strausbaugh, of, Western Carolina**
38. Eric Komatsu, of, Oxnard (Calif.) JC
39. Eric Thames, of, Pepperdine
40. Luke Murton, 1b, Georgia Tech
41. **Jake Shafer, rhp, Missouri State**
42. **Chris Raber, 1b, Coastal Carolina**
43. Jason Chowning, rhp, Texarkana (Texas) JC
44. Tyler Herriage, lhp, Weatherford (Texas) JC
45. Pat Venditte, rhp/lhp, Creighton
46. **Dan Kapala, rhp, Notre Dame**
47. Colin Arnold, of, Daytona Beach (Fla.) CC
48. Scott Bittle, rhp, Mississippi
49. Ken Toves, lhp, Carlsbad (Calif.) HS
50. **Larry Day, c, Connecticut**

OAKLAND ATHLETICS (26)

1. **James Simmons, rhp, UC Riverside**
1s. **Sean Doolittle, 1b/lhp, Virginia** (Supplemental choice—41st overall—for loss of Type A free agent Barry Zito)
1s. **Corey Brown, of, Oklahoma State** (Supplemental choice—59th overall—for loss of Type B free agent Frank Thomas)
2. **Grant Desme, of, Cal Poly** (Choice from Giants as compensation for Zito)
2. **Josh Horton, ss, North Carolina**
3. **Sam Demel, rhp, Texas Christian**
4. **Travis Banwart, rhp, Wichita State**
5. **Andrew Carignan, rhp, North Carolina**
6. **Scott Hodsdon, rhp, Azusa Pacific (Calif.)**
7. **Lance Sewell, lhp, San Diego State**

8. Daniel Schlereth, lhp, Arizona
9. Eric Berger, lhp, Arizona
10. **Danny Hamblin, 1b, Arkansas**
11. **Michael Richard, ss, Prairie View A&M**
12. Gary Brown, of/2b, Diamond Bar HS, Walnut, Calif.
13. **Justin Friend, rhp, Oklahoma State**
14. **Matt Smith, c, Texas Tech**
15. **Brad Hertzler, lhp, Maine**
16. **Brent Lysander, rhp, Sonoma State (Calif.)**
17. Stephen Hunt, lhp, Jesuit HS, Tampa
18. **Matt Ray, ss, Middle Tennessee State**
19. **Dusty Napoleon, c, Iowa**
20. **Dan Wentzell, of, George Fox (Ore.)**
21. Stephen Porlier, rhp, Oklahoma
22. **Aaron Jenkins, lhp, Northern Iowa**
23. **J.D. Pruitt, of, Montevallo (Ala.)**
24. **Raymond Rodriguez, c, Puerto Rico Baseball Academy, Guaynabo, P.R.**
25. **Jareck West, of, Delta State (Miss.)**
26. Tobias Streich, c, Johnsonburg (Pa.) HS
27. **Justin Frash, 3b, Hawaii**
28. **Lee Land, rhp, UNC Greensboro**
29. Collin Cowgill, of, Kentucky
30. **Chad Kerfoot, rhp, Delaware**
31. **Fabian Gomez, lhp, Rockford (Ill.)**
32. **Bryan Collins, rhp, Central Missouri State**
33. **John Quine, rhp, San Francisco**
34. Ryne Tacker, rhp, Rice
35. **Herbert Hudson, of, Mount San Jacinto (Calif.) JC**
36. Trent Abbott, rhp, Fullerton (Calif.) JC
37. Nick Longmire, of, Grossmont HS, El Cajon, Calif.
38. Kevin Rath, lhp, Silverado HS, Las Vegas
39. Stan Widmann, ss, Clemson
40. Daniel Magante, c, Campbell Hall HS, North Hollywood, Calif.
41. James Wemke, lhp, Troy HS, Fullerton, Calif.
42. Jonathan Johnston, c, Navy
43. Stephen Cochrane, c, Yavapai (Ariz.) JC
44. **Ben Barrone, c, Winona State (Minn.)**
45. Jeremy Wise, 1b/3b, Louisiana State
46. Conner Bernatz, of, Mater Dei HS, Santa Ana, Calif.
47. Seth Blair, rhp, Rock Falls (Ill.) HS
48. **Adam Klein, of, Cal State Los Angeles**
49. Josh Bowman, rhp, Northeast HS, St. Petersburg, Fla.
50. Steve Hagen, 3b, Peninsula HS, Gig Harbor, Wash.

PHILADELPHIA PHILLIES (19)

1. **Joe Savery, lhp, Rice**
1s. **Travis d'Arnaud, c, Lakewood (Calif.) HS** (Supplemental choice—37th overall—for loss of Type A free agent David Dellucci)
2. **Travis Mattair, ss/3b, Southridge (Wash.) HS**
3. Brandon Workman, rhp, Bowie (Texas) HS (Choice from Indians as compensation for Dellucci)
4. **Matt Spencer, of/lhp, Arizona State**
5. **Tyler Mach, 3b, Oklahoma State**
6. **Michael Taylor, of, Stanford**
7. **Matt Rizzotti, 1b, Manhattan**
8. **Tyson Brummett, rhp, UCLA**
9. **Chance Chapman, rhp, Oral Roberts**
10. **Chris Kissock, rhp, Lewis-Clark State (Idaho)**
11. **Joe Rocchio, rhp, Cal State Northridge**
12. **Justin DeFratus, rhp, Ventura (Calif.) JC**
13. **Julian Sampson, rhp, Skyline (Wash.) HS**
14. **Luke Wertz, rhp, Nebraska**
15. **Jesus Andino, ss, Porterville (Calif.) JC**
16. **Karl Bolt, 1b, Air Force**
17. **Brian Schlitter, rhp, College of Charleston**
18. **Zack Sterner, rhp, Tennessee Wesleyan**
19. Mark Adzick, rhp, William Penn Charter HS, Haverford, Pa.
20. **Cedric Johnson, of, Thatcher (Ariz.) HS**
21. Carlos Moncrief, of, Hillcrest Christian HS, Jackson, Miss.
22. **Adam Sorgi, 2b, Stanford**
23. **Jiwan James, rhp, Williston (Fla.) HS**
24. **Gerard Breslin, rhp, La Salle**
25. **Caleb Magnum, c, North Carolina State**
26. **Billy Harris, lhp, Delaware**
27. **Nolan Mulligan, rhp, Lynn (Fla.)**
28. **Rick Austin, rhp, Seton Hill (Pa.)**
29. **Chris Rhoads, rhp, Arkansas**
30. Derek Hall, c, El Dorado HS, Placentia, Calif.
31. **Jacob Diekman, lhp, Cloud County (Kan.) CC**
32. Jeff Richard, rhp, Central Michigan
33. **Kirk Bacsu, c, Evansville**
34. **Rich Prall, c, La Salle**
35. Brett Hambright, c, Temescal Canyon HS, Lake Elsinore, Calif.

35. Zach Cleveland, rhp, Golden (Colo.) HS
36. Kyle Benoit, rhp, Cardinal Leger SS, Brampton, Ontario
37. **Kyle Slate, rhp, Christian Brothers Academy, Lincroft, N.J.**
38. Joseph Paylor, of, Hillcrest HS, Dallas
39. Michael Branham, rhp, Florida
40. John Hinson, of/2b, Reynolds HS, Asheville, N.C.
41. Tyler Glider, rhp, Butte (Mont.) HS
42. James Mahler, rhp, Jordan HS, Sandy, Utah
43. Cory Vaughn, of, Jesuit HS, Carmichael, Calif.
44. Brandon Bonner, rhp, Lakewood HS, St. Petersburg, Fla.
45. Mike Morrison, 1b, Bishop Luers HS, Fort Wayne, Ind.
46. Damien Seguen, rhp, North Bergen (N.J.) HS
47. Joey Manning, of, Bartow (Fla.) HS
48. Cody Winiarski, rhp, Union Grove (Wis.) HS
49. Navarro Holland, of, Kennesaw Mountain HS, Kennesaw, Ga.
50. Jeremy Penn, of, All Saints Cathedral HS, St. Thomas, V.I.

PITTSBURGH PIRATES (4)

1. **Daniel Moskos, lhp, Clemson**
2. **Duke Welker, rhp, Arkansas**
3. **Brian Friday, ss, Rice**
4. **Quincy Latimore, of, Middle Creek HS, Apex, N.C.**
5. **Andrew Walker, c, Texas Christian**
6. **Matt Foust, rhp, Nebraska**
7. **Juan Garcia, c, Puerto Rico Baseball Academy, Guaynabo, P.R.**
8. **Maurice Bankston, rhp, Texarkana (Texas) JC**
9. **Tony Watson, lhp, Nebraska**
10. **Sean Giblin, rhp, Pearl River (N.Y.) HS**
11. Runey Davis, of, Georgetown (Texas) HS
12. **Erik Huber, rhp, Eastern Illinois**
13. **Butch Biela, c, Palatine (Ill.) HS**
14. **Kyle McPherson, rhp, Mobile (Ala.)**
15. Rey Cotilla, rhp, Miami Springs (Fla.) HS
16. **Zach Oliver, lhp, Paris (Texas) JC**
17. **Harrison Bishop, rhp, Washington**
18. **Marcus Davis, of, Alcorn State**
19. **Bobby Spain, 3b, Oklahoma City**
20. **Brian Tracy, rhp, UC Santa Barbara**
21. **Matt Cavagnaro, 2b, Penn State**
22. Nikko Navarro, c, Flanagan HS, Pembroke Pines, Fla.
23. Luis Penate, ss, Flanagan HS, Pembroke Pines, Fla.
24. **Chad Rice, ss, Virginia Military Institute**
25. **Keanon Simon, of, Oklahoma State**
26. Steven Neff, lhp, Lancaster (S.C.) HS
27. Bob Revesz, lhp, Grove City (Pa.) HS
28. Matt Clark, 3b, Riverside (Calif.) CC
29. Brian Harrison, ss, Hilton Head (S.C.) HS
30. Josh Hula, c, Miami (Ohio)
31. **Taylor Cameron, rhp, Point Loma Nazarene (Calif.)**
32. **Daniel Forrer, lhp, Auburn-Montgomery**
33. **Caleb Fields, 2b, Northwestern**
34. Cedric Pomerlee, lhp, Gentry HS, Indianola, Miss.
35. **Tom Boleska, rhp, High Point**
36. Andrew Crisp, ss, South Carolina
37. Cody Springer, rhp, Montgomery (Texas) HS
38. Pat McAnaney, lhp, Virginia
39. J.C. Menna, rhp, Red Bank (N.J.) Catholic HS
40. Chad Poe, rhp, Bossier Parish (La.) CC
41. Demetrius Washington, of, Silver Bluff HS, New Ellenton, S.C.
42. **Daniel Bomback, 2b, Florida Atlantic**
43. Cameron Rupp, c/1b, Prestonwood Christian Academy, Plano, Texas
44. Dustin Emmons, rhp, Crescenta Valley HS, La Crescenta, Calif.
45. Pernell Halliman, rhp, West Hills (Calif.) JC
46. Reyes Dorado, rhp, Riverside (Calif.) CC
47. Robbie Broach, rhp, Archbishop Rummel HS, Metairie, La.
48. **Gary Amato, rhp, Penn State**
49. Erik Morrison, ss, Kansas
50. Brandon Glover, of, San Diego State

ST. LOUIS CARDINALS (18)

1. **Pete Kozma, ss, Owasso (Okla.) HS**
1s. **Clayton Mortensen, rhp, Gonzaga** (Supplemental choice—36th overall—for loss of Type A free agent Jeff Suppan)
2. **David Kopp, rhp, Clemson** (Choice from Brewers as compensation for Suppan)
2. **Jess Todd, rhp, Arkansas**
3. **Daniel Descalso, 3b, UC Davis**
4. Kyle Russell, of, Texas
5. **Thomas Eager, rhp, Cal Poly**
6. **Oliver Marmol, ss, Charleston**
7. **Deryk Hooker, rhp, Mira Mesa HS, San Diego**
8. **Tyler Henley, of, Rice**
9. Mike Stutes, rhp, Oregon State
10. **Beau Riportella, of, JC of the Sequoias (Calif.)**

11. Adam Reifer, rhp, UC Riverside
12. Brett Zawacki, rhp, LaSalle-Peru Township HS, LaSalle, Ill.
13. Steven Hill, 1b, Stephen F. Austin State
14. Josh Dew, 1b, Troy
15. Chuck Fick, rhp, Cal State Northridge
16. Antone DeJesus, of, Kentucky
17. Matt Arburr, 1b/3b, Pace (N.Y.)
18. Andrew Brown, of, Nebraska
19. Nick Peoples, 2b, Texas
20. Brian Cartie, 3b, McNeese State
21. Brian Broderick, rhp, Grand Canyon (Ariz.)
22. Charlie Kingrey, of, McNeese State
23. Joey Hage, of, Douglas HS, Parkland, Fla.
24. Sam Freeman, lhp, North Central Texas CC
25. Jonathan Stambaugh, lhp, Brigham Young
26. Arnoldi Cruz, 3b, Palm Beach (Fla.) CC
27. Brian Buck, of, Santa Barbara (Calif.) CC
28. Ross Oeder, 2b, Wright State
29. Charlie Pelt, 1b, Georgia State
30. Nick Derba, c, Manhattan
31. Dylan Gonzalez, rhp, Pepperdine
32. Nick Vera, 3b, Trinity (Texas)
33. Josh Fritsche, lhp, Oklahoma State
34. Steve Hill, rhp, Southeastern (Fla.)
35. Mike Blazek, rhp, Arbor View HS, Las Vegas
36. Collin Fanning, of, Brigham Young
37. C.J. Ziegler, 1b, Arizona
38. Adron Chambers, of, Pensacola (Fla.) JC
39. Rigoberto Lugo, rhp, Puerto Rico Baseball Academy, Guaynabo, P.R.
40. Justin Dalles, c, St. Petersburg (Fla.) JC
41. Ramon Delgado, rhp, Pima (Ariz.) CC
42. Ateo Folli, 2b, Buffalo
43. Davis Bilardello, lhp, South Florida
44. Dan Thomas, rhp, South Florida
45. Jameson Maj, rhp, Abilene Christian (Texas)
46. Rob Sanzillo, c, Johns Hopkins (Md.)
47. Mateo Marquez, of, Cal State Dominguez Hills
48. Jason King, of, Jerome HS, Dublin, Ohio
49. Ronald Russell, rhp, Harmony Grove HS, Camden, Ark.
50. Stephen McCray, rhp, Young Harris (Ga.) JC

SAN DIEGO PADRES (23)

1. Nick Schmidt, lhp, Arkansas
1s. Kellen Kulbacki, of, James Madison (Supplemental choice—40th overall—for loss of Type A free agent Woody Williams)
1s. Drew Cumberland, ss, Pace HS, Milton, Fla. (Supplemental choice—46th overall—for loss of Type A free agent Dave Roberts)
1s. Mitch Canham, c, Oregon State (Supplemental choice—57th overall—for loss of Type B free agent Chan Ho Park)
1s. Cory Luebke, lhp, Ohio State (Supplemental choice—63rd overall—for loss of Type B free agent Alan Embree)
1s. Danny Payne, of, Georgia Tech (Supplemental choice—64th overall—for loss of Type B free agent Ryan Klesko)
2. Eric Sogard, 2b, Arizona State (Choice from Astros as compensation for Williams)
2. Brad Chalk, of, Clemson
3. Tommy Toledo, rhp, Alonso HS, Tampa
4. Corey Kluber, rhp, Stetson (Choice from Giants as compensation for Roberts)
4. Lance Zawadzki, ss, Lee (Tenn.)
5. Jeremy Hefner, rhp, Oral Roberts
6. Emmanuel Quiles, c, Delgado HS, Sabana Hoyo, P.R.
7. Justin Baum, 3b, Pacific
8. Matt Teague, lhp, Carson-Newman (Tenn.)
9. Wynn Pelzer, rhp, South Carolina
10. Christian Colon, ss/2b, Canyon HS, Canyon Country, Calif.
11. Shane Buschini, of, San Diego
12. Luis Martinez, c, Cumberland (Tenn.)
13. Allen Harrington, lhp, Lamar
14. Keith Conlon, of, Texas Christian
15. Ryan Hill, of, Rutgers
16. Robert Perry, of, Long Beach State
17. Brandon Gomes, rhp, Tulane
18. Robbie Blauer, 1b, UC Santa Barbara
19. Adam McDaniel, rhp, Georgia
20. Robert Woodard, rhp, North Carolina
21. Tyler Davis, rhp, Hawaii
22. Keoni Ruth, 2b, Concordia (Calif.)
23. Angel Mercado, of, Bethune-Cookman
24. Bryan Oland, rhp, Sonoma State (Calif.)
25. Hunter Ovens, of, Cardinal Mooney HS, Bradenton, Fla.
26. Andy Parrino, 2b, Le Moyne
27. Zach Brown, of, The Citadel
28. Shawn Olsen, rhp, Southern California

29. Brian Joynt, 3b, Oklahoma City
30. Dylan Axelrod, rhp, UC Irvine
31. Colt Hynes, lhp, Texas Tech
32. Anthony Renteria, ss, Great Oaks HS, Temecula, Calif.
33. A.J. Schugel, 3b, Mountain Vista HS, Highlands Ranch, Colo.
34. Joseph Pagan, 1b, Archbishop Curley-Notre Dame HS, Miami
35. Ross Wilson, ss, Hoover (Ala.) HS

SAN FRANCISCO GIANTS (10)

1. Madison Bumgarner, lhp, South Caldwell HS, Hudson, N.C.
1. Tim Alderson, rhp, Horizon HS, Scottsdale, Ariz. (Choice from Dodgers as compensation for Type A free agent Jason Schmidt)
1. Wendell Fairley, of, George County-Lucedale (Miss.) HS (Choice from Mets as compensation for Type A free agent Moises Alou)
1s. Nick Noonan, 2b, Parker HS, San Diego (Supplemental choice—32nd overall—for loss of Alou)
1s. Jackson Williams, c, Oklahoma (Supplemental choice—43rd overall—for loss of Schmidt)
1s. Charlie Culberson, 2b/ss, Calhoun (Ga.) HS (Supplemental choice—51st overall—for loss of Type B free agent Mike Stanton)
2. (Choice to Athletics as compensation for Type A free agent Barry Zito)
3. (Choice to Reds as compensation for Type A free agent Rich Aurilia)
4. (Choice to Padres as compensation for Type A free agent Dave Roberts)
5. Chance Corgan, rhp, Texas Christian
6. Michael Ambort, c, Lamar
7. Kyle Nicholson, rhp, Texas A&M
8. Daniel Turpen, rhp, Oregon State
9. Dan Runzler, lhp, UC Riverside
10. Joe Paterson, lhp, Oregon State
11. Evan McArthur, 3b, Cal State Fullerton
12. Andrew Davis, 3b, Kent State
13. Andy Reichard, rhp, Georgia College & State
14. Craig Clark, lhp, Penn State
15. Bruce Edwards, of, Auburn
16. Steve Edlefsen, rhp, Nebraska
17. John King, rhp, Lipscomb
18. Andy de la Garza, lhp, Coastal Carolina
19. Andy D'Alessio, 1b, Clemson
20. David Mixon, rhp, Louisiana-Monroe
21. Danny Otero, rhp, South Florida
22. Oliver Odle, rhp, Oklahoma State
23. Drew Bowlin, rhp, Chattanooga State Tech (Tenn.) CC
24. Brock Bond, 2b, Missouri
25. Casey Bond, of, Lipscomb
26. Ramon Corona, ss/2b, North Carolina State
27. Myles Schroder, of, Diablo Valley (Calif.) JC
28. Dan McDaniel, rhp, Chabot (Calif.) JC
29. Lars Knepper, rhp, Hawaii-Hilo
30. Johnny Monell, c, Seminole (Fla.) CC
31. Josh Kasel, ss, Lehigh (Pa.) Senior HS
32. Dom Duggan, of, Coastal Carolina
33. Mike Loberg, of, Augustana (S.D.)
34. Tyler Ladendorf, ss, Howard (Texas) JC
35. T.J. Brewer, rhp, Arkansas State
36. Paul Clemens, rhp, Louisburg (N.C.) JC
37. Jason Neitz, lhp, East Carolina
38. J.J. Pannell, rhp, George Mason
39. Tim Egart, rhp, Arkansas State
40. Ben Wilshire, rhp, Austin Peay State
41. Brandon Grabham, rhp, Grayson County (Texas) CC
42. Chad Rothford, 1b, Oral Roberts
43. Shane Jordan, of, Stetson
44. Joseph Edens, rhp, Samford
45. Phil Disher, c, South Carolina
46. John Rye, of, Florida State
47. Ryan Verdugo, lhp, Skagit Valley (Wash.) CC
48. Andrew Barbosa, lhp, South Florida (Fla.) CC
49. Trent Kline, c, South Carolina
50. Mike Loree, rhp, Villanova

SEATTLE MARINERS (11)

1. Phillippe Aumont, rhp, Ecole Du Versant, Gatineau, Que.
1s. Matt Mangini, 3b, Oklahoma State (Supplemental choice—52nd overall—for loss of Type B free agent Gil Meche)
2. Denny Almonte, of, Florida Christian HS, Miami
3. Danny Carroll, of, Valley View HS, Moreno Valley, Calif.
4. Nolan Gallagher, rhp, Stanford
5. Joe Dunigan, of, Oklahoma
6. James McOwen, of, Florida International
7. Nick Hill, lhp, Army
8. Donnie Hume, lhp, San Diego State
9. Aaron Brown, rhp, Houston
10. Keith Renaud, rhp, Franklin Pierce (N.H.)
11. Jeff Dunbar, c, UC Riverside

12. Ryan Moorer, rhp, Maryland
13. Shawn Kelley, rhp, Austin Peay
14. Brandon McKerney, rhp, Washington
15. Keith Meyer, rhp, Duquesne
16. Colin Buckborough, rhp, Stamford Collegiate SS, Niagara Falls, Ont.
17. Ryan Rodriguez, rhp, Nevada
18. Guy Welsh, 3b, UNC Greensboro
19. Robert Mena, ss, Tampa
20. Stephen Penney, rhp, UC Riverside
21. Travis Mortimore, lhp, Wayne State (Neb.)
22. Bryan Harris, rhp, Cal State Fullerton
23. Broadie Downs, rhp, Modesto (Calif.) JC
24. Matt Renfree, rhp, Nevada
25. Conrad Flynn, rhp, Lee HS, Midland, Texas
26. Jake Wild, rhp, Pacific
27. Brooks Mohr, rhp, Elida (Ohio) HS
28. Josh Satow, lhp, Arizona State
29. Javier Martinez, rhp, Fordham
30. Jason Nance, 1b, Blackford HS, Hartford City, Ind.
31. Rod Scurry, rhp, Nevada
32. Blake Trinkler, 2b, Modesto (Calif.) JC
33. Chris Pecora, of, North Carolina Wesleyan
34. Johnny DuRocher, rhp, Washington
35. Trent Rothlin, rhp, Foard HS, Newton, N.C.
36. Cole Cook, rhp, Palisades Charter HS, Pacific Palisades, Calif.
37. Donald Brown, of, Pepperdine
38. Chris Kupillas, rhp, Central Michigan
39. Michael Beltran, ss, St. John Bosco, Lakewood, Calif.
40. Josh Liles, c, Jackson (Tenn.) HS
41. Matthew Thomas, rhp, Chino Hills (Calif.) HS
42. Jack Peterson, 2b, La Jolla (Calif.) HS
43. Jason Buursma, rhp, Bucknell
44. Forrest Snow, rhp, Lakeside HS, Seattle
45. Clay Van Hook, 2b, Texas
46. Kyle Haas, rhp, Northeastern Oklahoma A&M
47. Brett Oberholtzer, lhp, Penn HS, New Castle, Del.
48. Eric Maupin, rhp, Galena HS, Reno, Nev.
49. David Carpenter, rhp, New Mexico JC
50. Nick Purdy, of, St. Mary SS, Hamilton, Ont.

TAMPA BAY DEVIL RAYS (1)

1. David Price, lhp, Vanderbilt
2. Will Kline, rhp, Mississippi
3. Nicholas Barnese, rhp, Simi Valley (Calif.) HS
4. David Newmann, lhp, Texas A&M
5. Dustin Biell, of, Inglemoor HS, Kenmore, Wash.
6. Emeel Salem, of, Alabama
7. Reid Fronk, 3b/of, North Carolina
8. Matt Moore, rhp, Moriarty (N.M.) HS
9. Cody Cipriano, 2b, UC Irvine
10. Greg Sexton, 3b, William & Mary
11. D.J. Jones, of, Gulf Shores (Ala.) HS
12. Stephen Vogt, 1b, Azusa Pacific (Calif.)
13. Brian Flores, lhp, Arizona State
14. Kyle Ayers, rhp, Oswego (Ill.) HS
15. Mike Southern, rhp, West Hills (Calif.) JC
16. Josh Johnson, rhp, Mississippi State
17. Will Harvill, rhp, Young Harris (Ga.) JC
18. Julius Dettrich, lhp, Arlington (Wash.) HS
19. Kevin Boggan, rhp, Boston College
20. Chris Luck, rhp, South Granville HS, Creedmoor, N.C.
21. Kevin Brophy, rhp, UCLA
22. Ryan Turner, rhp, Richland (Texas) HS
23. Joel Carranza, c, Flanagan HS, Pembroke Pines, Fla.
24. John Baird, rhp, Cincinnati
25. Justin Garcia, rhp, Western Nevada CC
26. Grimes Medlin, lhp, Young Harris (Ga.) JC
27. John Mollicone, c, Fordham
28. Ben Humphrey, 1b, Central Michigan
29. Robert Morey, rhp, Cape Henry HS, Virginia Beach
30. Joseph Cruz, rhp, East Los Angeles JC
31. Stephen Sauer, rhp, Western Nevada CC
32. Thad Griffen, c, Barbe HS, Lake Charles, La.
33. R.J. Preach, rhp, Brophy Prep, Phoenix
34. Kevin Chavez, rhp, St. Michaels HS, Santa Fe, N.M.
35. Joe Terdoslavich, c, Sarasota (Fla.) HS
36. Travis Stortz, lhp, Countryside HS, Clearwater, Fla.
37. Robert Della Grotta, rhp, Pepperdine
38. Jesse Darcy, rhp, Manhattan
39. Joe Staley, c, Decatur (Texas) HS
40. Will Smith, lhp, Northgate HS, Newnan, Ga.
41. Austin Hinkle, rhp, Coastal Carolina
42. Sean Green, rhp, Chesterton (Ind.) HS
43. Brad Buehler, rhp, St. Pius X HS, Festus, Mo.

44. Braden Degamo, c, Mariner HS, Everett, Wash.
45. Brett Miller, rhp, Montgomery HS, San Diego
46. Elliot Glynn, lhp, Wilson HS, Long Beach
47. Kyle Decater, of, Bellevue (Wash.) CC
48. Matt Evers, lhp, Stratford (Texas) HS
49. Ken Burdi, rhp, Kishwaukee (Ill.) CC
50. Mark Peterson, lhp, Lincoln Park Academy, Fort Pierce, Fla.

TEXAS RANGERS (16)

1. (Choice to Blue Jays as compensation for Type A free agent Frank Catalanotto)
1. **Blake Beavan, rhp, Irving (Texas) HS** (Choice from Astros as compensation for Type A free agent Carlos Lee)
1. **Michael Main, rhp/of, Deland (Fla.) HS** (Choice from Angels as compensation for Type A free agent Gary Matthews Jr.)
1s. **Julio Borbon, of, Tennessee** (Supplemental choice—35th overall—for loss of Lee)
1s. **Neil Ramirez, rhp, Kempsville (Va.) HS** (Supplemental choice—44th overall—for loss of Matthews)
1s. **Tommy Hunter, rhp, Alabama** (Supplemental choice—54th overall—for loss of Type B free agent Mark DeRosa)
2. **Matt West, 3b, Bellaire (Texas) HS**
3. **Evan Reed, rhp, Cal Poly**
4. Garrett Nash, ss/of, Jordan HS, Draper, Utah
5. John Gast, lhp, Lake Brantley HS, Altamonte Springs, Fla.
6. **Bobby Wilkins, rhp, Valhalla HS, El Cajon, Calif.**
7. **Tim Smith, of, Arizona State**
8. **Jonathan Greene, c, Western Carolina**
9. **Ralph Stoneburner, inf, James Madison**
10. **Andrew Laughter, rhp, Louisiana-Lafayette**
11. Anthony Ranaudo, rhp, St. Rose HS, Ocean Township, N.J.
12. Drew Pomeranz, lhp, Collierville (Tenn.) HS
13. **Kyle Ocampo, rhp, Poly HS, Riverside, Calif.**
14. **Matt Lawson, 2b, Missouri State**
15. **Hector Nelo, rhp, St. Thomas (Fla.)**
16. **Josh Lueke, rhp, Northern Kentucky**
17. **Mitch Moreland, 1b/lhp, Mississippi State**
18. **Ryan Tatusko, rhp, Indiana State**
19. **Kyle Murphy, of, Kansas**
20. **Kenny Smith, 2b, Western Carolina**
21. Erik Davis, rhp, Stanford
22. **Donnie Ecker, of, Lewis-Clark State (Idaho)**
23. **Jake Kaase, ss, Texas Lutheran**
24. **Chris Gradoville, c, Creighton**
25. Andy Wilkins, 3b/1b, Broken Arrow (Okla.) HS
26. Kevin Keyes, of, Connally HS, Austin, Texas
27. Drew Gray, c, Longview (Mo.) CC
28. **Mike Ortiz, 1b, Miami Palmetto Senior HS**
29. **Ryan Falcon, lhp, UNC Greensboro**
30. **Ben Henry, rhp, Loris (S.C.) HS**
31. **Anton Maxwell, rhp, Oregon State**
32. Gaspar Santiago, lhp, Puerto Rico Baseball Academy, Guaynabo, P.R.
33. **Jared Hyatt, rhp, Georgia Tech**
34. Chase Hutchingson, lhp, Fayetteville (Ark.) HS
35. Jeff Schaus, of, Barron Collier HS, Naples, Fla.
36. Brian Dupra, rhp, Greece Athena HS, Rochester, N.Y.
37. Bryan Salsbury, rhp, San Jacinto (Calif.) HS
38. Hunter Hill, rhp, Prestonwood Christian Academy, Plano, Texas
39. Tyler Fleming, rhp, Cowley County (Kan.) CC.
40. Sean Meehan, rhp, Centralia (Wash.) HS
41. Tom Edwards, 1b, Rutgers
42. **Jason Sowers, 1b, Cowley County (Kan.) CC**
43. Joey Rosas, lhp, Yavapai (Ariz.) JC
44. Kris Jiggitts, rhp, Colby (Kan.) CC
45. **Ryan Turner, lhp, Georgia Tech**
46. Yoandy Barroso, of, Miami Springs (Fla.) HS
47. Ben Petralli, c, Sacramento (Calif.) CC
48. Dillon Baird, ss, Yavapai (Ariz.) JC
49. Brandon Hayes, of, Sheldon HS, Sacramento
50. Paul Zarlengo, 1b, Marian Catholic HS, Chicago Heights, Ill.

TORONTO BLUE JAYS (21)

1. **Kevin Ahrens, 3b, Memorial HS, Houston** (Choice from Rangers as compensation for Type A free agent Frank Catalanotto)
1. **J.P. Arencibia, c/1b, Tennessee**
1s. **Brett Cecil, lhp, Maryland** (Supplemental choice—38th overall—for loss of Type A free agent Justin Speier)
1s. **Justin Jackson, ss, Roberson HS, Asheville, N.C.** (Supplemental choice—45th overall—for loss of Catalanotto)
1s. **Trystan Magnuson, rhp, Louisville** (Supplemental choice—56th overall—for loss of Type B free agent Ted Lilly)
2. **John Tolisano, 2b/of, Estero (Fla.) HS**
2. **Eric Eiland, of, Lamar HS, Houston** (Choice from Angels as compensation for Speier)

3. Alan Farina, rhp, Clemson
4. Brad Mills, lhp, Arizona
5. Marc Rzepcynski, lhp, UC Riverside
6. Mike McDade, 1b, Silverado HS, Las Vegas
7. Randy Boone, rhp, Texas
8. Scott Leffler, rhp, Tampa
9. Marcus Walden, rhp, Fresno (Calif.) CC
10. Joel Collins, c, South Alabama
11. Brad Emaus, 2b, Tulane
12. Steve Condotta, ss, Florida Tech
13. Jon Talley, c, Carlsbad (Calif.) HS
14. Cody Crowell, lhp, Vanderbilt
15. Nate Jennings, rhp, Texas-Tyler
16. Darin Mastroianni, 2b, Southern Indiana
17. Adalberto Santos, 2b, New Mexico JC
18. Chris Corrigan, rhp, San Jacinto (Texas) JC
19. Brian Letko, lhp, Embry-Riddle (Fla.)
20. Jake Hale, rhp, Ohio State
21. Cody Dunbar, rhp, Texas Christian
22. Matt Thompson, rhp, Santa Rosa (Calif.) JC
23. Frank Gailey, lhp, West Chester (Pa.)
24. Jimmy Dougher, rhp, SUNY Cortland
25. Jay Monti, rhp, Sacred Heart
26. Ross Buckwalter, rhp, Shippensburg (Pa.)
27. Kyle Gilligan, ss, Connors State (Okla.) JC
28. Xorge Carrillo, c, McClintock HS
29. Jonathan Runnels, lhp, Rice
30. Dave Kaye, rhp, Riverview HS, Oakmont, Pa.

WASHINGTON NATIONALS (6)

1. Ross Detwiler, lhp, Missouri State
1s. Josh Smoker, lhp, Calhoun (Ga.) HS (Supplemental choice—31st overall—for loss of Type A free agent Alfonso Soriano)
1s. Michael Burgess, of, Hillsborough HS, Tampa (Supplemental choice—49th overall—for loss of Type B free agent Jose Guillen)
2. Jordan Zimmermann, rhp, Wisconsin-Stevens Point (Choice from Cubs as compensation for Soriano)
2. Jake Smolinski, 3b, Boylan Catholic HS, Rockford, Ill.
3. Steven Souza, 3b, Cascade HS, Everett, Wash.
4. Derek Norris, c, Goddard (Kan.) HS
5. Brad Meyers, rhp, Loyola Marymount
6. Jack McGeary, lhp/1b, Roxbury Latin HS, West Roxbury, Mass.
7. P.J. Dean, rhp, New Caney (Texas) HS

8. Adrian Alaniz, rhp, Texas
9. Mark Gildea, of, Florida State
10. Patrick McCoy, lhp, Sahuaro HS, Tucson, Ariz.
11. Bill Rhinehart, of, Arizona
12. Craig Stinson, c, Texas A&M
13. Steve Shepard, rhp, Franklin Pierce (N.H.)
14. Dan Lyons, ss, Minnesota
15. Patrick Arnold, rhp, Huntington (W.Va.) HS
16. Chris Blackwood, of, Gloucester County (N.J.) JC
17. Luke Pisker, rhp, Virginia Commonwealth
18. Swain Carroll, 1b, Kentucky
19. Jeff Mandel, rhp, Baylor
20. Daniel Cook, of, Florida Atlantic
21. Anthony Benner, 3b, Southwestern (Calif.) JC
22. Jake Rogers, ss, South Dakota State
23. David Duncan, lhp, Georgia Tech
24. Rick Nolan, c, St. Leo (Fla.)
25. Chris Berroa, of, Pennsauken (N.J.) HS
26. Kelvin Clark, of, Redan HS, Stone Mountain, Ga.
27. Aaron Seuss, of, California Baptist
28. Boomer Whiting, of, Louisville
29. Justin Phillabaum, rhp, Florida Atlantic
30. Zach Pitts, rhp, Louisville
31. Dave Stewart, of, St. John Vianney HS, St. Louis
32. Dan Killian, c, Chippewa Hills HS, Remus Mich.
33. Jeff McCollum, rhp, Southern
34. Kenn Kasparek, rhp, Texas
35. Alex Floyd, of, Hillsborough (Fla.) CC
36. Martin Beno, rhp, Oklahoma State
37. Devin Drag, rhp, Chapman (Calif.)
38. Shane Erb, rhp, Hillsborough (Fla.) CC
39. Caleb Staudt, rhp, St. Mary's (Texas)
40. Kai Tuomi, lhp, Evansville
41. Iden Nazario, of/lhp, Southridge HS, Miami
42. Garrett Bass, of, Jacksonville State
43. Michael Martinez, lhp, Columbus HS, Miami
44. Clint Pridmore, 3b, Santa Rosa (Calif.) JC
45. Travis Reagan, c, Rice
46. Ryan Cisterna, c, Chandler-Gilbert (Ariz.) CC
47. Jeffrey Walters, rhp, St. Petersburg (Fla.) JC
48. Kyle Gunderson, rhp, Rice
49. Jake Dugger, of, Arkansas
50. Lindon Bond, of, Texas Southern

APPENDIX

■ **Bob Allen**, public-relations director for his hometown Milwaukee Braves from 1956-1965 and a longtime sportswriter, died May 2 in Brookfield, Wis. He was 75.

■ **Ed Bahr**, a righthander who pitched in two big league seasons for the Pirates and in 10 pro seasons overall, died April 6 in Seattle. He was 87.

■ **Steve Barber**, a lefthander who pitched for seven teams in 15 big league seasons, primarily with the Orioles, died Feb. 4 in Henderson, Nev. He was 67. Barber became the first 20-game winner in the franchise's Baltimore history in 1963, when he went 20-13, 2.75 in 259 innings.

■ **Hank Bauer**, a three-time all-star outfielder and member of seven World Series-winning Yankees clubs, died Feb. 9 in Shawnee Mission, Kan. He was 84. Bauer also spent eight seasons as a big league manager, guiding the Orioles to their first World Series title in 1966.

■ **Rod Beck**, a righthanded reliever who pitched for 13 seasons in the big leagues, compiling 286 saves, died June 23 in Scottsdale, Ariz. He was 38. Shooter, as Beck was known, made his major league debut in 1991 for the Giants, and the next season he became the Giants' closer. He had a club-record 48 saves in 1993 and held the closer job through 1997, when he signed with the Cubs as a free agent. Beck established a career high with 51 saves that season. After two and half seasons with the Red Sox, Beck signed with the Cubs in 2003. He pitched in 21 games for Triple-A Iowa, famously interacting with fans after games in his 36-foot RV beyond the center field wall at Sec Taylor Stadium in Des Moines. Beck finished his career with 38-45, 3.30 numbers and those 286 saves, a total that ranked 22nd all time at the time of his death.

■ **Milt Bocek**, an outfielder who was the oldest living former White Sox player, died April 29 in Brookfield, Ill. He was 94.

Nicknamed "Beltin' Bo from Cicero," Boceck signed with the White Sox at the end of the 1933 season after he had been playing semipro ball--and he went straight to the majors. He hit .267/.362/.350 in two big league seasons.

■ **Stew Bowers**, a righthander who pitched for the Red Sox in the 1930s as part of a seven-year career from 1935 to 1941, died Dec. 14, 2005, in Hagerstown, Pa. He was 90.

Bowers did not pitch a game in the minors before debuting for Boston in 1935, when the righthander went 2-1, 3.38 in 24 innings. Bowers, whose son Stewart also played professionally, played his final major league season in 1937.

■ **Clete Boyer**, a 16-year big league third baseman for the Kansas City Athletics, Yankees and Braves, died June 4 in Atlanta. He was 70. The Athletics signed the slick-fielding Boyer in 1955 as a bonus baby, and he didn't play a game in the minors until his third pro season. While he hit just .241 and .217 in his initial two big league seasons, a trade to the Yankees in June 1957 cemented his future. Teamed with Mickey Mantle, Roger Maris and Whitey Ford, Boyer played for five consecutive World Series teams from 1960 to 1964. A contemporary of Brooks Robinson's, Boyer would have to wait for his trade to the National League to win his first and only Gold Glove award, in 1969 with the Braves. Boyer also enjoyed his finest offensive season in the NL, in 1967, when he hit .245/.292/.423 for the Braves with 26 home runs and 96 RBIs. Boyer was one of four brothers to play professional baseball. His brothers Ken and Cloyd, a righthander, played in the major leagues, while Len and Ron played in the minors. Clete Boyer hit .242/.299/.372

in 1,725 career big league games with 162 home runs. His career fielding percentage (.965) and range factor (3.26) at third base ranked significantly higher than the league averages over that span (.951 and 2.75).

■ **Richard Belec**, former Baseball Canada president and a longtime developer of baseball in his home province of Quebec, died in April. He was 71. A 2003 inductee into the Canadian Baseball Hall of Fame, Belec served IBAF as vice president of the youth commission from 1980 to 1994, and was Baseball Canada president from 1994 to 1996.

■ **Ray Berres**, a backup catcher for the Brooklyn Dodgers, Pirates, Boston Braves and New York Giants in 11 big league seasons, died Feb. 1 in Kenosha, Wis. He was 99. Berres had an excellent defensive reputation and an exceptional throwing arm that assured him a steady job once he established himself in the majors. He had been the second-oldest living player at the time of his death.

■ **Marv Breeding**, a second baseman for the Orioles, Washington Senators and Dodgers in four big league seasons, died Dec. 31, 2006, in Decatur, Ala. He was 72. The Orioles signed Breeding in 1955 and he made his major league debut in 1960, hitting .267 in 551 at-bats for the Orioles. He was traded to the Senators in late 1962 and proceeded to split the 1963 season between Washington and the Los Angeles, in what would be his final big league season. Breeding hit .250/.288/.314 in 415 games major league games.

■ **Chris Brown**, a third baseman for the Giants, Padres and Tigers in six big league seasons, died Dec. 26, 2006, in Houston. He was 45. The Giants drafted Brown in the second round of the 1979 draft out of Crenshaw High in Los Angeles, where he had been a teammate of Darryl Strawberry. Brown hit .269/.333/.392 in 449 big league games.

■ **Lew Burdette**, a righthander who won 203 big league games for six teams and who won three games for the Milwaukee Braves in the 1957 World Series to take MVP honors, died Feb. 6 in Winter Garden, Fla. He was 80. Burdette joined Hall of Fame lefthander Warren Spahn in Milwaukee's rotation beginning in 1954 and the duo would attain fame as baseball's most notable pitching pair, and maybe the most effective. Burdette pitched very well in 1954-55, but for the six seasons from 1956 to 1961, Burdette was one of the league's most durable and effective starters. He was among the league leaders in wins, innings and fewest walks per nine innings in each of the six seasons. Burdette finished 11th in NL MVP voting in 1958 (and third in Cy Young voting) for going 20-10, 2.91 in 275 innings, and finished 12th in 1959 for going 21-15, 4.07 in 290 innings. But it was his 1956 season that might have been his finest. That year, Burdette, went 19-10, 2.70 with 110 strikeouts in 256 innings. His ERA was tops in the league as were his six shutouts. Burdette's defining accomplishment, though, was his masterful pitching for the Spahn and Hank Aaron-led 1957 Braves team which won the Braves only Milwaukee championship, against the Yankees no less. Burdette went 3-0, 0.67 in three World Series starts that fall, all three complete games. He struck out 13 Yankees batters while walking just four over his 27 innings of work. Burdette went 203-144, 3.66 in 3,067 big league innings, allowing a meager 1.84 walks per nine innings for his career.

■ **Sam Calderone**, a catcher who played in 91 games

in parts of three seasons for the New York Giants and Milwaukee Braves, died Nov. 28, 2006, in Mount Holly, N.J. He was 80.

■ **Sam Chapman**, an outfielder and veteran of 11 big league seasons who did not play a game in the minor leagues before debuting for the Philadelphia Athletics, died Dec. 22, 2006, near Tiburon, Calif. He was 90. Chapman was an All-American in both baseball and football at California and was drafted by the NFL's Washington Redskins in 1938, but he opted to sign with the Athletics and made his major league debut that May, shortly after graduation. Chapman hit an impressive .259/.353/.461 as a rookie with 17 home runs. He finished 12th in the 1941 AL MVP vote for hitting .322/.378/.543 with 25 homers and 106 RBIs. Chapman lost the better part of four prime seasons when he joined the Navy during World War II--from 1942 to 1944 and most of 1945--but returned to make the 1946 all-star team. He hit .266/.342/.438 with 180 home runs in 1,368 major league games.

■ **Mike Coolbaugh**, a slugging minor league third baseman who played briefly for the Brewers and Cardinals in a 17-year pro career, died July 22 in North Little Rock, Ark. He was 35. Coolbaugh was killed by a line drive while he was coaching first base for Double-A Tulsa in the Texas League. Coolbaugh, who's brother Scott is the hitting coach for the league's Frisco team, had joined the Drillers on July 3 as interim hitting coach. It was the first time in 33 years that someone on the field had been killed during a professional baseball game. The Blue Jays drafted the San Antonio native in the 16th round out of Roosevelt High School, where Coolbaugh was an all-city quarterback. Coolbaugh's minor league numbers speak for themselves: He hit .266/.337/.467 with 258 home runs. The Blue Jays took him in the 16th round of the 1990 draft, and his finest season came in 1997, when he hit .308/.369/.542 for Double-A Huntsville, leading the Southern League with 30 home runs and 132 RBIs. His brother Scott, who also played in the majors, is hitting coach for Double-A Frisco. Coolbaugh batted .183/.256/.329 in 44 big league games in 2001 and 2002.

■ **Scat Davis**, an outfielder who appeared in one game for the Brooklyn Dodgers as a pinch runner, as part of a seven-year pro career from 1942-1948, died July 23 in Clearwater, Fla. He was 86.

■ **Pat Dobson**, an all-star righthander and 20-game winner who pitched for six teams in 11 big league seasons, died Nov. 22, 2006, in San Diego. He was 64. Dobson signed with the Tigers in 1959, finally breaking in with the Tigers in 1967 by going 1-2, 2.94 in 49 innings. The Tigers traded Dobson to the Padres following the 1969 season. He struck out 185 batters in 251 innings in his sole season in San Diego, attracting the attention of the Orioles, to whom he was traded in 1970. With Baltimore, Dobson would have his finest seasons, going 20-8, 2.90 and 16-18, 2.65 in 1971 and 1972. The Orioles won the pennant in the former season and Dobson was an all-star in the latter, despite leading the league in losses. He split the 1973 season between the Braves and Yankees and had his last great season with New York in 1974, going 19-15, 3.07 in 281 innings that year. He would spend one more year with the Yankees and his final two with the Indians, retiring following the 1977 season. Dobson went 122-129, 3.54 in 2,120 big league innings. After his playing career, he served as pitching coach for the

Brewers (1982-1984), the Padres (1988-1990), the Royals (1991) and the Orioles (1996). He joined the Giants in 1997 as an advance scout. Dobson was a special assistant to general manager Brian Sabean at the time of his death.

■ **Dr. Barry Goldberg**, chairman of the USA Baseball medical/safety advisory committee, died in September. He had served in that capacity since 1993. In 1996, Goldberg was elected to the Little League Baseball International board of directors, where he worked to curb overuse of young baseball pitchers. In 2003, Goldberg was named to the medical advisory committee of Major League Baseball.

■ **Art Fowler**, a righthander who pitched for the Reds, Dodgers and Angels in a nine-year big league career and who went on to a career as pitching coach, died Jan. 29 in Spartanburg, S.C. He was 84. Fowler enjoyed a lengthy career, pitching from 1944 to 1970, though just nine of his 26 playing seasons were spent in the big leagues. He spent the 1969 season as a coach with the Twins and did not pitch, before returning for one last go-round with Denver (American Association) in 1970. Fowler went 54-51, 4.03 in 362 big league games.

■ **Owen Friend**, a second baseman who played in five major league seasons for five teams, died Oct. 14 in Wichita, Kan. He was 80. Friend made his major league debut in 1949 for the St. Louis Browns, although he appeared in just two games that season. He saw the most playing time of his career the following season with the Browns, when he hit .237/.312/.352 in 372 at-bats. Friend appeared sparingly in the majors the rest of his career, appearing in games for the Tigers, Indians, Red Sox and Cubs before his final major league season in 1956. In 598 major league at-bats, Friend hit .227/.295/.339. After his playing days, Friend was a minor league manager and a Kansas City Royals coach during their inaugural 1969 season.

■ **Irv Hall**, an infielder who hit .261/.302/.311 in 508 at-bats with the Philadelphia Athletics from 1943 to 1946, died Dec. 12, 2006, in Baltimore. He was 88.

■ **Josh Hancock**, a righthander who pitched for four teams in six big league seasons, died April 29 in St. Louis. He was 29. Drafted by the Red Sox in the fifth round of the 1998 draft, Hancock spent five seasons in the minors before a three-game audition with the Red Sox in 2002. Though the Red Sox would be Hancock's first team in 2002, he was traded to the Phillies that offseason for Jeremy Giambi. After stints with the Reds in 2004 and 2005, Hancock moved on to the Cardinals, where he received a World Series ring with the 2006 team. Hancock's death was the result of a car accident. For his career, he went 9-7, 4.20 in 178 big league innings.

■ **Bill Harman**, a righthander and catcher for the Phillies in 1941 and in the minors in 1942, died Sept. 27 in Greenville, Del. He was 88. With no previous pro experience, Harman debuted for the Phillies in 1941, seeing time in five games behind the plate and five more on the mound. He went 1-for-14 (.071) with a single as a batter, and put up a 4.85 ERA in five relief appearances spanning 13 innings.

■ **Mark Harris**, whose 1956 novel "Bang the Drum Slowly" set a new tone for baseball fiction, died May 30 in Goleta, Calif. He was 84.

■ **Bobby Herrera**, a righthander who pitched in 15 professional seasons from 1945 to 1958, including a three-game stint with the St. Louis Browns in 1951, died Aug. 23 in Mexico City. He was 81.

■ **Gomer Hodge**, who played for the Indians in 1971 and professionally in 12 other seasons from 1963 to 1976, died May 13 in Saluda, N.C. He was 63. Hodge also managed Waterloo of the Midwest League in 1981 and 1984, and managed Beloit of the same league from 1986 to 1987.

■ **Hal Jeffcoat**, a two-way player who appeared in a professional game in three different decades and played 12 seasons in the major leagues, died Aug. 30 in Tampa. He was 82. In 1948, Jeffcoat began his first of eight seasons with the Cubs. His rookie year was his best, as his 132 hits, 42 RBIs and .279 average all were career bests. After not appearing as a pitcher from 1947 to 1953, Jeffcoat returned to the mound in 1954 as a two-way player for the Cubs, tossing 104 innings.

■ **Sherman Jones**, a righthander who pitched in three big league seasons for the Giants, Reds and Mets, died Feb. 21 I Kansas City, Kan. He was 72. Jones went 2-6, 4.73 in 48 big league games, striking out 53 batters and walking 46 in 110 innings.

■ **Buddy Kerr**, a nine-year big league shortstop for the New York Giants and Boston Braves, died Nov. 7, 2006, in New York. He was 84. Kerr, who made his big league debut with his hometown Giants in 1943 at age 20, became the club's regular shortstop the following year. A well-regarded all-around shortstop in his day, Kerr received National League MVP consideration in both 1945 and 1946, when he finished 21st and 11th in the voting. Kerr also set the NL record for errorless games by a shortstop in 1947 (since broken) when he flawlessly handled 384 chances over 68 games.

■ **Ernie Koy**, an outfielder for four teams in five big league seasons, died Jan. 1 in Bellville, Texas. He was 97. Koy hit .299/.352/.468 with 11 homers and 15 steals for Brooklyn in 1938 and .278/.338/.445 with 11 stolen bases the next year, but spent his remaining three big league seasons bouncing from team to team. He joined the military and missed the 1943 through 1945 seasons and voluntarily retired in 1946. He hit .279/.332/.427 in 558 big league games.

■ **Al Kozar**, a second baseman who spent three seasons in the big leagues as part of an 11-year career that lasted from 1941 to 1954, died Sept. 6 in Palm Beach Gardens, Fla. He was 86. He finished with career .254/.321/.334 averages in 285 games.

■ **Lou Kretlow**, a righthander who pitched parts of ten seasons in the American League in a career that spanned 1946 to 1957, died Sept. 12 in Enid, Okla. He was 86. Kretlow had his finest big league season in 1954, posting a 4.37 ERA in a career-high 166 2/3 innings.

■ **Bowie Kuhn**, the fifth commissioner of baseball who served three terms from 1969-1984, died March 15 in Jacksonville, Fla. He was 80. Kuhn served as commissioner during one of baseball's most turbulent eras, a time that saw the introduction of free agency and five of the sport's eight work stoppages

■ **Clem Labine**, a righthander who pitched in 13 big leagues seasons, 11 of them for the Dodgers, died March 2 in Vero Beach, Fla. He was 80. Labine was with the team when it moved from Brooklyn to Los Angeles for the 1958 season and appeared in four World Series with the franchise. Beginning in 1952, Labine would become a fixture in the Dodgers' bullpen for the next eight and a half seasons. He pitched in the 1953, 1955-56 and 1959-60 World Series,

the first four for the Dodgers and the final for the Pirates. Only the 1953 and 1956 Dodgers failed to win the Series. Labine went 77-56, 3.63 with 96 saves in 513 big league games. In addition to the Dodgers and Pirates, he also pitched for the Tigers in 1960 and for the 1962 Mets.

■ **Max Lanier**, a lefthander who pitched in 14 big league seasons for the Cardinals, where he was a part of three World Series teams, New York Giants and Browns, died Jan. 30 in Dunnellon, Fla. He was 91.

Though he would see time with the Cardinals in 1938 and 1939, Lanier did not stick until 1940. It didn't take him long to become a regular contributor to the talented wartime Cardinals teams, however, winning nine and 10 games in 1940-41. Beginning in 1942, the Cardinals would win three straight NL pennants, with Lanier going 13-8, 2.96 in 161 innings; 15-7, 1.90 in 213 innings and 17-12, 2.65 in 224 innings. The Cardinals won two of three World Series in that span, with Lanier going a sparkling 2-1, 1.71 in four Series starts, including the Game 5 clincher against the cross-town Browns in 1944. Lanier went 108-82, 3.01 in 327 big league games. His son Hal was a 10-year major league shortstop and the Astros' manager from 1986-88.

■ **Bill Lefebvre**, a lefthander who pitched in 36 big league games in four seasons with the Red Sox and Senators, died Jan. 19 in Largo, Fla. He was 91. Lefebvre, who missed the 1945 season due to his military service, retired with 5-5, 5.03 numbers in 132 big league innings.

■ **Art Lopatka**, a lefthander whose big league career was cut short by injury after two seasons, died March 10 in Elk Grove Village, Ill. He was 87. Lopatka went 1-1, 6.35 in eight career big league games.

■ **Emil Mailho**, an outfielder who played in 21 games for the Philadelphia Athletics and who hit .300 or better in five Pacific Coast League seasons, died March 7 in Hayward, Calif. He was 98.

■ **Bob Malloy**, a righthanded reliever who pitched in five seasons for the Reds and St. Louis Browns, died Feb. 20 in Cincinnati. He was 88. While Malloy's big league career consisted of just 48 games over those five seasons, he pitched professionally for 12 seasons, mostly in the high minors. Malloy went 4-7, 3.26 in 48 big league games.

■ **Frank Mancuso**, a catcher who played for the St. Louis Browns and Washington Senators in a 19-year pro career that lasted from 1937 to 1955, died Aug. 4 in Houston. He was 89. Mancuso, who served in the military in 1943, had his best major league season in 1945, when he hit .268 ith 13 doubles and 38 RBIs in 365 at-bats.

■ **Jim Mangan**, a catcher who played in 45 games for the Pirates and New York Giants as part of a nine-year pro career that spanned 1949 to 1958, died July 19 in San Jose, Calif. He was 77. Mangan hit .153/.265/.153 in 45 big league games. He missed the 1953 season to military service.

■ **Charlie Marshall**, a catcher who appeared in one big league game but did not bat and who spent 13 seasons in the minors, died April 15 Wilmington, Del. He was 87.

■ **Marty Martinez**, a shortstop for seven big league teams in seven seasons, died March 15 in Santo Domingo, Dominican Republic. He was 65. A native of Havana, Martinez enjoyed his best season in 1969 in Houston, hitting .308/.340/.374 in 198 at-bats.

■ **Eddie Mayo**, a second and third baseman for four major league teams over nine seasons, died Nov. 27, 2006, in Banning, Calif. He was 96. Mayo's best work came for the Tigers in their World Series-winning 1945 campaign. He achieved practically every one of his career highlights that season: Mayo hit a career-best .285/.347/.405 with 10 home runs as Detroit's second baseman, he made the all-star team and was runner-up to teammate Hal Newhouser in the American League MVP race.

■ **Orlando McFarlane**, a catcher who played 14 pro seasons from 1958 to 1971, including parts of five in the major leagues, died July 18 in Ponce, P.R. He was 69. McFarlane, who was born in Cuba, made his major league debut in 1962 with the Pirates, appearing in eight games. McFarlane hit .240/.290/.332 in 124 big league games.

■ **Doug McMillan**, an area scout for the Nationals for the past six years, died May 23. He was 60.

McMillan oversaw the Northern California and Pacific Northwest regions. He spent 25 years in pro ball as a player and scout, and he signed current Washington prospects Kory Casto and Stephen Englund.

The Nationals selected McMillan's son Brett, a lefthanded-hitting first baseman, in the 14th round of the 2006 draft. The 23-year-old was playing with low Class A Hagerstown.

■ **Sammy Meeks**, who spent three seasons with the Reds and one with the Washington Senators in a 14-year professional career that spanned 1946 to 1959, died April 23 in Memphis. He had turned 84 that day.

Meeks appeared in 24 games for Washington in 1948, and 68 more for Cincinnati from 1949 to 1951. A utility-man who played primarily the middle infield, Meeks hit .251/.284/.337 in 199 career big league at-bats.

■ **Ox Miller**, a righthander who pitched for the Washington Senators, St. Louis Browns and Cubs as part of a 14-year pro career spanning 1937 to 1953, died Aug. 13 in Beeville, Texas. He was 92. Miller went 4-6, 6.38 with 27 strikeouts and 33 walks in 91 2/3 big league innings.

■ **Bob Milliken**, a righthander who pitched in two seasons for the Brooklyn Dodgers in their early-1950s heyday, died Jan. 4 in Clearwater, Fla. He was 80. Though his big league career amounted to 180 innings, Milliken made the most of them, going 13-6, 3.59 in 1953-54, while working mostly as a reliever.

■ **Pete Naktenis**, a lefthander who pitched 10 pro seasons from 1936 to 1945, including one for the Philadelphia Athletics and another for the Reds, died Aug. 1, 2003, in Singer Island, Fla. He was 89. Naktenis appeared in seven games for the A's in 1936 and just three more for the Reds in 1939. He went 0-1, 10.72 in 22 2/3 career innings.

■ **Don Nottebart**, a righthander who pitched in 296 big league games as part of 17-year career that spanned 1954 to 1970, died Oct. 4 in Houston. He was 71. Nottebart went 36-51, 3.65 with 525 strikeouts and 283 walks in 928 innings.

■ **Gene Oliver**, a catcher/first baseman who played in 10 major league seasons for five teams, died March 3 in Rock Island, Ill. He was 71. Oliver spent three times leading his minor league in home runs, Oliver didn't stick in the majors until the Cardinals gave him 345 at-bats in 1962, his seventh pro season. In 1959, Oliver would split the season between Rochester and St. Louis, seeing time in 59 games (mostly as an outfielder) for the Cardinals. In 1961, Oliver made such an impression with St. Louis--hitting .258/.352/.441 with 14 homers as a 27-year-old rookie catcher in 1962--that he was traded to the Milwaukee Braves for Lew Burdette in June 1963. It was with Milwaukee that Oliver delivered his finest big league season. While playing both catcher and first base

for the Braves in 1965, Oliver hit .270/.336/.482 with a personal-best 21 homers. Oliver was traded to the Phillies for Bob Uecker in 1967 and also spent time with the Red Sox and Cubs. Though he toiled in the minors for seven years, Oliver still managed to crack 93 big league home runs to go with .246/.315/.427 career averages in 786 games.

■ **Jimmy Outlaw**, a veteran of 10 major league seasons with the Reds, Boston Braves and Tigers, died April 9, 2006, in Jackson, Ala. He was 93. For his major league career, he hit .268/.333/.334 in 650 games.

■ **Jim Pisoni**, an outfielder who played in 103 major league games for four teams and who played professionally for 12 seasons, died Feb. 4 in Frisco, Texas. He was 77. Pisoni hit .212/.278/.354 in 189 big league at-bats.

■ **Sam Pollock**, the Blue Jays' chairman and CEO from 1995 to 2000, died Aug. 14 in Toronto. He was 81. Pollock had served as a member of the organization's board of directors in the early 1990s and had served in that capacity at the time of his death. He rose to prominence as VP and general manager of the NHL's Montreal Canadiens when they won nine Stanley Cups in a period of 14 years in the 1960s and 1970s.

■ **Phil Rizzuto**, Hall of Famer and the best shortstop in Yankees history before Derek Jeter came along, died Aug. 14 in West Oragne, N.J. He was 89. The Yankees signed Rizzuto in 1937, in the midst of the Joe DiMaggio-led dynasty. The slight, 5-foot-6 shortstop proceeded to hit .300 or better--peaking at .347 for Kansas City (American Association) in 1940--in each of his four minor league stops before debuting in the big leagues in 1941 at age 23. If baseball had had the Rookie of the Year award at that time, Rizzuto might have won it for his 1941 season. He hit .307/.343/.398 with 20 doubles and 14 steals in 515 at-bats for the World Series-winning Yankees. He was equally as good in 1942, but he would miss all of the 1943 through 1945 seasons--his age 25 to 27 years--while serving in World War II. Though Rizzuto struggled in his return season of 1946, he improved steadily over the next two years, finally breaking through for his two finest seasons in 1949 and 1950, at ages 31 and 32. Rizzuto played a key role in the Yankees' dynastic period that began in 1949 and included five consecutive World Series titles. Mickey Mantle would not join the team until 1951.

Rizzuto hit .275/.352/.358 with 65 RBIs and 18 stolen bases in 1949 to finish second in the AL MVP voting. He won the award in 1950 on the strength of his best season. Rizzuto set career highs by batting .324/.418/.439 with seven home runs, while adding 36 doubles and 12 stolen bases. Most impressively, Rizzuto's walk-to-strikeout ratio over his two best seasons was 2.2-to-1. He settled into something resembling his pre-peak years following the 1950 season and remained the Yankees' regular shortstop through 1953. Rizzuto struggled badly in 1954, hitting .195/.291/.251 in 307 at-bats, and played sparingly through the 1956 season, after which he retired after 13 years as a player. Rizzuto's post-playing career was as distinguished as his playing career. He was a Yankees broadcaster for 40 years, from 1957 to 1996, and was elected by the Veterans Committee to the Hall of Fame in 1994. He hit .273/.351/.355 in 1,661 games for the Yankees.

■ **Mel Roberts**, who was a coach with Danville (Appalachian) in 2007, died Sept. 1 in Danville, Va. He was 64.

A former professional outfielder, Roberts also served as a coach for the Phillies from 1992 to 1995.

■ **Bill Robinson**, an outfielder who played in 16 major league seasons in a pro career that spanned 1961 to 1983 and who was working as the Dodgers' minor league hitting coordinator, died July 29 in Las Vegas. He was 64. The right-handed-hitting Robinson played for the Braves, Yankees, Phillies and Pirates, mostly as a reserve outfielder. In the two seasons in which he played most every day, Robinson hit .304/.337/.525 with 26 home runs and 104 RBIs for the Pirates in 1977, and .246/.296/.411 with 14 homers and 80 RBIs in 1978.

Robinson hit .258/.300/.438 with 1,127 hits and 166 home runs in 1,472 games.

■ **Vern Ruhle**, a 13-year big league righthander and a successful pitching coach, died Jan. 20, 2007 in Houtson after a yearlong battle with cancer. He was 55. Ruhle pitched well for the Tigers in 1975-76--going 11-12, 4.03 in 199 innings and 9-12, 3.92 in 200 innings. Ruhle finished his career t 67-88, 3.73 in 1,411 career innings. After his playing days, Ruhle served as pitching coach for the Astros, Phillies, Mets and Reds. He had become Reds pitching coach in June 2005, but missed the 2006 season while he received treatment.

■ **Mickey Rutner**, a third baseman who played in 12 games for the Philadelphia Athletics in a 10-year career that spanned 1941 to 1953, died Oct. 17 in Georgetown, Texas. He was 88.

■ **Johnny Sain**, a workhorse righthander who pitched in 11 major league seasons and won 139 games for the Boston Braves, Yankees and Kansas City Athletics, died Nov. 7, 2006. He was 89. Sain made his big league debut for the Braves in 1942, going 4-7, 3.90 in 97 innings. He then spent 1943 to 1945 in military service. When he returned in 1946 at age 28, he teamed with Hall of Fame lefthander Warren Spahn to form one of the most formidable pitching combos in the league. He would go 20-14, 2.21 with a league-leading 24 complete games; 21-12, 3.52; and 24-12, 2.60 with league-leading totals for wins, complete games (28) and innings (315) in his first three seasons back. Sain finished fifth and second (to Stan Musial) in National League MVP balloting in 1946 and 1948, with the Braves edging the Cardinals for the pennant in the latter season. He made three all-star teams. While he would never reach the heights of 1946-1948, Sain would pitch effectively for the Braves for three more seasons before being traded to the Yankees for righthander Lew Burdette. With the Yankees, Sain, now primarily a reliever, would appear in games for three consecutive World Series winners from 1951 to 1953. Sain was equally well known in his post-playing days as a pitching coach from 1959 to 1978 for the A's—for whom he made his final 25 appearances in 1955—Yankees, Twins, Tigers, White Sox and Atlanta Braves. He bounced around frequently because he seldom saw eye-to-eye with his managers, general managers or owners. He would coach the pitching staffs of five of the 10 American League pennant winners of the 1960s.

■ **Reggie Sanders**, an outfielder/first baseman who played 12 seasons from 1968 to 1979, including 26 games with the Tigers in 1974, died Jan. 27, 2002, in Los Angeles. He was 52. Sanders hit .273/.308/.434 with three home runs in the big leagues.

■ **Willard Schmidt**, a righthander who pitched in seven

big league seasons with the Cardinals and Reds, died March 22 in Newcastle, Okla. He was 78. The Cardinals signed Schmidt in 1949 and he had a distinguished minor league career, winning one wins, two ERA and a two minor league strikeout titles on his way to St. Louis. Schmidt appeared in 18 games for the 1952 Cardinals, but his 5.14 ERA bought him a ticket to Rochester (International). He got another big league look in 1953, but was even worse with a 9.00 ERA. Something clicked when he returned to the Cardinals in 1955, as he went 7-6, 2.78 in 130 innings. He was effective in 1956, too, going 6-8, 3.84 in 148 innings. He tailed off a bit the next season, after which he was dealt to the Reds in a trade for outfielder Curt Flood. The Reds got two quality relief seasons from Schmidt--a 3.41 ERA in 140 innings. Schmidt went 31-29, 3.93 in 586 big league innings.

■ **Larry Sherry**, the 1959 World Series MVP and a right-handed reliever for the Dodgers, Tigers, Astros and Angels for 11 seasons, died Dec. 17, 2006, in Mission Viejo, Calif. He was 71. Sherry signed with the Dodgers in 1953, but did not make his big league debut until 1958, the Dodgers' first season in Los Angeles. The next year, 1959, Sherry factored in all four of the Dodgers' World Series wins (two wins, two saves) against the White Sox in the World Series, giving up one run in 12 2/3 innings. Sherry was traded to Detroit early in the 1964 season and enjoyed his last hurrah with fine 1965 and 1966 seasons. He was traded to Houston in 1967, and retired at age 32 following his 1968 season with the Angels. Sherry was the brother of Norm Sherry, a backup catcher for the Dodgers from 1959-62.

■ **Bunky Stewart**, a lefthander who pitched sporadically for the Washington Senators in the early 1950s, died Oct. 3 in Wilmington, N.C. He was 76. Stewart played professionally for 12 seasons, from 1951 to 1962. He led the Coastal Plain League in winning percentage (.882) and ERA in his debut by going 15-2, 1.16 with 142 strikeouts in 171 innings for New Bern. Stewart got his longest big league look in 1956, going 5-7, 5.57 in 105 innings for the Senators. For his career, he went 5-11, 6.01 in 72 games.

■ **Rollie Stiles**, a righthander who pitched 298 innings for the St. Louis Browns in a 13-year career that spanned 1928 to 1940, died July 28 in St. Louis. He was 100. Stiles went 6-7 in 1930 and 1931, his first two years with the Browns. After pitching for Milwaukee (American Association) and Longview (Texas) in 1932, Stiles returned to the Browns in 1933, posting a career high in innings (115) and a career low in ERA (5.01). For his major league career, Stiles went 9-14, 5.92.

■ **Bobby Sturgeon**, a middle infielder who played in six big league seasons for the Cubs and Boston Braves, died March 10 in San Dimas, Calif. He was 87. Sturgeon turned in his best big league season in 1946 as a shortstop and second baseman for Chicago. He hit .296/.319/.361 with his lone big league homer in 294 at-bats. He was similarly effective in 1947 and was traded to the Braves in March 1948, where he spent his final big league season. Sturgeon hit .257/.277/.318 in 1,220 big league at-bats.

■ **John Sullivan**, who collected 422 hits in six seasons in the American League, died Sept. 20 in Homewood, Ill. He was 86.

Sullivan began his professional career in 1941 with Thomasville (Georgia-Florida), where the shortstop hit .323 in 567 at-bats. In 1942, Sullivan split time between

Chattanooga (Southern Association) and the majors, appearing in 94 games for the Washington Senators.

Sullivan played shortstop for Washington for the next two seasons, setting career-best marks for RBIs (55) in 1942 and hits (111) in 1943. After serving in the military from 1945 to 1946, Sullivan returned to play for the Senators in 1947, when he hit .256 in 133 at-bats. After one more year with the Senators in 1948, Sullivan finished his major league career with the St. Louis Browns, for whom he hit .226 in 105 games.

Sullivan played four more seasons in the minors, including his final year in 1953 with Lynchburg (Piedmont) as a player/manager. He hit .230/.312/.270 in 605 major league games.

■ **Cecil Travis**, a hard-hitting shortstop and third baseman who played 12 seasons for the Washington Senators, died Dec. 16, 2006, in Fayetteville, N.C. He was 93. Though he was a regular on just one winning team (the 1936 Senators went 82-71), Travis made three all-star teams and twice finished in the top 10 in American League MVP balloting--finishing ninth in 1938 when he hit .335/.401/.432, and sixth in 1941 for his .359/.410/.520 effort in which he led the league with 218 hits. The lefthanded-hitting Travis also finished 11th in the 1937 MVP race. Travis, who enrolled in the military at the end of 1941 and missed the next three seasons--and most of 1945--suffered a bad case of frostbite in World War II's Battle of the Bulge that required surgery to prevent amputation of his feet. Travis was not the same player when he returned, though he was still just 31, and would play in just two more seasons, retiring in 1947. Travis hit .314/.370/.416 in 1,328 big league games and his average remains the all-time mark for AL shortstops and trails only Pirates' greats Honus Wagner (.327) and Arky Vaughan (.318) for the all-time lead.

■ **Jose Uribe**, a shortstop in 10 major league seasons for the Cardinals, Giants and Astros, died in an automobile accident Dec. 8, 2006, near Santo Domingo, Dominican Republic. He was 47. Uribe is best remembered as the Giants' starting shortstop from 1985 to 1990, but he had actually played for two organizations previous to his time in San Francisco. The Yankees signed Uribe in February 1977 then released him in July.

The Cardinals signed him up in 1980 and in their farm system Uribe toiled for four years--mostly at Louisville (American Association)--before making the major leagues in 1984. Uribe's time in St. Louis would be brief, however: just eight games. Packaged with three other Cardinals for Giants slugging first baseman Jack Clark in February 1985, Uribe would open the season as a regular in San Francisco and not look back. In his first two seasons in the Bay Area, Uribe was a standard-fare all-field, no-hit shortstop--though his walk-strikeout ratio was an eye-opening 61-76 in 1986. Uribe enjoyed his career season in 1987, when he established career highs with .291/.343/.424 marks--all three about 50 points above his career norms. The Giants lost to the Cardinals in that year's Championship Series. Somewhat ironically, Uribe would have his worst season the next time the Giants made the playoffs, 1989, when he hit a mere .221/.273/.280.

Uribe signed with the Astros in 1993, but appeared in just 45 games with Houston before retiring. He finished his career with .241/.300/.314 numbers in 1,038 games.

■ **John Vukovich**, a major league third baseman for three teams in parts of 10 seasons and a fixture with the Phillies as a coach and overall personality, died March 8 in Philadelphia. He was 59. The Phillies selected Vukovich in the first round (10th overall) of the January 1966 draft and he spent most of his four seasons in the minors before debuting for Philadelphia in 1970. Though he hit just .161/.203/.222 in 277 big league games for the Phillies, Brewers and Reds, Vukovich did play for the World Series-winning 1980 Phillies and his contributions to the organization extended well beyond his playing days. Vukovich went on to become the longest-tenured coach in Phillies history at 31 years and he was a special assistant to Phillies general manager Pat Gillick at the time of his death from an inoperable brain tumor.

■ **Bill Wight**, a lefthander who won 77 games for eight teams in 12 big league seasons, died May 17 in Shasta, Calif. He was 85. Wight, who joined the military in 1942 missed the entire 1943 to 1945 seasons, broke camp with the Yankees in 1946 and appeared in 14 games for the big club. That arrangement changed dramatically in 1947 when he pitched in only one big league game, spending most of the season with Kansas City (American Association). The well-traveled Wight moved on to the White Sox in 1949, then to the Red Sox in 1951, the Tigers in 1952, the Indians in 1953, the Orioles in 1955, the Reds in 1958 and, finally, to the Cardinals to finish the same 1958 season. He finished his career with Seattle (Pacific Coast), going 1-3, 7.31 in 16 innings. He went 77-99, 3.95 in 347 games, covering 1,563 innings.

■ **Archie Wilson**, who appeared in 51 major league games and spent 15 seasons as an outfielder in professional baseball, died April 28 in Decatur, Ala. He was 83. In 1952, Wilson appeared in 11 games for Louisville (American Association) and appeared in 47 games for the Yankees, Washington Senators and Red Sox. Wilson had one hit in two at-bats for the Yankees, 20 hits in 96 at-bats for the Senators and 10 hits in 38 at-bats for the Red Sox. Wilson never returned to the major leagues after 1952. In 1961 Wilson become a player/manager for Pensacola (Alabama-Florida) in 1961, his final season as a player. Wilson also spent two seasons as a non-playing manager in the Carolina League, managing Raleigh in 1962 and Newport News in 1963. Wilson hit .221/.268/.300 in 51 big league games.

■ **K.C. Wise**, a second baseman who played in four big league seasons for the Cubs, Milwaukee Braves and Tigers, died Feb. 20 in Naples, Fla. He was 74. Wise, who would become his hometown of Naples' first orthodontist after his playing days in 1968, began his pro career in 1953 playing for Sioux Falls (Northern). Wise got his Bachelors' of Science degree from the University of Florida in 1956, the same year he advanced to Los Angeles of the Pacific Coast League. He continued his strong play in the PCL--hitting .287 with a career-high seven home runs--which earned him his first big league look in 1957. In 1957 Wise began a four-year stretch in which he appeared in the big league in each season, though he would struggle to hold down a job. Wise played for the Cubs in 1957, then moved to the Braves in 1958, for whom he appeared in the Series against the Yankees. Wise batted .174/.243 126 major league games. His father Hugh was for the Braves who ran the club's minor league Waycross, Ga.

Give BA a tryout

The magazine for baseball insiders

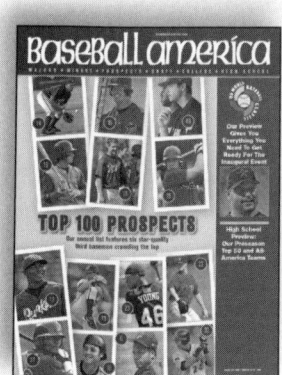

4 TRIAL ISSUES FOR **$4**

With a trial subscription
you'll discover what
makes our readers
so loyal!

**MAJORS
MINORS
PROSPECTS
DRAFT
COLLEGE
HIGH SCHOOL**

APPENDIX